STANDARD CATALOG OF AMERICAN
Light Duty TRUCKS

PICKUPS · PANELS · VANS · ALL MODELS 1896-1986

JOHN A. GUNNELL

EDITOR

Marque Researchers, Robert C. Ackerson, Jim Benjaminson, Don Bunn, James M. Flammang, Fred K. Fox, John Gunnell, Jeff Gillis, Bill Siuru, Charles Webb, Donald F. Wood, R. Perry Zavitz

CATALOG STAFF

PUBLISHER: Chester L. Krause

EDITOR: John A. Gunnell

PRICING: Ken Buttolph

PRODUCTION: Kathryn Hines

TYPESETTING: Sue Krause

GRAPHICS: Cheryl Kell
Larry Frank
Chris Mork

COVER DESIGN: Paul Tofte

COVER GRAPHICS: Barb Johnson

PROMOTIONS: Pat Klug

First Edition

First Printing

krause publications

700 East State St.   Iola, WI 54990

FORWARD

The concept behind Krause Publication's "Standard Catalogs" is to compile massive amounts of information about motor vehicles and present it in a standard format which the hobbyist, collector or professional dealer can use to answer some commonly asked questions.

These questions include: What year, make and model is the vehicle? What did it sell for when new? Is it original or modified? How rare is it? What's special about it? How much is it worth today?

Some answers are provided by illustrations in the catalogs; others by information found in the charts or text.

Each catalog represents the efforts of both professional research-historians and enthusiasts who collect facts and factory literature on one make or model.

The format we use calls for the following data: (1) a contributor's personal description of the vehicle's appearance; (2) where available, a list of standard factory equipment; (3) vehicle and/or engine identification codes and advice on how to interpret these; (4) a chart giving model codes, body type descriptions, original retail price, original shipping weight and available production totals; (5) engine specifications; (6) a description of chassis features in a concise, generalized manner; (7) some "technical" information about the drive train and running gear; (8) specific option lists or a description of accessories seen in original period photos of such vehicles; (9) a "thumbnail history" of the vehicle and/or manufacturer and, in many instances, (10) a "ballpark" estimate of current prices being paid for such (pre-1980) models in today's collector-vehicle market.

No claims are made about the catalogs being history textbooks or encyclopedias. They are not repair manuals or "bibles" for motor vehicle enthusiasts. They are intended as collectors' guides, much like the popular spotter's books, buyers' digests or pricing guides. How-ever, they are much larger in size, broader in scope and more deluxe in format. In addition, they represent the combined efforts of a large research team, rather than one individual's work.

All of the catalogs published to date reflect, to some degree, a balance between generalized research carried on by professional authors, and material prepared by individuals who know many facts about a single model or make through their personal hobby interests.

Part of the catalog concept is to coordinate future assignments in such a manner that each section in the book will ultimately feel both the skilled touch of the professional writer and the in-depth enthusiasm of the hobby expert. All contributors are requested to maintain an ongoing file of new research, corrections and additional photos which can be used to refine and expand future editions.

The long-range goal of Krause Publication's is to have a series of catalogs that are as near perfect as possible. We're told that these books provide many hobbyists with hours of enjoyable reading. Some also consider them essential guides to carry along when they travel to car shows, wrecking yards and swap meets. And, of course, they can be particularly useful to the hobbyist/collector when cruising the highways or backroads in search of new vehicle acquisitions. You will know, immediately, what type of vehicle you've found, how rare it is and how much it's worth when restored.

Other catalogs currently available include *The Standard Catalog of American Cars 1805-1942* and *The Standard Catalog of American Cars 1946-1972*. For ordering information and current prices on these books, write: **Krause Publications/Old Cars Weekly, 700 E. State St., Iola, WI 54990.**

CONTENTS

ABBREVIATIONS

A.A.A. .... American Automobile Assoc.
Adj. .... Adjustable
Air Cond. .... Air conditioning
A.K.A. .... Also known as
A.L.A.M. .... Assoc. of Licensed Automobile Manufacturers
AM .... Amplitude modulation (radio)
AMC .... American Motors Corp.
Amp. .... Amperes
Approx. .... Approximate
Auto. .... Automatic
Auxil. .... Auxiliary
Avail. .... Available
Avg. .... Average
Bbl. .... Barrel (in carburetor)
B.H.P. .... Brake horsepower
B.L. .... Bonus Load (pickup)
Bros. .... Brothers
BSW .... Black sidewall
Bus. .... Business
CA .... California (zip code)
Calif. .... California
Can. .... Canopy
Carb. .... Carburetor
CB .... Citizen's Band radio
C. Del. .... Custom Deluxe
C.F. .... Closed front
Chas. .... Chassis
Ch.-Cab .... Chassis & Cab
CIBA .... Cast iron block
C.I.D. .... Cubic inch diameter
CJ .... Civilian Jeep
Clsd. .... Closed
Co. .... Company
COBRA .... Copper Brazed Engine
C.O.E. .... Cab-over-engine
Comm. .... Commercial
Conv. .... Convertible
Col. .... Column
C.R. .... Compression ratio
CS .... Custom (Chevrolet)
CST .... Custom Sport Truck (Chevy)
Cu. In. .... Cubic Inch(es)
Cust. .... Custom
Cyl. .... Cylinder
Cw/C .... Chassis with cab
DB .... Dodge Brothers
Del. .... Deluxe
Dely. .... Delivery
Dia. .... Diameter
Dif. .... Differential
Div. .... Division
"Door(s)" .... Panel door model
Dr. (2-dr.) .... Door (two-door)
DRW .... Dual rear wheels
Dual Rear .... Dual rear wheels
Ea. .... Each
Econo. .... Econoline
EFI .... Electronic fuel injection
"Eight" .... Eight-cylinder engine
ELS .... Extra Luxurious Special (Ford)
En-bloc .... Cast in separate blocks
Endgt. .... End-Gate
EPA .... Enviornmental Protection Agency
Equip. .... Equipment
ESC .... Electronic speed control
Exc./Ex. .... Except
Exp. .... Express
Ext. .... Extended
E-Z-Eye .... Tinted glass
F (3F) .... Forward (three forward speeds)
FC .... Forward control
F.F. .... Flat-face cowl
F-head .... Vales in head and block
Flare. .... Flareside pickup (Ford)
Fleet .... Fleetside pickup (Chevy)
FM .... Frequency modulation (radio)
F.O.B. .... Free on board
"Four" .... Four-cylinder
4x4 .... Four-Wheel-Drive
4x2 .... Two-Wheel-Drive
4-dr. .... four-door
4-spd. .... four-speed
Frt. .... front
FS .... Fender-side pickup
Ft. .... Foot/feet
Ft.-Lbs. .... Foot-pounds
4V .... Four-barrel carburetor
4WD .... four-wheel-drive
Gal. .... gallon
"Gate" .... tailgate model
GBR .... Glass Belted Radial
GM .... General Motors
GMC .... General Motors Corporation, GM Truck & Bus, GM Truck & Coach
GMR .... GM Research Div.
GVW .... Gross Vehicle Weight
H-D .... Heavy-duty
HEI .... High-energy ignition
H.P. .... horsepower
Hr. .... hour
Hwy. .... highway
I .... Inline cylinder arrangement
ICC .... type of emergency flasher
I.D. .... Identification
IHC .... International Harvester Co.
In(s). .... Inch(es)
Inc. .... Incorporated
Incl. .... Included
Install. .... Installation
Int. .... Interior
I.P. .... Instrument Panel
Jr. .... Junior
L (L-head) .... side-valve engine
Lb(s). .... Pound(s)
Lbs.-Ft. .... pounds-feet
LCF .... Low Cab Forward
L-D .... Light-Duty
LE .... Luxury Edition
LG/LP/LPG .... Liquified Petroleum Gas
L-H/LH .... Left-hand
LHD .... Left-hand Drive
L-head .... side-valve engine
Ltd. .... Limited
LUV .... Light Utility Vehicle
LWB .... Long Wheelbase
Maint. .... Maintenance
Max. .... Maximum
Mfg. .... Manufacturing
M.M. .... Milimeters
M.P.G. .... Miles Per Gallon
M.P.H. .... Miles Per Hour
Mpx. .... Multiplex
N/A .... Not Available
N.A. .... Not Available
NACC .... National Automobile Chamber of Commerce
NC .... No charge
NADA .... National Automobile Dealers Assoc.
N.H.P. .... Net Horsepower
No. .... Number
O.F. .... Open front
OHC .... Overhead camshaft
OHV .... Overhead valves
OPEC .... Organization of Petroleum Exporting Countries
OPS .... Office of Price Stability
Opt. .... Optional
OSRV .... Outside rearview mirror
Oz. .... ounce
P .... Passenger
PDV .... Parcel Delivery Van
P. Frt. .... Power front
PMD .... Pontiac Motor Division
PR .... Ply-rated (tires)
Prod. .... Production
P.T.O. .... Power Take-Off
P.U. .... Pickup
Pwr. .... Power (power-assist)
Quad. .... four (quad shocks on 4x4)
Rad. .... radio
Rds./Rdstr. .... Roadster
Reg. .... Regular
Remote .... Remote Control
Req. .... Requires
RH/R-H .... Right-hand
RHD .... Right-hand drive
R.P.M. .... Revolutions per minute
R.P.O. .... Regular Production Option
RV .... Recreational Vehicle
RWL .... Raised White Letter
SAE .... Society of Automotive Engineers
SBR .... Steel-belted Radial Tires
SC .... Super Cab
"Screen" .... Screenside Delivery
SE .... Special Edition
Sed. .... Sedan
Sig. .... Signal
"Six" .... Six-cylinder
Spd. .... Speed
Spd. Reg. .... Speed regulator
Spec. .... Special
Spl. .... Special
Spt. .... Sport
Sq. In. .... Square Inch(es)
Sr. .... Senior
SRW .... Single Rear Wheel
SS .... Super Sport
Sta. Wag. .... Station Wagon
Std. .... Standard
Step. .... Stepside pickup (Chevy)
Style. .... Styleside pickup (Ford)
Sub. .... Suburban
SWB .... Short wheelbase
Tach. .... Tachometer
Tax. .... Taxable (horsepower)
TBI .... Throttle-Body Injection
Temp. .... Temperature
T-Head .... Type of valve layout
THM .... Turbo-Hydramatic transmission
3f/1R .... 3 speeds forward/ 1 reverse
3S .... Three-seat
Trans. .... Transmission
Trlr. .... Trailer
T.V. .... Television
2-dr. .... Two-door
2V .... Two-barrel (carburetor)
2WD .... Two-wheel-drive
U.S.A. .... United States of America
Util. .... Utility
V .... Venturi (carburetor)
V-6/8 .... Vee-block engines 6-/8-cyl.
VIN .... Vehicle identification number
V.P. .... Vice-president
V.V. .... Vision and ventilating
W/ .... With
Wag. .... Wagon
W.B. .... Wheelbase
Weap. Carr. .... Weapons Carrier
West. .... Westchester
Wgn. .... Wagon
WLT .... White-lettered tires
Wn. .... Winch
W/O .... Without
WS .... Wide-Side Pickup (GMC)
W/S .... Windshield (chassis with)
WSW .... White sidewall (tires)
W/WS .... With Windshield
Xport .... Export model

Many abbreviations are used in sales literature printed by truck manufacturers over the years. We have tried to minimize the use of different abbreviations. However, since original sales literature was used as a reference source by many contributors, some have asked to see abbreviations printed as they appear in factory printed materials. Thus, there will be slight variations in the use of abbreviations. For example, both 4x4 and 4WD have been approved factory abbreviations for four-wheel-drive trucks.

The above chart lists abbreviations found in this catalog, except those so common in usage that no special explanation is required.

INTRODUCTION

Take it from me, creating this catalog was more challenging, frustrating and nerve-wracking than any other book we've ever worked on. But it's been exciting to venture where no one has gone before; to create something significantly new.

Light-duty trucks are becoming a big part of the vehicle collecting hobby. You can still find them on the streets and buy them at affordable prices. For obvious reasons, they're cheaper to restore than cars. They have fewer parts, less chrome and easier-to-duplicate interiors. Yet, when nicely fixed-up, they demand high prices. This means there's a good margin for investment.

Collectors can paint their trucks nearly any color — like the factory did on special order. They can gold-leaf their names on the side, personalize the truck with countless options — even advertise a business. Yet, judges won't deduct for such things at a show.

Light-duty trucks have high utility value. They're built tough and they don't bruise easily. You can use them (with regular license plates) to work as well as play. Four-wheel-drive models will take you almost anywhere.

Other advantages in truck collecting include high availability of parts and simplicity of construction. Truck clubs tend to be multi-marque and somewhat low key. This adds extra fun to participation in hobby activities.

Not available — until now — was a comprehensive guide for light-duty truck collectors. That's exactly what this catalog is designed to be. It tells you many things about trucks up to one-ton models. This is a cut-off that some folks will debate and others will agree with, but we had to draw the line somewhere.

Section One of the catalog includes detailed, year-by-year coverage of 15 marques. These are presented in alphabetical order to make the data self-indexing. Following this, towards the rear of the catalog, Section Two is the "Illustrated Directory To Additional Light-Duty Truck Manufacturers." It is also self-indexing.

In addition to features, specifications and historical highlights, Section One contains estimates of current "ballpark" prices for collectable models more than seven years old. This is the point where standard "used car value guides" stop appraising vehicles. For newer models, these "used car value guides" should be referred to. They make quarterly priceupdates, which a catalog of this type cannot hope to do. Our interest is in "collector values," which change less frequently.

Price data for the pre-1980 trucks in Section One is broken down into value estimates for each model in five different condition classes. To find illustrations explaining the five condition classes, check the table of contents. You will also find "Body Style" and "Body I.D." illustrations, by artists Bob Lichty and Bob Hovorka, which show light-duty truck models and components.

In addition to pickups, panels, vans, utility vehicles and sedan deliveries, various other types of light-duty trucks and commercial cars have been covered. They include business coupes/sedans/roadsters, funeral vehicles, ambulances and certain station wagons. Truck collectors are interested in such models and this catalog is designed primarily as a guide for the efforts of serious collectors.

A great deal of the information in this catalog is what publishers call "virgin copy" — new information on a topic that's too long been ignored by automotive historians. Most of the data comes from sources such as older repair manuals, contemporary used car guides and trade journals published when the trucks were new.

There may be instances where such sources fall short, in an historic sense. For instance, a "blue book" published in April, 1934, may not list a series of new trucks introduced in June of the same year. Any first-time research efforts in a new field may encounter such ticklish problems.

Krause Publication's long-range plan is to use this catalog to expose available facts about light-duty trucks to scrutiny by hobbyists, collectors, historians and experts in car and truck literature. This may bring forth contributions of expanded information, new research and additional photos.

This particular edition is the result of two years work and planning by more than 12 marque researchers, two artists and scores of photo contributors. We feel it will answer a very strong need for information that light-duty truck enthusiasts require today. At the same time, we're sure it will raise questions and bring forth a flurry of facts that were not unearthed in the countless hours of study and proofreading by our editorial team. We invite every reader to provide us with the kind of feedback that will enhance future editions.

Above all else, I hope that all light-duty truck lovers will find this book fun to read, useful for answering questions and a good value for the commercial vehicle hobbyist. If so, the struggles involved in creating it will be well rewarded.

John "Gunner" Gunnell
Feb. 10, 1987

How to Use This Catalog

APPEARANCE AND EQUIPMENT: Word descriptions help identify light-duty trucks down to details such as styling features, trim and (where possible) interior appointments. Standard equipment lists begin with the lowest-priced models and, in subsequent data blocks, cover higher-priced models of the same year and make.

VEHICLE I.D. NUMBERS: The listings explain the basic serial numbering system used by light-duty truck manufacturers. These codes can help determine where, when and in what order your truck was built. Some codes also reveal body style, paint color and trim data.

SPECIFICATIONS CHART: The first column gives series/model numbers used on light-duty trucks. The second lists the chassis model and/or body styles. You may see additional body numbers or wheelbase and cargo box measurements accompanying these entries or codes like "SWB" (short wheelbase) or "LWB" (long wheelbase). Model names like SuperCab may appear in full or abbreviated form, based on space available. (A chart of abbreviations is in front of the catalog). Listed in the third column are original retail prices for the trucks. Factory shipping weights are found in column four. The fifth column provides production totals, where available for light-duty trucks. Dashes in any column indicate "information not available." Notes in any column are numbered to correspond with information appearing directly below that particular data chart in footnote form.

ENGINES: Engine data will be found below the price and weight charts for one series, or near the 'Chassis Features' data block when they apply to different series. Displacement, bore, stroke and horsepower are listed, plus a lot more data where available. Emphasis is heaviest on *base* engines.

CHASSIS: The main data compiled here consists of wheelbase measurements and tire sizes. Whenever it was obtainable, data on length, width, tread and other features was also included.

TECHNICAL: This includes basic information on type of transmission, clutch and axle used in each light-duty truck. In some cases, optional gear boxes and power train features are also listed. Braking system details and data on type of wheels was also included in the format. Since trucks have many more technical variations than cars, the simple approach has been used, emphasizing standard equipment on the base series.

OPTIONS: Extra-cost options are popular with truck collectors. These data blocks provide available information on what was offered and how much it cost. In some cases, option production totals or installation rates (in percents) show up, too.

HISTORICAL FOOTNOTES: Light-duty models are gaining recognition as an important part of America's trucking heritage. Revealing sales and production statistics; product innovations; important dates, places and personalities; performance milestones and other historical facts are highlighted in this data block.

PRICING: These charts show light-duty trucks and prices they bring in five conditions (Check index for 'Vehicle Classes' drawings). These are streamlined from complete model listings, as minor original variations may have no effect on collector values.

1939 STUDEBAKER

1939 Studebaker Coupe-Express (A&A)

MODEL L5 — SIX-CYLINDER: — For the second year in a row, the Coupe-Express front sheet metal was restyled to match the current year Studebaker car. As on Commanders and Presidents and, later, Champions, the headlights of the 1939 Coupe-Express were built into the front fenders. The front fenders were an all new design, although the high-mounted spare was retained in the right wheel well. The Commander/President split grille was also adopted on the Coupe-Express. The cab styling, pickup box and instrument panel remained unchanged from 1938 and the original 1937 rear fenders were retained. No significant mechanical changes were made from 1938. The L5 Suburban Car woody wagon and one-ton K10 Fast-Transport were continued. The K10 and larger Standard series trucks continued with the cab style introduced on the 1937 Coupe-Express. Edwards Iron Works, of South Bend, Ind., offered a small pickup box that could fit into the back of a Champion coupe with its trunk lid removed. Unlike the Coupe-Express box, the Edwards box had the "STUDEBAKER" name on the tailgate. Edwards called it both the Pick-Up Coupe and the Coupe-Delivery. Rated at only ¼-ton, the Coupe-Delivery did not really fall into the light-duty truck classification.

I.D. DATA: Serial number location: same as 1937-38. Engine number location: same as late 1938. The beginning serial numbers for the L5 Coupe-Express were L5-001 in South Bend and no 1939 Coupe-Express models were assembled in Los Angeles. The beginning engine number was H-42,501.

Model No.	Body Type	Factory Price ($)	Weight	GVW (lbs)	Prod. Total
L5 Series					
L5	Pickup	850	3250	4500	1200

ENGINE: Six-cylinder. L-head. Cast iron block. Displacement: 226.2 cu. in. Bore and stroke: 3-5/16 in. x 4⅜ in. Compression ratio: 6.0:1. Brake horsepower: 90 at 3400 R.P.M. Taxable horsepower: 26.35. Main bearings: Four. Valve lifters: Solid. Carburetor: Stromberg Model BXO-26 one-barrel.

CHASSIS & BODY: Wheelbase: 116.5 in. Overall length: 195.4 in. Height: 67.75 in. Width: 73 in. Interior pickup box dimensions: 77.25 in. long x 48.6 in. wide x 14.6 in. high. Front tread: 59.4 in. Rear tread: 59.6 in. Tires: 6.00 x 16.

TECHNICAL: Sliding gear transmission. Speeds: 3F/1R. Synchromesh in second and third. Floor or column shift controls. Single plate dry disc clutch. Planar independent front suspension. Hypoid semi-floating rear axle. Overall ratio: 4.55:1. Hydraulic brakes. Steel disc wheels. Two-stage rear springs. Front and rear Houdaille lever arm shocks. Variable ratio steering gear.

OPTIONS: Overdrive transmission. Automatic Hill Holder. Radio. Heater. Electric clock. Leather upholstery. Cigarette lighter. Rear axle: 4.82:1. Tires: 6.50 x 16. Cab-high tarpaulin pickup box cover. Locking gas cap. License plate frames. Spotlight. Clear road or amber fog lights. Wig-wag oscillating stop light. Windshield washer. Bumper and grille guards. Fender guide. Fabric radiator cover.

HISTORICAL: As in 1937 and 1938, no 1939 L5 Suburban Car woody wagons are known to have survived. The Suburban Car production is included in the Coupe-Express production figures and no breakdowns have been discovered. The economy took a definite upturn in 1939, but Coupe-Express sales only increased 20 percent over 1938 and were still way below the 1937 figure.

Pricing

	5	4	3	2	1
1939					
Model 9A, Commander Six					
Cpe Express	1350	2700	4500	6300	9000

VEHICLE CLASSES SCALE

You will find drawings below, and on the next few pages, which illustrate the *Old Cars Weekly* 1-to-5 collector vehicle grading scale. Next to the small drawings on the bottom of this page are word descriptions that explain each numbered grade of condition.

The 1-to-5 grading scale for collector vehicles was developed by Krause Publications over 10 years ago. These standard number-coded categories are currently being used by thousands of car and truck collectors throughout the world. According to this well-accepted system, the five classes used to establish the condition of vintage vehicles are:

1) Excellent; 2) Fine; 3) Very Good; 4) Good and 5) Restorable.

After you've determined the condition of the truck you own or want to buy, look it up under the proper make, model and year in the catalog. When you locate the proper page listing, you will find a "Pricing Chart" for your model. The left-hand column of each "Pricing Chart" includes the trucks offered that particular year. (Note: these are somewhat condensed from the complete model listings, since there may be no difference, in collector value, between a "light" three-quarter ton pickup and a "heavy" three-quarter ton pickup or between, say, Suburbans with end-gates or panel-style doors.)

Some body style descriptions may be abbreviated, such as 'Dely.' for 'delivery' truck. Elsewhere in *The Standard Catalog of American Light-Duty Trucks* you will find a chart of standard abbreviations used.

In addition to a listing of truck-lines and body styles, you will find five columns with single bold-faced numbers at the top of each column. The Number 5 column tells you the truck's 'ballpark' value in **RESTORABLE** condition. Next comes column Number 4, which gives the truck's approximate current worth in **GOOD** condition. The column headed Number 3 gives the average price in **VERY GOOD** condition. The Number 2 column is for trucks in **FINE** shape. If the truck looks as fresh and new as the day that it first left the factory, you'll find its 'ballpark' value in column Number 1 (**EXCELLENT**) at the right-hand side of the chart. These values are a good indication of retail prices that collectors might pay for such a truck in a range of different conditions.

Keep in mind that all prices listed herein are for complete vehicles that could be put back on the road. Trucks with pieces missing or those that are useful only for the obsolete parts on them may fall well below the value of a Number 5 vehicle. Modified trucks or those that are over-restored cannot be valued using our charts. However, if the modifications are slight, it may be possible to estimate a value by factoring-in the cost of taking the truck back to 100 percent original condition.

EXCELLENT CONDITION

FINE CONDITION

VERY GOOD CONDITION

GOOD CONDITION

RESTORABLE CONDITION   **VEHICLE CLASSES**

1) EXCELLENT: Restored to current professional standards of quality in every area; or original with all components operating and appearing as new.

2) FINE: Well-restored; or combination of superior restoration and excellent original; or extremely well maintained original showing very minimal wear.

3) VERY GOOD: Completely operable original or older restoration showing wear; or amateur restoration; all presentable and serviceable inside and out. Also combination of well-done restoration and good operable components; or partly restored car with all parts to complete and/or valuable NOS parts.

4) GOOD: A driveable vehicle needing no or only minor work to be functional; or a deteriorated restoration; or a very poor amateur restoration. All components may need restoration to be EXCELLENT, but mostly usable "as is."

5) RESTORABLE: Needs complete restoration of body, chassis, interior. Not driveable, but is not weathered, wrecked or stripped to the point of being useful only for parts salvage.

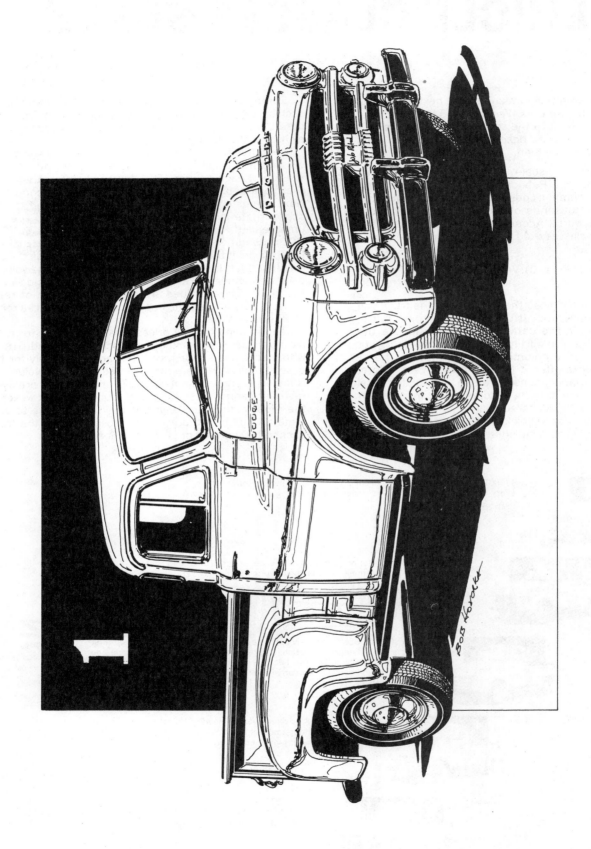

1

Bob Horocka

EXCELLENT CONDITION

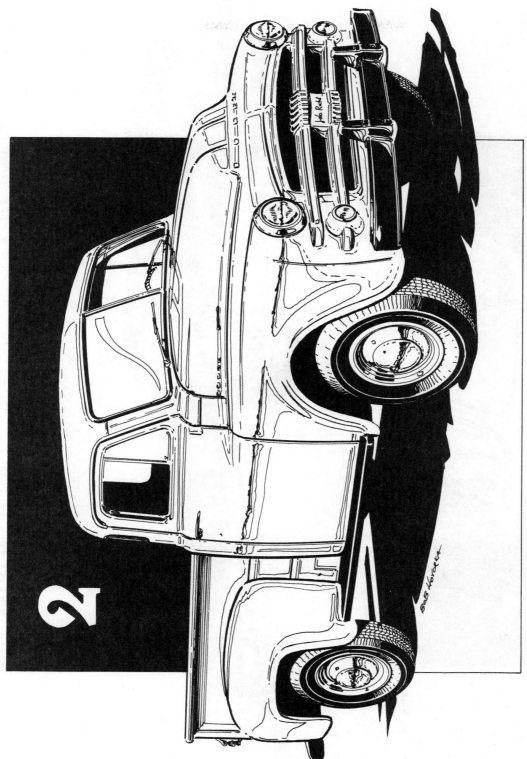

FINE CONDITION

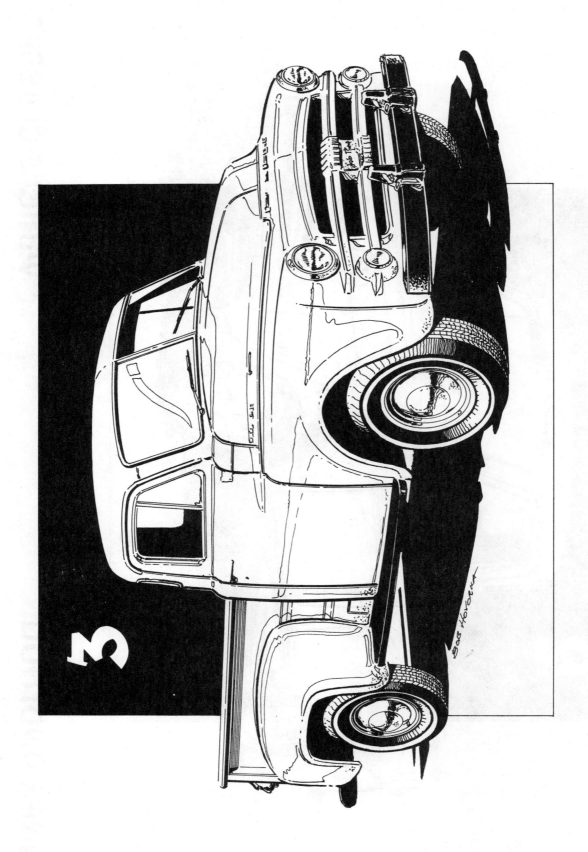

VERY GOOD CONDITION

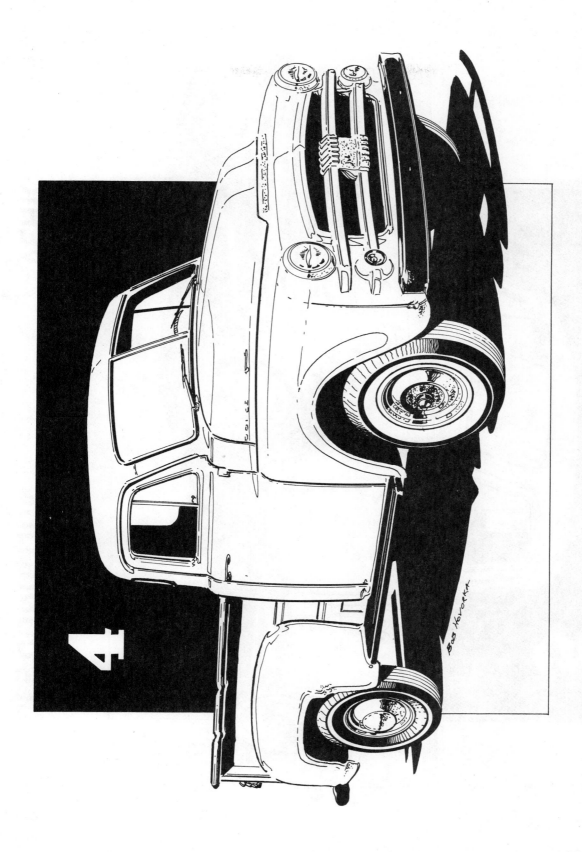

Bob Kovorka

4

GOOD CONDITION

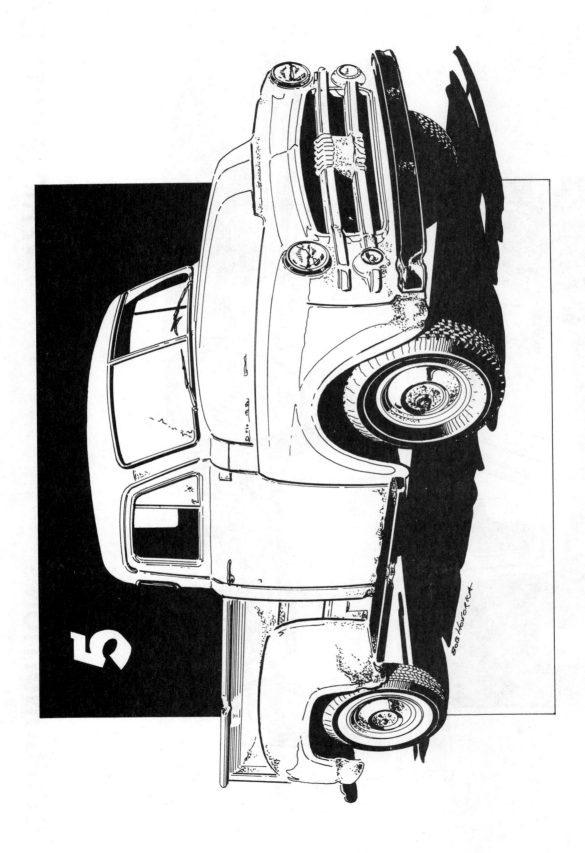

RESTORABLE CONDITION

BODY STYLES

Body style designations describe the shape and character of a truck. Over the years, truck-makers have exhibited great imagination in coining words to name their products. Here we have broken various types of trucks into five major groups: 1) Chassis; 2) Pickup; 3) Utility; 4) Delivery and 5) Station Wagon. A little background on each category is provided, along with illustrations, by artist Bob Lichty, showing representative examples. Of course, these descriptions and plates don't cover every possible variation. They are meant chiefly as a guide to the basic product lines offered by most light-duty truck manufacturers over the years.

CHASSIS MODELS: A glance at the available production break-outs in this catalog will prove that many ¾-ton or one-ton trucks (as well as a few lighter-duty models) left the factory as a bare or partially built-up chassis. These are supplied to one of the hundreds of vendors who supply purpose-built bodies to the light-duty truck industry. They may be sold as a chassis-only; chassis with flat-face cowl; chassis with cowl and windshield or chassis with all front end sheet metal except the cab. We have provided factory prices for such configurations, but have not included chassis-models in the charts of current "ballpark" values. You don't see many bare chassis in the collector's marketplace.

CHASSIS-ONLY: The term chassis-only is self-explanitory. This configuration dates back to the early days of the truck-building industry, when few manufacturers built their own commercial vehicle bodies. The chassis only is used for a wide variety of purpose-built trucks, as well as motorhomes, buses and an assortment of other vehicles. Most manufacturers worked in conjunction with "approved" body and equipment suppliers in merchandising their bare chassis. Chevrolet, for example, annually prints the *Silver Book*, an interesting piece of factory literature that describes the kinds of specialty bodies recommended for Chevrolet chassis-trucks.

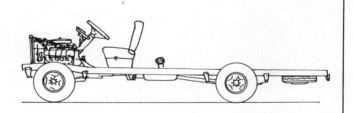

CHASSIS and CAB: The chassis and cab is the starting point for conventional pickups and many other light-duty truck models. At the start of pickup truck history, most manufacturers sold the various vehicle components as options for a buyer to add to his chassis and cab. For instance, as late as 1952, the IHC ½-ton chassis and cab was $1,375 and the buyer could then add a 6½ foot ($93); eight-foot ($108) or nine-foot ($127) cargo box body depending on whether the 115-, 127- or 134-inch wheelbase was ordered. For years, buying a pickup was like assembling a scale model.

PICKUP: Dictionaries define this type of vehicle as a small, open body delivery truck built on a chassis comparable to a passenger car. This seems slightly outdated when you think of a modern one-ton Crew Cab pickup with flared rear fenders, dual rear wheels and a fiberglass camper shell. Common among all pickups, however, is a box-like cargo container called an express box, pickup box, cargo box, dispatch box, grain box or any of several other names. Early pickups were known as "express" models. The term "pick-up" was adopted and, later, became "pickup."

FARM WAGON: Farmers used horsedrawn buckboards with cargo boxes before cars were even invented. Early motorized versions became known as farm wagons. Among the first to provide such a model were IHC and Sears, who offered cargo boxes for their high-wheeler autos. By about 1910, most car-makers could supply delivery boxes — often with flared-out sideboards — for installation on the chassis of a touring car with the rear tonneau removed. These were usually called delivery wagons, at first, and later became known as express trucks. Other names were also used by some companies.

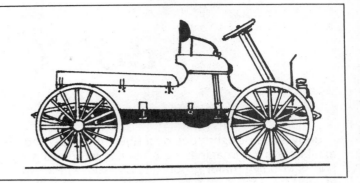

COUPE-EXPRESS: The coupe-express was more of a business car than a truck, although it fits the dictionary definition of a pickup perfectly. In many cases, this type of vehicle was originated in the late 1920s, when slip-in cargo boxes were released as optional equipment for business coupes. By the mid-1930s, the coupe-express (or coupe-pickup) was a regular model in numerous companies' commercial car-lines. The cargo box designs varied: some were bolted-on, some slipped into the trunk and others telescoped in-and-out like a dresser drawer. A few manufacturers preferred a fixed-position box, sometimes having a tailgate.

SEDAN PICKUP: In simple terms, this type of vehicle combines the front sheet metal of a two-door sedan with the cargo box of a pickup. But, describing trucks isn't "simple." For one thing, some coupe-express trucks are actually similar to sedan pickups. For another thing, a few of the best known sedan pickups have actually evolved from station wagons. Many compare these trucks to the "Utes" offered, for years, in Australia. However, American predecessors can also be found. Some historians prefer calling these vehicles pickup-cars or Sport pickups, since they heavily resemble automobiles and come with numerous sporty options.

FENDERSIDE PICKUP: Today, many trade names are used to describe the type of pickup on which the cargo box walls are flush with the *inside* of the rear wheels, with their fenders entirely outside the box. This permits the use of small running boards — or "steps" — between the lower rear corner of the cab and the back fenders. See the **Body I.D. Guide** illustrations for a list of the names that various manufacturers use to describe this body style. From the 1920s to the mid-1950s, virtually all pickup trucks were made this way. In recent years, there has been a revival in the popularity of fenderside pickup trucks.

SMOOTHSIDE PICKUP: The smoothside pickup features double-wall box construction, making the exterior walls of the box flush with the sides of the cab. This permits a wider box, except where the inner wheel wells protrude. A 25 percent increase in cargo capacity, over the fenderside model, is typical. Refer to the **Body I.D. Guide** illustrations for some of the trade names different truck-makers use to identify this type of truck. The smoothside pickup was popularized in the mid-1950s and has been the industry sales leader ever since. Some models come only in this form.

"COUNTRY CADILLACS:" This is the slang term often used to describe a big pickup truck with many heavy-duty options including an extra-long cargo box, flared rear fenders and dual rear wheels. In many cases, these will also be ordered with extended cabs providing either extra stowage or auxiliary seating. Often, these trucks come with slightly larger tires at the rear. Most also include optional interior and exterior trim packages, roof clearance marker lamps and West Coast type outside rearview mirrors.

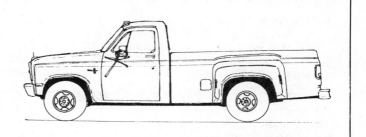

EXTENDED CAB PICKUP : Extra-long wheelbase pickups can be ordered with "stretched" cargo boxes and cabs. Shown here is the ultimate Crew Cab version with four-door styling and full rear passenger seat. Also available are Club Cab versions which have two-doors with a cab extension behind the seat. The added room may be utilized only for a secured storage area, or can be ordered with fixed or folding auxiliary seats for dual purpose use. In most cases, large "opera windows" will be added to the extended section of the cab.

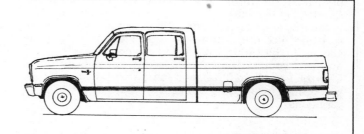

MINI-PICKUP: The "energy crunch" of the early 1970s popularized the mini-pickup, a down-sized version of the regular model. There were, however, several early minis such as the Austin, Bantam and Crosley pickups and Powell Sport Wagon. Today's minis have all of the big truck features including stretched cabs and extended wheelbases, although all are trimmer and lighter than comparable full-size models. This makes the use of smaller engines with fewer cylinders possible. In most cases, numerous sporty options are offered and look great on these pint-size pickups.

EXTENDED CAB MINI-PICKUP: Extended cab versions of the latest generation mini-pickups began to come on the market around 1982 and have been growing in popularity ever since. These trucks carry a ½-ton rating, just like their bigger brothers. They are roughly 10 inches shorter in wheelbase and some 2000 pounds lighter than a full-size extended cab model. The size and weight advantage adds up to improved efficiency, although the cargo carrying ability of these big "little" trucks is not that much less than a conventional light-duty pickup.

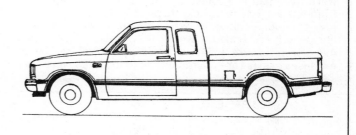

FORWARD-CONTROL PICKUP: These are pickups in which the operator sits ahead of, or above, the front wheels. In the early days of the trucking industry, this configuration was seen in Open Cab Express form. A glance at the "Illustrated Directory To Additional Light-Duty Truck Manufacturers" in this catalog will reveal photos of this format. For example, the 1915 American Argo Model K-10 Express shown on page 688. In the mid-fifties, Willys-Jeep revived this style of pickup in its famous FC-150/FC-170 series. These trucks were advanced in terms of styling and in their use of the 4x4 Jeep chassis. By the early 1960s, Chevrolet's Corvair spawned a truck-line that used the forward-control layout. It had a unique Rampside model with box sides that lowered to form a ramp. When the first compact vans appeared, in the mid-1960s, companies including Ford and Dodge had forward-control pickups among their offerings.

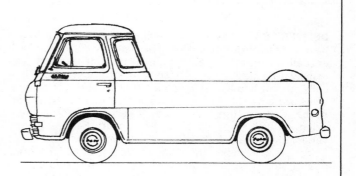

UTILITY VEHICLE: There is no dictionary definition of a Utility Vehicle. The term utility is defined as the "state or character of being useful." Thus, in truck industry terms, one must think of a vehicle that is useful in many different ways. This surely describes such dual-purpose models as the Jeep, Bronco, Scout, Jimmy, Trailduster, Ramcharger and Blazer, which can be used as cars, pickups or station wagons; for civilian or military purposes and for highway transportation or off-road use.

UTILITY PICKUP: Descriptions of this body style should start with a reading of the U.S. Army's specifications for a ¼-ton military reconaissance car it wished to have built prior to World War II. This became the Jeep, with Willys-Overland manufacturing the lion's share. After World War II, the Universal Jeep became the basis for a whole line of 4x4 and 4x2 utility models in all light-duty tonnage classes. In the 1960s, IHC refined this concept in its Scout and the Sports Utility Vehicle was born. Eventually, Chevrolet and Ford developed somewhat similar vehicles, which were followed by Dodge, Plymouth and AMC-Jeep variations.

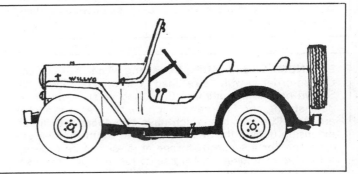

SPORT UTILITY WAGON: In addition to being available in a Jeep-like doorless configuration, IHC's original Scout also came with a variety of soft and hard top enclosures. The "hardtops" turned the Utility Pickup into a Utility Wagon. With the introduction of the Ford Bronco and Chevrolet Blazer, the popularity of this body type increased by leaps and bounds. Before long, Dodge, GMC and Plymouth were also offering Utility models in wagon form. Variations include fixed and removable tops and either tailgate/liftgate or tailgate-and-window rear end treatments.

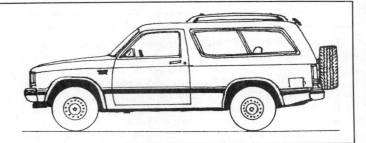

MINI-SPORT UTILITY: Like the mini-pickup, the downsized Sport Utility Wagon was a reaction to the energy crisis of the early 1970s. Some models, like the Scout II, were available in topless configuration, but most are fixed-top wagons featuring crisply tailored styling. Inline four-cylinder engines or V-6s are the power plants of choice in these scaled-down utility models. Both 4x2 and 4x4 drivetrains are available in this type of vehicle. Large expanses of glass are characteristic of the latest versions.

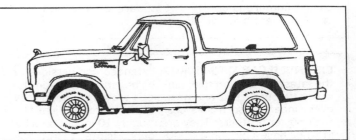

VANS and PANELS: Van is a British word that was used to describe both a railroad baggage car and a kind of vehicle, open or covered, used by tradesmen for carrying light goods. The primary dictionary definition is a "covered vehicle (usually of considerable size) for moving furniture or household effects." The term panel mainly describes a type of construction with a flat piece of material supported between girders. This is much more applicable to early auto (and truck) body building methods, but has come to mean any vehicle with panel sides.

DELIVERY CAR: This body style appeared very early in the history of light-duty trucking. The delivery car or van was actually the first type of panel truck, although it was usually on a car chassis. These vehicles are characteristically narrow and high. On some larger versions, the bodysides are bowed (or flared) outward to provide extra load space. Cabs on these trucks may be fully open or open-sided, as well as partly or fully enclosed. Early enclosed versions were called "vestibuled" delivery vans. On some "closed-cab" trucks, the roofs curved upward for higher headroom. The open cab models sometimes had a "C"-shape. Windows were often provided in the cab in various configurations.

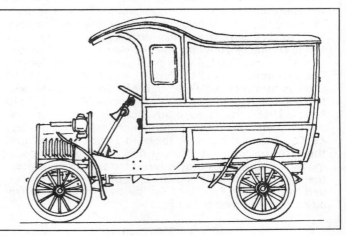

PANEL DELIVERY: The Panel Delivery or Panel truck characterizes the evolution of the Delivery Car type of body on a truck chassis. Most are lower and wider than their automobile-based ancestors. They utilize a conventional drive-train layout with the engine in front, transmission amidships and drive axle (typically) at the rear. During and after World War II, some 4x4 versions were offered, usually as an option. These are fairly rare. Panels have the front end sheet metal of trucks. Their cabs are nearly always fully enclosed.

SEDAN DELIVERY: This type of vehicle is built on either a standard or beefed-up passenger car (sometimes station wagon) chassis. Passenger car front end sheet metal is used in conjunction with a low, car-like roofline. Most sedan deliveries have panel sides, usually in place of station wagon windows. However, this name has also been used to identify commercial or business cars with two-door sedan bodies on which the rear seats are foldable, or removable, to provide a cargo stowage area. Most, if not all, sedan deliveries are two-door models.

PANEL DELIVERY VAN: These are known by a number of generic names such as Cargo Van or Commercial Van. They also go by manufacturer's trade names such as Econoline (Ford) or ChevyVan (Chevrolet). Basically, these trucks are forward-control (driver-up-front) models intended for use by tradesmen. They can have hinged or sliding cargo doors on one or both sides and usually have double panel doors at the rear. Since the late 1970s, it has been common to see long wheelbases, extended (''King-Size'') bodies, optional windows and protruding hoods (for better engine service access) on such models.

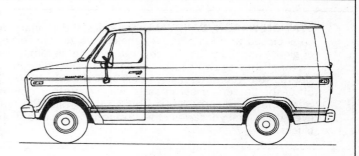

WALK-IN DELIVERY VAN: High, forward-control delivery vans are known by numerous names such as Walk-In, Door-to-door, All-purpose, Parcel Delivery, Metro or Step-Van trucks. Early milk and bakery vans of this type (usually electrics) were geared so that drivers could make door-to-door deliveries as the truck rolled slowly down the street. Bodies for such trucks are usually an aftermarket addition with many custom touches. They are of steel- or aluminum-panel construction. Dual rear wheels are a very common option. Small bus — and more recently camper — bodies are frequently seen on this type of chassis. Typical rear door configurations include double-panel and roll-up types.

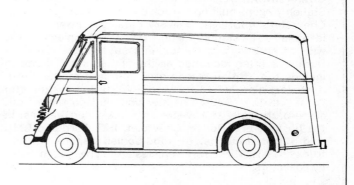

CUTAWAY DELIVERY VAN: This somewhat self-explanatory term is a good one to describe what's actually a van-based cab-and-chassis truck. Various types of bodies are essentially substituted for the ''cutaway'' rear portion of a standard van. Some have very large, high and wide cube-like cargo holds. Others are fitted with camper or mini-motorhome units. Ambulances, too, are built off the cutaway van type chassis. Steel bodies are predominant, but aluminum-body models are optional for their weight-saving advantages. In some cases, smaller models are marketed as semi-factory vehicles, while larger configurations have to be specially-ordered and purpose-built.

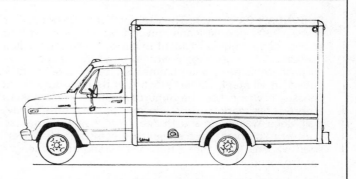

CANOPY DELIVERY: This body style dates back to the early days of light-duty trucking when express models were available with four- or eight-post tops and roll-down curtains for use in cold or stormy weather. These became popularly known as curtainside or canopied deliveries. This was a standard model, from nearly all manufacturers, for many years. In the 1930s, the same concept was used to create a version of the panel truck which had open sides to allow the display of items such as produce.

SCREENSIDE DELIVERY: Like the Canopy Delivery, the Screenside version allowed the businessman-owner to transport his goods to a location and display them to people when he got where he was going. However, in this case there were screens over the open sides. These were used either to keep merchandise from falling out or to foil would be thieves. This type of truck was also well-suited for police paddy wagon work and some services, like the Milwaukee Police Department, have restored such trucks to use in their safety and public affairs programs.

STATION WAGON/CARRYALL: The original dictionary definition of a Station Wagon is "an automobile having an enclosed wooden body of paneled design with removable seats behind the driver." The term Carryall — originally applied to a light, covered, one-horse family carriage, with two seats — later came to mean a closed motorcar having two passenger benches extending the length of the body. Station Wagons were usually considered to be commercial vehicles until the late 1930s. Thereafter, two types were often seen. One was built off of the passenger car chassis, while the other type was truck-chassis-based. Steel-bodied station wagons were known as carryall suburbans for a while. Passenger vans are sometimes called wagons, too. Whatever their idiosyncrasies, the "wagons" included in this book are basicaly passenger-carrying light-duty trucks.

COMMERCIAL STATION WAGON: This term describes Station Wagons built on a truck chassis. As early as 1920, Chevrolet's 490 Light Delivery catalog showed a truck identified as a "station wagon." It was a canopied express with three bench seats for nine passengers. Star, by Durant, is often identified as the first brand of truck to include the Station Wagon as a standard model. Ford, however, also called its Model A Station Wagon the "first." In the 1930s, Chrysler and Hudson turned out some particularly sturdy-looking truck-based wagons. In the postwar era, Dodge, Chevrolet, IHC, Ford and GMC sold a limited number of wood-bodied wagons on their truck chassis. These rare vehicles are highly sought after by collectors.

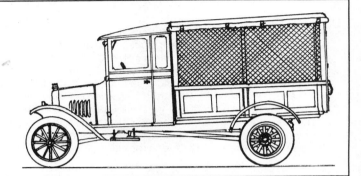

SUBURBAN CARRYALL: The Station Wagon grew popular in the 1930s as Americans moved from urban areas into smaller communities adjacent to cities. These were called "suburbs." Station Wagons were seen as the perfect dual-purpose vehicle for suburbanites. In 1935, Chevy introduced an all-steel Station Wagon on its light-duty truck chassis. It was called the Suburban. Other truck-makers entered this market with such models as the IHC Travelall, Jeep Wagoneer and Dodge Town Panel. Some use the term "carryall" to distinguish these somewhat oversized wagons from those that have standard passenger car proportions.

STANDARD PASSENGER VAN: The forward-control Volkswagen van was first seen in the early 1950s and grew increasingly popular, in the United States, as its society became more mobile. By the early 1960s, Chevrolet had developed the ''Corvan'' as a domestic counterpart. This truck-line included the Greenbriar passenger wagon. By the mid-1960s, nearly all major truck-makers were getting into the compact, forward-control van market. A natural evolution of the basic commercial cargo van was the passenger model with side windows, multiple seating arrangements and higher-level exterior and interior trim.

EXTENDED PASSENGER VAN: After the popularity of vans exploded in the 1960s, there came a time for refinements upon the theme. Hoods were extended for better engine accessibility and bodies were stretched to provide even more room for people and their luggage. These ''King-Size'' passenger vans had all of the features — windows, fancy trim, extra seats — of the standard Passenger Vans on a larger scale. Some could accomodate up to 15 passengers when equipped with special option packages.

STANDARD CATALOG CONTRIBUTORS MARQUE RESEARCHERS

ROBERT C. ACKERSON is a writer and automotive historian from Schenevus, New York. Ackerson wrote the Buick, Ford, Hudson and Lincoln sections in Krause Publication's Moto Award winning *Standard Catalog of American Cars 1805-1942*. He has also authored a number of books including *The Encyclopedia of the American Supercar* and *Ford Ranchero Source Book*. He is currently working on a new Cadillac title, soon to be released by Tab Books. Ackerson has received special recognition from the Society of Automotive Historians for material he contributed to the Cugnot Award-winning book *The Lincoln Motor Car: Sixty Years of Excellence*. The material covered the road racing Lincolns of the early 1950s. Mr. Ackerson is also the historical editor for *Keepin' Track of 'Vettes* magazine. He has done numerous articles for *Old Cars Weekly* and scores of other auto-related periodicals. His contributions to this catalog include the Chevrolet and GMC sections, plus those covering the Jeep under ownership of three different companies: Willys-Overland, Kaiser and AMC.

JIM BENJAMINSON has been active in the old car hobby since 1962, when his Aunt Clara gave him a 1932 Chevrolet pickup. This was followed, two years later, by a 1940 Plymouth. This car, which originally belonged to his father, was also a gift from Aunt Clara. The '40 was followed, that same year, by a '34 Plymouth purchased for $20. It matched a similar car his father had owned years earlier. This led to membership in the Plymouth 4 & 6 Cylinder Owners Club, in 1967, and the filling of Jim's garage with early Plymouths. Jim has been membership secretary of the ''Plymouth Club'' since 1974 and has served as editor of the club magazine — *The Plymouth Bulletin* — for the past seven years. Under his editorship the magazine received several ''Golden Quill'' awards from *Old Cars Weekly*. In 1984, Benjaminson received the M.J. Duryea award, from the Antique Automobile Club of America, for his article ''Automobile Manufacturing in North Dakota.'' Jim's articles and photos have appeared in *Old Cars Weekly*, *The Best of Old Cars Weekly*, *Special-Interest Autos* and numerous other old car and car club publications. He also founded the Powell Sport Wagon Registry in 1981. Jim researched the Fargo and Plymouth sections of this catalog.

DON BUNN researched the Dodge section of *The Standard Catalog of American Light-Duty Trucks*. He has lived in Minnesota all of his life and currently resides in Eden Prarie, a Minneapolis suburb, with his wife and son. When not involved in the old truck hobby, Don spends his time selling office furniture. He bought his first collector truck, a 1952 Dodge ½-ton pickup, during 1973 and restored it in 1980. Don still owns that Dodge, along with another, unrestored Dodge of 1951 vintage. Bunn's various old truck hobby activities included serving as President of the Light Commercial Vehicle Association. He is also the LCVA's Technical Advisor for 1948-1960 Dodge Trucks. In addition, Don writes a monthly column, entitled ''Light-Duty Trucking,'' for the leading collector tabloid *Old Cars Weekly*.

JAMES M. FLAMMANG is a full-time freelance writer/editor specializing in automobiles, computers and electronics. He has written extensively about automotive history and technology, the social impact of the motorcar, repair and restoration techniques and purchasing/ownership of both collectable and conventional vehicles. His interest in transportation dates back to childhood and encompasses just about everything that moves and carries passengers or cargo: not only trucks and cars, but also trains, buses and ships. Cars and pickup trucks of the 1930s through '50s rank as his favorites, along with vans and campers of the '60s. Flammang's latest book is *Understanding Automotive Specifications and Data*, published by Tab Books. In the late stages of production of this catalog, Jim assumed the re-writing and editing of the Dodge section, a project on which he did an outstanding job.

FRED K. FOX has been a collector vehicle enthusiast since seeing a restored Maxwell in a 1950 parade. He and wife Linda own 15 vehicles, including nine Studebakers. Fred is feature editor of *Turning Wheels*, the Studebaker Drivers Club's monthly publication, and former editor of the *Avanti Newsletter* and *The Milestone Car*. A 1985 recepient of the *Old Cars Weekly* ''Golden

(CONTINUED, page 775)

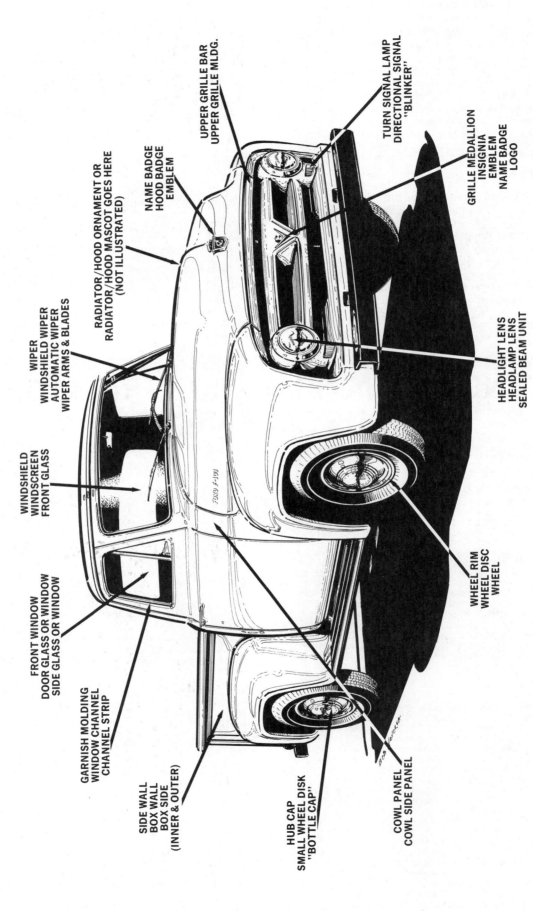

STANDARD CATALOG OF AMERICAN

Light Duty **TRUCKS**

BODY I.D. GUIDE

UPPER GRILLE BAR
UPPER GRILLE MLDG.

TURN SIGNAL LAMP
DIRECTIONAL SIGNAL
"BLINKER"

GRILLE MEDALLION
INSIGNIA
EMBLEM
NAME BADGE
LOGO

NAME BADGE
HOOD BADGE
EMBLEM

RADIATOR/HOOD ORNAMENT OR
RADIATOR/HOOD MASCOT GOES HERE
(NOT ILLUSTRATED)

WIPER
WINDSHIELD WIPER
AUTOMATIC WIPER
WIPER ARMS & BLADES

HEADLIGHT LENS
HEADLAMP LENS
SEALED BEAM UNIT

WINDSHIELD
WINDSCREEN
FRONT GLASS

FRONT WINDOW
DOOR GLASS OR WINDOW
SIDE GLASS OR WINDOW

WHEEL RIM
WHEEL DISC
WHEEL

GARNISH MOLDING
WINDOW CHANNEL
CHANNEL STRIP

SIDE WALL
BOX WALL
BOX SIDE
(INNER & OUTER)

HUB CAP
SMALL WHEEL DISK
"BOTTLE CAP"

COWL PANEL
COWL SIDE PANEL

xx

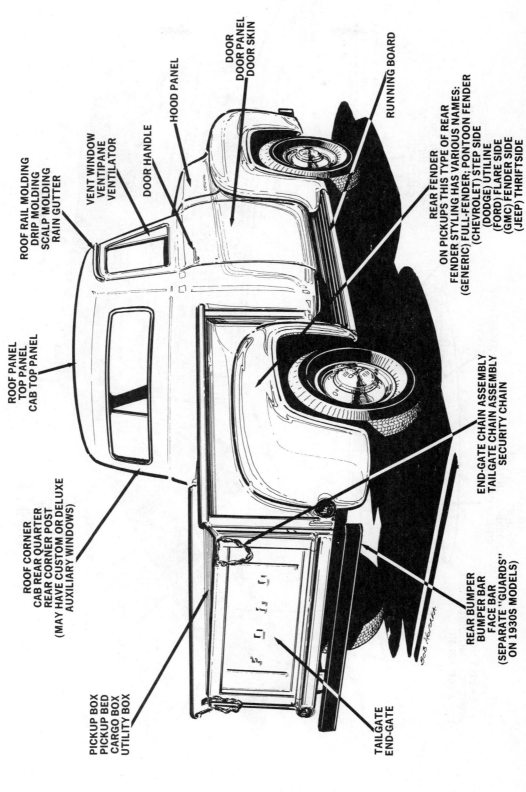

ROOF RAIL MOLDING
DRIP MOLDING
SCALP MOLDING
RAIN GUTTER

VENT WINDOW
VENTIPANE
VENTILATOR

DOOR HANDLE

HOOD PANEL

DOOR
DOOR PANEL
DOOR SKIN

RUNNING BOARD

ROOF PANEL
TOP PANEL
CAB TOP PANEL

ROOF CORNER
CAB REAR QUARTER
REAR CORNER POST
(MAY HAVE CUSTOM OR DELUXE
AUXILIARY WINDOWS)

REAR FENDER
ON PICKUPS THIS TYPE OF REAR
FENDER STYLING HAS VARIOUS NAMES:
(GENERIC) FULL-FENDER; PONTOON FENDER
(CHEVROLET) STEP SIDE
(DODGE) UTILINE
(FORD) FLARE SIDE
(GMC) FENDER SIDE
(JEEP) THRIFTSIDE

END-GATE CHAIN ASSEMBLY
TAILGATE CHAIN ASSEMBLY
SECURITY CHAIN

PICKUP BOX
PICKUP BED
CARGO BOX
UTILITY BOX

REAR BUMPER
BUMPER BAR
FACE BAR
(SEPARATE "GUARDS"
ON 1930S MODELS)

TAILGATE
END-GATE

STANDARD CATALOG OF AMERICAN

Light Duty **TRUCKS**

BODY I.D. GUIDE

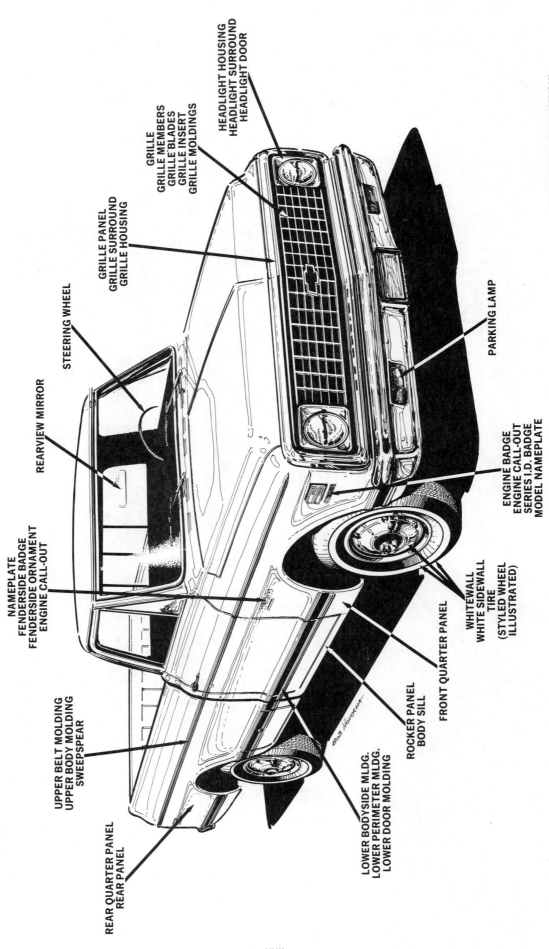

HEADLIGHT HOUSING
HEADLIGHT SURROUND
HEADLIGHT DOOR

GRILLE
GRILLE MEMBERS
GRILLE BLADES
GRILLE INSERT
GRILLE MOLDINGS

GRILLE PANEL
GRILLE SURROUND
GRILLE HOUSING

STEERING WHEEL

REARVIEW MIRROR

NAMEPLATE
FENDERSIDE BADGE
FENDERSIDE ORNAMENT
ENGINE CALL-OUT

UPPER BELT MOLDING
UPPER BODY MOLDING
SWEEPSPEAR

REAR QUARTER PANEL
REAR PANEL

PARKING LAMP

ENGINE BADGE
ENGINE CALL-OUT
SERIES I.D. BADGE
MODEL NAMEPLATE

WHITEWALL
WHITE SIDEWALL
TIRE
(STYLED WHEEL
ILLUSTRATED)

FRONT QUARTER PANEL

ROCKER PANEL
BODY SILL

LOWER BODYSIDE MLDG.
LOWER PERIMETER MLDG.
LOWER DOOR MOLDING

BODY I.D. GUIDE

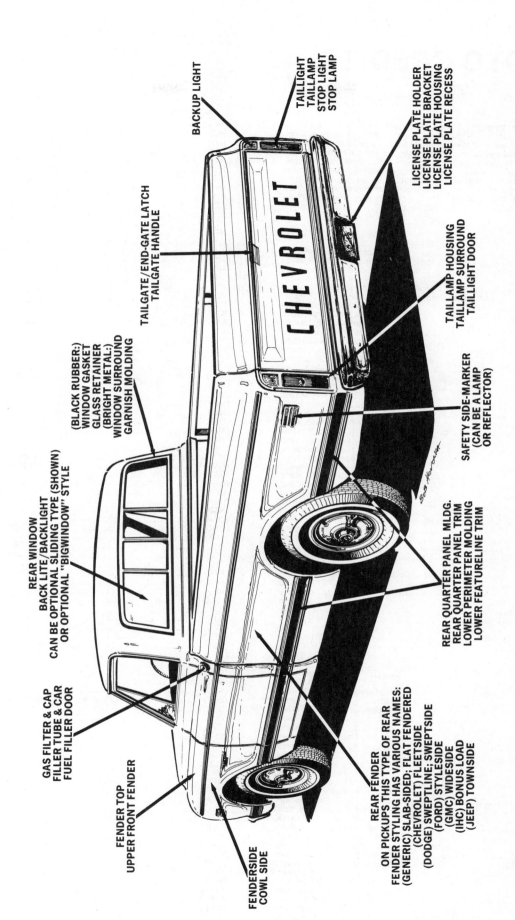

BACKUP LIGHT

TAILLIGHT
TAILLAMP
STOP LIGHT
STOP LAMP

LICENSE PLATE HOLDER
LICENSE PLATE BRACKET
LICENSE PLATE HOUSING
LICENSE PLATE RECESS

TAILGATE/END-GATE LATCH
TAILGATE HANDLE

TAILLAMP HOUSING
TAILLAMP SURROUND
TAILLIGHT DOOR

(BLACK RUBBER:)
WINDOW GASKET
GLASS RETAINER
(BRIGHT METAL:)
WINDOW SURROUND
GARNISH MOLDING

SAFETY SIDE-MARKER
(CAN BE A LAMP
OR REFLECTOR)

REAR WINDOW
BACK LITE/BACKLIGHT
CAN BE OPTIONAL SLIDING TYPE (SHOWN)
OR OPTIONAL "BIGWINDOW" STYLE

REAR QUARTER PANEL MLDG.
REAR QUARTER PANEL TRIM
LOWER PERIMETER MOLDING
LOWER FEATURELINE TRIM

GAS FILTER & CAP
FILLER TUBE & CAR
FUEL FILLER DOOR

REAR FENDER
ON PICKUPS THIS TYPE OF REAR
FENDER STYLING HAS VARIOUS NAMES:
(GENERIC) SLAB-SIDED; FLAT FENDERED
(CHEVROLET) FLEETSIDE
(DODGE) SWEPTLINE; SWEPTSIDE
(FORD) STYLESIDE
(GMC) WIDESIDE
(IHC) BONUS LOAD
(JEEP) TOWNSIDE

FENDER TOP
UPPER FRONT FENDER

FENDERSIDE
COWL SIDE

BODY I.D. GUIDE

STANDARD CATALOG OF AMERICAN
Light Duty TRUCKS

PHOTO CREDITS

Whenever possible, throughout the Catalog, we have strived to picture all light-duty trucks with photographs that show them in original form. Non-original features are noted, when necessary. Some photos show the full name (or first initial and last name) of hobbyists and collectors who are owners of light-duty trucks and contributed photos of their own vehicles. Photos contributed by other sources are identified with alphabetical codes corresponding to those in the list below. Double codes, separated by a slash mark, indicate the photo came from a collector who obtained it from another source. The double codes identify both sources. Photos without codes are from the *Old Cars Weekly* photo archives.

Photo Credits

(A&A) ... Applegate & Applegate
(ABA) ... Anheuser-Busch Archives
(ABE) ... American Body & Equipment Co.
(ACE) ... U.S. Army Corps of Engineers
(ACD) ... Auburn-Cord-Duesenberg Museum
(ACTHR) ... American Commercial Truck History & Research
(AHS) ... American Humane Society
(AMC) ... American Motors Corporation
(ASL) ... Akron-Summit County Library
(ASC) ... Antique Studebaker Club
(ATA) ... American Trucking Association
(ATC) ... Antique Truck Club of America
(ATHS) ... American Truck Historical Society
(BAC) ... Bill & Ann Clark
(BC/BCA) ... Blackhawk Classic Auto Collection
(BLHU) ... Baker Library, Harvard University
(BMM) ... Bill & Mary Mason
(BOR) ... U.S. Bureau of Reclaimation
(BS) ... Bob Strand
(BWA) ... Burkhart Wilson Associates
(BWW) ... B.W. Wine
(CAC) ... Crosley Automobile Club
(CC) ... Coca-Cola Company
(CCC) ... Crown Coach Corporation
(CDC) ... C.D. Clayton
(CE) ... Christine Eisenberg
(CHC) ... Chrysler Historical Collection
(CHP) ... California Highway Patrol
(CL) ... Carl Lirenzo
(CMD) ... Chevrolet Motor Division
(CMW) ... Christie, Manson & Woods Auctioneers
(CP) ... Crestline Publishing Company
(CPC) ... Calendar Promotions Company
(CPD) ... Chrysler-Plymouth Divisions
(CS) ... Curly Schreckenberg
(CSC) ... Cities Service Company
(CTA) ... California Trucking Association
(CW) ... Charles Webb
(CWC) ... Charles Wacker Body Company
(DB) ... Don Bunn
(DE) ... Doctor Eldoonie
(DFR) ... Durant Family Registry
(DFW) ... Donald F. Wood (SFU)
(DH) ... Don Hermany
(DHL) ... D.H. Landis
(DJE) ... David J. Entler
(DJS) ... Donald J. Summar
(DK) ... Dave Kostansek
(DNP) ... Dodge News Photo
(DPL) ... Detroit Public Library (NAHC)
(DS) ... Dennis Schrimpf
(DSM) ... Dunkirk (N.Y.) Swap Meet
(DSO) ... Daniel S. Olsen
(EK) ... Elliott Kahn
(ELC) ... Eli Lilly Company Archives
(FA) ... Firestone Archives
(FKF) ... Fred K. Fox
(FLP) ... Free Library of Philadelphia
(FLW) ... Franklin L. Walls
(FMC) ... Ford Motor Company
(FMCC) ... Ford Motor Company of Canada
(GC) ... Gillig Corporation
(GCC) ... Gast Classic Collection
(GEM) ... George E. Monroe
(GFC) ... General Foods Corporation
(GHB) ... George Heiser Body Company
(GHD) ... George H. Dammann
(GM) ... Giant Manufacturing Company
(GMC) ... General Motors Truck & Coach Division
(G-O) ... Grumman-Olsen
(GYTR) ... Goodyear Tire & Rubber Co.
(HAC) ... Harrah's Automobile Collection
(HACJ) ... Henry Austin Clark, Jr.
(HC) ... Hesse Corporation
(HCC) ... Horseless Carriage Club of America
(HCHS) ... Hobart County Historical Society
(HE) ... Hope Emerich
(HEPO) ... Hydro-Electric Power of Ontario
(HFM) ... Henry Ford Museum & Greenfield Village
(HSM) ... Hoosier Swap Meet & Auto Show
(HTM) ... Hays Truck Museum
(IBC) ... Interstate Brands Company
(IBT) ... Illinois Bell Telephone Co.
(ICS) ... Iola Car Show
(IHC) ... International Harvester Company
(IMSC) ... Indianapolis Motor Speedway Corp.
(IOA) ... Institute of Outdoor Advertising
(IPC) ... Imperial Palace Auto Collection
(JAG) ... John A. Gunnell Collection
(JAW) ... James A. Wren Automotive Research
(JB) ... Jim Benjaminson
(JB2) ... Jerry Beno (1928 Chevrolet)
(JB3) ... Jerry Bougher (1927 Pontiac)
(JBY) ... John B. Yetter
(JC) ... John Cox
(JCL) ... James C. Leake (Tulsa Auction)
(JE) ... Joe Egle
(JG) ... Jeff Gillis
(JHV) ... J.H. Valentine
(JL) ... Jon Lang
(JLB) ... James L. Bell
(JLC) ... Jefferson/Little Carlisle Auto Show
(JLM) ... Jack L. Martin
(JMS) ... John M. Sawruk
(JRH) ... J. Roddy Huft
(JS) ... John Scott
(KCMS) ... Kansas City Museum of Science
(KJC) ... Kaiser-Jeep Corporation
(KM/HW) ... Kissel Museum/Hardford, Wis.
(LC) ... Linda Clark
(LIAM) ... Long Island Automotive Museum
(LLD) ... Lewis L. Dandurand
(LOC) ... Library of Congress
(LS) ... Lorin Sorenson
(MBC/MPB) ... McCabe-Powers Body Company
(MC) ... Micheal Carbonella
(MCC) ... Mother's Cakes & Cookies, Co.
(MES) ... Missletoe Express Service
(MG) ... Mort Glashofer
(MM) ... Mike Margerum
(MPC) ... McCabe Powers Body Company
(MQ) ... Michael Querio
(MS) ... Mitch Stenzler
(MTFCA) ... Model T Ford Club of America
(MVMA) ... Motor Vehicle Manufacturer's Association
(NA) ... National Arcives
(NAHC) ... National Automotive History Collection (DPL)
(NDC) ... Nacy & Dean Cowan
(NIC) ... Navistar International Company (IHC)
(NSPC) ... National Steel Products Company
(OCW) ... Old Cars Weekly
(OHS) ... Oregon Historical Society
(PMD) ... Pontiac Motor Division
(POC) ... Plymouth 4 & 6 Cylinder Owners Club
(POCI) ... Pontiac Oakland Club International
(PS) ... Pierce-Arrow Society
(PTC) ... Pacific Telephone Company
(RAW) ... Raymond A. Wawrzyniak
(RB) ... Russell Brown
(RCK) ... Robert C. Krause
(RJ) ... Rolland Jerry
(RJT) ... Robert J. Theimer
(RLC) ... R.L. Carr
(RPZ) ... R. Perry Zavitz
(RSB) ... Rank & Sons Buick (Wally Rank)
(RT) ... Robert Trueax
(RVH) ... Richard Vander Haak
(RVM) ... Rearview Mirror Museum
(RWC) ... Ramsey Winch Company
(SAB) ... Saskatchewan Archives Board
(SBT) ... Southern Bell Telephone & Telegraph Company
(SCC) ... SCC Promotion Club (Tom Lutzi, V.P.)
(SI) ... Smithsonian Institute
(SM) ... Steve Mostowa
(SSP) ... Standard Steel Products Co.
(SWT) ... S. Ward Tiernan
(TDB) ... Tommy D. Bascom
(TL) ... Tom Lutzi
(TSC) ... The Stockland Company
(UPS) ... United Parcel Service
(USFS) ... United States Forest Service
(USPS) ... United States Park Service
(VCCA) ... Vintage Chevrolet Club of America
(VHTM) ... Van Horn's Truck Museum
(VVC) ... Vita's Vintage Collection
(VWC) ... Volvo-White Company, Inc.
(WAD) ... Walter A. Drew
(WEPS) ... Western Electric Photographic Services
(WJP) ... Willard J. Prentice
(WLB) ... William L. Bailey
(WOM) ... Walter O. McIlvain
(WPL) ... Wisconsin Power & Light Company
(WRHS) ... Western Reserve Historical Society
(WRL) ... Western Reserve Library
(WS) ... Wayne Sorenson

AMC-JEEP

By Robert C. Ackerson

American Motors purchased Jeep, from Kaiser Industries, in February, 1970. At first, AMC retained such established model designations as CJ (Civilian Jeep), Wagoneer, Gladiator and Jeepster Commando. Almost immediately, the new owner began a program of dressing-up its products and streamlining marketing techniques to widen the Jeep models' appeal.

By 1971, offerings had been pared-down from 38 to 22 models. The following season the venerable four-cylinder Jeep engine disappeared, too. In its place came AMC-built inline sixes and overhead valve V-8s, the top option being a 360 cubic inch (5.9-liter) V-8, offering up to 195 horsepower.

1970 AMC-Jeepster Commando Station Wagon (RPZ)

The die for the future was cast, in 1973, when the AMC-Jeep line was neatly divided into "truck" and "non-truck" models, all with name (rather than number) designations. The trucks came in single-wall Thriftside and double-wall Townside configurations. They were simply called Jeep Trucks and were no longer referred to as Gladiators. Jeep, Commando and Wagoneer labels were applied to other models. Wagoneers and four of the lighter-duty pickups had AMC's new "Quadra-Trac" full-time 4x4 setup wherein four-wheel-drive was always in use, but each wheel could spin at its own speed, making two-wheel-drive unnecessary.

1971 AMC-Jeep Super Wagoneer (RPZ)

Optional exterior woodgrain trims, bright bodyside moldings and new two-tone paint treatments were made available to spruce up appearances. Color-coded instrumentation, marked with international symbols, included two new types of gauges: an ammeter and a clock. A full-width "electric shaver" type grille was seen again, too.

AMC's first all-new offering, a two-door sports utility vehicle, bowed in the 1974 Cherokee. It replaced the Commando and was much better suited to slugging it out with Broncos and Blazers in the sales wars. By this time, the line was down to a pair each of Wagoneers, Cherokees and Jeeps, plus three Townside pickups. It totaled nine models, each with a distinct identity. There was just enough variety for practically everyone and a lot less confusion and crossover.

Calendar year registrations reflected the success that AMC's easier-to-understand marketing program was achieving. They stood at 36,354 vehicles in 1970, but leaped to 50,926 in 1972; 68,227 in 1973 and 96,835 for 1974. Model year production surpassed the magic 100,000 unit level during 1975, when some 62,000 CJs, 14,000 pickups, 17,000 Wagoneers and 16,000 Cherokees were built.

1983 AMC-Jeep Wagoneer Limited (RPZ)

Corporately, Jeep continued to operate as a wholly owned subsidiary of AMC, with operations still based in Toledo. W.H. Jean was plant manager; J.E. MacAfee was in charge of engineering; Charles Mashigan was styling chief and E.V. Amoroso headed-up sales. John A. Conde, today a well-known automotive historian, was director of public relations.

In the later '70s, there were a number of technical changes such as adopting power disc brakes (made standard equipment in 1977) and larger six- and eight-cylinder engines. A luxurious Wagoneer Limited model-option debuted in 1979 and all other vehicles were provided with a wide choice of trim options. There was the Renegade package for CJ models and Honcho or Golden Eagle assortments for pickups. "S" and "Chief" options could also be had on Cherokees. Such extras cost up to $1,300 in 1979. This made some rare, one reason they have strong appeal to collectors today.

Despite such steep prices, many high-optioned Jeeps performed well in the marketplace during this booming period for Jeep sales. Calendar year registrations went to 107,487 in 1976; 124,843 in 1977 and 168,548 in 1978. Even in off-year 1979 — a season of industrywide slack — Jeep saw 145,583 of its vehicles titled in the United States. Then came the early '80s.

1987 AMC-Jeep Wrangler (AMC)

The years 1980 to 1982 were disasterous, not only for Jeep, but for AMC and the entire American car and truck industry. By the fall of 1983, American Motors had registered its 14th consecutive business quarter with figures written in red ink. Despite crisp new styling touches and the release of a new Scrambler model (in 1981), registrations averaged no better than 67,400 units over this three-year period.

A high note was sounded at the beginning of 1984, when the down-sized Cherokee and Wagoneer Sport Wagons were added to the AMC lineup. By this time, the company had also inked an historic agreement to produce Jeeps in China on a joint-venture basis.

A two-wheel-drive version of the Cherokee was offered for the first time in 1985 and, for 1986, down-sized and modernized Commanche pickups took their place in a revitalized and expanded Jeep product stable. Entering the stage, in mid-1986 (as a 1987 model), was the totally revised Universal type Jeep known as the Wrangler. AMC claimed that this CJ-like new model "carries the illustrious badge of Jeep's off-road durability and ruggedness, but also holds out the promise of the smoothest on-road ride yet offered in a small sport utility."

1970 AMC/JEEP

1970 AMC-Jeep Gladiator Pickup (RPZ)

1970 AMC-Jeepster Commando Station Wagon (RPZ)

JEEP — 1970 SERIES — (ALL ENGINES): — After American Motors purchased Kaiser-Jeep from Kaiser Industries, in February, 1970, it renamed it the Jeep Corporation. With the acquisition of Jeep, which had sales of over $400 million, American Motors gained entry into the 4wd market, which had grown by almost 500 percent in the previous decade. Although Jeep's share of the market had fallen as other competitors had entered this field, its 20 percent share of the market was strong enough to serve as a base to re-establish Jeep as a sales leader. American Motors organized a new product development group which was assigned the long range task of developing completely new Jeep models while making improvements in the current line. For 1970 the most significant changes to be found were a new grille, for the Gladiator truck, as well as optional two-tone color combinations.

I.D. DATA: The VIN is located on the left front door hinge pillar and left firewall. The VIN has 13 symbols. The first five digits indicate series and body style. The sixth and seventh designate engine type. The last six digits are sequential serial numbers.

1970 AMC-Jeepster Commando Wagon Interior (RPZ)

Model	Body Type	Price	Weight	Prod. Total
CJ-5 — (¼-Ton) — (4x4) — (81 in. w.b.)				
	Jeep	2930	2212	—
CJ-6 — (101 in. w.b.)				
	Jeep	3026	2274	—
DJ-5 — (¼-Ton) — (2x2) — (81 in. w.b.)				
	Jeep	2396	1872	—
Jeepster — (¼-Ton) — (4x4) — (101 in. w.b.)				
	Pickup	3014	2659	—
Series J-2500 — (½-Ton) — (4x4)				
	Chassis & Cab	3361	3152	—
	Thriftside Pickup	3488	3447	—
	Townside Pickup	3516	3555	—
Series J-2600				
	Chassis & Cab	3483	3293	—
	Thriftside Pickup	3610	3588	—
	Townside Pickup	3638	3696	—
	Platform Stake	3804	3949	—
Series J-2700 — (¾-Ton) — (4x4)				
	Chassis & Cab	3649	3380	—
	Thriftside Pickup	3776	3675	—
	Townside Pickup	3804	3783	—
	Platform Stake	3790	4036	—
Series J-3500 — (½-Ton) — (4x4)				
	Chassis & Cab	3381	3176	—
	Townside Pickup	3544	3604	—
Series J-3600 — (½-Ton) — (4x4)				
	Chassis & Cab	3505	3314	—
	Townside Pickup	3667	3742	—
	Platform Stake	3860	4018	—
Series J-3700 — (¾-Ton) — (4x4)				
	Chassis & Cab	3668	3401	—
	Townside Pickup	3831	3829	—
	Platform Stake	4024	4105	—
Series J-3800 — (¾-Ton) — (4x4)				
	Chassis & Cab	4320	3792	—
Series J-4500 — (½-Ton) — (4x4)				
	Chassis & Cab	3381	3130	—
	Townside Pickup	3544	3558	—
Series J-4600				
	Chassis & Cab	3505	3268	—
	Townside Pickup	3668	3696	—

ENGINE (Optional all models except CJ-5, CJ-6, DJ-5, Jeepster): V-type. OHV. Eight-cylinder. Cast iron block. Bore & stroke: 4 x 3.25 in. Displacement: 327 cu. in. Compression ratio: 9.0:1. Brake horsepower: 250 at 4700 R.P.M. Max. Torque: 314 lb.-ft. at 2600 R.P.M. Five main bearings. Hydraulic valve lifters. Carburetor: Two-barrel.

ENGINE (Standard except CJ/DJ/Jeepster): Inline. OHV. Six-cylinder. Cast iron block. Bore & stroke: 3.75 x 3.51 in. Displacement: 232 cu. in. Compression ratio: 8.5:1. Brake horsepower: 145 at 4300 R.P.M. Torque: 215 lb.-ft. at 1600 R.P.M. Seven main bearings. Hydraulic valve lifters. Carburetor: Carter one-barrel model YF.

ENGINE (Standard CJ-5/CJ-6/DJ-5/Jeepster): Inline. F-head. Four-cylinder. Cast iron block. Bore & stroke: 3.125 x 4.375 in. Displacement: 134.2 cu. in. Compression ratio: 6.9:1. Brake horsepower: 72 at 4000 R.P.M. Torque: 114 lb.-ft. at 2000 R.P.M. Three main bearings. Mechanical valve lifters. Carburetor: Single one-barrel.

1970 AMC-Jeep CJ-5 Universal Jeep (RPZ)

ENGINE (Optional): Vee-block. Overhead valve. Six-cylinder. Cast iron block. Bore & stroke: 3.75 x 3.40 in. Displacement: 225 cu. in. Compression ratio: 9.0:1. Brake horsepower: 160 at 4200 R.P.M. Max Torque: 235 lb.-ft. at 2400 R.P.M. Hydraulic valve lifters. Carburetor: Two-barrel.

1970 AMC-Jeepster Commando Pickups (RPZ)

CHASSIS (CJ-5): Wheelbase: 81 in. Overall length: 133 in. Front tread: 48.25 in. Rear tread: 48.25 in. Tires: 6.00 x 16 in.

CHASSIS (CJ-6): Wheelbase: 101 in. Tires: 6.00 x 16 in.

CHASSIS (DJ-5): Wheelbase: 80 in. Overall length: 126 in. Front tread: 48.25 in. Rear tread: 48.25 in. Tires: 6.85 x 15 in.

CHASSIS: (Jeepster): Wheelbase: 101 in. Overall length: 168.40 in. Height: 64.2 in. Front tread: 50 in. Rear tread: 50 in. Tires: 7.35 x 15 in.

CHASSIS (J-2500/J-2600/J-2700): Wheelbase: 120 in. Overall length: 193.6 in. Front tread: 63.5 in. Rear tread: 63.8 in. Tires: (J-2500) 8.25 x 15 in.; (J-2600) 7.00 x 16 in.; (J-2700) 7.50 x 16 in.

CHASSIS (J-3500/J-3600/J-3700): Wheelbase: 126 in. Tires: (J-3500) 8.25 x 15 in.; (J-3600) 7.00 x 16 in.; (J-3700) 7.50 x 16 in.

CHASSIS (J-3800/J-4500/J-4600/J-4700): Wheelbase: 132 in. Overall length: 205.6 in. Front tread: 63.9 in. Rear tread: 64.4 in. Tires: (J-3800) 7.50 x 16 in.; (J-4500) 8.25 x 15 in.; (J-4600) 7.00 x 16 in.; (J-4700) 7.50 x 15 in.

1970 AMC-Jeep CJ-5 Universal Offroad Racer (RPZ)

TECHNICAL: Manual, synchromesh transmission. Speeds: 3F/1R. Column mounted gearshift. Dry plate clutch. (½-Ton Jeep models) semi-floating rear axle; (all others) full-floating rear axle. Hydraulic, four-wheel, drum brakes. Pressed steel wheels. Automatic transmission. Technical Options: Power steering. Four-speed manual transmission. Camper Package ($163).

OPTIONS: Rear bumper. Rear step bumper. AM radio. Clock. Camper Package ($163). West Coast mirror.

HISTORICAL: Introduced: Fall 1969. Calendar year sales: 30,842 (all series and models). Calendar year production: 45,805 (all series and models).

1970 AMC-Jeep Wagoneer Station Wagon (RPZ)

4

Pricing

	5	4	3	2	1
1970					
CJ-5	900	1800	3000	4200	6000
CJ-6	930	1860	3100	4350	6200
DJ-5	740	1470	2450	3350	4900
Jeepster	900	1800	3000	4200	6000
Series J-2500					
Thriftside Pickup	660	1320	2200	3100	4400
Townside Pickup	680	1350	2250	3150	4500
Series J-2600					
Thriftside Pickup	630	1250	2100	3000	4200
Townside Pickup	650	1300	2150	3050	4300
Platform Stake	600	1200	2000	2800	4000
Series J-2700					
Thriftside Pickup	600	1200	2000	2800	4000
Townside Pickup	620	1230	2050	2900	4100
Platform Stake	590	1170	1950	2700	3900
Series J-3500					
Townside Pickup	620	1230	2050	2900	4100
Series J-3600					
Townside Pickup	600	1200	2000	2800	4000
Platform Stake	570	1140	1900	2650	3800
Series J-3700					
Townside Pickup	590	1170	1950	2700	3900
Platform Stake	560	1100	1850	2600	3700
Series J-4500					
Townside Pickup	570	1140	1900	2650	3800
Series J-4600					
Townside Pickup	560	1100	1850	2600	3700

1971 AMC/JEEP

1971 AMC-Jeep Commando station wagon (OCW)

JEEP — 1971 SERIES — (ALL ENGINES): — No appearance changes were made for either the Jeep CJ or J-series trucks for 1971. Early in 1971 the AMC 304 and 360 cu. in. V-8 engines became optional for the J-series trucks, while the AMC 258 cu. in. six-cyl. became their standard power plant.

I.D. DATA: Unchanged from 1971.

Model	Body Type	Price	Weight	Prod. Total
CJ-5 — (¼-Ton) — (4x4)				
	Jeep	2886	2112	—
CJ-6 — (½-Ton) — (4x4)				
	Jeep	2979	2274	—
DJ-5 — (¼-Ton) — (2x2)				
	Open	2382	1872	—
Jeepster — (½-Ton)				
	Pickup	3291	2659	—
Series J-2500 — (½-Ton) — (4x4)				
	Chassis & Cab	3251	3125	—
	Thriftside Pickup (7-ft.)	3406	3420	—
	Townside Pickup (7-ft.)	3406	3528	—
Series J-3800 — (¾-Ton) — (4x4)				
	Chassis & Cab	4113	3792	—
	Townside Pickup	4264	4220	—

Model	Body Type	Price	Weight	Prod. Total
Series J-4500 — (½-Ton) — (4x4)				
	Chassis & Cab	3281	3151	—
	Townside Pickup (8-ft.)	3443	3579	—
Series J-4600 — (½-Ton) — (4x4)				
	Chassis & Cab	3405	3289	—
	Townside Pickup (8-ft.)	3567	3717	—
Series J-4700 — (¾-Ton) — (4x4)				
	Chassis & Cab	3567	3378	—
	Townside Pickup (8-ft.)	3729	3806	—
Series J-4800 — (¾-Ton) — (4x4)				
	Chassis & Cab	4218	3806	—
	Townside Pickup (8-ft.)	4370	4294	—

ENGINE (Standard CJ-5/CJ-6/DJ-5/Jeepster): Inline. F-head. Four-cylinder. Cast iron block. Bore & stroke: 3.125 x 4.375 in. Displacement: 134.2 cu. in. Compression ratio: 6.9:1. Brake horsepower: 72 at 4000 R.P.M. Torque: 114 lb.-ft. at 2000 R.P.M. Three main bearings. Mechanical valve lifters. Carburetor: One-barrel.

ENGINE (Standard: J-2500, J-4500, J-4600, J-4700): Inline. OHV. Six-cylinder. Cast iron block. Bore & stroke: 3.75 x 3.9 in. Displacement: 258 cu. in. Compression ratio: 8.0:1. Brake horsepower: 110 at 3500 R.P.M. Seven main bearings. Hydraulic valve lifters. Carburetor: Carter one-barrel model YF.

ENGINE (Standard: J-3807, J-4800): V-type. OHV. Eight-cylinder. Cast iron block. Bore & stroke: 4.08 x 3.44 in. Displacement: 360 cu. in. Brake horsepower: 175. Five main bearings. Hydraulic valve lifters. Carburetor: Two-barrel.

CHASSIS (Jeepster): Wheelbase: 101 in. Overall length: 168.40 in. Height: 64.2 in. Front tread: 50 in. Rear tread: 50 in. Tires: 7.35 x 15 in.

CHASSIS (J-2500): Wheelbase: 120 in. Overall length: 193.6 in. Front tread: 63.5 in. Rear tread: 63.8 in. Tires: 8.25 x 15 in.

CHASSIS (J-3800/J-4500/J-4600/J-4700/J-4800): Wheelbase: 132 in. Overall length: 205.6 in. Front tread: 63.9 in. Rear tread: 64.4 in. Tires: (J-4500) 8.25 x 15 in.; (J-4600) 7.00 x 16 in.; (J-4700) 7.50 x 16 in.; (J-4800) 7.50 x 16 in.

CHASSIS (CJ-5): Wheelbase: 81 in. Overall length: 133 in. Front tread: 48.25 in. Rear tread: 48.25 in. Tires: 6.00 x 16 in.

CHASSIS (CJ-6): Wheelbase: 101 in. Tires: 6.00 x 16 in.

CHASSIS (DJ-5): Wheelbase: 81 in. Overall length: 133 in. Tires: 6.85 x 15 in.

1971 AMC-Jeep Super Wagoneer (RPZ)

TECHNICAL: Manual, synchromesh transmission. Speeds: 3F/1R. Column mounted gearshift. Dry plate clutch. (½-Ton Trucks, all CJ-5/CJ-6/DJ-5) semi-floating rear axle; (all others) full-floating rear axle. Four-wheel hydraulic, drum brakes. Pressed steel wheels. Technical Options: Four-speed manual transmission. Power steering. Camper Package ($163).

OPTIONS: Rear bumper. Rear step bumper. AM radio. Clock. Cigar lighter. Camper Package ($163).

HISTORICAL: Introduced: Fall 1970. Calendar year sales: 38,979 (all series). Calendar year production: 54,480 (all series). At the same time the evidence was clear that American Motors' efforts to broaden Jeep appeal were paying off. For the first six months of 1971 Jeep wholesale sales were up 26 percent over the same 1970 period. Overall, sales for the same period totalled 17,878 compared to 14,186 in 1970.

Pricing

1971	5	4	3	2	1
CJ-5	900	1800	3000	4200	6000
CJ-6	930	1860	3100	4350	6200
DJ-5	750	1500	2500	3500	5000
Jeepster	800	1600	2650	3700	5300
Series J-2500					
Thriftside Pickup	740	1470	2450	3350	4900
Townside Pickup	720	1450	2400	3300	4800
Series J-3800					
Townside Pickup	700	1400	2350	3250	4700
Series J-4500					
Townside Pickup	690	1380	2300	3200	4600
Series J-4600					
Townside Pickup	680	1350	2250	3150	4500
Series J-4700					
Townside Pickup	660	1320	2200	3100	4400
Series J-4800					
Townside Pickup	650	1300	2150	3050	4300

1972 AMC/JEEP

1972 AMC-Jeep Commando station wagon (OCW)

JEEP — 1972 SERIES — (ALL ENGINES): — Leading the wave of change for 1972 at Jeep was a new line of engines for the CJ models. Although the vintage F-head four-cyl. was still offered for export, the "Dauntless" V-6 was no longer available. The standard CJ engine now was the AMC 232 cu. in. six-cyl. with the larger 258 cu. in. six-cyl. and 304 cu. in. V-8 engines available as options. The CJ-5 and CJ-6 retained their familiar look, but now had longer wheelbases and increased length. In addition, their front and rear treads were increased by 3 and 1.5 in. respectively.

Also adopted was a new Dana model 30 open-end front axle and a rear axle with a capacity of 3000 pounds, which was 500 pounds greater than the unit used in 1971. Use of a Dana model 20 transfer case reduced overall noise and provided a smoother shifting procedure. Appreciated by long time Jeep fans, was the latest model's larger diameter clutch, improved heater and suspended clutch and brake pedals. Numerous new options were listed for the CJ Jeeps including a fixed rear tailgate with a rear-mounted spare, a vinyl-coated full fabric top, 15 in. wheel covers and oil and ammeter gauges.

The Commando also had a longer w.b. and the same engine lineup as the CJ models. Its appearance was changed due to a new front end with a stamped steel grille that enclosed both the head and parking lights. The Commando, like the CJ Jeep, also was equipped with an open-ended front axle, larger brakes and increased capacity clutch. Changes to the Commando's interior included repositioned front seats and reshaped rear wheel housings.

The J-series trucks now could be ordered with a new 6000 GVW capacity on the 120 in. w.b. chassis. Common to all J-trucks were larger clutches and brakes. No styling changes were made in their appearance, but interiors featured new seat trim patterns.

I.D. DATA: Unchanged from 1971. The VIN consists of 13 symbols. The first letter identifies Jeep Corporation, the second indicates year of manufacture, the third letter indicates the transmission, drivetrain and power plant. The next two numbers identify vehicle series or model. The sixth symbol (letter) identifies body style. The seventh symbol (letter) indicates model type and GVM. The next letter identifies engine. The final five numbers are the sequential serial numbers.

Model	Body Type	Price	Weight	Prod. Total
CJ-5 — (¼-Ton) — (4x4)				
83050	Jeep	2955	2437	—
CJ-6 — (¼-Ton) — (4x4)				
84050	Jeep	3045	2499	—
DJ-5 — (¼-Ton) — (2x2)				
85050	Open	2475	2255	—

Model	Body Type	Price	Weight	Prod. Total
Commando — (½-Ton) — (4x4)				
8705H	Pickup	3284	2939	—
Series J-2500 — (½-Ton) — (4x4)				
2406W	Chassis & Cab	3181	3272	—
2406W	Thriftside Pickup	3328	3567	—
2406W	Townside Pickup	3328	3675	—
Series J-2600 — (½-Ton) — (4x4)				
2406X	Thriftside Pickup	3449	3689	—
2406X	Townside Pickup	3449	3797	—
Series J-4500 — (¾-Ton) — (4x4)				
3408W	Chassis & Cab	3210	3298	—
3408W	Townside Pickup	3365	3726	—
Series J-4600 — (¾-Ton) — (4x4)				
3408X	Chassis & Cab	3331	3436	—
3408X	Townside Pickup	3486	3864	—
Series J-4700 — (¾-Ton) — (4x4)				
3408Y	Chassis & Cab	3698	3732	—
3408Y	Townside Pickup	3853	4160	—
Series J-4800 — (¾-Ton) — (4x4)				
3407Z	Chassis & Cab	4107	4013	—
3407Z	Townside Pickup	4262	4441	—

ENGINE (Standard CJ-5/CJ-6/DJ-5/Commando): Inline. OHV. Six-cylinder. Cast iron block. Bore & stroke: 3.75 x 3.5 in. Displacement: 232 cu. in. Net horsepower: 100 at 3600 R.P.M. Torque: 185 lb.-ft. at 1800 R.P.M. Seven main bearings. Hydraulic valve lifters. Carburetor: One-barrel.

ENGINE (Standard: J-2500, J-2600, J-4500, J-4600): Inline. OHV. Six-cylinder. Cast iron block. Bore & stroke: 3.75 x 3.9 in. Displacement: 258 cu. in. Compression ratio: 8.0:1. Brake horsepower: 110 at 3500 R.P.M. Max torque: 195 lb.-ft. at 2000 R.P.M. Seven main bearings. Hydraulic valve lifters. Carburetor: Carter one-barrel model YF.

ENGINE (Optional J-2500, J-4500, J-4600, ($165): V-block. OHV. Eight-cylinder. Cast iron block. Bore & stroke: 3.75 x 3.44 in. Displacement: 304 cu. in. Compression ratio: 8.4:1. Net horsepower: 150 at 4400 R.P.M. Net torque: 245 lb.-ft. at 2500 R.P.M. Five main bearings. Hydraulic valve lifters. Carburetor: Autolite 2-barrel model 2100.

ENGINE (Standard J-4700, J-4800; Optional ($212): J-2500, J-2600, J-4500, J-4600): V-type. OHV. Eight-cylinder. Cast iron block. Bore & stroke: 4.08 x 3.44 in. Displacement: 360 cu. in. Compression ratio: 8.5:1. Net horsepower: 175 at 4000 R.P.M. Net torque: 285 lb.-ft. at 2400 R.P.M. Five main bearings. Hydraulic valve lifters. Carburetor: Autolite 2-barrel.

1972 AMC-Jeep Wagoneer (JAG)

CHASSIS (CJ-5): Wheelbase: 84 in. Overall length: 138.9 in. Front tread: 51.5 in. Rear tread: 50 in. Tires: 7.35 x 15 in.

CHASSIS (CJ-6): Wheelbase: 104 in. Overall length: 158.9 in. Front tread: 51.5 in. Rear tread: 50 in. Tires: 7.35 x 15 in.

CHASSIS (DJ-5): Wheelbase: 84 in. Overall length: 138.9 in. Tires: 7.35 x 15 in.

CHASSIS (J-4500/J-4600/J-4700/J-4800): Wheelbase: 132 in. Overall length: 205.6 in. Front tread: 63.9 in. Rear tread: 64.4 in. Tires: (J-4500) 8.25 x 15 in.; (J-4600) 7.00 x 16 in.; (J-4700) 7.50 x 16 in.; (J-4800) 7.50 x 16 in.

CHASSIS (Commando): Wheelbase: 104 in. Overall length: 174.5 in. Front tread: 51.5 in. Rear tread: 50 in. Tires: 7.35 x 15 in.

CHASSIS (J-2500/J-2600): Wheelbase: 120 in. Overall length: 193.6 in. Front tread: 63.5 in. Rear tread: 63.8 in. Tires: (J-2500) 8.25 x 15 in.; (J-2600) 7.00 x 16 in.

TECHNICAL (J-Series): Manual, synchromesh transmission. Speeds: 3F/1R (J-4800 4F/1R). Column (floor J-4800) mounted gearshift. Dry plate clutch. (½-Ton Trucks, DJ-5, CJ-5, CJ-6) semi-floating rear axle; (all others) full-floating rear axle. Hydraulic drum (four-wheel) brakes. Pressed steel wheels. Technical Options: Three-speed automatic transmission. Four-speed manual transmission. Power steering. Power brakes. Trac-Lok differential. Heavy-duty cooling system. Heavy-duty alternator. Heavy-duty battery. Semi-automatic front hubs. Reserve fuel tank. Fuel tank skid plate. Heavy-duty snow plow. Winches.

TECHNICAL (CJ-5, CJ-6): Manual synchromesh transmission. Speeds: 3F/1R. Floor mounted gearshift. Dry plate clutch. Technical Options: Four-speed manual transmission. Power brakes. Power steering. Heavy-duty springs. Heavy-duty shock absorbers. Trac-Lok differential. Semi-automatic front hubs. Heavy-duty cooling system.

TECHNICAL (Commando Series): Manual synchromesh transmission. Speeds: 3F/1R. Floor mounted gearshift. Dry plate clutch. Technical Options: Three-speed automatic transmission (column shift). 4-speed (floor shift) manual transmission. Power brakes. Power steering. Heavy-duty springs. Heavy-duty shock absorbers. Heavy-duty alternator. Heavy-duty battery. Trac-Lok differential. Semi-automatic. Heavy-duty cooling system. Heavy-duty snow plow. Winches. Power take-off.

Pricing

	5	4	3	2	1
1972					
CJ-5	900	1800	3000	4200	6000
CJ-6	930	1860	3100	4350	6200
DJ-5	750	1500	2500	3500	5000
Commando	800	1600	2650	3700	5300
Series J-2500					
Thriftside Pickup	740	1470	2450	3350	4900
Townside Pickup	720	1450	2400	3300	4800
Series J-2600					
Thriftside Pickup	720	1450	2400	3300	4800
Townside Pickup	700	1400	2350	3250	4700
Series J-4500					
Townside Pickup	690	1380	2300	3200	4600
Series J-4600					
Townside Pickup	680	1350	2250	3150	4500
Series J-4700					
Townside Pickup	660	1320	2200	3100	4400
Series J-4800					
Townside Pickup	650	1300	2150	3050	4300

1973 AMC/JEEP

1973 AMC-Jeep CJ-5 Universal (JAG)

JEEP — 1973 SERIES — (ALL ENGINES): — 1973 was the year that the full impact of American Motor's development plan was apparent in the design of Jeep vehicles. The J-series trucks had new double-wall side panels for the bed, a wider tailgate (operable with one hand) and a new mechanical clutch linkage that had a longer service life and required less maintenance. The interior was distinguished by a redesigned instrument panel with increased padding and easier-to-read gauges, including "direct-reading" oil and ammeter gauges. But, the big news for the J-trucks was the availability of the full-time Quadra-Trac 4wd option. This system, offered on J-2500/2600/4500 and 4600 models, included the 360 cu. in. V-8 and automatic transmission as standard equipment. An optional low range unit was available, either as a dealer-installed feature or as original equipment, direct from the factory. Quadra-Trac allowed all four wheels to operate at their own speeds, each receiving the proper portion of driving power. The key to this system was a limited-slip differential that transmitted power to the front and rear wheels.

The CJ Jeeps were given a new, more stylish instrument panel with a large center gauge encompassing the speedometer and the temperature and fuel gauges. Mounted to the left and right of this unit were the ammeter and oil pressure gauges. Beginning in January, 1973, the Jeep "Renegade" was available. It had a standard 304 cu. in. V-8, H78 x 16 tires on styled wheels, blacked-out hood, racing stripes, fender lip extensions, dual mirrors and visors, a custom vinyl interior, rear-mounted spare tire, plus transmission and fuel tank skid plates.

In its last year of production, the Commando was given standard upgraded tires and new axle joints.

1973 AMC-Jeep Gladiator Townside Pickup (CW)

I.D. DATA: Unchanged from 1972. The VIN consists of 13 symbols. The first letter identifies Jeep Corporation, the second indicates year of manufacture, the third letter indicates the transmission, drivetrain and power plant. The next two numbers identify vehicle series or model. The sixth symbol (letter) identifies body style. The seventh symbol (letter) indicates model type and GVM. The next letter identifies engine. The final five numbers are the sequential serial numbers.

Model	Body Type	Price	Weight	Prod. Total
CJ-5 — (¼-Ton) — (4x4)				
83	Jeep	3086	2450	—
CJ-6 — (¼-Ton) — (4x4)				
84	Jeep	3176	2510	—
DJ-5 — (¼-Ton) — (4x2)				
85	Jeep	2606	2270	—
Commando — (½-Ton) — (4x4)				
88	Pickup	3382	2950	—
Series J-2500 — (½-Ton) — (4x4)				
25	Thriftside Pickup	3353	3570	—
25	Townside Pickup	3353	3715	—
Series J-2600 — (½-Ton) — (4x4)				
26	Chassis & Cab	3327	3395	—
26	Thriftside Pickup	3474	3690	—
26	Townside Pickup	3474	3835	—
Series J-4500 — (¾-Ton) — (4x4)				
45	Chassis & Cab	3235	3300	—
45	Townside Pickup	3390	3760	—
Series J-4600 — (¾-Ton) — (4x4)				
46	Chassis & Cab	3356	3435	—
46	Townside Pickup	3511	3895	—
Series J-4700 — (¾-Ton) — (4x4)				
47	Chassis & Cab	3723	3730	—
Series J-4800 — (¾-Ton) — (4x4)				
48	Chassis & Cab	4132	4015	—
48	Townside Pickup	4287	4475	—

ENGINE (Standard: Commando/CJ-5/CJ-6): Inline. OHV. Six-cylinder. Cast iron block. Bore & stroke: 3.75 x 3.5 in. Displacement: 232 cu. in. Compression ratio: 8.0:1. Brake horsepower: 145 at 4300 R.P.M. Torque: 215 lb.-ft. at 1600 R.P.M. Net horsepower: 100 at 3600 R.P.M. Torque: 185 lb.-ft. at 1800 R.P.M. Seven main bearings. Hydraulic valve lifters. Carburetor: Single Carter one-barrel model YF.

ENGINE (Standard: J-2500/J-4500/J-4600; Optional: Commando/J-4800): Inline. Six-cylinder. Cast iron block. Bore & stroke: 3.75 x 3.9 in. Displacement: 258 cu. in. Compression ratio: 8.0:1. Net horsepower: 110 at 3500 R.P.M. Net torque: 195 lb.-ft. at 2000 R.P.M. Seven main bearings. Hydraulic valve lifters. Carburetor: Single Carter one-barrel model YF.

This $200.00 Cargo Cap at no extra cost

1973 AMC-Jeep Gladiator Townside pickup (JAG)

ENGINE (Optional: Commando/CJ-5/CJ-6; Standard: CJ-5/Renegade): V-type. OHV. Eight-cylinder. Cast iron block. Bore & stroke: 3.75 x 3.44 in. Displacement: 304 cu. in. Compression ratio: 8.4:1. Net horsepower: 150 at 4200 R.P.M. Net torque: 245 lb.-ft. at 2500 R.P.M. Five main bearings. Hydraulic valve lifters. Carburetor: Single two-barrel.

ENGINE (Optional: J-2500/J-2600/J-4500/J-4700/J-4800): V-type. OHV. Eight-cylinder. Cast iron block. Bore & stroke: 4.08 x 3.44 in. Displacement: 360 cu. in. Compression ratio: 8.5:1. Net horsepower: 175 at 4000 R.P.M. Net torque: 285 lb.-ft. at 2400 R.P.M. Five main bearings. Hydraulic valve lifters. Carburetor: Single two-barrel.

ENGINE (Optional: J-2500/J-2600/J-4500/J-4700/J-4800): V-type. OHV. Eight-cylinder. Cast iron block. Bore & stroke: 4.08 x 3.44 in. Displacement: 360 cu. in. Compression ratio: 8.5:1. Net horsepower: 195 at 4400 R.P.M. Net torque: 295 lb.-ft. at 2900 R.P.M. Five main bearings. Hydraulic valve lifters. Carburetor: Single four-barrel.

1973 AMC-Jeep Super Wagoneeer (JAG)

CHASSIS (Commando): Wheelbase: 104 in. Overall length: 174.5 in. Front tread: 51.5 in. Rear tread: 50.0 in. Tires: F78-15B in.

CHASSIS (J-2500): Wheelbase: 120 in. Overall length: 193.6 in. Front tread: 63.5 in. Rear tread: 63.8 in. Tires: F78-15 in.

CHASSIS (J-2600): Wheelbase: 120 in. Overall length: 193.6 in. Front tread: 63.5 in. Rear tread: 63.8 in. Tires: 7.00 x 16 in.

CHASSIS (J-4500): Wheelbase: 132 in. Overall length: 205.6 in. Front tread: 63.9 in. Rear tread: 64.4 in. Tires: F78-15 in.

CHASSIS (J-4600): Wheelbase: 132 in. Overall length: 205.6 in. Front tread: 63.9 in. Rear tread: 64.4 in. Tires: 7.00 x 16 in.

CHASSIS (J-4700): Wheelbase: 132 in. Overall length: 205.6 in. Front tread: 63.9 in. Rear tread: 64.4 in. Tires: 7.50 x 16 in.

CHASSIS (J-4800): Wheelbase: 132 in. Overall length: 205.6 in. Front tread: 63.9 in. Rear tread: 64.4 in. Tires: 7.50 x 16 in.

CHASSIS (CJ-5): Wheelbase: 84 in. Overall length: 138.9 in. Front tread: 51.5 in. Rear tread: 50.0 in. Tires: F78-15B, four-ply.

CHASSIS (CJ-6): Wheelbase: 104 in. Overall length: 158.9 in. Front tread: 51.5 in. Rear tread: 50.0 in. Tires: F78-15B, four-ply.

1973 AMC-Jeep Wagoneer (AMC)

TECHNICAL (CJ-5, CJ-6): Manual synchromesh transmission. Speeds: 3F/1R. Floor-mounted gearshift. Semi-floating rear axle. Hydraulic drum brakes. Pressed steel wheels. Technical options: Four-speed manual transmission. Power brakes. Power steering. Heavy-duty springs. Heavy-duty shock. Variety of tire sizes. Trac-Lok differential. Semi-automatic front hubs. Heavy-duty cooling system.

TECHNICAL (Commando): Synchronized, manual transmission. Speeds: 3F/1R. Floor-mounted gearshift. Semi-floating rear axle. Technical options: Automatic Transmission. Four-speed manual transmission. Power brakes. Power steering. Heavy-duty springs. Heavy-duty shock absorbers. Heavy-duty alternator. Heavy-duty battery. Trac-Lok differential. Semi-automatic front hubs. Heavy-duty cooling system. Power take-off. Reserve fuel tank (J-Series).

TECHNICAL (J-2500/J-2600/J-4500/J-4600/J-4700/J-4800): Synchronized, manual transmission. Speeds: 3F/1R (J-4800: 4F/1R). Column-mounted gearshift (J-4800: floor-mounted). Technical options: Automaitc Transmission. Power brakes. Power steering. Four-speed manual transmission. Trac-Lok differential. Heavy-duty cooling system. Heavy-duty alternator. Heavy-duty battery. Power-take-off. Semi-automatic hubs.

OPTIONS: Chrome front bumper (CJ). Chrome rear bumper (CJ). AM Radio. Electric clock. Cigar lighter. Wheel covers. Full-width split front seat (Commando). Tinted glass. Air conditioning. Special Decor Group (Commando). Bucket seats with center armrest (J-Series). West Coast Mirrors (J-Series). Courtesy lights. Custom Decor Group (J-Series). Outside passenger side mirror. Dual horns (J-Series). Tonneau cover (J-Series). Rear step bumper (J-Series). Two-tone paint (J-Series). Wood-grain trim (J-Series). Safari top (Commando Roadster/CJ). Meta top (CJ). Fabric top (CJ). Front bucket seats (CJ). Rear bench seat (Commando).

HISTORICAL: Introduced: Fall, 1972. Calendar year sales: (Jeep sales) 68,430. Calendar year production: (all models) 94,035.

Pricing

	5	4	3	2	1
1973					
CJ-5	900	1800	3000	4200	6000
CJ-6	930	1860	3100	4350	6200
Commando Pickup	800	1600	2650	3700	5300
Series J-2500					
Thriftside Pickup	750	1500	2500	3500	5000
Townside Pickup	770	1550	2550	3600	5100
Series J-2600					
Thriftside Pickup	740	1470	2450	3350	4900
Townside Pickup	750	1500	2500	3500	5000
Series J-4500					
Townside Pickup	720	1450	2400	3300	4800
Series J-4600					
Townside Pickup	700	1400	2350	3250	4700
Series J-4800					
Townside Pickup	690	1380	2300	3200	4600

1974 AMC/JEEP

1974 AMC-Jeep "Renegade" CJ-5 Universal (AMC)

JEEP — 1974 SERIES — (ALL ENGINES): — For 1974, the Quadra-Trac four-wheel-drive system was offered on all J-series trucks with either six- or eight-cyl. engines. Other improvements included larger brakes and a shorter turning radius for the J-trucks.

I.D. DATA: Unchanged from 1973. The VIN consists of 13 symbols. The first letter identifies Jeep Corporation, the second indicates year of manufacture, the third letter indicates the transmission, drivetrain and power plant. The next two numbers identify vehicle series or model. The sixth symbol (letter) identifies body style. The seventh symbol (letter) indicates model type and GVM. The next letter identifies engine. The final five numbers are the sequential serial numbers.

1974 AMC-Jeep Townside Pickup (CW)

Model	Body Type	Price	Weight	Prod. Total
CJ-5 — (¼-Ton) — (4x4)				
83	Jeep	3574	2540	—
CJ-6 — (¼-Ton) — (4x4)				
84	Jeep	3670	2600	—
J-10 — (½-Ton) — (4x4)				
25	Townside Pickup (SWB)	3776	3770	—
45	Townside Pickup (LWB)	3837	3820	—
J-20 — (¾-Ton) — (4x4)				
46	Townside Pickup (LWB)	4375	4390	—

ENGINE (Std.: J-10; Opt.: CJ-5/CJ-6): Inline. OHV. Six-cylinder. Cast iron block. Bore & stroke: 3.85 x 3.90 in. Displacement: 258 cu. in. Compression ratio: 8.0:1. Net horsepower: 110 at 3500 R.P.M. Torque: 195 lb.-ft. at 2000 R.P.M. Seven main bearings. Hydraulic valve lifters. Carburetor: Carter one-barrel model YF.

ENGINE (Std.: J-20; Opt.: J-10): V-type. OHV. Eight-cylinder. Cast iron block. Bore & stroke: 4.08 x 3.44 in. Displacement: 360 cu. in. Compression ratio: 8.5:1. Net horsepower: 175 at 4000 R.P.M. Net torque: 285 lb.-ft. at 2400 R.P.M. Five main bearings. Hydraulic valve lifters. Carburetor: Single two-barrel.

ENGINE (Opt.: J-10/J-20): V-type. OHV. Eight-cylinder. Cast iron block. Bore & stroke: 4.17 x 3.68 in. Displacement: 401 cu. in. Net horsepower: 235 at 4600 R.P.M. Five main bearings. Hydraulic valve lifters. Carburetor: Four-barrel.

ENGINE (Std.: CJ-5/CJ-6): Inline. OHV. Six-cylinder. Cast iron block. Bore & stroke: 3.75 x 3.50 in. Displacement: 232 cu. in. Compression ratio: 8.0:1. Net horsepower: 100 at 3600 R.P.M. Net torque: 185 lb.-ft. at 1800 R.P.M. Seven main bearings. Hydraulic valve lifters. Carburetor: Carter one-barrel model YF.

ENGINE (Opt.: CJ-5/CJ-6; Std.: "Renegade"): V-type. OHV. Eight-cylinder. Cast iron block. Bore & stroke: 3.75 x 3.44 in. Displacement: 304 cu. in. Compression ratio: 8.4:1. Net horsepower: 150 at 4200 R.P.M. Net torque: 245 lb.-ft. at 2500 R.P.M. Five main bearings. Hydraulic valve lifters. Carburetor: Autolite two-barrel model 2100.

1974 AMC-Jeep "Pioneer" Townside Pickup (AMC)

CHASSIS (CJ-5): Wheelbase: 84 in. Overall length: 138.9 in. Front tread: 51.5 in. Rear tread: 50.0 in. Tires: F78-15, four-ply.

CHASSIS (CJ-6): Wheelbase: 104 in. Overall length: 158.9 in. Front tread: 51.5 in. Rear tread: 50.0 in. Tires: F78-15, four-ply.

CHASSIS (J-10): Wheelbase: 118.7/130.7 in. Overall length: 192.5/204.5 in. Height: 69.3/69.1 in. Front tread: 63.3 in. Rear tread: 63.8 in. Tires: G78-15 in.

CHASSIS (J-20): Wheelbase: 130.7 in. Overall length: 204.5 in. Height: 70.7 in. Front tread: 63.3 in. Rear tread: 63.8 in. Tires: 8.00 x 16.5D in.

TECHNICAL (CJ-5, CJ-6, J-10, J-20): Same as 1973, except new option: Quadra-Trac full-time four-wheel-drive for J-10 and J-20 models.

OPTIONS: "258" engine in CJ-5/CJ-6 ($54). "360" engine in J-10 ($201). "401" engine, in J-10 ($295); in J-20 ($94). "304" engine in CJ-5/CJ-6, exc. "Renegade" ($126). Additional options same as 1973.

1974 AMC-Jeep Wagoneer Station Wagon (AMC)

HISTORICAL: Introduced: Fall, 1973. Calendar year sales: (all Jeep models) 67,110. Calendar year production: (all models) 96,645. Innovations: CJ-5 Renegade became a regular production model. Previously it had been available only in limited numbers. Quadra-Trac full-time four-wheel-drive available for all Jeep trucks.

Pricing

1974	5	4	3	2	1
CJ-5	930	1860	3100	4350	6200
CJ-6	930	1860	3100	4350	6200
Series J-10					
Townside Pickup	720	1450	2400	3300	4800
Townside Pickup (130.7" w.b.)	700	1400	2350	3250	4700
Series J-20					
Townside Pickup	690	1380	2300	3200	4600

1975 AMC/JEEP

1975 AMC-Jeep CJ-5 Renegade w/Levis Package (AMC)

JEEP — 1975 SERIES — (ALL ENGINES): — Leading the list of appearance changes for the 1975 CJ models was the availability of the Levi's vinyl front bucket and rear bench seat feature. This was standard for the Renegade model with optional for the CJ-5. The Renegade also had a new body stripe format. Added to the CJ option list was a factory-installed AM radio with a "weatherproof" case and a fixed length whip-type antenna. The full soft top was of a new design with improved visibility and larger door openings.

The J-Series pickup trucks were available with a new "Pioneer" trim package consisting of wood-grain exterior trim, deep pile carpeting, pleated fabric seats, chrome front bumpers, bright exterior window moldings, deluxe door trim pads, bright wheel covers (J-10), bright hub caps (J-20), dual horns, locking glove box, cigar lighter, wood-grain instrument cluster trim and bright armrest overlays.

I.D. DATA: Unchanged from 1974 except as follows: Sixth symbol (letter) indicates code model and GVW, last six numbers are sequential production numbers.

1975 AMC-Jeep J-20 "Pioneer" Townside Pickup (AMC)

Model	Body Type	Price	Weight	Prod. Total
CJ-5 — (¼-Ton) — (4x4) — (84 in. w.b.)				
83	Jeep	4099	2648	—
CJ-6 — (¼-Ton) — (4x4) — (104 in. w.b.)				
84	Jeep	4195	2714	—
J-10 — (½-Ton) — (4x4) — (119/131 in. w.b.)				
25	Townside Pickup (SWB)	4228	3712	—
45	Townside Pickup (LWB)	4289	3770	—
J-20 — (¾-Ton) — (4x4) — (131 in. w.b.)				
46	Townside Pickup	4925	4333	—

ENGINE (Std.: J-10; Opt.: CJ-5/CJ-6): Inline. OHV. Six-cylinder. Cast iron block. Bore & stroke: 3.75 x 3.9 in. Displacement: 258 cu. in. Compression ratio: 8.0:1. Net horsepower: 110 at 3500 R.P.M. Torque: 195 lb.-ft. at 2000 R.P.M. Seven main bearings. Hydraulic valve lifters. Carburetor: Single Carter one-barrel.

NOTE: This engine was not available in California where a four-barrel version of the "360" V-8 was standard.

1975 AMC-Jeep Cherokee Station Wagon (AMC)

ENGINE (Std.: J-20; Opt.: J-10): V-type. OHV. Eight-cylinder. Cast iron block. Bore & stroke: 4.08 x 3.44 in. Displacement: 360 cu. in. Compression ratio: 8.5:1. Net horsepower: 175 at 4000 R.P.M. Net torque: 285 lb.-ft. at 2400 R.P.M. Five main bearings. Hydraulic valve lifters. Carburetor: Single two-barrel.

ENGINE (Opt.: J-10/J-20): V-type. OHV. Eight-cylinder. Cast iron block. Bore & stroke: 4.08 x 3.44 in. Displacement: 360 cu. in. Net horsepower: 195 at 4400 R.P.M. Five main bearings. Hydraulic valve lifters. Carburetor: Single four-barrel.

ENGINE (Opt.: J-10/J-20): V-type. OHV. Eight-cylinder. Cast iron block. Bore & stroke: 4.17 x 3.68 in. Displacement: 401 cu. in. Net horsepower: 235 at 4600 R.P.M. Five main bearings. Hydraulic valve lifters. Carburetor: Single four-barrel.

ENGINE (Std.: CJ-5/CJ-6): Inline. OHV. Six-cylinder. Cast iron block. Bore & stroke: 3.75 x 3.50 in. Displacement: 232 cu. in. Compression ratio: 8.0:1. Net horsepower: 100 at 3600 R.P.M. Net torque: 185 lb.-ft. at 1800 R.P.M. Seven main bearings. Hydraulic valve lifters. Carburetor: Carter one-barrel model YF.

ENGINE (Std.: "Renegade"; Opt.: CJ-5/CJ-6): V-type. OHV. Eight-cylinder. Cast iron block. Bore & stroke: 3.75 x 3.44 in. Displacement: 304 cu. in. Compression ratio: 8.4:1. Net horsepower: 150 at 4200 R.P.M. Net torque: 245 lb.-ft. at 2500 R.P.M. Seven main bearings. Hydraulic valve lifters. Carburetor: Autolite two-barrel model 2100.

CHASSIS (CJ-5): Wheelbase: 84 in. Overall length: 138.9 in. Height: 69.5 in. Front tread: 51.5 in. Rear tread: 50.0 in. Tires: F78-15B in.

CHASSIS (CJ-6): Wheelbase: 104 in. Overall length: 158.9 in. Height: 68.3 in. Front tread: 51.5 in. Rear tread: 50.0 in. Tires: F78-15B in.

1975 AMC-Jeep Cherokee Chief Station Wagon (AMC)

CHASSIS (J-10 SWB): Wheelbase: 119.0 in. Overall length: 193.6 in. Height: 65.9 in. Front tread: 63.1 in. Rear tread: 64.9 in. Tires: H78-15B in.

CHASSIS (J-10/J-20 LWB): Wheelbase: 131.0 in. Overall length: 205.6 in. Height: 71.3 in. Front tread: 64.8 in. Rear tread: 66.1 in. Tires: (J-10) H78-15B; (J-20/6500-lb. GVW) 8.00 x 16.5; (J-20/7200-lb. GVW) 8.75 x 16.5 in.

TECHNICAL (CJ-5, CJ-6): Manual, synchromesh transmission. Speeds: 3F/1R. Floor-mounted gearshift. Single dry disc clutch. Semi-floating rear axle. Overall ratio: 3.73:1, (optional) 4.27:1. Manual four-wheel hydraulic drum brakes. Pressed steel, five-bolt design wheels. Technical options: Warn locking hubs. Winches (mechanical or electric). Four-speed manual transmission (with 258 cu. in., one-barrel engine only). Heavy-duty cooling system. Heavy-duty springs and shock absorbers (front and rear). Rear Trac-Lok differential. 70-amp battery. 62-amp alternator. Cold climate group. Draw bar. Helper springs.

TECHNICAL (J-10, J-20): Fully synchronized. Speeds: 3F/1R. Floor-mounted gearshift. Clutch: (J-10) 10.5 in., 106.75 sq. in. area, (J-20) 11.0 in., 110.96 sq. in. area. Semi-floating rear axle; (J-20) full-floating rear axle. Overall ratio: (J-10) 3.54, 4.09:1; (J-20) 3.73:1, 4.09:1 optional. Brakes: (J-10) Hydraulic, 11 in. x 2 in.; (J-20) front power disc, 12.5 in. Wheels: (J-10) 6-bolt; (J-20) 8-bolt steel disc. Technical options: Automatic transmission Turbo Hydra-Matic. Front power disc 12.0 in. brakes (J-10). Auxiliary fuel tank. Power steering. Quadra-Trac. Rear Trak-Lok Differential (not available with Quadra-Trac). Camper Special Package. Heavy-duty battery and alternator. Four-speed transmission. Heavy-duty cooling system. Cold climate group. Heavy-duty springs and shock absorbers. Helper springs.

OPTIONS (CJ-Series): Rear Bumperettes. Radio AM, Citizen's Band. Cigar lighter and ash tray. Swing-out tire carrier. Roll bar. Power brakes. Rear seat. Forged aluminum wheels (standard with Renegade Package). Padded instrument panel (standard with Renegade package). Passenger Safety Rail. Air conditioning. "360" engine in J-10 ($201). "360" four-barrel engine in J-10 ($295); in J-20 ($94). Tachometer. Metal top (full or half). Push bumper. Outside passenger mirror.

OPTIONS (J-10, J-20): Rear bumper. Rear step bumper. Bumper guards with nerf strips. Radio AM, AM/FM stereo. Air conditioning. Sliding rear window. Cruise control. Power steering. Sport steering wheel. Leather-wrapped steering wheel. Tilt steering wheel. Steel-belted radial tires (not available for J-20). Tinted glass. Custom trim package. Light group. Convenience group. Wheel hub caps (J-20). Wheel covers (J-10). Outside passenger mirror. Two-tone paint. Aluminum cargo cap.

HISTORICAL: Introduced: Fall, 1974. Calendar year sales: (Jeep sales) 69,834. Calendar year production: (all Jeep vehicles) 105,833, (Worldwide wholesale sales) 104,936. Innovations: Introduction of Levi's seat trim. New calendar year production mark. Use of electronic ignition system on J-Series.

1975 AMC-Jeep Wagoneer Station Wagon (AMC)

10

Pricing

	5	4	3	2	1
1975					
CJ-5	950	1900	3150	4400	6300
CJ-6	930	1860	3100	4350	6200
Series J-10					
Townside Pickup	720	1450	2400	3300	4800
Townside Pickup (LWB)	700	1400	2350	3250	4700
Series J-20					
Townside Pickup	690	1380	2300	3200	4600

1976 AMC/JEEP

1976 AMC-Jeep CJ-5 Renegade (JAG)

JEEP — 1976 SERIES — (ALL ENGINES): — The major story from Jeep for 1976 was the new CJ-7 model. It was described as "the most exciting vehicle to hit the four-wheel-drive market in years". With a 93.5 in. w.b., the CJ-7 offered more front and rear legroom, more cargo space and larger, 33.8 in.-wide, door openings. The smaller CJ-5 was also available. The CJ-7 made Jeep history by being the first CJ model available with an automatic transmission and Quadra-Trac.

The Renegade package, again available for both CJ models, was upgraded to include courtesy lights under the dash, an eight-in. day/night mirror, sports steering wheel, instrument panel overlay and bright rocker panel protection molding between the front and rear wheel wells.

The CJ frame was upgraded with splayed side rails (wider in front than back) to allow for wider spacing of the rear springs. In addition, the frame had stronger crossmembers and an integral skid plate. Other revisions included use of longer and wider multi-springs, new shock absorbers and new body hold-down mounts.

The J-series trucks also had a new frame with splayed rear side rails, body hold-down mounts, springs and shocks. Its crossmembers and box section side rails were also of stronger construction. All J-trucks were equipped with an improved windshield washer system having two spray nozzles.

In January, 1976 the "Honcho" package for J-10 short w.b. models was introduced. Its primary features included five 10 x 15 in. Tracker A-T Goodyear tires with raised white lettering mounted on eight-in. slotted wheels, gold striping on the bodyside, tailgate and fenders (with black and white accents), blue Levi's denim interior, a rear step bumper and a blue sports steering wheel. The Honcho was offered in a choice of six exterior colors.

1976 AMC-Jeep CJ-5 Renegade (JAG)

1976 AMC-Jeep CJ-7 Universal (JAG)

I.D. DATA: Same VIN symbol sequence as 1975.

Model	Body Type	Price	Weight	Prod. Total
CJ-5 — (¼-Ton) — (4x4) — (84 in. w.b.)				
83	Jeep	4199	2641	—
CJ-7 — (¼-Ton) — (4x4) — (94 in. w.b.)				
93	Jeep	4299	2683	—
J-10 — (½-Ton) — (4x4) — (119/131 in. w.b.)				
25	Townside Pickup (SWB)	4643	3773	—
45	Townside Pickup (LWB)	4704	3873	—
J-20 — (¾-Ton) — (4x4) — (131 in. w.b.)				
46	Townside Pickup	5290	4285	—

1976 AMC-Jeep CJ-7 Universal Hardtop (JAG)

ENGINE (J-10/J-20): Unchanged from 1975 except option price of 360 cu. in. V-8 (two-barrel) for J-10 is now $202. The option price for the 401 cu. in. V-8 for J-10 is $296 and $94 for the J-20.

ENGINE (CJ-Series): Unchanged from 1975. CJ-7 uses same standard engine and is available with same engine options as CJ-5.

1976 AMC-Jeep Townside pickup (AMC)

CHASSIS (CJ-5): Wheelbase: 83.5 in. Overall length: 138.5 in. Height: 67.6 in. Front tread: 51.5 in. Rear tread: 50.0 in. Tires: F78-15B in.

CHASSIS (CJ-7): Wheelbase: 93.5 in. Overall length: 147.9 in. Height: 67.6 in. Front tread: 51.5 in. Rear tread: 50.0 in. Tires: F78-15B in.

CHASSIS (J-10): Wheelbase: 118.7 in. Overall length: 192.5 in. Front tread: (J-10) 63.3 in., (Honcho) 65.4 in. Rear tread: (J-10) 63.8 in., (Honcho) 65.8 in. Tires: H78-15B in.

CHASSIS (J-10/J-20 LWB): Wheelbase: 130.7 in. Overall length: 204.5 in. Front tread: 64.6 in. Rear tread: 65.9 in. Tires: (J-10) H78-15B; (J-20/6500-lb. GVW) 8.00 x 16.5; (J-20/7200-lb. GVW) 9.50 x 16.5 in.

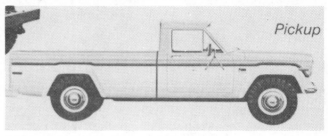

1976 AMC-Jeep Townside pickup (JAG)

TECHNICAL (J-10, J-20): Manual, synchromesh transmission. Speeds: 3F/1R. Floor-mounted gearshift. Clutch: (J-10) 10.5 in. dia., 106.75 sq. in., (J-20) 11.0 in. dia., 110.96 sq. in. Rear axle: (J-10) Semi-floating; (J-20) full-floating. Overall ratio: (J-10) 3.54:1 or 4.09:1; (J-20) 3.73:1. (J-10) Four-wheel hydraulic drum brakes. (J-20) Front disc/rear drum brakes with power assist. Pressed steel wheels. Technical Options: Automatic transmission Turbo Hydra-Matic. Four-speed manual transmission. Quadra-Trac (available with automatic transmission only). 12-in. power front disc brakes (J-10). Snow Boss plow package. Winches (mechanical or 12-volt). Auxiliary fuel tank (20 gallon, for long wheelbase only, not available for California). Rear Trac-Lok differential. Camper special package. Fuel tank skid plate. Heavy-duty battery and alternator. Heavy-duty shock absorbers. Heavy-duty springs. Heavy-duty cooling system. Cold climate package. Locking hubs (not available with Quadra-Trac). Trailer Towing Package.

1976 AMC-Jeep Cherokee (JAG)

TECHNICAL (CJ-Series): Manual, synchromesh transmission. Speeds: 3F/1R. Floor-mounted gearshift. Single dry disc clutch. Semi-floating rear axle. Overall ratio: 3.54:1. Manual, hydraulic brakes. Pressed steel, five-bolt wheels. Technical Options: Automatic Transmission. Turbo Hydro-Matic transmission. Quadra-Trac (available with automatic transmission only). Four-speed manual transmission. Extra-duty suspension system. Front stabilizer bar. Power drum brakes (available with "304" V-8 only). Low range for Quadra-Trac (available for CJ-7 only). Heavy-duty cooling system. Rear Trac-Lok differential. 70-amp battery. Heavy-duty alternator. Cold climate group. Steel belted radial ply tires. Winches. Snow plow. Free-running front hubs.

1976 AMC-Jeep Wagoneer (JAG)

OPTIONS (J-10, J-20): Front bumper guards with Nerf strips. Rear step bumper. Convenience group. Light group. Custom trim package. Radios: AM/FM stereo; Citizens Band; AM. Forged aluminum styled wheels (J-10 only). Bucket seats (Custom, Pioneer and Honcho only). Cruise control. Power steering. Tilt steering wheel. Sports steering wheel. Leather wrapped steering wheel. Sliding rear window. Dual low profile mirror. Aluminum cargo cap. Wheel covers. Honcho package. Pioneer package.

1976 AMC-Jeep Custom Wagoneer (JAG)

OPTIONS (CJ-Series): Rear step bumper. Roll bar. Full soft top. Carpeting. Convenience group. Decor group. Radios: AM or Citizens Band. Sports steering wheel. Leather wrapped sports steering wheel. Rear seat. Swing-out tire carrier. Passenger grab rail. Tachometer and Rally clock. Padded instrument panel. Removable top, injection-molded (CJ-7 only). Outside passenger mirror. Renegade package.

HISTORICAL: Introduced: Fall, 1975. Calendar year sales: (all models and series) 95,506. Calendar year production: (Worldwide wholesale sales) 125,879.

Pricing

	5	4	3	2	1
1976					
CJ-5	930	1860	3100	4350	6200
CJ-7	920	1850	3050	4300	6100
Series J-10					
Townside Pickup (SWB)	700	1400	2350	3250	4700
Townside Pickup (LWB)	690	1380	2300	3200	4600
Series J-20					
Townside Pickup (LWB)	680	1350	2250	3150	4500

1977 AMC/JEEP

1977 AMC-Jeep Honcho Townside pickup (JAG)

JEEP — 1977 SERIES — (ALL ENGINES): — This wasn't a year of dramatic appearance changes for Jeep vehicles. It was, however, a time when worthwhile and noteworthy technical improvements were made. For the first time the CJ models were available with factory air conditioning. Also debuting, as a CJ option, were power front disc brakes. To faciliate their use, the CJ Jeeps had stronger front axles and wheel spindles. Also revised was the frame. It now had fully boxed side rails. All rear body panels were also strengthened. The optional four-speed manual transmission had a new 6.32:1 low gear ratio. The popular Renegade package for the CJ-5 and CJ-7 models was continued. It now included new 9.00 x 15 "Tracker" Goodyear tires.

The most significant change made to the J-series trucks was their higher standard and optional GVW payload rating. The standard rating was increased to 6800 pounds from 6500 and the optional ratings were increased by 400 pounds to 7200 and 8000 pounds.

I.D. DATA: Same format as 1976.

Model	Body Type	Price	Weight	Prod. Total
CJ-5 —	(¼-Ton) — (4x4) — (84 in. w.b.)			
83	Jeep	4399	2659	—
CJ-7 —	(¼-Ton) — (4x4) — (94 in. w.b.)			
93	Jeep	4499	2701	—

Model	Body Type	Price	Weight	Prod. Total
J-10 —	(½-Ton) — (4x4) — (119/131 in. w.b.)			
25	Townside Pickup (SWB)	4995	3826	—
45	Townside Pickup (LWB)	5059	3926	—
J-20 —	(¾-Ton) — (4x4) — (131 in. w.b.)			
46	Townside Pickup	5607	4285	—

ENGINES: All CJ and J-Series engines were unchanged for 1977.

CHASSIS (CJ-5): Wheelbase: 83.5 in. Overall length: 138.5 in. Height: 67.6 in. Front tread: 51.5 in. Rear tread: 50.0 in. Tires: F78-15 in.

CHASSIS (CJ-7): Wheelbase: 93.5 in. Overall length: 147.9 in. Height: 67.6 in. Front tread: 51.5 in. Rear tread: 50.0 in. Tires: F78-15 in.

CHASSIS (J-10): Wheelbase: 118.7 in. Overall length: 192.5 in. Front tread: (J-10) 63.3 in.; (Honcho) 65.4 in. Rear tread: (J-10) 63.8 in.; (Honcho) 65.8 in. Tires: H78-15 in.

CHASSIS (J-10/J-20 LWB): Wheelbase: 130.7 in. Overall length: 204.5 in. Front tread: 64.6 in. Rear tread: 65.9 in. Tires: (J-10) F78-15; (J-20/6800 lb. GVW) 8.00 x 16.5; (J-20/7600-8200 lb. GVW) 9.50 x 16.5 in.

TECHNICAL (J-10, J-20): Same as 1976.

TECHNICAL (CJ-Series): Manual, synchromesh transmission. Speeds: 3F/1R. Floor-mounted gearshift. Single plate dry disc clutch. Semi-floating rear axle. Overall ratio: 3.54:1; 4.09:1. Manual, hydraulic four-wheel-drum brakes. Pressed steel wheels. Technical options: Automatic transmission Turbo Hydra-Matic. Quadra-Trac (available with Turbo Hydra-Matic only). Free-running front hubs ($95). Power steering ($166). Power front disc brakes ($73). Steering damper ($10). Front stabilizer bar ($27). Four-speed manual transmission (6.32:1 low gear). Extra-duty suspension system. Low-range for Quadra-Trac (CJ-7 only). Heavy-duty cooling system. Rear Trac-Lok differential. 70-amp. battery. Heavy-duty alternator. Cold climate group. Steel-belted radial ply tires. Winches. Snow plow.

OPTIONS (CJ-Series): Rear step bumper. Roll bar. Full soft top ($275). Carpeting ($63). Convenience group. Decor group. AM radio ($73). Citizens Band Radio. Cigar lighter and ash tray. Renegade package, CJ-5 ($839). Outside passenger mirror. Center console ($62). Air conditioning ($499). Tachometer and Rally clock ($73). Sports steering wheel. Leather wrapped sports steering wheel. Rear seat. Swing-out tire carrier. Padded instrument panel. Injection-molded removable top (CJ-7).

OPTIONS (J-10, J-20): Same as 1976 options.

HISTORICAL: Introduced: Fall, 1976. Calendar year sales: (all Jeep models and series) 115,079. Calendar year production: (Worldwide wholesales) 153,485. Innovations: Improved frame, brakes and suspension. New tires for Renegade series. Air conditioning made available for first time on CJs. "Golden Eagle" option introduced at mid-year. Historical notes: Jeep sales reached an all-time record high level in model year 1977.

Pricing

	5	4	3	2	1
1977					
CJ-5 Jeep	920	1850	3050	4300	6100
CJ-7 Jeep	900	1800	3000	4200	6000
Series J-10					
Townside Pickup (SWB)	690	1380	2300	3200	4600
Townside Pickup (LWB)	680	1350	2250	3150	4500
Series J-20					
Townside Pickup	660	1320	2200	3100	4400

NOTES: Add 10 percent for Renegade or Honcho.
Add 5 percent for hardtop.

1978 AMC/JEEP

JEEP — 1978 SERIES — (ALL ENGINES): — Technical and appearance changes for 1978 were limited. Continued into 1978, was the "Golden Eagle" option, which had been introduced in mid-1977. This year it was offered in a wider choice of colors and featured a large golden eagle decal on the hood, special striping on the grille and body, plus fender flares and gold-colored wheels. All CJ models were fitted with an improved heating system that distributed heat more efficiently, provided better fresh air ventilation and gave higher defroster temperatures. Engine efficiency was improved, due to a new ambient air intake system.

The J-series trucks also continued to be available with the Golden Eagle package. For the J-trucks it included a chrome front bumper; rear step bumper; gold eight inch spoked wheels (with black accents); 10 x 15 inch all-terrain tires; bright window frames; pickup box-mounted roll bar (with off-road driving lights); steel grille guard; Levi's bucket seats; custom interior and an engine-turned instrument cluster. Other interior appointments were tan carpeting, sports steering wheel and bright armrest overlays. A golden eagle decal was positioned on the hood and lower door panel. Gold, green and orange striping was found on the door, cab and upper box sides.

A new trim package, the "10-4" option was available for J-10 models on the short wheelbase chassis. It could be ordered in any of 10 body colors

1978 AMC-Jeep CJ-7 Renegade (JAG)

with two-tone orange and black accent striping. A two-tone orange "10-4" decal was located on the bodyside, just ahead of the rear wheels. Other features included 10 x 15 inch Tracker tires, white 15 x 8 inch wheels (with red pin striping), a bed-mounted roll bar and rear step bumper.

The J-series trucks had an additional 2.5 inch of legroom due to a modified toeboard and relocated accelerator. J-10 GVW rating for the J-10 was moved up to 6200 pounds.

I.D. DATA: Same format as 1977.

Model	Body Type	Price	Weight	Prod. Total
CJ-5 — (¼-Ton) — (4x4) — (84 in. w.b.)				
83	Jeep	5095	2738	—
CJ-7 — (¼-Ton) — (4x4) — (94 in. w.b.)				
93	Jeep	5195	2782	—
J-10 — (½-Ton) — (4x4) — (119/131 in. w.b.)				
25	Townside Pickup (SWB)	5675	3831	—
45	Townside Pickup (LWB)	5743	3898	—
J-20 — (¾-Ton) — (4x4) — (131 in. w.b.)				
46	Townside Pickup	6324	4269	—

ENGINES: Unchanged from 1978.

CHASSIS: All chassis measurements were the same as 1977. The CJ-5 and CJ-7 had new H78-15 size tires. The J-10 had the same new size tires.

TECHNICAL: Same as 1977.

OPTIONS: Most convenience and appearance options were unchanged for 1978. However, many items previously optional on the CJ models were now standard equipment. These included an ash tray and cigar lighters, passenger assist bar and passenger side exterior mirror. Standard tires were now H78-15 Suburbanite fiberglass belted types. Included in the convenience group option was an underhood light.

Added to the option list for the J-series pickups was the "10-4" appearance package.

New options for the J-trucks included an AM/FM Multiplex 8-track tape, 7-inch chrome-plated spoked steel wheels for J-10 models. A grille guard and a pickup bed mounted roll bar.

OPTIONS (J-Series): Bumper guards AM/FM stereo/Citizen's Band ($349). AM Radio ($86). AM/Citizen's Band ($229). AM/FM stereo ($229). AM/FM stereo w/tape player ($329). Sliding rear window ($79). Tinted glass ($32). "10-4" package ($619). Levis Fabric Bucket Seats ($175). Bucket seats ($155). Roll bar ($105). Air conditioning ($557). Brush guard ($69). Pickup box cap ($324). Convenience group ($83). Cruise control ($95). Custom package ($105). Golen Eagle Package, J-10 (SWB) only, with driving lights ($999); without ($974). Honcho Package, J-10 (SWB) only. Light group ($46).

OPTIONS (CJ-Series): AM radio ($86). Standard soft top ($253). Levis soft top ($292). Vinyl bucket Levis seats ($73). Vinyl bench seat ($35). Rear seat ($106). Moon roof for CJ-7 ($149). Roll bar ($70). Air conditioning ($529). Metal cab for CJ-5 ($471). Removable front carpet ($44). Removable front and rear carpet ($73). Convenience group ($27). Decor group ($105). Golden Eagle Package ($1249). Hardtop with doors, CJ-7 ($610). Renegade Package ($799).

HISTORICAL: Introduced: Fall, 1977. Calendar year sales: (all models and series) 161,912. Innovations: Many new options released. Legroom in the Jeep pickup trucks was increased. GVW ratings of Jeep trucks increased. Historical notes: To commemorate the 25th anniversary of the CJ-5 a limited edition "Silver Anniversary" CJ-5 was offered. A total of 3,000 copies were produced with a "Quick Silver" metallic finish, silver-toned Renegade accent striping black soft top, black vinyl bucket seats, silver accents and a special dashboard plaque.

Pricing

1978	5	4	3	2	1
CJ-5	920	1850	3050	4300	6100
CJ-7	900	1800	3000	4200	6000

	5	4	3	2	1
Series J-10					
Townside Pickup	690	1380	2300	3200	4600
Townside Pickup (LWB)	680	1350	2250	3150	4500
Series J-20					
Townside Pickup	660	1320	2200	3100	4400

NOTES: Add 10 percent for Renegade or Honcho.
Add 12 percent for "Golden Eagle".
Add 5 percent for hardtop.

1979 AMC/JEEP

1979 AMC-Jeep CJ-5 Renegade (RPZ)

JEEP — 1979 SERIES — (ALL ENGINES): — This was not a year of dramatic change for Jeep vehicles. The CJ series were carried over virtually unchanged. The Renegade package featured new exterior graphics. Revisions made in the J-series trucks consisted of a new front end appearance with rectangular headlights set in a grille with a slightly protruding center section and vertical blades. The front bumper no longer had a recessed middle portion. Available for all pickups was a new "high style" box enclosure. The Honcho package's body trim was also revised.

I.D. DATA: Same format as 1978.

1979 AMC-Jeep CJ-7 Renegade (RPZ)

Model	Body Type	Price	Weight	Prod. Total
CJ-5 — (¼-Ton) — (4x4) — (84 in. w.b.)				
83	Jeep	5588	2623	—
CJ-7 — (¼-Ton) — (4x4) — (94 in. w.b.)				
93	Jeep	5732	2666	—
J-10 — (½-Ton) — (4x4) — (119/131 in. w.b.)				
25	Townside Pickup (SWB)	6172	3693	—
45	Townside Pickup (LWB)	6245	3760	—
J-20 — (¾-Ton) — (4x4) — (131 in. w.b.)				
46	Townside Pickup	6872	4167	—

ENGINE (Std.: J-10/CJ-5/CJ-7): Inline. OHV. Six-cylinder. Cast iron block. Bore & stroke: 3.75 x 3.9 in. Displacement: 258 cu. in. Compression ratio: 8.0:1. Net horsepower: 110. Taxable horsepower: 33.75. Seven main bearings. Hydraulic valve lifters. Carburetor: Single two-barrel.

ENGINE (Std.: J-20; Opt.: J-10): Vee-block. OHV. Eight-cylinder. Cast iron block. Bore & stroke: 4.08 x 3.44 in. Displacement: 360 cu. in. Compression ratio: 8.25:1. Net horsepower: 175. Taxable horsepower: 53.27. Hydraulic valve lifters. Carburetor: Single two-barrel.

1979 AMC-Jeep Golden Eagle w/Hardtop (RPZ)

CHASSIS (J-10 SWB): Wheelbase: 118.7 in. Overall length: 192.5 in. Height: 69.3 in. Front tread: 63.3 in. Rear tread: 63.8 in. Tires: H78-15 in.

CHASSIS (J-10/J-20 LWB): Wheelbase: 130.7 in. Overall length: 204.5 in. Height: 69.1/70.7 in. Front tread: (J-10) 63.3 in., (J-20) 64.6 in. Rear tread: (J-10) 63.8 in., (J-20) 65.9 in. Tires: (J-10) H78-15, (J-20) 8.75 x 16.5 in.

CHASSIS (CJ-5): Wheelbase: 83.5 in. Overall length: 134.8 in. Height: 67.6 in. Front tread: 51.5 in. Rear tread: 50.0 in. Tires: H78-15 in.

CHASSIS (CJ-7): Wheelbase: 93.5 in. Overall length: 144.3 in. Height: 67.6 in. Front tread: 57.5 in. Rear tread: 50.0 in. Tires: H78-15 in.

1979 AMC-Jeep "Honcho" Townside Pickup (RPZ)

TECHNICAL (CJ-Series): Manual, synchronized transmission. Speeds: 3F/1R. Floor-mounted gearshift. Single dry disc clutch. Semi-floating rear axle. Four-wheel drum brakes. Pressed steel wheels. Options: Turbo-Hydramatic with Quadra-Trac (CJ-7 only). Four-speed manual transmission. Quadra-Trac low range. Rear Trac-Lok differential. Free-wheeling hubs. Heavy-duty cooling system. Extra-duty suspension package. Steering damper. Front stabilizer bar. Heavy-duty 70-amp. battery. Heavy-duty 63-amp. alternator. Cold Climate group.

1979 AMC-Jeep "Honcho" Townside Pickup (CW)

TECHNICAL (J-10, J-20): Fully synchronized manual transmission. Speeds: 3F/1R. Floor-mounted gearshift. Single dry disc clutch. (J-10) Semi-floating rear axle; (J-20) full-floating rear axle. Power front disc/rear drum brakes. Steel disc wheels. Options: Turbo-Hydramatic with Quadra-Trac. Four-speed manual transmission. Quadra-Trac low range. Rear Trac-Lok

differential. Free-wheeling hubs. Heavy-duty cooling system. Extra-duty suspension system. Heavy-duty shock absorbers. Front stabilizer bar. Heavy-duty 70-amp. battery. Heavy-duty 63-amp. alternator. Cold Climate group. "Snow Boss" package.

OPTIONS: Radios: AM, AM/FM, AM/CB, AM/FM/CB and AM/FM/Tape. Electric clock. Custom package ($126). Honcho package, SWB/J-10 ($824). Golden Eagle package, SWB/J-10 ($1224). "10-4" Package, SWB/J-10. 10-4 Package (J-10, 118.7 in. w.b. only). Soft feel sports steering wheel. Leather-wrapped sports steering wheel. Aluminum wheels (not available J-20). 15 inch wheel covers (not available J-20). Hub caps (J-20). Convenience group. Air conditioning. Tinted glass. Tilt steering wheel. Cruise control. Light group. Low profile mirrors. Bucket seats. Rear step bumper. Sliding rear window. Cargo cap. Roll bar. Fuel tank skid plate. Front bumper guards. Brush guards. Floor mats. Spare tire lock. Rear bumperettes. (CJ-5) Side-mounted spare and tailgate. (CJ-7) Swing-away spare tire carrier. Injection molded hardtop (CJ-7). Full metal cab (CJ-5). Removable carpet. AM radio. Moon roof (with hardtop only). Body side step. Power front disc brakes. Power steering. Tachometer and Rally clock. Tilt steering wheel. Air conditioning. Convenience group.

1979 AMC-Jeep Four-door Wagoneer Limited (RPZ)

OPTIONS (CJ Series): Renegade package ($825). Golden Eagle Package. Hardtop ($656). Decor group. 15 inch wheel covers. Soft feel steering wheel (black). Soft top. Padded instrument panel.

1979 AMC-Jeep Cherokee "S" Four-door (RPZ)

HISTORICAL: Introduced: Fall, 1978. Calendar year registrations: 145,583. Calendar year sales: (all models and series) 140,431. Calendar year production: (CJ Series) 74,878; (J-Series Pickups) 15,419. Innovations: New Renegade graphics. Jeep pickups get new front end treatment. Optional "high-style" box enclosure released.

1979 AMC-Jeep Cherokee Chief (RPZ)

	5	4	3	2	1
1979					
CJ-5 Jeep	920	1850	3050	4300	6100
CJ-7 Jeep	900	1800	3000	4200	6000
Series J-10					
Townside Pickup (SWB)	690	1380	2300	3200	4600
Townside Pickup (LWB)	680	1350	2250	3150	4500
Series J-20					
Townside Pickup	660	1320	2200	3100	4400

NOTES: Add 10 percent for Renegade or Honcho.
Add 12 percent for "Golden Eagle".
Add 5 percent for hardtop.

1980 AMC/JEEP

1980 AMC-Jeep Cherokee Police Special (JAG)

JEEP — 1980 SERIES — (ALL ENGINES): — American Motors' response to the dramatic upswing in gasoline prices and its inverse relationship to sales of off-road vehicle and four-wheel-drive light-duty trucks was pronounced. Throughout the Jeep line, transmissions were made more efficient and lighter in weight. Many models had free-wheeling front hubs and fuel conserving driveline designs. Quadra-Trac was improved by replacement of cone clutches with viscous drives.

For the CJ models, the most dramatic news was use of the General Motors 151 cubic inch, four-cylinder engine as standard power plant. Also new, was a standard, lightweight four-speed, close-ratio manual transmission. A new chassis design was adopted. It was both stronger and lighter than the unit it replaced. Free-wheeling front hubs were standard. Also installed on all CJ Jeeps was a roll bar. If the 258 cubic inch six-cylinder or 304 cubic inch V-8 were ordered for the CJ-7, they were available with a lightweight automatic transmission, part-time four-wheel-drive system and free-wheeling hubs.

Appearance changes were lead by a new soft top with steel doors and roll-up windows. Either CJ model was available with a new "Laredo" package. It included specially trimmed high-back bucket seats, chrome grille and accents, special striping and "Wrangler" radial tires.

For 1980, the J-trucks had a new lightweight, more efficient drivetrain, free-wheeling front hubs, front stabilizer bar and a high-density blow-molded fuel tank. Numerous new options were offered, including power windows and an electronic digital clock. Like the CJ models, the Jeep trucks were available with the improved Quadra-Trac, Laredo package an part-time four-wheel-drive (with either a standard four-speed manual or automatic transmission). The short-wheelbase Sportside model was available in an optional "highline" version with Honcho graphics, wooden cargo box rails and a styled roll bar.

I.D. DATA: Same format as 1979.

Model	Body Type	Price	Weight	Prod. Total
CJ-5 — (¼-Ton) — (4x4) — (84 in. w.b.)				
83	Jeep	6195	2439	—
CJ-7 — (¼-Ton) — (4x4) — (94 in. w.b.)				
93	Jeep	6445	2464	—
J-10 — (½-Ton) — (4x4) — (119/131 in. w.b.)				
25	Townside Pickup (SWB)	6874	3714	—
45	Townside Pickup (LWB)	6972	3776	—
J-20 — (¾-Ton) — (4x4) — (131 in. w.b.)				
46	Townside Pickup	7837	4246	—

ENGINE (Std.: J-10/CJ): Inline. OHV. Six-cylinder. Cast iron block. Bore & stroke: 3.75 x 3.90 in. Displacement: 258 cu. in. Compression ratio: 8.0:1. Net horsepower: 110. Taxable horsepower: 33.75. Seven main bearings. Hydraulic valve lifters. Carburetor: Single two-barrel.

ENGINE (Std.: CJ-20; Opt.: J-10): Vee-block. OHV. Eight-cylinder. Cast iron block. Bore & stroke: 4.08 x 3.44 in. Displacement: 360 cu. in. Compression ratio: 8.25:1. Net horsepower: 175. Taxable horsepower: 53.27. Five main bearings. Hydraulic valve lifters. Carburetor: Single two-barrel.

ENGINE (Std.: CJ): Inline. OHV. Four-cylinder. Cast iron block. Bore & stroke: 4.00 x 3.00 in. Displacement: 151 cu. in. Compression ratio: 8.2:1. Taxable horsepower: 21.70. Hydraulic valve lifters. Carburetor: Two-barrel.

ENGINE (Opt.: CJ): Vee-block. OHV. Eight-cylinder. Cast iron block. Bore & stroke: 3.75 x 3.44 in. Displacement: 304 cu. in. Compression ratio: 8.4:1. Net horsepower: 150. Taxable horsepower: 45. Five main bearings. Hydraulic valve lifters. Carburetor: Two-barrel.

CHASSIS (CJ-5): Wheelbase: 83.5 in. Overall length: 144.3 in. Height: 67.6 in. Front tread: 51.5 in. Rear tread: 50.0 in. Tires: H78-15 in.

CHASSIS (CJ-7): Wheelbase: 93.5 in. Overall length: 153.2 in. Height: 67.6 in. Front tread: 51.5 in. Rear tread: 50.0 in. Tires: H78-15 in.

CHASSIS (J-10 SWB): Wheelbase: 118.7 in. Overall length: 192.7 in. Height: 69.3 in. Front tread: 63.3 in. Rear tread: 63.8 in. Tires: H78-15 in.

CHASSIS (J-10/J-20 LWB): Wheelbase: 130.7 in. Overall length: 204.5 in. Height: 69.1/70.7 in. Front tread: (J-10) 63.3 in.; (J-20) 63.3 in. Rear tread: (J-10) 63.8 in.; (J-20) 64.9 in. Tires: (J-10) H78-15; (J-20) 8.75 x 16.5 in.

CHASSIS (J-10 Sportside): Wheelbase: 118.7 in. Overall length: 196.9 in. Height: 69.1 in. Front tread: 63.3 in. Rear tread: 63.8 in. Tires: H78-15 in.

TECHNICAL (CJ-Series): Manual, synchronized transmission. Speeds: 4F/1R. Floor-mounted gearshift. Single plate dry disc clutch. Semi-floating rear axle. Overall ratio: (4-cyl.) 3.73:1, (6-cyl.) 3.07:1, (V-8) 3.07:1. Manual front disc/rear drum brakes. Steel wheels. Technical Options: Automatic transmission (CJ-7). Quadra-Trac with automatic transmission (CJ-7). Heavy-duty shock absorbers. Steering stabilizer. Automatic hubs. Air overload kit. Heavy-duty cooling system. Snow plows.

TECHNICAL (J-Series): Fully synchronized, manual transmission. Speeds: 4F/1R. Floor-mounted gearshift. Single plate dry disc clutch. (J-10) Semi-floating rear axle; (J-20) full-floating rear axle. Front disc/rear drum brakes. Pressed steel wheels. Technical Options: Automatic transmission, column mounted. Quadra-Trac (with automatic transmission). Heavy-duty cooling system. Heavy-duty shock absorbers. Helper springs. Cruise control. Automatic hubs (not available with Quadra-Trac). Engine block heater. Extra-duty suspension package. Heavy-duty battery. Heavy-duty alternator. Cold climate group. Snow boss package.

OPTIONS: Chrome, painted rear bumper. Radios: AM/FM/CB. Digital clock. Custom trim package ($149). Model 25 Honcho trim package ($849). Model 25 Sportside trim package ($899). Model 25 Laredo trim package ($1600). Brush guards. Roll bar. Pickup box enclosure. Bumper Nerf strips. Tilt steering wheel. Remote mirrors. Driving lights. Automatic transmission ($333). "360" V-8 engine, J-10 ($420). Aluminum wheels. Chrome wheels. Cruise control. Running boards. Bed rails. Junior West Coast mirror. Tripod support mirror. Bodyside moldings. Splash guards. Model 25 Honcho Sportside package ($1325).

OPTIONS (CJ-5, CJ-7): Safari soft top. Skyviewer soft top. Top boot. Sun bonnet. M3 metal cab (CJ-5 only). Cab with vertical rear door (CJ-5 only). Deluxe M3 cab (CJ-5 only). Renegade package ($899). Golden Hawk package. Laredo package. Hardtop ($676). Hand held search light (all models). Assist handle. Ski rack. Bag screen. Automatic transmission ($333). "304" V-8 engine ($383). "258" six-cylinder engine ($129).

HISTORICAL: Introduced: Fall, 1979. Calendar year registrations: 81,923. Calendar year sales: (all models and series) 77,852 including: (CJ models) 47,304, (J Series Pickup) 8,656. Innovations: Four-cylinder engine returns to CJ Series. New top-of-the-line Laredo package available for pickup and CJ models. Historical notes: Jeep dealers recorded an average of 45 sales per outlet in 1980, down from an average of 77 sales per outlet in 1979 and 93 per outlet in 1978. Jeep vehicles continued to be produced exclusively in the company's Toledo, Ohio factory.

Pricing

	5	4	3	2	1
1980					
CJ-5 Jeep	900	1800	3000	4200	6000
CJ-7 Jeep	900	1800	3000	4200	6000
Series J-10					
Townside Pickup (SWB)	690	1380	2300	3200	4600
Townside Pickup (LWB)	680	1350	2250	3150	4500
Series J-20					
Townside Pickup	660	1320	2200	3100	4400

NOTES: Add 15 percent for Laredo or Honcho Sportside.
Add 10 percent for Honcho.
Add 5 percent for Sportside.
Add 5 percent for "360" V-8.

1981 AMC-Jeep Cherokee Chief (OCW)

Model	Body Type	Price	Weight	Prod. Total
CJ-5 — (¼-Ton) — (4x4) — (84 in. w.b.)				
85	Jeep	7240	2495	—
CJ-7 — (¼-Ton) — (4x4) — (94 in. w.b.)				
87	Jeep	7490	2520	—
Scrambler — (¼-Ton) — (4x4) — (104 in. w.b.)				
88	Jeep	7288	2650	—
J-10 — (½-Ton) — (4x4) — (119/131 in. w.b.)				
25	Townside Pickup (SWB)	7960	3702	—
26	Townside Pickup (LWB)	8056	3764	—
J-20 — (¾-Ton) — (4x4) — (131 in. w.b.)				
27	Townside Pickup	8766	4308	—

ENGINES: Same as 1980. Scrambler has all CJ engine options, except 304 cu. in. V-8.

CHASSIS: Same as 1980, plus:

CHASSIS (Scrambler): Wheelbase: 103.5 in. Overall length: 177.3 in. Height: 67.6 in. (70.5 w/hardtop). Front tread: 51.5 in. Rear tread: 50.0 in. Tires: H78-15 in.

TECHNICAL: Same basic specifications as comparable 1980 series. Scrambler specifications similar to those of CJ models.

1981 AMC-Jeep CJ-5 Renegade (OCW)

JEEP — 1981 SERIES — (ALL ENGINES): — CJ Jeeps for 1981 were fitted with a longer side step. CJ-7 models with the optional soft/metal top feature had a new vent window. The Renegade package, again available for either the CJ-5 or CJ-7 Jeeps, had a new graphics package in gradations of yellow, blue or red. All CJ models had a steering damper and a front anti-roll bar, plus a new front axle assembly with gas-filled upper and lower ball joint sockets.

The major physical change made to the J-trucks was a new lightweight, all-plastic slotted grille. Less noticeable, but important to the J-trucks' fuel economy, was a standard front air dam and the elimination of the pickup body's roof lip. The J-10 model was lowered by 1.25 inches, due to redesigned front and rear springs. Power steering was now standard on the J-10 models. All J-series models had low-drag brakes.

The Jeep's optional automatic transmission, which since 1980 had been the Chrysler TorqueFlite unit, now had a locking torque converter. The American Motors 258 cubic inch six-cylinder engine was redesigned to reduce its overall weight from 535 to 445 pounds.

An important addition to the Jeep line was the Scrambler pickup, which was depicted as an "import fighter."

1981 AMC-Jeep Scrambler pickup (OCW)

OPTIONS: (Jeep/Scrambler) Renegade package ($945). Laredo package ($2,049). SR Sport package ($775). Automatic transmission ($350). "304" V-8 engine ($345). "258" six-cyl. engine ($136). SL Sport package. Hardtop. Quadra Trac w/automatic transmission (CJ-7). CJ-7 wide-ratio automatic transmission (four-cyl.). Power front disc brakes. Power steering. Extra-duty suspension. Heavy-duty alternator. Heavy-duty battery. **(Jeep trucks)** Custom package ($157). Pioneer package ($559). Model 25 Honcho package ($892). Model 25, Laredo package ($1680). Model 25, Sportside package ($944). Model 25, Honcho Sportside package ($1392). Automatic transmission ($350). "360" V-8 engine ($345). Quadra Trac with automatic transmission. Heavy-duty cooling. Heavy-duty shocks. Helper springs. Cruise control. Automatic hubs (except w/Quadra Trac). Engine block heater. Extra-duty suspension. Heavy-duty battery. Heavy-duty alternator. Cold climate package. Snow Boss package.

HISTORICAL: Introduced: March 25, 1981 (Scrambler). Calendar year registrations: 58,257. Calendar year sales: (all models and series) 63,275 divided as follows: (CJ models) 30,564; (Scrambler) 7,840; (J-Series Pickups) 6,516. Innovations: Renegade package revised. Improvements to CJ front suspension. Jeep trucks restyled for fuel economy savings. Power steering becomes standard and on J-10. All-new "Scrambler" model introduced. Historical notes: AMC had a total of 1,589 dealers in 1981. The company posted a loss of $160.9 million for the year. Worldwide unit sales of Jeeps totaled $104,628 million. Jeep sales per outlet continued to fall, sliding to an average of 34 units.

1981 AMC-Jeep CJ-7 Laredo (OCW)

I.D. DATA: Location of Serial No.: The VIN is located on the top left surface of the instrument panel. There are 17 symbols in the VIN. The first three identify the manufacturer, make and vehicle type. The engine type is identified by the fourth character, which is a letter. For 1981, "B" identifies the 151 cu. in. 4-cyl.; "C" is the 258 cu. in. 6-cyl.; "N" is the 360 cu. in. V-8. The next letter identifies the transmission type. The series and body type are identified by the sixth and seventh characters respectively. These are the same as the model number. The eighth character identifies the GVW rating with the next serving as the check digit. Then follows the model year and assembly point codes. The last six digits are sequential production numbers.

1982 AMC/JEEP

1982 AMC-Jeep CJ-7 Laredo (RPZ)

1982 AMC-Jeep J-10 Honcho Pickup (RPZ)

ENGINE (Std.: J-20; Opt.: J-10): Vee-block. OHV. Eight-cylinder. Cast iron block. Bore & stroke: 4.08 x 3.44 in. Displacement: 360 cu. in. Compression ratio: 8.25:1. Net horsepower: 150 at 3400 R.P.M. Net torque: 205 lbs.-ft. at 1500 R.P.M. Five main bearings. Hydraulic valve lifters. Carburetor: Single two-barrel.

CHASSIS (CJ-5): Wheelbase: 83.4 in. Overall length: 144.3 in. Height: 69.1 in. Front tread: 52.4 in. Rear tread: 50.5 in. Tires: G78-15.

CHASSIS (CJ-7): Wheelbase: 93.4 in. Overall length: 153.2 in. Height: 69.1 in. Front tread: 55.8 in. Rear tread: 55.1 in. Tires: G78-15.

CHASSIS (Scrambler): Wheelbase: 103.4 in. Overall length: 177.2 in. Height: 69.2 in. Front tread: 55.8 in. Rear tread: 55.1 in. Tires: G78-15.

CHASSIS (J-10 SWB): Wheelbase: 118.8 in. Overall length: 194.0 in. Height: 68.5 in. Front tread: 63.3 in. Rear tread: 63.8 in. Tires: H78-15.

CHASSIS (J-10 LWB): Wheelbase: 130.8 in. Overall length: 206 in. Height: 68.3 in. Front tread: 63.3 in. Rear tread: 63.8 in. Tires: H78-15.

CHASSIS (J-10 Sportside): Wheelbase: 118.8 in. Overall length: 194 in. Height: 69.1 in. Front tread: 63.3 in. Rear tread: 63.8 in. Tires: H78-15.

CHASSIS (J-20): Wheelbase: 130.8 in. Overall length: 206 in. Height: 70.7 in. Front tread: 64.9 in. Rear tread: 65.9 in. Tires: 8.75 x 16.5.

JEEP — 1982 SERIES — (ALL ENGINES): — Both the CJ-7 and J-series trucks were offered in new trim packages for 1982. The most refined CJ model, the CJ-7 Limited, was depicted as the Jeep intended for "that special breed of drivers who want to blend an upgraded level of comfort and decor with their sports action on road and off." The Limited package included all base CJ-7 equipment, plus power steering and brakes; AM/FM radio with two speakers; a monochromatic paint scheme with color-keyed hardtop and wheel lip extensions; special dual-color bodyside striping; special grille panel; exterior "Limited" nameplates and a host of other features. Of these, the most controversial was the "special improved ride package" which gave the Limited a far softer ride than any other CJ in history.

Both the CJ-7 and Scrambler now had a wider front and rear tread. Respective increases were 3.4 inches and 4.6 inches. All models, except the CJ-5 with the 258 cubic inch six-cylinder engine, were available with a five-speed manual T5 transmission supplied by Warner Gear. All six-cylinder CJ Jeeps were also available with the wide-ratio, three-speed automatic transmission with a lock-up converter. CJs with manual transmissions were also available with cruise control.

The new Pioneer Townside package, available for both the J-10 and J-20, included all features found in the Custom package, plus upper bodyside scuff molding; tailgate stripes; "Pioneer" decals; dark argent-painted grille; carpeted cab floor; front bumper guards and full wheel covers (J-10 only), plus several other interior and exterior features. Otherwise, changes to the J-series trucks were extremely limited. The most important drivetrain development was the availability of the five-speed gear box.

The Scrambler was now delivered with a new Space-Saver spare tire mounted on the roll bar, instead of on the tailgate (as in 1981). The older arrangement, with a standard full-sized spare, was available as an option.

I.D. DATA: Location and format of VIN unchanged from 1981.

Model	Body Type	Price	Weight	Prod. Total
CJ-5 — (¼-Ton) — (4x4) — (84 in. w.b.)				
85	Jeep	7515	2489	—
CJ-7 — (¼-Ton) — (4x4) — (93.4 in. w.b.)				
87	Jeep	7765	2555	—
Scrambler — (½-Ton) — (4x4) — (103.4 in. w.b.)				
88	Pickup	7588	2093	—
J-10 — (½-Ton) — (4x4) — (119/131 in. w.b.)				
25	Townside Pickup (SWB)	8610	3656	—
26	Townside Pickup (LWB)	8756	3708	—
J-20 — (¾-Ton) — (4x4) — (131 in. w.b.)				
27	Townside Pickup	9766	4270	—

NOTE: J-10 Sportside option has 118.8 in. w.b.

ENGINE (Std.: J-10/Opt. Scrambler/CJ-5/CJ-7): Inline. OHV. Six-cylinder. Cast iron block. Bore & stroke: 3.75 x 3.90 in. Displacement: 258 cu. in. Compression ratio: 8.3:1. Net horsepower: 110 at 3000 R.P.M. Net torque: 205 lbs.-ft. at 1800 R.P.M. Seven main bearings. Hydraulic valve lifters. Carburetor: Single two-barrel.

ENGINE (Std.: Scrambler/CJ-5/CJ-7): Inline. OHV. Four-cylinder. Cast iron block. Bore & stroke: 4.00 x 3.00 in. Displacement: 151 cu. in. Compression ratio: 8.2:1. Net horsepower: 82 at 4000 R.P.M. Torque: 125 lbs.-ft. at 2600 R.P.M. Hydraulic valve lifters. Carburetor: Single Two-barrel.

1982 AMC-Jeep Cherokee Two-door Wagon (RPZ)

TECHNICAL: Selective synchromesh transmission. Speeds: 4F/1R. Floor-mounted gearshift. Single plate dry disc clutch. Shaft drive. Rear axle: (J-20) full-floating; (others) semi-floating. Overall drive ratio: 3.54:1. Four-wheel hydraulic front disc/rear drum power brakes. (* Power brakes optional on models 85/87/88). Steel disc wheels.

1982 AMC-Jeep Scrambler Pickup (RPZ)

1982 AMC-Jeep Wagoneer Limited (RPZ)

OPTIONS: "258" six-cylinder engine, models 85/87/88 ($150). "360" V-8 engine, standard w/J-20 ($351). Five-speed transmission, except J-20 ($199). Automatic transmission ($409). Automatic Quadra-Trac ($455). Air conditioning ($681). Heavy-duty alternator ($59). Optional axle ratio, w/o wide wheels ($33). Heavy-duty battery ($47). Power brakes, models 85/87/88 ($99). Bumper accessory package, models 85/87/88 ($113). Retractable cargo area cover ($75). Townside box cap for pickups ($684). Cold Climate group ($115). Heavy-duty cooling system ($49). Cruise control ($159). Custom package, Townside pickups ($169). Decor Group, models 85/87/88 ($86). Trac-Loc differential ($219). Doors for Scrambler/CJ-7 w/soft top ($229). California emissions system ($80). Tinted glass, pickups ($48). Chrome grille, pickups ($57). Halogen headlights on CJs ($56). Honcho Package, model 25 ($949). Honcho Sportside Package, J-10 Sportside ($470). Scrambler padded I.P. ($56). Laredo Package, model 25 ($1749). Laredo Package for CJ, w/soft top ($2149); w/hardtop ($2599). Light group, J-10/J-20 w/roll bar ($49); w/o roll bar ($71). CJ-7 Limited package ($2895). Pioneer package, on J-10 Townside ($599); on J-20 ($577); on Scrambler/CJ ($950). AM radio ($99). AM/FM stereo ($229). AM/FM stereo w/CB ($456). AM/FM w/cassette, pickups ($339). AM/FM ETR stereo w/cassette, pickups ($479). Premium audio system, Limited ($115). CJ Renegade package ($979). Roll bar on pickups ($135). Roll bar access package, CJs ($979). Scrambler "SL" package, w/soft top ($1,999); w/hardtop ($2,399). Scrambler "SR" Sport package ($799). Pickup cloth bench seat trim ($25). Cloth bucket seats, J-10 w/Pioneer package ($181); other pickups ($205). Vinyl bucket seats, Townside pickups ($181); Scrambler including Denim trim ($106). Dual low-profile mirrors (except Scrambler), w/visibility group ($26); w/o visibily group ($85). Dual electric remote mirrors (except Scrambler), w/visibility group ($83); w/o visibility group ($142). Heavy-duty shocks, regular ($35); w/dual fronts on J-10 ($119). Air adjustable rear shocks, except Scrambler and J-20 ($66). "Snow Boss" package, except Scrambler ($1,399). Scrambler spare tire lock ($9). Heavy-duty rear springs, pickups ($48). Heavy-duty front springs, pickups ($59). Extra heavy-duty front springs, pickups ($79). Power steering on Scrambler and CJs ($229). Tachometer and rally clock, Scrambler and CJs ($96). Hardtop with doors, Scrambler ($695); CJ ($775). Scrambler soft denim top ($300). Scrambler soft vinyl top ($280). CJ soft vinyl top ($330). Scrambler tonneau cover ($122). Visibility group, except Scrambler ($152). Wheel covers, all models ($55). Forged aluminum wheels, J-10 Townside ($399). Forged aluminum wheels, J-10 Honcho or Sportside ($200). Power side windows and door locks, J-10/J-20 ($288). Sliding rear window, J-10/J-20 ($97). Wood side rails, Scrambler ($92). Chrome styled wheels, models 85/87/88 ($349); J-10 ($150).

HISTORICAL: Introduced: Fall, 1981. Innovations: Wider tread for CJ and Scrambler models. New option packages released. Five-speed manual transmission available. Total calendar year production: 75,269 (includes Wagoneer and Cherokee). Calendar year registrations: 62,097 (includes Wagoneer and Cherokee). Calendar year production by model: (CJ) 37,221; (Pickups) 6,113; (Scrambler) 6,315. Calendar year sales: 67,646 (U.S. and Canada). Historical notes: W. Paul Tippett, Jr. became chairman of American Motors in 1982, replacing Gerald C. Meyers. Tippett was born Dec. 27, 1932 and graduated from Wabash College, in Cincinnati, Ohio. The company posted Jeep dollar sales of $90.7 million for Jeep vehicles in calendar 1982. AMC reported a net loss of $153.5 million on its cars and trucks during this period. Texans were the leading buyers of Jeep vehicles, based on the state's registration total of 6,492 vehicles. California was second with 4,132 registrations and Pennsylvania was third with 3,568 registration. Unit sales of Jeep vehicles, for the calendar year, were 67,646 for the U.S./Canadian market and an additional 23,083 for the international market.

1983 AMC/JEEP

JEEP — 1983 SERIES — (ALL ENGINES): — The most important developments for 1983 were technical in nature. A new full-time 4-wheel/2-wheel drive system, called "Selec-Trac", replaced Quadra-Trac, which had been introduced in 1973. Selec-Trac was optional on J-10 pickups with either six-cyl. or V-8 engines. Selec-Trac featured a two-speed capability in the transfer case for added torque. To engage either two- or four-wheel-drive, the driver of a Selec-Trac J-10 stopped the vehicle and activated a switch

on the instrument panel. A safety catch was provided to avoid accidental movement of the Selec-Trac switch.

Technical refinements to the 258 cu. in. six-cyl. engine included an increase in compression ratio to 9.2:1 from 8.6:1 and the addition of a fuel feedback system and knock sensor to improve performance and efficiency.

Appearance changes were held to a minimum. Both the Renegade package, for the CJ-5 and CJ-7, as well as the Scrambler's SR trim package, had new striping arrangements.

I.D. DATA: Location and code procedure unchaned from 1982.

1983 AMC-Jeep CJ-5 Renegade Universal (RPZ)

Model	Body Type	Price	Weight	Prod. Total
CJ-5 — (¼-Ton) — (4x4) — (83.4 in. w.b.)				
85	Jeep	7515	2099	—
CJ-7 — (¼-Ton) — (4x4) — (93.4 in. w.b.)				
87	Jeep	6995	2595	—
Scrambler — (½-Ton) — (4x4) — (103.4 in. w.b.)				
88	Pickup	6765	2733	—
J-10 — (½-Ton) — (4x4) — (119/131 in. w.b.)				
25	Townside Pickup (SWB)	9082	3728	—
26	Townside Pickup (LWB)	9227	3790	—
J-20 — (¾-Ton) — (4x4) — (131 in. w.b.)				
27	Townside Pickup	10,117	4336	—

1983 AMC-Jeep J-10 Laredo Townside Pickup (RPZ)

ENGINE (Std.: 88; Opt.: 85/87): Inline. OHV. Four-cylinder. Cast iron block. Bore & stroke: 4.0 x 3.0 in. Displacement: 151 cu. in. Compression ratio: 9.6:1. Net horsepower: 92. Five main bearings. Hydraulic valve lifters. Carburetor: Single two-barrel.

ENGINE (Std.: 85/25/26; Opt.: 88/87): Inline. OHV. Six-cylinder. Cast iron block. Bore & stroke: 3.75 x 3.90 in. Displacement: 258 cu. in. Compression ratio: 9.2:1. Net horsepower: 102 at 3000 R.P.M. Net Torque: 204 lbs.-ft. at 1650 R.P.M. Seven main bearings. Hydraulic valve lifters. Carburetor: Single Two-barrel.

ENGINE (Std.: 27; Opt.: 25/26): Vee-block. OHV. Eight-cylinder. Cast iron block. Bore & stroke: 4.08 x 3.44 in. Displacement: 360 cu. in. Brake horsepower: 170 at 4000 R.P.M. Taxable: 280 lbs.-ft. at 2400 R.P.M. Five main bearings. Hydraulic valve lifters. Carburetor: Two-barrel.

CHASSIS (CJ-5): Wheelbase: 83.4 in. Overall length: 142.9 in. Height: 69.3 in. Front tread: 52.4 in. (Styled Wheels 53.9 in.). Rear tread: 50.5 in. (Styled Wheels 51.9 in.). Tires: G78-15 in.

CHASSIS (CJ-7): Wheelbase: 93.4 in. Overall length: 153.5 in. Height: 69.3 in. Front tread: 55.8 in. Rear tread: 55.1 in. Tires: G78-15 in.

CHASSIS (Scrambler): Wheelbase: 103.4 in. Overall length: 168.9 in. Height: 69.5 in. Front tread: 55.8 in. Rear tread: 55.1 in. Tires: G78-15 in.

CHASSIS (Model 25): Wheelbase: 118.7 in. Overall length: 192.5 in. Height: 67.4 in. Front tread: 64.0 in. Rear tread: 63.8 in. Tires: P225 75R15 in.

CHASSIS (Model 26): Wheelbase: 130.7 in. Overall length: 204.5 in. Height: 67.5 in. Front tread: 66.0 in. Rear tread: 65.8 in. (with styled wheels). Tires: P225 x 75R15 in.

1983 AMC-Jeep Scrambler SL Sport Pickup (RPZ)

CHASSIS (Model 27): Wheelbase: 130.7 in. Overall length: 204.5 in. Height: 67.6 in. Front tread: 64.6 in. Rear tread: 65.9 in. Tires: 8.75 x 16.5 in.

TECHNICAL: Selective synchromesh transmission. Speeds: 4F/1R. Floor-mounted gearshift. Single plate dry disc clutch. Shaft drive. Rear axle: (J-20) full-floating; (others) semi-floating. Ratio: 3.54:1. Four-wheel hydraulic front disc/rear drum power brakes. (* Power brakes optional on models 85/87/88). Steel disc wheels.

OPTIONS: CJ: Renegade package ($1011). Laredo package ($2220). Limited package ($334). **(Scrambler):** "SR" Sport package ($825). "SL" Sport package ($2065). **(J10/J20):** Custom package ($175). Pioneer package ($619). Laredo package ($1807).

NOTE: Refer also to complete options list and option price listing in 1982 section. The partial list above gives an idea of price increase for options in 1983).

1983 AMC-Jeep Wagoneer Limited (RPZ)

HISTORICAL: Introduced: Fall, 1982. Innovations: New "Select-Trac" full-time four-wheel-drive system introduced. Higher compression, fuel feed-back system and knock sensor added to 258 cu. in. six-cyl. engine. Calendar year U.S. registrations: 76,453. Calendar year sales, U.S. and Canada: 93,169. U.S. Calendar year production: (total) 75,534; (CJ) 40,758; (Pickups) 4705; (Scrambler) 5407. Worldwide Calendar year production (Toledo plant): 113,263.

Company president was Paul W. Tippett, Jr. Historical notes: Sales of four-wheel-drive Jeep vehicles in 1983 were the best since 1979 and up 29 percent from the previous year. Chairman Tippett and president Jose J. Dedeurwaerder reported, in late 1983, that a particularly encouraging sign was the fact that "Jeep production at our Toledo plant is now higher than at any time since the plant was acquired from Kaiser in 1970." Worldwide wholesale unit sales of Jeeps totaled $113,443 million, up 25 percent from 1982. Worldwide unit sales of Jeeps, in the calendar year, peaked at 93,169 vehicles in the U.S. and Canada and 20,274 more for the international market. In state-by-state registrations, California leaped to second place with 6004 Jeeps registered for calendar 1982. Texas was still first with 6970 registrations.

On the international scene, the May, 1983 signing of an agreement with Beijing Jeep Corp. opened the door for a joint-venture in which AMC would help build Jeeps in the People's Republic of China. Efforts to strengthen the Latin American export market were also made by AMC-Jeep.

1984 AMC/JEEP

JEEP — 1984 SERIES — (ALL ENGINES): — The elimination of the CJ-5 from the Jeep lineup was of considerable historic importance, but equally significant to the future of Jeep vehicles was the introduction of the first four-cyl. engine ever produced by AMC. This 2.5-liter engine was the base power plant for both the CJ-7 and the Scrambler. Unlike many other contemporary truck engines the new four-cyl. was intended specifically for use in Jeep vehicles.

Jeep's 4.2-liter (258 cu. in.) inline six continued as base engine for the J-10 pickup. The J-20 three-quarter ton pickup continued to use the 5.9-liter (360 cu. in.) V-8 as its sole engine choice.

1984 AMC-Jeep CJ-7 Laredo (AMC)

GVWs for the various models were 4150-pounds for CJ-7s and Scramblers; 6200-pounds for the J-10 pickups and 7600-8400-pounds for the J-20s. The payload range for these models, in the same order, was: (CJ-7) 1227-pounds; (Scrambler) 1146-pounds; (J-10) 2156-pounds and (J-20) 3745-pounds.

I.D. DATA: Location and format unchanged from 1983.

Model	Body Type	Price	Weight	Prod. Total
CJ-7 — (¼-Ton) — (4x4) — (93.4 in. w.b.)				
87	Jeep	7563	2598	—
Scrambler — (½-Ton) — (4x4) — (103.4 in. w.b.)				
88	Pickup	7563	2679	—
J-10 Pickup — (½-Ton) — (4x4) — (118.8/130.7 in. w.b.)				
25	Townside Pickup (SWB)	9967	3724	—
26	Townside Pickup (LWB)	10,117	3811	—
J-20 Pickup — (¾-Ton) — (4x4) — (130.7 in. w.b.)				
27	Townside Pickup	11,043	4323	—

1984 AMC-Jeep Scrambler Pickup (OCW)

ENGINE (Std.: 87/88): Inline. OHV. Four-cylinder. Cast iron block. Bore & stroke: 3.875 x 3.188 in. Displacement: 150.4 cu. in. Compression ratio: 9.2:1. Taxable horsepower: 24.04. Net horsepower: 86 at 3650 R.P.M. Net torque: 132 lbs.-ft. at 3200 R.P.M. Five main bearings. Hydraulic valve lifters. Carburetor: One-barrel with electronic FFB.

ENGINE (Std.: J-10; Opt.: 87/88): Inline. OHV. Six-cylinder. Cast iron block. Bore & stroke: 3.75 x 3.90 in. Displacement: 258 cu. in. Compression ratio: 9.2:1. Taxable horsepower: 33.75. Net horsepower: 102 at 3000 R.P.M. Net Torque: 204 lbs.-ft. at 1650 R.P.M. Seven main bearings. Hydraulic valve lifters. Carburetor: Two-barrel.

1984 AMC-Jeep Laredo Scrambler Pickup (AMC)

1984 AMC-Jeep Townside Laredo Pickup (AMC)

ENGINE (Std.: 27; Opt.: J-10): Vee-block. OHV. Eight-cylinder. Cast iron block. Bore & stroke: 4.08 x 3.44 in. Displacement: 360 cu. in. Taxable horsepower: 53.27. Brake horsepower: 175. Five main bearings. Hydraulic valve lifters. Carburetor: Two-barrel.

CHASSIS (CJ-7): Wheelbase: 93.4 in. Width: 65.3 in. Overall length: 153.2 in. Height: 70.9 in. Front tread: 55.8 in. Rear tread: 55.1 in. Tires: P205/75R15 in.

CHASSIS (Scrambler): Wheelbase: 103.4 in. Width: 63.5 in. Overall length: 166.2 in. Height: 70.8 in. Front tread: 55.8 in. Rear tread: 55.1 in. Tires: P205/75R15 in.

CHASSIS (Model 25): Wheelbase: 118.8 in. Width: 78.9 in. Overall length: 194 in. Height: 69 in. Front tread: 64.0 in. Rear tread: 63.8 in. Tires: P225/75R15 in.

CHASSIS (Model 26): Wheelbase: 130.7 in. Width: 78.9 in. Overall length: 206 in. Height: 69 in. Front tread: 64.0 in. Rear tread: 63.8 in. Tires: P225/75R15 in.

CHASSIS (J-20): Wheelbase: 130.8 in. Width: 78.9 in. Overall length: 206 in. Height: 70 in. Front tread: 64.6 in. Rear tread: 65.9 in. Tires: 8.25 x 16.5 in.

TECHNICAL: Selective synchromesh transmission. Speeds: 4F/1R. Floor-mounted gearshift. Single dry clutch. Rear axle: (J-20) full-floating; (others) semi-floating. Overall ratio: 3.54:1. Power assisted hydraulic front disc/rear drum brakes. (* Power assist optional on CJ-7 and Scrambler). Steel disc wheels.

OPTIONS: (CJ-7): Renegade package ($1124). **(Scrambler):** "SR" Sport package ($932). Hardtop ($829). **(Pickups):** Pioneer package ($456). Laredo package ($2129).

NOTE: Refer also to complete options list and option price listing in 1982 section. The partial list above provides an idea of price increase for certain options between 1982 and 1984).

HISTORICAL: Introduced: Fall, 1983. Calendar year sales: 153,801 (all Series), includes: (CJ-7) 39,547; (Scrambler) 2846; (J-Series Pickup) 3404. Innovations: First four-cyl. AMC engine introduced. Historical notes: New Jeep Cherokee and Wagoneer Sport wagons were the first all-new Jeep line in 20 years. As a result of increased Jeep production, all laid-off employees were recalled at Toledo and the Jeep work force was increased by new hires.

1985 AMC/JEEP

JEEP — 1985 SERIES — (ALL ENGINES): — The latest CJ-7, available in base, Renegade and Laredo levels, had new, optional fold and tumble rear seats in place of the older fixed-back type. Both the Laredo and Renegade CJ-7 Jeeps featured new exterior tape stripe patterns, three new exterior colors and one new interior color. High-back bucket seats were now standard.

Highlights of the 1985 Scrambler included replacement of the SR Sport version by the Renegade and the introduction of the Scrambler Laredo, which filled the position previously occupied by the soft- and hard-top SL Sport. Both the Renegade and Laredo had new exterior and interior decor, a new interior color and new soft- and hard-top colors. All Scramblers, including the base model, had high-back bucket seats.

The J-series trucks were unchanged for 1985.

I.D. DATA: Location and format unchanged from 1984.

1985 AMC-Jeep CJ-7 Renegade (AMC)

Model	Body Type	Price	Weight	Prod. Total
CJ-7 — (¼-Ton) — (4x4) — (93.5 in. w.b.)				
87	Jeep	7282	2601	—
Scrambler — (½-Ton) — (4x4) — (103.5 in. w.b.)				
88	Jeep	7282	2701	—
J-10 Pickup — (½-Ton) — (4x4) — (131 in. w.b.)				
26	Pickup	10,311	3799	—
J-20 Pickup — (¾-Ton) — (4x4) — (131 in. w.b.)				
27	Pickup	11,275	4353	—

1985 AMC-Jeep Cherokee Chief (AMC)

ENGINE (Std.: 87/88): Inline. OHV. Four-cylinder. Cast iron block. Bore & stroke: 3.88 x 3.19 in. Displacement: 150 cu. in. Compression ratio: 9.2:1. Taxable horsepower: 24.04. Net horsepower: 86 at 3650 R.P.M. Net torque: 132 lbs.-ft. at 3200 R.P.M. Five main bearings. Hydraulic valve lifters. Carburetor: One-barrel.

ENGINE (Std.: 26; Opt.: 87/88): Inline. OHV. Six-cylinder. Cast iron block. Bore & stroke: 3.75 x 3.90 in. Displacement: 258 cu. in. Compression ratio: 9.2:1. Taxable horsepower: 33.75. Net horsepower: 102 at 3000 R.P.M. Net torque: 204 lbs.-ft. at 1650 R.P.M. Seven main bearings. Hydraulic valve lifters. Carburetor: Two-barrel.

ENGINE (Std.: 27): Vee-block. OHV. Eight-cylinder. Cast iron block. Bore & stroke: 4.08 x 3.44 in. Displacement: 360 cu. in. Compression ratio: 8.25:1. Taxable horsepower: 53.27. Five main bearings. Hydraulic valve lifters. Carburetor: Two-barrel.

1985 AMC-Jeep Wagoneer Limited (AMC)

CHASSIS (Scrambler): Wheelbase: 103.4 in. Overall length: 177.2 in. Height: 69.2 in. Front tread: 55.8 in. Rear tread: 55.1 in. Tires: P205/75R15 "Arriva".

CHASSIS (J-10/J-20): Wheelbase: 130.8 in. Overall length: 206.0 in. Height: 68.3/70.7 in. Front tread: (J-10) 63.3 in., (J-20) 64.6 in. Rear tread: (J-10) 63.8 in., (J-20) 65.9 in. Tires: (J-10) P225/75R15; (J-20) 9.50 x 16.5 in.

TECHNICAL (J-10): Selective synchromesh transmission. Speeds: 4F/1R. Floor-mounted gearshift. Single dry disc clutch. Shaft drive. Rear axle: semi-floating. Overall ratio: 2.73:1. Power front disc/rear drum brakes. 15 x 6 in. pressed steel wheels.

TECHNICAL (J-20): Automatic transmission. Speeds: 3F/1R. Column-mounted gearshift. Shaft drive. Rear axle: full-floating. Overall ratio: 3.73:1. Power front disc/rear drum brakes. 16.5 x 6 in. pressed steel wheels.

CHASSIS (CJ-7): Wheelbase: 93.4 in. Overall length: 153.2 in. Height: (hardtop) 71.0 in.; (open) 69.1 in. Front tread: 55.8 in. Rear tread: 55.1 in. Tires: P205/75R15 in. "Arriva", steel-belted.

1985 AMC-Jeep Grand Wagoneer (AMC)

TECHNICAL (CJ-7/Scrambler): Selective synchromesh transmission. Speeds: 4F/1R. Floor-shift. Single dry disc clutch. Shaft drive. Semi-floating rear axle. Overall ratio: 3.54:1. Manual front disc/rear drum brakes. 15 x 6 in., five-bolt pressed steel wheels.

OPTIONS: (CJ-7/Scrambler): Renegade package. Laredo package. Variable-ratio power steering (required with air conditioning. Five-speed manual transmission with overdrive. Power front disc brakes. Cold Climate Group. Heavy-duty alternator. Heavy-duty battery. Heavy-duty cooling system. Coolant recovery system. Automatic/part-time four-wheel-drive (not available with four-cyl.) Rear Trac-Lok differential. Heavy-duty shock absorbers. Extra-duty suspension package. Soft ride suspension (not available for base models). Front chrome bumper (Scrambler only, standard Laredo). Chrome rear step bumper (Scrambler only, standard Laredo). Painted rear step bumper (Scrambler only, not available Laredo). Bumper accessory package (not available for Laredo). Rear bumperettes (standard Laredo). Doors for soft and fiberglass tops. Outside passenger side mirror. Bodyside step. Full soft top. Vinyl soft tops. Radios: AM/AM-FM Stereo/AM-FM Stereo/Cassette player (require factory hard or soft top). Hardtop. Air conditioning (not available with four-cyl.) Cruise Control. Fog lamps (clear lens). Halogen headlamps. Extra Quiet Insulation (hardtop only). Styled steel chrome wheels. Styled steel painted wheels. Bumper accessory package (not available for Laredo). Carpeting (front and rear) (standard Laredo). Center Console (standard Laredo). Convenience Group (base model only, standard all others). Decor Group (standard Renegade, not available for Laredo). Roll Bar Accessory package. Fold and tumble rear seat (standard on Renegade and Laredo) CJ-7 only. Soft-feel sport steering wheel (standard on Renegade, not available for Laredo). Leather-wrapped steering wheel (standard on Laredo). Rear storage box. Tachometer and rally clock (standard on Laredo). Tilt steering wheel. Various wheel and tire combinations.

OPTIONS (Pickups): Heavy-duty alternator. Heavy-duty battery. Cold Climate Group. Heavy-duty cooling system. Heavy-duty GVW options: 8400 GVW (J-20); 6200 GVW (J-10). Rear Trac-Lok differential. Extra heavy-duty springs. Radios: AM/AM-FM Stereo/Electronically-tuned AM/FM with cassette. Automatic transmission. 5.9-liter V-8 engine. Pioneer package ($475). White styled wheels. Visibility Group. Tilt steering wheel (not available with manual transmission). Light Group. Insulation package. Protective floor mats. Grain vinyl bench seat (included in Pioneer package). Soft feel sport steering wheel. Leather-wrapped steering wheel. Chrome front grille. Dual low-profile exterior mirrors. Sliding rear window. Air conditioning. Convenience Group.

HISTORICAL: Introduced: Fall, 1984. Calendar year production: (all Jeep vehicles) 225,914. Includes: (CJ-Series) 46,553. (J-Series Pickup) 1953. Innovations: New Scrambler "Renegade" model introduced. CJ-7 gets new fold-and-tumble rear seat option. New trim packages. Historical notes: Paul W. Tippett continued as chairman of Renault/AMC/Jeep.

1986 AMC-Jeep Wrangler Laredo (OCW)

JEEP — 1986 SERIES — (ALL ENGINES): — An historic milestone in light-duty truck history was the end of production of the "CJ" Universal Jeep during model year 1986. At the start of the season, the 1986 sales brochure gave little hint that the CJ series would be phased-out. "CJ has always been special," said the promotional copy. "And for 1986 it makes more sense when you consider its long list of standard features, its exceptional fuel economy and its affordable price." The end came in Jan. 1986, closing 40 years of civilian production during which some 1.6 million units were built. Naturally, there were no significant changes in the 1986 CJ-7 model.

Its replacement, seen as early as February, at the Chicago Auto Show, carried a May 13, 1986 showroom release date. It was known as the "Wrangler" (or Jeep YJ in Canada). Although the basic Jeep CJ body silhouette was apparent in the Wrangler, the forward half of the vehicle, including hood and fender lines, as well as the grille, were more contemporary in appearance. Characteristics included a seven-slot, horizontally "veed" grille, square headlamps and parking lamps, a raised hood center panel, modern instrumentation and doors. It had a 93.4 in. w.b., 152-153 in. overall length, 66 in. width and 58 in. front/rear tread.

The Wrangler was actually merchandised as a 1987 model and came in base, Sport Decor and Laredo trim levels. Standard equipment included a fuel-injected version of AMC's 2.5-liter four-cyl. engine, five-speed manual transmission; power brakes; P215/75R-15 tires; high-back front bucket seats; fold-and-tumble rear seat; mini front carpet mat, column-mounted wiper/washer controls; padded roll bar with side bars extending to windshield frame; swing-away rear tailgate; soft top with metal half-doors and tinted windshield.

New — and promoted as a 1986 model — was the Comanche pickup truck. This slab-sided, sporty pickup was designed to meet the Japanese imports head-on. It had a grille with ten vertical segments between its rectangular headlamps and a sleek cab with trim panels on the rear corners. A Jeep uni-frame with 120 in. w.b. used a Quadra-link S.F.A. front suspension and Hotchkiss rear layout with semi-elliptical multi-leaf springs. Standard equipment included a throttle-body-injected 2.5-liter five-speed manual transmission, power assisted front disc/rear drum brakes and P195/75R15 steel radial tires. With 4x4 models, Jeep's "Command-Trac" shift-on-the-fly system was used.

"An enormous capacity for work" was promised, for 1986 buyers, in the J-10/20 Series of standard (now "large") pickups. These 4x4 only models had few appearance changes, other than new graphics treatments. They again had the Townside look set off by rectangular headlamps and a 13-slot "electric shaver" grille. Base engines were the 4.2-liter six in the half-ton J-10 and the 5.9-liter V-8 in the ¾-ton J-20.

I.D. DATA: Serial number located on top left-hand surface of I.P., visible through windshield. VIN has 17 symbols. The first 3 identify country, manufacturer and type of vehicle. Fourth designates engine; fifth represents model; sixth and seventh identify series; eighth gives GVW rating; ninth is check digit; tenth represents model year. The 11th symbol identifies the assembly plant. The last 6 digits are the sequential production numbers. Engine codes: "C" = 4.2-liter six-cyl.; "N" 5.9-liter V-8; "U" = 2.5-liter four; "W" = 2.8-liter V-6 and "B" = 2.1-liter four-cyl. diesel.

Model	Body Type	Price	Weight	Prod. Total
CJ-7 — (¼-Ton) — (4x4) — (93.5 in. w.b.)				
87	Jeep	7500	2596	—
Wrangler — (¼-Ton) — (4x2) — (93.4 in. w.b.)				
	Jeep	—	—	—
Wrangler — (¼-Ton) — (4x4) — (93.4 in. w.b.)				
	Jeep	—	—	—
Comanche — (½-Ton) — (4x2) — (120 in. w.b.)				
66	Pickup	7049	2931	—

21

Model	Body Type	Price	Weight	Prod. Total
Comanche — (½-Ton) — (4x4) — (120 in. w.b.)				
65	Pickup	8699	3098	—
J-10 — (½-Ton) — (4x4) — (131 in. w.b.)				
26	Pickup	10,870	3808	—
J-20 — (½-Ton) — (4x4) — (131 in. w.b.)				
27	Pickup	12,160	4388	—

ENGINE (Std.: Wrangler/66; 65; 87): Inline. OHV. Four-cylinder. Cast iron block. Bore & stroke: 3.88 x 3.19 in. Displacement: 150 cu. in./2.5L. Compression ratio: 9.2:1. Brake horsepower: 117 at 5000 R.P.M. Taxable horsepower: 24.04. Hydraulic valve lifters. Throttle Body Injection (EFI). Torque (Compression): 135 lbs.-ft. at 3500 R.P.M.

ENGINE (Std.: J-10; Opt.: 66/65/Wrangler)): Inline. OHV. Six-cylinder. Cast iron block. Bore & stroke: 3.75 x 3.9 in. Displacement: 258 cu. in./4.2L. Compression ratio: 9.2:1. Brake horsepower: 112 at 3000 R.P.M. Taxable horsepower: 33.75. Hydraulic valve lifters. Two-barrel carburetor. Torque (Compression) 210 lbs.-ft. at 3000 R.P.M.

ENGINE (Opt.: 65/66): Vee-block. Six-cylinder. Cast iron block. Bore & stroke: 3.5 x 2.99 in. Displacement: 173 cu. in./2.8L. Brake horsepower: 115 at 4800 R.P.M. Taxable horsepower: 29.45. Hydraulic valve lifters. Two-barrel carburetor. Torque (Compression) 150 lbs.-ft. at 2100 R.P.M.

ENGINE (Std.: 27; Opt.: 26): Vee-block. Eight-cylinder. Cast iron block. Bore & stroke: 4.08 x 3.44 in. Displacement: 360 cu. in./5.9L. Taxable horsepower: 53.27. Hydraulic valve lifters. Four-barrel carburetor.

ENGINE (Turbo Diesel; Opt.: 65/66): Inline. OHV. Four-cylinder. Cast iron block. Bore & stroke: 2.99 x 3.5 in. Displacement: 126 cu. in./2.1L. Taxable horsepower: 18.34. Hydraulic valve lifters. Turbo charged.

CHASSIS (CJ-7): Wheelbase: 93.5 in. Overall length: 153.2 in. Height: (hardtop) 71.0 in. Front tread: 55.8 in. Rear tread: 55.1 in. Tires: P205/75R-15 in.

CHASSIS (Wrangler): Wheelbase: 93.4 in. Overall length: 152 in. Height: (hardtop) 69.3 in. Front tread: 58 in. Rear tread: 58 in. Tires: P215/75R-15 in.

CHASSIS (Comanche): Wheelbase: 120 in. Tires: P195/75R-15 in.

CHASSIS (J-10): Wheelbase: 131 in. Overall length: 206 in. Height: 70.7 in. Front tread: 63.3 in. Rear tread: 63.8 in. Tires: P225/75R-15 in.

CHASSIS (J-20): Wheelbase: 131 in. Overall length: 206 in. Height: 70.7 in. Front tread: 63.3 in. Rear tread: 63.8 in. Tires: P225/75R-15 in.

NOTE: Comanche and Wrangler 4x4s use P225/75R-15 in. tires.

TECHNICAL: For carryover models, same as 1985.

TECHNICAL (Wrangler): Selective synchromesh transmission. Speeds: (std.) 5F/1R. Floor controls. Single dry disc clutch. Shaft drive. Semi-floating rear axle. Overall drive ratio: (std.) 4.11.1. Brakes: Disc front/drum rear with power assist. Wheels: 15 x 7.0 disc wheels.

NOTE: For std. 4x2 model w/2.5L four.

OPTIONAL: Chrysler A-3 automatic transmission available only with six-cyl. engine.

1986 AMC-Jeep Grand Wagoneer Limousine (OCW)

TECHNICAL (Comanche): Selective synchromesh transmission. Speeds: 5F/1R. Floor controls. Single dry disc clutch. Shaft drive. Hotchkiss solid rear axle. Overall drive ratio: 3.73:1. Brakes: Power assisted front disc/rear drum. Wheels: 15 x 6 in. five-bolt pressed steel wheels.

NOTE: For std. 4x2 model w/base engine.

OPTIONS: For carryover models, same as 1985 except body graphics treatments. **(Wrangler):** Carbureted 4.2L six-cyl. engine. Three-speed automatic transmission. Hardtop (standard w/Laredo). Tilt steering. **(Sport De Car Group):** includes, most standard features, plus AM/FM monaural radio; black side cowl carpet; special "Wrangler" hood decals; special "Wrangler" lower bodyside stripes; P215/75R15 Goodyear all-terrain Wrangler tires; conventional size spare with lock and convenience group. **(Laredo Hardtop Group):** richer interior trim; AM/FM monaural radio; Buffalo-grain vinyl upholstery; front and rear carpeting; center console; extra-quiet insulation; leather-wrapped Sport steering wheel; special door trim panels and map pockets; chrome front bumper; rear bumperettes; grille panel; headlamp bezels; tow hooks; color-keyed wheel flares; full-length mud guards; integrated body steps; deep tinted glass; OSRV door mirrors; bumper accessory package; special hood and bodyside stripes; convenience group; 15 x 7 in. aluminum wheels; P215/75R-15 Goodyear Wrangler OWL radial tires, spare tire and matching aluminum spare wheel. Rear trac-lok differential. Air conditioning. Extra-quiet insulation. Full-carpets. Halogen fog lamps. Power steering. Cruise Control (6-cyl. only). Leather-wrapped Sport steering wheel. Electric rear window defogger (hardtop). Heavy-duty suspension. Heavy-duty cooling. Aluminum wheels. Off-Road equipment package. Conventional spare tire. Metallic exterior body paints. **(Comanche):** "X" package. "XLS" package. 2.8L six-cyl. engine. 2.1L turbo diesel engine. 2205-pound payload package. Power steering w/17.5:1 ratio. P225/75R15 radial tires. 24-gallon fuel tank. Automatic transmission. Command-Trac 4x4 system (std. on 4x4 models). Selec-Trac 4x4 system (optional on 4x4 models). 4:11.1 rear axle ratio.

HISTORICAL: Introduced: Fall, 1985; (Wrangler) May, 1986. Innovations: New Comanche mini-pickup series. New Wrangler replaces CJ-Series in Jan., 1986 (considered a 1987 model). Historical notes: A California Jeep dealer launched an unsuccessful nationwide publicity campaign to "Save the Jeep CJ." Joseph E. Cappy became president of AMC during 1986. Cappy called the new Comanche AMC's "first state-of-the-art-product in the two-wheel-drive market, which accounts for 75 percent of the light truck market." Other names considered for the new compact pickup were Renegade, Commando, Wrangler and Honcho. AMC also announced that a total of five years had been spent in development of the 1987 Wrangler as an up-to-date replacement for the famous Jeep CJ.

CHEVROLET

By Robert C. Ackerson

Chevrolet's first trucks — a half-ton and one-ton — were made in 1918. From a start of 879 production units, the total number of Chevrolet trucks on the road grew to 8,179 by the end of 1919. By 1921, the company began installing outside-sourced bodies, on its truck chassis, in Chevrolet factories. An all-steel, enclosed cab and a panel truck were introduced in 1925.

Truck number 500,000 was made in 1929, when six-cylinder engines were adopted. By the end of that year, all-time sales hit 641,482 units. In 1930, hydraulic shocks, electric fuel gauges, vacuum wipers and outside mirrors became standard. Late that season, Martin-Parry Corp. — one of the world's largest truck bodymakers — was acquired. This led to the offering of complete ½-ton pickups, panels and canopied express trucks as factory models.

1919 Chevrolet Platform Stake (DFW/FLP)

1931 Chevrolet-Hercules Station Wagon (DFW/BC)

Passenger-car-like styling graced the trucks of 1937. Three-quarter ton and one-ton models joined the line. Race driver Harry Hartz traveled the country's perimeter in a Chevy truck. His gas bill was under one-cent per mile and he had no breakdowns. By 1939, Chevy offered 45 models on eight wheelbases. Cumulative output was up to two-million units. World War II halted production until 1946.

1920 Chevrolet Model T Curtain Top Express (BH)

1937 Chevrolet Utility-Box Pickup (WPL)

$510
F.O.B. Flint, Mich.
For Specifications
See page 13

1923 Chevrolet Superior Light Delivery (BH)

1937 Chevrolet Coupe w/Slip-in Box (DFW/MVMA)

Strong fleet sales, expanded color choices and a new synchromesh transmission helped the sale of trucks in the 1930s. Chevy's market share was 32.7 percent in 1930 and 50 percent in 1933 when the one-millionth unit was assembled. The Suburban appeared, in 1935, as an all-steel station wagon on the ½-ton truck chassis. The next year, one-piece steel cab roofs and hydraulic brakes were used on light-duties.

1949 Chevrole One-Ton Pickup (OCW)

A war-weary public gobbled-up nearly 260,000 Chevy trucks in 1947. They had 30 advanced features, including an alligator-jaw hood and "breathing" cab. A new body and column gear shifting bowed in 1948. The new design would last eight years with only modest changes like vent windows (1951), push-button door handles (1952), crossbar grilles (1954) and Hydra-Matic shifting (1954).

1952 Chevrolet Pickup (OCW)

1954 Chevrolet Pickup (OCW)

In mid-1955, the truck-line was revolutionized with wraparound windshields, 12-volt electrics, optional V-8 engines and a limited-edition "dream truck" called the Cameo. Its dispatch box had slab-side fiberglass outer skins for an all-new "fenderless" look. Chevy's six-millionth truck was built. During 1958, Chevy introduced dual headlamps and began a long-term association with Union Body Co. to produce Step-Van door-to-door delivery trucks.

1954 Chevrolet Produce Van (OCW)

1954 Chevrolet Sedan Delivery (OCW)

1954 Chevrolet Panel Truck (OCW)

The El Camino — a cross between car and truck — was a 1959 highlight. Positraction axles were introduced, too. Fleetside pickups took the Cameo's place in the line. In 1960, Chevy had a light-duty truck first — independent front suspension with torsion bars. A total body redesign was done and the 3100/3600/3800 series designations were switched to the C10/C20/C30 identifiers still in use today.

1954 Chevrolet Milk Delivery Truck (JAW)

1966 Chevrolet Fleetside Pickup (DFW)

Full-size El Caminos disappeared by 1961, the same year that a new line of forward-control trucks, using the Corvair platform and its air-cooled "pancake" six/transaxle setup, was introduced. Panels, passenger vans and pickups were available. One pickup had a drop-down box wall that doubled as a cargo loading ramp.

Chevy's eight millionth truck sale came in 1962. Two years later, the El Camino — now based on the mid-size Chevelle — reappeared. Full-size trucks featured self-adjusting brakes and 6000-mile chassis lubrication intervals. In mid-1964, a compact Chevy Van was phased-in as the Corvair truck's replacement. The nine millionth Chevy truck was retailed, too.

1974 Chevrolet Blazer 4x4 Utility Wagon (JAG)

A growing recreational vehicle market brought changes in 1965. They included a more powerful 327 cu. in. V-8. "Long Box" models with 8½- or 9-foot beds grew popular with buyers wishing to install camper-backs in pickup trucks. A "Camper Special" option package was also introduced. It had beefed-up power train and chassis components. Safety equipment was emphasized after 1966, becoming standard on all light-duty trucks. Chevy truck number 10 million left the factory that year.

A three-side-door Suburban bowed in 1967, when pickups got a redesign and new CS and CST trim packages. A 108 inch wheelbase Chevy Van was offered, along

1976 Chevrolet Panel Delivery Van (CP)

with a new, more rounded van body having a larger windshield. Safety side-markers were added to trucks in 1968, when the El Camino became a 116 inch wheelbase model with a "flying buttress" roofline. The following season, Chevy went one up on Ford with a full-size 4x4 utility truck named Blazer. Bucket seats and a center console became available as CST-level options in pickups. In 1970, Step-Vans adopted an "Easy Access" front end design.

Front disc brakes were standardized in 1971, when vans grew larger and gained coil spring front suspensions and sliding side doors. They also had a new, extended hood for easier servicing. A new P-30 Class A motorhome chassis was available, as well as a Panel Delivery version of Chevy's sub-compact Vega station wagon. Mini-pickups — sourced from Isuzu of Japan — bowed under the LUV name in 1972.

1978 Chevrolet LUV Pickup/Starlander Shell (DFW/TSC)

Half-ton and ¾-ton light-duties adopted optional full-time 4x4 systems in 1973, a year that saw the sale of Chevy's 15th millionth truck. Gas tanks were moved from in the cab and all-leaf rear suspensions were used. Trim levels were now called Custom, Custom DeLuxe, Cheyenne and Cheyenne Super (the last with wood grained exterior body panels). Sales zoomed to 923,189 units.

Light truck sales tapered off in 1973, due to the Arab Oil Embargo. Nevertheless, a new 454 cu. in. engine was released. Hi-Cube vans were a 1974 innovation. Silverado and Scottsdale trim packages bowed in 1975. By 1977, Chevy had gained domination of the 4x4 market as light-duty truck sales zoomed above the one-million-per-year level. A 5.7-litre diesel V-8 engine was 1978's big news. A 4x4 version of the LUV pickup was added in 1979, when Chevy announced a figure of 21,850,083 total sales of trucks since 1918.

1979 Chevrolet Fleetside Pickup (CP)

In mid-1980, Chevy abandoned the heavy-duty truck field to concentrate on light- and medium-duty sales. 1982 brought the compact S-10 pickup (replacing the LUV) and a new 6.2-liter diesel V-8. "Maxi-Cab" and 4x4 versions of the S-10 models were a headline happening for 1983. The 5.7-liter diesel was made available in El Caminos, while the full-size 4x2 Blazer was discontinued. Production of the down-sized Astro Van started in the summer of 1984, for 1985 model-year release.

1918 CHEVROLET

1918 Chevrolet Panel Delivery (DFW/OHS)

COMMERCIAL — MODEL 490/MODEL T — FOUR-CYLINDER: — Chevrolet began truck production in January, 1918. The Model 490 Light Delivery was a beefed-up version of the "490" passenger car chassis with heavier springs. It used the cowl and 15-degree backwards slanting windshield of open Chevrolet automobiles. Standard equipment included a speedometer, ammeter, tire pump, electric horn and demountable rims. Chevrolet manufactured only the chassis, fenders and cowl and included accessories like headlamps. Dealers or customers then had bodies built and installed by aftermarket firms. Martin-Parry Co., of Indianapolis, Ind., was one major supplier of commercial bodies for the Chevrolet chassis. The Light Delivery had a 1000-pound (½-ton) payload rating. Styling was simple and straightforward. Appearance features included semi-circular fenders and wood spoke wheels.

Also new for 1918 was the Model T, Chevrolet's one-ton worm drive truck, which was characterized by its honeycomb radiator with rounded Chevrolet "bow-tie" badge, sloping seven louver hood and cowl-mounted headlights. These lights had hand-grips on the back of them to aid driver entry into the cab. Three models were available: the chassis for $1,325; the Flare Board Express for $1,460 and Express with Eight Post Curtain Top for $1,545. The curtain top was supported, on each side, by four posts whose cross section was 1½ x 2 inches. It was removable by releasing the posts at the sill crossmembers. Mounted on the sides of the Model T were flare boards having a width of eight inches on the slope and overhanging the vertical sides of the body by approximately six inches. The flares were braced from the sill crossmembers to the undersides of the boards. Two compartments were provided, under the three-man seat — one to hold the gas tank and one for carrying purposes. Standard equipment included electric lights and starter (highest two-unit system); complete lamp equipment (including headlamp dimmers); electric horn; odometer; side curtains for driver's seat; windshield and complete tool equipment. The transmission was a selective type with three speeds forward and one reverse. Chevrolet's "FA" engine was used in this model in 1918.

1918 Chevrolet Model T Curtain Top Express (BH)

26

I.D. DATA: (Series T): Serial No. stamped on crossmember at left front of engine. (Series 490): Serial number located on dash nameplate. Engine numbers stamped on flywheel.

Model	Body Type	Price	Weight	Prod. Total
490	½-Ton Light Delivery	595	2170	Note 1
T	1-Ton Worm Drive Chassis	1325	3420	Note 2

NOTE 1: Production of the "490" light delivery was lumped in with production of "490" passenger cars.

NOTE 2: Model T production, through Sept. 23, 1919, was 359 units.

NOTE 3: See introductory text above for additional Model T prices.

ENGINE: (490) OHV. Inline. Four-cylinder. Cast-iron block (cylinders cast en-bloc). Bore & stroke: 3-11/16 x 4 in. Displacement: 170.9 cu. in. Compression ratio: 4.25:1. Brake horsepower: 26 at 1800 R.P.M. Net horsepower: 21.70. Three main bearings. Solid valve lifters. Carburetor: Zenith model "V" one-barrel.

ENGINE: (Model T) OHV. Inline. Four-cylinder. Cast iron block (cylinders cast en-bloc). Bore & stroke: 3-11/16 x 4 in. Displacement: 224 cu. in. Compression ratio: 4.25:1. Brake horsepower: 37 @ 2000 R.P.M. Net horsepower: 21.75. Three main bearings. Solid valve lifters. Carburetor: Zenith improved double jet.

CHASSIS: (Series 490) Wheelbase: 102 in. Tires: 30 x 3½.

CHASSIS: (Series T) Wheelbase: 125 in. Length of body from inside of tailboard to inside of headboard was 114½ inches. Width inside boards was 45¾ inches. Height of top from frame to highest point of top was 63¼ inches. Overall length of top: 156¼ inches. Tread: 56 inches. Tires: (Front) 31 x 4 in. pneumatic, clincher type, non-skid with wrapped tread. (Rear) 32 x 4 inches, solid.

1918 Chevrolet Model T with Express Body (BH)

TECHNICAL: (Series 490) Selective sliding gear transmission. Speeds: 3F/1R. Center-control floor shift. Cone clutch with adjustable compensating springs. Three-quarter floating rear axle with wheel bearing carried on wheel hub and in axle housing (not shaft). Hyatt roller bearings. Brakes: (emergency) internal-expanding type; (service) external-contracting type. 10-inch brake drums. Foot control. Wood artillery type wheels with demountable rims and large hub flanges.

TECHNICAL: Selective sliding gear transmission. Speeds: 3F/1R. Center floor-mounted gearshift. Cone clutch with adjustable compensating springs. Semi-floating rear axle. Brakes: Two sets internal-expanding type acting on rear wheel brake drums. Artillery type wheels of standard dimensions with 12 hickory spokes and front equipped with Timken tapered roller bearings of extra-large size.

OPTIONS: Front bumper. Rear bumper. Single sidemount. Heater. Spotlight. Cowl lamps. Rearview mirror.

HISTORICAL: Introduced: Late 1917. Calendar year sales: Chevrolet reported 879 truck sales. Calendar year production: (Model T) Model T truck production was 61 at Flint, Mich.; 270 at Tarrytown, N.Y. and 28 in Canada. Innovations: First Chevrolet commercial vehicles. Historical Notes: Chevrolet's four-cylinder engine had first been used in 1914 on its Baby Grand and Royal Mail passenger cars. It had a four inch stroke. The 5¼ inch stroke "FA" engine was introduced in 1918 for passenger cars and Model T trucks. The smaller "490" engine was used in Light Delivery models.

Pricing

1918	5	4	3	2	1
Series "490"					
½-Ton Light Delivery	1450	2850	4750	6650	9500
Series "T"					
1-Ton Flare Express	1010	2050	3400	4800	6800
1-Ton Covered Flare	1040	2070	3450	4850	6900

1919 CHEVROLET

1919 Chevrolet Model T Curtain Top Express (BH)

COMMERCIAL — MODEL 490/MODEL T — FOUR-CYLINDER: — Chevrolet's 1919 truck-line was largely unchanged. Several improvements were made to all "490" models, including the Light Delivery Wagon. The spare tire carrier was of the three-quarter circle type with a lever. Standard equipment included windshield, speedometer, ammeter, tire pump, electric horn and demountable rims.

The Model T one-ton worm drive truck was also much the same as in 1918. Chevy claimed its design combined graceful good looks with maximum utility. The cab was clean and simple with features including a gear shift lever and emergency brake lever positioned "right at hand" for the operator. Dash equipment consisted of a conveniently arranged speedometer, carburetor choke, ammeter, oil pressure guage, lighting and ignition switches. Chevrolet's "FB" engine was used this season. It had the same basic specs as the 1918 trucks' "FA" power plant. Its cylinders were cast en-bloc with the upper half of the crankcase. The cylinder head was detachable. Other mechanical features included a gear-driven oil pump, Remy ignition system, water pump, worm-and gear type steering, I-beam front axle, semi-floating rear axle, semi-elliptic front and rear springs and 13-gallon gas tank. Standard equipment was the same as 1918.

I.D. DATA: (Series T): Serial No. stamped on frame crossmember at left front of engine. Also on nameplate on dash. (Series 490): Serial number located on dash nameplate. Serial numbers: (Series T) 1-1082 to 1-2284; 2-1270 to 2-2201; 3-1000 to 3-1300; 6-1047 to 6-1644 and 9-029 to 9-355. Explanation of assembly plant code: The numerical prefix identifies manufacturing plant as follows, "1"=Flint; "2"=New York; "3"=St. Louis; "6"=Oakland (Calif.) and "9"=Oshawa (Ontario, Canada). These codes were unchanged thru 1923. Engine numbers: located on flywheel.

Model	Body Type	Price	Weight	Prod. Total
490	½-Ton Light Delivery Wagon	735	2170	Note 1
T	1-Ton Flareboard Express	1460	3420	3356

NOTE 1: "490" output lumped-in with passenger car production.

NOTE 2: Other Model T trucks listed in the factory sales catalog included: Chassis, $1,325/2840-lbs. and Express with Eight-post Curtain Top $1,545/3420-lbs.

ENGINE: (490) OHV. Inline. Four-cylinder. Cast iron block. Cylinders cast en-bloc. Bore & stroke: 3-11/16 x 4 in. Displacement: 170.9 cu. in. Compression ratio: 4.25:1. Brake horsepower: 26 at 1800 R.P.M. Net horsepower: 21.70. Three main bearings. Solid valve lifters. Carburetor: Zenith model "V" one-barrel.

ENGINE: (Model T) OHV. Inline. Four-cylinder. Cast iron block. Cylinder cast en-bloc. Bore & stroke: 3-11/16 x 5-1/4 in. Displacement: 224 cu. in. Compression ratio: 4.25:1. B.H.P.: 37 @ 2000 R.P.M. Net H.P.: 21.75. Three main bearings. Solid valve lifters. Carburetor: Zenith improved double jet.

CHASSIS: (Series 490) Wheelbase: 102 in. Frame thickness: 4 in. Front frame width: 30½ in. Rear frame width: 35⅛ in. Length behind seat: 109 in. Loaded frame height: 25 in. Springs: semi-elliptic, (front) 2¼ x 37½ in.; (rear) 2½ x 53 in. Tires: 30 x 3½.

CHASSIS: (Model T) Wheelbase: 125 in. Length of body from inside of tailboard to inside of headboard was 114½ in. Width inside boards was 45¾ in. Height of top from frame to highest point: 63¼ in. Overall length of top: 156¼ in. Tread: 56 in. Tires: (front) 31 x 4 in., pneumatic, non-skid with wrapped tread; (rear) 32 x 4 in.

TECHNICAL: (Both Models) Selective sliding gear transmission. Speeds: 3F/1R. Floor-mounted gearshift. Cone type clutches, same as 1918. (Model 490) Three-quarter floating rear axle; (Model T) semi-floating rear axle. External contracting mechanical rear wheel brakes. Wooden spoke wheels of same types as 1918. Model T driveshaft was of high-carbon seamless steel tubing 1⅝ in. in diameter. Center of driveshaft supported on double row of self-aligning ball bearings close to middle U-Joint. Bearing

housing filled with lubricant and fitted with compression grease cup for refilling. Worm gear drive: the steel worm was cut, hardened and finish-ground by special machine. The bronze gear was of special alloy, accurately cut, with teeth burnished to reduce friction. The gear ran in oil and acted as a pump which picked up and circulated oil over the worm and through the bearings. A governor was fitted on the Model T and set for 25 m.p.h. maximum speed, with a lock to prevent operator tampering.

OPTIONS: Front bumper. Rear bumper. Heater. Cowl lamps. Rearview mirror.

HISTORICAL: Introduced: Late 1918. Calendar year sales: Chevrolet recorded 8,179 truck sales. Calendar year production: (Model T) Model T truck production was 1,203 at Flint; 932 at Tarrytown; 301 at St. Louis; 597 at Oakland and 326 in Canada. Innovations: The popularity of Chevrolet trucks was starting to rise. Sales of Sampson (another GM branch) trucks and tractors were assigned to the Chevrolet dealer organization. Historical notes: Martin-Parry Co. continued as the major supplier of bodies for Chevrolet chassis. William C. Durant was in control of Chevrolet this year. The company was a branch of General Motors.

Pricing

1919	5	4	3	2	1
Series "490"					
½-Ton Light Delivery	1450	2850	4750	6650	9500
Series "T"					
1-Ton Flare Express	1010	2050	3400	4800	6800
1-Ton Covered Flare	1040	2070	3450	4850	6900

1920 CHEVROLET

1920 Chevrolet Model T Curtain Top Express (BH)

COMMERCIAL — MODEL 490/MODEL T — FOUR-CYLINDER: — "The Chevrolet Light Delivery Wagon was designed to meet the requirements of those who have need of a commercial car with slightly less capacity and of considerably lighter weight then is afforded by a one-ton truck," said Chevrolet's *Commercial Cars* sales catalog. "It is sturdily constructed and amply powered for all transportation needs. It is light enough to be speedy, easy riding and economical with fuel and tires." Appearance improvements to the "490" included use of a reverse curve fender line and full-crown fenders. Headlamps were mounted to the fenders, eliminating the tie-bar used previously. A couple of technical changes were made. Chevrolet still refrained from truck body building. However, the company put out a contract to source delivery wagon bodies from outside and install them at the factory level. In addition to the chassis & cowl, two models were cataloged with express bodies and four-post tops. The first included driver's seat and side curtains for use in cold or stormy weather. Two extra seats were provided in the second model (one at the extreme rear and one at the center of the express box) to make it useful for station wagon or other passenger transportation requirements. Standard equipment included: electric lights; self-starter; complete lamps (including adjustable headlamps); top and curtains; adjustable windshield; speedometer; electric horn; extra rim; tire carrier and complete tools including tire pump and jack.

Chevrolet's one-ton Model T truck (the worm drive system was now de-emphasized in sales literature) was also back in 1920. The *Commercial Car* sales catalog stressed the abilities of its "FB" power plant and sturdy ("insures maximum service and minimum wear") construction. Included with the basic chassis model were radiator, hood, cowl, front fenders, running board and a single driver's seat mounted atop a tall platform housing the gas tank and a storage compartment. Also available was a Flare Board Express body measuring 114½ inches long from the inside of the tailboard to inside of headboard, with 44 inches width inside the boards. A third model added an eight-post curtain top. The standard equipment list included electric lights and starter (highest two-unit system); complete lamp equipment (including headlamp dimmer); electric horn; odometer; side curtain for driver's seat; windshield and complete tool equipment.

I.D. DATA: Serial number stamped on frame crossmember at left front of engine. Also on nameplate on dash. Numbers used on 1920 Model T trucks were: 1-2285 to 4199; 2-2202 to 3616; 3-1301 to 1953; 6-1645 to 2362 and 9-356 to 9-847. Numbers used on "490" commercial vehicles 2-1000 to 2A-24086 and 9-115 and up. See 1923 for code explanation. Engine numbers located on flywheel.

1920 Chevrolet Light Delivery Express Body (BH)

Model Series "490" — (½-Ton)	Body Type	Price	Weight	Prod. Total
490	Light Delivery Chassis	685	2170	Note 1
490	Delivery Wagon (1-seat)	735	—	Note 1
490	Delivery Wagon (3-seat)	770	—	Note 1
Model "T" — (1-Ton)				
T	Chassis & Cowl	1325	3300	Note 2
T	Flareboard Express	1460	—	Note 2
T	Covered Flare	1545	—	Note 2

NOTE 1: Production unavailable.

NOTE 2: Series production was 5,288 units at all factories.

1920 Chevrolet Light Delivery Station Wagon (BH)

1920 Chevrolet Light Delivery Farm Wagon (BH)

ENGINE: (490) Inline. Cast en-bloc. OHV. Four-cylinder. Cast-iron block. Bore & stroke: 3-11/16 x 4 in. Displacement: 170.9 cu. in. Compression ratio: 4.25:1. Brake horsepower: 26 at 1800 R.P.M. Net horsepower: 21.70. Three main bearings. Solid valve lifters. Carburetor: Zenith model "V".

ENGINE: ("T") Inline. OHV. Cast en-bloc. Four-cylinder. Cast iron block. Bore & stroke: 3-11/16 x 5-1/4 in. Displacement: 224 cu. in. C.R.: 4.25:1; B.H.P.: 37 @ 2000 R.P.M. Net H.P.: 21.75. Three main bearings. Solid valve lifters. Carburetor: Zenith improved double-jet.

1920 Chevrolet Light Delivery Four-Post Top (BH)

CHASSIS: (Series 490) Wheelbase: 102 in. Tires: 30 x 3½ (front) in. Steering: Spur and gear type (adjustable for wear) with 15-inch steering wheel. See 1918-1919 section for other specifications.

CHASSIS: (Model T) Wheelbase: 125 in. Tires: (front) pneumatic 33 x 4 in. demountable S.S. type, non-skid with wrapped tread. (Rear) pneumatic 35 x 5 in. cord type. Steering: worm and gear type with 16-inch steering wheel. Steering arm of drop-forged steel, heat treated. See 1918-1919 for other specifications.

1920 Chevrolet Model T Chassis & Windshield (BH)

1920 Chevrolet Model T 1-Ton Express Wagon (BH)

TECHNICAL: (490) Selective sliding gear transmission. Speeds: 3F/1R. Floor-mounted center gearshift. Cone clutch with adjustable compensating springs. Three-quarter floating rear axle (wheel bearing carried on wheel hub in axle housing (not shaft). Hyatt roller bearings. Brakes (emergency) internal expanding type; (service) external contracting type with 10-inch brake drums and foot control. Wheels: Wood artillery type, demountable rim, large hub flanges.

TECHNICAL: ("T") Selective type transmission. Speeds: 3F/1R. Center floor-shift control. Leather-faced cone clutch with adjustable compensating springs. Governor provided and set and locked at 25 m.p.h. maximum speed. Semi-floating rear axle made of heat treated steel. Worm gear drive has cut and hardened, finish-ground steel worm requiring no adjustment at any time. Brakes: Same as 1918-1919. Wheels: Artillery spoke, standard dimensions, 12 hickory spokes, fronts equipped with Timken tapered roller bearings of extra large size.

OPTIONS: Front bumper. Rear bumper. Heater. Cowl lamps. Driver's seat ($50). Pair of auxiliary seats ($85). Rearview mirror.

1920 Chevrolet Model T Curtain Top Express (BH)

HISTORICAL: Introduced: January, 1920. Calendar year production: Model T production was 1,914 at Flint; 1,414 at Tarrytown; 652 at St. Louis; 717 at Oakland and 591 in Canada. Innovations: New fender treatment for "490" Series commercial cars. Factory-installed aftermarket bodies. Headlamp tie-bar eliminated on "490" models. Historical notes: W.C. Durant was forced out of General Motors by angry stock holders.

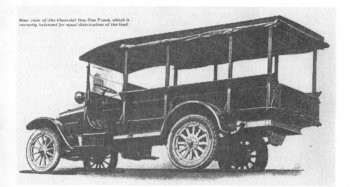

1920 Chevrolet Model T Curtain Top Express (BH)

Pricing

1920	5	4	3	2	1
Series "490"					
Light Delivery Wagon 1-Seat	1450	2850	4750	6650	9500
Light Delivery Wagon 2-Seat	1450	2850	4750	6650	9500
Model T					
Flareboard Express	1010	2050	3400	4800	6800
Covered Flare	1040	2070	3450	4850	6900

1921 CHEVROLET

1921 Chevrolet 490 Light Delivery Wagon (BH)

COMMERCIAL LINE — MODEL 490/MODEL G/MODEL T — FOUR-CYLINDER: — The "490" was basically unchanged. Chevrolet's copywriters described it as "a profitable investment for all light handling and delivery purposes." Standard equipment listed in the *Commercial Cars* catalog was the same as 1920, as were the base models. However, this piece of literature also promoted several of the more popular aftermarket (*) bodies including a station wagon, delivery wagon, express wagon and farm wagon.

An all-new commercial vehicle was the Model "G" Light Truck. It could be described as the front end of the "490" mated with the longer and heavier frame and rear axle of a truck. Chevy described it as "the product of years of experience" and said it was "built to supply the demand for a ¾-ton (**) truck whose strength and performance equal(s) cars of greater capacity." This model used the smaller "490" engine. Base model offerings included the chassis, chassis & cab, Open Express and Express with Curtain Top. Larger in size than the "490," the Model G had slanting hood louvers, reverse curve fenders and torpedo type front fender mounted headlamps. Body length was 97⅞ inches from tailboard to headboard, with a width of 46 inches between flare boards. Drive was from the left-hand side with center control. Spark and throttle were located under the steering wheel and there was a foot accelerator. Standard equipment included, electric lights and starter, highest two-unit system; complete lamp equipment; side curtains; adjustable windshield; speedometer; demountable rims; electric horn and complete tool equipment including pump and jack.

Cowl mounted headlamps remained a distinctive styling characteristic of the Model T one-tonner in 1921. The Model T had overall larger dimensions and a narrower cowl with scooped-out side. Aftermarket bodies depicted in the year's sales catalog included a passenger bus, fire engine, wholesale hauler, farm wagon and panel delivery. Standard equipment was the same as in 1920.

(*) All Chevrolet truck bodies were still "aftermarket" items, as they were sourced from outside supplier firms. However, some (as shown in the sales catalog) were mass-produced especially for delivery to and installation at Chevrolet factories. Others were purchased by dealers or buyers for "aftermarket" attachment to the Chevrolet chassis.

(**) *Branham Automobile Reference Book* called the "G" a one-ton model in 1921, but downrated it to 1500-pounds in 1922. Chevrolet literature and most other sources refer to it as a ¾-tonner for both years.

I.D. DATA: Serial number located on nameplate on dash. Series 490 numbers: 1-A-20821 to 57835; 2-A-24086 to 54564; or 2-3020 and up. Model G numbers: 1-13 to 1-384; 2-77 to 2-303; 3-58 to 3-122; 6-59 to 6-182; 9-115 to 9-194. Model T numbers: 1-4200 to 4454; 2-3617 to 2-3631; 3-1954 to 3-2081; 6-2363 to 6-2446 and 9-356 up. Engine numbers located on flywheel and left side of front motor support.

1921 Chevrolet 490 Light Express Wagon (BH)

Model	Body Type	Price	Weight	Prod. Total
Series "490" — (½-Ton)				
490	Chassis & Cowl	625	—	—
490	Open Express	820	1860	Note 1
490	3-Seat Covered Express	855	—	Note 1
Series G — (¾-Ton)				
G	Chassis - only	920*	2450	Note 2
G	Chassis & Flatface Cowl	995**	—	Note 2
G	Open Express	1030***	—	Note 2
G	Canopy Express	1095****	—	Note 2
Series T — (1-Ton)				
T	Chassis	1325	3300	Note 3
T	Open Express	1460	—	Note 3
T	Canopy Express	1545	—	Note 3
T	Canopy Express 3S	1595	—	Note 3

NOTE 1: "490" production lumped-in with passenger cars.

NOTE 2: "G" production was 855 units.

NOTE 3: "T" production was 478 units.

Additional Note: Prices for the Model Gs decreased during the year as follows, (*) $745; (**) $820; (***) $855 and (****) $920.

ENGINE: (490/"G") Inline. Cast en-bloc. OHV. Four-cylinder. Cast-iron block. Bore & stroke: 3-11/16 x 4 in. Displacement: 170.9 cu. in. Compression ratio: 4.25:1. Brake horsepower: 26 at 2800 R.P.M. Net horsepower: 21.70. Three main bearings. Solid valve lifters. Carburetor: Zenith model one-barrel.

ENGINE: ("T") Inline. Cast en-bloc. OHV. Four-cylinder. Cast iron block. Bore & Stroke: 3-11/16 x 5-1/4 in. Displacement: 224 cu. in. C.R.: 4.25:1 B.H.P.: 37 @ 2000 R.P.M. Net H.P.: 21.75. Three main bearings. Solid valve lifters. Carburetor: Zenith improved double jet.

CHASSIS: (490) Wheelbase: 102 in. Front axle: drop-forged I-beam. Springs: Cantilever type front and rear. Spur and gear steering, adjustable for wear. 15-inch steering wheel. Tires: 30 x 3½ non-skid front and rear.

CHASSIS: ("G") Wheelbase: 120 in. Front axle: drop-forged I-beam. Ample sized steering knuckles and steering arms (drop-forged and heat treated). Springs: cantilever front (21⅞ in. long x 1¾ in. wide); one-half elliptic rear (43¼ in. long x 2½ in. wide). Five inch deep frame. Front frame width: 28 in. Rear frame width: 37 in. Length in back of driver's seat: 76 in. Frame height: 23½ in. loaded. Tires: all-pneumatic; demountable type with wrapped tread, (front) 31 x 4 in.; (rear) 34 x 4½ in. All-weather tread. Gas tank: 10 gallons.

CHASSIS: ("T") Wheelbase: 125 in. Front axle: drop-forged I-beam. Springs: semi-elliptic front and rear: (front) 38 x 2¼ in. & (rear) 54 x 2½ in. Worm and gear steering. Steering arm of drop-forged, heat-treated steel, 16 inch wheel. Tires: (front) pneumatic, 33 x 4 in., demountable S.S. type, non-skid with wrapped tread; (rear) 35 x 5 in. pneumatic, cord type. Gas tank capacity: 13 gallons.

TECHNICAL: (490) Selective sliding gear transmission. Speeds: 3F/1R. Floor-mounted gearshift. Cone type clutch with adjustable compensating springs. Three-quarter floating rear axle with Hyatt roller bearings. Brakes: (emergency) internal expanding type; (service) external contracting type with 10 inch brake drums and foot control. Wood artillery wheels with demountable rims and large hub flanges.

TECHNICAL: ("G") Selective sliding gear transmission. Speeds: 3F/1R. Cone clutch with adjustable compensating springs. Semi-floating rear axle made of heat-treated nickel steel. Brakes: (emergency) internal expanding type; (service) external contracting type with 12 inch brake drums and foot control. Artillery type wheels of standard dimension with 12 hickory spokes (front wheels have Timken tapered roller bearings).

TECHNICAL: ("T") Selective sliding transmission. Speeds: 3F/1R. Governor, loackable, with 25 m.p.h. maximum speed. Leather-faced cone clutch with adjustable compensating springs. Semi-floating rear axle made of heat-treated steel. Worm drive. Artillery wheels of standard dimension with 12 hickory spokes (front wheels have Timken tapered roller bearings).

OPTIONS: Front bumper. Rear bumper. Single sidemount. Heater. Cowl lamps.

HISTORICAL: Introduced: January, 1921. Calendar year production: (Model G) 371 at Flint; 226 at Tarrytown; 64 at St. Louis; 123 at Oakland and 71 in Canada. (Model T) 255 at Flint; 14 at Tarrytown; 127 at St. Louis and 83 at Oakland. Innovations: New ¾-ton Model G. Historical notes: Colors for new Model G varied according to body style; it was painted black when sold without cowl and Chevrolet green when sold with cowl. "Standard" aftermarket bodies were again listed in the Chevrolet catalog.

Pricing

	5	4	3	2	1
1921					
Series "490"					
Open Express	1450	2850	4750	6650	9500
3S Canopy Express	1500	2900	4850	6800	9700
Series G					
Open Express	1200	2400	4000	5600	8000
Canopy Express	1200	2460	4100	5700	8200
Series T					
Open Express	1010	2050	3400	4800	6800
Canopy Express	1040	2070	3450	4850	6900

1922 CHEVROLET

$650
"192B Flint Sub
For specifications see page 18

1922 Chevrolet Model G Light Truck Chassis (BH)

30

COMMERCIAL LINE — MODEL 490/MODEL G/MODEL T — FOUR-CYLINDER: — The same three lines of Chevrolet trucks were back in 1922: the "490" Light Delivery Wagon, the Model "G" Light Delivery and the Mondel "T" one-tonner.

The 490 received a number of technical changes. Valve adjustment was moved to the rocker arms. Larger 9/16 inch king bolts replaced the previous 1/2 inch types. An emergency brake lever was introduced to replace the old ratchet on the rifht-hand foot pedal. The service brakes were now operated by the right-hand pedal and the left-hand pedal was for the clutch. A spiral type of ring gear and pinion replaced the old straight-cut type. Also, a new type of differential bearing was used. Standard equipment included: electric lights and starter, highest type two-unit system. Complete lamp equipment, including adjustable headlamps; four-post top; side curtains; adjustable windshield; speedometer; electric horn; extra rim; tire carrier and complete tool equipment including pump and jack. There were no major exterior design changes. Mifflinburg Body Co. of Pennsylvania supplied some models for the factory catalogs, including: Station Wagon; Delivery Wagon; Express Wagon and Farm Wagon.

For 1922, the Model G adopted a centrally mounted emergency brake lever and conventional clutch and brake pedals. Of the Model G, Chevrolet literature noted: "Chassis and body are balanced so as to make the utmost power available for the load itself and to reduce gasoline consumption to a minimum." The Model G again measure 97⅞ inches from tailboard to headboard, with 46 inches of width inside the boards. Standard equipment: Electric lights and starter, highest type two-unit system. Complete lamp equipment; side curtains; adjustable windshield; speedometer; demountable rims; electric horn; complete tool equipment including pump and jack.

New for the Model T truck, in 1922, was the provision of poured rod bearings in the "FB" engine. Also, the three exhaust port cylinder head, also used on FB autos, was adopted. As had been the case since 1920, pneumatic tires were used front and rear. The Series T continued to look typical of trucks of the era, with its headlamps mounted on the cowl. A cab was not used. Standard chassis features included a platform mounted seat and a windshield. Bodies sourced from outside suppliers often had tops designed to extend out to the windshield. The frame was four inch channel iron, 30½ inches wide in the front and 35⅛ inches wide at the rear. The front axle was of the drop-forged I-beam type. The rear axle was semi-floating with worm drive. The equipment consisted of a starter, generator, horn, headlamps (with dimmers), speedometer, ammeter, side curtains for driver's seat, complete tool equipment and a governor locked at 25 m.p.h. **Note:** Copies of a late 1922 Chevrolet sales catalog entitled *Chevrolet For Economical Transportation Commercial Cars* (supplied by Bob Hensel, of Chevy Acres, in Brillion, Wis.) does not include the 490 Light Delivery Wagon, but shows the "New Superior" Light Delivery truck instead. (It also includes the Model G and Model T trucks). This indicates that the Superior was available, in calendar 1922, perhaps as a mid-season release. However, most references treat the Superior Series as a 1923 line, a policy we will follow in this catalog.

1922 Chevrolet Superior Delivery Van (OCW)

I.D. DATA: Serial numbers stamped on frame crossmember at left front of engine. Serial number on the 490 is found on the dash-mounted nameplate. Serial numbers for the 490 commercials were 1-A-59934 to 928881; 2-A-55239 to 88858; 3-A-53242 to 87572; 6-A-54959 to 76001. Serial numbers for Model Ts were 1-4455 to 4792; 2-3632 to 4359; 3-2082 to 2107 and 6-2447 to 2631. Serial numbers for Model Gs were: 1-385 to 683; 2-304 to 623; 3-123 to 229; 6-183 to 6-386 and 9-195 to 202. See 1918 for factory code explanations. Engine number is stamped on the flywheel.

Model	Body Type	Price	Weight	Prod. Total
Series 490 — (½-Ton)				
490	Light Delivery Wagon	510	1860	Note 1
490	Panel Dely. (Mifflinburg)	—	2010	Note 1
490	Sta. Wag. (Mifflinburg)	—	—	Note 1
Series G — (¾-Ton)				
G	Chassis and Cowl	745	2450	Note 2
G	Chassis with Cab	820	—	Note 2
G	Express Body	855	2600	Note 2
G	Canopy Express	920	—	Note 2
Series T — (1-Ton)				
T	Chassis	1125	3300	Note 3
T	Open Express	1246	3450	Note 3
T	Canopy Express	1325	—	Note 3
T	Canopy Exp. w/curtains	1545	—	Note 3

1922 Chevrolet Closed Cab Canopy Express (L.Kuntz)

NOTE 1: Not available.

NOTE 2: Series production = 273 units.

NOTE 3: Series production = 1093 units.

ENGINE: (490/"G") Inline. Cast en-bloc. OHV. Four-cylinder. Cast iron block. Bore & stroke: 3-11/16 x 4 in. Displacement: 170.9 cu. in. Compression ratio: 4.3:1. Brake horsepower: 26 at 2000 R.P.M. Three main bearings. Mechanical valve lifters. Carburetor: Zenith one-barrel model.

ENGINE: ("T") Inline. Cast en-bloc. OHV. Four-cylinder. Cast iron block. Bore & stroke: 3-11/16 x 5-1/4 in. Displacement: 224 cu. in. Compression: 4.25:1. B.H.P.: 37 @ 2000 R.P.M. Net H.P.: 21.75. Three main bearings. Solid valve lifters. Carburetor: Zenith improved double jet.

CHASSIS: (490) Wheelbase: 102 in. Tires: 30 x 3½. See 1921 section for additional specifications.

CHASSIS: (G) Wheelbase: 120 in. Tires: All-pneumatic, demountable type, with wrapped tread: (front) 31 x 4 in.; (rear) 34 x 4½ in. See 1921 section for additional specifications.

CHASSIS: (T) Wheelbase: 125 in. Tires: (front) pneumatic 33 x 4 in. demountable S.S. type, non-skid, wrapped tread; (rear) 35 x 5 in. all-weather tread. See 1921 section for additional specifications.

TECHNICAL: (All) Selective sliding transmission. Speeds: 3F/1R. Floor-mounted gearshift. Cone type clutch. Rear axle: (490) Three-quarter floating; (G/T) semi-floating. Artillery type wood spoke wheels. Additional specifications same as 1921, except for changes indicated in descriptive text above.

OPTIONS: Front bumper. Rear bumper. Single sidemount. Heater. Cowl lamps. Motor Meter. Rearview mirror.

1922 Chevrolet Model T Chassis With Cowl (BH)

HISTORICAL: Introduced: January, 1922. Calendar year production: (Model G) Flint = 298; Tarrytown = 319; St. Louis = 106; Oakland = 203 and Canada = 7. (Model T) Flint = 337; Tarrytown = 727; St. Louis = 25 and Oakland = 184. Innovations: New clutch/brake pedal system. Lever-action parking brake. Historical notes: W.S. Knudsen became the new general manager of Chevrolet. The Janesville, Wis., factory where Sampsons were built, became a Chevrolet assembly plant.

Pricing

1922	5	4	3	2	1
Series 490					
Delivery Wagon	1450	2850	4750	6650	9500
Panel Delivery	1500	3000	5000	7000	10,000
Station Wagon	1800	3600	6000	8400	12,000
Series G					
Express	1200	2400	4000	5600	8000
Canopy Express	1200	2460	4100	5700	8200
Series T					
Open Express	1010	2050	3400	4800	6800
Canopy Express	1040	2070	3450	4850	6900
Canopy Express w/curtains	1050	2010	3500	4900	7000

1923 CHEVROLET

1923 Chevrolet-Hercules Panel Delivery (DFW/BC)

SUPERIOR — SERIES B/SERIES D — FOUR-CYLINDER: — The Series B and Series D trucks were identified by their raised hood lines, higher radiators with a flatter top surface and a narrower cowl section. Bodies were still sourced from outside firms, although some styles were included in Chevrolet truck catalogs as factory-installed models. Prices are listed for chassis and factory-installed body models only. The Utility Delivery had a large open flare board express box and closed cab. Standard features included a speedometer; ammeter; generator; starter; battery; drum type integral headlamps; dimmers; taillight; complete wiring system; oil pressure gauge; choke control; license brackets; motor hood; special combination dash and instrument board; front and rear fenders; running-boards with shields; demountable rims with extra front and rear rims; tire carrier; jack and complete tool equipment.

I.D. DATA: Serial numbers located on a plate found on the left side of the front seat frame. Serial numbers were 1-0-1000 to 1654; 2-D-1000 to 2236; 3-D-1000 to 2155 and 21-D-1000 to 1515. Note: Factory prefix "12" identifies Chevrolet's new Janesville, Wis. assembly plant. Engine numbers placed on the flywheel.

1923 Chevrolet Superior Commercial Chassis (BH)

Model	Body Type	Price	Weight	Prod. Total
Series B —	**(½-Ton)**			
B	Chassis	395	1860	—
B	Canopy Express	510	1965	—
B	Panel Delivery	—	—	—
B	Station Wagon	—	—	—
Series D —	**(1-Ton)**			
D	Chassis	375	1830(*)	—
D	Utility Delivery	—	2780	—
D	Cattle Body	—	—	—
D	Light Delivery	—	—	—

(*) Original source (Branham) indicates a lower weight for the one-ton this year only.

ENGINE: (All) Inline. OHV. Four-cylinder. Cast-iron block. Bore & stroke: 3-11/16 x 4 in. Displacement: 170.9 cu. in. Compression ratio: 4.3:1. Brake horsepower: 35 at 1900 R.P.M. Three main bearings. Mechanical valve lifters. Carburetor: Carter one-barrel.

CHASSIS: (Series B) Wheelbase: 103 in. Length: 142 in. Height: 74.25 in. Front tread: 58 in. Rear tread: 58 in. Tires: 30 x 3.5 in.

CHASSIS: (Series D) Wheelbase: 120 in. Tires: 31 x 4.0 in.

TECHNICAL: Manual, sliding gear transmission. Speeds: 3F/1R. Column-mounted gearshift. Cone type clutch. Semi-floating rear axle. Overall ratio: 3.77:1 (Series B). External contracting rear wheel brakes. Wooden spoke wheels.

OPTIONS: Front bumper. Rear bumper. Single sidemount. Heater. Cowl lamps. Motor Meter. Rearview mirror. Cattle body with "chute" type side ramps.

HISTORICAL: Introduced: January, 1923. Innovations: New 120 in. w.b. Historical notes: Alfred P. Sloan, Jr. took over as president of General Motors.

Pricing

	5	4	3	2	1
1923					
Series B Superior					
Canopy Express	1500	3000	5000	7000	10,000
Panel Delivery	1500	3000	5000	7000	10,000
Station Wagon	1800	3600	6000	8400	12,000
Series D Superior					
Utility Delivery (Express)	1010	2050	3400	4800	6800
Cattle Body (Stake)	1100	2200	3650	5100	7300
Delivery Wagon	1050	2100	3500	4900	7000
Panel Body	1130	2250	3750	5250	7500
Gravity Dump	1150	2310	3850	5400	7700
Petroleum Tanker	1170	2340	3900	5450	7800

1924 CHEVROLET

1924 Chevrolet Panel Delivery (WPL)

SUPERIOR/UTILITY — SERIES F/SERIES H — FOUR-CYLINDER: — The ½-Ton Superior Four line became the Series F this year. As usual, this was composed of smaller trucks riding a beefed-up version of the Chevrolet passenger car chassis. Available again was the Superior Utility Express line of one-tonners. These were now simply called "Utilities" and carried an H Series designation for 1924. Body-making was still an all-aftermarket operation, with some of the more popular styles available factory-installed. Standard equipment was similar to the 1923 list. References to a Series J one-ton model are found in some sources, although details about this series are not listed in *Branham Automobile Reference Book*.

I.D. DATA: Serial numbers located on either side of dash under cowl and seat frame. Numbers were: 1-D-1655 to 1-H-1307; 2-D-2237 to 2-H-2383; 3-D-2156 to 3-H-4177; 6-D-1818 to 6-H-1813; 9-D-1000 to 9-H-1372; 12-D-1000 to 12-H-1732 and 21-D-1516 to 21-H-2106. Note: The prefix "12" was used to identify the new Buffalo, N.Y. assembly plant opened in late 1923. Engine numbers located — same location as 1923.

Model	Body Type	Price	Weight	Prod. Total
Series F — (½-Ton)				
F	Chassis	395	1790	—
Series H — (1-Ton)				
H	Chassis	550	1850	—

ENGINE: (All) Inline. OHV. Four-cylinder. Cast-iron block. Bore & stroke: 3-11/16 x 4 in. Displacement: 170.9 cu. in. Compression ratio: 4.3:1. Net horsepower: 21.70. Brake horsepower: 35 at 1900 R.P.M. Three main bearings. Solid valve lifters. Carburetor: Carter one-barrel model.

CHASSIS: (Series F) Wheelbase: 103 in. Length: 142 in. Front tread: 58 in. Rear tread: 58 in. Tires: 30 x 3.5 in.

CHASSIS: (Series H) Wheelbase: 120 in. Front tread: 56 in. Rear tread: 56 in. Tires: (front) 30 x 3.5 in.; (rear) 30 x 5 in.

1924 Chevrolet Chemical Fire Wagon (DFW/WS)

TECHNICAL: Manual transmission. Speeds: 3F/1R. Floor-mounted gearshift. Cone type clutch. Semi-floating rear axle. Overall ratio: 3.82:1. External contracting mechanical rear brakes. Wooden spoke wheels.

OPTIONS: Front bumper. Rear bumper. Single sidemount. Heater. Rearview mirror. Panel body, ½-ton. Grain and stock body, 1-ton, open cab. Flareboard express body, 1-ton. Grain and stock body, 1-ton, fully-enclosed cab. Panel body, 1-ton. Coal truck body, 1-ton. Three-compartment tanker, 1-ton. Spare tires.

HISTORICAL: Introduced: August, 1923. Historical notes: Under W.S. Knudsen's direction, Chevrolet sales began to pickup at an unpredictable pace.

Pricing

	5	4	3	2	1
1924					
Series F					
Open Express	1450	2850	4750	6650	9500
Canopy Express	1500	3000	5000	7000	10,000
Panel Delivery	1500	3000	5000	7000	10,000
Station Wagon	1800	3600	6000	8400	12,000
Series H					
Open Cab Grain/Stock Body	1100	2200	3650	5100	7300
Closed Cab Grain/ Stock Body	1110	2220	3700	5200	7400
Flareboard Express	1050	2100	3500	4900	7000
Panel Body	1130	2250	3750	5250	7500
Dump/Coal Body	1150	2310	3850	5400	7700
Tanker (3 compartment)	1170	2340	3900	5450	7800

1925 CHEVROLET

SUPERIOR/UTILITY — SERIES M/SERIES K/SERIES R — FOUR-CYLINDER: — Introduced on the 1925 Series K Chevrolet truck models was a Fisher body with vertical ventilating windshield. This feature, along with a slightly-angled windshield position, contributed to a more modern appearance. During the year a longer, 124 inch wheelbase was used for the one-ton models. Major technical features were announced. The engine was substantially revised with new cylinder block, connecting rods and crankshaft. The rocker arms were now enclosed and a shorter intake manifold was installed. Replacing the old cone clutch was a single-disc dry plate type. The Series M appears to have been a late 1924 product, but historians regard it as a transitional 1925 Model. Later, the Series R one-ton was brought out. The "M" trucks used the same engine, clutch and transmission as the Series K Chevrolet passenger cars, but the rear axle was from the 1924 Series H truck. The "R" trucks had the Series K passenger car engine, transmission, clutch, hood, fenders, lights and radiator. However, the truck radiator was made of pressed steel, instead of the cast aluminum used for the car radiators. Standard equipment was the same as listed for 1923 models.

I.D. DATA: Serial number location: Same location as 1924. Serial numbers were: 1-H-1308 to 1-M-1812; 2-H-2384 to 2-M-4188; 3-H-4178 to 3-M-2496; 6-H-1814 to 6-M-1371; 9-H-1373 to 9-M-1719; 12-H-1733 to 12-M-2185 and 21-H-2107 to 21-M-1721. Engine numbers location: Same location as 1924.

Model	Body Type	Price	Weight	Prod. Total
Series M — (1-Ton)				
M	Chassis	550	1850	—
Series K — (½-Ton)				
K	Chassis	410	1380	—
Series R — (1-Ton)				
R	Chassis	Note 1	2035	—

NOTE 1: "Prices upon application" said Chevrolet literature.

ENGINE: (All) Inline. OHV. Four-cylinder. Cast-iron block. Bore & stroke: 3-11/16 x 4 in. Displacement: 170.9 cu. in. Compression ratio: 4.3:1. Brake horsepower: 35 at 1900 R.P.M. Net horsepower: 21.70. Three main bearings. Mechanical valve lifters. Carburetor: Carter one-barrel model RXO. Lubrication: Force feed and splash: Radiator: Cellular. Cooling: Water pump and fan. Ignition: Storage battery. Starting System: two-unit. Lighting System: Electric, six-volts. Gasoline System: Vacuum.

CHASSIS: (Series K) Wheelbase: 103 in. Length: 142 in. Front tread: 58 in. Rear tread: 58 in. Tires: 30 x 3.5 in.

CHASSIS: (Series M) Wheelbase: 120 in. Front tread: 56 in. Rear tread: 56 in. Tires: (front) 30 x 3.5 in.; (rear) 30 x 5 in.

CHASSIS: (Series R) Wheelbase: 124 in. Front tread: 56 in. Rear tread: 56 in. Tires: (front) 30 x 3.5 in.; (rear) 30 x 5 in.

TECHNICAL: Manual, sliding gear transmission. Speeds: 3F/1R. Floor-mounted gearshift. Single plate dry disc type clutch. Semi-floating rear axle. External contracting mechanical rear only brakes. Wooden spoke wheels.

OPTIONS: Front bumper. Rear bumper. Single sidemount. Heater. Rear-view mirror. Martin-Parry Co. Panel body. Springfield Panel body. Mifflinburg Station Wagon body. Spare tire(s), two required for one-ton front and rear.

HISTORICAL: Introduced: January, 1925. Innovations: Redesigned engine. Disc clutch. All-steel closed truck cabs introduced in late 1925 for 1926 model year. New 124 inch wheelbase series. Historical notes: A Chevrolet based U.S. Army Scout Car was supplied to the government this year. On June 3, 1925 the 100,000 Chevrolet built in Janesville, Wis. was assembled. It was a Series M one-ton Utility Express chassis. Series M trucks were the last Chevrolets to use quarter elliptic front springs.

Pricing

1925	5	4	3	2	1
Series M — (1924-25; 1-Ton)					
Flareboard Express	1050	2100	3500	4900	7000
Panel Body	1130	2250	3750	5250	7500
Series K — (½-Ton)					
Flareboard Express	1450	2850	4750	6650	9500
Panel Body	1500	3000	5000	7000	10,000
Station Wagon	1800	3600	6000	8400	12,000
Series R — (1-Ton)					
Flareboard Express	1050	2100	3500	4900	7000
Panel Body	1130	2250	3750	5250	7500
Grain Body	1110	2220	3700	5200	7400
Stake-Platform	1100	2200	3650	5100	7300
3-Compartment Tanker	1170	2340	3900	5450	7800
Dump Body	1150	2310	3850	5400	7700
Wrecker	1450	2850	4750	6650	9500

1926 CHEVROLET

1926 Chevrolet Capitol AA Pickup (L. Kemp/CPC)

SUPERIOR/UTILITY — SERIES V/SERIES X — FOUR-CYLINDER: — Chevrolet's Superior Series V was actually introduced in mid-1926 as a replacement for the Superior K. It included a chassis on which light-duty truck bodies could be installed. Most commonly seen in old photographs are "depot hack" type station wagons and "vestibule" type panel deliveries (the term "vestibule" referred to a fully-enclosed cab). More than

likely, express wagons (pickups) and other truck body styles were also built upon this chassis. Two new models were a roadster with cargo bed instead of rumble seat (Roadster Pickup) and another roadster with enclosed cargo box in the rear (Commercial Roadster). Such trucks were rated for ½-ton payloads. From serial numbers, it would appear that a substantial number of Series R trucks (one-ton) were also built and sold as 1926 models. This line was then replaced by the new Series X, which was technically similar. The Series X used the hood, fenders, lights and running gear of the late 1926 passenger cars. However, an innovation was the availability of a production-type lineup of truck bodies which were factory-built with all-steel enclosed cabs. This new series actually spanned two model years, with many "X" models sold as 1927 trucks. Standard equipment for 1926 models was about the same as the long list for the 1923 models.

I.D. DATA: Serial number location: Unchanged from 1925. (Series R-Early 1926 — Serial numbers) 1-R-1000 and up; 2-R-1000 and up; 3-R-1000 and up; 6-R-1000 and up; 9-R-1000 and up; 12-R-1000 and up and 21-R-1000 and up. Engine numbers location: Unchanged from 1925.

1926 Chevrolet Utility Express Chassis (OCW)

Model	Body Type	Price	Weight	Prod. Total
Series R — (1-Ton) — (1925-1926)				
R	Chassis	Note 1	1955	—
Series V — (½-Ton)				
V	Chassis	410	1520	—
Series X — (1-Ton) — (1926-1927)				
X	Chassis	—	—	—
X	Springfield Suburban	—	Note 2	—
X	Screenside Express	—	—	—

NOTE 1: "Prices upon application" said Chevrolet literature.

NOTE 2: This wood "station wagon" body weighed 725 pounds.

ENGINE: (All) Inline. OHV. Four-cylinder. Cast-iron block. Bore & stroke: 3-11/16 x 4 in. Displacement: 170.9 cu. in. Compression ratio: 4.3:1. Brake horsepower: 35 at 1900 R.P.M. Net horsepower: 21.7. Three main bearings. Mechanical valve lifters. Carburetor: Carter one-barrel model.

CHASSIS: (Series V) Wheelbase: 103 in. Length: 142 in. Front tread: 58 in. Rear tread: 58 in. Tires: 29 x 4.40 in.

CHASSIS: (Series X) Wheelbase: 120 in. Tires: (front) 30 x 5 in.; (rear) 30 x 3.5 in.

NOTE: See 1925 for R Series specs.

TECHNICAL: Manual, sliding gear transmission. Speeds: 3F/1R. Floor-mounted gearshift. Single plate, dry disc type clutch. Semi-floating rear axle. Overall ratio: 3.82:1 (V-series). Mechanical, external contracting rear brakes. Wooden spoke wheels.

1926 Chevrolet Open Cab Canopy Express (OCW)

OPTIONS: Front bumper. Rear bumper. Single sidemount. Heater. Side curtains. Spare tires. Rearview mirror. Optional bodies seen in old photos: (1) Springfield Panel with vestibule cab; (2) Suburban (Woodie) body, for Model X, by Springfield; (3) Gravity Dump body for coal delivery, by Proctor-Keefe Co.; (4) Mifflinburg combination Jitney/Express; (5) One-ton Rack Body by Springfield; (6) Hercules Vestibule Panel Delivery, for Model X.

HISTORICAL: Introduced: Mid-year 1926 (except Series R). Calendar year registrations: 113,682 (all Series). Innovations: New all-steel factory bodies on the Series X one-ton chassis. Bus-like depot wagons built for one-ton chassis. All-new series designations. Late in year, a new "Peddler's Wagon" is introduced to great popularity. Historical notes: A railcoach was built for a Louisiana Railroad using a Chevrolet Series X truck chassis. A panel version of the "X" was used by a Michigan college professor to search for rare fish in the northwestern United States. (Chevy donated the truck to him). An Australian bodied Series X bus made a 15-mile trip between Barwon Heads and Geelong, Australia, three times a day carrying up to 14 passengers.

Pricing

	5	4	3	2	1
1926					
Series V					
(Factory) Roadster Pickup	1450	2900	4800	6700	9600
(Factory) Commercial Roadster	1400	2800	4650	6500	9300
Hercules Panel Delivery	1500	3000	5000	7000	10,000
Springfield Country Club Suburban	1800	3600	6000	8400	12,000
Springfield Panel Delivery	1500	3000	5000	7000	10,000
Series X — (1926-1927)					
(Factory) Flareboard Express	1050	2100	3500	4900	7000
(Factory) Canopy Express	1130	2250	3750	5250	7500
(Factory) Screenside Express	1130	2250	3750	5750	7500
(Factory) Peddler's Wagon	1170	2340	3900	5450	7800
Mifflinburg Depot Hack	1500	3000	5000	7000	10,000
Springfield 12P Suburban	1500	3000	5000	7000	10,000
Proctor-Keefe Dump	1150	2310	3850	5400	7700
Mifflinburg Jitney/Express	1130	2250	3750	5750	7500
Platform Stake	1100	2200	3650	5100	7300
Rack Body w/Coach Front	1100	2200	3650	5100	7300

NOTE: See 1925 section for Series R pricing.

1927 CHEVROLET

1927 Chevrolet Panel Delivery (DFW/LOC)

CAPITOL — SERIES AA/SERIES LM — FOUR-CYLINDER: — Chevrolet's newest light-duty trucks were identified by their new radiator shell with a dipped center, bullet-shaped headlights with a black enamel finish with bright trim rings, and fuller crown fenders. The ½-ton Series AA was marketed as a commercial version of the passenger car chassis for aftermarket bodies. General Motors' bodies, for Chevrolet factory-installation, were used on the one-ton Series LM chassis. Of course, the bigger model could also be purchased as a chassis if the customer wished to add his or her own body.

I.D. DATA: Serial number located on right or left side of dash under the cowl and seat frame. Serial numbers unavailable. Engine numbers located on block ahead of fuel filter.

34

1927 Chevrolet Pickup (DFW/SAB)

Model	Body Type	Price	Weight	Prod. Total
Series Capitol AA — (½-Ton)				
AA	Chassis	495	2130	—
Series LM — (1-Ton)				
LM	(Factory) Panel Dely.	755	2850	—
LM	(Factory) Stake Bed	680	3045	—
LM	Chassis	550	1955	—

ENGINE: (All) Inline. OHV. Four-cylinder. Cast-iron block. Bore & stroke: 3-11/16 x 4 in. Displacement: 170.9 cu. in. Compression ratio: 4.3:1. Brake horsepower: 35 at 1900 R.P.M. Net horsepower: 21.8. Three main bearings. Mechanical valve lifters. Carburetor: Carter one-barrel model.

CHASSIS: (Series AA) Wheelbase: 103 in. Usable load space length: 64 in. (Panel). Width: 42 in. (Panel). Tires: 29 x 4.40 in.

1927 Chevrolet Commercial Depot Hack (OCW)

CHASSIS: (Series LM) Wheelbase: 124 in. Width: (Panel) 44* In.

* Hercules' standard panel body. Hercules also produced a flare side panel that had a 51 inch width and appropriate wheel cutouts. This larger panel was 94.5 inches long, compared to the standard panel's 93 inches. The factory type LM panel body was 42 inches wide by 45 inches high and had a usable load length of 102 inches.

TECHNICAL: Manual transmission. Speeds: 3F/1R. Floor-mounted gearshift. Single plate, dry disc type clutch. Semi-floating rear axle. Overall ratio: 3.82:1. External contracting, two-wheel rear brakes. Wooden spoke wheels.

1927 Chevrolet 1-Ton Gravity Dump Truck (OCW)

OPTIONS: Front bumper. Rear bumper. Single sidemount. Spare tire(s). Side curtains. Moto meter. Dual taillamps. Heater. Disc wheels (on commercials; std. passenger cars). Cowl lamps. Outside rearview mirror. Optional bodies from old photos: (1) Martin-Parry Dump; (2) Hercules dump; (3) Kentucky Wagon Works' Jitney Bus/School Bus; (4) Hercules Vestibule Panel (Standard or Flare side); (5) Hercules Cattle Body.

HISTORICAL: Introduced: January, 1927. Calendar year registrations: 104,832 (all Series). Innovations: New Capitol AA Light Delivery series. New LM one-ton series. New bullet headlights. Dipped style radiator shell adopted. Rectangular brake and clutch pedals. New coincidential lock. Historical notes: A South African built series LM one-ton truck carried supplies and communications equipment on a Cape Town to Stockholm (via Cairo and London) Chevrolet promotional tour in 1927.

Pricing

1927

	5	4	3	2	1
Capitol AA Series					
Roadster Pickup	1500	2950	4900	6850	9800
Commercial Roadster	1500	2950	4900	6850	9800
Open Express	1450	2850	4750	6650	9500
Station Wagon	1950	3900	6500	9100	13,000
Panel Delivery	1600	3150	5250	7300	10,500
Series LM					
Open Express	1130	2250	3750	5250	7500
Panel Delivery	1200	2400	4000	5600	8000
Dump	1200	2400	4000	5600	8000
Suburban (Station Wagon)	1800	3600	6000	8400	12,000
School Bus	1200	2400	4000	5600	8000
Peddler's Wagon	1300	2550	4250	5900	8500
Cattle Body/Stake	1130	2250	3750	5250	7500
Canopy Express	1200	2460	4100	5700	8200
Screenside Express	1200	2460	4100	5700	8200

1928 CHEVROLET

1928 Chevrolet Suburban Delivery (ATC)

NATIONAL — SERIES AB/SERIES LO/SERIES LP — FOUR-CYLINDER: — The 1928 Chevrolets were very similar to the models of the previous year. Four-wheel brakes were installed on light-duty models. The wheelbase was now 107 inches, up from 103 in 1927. Fenders were more crowned, headlights were larger and the cowl line was raised. With a higher compression ratio, larger valves, increased valve lift and a two-piece exhaust manifold the Chevrolet engine developed 35 horsepower at a higher 2200 R.P.M. Three series of trucks were marketed as 1928 models. The National AB was the ½-ton "commercial car" line. Transitional between 1927 and 1928, was the one-ton Series LO. The Series LP was a new one-ton line with a four-speed transmission and the four-wheel braking system (which the "LO" trucks lacked).

I.D. DATA: Serial numbers placed on front door heel board on either the left or right side. Also on nameplate on dash. Serial numbers for the AB series were 9-B-1000 and up. Engine number located on block just ahead of the oil filter, near fuel pump.

1928 Chevrolet Panel Delivery (DFW/MS)

Model	Body Type	Price	Weight	Prod. Total
Series National AB — (½-Ton)				
AB	Chassis	495	2130	—
AB	Pickup	—	—	—
AB	Canopy Delivery	—	—	—
AB	Screenside Dely.	—	—	—
AB	Panel Delivery	—	—	—
AB	Sedan Delivery	690	2450	1004
AB	Roadster Pickup	545	2130	—
AB	Commercial Roadster	575	2190	—
AB	Henney Hearse	1500	2800	—
AB	Henney Ambulance	1600	2800	—
Series LO — (1-Ton)				
LO	Chassis	520	—	—
Series LP — (1-Ton)				
LP	Chassis	520	—	—

1928 Chevrolet Depot Hack (FLW)

ENGINE: (All) Inline. OHV. Four-cylinder. Cast-iron block. Bore & stroke: 3-11/16 x 4 in. Displacement: 170.9 cu. in. Compression ratio: 4.5:1. Brake horsepower: 35 at 2200 R.P.M. Net horsepower: 21.7. Three main bearings. Mechanical valve lifters. Carburetor: Carter one-barrel model.

CHASSIS: (Series AB) Wheelbase: 107 in. Length: 156 in. Load Space: 72 in. Front tread: 56 in. Rear tread: 56 in. Tires: 30 x 4.50 in.

1928 Chevrolet Screenside Express (OCW)

1928 Chevrolet Pickup (JB)

CHASSIS: (Series LO) Wheelbase: 124 in.

CHASSIS: (Series LP) Wheelbase: 124 in.

TECHNICAL: Manual transmission. Speeds: 3F/1R. Floor-mounted gearshift. Single plate, dry disc type clutch. Semi-floating rear axle. Overall ratio: 3.82:1. Mechanical brakes. Wooden spoke or steel disc wheels.

OPTIONS: Front bumper. Rear bumper. Heater. Wood spoke wheels. Exterior rearview mirror. Slip-in pickup box for AB roadster. Commercial cargo box for AB roadster. (called "Panel Carrier")

HISTORICAL: Introduced: January, 1928. Calendar year registrations: 133,682 (all Series). Innovations: Four-wheel brakes. New four-speed transmission standard on Series LP (formerly an option). Refinements to engine (also last year for 170.9 cu. in. four-cylinder.) All-new sedan delivery body. Historical notes: Chevrolet was becoming a serious threat to Ford's sales leadership in both the car and truck markets.

Pricing

	5	4	3	2	1
1928					
Series National AB					
Roadster w/Slip-in Pickup					
Box	1500	3000	5000	7000	10,000
Roadster w/Panel Carrier	1500	3000	5000	7000	10,000
Pickup Express	1500	2900	4850	6800	9700
Canopy Delivery	1500	2950	4950	6900	9900
Screenside Delivery	1500	2950	4950	6900	9900
Panel Delivery	1600	3150	5250	7300	10,500
Sedan Delivery	1650	3300	5500	7700	11,000
Henney Hearse	1200	2400	4000	5600	8000
Henney Ambulance	1300	2550	4250	5900	8500
Series LO/LP					
Open Express Delivery	1150	2310	3850	5400	7700
Canopy Express	1250	2520	4200	5850	8400
Screenside Express	1250	2520	4200	5850	8400
Panel Delivery	1250	2500	4150	5800	8300
Platform Stake	1150	2310	3850	5400	7700
Dump Body	1200	2400	4000	5600	8000
Peddler's Wagon	1350	2650	4400	6150	8800
Tow Truck	1500	3000	5000	7000	10,000
Tank Truck	1500	3000	5000	7000	10,000

1929 CHEVROLET

INTERNATIONAL — SERIES AC — SIX-CYLINDER: — The 1929 Chevrolet light-delivery trucks had more rectangular radiators, fewer louvers at the rear side of the hood only, bullet-shaped headlights and full-crowned fenders. Of great importance was the introduction of the "Cast-Iron Wonder," Chevy's long-lived and extremely successful overhead valve six-cylinder engine. Models in both lines used passenger car sheet metal and the same black radiator shell as cars. "AC" was the ½-ton series or what Ford called commercial cars. "LQ" was the year's bigger truck line. However, it was a 1½-ton series, which doesn't fit into the scope of this study. Features of 1929 models included a standard side-mounted spare on the driver's side of sedan deliveries. A new Deluxe Panel Delivery (with Geneva body) was called the "Ambassador." It had wood body framing with steel outer paneling, imitation Spanish black leather upholstery, and multi-tone

1929 Chevrolet Roadster Pickup (OCW)

finish. The body was medium-light blue on upper portions and dark blue on the lower portions, black on hood, fenders and disc wheels and had an orange beltline panel.

I.D. DATA: Location of serial number: nameplate on dash. Starting number: AC-1000 and up. Engine number location: right side of cylinder block behind fuel pumps.

Model	Body Type	Price	Weight	Prod. Total
AC	Chassis	400	1815	—
AC	Sedan Dely.	595	2450	—
AC	Pickup	—	—	—
AC	Canopy or Screen	—	—	—
AC	Panel	—	—	9640

ENGINE: Inline. OHV. Six-cylinder. Cast-iron block. Bore & stroke: 3-5/16 x 3¾ in. Displacement: 194 cu. in. Compression ratio: 5.02:1. Brake horsepower: 46 at 2600 R.P.M. Net horsepower: 21.7. Three main bearings. Solid valve lifters. Carburetor: Carter one-barrel model 150S.

CHASSIS: (Series AC) Wheelbase: 107 in. Length: 156 in. Front tread: 56 in. Rear tread: 56 in. Tires: 20 x 4.50 in.

NOTE: Panel delivery load space was 72 inches long, 44 inches wide and 49 inches high.

1929 Chevrolet Roadster Pickup (MC)

TECHNICAL: Manual transmission. Speeds: 3F/1R. Floor-mounted gearshift. Single plate, dry disc type clutch. Semi-floating rear axle. Overall ratio: 3.82:1. Mechanical, four-wheel brakes. Disc wheels.

OPTIONS: Front bumper. Rear bumper. Single sidemount. Heater. Cigar lighter. Wire wheels. Exterior mirror. Slip-in pickup box for roadster. Cargo carrier for roadster.

HISTORICAL: Introduced: December, 1928. Calendar year registrations: 160,959 (all Series). Innovations: New six-cylinder engine. One-piece full crown fenders. New bullet type lamps. Electro lock. Banjo type rear axle. Chrome plated radiator shell. New multi-color finish with contrasting double belt panel. Longer 107 inch wheelbase. 17 inch rubber covered steering wheel. New line of panel bodies by Geneva Body Co. of Geneva, N.Y. Historical notes: The new six-cylinder engine was a strong selling point which carried Chevrolet's car and truck sales to record levels. During 1929, the company produced its 500,000th commercial vehicle and reported accumulated retail sales of 641,482 trucks since 1918, the majority of which were light-duty models of one-ton or less capacity.

1929	5	4	3	2	1
International Series AC					
Roadster w/Slip-in Cargo Box	1600	3150	5250	7300	10,500
Roadster w/Panel Carrier	1600	3150	5250	7300	10,500
Open Express	1500	2950	4950	6900	9900
Canopy Express	1500	3000	5000	7000	10,000
Sedan Delivery	1700	3450	5750	8050	11,500
Screenside Express	1500	3000	5000	7000	10,000
Panel Delivery	1650	3300	5500	7700	11,000
Ambassador Panel Delivery	1950	3900	6500	9100	13,000

1930 CHEVROLET

1930 Chevrolet Delivery Truck (DFW/ABA)

UNIVERSAL — SERIES AD — SIX-CYLINDER: — Chevrolet trucks for light-duty use, like the Chevrolet passenger cars, were fitted with a new instrument panel. An electric gasoline gauge was included in its array of circular gauges. The rear brakes were fully enclosed and Lovejoy hydraulic shock absorbers, plus a stronger rear axle, were now used.

The Chevrolet engine now developed 50 horsepower due primarily to a revised valve train with smaller exhaust and larger intake valves. Appearance-wise the latest Chevrolets had a slightly less vertical windshield. A new model was a Deluxe Delivery truck, which was a luxury version of the Sedan Delivery with carriage lamps just behind the doors. This year's Panel Delivery also came in standard and Deluxe versions, with the fancier edition having extra windows in the rear quarters of the cab section, plus lower and longer general lines.

I.D. DATA: Location of serial number: on dash-mounted nameplate. Starting number: AD-1000 and up. Engine number location: on right side of motor block behind fuel pump.

Model	Body Type	Price	Weight	Prod. Total
AD	Chassis	365	1815	—
AD	Sedan Delivery	595	2450	6522
AD	Panel Delivery	—	—	—
AD	Deluxe Delivery	—	—	—
AD	Deluxe Panel Body	—	—	—
AD	Pickup	—	—	—
AD	Canopy Delivery	—	—	—
AD	Screenside Delivery	—	—	—
AD	Roadster Pickup	—	—	—

1930 Chevrolet Popcorn Truck (R. Barbour/CPC)

1930 Chevrolet Huckster (MC)

ENGINE: Inline. OHV. Six-cylinder. Cast-iron block. Bore & stroke: 3-5/16 x 3¾ in. Displacement: 194 cu. in. Compression ratio: 5.02:1. Brake horsepower: 50 at 2600 R.P.M. Net horsepower: 26.3. Three main bearings. Mechanical valve lifters. Carburetor: Carter one-barrel model 150S.

CHASSIS: (Series AD) Wheelbase: 107 in. Tires: 19 x 4.75 in.

TECHNICAL: Manual transmission. Speeds: 3F/1F. Floor-mounted gearshift. Single plate type clutch. Shaft drive. Semi-floating rear axle. Overall ratio: 4.1:1. Internal, expanding four-wheel mechanical brakes. Wire or disc wheels.

OPTIONS: Front bumper. Rear bumper. Single sidemount. Side curtains. Right-hand taillamp. Special paint. Oversized tires. Cargo box-tarpaulin. Heater. Spare tire(s). Cigar lighter. Lettering stencils. External sun shade. Spotlight. Cowl lamps. Rearview mirror.

HISTORICAL: Introduced: January, 1930. Calendar year registrations: 118,253 (all Series). Innovations: More powerful six-cylinder engine. New Deluxe Sedan Delivery. New Roadster Pickup becomes a separate model, rather than roadster with slip-in cargo box. Historical notes: The U.S. Department of Agriculture maintained a large fleet of Chevrolet sedan deliveries for use in Midwestern states during a corn blight. A military gun wagon was constructed on a 1930 Series AD ½-ton chassis as a U.S. Army munitions experiment. It had an armored body, gun turret and 50 calibre machine gun.

Pricing

1930	5	4	3	2	1
Roadster Pickup	1600	3150	5250	7300	10,500
Pickup Express	1500	2950	4950	6900	9900
Panel Delivery	1650	3300	5500	7700	11,000
Deluxe Panel Delivery	1950	3900	6500	9100	13,000
Sedan Delivery	2050	4050	6750	9450	13,500
Deluxe Sedan Delivery	2100	4200	7000	9800	14,000
Canopy Express	1500	3000	5000	7000	10,000
Screenside Express	1500	3000	5000	7000	10,000

1931 CHEVROLET

1931 Chevrolet Depot Hack (OCW)

INDEPENDENCE — SERIES AE — SIX-CYLINDER: — The "Independence" series of Chevrolet trucks featured a longer set of side hood louvers than did the 1930 models. Early versions of the optional front and rear bumpers were of a two-piece design but this was changed during the model run to a single-piece design. Also apparent was a higher and larger radiator. The Sedan Delivery had a bright radiator shell, bright headlight buckets, wire wheels and a sidemount on the driver's side. It was shown in advertising literature with whitewall tires. Also available was the Light Delivery with a coupe-like driver's compartment and disc wheels. It had a load space 72 inches long by 45 inches wide and 48 inches high. Another half-tonner was the Light Delivery Canopy Express having similar body dimensions but open sides with curtain or screen side options. Its standard equipment included water-proof curtains for the sides and rear (screens were optional), a sedan-type roof, coupe-type cab and disc wheels. There was also an open cab pickup with a cargo box 66 inches long, 45 inches wide and 13 inches deep. Its body sides were designed to meet the floor at right angles. Equipment included a roadster-type cab and disc wheels.

I.D. DATA: Location of serial number: See 1930. Starting number: AE-1001 and up. Engine number location: See 1930.

1931 Chevrolet Deluxe Canopy Express (OCW)

Model	Body Type	Price	Weight	Prod. Total
AE	Chassis	355	1970	—
AE	Sedan Delivery	575	2675	—
AE	Panel Delivery	555	2800	—
AE	Pickup	565	2890	—
AE	Open Cab Pickup	440	2400	—

ENGINE: Inline. OHV. Six-cylinder. Cast-iron block. Bore & stroke: 3-5/16 x 3¾ in. Displacement: 194 cu. in. Compression ratio: 5.02:1. Brake horsepower: 50 at 2600 R.P.M. Net horsepower: 26.3. Three main bearings. Mechanical valve lifters. Carburetor: Carter one-barrel model 150S.

CHASSIS: (Series AE) Wheelbase: 109 in. Tires: 19 x 4.75 in.

TECHNICAL: Manual transmission. Speeds: 3F/1R. Floor-mounted gearshift. Single disc type clutch. Semi-floating rear axle. Overall ratio: 4.1:1. Internal, expanding mechanical (four-wheel) brakes. Steel disc or wire wheels.

OPTIONS: Front bumper. Rear bumper. Single sidemount. White sidewall tires. Sidemount cover(s). Wire wheels on pickup, panel or canopy express. Deluxe hood ornament. OSRV mirror. Heater. Right-hand taillight. Cigar lighter. Screen-sides for canopied express. Special paint colors. Stencils for company name application. Spotlight. Wheel trim rings. Deluxe equipment.

HISTORICAL: Introduced: November, 1930. Calendar year registrations: 99,600 (all Series). Innovations: New vibrator horn below left headlight. Revised hood louver design. Longer (by two inches) wheelbase. Enclosed brakes. Lovejoy shock absorbers on Deluxe models. New crankshaft vibration dampener. Historical notes: Late in 1930, Chevrolet purchased the Martin-Parry Co. of Indianapolis, Ind., which allowed the company to finally offer "factory" truck bodies. A new Deluxe ½-ton chassis was introduced using passenger car front end sheet metal. It became the basis of many station wagons, hearses, ambulances — and other special bodies where a non-truck appearance was preferable. This was the first year that a variety of finish colors were available. Before 1929, trucks were painted black. From 1929 to this year, Blue Bell blue was the standard color. Chevrolet had about 32.7 percent sales penetration in the light-truck market this year. The acquisition of Martin-Parry Co. would send this figure skyrocketing upwards.

Pricing

	5	4	3	2	1
1931					
Open Cab Pickup	1800	3600	6000	8400	12,000
Closed Cab Pickup	1500	2950	4950	6900	9900
Panel Delivery	1650	3300	5500	7700	11,000
Canopy Delivery (curtains)	1500	3000	5000	7000	10,000
Canopy Delivery (screens)	1500	3000	5000	7000	10,000
Sedan Delivery	2050	4050	6750	9450	13,500
Deluxe Station Wagon	1800	3600	6000	8400	12,000

NOTE: Add 5 percent for Deluxe ½-ton models.

1932 CHEVROLET

1932 Chevrolet Sedan Delivery (DFW/ABA)

CONFEDERATE — SERIES BB — SIX-CYLINDER: — The 1932 Chevrolet trucks with their 1931-Chevrolet passenger car front end appearance were now equipped with a "Silent Synchromesh" transmission. The Chevrolet engine, with a new downdraft carburetor, higher valve lift and compression ratio, now developed 60 horsepower. Other engine refinements included external ribbing for the block which was also increased in thickness. Replacing the three-point solid engine mounting system was a new four-point setup with rubber bushings. Standard trucks had flat-sided bodies and black-finished radiators and headlight buckets. Front bumpers and rear guards were not included as standard equipment on these models. Models with deluxe equipment were called "Specials" and had passenger car front end sheet metal. The Special Panel Delivery was the first Chevrolet to use a bright metal beltline molding. The Specials also had chrome headlamps and shock absorbers. Also, some Sedan Deliveries were produced with the door-type hood ventilators used on 1932 passenger cars.

I.D. DATA: Serial Number located: See 1930 section. Starting: BB-1001 and up. Engine numbers located: See 1930 section.

Model	Body Type	Price	Weight	Prod. Total
Confederate Series — (½-Ton)				
BB	Chassis	345	2020	—
BB	Special Chassis	365	2060	—
BB	Open Cab Pickup	430	2460	—
BB	Closed Cab Pickup	440	2555	—
BB	Canopied Express	500	2735	—
BB	Screenside Express	510	2735	—
BB	Panel Delivery	565	2755	—
BB	Spec. Panel Delivery	585	2820	—
BB	Sedan Delivery	575	2720	—

NOTE: Prices seem to have changed during the model year. Following are some other prices noted in sales literature: Half-ton Deluxe Panel ($595); Standard Panel ($560); Standard Canopy Express ($560); Standard Canopy Express with screen-sides ($579); Closed Cab Pickup ($470); Closed Cab Pickup with Canopy Top and Curtains ($500); Special Canopy Express ($580); Special Panel ($580); Open Cab Pickup with Canopy Top ($470). It is likely that the economic effects of the depression caused these changes and the addition of extra features (i.e. canopy tops on pickups) as a means of promoting more sales.

ENGINE: Inline. OHV. Six-cylinder. Cast-iron block. Bore & stroke: 3-5/16 x 3¾ in. Displacement: 194 cu. in. Compression ratio: 5.2:1. Brake horsepower: 60 at 3000 R.P.M. Net horsepower: 26.3. Three main bearings. Mechanical valve lifters. Carburetor: Carter one-barrel model 150S.

1932 Chevrolet Sedan Delivery (OCW)

CHASSIS: (Series BA) Wheelbase: 109 in. Tires: 18 x 5.24 in.

TECHNICAL: Manual, synchromesh (on light delivery models). Speeds: 3F/1R. Floor-mounted gearshift. Single plate type clutch. Semi-floating rear axle. Overall ratio: 4.1:1. Four wheel internal-expanding mechanical brakes. Wire wheels. Free-wheeling.

OPTIONS: Front bumper. Rear bumper. Single sidemount. Heater. Cowl lamps. Dual wipers. Fender well tire lock. Metal tire cover. Standard tire cover.

1932 Chevrolet Panel Delivery (DFW)

HISTORICAL: Introduced: December, 1931. Calendar year registrations: 60,784 (all Series). Innovations: Higher horsepower engine. First year for different styling appearance on cars and trucks. New 18 inch wire wheels standard for all models. Greater emphasis on marketing ''deluxe'' equipment for trucks. Historical notes: Chevrolet began placing great emphasis on improvements of its fleet sales program during this model-year. William S. Knudsen was general manager of Chevrolet from 1922 to 1932.

1932 Chevrolet Stand-up Delivery Van (DFW/SI)

Pricing

1932	5	4	3	2	1
Open Cab Pickup	1850	3750	6250	8750	12,500
Closed Cab Pickup	1500	3000	5000	7000	10,000
Canopied Express	1600	3150	5250	7300	10,500
Screen-Side Express	1600	3150	5250	7300	10,500
Panel Delivery	1700	3450	5750	8050	11,500
Special Panel Delivery	1850	3750	6250	8750	12,500
Sedan Delivery	2050	4050	6750	9450	13,500
Special Sedan Delivery	2100	4200	7000	9800	14,000

NOTE: Add 5 percent for Special Equipment on models other than those noted as ''Specials'' above.
Add 2 percent for Canopy Tops on both pickups.

1933 CHEVROLET

1933 Chevrolet Sedan Delivery (OCW)

EAGLE/MASTER EAGLE — SERIES CB — SIX-CYLINDER: — This was the last year Chevrolet used names such as ''Eagle'' and ''Master'' as well as letters to identify its truck models. Chevrolet continued the practice of fitting its light-duty trucks with a grille virtually identical to that introduced one year earlier on the Chevrolet passenger cars. The hood louver design, however, was still of the 1931 style. Providing 65 horsepower at 3000 R.P.M. was a new ''Blue Flame'' engine with a longer four-inch stroke resulting in a displacement of 206.8 cu. in. A four-speed transmission was now optional in light-duty models. Standard equipment varied by model. The Pickup truck came with a 66 x 45 x 13 inch cargo box, all-steel box construction, double security chains and left-hand sidemount spare. The standard Sedan Delivery had a load space 57 x 50 x 44.5 inches and 36 inch wide curbside opening rear door. Its sheet metal was truck-like, but bright metal headlamp shells, radiator shell and cowl molding were standard, as well as a left-hand sidemount. The Deluxe Sedan Delivery included coach lamps on the body rear quarters, sidemount cover, bright metal trim parts and, in some cases, the ventilator door style hood. The Special ½-ton Panel Delivery came with a recessed-panel body, chrome headlamps and radiator shell, bright metal headlight tie-bar, chromed bumpers and a bright OSRV mirror. Its load space was 72 x 45 x 48 inches. Insulation and a dome lamp were found inside. The canopy truck was similarsized with 18 inch deep steel sides, chrome trim parts and a slanted windshield. (*) Measurements given above are length x width x height.

I.D. DATA: Serial Number located: Same location as 1930. Starting: CB-1001 and up. Engine numbers located: Same location as 1930.

Model	Body Type	Price	Weight	Prod. Total
CB	Chassis	330	1995	—
CB	Special Chassis	345	2025	—
CB	Sedan Delivery	545	2775	3628
CB	Chassis Cab	420	2345	—
CB	Closed Cab Pickup	440	2565	—
CB	Panel Delivery	530	2750	—
CB	Special Panel Delivery	545	2885	—

NOTE 1: As the price of ''Special'' equipment appears to be $15, it's likely the Special Sedan Delivery sold for $560. The production figure given for this body style covers both trim variations. Figures for other body style's output are not available.

ENGINE: Inline. OHV. Six-cylinder. Cast-iron block. Bore & stroke: 3-5/16 x 4 in. Displacement: 206.8 cu. in. Compression ratio: 5.2:1. Brake horsepower: 65 at 2800 R.P.M. Net horsepower: 26.33. Three main bearings. Mechanical valve lifters. Carburetor: Carter one-barrel model W1.

1933 Chevrolet ''CB'' Canopy Express (R. Streval)

CHASSIS: (Series CB) Wheelbase: 109 in. Tires: 18 x 5.24 in.

TECHNICAL: Manual, synchromesh transmission. Speeds: 3F/1R. Floor-mounted gearshift. Single plate type clutch. Semi-floating rear axle. Over-all ratio: 4.11:1. Mechanical four wheel brakes. Wire spoke wheels.

OPTIONS: Front bumper. Rear bumper. Single sidemount. OSRV mirror. Special paint. Leatherette sidemount cover. Bumper guards. Right-hand taillight. Heater. Dual windshield wipers. Pedestal mirrors for sidemounts. Special paint. Seat covers. White sidewall tires. Lettering stencils. Spotlight. Coachlights (Sedan Delivery).

HISTORICAL: Introduced: December, 1932. Calendar year registrations: 99,880 (all Series). Innovations: New larger, more powerful "Blue Flame" six-cylinder engine. Completely new appearance with 1932 car-type radiator grille, fenders and headlights and 1931 car type hoods (except vent-door hoods optional on Deluxe Sedan Delivery). Historical notes: Factory built body availability and the strong sales to fleet operators and government agencies increased Chevrolet's penetration of the light-truck market to nearly 50 percent in 1933. The company produced its one-millionth commercial vehicle during the model-year. Chevrolet was now selling as many trucks in the ½-ton and 1½-ton weight classes as all other makers put together. M.E. Coyle took over as general manager of Chevrolet when William S. Knudsen was promoted to a GM Executive Vice-Presidency.

Pricing

	5	4	3	2	1
1933					
Sedan Delivery	1650	3300	5500	7700	11,000
Special Sedan Delivery	2050	4050	6750	9450	13,500
Closed Cab Pickup	1350	2700	4500	6300	9000
Panel Delivery	1300	3000	5000	7000	10,000
Special Panel Delivery	1600	3150	5250	7300	10,500
Canopy Express	1450	2850	4750	6650	9500
Special Canopy Express	1500	2950	4900	6850	9800
Screen-side Express	1500	2950	4950	6900	9900

NOTE: Add 2 percent for canopied pickups.

1934 CHEVROLET

1934 Chevrolet Pickup (DFW/SI)

HALF-TON TRUCK — SERIES DB — SIX-CYLINDER: — Dramatic new styling was a highlight of the latest Chevrolet trucks. Accentuating the smoother body contours and more fully-crowned fenders were two-tone color combinations available on most body styles. The elimination of the front tie-bar support for the headlights, plus the use of three curved vertical hood louvers, gave the Chevrolets a fresh contemporary look. Standard and Deluxe models used the same front end trim parts, but they were painted on lower-priced trucks and plated on the fancy ones. Dimensions for specific models, following the previous format, were: Pickup — 72 x 45 x 54 inches; Panel — 72 x 52 x 51 inches; Canopy — 72 x 52 x 54 inches. Wheelbase of the sedan delivery was five inches shorter than other models as it was based on Chevrolet's standard Series DC passenger car chassis, while other models used the Master DA Series car chassis with beefed up components for trucking.

I.D. DATA: Serial Number located: Same location as 1930. Starting: DB: DB-1001 and up. Engine numbers located: Same location as 1930. Starting: 3964078 and up.

Model	Body Type	Price	Weight	Prod. Total
DB	Chassis	355	2150	—
DB	Chassis Pickup	465	2850	—
DB	Canopy Top Pickup	495	2850	—
DB	Special Chassis	395	2150	—
DB	Special Chassis Cab	465	2485	—
DB	Special Pickup	485	2720	—
DB	Panel Delivery	575	2935	—
DB	Special Panel Delivery	615	2960	—
DB	Sedan Delivery	600	—	—

1934 Chevrolet Canopy Top Pickup (DFW/SI)

ENGINE: Same as 1933 engine.

CHASSIS: (Series DB) Wheelbase: (Sedan Delivery) 107 in.; (others) 112 in. Tires: 5.50 x 17 in.

TECHNICAL: Manual, synchromesh transmission. Speeds: 3F/1R. Floor-mounted gearshift. Semi-floating rear axle. Overall ratio: 4.11:1. Mechanical four wheel brakes. Wire spoke wheels.

OPTIONS: Front bumper. Rear bumper. Single sidemount. Dual sidemount. Sidemount (cover)s. Heater. Seat covers.

1934 Chevrolet Utility Pickup (DFW/USFS)

1934 Chevrolet Sedan Delivery (OCW)

HISTORICAL: Introduced: December, 1933. Calendar year registrations: 157,507 (all Series). Innovations: All-new styling. Sedan Delivery adopts shorter wheelbase. Engine moved further forward in chassis. Historical notes: For the first time since 1918, Chevrolet trucks had their own exclusive front sheet metal which was non-interchangeable with passenger car components.

Pricing

	5	4	3	2	1
1934					
Closed Cab Pickup	1300	2650	4350	6050	8700
Canopied Pickup	1350	2700	4500	6500	9000
Canopy Express w/Curtains	1400	2800	4600	6600	9200
Canopy Express w/Screens	1400	2800	4650	6650	9300
Panel Delivery	1450	2850	4750	6700	9500
Sedan Delivery	1600	3150	5250	7300	10,500

NOTE: Add 5 percent for "Special" models.

1935 CHEVROLET

1935 Chevrolet Parcel Delivery Van (JAW)

HALF-TON TRUCK — SERIES EB — SIX-CYLINDER: — Changes for 1935 were very minor, except for the introduction of a new model that would have great significance upon the light-duty truck field. This was the Suburban Carryall, an all-steel eight-passenger ''Station Wagon'' which was part of the upper-level Master series. An unusual thing about this truck was that it would eventually be sold with several entry-door configurations including two-, three- and four-doors. The original had two, plus a tailgate type rear load entrance. There were also some braking improvements in 1935. As in 1934, the Sedan Delivery had the chassis and sheet metal of Chevy's standard car-line, although the grille was plated and a right-hand sidemount was standard. Its hood also had three different sized horizontal louvers — smallest at bottom and largest at top. Other half-ton trucks had four curved vertical louvers on the rear most surface of the hoodsides. Wire wheels, chrome hub caps and a right-hand sidemount were standard. Chrome headlights, a chrome grille screen, radiator shell band, headlamp supports, spare tire hold-down and shock absorbers were part of the year's special equipment package. Rear bumpers were optional.

I.D. DATA: Serial Number located: on nameplate and dash. Starting numbers: (Sedan Delivery) EC-1001 and up; (others) EB-1001 and up. Engine numbers located: Same location as 1934. Starting: EB: 4708995 and up.

Model	Body Type	Price	Weight	Prod. Total
Series EB/EC — (½-Ton)				
EB	Commercial Chassis	355	2135	—
EB	Spec. Commercial Chassis	375	2235	—
EB	Chassis Cab Pickup	465	2585	—
EB	Panel Delivery	500	2920	—
EB	Special Panel Delivery	580	3035	—
EB	Chassis and Cab	445	2480	—
EB	Pickup	465	2700	—
EB	Spec. Pickup	485	2810	—
EB	Canopy Pickup	495	2795	—
EC	Sedan Delivery	515	2675	6192

ENGINE: Same as 1933-1934 engine, except: Compression ratio: 5.45:1. Brake horsepower: 80 at 3300 R.P.M. Carter Model 284S carburetor.

CHASSIS: (Series EB) Wheelbase: 112 in. Tires: 5.50 x 17 in.

CHASSIS: (Series EC) Wheelbase: 107 in. Tires: 17 x 5.25 in.

TECHNICAL: Same as 1934.

OPTIONS: Deluxe equipment. Rear bumper. Single sidemount. Metal sidemount covers. Fabric sidemount covers. Fender skirts. Bumper guards. Radio. Heater. Clock. Cigar lighter. Radio antenna. Seat covers. Foglights. Spotlight. Special paint. Wheel trim rings. Canopy top for pickup. License plate frames. Two-tone paint. Lettering stencils. Screen-sides for Canopy Express. Pickup box tarpaulin. OSRV mirror. Pedestal mirrors for sidemounts.

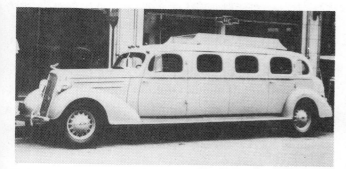

1935 Chevrolet Aerobus (DFW/DPL)

HISTORICAL: Introduced: December 15, 1934. Calendar year registrations: 167,129 (all Series). Innovations: All-new Suburban Carryall. Improved brakes. Historical notes: Suburban Carryall was first all-steel station wagon, although Checker produced a somewhat similar model in 1930-1931 period, as did Chrysler in its Fargo truck-line. However, both of these were more sedan-like than the new ''Suburban,'' as it came to be called later on.

Pricing

1935	5	4	3	2	1
Series EB					
Closed Cab Pickup	1300	2650	4350	6050	8700
Special Pickup	1425	2825	4650	6550	9150
Canopy Top Pickup	1350	2700	4500	6500	9000
Panel Delivery	1450	2850	4750	6700	9500
Special Panel Delivery	1325	2475	4975	6950	9950
Canopy w/Curtains	1400	2800	4600	6600	9200
Canopy w/Screens	1400	2800	4650	6650	9300
Series EC					
Sedan Delivery	1600	3150	5250	7300	10,500
Suburban	1500	3000	5050	7050	10,100

1936 CHEVROLET

1936 Chevrolet Pickup (DFW)

HALF-TON TRUCK — SERIES FB — SIX-CYLINDER: — Chevrolet began the model year with trucks little changed in appearance (exterior) from those of 1935. A new interior feature was a revamped dash closely patterned after that of the Chevrolet passenger cars. During the model year a model cab style was introduced that set the stage for the 1937 models. All 1936 Chevrolet trucks had horizontal hood louvers in place of the vertical openings found on the 1935 models. One new model was a Coupe Delivery which was essentially a five-window Business Coupe with cargo box built into its trunk (replacing the trunk lid) and a sidemounted spare. A trunk lid was supplied, too, and could be switched with the cargo box by loosening four bolts and substituting one accessory for the other. Step pads were also added to the rear bumper, allowing the user to reach into the rather deep box.

1936 Chevrolet Coupe-Express (DFW/DPL)

Serial Number located: Same location as 1935. Starting: FC: FC-1001 and up; FB: FB-1001 and up. Engine numbers located: Same location as 1935. Starting: FB: K-5500179 and up.

Model	Body Type	Price	Weight	Prod. Total
Series FC — (½-Ton)				
FC	Sedan Delivery	535	2705	9404
FC	Coupe Pickup	535	2760	3183
Series FB — (½-Ton)				
FB	Chassis	360	2095	—
FB	Chassis & Cab	450	2450	—
FB	Pickup	475	2075	—
FB	Panel Delivery	565	2895	—
FB	Spec. Panel Delivery	577	3000	—
FB	Suburban Carryall	685	3255	—

1936 Chevrolet Pickup (OCW)

ENGINE: Inline. OHV. Six-cylinder. Cast-iron block. Bore & stroke: 3-5/16 x 4 in. Displacement: 206.8 cu. in. Compression ratio: 6.0:1. Brake horsepower: 79 at 3200 R.P.M. Net horsepower: 26.3. Three main bearings. Mechanical valve lifters. Carburetor: Carter one-barrel model 319S.

CHASSIS: (Series FC) Wheelbase: 109 in.. Tires: 17 x 5.25 in.

CHASSIS: (Series FB) Wheelbase: 112 in. Tires: 5.50 x 17 in.

TECHNICAL: Manual, synchromesh transmission. Speeds: 3F/1R. Floor-mounted gearshift. Diaphragm type clutch. Semi-floating rear axle. Overall ratio: (FC) 4.11:1. Four-wheel hydraulic brakes. Short-spoke wheels.

OPTIONS: Deluxe equipment package. Rear bumper. Single sidemount. Pedestal mirrors for sidemounts. Sidemount cover(s). Fender skirts. Bumper guards. Radio. Heater. Clock. Cigar lighter. Radio antenna. Seat covers. Fog lamps. Spotlight. Screen-sides for canopy express. White side wall tires. Wheel trim rings. OSRV mirror. Special paint. Stencils for lettering. Pickup box tarpaulin. Pressed steel wheels. Deluxe radiator ornament. License plate frames. Dual windshield wipers. Side curtains. Right-hand taillight.

HISTORICAL: Introduced: November 2, 1935. Calendar year registrations: 204,344 (all Series). Innovations: Introduction of hydraulic brakes. New Carter carburetor. Coupe-pickup model bows. All new truck cabs with one-piece, all-steel construction brought out at mid-year. Historical notes: Dupont paint company sales representatives drove a fleet of standard Chevrolet Sedan Deliveries.

PRICING NOTE: For early 1936 models, refer to the 1935 price charts for the same or comparable body styles. For late 1936 models, refer to the 1937 price charts.

1937 CHEVROLET

LIGHT-DUTY TRUCK — SERIES GB/GC/GD/GE — SIX-CYLINDER: — Chevrolet offered many important new features for 1937 beginning with an all-steel cab and "steel stream styling". The result was a modern looking truck with rounded, fuller fenders and smoother lines. Replacing the older 207 cu. in. six-cylinder engine was a larger (216.5 cu. in.) and more powerful (78 horsepower) version. Important to Chevrolet's marketing strategy was the offering of ¾-ton models mid-way through the year, as well as a new one-ton series. Styling features for 1937 included straight side fenders. A streamline groove ran from the fenders onto the doors where it blended-in with the sheet metal on the sedan delivery and coupe delivery (pickup) models. Larger trucks lacked this design and had twin horizontal hood louvers and double-bead belt moldings with a scallop at the cowlside. A Chevrolet "bow-tie" was placed above the hoodside lou-

vers, except on the Carryall Suburban. The grille used on all models looked like a "waterfall" of vertical thin blades and was swept in on each side. There were three small "slashes" at the front upper corner ahead of the hood feature line. The GB sedan delivery had a 68 x 54 x 41 in. load space. Similar dimensions for the GC ½-ton Panel were 86 x 54 x 51 in. The ½-ton pickup box was 77 x 45 in. with 16 in. high sidewalls. Headlights on all models were torpedo-shaped and mounted on the side of the hood. A change was the spare tire carried under the floor of the sedan delivery.

I.D. DATA: Serial Number located: Same location as 1935. Starting: GB: GB-1001 and up; GC: GC-1001 and up; GD: GD-1001 and up; GE: GE-1001 and up. Engine numbers located: Same location as 1935. Starting: (GC) K-1 and up; (GD and GE) T-1 and up.

1937 Chevrolet Sedan Delivery (JAW)

Model	Body Type	Price	Weight	Prod. Total
Series GB — (½-Ton)				
GB	Sedan Delivery	595	2810	9404
Series GC — (½-Ton)				
GC	Chassis	390	2190	—
GC	Chassis & Cab	485	2575	—
GC	Pickup	515	2805	—
GC	Panel	605	3030	—
GC	Canopy Express	600	3050	—
GC	Carryall Suburban	725	3330	—
Series GD — (¾-Ton)				
GD	Chassis	460	2410	—
GD	Chassis & Cab	555	2780	—
GD	Pickup	595	3020	—
GD	Stake	630	3290	—
Series GE — (1-Ton)				
GE	Chassis	495	2585	—
GE	Chassis & Cab	590	2955	—
GE	Pickup	630	3195	—
GE	Stake	665	3465	—

NOTE: The Coupe Delivery (Pickup) was again available in the GB Series but price, weight and production total are not known.

ENGINE: Inline. OHV. Six-cylinder. Cast-iron block. Bore & stroke: 3.5 x 3.75 in. Displacement: 216.5 cu. in. Compression ratio: 6.25:1. Brake horsepower: 85 at 3200 R.P.M. Net horsepower: 29.4. Four main bearings. Mechanical valve lifters. Carburetor: Carter one-barrel model 838938 (W1).

CHASSIS: (Series GB) Wheelbase: 112¼ in. Tires: 6.00 x 16 in. (7.50 x 15 in. available).

CHASSIS: (Series GC) Wheelbase: 112 in.

CHASSIS: (Series GD, GE) Wheelbase: 122¼ in.

TECHNICAL: Manual, synchromesh transmission. Speeds: 3F/1R; (1-ton) 4F/1R. Floor-mounted gearshift. Diaphragm type clutch. (½-ton Models) Semi-floating rear axle; (all others) full-floating rear axle. Overall ratio: GC-4.11:1; 3.82:1. Hydraulic, four-wheel brakes. Pressed steel wheels.

OPTIONS: Same as 1936.

HISTORICAL: Introduced: November, 1936. Calendar year registrations: 183,674 (all Series). Innovations: New ¾-ton and 1-ton series. New "Diamond Crown" styling. Safety glass introduced. Trucks again share appearance features with current Chevrolet cars. Larger and more powerful "Blue Flame" six used. Historical notes: Chevrolet produced some unusual ½-ton Walk-In Panel Delivery vans on the ½-ton chassis. One used a body by Metro Body Co., which later become a part of International-Harvester Corp. Race driver Harry Hartz drove a ½-ton pickup on a "Round the Nation Economy Run" sponsored by Chevrolet under American Automobile Association (AAA) Sanction. Hartz was at the wheel of the truck as it rolled off the assembly line in Flint, Mich. The 72-day excursion covered 10,244.8 miles around the rim of America and did it, without mechanical failure, for less than a penny-a-mile.

Pricing

1938 CHEVROLET

1938 Chevrolet Pickup (DFW/C. Chasteen)

1938 Chevrolet Coupe w/Slip-in Box (DFW/BLHU)

Model	Body Type	Price	Weight	Prod. Total
Series HB — (½-Ton)				
HB	Coupe Pickup	689	2945	—
HB	Sedan Delivery	694	2835	5742
Series HC — (½-Ton)				
HC	Chassis	465	2200	—
HC	Chassis & Cab	562	2580	—
HC	Pickup	592	2805	—
HC	Panel	684	3015	—
HC	Canopy Express	678	3030	—
HC	Closed Suburban	834	3295	—
Series HD — (¾-Ton)				
HD	Chassis	543	2420	—
HD	Chassis & Cab	639	2785	—
HD	Pickup	680	3035	—
HD	Stake	716	3300	—
HD	Panel	792	3280	—
Series HE — (1-Ton)				
HE	Chassis	585	2575	—
HE	Chassis & Cab	681	2950	—
HE	Pickup	722	3200	—
HE	Stake	757	3440	—
HE	Panel	833	3445	—

LIGHT TRUCKS — SERIES HB/HC/HD/HE — SIX-CYLINDER: — The 1938 Chevrolet grille was made up of horizontal bars on either side of a vertical center divider. More massive horizontal bars were used to divide the thinner ones into six segments on each side. The top bar of the grille was lower and straighter than the 1937 style; on the same level as the horizontal feature line of the hood. The Coupe-Pickup and Sedan Delivery had long, horizontal louver vents similar to those of cars. These had sort of an "ice cube tray" look. Larger trucks had a different hoodside treatment with four, somewhat shorter horizontal louvers angled at the front. A Chevrolet bow-tie emblem was seen above them. Unlike the year's passenger cars, trucks had a flat, one-piece windshield. The double-bead belt molding with scalloped front was used on all, but the "HB" Series. The Coupe-Pickup had a cargo box measuring 66 x 38 x 12 in., compared to the half-ton pickup's 77 x 45 x 16 in. Measurements for the ½-ton Series HC Panel body were 86 x 56 x 51 and the rear door opening was 47 in. wide by 43 in. high.

I.D. DATA: Serial Number located for all models on nameplate positioned on firewall. Starting: (HB) HB-1001 and up; (HC) HC-1001 and up; (HD) HD-1001 and up; (HE) HE-1001 and up. Engine numbers located: Serial numbers for all models placed on right side of cylinder block behind fuel pump, and/or stamped on a milled pad on right side of engine at rear of distributor. Starting: (HB) 1187822 and up; (HC) K-1187822 and up; (HD) AT-1187822 and up; (HE) AT-1187822 and up.

ENGINE: Inline. OHV. Six-cylinder. Cast-iron block. Bore & stroke: 3½ x 3¾ in. Displacement: 216.5 cu. in. Compression ratio: 6.25:1. Brake horsepower: 90 at 3200 R.P.M. Net horsepower: 29.4. Four main bearings. Mechanical valve lifters. Carburetor: Carter one-barrel W-1 model 838938.

CHASSIS: (Series HB) Wheelbase: 112¼ in. Tires: 6.00 x 16 four-ply.

CHASSIS: (Series HC) Wheelbase: 112 in. Overall length: 188 in. Height: 71 in. Tires: 6.00 x 16 four-ply.

CHASSIS: (Series HD) Wheelbase: 122¼ in. Tires: 6.00 x 15 six-ply.

CHASSIS: (Series HE) Wheelbase: 122¼ in. Tires: 6.00 x 20 eight-ply, single rear.

TECHNICAL: Manual transmission. Speeds: 3F/1R; (1-ton) 4F/1R. Floor-mounted gearshift. Diaphragm type clutch. (½-ton Models) Semi-floating rear axle; (all others) full-floating rear axle. Overall ratio: Various. Four-wheel hydraulic brakes. Steel short spoke wheels. 4-speed heavy-duty transmission.

OPTIONS: Deluxe equipment. Rear bumper. Outside rearview mirror. Spotlight. Foglights. Cargo bed tarpaulin. Bumper guards. Radio. Heater. Clock. Cigar lighter. Radio antenna. Seat covers. External sun shade. Dual windshield wipers. Right-hand taillight. Side curtains (Canopy Delivery). White sidewall tires. Wheel trim rings. License plate frames. Screen-sides (Canopy Delivery). Sidemounted spare tire (special order). Two-tone paint. Special paint colors.

HISTORICAL: Introduced: October 23, 1937. Calendar year registrations: 119,479 (all Series). Innovations: Heavier valve springs. Larger water pump. New ball bearing water pump (mid-year). New diaphram spring type clutch. New voltage regulator and generator. Historical notes: M.E. Coyle was general manager of Chevrolet.

1938 Chevrolet Panel Delivery (OCW)

	5	4	3	2	1
1938					
Series HB					
Coupe Pickup	1200	2460	4100	5700	8200
Sedan Delivery	1550	3050	5150	7150	10,300
Series HC					
Pickup	1200	2460	4100	5700	8200
Panel	1200	2450	4050	5650	8100
Canopy Express	1130	2250	3750	5250	7500
Suburban	1140	2280	3800	5300	7600
Series HD					
Pickup	1130	2250	3750	5250	7500
Stake	980	1950	3250	4550	6500
Panel	1110	2220	3700	5200	7400
Series HE					
Pickup	980	1950	3250	4550	6500
Stake	900	1800	3000	4200	6200
Panel	950	1900	3150	4400	6300

1939 CHEVROLET

1939 Chevrolet ½-Ton Standard Pickup (J. Prodoehl)

LIGHT TRUCKS — SERIES JB/JC/JD/VA — SIX-CYLINDER: — Chevrolet used a new front end design with heavier horizontal members, and straighter vertical edges. Chevrolet script was found on the top grille bar. Chevrolet also adopted a two-piece v-shaped, rather than one-piece flat, windshield. The hood now had a single louver and a single side trim strip was used. The same image characterized all light-duty trucks, except the "JB" models. These had the passenger car's more rounded horizontal bar grille and "ice cube tray" hoodside vents. Models in this series — the Coupe-Pickup and Sedan Delivery — also had larger, more streamlined headlamp buckets. Popular models included the pickup with steel cargo box and wooden load floor, the box being the same size as last season; the Panel with a one-inch wider load space and the Surburban. This was again a two-door Carryall having a front seat on which the right third of the backrest folded forward for passenger ingress/egress. A new body with a straighter back was used for the Sedan Delivery, which had a 66 x 54 x 41 inch load space. Also somewhat changed was the Canopy Express, which gained a partition behind the driver's seat. This reduced the load space to a length of 80 inches, from last season's 86 inches.

1939 Chevrolet Sedan Delivery (MVMA)

1939 Chevrolet Utility Service Truck (J. Egle/NSPC)

I.D. DATA: Serial Number located on plate on right front side of body, under hood, JB, JD, JE — on plate on front of firewall. Serial numbers: (JB) JB-1001 to 33221; (JC) JC-1001 to 12094; (JD) JD -1001 to 12094; (VA) VA-1001 to 12094. Engine number located on right side of engine block behind fuel pump. Engine numbers: (JB-Cpe. P.U.) 1915447 to 2697267; (JB-Sed. Dely.) B-10503 to 105461; (JC-Chassis, Chassis Cab, P.U.) K-1915447 to 2697267; (JC-all others) B-10503 to 105461; (JD-Chassis, Chassis Cab, P.U.) AT-1915447 to 2697267; (JD-all others) B-10503 to 105461, (VA) - T-1915447 to 2697267.

NOTE: "B" prefix indicates motor built in Chevrolet's new plant in Buffalo, N.Y.

Model	Body Type	Price	Weight	Prod. Total
Series JB — (½-Ton)				
JB	Coupe Pickup	669	2925	—
JB	Sedan Delivery	673	2825	8090
Series JC — (½-Ton)				
JC	Chassis	450	2185	—
JC	Chassis Cab	542	2580	—
JC	Pickup	572	2785	—
JC	Panel	658	3030	—
JC	Canopy Express	714	3025	—
JC	Closed Suburban	808	3210	—
Series JD — (¾-Ton)				
JD	Chassis	528	2355	—
JD	Chassis Cab	619	2745	—
JD	Pickup	660	3035	—
JD	Stake	690	3305	—
JD	Panel	767	3275	—
Series VA — (1-Ton)				
VA*	Chassis	552	2920	—
VA	Chassis Cab	644	3295	—
VA	Panel	821	3975	—

NOTE *: VA-S designation for Kentucky, Pennsylvania, and North Carolina license. VA still used on chassis identification plate.

ENGINE: Inline. OHV. Six-cylinder. Cast-iron block. Bore & stroke: 3½ x 3¾ in. Displacement: 216.5 cu. in. Compression ratio: 6.25:1. Brake horsepower: 90 at 3200 R.P.M. Net horsepower: 29.4. Four main bearings. Mechanical valve lifters. Carburetor: Carter one-barrel model 838938.
420S.

CHASSIS: (Series JB) Wheelbase: 112¼ in. Tires: 6.00 x 16 four-ply.

CHASSIS: (Series JC) Wheelbase: 113½ in. Tires: 6.00 x 16 four-ply.

CHASSIS: (Series JD) Wheelbase: 123¾ in. Tires: 6.00 x 15 six-ply.

CHASSIS: (Series VA) Wheelbase: 133 in. Tires: 6.00 x 20 eight-ply, single rear.

1939 Chevrolet 1-Ton Wrecker (M. Gross)

1939 Chevrolet Model JD Stake Bed (A. Lovick/CPC)

TECHNICAL: Manual, synchromesh transmission. Speeds: 3F/1R; (1-ton) 4F/1R. Floor-mounted gearshift. Diaphragm type clutch. Shaft-drive. (½-ton Models) Semi-floating rear axle; (all others) full-floating rear axle. Four-wheel hydraulic brakes. Steel disc wheels.

OPTIONS: Deluxe equipment. Rear bumper. Outside rearview mirror. Spotlight. Foglights. Cargo bed tarpaulin. Bumper guards. Radio. Heater. Clock. Cigar lighter. Radio antenna. Seat covers. External sun shade. Dual windshield wipers. Right-hand taillight. Side curtains (Canopy Delivery). White sidewall tires. Wheel trim rings. License plate frames. Screen-sides (Canopy Delivery). Sidemounted sparetire (special order). Two-tone paint. Special paint colors.

HISTORICAL: Introduced: October, 1938. Calendar year registrations: 169,457 (all Series). Innovations: New carburetor. New Sedan Delivery body. Partition added to Canopy Express model. A vacuum gearshift option was available at $10 extra. Historical notes: Chevrolet built and sold its two millionth truck in the 1939 model year, which (including larger capacities) featured 45 models on eight wheelbases. A new 1½-ton C.O.E. truck was introduced this season.

Pricing

1939	5	4	3	2	1
Series JB					
Coupe Pickup	1200	2460	4100	5700	8200
Sedan Delivery	1550	3050	5150	7150	10,300
Series JC					
Pickup	1250	2520	4200	5850	8400
Panel	1200	2460	4100	5700	8200
Canopy Express	1200	2400	4000	5600	8000
Suburban	1200	2400	4000	5600	8000
Series JD					
Pickup	1150	2310	3850	5400	7700
Stake	980	1950	3250	4550	6500
Panel	1140	2280	3800	5300	7600
Series VA					
Panel	950	1900	3150	4400	6300

1940 CHEVROLET

1940 Chevrolet Pickup (DFW/R. McFarland)

LIGHT TRUCKS — SERIES KB/KH/KC/KD/KF/WA — SIX-CYLINDER: — Sealed beam headlights became a feature of 1940 Chevy trucks. Parking lights were now positioned on the fender. The top grille bar was wider than in 1939. A new dash panel, similar to that used on Chevrolet automobiles, was introduced for the trucks. Several new light-duty series were added. Technical improvements included a 4.55:1 rear axle for ¾-ton and 1-ton models. The pickup had a slightly longer, 78 inch load floor. Standard equipment on the Panel Delivery included an insulated roof and side panels, adjustable seat, wood floor with steel skid rails and latex-impregnated horse-hair seat padding. Both tailgates or double-doors could be had on the Suburban Carryall, while the Canopy Delivery came with a tailgate that latched automatically when slammed shut. Side curtains were standard on this model, but screen-sides were optional. This year's Sedan Delivery looked particularly handsome with its 1940 passenger car styling. It had a 65 x 55 x 41 inch cargo area and 34 x 34 inch rear door opening and could be had with Knee-Action suspension for the first time. Its counterpart, the Coupe-Pickup, was available with Master Deluxe trim on special order. A special left-hand taillight was required to show up when the removable box was carried. In its place, the conventional-looking turtledeck could be substituted.

1940 Chevrolet Pickup (DFW/ASL)

I.D. DATA: Serial Number located on plate on right side of cowl under hood; on plate on dash; on right or left side of seat frame, or on left-hinge pillar post. The numbers at start of serial number prefix indicate point of assembly. Following letters indicate model. Last indicates month of manufacture. Serial numbers: (KB): KB-1001 to 20946; (KH): KH-1001 to 37644; (KC): KC-1001 to 17658; (KP): KP-1001 to 17658; (KD): KD-1001 to 17658; (KF): KF-1001 to 17658; (WA) WA-1001 to 18041*. (*) was designation for Kentucky, Pennsylvania, North Carolina. Plate with letter "S" added. Engine number location same as 1939. Starting engine number: (KB, KH) 2697268 to 3665902; (KC) K-2697268 to 3665902; (KD) AT-2697268 to 3665902; (ATB) 105462 to 221935; (WA) T-2697268 to 3665902; (TB) 105462 to 221935.

NOTE: Series letters "KE" were used for ¾-ton special commercials with heavy-duty equipment.

Model	Body Type	Price	Weight	Prod. Total
Series KB — (½-Ton)				
KB	Sedan Delivery	694	2915	2590
KB	Coupe Pickup	699	3025	538
Series KH — (½-Ton)				
KH	Sedan Delivery	719	2970	—
KH	Coupe Pickup	725	3090	—
Series KC — (½-Ton)				
KC	Chassis	450	2195	—
KC	Chassis & Cab	541	2595	—
KC	Pickup	572	2840	—
KC	Panel	658	3050	—
KC	Canopy Express	694	3050	—
KC	Suburban	808	3300	—
Series KP "Double-Duty" — (½-Ton)				
KP	Package Delivery	1028	3650	—
Series KD — (¾-Ton)				
KD	Chassis	528	2355	—
KD	Chassis & Cab	619	2755	—
KD	Pickup	660	3110	—
KD	Platform	670	3150	—
KD	Stake	691	3330	—
KD	Panel	766	3325	—
Series KF — (¾-Ton)				
KF	Panel	813	3700	—
Series WA — (1-Ton)				
WA	Chassis	558	2940	—
WA	Chassis & Cab	649	3335	—
WA	Platform	704	3850	—
WA	Stake	730	4115	—
WA	Open Express	735	3835	—
WA	Panel	826	3985	—
WA	Canopy	867	3970	—

ENGINE: Inline. OHV. Six-cylinder. Cast-iron block. Bore & stroke: 3½ x 3¾ in. Displacement: 216.5 cu. in. Compression ratio: 6.25:1. Brake horsepower: 85 at 3400 R.P.M. Net horsepower: 29.4. Four main bearings. Mechanical valve lifters. Carburetor: Carter one-barrel model 838938.

1940 Chevrolet ½-Ton Standard Pickup (E.F. Higgins)

CHASSIS: (Series KB) Wheelbase: 113 in. Tires: 6.00 x 16 four-ply.

CHASSIS: (Series KH) Wheelbase: 113 in. Tires: 6.00 x 16 four-ply.

CHASSIS: (Series KC) Wheelbase: 113½ in. Overall length: 193 in. Tires: 6.00 x 16 four-ply.

CHASSIS: (Series WA) Wheelbase: 133 in. Tires: (front) 6.00 x 20 in., (rear, single) 6.00 x 32 eight-ply.

CHASSIS: (Series KD) Wheelbase: 123.75 in. Tires: 6.00 x 15 six-ply.

CHASSIS: (Series KF) Wheelbase: 133 in. Overall length: 208 in. Tires: 7.00 x 17 six-ply.

1940 Chevrolet Pickup (DFW)

TECHNICAL: Manual, synchromesh transmission. Speeds: 3F/1R; (1-ton) 4F/1R. Floor-shift controls. Diaphragm type clutch. Shaft-drive. (½-ton Models) Semi-floating rear axle; (all others) full-floating rear axle. Four-wheel hydraulic brakes. Pressed steel disc wheels.

1940 Chevrolet Sedan Delivery (OCW)

OPTIONS: Deluxe equipment. Rear bumper. Chrome trim rings. White sidewall tires. Screen-sides (Canopy Express). OSRV mirror(s). Bumper guards. Radio. Heater. Clock. Cigar lighter. Radio antenna. Seat covers. External sun shade. Spotlight. Two-tone paint. Special paint. Bumper step-pads (Coupe-Pickup). Master Deluxe trim (Coupe-Pickup). Oversize tires (standard on Suburban Carryall). "Knee-Action" (Coupe-Pickup and Sedan Delivery). Vacuum gear shift. Column-mounted gear control. License plate frames. Foglights. Panel doors in lieu of tailgate (on Suburban).

HISTORICAL: Introduced: October, 1939. Calendar year registrations: 185,636 (all Series). Innovations: New double-duty delivery truck added to ½-ton KP line. "Knee-Action" available on Sedan Delivery. Coupe-Pickup and Sedan Delivery have all-new styled body. Historical notes: The Foster Parents Plan for War Children purchased a number of Series KF 1-ton Panel Deliveries fitted with dual rear wheels and special interiors for Ambulance services and other wartime use in France and other parts of Europe.

Pricing

	5	4	3	2	1
1940					
Series KB					
Sedan Delivery	1650	3300	5500	7700	11,000
Coupe Pickup	1300	2600	4300	6000	8600
Series KH					
Sedan Delivery	1700	3450	5750	8050	11,500
Coupe Pickup	1350	2700	4500	6300	9000
Series KC					
Pickup	1250	2520	4200	5850	8400
Panel	1200	2460	4100	5700	8200
Canopy Express	1200	2400	4000	5600	8000
Suburban	1200	2450	4050	5650	8100
Series KP					
Panel	900	1800	3000	4200	6000
Series KD					
Pickup	1130	2250	3750	5250	7500
Platform	980	1950	3250	4550	6500
Stake	1000	2000	3300	4600	6600
Panel	1140	2280	3800	5300	7600
Series KF					
Panel	1050	2100	3500	4900	7000
Platform	900	1800	3000	4200	6000
Stake	920	1850	3050	4300	6100
Series WA					
Open Express	1050	2100	3500	4900	7000
Panel	950	1900	3150	4400	6300
Canopy	980	1950	3250	4550	6500

1941 CHEVROLET

1941 Chevrolet Master Deluxe Coupe-Pickup (BMM)

LIGHT TRUCKS — (ALL SERIES) — SIX-CYLINDER: — The 1941 models were easily identified by their new front end with fender mounted headlight pods which were crowned by swept-back parking lights. The grille had two distinct sections. The upper unit was similar to the 1940 version with two thick horizontal bars capped by a top bar with a thin divider and a bottom bar with Chevrolet lettering. The remaining grille elements consisted of broad vertical bars sweeping outward from a center post carrying a Chevrolet logo. No hood ornament was fitted. Side hood trim consisted of a single horizontal chrome stripe extending backward from the upper grille region and three shorter horizontal stripes trisecting the side hood louvers. This front end treatment was not found on the 1941 Coupe Pickup and Sedan Delivery, both of which used current passenger car sheet metal and trim. For an excellent detailed article on the 1941 Coupe Pickup see the January 1987 issue of *Cars & Parts* magazine.

I.D. DATA: Serial Number located on plate on right side of cowl under hood. Starting number: (AG) AG-1001 & up; (AJ) AJ-1001 & up; (AK) AK-1001 & up; (AL) AL-1001 & up; (AN) AN-1001 & up; (YR) YR-1001 & up; (AC) AC-1001 & up*; (AE) AE-1001 & up*; (AAN) AAN-1001 & up*; (AAN) AAN-1001 & up*; (AN) AN-1001 & up*. Engine number location: Same location as 1940. Starting engine number: (AG) AA-1001 & up; (AJ) AM-1001 & up; (AK) AD-1001 & up; (AL, AN) AAF-1001 & up; (YR) AF-1001 & up.

NOTE: YR-S designation for Kentucky, Pennsylvania, North Carolina. Plate with letter "S" added to YR Series Plate.

* - for trucks built at Tonawanda plant.

1941 Chevrolet Heiser Body Co. Sedan Delivery (DFW)

CHASSIS: (Series AN) Wheelbase: 134½ in. Tires: 7.00 x 17 six-ply.

CHASSIS: (Series YR) Wheelbase: 134½ in. Tires: (front) 6.00 x 20 six-ply, (rear) 6.50 x 20 eight-ply.

TECHNICAL: Manual, synchromesh transmission. Speeds: 3F/1R; (1-ton) 4F/1R. Floor-shift controls. Diaphragm: Single dry disc, 9⅛ in. clutch. Shaft-drive. (½-ton Models) Semi-floating rear axle; (all others) full-floating rear axle. Overall drive ratio: 3.73:1. Hydraulic, four-wheel brakes. Pressed steel disc wheels.

OPTIONS: Deluxe equipment. Rear bumper. Chrome trim rings. White sidewall tires. Screen-sides (Canopy Express). OSRV mirror(s). Bumper guards. Radio. Heater. Clock. Cigar lighter. Radio antenna. Seat covers. External sun shade. Spotlight. Two-tone paint. Special paint. Bumper step-pads (Coupe-Pickup). Master Deluxe trim (Coupe-Pickup). Oversize tires (standard on Suburban Carryall). "Knee-Action" (Coupe-Pickup and Sedan Delivery). Vacuum gear shift. Column-mounted gear control. License plate frames. Foglights. Panel doors in lieu of tailgate (on Suburban). Same as 1940, except the Suburban was available only with a tailgate this year.

HISTORICAL: Introduced: Sept., 1940. Calendar year registrations: 212,797 (all Series). Innovations: Knee-Action becomes standard on Sedan Delivery. Doubledoors no longer offered for Suburban Carryall. All-new grille design for trucks.

1941 Chevrolet ½-Ton Deluxe Pickup (OCW)

Model	Body Type	Price	Weight	Prod. Total
Series AG — (½-Ton)				
AG	Sedan Delivery	748	3045	9918
AG	Coupe Pickup	754	3195	1135
Series AJ — (½-Ton)				
AJ	Panel	1058	3665	—
Series AK — (½-Ton)				
AK	Chassis	478	2235	—
AK	Chassis & Cab	569	2630	—
AK	Pickup	600	2870	—
AK	Panel	686	3090	—
AK	Canopy	722	3090	—
AK	Suburban	837	3320	—
Series AL — (¾-Ton)				
AL(*)	Chassis	556	2400	—
AL	Chassis & Cab	648	2795	—
AL	Pickup	689	3120	—
AL	Platform	699	3205	—
AL	Stake	719	3355	—
AL	Panel	795	3355	—
Series AN — (¾-Ton)				
AN	Panel	848	3770	—
Series YR — (1-Ton)				
YR	Chassis	591	2910	—
YR	Chassis & Cab	683	3350	—
YR	Platform	739	3900	—
YR	Stake	765	4170	—
YR	Exp.	770	3865	—
YR	Panel	861	3995	—
YR	Canopy	902	4005	—

* AM designation for ¾-ton trucks with heavy-duty equipment.

ENGINE: Inline. OHV. Six-cylinder. Cast-iron block. Bore & stroke: 3½ x 3¾ in. Displacement: 216.5 cu. in. Compression ratio: 6.5:1. Brake horsepower: 90 at 3300 R.P.M. Net horsepower: 29.4. Torque: 174 lbs.-ft. at 1200-2000 R.P.M. Four main bearings. Mechanical valve lifters. Carburetor: Carter model W1-483S.

NOTE: Chevrolet introduced a 235.2 cu. in. six as an optional engine for the 1½-ton heavy-duty and C.O.E. trucks in 1941.

CHASSIS: (Series AG) Wheelbase: 116 in. Overall length: 195¾ in. Height: 65⅞ in. Front tread: 57⅝ in. Rear tread: 60.0 in. Tires: 6.00 x 16 four-ply.

CHASSIS: (Series AJ) Wheelbase: 115 in. Overall length: 195 in. Tires: 6.00 x 16 four-ply.

CHASSIS: (Series AK) Wheelbase: 115 in. Overall length: 195-198 in. Tires: 6.00 x 16 four-ply.

CHASSIS: (Series AL) Wheelbase: 125¼ in. Tires: 6.00 x 15 six-ply.

1941 Chevrolet Sedan Delivery (DFW/HTM)

Pricing

1941	5	4	3	2	1
Series AG					
Sedan Delivery	1650	3300	5500	7700	11,000
Coupe Pickup	1300	2600	4300	6000	8600
Series AG					
Panel Delivery	900	1800	3000	4200	6000
Series AK					
Pickup	1250	2520	4200	5850	8400
Panel Delivery	1200	2460	4100	5700	8200
Canopy	1200	2400	4000	5600	8000
Suburban	1200	2450	4050	5650	8100
Series AL					
Pickup	1130	2250	3750	5250	7500
Platform	980	1950	3250	4550	6500
Stake	1000	2000	3300	4600	6600
Panel Delivery	1140	2280	3800	5300	7600
Series AN					
Panel Delivery	1050	2100	3500	4900	7000
Platform	900	1800	3000	4200	6000
Stake	920	1850	3050	4300	6100
Express	1050	2100	3500	4900	7000
Panel Delivery	950	1900	3150	4400	6300
Series YR					
Canopy	980	1950	3250	4550	6500

1942 CHEVROLET

1942 Chevrolet "BK" Pickup (OCW)

LIGHT TRUCKS — SERIES BG/BJ/BK/BL/BN — SIX-CYLINDER: — Light-duty commercial vehicles in Chevrolet's BG Series had the same new "American Eagle" grille used on 1942 passenger cars. It was a heavier-looking design with lower and wider horizontal chrome bars. There was also a lower, longer and more massive body appearance; longer and deeper front fenders and a longer, larger hood. This line again included the Master Deluxe Coupe Pickup and Sedan Delivery. The balance of the light-duty trucks were virtually identical to 1941 models. Half-tonners included the BJ (5000 pounds GVW) and BK (4600 pounds GVW) Series models. The ¾-tonners were the BL (5200 pound GVW) and BN Series. There was no one-ton line for 1942. A rarely seen truck was the Double-Duty Package Delivery, which was the only model in the BJ Series. It was a walk-in style delivery truck, similar to an IHC Metro delivery van.

I.D. DATA: Serial Number located on plate on right side of cowl under hood or on plate on rear of dash. Serial numbers starting: (BG) 2AA-1001 and up; (BJ) 2AM-1001 and up; (BK) 2AD-1001 and up; (BL) 2AAF-1001 and up; (BN) 2AAF-1001 and up. Engine number location: On right side of engine block behind fuel pump. Starting engine number: (BG) BA-1001 and up; (BJ) BM-1001 and up; (BK) BD-1001 and up; (BL) ABF-1001 and up; (BN) ABF-1001 and up.

Model	Body Type	Price	Weight	Prod. Total
Series BG — (½-Ton)				
BG	Sedan Delivery	853	3080	2996
BG	Coupe Pickup	865	3230	206
Series BJ — (½-Ton)				
BJ	Package Delivery	1127	3665	—
Series BK — (½-Ton) — (Double-Duty)				
BK	Chassis	536	2235	—
BK	Chassis & Cab	629	2630	—
BK	Pickup	660	2870	—
BK	Panel Delivery	748	3090	—
BK	Canopy	785	3085	—
BK	Suburban	905	3320	—
Series BL — (¾-Ton)				
BL(*)	Chassis	617	2400	—
BL(*)	Chassis & Cab	710	2795	—
BL(*)	Pickup	752	3120	—
BL(*)	Platform	763	3205	—
BL(*)	Stake	783	3355	—
BL(*)	Panel Delivery	860	3355	—
Series BN — (¾-Ton)				
BN	Panel Delivery	915	3770	—

* BM designation was used for ¾-ton trucks with heavy-duty equipment.

ENGINE: Inline. OHV. Six-cylinder. Cast-iron block. Bore & stroke: 3½ x 3¾ in. Displacement: 216.5 cu. in. Compression ratio: 6.50:1. Brake horsepower: 90 at 3300 R.P.M. Net horsepower: 29.4. Four main bearings. Hydraulic valve lifters. Carburetor: Carter type W-1, downdraft, one-barrel Model 839534.

CHASSIS: (Series BG) Wheelbase: 116 in. Tires: 6.00 x 16 four-ply.

CHASSIS: (Series BJ) Wheelbase: 115 in. Tires: 6.00 x 16 six-ply.

CHASSIS: (Series BK) Wheelbase: 115 in. Tires: 6.00 x 16 four-ply.

CHASSIS: (Series BL) Wheelbase: 125.25 in. Tires: 6.00 x 15 six-ply.

CHASSIS: (Series BN) Wheelbase: 134.5 in. Tires: 7.00 x 16 six-ply.

TECHNICAL: Manual transmission. Speeds: 3F/1R. Floor-mounted gearshift. Diaphragm type clutch. (½-ton Models) Semi-floating rear axle; (all others) full-floating rear axle. Four-wheel hydraulic brakes. Steel disc wheels.

OPTIONS: Deluxe equipment. Rear bumper. Chrome trim rings. White sidewall tires. Screen-sides for canopy. OSRV mirror(s). Bumper guards. Radio. Heater. Clock. Cigar lighter. Radio antenna. Seat covers. External sun shade. Spotlight. Two-tone paint. Special paint. Bumper step-pads (Coupe Pickup). Master Deluxe trim (Coupe Pickup and Sedan Delivery). Oversize tires. Vacuum gearshift. Column-mounted gear control. License plate frames. Foglights. Panel doors instead of tailgate (for Suburban).

HISTORICAL: Introduced: October, 1941. Innovations: New body styling and trim for passenger car based commercial vehicles. Panel door option for Suburban reinstated. Black-out trim used on late-production models. Civilian truck production ended in January, 1942, with America's entry into World War II. It did not begin again until January, 1944, when production of trucks for high-priority civilian use began on a limited basis. All Chevrolet plants participated in the war effort, except the Saginaw service and manufacturing facility, which was used to supply replacement parts for trucks on the road at that time. This was the last year that the Coupe Pickup model was offered.

Pricing

	5	4	3	2	1
1942					
Series BG					
Sedan Delivery	1650	3300	5500	7700	11,000
Coupe Pickup	1300	2600	4300	6000	8600
Series BJ					
Double-Duty Package Delivery	900	1800	3000	4200	6000
Series BK					
Pickup	1250	2520	4200	5850	8400
Canopy	1200	2400	4000	5600	8000
Suburban	1200	2450	4050	5650	8100
Series BL					
Pickup	1130	2250	3750	5250	7500
Platform	980	1950	3250	4550	6500
Stake	1000	2000	3300	4600	6600
Panel Delivery	1140	2280	3800	5300	7600
Series BN					
Panel Delivery	1050	2100	3500	4900	7000

1944-1946 CHEVROLET

1946 Chevrolet Standard Pickup (OCW)

LIGHT TRUCKS — SERIES BK/DJ/CK — SIX-CYLINDER: — According to the N.A.D.A.'s 1950 Edition "Truck Reference Book" production of a limited line of Chevrolet trucks started up again in Jan. 1944. (Note: Other sources put this date at July 1944). The only light-duty model listed as being available at this time was the Series BK ½-ton Pickup. It had mostly the same specifications as the 1942 model except for a change to 6.50 x 16 six-ply tires, a painted grille, heavy-duty springs and four-speed transmission. These trucks had serial numbers BK-2127 and up. The "as delivered price" was up to $757, which was controlled by Office of Price Administration (OPA) regulations. In September, 1945, a larger selection of light-duty trucks became available. These were called "interim" 1946 models and there were two ½-ton Series with a total of 10 models. Interestingly, the Coupe Pickup was listed, although its generally believed that the last of these "car-trucks" was built and sold in 1942. The Series DJ models shared styling with 1946 Chevrolet passenger cars, while the Series CK models had no significant changes from the 1942 conventional half-tonners.

I.D. DATA: Serial Number located on plate on right side of cowl under hood or on plate on rear of dash (BK) BK-2127 and up; (DJ) DJ-1001 and up; (CK) CK-1001 and up.

Model Series BK	Body Type — (1944) — (½-Ton)	Price	Weight	Prod. Total
BK	Pickup	757	2870	—
Series DJ	**— (1945-1946) — (½-Ton)**			
DJ	Sedan Delivery	—	3060	—
DJ	Coupe Pickup	—	3210	—
Series CK	**— (1945-1946) — (½-Ton)**			
CK	Chassis	637	2235	—
CK	Chassis & Cab	727	2630	—
CK	Pickup	757	2870	—
CK	Panel Delivery	842	3090	—
CK	Suburban (door)	987	3320	—
CK	Suburban (gate)	987	3330	—
CK	Canopy	877	3085	—

1946 Chevrolet Deluxe Pickup (A. Kaylor)

ENGINE: Inline. OHV. Six-cylinder. Cast-iron block. Bore & stroke: 3½ x 3¾ in. Displacement: 216.5 cu. in. Compression ratio: 6.5:1. Brake horsepower: 90 at 3300 R.P.M. Net horsepower: 29.4. Four main bearings. Mechanical valve lifters. Carburetor: Downdraft one-barrel model W1-574S.

CHASSIS: (Series BK) Wheelbase: 115 in. Tires: 6.50 x 16 six-ply.

CHASSIS: (Series DJ) Wheelbase: 116 in. Tires: 6.00 x 16.

CHASSIS: (Series CK) Wheelbase: 115 in. Overall length: 198 in. (Suburban). Tires: 6.00 x 16.

TECHNICAL: Manual transmission. Speeds: 3F/1R. (Note: 4F/1R on 1944-1945 Series BK). Floor-mounted gearshift. (Model CK) Semi-floating rear axle; (all others) full-floating rear axle. Single disc clutch, 9⅛ in. Four-wheel hydraulic brakes. Pressed steel disc wheels.

OPTIONS: Rear bumper. Bumper guards. Radio. Heater. Clock. Cigar lighter. Radio antenna. Seat covers.

NOTE 1: Optional equipment production may have been restricted by OPA regulations. However, some of these models are known to have been sold by dealers who installed 1941 or 1942 accessories and options that were leftover in their dealer inventories.

NOTE 2: Wording in contemporary "Red Books" and "Blue Books" indicates that vehicle prices were fixed at 1942 levels by OPA regulations. However, additional charges for equipment variations between trucks of different model years were permitted. As a result, it appears that Chevrolet made certain equipment, previously sold as options, "mandatory" on the 1944-1946 trucks. This allowed the dealers to legally get higher prices for the trucks in the inflationary period immediately following the war. Mandatory options for these models included heavier-duty springs and tires, four-speed transmissions, etc.

HISTORICAL: Introduced: (BK) January, 1944; (DJ/CK) September 1945. Calendar year registrations: Included in 1946 totals. Innovations: Slightly revised styling for Sedan Delivery. Coupe Pickup model no longer available. Heavy-duty equipment made "mandatory" on some models. Historical notes: M.E. Coyle was elevated to a new position as executive vice-president of General Motors Corporation. Cadillac general manager Nicholas Dreystadt was appointed to Coyle's former position as president of Chevrolet.

Pricing

1944-1946 Series DJ	5	4	3	2	1
Sedan Delivery	1650	3300	5500	7700	11,000
Series BK/CK					
Pickup	1300	2600	4300	6000	8600
Panel	1250	2520	4200	5850	8400
Suburban	1300	2550	4250	5900	8500
Canopy	1300	2600	4300	6000	8600

NOTE 1: The Coupe Express was listed in the DJ Series, but none are believed to have been built. Therefore, no prices are given for this model.

1946 CHEVROLET

1946 Chevrolet Standard Pickup (P. George)

LIGHT TRUCKS — SERIES DJ/DP/DR/DS — SIX-CYLINDER: — Regular series production of civilian trucks began in May, 1946. The car-like DJ Series was carried over without change, except the Coupe Pickup no longer appeared on the models list. Conventional ½-tons were now designated as the Series DP trucks; ¾-tons were "DR" models and a one-ton line — designated Series DS — returned. These one-tons had the same 134½ in. w.b. used on 1½-ton models in 1942, but a lower GVW rating of 8800 pounds. (In contrast, the 1½-tons of 1942 had a 13,500 pound GVW). A sub-series for this new line was composed of three models, available with dual rear wheels, that had the same tonnage and GVW ratings as the single rear wheel trucks. In terms of appearance, the Sedan Delivery resembled the 1946 passenger cars and the other models looked like 1941-1942 trucks.

I.D. DATA: Serial Number located: Same as interim models. (DJ) DJ-1001 and up; (DP) DP-1001 and up; (DR) DR-1001 and up; (DS) DS-1001 and up. Engine number location: Same as interim models.

1946 Chevrolet Panel Truck (OCW)

49

1946 Chevrolet Pickup (OCW)

Model	Body Type	Price	Weight	Prod. Total
Series DJ — (½-Ton)				
DJ	Sedan Delivery	1173	3135	—
Series DP				
DP	Chassis	796	2300	—
DP	Chassis & Cab	922	2680	—
DP	Pickup	963	2925	—
DP	Panel Delivery	1077	3145	—
DP	Canopy	1126	3135	—
DP	Suburban (door)	1283	3370	—
DP	Suburban (gate)	1281	3385	—
Series DR — (¾-Ton)				
DR	Chassis	891	2495	—
DR	Chassis & Cab	1016	2890	—
DR	Pickup	1069	3215	—
DR	Panel Delivery	1212	3450	—
DR	Platform	1101	3300	—
DR	Stake	1127	3450	—
Series DS — (1-Ton)				
DS	Chassis	892	2835	—
DS	Express	1139	4095	—
DS	Panel Delivery	1264	4080	—
DS	Canopy Express	1318	4095	—
Series DS — (1-Ton w/Dual Rear Wheels)				
DS	Chassis & Cab	1106	3560	—
DS	Platform	1200	4065	—
DS	Stake	1235	4315	—

ENGINE: Inline. OHV. Six-cylinder. Cast-iron block. Bore & stroke: 3½ x 3¾ in. Displacement: 216.5 cu. in. Compression ratio: 6.5:1. Brake horsepower: 90 at 3300 R.P.M. Net horsepower: 29.4. Four main bearings. Mechanical valve lifters. Carburetor: Carter downdraft one-barrel model W1-574S.

CHASSIS: (Series DJ) Wheelbase: 116 in. Tires: 6.00 x 16 four-ply.

CHASSIS: (Series DP) Wheelbase: 115 in. Tires: 6.00 x 16 six-ply.

CHASSIS: (Series DR) Wheelbase: 125.25 in. Tires: 6.00 x 15 six-ply.

CHASSIS: (Series DS) Wheelbase: 134.50 in. Tires: 7.00 x 17 (dual wheel option available).

TECHNICAL: Manual transmission. Speeds: 3F/1R, (1-ton) 4F/1R. Floor-mounted gearshift. Single disc type clutch. (Model CK) Semi-floating rear axle. Hydraulic brakes. Pressed steel disc wheels.

OPTIONS: Deluxe equipment. Rear bumper. Chrome wheel trim rings. OSRV mirror(s). Floor mat. Screen-sides for Canopy. White sidewall tires. Radio. Heater. Clock. Cigar lighter. Radio antenna. Seat covers. External sun shade. Spotlight. Cowl lamps. Heavy-duty springs. Two-tone paint. Special paint. Oversize tires. License plate frame. Dual rear wheels (1-ton). Four-speed transmission. 93 horsepower engine. Dual windshield wipers. Directional signals. Dual taillights.

HISTORICAL: Introduced: May, 1946. Calendar year registrations: (all Series) 171,618. Innovations: One-ton series reintroduced; first since 1941. Suburban with panel doors and Suburban with tailgate now merchandised as separate models. Dual rear wheel series in 1-ton line. Historical notes: See 1944-1946 historical notes.

1946 Chevrolet bus (D. Gaser)

Pricing

	5	4	3	2	1
1946					
Series DJ					
Sedan Delivery	1650	3300	5500	7700	11,000
Series DP					
Pickup	1250	2500	4150	5800	8300
Panel	1200	2460	4100	5700	8200
Canopy	1180	2370	3950	5500	7900
Suburban	1250	2500	4150	5800	8300
Series DR					
Pickup	1140	2280	3800	5300	7600
Panel	1130	2250	3750	5250	7500
Platform	960	1920	3200	4500	6400
Stake	980	1950	3250	4550	6500
Series DS					
Express	1040	2070	3450	4850	6900
Panel	930	1860	3100	4350	6200
Canopy Express	960	1920	3200	4500	6400

1947 CHEVROLET

1947 Chevrolet Early Series Standard Pickup (EK)

LIGHT TRUCKS — SERIES 1500/3100/3600/3800 — SIX-CYLINDER:— Most 1947 Chevy trucks looked exactly like previous models. Then, in the summer of 1947, a series with new styling, stronger frames and revised interiors appeared. The new look was neat and uncluttered. The grille had five broad horizontal bars topped by a broad hood ornament containing a blue "Bow Tie" and red Chevrolet lettering. A Chevrolet nameplate was installed near the rear edge of the "Alligator" hood. Rectangular parking lights were set high in the outer grille regions. Deluxe models had chrome grille bars, but otherwise the bars were painted to match the body color. A two-piece, flat windshield was used. Front and rear fenders retained their individual forms. Their rounded shape, in conjunction with the rounded corners of the body, gave the Chevrolet an up-to-date appearance. The interior was highlighted by wider seats, improved vision through the larger windshield, side and rear windows and a redesigned instrument panel. The "EJ" (or 1500) Series had a 4100 pound GVW rating. The "EP" (or 3100) Series had a 4600 pound GVW rating. Both of these were half-ton lines. The "ER" (or 3600) Series included eight ¾-ton models with 5800 pound GVWs. The "ES" (or 3800) Series was a 1-ton line with ten 8800 pound GVW models. The sub-series with dual rear wheeled one-tonners was no longer listed.

1947 Chevrolet Early Series Pickup (OCW)

I.D. DATA: Serial Number located: Stamped on plate located on left door hinge pillar. Serial numbers: (Series 1500) EJ-1001 to EJ-33745; (Series 3100) EP-1001 and up; (Series 3600) ER-1001 and up; (Series 3800) ES-1001 and up. Engine numbers located: Stamped on boss on right side of cylinder block, to the rear of the distributor.

Model	Body Type	Price	Weight	Prod. Total
Series 1500 — (½-Ton)				
EJ	Sedan Delivery	1233	—	—
Series 3100 — (½-Ton)				
EP	Chassis	843	2420	—
EP	Chassis & Cab	1030	2915	—
EP	Pickup	1087	3205	—
EP	Panel	1238	3415	—
EP	Canopy Express	1289	3415	—
EP	Suburban	1474	3515	—
Series 3600 — (¾-Ton)				
ER	Chassis	941	2660	—
ER	Chassis & Cab	1128	3180	—
ER	Pickup	1201	3440	—
ER	Platform	1211	3560	—
ER	Stake Bed	1258	3720	—
Series 3800 — (1-Ton)				
ES	Chassis	988	2910	—
ES	Chassis & Cab	1176	3440	—
ES	Pickup	1279	3845	—
ES	Panel	1445	4220	—
ES	Canopy Express	1523	4210	—
ES	Platform	1295	3965	—
ES	Stake Bed	1362	4195	—

ENGINE: Inline. OHV. "Thrift-Master". Six-cylinder. Cast-iron block. Bore & stroke: 3½ x 3¾ in. Displacement: 216.5 cu. in. Compression ratio: 6.5:1. Brake horsepower: 90 at 3300 R.P.M. Max. Torque: 170 lb.-ft. at 1200-2000 R.P.M. Net horsepower: 29.4. Four main bearings. Mechanical valve lifters. Carburetor: Carter downdraft one-barrel model W1-574S.

CHASSIS: (Series 1500) Wheelbase: 116 in. Overall length: 207.5 in. Front tread: 57.6 in. Rear tread: 60 in. Tires: 6.00 x 16 in.

CHASSIS: (Series 3100) Wheelbase: 116 in. Overall length: 196.575 in. Tires: 6.00 x 16 in.

CHASSIS: (Series 3600) Wheelbase: 125.25 in. Overall length: 206 in. Tires: 6.00 x 15 in.

CHASSIS: (Series 3800) Wheelbase: 137 in. Overall length: 223.875 in. Tires: 7.00 x 17 in.

TECHNICAL: Manual transmission. Speeds: 3F/1R, (4F/1R Series 3800). Floor-mounted gearshift. Single disc, diaphragm spring clutch. (½-ton) Semi-floating hypoid rear axle, (others) full-floating rear axle. Hydraulic, four-wheel brakes. Drop center disc wheels. 4-spd. manual transmission (opt. Series 3100 and 3600) 3.73:1 rear axle (Series 1500).

OPTIONS: Rear bumper. Radio. Heater. Clock. Cigar lighter. Radio antenna. Seat covers. DeLuxe Cab. Rear Corner "Nu-Vue" windows.

HISTORICAL: Introduced: January, 1947. Calendar year registrations: (all Series) 235,803. Calendar year sales: (all Series) 259,533. Innovations: The all-new, completely restyled line featured "the cab that breathes," with 30 advanced design feature and an alligator-jaw hood opening to make servicing easier. Historical notes: Capacity of Chevrolet's commercial body plant at Indianapolis, Ind. was expanded to double production capacity this year. A new assembly plant in Flint, Mich. was also opened. Late in the year, a large new plant in Los Angeles began operations. A new manufacturing plant at Cleveland was also opened.

Pricing

1947	5	4	3	2	1
Series 1500					
Sedan Delivery	1700	3450	5750	8050	11,500
Series 3100					
Pickup	1130	2250	3750	5250	7500
Panel	1020	2050	3400	4800	6800
Canopy Express	1040	2070	3450	4850	6900
Suburban	1050	2100	3500	4900	7000
Series 3600					
Pickup	1050	2100	3500	4900	7000
Platform	930	1860	3100	4350	6200
Stake	930	1860	3100	4350	6200
Series 3800					
Pickup	980	1950	3250	4550	6500
Panel	950	1900	3150	4400	6300
Canopy Express	920	1850	3050	4300	6100
Platform	900	1800	3000	4200	6000
Stake	950	1900	3050	4300	6100

NOTE: Deduct 5 percent for painted bumpers and grille.

1948 CHEVROLET

1948 Chevrolet Thriftmaster One-Ton (K. Robbins)

LIGHT TRUCKS — SERIES 1500/3100/3600/3700/3800/3900 — SIX-CYLINDER: — After the introduction of the new "Advance Design" trucks in the summer of 1947, Chevrolet began the 1948 model year with an unchanged line of light-duty trucks. There were, however, two new series merchandised as DeLuxe chassis. These included the ¾-ton Series 3700 and the 1-ton Series 3900.

I.D. DATA: Serial Number located: Stamped on plate located on left door hinge pillar. Serial numbers: (Series 1500) FJ-1001 and up; (Series 3100) FP-1001 and up; (Series 3600) FR-1001 and up; (Series 3700) FT-1001 and up; (Series 3800) FS-1001 and up; (Series 3900) FU-1001 and up. Engine numbers located: Stamped on boss on right side of cylinder block, to the rear of the distributor.

Model	Body Type	Price	Weight	Prod. Total
Series 1500 — (½-Ton)				
FJ	Sedan Delivery	1361	3075	—
Series 3100 — (½-Ton)				
FP	Chassis	890	2430	—
FP	Chassis & Cab	1113	2960	—
FP	Pickup	1180	3215	—
FP	Panel Delivery	1377	3425	—
FP	Canopy Express	1429	3415	—
FP	Suburban	1627	3515	—
Series 3600 — (¾-Ton)				
FR	Chassis	1004	2660	—
FR	Chassis & Cab	1227	3180	—
FR	Pickup	1315	3460	—
FR	Platform	1320	3655	—
FR	Stake Bed	1378	3740	—
Series 3700 — (Deluxe ¾-Ton)				
FT	Deluxe Chassis	1097	2465	—
Series 3800 — (1-Ton)				
FS	Chassis	1087	3035	—
FS	Chassis & Cab	1310	3545	—
FS	Pickup	1425	3965	—
FS	Panel Delivery	1596	4220	—
FS	Canopy Express	1674	4210	—
FS	Platform	1440	4050	—
FS	Stake Bed	1513	4300	—
Series 3900 — (Deluxe 1-Ton)				
FU	Deluxe Chassis	1125	2630	—

1948 Chevrolet Pickup (OCW)

1948 Chevrolet Stylemaster Sedan Delivery (OCW)

ENGINE: Thriftmaster Six. Inline. OHV. Six-cylinder. Cast-iron block. Bore & stroke: 3½ x 3¾ in. Displacement: 216.5 cu. in. Compression ratio: 6.5:1. Brake horsepower: 90 at 3300 R.P.M. Net horsepower: 29.4. Four main bearings. Mechanical valve lifters. Carburetor: Carter downdraft one-barrel model W1-574S.

CHASSIS: Same as 1947.

TECHNICAL: Same as 1947, except column-mounted gearshift on all three-speed transmissions.

OPTIONS: Same as 1947 with addition of new DeLuxe exterior trim for the ½-ton Panel Delivery featuring chrome grille and chrome triple speed-line moldings on front and rear fender sides.

HISTORICAL: Introduced: January, 1948. Calendar year registrations: (all Series) 302,219. Calendar year sales: (all Series) 323,648. Innovations: Controls for three-speed transmission moved to steering column. New foot-type parking brake on ½-ton models. New DeLuxe chassis models introduced. Historical notes: Upon the death of Nicholas Dreystadt, W.F. Armstrong was temporarily named general manager of Chevrolet Motor Division. Later, T.H. Keating was promoted from the general sales manager's post to take over from Keating. On some 1948 Chevrolet trucks four-speed manual transmissions now featured synchronized gearing and optional two-speed axles were fitted with vacuum-operated shift controls.

1948 Chevrolet Pickup (OCW)

1949 Chevrolet Sedan Delivery (OCW)

LIGHT TRUCKS — SERIES 1508/3100/3600/3700/3800/3900 — SIX-CYLINDER: — For 1949, a major change was made in the Sedan Delivery, which took the lower, wider body of the first true postwar passenger cars. The Sedan Delivery's 115 in. w.b. was one inch shorter than the previous year. It had a load space that was 73 inches long, and looked much more streamlined than the 1948 models. Conventional trucks were little changed from the prior specifications. They still had painted bumpers and grilles as standard equipment. Again offered for specialty body builders were the ¾-ton and 1-ton delivery chassis. Aftermarket body builders also constructed special bodies on the ½-ton chassis-only or chassis and cab. Two interesting types included the Kurbmaster walk-in delivery by the Olsen Company and a commercial-chassis wood-bodied station wagon from Cantrell.

1949 Chevrolet Sedan Delivery (CHP)

I.D. DATA: Serial Number located: Same as 1948. As in 1947 and 1948, both numerical and alphabetical series designations were used. They were as follows: ½-ton sedan delivery (1508 or GJ); ½-ton trucks (3100 or GP); ¾-ton trucks (3600 or GR); ¾-ton delivery chassis (3700 or GT); 1-ton trucks (3800 or GS) and 1-ton delivery chassis (3900 or GU). Serial numbers: (GJ) GJ-1001 and up; (GP) GP-1001 and up; (GR) GR-1001 and up; (GT) GT-1001 and up; (GS) GS-1001 and up; (GU) GU-1001 and up. Engine numbers located: Same as 1948.

Pricing

	5	4	3	2	1
1948					
Series 1500					
Sedan Delivery	1600	3150	5250	7300	10,500
Series 3100					
Pickup	1130	2250	3750	5250	7500
Panel	1020	2050	3400	4800	6800
Canopy Express	1040	2070	3450	4850	6900
Suburban	1050	2100	3500	4900	7000
Series 3600					
Pickup	1050	2100	3500	4900	7000
Platform	930	1860	3100	4350	6200
Stake	950	1900	3150	4400	6300
Series 3800					
Pickup	980	1950	3250	4550	6500
Panel	950	1900	3150	4400	6300
Canopy Express	920	1850	3050	4300	6100
Platform	900	1800	3000	4200	6000
Stake	950	1850	3050	4300	6100

1949 Chevrolet Huckster (ATC)

1949 Chevrolet Suburban Carryall (OCW)

Model	Body Type	Price	Weight	Prod. Total
Series 1508 — (½-Ton)				
GJ	Sedan Delivery	1465	3050	9310
Series 3100 — (½-Ton)				
GP	Chassis	961	2430	—
GP	Chassis & Cab	1185	2920	—
GP	Pickup	1253	3185	—
GP	Panel	1450	3425	—
GP	Canopy Express	1502	3385	—
GP	Suburban	1700	3710	—
Series 3600 — (¾-Ton)				
GR	Chassis	1060	2750	—
GR	Chassis & Cab	1284	3170	—
GR	Pickup	1372	3520	—
GR	Platform	1378	3550	—
GR	Stake	1435	3725	—
Series 3700 — (¾-Ton Delivery)				
	Delivery Chassis	1076	2465	—
Series 3800 — (1-Ton)				
GS	Chassis	1134	3005	—
GS	Chassis & Cab	1357	3430	—
GS	Pickup	1471	3945	—
GS	Panel	1669	4220	—
GS	Canopy Express	1746	4180	—
GS	Platform	1487	3960	—
GS	Stake	1560	4215	—
Series 3900 — (1-Ton Delivery)				
GU	Delivery Chassis	1169	2700	—

1949 Chevrolet Pickup (OCW)

ENGINE: Thriftmaster Six. Inline. OHV. Six-cylinder. Cast-iron block. Bore & stroke: 3½ x 3¾ in. Displacement: 216.5 cu. in. Compression ratio: 6.5:1. Brake horsepower: 90 at 3300 R.P.M. Net horsepower: 29.4. Four main bearings. Mechanical valve lifters. Carburetor: Carter downdraft one-barrel model W1-684S.

1949 Chevrolet Suburban Carryall (OCW)

CHASSIS: (Series 1508) Wheelbase: 115 in. Overall length: 197.9 in. Tires: 6.70 x 15 four-ply.

CHASSIS: (other Series) Same as 1948.

TECHNICAL: Same as 1948.

OPTIONS: Same as 1948.

HISTORICAL: Introduced to dealers January, 1949. Calendar year registrations: (all Series) 345,519. Innovations: All-new styling for Sedan Delivery. New carburetor for all models. Compression increased slightly to 6.6:1. Sedan Delivery is marketed as a "Special" model. Historical notes: Cantrell wood-bodied station wagons and Olsen Kurbside delivery trucks were built on the Chevrolet chassis this year.

1949 Chevrolet Stake Truck (OCW)

Pricing

1949	5	4	3	2	1
Series 1500					
Sedan Delivery	1650	3300	5500	7700	11,000
Series 3100					
Pickup	1130	2250	3750	5250	7500
Panel Delivery	1020	2050	3400	4800	6800
Canopy Express	1040	2070	3450	4850	6900
Suburban Carryall	1050	2100	3500	4900	7000
Cantrell Station Wagon	1930	3900	6500	9100	13,000
Olsen Kurbside Van	600	1200	2000	2800	4000
Series 3600/3700					
Pickup	1050	2100	3500	4900	7000
Platform	930	1860	3100	4350	6200
Stake Bed	980	1950	3150	4400	6300
Series 3800/3900					
Pickup	980	1950	3250	4550	6500
Panel Delivery	950	1900	3150	4400	6300
Canopy Express	920	1850	3050	4300	6100
Platform	900	1800	3000	4200	6000
Stake Bed	920	1850	3050	4300	6100

NOTE: Deduct 5 percent for painted bumpers and grille.

1950 CHEVROLET

1950 Chevrolet Pickup (OCW)

LIGHT TRUCK — (ALL SERIES) — SIX-CYLINDER: — The passenger car-based Sedan Delivery was part of Chevrolet's Styleline Special series. It had a new frontal treatment with different hood ornaments and no vertical members in the lower section of the grille opening. The 73 in. cargo area gave a usable cargo area of 92.5 cu. ft. Conventional trucks looked the same as the previous models. All had improved seat cushion padding and larger, 56 in. wide seats. A new Suburban Carry-All with panel rear doors was introduced. The end-gate (tailgate) version was now available in all 12 colors that Chevrolet offered for its trucks. Suspension changes included new, direct double-action one-inch shock absorbers for the ½- and ¾-ton models. Eight-leaf front springs were made standard for ¾-tonners. Added to the regular production option list for one-tons were larger 1 ⅜ in. diameter rear shock absorbers and auxiliary leaf springs. Trucks in the 3942 and 3800 series were available with a larger Hydro-vac brake system. Panel and canopy models now had a one-piece floor made of ¾-inch thick, five-ply laminated wood. A revamped version of the "Thriftmaster" six was standard in 3100/3600/3800 models. It had a new "Powerjet" down-draft carburetor, larger exhaust valves and a straight-through muffler. A more powerful version of the "Loadmaster" six was used in medium- and heavy-duty models. Painted grilles and bumpers were standard on most ½-ton trucks, except the Sedan Delivery and DeLuxe Panel. The latter came with a chrome grille, bumpers and fender trim bars. Chrome grilles and bumpers could be had on other light-duty trucks at extra cost.

1950 Chevrolet Suburban Carryall (OCW)

ENGINE: (Standard Series 3700/3900) Inline. OHV. "Loadmaster". Six-cylinder. Cast-iron block. Bore & stroke: 3-9/16 x 3-15/16 in. Displacement: 235.5 cu. in. Compression ratio: 6.7:1. Brake horsepower: 92 at 3400 R.P.M. Net horsepower: 30.4. Four main bearings. Mechanical valve lifters. Carburetor: Single one-barrel model Carter Powerjet downdraft.

CHASSIS: Same as 1949.

TECHNICAL: Manual transmission. Speeds: 3F/1R (4F/1R on 1-ton). Column-mounted gearshift (floorshift with four-speed). Single dry disc clutch. Semi-floating rear axle. Overall ratio: 5.14:1 (Series 3600). Four-wheel hydraulic brakes. Steel disc wheels. 5.14:1 ratio offered as regular production option for Series 3600.

1950 Chevrolet Deluxe Cab Pickup (OCW)

I.D. DATA: Serial Number located on door hinge pillar post. Serial numbers were as follows: (Series 1500) HJ-1001 to 49801; (Series 3100) HP-1001 to 37721; (Series 3600) HR-1001 to 12078; (Series 3742) HT-1001 to 1600; (Series 3800) HS-1001 to 5611 and (Series 3942) HJ-1001 to 1408. Engine numbers located on right side of block near fuel pump; also stamped on crankcase near rear of distributor on right side of engine. Motor numbers were as follows: (Series 1500) HA-1001 to 1320152; (Series 3100) HB-1001 to 1320152; (Series 3600) HC-1001 to 1320152; (Series 3742/3800/3942) same as 3600 Series.

1950 Chevrolet Sedan Delivery w/custom wheels (DFW)

OPTIONS: Deluxe equipment package. White sidewall tires. Fender top clearance lamps. OSRV mirror(s). Chrome wheel trim rings. License plate frames. Bumper guards. Radio. Heater. Clock. Cigar lighter. Radio antenna. Seat covers. External sun shade. Spotlight. Fog lamps. Fender skirts (sedan delivery). Two-tone paint. Special colors. Oversize tires. Heavy-duty springs. Chrome bumper. Chrome grille. "Big Window" quarter-cab windows. Chrome fender trim moldings.

HISTORICAL: Dealer introduction: January, 1950. Calendar year registrations: (all Series) 414,496. Innovations: Improved engines. Suburban with panel doors reintroduced. Wider seats with improved padding. Historical notes: An all-time record for sales of the Sedan Delivery, to date, was established in 1950.

Model	Body Type	Price	Weight	Prod. Total
Series 1500 — (½-Ton)				
HJ	Sedan Delivery	1455	3105	—
Series 3100 — (½-Ton)				
HP	Chassis & Cab	1175	2910	—
HP	Pickup	1243	3175	—
HP	Panel Delivery	1440	3375	—
HP	Suburban (doors)	1690	3670	—
HP	Canopy Express	1492	3335	—
HP	Suburban (gate)	1690	3075	—
Series 3600 — (¾-Ton)				
HR	Chassis	1050	2710	—
HR	Chassis & Cab	1274	3170	—
HR	Pickup	1302	3515	—
HR	Platform	1308	3560	—
HR	Stake Bed	1425	3700	—
Series 3700 — ¾-Ton Delivery				
HT	Delivery Chassis	1066	2475	—
Series 3800 — (1-Ton)				
HS	Chassis	1124	2980	—
HS	Chassis & Cab	1347	3440	—
HS	Pickup	1461	3930	—
HS	Panel Delivery	1659	4190	—
HS	Canopy Express	1736	4145	—
HS	Platform	1477	4010	—
HS	Stake Bed	1550	4255	—
Series 3900 — (1-Ton)				
HU	Delivery Chassis	1159	2640	—

ENGINE: (Standard Series 1500/3100/3600/3800) Inline. OHV. "Thriftmaster". Six-cylinder. Cast-iron block. Bore & stroke: 3½ x 3¾ in. Displacement: 216.5 cu. in. Compression ratio: 6.6:1. Brake horsepower: 90 at 3300 R.P.M. Torque: 176 lb.-ft. at 1200-2000 R.P.M. Net horsepower: 29.4. Four main bearings. Mechanical valve lifters. Carburetor: Single one-barrel model Carter Powerjet downdraft.

1950 Chevrolet Panel Van (OCW)

1950 Chevrolet Panel Van (OCW)

1950 Chevrolet "3100" Pickup (P. Bachman)

Pricing

1950	5	4	3	2	1
Series 1500					
Sedan Delivery	1650	3300	5500	7700	11,000
Series 3100					
Pickup	1130	2250	3750	5250	7500
Panel Delivery	1020	2050	3400	4800	6800
Suburban Carry-All	1040	2070	3450	4850	6900
Canopy Express	1040	2070	3450	4850	6900
Series 3600/3700					
Pickup	1050	2100	3500	4900	7000
Platform	930	1860	3100	4350	6200
Stake Bed	950	1900	3150	4400	6300
Series 3800/3900					
Pickup	980	1950	3250	4550	6500
Panel Delivery	950	1900	3150	4400	6300
Platform	900	1800	3000	4200	6000
Stake Bed	920	1850	3050	4300	6100

NOTE: Deduct 5 percent for painted bumper and grille.

1951 CHEVROLET

LIGHT TRUCK — (ALL SERIES) — SIX-CYLINDER: — Chevrolet's new-for-1951 passenger car front end featured a lower grille that looked like a large "loop" of chrome running the entire width of the vehicle, with parking lamps at each end inside the loop. This was also used on the year's sedan delivery. Other trucks appeared mostly unchanged in exterior styling, but had minor technical changes. The front brake linings were larger and were bonded, instead of riveted. An improved foot-operated parking brake was standard on 3100/3600/3742/3942 models. This system was located near the driver's left foot and had a simplified release mechanism. A hand-operated emergency brake was, however, installed on trucks with a standard four-speed transmission. Each line of trucks carried a model designation on the engine hood: 3100 for ½-ton; 3600 for ¾-ton; 3742 for ¾-ton Forward Control; and 3800 for 1-ton. The 3942 trucks did not carry such a designation, however.

I.D. DATA: Serial Number located: (Forward Control) On chassis plate on temporary instrument panel support. (Flat face cowl) on plate attached to cowl left-hand inner panel. (All others) On plate attached to left-hand body hinge pillar. Numbers consisted of a series code in two letters and a sequence number starting at 00-1001 at each assembly plant. Starting numbers for 1951, by series, were: (1500) JJ-1001; (3100) JP-1001;

(3600) JR-1001; (3742) JT-1001; (3800) JS-1001 and (3942) JU-1001. Engine numbers located on right side of block behind distributor. Engine numbers were numbered in sequence, at each plant. Starting at 00-1001. Engine numbers for 1951, by series, were: (1500) JA-1001; (3100) JB-1001; (3600/3742/3800/3942) JC-1001.

1951 Chevrolet Pickup (OCW)

1951 Chevrolet Deluxe Panel Van (OCW)

Model	Body Type	Price	Weight	Prod. Total
Series 1500 — (½-Ton) — (Model JJ)				
JJ	Sedan Delivery	1532	4100	20,817
Series 3100 — (½-Ton) — (Model JP)				
JP	Chassis & F.F. Cowl	1035	2435	—
JP	Chassis, Cowl & W/S	1057	2420	—
JP	Chassis & Cab	1282	2880	—
JP/3104	Pickup	1353	3120	—
JP/3105	Panel Delivery	1556	3350	—
JP/3107	Canopy Express	1610	3325	—
JP/3106	Suburban (doors)	1818	3640	—
JP/3116	Suburban (gate)	1818	3635	—
Series 3600 — (¾-Ton)				
JP	Chassis & F.F. Cowl	1170	2650	—
JP	Chassis, Cowl & W/S	1190	2635	—
JP	Chassis & Cab	1417	3095	—
JP/3604	Pickup	1508	3470	—
JP/3608	Platform	1514	3510	—
JP/3608	Platform & Stake	1578	3690	—
Series 3742 — (¾-Ton) — (Forward Control)				
JT	Delivery Chassis	1190	2465	
Series 3800 — (1-Ton)				
JS	Chassis & F.F. Cowl	1258	2995	—
JS	Chassis, Cowl & W/S	1280	—	—
JS	Chassis & Cab	1505	3390	—
JS/3804	Pickup	1622	3930	—
JS/3808	Platform	1638	3955	—
JS/3808	Platform & Stake	1708	4205	—
JS/3805	Panel Delivery	1836	4185	—
JS/3807	Canopy Express	1916	4105	—
Series 3942 — (1-Ton) — (Forward Control)				
JU	Delivery Chassis	1296	2670	—

NOTE on Body Identification: Each Chevrolet commercial body was identified with a specific "Job Number." This consisted of seven digits, the last four in brackets — for example, number 026 (3104) for a 1951 half-ton pickup truck. The first three digits were a unique number. The first two digits inside the brackets identified the series. (3100 series in our example). The last two digits inside the brackets were a body style code ("04" meaning "pickup"). For 1951, the half-ton pickup was Job No. 026 (3104); the ¾-ton pickup was Job No. 028 (3604) and the one-ton pickup was Job No. 030 (3804). The last four digits for some trucks are shown in the first column of the chart above. However, it would be impossible to list this data in our format for all years. These numbers are usually listed in factory-issued "Master Parts Books" by Chevrolet, which may be useful to truck hobbyists researching the history of their Chevrolet trucks.

ENGINE: Inline. OHV. Six-cylinder. Cast iron block. Bore & stroke: 3½ x 3¾ in. Displacement: 216.5 cu. in. Compression ratio: 6.6:1. Brake horsepower: 92 at 3300 R.P.M. Net horsepower: 29.4 (SAE). Four main bearings. Solid valve lifters. Carburetor: GM Model B model no. 7002050.

NOTE: According to the 1949-1951 Chevrolet Truck Shop Manual all trucks, except two-tonners, used the 216.5 cu. in. "Thriftmaster" engine. The 235.5 cu. in. "Loadmaster" engine was standard in two-ton models and optional only in 1½-ton models. (Reprints of this manual, including the 1952 Supplement, are available from Crank 'N' Hope Publications of Blairsville, Pa.)

CHASSIS: (Series 1500) Wheelbase: 115 in. GVW: 4000 lbs. Tires: 6.70 x 15 four-ply.

CHASSIS: (Series 3100) Wheelbase: 116 in. GVW: 4200 lbs. Tires: 6.00 x 16 six-ply.

CHASSIS: (Series 3600) Wheelbase: 125¼ in. GVW: 5400 lbs. Tires: 15 in., six-ply.

CHASSIS: (Series 3742) Wheelbase: 125¼ in. GVW: 6200 lbs. Tires: 15 in., six-ply.

CHASSIS: (Series 3800) Wheelbase: 137 in. GVW: 6200 lbs. Tires: 7.00 x 17 six-ply.

CHASSIS: (Series 3942) Wheelbase: 137 in. GVW: 6700 lbs. Tires: 7.00 x 17 six-ply.

1951 Chevrolet Sedan Delivery (OCW)

TECHNICAL: Manual, synchromesh transmission. Speeds: (½-ton/¾-ton) 3F/1R; (1-ton) 4F/1R. Steering column-mounted gearshift (floorshift on one-tons). Single-plate, dry-disc type clutch. (½-ton) Semi-floating rear axle; (others) full-floating rear axle. Overall ratio: (½-ton) 4.11:1; (3600) 4.57:1; (others) 5.14:1. Four-wheel hydraulic brakes. Steel disc wheels.

OPTIONS: Deluxe "Big Window" Cab. Chrome grille. Chrome bumpers. Chrome hub caps. Chrome fender moldings (Panel, Suburban, Canopy). White sidewall tires. Chrome wheel trim rings. OSRV mirror (right-hand). Bumper guards. Right-hand inside sunvisor. Radio. Heater (standard or Deluxe). Clock. Cigar lighter. Radio antenna. Seat covers. External sun shade. Spotlight. Fender clearance lamps. Directional signals. Fog lamps. Auxiliary rear springs. Hydrovac. Heavy-duty springs. Six-ply tires (Sedan Delivery). Sixteen inch tires (3100 models). 7.00 x 17 six-ply tires (3600 models, requires two-stage, 8-leaf rear springs. 7.00 x 17 six-ply tires (3742 models). 7.00 x 17 eight-ply rear tires (3742 models). 7.50 x 17 eight-ply rear tires (3800 models). 7.00 x 18 eight-ply rear tires (3800 models). 7.00 x 18 eight-ply tires, single front/dual rear (3800 models, requires two-stage 8-leaf rear springs and hydro vac). 7.00 x 17 eight-ply rear tires (3942 models, requires double-acting rear shocks). 7.50 x 17 eight-ply rear tires (3942 models, requires above plus stabilizer). 7.00 x 18 eight-ply tires, single front/dual rear (3942 models, requires above plus two-stage, 8-leaf rear springs, auxiliary springs and hydrovac).

HISTORICAL: Introduced: January, 1951. Calendar year registrations: (all Series) 350,344. Innovations: Improved brake linings. Redesigned emergency brake. Historical notes: Well-known Chevrolet author George H. Dammann mentions, in his book *60 Years of Chevrolet*, his use of a 1951 Chevy truck for "workhorse" duty for many years.

1951 Chevrolet-National Ambulance (CP)

56

	5	4	3	2	1
1951					
Series 1500					
Sedan Delivery	1650	3300	5500	7700	11,000
Series 3100					
Pickup	1130	2250	3750	5250	7500
Panel Delivery	1020	2050	3400	4800	6800
Suburban Carry-All	1040	2070	3450	4850	6900
Canopy Express	1040	2070	3450	4850	6900
Series 3600/3700					
Pickup	1050	2100	3500	4900	7000
Platform	930	1860	3100	4350	6200
Stake Bed	950	1900	3150	4400	6300
Series 3800/3900					
Pickup	980	1950	3250	4550	6500
Panel Delivery	950	1900	3150	4400	6300
Platform	900	1800	3000	4200	6000
Stake Bed	920	1850	3050	4300	6100

NOTE: Deduct 5 percent for painted bumper and grille.

1952 CHEVROLET

LIGHT TRUCK — (ALL SERIES) — SIX-CYLINDER: — Chevrolet trucks were fitted with push-button door handles in 1952. The Sedan Delivery featured the year's new passenger car grille. It was basically similar to the 1951 style, except that there were five fins spaced across the main center bar. Hood ornaments were also redesigned on this model. Newly revised GM Model "B" carburetors were released for 1952 production and as a service part for retro-fitting to 1932-1951 models. A pressure type radiator cap which regulated cooling system pressure at 3½ to 4½ p.s.i. was also now installed on all Chevy trucks, except forward control models.

I.D. DATA: Serial Number located: Same as 1951. Serial numbers for 1952, by series were: (1500) KJ-1001 to 19,286; (3100) KP-1001 to 27,704; (3600) KR-1001 to 8,132; (3742) KT-1001 to 1430; (3800) KS-1001 to 5409 and (3942) KU-1001 to 1,300. Engine numbers located: Same as 1951. Engine numbers for 1952, by series, were: (1500) KA-1001 to 860,773; (3100) KB-1001 to 860,773; (3600/3742/3800/3942) KC-1001 to 860,773.

Job No.	Body Type	Price	Weight	Prod. Total
Model KJ — (Series 1500) — (½-Ton)				
1508	Sedan Delivery	1648	3100	9175
Model KP — (Series 3100) — (½-Ton)				
3102	Chassis & F.F. Cowl	1076	2435	—
3103	Chassis & Cab	1334	2880	—
3104	Pickup	1407	3120	—
3105	Panel	1620	3350	—
3107	Canopy Express	1676	3325	—
3112	Chassis & Cowl W/S	1099	—	—
3106	Suburban (doors)	1933	3640	—
3116	Suburban (doors)	1933	3635	—
Model KR — (Series 3600) — (¾-Ton)				
3602	Chassis & F.F. Cowl	1216	2655	—
3603	Chassis & Cab	1474	3095	—
3604	Pickup	1569	3470	—
3608	Platform	1575	3510	—
3609	Platform & Stake	1642	3690	—
3612	Chassis & Cowl & W/S	1238	2470	—
Model KT — (Series 3742) — (¾-Ton)				
3742	Delivery Chassis	1238	2470	—
Model KS — (Series 3800) — (1-Ton)				
3802	Chassis & F.F. Cowl	1312	3000	—
3803	Chassis & Cab	1570	3395	—
3804	Pickup	1692	3915	—
3805	Panel	1916	4140	—
3807	Canopy Express	2000	4110	—
3808	Platform	1709	3960	—
3809	Platform & Stake	1782	4240	—
3812	Chassis & Cowl & W/S	1335	—	—
Model KU — (Series 3900) — (1-Ton)				
3942	Delivery Chassis	1351	2670	—

NOTE: Last four digits of "Job Number" appear in the first column above. See 1951 footnote for specification chart.

ENGINE: (Standard, All) Inline. OHV. Six-cylinder. Cast iron block. Bore & stroke: 3½ x 3¾ in. Displacement: 216.5 cu. in. Compression ratio: 6.6:1. Brake horsepower: 92 at 3400 R.P.M. Net horsepower: 29.4 (SAE). Torque: 176 lbs.-ft. at 1200-2000 R.P.M. Four main bearings. Solid valve lifters. Carburetor: One-barrel model GM "B" (7002540).

ENGINE: (with Powerglide) Inline. OHV. Six-cylinder. Cast iron block. Bore & stroke: 3-9/16 x 3-15/16 in. Displacement: 235.5 cu. in. Compression ratio: 6.7:1. Brake horsepower: 105 at 3600 R.P.M. Net horsepower: 30.4 (SAE). Four main bearings. Hydraulic valve lifters. Carburetor: One-barrel model GM "B" (7003864).

NOTE: Powerglide availale in 1952 Sedan Delivery only.

1952 Chevrolet Sedan Delivery (OCW)

CHASSIS: (Series 1500) Wheelbase: 115 in. Overall length: 197.875 in. Height: 67.125 in. Tires: 6.70 x 15 four-ply.

CHASSIS: (Series 3100) Wheelbase: 116 in. Overall length: (Pickup) 191.31 in.; (others) 195.31 in. Height: (Panel) 80.68 in.; (Suburban) 79.5 in. Tires: 6.00 x 16 six-ply.

CHASSIS: (Series 3600) Wheelbase: 125¼ in. Overall length: (Pickup) 203.75 in.; (Stake) 209.437 in. Tires: 15 in., six-ply.

CHASSIS: (Series 3800) Wheelbase: 137 in. Overall length: (Pickup) 221.5 in.; (Panel) 229.7 in.; (Stake) 227.57 in. Height: (Panel) 86.437 in. Tires: (front) 7.00 x 17 six-ply; (rear) 7.00 x 17 eight-ply.

CHASSIS: (Series 3900) Wheelbase: 137 in. Overall length: 221.875 in. Front tread: 61.375 in. Rear tread: 61.75 in. Tires: 7.00 x 17 six-ply.

TECHNICAL: Same as 1951, except Powerglide automatic transmission available for Sedan Delivery.

OPTIONS: Same as 1951, plus: Grille guard. Powerglide transmission (Series 1500). Heavy-duty three-speed manual transmission. Heavy-duty four-speed manual tranmission. Right-hand door lock.

HISTORICAL: Introduced: January, 1952. Calendar year registrations: (all Series) 272,249. Innovations: New push-button door handles for conventional trucks. Improved carburetor. Pressure type radiator cap adopted. Feeler gauge slot removed from ½-ton brake drums. New 27 spline differential sidegears used in production.

1952 Chevrolet Panel Van (OCW)

Pricing

1952	5	4	3	2	1
Series 1500					
Sedan Delivery	1650	3300	5500	7700	11,000
Series 3100					
Pickup	1130	2250	3750	5250	7500
Panel Delivery	1020	2050	3400	4800	6800
Suburban Carry-All	1040	2070	3450	4850	6900
Canopy Express	1040	2070	3450	4850	6900
Series 3600/3700					
Pickup	1050	2100	3500	4900	7000
Platform	930	1860	3100	4350	6200
Stake Bed	950	1900	3150	4400	6300
Series 3800/3900					
Pickup	980	1950	3250	4550	6500
Panel Delivery	950	1900	3150	4400	6300
Platform	900	1800	3000	4200	6000
Stake Bed	920	1850	3050	4300	6100

NOTE: Deduct 5 percent for painted bumper and grille.

1953 CHEVROLET

1953 Chevrolet Government Van (RT)

LIGHT TRUCK — (ALL SERIES) — SIX-CYLINDER: — The most dramatic change in Chevrolet's truck line for 1953 was the new styling of the Sedan Delivery model which was patterned after that of the Chevrolet cars. Among its features was a one-piece windshield, an improved Powerglide automatic transmission option and a more powerful engine offering. The conventional trucks looked the same as they had since 1948, but a new option was a sidemounted spare tire. It replaced the regular spare carrier between the frame rails, directly under the tailgate. A special driver's side rear fender was required when this option was ordered.

I.D. DATA: Serial Number located: Same as 1951. For 1953 through 1955 second series models the serial number started with an alphabetical series code. This was followed by two digits indicating model year. Next came a letter code pinpointing the assembly plant. Finally, there were six digits representing the sequential production number. Series codes and assembly plant codes are listed below. Model year designations for 1953 were "53." See the sample below. Serial numbers for 1953, by series, were as follows: (1500) D53-001001 to 228961; (3100) H53-001001 to 49126; (3600) J53-001001 to 49126; (3742) K53-001001 to 49126; (3800) L53-001001 to 49126 and (3942) M53-001001 to 49126. Engine numbers located: Same as 1951. Each engine carried a letter code for model year, type and engine plant plus a production unit number. Example: LCS20737. All numbers were numbered at each source in sequence starting with 1001. Consult Chevrolet's "Special Information Catalog" for charts explaining engine codes more completely.

NOTE: (Series and factory Codes 1953-1955 models)

Factory Codes: A = Atlanta, B = Baltimore, F = Flint, J = Janesville, K = Kansas City; L = Los Angeles; N = Norwood, O = Oakland; S = St. Louis; T = Tarrytown and W = Willow Run.

Series Codes: H = 3100; J = 3600; K = 3700; L = 3800 and M = 3900.

1953 Chevrolet "3100" Pickup (G. Landry)

1953 Chevrolet Panel Delivery (OCW)

Job No.	Body Type	Price	Weight	Prod. Total
Model D — (Series 1500) — (½-Ton)				
1508	Sedan Delivery	1648	3160	15,523
Model H — (Series 3100) — (½-Ton)				
3102	Chassis & F.F. Cowl	1076	2440	—
3112	Chassis & Cowl & W/S	1099	2515	—
3103	Chassis & Cab	1334	2855	—
3104	Pickup	1407	3100	—
3105	Panel Delivery	1620	3335	—
3107	Canopy Express	1676	3305	—
3106	Suburban (doors)	1947	3625	—
3116	Suburban (gate)	1947	3635	—
Model J — (Series 3600) — (¾-Ton)				
3602	Chassis & F.F. Cowl	1216	2675	—
3612	Chassis & Cowl & W/S	1238	2780	—
3603	Chassis & Cab	1474	3110	—
3604	Pickup	1569	3480	—
3608	Platform	1575	3515	—
3609	Platform & Stake	1642	3700	—
Model K — (Series 3742) — (¾-Ton)				
3742	Delivery Chassis	1238	2480	—
Model M — (Series 3942) — (1-Ton)				
3942	Delivery Chassis	1351	2685	—
Model L — (Series 3800) — (1-Ton)				
3802	Chassis & F.F. Cowl	1312	3000	—
3812	Chassis & Cowl & W/S	1335	3080	—
3803	Chassis & Cab	1570	3405	—
3804	Pickup	1692	3920	—
3808	Platform	1709	3965	—
3809	Platform & Stake	1782	4210	—
3805	Panel Delivery	1916	4170	—
3807	Canopy Express	2000	4095	—

NOTE: Last four digits of "Job Number" appear in the first column above. See 1951 footnote.

ENGINE: (Standard Series 1500) Inline. OHV. Six-cylinder. Cast iron block. Bore & stroke: 3.5625 x 3.9375 in. Displacement: 235.5 cu. in. Compression ratio: 7.1:1. Brake horsepower: 108 at 3600 R.P.M. Net horsepower: 30.4. Four main bearings. Mechanical valve lifters. Carburetors: One-barrel model GM "B", Rochester 1-bbl. model B-7007181 or Carter 1-bbl. model 2101S.

ENGINE: (Optional Series 1500) Inline. OHV. Six-cylinder. Cast iron block. Bore & stroke: 3.5625 x 3.9375 in. Displacement: 235.5 cu. in. Compression ratio: 7.5:1. Brake horsepower: 115 at 3600 R.P.M. Net horsepower: 30.4. Four main bearings. Hydraulic valve lifters. Carburetors: Rochester BC 1-bbl. model 7007200 or Carter 1-bbl. model 2101S.

Chevrolet Deluxe Cab with Quarter Windows (Typical)

58

ENGINE: (Standard all Series except Series 1500) Inline. OHV. "Thriftmaster." Six-cylinder. Cast iron block. Bore & stroke: 3.5625 x 3.9375 in. Displacement: 235.5 cu. in. Compression ratio: 7.5:1. Brake horsepower: 112 at 3700 R.P.M. Four main bearings. Mechanical valve lifters. Carburetor: 1-bbl.

CHASSIS: (Series 1500) Wheelbase: 115 in. Overall length: 195.5 in. Height: 67.125 in. Front tread: 62 in. Rear tread: 62 in. Tires: 6.70 x 15 four-ply.

CHASSIS: (Series 3100) Wheelbase: 116 in. Overall length: (Pickup) 191.31 in.; (Panel, Suburban) 195.31 in. Height: (Panel) 80.68 in.; (Suburban) 79.5 in. Tires: 6.00 x 16 six-ply.

CHASSIS: (Series 3600) Wheelbase: 125.25 in. Overall length: (Pickup) 203.75 in.; (Stake) 209.437 in. Tires: 15 in., six-ply.

CHASSIS: (Series 3800) Wheelbase: 137 in. Overall length: (Pickup) 221.5 in.; (Panel) 229.57 in.; (Stake) 227.57 in. Height: (Panel) 86.437 in. Tires: (front) 7.00 x 17 six-ply; (rear) eight-ply.

CHASSIS: (Series 3742) Wheelbase: 125.25 in. Overall length: 197.125 in. Front tread: 62 in. Rear tread: 62.375 in. Tires: 7.00 x 17 in.

CHASSIS: (Series 3942) Wheelbase: 137 in. Overall length: 221.875 in. Front tread: 61.375 in. Rear tread: 61.75 in. Tires: 7.50 x 17 eight-ply or 7.50 x 18 eight-ply (Dual Rear Wheels).

TECHNICAL: Manual, synchromesh transmission. Speeds: 3F/1R (Series 3800 4F/1R). Column-mounted gearshift (floorshift in 3800). Single plate, dry disc clutch. (Series 1800, 3100) Semi-floating rear axle, (all others) full-floating rear axle. Overall ratio: (See 1951). Hydraulic, four-wheel brakes. Pressed steel wheels. Powerglide (Series 1500). Hydra-Matic. Heavy-duty 3-speed manual transmission. Heavy-duty 4-speed manual transmission. Heavy-duty rear springs. Extra-Output generators. Helper rear springs. Heavy-duty radiator.

OPTIONS: Deluxe "Big Window" Cab. Chrome grille. Chrome bumpers. Chrome hub caps. Chrome fender moldings (Panel, Suburban, Canopy). White sidewall tires. Chrome wheel trim rings. OSRV mirror (right-hand). Bumper guards. Right-hand inside sunvisor. Radio. Heater (standard or Deluxe). Clock. Cigar lighter. Radio antenna. Seat covers. External sun shade. Spotlight. Fender clearance lamps. Directional signals. Fog lamps. Auxiliary rear springs. Hydrovac. Heavy-duty springs. Six-ply tires (Sedan Delivery). Sixteen inch tires (3100 models). 7.00 x 17 six-ply tires (3600 models, requires two-stage, 8-leaf rear springs). 7.00 x 17 six-ply tires (3742 models). 7.00 x 17 eight-ply rear tires (3742 models). 7.50 x 17 eight-ply rear tires (3800 models). 7.00 x 18 eight-ply tires, single front/dual rear (3800 models, requires two-stage 8-leaf rear springs and hydro vac). 7.00 x 17 eight-ply rear tires (3942 models, requires double-acting rear shocks). 7.50 x 17 eight-ply rear tires (3942 models, requires above plus stabilizer). 7.00 x 18 eight-ply tires, single front/dual rear (3942 models, requires above plus two-stage, 8-leaf rear springs, auxiliary springs and hydrovac).

1953 Chevrolet Pickup (OCW)

HISTORICAL: Introduced: January, 1953. Calendar year registrations: (all Series) 327,960. Innovations: Completely new body style for Sedan Delivery. Black rubber gravel guards for Sedan Delivery. New side-mounted spare tire option for regular trucks. Historical notes: In factory terminology, the 1948-1953 Chevrolet trucks were classified as follows: The 3100 ½-ton line was called the "Light Delivery" series. The 3600 three-quarter-ton line was called "Conventional." The 3800 one-ton line was also called "Conventional," as well as "Medium-Duty." The 3742/3942 models were called "Forward Controls." In this catalog, all trucks of one-ton and under capacity are being considered Light-Duty Trucks.

1953 Chevrolet Pickup (JCL)

Pricing

1953	5	4	3	2	1
Series 1500					
Sedan Delivery	1650	3300	5500	7700	11,000
Series 3100					
Pickup	1130	2250	3750	5250	7500
Panel Delivery	1020	2050	3400	4800	6800
Suburban Carry-All	1040	2070	3450	4850	6900
Canopy Express	1040	2070	3450	4850	6900
Series 3600/3700					
Pickup	1050	2100	3500	4900	7000
Platform	930	1860	3100	4350	6200
Stake Bed	950	1900	3150	4400	6300
Series 3800/3900					
Pickup	980	1950	3250	4550	6500
Panel Delivery	950	1900	3150	4400	6300
Platform	900	1800	3000	4200	6000
Stake Bed	920	1850	3050	4300	6100

NOTE: Deduct 5 percent for painted bumper and grille.

1954 CHEVROLET

1954 Chevrolet Pickup (OCW)

LIGHT TRUCK — (ALL SERIES) — SIX-CYLINDER: — For 1954, the Sedan Delivery used the new-for-1953 body with a different treatment at front and rear. Up front, a new full-width grille had five "teeth" spaced across the main horizontal bar and the parking lamps wrapped around the body corners. Found at the rear were oblong taillights mounted in vertical housings with a "peak" or "fin" at the top. Other trucks had, what for them, was a major restyling with an open radiator grille. The opening was filled with a massive cross-bar arrangement with the main horizontal bar extending full-width of the body. Below it were rectangular parking lamps.

Also new was a one-piece windshield without vertical center molding. Numerous technical changes were introduced. They included a four-speed Hydra-Matic transmission, more rugged three-speed manual gear box and more durable clutch. Due to a reduced frame kickup at the rear axle, plus modified body mountings, the loading height of the pickup was reduced. Frame rigidity was increased by the use of a heavier crossmember at the rear of the engine. Series 3600 and 3800 models used a stronger driveline and universal joints. Deluxe models now came with painted grilles, and hub caps. Chrome fender trim strips were still seen as Deluxe equipment on some body styles. A switch to gray and maroon interiors was made for Suburban Carry-Alls. Juniper green body finish with Cream Medium striping and black wheels was standard finish for all models. Twelve other colors were optional. Deluxe models in solid colors had the wheels painted body color. With two-tone combinations, the wheels were done in the lower body color.

1954 Chrveolet Pickup (OCW)

I.D. DATA: Serial Number located: Same as 1951 and up. The coding system was the same one explained in the 1953 section. A ½-ton being the 90th truck built in Kansas City for model-year 1954 would have serial number H54K001090. Actual 1954 serial numbers, by series, were as follows: (1500) D54-001001 to 174684; (3100) H54-001001 to 52112; (3600) J54-001001 to 52112; (3700) K54-001001 to 52112; (3800) L54-001001 to 52112 and (3900) M54-001001 to 52112. Engine numbers located: Same as 1951 and up. Engine numbers by series were: (1500) 01001Z54 to 1024930; (3100) 01001X54 to 1024930; (3600) 01001X54 to 1024930; (3700) 01001T54 to 1024930; (3800) 01001X54 to 1024930 and (3900) 01001T54 to 1024930.

NOTE: For more complete information about 1954 Chevrolet truck serial numbers consult the "Chevrolet Special Information Catalog" which is available, in reprint form, from Crank 'N' Hope Publications of Blairsville, Pa.

1954 Chevrolet Pickup (DFW)

1954 Chevrolet Stake Truck (OCW)

1954 Chevrolet Panel (JCL)

Job No.	Body Type	Price	Weight	Prod. Total
Model D-54 — (Series 1500) — (½-Ton)				
1508	Sedan Delivery	1632	3195	8255
Model H-54 — (Series 3100) — (½-Ton)				
3102	Chassis & F.F. Cowl	1087	2430	—
3103	Chassis & Cab	1346	2870	—
3104	Pickup	1419	3145	—
3105	Panel Delivery	1631	3375	—
3107	Canopy Express	1688	3325	—
3112	Chassis & Cowl & W/S	1109	—	—
3106	Suburban (doors)	1958	3655	—
3116	Suburban (gate)	1958	3660	—
Model J-54 — (Series 3600) — (¾-Ton)				
3602	Chassis & F.F. Cowl	1227	2685	—
3603	Chassis & Cab	1486	3120	—
3604	Pickup	1582	3485	—
3608	Platform	1587	3540	—
3609	Platform & Stake	1654	3700	—
3612	Chassis & Cowl & W/S	1249	—	—
Model K-54 — (Series 3700) — (¾-Ton)				
3742	Delivery Chassis	1249	2460	—
Model M-54 — (Series 3900) — (1-Ton)				
3942	Delivery Chassis	1364	2700	—
Model L-54 — (Series 3800) — (1-Ton)				
3802	Chassis & F.F. Cowl	1325	3015	—
3803	Chassis & Cab	1582	3435	—
3804	Pickup	1705	3880	—
3805	Panel Delivery	1929	4170	—
3807	Canopy Express	2012	4130	—
3808	Platform	1722	3950	—
3809	Platform & Stake	1794	4200	—
3812	Chassis & Cowl & W/S	1347	—	—

NOTE: Job Numbers appear in first column above.

1954 Chevrolet Van (OCW)

1954 Chevrolet Panel Van (OCW)

1954 Chevrolet Sedan Delivery (MVMA)

ENGINE: Inline. OHV. Six-cylinder. Cast iron block. Bore & stroke: 3-9/16 x 3-15/16 in. Displacement: 235.5 cu. in. Compression ratio: 6.7:1. Gross horsepower: 112 at 3700 R.P.M. Net horsepower: 105 at 3600 R.P.M. SAE horsepower: 30.4. Four main bearings. Solid valve lifters. Carburetor: One-barrel model GM "B".

NOTE 1: Code X indicated "Thriftmaster 235" engine for 3100 / 3600 / 3800. Code U indicated "Thriftmaster 235" w/heavy-duty clutch for 3100/3600/3800. Code M indicated "Thriftmaster 235" w/Hydra-Matic for 3100/3600/3800. Code T indicated "Loadmaster 235" for 3700/3900. Code L indicated "Loadmaster 235" w/Hydra-Matic for 3700/3900.

NOTE 2: The "Loadmaster 235" used in 3700/3900 series model had a Gross Horsepower rating of 110 at 3600 R.P.M. and a Net Horsepower rating of 102 at 3600 R.P.M.

1954 Chevrolet Suburban w/end doors (OCW)

1954 Chevrolet "3100" Pickup (HSM)

CHASSIS: (Series 1500) Wheelbase: 115 in. Tires: 6.70 x 15 four-ply.

CHASSIS: (Series 3100) Wheelbase: 116 in. Tires: 6.00 x 16 six-ply.

CHASSIS: (Series 3600) Wheelbase: 125¼ in. Tires: (front) 7.00 x 17 six-ply; (rear) 7.00 x 17 eight-ply.

CHASSIS: (Series 3700) Wheelbase: 125¼ in. Tires: 15 inch, six-ply.

CHASSIS: (Series 3800) Wheelbase: 137 in. Tires: (front) 7.00 x 17 six-ply; (rear) 7.00 x 17 eight-ply.

CHASSIS: (Series 3900) Wheelbase: 137 in. Tires: 7.00 x 17 six-ply.

1954 Chevrolet "150" Sedan Delivery (OCW)

TECHNICAL: Selective synchromesh transmission. Speeds: (1-ton) 4F/1R; (others) 3F/1R. Column-mounted gearshift (floorshift on one-ton). Single plate, dry disc clutch. Overall ratio: (3100) 3.90:1; (3600) 4.57:1 or 5.14:1; (others) 5.14:1. Four-wheel hydraulic brakes. Steel disc wheels.

1954 Chevrolet "150" Sedan Delivery (JAW)

OPTIONS: Chrome front bumper. Rear bumper. Sidemount tire carrier. White sidewall tires. OSRV mirror(s). Deluxe two-tone finish. Bumper guards. Radio. Heater temperature-controlled and recirculating type. Clock. Cigar lighter. Radio antenna. Seat covers. Outside metal sunvisor. Spotlight. Fog lamps. Chrome wheel trim rings. Rail-type grille guard. Brush-type grille guard. Bumper upright grille guard. Stainless steel vent shades. Bumper step. Directional signals. High-tone horn. Windshield washer (foot-operated). Interior non-glare rearview mirror. Deluxe comfort master Cab. Rear corner windows. Optional Solid Colors: Mariner blue. Commercial red. Jet black. Ocean green. Transport blue. Omaha orange. Copper Tone. Autumn brown. Pure white. Medium cream. Yukon yellow. Bugandy maroon.

1954 Chevrolet Deluxe Panel Truck (OCW)

HISTORICAL: Introduced: December, 1953. Calendar year registrations: (all Series) 293,079. Innovations: Hydra-matic transmission. One-piece windshield. New front end styling for regular trucks. Historical notes: The 1954 style trucks were carried over into the first part of the 1955 model-year virtually without change. In mid-1955 an entirely new line of light-duty trucks would be introduced as "second series" models. The 1955 section of this catalog will cover only the "Second Series" models.

1954 Chevrolet Pickup (MVMA)

Pricing

1954	5	4	3	2	1
Series 1500					
Sedan Delivery	1650	3300	5500	7700	11,000
Series 3100					
Pickup	1150	2310	3850	5400	7700
Panel	1040	2070	3450	4850	6900
Suburban	1070	2150	3550	5000	7100
Canopy	1050	2100	3500	4900	7000
Series 3600					
Pickup	1070	2150	3550	5000	7100
Platform	950	1900	3150	4400	6300
Stake	960	1920	3200	4500	6400
Series 3800					
Pickup	1000	2000	3300	4600	6600
Panel	950	1900	3150	4400	6300
Canopy	960	1920	3200	4500	6400
Platform	930	1860	3100	4350	6200
Stake	950	1900	3150	4400	6300

1955 CHEVROLET

1955 Chevrolet Suburban (Cameo) Pickup (HSM)

LIGHT TRUCK — (ALL SERIES) — SIX-CYLINDER/V-8: — Chevrolet's "first series" 1955 trucks were introduced on October 28, 1954. With the exception of the Sedan Delivery, the trucks were the same as last year's models at prices about $11 higher. The Sedan Delivery had the new sheet metal of the 1955 passenger cars, with the main changes being a slab-sided body, hooded headlamps and a rectangular egg-crate grille. An all-new V-8 could be ordered for this model only. When the "second series" trucks debuted on March 25, 1955, the Sedan Delivery was unchanged, but just about everything else was all-new. From a collector's standpoint, the most exciting innovation was a pickup identified with Job Number 3124. Generically, his was known as the "Suburban Pickup," but most people relate to the term "Cameo Carrier" much better. This was a limited production, highly stylized half-tonner with slab-sided rear fender skins made of plastic, a special red-and-white color scheme (inside and out) and many luxury features. Other trucks shared new cab styling with the Cameo Carrier. Appearance revisions were headlined by hooded headlights, an egg-crate grille, fade-away front fenders and a panoramic wraparound windshield. Another styling innovation was the introduction of a Custom Cab with full-width rear window. The interior was highlighted by a wedge-shaped speedometer similar to that used on cars. Chevy now offered a V-8 engine, in addition to the time-proven six. Also new was a 12-volt electrical system and, on half-ton models, tubeless tires. Paint colors for "first series" models were unchanged from 1954. For the "second series" trucks there were 13 solid and 13 two-tone color combinations. Eleven of the two-tones used Bombay Ivory on the upper body. The others were Sand beige upper over Russet brown lower body and Commercial red upper over Bombay Ivory. Only "second series" models are covered in this section. Refer to the 1954 section for details about the "first series" models.

1955 Chevrolet Pickup (DFW)

I.D. DATA: Serial Number located: (Forward Control) left side of steering column. (F.F. Cowl) front face of cowl top panel; (all others) body hinge pillar. The serial number system was basically the same as in 1954. Model year codes were "55" for "first series" and "255" for "second series." New series identification letters were adopted for some "second series" models, as follows: M=3200 Series, F=3400 Series and G=3500 Series. Serial numbers for the later trucks (second series), were as follows: (1500) D255-001001 to 256218; (3100) H255-001001 to 60351; (3200) M255-001001 to 60351; (3400) F255-001001 to 60351; (3500) G255-001001 to 60351; (3700) K255-001001 to 60351; (3600) J255-001001-60351 and (3800) L255-001001 to 60351. Engine numbers located on right side of engine on boss at rear of distributor. "Second Series" engine numbers were: (1500) 01001Z55 to 0905907; (3100) 01001X55 to 0905907; (3200) 01001X55 to 0905907; (3400/3500/3700) 01001T55 to 0905907 and (3600/3800) 01001X55 to 0905907.

NOTE: These codes are for the base engine.

1955 Chevrolet Cameo Carrier Pickup (OCW)

1955 Chevrolet Deluxe Panel Delivery (DFW)

1955 Chevrolet Panel Delivery (DFW)

Job No.	Body Type	Price	Weight	Prod. Total
Model D255 — (Series 1500) — (½-Ton) — (115 in. w.b.)				
1508	Sedan Delivery	1699	3110	8811
Model H255 — (Series 3100) — (½-Ton) — (114 in. w.b.)				
3102	Chassis & F.F. Cowl	1156	2335	—
3103	Chassis & Cab	1423	2850	—
3104	Pickup	1519	3210	—
3105	Panel	1801	3440	—
3106	Suburban (doors)	2150	3715	—
3112	Chassis & Cowl & W/S	1193	2460	—
3116	Suburban (gate)	2150	3725	—
3124	Suburban Pickup (*)	1981	3355	5220
Model M255 — (Series 3200) — (½-Ton) — (123¼ in. w.b.)				
3204	L.W.B. Pickup	1540	3305	—
Model F255 — (Series 3400) — (¾-Ton) — (104 in. w.b.)				
3442	Delivery Chassis	1279	2600	—
Model G255 — (Series 3500) — (¾-Ton) — (125 in. w.b.)				
3542	Delivery Chassis	1317	2720	—
Model K255 — (Series 3700) — (¾-Ton) — (137 in. w.b.)				
3742	Delivery Chassis	1350	2730	—
Model J255 — (Series 3600) — (¾-Ton) — (123¼ in. w.b.)				
3602	Chassis & F.F. Cowl	1316	2730	—
3603	Chassis & Cab	1583	3205	—
3604	Pickup	1690	3625	—
3608	Platform	1711	3630	—
3609	Platform & Stake	1780	3815	—
3612	Chassis Cowl & W/S	1353	2815	—
Model L255 — (Series 3800) — (1-Ton) — (135 in. w.b.)				
3802	Chassis & F.F. Cowl	1444	3050	—
3803	Chassis & Cab	1711	3535	—
3804	Pickup	1844	3985	—
3805	Panel	2135	4300	—
3808	Platform	1859	4075	—
3809	Platform & Stake	1944	4360	—
3812	Chassis & Cowl & W/S	1481	3130	—

(*) Job Number 3124, the Suburban Pickup, is better known as the Cameo Carrier pickup. The Cameo Carrier was based on the regular 3100 Series pickup with a 114 in. w.b. and 78 in. cargo bed. Bolt-on quarter panels, made of fiberglass, brought the exterior width of the bed out flush with the cab. These panels had a sculptured line that carried the main body feature line to the rear. A gap between the cab and the bed was chrome-trimmed. The spare tire was concealed in a compartment below the tailgate, under the bed. The flush tailgate had concealed hinges and latch. The special color scheme was Bombay Ivory with red trim on the rear cab posts and the interior. Unique finned taillights and stylish full wheel covers were among its other standard equipment features.

1955 Chevrolet Sedan Delivery (Owner: D. Batten)

1955 Chevrolet IMS Fire Truck (IMSC/Jack Martin)

ENGINE: (Standard 3100/3200/3600/3800) Inline. OHV. Six-cylinder. Cast iron block. Bore & stroke: 3-9/16 x 3-15/16 in. Displacement: 235.5 cu. in. Compression ratio: 7.5:1. Gross horsepower: 123 at 3800 R.P.M. Net horsepower: 109 at 3600 R.P.M. SAE horsepower: 30.4. Four main bearings. Solid valve lifters. Carburetor: Single-barrel downdraft. Model: Rochester B-7004468.

NOTE: This was called the "New Thriftmaster 235" engine. It was available with a three-speed transmission; heavy-duty three-speed; overdrive; four-speed transmission or Hydra-Matic. When attached to Hydra-Matic the engine came with hydraulic valve lifters and produced 136 gross horsepower at 4200 R.P.M.

ENGINE: (Standard 3400/3500/3700) Inline. OHV. Six-cylinder. Cast iron block. Bore & stroke: 3-9/16 x 3-15/16 in. Displacement: 235.5 cu. in. Compression ratio: 7.5:1. Gross horsepower: 119 at 3600 R.P.M. Net horsepower: 105 at 3600 R.P.M. SAE horsepower: 30.4. Four main bearings. Solid valve lifters. Carburetor: Single-barrel downdraft. Model: Rochester "B".

NOTE: This was called the "Loadmaster 235" engine. It was available with all transmissions, except Overdrive. When attached to Hydra-Matic, hydraulic valve lifters were used.

ENGINE: (Optional 3100/3200/3600/3800) Vee-block. OHV. Eight-cylinders. Cast iron block. Bore & stroke: 3¾ x 3 in. Displacement: 265 cu. in. Compression ratio: 7.5:1. Gross horsepower: 145 at 4000 R.P.M. Net horsepower: 126 at 4000 R.P.M. Five main bearings. Solid valve lifters. Carburetor: Two-barrel downdraft. Model: Rochester 7008006.

NOTE: This was called the "Trademaster 265" engine. It was available with all transmissions. Hydraulic valve lifters were used with Hydra-Matic.

CHASSIS: (Series 1500) Wheelbase: 115 in. Overall length: 200.8 in. Front tread: 58 in. Rear tread: 58.9 in. Tires: 7.15 x 14 four-ply.

CHASSIS: (Series 3100) Wheelbase: 114 in. Overall length: 185.687 in. Front tread: 60.5 in. Rear tread: 61.0 in. Tires: 6.70 x 15 four-ply.

CHASSIS: (Series 3200) Wheelbase: 123.25 in. Overall length: 205.56 in. Tires: 6.70 x 15 four-ply.

CHASSIS: (Series 3442) Wheelbase: 104 in. Tires: 8 x 19.5 six-ply.

CHASSIS: (Series 3542) Wheelbase: 125 in. Tires: 8 x 19.5 six-ply.

CHASSIS: (Series 3742) Wheelbase: 137 in. Tires: 8 x 19.5 six-ply.

CHASSIS: (Series 3600) Wheelbase: 123.25 in. Overall length: 205.56 in. Tires: 7 x 17.5 six-ply.

CHASSIS: (Series 3800) Wheelbase: 135 in. Overall length: 215.81 in. Tires: (front) 8 x 17.5 six-ply; (rear) 8 x 17.5 eight-ply.

1955 Chevrolet Sedan Delivery-rear view (DFW)

TECHNICAL: Selective synchromesh transmission. Speeds: (3800) 4F/1R; (others) 3F/1R. Column-mounted gearshift (floorshift on 3800). Single dry disc clutch. (3600/3800) Full-floating rear axle; (Others) semi-floating rear axle. Overall ratio: (3100/3200) 3.90:1; (3400/3500/3700) 5.14:1; (3600) 4.57:1. Four-wheel hydraulic brakes. Steel disc wheels. Technical options: Heavy-duty three-speed manual transmission. Over-

drive transmission. Four-speed manual transmission. Hydra-Matic transmission. Rear axles. Heavy-duty clutch. Heavy-duty radiator. Oil bath air cleaner.

NOTE: Code "M" indicates Muncie three-speed or overdrive transmission.
Code "S" indicates Saginaw three-speed or overdrive transmission.
Code "W" indicates Borg-Warner heavy-duty three-speed transmission.

OPTIONS: Side spare mount. Electric windshield wipers. Two-tone exterior point. Radio. Heater (Standard and Deluxe). Clock. Cigar lighter. Radio antenna. Seat covers. External sun shade. Chrome grille. Chrome headlight shell. Chrome bumpers. Chrome hubcaps. Rear bumper (painted or chromed) Custom Cab (packages include either small or wide rear window, deluxe seat, chrome instrument knobs, cigarette lighter, dual visors, dual arm rests, two-tone interior color scheme). Directional signals. Full-view rear window. EZ eye glass. Air-matic seat. Front bumper guards (painted or chrome). Rear pull-down steps. Dual visors. Door locks. Spare tire lock. Outside mirrors. Extendable outside mirror. Spotlight with mirror. Cigarette lighter. Windshield washer. Roof-mounted sunvisor. Traffic viewer. Back-up lights. Electric parking brake signal. Chrome hood ornament. Dual fog lamps. Red reflex reflectors. Portable spotlight. AC/DC shaver. Stainless steel door edge guards. Stainless steel door vent shades. Chrome door handle shields. Tool kit. Illuminated compass. Underhood light. High note horn.

Solid-Color Paint Colors: Juniper green (BI). Commercial red (AS). Sand beige (BI). Jet black (BI). Omaha orange (BI). Granite gray (BI). Empire blue (BI). Cream Medium (BI). Yukon yellow (BI). Ocean green (BI). Crystal blue (BI). Russet brown (BI). Pure white. Note: The code in brackets indicates wheel stripe color; either Bombay Ivory (BI) or Argent silver (AS).

Two-Tone Colors: (All following lower body colors available with Bombay Ivory upper body color and same wheel stripe color as solid above) Juniper green. Commercial red. Jet black. Empire blue. Cream medium. Yukon yellow. Ocean green. Crystal blue. Granite gray. Omaha orange. Sand beige. Another choice was Sand beige on top, Russet brown on bottom and Bombay Ivory wheel stripe. Cameo Carrier available only with Commercial red upper, Bombay Ivory lower & red wheel stripes.

NOTES: Wheels were painted lower body color on all 3000 Series trucks (black on over one-ton models). Deluxe equipment and two-tone options not available on ½-ton Suburbans. Cameo Carrier had wheel stripes on 16 x 5K wheels only. Other models had above noted stripe colors on 15 x 5K or 16 x 5K wheels only.

HISTORICAL: Introduced: (1st Series) Oct. 28, 1954. (2nd Series) March 25, 1955. Calendar year registrations: (all Series) 329,791. Innovations: Completely restyled "second series" line. Panaramic windshield. New V-8 engine options. Limited-production Cameo Carrier with fiberglass bedliner introduced. 12-volt electrical systems. Tubeless tires. Historical notes: This was a milestone year for Chevrolet light-duty trucks due to sweeping styling revisions, technical changes and introduction of a V-8 engine.

Pricing

1955	5	4	3	2	1
First Series					
Series 3100					
Pickup	1150	2310	3850	5400	7700
Panel	1040	2070	3450	4850	6900
Suburban	1070	2150	3550	5000	7100
Canopy	1050	2100	3500	4900	7000
Series 3600					
Pickup	1070	2150	3550	5000	7100
Platform	950	1900	3150	4400	6300
Stake	960	1920	3200	4500	6400
Series 3800					
Pickup	1000	2000	3300	4600	6600
Panel	950	1900	3150	4400	6300
Canopy	960	1920	3200	4500	6400
Platform	930	1860	3100	4350	6200
Stake	950	1900	3150	4400	6300
Second Series					
Series 1500					
Sedan Delivery	1800	3600	6000	8400	12,000
Series 3100					
Pickup	1150	2310	3850	5400	7500
Custom Cab Pickup	1300	2550	4250	5900	8500
Panel Delivery	1200	2400	4000	5600	8000
Suburban	1200	2460	4100	5700	8200
Cameo Carrier	2250	4500	7500	10,500	15,000
Cantrell Station Wagon	1650	3300	5500	7700	11,000
Series 3400/3500/3700					
Walk-In Delivery Van	750	1500	2500	3500	5000
School Bus	600	1200	2000	2800	4000
Series 3200					
Long Box Pickup	980	1950	3250	4550	6500
Series 3600					
Pickup	900	1800	3000	4200	6000
Custom Cab Pickup	1000	2000	3300	4600	6600
Platform	750	1500	2500	3500	5000
Platform & Stake	830	1650	2750	3850	5500
Cantrell Station Wagon	1500	3000	5000	7000	10,000
Series 3800					
Pickup	870	1750	2900	4100	5800
Panel Delivery	1000	2000	3300	4600	6600
Platform	680	1350	2250	3150	4500
Platform & Stake	720	1450	2400	3300	4800

NOTE: 1955-up prices based on top of the line models.

1956 CHEVROLET

1956 Chevrolet Sedan Delivery (DFW)

LIGHT TRUCK — (ALL SERIES) — SIX-CYLINDER/V-8: — The Sedan Delivery was restyled along the lines of Chevrolet's passenger cars. Squared-off fenders more deeply hooded the headlamps. A cross-hatched grille insert ran the full-width of the car between new, ribbed trim plates that wrapped around the body corners. Larger, square parking lamps were seen at each end. Side moldings were of the "150" Series style, stopping behind the side doors. Changes for regular trucks were minor. Fenderside nameplates kept the same basic shape, but had a raised blade portion and center crease line. They were moved above the main body feature line, instead of below it. The hood emblem was redesigned so the "wings" on it extended out from near the bottom, instead of the top. There were again 13 solid colors. New ones included Forest green, Cardinal red, Golden yellow, Regal blue and Crystal blue. Twelve two-tones were available on all but the Suburbans and Cameo Pickup. Nine combinations featured Arabian Ivory upper body in conjunction with the other colors. New was a choice of Jet black over Golden yellow. Cardinal red over Sand beige was also available. Deluxe equipment and two-tones were not available for Suburbans. This year's Cameo Pickup (or Suburban Pickup) came in eight two-tone combinations: Cardinal red over Bombay Ivory; Arabian Ivory over Cardinal red; Jet black over Golden yellow; Cardinal red over Sand beige and Arabian Ivory over any of four other colors, which were Regal blue, Granite gray, Ocean green or Crystal blue. Actually, the secondary color was used only on the rear cab pillars and around the back window. The roof, windshield pillars and rest of the body were done in what was called the "upper" color.

1956 Chevrolet Sedan Delivery (OCW)

I.D. DATA: Serial Number located in the same locations. For 1956 through 1959 the first number and letter designate the series according to the following codes: (1500) D56; (3100) 3A; (3200) 3B; (3400) 3C; (3500) 3D; (3600) 3E; (3700) 3F; (3800) 3G. The next two numbers designated model year which was "56" for 1956. Next came a letter designating the assembly plant using the same codes as 1953-1955 models. Following this was a group of numerals indicating production sequence in the specific assembly plant. These numbers started at 100001 and up. Under this system, a truck bearing Serial Number 3E56F100092 would be a 3600 Series model, built in 1956, as the 92nd assembled unit at the Flint factory. The ending number for Sedan Deliveries was 220555; for other models 033691. Engine numbers located in the same locations. (Note: V-8 engine numbers were on top of the right-hand cylinder bank near front of truck.) Engine numbers consisted of an engine serial number, alphabetical factory code, two-digit model year code and letter indicating the type of truck and type of engine. For example, an engine with the number 0068025F56X would be a "235 Thriftmaster" in a 3100/3200/3600/3800 Series truck (code "X") made in 1956 (code "56") at the Flint plant (code "F") which had engine serial number 0068025. Other common codes for trucks in these

series were: (XG) for the Thriftmaster 235 with Hydra-Matic; (V) for the Thriftmaster 235 w/heavy-duty clutch; (A) for the Trademaster 265 V-8; (B) for the Trademaster 265 with Hydra-Matic; (M) for the Trademaster 265 w/heavy-duty clutch; (W) for the Thriftmaster 235 Special and (WA) for the Thriftmaster 235 Special with Hydra-Matic. Codes for 3400/3500/3700 trucks were (D) for Trademaster 265 V-8; (DA) for Trademaster 265 V-8 with Hydra-Matic and (DB) for Trademaster 265 V-8 with heavy-duty clutch.

Job No.	Body Type	Price	Weight	Prod. Total
Model D56 — (Series 1500) — (½-Ton) — (115 in. w.b.)				
1508	Sedan Delivery	1865	3145	—
Model 3A — (Series 3100) — (½-Ton) — (114 in. w.b.)				
3102	Chassis & F.F. Cowl	1303	2374	—
3103	Chassis & Cab	1567	2872	—
3104	Pickup	1670	3217	—
3105	Panel Delivery	1966	3457	—
3106	Suburban (doors)	2300	3736	—
3112	Chassis & Cowl & W/S	1341	2505	—
3116	Suburban (gate)	2300	3752	—
3124	Cameo Pickup	2144	3373	1452
Model 3B — (Series 3200) — (½-Ton) — (123¼ in. w.b.)				
3204	Long Box Pickup	1692	3323	—
Model 3C — (Series 3400) — (¾-Ton) — (114 in. w.b.)				
3442	Delivery Chassis	1499	2716	—
Model 3D — (Series 3500) — (¾-Ton) — (125 in. w.b.)				
3542	Delivery Chassis	1537	2764	—
Model 3F — (Series 3700) — (¾-Ton) — (137 in. w.b.)				
3742	Delivery Chassis	1569	2784	—
Model 3E — (Series 3600) — (¾-Ton) — (123¼ in. w.b.)				
3602	Chassis & F.F. Cowl	1481	2736	—
3603	Chassis & Cab	1745	3252	—
3604	Pickup	1858	3633	—
3609	Platform & Stake	1950	3834	—
3612	Chassis & Cowl & W/S	1519	2870	—
Model 3G — (Series 3800) — (1-Ton) — (135 in. w.b.)				
3802	Chassis & F.F. Cowl	1611	2945	—
3803	Chassis & Cab	1875	3503	—
3804	Pickup	2009	3939	—
3805	Panel Delivery	2327	4243	—
3809	Platform & Stake	2122	4285	—
3812	Chassis & Cowl & W/S	1649	3118	—

NOTE: Although all of these trucks fit the catalog definition of a "light-duty" model (one-ton and under), Chevrolet called the ¾-ton and one-ton models "medium duties."

1956 Chevrolet Panel Delivery w/modern tires (JLB)

ENGINE: (Standard 3100/3200/3600/3800) Inline. OHV. Six-cylinder. Cast iron block. Bore & stroke: 3-9/16 x 3-15/16 in. Displacement: 235.5 cu. in. Compression ratio: 8.0:1. Gross horsepower: 140 at 4200 R.P.M. Net horsepower: 123 at 4000 R.P.M. SAE horsepower: 30.4. Four main bearings. Solid valve lifters. Carburetor: Single-barrel downdraft. (Std.) Rochester 7007181. (Auto.) Rochester 7007200.

NOTE: This was the "Thriftmaster 235" engine. Transmissions: Three-speed; heavy-duty three-speed; four-speed; overdrive; Hydra-Matic. (Hydraulic valve lifters with Hydra-Matic.)

ENGINE: (Standard 3400/3500/3700) Inline. OHV. Six-cylinder. Cast iron block. Bore & stroke: 3-9/16 x 3-15/16 in. Displacement: 235.5 cu. in. Compression ratio: 8.0:1. Gross horsepower: 140 at 4200 R.P.M. Net horsepower: 120 at 3800 R.P.M. SAE horsepower: 30.4. Four main bearings. Hydraulic valve lifters. Carburetor: Rochester model B-7005140.

NOTE: This was called the "Thriftmaster Special" engine. It came with all transmission choices except overdrive.

ENGINE: (Optional, all) Vee-block. OHV. Eight-cylinders. Cast iron block. Bore & stroke: 3¾ x 3 in. Displacement: 265 cu. in. Compression ratio: 7.5:1. Gross horsepower: 155 at 4200 R.P.M. Net horsepower: 132 at 3800 R.P.M. Torque: 249 lbs.-ft. at 2200 R.P.M. Five main bearings. Hydraulic valve lifters. Carburetor: Rochester model 2G-7008397.

NOTE: This was called the "Trademaster 265" engine. It came with all transmissions.

CHASSIS: (Series 1500) Wheelbase: 115 in. Overall length: 200.8 in. Front tread: 58 in. Rear tread: 58.9 in. Tires: 7.50 x 14 four-ply.

1956 Chevrolet Panel Delivery (C.H. Horst)

CHASSIS: (Series 3100) Wheelbase: 114 in. Overall length: 185.687 in. (Cameo) 193.56 in. Front tread: 60.5 in. Rear tread: 61.0 in. Tires: 6.70 x 15 four-ply.

CHASSIS: (Series 3200) Wheelbase: 123¼ in. Overall length: 205.56 in. Front tread: 60.5 in. Rear tread: 61.0 in. Tires: 6.70 x 15 four-ply.

CHASSIS: (Series 3400/3500/3700) Wheelbase: 104/125/137 in. Tires: 8 x 19.5 six-ply.

CHASSIS: (Series 3600) Wheelbase: 123¼ in. Overall length: 205.56 in. Tires: 7 x 17.5 six-ply.

CHASSIS: (Series 3800) Wheelbase: 135 in. Overall length: 215.81 in. Tires: (front) 8 x 17.5 six-ply; (rear) 8 x 17.5 eight-ply.

TECHNICAL: Same as 1955.

OPTIONS: Side spare mount. Rear bumper (painted or chrome). Bumper guards. Radio. Heater (Standard and Deluxe). Clock. Cigar lighter. Radio antenna. Seat covers. External sun shade. Spotlight. Radiator insect screen. Electric windshield wipers. Two-tone exterior paint. Full view rear window. EZ eye tinted glass. Directional signals. Dual sunvisors. Dual arm rests. Exterior chrome appearance package. Windshield washer. Back-up lights. Fog lamps. High-note horn.

HISTORICAL: Introduced: Fall 1956. Calendar year production: (All Series) 399,772. Innovations: New paint colors and two-tone combinations. The "Thriftmaster 235" six-cylinder engine had a higher compression ratio and 17 more gross horsepower for 1956. The "Trademaster 265" V-8 engine gained 10 gross horsepower. Longer overall length and new styling for Sedan Delivery. Historical notes: After building its six-millionth truck in model year 1955, Chevrolet had a slight sales slump in 1956. The company sent a fleet of its larger "Taskmaster" trucks to special displays around the country this year.

Pricing

	5	4	3	2	1
1956					
Series 1500					
Sedan Delivery	1700	3450	5750	8050	11,500
Series 3100					
Pickup	1150	2310	3850	5400	7500
Custom Cab Pickup	1300	2550	4250	5900	8500
Panel Delivery	1200	2400	4000	5600	8000
Suburban	1200	2450	4050	5650	8100
Cameo Carrier	2150	4200	7000	9800	14,000
Cantrell Station Wagon	1650	3300	5500	7700	11,000
Series 3400/3500/3700					
Walk-In Delivery Van	750	1500	2500	3500	5000
School Bus	600	1200	2000	2800	4000
Series 3200					
Long Box Pickup	980	1950	3250	4550	6500
Series 3600					
Pickup	900	1800	3000	4200	6000
Custom Cab Pickup	1000	2000	3300	4600	6600
Platform	750	1500	2500	3500	5000
Platform & Stake	830	1650	2750	3850	5500
Cantrell Station Wagon	1500	3000	5000	7000	10,000
Series 3800					
Pickup	870	1750	2900	4100	5800
Panel Delivery	1000	2000	3300	4600	6600
Platform	680	1350	2250	3150	4500
Platform & Stake	720	1450	2400	3300	4800

NOTE: 1955-up prices based on top of the line models.

1957 Chevrolet Pickup w/custom wheels (DFW)

LIGHT TRUCKS — (ALL SERIES) — SIX-CYLINDER/V-8: — The "classic" look for Chevrolet's 1957 cars included an oval front bumper grille with bomb type bumperguards, a flatter hood with windsplit bulges, screened headlamp housings and broad, flat tailfins. The Sedan Delivery had these features with "150" series trim. A new grille was also featured on regular light trucks. Its outer moldings had a traphazoid shape. A slimmer traphazoid floated in the middle, supported by four vertical pieces above and below. Fenderside nameplates were now oval-shaped with the brand name and series number in a center depression. These were again positioned above the feature line. The hood badge was of the same general shape, but larger. The Cameo got the chrome version of the new grille, plus a contrast band running horizontally from behind the cab to the area between the rear bumper and taillights. This carried a Chevy bow-tie badge and "Cameo" script. With V-8s, a V-shaped badge adorned the doors. All trucks, except Cameos, could be had in 14 solid colors. New ones included Brewster green, Alpine blue, Royal blue, Indian turquoise and Sandstone beige. There were 13 two tones available on all models except Suburbans and Cameos. Most used Bombay Ivory for the "upper" color, but Ocean green over Brewster green, Alpine blue over Royal blue and Jet black over Golden yellow were distinctive. Cameo two tones were extended to nine choices. Cardinal red over Bombay Ivory, Bombay Ivory over Sand beige, Bombay Ivory over Cardinal red, Jet black over Golden yellow, Bombay Ivory over Indian turquoise, Bombay Ivory over Granite gray, Bombay Ivory over Ocean green, Bombay Ivory over Alpine blue and Bombay Ivory over Sandstone beige. All light-duty pickups and stake trucks had the "big window" treatment in 1957.

I.D. DATA: The serial number system was the same as 1956. Starting numbers consisted of the model code, model year code ("57"), assembly plant code and production sequence number starting at 100001 at each plant. Ending number for light-duty trucks in the 3000 series was 144196. Engine serial numbers were eliminated in 1957, except on heavier trucks

1957 Chevrolet "3200" Panel Delivery (MLC)

65

with the 322 cu. in. "Loadmaster" engine. The engine number now consisted of an alphabetical assembly plant (same) code, numerical month code ("1" for Jan.; "2" for Feb., etc.), two-digit day code (01 for first day of month) and letter designating type of engine. Type codes for trucks in the 3100/3200/3600/3800 Series were "H" for Thriftmaster; "HD" for Thriftmaster w/Hydra-Matic and "HE" for Thriftmaster with heavy-duty clutch. Code "L" was used for the V-8 and code "LB" for V-8 with heavy-duty clutch. Type codes for trucks in the 3400/3500/3700 Series included "J" for Thriftmaster; "JA" for Thriftmaster w/Hydra-Matic and "M" for Trademaster V-8. A new 283 cu. in V-8 was coded only for heavier trucks. It was, however, later made optional in smaller trucks.

1957 Chevrolet Cameo Carrier Pickup (ICS)

Job No.	Body Type	Price	Weight	Prod. Total
Model D57 — (Series 1500) — (½-Ton) — (115 in. w.b.)				
1508	Sedan Delivery	2020	3254	7273
Model 3A — (Series 3100) — (½-Ton) — (114 in. w.b.)				
3102	Chassis & F.F. Cowl	1433	2374	—
3103	Chassis & Cab	1697	2871	—
3104	Pickup	1800	3217	—
3105	Panel	2101	3458	—
3106	Suburban (doors)	2435	3738	—
3112	Chassis & Cowl & W/S	1471	2514	—
3116	Suburban (gate)	2435	3752	—
3124	Cameo Pickup	2273	3373	2244
Model 3B — (Series 3200) — (½-Ton) — (123¼ in. w.b.)				
3204	Long Box Pickup	1838	3322	—
Model 3C — (Series 3400) — (¾-Ton) — (114 in. w.b.)				
3442	Delivery Chassis	1613	2722	—
Model 3D — (Series 3500) — (¾-Ton) — (125 in. w.b.)				
3542	Delivery Chassis	1651	2764	—
Model 3F — (Series 3700) — (¾-Ton) — (137 in. w.b.)				
3742	Delivery Chassis	1683	2784	—
Model 3E — (Series 3600) — (¾-Ton) — (123¼ in. w.b.)				
3602	Chassis & F.F. Cowl	1616	2741	—
3603	Chassis & Cab	1880	3252	—
3604	Pickup	1993	3632	—
3609	Platform & Stake	2085	3876	—
3612	Chassis Cowl & W/S	1654	2881	—
Model 3G — (Series 3800) — (1-Ton) — (135 in. w.b.)				
3802	Chassis & F.F. Cowl	1763	2945	—
3803	Chassis & Cab	2027	3496	—
3804	Pickup	2160	3938	—
3805	Panel Delivery	2489	4243	—
3809	Platform & Stake	2274	4286	—
3812	Chassis & Cowl & W/S	1801	3079	—

ENGINE: (Standard all models) Inline. OHV. Six-cylinder. Cast iron block. Bore & stroke: 3.562 x 3.937 in. Displacement: 235.5 cu. in. Compression ratio: 8.0:1. Gross horsepower: 140 at 4200 R.P.M. Torque: 210 lb.-ft. at 2000 R.P.M. Net horsepower: 123 at 4000 R.P.M. Four main bearings. Hydraulic valve lifters. Carburetor: Rochester one-barrel model 7007181. Name: Thriftmaster Six.

1957 Chevrolet "1500" Sedan Delivery (H. Fies)

66

1957 Chevrolet Cameo Carrier Pickup (DFW)

ENGINE: (Optional, all Series 3100 / 3200 / 3400 / 3500 / 3600 / 3700 / 3800) Vee-block. OHV. Eight-cylinder. Cast iron block. Bore & stroke: 3.75 x 3 in. Displacement: 265 cu. in. Compression ratio: 8.0:1. Brake horsepower: 155 at 4200 R.P.M. Torque: 250 lb.-ft. at 2400 R.P.M. Net horsepower: 132 at 3800 R.P.M. Five main bearings. Hydraulic valve lifters. Carburetor: Carter or Rochester model two-barrel. Name: Trademaster V-8.

ENGINE: (Optional, Series 1500) V-type. OHV. Eight-cylinder. Cast iron block. Bore & stroke: 3.75 x 3 in. Displacement: 265 cu. in. Compression ratio: 8.0:1. Brake horsepower: 162 at 4400 R.P.M. Max. Torque: 257 lb.-ft. at 2200 R.P.M. Five main bearings. Hydraulic valve lifters. Carburetor: Rochester two-barrel model 7009909. Name: Turbo-Fire 265.

ENGINE: (Optional, Series 1500) V-type. OHV. Eight-cylinder. Cast iron block. Bore & stroke: 3.875 x 3 in. Displacement: 283 cu. in. Compression ratio: 8.5:1. Brake horsepower: 185 at 4600 R.P.M. Torque: 300 lb.-ft. at 3000 R.P.M. Five main bearings. Hydraulic valve lifters. Carburetor: Rochester two-barrel model 7012133. Name: Turbo-Fire 283.

ENGINE: (Optional, Series 1500) V-type. OHV. "Super Turbo-Fire". Eight-cylinder. Bore & stroke: 3.875 x 3 in. Displacement: 283 cu. in. Compression ratio: 9.5:1. Brake horsepower: 220 at 4800 R.P.M. Max. Torque: 300 lb.-ft. at 3000 R.P.M. Five main bearings. Hydraulic valve lifters. Carburetor: Rochester four-barrel. Name: Super Turbo-Fire 283.

1957 Chevrolet Sedan Delivery (OCW)

CHASSIS: (Series 1500) Wheelbase: 115 in. Overall length: 200 in. Front tread: 58 in. Rear tread: 58.8 in. Tires: 7.50.

CHASSIS: (Series 3200) Wheelbase: 123.25 in. Overall length: 205.56 in. Tires: 6.70 x 15 four-ply, available: 7 x 17.5 six-ply.

CHASSIS: (Series 3400) Wheelbase: 104 in. Tires: 8 x 19.5 six-ply.

CHASSIS: (Series 3500) Wheelbase: 125 in. Tires: 8 x 19.5 six-ply.

CHASSIS: (Series 3100) Wheelbase: 114 in. Overall length: 185.687 (193.56 Cameo). Front tread: 60.5 in. Rear tread: 61.0 in. Tires: 6.70 x 15 four-ply, available: 7 x 17.5 six-ply.

CHASSIS: (Series 3600) Wheelbase: 123.25 in. Overall length: 205.56 in. Tires: 7 x 17.5 six-ply, available: 8 x 19.5 eight-ply.

CHASSIS: (Series 3700) Wheelbase: 137 in. Tires: 8 x 19.5 six-ply.

CHASSIS: (Series 3800) Wheelbase: 135 in. Overall length: 215.81 in. Tires: (front) 8 x 17.5 six-ply; (rear) 8 x 17.5 eight-ply, available: 8 x 19.5 eight-ply.

TECHNICAL: Manual, synchromesh transmission. Speeds: 3F/1R (3800 models — 4F/1R). Column-mounted gearshift (3800 models — Floor). Diaphragm spring clutch. (Series 1500, 3100, 3200) Semi-floating rear axle, (Series 3600, 3800) Full-floating rear axle. Overall ratio: (Series 3100, 3200) 3.90:1; (Series 3600) 4.57.1; (Series 3800) 5.14:1. Hydraulic four-wheel brakes. Pressed steel disc wheels. Technical options: Four-speed Hydra-Matic, Powerglide. (Series 3100, 3200) Overdrive. Heavy-duty three-speed manual. Four-speed manual. 11 in. dia. clutch. Hydrovac power brakes. Governor. Direct Double Action Shock Absorbers (Series 3800). 3300 pound rating rear axle 4.11:1 ratio (Series 3100, 3200). Heavy-duty rear springs. Heavy-duty cooling system. Power steering. Heavy-duty 72 amp battery.

1957 Chevrolet Panel Delivery (DFW)

OPTIONS: Rear bumper. Bumper guards. Radio. Heater. Clock. Cigar lighter. Radio antenna. Seat covers. Deluxe full-view exterior mirror. Push-button windshield washer. Dual chrome hood ornaments. Custom Cab. Full-view rear window (standard Cameo Carrier). Radiator insert screen. Side spare mount. Electric windshield wipers.

HISTORICAL: Introduced: October, 1956. Model year production: (All Series) 359,098. Innovations: New 283 cu. in. V-8 available as optional equipment. Sedan Delivery redesigned like passenger cars. Regular trucks have new grille styling. Expanded solid color choices and two-tone color schemes. Historical notes: Factory-built 4x4 trucks were available for the first time from Chevrolet this year. All light pickups and stake body trucks used cabs with wraparound rear windows in 1957.

Pricing

	5	4	3	2	1
1957					
Series 1500					
Sedan Delivery	1950	3900	6500	9100	13,000
Series 3100					
Pickup	1150	2310	3850	5400	7500
Custom Cab Pickup	1300	2550	4250	5900	8500
Panel Delivery	1200	2400	4000	5600	8000
Suburban	1200	2450	4050	5650	8100
Cameo	2250	4500	7500	10,500	15,000
Cantrell Station Wagon	1650	3300	5500	7700	11,000
Series 3400/3500/3700					
Walk-In Delivery Van	750	1500	2500	3500	5000
School Bus	600	1200	2000	2800	4000
Series 3200					
Long Box Pickup	980	1950	3250	4550	6500
Series 3600					
Pickup	900	1800	3000	4200	6000
Custom Cab Pickup	1000	2000	3300	4600	6600
Platform	750	1500	2500	3500	5000
Platform & Stake	830	1650	2750	3850	5500
Cantrell Station Wagon	1500	3000	5000	7000	10,000
Series 3800					
Pickup	870	1750	2900	4100	5800
Panel Delivery	1000	2000	3300	4600	6600
Platform	680	1350	2250	3150	4500
Platform & Stake	720	1450	2400	3300	4800

NOTE: 1955-up prices based on top of the line models.

1958 CHEVROLET

1958 Chevrolet Apache Fleetside Pickup (OCW)

LIGHT TRUCKS — (ALL SERIES) — SIX-CYLINDER/V-8: — Chevrolet's 1958 trucks were called "Task Force" models. Two significant merchandising innovations took place this year. First, the promotional designation "Apache" was applied to fancier models. Secondly, buyers were presented with a choice of two types of pickups: the Stepside (with exposed rear fenders and standard width box) and the Fleetside (with slab-sided rear fenders and extra-wide box.) Also, the optional 4x4 driveline was available for 3100/3600/3800 models. The term "Cameo Carrier" was now applied to the "Cameo" Suburban Pickup. Styling-wise, the new Sedan Delivery was part of the lower-lever Del Ray passenger car series and had a new Job Number designation to reflect its totally revised appearance and chassis. General styling updates included dual headlamps in each hooded front fender, a "drawer pull" grille and gull-wing rear fender treatment with concave sculptured upper side panels. An all-new "Safety Girder" X-type frame with coil springs at all four corners was featured. In addition to previous stick-shift and Powerglide drivetrains, the Sedan Delivery could be optioned with the 1958 Turbo-Thrust V-8 and Turob-Glide automatic transmission. Regular trucks were modernized with quad type headlights (two in each fender), broader hood with sculpturing and a new grille. The grille consisted of two narrow horizontal bars just below the hood and a more massive lower bar extending out and under the headlamps. It had the "Chevrolet" name lettered across it and the outboard extensions surrounded the rectangular parking lamps. Standard trim models had the grille painted. Base-level Apaches also had a cream-painted grille, bumper and headlamp buckets and cream-colored hubcaps. Chrome-plated parts could be substituted at extra-cost. A rather large, jet-plane-shaped ornament, above the front fender feature line, carried the Apache name and series identification. Fleetside models had a missle-shaped bulge along the slab-sided bed exterior. Their boxes were 75 in. wide versus the Cameo Carrier's 48 inches. Although the general appearance of both was similar, the Fleetline did not use bolt-on plastic panels and a fiberglass bedliner to achieve its slab-sided look. Color choices for the year totaled 14 solids: Dawn blue, Marine blue, Kodiak brown, Glade green, Oriental green, Polar green and Tartan turquoise were new. Ten two-tones were available for 1958 Cameo Carriers. New ones included Golden yellow with Jet black, Jet black with Tartan turquoise, Kodiak brown with Bombay Ivory, Glade green with Polar green, Marine blue with Dawn blue (or the reverse) and Bombay Ivory with Oriental green. All other trucks except Suburbans and Fleetside pickups could be had in 13 two-tones. Distinctive choices among this group were Cardinal red with black, Jet black with Golden yellow and Bombay Ivory with Yukon yellow. With most two-tones, the wheels were painted lower body color. However, the "production" version of the Cameo had Cardinal red upper over Bombay Ivory lower with red wheels. Cast spoke wheels, finished in gray, were also available.

I.D. DATA: Serial Number located: Vehicle identification number plate located on driver-side windshield pillar. Vehicle GVW plate attached to left inner cowl panel. The serial numbering system was the same one adopted in 1956. Starting: 58-100001 and up. Engine numbers located — six-cylinder engine number stamped on right side of block, next to distributor. V-8 engine number stamped on forward edge of block, which protrudes from under right cylinder head. Engine serial numbers were no longer used, except on heavy-duty trucks with the "322" engine. Other engines were simply stamped with a source code, production date and prefix indicating type of engine. A typical number was F104J in which F = Flint, 1 = January, 04 = Fourth day of month and J = Thriftmaster 235 with three-speed manual transmission in 3100/3200/3600/3800 Series truck.

Job No.	Body Type	Price	Weight	Prod. Total
Model D58 — (Series 1500) — (½-Ton) — (117½ in. w.b.)				
1171	Sedan Delivery	2123	3529	—
Model 3A — (Series 3100) — (½-Ton) — (114 in. w.b.)				
3102	Chassis	1517	2401	—
3103	Chassis & Cab	1770	2910	—
3104	Stepside Pickup	1884	3273	—
3105	Panel Delivery	2185	3495	—
3106	Suburban (door)	2518	3794	—
3124	Cameo Carrier	2231	3423	1405
3116	Suburban (gate)	2518	3799	—
3134	Fleetside Pickup	1900		—
Model 3B — (Series 3200) — (½-Ton) — (123¼ in. w.b.)				
3203	Chassis & Cab	1808	3102	—
3204	Stepside Pickup (LB)	1922	3342	—
3234	Fleetside Pickup (LB)	1938		—
Model 3C — (Series 3400) — (¾-Ton) — (104 in. w.b.)				
3442	Delivery Chassis	1652	2687	—
3445	Walk-In Delivery	3047	4698	—
Model 3D — (Series 3500) — (¾-Ton) — (125 in. w.b.)				
3542	Delivery Chassis	1690	2754	—
3545	Walk-In Delivery	3132	4975	—
Model 3E — (Series 3600) — (¾-Ton) — (123¼ in. w.b.)				
3602	Chassis	1689	2751	—
3603	Chassis & Cab	1953	3270	—
3604	Stepside Pickup	2066	3674	—
3634	Fleetside Pickup	2082		—
3609	Stake Bed	2158	3894	—
Model 3F — (Series 3700) — (¾-Ton) — (137 in. w.b.)				
3742	Delivery Chassis	1722	2762	—
3745	Walk-In Delivery	3243	5223	—
Model 3G — (Series 3800) — (1-Ton) — (135 in. w.b.)				
3802	Chassis	1836	3030	—
3803	Chassis & Cab	2100	3496	—
3804	Stepside Pickup	2233	3973	—
3805	Panel Delivery	2561	4265	—
3809	Stake Bed	2346	4321	—

NOTE: The 4x4 option was available on all 3100/3600/3800 Series trucks, except Cameo Carrier.

1958 Chevrolet Apache w/custom wheels (RVM)

ENGINE: (Standard, Series 1100) Inline. OHV. Six-cylinder. Cast iron block. Bore & stroke: 3-9/16 x 3-15/16 in. Displacement: 235.5 cu. in. Compression ratio: 8.25:1. Gross horsepower: 145 at 4200 R.P.M. Torque: 215 lb.-ft. at 2400 R.P.M. Net horsepower: 125 at 4000 R.P.M. Four main bearings. Hydraulic valve lifters. Carburetor: Rochester two-barrel model 7012133. Name: Blue Flame Six.

ENGINE: (Standard, Series 3000) Inline. OHV. Six-cylinder. Cast iron block. Bore & stroke: 3-9/16 x 3-15/16 in. Displacement: 235.5 cu. in. Compression ratio: 8.25:1. Gross horsepower: 145 at 4200 R.P.M. Torque: 215 lb.-ft. at 2000 R.P.M. Net horsepower: 125 at 4000 R.P.M. Four main bearings. Hydraulic valve lifters. Carburetor: Rochester two-barrel model 7012127. Name: Thriftmaster Six.

ENGINE: (Optional, Series 1100 / 3100 / 3200 / 3400 / 3500 / 3600 / 3700 / 3800) Vee-block. OHV. Eight-cylinder. Cast iron block. Bore & stroke: 3⅞ x 3 in. Displacement: 283 cu. in. Compression ratio: 8.5:1. Gross horsepower: 160 at 4200 R.P.M. Torque: 275 lb.-ft. at 2400 R.P.M. Net horsepower: 137 at 3800 R.P.M. Five main bearings. Hydraulic valve lifters. Carburetor: Rochester two-barrel model 7012133. Name: Trademaster V-8.

NOTE: All engines for 1958 were available with all transmissions except overdrive. The sedan delivery had the same power team offerings as passenger cars.

CHASSIS: (Series 1100) Wheelbase: 117.5 in. Overall length: 209.1 in. Height: 57.4 in. Tires: 7.50 x 14 four-ply.

CHASSIS: (Series 3100) Wheelbase: 114 in. Overall length: 193.5625 in. Tires: 6.70 x 15 four-ply.

CHASSIS: (Series 3200) Wheelbase: 123.25 in. Overall length: 205.5625 in. Tires: 6.70 x 15 four-ply.

CHASSIS: (Series 3400) Wheelbase: 104 in. Tires: 7 x 17.5 six-ply.

CHASSIS: (Series 3500) Wheelbase: 125 in. Tires: 7 x 17.5 six-ply.

CHASSIS: (Series 3600) Wheelbase: 123.25 in. Overall length: 205.5625 in. Tires: 7 x 17.5 six-ply.

CHASSIS: (Series 3700) Wheelbase: 137 in. Tires: 7 x 17.5 six-ply.

CHASSIS: (Series 3800) Wheelbase: 135 in. Overall length: 215.9375 in. Tires: (front) 8 x 17.5 six-ply; (rear) 8 x 17.5 eight-ply.

TECHNICAL: Manual, synchromesh transmission. Speeds: 3F/1R (Series 3800 — heavy-duty 4-speed manual). Column-mounted gearshift. Diaphragm spring clutch. (Series 3100, 3200) 10 in. dia.; (Series 3600, 3800) 10.5 in. dia. (Series 1500, 3100, 3200) Semi-floating rear axle, (Series 3600, 3800) Full-floating rear axle. Overall ratio: (Series 3100, 3200) 3.90:1; (Series 3600) 4.57:1; (Series 3800) 5.14:1. Hydraulic, four-wheel drum brakes. Pressed steel disc wheels. Technical options: Powerglide ($199) (Sedan Delivery). Turboglide ($242) (Sedan Delivery). Four-wheel-drive (4x4). Power brakes. Power steering. Hydra-Matic transmission. Auxiliary rear springs. Heavy-duty four-speed manual transmission (all Series 3000 models). Heavy-duty three-speed manual transmission. Rear double-action shock absorbers (Series 3800). Two-stage rear springs (standard Series 3800). Heavy-duty battery.

OPTIONS: Rear bumper. Radio. Heater. Clock. Cigar lighter. Radio antenna. Seat covers. Cool pack air conditioning. Factory-installed seat belts. Dual, matched horns. Deluxe full-view outside mirror. Push-button windshield washer. Custom Cab. Two-tone exterior color combinations. Full-view rear window (standard model 3124).

HISTORICAL: Introduced: October, 1957. Model year production: (All Chevrolet Truck Series) 278,632. Innovations: First year for dual headlights. All-new Fleetside pickup with double-wall cargo-box construction introduced to replace the Cameo Carrier during the model year. Historical notes: Chevrolet's long association with Union Body Co., of Union City, Ind., began with the introduction of Step Van forward control (Walk-In Delivery) models.

1958 Chevrolet Sedan Delivery (DFW)

Pricing

1958	5	4	3	2	1
Series 1100					
Sedan Delivery	1450	2850	4750	6650	9500
Series 3100					
Pickup Stepside	1050	2100	3500	4900	7000
Pickup Fleetside	1080	2160	3600	5050	7200
Cameo Pickup	1950	3900	6500	9100	13,000
Panel	980	1950	3250	4550	6500
Suburban	1020	2050	3400	4800	6800
Series 3200					
Pickup Stepside Long Box	980	1950	3250	4550	6500
Pickup Fleetside Long Box	1010	2030	3350	4700	6700
Series 3400/3500					
Step-Van w/104 in. w.b.	900	1800	3000	4200	6000
Step-Van w/125 in. w.b.	920	1850	3050	4300	6100
Series 3600					
Pickup Stepside	900	1800	3000	4200	6000
Pickup Fleetside	930	1860	3100	4350	6200
Stake	770	1550	2550	3600	5100
Series 3700					
Step-Van w/137 in. w.b.	850	1700	2850	4000	5700
Series 3800					
Pickup	750	1500	2750	3850	5500
Panel	770	1550	2550	3600	5100
Stake	750	1500	2500	3500	5000

NOTE: 1955-up prices based on top of the line models.

1959 CHEVROLET

1959 Chevrolet Step Side Pickup (DFW)

LIGHT TRUCKS — (ALL SERIES) — SIX-CYLINDER/V-8: — Chevrolet's "Task-Force '59," models were changed moderately from the 1958 models. The most apparent change was use of a larger and more ornate hood emblem. Replacing the (1955-57) Cameo pickup as a super-styled Pickup was the first of the El Camino models which Chevrolet depicted as "more than a car — more than a truck." The El Camino had the general styling of Chevrolet's controversial passenger sedan models while possessing a load capacity of 1150 pounds. The box, which had a volume capacity of nearly 34 cu. ft., was of double wall design. Its steel floor had built-in skid strips over a ribbed and embossed sub-floor supported by four cross members. Standard for the El Camino was a six-cylinder engine but two V-8s of 185 and 230 horsepower were available as were Powerglide, Turboglide, and overdrive transmissions as alternatives to the standard three-speed manual gearbox. The El Camino was offered in 13 solid and 10 two-tone color combinations. The two-tone design consisted of one color on the roof, upper pillar area and upper rear deck, with the rest of the vehicle in the second color. As usual, the Sedan Delivery took the passenger car styling revisions.

I.D. DATA: Serial Number located: Unchanged from 1958. Starting: 3A59-100001 and up. Engine numbers located: Unchanged from 1958.

Job No.	Body Type	Price	Weight	Prod. Total
Series 1100 — (½-Ton) — (119 in. w.b.)				
1170	Sedan Delivery	2363	3590	—
1180	El Camino	2352	3605	—
Series 3100 — (½-Ton) — (114 in. w.b.)				
3102	Chassis	1580	2421	—
3103	Chassis & Cab	1834	2909	—
3104	Stepside Pickup	1948	3260	—
3105	Panel Delivery	2249	3490	—
3106	Suburban (doors)	2583	3778	—
3116	Suburban (gate)	2616	3796	—
3134	Fleetside Pickup	1964	3304	—
Series 3200 — (Long Box) — (½-Ton) — (123¼ in. w.b.)				
3203	Chassis & Cab	1872	2988	—
3204	Stepside Pickup	1986	3386	—
3234	Fleetside Pickup	2002	3381	—
Series 3400 — (¾-Ton Step-Van) — (104 in. w.b.)				
3442	Chassis	1716	2700	—
3445	Step-Van	3112	5042	—
Series 3500 — (125 in. w.b.)				
3542	Chassis	1754	2795	—
3545	Step-Van	3197	5247	—
Series 3600 — (¾-Ton) — (123¼ in. w.b.)				
3602	Chassis	1753	2780	—
3603	Chassis & Cab	2018	3275	—
3604	Stepside Pickup	2132	3669	—
3634	Fleetside Pickup	2148	3664	—
3609	Stake	2223	3844	—
Series 3700 — (¾-Ton) — (Step-Van) — (137 in. w.b.)				
3742	Chassis	1786	2823	—
3745	Step-Van	3308	5416	—
Series 3800 — (1-Ton) — (135 in. w.b.)				
3802	Chassis	1899	3020	—
3803	Chassis & Cab	2164	3501	—
3804	Stepside Pickup	2298	3954	—
3805	Panel Delivery	2626	4270	—
3809	Stake	2411	4294	—

1959 Chevrolet El Camino (OCW)

ENGINE: (Standard, Series 1100 / 3100 / 3200 / 3400 / 3500 / 3600 / 3700 / 3800) Inline. OHV. Six-cylinder. Cast iron block. Bore & stroke: 3.562 x 3.937 in. Displacement: 235.5 cu. in. Compression ratio: 8.25:1. Brake horsepower: 135 at 4000 R.P.M. Torque: 215 lb.-ft. at 2400 R.P.M. Four main bearings. Hydraulic valve lifters. Carburetor: Rochester two-barrel model 7013003. Name: Thriftmaster Six.

NOTE: Thriftmaster Special engine available with lower net horsepower and torque ratings.

ENGINE: (Optional, Series 1100) V-type. OHV. Eight-cylinder. Cast iron block. Bore & stroke: 3.875 x 3 in. Displacement: 283 cu. in. Compression ratio: 8.5:1. Brake horsepower: 185 at 4600 R.P.M. Max. Torque: 275 lb.-ft. at 2400 R.P.M. Five main bearings. Hydraulic valve lifters. Carburetor: Rochester two-barrel model 7013007. Name: Turbo-Fire V-8.

ENGINE: (Optional, Series 1100) V-type. OHV. Eight-cylinder. Cast iron block. Bore & stroke: 3.875 x 3 in. Displacement: 283 cu. in. Compression ratio: 9.5:1. Brake horsepower: 230 at 4800 R.P.M. Max. Torque: 300 lb.-ft. at 3000. Five main bearings. Hydraulic valve lifters. Carburetor: Rochester four-barrel. Name: Super Turbo-Fire V-8.

ENGINE: (Optional, Series 3100-3800) V-type. OHV. Eight-cylinder. Cast iron block. Bore & stroke: 3.875 x 3 in. Displacement: 238 cu. in. Compression ratio: 8.5:1. Brake horsepower: 160 at 4200 R.P.M. Torque: 270 lb.-ft. at 2000 R.P.M. Five main bearings. Hydraulic valve lifters. Carburetor: Rochester two-barrel. Name: Trademaster V-8.

1959 Chevrolet El Camino (OCW)

CHASSIS: (Same as 1958 except; Series 1100) Wheelbase: 119 in. Overall length: 210.9 in. Height: 56.3 in. Tires: 8.00 x 14 four-ply.

TECHNICAL: Same as 1958.

OPTIONS: Options for 1959 were basically the same as those for 1958. A new extra-cost feature, the posi-traction rear axle, was introduced.

1959 Chevrolet El Camino (JCL)

HISTORICAL: Introduced: October, 1958. Calendar year registrations: (all Series) 306,237. Calendar year production: (all Series) 326,102. Innovations: El Camino personal Pickup introduced. Posi-traction rear axle option made available. Longer 119 in. w.b. for Sedan Delivery and El Camino. Historical notes: Chevrolet sold its seventh millionth truck, since 1918, during the 1959 model run.

Pricing

1959	5	4	3	2	1
Series 1100					
Sedan Delivery	1400	2800	4600	6400	9200
El Camino	1450	2900	4850	6800	9700
Series 3100					
Pickup Stepside	1050	2100	3500	4900	7000
Pickup Fleetside	1080	2160	3600	5050	7200
Cameo Pickup	1950	3900	6500	9100	13,000
Panel	980	1950	3250	4550	6500
Suburban	1020	2050	3400	4800	6800
Series 3200					
Pickup Stepside	980	1950	3250	4550	6500
Pickup Fleetside	1010	2030	3350	4700	6700
Series 3400/3500					
Panel (104 in. w.b.)	900	1800	3000	4200	6000
Panel (125 in. w.b.)	920	1850	3050	4300	6100
Series 3600					
Pickup Stepside	900	1800	3000	4200	6000
Pickup Fleetside	930	1860	3100	4350	6200
Series 3700					
Panel (137 in. w.b.)	850	1700	2850	4000	5700
Series 3800					
Pickup	750	1500	2750	3850	5500
Panel	770	1550	2550	3600	5100
Stake	750	1500	2500	3500	5000

NOTE: 1955-up prices based on top of the line models.

1960 CHEVROLET

LIGHT TRUCK — (ALL SERIES) — SIX-CYLINDER/V-8: — Chevrolet continued to market two half-ton trucks based on the year's passenger cars with a beefed up chassis. Both of these, the El Camino and the Sedan Delivery, adopted the 1960 appearance changes. The grille was oval-shaped with two free-floating headlights at either end. A cross-bar arrangement of moldings held the Bow-tie emblem in a smaller oval at the center. They were backed by full-width horizontal bars. Parking lamps were underneath the redesigned bumper. The rear had angular ''gull-wing'' fins. Below them was a horizontal full width oval with two round taillamps at each end. The Sedan Delivery had a station wagon body with blanked-out sides. The El Camino had an integral cargo bed and cab roof with rear overhang. Exterior trim for the El Camino was similar to the Bel Air level. Sedan Deliveries looked a bit plainer. Other light-duty trucks were totally restyled from 1959 and most had longer wheelbases. Series designations were changed to the C10, C20, C30 type codes, still in use today. Alternate alphabetical prefixes were used, on paper, to identify delivery chassis, walk-in vans and four-wheel-drive (4x4) models. However, the numerical portion of the code was consistent: ''10'' meaning half-ton; ''20'' meaning ¾-ton and ''30'' meaning one-ton. Styling on these trucks, in profile, was characterized by a sculptured indentation that ran straight along the body sides from the top of the grille to top of the taillights. This indentation or crease ''pinched-in'' the body at the mid-belt level. The panels then flared out again, forming another sculptured crease at the upper beltline level. From here, they curved back inward. Thus, the entire upper beltline seemed to have a ''flattened bulge'' to it. In front, the fenders had this flat, bulged look which ended in oval shapes at the front. These ovals held the parking lamps above the grille. The center hood was somewhat lower and flatter. A ''Bow-Tie'' emblem was placed on its front surface, between the fender ovals. The lower grille consisted of full-width surround of rectangular oval shape housing dual headlamps at each end, plus four horizontal blades between them. The cab looked wider, flatter and lower than in the past, but still had a wraparound windshield and side ventipanes. The bumper was a massive, but plain, full-width wraparound unit. The lower bar of the main grille surround had the ''Chevrolet'' name stamped in it. Series and model identification was carried on the lower cowlside at the mid-body crease. Stepside pickups had runningboards between the cab and ''pontoon'' style rear fenders. On these models, the pinched-in crease ended behind the cab doors, and a separate crease line decorated the rear fender sides. Two-toning on Carryalls was done with the contrast color on the lower body under the ''pinch'' and on the rear of the roof. This made them look like a pickup with a camper back installed on the box. Suburbans again came with either panel doors or an end-gate. ''Long-box'' versions of the half-ton pickups were available on a foot longer wheelbase. Three-quarter ton Walk-In panels were offered on three wheelbases with Step Van bodies by Union Body Co. However, these chassis could be ordered separately for aftermarket body installations.

1960 Chevrolet Deluxe Apache Pickup (DFW)

I.D. DATA: Serial Number located on plate on windshield corner post. Numbers began at 100001 and up. Beginning in 1960, the light trucks were basically considered ''10'' (half-ton), ''20'' (¾-ton) or ''30'' (one-ton) series vehicles. Each of these basic lines had various sub-series codes such as ''14'', ''15'', ''25'', ''36'', etc. Any sub-series belonged to the main series indicated by its first digit. For example, a C14 or C15 was actually part of the ½-ton C-10 series, while a C-25 was actually part of the ¾-ton C20 series. The ''C'' indicated a conventional truck (pickup, panel, suburban, etc.), while a ''P'' indicated a panel delivery type such as a walk-in van. When equipped with four-wheel-drive, a truck would be identified as a ''K'' series unit in factory literature. However, the badges on the truck itself would still read ''C''. Engine numbers located: (Six-cylinder) Stamped on right-hand side of block next to distributor. (V-8s) Stamped on forward edge of block, protruding from under right cylinder head.

1960 Chevrolet ½-ton Long Box Pickup (IMSC)

NOTE: Each model continued to be identified by a Fisher/Chevrolet ''job number'' or ''body style'' code. The first symbol was a letter indicating the truck-line. The next two digits indicated series/sub-series (and tonnage). The final two digits indicated body type. For example, the number C1534 breaks down as follows: ''C''=C10 half-ton series with rear-wheel drive; ''15''=C15 (half-ton, long wheelbase) Sub-series; a ''34''=Fleetside pickup. The Chevy buff will recognize that this code then identifies the ½-ton Fleetside Pickup on the 127 in. w.b. This is popularly known as the ''Fleetside ½-ton Long Box Pickup.'' Study of our 1960 specifications chart below will help you understand how to identify different models by the model numbers. This same basic system was used for many years and will not be repeated again. However, changes in numbers and new codes will be explained.

Job No.	Body Type	Price	Weight	Prod. Total
Series 1100 (*) — (½-Ton) — (119 in. w.b.)				
1170	Sedan Delivery	2361	3605	—
1180	El Camino	2366	3545	—

(*) The ''1100'' Series designation identified the passenger car based trucks. In later years, the ''R1200'' designation would identify Corvair trucks and a ''13000'' designation would be used for Chevelle-based El Caminos.

Job No.	Body Type	Price	Weight	Prod. Total
Series C10/Sub-Series C14 (*) — (½-Ton) — (115 in. w.b.)				
C1402	Chassis	1623	2505	—
C1403	Chassis & Cab	1877	3035	—
C1404	Stepside Pickup	1991	3395	—
C1405	Panel	2308	3615	—
C1406	Suburban (doors)	2690	3960	—
C1416	Suburban (gate)	2723	3975	—
C1434	Fleetside Pickup	2007	3425	—

(*) C10 is the basic ½-ton Series designation. Factory literature designates the short wheelbase (Short Box) half-tonners (C10s) as C14s through 1966. In 1967, ''CS107'' was adopted for coding the same type of trucks. In 1968, ''CE107'' was adopted for coding these models. In 1973, ''CC107'' was adopted and used through at least 1983. Factory literature substitutes a ''K'' for the ''C'' to identify 4x4 trucks.

Job No.	Body Type	Price	Weight	Prod. Total
Series C10/Sub-Series C15 (*) — (½-Ton) — (127 in. w.b.)				
C1503	Chassis & Cab	1914	3090	—
C1504	Stepside Pickup	2028	3505	—
C1534	Fleetside Pickup	2044	3565	—

(*) C10 is the basic ½-ton series designation. Factory literature designates the long wheelbase (Long Box) half-tonners (C10s) as C15s through 1966. In 1967, ''CS109'' was adopted for coding the same type of trucks. In 1968, ''CE109'' was adopted for coding these models. In 1973, ''CC109'' was adopted and used through at least 1983. Factory literature substitutes a ''K'' for the (first) ''C'' to identify 4x4 trucks. (Note: The 4x4 trucks still have C10 badges on the exterior).

Job No.	Body Type	Price	Weight	Prod. Total
Series P20/Sub-Series P23 (**) — (¾-Ton) — (104 in. w.b.)				
P2342	Chassis	1687	2690	—
P2345	Walk-In Panel	3083	5030	—
Series P20/Sub-Series P25 (**) — (¾-Ton) — (125 in. w.b.)				
P2542	Chassis	1725	2740	—
P2545	Walk-In Panel	3168	5185	—
Series P20/Sub-Series P26 (**) — (¾-Ton) — (137 in. w.b.)				
P2642	Chassis	1758	2770	—
P2645	Walk-In Panel	3279	5365	—

(**) P20 is the basic ¾-ton Delivery Series designation. The ''P'' indicates the Step Van chassis or model; the ''20'' indicates ¾-ton. P23/P25/P26 indicate the small/medium/large wheelbases; respectively. In 1967, ''PS209'' was used in place of P23; ''PS213'' in place of P25 and ''PS215'' in place of P26. In 1968, ''PE'' was adopted as the first two symbols. In 1973, ''PC'' was adopted for the first two symbols and used through at least 1983.

Job No.	Body Type	Price	Weight	Prod. Total
Series C20/Sub-Series C25 (•) — (¾-Ton) — (127 in. w.b.)				
C2502	Chassis	1795	2785	—
C2503	Chassis & Cab	2059	3370	—
C2504	Stepside Pickup	2173	3790	—
C2509	Stake (8 ft.)	2264	4000	—
C2534	Fleetside Pickup	2189	3845	—

(•) C20 is the basic ¾-ton series designation. C25 was used as the first three symbols through 1966. In 1967, ''CS209'' was adopted; in 1968, ''CE209'' and in 1973 (through at least 1983) ''CC209''. Factory literature substituted a ''K'' for ''C'' on 4x4 trucks.

Job No.	Body Type	Price	Weight	Prod. Total
Series C30/Sub-Series C36 (━) — (1-Ton) — (133 in. w.b.)				
C3602	Chassis	1952	3095	—
C3603	Chassis & Cab	2216	3665	—
C3604	Stepside Pickup	2350	4120	—
C3605	Panel	2775	4405	—
C3609	Stake (9 ft.)	2463	4485	—

(━) C30 is the basic one-ton Series designation. C36 was used as the first three symbols through 1966; then ''CS310''; then ''CE310'' and finally, after 1973, ''CC310.'' Four-wheel-drive not available on 1960 one-tons.

Job No.	Body Type	Price	Weight	Prod. Total
Series 30/Sub-Series P33 — (1-Ton) — (104 in. w.b.)				
P3342	Chassis	1877	2865	—
P3345	Walk-In Panel	3273	5205	—
Series 30/Sub-Series P35 — (1-Ton) — (125 in. w.b.)				
P3542	Chassis	1915	2930	—
P3545	Walk-In Panel	3358	5375	—
Series 30/Sub-Series P36 — (1-Ton) — (137 in. w.b.)				
P3642	Chassis	1948	2960	—
P3645	Walk-In Panel	3469	5550	—

NOTE 1: New Series. ''30''=one-ton; ''P''=Walk-In Panel Delivery. The sub-series codes P33/P35/P36 became (1967) P309/P313/P315; (1968) PE309/PE313/PE315 and (1973) PC309/PC313/PC315.

NOTE 2: Hopefully, the Layman's explanation of series and model codes given in the notes above will help to unravel some confusion. These will not be repeated throughout the catalog, but new codes will be explained as necessary.

1960 Chevrolet Deluxe Panel Delivery (DFW)

ENGINE: (Standard, Series 1100 / C14 / C15 / P23 / P25 / P26 / P35 / P36) Inline. OHV. Six-cylinder. Cast iron block. Bore & stroke: 3.5625 x 3.9375 in. Displacement: 235.5 cu. in. Compression ratio: 8.25:1. Brake horsepower: 135 at 4000 R.P.M. Torque: 217 lb.-ft. at 2000 R.P.M. SAE horsepower: 30.4. Four main bearings. Hydraulic valve lifters. Carburetor: Rochester one-barrel model 87015011.

NOTE: "Thriftmaster" six-cylinder.

ENGINE: (Optional, Series C14 / K14 / C15 / C25 / K25 / C36) Vee-block. OHV. Eight-cylinder. Cast iron block. Bore & stroke: 3.875 x 3 in. Displacement: 283 cu. in. Net horsepower 160 at 4200 R.P.M. SAE horsepower: 48. Torque: 270 lb.-ft. at 2000 R.P.M. Five main bearings. Hydraulic valve lifters. Carburetor: Rochester two-barrel model 2G7015017.

NOTE: "Trademaster" V-8.

1960 Chevrolet Pickup w/custom wheels (DFW)

ENGINE: (Optional, Series 1100) Vee-block. OHV. Eight-cylinder. Cast iron block. Bore & stroke: 3.875 x 3 in. Displacement: 283 cu. in. Compression ratio: 8.50:1. Brake horsepower: 170 at 4200 R.P.M. Torque: 275 lb.-ft. at 2200 R.P.M. SAE horsepower: 48.0. Five main bearings. Hydraulic valve lifters. Carburetor: Rochester two-barrel.

NOTE: "Turbo-Fire" V-8.

ENGINE: (Optional, Series 1100) Vee-block. OHV. Eight-cylinder. Cast iron block. Bore & stroke: 3.875 x 3 in. Displacement: 283 cu. in. Compression ratio: 9.5:1. Brake horsepower: 230 at 4800 R.P.M. Torque: 300 lb.-ft. at 3000 R.P.M. SAE horsepower: 48.0. Five main bearings. Hydraulic valve lifters. Carburetor: Rochester four-barrel.

CHASSIS: (Series 1100) Wheelbase: 119 in. Overall length: 210.9 in. Height: 56.3 in. Tires: 8.00 x 14 four-ply.

1960 Chevrolet Carryall Suburban (BOR)

CHASSIS: (Series C14) Wheelbase: 115 in. Overall length: (Pickup) 186.75; (Suburban) 199.5 in. Tires: 6.70 x 15 four-ply.

CHASSIS: (Series C15) Wheelbase: 127 in. Overall length: 206.25 in. Tires: 6.75 x 15 four-ply.

CHASSIS: (Series P23) Wheelbase: 104 in. Tires: 7 x 17.5 six-ply.

CHASSIS: (Series C25) Wheelbase: 127 in. Overall length: 210.75 in. Tires: 7 x 17.5 six-ply.

CHASSIS: (Series P25) Wheelbase: 125 in. Tires: 7 x 17.5 six-ply.

CHASSIS: (Series P26) Wheelbase: 137 in. Tires: 7 x 17.5 six-ply.

CHASSIS: (Series P33) Wheelbase: 104 in. Tires: 8 x 19.5 six-ply.

CHASSIS: (Series P35) Wheelbase: 125 in. Tires: 8 x 19.5 six-ply.

CHASSIS: (Series P36) Wheelbase: 137 in. Tires: 8 x 17.5 six-ply.

CHASSIS: (Series C36) Wheelbase: 133 in. Overall length: 211.75 in. Tires: (front) 8 x 17.5 six-ply, (rear) 8 x 17.5 eight-ply.

1960 Chevrolet El Camino (OCW)

TECHNICAL: Selective synchromesh transmission. Speeds: 3F/1R (except one-ton 4F/1R). Column-mounted gearshift (except four-speed). 10 or 11 in. diaphragm spring type clutch. (1-ton) Full-floating rear axle; (others) Semi-floating rear axle. Overall ratio: (C14/C15/K14/K15) 3.90:1; (C25/K25) 4.57:1; (C36) 5.14:1. Four wheel hydraulic brakes. Options: Heavy-duty three-speed transmission. Four-speed manual transmission. Powerglide automatic, in Series 1100 ($188). Steel disc wheels. Turboglide automatic in Series 1100 ($210). Hydra-Matic, in others ($253).

OPTIONS: Chrome front bumper. Rear bumper. Chrome grille. Master grille guard. Chrome hub caps. Gray cast spoke wheels. Bumper guards. Two-tone paint. Special paint. OSRV mirror(s). Radio. Heater. Clock. Cigar lighter. Radio antenna. Seat covers. Tinted windshield. Tinted glass. Directional signals. Backup lamps. Auxiliary rear springs. Whitewall tires. Oversized tires. Custom comfort equipment (interior). Custom appearance equipment (exterior). Custom chrome equipment (exterior). Custom side molding equipment (exterior, Fleetside Pickups only).

NOTE: A host of factory approved special equipment supplied by aftermarket companies was included in the "Silver Book" published each year by Chevrolet. This included heaters, double gas tanks, snow plows, winches, wrecking truck booms; utility cabinets, body conversions and walk-in type delivery bodies.

1960 Chevrolet El Camino (OCW)

HISTORICAL: Introduced: Fall 1959. Calendar year production: (all Chevrolet trucks) 394,017. Innovations: All-new styling for pickups, panels and Suburbans. First independent front suspension system for trucks. (Light-duty models featured torsion bars in front and coil springs at rear). Historical notes: Chevrolet was America's number one truck-maker. Last year for Sedan Delivery. Last year for full-size El Camino.

Pricing

NOTE: 1955-up prices based on top of the line models.
Add 5 percent for 4x4.

1961 CHEVROLET

1961 Chevrolet Corvair Pickup Truck (DFW)

LIGHT TRUCK — 1961 SERIES — (ALL ENGINES): — Chevrolet's answer to the Volkswagen van was the all-new Corvair 95 line of trucks. These were driver-forward models built on the Corvair platform, with a rear-mounted air-cooled engine and transaxle. Dual headlamps, a small front grille with Chevrolet emblem and concave, sculptured contrast panel, all along the front and sides, were among styling characteristics. The fanciest model carried a "Greenbriar" script on its doors. It was actually a passenger van, but Chevy merchandised it as a station wagon, rather than a truck. Seating for six adults was standard. The panel version had steel sides in place of three side windows. There were two side load doors and double rear panel doors. It was merchandised as the "Corvan" and had Corvair 95 scripts on the front doors. A pickup was made by adding a cab panel-back and removing the upper body sheet metal at the rear. It had a cargo box that was 105 inches long and 43⅞ inches wide. It was called the "Loadside" model and featured fixed, double-wall box-side panel doors, just behind the cab. Also available was the "Rampside" version, which had a unique "door" that dropped to the ground to make a cargo loading ramp. Standard equipment on all Corvair 95s included: air-cooled six; three-speed synchromesh transmission; electric wipers; directional signals and five tubeless tires. Chrome hubcaps, chrome bumpers and a Custom interior/exterior appearance package were available.

For Chevrolet's regular light-duties, the most notable exterior change involved a revised front end appearance. The inserts for the parking light nacelles now had a distinct Chevrolet "bow-tie" form and the grille carried Chevrolet lettering in its center portion. Front fender model identification was positioned higher than on the 1960 models. Still offered were both Stepside (with pontoon rear fenders) and Fleetside (with slab type rear fenders) models in C10 (½-ton); C20 (¾-ton) and C30 (1-ton) series with a choice of wheelbases and box lengths. Factory literature referred to trucks with a 4x4 driveline with a "K" (instead of "C") prefix on the series designation.

I.D. DATA: Serial number stamped on plate mounted on windshield corner post. Twelve numbers were used. The first identified the 1961 model year, the next three the serial number. The body type was identified by the fifth number. The sixth designated the assembly plant. The final six digits represented the production sequence. Starting: 1 ( ) ( ) 100001 and up. Engine numbers located: (6-cyl.): stamped on right side of block next to distributor. (V-8s): stamped on forward edge of block, protruding from under right cylinder head.

1961 Chevrolet Corvair Pickup w/cust. wheels (CW)

Model	Body Type	Price	Weight	Prod. Total
Corvair Series 95				
R1244	Loadside Pickup	2079	2595	2,475
R1254	Rampside Pickup	2133	2605	10,787
Fleetside Models				
C1434	½-Ton 115 in. w.b.	2007	3425	—
C1534	½-Ton 127 in. w.b.	2007	3425	—
K1434	½-Ton 4x4 115 in. w.b.	2684	—	—
K1534	½-Ton 4x4 127 in. w.b.	2684	—	—
C2539	¾-Ton 127 in. w.b.	2189	3855	—
K2539	¾-Ton 4x4 127 in. w.b.	2866	—	—
Stepside Models				
C1404	½-Ton 115 in. w.b.	1991	3390	—
C1504	½-Ton 127 in. w.b.	1991	3390	—
K1404	½-Ton 4x4 115 in. w.b.	2668	—	—
K1504	½-Ton 4x4 127 in. w.b.	2668	—	—
C2504	¾-Ton 127 in. w.b.	2173	3810	—
K2504	¾-Ton 4x4 127 in. w.b.	2850	—	—
C3604	1-Ton 133 in. w.b.	2350	4110	—
Van/Panel Models				
Corvair 95 Series R-12				
R1205	Corvan 4-dr.	2289	2695	15,806
Series P-10				
P1345	Walk-In Panel 102 in. w.b.	2546	3904	—
Series C-14 — ½-Ton — 115 in. w.b.				
C1405	Panel 115 in. w.b.	2308	3665	—
C1406	Suburban (doors)	2669	3970	—
C1416	Suburban (gate)	2702	4000	—
K1405	Panel 4x4	2985	—	—
K1406	Suburban 4x4 (doors)	3346	—	—
K1416	Suburban 4x4 (gate)	3379	—	—
Series P-20				
P2345	Walk-In Van 137 in. w.b.	3083	5030	—
Series P-30				
P3345	Walk-In Van 104/137" w.b.	3273	5185	—
Series C-36				
C3605	Panel	2775	4490	—
Additional Body Choices				
C1403	½-Ton Ch.-Cab 115" w.b.	1877	3030	—
C1503	½-Ton Ch.-Cab 127" w.b.	—	—	—
C2503	¾-Ton Ch.-Cab 127" w.b.	2059	3395	—
C2509	¾-Ton Stake 8' 127" w.b.	2264	4020	—
C3603	1-Ton Ch.-Cab 133" w.b.	2216	3655	—
C3609	1-Ton Stake 9' 133" w.b.	2463	4485	—

ENGINE (Corvair Series 95): Opposed. OHV. "Turbo-Air". Six-cylinder. Aluminum block. Bore & stroke: 3.437 in. x 2.60 in. Displacement: 144.8 cu. in. Compression ratio: 8.0:1. Brake horsepower: 80 at 4400 R.P.M. Max. Torque: 128 lb. ft. at 2300 R.P.M. Four main bearings. Hydraulic valve lifters. Carburetor: Two Rochester 1-Bbl. model 7019101.

ENGINE (Standard: All except Series 95): Inline. OHV. "Thriftmaster". Six-cylinder. Cast iron block. Bore & stroke: 3-9/16 in. x 3-15/16 in. Displacement: 235.5 cu. in. Compression ratio: 8.25:1. Brake horsepower: 135 at 4000 R.P.M. Max. Torque: 217 lb. ft. at 2000 R.P.M. Four main bearings. Hydraulic valve lifters. Carburetor: Rochester 1-Bbl. model B7015011.

ENGINE (Optional All Series): Inline. OHV. Six-cylinder. Cast iron block. Bore & stroke: 3¾ in. x 3-15/16 in. Displacement: 261 cu. in. Compression ratio: 8.0:1. Brake horsepower: 150 at 4000 R.P.M. Max. Torque: 235 lb. ft. at 2000 R.P.M. Four main bearings. Hydraulic valve lifters. Carburetor: Rochester model 7015013.

1961 Chevrolet Apache 10 Custom Pickup (JLC)

ENGINE (Optional: All except Series 95): V-type. OHV. "Trademaster". Eight-cylinder. Cast iron block. Bore & stroke: 3⅞ in. x 3 in. Displacement: 283 cu. in. Compression ratio: 8.5:1. Brake horsepower: 160 at 4200 R.P.M. Max. Torque: 270 lb. ft. at 2000 R.P.M. Five main bearings. Hydraulic valve lifters. Carburetor: Rochester 2-Bbl. model 2G7015017.

CHASSIS (Series 95): Wheelbase: 95 in. Overall length: 179.7 in. Height: 68.5 in. Front tread: 58 in. Rear tread: 58 in. Tires: 7.00 x 14 in.

CHASSIS (Series C-14, K-14): Wheelbase: 115 in. Overall length: 206 (115 in. w.b.) Front tread: 63.1 in. Rear tread: 61 in. Tires: 6.70 x 15 in.

CHASSIS (Series C-15, K-15): Wheelbase: 127 in. Front tread: 63.1 in. Rear tread: 61.1 in. Tires: 6.70 x 15 in.

CHASSIS (Series C-25, K-25): Wheelbase: 127 in. Tires: 7 x 17.5 in.

CHASSIS (Series C-36): Wheelbase: 133 in. Tires: 8 x 17.5 in.

CHASSIS (Series P-10): Wheelbase: 102 in. Tires: 6.70 x 15 in.

CHASSIS (Series P-20): Wheelbase: 137 in. Tires: 7 x 17.5 in.

CHASSIS (Series P-30): Wheelbase: 104-137 in. Tires: 8 x 19.5 in.

TECHNICAL: Manual. Synchromesh. Speeds: 3F/1R. Column-mounted gear shift lever. Single plate; dry disc clutch. (½-ton) semi-floating, (¾-ton and 1-ton) full-floating rear axle. Overall ratio: (C14, C15, K14, K15) 3.73:1; (C25, K25) 5.14:1; (C36) 5.14:1. Hydraulic. 4-wheel brakes. Pressed steel wheels. Options: Trademaster 283 cu. in. V-8 ($118). Four-speed transmission. Jobmaster, 261 cu. in. six-cylinder. Powerglide automatic. Heavy-duty Borg-Warner three-speed transmission. Additional rear axle ratios. Auxiliary rear springs.

OPTIONS: Rear bumper. Radio. Heater. Clock. Cigar lighter. Radio antenna. Seat covers. **Corvair 95 Options:** Positraction. Front and rear chrome bumpers. Custom Equipment package. Left-hand body door (Corvan). Level pickup box floor. Gasoline heater/defroster. Direct-Air heater/defroster. Chrome hubcaps. Two-tone exterior. Radio. Full-width front seat. Single right-hand auxiliary seat. Whitewall tires. Six-ply rated tires. Four-speed manual transmission. Powerglide automatic transmission. Two-speed electric wipers and washers.

HISTORICAL: Introduced: Fall 1960. Calendar Year Production: (all 6-Cyl.) 294,194; (all V-8) 48,391; (total/all-Chevys) 342,658. Calendar year registrations: (6000-lbs. or less) 202,697; (6001-10,000 lbs.) 44,903. Innovations: All-new Corvair truck-line. Alternators available (instead of generator) in electrical system. Optional heavy-duty front suspension introduced. Diesel options introduced for medium-duty series (and heavy-duties). Historical Notes: Public acceptance of the styling and economy of the Corvair trucks was enthusiastic, but the lack of a single, smooth cargo load floor (due to rear engine location) proved to be a drawback to strong sales of these models. A fourth type of Corvair Van (Model R1206 Greenbriar) was merchandised as a station wagon. It had a price of $2,651 and a 2,895 pound curb weight. Production of this model, at 18,489, was the highest of all Corvair vans (total output was 47,557). Chevrolet was America's number one truck-maker in 1961, but only by the narrow margin of 3,670 units. Its 30.39 market share represented the production of 294,194 six-cylinder trucks and 48,391 V-8 powered units in calendar 1961 (totaling 342,658, down from 1960's 394,014 units). This was in contrast to production of 494,575 trucks (all sixes) in 1950! The company's great strength, at this time, was in the six-cylinder category. The Chevy six outsold its nearest competitor by nearly 100,000 units. J.E. Conlan was assistant general sales manager of the truck division.

Pricing

1961	5	4	3	2	1
Corvair Series 95					
Loadside	590	1170	1950	2700	3900
Rampside	630	1250	2100	3000	4200
Corvan Series					
Corvan Panel	570	1140	1900	2650	3800
Greenbriar Sportvan	680	1350	2250	3150	4500
Fleetside Pickups					
C-10 P.U. (short box)	1180	2370	3950	5500	7900
C-10 P.U. (long box)	1170	2340	3900	5450	7800
K-10 P.U. (short box)	1150	2310	3850	5400	7700
K-10 P.U. (long box)	1140	2280	3800	5300	7600
C-20 P.U. (long box)	980	1950	3250	4550	6500
K-20 P.U. (long box)	930	1860	3100	4350	6200

NOTE: "C" is conventional drive model. "K" is four-wheel drive (4x4) model. "10" is the ½-ton series. "20" is the ¾-ton series. "30" is the one-ton issue. "Short box" is 6½ ft. bed. "Long box" is 8 ft. bed.

Stepside Pickups	5	4	3	2	1
C-10 P.U. (short box)	1180	2370	3950	5450	7800
C-10 P.U. (long box)	1150	2310	3850	5400	7700
K-10 P.U. (short box)	1140	2280	3800	5300	7600
K-10 P.U. (long box)	1130	2250	3750	5250	7500
C-20 P.U. (long box)	960	1920	3200	4500	6400
K-20 P.U. (long box)	950	1850	3050	4300	6100
C-30 P.U. (8½ ft. bed)	900	1800	3000	4200	6000
Step Vans					
P-10 Walk-In	590	1170	1950	2700	3900
P-20 Walk-In	600	1200	2000	2800	4000
P-30 Walk-In	620	1230	2050	2900	4100
Panel/Suburban/Stake-Bed					
C-10 Panel	570	1140	1900	2650	3800
C-10 Suburban	750	1500	2500	3500	5000
C-20 Panel	530	1050	1750	2450	3500
C-20 Suburban	720	1450	2400	3300	4800
C-20 Stake	530	1050	1750	2450	3500
C-30 Panel (10½ ft.)	540	1080	1800	2500	3600
C-30 Stake	540	1080	1800	2500	3600

NOTE: 1955-up prices based on top of the line models.

1962 CHEVROLET

1962 Chevrolet Corvair 95 Rampside Pickup (OCW)

LIGHT TRUCK — 1962 SERIES — (ALL ENGINES): — The Corvair trucks were virtually unchanged, except, possibly, for color choices. The Greenbriar passenger van was again merchandised as a station wagon in the Corvair car-line. Other models included the Corvan panel and Loadside or Rampside pickups. The Loadsides were the rarest. A new option was a Positraction rear axle.

Chevrolet's C-series trucks adopted a new front end design for 1962 which featured two, rather than the four headlights used from 1958-1961. The ribbon headlight surrounds were very large and were separated by a center grille portion with nine sub-divisions. Chevrolet lettering was placed along its lower edge. The parking lights, along with two air intakes, were set in a beveled surface that extended around the truck body to give it a distinct upper and lower level. Deluxe models had a chrome grille, bumpers and hubcaps. Spare tires were mounted upright, behind the cab, on pickups.

I.D. DATA: Serial number stamped on plate mounted on windshield corner post. See 1961 for specifics. Example: 2C140 (A) 10001 and up. Engine numbers located (6-Cyl.) on right side of block next to distributor. (V-8) on forward edge of block, protruding from under right cylinder head.

Model	Body Type	Price	Weight	Prod. Total
Corvair Series 95				
R1244	Loadside Pickup	2084	2580	369
R1254	Rampside Pickup	2138	2660	4102
Fleetside Models				
C1434	½-Ton 115 in. w.b.	2027	3440	—
C1534	½-Ton 127 in. w.b.	2027	3440	—
K1434	½-Ton 4x4 115 in. w.b.	2678	—	—
K1534	½-Ton 4x4 127 in. w.b.	2678	—	—
C2534	¾-Ton 127 in. w.b.	2209	3905	—
K2534	¾-Ton 4x4 127 in. w.b.	2886	—	—
Stepside Models				
C1404	½-Ton 115 in. w.b.	2011	3385	—
C1504	½-Ton 127 in. w.b.	2011	3385	—
K1404	½-Ton 4x4 115 in. w.b.	2662	—	—
K1504	½-Ton 4x4 127 in. w.b.	2662	—	—
C2504	¾-Ton 127 in. w.b.	2193	3845	—
K2504	¾-Ton 4x4 127 in. w.b.	2870	—	—
C3604	1-Ton 133 in. w.b.	2372	4155	—
Van/Panel Models				
Corvair 95 Series R-12				
R1205	Corvan 4-dr.	2294	2820	13,491
Series P-10				
P1345	Walk-In Van 102 in. w.b.	2546	3695	—
Series C-14				
C1405	Panel 115 in. w.b.	2328	3650	—
C1406	Suburban (doors)	2623	3980	—
C1416	Suburban (gate)	2656	3990	—
K1405	Panel 4x4 115 in. w.b.	2979	—	—
Series K-14				
K1406	Suburban 4x4 (doors)	3274	—	—
K1416	Suburban 4x4 (gate)	3307	—	—
Series P-20				
P2345	Walk-In 104/137'' w.b.	3083	4945	—
Series P-30				
P3345	Walk-In 104/137'' w.b.	3275	5140	—
Series C-36				
C3605	Panel 10.5 ft.	2797	4525	—
Additional Body Choices				
C1403	½-Ton Ch-Cab 115'' w.b.	1897	3020	—
C1503	½-Ton Ch-Cab 127'' w.b.	—	—	—
C2503	¾-Ton Ch-Cab 127'' w.b.	2080	3405	—
C2509	¾-Ton Stake 8'/127'' w.b.	2284	4035	—
C3603	1-Ton Ch-Cab 133'' w.b.	2238	3700	—
C3609	1-Ton Stake 9'/133'' w.b.	2485	4530	—

1962 Chevrolet Fleetside Pickup (DFW)

ENGINE (Corvair Series 95): Opposed. OHV. Six-cylinder. Aluminum block. Bore & stroke: 3.437 in. x 2.60 in. Displacement: 144.8 cu. in. Compression ratio: 8.0:1. Brake horsepower: 80 at 4400 R.P.M. Max. Torque: 128 lb. ft. at 2300 R.P.M. Four main bearings. Hydraulic valve lifters. Carburetor: Two Rochester 1-Bbl. model 7019101.

ENGINE (Standard: All other Series): Inline. OHV. Six-cylinder. Cast iron block. Bore & stroke: 3-9/16 in. x 3-15/16 in. Displacement: 235 cu. in. Compression ratio: 8.25:1. Brake horsepower: 135 at 4000 R.P.M. Max. Torque: 217 lb. ft. at 2000 R.P.M. Four main bearings. Hydraulic valve lifters. Carburetor: Rochester 1-Bbl. model B7015011.

ENGINE (Optional: All except Series 95): Inline. OHV. Six-cylinder. Cast iron block. Bore & stroke: 3¾ in. x 3-15/16 in. Displacement: 261 cu. in. Compression ratio: 8.0:1. Brake horsepower: 150 at 4000 R.P.M. Max. Torque: 235 lb. ft. at 2000 R.P.M. Four main bearings. Hydraulic valve lifters. Carburetor: Rochester model 7015013.

ENGINE (Optional: All except Series 95): V-type. OHV. Eight-cylinder. Cast iron block. Bore & stroke: 3⅞ in. x 3 in. Displacement: 283 cu. in. Compression ratio: 8.5:1. Brake horsepower: 160 at 4200 R.P.M. Max. Torque: 270 lb. ft. at 2000 R.P.M. Five main bearings. Hydraulic valve lifters. Carburetor: Rochester model 2G7015017.

(NOTE: This engine was $118 extra)

1962 Chevrolet Fleetside Pickup (OCW)

CHASSIS (Series 95): Wheelbase: 95 in. Overall length: 179.7 in. Height: (Greenbriar) 68.5 in.; (Pickups) 70 in.; (Corvan) 70¾ in. Front tread: 58 in. Rear tread: 58 in. Tires: 7.00 x 14 in.

CHASSIS (Series C10, K10): Wheelbase: 115/127 in. Overall length: (C10/K10) 206 in.; (C14/K14) 198¼ in. Front tread: 63.1 in. Rear tread: 61.0 in. Tires: 6.70 x 15 in.

CHASSIS (Series C20, K20): Front tread: 63.1 in. Rear tread: 61.0 in. Tires: 6.70 x 15 in.

CHASSIS (Series C25, K25): Wheelbase: 127 in. Overall length: 200¼ in. Tires: 7 x 17.5 in.

CHASSIS (Series C36): Wheelbase: 133 in. Overall length: 211¾ in. Tires: 8 x 17.5 in.

CHASSIS (Series P10): Wheelbase: 102 in. Overall length: 167¼ in. Tires: 6.70 x 15 in.

CHASSIS (Series P20): Wheelbase: 137 in. Overall length: (P23) 184¼ in.; (P25) 208½ in.; (P26) 232¼ in. Tires: 7 x 17.5 in.

CHASSIS (Series P30): Wheelbase: 104-137 in. Overall length: Same as P20 for comparable models. Tires: 8 x 19.5 in.

TECHNICAL: Manual. Synchromesh. Speeds: 3F/1R. Column-mounted gear shift lever. Single plate; dry disc clutch. Rear axle: (½-ton) semi-floating; (¾-ton and 1-ton) full-floating. Overall ratio: (C-14, C-15, K-14, K-15) 3.73:1; (C-25, K-25) 5.14:1; (C-36) 5.14:1. Hydraulic four-wheel brakes. Pressed steel wheels. Options: Four-speed transmission. Trademaster 283 cu. in V-8 ($118). Jobmaster, 261 cu. in. six-cylinder. Powerglide automatic transmission. Heavy-duty Borg-Warner three-speed transmission. Additional rear axle ratios.

OPTIONS: (Corvair) Custom chrome, R1200 w/o wheel covers ($25.10). Custom Equipment, R1205 w/ std. seat ($17.56). Custom Equipment, R1205 w/full-width seat ($19.23). Custom Equipment, R1206 ($167.20). Custom Equipment, R1244/1254 ($19.23). Left Side Body Doors, R1205/1206 ($62.70). Floor level pickup box, R1244/1254 ($37.65). Laminated front door glass ($4.20). Direct Air heater ($57.69). Gasoline operated heater ($71.10). OSRV mirror, left or right ($3.77). Two-tone paint ($20.90). Two-tone paint, 1200 pickups ($25.10). Auxiliary front seat, R1205 ($31.78). Full Width seat, R1205 ($20.90). Third seat, R1206 ($29.30). H-D front springs ($8.40). H-D shock absorbers ($5.87). Whitewall tires, four-ply ($24.60). Blackwall tires, six-ply ($34.46). Whitewall tires, six-ply ($67.47). Full wheel covers, R1206 w/Custom ($6.73). Two-speed washers and wipers ($12.55). **(C10/C20/C30)** Add for 150 h.p. "261" six-cylinder ($50.20). Add for V-8 ($92). Oil bath air cleaner, six-cylinder w/governor ($1.72); w/o governor ($5.06). Positraction axle, C1400/1500 ($50.20). No-Spin rear axle, C2500 ($104.50). Optional rear axle ratios: 3.38:1 w/manual transmission ($5.06); 4.11:1 w/manual transmission; 4.11:1 w/Powerglide ($25.10). H-D battery ($5.87). Eleven-inch H-D clutch, 6-cyl. only ($4.20). Custom Appearance Option, Panels

1962 Chevrolet Stepside Pickup (DFW)

($33.45); others ($40.13). Custom Chrome Option, all w/chrome front bumper ($16.75); pickups with both bumpers chromed ($41.80); panels w/chrome bumpers ($25.10). Custom Comfort Option, panels ($9.21); other models ($42.66). Custom side moldings, Fleetsides ($16.75). Temperature control radiator fan ($16.75). 35-amp. generator ($5.87). 42-amp. Delcotron ($22.62). 52-amp. Delcotron ($29.30). All glass tinted ($11.74). Tinted windshield ($10.07). Deluxe heater ($53.11). Recirculating heater ($37.22). 17.5 inch OSRV mirror, except panels, left-hand ($1.72); right-hand ($3.77). 8-inch OSRV mirror, right-hand ($3.77). Oil filter, w/std. 6-cyl. ($2.96). "Tu-tone" paint, panels ($20.90); others ($12.55). H-D radiator, except w/Powerglide ($16.75). Radio ($37.22). Auxiliary seat, panels ($31.78). Full-Depth foam seat, except panels ($25.10). H-D shock absorbers, rear ($6.73); front — requires rears — ($5.87).H-D springs, C2500 front ($2.53); all models, rear ($5.06). H-D three-speed manual transmission, C1400 ($58.55); C1500 ($62.70) and C2500 ($71.10). H-D four-speed manual transmission, C1400 ($62.70); C1500 ($66.90) and C2500 ($72.25). Powerglide transmission, all models ($146.30). Full-View rear window, except panels ($33.45). Two-speed windshield wipers and washers ($12.55). Note: Prices above are "dealer cost" for 1962 options.

HISTORICAL: Introduced: Fall 1961. Calendar year registrations: (all Chevy trucks) 425,406. Calendar year production: (all Chevy trucks) 396,819. Of this total, 82 percent were six-cylinder models. Innovations: New styling for "C" Series models. First diesels in "big" Chevrolet trucks. Historical Notes: Chevy was America's number one truck-maker in 1962. The 8 millionth Chevy truck since 1918 was sold this season. J.E. Conlan remained in charge of Chevrolet's Truck and Fleet Sales Department. Model year production: 396,940.

1962 Chevrolet Crew Cab Pickup (VCCA)

Pricing

	5	4	3	2	1
1962					
Corvair Series 95					
Loadside	590	1170	1950	2700	3900
Rampside	630	1250	2100	3000	4200
Corvan Series					
Corvan Panel Van	570	1140	1900	2650	3800
Greenbriar Sportvan	680	1350	2250	3150	4500
Fleetside Pickups					
C10 Pickup (short box)	1180	2370	3950	5500	7900
C10 Pickup (long box)	1170	2340	3900	5450	7800
K10 Pickup (short box)	1150	2310	3850	5400	7700
K10 Pickup (long box)	1140	2280	3800	5300	7600
C20 Pickup (long box)	980	1950	3250	4550	6500
K20 Pickup (long box)	930	1860	3100	4350	6200

NOTES:
"C" is 4x2 model.
"K" is 4x4 model.
"10" is ½-Ton.
"20" is ¾-Ton.
"30" is 1-Ton.
"Short Box" has 6½-ft. box.
"Long Box" has 8-ft. box.

	5	4	3	2	1
Stepside Pickups					
C10 Pickup (short box)	1180	2370	3950	5450	7800
C10 Pickup (long box)	1150	2310	3850	5400	7700
K10 Pickup (short box)	1140	2280	3800	5300	7600
K10 Pickup (long box)	1130	2250	3750	5250	7500
C20 Pickup (long box)	960	1920	3200	4500	6400
K20 Pickup (long box)	950	1850	3050	4300	6100
C30 Pickup (8½ ft. bed)	900	1800	3000	4200	6000
Step Vans					
P10 Walk-In	590	1170	1950	2700	3900
P20 Walk-In	600	1200	2000	2800	4000
P30 Walk-In	620	1230	2050	2900	4100
Panel/Suburban/Stake-Bed					
C10 Panel	570	1140	1900	2650	3800
C10 Suburban	750	1500	2500	3500	5000
K10 Panel	530	1050	1750	2450	3500
K10 Suburban	720	1450	2400	3300	4800
C20 Stake	530	1050	1750	2450	3500
C30 Panel (10½ ft.)	540	1080	1800	2500	3600
C30 Stake	540	1080	1800	2500	3600

NOTE: 1955-up prices based on top of the line models.

1963 CHEVROLET

1963 Chevrolet Corvair 95 Rampside Pickup (OCW)

LIGHT TRUCK — SERIES R1200/C10/C20/K10/K20 — (ALL ENGINES): — Corvair trucks were again unchanged. Standard equipment was the same as 1962 and included the 145 cu. in./80 h.p. engine; three-speed Synchromesh transmission; 9⅛-inch diameter clutch; 3.89:1 rear axle; 11 x 2 inch hydraulic brakes with 167 cubic inches of lining area; 12-volt electrical system and 18½ gallon gas tank. Front suspension was fully independent with 1150-pound coil springs and 2500-pound capacity. The rear suspension had identical specifications. Also standard were single-speed dual electric windshield wipers; directional signals; five tubeless tires and 20.0:1 ball-gear ratio steering. The CVW rating was 4600 pounds. New tire options included truck type 7.00-14 6-PR or 8-PR sizes. Custom exterior/interior treatments, chrome bumpers and chrome hubcaps were available at extra cost.

The regular 1963 Chevrolet trucks had their series I.D. badges moved from above the front fender feature line to the fendersides, behind the front wheel openings. As in 1962, Deluxe models had a side spear from front to back. It branched into two moldings (with a contrast panel between them) from the center of the door to rear. Introduced this season were two engines that were destined for long production runs, the 230 and 292 cubic inch six-cylinder "high-torque" models. Externally the '63 Chevrolets were identified by their new front end which carried a wider grille with a mesh design. The headlights were positioned further outward than in 1962. As before, customers could select either a narrow or wide rear window. Power steering kits were now available, through Chevrolet dealers, for light-duty trucks.

I.D. DATA: Serial number stamped on plate mounted on windshield corner post on driver's side. Example: 3C 140 (A) 100001 and up. Engine numbers located (Six-cylinder) stamped on right side of block, next to distributor. (V-8) stamped on forward edge of block, protruding from under right cylinder head.

Model	Body Type	Price	Weight	Prod. Total
Corvair Series 95				
R1254	Rampside Pickup	2212	2800	2046
Fleetside Models				
C1434	½-Ton 115 in. w.b.	2025	3235	—
C1534	½-Ton 127 in. w.b.	2025	3235	—
K1434	½-Ton 4x4 115 in. w.b.	2676	—	—
K1534	½-Ton 4x4 127 in. w.b.	2676	—	—
C2534	¾-Ton 127 in. w.b.	2209	3760	—
K2534	¾-Ton 4x4 127 in. w.b.	2887	—	—
Stepside Models				
C1404	½-Ton 115 in. w.b.	2009	3190	—
C1504	½-Ton 127 in. w.b.	2009	3190	—
K1404	½-Ton 4x4 115 in. w.b.	2660	—	—
K1504	½-Ton 4x4 127 in. w.b.	2660	—	—
C2504	¾-Ton 127 in. w.b.	2193	3710	—
K2504	¾-Ton 4x4 127 in. w.b.	2871	—	—
C3604	1-Ton 133 in. w.b.	2371	3900	—
Van/Panel Models				
Corvair 95 Series R-12				
R1205	Corvan 4-dr.	2212	2800	11,161
Series P-10				
P1345	Walk-In Van 102 in. w.b.	2479	3450	—
Series C14 — 115 in. w.b.				
C1405	Panel 2-dr.	2326	3440	—
C1406	Suburban (doors)	2620	3720	—
C1416	Suburban (gate)	2653	3735	—
Series K14 — 115 in. w.b.				
K1405	Panel 4x4	2977	—	—
K1406	Suburban 4x4 (doors)	3271	—	—
K1416	Suburban 4x4 (gate)	3304	—	—
Series P20 — 104/137 in. w.b.				
P2345	¾-Ton Walk-In Panel	3082	4805	—

Model	Body Type	Price	Weight	Prod. Total
Series P30 — 104/137 in. w.b.				
P3345	1-Ton Walk-In Panel	3274	5020	—
Series C30				
C3605	1-Ton Panel 10.5 ft.	2795	4260	—
Additional Body Choices				
C1403	½-Ton Ch-Cab 115" w.b.	1895	2820	—
C1503	½-Ton Ch-Cab 127" w.b.	—	—	—
C2503	¾-Ton Ch-Cab 127" w.b.	2079	3280	—
C2509	¾-Ton Stake 127" w.b.	2284	3895	—
C3603	1-Ton Ch-Cab 133 " w.b.	2236	3430	—
C3609	1-T Stake 9 ft. 133" w.b.	2483	4230	—

NOTE: The Corvair Greenbriar was merchandised as a station wagon. It had a price of $2,655; weight of 2,990 pounds and production total of 13,761 units.

ENGINE (Std. C10/20/30-K10/20/30): Inline. OHV. Six-cylinder. Cast iron block. Bore & stroke: 3⅞ in. x 3¼ in. Displacement: 230 cu. in. Compression ratio: 8.5:1. Brake horsepower: 140 at 4400 R.P.M. Max. Torque: 220 lb. ft. at 1600 R.P.M. Net horsepower: 120 at 3600 R.P.M. Seven main bearings. Hydraulic valve lifters. Carburetor: Rochester 1-Bbl. model B-7023017. 1963 was the first year for Chevrolets use of the new 230 and 292 cu. in. engine. Engine Color Code 230 L-6 - Blue, 292 L-6 - Green, 283 V-8 - Gray.

1963 Chevrolet Fleetside Pickup (DFW)

ENGINE (Opt. C10/20/30-K10/20/30/230 Economy): Inline. OHV. Six-cylinder. Cast iron block. Bore & stroke: 3⅞ in. x 3¼ in. Displacement: 230 cu. in. Compression ratio: 8.5:1. Brake horsepower: 125 at 3400 R.P.M. Max. Torque: 210 lb. ft. at 1600 R.P.M. Net horsepower: 100 at 3200 R.P.M. Seven main bearings. Hydraulic valve lifters. Carburetor: Rochester 1-Bbl. model B-7023021.

ENGINE (Opt. C10/20/30-K10/20/30-$97): Inline. OHV. Six-cylinder. Cast iron block. Bore & stroke: 3⅞ in. x 4⅛ in. Displacement: 292 cu. in. Compression ratio: 8.0:1. Brake horsepower: 165 at 3800 R.P.M. Max. Torque: 280 lb. ft. at 1600 R.P.M. Net horsepower: 147 at 3600 R.P.M. Seven main bearings. Hydraulic valve lifters. Carburetor: Rochester 1-Bbl. model B-7023013.

ENGINE (Opt. C10/20/30-K10/20/30 ($118): V-type. OHV. Eight-cylinder. Cast iron block. Bore & stroke: 3⅞ in. x 3 in. Displacement: 283 cu. in. Compression ratio: 8.5:1. Brake horsepower: 175 at 4400 R.P.M. Five main bearings. Hydraulic valve lifters. Carburetor: Rochester 2-Bbl. model 2G-7023010.

ENGINE (Std. Series P10): Inline. OHV. Six-cylinder. Cast iron block. Bore & stroke: 3⅞ in. x 3¼ in. Displacement: 153.3 cu. in. Compression ratio: 8.5:1. Brake horsepower: 90 at 4000 R.P.M. Max. Torque: 152 lb. ft. at 2400 R.P.M. Five main bearings. Hydraulic valve lifters. Carburetor: Rochester 1-Bbl. model 7020103.

ENGINE (Std. Corvair): Opposed. OHV. Four-cylinder. Aluminum block. Bore & stroke: 3.437 in. x 2.60 in. Displacement: 144.8 cu. in. Compression ratio: 8.0:1. Brake horsepower: 80 at 4400 R.P.M. Max. Torque: 128 lb. ft. at 2300 R.P.M. Four main bearings. Hydraulic valve lifters. Carburetor: Two Rochester 1-Bbl. model 7019101.

CHASSIS (Series C10): Wheelbase: 115/127 in. Overall length: 206 (115 in. w.b.) Height: 71 in. Front tread: 63.1 in. Rear tread: 61.0 in. Tires: 6.70 x 15 in.

CHASSIS (Series 95): Wheelbase: 95 in. Overall length: 179.7 in. Height: 68.5 in. Front tread: 58 in. Rear tread: 58 in. Tires: 7.00 x 14 in.

CHASSIS (Series C14/K14): Wheelbase: 115 (with 6½ ft. bed)/127 in. (with 8-ft. bed). Tires: G70 x 15.

CHASSIS (Series C15/K15): Wheelbase: 127 in. Tires: 6.70 x 15 in.

CHASSIS (Series C20): Wheelbase: 127 in. Tires: 7 x 17.5.

CHASSIS (Series C30): Wheelbase: 133 in. (with 9-ft. bed) Tires: 8 x 17.5 in.

CHASSIS (Series P10): Wheelbase: 102 in. Tires: 6.70 x 15 in.

CHASSIS (Series P20): Wheelbase: 104-137 in. Tires: 7 x 17.5 in.

CHASSIS (Series P30): Wheelbase: 104-137 in. Tires: 8 x 19.5 in.

CHASSIS (Series C25): Wheelbase: 125 in. Tires: 7 x 17.5 in.

NOTE: Overall length of flat-face cowl models: (C14) 200¾ in.; (C25) 200 in.; (C36) 211¾ in.; (P13) 167¼ in.; (P23/P33) 184¼ in.; (P25/25) 208¼ in. and (P26/36) 232¼ in.

TECHNICAL: Manual, Chevrolet manufacture (Borg-Warner heavy-duty 3spd.-opt.) 3F/1R. Column-mounted gear shift lever. Single dry plate clutch. (½-ton) semi-floating, (¾-ton and 1-ton) full-floating rear axle. Overall ratio: 3.90 opt. 3.73, 3.07, 4.11 4 wheel drive 3.73. Technical options: Powerglide C-10 all engines 3.73, 4.11, C-20 all engines 4.57. Four-wheel hydraulic, drums, 11 x 2 in. (C-10, K-10), 11 x 2.75 in. (C-20), 12 x 2 in. (K-20). Steel, drop center wheels. Powerglide automatic transmission. Overdrive. Power steering $188. 292 cu. in. I-6 engine $97. 283 cu. in. V-8 engine $118. Four-speed transmission.

OPTIONS: (LIGHT-DUTY) Rear bumper. Radio. Heater. Clock. Cigar lighter. Radio antenna. Custom rear bumper. Outside mirror. (CORVAIR) Pre-oil bath cleaner ($17.25). Custom chrome: Greenbrier w/ wheel covers ($21.55); Greenbrier w/o wheel covers ($32.30). Custom Equipment: Corvan w/ std. seat ($22.60); Corvan w/full-width seat ($24.75); Greenbrier ($215.20); Rampside ($24.75). Left side body doors ($80.70). Laminated front door glass ($5.40). Level pickup floor ($48.45). OSRV mirros ($4.85). Two-tone paint, R1205/1206 ($26.90); R1254 ($32.30). Direct Air heater ($74.25). Gasoline operated heater $91.50). Manual radio ($47.90). Push-button radio and rear speaker ($69.95). Auxiliary front seat, R1205 ($40.90). Full-width seat, R1205 ($26.90). Third seat, R1205 ($53.90). H-D front shocks, R1205/1254 ($7.55). H-D front springs, R1206 ($10.80). Four-ply whitewall tires ($31.80). Six-ply black-wall tires ($44.30). Six-ply whitewall tires ($87.15). Powerglide transmission ($156.60). Four-speed manual transmission ($91.50). Full wheel covers, R1206 w/ Custom equip. ($8.65). Windshield washer and two-speed wipers ($16.15). Positraction ($37.70). Front driver seat belt ($10.25). Two front seat belts ($18.85)

HISTORICAL: Introduced: Sept. 28, 1962. Calendar Year Production Total: 483,119. (This was 33.01 percent share of total industry). In round numbers, the total included 500 four-cylinder powered trucks; 2,200 diesels; 378,000 six-cylinder models and 102,400 trucks with V-8 power plants. Calendar year registrations: 425,406. Corvair, total production for model year: 26,968 (including Greenbriar Sports Wagon). Innovations: New "High-Torque"230 and 292 cu. in. sixes. Light-duty trucks adopt ladder-type frame. Historical notes: Chevrolet commanded its largest share, ever, of the U.S. truck market in 1983. Over one-third of all trucks built this year had "bow-tie" badges. It was also the first time, since 1950, that truck deliveries went above 400,000 units. Leafing through a Chevrolet *Silver Book* for 1963 reveals some unusual "vocational equipment" available in the factory-approved aftermarket. This included roll-up doors for walk-in deliveries (from Overhead Door Corp., of Marion, Ohio); a Crew Cab conversion (from Orrville Metal Specialty Co., of Orrville, Ohio); a fan-belt-driven automatic snow plow from Monarch Road Machinery Co. (of Grand Rapids, Mich.) and pickup truck extension boom wrecker units from Canfield Tow Bar Co.)of Detroit. Winnebago Industries and Wolverine Camper Co. were among firms offering slide-in campers for pickups. Perhaps the ultimate conversion, however, was the "Go-Home" mobilehome (based on Corvair running gear) made by Ultra-Van Mfg. Co., of Oakland, Calif.

Pricing

1963	5	4	3	2	1
Corvair Series 95					
Loadside	590	1170	1950	2700	3900
Rampside	630	1250	2100	3000	4200
Corvan Series					
Corvan Panel Van	570	1140	1900	2650	3800
Greenbriar Sportvan	680	1350	2250	3150	4500
Fleetside Pickups					
C10 Pickup (short box)	1180	2370	3950	5500	7900
C10 Pickup (long box)	1170	2340	3900	5450	7800
K10 Pickup (short box)	1150	2310	3850	5400	7700
K10 Pickup (long box)	1140	2280	3800	5300	7600
C20 Pickup (long box)	980	1950	3250	4550	6500
K20 Pickup (long box)	930	1860	3100	4350	6200

NOTES:
"C" is conventional drive model.
"K" is four-wheel drive (4x4) model.
"10" is ½-ton series. "20" is ¾-ton series. "30" is one-ton series.
"Short box" is 6½ ft. bed.
"Long box" is 8 ft. bed.

Stepside Pickups					
C10 Pickup (short box)	1180	2370	3950	5450	7800
C10 Pickup (long box)	1150	2310	3850	5400	7700
K10 Pickup (short box)	1140	2280	3800	5300	7600
K10 Pickup (long box)	1130	2250	3750	5250	7500
C20 Pickup (long box)	960	1920	3200	4500	6400
K20 Pickup (long box)	950	1850	3050	4300	6100
C30 Pickup (8½ ft. bed)	900	1800	3000	4200	6000
Step Vans					
P10 Walk-In	590	1170	1950	2700	3900
P20 Walk-In	600	1200	2000	2800	4000
P30 Walk-In	620	1230	2050	2900	4100
Panel/Suburban/Stake-Bed					
C10 Panel	570	1140	1900	2650	3800
C10 Suburban	750	1500	2500	3500	5000
K10 Panel	530	1050	1750	2450	3500
K10 Suburban	720	1450	2400	3300	4800
C20 Stake	530	1050	1750	2450	3500
C30 Panel (10½ ft.)	540	1080	1800	2500	3600
C30 Stake	540	1080	1800	2500	3600

NOTE: 1955-up prices based on top of the line models.

1964 CHEVROLET

1964 Chevrolet El Camino (LC)

LIGHT TRUCK — 1964 SERIES — (ALL ENGINES): — The Corvair trucks were unchanged again, except for new paint colors. These included Meadow green; Bahama green; Daytona blue; Lagoon Aqua; Desert beige and Goldwood yellow. The slow-selling Loadside pickup was gone. The engine grew from 145 to 164 cubic inches and gained horsepower. A 110 horsepower option was offered, at least in Greenbriers.

For regular trucks, styling changes consisted of a grille with two massive horizontal bars. The Chevrolet name (in letters) was moved from the grille's lower edge to the top. The single headlight nacelles were now squared and had modest "eyelids".

Returning after a four-year hiatus was the El Camino which Chevrolet described as a "Personal Pickup". Built on the mid-size Chevelle's 115 in. wheelbase, the El Camino was available with many passenger-car options. It came with trim levels comparable to the "300" and Malibu series.

A low-priced, front-engined Chevy Van was released early in calendar 1964. It had the same general characteristics (body configuration and 90 inch wheelbase) as the Corvan, but utilized a water-cooled 153 cubic inch four-cylinder Chevy II engine. It was available in Carryall and Panel models. The Carryall had windows and six doors (with passenger seats available). The Commercial Panel had double right side cargo doors. Styling characteristics included five-segment vents on the front with a "bow-tie" underneath and an oval, horizontal-bar grille near the bottom of the front single headlights.

I.D. DATA: Serial number stamped on plate mounted on windshield corner post — driver's side. The VIN consists of 12 symbols, the first three identify the truck type and series. The fifth digit is model year. The sixth letter identifies the assembly plant with the last six digits indicating production number. Starting: 10001 and up. Engine numbers located — 6-cyl. stamped on right side of block next to distributor. V-8's stamped on forward edge of block, protruding from under right cylinder head.

Model	Body Type	Price	Weight	Prod. Total
El Camino Series 5000				
13380	Pickup (6-cyl.)	2267	2935	34,724
13480	Pickup (V-8)	2367	2935	—
13580	Custom Pickup (6-cyl.)	2342	2935	—
13680	Custom Pickup (V-8)	2442	—	—
Corvair Series R12				
R1254	Rampside Pickup	2136	2665	851
Fleetside Models				
C1434	½-Ton 115 in. w.b.	2023	3205	—
C1534	½-Ton 127 in. w.b.	2023	3205	—
K1434	½-Ton 4x4 115 in. w.b.	2674	—	—
K1534	½-Ton 4x4 127 in. w.b.	2674	—	—
C2534	¾-Ton 127 in. w.b.	2208	3710	—
K2534	¾-Ton 4x4 127 in. w.b.	2859	—	—
Stepside Models				
C1404	½-Ton 115 in. w.b.	2007	3175	—
C1504	½-Ton 127 in. w.b.	2007	3175	—
K1404	½-Ton 4x4 115 in. w.b.	2658	—	—
K1504	½-Ton 4x4 127 in. w.b.	2658	—	—
C2504	¾-Ton 127 in. w.b.	2192	3665	—
C3604	1-Ton 133 in. w.b.	2370	3880	—
Van/Panel Models				
Corvair Series R12				
R1205	Corvan 4-dr.	2212	2800	8147
Series G10				
G1205	Panel 2-dr.	2067	2735	—
Series P10				
P1345	Walk-In Panel 2-dr.	2477	3475	—
Series C10 — 115 in. w.b.				
C1405	Panel 7½ ft.	2324	3405	—
C1406	Suburban (doors)	2629	3695	—
C1416	Suburban (gate)	2662	3705	—
Series K10 — (4x4) — 115 in. w.b.				
K1405	Panel 7½ ft.	2975	—	—
K1406	Suburban (doors)	3280	—	—
K1416	Suburban (gate)	3313	—	—

Model	Body Type	Price	Weight	Prod. Total
Series P20				
P2345	¾-Ton Walk-In 104/137 w.b.	3081	4825	—
Series P30				
P3345	1-Ton Walk-In 104/137 w.b.	3274	5030	—
Series C30				
C3605	1-Ton Pnl. 10.5 ft.	2791	4240	—
Additional Body Choices				
C1403	½-Ton Ch-Cab 115" w.b.	1893	2810	—
C1503	½-Ton Ch-Cab 127" w.b.	—	—	—
C2503	¾-Ton Ch-Cab 127" w.b.	2078	3230	—
C2509	¾-Ton Stake	2283	3855	—
C3603	1-Ton Ch-Cab 133" w.b.	2235	3410	—
C3609	1-Ton Stake 9'/133" w.b.	2482	4240	—

1964 Chevrolet C10 Fleetside Pickup (OCW)

ENGINE (Standard C10/C20/C30/G1236/Opt. P10): Inline. OHV. Six-cylinder. Cast iron block. Bore & stroke: 3⅞ in. x 3¼ in. Displacement: 230 cu. in. Compression ratio: 8.5:1. Brake horsepower: 140 at 4400 R.P.M. Max. Torque: 220 lb. ft. at 1600 R.P.M. Net horsepower: 120 at 3600 R.P.M. Seven main bearings. Hydraulic valve lifters. Carburetor: Rochester model B-7023017. Engine Color Code 230 L-6 - Blue, 292 L-6 - Green, 283 V-8 - Gray.

ENGINE (230 Economy): Inline. OHV. Six-cylinder. Cast iron block. Bore & stroke: 3⅞ in. x 3¼ in. Displacement: 230 cu. in. Compression ratio: 8.5:1. Brake horsepower: 125 at 3400 R.P.M. Max. Torque: 210 lb. ft. at 1600 R.P.M. Net horsepower: 100 at 3200 R.P.M. Seven main bearings. Hydraulic valve lifters. Carburetor: Rochester model B-7023021.

ENGINE (Optional C10/C20/C30/K10/K20/K30): Inline. OHV. Six-cylinder. Cast iron block. Bore & stroke: 3⅞ in. x 4⅛ in. Displacement: 292 cu. in. Compression ratio: 8.0:1. Brake horsepower: 165 at 3800 R.P.M. Max. Torque: 280 lb. ft. at 1600 R.P.M. Net horsepower: 147 at 3600 R.P.M. Seven main bearings. Hydraulic valve lifters. Carburetor: Rochester 1-Bbl. model B-7023013.

ENGINE (Optional C10/C20/C30/K10/K20/K30): Inline. OHV. Six-cylinder. Cast iron block. Bore & stroke: 3⅞ in. x 4⅛ in. Displacement: 292 cu. in. Compression ratio: 8.0:1. Brake horsepower: 170 at 4000 R.P.M. Max. Torque: 275 lb. ft. at 1600 R.P.M. Net horsepower: 153 at 3600 R.P.M. Seven main bearings. Hydraulic valve lifters. Carburetor: Rochester model G-7024009.

ENGINE (Opt. El Camino:C10/C20/C30/K10/K20/K30): V-type. OHV. Eight-cylinder. Cast iron block. Bore & stroke: 3⅞ in. x 3 in. Displacement: 283 cu. in. Compression ratio: 9.0:1. Brake horsepower: 175 at 4400 R.P.M. Max. Torque: 275 lb. ft. at 2400 R.P.M. Net horsepower: 145 at 4200 R.P.M. Five main bearings. Hydraulic valve lifters. Carburetor: Rochester model 2G-7023010.

ENGINE (Standard Series G10): Inline. OHV. Four-cylinder. Cast iron block. Bore & stroke: 3⅞ in. x 3¼ in. Displacement: 153.1 cu. in. Compression ratio: 8.5:1. Brake horsepower: 90 at 4000 R.P.M. Max. Torque: 152 lb. ft. at 2400 R.P.M. Net horsepower: 75 at 4000 R.P.M. Five main bearings. Hydraulic valve lifters. Carburetor: Rochester 1-Bbl. model 7020103.

ENGINE (Standard Corvair Series 95): Opposed. OHV. Six-cylinder. Aluminum block. Bore & stroke: 3.437 in. x 2.938 in. Displacement: 163.6 cu. in. Compression ratio: 8.25:1. Brake horsepower: 95 at 3600 R.P.M. Four main bearings. Hydraulic valve lifters. Carburetor: Two Rochester 1-Bbl. model 7019101.

ENGINE (Optional, Greenbrier): Opposed. OHV. Six-Cylinder. Aluminum block. Bore & Stroke: 3.437 in. x 2.938 in. Displacement: 163.6 cu. in. Compression ratio: 9.0:1. Brake horsepower: 110 at 3600 R.P.M. Four main bearings. Hydraulic valve lifters. Carburetor: Two Rochester single-barrel. (This engine available with 3- or 4-speed manual transmissions only).

ENGINE (Standard El Camino Opt. G10): Inline. OHV. Six-cylinder. Cast iron block. Bore & stroke: 3-9/16 in. x 3¼ in. Displacement: 194 cu. in. Compression ratio: 8.5:1. Brake horsepower: 120 at 4400 R.P.M. Max. Torque: 177 lb. ft. at 2400 R.P.M. Seven main bearings. Hydraulic valve lifters. Carburetor: Rochester 1-Bbl. model 7023105.

1964 Chevrolet Corvair Rampside Pickup (OCW)

ENGINE (Optional El Camino): V-type. OHV. Eight-cylinder. Cast iron block. Bore & stroke: 3.875 in. x 3.0 in. Displacement: 283 cu. in. Compression ratio: 9.25:1. Brake horsepower: 195 at 4800 R.P.M. Five main bearings. Hydraulic valve lifters. Carburetor: Rochester 2-Bbl. model 7024101.

ENGINE (Optional El Camino): V-type. OHV. Eight-cylinder. Cast iron block. Bore & stroke: 3.875 in. x 3.0 in. Displacement: 283 cu. in. Compression ratio: 9.25:1. Brake horsepower: 220 at 4800 R.P.M. Five main bearings. Hydraulic valve lifters. Carburetor: Rochester 4-Bbl.

CHASSIS (Series 95): Wheelbase: 95 in. Overall length: 179.7 in. Height: 68.5 in. Front tread: 58 in. Rear tread: 58 in. Tires: 7.00 x 14 in.

CHASSIS (Series C10/K10): Wheelbase: 115/127 in. Overall length: 206 (115 in. w.b.) Height: 71 in. Front tread: 63.1 in. Rear tread: 61.1 in.

CHASSIS (Series El Camino): Wheelbase: 115 in. Overall length: 198¼ in. Front tread: 58 in. Rear tread: 58 in. Tires: 7.00 x 14 in.

CHASSIS (Series C20): Wheelbase: 127 in. Height: 71 in. Front tread: 63.1 in. Rear tread: 61.1 in. Tires: 7 x 17.5 in.

CHASSIS (Series C30): Wheelbase: 133 in.

CHASSIS (Series P10): Wheelbase: 102 in. Tires: 6.70 x 15 in.

CHASSIS (Series P20): Wheelbase: 104 in. Tires: 7 x 17.5 in.

CHASSIS (Series G10): Wheelbase: 90 in. Tires: 6.50 x 13 in.

TECHNICAL: Manual, Chevrolet manufacture (Borg-Warner heavy duty 3 spd. opt.) 3F/1R. Column-mounted gear shift lever. Single dry plate clutch (9⅛" dia. El Camino 6-cyl - 10 in. dia. El Camino V-8). (½-Ton) semi-floating, (¾-Ton and 1-Ton) full-floating rear axle. Overall ratio: 3.73:1; opt. 3.07:1, 4.11:1 (4 spd.-3.73) El Camino 6-cyl. 3.36, V-8-3.08. Hydraulic drums, 11 x 2 in. (C-10, K-10), 11 x 2.75 in. (C-20), 12 x 2 in. (K-20), 9½ x 2 in. (F) El Camino, 9½ x 2½ in. (R) El Camino. Kelsey-Hayes pressed steel wheels. Technical options: Powerglide automatic transmission. Free-wheeling hubs (4-wd). Hand throttle. Borg-Warner h-d, 3 spd. transmission. 4 spd. transmission. Power steering ($75.35). Heavy-duty 70 amp battery $7.55. Auxiliary rear springs $26.90. No-spin differential $64.60. Overdrive $108. Heavy duty generator (Dekotron). Heavy-duty radiator. Sintered metallic brake linings (El Camino).

OPTIONS: Corvair (wholesale prices): Custom Equipment Group, includes windshield molding; door inserts; nylon-and-vinyl seat; two-tone doors and steering wheel; right visor; left door armrest; cigar lighter and dispatch box trim plate: R1205 w/std. seat ($17.56); R1205 w/full-length ($19.23); R1254 ($1923). Greenbrier Equipment Group, includes all above, plus chromed bumpers and hubcaps; all armrests; dome light; sport wheel cover and rear ash trays, R1206 only ($167.20). 110 H.P. engine ($20.90). Four-speed manual transmission ($71.10). Powerglide ($127.60). Gas heater ($71.10). Direct Air heater ($57.69). Manual radio ($37.22). Passenger car type tires: 7.00x14-4PR whitewall ($24.70); 7.00x14-6PR blackwall ($34.16); 7.00x14-6PR whitewall ($54.65); 7.00x14. Custom Chrome Trim: w/wheel covers ($16.75); w/o wheel

1964 Chevrolet Corvair 95 Van (OCW)

covers ($25.10). Two-tone paint: pickups ($25.10); all others ($20.90). Wheelcovers: R1205/1254 ($8.40); Greenbrier Custom ($6.73); std. Greenbrier ($8.40). Auxiliary seat, R1205 ($31.78). Full-width front seat, R1206 ($20.90). Third seat, R1206 ($41.80). Air cleaner ($5.06). Positraction ($29.30). Body doors, R1205/1206 ($62.70). Level pickup box floor, R1254 ($37.65). 35 amp. generator ($29.30). Laminated front glass ($4.20). Rear door glass ($10.07). Dual OSRV mirrors ($7.54). Left- or right-hand fixed mirror ($3.77). Wire-control OSRV mirror ($4.20). H-D shocks, exc. R1206 ($5.87). H-D front springs — includes H-D shocks — exc. R1206 ($8.40). Windshield washer and two-speed wipers ($12.55). **Light-Duty Trucks** (wholesale prices): 292 cu. in. six-cylinder ($75.25). 230 cu. in./120 h.p. six-cylinder in Step-Van ($50.20). 283 cu. in. V-8 in C models and K20s ($92.00). Powerglide w/H-D radiator ($146.30). Step-Van, Warner 3-speed manual trans. ($60 avg.). 4-speed manual trans. ($68 avg.). H-D battery ($5.87). Air cleaner w/"230" 6-cyl. ($5.06). Air cleaner w/"292" 6-cyl. ($1.72). Custom Appearance Group: C10/30 and K10 ($33.45); C10/20/30 and K10/20 ($40.13). No-Spin axle ($104.50). Positraction axle ($50.20). Vacuum power brakes ($35.12). Painted rear bumper ($16.75). Painted front bumper ($4.20). Spare wheel carrier (avg. $11). Custom chrome package (high price:$41.80). Custom Comfort package (high price: $42.66). Economy equipment ($5.87). Fuel filter ($5.87). Gauge package ($5.87). 42-amp. generator ($16.75). 55-amp. generator ($23.43). 62-amp. generator ($69.43). Laminated glass, exc. Step-Vans ($4.20). Soft-Ray windshield, exc. Carryall/Step-Van ($10.07). E-Z-Eye windshield, P10 ($15.08). Soft-Ray glass, all windows, exc. Step-Van ($11.74). E-Z-Eye windshield, P20/30 ($16.75). Soft-Ray glass, all Carryall windows, ($15.08). Deluxe heater/defroster, exc. Step-Van ($53.11). Std. heater and defroster, exc. Step-Van ($41.80). Towing hooks ($10.07). Free Wheeling hubs ($61.03). Lamp group ($20.90). Locks: right door ($1.29); side spare wheel($5.06); both ($5.87). 17-inch mirrors: left ($1.72); right-extended type ($3.77). 6x11 inch mirrors ($4.20 each). 7x16 inch mirrors ($12.55 each). C10 Custom side moldings ($25.10). Two-tone paint: pickup/cab ($12.55); Panel/Carryall ($20.90). 8-ft. platform body ($117.05). 9-ft. platform body ($142.15). 12-ft. platform body ($167.20). H-D radiator ($16.75). Radio ($37.22). Folding auxiliary seat for panel truck ($31.78). Bostrom seat, exc. Step-Vans (high-price $96.15). Tachometer ($37.65). Wipers and washers ($12.55). Plus, more.

1964 Chevrolet El Camino Sport Pickup (OCW)

HISTORICAL: Introduced September 29, 1963. Model year production: 523,791. Calendar year registrations: 483,853. Innovations: Compact van series introduced mid-year. El Camino reintroduced on Chevelle platform. New features of full-size trucks include self-adjusting brakes and 6,000 mile chassis lube intervals. Historical note: The 9 millionth Chevrolet truck of all time was produced this season. Model year output of Corvair trucks was 15,199 units. This included 6,201 Greenbrier Sport Wagons, which were merchandised as a station wagon in the car-line and had a price of $2,666 and weight of 2,990 pounds.

Pricing

1964	5	4	3	2	1
El Camino					
Sport Pickup	1200	2460	4100	5700	8200
Custom Sport Pickup	1300	2550	4250	5900	8500
Corvair Series 95					
Loadside	590	1170	1950	2700	3900
Rampside	630	1250	2100	3000	4200
Corvan Series					
Panel Van	570	1140	1900	2650	3800
Greenbrier Sportvan	680	1350	2250	3150	4500
Fleetside Pickups					
C10 Short Box Pickup	1180	2370	3950	5500	7900
C10 Long Box Pickup	1170	2340	3900	5450	7800
K10 Short Box Pickup	1150	2310	3850	5400	7700
K10 Long Box Pickup	1140	2280	3800	5300	7600
C20 Long Box Pickup	980	1950	3250	4550	6500
K20 Long Box Pickup	930	1860	3100	4350	6200

NOTES:
"C" is conventional drive model.
"K" is four-wheel drive (4x4) model.
"10" is ½-ton series.
"20" is ¾-ton series.
"30" is one-ton series. "Short box" is 6½ ft. bed.
"Long box" is 8 ft. bed.

Stepside Pickups	5	4	3	2	1
C10 Short Box Pickup	1180	2370	3950	5450	7800
C10 Long Box Pickup	1150	2310	3850	5400	7700
K10 Short Box Pickup	1140	2280	3800	5300	7600
K10 Long Box Pickup	1130	2250	3750	5250	7500
C20 Long Box Pickup	960	1920	3200	4500	6400
C30 Pickup-8½-ft. bed	900	1800	3000	4200	6000
G10 Chevy Van Series					
Panel Van	630	1250	2100	3000	4200
Step Van Series					
P10 Walk-In	590	1170	1950	2700	3900
P20 Walk-In	600	1200	2000	2800	4000
P30 Walk-In	620	1230	2050	2900	4100
Panel/Suburban/Stake-Bed					
C10 Panel	570	1140	1900	2650	3800
C10 Suburban	750	1500	2500	3500	5000
K10 Panel	530	1050	1750	2450	3500
K10 Suburban	720	1450	2400	3300	4800
C20 Stake	530	1050	1750	2450	3500
C30 Panel-10½ ft.	540	1080	1800	2500	3600
C30 Stake	540	1080	1800	2500	3600

NOTE: 1955-up prices based on top of the line models.

1965 CHEVROLET

1965 Chevrolet Fleetside Pickup w/cus. whls. (DFW)

LIGHT TRUCK — 1965 SERIES — (ALL ENGINES): — The all-new, intermediate-sized El Camino had a new grille with a finer pattern and heavier horizontal center bar. Chevrolet's red, white and blue emblem was in the bar's mid-section. The front bumper was now slotted with the parking lamps being relocated to the long, horizontal slots. An AM/FM radio and simulated wire wheels were among new options. V-8 badges, on models so-equipped, were moved ahead of the front wheel cutouts.

The pickup/panel/suburban body was mostly unchanged, except for repositioning the I.D. badges high up on the cowl sides, above the main feature line (on '64s and '66s they were lower). Standard models still had painted bumpers, grilles and hubcaps. Heading the option list, this year, was a new factory air conditioning system. A new 327 cubic inch V-8 was available in some trucks, too. An auxiliary hot water heater was available for the rear compartment of Suburban Carry-Alls. In mid-year, a truck camper package (with chassis beefed-up for camper use) was released.

Chevy Vans and Step-Vans looked just like last year's models. The Chevy Van had an optional 230 cubic inch, 140 horsepower six replacing the smaller 120 horsepower offering.

I.D. DATA: Serial number stamped on plate mounted on windshield corner post — driver's side. Starting: example: 1445 ( ) 100001 and up (pickups) G-1255 ( ) 100001 and up (G-series vans) Engine numbers located 4-/6-cyl.: stamped on right side of block next to distributor. V-8: stamped on forward edge of block, protruding from under right cylinder head.

Model	Body Type	Price	Weight	Prod. Total
El Camino Series				
13380	Pickup (6-cyl.)	2272	2925	—
13480	Pickup (V-8)	2380	3060	—
13580	Custom Pickup (6-cyl.)	2353	2935	—
13680	Custom Pickup (V-8)	2461	3060	—
Fleetside Models				
Series C10				
C1434	½-Ton 115 in. w.b.	2023	3205	—
C1534	½-Ton 127 in. w.b.	2060	3315	—
Series K10				
K1434	½-Ton 4x4 115 in. w.b.	2675	—	—
K1534	½-Ton 4x4 127 in. w.b.	2712	—	—
Series C20				
C2534	¾-Ton 127 in. w.b.	2209	3705	—
Series K20				
K2534	¾-Ton 4x4 127 in. w.b.	2861	—	—

Model	Body Type	Price	Weight	Prod. Total
Stepside Models				
Series C10				
C1404	½-Ton 115 in. w.b.	2007	3190	—
C1504	½-Ton 127 in. w.b.	2044	3300	—
Series K10				
K1404	½-Ton 4x4 115 in. w.b.	2659	—	—
K1504	½-Ton 4x4 127 in. w.b.	2696	—	—
Series C20				
C2504	¾-Ton 127 in. w.b.	2192	3680	—
Series K20				
K2504	¾-Ton 127 in. w.b.	2844	—	—
Series C30				
C3604	1-Ton 133 in. w.b.	2370	3920	—

115 in. w.b. = 6½ ft. box
127 in. w.b. = 8 ft. box
133 in. w.b. = 9 ft. box

Model	Body Type	Price	Weight	Prod. Total
Van/Panel Models				
Series G12				
G1205	Panel	2105	2610	—
G1206	Sportvan	2355	2870	—
G1226	Sportvan Custom	2492	2970	—
G1236	Sportvan Deluxe	2717	3115	—
Series P10				
P1345	½-Ton Panel Step-Van	2518	3480	—
Series P20				
P2345	¾-Ton Step Van	3122	4830	—
Series P30				
P3345	1-Ton Panel Step Van	3314	5040	—
Series C10 — 115 in. w.b.				
C1405	½-Ton Panel (7½ ft.) w.b. 2-dr.	2324	3420	—
C1406	½-Ton Suburban	2630	3710	—
Series K10 — 115 in. w.b.				
K1405	½-Ton 4x4 Panel	2976	—	—
K1406	½-Ton 4x4 Suburban	3328	—	—
Series C-30				
C3605	1-Ton Panel 133 in. w.b. 2-dr.	2795	4250	—
Additional Body Choices				
C1403	½-Ton Ch-Cab 115 in. w.b.	1894	2830	—
C1503	½-Ton Ch-Cab 127 in. w.b.	—	—	—
C2503	¾-Ton Ch-Cab 127 in. w.b.	2079	3240	—
C2509	¾-Ton Stake 8'	2284	3870	—
C3609	1-Ton Stake 9'	2483	4255	—

ENGINE (P-10): Inline. OHV. Four-cylinder. Cast iron block. Bore & stroke: 3⅞ in. x 3¼ in. Displacement: 153.3 cu. in. Compression ratio: 8.5:1. Brake horsepower: 90 at 4400 R.P.M. Max. Torque: 152 lb.-ft. at 2400 R.P.M. Net horsepower: 75 at 4000 R.P.M. Five main bearings. Hydraulic valve lifters. Carburetor: Rochester 1-Bbl. model 7020103.

ENGINE (Standard: Sportvan/P20/P30/C10/C20/C30/K10/K20/ K30, Optional: G1205/G1206/G1226/El Camino-$27): Inline. OHV. Six-cylinder. Cast iron block. Bore & stroke: 3⅞ in. x 3¼ in. Displacement: 230 cu. in. Compression ratio: 8.5:1. Brake horsepower: 140 at 4400 R.P.M. Max. Torque: 220 lb.-ft. at 1600 R.P.M. Net horsepower: 120 at 3600 R.P.M. Seven main bearings. Hydraulic valve lifters. Carburetor: Rochester 1-Bbl. model B-7023017.

ENGINE (Optional C/10/C20/C30/K10/K20/K30-$97): Inline. OHV. Six-cylinder. Cast iron block. Bore & stroke: 3⅞ in. x 4⅛ in. Displacement: 292 cu. in. Compression ratio: 8.0:1. Brake horsepower: 170 at 4000 R.P.M. Max. Torque: 275 lb.-ft. at 1600 R.P.M. Net horsepower: 153 at 3600 R.P.M. Seven main bearings. Hydraulic valve lifters. Carburetor: Rochester model B-7024009.

ENGINE (Optional El Camino/C10/C20/C30/K10/K20/K30): V-type. OHV. Eight-cylinder. Cast iron block. Bore & stroke: 3⅞ in. x 3 in. Displacement: 283 cu. in. Compression ratio: 9.25:1. Brake horsepower: El Camino 195 at 4800 R.P.M., all others 175 at 4400 R.P.M. Five main bearings. Hydraulic valve lifters. Carburetor: Rochester 2-Bbl. model 7024101.

ENGINE (Optional El Camino, RPO L-30-$95): V-type. OHV. Eight-cylinder. Cast iron block. Bore & stroke: 4 in. x 3¼ in. Displacement: 327 cu. in. Compression ratio: 10.5:1. Brake horsepower: 250 at 4400 R.P.M. Max. Torque: 350 lb. ft. at 2800 R.P.M. Five main bearings. Hydraulic valve lifters. Carburetor: Rochester 4-Bbl.

1965 Chevrolet El Camino (DFW)

ENGINE (Standard El Camino/G1205/G1206/G1226): Inline. OHV. Six-cylinder. Cast iron block. Bore & stroke: 3-9/16 in. x 3¼ in. Displacement: 194 cu. in. Compression ratio: 8.5:1. Brake horsepower: 120 at 4400 R.P.M. Max. torque: 177 lb. ft. at 2400 R.P.M. Seven main bearings. Hydraulic valve lifters. Carburetor: Rochester 1-Bbl. model 7023105.

ENGINE (Optional El Camino): V-type. OHV. Eight-cylinder. Cast iron block. Bore & stroke: 4 in. x 3¼ in. Displacement: 327 cu. in. Compression ratio: 10.5:1. Brake horsepower: 300 at 5000 R.P.M. Max. torque: 360 lb. ft. at 3200 R.P.M. Five main bearings. Hydraulic valve lifters. Carburetor: Rochester 4-Bbl.

CHASSIS (El Camino 5000): Wheelbase: 115 in. Overall length: 197 in. Front tread: 58 in. Rear tread: 58 in. Tires: 7.35 x 14 in.

CHASSIS (Series C10/K10): Wheelbase: 115/127 in. Overall length: 206 (115 in. w.b.) in. Height: 71 in. Front tread: 63.1 in. Rear tread: 61.1 in. Tires: 7.75 x 15 in.

CHASSIS (Series P10): Wheelbase: 102 in. Tires: 7.75 x 15 in.

CHASSIS (Series C20): Wheelbase: 127 in. Tires: 7 x 17.5 in.

CHASSIS (Series C30): Wheelbase: 133 in. Tires: 8 x 17.5 in.

CHASSIS (Series P20): Wheelbase: 104 in. Tires: 7.75 x 15 in.

CHASSIS (Series G12): Wheelbase: 90 in. Tires: 6.50 x 13 in.

TECHNICAL: Manual, Chevrolet manufacture. Speeds: 3F/1R. Column-mounted gear shift lever. Single dry plate clutch. El Camino 9½ in. (6-cyl.); 10 in. (V-8). (½-Ton) semi-floating; (¾-Ton and 1-Ton) full-floating rear axle. Overall ratio: El Camino 3.36 (6-cyl.); 3.08 (V-8). Hydraulic 11 x 2 in. (C10/K10); 11 x 2.75 in. (C20); 12 x 2 in. (K20); 9½ x 2½ in. (F) El Camino, 9½ x 2 in (R) El Camino. Kelsey-Hayes pressed steel wheels. Options: Powerglide automatic transmission $188. Free-wheeling hubs (4x4). Borg-Warner heavy-duty, 3-spd. transmission. 4-spd. transmission. Power steering ($86). Heavy-duty 70 amp battery. Auxiliary rear springs. No-spin differential. Overdrive $108. Power brakes.

OPTIONS: 293 cu. in. V-8 ($92). 292 cu. in. 6-cyl. $75.25. Oil bath air cleaner ($5.06). Positraction ($50.20). No-Spin rear axle ($104.50). Rear axle, 3.07:1 ratio, w/stick ($10.07). Rear axle, 4.11:1 ratio, w/stick ($6.73). H-D battery ($5.87). Painted rear bumper on pickups with painted front bumper ($16.75). H-D 11 in. clutch with 6-cyl. only ($4.20). Custom Appearance option: panels ($33.45); others ($40.13). Custom Chrome option: pickups with chrome front bumper ($16.75); pickups with two chrome bumpers ($41.80); panels with two chrome bumpers ($25.10). Custom Comfort option, panels ($9.21); other trucks ($42.66). Fleetside Custom side moldings ($25.10). Delcotrons: 42-amp ($16.75); 52-amp ($23.43). Tinted glass ($11.74). Tinted windshield ($10.07). Deluxe heater ($53.11). Thrift-Air heater ($41.80). OSRV mirrors: 17¼ in. left, except panel ($1.72); right, except panel ($3.77); 6¼ in. right ($3.77). Tutone paint: panels ($20.90); other trucks ($12.55). H-D radiator, except w/Powerglide ($16.75). Radio ($37.22). Auxiliary panel truck seat ($31.78). Foam seat ($16.75). H-D front shocks (avg. $6). H-D rear shocks ($6.73). H-D front springs, C2500 ($2.53). H-D rear springs, all ($5.06). H-D three-speed transmission: C1400 ($58.55); C1500 ($62.70) and C2500 ($71.10). H-D four-speed transmission: C1400 ($62.70); C1500 ($66.90) and C2500 ($75.25). Powerglide, all ($146.30). Full-View rear window, except panel ($33.45). Two-speed windshield washers and wipers ($12.55).

HISTORICAL: Introduced: September 24, 1964. Model year production: 619,685. Calendar year registrations: 567, 473. Calendar year factory shipments by GVW class: (6000-lbs. and less) 427,100; (6001-10,000 lbs. 111,600. Retail sales: 574,120 units (up 15.6 percent). Innovations: Larger six-cylinder engine for vans. 327 cubic inch V-8 released. New truck-camper options. First year for factory air conditioning. Historical notes: Chevy showcased the Turbo Titan III, a gas-turbine powered experimental truck in 1965, calling it the "Truck of Tommorrow." The 1965 Chevrolet commercial vehicles were advertised as "Work Power" trucks. This was an all-time record season for America's number one truck-maker and the first in which registrations broke the 500,000 level. Chevrolet claimed that, by the end of 1965, there were 4,751,127 Chevrolet trucks operating in the United States.

Pricing

	5	4	3	2	1
1965					
El Camino					
Spt. P.U.	1200	2460	4100	5700	8200
Cust. Spt. P.U.	1300	2550	4250	5900	8500
Fleetside Pickups					
C-10 P.U. (short box)	1180	2370	3950	5500	7900
C-10 P.U. (long box)	1170	2340	3900	5450	7800
K-10 P.U. (short box)	1150	2310	3850	5400	7700
K-10 P.U. (long box)	1140	2280	3800	5300	7600
C-20 P.U. (long box)	980	1950	3250	4550	6500
K-20 P.U. (long box)	930	1860	3100	4350	6200

NOTE: "C" is conventional drive model. "K" is four-wheel drive (4x4) model. "10" is ½-ton series. "20" is ¾-ton series. "30" is one-ton series. "Short box" is 6½ ft. bed. "Long box" is 8 ft. bed.

	5	4	3	2	1
Stepside Pickups					
C-10 P.U. (short box)	1180	2370	3950	5450	7800
C-10 P.U. (long box)	1150	2310	3850	5400	7700
K-10 P.U. (short box)	1140	2280	3800	5300	7600
K-10 P.U. (long box)	1130	2250	3750	5250	7500
C-20 P.U. (long box)	960	1920	3200	4500	6400
C-30 P.U. (8½ ft. bed)	900	1800	3000	4200	6000
G-12 Chevy Van Series					
Panel Van	600	1200	2000	2800	4000
Spt. Van	620	1230	2050	2900	4100
Cust. Spt. Van	630	1250	2100	3000	4200
DeL. Spt. Van	650	1300	2150	3050	4300
Step Van Series					
P-10 Panel	590	1170	1950	2700	3900
P-20 Panel	600	1200	2000	2800	4000
P-30 Panel	620	1230	2050	2900	4100
Panel/Suburban/Stake-Bed					
C-10 Panel	570	1140	1900	2650	3800
C-10 Suburban	750	1500	2500	3500	5000
K-10 Panel	530	1050	1750	2450	3500
K-10 Suburban	720	1450	2400	3300	4800
C-20 Stake	530	1050	1750	2450	3500
C-30 Panel	540	1080	1800	2500	3600
C-30 Stake	540	1080	1800	2500	3600
Corvan Series					
Greenbriar Sportvan	680	1350	2250	3150	4500

* Greenbriar remained available through 1965.

NOTE: 1955-up prices based on top of the line models.

1966 CHEVROLET

1966 Chevrolet El Camino (DFW)

LIGHT TRUCK — 1966 SERIES — (ALL ENGINES): — This was the final year for the Pickup bodies introduced in 1960. The side emblem was moved to the same position as on the 1964 models.

Horizontal bars ran across the fine-finned an all-new Chevelle body was used for the El Camino. It had a slanted front end. The new grille was lower and wider. The front fenders had a wraparound design. There were new wheel covers, too. Options ranged from the standard model to a Custom trim level and the high-performance "SS" (Super Sport) package. The latter featured a blacked-out grille and "power bulge" type hood.

The Chevy van series lost its original four-cylinder engine. Carryover models included the panel, Sport and Custom vans. A new option was the Deluxe Sportvan. There was also a new pop-up camper option.

Standard equipment on all light-duties, effective this season, included seat belts, dual "long-arm" mirrors, two-speed wiper washers and backup lamps.

I.D. DATA: Serial number stamped on plate mounted on windshield corner post on driver's side. Starting: C-1446 ( ) 100001 and up (C series pickups), G-1256 ( ) 100001 and up (Vans). Engine numbers located 4-cyl./6-cyl.: stamped on right side of block, next to distributor; V-8s: stamped on forward edge of block, protruding from under right cylinder head.

Model	Body Type	Price	Weight	Prod. Total
El Camino Series				
13380	Pickup 6-cyl.	2318	2930	—
13480	Pickup V-8	2426	3075	—
13580	Custom Pickup 6-cyl.	2396	2930	—
13680	Custom pickup V-8	2504	3075	—
Fleetside Models				
Series C10				
C1434	½-Ton 115 in. w.b.	2066	3220	57,386
C1534	½-Ton 127 in. w.b.	2104	3225	178,752

Model	Body Type	Price	Weight	Prod. Total
Series K10				
K1434	½-Ton 4x4 115 in. w.b.	2718	—	678
K1534	½-Ton 4x4 127 in. w.b.	2756	—	1,976
Series C20				
C2534	¾-Ton 127 in. w.b.	2252	3700	55,855
Series K20				
K2534	¾-Ton 4x4 127 in. w.b.	2904	—	1,796
Stepside Models				
Series C10				
C1404	½-Ton 115 in. w.b.	2050	3195	59,947
C1504	½-Ton 127 in. w.b.	2087	3290	26,456
Series K10				
K1404	½-Ton 4x4 115 in. w.b.	2702	—	1,123
K1504	½-Ton 4x4 127 in. w.b.	2739	—	457
Series C20				
C2504	¾-Ton 127 in. w.b.	2236	3700	9,905
Series K20				
K2504	¾-Ton 4x4 127 in. w.b.	2888	—	924
Series C30				
C3604	1-Ton 133 in. w.b.	2414	3930	3,646
Cab and Chassis				
C1403	½-Ton 115 in. w.b.	1927	2835	3,030
C2503	¾-Ton 127 in. w.b.	2112	3265	6,520
C3603	1-Ton 133 in. w.b.	2269	3455	11,852
115 in. w.b. = 6½ ft. box				
127 in. w.b. = 8 ft. box				
133 in. w.b. = 9 ft. box				
Van, Panel and Stake Models				
Series G12				
G1205	Panel 2-dr.	2141	2755	28,180
G1206	Sportvan 2-dr.	2388	2965	4,209
G1226	Sportvan Custom 2-dr.	2521	3065	2,673
G1236	Sportvan Deluxe 2-dr.	2747	3125	2,341
Series P10				
P1335	½-Ton Panel 2-dr.	2658	3480	3,202
Series P20				
P2345	¾-Ton Panel 2-dr.	3237	4835	192
Series P30				
P3345	1-Ton Panel 2-dr.	3432	5040	61
Series C10 — ½-Ton — 115 in. w.b.				
C1403	Chassis & Cab	1927	2835	3,030
C1405	Panel Delivery	2361	3420	
C1406	Suburban (Doors)	2598	3710	6,717
Series K10 — ½-Ton — 115 in. w.b. — (4x4)				
K1403	Chassis & Cab	2579	—	40
K1405	Panel Delivery	3013	—	170
K1406	Suburban (Doors)	3250	—	530
Series C20 — ¾-Ton — 127 in. w.b.				
C2503	Chassis & Cab	2112	3265	6,520
C2509	8-ft. Platform Stake	2328	3890	1,499
Series C30 — 1-Ton — 133 in. w.b.				
C3603	Chassis & Cab	2269	3455	11,852
C3605	10½-ft. Panel Delivery	2832	4265	3,560
C3609	9-ft. Platform Stake	2527	4285	3,651

NOTE 1: Production totals from Chevrolet records are for model-year through August 5, 1966 and include all trucks built in U.S. factories for domestic/export/Canadian markets.

ADDITIONAL PRODUCTION: (C10) Model C1412 cowl w/windshield (10); Model C1402 cowl less windshield (15); Model C1416 End-gate Suburban (5334). Model C1503 Chassis & Cab (1155). **(K10)** Model K1416 End-gate Suburban (418). Model K1503 Chassis & cab (30). **(P10)** Model P1342 Chassis (107).

ENGINE (Std. Series P10/G12/El Camino): Inline. OHV. Six-cylinder. Cast iron block. Bore & stroke: 3-9/16 in. x 3¼ in. Displacement: 194 cu. in. Compression ratio: 8.5:1. Brake horsepower: 120 at 4400 R.P.M. Max. Torque: 220 lb. ft. at 1600 R.P.M. Seven main bearings. Hydraulic valve lifters. Carburetor: Rochester 1-Bbl. model 7023105.

ENGINE (Std. G1236/Opt. other G-12/and El Camino): Inline. OHV. Six-cylinder. Cast iron block. Bore & stroke: 3⅞ in. x 3¼ in. Displacement: 230 cu. in. Compression ratio: 8.5:1. Brake horsepower: 140 at 4400 R.P.M. Max. Torque: 220 lb. ft. at 1600 R.P.M. Net horsepower: 120 at 3600 R.P.M. Seven main bearings. Hydraulic valve lifters. Carburetor: Rochester 1-Bbl. model B-7023017.

ENGINE (Std. C10/K10/P20/C20/K20/P30/C30): Inline. OHV. Six-cylinder. Cast iron block. Bore & stroke: 3.875 in. x 3.53 in. Displacement: 250 cu. in. Compression ratio: 8.5:1. Brake horsepower: 155 at 4200 R.P.M. Seven main bearings. Hydraulic valve lifters. Carburetor: Downdraft 2-Bbl.

ENGINE (Opt. C10/C20/C30/K): Inline. OHV. Six-cylinder. Cast iron block. Bore & stroke: 3⅞ in. x 4½ in. Displacement: 292 cu. in. Compression ratio: 8.0:1. Brake horsepower: 170 at 4000 R.P.M. Max. Torque: 275 lb. ft. at 1600 R.P.M. Net horsepower: 153 at 3600 R.P.M. Seven main bearings. Hydraulic valve lifters. Carburetor: Rochester model B-7024009.

ENGINE (Opt. El Camino/C10/C20/C30/K): V-type. OHV. Eight-cylinder. Cast iron block. Bore & stroke: 3⅞ in. x 3 in. Displacement: 283 cu. in. Compression ratio: 9.25:1. Brake horsepower: 195 at 4800 R.P.M. Max. Torque: 285 lb. ft. at 2400 R.P.M. Five main bearings. Hydraulic valve lifters. Carburetor: Rochester 2-Bbl. model 7024101.

ENGINE (Opt. El Camino/C10/C20/C30): V-type. OHV. Eight-cylinder. Cast iron block. Bore & stroke: 4 in. x 3¼ in. Displacement: 327 cu. in. Compression ratio: 9.25:1. Brake horsepower: 220 at 4400 R.P.M. Max. Torque: 320 lb. ft. at 2800 R.P.M. Five main bearings. Hydraulic valve lifters. Carburetor: Rochester 4-Bbl. model 4G.

ENGINE (Opt. El Camino): V-type. OHV. Eight-cylinder. Cast iron block. Bore & stroke: 4 in. x 3¼ in. Displacement: 327 cu. in. Brake horsepower: 275 at 4800 R.P.M. Max. Torque: 355 lb. ft. at 3200 R.P.M. Five main bearings. Hydraulic valve lifters. Carburetor: Rochester 4-Bbl.

ENGINE (Opt. El Camino): V-type. OHV. Eight-cylinder. Cast iron block. Bore & stroke: 4.094 in. x 3.76 in. Displacement: 396 cu. in. Compression ratio: 10.25:1. Brake horsepower: 325 at 4800 R.P.M. Max. Torque: 410 lb. ft. at 3200 R.P.M. Five main bearings. Hydraulic valve lifters. Carburetor: Downdraft 4-Bbl.

ENGINE (Opt. El Camino): V-type. OHV. Eight-cylinder. Cast iron block. Bore & stroke: 4.094 in. x 3.76 in. Displacement: 396 cu. in. Compression ratio: 10.25:1. Brake horsepower: 360 at 5200 R.P.M. Max. Torque: 420 lb. ft. at 3600 R.P.M. Five main bearings. Hydraulic valve lifters. Carburetor: 4-Bbl.

CHASSIS (G12): Wheelbase: 90 in. Tires: 6.50 x 13 in.

CHASSIS (El Camino): Wheelbase: 115 in. Overall length: 197 in. Front tread: 58 in. Rear tread: 58 in. Tires: 7.35 x 14 in.

CHASSIS (Series P10): Wheelbase: 102 in. Tires: 7.75 x 15 in.

CHASSIS (Series C10/K10): Wheelbase: 115/127 in. Overall length: 206 (115 in. w.b.) Height: 71 in. Front tread: 63.1 in. Rear tread: 61.1 in. Tires: 7.75 x 15 in.; (Suburban) 8.15 x 15 in.

CHASSIS (Series C20/K20): Wheelbase: 127 in. Tires: 7 x 17.5 in.

CHASSIS (Series C30): Wheelbase: 133 in. Tires: 8 x 17.5 in.

TECHNICAL: Manual transmission. Speeds: 3F/1R. Column-mounted gear shift lever. Single dry plate clutch. Rear axle:(½-Ton) semi-floating; (¾-Ton and 1-Ton) full-floating rear axle. Overall ratio: El Camino: (6-cyl.) 3.36; (V-8) 3.08 or (396 V-8) 3.07. Four-wheel hydraulic brakes. Kelsey-Hayes pressed steel wheels. Technical options: Powerglide. Overdrive. Free-wheeling hubs with 4x4. Borg-Warner H-D three-speed transmission. Four-speed transmission. Power steering. H-D 70-amp. battery. Auxiliary rear springs. No-Spin differential. H-D clutch. Temperature-controlled radiator fan. 61-amp. and 62-amp. Delcotron.

OPTIONS: Rear bumper. Bumper guards. Radio (manual and push-button) AM/FM. Heater. Clock. Cigar lighter. Seat covers. Gauge package. Four-season air conditioning. Spare tire carrier. Custom Comfort Package. Full view rear cab window. El Camino Options: Custom seat belts. Tinted glass. Tri-volume electric horn. Statro-Ease headrests. Highway emergency kit. Transistorized ignition system. Automatic level control. Spare tire lock. Strato bucket seats. Sport walnut-grained steering wheel. Comfortilt steering wheel. Electric tachometer. Special front and rear suspension. Bright metal wheel covers. Mag-styled wheel covers. Simulated wheel covers.

HISTORICAL: Model year production: (all Chevy trucks) 621,354. Model Year Output by category/wheelbase: (Light-Duty/90 in. w.b.) 37,403; (Light-Duty/115 in. w.b.) 140,783; (4x4 Light-Duty/115 in. w.b.) 2,959; (4x4 Light-Duty/127 in. w.b.) 2,463; (Forward-Control/½-ton) 3,309; (¾-ton/127 in. w.b.) 73,825; (¾-ton 4x4/127 in. w.b.) 3,151; (Forward-Control/¾-ton) 4,793; (1-ton conventional/133 in. w.b.) 23,223; (1-ton Forward-Control/157 in. w.b.) 7,032. Light-Duty model year output by marketing category: (Domestic) 461,774; (U.S. built for export) 11,120; (U.S. built for Canada) 31,885; (Total) 504,779. Innovations: Safety equipment made standard in light-duty trucks. Expanded heavy-duty line made available. Historical note: Chevy clinched its 10 millionth truck sale, of all-time, this season.

Pricing

	5	4	3	2	1
1966					
El Camino					
Sport Pickup	1200	2400	4000	5600	8000
Custom Sport Pickup	1200	2460	4100	5700	8200
Fleetside Pickups Series C10/C20					
C14 Pickup (short box)	1180	2370	3950	5500	7900
C15 Pickup (long box)	1170	2340	3900	5450	7800
K14 Pickup (short box)	1150	2310	3850	5400	7700
K15 Pickup (long box)	1140	2280	3800	5300	7600
C25 Pickup (long box)	980	1950	3250	4550	6500
K25 Pickup (long box)	930	1860	3100	4350	6200
NOTE:					

"C" is conventional drive.
"K" is 4x4.
"14" is ½-ton short box (6½ ft. bed).
"15" is ½-ton long box (8 ft. bed).
"25" is ¾-ton.
"36" is 1-ton.

	5	4	3	2	1
Stepside Pickups Series C10/C20/C30					
C14 Pickup (short box)	1180	2370	3950	5450	7800
C15 Pickup (long box)	1150	2310	3850	5400	7700
K14 Pickup (short box)	1140	2280	3800	5300	7600
K15 Pickup (long box)	1130	2250	3750	5250	7500
C25 Pickup (long box)	960	1920	3200	4500	6400
K25 Pickup (long box)	920	1850	3050	4300	6100
1-Ton Pickup (8½ ft. bed)	900	1800	3000	4200	6000
Chevy Van Series					
G12 Panel Van	600	1200	2000	2800	4000
G12 Sportvan	620	1230	2050	2900	4100
G12 Custom Sportvan	630	1250	2100	3000	4200
G12 Deluxe Sportvan	650	1300	2150	3050	4300

	5	4	3	2	1
Step Van Series					
P10 Panel	590	1170	1950	2700	3900
P20 Panel	600	1200	2000	2800	4000
P30 Panel	620	1230	2050	2900	4100
Panel/Suburban/Stake-Bed					
C14 Panel	570	1140	1900	2650	3800
C14 Suburban	750	1500	2500	3500	5000
K14 Panel	530	1050	1750	2450	3500
K14 Suburban	720	1450	2400	3300	4800
C25 Stake	530	1050	1750	2450	3500
C36 Panel	540	1080	1800	2500	3600
C36 Stake	540	1080	1800	2500	3600

NOTE: 1955-up prices based on top of the line models.

1967 CHEVROLET

1967 Chevrolet El Camino (DFW)

LIGHT TRUCK — 1967 SERIES — (ALL ENGINES): — The 1967 truck-line was described by Chevrolet as possessing "the most significant cab and sheet metal styling change in Chevrolet history." The new styling reflected the importance of an attractive appearance in the light-duty truck field, as more and more were purchased for personal transportation and camper use. The major styling themes on the pickup combined an inner slant above the beltline with a side body molding nearly dividing the wheel wells into equal sections. The front end was very attractive with single headlights recessed into square receptacles at either end of a grille with a single wide center bar.

The 1967 Chevrolet truck's front sheet metal also featured greatly improved protection against corrosion. The use of smooth surfaced, undercoated, full fender skirts protected the fenders and other sheet metal from mud, water and salt. In addition, minimal use of coach joints and liberal use of spot weld sealers provided additional corrosion resistance.

All cab and pickups up to one-ton were available with an optional Custom Sport Truck package that included full-carpeting, bucket seats, extensive interior and exterior bright trim, chrome front bumper undercoating and a CST emblem on the doors.

The El Camino was restyled with wraparound taillights and new radiator grille, front bumpers, fenders and hood panel.

This year's Suburban was changed in that there were now three side doors, one on the driver's side and two on the passenger side. It was, however, still available with a choice of double panel rear doors or and endgate.

Chevy's Van-line had a more rounded configuration with a larger windshield. Added to the Chevy Van and Sportvan series were 108 inch wheelbase models in ½- and ¾-ton ratings. Their bodies were 18 inches longer than the 90 inch wheelbase models, which were continued. An additional 12 models with V-8 engines were offered in the Chevy Van and Sportvan series. Replacing the 194 cubic inch six was the 230 cubic inch six. The 250 cubic inch six was optional.

I.D. DATA: Combination GVW and serial number plate located on left door hinge pillar. The VIN consists of twelve symbols. The first (letter) identifies the chassis. The second (letter) designates the engine. The third (digit) indicates the model type. The model year is identified by the fifth (digit). The sixth (letter) identifies the assembly plant. The last six digits are the production sequence numbers. For example: GS-157 (   ) 10001 and up. The engine number indicated the manufacturing plant, month and day of manufacture and transmission type. On 6-cyl. engines the number is located on pad at right side of cylinder block at rear of distributor. For V-8 engines it is located on pad at front right side of cylinder block. Example: F1210FA=(F=Flint manufacture, 12=December, 10=tenth day, FA=transmission and engine type.)

Model	Body Type	Price	Weight	Prod. Total
El Camino Series — ½-Ton — (V-8)				
13480	Pickup	2613	3193	—
13680	Custom Pickup	2694	3210	—
Fleetside Models				
Series C10 — ½-Ton				
CS10734	Pickup 115 in. w.b.	2371	3333	43,940
CS10934	Pickup 127 in. w.b.	2408	3440	165,973
Series K10 — ½-Ton — (4x4)				
KS10734	Pickup 115 in. w.b.	—	—	1046
KS10934	Pickup 127 in. w.b.	—	—	2715

Model	Body Type	Price	Weight	Prod. Total
Series C20 — ¾-Ton				
CS20934	Pickup 127 in. w.b.	2550	3848	50,413
CS21034	Pickup 127 in. w.b. (8½' box)	2614	—	—
Series K20 — ¾-Ton — (4x4)				
KS20934	Pickup 127 in. w.b.	—	—	2773
KS21034	Pickup 127 in. w.b. (8½' box)	—	—	—
Series C30 — One-Ton				
CS31034	Pickup 133 in. w.b. (8½' box)	2755	—	See Note
Stepside Models				
Series C10 — ½-Ton				
CS10704	Pickup 115 in. w.b.	2333	3255	45,606
CS10904	Pickup 127 in. w.b.	2371	3345	19,969
Series C20 — ¾-Ton				
CS20904	Pickup 127 in. w.b.	2513	3753	7859
Series K20 — ¾-Ton (4x4)				
KS20904	Pickup 127 in. w.b.	—	—	872
Series C30 — One-Ton				
CS31004	Pickup 133 in. w.b. (9' box)	2695	3995	4026
Cab and Chassis				
CS10703	½-Ton 115 in. w.b.	2223	2914	2790
CS20903	¾-Ton 127 in. w.b.	2403	3346	6320
CS31003	1-Ton 133 in. w.b.	2561	3556	11,304

Note 1: 115 in. w.b. = 6½-ft. box
Note 2: 127 in. w.b. = 8-ft. box (except as noted)

Model	Body Type	Price	Weight	Prod. Total
Van, Panel and Stake Models				
Chevy Van 10 — ½-Ton — 90 in. w.b.				
GS11005	Panel	2331	2849	17,956
GS11006	Sportvan	2571	3035	2398
GS11026	Custom Sportvan	2699	3138	777
GS11036	DeLuxe Sportvan	2890	3174	535
Series P10				
PS10535	Step-Van 10 (102 in. w.b.)	2864	3559	2374
Chevy Van 20 — ¾-Ton - 108 in. w.b.				
GS21305	Panel	2618	3109	6013
GS21306	Sportvan	2848	3241	930
GS21326	Custom Sportvan	2975	3365	501
GS21336	DeLuxe Sportvan	3166	3409	508
Series P20				
PS20835	Step-Van (125-133")	3626	4970	203
PT30835	10' Step-Van (125") diesel	5648	5931	10
Series C10 — ½-Ton — 115 in. w.b.				
CS10905	Panel	2742	3502	3827
CS10906	Suburban	2986	3670	5164
Series C20 — ¾-Ton — 127 in. w.b.				
CS20909	8-ft. Stake	2606	3973	1415
CS20905	Panel	2884	3917	940
CS20906	Suburban	3170	4093	709
Series C30 — One-Ton — 133 in. w.b.				
CS31009	9-ft. Stake	2875	4390	3236

GENERAL NOTE: Production total column includes total trucks made at U.S. plants for domestic and export sale, plus trucks built here for sale in Canada, plus units imported from Canada for sale in U.S. These figures are for the model-year through July 31, 1967.

ADDITIONAL PRODUCTION: G10 w/108" w.b.: (panel van) 13,664; (Sportvan) 2,568; (Custom Sportvan) 1,603; (Deluxe Sportvan) 1,665. **C10 Series:** (Cowl less w/s) 15; (Cab & w/s) 6; (Chassis & Cab/127" w.b.) 1,066. **K10 Series (4x4):** (Chassis & Cab/118" w.b.) 39; (Stepside/115" w.b.) 1,229; (Chassis & Cab/127" w.b.) 41; (Stepside/127" w.b.) 500; (Panel) 30; (Suburban) 166. **P10 Step-Van:** (Chassis only) 140. **K20 Series (4x4):** (Chassis & Cab) 498; (Panel) 8; (Suburban) 120. **P20 Step-Van:** (Chassis-only) 151; (Panel/104" w.b.) 143; (Square Panel/125" w.b.) 1,313; (Chassis-only/125" w.b.) 400; (Square Panel/137" w.b.) 652; (Chassis-only/137" w.b.) 240; (Panel/137" w.b.) 76. **C30 Series:** (Cowl less w/s) 366; (Cowl & w/s) 8; (Chassis & Cab/157" w.b.) 4,488. **P30 Step-Van:** (Total gas) 6, 777; (Total diesel) 117.

ENGINE (Standard El Camino G10/P10/G20): Inline. OHV. Six-cylinder. Cast iron block. Bore & stroke: 3⅞ in. x 3¼ in. Displacement: 230 cu. in. Compression ratio: 8.5:1. Brake horsepower: 140 at 4400 R.P.M. Torque: 220 lbs.-ft. at 1600 R.P.M. Net horsepower: 120 at 3600 R.P.M. Seven main bearings. Hydraulic valve lifters. Carburetor: Rochester 1-Bbl. model 7028006/7028010.

ENGINE (Standard C10/C20/C30/P30, also all K-Series; Optional G10/P10): Inline. OHV. Six-cylinder. Cast iron block. Bore & stroke: 3⅞ in. x 3.53 in. Displacement: 250 cu. in. Compression ratio: 8.5:1. Brake horsepower: 155 at 4200 R.P.M. Torque: 235 lbs.-ft. at 1600 R.P.M. Seven main bearings. Hydraulic valve lifters. Carburetor: Rochester 1-Bbl. model 7028007/7028011.

ENGINE (Optional C10/C20/C30/P10/P20/P30): Inline. OHV. Six-cylinder. Cast iron block. Bore & stroke: 3⅞ in. x 4½ in. Displacement: 292 cu. in. Compression ratio: 8.1:1. Brake horsepower: 170 at 4000 R.P.M. Torque: 275 lbs.-ft. at 1600 R.P.M. Seven main bearings. Hydraulic valve lifters. Carburetor: Rochester 1-Bbl. model 7028012/7028013.

ENGINE (Optional: K Series/C10/C20/C30/El Camino): V-block. OHV. Eight-cylinder. Cast iron block. Bore & stroke: 3⅞ in. x 3 in. Displacement: 283 cu. in. Brake horsepower: 175 at 4400 R.P.M. Torque: 275 lbs.-ft. at 2400 R.P.M. Five main bearings. Hydraulic valve lifters.

ENGINE (Optional: C10/C20/C30/El Camino/K-Series): V-block. OHV. Eight-cylinder. Cast iron block. Bore & stroke: 4 in. x 3.25 in. Displacement: 327 cu. in. Compression ratio: 9.25:1. Brake horsepower: 220. Five main bearings. Hydraulic valve lifters. Carburetor: Rochester 4-Bbl. model 4G.

ENGINE (El Camino/Std. SS-396): V-block. OHV. Eight-cylinder. Cast iron block. Bore & stroke: 4-3/32 in. x 3.76 in. Displacement: 396 cu. in. Compression ratio: 10.25:1. Brake horsepower: 325 at 4800 R.P.M. Torque: 410 lbs.-ft. at 3200 R.P.M. Five main bearings. Hydraulic valve lifters. Carburetor: Rochester 4-Bbl. model Quadra-Jet.

ENGINE (Optional: El Camino SS-396): V-block. OHV. Eight-cylinder. Cast iron block. Bore & stroke: 4.09 in. x 3.76 in. Displacement: 396 cu. in. Compression ratio: 10.25:1. Brake horsepower: 350 at 5200 R.P.M. Torque: 415 lbs.-ft. at 3400 R.P.M. Five main bearings. Hydraulic valve lifters. Carburetor: Rochester 4-Bbl model Quadra-Jet.

CHASSIS (El Camino): Wheelbase: 115 in. Overall length: 197 in. Front tread: 58 in. Rear tread: 58 in. Tires: 7.35 x 14.

CHASSIS (Series G-10): Wheelbase: 90 in. Tires: 6.95 x 14.

CHASSIS (Series P-10): Wheelbase: 102 in. Tires: 8.15 x 15.

CHASSIS (Series G-20): Wheelbase: 108 in. Tires: 7.75 x 15.

CHASSIS (Series P-20): Wheelbase: 104 in. Tires: 7 x 17.5.

CHASSIS (Series P-30): Wheelbase: 104 in. Tires: 8 x 19.5.

CHASSIS (Series C-10/K-10): Wheelbase: 115/127 in. Overall length: 200.5 in. Height: 74.5 in. Tires: 8.15 x 15.

CHASSIS (Series C-20/K-20): Wheelbase: 127 in. Overall length: 200.5 in. Height: 74.5 in. Tires: 7 x 17.5.

CHASSIS (Series C-30/K-30): Wheelbase: 133 in. Height: 74.5 in. Tires: 8 x 17.5.

TECHNICAL: Three-speed, synchromesh. Speeds: 3F/1R. Column-mounted gear shift lever. Single-plate dry disc clutch (230/250 cu. in. engine), coil spring single dry plate (292/307/327/396 cu. in. engine). (½-Ton) semi-floating rear axle; (¾-Ton and 1-Ton) full-floating rear axle. Hydraulic, four-wheel brakes. Kelsey-Hayes pressed steel wheels. Options: Turbo Hydra-Matic transmission (½-Ton and El Camino). Powerglide transmission. Free wheeling hubs (4x4). Four-speed manual transmission. Auxiliary rear springs. No-spin differential. Heavy-duty suspension.

OPTIONS: Heavy-duty seat (6%). Rear seat (44%). Panoramic Cab (12%). Tinted glass (13%). Bucket seats. Level-Ride seat. One-passenger auxiliary seat (61%). Rear center seat belt (6%). Center and rear seat (59%). Deluxe shoulder harness (1%). Spare wheel lock (1%). Side trim moldings (34%). Single-speed wipers. Deluxe heater (88%). Air conditioning (3%). Junior West Coast mirror (32%). Senior West Coast mirror (12%). Long or short OSRV mirror (4%). Front crossview mirror. Platform and stake rack (3%). Platform equipment (1%). Pickup box mounting (7%). Floorboard (44%). Special heavy-duty frame (23%). 9,000-lb. front axle (16%). 5,000-4,000 lb. front axle (26%). 5,000-7,000 lb. front axle (14%). Heavy-duty front axle (16%). Front wheel locking hub (75%). Heavy rear springs (70%). Auxiliary springs (33%). Positraction (11%). No-Spin rear axle (8%). 3.07:1 rear axle (1%). 4.11:1 rear axle (3%). Vacuum gauge (74%). Heavy-duty air cleaner. Oil bath air cleaner (17%). Transistor ignition. 327 cu. in. V-8 (21%). Overdrive (1%). Four-speed transmission (21%). Heavy-duty four-speed transmission (2%). Powerglide transmission (10%). Three-speed automatic transmission (3%). Wheel trim cover (7%). Chrome hub caps (9%). Roof marker lamps (9%). Whitewall tires (8%). Speed warning indicator (2%). Speed warning indicator (2%). Tachometer (2%). Push-button radio (23%). Chrome bumper (17%). Rear painted bumpers (26%). Rear step bumper (9%). Custom Appearance equipment (17%). Custom Comfort and Convenience equipment (21%). Camper Special equipment (2%). Custom Sport Truck (CST) option package (3%). Two-tone paint (25%).

NOTE: The percentage figures after each option are from Chevrolet records. They indicate what percentage of ½-Ton to 2-Ton trucks that qualified for the particular option were factory-equipped with the option. For example, the figure of 75 percent for front wheel locking hubs would apply to 4x4 models only.

(**HISTORICAL:** Introduced September 11, 1966. Model Year Production (by series): **½-Tons:** (G10) 42,133; (C10) 288,356; (K10) 6,055 and (P10) 2,514. **¾-Tons:** (G20) 8,032; (C20) 67,681; (K20) 4,271; (P20/gas) 3,178 and (P20/diesel) 10. **One-Tons:** (C30) 23,428; (P30) 6,777 and (P30/diesel) 117. Model Year Production (by engine type): **½-Ton:** (six-cylinder) 207,720; (V-8) 131,338. **¾-Ton:** (six-cylinder) 41,583; (V-8) 41,589. **One-Ton:** (six-cylinder) 20,805; (V-8) 9,517. **Grand Total:** 452,552. (Note: Step-Vans were six-cylinder only models). Innovations: First year power steering was available for 4x4 models. New "three-door" Suburban styling. All trucks adopt 15 safety-related product improvements including dual cylinder brake systems, hazzard lights, brake system warning lamp, energy-absorbing steering column, padded instrument panel, padded sun visors, folding front seatback latch and thicker laminated windshield glass. Extensively restyled El Camino. First year for Chevy Vans with two wheelbase lengths. First year for V-8 power in vans. Historical notes: R.M. O'Connor was assistant general sales manager, truck & fleet sales, for Chevrolet Motor Division.

Pricing

	5	4	3	2	1
1967					
El Camino Series					
Sport Pickup	1200	2450	4050	5650	8100
Custom Sport Pickup	1250	2500	4150	5800	8300
Fleetside Pickups					
C10 Pickup (short box)	1200	2460	4100	5700	8200
C10 Pickup (long box)	1200	2400	4000	5600	8000
K10 Pickup (short box)	1180	2370	3950	5500	7900
K10 Pickup (long box)	1150	2310	3850	5400	7700
C20 Pickup (long box)	1050	2100	3500	4900	7000
C20 Pickup (8½-ft. box)	1040	2070	3450	4850	6900
K20 Pickup (long box)	1040	2070	3450	4850	6900
K20 Pickup (8½-ft. box)	1020	2050	3400	4800	6800
C30 Pickup (8½-ft. box)	900	1800	3000	4200	6000

NOTES: "C" = conventional drive.
"K" = four wheel drive (4x4)
"10" = ½-Ton.
"20" = ¾-Ton.
"30" = One-Ton
"Short Box" pickups have 6½-ft. box.
"Long Box" pickup have 8-ft. box.

Stepside Pickups					
C10 Pickup (short box)	1200	2400	4000	5600	8000
C10 Pickup (long box)	1170	2340	3900	5450	7800
C20 Pickup (long box)	1040	2070	3450	4850	6900
K20 Pickup (long box)	1020	2050	3400	4800	6800
C30 Pickup (8½-ft. box)	900	1800	3000	4200	6000
Chevy Van Series					
G10 Panel Van	600	1200	2000	2800	4000
G10 Sportvan	630	1250	2100	3000	4200
G10 Custom Sportvan	680	1350	2250	3150	4500
G10 DeLuxe Sportvan	720	1450	2400	3300	4800
G20 Panel Van	570	1140	1900	2650	3800
G20 Sportvan	600	1200	2000	2800	4000
G20 Custom Sportvan	630	1250	2100	3000	4200
G20 DeLuxe Sportvan	680	1350	2250	3150	4500
Step-Van Series (Code "P")					
P10 Steel Panel	600	1200	2000	2800	4000
P20 Steel Panel	590	1170	1950	2700	3900
P30 Steel Panel	570	1140	1900	2650	3800
Panel/Suburbans/Stakes					
C10 Panel	630	1250	2100	3000	4200
C10 Suburban	830	1650	2750	3850	5500
C20 Stake	660	1320	2200	3100	4400
C20 Panel	600	1200	2000	2800	4000
C20 Suburban	680	1200	2250	3150	4500
C30 Stake	680	1200	2250	3150	4500

NOTES: 1955-up prices based on top-of-the-line models.
Add five percent for 4x4.

1968 CHEVROLET

1968 Chevrolet El Camino SS-396 (OCW)

LIGHT TRUCK — 1968 SERIES — (ALL ENGINES): — For 1968, the El Camino was totally restyled on a 116 inch wheelbase. Its front end was patterned along the lines of the 1968 Chevelle. Features included a front bumper slotted behind the license plate only. The headlamps — two on each side — were set into squarish, bright metal housings. A fine mesh grille ran the full width of the body. It had a horizontal Chevrolet badge in its center. On SS-396 versions the grille was blacked-out and had an "SS" center badge. This option also included "power blisters" on the hood and blacked-out lower body perimeter, plus special styled wheels.

G10 vans again came on either a 90 or 108 inch wheelbase, while G20s were offered only with the longer stance. There was a large windshield. The upper body slanted down and out towards the sculptured feature line that encircled the entire truck. The grille had horizontal blades divided into four segments by a heavy vertical bar at the center and two thinner, vertical members running down the center of each half. Single, round headlamps were mounted at the outer ends with rectangular parking lamps branching towards the grille center. A "bow-tie" decorated the forward cowl. The vans had double side cargo doors and double rear panel doors. Passenger-carrying Sportvans came in standard, Custom and Deluxe trim levels.

Safety side-marker lamps were added to the front fender tips of Pickups, Panels and Suburban Carryalls. A modestly revamped which had slightly more brightwork. Badges on the side of the cowl carried C10, C20 or C30 designations for ½-ton, ¾-ton and one-ton, respectively. (On approximately four percent of production the badges read CS10, CS20 or CS30, indicating the buyer had selected the optional "Custom Sport" package.) The Custom Sport truck option was a notch above the Custom Comfort and Appearance option. The latter included bright windshield trim, rear window moldings and ventipane frames; Custom front fender nameplates; color-keyed vinyl floor mats; foam seats with color-keyed vinyl trim; cigarette lighter; bright dash knobs; cowl insulation and full-depth arm rests. The "CST" option had most of these items, plus a chrome front bumper; CS fender nameplates; full-width Western style vinyl seats; pedal trim; roof trim molding; carpeting and extra insulation.

The C10 and K10 (4x4) models came on 115 or 127 inch wheelbases. Suburbans again had the unique three-door body and could be had with double rear panel doors or an end-gate (tailgate). Pickups came in Stepside or Flareside variations and with six- or eight-foot dispatch boxes. The 127 inch wheelbase was used for all C20/K20 models, except the "long box" (8½-ft. bed) pickup, which came only as a Fleetside on the 133 inch wheelbase.

Four models made up the C30 Series. One was a chassis and cab on a 157 inch wheelbase, while the others had a 133 inch stance. The one-ton pickups included a Stepside with a nine-foot box and Fleetside with 8½-foot box. The C30 Platform Stake, with its nine-foot platform, was a foot longer than its C20 counterpart.

Forward Control delivery truck offerings included P10, P20 and P30 Step-Vans with a choice of chassis-only, steel panel bodies or aluminum panel bodies. Wheelbases were 102 inches for the ½-ton P10; 127 or 133 inches for the ¾-ton P20 and 125, 133 or 157 inches for the one-ton P30. P20/P30 Step-Vans could also be had with three-cylinder diesel engines, which are very rare. Also new was a coil spring front suspension, as the Step-Van chassis was now starting to find its way into the growing RV market.

I.D. DATA: Serial number located Combination GVW and serial number late found on left door hinge pillar. Starting: Example: (Van) GE158 ( ) 100001 and up. Engine number indicates manufacturing plant, month and day of manufacture and transmission type. 6-cyl.: located on pad at right-hand side of cylinder block at rear of distributor. 8-cyl.: located on pad at front, right-hand side of cylinder block.

Model	Body Type	Price	Weight	Prod. Total
El Camino Series				
13480	Pickup (V-8)	2590	3193	—
13680	Custom Pickup (V-8)	2671	3210	—
13380	Pickup (6-cyl.)	2482	—	—
13580	Custom Pickup (6-cyl.)	2563	—	—
13880	SS-396 Pickup	2926	—	—
Fleetside Models (I)				
Series C10				
CS10734	½-Ton 115 in. w.b.	2371	3333	46,483
CS10934	½-Ton 127 in. w.b.	2408	3440	204,236
Series K10				
KS10734	½-Ton 4x4 115 in. w.b.	—	—	1449
KS10934	½-Ton 4x4 127 in. w.b.	—	—	—
Series C20 — ¾-Ton — 127 in. w.b.				
CS20934	Pickup	2550	3848	60,646
CS21034	Pickup w/8½ ft. box	2614		
Series K20				
KS20934	4x4 Pickup	—	—	4705
KS21034	4x4 Pickup w/8½ ft. box	—	—	4705
Series C30				
CS31034	1-Ton 133" w.b. 8½ ft. box	2755		213
Stepside Models (I)				
Series C10				
CS10704	½-Ton 115 in. w.b.	2330	3255	46,322
CS10904	½-Ton 127 in. w.b.	2371	3345	18,632
Series K10				
KS10704	½-Ton 4x4-115 in. w.b.	—	—	1706
KS10904	½-Ton 4x4-127 in. w.b.	—	—	552
Series C20				
CS20904	¾-Ton 127 in. w.b.	2513	3753	7666
Series K20				
KS20904	¾-Ton 4x4-127 in. w.b.	—	—	1047
Series C30				
CS31004	1-Ton 133 in. w.b. 9 ft. box	2695	3995	2836
Cab and Chassis				
CS10703	½-Ton 115 in. w.b.	2223	2914	2735
CS20903	¾-Ton 127 in. w.b.	2403	3446	6636
CS31003	1-Ton 133 in. w.b.	2561	3556	11,948

115 in. w.b. = 6½ ft. box
127 in. w.b. = 8 ft. box (except as noted)

Van, Panel and Stake Models

Model	Body Type	Price	Weight	Prod. Total
Series G10 — ½-Ton — 90 in. w.b. (*)				
GS11005	Panel Van	2331	2849	18,617
GS11026	Sportvan	2571	3035	2153
GS11026	Custom Sportvan	2699	3138	685
GS11036	DeLuxe Sportvan	2890	3174	403
Series P10				
PS10535	½-Ton Panel 102 in. w.b.	2864	3559	2767

Model	Body Type	Price	Weight	Prod. Total
Series G20 — ¾-Ton — 108 in. w.b.				
GS21305	Panel Van	2618	3109	5504
GS21306	Sportvan	2848	3241	715
GS21326	Custom Sportvan	2975	3365	325
GS21336	Deluxe Sportvan	3166	3409	383
Series P20				
PS20835	¾-Ton Panel (125-133" w.b.)	3626	4970	2314
Diesel				
PT20835	¾-Ton 10-ft. Panel (125 in. 137" w.b.)	5568	5833	4
PT30835	1-Ton 10-ft. Panel (125 in. w.b.	5648	5931	2
Series P30 (Step-Van)				
PS30835	1-Ton Panel 125 in. w.b.	3806	5185	733
Series C10A — ½-Ton				
CS10905	Panel Delivery	2742	3502	4801
CS10906	Suburban (Doors)	2986	3670	11,004
Series C20A — ¾-Ton — 127 in. w.b.				
CS20909	8-ft. Platform Stake	2606	3973	1103
CS20905	Panel Delivery	2884	3917	1572
CS20906	Suburban (Doors)	3170	4093	1573
Series C30				
CS31009	1-Ton 9-ft. Stake	2875	4390	3272

* = 108 in. w.b. available
A = 4x4 versions available

NOTE: Production totals from Chevrolet records are for model-year through August 1, 1968 and include all trucks made in U.S. factories for domestic/export/Canadian markets.

ADDITIONAL PRODUCTION: G10/108 in. w.b.: (Panel van) 17, 569; (Sportvan) 2,961; (Custom Sportvan) 2,158; (Deluxe Sportvan) 1,681. **C10:** (cowl less windshield, 115 in. w.b.) 14; (chassis & cab 127 in. w.b.) 1,197. **K10:** (cab & chassis, 115 in. w.b.) 43; (cab & chassis, 127 in. w.b.) 41; (Panel) 59; (Suburban) 4,257. **P10:** (Chassis, 102 in. w.b.) 139. **C20:** (cowl less windshield, 127 in. w.b.) 12; (Fleetside, 133 in. w.b.) 1,902. **K20:** (cab) 498; (Panel) 68; (Suburban) 299. **P20:** (chassis, 125 in. w.b.) 404; (aluminum panel, 125 in. w.b.) 44; (steel panel, 133 in. w.b.) 735; (chassis, 133 in. w.b.) 188; (aluminum panel, 133 in. w.b.) 32; (chassis, 125 in. w/diesel) 1. **C30:** (cowl less windshield,133 in. w.b.) 238; (cab, 157 in. w.b.) 5,639. **P30:** (chassis, 125 in. w.b.) 759; (aluminum panel, 125 in. w.b.) 16; (steel panel, 133 in. w.b.) 1,401; (chassis, 133 in. w.b.) 1,043; (aluminum panel, 133 in. w.b.) 73; (steel panel, 157 in. w.b.) 655; (chassis, 157 in. w.b.) 853 and (aluminum panel, 157 in. w.b.) 1. **P30/Diesel:** (chassis, 125 in. w.b.) 10; (steel panel, 133 in. w.b.) 8; (chassis, 133 in. w.b.) 8; (steel panel, 157 in. w.b.) 1 and (chassis, 157 in. w.b.) 1.

P30: ENGINE (Std. G10/P10/G20/El Camino): Inline. OHV. Six-cylinder. Cast iron block. Bore & stroke: 3.875 in. x 3.25 in. Displacement: 230 cu. in. Compression ratio: 8.5:1. Brake horsepower: 140 at 4400 R.P.M. Net horsepower: 120 at 3600 R.P.M. Max. Torque: 220 lbs.-ft. at 1600 R.P.M. Seven main bearings. Hydraulic valve lifters. Carburetor: Rochester one-barrel model M: 7028006/7028010.

ENGINE (Std. P20/P30/C10/C20/C30/K10/K20/K30): Inline. OHV. Six-cylinder. Cast iron block. Bore & stroke: 3.875 in. x 3.53 in. Displacement: 250 cu. in. Compression ratio: 8.5:1. Brake horsepower: 155 at 4200 R.P.M. Max. Torque: 235 lbs.-ft. at 1600 R.P.M. Seven main bearings. Hydraulic valve lifters. Carburetor: Rochester one-barrel model M: 7028007/7028011.

ENGINE (Opt. C10/C20/C30/K10/K20/K30/P10/P20/P30): Inline. OHV. Six-cylinder. Cast iron block. Bore & stroke: 3⅞ in. x 4.12 in. Displacement: 292 cu. in. Compression ratio: 8.1:1. Brake horsepower: 170 at 4000 R.P.M. Max. Torque: 275 lbs.-ft. at 1600 R.P.M. Seven main bearings. Hydraulic valve lifters. Carburetor: Rochester one-barrel model M: 7028012/7028013.

ENGINE (Opt. P10/P20/P30/C10/C20/C30/K10/K20/K30/El Camino): V-type. OHV. Eight-cylinder. Cast iron block. Bore & stroke: 3⅞ in. x 3.25 in. Displacement: 307 cu. in. Compression ratio: 8.25:1. Brake horsepower: 180 at 4400 R.P.M. Max. Torque: 285 lbs.-ft. at 2400 R.P.M. Five main bearings. Hydraulic valve lifters. Carburetor: Rochester two-barrel model 26 (numbers vary).

ENGINE (Opt. P10/P20/P30/C10/C20/C30/K10/K20/K30): V-type. OHV. Eight-cylinder. Cast iron block. Bore & stroke: 4 in. x 3.25 in. Displacement: 327 cu. in. Compression ratio: 9.0:1. Brake horsepower: 200 at 4600 R.P.M. Max. Torque: 300 lbs.-ft. at 2400 R.P.M. Five main bearings. Hydraulic valve lifters. Carburetor: Rochester model four-barrel 4MV 702821.

ENGINE (Opt. C10/C20/C30/K10/K20/K30): V-type. OHV. Eight-cylinder. Cast iron block. Bore & stroke: 4.09 in. x 3.76 in. Displacement: 396 cu. in. Compression ratio: 9.1. Brake horsepower: 310 at 4800 R.P.M. Max. Torque: 400 lbs.-ft. at 3200 R.P.M. Five main bearings. Hydraulic valve lifters. Carburetor: Rochester model four-barrel 4MV 7028211.

ENGINE (Opt. El Camino/SS396): V-type. OHV. Eight-cylinder. Cast iron block. Bore & stroke: 4.09 in. x 3.76 in. Displacement: 396 cu. in. Compression ratio: 10.25:1. Brake horsepower: 350 at 5200 R.P.M. Max. Torque: 415 lbs.-ft. at 3400 R.P.M. Five main bearings. Hydraulic valve lifters. Carburetor: Rochester four-barrel model Quadra-Jet.

ENGINE (Std. El Camino/SS396): V-type. OHV. Eight-cylinder. Cast iron block. Bore & stroke: 4.09 in. x 3.76 in. Displacement: 396 cu. in. Compression ratio: 10.25:1. Brake horsepower: 325 at 4800 R.P.M. Five main bearings. Hydraulic valve lifters. Carburetor: four-barrel Rochester model Quadra-Jet.

1968 Chevrolet 3-door Suburban (JAG)

CHASSIS (El Camino): Wheelbase: 116 in. Overall length: 201 in. Front tread: 59 in. Rear tread: 59 in. Tires: 7.35 x 14.

CHASSIS (Series G10): Wheelbase: 90 in. Tires: 6.95 x 14.

CHASSIS (Series P10): Wheelbase: 102 in. Tires: 8.15 x 15.

CHASSIS (Series G20): Wheelbase: 108 in. Tires: 7.75 x 15.

CHASSIS (Series P20): Wheelbase: 125/133 in. Tires: 8 x 17.5.

CHASSIS (Series PT30835): Wheelbase: 125 in. Tires: 8 x 17.5.

CHASSIS (Series C10/K10): Wheelbase: 115/127 in. Overall length: 200.5 in. Height: 74.5 in. Tires: 8.15 x 15.

CHASSIS (Series C20/K20): Wheelbase: 127 in. Overall length: 200.5 in. Height: 74.5 in. Tires: 7 x 17.5.

CHASSIS (Series C30/K30): Wheelbase: 133 in. Height: 74.5 in. Tires: 8 x 17.5.

CHASSIS (Series PT20835): Wheelbase: 125/137 in. Tires: 8 x 17.5.

CHASSIS (Series P30): Wheelbase: 125 in. Tires: 8 x 17.5.

TECHNICAL: Three-speed synchromesh transmission. Speeds: 3F/1R. Column-mounted gear shift lever. Single-plate dry-disc clutch (230/250 cu. in. engines); coil spring single-plate dry (292/307/327/396 cu. in. engines). Rear axle: (½-Ton) semi-floating; (¾-Ton/1-Ton) full-floating. Hydraulic four-wheel-brakes. Kelsey-Hayes pressed steel wheels. Technical options: Overdrive. Turbo Hydra-Matic drive. Powerglide transmission. Free wheeling hubs (4x4). Four-speed transmission. Auxiliary rear springs. No-Spin differential. Power steering. Camper Package ($61). Heavy-duty suspension. Power brakes. Heavy-duty clutch.

OPTIONS AND INSTALLATION RATES: Heavy-dury seat (6%). Front center seat belt (2%). Rear seat (40%). Shoulder harnes (1%). Panoramic cab (19%). Bucket seats (2%). Custom bench seat (1%). One-passenger auxiliary seat (55%). Rear center seat belt (10%). Center and rear seat (41%). Shoulder harness (n/a). Spare wheel lock (2%). Upper bodyside molding (n/a). Door edge guards (6%). Side trim molding (36%). Heater deletion (12%). Air conditioning (3%). Roof mounted air conditioning (n/a). Front door armrest (2%). Jr. West Coast mirror (32%). Sr. West Coast mirror (3%). Non-glare inside mirror (16%). Body paint stripe (5%). Platform equipment (1%). Pickup box mounting (9%). Floorboard (28%). Front stabilizer (20%). Heavy front springs (18%). Front wheel locking hub (75%). Heavy rear spring (65%). Heavy shocks (11%). Heavy front axle (12%). Auxiliary springs (22%). H-D rear shocks (4%). Leaf springs (2%). Positraction (11%). No-Spin rear axle (7%). Pow-R-Lock rear axle (n/a). Optional gear ratio (16%). Cruise control (n/a). Oil bath air cleaner (10%). "327" V-8 engine (26%). "396-4V" engine (3%). "396-2V" engine (2%). Overdrive (1%). H-D three-speed manual transmission (9%). Four-speed manual transmission (21%). Powerglide transmission (9%). Three-speed automatic transmission (16%). Wheel trim covers (10%). Chrome hub caps (12%). Whitewall tires (9%). Roof marker lamps (2%). Speed warning indicator (n/a). Tachometer (1%). Push-button radio (25%). Special camper equipment (3%). Custom Sport Truck option (4%). Two-tone paint (32%). Full gauge package (55%). Custom Appearance package (3%). Custom comfort and convenience package (26%). Note: Partial list of options and installation rates based on Chevrolet cumulative model year records for ½-ton to 2-ton trucks built through August 1, 1968. Figures do not include El Camino which was considered a Chevelle for record-keeping purposes. The installation rate (%) shows the percent option useage in *those trucks qualifying for the particular option*. For example, front wheel locking hubs were used on 75% of Chevy's four-wheel-drive trucks; not 75% of total production.

HISTORICAL: Calendar Year production (all Chevy trucks): 680,499. Model Year production (light-duty only) by tonnage class and engine: ½-**ton:** (6-cyl.) 202,962; (V-8) 190,413; (Total) 393,375. ¾-**ton:** (6-cyl.) 35,645; (V-8) 62,731; (Total) 98,376. **One-ton:** (6-cyl.) 14,556; (V-8) 15,179; (Total) 29,735. **Grand Total:** 521,486. Innovations: First year for front and rear safety side-markers. New models included ¾- and 1-ton forward control Step-Vans equipped with independent front suspension, coil springs, power steering and V-8 engines for the first time. New 327 cu. in./200 h.p. and 396 cu. in./310 h.p. engines. Historical: Record sales and production marked Chevrolet's truck operations this season. Dealers

delivered 843,990 trucks of all sizes. Most Chevrolet trucks were built at St. Louis. The home plant, at Flint, Mich., was the second highest source, but the Freemont, Calif. factory was challenging for second-place. This was the first year that production of V-8 powered trucks (410,178 units) outpaced production of sixes (269,291 units). T.L. Pritchett, assistant general sales manager, was head of the truck division.

Pricing

1968	5	4	3	2	1
El Camino Series					
Sport Pickup	1200	2400	4000	5600	8000
Custom Sport Pickup	1200	2460	4100	5700	8200
"SS-396" option add 15%.					
Fleetside Pickups					
C10 Pickup (short box)	1200	2460	4100	5700	8200
C10 Pickup (long box)	1200	2400	4000	5600	8000
K10 Pickup (short box)	1180	2370	3950	5500	7900
K10 Pickup (long box)	1150	2310	3850	5400	7700
C20 Pickup (long box)	1050	2100	3500	4900	7000
C20 Pickup (8½ ft.)	1040	2070	3450	4850	6900
K20 Pickup (long box)	1040	2070	3450	4850	6900
K20 Pickup (8½ ft.)	1020	2050	3400	4800	6800

NOTE:
"C" = conventional drive.
"K" = 4x4.
"10" = ½-Ton.
"20" = ¾-Ton.
"30" = 1-Ton.
"Short Box" has 6½ ft. bed.
"Long Box" has 8-ft. ft. bed.

Stepside Pickups	5	4	3	2	1
C10 Pickup (short box)	1200	2400	4000	5600	8000
C10 Pickup (long box)	1170	2340	3900	5450	7800
K10 Pickup (short box)	1150	2310	3850	5400	7700
K10 Pickup (long box)	1140	2280	3800	5300	7600
C20 Pickup (long box)	1040	2070	3450	4850	6900
K20 Pickup (long box)	1020	2050	3400	4800	6800
C30 Pickup (8½ ft.)	900	1800	3000	4200	6000
Chevy Van Series					
G10 Panel Van	600	1200	2000	2800	4000
G10 Sportvan	630	1250	2100	3000	4200
G10 Custom Sportvan	680	1200	2250	3150	4500
G10 DeLuxe Sportvan	720	1450	2400	3300	4800
G20 Panel Van	570	1140	1900	2650	3800
G20 Sportvan	600	1200	2000	2800	4000
G20 Custom Sportvan	630	1250	2100	3000	4200
G20 DeLuxe Sportvan	680	1350	2250	3150	4500
Step Van Series					
P10 Panel	600	1200	2000	2800	4000
P20 Panel	590	1170	1950	2700	3900
P30 Panel	570	1140	1900	2650	3800
Panel/Suburban/Stake-Bed					
C10 Panel	630	1250	2100	3000	4200
C10 Suburban	830	1650	2750	3850	5500
C20 Stake	600	1200	2000	2800	4000
C20 Stake	680	1200	2250	3150	4500
C20 Stake	680	1200	2250	3150	4500

NOTE: 1955-up prices based on top-of-the-line models.

1969 CHEVROLET

1969 Chevrolet CST/10 Fleetside Pickup (CW)

LIGHT TRUCK — 1969 SERIES — (ALL ENGINES): — For 1969, the El Camino had a new face. The center bumper slot was larger, with the parking lamps inside it. Bright, horizontal bars ran across the fine-finned grille insert at its top, center and bottom. The middle bar held a Chevy emblem at its center. An El Camino script was on the left fendertop. On SS-396 models, the grille background and lower body perimeter were blacked-out. The "flying buttress" roofline was retained.

Both Chevy Van and Sportvan models offered two lengths, two wheelbases and two capacities, plus six-cylinder or V-8 power. Half-tons offered 209 cubic feet of payload space on a 90 inch wheelbase. The 256 cubic foot body, mounted on a 108 inch wheelbase, could be ordered with either ½-ton or ¾-ton chassis components. Standard features included "Stay-Tight" integral body-frame construction and durable, tapered leaf springs.

Attracting considerable attention was Chevrolet's entry into the expanding off-road, 4x4 vehicle field, the Blazer. Its suspension system consisted of single-leaf tapered front springs with a combination of multi-leaf and tapered springs at the rear. The ball-type steering unit had a 24:1 ratio and its standard engine was Chevrolet's 155 horsepower six-cylinder. The Blazer's single-unit body was joined to a heavy channel steel frame. The rear-mounted 23.5 gallon fuel tank was located inside the frame. Numerous options were offered for the Blazer including four-speed manual and automatic transmissions, V-8 engines, power steering, power brakes and a removable fiberglass top.

Pickups had a frontal re-do. An aluminum centerpiece, in the grille, was embossed with the Chevrolet name and had integral, rectangular parking lamps at each end, next to the square headlamp housings. A large "bowtie" was at the front center of the hood. Inside was a new "low-profile" steering wheel, new seatback construction and new foot-operated parking brake. Standard equipment on all pickups included: six-cylinder engine; self-adjusting four-wheel brakes; dual brake master cylinder; backup lights; directional signals; Panoramic rear window; side-marker reflectors; left- and right-hand OSRV mirrors; heater and defroster; padded dash; non-glare front instrument panel (I.P.) finish; padded sunshades; ash tray; push-button seat belt buckles; "low-profile" control knobs; two-speed electric washer/wipers; windshield defrosters; safety glass; flexible fuel filler neck; deep-dish steering wheel with telescoping shaft and thick laminate safety glass windshield. Sixteen paint colors were available.

Fleetside and Stepside models came with "short box" (6-foot bed) or "long box" (8½-foot bed) options. A big nine-foot box was also available, but only with Stepsides. C10/C20/C30 (½-ton/¾-ton/1-ton) truck-lines were offered with a total of eight wheelbases from 113 to 137 inches. Both Fleetside and Stepside pickups and chassis-cab models were available with four-wheel-drive in the ½-ton and ¾-ton lines with 115 or 127 inch wheelbases.

Standard "CE" cabs (the "E" did not appear on fender badges) came with a curved front windshield; Panoramic rear window; three-man adjustable bench seat; embossed vinyl upholstery; heater and defroster; dome light; rubber floor mat and dual sunshades. Seat colors were saddle, blue, green, red, black and turquoise.

An optional Custom Comfort and Appearance package included bright metal windshield moldings, rear window trim and ventipane frames; Custom ("CS") nameplates on front fenders; color-keyed vinyl-coated rubber floor mats; full-depth foam seat with color-keyed fabric and vinyl trim; vinyl trim door panels with bright upper retainers; a cigar lighter; Chevrolet "Custom" nameplate on dispatch box door; bright metal control knob inserts; cowl insulation and full-depth armrests.

Top trim level was the Custom Sport Truck option. It included most equipment in the "CS" package, plus a chrome front bumper; full-width vinyl seats; bright pedal frames; bright roof drip moldings; extra insulation; matching carpets and "CST" nameplates for the front fenders. Bucket seats with a center console were available on CST models.

"Underneath Suburban's station wagon style and comfort lies a rugged truck chassis," a Chevrolet catalog advised. This went for panel trucks, too. Both had coil springs on all four wheels and came as ½-ton or ¾-ton vehicles. Optional seats, in the Suburban, converted the 181 cubic foot payload space into a passenger compartment. Eight models in this sub-series were available with four-wheel-drive, a somewhat rare option.

Chevy's Step-Vans and forward control chassis were designed for door-to-door delivery service. Body lengths ranged from seven or eight feet for the Step-Van 7 series, up to 14½ feet for the one-ton Step-Van King. Features included independent coil spring front suspension; three six-cylinder engines; two optional V-8s, plus a three-cylinder Detroit diesel engine. Buyers could also get full-height doors; sliding side doors and double rear doors.

1969 Chevrolet El Camino (DFW)

I.D. DATA: Combination GVW and serial number plate found on left door hinge pillar. Starting: Example: (Pickup) CE149 (   ) 100001 and up. Engine number indicates manufacturing plant, month and day of manufacture, plus transmission type. (6-cyl.) located on pad at right-hand side of cylinder block at rear of distributor. (V-8) located on pad at front, right-hand side of cylinder block.

Model	Body Type	Price	Weight	Prod. Total
El Camino Series				
13380	Sport Pickup (6-cyl.)	2552	3192	48,400
13480	Sport Pickup (V-8)	2642	3320	48,400
13580	Custom Sport P.U. (6-cyl.)	2633	2219	48,400
13680	Custom Sport P.U. (V-8)	2723	3352	48,400
13880	"SS-396" Sport Pickup	3293	—	—
Blazer				
Series K10				
KS10514	4x4 Utility (104" w.b.)	2852	2947	4935
Fleetside Models (I)				
Series C10				
CS10734	½-Ton Pickup (115" w.b.)	2435	3407	54,211
CS10934	½-Ton Pickup (127" w.b.)	2473	3511	268,233
Series K10 — ½-Ton — 4x4				
KS10734	Pickup (115" w.b.)	3085	—	1649
KS10934	Pickup (127" w.b.)	3123	—	4937
Series C20 — ¾-Ton - 4x2				
CS20934	Pickup (127" w.b.)	2665	3901	74,894
CS21034	8½-ft. Pickup (133" w.b)	2730	3953	8797
Series K20				
KS20934	4x4 Pickup (127" w.b.)	3345	—	6124
Series C30 — One-Ton — 133 in. w.b.				
CS31034	8½ ft. Pickup	2822	4092	1300
Stepside Models (I)				
Series C10 — ½-Ton				
CS10704	Pickup (115" w.b.)	2397	3227	49,147
CS10904	Pickup (127" w.b.)	2435	3416	18,179
Series K10 — 4x4 — ½-Ton				
KS10704	Pickup (115" w.b.)	3047	—	1698
KS10904	Pickup (127" w.b.)	3085	—	521
I = 115 in. w.b., 6½ ft. box				
127 in. w.b., 8 ft. box (except as noted)				
Series C20 — ¾-Ton				
CS20904	Pickup (127" w.b.)	2627	3795	8090
Series K20 — 4x4 — ¾-Ton				
KS20904	Pickup (127" w.b.)	3307	—	1071
KS21034	8½ ft. Pickup (133" w.b.)	3410	—	—
Series C30 — One-Ton — 133 in. w.b.				
CS31004	9 ft. Box Pickup	2761	4011	2457
Cab and Chassis				
CS10703	½-Ton 115" w.b.	2286	2991	2343
CS20903	¾-Ton 127" w.b. (A)	2517	3396	8440
CS31003	1-Ton 133" w.b. (B)	2627	3580	16,828
Van/Panel/Stake				
Series G10 — ½-Ton — 90 in. w.b. (C)				
GS11005	Panel Van	2412	2945	18,456
GS11006	Sportvan	2622	3147	1730
GS11026	Custom Sportvan	2747	3255	526
GS11036	Deluxe Sportvan	2933	3293	270
Series P10				
PS10535	½-Ton Panel 102 in. w.b.	2944	3702	2819
Series G20 — ¾-Ton - 108 in. w.b.				
GS21305	Panel Van	2670	3182	6030
GS21306	Sportvan	2866	3343	625
GS21326	Custom Sportvan	2991	3466	382
GS21336	Deluxe Sportvan	3177	3509	306
Series P20				
PS20835	¾-Ton Panel 125 in. w.b.	3722	5082	1843
Series P30 — One-Ton — 125 in. w.b.				
PS30835	Steel Panel	3898	5229	855
PT30835	Steel Panel (Diesel)	5773	5923	—
Series C10 — ½-Ton — 115 in. w.b.				
CS10905	Panel Delivery	2863	3610	5492
CS10906	Suburban (doors)	3099	3699	14,056
Series K10 — ½-Ton — 4x4 — 115 in. w.b.				
KS10905	Panel Delivery	3513	—	
KS10906	Suburban (doors)	3749	—	1427
Series C20 — ¾-Ton — 127 in. w.b.				
CS20909	Platform Stake	2735	—	
CS20905	Panel Delivery	3075	3982	1779
CS20906	Suburban (doors)	3352	4086	2736
Series K20 — ¾-Ton — 4x4 — 127 in. w.b.				
KS20905	Panel Delivery	3755	—	
KS20906	Suburban (doors)	4032	—	545
Series C30 — One-Ton — 133 in. w.b.				
CS31009	Platform Stake	2966	—	

A = also available with 133 in. w.b.
B = also available with 157 in. w.b.
C = also available with 108 in. w.b.

ADDITIONAL PRODUCTION: G10/108 in. w.b.: (panel van) 20,730; (Sportvan) 3,065; (Custom Sportvan) 2,598; (Deluxe Sportvan) 1,758. C10/127 in. w.b.: (chassis & cab) 1,230. K10: (Chassis & cab/115 in. w.b.) 58; (chassis & cab/127 in. w.b.) 35. P10: (chassis) 125. K20: (chassis & cab/127 in. w.b.) 556. P20 - 124/133 in. w.b.: (SWB chassis) 616; (SWB aluminum panel) 68; (LWB steel panel) 950; (LWB chassis) 233; (LWB aluminum panel) 79. C30: (cowl less w/s) 236; (chassis & cab/157 in. w.b.) 8,290. P30: (chassis/125 in. w.b.) 3,447; (aluminum panel/125 in. w.b.) 46; (steel panel/133 in. w.b.) 1,600; (chassis/133 in. w.b.) 1,170; (aluminum panel/133 in. w.b.) 126; (steel panel/157 in. w.b.) 924; (chassis/157 in. w.b.) 1,607. (aluminum panel/157 in. w.b.) 86. P30 Diesel: Total-53.

ENGINE: (Std. G10/P10/G20/El Camino): Inline. OHV. Six-cylinder. Cast iron block. Bore & stroke: 3.875 x 3.25 in. Displacement: 230 cu. in. Compression ratio: 8.5:1. Brake horsepower: 140 at 4400 R.P.M. Max. Torque: 220 lbs.-ft. at 1600 R.P.M. Net horsepower: 120 at 3600 R.P.M. Seven main bearings. Hydraulic valve lifters. Carburetor: Rochester one-barrel model M: 7028006/7028010.

ENGINE (Std. P20/P30/C10/C20/C30/K10/K20/K30): Inline. OHV. Six-cylinder. Cast iron block. Bore & stroke: 3.875 in. x 3.53 in. Displacement: 250 cu. in. Compression ratio: 8.5:1. Brake horsepower: 155 at 4200 R.P.M. Max. Torque: 235 lbs.-ft. at 1600 R.P.M. Seven main bearings. Hydraulic valve lifters. Carburetor: Rochester one-barrel model M: 7028007/7028011.

ENGINE (Opt. C10/C20/C30/K10/K20/K30/P10/P20/P30): Inline. OHV. Six-cylinder. Cast iron block. Bore & stroke: 3⅞ in. x 4.12 in. Displacement: 292 cu. in. Compression ratio: 8.1:1. Brake horsepower: 170 at 4000 R.P.M. Max. Torque: 275 lbs.-ft. at 1600 R.P.M. Seven main bearings. Hydraulic valve lifters. Carburetor: Rochester one-barrel model M: 7028012/7028013.

ENGINE (Opt. P10/P20/P30/C10/C20/C30/K10/K20/K30/El Camino): V-type. OHV. Eight-cylinder. Cast iron block. Bore & stroke: 3⅞ in. x 3.25 in. Displacement: 327 cu. in. Compression ratio: 9.0:1. Brake horsepower: 200 at 4600 R.P.M. Max. Torque: 300 lbs.-ft. at 2400 R.P.M. Five main bearings. Hydraulic valve lifters. Carburetor: Rochester four-barrel model 4MV 702821.

ENGINE (Opt. C10/C20/C30/K10/K20/K30): V-type. OHV. Eight-cylinder. Cast iron block. Bore & stroke: 4.09 in. x 3.76 in. Displacement: 396 cu. in. Compression ratio: 9.1. Brake horsepower: 310 at 4800 R.P.M. Max. Torque: 400 lbs.-ft. at 3200 R.P.M. Five main bearings. Hydraulic valve lifters. Carburetor: Rochester model 4MV 7028211.

ENGINE (Std. El Camino/SS396): V-type. OHV. Eight-cylinder. Cast iron block. Bore & stroke: 4.09 in. x 3.76 in. Displacement: 396 cu. in. Compression ratio: 1.25:1. Brake horsepower: 325 at 4800 R.P.M. Max. Torque: 410 lbs.-ft. at 3200 R.P.M. Five main bearings. Hydraulic valve lifters. Carburetor: Rochester four-barrel model Quadra-Jet.

CHASSIS (C10/K10 Blazer): Wheelbase: 104 in. Overall length: 177.5 in. Height: 68.7 in. Front tread: 60.4 in. Rear tread: 60.4 in. Tires: 7.35 x 15.

CHASSIS (El Camino): Wheelbase: 116 in. Overall length: 201 in. Front tread: 59 in. Rear tread: 59 in. Tires: 7.35 x 14.

CHASSIS (G10): Wheelbase: 90 in. Tires: 6.95 x 14.

CHASSIS (P10): Wheelbase: 102 in. Tires: 8.25 x 15.

CHASSIS (G20): Wheelbase: 108 in. Tires: 7.75 x 15.

CHASSIS (P20): Wheelbase: 125 in. Tires: 8 x 16.5.

CHASSIS (P30): Wheelbase: 125 in. Tires: 8 x 16.5.

CHASSIS (C10/K10): Wheelbase: 115/127 in. Overall length: 200.5 in. Height: 74.5 in. Tires: 8.25 x 15.

CHASSIS (C20/K20): Wheelbase: 127/133 in. Overall length: 200.5 in. Height: 74.5 in. Tires: 8 x 16.5.

CHASSIS (C30): Wheelbase: 133 in. Height: 74.5 in. Tires: 8 x 16.5.

1969 Chevrolet Fleetside Pickup (OCW)

TECHNICAL: Three-speed synchromesh transmission. Speeds: 3F/1R. Column-mounted gear shift lever. Single-plate dry-disc clutch (230/250 cu. in. engines); coil-spring single-plate dry clutch (292/307/327/396 cu. in. engines). Rear axle: (½-Ton) semi-floating; (¾-Ton/1-Ton) full-floating. Hydraulic, four-wheel brakes. Kelsey-Hayes pressed steel wheels. Technical options: Turbo Hydra-Matic transmission ($240). Powerglide (avg. $195). Free-wheeling hubs (4x4). Four-speed transmission (avg. $100). Four-speed close-ratio transmission (El Camino). Auxiliary rear springs. No-spin differential. Power steering. Camper package. Heavy-duty suspension. Heavy duty three-speed transmission.

OPTIONS: El Camino: Strato-bucket seats. Speed and cruise control. Comfortilt steering wheel. Deluxe steering wheel. Wheel covers. Mag-style wheel covers. Simulated wire wheel covers. Rally wheels and trim. Concealed windshield wipers. Deluxe seat and shoulder belts. Appearance guard group. Console. Power door locks. Tinted glass. Tri-volume horn.

Special instrumentation. Auxiliary lighting. Vinyl roof cover. **Vans:** (with useage rates) Tinted windshield (15%). One-passenger auxiliary seat (27%). Heater deletion (2%). Jr. West Coast mirror (72%). R-H bodyside door (94%). Body paint stripe (1%). Non-glare inside mirror (n/a). Front stabilizer (68%). Heavy front springs (73%). Heavy rear springs (85%). Positraction (9%). Optional rear axles (27%). Hydraulic brake booster (10%). Ignition block heater (2%). Emission controls (9%). Oil bath air cleaner (4%). "250" six-cylinder engine (66%). Powerglide transmission (19%). Three-speed automatic transmission (16%). Whitewall tires (12%). H-D battery (16%). Dual electric horns (1%). Speed warning indicator (n/a). Heavy-duty radiator (5%). Chrome rear bumper (7%). Gauge package (30%). Custom equipment (3%). Two-tone paint (14%). Cargo door lock (8%). Swing-out rear door glass (7%). Tinted side door glass (26%). Tinted rear door glass (77%). Center seat (28%). Center and rear seat (26%). Stationary auxiliary seat (53%). **Other ½-Ton to 1-Ton Trucks:** (with useage rates) Heavy-duty seats (3%). Custom Sport Truck Option (6%). Chrome bumper (28%). Custom Comfort and Appearance option (28%). Blazer removable top, white (94%). Blazer removable top, black (6%). Full-foam seat (23%). Painted rear bumper (16%). Rear step bumper (16%). H-D cooling (1%). Chrome rear bumper (2%). Courtesy lights (99%). Push-button radio (41%). Tacometer (1%). Speed warning indicator (n/a). Side marker lamps (n/a). Cargo lamps (n/a). Camper wiring (2%). Roof marker lamps (2%). Whitewall tires (13%). Step-Van dual rear wheel conversion (71%). Side-mounted wheel carrier (11%). Chrome hub caps (11%). Wheel trim cover (19%). Hydraulic steering (21%). "350" medium-duty V-8 (8%). "350" light-duty V-8 (32%). "292" six-cylinder (14%). "SS-396 4V" V-8 (4%). H-D clutch (28%). Overdrive (1%). Four-speed manual transmission (17%). Type N heavy-duty four-speed manual transmission (1%). Powerglide transmission (5%). 300 Deluxe three-speed automatic transmission (10%). Hydraulic brake booster (14%). Positraction (7%). Pow-R-Lock rear axle (1%). No-Spin rear axle (6%). Positraction (7%): **Note:** Based on Chevrolet records for model year through December 31, 1969. Figures show percentage of option usage on truck qualified for the option. For example, Step-Van dual rear wheel option was used on 71% of all Step-Vans offering this equipment, not 71% of total Chevrolet production).

HISTORICAL: Introduced: Fall 1968. Model year production (all Chevrolet trucks): 684,748. Model year production by tonnage and engine type: ½-Ton: (6-cyl) 199,256; (V-8) 281,172; (Total) 480,428. ¾-Ton: (6-cyl.) 30,991; (V-8) 93,178; (Total) 124,169. 1-Ton: (6-cyl.) 16,617; (V-8) 22,408; (Total) 39,025. (Grand Total) 643,622. Production of Custom Sport Truck ("CST") option: 29,942. Production of "CS" option: 147,311. Innovations: All-new Blazer. New hinged hood on Step-Vans. New 350 cu. in. V-8 option. New LP gas engine conversions available. Historical notes: Chevrolet production records show a model number and listing for a 4x2 Blazer, but indicate that none were built in this model year. In 1969, Chevrolet became a full-line truck-maker sharing GMC's heavy over-the-road product line with Chevrolet nameplates.

Pricing

1969	5	4	3	2	1
El Camino Series					
Sport Pickup	1300	2550	4250	5900	8500
Custom Sport Pickup	1300	2650	4350	6050	8700
"SS-396" option add 15%					
Blazer Series — (4x4)					
Blazer	1080	2160	3600	5050	7200
Fleetside Series					
C10 Pickup (short box)	1300	2550	4250	5900	8500
C10 Pickup (long box)	1250	2500	4150	5800	8300
K10 Pickup (short box)	1200	2460	4100	5700	8200
K10 Pickup (long box)	1200	2400	4000	5600	8000
C20 Pickup (long box)	1050	2100	3500	4900	7000
C20 Pickup (long horn)	1020	2050	3400	4800	6800
K20 Pickup (long box)	1170	2340	3900	5450	7800
K20 Pickup (long horn)	1180	2370	3950	5500	7900
C30 Pickup (long horn)	900	1800	3000	4200	6000

NOTES:
"C" = conventional drive.
"K" = four wheel drive (4x4)
"10" = ½-Ton
"20" = ¾-Ton
"30" = 1-Ton
"Short Box" pickups have 6½ ft. bed and 115 in. w.b.
"Long Box" pickups have 8 ft. bed and 127 in. w.b.
"Long Horn" pickups have 8½-9 ft. bed and 133 in. w.b.
(Except as noted otherwise)

Stepside Series	5	4	3	2	1
C10 Pickup (short box)	1250	2520	4200	5850	8400
C10 Pickup (long box)	1200	2460	4100	5700	8200
K10 Pickup (short box)	1200	2450	4050	5650	8100
K10 Pickup (long box)	1180	2370	3950	5500	7900
C20 Pickup (long box)	1200	2400	4000	5600	8000
C20 Pickup (long horn)	1180	2370	3950	5500	7900
K20 Pickup (long box)	1180	2370	3950	5500	7900
K20 Pickup (long horn)	1170	2340	3900	5450	7800
C30 Pickup (long horn)	900	1800	3000	4200	6000
Chevy Van Series G10 — (½-Ton) — (90 in. w.b.)					
Panel Van	630	1250	2100	3000	4200
Sportvan	720	1450	2400	3300	4800
Custom Sportvan	700	1400	2350	3250	4700
DeLuxe Sportvan	740	1470	2450	3350	4900
Chevy Van Series G20 — (¾-Ton) — (108 in. w.b.)					
Panel Van	600	1200	2000	2800	4000
Sportvan	690	1380	2300	3200	4600
Custom Sportvan	680	1350	2250	3150	4500
DeLuxe Sportvan	700	1400	2350	3250	4700

	5	4	3	2	1
Series P10 — (102 in. w.b.)					
½-Ton Panel	600	1200	2000	2800	4000
Series P20 — (125 in. w.b.)					
Series P30 (Step-Van)					
1-Ton Panel	630	1250	2100	3000	4200
Panel/Suburban Series C10/K10 — (115 in. w.b.)					
C10 Panel	900	1800	3000	4200	6000
C10 Suburban	1130	2250	3750	5250	7500
K10 Panel	870	1750	2900	4100	5800
K10 Suburban	1100	2200	3650	5100	7300
Panel/Suburban Series C20/K20 — (127 in. w.b.)					
C20 Panel	870	1750	2900	4100	5800
C20 Suburban	980	1950	3250	4550	6500
K20 Panel	840	1680	2800	3900	5600
K20 Suburban	950	1900	3150	4400	6300

NOTE: 1955-up prices based on top of the line models.

1970 CHEVROLET

1970 Chevrolet El Camino (DFW)

LIGHT TRUCK — 1970 SERIES — (ALL ENGINES): — The "light-delivery trucks," as Chevrolet referred to its pickups, panels and suburbans, continued with the general 1969 styling, but the grille insert was modified. It now had 12 sets of small horizontal "fins" — six above and six below the aluminum centerpiece embossed with the Chevrolet name. Refinements included optional dress-up moldings with wood-grain vinyl or painted inserts for Fleetside pickups. Custom and Custom Sport Truck trim options were offered again. For the first time a 402 cu. in. V-8 (advertised as a 400 cu. in. V-8) was available. Chevy also had the "Longhorn." This was a fitting promotional name for the truck designed especially for king-size camper bodies. It was available in both ¾- and 1-ton sizes. Its cargo box was 8½ feet long on a 133 inch wheelbase.

The El Camino featured a new, more rounded front end. The "SS" option was readily identified by the exterior body logos and unique grille, which was divided into two sections by a prominent center-divider carrying "SS" lettering. All El Caminos featured a new dash with a wide rectangular-shaped speedometer and gauges. The "SS" dash used circular units.

Chevy Vans continued to feature "easy access" body design, which was popular with highly mobile businessmen. A three-range Turbo-Hydramatic transmission could be ordered. The styling — now in its last appearance — was unchanged from 1969.

For 1970, the Step-Van models got a front end designed for easy service access. They came in ½-ton, ¾-ton and 1-ton models with either steel or aluminum factory bodies or as a chassis suitable for many aftermarket body applications.

Blazers also took the new grille with six finned segments above and below the center strip with Chevy's name. The 4x2 version was produced this season, but less than 1,000 were made. the 4x4 version was more than ten times as popular.

I.D. DATA: Serial number located Combination GVW and serial number plate found on left door hinge pillar. Starting: Example: (Pickup) CE140 ( ) 100001 and up. Engine number indicates manufacturing plant, month and day of manufacture and transmission type. (6-cyl.) located on pad at right-hand side of cylinder block at rear of distributor. (8-cyl.) located on pad at front, right-hand side of cylinder block.

Model	Body Type	Price	Weight	Prod. Total
El Camino Series				
13380	Sedan P.U. (6-cyl.)	2679	3302	—
13480	Sedan P.U. (V-8)	2769	3418	—
13580	Sedan P.U. Custom (6-cyl.)	2760	3324	—
13680	Sedan P.U. Custom (V-8)	2850	3442	—
13880	Sedan P.U. SS396	3305	—	—
Blazer				
Series K10 — 4x4				
KS10514	½-Ton Util. (104 in. w.b.)	2956	3552	11,527
Fleetside Models (I)				
Series C10				
CS10734	½-Ton 115 in. w.b.	2558	3386	40,754
CS10934	½-Ton 127 in. w.b.	2595	3485	234,904

Model	Body Type	Price	Weight	Prod. Total
Series K10				
KS10734	½-Ton 4x4 115 in. w.b.	3128	—	2554
KS10934	½-Ton 4x4 127 in. w.b.	3165	—	7348
Series C20 — ¾-Ton — 127 in. w.b.				
CS20934	Pickup	2790	3871	70,880
CS21034	8½ ft. Pickup	2854	3912	5281
Series K20 — ¾-Ton (4x4) - 127 in. w.b.				
KS20934	Pickup	3540	8355	—
KS21034	8½ ft. Pickup	3604	8355	—
Series C30 — One-Ton — 133 in. w.b.				
CS31034	9 ft. Pickup	2935	4037	1404
Stepside Models (I)				
Series C10				
CS10704	½-Ton 115 in. w.b.	2520	3306	40,754
CS10904	½-Ton 127 in. w.b.	2558	3390	11,857
Series K10				
KS10704	½-Ton 4x4 115 in. w.b.	3090	—	1629
KS10904	½-Ton 4x4 127 in. w.b.	3128	—	464

I = 115 in. w.b., 6½ ft. box
127 in. w.b., 8 ft. box (except as noted)

Model	Body Type	Price	Weight	Prod. Total
Series C20				
CS20904	¾-Ton 127 in. w.b.	2752	3776	5856
KS20904	¾-Ton 4x4 127 in. w.b.	3500	—	—
Series C30				
CS31004	1-Ton 133 in. w.b. 9 ft. box	2874	3591	2101
Cab and Chassis				
CS10703	½-Ton 115 in. w.b.	2405	2970	2084
CS20903	¾-Ton 127 in. w.b. (A)	2652	3376	7277
CS31003	1-Ton 133 in. w.b. (B)	2736	3521	14,873
Van, Panel and Stake Models				
Series G10 (C)				
GS11005	½-Ton Panel	2489	2927	3933
GS11006	½-Ton Sportvan	2724	3123	277
GS11026	½-Ton Sportvan Custom	2849	3230	57
GS11036	½-Ton Sportvan Deluxe	3036	3268	42
Series P10 (Step-Van)				
PS10535	½-Ton Panel 102 in. w.b.	3139	3674	2526
Series G20 — ¾-Ton — 108 in. w.b.				
GS21305	Panel Van	2747	3161	1195
GS21306	Sportvan	2968	3313	134
GS21326	Custom Sportvan	3093	3443	61
GS21336	Deluxe Sportvan	3279	3489	45
Series P20 (Step-Van)				
PS20835	¾-Ton Panel 125 in. w.b.	3904	5040	1520
Series P30 (Step-Van)				
PS30835	1-Ton Panel 125 in. w.b.	4078	5213	743
PT30835	1-Ton Diesel Panel 125" w.b.	5780	5918	3
Series C10 — ½-Ton — 115 in. w.b.				
CS10905	Panel Delivery	3071	3598	3965
CS10906	Suburban (doors)	3279	3730	11,332
Series K20 — (4x4)				
KS10905	½-Ton Panel 115 in. w.b.	3975	—	—
KS10906	½-Ton Suburban 127" w.b.	4145	—	1877
Series C20 — ¾-Ton — 127 in. w.b.				
CS20905	Panel Delivery	3269	3991	1032
CS20906	Suburban (doors)	3441	4113	2224
Series K20 — ¾-Ton (4x4) — 127 in. w.b.				
KS20905	Panel Delivery	4019	—	—
KS20906	Suburban (doors)	4191	—	541
Series C30 — One-Ton — 133 in. w.b.				
CS31009	9 ft. Stake Bed	3075		

A = also available with 133 in. w.b.
B = also available with 157 in. w.b.
C = also available with 108 in. w.b.

ADDITIONAL PRODUCTION: G10/108 in. w.b.: (Panel) 3,069; (Sportvan) 422; (Custom Sportvan) 303; (Deluxe Sportvan) 158. **C10/127 in. w.b.:** (chassis & cab) 913. **K10:** (Blazer 4x2) 985; (chassis & cab/115 in. w.b.) 64; (chassis & cab/127 in. w.b.) 26. **K20:** (chassis & cab/127 in. w.b.) 582; (Stepside) 953. **P10:** (chassis/102 in. w.b.) 211. **P20:** (chassis/125 in. w.b.) 421; (aluminum panel/125 in. w.b.) 60; (steel panel/133 in. w.b.) 872; (aluminum panel/133 in. w.b.) 64; (chassis/133 in. w.b.) 184. **C30:** (cowl less w/s) 138. **P30:** (chassis/125 in. w.b.) 446; (aluminum panel/125 in. w.b.) 35; (steel panel/133 in. w.b.) 1,624; (chassis/133 in. w.b.) 1,758; (aluminum panel/133 in. w.b.) 68; (steel panel/157 in. w.b.) 1,027; (chassis/157 in. w.b.) 2,608; (aluminum panel/157 in. w.b.) 76; (diesel/all) 37. **Note:** Figures based on cumulative model year through August 31, 1970 including all trucks made in U.S. for domestic/export/Canadian markets.

ENGINE (Std. all models): Inline. OHV. Six-cylinder. Cast iron block. Bore & stroke: 3.875 in. x 3.53 in. Displacement: 250 cu. in. Compression ratio: 8.5:1. Brake horsepower: 155 at 4200 R.P.M. Seven main bearings. Hydraulic valve lifters. Carburetor: Rochester one-barrel model M: 7028007/7028011.

ENGINE (Opt. P10/P20/C10/C20/C30/K10/K20/K30): Inline. OHV. Six-cylinder. Cast iron block. Bore & stroke: 3⅞ in. x 4.12 in. Displacement: 292 cu. in. Compression ratio: 8.1:1. Brake horsepower: 170 at 4000 R.P.M. Max. Torque: 275 lbs.-ft. at 1600 R.P.M. Seven main bearings. Hydraulic valve lifters. Carburetor: Rochester one-barrel model M: 7028012/7028013.

ENGINE (Opt. El Camino/K10/G10/G20/P10/P20/C10/C20/C30/K20/K30): V-type. OHV. Eight-cylinder. Cast iron block. Bore & stroke: 3⅞ in. x 3¼ in. Displacement: 307 cu. in. Compression ratio: 8.25:1. Brake horsepower: 180 at 4400 R.P.M. Max. Torque: 285 lbs.-ft. at 2400 R.P.M. Five main bearings. Hydraulic valve lifters. Carburetor: Rochester two-barrel.

1970 Chevrolet CST/20 Fleetside Pickup (CW)

ENGINE (Opt. El Camino): V-type. OHV. Eight-cylinder. Cast iron block. Bore & stroke: 4 in. x 3.48 in. Displacement: 350 cu. in. Compression ratio: 9.0:1. Brake horsepower: 255 at 4800 R.P.M. Max. Torque: 365 lbs.-ft. at 3200 R.P.M. Five main bearings. Hydraulic valve lifters. Carburetor: Rochester two-barrel.

ENGINE (Opt. El Camino): V-type. OHV. Eight-cylinder. Cast iron block. Bore & stroke: 4.126 in. x 3.76 in. Displacement: 400 cu. in. Compression ratio: 8.5:1. Brake horsepower: 254 at 3700 R.P.M. Max. Torque: 400 lbs.-ft. at 3200 R.P.M. Five main bearings. Hydraulic valve lifters. Carburetor: Rochester two-barrel.

ENGINE (Std. El Camino SS396): V-type. OHV. Eight-cylinder. Cast iron block. Bore & stroke: 4.09 in. x 3.76 in. Displacement: 396 cu. in. Compression ratio: 10.25:1. Brake horsepower: 350 at 5200 R.P.M. Max. Torque: 445 lbs.-ft. at 3400 R.P.M. Five main bearings. Hydraulic valve lifters. Carburetor: Rochester four-barrel model Quadra-Jet.

ENGINE (Opt. El Camino/$321): V-type. OHV. Eight-cylinder. Cast iron block. Bore & stroke: 4.251 in. x 4.0 in. Displacement: 454 cu. in. Compression ratio: 10.25:1. Brake horsepower: 360 at 4400 R.P.M. Max. Torque: 500 lbs.-ft. at 3200 R.P.M. Five main bearings. Hydraulic valve lifters. Carburetor: Rochester four-barrel model Quadra-Jet.

CHASSIS (Series C10): Wheelbase: 115/127 in. Tires: 115 in. w.b.: G78-15B; 127 in. w.b.: H78-15B.

CHASSIS (Series C20): Wheelbase: 127/133 in. Tires: 8.75 x 16.5.

CHASSIS (Series C30): Wheelbase: 133 in. Tires: 8.75 x 16.5.

CHASSIS (El Camino): Wheelbase: 116 in. Overall length: 206.8 in. Height: 54.4 in. Front tread: 60.2 in. Rear tread: 59.2 in. Tires: F78-14B.

CHASSIS (Series K10): Wheelbase: 115/127 in. Tires: G78-15B (115 in. w.b.); H78-15B (127 in. w.b.).

CHASSIS (Series K20): Wheelbase: 127 in. Tires: 8.75 x 16.5.

CHASSIS (Series G10): Wheelbase: 90 in. Tires: 6.95 x 14.

CHASSIS (Series G20): Wheelbase: 108 in. Tires: 7.75 x 15.

CHASSIS (Series P10): Wheelbase: 102 in. Tires: G78-15B.

CHASSIS (Series P20): Wheelbase: 125 in. Tires: 8.75 x 16.5.

CHASSIS (Series P30): Wheelbase: 125 in. Tires: 8.75 x 16.5.

CHASSIS (Series K10 Blazer): Wheelbase: 104 in. Overall length: 177.5 in. Height: 68.7 in. Front tread: 60.4 in. Rear tread: 60.4 in. Tires: E78-15B.

TECHNICAL: Selective synchromesh transmission. Speeds: 3F/1R. Column-mounted gear shift lever. Single-plate dry-disc clutch (250 cu. in. engine); coil spring dry plate (all other engines). Rear axle: (½-Ton) semi-floating; (¾-Ton/1-Ton) full-floating. Hydraulic four-wheel brakes. Kelsey-Hayes pressed steel wheels. Technical options: Powerglide. Turbo Hydra-Matic (350 and 400). Wide-ratio Muncie three-speed manual transmission. Four-speed manual transmission with floor-mounted controls. Free-wheeling hubs (4x4). No-spin axle. Power brakes. Power steering. Front stabilizer bar. Rear leaf spring. 42 amp. Generator. Heavy-duty battery. Marker lights. Heavy-duty rear springs. Heavy-duty front shocks. Auxiliary fuel tank.

OPTION PRICES: (½-Ton): "292" six-cylinder engine ($95). "307" V-8 engine ($120). "307" V-8 engine ($120). "400" V-8 engine (avg. $160). "350" V-8 engine, for El Camino ($70). Four-speed manual transmission ($190). Powerglide transmission (avg. $195). Turbo-Hydramatic transmission ($280). Power brakes ($50). Power steering (avg. $115). Four-wheel-drive system ($570). (¾-Ton): "292" six-cilinder engine ($95). "307" V-8 engine ($95). "400" V-8 engine ($160). Powerglide transmission (avg. $190). Turbo-Hydramatic transmission (avg. $230). Power steering ($130). Four-speed manual transmission (avg. $100). Four-Wheel-Drive system ($705). (1-Ton): "307" V-8 engine ($100). "292" six-cylinder engine ($95). "350" V-8 engine ($40). "400" V-8 engine (avg. $160). LPG kit ($80). Turbo-Hydramatic transmission ($230). New Process transmission ($30). Nine-foot platform ($310). 12-foot platform ($370). 157 inch wheelbase ($40).

1970 Chevrolet Custom 10 Fleetside Pickup (OCW)

OPTIONS: (½-Ton to 1-Ton Trucks with useage rates) Rear seat (57%). Front center seat belt (1%). Tinted glass (28%). Bodyside belt molding (14%). Wide lower bodyside molding (46%). Door edge guards (12%). Air conditioning (16%). Roof mounted air conditioning (15%). Painted camper mirror (1%). Stainless camper mirror (2%). Jr. West Coast mirror, stainless (10%). Dual Sr. West Coast mirrors (3%). Jr. painted West Coast mirror (21%). Body paint stripe (5%). H-D shocks (14%). Front stabilizer (28%). Heavy front springs (24%). 4x4 front locking hubs (79%). Heavy rear springs (65%). Auxiliary springs (20%). Leaf spring suspension (20%). Positraction (10%). No-Spin rear axle (6%). Optional rear axles (11%). Hydraulic brake booster (23%). Oil bath air cleaner (5%). Engine block heater (3%). Manual throttle (3%). "292" six-cylinder engine (15%).

1970 Chevrolet Stepside Pickup (DFW)

1970 Chevrolet CST/10 Fleetside Pickup (OCW)

"396" four-barrel V-8 (5%). H-D clutch (21%). Four-speed manual trans-mission (17%). H-D close-ratio four-speed manual transmission (1%). Powerglide transmission (2%). Turbo Hydra-matic transmission (38%). Three-speed manual transmission (4%). 4x4 auxiliary fuel tank (1%). Hydraulic steering (33%). G78x15 whitewall tires (15%). H78x15B white-wall tires (3%). Wheel trim covers (25%). Chrome hub caps (11%). Tachometer (1%). Push-button radio (48%). Two-tone paint (30%). Spe-cial two-tone paint (15%). Custom Sport Truck option (10%). Special camper equipment (4%). Custom Comfort and Convenience option (24%). Chrome rear bumper (4%). Chrome bumper (6%). Painted rear bumper (11%). Rear step bumper (17%). Chrome front bumper (20%). **Note:** See notes for previous years.

1970 Chevrolet El Camino "SS" Sport Pickup (OCW)

HISTORICAL: Model year production (all Chevy trucks): 492,607. Model year production, light-duty, by tonnage and engine type: ½-Ton: (6-cyl.) 115,286; (V-8) 259,348; (Total) 374,634. ¾-Ton: (6-cyl.) 18,644; (V-8) 88,893; (Total) 107,537. 1-Ton: (6-cyl.) 10,350; (V-8) 25,552; (Total) 35,902. (Grand Total) 518,073. Production, Custom Sport Truck ("CST") option: 49,717; Custom ("CS") Cab option: 126,848; Camper Special: 20,900.

Pricing

1970	5	4	3	2	1
El Camino Series					
Sport Pickup	1300	2550	4250	5900	8500
Custom Sport Pickup	1300	2650	4350	6050	8700
"SS-396" option add 15%					
Blazer Series K10 — (4x4)					
Blazer	1080	2160	3600	5050	7200
Fleetside Pickups					
C10 Pickup (short box)	1300	2550	4250	5900	8500
C10 Pickup (long box)	1250	2500	4150	5800	8300
K10 Pickup (short box)	1200	2460	4100	5700	8200
K10 Pickup (long box)	1200	2400	4000	5600	8000
C20 Pickup (long box)	1050	2100	3500	4900	7000
C20 Pickup (long horn)	1020	2050	3400	4800	6800
K20 Pickup (long box)	1170	2340	3900	5450	7800
K20 Pickup (long horn)	1180	2370	3950	5500	7900
C30 Pickup (long horn)	900	1800	3000	4200	6000

NOTES:
"C" = conventional drive
"K" = four wheel drive (4x4)
"10" = ½-Ton
"20" = ¾-Ton
"30" = 1-Ton
"Short Box" pickups have 6½ ft. bed and 115 in. w.b.
"Long Box" pickups have 8 ft. bed and 127 in. w.b.
"Long Horn" pickups have 8½-9 ft. bed and 133 in. w.b.

Stepside Pickups	5	4	3	2	1
C10 Pickup (short box)	1250	2520	4200	5850	8400
C10 Pickup (long box)	1200	2460	4100	5700	8200
K10 Pickup (short box)	1200	2450	4050	5650	8100
K10 Pickup (long box)	1180	2370	3950	5500	7900
C20 Pickup (long box)	1200	2400	4000	5600	8000
K20 Pickup (long box)	1180	2370	3900	5500	7900
C30 Pickup (long horn)	900	1800	3000	4200	6000
Chevy Van Series G10 — (½-Ton) — (90 in. w.b.)					
Panel Van	630	1250	2100	3000	4200
Sportvan	720	1450	2400	3300	4800
Custom Sportvan	700	1400	2350	3250	4700
Deluxe Sportvan	740	1470	2450	3350	4900
Chevy Van Series G20 — (¾-Ton) — (108 in. w.b.)					
Panel Van	600	1200	2000	2800	4000
Sportvan	690	1380	2300	3200	4600
Custom Sportvan	680	1350	2250	3150	4500
Deluxe Sportvan	700	1400	2350	3250	4700
Series P10 — (102 in. w.b.)					
Step-Van	600	1200	2000	2800	4000

	5	4	3	2	1
Series P20 — (125 in. w.b.)					
Step-Van	620	1230	2050	2900	4100
Series P30 — (125 in. w.b.)					
Step-Van	630	1250	2100	3000	4200
Panel/Suburban Series C10/K10 — (115 in. w.b.)					
C10 Panel	900	1800	3000	4200	6000
C10 Suburban	1130	2250	3750	5250	7500
K10 Panel	870	1750	2900	4100	5800
K10 Suburban	1100	2200	3650	5100	7300
Panel/Suburban Series C20/K20 — (127 in. w.b.)					
C20 Panel	870	1750	2900	4100	5800
C20 Suburban	980	1950	3250	4550	6500
K20 Panel	840	1680	2800	3900	5600
K20 Suburban	950	1900	3150	4400	6300
Series C30 — (133 in. w.b.)					
1-Ton Stake (9 ft.)	750	1560	2500	3500	5000

NOTE: 1955-up prices based on top of the line models.

1971 CHEVROLET

1971 Chevrolet Cheyenne Fleetside Pickup (JLC)

LIGHT TRUCK — 1971 SERIES — (ALL ENGINES): — New for 1971 was a Panel Express version of the sub-compact Vega. It was based on the Kammback wagon, with the rear side windows blanked-out. Chevy described it as the "kinky way to haul around your surfboard." It came only with the standard all-vinyl interior, less passenger bucket seat, and only with black or green upholstery. The Custom interior option was not available. Standard equipment included the four-cylinder aluminum block engine, three-speed manual transmission, front disc brakes, two separate stowage compartments below the floor, many safety features and a choice of 10 colors. It had a 67.4 inch floor length, 42.6 inches between the wheelhousings and a 68.7 cubic foot cargo volume. Payload capacity was 650 pounds.

Pickups, Panels and Suburbans featured a more "macho" looking egg-crate grille. It had five horizontal blades and 15 vertical members, plus a bow-tie in the center. The parking/directional lights were moved from their previous location in the grille to positions within the front bumper. For the first time the Cheyenne trim package was offered. Also available was a Cheyenne Super option, plus "CS" (Custom) and "CST" (Custom Sport Truck) packages. The latter added $364 to the price tag. Suburbans continued to feature two doors on the passenger side, but only one on the left. Their usable floor space was nine feet long. With second and third seats removed, cargo space totaled 190 cubic feet. Four-wheel-drive was available for a price of just over $500.

The Chevrolet van models were attractively re-styled. They had new 110/125 inch wheelbases, plus an extended front hood that made 26 ser-vice areas readily accessible. For the first time ever, buyers could order a G30 (one-ton) van. The van grilles consisted of seven horizontal bars with a center-mounted Chevrolet emblem. The new "Beauville" version of the Sportvan offered "travel space for 12." Other innovations included inde-pendent front suspension and a sliding door option. A Custom Appearance package was available, as well as Custom and Convenience interior equip-ment.

The El Camino models had a new look due to the use of single-unit "Power Beam" headlamps and stacked parking lamps which angled around the body corners. The grille also had a stacked horizontal theme with sections that angled in-and-out around the "veed" center. Super Sport equipment was available for $365 extra. The performance model had "SS" badges behind the front wheel cutouts and a "power blister" hood. A 454 cubic inch V-8 replaced the "396." There was a custom inte-rior option.

Chevy's Blazer also adopted the new, egg-crate grille. Some sources say that the 4x2 version was introduced this year, although factory records show nearly 1,000 of these were made in *model year* 1970.

I.D. DATA: Serial number located Combination GVW and serial number plate located on left door hinge pillar. Starting: ( ) ( ) ( ) 4 ( ) 600001 or 800001 at each assembly plant regardless of series. Engine numbers located (6-cyl) stamped on a boss right side of block to rear of distributor; (V-8) stamped on a boss right front side of block.

Model	Body Type	Price	Weight	Prod. Total
Vega Series				
14105	½-Ton Panel Express	2159	2142	7,800
El Camino (307 cu. in. V-8)				
13480	½-Ton Sport Pickup	2988	3340	—
13680	½-Ton Custom Sport Pickup	3074	3356	—
Blazer (307 cu. in. V-8)				
Series K10				
KE10514	½-Ton 4x4 Utility	3358	3719	17,220
Fleetside Models				
Series C10				
CE10734	½-Ton 115 in. w.b.	2930	3618	32,865
CE10934	½-Ton 127 in. w.b.	2967	3711	206,313
Series K10				
KE10734	½-Ton 4x4 115 in. w.b.	3500	—	3068
KE10934	½-Ton 4x4 127 in. w.b.	3537	—	9417
Series C20 — ¾-Ton				
CE20934	Pickup 127 in. w.b.	3172	4042	62,465
CE21034	8½ ft. Pickup 133" w.b.	3236	4090	3331
Series K20 — ¾-Ton (4x4)				
KE20934	Pickup 127 in. w.b.	3852	—	10,066
KE21034	8½ ft. Pickup 133" w.b.	—	—	
Series C30 — 1-Ton				
CE31034	8½ ft. Pickup 133" w.b.	3316	4201	1479
Stepside Models				
Series C10				
CE10704	½-Ton 115 in. w.b.	2930	3533	19,041
CE10904	½-Ton 127 in. w.b.	2967	3616	7269
Series K10				
CK10704	½-Ton 4x4 115 in. w.b.	3500	—	1438
CK10904	½-Ton 4x4 127 in. w.b.	3537	—	364
Series C20				
CE20904	¾-Ton 127 in. w.b.	3172	3947	3406
Series K20				
KE20904	¾-Ton 4x4 127 in. w.b.	3852	—	674
Series C30				
CE31004	1-Ton 133 in. w.b. 9 ft. box	3255	4118	1557
Van/Panel				
Series G10 — ½-Ton — 110 in. w.b. (307 cu. in. V-8)*				
GE11005	Panel Van	3053	3387	15,012
GE11006	Sportvan	3503	3831	1846
GE11036	Beauville Sportvan	3790	3937	481
Series G20 — ¾-Ton — 110 in. w.b. (350 cu. in. V-8)*				
GE21005	Panel Van	3196	3577	5901
GE21006	Sportvan	3581	3925	1774
GE27036	Beauville Sportvan	3868	4032	345
Series G30 — 1-Ton — 110 in. w.b. (350 cu. in. V-8)*				
GE31305	Panel Van	3447	4039	624
GE31306	Sportvan	3824	4369	9
GE31336	Beauville Sportvan	4111	4522	8
Series P10				
PS10535	½-Ton Steel Panel	3415	3777	1905
Series P20				
PE20835	¾-Ton Steel Panel	4312	5200	819
Series P30				
PE30835	1-Ton Steel Panel	4486	5385	561
Series C10 — ½-Ton — (307 cu. in. V-8)				
CE10906	Suburban (doors)	3709	3975	9945
Series K10 — ½-Ton — (V-8)				
KE10906	4x4 Suburban (doors)	4279	—	1625
Series C20 — ¾-Ton — (V-8)				
CE20906	Suburban (doors)	3870	4300	2546
Series K20				
KE20906	4x4 Suburban (doors)	4550	—	609
(* 125 in. w.b. also available)				
Additional Body Choices (w/"307" V-8)				
Series C10				
CE10703	½-Ton Ch-Cab 115" w.b.	2770	3200	1476
Series C20				
CE20903	¾-Ton Ch-Cab 115" in. w.b.	3011	3545	4523
	¾-Ton Stake 8 ft.	3319	—	
Series K20				
KE10903	¾-Ton 4x4 Ch-Cab 127" w.b.	3691	—	509
Series C30				
CE31003	1-Ton Ch-Cab 133" w.b.	3102	3686	11,438
	1-Ton Stake 9 ft.	3530	—	

ADDITIONAL PRODUCTION: G10/125 in w.b.: (Panel) 15,013; (Sportvan) 2,011; (Beauville) 1,146. **Blazer 4x2:** (Utility) 1,277. **C10/127 in. w.b.:** (Chassis & Cab) 588. **P10:** (delivery chassis) 229. **G20/125 in. w.b.:** (Panel) 14,027; (Sportvan) 2,796; (Beauville) 3,568. **P20:** (125" chassis) 288; (125" aluminum panel) 48; (133" chassis) 167; (133" aluminum panel) 37. **G30:** (Panel) 9,518; (Sportvan) 1,834; (Beauville) 1,552. **C30:** (cowl less w/s) 139; (157" chassis & cab) 6,071. **P30:** (125" chassis) 278; (125" aluminum panel) 71; (133" chassis) 1,378; (133" aluminum panel) 107; (157" steel panel) 1,052; (157" chassis) 1,669; (137" aluminum panel) 70; (137" motorhome chassis) 788 and (157" motorhome chassis) 821. **Note:** Figures based on cumulative model year through August 31, 1971 including all trucks made in U.S. factories for domestic/Canadian/export markets. Figures do not include El Caminos (counted with autos). Suburban totals combine panel-door and end-gate model production; model number shown is that of the panel-door version.

1971 Chevrolet Vega Panel Express (OCW)

ENGINE (Std.: all models, exc. Vega): Inline. OHV. Six-cylinder. Cast iron block. Bore & stroke: 3.9 in. x 4.5 in. Displacement: 250 cu. in. Compression ratio: 8.5:1. Brake horsepower: 145 at 4200 R.P.M. Max. Torque: 230 lbs.-ft. at 1600 R.P.M. Net horsepower: 110 at 4000 R.P.M. Seven main bearings. Mechanical valve lifters. Carburetor: Rochester one-barrel.

ENGINE (Opt.): Inline. OHV. Six-cylinder. Cast iron block. Bore & stroke: 3⅞ in. x 4⅛ in. Displacement: 292 cu. in. Compression ratio: 8.0:1. Brake horsepower: 165 at 4000 R.P.M. Max. Torque: 270 lbs.-ft. at 1600 R.P.M. Net horsepower: 125 at 3600 R.P.M. Seven main bearings. Hydraulic valve lifters. Carburetor: Rochester one-barrel.

ENGINE (Opt.): V-block. OHV. Eight-cylinder. Cast iron block. Bore & stroke: 3.875 in. x 3.25 in. Displacement: 307 cu. in. Compression ratio: 8.5:1. Brake horsepower: 200 at 4600 R.P.M. Max. Torque: 300 lbs.-ft. at 2400 R.P.M. Net horsepower: 135 at 4000 R.P.M. Five main bearings. Hydraulic valve lifters. Carburetor: Rochester two-barrel.

ENGINE (Opt. Series 20): V-block. OHV. Eight-cylinder. Cast iron block. Bore & stroke: 3.875 in. x 3.25 in. Displacement: 307 cu. in. Compression ratio: 8.5:1. Brake horsepower: 215 at 4800 R.P.M. Max. Torque: 305 lbs.-ft. at 2800 R.P.M. Net horsepower: 135 at 4000 R.P.M. Five main bearings. Hydraulic valve lifters. Carburetor: Rochester two-barrel.

ENGINE (Opt. 350 V-8): V-block. OHV. Eight-cylinder. Cast iron block. Bore & stroke: 4.0 in. x 3.5 in. Displacement: 350 cu. in. Compression ratio: 8.5:1. Brake horsepower: 250 at 4600 R.P.M. Max. Torque: 350 lbs.-ft. at 3000 R.P.M. Net horsepower: 170 at 3600 R.P.M. Five main bearings. Hydraulic valve lifters. Carburetor: Rochester two-barrel.

ENGINE (Opt. 400 V-8): V-block. OHV. Eight-cylinder. Cast iron block. Bore & stroke: 4.125 in. x 3.75 in. Displacement: 402 cu. in. Compression ratio: 8.5:1. Brake horsepower: 300 at 4800 R.P.M. Net horsepower: 240 at 4400 R.P.M. Five main bearings. Hydraulic valve lifters. Carburetor: Rochester four-barrel.

ENGINE (Std. Vega): Inline. OHV. Four-cylinder. Aluminum block. Bore & stroke: 3.501 in. x 3.625 in. Displacement: 140 cu. in. Compression ratio: 8.0:1. Brake horsepower: 90 at 4600-4800 R.P.M. Net horsepower: 72 at 4200 R.P.M. Max. Torque: 115 lbs.-ft. at 2400 R.P.M. Five main bearings. Hydraulic valve lifters. Carburetor: one-barrel.

ENGINE (Opt. El Camino/SS): V-block. OHV. Eight-cylinder. Cast iron block. Bore & stroke: 4.251 in. x 4.00 in. Displacement: 454 cu. in. Compression ratio: 8.5:1. Brake horsepower: 365 at 4800 R.P.M. Max. Torque: 465 lbs.-ft. at 3200 R.P.M. Net horsepower: 285. Five main bearings. Hydraulic valve lifters. Carburetor: four-barrel.

ENGINE (Opt. El Camino/SS): V-block. OHV. Eight-cylinder. Cast iron block. Bore & stroke: 4.251 in. x 4.00 in. Displacement: 454 cu. in. Compression ratio: 9.0:1. Brake horsepower: 425 at 5600 R.P.M. Max. Torque: 475 lbs.-ft. at 4000 R.P.M. Five main bearings. Hydraulic valve lifters. Carburetor: four-barrel.

CHASSIS (C10): Wheelbase: 115/127 in. Tires: (115 in. w.b.) G78-15B; (127 in. w.b.) H78-15B.

CHASSIS (C20): Wheelbase: 127/133 in. Tires: 8.75 x 16.5 six-ply.

CHASSIS (C30): Wheelbase: 133 in. Tires: 8.75 x 16.5.

CHASSIS (K10): Wheelbase: 115/127 in. Tires: (115 in. w.b.) G78-15B; (127 in. w.b.) H78-15B.

CHASSIS (K20): Wheelbase: 127 in. Tires: 8.75 x 16.5, six-ply.

CHASSIS (G10): Wheelbase: 110/125 in. Overall length: 178/202.2 in. Height 80 in. Tires: F78-4B.

CHASSIS (G20): Wheelbase: 110/125 in. Overall length: 178/202.2 in. Height: 80 in. Tires: G78-15B.

CHASSIS (G30): Wheelbase: 110/125 in. Overall length: 178/202.2 in. Height: 80 in. Tires: 8 x 16.5.

CHASSIS (P10): Wheelbase: 102 in. Height: 75 in. Tires: G78-15B.

CHASSIS (P20): Wheelbase: 125/133 in. Overall length: 220.75/244.75 in. Tires: 8.75 x 16.5.

CHASSIS (P30): Wheelbase: 125/157 in. Overall length: 220.75/265.75 in. Tires: 8.75 x 16.5.

CHASSIS (Vega): Wheelbase: 97 in. Overall length: 176 in. Height: 51.8 in. Front tread: 54.8 in. Rear tread: 53.6 in. Tires: 6.00-13B.

CHASSIS (Blazer): Wheelbase: 104 in. Overall length: 177.5 in. Height: 68.7 in. Front tread: 60.4 in. Rear tread: 60.4 in. Tires: E78-15B.

CHASSIS (El Camino): Wheelbase: 116 in. Overall length: 206.8 in. Height: 54.4 in. Front tread: 60.2 in. Rear tread: 59.2 in. Tires: E78-14B.

TECHNICAL: Saginaw manual, fully-synchronized, transmission. Speeds: 3F/1R. Column-mounted gear shift lever. Single plate dry disc clutch (250 cu. in. engine); coil spring single dry plate (292/307/350/402/454 cu. in. engine). Rear axle: ½-Ton) semi-floating; ¾-Ton and 1-Ton) full-floating rear axle. Hydraulic, four-wheel brakes. Kelsey-Hayes pressed steel wheels. Technical options: Powerglide, THM 350 and THM 400 transmissions. Wide-ratio Muncie, three-speed manual or four-speed manual transmission w/floor shifter. Free-wheeling hubs (4x4). Positraction. No-Spin axle. Power brakes. Power steering. Front stabilizer ($19.40). Rear-leaf springs ($16.15). 42 Amp generator ($23.70). 9.50 x 165 x 8 tires ($52.05). Heavy duty battery ($17.25). Marker lights ($26.90). Heavy-duty rear springs ($19.40). Heavy-duty front shocks ($8.10). 4.10 axle ($10.95). 402 cu. in. V-8 ($177.55). Auxil. fuel tank ($80.70).

OPTIONS & PRICES: Rear bumper ($53.80). Extra wheel ($31.50). Radio ($69.95). Clock. Air conditioning. Deluxe heater. Gauge package (Ammeter, oil, temp. $12.95). Tilt wheel. Shoulder belts. Tinted glass ($19.40). Dual outside mirrors ($21.00). Dome light switch ($4.35). Side wheel carrier ($15.10). Full foam seat ($30.15). (½-Tons) — "292" six-cylinder engine ($95). "307" V-8 engine ($120). "400" V-8 engine (avg. $160). "350" V-8 in El Camino ($70). Four-speed transmission ($190). Powerglide transmission ($195). THM transmission (avg. $280). Power brakes (avg. $50). Power steering (avg. $115). Four-wheel-drive system (avg. $570). (¾-Tons) — "292" six-cylinder engine ($95). "307" V-8, over base six ($120). "400" V-8 over "307" ($175). Powerglide (avg. $210). THM transmission (avg. $245). Four-speed transmission (avg. $120). Power steering (avg. $140). Four-wheel-drive system (avg. $680). (1-Tons) — "307" V-8 over base six ($120). "292" six-cylinder engine ($95). "350" V-8 engine, over "307" ($45). "400" V-8 engine, over "350." LPG kit ($95). THM transmission ($245). New Process transmission ($30). Vacuum brakes ($45). Power steering (avg. $135). Nine-foot platform equipment ($425). 12-foot platform equipment ($484). 157 inch wheelbase ($30).

OPTIONS/USEAGE: Tinted glass, van (27%). Cargo door lock, van (8%). Body glass, van (10%). Right side body glass, van (7%). Side door window glass, panel (1%). All tinted glass, light trucks (30%). Rear door glass, van (64%). Sliding rear window, light truck (3%). Bucket seats, light truck (3%). Custom bench seat (used on 967 light trucks). Bodyside belt molding , light truck (27%). Wide lower bodyside molding, light truck (28%). Upper bodyside molding, light truck (37%). Door edge guards, light truck (12%). Bodyside molding, van (1%). Deluxe air conditioning, light truck (25%). Roof air conditioning, light truck (25%). Front air conditioning, van (3%). Rear air conditioning, van (1%). Painted camper mirror, light truck (3%). Stainless camper mirror, light truck (3%). West Coast Jr. mirror, stainless, light truck (10%); van (13%). Dual West Coast Sr. mirror, light truck (41%). Painted West Coast Jr. mirror, light truck (19%); van (50%). Body paint stripe, light truck (8%). Platform and Stake Rack Equipment, light truck (14%). Positraction, light truck (11%); van (12%); Step-Van (7%). Oil bath air cleaner, light truck (3%); van (5%). "350" light-duty V-8 engine, light truck (65%); van (49%). "292" six-cylinder engine, light truck (14%); van (68%). "396" V-8 engine, Step-Van (8%); light truck (6%). LPG engine package (used on only 387 light trucks and six vans). Four-speed transmission, light truck (14%); van (24%). Heavy-duty, close-ratio, four-speed manual transmission (used on 1,122 light trucks). Powerglide transmission, light truck (1%); van (7%); Step-Van (6%). M-38 THM transmission, light truck (45%); van (49%); Step-Van (22%). M-49 THM transmission, light truck (6%); van (17%); Step-Van (17%). Tilt steering wheel, light truck (2%). Power steering, light truck (43%); van (9%); Step-Van (17%). Wheel trim cover, light truck (53%); van (37%). AM/FM push-button radio, light truck (1%). Chrome rear bumper, light truck (3%). Chrome front bumper, light truck (22%). Cheyenne Super package, light truck (2%). Removable hardtop, Blazer/light truck, black (78%); white (21%). Custom Appearance package, van (9%). Custom Comfort and Convenience package, light truck (21%); van (10%). Camper Special package, light truck (18%). "CST" package, light truck (16%). **Notes:** A total of 72,609 light trucks were equipped with the "CST" trim package. A total of 7,190 vans were equipped with Custom Appearance features. A total of 20,501 pickups got the "Camper Special" option. A total of 9,867 trucks were Cheyenne Super models. "CS" (Custom) equipment was added to 8,686 vans and 98,895 light trucks. Over 50 percent of the light duty trucks were two-toned in standard colors or special colors. One two-tone paint combination ending with code "73" was used on only three trucks.

HISTORICAL: Introduction: The 1971 Chevy Van and Sportvan were introduced in May 1970. Production startup date for other '71s was Aug. 21, 1970. They hit the showrooms one month and eight days later (Sept. 29). Calendar year registrations, by weight class: (6000-lbs. and less) 450,354; (6001 to 10,000-lbs.) 145,358. Calendar year production was 739,478 units, outpacing the previous (1969) record of 683,694. This included 599,207 trucks with V-8 engines; 128,660 with inline six-cylinder engines; 345 with V-6s; 9,120 Vega Panels with the four-cylinder engine and 2,146 diesels. Note: El Caminos are most likely not included in many production totals, as they were sometimes counted in Chevelle passenger cars. Also, 15,670 vans were considered "Nova Sportsvans" and included with passenger car production total. Innovations: All 1971 Chevy truck engines were modified to operate on unleaded gasoline. Front disc brakes were standard on all conventional light duty models and Step-Vans. Independent front suspension was adopted for vans. The fuel evaporative system, formerly optional in California, became standard in all ½-tons. Historical notes: A big recovery from strike-year 1970, made this a banner season.

Several truck factories ran six days a week, all year, to keep up with demand. A.T. Olson was assistant general sales manager of the truck division.

Pricing

	5	4	3	2	1
1971					
Vega Panel Series					
Panel Express	400	840	1400	1950	2800
El Camino (V-8)					
Sport Pickup	1300	2550	4250	5900	8500
Custom Sport Pickup	1300	2650	4350	6050	8700
Blazer Series K10 (4x4)					
Blazer	1100	2220	3700	5200	7400
Fleetside Pickups					
C10 Pickup (short box)	1400	2800	4650	6500	9300
C10 Pickup (long box)	1350	2700	4500	6300	9000
K10 Pickup (short box)	1300	2650	4350	6050	8700
K10 Pickup (long box)	1300	2550	4250	5900	8500
C20 Pickup (long box)	1200	2400	4000	5600	8000
C20 Pickup (long horn)	1150	2310	3850	5400	7700
K20 Pickup (long box)	1170	2340	3900	5450	7800
K20 Pickup (long horn)	1180	2370	3950	5500	7900
C30 Pickup (long horn)	900	1800	3000	4200	6000

NOTE: See notes for 1969-1970 model nomenclature.

	5	4	3	2	1
Stepside Pickups					
C10 Pickup (short box)	1350	2700	4500	6300	9000
C10 Pickup (long box)	1350	2700	4450	6250	8900
K10 Pickup (short box)	1350	2650	4400	6150	8800
K10 Pickup (long box)	1300	2550	4250	5900	8500
C20 Pickup (long box)	1300	2550	4250	5900	8500
K20 Pickup (long box)	1250	2520	4200	5850	8400
C30 Pickup (long horn)	1130	2250	3750	5250	7500
Chevy Van Series G10 — (½-Ton) — (110 in. w.b.)					
Panel Van	780	1560	2600	3600	5200
Sportvan	830	1650	2750	3850	5500
Beauville	900	1800	3000	4200	6000
Chevy Van Series G20 — (¾-Ton) — (110 in. w.b.)					
Sportvan	750	1560	2600	3600	5300
Beauville	830	1650	2750	3850	5500
Chevy Van Series G30 — (1-Ton) — (110 in. w.b.)					
Panel Van	680	1350	2250	3150	4500
Sportvan	700	1400	2350	3250	4700
Beauville	750	1500	2500	3500	5000
Step-Vans					
P10 Step Van	630	1250	2100	3000	4200
P20 Step Van	650	1300	2150	3050	4300
P30 Step Van	660	1320	2200	3100	4400
Panels and Suburbans					
C10 Suburban	1050	2100	3500	4900	7000
K10 Suburban	980	1950	3250	4550	6500
C20 Suburban	980	1950	3250	4550	6500
K20 Suburban	900	1800	3000	4200	6000
C20 Stake	750	1500	2500	3500	5000
C30 Stake	750	1500	2500	3500	5000

NOTE: 1955-up prices based on top of the line models.

1972 CHEVROLET

1972 Chevrolet El Camino (DFW)

LIGHT TRUCK — 1972 SERIES — (ALL ENGINES): — The Vega Panel Express was available, again, in 1972. Its grille was finished in a manner that made the vertical elements slightly less prominent. A model emblem was seen on the cowl. Otherwise, there was very little change.

Larger, one-piece corner lights were seen on the El Camino. Four bright moldings now split the grille into three horizontal segments. The center "bow-tie" emblem of 1971 was replaced with "Chevrolet" letters at the left-hand side of the lower grille segment. The "SS" package included cowl badges, hood locking pins, styled wheels, special vertically pleated door panels, round I.P. gauges and other extras.

Light trucks, including Blazers, looked similar to the previous year's model, except that the border of the grille surround was no longer black-finished. The Panel Delivery model was no longer offered. A new "Highlander" interior option was available on Pickups and Suburbans with the Custom Deluxe package and Blazers with the CST package. These options (CS and CST) added a cigarette lighter, door-operated dome light, bright trim on doors and instrument panel and bright window framing all around. The Highlander option added plaid upholstery in four combinations of orange, avacado, blue and gray colors and thick-pile carpeting in rich-looking black nylon blend. The Blazer came in 4x2 or 4x4 Sportabout versions and with some wild new decal packages. Fleetside pickups, in three different wheelbases, came in 16 models, plus Stepsides, chassis-cabs or stake truck, with 4x2 or 4x4 options. The Suburban was still a "three-door" with rear panel-door or end-gate options.

Chevy Vans continued to come in three basic models: Panel, Sportvan and Beauville. In the G10/G20 lines, all could be had on a 110 or 125 inch wheelbase. In the one-ton (G30) line, only the Panel was available with the shorter wheelbase, while all three came with the 125 inch stance. Base engine in the ½-ton Beauville was the 307 cubic inch/200 horsepower V-8; in the ¾- and one-ton the 350 cubic inch/250 horsepower V-8. Panels and Sportvans in all lines used the 250 cubic inch/145 horsepower inline six as base power plant.

Step-Vans looked identical to 1971 versions. The ½-ton (P10) models were sold in chassis and steel panel models on a 102 inch wheelbase. These were advertised as "Step Van 7" models (due to their seven-foot long bodies). The grilles had single round headlights in the *top* of the housings, with rectangular parking lamps below. The ¾-ton (P20) models offered 125 or 133 inch wheelbases and came in Step-Van chassis form or as "Step-Van King" steel or aluminum panel bodies. Step-Van King" did not refer to the wheelbase, but to body height and width. The "Kings" had their round headlamps *below* the rectangular parking lamps. The P30 models were the same sizes as the P20s, but had much higher GVW ratings — 7300 to 14,000 pounds, versus the ¾-ton's 6500-7500. More and more of these forward control chassis were being used for motorhome conversions.

An all-new LUV pickup truck was introduced in March 1972 as a "captive import" sourced from Isuzu Motors of Japan. The '72 is readily identifiable by its '55 Chevy-like egg-crate grille and of eight round reflectors and lights on the rear end. The name LUV stood for "Light Utility Vehicle." A total of 21,098 of these trucks were sold from March to December.

I.D. DATA: Serial number stamped on left door pillar. The VIN consists of 13 symbols. The first letter designates Chevrolet Motor Division. The second symbol (letter) indicates vehicle type. The third, a letter, identifies the engine. Starting: ( ) ( ) ( ) 2 ( ) 100001 and up. Engine numbers located: (6-cyl.) stamped on a boss, right side of block to rear of distributor. (V-8) stamped on a boss, right front of block. Serial number type, the fourth symbol, a number indicates tonnage. The fifth symbol reflects model type. The sixth symbol is model year. The seventh identifies the assembly plant with the last six digits serving as the vehicle production numbers.

Model	Body Type	Price	Weight	Prod. Total
Vega Series				
14105	½-Ton Panel Express	2079	2190	4114
LUV Series				
82	½-Ton Pickup	2196	2360	21,098
El Camino — ½-Ton — (307 cu. in. V-8)				
13480	Sport Pickup	2881	3340	—
13680	Custom Sport Pickup	2960	3350	—
Blazer (307 cu. in. V-8)				
Series K10				
KE10514	½-Ton 4x4 Utility	3258	3790	44,266
CE10514	½-Ton 4x2 Utility	2700	3506	3357
Fleetside Models				
Series C10				
CE10734	½-Ton 115 in. w.b.	2796	3560	39,730
CE10934	½-Ton 127 in. w.b.	2832	3720	273,249
Series K10				
KE10734	½-Ton 4x4 115 in. w.b.	3371	—	6069
KE10934	½-Ton 4x4 127 in. w.b.	3407	—	18,431
Series C20 — ¾-Ton — 127/133 in. w.b.				
CE20934	Pickup (SWB)	3027	4030	94,458
CE21034	Longhorn Pickup (LWB)	3088	3950	3328
Series K20				
KE20934	¾-Ton 4x4 127 in. w.b.	3687	—	19,648
KE21034	¾-Ton 4x4 133 in. w.b.	3748	—	—
Series C30 — 1-Ton — 133 in. w.b				
CE31034	Longhorn Pickup	3164	4180	2450
Stepside Models				
Series C10				
CE10704	½-Ton 115 in. w.b.	2796	3560	22,042
CE10904	½-Ton 127 in. w.b.	2832	3640	7538
Series K10				
KE10704	½-Ton 4x4 115 in. w.b.	3371	—	1736
KE10904	½-Ton 4x4 127 in. w.b.	3407	—	407
Series C20				
CE20904	¾-Ton 127 in. w.b.	3027	3940	3973
Series K20				
KE20904	¾-Ton 4x4 127 in.	3687	—	755
Series C30				
CE31004	1-Ton in. w.b. 9 ft. box	3105	4090	1542
Vans/Panels				
Series G10 — ½-Ton — 110 in. w.b. (307 cu. in. V-8)*				
GE11005	Panel Van	2897	3550	12,205
GE11006	Sportvan	3405	3830	1346
GE11036	Beauville Sportvan	3684	3990	433
Series G20 — ¾-Ton — 110 in. w.b — (350 cu. in. V-8)*				
GE21005	Panel Van	3034	3640	4618
GE21006	Sportvan	3480	3910	605
GE21036	Beauville Sportvan	3759	4070	345

Model	Body Type	Price	Weight	Prod. Total
Series G30 — 1-Ton — 110 in. w.b. — (350 cu. in. V-8)*				
GE31005	Panel Van	3142	3900	623
GE31306	Sportvan	3718	4390	2036
GE31336	Beauville Sportvan	3997	4560	2020
Series P10				
PS10535	½-Ton Panel 7 ft.	3259	3810	2063
Series P20				
PE20835	¾-Ton Panel 10'/125" w.b.	4113	5240	1706
Series P-30				
PE30835	1-Ton Panel 10'/125" w.b.	4278	5400	559
Series C10				
CE10906	½-Ton Suburban (doors)	3610	4000	17,505
Series K10				
KE10906	½-Ton 4x4 Suburban (doors)	4185	—	3144
Series C20				
CE20906	¾-Ton Suburban (doors)	3767	4470	5277
Series K20 — (4x4)				
KE20906	¾-Ton Suburban (doors)	4427	—	1382

* 125 in. w.b. also available

Model	Body Type	Price	Weight	Prod. Total
Additional Models (all w/307 cu. in. V-8)Series C10				
CE10703	½-Ton Ch-Cab 115" w.b.	2645	3220	1640
Series K10				
KE10703	½-Ton 4x4 Ch-Cab 115" w.b.	3220	—	—
Series C20				
CE20903	¾-Ton Ch-Cab 127" w.b.	2875	3540	5974
	¾-Ton 8' Stake 127" w.b.	3168	4163	
Series C30				
CE31003	1-Ton Ch-Cab 133" w.b.	2962	3660	14,988

115 in. w.b. — 6½ ft. bed
127 in. w.b. — 8 ft. bed
133 in. w.b. — 9 ft. bed

ADDITIONAL PRODUCTION: G10/125 in. w.b.: (Panel 14,044; (Sportvan) 1,593; (Beauville) 997. **C10/127 in. w.b.:** (chassis & cab) 717. **P10/102 in. w.b.:** (Delivery chassis) 196. **G20/125 in. w.b.:** (Panel) 16,084; (Sportvan) 3,310; (Beauville) 5,581. **K20:** (4x4 chassis & cab) 676. **P20:** (125" chassis) 343; (125" aluminum panel) 52; (133" steel panel) 989; (133" chassis) 189; (133" aluminum panel) 42. **C30:** (cowl less w/s) 127; (chassis & cab w/157 in. w.b.) 8,944. **P30:** (125" chassis) 441; (125" aluminum panel) 125; (133" steel panel) 1,710; (133" chassis) 967; (133" aluminum panel) 127; (157" steel panel) 1,702; (157" chassis) 1,899; (157" aluminum panel) 231; (137" motorhome chassis) 2,267; (157" motorhome chassis) 2,942. **G30/125 in. w.b.:** (Panel van) 12,545.

ENGINE (Std. all except LUV/Vega): Inline. OHV. Six-cylinder. Cast iron block. Bore & stroke: 3.9 in. x 4.5 in. Displacement: 250 cu. in. Compression ratio: 8.5:1. Brake horsepower: 145 at 4200 R.P.M. Max. Torque: 230 lbs.-ft. at 1600 R.P.M. Net horsepower: 110 at 4000 R.P.M. Seven main bearings. Hydraulic valve lifters. Carburetor: Rochester one-barrel model 1.

ENGINE (Optional): Inline. OHV. Six-cylinder. Cast iron block. Bore & stroke: 3.875 in. x 4.125 in. Displacement: 292 cu. in. Compression ratio: 8.0:1. Brake horsepower: 165 at 4000 R.P.M. Max. Torque: 270 lbs.-ft. at 1600 R.P.M. Net horsepower: 125 at 3600 R.P.M. Seven main bearings. Hydraulic valve lifters. Carburetor: Rochester one-barrel.

ENGINE (Optional): V-block. OHV. Eight-cylinder. Cast iron block. Bore & stroke: 3.875 in. x 3.25 in. Displacement: 307 cu. in. Compression ratio: 8.5:1. Brake horsepower: 200 at 4600 R.P.M. Max. Torque: 300 lbs.-ft. at 2400 R.P.M. Net horsepower: 135 at 4000 R.P.M. Five main bearings. Hydraulic valve lifters. Carburetor: Rochester two-barrel.

ENGINE: (Optional): V-block. OHV. Eight-cylinder. Cast iron block. Bore ans Stroke: 4.0 x 3.5 in. Displacement: 350 cu. in. Compression ratio: 8.5:1. Brake horsepower: 250 at 4600 R.P.M. Torque: 350 lbs.-ft. at 3000 R.P.M. Net horsepower: 170 at 3600 R.P.M. Five main bearings. Hydraulic valve lifters. Carburetor: Rochester two-barrel.

ENGINE (Optional): V-block. OHV. Eight-cylinder. Cast iron block. Bore & stroke: 4.125 in. x 3.75 in. Displacement: 402 cu. in. Compression ratio: 8.5:1. Brake horsepower: 300 at 4800 R.P.M. Net horsepower: 240 at 4400 R.P.M. Five main bearings. Hydraulic valve lifters. Carburetor: Rochester four-barrel.

ENGINE (Opt. El Camino SS-RPO LS5): V-block. OHV. Eight-cylinder. Cast iron block. Bore & stroke: 4.251 in. x 4.00 in. Displacement: 454 cu. in. Compression ratio: 8.5:1. Net horsepower: 270 at 4000 R.P.M. Max. Torque: 390 lbs.-ft. at 3200 R.P.M. Five main bearings. Hydraulic valve lifters. Carburetor: Rochester four-barrel.

ENGINE: (Std. Vega): Inline. OHV. Four-cylinder. Aluminum block. Bore & stroke: 3.501 in. x 3.625 in. Displacement: 140 cu. in. Compression ratio: 8.0:1. Brake horsepower: 90 at 4600-4800 R.P.M. Net horsepower: 72 at 4200 R.P.M. Max. Torque: 115 lbs.-ft. at 2400 R.P.M. Five main bearings. Hydraulic valve lifters. Carburetor: one-barrel.

ENGINE (Opt. Vega): Inline. OHV. Four-cylinder. Aluminum block. Bore & stroke: 3.501 in. x 3.625 in. Displacement: 140 cu. in. Compression ratio: 8.0:1. Net horsepower: 85 at 4400 R.P.M. Max. Torque: 122 lbs.-ft. at 2400 R.P.M. Five main bearings. Hydraulic valve lifters. Carburetor: Staged two-barrel.

ENGINE (Std. LUV): Inline. OHV. Four-cylinder. Cast iron block. Bore & stroke: 3.31 in. x 3.23 in. Displacement: 110.8 cu. in. Compression ratio: 8.5:1. Net horsepower: 75 at 5000 R.P.M. Max. Torque: 88 lbs.-ft at 3000 R.P.M. Five main bearings. Hydraulic valve lifters. Carburetor: two-barrel.

CHASSIS (Series G10): Wheelbase: 110/125 in. Overall length: 178/202.2 in. Height 80 in. Tires: E78-14B.

CHASSIS (Series G20): Wheelbase: 110/125 in. Overall length: 178/202.2 in. Height: 80 in. Tires: G78-15B.

CHASSIS (Series G30): Wheelbase: 110/125 in. Overall length: 178/202.5 in. Height: 80 in. Tires: 8.75 x 16.5C.

CHASSIS (Series P10): Wheelbase: 102 in. Height: 75 in. Tires: G78-15B.

CHASSIS (Series P20): Wheelbase: 125/133 in. Overall length: 220.75/244.75 in. Tires: 8.75 x 16.5C.

CHASSIS (Series P30): Wheelbase: 125/157 in. Overall length: 220.75/265.75 in. Tires: 8.75 x 16C.

CHASSIS (LUV): Wheelbase: 102.4 in. Overall length: 173.8 in. Height: 59.3 in. Front tread: 54 in. Rear tread: 52.2 in. Tires: 6.00-14C.

CHASSIS (Series C10): Wheelbase: 115/127 in. Overall length: 200.5 in. Height: 74.5 in. Tires: (115 in. w.b.) G78-15B; (127 in. w.b.) H78-15B.

CHASSIS (Series C20): Wheelbase: 127/133 in. Overall length: 200.5 in. Height: 74.5 in. Tires: 8.75 x 16.5C.

CHASSIS (Series C30): Wheelbase: 133 in. Tires: 8.75 x 16.5.

CHASSIS (Series K10): Wheelbase: 115/127 in. Tires: (115 in. w.b.) G78-15B; (127 in. w.b.) H78-15B.

CHASSIS (Series K20): Wheelbase: 127 in. Tires: 8.75 x 16.5.

CHASSIS (Blazer): Wheelbase: 104 in. Overall length: 177.5 in. Height: 67.7 in. Front tread: 60.4 in. Rear tread: 60.4 in. (4x4). Tires: E78-15B.

CHASSIS (El Camino): Wheelbase: 116 in. Overall length: 206.8 in. Height: 54.4 in. Front tread: 60.2 in. Rear tread: 59.2 in. Tires: E78-14B.

CHASSIS (Vega): Wheelbase: 97 in. Overall length: 176 in. Height: 51.8 in. Front tread: 54.8 in. Rear tread: 53.6 in. Tires: E78-14A.

TECHNICAL: Three speed synchromesh. 3F/1R. Column-mounted gear shift lever. Single plate dry disc clutch (250 cu. in. engine); coil spring single dry plate (292/307/350/402 cu. in. engine). (½-Ton) semi-floating, (¾-Ton and 1-Ton) full-floating, rear axles Hydraulic four-wheel brakes. Kelsey-Hayes pressed steel wheels. Technical options: Turbo Hydramatic transmission. Powerglide transmission. Free-wheeling hubs (4x4). Four-speed transmission. Four-speed close-ratio transmission (El Camino). Auxiliary rear springs. No-Spin differential. Power steering. Camper package. Heavy-duty suspension. Heavy-duty three-speed transmission.

OPTION PRICES: (½-Ton) "292" six-cylinder engine ($90). "307" V-8 engine ($120). "400" V-8 engine (avg. $173). "350" V-8 engine, El Camino ($70). Four-speed transmission ($190). Powerglide transmission (avg. $195). THM transmission ($242). Power brakes ($50). Power steering (avg. $140). Four-wheel-drive ($575). (¾-Ton) "292" six-cylinder engine ($120). "307" V-8 engine, over six-cylinder ($120). "400" V-8 engine over "307" ($170). Powerglide transmission (avg. $210). THM transmission (avg. $210). Four-speed manual transmission ($105). Power steering (avg. $140). Four-wheel-drive ($660). (1-Ton) "307" V-8 engine over six-cylinder ($120). "292" six-cylinder engine ($97). "350" V-8 engine over "307" ($45). "400" V-8 engine ($177). LPG kit ($97). THM transmission ($248). Power steering ($135). Nine-foot platform ($425). 12-foot platform ($487). 157 inch wheelbase ($40).

OPTIONS: (½-Ton to 1-Ton Trucks with useage rates). **(Light Trucks)** Bodyside belt molding (33%). Wide lower belt molding (54%). Upper bodyside molding (46%). Door edge guards (17%). Deluxe air conditioning (33%). Roof-mounted air conditioning (34%). Custom Comfort & Appearance group (24%). Camper Special package (19%). Removeable top for Blazer, black (23%); (white) 76%. Gauge package (81%). Cheyenne Super package (7%). Custom Sport Truck option (22%). Chrome front bumper (22%). V37 chrome bumper (7%). Rear step bumper (20%). Full foam seat (21%). Painted rear bumper (7%). Tachometer (2%). Push-button radio (60%). AM/FM radio (3%). VF1 rear chrome bumper (3%). Tool and storage box (6%). Camper wiring harness (4%). Cargo lamp (5%). Wheel trim cover (31%). Chrome hub caps (16%). Tilt steering (9%). Blazer and 4x4 skid plate (26%). Power steering (58%). Deluxe wheel covers (8%). M-38 THM transmission (55%). M49 THM transmission (28%). Four-speed manual transmission (13%). LPG engine kit (used on 1,429 trucks). "396" V-8 engine (8%). "292" six-cylinder engine (8%). "350" V-8 engine (79%). 4x4 front locking hubs (86%). Positraction (15%). Bucket seats (4%). Front stabilizer (35%). Body paint stripe (6%). Platform and stake rack (13%). **(Vans):** Bodyside trim molding (1%). Front air conditioning (12%). Rear air conditioning (4%). Camper conversion (113 units). Custom Appearance package (9%). Custom Comfort and Convenience option (11%). Gauge package (60%). Rear chrome bumper (14%). Push-button radio (42%). Chrome hub caps (4%). Tilt steering (3%). M38 THM trans-

mission (65%). "350" V-8 engine (33%). Positraction (12%). Front stabilizer (57%). Jr. West Coast mirror, stainless (14%); painted (50%). Rear door glass (57%). Side door glass (28%). Swing-out rear door glass (22%). Stationary auxiliary seat (87%). Side rear door trim panel (used on 13 units). Rear door trim panel (used in 14 units). H-D rear springs (64%). No-Spin rear axle (8%). 3.73:1 rear axle (3%). 3.40:1 rear axle (32%). **(Step-Vans)** Body insulation (6%). Roof insulation (5%). Gauge package (96%). Cargo lamp (37%). Dual rear wheel conversion (88%). Roof marker clearance lamps (10%). Roof marker cluster bar (5%). M-38 THM transmission (7%). M49 THM transmission (15%). Four-speed manual transmission (19%). LPG engine kit (nine units). "396" V-8 engine (51%). "292" six-cylinder engine (79%). "350" V-8 engine (100%). Positraction (3%). 74-inch rear doors w/piano hinges (4%); w/straps (7%). **Note:** All production and options use information in this section is based on Chevrolet records covering cumulative model year through July 31, 1972. Figures indicate what percentage of trucks eligible for an option were built with it. For example, the 396 cubic inch V-8 was not available in all Step-Vans so the 77% figure does not apply to total Step-Van output; only to those Step-Vans available with the 396 V-8. The "production total" for LUV pickups is actually the number *sold* between March and December 1972.

HISTORICAL: Introduced: (LUV) March 1972; (others) Sept. 21, 1971. Calendar year registrations: (Nova Sportvan) 16,839. (Others) 774,871 including 165,829 Chevy Van/El Caminos/Blazer/Vega panel/LUV. Calendar year registrations by weight class: (6000 lbs. and less) 539,242; (6000-10,000 lbs.) 722,379. Calendar year production: 770,773 units or 31.10% share of total truck market. Calendar year sales: 748,478. Model year production by tons and engine: ½-Ton: (4/6-cyl.) 85,120; (V-8) 387,582; (both) 472,702. ¾-Ton: (4/6-cyl.) 15,952; (V-8) 153,383; (both) 169,335. 1-Ton: (4/6-cyl.) 8,316; (V-8) 49,929; (both) 58,245. **Grand Total:** 700,282 units. **Additional production breakouts:** (Camper Specials) 32,226; (Light truck w/Custom Comfort and Convenience) 156,391; (Van w/Custom Comfort and Convenience) 8,993; (Van w/Custom Appearance pkg.) 7,379. (Factory van-campers) 113; (Custom Sport Trucks) 142,636; (Cheyenne Supers) 40,636. Innovations: Front disc brakes made standard in light-duty trucks. Sliding load door made standard on vans. New cab trim and stain-resistant acrylic enamel paint finish. Stellite-faced exhaust valves in 350 and 400 cu. in. engines. Exhaust valve rotators added to 307/350/400 cu. in. V-8s. Four-barrel 350 cu. in. V-8 optional in ½-ton vans. All-new LUV pickup introduced. Highs in production (828,961 units) and sales (845,000) for 1972 broke 1971's records. During 1972, Chevrolet predicted that it would have its first one-million truck year in 1973. A.T. Olson was assistant general sales manager, the top spot in the truck division.

Pricing

1972	5	4	3	2	1
Vega (½-Ton)					
Panel Express	400	840	1400	1950	2800
LUV Pickup (½-Ton)					
Pickup	440	870	1450	2050	2900
El Camino (V-8)					
Sport Pickup	1300	2550	4250	5900	8500
Custom Sport Pickup	1300	2650	4350	6050	8700
Blazer (4x4)					
C10 Blazer	1070	2150	3500	4900	7000
K10 Blazer	1130	2250	3750	5250	7500
Fleetside Pickups					
C10 Short Box Pickup	1450	2850	4750	6650	9500
C10 Long Box Pickup	1400	2850	4700	6600	9400
K10 Short Box Pickup	1350	2700	4500	6300	9000
K10 Long Box Pickup	1300	2650	4350	6050	8700
C20 Short Box Pickup	1200	2400	4000	5600	8000
C20 Long Box Pickup	1200	2460	4100	5700	8200
K20 Short Box Pickup	1170	2340	3900	5450	7800
K20 Long Box Pickup	1180	2370	3950	5500	7900
C30 Longhorn Pickup	900	1800	3000	4200	6000
Stepside Pickups					
C10 Short Box Pickup	1400	2800	4600	6400	9200
C10 Long Box Pickup	1400	2750	4550	6350	9100
K10 Short Box Pickup	1350	2700	4500	6300	9000
K10 Long Box Pickup	1300	2650	4350	6050	8700
C20 Short Box Pickup	1350	2700	4500	6300	9000
K20 Long Box Pickup	1300	2550	4250	5900	8500
C30 Longhorn Pickup	1130	2250	3750	5250	7500
Chevy Van					
G10 Panel Van	780	1560	2600	3600	5200
G10 Sportvan	830	1650	2750	3850	5500
G10 Beauville	900	1800	3000	4200	6000
G20 Panel Van	750	1500	2500	3500	5000
G20 Sportvan	780	1560	2600	3600	5200
G20 Beauville	530	1650	2750	3850	5500
Step-Van					
P10 Step-Van	600	1200	2000	2800	4000
P20 Step-Van	570	1140	1900	2650	3800
P30 Step-Van	540	1080	1800	2500	3600
Suburban					
C10 Suburban	1050	2100	3500	4900	7000
K10 Suburban	980	1950	3250	4550	6500
C20 Suburban	980	1950	3250	4550	6500
K20 Suburban	900	1800	3000	4200	6000
Stake Bed					
C20 Stake	750	1500	2500	3500	5000
C30 Stake	750	1500	2500	3500	5000

NOTE: 1955-up prices based on top of the line models.

1972 Chevrolet Custom 10 Fleetside Pickup (OCW)

1972 Chevrolet El Camino Sport Pickup (OCW)

1972 Chevrolet LUV Pickup (OCW)

1972 Chevrolet C20 Fleetside Pickup (OCW)

1972 Chevrolet Blazer Convertible (OCW)

1972 Chevrolet Cargo Delivery Van (OCW)

1972 Chevrolet 3-Door Suburban (OCW)

1972 Chevrolet C30 'Camper Special' Pickup

1972 Chevrolet Custom 10 Fleetside Pickup (OCW)

95

1973 CHEVROLET

1973 Chevrolet Cheyenne Fleetside Pickup (CP)

LIGHT TRUCK — 1973 SERIES — (ALL ENGINES): — The 1973 Chevrolet light trucks were radically changed in appearance from previous models. Major styling features consisted of curved side glass, doors that opened into the roofline and the elimination of roof drip rails. Running along the beltline was a sculptured cove. Along with the very wide and flat load box, it gave the new model very clean and distinctive lines. Also contributing to the Chevrolet's good looks was a simple egg-crate grille, suggestive of the 1955 passenger cars. The wider interior featured a powered, flow-through ventilation system.

A redesigned dash, with all instruments and controls placed in a semi-circular cluster within easy reach and view of the driver, was adopted. The steering wheel was also reduced in diameter. Technical changes were numerous. One-half ton models used rubber control arm bushings for a quieter and smoother ride. Leaf-springs replaced the rear coil springs used in 1972 on ½- and ¾-ton models. Four-wheel drive-models were fitted with longer front springs and a standard front stabilizer bar. All of the pickups now used a Salisbury rear end, as only the C10 had before. On C20 and C30 pickups, an Eaton locking differential was optional. It locked in upon a 100 rpm difference in the rear axles and had a governor to keep it from locking at above 15 m.p.h. Gas tanks were moved from inside the cabs to under them, at the rear. Full-time four-wheel-drive was introduced. It was available with only the V-8/Turbo-Hydramatic powertrain.

All earlier models were continued, except the Longhorns, the flat-face cowl and the nine-foot Stepside. The small-size C10 was named the "Fleetwood." Available trim levels included Custom, Custom Deluxe, Cheyenne and Cheyenne Super. Crew cabs, seating six, could be had on all ¾-ton and one-ton pickups. A new offering was the C30 pickup with dual rear wheels.

The Blazers had the full-time 4x4 system. Those with Cheyenne trim had a chrome circle on the rear fender. The tailgate came two ways. With the open Utility body, it was like the Fleetwood pickup's gate. When the optional hardtop was ordered, the gate had a manually operated roll-up window. This eliminated the lift-gate that had been used in older tops.

Chevy Vans had no exterior changes, except that the blue Chevy badge was now painted Ochre. The G10s and G20s had rubber bushings on the inner pivots of their front suspension for a quieter ride. The G30s had a new, 5700-lb. Salisbury axle.

The El Camino received its first new body since 1968. Accentuating its appearance, which was essentially that of the Chevelle, were two new trim packages: Estate and Conquista. The former was available on the standard El Camino and included a two-tone paint scheme and special body moldings. The Estate version could be ordered only on the Classic model. It consisted of full bodyside and tailgate accents with a wood-grain vinyl trim. In addition, the base El Camino had its own bodyside, tailgate, drip rail and wheel opening moldings.

1973 Chevrolet Cheyenne Fleetside Pickup (DFW/TSC)

Beginning early in 1973 the LUV model adopted rectangular-shaped headlamps in place of the circular units used since its 1972 introduction. The grille appeared to have a slightly finer gridwork. A unique feature of this mini-model was a crank-down spare lowered by a chain-and-winch system.

I.D. DATA: Serial number located. Combination VIN and rating plate located on left door pillar. Third letter identifies engine as follows: Q: 250 cu. in., L-6/1-bbl.; T: 292 cu. in., L-6/1-bbl.; X: 307 cu. in. V-8/2-bbl.; Y: 350 cu. in. V-8/4-bbl.; 2: 454 cu. in. V-8/4-bbl. Starting number: CC ( ) 143 ( ) 10001 and up. Engine numbers located: (6-cyl.) located on pad at right hand side of cylinder block at rear of distributor; (V-8) located on pad at front, right side of cylinder block. Starting: CC ( ) 143 ( ) 10001 and up (same as serial number).

Model	Body Type	Price	Weight	Prod. Total
Vega Series				
IHV05	½-Ton Panel Express	2107	2206	—
LUV Series — ½-Ton — 102.4 in. w.b.				
82	Mini Pickup	2406	2360	18,771
El Camino — ½-Ton — (307 cu. in. V-8)				
IAC80	Sport Pickup	2976	3625	—
IAD80	Custom Sport Pickup	3038	3635	—
Blazer (307 cu. in. V-8)				
Series K10				
CK10514	½-Ton 4x4 Utility	3319	3892	44,841
CC10514	½-Ton 4x2 Utility	2755	3227	3342
Fleetside Models				
Series C10				
CC10703	½-Ton 117.5 in. w.b.	2882	3741	43,987
CC10903	½-Ton 131.5 in. w.b.	2918	3843	339,089
Series K10				
CK10703	½-Ton 4x4 117.5 in. w.b.	3510	—	9605
CK10903	½-Ton 4x4 131.5 in. w.b.	3546	—	29,197
Series C20 — ¾-Ton — 131.5/164.5 in. w.b.				
CC20903	Pickup (SWB)	3119	4170	131,621
CC20963	6P Crew Cab Pickup (LWB)	4153	4947	7137
Series K20 — ¾-Ton (4x4) — 131.5/164.5 in. w.b.				
CK20903	Pickup (SWB)	3747	—	29,769
CK20963	6P Crew Cab Pickup (LWB)	4881	—	—
Series C30 — 1-Ton — 131.5/164.5 in. w.b.				
CC30903	Pickup (SWB)	3207	4326	7281
CC30963	6P Crew Cab Pickup (LWB)	4226	4944	2925
Stepside Models				
Series C10				
CC10703	½-Ton 117.5 in. w.b.	2882	3622	19,408
CC10903	½-Ton 131.5 in. w.b.	2918	3718	7040
Series K10				
CK10703	½-Ton 4x4 117.5 in. w.b.	3510	—	2112
CK10903	½-Ton 4x4 131.5 in. w.b.	3546	—	417
Series C20				
CC20903	¾-Ton 131.5 in. w.b.	3119	4045	4894
Series K20				
CK20903	¾-Ton 4x4 131.5 in. w.b.	3747	—	925
Series C30				
CC30903	1-Ton 131.5 in. w.b.	3207	4236	1939
Van/Panel				
Series G10 — ½-Ton — 110 in. w.b. (307 cu. in. V-8)*				
CG11005	Panel Van	2942	3518	13,408
CG11006	Sportvan	3451	3822	1111
CG11006	Beauville	3785	3985	475
Series G20 — ¾-Ton — 110 in. w.b. (350 cu. in. V-8)*				
CG21005	Panel Van	3079	3658	5988
CG21006	Sportvan	3531	3901	552
CG21006	Beauville	3861	4064	299
Series G30 — 1-Ton — 110 in. w.b. (350 cu. in. V-8)*				
CG31005	Panel Van	3188	3962	13,420
CG31006	Sportvan	3772	4358	2397
CG31306	Beauville	4102	4478	1999
Series P10				
CP10542	½-Ton Steel Panel 7 ft.	3453	4040	2877
Series P20				
CP20842	¾-Ton Steel Panel 10 ft.	4234	5278	2099
Series P30				
CP30842	1-Ton Steel Panel 10 ft.	4402	5448	631
Series C10				
CC20906	½-Ton Suburban (gate)	3710	4667	24,100
Series K10				
CK20906	½-Ton 4x4 Suburban (gate)	4338	—	—
Series C20				
CC20906	¾-Ton Suburban (gate)	4153	4947	9792
Series K20				
CK20906	¾-Ton 4x4 Suburban (gate)	4781	—	2642

* 125 inch wheelbase also available

Additional Body Choices

Series C10				
CC10703	½-Ton Ch-Cab 117.5" w.b.	2696	3296	1922
Series C20				
CC20903	¾-Ton Ch-Cab 131.5" w.b.	2934	3650	877
Series K10				
KC10703	½-Ton 4x4 Ch-Cab 117" w.b.	3334	—	—
Series K20				
KC20903	¾-Ton Ch-Cab 131.5" w.b.	3562	—	880
Series C20				
	¾-Ton Stake 131.5" w.b.	3327	4273	—
Series C30				
CC30903	1-Ton Ch-Cab 131.5" w.b.	3023	3810	475

1973 Chevrolet El Camino SS (CP)

ADDITIONAL PRODUCTION: G10/125 in. w.b.: (Chevy Van) 13,956; (Sportvan) 1,936; (Beauville) 1,043. **P10:** (chassis) 281. **G20/125 in. w.b.:** (Chevy Van) 20,515; (Sportvan) 3,966; (Beauville) 7,750. **C20:** (chassis and Crew Cab) 112. **P20:** (133'' steel panel) 1,282; (125'' aluminum panel) 107; (133'' aluminum panel) 58; (125'' chassis only) 409; (133'' chassis only) 4,151. **C30:** (135.5'' chassis and cab) 17,422; (159.5 inch chassis and cab) 12,088; (164.5'' chassis and Crew Cab) 80. **P30:** (133'' steel panel) 1,282; (125'' aluminum panel) 107; (133'' aluminum panel) 98; (125'' chassis only) 409; (133'' chassis only) 156. **NOTE:** Figures on based on records of Chevrolet cumulative model year production through Aug. 31, 1973.

ENGINE (Std: all, except El Camino/LUV/Vega/K20-30/ C20): Inline. OHV. Six-cylinder. Cast iron block. Bore & stroke: 3⅞ in. x 3½ in. Displacement: 250 cu. in. Compression ratio: 8.25:1. Net horsepower: 100 at 3600 R.P.M. Max. Torque: 175 lbs.-ft. at 2000 R.P.M. Seven main bearings. Hydraulic valve lifters. Carburetor: Rochester one-barrel.

1973 Chevrolet Blazer (JAG)

ENGINE (Opt: C10/Blazer/G10/P Series; Std. El Camino): V-block. OHV. Eight-cylinder. Cast iron block. Bore & stroke: 3⅞ in. x 3¼ in. Displacement: 307 cu. in. Compression ratio: 8.5:1. Net horsepower: 115 at 3600 R.P.M. Max. Torque: 205 lbs.-ft. at 2000 R.P.M. Five main bearings. Hydraulic valve lifters. Carburetor: two-barrel.

ENGINE (Opt: C/K Series/P20-30): Inline. OHV. Six-cylinder. Cast iron block. Bore & stroke: 3⅞ in. x 4⅛ in. Displacement: 292 cu. in. Compression ratio: 8.0:1. Net horsepower: 120 at 3600 R.P.M. Max. Torque: 225 lbs.-ft. at 2000 R.P.M. Seven main bearings. Hydraulic valve lifters. Carburetor: one-barrel.

ENGINE (Std: C20/K20/K30; Opt: G10/G20/G30/P Series/ El Camino): V-block. OHV. Eight-cylinder. Cast iron block. Bore & stroke: 4 in. x 3.48 in. Displacement: 350 cu. in. Compression ratio: 8.5:1. Net horsepower: 155 at 4000 R.P.M. Max. Torque: 255 lbs.-ft. at 2400 R.P.M. Five main bearings. Hydraulic valve lifters. Carburetor: two-barrel.

ENGINE (Opt: El Camino/C20/C30/Suburban 4x2/ P30): V-block. OHV. Eight-cylinder. Cast iron block. Bore & stroke: 4.251 in. x 4.0 in. Displacement: 454 cu. in. Compression ratio: 8.25:1. Net horsepower: 240 at 4000 R.P.M. Max. Torque: 355 lbs.-ft. at 2800 R.P.M. Five main bearings. Hydraulic valve lifters. Carburetor: Rochester model Quadra-Jet, four-barrel.

ENGINE (Opt: El Camino): V-block. OHV. Eight-cylinder. Cast iron block. Bore & stroke: 4 in. x 3.48 in. Displacement: 350 cu. in. Compression ratio: 8.5:1. Net horsepower: 175 at 4000 R.P.M. Max. Torque: 260 lbs.-ft. at 2800 R.P.M. Five main bearings. Hydraulic valve lifters. Carburetor: Rochester model Quadra-Jet, four-barrel.

1973 Chevrolet 4-door Suburban Cheyenne (CP)

ENGINE (Std: Vega): Inline. OHV. Four-cylinder. Aluminum block. Bore & stroke: 3.501 in. x 3.625 in. Displacement: 140 cu. in. Compression ratio: 8.0:1. Net horsepower: 72 at 4200 R.P.M. Max. Torque: 115 lbs.-ft. at 2400 R.P.M. Five main bearings. Hydraulic valve lifters. Carburetor: one-barrel.

ENGINE (Opt: Vega): Inline. OHV. Four-cylinder. Aluminum block. Bore & stroke: 3.501 in. x 3.625 in. Displacement: 140 cu. in. Compression ratio: 8.0:1. Net horsepower: 85 at 4400 R.P.M. Max. Torque: 122 lbs.-ft. at 2400 R.P.M. Five main bearings. Hydraulic valve lifters. Carburetor: Staged two-barrel.

ENGINE (Std: LUV): Inline. OHV. Four-cylinder. Cast iron block. Bore & stroke: 3.31 in. x 3.23 in. Displacement: 110.8 cu. in. Compression ratio: 8.5:1. Net horsepower: 75 at 5000 R.P.M. Max. Torque: 88 lbs.-ft. at 3000 R.P.M. Five main bearings. Carburetor: two-barrel.

CHASSIS (Series C10): Wheelbase: 117.5/131.5 in. Overall length: 191.2/212 in. Height: 69.8 in. Front tread: 65.8 in. Rear tread: 62.7 in. Tires: G78-15B.

CHASSIS (Series C20): Wheelbase: 117.5/131.5/164.5 in. Overall length: 191.5/212/244.43 in. Height: 69.8 in. Front tread: 65.8 in. Rear tread: 62.7 in.

CHASSIS (Series C30): Wheelbase: 131.5/164.5 in. Overall length: 212/244.43 in. Height: 71.8 in. Front tread: 65.8 in. Rear tread: 62.7 in. Tires: (Regular cab) 8.75 x 16.5C; (Crew Cab) 9.50 x 16.5E.

CHASSIS (Series K10): Wheelbase: 117.5/131.5 in. Overall length: 191.3/212 in. Height: 72 in. Front tread: 65.8 in. Rear tread: 62.7 in. Tires: G78-15B.

CHASSIS (Series K20): Wheelbase: 117.5/131.5 in. Overall length: 191.3/212 in. Height: 73.9 in. Front tread: 65.8 in. Rear tread: 62.7 in. Tires: 8.75 x 16.5C.

CHASSIS (Blazer): Wheelbase: 106.5 in. Overall length: 184.5 in. Height: (4x2 w/o top) 67.5 in.; (4x2 w/top) 69.5; (4x4 w/o top) 69.5; (4x4 w/top) 71.5. Front tread: 64.5 in. Rear tread: 63.0 in. — 2-wd. Front tread: 65.75 in. Rear tread: 62.75 in. Tires: E78-15B.

1973 Chevrolet Custom Deluxe 10 Suburban (IMSC/JLM)

CHASSIS (El Camino): Wheelbase: 116 in. Overall length: 201.6 in. Height: 53.8 in. Front tread: 58.5 in. Rear tread: 57.8 in. Tires: G78-14B.

CHASSIS (LUV): Wheelbase: 102.4 in. Overall length: 173.8 in. Height: 59.3 in. Front tread: 54 in. Rear tread: 52.2 in. Tires: A78-13B.

CHASSIS (Vega): Wheelbase: 97 in. Overall length: 176 in. Height: 51.8 in. Front tread: 54.8 in. Rear tread: 53.6 in. Tires: A78-13B.

CHASSIS (Series G10): Wheelbase: 110/125 in. Overall length: 178/202.2 in. Tires: E78-14A.

CHASSIS (Series G20): Wheelbase: 110/125 in. Overall length: 178/202.2 in. Tires: G78-15B.

CHASSIS (Series G30): Wheelbase: 110/125 in. Overall length: 178/202.2 in. Tires: 8.00 x 16.5C.

CHASSIS (Series P10): Wheelbase: 102 in. Height: 75 in. Tires: G78-15B.

CHASSIS (Series P20): Wheelbase: 125/133 in. Overall length: 220.75/244.75 in. Tires: 8.75 x 16.5C.

CHASSIS (Series P30): Wheelbase: 125/157 in. Overall length: 220.75/265.75 in. Tires: 8.75 x 16.5C.

OPTIONS: Front chrome bumper. Radio AM, AM/FM. Clock. Power steering. Custom deluxe interior. Cheyenne interior. Cheyenne super interior. Below-Eye-Line mirrors. Drip moldings. Sliding rear window. Cargo lamp. Gauge package. Air conditioning. Tachometer. Comfortilt steering wheel. Chrome bumper. Exterior tool and storage compartment. Wheel covers. White wall tires. Special trim molding. Wood-grain exterior trim. Rear-step bumper. Glide-out spare tire carrier. Additional Vega options: Special ride and handling package. Rear window air deflector.

HISTORICAL: Calendar year sales: 923,189. First year for 454 cu. in. V-8 option for standard trucks. Salisbury rear axle adopted. Six passenger model introduced. Fuel tank re-located outside cab to a position on the right frame rail. New energy-absorbing steering column.

1973 Chevrolet Vega Panel Express (CP)

Pricing

1974 Chevrolet 4x4 Fleetside Pickup (JAG)

1973	5	4	3	2	1
Vega					
Panel	380	750	1250	1750	2500
LUV					
Pickup	420	840	1400	1950	2800
El Camino					
Pickup	750	1500	2500	3500	5000
Custom Pickup	830	1650	2750	3850	5500
Blazer K-10					
Blazer 2-wd	830	1650	2750	3850	5500
Blazer 4-wd	980	1950	3250	4550	6500
C-10 (½-Ton)					
Stepside short box	810	1620	2700	3800	5400
Stepside long box	830	1650	2750	3850	5500
Fleetside short box	840	1680	2800	3900	5600
Fleetside long box	850	1700	2850	4000	5700
Suburban	830	1650	2750	3850	5500
K-10 4-wd (½-Ton)					
Stepside short box	780	1560	2600	3600	5200
Stepside long box	800	1600	2650	3700	5300
Fleetside short box	810	1620	2700	3800	5400
Fleetside long box	830	1650	2750	3850	5500
Suburban	800	1600	2650	3700	5300
C-20 (¾-Ton)					
Stepside long box	750	1500	2500	3500	5000
Fleetside long box	780	1560	2600	3600	5200
Long box 6P	720	1450	2400	3300	4800
Suburban	770	1550	2550	3600	5100
K-20 4-wd (¾-Ton)					
Stepside long box	800	1600	2650	3700	5300
Fleetside long box	810	1620	2700	3800	5400
Long box 6P	750	1500	2500	3500	5000
Suburban	800	1600	2650	3700	5300
C-30 (1-Ton)					
Stepside long box	720	1450	2400	3300	4800
Fleetside long box	750	1500	2500	3500	5000
Long box 6P	700	1400	2350	3250	4700
Series CG Panels & Vans (½-Ton)					
Panel	600	1200	2000	2800	4000
Sport Van	750	1500	2500	3500	5000
Beauville Van	780	1560	2600	3600	5200
Series CG Panels & Vans (¾-Ton)					
Panel	570	1140	1900	2650	3800
Sport Van	720	1450	2400	3300	4800
Beauville Van	750	1500	2500	3500	5000
Series CG Panels & Vans (1-Ton)					
Panel	540	1080	1800	2500	3600
Sport Van	700	1400	2300	3200	4600
Beauville Van	720	1450	2400	3300	4800
Series P-10, P-20, P-30 Panels					
P-10 Panel	530	1050	1750	2450	3500
P-20 Panel	520	1020	1700	2400	3400
P-30 Panel	500	1000	1650	2300	3300

NOTE: 1955-up prices based on top of the line models.

LIGHT TRUCK — 1974 SERIES — (ALL ENGINES): — The LUV, for 1974, adopted vertical taillights with a square back-up light lens at the bottom. A "Mikado" trim package — with striped upholstery and a sporty three-spoke steering wheel — was available.

After being totally re-styled in 1973, the latest Chevrolet pickups and Suburbans were visually virtually unchanged. Exterior changes were highlighted by four new colors, improved below-eye-line mirrors and new optional bright roof drip moldings. Technical developments included use of a full-time unit on all V-8 engined 4x4 drive models and the computer matching of all brake systems to the GVW rating of each truck. The new braking system included a lining sensor on the front disc brakes. It sounded an audible signal when the pads needed replacement. In addition, all pickups had larger front disc and rear drum brakes as well as a new hydraulic booster power assist called "Hydro-Boost." Interior refinements included foam instrument panel padding with all trim levels. All models had an energy absorbing steering column and, on all models with automatic transmission, an anti-theft ignition system was used.

The El Camino continued to be a model of the Malibu series and carried a grille with obvious Mercedes-Benz overtones. The grille was split into six horizontal segments, three on each side of a vertical center molding. A new Classic model was added to the El Camino line. It featured a bright lower body sill molding, a full-width custom seat with a fold-down center arm rest, door panel trim, deluxe vinyl-coated headlines and a black-finished rearview mirror.

Chevy Vans and Sportvans were offered with a new two-tone paint treatment, improved optional below-eye-line mirrors and new optional bright roof drip moldings. Both models also had a restyled instrument cluster and panel as well as a new optional air conditioning system with air out-lets designed into the instrument panel. An AM/FM radio, not previously available, was new for 1974. All Vans now had a coolant recovery system, too.

The Vega Panel Express had a new front end with a divided four-slot grille and recessed headlamps. The front and rear sidemarker lamps were raised above bumper level and the rear license plate was now housed in the tailgate center, instead of below the bumper (the bumper was a thicker, 5-m.p.h. crash test type). The Panel Express had the same large swing-out tailgate arrangement as the Kammback wagon. The Chevrolet brochure described it as "our economy truck." It still came with just one bucket seat, rubber floor coverings and without side windows. Maximum cargo capacity was 50,.2 cubic feet. All 14 Vega color combinations were available. The Panel Express used the standard interior (without dash grab handle) in choices of black, neutral, green, saddle, red and chamois colors. Technical improvements included front brake lining wear sensors, electric windshield washer and a new 16-gallon gas tank, five gallons larger than in 1973. Interestingly, Chevy used the same artwork in the catalog illustration both years, airbrushing in the minor changes and adding "T. Tonies Bakery" lettering in the panel sides.

1974 Chevrolet El Camino Classic Sport Pickup (OCW)

I.D. DATA: Combination VIN and rating plate located on left door pillar. Third letter identifies engine as follows: 2=250 cu. in., L-G/1-bbl., T: 292 cu. in., L-G/1-bbl., Y: 350 cu. in. V-8/4-bbl., Z: 454 cu. in. V-8/4-bbl. There were 13 symbols. See 1972 section for full explanation. Starting: CC ( ) 134F 100001 and up. Engine numbers located: (6-cyl) on pad at right-hand side of cylinder block at rear of distributor; (V-8) on pad at front, right side of cylinder block. Starting: CC ( ) 134 ( ) 100001 and up (same as serial number).

Model	Body Type	Price	Weight	Prod. Total
Vega Series — ½-Ton				
IHV05	Panel Express	2404	2402	4289
LUV Series — ½-Ton				
CL10503	Pickup	2406	2360	Note 1
El Camino — ½-Ton — (350 cu. in. V-8)				
IAC80	Sport Pickup	3139	3817	Note 2
IAD80	Classic Pickup	3277	3832	Note 2
Blazer				
Series K10				
CK10514	½-Ton 4x4 Utility	3798	3954	Note 2
CC10514	½-Ton 4x2 Utility	3082	3759	Note 2
Fleetside Models				
Series C10				
CC10703	½-Ton 117.5 in. w.b.	3117	3757	Note 2
CC10903	½-Ton 131.5 in. w.b.	3153	3871	Note 2
Series K10				
CK10703	½-Ton 4x4 117.5 in. w.b.	3937	—	Note 2
CK10903	½-Ton 4x4 131.5 in. w.b.	3973	—	Note 2
Series C20 — ¾-Ton — 131.5/164.5 in. w.b.				
CC20903	Pickup (SWB)	3434	4219	Note 2
CC20963	Open Crew Cab Pickup (LWB)	4544	4967	Note 2
Series K20				
CK20903	¾-Ton 4x4 131.5 in. w.b.	4254	—	Note 2
Series C30				
CC30903	1-Ton 131.5 in. w.b.	3531	4304	Note 2
CC30963	1-Ton Crew Cab 164.5'' w.b.	4626	5002	Note 2
Stepside Models				
Series C10				
CC10703	½-Ton 117.5 in. w.b.	3117	3653	Note 2
CC10903	½-Ton 131.5 in. w.b.	3153	3761	Note 2
Series C20				
CC20903	¾-Ton 131.5 in. w.b.	3434	4109	Note 2
Series K10				
CK10703	½-Ton 4x4 117.5 in. w.b.	3937	—	Note 2
CK10903	½-Ton 4x4 131.5 in. w.b.	3973	—	Note 2
Series K20				
CK20903	¾-Ton 131.5 in. w.b.	4254	—	Note 2
Series C30				
CC30903	1-Ton 131.5 in. w.b.	3531	4304	Note 2

117.5 in. w.b. = 6.5 ft. box
131.5 in. w.b. = 8 ft. box
164.5 in. w.b. = Crew Cab (6 passenger)

Model	Body Type	Price	Weight	Prod. Total
Van/Panel				
Series G10 — ½-Ton — 110 in. w.b. (350 cu. in. V-8)*				
CG11005	Panel	3238	3516	Note 2
CG11006	Sportvan	3867	3833	Note 2
CG11006	Beauville	4232	3996	Note 2
Series G20 — ¾-Ton — 110 in. w.b. (350 cu. in. V-8)*				
CG21005	Panel	3377	3615	Note 2
CG21006	Sportvan	3965	3891	Note 2
CG21006	Beauville	4330	4054	Note 2
Series G30 — 1-Ton — 110 in. w.b. (350 cu. in. V-8)*				
CG31005	Panel	3495	3904	Note 2
CG31306	Sportvan	4200	4364	Note 2
CG31306	Beauville	4565	4577	Note 2
Series P10				
CP10542	½-Ton Steel Pnl. 7 ft.	3763	4064	Note 2
Series P20				
CP20842	¾-Ton Steel Pnl. 10 ft.	4634	5306	Note 2
Series P30				
CP30842	1-Ton Steel Pnl. 10 ft.	4842	5485	Note 2
Series C10				
CC10906	½-Ton Suburban (gate)	4026	4211	Note 2
Series K10				
CK10906	½-Ton 4x4 Suburban (gate)	4846	—	Note 2
Series C20				
CC20906	¾-Ton Suburban (gate)	4933	4946	Note 2
Series K20				
CK20906	¾-Ton 4x4 Suburban (gate)	5753	—	Note 2
Additional Body Choices				
Series C20				
CC20903	¾-Ton Ch-Cab 131.5'' w.b.	3267	3714	Note 2
Series K20				
KC20903	¾-Ton 4x4 Ch-Cab 131.5'' w.b.	4087	—	—
Series C20				
	¾-Ton Stake 131.5'' w.b.	3580	4342	—
Series K20				
	¾-Ton 4x4 Stake 131.5'' w.b.	4400	—	—
Series C30				
CC30903	1-Ton Ch-Cab 131.5'' w.b.	3364	3878	—

* 125 in. w.b. also available

NOTE 1: Calendar year sales of LUV pickups were 39,422 units in 1973 and 30,328 units in 1974.

1974 Chevrolet Fleetside Pickup (CP)

NOTE 2: Model year production by series was as follows: **(C10):** 445,699; **(C20):** 178,829; **(C30):** 39,964; **(P-Series):** 19,759; **(El Camino):** 51,223; **(Blazer):** 56,798; **(Suburban):** 41,882; **(Chevy Van):** 70,763; **(Sportvan):** 20,779; **(TOTAL):** 925,696. Note: Includes units built in Canada for the U.S. market.

ENGINE (Std. all except El Camino/LUV/Vega): Inline. OHV. Six-cylinder. Cast iron block. Bore & stroke: 3⅞ in. x 3½ in. Displacement: 250 cu. in. Compression ratio: 8.25:1. Net horsepower: 100 at 3600 R.P.M. Max. Torque: 175 lbs.-ft. at 1800 R.P.M. Seven main bearings. Hydraulic valve lifters. Carburetor: one-barrel.

ENGINE (Opt. C20/C30/K20; Std. G20/G30): Inline. OHV. Six-cylinder. Cast iron block. Bore & stroke: 3⅞ in. x 4.12 in. Displacement: 292 cu. in. Compression ratio: 8.0. Net horsepower: 120 at 3600 R.P.M. Max. Torque: 215 lbs. ft. at 2000 R.P.M. Seven main bearings. Hydraulic valve lifters. Carburetor: one-barrel.

1974 Chevrolet "Big Dooley" Crew Cab Pickup (CP)

ENGINE (Opt. C10/G10; Std. El Camino): Inline. OHV. Eig)ht-cylinder. Cast iron block. Bore & stroke: 4 in. x 3.48 in. Displacement: 350 cu. in. Compression ratio: 8.5. Brake horsepower: 145 at 3800 R.P.M. Net horsepower: 145 at 3600 R.P.M. Max. Torque: 250 lbs.-ft. at 2200 R.P.M. Five main bearings. Hydraulic valve lifters. Carburetor: two-barrel.

ENGINE (Optional: C10/C20/C30/K10/K20/G10/G20/G30/El Camino): Inline. OHV. Eight-cylinder. Cast iron block. Bore & stroke: 4 in. x 3.48 in. Displacement: 350 cu. in. Compression ratio: 8.5. Brake horsepower: 245 at 3800 R.P.M. Net horsepower: 160 at 3800 R.P.M. Max. Torque: 255 lbs.-ft. at 2400 R.P.M. Five main bearings. Hydraulic valve lifters. Carburetor: four-barrel.

ENGINE (Opt. C10/C20/C30/El Camino): Inline. OHV. Eight-cylinder. Cast iron block. Bore & stroke: 1¼ in. x 4 in. Displacement: 454 cu. in. Compression ratio: 8.5. Brake horsepower: 5. Net horsepower: 245 at 4000 R.P.M. Max. Torque: 365 lbs.-ft. at 2800 R.P.M. Five main bearings. Hydraulic valve lifters. Carburetor: Rochester four-barrel model Quadra-Jet.

ENGINE (Std. LUV): Inline. OHV. Four-cylinder. Cast iron block. Bore & stroke: 3.31 in. x 3.23 in. Displacement: 110.8 cu. in. Compression ratio: 8.5:1. Net horsepower: 75 at 5000 R.P.M. Max. Torque: 88 lbs.-ft at 3000 R.P.M. Five main bearings. Hydraulic valve lifters. Carburetor: two-barrel.

ENGINE (Std. Vega): Inline. OHV. Four-cylinder. Aluminum block. Bore & stroke: 3.501 in. x 3.625 in. Displacement: 140 cu. in. Compression ratio: 8.0:1. Net horsepower: 75 at 4200 R.P.M. Max. Torque: 115 lbs.-ft. at 2400 R.P.M. Five main bearings. Hydraulic valve lifters. Carburetor: one-barrel.

1974 Chevrolet Custom Deluxe 10 Fleetline (IMSC/JLM)

ENGINE (Opt. Vega): Inline. OHV. Four-cylinder. Aluminum block. Bore & stroke: 3.50 in. x 3.625 in. Displacement: 140 cu. in. Compression ratio: 8.0:1. Net horsepower: 85 at 4400 R.P.M. Max. Torque: 122 lbs.-ft. at 2400 R.P.M. Five main bearings. Hydraulic valve lifters. Carburetor: Staged two-barrel.

CHASSIS (Blazer): Wheelbase: 106.5 in. Overall length: 184.5 in. Height: **(4x2):** 67.5 in. (w/o top); 69.5 in. (w/top). **(4x4):** 69.5 in. (w/o top); 71.5 in. (w/top). Front tread: 64.5 in. Rear tread: 63.0 in. (4x2). Front tread: 65.75 in. Rear tread: 62.75 in. (4x4). Tires: E78-15B.

CHASSIS (El Camino): Wheelbase: 116 in. Overall length: 201.6 in. Height: 53.8 in. Front tread: 58.5 in. Rear tread: 57.8 in. Tires: GR78-14B.

1974 Chevrolet Blazer (CP)

CHASSIS (LUV): Wheelbase: 102.4 in. Overall length: 173.8 in. Height: 59.3 in. Front tread: 54 in. Rear tread: 52.2 in. Tires: A78-13B.

CHASSIS (Vega): Wheelbase: 97 in. Overall length: 176 in. Height: 51.8 in. Front tread: 54.8 in. Rear tread: 53.6 in. Tires: A78-13B.

CHASSIS (Series G10): Wheelbase: 110/125 in. Overall length: 178/202.2 in. Tires: E78-14A.

CHASSIS (Series G20): Wheelbase: 110/125 in. Overall length: 178/202.2 in. Tires: G78-15B.

CHASSIS (Series G30): Wheelbase: 110/125 in. Overall length: 178/202.2 in. Tires: 8.00 x 16.5C.

CHASSIS (Series P10): Wheelbase: 102 in. Height: 75 in. Tires: G78-15B.

CHASSIS (Series P20): Wheelbase: 125/133 in. Overall length: 220.75/244.75 in. Tires: 8.75 x 16.5C.

CHASSIS (Series P30): Wheelbase: 125/157 in. Overall length: 220.75/265.75 in. Tires: 8.75 x 16.5C.

1974 Chevrolet 4x4 Suburban (JAG)

100

1974 Chevrolet G10 Step Van (CP)

CHASSIS (Series C10): Wheelbase: 117.5/131.5 in. Overall length: 191.2/211.25 in. Height: 69.8 in. Front tread: 65.8 in. Rear tread: 62.7 in. Tires: G78-15B.

CHASSIS (Series C20): Wheelbase: 117.5/131.5/164.5 in. Overall length: 191.5/212/244.43 in. Height: 69.8 in. Front tread: 65.8 in. Rear tread: 62.7 in. Tires: 8.75 x 16.5C. (Crew Cab: 9.50 x 16.5D.)

CHASSIS (Series C30): Wheelbase: 131.5/164.5 in. Overall length: 212/244.43 in. Height: 71.8 in. Front tread: 65.8 in. Rear tread: 62.7 in. Tires: 8.75 x 16.5C. (Crew Cab: 9.50 x 16.5E.)

CHASSIS (Series K10): Wheelbase: 117.5/131.5 in. Overall length: 191.3/212 in. Height: 72 in. Front tread: 65.8 in. Rear tread: 62.7 in. Tires: G78-15B.

CHASSIS (Series K20): Wheelbase: 117.5/131.5 in. Overall length: 191.3/212 in. Height: 73.9 in. Front tread: 65.8 in. Rear tread: 62.7 in. Tires: 8.75 x 16.5C.

TECHNICAL: See 1972.

1974 Chevrolet Vega Panel Express (DFW)

OPTIONS: Radio AM, AM/FM. Power steering. Custom deluxe interior. Cheyenne interior. Cheyenne super interior. Below-Eye-Line mirrors. Drip molding. Sliding rear window. Cargo lamp. Gauge package. Air conditioning. Tachometer. Comfortilt steering wheel. Chrome bumpers. Chromed front bumper with rubber impact strips. Exterior tool and storage compartment. Wheel covers. White wall tires. Special trim molding. Wood-grain exterior trim. Rear-step bumper. Glide-out spare tire carrier. Additional El Camino options: SS package ($215). Conquista package. Estate package (Classic models only). Deluxe bumpers. Power door locks. Dual sport mirrors. Turbine I wheels. Wire wheel covers. Additional Vega Panel Express options: Variable ratio power steering. Electro-clear rear window. Defroster.

1974 Chevrolet El Camino SS (DFW)

1974 Chevrolet Beauville Sportvan (CP)

OPTION INSTALLATION RATES: (C10): Automatic transmission (63.4%). Manual disc brakes (58.5%). Power disc brakes (41.4%). Power steering (63.3%). AM radio (71.6%). AM/FM stereo radio (3.6%). Small V-8 (74.4%). Large V-8 (5.9%). Air conditioning (33.3%). Limited slip differential (3.3%). Tinted glass (38.9%). Steel-belted radial tires (1.2%). Wheel covers (29.3%). Interior trim package (47.3%). Exterior trim package (47.3%). Four-wheel-drive (9.8%). **(C20):** Automatic transmission (66.9%). Power disc brakes (100%). Power steering (85.5%). AM radio (74.5%). AM/FM Stereo radio (3.7%). Small V-8 (78.6%). Large V-8 (15.8%). Air conditioning (30.7%). Limited slip differential (14.3%). Tinted glass (40.5%). Interior trim package (47.3%). Exterior trim package (47.3%). Four-wheel-drive (21.6%). **(C30):** Automatic transmission (28.9%). Power steering (68.9%). AM radio (49.4%). AM/FM stereo radio (3.9%). Small V-8 engine (64.4%). Large V-8 engine (23.8%). Air conditioning (20%). Limited slip differential (10.1%). Dual rear wheels (75.6%). Tinted glass (29.5%). Wheel covers (1.8%). Interior trim package (22.6%). Exterior trim package (22.6%). **(P-Series):** Automatic transmission (56.2%). Manual disc brakes (9.2%). Power disc brakes (90.8%). Power steering (42%). Small V-8 (57.6%). Large V-8 (7%). Air conditioning (2.1%). Limited slip differential (1%). Dual rear wheels (56.1%). Tinted glass (11.5%). Wheel covers (1.7%). **(El Camino):** Automatic transmission (95.8%). Power steering (97.3%). AM radio (77.5%). AM/FM stereo radio (16.4%). Small V-8 (66.4%). Large V-8 (33.1%). Air conditioning (72.4%). Limited slip differential (9.9%). Tinted glass (90.9%). Steel-belted radial tires (16.8%). Wheel covers (70.3%). Interior trim package (44.5%). Exterior trim package (44.5%). **(Blazer):** Automatic transmission (81.5%). Power steering (95%). AM radio (77.4%). AM/FM stereo radio (11.8%). Small V-8 (96%). Air conditioning (47.4%). Limited slip differential (8.6%). Tinted glass (63.7%). Steel-belted radial tires (3.8%). Wheel covers (34.2%). Interior trim package (59.5%). Exterior trim package (59.5%). Four-wheel-drive (94.6%). **(Suburban):** Automatic transmission (89.3%). Power steering (71.5%). AM radio (67.7%). AM/FM stereo radio (12.5%). Small V—8 (62.7%). Large V-8 (33.7%). Air conditioning (76%). Limited slip (13%). Tinted glass (68.2%). Steel-belted radial tires (6.4%). Wheel covers (24.1%). Interior trim package (72.5%). Exterior trim package (72.5%). **(Chevy Van):** Automatic transmission (73.5%). Manual disc brakes (23.3%). Power disc brakes (76.7%). Power steering (41.8%). AM radio (43.4%). AM/FM stereo radio (2.4%). Small V-8 (77%). Air conditioning (11.6%). Limited slip (3.6%). Tinted glass (28.3%). Interior trim package (21.6%). Exterior trim package (21.6%). **(Sportvan):** Automatic transmission (91.5%). Power steering (89.1%). AM radio (69%). AM/FM stereo radio (10.3%). Small V-8 (94.2%). Air conditioning (64%). Limited slip (5.1%). Tinted glass (73.4%). Steel-belted radial tires (6.3%). Interior trim package (17%). Exterior trim package (17%). **Note:** "Small V-8" means 350 cu. in. or less; "large V-8" means over 350 cu. in.

HISTORICAL: Introduced September 2, 1973. Calendar year registrations: 803,864. Calendar year registrations by weight class: (6000-lbs. and less) 575,348; (6000 to 10,000 lbs.) 228,516. Calendar year production: 838,959 units or 29.44 percent of the U.S. truck market. On a calendar year basis, this was Chevrolet's second best year in truck sales in history with sales of 885,362 units and production of 896,130. The model year figures were, however, even more impressive with sales of 975,257 and 925,696 trucks built to 1974 specifications. This production total includes trucks built in Canada for sale here, but does not include LUVs (which *are* included in the sales total). An all-time production record, for the Flint, Mich. factory (339,678 trucks) was set. On a calendar year basis, 85.5% of Chevy's truck output was V-8 powered; 15.1% had six-cylinder engines and a mere 0.4% were diesel engined.

Pricing

1974	5	4	3	2	1
Vega					
Panel	380	750	1250	1750	2500
LUV					
Pickup	420	840	1400	1950	2800
El Camino					
Pickup	750	1500	2500	3500	5000
Custom Pickup	830	1650	2750	3850	5500
Blazer K10					
Blazer 2wd	830	1650	2750	3850	5500
Blazer 4wd	980	1950	3250	4550	6500

	5	4	3	2	1
C10 (½-Ton)					
Stepside short box	810	1620	2700	3800	5400
Stepside long box	830	1650	2750	3850	5500
Fleetside short box	840	1680	2800	3900	5600
Fleetside long box	850	1700	2850	4000	5700
Suburban	830	1650	2750	3850	5500
K10 4x4 (½-Ton)					
Stepside short box	780	1560	2600	3600	5200
Stepside long box	800	1600	2650	3700	5300
Fleetside short box	810	1620	2700	3800	5400
Fleetside long box	830	1650	2750	3850	5500
Suburban	800	1600	2650	3700	5300
C20 (¾-Ton)					
Stepside long box	750	1500	2500	3500	5000
Fleetside long box	780	1560	2600	3600	5200
Long box 6P	720	1450	2400	3300	4800
Suburban	770	1550	2550	3600	5100
K20 4x4 (¾-Ton)					
Stepside long box	800	1600	2650	3700	5300
Fleetside long box	810	1620	2700	3800	5400
Long box 6P	750	1500	2500	3500	5000
Suburban	800	1600	2650	3700	5300
C30 (1-Ton)					
Stepside long box	720	1450	2400	3300	4800
Fleetside long box	750	1500	2500	3500	5000
Long box 6P	700	1400	2350	3250	4700
Series CG Panels/Vans (½-Ton)					
Panel	600	1200	2000	2800	4000
Sport Van	750	1500	2500	3500	5000
Beauville Van	780	1560	2600	3600	5200
Series CG Panels/Vans (¾-Ton)					
Panel	570	1140	1900	2650	3800
Sport Van	720	1450	2400	3300	4800
Beauville Van	750	1500	2500	3500	5000
Series CG Panels/Vans (1-Ton)					
Panel	540	1080	1800	2500	3600
Sport Van	700	1400	2300	3200	4600
Beauville Van	720	1450	2400	3300	4800
Series P10/P20/P30 Step-Van					
P-10 Panel	530	1050	1750	2450	3500
P-20 Panel	520	1020	1700	2400	3400
P-30 Panel	500	1000	1650	2300	3300

NOTE: 1955-up prices based on top of the line models.

1975 CHEVROLET

1975 Chevrolet Fleetside Pickup (CP)

LIGHT TRUCK — 1975 SERIES — (ALL ENGINES): — The 1975 Chevrolet El Camino continued the basic 1974 look, but had a slightly revised grille. It was vertically segmented with nine prominent members. There was now a built-in license plate holder at the center of the bumper.

Light-duty trucks were promoted as having newly designed engine with increased efficiency. However, one truck enthusiast publication recommended that "since the catalytic converter adds to the cost of the truck, it's a good idea to specify chassis equipment sufficiently heavy-duty to exceed 6000-pounds (GVW) on C10s, K10s and Blazers." (With the heavy-duty options, the converter wasn't required.) The "Big Dualie" package (later called "Big Dooley") was one of several expanded optional equipment offerings. There were revised appearances, both inside and out.

Custom Deluxe was the base interior. It included plaid, foam-padded seats, a body-color headliner; padded armrests and plaid vinyl trim in a choice of four colors. The next-step-up was Scottsdale trim ($137-$199 extra), which included woodgrain door trim inserts, a cigarette lighter, courtesy lamps, color-keyed rubber floor mats, a little bit more exterior brightwork and seats covered with upholstery of nylon cloth and vinyl. Cheyenne trim ($258-$315) was the next notch on the totem pole and added more woodgraining, door pockets, headliner, nylon carpeting, the Deluxe steering wheel and more insulation. Top-of-the-line was the Silverado option ($312-$531) featuring seven-inch thick seat foam, richer upholstering (including Buffalo hide vinyl), full gauges and more exterior goodies.

Two types of 4x4 systems were optionally available in 1975. In combination with a V-8 and THM transmission, buyers got full-time 4x4. With a six-cylinder engine or manual gear box, a conventional 4x4 drivetrain was provided. This applied to both pickups/Suburbans and Blazers. According to *Four-Wheeler* magazine's June '75 issue, you could not order a V-8 powered 4x4 with manual transmission. The magazine said, "In 1974, they did build some that way and had many problems with the New Process full-time 4x4 system. The full-time transfer case just didn't want to work with the manual transmission."

Trucks under 6,001 lbs. GVW, except LUV, were equipped with catalytic converters. They significantly reduced hydrocarbon and carbon monoxide emissions to meet 1975 EPA standards. Introduced on all engines, except the LUV's, was a high-energy ignition (HEI) system, which delivered a hotter and more consistent spark for better starting power. Also introduced was an outside air carburetion intake and an early fuel evaporation system which provided faster engine warmup after cold start. Chevy's stalwart 250 cubic inch, six-cylinder engine had a new, integrally-cast cylinder head, with improved-flow intake manifold. All half-ton models with this engine had a larger standard clutch.

Specific styling changes for light-duty trucks (Bronco/pickup/Suburban) were headed by a revamped grille with a larger gridwork, clear-lensed parking lights and new front fender model identification combining model nameplates and series with a plaque. A restyled tailgate, with a quick-release control, was found on Fleetside pickups. All pickups could be equipped with an optional glide-out spare tire carrier.

Suburbans came with the Custom DeLuxe, Scottsdale or Silverado (not Cheyenne) packages. An "Estate" option, with woodgrain exterior paneling, was offered, too. A removable rear seat was available at extra-cost. Buyers still had a choice of end-gate or double panel-door rear styling.

The LUV truck again offered the "Mikado" trim package including striped upholstery, a fancier steering wheel, finer seat cloth, carpets and upgraded trim throughout.

1975 Chevrolet Pickup (CP)

Model	Body Type	Price	Weight	Prod. Total
Series C30				
CC30903	1-Ton 131.5" w.b.	4163	4379	Note 1
CC30963	1-Ton CrewCab 164.5" w.b.	5135	4987	Note 1
Stepside Pickups (V-8)				
Series C10				
CC10703	½-Ton 117.5 in. w.b.	3609	3649	Note 1
CC10903	½-Ton 131.5 in. w.b.	3652	3774	Note 1
Series K10				
CK10703	½-Ton 4x4 117.5" w.b.	4698	—	Note 1
CK10903	½-Ton 4x4 131.5" w.b.	4741	—	Note 1
Series C20				
CC20903	¾-Ton 131.5" w.b.	4030	4137	Note 1
CC20943	¾-Ton BonusCab 164.5" w.b.	4613	—	Note 1
CC20963	¾-Ton CrewCab 164.5" w.b.	5002	4861	Note 1
CC20943	¾-Ton BonusCab 164.5" w.b.	4613	—	Note 1
CC20963	¾-Ton BonusCab 164.5" w.b.	4446	—	Note 1
CC20963	¾-Ton CrewCab 164.5" w.b.	5002	4935	Note 1
Series C30				
CC30903	1-Ton 131.5" w.b.	4163	4344	Note 1
Vans/Panels				
Series G10 — ½-Ton — 110 in. w.b. (*) — "350" V-8				
CG11005	Panel Van	3443	3584	Note 1
CG11006	Sportvan	4103	3925	Note 1
CG11006	Beauville	4506	4088	Note 1
Series G20 — ¾-Ton — 110 in. w.b. (*) — "350" V-8				
CG21005	Panel Van	3653	3625	Note 1
CG21006	Sportvan	4275	3910	Note 1
CG21006	Beauville	4678	4073	Note 1

117.5 in. w.b. = 6.5 ft. box.
131.5 in. w.b. = 8 ft. box.
164.5 in. w.b. on 6-passenger CrewCab

Model	Body Type	Price	Weight	Prod. Total
Series G30 — 1-Ton — 110 in. w.b. (*) — "350" V-8				
CG31005	Panel Van	3743	3917	Note 1
CG31306	Sportvan	4477	4369	Note 1
CG31306	Beauville	4880	4583	Note 1

* 125 in. w.b. also available

Model	Body Type	Price	Weight	Prod. Total
Series G30 Hi-Cube Vans — 1-Ton — 125 in. w.b.				
CG31303	10-ft. Steel Panel	4970	4998	Note 1
CG31603	12-ft. Steel Panel	5418	5730	Note 1
P10 STEP-VAN — ½-Ton — 102 in. w.b.				
CP10542	7-ft. Steel Panel	4532	4220	Note 1
P20 STEP-VAN — ¾-Ton - 125 in. w.b.				
CP20842	10-ft. Steel Panel	5242	5382	Note 1
P30 STEP-VAN — 1-Ton - 125 in. w.b.				
CP30842	10-ft. Steel Panel	5499	5588	Note 1
Series C10 — ½-Ton — 117.5 in. w.b.				
CC10906	Suburban (gate)	4707	4336	Note 1
Series K10 — ½-Ton — 117.5 in. w.b.				
CK10906	4x4 Suburban (gate)	5796	—	Note 1
Series C20 — ¾-Ton — 129.5 in. w.b.				
CC20906	Suburban (gate)	5045	4464	Note 1—
Series K20 — ¾-Ton — 129.5 in. w.b.				
CK20906	4x4 Suburban (gate)	6054	—	Note 1
Additional Body Choices				
Series C10				
CC10703	½-Ton Chassis-Cab 117.5"	3676	3318	Note 1
Series K10 — ½-Ton — 4x4 — 117.5 in. w.b.				
CK10703	Chassis-Cab	4765	—	Note 1

1975 Chevrolet 'Big Dooley' Crew Cab Pickup (CP)

I.D. DATA: Combination VIN and rating plate located on left door pillar. Third letter identifies engine as follows: Q=250 cu. in., L-G/1-bbl., T: 292 cu. in., L-G/1-bbl., V: 350 cu. in. V-8/2-bbl., Y: 350 cu. in. V-8/4-bbl. M: 400 cu. in. V-8/4-bbl., Z: 454 cu. in. V-8/4-bbl. (6,000 under GVMR) L: 454 cu. in. V-8/4-bbl. (over 6,000 GVMR) Starting: CC ( ) 145(F) 10001 and up. Engine numbers located: (6-cyl.) on pad at right side of cylinder block at rear of distributor. (V-8) on pad at front, right side of cylinder block. Same as VIN.

Model	Body Type	Price	Weight	Prod. Total
Vega Series				
1HV05	½-Ton Panel Express	2822	2401	1,525
LUV Series				
CL10503	½-Ton Pickup	2976	2380	Note 1
El Camino (350 cu. in. V-8)				
1AC80	½-Ton Sport Pickup	3828	3706	Note 1
1AD80	½-Ton Classic Pickup	3966	3748	Note 1
Blazer				
Series K10 — ½-Ton Utility Vehicle — V-8				
CK10514	Open 4x4 Pickup	4569	4026	Note 1
CK10516	4x4 Hardtop	4998	4313	Note 1
CC10514	Open 4x2 Pickup	3497	3770	Note 1
CC10516	4x2 Hardtop	3926	4057	Note 1
Fleetside Pickups (V-8)				
Series C10				
CC10703	½-Ton 117.5 in. w.b.	3609	3713	Note 1
CC10903	½-Ton 131.5 in. w.b.	3652	3844	Note 1
Series K10				
CK10703	½-Ton 4x4 117.5 in. w.b.	4698	—	Note 1
CK10903	½-Ton 4x4 131.5 in. w.b.	4741	—	Note 1
Series C20				
CC20903	¾-Ton 131.5 in. w.b.	4030	4207	Note 1
Series K20				
CK20903	¾-Ton 4wd 131.5 in. w.b.	5119	—	Note 1

Model	Body Type	Price	Weight	Prod. Total
Series C20 — ¾-Ton — 131.5/164.5 in. w.b.				
CC20903	Chassis-Cab (SWB)	3863	3737	Note 1
CC20943	Bonus Cab Chassis (LWB)	4446	—	Note 1
CC20963	Crew Cab Chassis (LWB)	4835	4461	Note 1
Series K20 — ¾-Ton — (4x4) — 131.5/164.5 in. w.b.				
CK10703	Chassis-Cab (SWB)	4872	—	Note 1
CK20943	Bonus Cab Chassis	5455	—	Note 1
CK20963	Crew Cab Chassis	5844	—	Note 1
Series C30 — 1-Ton — 131.5/164.5 in. w.b.				
CC30903	Chassis-Cab (SWB)	3996	3913	Note 1
CC30963	Crew Cab (LWB)	4988	4517	Note 1

NOTE 1: Industry records show the following 1974 Chevy light-duty truck model year production break-outs: (C10/K10 Pickup) 318,234; (C20/K20 Pickup) 144,632; (C30/K30 Pickup) 44,929; (All Suburban) 30,032; (All Step-Van) 16,877; (All El Camino) 33,620; (Blazer) 50,548; (Sportvan) 21,326 and (Chevy Van) 87,290; (Grand Total) 747,488.

1975 Chevrolet El Camino (CP)

ENGINE (Std. C10/K10/Blazer/El Camino/G10): Inline. Gasoline. Six-cylinder. Cast iron block. Bore & stroke: 3⅞ in. x 3½ in. Displacement: 250 cu. in. Compression ratio: 8.25:1. Net horsepower: 105 at 3800 R.P.M. Max. Torque: 185 lbs.-ft. at 1200 R.P.M. Seven main bearings. Hydraulic valve lifters. Carburetor: one-barrel.

ENGINE (Opt. C10/El Camino): V-block. Gasoline. Eight-cylinder. Cast iron block. Bore & stroke: 4 in. x 3½ in. Displacement: 350 cu. in. Compression ratio: 8.5:1. Net horsepower: 145 at 3800 R.P.M. Max. Torque: 250 lbs.-ft. at 2200 R.P.M. Five main bearings. Hydraulic valve lifters. Carburetor: two-barrel.

ENGINE (Std. C20/C30/K20/P10/P20/P30/G20/G30): Inline. OHV. Six-cylinder. Cast iron block. Bore & stroke: 3⅞ in. x 4⅛ in. Displacement: 292 cu. in. Compression ratio: 8.0:1. Net horsepower: 120 at 3600 R.P.M. Max. Torque: 215 lbs.-ft. at 2000 R.P.M. Seven main bearings. Hydraulic valve lifters. Carburetor: one-barrel.

ENGINE (Opt. all except Vega/LUV): V-block. Gasoline. Eight-cylinder. Cast iron block. Bore & stroke: 4 in. x 3½ in. Displacement: 350 cu. in. Net horsepower: 160 at 3800 R.P.M. Max. Torque: 250 lbs.-ft. at 2400 R.P.M. Five main bearings. Hydraulic valve lifters. Carburetor: four-barrel.

ENGINE (Opt. C10/C20/C30/El Camino — $340): V-block. OHV. Eight-cylinder. Cast iron block. Bore & stroke: 4⅛ in. x 4 in. Displacement: 454 cu. in. Compression ratio: 8.25:1. Net horsepower: 245 at 4000 R.P.M. Max. Torque: 355 lbs.-ft. at 2800 R.P.M. Five main bearings. Hydraulic valve lifters. Carburetor: Rochester four-barrel Quadra-Jet.

ENGINE (Opt. K10/K20/El Camino — $113): V-block. OHV. Eight-cylinder. Cast iron block. Bore & stroke: 4⅛ in. x 4 in. Displacement: 400 cu. in. Compression ratio: 8.5:1. Net horsepower: 175 at 3600 R.P.M. Five main bearings. Hydraulic valve lifters. Carburetor: four-barrel.

ENGINE (LUV): Inline. OHV. Four-cylinder. Cast iron block. Bore & stroke: 3.31 in. x 3.23 in. Displacement: 110.8 cu. in. Compression ratio: 8.5:1. Net horsepower: 75 at 5000 R.P.M. Max. Torque: 88 lbs.-ft. at 3000 R.P.M. Five main bearings. Hydraulic valve lifters. Carburetor: two-barrel.

ENGINE (Opt. Vega): Inline. OHV. Four-cylinder. Aluminum block. Bore & stroke: 3.501 in. x 3.625 in. Displacement: 140 cu. in. Compression ratio: 8.0:1. Net horsepower: 87 at 4200 R.P.M. Five main bearings. Hydraulic valve lifters. Carburetor: Staged two-barrel.

ENGINE (Std. Vega): Inline. OHV. Four-cylinder. Aluminum block. Bore & stroke: 3.501 in. x 3.625 in. Displacement: 140 cu. in. Compression ratio: 8.0:1. Net horsepower: 78 at 4200 R.P.M. Five main bearings. Hydraulic valve lifters. Carburetor: one-barrel.

CHASSIS (Series C10): Wheelbase: 117.5/131.5 in. Overall length: Fleetside: 191¼/211¼ in.; Stepside: 190¼/210¼ in. Height: 69.8 in. Front tread: 65.8 in. Rear tread: 62.7 in. Tires: G78-15B. (Larger size tubeless and tube-type tires available for all models and series.)

CHASSIS (Series C20): Wheelbase: 117.5/131.5/164.5 in. Overall length: Fleetside: 191¼/211¼/244¼ in.; Stepside: 210¼/244¼ in. Height: 69.8 in. Front tread: 65.8 in. Rear tread: 62.7 in. Tires: 8.75 x 16.5C. (Crew Cab 9.50 x 16.5D)

CHASSIS (Series C30): Wheelbase: 131.5/164.5 in. Overall length: Fleetside: 211¼/244¼ in.; Stepside: 210¼/244¼ in. Height: 71.8 in. Front tread: 65.8 in. Rear tread: 62.7 in. Tires: 8.75 x 16.5C in. (Crew Cab — 9.50 x 16.5E)

CHASSIS (Series K10): Wheelbase: 117.5/131.5 in. Overall length: Fleetside: 191¼/211¼ in.; Stepside: 190¼/210¼ in. Height: 72 in. Front tread: 65.8 in. Rear tread: 62.7 in. Tires: G78-15B.

CHASSIS (Series K20): Wheelbase: 131.5 in. Overall length: Fleetside: 211¼ in.; Stepside: 210¼ in. Height: 73.9 in. Front tread: 65.8 in. Rear tread: 62.7 in. Tires: 8.75 x 16.5C.

CHASSIS (El Camino): Wheelbase: 116 in. Overall length: 201.60 in. Height: 53.8 in. Front tread: 58.5 in. Rear tread: 57.8 in. Tires: GR78-15B.

CHASSIS (Series G10): Wheelbase: 110/125 in. Overall length: 178/202.2 in. Height: 78.8 x 81.2 in. Tires: E78-14A.

CHASSIS (Series G20): Wheelbase: 110/125 in. Overall length: 178/202.2 in. Height: 78.8 x 81.2 in. Tires: G78-15B.

CHASSIS (Series G30): Wheelbase: 125/146 in. Tires: 8.00 x 16.5C.

CHASSIS (Series P10): Wheelbase: 102 in. Height: 75 in. Tires: G78-15B.

CHASSIS (Series P20): Wheelbase: 125/133 in. Overall length: 220.75/244.75 in. Tires: 8.75 x 16.5C.

CHASSIS (Series P30): Wheelbase: 125/157 in. Overall length: 220.75/268.75 in. Tires: 8.75 x 16.5C.

CHASSIS (LUV): Wheelbase: 102.4 in. Overall length: 173.8 in. Height: 59.3 in. Front tread: 54 in. Rear tread: 52.2 in. Tires: 6.00 x 14C.

CHASSIS (Vega): Wheelbase: 97 in. Overall length: 176 in. Height: 51.8 in. Front tread: 54.8 in. Rear tread: 53.6 in. Tires: A78-13B.

CHASSIS (Blazer): Wheelbase: 106.5 in. Overall length: 184.5 in. Height: 66.75 in. (w/o top), 68.75 in. (w/top) — 4x2, 69 in. (w/o top), 71 in. (w/top), — 4x4. Front tread: 64.5 in. Rear tread: 63 in. 2-wd, Front tread: 65.75 in. Rear tread: 62.75 in. — 4x4. Tires: E78-15B — 6-cyl. models. H78-15B — V-8. models.

TECHNICAL (Selected Specifications): (C10) Three-speed manual transmission or THM transmission w/454 cu. in. V-8. (C20) Same as C10 except THM w/Crew Cab also. (K10/K20) Three-speed manual transmission or THM w/400 cu. in. V-8. New Process transfer case w/4x4 trucks. Single plate dry disc clutch (w/base six-cylinder). Rear axle ratio (w/base six-cylinder) 3.73:1 on C10s and 4.10:1 on C20s. Front disc/rear drum brakes. Standard equipment incl. steel disc wheels.

OPTIONS: Radio: AM or AM/FM. Windshield embedded antenna. Gauge package (ammeter, oil pressure, temperature) available with either tachometer or clock or with Exomomindior gauge only. Tachometer. Drip

1975 Chevrolet LUV Pickup (CP)

1975 Chevrolet Cheyenne Blazer (CP)

molding. Exterior tool and storage compartment. Air conditioning. Stainless steel wheel covers. White sidewall tires (Series 10 only). Below-Eyeline mirrors. Comfortilt steering wheel. Rear step bumper. Special trim molding (Fleetside only). Chrome bumpers. Chrome front bumper with rubber impact strips. Wood grain exterior trim (Fleetside only). Sliding rear window. Cargo area lamp. Box-mounted spare tire. Glide-out spare tire carrier.

HISTORICAL: Introduced September 1, 1974. Calendar year sales: 771,518. High-energy ignition standard. Six-cylinder more efficient and powerful. Extended maintenance schedules. Catalytic converters now standard on pickups under 6,001 lbs. GVW.

Pricing

	5	4	3	2	1
1975					
Vega					
Panel	380	750	1250	1750	2500
LUV					
Pickup	420	840	1400	1950	2800
El Camino					
Pickup	750	1500	2500	3500	5000
Custom Pickup	830	1650	2750	3850	5500
Blazer K10					
Blazer 4x2	830	1650	2750	3850	5500
Blazer 4x4	980	1950	3250	4550	6500
C10 (½-Ton)					
Stepside short box	810	1620	2700	3800	5400
Stepside long box	830	1650	2750	3850	5500
Fleetside short box	840	1680	2800	3900	5600
Fleetside long box	850	1700	2850	4000	5700
Suburban	830	1650	2750	3850	5500
K10 4x4 (½-Ton)					
Stepside short box	780	1560	2600	3600	5200
Stepside long box	800	1600	2650	3700	5300
Fleetside short box	810	1620	2700	3800	5400
Fleetside long box	830	1650	2750	3850	5500
Suburban	800	1600	2650	3700	5300
C20 (¾-Ton)					
Stepside long box	750	1500	2500	3500	5000
Fleetside long box	780	1560	2600	3600	5200
Long box 6P	720	1450	2400	3300	4800
Suburban	770	1550	2550	3600	5100
K20 4x4 (¾-Ton)					
Stepside long box	800	1600	2650	3700	5300
Fleetside long box	810	1620	2700	3800	5400
Long box 6P	750	1500	2500	3500	5000
Suburban	800	1600	2650	3700	5300
C30 (1-Ton)					
Stepside long box	720	1450	2400	3300	4800
Fleetside long box	750	1500	2500	3500	5000
Long box 6P	700	1400	2350	3250	4700
Panels/Vans (½-Ton)					
Panel	600	1200	2000	2800	4000
Sport Van	750	1500	2500	3500	5000
Beauville Van	780	1560	2600	3600	5200
Panels/Vans (¾-Ton)					
Panel	570	1140	1900	2650	3800
Sport Van	720	1450	2400	3300	4800
Beauville Van	750	1500	2500	3500	5000
Panels/Vans (1-Ton)					
Panel	540	1080	1800	2500	3600
Sport Van	700	1400	2300	3200	4600
Beauville Van	720	1450	2400	3300	4800
Step-Vans					
P-10 Panel	530	1050	1750	2450	3500
P-20 Panel	520	1020	1700	2400	3400
P-30 Panel	500	1000	1650	2300	3300

NOTE: 1955-up prices based on top of the line models.

1976 CHEVROLET

1976 Chevrolet Crew Cab Pickup (CP)

104

LIGHT TRUCK — 1976 SERIES — (ALL ENGINES): — Model year 1976 marked the discontinuance of the Vega Panel Express truck.

In "LUV-land," changes included a new three-speed Hydramatic transmission option and plaid upholstery with the extra-cost Mikado trim package. The EPA mileage rating for the mini pickup was 33 Hwy/23 City versus the 1975 model's 29/19 rating.

This season's standard El Camino had single round headlights. Classic models used dual square headlamps stacked vertically at either side. The standard grille had a tight cross-hatched pattern. Others used a mesh insert. Returning to the center of the grille was a "bow-tie" badge. The performance edition had its "SS" emblem at the lower left-hand grille corner.

Although no changes of any consequence were made in Chevrolet's appearance, a new two-tone paint scheme combined main body colors with selected secondary colors to give Fleetsides a fresh new look. Stepside models with the 6½-foot box were not ignored; they were available with a new trim package including special striping, chromed bumpers, Rally wheels and white-lettered tires. It was offered in four body colors: blue, orange, red or black.

A new body design for the 1976 model was introduced as a major change for Blazers. It featured a steel cab with an integral roll bar built into the steel front compartment roof and lock pillar structures.

1976 Chevrolet El Camino Classic Pickup (CP)

I.D. DATA: Combination VIN and rating plate located on left door pillar. Third letter identifies engine as follows: D: 250 cu. in. L-G/1-bbl., T: 292 cu. in., L-G/1-bbl., V: 350 cu. in. V-8/2-bbl., L: 350 cu. in. V-8/4-bbl. U: 400 cu. in. V-8/4-bbl., S: 454 cu. in. V-8/4-bbl. (6,000 lbs and under GVMR) Y: 454 cu. in. V-8/4-bbl. (over 6,000 lbs. GVMR) Starting: CC ( ) 146F 100001 and up. Engine numbers located (6-cyl.) on pad at right side of cylinder block at rear of distributor. (V-8) on pad at front, right side of cylinder block.

Blazer's wagon-type tailgate

1976 Chevrolet Blazer (CP)

Model	Body Type	Price	Weight	Prod. Total
LUV Series				
CL10503	½-Ton Pickup	3285	2460	Note 1
El Camino (305 cu. in. V-8)				
IAC80	½-Ton Sport Pickup	4333	3791	Note 1
IAD80	½-Ton Classic Pickup	4468	3821	Note 1
Blazer				
Series K10				
CK10516	½-Ton 4x4 Utility	5365	4017	Note 1

Model	Body Type	Price	Weight	Prod. Total
Fleetside Models				
Series C10				
CC10703	½-Ton 117.5 in. w.b.	3863	3848	Note 1
CC10903*	½-Ton 131.5 in. w.b.	3908	3953	—
Series K10				
CK10703	½-Ton 4x4 117.5 in. w.b.	4980	—	Note 1
CK10903	½-Ton 4x4 131.5 in. w.b.	5055	—	Note 1
Series C20 — ¾-Ton — 131.5/164.5 in. w.b.				
CC20903	¾-Ton Pickup (SWB)	4306	4128	Note 1
CC20963	¾-Ton Crew Cab (LWB)	5327	4919	Note 1
CC20943	¾-Ton Bonus Cab (LWB)	4953	4676	Note 1
Series K20				
CK20903	¾-Ton 4x4 131.5 in. w.b.	5372	—	Note 1
Series C30				
CC30903	1-Ton 131.5 in. w.b.	4279	3887	Note 1
CC30943	1-Ton 164.5 in. w.b.	5210	4420	Note 1
CC30963	1-Ton 164.5 in. w.b.	5320	4497	Note 1

* becomes ½-Ton as C10/F4Y

Stepside Models				
Series C10				
CC10703	½-Ton 117.5 in. w.b.	3863	3780	Note 1
CC10903	½-Ton 131.5 in. w.b.	3908	3877	Note 1
Series C20				
CC20903	¾-Ton 131.5 in. w.b.	4306	4128	Note 1
Series K10				
CK10703	½-Ton 4x4, 117.5 in. w.b.	4980	—	Note 1
CK10903	½-Ton 131.5 in. w.b.	5055	—	Note 1
Series K20				
CK20903	¾-Ton 131.5 in. w.b.	5372	—	Note 1
Series C30				
CC30903	¾-Ton 131.5 in. w.b.	4446	4316	Note 1

117.5 in. w.b. = 6.5 ft. box
131.5 in. w.b. = 8 ft. box
164.5 in. w.b. Crew Cab (6 pass.)

Vans/Panels				
Series G10 - ½-Ton — 110 in w.b. (350 cu. in. V-8)*				
CG11005	Panel Van	3811	3593	Note 1
CG11006	Sportvan	4509	3917	Note 1
CG11006	Beauville	5102	4293	Note 1
Series G20 — ¾-Ton — 110 in. w.b. (350 cu. in. V-8)*				
CG21005	Panel Van	4022	3620	Note 1
CG21006	Sportvan	4682	3903	Note 1
CG21306	Beauville	5220	4259	Note 1
Series G30 — 1-Ton — 110 in. w.b. (350 cu. in. V-8)*				
CG31005	Panel Van	4143	3861	Note 1
CG31306	Sportvan	4915	4321	Note 1
CG31306	Beauville	5318	4508	Note 1
Series G30 - 1—Ton — 125 in. w.b. (350 cu. in. V-8)				
CG31303	10-ft. Hi-Cube Van	5405	4990	Note 1
CG31603	12-foot High-Cube	5883	5732	Note 1
Series P10 — Step-Van — ½-Ton — 102 in. w.b.				
CP10542	7-ft. Steel Panel	4855	4204	Note 1
Series P20 — Step-Van — ¾-Ton — 125 in. w.b.				
CP20842	10-ft. Steel Panel	5563	5300	Note 1
Series P30 — Step-Van — 1-Ton — 125 in. w.b.				
CP30842	10-ft. Steel Panel	5864	5506	Note 1
Series C10				
CC10906	½-Ton Suburban (gate)	5087	4335	
Series K10				
CK10906	½-Ton 4x4 Suburban (gate)	6234	—	Note 1
Series C20				
CC20906	¾-Ton Suburban (gate)	5375	4717	
Series K20				
CK20904	¾-Ton 4x4 Suburban (gate)	6441	—	Note 1
Additional Body Choices				
Series C10				
CC10703	½-Ton Ch-Cab 117.5''	3957	3449	Note 1
Series C20 — ¾-Ton — 131.5/164.5 in. w.b.				
CC20903	Ch-Cab (SWB)	4139	3730	Note 1
CC20943	Bonus Cab Chassis (LWB)	4786	4198	Note 1
CC20963	Crew Cab Chassis (LWB)	5160	4441	Note 1
Series C30 — 1-Ton — 134.5/164.5 in. w.b.				
CC30903	Chassis-Cab (SWB)	4279		Note 1
CC30943	Bonus Cab Chassis (LWB)	5210	4497	Note 1
CC30963	Crew Cab Chassis (LWB)	5320	4497	Note 1
Series K10				
CK10703	½-Ton Ch-Cab 117.5''	5104	—	Note 1
Series K20				
CK20903	¾-Ton 4x4 Ch-Cab 131.5''	5205	—	Note 1

NOTE 1: Chevrolet records show the following production break-out for model year 1976: (C10/K10 Pickups) 458,424; (C20/K20 Pickups) 172,419; (C30/K30 Pickups) 45,299; (Step-Vans) 20,043; (Blazer) 74,389; (Suburban) 44,977; (El Camino) 44,890; (Sportvan) 26,860 and (Chevy Van) 125,695. (Total) 1,012,996. **Note:** These totals include trucks built in Canada for sale in the United States. Calendar year sales of the LUV pickup were 45,670 units.

ENGINE (Std. C10/K10/C10-F44/El Camino/Blazer/Vans): Inline. OHV. Six-cylinder. Cast iron block. Bore & stroke: 3⅞ in. x 3½ in. Displacement: 250 cu. in. Compression ratio: 8.25:1. Net horsepower: 100 at 3600 R.P.M. Max. Torque: 175 lbs.-ft. at 1800 R.P.M. Seven main bearings. Hydraulic valve lifters. Carburetor: one-barrel.

ENGINE (Std. C20/C30/K20/Step-Van): Inline. OHV. Six-cylinder. Cast iron block. Bore & stroke: 3⅞ in. x 4⅛ in. Displacement: 292 cu. in. Compression ratio: 8.0:1. Net horsepower: 120 at 3600 R.P.M. Max. Torque: 215 lbs.-ft. at 2000 R.P.M. Seven main bearings. Hydraulic valve lifters. Carburetor: one-barrel.

1976 Chevrolet Fleetside Pickup w/Camper (CP)

ENGINE (Opt.: all except LUV - $30): V-block. OHV. Eight-cylinder. Cast iron block. Bore & stroke: 4 in. x 3½ in. Displacement: 350 cu. in. Compression ratio: 8.5:1. Net horsepower: 165 at 3800 R.P.M. Max. Torque: 255 lbs.-ft. at 2800 R.P.M. Five main bearings. Hydraulic valve lifters. Carburetor: Rochester Quadrajet four-barrel.

ENGINE (Opt. C10): V-block. OHV. Eight-cylinder. Cast iron block. Bore & stroke: 4 in. x 3½ in. Displacement: 350 cu. in. Compression ratio: 8.5:1. Net horsepower: 145 at 3800 R.P.M. Max. Torque: 250 lbs.-ft. at 2200 R.P.M. Five main bearings. Hydraulic valve lifters. Carburetor: two-barrel.

ENGINE (Opt. C10/C20/C30-$423): V-block. OHV. Eight-cylinder. Cast iron block. Bore & stroke: 4¼ in. x 4 in. Displacement: 454 cu. in. Compression ratio: 8.25:1. Net horsepower: 240 at 3800 R.P.M. Max. Torque: 370 lbs.-ft. at 2800 R.P.M. Five main bearings. Hydraulic valve lifters. Carburetor: Rochester Quadrajet four-barrel.

ENGINE (Opt. K10/K20/Vans/Blazer-$144/El Camino-$148): V-block. OHV. Eight-cylinder. Cast iron block. Bore & stroke: 4⅛ in. x 4 in. Displacement: 400 cu. in. Compression ratio: 8.5:1. Net horsepower: 175 at 3600 R.P.M. Max. Torque: 290 lbs.-ft. at 2800 R.P.M. Five main bearings. Hydraulic valve lifters. Carburetor: Rochester four-barrel Quadrajet.

1976 Chevrolet Fleetside Pickup (CP)

ENGINE (Std. LUV): Inline. OHV. Four-cylinder. Cast iron block. Bore & stroke: 3.31 in. x 3.23 in. Displacement: 110.8 cu. in. Compression ratio: 8.5:1. Net horsepower: 75 at 5000 R.P.M. Max. Torque: 88 lbs.-ft. at 3000 R.P.M. Five main bearings. Hydraulic valve lifters. Carburetor: Rochester Quadrajet four-barrel.

CHASSIS (Series C10/C10-F44): Wheelbase: 117.5/131.5 in. Overall length: Fleetside: 191.5/211.40 in.; Stepside: 190.75/210.50 in. Height: 69.8 in. Front tread: 65.8 in. Rear tread: 62.7 in. Tires: G70-15B. C10/F44: L78-15B (6-cyl.); L78-15C (V-8).

CHASSIS (Series C20): Wheelbase: 131.5/164.5 in. Overall length: Fleetside: 211.40/244.40 in.; Stepside: 210.50 in. Height: 69.8 in. Front tread: 65.8 in. Rear tread: 62.7 in. Tires: 8.75 x 16.5C. Bonus Cab tires: 8.75 x 16.5C (Front); D (Rear). Crew Cab tires 9.50 x 16.5D.

CHASSIS (Series C30): Wheelbase: 131.5/164.5 in. Overall length: Fleetside: 211.40/244.40 in.; Stepside: 210.50 in. Height: 71.8 in. Front tread: 65.8 in. Rear tread: 62.7 in. Tires: 8.75 x 16.5C. Bonus and Crew Cab tires: 9.50 x 16.5E.

1976 Chevrolet "Big 10" Fleetside Pickup (CP)

CHASSIS (Series K10): Wheelbase: 117.5/131.5 in. Overall length: Fleetside: 192.10/212 in.; Stepside: 191.30/211.20 in. Height: 72 in. Front tread: 65.8 in. Rear tread: 62.7 in. Tires: L78-15B.

CHASSIS (Series K20): Wheelbase: 131.5 in. Overall length: Fleetside: 212 in.; Stepside: 211.20 in. Height: 73.9 in. Front tread: 65.8 in. Rear tread: 62.7 in. Tires: 8.75 x 16.5C.

CHASSIS (El Camino): Wheelbase: 116 in. Overall length: 201.6 in. Height: 53. 8. Front tread: 58.5 in. Rear tread: 57.8 in. Tires: GR78-15B.

CHASSIS (Series G10): Wheelbase: 110/125 in. Overall length: 178/202.2 in. Height: 78.8 x 81.2 in. Tires: E/F78 x 15B.

CHASSIS (Series G20): Wheelbase: 110/125 in. Overall length: 178/202.2 in. Height: 78.8 x 81.2 in. Tires: J78-15B.

CHASSIS (Series G30): Wheelbase: 125/146 in. Tires: 8.00 x 16.5C.

CHASSIS (Series P10): Wheelbase: 102 in. Tires: L78-15B.

CHASSIS (Series P20): Wheelbase: 125/133 in. Overall length: 220.75/244.75 in. Tires: 8.75 x 16.5C.

CHASSIS (Series P30): Wheelbase: 125/157 in. Overall length: 220.75/268.75 in. Tires: 8.75 x 16.5C.

1976 Chevrolet LUV Pickup (CP)

CHASSIS (LUV): Wheelbase: 102.4 in. Overall length: 173.8 in. Height: 59.3 in. Front tread: 54 in. Rear tread: 52.2 in. Tires: E78 x 14B.

CHASSIS (Blazer): Wheelbase: 106.5 in. Overall length: 184.5 in. Height: 4x2: 66.75 in. (w/o top); 68.75 in. (w/top). 4x4: 69 in. (w/o top); 71 in. (w/top). Front tread: 64.5 in. Rear tread: 63 in. (4x2). Front tread: 65.75 in. Rear tread: (4x4) 62.75 in. Tires: (6-cyl.) E78-15B; (V-8) H78-15B.

TECHNICAL: See 1975 section.

OPTIONS: El Camino: "SS" equipment package ($226). "Conquista" package for Classic ($128). "350" V-8 ($30). "400" V-8 ($148). Blazer: "Cheyenne" package ($626). "400" 4V V-8 engine ($144). Pickups/Suburbans: "400" V-8 engine ($144). C20 eight-foot stake equipment ($595). C30 nine-foot stake equipment ($695). C10 4x4 option ($1,147). C20 4x4 option ($1,066). Chevy Van: "350" 4V V-8 for G10 ($17). M40 THM transmission ($246). Optional axle ratios ($13). Limited-

slip axle ($137). Polywrap air cleaner ($11). Air conditioning ($527). Front and rear air conditioning ($840). H-D battery ($16). Power brakes, G10 ($50). Chrome bumpers ($33). H-D clutch ($7). H-D radiator ($24). Push-button radio ($67). AM/FM radio ($145). Painted OSRV mirror ($19.50). Stainless OSRV mirror ($31). Back door glass ($45). Extra H-D cooling ($48). Custom Deluxe trim package ($14). Gauge package ($13). 42-amp. generator ($25). Tinted glass ($14). Body moldings ($55). Auxiliary seat ($67). H-D shocks ($16). Comfort-tilt steering ($58). 50-gallon fuel tank ($50). Rally wheels ($70). Custom Appearance package ($99). Step-Van: 11,000-pound rear axle ($152). "454" V-8 engine ($452). Radios: AM; AM/FM ($151.00). Tachometer. Sliding rear window. Speed and cruise control. Cargo area lamp. Below-Eyeline mirrors. Bucket seats. Two-tone paint combinations. Pickup box side rails. Rear chromed step bumper. Deluxe chromed bumper. Stainless steel wheel covers. White-stripe or white lettered tires, Series 10 only ($187.55). Glide-out spare tire carrier. Silverado trim package ($172.00). Scottsdale trim package.

1976 Chevrolet Beauville Sportvan (CP)

HISTORICAL: Introduced: Oct. 2, 1975. Calendar year sales: 1,048,135. Model year sales: (Light-duty Pickups) 682,039; (Vans) 128,040; (Blazer) 66,368; (El Camino) 43,595; (LUV) 41,693; (Suburban) 40,122; (Medium- and heavy-duty) 43,312. (Total) 1,045,169. Innovations: All-new Blazer with "station wagon" type body. New trim packages and options. Historical notes: J.T. Riley was sales manager for Chevrolet Motor Division's truck group. All-time high output of Blazers, Vans and Suburbans in calendar year 1976. Chevrolet was America's leading truck-maker with its strong 35.02 percent market share for calendar 1976.

Pricing

1976	5	4	3	2	1
LUV					
Pickup	420	840	1400	1950	2800
El Camino					
Pickup	750	1500	2500	3500	5000
Custom Pickup	830	1650	2750	3850	5500
Blazer K10					
Blazer 4x2	830	1650	2750	3850	5500
Blazer 4x4	980	1950	3250	4550	6500
C10 (½-Ton)					
Stepside short box	810	1620	2700	3800	5400
Stepside long box	830	1650	2750	3850	5500
Fleetside short box	840	1680	2800	3900	5600
Fleetside long box	850	1700	2850	4000	5700
Suburban	830	1650	2750	3850	5500
K10 4x4 (½-Ton)					
Stepside short box	780	1560	2600	3600	5200
Stepside long box	800	1600	2650	3700	5300
Fleetside short box	810	1620	2700	3800	5400
Fleetside long box	830	1650	2750	3850	5500
Suburban	800	1600	2650	3700	5300
C20 (¾-Ton)					
Stepside long box	750	1500	2500	3500	5000
Fleetside long box	780	1560	2600	3600	5200
Long box 6P	720	1450	2400	3300	4800
Suburban	770	1550	2550	3600	5100
K20 4x4 (¾-Ton)					
Stepside long box	800	1600	2650	3700	5300
Fleetside long box	810	1620	2700	3800	5400
Long box 6P	750	1500	2500	3500	5000
Suburban	800	1600	2650	3700	5300
C30 (1-Ton)					
Stepside long box	720	1450	2400	3300	4800
Fleetside long box	750	1500	2500	3500	5000
Long box 6P	700	1400	2350	3250	4700
Panels/Vans (½-Ton)					
Panel	600	1200	2000	2800	4000
Sport Van	750	1500	2500	3500	5000
Beauville Van	780	1560	2600	3600	5200
Panels/Vans (¾-Ton)					
Panel	570	1140	1900	2650	3800
Sport Van	720	1450	2400	3300	4800
Beauville Van	750	1500	2500	3500	5000
Panels/Vans (1-Ton)					
Panel	540	1080	1800	2500	3600
Sport Van	700	1400	2300	3200	4600
Beauville Van	720	1450	2400	3300	4800
P10/P20/P30 Step-Vans					
P10 Steel Panel	530	1050	1750	2450	3500
P20 Steel Panel	520	1020	1700	2400	3400
P30 Steel Panel	500	1000	1650	2300	3300

NOTE: 1955-up prices based on top of the line models.

1976 Chevrolet Silverado Suburban (CP)

1977 Chevrolet Cheyenne Fleetside Pickup (CP)

LIGHT TRUCK — 1977 SERIES — (ALL ENGINES): — Chevrolet's Luv pickup for 1977 was merchandised in chassis & cab form for the first time. The main reason for this was to provide a mini-motorhome chassis. Platform and stake models were also seen. The "Mighty Mike" package came with a new, wide tape stripe running from doors to the rear. A "spectrum" style color treatment was featured at the beginning of the decal, on the doors. At the rear, reversed-out lettering identified the package, which included white spoke wheels and fat white-letter tires.

Standard El Camino continued to feature single headlights and a cross-shatched grille insert. Classic models had a vertical members grille and dual stacked headlights. The grille surround molding was a much thicker piece of chrome. Classics carried a model identification script below the front fender's "El Camino" lettering. Their rocker panels had bright metal underscores. The sporty package included "SS" identification letters for the lower left-hand grille corner, plus "'SS' decals for the cowlsides. Twin tape stripes ran from behind the decal to the rear. Styled wheels and white-letter tires were other extras.

Blazers got the same new grille described below for pickups. Color-keyed tape treatments on front fender tops were part of an Exterior Decor Package that included two toning with hood done in the secondary color and a standup hood ornament. It was available only on units with white bed tops. A bi-level "Chalet" tent-top camper option was available.

The 1977 Chevrolet pickups were identified by the new grille arrangement which used four rather than eight vertical dividers and two, instead of three horizontal bars. In addition, the 1977 model grille had a secondary mesh placed behind the major sections. Single unit combination tail-stop-backup lights replaced the former separate units on Stepside models. A new pickup truck option was the Sport Package with special hood and side striping and white-spoke or Rally wheels. The tape stripes followed the body feature lines and continued in tiara fashion across the roof. Chevy Sport lettering appeared on the upper box sides of Fleetlines and the rear spare tire cover on Stepsides.

Also offered was a new optional Exterior Decor package that included a spring-loaded hood emblem, two-tone paint and color-coordinated hood striping. Six new two-tone color schemes were offered in this package. They featured a secondary color on the hood, between body side moldings and on the pickup roof. Appearance changes to the interior consisted of new seat trim colors, fabrics and woodgrain trim. For the first time C30 one-ton trucks were available as K3- four-wheel-drive models. These carried a heavier capacity 4,500 pound front driving axle in contrast to the 3,800 pound axle on ¾-ton models. Other equipment on the K30 models included a modified 7,500 pound rear axle, power steering and a standard four-speed manual transmission.

Joining the optional equipment list was an Operating Convenience Package of power windows and power door locks. These could also be ordered separately and represented a first in the truck industry. Also offered were new wheel trim covers for ½-ton models and an inside hood release.

The big 454 cu. in. V-8 was now fitted with double-honed piston walls and modified rings for improved oil consumption. Also debuting was a new method of gasketing rocker covers and altered distributor cap and rotor.

Chevy Vans were virtually unchanged from 1976.

I.D. DATA: Combination VIN and rating plate located on left door pillar. **LUV:** Number has 13 symbols. First indicates Chevrolet. Second = vehicle type. Third = engine type. Fourth = tonnage. Fifth = body type. Sixth = series. Seventh = factory. Last six are sequential number. **EL CAMINO:** Also 13 symbols. First indicates Chevrolet. Second = series. Third and fourth = body style. Fifth = engine. Sixth = year. Seventh = factory. Last six are sequential number. **LIGHT TRUCK:** Also 13 symbols. First indicates Chevrolet. Second = vehicle type. Third = engine. Fourth = tonnage (in 1979 and 1980 models 50-80 indicate cab type). Fifth = model type. Sixth = year. Seventh = factory. Last six are sequential number. This system is used for all 1977-1980 models. Engine number locations: (six-cylinder) on pad at right side of cylinder block at rear of distributor; (V-8) on pad at front right side of cylinder block. **ENGINE TYPE CODES:** "250" 6-cyl. (D); "292" 6-cyl. (T); "305" V-8 (U); "350" V-8 (L); "400" V-8 (R) and "454" V-8 (S).

Model	Body Type	Price	Weight	Prod. Total
LUV Series — (½-Ton) — (102.4 in. w.b.)				
CL10503	Chassis & Cab	3084	2380	—
CL10503	Pickup	3284	2380	—
El Camino Series — (½-Ton) — (116 in. w.b.) — (V-8)				
1AC80	Sedan Pickup	4268	3797	—
1AD80	Classic Sedan Pickup	4403	3763	—
1AD80	Super Sport Pickup	4647	3800	—
—	Conquista Pickup	4406		—
K10 Blazer Series — (½-Ton) — (4x4) — (106.5 in. w.b.) — (V-8)				
CK10516	Utility w/Hardtop	5603	4268	—
CK10516	Convertible Utility	5503	—	—

NOTE: 4x2 Blazer available.

Model	Body Type	Price	Weight	Prod. Total
G10 Chevy Van — (½-Ton) — (110/125 in. w.b.) — (V-8)				
CG11005	Panel	4112	3586	—
CG11006	Sportvan	4885	3913	—
CG11306	Beauville	5548	4314	—
G20 Chevy Van — (¾-Ton) — (110/125 in. w.b.) — (V-8)				
CG21005	Panel	4375	3607	—
CG21006	Sportvan	5110	3890	—
CG21306	Beauville	5871	4508	—
G30 Chevy Van — (1-Ton) — (110/125 in. w.b.) — (V-8)				
CG31005	Panel	4496	3840	—
CG31006	Sportvan	5368	4300	—
CG31306	Beauville	5871	4508	—
G30 Hi-Cube Van — (1-Ton) — (125/146 in. w.b.) — (V-8)				
CG31303	10-ft. Van	6410	4961	—
CG31603	12-ft. Van	6593	5727	—
Step-Vans Series 10/20/30				
CP10542	Panel (102 in. w.b.) (6)	5391	4176	—
CP20842	Panel (125 in. w.b.) (V-8)	6287	5273	—
CP30842	Panel (125 in. w.b.) (V-8)	6603	5493	—
Series C10 — (½-Ton) — (117.5/131.5 in. w.b.) — (V-8)				
CC10703	Chassis & Cab (SWB)	4116	3251	—
CC10703	Stepside (SWB)	4122	3585	—
CC10703	Fleetside (SWB)	4122	3645	—
CC10903	Stepside (LWB)	4172	3700	—
CC10903	Fleetside (LWB)	4172	3791	—
CC10906	Suburban (gate)	5248	4315	—

NOTE: 4x4 available on all C10 for $1100.
"CK" prefix on 4x4 model numbers.

Model	Body Type	Price	Weight	Prod. Total
Series C20 — (¾-Ton) — (131.5/164.5 in. w.b.) — (V-8)				
CC20903	Chassis & Cab	4399	3662	—
CC20903	Stepside (SWB)	4624	4051	—
CC20903	Fleetside (SWB)	4624	4142	—
CC20943	Chassis & Bonus Cab (LWB)	5046	4164	—
CC20943	Fleetside & Bonus Cab (LWB)	5271	4644	—
CC20943	Chassis & Crew Cab (LWB)	5420	4850	—
CC20943	Fleetside & Crew Cab (LWB)	5645	4880	—
CC20906	Suburban (gate)	5775	4671	—

NOTE: 4x4 available on all C20 for $1076.
"CK" prefix on 4x4 model numbers.

Model	Body Type	Price	Weight	Prod. Total
Series C30 — (1-Ton) — (131.5/164.5 in. w.b.) — (V-8)				
CC30903	Chassis & Cab	4539	3803	—
CC30903	Stepside (SWB)	4764	4192	—
CC30903	Fleetside (SWB)	4764	4283	—
CC30943	Chassis & Bonus Cab (LWB)	5470	4444	—
CC30943	Fleetside & Bonus Cab (LWB)	5695	4924	—
CC30943	Chassis & Crew Cab (LWB)	5580	5475	—
CC30943	Fleetside Crew Cab (LWB)	5805	5015	—

NOTE: 4x4 available on all C30 for approximately $1050.
"CK" prefix on 4x4 model numbers.

1977 Chevrolet Blazer (CP)

107

GENERAL NOTE: "SWB" is shortest wheelbase given above each series listing. "LWB" is longest wheelbase given above each series listing. (Example: C10 Stepside (SWB) is "Stepside Short Box" with 117.5 in. w.b.)

ENGINE: (Standard C10/C10/F44/K10/El Camino): Inline. OHV. Six-cylinder. Cast iron block. Bore & stroke: 3.9 x 3.5 in. Displacement: 250 cu. in. Compression ratio: 8.3:1 (8.0:1 on models above 6001 lb. GVW). Net horsepower: 110 at 3800 R.P.M. Torque: 195 lb.-ft. at 1600 R.P.M. 100 at 3600 R.P.M. Torque: 175 lb.-ft. at 1800 R.P.M. (models above 6001 lb. GVW). Seven main bearings. Hydraulic valve lifters. Carburetor: One-barrel.

ENGINE: (Standard C20/C30/K20/P10) Inline. OHV. Six-cylinder. Cast iron block. Bore & stroke: 3.9 x 4.1 in. Displacement: 292 cu. in. Compression ratio: 8.0:1. Net horsepower: 120 at 3800 R.P.M. Net torque: 215 lb.-ft. at 2000 R.P.M. Seven main bearings. Hydraulic valve lifters. Carburetor: One-barrel.

ENGINE: (Optional C10) V-type. OHV. Eight-cylinder. Cast iron block. Bore & stroke: 3.74 x 3.48 in. Displacement: 305 cu. in. Compression ratio: 8.5:1. Net horsepower: 145 at 3800 R.P.M. Net torque: 245 lb.-ft. at 2400 R.P.M. Five main bearings. Hydraulic valve lifters. Carburetor: Two-barrel.

NOTE: Not available in California.

ENGINE: (Optional, all models except LUV) V-type. OHV. Eight-cylinder. Cast iron block. Bore & stroke: 4.0 x 3.5 in. Displacement: 350 cu. in. Compression ratio: 8.5:1. Net horsepower: 165 at 3800 R.P.M. Net torque: 260 lb.-ft. at 2400 R.P.M. (255 lb.-ft. for models above 6001 - GVW). Five main bearings. Hydraulic valve lifters. Carburetor: Four-barrel model Quad.

ENGINE: (Optional K20/K30) V-type. OHV. Eight-cylinder. Cast iron block. Bore & stroke: 4.1 x 3.8 in. Displacement: 400 cu. in. Compression ratio: 8.5:1. Net horsepower: 175 at 3600. Net torque: 290 lb.-ft. at 2800 R.P.M. Five main bearings. Hydraulic valve lifters. Carburetor: Four-barrel model Quad.

ENGINE: (Optional C10/C10/F44/C20/C30, all P Series (not available in California ($380) V-type. OHV. Eight-cylinder. Cast iron block. Bore & stroke: 4.3 x 4.0 in. Displacement: 454 cu. in. Compression ratio: 8.25:1 (on models under 6000 lb. GVW) above 8.15:1 — C10/F44 — 8.25:1. Net torque: 245 at 3800 R.P.M., 240 horsepower at 3800 R.P.M. (Models above 6001 lb. GVW). 250 horsepower at 3800 R.P.M. (California). Net horsepower: 365 lb.-ft. at 2800 R.P.M. (370 lb.-ft. at 2800 R.P.M. for models above 6001 lb. GVW). 385 lb.-ft. at 3800 R.P.M. — California. Five main bearings. Hydraulic valve lifters. Carburetor: Four-barrel model Quad.

ENGINE: (Standard LUV) Inline. OHV. Four-cylinder. Cast iron block. Bore & stroke: 3.31 x 3.23 in. Displacement: 110.8 cu. in. Compression ratio: 8.5:1. Net horsepower: 75 at 5000 R.P.M. Max. Torque: 88 lb. ft at 3000 R.P.M. Five main bearings. Hydraulic valve lifters. Carburetor: Two-barrel.

1977 Chevrolet Classic Pickup El Camino (CP)

CHASSIS: (El Camino) Wheelbase: 117.1 in. Overall length: 201.6 in. Height 53.8 in. Front tread: 58.5 in. Rear tread: 57.8 in. Tires: GR78 x 15B in.

CHASSIS: (Series G10) Wheelbase: 110/125 in. Overall length: 178/202.2 in. Height: 78.8/81.2 in. Tires: E/F 78 x 15B in.

CHASSIS: (Series G20) Wheelbase: 110/125 in. Overall length: 178/202.2 in. Height: 78.8/81.2 in. Tires: J78 x 15B in.

CHASSIS: (Series G30) Wheelbase: 125/146 in. Tires: 8.00 x 16.5D in.

CHASSIS: (Series P10) Wheelbase: 102 in. Overall length: 175 in. Tires: L78-15B in.

CHASSIS: (Series P20) Wheelbase: 125/133 in. Overall length: 220¾/244¾ in. Tires: 8.75 x 16.5C in.

CHASSIS: (Series P30) Wheelbase: 125/157 in. Overall length: 220¾/268¾ in. Tires: 8.75 x 16C in.

CHASSIS: (LUV) Wheelbase: 102.4 in. Overall length: 173.8 in. Height: 59.3 in. Front tread: 54 in. Rear tread: 52.2 in. Tires: E78 x 14B in.

CHASSIS: (Series C10, C10/F44) Wheelbase: 117.5/131.5 in. Overall length: 191.3/212 in. Height: 69.8 in. Front tread: 65.8 in. Rear tread: 62.7 in. Tires G78 x 15B in., L78 x 15B in. (C10/F44)

CHASSIS: (Series C20) Wheelbase: 117.5/131.5/164.5 in. Overall length: 191.3/212/244.43 in. Height: 69.8 in. Front tread: 65.8 in. Rear tread: 62.7 in. Tires: 8.75 x 16.5C in. Bonus Cab: 8.75 x 16.5 in. (Front C, Rear D). Crew Cab: 9.50 x 16.5D in.

CHASSIS: (Series C30) Wheelbase: 131.5/164.5 in. Overall length: 212/244.43 in. Height: 71.8 in. Front tread: 65.8 in. Rear tread: 62.7 in. Tires: 8.75 x 16.5C in. Bonus/Crew Cab: 9.50 x 16.5E in.

CHASSIS: (Series K10) Wheelbase: 117.5/131.5 in. Overall length: 191.3/212 in. Height: 72 in. Front tread: 65.8 in. Rear tread: 62.7 in. Tires: L78 x 15B in.

CHASSIS: (Series K20) Wheelbase: 131.5 in. Overall length: 212 in. Height: 73.9 in. Front tread: 65.8 in. Rear tread: 62.7 in. Tires: 8.75 x 16.5C in.

CHASSIS: (Series K30) Wheelbase: 131.5/164.5 in. Overall length: 212/244.43 in. Height: 74.7/75 in. Front tread: 65.8 in. Rear tread: 62.7 in. Tires: 9.50 x 16.5D in.

CHASSIS: (Series K10 Blazer) Wheelbase: 106.5 in. Overall length: 184.4 in. Height: 69.8 in. Front tread: 66.7 in. Rear tread: 63.7 in. Tires: H78 x 15B in.

TECHNICAL: (With Base Six-cylinder engine) Selective synchromesh transmission. Speeds: 3F/1R (one-ton, 4F/1R). Column-mounted gearshift. Single-plate dry disc clutch. Salisbury rear axle. Overall ratio: (C10) 3.73:1; (C20) 4.10:1. Power front disc/rear drum brakes. Steel disc wheels. Drivetrain options: 11,000 lb. rear axle, P30 ($272). "454" V-8 engine, P30 ($380). "350" V-8 engine, C10 ($90). "Big Dualie" package, C30 ($510). M-38 Turbo Hydramatic transmission. M-49 Turbo Hydramatic transmission.

1977 Chevrolet Beauville Sportvan (CP)

OPTIONS: El Camino: "305" two-barrel V-8 ($120). "350" four-barrel V-8 ($210). Turbo Hydramatic ($282). Power steering ($146). Power windows ($108). Front air conditioning ($499). All tinted glass ($54). AM radio ($72). AM/FM radio ($137). Stereo tape w/AM radio ($209). Stereo tape with AM/FM radio ($324). Performance axle ($14). Positraction ($54). Heavy-duty battery ($17). Heavy-duty radiator ($29). Conguista package ($138). Box tonneau ($96). Box rails ($68). "SS" equipment package ($244). Tie down cargo box ($14). Speed and cruise control ($80). Vinyl roof ($65). Econo gauges ($47). Exterior decor package, with vinyl roof ($20); w/o vinyl roof ($46). Swing-out vinyl bucket seats ($129). Power seat ($137). **Chevy Vans:** "305" two-barrel V-8 ($120). "350" four-barrel V-8, G10 ($210). G20 ($135). "400" four-barrel V-8 ($319). Turbo Hydramatic ($315). Power steering ($146). Power brakes ($62). Heavy-duty vacuum power brakes ($53). Front air conditioning ($601). All tinted glass, Nomad ($43); other vans ($60). AM radio ($79). AM/FM radio ($155). Rear speaker ($36). Optional axle ratio ($16). Locking differential ($160). Heavy-duty battery ($31). Heavy-duty radiator ($29). Beauville trim, with "Caravan" ($173); w/o "Caravan" ($295). Caravan package, G10/SWB ($938); G10/LWB ($990); G20/SWB ($830); G20/LWB ($882). Custom Appearance Package ($104). Custom Comfort and Convenience, Chevy Van ($141); Sportvan ($320); Sportvan/LWB ($363). Custom vinyl bucket seats, w/o "Caravan" ($365). Custom cloth bucketseats, w/o "Caravan" ($365). 12-passenger seating option, Sportvan ($363). Front and rear air conditioning ($964). **Blazer:** "305" two-barrel V-8 ($120). "350" four-barrel V-8 ($210). "400" four-barrel V-8 ($369). Turbo Hydramatic ($282). Four-speed manual transmission ($142). Power steering, w/4x2 ($169); w/4x4 ($188). Front air conditioning ($509). All windows tinted ($43). Tinted sliding side window w/hardtop ($156). AM radio ($79). AM/FM radio ($155). Rear speaker ($36). Optional axle ratio ($16). Locking differential ($160). Heavy-duty battery ($31). Auxiliary battery ($88). Heavy-duty radiator ($34). Wood grain exterior trim, with "Cheyenne" ($126); w/o "Cheyenne" ($266). Cold climate package, with "trailer special" ($89); w/o ($120). Cheyenne package, w/16 inch tires ($713); w/o ($735). Custom vinyl seats, w/"Cheyenne" one-seater (NC); w/"Cheyenne" two-seater ($38); regular one-seater ($222); regular two-seater ($260). 3-passenger rear seat ($179). Trailering special package, w/4x2 ($200); w/4x4 ($219). **Suburban:** "305" V-8, C10 ($120). "350" V-8, C10 ($210); others ($249). "400" V-8, C10 ($465); C20 ($335). Turbo Hydramatic w/"454" V-8 ($330); w/o "454" V-8 ($315). Four-speed manual transmission ($142). Power steering, w/4x2 ($169); w/4x4 ($188). Front air conditioning, Scottsdale/Silverado ($500); others ($599). Front/rear air conditioning ($780). All tinted glass ($50). AM radio ($79). AM/FM radio ($155). Rear speaker ($36). Optional axle ratio ($16). Locking differential ($160). Heavy-duty battery ($31). Auxiliary battery ($88). Heavy-duty radiator ($34). Woodgrain exterior trim, Silverado ($208); Scottsdale ($210); others ($266). Scottsdale package, w/4x2 ($315); w/4x4 ($318). Silverado package, w/4x2 ($591); w/4x4 ($582). Custom vinyl seats, w/Silverado ($103 or $141 depending on number of seats); w/Scottsdale ($38, $88 or $216 depending on number/type of seats). Center rear seat ($265); center and rear seats, C10 ($466); K10/C20/K20 ($444). Trailering Special, 4x2 ($200); 4x4 ($219). Special Custom cloth seat, (same prices as Custom Vinyl seat options). **Pickups:** "305" V-8 ($120). "350" V-8 ($210); 20 Series ($90). "400" V-8, K10 ($369); K20 ($294). "454" V-8, C10 ($465); C20 ($380). Turbo Hydramatic, w/o "454" V-8 ($315); w/"454" V-8 ($330). Four-speed manual transmission ($142). Power steering, w/4x2 ($169); w/4x4 ($188). Power brakes ($62). Heavy-duty vacuum power brakes, 20 Series ($53). Power windows ($121). Power sliding rear window ($62). Front air conditioning ($509). All tinted glass, Bonus/Crew Cabs ($34); others ($27). AM radio ($79). AM/FM radio ($155). Optional axle ratio ($16). Locking differential ($160). Heavy-duty battery ($31). Auxiliary battery ($88). Heavy-duty radiator ($34). Speed and Cruise Control ($80). 8-foot pickup box floor ($63). **Scottsdale Package** (w/o dual rear wheels unless noted otherwise): C10/C20 Stepside w/bench seat ($236); w/bucket seats ($205), K10/K20 Stepside w/bench seat ($239); w/bucket seats ($208), C10/C20 Fleetside w/bench seat ($286); w/bucket seats ($255). Fleetside C20 Bonus Cab, ($236); Crew Cab ($255). Fleetside K10/K20 w/bench seat ($289); w/bucket seat ($258). Chassis-Cab C10/C20 w/bench seat ($236); w/bucket seat ($205). C20 Chassis w/Bonus Cab ($180); w/Crew Cab ($210). K10/K20 Chassis and Regular Cab, w/bench seat ($239); w/bucket seats ($208). C20 Crew Cab w/dual rear wheels ($195). **Silverado Package** (w/o dual rear wheels): C10/C20 Stepside w/bench ($431); w/buckets ($400). K10/K20 Stepside w/bench ($422); w/buckets ($391). C10/C20 Fleetside, w/buckets ($554); w/bench ($585). C20 Bonus Cab ($641); Crew Cab ($720). K10/K20 Fleetside, w/buckets ($545); w/o buckets ($575). Chassis-Cab, C10/C20 w/bench ($431). C20 Chassis and Bonus Cab ($487); Crew Cab ($566). K10/K20 Chassis-Cab, w/bench ($422); with buckets ($391). K10/K20 Chassis and Bonus Cab ($477); Crew Cab ($556). **Cheyenne Package:** (w/o dual rear wheels unless otherwise noted) C10/C20 Stepside, w/bench ($350); w/buckets ($319). C10/C20 Fleetside, w/bench ($422); w/buckets ($391). K10/K20 Stepside w/bench ($341); w/buckets ($310). K10/K20 Fleetside, w/bench ($413). C10/C20 Chassis-Cab, w/bench ($341); w/buckets ($319). K10/K20 Chassis-Cab, w/bench ($341); w/buckets ($382). Fleetside K10/K20, dual rear wheels, w/bench ($341); w/buckets ($310). Chassis-Cab, K10/K20 with dual rear wheels and bucket seats ($310). "Operating Convenience Group", includes power windows ($206). Custom vinyl bucket seats, w/"Scottsdale" ($169); w/"Cheyenne" or "Silverado" ($136); others ($207). Knit vinyl bench seat ($38). Special Custom bench seat, w/"Scottsdale" and Bonus Cab ($38); Crew Cab ($76). Folding seat back ($23). Trailering Special, includes powersteering, C10/C20 ($200); K10/K20 ($219). C20 eight-foot stake body w/regular cab ($640). **LUV:** "Mikado" package. "Mighty Mike" package.

HISTORICAL: Introduced: Fall 1976. Calendar year registrations: (all Series) 1,133,201. Innovations: New grilles on most models. First year for one-ton with 4x4 chassis. New Sport Truck pickup option. Improvements in 454 cu. in. V-8.

1977 Chevrolet Scottsdale Crew Cab Pickup

Pricing

1977

	5	4	3	2	1
LUV					
Pickup	400	800	1350	1900	2700
El Camino					
Pickup	780	1560	2600	3600	5200
Custom Pickup	850	1700	2850	4000	5700
Super Sport Pickup	1040	2070	3450	4850	6900
Blazer					
4x4 Blazer	1010	2030	3350	4700	6700
Chevy Van 10					
Panel	630	1250	2100	3000	4200
Sportvan	780	1560	2600	3600	5200
Beauville Sportvan	830	1650	2750	3850	5500
Chevy Van 20					
Panel	600	1200	2000	2800	4000
Sportvan	750	1500	2500	3500	5000
Beauville Sportvan	780	1560	2600	3600	5200

	5	4	3	2	1
Chevy Van 30					
Panel	590	1170	1950	2700	3900
Sportvan	740	1470	2450	3350	4900
Beauville Sportvan	770	1550	2550	3600	5100
Cube Van	570	1140	1900	2650	3800
P10 Step Van					
Van	540	1080	1800	2500	3600
P20 Step Van					
Van	530	1050	1750	2450	3500
P30 Step Van					
Van	480	975	1600	2250	3200
C10					
Stepside Sport Box Pickup	830	1650	2750	3850	5500
Fleetside Short Box Pickup	840	1680	2800	3900	5600
Stepside Long Box Pickup	840	1680	2800	3900	5600
Fleetside Long Box Pickup	850	1700	2850	4000	5700
Suburban	870	1750	2900	4100	5800
C20					
Stepside Pickup	780	1560	2600	3600	5200
Fleetside Pickup	810	1620	2700	3800	5400
Bonus Cab Pickup	800	1600	2650	3700	5300
Crew Cab Pickup	780	1560	2600	3600	5200
Suburban	810	1620	2700	3800	5400
C30					
Stepside Pickup	750	1500	2500	3500	5000
Fleetside Pickup	780	1560	2600	3600	5200
Bonus Cab Pickup	770	1550	2550	3600	5100
Crew Cab Pickup	750	1500	2500	3500	5000

NOTE: 1955-up prices based on top of the line models. Add 5 percent for 4x4 Pickups & Suburbans.

1978 CHEVROLET

1978 Chevrolet El Camino (CMD)

LIGHT TRUCKS — 1978 SERIES — (ALL ENGINES): — All Chevrolet pickup trucks available during the 1977 model year were retained for 1978 with no additions or deletions. The C30 dual rear wheel option was now called the "Big Dooley" option. Chevrolet introduced a new GM-built 5.7-litre V-8 diesel engine for use in the C10 ½-ton two-wheel-drive pickup. Among its design features were aluminum alloy pistons with three rings, a cast iron regrindable crankshaft, three-inch-diameter main bearings, rotary fuel injection plug, electric glow plugs and a seven-quart oil pump.

The El Camino underwent its most extensive re-design since 1964. The 1978 model was on a longer 117.1 in. w.b., but overall length was reduced to 201.6 in. or 11.7 in. less than in 1977. A V-6 engine was now the base powerplant. Key styling features included a sweeping roofling small side quarter windows, a wraparound rear window and single rectangular headlights. Curb weight was reduced by nearly 600 pounds, but load capacity, at 800 pounds, was unchanged. The standard 3.3-litre V-6 was a derivative of the Chevrolet small block V-8. It weighed almost 80 pounds less than the six-cylinder engine it replaced. A second V-6, with a 3.8-litre displacement, was mandatory for California.

The imported LUV model moved into its "Series 8" mode, which provided a new grille with horizontal bars and a re-designed instrument panel. Two box lengths, six- and 7½-feet, were offered. The wheelbase on the latter extended to 117.9 in.

Chevy Van's had a "facial." A new grille resembled the egg-crate version of other models. However, the headlight housings were distinct. They were sort of "D"-shaped and had a square headlight at top and a rectangular parking lamp on botom. The Beauville continued to come only on the longer wheelbase with standard V-8 power. A new model was the Sporty Nomad, available only in the G20 line. It was essentially a factory custom van.

I.D. DATA: Serial Number located: Combination VIN and rating plate located on left door pillar. See 1977 for breakdown of codes. Engine number located: Same as 1977. The engine number indicates manufacturing plant, month and day of manufacturing and transmission type. Example: F1210TFA, F=Flint, 12=Dec., 10=tenth day of month, FA=Trans. and engine type (etc.)

1978 Chevrolet Cheyenne Blazer (CP)

Model	Body Type	Price	Weight	Prod. Total
LUV — (½-Ton) — (102.4/117.9 in. w.b.) — (4-cyl.)				
CL10503	Chassis & Cab	3721	2095	—
CL10503	Pickup	3885	2315	—
El Camino — (½-Ton) — (117.1 in. w.b.) — (V-6)				
1AW80	Pickup	3807	—	—
1AW80	Super Sport Pickup	3956	—	—
El Camino — (½-Ton) — (117.1 in. w.b.) — (V-8)				
1AW80	Pickup	4843	3076	—
1AW80	Super Sport Pickup	5022	3076	—
Blazer — (½-Ton) — (106.5 in. w.b.) — (V-8) — (4x4)				
CK10516	Hardtop	6397	3928	—
CK10516	Softtop	6297	3780	—
Chevy Van 10 — (½-Ton) — (110/125 in. w.b.) — (V-8)				
CG11005	Panel (SWB)	4609	3652	—
CG11006	Sportvan (SWB)	5468	5468	—
CG11306	Beauville (LWB)	6296	4323	—
Chevy Van 10 — (½-Ton) — (110/125 in. w.b.) — (6-cyl.)				
CG11305	Panel (LWB)	4584	—	—
CG11306	Sportvan (LWB)	5443	—	—
Chevy Van 20 — (¾-Ton) — (110/125 in. w.b.) — (V-8)				
CG21005	Panel (SWB)	4904	3661	—
CG21006	Sportvan (SWB)	5726	3944	—
CG21306	Beauville (LWB)	6439	4282	—
CG21305	Nomad (LWB)	6334	3801	—
Chevy Van 20 — (¾-Ton) — (110/125 in. w.b.) — (6-cyl.)				
CG21305	Panel (LWB)	3429	—	—
CG21306	Sportvan (LWB)	5641	—	—
Chevy Van 30 — (1-Ton) — (110/125 in. w.b.) — (V-8)				
CG31005	Panel (SWB)	5055	3896	—
CG31306	Sportvan (LWB)	6037	4357	—
CG31306	Beauville (LWB)	6590	4530	—
Hi-Cube Van 30 — (1-Ton) — (125/146 in. w.b.) — (V-8)				
CG31303	10-ft. Van (SWB)	6857	5047	—
CG31603	12-ft. Van (LWB)	7157	5153	—
Step-Van 10/20/30 — (V-8)				
CP10542	Panel (102.6 in. w.b.)	5771	4172	—
CP20842	Panel (133 in. w.b.)	6753	5283	—
CP30842	Panel (133 in. w.b.)	6978	5503	—
C10 — (½-Ton) — (117.5/131.5 in. w.b.) — (V-8)				
CC10703	Chassis & Cab (SWB)	4428	3246	—
CC10703	Stepside (SWB)	4418	3579	—
CC10703	Fleetside (SWB)	4418	3639	—
CC10903	Stepside (LWB)	4493	3694	—
CC10903	Fleetside (LWB)	4493	3775	—
CC10906	Suburban (Gate)	5810	4257	—
K10 — (½-Ton) — (117.5/131.5 in. w.b.) — (6-cyl.) — (4x4)				
CK10703	Stepside (SWB)	5483	—	—
CK10703	Fleetside (SWB)	5483	—	—
CK10703	Chassis & Cab (SWB)	5124	—	—
CK10903	Stepside (LWB)	5558	—	—
CK10903	Fleetside (LWB)	5558	—	—
CK10903	Chassis & Cab (LWB)	5199	—	—
C20 — (¾-Ton) — (131.5/164.5 in. w.b.) — (V-8)				
CC20903	Chassis & Cab (SWB)	4813	3665	—
CC20903	Stepside (SWB)	5038	4054	—
CC20903	Fleetside (SWB)	5038	4135	—
CC20943	Chassis & Bonus Cab (LWB)	5512	4176	—
CC20943	Bonus Cab Fleetside (LWB)	5737	4646	—
CC20943	Chassis & Crew Cab (LWB)	5886	4233	—
CC20943	Crew Cab Fleetside (LWB)	6111	4703	—
K20 — (¾-Ton) — (131.5/164.5 in. w.b.) — (6-cyl.)				
CK20903	Stepside (SWB)	5916	—	—
CK20903	Fleetside (SWB)	5916	—	—
CK20903	Chassis Cab (SWB)	5691	—	—
CK20906	Suburban (gate)	6381	4620	—
C10 Diesel — (½-Ton) — (117.5/131.5 in. w.b.) — (V-8)				
CC10703	Stepside (SWB)	6228	3765	—
CC10703	Fleetside (SWB)	6228	3824	—
CC10903	Stepside (LWB)	6303	3841	—
CC10903	Fleetside (LWB)	6303	3962	—
C30 — (1-Ton) — (131.5/164.5 in. w.b.) — (V-8) *				
CC30903	Chassis & Cab (SWB)	5055	3792	—
CC30903	Stepside (SWB)	5280	4181	—
CC30903	Fleetside (SWB)	5280	4262	—
CC30943	Chassis & Cab (LWB)	5937	4439	—
CC30943	Bonus Cab Fleetside(LWB)	6162	4909	—
CC30943	Chassis & Crew Cab (LWB)	6047	4772	—
CC30943	Fleetwood Crew Cab (LWB)	6272	4941	—

*: C30 also available with 4x4; prices unavailable; "CK" prefix on 4x4.

110

1978 Chevrolet El Camino "SS" (CP)

GENERAL NOTE: "SWB" is shortest wheelbase given above each series listing. "LWB" is longest wheelbase given above each series listing. (Example: In C10 Series The Stepside Pickup (SWB) is the "Short Box" model with 117.5 in. w.b.). Prices for six-cylinder El Camino and 4x4 models are from a different reference source that does not provide shipping weights.

ENGINE: (Standard: C10, Big 10, K10): Inline. OHV. Six-cylinder. Cast iron block. Bore & stroke: 3.876 x 3.530 in. Displacement: 250 cu. in. Compression ratio: 8.25:1. Net horsepower: 115 at 3800 R.P.M. Torque: 195 lb.-ft. at 1800 R.P.M. Seven main bearings. Hydraulic valve lifters. Carburetor: Mono-jet model 1ME. R.P.O. Code: LD4.

ENGINE: (Standard: C20, C30, K20, K30): Inline. OHV. Six-cylinder. Cast iron block. Bore & stroke: 3.8764 x 4.120 in. Displacement: 292 cu. in. Compression ratio: 8.0:1. Net horsepower: 120 at 3600 R.P.M. Net torque: 215 lb.-ft. at 2000 R.P.M. Seven main bearings. Hydraulic valve lifters. Carburetor: One-barrel. R.P.O. Code: L25.

ENGINE: (Optional: C10, El Camino) Vee-block. OHV. Eight-cylinder. Cast iron block. Bore & stroke: 3.736 x 3.480 in. Displacement: 305 cu. in. Compression ratio: 8.5:1. Net horsepower: 145 at 3800 R.P.M. Net torque: 245 lb.-ft. at 2400 R.P.M. Five main bearings. Hydraulic valve lifters. Carburetor: Two-barrel model 2GC. R.P.O. Code: LG9.

ENGINE: (Optional: all models) V-type. OHV. Eight-cylinder. Cast iron block. Bore & stroke: 4.0 x 3.480 in. Displacement: 350 cu. in. Compression ratio: 8.5:1. Net horsepower: 165 at 3800 R.P.M. Net torque: 260 lb.-ft. at 2400 R.P.M. Five main bearings. Hydraulic valve lifters. Carburetor: Four-barrel model M4MC/MV. R.P.O. Code: LS9.

ENGINE: (Optional: K10, K20, K30) V-type. OHV. Eight-cylinder. Cast iron block. Bore & stroke: 4.125 x 3.750 in. Displacement: 400 cu. in. Compression ratio: 8.5:1. Net horsepower: 175 at 3600 R.P.M. Net torque: 290 lb.-ft. at 2800 R.P.M. Five main bearings. Hydraulic valve lifters. Carburetor: Four-barrel model M4MC/MV. R.P.O. Code: LF4.

ENGINE: (Optional: C1500, C2500, C3500 ($235) V-type. OHV. Eight-cylinder. Cast iron block. Bore & stroke: 4.250 x 4.0 in. Displacement: 454 cu. in. Compression ratio: 8.5:1 Net horsepower: 205 at 3600 R.P.M. Net torque: 355 lb.-ft. at 2800 R.P.M. Five main bearings. Hydraulic valve lifters. Carburetor: Four-barrel model M4MC/MV. R.P.O. Code: LF8.

ENGINE: (Optional: C10, Big 10) V-type. OHV diesel. Eight-cylinder. Cast iron block. Bore & stroke: 4.057 x 3.385 in. Displacement: 350 cu. in. Compression ratio: 20.5:1. Net horsepower: 120 at 3600 R.P.M. Net torque: 222 lb.-ft. at 1900 R.P.M. Five main bearings. Hydraulic valve lifters. R.P.O. Code: LF9.

1978 Chevrolet Cheyenne Flee)tside Pickup (CP)

ENGINE: (Standard LUV) Inline. OHV. Four-cylinder. Cast iron block. Bore & stroke: 3.31 x 3.23 in. Displacement: 110.8 cu. in. Compression ratio: 8.5:1. Net horsepower: 80 at 4800 R.P.M. Max. Torque: 95 lb. ft at 3000 R.P.M. Five main bearings. Hydraulic valve lifters. Carburetor: One-barrel.

ENGINE: (Standard El Camino) Vee-block. OHV. Six-cylinder. Cast iron block. Bore & stroke: 3.50 x 3.48 in. Displacement: 200 cu. in. Compression ratio: 8.2:1. Net horsepower: 95 at 3800 R.P.M. Max. Torque: 160 lb.-ft at 2000 R.P.M. Hydraulic valve lifters. Carburetor: Rochester two-barrel.

ENGINE: (Optional: El Camino) (Standard for California delivery) Available only automatic transmission. V-type. OHV. Six-cylinder. Cast iron block. Bore & stroke: 3.80 x 3.40 in. Displacement: 231 cu. in. Compression ratio: 8.0:1. Net horsepower: 105 at 3400 R.P.M. Net Torque: 185 lb.-ft at 2000 R.P.M. Carburetor: Rochester two-barrel.

CHASSIS: (Series C10, C10, Big 10) Wheelbase: 117.5/131.5 in. Overall length: 191.3/212 in. Height 69.8 in. Front tread: 65.8 in. Rear tread: 62.7 in. Tires: G78 x 15B in. (C10, Big 10), L78 x 15B in.

CHASSIS: (Series C20) Wheelbase: 117.5/131.5/164.5 in. Overall length: 191.3/212/244.43 in. Height: 69.8 in. Front tread: 65.8 in. Rear tread: 62.7 in. Tires: 8.75 x 16.5C in., (Bonus Cab) 8.75 x 16.5 in., (F-C, R-D), (Crew Cab) 9.50 x 16.5D in.

CHASSIS: (Series C30) Wheelbase: 131.5/164.5 in. Overall length: 212/244.43 in. Height: 71.8 in. Front tread: 65.8 in. Rear tread: 62.7 in. Tires: 8.75 x 16.5C in., (Bonus/Crew Cab) 9.50 x 16.5E in.

CHASSIS: (Series K10) Wheelbase: 117.5/131.5 in. Overall length: 191.3/212 in. Height: 72 in. Front tread: 65.8 in. Rear tread: 62.7 in. Tires: L78 x 15B in.

CHASSIS: (Series K20) Wheelbase: 131.5 in. Overall length: 212 in. Height: 73.9 in. Front tread: 65.8 in. Rear tread: 62.7 in. Tires: 8.75 x 16.5C in.

CHASSIS: (Series K10 Blazer) Wheelbase: 106.5 in. Overall length: 184.8 in. Height: 73.4 in. Front tread: 66.1 in. Rear tread: 63 in. Tires: H78 x 15B in.

1978 Chevrolet ChevyVan Panel (CP)

CHASSIS: (Series K30) Wheelbase: 131.5/164.5 in. Overall length: 212/244.43 in. Height: 74.7/75 in. Front tread: 65.8 in. Rear tread: 62.7 in. Tires: 9.50 x 16.5D in.

CHASSIS: (LUV) Wheelbase: 102.4/117.9 in. Overall length: 173.8/190.9 in. Front tread: 54 in. Rear tread: 52.2 in. Tires: E78 x 14B in.

CHASSIS: (Series G10) Wheelbase: 110/125 in. Overall length: 178.2/202.2 in. Tires G78 x 15B in.

CHASSIS: (Series G20) Wheelbase: 110/125 in. Overall length: 178.2/202.2 in. Tires: J78 x 15B in.

CHASSIS: (Series G30) Wheelbase: 110/125 in. Overall length: 178.2/202.2 in. Tires: 8.00 x 16.5 in.

CHASSIS: (Series P30) Wheelbase: 125/157 in. Tires: 8.75 x 6.5 in.

CHASSIS: (El Camino) Wheelbase: 117.1 in. Overall length: 201.6 in. Height: 53.8 in. Front tread: 58.5 in. Rear tread: 57.8 in. Tires: P205/75R x 14 in.

CHASSIS: (Series P10) Wheelbase: 102 in. Tires: L78 x 15B in.

CHASSIS: (Series P20) Wheelbase: 125/133 in. Tires: 8.75 x 16.5C in.

TECHNICAL: Same as 1977.

OPTIONS: Rear bumper. Rear-mounted spare tire. Chevy Van Custom Appearance package ($92). Chevy Van Custom Comfort package ($342). Bumper guards. Radio AM; AM/FM. Heater (deletion). Electric clock. Cigar lighter. Radio antenna. Chevy Van Caravan package ($980 to $1,050). "454" V-8 in Step-Van ($235). F44 "Big 10" package. Chevy Van Sport Package ($497). Scottsdale trim package, light trucks ($251). Cheyenne trim package, light trucks. Silverado trim package, light trucks ($781). Short-box Stepside Sport Package. Short-box Fleetside sport package. Rear step bumper. Cargo area lamp. Power windows. Power door locks. Glide-out spare tire carrier. Rally wheels. Styled wheels. Exterior Decor Package with Silverado package only. Comfortilt steering wheel. C20 8-ft.

1978 Chevrolet Scottsdale Suburban (CP)

stake body ($728). El Camino "Conquista" Package ($146). Sliding rear window. Pickup box side rails. Speed and cruise controls. Bucket seats/center console. Gauges. Air conditioning. Tachometer. Whitewall tires. Bumper guards. Auxiliary fuel tank. Chromed front and rear bumpers. Below-Eye-Line mirrors. Color-keyed floor mats. Intermittent windshield wipers. Inside hoodlock release. Simulated wood grain. Exterior trim, Blazer and Suburban. Special two-tone paint. Spare tire cover (Blazer and Suburban). Rear radio speaker (Blazer and Suburban). Soft-Ray tinted glass. **LUV Options:** Mikado interior. High-back bucket seats. "Mighty Mike" decal package. Decor package. Sliding rear window. E78 x 14B Steel-belted whitewall tires. Mud flaps. Below-Eye-Line mirrors. Right-hand exterior mirror.

HISTORICAL: Introduced: Fall 1977. Calendar year registrations: 1,275,787. Calendar year sales: (all Series) 1,233,932. Innovations: El Camino down-sized. New V-8 engines introduced. "Big Dooley" name replaces "Big Dualie." New 5.7-litre V-8 diesel in half-ton pickups. Historical notes: Chevrolet reported an all-time record of 1.34 million truck sales in 1978. The number of trucks registered by Chevrolet dealers, per sales outlet, was 215 units, up from 187 in 1977.

Pricing

1978	5	4	3	2	1
LUV					
Pickup	400	800	1350	1900	2700
Long Box	420	840	1400	1950	2800
El Camino — (V-8)					
Pickup	780	1560	2600	3600	5200
Super Sport Pickup	850	1700	2850	4000	5700
Blazer — (V-8)					
4x4 Blazer	1010	2030	3350	4700	6700
Chevy Van 10					
Panel	630	1250	2100	3000	4200
Sportvan	780	1560	2600	3600	5200
Beauville Sportvan	830	1650	2750	3850	5500
Chevy Van 20					
Panel	600	1200	2000	2800	4000
Sportvan	750	1500	2500	3500	5000
Beauville Sportvan	780	1560	2600	3600	5200
Chevy Van 30					
Panel	590	1170	1950	2700	3900
Sportvan	740	1470	2450	3350	4900
Beauville Sportvan	770	1550	2550	3600	5100
Hi-Cube	570	1140	1900	2650	3800
P10 Step Van					
Van	540	1080	1800	2500	3600
P20 Step Van					
Van	530	1050	1750	2450	3500
P30 Step Van					
Van	480	975	1600	2250	3200
C10					
Stepside Sport Box Pickup	830	1650	2750	3850	5500
Fleetside Short Box Pickup	840	1680	2800	3900	5600
Stepside Long Box Pickup	840	1680	2800	3900	5600
Fleetside Long Box Pickup	850	1700	2850	4000	5700
Suburban	870	1750	2900	4100	5800
C20					
Stepside Pickup	780	1560	2600	3600	5200
Fleetside Pickup	810	1620	2700	3800	5400
Bonus Cab Pickup	800	1600	2650	3700	5300
Crew Cab Pickup	780	1560	2600	3600	5200
Suburban	810	1620	2700	3800	5400
C30					
Stepside Pickup	750	1500	2500	3500	5000
Fleetside Pickup	780	1560	2600	3600	5200
Bonus Cab Pickup	770	1550	2550	3600	5100
Crew Cab Pickup	750	1500	2500	3500	5000
"Big Dooley"	850	1700	2850	4000	5700

NOTE: 1955-up prices based on top of the line models. Add 5 percent for 4x4 models.

1979 Chevrolet LUV 4x4 Pickup (OCW)

1979 Chevrolet LUV Pickup (CP)

LIGHT TRUCK — 1979 SERIES — (ALL ENGINES): — Chevrolet's captive import, the LUV truck, looked the same in 1979 as it did the year before. Until you started adding some new options, that is. Four-wheel-drive was now available at extra-cost. Trucks so-equipped were seen with wide striping and 4x4 decals on the sides of their cargo boxes.

El Caminos featured a new grille with eight distinct horizontal segments formed by the bright metal molding. The moldings ran three across, with a thin one down the center. A "Royal Knight" dress-up package featured two dragon decals on its hood, styled wheels and other goodies. A new item was a 267 cu. in. V-8 for all non-California trucks. The Super Sport was again merchandised as a model-option rather than an individual package.

Light-duty trucks had a grille that was slightly narrower top-to-bottom, but of the same basic design as last year's style. The slotted area, directly below the grille was now bright metal. An optional sport grille had only two full-width horizontal members and a center bow-tie, the background being blacked-out. Custom Deluxe, Cheyenne, Scottsdale and Silverado packages were offered again.

Vans and Step-Vans were available in various configurations. Appearance updates were mainly in terms of new decal and paint treatments. On most vans, the grille had more of a horizontal theme due to the method of finishing the grille bars with paint.

I.D. DATA: See 1977 and 1978 serial number data.

Model	Body Type	Price	Weight	Prod. Total
LUV — (½-Ton) — (102.4/117.9 in. w.b.) — (4-cyl.)				
CL10503	Chassis & Cab (SWB)	4132	2095	—
CL10503	Pickup (SWB)	4276	2345	—
CL10803	Pickup (LWB)	4486	2405	—

NOTE 1: Add $971 for 4x4.

Model	Body Type	Price	Weight	Prod. Total
El Camino — (½-Ton) — (117.1 in. w.b.) — (V-8)				
1AW80	Pickup	5377	3242	—
Z15	"SS" Pickup	5579	3242	—
1AW80	Conquista	5532	3242	—
Blazer — (½-Ton) — (106.5 in. w.b.) — (V-8) — (4x4)				
CK10516	Hardtop	7373	4371	—
CK10516	Softtop	7273	—	—
Chevy Van 10 — (½-Ton) — (110/125 in. w.b.) — (V-8)				
CG11005	Panel	5312	3693	—
CG11006	Sportvan	6229	3998	—
CG11306	Beauville	7030	4367	—
Chevy Van 20 — (¾-Ton) — (110/125 in. w.b.) — (V-8)				
CG21005	Panel	5606	3689	—
CG21006	Sportvan	6397	3970	—
CG21306	Beauville	7198	4318	—
CG21305	Nomad	7108	3830	—
Chevy Van 30 — (1-Ton) — (110/125 in. w.b.) — (V-8)				
CG31005	Panel	5822	3914	—
CG31306	Sportvan	6474	4378	—
CG31306	Beauville	7410	4556	—
Hi-Cube Van — (1-Ton) — (125/146 in. w.b.) — (V-8)				
CG31303	10-ft. Panel	7662	—	—
CG31603	12-ft. Panel	7828	—	—
Step-Van — (P10/20/30) — (V-8)				
CP10542	Steel Panel (102 in. w.b.)	6189	4226	—
CP20842	Steel Panel (125/133 in. w.b.)	7287	5311	—
CP30842	Steel Panel (125/157 in. w.b.)	7487	5485	—

NOTE 2: Fifth symbol in Step-Van model number indicates wheelbase; "5"=102 in. w.b., "8"=125 in. w.b.; "0"=133 in. w.b., etc. Prices and weights for P20/P30 models above are for 125 in. w.b.

Model	Body Type	Price	Weight	Prod. Total
C10 — (½-Ton) — (117.5/131.5 in. w.b.) — (V-8)				
CC10703	Chassis & Cab (SWB)	4943	3406	—
CC10703	Stepside Pickup (SWB)	5091	3570	—
CC10703	Fleetside Pickup (SWB)	5091	3629	—
CC10903	Stepside Pickup (LWB)	5171	3693	—
CC10903	Fleetside Pickup (LWB)	5171	3767	—
CC10906	Suburban w/gate (LWB)	6614	4285	—

NOTE 3: Add for 4x4 (CK prefix).
NOTE 4: Add $1758 and 295 pounds for C-10 diesel.

Model	Body Type	Price	Weight	Prod. Total
C20 — (¾-Ton) — (131.5/164.5 in. w.b.) — (V-8)				
CC20903	Chassis & Cab (SWB)	5481	3693	—
CC20903	Stepside Pickup (SWB)	5777	4077	—
CC20903	Fleetside Pickup (SWB)	5777	4151	—
CC20943	Chassis & Bonus Cab (LWB)	6233	4224	—
CC20943	Bonus Cab Pickup (LWB)	6516	4682	—
CC20943	Chassis & Crew Cab (LWB)	6634	—	—
CC20943	Crew Cab Pickup (LWB)	6918	—	—
CC20906	Suburban w/gate (SWB)	7075	—	—

NOTE 5: Add for 4x4 (CK prefix).

Model	Body Type	Price	Weight	Prod. Total
C30 — (1-Ton) — (131.5/164.5 in. w.b.) (V-8)				
CC30903	Chassis & Cab (SWB)	5941	3899	—
CC30903	Stepside Pickup (SWB)	6237	4283	—
CC30903	Fleetside Pickup (SWB)	6237	4358	—
CC30943	Chassis-Bonus Cab (LWB)	6740	4453	—
CC30943	Chassis-Crew Cab (LWB)	7023	4911	—
CC30943	Bonus Cab Pickup (LWB)	6900	—	—
CC30943	Crew Cab Pickup (LWB)	7183	—	—

NOTE 6: Add for 4x4 (CK prefix).

1979 Chevrolet El Camino Royal Knight (OCW)

GENERAL NOTE: "SWB" is shortest wheelbase given above each series listing. "LWB" is longest wheelbase given above each series listing. (Example: In C10 Series the Stepside Pickup (SWB) is the "Short-Box" model with 117.5 in. w.b.)

ENGINE: (Standard: C10/Big 10/K10): Inline. OHV. Six-cylinder. Cast iron block. Bore & stroke: 3.876 x 3.530 in. Displacement: 250 cu. in. Compression ratio: 8.3:1. Net horsepower: 130 at 3800 R.P.M. Torque: 210 lb.-ft. at 2400 R.P.M. Seven main bearings. Hydraulic valve lifters. Carburetor: Two-barrel.

NOTE: (Base engine in California) 125 horsepower at 4000 R.P.M. Torque: 205 lbs.-ft. at 2000 R.P.M.

ENGINE: (Standard: C20/C30/K20/K30) Inline. OHV. Six-cylinder. Cast iron block. Bore & stroke: 3.876 x 4.120 in. Displacement: 292 cu. in. Compression ratio: 8.0:1. Net horsepower: 115 at 3400 R.P.M. Net torque: 215 lb.-ft. at 3400 R.P.M. Seven main bearings. Hydraulic valve lifters. Carburetor: Rochester one-bbl.

1979 Chevrolet Blazer (CP)

ENGINE: (Optional C10) V-type. OHV. Eight-cylinder. Cast iron block. Bore & stroke: 3.736 x 3.480 in. Displacement: 305 cu. in. Compression ratio: 8.4:1. Net horsepower: 140 at 4000 R.P.M. Net torque: 235 lb.-ft. at 2000 R.P.M. Five main bearings. Hydraulic valve lifters. Carburetor: Rochester two-bbl. model 2GC.

NOTE: (Base engine in California) 155 horsepower at 3600 R.P.M. Torque: 260 lb.-ft. at 2000 R.P.M. (Four-barrel California engine) 155 horsepower at 4000 R.P.M. Torque: 260 lbs.-ft. at 2000 R.P.M.

ENGINE: (Optional: all models except LUV) V-type. OHV. Eight-cylinder. Cast iron block. Bore & stroke: 4.0 x 3.48 in. Displacement: 350 cu. in. Compression ratio: 8.2:1. Net horsepower: 165 at 3600 R.P.M. Net torque: 270 lb.-ft. at 2700 R.P.M. Five main bearings. Hydraulic valve lifters. Carburetor: Rochester four-bbl. model M4 MC/MV.

ENGINE: (Optional: K10/K20/K30) V-type. OHV. Eight-cylinder. Cast iron block. Bore & stroke: 4.125 x 3.750 in. Displacement: 400 cu. in. Compression ratio: 8.5:1. Net horsepower: 185 at 3600 R.P.M. Net torque: 300 lb.-ft. at 2400 R.P.M. Five main bearings. Hydraulic valve lifters. Carburetor: Rochester four-bbl. model M4 MC/MV.

ENGINE: (Optional: all models except Blazer, El Camino, LUV) V-type. OHV. Eight-cylinder. Cast iron block. Bore & stroke: 4.250 x 4.0 in. Displacement: 454 cu. in. Compression ratio: 7.6:1. Net horsepower: 245 at 4000 R.P.M. Net torque: 380 lb.-ft. at 2500 R.P.M. Five main bearings. Hydraulic valve lifters. Carburetor: Rochester four-bbl. model M4 MC/MV.

ENGINE: (Optional: C10/Big 10) V-type. OHV diesel. Eight-cylinder. Cast iron block. Bore & stroke: 4.057 x 3.385 in. Displacement: 350 cu. in. Compression ratio: 20.5:1. Net horsepower: 120 at 3600 R.P.M. Net torque: 222 lb.-ft. at 1900 R.P.M. Five main bearings. Hydraulic valve lifters.

ENGINE: (Standard LUV) Inline. OHV overhead camshaft. Four-cylinder. Cast iron block. Bore & stroke: 3.31 x 3.23 in. Displacement: 110.8 cu. in. Compression ratio: 8.5:1. Net horsepower: 80 at 4800 R.P.M. Max. Torque: 95 lb.-ft at 3000 R.P.M. Five main bearings. Hydraulic valve lifters. Carburetor: One-barrel.

ENGINE: (Standard El Camino) V-type. OHV. Six-cylinder. Cast iron block. Bore & stroke: 3.5 x 3.48 in. Displacement: 200 cu. in. Compression ratio: 8.2:1. Net horsepower: 95. Four main bearings. Carburetor: Rochester two-bbl. model 210.

ENGINE: (Optional: El Camino) V-type. OHV. Six-cylinder. Cast iron block. Bore & stroke: 3.8 x 3.4 in. Displacement: 231 cu. in. Compression ratio: 8.0:1. Net horsepower: 105. Four main bearings. Carburetor: Rochester two-bbl. model 2GC.

ENGINE: (Optional El Camino) V-type. OHV. Eight-cylinder. Cast iron block. Bore & stroke: 3.5 x 3.48 in. Displacement: 267 cu. in. Five main bearings. Hydraulic valve lifters. Carburetor: two-bbl.

ENGINE: (Optional El Camino) V-type. OHV. Eight-cylinder. Cast iron block. Bore & stroke: 3.736 x 3.480 in. Displacement: 305 cu. in. Compression ratio: 8.4:1. Net horsepower: 145/135*. Five main bearings. Hydraulic valve lifters. Carburetor: Rochester two-bbl. model 2GC.

* California rating.

ENGINE: (Optional El Camino) V-type. OHV. Eight-cylinder. Cast iron block. Bore & stroke: 4.0 x 3.48 in. Displacement: 350 cu. in. Compression ratio: 8.2:1. Net horsepower: 170/160* at 3800 R.P.M. Max. torque: 270 lb.-ft. at 2400 R.P.M. Five main bearings. Hydraulic valve lifters. Carburetor: Rochester four-bbl. model M4 MC/MV.

* California rating.

CHASSIS: (Series K10) Wheelbase: 117.5/131.5 in. Overall length: 191.3/212 in. Height: 72 in. Front tread: 65.8 in. Rear tread: 62.7 in. Tires: L78 x 15B in.

CHASSIS: (Series K20) Wheelbase: 131.5 in. Overall length: 212 in. Height: 73.9 in. Front tread: 65.8 in. Rear tread: 62.7 in. Tires: 8.75 x 16.5C in.

CHASSIS: (Series K10 Blazer) Wheelbase: 106.5 in. Overall length: 184.8 in. Height: 73.4 in. Front tread: 66.1 in. Rear tread: 63 in. Tires: H78 x 15B in.

1979 Chevrolet Blazer (CP)

CHASSIS: (Series G20) Wheelbase: 110/125 in. Overall length: 178.2/202.2 in. Tires: J78 x 15B in.

CHASSIS: (Series G30) Wheelbase: 110/125 in. Overall length: 178.2/202.2 in. Tires: 8.00 x 16.5 in.

CHASSIS: (Series P30) Wheelbase: 125/157 in. Tires: 8.75 x 6.5 in.

CHASSIS: (Series K30) Wheelbase: 131.5/164.5 in. Overall length: 212/244.43 in. Height: 74.7/75 in. Front tread: 65.8 in. Rear tread: 62.7 in. Tires: 9.50 x 16.5D in.

CHASSIS: (LUV) Wheelbase: 102.4/117.9 in. Overall length: 173.8/190.9 in. Front tread: 54 in. Rear tread: 52.2 in. Tires: E78 x 14B in.

CHASSIS: (Series G10) Wheelbase: 110/125 in. Overall length: 178.2/202.2 in. Tires: G78 x 15B in.

1979 Chevrolet 'Old Cars Weekly' Scottsdale Suburban

CHASSIS: (Series C10, C10/Big 10) Wheelbase: 117.5/131.5 in. Overall length: 191.3/212 in. Height 69.8 in. Front tread: 65.8 in. Rear tread: 62.7 in. Tires: (C10) G78 x 15B in. (Big 10), L78 x 15B in.

CHASSIS: (Series C20) Wheelbase: 117.5/131.5/164.5 in. Overall length: 191.3/212/244.43 in. Height: 69.8 in. Front tread: 65.8 in. Rear tread: 62.7 in. Tires: (Pickup) 8.75 x 16.5C in., (Bonus Cab) Front, 8.75 x 16.5C in.; Rear, 8.75 x 16.5D in.; (Crew Cab) 9.50 x 16.5D in.

CHASSIS: (Series C30) Wheelbase: 131.5/164.5 in. Overall length: 212/244.43 in. Height: 71.8 in. Front tread: 65.8 in. Rear tread: 62.7 in. Tires: (Pickup) 8.75 x 16.5C in., (Bonus/Crew Cab) 9.50 x 16.5E in.

CHASSIS: (Series P30) Wheelbase: 125/157 in. Tires: 8.75 x 6.5 in.

CHASSIS: (El Camino) Wheelbase: 117.1 in. Overall length: 201.6 in. Height: 53.8 in. Front tread: 58.5 in. Rear tread: 57.8 in. Tires: P205/75R x 14 in.

CHASSIS: (Series C10, C10/Big 10) Wheelbase: 117.5/131.5 in. Overall length: 191.3/212 in. Height: 69.8 in. Front tread: 65.8 in. Rear tread: 62.7 in Tires: (Pickup) G78 x 15B in.; (Big 10) L78 x 15B in.

CHASSIS: (Series C20) Wheelbase: 117.5/131.5/164.5 in. Overall length: 191.3/212/244.43 in. Height: 65.8 in. Rear tread: 62.7 in. Tires: (Pickup) 8.75 x 16.5C in.; (Bonus Cab) Front, 8.75 x 16C in.; Rear, 8.75 x 16D in.; (Crew Cab) 9.50 x 16.5D in.

CHASSIS: (Series C30) Wheelbase: 131.5/164.5 in. Overall length: 212/244.43 in. Height: 71.8 in. Front tread: 65.8 in. Rear tread: 62.7 in. Tires: (Pickup) 8.75 x 16.5C in.; (Bonus/Crew Cab) 9.50 x 16.5E in.

1979 Chevrolet Stepside Pickup (CP)

CHASSIS: (El Camino) Wheelbase: 117.1 in. Overall length: 201.6 in. Height: 53.8 in. Front tread: 58.5 in. Rear tread: 57.8 in. Tires: P205/75R x 14 in.

CHASSIS: (P10 Step-Van) Wheelbase: 102 in. Tires: L78 x 15B in.

CHASSIS: (P20 Step-Van) Wheelbase: 125/133 in. Tires: 8.75 x 16.5C in.

TECHNICAL: Selective synchromesh transmission (Diesel w/THM only). Speeds: 3F/1R (LUV includes 4F/1R transmission). Column-mounted gearshift, except LUV. Single dry disc type clutch. Salisbury rear axle. Overall ratio: (C10) 3.07:1; (K10) 4.11:1; (C20) 4.10:1. Front disc/rear drum brakes. Pressed steel wheels. Drivetrain options: Turbo hydramatic transmission ($370). Locking differential and 3.73: axle ($210). Freedom battery ($39). Engine oil cooler ($91). Heavy-duty springs and shocks ($71). Blazer towing device ($30). Dead-weight trailer hitch ($43). Uni-Royal "Land Trac" tires, 10.00 x 15 ($362.85). Blazer rear roll bar ($105). "Big 10" package ($375).

1979 Chevrolet Fleetside Pickup (OCW)

OPTIONS: Chrome front bumper ($33). Electric clock ($55). Chevy Van Caravan package. Custom comfort package. Chevy Sport package. F44 "Big 10" package ($375). Scottsdale package. C20 Stake, 8-ft. Air conditioning ($574). Color-keyed floor mats ($11). Tinted glass ($49). Chromed grille ($29). Exterior eye-level mirror ($55). Convenience package ($231). Comfortilt steering wheel ($78). Rally wheels ($84). Intermittent wipers ($33). Sliding side window glass, Blazer ($176). Folding rear seat, Blazer ($260). Electric tailgate window, Blazer ($65).

HISTORICAL: Introduced: Fall 1978. Calendar year registrations: 1,085,855. Calendar year sales: (Light Trucks/Pickups) - 644,775; (Vans) - 166,850; (Suburbans) - 37,215; (Blazers) - 57,734; (LUV) - 100,192; (El Camino) - 52,803; (Sportvan) - 30,135, (Total) — 1,090,204. Innovations: New El Camino "Black Knight" model - option. 4x4 introduced for LUV pickup. New 267 cu. in. V-8.

1979 Chevrolet Beauville Sportvan (OCW)

114

1979 Chevrolet Silverado Suburban (CP)

1979 Chevrolet Silverado Suburban (OCW)

Pricing

	5	4	3	2	1
1979					
LUV					
Pickup	400	800	1350	1900	2700
Long Bed	420	840	1400	1950	2800
El Camino — (V-8)					
Pickup	780	1560	2600	3600	5200
Custom Pickup	850	1700	2850	4000	5700
Super Sport	870	1750	2900	4100	5800
Blazer — (V-8)					
4x4 Blazer	1010	2030	3350	4700	6700
Chevy Van 10					
Panel	630	1250	2100	3000	4200
Sportvan	780	1560	2600	3600	5200
Beauville Sportvan	830	1650	2750	3850	5500
Chevy Van 20					
Panel	600	1200	2000	2800	4000
Sportvan	750	1500	2500	3500	5000
Beauville Sportvan	780	1560	2600	3600	5200
Caravan	850	1700	2850	4000	5700
Chevy Van 30					
Panel	590	1170	1950	2700	3900
Sportvan	740	1470	2450	3350	4900
Beauville Sportvan	770	1550	2550	3600	5100
Hi-Cube Van	570	1140	1900	2650	3800
P10 Step Van					
Van	540	1080	1800	2500	3600
P20 Step Van					
Van	530	1050	1750	2450	3500
P30 Step Van					
Van	480	975	1600	2250	3200
C10 — (V-8)					
Stepside Sport Box Pickup	830	1650	2750	3850	5500
Fleetside Short Box Pickup	840	1680	2800	3900	5600
Stepside Long Box Pickup	840	1680	2800	3900	5600
Fleetside Long Box Pickup	850	1700	2850	4000	5700
Suburban	870	1750	2900	4100	5800
C20 — (V-8)					
Stepside Pickup	780	1560	2600	3600	5200
Fleetside Pickup	810	1620	2700	3800	5400
Bonus Cab Pickup	800	1600	2650	3700	5300
Crew Cab Pickup	780	1560	2600	3600	5200
Suburban	810	1620	2700	3800	5400
C30 — (V-8)					
Stepside Pickup	750	1500	2500	3500	5000
Fleetside Pickup	780	1560	2600	3600	5200
Bonus Cab Pickup	770	1550	2550	3600	5100
Crew Cab Pickup	750	1500	2500	3500	5000
Big Dooley	870	1750	2900	4100	5800

NOTE: 1955-up prices based on top of the line models. Add 5 percent for 4x4 models.

1980 CHEVROLET

1980 Chevrolet Sportvan (CP)

LIGHT TRUCK — 1980 SERIES — (ALL ENGINES): — Biggest change in the 1980 El Camino was the grille. It had 21 fine vertical members on either side of a slightly heavier vertical center molding. Base powertrain was a 229 cu. in. (3.8 liter) V-6 and three-speed manual transmission. The ribbed steel, six-foot cargo box provided 35.5 cu. ft. of room and a gross payload of 1250 pounds including passengers. Contrasting lower body perimeter finish with "Super Sport" shadow graphics along the door bottoms identified this model-option. Other "SS" features included Rally wheels, large front airdam, body color sport mirrors, white-letter tires and Super Sport tailgate decals. The "Royal Knight" option included the double-dragon hood decal, large front airdam, Rally wheels and painted sport mirrors.

The 1980 LUV pickup looked just like the 1979 model. New, under the hood, was an 80 horsepower engine.

Vans and light-duty trucks had a new "ice cube tray" grille with eleven horizontal and three vertical segments and a bow-tie emblem in the center. Unless you ordered a C10 diesel (it had round headlamps for some reason), the headlamps were rectangular and stacked on slightly narrower rectangular parking lamps.

Model-options included Caravan and Chevy Sport packages for the forward control trucks and Cheyenne, Scottsdale, Silverado, Chevy Sport and Camper Deluxe equipment for pickups and Suburbans. One-ton vans no longer used the 110 in. w.b. The 125 in. w.b. was standard for these models and a new "long wheelbase" (146 in.) version was offered.

I.D. DATA: See 1977 and 1978 sections for explanation of serial number and engine number systems. Locations of numbers were unchanged in 1980.

1980 Chevrolet Suburban (CP)

Model	Body Type	Price	Weight	Prod. Total
LUV — (½-Ton) — (102.4/117.9 in. w.b.) — (4-cyl.)				
CL10503	Chassis & Cab	4448	2095	—
CL10503	Pickup	4612	2315	—
CL10803	Long-Box Pickup	4787	2405	—
El Camino — (½-Ton) — (117.1 in. w.b.) — (V-8)				
1AW80	Pickup	5911	3238	—
w/Z15	Super Sport Pickup	6128	3238	—
Blazer — (½-Ton) — (106.5 in. w.b.) — (V-8) — (4x4)				
CK10516	Hardtop	8233	4429	—
CK10516	Softtop	8130	—	—
Chevy Van 10 — (½-Ton) — (110/125 in. w.b.) — (V-8)				
CG11005	Panel	5748	3652	—
CG11006	Sportvan	6747	3971	—
CG11306	Beauville	7854	4203	—
Chevy Van 20 — (¾-Ton) — (110/125 in. w.b.) — (V-8)				
CG21005	Panel	6183	3756	—
CG21006	Sportvan	7023	4012	—
CG21306	Beauville	7975	4901	—
CG21305	Nomad	7864	3915	—

1980 Chevrolet Fleetside Pickup (CP)

Model	Body Type	Price	Weight	Prod. Total
Chevy Van 30 — (1-Ton) — (125/146 in. w.b.) — (V-8)				
CG31305	Panel	7060	4154	—
CG31306	Sportvan	7901	4450	—
CG31306	Beauville	8680	4450	—
Hi-Cube Van — (C30/1-Ton) — (125/146 in. w.b.) — (V-8)				
CG31303	10-ft. Panel & Cab	7666	3524	—
CG31603	12-ft. Panel & Cab	8793	8793	—
Step-Van — (P10/20/30) — (102/157 in. w.b.) — (V-8)				
CP10542	7-ft. Steel Panel	6681	4226	—
CP20842	10-ft. Steel Panel	8021	5346	—
CP20842	12-ft. Steel Panel	8287	5522	—
C10 — (½-Ton) — (117.5/131.5 in. w.b.) — (V-8)				
CC10703	Chassis & Cab	5785	3243	—
CC10703	Stepside (SWB)	5505	3550	—
CC10703	Fleetside (SWB)	5505	3609	—
CC10903	Stepside (LWB)	5590	3692	—
CC10903	Fleetside (LWB)	5590	3767	—
CC10906	Suburban	7456	4242	—
C20 — (¾-Ton) — (131.5/164.5 in. w.b.) — (V-8)				
CC20903	Chassis & Cab	6216	3585	—
CC20903	Stepside (SWB)	2326	3969	—
CC20903	Fleetside (SWB)	6326	4044	—
CC20943	Chassis Bonus Cab	6964	4330	—
CC20943	Fleetside Bonus Cab	7241	4789	—
CC20943	Chassis & Crew Cab	7218	—	—
CC20943	Fleetside Crew Cab	7495	—	—
CC20906	Suburban	7923	4538	—
C30 — (1-Ton) — (131.5/164.5 in. w.b.) (V-8) *				
CC30903	Chassis & Cab	6399	3848	—
CC30903	Stepside (SWB)	6687	4232	—
CC30903	Fleetside (SWB)	6687	4307	—
CC30943	Chassis-Bonus Cab	7120	4364	—
CC30943	Fleetside Bonus Cab	7397	—	—
CC30943	Chassis-Crew Cab	7374	—	—
CC30943	Fleetside Crew Cab	7651	—	—

NOTE 1: 4x4 running gear available for C10/C20/C30 models. The difference in price for a ¾-ton (K20) pickup with 350 cu. in. V-8 engine was approximately $1,120. "CK" prefix for 4x4 trucks.

GENERAL NOTE: "SWB" means shortest wheelbase listed above each series. "LWB" means longest wheelbase listed above each series. (Example: In C30 Series the "Stepside [SWB]" is the Stepside with a 131.5 in. w.b.; in the C10 series the "Stepside [SWB]" is the Stepside with a 117.5 in. w.b.)

1980 Chevrolet ChevyVan w/Sport package (CP)

ENGINE: (Standard: C10/Big 10/K10): Inline. OHV. Six-cylinder. Cast iron block. Bore & stroke: 3.876 x 3.530 in. Compression ratio: 8.3:1. Net horsepower: 130 at 3800 R.P.M. Torque: 210 lb.-ft. at 2400 R.P.M. Seven main bearings. Hydraulic valve lifters. Carburetor: Two-barrel model Rochester.

NOTE: (All Engines) Horsepower and torque may vary in California.

ENGINE: (Standard: C20/C30/K20/K30) Inline. OHV. Six-cylinder. Cast iron block. Bore & stroke: 3.876 x 4.120 in. Displacement: 292 cu. in. Compression ratio: 8.0:1. Net horsepower: 115 at 3400 R.P.M. Torque: 215 lb.-ft. at 3400 R.P.M. Seven main bearings. Hydraulic valve lifters. Carburetor: Rochester model one-bbl.

ENGINE: (Optional C10) Vee-block. OHV. Eight-cylinder. Cast iron block. Bore & stroke: 3.736 x 3.480 in. Displacement: 305 cu. in. Compression ratio: 8.4:1. Net horsepower: 140 at 4000 R.P.M. Net torque: 235 lb.-ft. at 2000 R.P.M. Five main bearings. Hydraulic valve lifters. Carburetor: Rochester two-bbl. model 2GC.

ENGINE: (Optional: all models except LUV) Vee-block. OHV. Eight-cylinder. Cast iron block. Bore & stroke: 4.0 x 3.48 in. Displacement: 350 cu. in. Compression ratio: 8.2:1. Net horsepower: 165 at 3600 R.P.M. Net torque: 270 lb.-ft. at 2700 R.P.M. Five main bearings. Hydraulic valve lifters. Carburetor: Rochester four-bbl. model M4 MC/MV.

ENGINE: (Optional: K10/K20/K30) Vee-block. OHV. Eight-cylinder. Cast iron block. Bore & stroke: 4.125 x 3.750 in. Displacement: 400 cu. in. Compression ratio: 8.5:1. Net horsepower: 185 at 3600 R.P.M. Net torque: 300 lb.-ft. at 2400 R.P.M. Five main bearings. Hydraulic valve lifters. Carburetor: Rochester four-bbl. model M4 MC/MV.

ENGINE: (Optional: all models except Blazer, El Camino, LUV) Vee-block. OHV. Eight-cylinder. Cast iron block. Bore & stroke: 4.250 x 4.0 in. Displacement: 454 cu. in. Compression ratio: 7.6:1. Net horsepower: 245 at 4000 R.P.M. Net torque: 380 lb.-ft. at 2500 R.P.M. Five main bearings. Hydraulic valve lifters. Carburetor: Rochester four-bbl. model M4 MC/MV.

1980 Chevrolet El Camino Royal Knight (CP)

ENGINE: (Optional: C10/Big 10) V-type. OHV Diesel. Eight-cylinder. Cast iron block. Bore & stroke: 4.057 x 3.385 in. Displacement: 350 cu. in. Compression ratio: 20.5:1. Net horsepower: 120 at 3600 R.P.M. Net torque: 222 lb.-ft. at 1900 R.P.M. Five main bearings. Hydraulic valve lifters.

ENGINE: (Standard LUV) Inline. OHV. OHC. Four-cylinder. Cast iron block. Bore & stroke: 3.31 x 3.23 in. Displacement: 110.8 cu. in. Compression ratio: 8.5:1. Net horsepower: 80 at 4800 R.P.M. Max. Torque: 95 lb.-ft at 3000 R.P.M. Five main bearings. Hydraulic valve lifters. Carburetor: One-barrel.

ENGINE: (Standard El Camino) Vee-block. OHV. Six-cylinder. Cast iron block. Bore & stroke: 3.5 x 3.48 in. Displacement: 200 cu. in. Compression ratio: 8.2:1. Net horsepower: 95. Four main bearings. Hydraulic valve lifters. Carburetor: Rochester two-bbl. model 210.

ENGINE: Vee-block. OHV. Six-cylinder. Cast iron block. Bore & stroke: 3.8 x 3.4 in. Displacement: 231 cu. in. Compression ratio: 8.0:1. Net horsepower: 105. Four main bearings. Hydraulic valve lifters. Carburetor: Rochester two-bbl. model 2GC.

ENGINE: (Optional El Camino) Vee-block. OHV. Eight-cylinder. Cast iron block. Bore & stroke: 3.5 x 3.48 in. Displacement: 267 cu. in. Five main bearings. Hydraulic valve lifters. Carburetor: two-bbl.

ENGINE: (Optional El Camino) Vee-block. OHV. Eight-cylinder. Cast iron block. Bore & stroke: 3.736 x 3.480 in. Displacement: 305 cu. in. Compression ratio: 8.4:1. Net horsepower: 145/135*. Five main bearings. Hydraulic valve lifters. Carburetor: Rochester two-bbl. model 2GC.

* California rating.

ENGINE: V-type. OHV. Eight-cylinder. Cast iron block. Bore & stroke: 4.0 x 3.48 in. Displacement: 350 cu. in. Compression ratio: 8.2:1. Net horsepower: 170/160 at 3800 R.P.M. Max. torque: 270 lb.-ft. at 2400 R.P.M. Five main bearings. Hydraulic valve lifters. Carburetor: Rochester four-bbl. model M4 MC/MV.

CHASSIS: (LUV) Wheelbase: 102.4/117.9 in. Overall length: 173.8/190.9 in. Front tread: 54 in. Rear tread: 52.2 in. Tires: E78 x 14B in.

CHASSIS: (El Camino) Wheelbase: 117.1 in. Overall length: 201.6 in. Height: 53.8 in. Front tread: 58.5 in. Rear tread: 51.8 in. Tires: P205/75R x 14 in.

CHASSIS: (Blazer) Wheelbase: 106.5 in. Overall length: 184.8 in. Height: 73.4 in. Front tread: 66.1 in. Rear tread: 63 in. Tires: P215/75R x 15 in.

CHASSIS: (Chevy Van 10) Wheelbase: 110/125 in. Overall length: 178/202.2 in. Height: 78.8/81.2 in. Front tread: 69.5 in. Rear tread: 69.7 in. Tires: GR78 x 15B in.

CHASSIS: (Chevy Van 20) Wheelbase: 110/125 in. Overall length: 178.2/202.2 in. Height: 78.8/81.2 in. Front tread: 69.5 in. Rear tread: 69.7 in. Tires: JR78 x 15B in.

CHASSIS: (Chevy Van 30) Wheelbase: 125/146 in. Overall length: 207.6/231.3 in. Tires: 8.75 x 16.5E in.

CHASSIS: (Step-Van 10) Wheelbase: 102 in. Tires: L78 x 15B in.

CHASSIS: (Step-Van 20) Wheelbase: 125/133 in. Tires: 8.75 x 16.5 in.

CHASSIS: (Step-Van 30) Wheelbase: 125/157 in. Tires: 8.75 x 16.5 in.

CHASSIS: (Series C10/K10) Wheelbase: 117.5/131.5 in. Overall length: 193.3/212 in. Height: 72 in. Front tread: 65.8 in. Rear tread: 62.7 in. Tires: GR78 x 15B in.

CHASSIS: (Series C20/K20) Wheelbase: 131.5 in. Overall length: 212 in. Height: 73.9 in. Front tread: 65.8 in. Rear tread: 62.7 in. Tires: 8.75 x 16.5C in.

TECHNICAL: Basically the same as 1980.

OPTIONS: Chrome front bumper ($33). Radio AM, AM/FM. Electric clock ($55). Caravan package (Van). Custom comfort package. Chevy Sport package. F44 "Big 10" package ($375). Scottsdale package. C20 Stake, 8-ft. Air conditioning ($574). Color-keyed floor mats ($11). Tinted glass ($49). Chromed grille ($29). Exterior below eye-level mirror ($55). Convenience package ($23). Comfortilt steering wheel ($78). Rally wheels ($84). Intermittent wipers ($33). Sliding side window glass ($176). Folding rear seat, Blazer ($260). Electric tailgate window, Blazer ($65).

HISTORICAL: Introduced: Fall 1979. Calendar year registrations: (all Chevy trucks) 737,788. Calendar year sales: (Pickups) - 403,487; (Vans) - 86,727; (Suburbans) - 19,518; (Blazer) - 21,399; (LUV) - 61,724; (El Camino) - 33,086; (Sportvan) - 13,576; (Total) — 724,330. Innovations: New grilles for all series, except LUV. One-ton Chevy vans adopt a new 146 in. "long" w.b. and no longer come on 110 in. chassis.

Rising gasoline prices and a slackening economy made this a poor year for truck sales. At Chevrolet, calendar year registrations dropped below the one-million level for the first time since 1976. In mid-year, Chevy discontinued its heavy, over-the-road type trucks to concentrate on the light-duty and medium-duty market products.

Pricing

1980	5	4	3	2	1
LUV					
Pickup	420	840	1400	1950	2800
Long Bed Pickup	440	870	1450	2050	2900
El Camino — (V-8)					
Pickup	800	1600	2650	3700	5300
Custom Pickup	870	1750	2900	4100	5800
Super Sport	890	1770	2950	4150	5900
Blazer — (V-8)					
4x4 Blazer	1020	2050	3400	4800	6800
C10 — (V-8)					
Stepside Short Box Pickup	840	1680	2800	3900	5600
Fleetside Short Box Pickup	850	1700	2850	4000	5700
Stepside Long Box Pickup	850	1700	2850	4000	5700
Fleetside Long Box Pickup	870	1750	2900	4100	5800
Suburban	890	1770	2950	4150	5900
C20 — (V-8)					
Stepside Pickup	800	1600	2650	3700	5300
Fleetside Pickup	830	1650	2750	3850	5500
Bonus Cab Pickup	810	1620	2700	3800	5400
Crew Cab Pickup	800	1600	2650	3700	5300
Suburban	830	1650	2750	3850	5500
C30 — (V-8)					
Stepside Pickup	750	1500	2500	3500	5000
Fleetside Pickup	780	1560	2600	3600	5200
Bonus Cab Pickup	770	1550	2550	3600	5100
Crew Cab Pickup	750	1500	2500	3500	5000
Big Dooley	830	1650	2750	3850	5500
Chevy Van 10 — (V-8)					
Panel	630	1250	2100	3000	4200
Sportvan	780	1560	2600	3600	5200
Beauville Sportvan	830	1650	2750	3850	5500

1980 LUV Pickup (DFW)

	5	4	3	2	1
Chevy Van 20 — (V-8)					
Panel	600	1200	2000	2800	4000
Sportvan	750	1500	2500	3500	5000
Beauville Sportvan	780	1560	2600	3600	5200
Nomad	830	1650	2750	3850	5500
Chevy Van 30 — (V-8)					
Panel	590	1170	1950	2700	3900
Sportvan	740	1470	2450	3350	4900
Beauville Sportvan	770	1550	2550	3600	5100
Hi-Cube Van	570	1140	1900	2650	3800
Step-Vans (V-8)					
½-Ton Step-Van	540	1080	1800	2500	3600
¾-Ton Step-Van	530	1050	1750	2450	3500
1-Ton Step-Van	480	975	1600	2250	3200

NOTE: 1955-up prices based on top of the line models.
Add 5 percent for 4x4 models.

1981 CHEVROLET

1981 Chevrolet Stepside Pickup (CP)

LIGHT TRUCK — 1981 SERIES — (ALL ENGINES): — New Aerodynamic styling was seen inside and outside this year's Series 11 LUV imported compact truck. The hood was smoother and the new cab provided a larger glass area. A curved rear window was used. A major functional change added some 2½ in. of leg room and about an inch of shoulder room. Wheelbase was increased to 104.3 in. with a new frame design. The grille was of egg-crate style, with a larger Chevy bow-tie in its center. Bumper slots again numbered four, but those near the center were now the widest, while the smaller outer pair housed the parking lamps. Headlamp housings could no longer be seen in profile. The bodysides were now smoothly curved with a sculptured feature line near the bottom rather than the belt. Chevrolet medallions were positioned on the side roof panel and load tie-downs, now located on the inner side of the box. Interiors featured a restyled, color-keyed instrument panel and pad with a new instrument cluster, color-keyed steering wheel, new seat trim material, door and window regulator handles, headliner, door trim panel materials and redesigned steering column. The "Mikado" package was revised with new seat trim, door trim panels, steering wheel and instrument panel trim. A new color-keyed floor console was standard with automatic transmission. Realigned cab door openings made for easier exit and entry. Other improvements included weight reduction, heavier payload capacities, improved

4x2 front suspension, larger front brake area and power brake booster, improved heating/ventilation system and new electronic ignition system.

The El Camino featured a new grille of horizontal design with bright upper and lower moldings. A Chevrolet name was at the lower left-hand corner of the grille, while El Camino lettering decorated the lower rear body quarter, above the feature line. Attractive new wheel covers with a turbine-fin look around a plain center disc were introduced. Inside was a redesigned instrument panel with a new pad and glossy applique, convenient door-pull straps, new seat trim and international symbols on the controls. A new 55/45 split front seat was optional, with single folding arm rests. A "Resume" function was added to the optional automatic speed control. Standard tires were now high-pressure P205/75R models with reduced rolling resistance for better mileage. A side-lift jack replaced the former bumper type. Powertrains were carried over, but all engines were now equipped with GM's Computer Command Control (CCC) emissions system. This utilized an on-board computer for precise fuel-air ratio control. Option packages included the Conquista and Royal Knight equipment groups, while the Super Sport version was merchandised as a separate model-option, rather than individual package. New-for-1981 options also included a trip odometer.

Blazers, for 1981, had an aerodynamically restyled front end. The smoother new hood and fenders, together with a front bumper mounted air dam, were designed to improve fuel economy. A handsome new grille (also used on pickups) continued the "ice cube tray" look with 16 taller openings running across the truck between the stacked square headlamps. A wide center horizontal molding — bright-finished with a bow-tie in the middle — spanned the full width of the front end. Rectangular parking lamps/turn signals were placed in the new front bumper, directly beneath the headlamps. On the bodysides, the belt-level feature line ran the length of the Blazer and blended more smoothly into the fender edge at the front. Two-tone paint treatments were now separated at the lower perimeter feature line. New front fender skirts with attached shields helped reduce engine compartment splash. Standard engine was still the "250" six-cylinder. A new 305 cu. in. V-8 with electronic spark control (ESC) was optional, except in California. 4x4 models had a new aluminum transfer case and automatic locking hubs. Other technical improvements included bumpers made of lighter-weight high-strength/low-alloy steel, and a new "front quad shock" package. A Custom trim package included an exterior decor package or special two-tone paint. Also available were the Deluxe and Silverado options and new "Deluxe Front Appearance" package.

1981 Chevrolet Fleetside Pickup (CP)

Chevy Vans were essentially unchanged in appearance. This went for Hi-Cube vans and Step-Vans, as well. A new Chevy Van model-option was the Bonaventure van. This was a mid-level passenger van with special identification nameplates, high-back bucket seats (standard in Sportvans), Custom vinyl trim, a full-length headliner, door and sidewall trim panels and deluxe instrument panel. It was available in all tonnage classes, on the 125 in. w.b. Offered for the first time in a Chevrolet factory van was a travel bed package consisting of a three-passenger bench seat with folding back rest and hinged extension which unfolded into a travel bed. Technical changes included improvements to the base six-cylinder engine; a new high-compression 5-liter V-8 with ESC (not available in California with ESC); and better corrosion protection measures. Anti-rust measures were the use of new, two-sided galvanized steel for rear door outer panels and the use of zinc-rich paints on brake and fuel lines.

Suburbans were restyled, along the lines of the Blazer, at the front. Like other 1981 trucks, they had reduced weights (about 200-300 pounds). A new standard 305 cu. in. V-8 was featured outside California. Half-tons had new drag-free disc brakes and quick-takeup master cylinder, plus lighter weight rear springs. Due to the use of new automatic-locking front hubs, Suburbans with 4x4 drive could be shifted into the 4x4 mode at speeds up to 20 m.p.h.

Chevy's 1981 pickups were 87 to 300 pounds lighter than their 1980 counterparts, while retaining the same cab size and bed size as before. They received the same new grille and sheet metal treatments described above for Blazers. The grille could be had with the square headlamps only in the top level or with a "Halogen High-Beam" option in which both grille levels held a square lamp unit at each end. A new one-piece I.P. trim panel was used on the dash eliminating the vertical seam between the banks of gauges. Collectible trim options include the Chevy Sport, Cheyenne, Scottsdale and Silverado packages. Custom and Custom Deluxe trims were more commonly seen. Among light-duty powerplants was a new high-compression 5.0-liter V-8 with ESC (not used in California) that was designed to give both economy and performance improvements. Also new for the season were improved corrosion resistance; low-drag disc brakes; new 6000-pound semi-floating axle (specific models); "Resume Speed" cruise controls; "Quad shock" 4x4 front suspension; heavier-duty rear springs and a water-in-fuel warning lamp for diesel-powered trucks. K20s and K10s adopted the new automatic locking hubs and shot-peened rear springs. Standard on all models were high-efficiency radiators and Delco Freedom II battery.

I.D. DATA: Serial Numbers in same locations. All 1981 to 1983 models had a VIN with 17 symbols. The first three identified the manufacturer, make and type of vehicle. The fourth, a letter, designates GVW range. The fifth, sixth and seventh identify series, nominal rating and body style. Eight=engine. Ninth=check digit. Tenth=model year. Eleventh=factory. Last six are sequential production numbers. Example: 1GCC14G(X)B(A) 100001 and up: 1=Chevrolet; G=General Motors; C=truck; C=light-duty; 1="10" series; 0=4900-6800 lb. GVW and G=Chevy Van; (X)=5.7 litre V-8; B=check digit; (A)=1981 and 100001=sequential number. Engine numbers in same locations.

Model	Body Type	Price	Weight	Prod. Total
LUV — (½-Ton) — (104.3/117.9 in. w.b.) — (4-cyl.)				
CL10503	Chassis & Cab	5913	—	—
CL10503	Pickup (SWB)	6586	2315	—
CL10803	Pickup (LWB)	6795	2405	—
El Camino — (½-Ton) — (117.1 in. w.b.) — (V-6)				
A1AW80	Pickup	6988	3181	—
w/Z15	Super Sport Pickup	7217	3188	—
Blazer — (½-Ton) — (106.5 in. w.b.) — (6-cyl.) — (4x4)				
CK10516	Hardtop	8856	4087	—
CK10516	Softtop	8750	—	—
Chevy Van 10 — (½-Ton) — (110/125 in. w.b.) — (6-cyl.)				
CG11005	Panel	6434	3577	—
CG11006	Sportvan	7465	3907	—
CG11306	Bonaventure	8305	4016	—
CG11306	Beauville	8515	4016	—
Chevy Van 20 — (¾-Ton) — (110/125 in. w.b.) — (6-cyl.)				
CG21005	Panel	6756	3631	—
CG21006	Sportvan	7617	3928	—
CG21306	Bonaventure	8457	—	—
CG21306	Beauville	8667	—	—
CG21305	Nomad	8644	—	—
Chevy Van 30 — (1-Ton) — (125/146 in. w.b.) — (V-8)				
CG31305	Panel	8056	4285	—
CG31306	Sportvan	8997	4602	—
CS31306	Bonaventure	9653	—	—
CG31306	Beauville	9863	—	—
Hi-Cube Van — (1-Ton) — (125/146 in. w.b.) — (V-8)				
CG31303	10-ft. Panel & Cab	8921	—	—
CG31603	12-ft. Panel & Cab	10,257	—	—
Step-Van — (P20/P30) — (6-cyl.)				
CP20842	10-ft. Steel Panel (125 in. w.b.)	9536	5472	—
CP30842	10-ft. Steel Panel (125 in. w.b.)	9784	5671	—
C10 — (½-Ton) — (117.5/131.5 in. w.b.) — (6-cyl.)				
CC10703	Stepside (SWB)	6012	3328	—
CC10703	Fleetside (SWB)	6012	3391	—
CC10903	Stepside (LWB)	6099	3457	—
CC10903	Fleetside (LWB)	6099	3518	—
CC10906	Suburban (V-8)	8517	4276	—
CK10703	Fleetside 4x4 (SWB)	7762	3880	—
CK10703	Stepside 4x4 (SWB)	7762	4016	—

NOTE: Add $1750 for 4x4 w/Suburban and long wheelbase pickups.

Model	Body Type	Price	Weight	Prod. Total
C20 — (¾-Ton) — (131.5/164.5 in. w.b.) — (6-cyl.)				
CC20903	Chassis & Cab	6605	3326	—
CC20903	Stepside (SWB)	7109	3710	—
CC20903	Fleetside (SWB)	7109	3771	—
CC20943	Chassis & Bonus Cab (LWB)	7447	4246	—
CC20943	Bonus Cab Fleetside (LWB)	7935	—	—
CC20943	Chassis & Crew Cab	7737	—	—
CC20943	Fleetside Crew Cab	8225	—	—
CC20906	Suburban (V-8)	8771	4596	—
CK20903	Fleetside (4x4) (SWB)	8479	4227	—

NOTE: Add $1370 for other 4x4 models ("CK" prefix w/4x4).

Model	Body Type	Price	Weight	Prod. Total
C30 — (1-Ton) — (131.5/164.5 in. w.b.) (6-cyl.)				
CC30903	Chassis & Cab	6720	3893	—
CC30903	Stepside (SWB)	7214	4251	—
CC30903	Fleetside (SWB)	7214	4310	—
CC30943	Chassis-Bonus Cab (LWB)	7625	4327	—
CC30943	Bonus Cab Fleetside (LWB)	8114	—	—
CC30943	Chassis-Crew Cab (LWB)	7915	—	—
CC30943	Crew Cab Fleetside	8404	—	—

NOTE: Add for K30 4x4 models; price not available.

GENERAL NOTES: "SWB" means shortest wheelbase listed above each series. "LWB" means longest wheelbase listed above each series. (Example: The C10 "Stepside SWB" has the 117.5 in. w.b.; the C20 "Stepside SWB" has the 131.5 in. w.b.).

Step-Vans also available with 133- and 157-in. w.b. and with optional aluminum bodies.

ENGINE: (Standard: C10/C20/K10/G10/G20/G30/Blazer): Inline. OHV. Six-cylinder. Cast iron block. Bore & stroke: 3.9 x 4.5 in. Displacement: 250 cu. in. Compression ratio: 8.3:1. Net horsepower: 115 at 3600 R.P.M. Torque: 200 lb.-ft. at 2000 R.P.M. Seven main bearings. Hydraulic valve lifters. Carburetor: Rochester model Staged two-barrel.

1981 Chevrolet Beauville Sportvan (CP)

NOTE: Order Code LE3(A).

NOTE: Versions of some engines used in trucks for California sale have different horsepower and torque ratings.

ENGINE: (Standard: C20 HD (C6P), C20 Bonus/Crew Cab, C30, C30 Bonus/Crew Cab, K20 HD (P6) Inline. OHV. Six-cylinder. Cast iron block. Bore & stroke: 3.876 x 4.12 in. Displacement: 292 cu. in. Compression ratio: 7.8:1. Net horsepower: 115 at 3400 R.P.M. Max. torque: 215 lb.-ft. at 1600 R.P.M. Five main bearings. Hydraulic valve lifters. Carburetor: Rochester model one-bbl.

NOTE: Order Code L25(B).

ENGINE: (Optional C10, C20, K10, Blazer) Vee-block. OHV. Eight-cylinder. Cast iron block. Bore & stroke: 3.736 x 3.480 in. Displacement: 305 cu. in. Compression ratio: 8.5:1. Net horsepower: 130 at 4000 R.P.M. Max torque: 240 lb.-ft. at 2000 R.P.M. Five main bearings. Hydraulic valve lifters. Carburetor: Rochester model Staged two-barrel.

NOTE: Order Code LG9(C).

ENGINE: (Optional C10, C20, K10, Blazer) Vee-block. OHV. Eight-cylinder. Cast iron block. Bore & stroke: 3.736 x 3.480 in. Displacement: 305 cu. in. Compression ratio: 9.2:1. Net horsepower: 160 at 4400 R.P.M. Max torque: 235 lb.-ft. at 2000 R.P.M. Five main bearings. Hydraulic valve lifters. Carburetor: Rochester model Staged four-barrel with Electronic Spark Control.

NOTE: Order Code LE9(C). Not available for California.

ENGINE: (Optional: C10, C20, K10, G10, G20) Vee-block. OHV. Eight-cylinder. Cast iron block. Bore & stroke: 3.736 x 3.480 in. Displacement: 305 cu. in. Compression ratio: 8.6:1. Net horsepower: 150 at 4200. Max torque: 240 lb.-ft. at 2000 R.P.M. Five main bearings. Hydraulic valve lifters. Carburetor: Rochester model Staged four-barrel.

NOTE: Order Code LF3(C).

ENGINE: (Standard: G30, C20, K10, K20 Suburban) (Optional: C20, K20, K20 HD (CP6), K30, C10 Suburban) Vee-block. OHV. Eight-cylinder. Cast iron block. Bore & stroke: 4.3 x 3.5 in. Displacement: 350 cu. in. Compression ratio: 8.2:1. Five main bearings. Hydraulic valve lifters. Carburetor: Rochester model four-bbl.

NOTE: Order Code L59(A).

1981 Chevrolet Silverado Suburban (CP)

ENGINE: (Optional: C10) Vee-block. OHV Diesel. Eight-cylinder. Cast iron block. Bore & stroke: 4.06 x 3.38 in. Displacement: 350 cu. in. Compression ratio: 22.5:1. Net horsepower: 125 at 3600 R.P.M. Max torque: 225 lb.-ft. at 1600 R.P.M. Five main bearings. Hydraulic valve lifters. Carburetor: Fuel injectors.

NOTE: Order Code LS9(A).

ENGINE: (Optional: C20, C20 HD (CP6), C30) Vee-block. OHV. Eight-cylinder. Cast iron block. Bore & stroke: 4.250 x 4.0 in. Displacement: 454 cu. in. Compression ratio: 7.9:1. Net horsepower: 210 at 3800 R.P.M. Max. Torque: 340 lb.-ft at 2800 R.P.M. Five main bearings. Hydraulic valve lifters. Carburetor: Rochester model four-barrel.

NOTE: Order Code LE8(A).

ENGINE: (Standard: LUV) INline. OHV. OHC. Four-cylinder. Cast iron block. Bore & stroke: 3.31 x 3.23 in. Displacement: 110.8 cu. in. Compression ratio: 8.5:1. Net horsepower: 80 at 4800 R.P.M. Max torque: 95 lb.-ft. at 3000 R.P.M. Five main bearings. Hydraulic valve lifters. Carburetor: Single one-barrel.

ENGINE: (Standard: El Camino (Except California) Vee-block. OHV. Six-cylinder. Cast iron block. Bore & stroke: 3.7 x 3.48 in. Displacement: 229 cu. in. Compression ratio: 8.6:1. Net horsepower: 110 at 4200 R.P.M. Max torque: 170 lb.-ft. at 2000 R.P.M. Four main bearings. Hydralic valve lifters.

NOTE: Order Code LC3(A).

ENGINE: (Optional (except California): El Camino) Vee-block. OHV. Eight-cylinder. Cast iron block. Bore & stroke: 3.5 x 3.48 in. Displacement: 267 cu. in. Compression ratio: 8.3:1. Net horsepower: 115 at 4000 R.P.M. Max torque: 200 lb.-ft. at 2400 R.P.M. Five main bearings. Hydraulic valve lifters. Carburetor: Rochester model Staged two-barrel.

NOTE: Order Code L39(B).

ENGINE: (Optional El Camino) Vee-block. OHV. Eight-cylinder. Cast iron block. Bore & stroke: 3.7 x 3.48 in. Displacement: 305 cu. in. Compression ratio: 8.6:1. Net horsepower: 145 at 3800 R.P.M. Max torque: 248 lb.-ft. at 2400 R.P.M. Five main bearings. Hydraulic valve lifters. Carburetor: Rochester model Staged four-barrel.

NOTE: Order Code LG4(B).

ENGINE: (Standard: El Camino (California only) Vee-block. OHV. Eight-cylinder. Cast iron block. Bore & stroke: 3.8 x 3.4 in. Displacement: 231 cu. in. Compression ratio: 8.0:1. Net horsepower: 110 at 3800 R.P.M. Max. torque: 190 lb.-ft. at 1600 R.P.M. Four main bearings. Hydraulic valve lifters.

NOTE: Order Code LD5(C).

1981 Chevrolet Blazer (CP)

CHASSIS: (LUV) Wheelbase: 104.3/117.9 in. Overall length: 174.5/191.6 in. Height: (4x2) 59.3 in.; (4x4) 61.0 in. Front tread: (4x2) 53.8 in.; (4x4) 54.2 in. Rear tread: (4x2) 51.2 in.; (4x4) 52.7 in. Tires: (4x2) E78 x 14B in.; (4x4) F70 x 14B in. white-lettered.

CHASSIS: (El Camino) Wheelbase: 117.1 in. Overall length: 201.6 in. Height: 53.8 in. Front tread: 58.5 in. Rear tread: 57.8 in. Tires: P205/75R x 14 in.

CHASSIS: (Blazer 4x4) Wheelbase: 106.5 in. Overall length: 184.8 in. Height: 73.4 in. Front tread: 66.1 in. Rear tread: 63 in. Tires: (4x2) P215/75R x 15 in.; (4x4) P215/75R x 15 in.

CHASSIS: (Chevy Van 10) Wheelbase: 110/125 in. Overall length: 178.2/202.2 in. Height: 78.8/81.2 in. Front tread: 69.5 in. Rear tread: 69.7 in. Tires: FR78 x 15B in.

CHASSIS: (Chevy Van 20) Wheelbase: 110/125 in. Overall length: 178.2/202.2 in. Height: 78.8/81.2 in. Front tread: 69.5 in. Rear tread: 69.7 in. Tires: P225/75R x 15 in.

1981 Chevrolet El Camino Royal Knight (CP)

CHASSIS: (Chevy Van 30) Wheelbase: 125/146 in. Tires: 8.75 x 16.5E in.

CHASSIS: (Hi-Cube Van): Wheelbase: 125/146 in. Overall length: 207.3/231.3 in. Tires: (front) 8.75 x 16 in.; (rear) 8.00 x 16 in.

CHASSIS: (P20 Step-Van) Wheelbase: 125/133 in. Tires: 8.75 x 16.5C in.

CHASSIS: (P30 Step-Van) Wheelbase: 125/157 in. Tires: 8.75 x 16.5 in.

CHASSIS: (Suburban, C20) Wheelbase: 129.5 in. Overall length: 218.7 in. Height: 71.8 in. Tires: 8.75R x 16.5 in.

CHASSIS: (C10 Pickups) Wheelbase: 117.5/131.5 in. Overall length: 192.2/211.4 in. Height: (Fleetside) 69.8 in.; (Stepside) 71.9 in. Tires: FR78 x 15B in.

CHASSIS: (C20 Pickup) Wheelbase: 131.5/164.5 in. Overall length: (SWB Fleetside C10) 211.4 in.; (SWB Fleetside K10) 212.1 in. Height: (4x2) 70.8 in.; (4x4) 73.9 in. Tires: 8.75R x 16.5C in.

CHASSIS: (C30 Pickup) Wheelbase: 131.5/164.5 in. Overall length: (SWB Fleetside) 211.4 in. Height: (SWB Fleetside 4x2) 70.9 in. Tires: 8.75 x 16.5C in.

TECHNICAL: Selective, synchromesh transmission. Speeds: 3F/1R (LUV and "30" have 4F/1R speeds). Column-mounted gearshift (except LUV). Single disc type clutch. Salisbury rear axle. Overall ratio: various. Power front disc/rear drum brakes. Pressed steel wheels.

NOTE: Specific technical features varied by type and series.

1981 Chevrolet LUV Pickup (CP)

OPTIONS: (LUV): Air conditioning ($603). Chrome rear step bumper ($122); Painted ($122). Chrome front bumper guards ($38). Sport stripe decals ($45). Decals and stripes ($111). California emissions ($111). Exterior Decor package, includes chrome center hubcaps and moldings for beltline, windshield and roof rails ($98). Mikado trim, w/bench seat ($228); w/bucket seat ($354). Stainless below-eyeline mirrors ($61). Solid paint, metallic ($75). AM radio ($98). AM/FM radio ($176). Passenger type whitewall tires, front ($19); rear ($19); spare ($10). Automatic transmission ($420). Sliding rear window ($92). **Blazer Options:** Silverado ($881). Custom high-back vinyl bucket seats, w/o Silverado and rear seat ($170); two seats w/o Silverado ($212); one seat w/Silverado (no charge); two seats w/Silverado ($42). Custom cloth high-back bucket seats, w/o rear seat (no charge); w/rear seat ($42). Special two-tone, w/o Silverado ($314); w/Silverado ($130). Exterior Decor package, w/o Silverado ($430); w/Silverado ($246). 5.0-liter two-barrel V-8 ($295). 5.0-liter four-barrel V-8 ($345). 5.0-liter four-barrel V-8 w/ESC ($345). Four-speed manual transmission ($170). Automatic transmission ($384).

Optional axle ($26). High-altitude 3.73:1 rear axle ($26). Air conditioning ($591). Deluxe front ($88). Locking differential ($191). Auxiliary battery ($101). Heavy-duty battery ($40). Chromed bumpers ($58). Deluxe chrome bumpers, w/Silverado ($38); w/o Silverado ($96). Front bumper guards ($34). Quartz electric clock ($60). Power door locks ($98). Halogen high-beams ($26). Sliding side window ($184). One-way glass ($147). Below eyeline mirror, stainless ($63); painted ($39); camper ($74). Body side moldings ($92). Operating Convenience package ($243). Rally wheels ($88). Aluminum forged wheels ($360). Styled wheels ($176). Power windows ($145). Tailgate ($67). Power steering ($205). Fuel tank shield ($135). AM/FM w/8-track stereo ($320). Roll bar ($108). And others.
Chevy Van Options: Custom vinyl high-back bucket seats ($34). Custom cloth swivel bucket seats ($420). Special two-tone paint ($185). Deluxe two-tone paint ($195). 5.0-liter two-barrel V-8 ($345). 5.7-liter four-barrel V-8 ($345). Automatic transmission ($384). Axle options ($26). Air conditioning, front ($696); front and rear ($1,138). Locking differential ($191). Heavy-duty battery ($40). Heavy-duty powerbrakes ($63). Chrome bumpers front/rear ($58). Front chrome bumper guards ($34). Electric clock ($27). Engine oil cooler ($95). Heavy-duty cooling ($42). Spare tire cover ($26). Power door locks ($147). California emissions ($80). Side rear door extender link ($29). All glass tinted ($75). Windshield tinted ($25). One-way glass ($296). Rear heater, w/o air conditioner ($189); with ($156). Cigar lighter ($19). Auxiliary lighting ($77). Below eyeline mirrors, painted ($39); stainless ($63). Bodyside moldings ($102). Door edge guards ($13). Wheel opening moldings ($57). Operating Convenience package, includes power door locks and windows ($292). Passenger seats, eight-man ($219); 12-man ($467). Swivel bucket seats ($426). Travel bed w/8-passenger ($770); regular ($561). Heavy-duty shocks ($27). Automatic speed control ($132). Power steering ($217). Comfort tilt steering wheel ($81). Custom steering wheel ($21). Rear door stop ($29). Front seat storage compartment ($29). Body striping ($56). Large 33-gallon fuel tank ($68). Theft deterrent system ($148). Dead-weight trailer hitch ($145). Roof ventilator ($62). Special wheel covers ($51). Forged aluminum wheels ($360). Rally wheels w/trim rings ($88). Styled wheels ($176). Power windows ($145). Windshield wiper system, intermittent ($34). Deluxe front appearance ($59). Beauville trim for cargo van ($516). Trailering special ($456). Gauge package ($29). Custom vinyl high-back bucket seats in Cargo van, w/auxiliary seat ($50); w/o auxiliary seat ($25). 5.0-liter two-barrel V-8 in cargo van ($295). Automatic transmission in G30 one-ton vans ($399). Heavy-duty transmission oil cooler ($47). Carpeting, floor and wheelhouse, in Sportvans ($145). 42 amp generator ($33). 55 amp generator, w/rear heater ($14); w/o ($47). Sliding cargo door ($88). **El Camino Options:** Cloth bucket seats ($91). Cloth 55/45 seat ($181). Vinyl bench seat ($91). Vinyl bucket seats ($91). Vinyl 55/45 seat ($209). 4.4-litre two-barrel V-8 ($50). 5.0-litre four-barrel V-8 ($50). Performance ratio rear axle ($19). Limited-slip axle ($67). Air conditioning ($585). Heavy-duty battery ($20). Bumper rub strips ($43). Bumper guards ($48). Electric clock, w/gauge package or instrumentation (no charge); w/o ($23). Conquista package ($161). Heavy-duty cooling, w/air conditioning ($34); w/o air conditioning ($61). Cargo box tonneau cover ($113). Power door locks ($93). California emissions system ($46). Color-keyed mats ($13). Gauge package w/trip odometer ($92). 63-amp generator, w/air conditioning ($6); w/o air conditioning ($34). All glass tinted ($75). Halogen headlamps ($36). Special instrumentation ($159). Auxiliary lighting ($26). OSRV mirrors, Left-hand remote ($19); Left-and right-hand Sport type, remote on left ($47); twin Sport, remote ($73). Moldings, deluxe body side ($53); door edge guard ($13); front fender, bodyside and tailgate ($28). Cargo box side rails ($77). Royal Knight trim package ($71). Electric six-way power driver's seat ($173). Automatic speed control ($132). Comfortilt steering wheel ($81). Sport suspension ($13). 22-gallon fuel tank ($22). Cargo box tie-downs ($20). Four-speed manual transmission ($141). Automatic transmission ($349). Sport silver wheel covers ($55). Sport gold wheel covers ($55). Wire wheel covers ($135). Rally wheels ($49). Wheel cover locking package ($34). Power windows ($140). Intermittent windshield wipers ($41). Note: See pickups for sound equipment options and prices.

NOTE: The following option prices apply to C10 Fleetside Pickup equipment. Some equipment was slightly less expensive on Stepsides and slightly more expensive on Suburbans and larger pickups.

Pickup/Suburban Options: (Fleetside) Scottsdale, w/bucket seats ($290); w/o ($310). Cheyenne, w/o decor and buckets ($452); w/o decor w/buckets ($394); w/decor w/o buckets ($395); w/decor and buckets ($338). Silverado, w/o decor and buckets ($718); w/o decor w/buckets ($668); w/decor w/o buckets ($693) and w/buckets and decor ($642). Regular two-tone paint, w/Cheyenne or Silverado ($37); w/o Cheyenne or Silverado ($61). Special two-tone paint, w/o Scottsdale-Silverado-Cheyenne ($256); w/Scottsdale ($153); w/Silverado ($130); w/Cheyenne ($222). 4.1-liter two-barrel six (no charge). 5.0-liter two-barrel V-8 ($295). 5.0-liter four-barrel V-8 w/ESC ($345). 5.0-liter four-barrel V-8 ($345). 5.7-liter four-barrel V-8 ($315). 7.4-liter four-barrel V-8 ($425). Automatic transmission ($384). Four-speed manual transmission ($170). Deluxe two-tone paint ($288); with Scottsdale ($185); w/Silverado ($138); w/Cheyenne ($230). Air conditioning ($591). Chrome bumpers ($111); w/Scottsdale/Cheyenne/Silverado ($82). Chrome rear step bumper ($151); w/Chevy Sport ($98). Chrome bumper w/rub strip ($149); w/Scottsdale/Cheyenne/Silverado ($120). Chevy Sport, w/buckets ($722); w/o buckets ($767). AM radio ($90). AM/FM rado ($141). AM/FM stereo ($224); w/8-track ($320); w/cassette tape ($325). AM/FM/CB radio w/triband mast antenna ($420). Auxiliary rear speaker ($19). Tachometer, w/Silverado ($90); w/o ($61). Cargo lamps, w/Scottsdale/Silverado/Cheyenne/Chevy Sport ($28); w/o ($49). Pickup box siderails ($77). Heavy-duty springs, front ($112); rear ($44). One-inch front stabilizer bar ($27). Trim rings ($45). Wheel covers ($69). Sliding gear window ($88). Basic camper group C20/C30 ($48). Deluxe camper group for C20/C30 w/cabover camper bodies ($292). **Scottsdale Package:** includes front and rear bumpers; black bodyside moldings; cigarette lighter; headliner and dome lamp. **Silverado Package:** include front and rear bumpers, wheel opening trim; deluxe molding package; visor mirror; bright bodyside moldings; deluxe front appearance headliner; carpeting; Custom steering wheel; cigarette lighter; domelamp; voltmeter; temperature and oil pressure gauges.

HISTORICAL: Introduced: Fall 1980. Calendar year registrations: 650,460. Calendar year sales: (Pickups) - 403,487; (S-10) - 15,473; (Van) - 86,727; (Suburban) - 19,518; (Blazer) - 21,399; (LUV) - 61,724; (El Camino) - 33,086; (Sportvan) - 13,576; (Total) — 654.990. Innovations: Low-alloy steel body panels. New light-weight window glass. Aerodynamic body styling. Electronic spark control. Historical notes: The fuel crisis and high-interest rates continued to have a negative effect on Chevrolet's light-duty truck sales.
* S-10 introduced in mid-1981 as a 1982 model.

1982 CHEVROLET

1982 Chevrolet S-10 Indy 500 Pickup (IMSC/JLM)

LIGHT TRUCK — 1982 SERIES — (ALL ENGINES): — An important extension of the Chevy truck line was accomplished by introduction of the S10 Series. It was a new-sized compact pickup, larger than a LUV, but smaller than a C10. Styling was in the big truck mold, but with flatter bodysides. Single, rectangular headlamps were featured. They had parking lamps on the outer ends that went around the body corners while the inner edge was slanted to complement the grille design. The grille was formed with three rows of six rectangular segments, each row a little narrower than the one above. This gave an inverted traphazoid shape to overall arrangement. A Chevy bow-tie was in the center. Bumper mounted turn signals and vertical taillights were other touches. Standard equipment included a 1.9-liter four-cylinder engine, four-speed manual transmission, bench seat and dual OSRV mirrors. Trim levels included standard, Sport and top-of-the-line Durango.

The Series 12 LUV pickups were similar to 1981 models. A new four-cylinder diesel engine was listed as the only powertrain for the 4x2 models in Chevrolet catalogs; which all offered gasoline and diesel 4x4s. However, at least one magazine received a gas-engined 4x2 model as a road test truck. This particular unit had the Mikado trim option with cloth/vinyl seat upholstery, full carpeting, deluxe steering wheel and other goodies.

El Caminos adopted a new cross-hatched grille and guadruple rectangular headlights. Standard equipment included a 3.8-litre V-6 engine, three-speed automatic transmission, powerbrakes, cloth bench seat and carpeting. The Super Sport model-option added dual Sport mirrors, front air dam, accent color on lower body and rally wheels.

New for '82 Blazers was a 6.2-liter (379 cu. in.) Chevy-built diesel V-8 and four-speed overdrive transmission, both costing extra. Appearance features were virtually identical to last season. Standard equipment included the 4.1-liter six, three-speed manual transmission (four-speed on 4x4 models), power brakes, vinyl bucket-seats, chrome bumpers, automatic locking hubs and on, 4x4s, power steering.

Since they were, more or less, longer wheelbase versions of the Blazer, Chevy standard size pickups had the same type of appearance and same new options. Standard equipment included the same 250 cu. in. six (292 cu. in. on C30/K20/K30); column-mounted three-speed gear box (four-speed on "30s"); power brakes (except C10/C20); chrome bumpers and a bench seat. Four-wheel-drive models came with standard power steering and the K30s featured a two-speed transfer case.

Hi-Cube vans, Chevy Vans and Step Vans were also pretty much devoid of any earth shaking differences from 1981.

I.D. DATA: Location of Serial Number: The VIN is stamped on a plate attached to the left top of the instrument panel on C, K and G Series. On P Series the plate is attached to the front of the dash and the panel to the left of the steering column. See 1981 for code explanation. Starting No. 10001 and up. Engine Number Location: (6-cyl.) — located on pad at right-hand side of cylinder block at rear of distributor. (V-8) — located on pad at right front side of cylinder block.

Model	Body Type	Price	Weight	Prod. Total
LUV — (½-Ton) — (104.3/117.9 in. w.b.) — (4-cyl.)				
CL10503	Pickup (SWB)	6256	2375	—
CL10803	Pickup (LWB)	6465	2470	—
El Camino — (½-Ton) — (117.1 in. w.b.) — (V-6)				
1GW80	Sedan Pickup	7995	3294	—
1GW80	Super Sport Pickup	8244	3300	—
Blazer — (½-Ton) — (106.5 in. w.b.) — (6-cyl.)				
CK10516	Hardtop (4x4)	9874	4294	—
CK10516	Hardtop (4x2)	8533	—	—

Model	Body Type	Price	Weight	Prod. Total
S10 — (½-Ton) — (108.3/118 in. w.b.) — (V-6)				
CS10803	Chassis & Cab (LWB)	—	2878	—
CS10603	Pickup (SWB)	6600	2476	—
CS10803	Pickup (LWB)	6750	2552	—
CS10803	Utility (LWB)	—	3276	—
C10 — (½-Ton) — (117.5/131.5 in. w.b.) — (6-cyl.)				
CC10703	Stepside (SWB)	6689	3418	—
CC10703	Fleetside (SWB)	6564	3461	—
CC10903	Fleetside (LWB)	6714	3613	—
CC10906	Suburban ("305" V-8)	9744	4295	—

NOTE: Add $2185 for 4x4 ("CK" prefix with 4x4s).

C20 — (¾-Ton) — (131.5/164.5 in. w.b.) — (6-cyl.)				
CC20903	Chassis & Cab (SWB)	7865	3661	—
CC20903	Stepside (SWB)	7857	3956	—
CC20903	Fleetside (SWB)	7732	3999	—
CC20943	Bonus Cab (LWB)	9123	4748	—
CC20943	Crew Cab (LWB)	9439	4809	—
CC20906	Suburban ("350" V-8)	9978	4677	—

NOTE: Add $1974 for 4x4 ("CK" prefix with /4x4s); Stepside 4x4 is $1849.

C30 — (1-Ton) — (131.5/164.5 in. w.b.) (6-cyl.)				
CC30903	Chassis & Cab (SWB)	7990	3973	—
CC30903	Stepside (SWB)	8474	4323	—
CC30903	Fleetside (SWB)	8349	4394	—
CC30943	Chassis-Bonus Cab (LWB)	8943	4400	—
CC30943	Bonus Cab Pickup (LWB)	9286	4817	—
CC30943	Chassis-Crew Cab (LWB)	9259	4461	—
CC30943	Crew Cab Pickup (LWB)	9602	4878	—
Chevy Van 10 — (110/125 in. w.b.) — (6-cyl.)				
CG11005	Panel (SWB)	6908	3708	—
CG11006	Sportvan (SWB)	8122	4039	—
CG11306	Bonaventure (LWB)	9040	—	—
CG11306	Beauville (LWB)	9268	—	—
Chevy Van 20 — (110/125 in. w.b.) — (6-cyl.)				
CG21005	Panel (SWB)	7256	3782	—
CG21306	Sportvan (LWB)	8486	4251	—
CG21306	Bonaventure (LWB)	9204	—	—
CG21306	Beauville (LWB)	9432	—	—
Chevy Van 30 — (125/146 in. w.b.) — (6-cyl.)				
CG31305	Panel (SWB)	8494	4251	—
CG31306	Sportvan (LWB)	10,228	4608	—
CG31306	Bonaventure (LWB)	10,946	—	—
CG31306	Beauville (LWB)	11,174	—	—
G30 Hi-Cube Van — (125/146 in. w.b.) — (V-8)				
CG31303	Hi-Cube Panel 10.-ft.	10,141	5515	—
CG31603	Hi-Cube Panel 12-ft.	11,607	5848	—
P20 Step-Van — (¾-Ton) — (6-cyl.)				
CP20842	Steel Panel 10.5-ft.	11,744	5777	—
P30 Step-Van — (1-Ton) — (6-cyl.)				
CP30842	Steel Panel 10.5-ft.	11,820	5939	—

1982 Chevrolet El Camino Conquista (CP)

ENGINE: (Standard: C10/C20/K10/G10/G20/G30): Inline. OHV. Six-cylinder. Cast iron block. Bore & stroke: 3.9 x 4.5 in. Displacement: 250 cu. in. Compression ratio: 8.3:1. Net horsepower: 110 at 3600 R.P.M. Torque: 195 lb.-ft. at 2000 R.P.M. Seven main bearings. Hydraulic valve lifters. Carburetor: Rochester Staged two-barrel.

NOTE: Order Code LE3(A).

NOTE: Horsepower and torque ratings may vary with specific applications or in certain marketing areas.

ENGINE: (Standard: C20 HD (C6P), C20, C30, K20 HD (C6P), K30, P20, P30) Inline. OHV. Six-cylinder. Cast iron block. Bore & stroke: 3.876 x 4.12 in. Displacement: 292 cu. in. Compression ratio: 7.8:1. Net horsepower: 115 at 3400 R.P.M. Max. torque: 215 lb.-ft. at 1600 R.P.M. Seven main bearings. Hydraulic valve lifters. Carburetor: Rochester one-bbl.

NOTE: Order Code L25(B).

ENGINE: (Optional C10, C20, K10) Vee-block. OHV. Eight-cylinder. Cast iron block. Bore & stroke: 3.736 x 3.480 in. Displacement: 305 cu. in. Compression ratio: 9.2:1. Net horsepower: 160 at 4400 R.P.M. Max torque: 235 lb.-ft. at 2000 R.P.M. Five main bearings. Hydraulic valve lifters. Carburetor: Rochester Staged four-barrel Electronic Spark Control.

NOTE: Order Code LE9(C). Not available in California.

ENGINE: (Optional C20, C20 HD (C6P), C30, K20 HD (C6P), K30, P20, P30, G10, G20) Vee-block. OHV. Eight-cylinder. Cast iron block. Bore & stroke: 4.0 x 3.5 in. Displacement: 350 cu. in. Compression ratio: 8.2:1. Net horsepower: 165 at 3800 R.P.M. Max torque: 275 lb.-ft. at 1600 R.P.M. Five main bearings. Hydraulic valve lifters. Carburetor: Rochester four-bbl.

NOTE: Order Code LS9(A). Not available in California.

ENGINE: (Optional C20 HD (C6P), C20, C30, K30, C20 Suburban) Vee-block. OHV. Eight-cylinder. Cast iron block. Bore & stroke: 4.25 x 4 in. Displacement: 454 cu. in. Compression ratio: 7.9:1. Net horsepower: 210 at 3800 R.P.M. Max torque: 340 lb.-ft. at 2800 R.P.M. Five main bearings. Hydraulic valve lifters. Carburetor: Rochester four-barrel.

NOTE: Order Code LE8(A).

ENGINE: (Optional C10, C20, C30, K10, K20, K30, C20 HD (C6P), K20 HD (C6P), all Suburbans) Vee-block. OHV. Diesel. Eight-cylinder. Cast iron block. Bore & stroke: 3.98 x 3.80 in. Displacement: 379 cu. in. Compression ratio: 21.5:1. Net horsepower: 130 at 3600 R.P.M. Max torque: 240 lb.-ft. at 2000 R.P.M. Hydraulic valve lifters. Carburetor: fuel injection.

NOTE: Order Code LH6(A).

ENGINE: (Standard: 4x2 LUV models; Optional: 4x4) Inline. OHV Diesel. Four-cylinder. Cast iron block. Displacement: 136.6 cu. in. Compression ratio: 21:1. Net horsepower: 58 at 4300 R.P.M. Max torque: 93 lb.-ft. at 2200 R.P.M. Hydraulic valve lifters.

NOTE: Order Code LQ7.

ENGINE: (Standard: 4x4 LUV) Inline. OHV. OHC. Four-cylinder. Cast iron block. Bore & stroke: 3.31 x 3.23 in. Displacement: 110.8 cu. in. Compression ratio: 8.5:1. Net horsepower: 80 at 4800 R.P.M. Max. lb.-ft at 3000 R.P.M. Five main bearings. Hydraulic valve lifters. Carburetor: one-barrel.

NOTE: Order Code L10.

ENGINE: (Standard: El Camino (except California) Vee-block. OHV. Six-cylinder. Cast iron block. Bore & stroke: 3.7 x 3.48 in. Displacement: 229 cu. in. Compression ratio: 8.6:1. Net horsepower: 110 at 4200 R.P.M. Max torque: 170 lb.-ft. at 2000 R.P.M. Four main bearings. Hydraulic valve lifters.

NOTE: Order Code LC3(A).

ENGINE: (Optional: El Camino (except California) Vee-block. OHV. Eight-cylinder. Cast iron block. Bore & stroke: 3.5 x 3.48 in. Displacement: 267 cu. in. Compression ratio: 8.3:1. Net horsepower: 115 at 4000 R.P.M. Max torque: 200 lb.-ft. at 2400 R.P.M. Five main bearings. Hydraulic valve lifters. Carburetor: Rochester staged two-bbl.

NOTE: Order Code L39(B).

ENGINE: (Optional El Camino) Vee-block. OHV. Eight-cylinder. Cast iron block. Bore & stroke: 3.7 x 3.48 in. Displacement: 305 cu. in. Compression ratio: 8.6:1. Net horsepower: 150 at 3800 R.P.M. Max torque: 240 lb.-ft. at 2400 R.P.M. Five main bearings. Hydraulic valve lifters. Carburetor: Rochester Staged four-barrel.

NOTE: Order Code LG4(B).

ENGINE: (Optional El Camino (California only) Vee-block. OHV. Six-cylinder. Cast iron block. Bore & stroke: 3.8 x 3.4 in. Displacement: 231 cu. in. Compression ratio: 8.0:1. Net horsepower: 110 at 3800 R.P.M. Max torque: 190 lb.-ft. at 1600 R.P.M. Five main bearings. Hydraulic valve lifters. Carburetor: Rochester two-barrel.

NOTE: Order Code LO5(C).

ENGINE: (Standard: S10) Inline. OHV. OHC. Four-cylinder. Cast iron block. Bore & stroke: 3.42 x 3.23 in. Displacement: 119 cu. in. Compression ratio: 8.4:1. Net horsepower: 82 at 4600 R.P.M. Max. torque: 101 lb.-ft. at 3000 R.P.M. Hydraulic valve lifters.

NOTE: Order Code LR1.

ENGINE: (Optional S10) Vee-block. OHV. Six-cylinder. Cast iron block. Bore & stroke: 3.50 x 2.99 in. Displacement: 173 cu. in. Compression ratio: 8.5:1. Net horsepower: 110 at 4800 R.P.M. Max torque: 148 lb.-ft. at 2000 R.P.M. Hydraulic valve lifters.

NOTE: Order Code LR2.

CHASSIS: (Suburban) Wheelbase: 129.5 in. Overall length: 218.7 in. Height: 75.4 in. Front tread: 66.7 in. Rear tread: 63.0 in. Tires: (C10) P235/75R15; (C20) 9.50 x 16.5 in.; (K10) P215/75R15; (K20) 9.50 x 16.5 in.

CHASSIS: (LUV) Wheelbase: (4x2) 104.3/117.9 in.; (4x4) 104.3 in. Overall length: 174.5/191.6 in. Height: (4x2) 59.3 in.; (4x4) 61.0 in. Front tread: (4x2) 53.8 in.; (4x4) 54.2 in. Rear tread: (4x2) 51.2 in.; (4x4) 52.7 in. Tires: (4x2) E78 x 14B in.; (4x4) F70 x 14B in. white-lettered.

CHASSIS: (El Camino) Wheelbase: 117.1 in. Overall length: 201.6 in. Height: 53.8 in. Front tread: 58.5 in. Rear tread: 57.8 in. Tires: P205/75R x 14 in.

CHASSIS: (C10) Wheelbase: 117.5/131.5 in. Overall length: 191.3/212 in. Height: 69.8 in. Front tread: 65.8 in. Rear tread: 62.7 in. Tires: FR78 x 15B in.

CHASSIS: (C20) Wheelbase: 117.5/131.5/164.5 in. Overall length: 191.3/212/244.43 in. Height: 69.8 in. Front tread: 65.8 in. Rear tread: 62.7 in. Tires: 8.75R x 16.5C in.; (front) 9.50 x 16.5D in.; (rear) 9.50 x 16.5E in.; C20 HD (C6P)

CHASSIS: (C30) Wheelbase: 131.5/164.5 in. Overall length: 212/244.43 in. Height: 77.8 in. Front tread: 65.8 in. Rear tread: 62.7 in. Tires: 9.50 x 16.5D in.; (Bonus/Crew) 9.50 x 16.5E in.

CHASSIS: (K10) Wheelbase: 117.5/131.5 in. Overall length: 191.3/212 in. Height: 72 in. Front tread: 65.8 in. Rear tread: 62.7 in. Tires: P235/75R x 15 in.

CHASSIS: (K20) Wheelbase: 131.5 in. Overall length: 212 in. Height: 73.9 in. Front tread: 65.8 in. Rear tread: 62.7 in. Tires: 8.75R x 16.5C in.; 9.50 x 16.5D in. (front) E (rear) K20HD (CP6)

CHASSIS: (K30) Wheelbase: 131.5/164.5 in. Overall length: 212/244.43 in. Height: 74.7/75 in. Front tread: 65.8 in. Rear tread: 62.7 in. Tires: 9.50 x 16.5D in.

CHASSIS: (K10, Blazer) Wheelbase: 106.5 in. Overall length: 184.8 in. Height: 73.4 in. Front tread: 66.1 in. Rear tread: 63 in. Tires: (2wd) P215/75R x 15 in.; (4wd) P215/75R x 15 in. Larger sizes available.

CHASSIS: (G10) Wheelbase: 110/125 in. Overall length: 178.2/202.2 in. Height: 78.8/81.2 in. Front tread: 69.5 in. Rear tread: 69.7 in. Tires: FR78 x 15B in.

CHASSIS: (G20) Wheelbase: 110/125 in. Overall length: 178.2/202.2 in. Height: 78.8/81.2 in. Front tread: 69.5 in. Rear tread: 69.7 in. Tires: P225/75R x 15 in.

CHASSIS: (G30) Wheelbase: 110/125 in. Overall length: 178.2/202.2 in. Height: 78.8/81.2 in. Front tread: 69.5 in. Rear tread: 69.7 in. Tires: 8.75 x 16.5E in.

CHASSIS: (G30 Hi-Cube) Wheelbase: 125/146 in. Overall length: 207.3/231.3 in. Tires: (front) 8.75 x 16 in.; (rear) 8.00 x 16.5C in.

CHASSIS: (P20) Wheelbase: 125/133 in. Tires: 8.75 x 16.5C in.

CHASSIS: (P30) Wheelbase: 125/157 in. Tires: 8.75 x 16.5 in.

CHASSIS: (S10) Wheelbase: 108.3/117.9 in. Overall length: 178.2/194.1 in. Height: 59 in. Front tread: 64.7 in. Rear tread: 64.7 in. Tires: P195/75R x 14 in. Fiberglass-belted.

TECHNICAL: Same as 1981 except for S-10. This model has a selective synchromesh transmission with four-speeds forward/one reverse; floorshift; single dry disc clutch; 2.73:1 final drive ratio; front disc/rear drum brakes and pressed steel wheels.

OPTIONAL EQUIPMENT:
Engines:
2.8-liter (173 cu. in.) V-6, S-10 ($215). 4.4-liter (267 cu. in.) V-8, El Camino ($70). 5.0-liter (305 cu. in.) V-8, El Camino ($70). 5.0-liter (305 cu. in.) V-8, electronic spark control, Blazer/Pickups w/o Special Economy Package ($170); Pickups w/Special Economy Package ($170). 5.0-liter (305 cu. in.) V-8 four-barrel, Blazer/Pickups ($170). 5.7-liter (350 cu. in.) V-8, LS9/Blazer/Pickups ($345). 5.7-liter (350 cu. in.) V-8, LT9/Pickups ($315). 6.2-liter (379 cu. in.) diesel V-8, K-20 pickup ($1164)/Blazer/C-10/K-10/C-20 Pickups ($1334) and 7.4-liter (454 cu. in.) V-8, Pickups ($425)
Transmissions:
Four-speed manual, C-10 pickup ($198); four-speed overdrive manual C-10 pickup w/Special Economy Package ($273); C-20, K-10/K-20 pickups ($75); three-speed automatic S-10, C-10 pickup ($438); C/K-20, 30 pickup ($455); four-speed automatic C-10 Blazer ($199); K-10 Blazer, C & K-10, 20 pickups ($637)
Air Conditioning:
Pickups w/o diesel equipment package, exc. K-30 ($677); Pickups w/diesel equipment package, K-30 ($619); S-10, Blazer w/o diesel equipment package ($677); Blazer w/diesel equipment package ($619); Deluxe front appearance package, Blazer, pickups ($100); Limited-slip rear axle, El Camino ($76); Locking axle/differential (N/A El Camino) ($217)
Optional Axle Ratio:
El Camino ($21); Others ($35); Auxiliary battery, Blazer, pickups ($118)
Heavy-Duty Battery:
El Camino ($25), Others ($45); Power brakes, pickup, S-10 ($87)
Heavy-Duty Power Brakes:
C-10 pickup w/o diesel equipment package ($159); C-10 pickup w/diesel equipment package ($72); C & K-20 pickups ($82); Chrome rear bumper, pickups ($97); Painted rear step bumper, pickups ($106); Chromed rear step bumper, pickups ($177); Color-keyed front bumper, S-10 ($56); Color-keyed rear step bumper, S-10 ($127); Deluxe chromed front and rear bumpers, Blazer ($44); Glide-out spare carrier, pickups ($27); Slide-mount spare carrier, pickups ($39)
Electric Quartz Clock:
El Camino ($32); Blazer/Pickups w/o Silverado ($70); Blazer/Pickups w/Silverado ($36); Electric digital clock, S-10 ($60)
Cold Climate:
Conquisa package, El Camino ($183); Console, S-10 ($96); Engine oil cooler, not on El Camino ($112)
Transmission Oil Cooler:
S-10 w/o air conditioning ($103); S-10 w/air conditioning, others exc. El Camino ($55)
Heavy-Duty Cooling System
El Camino w/o air conditioning ($70); El Camino w/air conditioning ($40); Others ($48); Cargo box cover (Tonneau), El Camino ($129)
Diesel Equipment Package:
Blazer ($1125); C-10 pickup ($1287); C-20 pickup ($1723); C-30 pickup ($1073); K-10 and 20 pickups ($1041); K-20 pickup ($783)

1982 Chevrolet Silverado Blazer (CP)

Power Door Locks:
El Camino ($106); Others ($115); Dual exhaust system, pickups ($48)
Exterior Decor Package:
Blazer w/o Silverado package ($423); Blazer w/Silverado package ($279); Pickup w/o Scottsdale or Silverado ($503); Pickup w/Scottsdale package ($385); Pickup w/Silverado package ($359)
Fuel Tanks:
20 gal., S-10 ($39); 22 gal., El Camino ($25); 31 gal., Blazer ($39); Auxiliary 16 gal., C/K-10 & 20 pickups ($208)
Gauges:
S-10 ($51); El Camino ($111); Others ($34)
Tinted Glass:
El Camino ($88); Pickups, S-10 ($40); Deep tinted glass w/tinted rear, Blazer ($119); Deep tinted glass, Blazer ($168); Chromed grille, S-10 ($53); Durango equipment group, S-10 ($325); Sport equipment group, S-10 ($775); Camper body wiring harness, pickups ($37); Trailer wiring harness, Blazer ($42); 5-lead trailer wiring harness, S-10 ($37)
Halogen Headlamps:
High/low beam (NA El Camino) ($20); High beam El Camino ($10); Others ($15); Headlamp warning buzzer, Blazer ($11); Headliner, Blazer ($74); Instrumentation package, El Camino ($187); Cargo area light, pickups ($56); Dome light, pickups ($24); Roof marker lights, pickups ($46)
Auxiliary Lighting:
El Camino ($30); S-10 w/o Durango or Sport package ($87); S-10 w/Durango or Sport package ($45)
Mirrors:
Left remote, El Camino ($22); Sport, left remote, right manual, El Camino ($55); Camper-type L & R, pickups ($86); 6½ in. x 9 in. dual, painted (NA El Camino) ($44); Stainless (NA El Camino) ($72); Sr. West Coast, pickups ($59)
Custom Molding Package:
Pickups w/o Scottsdale, Blazer ($144); Pickups w/Scottsdale ($26); Deluxe molding package ($157); Operating convenience group, Blazer, pickups ($281)
Two-Tone Paint
Pickups w/o Silverado ($69); Pickups w/Silverado ($42)
Special Two-Tone Paint
Pickups w/o Scottsdale or Silverado ($291); Pickups w/Scottsdale ($173); Pickups and Blazer w/Silverado ($147); Blazer w/o Silverado ($291); S-10 ($275)
Deluxe Two-Tone Paint
Pickups w/o Scottsdale or Silverado ($328); Pickups w/Scottsdale ($210); Pickups w/Silverado ($157); Sport two-tone paint, S-10 ($135); Payload capacity package, 1500 lb., S-10 ($173)
Radio Equipment:
AM El Camino ($111); S-10 ($104); Others ($92)
AM/FM
El Camino ($165); S-10 ($173); Others ($143)
AM/FM Stereo
El Camino ($196); S-10 ($256); Others ($226)
AM/FM Stereo w/8-Track Tape
El Camino ($282); Others ex. S-10 ($322)
AM/FM Stereo w/Cassette Tape
El Camino ($283); Others ex. S-10 ($327); AM/FM stereo w/cassette and clock, S-10 ($425); AM/FM/CB w/power antenna, pickups, Blazer ($559); AM/FM stereo/CB, Blazer, pickups ($559); Windshield antenna (NA S-10, El Camino) ($31); Power antenna, El Camino ($55); Cargo box rails, El Camino ($81); Roll bar, Blazer ($123)
Scottsdale Package:
Stepside pickup ($208); Fleetside pickup w/o dual rear wheels ($318); Fleetside pickup w/dual rear wheels ($217)
Folding Rear Seats:
Blazer w/o custom trim ($308); Blazer w/custom trim ($334)
Seats/Trim:
Custom Vinyl High-Back Buckets:
Blazer w/o Silverado or rear seat ($193); Blazer w/o Silverado, w/rear seat ($241); Blazer w/Silverado w/o rear seat (NC); Blazer w/Silverado and rear seat ($48); S-10 w/o Durango or Sport package ($166); S-10 w/Durango or Sport package ($118);
Custom Cloth High-Back Buckets:
Blazer w/rear seat (NC); Blazer w/o rear seat ($48); Special custom cloth bench, pickups (NC)
Custom Vinyl Bench:
Pickup w/o Scottsdale or Silverado ($48); S-10 w/o High Sierra or Gypsy package ($48)
Fuel Tank Shield:
C-10 Blazer; C-Series pickups w/auxiliary fuel tank ($115); K-10 Blazer, K-Series pickups w/auxiliary fuel tank ($154); C-Series pickups w/o auxiliary fuel tank ($45); K-Series pickups w/o auxiliary fuel tank ($84); Heavy-duty shock absorbers, F & R (NA El Camino) ($31); Quad. front shock absorbers, Blazer, K-10 & 20 pickups ($117); Pickup box side rails, pickups ($88)

Silverado Package:

Blazer ($931); Stepside Pickups ($614); Fleetside pickups w/o exterior decor package or dual rear wheels ($780); Fleetside pickups w/exterior decor package w/o dual rear wheels ($753); Fleetside w/o Special Big Dooley package ($640); Fleetside w/o special Big Dooley package and dual rear wheels ($596).

Special Big Dooley Two-Tone Paint Package

Pickups w/o Scottsdale package ($429); Pickups w/Scottsdale package ($412); Fleetside pickup add to above ($27).

Automatic Speed Control:

El Camino ($155); Others w/manual transmission ($169); Others w/automatic transmission ($159).

Heavy-Duty Front Springs:

Blazer, K-10 & 20 pickups w/o quad shocks ($84); Blazer, K-10 & 20 pickups w/quad shocks ($53); C-10 & 20 pickups ($14); Heavy-duty rear springs, C-10 & 20 pickups ($51); Extra capacity rear springs, C-10 pickup ($66); Main and auxiliary rear springs, pickups ($91); Front stabilizer bar (NA El Camino) ($31); Heavy-duty front stabilizer bar, C-Series pickups ($51); Power steering, Blazer, S-10, C-Series pickups ($234); Tahoe equipment, S-10 ($550); Tilt steering wheel ($95); Sport suspension, El Camino ($15).

Tachometer:

S-10 w/o Sport package ($105); S-10 w/Sport package ($54); Cargo box tie downs ($23); Towing device (NA S-10, El Camino) ($34); Trailer Hitch Deadweight, Blazer ($53); Weight distribution platform, Blazer ($145).

Heavy-Duty Trailering Special Package:

C-20, 30 pickup w/o air or diesel equipment ($646); C-20, 30 pickup w/air w/o diesel equipment ($588); K-20 pickup w/o air or diesel equipment ($412); K-20 pickup w/air w/o diesel equipment ($354); K-30 pickup w/o diesel equipment ($354); Blazer and pickups w/diesel equipment ($242); S-10 ($187); C-10 Blazer w/o air conditioning ($677); C-10 Blazer w/air conditioning ($619); K-10 Blazer w/o air or diesel equipment ($412); K-10 blazer w/air w/o diesel equipment ($354); Wheel cover lock package, El Camino ($39); Bright wheel covers, Blazer C/K-10 pickups, S-10 w/o Durango ($38).

Sport Wheel Covers:

El Camino base ($62); El Camino Super Sport ($6); Wire wheel covers, El Camino ($153); Wheel trim rings, pickups, Blazer ($52).

Rally Wheels:

Base El Camino ($56); S-10 w/o Durango or Sport ($83); S-10 w/Durango ($31); Others ($103); Styled wheels (NA S-10, El Camino) ($201); Forged aluminum wheels (NA El Camino) ($411).

Dual Rear Wheels:

C-30 Fleetside w/o air or diesel equipment ($677); C-30 Fleetside w/air or diesel equipment ($619); K-30 pickups w/o air or diesel equipment ($644); K-30 pickups w/air or diesel equipment ($606); Sliding rear window, pickups ($100); Power windows ($166); Power tailgate window, Blazer ($79).

Intermittent Wipers:

El Camino ($47); Others ($45).

LUV Optional Equipment:

Air conditioning ($677); Chrome rear step bumper ($131); Painted rear step bumper ($106); Front bumper guards ($38).

Sport Stripe Decals:

104.3 in. w.b. 4x2 ($45); 117.9 in. w.b. 4x2 ($50); 104.3 in. w.b. 4x4 ($119); Exterior decor package ($105).

Mikado Package:

W/bench seats ($244); w/bucket seats ($379); Dual mirrors ($61); Metallic paint ($80).

Radio Equipment:

AM ($104); AM/FM ($176); Power steering ($325); Sliding rear window ($100).

Tires:

E78-14B whitewall, 2 front or 2 rear ($20); E78-14B whitewall, spare ($10).

HISTORICAL: Introduced: Fall 1981. Calendar year registrations: 758,107. Calendar year sales: (Vans) 101,932; (Sportvan) 15,843; (S-10) 177,758; (S-10 Blazer) 8,161; (LUV) 22,304; (El Camino) 22,732; (Blazer) 24,103; (Suburban) 28,004; (Pickups) 393,277. Calendar year production at U.S. Factories: (Blazer) 24,238; (El Camino) 22,621; (Pickups) 268,080; (Chevy Van/Sportvan) 98,764; (Suburban) 34,846; (Compact Pickups) 209,517; (Total) 658,066. Innovations: New-sized compact S-10 line introduced. LUV comes with 4-cyl. diesel as standard powerplant. New 6.2-Liter Chevy-built diesel V-8 for larger trucks. Historical Notes: **Consumer Guide** gave the 1982 Blazer 68 out of a possible 100 points in its road test covering performance, interior, utility and finish characteristics. The new S-10 pickups scored 69 points on the same scale, while the standard C10 pickup racked up 70 points. The 1982 LUV pickup earned 65 points. Chevrolet truck sales started on an upswing this season, but Ford Motor Company was beginning to again threaten Chevrolet's ranking as the number one truck-maker. Chevrolet had held the number one position steadily from 1951 to 1968. From 1969 to 1974, Ford was on top. In 1975 and 1976, Chevrolet was back in first position again. The next five years were counted in Ford's favor. The final totals for calendar year registrations in 1982 were 758,107 for Chevy versus 733,120 for Ford.

1983 CHEVROLET

LIGHT TRUCK — 1983 SERIES — (ALL ENGINES): — Chevrolet entered what it called "Year II of a New Era for Chevy trucks" with new four-wheel-drive, extended-cab and Blazer models added to the S-10 line. All S-10

models, except chassis and utility cars, were available in four-wheel-drive. The S-10 Blazer, compared to the 13-year-old full-size Blazer, was 15.3 in. shorter and 14.8 in. narrower. Its total floor space was only 4.8 square feet less. The S-10 Extended-Cab, the first such configuration ever offered by Chevrolet, added 14.5 inches to regular cab length. Added to the S-10 engine lineup was a new 2.0 liter 83 h.p. L-4/ Four-wheel-drive models had a new independent front suspension utilizing computer-matched torsion bars.

The conventional C and K pickups, except for revised grille treatment and parking lamp placement were unchanged in appearance from 1982. Added corrosion protection was provided due to the use of galvinized steel in the pickup box front panel and a Zincrometal hood inner liner.

For the first times G-20 and G-30 vans and Sportvans were available with the 6.2 liter diesel engine, as well as a four-speed overdrive automatic transmission. Other changes in the 1983 vans included a steering column angle approximating that used on pickups, floor-mounted manual transmission shift lever, "Wet Arms" windshield washers (with nozzles located on the wiper arms). Tiltsteering was available with manual transmission. There was an anti-chip coating along lower body from front wheel wells, to rear doors, a new rear pivot hinge, rear latch and a floating roller mechanism for the sliding door and an inside hood release.

This was also the first year the El Camino could be ordered with a 5.7 liter diesel V-8.

1983 Chevrolet S-10 'Short Box' Pickup (CMD)

I.D. DATA: Location of Serial Number: The VIN is stamped on a plate which is attached to the left top of the instrument panel. (See 1981 for additional code explanations). Engine Number Location: (6-cyl.) — located on pad at right-hand side of cylinder block at rear of distributor. (V-8) — located on pad at front right side of cylinder block. Same sequence as Serial Numbers.

Model	Body Type	Price	Weight	Prod. Total
El Camino	**— (½-Ton) — (117.1 in. w.b.) — (V-6)**			
1GW80	Sedan Pickup	8191	3332	24,010
1GW80	Super Sport Pickup	8445	3337	24,010
K10 Blazer	**— (½-Ton) — (106.5 in. w.b.) — (V-8/4x4)**			
CK10516	Hardtop	10287	4426	31,282
S10 Blazer	**— (½-Ton) — (100.5 in. w.b.) — (6-cyl./4x4)**			
CT10516	Hardtop (gate)	9433	3106	106,214
Chevy Van 10	**— (½-Ton) — (110/125 in. w.b.) — (6-cyl.)**			
CG11005	Panel (SWB)	7101	3711	—
CG11006	Sportvan (SWB)	8596	4039	—
CG11306	Bonaventure (LWB)	9533	—	—
CG11306	Beauville (LWB)	9789	—	—
Chevy Van 20	**— (¾-Ton) — (110/125 in. w.b.) — (6-cyl.)**			
CG21005	Panel (SWB)	7714	3812	—
CG21306	Sportvan (LWB)	8968	4278	—
CG21306	Bonaventure (LWB)	9701	—	—
CG21306	Beauville (LWB)	9957	—	—
Chevy Van 30	**— (1-Ton) — (125 in. w.b.) — (6-cyl.)**			
CG31305	Panel	8718	4399	14,575
CG31306	Sportvan	11,371	4719	18,178
CG31306	Bonaventure	12,104	—	—
CG31306	Beauville	12,360	—	—
G30 Hi-Cube Van	**— (1-Ton) — (125/146 in. w.b.) — (V-8)**			
CG31303	Hi-Cube Panel 10-ft.	11,151	5052	—
CG31603	Hi-Cube Panel 12-ft.	12,388	5881	—
P20 Step-Van	**— (P20/P30) — (125-157 in. w.b.) — (6-cyl.)**			
CP20842	Steel Panel 10.5-ft.	12,031	5801	—
CP30842	Steel Panel 10.5-ft.	12,071	5946	—
S10 Series	**— (½-Ton) — (108.3/122.0 in. w.b.) — (6-cyl.)**			
CS10603	Pickup (SWB)	6343	2537	—
CS10803	Pickup (LWB)	6496	2618	—
CS10653	Extended Pickup (LWB)	6725	2647	—
C10 Series	**— (½-Ton) — (117.5/131.5 in. w.b.) — (6-cyl.)**			
CC10703	Stepside (SWB)	6835	3408	—
CC10703	Fleetside (SWB)	6707	3471	—
CC10903	Fleetside (LWB)	6860	3633	—
CC10906	Suburban (V-8)	9951	4293	—
C20 Series	**— (¾-Ton) — (131.5/164.5 in. w.b.) — (6 cyl.)**			
CC20903	Chassis and Cab (SWB)	8032	3614	—
CC20903	Stepside (SWB)	8525	3964	—
CC20903	Fleetside (SWB)	8397	4025	—
CC20943	Bonus Cab Pickup (LWB)	9315	4745	—
CC20943	Crew Cab Pickup (LWB)	9637	4806	—
CC20906	Suburban (V-8)	10,187	4697	—
C30 Series	**— (1-Ton) — (131.5/164.5 in. w.b.) — (6 cyl.)**			
CC30903	Chassis and Cab (SWB)	8160	3965	—
CC30903	Stepside (SWB)	8654	4319	—
CC30903	Fleetside (SWB)	8526	4380	—
CC30943	Chassis Bonus Cab (LWB)	9131	4406	—
CC30943	Bonus Cab Pickup (LWB)	9481	4817	—
CC30943	Chassis Crew Cab (LWB)	9453	4467	—
CC30943	Crew Cab Pickup (LWB)	9803	4878	—

NOTE: Add for 4x4 ("CK" prefix on 4x4s).

1983 Chevrolet Suburban w/Panel Doors (OCW)

GENERAL NOTE: "SWB" means shortest wheelbase above each series listing. "LWB" means longer wheelbase above each series listing. (Example: Chevy Van 10 Sportvan SWB has 110 in..w.b. and Chevy Van 20 Sportvan SWB has 125 in. w.b.).

ENGINE: (Standard: El Camino): Vee-block. OHV. Six-cylinder. Cast iron block. Bore & stroke: 3.7 x 3.48 in. Displacement: 229 cu. in. Compression ratio: 8.6:1. Net horsepower: 110 at 4200 R.P.M. Torque: 170 lb.-ft. at 2000 R.P.M. Four main bearings. Hydraulic valve lifters. Carburetor: Rochester two-barrel.

NOTE: Horsepower and torque ratings of specific engines will vary in accordance with factors such as GVW rating, transmission type and marketing area.

ENGINE: (Optional: El Camino). Vee-block. OHV. Diesel. Eight-cylinder. Cast iron block. Bore & stroke: 4.0 x 3.5 in. Displacement: 350 cu. in. Net horsepower: 105 R.P.M. Five main bearings. Fuel-injected.

ENGINE: (Standard C10, C20, K10). Inline. OHV. Six-cylinder. Cast iron block. Bore & stroke: 3.9 x 3.5 in. Displacement: 4.1 liter (250 cu. in.) Compression ratio: 8.3:1. Net horsepower: (C10) 120 at 4000 R.P.M. Torque 205 lb.-ft. at 2000 R.P.M. Seven main bearings. Hydraulic valve lifters. Carburetor: Rochester two-barrel.

NOTE: Order Code LE3(A).

ENGINE: (Optional C10, C20 K10, El Camino). Vee-block. OHV. Eight-cylinder. Cast iron block. Bore & stroke: 3.74 x 3.48 in. Displacement: 5 liters (305 cu. in.) Compression ratio: 9.2:1. Net horsepower: (C10) 165 at 4400 R.P.M. Torque: 240 lb.-ft. at 2000 R.P.M. Five main bearings. Hydraulic valve lifters. Carburetor: Rochester four-barrel.

NOTE: Order Code LE9(C).

ENGINE: (Optional: C20, C20 HD, C30, K10, K20, K20 HD, K30) Vee-block. OHV. Eight-cylinder. Cast iron block. Bore & stroke: 4.0 x 3.5 in. Displacement: 5.7 liters (350 cu. in.) Compression ratio: 8.2:1. Net horsepower: 165 at 3800 R.P.M. Torque: 275 lb.-ft. at 1600 R.P.M. Five main bearings. Hydraulic valve lifters. Carburetor: Rochester four-barrel.

NOTE: Order Code LS9(A).

1983 Chevrolet S-10 Blazer (CMD)

1983 Chevrolet S-10 Bonus Cab 'Long Box' Pickup (CMD)

ENGINE: (Optional: C10, C20, C20 HD, C30, K10, K20, K20 HD, K30) Vee-block. OHV. Diesel. Eight-cylinder. Cast iron block. Bore & stroke: 3.98 x 3.80 in. Displacement: 6.2 liters (379 cu. in.) Compression ratio: 21.3:1. Net horsepower: 130 at 3600 R.P.M. Torque: 240 lb.-ft. at 2000 R.P.M.

NOTE: Order Code LH6(D).

ENGINE: (Optional: C20 HD, C20, C30, K20 HD, K301) Inline. OHV. Six-cylinder. Cast iron block. Bore & stroke: 3.9 x 4.1 in. Displacement: 4.8 liters (292 cu. in.) Compression ratio: 7.8:1. Net horsepower: 115 at 3600 R.P.M. Net torque: 215 lb.-ft. at 1600 R.P.M. Five main bearings. Hydraulic valve lifters. Carburetor: Rochester one-barrel.

NOTE: Order Code L25(B).

ENGINE: (Optional: C20 HD, C20, C30, K30) V-block. OHV. Eight-cylinder. Cast iron block. Bore & stroke: 4.3 x 4.0 in. Displacement: 7.4 liters (454 cu. in. Compression ratio: 7.9:1. Net horsepower: 230 at 3800 R.P.M. Net. Torque: 360 lb.-ft. at 2800 R.P.M. Five main bearings. Hydraulic valve lifters. Carburetor: four-barrel.

NOTE: Order Code LE8(A).

ENGINE: (Standard: S10 Ordering) Inline. OHV. OHC. Four-cylinder. Cast iron block. Bore & stroke: 3.42 x 3.23 in. Displacement: 119 cu. in. Compression ratio: 8.4:1. Net horsepower: 82 at 4600 R.P.M. Max torque: 101 lb.-ft. at 3000 R.P.M. Hydraulic valve lifters.

NOTE: Order Code LR1.

ENGINE: (Standard: S10 Blazer, optional extended cab S10 models). Inline. OHV. Four-cylinder. Cast iron block. Bore & stroke: 3.50 x 3.15 in. Displacement: 121 cu. in. Compression ratio: 9.3:1. Net horsepower: 83 at 4000 R.P.M. Max torque: 108 lb.-ft. at 2400 R.P.M. Hydraulic valve lifters. Carburetor: Rochester two-barrel.

NOTE: Order Code LQ2.

1983 Chevrolet El Camino (CMD)

ENGINE: (Optional S10, S10 Blazer) Inline. OHV. Diesel. Four-cylinder. Cast iron block. Bore & stroke: 3.46 x 3.62 in. Displacement: 136.6 cu. in. Net horsepower: 62 at 4300 R.P.M. Max torque: 96 lb.-ft. at 2200 R.P.M. Hydraulic valve lifters.

NOTE: Order Code LQ7.

ENGINE: (Optional S10, S10 Blazer) Vee-block. OHV. Six-cylinder. Cast iron block. Bore & stroke: 3.50 x 2.99 in. Displacement: 173 cu. in. Compression ratio: 8.5:1. Net horsepower: 110 at 4800 R.P.M. Max torque: 145 lb.-ft. at 2100 R.P.M. Hydraulic valve lifters.

CHASSIS: Same as 1982, except for S10 models, as follows: (S10 Blazer) Wheelbase: 100.5 in. Overall length: 170.3 in. Height: 65 in. Front tread: 55.6 in. Rear tread: 55.1 in. Tires: D195/75R x 15 in.

1983 Chevrolet S-10 Blazer (CMD)

CHASSIS: (S10 Extended Cab Pickup) Wheelbase: 122.9 in.; Height: 59.4 in. Front tread: 64.7 in. Rear tread: 64.7 in.; Tires: D195/75R x 14 in.

TECHNICAL: Manual, synchromesh. 3F/1R (most models). Controls located: Column (most). Single dry disc type clutch. Shaft drive. Salisbury rear axle. Front disc/rear drum (power on most). Pressed steel disc wheels.

OPTIONS: Engine oil cooler. Heavy-duty automatic transmission. Heavy-duty battery. Heavy-duty radiator. Camper chassis equipment. Fuel tank shield. 66 amp generator (std. on K30). Heavy-duty automatic transmission cooler. Four-speed manual transmission. Four-speed overdrive transmission. Four-speed automatic with overdrive. Three-speed automatic. Locking differential. Cruise control. Chromed front bumper. Rear bumper (chromed or painted). Radio, AM; AM/FM; AM/FM with cassette. Cigar lighter. Chromed rear step bumper. Sidemounted spare tire carrier. Spare tire carrier — Glide-out (Fleetside only). Cargo area lamp. Color keyed floor mats. Comfortilt steering wheel. Deluxe front appearance package. Dome lamp. Quartz electric clock. Air conditioning. Gauge package (voltmeter, temperature, oil pressure). Halogen headlamps. Intermittent windshield wipers. Tinted glass. OSRV mirrors (painted or stainless steel; below eyeline; stainless steel camper mirror; West Coast, painted). Sliding rear window. Durango equipment (S10). Tahoe equipment (S10). Sport equipment (S10). Body moldings; black; bright; custom package, black or bright (Fleetside only). Paint options: Conventional two-tone. (Fleetside only). Deluxe two-tone. Exterior decor. Special two-tone paint. Pickup body side rails. Power door locks. Power windows. Roof marker lamps. Rally wheels. Styled wheels. Bright metal wheel covers. Special bright metal wheel covers. Conquista package, El Camino ($189).

HISTORICAL: Introduced: Sept. 14, 1982. Calendar year registrations: (all Chevy trucks) 904,672. Calendar year sales. (Vans) 141,575; (Sportvan) 18,178; (S10) 198,222; (S10 Blazer) 106,214; (El Camino) 24,010; (Blazer) 31,282; (Suburban) 37,222; (Pickups) 412,533. (low ser.) Calendar year production: (Blazer) 35,179; (El Camino) 28,322; (2 series) (Pickups) 280,209; (Chevy Van/Sportvan) 142,555; (Suburban) 41,261; (3 series) and (S10) 321,054; (Total) 848,580. Innovations: New S10 Blazer introduced. Extend cab pickups added to S10 pickup series. Full-size 4x4s now use 15 inch wheels and tires. Historical notes: Chevrolet dealers recorded 176 registrations per outlet in 1983, compared to 156 the previous season. Chevrolet slipped behind Ford Motor Company in calendar year registrations for all types of trucks. In van and light truck production (calendar year) in U.S. factories, Chevy was also behind Ford's output of 848,580 units. The big news, however, was the auto and truck industry's general recovery from the bleak period of the early 1980s. Chevrolet's overall market penetration in the light truck and van field was up 1.58% to a 39.72% shore of industry.

1984 CHEVROLET

1984 Chevrolet Fleetside Pickup (CP)

LIGHT TRUCK — 1984 SERIES — (ALL ENGINES): — The El Camino, for 1984, was a very luxurious vehicle. Standard equipment included an automatic transmission, power steering, air adjustable rear shocks, notch back seat with armrest, and color-keyed cut-pile carpeting. Both the Super Sport model-option and Conquista package were available again. The base El Camino had dual square headlamps on either side of a cross-hatch grille with long, narrow parking lights directly below the headlamps.

Disappearance of the LUV pickups made the S-10 Chevy's small truck entry. While styling was unaltered, new features included a Sport suspension for regular cab 4x2 models, new quiet-set trip odometer, new ignition warning buzzer and an hydraulic — rather than cable-type - clutch. Gasoline 4x2 and 4x4 models, plus the diesel 4x2 came on the short 108.3 in. w.b. with either the 73.1 in. short box or 89 in. long box. Gas and diesel 4x2s and gas 4x4 with the extended Maxi-cab used the 122.9 in. w.b. with short box only. The gas 4x2 chassis-cab was on the 117.9 in. stance. Standard equipment varied by trim level. Durango added such things as color-keyed floor mats, courtesy lights and custom cloth/vinyl or Special Custom cloth bench seats. The Tahoe package added carpeting, I.P. gauges and a right-hand visor mirror. Including all Tahoe features, plus a Sport steering wheel and Sport cloth bucket-seats (with console) was the highest-priced Sport package. The standard interior was vertically pleated vinyl. Durango's interior featured rectangular pleats in three rows on each end of the seat with a plain center section. Sport upholstery used vinyl backs and bolsters with a textured woven cloth on the seat cushions and backs. Side-mounted vertically pleated jump seats were optional for Maxi-cab models.

After being selected "Four wheeler of the Year" in 1983, the S-10 Blazer was back with such new features as an optional off-road package with gas-pressure shock absorbers and an hydraulic clutch. Both the 4x2 and 4x4 versions used a 2.0-liter four and four-speed gearbox as standard. The only options featured on standard S-10 Blazers included a cigar lighter, chrome grille and dome lamp. The Tahoe package added a right-hand visor mirror, bodyside and wheelhouse moldings, spare tire cover and wheel trim rings. On top of this, the Sport model came with a color-keyed front bumper, center console and black wheel opening moldings. Interiors included the standard type with high back vinyl "memory" bucket seats and other niceties; Tahoe with Custom vinyl or Special Custom Cloth upholstery, side window defoggers and gauges; and the Sport type with reclining seats in charcoal or Saddle tan Sport cloth or optional High Country Sheepskin front buckets.

1984 Chevrolet Fleetside Pickup (CP)

Sales catalogs for '84 actually included the full-size Blazer 4x4 as a "wagon." The big Blazer also had its own separate catalog, too. It mentioned that the Army Tank Automotive Command recently placed an order for 23,000 diesel powered Blazers. A bold new grille had a bi-level design with three black-finished horizontal bars and square headlamps in both sections, (optional), parking lamps behind the bars on the body color strip in the middle and a yellow bow-tie on the body color strip in the middle. Only 4x4 models were available. The Custom Deluxe standard interior offered foam-padded seats (front buckets) in vinyl with color-keyed door trim panels, integrated armrests and I.P. pad. A rear seat was optional. With the upscale Silverado package, Custom vinyl or cloth upholstery was added. Fender badges now identified these trucks as K-5 models, although the series designation was K10. Scottsdale versions carried an I.D. badge on the rear fender sides near the taillights.

The Chevy Van grille also had the bi-level arrangement with quad Halogen headlamps optional. Upper and lower sections of the grille each contained three horizontal blades and seven vertical members. A body-colored horizontal centerpiece held a yellow bow-tie in the middle. (Note: If the halogen headlamp option wasn't ordered, the rectangular parking lamps were used in the lower grille section under the regular rectangular headlamps; if the option was ordered, the parking lamps were mounted behind the lower grille). The G10 and G20 models offered a choice of 110 or 125 in. w.b. G30s came only on the larger chassis. A 146 in. w.b. was also available for G30 RV, commercial and Hi-Cube applications. Power steering and heavy-duty power brakes were standard on the G20/G30 vans. RV versions of the Chevy Van 30 also came with chromed front bumpers, cigar lighters and ash trays standard, which Hi-Cube versions included an extended-arm OSRV mirror. In November, 1983, a new 60/40 swing-out side door option was introduced. Standard interiors featured striped vinyl low-back bucket seats. Custom trim included high-back in vinyl or Custom vinyl.

Chevy issued separate 1984 sales catalogs for steel-bodied and aluminum-bodied Step-Vans and High-Cube Vans. Steel models came on 125 in. (CP208/CP308), 133 in. (CP210/CP310) and 157 in. (CP314) w.b. Aluminum-body models could be had in the same configurations, plus a 178 in. (CP318) version. Load lengths were: (CP208/CP308) 129.6 in.; (CP210/CP310) 153.6 in.; (CP314) 177.6 in. and (CP318) 178 in. Hi-Cube models (all series 30) came in 10 foot models on the 125 in. w.b. or a 12 foot model on the 146 in. stance.

Chevy's full-sized pickups also had the bi-level grille, as used on the big Blazer. There were three horizontal bars showing prominently in each section, with seven vertical members less prominent behind them. When bright-plated, the grille had a cross-hatch look; when black-finished, it appeared more horizontal. Halogen quad headlamps were an option. New for the season were two galvanized steel interior door panels for better rust protection. Also new were semi-metallic front brake linings on 10 and 20 series trucks; new non-asbestos rear brake linings on most models and plastic fuel tank stone shields for all pickups and chassis-cabs. This was the first year for optional power windows and door locks on Bonus and Crew Cab models, both of which came on a 164.5 in. w.b. with Fleetside boxes. Trucks with Deluxe two-tone paint had the cab and lower perimeter finished in the secondary color. Special two-toning meant only the lower perimeter was in the secondary color and there was bright trim on the bodyside and wheel openings. The Exterior Decor package included dual-tone bodyside finish and a rear tape stripe keyed to body colors plus a hood ornament. The secondary color was used between the decal stripes and moldings. Interior options included Custom Deluxe (Standard), Scottsdale and Silverado. There were 39 models all total. C10 and K10 pickups came in short box Stepside and long box Stepside and Fleetside models. C20 and K20 models came in Stepside or Fleetside form, only with the 8-foot long box. The heavy-duty C20 added chassis-cab, Bonus Cab and Crew Cab models, but heavy-duty K10s came as Fleetsides and Stepsides with the long box. The C30 heavies offered three 4x2 and four 4x4 configurations in chassis-cab form for commercial and RV applications.

I.D. DATA: The serial numbering system used in 1984 was the same one adopted in 1981. The tenth symbol, a letter designating model year, was changed to an "E" for 1985. A slightly different system was used on certain models which Chevrolet considered "medium-duty" trucks. On these vehicles the first of 17 symbols identified the country of origin, the second identified the manufacturer and the third designated the type of truck. Next came a symbol indicating GVW range. The fifty symbol designated series and the sixth designated the line and cab type. The seventh designated chassis type. The balance of the number was the same as on light-duty models.

Model	Body Type	Price	Weight	Prod. Total
El Camino — **½-Ton** — **(117.1 in. w.b.)** — **(V-6)**				
W80	Pickup	8522	3298	—
W80	Super Sport Pickup	8781	3305	—
Full-Size Blazer — **½-Ton** — **(106.5 in. w.b.)** — **(V-8)**				
K10	4x4 Hardtop	10,819	4409	—
S10 Blazer — **½-Ton** — **(100.5 in. w.b.)** — **(6-cyl.)**				
T10	4x4 Hardtop	9685	3146	—
Chevy Van 10 — **½-Ton** — **(110/125 in. w.b.)** — **(6-cyl.)**				
G11	Panel (SWB)	7541	3732	—
G11	Sportvan (SWB)	9089	4085	—
G11	Bonaventure (LWB)	10,062	—	—
G11	Beauville (LWB)	10,327	—	—
Chevy Van 20 — **¾-Ton** — **(110/125 in. w.b.)** — **(6-cyl.)**				
G21	Panel (SWB)	8176	3813	—
G21	Sportvan (LWB)	9477	4276	—
G21	Bonaventure (LWB)	10,238	—	—
G21	Beauville (LWB)	10,503	—	—
Hi-Cube and Chevy Van 30 — **1-Ton** — **(125/146 in. w.b.)** — **(6-cyl./V-8)**				
G31	Panel (SWB)	9212	4305	—
G31	Sportvan (SWB)	11,964	4984	—
G31	Bonaventure (V-8/SWB)	12,724	—	—
G31	Beauville (V-8/SWB)	12,990	—	—
G31	Cutaway Van (SWB)	8584	3731	—
G31303	10-ft. Hi-Cube (V-8/SWB)	11,624	5423	—
G31603	12-ft. Hi-Cube (V-8/SWB)	12,894	5891	—
Step-Vans — **¾-Ton/ (20)/1-Ton (30)** — **(10.5-ft. Body)** — **(6-cyl.)**				
P20	Steel Panel Step Van (125 in. w.b.)	12,588	5860	—
P30	Steel Panel (146 in. w.b.)	12,666	5998	—

NOTE: Add for 12.5-ft. and 14.5-ft. Step-Van bodies.

Model	Body Type	Price	Weight	Prod. Total
S-10 Pickups — **½-Ton** — **(108.3/122.9 in. w.b.)** — **(6-cyl.)**				
S10	Pickup (SWB)	6398	2574	—
S10	Pickup (LWB)	6551	2649	—
S10	Maxi-Cab Pickup (LWB)	6924	2705	—
Series C10 — **½-Ton** — **(117.5/131.5 in. w.b.)** — **(6-cyl.)**				
C10	Stepside (SWB)	7101	3434	—
C10	Fleetside (SWB)	6970	3481	—
C10	Fleetside (LWB)	7127	3644	—
C10	Suburban (V-8/LWB)	10,368	4310	—
Series C20 — **¾-Ton** — **(131.5/164.5 in. w.b.)** — **(6-cyl.)**				
C20	Chassis & Cab	8342	3617	—
C20	Stepside (SWB)	8319	3977	—
C20	Fleetside (SWB)	8188	4039	—
C20	Bonus Cab (LWB)	9645	4742	—
C20	Crew Cab (LWB)	9975	4803	—
C20	Suburban (V-8/LWB)	10,579	4698	—
Series C30 — **1-Ton** — **(131.5/164.5 in. w.b.)** — **(6-cyl.)**				
C30903	Chassis & Cab (SWB)	8474	3990	—
C30903	Stepside (SWB)	8966	4342	—
C30903	Fleetside (SWB)	8834	4404	—
C30943	Chassis & Bonus Cab (LWB)	9471	4412	—
C30943	Bonus Cab (LWB)	9815	4822	—
C30943	Chassis-Crew Cab (LWB)	9802	4473	—
C30943	Crew Cab (LWB)	10,146	4883	—

1984 Chevrolet S-10 Blazer 4x4 (CP)

NOTE 1: Chassis-cab models were also available on 135.5 in. and 159.5 in. w.b. for RV and commercial applications.
NOTE 2: Add for 4x4 models (4x4 models have CK prefix).

GENERAL NOTE: "SWB" means shortest wheelbase above each series listing. "LWB" means longest wheelbase above each series listing. (Example: The shortest wheelbase for C10 models is 117.5 in., while the shortest wheelbase for C20 and C30 models is 131.5 in.).

ENGINE: (Standard: El Camino) Vee-block. OHV. Six-cylinder. Cast iron block. Bore & stroke: 3.7 x 3.48 in. Displacement: 229 cu. in. Net horsepower: 110 at 4000 R.P.M. Torque: 190 lb.-ft. at 1600 R.P.M. Four main bearings. Hydraulic valve lifters. Carburetor: Two-barrel.

ENGINE: (Optional: El Camino) Vee-block. OHV. Eight-cylinder. Cast iron block. Bore & stroke: 3.7 x 3.48 in. Displacement: 305 cu. in. Compression ratio: 9.2:1. Net horsepower: 160 at 4400 R.P.M., 235 lb.-ft. at 2000 R.P.M. Five main bearings. Hydraulic valve lifters. Carburetor: Rochester model four-barrel.

ENGINE: (Optional El Camino) Vee-block. OHV. Diesel. Eight-cylinder. Cast iron block. Bore & stroke: 4.0 x 3.5 in. Displacement: 350 cu. in. Net horsepower: 105. Five main bearings. Hydraulic valve lifters. Fuel injection.

ENGINE: (Standard C10, C20, K10, G10, G20, G30) Inline. OHV. Six-cylinder. Cast iron block. Bore & stroke: 3.9 x 3.5 in. Displacement: 250 cu. in. Compression ratio: 8.3:1. Net horsepower: 115 at 3600 R.P.M. Max torque: 200 lb.-ft. at 2000 R.P.M. Seven main bearings. Hydraulic valve lifters. Carburetor: Rochester staged two-bbl.

NOTE: Order Code LE3(A).

ENGINE: (Optional C10, C20 K10, G10, G20; Standard: K10 Blazer, C10 Suburban) Vee-block. OHV. Eight-cylinder. Cast iron block. Bore & stroke: 3.736 x 3.480 in. Displacement: 305 cu. in. Compression ratio: 9.2:1. Net horsepower: 160 at 4400 R.P.M. Max torque: 235 lb.-ft. at 2000 R.P.M. Five main bearings. Hydraulic valve lifters. Carburetor: Rochester staged four-bbl. (ESC).

NOTE: Order Code LE9(C).

ENGINE: (Standard Hi-Cube Vans and Suburbans/Optional in specific other Series 10/20/30 models) V-8. OHV. Eight-cylinder. Cast iron block. Bore & stroke: 4.0 x 3.5 in. Displacement: 350 cu. in. Compression ratio: 8.2:1. Net horsepower: 165 at 3800 R.P.M. Max torque: 275 lb.-ft. at 1600 R.P.M. Five main bearings. Hydraulic valve lifters. Carburetor: Rochester four-bbl.

NOTE: Order Code LS9(A).

ENGINE: (Optional: All 4x2/4x4, Full Size Pickups, Suburbans, K10 Blazer, G20, G30/C6P) Vee-block. OHV. Diesel. Eight-cylinder. Cast iron block. Bore & stroke: 3.98 x 3.80 in. Displacement: 379 cu. in. Compression ratio: 21.3:1. Net horsepower: 130 at 3600 R.P.M. Max torque: 240 lb.-ft. at 2000 R.P.M. Hydraulic valve lifters.

NOTE: Order Code LH6(D).

ENGINE: (Standard: C20 HD (C6P), C20 Bonus/Crew, C30, K20 HD (C6P), K30) Inline. OHV. Six-cylinder. Cast iron block. Bore & stroke: 3.876 x 4.12 in. Displacement: 292 cu. in. Compression ratio: 7.8:1. Net horsepower: 115 at 3600 R.P.M. Max torque: 215 lb.-ft. at 1600 R.P.M. Five main bearings. Hydraulic valve lifters. Carburetor: Rochester one-bbl.

NOTE: Order Code L25(B).

ENGINE: (Optional: C20 HD (C6P), C20, C30, K30) Vee-block. OHV. Eight-cylinder. Cast iron block. Bore & stroke: 4.250 x 4 in. Displacement: 454 cu. in. Compression ratio: 7.9:1. Net horsepower: 230 at 3800 R.P.M. Max torque: 360 lb.-ft. at 2800 R.P.M. Five main bearings. Hydraulic valve lifters. Carburetor: Rochester four-bbl.

NOTE: Order Code LE8(A).

ENGINE: (Standard: 108.3 in. w.b. regular cab S-10 models and all models with California emissions) Inline. OHV. OHC. Four-cylinder. Cast iron block. Bore & stroke: 3.42 x 3.23 in. Displacement: 119 cu. in. Compression ratio: 8.4:1. Net horsepower: 82 at 4000 R.P.M. Max torque: 101 lb.-ft. at 3000 R.P.M.

1984 Chevrolet S-10 Blazer 4x2 (CP)

NOTE: Order Code LR1(A).

ENGINE: (Standard: All S10 models except short wheelbase regular cab models not available: California) Inline. OHV. Four-cylinder. Cast iron block. Bore & stroke: 3.50 x 3.15 in. Displacement: 121 cu. in. Compression ratio: 9.3:1. Net horsepower: 83 at 4600 R.P.M. Max torque: 108 lb.-ft. at 2400 R.P.M.

NOTE: Order Code LQ2(B).

ENGINE: (Optional S10 4x2 regular and Maxi-Cab models) Inline. OHV. Diesel. Four-cylinder. Cast iron block. Bore & stroke: 3.46 x 3.62 in. Displacement: 137 cu. in. Compression ratio: 21:1. Net horsepower: 62 at 4300 R.P.M. Max torque: 96 lb.-ft. at 2200 R.P.M.

NOTE: Order Code LQ7(B).

ENGINE: (Optional All S-10 models) Vee-block. OHV. Six-cylinder. Cast iron block. Bore & stroke: 3.50 x 2.99 in. Displacement: 173 cu. in. Compression ratio: 8.5:1. Net horsepower: 110 at 4800 R.P.M. Max torque: 145 lb.-ft. at 2100 R.P.M.

NOTE: Order Code LR2(B).

CHASSIS: (Series C20) Wheelbase: 131.5/164.5 in. (129.5 in Suburban). Overall length: 212/244.43 in. Height: 69.8 in. Tires: LT215/85R x 16C in.; Bonus/Crew: LT235/85R x 16D in. (rear E).

CHASSIS: (Series C30) Wheelbase: 131.5/164.5 in. Overall length: 212/244.43 in. Height: 77.8 in. Front tread: 65.8 in. Rear tread: 62.7 in. Tires: LT235/85R x 16D in.

CHASSIS: (El Camino) Wheelbase: 117.1 in. Overall length: 201.6 in. Height: 53.8 in. Front tread: 58.5 in. Rear tread: 57.8 in. Tires: P205/75R x 14 in.

CHASSIS: (K10 Blazer) Wheelbase: 106.5 in. Overall length: 184.8 in. Height: 73.4 in. Front tread: 66.1 in. Rear tread: 63 in. Tires: P21/75R x 15 in.

CHASSIS: (S10 Blazer) Wheelbase: 100.5 in. Overall length: 170.3 in. Height: 65 in. Front tread: 55.6 in. Rear tread: 55.1 in. Tires: P195/75R x 15 in.

CHASSIS: (G10) Wheelbase: 110/125 in. Overall length: 178.2/202.2 in. Height: 78.8/81.2 in. Front tread: 69.5 in. Rear tread: 69.7 in. Tires: P205/75R x 15 in.

CHASSIS: (G20) Wheelbase: 110/125 in. Overall length: 178.2/202.2 in. Height: 78.8/81.2 in. Front tread: 69.5 in. Rear tread: 69.7 in. Tires: P225/75R x 15 in.

CHASSIS: (G30) Wheelbase: 125 in. Overall length: 202.2 in. Height: 81.2 in. Front tread: 69.5 in. Rear tread: 69.7 in. Tires: 8.75R x 16.5D in.

CHASSIS: (G30 Hi-Cube) Wheelbase: 125/146 in. Overall length: 207.3/231.3 in. Tires: 8.75 x 16.5 in.

1984 Chevrolet C10 Suburban Silverado (CP)

CHASSIS: (P20) Wheelbase: 125/133 in. Tires: LT215/85R x 16C in.

CHASSIS: (P30) Wheelbase: 125/178 in. Tires: LT215/85R x 16C in.

CHASSIS: (S10) Wheelbase: 108.3/117.9/122.9 in. Overall length: 178.2/194.1 in. Height: 59.4 in. Front tread: 64.7 in. Rear tread: 64.7 in. Tires: P195/75R x 14 in.

CHASSIS: (C10) Wheelbase: 117.5/131.5 in. (129.5 Suburban). Overall length: 191.3/212 in. Height: 69.8 in. Front tread: 65.8 in. Rear tread: 62.7 in. Tires: P195/75R x 15 in.; Suburban P235/75R x 15 in.

TECHNICAL: Selective synchromesh transmission (Automatic on Suburban and some vans). Speeds: 3F/1R (four-speed manual in "20" and "30" Series and S10s). Steering column-mounted gearshift (or four-speed on floor). Single dry disc type clutch. Semi-floating rear axle (C30/K30/Crew and Bonus Cabs have full-floating) rear axle. Overall ratio: various. Power front disc/rear drum brakes. Pressed steel wheels. Drivetrain options: See options section.

OPTIONS

S-10 Pickup: Color-keyed bumper. Air conditioning. Rear step bumper, chrome or black. Chrome bumpers with rub strip. Black front bumper guards. Console. Chrome grille. Cigarette lighter. Color-keyed floor mats. Comfortilt steering wheel. Tinted glass. Deep tinted glass. Intermittent wipers. Auxiliary lighting. Cargo area lamp. Dome lamp. Halogen headlamps. Dual eyeline mirrors, painted or chrome. RH visor mirror. Black bodyside/bright wheel opening moldings. Bright door edge moldings. Black or bright wheel opening moldings. Power windows. Power door locks. Special two-tone. Sport two-tone. AM radio. AM/FM stereo radio. AM/FM stereo radio w/cassette and clock; same w/seek-and-scan. Premium rear speakers. High-back bucket seats, w/Custom vinyl; w/High-Country Sheepskin; w/Special Custom cloth; w/adjustable seatbacks. Rear jump seats in Maxi-cab. Tinted sliding rear window. Swing-out rear quarter windows. Cast aluminum wheels. Styled wheels. Wheel trim rings. Wheel trim covers. "Resume" cruise control. Sport suspension. 2.2-liter diesel engine. Insta-Trac 4x4 system. Off-road package. P235/75R x 15 steel-belted radial tires. Heavy-duty trailering package (with V-6). Heavy-duty battery. Vacuum power brakes. Cold climate package. Engine and oil cooler (V-6 only). Radiator and transmission oil cooler (V-6 only). 20-gallon fuel tank. Gauge package. Tachometer. 66-amp generator. Fuel tank shield. Transfer case and differential shield. Locking rear axle differential. Heavy-duty shocks. Heavy-duty springs. Front stabilizer bar. Power steering. Two front tow hooks. Trailering wiring harness. Three-speed automatic transmission (California only). 1.9 liter 4-cyl. engine (California only; standard in California). Four-speed automatic overdrive transmission. Fully-synchronized five-speed manual transmission with overdrive. Snowplow (special order). 2.8-liter V-6 engine. Stake body (chassis-cab). Durango interior trim. Tahoe interior trim. Sport interior trim. Exterior colors: Silver Metallic; Frost white; Light Blue Metallic; Galaxy Blue Metallic; Doeskin Tan; Indian Bronze Metallic, Desert Sand Metallic; Apple Red; Cinnamon Red and Satin Black (secondary). **S-10 Blazer:** Air conditioning. Color-keyed front bumper (requires two-tone). Black front bumper guards. Console. Chromed grille. Cigarette lighter. Color-keyed floor mats. Comfortilt steering wheel. Rear window defogger. Digital clock (requires radio). Deep-tint glass. Deep-tint w/light tint rear window. Sliding rear quarter windows. Intermittent wipers. Engine compartment lamp. Dome lamp. Halogen headlamps. Luggage carrier and rear air deflector. Dual painted below-eyeline mirrors. Chrome below-eyeline mirrors. RH visor mirror. Bodyside and wheel opening moldings. Door edge guards. Separate wheel opening moldings, black or bright. Operating Convenience Package. Special two-tone. Sport two-tone. Striping (req. solid paint). AM radio. AM/FM radio. AM/FM stereo w/cassette and clock. Same with seek-and-scan. Premium rear speakers. Folding rear bench seat. Sliding rear tinted quarter window. Spare tire cover. 4x2 styled wheels. 4x4 cast aluminum wheels. Bright wheel trim rings. Insta-Trac 4x4 system. Cold climate package. Heavy-duty cooling w/transmission oil cooler. Cruise Control. 20-gallon fuel tank. Gauges. 66-amp generator. Heavy-duty battery. Heavy-duty front/rear shocks. Locking rear axle differential. Off-Road chassis equipment. Power steering. Tachometer. Tailgate window release. Trailering Special equipment. Transfer case shield (4x4). 1.9-liter four-cylinder engine (California only). 2.8-liter V-6. Five-speed manual transmission. Four-speed automatic overdrive transmission. Larger size tubeless tires. Dealer-installed black-finish brush guard. Tahoe interior trim (Custom vinyl/Special Custom cloth/High-Country Sheepskin). Sport cloth interior. Paint colors: same as S-10 pickups. Snowplow (special order). **Full-Size Blazer:** Air cleaner. Air conditioning. Bright wheel covers. Chrome front bumper guards. Deluxe bumpers. Cigarette lighter. Color-keyed floor mats. Comfortilt steering wheel. Deluxe front appearance. Electric Quartz clock. Deep-tint glass. Sliding side window. Halogen headlamps. Headlight warning buzzer. Full-length headliner. Intermittent wipers. Painted below-eyeline mirrors. Stainless below-eyeline mirrors. Black bodyside moldings. Bright bodyside moldings. Black molding package. Bright molding package. Door edge guards. Operating Convenience package. Power door locks. Power windows. Special two-tone paint. Exterior decor package. AM radio. AM/FM radio. AM/FM stereo radio. AM/FM stereo w/cassette. Windshield antenna. Folding rear seat. Electric tailgate window. Rally wheels. Styled wheels. Cold Climate package. Engine oil cooler. Transmission oil cooler. Cruise control. Deadweight trailer hitch. Front quad shocks. Front stabilizer bar. Front tow hooks. 31-gallon fuel tank. Fuel tank stoneshield. Gauges. 66-amp generator. Heavy-duty battery. Heavy-duty springs. Heavy-duty radiator. Locking differential. Trailering Special equipment. Weight distributing hitch. Four-speed overdrive automatic. 5.0-liter V-8 engine (w/ESC; not in Calif.). 5.7-liter V-8 engine (Calif. only). 6.2-liter Diesel V-8. Dealer installed brush guard. Silverado interior trim. Silverado Custom cloth trim. Full-length black top. ¾-length black top. Paint colors: Frost White; Silver Metallic; Midnight Black; Light Blue Metallic; Midnight Blue; Colonial Yellow; Doeskin Tan; Desert Sand Metallic; Indian Bronze Metallic and Apple Red. **Chevy Vans:** Front air conditioning. Front and rear air conditioning. "Resume" Speed Control. Auxiliary lighting package. Auxiliary rear heater. Chrome bumpers. Front bumper guards. Cigar lighter & ash tray light. Comfortilt steering wheel. Custom steering wheel. Deluxe

127

1984 Chevrolet K20 Suburban Silverado (CP)

front appearance. Quartz electric clock. Floor carpeting. All windows tinted. Tinted windshield. Halogen headlights. Intermittent windshield wipers. Fixed extended arm mirrors; painted or stainless. Below eyeline mirrors; painted or stainless. Black bodyside moldings. Wheel opening moldings. Operating Convenience Package. Power door locks. Power windows. Special two-tone paint. Power brakes. Deluxe two-tone paint. Rear door stop. AM radio. AM/FM stereo. AM/FM stereo w/cassette. Roof ventilator. Front auxiliary seat. High-back front bucket seat. Sliding door extender link. Special exterior trim. Special interior trim. RH sunshade. Rally wheels. Bright wheel covers. Inside spare container. Spare tire cover. Side and rear windows. Auxiliary battery. Engine oil cooler. Transmission oil cooler. Dual rear wheels (cutaway Vans). Voltmeter. Temperature gauge. Oil pressure gauge. 66-amp generator. Heavy-duty battery. Heavy-duty power brakes. Heavy-duty cooling. Heavy-duty front springs. Heavy-duty front/rear shocks. Heavy-duty rear springs. Locking differential. Power steering (G10). School bus equipment (G30). Dead-weight trailer hitch. Weight distributing hitch. Heavy-duty Trailering Special equip. Light-duty Trailering Special equipment. 250 cu. in. six-cylinder engine. 5.0-liter V-8 engine (W/ESC) (not in Calif.). 5.0-liter V-8 (Calif. only). 5.7-liter V-8 engine. 6.2-liter Diesel V-8 engine. Four-speed automatic overdrive transmission. Four-speed manual overdrive transmission. Oversize tires. Paint colors: Galaxy Blue, Metallic; Colonial Yellow; Doeskin tan; Desert Sand Metallic; Indian Bronze Metallic; Apple Red Metallic; Autumn Red Metallic; Frost white; Silver Metallic; Light Blue Metallic and (cutaway vans only) Polar White. **Step-Vans:** 4.8-liter one-barrel LG engine (standard). 5.7-liter four-barrel V-8 engine. 6.2-liter diesel V-8 engine. Four-speed manual transmission (standard). Three-speed automatic transmission (optional, except P20 w/standard six-cylinder). 125 in. w.b. (standard). 133 in. and 157 in. w.b. (optional). Steel panel bodies, 10½-ft.; 12½-ft. and 14½-ft. Wide (74 in.) rear doors. Aluminum panel bodies (same sizes as above, plus 14-ft. 10 in.). X-950 aluminum bodies. Merchandise shelf interior. Snack food interior. Bakery pallet rack interior. Industrial laundry interior. Fiberglass skylight. Step-type bumper w/recessed lights. Deluxe high-back bucket seat. Auxiliary seats with arm-rests. Expanded metal partition. Plywood interior lining. Right-hand sliding panel w/key-locking handle. Special Custom cloth interior. All-Weather air conditioning. RH inside spare tire carrier. 66-in. wide overhead door. 60-in. wide rear door opening. Dual rear wheels. Larger size tubeless tires. P30 Step-Van 18-ft. aluminum body. **High-Cube Vans:** 5.7-liter V-8 engine (standard). 6.2-liter Diesel V-8 engine. Overhead rear door. Hi-back bucket seats. Three-speed automatic (w/column shift) transmission (standard). Dual rear wheels on 125 in. w.b. (Standard with extra-cost 6200-pound rear axle). 7500-pound rear axle also available. Load space skylight. Step-type rear bumper. Plywood interior lining. Expanded metal partition. RH sliding panel w/key-locking handle; custom cloth interior trim. Inside spare tire carrier. Plywood partition w/center sliding panel. **C/K-10/20/30: (Suburban-only):** Electric tailgate window. Tailgate window defogger. Front and rear air conditioning. Bucket seats. Deluxe front and rear bumpers. Rear heater. Three-passenger folding center seat. Three-passenger center and rear seats. 60-in. wide double panel doors. Wagon type rear tailgate. Standard transmissions for Suburbans were as follows: C10 (gas)=four-speed automatic w/overdrive; C20 (gas)=three-speed automatic; K10 (gas)=same as C10; K20 (gas) same as C20. With Diesel engines the C10 came with four-speed automatic w/overdrive and all other models came with four-speed manual, (as standard equipment). 40-gallon or 31-gallon fuel tanks. Headlamp warning buzzer. Full-length head-liner. **(Pickups Only):** Chromed rear bumper. Chromed rear step bumper, (Fleetside). Painted rear step bumper. Cargo area lamp. Dome lamp. Gauges. Conventional two-tone. Deluxe two-tone paint (Fleetside only). Sliding rear window. Side-mounted spare tire carrier (Fleetside only). Auxiliary fuel tank. Engine oil cooler. Heavy-duty automatic transmission cooler. Vacuum power brakes. Extra-capacity rear springs. G50 heavy-duty rear springs. G60 main and auxiliary rear springs. Special Camper Chassis equipment. Special commercial chassis equipment. Heavy-duty 4.8-liter six-cylinder engine (heavy-duty emissions trucks). Standard 4.1-liter six-cylinder engine. Special bright metal wheel covers. Pickup box side rails. Painted West Coast mirrors. Glide-out spare tire carrier. **(Suburbans and Pickups):** Front air conditioning. Chromed front bumper guards. Cigarette lighter. Color-keyed floor mats. Comfortilt steering wheel. Deluxe front appearance. Quartz electric clock. Deep tinted glass. Deluxe molding package, bright (Fleetside only pickups). Door edge guards. Power door locks. Power windows. Operating convenience package. Special two-tone (Fleetside only on pickups). Exterior decor package (Fleetside only on pickups). AM radio. AM/FM radio. AM/FM stereo with cassette. Windshield antenna. High-beam Halogen headlamps. Intermittent windshield wipers. Painted below-eyeline mirrors. Stainless below-eyeline mirrors. Stainless camper mirrors. Black bodyside moldings (Fleetside only on pickups). Bright bodyside moldings (Fleetside only on pickups). Roof marker lamps. Rally wheels. Styled wheels. Bright wheel covers. Precleaner air cleaner. Locking differential. Cold Climate package.

Electronic speed control. Front quad shocks. Front stabilizer bar. Heavy-duty front stabilizer. Front tow hooks. Stone shield. Gauges. 66-amp generator. Heavy-duty battery. Heavy-duty shocks. Heavy-duty front springs. Heavy-duty radiator. Power steering. Trailer wiring. Trailer hitches. 5.0-liter V-8 w/ESC (not in California). 5.7-liter V-8. 6.2-liter Diesel V-8. 7.4-liter V-8 (Suburban and heavy-duty emissions pickups). Scottsdale interior trim. Silverado interior trim. Paint colors: Frost White; Silver Metallic; Midnight Black; Light Blue Metallic; Midnight Blue; Colonial Yellow; Doeskin Tan; Desert Sand Metallic; Indian Bronze Metallic and Apple Red.

HISTORICAL: Introduced: Fall, 1983. Calendar year sales: (all models) 1,111,839. (El Camino) 22,997. (K10 Blazer) 46,919. (S-10 Blazer) 150,599. (Chevy Van) 155,421. (Sportvan) 21,902. (S-10 Pickup) 199,631. (C20 Pickups) 50,823. Calendar year production: (Chevy Van/Sportvan) 120,878; (Suburban) 57,286; (Pickups) 332,404 and (Step-Van/Hi-Cube/Cutaway) 53,097. (Total) 563,665. Innovations: Newly designed grilles. S-10 trucks feature hydraulic clutch in place of cable type. Improved rust protection on pickups. Improved brake linings for Blazers, Suburbans and Pickups. Step-Vans feature new exterior Velvac OSRV mirrors, new rotary side door latches and new key-locking push-button side door handles. Historical notes: Chevrolet products were named as the official cars and trucks of the XIV Olympic winter games in Sarajevo. Chevy advertised the U.S. Army's purchase of nearly 30,000 full-size Chevy 4x4 pickups and over 23,000 full-size Blazers with 6.2-liter diesel V-8 engines. These trucks were said to be "regular production trucks like the ones you can get except for a few specialized military adaptions like a special electrical system."

1985 CHEVROLET

1985 Chevrolet S-10 Pickup (CP)

LIGHT TRUCK — 1985 SERIES — (ALL ENGINES): — Chevrolet's all-new Astro was a compact van featuring a standard V-6 engine, five-speed manual transmission and rear drive axle. The mini-van body featured a sloping hood and aerodynamically rounded front end with wraparound parking lamps, single rectangular headlights and a grille with seven horizontal bars. Each bar decreased slightly in width, from top to bottom. A yellow bow-tie badge was in the center. Additional standard equipment included an engine cover storage box, front arm rests, swing-out side windows, black rubber floor covering, high-back bucket seats, five-passenger seating and P195/75R15 all-season steel-belted radial tires. "CS" trim added color-keyed floor coverings, side window defoggers, inside fuel door release, lighted vanity mirrors and an under-the-floor spare tire carrier. The optional "CL" package included added features, such as bumper rub strips, a tripodometer, gauges, custom steering wheel, wheel trim rings, auxiliary lighting, cigar lighter and carpets. Cargo van versions had a standard low-back driver's seat in saddle tan, black rubber floor covering, solid panel bodysides and the same arrangement of a sliding right-hand side cargo door and double panel type rear doors. Custom cloth upholstery was optional. Paint treatments included 10 solid colors; special two-tone (with decal strips at beltline and secondary color below the belt) and sport two-tone (with secondary color on lower body perimeter). The Astro name appeared on both entry doors, just behind the front wheel openings. Tail-lamps were vertical units positioned on the rear body corners, just below the beltline. The rear doors of all models had large windows.

In addition to last year's standard features, the '85 El Camino had a new 4.3-litre V-6 base engine. Standard grille was the same as last year. Also back was the El Camino SS and the Conquista. The SS had an aero-style nose cap like the Monte Carlo SS. A non-functional "power blister" hood, dummy side pipes and pickup bed rails were optional. Model I.D. decals were used on the doors, above the lower feature line. Conquista and SS Sport decors each included five distinctive two-tones.

The easiest way to spot a 1985 S10 was by its larger and more stylized fender badges with the "S" done in red (the hyphen between the letter and the numbers was gone). At the rear, the taillights were framed in chrome and the large Chevrolet name (formerly running across the tailgate center) was changed to a smaller name at the right-hand side of a tailgate trim panel. A new 2.5-litre engine with EFI (electronic fuel-injection) was standard in 4x4 models. Standard, Durango, Tahoe and Sport trim treatments were available again. Trim options included Custom two-tone (second color below belt); Sport two-tone (second color on bottom below four-stripe decals or moldings) and Special two-tone (second color between beltline and lower feature line).

1985 Chevrolet Fleetside and Stepside Pickups (CP)

Also standard in S10 Blazers was the 2.5-litre four-cylinder EFI engine. A "new" Custom vinyl interior amounted to little more than wider door panel pleats and brushed aluminum door panel trim plates. Much of the artwork used in the 1984 and 1985 sales catalogs is close to identical and even the 10 colors available (not counting satin black) were the same. As in 1984, Satin Black could only be ordered as a secondary color. Custom two-toning (with beltline decal and second color below it) was, however, new for 1985.

Full-size '85 Blazers were easier to spot. They had a much wider body-color panel between upper and lower grilles and the grilles had only a single horizontal bar intersected by seven vertical bars. The head light housing had more of a vertical look than last year's, although the rectangular lamps were stacked atop each other again. An amber-colored parking lamp was standard on the bottom, but when Halogen high-beams were ordered, the parking lamps moved behind the lower grille. New features included fluidic wiper arms with built-in washers and standard color-keyed tops in a choice of four new colors plus the old black and white. Custom Deluxe interiors were standard, with Silverado trim available at extra cost. Special two-tone and Exterior Decor packages were optional. Colonial Yellow and Desert Sand Metallic finishes were no longer offered. Engine and transmission selections were unchanged.

Chevy Vans had new grilles of the same design described above for Blazers. Model I.D. nameplates featured somewhat smaller and thinner lettering. Chrome trim around the taillights was no longer used. Chevy's new 4.3-litre "Vortec" V-6 was base equipment in G10/G20/G30 models, while the 6.2-litre diesel V-8 was available in G20/G30-CP6 series vans. The 5.7-litre V-8 could also be had in G30/CP6 (cutaway van) versions. Custom vinyl seats now used a four-pleat pattern. 60/40 style side doors were now regularly available, at no extra cost, in place of the sliding right-hand side load door. G30 Hi-cube vans again come in 10-foot (125 inch wheelbase) and 12-foot (146 inch wheelbase) models, with RV and Commercial Cutaway vans available on both of these chassis as well. All manual transmissions (three-speed type standard in G10/G20) came with floor-mounted gearshifts.

Suburbans also had the new-for-'85 wide center panel grille styling. Also standard were fluidic arm window washer/wipers. Custom Deluxe trim was standard. Scottsdales had color-keyed floor mats and added cowl and headliner insulation. Door-to-door carpeting and velour or grained vinyl upholstery were featured with Silverado interiors. Special two-tone and Exterior Decor finish options were available. The latter included a hood ornament. End-gate and panel-door options were still cataloged. Standard engines were all V-8s.

Full-sized pickups shared the new 1985 grille with Blazers and Suburbans. A new Custom two-tone treatment used the secondary color above the beltline on the (Fleetside) box, on only the rear of the cab and on the doors and fender sides above the belt (but not on the hood or window frames). This gave a sportier look — something like a tapering racing stripe — to the cab and fender sides. Under the hood, as standard equipment, was the Vortec six. The trucks continued to come in a wide range of choices including ½, ¾ and 1-ton series with long or short cargo boxes; Fleetside or Stepside styling; Crew Cab or Bonus Cab models and 4x2 or 4x4 drive. A real "Country Cadillac" was the Crew Cab "Big Dooley" with its flared rear fenders and dual rear wheels. Custom Deluxe, Scottsdale and Silverado trims were again available.

I.D. DATA: Same as 1984.

1985 Chevrolet Astro Van (CP)

Model	Body Type	Price	Weight	Prod. Total
El Camino — (½-Ton) — (117.1 in. w.b.) — (V-6)				
1GW80	Sedan Pickup	9058	3252	—
1GW80	Super Sport Pickup	9327	3263	—
K10 Blazer — (½-Ton) — (106.5 in. w.b.) — (V-8)				
K10516	4x4 Hardtop Utility	11,223	4462	—

NOTE: Add $2,730 and 375 pounds for diesel.

Model	Body Type	Price	Weight	Prod. Total
S10 Blazer — (½-Ton) — (100.5 in. w.b.) — (V-6)				
CT10516	4x4 Hardtop Utility	10,134	3151	—
CS10516	4x2 Hardtop Utility	8881	2894	—
Astro Van — (½-Ton) — (111 in. w.b.) — (4-cyl.)				
CM10905	Cargo Van	7821	3048	—
CM10906	Passenger Van	8195	3277	—
CM10906	"CS" Passenger Van	8623	3277	—
CM10906	"CL" Passenger Van	9359	3277	—
Chevy Van 10 — (½-Ton) — (110/125.5 in. w.b.) — (V-6)				
CG11006	Panal Van (SWB)	9650	4802	—
CG11306	Sportvan (LWB)	9870	4966	—
CG11306	Bonaventure (LWB)	10,661	5067	—
CG11306	Beauville (LWB)	10,979	5110	—
Chevy Van — (¾-Ton) — (110/125 in. w.b.) — (V-6)				
CG21006	Panel Van (SWB)	8581	3811	—
CG21306	Sportvan (LWB)	10,054	4994	—
CG21306	Bonaventure (LWB)	10,845	5095	—
CG21306	Beauville (LWB)	11,161	5138	—
Chevy Van 30 — (1-Ton) — (125 in. w.b.) — (V-8)				
CG31306	Panel	10,342	4402	—
CG31306	Sportvan	12,463	6915	—
CG31306	Bonaventure	13,254	7016	—
CG31306	Beauville	13,569	7059	—
Chevy Van 30 — (1-Ton) — (125 in. w.b.) — (Diesel V-8)				
CG31306	Sportvan	13,545	5971	—
CG31306	Bonaventure	14,350	6070	—
CG31306	Beauville	14,587	6113	—
Hi-Cube Vans 30 — (1-Ton) — (125 in./146 in. w.b.) — (V-8)				
CG31	10-ft. Steel Panel (SWB)	12,097	5054	—
	12-ft. Steel Panel (LWB)	13,351	5891	—

NOTE: Also available were 10-ft. aluminum and 12-ft. aluminum Hi-Cube G30 Vans, plus RV Cutaway and Commercial Cutaway models on a choice of 125 or 146 in. w.b.

Model	Body Type	Price	Weight	Prod. Total
Step-Van — (P20/P30) — (125/133/178 in. w.b.) — (6-cyl.)				
P20	¾-Ton 10.5-ft. Steel Panel	13,038	5860	—
P30	1-Ton 10.5-ft. Steel Panel	13,119	5998	—

NOTE: Other models available; see 1984 section text and chart.

Model	Body Type	Price	Weight	Prod. Total
S-10 Pickup — (½-Ton) — (108.3/122.9 in. w.b.) — (V-6)				
CS10603	4x2 Pickup (SWB)	5999	2561	—
CS10803	4x2 Pickup (LWB)	6702	2623	—
CS10653	4x2 Maxi-Cab Pickup (LWB)	7167	3030	—
CT10603	4x4 Pickup (SWB)	8258	2898	—
CT10803	4x4 Pickup (LWB)	8412	2623	—
CT10653	4x4 Maxi-Cab Pickup (LWB)	8756	3030	—
CS10803	4x2 Chassis Cab (LWB)	6500	2954	—
C10 — (½-Ton) — (117.5/131.5 in. w.b.) — (V-6)				
CC10703	Stepside Pickup (SWB)	7532	3844	—
CC10703	Fleetside Pickup (SWB)	7397	3891	—
CC10903	Fleetside Pickup (LWB)	7565	4060	—

NOTE 1: Add $2322 for CK10 (4x4) pickups with Vortec six engine.
NOTE 2: Add $2913 for 6.2-litre diesel V-8 option.

Model	Body Type	Price	Weight	Prod. Total
C10 Suburban — (½-Ton) — (131.5 in. w.b.) — (V-8)				
CC10906	Suburban (doors)	10,812	4755	—
CC10916	Suburban (tailgate)	10,850	4790	—

NOTE 1: Add $2322 for 4x4 Suburban with larger 350 cu. in. V-8.
NOTE 2: Add $2557 for 6.2-litre diesel V-8 option.

Model	Body Type	Price	Weight	Prod. Total
C20 — (¾-Ton) — (131.5/164.5 in. w.b.) — (V-6)				
CC20903	Stepside Pickup (SWB)	8798	4417	—
CC20903	Fleetside Pickup (SWB)	8663	4479	—
CC20943	Bonus Cab Pickup (LWB)	10,584	5258	—
CC20943	Crew Cab Pickup (LWB)	10,920	5258	—
CC20903	Heavy-duty Stepside Pickup (SWB)	9756	4417	—
CC20903	Heavy-duty Fleetside Pickup (SWB)	9622	4479	—
CC20903	Chassis & Cab (SWB)	9198	4057	—
CC20906	Door Suburban w/V-8 (SWB)	10,953	4705	—
CC20916	End-gate Suburban w/V-8 (SWB)	10,991	4740	—

NOTE 1: Add $1525 for CK20 (4x4) pickups with 350 cu. in. V-8.
NOTE 2: Add $1479 for CK20 (4x4) Suburban with larger 350 cu. in. V-8.
NOTE 3: Add $2276 for 6.2-litre diesel V-8 option on C20 Pickups.
NOTE 4: Add $2196 for 6.2-litre diesel V-8 option on C20 Suburbans.

Model	Body Type	Price	Weight	Prod. Total
C30 — (1-Ton) — (131.5/164.5 in. w.b.) — (6-cyl.)				
CC30903	Chassis-Cab (SWB)	9332	4485	—
CC30903	Stepside Pickup (SWB)	9849	4838	—
CC30903	Fleetside Pickup (SWB)	9715	4900	—
CC30943	Chassis-Bonus Cab (LWB)	10,349	4912	—
CC30943	Bonus Cab Pickup (LWB)	10,715	5323	—
CC30943	Chassis-Crew Cab (LWB)	9446	4520	—
CC30943	Crew Cab Pickup (LWB)	11,053	5323	—

NOTE 1: Add $2344 average for CK30 (4x4) models with six-cylinder engine.
NOTE 2: Add $1800 average for 6.2-litre diesel V-8 option on C30 models.

GENERAL NOTE: "SWB" indicates shortest wheelbase above each series listing. "LWB" indicates longest wheelbase above each series listing. (Example: For C10 models "SWB" indicates 117.1 in. w.b.; for C20 models "LWB" indicates 131.5 in. w.b.) Prices for four-wheel-drive and diesel options are averages. Each option combination actually had its own individual price and Chevrolet price sheets contained nearly 150 separate list prices for 1985 light-duty trucks.

ENGINE: Vee-block. OHV. Six-cylinder. Cast iron block. Bore & stroke: 4.0 x 3.48 in. Displacement: 262 cu. in. Compression ratio: 9.3:1. Net horsepower: 155 at 4000 R.P.M. Torque: 230 lb.-ft. at 2400 R.P.M. Hydraulic valve lifters. Carburetor: Single four-barrel.

NOTE: Ordering Code LB1.

ENGINE: Inline. OHV. Four-cylinder. Cast iron block. Bore & stroke: 3.42 x 3.23 in. Displacement: 119 cu. in. Compression ratio: 8.4:1. Net horsepower: 82 at 4600 R.P.M. Net torque: 101 lb.-ft. at 3000 R.P.M.

NOTE: Ordering Code LR1

ENGINE: Inline. OHV. Diesel Four-cylinder. Cast iron block. Bore & stroke: 3.46 x 3.62 in. Displacement: 137 cu. in. Compression ratio: 21:1. Net horsepower: 62 at 4300 R.P.M. Net torque: 96 lb.-ft. at 2200 R.P.M.

NOTE: Ordering Code LQ7.

ENGINE: Vee-block. OHV. Six-cylinder. Cast iron block. Bore & stroke: 3.50 x 2.99 in. Displacement: 173 cu. in. Compression ratio: 8.5:1. Net horsepower: 110 at 4800 R.P.M. Net torque: 145 lb.-ft. at 2100 R.P.M. Electronic fuel injection.

ENGINE: Inline. OHV. Four-cylinder. Cast iron block. Bore & stroke: 4 x 3.00 in. Displacement: 151 cu. in. Compression ratio: 9.0:1. Net horsepower: 92 at 4400 R.P.M. Net torque: 132 lb.-ft. at 2800 R.P.M. Electronic fuel injection.

NOTE: Ordering Code LN8.

ENGINE: Vee-block. OHV. Eight-cylinder. Cast iron block. Bore & stroke: 3.74 x 3.48 in. Displacement: 305 cu. in. Compression ratio: 9.5:1. Net horsepower: 150 at 4000 R.P.M. Net torque: 240 lb.-ft. at 2000 R.P.M. Five main bearings. Hydraulic valve lifters. Carburetor: Single 4-barrel.

NOTE: Ordering Code LG4

ENGINE: Vee-block. OHV. Six-cylinder. Cast iron block. Bore & stroke: 4.0 x 3.48 in. Displacement: 202 cu. in. Compression ratio: 9.3:1. Net horsepower: 130 at 3600 R.P.M. 210 lb.-ft. at 2000 R.P.M. Hydraulic valve lifters. Electronic fuel injection.

NOTE: Ordering Code LB4.

ENGINE: Inline. Diesel. OHV. Eight-cylinder. Cast iron block. Bore & stroke: 3.98 x 3.80 in. Displacement: 379 cu. in. Compression ratio: 21.3:1. Net horsepower: 151 at 3600 R.P.M. Net Torque: 248 lb.-ft at 2000 R.P.M. Hydraulic valve lifters. Fuel-injection.

NOTE: Ordering Code LL4.

ENGINE: Vee-block. OHV. Eight-cylinder. Cast iron block. Bore & stroke: 4.3 x 4.0 in. Displacement: 454 cu. in. Compression ratio: 7.9:1. Net horsepower: 230 at 3800 R.P.M. Net torque: 360 lb.-ft. at 2800 R.P.M. Five main bearings. Carburetor: Rochester single 4-barrel.

NOTE: Ordering Code LE8

ENGINE: Vee-block. OHV. Eight-cylinder. Cast iron block. Bore & stroke: 4.0 x 3.5 in. Displacement: 350 cu. in. Compression ratio: 8.3:1. Net horsepower: 160 at 3800 R.P.M. Net torque: 250 lb.-ft. at 2800 R.P.M. Five main bearings. Hydralic valve lifters. Carburetor: Rochester four-barrel.

NOTE: Ordering Code LT9.

ENGINE: Vee-block. OHV. Eight-cylinder. Cast iron block. Bore & stroke: 3.74 x 3.48 in. Displacement: 305 cu. in. Compression ratio: 9.2:1. Net horsepower: 160 at 4400 R.P.M. Net torque: 235 lb.-ft. at 2000 R.P.M. Four main bearings. Hydraulic valve lifters. Carburetor: Rochester single four-barrel.

NOTE: Ordering Code LE9.

ENGINE: Vee-block. OHV. Diesel Eight-cylinder. Cast iron block. Bore & stroke: 3.98 x 3.82 in. Displacement: 379 cu. in. Compression ratio: 21.3:1. Net horsepower: 130 at 3600 R.P.M. Net torque: 240 lb.-ft. at 2000 R.P.M. Hydraulic valve lifters. Fuel injection.

NOTE: Ordering Code LH6.

ENGINE: Vee-block. OHV. Eight-cylinder. Cast iron block. Bore & stroke: 4.0 x 3.48 in. Displacement: 350 cu. in. Compression ratio: 8.2:1. Net horsepower: 165 at 3800 R.P.M. Net torque: 275 lb.-ft. at 1600 R.P.M. Carburetor: Rochester single 4-barrel.

NOTE: Ordering Code LS9.

ENGINE: Inline. OHV. Six-cylinder. Cast iron block. Bore & stroke: 3.9 x 4.1 in. Displacement: 292 cu. in. Compression ratio: 7.8:1. Net horsepower: 115 at 3600 R.P.M. Net torque: 215 lb.-ft. at 1600 R.P.M. Seven main bearings. Hydraulic valve lifters. Carburetor: Rochester single 1-barrel.

NOTE: Ordering Code L25.

1985 Chevrolet El Camino (CP)

CHASSIS: (El Camino) Wheelbase: 117.1 in. Tires: P205/75R14.

CHASSIS: (K10 Blazer) Wheelbase: 106.5 in. Tires: P215/75R15.

CHASSIS: (S10 Blazer) Wheelbase: 100.5 in.; Tires P195/75R15.

CHASSIS: (Astro) Wheelbase: 111 in. Tires P195/75R15.

CHASSIS: (Chevy Van 10) Wheelbase: 110 in. Tires: P195/75R15.

CHASSIS: (Sportvan 10) Wheelbase: 125 in. Tires: P205/75R15.

CHASSIS: (Chevy Van 20) Wheelbase: 110 in. Tires: P225/75R15.

CHASSIS: (Sportvan 20) Wheelbase: 125 in. Tires: P225/75R15.

CHASSIS: (Chevy Van 30) Wheelbase: 125 in. Tires: 8.75R-16.5C.

CHASSIS: (Sportvan 30) Wheelbase: 125 in. Tires: 8.75R-16.5D.

CHASSIS: (10 ft. Hi-Cube Van) Wheelbase: 125 in. Tires: 8.00-16.5D.

CHASSIS: (12 ft. Hi-Cube Van) Wheelbase: 146 in. Tires: 8.75-16.5D.

CHASSIS: (P20 Step-Van) Wheelbase: 125/133 in. Tires: LT215/85R16C.

CHASSIS: (P30 Step-Van) Wheelbase: 125/178 in. Tires: LT215/85R16C.

CHASSIS: (S10 Pickup) Wheelbase: 108.3/122.9 in. Tires: P195/75R14.

CHASSIS: (C10 Pickup) Wheelbase: 117.5/131.5 in. Tires: 195/75R15.

CHASSIS: (C10 Suburban) Wheelbase: 129.5 in. Tires: P233/75R15.

CHASSIS: (C20 Pickup) Wheelbase: 131.5 in. Tires: LT215/85R16C.

CHASSIS: (C20 Pickup) Wheelbase: 164.5 in. Tires: LT235/85R16D (Rear E).

CHASSIS: (C20 Suburban) Wheelbase: 129.5. Tires: LT235/85R16D (Rear E).

CHASSIS: (C30 Pickup) Wheelbase: 131.5/164.5. Tires: LT235/85R16D (Rear E).

TECHNICAL: (Series: G10, G20) Synchromesh, manual transmission. Speeds: 3 F/1 R. Column-mounted gearshift. Semi-floating rear axle. Hydraulic front disc, rear drum brakes. Pressed steel wheels.

TECHNICAL: (Series G30) Automatic/overdrive transmission. Speeds: 4 F/1R. Column-mounted gearshift. Full-floating rear axle. Overall ratio: 3.73, 4.10:1. Power front disc, rear drum brakes. Pressed steel wheels.

TECHNICAL: (Suburban) Automatic with overdrive transmission. Speeds: 4 F/1 R. Column-mounted gearshift. Semi-floating rear axle. Overall ratio: 3.21, 3.42, 3.73, 4.10, 3.56:1. Power hydraulic front disc, rear drum brakes. Pressed steel wheels.

TECHNICAL: (Suburban) Manual, synchromesh (standard on C20, K10, K20) transmission. Speeds: 4 F/1 R. Floor-mounted gearshift. Semi-floating (full-floating with 454 V-8) rear axle. Overall ratio: 3.21, 3.42, 3.73, 4.10, 4.56:1. Power hydraulic front disc, rear drum brakes. Pressed steel wheels.

TECHNICAL: (All C Series, except C10) Manual, synchromesh transmission. Speeds: 4 F/1 R. Floor-mounted gearshift. Semi-floating (all except C30, K30), full-floating (C30, K30) rear axle. Overall ratio: 3.23, 3.42, 3.73, 4.10, 4.56:1 (LE 8 engine and locking differential: 3.21:1).

TECHNICAL: (C10) Manual, synchromesh transmission. Speeds: 3 F/1 R. Column-mounted gearshift. Semi-floating rear axle. Overall ratio: 2.73, 3.08, 3.42, 3.73:1. Hydraulic front disc, rear drum brakes. Pressed steel, 6.00 in. wide wheels.

TECHNICAL: (Astro) Manual, synchromesh transmission. Speeds: 4 F/1 R. Floor-mounted gearshift. Semi-floating rear axle. Overall ratio: 2.56, 2.73, 3.08, 3.42, 3.73, 4.11:1. Hydraulic disc front, rear drum brakes. Pressed steel wheels.

TECHNICAL: (S10) Manual, synchromesh transmission. Speeds: 4 F/1 R. Floor-mounted gearshift. Semi-floating rear axle. Overall ratio: 3.08, 3.42, 3.73, 4.11:1. Hydraulic, front disc, rear drum brakes. Pressed steel wheels.

1985 Chevrolet C10 Stepside Pickup (CP)

TECHNICAL: (S10 Blazer) Manual, synchromesh transmission. Speeds: 4 F/1 R. Floor-mounted gearshift. Semi-floating rear axle. Overall ratio: 2.73, 3.08, 3.42, 3.73. Hydraulic power front disc, rear drum brakes. Pressed steel, 6 in. wheels.

TECHNICAL: (El Camino) Automatic transmission. Speeds: 3 F/1 R. Floor-mounted gearshift. Semi-floating rear axle. Overall ratio: 2.41, 2.56, 2.73, 3.08:1. Hydraulic power front disc, rear drum brakes. Pressed steel wheels.

OPTIONS: Optional equipment for 1985 models was approximately the same as that available in 1984, except for certain power teams and Astro options. The following data gives a complete list of Astro options and prices, plus available prices for equipment offered on certain other models.

ASTRO: Four-speed automatic transmission ($520). Four-passenger seating CL ($552); others ($634). Seven-passenger seating, CL ($1195); others ($1277). Eight-passenger seating, CL ($643); others ($643). Seat-back recliner and dual arm rests ($230). Custom high-back buckets, 8-passenger ($150); 5-passenger ($100). Front air conditioning, base ($740); CL/CS ($697). Front and rear air conditioning, CL/CS ($1249). Deluxe front/rear bumpers, base/CS ($122); CL ($72). Color-keyed bumpers, base/CS ($50). Increased cargo capacity, reg. 4/5 pass. seats ($314). Heavy-duty radiator ($53); w/trans. cooler ($112); w/trans. cooler and A/C ($171). Remote fuel filler release ($25). Rubber floor covering, base ($43). Gauge package, base/CS ($58). 100-amp alternator ($30). Tinted glass, complete ($98); standard ($71). Deluxe grille, base/CS ($25). Halogen headlamps ($22). Engine block heater ($31). Rear heater ($256). Deluxe heater ($43). Special two-tone ($237). Sport two-ton ($162). Calif. emissions ($99). Optional axle ratio ($36). Locking differential ($238). Heavy-duty battery ($53). Sparetire carrier, base ($21). Engine oil cooler ($120). Roof console ($79). Power door locks ($198). Carpeting in CS ($111). Rear heater ($256). Complete body glass ($121). Tinted windshield ($38). Swingout door glass ($55). Trailer wiring harness ($39). Dome and reading lamps ($31). Auxiliary lighting, base ($142); CS ($121). Dual deluxe mirrors ($50). Black body side moldings, base/CS ($55). Power windows and door locks ($388). Door edge guards ($17). RH visor mirror, base ($48); CL/SC ($41). Protective interior panels ($25). AM radio ($112). AM/FM stereo, base ($243); CL/CS ($283). AM/FM stereo w/ET, base ($424); CL/CS ($464). Above w/quadraphonic, base ($574); CL/CS ($614). Heavy-duty front/rear shocks ($34). Cruise control ($195). Front stabilizer bar ($38). Power steering ($276). Tilt steering column ($129). Custom steering wheel, base/CS ($26). Power windows ($190). Positive stop rear door, base ($35). LH front seat storage compartment ($35). LH/RH front seat storage compartments ($70). Body striping ($75). 27-gallon fuel tank ($66). Cargo tiedowns ($30). Dead weight trailer hitch ($64). Heavy-duty trailering pkg., w/f&r A/C ($471); w/o f&r A/C ($524). Light-duty trailering package ($103). Wheel trim rings, base/CS ($56). Rally wheels, base/CS ($88); CL ($48). Cast aluminum wheels, base/CS ($299); CL ($259). Intermittent wipers ($55). Tahoe/Sierra classic equipment, S10 ($595). Sport gypsy equipment, S10 ($972). Seat Trim, S10 ($24). High country bucket seats, S10 ($295). Custom two-tone paint, S10 ($200). Special

two-tone paint, S10 ($311). Sport two-tone paint, S10 ($227). Air conditioning, S10 ($705). Console, S10 ($108). Rear step bumper C-K Series, Fleetside ($189). Chromed front bumper guards C-K Series ($41). Exterior mirrors C-K Series ($50-$94). Body side molding package C-K Series ($115-$173). Rally wheels C10, K10, K Blazer ($115). Styled wheels C10, K10, K Blazer ($174). Cast aluminum wheels C10, K10, K Blazer ($299). Gage package, S10 ($55-$113). Tinted glass, S10 ($135-$190). Exterior mirrors, S10 ($50-$83). Speed control, S10 ($195). Radio: AM, AM/FM, AM/FM/clock, AM/FM stereo and stereo cassette, AM stereo/FM stereo/seek and scan ($112-$594). Scottsdale/High Sierra C-K Series ($250). Silverado/Sierra Classic C-K Series ($671). Conventional two-tone C-K Series ($72). Special two-tone C-K Series ($327). Deluxe two-tone C-K Series, Fleetside ($184-$370). Custom two-tone C-K Series, Fleetside ($531). Special Big Dooley two-tone Fleetside, dual wheels ($426-$444). Deluxe front appearance package C-K Series ($109). All-weather Air Conditioning C-K Series ($678-740). Chromed rear bumper C-K Series ($103). Silverado/Sierra classic package K Blazer ($1015). Special two-tone paint K Blazer ($170-$327). Exterior decor package K Blazer ($314-$471). Deluxe front appearance K Blazer ($109). Deluxe chromed bumpers K Blazer ($49). Body side moldings K Blazer ($115-$173). Scottsdale/High Sierra Suburban ($311-$459). Silverado/Sierra Classic ($1111-$1259). Conquista package El Camino ($195). Air conditioning El Camino ($750). Gage package El Camino ($115). Sport mirrors El Camino ($61). Rally wheels El Camino ($56). Wire wheel covers El Camino ($199).

HISTORICAL: Introduced September 21, 1984. Calendar year production: (all models) 1,325,491. Total pickup: 430,600. Total P-series: 46,978. Total Van/Sportvan: 171,329. Innovations: New Astro Van truck-line introduced. El Camino has new 4.3-litre base V-6. New 2.5-litre base engine for S-10 trucks with 4x4 drive. Custom two-toning extended to S-10 pickups. New 4.3-litre "Vortec Six" also used in Chevy Vans as standard engine. Full-sized trucks adopt new grille styling. Historical notes: Every new 1985 light-duty Chevy truck delivered by a Chevrolet dealer in the U.S. came with a one-year, $10,000 seat belt insurance certificate from MIC General Insurance Corp. at no additional charge. Under the policy, $10,000 would be paid to the estate of any occupant suffering fatal injuries as a result of an accident involving that vehicle while wearing a GM seat belt. The 1985 sales catalog also stated, "For three and a half decades there have been more Chevy trucks in use than any other make."

1986 CHEVROLET

1986 Chevrolet Silverado Fleetside Pickup (CMD)

LIGHT TRUCK — 1986 SERIES — (ALL ENGINES): — For 1986, Chevrolet's light-duty trucks were little changed in terms of styling and trim packages. However, a number of technical refinements were made in practically all of the product lines.

The El Camino featured a new instrument panel and revised gauge cluster graphics to modernize it. It continued to offer 35.5 cu. ft. of cargo capacity and a 1,250-pound payload. A four-speed automatic transmission with overdrive was made available with the standard 4.3-litre V-6. Both it and the three-speed manual gearbox were offered with this engine or the optional 5.0-litre V-8.

Also having a new high-tech instrument cluster was the compact S-10 pickup. Both the standard 2.5-litre EFI engine or the optional 2.8-litre V-6 were changed for improved performance, fuel economy and durability. A Throttle Body Injection (TBI) system, optional for the V-6, was another mechanical update. In boosted the horsepower rating by nine percent.

New for the S-10 Blazer was a redesigned instrument cluster, Throttle Body Injected V-6, low-pressure Delco/Bilstein gas shocks and new paint and trim options. Chevy advised that the 4x2 model was rising in popularity. The 4x4 mini-Blazer came with the Insta-Trac system, which let the driver shift from 4x2 to 4x4 high, and back again, without stopping.

Sportvans and Chevy Vans were again offered in G10/G20/G30 Series, with engines including the Vortec Six, a choice of two gas V-8s and Chevy's 6.2-litre diesel V-8 on G20/G30 models. One change for the season was that the conventional sliding door could be replaced, at no extra cost, by the 60/40 swing-out type incorporating a new sliding 90-degree door-check system. This change prevented door fouling between the right front side door and the forward side swing-out door.

1985 El Camino "Designer Series" Pickup

Full-size Blazers, for 1986, had new molded front bucket seats with folding seat backs. The cloth trim option included a reclining seat back feature and the passenger seat had the same slide-forward, easy entry system previously used on the S-10 Blazer. Three new paint colors — Canyon Copper Metallic, Nevada Gold Metallic and Steel Gray Metallic — were released. A new, Steel Gray top was designed expressly to go with the third added paint scheme.

Chevy's Suburban began its second half-century in 1986. The same three new colors available for the big Blazer were offered for the Suburban as well. New outboard arm rests were made a part of the year's reclining bucket seat option. According to Chevy, the Suburban could hold nine passengers and 40.8 cu. ft. of luggage behind the third seat when outfitted for use as a station wagon. With the second seat folded and the optional rear seat removed, it became a truck with a 167 cu. ft. cargo area and payload capacity up to 3,911 pounds.

Continuing as standard equipment on full-size Chevy pickups was the Vortec Six. Swirl-port cylinder heads helped it pump out 155 horsepower and 230 lbs.-ft. of torque. "It is the most powerful standard engine ever offered in a Chevy pickup" advised a press release. An electric booster fan, mounted ahead of the radiator, was a new feature used with the optional 7.4-litre V-8. The 5.0-litre and 5.7-litre gas V-8s, as well as the 6.2-litre diesel V-8, were used again. The diesel trucks came with a 50,000 mile warranty and had up to 148 horsepower (on trucks with over 8,500 pound GVW ratings.)

The Astro Van was back, with practically no obvious changes. Standard power for the commercial versions was Chevy;s 2.5-litre "Tech IV" power plant with EFI. The Vortec Six, with TBI and a five-speed manual transmission, was the standard power team for the Astro passenger van in 1986. This made it the most powerful of any down-sized van available in America. The Vortec six developed 155 horsepower, a five percent increase over 1985. With all auxiliary seats removed, the Astro passenger van provided 151.8 cu. ft. of cargo capacity, while the commercial version maxed-out at 183 cu. ft. Many industry observers felt that this model's rear-drive configuration made it better suited to commercial use than other mini-vans available from competing manufacturers.

I.D. DATA: The VIN has 17 symbols. The first three identify the country, manufacturer and type of vehicle. The fourth designates GVW range. The fifth, sixth and seventh identify the series, nominal rating and body style. The eighth identifies the engine. The ninth is the check digit. The tenth represents model year. The eleventh identifies the assembly plant. The last six are sequential production numbers.

Model	Body Type	Price	Weight	Prod. Total
El Camino — (½-Ton) — (117.1 in. w.b.) — (V-6)				
W80	Sedan Pickup	9572	3234	—
W80	Super Sport Pickup	9885	3239	—
K10 Blazer (4x4) — (½-Ton) — (106.5 in. w.b.) — (V-8)				
K18	Utility wagon	12,034	4444	—
S10 Blazer (4x4) — (½-Ton) — (100.5 in. w.b.) — (V-6)				
T18	Utility wagon	10,698	3152	—
Astro — (½-Ton) — (111 in. w.b.) — (V-6)				
M15	Cargo Van	8431	3258	—
M15	Passenger Van	9037	3434	—
M15	"CS" Passenger Van	9492	3509	—
M15	"CL" Passenger Van	10,216	3569	—
Chevy Van 10 — (½-Ton) — (110/125 in. w.b.) — (V-6)				
G15	Chevy Van (SWB)	8626	3700	—
G15	Sportvan (SWB)	10,232	4052	—
G15	Bonaventure (LWB)	11,290	4153	—
G15	Beauville (LWB)	11,622	4196	—
Chevy Van 20 — (¾-Ton) — (110/125 in. w.b.) — (V-6)				
G25	Chevy Van (SWB)	9257	3786	—
G25	Sportvan (LWB)	10,655	4244	—
G25	Bonaventure (LWB)	11,482	4345	—
G25	Beauville (LWB)	11,813	4388	—
Chevy Van 30 — (1-Ton) — (125 in. w.b.) — (V-8)				
G35	Chevy Van (V-6)	11,128	4526	—
G35	Sportvan	13,173	5117	—
G35	Bonaventure	14,001	5218	—
G35	Beauville	14,331	5261	—
G35	Cutaway Van	10,204	3906	—
Hi-Cube Van — (1-Ton) — (125/146 in. w.b.) — (V-8)				
G31	10-ft. Hi-Cube	13,492	5209	—
G31	12-ft. Hi-Cube	14,803	5886	—
Step-Vans — (125/133/178 in. w.b.) — (6 cyl.)				
P22	¾-Ton Steel Panel	14,338	5869	—
P32	1-Ton Steel Panel	14,422	6022	—
S-10 Pickup — (½-Ton) — (108.3/122.9 in. w.b.) — (V-6)				
S14	Fleetside "EL" (SWB)	5990	—	—
S14	Fleetside (SWB)	6999	2574	—
S14	Fleetside (LWB)	7234	2645	—
S14	Maxi-Cab (LWB)	7686	2713	—
C10 Pickup — (½-Ton) — (117.5/131.5 in. w.b.) — (V-6)				
C14	Stepside (SWB)	7904	3385	—
C14	Fleetside-6½-ft. (SWB)	7764	3432	—
C14	Fleetside-8-ft. (LWB)	7938	3595	—
C16	Suburban (LWB)	11,476	4279	—
C20 Pickup — (¾-Ton) — (131.5/164.5 in. w.b.)				
C24	Chassis & Cab (SWB/V-6)	9667	3570	—
C24	Stepside (SWB/V-6)	9253	3930	—
C24	Fleetside (SWB/V-6)	9113	3992	—
C24	Bonus Cab Pickup (LWB/L6)	11,103	4773	—
C24	Crew Cab Pickup (LWB/L6)	11,451	4834	—
C24	Suburban (LWB/V-8)	12,297	4771	—

NOTE: All C20s have eight-foot dispatch boxes.

Model	Body Type	Price	Weight	Prod. Total
C30 Pickup — (1-Ton) — (131.5/164.5 in. w.b.) (6-cyl.)				
C34	Chassis & Cab (SWB)	9843	4011	—
C34	Stepside (SWB)	10,381	4426	—
C34	Fleetside (SWB)	10,242	4426	—
C34	Chassis-Bonus Cab (LWB)	10,901	4451	—
C33	Bonus Cab Pickup (LWB)	11,282	4862	—
C33	Chassis-Crew Cab (LWB)	11,253	4512	—
C33	Crew Cab Pickup (LWB)	11,633	4923	—

NOTE: All C30s have eight-foot dispatch boxes.

GENERAL NOTE: "SWB" is shortest wheelbase listed above each series. "LWB" is longest wheelbase listed above each series. (Example: C30 Stepside (SWB) has 131.5 in. w.b., while C30 Bonus Cab Pickup (LWB) has 164.5 in. w.b.)

ENGINE: (Gas). Vee-block. OHV. Eight-cylinder. Cast iron block. Bore & stroke: 4.0 x 3.48 in. Displacement: 350 cu. in. (5.7-litre). Compression ratio: 8.3:1. Brake horsepower: 160 at 3800 R.P.M. Tax. horsepower: 51.2. Torque: 275 lbs.-ft. at 2400 R.P.M. Hydraulic valve lifters. Carburetor: Four-barrel.

NOTE: VIN Code "A". This engine manufactured by various GM divisions. Optional in Pickups, full-size Blazer and Suburbans w/heavy-duty emissions.

ENGINE: (Gas). Vee-block. OHV. Six-cylinder. Cast iron block. Bore & stroke: 3.5 x 2.99 in. Displacement: 173 cu. in. (2.8-litre). Compression ratio: 8.5:1. Brake horsepower: 125 at 4800 R.P.M. Tax. horsepower: 29.4. Torque: 150 lbs.-ft. at 2200 R.P.M. Hydraulic valve lifters. Induction system: TBI.

NOTE: VIN Code "B". Manufactured by Chevrolet. Optional in S10 Blazer and Pickups.

ENGINE: (Gas). Inline. OHV. Four-cylinder. Cast iron block. Bore & stroke: 4.0 x 3.0 in. Displacement: 151 cu. in. (2.5-litre). Compression ratio: 9.0:1. Brake horsepower: 92 at 4400 R.P.M. Tax. horsepower: 25.6. Torque: 134 lbs.-ft. at 2800 R.P.M. Hydraulic valve lifters. Carburetor: Two-barrel.

NOTE: VIN Code "E"; manufactured by Pontiac. Standard in S-10 Blazers and Pickups. Also standard in Astro commercial vans.

1986 Chevrolet Fleetside Pickup (OCW)

ENGINE: (Gas). Vee-block. OHV. Eight-cylinder. Cast iron block. Bore & stroke: 3.74 x 3.48 in. Displacement: 305 cu. in. (5.0 litre). Compression ratio: 8.6:1. Brake horsepower: 155 at 4000 R.P.M. Tax. horsepower: 44.76. Torque: 245 lbs.-ft. at 1600 R.P.M. Hydraulic valve lifters. Carburetor: Four-barrel.

NOTE: VIN Code "F". Manufactured by Chevrolet. Optional in full-size Pickups, Blazers, Suburban and El Camino. Also optional in light-duty vans with under 8500-lb. GVWs and El Camino.

ENGINE: (Gas). Vee-block. OHV. Eight-cylinder. Cast iron block. Bore & stroke: 3.74 x 3.48 in. Displacement: 305 cu. in. (5.0-litre). Brake horsepower: 160 at 4400 R.P.M. Tax. horsepower: 44.76. Torque: 235 lbs.-ft. at 2000 R.P.M. Hydraulic valve lifters. Carburetor: Four-barrel.

NOTE: VIN Code "H". Manufactured by Chevrolet. Optional in full-sized pickups, Blazer, Suburban and El Camino. Also optional in light-duty vans with under 8500-lb. GVW.

ENGINE: (Gas). Vee-block. OHV. Eight-cylinder. Cast iron block. Bore & stroke: 4.0 x 3.48 in. Displacement: 350 cu. in. (5.7-litre). Compression ratio: 8.2:1. Brake horsepower: 165 at 3800 R.P.M. Tax. horsepower: 51.2. Torque: 275 lbs.-ft. at 1600 R.P.M. Hydraulic valve lifters. Carburetor: Four-barrel.

NOTE: VIN Code "L". Manufactured by Chevrolet. Optional in full-size pickups and Blazers; Suburbans. Also optional in light-duty vans under 8500-lb. GVW.

ENGINE: (Gas). Vee-block. OHV. Eight-cylinder. Cast iron block. Bore & stroke: 4.0 x 3.48 in. Displacement: 350 cu. in. (5.7 litre). Brake horsepower: 185 at 4000 R.P.M. Tax. horsepower: 51.2. Torque: 285 lbs.-ft. at 2400 R.P.M. Hydraulic valve lifters. Carburetor: Four-barrel.

NOTE: VIN Code "M". Manufactured by Chevrolet. Optional in full-size pickups, Blazers and Suburbans.

ENGINE: (Gas). Vee-block. OHV. Six-cylinder. Cast iron block. Bore & stroke: 4.0 x 3.48 in. Displacement: 262 cu. in. (4.3-litre). Compression ratio: 9.5:1. Brake horsepower: 155 at 4000 R.P.M. Tax. horsepower: 38.4. Torque: 230 lbs.-ft at 2400 R.P.M. Hydraulic valve lifters. Induction system: TBI.

NOTE: VIN Code "N". Manufactured by Chevrolet. Standard in full-size pickups and Blazer and Suburbans and Vans.

ENGINE: (Gas). Inline. OHV. Six-cylinder. Cast iron block. Bore & stroke: 3.88 x 4.12 in. Displacement: 292 cu. in. (4.8-litre). Brake horsepower: 115 at 4000 R.P.M. Tax. horsepower: 36.13. Torque: 210 lbs.-ft. at 2800 R.P.M. Hydraulic valve lifters. Carburetor: Two-barrel.

NOTE: VIN Code "T". Manufactured by Chevrolet. Standard in Step-Vans and Crew Cab/Bonus Cab Pickups.

ENGINE: (Gas). Vee-block. OHV. Eight-cylinder. Cast iron block. Bore & stroke: 4.25 x 4.0 in. Displacement: 454 cu. in. (7.4-litre). Brake horsepower: 240 at 3800 R.P.M. Tax. horsepower: 57.8. Torque: 375 lbs.-ft. at 3200 R.P.M. Hydralic valve lifters. Carburetor: Four-barrel.

NOTE: VIN Code "W". Manufactured by Chevrolet. Available for motorhome chassis.

ENGINE: (Gas). Vee-block. OHV. Six-cylinder. Cast iron block. Bore & stroke: 4.0 x 3.48 in. Displacement: 262 cu. in. (4.3-litre). Compression ratio: 9.3:1. Brake horsepower: 140 at 4000 R.P.M. Tax. horsepower: 38.4. Torque: 225 lbs.-ft. at 2000 R.P.M. Hydraulic valve lifters. Carburetor: Two-barrel.

NOTE: VIN Code "Z". Manufactured by Chevrolet. Standard in El Camino.

ENGINE: (Diesel). Vee-block. OHV. Eight-cylinder. Cast iron block. Bore & stroke: 3.98 x 3.82 in. Displacement: 379 cu. in. (6.2-litre). Brake horsepower: 130 at 3600 R.P.M. Tax. horsepower: 50.69. Torque: 240 lbs.-ft. at 2000 R.P.M. Hydraulic valve lifters. Carburetor: Four-barrel.

NOTE: VIN Code "C". Manufactured by Chevrolet. Diesel option.

ENGINE: (Diesel). Vee-block. OHV. Eight-cylinder. Cast iron block. Bore & stroke: 3.98 x 3.82 in. Displacement: 379 cu. in. (6.2-litre). Brake horsepower: 148 at 3600 R.P.M. Tax. horsepower: 50.69. Torque: 246 lbs.-ft. at 2000 R.P.M. Hydraulic valve lifters. Carburetor: Four-barrel.

NOTE: VIN Code "J". Manufactured by Chevrolet. Diesel option.

ENGINE: (Diesel). Inline. OHV. Four-cylinder. Cast iron block. Bore & stroke: 3.46 x 3.62 in. Displacement: 137 cu. in. (2.2-litre). Brake horsepower: 62 at 4300 R.P.M. Tax. horsepower: 19.50. Torque: 96 lbs.-ft. at 2200 R.P.M. Hydraulic valve lifters.

NOTE: VIN Code "S". Manufactured by Isuzu of Japan. Diesel optional in S-10 Pickups and Blazers.

CHASSIS: (El Camino) Wheelbase: 117.1 in. Overall length: 201.6 in. Height: 53.8 in. Tires: P205/75R14

CHASSIS: (K10 Blazer) Wheelbase: 106.5 in. Overall length: 184.8 in. Height: 73.8 in. Tires: P215/75R15.

CHASSIS: (S10 Blazer) Wheelbase: 100.5 in. Overall length: 170.3 in. Height: 64.7 in. P195/75R15.

CHASSIS: (G10 Vans) Wheelbase: 110/125 in. Overall length: 178.2/202.2 in. Height: 79.4 in. Tires: (Chevy Van) P195/75R-15; (others) P205/75R15.

CHASSIS: (G20 Vans) Wheelbase: 110/125 in. Overall length: 178.2/202.2 in. Height: 79.4 in. Tires: (Chevy Van) P225/75R15; (others) P235/75R15.

CHASSIS: (G30 Vans) Wheelbase: 125 in. Overall length: 202.2 in. Height: 79.4 in. Tires: (Chevy Van) 8.75R-16.5C; (others) 8.75R-16.5D.

1986 Chevrolet Fleetside Indy 500 Pickup

CHASSIS: (Astro Van) Wheelbase: 111 in. Overall length: 176.8 in. Height: 74.5 in. Tires: P195/75R15.

CHASSIS: (Hi-Cube Van) Wheelbase: 125/146 in. Tires: 8.75 x 16.5D.

CHASSIS: (Stepvans) Wheelbase: 125/133/178 in. Tires: LT215/85R16C.

CHASSIS: (S10 Pickup) Wheelbase: 108.3/122.9 in. Overall length: 178.2/194.2 in. Height: 61.3 in. Tires: P195/75R14.

CHASSIS: (C10 Series) Wheelbase: 117.5/131.5 in. Overall length: 193.5/212.2 in. Height: 69.2 in. Tires: (Pickups) P195/74R15; (Suburban) P235/75R15.

CHASSIS: (C20/C30 Series) Wheelbase: 131.5/164.5 in. Overall length: 212.2/246.4 in. Height: 72.2 in. Tires: (C20 Pickups) LT235/85R16C; (C20 Suburbans/Bonus/Crew) LT235/85R16D (Rear E). The C30 pickups also use the latter sizes.

TECHNICAL: Same as 1985 except that the El Camino now offers both the three-speed and four-speed (with overdrive) automatic transmission with both the 4.3-litre V-6 and optional 5.0-litre V-8. The 4.3-litre engine and four-speed automatic with overdrive was standard. Also, the five-speed manual transmission (made available in May 1985) was now standard in Astro passenger vans.

SELECTED OPTIONS: (Retail Values) — Cab type air conditioning ($750). Van type air conditioning ($800). Dual air conditioning ($1100). Power door locks ($100). Power windows ($125). Cruise control ($100). Tilt steering ($100). Swivel bucket seats ($275). AM/FM stereo ($175). AM/FM stereo w/tape ($200). AM/FM stereo w/C.B. ($275). Sliding rear window ($175). Sunscreen glass ($200). Auxiliary fuel tank ($275). Custom wheels ($125). Dual rear wheels ($525). Aluminum pickup cap ($250). Fiberglass pickup cap ($350). Aluminum Stepvan body/Hi-Cube body ($1100). Trailering package ($175). Camping package ($225). Stake body ($1000). Long wheelbase van ($150). Eight-passenger package ($200). 12-passenger package ($350). Custom paint ($150). Two-tone paint ($100). Four-wheel-drive ($1500).

NOTE: These are not factory prices. They represent the approximate additional value these options will add to the retail price of a 1986 model truck at the time this catalog was published.

HISTORICAL: Introduced Fall 1985. Sales: (Nov. 1985-Nov. 1986). Chevy Van (139,338); Sportvan (19,455); (Astro) 95,701; S-10 (195,620); S-10 Blazer (170,742); El Camino (19,231); Blazer (41,866); Suburban (53,842); Pickups (438,422); (Total Chevrolet) 1,174,217. Innovations: Electronic fuel injection used for 2.8-litre gas V-6 for nine percent horsepower boost. New "high-tech" instrument cluster for many models. Vortec Six has increased horsepower. Diesel V-8 gets durable steel crankshaft, modular iron crankshaft, cast-aluminum pistons and glow-plug system for fast cold-engine starts. Five-speed manual transmission standardized for Astro. New sliding 90-degree door check system made no-cost option on vans. Historical Notes: Chevy Astro Van was included in a special "Century of the Automobile" display at the 1986 Iola Old Car Show. Chevrolet kicked-off a year-long celebration of its 75th year as an auto-maker in 1986.

CROSLEY

By William D. Siuru, Jr.

In 1939, multi-millionaire Powell Crosley started his automobile company. Crosley was building two-cylinder, air-cooled mini-cars in the days of 25¢-a-gallon gasoline and $700 Fords and Chevys. Thus, they were not an overnight success. By 1940, light-duty trucks were added to the line.

"Here's the truck that makes sense and makes money on service and deliveries," read the sales literature. "Low cost, low operating cost...parks where no other truck can park. Gives you 35 to 50 miles on a gallon of gasoline."

1941 Crosley (Commercial) Station Wagon (OCW)

Introduced in mid-1939 (as a 1940 model) was a fancy Parkway Delivery truck. There was also a station wagon, which was then considered a commercial vehicle. By the time the 1941 line bowed, in mid-1940, a Pick-Up, Panel Delivery and the Covered Wagon had been added for truck buyers. These, like the cars were powered by the twin cylinder Waukesha engine and rode a diminutive 80 inch wheelbase.

Critics scoffed. They said the little trucks were unsuitable for cargo carrying chores, but Crosley saw them as the modern replacement for the basket-equipped delivery bikes used by many small businesses. Light-duty hauling, Powell Crosley felt, had its place in the nation's commerce system.

Crosley was a good promoter. He introduced the Covered Wagon at Macy's department store in New York City. Cannonball Baker drove one of these on a cross-country endurance run. Nevertheless, despite fame and fanfare, this model found few buyers and was dropped in 1942 (by which time it had been renamed the "Garden Wagon.")

Shortly after the outbreak of World War II, Crosley took a shot a making a prototype military vehicle in hopes of landing some lucrative government contracts. It was, more or less, based on the U.S. Army specifications for a ¼-ton reconaissance car (which ultimately led to development of the Jeep). Crosley's version — called the "Pup" — was intended for use by the U.S. Navy. The few that were made are now considered collectable items.

1947 Crosley Pick-Up Truck (OCW)

During the war, Crosley stopped car and truck production and switched to war goods manufacturing. The company developed a four-cylinder, overhead camshaft engine for the navy. It had unusual block construction of brazed copper and sheet metal and was used in refrigeration, air conditioning and aircraft applications. This "Cobra" engine was put in some early postwar cars and trucks. It was soon discovered to be prone to electrolysis problems which could cause holes to form in the cylinders. A new CIBA (Cast Iron Block) engine was phased-in during 1946.

1947 Crosley Pick-Up Truck (rear view)

Trucks were not included in Crosley's 1946 model offerings, but returned in force the next season. They were, like the cars, completely revised, albeit still very small vehicles. The body was all-new, as was the more conventional CIBA water-cooled power plant, running gear and chassis components.

The postwar truck-line consisted of Pick-Up and Panel (it was no more than a station wagon with blanked-out rear side windows), plus two configurations (chassis-and-flatface cowl or cab-and-chassis) that could be customized to the needs of the customer. A relatively popular example of the latter were miniature fire engines built for use in industrial factories.

Even though Crosley trucks weighed about one-third as much as contemporary full-sized models from other makers, they were rated at a full quarter-ton capacity. Where they came up short, however, was in the cargo capacity department. Being over 15 inches shorter than a Volkswagen Beetle, they were limited in the size of load they could carry.

1948 Crosley Fire Truck (OCW)

1948 Crosley Pick-Up Truck (rear view)

Powell Crosley was the first to admit that his trucks were designed for inner-city use by commercial buyers whose demands were small: grocers, repairmen and flower shops. They turned in a mere 15-foot radius circle and required half as much parking space as a full-sized truck. Their economy benefits couldn't be bettered and intial prices were as low as $800.

1948 Crosley Sports Utility (OCW)

A major restyling took place in 1949. It was seen on the two trucks — Pick-Up and Panel — offered that year. A sales brochure described the Panel as the "most practical delivery truck on the streets" due to its ability to move through traffic with ease. Both models were rated for ¼-ton payloads and sold for under $900. By way of comparison, a 1949 Chevrolet ½-ton pickup listed for $1,253, a Dodge for $1,213 and a Ford for $1,302.

A new creation called the Farm-O-Road joined the line in 1950. This was an improved version of the Pup and had a 63 inch wheelbase, fold-down windshield and open two-passenger utility body. It came in Pick-Up or Dump models with hydraulic assist on the draw-bar available as a $150 option. Power-take-off attachments were provided front and rear. The Warner gear transmission featured six forward speeds. As the name implies, it could be used as a farm tractor or for road work. Only about 2,000 of these were sold.

1948 Crosley Panel Delivery (OCW)

In mid-1952, Crosley was sold to General Tire and Rubber Company. Apparently, a few leftover vehicles, including trucks, were sold and titled as 1953 models. Instead of continuing production, the new owner later wrote the acquisition off as a tax loss and sold its rights on several patents to other firms. Eventually, Crofton Diesel Engine Co. purchased rights to the power plant.

1951 Crosley Panel Delivery (Crosley Club)

W.B. Crofton hired a man named Robert W. Jones to work out a complete redesign of the Farm-O-Road. The result was an improved version of the utility vehicle. From 1959 to 1961, some 200 of these new Crofton "Bugs" were produced and sold by the San Diego, California company.

1953 Crosley "Pup" Utility (CAC)

Powell Crosley, Jr., passed away in 1961, about the same time that the last Crofton Bugs were available. In his 74 years he had been involved in many businesses — appliances, broadcasting, baseball and auto-making. Unfortunately, his light-duty truck venture seems to have taken a back seat to the others. Nevertheless, Crosley trucks are very popular with commercial vehicle collectors today — especially those with limited storage room!

1940 CROSLEY

1940 Crosley "Official Speedway" Pickup (IMSC/JLM)

CROSLEY — COMMERCIAL SERIES — TWO-CYLINDER: — In 1939 Powell Crosley, who had made millions in the radio and appliance business, embarked on building cars. The Crosley was the ultimate in economy transportation. It was powered by a two-cylinder, air-cooled Waukesha engine. The car sold for a mere $325. It was first offered in department stores, alongside Crosley radios and refrigerators. In 1940, the first Crosley aimed at the commercial market was offered. This was the "Parkway Delivery," designed for light, in-town delivery service by owners such as grocers and florists. It was rated at 350 pounds capacity. Besides being economical to purchase it was cheap to operate with fuel consumption in the 45 to 50 m.p.g. range. Top speed was under 50 m.p.h.

I.D. DATA: Serial number located in engine compartment below battery shelf. Starting: 20000 (For all 1940 Crosleys). Ending: 30000. Engine numbers located: On engine block. Starting: 12500 (For all 1940 Crosleys). Ending: 21000.

Model	Body Type	Price	Weight	Prod. Total
A	2-dr. Panel	324	990	—

ENGINE: Waukesha, L-head. Horizontally-opposed. Air-cooled. Two-cylinder. Bore & stroke: 3 in. x 2.75 in. Displacement: 38.9 cu. in. Compression ratio: 5.6:1. Brake horsepower: 12 at 4000 R.P.M. Net horsepower: 7.2. Solid valve lifters. Carburetor: Tillotson, downdraft, one-barrel.

CHASSIS: Wheelbase: 80 in. Length: 120 in. Height: 56 in. Front tread: 40 in. Rear tread: 40 in. Tires: 4.25 x 12 in.

TECHNICAL: Three-speed manual, synchromesh transmission. Speeds: 3F/1R. Floor-mounted gearshift lever. 6 inch diameter, single, dry-plate clutch. Torque tube drive. Semi-floating rear axle. Overall ratio: 5.57:1. Four-wheel mechanical brakes, cable activated. Pressed steel, drop center wheels.

OPTIONS: Heater ($13). Crosley 5-tube radio ($30).

HISTORICAL: Introduced: October 1939. Calendar year production: 422 (all Crosleys).

Pricing

	5	4	3	2	1
1940 **Crosley Commercial**					
Panel Delivery	470	950	1550	2200	3100

1941 CROSLEY

CROSLEY — COMMERCIAL SERIES — TWO-CYLINDER: — Several new models were added to Crosley's commercial series to join the Parkway Delivery. These included the Pickup Delivery and Panel Delivery. The Panel Delivery was like the station wagon. Its steel body had wooden side panels, but the side windows were omitted for the Panel Delivery. A chassis model consisting of hood, cowl, front fenders, square doors, windshield front seat, front floor pan and running gear was available on special order. All commercial cars were equipped with 500 pound capacity springs, except the Parkway Delivery, which came with 350 pound capacity springs. The stroke of the engine was reduced for 1941 by 0.25 inch to solve a weak crankshaft problem. Aslo, larger main bearings, improved oil cooling and a U-joint in the driveline were used. Floating brakes shoes were replaced by conventional ones.

I.D. DATA: Serial number located in engine compartment below battery shelf. Starting: 30700 (all Crosleys). Ending: 31999. Engine numbers located: On block. Starting: 21000 (all 1940 Crosleys). Ending: 24999.

Model	Body Type	Price	Weight	Prod. Total
CB-41-V	2-dr. Pickup Delivery	385	1100	—
CB-41-Y	2-dr. Parkway Delivery	375	1030	—
CB-41-P	2-dr. Panel Delivery	435	1125	—
CB-41-W	Chassis	—	—	—

ENGINE: Waukesha, L-head. Horizontally-opposed. Air-cooled. Two-cylinder. Bore & stroke: 3 in. x 2.5 in. Displacement: 35.3 cu. in. Compression ratio: 5.6:1. Brake horsepower: 12 at 4000 R.P.M. Net horsepower: 7.20. Two main bearings. Carburetor: Tillotson downdraft, single-barrel.

CHASSIS: Wheelbase: 80 in. Length: 120 in. Height: 56 in. Front tread: 40 in. Rear tread: 40 in. Tires: 4.25 x 12.

TECHNICAL: Three-speed manual, transmission. Speeds: 3F/1R. Floor-mounted gearshift lever. Six inch diameter, single disc dry-plate clutch. Semi-floating rear axle. Overall ratio: 5.57:1. Four-wheel, mechanical brakes. Pressed steel wheels.

OPTIONS: Heater ($13). Crosley 5-tube radio ($30).

HISTORICAL: Introduced: October 1940. Calendar year production: 2,289 (all Crosleys).

1941 Crosley Station Wagon

Pricing

	5	4	3	2	1
1941 **Crosley Commercial**					
Pickup Delivery	470	950	1550	2200	3100
Parkway Delivery	470	950	1550	2200	3100
Panel Delivery	480	975	1600	2250	3200

1942 CROSLEY

CROSLEY — COMMERCIAL SERIES — TWO-CYLINDER: — The Crosley line was the same in 1942 as in 1941.

I.D. DATA: Serial number located inside flange of right-hand cowl panel. Starting: 32000 (all Crosleys). Ending: 35050. Engine numbers located on engine block. Starting: 25000 (all Crosleys). Ending: 27179.

Model	Body Type	Price	Weight	Prod. Total
CB-42-P	2-dr. Panel Delivery	548	1080	—
CB-42-V	2-dr. Pickup Delivery	493	1100	—
CB-42-Y	2-dr. Parkway Delivery	493	1030	—
CB-42-W	Chassis	—	—	—

ENGINE: Waukesha, L-head. Horizontally-opposed. Air-cooled. Two-cylinder. Bore & stroke: 3 in. x 2.5 in. Displacement: 35.3 cu. in. Compression ratio: 5.6:1. Brake horsepower: 12 at 4000 R.P.M. Two main bearings. Solid valve lifters. Carburetor: Tillotson downdraft. Single-barrel.

CHASSIS: Wheelbase: 80 in. Length: 120 in. Height: 56 in. Front tread: 40 in. Rear tread: 40 in. Tires: 4.25 x 12.

TECHNICAL: Three-speed manual, synchromesh transmission. Speeds: 3F/1R. Floor-mounted gearshift lever. Six inch single-disc, dry plate clutch. Torque tube drive. Semi-floating rear axle. Overall ratio: 5.57:1. Four-wheel, mechanical brakes. Pressed steel wheels.

OPTIONS: Heater ($13). 5-tube Crosley Radio ($30).

HISTORICAL: Introduced: August 1, 1941. Calendar year production: 1,029 (all Crosleys).

Pricing

1942 Crosley Commercial	5	4	3	2	1
Pickup Delivery	470	950	1550	2200	3100
Parkway Delivery	470	950	1550	2200	3100
Panel Delivery	480	975	1600	2250	3200

1947 CROSLEY

1947 Crosley Pickup Truck (OCW)

CROSLEY — COMMERCIAL SERIES — FOUR-CYLINDER: — Unlike most other United States auto-makers, Crosley completely redesigned its post-war cars and trucks. While cars were made in model year 1946, commercial vehicles did not appear until early 1947. The slab-sided body styling was completely new. Originally, the Crosley was to have used an aluminum body. The 80-inch wheelbase was still used. Power came from Crosley's unique "Cobra Four" overhead cam engine that had a block made of sheet metal stampings copper-brazed together. This engine was developed during World War II and used for a variety of applications, such as in aircraft and PT boat generators. The Cobra Four was much less successful in the Crosley, because electrolysis problems set in after extended periods of use. After 1949, a cast-iron block was offered and many earlier models were retrofitted with this engine. Crosley's commercial line for 1947 included a Pickup, Cab-and-Chassis and Chassis model.

I.D. DATA: Serial number located in engine compartment on firewall. (January 1947 to October 10, 1947) Starting: CC47-10000. Ending: CC47-26999. (October 10, 1947 to December 1947) Starting: CC-27000. Ending: CC-31999. Engine numbers located on left front side of crankcase (January 1947 to September 24, 1947) Starting: CE7-5587. Ending: CE7-21999. (September 24, 1947 to December 1947) Starting: 22000. Ending: 28803.

Model	Body Type	Price	Weight	Prod. Total
CC-47	2-dr. Pickup	839	1180	—
CC-47	2-dr. Chassis & Cab	819	1110	—

ENGINE: Inline. Water-cooled. Four-cylinder. Stamped sheet metal block with copper brazing. Bore & stroke: 2.5 in. x 2.25 in. Displacement: 44.2 cu. in. Compression ratio: 7.5:1. Brake horsepower: 26.5 at 5400 R.P.M. Net horsepower: 10. Five main bearings. Overhead cam. Carburetor: Tillotson one-barrel model DV-9B.

CHASSIS: Wheelbase: 80 in. Length: 145 in. Height: 57 in. Front tread: 40 in. Rear tread: 40 in. Tires: 4.5 x 12.

TECHNICAL: Three-speed, non-synchromesh transmission. Speeds: 3F/1R. Floor-mounted gearshift lever.

OPTIONS: Radio and Antenna. Seat covers. Bumper guards.

HISTORICAL: Introduced: Pickup Truck: Jan. 1947; Cab & Chassis: June 1947. Innovations: New Cobra engine with brazed sheet metal construction. Overhead cam. "High" compression ratio.

Pricing

1947 Crosley Commercial	5	4	3	2	1
Pickup	440	870	1450	2050	2900

1948 CROSLEY

1948 Crosley Pickup Truck (DFW)

CROSLEY — COMMERCIAL SERIES — FOUR-CYLINDER: — 1948 was the best year for Crosley sales, including commercial models. Added to the line was a Panel Delivery and a Flat-face Cowl model. The Panel Delivery was essentially a two-door wagon without rear side windows. The Station Wagon was by far the most popular 1948 Crosley model. Economy was the key word in advertisements for Crosley trucks. Mileage claims were in the 35 to 50 m.p.g. range and overall operating cost were touted as being half of a full-sized vehicle's. The 15-inch turning circle was great for congested city traffic. The trucks were rated at a full quarter-ton capacity. The ads also made a point of "Prompt Delivery," a key factor in the car-starved early postwar years.

I.D. DATA: Serial number located on firewall in engine compartment. Starting: CC-32000. Ending: CC-61256. Engine numbers located on front left side of crankcase. Starting: 28804 (other numbers from 27270 to 28803 were used).

1948 Crosley Pickup Truck (CAC)

137

1948 Crosley Pickup Truck (BMM)

Model	Body Type	Price	Weight	Prod. Total
CC	2-dr. Pickup	839	1223	—
CC	2-dr. Panel Delivery	899	1265	—
CC	2-dr. Chassis & Cab	819	1110	—
CC	Chassis	729	—	—
CC	Flat Face Cowl	791	920	—

ENGINE: Inline. Water-cooled. Four-cylinder. Stamped sheet metal block with copper brazing. Bore & stroke: 2.5 in. x 2.25 in. Displacement: 44.2 cu. in. Compression ratio: 7.5:1. Brake horsepower: 26.5 at 5400 R.P.M. Net horsepower: 10. Five main bearings. Overhead cam. Carburetor: Tillotson, one-barrel.

CHASSIS: Wheelbase: 80 in. Length: 145 in. Height: 57 in. Front tread: 40 in. Rear tread: 40 in. Tires: 4.5 x 12 in.

TECHNICAL: Manual, non-synchromesh, transmission. Speeds: 3F/1R. Floor-mounted gearshift lever.

OPTIONS: Radio and antenna. Seat covers. Bumper guards. Cast iron engine.

HISTORICAL: Introduced: January 1948. Calendar year registrations: 2411.

Pricing

1948 Crosley Commercial	5	4	3	2	1
Pickup	440	870	1450	2050	2900
Panel	450	900	1500	2100	3000

1949 CROSLEY

1949 Crosley Panel Truck (DFW/MVMA)

138

COMMERCIAL — SERIES CD — FOUR-CYLINDER: — The Crosley was restyled for 1949. For the trucks this meant, essentially, a new front end. It included a flatter hood, revised grille, wraparound bumper, squarer front fenders, re-shaped wheel openings and headlamps that were spaced more widely apart. Crosley sales started on their downward spiral and only the Pickup and Panel were offered for commercial buyers. While the "Cobra Four" was standard until January 1949, the "CIBA" cast-iron block, with the same internal dimensions, replaced it after January 1, 1949 as standard equipment on all Crosleys.

I.D. DATA: Serial number located on firewall in engine compartment. Starting: CD-100001. Ending: CD-108628. Engine numbers located on front left side of crankcase. Starting: Engine numbers continued from 1948.

Model	Body Type	Price	Weight	Prod. Total
CD	2-dr. Pickup	849	1310	—
CD	2-dr. Panel Delivery	879	1343	—

ENGINE (Cobra Four): Inline. Water-cooled. Four-cylinder. Brazed copper/sheet metal block. Bore & stroke: 2.5 in. x 2.25 in. Displacement: 44 cu. in. Compression ratio: 7.8:1. Brake horsepower: 26.5 at 5400 R.P.M. Net horsepower: 10. Five main bearings. Overhead cam. Carburetor: Tillotson, one-barrel, model DY-9C.

ENGINE (Ciba Four): Inline. Water-cooled. Four-cylinder. Cast-iron block. Bore & stroke: 2.5 in. x 2.25 in. Displacement: 44 cu. in. Compression ratio: 7.8:1. Brake horsepower: 26.5 at 5400 R.P.M. Five main bearings. Overhead cam. Carburetor: Tillotson, one-barrel, model DY-9C.

CHASSIS: Wheelbase: 80 in. Length: 145 in. Height: 57 in. Front tread: 40 in. Rear tread: 40 in. Tires: 4.5 x 12.

TECHNICAL: Three-speed manual, non-synchromesh transmission. Speeds: 3F/1R. Floor-mounted gearshift lever.

OPTIONS: Crosley radio and antenna. Bumper guards. Heater and defroster. Turn signal indicators. Seat covers.

HISTORICAL: Introduced: November 1948. Calendar year registrations: 871.

Pricing

1949 Series CD	5	4	3	2	1
Pickup	450	900	1500	2100	3000
Panel	470	950	1550	2200	3100

1950 CROSLEY

1950 Crosley Pickup Truck (OCW)

COMMERCIAL — SERIES CD — FOUR-CYLINDER: — Sales of Crosleys continued their downward trend. Changes to 1950 models, over the previous year, were minor. A Pickup and Panel Delivery, rated at quarter-ton capacity, were still offered. At mid-year, Crosley offered its Jeep-like Farm-O-Road, which was aimed at the small farm market. Crosley even offered farm implements as options. It came in several versions including pickup, dump-truck and buckboard for four-person capacity. The Farm-O-Road had individual rear wheel braking that allowed it to turn around, essentially, in its own length.

I.D. DATA (Pickup and Panel Delivery): Serial number located on firewall in engine compartment. Starting: CD-200001. Ending: CD-206685. Engine numbers located on left front side of crankcase. Numbers continued from 1946.

1950 Crosley Farm-O-Road (CAC)

Model	Body Type	Price	Weight	Prod. Total
CD	2-dr. Pickup	769	1310	—
CD	2-dr. Panel Delivery	799	1343	—
—	Farm-O-Road	835	1100	—

ENGINE: Inline. Water-cooled. CIBA. Four-cylinder. Cast-iron block. Bore & stroke: 2.5 in. x 2.25 in. Displacement: 44 cu. in. Compression ratio: 7.8:1. Brake horsepower: 26.5 at 5400 R.P.M. Net horsepower: 10. Five main bearings. Overhead cam. Carburetor: Tillotson, one-barrel, model DY-9C.

CHASSIS (Trucks): Wheelbase: 80 in. Length: 145 in. Height: 57 in. Front tread: 40 in. Rear tread: 40 in. Tires: 4.5 x 12.

CHASSIS (Farm-O-Road): Wheelbase: 63 in. Length: 91.5 in. Height: 58 in. Front tread: 40 in. Rear tread: 40 in.

TECHNICAL: Non-synchromesh transmission. Speeds: 3F/1R. Four-wheel hydraulic disc brakes. Floor-mounted gearshift lever.

NOTE: Farm-O-Road has compound transmission with speeds of 6F/2R.

1950 Crosley Sedan Delivery (OCW)

OPTIONS: Crosley radio and antenna. Heater and defroster. Bumper guards. Seat covers. Turn signal indicators. Hydraulic drawbar and power-take-off. Farm-O-Road ($150). Plow for Farm-O-Road ($35). Cultivator/Harrow for Farm-O-Road ($50).

HISTORICAL: Introduced: (Trucks): October 1949. (Farm-O-Road): August 1950. Calendar year registrations: 422 (Trucks). Innovations: Hydradisc brakes were a first for the industry, although disc brakes were also used on 1950 Chrysler Town & Country Newports.

Pricing

1950 Crosley Commercial Series CD	5	4	3	2	1
Pickup	450	900	1500	2100	3000
Panel	470	950	1550	2200	3100
Farm-O-Road	420	840	1400	1950	2800

1951 CROSLEY

1951 Crosley Farm-O-Road (OCW)

COMMERCIAL — SERIES CD — FOUR-CYLINDER: — The Crosley line was given a face-lift. It consisted of a grille with a spinner in the center and V-shaped bumpers that increased the length by over three inches. The Pickup and Panel Delivery were now available as Super series models. Their main exterior feature, when so ordered, was a bodyside molding on the front fender and door.

I.D. DATA: Serial number located on firewall in engine compartment. Starting: CD-300001. Ending: CD-306958. Engine numbers located on front left side of crankcase. Numbers continued from 1950.

Model	Body Type	Price	Weight	Prod. Total
CD	2-dr. Super Pickup	870	1400	—
CD	2-dr. Super Panel Dely.	900	1400	—
—	Cab & Chassis	849	—	—
—	Farm-O-Road	—	1100	—

ENGINE: Inline. Water-cooled. CIBA. Four-cylinder. Cast-iron block. Bore & stroke: 2.5 in. x 2.25 in. Displacement: 44 cu. in. Compression ratio: 8.0:1. Brake horsepower: 26.5 at 5400 R.P.M. Net horsepower: 10. Five main bearings. Overhead cam. Carburetor: Tillotson, one-barrel, model DY-9C.

CHASSIS (Trucks): Wheelbase: 80 in. Length: 148 in. Height: 57 in. Front tread: 40 in. Rear tread: 40 in. Tires: 4.5 x 12.

CHASSIS (Farm-O-Road): Wheelbase: 63 in. Length: 91.5 in. Height: 58 in. Front tread: 40 in. Rear tread: 40 in.

TECHNICAL: Same as 1950.

1951 Crosley Pickup Truck (EK)

OPTIONS: Crosley radio and indicator. Heater and defroster. Bumper guards. Seat covers. Plow, cultivator, harrow (Farm-O-Road).

HISTORICAL: Introduced: October 1950. Calendar year registrations: 434 (trucks). Historical note: Crosley returned to conventional drum brakes after experiencing problems with the Hydradisc units.

1952 CROSLEY

1952 Crosley Sedan Delivery (EK)

COMMERCIAL — SERIES CD — FOUR-CYLINDER: — 1952 would be the last year for the Crosley marque. After losing, reportedly, millions of his own dollars on this automotive venture, Powell Crosley ceased producing cars in July 1952. Crosley Motors became part of the General Tire & Rubber Company industrial empire when it merged with the Aerojet Engineering Company. The Fageol Company obtained the rights to the Crosley engine and, for a while, sold an inboard boat engine based on the Crosley design. Later, rights to build the power plant were transferred to other companies like the Homelite Corporation, Fisher Pierce, Co. and Crofton Diesel Engine Co. The latter company produced a few hundred of its version of the Farm-O-Road calling it the "Bug." The slightly more than two-thousand Crosleys sold in 1952 were virtually identical to the previous year, except a Carter carburetor was now used.

I.D. DATA: Serial number located on firewall just below the hood. Starting: CD-400001 and up. Engine numbers located: Behind the distributor. Continued from previous year.

Model	Body Type	Price	Weight	Prod. Total
CD	2-dr. Super Pickup	870	1310	—
CD	2-dr. Super Panel Dely.	900	1343	—
CD	Farm-O-Road	—	1100	—

ENGINE: Inline. Water-cooled. Four-cylinder. Cast-iron block. Bore & stroke: 2.5 in. x 2.25 in. Displacement: 44 cu. in. Compression ratio: 8.0:1. Brake horsepower: 25.5 at 5200 R.P.M. Net horsepower: 10. Five main bearings. Carburetor: Carter, one-barrel, model WO-870S.

CHASSIS (Trucks): Wheelbase: 80 in. Length: 148 in. Height: 57 in. Front tread: 40 in. Rear tread: 40 in. Tires: 4.5 x 12 in.

CHASSIS (Farm-O-Road): Wheelbase: 63 in. Length: 91.5 in. Height: 58 in. Front tread: 40 in. Rear tread: 40 in.

TECHNICAL: Manual transmission. Non-synchromesh. Speeds: 3F/1R. Four-wheel hydraulic drum brakes.

OPTIONS: Crosley radio and antenna. Heater and defroster. Bumper guards. Seat covers. Plow, cultivator, harrow (Farm-O-Road).

HISTORICAL: Introduced: November 1951. Calendar year registrations: Trucks 243 in 1952; 32 in 1953.

Pricing

1952	5	4	3	2	1
Crosley Commercial Series CD					
Pickup	450	900	1500	2100	3000
Panel	470	950	1550	2200	3100
Farm-O-Road	420	840	1400	1950	2800

1959-1962 CROSLEY-CROFTON

1960 Crofton-Bug Utility (Reggie Rapp)

CROFTON — "BUG" SERIES — FOUR-CYLINDER: — After Crosley ceased production in 1952, other companies picked up the rights to produce the Crosley engine for industrial and marine applications. In addition, Crofton Marine Engineering Co. of San Diego, Calif., manufactured a slightly revised version of the Crosley Farm-O-Road, calling it the "Bug." The main modifications came in the way of higher performance from the Crosley designed engine, a longer overall length to handle more cargo and some interior and exterior styling changes. Crofton aimed the Bug at the commercial market and off-road sportsmen. A upgraded version called the "Brawny Bug" included a six-speed transmission, limited-slip differential, full crash pan and either high-flotation or cleated tires as standard equipment.

I.D. DATA: Serial numbers not available. Engine numbers not available.

Model	Body Type	Price	Weight	Prod. Total
—	Bug Utility	1350	1100	—
—	Brawny Bug Utility	1800	1300	—

NOTE: All information in this section based on 1961 sales catalog.

ENGINE: Crosley. Inline. Water-cooled. Four-cylinder. Cast iron block. Bore & stroke: 2.5 in. x 2.25 in. Displacement: 44 cu. in. Compression ratio: 9.0:1. Brake horsepower: 35 at 5200 R.P.M. Five main bearings. Overhead Cam.

CHASSIS: Wheelbase: 63 in. Length: 105 in. Height: 59 in. Front tread: 40 in. Rear tread: 40 in. Tires: 5.3 x 12 (Bug); 9.00 x 10 "high-flotation" or 7.5 x 10 cleated (Brawny Bug).

TECHNICAL: Synchromesh transmission. Speeds: 3F/1R. Floor-mounted gearshift lever. 6.5 inch single-plate clutch. Overall ratio: 5.38:1. Four-wheel, hydraulic drum brakes. Drivetrain options: Six-speed compound transmission with two-speed reverse ($100). Power-Lok differential ($40).

OPTIONS: Tow bar assembly ($28.50). Snowplow ($160). Bumper jack ($5.95). Wheel lug wrench ($1.44). Rubber front floor mat ($4.50). Tinted windshield ($10). Rear seats each ($26.65). Spare tire and wheel, 5.30 x 12 in. ($23.50). Spare tire and wheel, 6.00 x 13 in. ($39.65). Spare tire and wheel, 9.00 x 10 in. ($53.85). Dual rear wheels with wider rear fenders ($90). Folding canvas top ($100). All weather enclosure ($196). Hot water heater ($48.50). Deluxe high back seats each ($10). Optional paint color ($20). Power-take-off unit ($150). Right side windshield wiper ($9.95). Oil Filter ($12). Towing eye ($4.50). Trailer hitch ($8.50). Pintle hook ($18.50). Set of 6.00 x 9 tires ($60). Set of 6.00 x 13 tires ($55). Enginair tire pump ($10.40). Electric winch ($122.50).

HISTORICAL: Total production of Bugs and Brawny Bugs is estimated to be between 200 and 250. Listed in Crofton catalog as late as 1963.

Pricing

1959-1962	5	4	3	2	1
Crofton Bug Series					
Bug Utility	530	1050	1750	2450	3500
Brawny Bug Utility	570	1140	1900	2650	3800

DODGE

By Don Bunn (1917-1980)
Charles Webb (1981-86)

Edited by James M. Flammang

The first Dodge Brothers car was built on November 14, 1914. One day later, the first Dodge commercial chassis rolled off a production line. A Dodge dealer in Brooklyn, New York fitted it with a utility body.

An article in the November 29, 1916 issue of *Motor Traction* magazine described a Dodge Brothers van in London, a full year before Dodge produced such a vehicle here. It called this light-duty truck "a smart looking vehicle rated at 12 cwt load capacity." Bare chassis were shipped to Britain. The body was built by Charles Jarrott & Hetts Ltd., Dodge representatives in London.

1926 Dodge Commercial Car Express (JAW)

The American factory was continuously asked to produce such a vehicle based on the car chassis. Demand for the Dodges ran at such a torrid pace, though, that the factory was reluctant to attempt a commercial model. Eventually, dealer insistence and the United States Army forced the Dodge Brothers to enter the commercial field.

1930 Dodge ½-Ton Pickup (JAW)

The rugged Dodge car made its military mark in 1916, serving with General Pershing during the Mexican expedition against Pancho Villa. Pershing was so impressed by the Dodge's performance that he ordered his staff to use only Dodge cars. As a result, just a few years later, Dodge Brothers began building the first of thousands of commercial vehicles for World War I use as troop carriers, ambulances and light utility trucks. The first civilian Dodge commercial vehicle, produced in 1917, was virtually a duplicate of the screenside panel built for the army.

1932 Dodge Express (JAW)

The commercial vehicle differed from the car in its use of heavier springs, higher-angled steering column, under-seat gas tank and screen delivery type body. A Panel was added in 1918. The Screenside, Panel and a chassis-only made up the line until 1926.

1937 Dodge pickup truck (OCW)

Historians identify four series of early "commercial cars." In 1921, Dodge signed an agreement with Graham Brothers to source parts for Graham trucks to be marketed through Dodge dealers. The second series Dodge/Graham trucks used Dodge passenger car front styling and were made in 1923 only. Third series models (1924-1925) had longer wheelbases. On July 7, 1925, the fourth series — with totally enclosed cab and roll-up windows — appeared and lasted through 1926.

1939 Dodge Fire Department Brush Truck (OCW)

141

1954 Dodge 1-Ton Pickup (R. Perry Zavitz)

Walter P. Chrysler purchased Dodge Brothers on June 1, 1928. He immediately changed the name of all products — including light-duty trucks — back to Dodge Brothers. He substituted the four-cylinder engine from his new Plymouth and added a six-cylinder. Nevertheless, the truck-line continued, until 1933, generally as before.

1955 Dodge Power Wagon Fire Truck (Elliott Kahn)

The 1933 models were Chrysler Corporation's first totally revised ones; new from the wheels up. Included was Chrysler's inline six-cylinder engine (standard power plant through 1960), attractive modernized styling and the famous "humpback" type panel truck.

1956 Dodge Military Type Power-Wagon (DB)

In 1936, styling was changed to echo cars of that year. A ladder-type frame was adopted, converting the commercial cars into full-fledged trucks. The Commercial Sedan was the surviving model built on a beefed-up car chassis. Dodge's first-ever, specifically-designed ¾-ton was seen in 1937. Last year for the raised roof was 1938.

All-new styling ushered in 1939. This was the first year pickup box floors were of oak with steel skid strips. A new truck plant opened. Parking lights on 1940 models moved

to the top of the headlamp housings due to a change to sealed-beam lenses. In 1941, they moved to the cowl. Engine lineups were changed in 1942.

1956 Dodge Postal Delivery Van (C. Jester)

1957 Dodge Sweptline Pickup (OCW)

1959 Dodge Forward Control Walk-in Van (OCW)

The Power-Wagon, an adaption of the ¾-ton military 4x4 made for World War II, joined the line in 1946. No changes were apparent in 1947 models. Announcement date for Dodge's first all-new postwar models was January 1948. These B-1 models were revised from the frame up. A Route-Van was a mid-year introduction.

Fluid Drive for all light-duties arrived in 1950, along with steering column gearshifting for three-speed manual transmissions. A "lowside" box became available for ½-ton pickups. New grilles, hoods and instrument panels characterized the 1951-'52 B-3s, which also had double-acting Oriflow shocks for improved ride quality.

The B-4 Series of 1953 brought an era to a close. Dodge made its first attempts to target light-duty truck marketing efforts towards women by upgrading interior quality and comfort and adding an automatic transmission. Only two of the early postwar years — 1950 and 1953 — showed drops in market share. Years 1946 and 1947 were outstanding; not until 1968 would sales of Dodge trucks exceed the 1947 figures!

1965 Dodge A-100 Pickup (OCW)

In 1954, the Dodge C-1 series featured all-new cab styling with a one-piece curved windshield and redesigned instrument panel. It continued until April, 1955, when the C-3 line replaced it. Highlights of the C-3 were a wrap-around windshield, full-width rear window and further interior upgrades. The Town Wagon, a "suburban" type vehicle, was added in 1956, as was a roof-mounted radio.

1968 Dodge Sweptline Pickup (CW)

1957 was an important year in Dodge's truck history. Frontal styling was changed; the Sweptside D100 pickup was introduced; V-8s grew to 315 cu. in.; Power-Wagons with conventional cabs were added; push-button Load-Flite automatic appeared and a one-piece alligator hood was adopted. In 1958, full-width hoods and double head-lights were among innovations. A new Sweptline "cab-wide" pickup was added in 1959, but the Sweptside D100 disappeared in mid-year. Also new were suspended brake and clutch pedals, concealed running boards, an hydraulically-operated clutch, 318 cu. in. V-8 and restyled instrument panel. Changes were very minor in 1960.

Dodge lost market share in virtually every late '50s year, except 1959. Sales fell again, in 1960, and hit an all-time low (in terms of market share) the next season. After 1961, the trend was reversed.

1980 Dodge Power-Wagon Utiline Pickup (CW)

Dodge built a vast range of products between 1961 and 1971, becoming a true full-line light-duty truck-maker. This period started with use of the one-year-only Dart name. Cabs were seven inches lower, four inches wider and mounted on all-new frames with changed wheel-bases. Two slant-six engines replaced the old inlines as base equipment. An alternator was an industry first.

1983 Dodge Rampage 2.2L Sport Pickup (OCW)

Revisions to grilles and nameplates were the only changes for 1962. In mid-year, Dodge announced it would no longer make model-year changes and there were none for 1963. A Custom Sports Special was among the news of 1964. It included racing stripes and could be ordered with V-8s up to 426 cu. in. In mid-year, the A100 forward-control compact van line was released. It included pickup and (passenger) wagon models.

1983 Dodge Ram Maxi-Wagon Van (DNP)

January 1965 saw a return to single headlights, the use of a new grille and the adoption of double-wall box construction. Additional emphasis was placed on impacting the growing RV and camping market. A dash-mount lever was now used for gear selection with automatic transmissions. Among technical changes of 1966 was a close-ratio four-speed manual gear box.

Mid-1967 saw introduction of a 108 in. wheelbase A100 van. The "273" V-8 was dropped in favor of the "318" as a van option. The 383 cu. in. V-8 became available for all other light-duties. Dodge combined work with pleasure in the new-for-1968 high-styled Adventurer pickup. An

1986 Dodge Ram Sweptline Pickup (DNP)

attractive grille and vinyl top were among new options. This was the final season for the military-type Power-Wagon as a domestic offering. After all this excitement, 1969 was another "no change" year.

Dodge's second-generation van models were introduced in 1970. They had engines moved forward, improved front suspensions and new looks. They now came in all three light-duty weight classes in two wheelbase lengths and three body sizes. A 198 cu. in. slant-six became base engine. Dodge was the industry's leading van-maker. Standard pickups got a facelift. The Adventurer was heavily promoted. And all of this was carried over for 1971.

All-new 1972 models featured independent front suspension, lower and wider cabs, all-new interior and dash trims and a growing options list. Electronic ignition was added to the list at mid-season; the first ever for a light-duty truck. A landmark innovation of 1973 was the industry's first (extended) Club Cab model. A new grille graced the 1974 trucks and the Ramcharger 4x4 sport utility was launched. Vans had sliding cargo doors and the Club Cab option was available teamed with 4x4.

Innovations of the late-1970s included the release of full-time 4x4 systems and a 4x2 Ramcharger in 1975; a

dual rear wheel option for one-ton pickups in 1976; the introduction of the Dodge "Street Van" package (also in 1976); an "adult toys" marketing program for 1977 and the availability of the "L'il Red Truck" in 1978. Some annual changes in grilles and trim were seen, too. Quad rectangular headlamps characterized the 1979 models, which also had new hoods, new front ends and an optional Mitsubishi-built diesel engine option. Dodge began importing two small pickups from this Japanese maker.

There were no major changes in the 1980 lineup. For 1981, Chrysler's new chairman, Lee Iacocca, made more news than the change to single quad headlights and egg-crate grilles in regular Dodge trucks. A "new" accessory was a ram's head hood ornament.

1987 Dodge Rod Hall Edition Pickup (DTD)

In general, the 1981-1986 period has been marked by aerodynamic styling and the down-sizing of products in order to make Dodge trucks more efficient. At the same time, sports-performance model-options like the Rampage 2.2 package have returned a missing touch of excitement to the line. Highlights of this period include the release of the Miser package in 1983, the appearance of the mini-Ram Van wagon, the introduction of a shift-on-the-go feature for 4x4 Ramchargers and the all-new front-wheel drive Caravan series. In these same years, the Ram 50 mini-pickup gained a reputation for being one of the best trucks of its type in America.

1917 DODGE

1917 Dodge Screenside Commercial Car (DFW/SI)

½-TON DELIVERY — SERIES ONE — FOUR-CYLINDER: — The first Dodge Brothers screenside commercial car was driven off the line on October 18, 1917, with all-steel body built by Budd. Wheelbase was identical to passenger cars, but the chassis was longer, heavier and sturdier. *Automobile Topics* magazine best described the debut: "Frequent and increasing demands for its passenger car chassis to be used for commercial purposes has resulted in the production by Dodge Brothers, Detroit, of a light commercial car with pressed steel panel body with a black enamel finish, similar to that of the passenger models. The car has a standing roof with removable wire screen sides, a set of substantial oiled duck side curtains for both sides and the rear of the body, as well as for both sides and rear of the driver's seat, and, all told, it is precisely the kind of light delivery car that one would expect Dodge Brothers to build." Series One styling from the front bumper to the windshield was exactly the same as the Dodge Bros. car. So were the engine, transmission and axles. Springs were heavier, and the tire size was increased to 33 x 4. The steering column sat at a higher angle and the gas tank was under the driver's seat, which was upholstered in genuine leather. Driver's doors were roadster type. An extra rim was carried outside, on the left side just back of the driver's seat. Payload capacity was 1000 pounds. Body loading space was 72 x 43 inches wide, with 54-inch inside height. Standard equipment included oiled duck curtains for complete enclosure; two wire screens; electric horn; license brackets; tire pump, jack and tool kit; plus complete instrument panel with 60-mph speedometer, total/trip mileage recorder, oil pressure gauge, current indicator, locking ignition and lighting switch, choke, and instrument light.

I.D. DATA: Serial numbers on Commercial cars ran concurrently with those on Dodge passenger cars. The serial numbers were die-cut on a 2¾ x 5 in. aluminum plate attached to the right front upper toe-board. They were also stamped into the chassis on the center cross-member, under the front floorboard and near the right front door. Starting Serial No.: 116339. Ending: 217925. Engine numbers were stamped on a pad above the carburetor, on the left side of the cylinder block. Engine numbers are not available.

Model (½-Ton) — (114 in. w.b.)	Body Type	Price	Weight	Prod. Total
Comm. Car	Screenside	885	2610	Note 1

NOTE 1: Commercial cars were built on the same line as passenger cars; no production records available by type. Total calendar year shipments to dealers: 720 units.

ENGINE: Inline. L-Head. Four-cylinder. Cast iron block. Bore & stroke: 3⅞ x 4½ in. Displacement: 212.3 cu. in. Compression ratio: 4.0:1. Brake horsepower: 35 at 2000 R.P.M. Net (Taxable) horsepower: 24.03. Four main bearings. Solid valve lifters. Carburetor: Special design 7-6-24 Stewart.

CHASSIS: Wheelbase: 114 in. Tread: 56 in. Tires: 33 x 4 in.

TECHNICAL: Selective sliding gear transmission. Speeds: 3F/1R. Floor shift control. Dry plate disc clutch. Full-floating rear axle; spiral bevel gears. Shaft drive. Two-wheel mechanical brakes. Springs: (front) semi-elliptic; (rear) three-quarters elliptic. Vacuum feed fuel system. 12-volt North East single-unit starter-generator. Wheels: 12 hickory spokes (front and rear).

HISTORICAL: Introduced: November, 1917. Innovations: Passenger car styling on heavy-duty chassis. Historical notes: Commercial Car production began in late October, 1917. Deliveries to dealers began in November. These first Commercial Cars were considered 1918 models, since the Dodge Bros. model year ran from July 1 through June 30. Dodge Bros. also built thousands of vehicles for the U.S. Army during 1917, including touring cars, ambulances, screensides, troop carriers, and light repair

trucks. During World War I, the company also erected a plant to build recoil mechanisms for the French 155mm field piece after two other manufacturers failed. Dodge engineered the pieces, built the machines and plant, and produced the product. The Dodge Bros. factory was in Hamtramck, Michigan. Dodge was the fifth largest U.S. automaker in 1917.

Pricing

	5	4	3	2	1
1917 **Commercial Car — (½-Ton)**					
Screenside	890	1770	2950	4150	5900

1918 DODGE

1918 Dodge Express Truck (DFW/FLP)

½-TON DELIVERY — SERIES ONE — FOUR-CYLINDER: — Series One Commercial Cars continued basically unchanged except for mechanical improvements from 1917 to 1922. The Dodge Brothers did not believe in annual model introductions, or change for change's sake. Instead, they stated that improvements would be made at any time. The annual series for registration purposes ran from July 1 through the following June 30. On March 26, the first panel model was built, with chassis details and body size duplicating the screenside. Dodge called the panel a Business Car and the screenside a Commercial Car.

I.D. DATA: Serial numbers were in same locations as 1917. Starting: 217,926. Ending: 303,126. Engine numbers not available.

Model (½-Ton) — (114 in. w.b.)	Body Type	Price	Weight	Prod. Total
Comm. Car	Screenside	985	2610	2335
Bus. Car	Panel	1085	2640	1728

NOTE: Calendar year shipments to dealers. Production figures by type not available.

ENGINE: Specifications same as 1917.

CHASSIS: Same as 1917.

TECHNICAL: Same as 1917.

HISTORICAL: Introduced: Continuation of model year that began in October, 1917. Calendar year shipments to dealers: 10,271 (including chassis alone). Innovations: Heavier engine crankshaft. Roadster-type door curtains, with curved rod that opened with the door, replaced the original roll curtains over driver's door in June, 1918. Historical notes: In addition to screen and panel models, Dodge Brothers continued to produce a commercial chassis only, on which customers could mount their own bodies. This dependable chassis soon became a favorite with custom body builders. They used the Dodge chassis for many special-duty vehicles, including hearses, Hucksters, ambulances, station buses, suburbans, carry-alls, fire engines, paddy wagons, and light delivery vehicles. A total of 6133 commercial chassis were shipped in calendar year 1917. Dodge continued to rank fifth in auto sales.

Pricing

	5	4	3	2	1
1918 **Commercial/Business Car — (½-Ton)**					
Screenside	890	1770	2950	4150	5900
Panel	870	1750	2900	4100	5800

1919 DODGE

½-TON DELIVERY — SERIES ONE — FOUR-CYLINDER: — Screenside and panel trucks were unchaged in appearance for 1919. The Dodge Brothers were convinced that their policy of no annual model changes contributed heavily to the company's success. Hub caps were changed to a light aluminum stamping with the Dodge Bros. monogram on their faces. Cab floorboards were now covered with durable linoleum, and the four floorboard sections were individually bound on each edge with heavy aluminum strips.

I.D. DATA: Serial numbers were in the same locations as 1917-18. Starting: 303,127. Ending: 378,971. Engine numbers are not available.

Model (½-Ton) —	Body Type (114 in. w.b.)	Price	Weight	Prod. Total
Comm. Car	Screenside	1085	2610	8055
Bus. Car	Panel	1085	2640	2715

NOTE: Calendar year shipments to dealers. Production figures by type not available.

ENGINE: Same as 1917-18; see previous specifications.

CHASSIS: Same as 1917-18.

TECHNICAL: Same as 1917-18.

HISTORICAL: Model year began July 1, 1918. Total calendar year shipments to dealers: 15,612 (including chassis alone). Historical notes: The first Dodge Brothers taxi was built on September 9, 1919; the first limousine in October. Total vehicle production (passenger and commercial) climbed to 105,398. The Dodges won their long-standing lawsuit against Henry Ford and were paid $25 million for their stock, which had originally been purchased for $10,000. Dodge ended the year fourth in automobile sales.

Pricing

1919	5	4	3	2	1
Commercial/Business Car — (½-Ton)					
Screenside	870	1750	2900	4100	5800
Panel	850	1700	2850	4000	5700

1920 DODGE

1920 Dodge Business Car (DFW/OHS)

½-TON DELIVERY — SERIES ONE — FOUR-CYLINDER: — A sales brochure for 1920 claimed that ''Dodge Brothers Business Cars offer a definite solution of the light transportation problem.'' The public must have agreed, as they purchased every unit the Dodges could push through their strained factory. Apart from the adoption of Kelsey steel-felloe wheels, product changes were minimal. Late in the model year, wheel size was reduced to 32 x 4. Standard equipment was the same as before.

I.D. DATA: Serial numbers were in the same locations as 1917-19. Starting: 378,972. Ending: 569,548. Engine numbers are not available.

1920 Dodge Commercial Car (DB)

Model (½-Ton) —	Body Type (114 in. w.b.)	Price	Weight	Prod. Total
Comm. Car	Screenside	1270	2610	9064
Bus. Car	Panel	1330	2640	5106

NOTE: Calendar year shipments to dealers. Production figures by type are not available.

ENGINE: Same as 1917-19; see previous specifications.

CHASSIS: Same as 1917-19 except for late change to 32 x 4 wheels.

TECHNICAL: Same as 1917-19.

HISTORICAL: Model year began July 1, 1919. Total calendar year shipments to dealers: 16,198 (including chassis alone). Historical notes: Business was very good for Dodge Brothers. During late 1919, the plants were hard pressed to turn out enough vehicles to meet the demand. Production continued to include chassis alone, as well as screen and panel models. John Dodge caught pneumonia and died January 14, 1920 at the Ritz-Carlton Hotel, where the brothers were staying while attending the New York auto show. Horace Dodge died in December of the same year, a victim of influenza while visiting Palm Beach, Florida. One of the brothers' last accomplishments was a plant expansion project that would double production capacity at Hamtramck, from 300 to 600 vehicles per day. Dodge rose to America's second best selling automobile in 1920.

Pricing

1920	5	4	3	2	1
Commercial/Business Car — (½-Ton)					
Screenside	840	1680	2800	3900	5600
Panel	830	1650	2750	3850	5500

1921 DODGE

1921 Dodge Commercial Car (OCW)

½-TON DELIVERY — SERIES ONE — FOUR-CYLINDER: — Frederick J. Haynes became the new company president on January 11, 1921, following the death of Horace Dodge. Haynes continued the Dodge family's policies. A severe economic depression cut deeply into the car market. Even though the Dodge work force would be drastically reduced by March, two million dollars in bonuses were paid to employees in January, 1921. One of Haynes' first official acts was to work out an agreement whereby Dodge would become the exclusive distributor of Graham Brothers trucks and buses. The Graham company agreed to use only Dodge engines, transmissions and front-end assemblies. Graham benefitted from Dodge Brothers' excellent dealer and parts organization, and consumer confidence in Dodge products. Dodge Brothers, in return, gained the experience, management and engineering skills of the Graham brothers. So Dodge became an instant full-line truck manufacturer without diluting its own management and engineering staff. Meanwhile, the half-ton screenside and panel commercial cars continued with minor changes. Top and windshield supports were added to the screenside in March. And in May, both received redesigned fenders, runningboards and splash shields. A heater was also added.

I.D. DATA: Serial numbers were located on a small plate fastened to the upper toe-board in the truck's front compartment. They were also stamped on the right side member of the frame, under the front fender, near the front spring's rear bracket. Starting: 569,549. Ending: 663,096. Engine numbers are not available.

Model (½-Ton) — (114 in. w.b.)	Body Type	Price	Weight	Prod. Total
Comm. Car	Screenside	1270	2610	5915
Bus. Car	Panel	1330	2640	3073

NOTE: Calendar year shipments to dealers. Production figures by type are not available.

ENGINE: Same as 1917-20; see previous specifications.

CHASSIS: Same as 1920.

TECHNICAL: Same as 1917-20.

1921 Dodge Panelside Business Car (OCW)

HISTORICAL: Model year began July 1, 1920. Total calendar year shipments of half-ton trucks: 10,731 (including chassis alone). Innovations: Heater available. Historical notes: A March, 1920 article in *Automobile Industries* announced a new Graham Bros. truck model, a 1½-tonner on a 130 in. w.b., powered by a four-cylinder Continental engine. In August, *Automobile Trade Journal* reported a new 18-passenger bus built on the Graham Brothers 1½-ton chassis. Graham Brothers produced and sold 1086 trucks and buses using Dodge engines, transmissions and front-end sheet metal. That pattern, which gave Graham success with their assembled trucks, would last until Chrysler Corp. purchased Dodge Brothers in 1928. Light commercials, screenside and panel models would be built by Dodge Brothers while heavier trucks were made by the Graham Brothers. Upon signing the agreement with Dodge, Graham Brothers immediately moved to Detroit and built a modern new factory. Dodge produced a total of 81,000 vehicles in 1921, ranking third in sales for the U.S. auto industry.

Graham Background: Born on a farm in Indiana, the three Graham brothers were originally in the glass-making business. They became very successful after developing a method to blow glass bottles that made the neck very strong. Bottles of the day had weak necks that were prone to break. In 1919, Ray Graham, the youngest brother, had invented a kit which converted the Model T Ford car into a serviceable little truck. After selling the glass business, the Grahams had time and money to spend on producing trucks.

Pricing

1921 Commercial/Business Car — (½-Ton)	5	4	3	2	1
Screenside	850	1700	2850	4000	5700
Panel	840	1680	2800	3900	5600

1922 DODGE

1922 Dodge open-cab pickup (DFW/JRH)

½-TON DELIVERY — SERIES ONE — FOUR-CYLINDER: — Early in the new year, the panel model received the new top and windshield supports given to the screenside in 1921. Tire size was changed to 33 x 4½ in November, 1921. Headlight lenses went from plain glass to rippled or fluted type. A major appearance change occurred on all Dodge Bros. cars in April, 1922, consisting of a 3½ in. higher radiator, hood and cowl. The higher hood went on the panel Business Car beginning with serial number 725468, on May 31; and on the screenside starting with number 725961, on June 5. Semi-floating rear axles replaced the full-floating type in a gradual phase-out that began on May 8. Finally, a North East speedometer replaced the Johns-Manville unit on June 20. Standard equipment also included an ammeter, windshield, electric horn, ignition-theft lock, demountable rims and tire pump.

I.D. DATA: Serial numbers were in the same location as in 1921. Starting: 663,097. Ending: 826,400. Engine numbers are not available.

Model (½-Ton) — (114 in. w.b.)	Body Type	Price	Weight	Prod. Total
Comm. Car	Screenside	1035	2610	9810
Bus. Car	Panel	1135	2640	5845

NOTE: Calendar year shipments to dealers. Production figures by type are not available.

ENGINE: Same as 1917-21; see 1917 specifications.

CHASSIS: Wheelbase: 114 in. Tires: 33 x 4 in. (33 x 4½ beginning in November, 1921). Wood-spoke wheels. Gross Weight Rating: 3850 lbs. (including chassis, body and payload).

TECHNICAL: Selective sliding gear transmission. Speeds: 3F/1R. Dry disc clutch. Semi-floating rear axle, spiral bevel gear drive. Rear-wheel mechanical brakes; emergency brake on rear wheels. Worm and worm wheel steering gear. Tubular radiator. Single-unit starter-generator. 12-volt electric system. Vacuum feed fuel system.

HISTORICAL: Model year began July 1, 1921. Total calendar year shipments of ½-ton trucks: 18,595 (including chassis alone). Model year vehicle production (passenger and commercial): 152,673. Historical notes: This was a very good year for Dodge Brothers as the company maintained third place in sales. Dodge's business coupe was the first all-steel enclosed-type body ever marketed by any automaker in the world. This was the final year for Series One commercial models. Dodge continued to supply Graham Brothers with chassis and engines. Graham produced 3401 trucks and buses using Dodge components: a 1-ton and 1½-ton, both on 140 in. w.b.

1922 Dodge Cantrell Station Wagon (CHC)

1923 DODGE

¾-TON DELIVERY — SERIES TWO — FOUR-CYLINDER: — More changes hit Dodge Brothers' commercial vehicles in the 1923 model year than anytime since production began. Beginning with serial number 723615, all commercial vehicles were rated at ¾-ton capacity. Early in the model year, the radiator was enlarged. In October, 1922, a new caution plate was affixed to all commercial cars. Appearance changes included slanting windshields and outside handles on drivers' doors. Panel models were made with one continuous side panel, eliminating the vertical half-round molding, which had been located in back of the driver's door. Steel runningboards replaced the original wooden boards, the horn button moved from the left front door to the steering wheel center, and the steering wheel's style was changed. Series Two vehicles were built only during this one model year. The 114 in. w.b. trucks began to be phased out just before the model year ended, on June 26, 1923. The last 114 in. units were serial number 927227 (panel) and 928100 (screenside). Standard equipment included a speedometer, ammeter, electric horn, ignition-theft lock, windshield wiper, demountable rims, rear wheel puller, and tire pump.

I.D. DATA: Serial numbers were in the same location as in 1921-22. Starting: 826401. Ending: 928140. Engine numbers are not available.

Model (¾-Ton) —	Body Type (114 in. w.b.)	Price	Weight	Prod. Total
Comm.				
Car	Screenside	880	2735	10,732
Bus. Car	Panel	980	2695	6737

NOTE: Calendar year shipments to dealers. Production figures by type are not available.

ENGINE: Inline. L-head. Four-cylinder. Cast iron block. Bore & stroke: 3⅞ x 4½ in. Displacement: 212.3 cu. in. Compression ratio: 4.0:1. Brake horsepower: 35 at 2000 R.P.M. Net (Taxable) horsepower: 24.03. Three main bearings. Solid valve lifters. Carburetor: Stewart.

CHASSIS: Wheelbase: 114 in. Tires: 32 x 4 pneumatic (cord). Tread: 56 in. Gross Weight Rating: 4405 lbs.

TECHNICAL: Selective sliding gear transmission. Speeds: 3F/1R. Dry disc clutch. Floor shift control. Semi-floating rear axle with spiral bevel drive. Rear-wheel mechanical (contracting) brakes; emergency brakes (expanding) on rear wheels. Worm and worm wheel steering. 12-volt electrical system. Engine lubrication: splash with circulating pump. Water pump cooling. Vacuum feed fuel system.

HISTORICAL: Model year began July 1, 1922. Total calendar year shipments of ¾-ton trucks (including chassis alone): 21,681. Calendar year sales (screenside and panel): 18,427. Innovations: Slanting windshields. Steel runningboards. Horn button on steering wheel. Historical notes: For the first time, Dodge Brothers advertising began to use the famous word "Dependable." Customers regularly told the factory how they could depend on Dodge cars, which led the ad writers to "Dodge Dependability." They also boasted that since production of commercial vehicles began, Dodge had sold "the unusual total of 102,000 units." Graham Brothers built and sold 6971 trucks and buses using Dodge engines and transmissions. Though constructed mainly of Dodge components, Graham truck chassis were built to carry heavier loads. They now had radiator and hub caps of their own design rather than the former Dodge style. This year, too, Graham began stamping Dodge serial numbers on the chassis under the right front fender, at the spring shackle. Graham Brothers trucks also carried the Dodge number on an aluminum toe-board plate, as on Dodge vehicles. Graham built seven truck series and three bus series of one and 1½-ton capacity. America's greatest World War I hero, Sergeant Alvin York, acquired a Dodge dealership in his native state of Tennessee. Dodge dropped to sixth place in car sales in 1923.

Pricing

	5	4	3	2	1
1923					
Commercial/Business Car — (¾-Ton)					
Screenside	870	1750	2900	4100	5800
Panel	850	1700	2850	4000	5700

148

1924 DODGE

1924 Dodge Commercial Station Wagon (OCW)

¾-TON DELIVERY — SERIES THREE — FOUR-CYLINDER: — Built only during the 1924 and 1925 model years, the Series Three retained most of the basic Dodge Brothers characteristics. Appearance changes included a taller radiator and higher hood line. Hoods were louvered. Headlamps were the popular drum-style. The tail lamp housing included a brake light, and was combined with a license plate bracket. Front fenders and runningboards were new. Wheelbase grew to 116 in. Rear springs were now underslung semi-elliptic rather than ¾-elliptic, lengthened to 55 in. Front springs were longer too, with thinner and wider leaves. Engine, transmission and rear axle remained as before. Gearshift and parking brake hand levers were relocated farther forward, while steering column angle was lowered. Overall vehicle weight was increased, but the center of gravity was lowered. The screenside cargo box was enlarged to 84 cu. ft. of loading space and 1500-pound payload capacity. Brake and clutch pedal pads were now rectangular rather than oval. Rubber floor mats were new and the driver's seat back gained coil spring construction. Standard equipment was the same as in 1923.

I.D. DATA: Serial numbers were in the same locations. During the model year, a new numbering system began, beginning with A-1001. [Early series] Starting: 930312. Ending: 982625. [New series] Starting: A-2386.

Model (¾-Ton) —	Body Type (116 in. w.b.)	Price	Weight	Prod. Total
Comm.				
Car	Screenside	895	2847	10,198
Bus. Car	Panel	995	2794	5151

NOTE: Calendar year shipments to dealers. Production figures by type are not available.

ENGINE: Same as 1923; see previous specifications.

CHASSIS: Wheelbase: 116 in. Tires: 32 x 4 (cord). Tread: 56 in. Gross Weight Rating: 4405 lbs.

TECHNICAL: Same as 1923; see previous specifications.

HISTORICAL: Model year began July 1, 1923. Total calendar year shipments of ¾-ton trucks (including chassis alone): 20,525. Model year production (passenger and commercial): 207,687. Historical notes: Dodge Brothers invested heavily in production facilities during 1924, spending $5 million to increase capacity. This would allow daily production of 1000 vehicles — about 200 more than the peak reached early in the year. On December 12, 1923, the one-millionth Dodge Brothers vehicle (a touring car) was built. Dodge had a great year, as demand outstripped production even after the plant expansion. Their reputation for quality continued to grow, as the company regained third place among U.S. automakers. A total of 141,662 Dodge commercial vehicles had been built and sold since 1917, not including the bare chassis on which other companies mounted special bodies. Graham Brothers had its best year ever, selling 10,743 vehicles. The line consisted of 13 truck and 12 bus models, rated one or 1½-tons. All Graham trucks used the standard Dodge four-cylinder engine.

Pricing

	5	4	3	2	1
1924					
Commercial/Business Car — (¾-Ton)					
Screenside	870	1750	2900	4100	5800
Panel	850	1700	2850	4000	5700

1925 DODGE

1925 Dodge 96-in. panel commercial car (DFW/WRL)

¾-TON DELIVERY — SERIES THREE — FOUR-CYLINDER: — Series Three commercial cars continued with little change, again offered in screenside and panel models as well as the basic chassis. Improvements included automatic windshield wipers, cowl vents, one-piece windshield, silchrome exhaust valves, oil drain piston rings, and balloon tires.

I.D. DATA: Serial numbers were in the same locations as in 1921-24. Starting: A-132707. Engine numbers were in the same locations. Starting Engine no.: A-205208.

Model (¾-Ton) —	Body Type (116 in. w.b.)	Price	Weight	Prod. Total
Comm. Car	Screenside	910	2847	13,215
Bus. Car	Panel	995	2794	8754

NOTE: Calendar year shipments to dealers. Production figures by type are not available.

1925 Dodge huckster wagon (DFW/WAD)

ENGINE: Same as 1923-24; see 1923 specifications.

CHASSIS: Wheelbase: 116 in. Tires: 32 x 4 (cord). Tread: 56 in. Gross Weight Rating: 4405 lbs.

TECHNICAL: Same as 1923-24; see 1923 specifications.

HISTORICAL: Introduced: July 1, 1924. Total calendar year shipments to dealers of ¾-ton trucks (including chassis alone): 26,696. Historical notes: Dodge was the fifth best-selling car in 1925, but the year's major event had to do with the organization rather than the product. On May 1, 1925, ownership of Dodge Brothers Inc. passed to Dillon, Read and Company, a New York banking syndicate. The widows of John and Horace Dodge were paid $146 million. Stock went public, but control remained in the hands of Dillon, Read and Co. Officers, management and policies remained as before. Robert C. Graham was named director of the Commercial Car and Truck Division. Earlier in the model year, in fact, a stronger bond between Graham and Dodge had been announced. On October 6, 1924, Graham Brothers became a division of Dodge Brothers Inc., while maintaining its own organization and product identity. Graham Brothers continued to operate its factory in Detroit and a body plant in Evansville, Indiana. Graham had another great year, nearly doubling 1924 production with a total of 24,298 trucks and buses built and sold. The 12 truck and 12 bus models were all either 1-ton or 1½-ton capacity. Beginning in May, 1925, Graham Brothers' frame serial numbers carried a "D", "E" or "S" prefix, denoting where the truck was assembled: Detroit, Michigan; Evansville, Indiana, or Stockton, California.

1925 Dodge panel commerical car (OCW)

Pricing

1925 Commercial/Business Car — (¾-Ton)	5	4	3	2	1
Screenside	870	1750	2900	4100	5800
Panel	850	1700	2850	4000	5700

1926 DODGE

1926 Dodge screen commercial car (OCW)

¾-TON DELIVERY — SERIES FOUR — FOUR-CYLINDER: — The new model year ushered in the first Dodge commercial cars with a totally enclosed cab. Dodge Brothers' policy from the beginning had been to make running changes at any time rather than to coincide with the new model year. A 140 in. w.b. chassis with 96 in. panel body was added to the shorter w.b. models in the lineup. Intended for businesses that handled large, bulky loads, the new panel had the same payload rating as the smaller trucks. Radiators were larger this year and the spare tire carrier was underslung.

I.D. DATA: Serial numbers were in the same locations. Starting: A-372475. Ending: A-702242. No engine numbers are available.

Model (¾-Ton) —	Body Type (116 in. w.b.)	Price	Weight	Prod. Total
Comm. Car	Screenside	885	2929	14,318
Bus. Car	72 in. Panel	960	2952	11,354
(140 in. w.b.)				
Bus. Car	96 in. Panel	1225	3208	591

NOTE 1: Calendar year shipments to dealers. Production figures by type are not available.

ENGINE: Same as 1923-25; see 1923 specifications.

CHASSIS: Same as 1924-25.

TECHNICAL: Same as 1925; see previous specifications.

HISTORICAL: Introduced: July 1, 1925. Total calendar year shipments to dealers of ¾-ton trucks (including chassis alone): 29,830. Calendar year production of all commercial vehicles (except Graham): 24,281. Model year production (passenger and commercial): 249,869. Innovations: Change to S.A.E. standard gearshift pattern. Disc wheels with balloon

1926 Dodge panel commercial car (OCW)

tires. Oil drain piston rings. Change from 12-volt to 6-volt electrical system. Separate starter and generator made standard. Historical notes: In November, 1925, Dodge Brothers bought a majority interest in the Graham Brothers company. Dodge President Frederick J. Haynes took on the additional job of chairman of the executive committee while E.G. Wilmer became chairman of the board. Joseph B. and Robert C. Graham were elected to the Dodge board, while Ray A. Graham became general manager of Dodge Brothers Inc. Graham continued to operate its truck division independently, selling through Dodge dealers. Early in 1926 Graham added a new factory in Stockton, California. Joseph was named Vice President of manufacturing in January, 1926. The Graham lineup consisted of 17 trucks and four buses rated 1-, 1½- and 2-ton capacity. Graham built and sold 37,463 vehicles during 1926. Early in the model year, work began on an $8 million plant expansion. By February, daily production reached 1500 vehicles, but couldn't meet the goal of 2000. Thus, production still lagged behind demand. Early in 1926, Dodge Bros. began the practice of allowing dealers to sit on its board, an industry "first." Late in the model year, all three Grahams resigned from their posts to start a new firm, Graham-Paige. Dodge Bros. purchased all the Graham stock. Wilmer became president, Haynes chairman. This was the last year that light delivery vehicles were marketed under the Dodge Bros. name by the original Dodge company. All trucks built in 1927 and 1928 would be sold as Graham Bros. trucks, even though Dodge wholly owned the Graham company, which actually built the vehicles. Dodge was the auto industry's fourth largest producer in 1926.

1926 Dodge screen commercial car (DFW/JC)

Pricing

1926	5	4	3	2	1
Commercial/Business Car — (¾-Ton) — (116 in. w.b.)					
Screenside	850	1700	2850	4000	5700
Panel (72 in.)	830	1650	2750	3850	5500
Business Car — (¾-Ton) — (140 in. w.b.)					
Panel (96 in.)	810	1620	2700	3800	5400

1927 DODGE

¾-TON DELIVERY — GRAHAM BROTHERS DC SERIES — FOUR-CYLINDER: — For the first time, Graham Brothers took over all truck production under its own name, even though the company was now wholly owned by Dodge. Graham Brothers' truck line consisted of a new ¾-ton series,

which was basically the former Dodge ¾-ton panel and screenside; two 1-ton series; plus 1½- and 2-ton truck and bus models. All used Dodge Brothers engines, transmissions and front-end sheet metal. Appearance changes of the ¾-tonners now wearing the Graham nameplate were minimal, except that the roof line extended over the windshield to form a sun shade. Windshields were one-piece and a double belt molding was added to cab doors. The major styling difference between new and former ¾-ton trucks was the oblong quarter window Graham Brothers added directly in back of the driver's door. That helped light the load compartment and contributed to safety by giving better visibility. In addition, quarter windows gave all Graham Brothers models a "big truck" look. This year also brought a reworking of the venerable old Dodge four-cylinder engine. A five-bearing crankshaft contributed to smoother performance. Bore and stroke remained the same, and developed horsepower remained at 35. All five-bearing engines had a "C" prefix with the engine number. On March 22, 1927, a new Morse chain drive replaced the timing gears, the oil pump was moved inside the crankcase, and both manifolds were placed on the engine's right side. Water pump, generator and distributor were also relocated. The new engine was designated the "124." Graham Brothers' trucks first received this engine on April 14, 1927. Beginning on January 3, 1927, a single plate Borg and Beck clutch replaced the Dodge-built dry disc type. Engines with the new clutch had a "D" prefix to their engine number. "D" models were known as series 126, the first series designation ever officially given to a line of Dodge Brothers vehicles. Standard equipment included a speedometer, ammeter, electric head and tail lamps, electric horn, air cleaner, automatic tire pump, jack, tools and tool box. Upholstery was leather over curled hair and coil springs.

1927 Graham Brothers Enclosed Cab Pickup (OCW)

1-TON — GRAHAM BROTHERS BD/ID SERIES — FOUR-CYLINDER: — Introduced by Graham in 1926 as the famous "G-Boy" series, the BD continued essentially unchanged for 1927. The only difference was company ownership. Graham Brothers' truck division had been totally taken over by Dodge. However, Dodge Brothers continued to build trucks in the Graham factories and sold them under the Graham name. Appearance was much like the ¾-ton line, except that one-tonners were built on two longer w.b. chassis and were equipped with steel spoke wheels. Standard equipment was the same as the ¾-ton models.

I.D. DATA: Serial numbers were located on the left side member of the frame, just back of the front spring's front bracket. Starting: A-702243. Ending serial number not available. Engine numbers not available.

Model (¾-Ton)	Body Type (116 in. w.b.)	Price	Weight	Prod. Total
DC	Chassis	670	4495	2742
DC	Canopy	870	4495	1012
DC	Express	845	4495	1473
DC	Panel	895	4495	8986
DC	Screen	885	4495	6757
(1-Ton)	**(126 in. w.b.)**			
BD	Chassis	895	5415	Note 2
BD	Canopy	1120	5415	Note 2
BD	Express	1085	5415	Note 2
BD	Farm Box	1115	5415	Note 2
BD	Panel	1160	5415	Note 2
BD	Stake	1115	5415	Note 2
(137 in. w.b.)				
ID	Chassis	980	5415	Note 2
ID	Canopy	1275	5415	Note 2
ID	Express	1240	5415	Note 2
ID	Panel	1320	5415	Note 2

NOTE 1: Calendar year shipments to dealers.

NOTE 2: Total calendar year shipments to dealers of 1-ton trucks: 16,992.

NOTE 3: Weights shown are GVW rating.

ENGINE: Inline. L-head. Four-cylinder. Cast iron block. Bore & stroke: 3⅞ x 4½ in. Displacement: 212.3 cu. in. Compression ratio: 4.0:1. Brake horsepower: 35 at 2000 R.P.M. Net (Taxable) horsepower: 24.03. Five main bearings. Solid valve lifters. Carburetor: Stewart.

CHASSIS (¾-Ton): Wheelbase: 116 in. Tires: 31 x 5.25 balloon on wood wheels.

CHASSIS (Series BD): Wheelbase: 126 in. Tires: 30 x 5 pneumatic on steel-spoke wheels.

CHASSIS (Series ID): Wheelbase: 137 in. Tires: Same as Series BD.

1927 Graham Brothers Model SD-770 Panel (HACJ)

TECHNICAL: Selective sliding gear transmission. Speeds: 3F/1R. Floor shift control. Dry multiple-disc clutch (later, single plate Borg & Beck). Semi-floating rear axle. Rear-wheel mechanical brakes. Hand brake (expanding) on rear wheels. Worm and wheel steering. Shaft drive. Springs: (front) semi-elliptic; (rear) semi-elliptic, underslung. Vacuum feed fuel system. 6-volt electrical system.

HISTORICAL: Introduced: July 1, 1926. Calendar year sales (Graham Brothers trucks): 42,359. Calendar year shipments to dealers: (¾-Ton) 20,969; (1-Ton) 16,992. Model year production (cars and trucks): 146,001. Innovations: Five-bearing crankshaft. Two-unit 6-volt electrical system. Single plate clutch. Four-point engine suspension. Convertible ¾-ton bodies used standardized parts, so owners could switch easily to another body type. Historical notes: Dodge ranked seventh in U.S. car sales and third in trucks. Graham Brothers built a wide range of truck bodies in its own plants, in Detroit, Evansville, and Stockton, California. The lineup included 13 truck models in 1½- and 2-ton capacity, plus three bus models. Dodge Brothers began to sell a commercial conversion for its sedan, coupe and roadster. Coupe/roadster conversions, offered in box and sliding-drawer form for the rear deck compartment, could be dealer-installed or ordered from the factory. Sedan conversions were available only from the Millspaugh and Irish Company. A removable rear seat was installed and the rear end was fitted with a single door, as in a panel or sedan delivery.

1927 Graham Brothers 1-Ton Panel Delivery (OCW)

1928 DODGE

1928 Graham Brothers ¾-Ton Panel Delivery (OCW)

½-TON — SERIES SD — FOUR-CYLINDER: — The all new SD panel delivery was based on Dodge Brothers' Fast Four automobile, which had been introduced in July, 1927 for the 1928 model year. Much lighter in weight, with w.b. shortened to 108 in., that Fast Four using the Dodge Brothers four-cyl. engine. Production of the SD, or Merchant's Express, began in September, 1927 and ran until July, 1928. Its handsome, low panel body featured a smart "cadet" front and sunvisor. The spare tire sat in the recessed left front fender. Built in the Graham Brothers factories and carrying that name, the SD was promoted for its ability to make prompt deliveries, with fast getaways and high speed runs. Standard equipment included front and rear fenders, front bumper, spare rim, air cleaner, electric head and taillights, stoplight horn, speedometer and ammeter, windshield wipers, rearview mirrors, and a tire pump.

¾-TON — SERIES DD — FOUR-CYLINDER: — Carried over unchanged from 1927, the DD was powered by the improved Dodge Brothers four-cylinder, five-bearing engine. Outselling all other Graham Brothers trucks, the panel body was padded to reduce road rumble. Convertible bodies were featured. Any standard body could be changed easily by adding or removing various standard units. If the owner of a pickup truck wanted to convert it into a canopy type, a standard canopy top could be mounted on the pickup body. The pickup could also be used as the basis for a panel or screen truck. Equipment was the same as the ½-ton model.

1-TON — SERIES BD/ID — FOUR-CYLINDER: — Both the BD (126 in. w.b.) and ID (137 in.) continued unchanged from 1927, powered by the improved Dodge four-cylinder engine. The BD was available as a chassis only, or a canopy, express, farm box, panel and stake body truck. The ID came in chassis form plus canopy, express and panel bodies. All bodies were convertible, like the DD series. Trucks were built in Graham Brothers plants and carried that nameplate. Equipment was the same as the ½-ton SD.

I.D. DATA: Serial numbers were in the same locations as 1927. (Detroit) Starting: D-151237. Ending: D-175589. (Evansville) Starting: E-127500. Ending: E-133096. (Stockton) Starting: S-107181. Ending: S-109834. Engine numbers not available.

Pricing

	5	4	3	2	1
1927					
Series DC — (¾-Ton) — (116 in. w.b.)					
Express	850	1700	2850	4000	5700
Canopy	840	1680	2800	3900	5600
Panel	800	1600	2650	3700	5300
Screen	850	1700	2850	4000	5700
Series BD — (1-Ton) — (126 in. w.b.)					
Express	750	1500	2500	3500	5000
Farm Box	690	1380	2300	3200	4600
Canopy	740	1470	2450	3350	4900
Panel	720	1450	2400	3300	4800
Stake	690	1380	2300	3200	4600
Series ID — (1-Ton) — (137 in. w.b.)					
Express	740	1470	2450	3350	4900
Canopy	720	1450	2400	3300	4800
Panel	700	1400	2350	3250	4700

1928 Graham Brothers 1-Ton Panel Delivery (OCW)

151

Model	Body Type	Price	Weight	Prod. Total
(½-Ton) — (108 in. w.b.)				
SD	Panel	770	3780	—
(¾-Ton) — (116 in. w.b.)				
DD	Chassis	670	2170	—
DD	Pickup	845	4570	—
DD	Panel	895	4570	—
(1-Ton) — (126 in. w.b.)				
BD	Chassis	895	2530	—
BD	Canopy	1130	5415	—
BD	Pickup	1095	5415	—
BD	Farm Box	1125	5415	—
BD	Panel	1170	5415	—
BD	Stake	1125	5415	—
(1-Ton) — (137 in. w.b.)				
ID	Chassis	980	2860	—
ID	Canopy	1235	5415	—
ID	Pickup	1200	5415	—
ID	Panel	1280	5415	—

NOTE: All weights except chassis alone are GVW.

ENGINE (All Models): Inline. L-head. Four-cylinder. Cast iron block. Bore & stroke: 3⅞ x 4½ in. Displacement: 212.3 cu. in. Compression ratio: 4.1:1. Brake horsepower: 35. Net horsepower: 24.03. Five main bearings. Solid valve lifters. Carburetor: Stewart.

CHASSIS (Series SD): Wheelbase: 108 in. Tires: 29 x 5.00 balloon. Payload: 1000 lbs.

CHASSIS (Series DD): Wheelbase: 116 in. Tires: 31 x 5.25 in. Payload: 1500 lbs.

CHASSIS (Series BD): Wheelbase: 126 in. Tires: 30 x 5 in. Payload: 2000 lbs.

CHASSIS (Series ID): Wheelbase: 137 in. Tires: 30 x 5 in. Payload: 2000 lbs.

TECHNICAL: Selective sliding gear transmission. Speeds: 3F/1R. Floor shift control. Single plate dry disc clutch. Semi-floating rear axle. Two-wheel mechanical brakes. Hand brake: (SD) contracting on propellor shaft; (others) expanding on rear wheels. Steering: (SD) worm and sector; (others) cam and lever. Vacuum fuel feed. Wood-spoke wheels.

HISTORICAL: Introduced: September, 1927. Calendar year registrations (all Graham Bros. trucks and buses: 36,542). Production figures not available. Dodge/Graham ranked third in sales among U.S. truck producers. Innovations: Hotchkiss drive replaced torque tube drive. New spiral bevel-gear rear axle was again semi-floating type. Millspaugh and Irish Corp. developed an All-Purpose Sedan Commercial Conversion for the Fast Four car. A new six-cylinder Dodge car engine was used in Graham Brothers 2- and 3-ton trucks and buses; it would be ready for smaller trucks in the next model year. This was the final production year for the Dodge Brothers Company. On July 30, 1928, Walter Chrysler — who had wanted the company for years — purchased Dodge Bros. for a $170 million exchange of stock. Chrysler wanted a car to compete with Ford, plus the excellent Dodge dealer network and huge manufacturing capabilities. On the night the deal was closed, Chrysler's people moved into the Dodge Bros. factories, taking over completely and dismissing staff, including president Wilmer. K.T. Keller was then appointed as the new president of Dodge Division. Dodge Bros. began producing six-cylinder cars in February, 1928 and the last four were built on July 27, 1928.

Pricing

	5	4	3	2	1
1928					
Series SD — (½-Ton)					
Panel	830	1650	2750	3850	5500
Series DD — (¾-Ton)					
Pickup	840	1680	2800	3900	5600
Panel	780	1560	2600	3600	5200
Series BD — (1-Ton)					
Pickup	750	1500	2500	3500	5000
Panel	720	1450	2400	3300	4800
Canopy	740	1470	2450	3350	4900
Farm Box	680	1350	2250	3150	4500
Stake	660	1320	2200	3100	4400
Series ID — (1-Ton)					
Pickup	740	1470	2450	3350	4900
Panel	700	1400	2350	3250	4700
Canopy	720	1450	2400	3300	4800

1928-1929 DODGE

½-TON MERCHANT'S EXPRESS — MODEL SE — SIX-CYLINDER: — After Dodge Bros. was sold to Chrysler Corp. in July, 1928, the new management had little time to plan, prepare and introduce new trucks for the 1929 model year. The ½-ton SD panel was discontinued in April, 1928, and immediately replaced by a Merchant's Express SE with 110 in. w.b. — 2 in.

longer than before. Essentially the same as its predecessor, the SE had a 6-cyl. engine, developed from the Victory Six car line, to replace the familiar old Dodge Bros. four. Only a panel body was offered, with loading space 67¾ in. long, 44½ in. wide (48¾ in. at beltline) and 44 in. high. The radiator shell, front bumper and filler cap were nickel plated. Standard equipment included full-length runningboards, spare tire carrier with extra rim, oil filter, air cleaner, electric horn, tail/stop light, instrument light, rearview mirror, windshield wipers, and tool kit.

¾-TON COMMERCIAL TRUCK — SERIES DA-120 — SIX-CYLINDER: — This new model appeared late in the model year to replace the Series DD. Appearance was similar to the DD, but the new truck sat on a longer 120 in. w.b. and was powered by a 6-cyl. engine rather than the original Dodge Bros. four. Model availability was expanded to include stake and platform styles. Painted in blue lacquer with gold moldings and cream-colored wheels, the ¾-ton had a chrome-plated radiator shell and filler cap. Standard equipment included full-length runningboards, front bumper, electric starter and horn, tail/stop light, dash light, oil filter, radiator shutter, speedometer, oil pressure and temperature gauges, ammeter, choke, locking ignition switch, license bracket, and tool kit. A spare rim sat in a tire carrier under the frame at rear.

1-TON — SERIES DA-130 and DA-140 — SIX-CYLINDER: — The DA-130 (130 in. w.b.) and DA-140 (140 in.) trucks were identical in appearance, except for the lengthened w.b., to the BD and ID models of 1928 that they replaced. Both were powered by the new 6-cyl. engine. The 130 in. chassis held an 8-ft. body, while the longer one mounted a 9-ft. body. Model availability of the smaller truck was the same as in 1928, but the DA-140 added side door panel, platform and stake bodies. Standard equipment was identical to the DA-120 but with short runningboards and a thermostat.

I.D. DATA: Serial numbers were on the left side member of the frame, just back of the front spring's front bracket. (Model SE) (Detroit) Starting: D-203830. (Evansville) Starting: E-141527. (Stockton) Starting: S-112553. (¾- and 1-ton) (Detroit) Starting: D-175590 (April, 1928). Ending: D-237361 (January, 1932). (Evansville) Starting: E-133097 (May, 1928). Ending: E-151171 (May, 1932). (Stockton) Starting: S-109835 (June, 1928). Ending: S-116399 (November, 1932). Engine numbers were located on the left front corner of cylinder block. (Model SE) Starting: J-31810. (¾- and 1-ton) Starting: M-120553.

1928 Dodge 1-Ton Panel Delivery (JAW)

Model	Body Type	Price	Weight	Prod. Total
(½-Ton) — (110 in. w.b.)				
SE	Chassis	665	1965	—
SE	Panel	845	—	—
(¾-Ton) — (120 in. w.b.)				
DA-120	Chassis	775	2510	—
DA-120	Chassis Cab	920	—	—
DA-120	Canopy	970	—	—
DA-120	Express	955	—	—
DA-120	Panel	995	—	—
DA-120	Screen	985	—	—
DA-120	Platform	975	—	—
DA-120	Stake	1020	—	—
(1-Ton) — (130 in. w.b.)				
DA-130	Chassis	995	2920	—
DA-130	Chassis Cab	1140	—	—
DA-130	Canopy	1240	—	—
DA-130	Express	1205	—	—
DA-130	Panel	1280	—	—
DA-130	Screen	1265	—	—
DA-130	Farm	1245	—	—
DA-130	Platform	1205	—	—
DA-130	Stake	1250	—	—
(1-Ton) — (140 in. w.b.)				
DA-140	Chassis	1065	2955	—
DA-140	Chassis Cab	1130	—	—
DA-140	Canopy	1330	—	—
DA-140	Carryall	1385	—	—
DA-140	Express	1295	—	—
DA-140	Panel	1375	—	—
DA-140	Side Door Panel	1425	—	—
DA-140	Screen	1365	—	—
DA-140	Platform	1280	—	—
DA-140	Stake	1330	—	—

ENGINE (All Models): Inline. L-head. Six-cylinder. Cast iron block. Bore & stroke: 3⅜ x 3⅞ in. Displacement: 208 cu. in. Compression ratio: 5.18:1. Brake horsepower: 63. Net horsepower: 27.34. Seven main bearings. Solid valve lifters. Carburetor: Stromberg or Stewart (buyer's choie).

CHASSIS (Model SE): Wheelbase: 110 in. Tires: 29 x 5.00 balloon (6-ply). Payload: 1000 lbs.

CHASSIS (Series DA-120): Wheelbase: 120 in. Tires: 31 x 5.25 balloon (6-ply) on 21 x 4 rims. Payload: 1500 lbs.

CHASSIS (Series DA-130): Wheelbase: 130 in. Tires: 30 x 5 (8-ply) on 20 x 5 rims. Payload: 2000 lbs.

CHASSIS (Series DA-140): Wheelbase: 140 in. Tires: 30 x 5 (8-ply) on 20 x 5 rims. Payload: 2000 lbs.

TECHNICAL: Selective sliding gear transmission. Speeds: (SE and DA-120) 3F/1R. (DA-130/140) 4F/1R with provision for power takeoff. Floor shift control. Single plate dry disc clutch. Semi-floating rear axle. Overall ratio: (SE) 4.455:1; (others) 5.1:1 (5.667:1 optional on DA-130/140). Spiral bevel gear drive. Four-wheel brakes: (SE) Steeldraulic mechanical with 2 x 12 in. drums; (others) Lockheed hydraulic. Hand brake on propeller shaft. Semi-elliptical springs: (SE) front 1¾ x 37 in., 9 leaves, rear 2 x 54 in., 8 leaves. (DA-120) front 2 x 39 in., 8 leaves; rear 2½ x 48 in., 9 leaves. (DA-130/140) front 2 x 39 in., 8 leaves; rear 2½ x 48 in., 10 leaves. Steering: (SE) worm and sector; (others) cam and lever (varying ratio). Fuel: (DA-120/130/140) vacuum feed; air cleaner and gas filter; 15-gallon gas tank under driver's seat. Allowable speed: (DA-120/130/140) 35 mph. Drop forged I-beam front axle. Wheels: (SE and DA-120) wood-spoke with steel felloes on demountable rims; (others) malleable iron spoke.

OPTIONS: (DA-120) 33 x 4½ high-pressure tires, front and rear ($15). 30 x 5 8-ply tires, front and rear ($55). Screen section hinged at top for rear end above tailgate ($15). (DA-130/140) 33 x 5 tires, front and rear ($35). 32 x 6 8-ply tires, front and rear ($45). 32 x 6 10-ply tires, front and rear ($125). Power tire pump ($12). Heavy-duty power tire pump ($12.50). Screen section hinged at top for rear end above tailgate ($15). Extra farm sides for 8-ft. stake ($40). Extra standard stake sides for 8-ft. Farm Box body ($45).

HISTORICAL: Introduced: (Model SE) April, 1928. (Series DA-120, DA-130, DA-140) late in 1927 model year. Calendar year production (1929): 47,014. Calendar year registrations (1929): 28,759. Production figures by model year and type not available. Innovations: four-wheel brakes (hydraulic on larger trucks). One effect of the new Chrysler Corp. influence was the abandonment of the Graham Bros. name on trucks. Beginning on January 1, 1929, all trucks, buses and motor coaches would carry the Dodge Bros. nameplate. That Dodge name was thought to have wider public acceptance and be more generally known. Besides that, the Graham Brothers were back in business building cars after a merger with the Paige-Detroit Co.

Pricing

1928-1929	5	4	3	2	1
Series SE — (½-Ton)					
Panel	810	1620	2700	3800	5400
Series DA-120 — (¾-Ton)					
Pickup Express	830	1650	2750	3850	5500
Panel Dely.	780	1560	2600	3600	5200
Canopy Dely.	800	1600	2650	3700	5300
Screen Dely.	810	1620	2700	3800	5400
Platform	750	1500	2500	3500	5000
Stake	740	1470	2450	3350	4900
Series DA-130 — (1-Ton)					
Pickup Express	750	1500	2500	3500	5000
Panel Dely.	700	1400	2350	3250	4700
Canopy Dely.	720	1450	2400	3300	4800
Screen Dely.	740	1470	2450	3350	4900
Platform	680	1350	2250	3150	4500
Stake	660	1320	2200	3100	4400
Farm	680	1350	2250	3150	4500
Series DA-140 — (1-Ton)					
Pickup Express	740	1470	2450	3350	4900
Panel Dely.	690	1380	2300	3200	4600
Canopy Dely.	700	1400	2350	3250	4700
Screen Dely.	720	1450	2400	3300	4800
Platform	660	1320	2200	3100	4400
Stake	660	1320	2200	3100	4400
Carryall	690	1380	2300	3200	4600
Side Door Panel	680	1350	2250	3150	4500

1929 DODGE

½-TON PANEL — MERCHANT'S EXPRESS — FOUR-CYLINDER: — In May 1929, the first all-new truck designed and built by Chrysler Corp. was introduced. This ½-ton panel used a Plymouth four-cylinder, 175.4 cu. in. engine. At $545, this was the lowest-priced chassis ever offered by Dodge for commercial use. In less than one model year, Dodge ½-ton production

1929 Dodge panel commercial car (OCW)

went from a 108 in. w.b. model with Dodge Bros. four, to a 110 in. SE with a six, to this 109 in. version powered by a smaller four. The new Merchant's Express was an attractive little truck with forward-sweeping roof line and "cadet" type overhanging sun shield. Front end appearance borrowed much from Chrysler's passenger cars. The windshield was flat and vertical, and the spare was carried in the left front fender. Two full-length rear doors gave access to cargo space. Interior dimensions were slightly larger than the SE it replaced: 72 in. long, 45½ in. between wheel wells (50 in. at the belt line), and 50 in. high, for a total of 102 cu. ft. Brakes were hydraulic. The 6-foot panel body was painted Blue, with Gray interior. Wood-spoke wheels were Cream with Black hubs; fenders were Black. Radiator shell and headlight rims were chrome plated. Standard equipment included full-length running boards, tail/stop light, panel light, automatic wipers, electric horn, electric starter, speedometer, oil pressure gauge, ammeter, choke, locking ignition switch, license bracket, and tool kit.

I.D. DATA: Serial number was located on left side member of frame, just back of the front spring's front bracket. Starting: P-1001. Engine number was on the left front corner of the cylinder block. Starting: UT-1001.

1929 Dodge Commercial Suburban Carryall (CHC)

Model (½-Ton) — (109 in. w.b.)	Body Type	Price	Weight	Prod. Total
Merch. Express	Chassis	545	1900	—
Merch. Express	Panel	795	2850	—

ENGINE: Inline. L-head. Four-cylinder. Cast iron block. Bore & stroke: 3⅝ in. x 4¼ in. Displacement: 175.4 cu. in. Compression ratio: 4.6:1. Brake horsepower: 45 at 2800 R.P.M. Net horsepower: 21.03. Three main bearings. Solid valve lifters. Carburetor: plain tube.

CHASSIS: Wheelbase: 109 in. Tires: 29 x 4.75 (6-ply) on 20 in. wheels. Payload: 1000 lbs.

153

TECHNICAL: Selective sliding gear transmission. Speeds: 3F/1R. Floor shift control. Single plate dry disc clutch. Semi-floating rear axle. Overall ratio: 4.7:1. Spiral bevel gear drive. Hydraulic four-wheel brakes; 1½ x 11 in. drums. Hand brake on propeller shaft. Springs: front 1¾ x 35½ in., 9 leaves; rear 1¾ x 53½ in., 13 leaves. Drop forged I-beam front axle. Worm and sector steering. Vacuum feed fuel system. Air cleaner. 11-gallon gas tank under frame at rear. Allowable speed: 40 mph. Wood-spoke wheels with steel felloes on demountable rims.

OPTIONS: Extra seat ($20). Bumpers, front and rear ($15).

HISTORICAL: Introduced: May 1929. Calendar year production (1929): 47,014. Calendar year sales (1929): 28,759. Production figures by model type not available. Innovations: hydraulic brakes. The new Merchant's Express, designed and engineered by Chrysler, began a trend that has lasted to the present time: Dodge trucks powered by one of the corporate engines. The ½-ton was powered by a Plymouth four, while ¾ and 1-ton models carried the Dodge car's six-cylinder engine. Dodge built a full line of trucks, up to 3-ton capacity, which were basically the former Graham Bros. trucks with a new nameplate. Dodge trucks ranked fourth in sales for 1929.

Pricing

	5	4	3	2	1
1929					
Merchant's Express — (½-Ton) — (109 in. w.b.)					
Panel	830	1650	2750	3850	5500

1930 DODGE

1930 Dodge Cantrell Commercial Station Wagon (CHC)

½-TON MERCHANT'S EXPRESS — SERIES UI-A-109 — FOUR-CYLINDER:
— The four-cylinder Merchant's Express entered its second year without appearance changes or engineering refinements. Three new body styles were added, including the first ½-ton pickup available from Dodge truck. That perky little pickup was constructed with cab integral to body, and featured two small, rectangular rear cab windows. Solid-panelled wood box sides were covered outside by sheet metal. Full-length flare boards and a full-width tailgate were constructed in the same manner. The pickup's cab shared with its larger mates the traditional Graham Bros. type rear quarter windows, which enhanced its businesslike good looks. Pickups were painted Dodge Blue with Yellow moldings, Black stripes, and Cream-colored wood-spoke wheels. Other models used the same scheme, except for Gold stripes on the screen truck. Pickup box inside dimensions were 60½ in. long by 45⅛ in. wide and 13¼ in. high. New screen and canopy models measured the same as the panel body, which continued without change. Standard equipment was the same as in 1929.

¾-TON COMMERCIAL TRUCK — SERIES UI-B-124 — FOUR-CYLINDER:
— An all-new ¾-ton truck with 124 in. w.b. — 4 in. longer than the previous version — came with hydraulic brakes and a choice of four or six-cylinder engine. Appearance reflected the corporate styling: cleaner and crisper than the former Graham Bros. look. The ¾-ton looked much like a large version of the Merchant's Express. Six body styles were available. Roomy, comfortable cabs had larger windshields and slender steel corner posts. Upholstery was leather. Paint scheme was Dodge Blue with Yellow moldings, Black stripes, and Cream wheels. Standard equipment included a chrome-plated radiator shell and filler cap, full-length running boards, spare rim under frame at rear, electric horn and starter, tail/stop light, air cleaner, crankcase ventilator, speedometer, oil pressure gauge, ammeter, choke, locking ignition switch, license brackets, and tool kit.

¾-TON COMMERCIAL TRUCK — SERIES DA1-B-124 — SIX-CYLINDER — Same as UI-B-124, but with six-cylinder engine.

1-TON — SERIES UI-C-133 — FOUR-CYLINDER — Dodge 1-ton trucks for 1930 mixed the new with the old. At 133 in. w.b. length, the new four was a stretched version of the ¾-tonner, with an 8-foot body rather than 7-foot. Priced lower than any 1-ton in Dodge history, it used the same Plymouth-based four-cylinder engine as the smaller trucks. Radiator shell and

filler cap were chrome plated. Standard equipment included a cowl ventilator, short or long running boards (depending on body type), spare rim under frame at rear, electric horn and starter, tail/stop light, thermostat, speedometer, oil pressure gauge, ammeter, locking ignition switch, choke, license brackets, governor, and tool kit.

1-TON — SERIES DA1-C-133 and DA1-C-140 — SIX-CYLINDER — Six-cylinder engines came in a 133 in. or 140 in. w.b. truck. The 140 in. models were carried over unchanged from 1929, continuing the old Graham Bros. styling with distinctive rear quarter cab windows. Standard equipment was the same as the four-cylinder.

I.D. DATA: Continuation of 1929 serial and engine numbers. See 1929 listing for details.

Model	Body Type	Price	Weight	Prod. Total
(½-Ton)	**— (109 in. w.b.)**			
UI-A	Chassis	545	1900	—
UI-A	Pickup	754	—	—
UI-A	Canopy	770	—	—
UI-A	Screen	795	—	—
UI-A	Panel	795	—	—
(¾-Ton)	**— (124 in. w.b.)**			
UI-B	Chassis	695	2260	—
UI-B	Chassis Cab	845	—	—
UI-B	Platform	905	—	—
UI-B	Pickup	935	—	—
UI-B	Canopy	960	—	—
UI-B	Stake	955	—	—
UI-B	Screen	985	—	—
UI-B	Panel	985	—	—
DA1-B	Chassis	795	2360	—
DA1-B	Chassis Cab	945	—	—
DA1-B	Platform	1005	—	—
DA1-B	Express	1035	—	—
DA1-B	Canopy	1060	—	—
DA1-B	Stake	1055	—	—
DA1-B	Screen	1085	—	—
DA1-B	Panel	1085	—	—
(1-Ton)	**— (133 in. w.b.)**			
UI-C	Chassis	795	2590	—
UI-C	Chassis Cab	945	—	—
UI-C	Platform	1015	—	—
UI-C	Farm	1055	—	—
UI-C	Stake	1065	—	—
UI-C	Express	1087.50	—	—
UI-C	Canopy	1102.50	—	—
UI-C	Screen	1152.50	—	—
UI-C	Panel	1152.50	—	—
DA1-C	Chassis	895	2690	—
DA1-C	Chassis Cab	1045	—	—
DA1-C	Platform	1115	—	—
DA1-C	Farm	1155	—	—
DA1-C	Stake	1165	—	—
DA1-C	Express	1187.50	—	—
DA1-C	Canopy	1202.50	—	—
DA1-C	Screen	1252.50	—	—
DA1-C	Panel	1252.50	—	—
(1-Ton)	**— (140 in. w.b.)**			
DA1-C	Chassis	1095	2955	—
DA1-C	Chassis Cab	1255	—	—
DA1-C	Platform	1335	—	—
DA1-C	Express	1385	—	—
DA1-C	Stake	1385	—	—
DA1-C	Canopy	1410	—	—
DA1-C	Screen	1440	—	—
DA1-C	Panel	1440	—	—
DA1-C	Carryall	1470	—	—
DA1-C	Side Door Panel	1475	—	—

ENGINE (UI-A-109, UI-B-124 and UI-C-133) Inline. L-head. Four cylinder. Cast iron block. Bore & stroke: 3⅝ in. x 4¼ in. Displacement: 175.4 cu. in. Compression ratio: 4.6:1. Brake horsepower: 45 at 2800 R.P.M. Net horsepower: 21.03. Three main bearings. Solid valve lifters. Carburetor: Carter.

ENGINE (DA1-B-124, DA1-C-133 and DA1-B-140) Inline. L-head. Six cylinder. Cast iron block. Bore & stroke: 3⅜ in. x 3⅞ in. Displacement: 208 cu. in. Compression ratio: 5.18:1. Brake horsepower: 63 at 3000 R.P.M. Net horsepower: 27.34. Seven main bearings. Solid valve lifters. Carburetor: (DA1-B-124) Zenith. (DA1-C-140) Stewart.

CHASSIS (UI-A-109) Wheelbase: 109 in. Tires: 20 x 5 (6-ply). Payload: 1000 lbs.

CHASSIS (UI-B-124, DA1-B-124) Wheelbase: 124 in. Tires: 20 x 5.50 (6-ply). Body length: 7 feet. Payload: 1500 lbs.

CHASSIS (UI-C-133 and DA1-C-133) Wheelbase: 133 in. Tires: 20 x 6.00 (6-ply) front and 32 x 6 (8-ply) rear. Payload: 2000 lbs.

CHASSIS (DA1-C-140) Wheelbase: 140 in. Tires: 30 x 5 (8-ply).

TECHNICAL: Selective sliding gear transmission. Speeds (½ and ¾-ton) 3F/1R; (1-ton) 4F/1R with provision for power takeoff. Floor shift control. Single plate dry disc clutch. Semi-floating rear axle. Spiral bevel gear drive. Overall ratio: (½-ton) 4.7:1; (¾-ton) 5.63:1 (6.00:1 and 5.11:1 optional); (1-ton) (UI-C-133, DA1-C-133) 5.6:1 (5.1:1 and 6.375:1 optional); (DA1-C-140) 5.1:1 (5.667:1 optional). Hydraulic four-wheel brakes. Hand brake on propellor shaft. Semi-elliptic springs: (½-ton) front 35 in., 9 leaves; rear 53½ in., 13 leaves. (¾-ton) front 39 in., 8 leaves; rear 48 in., 9 leaves. (1-ton) front 39 in., 8 leaves; rear 48 in., 11 leaves. Steering: (½-ton) worm and sector; (others) nut and lever (varying ratio). Vacuum feed fuel system. Air cleaner. Gas tank: (½-ton) 11-gallon, under frame at rear; (others) 15-gallon, under driver's seat. Allowable speed: 40 mph except DA1-C-140, 35 mph. Wood-spoke wheels with steel felloes on demountable rims except DA1-C-140, malleable iron spoke.

OPTIONS: (½-ton) Extra seat ($20). Bumpers, front and rear ($15). Front bumper only ($8.50). Rear bumper only ($6.50). (¾-ton) 33 x 4½ 6-ply tires with wood wheels ($17.50). 30 x 5 8-ply tires with metal spoke wheels ($50). Front bumper ($8.50). (1-ton) 30 x 5 8-ply tires on metal spoke wheels ($15). 20 x 6 6-ply tires front, 32 x 6 8-ply rear, with metal spoke wheels ($12). 20 x 6 6-ply front, 32 x 6 10-ply rear tires on metal spoke wheels ($32.50). Extra farm box sides for 8-foot stake body ($40). Extra standard stake sides for 8-foot farm box body ($50). Front bumper ($8.50). Long running boards and rear fenders for chassis only ($12.50). Power tire pump ($18.50).

HISTORICAL: Introduced: (UI-C-133) September 1929. Calendar year production: 23,316. Calendar year registrations: 15,558. Production figures not available by model year or type. Innovations: (4-cylinder) Fuel vacuum from oil pump rather than intake manifold. A 22 percent drop in U.S. truck registrations signalled the beginning of the Great Depression. Dodge suffered even worse, dropping 45.9 percent from 1929, yet ranking fourth in the truck sales race. The full Dodge line included four and six-cylinder engines, but only sixes were used to power 1½ to 3-ton trucks. As before, Dodge trucks were built at factories in Detroit; Evansville, Indiana; and Stockton, California.

Pricing

	5	4	3	2	1
1930					
Series UI-A-109 — (½-Ton)					
Pickup	830	1650	2750	3850	5500
Canopy	800	1600	2650	3700	5300
Screen	810	1620	2700	3800	5400
Panel	780	1560	2600	3600	5200
Series UI-B-124 — (4-cylinder) — (¾-Ton)					
Platform	600	1200	2000	2800	4000
Pickup	750	1500	2500	3500	5000
Canopy	720	1450	2400	3300	4800
Stake	630	1256	2100	3000	4200
Screen	740	1470	2450	3350	4900
Panel	700	1400	2350	3250	4700
Series DA1-B-124 — (6-cylinder) — (¾-Ton) — (Note 1)					
Series UI-C-133 — (4-cylinder) — (1-Ton)					
Platform	590	1170	1950	2700	3900
Farm	620	1230	2050	2900	4100
Stake	620	1230	2050	2900	4100
Express	740	1470	2450	3350	4900
Canopy	700	1400	2350	3250	4700
Screen	720	1450	2400	3300	4800
Panel	690	1380	2300	3200	4600
Series DA1-C-133 — (6-cylinder) — (1-Ton) — (Note 2)					
Series DA1-C-140 — (140 in. w.b.) — (1-Ton)					
Platform	590	1170	1950	2700	3900
Express	620	1230	2050	2900	4100
Stake	620	1230	2050	2900	4100
Canopy	700	1400	2350	3250	4700
Screen	720	1450	2400	3300	4800
Panel	690	1380	2300	3200	4600
Carryall	720	1450	2400	3300	4800
Side Door Panel	680	1350	2250	3150	4500

NOTE 1: For six-cylinder models, deduct five percent from figure given for equivalent four-cylinder (UI-B-124).

NOTE 2: For six-cylinder models, deduct five percent from figures given for equivalent four-cylinder (UI-C-133).

1931 DODGE

1931 Dodge with open passenger body (DFW/CCC)

½-TON — SERIES UF-10 — FOUR-CYLINDER / ½-TON — SERIES F-10 — SIX-CYLINDER: — Dodge entered the second year of the Great Depression fighting for sales. Two steps were taken in the ½-ton series to strengthen its position in the marketplace. First was the addition of a six-cylinder model, the F-10. Second was a substantial price cut of $110 for each model. The new series was identical in appearance to the 1930 Merchant's Express. Technical features varied only slightly, and all body types were carried over. Radiator shell was Black enamel, with chrome plated cap. Standard equipment included full-length running boards, cowl vent, automatic wipers, electric horn and starter, tail/stop light, speedometer, oil pressure gauge, ammeter, locking ignition switch, choke, thermostat, rear-view mirror, license brackets, spare rim in right front fender well, and tool kit.

¾-TON — SERIES UI-B-124 — FOUR-CYLINDER / ¾-TON — SERIES DA1-B-124 — SIX-CYLINDER: — These trucks were carried over from 1930 without change in either appearance or engineering specifications. Unlike the ½-ton and 1-ton models, their prices were not reduced. Body types and standard equipment were the same as before.

1-TON — SERIES UI-C-133 — FOUR-CYLINDER / 1-TON — SERIES DA1-C-133 — SIX-CYLINDER: — No changes were made in the carryover 1-ton trucks, except that the 140 in. w.b. model was discontinued and prices for the others were cut substantially. Standard equipment was the same as 1930.

I.D. DATA: (½-ton) Serial numbers were stamped on the left side member of the frame, just back of the front spring's front bracket. They were also on a serial number plate on the engine side of the cowl. (UF-10) Starting: 8000001 (August 1930). Ending: 8007264 (December 1932). Starting: 9200001 (December 1930). Ending 9200313 (October 1932). (F-10) Starting: 8100001 (August 1930). Ending: 8102959 (January 1933). Starting: 9212501 (January 1931). Ending: 9212717 (January 1933). Engine numbers were stamped on the top left front of the engine block. (UF-10) Starting Engine Number: UT21101. (F-10) Starting Engine Number: DD2T1001. (¾-ton) Serial numbers same as 1930. (1-ton) Serial numbers same as 133 in. w.b. models of 1930.

Model	Body Type	Price	Weight	Prod. Total
(½-Ton) — (109 in. w.b.)				
UF-10	Chassis	435	1900	—
UF-10	Pickup	644	—	—
UF-10	Canopy	660	—	—
UF-10	Screen	685	—	—
UF-10	Panel	685	—	—
F-10	Chassis	535	2000	—
F-10	Pickup	744	—	—
F-10	Canopy	760	—	—
F-10	Screen	785	—	—
F-10	Panel	785	—	—
(¾-Ton) — (124 in. w.b.)				
UI-B	Chassis	695	2260	—
UI-B	Chassis Cab	845	—	—
UI-B	Platform	905	—	—
UI-B	Pickup	935	—	—
UI-B	Canopy	960	—	—
UI-B	Stake	955	—	—
UI-B	Screen	985	—	—
UI-B	Panel	985	—	—
DA1-B	Chassis	795	2360	—
DA1-B	Chassis Cab	945	—	—
DA1-B	Platform	1005	—	—
DA1-B	Express	1035	—	—
DA1-B	Canopy	1060	—	—
DA1-B	Stake	1055	—	—
DA1-B	Screen	1085	—	—
DA1-B	Panel	1085	—	—
(1-Ton) — (133 in. w.b.)				
UI-C	Chassis	495	2590	—
UI-C	Chassis Cab	645	—	—
UI-C	Platform	715	—	—
UI-C	Farm	755	—	—
UI-C	Stake	765	—	—
UI-C	Express	787.50	—	—
UI-C	Canopy	802.50	—	—
UI-C	Screen	852.50	—	—
UI-C	Panel	852.50	—	—
DA1-C	Chassis	595	2690	—
DA1-C	Chassis Cab	745	—	—
DA1-C	Platform	815	—	—
DA1-C	Farm	855	—	—
DA1-C	Stake	865	—	—
DA1-C	Express	887.50	—	—
DA1-C	Canopy	902.50	—	—
DA1-C	Screen	952.50	—	—
DA1-C	Panel	952.50	—	—

ENGINE (UF-10): Inline. L-head. Four cylinder. Cast iron block. Bore & stroke: 3⅝ in. x 4¾ in. Displacement: 196.1 cu. in. Compression ratio: 4.6:1. Brake horsepower: 48 at 2800 R.P.M. Net horsepower: 21.02. Max. torque: 124 ft.-lbs. at 1200 R.P.M. Three main bearings. Solid valve lifters. Carburetor: Carter.

ENGINE (F-10): Inline. L-head. Six cylinder. Cast iron block. Bore & stroke: 3⅛ in. x 4⅛ in. Displacement: 189.8 cu. in. Compression ratio: 5.2:1. Brake horsepower: 60 at 3400 R.P.M. Net horsepower: 23.4. Max. torque: 120 ft.-lbs. at 1200 R.P.M. Four main bearings. Solid valve lifters. Carburetor: Carter. (¾ and 1-ton) Same as 1930 models.

CHASSIS: (½-Ton) Wheelbase: 109 in. Tires: 19 x 5.00 (4-ply). Payload: 1200 lbs.

CHASSIS: (¾-Ton) Wheelbase: 124 in. Tires: 20 x 5.50 (6-ply). Payload: 1500 lbs.

CHASSIS: (1-Ton) Wheelbase: 133 in. Tires: 20 x 6 (6-ply) front and 32 x 6 (8-ply) rear. Payload: 2000 lbs.

TECHNICAL: (½-Ton) Selective sliding gear transmission. Speeds: 3F/1R. Single plate dry disc clutch (9 in.) Semi-floating rear axle. Overall ratio: 4.66:1. Spiral bevel gear drive. Hydraulic 4-wheel brakes; 11 in. drums. Handbrake on propeller shaft. Semi-elliptical springs: front 1¾ x 35½ in., 8 leaves; rear 1 11/16 x 53½ in., 15 leaves. Semi-irreversible worm and sector steering. I-beam front axle. Gas filter. Fuel pump. 12-gallon gas tank under frame at rear. Allowable speed: 40 mph. Wood-spoke wheels with steel felloes on demountable rims. (¾ and 1-ton) Same as 1930 models.

OPTIONS: (½-Ton) Chrome plated spring-type front and rear bumpers. (¾ and 1-Ton) Same as 1930 models.

HISTORICAL: Introduced: September 1930. Calendar year production: 17,509. Calendar year registrations: 13,518. Production figures by model year and type not available. Innovations: Fuel pump replaced vacuum feed on ½-ton models. All except ½-ton had full floating rear axle. Dodge began for 1931 to divide its truck line into two categories. The Standard Line included ½, ¾, 1 and 1½-ton models, powered by four and six-cylinder engines. The Heavy Duty Line consisted of 2-ton and 3-ton trucks, all with sixes. This separation allowed more effective competition in the marketplace. The ½-ton had been developed along passenger car lines, following the modern trend. As the Depression strengthened its grip on the economy, Dodge sales fell 13.1 percent. But total industry sales dropped 23.6 percent, so Dodge still captured fourth place in U.S. truck sales.

Pricing

	5	4	3	2	1
1931					
Series UF-10 — (½-Ton) — (4-cylinder)					
Pickup	870	1750	2900	4100	5800
Canopy	840	1680	2800	3900	5600
Screen	850	1700	2850	4000	5700
Panel	830	1650	2750	3850	5500
Series F-10 — (½-Ton) — (6 cylinder) Note 1.					
Series UI-B-124 — (¾-Ton) — (4 cylinder).					
Platform	600	1200	2000	2800	4000
Pickup	750	1500	2500	3500	5000
Canopy	720	1450	2400	3300	4800
Stake	630	1256	2100	3000	4200
Screen	740	1470	2450	3350	4900
Panel	700	1400	2350	3250	4700
Series DA1-B-124 — (¾-Ton) — (6 cylinder) Note 2.					
Series UI-C-133 — (1-Ton) — (4 cylinder)					
Platform	590	1170	1950	2700	3900
Farm	620	1230	2050	2900	4100
Stake	620	1230	2050	2900	4100
Express	740	1470	2450	3350	4900
Canopy	700	1400	2350	3250	4700
Screen	720	1450	2400	3300	4800
Panel	690	1380	2300	3200	4600
Series DA1-C-133 — (1-Ton) — (6 cylinder) Note 3					

NOTE 1: For six-cylinder model F-10, deduct five percent from figure given for equivalent four-cylinder (UF-10).
NOTE 2: For six-cylinder model DA1-B-124, deduct five percent from figure given for equivalent four-cylinder (UI-B-124).
NOTE 3: For six-cylinder model DA1-C-133, deduct five percent from figure given for equivalent four-cylinder (UI-C-133).

1932 DODGE

1932 Dodge panel truck (DFW/CHC)

½-TON — SERIES UF-10 — FOUR-CYLINDER / ½-TON — SERIES F-10 — SIX-CYLINDER: — Introduced for 1931, the two ½-ton Dodge trucks continued into their second year without appearance changes or engineering refinements. Prices were again reduced as the Depression continued its hold on the economy. Standard equipment was the same as in 1931.

¾-TON — SERIES UI-B-124 — FOUR-CYLINDER / ¾-TON — SERIES DA1-B-124 — SIX-CYLINDER: — Except for price cuts to meet the lowered demand, these trucks entered 1932 unchanged.

1-TON — SERIES UI-C-133 — FOUR-CYLINDER / 1-TON — SERIES DA1-C-133 — SIX-CYLINDER: — Additional price cuts, beyond the substantial reductions of 1931, were the only changes for the Dodge 1-ton lineup.

I.D. DATA: Continuation of serial numbers that began in 1930-31. See 1931 listing for details.

Model (½-Ton) — (109 in. w.b.)	Body Type	Price	Weight	Prod. Total
UF-10	Chassis	375	1900	—
UF-10	Pickup	584	—	—
UF-10	Canopy	600	—	—
UF-10	Screen	625	—	—
UF-10	Panel	625	—	—
F-10	Chassis	475	2000	—
F-10	Pickup	684	—	—
F-10	Canopy	700	—	—
F-10	Screen	725	—	—
F-10	Panel	725	—	—
(¾-Ton) — (124 in. w.b.)				
UI-B	Chassis	490	2260	—
UI-B	Chassis Cab	640	—	—
UI-B	Platform	700	—	—
UI-B	Pickup	730	—	—
UI-B	Canopy	755	—	—
UI-B	Stake	750	—	—
UI-B	Screen	780	—	—
UI-B	Panel	780	—	—
DA1-B	Chassis	595	2360	—
DA1-B	Chassis Cab	745	—	—
DA1-B	Platform	805	—	—
DA1-B	Express	835	—	—
DA1-B	Canopy	860	—	—
DA1-B	Stake	855	—	—
DA1-B	Screen	885	—	—
DA1-B	Panel	885	—	—
(1-Ton) — (133 in. w.b.)				
UI-C	Chassis	495	2590	—
UI-C	Chassis Cab	645	—	—
UI-C	Platform	715	—	—
UI-C	Farm	755	—	—
UI-C	Stake	765	—	—
UI-C	Express	787.50	—	—
UI-C	Canopy	802.50	—	—
UI-C	Screen	852.50	—	—
UI-C	Panel	852.50	—	—
DA1-C	Chassis	595	2690	—
DA1-C	Chassic Cab	745	—	—
DA1-C	Platform	815	—	—
DA1-C	Farm	855	—	—
DA1-C	Stake	865	—	—
DA1-C	Express	887.50	—	—
DA1-C	Canopy	902.50	—	—
DA1-C	Screen	952.50	—	—
DA1-C	Panel	952.50	—	—

ENGINE: Same as 1931 models.

CHASSIS: Same as 1931 models.

TECHNICAL: Same as 1931 models.

OPTIONS: Same as 1931 models.

HISTORICAL: Introduced: Calendar year production: 10,713. Calendar year registrations: 8744. Production figures for model year and type not available. This was the all-time record low year for both the truck industry and Dodge truck sales, as truck makers tried to weather the storm of the Depression. Industry sales were down 42.5 percent, to only 180,413. Dodge fell 35.3 percent from 1931. Beginning in 1933, sales would again begin an upward climb. Dodge made no changes in its light-duty line for 1932, planning all new products for 1933. An 8-cylinder engine went into one of the Heavy-duty models, and two new 1½-ton models were introduced. The new G-80 8-cylinder chassis handled a 15,000-pound payload or 50,000-pound GCW. It also had automatic chassis lubrication from Alemite, providing constant oil to the chassis when the truck was in motion.

Pricing

	5	4	3	2	1
1932					
Series UF-10 — (½-Ton) — (4-cylinder)					
Pickup	870	1750	2900	4100	5800
Canopy	840	1680	2800	3900	5600
Screen	850	1700	2850	4000	5700
Panel	830	1650	2750	3850	5500

	5	4	3	2	1
Series F-10 — (½-Ton) — (6-cylinder) — (Note 1)					
Series UI-B-124 — (¾-Ton) — (4-cylinder)					
Platform	600	1200	2000	2800	4000
Pickup	750	1500	2500	3500	5000
Canopy	720	1450	2400	3300	4800
Stake	630	1256	2100	3000	4200
Screen	740	1470	2450	3350	4900
Panel	700	1400	2350	3250	4700
Series DA1-B-124 — (¾-Ton) — (6-cylinder) — (Note 2)					
Series UI-C-133 — (1-Ton) — (4-cylinder)					
Platform	590	1170	1950	2700	3900
Farm	620	1230	2050	2900	4100
Stake	620	1230	2050	2900	4100
Express	740	1470	2450	3350	4900
Canopy	700	1400	2350	3250	4700
Screen	720	1450	2400	3300	4800
Panel	690	1380	2300	3200	4600
Series DA1-C-133 — (1-Ton) — (6-cylinder) — (Note 3)					

NOTE 1: For six-cylinder model F-10, deduct five percent from figure given for equivalent four-cylinder (UF-10).

NOTE 2: For six-cylinder model DA1-B-124, deduct five percent from figure given for equivalent four-cylinder (UI-B-124).

NOTE 3: For six-cylinder model DA1-C-133, deduct five percent from figure given for equivalent four-cylinder (UI-C-133).

1933 DODGE

1933 Dodge commercial sedan (DFW/WRL)

½-TON — COMMERCIAL SERIES HC — SIX-CYLINDER: — An all-new, fully restyled, modern Commercial Series was announced in January 1933. Front end appearance was similar to the new Dodge passenger cars, with a sloping V-shaped radiator front, chrome-plated radiator shell, chromed windshield frame with rounded headers, fenders that concealed the chassis, and a hood that extended almost to the windshield base. Narrow, yet rigid cowl posts gave improved visibility. Doors were also passenger type, hinged at the rear, with a large window operated by hand crank. The Sedan Delivery featured a full-size rear door with large rectangular glass window, which allowed easy access to the load compartment. Inside, ⅛ in. thick rubber matting covered a heavy plywood floor. The body interior was finished in mahogany-look plywood veneer, illuminated by a dome light. The driver's seat and steering column were adjustable, and the hinged right-hand seat could be pushed forward out of the way. Body dimensions of the Commercial Sedan were 53 in. long, 44¾ in. wide and 44 in. high. Door opening was 35 in. wide by 37 in. high, and the floor was 26 in. above ground. The Commercial Pickup had a load space 63 in. long, 45¾ in. wide on the floor (50 in. at top), and 15½ in. high. Loading height was also 26 inches. The spare tire sat in a right front fender well.

½-TON — COMMERCIAL SERIES HCL — SIX-CYLINDER: — The 119 in. w.b. HCL lineup consisted of a chassis alone, chassis with cab, and Commercial Panel body. That panel model was the first of the famous Dodge "humpback" panels, with cab roof lower than the load compartment. Loading dimensions were 81 in. long at beltline (73 in. on floor), 57 in. wide at beltline (44¾ in. between wheelhouses), and 50⅝ in. high. Floor height was 26 inches. Wheelbase was the only difference between the HC and HCL series.

½-TON — SERIES UF-10 — FOUR-CYLINDER: — This would be the last four-cylinder Dodge for many years, carried over unchanged from 1932.

½-TON — SERIES F-10 — SIX-CYLINDER: — Continued into 1933 without change, the F-10 was also facing its final year in the Dodge lineup.

¾-1-TON — SERIES H-20 — SIX-CYLINDER: — Another new series, rated ¾ to 1-ton, was introduced in October 1932. Available only with panel body, it was a special model built down from the H-30 1½-ton line. Wheelbase was 131 in., gross weight rating 6000 lbs. It had a four-speed transmission and 203.1 cu. in. engine.

¾-1-TON — SERIES UG-20, UG-21 — FOUR-CYLINDER / ¾-1-TON — SERIES G-20, G-21 — SIX-CYLINDER: — These 131 in. and 157 in. w.b. trucks were carried over basically unchanged from 1932.

I.D. DATA: Serial numbers were located on a number plate on the engine side of the cowl. (HC) Starting: 8007301. Ending: 8017443. (HCL) Starting: 9201001. Ending: 9201576. (UF-10) (Detroit) Starting: 9200300. Ending: 9300313. (Evansville) Starting: 8007133. Ending: 8007264. (Los Angeles) Starting: 8102731. Ending: 8102959. (F-10) (Detroit) Starting: 9212689. Ending: 9212724. (H-20) Starting: 8483101. Ending: 8492872. (UG-20, UG-21) (Detroit) Starting: 8351688. (Los Angeles) Starting: 9243544. (G-20, G-21) (Detroit) Starting: 8481871. (Los Angeles) 9258645. Engine numbers were stamped on top left side of block, between cylinders one and two. (HC) Starting: TPD1001. (HCL) Starting: DTPP-1001. (UF-10) Starting: UT-21101. (F-10) Starting: DD-2-T1001. (H-20) Engine numbers not available.

Model	Body Type	Price	Weight	Prod. Total
HC Commercial Series — (½-Ton) — (111¼ in. w.b.)				
HC	Chassis & Cab	430	1775	—
HC	Pickup	450	2465	—
HC	Canopy	535	2525	—
HC	Commercial Sedan	555	2600	—
HC	Panel	—	—	—
HCL Commercial Series — (½-Ton) — (119 in. w.b.)				
HCL	Chassis & Cowl	365	2015	—
HCL	Chassis & Cowl	455	—	—
HCL	Panel	545	—	—
UF-10 Series — (½-Ton) — (109 in. w.b.)				
UF-10	Chassis	375	1925	—
UF-10	Screen	570	—	—
UF-10	Pickup	500	—	—
UF-10	Canopy	570	—	—
UF-10	Panel	570	—	—
F-10 Series — (½-Ton) — (109 in. w.b.)				
F-10	Chassis	445	1975	—
F-10	Screen	655	—	—
F-10	Pickup	580	—	—
F-10	Canopy	655	—	—
F-10	Panel	655	—	—
H-20 Series — (¾-1-Ton) — (131 in. w.b.)				
H-20	Chassis	502	2559	—
H-20	Panel	765	—	—
UG-20 Series — (¾-1-Ton) — (131 in. w.b.)				
UG-20	Chassis	537	2450	—
UG-20	Pickup	—	—	—
UG-20	Canopy	—	—	—
UG-20	Panel	—	—	—
UG-20	Sedan Delivery	—	—	—
G-20 Series — (¾-1-Ton) — (131 in. w.b.)				
G-20	Chassis	597	2520	—
G-20	Pickup	—	—	—
G-20	Canopy	—	—	—
G-20	Panel	—	—	—
G-20	Sedan Delivery	—	—	—

1933 Dodge Brothers 1-Ton Armored Cars (JE/NSPC)

ENGINE (Series HC/HCL): Inline. L-head. Six-cylinder. Cast iron block. Bore & stroke: 3⅛ in. x 4⅛ in. Displacement: 189.8 cu. in. Compression ratio: 5.5:1. Brake horsepower: 70 at 3600 R.P.M. Net horsepower: 23.44. Torque 130 lbs.-ft. at 1200 R.P.M. Four main bearings. Solid valve lifters. Carburetor: Downdraft.

ENGINE (UF-10 and F-10): Same as 1930-31 models.

ENGINE (H-20): Inline. L-head. Six-cylinder. Cast iron block. Bore & stroke: 3⅛ x 4⅜ in. Displacement: 201.3 cu. in. Compression ratio: 5.8:1. Brake horsepower: 62 at 3000 R.P.M. Net horsepower: 23.5. Torque: 132 lbs.-ft. at 1000 R.P.M. Four main bearings. Solid valve lifters.

CHASSIS (Series HC): Wheelbase: 111¼ in. Tires: 5.25 x 17 4-ply non-skid balloon (front/rear).

CHASSIS (Series HCL): Wheelbase: 119 in. Tires: 5.25 x 17 4-ply (front/rear).

CHASSIS (Series UF-10, F-10): Wheelbase: 109 in. Tires: 5.00 x 19 4-ply. Payload: 1200 lbs.

CHASSIS (Series H-20): Wheelbase: 131 in. Tires: 7.50 x 17.

TECHNICAL: Selective sliding gear transmission. Speeds: 3F/1R except (H-20) 4F/1R. Floor shift control. Single plate dry disc clutch: (HC/HCL) 9-inch. Semi-floating rear axle except (H-20) full-floating. Overall ratio: (HC/HCL) 4.37:1; (UF-10, F-10) 4.66:1. Hotchkiss drive. Hydraulic 4-wheel brakes: (HC/HCL) 10-inch drums with 1½ in. linings; (UF-10, F-10) 11-inch. Semi-elliptic springs: (HC/HCL) (front) 36 in. long, 7 leaves; (rear) 53½ in., 8 leaves; (UF-10, F-10) (front) 35½ in. long, 8 leaves; (rear) 53½ in., 15 leaves. Steering: Semi-irreversible worm and sector. Front axle: (HC/HCL) Tubular; (UF-10, F-10) I-beam. Gas tank: (HC/HCL) 15-gallon rear-mounted. Air cleaner. Mechanical fuel pump. Foot headlight dimmer. Wheels: (HC/HCL) Demountable wire wheels with drop-center rims; (H-20) Wire.

OPTIONS: (Series HC/HCL) Chrome front bumper ($7.50). Chrome rear bumper ($7.50). Allowance for Commercial Sedan body in primer ($8.00 net); Panel body ($6.00 net). Duplate safety plate glass on sedan, panel or cab ($14.50). Auxiliary seat for panel or canopy ($10.00). Screen sides for canopy model ($12.50). Rear screen lift for canopy ($14.00). Double screen rear doors ($15.00). Dual trumpet horns ($12.50). Dual taillights ($5.00). Auxiliary windshield wiper ($4.50). Metal tire cover ($5.00 ea.). Inside sun visor ($2.00 ea.). Free-wheeling ($8.00). Free-wheeling and automatic clutch ($17.50). Duplex air cleaner ($5.00). Vortex air cleaner ($16.00). Crankcase to air intake vent ($3.50). Monarch governor ($8.50). Hardy governor ($15.00). Duplate safety plate glass windshield ($3.50). Ornamental radiator cap ($2.00). Tire lock ($1.20). Side-mounted coach lamps for Commercial Sedan ($8.00). Chrome-plated radiator shell and headlamps ($5.00). Shock absorbers: double acting hydraulic, front/rear ($10.00). (Note on HC/HCL options: Unless dealer's order specified otherwise, ornamental radiator cap and tire lock were shipped. Bumper equipment was shipped as follows: on Commercial Sedan, front and rear bumpers; on pickup and canopy, front only; on panel, front and rear bumpers.) (UF-10, F-10) Chrome plated spring-type front and rear bumpers.

HISTORICAL: Introduced: (HC) January 1933; (H-20) October 1932. Model year began October 1, 1932. Calendar year registrations: 28,034. Calendar year production: 38,841. Production figures by model year or series not available. Innovations: Passenger car styling on Commercial series. First "humpback" Dodge panel model (HCL). Free-wheeling and automatic clutch. This was a transitional year for Dodge truck. Several new series of totally redesigned trucks, ranging in size from ½ to 2 tons, were brought to market over a period of several months. Designated the Standard Line, they included five series: the HC and HCL ½-ton Commercial series, the H-20 ¾-1-ton, H-30 1½-ton models, and H-43 2-ton trucks. In the light duty lineup, the UF-10 and F-10 ½-ton series and G/UG-20 ¾-1-ton models were carried over basically unchanged. Those two series retained their 1920s styling, with the old Graham Bros. look. Seven different six-cylinder engine sizes were offered. Larger 3-ton and 4-ton models were also carried over from 1932. Dodge bounced back with the new lineup to recapture third place in the truck sales race. The truck industry as a whole also recovered nicely, gaining 36.3 percent in registrations while Dodge truck rose a whopping 321 percent. Dodge trucks were manufactured in Hamtramck, Michigan.

Pricing

	5	4	3	2	1
1933					
Series HC — (½-Ton) — (111¼ in. w.b.)					
Pickup	870	1750	2900	4100	5800
Canopy	840	1680	2800	3900	5600
Comm. Sedan	850	1700	2850	4000	5700
Panel	830	1650	2750	3850	5500
Series HCL — (½-Ton) — (119 in. w.b.)					
Panel	810	1620	2700	3800	5400
Series UF-10 — (½-Ton) — (109 in. w.b.)					
Pickup	890	1770	2950	4150	5900
Canopy	850	1700	2850	4000	5700
Screen	870	1750	2900	4100	5800
Panel	840	1680	2800	3900	5600
Series F-10 — (½-Ton) — (109 in. w.b.) Note 1					
Series H-20 — (¾-1-Ton) — (131 in. w.b.)					
Panel	800	1600	2650	3700	5300
Series UG-20 — (¾-1-Ton) — (131 in. w.b.)					
Pickup	830	1650	2750	3850	5500
Canopy	810	1620	2700	3800	5400
Panel	780	1560	2600	3600	5200
Sedan Delivery	850	1700	2850	4000	5700
Series G-20 — (¾-1-Ton) — (131 in. w.b.) Note 2					

NOTE 1: For 6-cyl. model F-10, add 5 percent to figure given for equivalent 4-cyl. (UF-10).
NOTE 2: For 6-cyl. model G-20, add 5 percent to figure given for equivalent 4-cyl. (UG-20).

1934 DODGE

½-TON — COMMERCIAL SERIES KC — SIX-CYLINDER: — All new in 1933, the Commercial Series continued with only two changes. A drop-forged I-beam front axle replaced the former tubular type, and engine size was increased to 201.3 cu. in., now rated 75 horsepower. New canopy and screen models were added.

1934 Dodge commercial sedan (OCW)

½-TON — COMMERCIAL SERIES KCL — SIX-CYLINDER: — The longer-wheelbase (119 in.) Commercial Series continued with the same two changes as the KC. Only a panel body and basic chassis were offered.

¾-TON — SERIES K-20 — SIX-CYLINDER / 1-TON — SERIES K-20X — SIX-CYLINDER / 1-TON — SERIES K-30 — SIX-CYLINDER: — All ¾- and 1-ton trucks were carried over for 1934, with a greatly expanded lineup. Only a panel body had been available in 1933. Pickup, canopy and screen models were added in May 1934. The panel was again the popular "humpback" style, while canopy and screen bodies were not. 1-ton models differed only in optional tire equipment and rear axle ratio. All were powered by the 217.7 cu. in. engine. An underslung tire carrier was standard on all models. Standard equipment included a cowl vent, black-enamel radiator shell, chrome filler cap, crown front fenders, short runningboards (long on panel, canopy and screen), spare wheel, electric horn, stop/taillight, dash light, gas gauge, speedometer, ammeter, oil pressure gauge, heat indicator, locking ignition switch, choke, throttle, license brackets, and tool kit.

I.D. DATA: Serial numbers were in the same location as 1933. (Series KC) Starting: 8023001. Ending: 8048626. (KCL) Starting: 9202001. Ending: 9203885. (K-20) Starting: 8103001. Ending: 8105509. (K-20X, K-30) Starting: 9260001. Ending: 9260137. Engine numbers were in the same location. (Series KC) Starting: T5-1001. (KCL) DT5-1001. (K-20, K-20X, K-30) Starting: T6-1000.

Model	Body Type	Price	Weight	Prod. Total
Commercial Series KC — (½-Ton) —		**(111¼ in. w.b.)**		
KC	Chassis & Cowl	385	1775	—
KC	Chassis & Cab	480	—	—
KC	Pickup	500	2465	—
KC	Comm. Sedan	595	2600	—
KC	Canopy	610	2525	—
KC	Screen	630	2550	—
Commercial Series KCL — (½-Ton) —		**(119 in. w.b.)**		
KCL	Chassis & Cowl	415	2015	—
KCL	Chassis & Cab	510	—	—
KCL	Panel	630	2860	—
Series K-20 — (¾-Ton) —		**(131 in. w.b.)**		
K-20	Chassis	540	2800	—
K-20	Chassis & Cab	635	3260	—
K-20	Canopy	810	3575	—
K-20	Screen	830	3650	—
K-20	Panel	820	4050	—
K-20	Pickup	715	—	—

NOTE: K-20X and K-30 1-ton models were priced the same as equivalent K-20 series ¾-ton models.

ENGINE (Series KC/KCL): Inline. L-head. Six-cylinder. Cast iron block. Bore & stroke: 3⅛ x 4⅜ in. Displacement: 201.3 cu. in. Compression ratio: 5.8:1. Brake horsepower: 75 at 3600 R.P.M. Net horsepower: 23.44. Torque: 138 lbs.-ft. at 1200 R.P.M. Four main bearings. Solid valve lifters.

ENGINE (Series K-20, K-20X, K-30): Inline. L-head. Six-cylinder. Cast iron block. Bore & stroke: 3¼ x 4⅜ in. Displacement: 217.76 cu. in. Compression ratio: 5.6:1. Brake horsepower: 70 at 3000 R.P.M. Net horsepower: 25.35. Torque: 150 lbs.-ft. at 1200 R.P.M. Four main bearings. Solid valve lifters.

CHASSIS (Series KC): Wheelbase: 111¼ in. Tires: 5.25 x 17 four-ply (front/rear). Payload: 1000 lbs.

CHASSIS (Series KCL): Wheelbase: 119 in. Tires: 5.25 x 17 four-ply (front/rear). Payload: 1200 lbs.

CHASSIS (Series K-20, K-20X, K-30): Wheelbase: 131 in. Tires: (front) 6.00 x 20 six-ply; (rear) 32 x 6 eight-ply except panel, 7.50 x 17 (front/rear). Max. GVW: (K-20) 5500 lbs.; (K-20X) 6075 lbs.; (K-30) 8400 lbs.

TECHNICAL: (Series KC/KCL) Same as HC/HCL series of 1933, except front axle was now reverse Elliott type drop-forged I-beam and overall axle ratio was 4.11:1. (K-20, K-20X, K-30) Selective sliding gear transmission. Speeds: 4F/1R. Floor shift control. Single plate dry disc 10 in. clutch. Full-floating rear axle. Overall ratio: 4.875:1. Hydraulic four-wheel brakes with 12 in. front and 14 in. rear drums. Roller tooth steering. Drop-forged I-beam front axle. Semi-elliptic Silico Manganese springs: (front) 36 in. long, 8 leaves; (rear) 48 in. long, 8 leaves. 15-gallon gas tank under driver's seat. Fuel pump. Ventilated disc steel wheels (wire wheels standard on panel model).

OPTIONS: (Series KC/KCL) Chrome front bumper ($6). Chrome rear bumper ($7). Dual trumpet horns, dual taillights and auxiliary windshield wiper ($20). Auxiliary wiper alone ($4). Inside sunvisor ($2 each). Metal tire cover ($6.50 each). Free-wheeling ($11.50). Free-wheeling and automatic clutch ($20). Duplate safety windshield ($5). Duplate safety glass throughout ($14). Auxiliary seat for panel body ($10). Side-mounted coach lamps for Commercial Sedan ($8). Ornamental radiator cap ($2). Tire lock ($1.20). Chrome-plated radiator shell and headlamps, plus single-acting hydraulic shock absorbers front/rear ($15). Duplex air cleaner ($2.50). Long-arm rearview mirror ($2.50). Five wood wheels with four 5.25 x 17 four-ply tires ($10). Six wood wheels with four 5.25 x 17 four-ply tires, extra fender well and tire lock ($20). Six wire wheels with four 5.25 x 17 four-ply tires, extra fender well and tire lock ($10). Five wire wheels with four 6.00 x 16 four-ply tires ($20). Six wire wheels with four 6.00 x 16 four-ply tires, extra fender well and tire lock ($25). Five steel spoke wheels with four 6.00 x 16 four-ply tires ($20). Six steel spoke wheels with four 6.00 x 16 four-ply tires, extra fender well and tire lock ($30). (Series K-20, K-20X, K-30) Black enamel front bumper ($5). Chrome front bumper ($7). Chrome rear bumper for panel model ($12). Auxiliary seat for panel or canopy ($10). Tire carrier for chassis or chassis/cab ($3.50). Chrome-plated radiator shell ($6). Chrome-plated headlights ($3). Duplate safety glass windshield ($5). Duplate safety glass throughout ($14). Auxiliary windshield wiper ($4). Long-arm rearview mirror ($2.50). Ornamental radiator cap ($2). Double-acting shock absorbers, front or rear ($10/pair). Duplex air cleaner ($2). Coach type lamps for panel ($8). Monarch governor ($8.50). 7.50 x 17 six-ply tires front/rear with wire wheels ($13.50). 6.00 x 20 six-ply front and 32 x 6 ten-ply rear tires ($25). 7.00 x 20 eight-ply front and 7.00 x 20 eight-ply rear tires ($26.50). 6.50 x 20 six-ply tires front/rear (no charge). Dual rear wheels were not available.

HISTORICAL: Introduced: October, 1933. Calendar year registrations: 48,252. Calendar year production: 68,469. Production figures by model year or series not available. Dodge Division reorganized and split the truck line completely from automobile operations. Four-cylinder engines were out of the lineup, but an eight powered the largest models — the final year for an inline eight in a Dodge truck. Dodge again placed third in truck sales, with registrations up 72 percent over 1933. The truck industry continued its recovery from the Depression depths, with a 64.3 percent gain in registrations. This was the first year for the famous Dodge Airflow trucks: monstrous model K-52 4-ton fuel tankers, powered by a 310 cu. in. six with 3⅝ in. bore and 5 in. stroke. Their distinctive styling is a favorite with truck lovers — once seen, never forgotten. All Dodge trucks were built in Hamtramck, the last time for many years that all trucks were Michigan-made.

Pricing

1934	5	4	3	2	1
Series KC — (½-Ton) — (111¼ in. w.b.)					
Pickup	870	1750	2900	4100	5800
Canopy	840	1680	2800	3900	5600
Comm. Sedan	850	1700	2850	4000	5700
Panel	830	1650	2750	3850	5500
Series KCL — (½-Ton) — (119 in. w.b.)					
Panel	810	1620	2700	3800	5400
Series K-20 — (¾-Ton) — (131 in. w.b.)					
Pickup	890	1770	2950	4150	5900
Canopy	850	1700	2850	4000	5700
Screen	870	1750	2900	4100	5800
Panel	840	1680	2800	3900	5600
Series K-20X — (1-Ton) — (131 in. w.b.)					
Pickup	830	1650	2750	3850	5500
Canopy	810	1620	2700	3800	5400
Screen	830	1650	2750	3850	5500
Panel	800	1600	2650	3700	5300
Series K-30 — (1-Ton) — (131 in. w.b.)					
Pickup	830	1650	2750	3850	5500
Canopy	810	1620	2700	3800	5400
Screen	830	1650	2750	3850	5500
Panel	800	1600	2650	3700	5300

1935 DODGE

½-TON — COMMERCIAL SERIES KC — SIX-CYLINDER: — The very attractive, good selling KC series entered another year without change. Pickup, canopy, screen and sedan bodies again were offered. When introduced in 1933, the Commercial Series front end looked the same as that used on Dodge passenger cars. But by 1935, the car lines had changed to keep up with the dictates of fashion, while truck sheet metal continued as before. One new body style was added: the wood-bodied Suburban Sedan (station wagon), built by U.S. Body and Forging Co. in Tell City, Indiana. Suburban Sedan styling was car-like, but they were actually considered trucks. Sheet metal from the cowl forward was shared with other commercial models, except that its radiator shell and headlight housings were chrome plated.

½-TON — COMMERCIAL SERIES KCL — SIX-CYLINDER: — Differing from the KC only in its longer (119 in.) w.b., the KCL also continued unchanged. Only the basic chassis and panel models were available.

1935 Dodge Model KC ½-Ton Pickup (M. Magnuson)

¾-TON — SERIES KH-15, KH-16, KH-17, KH-18 — SIX-CYLINDER / 1-TON — SERIES KH-20, KH-21, KH-22, KH-23 — SIX-CYLINDER: — The ¾-ton and 1-ton truck lineup expanded substantially for 1935. Trucks with 131 in. w.b. (KH-15 and -20) were the K-20 and K-20X models of 1934. Those with 136, 148 and 161 in. w.b. were 1½-ton trucks scaled down to ¾- and 1-ton capacities through the use of smaller wheels and tires, as well as lighter springs and axles. Powered by the same engine as KC/KCL trucks, these series would run only in the 1935 model year. No appearance or mechanical changes were made, but factory list prices were cut considerably. Standard equipment was the same as in 1934.

I.D. DATA: Serial numbers were in the same location. (Series KC) Starting: 8048701. Ending: 8072550. (KCL) Starting: 9203901. Ending: 9206587. (Series KH) Starting: 8220101. Ending: 8234001. Engine numbers were in the same location. (Series KC and KCL) Starting: T12-1001. (Series KH) Starting:T17-1001.

Model	Body Type	Price	Weight	Prod. Total
Commercial Series KC — (½-Ton) — (111¼ in. w.b.)				
KC	Chassis & Cowl	365	1775	—
KC	Chassis & Cab	460	—	—
KC	Pickup	480	2465	—
KC	Canopy	590	2525	—
KC	Screen	610	2550	—
KC	Comm. Sedan	595	2600	—
KC	Suburban Sedan	715	2996	—
KC	Suburban (Note 1)	735	2996	—
Commercial Series KCL — (½-Ton) — (119 in. w.b.)				
KCL	Chassis & Cowl	395	2015	—
KCL	Chassis & Cab	490	2800	—
KCL	Panel	595	2860	—
Series KH-15 — (¾-Ton) — (131 in. w.b.)				
KH-15	Chassis	490	2800	—
KH-15	Chassis & Cab	585	3260	—
KH-15	Pickup	665	—	—
KH-15	Canopy	720	3575	—
KH-15	Screen	740	3650	—
KH-15	Panel	740	4050	—
Series KH-16 — (¾-Ton) — (136 in. w.b.)				
KH-16	Chassis	490	—	—
KH-16	Chassis & Cab	585	—	—
Series KH-17 — (¾-Ton) — (148 in. w.b.)				
KH-17	Chassis	520	—	—
KH-17	Chassis & Cab	615	—	—
Series KH-18 — (¾-Ton) — (161 in. w.b.)				
KH-18	Chassis	520	—	—
KH-18	Chassis & Cab	615	—	—
Series KH-20, KH-21, KH-22, KH-23 (Note 2)				

NOTE 1: Suburban Sedan with movable glass windows in front doors.

NOTE 2: 1-ton models were priced the same as equivalent ¾-ton models KH-15, KH-16, KH-17 and KH-18, repsectively.

ENGINE: Inline. L-head. Six-cylinder. Cast iron block. Bore & stroke: 3⅛ x 4⅜ in. Displacement: 201.3 cu. in. Compression ratio: 5.8:1. Brake horsepower: 70 at 3600 R.P.M. Net horsepower: 23.44. Torque: 138 lbs.-ft. at 1200 R.P.M. Four main bearings. Solid valve lifters. Carburetor: Carter.

1935 Dodge ½-Ton Pickup (Daniel S. Olsen)

1935 Dodge Pickup (S. Glasbrenner)

CHASSIS (Series KC): Wheelbase: 111¼ in. Tires: 5.25 x 17 four-ply (front/rear). Payload: 1000 lbs.

CHASSIS (Series KCL): Wheelbase: 119 in. Tires: 5.25 x 17 four-ply (front/rear). Payload: 1200 lbs.

CHASSIS (Series KH-15, KH-20): Wheelbase: 131 in.

CHASSIS (Series KH-16, KH-21): Wheelbase: 136 in.

CHASSIS (Series KH-17, KH-22): Wheelbase: 148 in.

CHASSIS (Series KH-18, KH-23): Wheelbase: 161 in.

TECHNICAL: Selective sliding gear transmission. Speeds: (KC/KCL) 3F/1R; (KH) 4F/1R. Floor shift control. Single plate dry disc clutch. Rear axle: (KC/KCL) Semi-floating; (KH) full-floating. Overall ratio: (KC/KCL) 3.7:1 and 4.125:1; (KH) 4.875:1. Hydraulic four-wheel brakes. Semi-elliptic springs: (KC/KCL) (front) 36 in. long, 7 leaves; (rear) 53½ in., 8 leaves; (KH) (front) 36 in. long, 8 leaves; (rear) 48 in., 8 leaves. Drop-forged I-beam front axle. Steering: (KC/KCL) Semi-irreversible worm and sector; (KH) Roller tooth. 15-gallon gas tank: (KC/KCL) at rear; (KH) under driver's seat. Fuel pump. Wheels: (KC/KCL) Demountable wire wheels with drop-center rims; (KH) Ventilated disc steel except panel model.

OPTIONS: Same as equivalent 1934 models.

1935 Dodge high-headroom panel truck (OCW)

HISTORICAL: Introduced: October, 1934. Calendar year registrations: 61,488. Calendar year production: 83,701. Innovations: Wood-bodied station wagon added to line. This was another strong year for the truck industry, with sales close to 1929, when the all-time record was set. Total industry sales came to 510,683 trucks, up 26.2 percent over 1934. Dodge also had a very good year, with registrations up 27.4 percent. Truck production began in Los Angeles and Canada. Of the total trucks built, 5766 were made in California and 1500 in Canada. Once again, Dodge marketed three truck lines: the ½-ton Commercial Series, the 1½- to 2-ton mid-range standard series, and the 3- and 4-ton heavy-duty units. Those heavy-duty trucks still had the familiar old Graham styling of the late 1920s. In July, 1935, Dodge announced an all-new 3-ton series with modern styling. A 4-tonner was no longer available. As in 1934, all Dodge trucks were powered by 6-cyl. engines. The U.S. Government ordered over 5,000 Dodge trucks for Army use, including ½-ton panels and 1½-ton cargo trucks — some with four-wheel-drive.

Pricing

1935	5	4	3	2	1
Series KC — (½-Ton) — (111¼ in. w.b.)					
Pickup	870	1750	2900	4100	5800
Canopy	840	1680	2800	3900	5600
Screen	850	1700	2850	4000	5700
Comm. Sedan	830	1650	2750	3850	5500
Suburban Sedan	890	1770	2950	4150	5900

	5	4	3	2	1
Series KCL — (½-Ton) — (119 in. w.b.)					
Panel	920	1800	3000	4200	6000
Series KH-15 — (¾-Ton) — (131 in. w.b.)					
Pickup	890	1770	2950	4150	5900
Canopy	850	1700	2850	4000	5700
Screen	870	1750	2900	4100	5800
Panel	840	1680	2800	3900	5600
Series KH-20 — (1-Ton) — (131 in. w.b.)					
Pickup	830	1650	2750	3850	5500
Canopy	810	1620	2700	3800	5400
Screen	830	1650	2750	3850	5500
Panel	800	1600	2650	3700	5300

1936 DODGE

1936 Dodge pickup truck (DFW/BLHU)

½-TON — COMMERCIAL SERIES LC — SIX-CYLINDER / ½-TON — COMMERCIAL SEDAN MODEL D2 — SIX-CYLINDER: — An all-new line of trucks, including a new commercial series, was announced for 1936. The new trucks featured beautiful styling and Amola springs, plus "fore point" load distribution. That meant the engine and cab had been shifted forward, putting more payload weight on the front axle and wheels. The longer cab-to-rear-axle distance also permitted the use of longer bodies. One welcome styling change was the adoption of front-hinged doors. All Commercial Series models sat on a 116 in. w.b., rather than the two w.b. choices of 1935. The unchanged six-cylinder engine was mounted on Chrysler's famous three-point suspension system, cushioned with rubber. Springs were all made of Amola steel, a recent metallurgical development from Chrysler engineering. The series consisted of a Pickup, Panel, Screen, Canopy and Westchester station wagon, plus the Commercial Sedan, which was the only model built on a passenger-car chassis. For the first time, the balance of the series used a truck-type double-drop chassis. The Commercial Sedan used a 218 cu. in. engine rather than the 201 six in other LC models. The spare tire sat in the right side fender well. Standard equipment included an ammeter, speedometer, fuel gauge, oil pressure gauge, heat indicator, glove compartment, choke, throttle, and vacuum wiper. The 17 in. three-spoke steering wheel was height-adjustable. Sedan, Panel, Screen and Canopy models had only one bucket seat.

¾-TON — SERIES LE-15, LE-16, LE-17 — SIX-CYLINDER / 1-TON — SERIES LE-20, LE-21, LE-22 — SIX-CYLINDER: — Like the smaller trucks, the LE series was totally restyled for 1936. More massive and rugged in appearance, the ¾- and 1-ton models looked more truck-like than the LC. Three w.b. lengths were available: 129, 136 or 162 in. Doors now hinged at the front. "Fore point" load distribution shifted the engine and cab forward. Only in the 136 in. size were all body types available. As before, the ¾- and 1-ton trucks were basically 1½-ton models, built down by using smaller wheels and lighter springs. Standard equipment included a cowl vent, painted radiator shell, electric horn, tail/stop light, dash light, gas gauge, speedometer, ammeter, oil pressure gauge, heat indicator, choke, throttle, license bracket, and tool kit. The 17½ in. three-spoke steering wheel had an adjustable column.

1936 Dodge "dog-catcher" truck (DFW/AHS)

I.D. DATA: Serial numbers were again on a number plate on the engine side of the cowl. (Series LC) (Detroit) Starting: 8105601. Ending: 8156402. (Los Angeles) Starting: 9287701. Ending: 9293583. (D2) (Detroit) Starting: 4015051. Ending: 8263157. (LE-15, LE-20) (Detroit) Starting: 8242801. Ending: 8242801. (LE-16, LE-21) (Detroit) Starting: 8378051. Ending: 8380000. (LE-17, LE-22) (Los Angeles) Starting: 9260551. Ending: 9264974. Engine numbers were stamped on top left side of block, between cylinders one and two. (LC/D2) Starting: T23-1001. (LE) Starting: T25-1001.

Model	Body Type	Price	Weight	Prod. Total
Commercial Series LC/D2 — (½-Ton) — (116 in. w.b.)				
D2	Commercial Sedan	665	2844	—
LC	Chassis & Cowl	370	1935	—
LC	Chassis & Cab	470	2450	—
LC	Pickup	500	2685	—
LC	Canopy	600	2735	—
LC	Screen	620	2755	—
LC	Panel	585	2985	—
LC	Westchester Sub.	725	2985	—
LC	West. (Note 1)	750	2990	—

NOTE: LC/D2 calendar year shipments, U.S. only: (Domestic) 51,229; (Government) 1214; (Export) 4783; (Total) 57,226.

Series LE-15 — (¾-Ton) — (129 in. w.b.)				
LE-15	Chassis only	550	—	—
LE-15	Chassis & Cab	657	—	—
Series LE-16 — (¾-Ton) — (136 in. w.b.)				
LE-16	Chassis only	550	—	—
LE-16	Chassis & Cab	657	—	—
LE-16	Pickup	734	—	—
LE-16	Canopy	799	—	—
LE-16	Screen	819	—	—
LE-16	Panel	824	—	—
LE-16	Platform	709	—	—
LE-16	Stake	739	—	—
Series LE-17 — (¾-Ton) — (162 in. w.b.)				
LE-17	Chassis only	580	—	—
LE-17	Chassis & Cab	687	—	—
LE-17	Platform	759	—	—
LE-17	Stake	799	—	—
Series LE-20, LE-21, LE-22 (Note 2)				

NOTE 1: Westchester Suburban with roll-up windows in front doors.
NOTE 2: 1-ton models were priced the same as equivalent ¾-ton models LE-15, LE-16, and LE-17, repsectively.
NOTE 3: LE series calendar year shipments, U.S. only: 2399 (804 ¾-ton trucks and 1595 1-ton).

1936 Dodge ½-Ton Pickup (JAW)

ENGINE (Series LC and LE): Inline. L-head. Six-cylinder. Cast iron block. Bore & stroke: 3⅛ x 4⅜ in. Displacement: 201.3 cu. in. Compression ratio: 5.8:1. Brake horsepower: 70 at 3000 R.P.M. Net horsepower: 23.44. Torque: 138 lbs.-ft. at 1200 R.P.M. Four main bearings. Solid valve lifters. Carburetor: Downdraft.

ENGINE (D2 Commercial Sedan only): Inline. L-head. Six-cylinder. Cast iron block. Bore & stroke: 3¼ x 4⅜ in. Displacement: 217.8 cu. in. Compression ratio: 6.5:1. Brake horsepower: 87 at 3600 R.P.M. Net horsepower: 25.35. Torque: 155 lbs.-ft. at 1200 R.P.M. Four main bearings. Solid valve lifters.

CHASSIS (Series LC/D2): Wheelbase: 116 in. Tires: 6.00 x 16 four-ply (front/rear). Payload: 1000 lbs.

CHASSIS (Series LE-15, LE-20): Wheelbase: 129 in. Tires: (front) 6.00 x 20 six-ply; (rear) 32 x 6 eight-ply on chassis, chassis & cab, platform and stake; 6.50 x 20 six-ply front/rear on panel, pickup, canopy and screen models.

CHASSIS (Series LE-16, LE-21): Wheelbase: 136 in. Tires: same as LE-15.

CHASSIS (Series LE-17, LE-22): Wheelbase: 162 in. Tires: same as LE-15.

TECHNICAL: Transmission: (LC/D2) Synchro-silent shift; (LE) Selective sliding gear. Speeds: (LC/D2) 3F/1R; (LE) 4F/1R with power takeoff on right side of case. Floor shift control. Single plate dry disc clutch. Rear axle: (LC/D2) Semi-floating; (LE) full-floating. Overall ratio: 4.1:1 (3.7:1 optional at no extra cost); (LE) 4.875:1 (5.428:1 and 5.857:1 optional). Spiral bevel gear drive. Hydraulic four-wheel brakes: (LC/D2)

10 in. drums, 2 in. lining; (LE) 14⅛ in. drums, 1¾ in. lining. Steering: (LC/D2) Semi-irreversible worm and roller gear; (LE) Worm and sector type. Reverse Elliott type I-beam front axle. Semi-elliptic springs; (LC/D2) (front) 36 in., 8 leaves; (rear) 48 in., 8 leaves; (LE) (front) 1¾ x 39 in., 7 leaves; (rear) 2¼ x 48 in., 8 or 9 leaves. 15-gallon gas tank. Wheels: (LC/D2) Pressed steel spoke; (LE) Ventilated disc.

OPTIONS: (Series LC/D2) Chrome-plated front bumper ($6). Chrome-plated rear bumper ($7). Chrome radiator shell and headlamps ($7.50). Safety glass in windshield ($4). Safety glass throughout for cab, panel, canopy or screen ($7.50). Auxiliary seat for panel, canopy or screen body ($10). Inside sunvisor ($2 each). Auxiliary windshield wiper ($4). Oil-bath air cleaner ($2.50). Vortex air cleaner with standard breather cap ($17.50). Vortex air cleaner with vortex cap ($19.50). Crankcase ventilator ($3.50). Governor ($10). Coach lamps for panel ($8). Oil filter ($2.75). Metal tire cover ($6.50 each). Tire lock ($1.20). Rearview mirror, long arm ($1). Adjustable mirror ($2.50). Shock absorbers, front and rear ($10). Six steel spoke wheels with four 6.00 x 16 four-ply tires, tire lock ($10). Five 20 in. wheels with four 5.25 x 20 four-ply tires, 4.875:1 rear axle and shock absorbers ($25). Six 20 in. wheels with four 5.25 x 20 four-ply tires, 4.875:1 rear axle, shocks, extra fender well and tire lock ($35). (Series LE) Chrome bumper ($2 adder). Chrome radiator shell ($6). Rearview mirror, long arm ($1). Adjustable mirror ($2.50). Black front bumper ($5). Tire carrier ($3.50). Safety glass throughout ($7.50). Auxiliary windshield wiper ($4). Long runningboards with rear fenders: 126 or 136 in. ($16.50); 162 in. ($27). Governor ($5). Oil-bath air cleaner ($2.50). Shock absorbers, double-acting, front or rear ($10 pair). Auxiliary springs ($10).

1936 Dodge pickup truck (OCW/DSM)

HISTORICAL: Introduced: November, 1935. Calendar year registrations: 85,295. Calendar year production: 109,392 (8599 in Los Angeles and 2764 in Canada). Innovations: Front-hinged doors for safety. Once again, Dodge ranked third in truck sales, with a production gain of 31 percent over 1935. All U.S. trucks were made either in Hamtramck, Michigan or Los Angeles. Trucks up to 3-ton capacity made up the standard line, and a 4-ton Airflow was also produced. All trucks were powered by 6-cyl. engines. Truck registrations were up 38.7 percent. The year's totals included 4783 ½-ton trucks exported and 1214 shipped to the government. Rapidly-growing truck sales had made necessary two plant expansions in the previous two years. In Detroit, Dodge had the capacity to build 500 units a day, in 546,000 square feet of floor space. A rumor circulated that Dodge was ready to announce a diesel-powered truck, but that was not to happen until 1939.

Pricing

1936	5	4	3	2	1
Series LC/D2 — (½-Ton)					
Comm. Sedan	890	1770	2950	4150	5900
Pickup	920	1850	3050	4300	6100
Canopy	850	1700	2850	4000	5700
Screen	870	1750	2900	4100	5800
Panel	840	1680	2800	3900	5600
Westchester Sub.	930	1860	3100	4350	6200
Series LE-16 — (¾-Ton) — (136 in. w.b.)					
Pickup	890	1770	2950	4150	5900
Canopy	840	1680	2800	3900	5600
Screen	850	1700	2850	4000	5700
Panel	830	1650	2750	3850	5500
Platform	720	1450	2400	3300	4800
Stake	750	1500	2500	3500	5000
Series LE-17 — (¾-Ton) — (162 in. w.b.)					
Platform	680	1350	2250	3150	4500
Stake	720	1450	2400	3300	4800
Series LE-21 — (1-Ton) — (136 in. w.b.)					
Pickup	850	1700	2850	4000	5700
Canopy	830	1650	2750	3850	5500
Screen	840	1680	2800	3900	5600
Panel	810	1620	2700	3800	5400
Platform	630	1250	2100	3000	4200
Stake	680	1350	2250	3150	4500
Series LE-22 — (1-Ton) — (162 in. w.b.)					
Platform	600	1200	2000	2800	4000
Stake	650	1300	2150	3050	4300

1937 DODGE

1937 Dodge high-headroom Panel Delivery (ATC)

½-TON — COMMERCIAL SERIES MC — SIX-CYLINDER: — Commercial Series trucks were carried over from 1936 basically unchanged in appearance. Model offerings remained the same, including a Commercial Sedan and Westchester Suburban station wagon. Only the Commercial Sedan was built on a passenger car chassis; all others shared a 116 in. w.b. truck-type chassis. The only difference between the Panel and Commercial Sedan was the Panel's familiar raised-roof style. A new 218 cu. in., 75 horsepower engine replaced the former 201 cu. in. six. A chromed front bumper was standard. Chrome-plated front and rear bumpers came on the Commercial Sedan, while the Westchester Suburban carried a chrome front bumper and shock absorbers all around. The spare wheel sat in a right side fender well. Standard equipment was the same as in 1936.

¾-TON and 1-TON — SERIES MD/ME — SIX-CYLINDER: — All-new appearance highlighted the ¾- and 1-ton lineup, due to sharing sheet metal with the MC ½-ton series rather than the 1½-tonners. Dodge called this series its "In-Between" trucks: between the light Commercial Series and the larger 1½-ton models. Prior to this year, a 1½-ton series had been built by reducing spring capacity and substituting smaller tires to carry bulky, but not heavy, loads. Only two wheelbases were now available: 120 and 136 in. The 120 in. w.b. series carried 7-ft. bodies, while the 136 in. had 9-footers. All used the same new 218 cu. in. engine as the MC. The 17 in. steering wheel had an adjustable column. Standard equipment included a cowl ventilator, glove compartment, hood ornament, electric horn, tail/stop lamp, dash light, gas gauge, ammeter, oil pressure gauge, heat indicator, speedometer, choke, throttle, license bracket, vacuum windshield wiper and tool kit, plus a chrome front bumper. The Panel model had chrome bumpers front and rear. Dual wheels were not available.

I.D. DATA: Serial numbers were located on a plate on the right front door pillar. (MC) (Detroit) Starting: 8156701. Ending: 8186617. (Los Angeles) Starting: 9247201. Ending: 9250807. (MD/ME) (Detroit) Starting: 8072601. Ending: 8082022. (Los Angeles) Starting: 9282601. Ending: 9283704. Engine numbers were on the top front, left side of the block between cylinders one and two. (MC) Starting: T38-1001. (MD/ME) Starting: T30-1001.

Model	Body Type	Price	Weight	Prod. Total
Series MC — (½-Ton) — (116 in. w.b.)				
MC	Chassis & Cowl	410	1975	—
MC	Chassis & Cab	510	2450	—
MC	Pickup	540	2700	—
MC	Panel	625	2975	—
MC	Canopy	640	2695	—
MC	Screen	660	2710	—
MC	Commercial Sedan	670	2845	—
MC	Westchester Suburban	755	2915	—

NOTE: MC Series calendar year shipments, U.S. only: (Domestic) 52,610; (Government) 80; (Export) 6973; (Total) 59,663.

Series MD — (¾-Ton) — (120 in. w.b.)				
MD-15	Chassis & Cowl	505	2425	—
MD-15	Chassis & Cab	605	2900	—
MC-15	Pickup (7-ft.)	685	3200	—
MD-15	Stake (7-ft.)	685	3500	—
MD-15	Platform (7-ft.)	655	3225	—
(136 in. w.b.)				
MD-16	Chassis & Cowl	520	2450	—
MD-16	Chassis & Cab	620	2925	—
MD-16	Panel	800	3565	—
MD-16	Canopy	765	3310	—
MD-16	Screen	785	3330	—
MD-16	Pickup (9-ft.)	700	3275	—
MD-16	Stake (9-ft.)	705	3675	—
MD-16	Platform (9-ft.)	675	3500	—
MD-20 and MD-21 1-Ton (Note 1)				

NOTE 1: 1-Ton models were priced the same as equivalent ¾-ton models MD-15 and MD-16, respectively.

NOTE 2: MD Series calendar year shipments, U.S. only: (Domestic) 12,076; (Government) 2; (Export) 1556; (Total) 13,634.

ENGINE: Inline. L-head. Six-cylinder. Cast iron block. Bore & stroke: 3⅜ x 4-1/16 in. Displacement: 218.06 cu. in. Compression ratio: 6.5:1. Brake horsepower: 75 at 3000 R.P.M. Net horsepower: 27.34. Torque: 155 lbs.-ft. Four main bearings. Solid valve lifters. Carburetor: Carter.

CHASSIS (Series MC): Wheelbase: 116 in. Tires: 6.00 x 16 four-ply (front/rear). Payload: 1000 lbs.

CHASSIS (Series MD-15, MD-20): Wheelbase: 120 in. Tires: (front) 7.00 x 16 six-ply; (rear) 7.50 x 16 six-ply.

CHASSIS (Series MD-16, MD-21): Wheelbase: 136 in. Tires: same as MD-15.

TECHNICAL: Transmission: (Series MC) Synchro-silent shift; (MD) Selective sliding gear. Speeds: (MC) 3F/1R; (MD) 3F/1R with power takeoff opening on right side of case. Floor shift control. Single plate dry disc clutch. Semi-floating rear axle. Overall ratio: (MC) 4.1:1 (3.7:1 optional); (MD) 4.3:1 (3.9:1 and 4.78:1 optional at no extra cost). Hotchkiss drive. Hydraulic four-wheel brakes: (MC) 10 in. drums, 2 in. lining; (MD) 11 in. front and 13 in. rear drums, 2 in. lining. Steering: (MC) Semi-irreversible worm and roller gear; (MD) Worm and sector. Reverse Elliott I-beam front axle. Semi-elliptic springs: (MC) (front) 36 in. long; (rear) 48 in., 8 leaves; (MD) (front) 1¾ x 36 in., 12 leaves; (rear) 1¾ x 52 in., 11 leaves. 16-gallon gas tank under left side of seat (MD). 17 in. cooling fan (MD). Pressed steel disc wheels.

OPTIONS: (All Models) Chrome rear bumper ($8.50). Dual horns ($7.50). Coach lamps ($8). Stationary rearview mirror ($1.50). Adjustable mirror ($2.50). Auxiliary seat ($10). Inside sunvisor ($2 each). Tire lock, except 136 in. w.b. ($2.50). Auxiliary windshield wiper ($4). Double-acting hydraulic shock absorbers, front or rear ($4.75/pair). Four-speed transmission ($25). Oil-bath air cleaner ($3.25). Oil filter ($3.25). Leibing governor ($5). Monarch governor ($7.50). Handy governor ($10). (½-ton only) Bumper guards ($1.50/pair). Metal tire cover ($6.50 each). 6.00 x 16 six-ply tires, front and rear ($11.40). Five 20 in. wheels with 5.25 x 20 six-ply tires, 4.78:1 rear axle ratio and front/rear shock absorbers ($40). (¾- and 1-ton only) Underslung tire carrier for 136 in. w.b. ($3.50). 7.00 x 16 six-ply tires front and rear ($15 net allowance). 7.00 x 16 six-ply front and 7.50 x 16 eight-ply rear tires ($7.50). 7.50 x 16 six-ply tires front and rear ($20.50). 7.50 x 16 six-ply front and 7.50 x 16 eight-ply rear tires ($28).

1937 Dodge Staion Wagon Built For Clark Gable (CHA)

HISTORICAL: Introduced: December, 1936. Calendar year registrations: 64,098. Calendar year production: 121,917. Production figures by model year and type not available. Dodge truck registrations fell by 24.8 percent while total industry sales were up slightly, so Dodge slipped down to fourth position, even though total production actually increased. Of the total production, 7409 trucks were made in Los Angeles and 5383 in Canada. Sizes ranged from ½- to 3-tons in the standard line, plus 4-ton Airflow trucks. All were 6-cyl. powered. For the first time, Dodge offered a cab-over-engine model, a conversion made for Dodge by the Montpelier Company in 1½- and 3-ton ratings. Plymouth marketed a line of ½-ton pickups this year, based on the Dodge MC series.

Pricing

1937	5	4	3	2	1
Series MC — (½-Ton) — (116 in. w.b.)					
Pickup	1170	2340	3900	5450	7800
Canopy	1080	2160	3600	5050	7200
Screen	1100	2200	3650	5100	7300
Panel	1110	2220	3700	5200	7400
Commercial Sedan	930	1860	3100	4350	6200
Westchester Suburban	1010	2030	3350	4700	6700
Series MD — (¾-Ton) — (120 in. w.b.)					
Pickup	1080	2160	3600	5050	7200
Platform	980	1950	3250	4550	6500
Stake	900	1800	3000	4200	6000

	5	4	3	2	1
Series MD — (¾-Ton) — (136 in. w.b.)					
Pickup	1050	2100	3500	4900	7000
Canopy	960	1920	3200	4500	6400
Screen	980	1950	3250	4550	6500
Panel	1000	2000	3300	4600	6600
Platform	750	1500	2500	3500	5000
Stake	800	1600	2650	3700	5300
Series MD — (1-Ton) — (120 in. w.b.)					
Pickup	980	1950	3250	4550	6500
Stake	900	1800	3000	4200	6000
Platform	870	1750	2900	4100	5800
Series MD — (1-Ton) — (136 in. w.b.)					
Pickup	850	1700	2850	4000	5700
Canopy	830	1650	2750	3850	5500
Screen	840	1680	2800	3900	5600
Panel	810	1620	2700	3800	5400
Platform	630	1250	2100	3000	4200
Stake	680	1350	2250	3150	4500

1938 DODGE

1938 Dodge ½-Ton Pickup (DFW)

½-TON — COMMERCIAL SERIES RC — SIX-CYLINDER: — Only appearance changes hit the 1938 half-tons. A new grille following Dodge car styling gave the series a fresh new look. Though similar in appearance, Dodge cars and light trucks were not identical. Car headlights were now fender-mounted, while bullet-shaped truck lamps sat alongside the radiator shell. Dropped this year was the Westchester Suburban wagon, which was offered instead as a passenger car, using auto front end sheet metal and chassis. All other Commercial body types remained the same, as did engine and mechanical components, including the frame. Dodge was busy preparing an all-new line for 1939, so could afford only a quick cosmetic facelift this year. Bodies were 6-ft. long. Standard equipment included an ammeter, speedometer, fuel gauge, oil pressure gauge, heat indicator, glove compartment, choke, throttle, and vacuum windshield wiper. Sedan, Panel, Screen and Canopy models had only one bucket seat.

¾-TON and 1-TON — SERIES RD — SIX-CYLINDER: — Like the smaller trucks, the RD line continued with only front end sheet metal appearance changes. Body types, engine and mechanical equipment were the same as 1937 models. The ¾-ton models differed from the 1-ton only in tire size and spring capacities, which affected total Gross Vehicle Weight ratings. The 120 in. w.b. RD-15 and RD-20 carried 7-ft. bodies; the 136 in. RD-16 and RD-21, 9-ft. Standard equipment was the same as 1937. All models included a chrome front bumper, but the Panel had chrome bumpers front and rear. Prices included a spare tire and tube, in the rear tire's size and ply.

I.D. DATA: Serial numbers were in the same location as 1937. (Series RC) (Detroit) Starting: 8186701. Ending: 8204334. (Los Angeles) Starting: 9251001. Ending: 9252540. (Series RD) (Detroit) Starting: 8082101. Ending: 8087863. (Los Angeles) Starting: 9283801. Ending: 9284247. Engine numbers were in the same location as 1937. (Series RC) Starting: T58-1001. (Series RD) Starting: T60-1001.

Model	Body Type	Price	Weight	Prod. Total
Series RC — (½-Ton) — (116 in. w.b.)				
RC	Chassis & Cowl	475	1975	—
RC	Chassis & Cab	575	2450	—
RC	Pickup (6-ft.)	600	2700	—
RC	Canopy	690	2695	—
RC	Screen	710	2710	—
RC	Panel	695	2975	—
RC	Commercial Sedan	710	2845	—

NOTE: RC Series calendar year shipments, U.S. only: (Domestic) 17,299; (Government) 242; (Export) 3236; (Total) 20,777.

Model	Body Type	Price	Weight	Prod. Total
Series RD — (¾-Ton) — (120 in. w.b.)				
RD-15	Chassis & Cowl	584	2475	—
RD-15	Chassis & Cab	682	2900	—
RD-15	Pickup (7-ft.)	725	3200	—
RD-15	Platform (7-ft.)	725	3250	—
RD-15	Stake (7-ft.)	758	3525	—
(136 in. w.b.)				
RD-16	Chassis	635	2450	—
RD-16	Chassis & Cab	733	2925	—
RD-16	Pickup (9-ft.)	776	3275	—
RD-16	Platform (9-ft.)	776	3525	—
RD-16	Stake (9-ft.)	809	3700	—
RD-16	Canopy	858	3310	—
RD-16	Screen	878	3330	—
RD-16	Panel	885	3565	—
Series RD-20 and RD-21 1-Ton (Note 1)				

NOTE 1: 1-Ton models were priced the same as equivalent ¾-ton trucks RD-15 and RD-16, respectively.

NOTE 2: RD Series calendar year shipments, U.S. only: (Domestic) 4988; (Government) 13; (Export) 760; (Total) 5761.

ENGINE: Same as 1937.

CHASSIS (Series RC): Wheelbase: 116 in. Tires: 6.00 x 16 four-ply. Payload: 1000 lbs.

CHASSIS (Series RD-15, RD-20): Wheelbase: 120 in. Tires: (front) 7.00 x 16 six-ply; (rear) 7.50 x 16 six-ply.

CHASSIS (Series RD-16, RD-21): Wheelbase: 136 in. Tires: same as RD-15.

TECHNICAL: Same specifications as 1937 models.

1938 Dodge light-duty chassis & cab (DFW/FLP)

OPTIONS: (½-Ton) Chrome rear bumper ($8.50). Chrome-plated headlamps ($2.75). Dual horns ($7.50). Chrome-plated radiator shell ($6). Coach lamps ($8.50). Full-width partition behind driver's seat on canopy, screen, panel models ($15). Auxiliary seat ($10). Stationary rearview mirror ($1.50). Adjustable mirror ($2.50). Inside sunvisors ($2 each). Auxiliary windshield wiper ($4). Oil-bath air cleaner ($3.75). Shock absorbers, front or rear ($4.75). Leibing governor ($5.00). Monarch governor ($5). Handy governor ($10). Four-speed transmission ($25). Five 6.00 x 16 six-ply tires ($14.68). Six steel disc wheels with five 6.00 x 14 four-ply tires, extra fender well and tire lock ($10.30). Five 20 in. wheels with 5.25 x 20 four-ply tires and 4.78:1 rear axle ratio ($10.82). Five 20 in. wheels with 5.25 x 20 six-ply tires and 4.78:1 axle ($31.42). Six 20 in. wheels with five 5.25 x 20 four-ply tires, 4.78:1 axle, extra fender well and tire lock ($26.27). Six 20 in. wheels with five 5.25 x 20 six-ply tires, 4.78:1 axle, extra fender well and tire lock ($41.72). (¾- and 1-ton) Same as 1937, except: 7.00 x 16 six-ply front and 7.50 x 16 eight-ply rear tires ($10). 7.50 x 16 six-ply tires, front and rear ($24). 7.50 x 16 six-ply front and 7.50 x 16 eight-ply rear tires ($34).

HISTORICAL: Calendar year registrations: 33,676. Calendar year production: 53,613. Production figures by model year and type not available. 1938 was a disastrous year for Dodge truck sales as registrations plummeted 47.5 percent. Total industry sales were little better, down 40.9 percent. The Depression was still very much alive, though this would be the last truly lean year. Of the total production, 2563 trucks were made in Los Angeles, 5704 in Canada, and the remainder at Hamtramck, Michigan. The truck lineup ranged from ½- to 3-ton ratings, including 2- and 3-ton Montpelier cab-over-engine conversions. Airflow 4-tonners were custom-built. This would be the last year for the famous and popular raised-roof (humpback) Panel model. Dodge finished fourth in the truck sales race.

Pricing

1938	5	4	3	2	1
Series RC — (½-Ton) — (116 in. w.b.)					
Pickup	1170	2340	3900	5450	7800
Canopy	1080	2160	3600	5050	7200
Screen	1100	2200	3650	5100	7300
Panel	1110	2220	3700	5200	7400
Comm. Sed.	930	1860	3100	4350	6200
Westchester Sub.	1010	2030	3350	4700	6700

	5	4	3	2	1
Series RD-15 — (¾-Ton) — (120 in. w.b.)					
Pickup	1080	2160	3600	5050	7200
Platform	980	1950	3250	4550	6500
Stake	900	1800	3000	4200	6000
Series RD-16 — (¾-Ton) — (136 in. w.b.)					
Pickup	1050	2100	3500	4900	7000
Canopy	960	1920	3200	4500	6400
Screen	980	1950	3250	4550	6500
Panel	1000	2000	3300	4600	6600
Platform	750	1500	2500	3500	5000
Stake	800	1600	2650	3700	5300
Series RD-20 — (1-Ton) — (120 in. w.b.)					
Pickup	980	1950	3250	4550	6500
Stake	900	1800	3000	4200	6000
Platform	870	1750	2900	4100	5800
Series RD-21 — (1-Ton) — (136 in. w.b.)					
Pickup	850	1700	2850	4000	5700
Canopy	830	1650	2750	3850	5500
Screen	840	1680	2800	3900	5600
Panel	810	1620	2700	3800	5400
Platform	630	1250	2100	3000	4200
Stake	680	1350	2250	3150	4500

1939 DODGE

1939 Dodge 1-ton panel bread van (OCW)

1939 Dodge furniture delivery truck (DFW/HC)

LIGHT TRUCK — TC SERIES — ½-TON — SIX-CYLINDER: — Dodge called it "The truck of the year". For Dodge truck 1939 was "The year of the truck". In addition to a totally redesigned truck line, Dodge also opened the world's largest exclusive truck factory. This modern new facility cost over $6,000,000. It was built to be an exclusive truck building facility. This plant is located in Warren, Mich. and is still the home of Dodge trucks today. The ½-ton truck TC sported all new sheet metal on the previous model's 116 in. w.b. Gone were the Commercial sedan, Westchester Suburban and the raised roof panel. The new line consisted of pickup, panel, canopy and screen models. There was a family resemblance between the Dodge car and truck lines, but trucks were definitely acquiring a look of their own. The new trucks were particularly handsome and modern looking. The ½-ton truck engine for 1939 actually took a backward step as it was reduced from 218 cu. in. to 201 cu. in. Dodge continued to refer to the ½-ton series as the Commercial series, but at long last Dodge was beginning to recognize the popular tonnage classification of ½-, ¾-, 1-½, 2-, 2-½ and 3-ton models and designate them that way. Standard equipment: Shocks front and rear. Spare tire and tube. Front bumper. Rear bumper on Panel models. Hood ornament. Safety glass. Electric horn. Combination stop and tail lamp. License brackets. Tool kit. Speedometer. Fuel gauge. Oil pressure gauge. Ammeter. Engine temperature indicator. Choke. Throttle. High-low beam headlights. Glove compartment. Cowl vent. Vacuum windshield wipers. Panel, Canopy and Screen models, one bucket seat only.

I.D. DATA (Series TC): Serial number plate is located on the right front door hinge pillar. Engine number is stamped on a pad on left side of cylinder block between cylinder numbers one and two. Beginning serial numbers Detroit 8520301, ending 8542929. Los Angeles 9252601, ending 9254160. Engine numbers T81-1001 and up.

Model	Body Type	Price	Weight	Prod. Total
Model TC				
TC	½-Ton Chassis Flat Face Cowl	465	2375	—
TC	½-Ton Chassis Cab	560	2775	—
TC	½-Ton Pickup	590	2975	—
TC	½-Ton Panel	680	3175	—
TC	½-Ton Canopy	690	3000	—
TC	½-Ton Screen	710	3020	—

NOTE 1: Shipments, U.S. Only (Calendar Year) (Domestic) 30,536; (Government) 905; (Export) 3,017; (Total) 34,458.

ENGINE (Series TC): Inline. L-head. Six-cylinder. Cast iron block. Bore & stroke: 3⅛ in. x 4⅜ in. Displacement: 201.3 cu. in. Compression ratio: 6.7:1. Taxable horsepower: 23.44. Brake horsepower: 70 at 3000 R.P.M. Max. Torque: 148 lbs. ft. at 1200 R.P.M. Four main bearings. Solid valve lifters.

CHASSIS (Series TC): Wheelbase: 116 in. Wheels: five steel disc with five 6.00 x 16, four-ply tires with underslung tire carrier for spare wheel and tire. Payload 1000 pounds.

LIGHT TRUCK — SERIES TD-15 — ¾-TON — SIX-CYLINDER: — For the first time since the early thirties Dodge built a ¾-ton series. The series consisted of pickup, platform and stake, all with 7½ foot bodies on a 120 in. w.b. Styling of the TD-15 Series was the same as the TC as they essentially shared all the same sheet metal from front bumper to back of cab. Pickup bodies were similar, only longer. Mechanicals were shared with the TC line except TD had a larger engine 218 cu. in. vs. 201 cu. in.

I.D. DATA (Series TD-15): Beginning serial number Detroit 8204401, ending 8207021, Los Angeles 9200321, ending 9200465. Engine numbers T70-1001 and up (Engine number and serial number locations same as TC).

Model	Body Type	Price	Weight	Prod. Total
Model TD-15				
TD-15	Chassis/Flat Face Cowl	535	2525	—
TD-15	Chassis Cab	630	2925	—
TD-15	Pickup 7½ ft.	670	3225	—
TD-15	Stake 7½ ft.	705	3550	—
TD-15	Platform 7½ ft.	680	3325	—

NOTE 1: Shipments, U.S. Only (Calendar Year) (Domestic) 2,878; (Government) 40; (Export) 111; (Total) 3,029.

ENGINE (Series TD-15): Inline. L-head. Six-cylinder. Cast iron block. Bore & stroke: 3¼ in. x 4⅜ in. Displacement: 217.76 cu. in. Compression ratio: 6.5:1. Taxable horsepower: 25.35. Brake horsepower: 77 at 3000 R.P.M. Max. Torque: 158 lbs. ft. at 1200 R.P.M. Four main bearings. Solid valve lifters.

CHASSIS (Series TD-15): Wheelbase: 120 in. Standard wheels are five steel disc with five TA-15, six-ply tires front and rear. Underslung tire carrier for the spare wheel and tire. Gross weight: 5000 lbs. Payload 1500 lbs.

LIGHT TRUCK — SERIES TD-20/TD-21 — ONE-TON — SIX-CYLINDER: — The one ton series completed the new light truck line-up for 1939. One ton trucks were available in two wheelbase lengths, 120 in. TD-20 and 133 in. TD-21. The TD-20 series was basically the ¾-ton series with beefier wheels and springs increasing payload by 500 pounds to 2,000 pounds total. Model offerings in the TD-20 line were the same as the ¾-ton line, 7-½ foot pickup, stake and platform. The longer wheelbase TD-21 series mirrored the model offerings of the ½-ton series, plus added platform and stake models. Both one ton series used the same 218 cu. in. engine which they shared with the ¾-ton trucks. Cabs and mechanicals used on one tonners were the same as ½-ton and ¾-ton models.

I.D. DATA (Series TD-20/TD-21): Beginning serial numbers for TD-20 and TD-21 series, Detroit 8087901, ending 8093438, Los Angeles 9284301, ending 9284669. Engine numbers T72-1001 and up. Engine and serial number locations same as TC series.

Model	Body Type	Price	Weight	Prod. Total
Model TD-20/TD-21				
TD-20	Chassis/Flat Face Cowl	580	2825	—
TD-20	Chassis Cab	675	3250	—
TD-20	Pickup 7½ ft.	715	3600	—
TD-20	Stake 7½ ft.	750	3850	—
TD-20	Platform 7½ ft.	725	3265	—
TD-21	Chassis/Flat Face Cowl	620	2850	—
TD-21	Chassis Cab	715	3275	—
TD-21	Panel	855	3850	—
TD-21	Canopy	840	—	—
TD-21	Screen	860	—	—
TD-21	Pickup 9 ft.	765	3675	—
TD-21	Stake 9 ft.	790	4025	—
TD-21	Platform 9 ft.	760	3750	—

NOTE 1: Shipments, U.S. Only (Calendar Year) (Domestic) 5,414; (Government) 193; (Export) 980; (Total) 6,587.

1939 Dodge panel delivery (OCW)

CHASSIS (Series TD-20/TD-21): Wheelbase: 120/133 in. Wheels and tires for both: steel disc with semi-drop center rim. Tires: 7.00/16 six-ply front, 7.50/16 six-ply rear. Spare underslung at rear of frame. Gross weight rating 6000 pounds both series. Payload 2000 pounds both series. Rear axle ratios 4.3, 3.9 or 4.89 to 1.

TECHNICAL (Series TC/TD-15/TD-20/TD-21): Maximum gross weight: Dodge said "has no gross rating but will carry 1000 pounds payload." Mechanical fuel pump fed from 18 gallon gas tank mounted inside frame at left side. Air cleaner and gas filter. Dry, single plate clutch. Selective sliding gear transmission. Speeds: 3F/1R. Hotchkiss drive. Tubular steel propeller shaft. Reverse Elliot type front axle, I-beam section. Rear axles on ½ and ¾-ton models have hypoid drive gears, one-ton model has spiral bevel drive gears. Worm and sector gears steering. 17 in. three spoke steering wheel, adjustable for height. Four wheel hydraulic brakes. Independent handbrake operating on propeller shaft. Amola steel springs. Rear axle ratios: Standard 4.1, 3.73, 4.3 or 4.78 to 1.

OPTIONS: Oil bath air cleaner ($3.25). Rear bumper ($6). Generator for slow speed operation ($27.50). Governors: Leibing ($5), Monarch ($5), Handy ($10). Chrome headlamps ($2.75). Dual horns ($7.50). 6.00 x 16 6-ply tires front and rear ($14.50). 6.50 x 16 6-ply tires front and rear ($28.25). 5.25 x 20 4-ply tires front and rear and 20 in. wheels ($18). 5.25 x 20 6-ply tires front and rear and 20 in. wheels ($35). Coach lamps ($8.50). Oil filter ($3.25). Partition behind driver's seat: Panel, screen and canopy ($15). Stationary rear view mirror ($1.50). Adjustable rear view mirror ($2.50). Auxiliary seat ($10). Sun visors interior each ($2). Auxiliary taillight ($4). Four speed transmission ($17.50). Chrome windshield frame ($3). Auxiliary windshield wiper - vacuum ($4). Dual electric wipers ($8).

HISTORIAL: Model year began Dec. 1, 1938. Dodge truck sales rebounded significantly from the low of 1938 gaining 42.8 percent in sales. Total registrations were 48,049. Total production was 89,364 of which 3,403 were built in Los Angeles and 5,704 were built in Canada. Dodge exported 19,336 trucks of all sizes and delivered 5,997 trucks to the government. Of the government sales 905 were ½-ton, 40 three-quarter-ton and 193 one-tonners. Dodge came in fourth in the U.S. truck sales race while the car division came in fifth place in the car sales race. Dodge startled the truck industry by announcing a Dodge built Diesel engine for use in their heavy duty 2½ and three-ton models. This engine was developed and built in house. Dodge, as did Ford and Chevrolet, offered an economy model again for 1939 on the ½, ¾ and one-ton series. Economy models were supplied with a smaller carburetor. Dodge also introduced two series of forward control panel delivery models built on ¾ and one-ton chassis. Body builders were Metroplitan and Montpelier. Dodge for 1939 continued to build trucks ranging from ½ to three-tons. Montpelier continued, to produce a Dodge Cab-over engine conversion and Dodge continued their popular, but low volume four-ton Airflow truck line.

1939 Dodge 1-ton long-wheelbase panel delivery.

1939	5	4	3	2	1
Series TC — (½-Ton) — (116 in. w.b.)					
Pickup	1300	2550	4250	5900	8500
Panel	1350	2650	4400	6150	8800
Canopy	1300	2600	4300	6000	8600
Screen	1300	2600	4300	6000	8600
Series TD — (¾-Ton) — (120 in. w.b.)					
Pickup	1150	2310	3850	5400	7700
Stake	1110	2220	3700	5200	7400
Platform	1110	2220	3700	5200	7400
Series TD-20 — (1-Ton) — (120 in. w.b.)					
Pickup	1130	2250	3750	5250	7500
Stake	1070	2150	3550	5000	7100
Platform	1070	2150	3550	5000	7100
Series TD-21 — (1-Ton) — (133 in. w.b.)					
Panel	1150	2310	3850	5450	7800
Canopy	1130	2250	3750	5250	7500
Screen	1140	2280	3800	5300	7600
Pickup	1130	2250	3750	5250	7500
Stake	1070	2150	3550	5000	7100
Platform	1070	2150	3550	5000	7100

1940 DODGE

1940 Dodge ½-Ton Sedan Delivery (CHC)

LIGHT TRUCK — VC SERIES — ½-TON — SIX-CYLINDER: — The ½-ton TC series, began in 1939, continued as is with very minimal changes. Series designation changed to VC. Engine gross horsepower was increased to 79 from 70 and maximum engine torque increased to 154 lbs.-ft. from 148 lbs.-ft. Sealed beam headlights were new, as well as a new 35 ampere capacity generator to power them. Maximum gross allowable weight was increased from 4,000 pounds to 4,200 pounds. Another new feature was a new wheel attaching bolt which was made in right-and left-hand threads to prevent loosening. Front end appearance was changed by redesigning the chrome strips on the "V" shaped grille. The chrome strips were moved upward, to give a better balanced overall look. Dodge nameplates were removed from the grille sides and replaced with the Dodge name embossed and painted on the front chrome strip. Model lineups remained as before. Standard Equipment: Same as 1939 TC except add sealed beam headlights and 35 ampere generator.

I.D. DATA (Series VC): Engine numbers and serial numbers in same locations as 1939 TC series. Beginning serial numbers Detroit 8543001, ending 8562183, Los Angeles 9254201, ending 9256160. Engine numbers T105-1001 and up.

Model Model VC	Body Type	Price	Weight	Prod. Total
VC	Chassis F.F. Cowl	465	2375	—
VC	Chassis Cab	560	2775	—
VC	Pickup	590	2975	—
VC	Panel	680	3175	—
VC	Canopy	690	3000	—
VC	Screen	710	3020	—

Shipments, U.S. Only (Calendar Year) (Domestic) 36,583; (Government) 10,107; (Export) 3,022; (Total) 49,712.

ENGINE (Series VC): Inline. L-head. Six-cylinder. Cast iron block. Bore & stroke: 3⅛ in. x 4⅜ in. Displacement: 201.3 cu. in. Compression ratio: 6.7:1. Taxable horsepower: 23.44. Brake horsepower: 79 at 3000 R.P.M. Max. Torque: 154 lbs. ft. at 1200 R.P.M. Four main bearings. Solid valve lifters.

CHASSIS (Series VC): (Same as 1939 TC models).

TECHNICAL: Same as 1939 TC.

LIGHT TRUCK — SERIES VD-15 — ¾-TON — SIX-CYLINDER: — This series was carried over with but few changes. The engine maximum gross horsepower was increased to 82 from 77 and maximum torque increased from 158 lbs.-ft. to 166 lbs.-ft. at 1,200 R.P.M. Front end styling treatment was changed as per VC series; sealed beam headlights and 35-ampere generator were added. Maximum gross weight remained unchanged at 5,000 pounds.

I.D. DATA (Series VD-15): Engine number and serial number locations same as 1939 TD models. Beginning serial number: Detroit 8207101, ending 8210295. Los Angeles 9200471, ending 9200755. Engine numbers T94-1001 and up.

Model	Body Type	Price	Weight	Prod. Total
Model VD-15				
VD-15	Chassis/Flat Face Cowl	535	2525	—
VD-15	Chassis & Cab	630	2925	—
VD-15	Pickup 7½ ft.	670	3225	—
VD-15	Stake 7½ ft.	705	3550	—
VD-15	Platform 7½ ft.	680	3325	—

NOTE 1: Shipments, U.S. Only (Calendar Year). (Domestic) 4,433; (Government) none; (Export) 81; (Total) 4,514

ENGINE (Series VD-15/VD-20/VD-21): Inline. L-head. Six-cylinder. Cast iron block. Bore & stroke: 3¼ in. x 4⅜ in. Displacement: 217.76 cu. in. Compression ratio: 6.5:1. Taxable horsepower: 25.35. Brake horsepower: 82 at 3000 R.P.M. Max. Torque: 166 lbs. ft. at 1200 R.P.M. Four main bearings. Solid valve lifters.

CHASSIS: Same as 1939 TD series.

TECHNICAL: Same as 1939 TD series.

LIGHT TRUCK — SERIES VD-20/VD-21 — ONE-TON — SIX-CYLINDER: — The one ton series was also carried over from 1939 with minimum changes. Maximum gross weight was increased from 6,000 pounds to 6,400 pounds. Engine gross horsepower was increased from 77 to 82 at 3,000 R.P.M. and maximum torque increased from 158 lbs.-ft. to 166 lbs.-ft. and feet at 1,200 R.P.M. The rear axle was changed to a new hypoid type with a new barrel type differential. This permitted the use of larger and stronger differential gears. Sealed beam headlights and a 35-ampere generator were also added. The same front end appearance changes as made on the VC models were also made on the VD series.

I.D. DATA (Series VD-20/VD-21): Engine numbers and serial number locations same as TD models of 1939. Beginning serial numbers Detroit 8093476, ending 8098913. Los Angeles 9284701, ending 9285132. Engine numbers T96-1001 and up.

Model	Body Type	Price	Weight	Prod. Total
Model VD-20/VD-21				
VD-20	Chassis/Flat Face Cowl	580	2825	—
VD-20	Chassis Cab	675	3250	—
VD-20	Pickup 7½ ft.	715	3600	—
VD-20	Stake 7½ ft.	750	3850	—
VD-20	Platform 7½ ft.	725	3265	—
VD-21	Chassis/Flat Face Cowl	620	2850	—
VD-21	Chassis Cab	715	3275	—
VD-21	Panel	855	3850	—
VD-21	Canopy	840	—	—
VD-21	Screen	860	—	—
VD-21	Pickup 9 ft.	765	3675	—
VD-21	Stake 9 ft.	790	4025	—
VD-21	Platform 9 ft.	760	5750	—

Shipments, U.S. Only (Calendar Year) (Domestic) 6,666; (Government) 23; (Export) 834; (Total) 7,523.

ENGINE: Same as VD-15 series.

CHASSIS: All same except gross weight rating increased to 6,400 from 6,000 pounds.

TECHNICAL: Same as 1939 TD series.

OPTIONS: (Same list and prices as 1939.)

HISTORIAL: Model year began Oct. 1, 1939. Dodge truck sales for 1940 were up by 13.1 percent to 54,323 keeping Dodge in fourth place in the truck sales race. Total production was 117,588 of which 4,860 were produced in Los Angeles and 7,790 were produced in Canada. Government sales in 1940 were very good as the Army geared itself up for the European War. Dodge sold 10,107 half-ton models, 23 one-ton models, 8,006 1½-tons and 22 two-ton models to the government. Export sales were also very good, totalling 17,599 from ½- to three-ton capacity. Dodge continued to produce a full line of trucks including Diesels. Dodge also began producing their own line of cab-over-engine trucks this year. In February 1940 the last Airflow model was built. The DeKalb Wagon Company of DeKalb, Ill. produced a Brooks Stevens designed Urban Delivery for Dodge for use on its 120 inch ¾-ton chassis. This ultra-modern designed truck was the smartest looking truck on the road featuring an egg-shaped body and two-tone paint schemes.

166

	5	4	3	2	1
1940					
Series VC — (½-Ton) — (116 in. w.b.)					
Pickup	1300	2550	4250	5900	8500
Panel	1350	2650	4400	6150	8800
Canopy	1300	2600	4300	6000	8600
Screen	1300	2600	4300	6000	8600
Series VD-15 — (¾-Ton) — (120 in. w.b.)					
Pickup	1150	2310	3850	5400	7700
Stake	1110	2220	3700	5200	7400
Platform	1110	2220	3700	5200	7400
Series VD-20 — (1-Ton) — (120 in. w.b.)					
Pickup	1130	2250	3750	5250	7500
Stake	1070	2150	3550	5000	7100
Platform	1070	2150	3550	5000	7100
Series VD-21 (1-Ton) — (133 in. w.b.)					
Pickup	1130	2250	3750	5250	7500
Stake	1070	2150	3550	5000	7100
Platform	1070	2150	3550	5000	7100
Panel	1150	2310	3850	5450	7800
Canopy	1130	2250	3750	5250	7500
Screen	1140	2280	3800	5300	7600

1941 DODGE

1941 Dodge canopy express (DFW/DPL)

LIGHT TRUCK — WC SERIES — ½-TON — SIX-CYLINDER: — Minimal changes were made in the 1941 WC series. Appearance changes included moving the headlight mountings to a pocket formed in the front fenders, and new style parking lights mounted on the cowl. Also, all ½, ¾ and one-ton models were available in a score of two-tone paint finishes at no extra cost. Standard Dodge truck paint colors remained the same since 1939. They were Light Blue, Dark Blue, Orange, Dark Green, Gray, Red and Black. Engine horsepower and torque was increased by addition of a new high-lift camshaft. Oil bath air cleaners were made standard equipment and a second fuel filter was mounted at the carburetor. Also, a floating-type oil pump screen was new. The hinged intake screen floated just below the surface of the oil in the crankcase. Models available in the ½-ton series remained the same 1940. WC Standard Equipment: Sealed-beam headlights. Two-tone color combinations. 35-ampere generator. Oil bath air cleaner. Front and rear shocks. Spare wheel and tire. Front bumper. Hood ornament. Horn. Combination stop and taillamp. Tool kit. Speedometer. Choke. Fuel gauge. Oil pressure indicator. Ammeter. Throttle. Cowl vent. Vacuum wipers. Panel, canopy and screen models have one bucket seats only.

I.D. DATA (Series WC): Serial numbers and engine numbers found in same locations as 1939 TC models. Beginning serial numbers Detroit 8562201, ending in 1947 8584879. Los Angeles beginning 9212801, ending in 1947 9215035. Starting engine number T125-1001.

Model	Body Type	Price	Weight	Prod. Total
Series WC				
WC	Chassis & Cowl	500	2375	—
WC	Chassis & Cab	595	2775	—
WC	Pickup (6½ ft.)	630	2975	—
WC	Canopy	740	3000	—
WC	Panel	730	3175	—
WC	Screen	760	3020	—

NOTE 1: Shipments, U.S. Only (Calendar Year) (Domestic) 32,617; (Government) 54,235; (Export) 2,051; (Total) 88,903.

ENGINE (Series WC): Inline. L-head. Six-cylinder. Cast iron block. Bore & stroke: 3⅛ in. x 4⅜ in. Displacement: 201.3 cu. in. Compression ratio: 6.7:1. Brake horsepower: 82.5 at 3000 R.P.M. Net horsepower: 23.44. Max. Torque: 160 lbs. ft. at 1200 R.P.M. Four main bearings. Solid valve lifters.

CHASSIS (Series WC): Same as 1940 VC models. Tires: 6.00 x 16 4-ply (front and rear).

TECHNICAL: Clutch 10 inch single dry plate. Selective sliding transmission 3F/1R. Drop forged I-Beam front axle. Rear axle semi-floating with hypoid gears. Front springs 39 in. x 1¾ in.; quantity eight. Rear springs 52 in. x 1¾ in. quantity nine for WC, 10 for WD-15 and 11 WD-20-21. Hotchkiss drive. Steering ratio 17:1. Fuel tank 18 gallons, located inside left frame rail.

LIGHT TRUCK — SERIES WD-15 — ¾-TON — SIX-CYLINDER: — Carried over from 1940 with the same changes as WC series. Standard equipment: Same as WC series.

I.D. DATA (Series WD-15): Engine number and serial number locations same as WC series. Beginning serial number: Detroit 8210351, ending in 1947 82147541. Los Angeles 9199101, ending in 1947 9199515. Engine numbers T114-1001.

Model Series WD	Body Type	Price	Weight	Prod. Total
WD-15	Chassis & Cowl	570	2525	—
WD-15	Chassis & Cab	665	2925	—
WD-15	Pickup 7½ ft.	705	3225	—
WD-15	Platform 7½ ft.	715	3325	—
WD-15	Stake 7½ ft.	740	3550	—

NOTE 1: Shipments, U.S. Only (Calendar Year). (Domestic) 5,692; (Export) 149; (Total) 5,841.

ENGINE (Series WD-20/WD-21): Inline. L-head. Six-cylinder. Cast iron block. Bore & stroke: 3¼ in. x 4⅜ in. Displacement: 217.76 cu. in. Compression ratio: 6.5:1. Brake horsepower: 85 at 3000 R.P.M. Net horsepower: 25.35. Max. Torque: 170 lbs. ft. at 1200 R.P.M. Four main bearings. Solid valve lifters.

CHASSIS: Same as 1940 VD series. Tires: TA-15 six-ply (front & rear).

TECHNICAL: Same as WC series.

LIGHT TRUCK — SERIES WD-20/WD-21 — ONE-TON — SIX-CYLINDER: — Both one-ton series were carried over intact from 1940 with the same changes as outlined above for the WC models. One-ton models were now available with dual rear wheels. On panel, canopy and screen models dual rear fenders were supplied when dual wheels were specified. On platform and stake models bodies were six in. wide when ordered with dual wheels. Standard equipment same as WC series.

I.D. DATA: WD-20 Series beginning serial number: Detroit 81200101, ending in 1947 81207016. Los Angeles beginning in 1947 9285201, ending in 1947 9285810. Beginning engine number T116-1001 WD-21 series beginning serial number Detroit 81200101, ending in 1947 81207016. Los Angeles 9285201, ending 81207016. Beginning engine number T116-1001.

Model Model WD-20/WD-21	Body Type	Price	Weight	Prod. Total
WD-20	Chassis & Cowl	635	2825	—
WD-20	Chassis & Cab	730	3250	—
WD-20	Pickup 7½ ft.	770	3600	—
WD-20	Platform 7½ ft.	780	3625	—
WD-20	Stake 7½ ft.	805	3850	—
Series WD-21				
WD-21	Chassis & Cowl	655	2850	—
WD-21	Chassis & Cab	750	3275	—
WD-21	Pickup	800	3675	—
WD-21	Canopy	895	3400	—
WD-21	Panel	890	3850	—
WD-21	Platform	805	3750	—
WD-21	Stake	825	4025	—
WD-21	Screen	915	3420	—

NOTE 1: Shipments, U.S. Only (Calendar Year) (Domestic) 7,837; (Export) 756; (Total) 8,593.

1941 Dodge Power Wagon staff car (OCW)

ENGINE: See WD-15 engine data above.

CHASSIS: Both the WD-20 and WD-21 models used 6.50 x 16 (six-ply) tires in front and 7.00 x 16 (six-ply) tires in the rear. Other chassis specifications same as VD-20/VD-21 Series of 1940.

TECHNICAL: Same as WC series.

OPTIONS: Inside rear view mirror ($1). Long arm type rear view mirror ($1.50). Long arm adjustable types ($2.50). Auxiliary seat ($12). Adjustable auxiliary seat ($14.50). Sun visors each ($2). Auxiliary taillight ($2.50). Tow hooks (two front only) ($4). Four- speed transmission ($17.50). Chrome plated windshield frame ($3). Auxiliary vacuum wiper ($4). Dual electric ($13). Single auxiliary electric wiper ($8). Air Cleaners: Vortox ($17.50), Vortox with Vortox breather cap ($19.50). Airfoam seat cushion and back ($10). Battery 119 ampere hours ($2.50). Rear bumper ($6). DeLuxe Cab Equipment consisting of: leather upholstery, air foam seat and back cushions, arm rest on left door, single electric windshield wiper, dome light, one interior sun visor and chrome windshield frame ($25). Dome light in cab ($2.50). Generator for slow operations ($8). Glove compartment door lock ($1.50). Governor ($5). Chrome headlight and parking lights ($3.50). Heater and defroster ($25). Dual horns ($2.50). Coach lights ($8.50). Oil filter ($3.25). Cartridge type oil filter ($6). Partition behind drivers seat ($20). Partition behind drivers seat with full width seat ($25). Grille guard ($7.50).

HISTORICAL: Model year began Sept. 1, 1940. Total registrations were 62,925 or a 15.8 percent increase over 1940. However, total production increased to 166,602 of which 7,164 were built in Los Angeles and 12,376 were built in Canada. This was a very good year for Government business as the army continued to prepare for war. Dodge delivered to the government 57,692 trucks; 54,235 were ½-ton models and 3,457 were 1½-ton models. In addition to the government business Dodge exported 18,592 trucks most of which were 1½-ton models. Dodge ended in fourth place in United States truck sales this year while the car division came in seventh place. Dodge continued to produce a full line of trucks from ½ to three-ton capacity including a diesel model. Dodge also cataloged an Urban Panel Delivery a forward control truck built on either a ¾ or one-ton chassis. The body was custom built by Montpelier Manufacturing Company of Montpelier, Ohio. This was also the first year in which Dodge used their famous "Job-Rated" advertising slogan. An advertising scheme they would use for many years.

Pricing

1941	5	4	3	2	1
Series WC (½-Ton)					
Pickup	1000	2000	3300	4600	6600
Canopy	1010	2030	3350	4700	6700
Panel	930	1860	3100	4350	6200
Screen	1020	2040	3400	4850	6800
Series WD (¾-Ton)					
Pickup	920	1850	3050	4300	6100
Platform	870	1750	2900	4100	5800
Stake	890	1770	2950	4150	5900
Series WD-20 (1-Ton)					
Pickup	850	1700	2850	4200	6000
Platform	840	1680	2800	3900	5600
Stake	850	1700	2850	4000	5700
Series WD-21 (1-Ton)					
Pickup	850	1700	2850	4000	5700
Canopy	900	1800	3000	4200	6000
Panel	850	1700	2850	4000	5700
Platform	720	1450	2400	3300	4800
Stake	830	1650	2750	3850	5500
Screen	930	1860	3100	4350	6200

1942 DODGE

LIGHT TRUCK — WC SERIES — ½-TON — SIX-CYLINDER: — This series was now in its fourth year and still selling well. For 1942 it was carried over without major change. A new larger 217 cu. in. engine was made standard in the WC series boosting horsepower from 82 to 90. Clutch housings on all models ½-ton through two-ton capacity were made stronger through the use of reinforcing ribs. Frames of the WC series were strengthened by an increase in stock thickness. Bumpers on ½-ton and ¾-ton models were now painted gray or black enamel in place of the former aluminum color. A redesigned radiator core on ½-ton models provided for more efficient cooling. This was the first year of this series in which the series designation was carried over without change from the previous year. No appearance changes were made. No further appearance changes would be made to the W Series through the 1947 model year. Standard Equipment: Same as 1941.

I.D. DATA (Series WC): Engine numbers and serial numbers found in same locations as 1941 models. Beginning serial number Detroit 81100101, ending in 1947 81115301. Los Angeles beginning 9215036, ending in 1947 9216935. Beginning engine number T112-42001.

1942 Dodge WC-23 command car (ATC)

Model	Body Type	Price	Weight	Prod. Total
Series WC				
WC	Chassis & Cowl	522	2375	—
WC	Chassis & Cab	617	2775	—
WC	Pickup (6½ ft.)	651	2975	—
WC	Canopy	762	3000	—
WC	Panel	751	3175	—

NOTE 1: Shipments, U.S. Only (Calendar Year) (Domestic) 2,466; (Government) 19,600; (Export) 566; (Total) 22,572.

ENGINE (Series WC): Inline. L-head. Six-cylinder. Cast iron block. Bore & stroke: 3¼ in. x 4⅜ in. Displacement: 217.76 cu. in. Compression ratio: 6.8:1. Brake horsepower: 95 at 3600 R.P.M. Net horsepower: 25.35. Max. Torque: 172 lbs. ft. at 1200 R.P.M. Four main bearings. Solid valve lifters.

LIGHT TRUCK — SERIES WD-15 — ¾-TON — SIX-CYLINDER: — As with the WC series the WD-15 series was carried forward with very little change. The WD series also received the same new engine as did the WC series. A pattern of using the 218 cu. in. in the ½ and ¾-ton trucks was now set and would last well into the 1950s. No appearance changes were made. Standard Equipment: Same as 1941.

I.D. DATA (Series WD-15): Engine number and serial number location same as 1941. Beginning serial number: Detroit 8214755, ending in 1947 8217538. Los Angeles beginning 9199516, ending in 1947 9199890. Beginning engine number T112-42001.

Model	Body Type	Price	Weight	Prod. Total
Series WD-15				
WD-15	Chassis & Cowl	571	2525	—
WD-15	Chassis & Cab	666	2925	—
WD-15	Pickup 7½ ft.	705	3225	—
WD-15	Platform 7½ ft.	716	3325	—
WD-15	Stake 7½ ft.	742	3550	—

NOTE 1: Shipments, U.S. Only (Calendar Year). (Domestic) 640; (Government) 77,046; (Export) 8; (Total) 77,694.

ENGINE: See WC Series engine data above.

LIGHT TRUCK — SERIES WD-20/WD-21 — ONE-TON — SIX-CYLINDER: — One-ton models were carried over without appearance changes and with but few mechanical changes. However, a new engine displacing 230.2 cu. in. and producing 105 horsepower gave the new models added performance. Other mechanical changes were a strengthened clutch housing and a larger diameter radiator fan. The 230.2 cu. in engine was used in one-ton trucks through the 1950s.

I.D. DATA: Location same as 1941. WD-20 Series beginning serial number: Detroit 81207017, ending in 1947 81210967. Beginning Los Angeles 9285811, ending in 1947 9286180. Beginning engine number T116-42001. WD-21 Series beginning serial number: Detroit 81207017, ending in 1947 81210967. Beginning Los Angeles 9285811, ending in 1947 9286180. Beginning engine number T116-42001.

Model	Body Type	Price	Weight	Prod. Total
Series WD-20				
WD-20	Chassis & Cowl	651	2825	—
WD-20	Chassis & Cab	746	3250	—
WD-20	Pickup 7½ ft.	787	3600	—
WD-20	Platform 7½ ft.	796	3625	—
WD-20	Stake 7½ ft.	821	3850	—
Series WD-21				
WD-21	Chassis & Cowl	672	2850	—
WD-21	Chassis & Cab	767	3275	—
WD-21	Pickup (9 ft.)	817	3675	—
WD-21	Canopy	912	3400	—
WD-21	Panel	907	3850	—
WD-21	Platform (9 ft.)	821	3750	—
WD-21	Stake (9 ft.)	842	4025	—

NOTE 1: Shipments, U.S. Only (Calendar Year) (Domestic) 978; (Government) 3; (Export) 157; (Total) 1,138.

ENGINE: Inline. L-head. Six-cylinder. Cast iron block. Bore & stroke: 3¼ in. x 4⅝ in. Displacement: 230.2 cu. in. Compression ratio: 6.8:1. Brake horsepower: 105 at 3600 R.P.M. Net horsepower: 25.35. Max. Torque: 184 lbs. ft. at 1200 R.P.M. Four main bearings. Solid valve lifters.

CHASSIS (Series WC): Wheelbase: 116 in. Tires: 6.00 x 16 (four-ply) (front & rear).

CHASSIS (Series WD-15): Wheelbase: 120 in. Tires: TA15 six-ply (front & rear).

CHASSIS (Series WD-20/WD-21): Wheelbase: 120/133 in. Tires: (front) 6.50 x 16 six-ply; (rear) 7.00 x 16 six-ply.

TECHNICAL: Same as 1941.

OPTIONS: Extra Equipment: Same list, same prices as 1941.

HISTORICAL: Model year began Sept. 1, 1941. Registration figures for 1942 are not available. Civilian truck production ceased on Apr. 30, 1942. Total production for the calendar year, however, was very good due to purchases by the military. Total production was 169,837 of which 2,420 were built in Los Angeles and 41,665 were built in Canada. Total government purchases were 109,665. Which breaks down as follows: ½-ton 19,600, ¾-ton 77,046, one-ton 3, 1½-ton 12,919, two-ton 39, and three ton 58. Also, 4,445 trucks were exported. Much of the Canadian production were military vehicles delivered to the Canadian government. Dodge built a full line of civilian trucks this year consisting of 112 standard chassis and body models on 18 wheelbase lengths ranging in size from ½ to three-tons. This was the last year for the Dodge built Diesel engine. Civilian auto production at Chrysler ceased on Jan. 31, 1942. Dodge cars came in sixth place in the U.S. car sale race.

Pricing

	5	4	3	2	1
1942					
Series WC (½-Ton)					
Pickup	1000	2000	3300	4600	6600
Canopy	1010	2030	3350	4700	6700
Panel	930	1860	3100	4350	6200
Screen	1020	2040	3400	4800	6800
Series WD (¾-Ton)					
Pickup	920	1850	3050	4300	6100
Platform	870	1750	2900	4100	5800
Stake	890	1770	2950	4150	5900
Series WD-20 (1-Ton)					
Pickup	850	1700	2850	4200	6000
Platform	840	1680	2800	3900	5600
Stake	850	1700	2850	4000	5700
Series WD-21 (1-Ton)					
Pickup	850	1700	2850	4000	5700
Canopy	900	1800	3000	4200	6000
Panel	850	1700	2850	4000	5700
Platform	720	1450	2400	3300	4800
Stake	830	1650	2750	3850	5500
Screen	930	1860	3100	4350	6200

Brief History — World War II Dodge All-Wheel-Drive Trucks

(Military section: John Zentmyer)

World War II Dodge all-wheel-drive trucks were the result of experience with several 4x4 trucks that Dodge had developed in the thirties. The 1940 ½-ton 4x4 VC series was the first of the World War II light trucks; these vehicles had civilian front-end sheet metal. They were followed by the ½-ton 4x4 WC series, which had all-military design sheet metal and improved running gear. Next came probably the best of the World War II light trucks, the ¾-ton 4x4 WC series. From these trucks was developed a very close cousin, the 1½-ton 6x6, which is included after the ¾-ton trucks because it essentially is a ¾-ton truck with a two-speed transfer case and another rear end. Many of these WC-series trucks were shipped to England, Russia, and other countries as a part of the Lend-Lease program.

As each Dodge military truck entered the design / maufacturing system, it received an Engineering Code for company use that began with a letter and three digits (T-207-, for example). In general, the beginning of the engineering code also was used as the prefix for the engine number. This code usually was changed when a major engine or chassis change was made, although in at least one instance the engine was changed but the engineering code was not changed until the completion of the series run (½-ton 4x4 T-211). Beginning in 1937 with the T-200 (model RF-40-X-4) and continuing on into the fifties, all of the military-design vehicles had engineering codes that were in the T-200 series.

The model codes (VC-1, WC-25, etc.) simply were an outgrowth of the standard civilian codes. The letter "V" denoted 1940 and "W" 1941; the letter "C" denoted the ½-ton weight class. Thus, a "VC" model was the standard civilian 1940 ½-ton truck and a "WC" model was the 1941 ½-ton truck. When the military ½-ton 4x4 chassis and various body styles were designed, a numerical suffix (-1, -25, etc.) was added to the ½-ton civilian model code to differentiate the various military styles. A common misconception is that "WC" stood for "Weapons Carrier," when in fact it simply was the model designation for a 1941 ½-ton truck. When the later ¾-ton and 1½-ton trucks were produced, the earlier ½-ton "WC" model prefix simply was continued.

Several sources were consulted for production quantities, including serial number range, monthly production figures, U.S.A. registration numbers, and acceptance by the Army Service Forces. The serial number range is believed to be the most accurate. Published sources reported the registration numbers contained some errors that were found by comparison to the acceptance figures. The "body type and end use N/A" vehicles were believed to have been made but were not included in acceptance figures by the Army Service Forces.

1940 ½-Ton Dodge 4x4 Carryall

MODELS VC-1 through VC-6 — SIX-CYLINDER: Dodge's first production ½-ton-rated 4x4 light trucks for the U.S. Army were models VC-1 through VC-6 (engineering code T-202). These vehicles were based on 1-ton commercial truck components to which were added a one-speed transfer case and a gear-driven front end to produce a ½-ton off-road rated vehicle. Interestingly enough, these trucks could only be shifted into first or reverse with the transfer case lever in the 4WD position. Several different body styles were produced using standard commercial front-end sheet metal to which was added a brush guard. The VC series trucks were not equipped with winches.

I.D. DATA: Serial numbers are stamped in the frame side rail on the driver's side slightly forward of the front axle and on a data plate on the dashboard. Starting and ending: see table. Serial numbers were assigned without regard to body type as each truck came down the production line. The numbers were assigned by blocks, with no known record kept of body types within each block. Army series no.: G-505. Starting engine no.: T-202-1001.

T-202-201.3 cu. in. flathead six; 79 bhp at 3000 R.P.M.

Model	Type	WB	Wt	Starting	Ending	Quan
VC-1	Command Reconnaissance	116	4275	8640001	8644641	2129
VC-2	Command Radio	—	4275	—	—	60
VC-3	Closed Cab Pickup w/troop seats	—	4620	—	—	816
VC-4	Closed Cab Pickup w/o troop seats	—	4620	—	—	4
VC-5	Weapons Carrier (Open-Cab Pickup)	—	4220	—	—	1608
VC-6	Carryall	—	4595	—	—	24
	Total World War II Production					4641

TECHNICAL: Spur gear (non-synchro) transmission. Speeds: 4F/1R. One-speed transfer case. Parking brake: External contracting band on transmission. Floor controls for all functions. Single plate dry disc clutch. Hypoid front and rear third members (interchangeable). Overall ratio: 4.89:1. 8¾ in. diameter ring gear. Semi-floating rear axle; Bendix-Weiss drive front axle. Hydraulic internal expanding brakes. Five-hole concave solid disc wheels (Budd). Tires: 7.50 x 16 eight-ply.

1941 ½-Ton Dodge 4x4 Weapons Carrier (Open-Cab Pickup)

MODELS WC-1 - 27, 40 - 43 (no WC-2) — SIX-CYLINDER: Re-designed sheet metal and rear axle, slightly different engines and some models with winch comprised the WC ½-ton-rated 4x4 trucks. Models WC 36 - 39 and 47 - 50 were 4x2 vehicles having the same body styles as some of the other WC models but with 1941-pattern commercial sheet metal. Missing WC numbers were not assigned. The 4x4 trucks were produced in three engineering code groups — T-207, T-211 and T-215. They were made for the Quartermaster Corps on several contracts, with changes being made for each group. The main differences were:

1. The T-207 vehicles had smaller rear brakes than did the T-211 and T-215 vehicles.

2. The T-211 vehicles were not equipped with winches. Some T-207 and T-215 vehicles were so equipped. The frames for the winch vehicles were specially made for the purpose and did not simply have extensions added.

3. Some T-211 and T-215 vehicles were equipped with Rzeppa drive front axles, although the Bendix-Weiss type was the most common. The T-207 vehicles were exclusively equipped with the Bendix-Weiss type.

4. The T-215 vehicles were equipped with a larger engine that actually was introduced during the T-211 model run.

I.D. DATA: Serial numbers are stamped in the frame side rail on the driver's side slightly forward of the front axle and on a data plate on the dashboard. Starting and ending: see table. Serial numbers were assigned without regard to body type as each truck came down the production line. The numbers were assigned by blocks for each contract, with no known record kept of body types within each block. Months of manufacture are approximate. Army series no.: G-505. Starting engine nos.: T-207-1001; T-211-1001, 42001; T-215-1001.

T-207 — Models WC-1 through WC-11 No WC-2)

217.8 cu. in. flathead six; 85 bhp at 3000 R.P.M. (9/40 thru 5/41). Beginning S/N 8644701; ending S/N 8676719. (8666217-8666300 not assigned)

T-211 — Models WC-12 through WC-20

217.8 cu. in. flathead six; 85 bhp at 3000 R.P.M. (T-211-1001; 6/41, 7/41). 230.2 cu. in. flathead six; 92 bhp at 3100 R.P.M. (T-211-42001; 8/41, 9/41). Beginning S/N 8676901; ending S/N 8694193

T-215 — Models WC-21 through WC-27, WC-40 through WC-43

230.2 cu. in. flathead six; 92 bhp at 3100 R.P.M. (10/41 thru 6/42). Beginning S/N 81500001; ending S/N 81528537.

Body Type/ Model Number	WB	Wt	T-207	T-211	T-215	Total
Ambulance — WC-9, 18, 27	123	5340	2288	1555	2579	6422
Carryall — WC-10, 17, 26	116	4850	1643	274	2899	4816
Clsd. Cab P/U — WC-1, 5; 12, 14; 40	116	4640	2633	6048	275	8956
Command w/o wn. — WC-6, 15, 23	116	4640	9365	3980	3409	16754
Command w/wn. — WC-7, 24	116	4975	1438	none	1412	2850
Command Radio — WC-8, 16, 25	116	4770	548	1284	873	2705
Emergency Repair — WC-20, 41	123	5120	none	30	383	413
Panel Body — WC-11, 19	116	4470	642	103	none	745
Panel Radio — WC-42	116	4510	none	none	650	650
Telephone Installation — WC-43	116	N/A	none	none	370	370
Weap. Carr. w/o wn. — WC-3, 13, 21	116	4440	7808	4019	13787	25614
Weap. Carr. w/wn. — WC-4, 22	116	4775	5570	none	1900	7470
Total World War II Production			31935	17293	28537	77765

TECHNICAL: Spur gear (non-synchro) transmission. Speeds: 4F/1R. One-speed transfer case. Parking brake: External contracting band on transmission. Floor controls for all functions. Single plate dry disc clutch. Hypoid front and rear third members (interchangeable). Overall ratio: 4.89:1. 8¾ in. diameter ring gear. Full-floating rear axle; Bendix-Weiss or Rzeppa drive front axle. Five-hole wheels (Budd). Tires: 7.50 x 16 eight-ply highway or directional (chevron) tread.

HISTORICAL: Production began in September, 1940. 5332 vehicles were manufactured by the end of that year. The last of these vehicles were produced in June, 1942, when five were made.

1941 ½-Ton Dodge 4x2 Panel Truck

The following models are the 4x2 vehicles with commercial sheet metal referred to above. Army series no.: G-613. Starting engine no.: T-112-42001.

T-112 — 217.8 cu. in. flathead six; 85 bhp at 3000 R.P.M.

Model	Type	WB	Wt	Starting	Ending	Quan
WC-36	Carryall	116	3800	81003700	81104468	400
WC-37	Panel	—	3400	—	—	6
WC-38	Closed Cab Pickup	—	3365	—	—	362
WC-39	Closed Cab w/telephone install. body	—	N/A	—	—	1
	Total					769
WC-47	Closed Cab Pickup	—	3365	81113001	81113773	390
WC-48	Carryall	—	3800	—	—	374
WC-49	Panel	—	3400	—	—	8
WC-50	Closed Cab w/telephone install. body	—	N/A	—	—	1
	Total					773
	Total World War II Production					1542

TECHNICAL: Helical gear (second and third synchro) transmission. Speeds: 3F/1R. Parking brake: External contracting band on transmission. Floor controls for all functions. Single plate 10-inch dry disc clutch. Hypoid rear differential unit. Overall ratio: 4.1:1. Semi-floating rear axle. Hydraulic internal expanding brakes. Five-hole wheels. Tires: 6.50 x 16 six-ply.

1941 ¾-Ton Dodge 4x4 Weapons Carrier

MODELS WC-51 through WC-61 and WC-64 — SIX-CYLINDER: These trucks were among the best vehicles produced during World War II. They were lower, wider, had high-flotation tires and heavier-duty components than did the ½-ton 4x4 models. They were procured by all services and saw service in all theaters. They also were supplied to the Allies on the Lend-Lease program. The civilian Power Wagon (1945-1968) essentially was a ¾-ton Weapons Carrier with different sheet metal, as was the Korean War M37 series. Thus, the venerable World War II design survived basically intact for many years after the close of the war.

I.D. DATA: Serial numbers are stamped in the frame side rail on the driver's side slightly forward of the front axle and on a data plate on the dashboard. Starting and ending: see table. Serial numbers were assigned without regard to body type as each truck came down the production line, with the exception of the WC-55s. The numbers were assigned by blocks for each contract, with no known record kept of body types within each block. Army series no.: G-502. Starting engine no.: T-214-1001.

T-214 — 230.2 cu. in. flathead six; 92 bhp at 3200 R.P.M.

Model	Type	WB	Wt	Starting	Ending	Quan
WC-51	Weapons Carrier	98	5250	81523481	81784196	123541
WC-52	Weapons Carrier w/winch	98	5550	—	—	59118
WC-53	Carryall (Completed 9/43)	114	5750	—	—	8402
WC-54	Ambulance (Declared ltd. std. 4/44)	121	5920	—	—	26002
WC-55	Gun Motor Carriage M6 (37-mm anti-tank)	98	6621	81529001	81534380	5380
WC-56	Command Reconnaissance	98	5375	81534381	81784196	18812
WC-57	Command Reconnaissance w/winch	98	5675	—	—	6010
WC-58	Command Radio w/o winch)	98	5375	—	—	2344
WC-59	Telephone Maint. (Signal Corps K-50)	121	5400	—	—	549
WC-60	Emergency Repair M2 (Series #G-61)	121	5580	—	—	300
WC-61	Phone Maint. w/wn (Sig. Corps. K-50B)	121	5700	—	—	58
----	Phone Maint. w/o wn (Sig. Corps. K-50B)	121	5400	—	—	
WC-64	KD (Knockdown) Ambulance (air xport)	121	6755	—	—	3500
----	Body type and end use N/A	—	—	—	—	1180
Total World War II Production 255196						

TECHNICAL: Spur gear (non-synchro) transmission. Speeds: 4F/1R. One-speed transfer case. Parking brake: External contracting band on transmission. Floor controls for all functions. Single plate dry disc clutch. Hypoid front and rear third members (interchangeable). Overall ratio: 5.83:1. 8¾ in. diameter ring gears in early models, 9⅝ in. gears in later vehicles. Full-floating rear axle; Bendix-Weiss drive front axle. Hydraulic internal expanding brakes. Five-hole bolted-together combat wheels (Budd). Tires: 9.00 x 16 eight-ply.

HISTORICAL: Production began in April, 1942 with 12 vehicles and continued through August, 1945, when 1146 were built. The Carryall was too distinctive a vehicle and was declared obsolete in April, 1943. The WC-54 ambulance was declared limited standard in April, 1944, and was replaced by the WC-64 KD (KnockDown) ambulance as standard. Production on these ambulances began in January, 1945.

1943 1½-Ton Dodge 6x6 Cargo Truck

MODELS WC-62 and WC-63 — SIX-CYLINDER: These trucks were ¾-ton weapons carriers to which were added a two-speed transfer case and another rear end assembly to produce a 1½-ton rated 6x6.

I.D. DATA: Serial numbers are stamped in the frame side rail on the driver's side slightly forward of the front axle and on a data plate on the dashboard. Starting and ending: see table. Serial numbers were assigned without regard to whether or not a winch was installed as each truck came down the production line. No known record was kept of truck type correlated to serial number. Army series no.: G-507. Starting engine no.: T-223-1001.

T-223-230.2 cu. in. flathead six; 92 bhp at 3200 R.P.M.

Model	Type	WB	Wt	Starting	Ending	Quan
WC-62	Open Cab with cargo bed	125	7250	82000001	82043278	23092
WC-63	Open Cab with cargo bed and winch	—	7550	—	—	20132
----	Body type and end use N/A	—	—	—	—	54
Total World War II Production 43278						

1943 Dodge U.S. Army Command Car

TECHNICAL: Spur gear (non-synchro) transmission. Speeds: 4F/1R. Two-speed transfer case (1.5:1 and 1.0:1). Parking brake: External contracting band on transfer case. Floor controls for all functions. Single plate dry disc clutch. Hypoid front and rear third members (interchangeable). Ratio: 5.83:1. 9⅝ in. diameter ring gear. Full-floating rear axles; Bendix-Weiss drive front axle. Hydraulic internal expanding brakes. Five-hole bolted-together combat wheels (Budd). Tires: 9.00 x 16 eight-ply.

HISTORICAL: Production began in March, 1943, with five vehicles, and continued through August, 1945, when 1517 were made. 45,000 vehicles had been ordered; 43,278 were built and the remaining 1722 cancelled at the end of the war.

1943 Dodge weapons carrier (DB/CHC)

Model	Contract No.	U.S.A. Registration Nos.	WB	Wt	Starting	Ending	Quan
WC-1	W-398-QM-8039	24615 thru 25789	116	4640	8644701	8666216	1175
	W-398-QM-8286	25792 thru 27189	—	—	—	—	1398
	Total Closed Cab Pickup w/o winch, w/longitudinal troop seats						2573
WC-2	(Not assigned)						0
WC-3	W-398-QM-8286	27190 thru 29999	116	4240	8644701	8666216	2810
		210000 thru 214671	—	—	—	—	4672
		215536 thru 215861	—	—	—	—	326
	Total Weapons Carrier w/o winch, w/transverse troop seats						7808
WC-4	W-398-QM-8286	214672 thru 215418	116	4775	8644701	8666216	747
		215862 thru 216056	—	—	—	—	195
	W-398-QM-9140	217349 thru 221976	—	—	8666301	8676719	4628
	Total Weapons Carrier w/winch, w/transverse troop seats						5570
WC-5	W-398-QM-8286	001332 thru 001391	116	5920	8644701	8666216	60
	Total Closed Cab Pickup w/o winch, w/o troop seats						60
WC-6	W-398-QM-8286	206490 thru 209867	116	4640	8644701	866216	3378
		2010913 thru 2015119	—	—	—	—	4207
	W-398-QM-9140	2020437 thru 2022216	—	—	8666301	8676719	1780
	Total Command Reconnaissance w/o winch						9365
WC-7	W-398-QM-8286	2010209 thru 2010500	116	4975	8644701	8666216	292
		2015244 thru 2015297	—	—	—	—	54
	W-398-QM-9140	2022217 thru 2023308	—	—	8666301	8676719	1092
	Total Command Reconnaissance w/winch						1438

Model	Contract No.	U.S.A. Registration Nos.	WB	Wt	Starting	Ending	Quan
WC-8	W-398-QM-8038	60473 thru 60479	116	4770	8644701	8666216	7
	W-398-QM-8286	605100 thru 605304	—	—	—	—	205
	W-398-QM-9140	606021 thru 606356	—	—	8666301	8676719	336
	Total Command Radio (w/o winch)						548
WC-9	W-398-QM-8286	71077 thru 71973	123	5340	8644701	8666216	897
		71975 thru 72249	—	—	—	—	275
	W-398-QM-9140	72256 thru 73371	—	—	8666301	8676719	1116
	Total WC-9 Ambulance						2288
WC-10	W-398-QM-8286	209868 thru 209999	116	4850	8644701	8666216	132
		2010000 thru 2010208	—	—	—	—	209
		2015120 thru 2015243	—	—	—	—	124
	W-398-QM-9140	2023309 thru 2024486	—	—	8666301	8676719	1178
	Total Carryall						1643
WC-11	W-398-QM-8286	215419 thru 215478	116	4510	8644701	8666216	60
		216057 thru 216349	—	—	—	—	293
	W-398-QM-9140	221977 thru 222265	—	—	8666301	8676719	289
	Total Panel						642
	Total T-207 trucks manufactured (S/N 8666217-8666300 not assigned)						31935
WC-12	W-390-QM-9388	80766 thru (no body)	116	4640	8676901	8694193	1
		222266 thru 226218	—	—	—	—	3953
		226219 thru 227043	—	—	—	—	825
		231275 thru 232274	—	—	—	—	1000
	Total Closed Cab Pickup w/o winch, w/ longitudinal troop seats						5579
WC-13	W-398-QM-9388	227044 thru 229817	116	4240	8676901	8694193	2774
		229818 thru 230130	—	—	—	—	313
		232275 thru 233206	—	—	—	—	932
	Total Weapons Carrier w/o winch, w/transverse troop seats						4019
WC-14	W-398-QM-9388	003856 thru 004123	116	4640	8676901	8694193	268
	Total Closed Cab Pickup w/o winch, w/o troop seats						268
WC-15	W-398-QM-9388	2024487 thru 2025966	116	4640	8676901	8694193	1480
		2026644 thru 2027937	—	—	—	—	1294
		2027938 thru 2029143	—	—	—	—	1206
	Total Command Reconnaissance w/o winch						3980
WC-16	W-398-QM-9388	606357 thru 607238	116	4770	8676901	8694193	882
		607239 thru 607383	—	—	—	—	145
		607687 thru 607943	—	—	—	—	257
	Total Command Radio (w/o winch)						1284
WC-17	W-398-QM-9388	2025967 thru 2026129	116	4850	8676901	8694193	163
		2026533 thru 2026643	—	—	—	—	111
	Total Carryall						274
WC-18	W-398-QM-9388	73372 thru 74241	123	5340	8676901	8694193	870
		74242 thru 74631	—	—	—	—	390
		74733 thru 75027	—	—	—	—	295
	Total WC-18 Ambulance						1555
WC-19	W-398-QM-9388	230519 thru 230621	116	4510	8676901	8694193	103
	Total Panel						103
WC-20	W-398-QM-9388	003759 thru 003788	116	—	8676901	8694193	30
	Total Closed Cab — no body (Emergency Repair, Oil Service added)						30
	Total T-211 trucks manufactured (includes one truck, type N/A)						17293
WC-21	W-398-QM-10327	234379 thru 238778	116	4240	81500001	81528537	4400
		240179 thru 242178	—	—	—	—	2000
	W-398-QM-DA-28	none	—	—	81501667	81503563	500
	DAW-398-QM-129	none	—	—	81516231	—	352
	W-398-QM-11592	247219 thru 252141	—	—	81517694	—	4923
	DAW-398-QM-210		—	—			1612
	Total Weapons Carrier w/o winch, w/transverse troop seats						13787
WC-22	W-398-QM-10327	238779 thru 240178	116	4775	81500001	81528537	1400
		242179 thru 242678	—	—	—	—	500
	Total Weapons Carrier w/winch, w/transverse troop seats						1900
WC-23	W-398-QM-10327	2050397 thru 2051696	116	4640	81500001	81528537	1300
		2052047 thru 2052246	—	—	—	—	200
	(Above figures include one truck on contract W-398-QM-DA-228)						
	W-3980QM-11592	2071355 thru 2072099	—	—	81517694	—	745
	W-398-QM-DA-28	none	—	—			700
	DAW-398-QM-210	none	—	—	81517694	—	464
	Total Command Reconnaissance w/o winch						3409
WC-24	W-398-QM-10327	2051697 thru 2052046	116	4975	81500001	81528537	350
		2052247 thru 2052396	—	—	—	—	150
	DAW-398-QM-86	none	—	—	81516783	—	512
	DAW-398-QM-210	none	—	—	81517694	—	400
	Total Command Reconnaissance w/winch						1412
WC-25	W-398-QM-10327	608358 thru 608857	116	4770	81500001	81528537	500
		608858 thru 609000	—	—	—	—	143
	DAW-398-QM-125	none	—	—	81517445	—	64
	DAW-398-QM-210	none	—	—			166
	Total Command Radio (w/o winch)						873
WC-26	W-398-QM-10327	2052397 thru 2053446	116	4850	81500001	81528537	1050
		2053447 thru 2053496	—	—	—	—	50
	(Above figures include two trucks on contract W-398-QM-DA-225)						
	W-398-QM-DA-28	none	—	—	—	—	300
	W-398-QM-11592	2069855 thru 2071353	—	—	81517694	—	1499
	Total Carryall						2899
WC-27	W-398-QM-10327	75400 thru 77080	123	5340	81500001	81528537	1681
	W-398-QM-DA-28	none	—	—	—	—	260
	DAW-398-QM-129	none	—	—	81517509	—	35
	W-398-QM-11592	77341 thru 77840	—	—	81717694	—	500
	DAW-398-QM-210	none	—	—	—	—	103
	Total WC-27 Ambulance						2579
WC-40	W-398-QM-10327	005371 thru 005645	116	4640	81500001	81528537	275
	Total Closed Cab Pickup w/o troop seats (bullet sealing tubes)						275
WC-41	W-398-QM-10327	005646 thru 005858	123	5120	81500001	81528537	213
		005859 thru 005912	—	—	—	—	54
	W-398-QM-11244	006868 thru 006906	—	—	81517648	—	39
	W-398-QM-11592	008608 thru 008684	—	—	81517694	—	77
	Total WC-27 Closed Cab — no body (Emergency Repair)						383
WC-42	W-398-QM-DA-28	none	116	4510	81512931	81513580	650
	Total Panel Radio						650

Model	Contract No.	U.S.A. Registration Nos.	WB	Wt	Starting	Ending	Quan
WC-43	W-398-QM-11592	007539 thru 007908	116	4480	81517694	81528537	370
	Total Telephone Installation (Signal Corps K-50)						370
	Total T-215 trucks manufactured						28537
	Grand Total — T-207, T-211, T-215 trucks manufactured						77765
	(WC thru 1940 — 5332)						
WC-51	W-374-ORD-2740	252293 thru 254792	98	5250	81534381	81784196	2500
	W-374-ORD-2741	259135 thru 289212	—	—	—	—	30078
	W-374-ORD-2799	291910 thru 291992	—	—	—	—	83
		293685 thru 294209	—	—	—	—	525
	W-374-ORD-2864	2110000 thru 2135113	—	—	81601050	—	25114
		2232075 thru 2233424	—	—	—	—	1350
	W-374-ORD-6322	N/A	—	—	81534381	—	40727
	W-20-018-ORD-8301		—	—	—	—	23164
	Total WC-51 Weapons Carrier w/o winch manufactured*						123541
WC-52	W-374-ORD-2740	245845 thru 246394	98	5550	81534381	—	550
	W-374-ORD-2741	289213 thru 291384	—	—	—	—	2172
	W-374-ORD-2799	291993 thru 292508	—	—	—	—	516
		292509 thru 292512	(no body)	—	—	—	4
	W-374-ORD-2864	2160419 thru 2179292	—	—	81601050	—	18874
		2180276 thru 2189555	—	—	—	—	9280
	W-374-ORD-6322	N/A	—	—	81534381	—	16896
	W-20-018-ORD-8301		—	—	—	—	10826
	Total WC-52 Weapons Carrier w/winch manufactured*						59118
WC-53	W-374-ORD-2740	2072128 thru 2073327	114	5750	81534381	—	1200
	DAW-398-QM-505	2089156 thru 2089175	—	—	—	—	20
	DAW-398-QM-521	2089176 thru 2089947	—	—	—	—	772
	W-374-ORD-2799	2089952 thru 2091083	—	—	—	—	1132
	W-2425-QM-201	2092777 thru 2092778	—	—	—	—	2
	W-374-ORD-2741	20163146 thru 20167956	—	—	—	—	4811
	W-374-ORD-2864	20260793 thru 20261257	—	—	81601050	—	465
	Total WC-53 Carryall manufactured (completed by April, 1943)						8402
WC-54	W-374-ORD-2740	77841 thru 78690	121	5920	81534381	—	850
	W-374-ORD-2741	78691 thru 79999	—	—	—	—	1309
		710000 thru 718635	—	—	—	—	8636
	W-374-ORD-2799	718636 thru 719045	—	—	—	—	410
	W-374-ORD-2864	721000 thru 732635	—	—	81601050	—	11636
	DAW-398-QM-448	750068 thru 750083	—	—	81534381	—	16
	W-374-ORD-6322	N/A	—	—	—	—	3145
	Total WC-54 Ambulance manufactured (limited std. in April, 1944)*						26002
WC-55	W-374-ORD-1316	6016072 thru 6021066	98	6621	81529001	81534380	4995
		6022453 thru 6022776	—	—	—	—	324
	W-374-ORD-1939	6039733 thru 6039793	(Dedicated S/N block)				61
	Total M6 Gun Motor Carriage manufactured (completed by 9/42)						5380
WC-56	W-374-ORD-2799	2091084 thru 2091983	98	5375	81534381	81784196	900
	W-374-ORD-2741	20167957 thru 20182608	—	—	—	—	14652
	W-374-ORD-6322	N/A	—	—	—	—	3260
	Total WC-56 Command Reconnaissance w/o winch manufactured*						18812
WC-57	W-374-ORD-2799	2092119 thru 2092618	98	5675	81534381	—	500
	W-374-ORD-2741	20184953 thru 20185868	—	—	—	—	916
	W-374-ORD-2864	20291158 thru 20295751	—	—	81601050	—	4594
	Total WC-57 Command Reconnaissance w/winch manufactured						6010
WC-58	W-374-ORD-2741	20182609 thru 20184952	98	5375	81534381	—	2344
	Total WC-58 Command Radio (w/o winch) manufactured						2344
WC-59	W-374-ORD-2799	0015366 thru 0015914	121	5400	81534381	—	549
	Total WC-59 Signal Corps K-50 Telephone Maintenance manufactured						549
WC-60	W-374-ORD-2799	0015915 thru 0015986	121	5580	81534381	—	72
	W-374-ORD-2864	0026383 thru 0026606	—	—	81601050	—	224
	W-374-ORD-6322	N/A	—	—	81534381	—	4
	Total WC-60 M2 Emergency Repair manufactured*						300
WC-61	W-374-ORD-2799	0051312 thru 1151369	121	5700	81601050	—	58
			—	5400	—	—	
	Total WC-61 Signal Corps K-50B Telephone Maintenance (w, w/o winch)						58
WC-64	W-20-018-ORD-8301	N/A	121	6755	81529001	—	3500
	Total WC-64 KD (KnockDown) Ambulance manufactured (beginning 1/45)						3500

Total ¾-ton 4x4 trucks manufactured (above totals) 254014
Total for body type and end use N/A* 1180

Total World War II Production 255196

---

* Some discrepancies exist among sources reporting production quantities. The numbers without asterisks are believed to be correct, with a small latitude possible on some of the others. The numbers without asterisks agree as to quantity by U.S.A. registration numbers assigned, quantity as reported by Chrysler, and acceptance by the Army Service Forces.

The sources and the numbers reported are:

1. Total from Acceptance of Tank-Automotive Material, 1940-1945 254014
2. Total by monthly production figures, 4/42 - 8/45 255193
3. Total by vehicle serial numbers (believed to be the most accurate) 255196

Model	Type	SUMMARY WB	Wt	Starting	Ending	Quan
	T-214 — 230.2 cu. in. flathead six; 92 bhp at 3200 R.P.M.					
WC-51	Weapons Carrier	98	5250	81523481	81784196	123541
WC-52	Weapons Carrier w/winch	98	5550	—	—	59118
WC-53	Carryall (Completed 9/43)	114	5750	—	—	8402
WC-54	Ambulance (Declared ltd. std. 4/44)	121	5920	—	—	26002

Model	Type	SUMMARY WB	Wt	Starting	Ending	Quan
WC-55	Gun Motor Carriage M6 (37-mm anti-tank)	98	6621	81529001	81534380	5380
WC-56	Command Reconnaissance	98	5375	81534381	81784196	18812
WC-57	Command Reconnaissance w/winch	98	5675	—	—	6010
WC-58	Radio Reconnaissance	98	5375	—	—	2344
WC-59	Telephone Maint. (Signal Corps K-50)	121	5400	—	—	549
WC-60	Emergency Repair M2 (Series #G-61)	121	5580	—	—	300
WC-61	Phone Maint. w/wn (Sig. Corps K-50B)	121	5700	—	—	58
----	Phone Maint. w/o wn (Sig. Corps K-50B)	121	5400	—	—	—
WC-64	KD (Knockdown) Ambulance (air xport)	121	6755	—	—	3500
----	Body type and end use N/A	—	—	—	—	1180
	Total World War II Production					255196

1942 Dodge ½-Ton Command Car (A. Gandy)

1943 Dodge ¾-Ton Military Ambulance (MVCC)

1944 Dodge 4x4 weapons carrier (DB/CHC)

1945 Dodge Model VC Carryall (DB/CHC)

1946 DODGE

1946 Dodge Pickup (Mel Kay)

LIGHT TRUCK — SERIES WC — ½-TON — SIX-CYLINDER: — To meet the pent up demand for trucks after World War II, Dodge continued its dependable proven models rather than design a new series. The WC Series continued with very minimal changes. No appearance changes were made. Seat cushions and backs were of a new design and equipped with a manually-operated air control valve by which the driver could regulate the amount of air in the seat cushion according to his weight. New spring construction in seats and backs afforded more comfort. Steering gear was improved and made heavier. Steering gear ratios were increased. Axle shafts were made larger in diameter for added strength. The WC series was given a new four pinion type differential replacing the former two pinion type. No changes were made to the engine. Models available continued unchanged from 1942. Standard Equipment: Same as 1942. Power Wagon Colors: Seawolf Submarina Green was standard. Also available at no extra cost were Red, Dark Blue and Dark Green.

I.D. DATA (Series WC): Serial numbers and engine numbers same locations as 1942. Beginning serial number Detroit 81121158, ending 81172528. Beginning Los Angeles 9217001, ending 9221269. Beginning engine number not available.

Model Series WC	Body Type	Price	Weight	Prod. Total
WC	Chassis & Cowl	682	2375	—
WC	Chassis & Cab	813	2775	—
WC	Pickup (6½ ft.)	861	2975	—
WC	Canopy	1008	3000	—
WC	Panel	995	3175	—

NOTE 1: Shipments, U.S. Only (Calendar Year) (Domestic) 42,404; (Export) 3,108; (Total) 45,512.

1946 Dodge ½-Ton Pickup Truck (Mel Kay)

ENGINE (Series WC/WD-15): Inline. L-head. Six-cylinder. Cast iron block. Bore & stroke: 3¼ in. x 4⅜ in. Displacement: 217.76 cu. in. Compression ratio: 6.6:1. Brake horsepower: 95 at 3600 R.P.M. Net horsepower: 25.35. Max. Torque: 172 lbs. ft. at 1200 R.P.M. Four main bearings. Solid valve lifters. Carburetor: Stromberg model BXV-3.

LIGHT TRUCK — SERIES WD-15 — ¾-TON — SIX-CYLINDER: — No changes were made to the WD-15 series except those noted for WC series. Engine remained the same 218 cu. in. L-6 as in 1942. No changes in model lineup. Standard Equipment: Same as 1942.

I.D. DATA (Series WD-15): Engine number and serial numbers found same locations as 1942. Beginning serial number: Detroit 83300001, ending 83303424. Beginning Los Angeles 85500001, ending 85500431. Beginning engine number T112-7001.

Model	Body Type	Price	Weight	Prod. Total
Series WD-15				
WD-15	Chassis & Cowl	768	2525	—
WD-15	Chassis & Cab	900	2925	—
WD-15	Pickup (7½ ft.)	954	3225	—
WD-15	Platform (7½ ft.)	973	3325	—
WD-15	Stake (7½ ft.)	1012	3550	—

NOTE 1: Shipments, U.S. Only (Calendar Year). (Domestic) 3,834; (Export) 1; (Total) 3,835.

ENGINE: Same as WC Series.

LIGHT TRUCK — SERIES WD-20/WD-21 — ONE-TON — SIX-CYLINDER: — As with the ¾ ton series, no changes except those noted for WC series were made. Engine and model line up remained the same. Standard equipment: Same as 1942.

I.D. DATA: Engine numbers and serial numbers found same locations as 1942. Beginning serial number Detroit 81211001, ending 81224002. Beginning Los Angeles 86000001, ending 86001388. Beginning engine number T116-69200.

Model	Body Type	Price	Weight	Prod. Total
Series WD-20				
WD-20	Chassis & Cowl	849	2825	—
WD-20	Chassis & Cab	981	3250	—
WD-20	Pickup (7½ ft.)	1036	3600	—
WD-20	Platform (7½ ft.)	1053	3625	—
WD-20	Stake (7½ ft.)	1093	3850	—
Series WD-21				
WD-21	Chassis & Cowl	877	2850	—
WD-21	Chassis & Cab	1008	3275	—
WD-21	Pickup (9½ ft.)	1076	3675	—
WD-21	Platform (9½ ft.)	1091	3750	—
WD-21	Stake (9½ ft.)	1123	4025	—
WD-21	Canopy	1203	3400	—
WD-21	Panel	1197	3850	—

NOTE 1: Shipments, U.S. Only (Calendar Year) (Domestic) 15,784; (Export) 1,615; (Total) 17,399.

ENGINE: Inline. L-head. Six-cylinder. Cast iron block. Bore & stroke: 3¼ in. x 4⅝ in. Displacement: 230.2 cu. in. Compression ratio: 6.7:1. Brake horsepower: 102 at 3600 R.P.M. Net horsepower: 25.35. Max. Torque: 184 lbs. ft. at 1200 R.P.M. Four main bearings. Solid valve lifters. Carburetor: Stromberg.

CHASSIS (Series WC): Wheelbase: 116 in. Tires: 6.00 x 16 four-ply (front & rear).

CHASSIS (Series WD-15): Wheelbase: 120 in. Tires: TA15 six-ply (front & rear).

CHASSIS (Series WD-20/WD-21): Wheelbase: 120/133 in. Tires: (front) 6.50 x 16 six-ply; (rear) 7.00 x 16 six-ply.

TECHNICAL: Same as 1942.

OPTIONS: Options for the WC, WD-15 Series and WD-20/WD-21 were basically the same as in 1942.

LIGHT TRUCK — SERIES WDX — ONE-TON POWER-WAGON — SIX-CYLINDER: — The famous Dodge Power-Wagon was, in reality, a civilian adaptation of the four-wheel drive ¾ ton military vehicle which Dodge built in great numbers during World War II. Dodge engineered the Power-Wagon to be a self-propelled power plant capable of a wide range of industrial and agricultural power needs. Dodge engineers set out to create the most useful and versatile vehicle ever manufactured. The Power-Wagon was capable of carrying a 3,000 pound payload in off-highway service. In addition the Power-Wagon provided power for driving various items of auxiliary equipment. A transmission power-take-off was available with front and rear drive shafts. The Power-Wagon was equipped with a four-speed transmission and a two-speed transfer case, providing a total of eight speeds forward and two reverse. The Power-Wagon was powered by Dodge's 230 cu. in. six as used in all one ton trucks. Standard equipment: Heavy duty shocks in front. One quart oil bath air cleaner. Front bumper. Channel type reinforcements inside frame side-rails. Velocity type engine governor set at 3,200 RPM. Dual vacuum windshield wipers. Interior sun visor on left side. DeLuxe seat cushion and back. Rear axle gear ratio 4.89:1 with 7.50 x 16 eight-ply tires, 5.83:1 with 9.00 x 16 eight-ply tires.

I.D. DATA: Engine numbers and serial numbers found in same locations as on other series. Beginning serial number Detroit 83900001, beginning Los Angeles 88750001. Ending numbers not available. Engine numbers not available.

Model	Body Type	Price	Weight	Prod. Total
Series WDX Power-Wagon				
WDX	Chassis & Cab	1555	4475	—
WDX	Pickup	1627	4900	—

ENGINE: Inline. L-head. Six-cylinder. Cast iron block. Bore & stroke: 3¼ in. x 4⅝ in. Displacement: 230.2 cu. in. Compression ratio: 6.7:1. Brake horsepower: 94 at 3200 R.P.M. Net horsepower: 25.35. Max. Torque: 185 lbs. ft. at 1200 R.P.M. Four main bearings. Solid valve lifters. Carburetor: Stromberg.

CHASSIS (Series WDX/Power-Wagon): Wheelbase: 126 in. Tires: (16 x 5.50 wheels) 7.50 x 16 eight-ply. (16 x 6.50 wheels) 9.00 x 16 eight-ply.

1946 Dodge Power Wagon wrecker

TECHNICAL: Front and rear axles were of full floating hypoid-drive type. Ratio 5.83 to 1. Springs are semi-elliptic type. Front 11-leaves, 39 inches long by 1¾ inches wide. Rear 14-leaves, 52¼ inches long by 1¾ inch wide. Hotchkiss drive. Heavy duty double acting telescopic type shocks on front (extra cost on rear). Mud and snow all-service tread. Spare wheel and tire carrier mounted vertically on right side of pickup body, immediately behind cab. Single-plate 10 inch diameter clutch. Selective sliding gear type transmission with two-speed transfer case gives 8F/2R. Steering worm-and-sector type, 23.2:1 ratio with 17 inch diameter steering wheel. Electrical: 6-volt system with 35-ampere generator. Fuel tank 18 gallons. Maximum gross weight rating with 7.50 x 16 eight-ply tires was 7,600 pounds; with 9.00 x 16 eight-ply tires 8,700 pounds.

OPTIONS (Truck): Air cleaner - one quart instead of standard one pint ($.70). Rear bumper ($6.35). Cab-deluxe equipment includes hair pad seat cushion and back, arm rest (left side), dome light, dual vacuum windshield wipers, one sun visor, plastic coated trim ($26.65). Generator 230 watt, 6-8 volt, 32 ampere hour. High charging at low engine speed ($8.30). Governor ($5.15). Oil Filter - replaceable cartridge type ($6.35). Rear view mirror: Long arm adjustable-left side ($1.50); Long arm adjustable-right side ($2.60). Transmission - four speed ($31.45). Auxiliary vacuum windshield wiper ($4.10).

OPTIONS (Power-Wagon): Power take-off mounted on left side of transmission. Transfers power forward to winch or to tail shaft. Power winch - 7,500 pounds capacity. Mounted directly on frame in front of radiator. Provided with 250' of 7/16 inch steel cable. Tail shaft - consisted of two tubular drive shafts and one pillow block shaft. Pillow block attached to center of frame cross-member. Pulley Drive - Mounted on pillow block at center of frame rear cross-member. Pulley was nine inch diameter x 6⅝ inch wide. Mechanical Govenor. Deluxe Cab Equipment: Same as WC and WD models. Draw Bar. Pintle Hook. Front tow hooks.

HISTORICAL: Model year started December, 1945. Sales for 1946 hit an all-time record high for Dodge, topping off at 96,490. This moved Dodge into third place in United States truck sales. Dodge truck production, at 144,968, was not a record-setter, because government sales slowed down to a trickle with the war over. Of the total produced, 12,919 were built in Canada and 9,251 were built in Los Angeles. The government purchased 2,076 three ton trucks and 22,099 trucks were exported. For the industry as a whole, 1946 sales were below the level of 1941. However, Dodge sales were up 53.3 percent. Civilian trucks sales, unlike car sales, did not completely cease during World War II. A number of civilian trucks were produced to meet the requirements of those industries deemed vital to the war effort. Dodge built 1,580 civilian trucks in 1942, after general sales to the public ceased. Nine were built in 1943; 7,983 in 1944 and, in 1945 before restrictions were lifted, 28,405 civilian trucks were built (alongside military trucks on the same production lines.) Dodge was very proud of the fact that, two hours after the last military truck rolled off the line, they had the Detroit truck plant reconverted for volume output of civilian trucks. Dodge built 400,000 military trucks during World War II. Dodge began the 1946 model year building trucks of ½ to two ton capacity and, as a mid-year introduction, brought out a redesigned 2½ and three ton series. The new heavy-duty series featured a redesigned grille, which gave these trucks a more massive appearance.

Pricing

	5	4	3	2	1
1946					
Series WC — (½-Ton) — (116 in. w.b.)					
Pickup (6½ ft.)	1000	2000	3300	4600	6600
Canopy	1010	2030	3350	4700	6700
Panel	930	1860	3100	4350	6200
Series WD-15 — (¾-Ton) — (120 in. w.b.)					
Pickup (7½ ft.)	920	1850	3050	4300	6100
Platform	870	1750	2900	4100	5800
Stake	890	1770	2950	4150	5900
Series WD-20 — (1-Ton) — (120 in. w.b.)					
Pickup	870	1750	2900	4100	5800
Pickup (7½ ft.)	900	1800	3000	4200	6000
Platform	840	1680	2800	3900	5600
Stake	850	1700	2850	4000	5700
Series WD-21 (1-Ton) — (133 in. w.b.)					
Pickup (9½ ft.)	850	1700	2850	4000	5700
Platform	720	1450	2400	3300	4800
Stake	830	1650	2750	3850	5500
Canopy	900	1800	3000	4200	6000
Panel	850	1700	2850	4000	5700
Power-Wagon WDX (1-Ton) — (126 in. w.b.)					
Chassis & Cab	900	1800	3000	4200	6000
Pickup	1130	2250	3750	5250	7500

1947 DODGE

1947 Dodge WC Series ½-Ton Pickup (J. Owens)

½-TON — SERIES WC — SIX-CYLINDER: — The only change in the ½-ton line was an across-the-board price increase. All models were carried over untouched. Standard equipment was the same as in 1946.

¾-TON — SERIES WD-15 — SIX-CYLINDER / 1-TON — SERIES WD-20/21 — SIX-CYLINDER / 1-TON POWER WAGON — SERIES WDX — SIX-CYLINDER: — All ¾ and 1-ton models were carried over without change.

I.D. DATA: Serial numbers were in the same location as 1946 models.

Series	Detroit		Los Angeles	
	Starting	Ending	Starting	Ending
WC	81172529	84506112	9221270	9225013
WD-15	83303425	83312388	85500432	85501169
WD-20	81224003	81243970	86001389	86002923
WD-21	81224003	81243970	86001389	86002923
WDX	83902666	83906216	88750226	88750894

Engine numbers not available.

Model Series WC — (½-Ton) — (116 in. w.b.)	Body Type	Price	Weight	Prod. Total
WC	Chassis	789	2375	Note 1
WC	Chassis & Cab	944	2775	Note 1
WC	Pickup (6½-ft.)	989	2975	Note 1
WC	Canopy	1119	3000	Note 1
WC	Panel	1184	3175	Note 1

NOTE 1: Total U.S. calendar year production, WC Series: (Domestic) 37,532; (Export) 5010; (Total) 42,542.

Series WD-15 — (¾-Ton) — (120 in. w.b.)				
WD-15	Chassis & Cowl	886	2525	Note 2
WD-15	Chassis & Cab	1041	2925	Note 2
WD-15	Pickup (7½-ft.)	1096	3225	Note 2
WD-15	Platform (7½-ft.)	1121	3325	Note 2
WD-15	Stake (7½-ft.)	1166	3550	Note 2

NOTE 2: Total U.S. calendar year production, Series WD-15: 9992.

Series WD-20 — (1-Ton) — (120 in. w.b.)				
WD-20	Chassis & Cowl	952	2825	Note 3
WD-20	Chassis & Cab	1107	3250	Note 3
WD-20	Pickup (7½-ft.)	1162	3600	Note 3
WD-20	Platform (7½-ft.)	1187	3625	Note 3
WD-20	Stake (7½-ft.)	1232	3850	Note 3
Series WD-21 — (1-Ton) — (133 in. w.b.)				
WD-21	Chassis	972	2850	Note 3
WD-21	Chassis & Cab	1127	3275	Note 3
WD-21	Pickup	1187	3675	Note 3
WD-21	Platform	1222	3750	Note 3
WD-21	Stake	1272	4025	Note 3
WD-21	Canopy	1352	3400	Note 3

NOTE 3: Total U.S. calendar year production, Series WD-20/21: (Domestic) 24,615; (Export) 3158; (Total) 27,773.

Series WDX — (1-Ton) — (126 in. w.b.)				
WDX	Chassis & Cab	1679	4475	—
WDX	Pickup	1764	4900	—

ENGINE (Series WC, WD-15): Inline. L-head. Six-cylinder. Cast iron block. Bore & stroke: 3¼ x 4⅜ in. Displacement: 217.76 cu. in. Compression ratio: 6.6:1. Brake horsepower: 95 at 3600 R.P.M. Net horsepower: 25.35. Torque: 172 lbs.-ft. at 1200 R.P.M. Four main bearings. Solid valve lifters.

ENGINE (Series WD-20/21): Inline. L-head. Six-cylinder. Cast iron block. Bore & stroke: 3¼ in. x 4⅜ in. Displacement: 230.2 cu. in. Compression ratio: 6.7:1. Brake horsepower: 102 at 3600 R.P.M. Net horsepower: 25.35. Torque: 184 lbs.-ft. at 1200 R.P.M. Four main bearings: Solid valve lifters.

ENGINE (Series WDX): Same as WD-20 except Brake horsepower: 94 at 3200 R.P.M. Torque: 185 lbs.-ft. at 1200 R.P.M.

1947 Dodge Screenside Delivery

CHASSIS (Series WC): Wheelbase: 116 in. Tires: 6.00 x 16 4-ply. Body: 6½ ft.

CHASSIS (Series WD-15): Wheelbase: 120 in. Tires: TA-15 6-ply. Body: 7½ ft.

CHASSIS (Series WD-20): Wheelbase: 120 in. Tires: (front) 6.50 x 16 6-ply; (rear) 7.00 x 16 6-ply. Body: 7½ ft.

CHASSIS (Series WD-21): Wheelbase: 133 in. Tires: (front) 6.50 x 16 6-ply; (rear) 7.00 x 16 6-ply. Body: 9 ft.

CHASSIS (Series WDX): Wheelbase: 126 in. Tires: 7.50 x 16 8-ply.

TECHNICAL: Some specifications as 1946 models.

OPTIONS: Same as 1946 models.

HISTORICAL: Introduced: December 1946. Calendar year registrations: 126,736. Calendar year production: 183,953. History: Dodge trucks sales were up 31.3 percent over 1946, just a trifle better than the overall industry increase. This was Dodge truck's best year ever for both sales and production. Of the total, 17,378 trucks were Canadian built and 13,320 were made in California. No trucks were shipped to the government, but 32,907 were exported. Dodge placed third in truck sales, claiming that its full line from ½ to 3-tons satisfied 97 percent of the truck market. The Job-Rated advertising that began in 1941 continued this year.

1947 Dodge Panel Delivery

Pricing

1947	5	4	3	2	1
Series WC — (½-Ton) — (116 in. w.b.)					
Pickup	1000	2000	3300	4600	6600
Canopy	1010	2030	3350	4700	6700
Panel	930	1860	3100	4350	6200
Series WD-15 — (¾-Ton) — (120 in. w.b.)					
Pickup	920	1850	3050	4300	6100
Platform	870	1750	2900	4100	5300
Stake	890	1770	2950	4150	5900
Series WD-20 — (1-Ton) — (120 in. w.b.)					
Pickup	870	1750	2900	4100	5800
Platform	840	1680	2800	3900	5600
Stake	850	1700	2850	4000	5700
Series WD-21 — (1-Ton) — (133 in. w.b.)					
Pickup	850	1700	2850	4000	5700
Platform	720	1450	2400	3300	4800
Stake	830	1650	2750	3850	5500
Canopy	900	1800	3000	4200	6000
Series WDX — Power-Wagon — (1-Ton)					
Pickup	1130	2250	3750	5250	7500

1948-49 DODGE

1948 Dodge ½-Ton Pickup (H. Kruger)

½-TON — SERIES B-1-B — SIX-CYLINDER / ¾-TON — SERIES B-1-C — SIX-CYLINDER / 1-TON — SERIES B-1-D — SIX-CYLINDER / 1-TON POWER-WAGON — SERIES B-1-PW — SIX-CYLINDER: Dodge introduced a completely new truck line, the first new models since 1939. The lineup totalled 248 basic chassis models, ranging from 4250 to 23,000 pounds GVW. Front axles were moved back and engines forward, to place more weight on the front axle and improve weight distribution. Wheelbases for conventional models through 2-ton size were reduced by 8 in. The new trucks were engineered so that even with shorter w.b., their cab-to-axle dimensions remained the same, permitting the same body lengths as before.

Ease of handling and driving was provided by the shorter w.b. and a wide-tread front axle, plus cross steering — a new feature on all conventional cab models. Cross steering allowed a 37-degree turning angle, both right and left. Turning diameter was as tight as 38 feet. Road shock through the steering wheel was greatly reduced, as cross steering had the drag link running parallel with the axle.

Standard, deluxe and custom cabs gave the driver more room, visibility, safety and comfort. Deluxe and custom cabs offered "360-degree vision" through increased glass area, including rear quarter windows. Windshield and windows of the new "Pilot House Cabs" were higher and wider. Comfort in any season was provided by an all-weather heating/ventilating system — a combination of truck heater, defroster, vent windows, cowl vent, and fresh air intake. Braking systems were larger and improved. Front and rear axles had increased load capacity. Front springs were longer. Redesigned radiator cores gave better cooling and the frame was made heavier.

1948 Dodge 1-Ton Truck Cab (RPZ)

One major improvement was a much larger pickup body with sides 7-5/16 in. higher than before as well as wider and longer, totalling a 40 percent increase in cu. ft. capacity. Pickup styling used simple, cycle-type rear fenders that were easy and inexpensive to repair or replace. Drive lines, engines, clutches, transmissions and rear axles were carried over virtually unchanged from 1947. The Power-Wagon was unchanged except for a new model number. Discontinued models included the 1-ton panel, plus ½ and 1-ton canopy express. Standard, DeLuxe and Custom cabs were not separate series, but optional extra-cost upgrades.

1-TON — SERIES B-1-DU/EU ROUTE-VAN — SIX-CYLINDER: — Introduced late in 1948, the all new Route-Van had many industry "firsts". Foremost was the first use of Fluid Drive in a volume-production truck, making the driver's job easier as well as increasing vehicle life and cutting maintenance costs. Route-Vans had two rear axles — one to support the load and another to move it. The sole function of the driving axle was to drive the wheels. Its differential assembly was rubber-mounted on the chassis frame, moving up and down with the frame and body rather than the wheels. It connected to the wheels by open-type axle shafts and universal joints. Axle shaft length and angularity changed with the deflection of the springs. The two shafts "telescoped" to compensate for loads, with two "U" joints on each adjusting for angular fluctuations. An electro-hydraulic service brake holder, available on all models, made it unnecessary for the driver to reach for the hand brake at every door-to-door stop. He merely flicked a switch on the steering column to apply the brakes. Extremely low floor and step heights, large door openings, 76 in. inside headroom and 72 in. width, and a windshield with 1870 sq. in. of unobstructed vision, all combined to make the delivery man's job easier. The Route-Van's floor was about 10 in. closer to the pavement than other vehicles', due to the Dodge-designed rear driving axle. The engine was off-set to the right to permit better use of front-end space. Gas, oil and water intakes, and the oil level indicator, were easily reached by raising the front hood. An engine hood inside the body gave access for service and adjustments. All Route-Van bodies were Dodge-built.

I.D. DATA: Serial numbers were located on a plate on left front door hinge post.

1949 Dodge Pickup (R. Cenowa/DB)

| Model | Year | Starting Serial Numbers | | Ending | |
		Detroit	California	Detroit	California
B-1-B	1948	82044001	9227001	82092128	9234691
	1949	82092129	9234692	82127008	9238500
B-1-C	1948	83314001	85502001	83323945	85503862
	1949	83323946	85503863	83332940	85505264
B-1-D	1948	81245001	86003501	81268731	86006645
	1949	81268732	86006646	81278472	86007552
B-1-DU		84202001	—	84202693	—
B-1-DU	1948	84202694	—	84204553	—
B-1-EU	and	84000001	—	84000167	—
B-1-EUF	1949	84000168	—	84000911	—
B-1-PW	1948	83907001	88759501	83911548	88759912
	and	83911549	88759913	83915078	88760162
	1949				

Engine numbers were on top left side of block between cylinders 2 and 3. The first letter and three digits of the engine number were the Engineering Code numbers. Engine numbers not available.

Model	Body Type	Price	Weight	Prod. Total
Series B-1-B — (½-Ton) — (108 in. w.b.)				
B-1-B	Chassis & Cowl	987	2475	Note 1
B-1-B	Chassis (Note 4)	1032	—	Note 1
B-1-B	Chassis & Cab	1197	2975	Note 1
B-1-B	Pickup (6½-ft.)	1263	3275	Note 1
B-1-B	Panel	1448	3375	Note 1

NOTE 1: Total U.S. calendar year production, 1948-49, Series B-1-B: (Domestic) 106,794; (Export) 11,570; (Total) 118,364.

Model	Body Type	Price	Weight	Prod. Total
Series B-1-C — (¾-Ton) — (116 in. w.b.)				
B-1-C	Chassis & Cowl	1070	2650	Note 2
B-1-C	Chassis (Note 4)	1115	—	Note 2
B-1-C	Chassis & Cab	1280	3150	Note 2
B-1-C	Pickup (7½-ft.)	1371	3525	Note 2
B-1-C	Platform (7½-ft.)	1377	3475	Note 2
B-1-C	Stake (7½-ft.)	1430	3700	Note 2

NOTE 2: Total U.S. production, calendar years 1948-49, Series B-1-C: (Domestic) 29,686.

Model	Body Type	Price	Weight	Prod. Total
Series B-1-D — (1-Ton) — (116 in. w.b.)				
B-1-D	Chassis & Cowl	1134	2900	Note 3
B-1-D	Chassis (Note 4)	1179	—	Note 3
B-1-D	Chassis & Cab	1344	3375	Note 3
B-1-D	Pickup (7½-ft.)	1435	3725	Note 3
B-1-D	Platform (7½-ft.)	1441	3725	Note 3
B-1-D	Stake (7½-ft.)	1494	3905	Note 3
Series B-1-D — (1-Ton) — (126 in. w.b.)				
B-1-D	Chassis & Cowl	1154	2950	Note 3
B-1-D	Chassis (Note 4)	1199	—	Note 3
B-1-D	Chassis & Cab	1364	3375	Note 3
B-1-D	Pickup (9-ft.)	1465	3800	Note 3
B-1-D	Platform (9-ft.)	1473	3825	Note 3
B-1-D	Stake (9-ft.)	1539	4055	Note 3
Series B-1-PW Power-Wagon — (1-Ton) — (126 in. w.b.)				
B-1-PW	Chassis & Cowl	1790	4075	Note 3
B-1-PW	Chassis & Cab	1940	4675	Note 3
B-1-PW	Pickup (8-ft.)	2045	5100	Note 3
Series B-1-DU/EU Route-Van — (1-Ton) — (102 in. w.b.)				
B-1-DU	Cab & Body (7-ft.)	2595	4150	Note 3
(1-Ton) — (117 in. w.b.)				
B-1-DU	Cab & Body (9½-ft.)	2690	4950	Note 3
(1-Ton) — (102 in. w.b.)				
B-1-EU	Cab & Body (7-ft.)	2755	4855	Note 3
(1-Ton) — (117 in. w.b.)				
B-1-EU	Cab & Body (9½-ft.)	2850	5280	Note 3
(1-Ton) — (142 in. w.b.)				
B-1-EU	Cab & Body (12½-ft.)	2990	5845	Note 3

NOTE 3: Total U.S. production, calendar years 1948-49, all 1-ton series B-1-D, B-1-PW and B-1-DU/EU: (Domestic) 45,272; (Export) 9483; (Total) 54,755.

NOTE 4: Chassis with windshield and cowl.

1949 Dodge Pickup (L. Anderson)

ENGINE (Series B-1-B, B-1-C): Inline. L-head. Six-cylinder. Cast iron block. Bore & stroke: 3¼ x 4⅜ in. Displacement: 217.8 cu. in. Compression ratio: 6.6:1. Brake horsepower: 95 at 3600 R.P.M. Net horsepower: 25.35. Torque: 172 lbs.-ft. at 1200 R.P.M. Four main bearings. Solid valve lifters. Carburetor: Carter.

ENGINE (All 1-Ton): Inline. L-head. Six-cylinder. Cast iron block. Bore & stroke: 3¼ x 4⅝ in. Displacement: 230.2 cu. in. Compression ratio: 6.7:1. Brake horsepower: 102 at 3600 R.P.M. Net horsepower: 25.35. Torque: 184 lbs.-ft. at 1200 R.P.M. Four main bearings. Solid valve lifters. Carburetor: Stromberg.

CHASSIS (Series B-1-B — ½-Ton): Wheelbase: 108 in. Tires: 6.00 x 16 four-ply front and rear, on 4.00 drop-center safety-rim wheels. GVW: 4200 lbs. (4500 lbs. with 6.50 x 16 six-ply tires; 4800 lbs. with 6.50 x 16 six-ply tires on 4.50 wheels).

CHASSIS (Series B-1-C — ¾-Ton): Wheelbase: 116 in. Tires: 7.00 x 15TA six-ply on 5.50 drop-center rims. GVW: 5500 lbs. (5500 lbs. with 6.00 x 16 six-ply front tires on 4.50 semi-drop center rims and 7.00 x 16 six-ply rear tires on 5.50 rims; 6000 lbs. with 7.00 x 16 six-ply front and 7.50 x 16 six-ply front tires on 5.50 semi-drop center rims. Only single rear wheels available.

CHASSIS (Series B-1-D-116): Wheelbase: 116 in. Tires: (front) 6.00 x 16 six-ply on 4.50 semi-drop-center rims; (rear) 7.00 x 16 six-ply on 5.50 rims. GVW: 5500 lbs. (6800 lbs. with 6.00 x 16 six-ply front tires and dual rears on 4.50 rims; 7500 lbs. with 6.50 x 16 six-ply front and dual rear tires on 4.50 rims).

1948 Dodge Panel Delivery (OCW)

CHASSIS (Series B-1-D-126): Wheelbase: 126 in. Tires: (front) 6.00 x 16 six-ply; (rear) 7.00 x 16 six-ply. GVW: 6000 lbs. with 7.00 x 16 six-ply front and 7.50 x 16 six-ply single rear tires on 5.50 rims; 6800 lbs. with 6.00 x 16 six-ply front and dual rear tires on 4.50 rims; 7500 lbs. with 6.50 x 16 six-ply front and dual rear tires on 4.50 rims with 2300-lb. rear springs.

CHASSIS (Series B-1-PW-126 Power Wagon): Wheelbase: 126 in. Tires: 7.50 x 16 eight-ply front and rear on 5.50 wheels. GVW: 7600 lbs. (8700 lbs. with 9.00 x 16 eight-ply tires on 6.50 rims).

CHASSIS (Series B-1-DU-102 and 117 Route-Van): Wheelbase: 102 and 117 in. Tires: 7.00 x 16 six-ply, front and rear. GVW: 6200 lbs. (6900 lbs. with 7.00 x 16 front and 7.50 x 16 six-ply rear tires; 7500 lbs. with 7.50 x 16 eight-ply front and rear; 7900 lbs. with 8.25 x 16 eight-ply tires front and rear).

CHASSIS (Series B-1-EU-102 and 117): Wheelbase: 102 and 117 in. Tires: 7.50 x 16 six-ply front and 8.25 x 16 eight-ply rear. GVW: 8000 lbs. with 8.25 x 16 eight-ply tires front and rear; 8700 lbs. with 9.00 x 16 eight-ply front and rear; 9600 lbs. with 9.00 x 16 ten-ply front and rear.

CHASSIS (Series B-1-EU-142): Wheelbase: 142 in. Tires: (front) 7.50 x 16 six-ply; (rear) 8.25 x 16 eight-ply. GVW: 8500 lbs. with 8.25 x 16 eight-ply front and rear; 9200 lbs. with 9.00 x 16 eight-ply front and rear; 10,100 lbs. with 9.00 x 16 ten-ply front and rear.

1949 Dodge Panel Delivery (MC)

TECHNICAL: (Series B-1-B/C, ½ and ¾-Ton). Selective sliding gear transmission. Speeds: 3F/1R; optional 4F/1R with power takeoff. Floor shift control. Single plate dry disc clutch, 10-in. diameter (11-in. optional). Semi-floating rear axle. Rear axle ratio: 4.1:1 (4.78:1 optional). Hotchkiss drive with hypoid drive gears. Hydraulic four-wheel brakes. Parking brake: band and drum type, mounted at rear of transmission. Worm and roller steering. Shock absorbers front and rear. (Series B-1-D 1-Ton). Speeds: 3F/1R standard; 4F/1R optional. Rear axle ratio: 3.9 or 4.89:1. All other specs same as ½-ton. (Route Van) Speeds: (DU) 3F/1R (4F/1R optional); (EU) 4F/1R only. Floor shift control. Single plate dry disc clutch: (DU) 10-inch; (EU) 11-in. Full-floating, single-speed rear drive axle with hypoid gears; frame-mounted differential; open-type telescoping driveshafts to wheels with two cross-and-trunnion "U" joints on each side. Hotchkiss drive. Rear axle ratios: (DU) 4.89:1; (EU) 5.83:1. Semi-elliptic springs front and rear. Reverse Elliott I-beam front axle. Steel I-beam rear supporting axle. Worm and roller steering. (Note: other axle ratios supplied with optional heavy-duty tires).

OPTIONS: (Installed at Factory for B-1-B/C/D ½, ¾ and 1-ton models). Rear bumper for pickup ($7). Deluxe cab equipment consisting of vent wings in cab door and rear quarter windows ($25). Custom cab equipment: vent wings in cab door and rear quarter windows, deluxe seat cushion and back, dome light, left armrest, dual interior sun visors and dual

1948 Dodge Commercial Station Wagon (DB)

electric windshield wipers ($46). Deluxe panel equipment: vent wings in cab door windows, left armrest, dual sun visors, dual electric wipers ($30). Bumper guards, set of three ($5). Rear view mirror, long arm adjustable: left side ($2); right side ($3.00). Dual electric horns ($12). Auxiliary seat, stationary type, panels only ($27). Seat cushion with special air foam padding, cab models only ($10). Paint: pickup body and rear fenders painted to match cab, Dodge Truck Red or Armour Yellow only ($5). Oil-bath air cleaner, one-quart ($1.75). Oil filter with replaceable element ($8.50). Clutch, 11-inch diameter, replacing standard ($6.50). Generator: 256 watt, 32 ampere-hour ($9.50). Engine governor ($7). Rear springs, 750-pound nominal capacity each (no charge). Tail lamp, right side ($6). Four-speed transmission replacing standard three-speed ($30). (Note: Replaceable-element oil filter was standard on heavy-duty models with optional tires and high GVW ratings). (Installed at Factory for Route-Van models). Rear bumper with step-plate. Radiator grille (bumper) guards, set of three. Rear view mirror (left or right). Ventilating wings in driver compartment side windows. Windshield header roof cap. Jackknife type side doors, left and right. Jackknife type rear doors. Interior lining and insulation equipment: complete roof steel liner, ½ in. roof insulation, steel side liners above beltline, and dome light in driver's section. Side rub rails. Driver's seat assembly, stationary type, with standard seat cushion or air foam padding. Dual auxiliary tail lamps. Tire carrier inside body above wheelhouse, right or left side. Undercoating. Paint: body and fenders Ecuador Blue, Judson Green, Charlotte Ivory, or Black; wheels Black; all body sizes (standard paint was primer). Windshield wiper: vacuum, right side; electric, left and right side. Oil-bath air cleaner (one-quart capacity). Oil filter (replaceable element type). Battery: 120 ampere-hour capacity. Generator: 280 watt, 35-ampere, for high charging at low engine speeds. Governor (engine velocity type). Shock absorbers, front and rear. Tool kit (wheel wrench, jack and handle in cloth bag). Four-speed transmission with 10-inch clutch, fluid drive and auxiliary parking brake. (Installed at Factory for Power-Wagon models). Deluxe cab equipment: vent wings in cab door windows, dome light, left armrest, dual interior sun visors and dual electric windshield wipers ($40). Rear view mirror, long arm adjustable, left side ($2); right side ($3). Tail lamp, right side ($6). Generator: 256 watt, 32 ampere-hour ($18.50). Governor, mechanical, for use with rear drive shaft assembly ($63). Oil filter, replaceable element type ($7). Radiator overflow tank ($6). Shock absorbers, telescopic type, rear ($31). Draw bar ($20). Pintle hook ($10). Power take-off assembly ($65). Pulley drive — pulley unit only ($73). Rear drive shaft assembly only ($72). Tow hooks, front only ($5.00/pair). Winch assembly: front winch and drive shaft ($200). (Note: since the majority of orders for Power-Wagons specified Deluxe cab equipment, it was decided that, to expedite production, Deluxe equipment would be furnished on all cab and/or pickup models at the established prices). (Dealer installed — All Models). Recirculating hot water heater. Defroster package. Fresh air intake heater. Radio. Fog lamps. Cigar lighter. Fire extinguisher. Flares. Grille guards. Windshield washers. Rear fender step plate (for pickups). Directional signal lamps. (All these items from Mopar.)

HISTORICAL: Introduced: December 1947 except Route-Van, October 1948. Calendar year registrations: (1948) 114,431. (1949) 116,956. Calendar year production: (1948) 172,020. (1949) 151,513. Production breakdown by size. ½-Ton: (1948) (Domestic) 45,196; (Export) 6898; (Total) 52,094. (1949) (Domestic) 61,598; (Export) 4672; (Total) 66,270. ¾-Ton: (Domestic only) (1948) 11,279. (1949) 18,407. 1-Ton (including Power-Wagon and Route-Van): (1948) (Domestic) 26,288; (Export) 4822;

1948 Dodge B-108 Panel Delivery (OCW)

178

(Total) 31,110. (1949) (Domestic) 18,984; (Export) 4661; (Total) 23,645. (Note: Power-Wagon production for 1949 was 8198 units). Innovations: Cross steering for tight turning angle. Route-Van had Fluid Drive, an electro-hydraulic service brake switch, separate drive and support rear axles, "telescoping" axle shafts, offset engine, and very low floor/step heights. History: B-1 Series trucks continued unchanged through the 1948-49 period. Dodge ranked fourth in industry sales in 1948, rising to third the next year. The U.S. Government purchased 377 Power-Wagons for various agencies. Dodge opened a new truck and car assembly plant in San Leandro, California. L.L. Colbert was President of Dodge Division and L.J. Purdy was Vice President in charge of trucks.

NOTE: Some station wagons with the 1947 styling were registered as 1948 models.

Pricing

	5	4	3	2	1
1948-49					
Series B-1-B — (½-Ton) — (108 in. w.b.)					
Pickup	900	1800	3000	4200	6000
Panel	830	1650	2750	3850	5500
Series B-1-C — (¾-Ton) — (116 in. w.b.)					
Pickup	870	1700	2850	4000	5700
Platform	750	1500	2500	3500	5000
Stake	770	1550	2550	3600	5100
Series B-1-D — (1-Ton) — (116 in. w.b.)					
Pickup	810	1620	2700	3800	5400
Platform	700	1400	2350	3250	4700
Stake	720	1450	2400	3300	4800
Series B-1-D — (1-Ton) — (126 in. w.b.)					
Pickup	800	1600	2650	3700	5300
Platform	690	1380	2300	3200	4600
Stake	700	1400	2350	3250	4700
Series B-1-PW — (1-Ton) — (126 in. w.b.)					
Pickup	1130	2250	3750	5250	7500
Series B-1-DU — (1-Ton) (102 in. w.b.)					
7-ft. body	570	1140	1900	2650	3800
Series B-1-DU — (1-Ton) — (117 in. w.b.)					
9½-ft. body				2600	3700
Series B-1-EU — (1-Ton) — (102 in. w.b.)					
7-ft.	570	1140	1900	2650	3800
Series B-1-EU — (1-Ton) — (117 in. w.b.)					
9½-ft.	560	1100	1850	2600	3700
Series B-1-EU — (1-Ton) — (142 in. w.b.)					
12½-ft.	540	1080	1800	2500	3600

1950 DODGE

1950 Dodge Light-Duty Truck Cab (D. Sagvold)

½-TON — SERIES B-2-B — SIX-CYLINDER / ¾-TON — SERIES B-2-C — SIX-CYLINDER / 1-TON — SERIES B-2-D — SIX-CYLINDER / 1-TON POWER-WAGON — SERIES B-2-PW / 1-TON ROUTE-VAN — SERIES B-2-DU — SIX-CYLINDER: The first improvements to the B-series came on the 1950 models. Cycle bonded brake linings, previously offered only on ½-tons, were made standard on all models. Brake shoes were attached without rivets. The three-speed transmission now had a steering column gearshift handle. A "Right Spot" hand-pull parking brake control sat under the dash to the right of the steering wheel. A new standard ½-ton pickup body had 17 in. high sides, reduced from 22 7/16 in. The two pickup bodies were called "high side" and "low side," the latter identical to that on the W-series pickups offered through 1947. Starting in spring 1950, Fluid Drive was offered as an extra-cost option on all ½, ¾ and 1-ton trucks, a response to its popularity on the Route-Van. No appearance changes were made. Power-Wagon and Route-Van models continued unchanged. Model availability was the same as the B-1 series, as were the two light-duty truck engines. Standard equipment was also the same as in 1948-49.

I.D. DATA: Serial and engine numbers were in the same locations as series B-1.

Model	Serial Numbers Starting	Ending	Place of Manuf.	Starting Engine No.
B-2-B	82140001	82212862	Detroit	T172-1001
	85300001	85307000	Los Angeles	T172-1001
B-2-C	83340001	83361096	Detroit	T174-1001
	85506001	85508219	Los Angeles	T174-1001
B-2-D	81280001	81295887	Detroit	T176-1001
	86008501	86009522	Los Angeles	T176-1001
B-2-PW	83917001	83921140	Detroit	T137-1001
	88766001	88766296	Los Angeles	T137-1001
B-2-DU	84204554	84206127	Detroit	T164-1001
B-2-EU	84000912	84001405	Detroit	T165-1001

Model	Body Type	Price	Weight	Prod. Total
Series B-2-B	**(½-Ton)**	**(108 in. w.b.)**		
B-2-B	Chassis & Cowl	937	2475	Note 1
B-2-B	Chassis (Note 4)	982	—	Note 1
B-2-B	Chassis & Cab	1147	2975	Note 1
B-2-B	Pickup (6½-ft.)	1213	3275	Note 1
B-2-B	Panel	1398	3375	Note 1

NOTE 1: Total U.S. calendar year production: (Domestic) 46,950; (Export) 4300; (Total) 51,250.

Series B-2-C	**(¾-Ton)**	**(116 in. w.b.)**		
B-2-C	Chassis & Cowl	1030	2650	Note 2
B-2-C	Chassis (Note 4)	1075	—	Note 2
B-2-C	Chassis & Cab	1240	3150	Note 2
B-2-C	Pickup (7½-ft.)	1331	3525	Note 2
B-2-C	Platform (7½-ft.)	1337	3475	Note 2
B-2-C	Stake (7½-ft.)	1390	3700	Note 2

NOTE 2: Total U.S. calendar year production: (all Domestic) 14,928.

Series B-2-D	**(1-Ton)**	**(116 in. w.b.)**		
B-2-D	Chassis & Cowl	1084	2900	Note 3
B-2-D	Chassis (Note 4)	1129	—	Note 3
B-2-D	Chassis & Cab	1294	3375	Note 3
B-2-D	Pickup (7½-ft.)	1385	3725	Note 3
B-2-D	Platform (7½-ft.)	1391	3725	Note 3
B-2-D	Stake (7½-ft.)	1444	3905	Note 3
(126 in. w.b.)				
B-2-D	Chassis & Cowl	1104	2950	Note 3
B-2-D	Chassis (Note 4)	1149	—	Note 3
B-2-D	Chassis & Cab	1314	3375	Note 3
B-2-D	Pickup (9-ft.)	1415	3800	Note 3
B-2-D	Platform (9-ft.)	1423	3825	Note 3
B-2-D	Stake (9-ft.)	1489	4055	Note 3
Series B-2-PW Power Wagon	**(1-Ton)**	**(126 in. w.b.)**		
B-2-PW	Chassis & Cowl	1750	4075	Note 3
B-2-PW	Chassis (Note 4)	1790	—	Note 3
B-2-PW	Chassis & Cab	1940	4675	Note 3
B-2-PW	Pickup (8-ft.)	2045	5100	Note 3
Series B-2-DU/EU Route-Van	**(1-Ton)**	**(102 in. w.b.)**		
B-2-DU	7-ft. Panel Body	2295	—	—
B-2-DUF	7-ft. (Note 5)	2350	—	—
(117 in. w.b.)				
B-2-DU	9½-ft. Panel Body	2380	—	—
B-2-DUF	9½-ft. (Note 5)	2435	—	—
(142 in. w.b.)				
B-2-EUF	12½-ft. (Note 5)	2725	—	—
B-2-EU	12½-ft. Body	2670	—	—

NOTE 3: Total U.S. calendar year production, 1-Ton models with 116 and 126 in. w.b.: (Domestic) 11,640; (Export) 3221; (Total) 14,861.

NOTE 4: Chassis with cowl and windshield.

NOTE 5: With Fluid Drive.

ENGINE: Same as 1948-49 models.

CHASSIS (Series B-2-B): Wheelbase: 108 in. Tires: 6.00 x 16 four-ply front and rear; disc wheels with 4.00 drop-center rims. Underslung tire carrier.

CHASSIS (Series B-2-C): Wheelbase: 116 in. Tires: 7.00 x 15 six-ply front and rear; disc wheels with 5.50 drop-center rims. Underslung tire carrier.

CHASSIS (Series B-2-D): Wheelbase: 116 and 126 in. Tires: (front 6.00 x 16 six-ply; (rear) 7.00 x 16 six-ply. Disc wheels on 4.50 semi-drop-center rims (front); 5.50 (rear and spare). Underslung tire carrier.

TECHNICAL: Same as 1948-49 B-1 Series.

OPTIONS: (Dealer-installed) Same as 1948-49 B-1 Series.

HISTORICAL: Introduced: October, 1949. Calendar year registrations: 99,716. Calendar year production: 122,324 (U.S. only). Model year figures not available. Innovations: Bonded brake linings on all light-duty trucks. Steering column three-speed gearshift. History: Sales dropped by 14.7 percent for 1950. Dodge offered 396 models rated ½ to 4-tons. Of the total production, 9471 trucks were built in San Leandro, California. Dodge sold 400 ½-ton panel trucks and 3750 special-bodied 1-tons to the Post Office. Early in 1950, Dodge announced a new line of 4-ton trucks in five w.b., powered by a huge 337 cu. in. L-head six. They had GVW ratings of 28,000 pounds and combined GVW of 50,000 lbs. Chrysler Corp. suffered a 100-day labor strike from January to April 1950. Stepped-up production after the strike ended could not make up for the loss. On January 10, 1950, Dodge cut truck prices by $40 to $125.

Pricing

1950	5	4	3	2	1
Series B-2-B — (½-Ton) — (108 in. w.b.)					
Pickup	900	1800	3000	4200	6000
Panel	830	1650	2750	3850	5500
Series B-2-C — (¾-Ton) — (116 in. w.b.)					
Pickup	870	1700	2850	4000	5700
Platform	750	1500	2500	3500	5000
Stake	770	1550	2550	3600	5100
Series B-2-D — (1-Ton) — (116 in. w.b.)					
Pickup	810	1620	2700	3800	5400
Platform	700	1400	2350	3250	4700
Stake	720	1450	2400	3300	4800
Series B-2-D — (1-Ton) — (126 in. w.b.)					
Pickup	800	1600	2650	3700	5300
Platform	690	1380	2300	3200	4600
Stake	700	1400	2350	3250	4700
Series B-2-PW Power-Wagon — (1-Ton) — (126 in. w.b.)					
Pickup	1130	2250	3750	5250	7500
Series B-2-DU/EU Route-Van — (1-Ton) — (102 in. w.b.)					
7-ft. body	570	1140	1900	2650	3800
(117 in. w.b.)					
9-½ ft. body	560	1100	1850	2600	3700
(142 in. w.b.)					
12½-ft. body	540	1080	1800	2500	3600

NOTE: Add 3 percent for Fluid Drive.

1951 DODGE

½-TON — SERIES B-3-B — SIX-CYLINDER / ¾-TON — SERIES B-3-C — SIX-CYLINDER / 1-TON — SERIES B-3-D — SIX-CYLINDER: Restyling of the grille and hood gave an all-new appearance to the B-Series front end. Inside, the dash was also restyled. Instruments were moved from the center of the panel to directly in front of the driver. Cab trim details and colors were improved, while the steering wheel was given an attractive horn ring and turn signal switch. Engine horsepower and torque increased, due to a boost in compression ratio to 7:1. Chrysler's double-acting Oriflow shock absorbers improved the ride quality. Both ¾ and 1-ton pickups were now available with either high side or low side bodies. Low sides were now standard for all pickups; high side bodies cost extra. A new narrow wedge fan belt gave the B/C engine quieter running and longer belt life.
Anodized brake cylinders cut rust and corrosion. Standard equipment included hydraulic shocks front and rear (front only on 1-ton), front bumper, underslung tire carrier, left-side outside mirror, oil-bath air cleaner (one pint capacity), dual vacuum windshield wipers, and an interior sun visor on the left side. This would be the first time for many years that the Dodge Ram hood ornament, used from 1948-50, was not standard equipment, though it was still available as an extra-cost dealer-installed option. All models were carried over from 1950.

1-TON POWER-WAGON — SERIES B-3-PW — SIX-CYLINDER: — Several improvements reached the Power-Wagon. Front axle capacity was raised to 3750 pounds from 3500; rear axle to 6500 pounds from 5500. Instruments were changed to the B-2 Series type, rather than the style used in the old W-Series of 1947. The pickup body was totally redesigned so it was very much like conventional B-Series pickups. A quieter 4-blade radiator fan replaced the former 6-blade unit. The Power-Wagon engine did not get a compression ratio boost, but it did receive improved "floating power" mountings.

1-TON ROUTE-VAN — SERIES B-3-DU/EU — SIX-CYLINDER: — Route-Van models continued unchanged, except for the addition of the improved 230 cu. in. engine. They kept the old B-1 Series grille design.

I.D. DATA: Serial and engine numbers were in the same locations as 1950 models.

Model	Serial Numbers Starting	Serial Numbers Ending	Place of Manuf.	Starting Engine No.
B-3-B	82215001	82256916	Detroit	T306-1001
B-3-B	85308001	85313574	California	T306-1001
B-3-C	83362001	83372821	Detroit	T308-1001
	85510001	85511859	California	T308-1001
B-3-D	81435001	81446940	Detroit	T310-1001
	86010001	86011065	California	T310-1001
B-3-PW	83922501	83926471	Detroit	T137-1001
	88766501	88766833	California	T137-1001
B-3-DU	84206501	84207490	Detroit	T164-1001
B-3-EU	84001701	84002151	Detroit	T165-1001

Model	Body Type	Price	Weight	Prod. Total
Series B-3-B — (½-Ton) — (108 in. w.b.)				
B-3-B	Chassis & Cowl	1017	2475	Note 1
B-3-B	Chassis (Note 4)	1062	—	Note 1
B-3-B	Chassis & Cab	1227	2975	Note 1
B-3-B	Pickup (6½-ft.)	1293	3275	Note 1
B-3-B	Panel	1493	3375	Note 1

NOTE: Calendar year production of ½-ton trucks, U.S. only: (Domestic) 53,563; (Export) 5429; (Total) 58,992.

Model	Body Type	Price	Weight	Prod. Total
Series B-3-C — (¾-Ton) — (116 in. w.b.)				
B-3-C	Chassis & Cowl	1140	2650	Note 2
B-3-C	Chassis (Note 4)	1185	—	Note 2
B-3-C	Chassis & Cab	1350	3150	Note 2
B-3-C	Pickup (7½-ft.)	1441	3525	Note 2
B-3-C	Platform (7½-ft.)	1457	3425	Note 2
B-3-C	Stake (7½-ft.)	1515	3700	Note 2

NOTE 2: Calendar year production of ¾-ton trucks, U.S. only: (Domestic) 15,619; (Government) 11,246; (Total) 26,865.

Model	Body Type	Price	Weight	Prod. Total
SERIES B-3-D — (1-Ton) — (116 in. w.b.)				
B-3-D	Chassis & Cowl	1199	2900	Note 3
B-3-D	Chassis (Note 4)	1244	—	Note 3
B-3-D	Chassis & Cab	1409	3375	Note 3
B-3-D	Pickup (7½-ft.)	1500	3725	Note 3
B-3-D	Platform (7½-ft.)	1516	3725	Note 3
B-3-D	Stake (7½-ft.)	1574	3905	Note 3
(126 in. w.b.)				
B-3-D	Chassis & Cowl	1219	2950	Note 3
B-3-D	Chassis (Note 4)	1264	—	Note 3
B-3-D	Chassis & Cab	1429	3375	Note 3
B-3-D	Pickup (9-ft.)	1530	3800	Note 3
B-3-D	Platform (9-ft.)	1548	3825	Note 3
B-3-D	Stake (9-ft.)	1619	4055	Note 3
Series B-3-PW Power-Wagon — (1-Ton) — (126 in. w.b.)				
B-3-PW	Chassis & Cowl	1875	4075	Note 3
B-3-PW	Chassis (Note 4)	1915	—	Note 3
B-3-PW	Chassis & Cab	2065	4675	Note 3
B-3-PW	Pickup (8-ft.)	2170	5100	Note 3

NOTE 3: Calendar year production of 1-ton models (including Power Wagon), U.S. only: (Domestic) 17,489; (Export) 5947; (Total) 23,436. Power-Wagon production for 1951-52 model years: 10,693 units.

NOTE 4: Chassis with cowl and windshield.

Model	Body Type	Price	Weight	
Series B-3-DU/EU Route-Van — (1-Ton) — (102 in. w.b.)				
B-3-DU	7-ft. Panel Body	2587	—	451
B-3-EU	7-ft. Panel	2826	—	85
(117 in. w.b.)				
B-3-DU	9½-ft. Panel	2679	—	913
B-3-EU	9½-ft. Panel	2920	—	131
(142 in. w.b.)				
B-3-EU	12½-ft. Panel	3063	—	436

NOTE: Combined production total, 1951-52 model years.

ENGINE (Series B-3-B, B-3-C): Inline. L-head. Six-cylinder. Bore & stroke: 3¼ x 4⅜ in. Displacement: 217.8 cu. in. Compression ratio: 7.0:1. Brake horsepower: 97 at 3600 R.P.M. Net horsepower: 25.35. Torque: 175 lbs.-ft. at 1600 R.P.M. Four main bearings. Solid valve lifters.

ENGINE (Series B-3-D): Inline. L-head. Six-cylinder. Bore & stroke: 3¼ x 4⅝ in. Displacement: 230.2 cu. in. Compression ratio: 7.0:1. Brake horsepower: 103 at 3600 R.P.M. Net horsepower: 25.35. Torque: 190 lbs.-ft. at 1600 R.P.M. Four main bearings. Solid valve lifters.

ENGINE (Series B-3-PW): Inline. L-head. Six-cylinder. Bore & stroke: 3¼ x 4⅝ in. Displacement: 230.2 cu. in. Compression ratio: 6.7:1. Brake horsepower: 94 at 3200 R.P.M. Net horsepower: 25.35. Torque: 186 lbs.-ft. at 1200 R.P.M. Four main bearings. Solid valve lifters.

ENGINE (Route-Van): Same as B-3-D except Horsepower: 99 at 3600 R.P.M.

CHASSIS: Same as 1950. Front axle capacity: (½-ton) 2200 lbs.; (¾ and 1-ton) 2500 lbs. Rear axle capacity: (½-ton) 3300 lbs; (¾-ton) 3600 lbs; (1-ton) 5800 lbs. Gross Vehicle Weight Rating: (½-ton) 4850 lbs; (¾-ton) 5800 lbs; (1-ton) 8000 lbs.

TECHNICAL: Same as B-1 Series models of 1948-49, except for rear axle ratios as follows: (½-ton) 3.73:1, 4.1:1 and 4.78:1; (¾-ton) 4.1:1 and 4.78:1; (1-ton) 3.9:1, 4.3:1 and 4.89:1.

OPTIONS: (Standard ½, ¾ and 1-ton models) Rear bumper ($8). Deluxe cab equipment ($30). Custom cab equipment ($56). Deluxe panel equipment ($30). High side pickup body ($7). Bumper guards ($3.50/pair). Chrome grab handles ($8). Long rear-view mirror, left side ($2); right side ($3). Stainless steel grille panel moldings ($10). Dual electric horns ($12). Auxiliary seat for panel ($30). Air foam seat cushion ($10). Dual electric windshield wipers ($8). Door ventilating wings ($15). Auxiliary tail light for panel ($3); for other models ($6). Ash tray ($2). Oil-bath air cleaner, one-quart ($1.75). Sealed-type oil filter ($5). Battery: 120 ampere-hour ($5). Fluid Drive ($38). Electric fuel pump ($13). Governor ($7). 11-in. clutch ($7.50). Four-speed transmission ($50). Rear shock absorbers for 1-ton models ($11). Dome light ($5).

HISTORICAL: Introduced: December 1950. Calendar year registrations: 106,600. Calendar year production, U.S. only: 169,088. Model year production (combined 1951-52): (Series B-3-B) 118,094; (Series B-3-C) 27,194; (Series B-3-D-116) 9085; (Series B-3-D-126) 25,704; (Total) 192,886. History: Truck production rose 38.2 percent over 1950 output. Of the total, 14,081 trucks were built in San Leandro, California. Canadian plants turned out 20,876 trucks. Dodge began producing military trucks for the Korean War on January 15, 1951, using the same assembly lines as civilian models. Four types, all 4x4 with ¾-ton capacity, were built: the M-37 cargo vehicle, a telephone and maintenance truck, M-42 Command Utility truck, and M-43 field ambulance. In all, 11,246 military trucks were made in 1951. Dodge also exported 28,772 trucks. A new truck engine plant at Trenton, Michigan was completed in November. A six-week strike at Midland Steel caused production loss of 7500 vehicles, due to shortages of frames. Six of nine ATA Roadeo winners drove Dodge trucks in the 1951 driving competition.

Pricing

1951	5	4	3	2	1
Series B-3-B — (½-Ton) — (108 in. w.b.)					
Pickup	890	1770	2950	4150	5900
Panel	810	1620	2700	3800	5400
Series B-3-C — (¾-Ton) — (116 in. w.b.)					
Pickup	840	1680	2800	3900	5600
Platform	740	1470	2450	3350	4900
Stake	750	1500	2500	3500	5000
Series B-3-D — (1-Ton) — (116 in. w.b.)					
Pickup	800	1600	2650	3700	5300
Platform	690	1380	2300	3200	4600
Stake	700	1400	2350	3250	4700
(126 in. w.b.)					
Pickup	780	1560	2600	3600	5200
Platform	680	1350	2250	3150	4500
Stake	690	1380	2300	3200	4600
Series B-3-PW — (1-Ton) — (126 in. w.b.)					
Pickup	1130	2250	3750	5250	7500
Series B-3-DU/EU — (102 in. w.b.)					
7-ft. Body	570	1140	1900	2650	3800
(117 in. w.b.)					
9½-ft. Body	560	1100	1850	2600	3700
(142 in. w.b.)					
12½-ft. Body	540	1080	1800	2500	3600

NOTE: Add 3 percent for Fluid Drive.

1952 DODGE

1952 Dodge 1-Ton Platform Stake Body (D. Sagvold)

½-TON — SERIES B-3-B — SIX-CYLINDER / ¾-TON — SERIES B-3-C — SIX-CYLINDER / 1-TON — SERIES B-3-D — SIX-CYLINDER: — The entire B-3 Series was carried over without change in appearance, model availability, equipment, or mechanical details. The only exterior clue to identify model year is that the 1951 models used a chrome-finished medallion in the center of the grille, while in 1952 the medallion was painted argent. Standard colors were the same as 1948-52: Armour Yellow, Dodge Truck Red or Dark Green, Deep Blue, and Black. Gray was discontinued. Pickup bodies, including rear fenders, were Black regardless of cab color. Only for additional cost would pickup bodies and rear fenders be painted cab color. Running boards and bumpers were always Black, wheels Dodge Truck Cream (Black optional).

1-TON — POWER—WAGON SERIES B-3-PW — SIX-CYLINDER / 1-TON ROUTE-VAN — SERIES B-3-DU/EU — SIX-CYLINDER: — Power-Wagons and Route-Vans continued unchanged for 1952.

I.D. DATA: Serial and engine numbers were in the same locations as 1950-51.

Model	Serial Numbers Starting	Ending	City of Manuf.	Starting Engine No.
B-3-B	83373001	83388000	Detroit	T306-1001
B-3-B	85512001	85515000	Los Angeles	T306-1001
B-3-C	81447301	81463000	Detroit	T308-1001
B-3-C	86011201	86013000	Los Angeles	T308-1001
B-3-D	81447301	81463000	Detroit	T310-1001
B-3-D	86011201	86013000	Los Angeles	T310-1001
B-3-PW	83926501	83934000	Detroit	T137-1001
B-3-PW	88766901	88767500	Los Angeles	T137-1001
B-3-DU	84207601	84208500	Detroit	T164-1001
B-3-EU	84002201	84003000	Detroit	T165-1001

Model	Body Type	Price	Weight	Prod. Total
Series B-3-B — (½-Ton) — (108 in. w.b.)				
B-3-B	Chassis & Cowl	1125	2475	Note 1
B-3-B	Chassis & Cab	1365	2975	Note 1
B-3-B	Pickup (6½-ft.)	1440	3275	Note 1
B-3-B	Panel	1650	3375	Note 1

NOTE 1: Calendar year production of ½-ton trucks, U.S. only: (Domestic) 48,497; (Export) 3675; (Total) 52,172.

Model	Body Type	Price	Weight	Prod. Total
Series B-3-C — (¾-Ton) — (116 in. w.b.)				
B-3-C	Chassis & Cowl	1235	2650	Note 2
B-3-C	Chassis & Cab	1473	3150	Note 2
B-3-C	Pickup (7½-ft.)	1578	3525	Note 2
B-3-C	Platform (7½-ft.)	1585	3475	Note 2
B-3-C	Stake (7½-ft.)	1646	3700	Note 2

NOTE 2: Calendar year production of ¾-ton trucks, U.S. only: (Domestic) 14,420; (Government) 26,143; (Total) 40,563.

Model	Body Type	Price	Weight	Prod. Total
Series B-3-D — (1-Ton) — (116 in. w.b.)				
B-3-D	Chassis & Cowl	1293	2900	Note 3
B-3-D	Chassis & Cab	1531	3375	Note 3
B-3-D	Pickup (7½-ft.)	1636	3725	Note 3
B-3-D	Platform (7½-ft.)	1642	3725	Note 3
B-3-D	Stake (7½-ft.)	1702	3905	Note 3
Series B-3-D — (1-Ton) — (126 in. w.b.)				
B-3-D	Chassis & Cowl	1315	2950	Note 3
B-3-D	Chassis & Cab	1555	3375	Note 3
B-3-D	Pickup (9-ft.)	1669	3800	Note 3
B-3-D	Platform (9-ft.)	1678	3825	Note 3
B-3-D	Stake (9-ft.)	1755	4055	Note 3
Series B-3-PW Power-Wagon — (1-Ton) — (126 in. w.b.)				
B-3-PW	Chassis & Cab	2232	4675	Note 3
B-3-PW	Pickup (8-ft.)	2353	5100	Note 3

NOTE 3: Calendar year production of 1-ton trucks (including Power-Wagon and Route-Van), U.S. only: (Domestic) 14,282; (Export) 5997; (Total) 20,279.

Model	Body Type	Price	Weight	Prod. Total
Series B-3-DU/EU — (1-Ton) — (102 in. w.b.)				
B-3-DU	7-ft. Panel Body	2692	—	Note 4
B-3-EU	7-ft. Panel Body	—	—	Note 4
Series B-3-DU/EU — (1-Ton) — (117 in. w.b.)				
B-3-DU	9½-ft. Panel	2788	—	Note 4
B-3-EU	9½-ft. Panel	—	—	Note 4
Series B-3-EU — (1-Ton) — (142 in. w.b.)				
B-3-EU	12½-ft. Panel	3186	—	Note 4

NOTE 4: See 1951 listing for combined production figures.

ENGINE: Same as 1951; see previous specifications.

CHASSIS: Same as 1950-51; see previous specifications.

TECHNICAL: Same as 1951.

OPTIONS: Rear bumper ($8.25). Deluxe cab equipment ($30.59). Custom cab equipment ($69.36). Deluxe panel equipment ($40.73). High side pickup body ($8.27). Bumper guards ($4.44). Long-arm adjustable mirror, left ($2.10); right ($3.23). Dual electric horns ($12.42). Auxiliary seat for panel ($31.36). Air foam seat cushion ($9.52). Pickup body and rear fenders painted to match cab ($6.44). Auxiliary tail lamp ($6.63). Ash tray ($1.53). Oil-bath air cleaner, one-quart ($1.47). Oil filter ($9.27). Electric fuel pump ($13.96). High-charging generator ($10.38). Governor ($7.17). Fluid Drive ($43.14). Four-speed transmission ($61.01).

1952 Dodge Power Wagon (J.C. Lowe)

HISTORICAL: Introduced: October 15, 1951. Calendar year registrations: 102,129. Calendar year production: 127,716. See 1951 for combined model year production figures. History: Dodge produced a full line of trucks from ½ to 4-ton capacity, including a six-wheeler and 26,143 ¾-ton 4x4 trucks for the Army. Due to the Korean War, the Government, through the National Production Authority, limited car and truck output to ensure availability of vital war equipment. The NPA assigned a quota of civilian trucks to each manufacturer by weight class. Dodge's NPA percentages were a bit over 13 percent of total industry output for each category. In spite of the NPA, U.S. truck production was only 14 percent less than 1951. Dodge's sales and production figures fell modestly. During 1952, Dodge created two new executive posts: Sales Manager for Cars, and Sales Manager for Trucks.

Pricing

	5	4	3	2	1
1952					
Series B-3-B — (½-Ton) — (108 in. w.b.)					
Pickup	890	1770	2950	4150	5900
Panel	810	1620	2700	3800	5400
Series B-3-C — (¾-Ton) — (116 in. w.b.)					
Pickup	840	1680	2800	3900	5600
Platform	740	1470	2450	3350	4900
Stake	750	1500	2500	3500	5000
Series B-3-D — (1-Ton) — (116 in. w.b.)					
Pickup	800	1600	2650	3700	5300
Platform	690	1380	2300	3200	4600
Stake	700	1400	2350	3250	4700
Series B-3-D — (1-Ton) — (126 in. w.b.)					
Pickup	780	1560	2600	3600	5200
Platform	680	1350	2250	3150	4500
Stake	690	1380	2300	3200	4600
Series B-3-PW Power-Wagon — (1-Ton) — (126 in. w.b.)					
Pickup	1130	2250	3750	5250	7500
Series B-3-DU/EU Route-Van — (102 in. w.b.)					
7-ft. Body	570	1140	1900	2650	3800
Series B-3-DU/EU Route-Van — (117 in. w.b.)					
9½-ft. Body	560	1100	1850	2600	3700
Series B-3-EU Route-Van — (142 in. w.b.)					
12½-ft. Body	540	1080	1800	2500	3600

NOTE: Add 3 percent for Fluid Drive.

1953 DODGE

1953 Dodge ½-Ton Pickup (DB)

½-TON — SERIES B-4-B — SIX-CYLINDER / ¾-TON — SERIES B-4-C — SIX-CYLINDER / 1-TON — SERIES B-4-D — SIX-CYLINDER: — Extensive changes were made for this final year of the B-Series. A new Dodge nameplate on the front featured modern, wider-spaced letters connected by a Red stripe. Chrome headlight rims replaced the Black enameled ones. Parking light rims were also chrome. Striping was omitted from the grille moulding. Pickup rear fenders were redesigned to a modern, streamlined look. These fenders, in fact, were used on Dodge pickups up to 1985. Dual-wheeled 1-ton pickups kept the previous rear fenders. Hub caps, changed for the first time since 1948, were now stainless steel with a raised circular flange, inset with Red Dodge letters. Dual taillamps were now standard on the panel model. Inside the cab, seat trim fabrics sported a new Maroon/Grey color combination. All accessories including armrests, sun visors and door handle escutcheons were color-matched. For the first time in the B-Series, the Dodge nameplate stood on the instrument panel. An industry "first" was the addition of a new ½-ton pickup with 90 in. box, for customers who needed to haul light but bulky loads. Built on a 116 in. w.b. chassis like the ¾-ton pickups, this model also had the highside body. Only the short-box ½-ton pickup carried a lowside body. Dodge offered another industry "first" in its automatic transmission, optional on all light-duty models. Truck-O-Matic was similar in operation to the automatic used in DeSoto and Chrysler cars. This was also the first year Dodge offered tinted windows. Engines were unchanged, and standard equipment was the same as in 1952.

1-TON POWER-WAGON — SERIES B-4-PW — SIX-CYLINDER / 1-TON ROUTE-VAN — SERIES B-4-DU/EU — SIX-CYLINDER: — Route-Vans continued without change. The Power-Wagon engine received a boost in compression ratio, to 7.0:1 from 6.7:1, plus a new carburetor. Horsepower and torque ratings were increased.

I.D. DATA: Serial and engine numbers were in the same locations as 1950-52.

Model	Serial Numbers Starting	Serial Numbers Ending	City of Manuf.	Starting Engine No.
B-4-B	82302001	82335036	Detroit	T306-1001
B-4-B	85322001	85327718	Los Angeles	T306-1001
B-4-C	83388001	83396360	Detroit	T308-1001
B-4-C	85515001	85516395	Los Angeles	T308-1001
B-4-D	81463001	81470822	Detroit	T310-1001
B-4-D	86013001	86013850	Los Angeles	T310-1001
B-4-PW	83934001	83937729	Detroit	T137-1001
B-4-PW	88767501	88767693	Los Angeles	T137-1001
B-4-DU	84208501	84208886	Detroit	T164-1001
B-4-EU	84003001	84003150	Detroit	T165-1001

Model	Body Type	Price	Weight	Prod. Total
Series B-4-B — (½-Ton) — (108 in. w.b.)				
B-4-B	Chassis & Cowl	1028	2425	Note 1
B-4-B	Chassis & Cab	1265	2975	Note 1
B-4-B	Pickup (6½-ft.)	1344	3275	Note 1
B-4-B	Panel	1541	3375	Note 1
Series B-4-B — (½-Ton) — (116 in. w.b.)				
B-4-B	Chassis & Cowl	1043	2650	Note 1
B-4-B	Chassis & Cab	1280	3150	Note 1
B-4-B	7½-ft. Pickup	1379	3525	Note 1

NOTE 1: Calendar year production of ½-ton trucks, U.S. only: (Domestic) 32,506; (Export) 3903; (Total) 36,409.

Model	Body Type	Price	Weight	Prod. Total
Series B-4-C — (¾-Ton) — (116 in. w.b.)				
B-4-C	Chassis & Cowl	1119	2650	Note 2
B-4-C	Chassis & Cab	1358	3150	Note 2
B-4-C	7½-ft. Pickup	1471	3525	Note 2
B-4-C	Platform	1469	3475	Note 2
B-4-C	Stake	1528	3200	Note 2

NOTE 2: Calendar year production of ¾-ton trucks, U.S. only: (Domestic) 9702; (Export) 15; (Government) 20,207; (Total) 29,924.

Model	Body Type	Price	Weight	Prod. Total
Series B-4-D — (1-Ton) — (116 in. w.b.)				
B-4-D	Chassis & Cowl	1182	2900	Note 3
B-4-D	Chassis & Cab	1417	3375	Note 3
B-4-D	7½-ft. Pickup	1536	3725	Note 3
B-4-D	7½-ft. Platform	1527	3725	Note 3
B-4-D	7½-ft. Stake	1586	3905	Note 3
Series B-4-D — (1-Ton) — (126 in. w.b.)				
B-4-D	Chassis & Cowl	1204	2950	Note 3
B-4-D	Chassis & Cab	1441	3375	Note 3
B-4-D	9-ft. Pickup	1568	3800	Note 3
B-4-D	9-ft. Platform	1562	3825	Note 3
B-4-D	Stake	1638	4055	Note 3

NOTE 3: Calendar year production of 1-ton models (including Power-Wagon and Route-Van), U.S. only: (Domestic) 8231; (Export) 4921; (Total) 13,152.

Model	Body Type	Price	Weight	Prod. Total
Series B-4-PW Power-Wagon — (1-Ton) — (126 in. w.b.)				
B-4-PW	Chassis & Cab	2190	4675	Note 4
B-4-PW	8-ft. Pickup	2307	5100	Note 4

NOTE 4: Model year production of Power-Wagons: (Domestic) 1215; (Export) 2781; (Total) 3996.

Model	Body Type	Price	Weight	Prod. Total
Series B-4-DU/EU Route-Van — (1-Ton) — (102 in. w.b.)				
B-4-DU	7-ft. Panel	2692	—	47
Series B-4-DU/EU Route-Van — (1-Ton) — (117 in. w.b.)				
B-4-DU	9½ ft. Panel	2788	—	345
Series B-4-DU/EU Route-Van — (1½-Ton) — (117 in. w.b.)				
B-4-EU	9½-ft. Panel	—	—	27
Series B-4-DU/EU Route-Van — (1½-Ton) — (142 in. w.b.)				
B-4-EU	12½-ft. Panel	3186	—	125

182

1953 Dodge Model 4B Pickup (R.L. Miracle)

ENGINE (Series B-4-B, B-4-C): Inline. L-head. Six-cylinder. Cast iron block. Bore & stroke: 3¼ x 4⅜ in. Displacement: 217.8 cu. in. Compression ratio: 7.1:1. Brake horsepower: 100 at 3600 R.P.M. Net horsepower: 25.35. Torque: 177 lbs.-ft. at 1600 R.P.M. Four main bearings. Solid valve lifters.

ENGINE (Series B-4-D): Inline. L-head. Six-cylinder. Cast iron block. Bore & stroke: 3¼ x 4⅝ in. Displacement: 230.2 cu. in. Compression ratio: 7.0:1. Brake horsepower: 103 at 3600 R.P.M. Net horsepower: 25.35. Torque: 190 lbs.-ft. at 1200 R.P.M. Four main bearings. Solid valve lifters.

ENGINE (Series B-4-PW): Inline. L-head. Six-cylinder. Cast iron block. Bore & stroke: 3¼ x 4⅝ in. Displacement: 230.2 cu. in. Compression ratio: 7.0:1. Brake horsepower: 99 at 3600 R.P.M. Net horsepower: 25.35. Torque: 190 lbs.-ft. at 1200 R.P.M. Four main bearings. Solid valve lifters.

CHASSIS (Series B-4-B): Wheelbase: 108 in. or 116 in. Tires: 6.00 x 16 four-ply. GVW: 4900 lbs.

CHASSIS (Series B-4-C): Wheelbase: 116 in. Tires: 7.00 x 15 six-ply. GVW: 5800 lbs.

CHASSIS (Series B-4-D): Wheelbase: 116 in. or 126 in. Tires: (front) 6.00 x 16 six-ply; (rear) 7.00 x 16 six-ply. GVW: 8000 lbs.

CHASSIS (Power-Wagon): Wheelbase: 126 in. Tires: 7.50 x 16 eight-ply. GVW: 8700 lbs.

TECHNICAL: Same as 1951-52; see previous specifications.

FACTORY OPTIONS: Same as 1952, with the addition of the following: Dodge-Tint glass on all cab models, all glass areas ($12.30); on panel model ($10.20). Truck-O-Matic transmission ($110). Rear quarter windows for standard and Deluxe models ($12.33).

HISTORICAL: Introduced: December 4, 1952. Calendar year registrations: 82,345. Calendar year production: 105,208. Model year production: (Series B-4-B-108) 40,412; (Series B-4-B-116) 9002; (Series B-4-C) 9760; (Series B-4-D-116) 967; (Series B-4-D-126) 11,178; (Total) 75,859. Innovations: Automatic transmission. Tinted glass. Long-box ½-ton pickup model. History: Prices of the new B-4 were reduced from 1952, and cut again in March 1953. In February 1953, the government removed the National Production Authority restrictions on civilian truck manufacturing. This action didn't help Dodge, as 1953 was a disaster. Sales fell 19.4 percent, in a year when industry sales increased by 14.6 percent. Production dropped 35.2 percent. Dodge sunk from third to fifth place in the industry's ranking. The Army purchased 20,207 4x4 military ¾-ton trucks. Light-duty exports totalled 8,839. Of the total U.S. production, 8,122 trucks were built at San Leandro, California; the remainder at the main truck plant in Warren, Michigan. Canadian production was 16,535. Dodge truck plants worked four-day weeks in February-March 1953. The 4-ton model, raised to 60,000 pounds maximum GCW, gained a new 413 cu. in. six-cylinder engine with dual carburetors and exhausts.

1953 Dodge ½-Ton Town Panel (Al Doerman)

Pricing

1953

	5	4	3	2	1
Series B-4-B — (½-Ton) — (108 in. w.b.)					
Pickup	890	1770	2950	4150	5900
Panel	810	1620	2700	3800	5400
Series B-4-B — (½-Ton) — (116 in. w.b.)					
Pickup	870	1750	2900	4100	5800
Series B-4-C — (¾-Ton) — (116 in. w.b.)					
Pickup	840	1680	2800	3900	5600
Platform	740	1470	2450	3350	4900
Stake	750	1500	2500	3500	5000
Series B-4-D — (1-Ton) — (116 in. w.b.)					
Pickup	800	1600	2650	3700	5300
Platform	690	1380	2300	3200	4600
Stake	700	1400	2350	3250	4700
Series B-4-D — (1-Ton) — (126 in. w.b.)					
Pickup	780	1560	2600	3600	5200
Platform	680	1350	2250	3150	4500
Stake	690	1380	2300	3200	4600
Series B-4-PW Power-Wagon — (1-Ton) — (126 in. w.b.)					
Pickup	1130	2250	3750	5250	7500
Series B-4-DU/EU Route-Van — (102 in. w.b.)					
7-ft. Body	570	1140	1900	2650	3800
Series B-4-DU/EU Route-Van — (117 in. w.b.)					
9½-ft. Body	560	1100	1850	2600	3700
Series B-4-DU/EU Route-Van — (142 in. w.b.)					
12½-ft. Body	540	1080	1800	2500	3600

NOTE: Add 3 percent for Fluid Drive.

1954 DODGE

1954 Dodge Speedway Emergency Truck (IMSC/JLM)

½-TON — SERIES C-1-B — SIX-CYLINDER / ¾-TON — SERIES C-1-C — SIX-CYLINDER / 1-TON — SERIES C-1-D — SIX-CYLINDER: — Dodge brought an all-new truck to market for 1954, with new frames and cab styling plus a curved one-piece windshield. Wheelbases and model lineups remained the same as the B-4 Series. Restyled cab interiors gave more driver comfort. Cabs were available in three trim levels: Standard, Deluxe, and Custom. All were trimmed in attractive two-tone grey, including headliners and door trim panels. Cabs sat lower on the frame, to make entry and exit easier. Rear quarter windows, begun in 1948, continued but in a larger size. Brake and clutch pedals were now frame-mounted to reduce vibration. All dials on the new instrument panel were positioned in front of the driver, with a centered glove box. Control buttons were conveniently placed on the driver's right. Engines in the light-duty line carried over unchanged. V-8 engines, new for 1954, came only in medium and heavy-duty models, though a 241 cu. in. V-8 did become available for ½-, ¾-, and 1-ton trucks very late in the model year (August, 1954). At that time, the venerable old 218 cu. in. six was dropped, and a higher output 230 cu. in. six became the base engine for light-duty models. New standard paint colors were: Armour Yellow, Banner Green, Sonora Blue, Black, Dodge Truck Red, Dodge Truck Ponchartrain Green, and Ecuador Blue. Wheels were painted chrome metallic. Half-ton rear fenders and pickup boxes were black, regardless of cab color. Pickup bodies painted cab color were standard on ¾- and 1-ton models, but an extra-cost option on ½-tons. Lowside bodies were standard on ½-ton pickups; highside available at extra cost. The Town Panel was restyled extensively, much sleeker and more modern with smooth, flowing lines. It featured dual rounded taillights, larger rear doors, smaller wheel housings, and a longer floor. Since Dodge did not make a Sedan Delivery, the Town Panel had to fill that role. An inside-mounted tire carrier was available for Town Panels, and a side-mounted carrier on pickups. Standard equipment included a front bumper, front and rear shocks, oil-bath air cleaner, dual vacuum windshield wipers, vent wings in cab doors, left side sunvisor, and a dome light (Town Panel only).

½-TON, ¾-TON and 1-TON — SERIES C-1-B/C/D — EIGHT-CYLINDER: — V-8 versions were offered in August, 1954, as the model year drew to a close.

1954 Dodge Town-Panel (OCW)

1-TON POWER-WAGON — SERIES C-1-PW — SIX-CYLINDER / 1-TON ROUTE-VAN — SERIES C-1-DU/EU — SIX-CYLINDER: — A V-8 engine was not available for the Power-Wagon or Route-Van, which continued unchanged. The Route-Van retained its 1948 styling, while the Power-Wagon's cab style continued without significant change from 1946 through 1968.

I.D. DATA: Serial numbers were located on the left side of the cowl, under the hood. Engine numbers were stamped on a pad on the left side of the cylinder block, between cylinders two and three.

Model	Engine	Serial Numbers Starting	Ending	Place of Manuf.	Starting Engine No.
C-1-B	Six	82338001	82372344	Detroit	T334-1001
C-1-B	Six	85328001	85330985	Calif.	
C-1-B	Eight	84250001	84262923	Detroit	VT334-1001
C-1-B	Eight	86100001	86100446	Calif.	
C-1-C	Six	83398001	83404307	Detroit	T336-1001
C-1-C	Six	85517001	85517631	Calif.	
C-1-C	Eight	84650001	84652998	Detroit	VT336-1001
C-1-C	Eight	86300001	86300105	Calif.	
C-1-D	Six	81472001	81481925	Detroit	T338-1001
C-1-D	Six	86014001	86014376	Calif.	
C-1-D	Eight	84800001	84802208	Detroit	VT338-1001
C-1-D	Eight	86400001	86400055	Calif.	
C-1-PW	Six	83938001	83943347	Detroit	T137-1001
C-1-PW	Six	88768001	88768126	Calif.	
C-1-DU					

Model	Body Type	Price	Weight	Prod. Total
Series C-1-B — (½-Ton) — (108 in. w.b.) — (6-cyl.)				
C-1-B6	Chassis & Cowl	1017	2475	Note 1
C-1-B6	Chassis & Cab	1252	2975	Note 1
C-1-B6	Pickup (6½-ft.)	1331	3275	Note 1
C-1-B6	Town Panel	1528	3375	Note 1
(116 in. w.b.)				
C-1-B6	Chassis & Cowl	1032	2650	Note 1
C-1-B6	Chassis & Cab	1267	3150	Note 1
C-1-B6	Pickup (7½-ft.)	1357	3525	Note 1

NOTE: Calendar year production, ½-ton trucks; (Domestic) 26,973; (Export) 8697; (Total) 35,670. Model year production (Total): 108 in., 35,862; 116 in. 6570.

Series C-1-C — (¾-Ton) — (116 in. w.b.) — (6-cyl.)				
C-1-C6	Chassis & Cowl	1114	2650	Note 2
C-1-C6	Chassis & Cab	1349	3150	Note 2
C-1-C6	Pickup (7½-ft.)	1462	3525	Note 2
C-1-C6	Platform	1459	3475	Note 2
C-1-C6	Stake (7½-ft.)	1518	3700	Note 2

NOTE 2: Calendar year production, ½-ton trucks: (Domestic) 6639; (Export) 166; (Government) 5586; (Total) 12,391. Model year production (Total): 6808.

SERIES C-1-D — (1-Ton) — (116 in. w.b.) — (6-cyl.)				
C-1-D6	Chassis & Cowl	1182	2900	Note 3
C-1-D6	Chassis & Cab	1417	3375	Note 3
C-1-D6	Pickup (7½-ft.)	1536	3725	Note 3
C-1-D6	Platform	1527	3725	Note 3
C-1-D6	Stake (7½-ft.)	1586	3905	Note 3
(126 in. w.b.)				
C-1-D6	Chassis & Cowl	1206	2950	Note 3
C-1-D6	Chassis & Cab	1441	3375	Note 3
C-1-D6	Pickup (9-ft.)	1568	3800	Note 3
C-1-D6	Platform	1562	3825	Note 3
C-1-D6	Stake (9-ft.)	1638	4055	Note 3

NOTE 3: Calendar year production, 1-ton trucks: (Domestic) 7711; (Export) 6195; (Total) 13,906. Model year production (Total): 116 in., 1616; 126 in., 10,597.

SERIES C-1-PW POWER-WAGON — (1-Ton) — (126 in. w.b.)				
C-1-PW6	Chassis & Cowl	1955	4075	Note 4
C-1-PW6	Chassis & Cab	2190	4675	Note 4
C-1-PW6	Pickup (8-ft.)	2307	5100	Note 4

NOTE 4: Model year production: 5601.

1954 Dodge Panel Delivery (OCW)

NOTE 5: V-8 equipped trucks, available at the end of the model year, had a D8 (rather than D6) designation in their model number.

SERIES C-1-DU/EU ROUTE-VAN — (1-Ton) — (102 in. w.b.)			
C-1-DU Panel (7-ft.)	—	—	61
(117 in. w.b.)			
C-1-DU Panel (9½-ft.)	—	—	458
(1½-Ton) — (102 in. w.b.)			
C-1-EU Panel (7-ft.)	—	—	32
(1½-Ton) — (117 in. w.b.)			
C-1-EU Panel (9½-ft.)	—	—	2
(142 in. w.b.)			
C-1-EU Panel (12½-ft.)	—	—	205

ENGINE (C-1-B, C-1-C): Inline. L-head. Six-cylinder. Cast iron block. Bore & stroke: 3¼ x 4⅜ in. Displacement: 217.8 cu. in. Compression ratio: 7.1:1. Brake horsepower: 100 at 3600 R.P.M. Net horsepower: 25.35. Torque: 177 lbs.-ft. at 1600 R.P.M. Four main bearings. Solid valve lifters.

ENGINE (Series C-1-D): Inline. L-head. Six-cylinder. Cast iron block. Bore & stroke: 3¼ x 4⅝ in. Displacement: 230.2 cu. in. Compression ratio: 7.25:1. Brake horsepower: 110 at 3600 R.P.M. Net horsepower: 25.35. Torque: 194 lbs.-ft. at 1600 R.P.M. Four main bearings. Solid valve lifters.

ENGINE (Power-Wagon): Inline. L-head. Six-cylinder. Cast iron block. Bore & stroke: 3¼ x 4⅝ in. Displacement: 230.2 cu. in. Compression ratio: 7.0:1. Brake horsepower: 99 at 3600 R.P.M. Net horsepower: 25.35. Torque: 190 lbs.-ft. at 1200 R.P.M. Four main bearings. Solid valve lifters.

ENGINE (C-1-B/C/D, Late): V-8. Overhead valve. Eight-cylinder. Cast iron block. Bore & stroke: 3-7/16 x 3¼ in. Displacement: 241.4 cu. in. Compression ratio: 7.5:1. Brake horsepower: 145 at 4400 R.P.M. Net horsepower: 37.8. Torque: 215 lbs.-ft. at 2400 R.P.M. Five main bearings. Hydraulic valve lifters.

CHASSIS (Series C-1-B): Wheelbase: 108 or 116 in. Tires: 6.00 x 16 four-ply. GVW: 4900 lbs. Rear axle rating: 3300 lbs. Front axle rating: 2200 lbs.

CHASSIS (Series C-1-C): Wheelbase: 116 in. Tires: 7.00 x 15 six-ply. GVW: 5800 lbs. Rear axle rating: 3600 lbs. Front axle rating: 2500 lbs.

CHASSIS (Series C-1-D): Wheelbase: 116 or 126 in. Tires: (front) 6.00 x 16 six-ply; (rear) 7.00 x 16 six-ply. GVW: 8000 lbs. Rear axle rating: 5800 lbs. Front axle rating: 2500 lbs.

CHASSIS (Power-Wagon): Wheelbase: 126 in. Tires: 7.50 x 16 eight-ply. GVW: 8700 lbs.

TECHNICAL: Selective sliding gear transmission. Speeds: 3F/1R; optional 4F/1R. Column or floor shift. Single plate dry disc clutch: 10 in., except 11 in. with optional four-speed transmission. Fluid Drive optional with three-speed transmission on ½- and ¾-ton models; with four-speed on 1-ton models. Automatic transmission optional on ½- and ¾-ton models. Rear axle ratio: (½- and ¾-ton) 4.1:1 and 4.78:1; (1-ton) 4.1:1 and 4.89:1. I-beam front axle. Worm and roller steering. Hydraulic four-wheel brakes.

1954 Dodge ½-Ton Town Panel (RPZ)

OPTIONS (Factory Installed): Rear bumper ($8.25). Bumper guards ($4.40). Highside pickup body: 6½-ft. ($8.25); 7½-ft. ($9). Deluxe cab equipment ($23.50). Custom cab equipment ($49). Deluxe panel equipment ($20). Door armrest ($3). Dodge Tint glass: all cabs ($12.30); panel ($10.20). Turn signals: panel ($11); pickup ($16). Dome light ($4.15). Auxiliary taillight ($6.60). Rear quarter windows ($12.30). Dual electric wipers ($8.40). Dual horns ($12.40). Horn ring on steering wheel ($2.50). Long arm mirror: right ($3.20); left ($2.10). Inside rearview mirror ($2.75). Set of stainless wheel covers ($13). Bright finish hub caps ($1.50). Bright metal grille moldings ($2.75). Bright metal moldings for Town Panel ($13). Inside sunvisor ($2.55). Auxiliary seat for Town Panel: standard ($31.35); deluxe ($39.90). Deluxe seat back padding: standard cab ($11.50); deluxe cab ($7.50). Deluxe seat cushion ($9). Heater: standard ($40); deluxe ($60). Paint to match pickup body with cab ($6.40). One-quart air cleaner ($1.45). Oil filter ($9.25). Electric fuel pump ($13.95). Governor ($7.15). Hand throttle ($2.50). Ash tray ($1.50). Heavy-duty three-speed transmission ($20). Three-speed transmission with Fluid Drive ($63). Four-speed transmission ($71.90). Truck-O-Matic transmission ($110).

HISTORICAL: Introduced: October, 1953. Calendar year sales: 60,658. Calendar year production: 94,887. Model year production, light trucks with six-cylinder engines: (Total) 67,812 (including Power-Wagons and Route-Vans); (Domestic only) 41,603. Innovations: Curved one-piece windshield. V-8 engine. Frame-mounted brake and clutch pedals. Historical notes: Despite the major product changes, 1954 was not a good year for Dodge truck. Sales were down 26.3 percent, well beyond the industry drop of 10.9 percent. Dodge's market share eroded to 7.3 percent. Of the total U.S. production, 3,690 trucks were made in California. Canadian production also dropped drastically, down to 7,201. Dodge exported 15,058 trucks and sold 5,586 to the government. The V-8 engine introduced on light-duty trucks in August, 1954 was not a hemi. The V-8 with hemispherical combustion chambers was used only in medium and heavy-duty trucks. To publicize the light-duty V-8, Dodge ran a ½-ton pickup 50,198 miles in 50 days on the Chrysler Proving Grounds, setting a world endurance record. Dodge advertised the new ½-ton V-8 as the most powerful low-tonnage engine in the world. In November, 1954, the AAA certified the V-8's gas economy at 22.21 miles per gallon. Dodge also began development work on an all-aluminum Army truck. In December, the Post Office purchased 1,890 Dodge trucks. The largest Dodge models continued to use the monster 413 cu. in. six, which debuted in 1953.

Pricing

	5	4	3	2	1
1954					
Series C-1-B — (½-Ton) — (108 in. w.b.)					
Pickup	920	1850	3050	4300	6100
Town Panel	840	1680	2800	3900	5600
Series C-1-B — (½-Ton) — (116 in. w.b.)					
Pickup	900	1800	3000	4200	6000
Series C-1-C — (¾-Ton) — (116 in. w.b.)					
Pickup	840	1680	2800	3900	5600
Platform	740	1470	2450	3350	4900
Stake	750	1500	2500	3500	5000
Series C-1-D — (1-Ton) — (116 in. w.b.)					
Pickup	800	1600	2650	3700	5300
Platform	690	1380	2300	3200	4600
Stake	700	1400	2350	3250	4700
Seris C-1-D — (1-Ton) — (126 in. w.b.)					
Pickup	780	1560	2600	3600	5200
Platform	680	1350	2250	3150	4500
Stake	690	1380	2300	3200	4600
Series C-1-PW Power-Wagon — (1-Ton) — (126 in. w.b.)					
Pickup	1130	2250	3750	5250	7500
Series C-1-DU/EU Route-Van — (102 in. w.b.)					
7-ft. Body	570	1140	1900	2650	3800
(117 in. w.b.)					
9½-ft. Body	560	1100	1850	2600	3700
(142 in. w.b.)					
12½-ft. Body	540	1080	1800	2500	3600

NOTE: Add 15 percent for V-8 engine.
Add 5 percent for automatic transmission.
Add 5 percent for Fluid Drive.

1955 DODGE

½-, ¾- and 1-TON — SERIES C-1-B/C/D — SIX and EIGHT-CYLINDER: — The model year began by continuing the C-1 Series without change. Early in 1955, truck manufacturing was terminated at the San Leandro, California facility. Further production came from the Warren truck plant in Detroit. That factory was changed over and the new C-3 Series trucks were unveiled on April 11, 1955.

½-TON — SERIES C-3-B — SIX and EIGHT-CYLINDER / ¾-TON — SERIES C-3-C — SIX and EIGHT-CYLINDER / 1-TON — SERIES C-3-D — SIX and EIGHT-CYLINDER: — The C-3 Series featured a new cab, called "Pilot-House" because of its excellent 360-degree visibility. Wraparound windshields and rear windows gave almost unobstructed vision in all directions. Interior appointments were more deluxe, featuring colorful woven Saron and nylon fabrics trimmed in vinyl. Seat construction was upgraded through the use of coil springs and foam rubber padding. Cabs were available with three upholstery color schemes, in four trim levels: Standard, Deluxe, Custom, and Custom Regal. Body paint colors were carried over, but the Custom Regal added chrome exterior accents. New models included a lower-priced ½-ton, 108 in. w.b. pickup, available only with a 6-cyl. engine and limited options. Other new models, never available before from Dodge, were ½-ton, 116 in. w.b. stake and platform trucks. The 6-cyl. engine was unchanged, but the V-8 was enlarged to 259 cu. in. (from 241 cu. in.). Two new tranmissions were available: a three-speed with overdrive, and a new Powerflite automatic. Truck-O-Matic and Fluid Drive were discontinued. Standard equipment included front and rear shock absorbers, front bumper, rear bumper (panel models only), underslung tire carrier, one-pint oil-bath air cleaner, dual vacuum wipers, inside sunvisor, plus dome light and dual tail lamps (panel model only).

1-TON POWER-WAGON — SERIES C-3-PW — SIX-CYLINDER: — The Power-Wagon continued without change, but Route-Vans were no longer available.

I.D. DATA: Serial numbers were on a plate on the left side of the cowl, under the hood. Engine numbers were stamped on a pad on the left side of the cylinder block, between cylinders two and three.

Model	Engine	Serial Numbers Starting	Ending	Starting Engine Nos.
C-3-B	Six	82373001	82397181	T334-1001
C-3-B	Eight	84265001	84284000	VT334-1001
C-3-C	Six	83405001	83409905	T336-1001
C-3-C	Eight	84654001	84658200	VT336-1001
C-3-D	Six	81483001	81489600	T338-1001
C-3-D	Eight	84803001	84806500	VT338-1001
C-3-PW	Six	83744001	83749000	T137-1001

NOTE: First (C-1) Series was continued from 1954.

Model	Body Type	Price	Weight	Prod. Total
Series C-3-B — (½-Ton) — (108 in. w.b.) — (6-cyl.)				
C-3-BL6	Pickup (Lowside)	1367	2175	Note 1
C-3-B6	Chassis & Cowl	1084	2200	Note 1
C-3-B6	Chassis & Cab	1321	2675	Note 1
C-3-B6	Pickup (Lowside)	1407	2975	Note 1
C-3-B6	Pickup (Highside)	1420	3025	Note 1
C-3-B6	Panel	1630	3150	Note 1
(116 in. w.b.)				
C-3-B6	Chassis & Cowl	1098	2225	Note 1
C-3-B6	Chassis & Cab	1334	2700	Note 1
C-3-B6	Pickup (Lowside)	1433	3025	Note 1
C-3-B6	Pickup (Highside)	1446	3075	Note 1
C-3-B6	Platform	1446	—	Note 1
C-3-B6	Stake (7½-ft.)	1512	3250	Note 1

NOTE 1: Calendar year production: (Domestic) 29,553; (Export) 8214; (Total) 37,767. Model year production (Total): 6-cyl, 108 in., 26,067; 116 in., 3197.

SERIES C-3-B8 — (V-8): — V-8 equipped models carried a B8 (rather than B6) designation and were priced $120 higher than equivalent 6-cyl. models. Total model year production: 108 in., 6595; 116 in., 8704.

Model	Body Type	Price	Weight	Prod. Total
Series C-3-C — (¾-Ton) — (116 in. w.b.) — (6-cyl.)				
C-3-C6	Chassis & Cowl	1183	2325	Note 2
C-3-C6	Chassis & Cab	1420	2800	Note 2
C-3-C6	Pickup (7½-ft.)	1532	3175	Note 2
C-3-C6	Platform	1532	3150	Note 2
C-3-C6	Stake (7½-ft.)	1598	3350	Note 2

NOTE 2: Calendar year production: (Domestic) 6600; (Export) 422; (Government) 7; (Total) 7029. Model year production (Total 6-cyl.): 5122.

SERIES C-3-C8 — (V-8): — V-8 equipped ¾-ton models carried a C8 designation and were priced $120 higher than equivalent 6-cyl. models. Total model year production: 4083.

Model	Body Type	Price	Weight	Prod. Total
Series C-3-D — (1-Ton) — (116 in. w.b.) — (6-cyl.)				
C-3-D6	Chassis & Cowl	1236	2625	Note 3
C-3-D6	Chassis & Cab	1473	3100	Note 3
C-3-D6	Pickup (7½-ft.)	1584	3475	Note 3
C-3-D6	Platform	1584	3450	Note 3
C-3-D6	Stake (7½-ft.)	1650	3650	Note 3
(126 in. w.b.)				
C-3-D6	Chassis & Cowl	1262	2650	Note 3
C-3-D6	Chassis & Cab	1499	3125	Note 3
C-3-D6	Pickup (9-ft.)	1624	3550	Note 3
C-3-D6	Platform	1624	3600	Note 3
C-3-D6	Stake (9-ft.)	1690	3775	Note 3

NOTE 3: Calendar year production (including Power-Wagons): (Domestic) 8257; (Export) 7025; (Total) 15,282. Model year production (Total 6-cyl.): 116 in., 314; 126 in., 236.

SERIES C-3-D8 — (V-8): — V-8 equipped 1-ton models carried a D8 designation and were priced $120 higher than equivalent 6-cyl. models. Total model year production: 116 in., 252; 126 in., 3100.

Model	Body Type	Price	Weight	Prod. Total
Series C-3-PW Power-Wagon — (1-Ton) — (126 in. w.b.)				
C-3-PW	Chassis & Cowl	1965	4075	Note 4
C-3-PW	Chassis & Cab	2200	4675	Note 4
C-3-PW	Pickup (8-ft.)	2317	5100	Note 4

NOTE 4: Model year production: 5058.

ENGINE (First C-1 Series): Same as 1954; see previous specifications.

1955 Dodge Town Wagon (DB)

ENGINE (Second C-3 Series): Inline. L-head. Six-cylinder. Cast iron block. Bore & stroke: 3.25 x 4.625 in. Displacement: 230.2 cu. in. Compression ratio: 7.6:1. Brake horsepower: 115 at 3600 R.P.M. Net horsepower: 25.35. Torque: 201 lbs.-ft. at 1600 R.P.M. Four main bearings. Solid valve lifters.

ENGINE (Second C-3 Series): V-8. Overhead valves. Eight-cylinder. Cast iron block. Bore & stroke: 3.563 x 3.25 in. Displacement: 259.2 cu. in. Compression ratio: 7.6:1. Brake horsepower: 169 at 4400 R.P.M. Net horsepower: 40.6. Torque: 243 lbs.-ft. at 2400 R.P.M. Five main bearings. Hydraulic valve lifters.

ENGINE (C-3-PW Power-Wagon): Inline. L-head. Six-cylinder. Cast iron block. Bore & stroke: 3.25 x 4.625 in. Displacement: 230.2 cu. in. Compression ratio: 7.6:1. Brake horsepower: 111 at 3600 R.P.M. Net horsepower: 25.35. Torque: 198 lbs.-ft. at 1600 R.P.M. Four main bearings. Solid valve lifters.

CHASSIS (Series C-1): Same as 1954.

CHASSIS (Series C-3-BL6): Wheelbase: 108 in. Tires: 6.70 x 15 four-ply (front and rear). GVW: 4250 lbs.

CHASSIS (Series C-3-B): Wheelbase: 108 in. and 116 in. Tires: 6.70 x 15 four-ply (front and rear). GVW: 5100 lbs. Front axle capacity: 2500 lbs. Rear axle capacity: 3300 lbs.

CHASSIS (Series C-3-C): Wheelbase: 116 in. Tires: 7.00 x 15 six-ply (front and rear). GVW: 5800 lbs. Front axle capacity: 2500 lbs. Rear axle capacity: 3300 lbs.

CHASSIS (Series C-3-D): Wheelbase: 116 in. and 126 in. Tires: (front) 6.00 x 16 six-ply; (rear) 7.00 x 16 six-ply. GVW: 8800 lbs. Front axle capacity: 2800 lbs. Rear axle capacity: 3600 lbs.

CHASSIS (Series C-3-PW Power-Wagon): Wheelbase: 126 in. Tires: 7.50 x 16 eight-ply (front and rear). GVW: 9500 lbs.

TECHNICAL: Selective sliding gear transmission. Speeds: 3F/1R; optional 4F/1R, or 3F/1R with overdrive. Column or floor shift. Automatic transmission optional. Single plate dry disc clutch: 10 in., except 11 in. with optional heavy-duty or four-speed transmission. Rear axle ratio: (¾-ton) 3.73:1 and 4.78:1, (1-ton) 4.1:1 and 4.89:1. Hydraulic four-wheel brakes.

1955 Dodge Pickup (DB)

OPTIONS (Factory Installed): Rear bumper ($11.25). Bumper guards ($5.50). Deluxe cab equipment ($26). Custom equipment ($51). Custom Regal equipment ($79). Left door armrest ($3.30). Town Panel equipment ($22.50); Custom Regal equipment ($51). Long arm mirror: left side ($2.50); right side ($3.95). Inside rearview mirror ($3). Bright metal molding package for Town Panel ($14.50). Dodge Tint glass, all models ($17.50). Right inside sunvisor ($3). Auxiliary taillamp ($7.25). Dual electric horns ($14.50). Horn ring ($3). Cab corner marker lights ($10). Set of four bright hub caps ($1.65); set of five ($3). Set of four 15 in. wheel covers ($16.50). Dome light ($5.50). Heater: standard ($41.50); Deluxe ($62). Deluxe seat for Panel ($11.25). Auxiliary seat for Panel ($45). Deluxe seat back and cushion ($11.25 each). Dual electric wipers ($11.25). Wraparound rear window ($29). Inside tire carrier, Panel ($6). Side tire carrier for pickup ($10.25). Hand throttle control ($3). One-quart oil-bath air cleaner: 6-cyl. ($1.65); 8-cyl. ($3.95). Increased cooling capacity ($10). Ash tray ($1.65). Oil filter ($12). Electric fuel pump ($16). Three-speed transmission with overdrive ($100). Heavy-duty three-speed transmission with 10 in. clutch ($40); with 11 in. clutch ($45). Four-speed transmission ($70). PowerFlite automatic transmission ($165). Governor ($10). (C-3-BL6-108 Model Only) Rear bumper ($11.25). Increased cooling capacity ($10). Turn signals ($23.50). Heater ($41.50). Oil filter ($12). Auxiliary taillight ($7.25). (Power-Wagon Only) Deluxe cab equipment ($10). Turn signals ($30.50). Dodge Tint glass ($17.50). Long arm mirror: left side ($2.50); right ($3.95). Inside mirror ($3). Front and rear fenders painted cab color ($7.50). Auxiliary taillight ($8.75). Brake booster with 7½ in. diaphragm ($42.50). Governor ($69.10). Draw bar ($23.05). Heater ($41.50). Oil filter ($12). Pintle hook ($12.50). Power take-off ($75.70). Pulley drive ($85.55). Radiator overflow tank ($10). Rear drive shaft assembly ($85.55). Rear shock absorbers ($34.90). Front springs with 1600-pound capacity ($7.90). Rear main springs, 3000-pound ($8.75). Front tow hooks ($8.25/pair). Winch assembly ($243.45).

HISTORICAL: Introduced: (Series C-3) April, 1955. (Series C-1) carried over from 1954. Calendar year sales: 66,208. Calendar year production: 95,430. Model year production: (6-cyl.) 40,246; (V-8) 22,734; (Total C-3 light-duty) 62,980. Model year production (U.S. only): (6-cyl.) 24,626; (V-8) 21,538; (Total) 46,164. Innovations: "Pilot-House" cabs with wraparound windshield and rear window. Basic low-cost pickup model. Enlarged V-8 engine. PowerFlite automatic transmission. Historical notes: Dodge truck sales improved by 9.1 percent over 1954, as production gained slightly. All trucks were now built at the Warren plant in Detroit. Canadian production totaled 11,054 units. This was the end of Korean War truck production, as only seven ¾-ton 4x4s were made in January, 1955. A total of 15,661 trucks were built for export. Dodge models met 98 percent of all hauling needs, with a total of seven 6-cyl. and V-8 engines, covering a GVW range from 4,250 up to 60,000 pounds (GCW rating). For the first time, Dodge produced a clutchless automatic transmission for light-duty trucks, and also built medium-duty trucks with automatic shift.

Pricing

	5	4	3	2	1
1955					
Series C-3-BL — (½-Ton) — (108 in. w.b.)					
Lowside Pickup	930	1860	3100	4350	6200
Series C-3-B — (½-Ton) — (108 in. w.b.)					
Lowside Pickup	920	1850	3050	4300	6100
Highside Pickup	930	1860	3100	4350	6200
Panel	850	1700	2850	4000	5700
(116 in. w.b.)					
Lowside Pickup	900	1800	3000	4200	6000
Highside Pickup	920	1850	3050	4300	6100
Platform	750	1500	2500	3500	5000
Stake	770	1550	2550	3600	5100
Series C-3-C — (¾-Ton) — (116 in. w.b.)					
Pickup	890	1770	2950	4150	5900
Platform	740	1470	2450	3350	4900
Stake	750	1500	2500	3500	5000
Series C-3-D — (1-Ton) — (116 in. w.b.)					
Pickup	830	1650	2750	3850	5500
Platform	720	1450	2400	3300	4800
Stake	740	1470	2450	3350	4900
(126 in. w.b.)					
Pickup	750	1500	2500	3500	5000
Platform	680	1350	2250	3150	4500
Stake	690	1380	2300	3200	4600
Series C-3-PW Power-Wagon — (1-Ton) — (126 in. w.b.)					
Pickup	1130	2250	3750	5250	7500

NOTE: Add 15 percent for V-8 engine.
Add 5 percent for automatic transmission.

1956 DODGE

½-TON — SERIES C-4-B — SIX-CYLINDER and V-8 / ¾-TON — SERIES C-4-C — SIX-CYLINDER and V-8 / 1-TON — SERIES C-4-D — SIX-CYLINDER and V-8: — All models, engines and options of the C-3 Series, introduced in April 1955, continued without change for the C-4 Series. In January 1956, Dodge announced a new addition to the line: the Town Wagon, which was created by adding sliding glass windows and seats to the Town Panel. This versatile half-tonner could take the place of a sta-

1956 Dodge Town Wagon (DFW)

tion wagon, hauling up to eight people on three seats plus luggage — or six people on two seats, with even more luggage. With both rear seats removed, it served as a truck, rated for 1650-pound payload. In Custom Regal trim, the Town Wagon was a luxurious and beautiful people/cargo hauler. PowerFlite automatic and overdrive transmissions were available. Four new paint colors were added: Chilean Beige, Rackham Blue, Terra Cotta, and Canyon Coral. Sonora Blue was dropped. Standard equipment was the same as in 1955.

1-TON POWER-WAGON — SERIES C-4-PW — SIX-CYLINDER: — The 4x4 Power-Wagon continued unchanged, powered only by the six-cylinder engine.

I.D. DATA: Serial and engine numbers were in the same locations as in 1955.

Model	Engine	Serial Numbers Starting	Serial Numbers Ending	Starting Engine Nos.
C-4-B	Six	82398001	82407868	T434-1001
C-4-B	V-8	84284001	84287960	VT434-1001
C-4-C	Six	83411001	83413368	T436-1001
C-4-C	V-8	84660001	84661053	VT436-1001
C-4-D	Six	81490001	81492874	T438-1001
C-4-D	V-8	84807001	84808342	VT438-1001
C-4-PW	Six	83949001	83951794	T137-1001

Model	Body Type	Price	Weight	Prod. Total
C-4-B — (6-cyl.) — (½-Ton) — (108 in. w.b.)				
C-4-BL6	Pickup (Lowside)	1446	—	Note 1
C-4-B6	Chassis & Cowl	1164	—	Note 1
C-4-B6	Chassis & Cab	1400	—	Note 1
C-4-B6	Pickup (Lowside)	1436	—	Note 1
C-4-B6	Pickup (Highside)	1499	—	Note 1
C-4-B6	Panel	1729	—	Note 1
(½-Ton) — (116 in. w.b.)				
C-4-B6	Chassis & Cowl	1177	—	Note 1
C-4-B6	Chassis & Cab	1413	—	Note 1
C-4-B6	Pickup (Lowside)	1512	—	Note 1
C-4-B6	Pickup (Highside)	1525	—	Note 1
C-4-B6	Platform	1532	—	Note 1
C-4-B6	Stake (7½-ft.)	1598	—	Note 1

NOTE 1: Calendar year production: (Domestic) 27,498; (Export) 5346; (Total) 32,844. Model year production: (Total 6-cyl.): 108-inch, 11,285; 116-inch, 2782.

SERIES C-4-B8 — (V-8): — V-8 equipped models carried a B8 (rather than B6) designation and were priced $120 higher than equivalent 6-cyl. models. Total model year production: 108-inch, 1765; 116-inch, 2530.

Series C-4-C — (¾-Ton) — (116 in.w.b.) — (6-cyl.)				
C-4-C6	Chassis & Cowl	1269	—	Note 2
C-4-C6	Chassis & Cab	1505	—	Note 2
C-4-C6	Pickup (7½-ft.)	1617	—	Note 2
C-4-C6	Platform	1624	—	Note 2
C-4-C6	Stake (7½-ft.)	1690	—	Note 2

NOTE 2: Calendar year production: (Domestic) 9100; (Export) 452; (Government) 7; (Total) 9552. Model year production (Total 6-cyl.): 1406 (plus 1089 special models).

SERIES C-4-C8 — (V-8): — V-8 equipped ¾-ton models carried a C8 designation and were priced $120 higher than equivalent 6-cyl. models. Total model year production: 1171.

Series C-4-D — (1-Ton) — (116 in. w.b.) — (6-cyl.)				
C-4-D6	Chassis & Cowl	1327	—	Note 3
C-4-D6	Chassis & Cab	1563	—	Note 3
C-4-D6	Pickup (7½-ft.)	1675	—	Note 3
C-4-D6	Platform	1682	—	Note 3
C-4-D6	Stake (7½-ft.)	1748	—	Note 3
(126 in. w.b.)				
C-4-D6	Chassis & Cowl	1353	—	Note 3
C-4-D6	Chassis & Cab	1589	—	Note 3
C-4-D6	Pickup (9-ft.)	1714	—	Note 3
C-4-D6	Platform	1734	—	Note 3
C-4-D6	Stake (9-ft.)	1800	—	Note 3

NOTE 3: Calendar year production (including Power-Wagons): (Domestic) 7702; (Export) 6592; (Total) 14,294. Model year production (Total 6-cyl.): 116 in., 631; 126 in., 3434.

SERIES C-4-D8 — (V-8): — V-8 equipped 1-ton models carried a D8 designation and were priced $120 higher than equivalent 6-cyl. models. Total model year production: 116 in., 132; 126 in., 1353.

Series C-4-PW Power-Wagon — (1-Ton) — (126 in. w.b.)

C-4-PW	Chassis & Cowl	2096	4075	Note 4
C-4-PW	Chassis & Cab	2332	4675	Note 4
C-4-PW	Pickup (8-ft.)	2449	5100	Note 4

NOTE 4: Model year production: 2730.

ENGINE: Same as 1955; see previous specifications.

CHASSIS: Same as 1955; see previous specifications.

TECHNICAL: Same as 1955; see previous specifications.

OPTIONS: Same as 1955; see previous list and prices.

HISTORICAL: Introduced: continuation of C-3 series. Calendar year sales: 57,651. Calendar year sales: 91,383. Model year production: (6-cyl.) 23,795; (V-8) 6982; (Total light-duty C-4 Series) 30,777. Model year production (U.S. only): (6-cyl.) 12,631; (V-8) 6249; (Total) 18,880. Historical notes: Dodge truck sales fell 12.9 percent from their 1955 level, more than the industry drop of 6.5 percent. Total exports came to 12,390. In January 1956, Dodge received an order for 2,000 special sit/stand ¾-ton trucks for the Post Office. Equipped with automatic transmissions, their bodies were built by Twin Coach. Dodge also built a line of one and 1½-ton forward control chassis-only models, powered by a six or V-8, with bodies supplied by other companies. This was a period of rising demand for heavy-duty trucks, due to the multi-billion dollar federal highway building program which would put a national freeway system in place. To capitalize on this trend, Dodge discontinued the 413 cu. in. six in its 4-ton series, replacing it with a 354 cu. in. hemi-head V-8. Two new V-8s were also made available to Dodge's cab-over-engine models, a 269.6 cu. in. and a 331 cu. in. hemi. A 2-ton 4WD truck was added to the Power-Wagon line, powered by a 265 cu. in. six.

Pricing

	5	4	3	2	1
1956					
Series C-4-BL — (½-Ton) — (108 in. w.b.)					
Lowside Pickup	930	1860	3100	4350	6200
Series C-4-B — (½-Ton) — (108 in. w.b.)					
Lowside Pickup	920	1850	3050	4300	6100
Highside Pickup	930	1860	3100	4350	6200
Panel	850	1700	2850	4000	5700
Series C-4-B — (½-Ton) — (116 in. w.b.)					
Lowside Pickup	900	1800	3000	4200	6000
Highside Pickup	920	1850	3050	4300	6100
Platform	750	1500	2500	3500	5000
Stake	770	1550	2550	3600	5100
Series C-4-C — (¾-Ton) — (116 in. w.b.)					
Pickup	890	1770	2950	4150	5900
Platform	740	1470	2450	3350	4900
Stake	750	1500	2500	3500	5000
Series C-4-D — (1-Ton) — (116 in. w.b.)					
Pickup	830	1650	2750	3850	5500
Platform	720	1450	2400	3300	4800
Stake	740	1470	2450	3350	4900
Seris C-4-D — (1-Ton) — (126 in. w.b.)					
Pickup	750	1500	2500	3500	5000
Platform	680	1350	2250	3150	4500
Stake	690	1380	2300	3200	4600
Series C-4-PW Power-Wagon — (1-Ton) — (126 in. w.b.)					
Pickup	1130	2250	3750	5250	7500

NOTE: Add 15 percent for V-8 engine.
Add 5 percent for automatic transmission.

1957 DODGE

½-TON — K SERIES D100 — SIX-CYLINDER and V-8 / ¾-TON — K SERIES D200 — SIX-CYLINDER and V-8 / 1-TON — K SERIES D300 — SIX-CYLINDER and V-8: — Beginning with 1957, Dodge used a new identifying system. A letter indicated the series (K for 1957), while a number ranked the individual models according to truck size: 100, 200, 300 and up to 900. Model types were identified by a letter preceding that number. The letter D indicated a conventional cab; C, cab-over-engine; T, tandem axle; P, forward control; and W, 4wd. To keep styling pace with Dodge cars, the 1957 trucks were given the "Forward Look." The front fender line extended forward with a "Frenched" headlight, giving a feeling of motion even while the truck was at rest. The entire front clip was redesigned, as were the hood and front bumper. For the first time, Dodge used an alligator type, rear-hinged hood. It had two positions: 45 degrees for engine servicing, and 90 degrees for full accessbility. Pull-type door handles, safety door latches, locks on both doors, adjustable tilting seat back and chrome grille bars were all new. The hand brake could be adjusted from inside the cab by turning a knob at the end of the handle. Two basic cabs

1957 Dodge Pickup (DFW)

were available: Standard and Custom. Standard cab equipment included dual electric wipers, ashtray, dome light, left armrest, sound-deadened door panels, rubber floor mats, left side mirror and sunvisor, and two-tone interior trim. Custom cabs added a glove box lock, Saron and Rayon seat covering, foam rubber seat cushion, right sunvisor, wraparound rear window, and two-speed wipers. New colors were: Stone Grey, Mojave Beige, Pacific Blue, Bermuda Coral, Bayview Green, and Omaha Orange. Six old colors were dropped. Beginning this year, all pickup boxes were painted cab color; wood pickup box floors were black. Pushbutton three-speed PowerFlite automatic transmission was an extra-cost option on D100, D200 and D300 models. The base 6-cyl. engine gained a horsepower boost by raising its compression ratio to 8.0:1. An all new, larger V-8, 315 cu. in. and rated 204 horsepower, was now standard — the largest engine in the light truck field. A mid-year addition entered the lineup in May, 1957. The famous Sweptside D100 pickup was the Dodge answer to Chevrolet's Cameo Carrier of 1955 and Ford's 1957 Ranchero. Dodge created the Sweptside by grafting rear fenders from its two-door station wagon onto the sides of a ½-ton, 116 in. w.b. pickup's long box. The wagon's rear bumper was also used. In addition, the Sweptside got side moldings to complete the lines running forward from the station wagon fenders. Sweptside cabs were Custom type. All models had shock absorbers front and rear.

½-TON 4WD — K SERIES W100 — SIX-CYLINDER and V-8 / ¾-TON 4WD — K SERIES W200 — SIX-CYLINDER and V-8 / 1-TON POWER-WAGON — K SERIES W300 — SIX-CYLINDER: — The Power-Wagon had proven so successful that customers were demanding additional models. So Dodge now offered ½-ton and ¾-ton conventional cab 4wd models, in all body types from pickups through Town Wagons. All had shock absorbers in front only. After 1957, the Power-Wagon would be designated WM300, and W300 would denote a contentional cab 4wd 1-ton truck. Power-Wagon front and rear fenders were painted black, regardless of cab color.

I.D. DATA: Serial number information was found on a ticket in the glove box. Starting Serial Numbers: (D100 Six) 82413001; (D100 V-8) 84289001; (D200 Six) 83414001; (D200 V-8) 84662001; (D300 Six) 81494001; (D300 V-8) 84809001; (W100 Six) 8191001; (W100 V-8) 82901001; (W200 Six) 82701001; (W200 V-8) 83250001; (W300) 83952001. 6-cyl. engine numbers were located on the left side of the block at the front, below the cylinder head. 8-cyl. engine numbers were on top of the cylinder block, behind the water pump. Starting Engine Numbers: (D100 Six) T534-1001; (D100 V-8) VT534-1001; (D200 Six) T536-1001; (D200 V-8) VT536-1001; (D300 Six) T538-1001; (D300 V-8) VT538-1001; (W100 Six) T500-1001; (W100 V-8) VT500-1001; (W200 Six) T502-1001; (W200 V-8) VT502-1001; (W300) T137-1001. Ending serial and engine numbers are not available.

1957 Dodge Town Wagon (OCW)

187

1957 Dodge Sweptside Pickup (OCW)

Model	Body Type	Price	Weight	Prod. Total
K6-D100 Series — (½-Ton) — (108 in. w.b.)				
K6-D100	Chassis & Cowl	1279	2400	—
K6-D100	Chassis & Cab	1524	2875	—
K6-D100	Pickup (6½-ft.)	1620	3225	—
K6-D100	Panel (7½-ft.)	1873	3825	—
K6-D100	Town Wagon (6-pass.)	2164	3925	—
K6-D100	Town Wagon (8-pass.)	2210	3975	—
(116 in. w.b.)				
K6-D100	Chassis & Cowl	1295	2425	—
K6-D100	Chassis & Cab	1540	2900	—
K6-D100	Pickup (7½-ft.)	1646	3250	—
K6-D100	Platform	1665	3250	—
K6-D100	Stake (7½-ft.)	1731	3450	—
K6-D200 Series — (¾-Ton) — (116 in. w.b.)				
K6-D200	Chassis & Cowl	1449	2925	—
K6-D200	Chassis & Cab	1694	3400	—
K6-D200	Pickup	1800	3775	—
K6-D200	Platform	1819	3750	—
K6-D200	Stake	1885	3950	—
K6-D300 Series — (1-Ton) — (126 in. w.b.)				
K6-D300	Chassis & Cowl	1482	3025	—
K6-D300	Chassis & Cab	1727	3500	—
K6-D300	Pickup	1852	3925	—
K6-D300	Platform	1881	3900	—
K6-D300	Stake	1947	4150	—
K6-W100 Series 4x4 — (½-Ton) — (108 in. w.b.)				
K6-W100	Chassis & Cowl	2253	3100	—
K6-W100	Chassis & Cab	2489	3575	—
K6-W100	Pickup (6½-ft.)	2594	3925	—
K6-W100	Town Panel	2865	4525	—
K6-W100	Town Wagon (6-pass.)	3143	4625	—
K6-W100	Town Wagon (8-pass.)	3189	4675	—
(116 in. w.b.)				
K6-W100	Chassis & Cowl	2289	3125	—
K6-W100	Chassis & Cab	2524	3600	—
K6-W100	Pickup (7½-ft.)	2629	3950	—
K6-W100	Platform	2660	3950	—
K6-W100	Stake (7½-ft.)	2715	4150	—
K6-W200 Series 4x4 — (¾-Ton) — (116 in. w.b.)				
K6-W200	Chassis & Cowl	2397	3975	—
K6-W200	Chassis & Cab	2641	4450	—
K6-W200	Pickup (7½-ft.)	2747	4875	—
K6-W200	Platform	2777	4850	—
K6-W200	Stake (7½-ft.)	2832	5100	—
K6-W300 Power-Wagon — (1-Ton) — (126 in. w.b.)				
K6-W300	Chassis & Cowl	2266	4650	—
K6-W300	Chassis & Cab	2511	5075	—
K6-W300	Pickup	2636	5450	—

NOTE 1: Weights and prices shown are for 6-cyl. trucks. For V-8 equipped models (prefix K8), add 100 pounds to weight and $105.30 to price.

NOTE 2: Production figures by model and series not available.

ENGINE (All models except Power-Wagon): Inline. L-head. Six-cylinder. Cast iron block. Bore & stroke: 3.25 x 4.625 in. Displacement: 230.2 cu. in. Compression ratio: 8.0:1. Brake horsepower: 120 at 3600 R.P.M. Net horsepower: 25.35. Torque: 202 lbs.-ft. at 1600 R.P.M. Four main bearings. Solid valve lifters.

ENGINE (All models except Power-Wagon): V-8. Overhead valve. Eight-cylinder. Cast iron block. Bore & stroke: 3.63 x 3.80 in. Displacement: 314.6 cu. in. Compression ratio: 8.5:1. Brake horsepower: 204 at 4400 R.P.M. Net horsepower: 42.16. Torque: 290 lbs.-ft. at 2400 R.P.M. Five main bearings. Hydraulic valve lifters.

ENGINE (Power-Wagon): Inline. L-head. Six-cylinder. Cast iron block. Bore & stroke: 3.25 x 4.625 in. Displacement: 230.2 cu. in. Compression ratio: 7.9:1. Brake horsepower: 113 at 3600 R.P.M. Net horsepower: 25.35. Torque: 198 lbs.-ft. at 1600 R.P.M. Four main bearings. Solid valve lifters.

CHASSIS (D100-108): Wheelbase: 108 in. Tires: 6.70 x 15 four-ply; tubeless passenger-car type (front and rear). GVW: 4250 lbs. Front axle capacity: 2500 lbs. Rear axle: 3600 lbs. Front spring capacity: 900 lbs. Rear spring: 1200 lbs.

CHASSIS (D100-116): Wheelbase: 116 in. Tires and capacities: same as D100-108 except 5100 lbs. GVW.

CHASSIS (D200): Wheelbase: 116 in. Tires: 7 x 17.5 six-ply (front and rear); tubeless truck type. GVW: 7500 lbs. Front axle capacity: 2800 lbs. Rear axle: 6500 lbs. Front spring capacity: 1000 lbs. Rear spring: 1950 lbs.

CHASSIS (D300): Wheelbase: 126 in. Tires and capacities: same as D200 except 8800 lbs. GVW.

CHASSIS (W100): Wheelbase: 108 in. and 116 in. Tires: 7 x 17.5 six-ply (front and rear). GVW: 5100 lbs. Front axle capacity: 3000 lbs. Rear axle: 3600 lbs. Front spring capacity: 1050 lbs. Rear springs: 1250 lbs.

CHASSIS (W200): Wheelbase: 116 in. Tires: 7 x 17.5 six-ply (front and rear). GVW: 8000 lbs. Front axle capacity: 3000 lbs. Rear axle: 6500 lbs. Front spring capacity: 1050 lbs. Rear springs: 1750 lbs.

CHASSIS (W300 Power-Wagon): Wheelbase: 126 in. Tires: 7.50 x 16 eight-ply (front and rear). GVW: 9500 lbs. Front axle capacity: 3750 lbs. Rear axle: 6500 lbs. Front spring capacity: 1150 lbs. Rear springs: 2500 lbs.

TECHNICAL: Selective sliding gear transmission. Speeds: 3F/1R (heavy-duty on ¾- and 1-ton). Four-speed, overdrive and automatic transmissions available. Single plate dry disc clutch (11 in.). Column shift control (push-button automatic). One-pint oil bath air cleaner. Standard rear axle ratio: 4.1:1. Optional axle ratios: (½-ton) 3.73:1, (¾- and 1-ton) 4.89:1. Hydraulic four-wheel brakes. Five disc wheels. (½-ton) 5.25 in. Same, except two-speed transfer case with three-speed transmission. (W100, W200) Same. Standard axle ratio: 4.09:1 front, 4.11:1 rear, or 4.89:1 front and rear. Six-hole 5.25 in. wheels. (W300 Power-Wagon) Four-speed transmission. Front/rear axle ratio: 4.89:1 with 7.50 x 16 tires; 5.83:1 with 9.00 x 16 tires. Two-speed transfer case. Velocity-type governor. One-quart oil bath air cleaner. Five 5.50 in. wheels.

1957 Dodge Sweptside Pickup (DB)

OPTIONS (Factory Installed): (D100, D200, D300, W100, W200) Chrome front bumper ($13.20). Painted rear bumper ($19.20). Chrome plated rear bumper ($25). Bumper guards: painted ($5.30); chrome ($11.90). Bright hub caps, set of our ($7.30); set of five for pickup with side tire carrier ($8.70). Chrome wheel covers, set of four ($16.50); set of five ($20.60). Custom equipment ($46.10). Turn signals ($23.10). Dodge Tint glass ($17.20). Chrome headlight doors ($2). Cab corner marker lights ($9.90). Dual electric horns ($14.50). Horn ring ($3). Cigar lighter ($4.70). Glove box lock ($4). Inside rearview mirror ($3). Adjustable mirror: left side ($2.40); right side ($4.30). Bright metal windshield molding ($7). Grab handles ($8.50). Two-tone paint ($15.20). Wraparound rear window ($29). Dual electric wipers ($7.20). Windshield washer ($11.60). Auxiliary taillamp ($7.30). Right side sunvisor ($3). Foam padded seat back ($11.20); seat cushion ($11.20). Rear shocks for D200 or D300 ($17.80). Tire carrier on side of pickup ($10.20). Hand throttle on dash ($3). One-quart oil bath air cleaner: 6-cyl. ($1.70); V-8 ($4). Right door armrest ($3.30). One-quart oil filter ($11.90); two-quart ($15.80). Electric fuel pump ($25). Increased cooling capacity ($9.90). Vacuum brake booster ($42.50). Velocity type governor, manual transmission only ($9.90). Perforated headliner ($5.60). Heater ($46.10). Deluxe heater ($65.80). Power steering ($112). V-8 engine ($105.30). Three-ton jack ($7.90). Heavy-duty three-speed transmission ($57). Three-speed with overdrive transmission, D100 only ($100). Four-speed transmission: D100 ($65); D200 or D300 ($46.20). Three-speed automatic transmission with push-button control ($203.75). (Town Panel and Town Wagon only) Chrome plated rear bumper ($13.20). Custom Town Panel equipment ($19.80). Turn signals ($18.50). Headliner roof insulation ($7.20). Recessed rear license plate light ($8.60). Bright metal molding package ($14.50). Two-tone paint ($25). Auxiliary seat, standard panel ($34.90). Auxiliary seat, custom panel ($46.10). Tire carrier inside body ($6). Side windows in panel, stationary clear glass ($50). Dodge tint glass ($56.60). (W300 Power-Wagon) Deluxe cab equipment ($19). Dodge Tint glass ($17.20). Turn signals ($30.30). Grab handles ($8.50/pair). Inside rearview mirror ($3). Long arm adjustable mirror: left side ($2.40); right ($4.30). Heater ($46.10). Front and rear fenders painted to match cab color ($13.20). Auxiliary taillight ($7.30). Windshield washer ($11.60). Vacuum brake booster, 7½ in. diaphragm ($42.50). Draw bar ($23.10). Oil filter, two-quart ($6). Pintle hook ($12.50). Power take-off ($75.20). Pulley drive ($85.60). Rear drive shaft assembly ($85.60). Rear shocks ($34.90). Springs, 1600-pound capacity ($164.50). Winch ($243.45). Three-ton jack ($7.90).

HISTORICAL: Introduced: October 30, 1956. Calendar year sales: 49,431. Calendar year production: 76,601. Innovations: 12-volt electrical system. Ignition key starter switch. "Forward Look" styling taken from Chrysler Corp. passenger cars. Half- and ¾-ton 4wd models. Sweptside pickup, mating station wagon and pickup panels. Historical notes: Sales fell again this year, by 14.2 percent; some 10 percent more than the total industry drop. Dodge ranked fifth in truck sales, with 7 percent of the total manufacturing output. V-8 truck sales rose from 38 percent in 1954 to 54 percent in 1957. In March, Chrysler Corp. received over $12 million in defense contracts. One was for 2,900 4x4 trucks; another for $3.5 million worth of spare parts for World War II type military trucks. Also in March, Dodge offered for commercial sale a modification of the compact Post Office truck, for door-to-door delivery use. This forward-control truck was built on a D100 or D200 chassis, shortened to 95 in. w.b. and powered by a 6-cyl. engine with pushbutton automatic transmission. Other forward-control chassis were in the regular lineup, in 4 w.b. lengths of the P300 or P400 series (¾- or 1-ton). Dodge made significant inroads into the heavy-duty market, due to the outstanding performance of their hemi-head V-8s. Advertisements proclaimed the 1957 Dodge truck line as "Power Giants."

Pricing

	5	4	3	2	1
1957					
K6-D100 Series — (½-Ton) — (108 in. w.b.)					
Pickup	950	1900	3150	4400	6300
Panel	870	1750	2900	4100	5800
6-pass. Wagon	890	1770	2950	4150	5900
8-pass. Wagon	890	1770	2950	4150	5900
(116 in. w.b.)					
Pickup	930	1860	3100	4350	6200
Platform	780	1560	2600	3600	5200
Stake	800	1600	2650	3700	5300
K6-D200 Series — (¾-Ton) — (116 in. w.b.)					
Pickup	900	1800	3000	4200	6000
Platform	770	1550	2550	3600	5100
Stake	780	1560	2600	3600	5200
K6-D300 Series — (1-Ton) — (126 in. w.b.)					
Pickup	840	1680	2800	3900	5600
Platform	690	1380	2300	3200	4600
Stake	700	1400	2350	3250	4700
K6-W100 Series 4x4 — (½-Ton) — (108 in. w.b.)					
Pickup	980	1950	3250	4550	6500
Panel	900	1800	3000	4200	6000
6-pass. Wagon	920	1850	3050	4300	6100
8-pass. Wagon	920	1850	3050	4300	6100
(116 in. w.b.)					
Pickup	960	1920	3200	4500	6400
Platform	810	1620	2700	3800	5400
Stake	830	1650	2750	3850	5500
K6-W200 Series 4x4 — (¾-Ton) — (116 in. w.b.)					
Pickup	930	1860	3100	4350	6200
Platform	800	1600	2650	3700	5300
Stake	810	1620	2700	3800	5400
K6-W300 Series — (1-Ton) — (126 in. w.b.)					
Pickup	1050	2100	3500	4900	7000

NOTE: Add 10 percent for V-8 engine.
Add 5 percent for automatic transmission.

1958 DODGE

1958 Dodge D100 Sweptside Pickup w/camper (OCW)

½-TON — L SERIES D100 — SIX-CYLINDER and V-8 / ¾-TON — L SERIES D200 — SIX-CYLINDER and V-8 / 1-TON — L SERIES D300 — SIX-CYLINDER and V-8: — Dodge's 1958 Power Giant truck line featured all new styling from the cowl forward — full width hood, quad headlights, new grille, and heavy-duty bumper. New fender housings and two-piece splash shields created an engine compartment as wide as possible. Engine access was greatly improved. The battery was moved from under the driver's floor to under the hood. Light-duty engines remained the same as in 1957. The 230.2 cu. in. inline six remained the base engine, with the 315 cu. in. V-8 optional. All models available in 1957 were carried forward, including the Sweptside pickup. One new body, the Tradesman utility, was available on D100 and D200 chassis. It featured two large horizontal storage compartments and one vertical compartment on each side, all lockable. Tradesman bodies were a favorite with utility companies. New progressive-type rear springs and redesigned front springs with lowered deflection rates improved D100 ride quality. Those rear springs gave a smoother ride while the truck was empty, stiffening as the load increased for support and smoothness. A new chrome trim package was optional, including chromed grille bars, sweeping side moldings, chromed hood ornament, and anodized headlight trim plates. Thirteen body colors were available, plus 12 two-tone combinations. New colors were Marlin Blue, Arctic Blue, Valley Green, Bell Green, Ranch Brown, Alaska White, Angus Black, Klondike Yellow, and Sahara Beige. Two-tones had Sahara Beige at the top. Standard and Custom cabs were available. Cabs featured new colors, a hooded instrument panel to reduce glare, red warning lights replacing ammeter and oil pressure gauge, deep-dish steering wheel, a turn-signal switch integral with steering column, and an available roof-mounted transistor radio. Standard equipment was the same as in 1957.

½-TON 4x4 — L SERIES W100 — SIX-CYLINDER and V-8 / ¾-TON 4x4 — L SERIES W200 — SIX-CYLINDER and V-8 / 1-TON 4x4 — L SERIES W300 — SIX-CYLINDER and V-8: — No change occurred in the 4x4 W Series, except for the addition of a 1-ton model. Standard equipment was the same as the D Series.

1-TON POWER-WAGON — L SERIES W300M — SIX-CYLINDER: — Power-Wagons continued without change. The M suffix meant military style. Only the 6-cyl. engine was available.

1958 Dodge Sweptside Pickup (JAW)

I.D. DATA: Serial numbers were on a plate on the left door hinge pillar. Starting Serial Numbers: (D100 Six) L6D10-L01001; (D100 V-8) L8D10-L01001; (D200 Six) L6D20-L01001; (D200 V-8) L8D20-L01001; (D300 Six) L6D30-L01001; (D300 V-8) L8D30-L01001; (W100 Six) L6W10-L01001; (W100 V-8) L8W10-L01001; (W200 Six) L6W20-L01001; (W200 V-8) L8W20-L01001; (W300 Six) L6W30-L01001; (W300 V-8) L8W30-L01001; (W300M Power-Wagon) L6WM30-L01001. Engine numbers were in the same locations as 1957. Starting Engine Numbers: (D100 Six) L6-D1-1001; (D100 V-8) L8-D1-1001; (D200 Six) L6-D2-1001; (D200 V-8) L8-D2-1001; (D300 Six) L6-D3-1001; (D300 V-8) L8-D3-1001; (W100 Six) L6-W1-1001; (W100 V-8) L8-W1-1001; (W200 Six) L6-W2-1001; (W200 V-8) L8-W2-1001; (W300 Six) L6-W3-1001; (W300 V-8) L8-W3-1001; (W300M Power-Wagon) L6-WM3-1001. Ending serial and engine numbers are not available.

1958 Dodge Compact Mini-Van (James A. Wren)

Model	Body Type	Price	Weight	Prod. Total
Series L6-D100 — (½-Ton) — (108 in. w.b.)				
L6-D100	Chassis & Cowl	1373	2400	Note 1
L6-D100	Chassis & Cab	1608	2875	Note 1
L6-D100	Pickup	1714	3225	Note 1
L6-D100	Town Panel	1985	3350	Note 1
L6-D100	Town Wgn (6-pass.)	2262	3575	Note 1
L6-D100	Town Wgn (8-pass.)	2308	3575	Note 1
(116 in. w.b.)				
L6-D100	Chassis & Cowl	1411	2450	Note 2
L6-D100	Chassis & Cab	1647	2925	Note 2
L6-D100	Pickup	1752	3300	Note 2
L6-D100	Platform	1782	3300	Note 2
L6-D100	Stake	1837	3475	Note 2
L6-D100	Sweptside Pickup	2124	3425	Note 2

NOTE 1: Model year production, D100-108: (six) 11,862; (V-8) 2435.

NOTE 2: Model year production, D100-116: (six) 4199; (V-8) 6067.

Series L6-D200 — (¾-Ton) — (116 in. w.b.)				
L6-D200	Chassis & Cowl	1595	2875	Note 3
L6-D200	Chassis & Cab	1840	3350	Note 3
L6-D200	Pickup	1945	3725	Note 3
L6-D200	Platform	1975	3725	Note 3
L6-D200	Stake	2031	3900	Note 3

NOTE 3: Model year production: (six) 1899; (V-8) 1508.

Series L6-D300 — (1-Ton) — (126 in. w.b.)				
L6-D300	Chassis & Cowl	1631	3025	Note 4
L6-D300	Chassis & Cab	1875	3500	Note 4
L6-D300	Pickup	2000	3925	Note 4
L6-D300	Platform	2041	3950	Note 4
L6-D300	Stake	2106	4150	Note 4

NOTE 4: Model year production: (six) 2973; (V-8) 2148.

Series L6-W100 4x4 — (½-Ton) — (108 in. w.b.)				
L6-W100	Chassis & Cowl	2253	3100	Note 5
L6-W100	Chassis & Cab	2489	3575	Note 5
L6-W100	Pickup	2594	3925	Note 5
L6-W100	Town Panel	2865	4050	Note 5
L6-W100	Town Wgn (6-pass.)	3143	4275	Note 5
L6-W100	Town Wgn (8-pass.)	3189	4300	Note 5
(½-Ton) — (116 in. w.b.)				
L6-W100	Chassis & Cowl	2289	3125	Note 6
L6-W100	Chassis & Cab	2524	3600	Note 6
L6-W100	Pickup	2629	3975	Note 6
L6-W100	Platform	2660	3975	Note 6
L6-W100	Stake	2715	4150	Note 6

NOTE 5: Model year production: (six) 406; (V-8) 290.

NOTE 6: Model year production: (six) 196; (V-8) 564.

Series L6-W200 4x4 — (¾-Ton) — (116 in. w.b.)				
L6-W200	Chassis & Cowl	2397	3400	Note 7
L6-W200	Chassis & Cab	2641	3875	Note 7
L6-W200	Pickup	2747	4250	Note 7
L6-W200	Platform	2777	4250	Note 7
L6-W200	Stake	2832	4425	Note 7

NOTE 7: Model year production: (six) 396; (V-8) 331.

Series L6-W300 4x4 — (1-Ton) — (129 in. w.b.)				
L6-W300	Chassis & Cowl	2803	3975	Note 8
L6-W300	Chassis & Cab	3048	4450	Note 8
L6-W300	Pickup	3173	4875	Note 8
L6-W300	Platform	3214	4900	Note 8
L6-W300	Stake	3278	5100	Note 8

NOTE 8: Model year production: (six) 143; (V-8) 194.

Series L6-W300M Power-Wagon — (1-Ton) — (126 in. w.b.)				
L6-W300M	Chassis & Cowl	2481	4600	Note 9
L6-W300M	Chassis & Cab	2725	5025	Note 9
L6-W300M	Pickup	2850	5400	Note 9

NOTE 9: Model year production, Power-Wagon: 2387.

NOTE 10: Weights and prices shown are for 6-cyl. models. For V-8 equipped trucks (prefix L8) add 100 pounds to weight and $105.30 to price.

ENGINES (D100, D200, D300, W100, W200) Inline. L-head. Six-cylinder. Cast iron block. Bore & stroke: 3.25 in. x 4.625 in. Displacemen. in. Compression ratio.: 7.9:1. Brake Horsepower: 120 @ 3600 R.P.M. Net (Taxable) horsepower.: 25.35. Torque: 202 lbs.-ft. @ 1600 R.P.M. Four main bearings. Solid valve lifters.

ENGINE (W300) Inline. L-head. Six-cylinder. Cast iron block. Bore & stroke: 3.437 in. x 4.5 in. Displacement: 250.6 cu. in. Compression ratio: 7.1:1. Brake horsepower: 125 @ 3600 R.P.M. Net Horsepower: 28.35. Torque: 216 lbs.-ft. @ 1600 R.P.M. Four main bearings. Solid valve lifters.

ENGINE (Power-Wagon) Same as D100 except — Brake horsepower: 113 @ 3600 R.P.M. Torque: 198 lbs.-ft. @ 1600 R.P.M.

1958 Dodge D100 Sweptside Pickup (OCW)

ENGINE (Optional, all models except Power-Wagon) V-8. Overhead valves. Eight-cylinder. Cast iron block. Bore & stroke: 3.63 in. x 3.8 in. Displacement: 314.6 cu. in. Compression ratio: 8.1:1. Brake horsepower: 204 @ 4400 R.P.M. Net horsepower: 42.16. Torque: 290 lbs.-ft. @ 2400 R.P.M. Five main bearings. Hydraulic valve lifters.

CHASSIS (D100) Wheelbase: 108 in. and 116 in. Tires: 6.70 x 15 four-ply (front and rear). GVW: 5100 lbs. Axle capacity: (front) 2500 lbs.; (rear) 3600 lbs.

CHASSIS (D200) Wheelbase: 116 in. Tires: 7-17.5 six-ply (front and rear). GVW: 7500 lbs. Axle capacity: (front) 2800 lbs.; (rear) 6500 lbs.

CHASSIS (D300) Wheelbase: 126 in. Tires: 7-17.5 six-ply (front and rear). GVW: 9000 lbs. Axle capacity: (front) 2800 lbs.; (rear) 6500 lbs.

CHASSIS (W100) Wheelbase: 108 in. and 116 in. Tires: 7-17.5 six-ply (front and rear). GVW: 5100 lbs. Axle capacity: (front) 3000 lbs.; (rear) 3600 lbs.

CHASSIS (W200) Wheelbase: 116 in. Tires: 7-17.5 six-ply (front and rear). GVW: 8000 lbs. Axle capacity: (front) 3000 lbs.; (rear) 6500 lbs.

CHASSIS (W300) Wheelbase: 129 in. Tires: 8-19.5 eight-ply (front and rear). GVW: 10,000 lbs. Axle capacity: (front) 4500 lbs.; (rear) 8000 lbs.

CHASSIS (Power-Wagon) Wheelbase: 126 in. Tires: 7.50 x 16 eight-ply (front and rear). GVW: 9500 lbs. Axle capacity: (front) 3750 lbs.; (rear) 6500 lbs.

TECHNICAL: Selective sliding gear transmission. Speeds: 3F/1R except W300 and W300M, 4F/1R. Column or floor shift. Automatic transmission and overdrive optional. Overall axle ratio: (D100) 3.73:1, 4.1:1 and 4.89:1; (D200/300) 4.1:1 and 4.89:1; (W100/200) 4.11:1 and 4.89:1; (W300) 4.88:1 and 5.87:1 (front and rear); (W300M) 4.89:1 and 5.83:1 (front and rear). Single plate dry disc clutch: 11 in. Hydraulic four-wheel brakes: (D100) 11 in. drums; (D200, D300, W200) 12⅛ in.; (W100) 11 in. (front) and 13 in. (rear); (W300) 13 in.; (W300M) 14⅛ in. Fuel tank: 17.4 gallons except W100/200 and W300M, 18-gallon; W300, 25-gallon. Wheels: (D100) 15 x 4.50; (W300) 19.5 x 5.25; (W300M) 16 x 5.50; (others) 17.5 x 5.25. One-pint oil bath air cleaner.

OPTIONS: (D100, D200, D300) Same list and prices as 1957, plus the following: Chrome trim package, all models except Sweptside (32.90). Hood ornament for Sweptside (2.40). Electric tachometer (52.00). Full-traction differential for D100 only (46.10). (All W Series) Same list and prices as 1957.

HISTORICAL: Introduced: October 31, 1957. Calendar year sales: 36,972. Calendar year production: 58,668. Model year production: (six-cylinder) 28,276; (V-8) 13,610; (Total) 41,886. Model year production (U.S. only): (six) 25,760; (V-8) 12,180; (Total) 37,940. Innovations: Quad headlights. Tradesman utility body. Hooded instrument panel. Oil/amp warning lights. Historical notes: For the first time, Dodge styled three distinct front end appearances: one for light and medium-duty, another for heavy-duty, and

1958 Dodge Town Panel (OCW)

a third for cab-over-engine models. Production fell 23.4 percent, to the lowest total since World War II. Sales suffered a similar decrease. As a result of the general business recession, total industry sales were down 15.4 percent. Foreign trucks (mainly Volkswagen) became a factor for the first time, capturing nearly 4 percent of total U.S. sales. Dodge extended a new six-speed automatic transmission to medium and heavy-duty trucks. The full line included trucks from 4,250 to 46,000 pounds GVW, and 65,000 pounds GCW. Four six-cylinder engines and three V-8s were available. A 315 cu. in. hemi powered medium-tonnage models; a 354 with dual carburetion and exhaust went into heavy trucks. During 1958, Dodge opened 13 new truck centers, bringing the nationwide network total to 23. Chrysler Corp. previewed its new car and truck line at the Americana Hotel in Bal Harbour, Florida in September — the first full line preview outside of Detroit.

Pricing

1958	5	4	3	2	1
L6-D100 Series — (½-Ton) — (108 in. w.b.)					
Pickup	960	1920	3200	4500	6400
Town Panel	890	1770	2950	4150	5900
6-pass. Wagon	900	1800	3000	4200	6000
8-pass. Wagon	900	1800	3000	4200	6000
L6-D100 Series — (½-Ton) — (116 in. w.b.)					
Pickup	950	1900	3150	4400	6300
Sweptside Pickup	1020	2050	3400	4800	6800
Platform	780	1560	2600	3600	5200
Stake	800	1600	2650	3700	5300
L6-D200 Series — (¾-Ton) — (116 in. w.b.)					
Pickup	900	1800	3000	4200	6000
Platform	770	1550	2550	3600	5100
Stake	780	1560	2600	3600	5200
L6-D300 Series — (1-Ton) — (126 in. w.b.)					
Pickup	840	1680	2800	3900	5600
Platform	690	1380	2300	3200	4600
Stake	700	1400	2350	3250	4700
L6-W100 Series 4x4 — (½-Ton) — (108 in. w.b.)					
Pickup	980	1950	3250	4550	6500
Town Panel	900	1800	3000	4200	6000
6-pass. Wagon	920	1850	3050	4300	6100
8-pass. Wagon	920	1850	3050	4300	6100
L6-W100 Series 4x4 — (½-Ton) — (116 in. w.b.)					
Pickup	960	1920	3200	4500	6400
Platform	810	1620	2700	3800	5400
Stake	830	1650	2750	3850	5500
L6-W200 Series 4x4 — (¾-Ton) — (116 in. w.b.)					
Pickup	930	1860	3100	4350	6200
Platform	800	1600	2650	3700	5300
Stake	810	1620	2700	3800	5400
L6-W300 Series 4x4 — (1-Ton) — (129 in. w.b.)					
Pickup	900	1800	3000	4200	6000
Platform	770	1550	2550	3600	5100
Stake	780	1560	2600	3600	5200
L6-W300M Power-Wagon — (1-Ton) — (126 in.w.b.)					
Pickup	1050	2100	3500	4900	7000

NOTE: Add 10% for V-8 engine.
Add 5% for automatic transmission.

1959 DODGE

1959 Dodge Sweptline Pickup (OCW)

½-TON — M SERIES D100 — SIX-CYLINDER and V-8 / ¾-TON — M SERIES D200 — SIX-CYLINDER and V-8 / 1-TON — M SERIES D300 — SIX-CYLINDER and V-8: — An all new, smooth-sided pickup called the Sweptline was the only major change for 1959. Sweptlines, offered on all three chassis, featured a cab-wide pickup body for greater hauling ability and cleaner, more modern styling. The traditional fender-sided pickup, now called Utiline, was available on both D and W Series chassis. Utiline pickups would remain in the line until mid-1985. Other styling changes included a new Dodge nameplate above a cleaner one-piece grille, plus new concealed runningboards. New features included a hydraulically operated clutch, suspended brake and clutch pedals, and a 318 cu. in. V-8 engine. All gauges on the new dash sat directly in front of the driver, and the glove box moved to the far right from the center. Four body colors were added: Heron Gray, Buckskin Tan, Vista Green, and Sand Dune White. Four colors were dropped, but 13 solid colors were still available. Two-tones featured Sand Dune White at the top. Hub caps were also Sand Dune White. All 1958 models were continued, including the Tradesman, Town Panel and Town Wagon, and ¾-ton Forward-Control chassis. The Sweptside D100 pickup was dropped in January, 1959. New this year was the Minivan package delivery vehicle, only 169 in. long on a 95 in. w.b. but with 164 cu. ft. of load space. LoadFlite pushbutton automatic transmission was standard on the Minivan. Standard equipment included the 230 cu. in. 6-cyl. engine, underslung tire carrier, a short-arm outside mirror, dual electric single-speed wipers, and front and rear shock absorbers (front only on 1-ton).

½-TON 4x4 — M SERIES W100 — SIX-CYLINDER and V-8 / ¾-TON 4x4 — M SERIES W200 — SIX-CYLINDER and V-8 / 1-TON 4x4 — M SERIES W300 — SIX-CYLINDER and V-8: — 4wd models continued unchanged. Standard equipment was the same as the D Series, but with two-speed transfer case, and tire carrier inside pickup box.

1-TON POWER-WAGON — M SERIES W300M — SIX-CYLINDER: — Power-Wagons continued without change. Standard equipment included an oil filter, single taillight, side-mounted tire carrier, four-speed transmission and two-speed transfer case, and front bumper. Only the 230 cu. in. six was available.

1959 Dodge D100 Sweptside Pickup (OCW)

I.D. DATA: Serial numbers were on a plate on the left lock pillar post. Starting Serial numbers: (D100 Six) M6D1-L01001; (D100 V-8) M8D1-L01001; (D200 Six) M6D2-1001; (D200 V-8) M8D2-L01001; (D300 Six) M6D3-L01001; (D300 V-8) M8D3-L01001; (W100 Six) M6W1-L01001; (W100 V-8) M8W1-L01001; (W200 Six) M6W2-L01001; (W200 V-8) M8W2-L01001; (W300 Six) M6W3-L01001; (W300 V-8) M8W3-L01001; (W300M Power-Wagon) M6W3M-L01001. Engine numbers were in the same locations as 1957-58. Starting Engine Numbers: (D100 Six) M6-D1-1001; (D100 V-8) M8-D1-1001; (D200 Six) M6-D2-1001; (D200 V-8) M8-D2-1001; (D300 Six) M6-D3-1001; (D300 V-8) M8-D3-1001; (W100 Six) M6-W1-1001; (W100 V-8) M8-W1-1001; (W200 Six) M6-W2-1001; (W200 V-8) M8-W2-1001; (W300 Six) M6-W3-1001; (W300 V-8) M8-W3-1001; (W300M Power-Wagon) M6-W3M-1001. Ending serial and engine numbers are not available.

1959 Dodge D100 Sweptline Pickup (S. Soloy)

Model	Body Type	Price	Weight	Prod. Total
M6-D100 Series — (½-Ton) — (108 in. w.b.)				
M6-D100	Chassis & Cowl	1440	2475	—
M6-D100	Chassis & Cab	1675	2950	—
M6-D100	Utiline Pickup	1781	3250	—
M6-D100	Sweptline Pickup	1797	3325	—
M6-D100	Town Panel	2062	3425	—
M6-D100	Town Wagon (6-pass.)	2336	3650	—
M6-D100	Town Wagon (8-pass.)	2382	3700	—
(116 in. w.b.)				
M6-D100	Chassis & Cowl	1475	2500	—
M6-D100	Chassis & Cab	1711	2975	—
M6-D100	Utiline Pickup	1816	3325	—
M6-D100	Sweptline Pickup	1832	3425	—
M6-D100	Sweptside Pickup	2189	3475	—
M6-D100	Platform	1852	3175	—
M6-D100	Stake	1902	3375	—
M6-D200 Series — (¾-Ton) — (116 in. w.b.)				
M6-D200	Chassis & Cowl	1549	2950	—
M6-D200	Chassis & Cab	1794	3425	—
M6-D200	Utiline Pickup	1899	3775	—
M6-D200	Sweptline Pickup	1915	3875	—
M6-D200	Platform	1935	3625	—
M6-D200	Stake	1985	3825	—
M6-D300 Series — (1-Ton) — (126 in. w.b.)				
M6-D300	Chassis & Cowl	1693	3125	—
M6-D300	Chassis & Cab	1937	3600	—
M6-D300	Utiline Pickup	2062	4000	—
M6-D300	Sweptline Pickup	2078	4025	—
M6-D300	Platform	2108	3875	—
M6-D300	Stake	2168	4075	—
M6-W100 Series 4x4 — (½-Ton) — (108 in. w.b.)				
M6-W100	Chassis & Cowl	2248	3275	—
M6-W100	Chassis & Cab	2483	3750	—
M6-W100	Utiline Pickup	2589	4050	—
M6-W100	Town Panel	2870	4225	—
M6-W100	Town Wagon (6-pass.)	3144	4450	—
M6-W100	Town Wagon (8-pass.)	3190	4500	—
(116 in. w.b.)				
M6-W100	Chassis & Cowl	2283	3300	—
M6-W100	Chassis & Cab	2519	3775	—
M6-W100	Utiline Pickup	2624	4125	—
M6-W100	Platform	2660	3975	—
M6-W100	Stake	2710	4175	—
M6-W200 Series 4x4 — (¾-Ton) — (116 in. w.b.)				
M6-W100	Chassis & Cowl	2379	3475	—
M6-W100	Chassis & Cab	2624	3950	—
M6-W100	Utiline Pickup	2729	4300	—
M6-W100	Platform	2765	4150	—
M6-W100	Stake	2815	4350	—
M6-W300 Series 4x4 — (1-Ton) — (129 in. w.b.)				
M6-W300	Chassis & Cowl	2932	4050	—
M6-W300	Chassis & Cab	3177	4525	—
M6-W300	Utiline Pickup	3302	4925	—
M6-W300	Platform	3348	4800	—
M6-W300	Stake	3407	5000	—
M6-W300M Series Power-Wagon — (1-Ton) — (126 in. w.b.)				
M6-W300M	Chassis & Cowl	2811	4600	—
M6-W300M	Chassis & Cab	3056	5025	—
M6-W300M	Utiline Pickup	3197	5400	—

NOTE 1: Weights and prices shown are for 6-cyl. trucks. For V-8 equipped trucks (prefix M8) add $120.75 to price.

NOTE 2: Production figures by model and series are not available.

1959 Dodge D200 with Milk Truck body (DFW)

ENGINE: Six-cylinder: same as 1958; see previous specifications.

ENGINE (Optional, D100, D200, D300, W100, W200): 90-degree, overhead valve. Eight-cylinder. Cast iron block. Bore & stroke: 3.91 x 3.312 in. Displacement: 318.1 cu. in. Compression ratio: 8.25:1. Brake horsepower: 205 at 4400 R.P.M. Net (Taxable) horsepower: 42.16. Torque: 290 lbs.-ft. at 2400 R.P.M. Five main bearings. Hydraulic valve lifters.

1959 Dodge 1-Ton Walk-in Delivery Van (DFW)

ENGINE (Optional, W300): Same as V-8 above, but with heavy-duty features to meet demands of more rugged use. Brake horsepower: 207 at 4400 R.P.M. Torque: 292 lbs.-ft. at 2400 R.P.M.

CHASSIS (D100): Wheelbase: 108 in. and 116 in. Tires: 6.70 x 15 four-ply tubeless (front/rear). GVW: 5100 lbs. Rear axle capacity: 3600 lbs. Front axle: 2800 lbs.

CHASSIS (D200): Wheelbase: 116 in. Tires: 6.50 x 16 six-ply tubeless (front/rear). GVW: 7500 lbs. Rear axle: 5500 lbs. Front axle: 2800 lbs.

CHASSIS (D300): Wheelbase: 126 in. Tires: 7 x 17.5 six-ply tubeless (front/rear). GVW: 9000 lbs. Rear axle: 6500 lbs. Front axle: 2800 lbs.

CHASSIS (W100): Wheelbase: 108 in. and 116 in. Tires: 7 x 17.5 six-ply tubeless (front/rear). GVW: 6000 lbs. Axle capacity: (front) 3000 lbs.; (rear) 4500 lbs.

CHASSIS (W200): Wheelbase: 116 in. Tires: 7 x 17.5 six-ply tubeless (front/rear). GVW: 8000 lbs. Axle capacity: (front) 3000 lbs.; (rear) 6500 lbs.

CHASSIS (W300): Wheelbase: 129 in. Tires: 8 x 19.5 eight-ply tubeless (front/rear). GVW: 10,000 lbs. Axle capacity: (front) 4500 lbs.; (rear) 7500 lbs.

CHASSIS (Power-Wagon): Wheelbase: 126 in. Tires: 7.50 x 16 eight-ply tubeless (front/rear). GVW: 9500 lbs. Axle capacity: (front) 3750 lbs.; (rear) 6500 lbs.

TECHNICAL: Selective sliding gear transmission. Speeds: 3F/1R except 1-ton models, 4F/1R. Column or floor shift. Automatic transmission optional. Single plate dry disc clutch: 11 in. Overall axle ratio: (D100) 3.54:1, 4.1:1 or 4.89:1; (D200, W100) 4.1:1 or 4.88:1; (D300, W200) 4.1:1 or 4.89:1; (W300) 4.88:1 or 5.87:1; (Power-Wagon) 4.89:1 or 5.83:1. Hydraulic four-wheel brakes. Oil bath air cleaner: (W300M) one quart; (others) one pint. Fuel tank: (D Series) 17.4 gallon mounted inside frame; (W100-300) 17.4 gallon mounted outboard on right side; (Power-Wagon) 18 gallon, at rear of frame. Governor: (Power-Wagon) velocity type. Wheels: (D100) 5-stud disc; (D200, W100) 8-stud disc; (Power-Wagon) 5-stud ventilated disc; (others) 6-stud disc.

OPTIONS: (All models except Power-Wagon) Chromed front bumper ($13.20). Rear bumper ($20.40). Chrome rear bumper ($33.60). Bumper guards ($5.30). Chrome bumper guards ($11.85). Chrome hub caps: set

1959 Dodge Power Wagon (OCW)

of four ($5.95); five ($9.35). Painted hub caps for D200: four ($8.60); five ($10.70). Chrome wheel covers for panel and wagon ($16.45); for other D100 models ($22.40). Custom cab equipment ($36.85). Armrest, left or right ($3.70). Dodge-Tint glass ($19.25). Interior lining package, Town Panel ($39.50). Glove box lock ($3.95). Inside rearview mirror ($3). Adjustable long-arm mirror: left ($2.35); right ($5.95). 5 x 7 in. mirror: left ($11.85); right ($15.50). Right sunvisor ($2.65). Chrome trim package No. 1, pickups ($23.05). Chrome trim package No. 2, Town Wagons and Panels ($39.50). Wraparound rear window ($40.15). Side glass in panel ($50). Dual electric variable-speed wipers ($7.15). Windshield washer ($11.85). Turn signals ($26.35). Heater: standard ($46.10); deluxe ($63.20). Hood ornament ($4.65). Dual electric horns ($14.50). Grab handles ($8.50). Heavy-duty instrument cluster ($59.25). Cab corner marker lights ($9.90). Bright metal moldings, Town Panel and Wagon ($14.50); Sweptline pickup ($19.75). Bright windshield molding ($6.95). Roof-mounted radio ($55.30). Auxiliary seat: standard panel ($38.20); Custom panel ($46.10). Foam padding, seat back or bottom ($15.80 each). Auxiliary taillight ($7.25). Electric tachometer ($52). Hand throttle control ($4.90). Dual rear fender for D300 Utiline ($27.65). Two-tone paint: Town Panel or Wagon ($25); others, except Sweptside ($31.60). Inside tire carrier for panel or pickup, or outside for Utiline ($8.60). One-quart oil bath air cleaner: 6-cyl. ($3.95); V-8 ($5.60). Oil filter: one-quart ($8.60); two-quart ($12.05); all V-8 ($3.50). Electric fuel pump ($25). Vacuum brake booster ($39.50). Power steering ($111.85). Rear shocks, D300 ($25). Full-traction differential, D100 ($59.25). V-8 engine ($120.75). Governor ($10.20). 3-ton jack ($9.90). Increased cooling capacity ($9.90). Heavy-duty three-speed transmission ($5.30). LoadFlite automatic transmission ($221.10). (Power-Wagon only) Vacuum brake booster ($42.15). Deluxe cab equipment ($19.75). Forced-draft crankcase vent system ($19.75). Heater ($46.10). Fenders painted to match cab ($13.20). Draw bar ($23.05). Governor for rear drive shaft ($98.70). Two-quart oil filter ($12.05). Drive pulley ($85.55). Rear drive shaft assembly ($85.55). Winch assembly ($251.35). Heavy-duty springs: 1600-pound front ($7.90); 3000-pound rear ($10.70).

HISTORICAL: Introduced: October 24, 1958. Calendar year sales: 52,107. Calendar year production: 71,680. Model year production figures not available. Innovations: Cab-wide pickup body (Sweptline). Hydraulic clutch. Suspended pedals. Large-capacity Minivan. Historical notes: "Today it's real smart to choose Dodge trucks" was the new advertising slogan. Dodge dropped the terms "Power Giant" and "Job-Rated" in ads. Truck sales bounced back from their 1958 low, chalking up a gain of 40.7 percent. Production gained 22.2 percent, giving Dodge a 6.29 percent share of total industry production and 5.55 percent of total sales. Dodge cut production on 21 of its basic 1959 model trucks. The full Dodge truck line covered 98 percent of the market. Prices ranged from $1440 for a D100 chassis to $10,474 for a 4-ton tandem. Engines rated 113 to 234 horsepower were available.

Pricing

1959

	5	4	3	2	1
M6-D100 Series — (½-Ton) — (108 in. w.b.)					
Utiline Pickup	960	1920	3200	4500	6400
Sweptline Pickup	1010	2030	3350	4700	6700
Town Panel	890	1770	2950	4150	5900
6-pass. Wagon	900	1800	3000	4200	6000
8-pass. Wagon	900	1800	3000	4200	6000
M6-D100 Series — (½-Ton) — (116 in. w.b.)					
Utiline Pickup	950	1900	3150	4400	6300
Sweptline Pickup	1020	2050	3400	4800	6800
Sweptside Pickup	1080	2160	3600	5050	7200
Platform	780	1560	2600	3600	5200
Stake	800	1600	2650	3700	5300
M6-D200 Series — (¾-Ton) — (116 in. w.b.)					
Utiline Pickup	900	1800	3000	4200	6000
Sweptline Pickup	930	1860	3100	4350	6200
Platform	770	1550	2550	3600	5100
Stake	780	1560	2600	3600	5200
M6-D300 Series — (1-Ton) — (126 in. w.b.)					
Utiline Pickup	840	1680	2800	3900	5600
Sweptline Pickup	870	1750	2900	4100	5800
Platform	690	1380	2300	3200	4600
Stake	700	1400	2350	3250	4700
M6-W100 Series 4x4 — (½-Ton) — (108 in. w.b.)					
Utiline Pickup	980	1950	3250	4550	6500
Town Panel	900	1800	3000	4200	6000
6-pass. Wagon	920	1850	3050	4300	6100
8-pass. Wagon	920	1850	3050	4300	6100
M6-W100 Series 4x4 — (½-Ton) — (116 in. w.b.)					
Utiline Pickup	960	1920	3200	4500	6400
Platform	810	1620	2700	3800	5400
Stake	830	1650	2750	3850	5500
M6-W200 Series 4x4 — (¾-Ton) — (116 in. w.b.)					
Utiline Pickup	930	1860	3100	4350	6200
Platform	800	1600	2650	3700	5300
Stake	810	1620	2700	3800	5400
M6-W300 Series 4x4 — (1-Ton) — (129 in. w.b.)					
Utiline Pickup	900	1800	3000	4200	6000
Platform	770	1550	2550	3600	5100
Stake	780	1560	2600	3600	5200
M6-W300M Series Power-Wagon — (1-Ton) — (126 in. w.b.)					
Pickup	1050	2100	3500	4900	7000

NOTE: Add 10 percent for V-8 engine.
Add 5 percent for automatic transmission.

1960 DODGE

1960 Dodge D100 Sweptline Pickup (S. Soloy)

½-TON — P SERIES D100 — SIX-CYLINDER and V-8 / ¾-TON — P SERIES D200 — SIX-CYLINDER and V-8 / 1-TON — P SERIES D300 — SIX-CYLINDER and V-8 — Dodge marked time in 1960, preparing for an all new line of light-duty trucks that would be unveiled for the next model year. A new bright-finished grille was the only appearance change. Cabs, engines, mechanical details and model availability were unchanged. The Minivan was dropped. Six new colors brought the total to 14: Nile Green, Mustang Gray, Toreador Red, Indian Turquoise, Pine Green, and School Bus Chrome Yellow. Body colors dropped were Heron Gray, Alaska White, Buckskin Tan, Vista Green, and Ponchartrain Green. Two-tones combined Sand Dune White with any of the other 13 colors. Standard equipment was the same as in 1959.

½-TON 4x4 — P SERIES W100 — SIX-CYLINDER and V-8 / ¾-TON 4x4 — P SERIES W200 — SIX-CYLINDER and V-8 / 1-TON 4x4 — P SERIES W300 — SIX-CYLINDER and V-8 / 1-TON POWER-WAGON — P SERIES WM200 — SIX-CYLINDER — W Series 4x4s received the new grille design, while the familiar Power-Wagon continued without change. So did the 1-ton Forward Control chassis.

I.D. DATA: Serial numbers were on a plate on the left door lock pillar. The first digit indicates model year ("0" = 1960, "1" = 1961, etc.); the second digit reveals number of cylinders; the next letter indicates model ("D" for conventional, "W" for 4wd, etc.); next is the nominal weight rating ("1" for ½-ton, "2" for ¾-ton, "3" for 1-ton); next is "L" (light duty), "M" (medium) or "H" (heavy); and the final six digits are the sequence number. Starting Serial Numbers: (D100 Six) 06D1-L100001; (D100 V-8) 08D1-L100001; (D200 Six) 06L2-L100001; (D200 V-8) 08D2-L100001; (D300 Six) 06D3-L100001; (D300 V-8) 08D3-L100001; (W100 Six) 06W1-L100001; (W100 V-8) 08W1-L100001; (W200 Six) 06W2-L100001; (W200 V-8) 08W2-L100001; (W300 Six) 06W3-L100001; (W300 V-8) 08W3-L100001; (WM300) 06WM3-L100001. Six-cylinder engine numbers were on the left side of the block at the front, below the cylinder head; V-8 numbers were on the left front of the block. A new engine numbering system began with the P-Series. The first two letters designate the series ("T" stands for truck, "P" for P-Series); the next two digits indicate engine displacement ("23" means 230.2 cu. in.); the next two digits show the month and date of manufacture; and the final digits are the sequence number. (Note: The 318 cu. in. V-8 uses three digits to designate its size). Starting Engine Numbers: (230.2 cu. in. Six) TP-23-8-3-1001; (251 cu. in. Six) TP-25-8-3-1001; (318 cu. in. V-8) TP-318-8-3-1001. Ending serial and engine numbers are not available.

Model	Body Type	Price	Weight	Prod. Total
P6-D100 Series — (½-Ton) — (108 in. w.b.)				
P6-D100	Chassis & Cowl	1471	2475	Note 1
P6-D100	Chassis & Cab	1706	2950	Note 1
P6-D100	Utiline Pickup	1812	3250	Note 1
P6-D100	Sweptline Pickup	1826	3325	Note 1
P6-D100	Town Panel	2119	3425	Note 1
P6-D100	Town Wagon (6-pass.)	2384	3650	Note 1
P6-D100	Town Wagon (8-pass.)	2431	3700	Note 1
(116 in. w.b.)				
P6-D100	Chassis & Cowl	1506	2500	Note 2
P6-D100	Chassis & Cab	1740	2975	Note 2
P6-D100	Utiline Pickup	1847	3325	Note 2
P6-D100	Sweptline Pickup	1860	3425	Note 2
P6-D100	Platform	1883	3175	Note 2
P6-D100	Stake	1931	3375	Note 2

NOTE 1: Total model year production: (six-cylinder) 12,983; (V-8) 2837.

NOTE 2: Total model year production: (six-cylinder) 10,712; (V-8) 6922.

Model	Body Type	Price	Weight	Prod. Total
P6-D200 Series — (¾-Ton) — (116 in. w.b.)				
P6-D200	Chassis & Cowl	1602	2950	Note 3
P6-D200	Chassis & Cab	1846	3425	Note 3
P6-D200	Utiline Pickup	1952	3775	Note 3
P6-D200	Sweptline Pickup	1966	3875	Note 3
P6-D200	Platform	1988	3625	Note 3
P6-D200	Stake	2036	3825	Note 3

NOTE 3: Total model year production: (six-cylinder) 3031; (V-8) 1578.

Model	Body Type	Price	Weight	Prod. Total
P6-D300 Series — (1-Ton) — (126 in. w.b.)				
P6-D300	Chassis & Cowl	1727	3125	Note 4
P6-D300	Chassis & Cab	1971	3600	Note 4
P6-D300	Utiline Pickup	2096	4000	Note 4
P6-D300	Sweptline Pickup	2110	4025	Note 4
P6-D300	Platform	2143	3875	Note 4
P6-D300	Stake	2202	4075	Note 4

NOTE 4: Total model year production: (six-cylinder) 3737; (V-8) 2468.

Model	Body Type	Price	Weight	Prod. Total
P6-W100 Series 4x4 — (½-Ton) — (108 in. w.b.)				
P6-W100	Chassis & Cowl	2236	3275	Note 5
P6-W100	Chassis & Cab	2471	3750	Note 5
P6-W100	Utiline Pickup	2578	4050	Note 5
P6-W100	Sweptline Pickup	2591	4125	Note 5
P6-W100	Town Panel	2884	4225	Note 5
P6-W100	Town Wagon (6-pass.)	3150	4450	Note 5
P6-W100	Town Wagon (8-pass.)	3196	4500	Note 5
(116 in. w.b.)				
P6-W100	Chassis & Cowl	2271	3300	Note 6
P6-W100	Chassis & Cab	2506	3775	Note 6
P6-W100	Utiline Pickup	2612	4125	Note 6
P6-W100	Sweptline Pickup	2626	4150	Note 6
P6-W100	Platform	2648	3975	Note 6
P6-W100	Stake	2696	4175	Note 6

NOTE 5: Total model year production: (six-cylinder) 352; (V-8) 165.

NOTE 6: Total model year production: (six-cylinder) 189; (V-8) 262.

Model	Body Type	Price	Weight	Prod. Total
P6-W200 Series 4x4 — (¾-Ton) — (116 in. w.b.)				
P6-W200	Chassis & Cowl	2368	3475	Note 7
P6-W200	Chassis & Cab	2612	3950	Note 7
P6-W200	Utiline Pickup	2719	4300	Note 7
P6-W200	Sweptline Pickup	2732	4400	Note 7
P6-W200	Platform	2755	4150	Note 7
P6-W200	Stake	2803	4350	Note 7

NOTE 7: Total model year production: (six-cylinder) 262; (V-8) 150.

Model	Body Type	Price	Weight	Prod. Total
P6-W300 Series 4x4 — (1-Ton) — (129 in. w.b.)				
P6-W300	Chassis & Cowl	2928	4050	Note 8
P6-W300	Chassis & Cab	3172	4525	Note 8
P6-W300	Utiline Pickup	3299	4925	Note 8
P6-W300	Sweptline Pickup	3346	5050	Note 8
P6-W300	Platform	3405	4800	Note 8
P6-W300	Stake	—	5000	Note 8

NOTE 8: Total model year production: (six-cylinder) 141; (V-8) 171.

Model	Body Type	Price	Weight	Prod. Total
P6-WM300 Series Power-Wagon — (1-Ton) — (126 in. w.b.)				
P6-WM300	Chassis & Cowl	2848	4600	Note 9
P6-WM300	Chassis & Cab	3096	5025	Note 9
P6-WM300	Utiline Pickup	3239	5425	Note 9

NOTE 9: Total model year production: 1517.

NOTE 10: Weights and prices shown are for six-cylinder models. For V-8 equipped trucks (prefix P8) add $120.75 to price.

ENGINE: Six-cylinder: same as 1957-58; see previous specifications.

ENGINES (Optional, D100, D200, D300, W100, W200): 90-degree, overhead valve. Eight-cylinder. Cast iron block. Bore & stroke: 3.91 in. x 3.312 in. Displacement: 318.1 cu. in. Compression ratio: 8.25:1. Brake horsepower: 200 at 3900 R.P.M. Net (Taxable) horsepower: 48.92. Torque: 286 lbs.-ft. at 2400 R.P.M. Five main bearings. Hydraulic valve lifters.

ENGINE (Optional, W300): Same as V-8 above, but heavy-duty. Brake horsepower: 202 at 3900 R.P.M. Torque: 288 lbs.-ft. at 2400 R.P.M.

CHASSIS: Same as 1959; see previous specifications.

TECHNICAL: Same as 1959; see previous specifications.

OPTIONS: Same list and prices as 1959, plus a 20-inch diameter steering wheel ($4) for "D" models.

HISTORICAL: Introduced: October 9, 1959. Calendar year sales: 44,998. Calendar year production: 70,305. Model year production: (Six-cylinder) 33,408; (V-8) 14,591; (Total) 47,999. Model year production, U.S. only: (Six-cylinder) 31,522; (V-8) 13,454; (Total) 44,976. History: Dodge's advertising theme for 1960 was "You Can Depend on Dodge to Save You Money in Trucks." Despite a 20 percent increase in advertising budget, sales dropped 13.6 percent. While the light-duty line stood still, Dodge in May 1959 introduced a new series of medium and heavy-duty cab-forward trucks, featuring "Servi-Swing" fenders that swung out at 110 degrees for easy service access. The new cab-forward C line had a short (89¾ in.)

bumper-to-back-of-cab dimension, able to pull the maximum length trailers allowed by law. Gone were the hemi-head engines, replaced by a whole new series of 361 and 413 cu. in. V-8s. Available for the first time were four turbocharged Cummins diesels. GCW ratings ranged all the way to 76,800 pounds. The expanding federal highway construction program continued to be a good market for trucks. The Pennsylvania State Highway Dept. ordered 250 heavy-duty D700 models. Dodge also received a contract from the Army to test Chrysler's gas turbine engine in a 14,000-pound GVW Dodge truck. Dodge announced in March 1960 a nationwide sales campaign based on the theme: "Take 5 to Drive the New Dodge Sweptline." This campaign, supported by national newspaper advertising, local billboards and direct mail, was intended to encourage five-minute demonstration drives.

Pricing

	5	4	3	2	1
1960					
P6-D100 Series — (½-Ton) — (108 in. w.b.)					
Utiline Pickup	960	1920	3200	4500	6400
Sweptline Pickup	1010	2030	3350	4700	6700
Town Panel	890	1770	2950	4150	5900
6-pass. Wagon	900	1800	3000	4200	6000
8-pass. Wagon	900	1800	3000	4200	6000
P6-D100 Series — (½-Ton) — (116 in. w.b.)					
Utiline Pickup	950	1900	3150	4400	6300
Sweptline Pickup	1020	2050	3400	4800	6800
Platform	780	1560	2600	3600	5200
Stake	800	1600	2650	3700	5300
P6-D200 Series — (¾-Ton) — (116 in. w.b.)					
Utiline Pickup	900	1800	3000	4200	6000
Sweptline Pickup	930	1860	3100	4350	6200
Platform	770	1550	2550	3600	5100
Stake	780	1560	2600	3600	5200
P6-D300 Series — (1-Ton) — (126 in. w.b.)					
Utiline Pickup	840	1680	2800	3900	5600
Sweptline Pickup	870	1750	2900	4100	5800
Platform	690	1380	2300	3200	4600
Stake	700	1400	2350	3250	4700
P6-W100 Series 4x4 — (½-Ton) — (108 in. w.b.)					
Utiline Pickup	980	1950	3250	4550	6500
Sweptline Pickup	1010	2030	3350	4700	6700
Town Panel	900	1800	3000	4200	6000
6-pass. Wagon	920	1850	3050	4300	6100
8-pass. Wagon	920	1850	3050	4300	6100
P6-W100 Series 4x4 — (½-Ton) — (116 in. w.b.)					
Utiline Pickup	960	1920	3200	4500	6400
Sweptline Pickup	1000	2000	3300	4600	6600
Platform	810	1600	2700	3800	5400
Stake	830	1650	2750	3850	5500
P6-W200 Series 4x4 — (¾-Ton) — (116 in. w.b.)					
Utiline Pickup	930	1860	3100	4350	6200
Sweptline Pickup	960	1920	3200	4500	6400
Platform	800	1600	2650	3700	5300
Stake	810	1620	2700	3800	5400
P6-W300 Series — (1-Ton) — (129 in. w.b.)					
Utiline Pickup	900	1800	3000	4200	6000
Sweptline Pickup	930	1860	3100	4350	6200
Platform	770	1550	2550	3600	5100
Stake	780	1560	2600	3600	5200
P6-WM300 Series Power-Wagon — (1-Ton) — (126 in. w.b.)					
Utiline Pickup	1050	2100	3500	4900	7000

NOTE: Add 5 percent for automatic transmission.
Add 10 percent for V-8 engine.

1961 DODGE

1961 Dodge Dart Sweptside Pickup (OCW)

½-TON — R SERIES D100 — SIX-CYLINDER and V-8 / ¾-TON — R SERIES D200 — SIX-CYLINDER and V-8 / 1-TON — R SERIES D300 — SIX-CYLINDER and V-8: — For the first time since 1954, Dodge announced an all new light and medium duty truck line. The heavy-duty line had been redesigned and reengineered for 1960. This year, the light-duty lineup was truly new from the ground up. New styling lowered overall heights by up to 7 inches, while widths grew by 4 inches. The new Dart pickup had a low, wide silhouette with clean lines that flowed smoothly from front to rear. Dodge aimed for passenger-car styling and handling characteristics in its new truck lineup. Even the name Dart was borrowed from Dodge's popular new car line — though it lasted only one season in the truck division. All the basic 1960 models were carried over, including the Town Panel and Wagon. The only new model was a ¾-ton Forward-Control chassis to round out that line. New drop-center frames in ½-ton and ¾-ton models lowered the center of gravity and cab position. Rear cross-members provided greater frame strength and rigidity. 1-ton models had a new straight frame at SAE standard 34 in. width, combined with heavier front and rear axles to produce a 10,000 pound GVW rating. Tread was widened and w.b. lengths stretched, to improve stability. New front and rear springs were longer and wider, for a "passenger car" ride. A new heavy-duty New Process A745 transmission was made standard for ½-ton and ¾-ton models. New alternators replaced the old generators, at no increase in cost, producing a charge even while idling. Cabs were available with Standard or Custom equipment. Increased cab width made the seat 4 in. wider, while the 7 in. reduced height made entry easier, with no loss of ground clearance. Once again, both Utiline (fender side) and Sweptline pickups were available. Sweptline boxes gained 4 in. wider, gaining 10 percent more load space. Base engine was now an overhead-valve 225 cu. in. slant six-cylinder, tilted 30 degrees to reduce its height. This provided space for individual branch intake manifolding and lowered the center of gravity. In standard form, the slant six was rated 140 horsepower, developing 215 lbs.-ft. of torque. D100 models intended for extra-light duty, such as stop-and-go delivery, could have a smaller 170-cu. in. version. The familiar old L-head 230-cu. in six was gone. The 318-cu. in. V-8 continued as an extra-cost option. Fourteen paint colors were again standard, including three new ones: Desert Turquoise, Sunset Yellow, and Turf Green. Wheels and bumpers were painted Sand Dune White; hub caps Gray Metallic. Two-tone combinations on the Town Panel and Town Wagon used Sand Dune White at the top. Other two-tone options used Mustang Gray or Angus Black as the upper color. All inside cab surfaces matched the body color. Steering wheel and column, hand brake control, gearshift lever, seat frame and riser were painted Black. Town Panel and Town Wagon models continued without appearance change, not receiving the new styling. Only minor trim changes differentiated the 1961 models from 1960, though their w.b. were stretched to 114 in. like other D100 models. Load capacity remained the same.

½-TON 4x4 — R SERIES W100 — SIX-CYLINDER and V-8 / ¾-TON 4x4 — R SERIES W200 — SIX-CYLINDER and V-8 / 1-TON 4x4 — R SERIES W300 — SIX-CYLINDER and V-8: — All W-Series models were carried over, but with the new w.b., frame construction and styling of the D models. A 251 cu. in. L-head six, used for many years in medium-duty models, became the base engine for the W300.

1-TON POWER-WAGON — R SERIES W300M — SIX-CYLINDER: — Power-Wagons continued basically unchanged, except for the new 251 cid L-head six-cylinder engine, which was 3 inches longer than the former 230 cid engine.

I.D. DATA: Serial numbers were on an identification plate on the left door lock pillar. Code was the same as on 1960 models. Starting Serial Numbers: (D100 Six) 16D1-100001; (D100 V-8) 18D1-L100001; (D200 Six) 16D2-L100001; (D200 V-8) 18D2-L100001; (D300 Six) 16D3-L100001; (D300 V-8) 18D3-L100001; (W100 Six) 16W1-L100001; (W100 V-8) 18W1-L100001; (W200 Six) 16W2-L10000; (W200 V-8) 18W2-L100001; (W300 Six) 16W3-L100001; (W300 V-8) 18W3-L100001; (W300M) 16WM3-L100001. Six-cylinder engine numbers were on the left side of the block at the front, below the cylinder head. V-8 engine numbers were at the left front of the block. Code was the same as on 1960 models. Starting Engine Numbers: (225 cu. in. Six) TR-22-8-3-1001; (251 cu. in. Six) TR-25-8-3-1001; (318 cu. in. V-8) TR-318-8-3-1001.

Model	Body Type	Price	Weight	Prod. Total
R6-D100 Series — (½-Ton) — (114 in. w.b.)				
R6-D100	Chassis & Cowl	1471	2540	Note 1
R6-D100	Chassis & Cab	1706	3095	Note 1
R6-D100	Dart Utiline	1812	3405	Note 1
R6-D100	Dart Sweptline	1826	3505	Note 1
R6-D100	Town Panel	2119	3565	Note 1
R6-D100	Town Wagon (6-pass.)	2384	3795	Note 1
R6-D100	Town Wagon (8-pass.)	2435	3845	Note 1
(122 in. w.b.)				
R6-D100	Chassis & Cowl	1506	2565	Note 2
R6-D100	Chassis & Cab	1740	3120	Note 2
R6-D100	Dart Utiline	1847	3470	Note 2
R6-D100	Dart Sweptline	1860	3600	Note 2
R6-D100	Platform	1883	3495	Note 2
R6-D100	Stake	1931	3695	Note 2

NOTE 1: Total model year production: (six-cylinder) 15,499; (V-8) 2930.

NOTE 2: Total model year production: (six-cylinder) 8981; (V-8) 4298.

Model	Body Type	Price	Weight	Prod. Total
R6-D200 Series — (¾-Ton) — (122 in. w.b.)				
R6-D200	Chassis & Cowl	1602	3060	Note 3
R6-D200	Chassis & Cab	1846	3615	Note 3
R6-D200	Utiline Pickup	1952	3965	Note 3
R6-D200	Sweptline Pickup	1966	4095	Note 3
R6-D200	Platform	1988	3790	Note 3
R6-D200	Stake	2036	4190	Note 3

NOTE 3: Total model year production: (six-cylinder) 2527; (V-8) 1304.

Model	Body Type	Price	Weight	Prod. Total
R6-D300 Series — (1-Ton) — (133 in. w.b.)				
R6-D300	Chassis & Cowl	1760	3220	Note 4
R6-D300	Chassis & Cab	2004	3775	Note 4
R6-D300	Utiline Pickup	2130	4175	Note 4
R6-D300	Platform	2176	4475	Note 4
R6-D300	Stake	2235	4675	Note 4

NOTE 4: Total model year production: (six-cylinder) 3894; (V-8) 1689.

Model	Body Type	Price	Weight	Prod. Total
R6-W100 Series 4x4 — (½-Ton) — (114 in. w.b.)				
R6-W100	Chassis & Cowl	2427	3900	Note 5
R6-W100	Dart Utiline	2534	4210	Note 5
R6-W100	Dart Sweptline	2547	4310	Note 5
R6-W100	Town Panel	2840	4380	Note 5
R6-W100	Town Wagon (6-pass.)	3106	4600	Note 5
R6-W100	Town Wagon (8-pass.)	3152	4640	Note 5

NOTE 5: Total model year production: (six-cylinder) 516; (V-8) 281.

Model	Body Type	Price	Weight	Prod. Total
R6-W200 Series 4x4 — (¾-Ton) — (122 in. w.b.)				
R6-W200	Chassis & Cab	2479	4070	Note 6
R6-W200	Utiline Pickup	2586	4420	Note 6
R6-W200	Sweptline Pickup	2599	4550	Note 6
R6-W200	Platform	2622	4445	Note 6
R6-W200	Stake	2670	4645	Note 6

NOTE 6: Total model year production: (six-cylinder) 273; (V-8) 258.

Model	Body Type	Price	Weight	Prod. Total
R6-W300 Series 4x4 — (1-Ton) — (133 in. w.b.)				
R6-W300	Chassis & Cowl	2934	4090	Note 7
R6-W300	Chassis & Cab	3178	4645	Note 7
R6-W300	Utiline Pickup	3304	5045	Note 7
R6-W300	Platform	3351	5345	Note 7
R6-W300	Stake	3411	5545	Note 7

NOTE 7: Total model year production: (six-cylinder) 239; (V-8) 215.

Model	Body Type	Price	Weight	Prod. Total
R6-WM300 Series Power-Wagon — (1-Ton) — (126 in. w.b.)				
R6-WM300	Chassis & Cowl	3124	4095	Note 8
R6-WM300	Chassis & Cab	3372	4645	Note 8
R6-WM300	Utiline Pickup	3515	4920	Note 8

NOTE 8: Total model year production: 1367.

NOTE 9: Weights and prices shown are for six-cylinder models. For V-8 engine (prefix R8) add $130 to price.

ENGINE (D100 extra-light duty): Inline. Overhead valves. Slant six-cylinder. Cast iron block. Bore & stroke: 3.4 x 3.125 in. Displacement: 170.2 cu. in. Compression ratio: 8.6:1. Brake horsepower: 101 at 4000 R.P.M. Net (Taxable) horsepower: 27.70. Torque: 136 lbs.-ft. at 1600 R.P.M. Four main bearings. Solid valve lifters.

ENGINE (D100, D200, D300, W100, W200): Inline. Overhead valve. Slant six-cylinder. Cast iron block. Bore & stroke: 3.4 x 4.125 in. Displacement: 224.7 cu. in. Compression ratio: 8.2:1. Brake horsepower: 140 at 3900 R.P.M. Net horsepower: 27.70. Torque: 201 lbs.-ft. at 2000 R.P.M. Four main bearings. Solid valve lifters.

ENGINE (W300, WM300): Inline. L-head. Six-cylinder. Cast iron block. Bore & stroke: 3.437 x 4.5 in. Displacement: 250.6 cu. in. Compression ratio: 7.1:1. Brake horsepower: 125 at 3600 R.P.M. Net horsepower: 28.35. Torque: 216 lbs.-ft. at 1600 R.P.M. Four main bearings. Solid valve lifters.

ENGINE (Optional V-8): Same as 1960; see previous specifications.

CHASSIS (D100): Wheelbase: 114 in. or 122 in. Tires: 6.70 x 15 four-ply; tubeless (front and rear). GVW: 4300-5100 lbs. Axle capacity: (front) 2500 lbs; (rear) 3600 lbs.

CHASSIS (D200): Wheelbase: 122 in. Tires: 8 x 19.5 eight-ply tubeless (front and rear). GVW: 5200-7500 lbs. Axle capacity: (front) 2800 lbs; (rear) 5500 lbs.

CHASSIS (D300): Wheelbase: 133 in. Tires: 7 x 17.5 six-ply tubeless (front and rear). GVW: 6300-9000 lbs. Axle capacity: (front) 3800 lbs; (rear) 7500 lbs.

CHASSIS (W100): Wheelbase: 114 in. Tires: 7 x 17.5 six-ply tubeless (front and rear). GVW: 5100-6000 lbs. Axle capacity: (front) 3000 lbs; (rear) 4500 lbs.

CHASSIS (W200): Wheelbase: 122 in. Tires: 8 x 19.5 eight-ply (front and rear). GVW: 6000-8000 lbs. Axle capacity: (front) 3500 lbs. (rear) 5500 lbs.

CHASSIS (W300): Wheelbase: 133 in. Tires: 7.50 x 16 six-ply (front and rear). GVW: 8500-10,000 lbs. Axle capacity: (front) 4500 lbs; (rear) 7500 lbs.

CHASSIS (WM300): Wheelbase: 126 in. Tires: 9.00 x 16 ten-ply (front and rear). GVW: 8700-9500 lbs. Axle capacity: (front) 3750 lbs; (rear) 6500 lbs.

TECHNICAL: Selective sliding gear transmission. Speeds: 3F/1R except 1-ton models, 4F/1R; 4wd models, two-speed two-lever transfer case. Column or floor shift. Automatic transmission optional. Single plate dry disc clutch: (D100/200) 10 in. hydraulic; (D200, W100-300) 11 in. hydraulic;

(WM300) 11 in. mechanical. Overall axle ratio: (D100) 3.58:1, 3.91:1 or 4.56:1; (D200, W100, W200) 4.1:1 or 4.88:1; (W300) 4.88:1 or 5.87:1 (front and rear); (Power-Wagon) 5.83:1 (front and rear). Hydraulic four-wheel brakes: (D100) 11 in. drums; (D200, W100-200) 12⅛ in; (D300) 12⅛ in. front, 13 in. rear; (W300) 14⅛ in. front, 13 in. rear. Recirculating ball steering except (W300) worm and roller; (WM300) worm and sector. 35-amp alternator. One-pint oil bath air cleaner. 18-gallon gas tank inside, behind rear axle. Wheels: (D100) 15 x 5.00; (D200, W100) 16 x 6.00; (W200, D300) 17.5 x 5.25; (W300) 19.5 x 5.25; (WM300) 16 x 6.50.

OPTIONS (Factory Installed): Painted rear bumper. Bright rear bumper. Custom cab equipment. Bright hub caps (D100 only). Tinted windows. Dual electric horns. Cab corner marker lights. Inside rear-view mirror. Right sun visor. Dual electric variable-speed wipers. Windshield washer. Full-width rear window. Dual wheel rear fenders. Two-tone paint. Cigar lighter. Left armrest. Radio. Heater. Heavy-duty instruments. Foam rubber seat cushion. Auxiliary seat. Hand throttle. Rear shock absorbers. Vacuum power brake. Power steering. One-quart oil bath air cleaner. 40-amp alternator. Increased cooling capacity (manual transmission). Anti-spin rear axle. 170 cu. in. slant six engine (D100 only). 318 cu. in. V-8 engine. Oil pressure gauge. Oil filter. Engine governor. Four-speed synchromesh transmission. LoadFlite three-speed automatic transmission. Heavy-duty springs, front or rear. Three-ton hydraulic jack. (W Series 4x4 models only) Pintle hook. Power take-off. Winch, 8000-pound. (Power-Wagon only) Combined fuel/vacuum pump. Radiator overflow tank. Tow hooks. Winch, 10,000-pound.

HISTORICAL: Introduced: October 1960. Calendar year sales: 40,147. Calendar year production: 64,886. Model year production: (six-cylinder) 38,021; (V-8) 10,975; (Total) 48,996. Innovations: Reduced-height design. Slant six engine. Alternator charging system. History: Dodge ranked fifth in truck sales, as total sales fell 7.9 percent from 1959. Truck production was hindered by a December strike at the Warren plant. In August 1961, Dodge was awarded government contracts for 10,254 trucks: 8,503 military vehicles (trucks, ambulances and weapons carriers) and 1,751 walk-in, forward-control trucks for the Post Office. The postal trucks had a slant six and automatic transmission, plus plastic skylights in their roof panels. The full Dodge line of 140 basic models ranged from 4250 pounds GVW to 76,800 pounds GCW. It included conventional, cab-forward, 4wd, forward-control, school bus chassis, and tandem units.

Pricing

	5	4	3	2	1
1961					
R6-D100 Series — (½-Ton) — (114 in. w.b.)					
Utiline Pickup	850	1700	2850	4000	5700
Sweptline Pickup	840	1680	2800	3900	5600
Town Panel	870	1750	2900	4100	5800
6-pass. Wagon	890	1770	2950	4150	5900
8-pass. Wagon	890	1770	2950	4150	5900
R6-D100 Series — (½-Ton) — (122 in. w.b.)					
Utiline Pickup	840	1680	2800	3900	5600
Sweptline Pickup	870	1750	2900	4100	5800
Platform	750	1500	2500	3500	5000
Stake	770	1550	2550	3600	5100
R6-D200 Series — (¾-Ton) — (122 in. w.b.)					
Utiline Pickup	800	1600	2650	3700	5300
Sweptline Pickup	830	1650	2750	3850	5500
Platform	740	1470	2450	3350	4900
Stake	750	1500	2500	3500	5000
R6-D300 Series — (1-Ton) — (133 in. w.b.)					
Utiline Pickup	750	1500	2500	3500	5000
Platform	720	1450	2400	3300	4800
Stake	740	1470	2450	3350	4900
R6-W100 Series 4x4 — (½-Ton) — (114 in. w.b.)					
Utiline Pickup	870	1750	2900	4100	5800
Sweptline Pickup	850	1700	2850	4000	5700
Town Panel	890	1770	2950	4150	5900
6-pass. Wagon	930	1860	3100	4350	6200
8-pass. Wagon	930	1860	3100	4350	6200
R6-W200 Series 4x4 — (¾-Ton) — (122 in. w.b.)					
Utiline Pickup	830	1650	2750	3850	5500
Sweptline Pickup	850	1700	2850	4000	5700
Platform	770	1550	2550	3600	5100
Stake	780	1560	2600	3600	5200
R6-W200 Series 4x4 — (1-Ton) — (133 in. w.b.)					
Utiline Pickup	780	1560	2600	3600	5200
Platform	740	1470	2450	3350	4900
Stake	770	1550	2550	3600	5100
R6-WM300 Series — (1-Ton) — (126 in. w.b.)					
Pickup	980	1950	3250	4550	6500

NOTE: Add 10 percent for V-8 engine.
Add 5 percent for automatic transmission.

1962 DODGE

½-TON — S SERIES D100 — SIX-CYLINDER and V-8 / ¾-TON — S SERIES D200 — SIX-CYLINDER and V-8 / 1-TON — S SERIES D300 — SIX-CYLINDER and V-8: — Beginning with the 1961 R Series, Dodge Truck

reverted to a policy the Dodge Brothers had established when they made their first car back in 1914. There would be no annual model changes just for the sake of change. Instead, improvements came as soon as they were approved, rather than waiting for the next model year. The basic 1961 body styling would continue with only minor appearance changes through the 1971 model year, though many other changes would arrive during that decade. Improvements for the 1962 S Series included a new one-piece steel grille for conventional cab models, painted Sand Dune White with standard cabs but chrome plated for Custom cabs. Dodge nameplates were attached to the upper rear of the front fenders. A model number plate sat at the center of the grille. Solid vinyl, heavy-duty upholstery fabrics gave longer life in conventional cab, Town Panel and Town Wagon models. Both doors on Custom cab, Town Panels and Wagons had key locks. D100 Town Panel/Wagon models gained dual electric variable-speed wipers. A new LoadFlite automatic transmission, available with any engine, had 10 percent more torque capacity. Conventional cabs had a wide, easy-to-read speedometer with black numbers against a white background for greater visibility. Sealing against air, dust and water was improved. Point life was virtually doubled by a ventilated-point distributor and more efficient condenser. A new heavy-duty solenoid-shift starter was standard on all gas models (except the Power-Wagon). Both 170 and 225 cu. in. slant six engines and the 318 cu. in. V-8 continued without change. The only new model was a ½-ton Forward-Control chassis, making that line complete from ½- to 1½-tons. A six-man crew cab pickup arrived in mid-year (see 1963 listing). Standard paint colors were carried over from 1961. This was the first year for Dodge's 5-year, 50,000-mile warranty.

1962 Dodge D100 Sweptline Pickup (OCW)

½-TON 4x4 — S SERIES W100 — SIX-CYLINDER and V-8 / ¾-TON 4x4 — S SERIES W200 — SIX-CYLINDER and V-8 / 1-TON 4x4 — S SERIES W300 — SIX-CYLINDER and V-8 / 1-TON POWER-WAGON — S SERIES WM300 — SIX-CYLINDER: — A closed-crankcase ventilating system was made standard on V-8 4wd models, and on the WM300. Power-Wagon front and rear fenders were now painted body color. Otherwise, these models continued with little change.

1962 Dodge D200 Sweptline Pickup (OCW)

1962 Dodge D100 Tradesman Utility Body (OCW)

I.D. DATA: Serial numbers were in the same locations as in 1961. Starting Serial Numbers: (D100 Six) 26D1-L100001; (D100 V-8) 28D1-L100001; (D200 Six) 26D2-L100001; (D200 V-8) 28D2-L100001; (D300 Six) 26D3-L100001; (D300 V-8) 28D3-L100001; (W100 Six) 26W1-L100001; (W100 V-8) 28W1-L100001; (W200 Six) 26W2-L100001; (W200 V-8) 28W2-L100001; (W300 Six) 26W3-L100001; (W300 V-8) 28W3-L100001; (WM300) 26WM3-L100001. Engine numbers were in the same locations as in 1961. Starting Engine Numbers: (225 cu. in. Six) TS-22-8-3-1001; (251 cu. in. Six) TS-25-8-3-1001; (318 cu. in. V-8) TS-318-8-3-1001. Ending serial and engine numbers are not available.

Model	Body Type	Price	Weight	Prod. Total
S6-D100 Series — (½-Ton) — (114 in. w.b.)				
S6-D100	Chassis & Cowl	1459	2540	Note 1
S6-D100	Chassis & Cab	1694	3095	Note 1
S6-D100	Utiline Pickup	1800	3405	Note 1
S6-D100	Sweptline Pickup	1814	3505	Note 1
S6-D100	Town Panel	1990	3565	Note 1
S6-D100	Town Wagon (6-pass.)	2263	3795	Note 1
S6-D100	Town Wagon (8-pass.)	2310	3845	Note 1
(122 in. w.b.)				
S6-D100	Chassis & Cowl	1494	2565	Note 2
S6-D100	Chassis & Cab	1728	3120	Note 2
S6-D100	Utiline Pickup	1835	3470	Note 2
S6-D100	Sweptline Pickup	1848	3600	Note 2
S6-D100	Platform	1871	3495	Note 2
S6-D100	Stake	1919	3695	Note 2

NOTE 1: Total model year production: (six) 16,019; (V-8) 2824.

NOTE 2: Total model year production: (six) 8770; (V-8) 4752.

Model	Body Type	Price	Weight	Prod. Total
S6-D200 Series — (¾-Ton) — (122 in. w.b.)				
S6-D200	Chassis & Cowl	1590	3060	Note 3
S6-D200	Chassis & Cab	1838	3615	Note 3
S6-D200	Utiline Pickup	1940	3965	Note 3
S6-D200	Sweptline Pickup	1954	4095	Note 3
S6-D200	Platform	1976	3990	Note 3
S6-D200	Stake	2024	4190	Note 3

NOTE 3: Total model year production: (six) 3789; (V-8) 2161.

Model	Body Type	Price	Weight	Prod. Total
S6-D300 Series — (1-Ton) — (133 in. w.b.)				
S6-D300	Chassis & Cowl	1748	3220	Note 4
S6-D300	Chassis & Cab	1992	3775	Note 4
S6-D300	Utiline Pickup	2118	4175	Note 4
S6-D300	Platform	2164	4475	Note 4
S6-D300	Stake	2223	4675	Note 4

NOTE 4: Total model year production: (six) 4358; (V-8) 1983.

Model	Body Type	Price	Weight	Prod. Total
S6-W100 Series 4x4 — (½-Ton) — (114 in. w.b.)				
S6-W100	Chassis & Cab	2367	3900	Note 5
S6-W100	Utiline Pickup	2474	4210	Note 5
S6-W100	Sweptline Pickup	2487	4310	Note 5
S6-W100	Town Panel	2780	4370	Note 5
S6-W100	Town Wagon (6-pass.)	3046	4600	Note 5
S6-W100	Town Wagon (8-pass.)	3092	4640	Note 5

NOTE 5: Total model year production: (six) 490; (V-8) 297.

Model	Body Type	Price	Weight	Prod. Total
S6-W200 Series 4x4 — (¾-Ton) — (122 in. w.b.)				
S6-W200	Chassis & Cab	2418	4070	Note 6
S6-W200	Utiline Pickup	2525	4420	Note 6
S6-W200	Sweptline Pickup	2538	4550	Note 6
S6-W200	Platform	2561	4445	Note 6
S6-W200	Stake	2609	4645	Note 6

NOTE 6: Total model year production: (six) 805; (V-8) 375.

Model	Body Type	Price	Weight	Prod. Total
S6-W300 Series 4x4 — (1-Ton) — (133 in. w.b.)				
S6-W300	Chassis & Cowl	2934	4090	Note 7
S6-W300	Chassis & Cab	3178	4645	Note 7
S6-W300	Utiline Pickup	3304	5045	Note 7
S6-W300	Platform	3351	5345	Note 7
S6-W300	Stake	3411	5545	Note 7

NOTE 7: Total model year production: (six) 221; (V-8) 280.

1962 Dodge W200 Sweptline Power Wagon (OCW)

Model	Body Type	Price	Weight	Prod. Total
S6-WM300 Series Power-Wagon — (1-Ton) — (126 in. w.b.)				
S6-WM300	Chassis & Cowl	3124	4095	Note 8
S6-WM300	Chassis & Cab	3372	4645	Note 8
S6-WM300	Utiline Pickup	3515	4920	Note 8

NOTE 8: Total model year production: 2141 (plus 1544 M.D.A.P.).

NOTE 9: Weights and prices shown are for 6-cyl. models. For V-8 engine (prefix S8) add $120 to price.

1962 Dodge W300 Utiline Power Wagon (OCW)

ENGINE (D100 extra-light duty): Inline. Overhead valves. Slant six-cylinder. Cast iron block. Bore & stroke: 3.4 x 3.125 in. Displacement: 170.2 cu. in. Compression ratio: 8.6:1. Brake horsepower: 101 at 4000 R.P.M. Net (Taxable) horsepower: 27.70. Torque: 145 lbs.-ft. at 1600 R.P.M. Four main bearings. Solid valve lifters.

1962 Dodge D300 Sweptline Power Wagon Wrecker

ENGINE (D100, D200, D300, W100, W200): Inline. Overhead valves. Slant six-cylinder. Cast iron block. Bore & stroke: 3.4 x 4.125 in. Displacement: 224.7 cu. in. Compression ratio: 8.2:1. Brake horsepower: 140 at 3900 R.P.M. Net horsepower: 27.70. Torque: 215 lbs.-ft. at 1600 R.P.M. Four main bearings. Solid valve lifters.

1962 Dodge WM300 Military Type Power Wagon (OCW)

ENGINE (W300, WM300): Inline. L-head. Six-cylinder. Cast iron block. Bore & stroke: 3.437 x 4.5 in. Displacement: 250.6 cu. in. Compression ratio: 7.1:1. Brake horsepower: 125 at 3600 R.P.M. Net horsepower: 28.35. Torque: 216 lbs.-ft. at 1600 R.P.M. Four main bearings. Solid valve lifters.

ENGINE (Optional V-8): Same as 1960-61; see previous specifications.

CHASSIS: Same as 1961; see previous specifications.

TECHNICAL: Same as 1961; see previous specifications.

OPTIONS: Same list and prices as 1961.

197

1962 Dodge D100 6/8-Passenger Town Wagon (OCW)

1962 Dodge D100 7½-foot Town Panel (OCW)

HISTORICAL: Introduced: September 28, 1961. Calendar year sales: 59,118. Calendar year production: 96,102. Model year production: (6-cyl.) 53,542; (V-8) 12,672; (Total) 66,214. Historical notes: Dodge Truck had a very good year as production rose 48.1 percent. A heavy-duty version of the 225 cu. in. slant six arrived in medium-duty trucks. Also new was a light weight 6-cyl. diesel from Dodge-Perkins, introduced in spring 1962. Dodge produced 1000 diesel-powered trucks. Of the gasoline-powered trucks, 69.5 percent were 6-cyl., whereas the V-8 was most popular in passenger cars. Heavy-duty truck warranty coverage on major gas engine components was extended to 100,000 miles. No appearance changes came to the medium and high-tonnage low-cab-forward (LCF) models. Dodge exhibited its gas turbine powered truck at the Chicago Automobile Show in February. The 1962 line consisted of 141 basic models from ½- to 5-ton capacity, all built in the Warren, Michigan truck plant.

1962 Dodge W100 Town Power Wagon (OCW)

1962 Dodge D300 9-foot body Platform Stake (OCW)

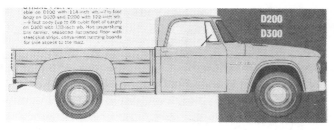

1962 Dodge D200 Utiline Pickup (OCW)

198

Pricing

1962	5	4	3	2	1
S6-D100 Series — (½-Ton) — (114 in. w.b.)					
Utiline Pickup	850	1700	2850	4000	5700
Sweptline Pickup	840	1680	2800	3900	5600
Town Panel	870	1750	2900	4100	5800
6-pass. Wagon	890	1770	2950	4150	5900
8-pass. Wagon	890	1770	2950	4150	5900
S6-D100 Series — (½-Ton) — (122 in. w.b.)					
Utiline Pickup	840	1680	2800	3900	5600
Sweptline Pickup	870	1750	2900	4100	5800
Platform	750	1500	2500	3500	5000
Stake	770	1550	2550	3600	5100
S6-D200 Series — (¾-Ton) — (122 in. w.b.)					
Utiline Pickup	800	1600	2650	3700	5300
Sweptline Pickup	830	1650	2750	3850	5500
Platform	740	1470	2450	3350	4900
Stake	750	1500	2500	3500	5000
S6-D300 Series — (1-Ton) — (133 in. w.b.)					
Utiline Pickup	750	1500	2500	3500	5000
Platform	720	1450	2400	3300	4800
Stake	740	1470	2450	3350	4900
S6-W100 Series 4x4 — (½-Ton) — (114 in. w.b.)					
Utiline Pickup	870	1750	2900	4100	5800
Sweptline Pickup	850	1700	2850	4000	5700
Town Panel	890	1770	2950	4150	5900
6-pass. Wagon	930	1860	3100	4350	6200
8-pass. Wagon	930	1860	3100	4350	6200
S6-W200 Series 4x4 — (¾-Ton) — (122 in. w.b.)					
Utiline Pickup	8300	1650	2750	3850	5500
Sweptline Pickup	850	1700	2850	4000	5700
Platform	770	1550	2550	3600	5100
Stake	780	1560	2600	3600	5200
S6-W300 Series 4x4 — (1-Ton) — (133 in. w.b.)					
Utiline Pickup	780	1560	2600	3600	5200
Platform	740	1470	2450	3350	4900
Stake	770	1550	2550	3600	5100
S6-WM300 Power-Wagon — (1-Ton) — (126 in. w.b.)					
Pickup	980	1950	3250	4550	6500

NOTE: Add 10 percent for V-8 engine.
Add 5 percent for automatic transmission.

1963 DODGE

1963 Dodge D200 Sweptline Power Wagon (OCW)

½-TON — T SERIES D100 — SIX-CYLINDER and V-8 / ¾-TON — T SERIES D200 — SIX-CYLINDER and V-8 / 1-TON — T SERIES D300 — SIX-CYLINDER and V-8: — Dodge Truck continued its policy of product improvements whenever possible throughout the year, instead of automatic annual styling changes. Appearance was identical to 1962 models, including standard paint colors. Crew cab (6-man) models on 146 in. w.b., introduced midway in the 1962 model year, were available in D200 ¾-ton capacity with 6½-ft. Utiline or Sweptline pickup boxes. Crew cabs were also offered in medium-tonnage models D400 through D700. Improvements included a new, more efficient oil cooler for the LoadFlite automatic transmission. Seat cushions offered more comfort and longer wear on conventional cab and cab-forward models. Full-depth foam cushioning was now standard on Custom cab seat and optional for standard cabs. Driver's side armrests became standard on Custom cabs, but passenger armrests cost extra. All cabs now had locks on both doors, operated by the ignition key. All models in light, medium and heavy-tonnage carried over. No changes were made to Town Panel, Town Wagon or Forward-Control chassis models. Standard equipment was unchanged except for the addition of a one-quart oil-filter.

½-TON 4x4 — T SERIES W100 — SIX-CYLINDER and V-8 / ¾-TON 4x4 — T SERIES W200 — SIX-CYLINDER and V-8 / 1-TON 4x4 — T SERIES W300 — SIX-CYLINDER and V-8 / 1-TON POWER-WAGON — T SERIES WM300 — SIX-CYLINDER: Crew cab models were available in the W200 series with Utiline or Sweptline pickup boxes, as well as in the heavier W500 4wd series. Other changes were the same as the D Series. Power-Wagons carried on without change. W300 models now carried a 225 cu. in. six as standard equipment.

I.D. DATA: Serial numbers were stamped on a plate on the left door lock pillar. New serial number coding produced a 10-digit number. The first two digits indicated the Model Code; the third digit showed number of cylinders; and the last seven digits were the sequence number. Model Codes were as follows: (D100) 11; (D200) 12; (D300) 13; (W100) 21; (W200) 22; (W300) 23; (WM300) 24; (P100/200/300 Forward-Control) 30, 31 and 32. Example: 116 1,230,000 indicates model D100 with 6-cyl. engine, sequence number 1,230,000. Starting Serial (Sequence) Number: 1,230,000. Ending serial numbers are not available. Engine numbers were located as follows: (170 and 225 cu. in. Six) right side of block, on top of boss directly behind coil; (251 cu. in. Six) left front of block, at top; (318 cu. in. V-8) left front of block, under cylinder head. The first two letters designated the Series (TT, VT, AT, B, BT, C or CT). The next two digits indicated engine displacement. Third and fourth digits showed the month and date of manufacture. Then came the sequence number. Starting and ending numbers are not available.

1963 Dodge D100 Sweptline Pickup (D. Sagvold)

Model	Body Type	Price	Weight	Prod. Total
T6-D100 Series — (½-Ton) — (114 in. w.b.)				
T6-D100	Chassis & Cowl	1468	2540	Note 1
T6-D100	Chassis & Cab	1703	3095	Note 1
T6-D100	Utiline Pickup	1809	3405	Note 1
T6-D100	Sweptline Pickup	1823	3505	Note 1
T6-D100	Town Panel	2007	3565	Note 1
T6-D100	Town Wagon (6-pass.)	2272	3795	Note 1
T6-D100	Town Wagon (8-pass.)	2319	3845	Note 1
(122 in. w.b.)				
T6-D100	Chassis & Cowl	1503	2565	Note 2
T6-D100	Chassis & Cab	1737	3120	Note 2
T6-D100	Utiline Pickup	1844	3470	Note 2
T6-D100	Sweptline Pickup	1857	3600	Note 2
T6-D100	Platform	1880	3495	Note 2
T6-D100	Stake	1928	3695	Note 2

NOTE 1: Total model year production: (six) 19,375; (V-8) 4166.

NOTE 2: Total model year production: (six) 12,920; (V-8) 7392.

T6-D200 Series — (¾-Ton) — (122 in. w.b.)				
T6-D200	Chassis & Cowl	1599	3070	Note 3
T6-D200	Chassis & Cab	1843	3625	Note 3
T6-D200	Utiline Pickup	1949	3975	Note 3
T6-D200	Sweptline Pickup	1963	4105	Note 3
T6-D200	Platform	1985	4000	Note 3
T6-D200	Stake	2033	4200	Note 3
T6-D200 Crew Cab Series — (¾-Ton) — (146 in. w.b.)				
T6-D200	Chassis	2451	3973	—
T6-D200	Utiline Pickup	2557	4285	—
T6-D200	Sweptline Pickup	2571	4385	—

NOTE 3: Total model year production: (six) 7324; (V-8) 4639.

T6-D300 Series — (1-Ton) — (133 in. w.b.)				
T6-D300	Chassis & Cowl	1757	3220	Note 4
T6-D300	Chassis & Cab	2021	3775	Note 4
T6-D300	Utiline Pickup	2147	4175	Note 4
T6-D300	Platform	2193	4475	Note 4
T6-D300	Stake	2252	4675	Note 4

NOTE 4: Total model year production: (six) 4571; (V-8) 2930.

Model	Body Type	Price	Weight	Prod. Total
T6-W100 Series 4x4 — (½-Ton) — (114 in. w.b.)				
T6-W100	Chassis & Cab	2379	3900	Note 5
T6-W100	Utiline Pickup	2486	4210	Note 5
T6-W100	Sweptline Pickup	2499	4310	Note 5
T6-W100	Town Panel	2792	4370	Note 5
T6-W100	Town Wagon (6-pass.)	3058	4600	Note 5
T6-W100	Town Wagon (8-pass.)	3104	4640	Note 5

NOTE 5: Total model year production: (six) 951; (V-8) 445.

T6-W200 Series 4x4 — (¾-Ton) — (122 in. w.b.)				
T6-W200	Chassis & Cab	2430	4070	Note 6
T6-W200	Utiline Pickup	2537	4420	Note 6
T6-W200	Sweptline Pickup	2550	4550	Note 6
T6-W200	Platform	2573	4445	Note 6
T6-W200	Stake	2621	4645	Note 6
T6-W200 Crew Cab Series 4x4 — (¾-Ton) — (146 in. w.b.)				
T6-W200	Chassis	3149	4259	—
T6-W200	Utiline Pickup	3256	4569	—
T6-W200	Sweptline Pickup	3269	4669	—

NOTE 6: Total model year production: (six) 2385; (V-8) 764.

T6-W300 Series 4x4 — (1-Ton) — (133 in. w.b.)				
T6-W300	Chassis & Cowl	2943	4090	Note 7
T6-W300	Chassis & Cab	3187	4645	Note 7
T6-W300	Utiline Pickup	3313	5045	Note 7
T6-W300	Platform	3360	5345	Note 7
T6-W300	Stake	3420	5545	Note 7

NOTE 7: Total model year production: (six) 298; (V-8) 335.

T6-WM300 Series Power-Wagon — (1-Ton) — (126 in. w.b.)				
T6-WM300	Chassis & Cowl	3140	4095	Note 8
T6-WM300	Chassis & Cab	3388	4520	Note 8
T6-WM300	Utiline Pickup	3531	4920	Note 8

NOTE 8: Total model year production: 3386 (plus 1302 M.D.A.P. models).

NOTE 9: Weights and prices shown are for 6-cyl. models. For V-8 engine (prefix S8) add $120 to price.

1963 Dodge D100 Sweptline Pickup (D. Sagvold)

ENGINE (D100 extra-light duty): Inline. Overhead valves. Slant six-cylinder. Cast iron block. Bore & stroke: 3.4 x 3.125 in. Displacement: 170.2 cu. in. Compression ratio: 8.6:1. Brake horsepower: 101 at 4000 R.P.M. Net (Taxable) horsepower: 27.70. Torque: 145 lbs.-ft. at 1600 R.P.M. Four main bearings. Solid valve lifters.

ENGINE (D100, D200, D300, W100, W200): Inline. Overhead valves. Slant six-cylinder. Cast iron block. Bore & stroke: 3.4 x 4.125 in. Displacement: 224.7 cu. in. Compression ratio: 8.2:1. Brake horsepower: 140 at 3900 R.P.M. Net horsepower: 27.70. Torque: 215 lbs.-ft. at 1600 R.P.M. Four main bearings. Solid valve lifters.

ENGINE (W300): Same as W200, but heavy-duty version to meet rugged demands.

ENGINE (WM300): Inline. L-head. Six-cylinder. Cast iron block. Bore & stroke: 3.437 x 4.5 in. Displacement: 250.6 cu. in. Compression ratio: 7.1:1. Brake horsepower: 125 at 3600 R.P.M. Net horsepower: 28.35. Torque: 216 lbs.-ft. at 1600 R.P.M. Four main bearings. Solid valve lifters.

ENGINE (Optional: D100, D200, D300, W100, W200): 90-degree, overhead valve. Eight-cylinder. Cast iron block. Bore & stroke: 3.91 x 3.312 in. Displacement: 318.1 cu. in. Compression ratio: 8.25:1. Brake horsepower: 200 at 3900 R.P.M. Net horsepower: 48.92. Torque: 286 lbs.-ft. at 2400 R.P.M. Five main bearings. Hydraulic valve lifters.

ENGINE (Optional, W300): Same as V-8 above, but heavy-duty. Brake horsepower: 202 at 3900 R.P.M. Torque: 288 lbs.-ft. at 2400 R.P.M. Compression ratio: 7.5:1.

199

CHASSIS (D100): Wheelbase: 114 in. or 122 in. Tires: 6.70 x 15 four-ply tubeless (front and rear). GVW: 4300-5100 lbs.

CHASSIS (D200): Wheelbase: 122 in. or 146 in. (Crew Cab). Tires: 7 x 17.5 six-ply tubeless (front and rear). GVW: 5200-7500 lbs.

CHASSIS (D300): Wheelbase: 133 in. Tires: 7 x 17.5 six-ply tubeless (front and rear). GVW: 6300-9000 lbs.

CHASSIS (W100): Wheelbase: 114 in. Tires: 7 x 17.5 six-ply tubeless (front and rear). GVW: 5100-6000 lbs.

CHASSIS (W200): Wheelbase: 122 in. or 146 in. (Crew Cab). Tires: 8 x 19.5 eight-ply (front/rear) except Crew Cab, 7 x 17.5 six-ply. GVW: 6000-8000 lbs.

CHASSIS (W300): Wheelbase: 133 in. Tires: 7.50 x 16 six-ply (front/rear). GVW: 8500-10,000 lbs.

CHASSIS (WM300): Wheelbase: 126 in. Tires: 9.00 x 16 ten-ply (front/rear). GVW: 8700-9500 lbs.

TECHNICAL: Same as 1961-62; see previous specifications.

OPTIONS (Factory-Installed): No. 1 trim package for D Series Utiline pickup, platform or stake: bright metal moldings on hood, cowl, door and cab back. No. 2 Trim Package for D100/200 Sweptline pickup: bright metal bumper; molding on hood, cowl, door, cab back and bodysides. Left side armrest (D/W100 panel, standard cab). Right and left armrest (D/W100 panel, standard cab). Right side armrest (Custom cab). 318 cu. in. V-8 engine ($120). Vacuum power brakes ($45). Anti-spin rear axle ($65). LoadFlite 3-speed automatic transmission ($220). Three-speed transmission on D300 ($35). Four-speed transmission on 100/200 models ($85). Undercoating.

HISTORICAL: Introduced: October, 1962. Calendar year sales: 75,025. Calendar year production: 110,987. Model year production: (6-cyl.) 67,685; (V-8) 20,671; (Total) 88,356. Innovations: Crew Cab 4-dr. pickup model. Historical notes: Dodge Truck had its best year since 1952, with a production gain of 15.5 percent and sales increase of 35 percent. Exports and government sales were substantial. Dodge produced 2,137 diesel trucks, all 6-cyl., recording an impressive sales gain. Of the total gasoline-powered trucks produced, 70,996 were 6-cyl. and 37,854 were V-8 powered.

Pricing

1963	5	4	3	2	1
T6-D100 Series — (½-Ton) — (114 in. w.b.)					
Utiline Pickup	850	1700	2850	4000	5700
Sweptline Pickup	840	1680	2800	3900	5600
Town Panel	870	1750	2900	4100	5800
6-pass. Wagon	890	1770	2950	4150	5900
8-pass. Wagon	890	1770	2950	4150	5900
T6-D100 Series — (½-Ton) — (122 in. w.b.)					
Utiline Pickup	840	1680	2800	3900	5600
Sweptline Pickup	870	1750	2900	4100	5800
Platform	750	1500	2500	3500	5000
Stake	770	1550	2550	3600	5100
T6-D200 Series — (¾-Ton) — (122 in. w.b.)					
Utiline Pickup	800	1600	2650	3700	5300
Sweptline Pickup	830	1650	2750	3850	5500
Platform	740	1470	2450	3350	4900
Stake	750	1500	2500	3500	5000
T6-D200 Crew Cab — (¾-Ton) — (146 in. w.b.)					
Utiline Pickup	770	1550	2550	3600	5100
Sweptline Pickup	780	1560	2600	3600	5200
T6-D300 Series — (1-Ton) — (133 in. w.b.)					
Utiline Pickup	750	1500	2500	3500	5000
Platform	720	1450	2400	3300	4800
Stake	740	1470	2450	3350	4900
T6-W100 Series 4x4 — (½-Ton) — (114 in. w.b.)					
Utiline Pickup	870	1750	2900	4100	5800
Sweptline Pickup	850	1700	2850	4000	5700
Town Panel	890	1770	2950	4150	5900
6-pass. Wagon	930	1860	3100	4350	6200
8-pass. Wagon	930	1860	3100	4350	6200
T6-W200 Series 4x4 — (¾-Ton) — (122 in. w.b.)					
Utiline Pickup	830	1650	2750	3850	5500
Sweptline Pickup	850	1700	2850	4000	5700
Platform	770	1550	2550	3600	5100
Stake	780	1560	2600	3600	5200
T6-W200 Crew Cab — (¾-Ton) — (146 in. w.b.)					
Utiline Pickup	750	1500	2500	3500	5000
Sweptline Pickup	770	1550	2550	3600	5100
T6-W300 Series — (1-Ton) — (133 in. w.b.)					
Utiline Pickup	780	1560	2600	3600	5200
Platform	740	1470	2450	3350	4900
Stake	770	1550	2550	3600	5100
T6-WM300 Power-Wagon — (1-Ton) — (126 in. w.b.)					
Utiline Pickup	980	1950	3250	4550	6500

NOTE: Add 10 percent for V-8 engine.
       Add 5 percent for automatic transmission.

1964 DODGE

½-TON COMPACT — V SERIES A100 — SIX-CYLINDER / ½-TON — V SERIES D100 — SIX-CYLINDER and V-8 / ¾-TON — V SERIES D200 — SIX-CYLINDER and V-8 / 1-TON — V SERIES D300 — SIX-CYLINDER and V-8: — No changes were made in this third year of the V-Series light-duty conventional trucks, in either appearance or specifications. Only in standard paint colors was there a change, as Sand Dune White was replaced by Dodge Truck White. All efforts went toward developing two mid-year introductions, which began production in February, 1964. One was a high-tonnage tilt-cab diesel, with and without sleeper. The second new entry was the compact A100 series — a light-duty, forward-control pickup, van and wagon. With a level load floor and simple, utilitarian styling, the 90 in. w.b. A100 van was shorter, wider and higher than a Ford or Chevrolet Greenbriar. It weighed about the same as a Greenbriar and 200 pounds more than a Ford Econoline. Total load space was 213 cu. ft. An A100 wagon could carry 9 passengers. Both 170 and 225 cu. in. slant sixes were available. The 225 was the largest engine in the compact truck field. Three-speed manual shift was standard, while three-speed LoadFlite automatic transmission, its shift lever conveniently located on the dash, was an option. A100 driving position was termed excellent, its front bucket seats firm and form-fitting. Dodge also introduced the Camper Wagon, an A100 Sportsman wagon specially equipped by Travel Equipment Corp. with pop-up roof and living facilities for up to six people. Recognizing the tremendous growth in popularity of pickup trucks, Dodge built the first sports-type truck, the Custom Sports Special. Available as an option package with either a Utiline or Sweptline box in D100 or D200 capacity, the Custom Sports carried a long list of features that set it apart from standard pickups. Those extras included black vinyl upholstered bucket seats (from a Dart GT), plush carpeting from firewall to top of gas tank behind the seat, dual armrests, a between-seat console (from Polara 500) with lighter and map light, four hood stripes, chrome front bumper and grille, chrome hub caps, whitewall tires, twin sunvisors, insulated headlining, and heat/noise insulation. In addition to the slant six or 318 cu. in. V-8, the Custom Sports could have an optional 426 cu. in. high-performance V-8 engine. All Custom Sports engines had chrome air cleaners and valve covers.

½-TON 4x4 — V SERIES W100 — SIX-CYLINDER and V-8 / ¾-TON 4x4 — V SERIES W200 — SIX-CYLINDER and V-8 / 1-TON 4x4 — V SERIES W300 — SIX-CYLINDER and V-8 / 1-TON POWER-WAGON — V SERIES WM300 — SIX-CYLINDER: — The Custom Sports Package described above was also available on W100 and W200 pickups. Power-Wagons entered yet another year in their long history without change.

I.D. DATA: Serial numbers were in the same locations as 1963, with the same coding. Model Codes were as follows: (D100) 11; (D200) 12; (D300) 13; (A100 Pickup) 18; (A100 Van) 19; (A100 Wagon) 20; (W100) 21; (W200) 22; (W300) 23; (WM300) 24. Starting Serial Number: (A100 models) 2,000,001; (all others) 1,315,000. Ending serial numbers are not available. Engine numbers were in the same location as 1963. Starting and ending numbers are not available.

Model	Body Type	Price	Weight	Prod. Total
V6-A100 Series — (½-Ton) — (90 in. w.b.)				
V6-A100	Pickup	—	—	Note 1
V6-A100	Van	—	—	Note 1
V6-A100	Wagon	—	—	Note 1

NOTE 1: Total model year production: 11,046.

Model	Body Type	Price	Weight	Prod. Total
V6-D100 Series — (½-Ton) — (114 in. w.b.)				
V6-D100	Chassis & Cowl	1468	2540	Note 2
V6-D100	Chassis & Cab	1703	3095	Note 2
V6-D100	Utiline Pickup	1809	3405	Note 2
V6-D100	Sweptline Pickup	1823	3505	Note 2
V6-D100	Town Panel	2007	3565	Note 2
V6-D100	Town Wagon (6-pass.)	2272	3795	Note 2
V6-D100	Town Wagon (8-pass.)	2319	3845	Note 2
(122 in. w.b.)				
V6-D100	Chassis & Cowl	1503	2565	Note 3
V6-D100	Chassis & Cab	1737	3120	Note 3
V6-D100	Utiline Pickup	1844	3470	Note 3
V6-D100	Sweptline Pickup	1857	3600	Note 3
V6-D100	Platform	1880	3495	Note 3
V6-D100	Stake	1928	3695	Note 3

NOTE 2: Total model year production: (six) 24,022; (V-8) 4564.

NOTE 3: Total model year production: (six) 14,469; (V-8) 11,917.

Model	Body Type	Price	Weight	Prod. Total
V6-D200 Series — (¾-Ton) — (122 in. w.b.)				
V6-D200	Chassis & Cowl	1599	3070	Note 4
V6-D200	Chassis & Cab	1843	3625	Note 4
V6-D200	Utiline Pickup	1949	3975	Note 4
V6-D200	Sweptline Pickup	1963	4105	Note 4
V6-D200	Platform	1985	4000	Note 4
V6-D200	Stake	2033	4200	Note 4
V6-D200 Crew Cab Series — (¾-Ton) — (146 in. w.b.)				
V6-D200	Chassis	2451	3973	—
V6-D200	Utiline Pickup	2557	4285	—
V6-D200	Sweptline Pickup	2571	4385	—

NOTE 4: Total model year production: (six) 6435; (V-8) 7117.

Model	Body Type	Price	Weight	Prod. Total
V6-D300 Series — (1-Ton) — (133 in. w.b.)				
V6-D300	Chassis & Cowl	1757	3220	Note 5
V6-D300	Chassis & Cab	2021	3775	Note 5
V6-D300	Utiline Pickup	2147	4175	Note 5
V6-D300	Platform	2193	4475	Note 5
V6-D300	Stake	2252	4675	Note 5

NOTE 5: Total model year production: (six) 4263; (V-8) 3263.

Model	Body Type	Price	Weight	Prod. Total
V6-W100 Series 4x4 — (½-Ton) — (114 in. w.b.)				
V6-W100	Chassis & Cab	2379	3900	Note 6
V6-W100	Utiline Pickup	2486	4210	Note 6
V6-W100	Sweptline Pickup	2499	4310	Note 6
V6-W100	Town Panel	2792	4370	Note 6
V6-W100	Town Wagon (6-pass.)	3058	4600	Note 6
V6-W100	Town Wagon (8-pass.)	3104	4640	Note 6

NOTE 6: Total model year production: (six) 955; (V-8) 504.

Model	Body Type	Price	Weight	Prod. Total
V6-W200 Series 4x4 — (¾-Ton) — (122 in. w.b.)				
V6-W200	Chassis & Cab	2430	4070	Note 7
V6-W200	Utiline Pickup	2537	4420	Note 7
V6-W200	Sweptline Pickup	2550	4550	Note 7
V6-W200	Platform	2573	4445	Note 7
V6-W200	Stake	2621	4645	Note 7
V6-W200 Crew Cab Series 4x4 — (¾-Ton) — (146 in. w.b.)				
V6-W200	Chassis	3149	4259	—
V6-W200	Utiline Pickup	3256	4569	—
V6-W200	Sweptline Pickup	3269	4669	—

NOTE 7: Total model year production: (six) 2058; (V-8) 989.

Model	Body Type	Price	Weight	Prod. Total
V6-W300 Series 4x4 — (1-Ton) — (133 in. w.b.)				
V6-W300	Chassis & Cowl	2943	4090	Note 8
V6-W300	Chassis & Cab	3187	4645	Note 8
V6-W300	Utiline Pickup	3313	5045	Note 8
V6-W300	Platform	3360	5345	Note 8
V6-W300	Stake	3420	5545	Note 8

NOTE 8: Total model year production: (six) 289; (V-8) 333.

Model	Body Type	Price	Weight	Prod. Total
V6-WM300 Series Power-Wagon — (1-Ton) — (126 in. w.b.)				
V6-WM300	Chassis & Cowl	3140	4095	Note 8
V6-WM300	Chassis & Cab	3388	4520	Note 8
V6-WM300	Utiline Pickup	3531	4920	Note 8

NOTE 8: Total model year production: 5428 (plus 486 M.D.A.P. models).

NOTE 9: Weights and prices shown are for 6-cyl. models. For V-8 engine (prefix S8) add $120 to price.

ENGINE (A100 and D100 extra-light duty): Inline. Overhead valves. Slant six-cylinder. Cast iron block. Bore & stroke: 3.4 x 3.125 in. Displacement: 170.2 cu. in. Compression ratio: 8.5:1. Brake horsepower: 101 at 4000 R.P.M. Net (Taxable) horsepower: 27.70. Torque: 145 lbs.-ft. at 1600 R.P.M. Four main bearings. Solid valve lifters.

ENGINE (A100, D100, D200, D300, W100, W200): Inline. Overhead valves. Slant six-cylinder. Cast iron block. Bore & stroke: 3.4 x 4.125 in. Displacement: 224.7 cu. in. Compression ratio: 8.4:1. Brake horsepower: 140 at 3900 R.P.M. Net horsepower: 27.70. Torque: 215 lbs.-ft. at 1600 R.P.M. Four main bearings. Solid valve lifters.

ENGINE (W300): Same as W200, but premium heavy-duty version to meet rugged demands.

ENGINE (WM300): Same as 1963, see previous specifications.

ENGINE (Optional 318 cu. in. V-8): Same as 1963, see previous specifications.

ENGINE (Custom Sports Package: D100, D200, W100, W200): 90-degree, overhead valve, single rocker. Eight-cylinder. Cast iron block. Bore & stroke: 4.25 x 3.75 in. Displacement: 426 cu. in. Compression ratio: 10.3:1. Brake horsepower: 365 at 4800 R.P.M. Net (Taxable) horsepower: 57.8. Torque: 470 lbs.-ft. at 3200 R.P.M. Five main bearings. Hydraulic valve lifters. Carburetor: Single 4-barrel.

CHASSIS (A100): Wheelbase: 90 in. Tires: 6.50 x 13 four-ply. GVW: 3800 lbs. Axle Capacity: (front) 2200 lbs.; (rear) 3000 lbs.

CHASSIS (D100): Wheelbase: 114 in. or 122 in. Tires: 6.70 x 15 four-ply. GVW: 4300-5100 lbs. Axle Capacity: (front) 2500 lbs.; (rear) 3600 lbs.

CHASSIS (D200): Wheelbase: 122 in. or 146 in. Tires: 6.50 x 16 six-ply. GVW: 5200-7500 lbs. Axle Capacity: (front) 2800 lbs.; (rear) 5500 lbs.

CHASSIS (D300): Wheelbase: 133 in. Tires: 8 x 17.5 six-ply. GVW: 6300-9000 lbs. Axle Capacity: (front) 3800 lbs.; (rear) 7500 lbs.

CHASSIS (W100): Wheelbase: 114 in. Tires: 6.50 x 16 six-ply. GVW: 5100-6000 lbs. Axle Capacity: (front) 3000 lbs.; (rear) 4500 lbs.

CHASSIS (W200): Wheelbase: 122 in. or 146 in. (Crew Cab). Tires: 7 x 17.5 six-ply. GVW: 6000-8000 lbs. Axle Capacity: (front) 3000 lbs.; (rear) 5500 lbs.

CHASSIS (W300): Wheelbase: 133 in. Tires: 8 x 19.5 eight-ply. GVW: 8500-10,000 lbs. Axle Capacity: (front) 4500 lbs.; (rear) 7500 lbs.

CHASSIS (WM300): Wheelbase: 126 in. Tires: 9.00 x 16 eight-ply. GVW: 8700-9500 lbs. Axle Capacity: (front) 3750 lbs.; (rear) 6500 lbs.

TECHNICAL: Selective sliding gear transmission. Speeds: 3F/1R except 1-ton models, 4F/1R. Column or floor shift control. Transfer Case: (W models) Two-speed, two-lever. Three-speed automatic transmission optional. Single plate dry disc clutch: (A100) 9⅛ in.; (D100/D200) 10 in.; (others) 11 in. Rear axle ratio: (A100) 3.55:1 or 3.91:1, (D100) 3.55:1, 3.91:1 or 4.56:1; (D200, W100, W200) 4.1:1 or 4.88:1; (D300, W200) 4.88:1 or 5.87:1; (WM300) 5.83:1. Hydraulic four-wheel brakes. Oil bath air cleaner. Fuel tank: (A100) 21 gallon; (others) 18 gallon. Alternator: (A100) 30-amp; (others) 35-amp. Shock absorbers: front and rear except 300 models, front only. Wheels: (A100) 13 x 4.50; (D100) 15 x 5.00; (D200, W100) 16 x 6.00; (D300, W200) 17.5 x 5.25; (W300) 19.5 x 5.25; (WM300) 16 x 6.50.

1964 Dodge A100 Forward Control Pickup (LLD)

OPTIONS (Factory-Installed): Chrome front bumper (A100, D100/200). Rear bumper (100/200). Bumper guards (A100). Chrome hub caps (A100, D100/200). Custom cab equipment (D/W models). Left armrest. Right armrest (A/D models). Radio (except WM300). Heater. Cigar lighter (except WM300). Inside mirror. Seat belts. Dual horns (except WM300). Oil pressure gauge (except WM300). Undercoating. Windshield washers. Dual electric variable-speed wipers (except WM300). Tinted glass (D/W models). Heavy-duty instruments (D/W). Cab marker lights (D/W). Auxiliary taillight (D/W/WM). Auxiliary seat (D100). Right sunvisor (D/W). Full-width rear window (D/W). No. 1 Trim Package: chrome moldings on hood, cowl, door and cab back (D100-300 Utiline, platform, stake). No. 2 Trim Package: chrome front bumper; moldings on hood, cowl, doors, cab back and bodysides (D100/200 Sweptline). Full-depth foam padded seats (D models). Turn signals. Hand throttle (D/W/WM). One-quart oil bath air cleaner (except WM300). 40-amp alternator. 3000- or 3600-pound rear axle. Two-tone paint (except WM300). Increased cooling capacity (D/W). Anti-spin rear axle (D100-300, W100/200). Engine governor (D/W). 3-ton jack (except A100). Heavy-duty front springs (D/W). Heavy-duty rear springs (D/W). Power steering (D models). Heavy-duty three-speed manual transmission (A100). LoadFlite automatic transmission (A/D models). 170 cu. in. engine (D100). 225 cu. in. engine (A100). 318 cu. in. V-8 engine (D/W models). Four-speed transmission (D100/200, W100/200). Vacuum power brake (all except A100 and D100). Rear shock absorbers (D/W/WM300). Front wheel locking hubs (W/WM). Pintle hook (W/WM). Power take-off (W/WM). 8000-lb. winch (W models). Spare wheel (W300 dual-wheel models). Front tow hooks (WM300). 10,000-lb. winch (WM300). Fuel/vacuum pump (WM300). Radiator overflow tank (WM300).

NOTE: High performance 426 cu. in. V8 in Custom Sports Package had to be ordered with: dual exhausts, rear axle struts, power steering, heavy-duty instrument cluster, LoadFlite automatic transmission, power brakes and tachometer. (Options for Custom Sports Package) Chrome rearview mirror (left). Trim package: bright moldings on hood, cowl, doors, cab back and bodysides. Chrome rear bumper.

HISTORICAL: Introduced: October, 1963. Calendar year sales: 101,072. Calendar year production: 135,630. Model year production: (6-cyl.) 76,075; (V-8) 28,687; (Total) 104,762. Innovations: Compact van (90 in. w.b.). Sports-type pickup, available with 426 cu. in. V-8 engine. Historical notes: Truck sales rose 31 percent over 1963 — the best performance since 1953. Dodge increased its share of the U.S. market from 7.7 to 8.8 percent. Of the 141,393 gasoline-powered trucks, 64 percent had 6-cyl. engines. Diesel engine production was down slightly. Dodge built 7,852 A100 wagons that were registered as passenger cars. In addition to the light-duty engines, 361 and 413 cu. in. V-8s were available in medium- and heavy-tonnage models. Dodge opened a series of truck branch offices throughout the country, specializing in the sale of trucks over 10,000 pounds Gross Vehicle Weight.

Pricing

	5	4	3	2	1
V6-A100 Series — (½-Ton) — (90 in. w.b.)					
Pickup	840	1680	2800	3900	5600
Van	780	1560	2600	3600	5200
Wagon	850	1700	2850	4000	5700
V6-D100 Series — (½-Ton) — (114 in. w.b.)					
Utiline Pickup	850	1700	2850	4000	5700
Sweptline Pickup	840	1680	2800	3900	5600
Town Panel	870	1750	2900	4100	5800
Wagon 6-pass.	890	1770	2950	4150	5900
Wagon 8-pass.	890	1770	2950	4150	5900
(122 in. w.b.)					
Utiline Pickup	840	1680	2800	3900	5600
Sweptline Pickup	870	1750	2900	4100	5800
Platform	750	1500	2500	3500	5000
Stake	770	1550	2550	3600	5100
V6-D200 Series — (¾-Ton) — (122 in. w.b.)					
Utiline Pickup	800	1600	2650	3700	5300
Sweptline Pickup	830	1650	2750	3850	5500
Platform	740	1470	2450	3350	4900
Stake	750	1500	2500	3500	5000
V6-D200 Crew Cab — (¾-Ton) — (146 in. w.b.)					
Utiline Pickup	770	1550	2550	3600	5100
Sweptline Pickup	780	1560	2600	3600	5200
V6-D300 Series — (1-Ton) — (133 in. w.b.)					
Utiline Pickup	750	1500	2500	3500	5000
Platform	720	1450	2400	3300	4800
Stake	740	1470	2450	3350	4900
V6-W100 Series 4x4 — (½-Ton) — (114 in. w.b.)					
Utiline Pickup	870	1750	2900	4100	5800
Sweptline Pickup	850	1700	2850	4000	5700
Town Panel	890	1770	2950	4150	5900
Wagon 6-pass.	930	1860	3100	4350	6200
Wagon 8-pass.	930	1860	3100	4350	6200
V6-W200 Series 4x4 — (¾-Ton) — (122 in. w.b.)					
Utiline Pickup	830	1650	2750	3850	5500
Sweptline Pickup	850	1700	2850	4000	5700
Platform	770	1550	2550	3600	5100
Stake	780	1560	2600	3600	5200
V6-W200 Crew Cab 4x4 — (¾-Ton) — (146 in. w.b.)					
Utiline Pickup	750	1500	2500	3500	5000
Sweptline Pickup	770	1550	2550	3600	5100
V6-W300 Series 4x4 — (1-Ton) — (133 in. w.b.)					
Utiline Pickup	780	1560	2600	3600	5200
Platform	740	1470	2450	3350	4900
Stake	770	1550	2550	3600	5100
V6-WM300 Power-Wagon — (1-Ton) — (126 in. w.b.)					
Utiline Pickup	980	1950	3250	4550	6500

NOTE: Add 10 percent for V-8 engine.
Add 5 percent for automatic transmission.
Add 4 percent for power winch.

1965 DODGE

1965 Dodge Custom Sweptline Pickup (OCW)

½-TON COMPACT — A SERIES A100 — SIX-CYLINDER and V-8: — The A100 lineup carried over largely unchanged into its second year. Although Sportsman and Custom Sportsman wagon models were available, they were considered part of the Dodge car line. The 170 cu. in. slant six was standard; 225 cu. in. slant six and 273.5 cu. in. V-8 were optional. Dodge was the only compact van offering a V-8. Three GVW ratings were available: 3800, 4600 and 5200 pounds, depending on equipment options.

½-TON — A SERIES D100 — SIX-CYLINDER and V-8 / ¾-TON — A SERIES D200 — SIX-CYLINDER and V-8 / 1-TON — A SERIES D300 — SIX-CYLINDER and V-8: — Dodge began the model year selling an unchanged truck line. By spring 1965, in keeping with the policy of making

product improvements at any time, Dodge introduced an improved line of light-duty trucks. Exterior appearance changes included a new full-width grille and headlight treatment, which gave a lower, wider look. A new full-length molding was optional on Sweptline pickups only. The "series" designation plate moved from the grille to the rear section of both front fenders. A wider tailgate with single-latch opening mechanism operated easily with one hand. Taillights were newly styled, slim and vertical in shape. Sweptline boxes were now perfectly vertical at the rear, better to hold an add-on camper. To improve weight distribution for big loads (such as pickup campers) the old 122 in. w.b. models were stretched to 128 in. A new 8-ft. Utiline box replaced the 7½-footer on the longer chassis. Sweptline pickup boxes had new double wall construction, plus a flat top on both wheelhousings. Custom cab options were now available in two packages — one for comfort, another for appearance. (See 1964 option list for details.) Turn signals were made standard equipment in the new models. Half- and ¾-ton models had self-adjusting brakes. Prices did not increase when the new models arrived.

1965 Dodge Custom Sweptline Pickup (OCW)

½-TON 4x4 — A SERIES W100 — SIX-CYLINDER and V-8 / ¾-TON 4x4 — A SERIES W200 — SIX-CYLINDER and V-8 / 1-TON 4x4 — A SERIES W300 — SIX-CYLINDER and V-8 / 1-TON POWER-WAGON — A SERIES WM300 — SIX-CYLINDER: — 4wd models continued as before, except for the changes noted in the D series. W200 models grew to 128 in. w.b. at mid-year.

I.D. DATA: Serial numbers were in the same location, with the same coding, as 1964. Starting Serial Numbers: (A100) 2,015,000; (all others) 1,430,000. Ending serial numbers are not available. Engine numbers were in the same location as 1963-64. Starting and ending numbers are not available.

1965 Dodge Sportsman Wagon (OCW)

Model	Body Type	Price	Weight	Prod. Total
A6-A100 Compact Series — (½-Ton) — (90 in. w.b.)				
A6-A100	Pickup	1756	2910	Note 1
A6-A100	Panel Van	1897	2910	Note 1
A6-A100	Van (side/rear doors)	1947	2930	Note 1
A6-A100	Sportsman Wagon	2129	—	—
A6-A100	Custom Sportsman	2434	—	—

NOTE 1: Total model year production: (six) 36,535; (V-8) 5810.

Model	Body Type	Price	Weight	Prod. Total
A6-D100 Series — (½-Ton) — (114 in. w.b.)				
A6-D100	Chassis & Cowl	1482	2540	Note 2
A6-D100	Chassis & Cab	1727	3095	Note 2
A6-D100	Utiline Pickup	1833	3405	Note 2
A6-D100	Sweptline Pickup	1847	3505	Note 2
A6-D100	Town Panel	2088	3565	Note 2
A6-D100	Town Wagon (6-pass.)	2378	3795	Note 2
A6-D100	Town Wagon (8-pass.)	2424	3845	Note 2
(128 in. w.b.)				
A6-D100	Chassis & Cowl	1517	2590	Note 3
A6-D100	Chassis & Cab	1761	3110	Note 3
A6-D100	Utiline Pickup	1868	3600	Note 3
A6-D100	Sweptline Pickup	1881	3660	Note 3
A6-D100	Platform	1904	3535	Note 3
A6-D100	Stake	1952	3735	Note 3

NOTE 2: Total model year production: (six) 21,589; (V-8) 6418.

NOTE 3: Total model year production: (six) 8081; (V-8) 6789. Model year production of early 122 in. w.b. D100: (six) 9206; (V-8) 7385.

Model	Body Type	Price	Weight	Prod. Total
A6-D200 Series — (¾-Ton) — (128 in. w.b.)				
A6-D200	Chassis & Cowl	1613	3095	Note 4
A6-D200	Chassis & Cab	1867	3650	Note 4
A6-D200	Utiline Pickup	1973	4090	Note 4
A6-D200	Sweptline Pickup	1987	4150	Note 4
A6-D200	Platform	2009	4025	Note 4
A6-D200	Stake	2057	4225	Note 4

NOTE 4: Total model year production: (six) 3767; (V-8) 4366. Model year production of early 122 in. w.b.: (six) 3708; (V-8) 4713.

Model	Body Type	Price	Weight	Prod. Total
A6-D200 Crew Cab Series — (¾-Ton) — (146 in. w.b.)				
A6-D200	Chassis	2475	3973	—
A6-D200	Utiline Pickup	2581	4285	—
A6-D200	Sweptline Pickup	2595	4385	—
A6-D300 Series — (1-Ton) — (133 in. w.b.)				
A6-D300	Chassis & Cowl	1771	3220	Note 5
A6-D300	Chassis & Cab	2045	3775	Note 5
A6-D300	Utiline Pickup	2170	4175	Note 5
A6-D300	Platform	2217	4475	Note 5
A6-D300	Stake	2276	4675	Note 5

NOTE 5: Total model year production: (six) 4961; (V-8) 4155.

Model	Body Type	Price	Weight	Prod. Total
A6-W100 Series 4x4 — (½-Ton) — (114 in. w.b.)				
A6-W100	Chassis & Cab	2403	3900	Note 6
A6-W100	Utiline Pickup	2510	4210	Note 6
A6-W100	Sweptline Pickup	2523	4310	Note 6
A6-W100	Town Panel	2813	4370	Note 6
A6-W100	Town Wagon (6-pass.)	3079	4600	Note 6
A6-W100	Town Wagon (8-pass.)	3125	4640	Note 6

NOTE 6: Total model year production: (six) 843; (V-8) 631.

Model	Body Type	Price	Weight	Prod. Total
A6-W200 Series 4x4 — (¾-Ton) — (128 in. w.b.)				
A6-W200	Chassis & Cab	2454	3945	Note 7
A6-W200	Utiline Pickup	2561	4385	Note 7
A6-W200	Sweptline Pickup	2574	4445	Note 7
A6-W200	Platform	2579	4320	Note 7
A6-W200	Stake	2645	4520	Note 7

NOTE 7: Total model year production: (six) 607; (V-8) 759. Model year production of early 122 in. w.b.: (six) 776; (V-8) 550.

Model	Body Type	Price	Weight	Prod. Total
A6-W200 Crew Cab Series 4x4 — (¾-Ton) — (146 in. w.b.)				
A6-W200	Chassis	3173	4259	—
A6-W200	Utiline Pickup	3280	4569	—
A6-W200	Sweptline Pickup	3293	4669	—
A6-W300 Series 4x4 — (1-Ton) — (133 in. w.b.)				
A6-W300	Chassis & Cowl	2957	4090	Note 8
A6-W300	Chassis & Cab	3211	4645	Note 8
A6-W300	Utiline Pickup	3337	5045	Note 8
A6-W300	Platform	3384	5345	Note 8
A6-W300	Stake	3444	5545	Note 8

NOTE 8: Total model year production: (six) 223; (V-8) 573.

Model	Body Type	Price	Weight	Prod. Total
A6-WM300 Series Power-Wagon — (1-Ton) — (126 in. w.b.)				
A6-WM300	Chassis & Cowl	3154	4095	Note 9
A6-WM300	Chassis & Cab	3412	4520	Note 9
A6-WM300	Utiline Pickup	3555	4920	Note 9

NOTE 9: Total model year production: 2397 (plus 2496 M.D.A.P. models).

NOTE 10: Weights and prices shown are for 6-cyl. models. For V-8 engine (prefix AB) add $120 to price.

1965 Dodge Sweptline 'Indy' Pickup (IMSC/JLM)

ENGINES: (170 and 225 cu. in. slant six; 251 cu. in. L-head six; 318 cu. in. V-8) Same as 1964; see previous specifications. (Optional: A100) 90-degree, overhead valve. Eight-cylinder. Cast iron block. Bore & stroke: 3.63 x 3.31 in. Displacement: 273.8 cu. in. Compression ratio: 8.8:1. Brake horsepower: 174 at 3900 R.P.M. Net hosepower: 42.2. Torque: 246 lbs.-ft. at 2000 R.P.M. Five main bearings. Solid valve lifters.

1965 Dodge A-100 Pickup (OCW)

CHASSIS (A100): Wheelbase: 90 in. Tires: 6.95 x 14-2 four-ply. GVW: 4600 lbs. except Sportsman, 5200 lbs. maximum.

CHASSIS (D100): Wheelbase: 114 in., 122 in. or 128 in. Tires: 6.70 x 15 four-ply except Town Panel/Wagon models, 7.10 x 15. GVW: 5200 lbs. maximum.

CHASSIS (D200): Wheelbase: 122 in., 128 in. or 146 in. Tires: (122 in.) 6.50 x 16 six-ply; (others) 7 x 17.5 six-ply. GVW: 7500 lbs. maximum.

CHASSIS (D300): Wheelbase: 133 in. Tires: 7 x 17.5 six-ply. GVW: 9000 lbs. maximum.

CHASSIS (W100): Wheelbase: 114 in. Tires: 7 x 17.5 six-ply. GVW: 6000 lbs. maximum.

CHASSIS (W200): Wheelbase: 122 in., 128 in. or 146 in. Tires: 7 x 17.5 six-ply except 128 in., 8 x 19.5 eight-ply. GVW: 8000 lbs. maximum (Crew Cab, 6000 lbs.)

CHASSIS (W300): Wheelbase: 133 in. Tires: 7.50 x 16 six-ply. GVW: 10,000 lbs. maximum.

CHASSIS (WM300): Wheelbase: 126 in. Tires: 9.00 x 16 ten-ply. GVW: 9500 lbs. maximum.

TECHNICAL: Same as 1964; see previous specifications.

OPTIONS: Same list and prices as 1964, including Custom Sports Package for D/W100/200 pickups.

HISTORICAL: Introduced: October, 1964. (128 in. models midway through model year). Calendar year sales: 119,365. Calendar year production: 143,452. Model year production: (six) 97,853; (V-8) 42,149; (Total) 140,002. Innovations: V-8 engine in compact van. Double wall Sweptline pickup box construction. Historical notes: Dodge had a very good year as sales rose 19 percent. Only in 1947 and 1949 had Dodge sold more trucks. Dodge ranked fourth in U.S. production. Of the total gasoline-powered trucks sold, 58.8 percent still had 6-cyl. engines. Diesel sales came to 2,100. A new 860,000 sq. ft. assembly plant, to be built in St. Louis, was announced in 1965. It would turn out 200 trucks per day, with the potential for 400. A100 sales amounted to 21,333 pickups and vans. For the first time, industry sales of light trucks (6000 lbs. or less) hit the one million mark.

1965 Dodge A100 Forward Control Pickup (Louderbough)

Pricing

1965

	5	4	3	2	1
A6-A100 Compact — (½-Ton) — (90 in. w.b.)					
Pickup	840	1680	2800	3900	5600
Panel Van	800	1600	2650	3700	5300
Van	780	1560	2600	3600	5200
Sportsman	850	1700	2850	4000	5700
Custom Sportsman	870	1750	2900	4100	5800
A6-D100 Series — (½-Ton) — (114 in. w.b.)					
Utiline Pickup	850	1700	2850	4000	5700
Sweptline Pickup	840	1680	2800	3900	5600
Town Panel	870	1750	2900	4100	5800
6-pass. Wagon	890	1770	2950	4150	5900
8-pass. Wagon	890	1770	2950	4150	5900
A6-D100 Series — (½-Ton) — (122 in. or 128 in. w.b.)					
Utiline Pickup	840	1680	2800	3900	5600
Sweptline Pickup	870	1750	2900	4100	5800
Platform	750	1500	2500	3500	5000
Stake	770	1550	2550	3600	5100
A6-D200 Series — (¾-Ton) — (122 in. or 128 in. w.b.)					
Utiline Pickup	800	1600	2650	3700	5300
Sweptline Pickup	830	1650	2750	3850	5500
Platform	740	1470	2450	3350	4900
Stake	750	1500	2500	3500	5000
A6-D200 Crew Cab — (¾-Ton) — (146 in. w.b.)					
Utiline Pickup	770	1550	2550	3600	5100
Sweptline Pickup	780	1560	2600	3600	5200
A6-D300 Series — (1-Ton) — (133 in. w.b.)					
Utiline Pickup	750	1500	2500	3500	5000
Platform	720	1450	2400	3300	4800
Stake	740	1470	2450	3350	4900
A6-W100 Series 4x4 — (½-Ton) — (114 in. w.b.)					
Utiline Pickup	870	1750	2900	4100	5800
Sweptline Pickup	850	1700	2850	4000	5700
Town Panel	890	1770	2950	4150	5900
6-pass. Wagon	930	1860	3100	4350	6200
8-pass. Wagon	930	1860	3100	4350	6200
A6-W200 Series 4x4 — (¾-Ton) — (122 in. or 128 in. w.b.)					
Utiline Pickup	830	1650	2750	3850	5500
Sweptline Pickup	850	1700	2850	4000	5700
Platform	770	1550	2550	3600	5100
Stake	780	1560	2600	3600	5200
A6-W200 Crew Cab 4x4 — (¾-Ton) — (146 in. w.b.)					
Utiline Pickup	750	1500	2500	3500	5000
Sweptline Pickup	770	1550	2550	3600	5100
A6-W300 Series 4x4 — (1-Ton) — (133 in. w.b.)					
Utiline Pickup	780	1560	2600	3600	5200
Platform	740	1470	2450	3350	4900
Stake	770	1550	2550	3600	5100
A6-WM300 Power-Wagon — (1-Ton) — (126 in. w.b.)					
Utiline Pickup	980	1950	3250	4550	6500

NOTE: Add 10 percent for V-8 engine.
Add 5 percent for automatic transmission.
Add 4 percent for power winch.

1966 DODGE

1966 Dodge Sweptline 'Camper Special' Pickup (JAG)

204

½-TON COMPACT — B SERIES A100 — SIX-CYLINDER and V-8 — Compact vans, wagons and pickups entered their third year without change. Calendar year production increased by 1,015, to 22,348 units.

½-TON — B SERIES D100 — SIX-CYLINDER and V-8 / ¾-TON — B SERIES D200 — SIX-CYLINDER and V-8 / 1-TON — B SERIES D300 — SIX-CYLINDER and V-8 / ½-TON 4x4 — B SERIES W100 — SIX-CYLINDER and V-8 / ¾-TON 4x4 — B SERIES W200 — SIX-CYLINDER and V-8 / 1-TON 4x4 — B SERIES W300 — SIX-CYLINDER and V-8 — The restyling and other improvements made during the 1965 model year continued into 1966 with no further change. All models, engines and specifications carried on. Prices remained the same as in 1965. Standard equipment included a dome light, door locks, left sunvisor, painted hub caps and front bumper, glove box, seat belts, dual variable-speed wipers and dual jet washers, inside mirror, left outside mirror, front and rear shocks (front only on 1-ton), and 6-cyl. engine.

1-TON POWER-WAGON — B SERIES WM300 — SIX-CYLINDER: — Power-Wagons carried on again without change.

I.D. DATA: Serial numbers were in the same location, with the same coding, as 1964-65. Starting Serial Numbers: (A100) 2,055,000; (all other models) 1,548,000. Ending numbers are not available. Engine numbers were in the same location as 1963-65. Engine numbers are not available.

1966 Dodge A100 Forward Control Pickup (JAG)

Model	Body Type	Price	Weight	Prod. Total
B6-A100 Compact Series — (½-Ton) — (90 in. w.b.)				
B6-A100	Pickup	1756	2910	Note 1
B6-A100	Panel Van	1897	2910	Note 1
B6-A100	Van (side/rear doors)	1947	2930	Note 1
B6-A100	Sportsman Wagon	2129	—	—
B6-A100	Custom Sportsman	2434	—	—

NOTE 1: Total model year production: (six) 35,190; (V-8) 9536.

B6-D100 Series — (½-Ton) — (114 in. w.b.)				
B6-D100	Chassis & Cowl	1482	2540	Note 2
B6-D100	Chassis & Cab	1727	3095	Note 2
B6-D100	Utiline Pickup	1833	3405	Note 2
B6-D100	Sweptline Pickup	1847	3505	Note 2
B6-D100	Town Panel	2088	3565	Note 2
B6-D100	Town Wagon (6-pass.)	2378	3795	Note 2
B6-D100	Town Wagon (8-pass.)	2424	3845	Note 2
(128 in. w.b.)				
B6-D100	Chassis & Cowl	1517	2590	Note 3
B6-D100	Chassis & Cab	1761	3110	Note 3
B6-D100	Utiline Pickup	1868	3600	Note 3
B6-D100	Sweptline Pickup	1881	3660	Note 3
B6-D100	Platform	1904	3535	Note 3
B6-D100	Stake	1952	3735	Note 3

NOTE 2: Total model year production: (six) 17,512; (V-8) 5167.

NOTE 3: Total model year production: (six) 17,870; (V-8) 15,991.

B6-D200 Series — (¾-Ton) — (128 in. w.b.)				
B6-D200	Chassis & Cowl	1613	3095	Note 4
B6-D200	Chassis & Cab	1867	3650	Note 4
B6-D200	Utiline Pickup	1973	4090	Note 4
B6-D200	Sweptline Pickup	1987	4150	Note 4
B6-D200	Platform	2009	4025	Note 4
B6-D200	Stake	2057	4225	Note 4

NOTE 4: Total model year production: (six) 11,224; (V-8) 13,871.

B6-D200 Crew Cab Series — (¾-Ton) — (146 in. w.b.)				
B6-D200	Chassis	2475	3973	—
B6-D200	Utiline Pickup	2581	4285	—
B6-D200	Sweptline Pickup	2595	4385	—
B6-D300 Series — (1-Ton) — (133 in. w.b.)				
B6-D300	Chassis & Cowl	1771	3220	Note 5
B6-D300	Chassis & Cab	2045	3775	Note 5
B6-D300	Utiline Pickup	2170	4175	Note 5
B6-D300	Platform	2217	4475	Note 5
B6-D300	Stake	2276	4675	Note 5

NOTE 5: Total model year production: (six) 4042; (V-8) 5037.

Model	Body Type	Price	Weight	Prod. Total
B6-W100 Series 4x4 — (½-Ton) — (114 in. w.b.)				
B6-W100	Chassis & Cab	2403	3900	Note 6
B6-W100	Utiline Pickup	2510	4210	Note 6
B6-W100	Sweptline Pickup	2523	4310	Note 6
B6-W100	Town Panel	2813	4370	Note 6
B6-W100	Town Wagon (6-pass.)	3079	4600	Note 6
B6-W100	Town Wagon (8-pass.)	3125	4640	Note 6

NOTE 6: Total model year production: (six) 1528; (V-8) 820.

Model	Body Type	Price	Weight	Prod. Total
B6-W200 Series 4x4 — (¾-Ton) — (128 in. w.b.)				
B6-W200	Chassis & Cab	2454	3945	Note 7
B6-W200	Utiline Pickup	2561	4385	Note 7
B6-W200	Sweptline Pickup	2574	4445	Note 7
B6-W200	Platform	2579	4320	Note 7
B6-W200	Stake	2645	4520	Note 7

NOTE 7: Total model year production: (six) 1055; (V-8) 2258.

Model	Body Type	Price	Weight	Prod. Total
B6-W200 Crew Cab Series 4x4 — (¾-Ton) — (146 in. w.b.)				
B6-W200	Chassis	3173	4259	—
B6-W200	Utiline Pickup	3280	4569	—
B6-W200	Sweptline Pickup	3293	4669	—
B6-W300 Series 4x4 — (1-Ton) — (133 in. w.b.)				
B6-W300	Chassis & Cowl	2957	4090	Note 8
B6-W300	Chassis & Cab	3211	4645	Note 8
B6-W300	Utiline Pickup	3337	5045	Note 8
B6-W300	Platform	3384	5345	Note 8
B6-W300	Stake	3444	5545	Note 8

NOTE 8: Total model year production: (six) 220; (V-8) 625.

Model	Body Type	Price	Weight	Prod. Total
B6-WM300 Series Power-Wagon — (1-Ton) — (126 in. w.b.)				
B6-WM300	Chassis & Cowl	3154	4095	Note 9
B6-WM300	Chassis & Cab	3412	4520	Note 9
B6-WM300	Utiline Pickup	3555	4920	Note 9

NOTE 9: Total model year production: 1245 (plus 3371 M.D.A.P. models).

NOTE 10: Weights and prices shown are for 6-cyl. models. For V-8 engine (prefix S8) add $120 to price.

1966 Dodge D200 Crew Cab Sweptline Pickup (JAG)

ENGINE (A100): Inline. Overhead valves. Slant six. Cast iron block. Bore & stroke: 3.4 x 3.125 in. Displacement: 170.2 cu. in. Compression ratio: 8.5:1. Brake horsepower 101 at 4000 R.P.M. Net (Taxable) horsepower: 27.70. Torque: 145 lbs.-ft. at 1600 R.P.M. Four main bearings. Solid valve lifters.

ENGINE (D100, D200, D300, W100, W200): Inline. Overhead valves. Slant six-cylinder. Cast iron block. Bore & stroke: 3.4 x 4.125 in. Displacement: 224.7 cu. in. Compression ratio: 8.4:1. Brake horsepower: 140 at 3900 R.P.M. Net horsepower: 27.70. Torque: 215 lbs.-ft. at 1600 R.P.M. Four main bearings. Solid valve lifters.

ENGINE (W300): Same as W200, but premium heavy-duty version to meet rugged demands.

ENGINE (WM300): Inline. L-head. Six-cylinder. Cast iron block. Bore & stroke: 3.437 x 4.5 in. Displacement: 250.6 cu. in. Compression ratio: 7.1:1. Brake horsepower: 125 at 3600 R.P.M. Net horsepower: 28.35. Torque: 216 lbs.-ft. at 1600 R.P.M. Four main bearings. Solid valve lifters.

ENGINE (Optional: D100, D200, D300, W100, W200): 90-degree, overhead valve. Eight-cylinder. Cast iron block. Bore & stroke: 3.91 x 3.312 in. Displacement: 318.1 cu. in. Compression ratio: 8.25:1. Brake horsepower: 200 at 3900 R.P.M. Net horsepower: 48.92. Torque: 286 lbs.-ft. at 2400 R.P.M. Five main bearings. Hydraulic valve lifters.

ENGINE (Optional: W300): Same V-8 as above but with premium heavy-duty features for rugged use.

ENGINE (Optional: A100): 90-degree, overhead valve. Eight-cylinder. Cast iron block. Bore & stroke: 3.63 x 3.31 in. Displacement: 273.8 cu. in. Compression ratio: 8.8:1. Brake horsepower: 174 at 3900 R.P.M. Net horsepower: 42.2. Torque: 246 lbs.-ft. at 2000 R.P.M. Five main bearings. Solid valve lifters.

1966 Dodge D100 Sweptline Pickup (E.H. Terry)

CHASSIS (A100): Wheelbase: 90 in. Tires: 6.50 x 13 four-ply. GVW: 3800-4600 lbs. Axle Capacity: (front) 2200 lbs.; (rear) 3000 lbs.

CHASSIS (D100): Wheelbase: 114 in. or 128 in. Tires: 6.70 x 15 four-ply except Town Panel/Wagon, 7.10 x 15. GVW: 4300-5200 lbs. Axle Capacity: (front) 2500 lbs.; (rear) 3600 lbs.

CHASSIS (D200): Wheelbase: 128 in. or 146 in. Tires: 6.50 x 16 six-ply. GVW: 5200-7500 cu. in. Axle Capacity: (front) 2800 lbs.; (rear) 5500 lbs.

CHASSIS (D300): Wheelbase: 133 in. Tires: 8 x 17.5 six-ply. GVW: 6300-9000 lbs. Axle Capacity: (front) 3800 lbs.; (rear) 7500 lbs.

CHASSIS (W100): Wheelbase: 114 in. Tires: 6.50 x 16 six-ply. GVW: 5100-6000 lbs. Axle Capacity: (front) 3000 lbs.; (rear) 4500 lbs.

CHASSIS (W200): Wheelbase: 128 in. or 146 in. Tires: 7 x 17.5 six-ply. GVW: 6000-8000 lbs. Axle Capacity: (front) 3000 lbs.; (rear) 5500 lbs.

CHASSIS (W300): Wheelbase: 133 in. Tires: 8 x 19.5 eight-ply. GVW: 8500-10,000 lbs. Axle Capacity: (front) 4500 lbs.; (rear) 7500 lbs.

CHASSIS (WM300): Wheelbase: 126 in. Tires: 9.00 x 16 eight-ply. GVW: 8700-9500 lbs. Axle Capacity: (front) 3750 lbs.; (rear) 6500 lbs.

TECHNICAL: Selective sliding gear transmission. Speeds: 3F/1R except 1-ton models, 4F/1R. Column or floor shift control. Transfer Case: (W models) Two-speed, two-lever. Single plate dry disc clutch: (A100) 9⅛ in.; (D100/D200) 10 in.; (others) 11 in. Rear axle ratio: (A100) 3.23:1, 3.55:1 or 3.91:1, (D200) 3.54:1, 4.1:1 or 4.88:1; (D300) 4.1:1, 4.88:1 or 5.87:1; (W100/200) 4.1:1 or 4.88:1; (W300) 4.88:1 or 5.87:1; (WM300) 5.83:1. Hydraulic four-wheel brakes. Fuel tank: (A100) 21 gallon; (others) 18 gallon. Oil filter. Alternator: (A100) 30-amp; (others) 35-amp. Wheels: (A100) 13 x 4.50; (D100) 15 x 5.00; (D200, W100) 16 x 6.00; (D300, W200) 17.5 x 5.25; (W300) 19.5 x 5.25; (WM300) 16 x 6.50.

OPTIONS (Factory-Installed): Chrome front bumper (A100, D100/200). Rear bumper (all except D300, WM300). Bumper guards: painted or chrome (A100). Chrome hub caps (A/D100). Chrome wheel covers (A/D100). Spare tire carrier (D/W100/200). Appearance package (D/W100-300). Comfort package (D/W100-300). Tinted glass (except WM300). Left or right armrest (except WM300). Radio (except WM300). Heater/defroster. Cigar lighter (except WM300). Outside mirrors (except A100). Cab marker lights (D/W100-300). Dual electric horns (except WM300). Heavy-duty instruments (D/W100-300). Full-width rear window (D/W100-300). Custom equipment package (A100). Rear quarter cab window (A100). Right sunvisor. Fenders for dual rear wheels (D/W300). Chrome trim (D/W100/200 Sweptline). Two-tone paint (except WM300). Traffic hazard switch (except A100). Hand throttle (D/W100-300). Foam padded seat (D/W100-300). Oil pressure gauge (except WM300). Power steering (D models). Vacuum power brakes (D200, W100-300, W300). Heavy-duty front springs (except WM300). Heavy-duty rear springs (A and D models). 5200-lb. GVW package (A100). Rear shock absorbers (300 models). Positive crankcase ventilation system (W100-300). Cleaner air package (A/D100). One-quart oil bath air cleaner (except W/WM300). 46 or 59-amp alternator (except WM300). Increased cooling capacity (except WM300). 225 cu. in. engine (A100). 273.8 cu. in. V-8 engine (A100). 318 cu. in. V-8 engine (D/W100-300). Heavy-duty clutch: 10 in. (A100); 11 in. (D100/200); 12 in. (W300). Governor (D/W100-300). Four-speed manual transmission (D/W100-200). LoadFlite three-speed automatic transmission (A/D models). Three-speed heavy-duty transmission (A100). Anti-spin rear axle (except WM300). Undercoating. Three-ton jack (except A100). Locking front wheel hubs (W/WM). Pintle hook (W/WM). Radiator overflow tank (WM300). Power take-off assembly (W/WM). Front tow hooks, pair (W/WM300). Spare wheel (W300). Fuel/vacuum pump (WM300). 8000-lb. winch (W100-300). 10,000-lb. winch (WM300).

HISTORICAL: Introduced: October, 1965. Calendar year sales: 119,777. Calendar year production: 153,159. Model year production: (six) 96,443; (V-8) 53,305; (Total) 149,748. Historical notes: Truck production rose 6.8 percent, giving Dodge 8.7 percent of the industry total. Dodge ranked fourth in the truck industry, with its best production year since 1952. Sales increased only slightly over 1965. Dodge showed a good gain on both light and heavy-duty trucks. V-8 engines made up 47.5 percent of gasoline truck sales, while diesel sales fell to 1900 units. Dodge introduced two L Series medium-duty tilt cab models, which used A100 cabs plus a new D800 heavy-duty conventional gas model. The full line, ranging from the 90 in. w.b. A100 up to a diesel tandem axle tilt-cab with 50,000-pound GVW, met nearly 97 percent of truck needs. Forward-control models remained in the lineup. The only major model introduction yet to come would be the 108 in. w.b. van, available late in 1966 as a 1967 model. To meet demand, Dodge added 40,000 square feet to its Warren, Michigan truck plant. Production also began at the new St. Louis facility.

Pricing

1966

	5	4	3	2	1
B6-A100 Compact — (½-Ton) — (90 in. w.b.)					
Pickup	840	1680	2800	3900	5600
Panel Van	800	1600	2650	3700	5300
Van	780	1560	2600	3600	5200
Sportsman	850	1700	2850	4000	5700
Custom Sportsman	870	1750	2900	4100	5800
B6-D100 Series — (½-Ton) — (114 in. w.b.)					
Utiline Pickup	850	1700	2850	4000	5700
Sweptline Pickup	840	1680	2800	3900	5600
Town Panel	870	1750	2900	4100	5800
6-pass. Wagon	890	1770	2950	4150	5900
8-pass. Wagon	890	1770	2950	4150	5900
B6-D100 Series — (½-Ton) — (122 in. or 128 in. w.b.)					
Utiline Pickup	840	1680	2800	3900	5600
Sweptline Pickup	870	1750	2900	4100	5800
Platform	750	1500	2500	3500	5000
Stake	770	1550	2550	3600	5100
B6-D200 Series — (¾-Ton) — (122 in. or 128 in. w.b.)					
Utiline Pickup	800	1600	2650	3700	5300
Sweptline Pickup	830	1650	2750	3850	5500
Platform	740	1470	2450	3350	4900
Stake	750	1500	2500	3500	5000
B6-D200 Series Crew Cab — (¾-Ton) — (146 in. w.b.)					
Utiline Pickup	770	1550	2550	3600	5100
Sweptline Pickup	780	1560	2600	3600	5200
B6-D300 Series — (1-Ton) — (133 in. w.b.)					
Utiline Pickup	750	1500	2500	3500	5000
Platform	720	1450	2400	3300	4800
Stake	740	1470	2450	3350	4900
B6-W100 Series 4x4 — (½-Ton) — (114 in. w.b.)					
Utiline Pickup	870	1750	2900	4100	5800
Sweptline Pickup	850	1700	2850	4000	5700
Town Panel	890	1770	2950	4150	5900
6-pass. Wagon	930	1860	3100	4350	6200
8-pass. Wagon	930	1860	3100	4350	6200
B6-W200 Series 4x4 — (¾-Ton) — (122 in. or 128 in. w.b.)					
Utiline Pickup	830	1650	2750	3850	5500
Sweptline Pickup	850	1700	2850	4000	5700
Platform	770	1550	2550	3600	5100
Stake	780	1560	2600	3600	5200
B6-W200 Crew Cab 4x4 — (¾-Ton) — (146 in. w.b.)					
Utiline Pickup	750	1500	2500	3500	5000
Sweptline Pickup	770	1550	2550	3600	5100
B6-W300 Series 4x4 — (1-Ton) — (133 in. w.b.)					
Utiline Pickup	780	1560	2600	3600	5200
Platform	740	1470	2450	3350	4900
Stake	770	1550	2550	3600	5100
B6-WM300 Power-Wagon — (1-Ton) — (126 in. w.b.)					
Utiline Pickup	980	1950	3250	4550	6500

NOTE: Add 10 percent for V-8 engine.
Add 5 percent for automatic transmission.
Add 4 percent for power winch.

1967 DODGE

1967 Dodge A108 King-Size Forward Control Van (JAG)

½-TON COMPACT — C SERIES A100 — SIX-CYLINDER and V-8 / ½-TON COMPACT — C SERIES A108 — SIX-CYLINDER and V-8: — An extended-wheelbase (108 in.) van and Sportsman, offering 43 cu. ft. more cargo space, were added to round out the compact truck lineup. Available Gross Vehicle Weights for both models were now 4000, 4800 or 5400 pounds. The 318 cu. in. V-8 was made optional, replacing the 273. Both 170 and 225 cu. in. slant sixes were still available. Transmission options remained as before: an A903 three-speed manual, only for the 170 six; heavy-duty three-speed manual (Model A745) for the 225 cu. in. six and 318 V-8; and three-speed automatic LoadFlite for any engine.

½-TON — C SERIES D100 — SIX-CYLINDER and V-8 / ¾-TON — C SERIES D200 — SIX-CYLINDER and V-8 / 1-TON — C SERIES D300 — SIX-CYLINDER and V-8 / ½-TON 4x4 — C SERIES W100 — SIX-CYLIN-DER and V-8 / ¾-TON 4x4 — C SERIES W200 — SIX-CYLINDER and V-8 / 1-TON 4x4 — C SERIES W300 — SIX-CYLINDER and V-8: — All models continued without appearance changes, but the Town Panel and Wagon were dropped. Both a 383 cu. in. V-8 and the former 318 V-8 engine were available at extra cost on all models. The 383 was the largest engine available for the Custom Sports Special pickup, replacing the 426. Dodge continued aggressive tactics in the pickup camper business, offering "Camper Special" packages for the entire pickup line. One interesting development was the NP435 four-speed manual transmission. Originally designed for camper use, it worked well in all pickups, offering unique spacing between 2nd and 3rd gear. A driver could shift down into 3rd at highway speed and maintain speeds as high as 60 mph while pulling a load up a moderate grade. Introduced at mid-year was a new, specially applied paint for cab roofs, stippled to create a grain effect. Viewed from a distance, it looked like a vinyl roof. Standard equipment was the same as 1966.

1-TON POWER-WAGON — C SERIES WM300 — SIX-CYLINDER: — Once again, Power-Wagons continued with minimal change.

I.D. DATA: Serial numbers were in the same location, with the same coding, as 1964-66. Starting Serial Numbers: (A100/108) 2,098,000 (Michigan); 7,000,000 (Missouri). (all others) 1,668,000 (Michigan); 7,000,000 (Missouri). Ending serial numbers are not available. Engine numbers were in the same location as 1963-66. Engine numbers are not available.

Model	Body Type	Price	Weight	Prod. Total
A100/A108 Compact Series — (½-Ton) — (90 in. w.b.)				
A100	Pickup	1989	2910	Note 1
A100	Panel Van (Note 3)	2076	2910	Note 1
A100	Van	2126	2930	Note 1
(108 in. w.b.)				
A108	Panel Van (Note 3)	2232	3125	Note 2
A108	Van	2282	3145	Note 2

NOTE 1: Total model year production: (six) 22,182; (V-8) 6352.

NOTE 2: Total model year production: (six) 6599; (V-8) 7373.

NOTE 3: Rear doors only.

Model	Body Type	Price	Weight	Prod. Total
D100 Series — (½-Ton) — (114 in. w.b.)				
D100	Chassis & Cowl	1537	2540	Note 4
D100	Chassis & Cab	1914	3095	Note 4
D100	Utiline Pickup	2019	3405	Note 4
D100	Sweptline Pickup	2045	3505	Note 4
(128 in. w.b.)				
D100	Chassis & Cowl	1572	2590	Note 5
D100	Chassis & Cab	1948	3110	Note 5
D100	Utiline Pickup	2055	3600	Note 5
D100	Sweptline Pickup	2080	3660	Note 5
D100	Platform	2105	3535	Note 5
D100	Stake	2153	3735	Note 5

NOTE 4: Total model year production: (six) 9532; (V-8) 3342.

NOTE 5: Total model year production: (six) 13,419; (V-8) 15,770.

Model	Body Type	Price	Weight	Prod. Total
D200 Series — (¾-Ton) — (128 in. w.b.)				
D200	Chassis & Cowl	1667	3095	Note 6
D200	Chassis & Cab	2053	3650	Note 6
D200	Utiline Pickup	2158	4090	Note 6
D200	Sweptline Pickup	2186	4150	Note 6
D200	Platform	2209	4025	Note 6
D200	Stake	2257	4225	Note 6

NOTE 6: Total model year production: (six) 6556; (V-8) 13,469.

Model	Body Type	Price	Weight	Prod. Total
D200 Crew Cab Series — (¾-Ton) — (146 in. w.b.)				
D200	Chassis	2724	3973	—
D200	Utiline Pickup	2841	4285	—
D200	Sweptline Pickup	2855	4385	—
D300 Series — (1-Ton) — (133 in. w.b.)				
D300	Chassis & Cowl	1781	3220	Note 7
D300	Chassis & Cab	2187	3775	Note 7
D300	Utiline Pickup	2324	4175	Note 7
D300	Platform	2373	4475	Note 7
D300	Stake	2432	4675	Note 7

NOTE 7: Total model year production: (six) 3676; (V-8) 4577.

Model	Body Type	Price	Weight	Prod. Total
W100 Series 4x4 — (½-Ton) — (114 in. w.b.)				
W100	Chassis & Cab	2559	3900	Note 8
W100	Utiline Pickup	2678	4210	Note 8
W100	Sweptline Pickup	2691	4310	Note 8

NOTE 8: Total model year production: (six) 570; (V-8) 530.

Model	Body Type	Price	Weight	Prod. Total
W200 Series 4x4 — (¾-Ton) — (128 in. w.b.)				
W200	Chassis & Cab	2659	3945	Note 9
W200	Utiline Pickup	2778	4385	Note 9
W200	Sweptline Pickup	2791	4445	Note 9
W200	Platform	2815	4320	Note 9
W200	Stake	2865	4520	Note 9

NOTE 9: Total model year production: (six) 2099; (V-8) 1997.

Model	Body Type	Price	Weight	Prod. Total
W200 Crew Cab Series 4x4 — (¾-Ton) — (146 in. w.b.)				
W200	Chassis	3416	4375	—
W200	Utiline Pickup	3534	4775	—
W200	Sweptline Pickup	3547	4785	—

Model	Body Type	Price	Weight	Prod. Total
W300 Series 4x4 — (1-Ton) — (133 in. w.b.)				
W300	Chassis & Cowl	3011	4090	Note 10
W300	Chassis & Cab	3395	4645	Note 10
W300	Utiline Pickup	3534	5045	Note 10
W300	Platform	3584	5345	Note 10
W300	Stake	3644	5545	Note 10

NOTE 10: Total model year production: (six) 214; (V-8) 528.

Model	Body Type	Price	Weight	Prod. Total
WM300 Series Power-Wagon — (1-Ton) — (126 in. w.b.)				
WM300	Chassis & Cowl	3662	4095	Note 11
WM300	Chassis & Cab	4033	4520	Note 11
WM300	Utiline Pickup	4184	4920	Note 11

NOTE 11: Total model year production: 974 (plus 2303 M.D.A.P. models).

NOTE 12: Weights and prices shown are for 6-cyl. models. For V-8 engine, add $120 to price.

ENGINE (A100/108): Inline. Overhead valves. Slant six. Cast iron block. Bore & stroke: 3.4 x 3.125 in. Displacement: 170.2 cu. in. Compression ratio: 8.5:1. Brake horsepower 101 at 4000 R.P.M. Net (Taxable) horsepower: 27.70. Torque: 145 lbs.-ft. at 1600 R.P.M. Four main bearings. Solid valve lifters.

ENGINE (D100-300, W100-300; optional A100/108): Inline. Overhead valves. Slant six-cylinder. Cast iron block. Bore & stroke: 3.4 x 4.125 in. Displacement: 224.7 cu. in. Compression ratio: 8.4:1. Brake horsepower: 140 at 3900 R.P.M. Net horsepower: 27.70. Torque: 215 lbs.-ft. at 1600 R.P.M. Four main bearings. Solid valve lifters.

ENGINE (WM300): Inline. L-head. Six-cylinder. Cast iron block. Bore & stroke: 3.437 x 4.5 in. Displacement: 250.6 cu. in. Compression ratio: 7.1:1. Brake horsepower: 125 at 3600 R.P.M. Net horsepower: 28.35. Torque: 216 lbs.-ft. at 1600 R.P.M. Four main bearings. Solid valve lifters.

ENGINE (Optional: D100-300, W100-300, A100/108): 90-degree, overhead valve. Eight-cylinder. Cast iron block. Bore & stroke: 3.91 x 3.312 in. Displacement: 318.1 cu. in. Compression ratio: 8.5:1. Brake horsepower: 210 at 4000 R.P.M. Net horsepower: 48.92. Torque: 280 lbs.-ft. at 2400 R.P.M. Five main bearings. Hydraulic valve lifters.

ENGINE (D100-300, W100-200): 90-degree, overhead valve. Eight-cylinder. Cast iron block. Bore & stroke: 4.25 x 3.38 in. Displacement: 383 cu. in. Compression ratio: 9.2:1. Brake horsepower: 258 at 4400 R.P.M. Net horsepower: 57.8. Torque: 323 lbs.-ft. at 2400 R.P.M. Five main bearings. Hydraulic valve lifters.

CHASSIS (A100): Wheelbase: 90 in. Tires: 6.95 x 14-2 four-ply. (4000-lb. GVW); 8.15 x 15 four-ply (4800-lb. GVW); 8.15 x 15 eight-ply (5400-lb. GVW).

CHASSIS (A108): Wheelbase: 108 in. Tires: 6.95 x 14-4 eight-ply. (4000-lb. GVW); 8x15 x 15 four-ply (4800-lb. GVW); 8.15 x 15 eight-ply (5400-lbs. GVW).

CHASSIS (D100): Wheelbase: 114 in. or 128 in. Tires: 6.70 x 15 four-ply. GVW: 5200 lbs. max.

CHASSIS (D200): Wheelbase: 128 in. or 146 in. Tires: 7 x 17.5 six-ply. GVW: 7500 lbs. maximum.

CHASSIS (D300): Wheelbase: 133 in. Tires: 7 x 17.5 six-ply. GVW: 9000 lbs. max.

CHASSIS (W100): Wheelbase: 114 in. Tires: 7 x 17.5 six-ply. GVW: 6000 lbs. max.

CHASSIS (W200): Wheelbase: 128 in. or 146 in. Tires: 8 x 19.5 eight-ply. GVW: 8000 lbs. maximum.

CHASSIS (W300): Wheelbase: 133 in. Tires: 7.50 x 16 six-ply. GVW: 10,000 lbs. maximum.

CHASSIS (WM300): Wheelbase: 126 in. Tires: 9.00 x 16 ten-ply. GVW: 9500 lbs. maximum.

TECHNICAL: Same as 1966; see previous specifications.

OPTIONS: Same as 1966; see previous list. Custom Sports Package included: bucket seats; custom carpeting; 1 in. tape stripes; bright mylar molding around windshield and rear window; Dodge Delta emblems on "B" posts; bright molding on instrument panel; textured metal door trim panels; left and right armrests; left and right sunvisors; additional insulation; console with lighter and map light; black carpet over gas tank cover; bright grille; bright drip molding; custom nameplates; bright trim on instrument cluster; hood around dials and knobs; white steering wheel with bright horn ring; bright finish front bumper. Custom Sports Package option: short arm stationary 5 in. chromed outside mirrors (left and right).

NOTE: Custom Sports Package was available on all conventional cab pickups.

HISTORICAL: Introduced: October, 1966. Calendar year sales: 101,436. Calendar year production: 141,865. Model year production: (six) 74,794; (V-8) 53,938; (Total) 128,732. Historical notes: Dodge placed fourth in the truck industry production race, increasing its market share slightly though total production was down 7.4 percent from 1966. This was Dodge's Golden Anniversary as a truck builder. In a half-century, the company had built about 4.7 million commercial vehicles. The Warren, Michigan plant produced 111,198 trucks, while 30,667 came out of St. Louis. Nearly half

the trucks made carried a V-8 engine. Diesel sales rose significantly. Total industry truck shipments declined for the second straight year. Dodge exhibited an experimental truck, called Deora, at various auto shows during 1967. Based on the A100 chassis and power train, this "dream truck" was a fully operating prototype. Combining the creature comforts of a luxurious town sedan with the utility of a pickup truck, the Deora anticipated the tremendous future upsurge in sales of vehicles based on the pickup format.

Pricing

1967	5	4	3	2	1
A100 Compact — (½-Ton) — (90 in. w.b.)					
Pickup	840	1680	2800	3900	5600
Panel Van	780	1560	2600	3600	5200
Van	770	1550	2550	3600	5100
A108 Compact — (½-Ton) — (108 in. w.b.)					
Panel Van	800	1600	2650	3700	5300
Van	780	1560	2600	3600	5200
D100 Series — (½-Ton) — (114 in. w.b.)					
Utiline Pickup	870	1750	2900	4100	5800
Sweptline Pickup	890	1770	2950	4150	5900
D100 Series — (½-Ton) — (128 in. w.b.)					
Utiline Pickup	850	1700	2850	4000	5700
Sweptline Pickup	870	1750	2900	4100	5800
Platform	750	1500	2500	3500	5000
Stake	770	1550	2550	3600	5100
D200 Series — (¾-Ton) — (128 in. w.b.)					
Utiline Pickup	830	1650	2750	3850	5500
Sweptline Pickup	840	1680	2800	3900	5600
Platform	740	1470	2450	3350	4900
Stake	750	1500	2500	3500	5000
D200 Crew Cab — (¾-Ton) — (146 in. w.b.)					
Utiline Pickup	810	1620	2700	3800	5400
Sweptline Pickup	830	1650	2750	3850	5500
D300 Series — (1-Ton) — (133 in. w.b.)					
Utiline Pickup	750	1500	2500	3500	5000
Platform	720	1450	2400	3300	4800
Stake	740	1470	2450	3350	4900
W100 Series 4x4 — (½-Ton) — (114 in. w.b.)					
Utiline Pickup	890	1770	2950	4150	5900
Sweptline Pickup	900	1800	3000	4200	6000
W200 Series 4x4 — (¾-Ton) — (128 in. w.b.)					
Utiline Pickup	850	1700	2850	4000	5700
Sweptline Pickup	870	1750	2900	4100	5800
Platform	750	1500	2500	3500	5000
Stake	770	1550	2550	3600	5100
W200 Crew Cab 4x4 — (¾-Ton) — (146 in. w.b.)					
Utiline Pickup	770	1550	2550	3600	5100
Sweptline Pickup	780	1560	2600	3600	5200
W300 Series 4x4 — (1-Ton) — (133 in. w.b.)					
Utiline Pickup	770	1550	2550	3600	5100
Platform	740	1470	2450	3350	4900
Stake	750	1500	2500	3500	5000
WM300 Power-Wagon — (1-Ton) — (126 in. w.b.)					
Utiline Pickup	980	1950	3250	4550	6500

NOTE: Add 10 percent for V-8 engine.
Add 5 percent for automatic transmission.
Add 4 percent for power winch.

1968 DODGE

1968 Dodge D100 Adventurer Sweptline Pickup (JAG)

½-TON COMPACT — A100/108 SERIES — SIX-CYLINDER and V-8: — Compacts carried forward with no change in appearance, models, major mechanicals, or engine options. But they shared much of the increased glamour given to the conventional light-duty models. Dodge now offered color-keyed interiors as standard equipment. Two-tone paint schemes were available. Dodge also picked up and expanded a concept begun several years earlier, called the Tradesman. Replacing a conventional pickup, the Tradesman utility body contained lockable, easy-access storage compartments on both sides. Starting with 1968, Dodge applied the idea to its compact vans, targeting the service trades — TV and appliance repair, air conditioning, plumbing/heating, etc. Dodge offered "Job-Mated" interiors to allow these tradespeople to make best use of van interiors for tools and equipment. Eighteen factory-installed extra equipment packages were available, which consisted of shelves, locks, drawers, hanging bars and partitions. These packages were available for both 90 in. and 108 in. w.b. vans, helping Dodge to strengthen its leadership position in the compact van market. Dodge captured an industry "first" by offering power steering on compact vans and wagons with automatic transmission. Passenger vans were considered station wagons, not trucks.

½-TON — D100 SERIES — SIX-CYLINDER and V-8 / ¾-TON — D200 SERIES — SIX-CYLINDER and V-8 / 1-TON — D300 SERIES — SIX-CYLINDER and V-8 / ½-TON 4x4 — W100 SERIES — SIX-CYLINDER and V-8 / ¾-TON 4x4 — W200 SERIES — SIX-CYLINDER and V-8 / 1-TON 4x4 — W300 SERIES — SIX-CYLINDER and V-8: — Front end appearance changes set the 1968 models apart from their predecessors. A new one-piece, full-width grille, which enclosed the wide-spaced headlights and new vertical parking lights, gave a fresh new look. Gone was the plush Custom Sports Special, replaced by the even plusher Adventurer. A special sports-type Sweptline, the Adventurer featured vinyl bucket seats, a center console, vinyl roof, chrome moldings that swept from hood to tailgate, and color-keyed custom carpeting. Increased comfort, appearance, glamour and prestige, available through optional custom features, was the main marketing thrust this year. Dodge made a real effort to give light-duty trucks better looks and convenience, to add sales appeal and build in more resale value and owner satisfaction. Four color-keyed interiors were available, plus 13 body colors. Engines and models remained the same as 1967. Standard equipment included a dome light, painted front bumper and hubcaps, padded dash, backup lights, emergency flasher, heater/defroster, side reflectors, variable-speed electric wipers and dual jet washers, front and rear shocks (front only on 1-ton), and a 225-cu. in. 6-cyl. engine.

1-TON POWER-WAGON — WM300 SERIES — SIX-CYLINDER: — After a lengthy "career," this would be the final year for the military-style Power-Wagon. From 1969 through the late 1970s, it would be produced for export only.

I.D. DATA: Serial numbers were in the same location, with the same coding, as 1964-67. Starting Serial Numbers: (A100/108) 2,135,000 (Michigan); 7,020,000 (Missouri). (all others) 1,780,000 (Michigan); 7,020,000 (Missouri); 6,000,000 (Canada). Ending serial numbers are not available. A new engine numbering system began this year. The first two letters designated the manufacturing plant: PM (Mound Road); PT (Trenton); or DW (Windsor). The next three digits indicated displacement: 170, 225, 318, etc. The next letter designated model: R (regular gas); L (low compression); T (standard-duty); or H (heavy-duty). The next four digits designated the date of manufacture, based on a 10,000-day calendar. Last came a four-digit sequence number for each day's production, starting with 0000 for LA318 engines and 5000 for all others. Example: PT318T22040008. This engine would be made in Trenton, with 318 cu. in. displacement, standard compression, the eighth engine built on day no. 2204.

NOTE: No compact vans were built in Canada.

Model	Body Type	Price	Weight	Prod. Total
A100/A108 Compact Series — (½-Ton) — (90 in. w.b.)				
A100	Pickup	2047	2910	Note 1
A100	Panel Van (Note 3)	2132	2910	Note 1
A100	Van	2183	2930	Note 1
(108 in. w.b.)				
A108	Panel Van (Note 3)	2291	3125	Note 2
A108	Van	2342	3145	Note 2

NOTE 1: Total model year production: (six) 18,756; (V-8) 2613.

NOTE 2: Total model year production: (six) 17,548; (V-8) 16,248.

NOTE 3: Rear doors only.

Model	Body Type	Price	Weight	Prod. Total
D100 Series — (½-Ton) — (114 in. w.b.)				
D100	Chassis & Cowl	1656	2540	Note 4
D100	Chassis & Cab	2056	3090	Note 4
D100	Utiline Pickup	2163	3470	Note 4
D100	Sweptline Pickup	2189	3520	Note 4
(128 in. w.b.)				
D100	Chassis & Cowl	1691	2590	Note 5
D100	Chassis & Cab	2090	3110	Note 5
D100	Utiline Pickup	2200	3600	Note 5
D100	Sweptline Pickup	2225	3660	Note 5
D100	Platform	2251	3535	Note 5
D100	Stake	2300	3735	Note 5

NOTE 4: Total model year production: (six) 10,126; (V-8) 3930.

NOTE 5: Total model year production: (six) 18,505; (V-8) 27,384.

Model	Body Type	Price	Weight	Prod. Total
D200 Series — (¾-Ton) — (128 in. w.b.)				
D200	Chassis & Cowl	1756	3095	Note 6
D200	Chassis & Cab	2165	3650	Note 6
D200	Utiline Pickup	2273	4090	Note 6
D200	Sweptline Pickup	2301	4150	Note 6
D200	Platform	2325	4025	Note 6
D200	Stake	2374	4225	Note 6

NOTE 6: Total model year production: (six) 7451; (V-8) 20,422.

Model	Body Type	Price	Weight	Prod. Total
D200 Crew Cab Series — (¾-Ton) — (146 in. w.b.)				
D200	Chassis	2859	3973	—
D200	Utiline Pickup	2979	4335	—
D200	Sweptline Pickup	2993	4385	—
D300 Series — (1-Ton) — (133 in. w.b.)				
D300	Chassis & Cowl	1876	3220	Note 7
D300	Chassis & Cab	2305	3775	Note 7
D300	Utiline Pickup	2446	4355	Note 7
D300	Platform	2496	4560	Note 7
D300	Stake	2556	4760	Note 7

NOTE 7: Total model year production: (six) 3394; (V-8) 6979.

Model	Body Type	Price	Weight	Prod. Total
W100 Series 4x4 — (½-Ton) — (114 in. w.b.)				
W100	Chassis & Cab	2696	3735	Note 8
W100	Utiline Pickup	2818	4095	Note 8
W100	Sweptline Pickup	2831	4145	Note 8

NOTE 8: Total model year production: (six) 721; (V-8) 752.

Model	Body Type	Price	Weight	Prod. Total
W200 Series 4x4 — (¾-Ton) — (128 in. w.b.)				
W200	Chassis & Cab	2800	3945	Note 9
W200	Utiline Pickup	2922	4385	Note 9
W200	Sweptline Pickup	2935	4445	Note 9
W200	Platform	2960	4320	Note 9
W200	Stake	3011	4520	Note 9

NOTE 9: Total model year production: (six) 2759; (V-8) 3178.

Model	Body Type	Price	Weight	Prod. Total
W200 Crew Cab Series 4x4 — (¾-Ton) — (146 in. w.b.)				
W200	Chassis	2582	4375	—
W200	Utiline Pickup	3703	4735	—
W200	Sweptline Pickup	3716	4785	—
W300 Series 4x4 — (1-Ton) — (133 in. w.b.)				
W300	Chassis & Cowl	3100	4090	Note 10
W300	Chassis & Cab	3508	4645	Note 10
W300	Utiline Pickup	3649	5140	Note 10
W300	Platform	3700	5345	Note 10
W300	Stake	3762	5545	Note 10

NOTE 10: Total model year production: (six) 175; (V-8) 693.

Model	Body Type	Price	Weight	Prod. Total
WM300 Series Power-Wagon — (1-Ton) — (126 in. w.b.)				
WM300	Chassis & Cowl	3761	4095	Note 11
WM300	Chassis & Cab	4141	4520	Note 11
WM300	Utiline Pickup	4295	4920	Note 11

NOTE 11: Total model year production: 2461 (plus 1958 M.D.A.P.).

NOTE 12: Weights and prices shown are for 6-cyl. engines. For V-8 engine, add $120 to price.

ENGINE: Same as 1967; see previous specifications.

CHASSIS (A100): Wheelbase: 90 in. Tires: 6.95 x 14 four-ply. GVW: 3800-4600 lbs. Axle Capacity: (front) 2200 lbs.; (rear) 3000 lbs.

CHASSIS (A108): Wheelbase: 108 in. Tires: 8.15 x 15-2 four-ply. GVW: 3800-4800 lbs. Axle Capacity: (front) 2200 lbs.; (rear) 3000 lbs.

CHASSIS (D100): Wheelbase: 114 in. or 128 in. Tires: 8.15 x 15 eight-ply. GVW: 4300-5200 lbs. Axle Capacity: (front) 2500 lbs.; (rear) 3600 lbs.

CHASSIS (D200): Wheelbase: 128 in. or 146 in. Tires: 8 x 19.5 eight-ply. GVW: 5200-7500 lbs. Axle Capacity: (front) 2800 lbs.; (rear) 5500 lbs.

CHASSIS (D300): Wheelbase: 133 in. Tires: 8 x 17.5 six-ply. GVW: 6700-10,000 lbs. Axle Capacity: (front) 3800 lbs.; (rear) 7500 lbs.

CHASSIS (W100): Wheelbase: 114 in. Tires: 7 x 17.5 six-ply. GVW: 5100-6000 lbs. Axle Capacity: (front) 3000 lbs.; (rear) 4500 lbs.

CHASSIS (W200): Wheelbase: 128 in. or 146 in. Tires: 8 x 19.5 eight-ply. GVW: 6000-8000 lbs. Axle Capacity: (front) 3000 lbs.; (rear) 5500 lbs.

CHASSIS (W300): Wheelbase: 133 in. Tires: 7.50 x 16 six-ply. GVW: 10,000 lbs. maximum. Axle Capacity: (front) 4500 lbs.; (rear) 7500 lbs.

CHASSIS (WM300): Wheelbase: 126 in. Tires: 9.00 x 16 ten-ply. GVW: 8200-9500 lbs. Axle Capacity: (front) 3750 lbs.; (rear) 6500 lbs.

TECHNICAL: Selective sliding gear transmission. Speeds: 3F/1R except 1-ton models, 4F/1R. Column or floor shift control. Single plate dry disc clutch: (A100) 9⅛ in.; (D100/D200) 10 in.; (others) 11 in. Rear axle ratio: (A100) 3.27:1, 3.55:1, 3.91:1 or 4.56:1; (D100) 3.23:1, 3.55:1 or 3.91:1; (D200, W100-200) 3.54:1, 4.1:1 or 4.88:1; (D300) 4.1:1 or 5.87:1; (W300) 4.88:1 or 5.87:1; (WM300) 5.83:1. Hydraulic four-wheel brakes. Fuel tank: (A100) 23 gallon; (others) 18 gallon. One-quart oil filter. Air cleaner: (A100, D100-200) dry; (others) oil bath. Alternator: (A100) 30-amp; (others) 37-amp. Wheels: (A100) 14 x 5.00; (D100) 15 x 5.50; (D200, W100) 16 x 6.00; (D300, W200) 17.5 x 5.25; (W300) 19.5 x 5.25; (WM300) 16 x 6.5.

OPTIONS (Factory-Installed): Chrome front-bumper (A100, D100-200). Rear bumper (except WM300). Bumper guards (A100). Wheel covers (A100, D100). Chrome hubcaps (A100, D100-200). Spare tire carrier (D/W100-300). Adventurer package (D100-200). Appearance package (D/W100-300). Comfort package (D/W100-300). Tinted glass (except WM300). Radio (except WM300). Auxiliary heater (D100-300, W300). Cigar lighter (except WM300). Outside mirrors. Cab marker lights (D/W100-200). Dual horns (D/W100-300). Heavy-duty instruments (D/W100-300). Rear quarter cab windows (A100). Undercoating. Camper Special package (D/W200). Camper Custom package (D200). Trim molding package (D/W100-200). Two-tone paint (except WM300). Textured vinyl roof (D100). Bucket seat No. 1 or No. 2 (D100-200). Foam padded seat (D/W100-300). Third seat belt (except A100). Shoulder belt (D/W100-300). Three-ton jack (except A100). Heavy-duty front or rear springs (except WM300). Extra-heavy-duty rear springs (D100-300). Oil pressure gauge (except WM300). Power steering (D100-300). Vacuum power brake booster (D200-300, W100-300). Hand throttle (D/W100-300). Horn ring (A100). 7500-lb. rear axle (D300). Fenders for dual rear wheels (D/W300). Rear shock absorbers (D300). 3500-lb. front axle (W200). Spare wheel for dual axes (D/W300). Increased cooling capacity (D200-300, W100-300). One-quart oil bath air cleaner (except W/WM300). 46 or 60-amp alternator (except A100). 37, 46 or 60-amp alternator (A100). 10 in. clutch (A100). 11 in. clutch (D100-200). Anti-spin rear axle (except WM300). Governor (D/W100-300). 225 cu. in. engine (A100). 318 cu. in. V-8 engine (except WM300). 383 cu. in. V-8 engine (D100-300, W100-200). Four-speed manual transmission, close or wide spaced ratios (D/W100-200); close only (D300). LoadFlite automatic transmission (D models). Locking front hubs (W/WM models). Pintle hook (W/WM models). Power take-off (W/WM models). Fuel/vacuum pump (WM300). Radiator overflow tank (WM300). Rear shocks (W/WM300). Tow hooks (W/WM300). 8000-lb. winch (W100-300). 10,000-lb. winch (WM300).

HISTORICAL: Introduced: August, 1967. Calendar year sales: 138,205. Calendar year production: 173,769. Model year production: (six) 96,778; (V-8) 86,237; (Total) 183,015. Innovations: Car-like, color-keyed interiors. Tradesman compact vans with "Job-Mated" interiors. Power steering on compact vans. Historical notes: The U.S. truck industry had its best year ever, producing 1,950,713 units. Dodge shared in this record-setting feat, posting its highest production total in history. All-time record sales gained 36.2 percent over 1967. Trucks were built at three plants: Warren, Michigan (105,921 units); St. Louis (52,790); and the balance at Burt Road, Detroit. Well over half (56 percent) of Dodge trucks had V-8 engines. Dodge also built 3,488 diesel models. Dodge continued to produce a full line, from compacts to heavy-duty tilt cab diesels.

Pricing

1968

	5	4	3	2	1
A100 Compact — (½-Ton) — (90 in. w.b.)					
Pickup	840	1680	2800	3900	5600
Panel Van	780	1560	2600	3600	5200
Van	770	1550	2550	3600	5100
A108 Compact — (½-Ton) — (108 in. w.b.)					
Panel Van	800	1600	2650	3700	5300
Van	780	1560	2600	3600	5200
D100 Series — (½-Ton) — (114 in. w.b.)					
Utiline Pickup	870	1750	2900	4100	5800
Sweptline Pickup	890	1770	2950	4150	5900
D100 Series — (½-Ton) — (128 in. w.b.)					
Utiline Pickup	850	1700	2850	4000	5700
Sweptline Pickup	870	1750	2900	4100	5800
Platform	750	1500	2500	3500	5000
Stake	770	1550	2550	3600	5100
D200 Series — (¾-Ton) — (128 in. w.b.)					
Utiline Pickup	830	1650	2750	3850	5500
Sweptline Pickup	840	1680	2800	3900	5600
Platform	740	1470	2450	3350	4900
Stake	750	1500	2500	3500	5000
D200 Crew Cab — (¾-Ton) — (146 in. w.b.)					
Utiline Pickup	810	1620	2700	3800	5400
Sweptline Pickup	830	1650	2750	3850	5500
D300 Series — (1-Ton) — (133 in. w.b.)					
Utiline Pickup	750	1500	2500	3500	5000
Platform	720	1450	2400	3300	4800
Stake	740	1470	2450	3350	4900
W100 Series 4x4 — (½-Ton) — (114 in. w.b.)					
Utiline Pickup	890	1770	2950	4150	5900
Sweptline Pickup	900	1800	3000	4200	6000
W200 Series 4x4 — (¾-Ton) — (128 in. w.b.)					
Utiline Pickup	850	1700	2850	4000	5700
Sweptline Pickup	870	1750	2900	4100	5800
Platform	750	1500	2500	3500	5000
Stake	770	1550	2550	3600	5100
W200 Crew Cab 4x4 — (¾-Ton) — (146 in. w.b.)					
Utiline Pickup	770	1550	2550	3600	5100
Sweptline Pickup	780	1560	2600	3600	5200
W300 Series 4x4 — (1-Ton) — (133 in. w.b.)					
Utiline Pickup	770	1550	2550	3600	5100
Platform	740	1470	2450	3350	4900
Stake	750	1500	2500	3500	5000
WM300 Power-Wagon — (1-Ton) — (126 in. w.b.)					
Utiline Pickup	980	1950	3250	4550	6500

NOTE: Add 10 percent for V-8 engine.
Add 5 percent for automatic transmission.
Add 4 percent for power winch.

1969 DODGE

1969 Dodge D200 Adventurer Sweptline Pickup (JAG)

½-TON COMPACT — A100/108 SERIES — SIX-CYLINDER and V-8: — Both wheelbases carried on without change. Dodge continued to promote the versatility of its Job-Mated Tradesman van. Seventeen basic Tradesman packages were available from the factory, to suit nearly every need. In the Sportsman Wagon series, a unique mobile office called the "Executive Suite" was available, as was a living room on wheels called the "Host Wagon."

½-TON — D100 SERIES — SIX-CYLINDER and V-8 / ¾-TON — D200 SERIES — SIX-CYLINDER and V-8 / 1-TON — D300 SERIES — SIX-CYLINDER and V-8 / ½-TON 4x4 — W100 SERIES — SIX-CYLINDER and V-8 / ¾-TON — W200 SERIES — SIX-CYLINDER and V-8 / 1-TON 4x4 — W300 SERIES — SIX-CYLINDER and V-8: — Styling for 1969 did not change, as even the new grille from 1968 carried forward. Yet quite a few improvements were made. D100 and D200 models got an improved front suspension called "Cushioned-Beam." The old reliable I-beam front axle was still used, but a new sway bar took out some of the body lean while cornering and contributed to easier steering. All models except the military style Power-Wagon carried over, with the same engines. Transmission options also stayed the same, except on D100-300 models with 3-speed LoadFlite automatic transmission, the shift lever was now conveniently column-mounted. 4x4 models gained a simplified single-lever control for the transfer case. A driver could shift into and out of 4wd with a flick of the wrist. Gone was the old two-lever control. Air conditioning changed from under-dash to dash-integral mounting on all models.

I.D. DATA: Serial numbers were on a plate on the left door lock pillar. The 10-character number consisted of four elements. The first two digits gave model code; the third digit was number of cylinders (6 or 8). The fourth digit showed assembly plant (1 for Warren Truck; 2 for Warren heavy-duty; 6 for Windsor; or 7 for Missouri). The final six digits made up the sequence number. Model codes were as follows: 11 (D100); 12 (D200); 13 (D300); 18 (A100 Pickup); 19 (A100 Van); 20 (A100 Wagon); 21 (W100); 22 (W200); 23 (W300); 24 (WM300 — export only); 30 to 32 (P100-300 forward control). Starting and ending sequence numbers are not available. Engine numbers were located as follows: (six) right side of block, below no. 1 spark plug; (318 V-8) left side of block, below cylinder head; (383 V-8) right side of block, adjacent to distributor. Two engine numbering systems were used. The 170 and 225 cu. in. six-cylinder and 318 cu. in. V-8 engines were identified as follows: First two letters indicated manufacturing plant (GM, Mound Road; GT, Trenton; NM, Marysville; GW, Windsor). Next three digits showed displacement. Next letter gave engine type (R, regular 318; T, standard 225; H, premium 225). Next came a four-digit manufacturing date code based on a 10,000-day calendar. The final four digits were the sequence number, which began with 0001 for each day. 383 cu. in. and other engines were identified as follows: First letter indicated model year; next letter, engine type (T, standard; H, premium); next three digits, displacement; next digit, assembly plant shift; next four digits, manufacture date; next two letters, non-standard engine indicator; followed by four-digit sequence number. Starting and ending engine numbers are not available.

Model	Body Type	Price	Weight	Prod. Total
A100/A108 Compact Series — (½-Ton) — (90 in. w.b.)				
A100	Pickup	2363	2810	Note 1
A100	Panel Van (Note 3)	2435	2795	Note 1
A100	Van	—	—	Note 1
(108 in. w.b.)				
A108	Panel Van (Note 3)	2591	3005	Note 2
A108	Van	—	—	Note 2

NOTE 1: Total model year production: (six) 14,609; (V-8) 2235.

NOTE 2: Total model year production: (six) 14,453; (V-8) 16,354.

NOTE 3: Rear doors only.

Model	Body Type	Price	Weight	Prod. Total
D100 Series — (½-Ton) — (114 in. w.b.)				
D100	Chassis & Cowl	—	—	Note 4
D100	Chassis & Cowl	—	—	Note 4
D100	Utiline Pickup	—	—	Note 4
D100	Sweptline Pickup	2442	3432	Note 4
(128 in. w.b.)				
D100	Chassis & Cowl	—	—	Note 5
D100	Chassis & Cab	—	—	Note 5
D100	Utiline Pickup	—	—	Note 5
D100	Sweptline Pickup	2479	3572	Note 5
D100	Platform	—	—	Note 5
D100	Stake	2527	3645	Note 5

NOTE 4: Total model year production: (six) 10,860; (V-8) 4587.

NOTE 5: Total model year production: (six) 14,146; (V-8) 27,140.

D200 Series — (¾-Ton) — (128 in. w.b.)				
D200	Chassis & Cowl	—	—	Note 6
D200	Chassis & Cab	—	—	Note 6
D200	Utiline Pickup	—	—	Note 6
D200	Sweptline Pickup	2625	3807	Note 6
D200	Platform	—	—	Note 6
D200	Stake	2674	3880	Note 6

NOTE 6: Total model year production: (six) 4282; (V-8) 17,148.

D200 Crew Cab Series — (¾-Ton) — (146 in. w.b.)				
D200	Chassis	—	—	Note 7
D200	Utiline Pickup	—	—	Note 7
D200	Sweptline Pickup	3341	4135	Note 7

NOTE 7: Total model year production: (six) 857; (V-8) 1707.

D300 Series — (1-Ton) — (133 in. w.b.)				
D300	Chassis & Cowl	—	—	Note 8
D300	Chassis & Cab	2806	3715	Note 8
D300	Utiline Pickup	2722	4050	Note 8
D300	Platform	—	—	Note 8
D300	Stake	—	—	Note 8

NOTE 8: Total model year production: (six) 2390; (V-8) 6136.

D300 Crew Cab Series — (1-Ton) — (159 in. w.b.)				
D300	Chassis & Cab	2641	3810	Note 9
D300	Utiline Pickup	—	—	Note 9
D300	Sweptline Pickup	3389	4505	Note 9

NOTE 9: Total model year production: (six) 245; (V-8) 1596.

W100 Series 4x4 — (½-Ton) — (114 in. w.b.)				
W100	Chassis & Cab	—	—	Note 10
W100	Utiline Pickup	—	—	Note 10
W100	Sweptline Pickup	—	—	Note 10
(128 in. w.b.)				
W100	Chassis & Cab	—	—	Note 11
W100	Utiline Pickup	—	—	Note 11
W100	Sweptline Pickup	—	—	Note 11

NOTE 10: Total model year production: (six) 766; (V-8) 1007.

NOTE 11: Total model year production: (six) 218; (V-8) 878.

W200 Series 4x4 — (¾-Ton) — (128 in. w.b.)				
W200	Chassis & Cowl	—	—	Note 12
W200	Utiline Pickup	—	—	Note 12
W200	Sweptline Pickup	—	—	Note 12
W200	Platform	—	—	Note 12
W200	Stake	—	—	Note 12

NOTE 12: Total model year production: (six) 1091; (V-8) 3427.

W200 Crew Cab Series 4x4 — (¾-Ton) — (146 in. w.b.)				
W200	Chassis	—	—	Note 13
W200	Utiline Pickup	—	—	Note 13
W200	Sweptline Pickup	—	—	Note 13

NOTE 13: Total model year production: (six) 698; (V-8) 438.

W300 Series 4x4 — (1-Ton) — (133 in. w.b.)				
W300	Chassis & Cowl	—	—	Note 14
W300	Chassis & Cab	—	—	Note 14
W300	Utiline Pickup	—	—	Note 14
W300	Platform	—	—	Note 14
W300	Stake	—	—	Note 14

NOTE 14: Total model year production: (six) 749; (V-8) 901.

NOTE 15: Weights and prices shown are for V-8 models, except A100/108, 6-cyl.

ENGINE (A100/108): Inline. Overhead valves. Slant six. Cast iron block. Bore & stroke: 3.4 x 3.125 in. Displacement: 170.2 cu. in. Compression ratio: 8.5:1. Brake horsepower: 101 at 4000 R.P.M. Net (Taxable) horsepower: 27.70. Torque: 136 lbs.-ft. at 1600 R.P.M. Four main bearings. Solid valve lifters.

ENGINE (D100-300, W100-300; optional A100/108): Inline. Overhead valves. Slant six. Cast iron block. Bore & stroke: 3.4 x 4.125 in. Displacement: 224.7 cu. in. Compression ratio: 8.4:1. Brake horsepower: 140 at 3900 R.P.M. Net horsepower: 27.70. Torque: 215 lbs.-ft. at 1600 R.P.M. Four main bearings. Solid valve lifters.

210

ENGINE (Optional, all models): 90-degree, overhead valve. V-8. Cast iron block. Bore & stroke: 3.91 x 3.312 in. Displacement: 318.1 cu. in. Compression ratio: 8.5:1. Brake horsepower: 210 at 4000 R.P.M. Net horsepower: 48.92. Torque: 318 lbs.-ft. at 2800 R.P.M. Five main bearings. Hydraulic valve lifters.

ENGINE (Optional: D100-300, W100-200): 90-degree, overhead valve. V-8. Cast iron block. Bore & stroke: 4.25 x 3.38 in. Displacement: 383 cu. in. Compression ratio: 9.2:1. Brake horsepower: 258 at 4400 R.P.M. Net horsepower: 57.8. Torque: 375 lbs.-ft. at 2800 R.P.M. Five main bearings. Hydraulic valve lifters.

CHASSIS: Same as 1968 except as follows:

CHASSIS (W100): Tires 8.15 x 15 four-ply on 5.50 wheels. Rear axle capacity, 3000 lbs.

CHASSIS (W300): Tires 8.75 x 16.5 ten-ply on 6.75 wheels.

TECHNICAL: Selective sliding gear transmission. Speeds: 3F/1R except 1-ton models, 4F/1R; (A100/108) V-8 has heavy-duty 3-speed transmission. Column or floor shift control. Single plate dry disc clutch: (A100 six) 9⅛ in.; (A100 V-8, D100-200 six) 10 in.; (others) 11 in. Rear axle ratios: (A100) 3.27:1, 3.55:1, 3.91:1 or 4.56:1; (D100) 3.23:1, 3.55:1 or 3.91:1; (D/W200) 3.54:1, 4.1:1 or 4.88:1; ((W100) 3.54:1 or 4.1:1; (D300) 4.1:1, 4.88:1 or 5.87:1; (W300) 4.88:1 or 5.87:1. Hydraulic four-wheel brakes. Fuel tank: (A100) 23 gallon; (others) 18 gallon. One-quart oil filter. Air cleaner: (A100 and D300 V-8) dry; (others) oil bath. Alternator: (A100) 30-amp; (others) 37-amp. Wheels: (A100) 14 x 5.00; (D/W100) 15 x 5.50; (D200) 16 x 6.00; (D200, W200) 17.5 x 5.25; (W300) 16.5 x 6.75.

OPTIONS: Same as 1968, except for changes as follows: (A100) Standard heater dropped. (D100) Standard heater dropped. Air conditioner added. Packages changed to the following: Bucket seat package with Adventurer pickup; with standard cab; or with custom interior package on standard cab models. Custom exterior package. Custom interior package. Insulation package. Bodyside molding package. Wheel lip and sill molding package. Adventurer package (with Adventurer only). Paint stripe (with Adventurer only). (D200) Standard heater dropped. Air conditioner added. Packages changed to the following: Adventurer package for 128 in. Sweptline only. Bucket seat package for Adventurer; for standard cab; or with custom interior for standard cab. Camper Special. Custom Special. Custom interior. Custom exterior. Insulation. Bodyside moldings. Wheel lip and sill moldings. Black or white paint stripe (Adventurer only). (D300) Standard heater dropped. Air conditioner added. Custom interior package. Custom exterior package. (W100-300) Standard heater dropped. Air conditioner added. Custom exterior package. Camper package (W200 only). Custom interior package. Insulation package (W200 only). Bodyside trim molding package (W100-200 only). Wheel lip and sill trim molding package (W100-200 only).

HISTORICAL: Introduced: August, 1968. Calendar year sales: 177,308. Calendar year production: 165,133. Model year production: (six) 71,266; (V-8) 103,288; (Total) 174,554. Innovations: "Cushioned-Beam" front suspension. Historical notes: Total production fell from the record set in 1968. Sales dropped too, but this was still the second best year in Dodge truck history. Trucks were produced in four factories: Warren, Michigan; Burt Road, Detroit; St. Louis; and Windsor, Ontario. The Canadian plant built 7,175 trucks for sale in the U.S. market. V-8 engines accounted for 63 percent of total output. Diesel engine sales fell to just 2,512. Dodge also sold 14,739 Sportsman vans, but they were considered station wagons (passenger cars).

Pricing

	5	4	3	2	1
1969					
A100 Compact — (½-Ton) — (90 in. w.b.)					
Pickup	840	1680	2800	3900	5600
Panel Van	780	1560	2600	3600	5200
Van	770	1550	2550	3600	5100
A108 Compact — (½-Ton) — (108 in. w.b.)					
Panel Van	800	1600	2650	3700	5300
Van	780	1560	2600	3600	5200
D100 Series — (½-Ton) — (114 in. w.b.)					
Utiline Pickup	870	1750	2900	4100	5800
Sweptline Pickup	890	1770	2950	4150	5900
(128 in. w.b.)					
Utiline Pickup	850	1700	2850	4000	5700
Sweptline Pickup	870	1750	2900	4100	5800
Platform	750	1500	2500	3500	5000
Stake	770	1550	2550	3600	5100
D200 Series — (¾-Ton) — (128 in. w.b.)					
Utiline Pickup	830	1650	2750	3850	5500
Sweptline Pickup	840	1680	2800	3900	5600
Platform	740	1470	2450	3350	4900
Stake	750	1500	2500	3500	5000
D200 Crew Cab — (¾-Ton) — (146 in. w.b.)					
Utiline Pickup	810	1620	2700	3800	5400
Sweptline Pickup	830	1650	2750	3850	5500
D300 Series — (1-Ton) — (133 in. w.b.)					
Utiline Pickup	750	1500	2500	3500	5000
Platform	720	1450	2400	3300	4800
Stake	740	1470	2450	3350	4900
D300 Crew Cab — (1-Ton) — (159 in. w.b.)					
Utiline Pickup	770	1550	2550	3600	5100
Sweptline Pickup	780	1560	2600	3600	5200
W100 Series 4x4 — (½-Ton) — (114 in. w.b.)					
Utiline Pickup	890	1770	2950	4150	5900
Sweptline Pickup	900	1800	3000	4200	6000

W200 Series 4x4 — (¾-Ton) — (128 in. w.b.)	5	4	3	2	1
Utiline Pickup	770	1550	2550	3600	5100
Sweptline Pickup	780	1560	2600	3600	5200
Platform	740	1470	2450	3350	4900
Stake	750	1500	2500	3500	5000
W200 Crew Cab 4x4 — (¾-Ton) — (146 in. w.b.)					
Utiline Pickup	750	1500	2500	3500	5000
Sweptline Pickup	770	1550	2550	3600	5100
W300 Series 4x4 — (1-Ton) — (133 in. w.b.)					
Utiline Pickup	770	1550	2550	3600	5100
Platform	720	1450	2400	3300	4800
Stake	740	1470	2450	3350	4900

NOTE: Add 10 percent for V-8 engine.
Add 5 percent for automatic transmission.
Add 4 percent for power winch.

1970 DODGE

1970 Dodge Pickup (DFW)

½-TON COMPACT — A100/108 SERIES — SIX-CYLINDER and V-8: — No styling changes hit the compact bodies in their final year. V-8 models now had a new three-speed, fully synchronized manual transmission. A new 198 cid slant six replaced the 170 as standard engine; the 225 cid slant six and 318 V-8 remained optional. Job-Mated Tradesman van interiors were still available from the factory. Travco Corp. of Warren, Michigan continued its Host Wagon and Executive Suite conversions. The A100/108 series was discontinued in April 1970, when an all-new B Series van (considered a 1971 model) was introduced.

½-TON — D100 SERIES — SIX-CYLINDER and V-8 / ¾-TON — D200 SERIES — SIX-CYLINDER and V-8 / 1-TON — D300 SERIES — SIX-CYLINDER and V-8 / ½-TON 4x4 — W100 SERIES — SIX-CYLINDER and V-8 / ¾-TON 4x4 — W200 SERIES — SIX-CYLINDER and V-8 / 1-TON 4x4 — W300 SERIES — SIX-CYLINDER and V-8: — For the second year in a row, light-duty trucks received a new grille. This one was anodized aluminum, with horizontal lines that made the front end appear wider and lower. Parking lights within the grille changed to horizontal style. Bright finish Junior West Coast mirrors were now available. Inside the cab, three different instrument cluster faceplates marked standard, Custom or Adventurer models. Standard had silver and black plastic; Custom, bright chrome trim; while woodgraining went in the Adventurer faceplate. Several major engineering changes were achieved. For the first time, 4x4 models W100 and W200 were available with LoadFlite three-speed automatic transmission. A new three-speed, fully synchronized manual gearbox was made standard on all ½- and ¾-ton conventional trucks, and on 6-cyl. W100-200 models. Dodge also designed the industry's first "easy-off" tailgate, held by retaining straps and removable without tools, for the convenience of pickup camper owners. The tailgate could be installed by one person just as quickly as it could be removed. Camper Special models got a new hookup of the camper's electrical system to the chassis harness, plus a standard 25-gallon fuel tank. An auxiliary 23-gallon tank was optional. Tire tools were relocated to an under-hood storage area, strapped down so they wouldn't bounce around.

I.D. DATA: Serial numbers were on a plate on the left door lock pillar. The 13-character number consisted of seven elements: first two characters, Model Code; next digit, Body Code; next letter indicated GVW rating (A, 6000 lbs. or less; B, 6001 to 10,001 lbs.; C, 10,001 to 14,000 lbs.); next letter indicated engine displacement; next digit showed model year; next letter was assembly plant; and final six digits were the sequence number. Model Code Index: A1 (A100); B1 (B100); B2 (B200); B3 (B300); D1 (D100); D2 (D200); D3 (D300); E1 (W100); E2 (W200); E3 (W300). Body

Code Index: 1 (conventional cab; compact and pickup); 2 (crew cab; Tradesman van); 3 (Utiline; Low line wagon); 4 (Sweptline; Hi line wagon); 5 (Crew Utiline; Mid line wagon); 6 (crew cab Sweptline); 7 (flat face cowl); 8 (cowl with windshield). Engine Index: A (198 cid); B (225-1); C (225-2); D (251); E (LA318-1); F (360); G (LA318-3); J (383); W (230); X (Special 6-cyl.); Y (Special V-8). Assembly Plant Index: J (Canada); N (Burt Road); S (Warren No. 1); T (Warren No. 2); U (Missouri); V (Warren compact, 1971 on). Sequence numbering: 100,001 to 300,000. Engine numbers were the same as 1969. Starting and ending numbers are not available.

Model	Body Type	Price	Weight	Prod. Total
A100/A108 Compact Series — (½-Ton) — (90 in. w.b.)				
A100	Pickup	2454	2834	Note 1
A100	Panel Van (Note 3)	2530	2834	Note 1
A100	Van	—	—	Note 1
(108 in. w.b.)				
A108	Panel Van (Note 3)	2663	3044	Note 2
A108	Van	—	—	Note 2

NOTE 1: Total model year production: 7273.

NOTE 2: Total model year production: 11,235.

NOTE 3: Rear doors only.

Model	Body Type	Price	Weight	Prod. Total
D100 Series — (½-Ton) — (114 in. w.b.)				
D100	Chassis & Cowl	—	—	Note 4
D100	Chassis & Cab	—	—	Note 4
D100	Utiline Pickup	—	—	Note 4
D100	Sweptline Pickup	2667	3477	Note 4
(128 in. w.b.)				
D100	Chassis & Cowl	—	—	Note 5
D100	Chassis & Cab	—	—	Note 5
D100	Utiline Pickup	—	—	Note 5
D100	Sweptline Pickup	2703	3617	Note 5
D100	Platform	—	—	Note 5
D100	Stake	2778	3822	Note 5

NOTE 4: Total model year production: 15,978.

NOTE 5: Total model year production: 38,857.

Model	Body Type	Price	Weight	Prod. Total
D200 Series — (¾-Ton) — (128 in. w.b.)				
D200	Chassis & Cowl	—	—	Note 6
D200	Chassis & Cab	—	—	Note 6
D200	Utiline Pickup	—	—	Note 6
D200	Sweptline Pickup	2915	3902	Note 6
D200	Platform	—	—	Note 6
D200	Stake	2991	4107	Note 6

NOTE 6: Total model year production: 19,911.

Model	Body Type	Price	Weight	Prod. Total
D200 Crew Cab Series — (¾-Ton) — (146 in. w.b.)				
D200	Chassis	—	—	Note 7
D200	Utiline Pickup	—	—	Note 7
D200	Sweptline Pickup	3663	4227	Note 7
(160 in. w.b.)				
D200	Chassis	—	—	Note 8
D200	Utiline Pickup	—	—	Note 8
D200	Sweptline Pickup	3825	4382	Note 8

NOTE 7: Total model year production: 2002.

NOTE 8: Total model year production: 678.

Model	Body Type	Price	Weight	Prod. Total
D300 Series — (1-Ton) — (133 in. w.b.)				
D300	Chassis & Cowl	—	—	Note 9
D300	Chassis & Cab	3018	3704	Note 9
D300	Utiline Pickup	2995	4087	Note 9
D300	Platform	—	—	Note 9
D300	Stake	—	—	Note 9

NOTE 9: Total model year production: 7460.

Model	Body Type	Price	Weight	Prod. Total
D300 Crew Cab Series — (1-Ton) — (159 in. w.b.)				
D300	Chassis & Cab	3058	3799	Note 10
D300	Utiline Pickup	—	—	Note 10
D300	Sweptline Pickup	3770	4562	Note 10

NOTE 10: Total model year production: 2300.

Model	Body Type	Price	Weight	Prod. Total
W100 Series 4x4 — (½-Ton) — (114 in. w.b.)				
W100	Chassis & Cab	—	—	Note 11
W100	Utiline Pickup	—	—	Note 11
W100	Sweptline Pickup	—	—	Note 11
(128 in. w.b.)				
W100	Chassis & Cab	—	—	Note 12
W100	Utiline Pickup	—	—	Note 12
W100	Sweptline Pickup	—	—	Note 12

NOTE 11: Total model year production: 1500.

NOTE 12: Total model year production: 1897.

Model	Body Type	Price	Weight	Prod. Total
W200 Series 4x4 — (¾-Ton) — (128 in. w.b.)				
W200	Chassis & Cab	—	—	Note 13
W200	Utiline Pickup	—	—	Note 13
W200	Sweptline Pickup	—	—	Note 13
W200	Platform	—	—	Note 13
W200	Stake	—	—	Note 13

NOTE 13: Total model year production: 5719.

Model	Body Type	Price	Weight	Prod. Total
W200 Crew Cab Series 4x4 — (¾-Ton) — (146 in. w.b.)				
W200	Chassis	—	—	Note 14
W200	Utiline Pickup	—	—	Note 14
W200	Sweptline Pickup	—	—	Note 14

NOTE 14: Total model year production: 914.

W300 Series 4x4 — (1-Ton) — (133 in. w.b.)				
W300	Chassis & Cowl	—	—	Note 15
W300	Chassis & Cab	—	—	Note 15
W300	Utiline Pickup	—	—	Note 15
W300	Platform	—	—	Note 15
W300	Stake	—	—	Note 15

NOTE 15: Total model year production: 1053.

NOTE 16: Weights and prices shown are for V-8 models, except A100/108, 6-cyl.

ENGINE (A100/108): Inline. Overhead valve. Slant six. Cast iron block. Bore & stroke: 3.4 x 3.64 in. Displacement: 198.3 cu. in. Compression ratio: 8.4:1. Brake horsepower: 120 at 4000 R.P.M. Net (Taxable) horsepower: 27.70. Torque: 182 lbs.-ft. at 1600 R.P.M. Four main bearings. Solid valve lifters.

(225 cid slant six, 318 cid V-8 and 383 cid V-8) Same specifications and availability as in 1969; see previous specifications.

CHASSIS: Same as 1969; see previous specifications.

TECHNICAL: Same as 1969; see previous specifications.

OPTIONS: Same as 1969; see previous list.

HISTORICAL: Introduced: August, 1969. Calendar year sales: 137,509. Calendar year production: (Total) 188,632; (U.S. only) 178,584. Model year production: (Total) 161,015. Innovations: Junior West Coast mirrors available. Automatic transmission on 4wd models. Fully synchronized manual transmission. "Easy-off" pickup tailgate. Historical notes: This was the best year in Dodge truck history, as production gained 8.1 percent and Dodge captured more than 10 percent of the industry total. Sales rose 5.4 percent, to slightly below the 1968 record. Dodge was the only truck maker to show a gain, placing third in sales. V-8 engines went into more than two-thirds of Dodge gas trucks. Diesel production rose to 3,384, giving Dodge 4.7 percent of that market. Dodge continued its leadership in the camper business by adding a 413 cid engine to the motor home chassis. New engines of 478 and 549 cid went into the heavy-duty truck lineup.

Pricing

1970		5	4	3	2	1
A100 Compact — (½-Ton) — (90 in. w.b.)						
Pickup		840	1680	2800	3900	5600
Panel Van		780	1560	2600	3600	5200
Van		770	1550	2550	3600	5100
A108 Compact — (½-Ton) — (108 in. w.b.)						
Panel Van		800	1600	2650	3700	5300
Van		780	1560	2600	3600	5200
D100 Series — (½-Ton) — (114 in. w.b.)						
Utiline Pickup		870	1750	2900	4100	5800
Sweptline Pickup		890	1770	2950	4150	5900
D100 Series — (½-Ton) — (128 in. w.b.)						
Utiline Pickup		850	1700	2850	4000	5700
Sweptline Pickup		870	1750	2900	4100	5800
Platform		750	1500	2500	3500	5000
Stake		770	1550	2550	3600	5100
D200 Series — (¾-Ton) — (128 in. w.b.)						
Utiline Pickup		830	1650	2750	3850	5500
Sweptline Pickup		840	1680	2800	3900	5600
Platform		740	1470	2450	3350	4900
Stake		750	1500	2500	3500	5000
D200 Crew Cab — (¾-Ton) — (146 in. w.b.)						
Utiline Pickup		810	1620	2700	3800	5400
Sweptline Pickup		830	1650	2750	3850	5500
D300 Series — (1-Ton) — (133 in. w.b.)						
Utiline Pickup		750	1500	2500	3500	5000
Platform		720	1450	2400	3300	4800
Stake		740	1470	2450	3350	4900
D300 Crew Cab — (1-Ton) — (159 in. w.b.)						
Utiline Pickup		770	1550	2550	3600	5100
Sweptline Pickup		780	1560	2600	3600	5200
W100 Series 4x4 — (½-Ton) — (114 in. w.b.)						
Utiline Pickup		890	1770	2950	4150	5900
Sweptline Pickup		900	1800	3000	4200	6000
W100 Series 4x4 — (½-Ton) — (128 in. w.b.)						
Utiline Pickup		900	1800	3000	4200	6000
Sweptline Pickup		920	1850	3050	4300	6100
W200 Series 4x4 — (¾-Ton) — (128 in. w.b.)						
Utiline Pickup		770	1550	2550	3600	5100
Sweptline Pickup		780	1560	2600	3600	5200
Platform		740	1470	2450	3350	4900
Stake		750	1500	2500	3500	5000
W200 Crew Cab 4x4 — (¾-Ton) — (146 in. w.b.)						
Utiline Pickup		750	1500	2500	3500	5000
Sweptline Pickup		770	1550	2550	3600	5100
W300 Series 4x4 — (1-Ton) — (133 in. w.b.)						
Utiline Pickup		770	1550	2550	3600	5100
Platform		720	1450	2400	3300	4800
Stake		740	1470	2450	3350	4900

NOTE: Add 10 percent for V-8 engine.

212

1971 DODGE

1971 Dodge D100 Sweptline Pickup (Alvin Teeter)

½-TON VAN — B100 SERIES — SIX-CYLINDER and V-8 / ¾-TON VAN — B200 SERIES — SIX-CYLINDER and V-8 / 1-TON VAN — B300 SERIES — SIX-CYLINDER and V-8: — Introduced in April, 1970 as 1971 models, the much larger "second generation" vans replaced the original A100/108 series, which dated back to 1964. The new series was developed after many interviews with the buying public. Refinements over the original vans included: larger cargo area and increased load capacity; engine access from outside for routine maintenance; independent front suspension; longer wheelbases; wider front and rear track. Exterior styling was completely new. All-new interiors had passenger car style seats and instruments. Wheelbases were 109 and 127 inches, but overall lengths increased only 5 in. over prior models, to 176 and 194 in. Cargo capacities were 206 and 246 cu. ft. Passenger vans were also available. Base engine was the 198 cu. in. slant six. Options were the 225 cu. in. slant six and 318 V-8. Standard equipment included dual armrests, left sunvisor, two-speed wipers and washers, driver's seat, brake warning light, emergency flashers, turn signals, painted bumpers, solid cargo doors, locks on all doors, glove box, heater, painted hubcaps, driver's and cargo dome light, side marker lights, backup lights, and painted outside mirrors.

½-TON — D100 SERIES — SIX-CYLINDER and V-8 / ¾-TON — D200 SERIES — SIX-CYLINDER and V-8 / 1-TON — D300 SERIES — SIX-CYLINDER and V-8 / ½-TON 4x4 — W100 SERIES — SIX-CYLINDER and V-8 / ¾-TON 4x4 — W200 SERIES — SIX-CYLINDER and V-8 / 1-TON 4x4 — W300 SERIES — SIX-CYLINDER and V-8: — This was the final year for the standard light-duty series, which had begun in 1961 and run without major changes in styling or engineering features. Dodge merchandised its pickups in six lines. Standard models were now called Custom. New for 1971 were: light argent paint on grille insert; fender side "Custom 100" or "Custom 200" decal on right corner of tailgate; new "Dodge" decal on right corner of tailgate. The standard instrument cluster faceplace was bright and black, while standard 5x7 in. mirrors were painted. Automatic choke was standard. D100 models had a new evaporative emission control system. One new pickup model was offered at the lowest end of the lineup. Built only on a 114 in. w.b., the D100 Sweptline Special was only available with the 198 cu. in. slant six and 3-speed manual transmission. It had a painted grille, black wheels, 5 in. round mirror, black and argent paint on instrument cluster, and black vinyl interior, with no options available. Next up the line were the Utiline (fenderside) D100 and D200 models. Standard trim included a bright grille with insert; black rubber windshield and rear window molding; Dodge decal on tailgate; painted front bumper, hubcaps, gas cap and 5x7 in. mirror. Next came the similarly equipped Custom series, on 114 or 128 in. Sweptline or Utiline models. The Adventurer was now available in three series. The basic Adventurer, offered on all models, sported bright windshield moldings, bodyside molding package (Sweptline pickups only), and Adventurer nameplate on pickup box. Next highest, the Adventurer Sport (on Sweptline models only), included bright windshield and window moldings, drip moldings, wheel lip and sill moldings; white or black paint stripe; plain tailgate with bright plaque and "Dodge" identification; Delta hood ornament; bright front bumper, hub caps, gas cap and mirror; Dodge 100 nameplate; and Adventurer Sport nameplate on pickup box. Top-of-the-line on 128 in. Sweptlines only was the Adventurer S.E., which included: bright windshield and rear window moldings, drip molding, wheel lip and sill molding; tailgate with bright woodgrain-filled plaque and "Dodge" nameplate; Delta hood ornament; bright front bumper, hubcaps, gas cap and mirror; Adventurer S.E. nameplate on pickup box; plus lower body side woodgrain applique and molding. Engine lineup remained as before, adding the 198 cu. in. slant six, which was available only in the D100 Sweptline Special pickup. Standard equipment included a heater/defroster, full instruments, dome and courtesy lights, side markers, backup lights, 4-way flashers, armrests, rubber floor mats, two-speed wipers, and full-width rear window.

I.D. DATA: Serial numbers were in the same locations, with the same coding, as 1970. Sequence numbers for the 1971 production year began with: 300,001. Ending numbers are not available. Engine numbers were the same as 1969-70. Starting and ending numbers are not available.

Model	Body Type	Price	Weight	Prod. Total
B100-300 Series Van — (½-Ton) — (109 in. w.b.)				
B100-6	Van	2890	—	7673
(¾-Ton)				
B200-6	Van	2985	—	8610
(1-Ton)				
B300-6	Van	3116	—	591
(½-Ton) — (127 in. w.b.)				
B100-6	Van	3027	—	6020
(¾-Ton)				
B200-6	Van (Note 1)	3451	—	23,406
(1-Ton)				
B300-6	Van (Note 2)	3253	—	19,984

NOTE 1: Add $205 to price for B200 Maxivan.

NOTE 2: Add $240 to price for B300 Maxivan.

D100 Series — (½-Ton) — (114 in. w.b.)				
D100	Chassis & Cab	2652	3095	Note 3
D100	Utiline Pickup	2811	3450	Note 3
D100	Sweptline Pickup	2811	3505	Note 3
(128 in. w.b.)				
D100	Chassis & Cab	—	—	Note 4
D100	Utiline Pickup	—	—	Note 4
D100	Sweptline Pickup	—	—	Note 4

NOTE 3: Total model year production, 114 in.: 19,444.

NOTE 4: Total model year production, 128 in.: 33,487.

D200 Series — (¾-Ton) — (128 in. w.b.)				
D200	Chassis & Cab	3115	3430	Note 5
D200	Utiline Pickup	3275	3870	Note 5
D200	Sweptline Pickup	3275	3930	Note 5

NOTE 5: Total model year production: 14,094.

D200 Crew Cab Series — (¾-Ton) — (146 in. w.b.)				
D200	Chassis	3678	3845	Note 6
D200	Utiline Pickup	3837	4205	Note 6
D200	Sweptline Pickup	3837	4255	Note 6
(160 in. w.b.)				
D200	Chassis	—	—	Note 6
D200	Utiline Pickup	—	—	Note 6
D200	Sweptline Pickup	—	—	Note 6

NOTE 6: Total model year production: (146 in.) 1945; (160 in.) 446.

D300 Series — (1-Ton) — (133 in. w.b.)				
D300	Chassis & Cab	2755	3645	Note 7
D300	Utiline Pickup	2870	4140	Note 7
(159 in. w.b.)				
D300	Crew — Chassis	—	—	Note 7
D300	Crew — Utiline	—	—	Note 7

NOTE 7: Total model year production: (133 in.) 8904; (159 in.) 1764.

W100 Series 4x4 — (½-Ton) — (114 in. w.b.)				
W100	Chassis & Cab	3115	3555	Note 8
W100	Utiline Pickup	3275	3915	Note 8
W100	Sweptline Pickup	3275	3965	Note 8
(128 in. w.b.)				
W100	Chassis & Cab	—	—	Note 8
W100	Utiline Pickup	—	—	Note 8
W100	Sweptline Pickup	—	—	Note 8

NOTE 8: Total model year production: (114 in.) 1626; (128 in.) 2026.

W200 Series 4x4 — (¾-Ton) — (128 in. w.b.)				
W200	Chassis & Cab	3618	3785	Note 9
W200	Utiline Pickup	3777	4225	Note 9
W200	Sweptline Pickup	3777	4285	Note 9
(146 in. w.b.)				
W200	Crew — Chassis	4505	4260	Note 9
W200	Crew — Utiline	4664	4620	Note 9
W200	Crew — Sweptline	4664	4670	Note 9

NOTE 9: Total model year production: (128 in.) 4814; (146 in.) 334.

W300 Series 4x4 — (1-Ton) — (133 in. w.b.)				
W300	Chassis & Cab	4075	4665	Note 10
W300	Utiline Pickup	4185	5160	Note 10
W300	Platform	4395	5325	Note 10
W300	Stake	4450	5625	Note 10

NOTE 10: Total model year production: 783.

NOTE 11: Prices and weights are for 6-cyl. models. For V-8 engine, add $130-150 to price.

ENGINE (Standard: B100, B200, D100): Inline. Overhead valve. Slant six. Cast iron block. Bore & stroke: 3.4 x 3.64 in. Displacement: 198.3 cu. in. Compression ratio: 8.4:1. Brake horsepower: 120 at 4000 R.P.M. Net (Taxable) horsepower: 27.70. Torque: 180 lbs.-ft. at 1600 R.P.M. Four main bearings. Solid valve lifters.

ENGINE (Standard: B300, D200-300, W100-300): Inline. Overhead valve. Slant six. Cast iron block. Bore & stroke: 3.4 x 4.125 in. Displacement: 224.7 cu. in. Compression ratio: 8.4:1. Brake horsepower: 140 at 3900 R.P.M. Net horsepower: 27.70. Torque: 215 lbs.-ft. at 1600 R.P.M. Four main bearings. Solid valve lifters.

ENGINE (Optional, all models): 90-degree, overhead valve. V-8. Cast iron block. Bore & stroke: 3.91 x 3.312 in. Displacement: 318.1 cu. in. Compression ratio: 8.8:1. Brake horsepower: 210 at 4000 R.P.M. Net horsepower: 48.92. Torque: 318 lbs.-ft. at 2800 R.P.M. Five main bearings. Hydraulic valve lifters.

ENGINE (Optional: D100-300, W100-200): 90-degree, overhead valve. V-8. Cast iron block. Bore & stroke: 4.25 x 3.38 in. Displacement: 383 cu. in. Compression ratio: 8.7:1. Brake horsepower: 258 at 4400 R.P.M. Net horsepower: 57.80. Torque: 375 lbs.-ft. at 2800 R.P.M. Five main bearings. Hydraulic valve lifters.

CHASSIS (B100): Wheelbase: 109 in. or 127 in. Tires: E78 x 14-B four-ply. Max. GVW: 4200-4800 lbs. Axle Capacity: 2700 lbs.

CHASSIS (B200): Wheelbase: 109 in. or 127 in. Tires: G78 x 15-B four-ply. Max. GVW: 5200-5500 lbs. Axle Capacity: (front) 3000 lbs.; (rear) 3300 lbs.

CHASSIS: (B300): Wheelbase: 109 in. or 127 in. Tires: 8.00 x 16.5-C six-ply or 8.00 x 16.5D eight-ply. Max. GVW: 6100-7700 lbs. Axle Capacity: (front) 3300 lbs.; (rear) 3500 lbs.

CHASSIS (D100): Wheelbase: 114 in. or 128 in. Tires: G78 x 15-B-5. Max. GVW: 4300-5200 lbs. Axle Capacity: (front) 2800 lbs.; (rear) 3600 lbs.

CHASSIS (D200): Wheelbase: 128 in., 146 in. or 160 in. Tires: 8.00 x 16.5-D-4. Max. GVW: 6100-7500 lbs. Axle Capacity: (front) 3000 lbs.; (rear) 5500 lbs.

CHASSIS (D300): Wheelbase: 133 in. or 159 in. Tires: 8.00 x 16.5-D eight-ply. Max. GVW: 6600-10,000 lbs. Axle Capacity: (front) 3800 lbs.; (rear) 7500 lbs.

CHASSIS (W100): Wheelbase: 114 in. or 128 in. Tires: G78 x 15-B four-ply. Max. GVW: 5100-5600 lbs. Axle Capacity: (front) 3000 lbs.; (rear) 3600 lbs.

CHASSIS (W200): Wheelbase: 128 in. or 146 in. Tires: 8.00 x 16.5-D eight-ply. Max. GVW: 6000-8000 lbs. Axle Capacity: (front) 3000 lbs.; (rear) 5500 lbs.

CHASSIS (W300): Wheelbase: 133 in. Tires: 8.75 x 16.5-D ten-ply. Max. GVW: 8500 lbs. Axle Capacity: (front) 4500 lbs.; (rear) 7500 lbs.

TECHNICAL: Selective sliding gear transmission. Speeds: 3F/1R except D/W300 1-ton models, 4F/1R; (B vans) V-8 had heavy-duty 3-speed transmission. Column (3-speed) or floor shift control. Single plate dry disc clutch: (B100 six) 9.25 in.; (B200 and D100-300 six) 10 in.; (all V-8) 11 in. Hydraulic four-wheel brakes. Fuel tank: (B vans) 26 gallon; (D100) 23 gallon; (others) 25 gallon. Rear Spring Capacity: (B100) 1000/1170 lbs.; (B200) 1375/1550 lbs.; (B300) 1700/1870 lbs.; (D100) 1100/1300 lbs.; (D200) 1650/1900 lbs.; (D300) 2050/2400 lbs.; (W100) 1350/1600 lbs.; (W200) 1750/2000 lbs.; (W300) 3250/3600 lbs. Alternator: 37 amp. Wheels: (B100) five 14 x 5.5; (B200, D100) 15 x 5.5; (B300, D200-300) 16.5 x 6.

OPTIONS (Factory-Installed): (B Series Vans) Chrome hubcaps. Chrome wheel covers (except B300). Chrome bumpers, front and rear. Door check arms or straps. Tinted glass. Glove box door. Bright finish grille. Outside mirror. Inside mirror. Convenience package. Radio (AM or AM/FM). Heater. Insulation package. Lock package. Dual horns. Horn bar. Cigar lighter. Air conditioner. Deluxe driver's bucket seat. Passenger bucket seat. Shoulder belts. Undercoating. Window glass (side, rear, vision van, or vision van curb side). Two-tone paint. Exterior moldings: upper side package; lower side rear package; upper side and rear and lower side package. Cargo area headliner. Oil pressure gauge. Oil-wetted air cleaner. 50 or 60-amp alternator. Cruise control. Increased cooling capacity. One-quart oil filter. Emission control system (except B300). Padded dash. Front disc brakes (except B300). Vacuum brake booster. Power steering. Anti-spin rear axle (B300 only). 10 in. clutch (B100 with 198 cu. in. engine). 11 in. clutch (225 cu. in. engine). Heavy-duty shock absorbers (front and rear). Heavy-duty springs (front or rear). 3-speed automatic transmission A727. 225 cu. in. slant six engine (B100-200). 318 cu. in. V-8 engine. (D100-300 and W100-300) Chrome bumper (front or rear). White rear bumper. Step-type rear bumper. Spare tire carrier: inside (Sweptlines) or outside (Utilines). Wheel covers (except 300 models). Chrome hubcaps (except 300 models). Tinted glass. Dual horns. Textured vinyl roof. Two-tone paint. Radio. Air conditioner. Cigar lighter. Heavy-duty instruments. Marker lights. Outside mirrors. Oil pressure gauge. Foam padded seat. Third seat-belt. Shoulder belts (pair). Hand throttle. Undercoating. Adventurer package (except 300 models). Adventurer Sport package (except 300 models). Adventurer SE package (except 300 models). Bucket seat package (except W300). Camper package (D/W200). "Dude" package (except 300 models). Insulation package. Exterior trim: upper bodyside molding, or wheel lip and sill molding (except 300 models). NP435 4-speed transmission (except 300 models). NP445B 4-speed transmission (except W300). A727 3-speed automatic transmission. Power steering. Anti-spin rear axle. One-quart oil bath air cleaner (D/W200-300). 50 or 60-amp alternator. Heavy-duty (11 in.) clutch (for 225 cu. in. engine). Auxiliary 23-gallon fuel tank. Increased cooling capacity. 3-ton jack. One-quart oil filter. Heavy-duty springs (front or rear). Heavy-duty shock absorbers (front and rear). Auxiliary springs, rear (except D100). 318 cu. in. V-8 engine. 383 cu. in. V-8 engine.

HISTORICAL: Introduced: August, 1970 (B Series Vans, April, 1970). Calendar year sales: 159,055. Calendar year production: (U.S. only) 204,766; (including Canada) 218,337. Model year production: 175,588. Innovations: Enlarged "second generation" vans. Historical notes: Dodge had another record year in both sales and production — the third straight year of record-setting sales. Canadian production for the U.S. market totalled 13,571 trucks. Dodge also built 25,709 Spotsman vans, which were counted as station wagons. V-8 engines accounted for nearly 70 percent of all gasoline engine production. Diesel sales came to 2835 units.

Pricing

	5	4	3	2	1
1971					
B100 Series Van — (½-Ton) — (109 or 127 in. w.b.)					
(109 in.) Van	590	1170	1950	2700	3900
(127 in.) Van	620	1230	2050	2900	4100
B200 Series Van — (¾-Ton) — (109 or 127 in. w.b.)					
(109 in.) Van	560	1100	1850	2600	3700
(127 in.) Van	590	1170	1950	2700	3900
B300 Series Van — (1-Ton) — (109 or 127 in. w.b.)					
(109 in.) Van	540	1080	1800	2500	3600
(127 in.) Van	570	1140	1900	2650	3800
D100 Series — (½-Ton) — (114 in. w.b.)					
Utiline Pickup	870	1750	2900	4100	5800
Sweptline Pickup	890	1770	2950	4150	5900
D100 Series — (½-Ton) — (128 in. w.b.)					
Utiline Pickup	850	1700	2850	4000	5700
Sweptline Pickup	870	1750	2900	4100	5800
D200 Series — (¾-Ton) — (128 in. w.b.)					
Utiline Pickup	830	1650	2750	3850	5500
Sweptline Pickup	840	1680	2800	3900	5600
D200 Crew Cab — (¾-Ton) — (146 or 160 in. w.b.)					
(146 in.) Utiline Pickup	740	1470	2450	3350	4900
(146 in.) Sweptline Pickup	750	1500	2500	3500	5000
(160 in.) Utiline Pickup	680	1350	2350	3250	4700
(160 in.) Sweptline Pickup	740	1470	2450	3350	4700
D300 Series — (1-Ton) — (133 or 159 in. w.b.)					
(133 in.) Utiline Pickup	750	1500	2500	3500	5000
Crew Utiline	720	1450	2400	3300	4800
W100 Series 4x4 — (½-Ton) — (114 in. w.b.)					
Utiline Pickup	890	1770	2950	4150	5900
Sweptline Pickup	900	1800	3000	4200	6000
W100 Series 4x4 — (½-Ton) — (128 in. w.b.)					
Utiline Pickup	900	1800	3000	4200	6000
Sweptline Pickup	920	1850	3050	4300	6100
W200 Series 4x4 — (¾-Ton) — (128 in. w.b.)					
Utiline Pickup	770	1550	2550	3600	5100
Sweptline Pickup	780	1560	2600	3600	5200
W200 Crew Cab 4x4 — (¾-Ton) — (146 in. w.b.)					
Utiline Pickup	750	1500	2500	3500	5000
Sweptline Pickup	770	1550	2550	3600	5100
W300 Series 4x4 — (1-Ton) — (133 in. w.b.)					
Utiline Pickup	770	1550	2550	3600	5100
Platform	720	1450	2400	3300	4800
Stake	740	1470	2450	3350	4900

NOTE: Add 10 percent for V-8 engine.
Add 10 percent for Maxivan package.

1972 DODGE

1972 Dodge Adventurer Special Edition Pickup (DNP)

½-TON VAN — B100 SERIES — SIX-CYLINDER and V-8 — ¾-TON VAN — B200 SERIES — SIX-CYLINDER and V-8 — 1-TON VAN — B300 SERIES — SIX-CYLINDER and V-8: — Dodge "second generation" vans changed very little in their second year. The 198 cid slant six was dropped, while the 225 cid six became standard for all vans. A 318 cid V-8 or new 360 V-8 were options. All models, sizes and options carried forward, as did the Sportsman Wagon lineup of passenger vans, which were counted as station wagons. Standard van equipment included painted bumpers and hubcaps, heater/defroster, locks on all doors, dome light (driver's and cargo area), 4-way flashers, dual 5x7 in. mirrors, padded driver's sunvisor, two-speed wipers/washers, twin armrests, and a bumper jack (axle jack for B300).

½-TON — D100 SERIES — SIX-CYLINDER and V-8 / ¾-TON — D200 SERIES — SIX-CYLINDER and V-8 / 1-TON — D300 SERIES — SIX-CYLINDER and V-8 / ½-TON 4x4 — W100 SERIES — SIX-CYLINDER and V-8 / ¾-TON 4x4 — W200 SERIES — SIX-CYLINDER and V-8 / 1-TON 4x4 — W300 SERIES — SIX-CYLINDER and V-8: As 1971 was the last of an era (1961-71), 1972 heralded the beginning of an even longer era — an all

new line of light-duty Dodge trucks. The policy of no major yearly styling changes, ushered in with the 1961 models, would continue with the new 1972 trucks. Neither would basic chassis and mechanical components be altered on an annual basis. Light-duty trucks contributed heavily to total corporate profitability. Management was aware that the typical buyer did not expect big changes from year to year, but was more comfortable with traditional, proven appearances. Naturally, the policy of limited change, with longer runs from original tooling and development costs, added greatly to profits. Minor styling updates and engineering improvements, plus standard and optional equipment changes, would appear over the years; but the basic package would remain unchanged well into the 1980s. Dodge's new 1972 line was designed to incorporate more passenger car-like comfort and convenience, with no loss of truck function. Continued were the three basic load capacities. 2wd versions were basically as before, but 4wd models received beefier chassis components — a larger clutch, wider rear brake shoes and drums, heavier front axle, and front leaf springs rather than coils. Standard wheelbase lengths across the line grew from 1 to 5 in. for better load carrying capacity. Bigger windshields and back windows improved vision. Curved side windows added 4 in. to the cab's shoulder room. Doors were 2 in. longer and hinged to swing farther out, for easier entry and exit. Cab interiors were updated for comfort, convenience and serviceability. Dashboard design put function paramount, with round gauges recessed to prevent glare. All gauges could be serviced from the front of the dash. Both the fuse box and emergency flashers were behind the glove box door for easy service. Pedal pads and glove compartments were larger; sunvisors became full-width. Enlarged seats were mounted higher. Cab noise level diminshed with increased insulation, and by moving the heater and windshield wiper motors to the underhood area. Door latches were quieter too. Larger vents and cowl side openings for fresh air intake improved interior airflow. Base engine remained the 225 cu. in. slant six, while 318, 360 and 400 cu. in. V-8s were optional. The 383 V-8 was dropped, and the 400 was not available in 4x4 models. Suspension was all new, with coil springs and independent suspension in front (except 4x4), and long, wide-leaf springs in the rear. Front and rear track widths increased with the wheelbases, to provide better handling and load capacity. The new front end could be adjusted on standard alignment equipment. Brakes were larger, and a step-on parking brake became standard. Both Utiline and Sweptline pickup boxes were available on all models. Basic body was the Custom, with three appearance/trim packages optional: Adventurer, Adventurer Sport, and Adventurer Special Edition. Two Camper packages, a Heavy-Duty package, and a Trailer-Towing package also were available. Standard equipment included dual armrests, chrome front bumper and grille, heater/defroster, dome and courtesy lights, 5x7 in. chrome mirrors outside and day/night mirror inside, and two-speed wipers. New options included power-assisted disc brakes, integral power steering, cruise control, and a new integral air conditioning system.

I.D. DATA: Serial numbers were on a plate on the left door lock pillar. The seven-element serial numbers consisted of 13 alpha-numeric characters. First came a two-character Model Code. The next digit indicated Body Code. Next came a letter indicating GVW: A (6000 lbs. or less); B (6001 to 10,000 lbs.; C (10,001 to 14,000 lbs.; or D (14,001 to 16,000 lbs.) Next, one letter indicating Engine type. The next digit showed model year (2=1972). The sixth element was a letter indicating assembly plant; J (Windsor); N (Burt Road, Detroit); S (Warren Truck No. 1); T (Warren Truck No. 2); U (St. Louis); or V (Warren compact). Finally came the six-digit sequence number. Eash assembly plant began the 1972 model year with number 500001. Model Code Index: B1 (B100 van); B2 (B200 van); B3 (B300 van); D1 (D100); D2 ((D200); D3 (D300); G1 (Post Office); M3 (M300); P2 (P200); P3 (P300); W1 (W100); W2 (W200); W3 (W300); X3 (WM300 export). Body Code Index: 1 = compact van (Tradesman); conventional cab; LCF cab; standard heavy-duty tilt cab. 2 = compact heavy-duty tilt cab; long sleeper heavy-duty tilt cab. 3 = compact mid-line wagon (Custom Sportsman); crew cab; long sleeper heavy-duty tilt cab. 3 = compact mid-line wagon (Custom Sportsman); conventional Utiline. 4 = compact hi-line wagon (Royal Sportsman); conventional Sweptline. 5 = compact Maxivan (Tradesman); Utiline crew cab. 6 = compact low-line Maxiwagon (Sportsman); Sweptline crew cab. 7 = compact mid-line Maxiwagon (Custom Sportsman); flat face cowl. 8 = compact hi-line Maxiwagon (Royal Sportsman); windshield cowl. 9 = forward control or motor home; incomplete vehicle. Gas Engine Index: B (225-1); C (225-2); E (LA318-1); F (360); G (LA318-3); J (400). Engine numbers were located as follows: (225 cu. in.) right side of block below No. 1 spark plug; (318 and 360 cu. in. V-8) left front of block, below cylinder head; (400 cu. in. V-8) right side of block, adjacent to distributor. Engine numbers had five elements. The first two letters indicated manufacturing plant (PM = Mound Rock; PT = Trenton; NN = Marysville; GW = Windsor). The next three digits gave displacement in cu. in. The next letter showed engine type (R = regular fuel; T =standard; H =premium). Next came a four-digit build date code, based on a 10,000-day calendar. The final four digits were the sequence number, which began with 0001 for each day's production.

1972 Dodge Adventurer Special Edition Pickup (DNP)

Model	Body Type	Price	Weight	Prod. Total
B100-300 Series Van — (½-Ton) — (109 in. w.b.)				
B100-6	Van	2769	3470	13,686
(127 in. w.b.)				
B100-6	Van	2898	3570	9717
(¾-Ton) — (109 in. w.b.)				
B200-6	Van	2861	3460	12,923
(127 in. w.b.)				
B200-6	Van	2983	3570	35,919
B200-6	Maxivan	3179	3715	—
(1-Ton) — (109 in. w.b.)				
B300-6	Van	2988	3695	734
(127 in. w.b.)				
B300-6	Van	3117	3810	41,270
B300-6	Maxivan	3346	3985	—
D100 Series — (½-Ton) — (115 in. w.b.)				
D100	Chassis & Cab	2573	3065	Note 1
D100	Utiline Pickup	2732	3410	Note 1
D100	Sweptline Pickup	2732	3470	Note 1
(131 in. w.b.)				
D100	Chassis & Cab	2607	3105	Note 1
D100	Utiline Pickup	2765	3535	Note 1
D100	Sweptline Pickup	2765	3565	Note 1

NOTE 1: Total model year production, (115 in.): 18,370; (131 in.) 73,542.

Model	Body Type	Price	Weight	Prod. Total
D200 Series Custom — (¾-Ton) — (131 in. w.b.)				
D200	Chassis & Cab	2809	3245	Note 2
D200	Utiline Pickup	2966	3675	Note 2
D200	Sweptline Pickup	2966	3705	Note 2

NOTE 2: Total model year production: 23,902.

Model	Body Type	Price	Weight	Prod. Total
D200 Crew Cab Series Custom — (¾-Ton) — (149 in. w.b.)				
D200	Chassis & Cab	3566	3775	Note 3
D200	Utiline Pickup	3723	4120	Note 3
D200	Sweptline Pickup	3723	4160	Note 3
(165 in. w.b.)				
D200	Chassis & Cab	3651	3950	Note 3
D200	Utiline Pickup	3816	4380	Note 3
D200	Sweptline Pickup	3816	4410	Note 3

NOTE 3: Total model year production: (149 in.) 1881; (165 in.) 1057.

Model	Body Type	Price	Weight	Prod. Total
D300 Series Custom — (1-Ton) — (135 in. w.b.)				
D300	Chassis & Cab	2960	3795	Note 4
D300	Utiline Pickup	3077	4290	Note 4
(159 in. w.b.)				
D300	Chassis & Cab	2998	3890	2735
(165 in. w.b.)				
D300	Crew — Chassis/Cab	3868	4750	115

NOTE 4: Total model year production: (135 in.) 5681.

Model	Body Type	Price	Weight	Prod. Total
W100 Series 4x4 — (½-Ton) — (115 in. w.b.)				
W100	Chassis & Cab	3023	3510	Note 5
W100	Utiline Pickup	3180	3855	Note 5
W100	Sweptline Pickup	3180	3893	Note 5
(131 in. w.b.)				
W100	Chassis & Cab	3056	3565	Note 5
W100	Utiline Pickup	3217	3994	Note 5
W100	Sweptline Pickup	3217	4023	Note 5

NOTE 5: Total model year production: (115 in.) 2978; (131 in.) 4389.

Model	Body Type	Price	Weight	Prod. Total
W200 Series 4x4 Custom — (¾-Ton) — (131 in. w.b.)				
W200	Chassis & Cab	3508	3810	Note 6
W200	Utiline Pickup	3666	4240	Note 6
W200	Sweptline Pickup	3666	4270	Note 6
(149 in. w.b.)				
W200	Crew — Chassis/Cab	4365	4145	Note 6
W200	Crew — Utiline	4523	4490	Note 6
W200	Crew — Sweptline	4523	4530	Note 6

NOTE 6: Total model year production: (131 in.) 7886; (149 in. Crew Cab) 1067.

Model	Body Type	Price	Weight	Prod. Total
W300 Series 4x4 Custom — (1-Ton) — (135 in. w.b.)				
W300	Chassis & Cab	4227	4320	Note 7
W300	Utiline Pickup	4338	4515	Note 7
W300	Platform	4640	5325	Note 7
W300	Stake	4660	5625	Note 7

NOTE 7: Total model year production: 943.

NOTE 8: Weights and prices shown are for 6-cyl. models. For V-8 engine, add $118 to $167 to price (depending on series).

ENGINE (Standard: All Models): Inline. Overhead valve. Slant six. Cast iron block. Bore & stroke: 3.4 x 4.125 in. Displacement: 224.7 cu. in. Compression ratio: 8.4:1. Brake horsepower: 140 gross at 3900 R.P.M. (110 net at 4000 R.P.M.) Taxable horsepower: 27.70. Torque: 215 lbs.-ft. gross at 1600 R.P.M. (185 lbs.-ft. net at 2000 R.P.M.) Four main bearings. Solid valve lifters.

ENGINE (Standard V-8: All Models): 90-degree, overhead valve. V-8. Cast iron block. Bore & stroke: 3.91 x 3.312 in. Displacement: 318.1 cu. in. Compression ratio: 8.8:1. Brake horsepower: 210 gross at 4000 R.P.M. Taxable horsepower: 48.92. Torque: 318 lbs.-ft. gross at 2800 R.P.M. (245 lbs.-ft. net at 1600 R.P.M.) Five main bearings. Hydraulic valve lifters.

ENGINE (Optional: All Models): 90-degree, overhead valve. V-8. Cast iron block. Bore & stroke: 4.00 x 3.58 in. Displacement: 359.9 cu. in. Compression ratio: 8.7:1. Brake horsepower: 180 (net) at 4000 R.P.M. Taxable horsepower: 51.2. Torque: 295 lbs.-ft. (net) at 2400 R.P.M. Five main bearings. Hydraulic valve lifters.

ENGINE (Optional: D100-300 only): 90-degree, overhead valve. V-8. Cast iron block. Bore & stroke: 4.34 x 3.37 in. Displacement: 400 cu. in. Compression ratio: 8.2:1. Brake horsepower: 200 (net) at 4400 R.P.M. Taxable horsepower: 60.3. Torque: 320 lbs.-ft. (net) at 2400 R.P.M. Five main bearings. Hydraulic valve lifters.

NOTE: Beginning in 1972, advertised brake horsepower and torque ratings were normally given as "SAE net," with normal parts attached to the engine; prior "gross" ratings were measured with a bare engine.

CHASSIS (B100 Van): Wheelbase: 109 in. or 127 in. Tires: E78 x 14-B four-ply. GVW: (109) 4600 lbs.; (127) 4800 lbs. Axle Capacity: 2700 lbs. (front and rear).

CHASSIS (B200 Van): Wheelbase: 109 in. or 127 in. Tires: G78 x 15-B four-ply. GVW: 5500 lbs. max. Axle Capacity: (front) 3000 lbs.; (rear) 3300 lbs.

CHASSIS: (B300 Van): Wheelbase: 109 in. or 127 in. Tires: 8.00 x 16.5-C six-ply except Maxivan, 8.00 x 16.5-D eight-ply. GVW: 6200 to 7700 lbs. Axle Capacity: (front) 3300 lbs.; (rear) 5500 lbs.

CHASSIS (D100): Wheelbase: 115 in. or 131 in. Tires: G78 x 15-D four-ply. GVW: 4600 lbs. Axle Capacity: (front) 3000 lbs.; (rear) 3300 lbs.

CHASSIS (D200): Wheelbase: 131 in., 149 in. or 165 in. Tires: 8.00 x 16.5-D eight-ply. GVW: 6200-7500 lbs. Axle Capacity: (front) 3300/3800 lbs.; (rear) 5000/6200 lbs.

CHASSIS (D300): Wheelbase: 135 in., 159 in. or 165 in. Tires: 8.00 x 16.5-D eight-ply except dual rear wheel crew cab, 8.00 x 16.5-C six-ply. GVW: 6600-10,000 lbs. Axle Capacity: (front) 3800 lbs.; (rear) 7500 lbs.

CHASSIS (W100): Wheelbase: 115 in. or 131 in. Tires: G78 x 15-B four-ply. GVW: 5100 lbs. Axle Capacity: 3300 lbs. (front and rear).

CHASSIS (W200): Wheelbase: 131 in. or 149 in. Tires: 8.00 x 16.5-D eight-ply. GVW: 6500 lbs. Axle Capacity: (front) 3500 lbs.; (rear) 5500 lbs.

CHASSIS (W300): Wheelbase: 135 in. Tires: 8.75 x 16.5-E ten-ply. GVW: 8500 lbs. Axle Capacity: (front) 4500 lbs.; (rear) 7500 lbs.

TECHNICAL: Selective sliding gear transmission. Speeds: 3F/1R except (D300, W300 and 165 in. w.b. D200) 4F/1R. Column (3-speed) or floor shift control. Single disc dry clutch: (6-cyl.) 10 in.; (V-8) 11 in. Hydraulic four-wheel brakes: (B100) 10 x 2½ in. (front/rear); (B200) 10 x 2½ (rear), 11 x 3 (front); (B300) 12 x 2½ (rear), 12 x 3 (front); (D100) 10 x 2½ (rear), 11 x 2¾ (front); (D200) 12⅛ x 2; (D/W300) 12 x 3; (W100) 11 x 2; (W200) 12 x 2½ (rear); 12⅛ x 2 (front). Fuel tank: 25-gallon except vans, 26-gallon. Alternator: (vans) 48 amp; (others) 41 amp. Automatic transmission optional.

OPTIONS (Factory-Installed): (Vans) Chrome bumpers. Chrome grille. Chrome hubcaps. Chrome wheel covers. Tinted glass. Dual horns. Horn bar. Radio (AM or AM/FM). Cigar lighter. Deluxe heater. Cargo area heater. Cargo area headliner. Padded dash. Convenience package. Insulation package. Lock package. Trailer-towing package. Exterior moldings: upper side package; lower side and rear package; or upper side/rear and lower side/rear package. Oil pressure gauge. Door check arms (side and rear). Door check straps (side). Glove box door. Light switch (cargo door operated). Manual dome light switch. Chrome 5x7 in. outside mirrors. Dual Junior West Coast mirrors: painted or chrome. Two-tone paint. Bucket seat (passenger). Deluxe bucket seat (driver's, or driver and passenger). Undercoating. Window combinations: side glass, rear glass, vision van, or curbside vision van. Oil-wetted air cleaner. 50 or 60-amp alternator. Anti-spin rear axle (B100-200 with 3.2:1, 3.55:1 or 3.91:1 ratio; or B300 with 4.1:1 ratio). Cruise control. Front disc brakes. Vacuum booster power brakes (standard on B200-300). 11 in. clutch (for 225 cu. in.). Increased cooling capacity. Engine block heater. Air conditioner. Heavy-duty shock absorbers. Heavy-duty springs (front or rear). Power steering. 3-speed automatic transmission (A727). 360-cu. in. V-9 engine. (D100-300, W100-300) Painted rear bumper. Chrome rear bumper (D100-200). Step rear bumper. Front bumper guards. Spare tire carrier: inside body (D100-200 Sweptline); outside (Utiline); underslung (except D100). Chrome hubcaps (D100-200). Wheel covers (except D200). Sliding rear window. Undercoating. Tinted glass. Two-tone paint. Textured vinyl roof. Dual electric horns. Cab marker lights. Chrome 5x7 in. outside mirrors (short or long arm). Dual Junior West Coast mirrors. Radio (AM or AM/FM). Cigar lighter. Clock. Air conditioner. Heater/defroster. Deluxe foam rubber seat assembly. Shoulder belts. Adventurer package. Adventurer Sport package (131 in. w.b.). Adventurer SE package (131 in. w.b.). Bucket seat package. Convenience package. Heavy-duty package (D/W200, 131 in. w.b.). Trailer-towing package. Power steering. Electric tachometer. Hand throttle control. Oil pressure gauge. One-quart oil bath air cleaner (except D100). 50 or 60-amp alternator. Anti-spin rear axle: D100 with 3.2:1, 3.55:1 or 3.91:1 ratio; others with 3.54:1, 4.1:1 or 4.56:1 ratio. Power drum brakes (D100). Power front disc, rear drum brakes. 11 in. clutch (225 cu. in.). Increased cooling capacity. Auxiliary 25-gallon fuel tank. Engine block heater. Spare tire and wheel (except D100). Heavy-duty shock absorbers. Heavy-duty springs (front or rear). Auxiliary 500-lb. rear springs (D100-300, W300). Front stabilizer bar (D models). NP435 4-speed manual transmission (D/W100-200). NP445B 4-speed transmission. A727 3-speed automatic transmission. 360 cu. in. V-8 engine (D models). 400 cu. in. V-8 engine (D models). Tool storage box (D100-200 on 131 or 165 in. w.b.)

HISTORICAL: Introduced: August, 1971. Calendar year sales: 260,002. Calendar year production: 325,726 (U.S. only). Model year production: 296,397. Innovations: Curved side windows. Recessed gauges. Independent front suspension. Electronic ignition system. Historical notes: Dodge spent a record $50 million to completely re-engineer and restyle its line of light-duty trucks for 1972. Bolstered by a strong general economy, the U.S. truck industry produced a record 2,475,000 trucks and buses. Dodge production and sales also established new records, as the company's market share shot up to 13.2 percent (from less than 10 percent in 1971). Sales gained 63.5 percent over the previous year. For the first time, over 2 million V-8 gasoline powered trucks were sold by all manufacturers. For the model year, 71.4 percent of light-duty Dodge trucks were V-8 powered; 74.5 percent had automatic transmissions; 61.8 percent had power steering; 79.9 percent power brakes; and 15.5 percent carried air conditioners. Dodge built 216,345 trucks in its Warren, Michigan plant and 109,381 at St. Louis. Medium and heavy-duty models were unchanged from 1971. In spring 1972, Dodge introduced its mammoth new heavy-duty conventional model, called Big Horn. Also at mid-year, Dodge offered — for the first time in the industry — a fully electronic ignition system on light-duty trucks, vans and motor homes with V-8 engines and automatic transmissions. Dodge continued its leadership role in vans and motor homes.

Pricing

	5	4	3	2	1
1972					
B100 Series Van — (½-Ton)					
109 in. w.b.	540	1080	1800	2500	3600
127 in. w.b.	570	1140	1900	2650	3800
B200 Series Van — (¾-Ton)					
109 in. w.b.	520	1020	1700	2400	3400
127 in. w.b.	540	1080	1800	2500	3600
Maxivan	570	1140	1900	2650	3800
B300 Series Van — (1-Ton)					
109 in. w.b.	480	975	1600	2250	3200
127 in. w.b.	520	1020	1700	2400	3400
Maxivan	540	1080	1800	2500	3600
D100 Series — (½-Ton) — (115 in. w.b.)					
Utiline Pickup	770	1550	2550	3600	5100
Sweptline Pickup	780	1560	2600	3600	5200
D100 Series — (131 in. w.b.)					
Utiline Pickup	780	1560	2600	3600	5200
Sweptline Pickup	800	1600	2650	3700	5300
D200 Series — (¾-Ton) — (131 in. w.b.)					
Utiline Pickup	750	1500	2500	3500	5000
Sweptline Pickup	770	1550	2550	3600	5100
D200 Crew Cab — (¾-Ton) — (149 or 165 in. w.b.)					
(149 in.) Utiline Pickup	720	1450	2400	3300	4800
(149 in.) Sweptline Pickup	740	1470	2450	3350	4900
(165 in.) Utiline Pickup	690	1380	2300	3250	4700
(165 in.) Sweptline Pickup	720	1450	2400	3300	4800
D300 Series — (1-Ton) — (135 in. w.b.)					
Utiline Pickup	680	1350	2250	3150	4500
W100 Series 4x4 — (½-Ton) — (115 in. w.b.)					
Utiline Pickup	810	1620	2700	3800	5400
Sweptline Pickup	830	1650	2750	3850	5500
W100 Series 4x4 — (½-Ton) — (131 in. w.b.)					
Utiline Pickup	800	1600	2650	3700	5300
Sweptline Pickup	810	1620	2700	3800	5400
W200 Series 4x4 — (¾-Ton) — (131 in. w.b.)					
Utiline Pickup	770	1550	2550	3600	5100
Sweptline Pickup	780	1560	2600	3600	5200
W200 Crew Cab 4x4 — (¾-Ton) — (149 in. w.b.)					
Utiline Pickup	750	1500	2500	3500	5000
Sweptline Pickup	770	1550	2550	3600	5100
W300 Series 4x4 — (1-Ton) — (135 in. w.b.)					
Utiline Pickup	740	1470	2450	3350	4900
Platform	690	1380	2300	3200	4600
Stake	680	1350	2350	3250	4700

NOTE: Add 10 percent for V-8 engine.

1973 DODGE

½-TON VAN — B100 SERIES — SIX-CYLINDER and V-8 / ¾-TON VAN — B200 SERIES — SIX-CYLINDER and V-8 / 1-TON VAN — B300 SERIES — SIX-CYLINDER and V-8: — "Second generation" Dodge vans entered their third year without change in appearance or engineering features. Electronic ignition was now standard equipment on B100 and B200 vans, and optional on the B300. New this year was the innovative Dodge Kary Van, with a 10-ft. body on the 127 in. w.b. chassis. Rated up to 8200 pounds GVW, its 6 ft. 2 in. height gave walk-in roominess. Three rear door styles were available. All optional equipment offered on the Tradesman Van was available for the Kary Van. Its interior was readily adaptable to do-it-yourself alterations. Base engine remained the 225 cu. in. slant six, with 318 and 360 cu. in. V-8s optional. All models now had power brakes.

1973 Dodge Adventurer Special Edition Pickup (DNP)

½-TON — D100 SERIES — SIX-CYLINDER and V-8 / ¾-TON — D200 SERIES — SIX-CYLINDER and V-8 / 1-TON — D300 SERIES — SIX-CYLINDER and V-8 / ½-TON 4x4 — W100 SERIES — SIX-CYLINDER and V-8 / ¾-TON 4x4 — W200 SERIES — SIX-CYLINDER and V-8 / 1-TON 4x4 — W300 SERIES — SIX-CYLINDER and V-8: — Biggest news in 1973 pickups was the unique treatment Dodge gave to its standard cab, called the Club Cab. Lengthening the cab behind the rear seat added 18 in. of interior cargo or passenger space. Two windows in the rear quarter panels gave additional visibility. Two optional jump seats, normally facing forward, fit into depressions in the side trim panel when not in use. The Club Cab was available on a D100 chassis of 133 in. w.b. with 6½-ft. Sweptline box, a 149 in. D100 chassis with 8-ft. Sweptline box, or the D200 chassis with 8-ft. Sweptline body. Club Cabs were not available on 4x4 models. Electronic ignition, introduced as an option on V-8 engines during 1972, was now available at extra cost for all engines. Since it eliminated breaker points and condensers, electronic ignition was essentially maintenance-free. A new extra-cost option, only on D100 and D200 Sweptline 8-ft. pickups, was a tool storage compartment under the pickup box, between the cab and rear wheel on the right side. All other 1972 models carried forward without change in styling, engines, transmissions, or engineering features. Four trim levels, as introduced for 1970, continued unchanged. They ranged from the low-end Custom up to the Adventurer, the Adventurer Sport, and the top-of-the-line Adventurer Special Edition (SE).

I.D. DATA: Serial and engine numbers were in the same locations, with the same coding, as in 1972.

1973 Dodge Club Cab Pickup (DNP)

Model	Body Type	Price	Weight	Prod. Total
B100-300 Series Tradesman Van — (½-Ton) — (109 in. w.b.)				
B100-6	Van	2914	3470	26,980
(127 in. w.b.)				
B100-6	Van	3043	3570	17,995
(¾-Ton) — (109 in. w.b.)				
B200-6	Van	3049	3460	12,528
(127 in. w.b.)				
B200-6	Van	3171	3570	55,201
B200-6	Maxivan	—	3715	—
(1-Ton) — (109 in. w.b.)				
B300-6	Van	3151	3695	567
(127 in. w.b.)				
B300-6	Van	3280	3810	73,184
B300-6	Maxivan	—	3985	—
CB300	Kary Van	—	—	—
D100 Series — Custom — (½-Ton) — (115 in. w.b.)				
D100	Chassis & Cab	2758	3065	Note 1
D100	Utiline Pickup	2914	3410	Note 1
D100	Sweptline Pickup	2914	3470	Note 1
(131 in. w.b.)				
D100	Chassis & Cab	—	3105	Note 1
D100	Utiline Pickup	—	3535	Note 1
D100	Sweptline Pickup	—	3565	Note 1

NOTE 1: Total model year production, (115 in.): 14,485; (131 in.) 61,428.

D100 Series Club Cab — Custom — (133 in. w.b.)				
D100	Sweptline Pickup	—	—	4404
(149 in. w.b.)				
D100	Sweptline Pickup	—	3935	27,652

1973 Dodge Crew Cab USAC Fire-Rescue (IMSC/JLM)

Model	Body Type	Price	Weight	Prod. Total
D200 Series — Custom — (¾-Ton)		**(131 in. w.b.)**		
D200	Chassis & Cab	2984	3245	Note 2
D200	Utiline Pickup	3141	3675	Note 2
D200	Sweptline Pickup	3141	3705	Note 2

NOTE 2: Total model year production: 22,221.

Model	Body Type	Price	Weight	Prod. Total
D200 Series Club Cab — Custom — (¾-Ton)		**(149 in. w.b.)**		
D200	Sweptline Pickup	—	3935	Note 3
D200 Crew Cab — Custom — (¾-Ton)		**(149 in. w.b.)**		
D200	Chassis & Cab	3753	3775	Note 3
D200	Utiline Pickup	3910	4120	Note 3
D200	Sweptline Pickup	3910	4160	Note 3
(165 in. w.b.)				
D200	Chassis & Cab	—	3950	Note 3
D200	Utiline Pickup	—	4380	Note 3
D200	Sweptline Pickup	—	4410	Note 3

NOTE 3: Total model year production: (149 in., Club Cab and Crew Cab) 18,120; (165 in. Crew Cab) 1325.

Model	Body Type	Price	Weight	Prod. Total
D300 Series — Custom — (1-Ton)		**(135 in. w.b.)**		
D300	Chassis & Cab	3104	3795	Note 4
D300	Utiline Pickup	3221	4290	Note 4
(159 in. w.b.)				
D300	Chassis & Cab	—	3890	2888
(165 in. w.b.)				
D300	Crew — Chassis/Cab	—	4750	151

NOTE 4: Total model year production: (135 in.) 5856.

Model	Body Type	Price	Weight	Prod. Total
W100 Series 4x4 — Custom — (½-Ton)		**(115 in. w.b.)**		
W100	Chassis & Cab	3257	3510	Note 5
W100	Utiline Pickup	3414	3855	Note 5
W100	Sweptline Pickup	3414	3893	Note 5
(131 in. w.b.)				
W100	Chassis & Cab	—	3565	Note 5
W100	Utiline Pickup	—	3994	Note 5
W100	Sweptline Pickup	—	4023	Note 5

NOTE 5: Total model year production: (115 in.) 5889; (131 in.) 10,310.

Model	Body Type	Price	Weight	Prod. Total
W200 Series 4x4 — Custom — (¾-Ton)		**(131 in. w.b.)**		
W200	Chassis & Cab	3760	3810	Note 6
W200	Utiline Pickup	3914	4240	Note 6
W200	Sweptline Pickup	3914	4270	Note 6
(149 in. w.b.)				
W200	Crew — Chassis/Cab	4554	4145	Note 6
W200	Crew — Utiline	4707	4490	Note 6
W200	Crew — Sweptline	4707	4530	Note 6

NOTE 6: Total model year production: (131 in.) 13,948; (149 in.) 1023.

Model	Body Type	Price	Weight	Prod. Total
W300 Series 4x4 — Custom — (1-Ton)		**(135 in. w.b.)**		
W300	Chassis & Cab	4442	4320	Note 7
W300	Utiline Pickup	4553	4515	Note 7
W300	Platform (9½-ft.)	4860	4977	Note 7
W300	Stake (9½-ft.)	4879	5275	Note 7

NOTE 7: Total model year production: 1243,

NOTE 8: Weights and prices shown are for 6-cyl. models.

ENGINES: Same as 1972; see previous specifications, except 360-cu. in. V-8 now had 8.4:1 compression ratio.

CHASSIS: Same as 1972; see previous specifications, except B100 van now had E78 x 15-B four-ply tires.

TECHNICAL: Same as 1972; see previous specifications.

OPTIONS: Same as 1972, with the addition of the following: (B series Vans) Front disc brakes. Low-mount mirrors (painted or chrome). In-cab hood release lock. (D100-300, W100-300) Carpeting on Club Cabs, black only (D100-200). Inside hood release. Camper 7500 and 9000 package (D/W200).

1973 Dodge Townsman KaryVan (OCW)

HISTORICAL: Introduced: August, 1972. Calendar year sales: 332,751. Calendar year production: 377,555. Model year production: 414,709 (including 51,154 passenger vans and 16,862 D200 Club Cab models). Innovations: Roomy Club Cab model. Tall Kary Van. Historical notes: Despite a severe parts shortage and 10-day strike in the fourth quarter, Dodge set new truck sales and production records for the third straight year. Calendar year production gained almost 16 percent, while sales were up 15.2 percent. Still, Dodge's market share slipped a bit, to 12.56 percent. The Warren, Michigan factory produced 282,136 trucks; the Fenton, Missouri plant turned out 137,310 units; and 22,570 were built in Windsor, Ontario. Gasoline V-8 engines accounted for 88.6 percent of total gas engine production. Only 3,103 diesel engines were installed in 1973. Dodge continued its leadership role in manufacturing motor home chassis, completing 300 special nationwide Recreational Vehicle Service Centers. Dodge also put on the road five mobile emergency RV service vans, which operated in key camping areas to provide free servicing. Truck dealers offered a free pickup truck cap on some specially-equipped D100 Adventurer models with 131 in. w.b. During the year, George F. Butts, who had been with Chrysler Corp. since 1949, was appointed General Manager of Dodge Truck operations.

1973 Dodge Sportsman Passenger Van (OCW)

1973 Dodge Royal Sportsman Van (DNP)

Pricing

1973	5	4	3	2	1
B100 Series Van — (½-Ton)					
109 in. w.b.	540	1080	1800	2500	3600
127 in. w.b.	570	1140	1900	2650	3800

	5	4	3	2	1
B200 Series Van — (¾-Ton)					
109 in. w.b.	520	1020	1700	2400	3400
127 in. w.b.	540	1080	1800	2500	3600
Maxivan	570	1140	1900	2650	3800
B300 Series Van — (1-Ton)					
109 in. w.b.	480	975	1600	2250	3200
127 in. w.b.	520	1020	1700	2400	3400
Maxivan	540	1080	1800	2500	3600
Kary Van	560	1100	1850	2600	3700
D100 Series — (½-Ton) — (115 in. w.b.)					
Utiline Pickup	770	1550	2550	3600	5100
Sweptline Pickup	780	1560	2600	3600	5200
D100 Series — (½-Ton) — (131 in. w.b.)					
Utiline Pickup	780	1560	2600	3600	5200
Sweptline Pickup	800	1600	2650	3700	5300
D200 Series — (¾-Ton) — (131 in. w.b.)					
Utiline Pickup	750	1500	2500	3500	5000
Sweptline Pickup	770	1550	2550	3600	5100
D200 Cab — (¾-Ton) — (149 or 165 in. w.b.)					
(149 in.) Utiline	720	1450	2400	3300	4800
(149 in.) Sweptline	740	1470	2450	3350	4900
(165 in.) Utiline	690	1380	2300	3250	4700
(165 in.) Sweptline	720	1450	2400	3300	4800
D100 Club Cab — (½-Ton) — (133 or 149 in. w.b.)					
Sweptline (133 in.)	720	1450	2400	3500	5000
Sweptline (149 in.)	770	1550	2550	3600	5100
D200 Club Cab — (¾-Ton) — (149 in. w.b.)					
Sweptline	740	1470	2450	3350	4900
D300 Series — (1-Ton) — (135 in. w.b.)					
Utiline Pickup	680	1350	2250	3150	4500
W100 Series 4x4 — (½-Ton) — (115 in. w.b.)					
Utiline Pickup	810	1620	2700	3800	5400
Sweptline Pickup	830	1650	2750	3850	5500
W100 Series 4x4 — (½-Ton) — (131 in. w.b.)					
Utiline Pickup	800	1600	2650	3700	5300
Sweptline Pickup	810	1620	2700	3800	5400
W200 Series 4x4 — (¾-Ton) — (131 in. w.b.)					
Utiline Pickup	770	1550	2550	3600	5100
Sweptline Pickup	780	1560	2600	3600	5200
W200 Crew Cab 4x4 — (¾-Ton) — (149 in. w.b.)					
Utiline Pickup	750	1500	2500	3500	5000
Sweptline Pickup	770	1550	2550	3600	5100
W300 Series 4x4 — (1-Ton) — (135 in. w.b.)					
Utiline Pickup	740	1470	2450	3350	4900
Platform	690	1380	2300	3200	4600
Stake	680	1350	2350	3250	4700

NOTE: Add 10 percent for V-8 engine.

1974 DODGE

1974 Dodge Club Cab Pickup (JAG)

½-TON VAN — B100 SERIES — SIX-CYLINDER and V-8 / ¾-TON VAN — B200 SERIES — SIX-CYLINDER and V-8 / 1-TON VAN — B300 SERIES — SIX-CYLINDER and V-8 / 1-TON KARY VAN — CB300 SERIES — SIX-CYLINDER and V-8: — No major change hit the van lineup for 1974, other than the addition of a sliding side door for 127 in. w.b. and Maxivan models. A redesigned grille gave a new frontal appearance, and vans were available in nine new colors. As before, base engine was the 225 cu. in. slant six, with 318 and 360 cu. in. V-8 engines optional. The Kary Van continued as introduced in 1973, with the same new features as other vans. Vacuum booster brakes with 9 in. dual diaphragm were standard on B200 and B300 models, optional on the ½-ton.

½-TON — D100 SERIES — SIX-CYLINDER and V-8 / ¾-TON — D200 SERIES — SIX-CYLINDER and V-8 / 1-TON — D300 SERIES — SIX-CYLINDER and V-8 / ½-TON 4x4 — W100 SERIES — SIX-CYLINDER and V-8 / ¾-TON 4x4 — W200 SERIES — SIX-CYLINDER and V-8 / 1-TON 4x4 — W300 SERIES — SIX-CYLINDER and V-8: — Dodge had completely redesigned its light truck line two years before, so little was new for 1974. The very popular Club Cab, introduced in 1973, was now also available on W100 and W200 4wd models. A new grille changed appearance slightly,

1974 Dodge D100 Sweptline Pickup (RPZ)

and nine new paint colors were added. An optional 440 cu. in. V-8 engine replaced the 400 cu. in. Electronic ignition was now standard on all models. The fuel tank on D models, formerly behind the seat, was now mounted inside the frame rail, just ahead of the wheel well on the left side. An optional fuel tank went behind the seat. Adventurer and Adventurer Sport trim packages now had an all-vinyl seat available as an option. Conventional seats featured full foam construction. A new coolant recovery system was optional. Base engine remained the 225 cu. in. slant six, with three V-8 options: 318, 360 and 440 cu. in. Four trim options were available, as before: Custom, Adventurer, Adventurer Sport, and Adventurer Special Edition (SE). In spring 1974, a new dual-wheel 1-ton pickup was announced, with Sweptline box. Rated 10,000 pounds GVW, it came with conventional cab on 131 in. w.b. or Club Cab on 149 in. w.b., with payload rating up to 5,200 pounds.

½-TON RAMCHARGER 4WD — AW100 SERIES — V-8: — The long-awaited Dodge sport-utility vehicle arrived in March 1974. Called the Rhino during development stages, it became Ramcharger as marketers feared the original name would not suggest an agile, nimble, go-anywhere vehicle. Designed for commuting and personal use, the Ramcharger was a sporty and luxurious vehicle, appealing to affluent suburban drivers. Research showed that only 10-15 percent of buyers would take their vehicles off-road. High priority was placed on comfort, handling and riding quality, as well as such luxury accessories as automatic transmission and air conditioning. As many existing, proven components as possible were used, to cut costs and shorten the development cycle. All front-end sheetmetal, dashboard and other parts came from Dodge pickups. Considerable off-road ability was also included, in the form of full-time 4wd. Dodge used the NP203 full-time, 2-speed transfer case from Chrysler's New Process Division. Dodge's product development people, expecting Ramchargers to be driven by women, directed that the styling look rugged but not too truck-like. Ramchargers rode on a 106 in. w.b. chassis and featured the biggest V-8 (440 cu. in.) available in any sport-utility vehicle. The slant six engine was not available. Standard equipment included twin armrests, ashtray, power brakes, front disc brakes, chrome bumpers, 318 cu. in. base V-8 engine, chrome grille, glove box door, heater/defroster, painted hubcaps, padded dash, 5x7 in. chrome mirrors, day/night inside mirror, driver's bucket seat and color-keyed sunvisor, and two-speed wipers.

I.D. DATA: Serial and engine numbers were in the same locations, with the same coding, as in 1972-73.

1974 Dodge Crew Cab Sweptline Power Wagon (RPZ)

KARY VAN

1974 Dodge Forward Control Kary Van (RPZ)

Model	Body Type	Price	Weight	Prod. Total
AW100 Ramcharger 4wd — (½-Ton) — (106 in. w.b.)				
AW100	No top	4077	4085	15,810
B100-300 Series Van — (½-Ton) — (109 in. w.b.)				
B100-6	Van	3113	3435	39,684
(127 in. w.b.)				
B100-6	Van	3242	3550	21,364
(¾-Ton) — (109 in. w.b.)				
B200-6	Van	3238	3485	13,271
(127 in. w.b.)				
B200-6	Van	3360	3610	62,257
B200-6	Maxivan	3556	—	—
(1-Ton) — (109 in. w.b.)				
B300-6	Van	3369	3675	835
(127 in. w.b.)				
B300-6	Van	3498	3805	42,652
B300-6	Maxivan	3727	4000	—
CB300	(10-ft.) Kary Van	4346	4660	5332
(145 in. w.b.)				
CB300	(12-ft.) Kary Van	4618	5110	1267
D100 Series — Custom — (½-Ton) — (115 in. w.b.)				
D100	Chassis & Cab	2947	3145	Note 1
D100	Utiline Pickup	3103	3490	Note 1
D100	Sweptline Pickup	3103	3515	Note 1
(131 in. w.b.)				
D100	Chassis & Cab	2982	3160	Note 1
D100	Utiline Pickup	3137	3490	Note 1
D100	Sweptline Pickup	3137	3620	Note 1

NOTE 1: Total model year production, (115 in.): 16,852; (131 in.) 55,782.

Model	Body Type	Price	Weight	Prod. Total
D100 Series Club Cab — Custom — (½-Ton) — (133 in. w.b.)				
D100	Sweptline Pickup	3349	3730	3657
(149 in. w.b.)				
D100	Sweptline Pickup	3383	3870	17,173
D200 Series — Custom — (¾-Ton) — (131 in. w.b.)				
D200	Chassis & Cab	3291	3325	Note 2
D200	Utiline Pickup	3448	3755	Note 2
D200	Sweptline Pickup	3448	3785	Note 2

NOTE 2: Total model year production: 19,924.

Model	Body Type	Price	Weight	Prod. Total
D200 Series Club Cab — Custom — (¾-Ton) — (149 in. w.b.)				
D100	Sweptline Pickup	3694	3955	Note 3
D200 Crew Cab — Custom — (¾-Ton) — (149 in. w.b.)				
D200	Chassis & Cab	4060	3725	Note 3
D200	Utiline Pickup	4217	4070	Note 3
D200	Sweptline Pickup	4217	4095	Note 3
(165 in. w.b.)				
D200	Chassis & Cab	4290	4095	Note 3
D200	Utiline Pickup	4455	4525	Note 3
D200	Sweptline Pickup	4455	4555	Note 3

NOTE 3: Total model year production: (149 in., Club Cab and Crew Cab) 14,244; (165 in. Crew Cab) 1400.

Model	Body Type	Price	Weight	Prod. Total
D300 Series — Custom — (1-Ton) — (135 in. w.b.)				
D300	Chassis & Cab	3467	3735	Note 4
D300	Utiline Pickup	3584	—	Note 4
(149 in. w.b.)				
D300	Club — Chassis/Cab	3960	—	461
(159 in. w.b.)				
D300	Chassis & Cab	3505	3880	3990
(165 in. w.b.)				
D300	Crew — Chassis/Cab	4425	—	197

NOTE 4: Total model year production: (135 in.) 7198.

Model	Body Type	Price	Weight	Prod. Total
W100 Series 4x4 — Custom — (½-Ton) — (115 in. w.b.)				
W100	Chassis & Cab	3588	3780	Note 5
W100	Utiline Pickup	3745	4125	Note 5
W100	Sweptline Pickup	3745	4150	Note 5
(131 in. w.b.)				
W100	Chassis & Cab	3621	3790	Note 5
W100	Utiline Pickup	3782	4220	Note 5
W100	Sweptline Pickup	3782	4250	Note 5

NOTE 5: Total model year production: (115 in.) 7036; (131 in.) 11,923.

Model	Body Type	Price	Weight	Prod. Total
W100 Series Club Cab 4x4 — (Custom) — (½-Ton) — (133 in. w.b.)				
W100	Sweptline Pickup	3991	—	1830
(149 in. w.b.)				
W100	Sweptline Pickup	4028	—	3031
W200 Series 4x4 — Custom — (¾-Ton) — (131 in. w.b.)				
W200	Chassis & Cab	4083	3845	Note 6
W200	Utiline Pickup	4237	4275	Note 6
W200	Sweptline Pickup	4237	4305	Note 6
(149 in. w.b.)				
W200	Club — Sweptline	4483	4505	Note 7
W200 Crew Cab 4x4 — Custom — (¾-Ton) — (149 in. w.b.)				
W200	Chassis & Cab	4952	4245	Note 7
W200	Utiline Pickup	5105	4590	Note 7
W200	Sweptline Pickup	5105	4615	Note 7

NOTE 6: Total model year production: (131 in.) 14,549.

NOTE 7: Total model year production: (149 in. Club Cabs and Crew Cabs): 5895.

Model	Body Type	Price	Weight	Prod. Total
W300 Series 4x4 — Custom — (1-Ton) — (135 in. w.b.)				
W300	Chassis & Cab	4888	4380	Note 8
W300	Utiline Pickup	4999	—	Note 8

NOTE 8: Total model year production: 1867,

NOTE 9: Weights and prices shown are for 6-cyl. models. For V-8 engine (318 cu. in.) add 100 pounds to weight and $113 to $167 to price (depending on series).

1974 Dodge D100 Utiline Pickup (RPZ)

ENGINE (Standard: All models except AW100): Inline. Overhead valve. Slant six. Cast iron block. Bore & stroke: 3.4 x 4.125 in. Displacement: 224.7 cu. in. Compression ratio: 8.4:1. Brake horsepower: 110 (net) at 4000 R.P.M. Taxable horsepower: 27.70. Torque: 185 lbs.-ft. (net) at 2000 R.P.M. Four main bearings. Solid valve lifters.

ENGINE (Standard V-8: all models): 90-degree, overhead valve. V-8. Cast iron block. Bore & stroke: 3.91 x 3.31 in. Displacement: 318.1 cu. in. Compression ratio: 8.8:1. Brake horsepower: 150 (net) at 4000 R.P.M. Taxable horsepower: 48.92. Torque: 245 lbs.-ft. (net) at 1600 R.P.M. Five main bearings. Hydraulic valve lifters.

ENGINE (Optional: all models): 90-degree, overhead valve. V-8. Cast iron block. Bore & stroke: 4.00 x 3.58 in. Displacement: 359.9 cu. in. Compression ratio: 8.4:1. Brake horsepower: 180 (net) at 4000 R.P.M. Taxable horsepower: 51.2. Torque: 295 lbs.-ft. (net) at 2400 R.P.M. Five main bearings. Hydraulic valve lifters.

1974 Dodge Club Cab Pickup (JAG)

ENGINE (Optional: AW100 only): 90-degree, overhead valve. V-8. Cast iron block. Bore & stroke: 4.34 x 3.38 in. Displacement: 400 cu. in. Compression ratio: 8.2:1. Brake horsepower: 185 (net) at 4000 R.P.M. Taxable horsepower: 60.3. Torque: 305 lbs.-ft. (net) at 2400 R.P.M. Five main bearings. Hydraulic valve lifters.

ENGINE (Optional: AW100, D100-300): 90-degree, overhead valve. V-8. Cast iron block. Bore & stroke: 4.32 x 3.75 in. Displacement: 440 cu. in. Compression ratio: 8.12:1. Brake horsepower: 230 (net) at 4000 R.P.M. Taxable horsepower: 59.7. Torque: 350 lbs.-ft. (net) at 3200 R.P.M. Five main bearings. Hydraulic valve lifters.

CHASSIS (B100 Van): Wheelbase: 109 in. or 127 in. Tires: E78 x 15-B four-ply. GVW: 4600 lbs.

CHASSIS (B200 Van): Wheelbase: 109 in. or 127 in. Tires: G78 x 15-B four-ply except (Maxivan) H78 x 15-B four-ply. GVW: 5500 lbs.

1974 Dodge B200 Tradesman Maxivan (RPZ)

1974 Dodge Ramcharger S.E. Utility Wagon (CHC)

CHASSIS: (B300 Van): Wheelbase: 109 in. or 127 in. Tires: 8.00 x 16.5-C six-ply except (Maxivan) 8.00 x 16.5-D eight-ply. GVW: 6400 lbs.

CHASSIS (CB300 Kary Van): Wheelbase: 127 in. or 145 in. Tires: 8.75 x 16.5-E ten-ply. GVW: 7700 lbs.

CHASSIS (D100): Wheelbase: 115 in. or 131 in. (Club Cab, 133 in. and 149 in.). Tires: G78 x 15-D four-ply. GVW: 5000 lbs.

CHASSIS (D200): Wheelbase: 131 in., 149 in. (Crew Cab), or 165 in. Tires: 8.00 x 16.5-D eight-ply. GVW: 6200 lbs.

CHASSIS (D300): Wheelbase: 135 in., 149 in. (Club Cab), 159 in. or 165 in. (Crew Cab). Tires: (135 in.) 8.00 x 16.5-D eight-ply; (others) 8.00 x 16.5-C eight-ply. GVW: 6600 lbs.

CHASSIS (W100): Wheelbase: 115 in. or 131 in. (Club Cab, 133 in. or 149 in.). Tires: H78 x 15-B or G78 x 15-B. GVW: 5400 lbs.

CHASSIS (W200): Wheelbase: 131 in. or 149 in. (Club or Crew Cab). Tires: 8.00 x 16.5-D eight-ply. GVW: 6500 lbs.

CHASSIS (W300): Wheelbase: 135 in. Tires: 8.75 x 16.5-E ten-ply. GVW: 8500 lbs.

CHASSIS (AW100 Ramcharger): Wheelbase: 106 in. Tires: E78 x 15-B four-ply. GVW: 4900 lbs.

1974 Dodge Sportsman Van (JAG)

TECHNICAL: Selective sliding gear transmission. Speeds: 3F/1R except (D300, W300 and 165 in. w.b. D200) 4F/1R. Column or floor (4-speed) shift control. Single disc dry clutch: (6-cyl.) 10 in.; (V-8) 11 in. Rear axle ratio: (AW100 Ramcharger) 3.90:1 (318 cu. in. V-8 only); 3.55:1 or 3.23:1. Hydraulic four-wheel brakes: front disc, rear drum. Fuel tank: (B vans) 23-gallon; (AW100) 24-gallon; (others) 22-gallon. Alternator: (Vans, AW100) 48 amp; (others) 41 amp. Automatic 3-speed transmission optional.

OPTIONS: Same as 1972-73, except for the addition of the following: (B Vans) Brake vacuum booster (B100). Sliding cargo door. Banded glass in front doors and wing vents (B200-300). Glove box door and light. Heavy-duty package (B300). Chrome wheel covers (B100-200). (D100-300, W100-300) Power brakes (D100). Heavy-duty drum brakes (D/W200-300 with 131 or 149 in. w.b.) 440 cu. in. V-8 engine (D100-200). Chrome grip rails atop pickup box (D100-200 8-ft. Sweptline only). Two-tone paint (3 different procedures). Flip-type seat (D/W100-200 Club Cabs). (AW100 Ramcharger) Front bumper guards. Step rear bumper. Air conditioner. Cigarette lighter. Electric clock. Console. Deluxe trim. Color-keyed carpet. Tinted windshield. Tinted glass. Vented, tinted glass. Inside hood latch release. Dual horns. Chrome hubcaps. 7½ x 10½ in. chrome mirrors. Oil pressure gauge. Removable hardtop roof: body color, white, or vinyl-textured white. Convenience package. Exterior trim molding package. SE package. Trailer-towing package. Monotone paint. Two-tone paint. Radio (AM or AM/FM). Power steering. Roll bar. Vinyl textured black roof. Passenger's bucket seat. Two deluxe front bucket seats. Passenger bucket seat and rear bench seat. Deluxe bucket seats and rear bench seat. Shoulder belts (driver's or pair). Skid plates (fuel tank or transfer case). Cruise control. Heavy-duty shock absorbers (front and rear). Electric tachometer. Hand throttle. Outside-mounted spare tire. Chrome wheel covers. 55 or 72-amp alternator. Anti-spin rear axle (3.55:1 or 3.90:1 ratio).

Increased cooling capacity. 35-gallon fuel tank. Engine block heater. 360-cu. in. V-8 engine. 400-cu. in. V-8 engine. 440-cu. in. V-8 engine. NP435 4-speed manual transmission. NP445 4-speed transmission. A727 3-speed automatic transmission.

HISTORICAL: Introduced: August, 1973. (Ramcharger, March, 1974). Calendar year sales: 292,213. Calendar year production: 362,008. Model year production: 404,619 (including 58,669 passenger vans, 5,025 Plymouth Traildusters, and 12,609 D200 Club Cabs). Innovations: Ramcharger sport-utility model. Historical notes: Dodge truck sales and production saw a downturn in 1974, due to the petroleum crisis and a general slowdown in the economy. Dodge had been the industry leader in supplying chassis to the recreational vehicle industry. When the RV business collapsed because of high gas prices, Dodge lost its 85 percent share of that market. By year's end, most of the small camper manufacturers were out of business. Calendar year truck sales declined 10.1 percent; production 4.1 percent. Dodge's biggest loss was in the 10,000 to 14,000-pound GVW class: 1974 production fell to 6,841, from 40,086 the year before. Because of the fuel crisis, the 6-cyl. engine made a comeback, increasing from 9.3 percent of total gas engine sales in 1973 to 17.5 percent in 1974. 4wd production was good, as this market remained strong. Dodge built a total of 43,324 4wd trucks, plus 10,037 Ramchargers (which counted as passenger cars). Another 57,500 Dodge Sportsman and Plymouth Voyager passenger vans were made in 1974, also counted as passenger cars. Dodge produced many trucks at its Windsor, Ontario facility (25,328 in 1974), because of a trade agreement between the two countries. Truck makers could assemble some vehicles north of the border for sale in the U.S., and could then sell U.S.-made trucks in Canada, without paying duties either way. All Dodge medium-duty trucks were made in Canada. The Warren, Michigan factory turned out 246,119 trucks; the Sherwood Avenue (Detroit) facility built 4,995 conventional trucks; 77,899 came from Fenton, Missouri; and another 17,416 "knockdown" units for export were built. Dodge introduced an all new, contemporary styled medium-duty truck line. Vans and the new sport-utility vehicle were also sold by Plymouth dealers, carrying the Plymouth nameplate. They differed from Dodge models only in trim details. Dodge began work on a new truck facility in Pennsylvania, but shelved it because of uncertainty due to the oil crisis.

Pricing

1974	5	4	3	2	1
AW100 Ramcharger 4wd — (½-Ton) — (106 in. w.b.)					
Sport	870	1750	2900	4100	5800
B100 Series Van — (½-Ton) — (109 or 127 in. w.b.)					
109 in. w.b.	540	1080	1800	2500	3600
127 in. w.b.	570	1140	1900	2650	3800
B200 Series Van — (¾-Ton) — (109 or 127 in. w.b.)					
109 in. w.b.	520	1020	1700	2400	3400
127 in. w.b.	540	1080	1800	2500	3600
Maxivan	570	1140	1900	2650	3800
B300 Series Van — (1-Ton) — (109 or 127 in. w.b.)					
109 in. w.b.	480	975	1600	2250	3200
127 in. w.b.	520	1020	1700	2400	3400
Maxivan	540	1080	1800	2500	3600
CB Series Kary Van — (1-Ton) — (127 or 145 in. w.b.)					
10-ft. Body	560	1100	1850	2600	3700
12-ft. Body	540	1080	1800	2500	3600
D100 Series Pickup — (½-Ton) — (115 or 131 in. w.b.)					
Utiline (115 in.)	770	1550	2550	3600	5100
Sweptline (115 in.)	780	1560	2600	3600	5200
Utiline (131 in.)	780	1560	2600	3600	5200
Sweptline (131 in.)	800	1600	2650	3700	5300
D100 Series Club Cab — (½-Ton) — (133 or 149 in. w.b.)					
Sweptline (133 in.)	720	1450	2400	3500	5000
Sweptline (149 in.)	770	1550	2550	3600	5100
D200 Series Pickup — (¾-Ton) — (131 in. w.b.)					
Utiline	720	1450	2400	3500	5000
Sweptline	770	1550	2550	3600	5100
D200 Club Cab Pickup — (¾-Ton) — (149 in. w.b.)					
Sweptline	740	1450	2450	3350	4900
D200 Crew Cab Pickup — (¾-Ton) — (149 or 165 in. w.b.)					
Utiline (149 in.)	720	1450	2400	3300	4800
Sweptline (149 in.)	740	1470	2450	3350	4900
Utiline (165 in.)	690	1380	2300	3250	4700
Sweptline (165 in.)	720	1450	2400	3300	4800
D300 Series Pickup — (1-Ton) — (135 in. w.b.)					
Utiline	680	1350	2250	3150	4500
W100 Series 4x4 Pickup — (½-Ton) — (115 or 131 in. w.b.)					
Utiline (115 in.)	810	1620	2700	3800	5400
Sweptline (115 in.)	830	1650	2750	3850	5500
Utiline (131 in.)	800	1600	2650	3700	5300
Sweptline (131 in.)	810	1620	2700	3800	5400
W100 Series Club Cab 4x4 — (½-Ton) — (133 or 149 in. w.b.)					
Sweptline (133 in.)	800	1600	2650	3700	5300
Sweptline (149 in.)	770	1550	2550	3600	5100
W200 Series 4x4 Pickup — (¾-Ton) — (131 or 149 in. w.b.)					
Utiline (131 in.)	770	1550	2550	3600	5100
Sweptline (131 in.)	780	1560	2600	3600	5200
Sweptline Club Cab	800	1600	2650	3700	5300
W200 Series Crew Cab 4x4 — (¾-Ton) — (149 in. w.b.)					
Utiline	750	1500	2500	3500	5000
Sweptline	770	1550	2550	3600	5100
W300 Series 4x4 Pickup — (1-Ton) — (135 in. w.b.)					
Utiline	740	1470	2450	3350	4900

NOTE: Add 10 percent for V-8 engine.
Add 12 percent for 440 cu. in. V-8.

1975 DODGE

1975 Dodge Ramcharger SE (DNP)

½-TON VAN — B100 SERIES — SIX-CYLINDER and V-8 / ¾-TON VAN — B200 SERIES — SIX-CYLINDER and V-8 / 1-TON VAN — B300 SERIES — SIX-CYLINDER and V-8 / 1-TON KARY VAN — CB300 SERIES — SIX-CYLINDER and V-8: — Changes to the van line were minimal. A new optional one-piece rear door gave the back of the van an uncluttered look, made loading easier, and offered the driver a better view of the road behind. A package of more durable, heavy-duty interior trim materials was offered as an option to those owners who gave their van interiors hard service. Dodge offered a system of 50 codeable Gross Vehicle Weight packages, covering vans as well as D and W series trucks and Ramchargers. These packages were designed to eliminate the need for dealers to specify in detail each new unit ordered from the factory. Instead, each truck ordered with a specific GVW package came equipped with the correct tires, springs, and other required components. If the buyer desired or required a part different from that in a standard package, that item could be individually coded.

½-TON — D100 SERIES — SIX-CYLINDER and V-8 / ¾-TON — D200 SERIES — SIX-CYLINDER and V-8 / 1-TON — D300 SERIES — SIX-CYLINDER and V-8 / ½-TON 4x4 — W100 SERIES — SIX-CYLINDER and V-8 / ¾-TON 4x4 — W200 SERIES — SIX-CYLINDER and V-8 / 1-TON 4x4 — W300 SERIES — SIX-CYLINDER and V-8: — For the first time in five years, Dodge did not introduce a major new light-duty truck. Between 1971 and 1974, Dodge had introduced a new van line, an all new light-duty line, the Club Cab pickup and, finally, the Ramcharger. This year's emphasis went toward refining an already broad light-duty lineup. A new instrument panel appeared on pickups. Appearance changes included new bodyside moldings. Club Cab pickups, formerly offered in a choice of three interior trim colors, now had five. Full time 4wd from Chrysler's New Process Gear Division was made standard on all W Series pickups. W100 and W200 suspensions were completely reworked to give a much more pleasant, smooth and easy ride. This was accomplished by changing spring geometry to more closely coincide with that of the Ramcharger. In addition, longer front springs were used, spring rates were softer, and new shocks were added. Vehicle height was reduced one inch. A new optional sway bar was also available for 4x4s, to reduce body lean and increase understeer for better control through turns. The big 440 cu. in. V-8 became optional for 4x4s. All 1975 Dodge trucks with a GVW rating below 6000 pounds carried a catalytic converter to meet new EPA emission standards.

½-TON RAMCHARGER 2WD — AD100 SERIES — SIX-CYLINDER and V-8 / ½-TON RAMCHARGER 4x4 — AW100 SERIES — SIX-CYLINDER and V-8: — For 1975, a 2wd Ramcharger was added, on the same 106 in. w.b. but 2½ in. lower than the 4x4. Ramchargers also received the pickup's new instrument panel, which could accommodate an optional clock, tachometer, or combination vacuum-voltmeter gauges. To improve instrument readability, the cluster was wing-shaped, its hood redesigned to minimize glare. New interior door trim panels in high-line models included map pockets. The standard Ramcharger had a single driver's seat; a rear bench seat was optional. The SE package included carpeting, simulated woodgrain inserts, vinyl map pockets, front bucket seats — plus a lockable center console with removable canned-drink ice chest and storage area for cups, pencils, coins and maps. The slant six was made the base engine. Ramcharger roofs were optional. A dealer-installed soft top could be lowered, or its rear and side panels would roll up. A removable steel roof could be ordered in white, or to match any of the 14 standard body colors.

I.D. DATA: Serial numbers were on a vehicle identification plate attached to the driver's door body latch post. Vehicle Identification Numbers (VIN) consisted of 13 letters and numbers, divided into 7 elements. The first two characters indicated Model Code. The next digit showed Body Type. The next letter designated GVW rating. Next came a letter for Engine Type. The next digit gave model year (5 = 1975, 6 = 1976, etc.). The next letter indicated assembly plant (J = Windsor; S = Warren Plant No. 1; T = Warren Plant No. 2; X = Missouri). At the end came a six-digit sequence number at that assembly plant; all models began with sequence number 000,001. Model Code index: D1 (D100); D2 (D200); D3 (D300); W1 (W100); W2 (W200); W3 (W300); B1 (B100); B2 (B200); B3 (B300); P1, P2 or P3 (P100, P200 or P300 forward-control). Body Type Index: 0 = forward-con-

trol chassis; 1 = conventional cab; 2 = crew cab; 3 = Utiline conventional cab; 4 = Sweptline conventional cab; 5 = Utiline crew cab; 6 = Sweptline crew cab; 7 = flat face cowl or Sweptline club cab; 8 = club cab. GVW index: A (6000 lbs. or less); B (6001 to 10,000); C (10,001 to 14,000); D (14,000 to 16,000) etc. Engine Type Index: B (225-1); C (225-2); D (440-1); E (318-1); F (360); G (318-3); X (Special 6); Y (Special 8). Engine numbers were located as follows: (225 cu. in. six) Right side of block, below No. 1 spark plug; (318 or 360 cu. in. V-8) Left front of block, below cylinder head; (440 V-8) Left side of block, adjacent to front tappet rail. The first digit gave model year. The next letter indicated assembly plant (M = Mound Road). The next three digits showed displacement in cu. in. Next came a four-digit date code, followed by a four-digit sequence number. Starting engine numbers are not available.

Model	Body Type	Price	Weight	Prod. Total
AD100/AW100 Ramcharger — (½-Ton) — (106 in. w.b.)				
AD100	2wd — no top	—	3560	1674
AW100	4wd — no top	—	4075	11,361
B100-300 Series Van — (½-Ton) — (109 in. w.b.)				
B100-6	Van	3202	3435	31,516
(127 in. w.b.)				
B100-6	Van	3335	3435	12,522
(¾-Ton) — (109 in. w.b.)				
B200-6	Van	3331	3485	22,431
(127 in. w.b.)				
B200-6	Van	3456	3610	22,998
B200-6	Maxivan	3658	—	11,926
(1-Ton) — (109 in. w.b.)				
B300-6	Van	3465	3675	850
(127 in. w.b.)				
B300-6	Van	3598	3805	6638
B300-6	Maxivan	3834	4000	10,071
CB300	(10-ft.) Kary Van	4776	4660	889
(145 in. w.b.)				
CB300	(12-ft.) Kary Van	5056	5110	2239
D100 Series — Custom — (½-Ton) — (115 in. w.b.)				
D100	Chassis & Cab	3051	3145	Note 1
D100	Utiline Pickup	3212	3490	Note 1
D100	Sweptline Pickup	3212	3515	Note 1
(131 in. w.b.)				
D100	Chassis & Cab	3087	3160	Note 1
D100	Utiline Pickup	3247	3490	Note 1
D100	Sweptline Pickup	3247	3620	Note 1

NOTE 1: Total model year production, (115 in.): 20,921; (131 in.) 47,226.

D100 Series Club Cab — Custom — (½-Ton) — (133 in. w.b.)				
D100	Sweptline Pickup	3465	3730	2166
(149 in. w.b.)				
D100	Sweptline Pickup	3500	3870	10,025
D200 Series — Custom — (¾-Ton) — (131 in. w.b.)				
D200	Chassis & Cab	3385	3325	Note 2
D200	Utiline Pickup	3547	3755	Note 2
D200	Sweptline Pickup	3547	3785	Note 2

NOTE 2: Total model year production: 17,056.

D200 Series Club Cab — Custom — (¾-Ton) — (149 in. w.b.)				
D100	Sweptline Pickup	3800	3955	7152
D200 Crew Cab — Custom — (¾-Ton) — (149 in. w.b.)				
D200	Chassis & Cab	4176	3725	Note 3
D200	Utiline Pickup	4338	4070	Note 3
D200	Sweptline Pickup	4338	4095	Note 3
(165 in. w.b.)				
D200	Chassis & Cab	4413	4095	Note 3
D200	Utiline Pickup	4583	4525	Note 3
D200	Sweptline Pickup	4583	4555	Note 3

NOTE 3: Total model year production: (149 in.) 1935; (165 in.) 1731.

D300 Series — Custom — (1-Ton) — (131 in. w.b.)				
D300	Sweptline Pickup	4230	—	570
(135 in. w.b.)				
D300	Chassis & Cab	3556	3735	Note 4
D300	Utiline Pickup	3687	—	Note 4
(149 in. w.b.)				
D300	Club — Chassis/Cab	4073	—	Note 4
D300	Club — Sweptline	4483	—	Note 4
(159 in. w.b.)				
D300	Chassis & Cab	3605	3880	2770
(165 in. w.b.)				
D300	Crew — Chassis/Cab	4552	—	197

NOTE 4: Total model year production: (135 in.) 6560; (149 in.) 687.

W100 Series 4x4 — Custom — (½-Ton) — (115 in. w.b.)				
W100	Chassis & Cab	3784	3780	Note 5
W100	Utiline Pickup	3945	4125	Note 5
W100	Sweptline Pickup	3945	4150	Note 5
(131 in. w.b.)				
W100	Chassis & Cab	3818	3790	Note 5
W100	Utiline Pickup	3983	4220	Note 5
W100	Sweptline Pickup	3983	4250	Note 5

NOTE 5: Total model year production: (115 in.) 10,652; (131 in.) 10,974.

W100 Series Club Cab 4x4 — (Custom) — (½-Ton) — (133 in. w.b.)				
W100	Sweptline Pickup	4198	—	1868
(149 in. w.b.)				
W100	Sweptline Pickup	4236	—	2776

221

Model	Body Type	Price	Weight	Prod. Total
W200 Series 4x4 — Custom — (¾-Ton) — (131 in. w.b.)				
W200	Chassis & Cab	4280	3845	Note 6
W200	Utiline Pickup	4438	4275	Note 6
W200	Sweptline Pickup	4438	4305	Note 6
(149 in. w.b.)				
W200	Club — Sweptline	4691	4505	4179

NOTE 6: Total model year production (131 in.) 13,615.

Model	Body Type	Price	Weight	Prod. Total
W200 Crew Cab 4x4 — Custom — (¾-Ton) — (149 in. w.b.)				
W200	Chassis & Cab	5174	4245	Note 7
W200	Utiline Pickup	5331	4590	Note 7
W200	Sweptline Pickup	5331	4615	Note 7

NOTE 7: Total model year production: 1683.

Model	Body Type	Price	Weight	Prod. Total
W300 Series 4x4 — Custom — (1-Ton) — (135 in. w.b.)				
W300	Chassis & Cab	5108	4380	Note 8
W300	Utiline Pickup	5222	—	Note 8

NOTE 8: Total model year production: 2183.

NOTE 9: Weights and prices shown are for 6-cyl. models. For V-8 engine (318 cu. in.) add 100 pounds to weight and $116 to $172 to price (depending on series).

ENGINE (Standard: All models): Inline. Overhead valve. Slant six. Cast iron block. Bore & stroke: 3.4 x 4.125 in. Displacement: 224.8 cu. in. Compression ratio: 8.4:1. Brake horsepower: 95 (net) at 3600 R.P.M. Taxable horsepower: 27.70. Torque: 175 lbs.-ft. (net) at 2000 R.P.M. Four main bearings. Solid valve lifters.

ENGINE (Standard V-8: all models): 90-degree, overhead valve. V-8. Cast iron block. Bore & stroke: 3.91 x 3.31 in. Displacement: 318.3 cu. in. Compression ratio: 8.6:1. Brake horsepower: 150 (net) at 4000 R.P.M. Taxable horsepower: 48.92. Torque: 255 lbs.-ft. (net) at 2000 R.P.M. Five main bearings. Hydraulic valve lifters.

ENGINE (Optional V-8: all except B100): 90-degree, overhead valve. V-8. Cast iron block. Bore & stroke: 4.00 x 3.58 in. Displacement: 360 cu. in. Compression ratio: 8.4:1. Brake horsepower: 175 (net) at 4000 R.P.M. Taxable horsepower: 51.2. Torque: 285 lbs.-ft. (net) at 2400 R.P.M. Five main bearings. Hydraulic valve lifters.

ENGINE (Optional V-8: D100-300, W100-300, AW100): 90-degree, overhead valve. V-8. Cast iron block. Bore & stroke: 4.32 x 3.75 in. Displacement: 440 cu. in. Compression ratio: 8.2:1. Brake horsepower: 235 (net) at 4000 R.P.M. Taxable horsepower: 58.55. Torque: 340 lbs.-ft. (net) at 2400 R.P.M. Five main bearings. Hydraulic valve lifters.

CHASSIS: Same as 1975, except for Ramcharger as follows:

CHASSIS (AD100 2wd): Wheelbase: 106 in. Tires: (six) H78 x 15-B four-ply; (V-8) E78 x 15-B four-ply. GVW: 4900 lbs.

CHASSIS (AW100 4wd): Same as above except 6-cyl. model rated 6100 lbs. GVW.

TECHNICAL: Selective sliding gear transmission. Speeds: 3F/1R except (D300, W300 and 165 in. w.b. D200) 4F/1R. Column or floor (4-speed) shift control. Automatic 3-speed transmission optional. Single disc dry clutch: (6-cyl.) 10 in.; (V-8) 11 in. Rear axle ratio: (AW100 Ramcharger) 3.23:1, 3.55:1 or 3.90:1. Hydraulic four-wheel brakes: front disc, rear drum. Fuel tank: (B vans) 23-gallon; (AW100) 24-gallon; (others) 22-gallon. Alternator: 48 amp.

OPTIONS: Same list as 1974, with the addition of the following: (B Vans) Door edge protectors (front only). Single rear door with fixed glass. 36-gallon fuel tank. Full-length scuff pads (side step sill). Styled road wheels (B100-200, 15 in.). Premium wheel covers (B100-200). (D100-300, W100-300) Carpeting (conventional cabs). Transmission oil cooler. 21-gallon auxiliary fuel tank, behind rear axle. 24-gallon auxiliary tank, in cab behind seat. Chrome styled road wheels (D100). Premium wheel covers (D100). (Ramcharger) Transmission cooler. SE package. Protection package. Convenience package. Exterior trim molding package. Sno-fiter package. Trailer-towing package. Heavy-duty trailer-towing package. Plow lights. Deluxe wheel covers.

HISTORICAL: Introduced: August, 1974. Calendar year sales: 286,656. Calendar year production: 344,769 (in U.S. plants); 369,484 (total). Model year production: 336,946. Historical notes: Early in 1975, Dodge announced that it was pulling out of the heavy-duty truck market. Sales volume could not justify the expense needed to meet new or proposed federal regulations governing heavy-duty trucks. The 10 heavy-duty models dropped amounted to only 1.2 percent of all trucks produced. Despite this loss, then, 1975 was Dodge's second best production year in history. In addition to the 344,769 units produced in the U.S., 24,715 were built at Windsor, Ontario; and 52,330 Sportsman and Voyager passenger vans were counted as passenger cars. A total of 23,988 "knockdown" units were made for export. Dodge ranked number three in truck sales. Ramcharger 4x4 production for 1975 was 7,382, down from 10,037 in 1974; but sales rose to 10,547. 6-cyl. engines accounted for 15.8 percent of total truck sales. The U.S. Army adopted a plan to buy regular pickup trucks for military use. For years, the military had specified highly specialized vehicles, at considerable extra cost, for such non-military purposes as shuttling around Army bases in the U.S. Dodge won the first order under his new program, for 33,759 trucks. Normally list priced at around $5200, the Army bought these trucks for $3825 apiece.

Pricing

1975	5	4	3	2	1
AD100/AW100 Ramcharger — (½-Ton) — (106 in. w.b.)					
2wd	780	1560	2600	3600	5200
4wd	870	1750	2900	4100	5800
B100 Series Van — (½-Ton) — (109 or 127 in. w.b.)					
109 in.	540	1080	1800	2500	3600
127 in.	570	1140	1900	2650	3800
B200 Series Van — (¾-Ton) — (109 or 127 in. w.b.)					
109 in.	520	1020	1700	2400	3400
127 in.	540	1080	1800	2500	3600
Maxivan	570	1140	1900	2650	3800
B300 Series Van — (1-Ton) — (109 or 127 in. w.b.)					
109 in.	480	975	1600	2250	3200
127 in.	520	1020	1700	2400	3400
Maxivan	540	1080	1800	2500	3600
CB Series Kary Van — (1-Ton) — (127 or 145 in. w.b.)					
10-ft. Body	560	1100	1850	2600	3700
12-ft. Body	540	1080	1800	2500	3600
D100 Series Pickup — (½-Ton) — (115 or 131 in. w.b.)					
Utiline (115 in.)	770	1550	2550	3600	5100
Sweptline (115 in.)	780	1560	2600	3600	5200
Utiline (131 in.)	780	1560	2600	3600	5200
Sweptline (131 in.)	800	1600	2650	3700	5300
D100 Series Club Cab — (½-Ton) — (133 or 149 in. w.b.)					
Sweptline (133 in.)	720	1450	2400	3500	5000
Sweptline (149 in.)	770	1550	2550	3600	5100
D200 Series Pickup — (¾-Ton) — (131 in. w.b.)					
Utiline	720	1450	2400	3500	5000
Sweptline	770	1550	2550	3600	5100
Sweptline Club Cab	740	1450	2450	3350	4900
D200 Crew Cab Pickup — (¾-Ton) — (149 or 165 in. w.b.)					
Utiline (149 in.)	720	1450	2400	3300	4800
Sweptline (149 in.)	740	1470	2450	3350	4900
Utiline (165 in.)	690	1380	2300	3250	4700
Sweptline (165 in.)	720	1450	2400	3300	4800
D300 Series Pickup — (1-Ton) — (135 in. w.b.)					
Utiline	680	1350	2250	3150	4500
W100 Series 4x4 Pickup — (½-Ton) — (115 or 131 in. w.b.)					
Utiline (115 in.)	810	1620	2700	3800	5400
Sweptline (115 in.)	830	1650	2750	3850	5500
Utiline (131 in.)	800	1600	2650	3700	5300
Sweptline (131 in.)	810	1620	2700	3800	5400
W100 Series Club Cab 4x4 — (½-Ton) — (133 or 149 in. w.b.)					
Sweptline (133 in.)	800	1600	2650	3700	5300
Sweptline (149 in.)	770	1550	2550	3600	5100
W200 Series 4x4 Pickup — (¾-Ton) — (131 or 149 in. w.b.)					
Utiline (131 in.)	770	1550	2550	3600	5100
Sweptline (131 in.)	780	1560	2600	3600	5200
Sweptline Club Cab	800	1600	2650	3700	5300
W200 Series Crew Cab 4x4 — (¾-Ton) — (149 in. w.b.)					
Utiline	750	1500	2500	3500	5000
Sweptline	770	1550	2550	3600	5100
W300 Series 4x4 Pickup — (1-Ton) — (135 in. w.b.)					
Utiline	740	1470	2450	3350	4900

NOTE: Add 10 percent for V-8 engine.
Add 12 percent for 440 cu. in. V-8.

1976 DODGE

1976 Dodge Champion Sportsman mini-motorhome

½-TON VAN — B100 SERIES — SIX-CYLINDER and V-8 / ¾-TON VAN — B200 SERIES — SIX-CYLINDER and V-8 / 1-TON VAN — B300 SERIES — SIX-CYLINDER and V-8 / 1-TON KARY VAN — CB300 SERIES — SIX-CYLINDER and V-8: — Van models, though unchanged in appearance, gained a major improvement in ride quality through suspension system alterations and better noise suppression with an optional heavy-duty insulation package. A new transistorized system flashed a warning light when transmission fluid was low or overheated. To benefit from the large youth market for vans, a new Street Van appeared. It featured wide tires on sport wheels, cloth-and-vinyl Boca Raton upholstery on high-back bucket seats, carpeting, and a deluxe instrument panel with woodgrained inserts. Buyers also got a Customizing Idea Kit. This kit contained suggestions for exterior paint designs and color combinations, interior design schemes, stereo installation instructions, and a list of suppliers of portholes, roof vents, fender flares, and other accessories.

½-TON PICKUP — D100 SERIES — SIX-CYLINDER and V-8 / ¾-TON PICKUP — D200 SERIES — SIX-CYLINDER and V-8 / 1-TON PICKUP — D300 SERIES — SIX-CYLINDER and V-8 / ½-TON 4x4 — W100 SERIES — SIX-CYLINDER and V-8 / ¾-TON 4x4 — W200 SERIES — SIX-CYLINDER and V-8 / 1-TON 4x4 — W300 SERIES — SIX-CYLINDER and V-8: — The basic light-duty truck line, introduced in 1972, carried over for the fifth year with few changes. New bodyside moldings and restyled grille from 1975 saw another year's service. Engineering improvements included raising the fuel tank up between the frame rails, ahead of the rear axle, from its former hanging position where it had been at risk of puncture. Pickup rear suspensions were reworked to prevent the cargo box from tilting toward the back when fully loaded. Tie rods on all 4x4 models were raised to give greater ground clearance for off-road driving. Sweptline pickup boxes received more corrosion protection. The seat back on bench-seat models was hinged for access to storage space behind the seat. A glide-out spare tire carrier was mounted under the pickup box. Dodge continued to build a full line of light-duty trucks, including conventional cab, Club Cab, and Crew Cab models. Base engine remained the 225 cu. in. slant six, with 318, 360, 400 and 440 cu. in. V-8s optional. An optional overdrive 4-speed manual transmission for trucks under 5500 pounds GVW improved fuel economy.

½-TON RAMCHARGER 2WD — AD100 SERIES — SIX-CYLINDER and V-8 / ½-TON RAMCHARGER 4x4 — AW100 SERIES — SIX-CYLINDER and V-8: — Unchanged in appearance, Ramcharger continued as a topless sport-utility vehicle, with either a soft top or steel top available as an option. Both two-wheel and four-wheel drive models were offered. Tie rods were raised for greater ground clearance and the spare moved from a horizontal to a vertical position behind the rear seat. An optional external, swing-out spare tire mount was added. Most important was the re-engineered suspension, which delivered improved handling for both highway and off-road driving.

I.D. DATA: Serial and engine numbers were in the same locations, with the same coding, as in 1975.

1976 Dodge Royal Sportsman SE Van (DNP)

Model	Body Type	Price	Weight	Prod. Total
AD100/AW100 Ramcharger — (½-Ton) — (106 in. w.b.)				
AD100	2wd — no top	3702	3560	1700
AW100	4wd — no top	4640	4075	12,101
B100-300 Series Van — (½-Ton) — (109 in. w.b.)				
B100	Van	3876	3435	28,692
(127 in. w.b.)				
B100	Van	4009	3550	11,581
(¾-Ton) — (109 in. w.b.)				
B200	Van	3943	3485	28,257
(127 in. w.b.)				
B200	Van	4083	3610	27,714
B200	Maxivan	4300	—	13,567
(1-Ton) — (109 in. w.b.)				
B300	Van	4156	3675	262
(127 in. w.b.)				
B300	Van	4279	3805	5650
B300	Maxivan	4509	4000	9536
CB300	(10-ft.) Kary Van	5594	4660	863
(145 in. w.b.)				
CB300	(12-ft. x 80 in.) Kary Van	—	5110	2194
CB300	(12-ft. x 94 in.) Kary Van	6683	—	Note 1

NOTE 1: 12-ft. x 94 in. Kary Van was available only with V-8.

D100 Series — Custom — (½-Ton) — (115 in. w.b.)				
D100	Chassis & Cab	3512	3145	Note 2
D100	Utiline Pickup	3677	3490	Note 2
D100	Sweptline Pickup	3677	3515	Note 2
(131 in. w.b.)				
D100	Chassis & Cab	3556	3160	Note 2
D100	Utiline Pickup	3721	3490	Note 2
D100	Sweptline Pickup	3721	3620	Note 2

NOTE 2: Total model year production: (115 in.) 26,153; (131 in.) 54,585.

Model	Body Type	Price	Weight	Prod. Total
D100 Series Club Cab — Custom — (½-Ton) — (133 in. w.b.)				
D100	Sweptline Pickup	3975	3730	1816
(149 in. w.b.)				
D100	Sweptline Pickup	4009	3870	8049
D200 Series — Custom — (¾-Ton) — (131 in. w.b.)				
D200	Chassis & Cab	4010	3325	Note 3
D200	Utiline Pickup	4174	3755	Note 3
D200	Sweptline Pickup	4174	3785	Note 3

NOTE 3: Total model year production: 14,414.

D200 Series Club Cab — Custom — (¾-Ton) — (149 in. w.b.)				
D200	Sweptline Pickup	4463	3955	7007
D200 Series Crew Cab — Custom — (¾-Ton) — (149 in. w.b.)				
D200	Chassis & Cab	4705	3725	Note 4
D200	Utiline Pickup	4849	4070	Note 4
D200	Sweptline Pickup	4849	4095	Note 4
(165 in. w.b.)				
D200	Chassis & Cab	4932	4095	Note 4
D200	Utiline Pickup	5085	4525	Note 4
D200	Sweptline Pickup	5085	4555	Note 4

NOTE 4: Total model year production: (149 in.) 7007 including Club Cab models above; (165 in.) 1103.

D300 Series — Custom — (1-Ton) — (131 in. w.b.)				
D300	Sweptline Pickup	4777	—	711
(135 in. w.b.)				
D300	Chassis & Cab	4139	3775	6119
(149 in. w.b.)				
D300	Club — Chassis/Cab	4667	—	Note 5
D300	Club — Sweptline	5066	—	Note 5
(159 in. w.b.)				
D300	Chassis & Cab	4177	3880	1700
(165 in. w.b.)				
D300	Crew — Chassis/Cab	5213	—	163

NOTE 5: Total model year production: (149 in.) 888 units.

W100 Series 4x4 — Custom — (½-Ton) — (115 in. w.b.)				
W100	Chassis & Cab	4419	3780	Note 6
W100	Utiline Pickup	4585	4125	Note 6
W100	Sweptline Pickup	4585	4150	Note 6
(131 in. w.b.)				
W100	Chassis & Cab	4462	3790	Note 6
W100	Utiline Pickup	4628	4220	Note 6
W100	Sweptline Pickup	4628	4250	Note 6

NOTE 6: Total model year production: (115 in.) 10,580; (131 in.) 9005.

W100 Series Club Cab 4x4 — (Custom) — (½-Ton) — (133 in. w.b.)				
W100	Sweptline Pickup	4879	—	1440
(149 in. w.b.)				
W100	Sweptline Pickup	4917	—	1921
W200 Series 4x4 — Custom — (¾-Ton) — (131 in. w.b.)				
W200	Chassis & Cab	5085	3845	Note 7
W200	Utiline Pickup	5251	4275	Note 7
W200	Sweptline Pickup	5251	4305	Note 7
(149 in. w.b.)				
W200	Club — Sweptline	5661	4605	Note 8
W200 Crew Cab 4x4 — Custom — (¾-Ton) — (149 in. w.b.)				
W200	Chassis & Cab	6078	4245	Note 8
W200	Utiline Pickup	6244	4590	Note 8
W200	Sweptline Pickup	6244	4615	Note 8

NOTE 7: Total model year production (131 in.): 20,507.

NOTE 8: Total model year production (all 149 in. models): 3325.

W300 Series 4x4 — Custom — (1-Ton) — (135 in. w.b.)				
W300	Chassis & Cab	6039	4380	1522

NOTE 9: Weights and prices shown are for 6-cyl. models. For 318 cu. in. V-8 engine, add 100 pounds to weight and $90 to $193 (depending on series) to price; for W200 Crew Cab models, add $370 to price.

ENGINES (Standard: all models): Inline. Overhead valve. Slant six. Cast iron block. Bore & stroke: 3.4 x 4.125 in. Displacement: 224.8 cu. in. Compression ratio: 8.4:1. Brake horsepower: 105 (net) at 3600 R.P.M. Taxable horsepower: 27.70. Torque: 175 lbs.-ft. (net) at 2000 R.P.M. Four main bearings. Solid valve lifters.

ENGINE (Standard V-8: all models): 90-degree, overhead valve. V-8. Cast iron block. Bore & stroke: 3.91 x 3.31 in. Displacement: 318.3 cu. in. Compression ratio: 8.6:1. Brake horsepower: 150 (net) at 4000 R.P.M. Taxable horsepower: 48.92. Torque: 255 lbs.-ft. (net) at 2000 R.P.M. Five main bearings. Hydraulic valve lifters.

ENGINE (Optional V-8: all models): 90-degree, overhead valve. V-8. Cast iron block. Bore & stroke: 4.00 x 3.58 in. Displacement: 360 cu. in. Compression ratio: 8.4:1. Brake horsepower: 185 (net) at 4000 R.P.M. Taxable horsepower: 50.2. Torque: 290 lbs.-ft. (net) at 2400 R.P.M. Five main bearings. Hydraulic valve lifters.

ENGINE (Optional 400 V-8: all except B100): 90-degree, overhead valve. V-8. Cast iron block. Bore & stroke: 4.34 x 3.38 in. Displacement: 400 cu. in. Compression ratio: 8.2:1. Brake horsepower: 165 (net) at 4000 R.P.M. Taxable horsepower: 60.3. Torque: 290 lbs.-ft. (net) at 2400 R.P.M. Five main bearings. Hydraulic valve lifters.

ENGINE (Optional 440 V-8: D100-300, W100-300, B200-300, AW100): 90-degree, overhead valve. V-8. Cast iron block. Bore & stroke: 4.32 x 3.75 in. Displacement: 440 cu. in. Compression ratio: 8.2:1. Brake horsepower: 220 (net) at 4000 R.P.M. Taxable horsepower: 58.55. Torque: 330 lbs.-ft. (net) at 2400 R.P.M. Five main bearings. Hydraulic valve lifters.

CHASSIS (AD100/AW100): Wheelbase: 106 in. Tires: E78 x 15-B four-ply. GVW: 4900 lbs.

CHASSIS (B100): Wheelbase: 109 in. or 127 in. Tires: E78 x 15-B four-ply. GVW: 4600 lbs.

CHASSIS (B200): Wheelbase: 109 in. or 127 in. Tires: G78 x 15-B four-ply except (Maxivan) H78 x 15-B four-ply. GVW: 5500 lbs.

CHASSIS: (B300): Wheelbase: 109 in. or 127 in. Tires: 8.00 x 16.5-C six-ply except (Maxivan) 8.00 x 16.5-D eight-ply. GVW: 6400 lbs.

CHASSIS (CB300): Wheelbase: 127 in. or 145 in. Tires: 8.75 x 16.5-E ten-ply. GVW: 7700 lbs.

CHASSIS (D100): Wheelbase: 115 in. or 131 in. (Club Cab, 133 or 149 in.). Tires: G78 x 15-D four-ply. GVW: 5000 lbs.

CHASSIS (D200): Wheelbase: 131 in., 149 in. or 165 in. Tires: 8.00 x 16.5-D eight-ply. GVW: 6200 lbs.

CHASSIS (D300): Wheelbase: 131 in., 135 in., 149 in., 159 in. or 165 in. Tires: (131 in. and 135 in.), 8.00 x 16.5-D eight-ply; (others) 8.00 x 16.5-C eight-ply. GVW: 6600 lbs.

CHASSIS (W100): Wheelbase: 115 in. or 131 in. (Club Cab, 133 in. or 149 in.). Tires: (six) H78 x 15-B, (V-8) G78 x 15-B. GVW: 5400 lbs.

CHASSIS (W200): Wheelbase: 131 in. or 149 in. Tires: 8.00 x 16.5-D eight-ply. GVW: 6500 lbs.

CHASSIS (W300): Wheelbase: 135 in. Tires: 8.75 x 16.5-E ten-ply. GVW: 8500 lbs.

TECHNICAL: Same as 1975; see previous specifications.

OPTIONS: Same as 1975 list, but with the addition of the following: (B200-300 Vans) 400 cu. in. V-8 engine. 440 cu. in. V-8 engine. (Trucks under 5500-lb. GVW) Overdrive manual 4-speed transmission.

1976 Dodge Ramcharger SE w/4x4 (DNP)

HISTORICAL: Introduced: August, 1975. Model year sales: 406,654. Sales breakdown: 195,864 light conventional trucks; 184,583 vans; 11,905 Ramchargers; 4,711 Trail Dusters; and 9,591 medium-duty. Calendar year production: 441,769. Model year production: 360,080. Innovations: Youth-oriented Street Van with Customizing Idea Kit. Glide-out spare tire carrier on pickups. Historical notes: This was a year of real recovery for Dodge trucks. A combination of an improved economy and stabilized fuel prices resulted in vastly increased sales of vans and 4wd vehicles. Production rose 28 percent over 1975, while sales gained 42.9 percent. Dodge set sales records in vans, Ramchargers and medium-duty trucks. Pickup sales were up, yet below the 1973 record. Sales increased in every category except Trail Dusters, which were built by Dodge but sold by Plymouth dealers. Dodge Sportsman and Plymouth Voyager wagons were counted as passenger car sales. Dodge attributed the sales records in large measure to trucks tailored to handle specialized jobs, as well as to vehicles with special trim and option packages. Dodge offered one run of pickups with special trim and accessories for the Los Angeles market, and another package in the San Francisco area.

Pricing

	5	4	3	2	1
1976					
AD100/AW100 Ramcharger — (½-Ton) — (106 in. w.b.)					
2wd	750	1500	2500	3500	5000
4wd	840	1680	2800	3900	5600
B100 Series Van — (½-Ton) — (109 or 127 in. w.b.)					
109 in.	530	1050	1750	2450	3500
127 in.	560	1100	1850	2600	3700
B200 Series Van — (¾-Ton) — (109 or 127 in. w.b.)					
109 in.	480	975	1600	2250	3200
127 in.	520	1020	1700	2400	3400
Maxivan	540	1080	1800	2500	3600

	5	4	3	2	1
B300 Series Van — (1-Ton) — (109 or 127 in. w.b.)					
109 in.	450	900	1500	2100	3000
127 in.	480	975	1600	2250	3200
Maxivan	520	1020	1700	2400	3400
CB300 Series Kary Van — (1-Ton) — (127 or 145 in. w.b.)					
10-ft. Body	500	1000	1650	2300	3300
12-ft. x 80 in. Body	520	1020	1700	2400	3400
12-ft. by 94 in. Body	540	1080	1800	2500	3600
D100 Series Pickup — (½-Ton) — (115 or 131 in. w.b.)					
Utiline (115 in.)	740	1470	2450	3350	4900
Sweptline (115 in.)	750	1500	2500	3500	5000
Utiline (131 in.)	750	1500	2500	3500	5000
Sweptline (131 in.)	770	1550	2550	3600	5100
D100 Club Cab Pickup — (½-Ton) — (133 or 149 in. w.b.)					
Sweptline (133 in.)	720	1450	2400	3300	4800
Sweptline (149 in.)	740	1470	2450	3350	4900
D200 Series Pickup — (¾-Ton) — (131 or 149 in. w.b.)					
Utiline (131 in.)	700	1400	2350	3250	4700
Sweptline (131 in.)	720	1450	2400	3300	4800
Sweptline Club	750	1500	2500	3500	5000
D200 Crew Cab Pickup — (¾-Ton) — (149 or 165 in. w.b.)					
Utiline (149 in.)	680	1350	2250	3150	4500
Sweptline (149 in.)	690	1380	2300	3200	4600
Utiline (165 in.)	660	1320	2200	3100	4400
Sweptline (165 in.)	680	1350	2250	3150	4500
D300 Series Pickup — (1-Ton) — (131 or 149 in. w.b.)					
Sweptline (131 in.)	630	1250	2100	3000	4200
Sweptline Club	660	1320	2200	3100	4400
W100 Series 4x4 Pickup — (½-Ton) — (115 or 131 in. w.b.)					
Utiline (115 in.)	800	1600	2650	3700	5300
Sweptline (115 in.)	830	1650	2750	3850	5500
Utiline (131 in.)	810	1620	2700	3800	5400
Sweptline (131 in.)	840	1680	2800	3900	5600
W100 Club Cab 4x4 Pickup — (½-Ton) — (133 or 149 in. w.b.)					
Sweptline (133 in.)	740	1470	2450	3350	4900
Sweptline (149 in.)	720	1450	2400	3300	4800
W200 Series 4x4 Pickup — (¾-Ton) — (131 or 149 in. w.b.)					
Utiline (131 in.)	690	1380	2300	3250	4700
Sweptline (131 in.)	720	1450	2400	3300	4800
Sweptline Club	740	1470	2450	3350	4900
W200 Crew Cab 4x4 Pickup — (¾-Ton) — (149 in. w.b.)					
Utiline	720	1450	2400	3300	4800
Sweptline	740	1470	2450	3350	4900

NOTE: Add 10 percent for V-8 engine.
Add 12 percent for 440 cu. in. V-8 engine.

1977 DODGE

1977 Dodge Adventurer SE Pickup (DNP)

½-TON VAN — B100 SERIES — SIX-CYLINDER and V-8 / ¾-TON VAN — B200 SERIES — SIX-CYLINDER and V-8 / 1-TON VAN — B300 SERIES — SIX-CYLINDER and V-8 / 1-TON KARY VAN — CB300 SERIES — SIX-CYLINDER and V-8: — Though unchanged in appearance for 1977, B Series vans received several interior improvements. New convenience/comfort features included high-back swivel bucket seats, improved carpeting, a quick-release mechanism for bench seats, and grey-tinted privacy glass. The single rear door became standard, but dual doors were a no-cost option. The Fuel Pacer System was now offered on vans. Five new metallic body colors were available, and the Street Van option continued. The factory offered paint schemes with six different graphic designs, plus fat tires on either five-slot chrome disc wheels or eight-spoke painted wheels. Included with each 1977 Street Van was a free membership in Mopar's Van Clan Club. Base engine remained the 225 cid slant six (except in the B300 series); options were 318, 360, 400 and 440 cid V-8s. Transmission choices included 3-speed manual or automatic on all models, or 4-speed overdrive on the B100 only.

1977 Dodge Power Wagon Sweptline Pickup (JAG)

½-TON — D100 SERIES — SIX-CYLINDER and V-8 / HEAVY ½-TON — D150 SERIES — SIX-CYLINDER and V-8 / ¾-TON — D200 SERIES — SIX-CYLINDER and V-8 / 1-TON — D300 SERIES — SIX-CYLINDER and V-8 / ½-TON 4x4 — W100 SERIES — SIX-CYLINDER and V-8 / HEAVY ½-TON 4x4 — W150 SERIES — SIX-CYLINDER and V-8 / ¾-TON 4x4 — W200 SERIES — SIX-CYLINDER and V-8 / 1-TON 4x4 — W300 SERIES — SIX-CYLINDER and V-8: — The era of "adult toy trucks," "macho trucks" and factory customized "street trucks" began with the 1977 model year. Dodge's Warlock, the first entry in this new era, was available in either a 2wd or 4x4 version. Colors offered were bright red, medium green, sunfire metallic, and black sunfire metallic. Accent in the form of gold painted spoke wheels, gold pinstriping and chrome-plated mini runningboards made the Warlock a real standout. Warlocks were also equipped with real oak sideboards and wide tires with raised white letters. Inside were black bucket seats and gold paint accents. Warlocks sat on a 115 w.b. D100 or W100 chassis with Utiline 6½-ft. box. Standard engines were the 225 cid slant six and 318 cid V-8, both with two-barrel carburetors. A 3-speed column shift manual transmission was standard. Optional were automatic transmission, a 360 cid V-8 (two-barrel), 400 cid V-8 (two-barrel), or a big 440 V-8 with four-barrel carburetor. A new pickup grille incorporated rectangular parking lights, with the Dodge nameplate pressed into the top grille bar. New bodyside moldings completed the appearance changes. Three trim levels were now available on pickups: Custom, Adventurer, and Adventurer SE. Gone was the Adventurer Sport. Two-tone instrument panels on all models added a more luxurious look. Interior refinements included new seat trim and style, new door trim panels, and new colors. Five metallic and five non-metallic body colors were added. An optional Fuel Pacer System conserved fuel by alerting the driver — via a dash indicator light — that he was running an overly rich mixture. For improved performance, the 225 cid slant six was available with two-barrel carburetor, which produced an additional 10 horsepower. This new "Super Six" was developed to combine the good fuel economy of a six with the performance and "feel" of a V-8. The overdrive 4-speed manual transmission, introduced late in the 1976 model year, continued for models up to 5500 pounds GVW. Fourth gear was a 27 percent overdrive. Dodge offered additional factory custom models in mid-year, at a special Press introduction at the Ontario Motor Speedway in Ontario, California. New models included the "True Spirit," a D100 pickup with 318 V-8; a "Power Wagon" W100 4x4 pickup with 400 cid V-8 and four-barrel carburetor; and "Street Van," a fully-tricked-out Maxivan. Dodge management was well aware of the truck boom and sought to create "adult toys" for a great many pickup, van and 4wd enthusiasts. Dodge was intent on marketing factory custom, or high volume custom content, special models to enter the trick truck market. Optional factory personalization of utility vehicles attracted many a recreation-oriented buyer. Optional this year was a removable tinted glass SkyLite roof. Introduced at mid-year 1977 were D150 and W150 heavy ½-ton models, with GVW ratings above 6000 pounds.

½-TON RAMCHARGER 2WD — AD100 SERIES — SIX-CYLINDER and V-8 / ½-TON RAMCHARGER 4x4 — AW100 SERIES — SIX-CYLINDER and V-8: — New two-tone paint and upper body side moldings gave Ramchargers a new look. They also received the same new grille as the pickups, with vertical rectangular parking lights. Dodge's exclusive high-back swivel bucket seats with movable armrests were available in the SE

model. Full time 4wd was standard. Transmission options on 2wd models were limited to 3-speed manual or automatic; but 4wd Ramchargers could have a close ratio or wide ratio 4-speed (except with 440 V-8). Engine choices ranged from the 225 cid slant six to 318, 360 and 400 cid V-8s; plus the 440 V-8 on 4wd models only. Tops were again optional. The steel top's tailgate was operated by two pneumatic cylinders. Power brakes were standard.

I.D. DATA: Serial and engine numbers were in the same locations, with the same coding, as in 1975-76.

1977 Dodge Adventurer SE Club Cab Pickup (DNP)

Model	Body Type	Price	Weight	Prod. Total
AD100/AW100 Ramcharger Sport-Utility — (½-Ton) — (106 in. w.b.)				
AD100	2wd — no top	4377	3560	2538
AW100	4wd — no top	5392	4075	17,120
B100-300 Series Tradesman Vans — (½-Ton) — (109 in. w.b.)				
B100	Van	4589	3435	51,602
(127 in. w.b.)				
B100	Van	4747	3550	24,723
(¾-Ton) — (109 in. w.b.)				
B200	Van	4741	3485	56,306
(127 in. w.b.)				
B200	Van	4896	3610	91,174
B200	Maxivan	5045	—	39,086
(1-Ton) — (109 in. w.b.)				
B300	Van	4888	3675	517
(127 in. w.b.)				
B300	Van	5011	3805	11,465
B300	Maxivan	5241	4000	22,567
CB300	(10-ft.) Kary Van	5697	4525	1648
(145 in. w.b.)				
CB300	(12-ft.) Kary Van	6245	5200	5519
D100 Series — (½-Ton) — (115 in. w.b.)				
D100	Chassis & Cab	4212	3145	Note 1
D100	Utiline Pickup	4394	3490	Note 1
D100	Sweptline Pickup	4394	3515	Note 1
(131 in. w.b.)				
D100	Chassis & Cab	4261	3160	Note 1
D100	Utiline Pickup	4443	3490	Note 1
D100	Sweptline Pickup	4443	3620	Note 1

NOTE 1: Total D100 model year production: (115 in.) 32,276; (131 in.) 66,191.

D100 Series Club Cab — (½-Ton) — (133 in. w.b.)				
D100	Sweptline Pickup	4737	3730	2459
(149 in. w.b.)				
D100	Sweptline Pickup	4773	3870	9488
D150 Series — (H-D ½-Ton) — (115 in. w.b.)				
D150	Chassis & Cab	4424	—	—
D150	Utiline Pickup	4606	—	—
D150	Sweptline Pickup	4606	—	—
(131 in. w.b.)				
D150	Chassis & Cab	4473	—	—
D150	Utiline Pickup	4655	—	—
D150	Sweptline Pickup	4655	—	—
(133 in. w.b.)				
D150	Club — Sweptline	4945	—	—
(149 in. w.b.)				
D150	Club — Sweptline	4985	—	—
D200 Series — (¾-Ton) — (131 in. w.b.)				
D200	Chassis & Cab	4722	3325	Note 2
D200	Utiline Pickup	4983	3755	Note 2
D200	Sweptline Pickup	4983	3785	Note 2

NOTE 2: Total model year production: 18,025.

D200 Series Club Cab — (¾-Ton) — (149 in. w.b.)				
D200	Sweptline Pickup	5307	3955	Note 3
D200 Series Crew Cab — (¾-Ton) — (149 in. w.b.)				
D200	Chassis & Cab	5474	3725	Note 3
D200	Utiline Pickup	5708	4070	Note 3
D200	Sweptline Pickup	5708	4095	Note 3
(165 in. w.b.)				
D200	Chassis & Cab	5701	4095	Note 3
D200	Utiline Pickup	5944	4525	Note 3
D200	Sweptline Pickup	5944	4555	Note 3

NOTE 3: Total model year production: (149 in. Club Cab and Crew Cab) 7270; (165 in. Crew Cab) 1257.

1977 Dodge Custom "Warlock" Utiline Pickup (OCW)

225

1977 Dodge Pathfinder 4x4 Custom Sportsman Van

Model	Body Type	Price	Weight	Prod. Total
D300 Series — (1-Ton) — (131 in. w.b.)				
D300	Sweptline Pickup	—	—	689
(135 in. w.b.)				
D300	Chassis & Cab	—	3775	5921
(149 in. w.b.)				
D300	Club — Chassis/Cab	—	—	Note 4
D300	Club — Sweptline	—	—	Note 4
(159 in. w.b.)				
D300	Chassis & Cab	—	3880	2048
(165 in. w.b.)				
D300	Crew — Chassis/Cab	—	—	178

NOTE 4: Total model year production: (149 in.) 1266.

Model	Body Type	Price	Weight	Prod. Total
W100 Series 4x4 — (½-Ton) — (115 in. w.b.)				
W100	Chassis & Cab	5256	3780	Note 5
W100	Utiline Pickup	5477	4125	Note 5
W100	Sweptline Pickup	5477	4150	Note 5
(131 in. w.b.)				
W100	Chassis & Cab	5305	3790	Note 5
W100	Utiline Pickup	5525	4220	Note 5
W100	Sweptline Pickup	5525	4250	Note 5

NOTE 5: Total model year production: (115 in.) 17,523; (131 in.) 13,339.

Model	Body Type	Price	Weight	Prod. Total
W100 Series Club Cab 4x4 — (½-Ton) — (133 in. w.b.)				
W100	Sweptline Pickup	—	—	1956
(149 in. w.b.)				
W100	Sweptline Pickup	—	—	2336
W150 Series — (H-D ½-Ton) — (4x4) — (115 in. w.b.)				
W150	Chassis & Cab	5380	—	—
W150	Utiline Pickup	5601	-	—
W150	Sweptline Pickup	5601	—	—
(131 in. w.b.)				
W150	Chassis & Cab	5429	—	—
W150	Utiline Pickup	5649	—	—
W150	Sweptline Pickup	5649	—	—
(133 in. w.b.)				
W150	Club — Sweptline	5848	—	—
(149 in. w.b.)				
W150	Club — Sweptline	—	—	—
W200 Series 4x4 — (¾-Ton) — (131 in. w.b.)				
W200	Chassis & Cab	5713	3845	Note 6
W200	Utiline Pickup	5970	4275	Note 6
W200	Sweptline Pickup	5970	4305	Note 6
(149 in. w.b.)				
W200	Club — Sweptline	6287	4605	Note 7
W200 Crew Cab 4x4 — (¾-Ton) — (149 in. w.b.)				
W200	Chassis & Cab	6648	4245	Note 7
W200	Utiline Pickup	6900	4590	Note 7
W200	Sweptline Pickup	6900	4615	Note 7

NOTE 6: Total model year production (131 in.): 37,292.

NOTE 7: Total model year production (all 149 in. models): 4322.

Model	Body Type	Price	Weight	Prod. Total
W300 Series 4x4 — (1-Ton) — (135 in. w.b.)				
W300	Chassis & Cab	—	4380	2365

NOTE 8: Weights and prices shown are for 6-cyl. models. For 318 cid V-8 engine, add 100 pounds to weight and $68 to $168 to price (depending on series).

ENGINES (Standard six: all models): Inline. Overhead valve. Slant six. Cast iron block. Bore & stroke: 3.4 x 4.125 in. Displacement: 224.8 cu. in. Compression ratio: 8.4:1. Brake horsepower: 100 at 3600 R.P.M. (110 at 3600 with two-barrel carburetor). Taxable horsepower: 27.70. Torque: 175 lbs.-ft. at 1600 R.P.M. (175 lbs.-ft. at 2000 with two-barrel carb). Four main bearings. Solid valve lifters.

ENGINE (Standard 318 V-8: all models): 90-degree, overhead valve. V-8. Cast iron block. Bore & stroke: 3.91 x 3.31 in. Displacement: 318.3 cu. in. Compression ratio: 8.6:1. Brake horsepower: 150 at 4000 R.P.M. Taxable horsepower: 48.92. Torque: 230 lbs.-ft. at 2400 R.P.M. Five main bearings. Hydraulic valve lifters.

1977 Dodge Sportsman Passenger Van (DNP)

ENGINE (Optional 360 V-8: all models): 90-degree, overhead valve. V-8. Cast iron block. Bore & stroke: 4.00 x 3.58 in. Displacement: 360 cu. in. Compression ratio: 8.4:1. Brake horsepower: 170 at 4000 R.P.M. Taxable horsepower: 50.2. Torque: 280 lbs.-ft. at 2400 R.P.M. Five main bearings. Hydraulic valve lifters.

ENGINE (Optional 400 V-8: all except B100 and D100): 90-degree, overhead valve. V-8. Cast iron block. Bore & stroke: 4.34 x 3.38 in. Displacement: 400 cu. in. Compression ratio: 8.2:1. Brake horsepower: 165 at 4000 R.P.M. Taxable horsepower: 60.3. Torque: 290 lbs.-ft. at 2400 R.P.M. Five main bearings. Hydraulic valve lifters.

1977 Dodge Ramcharger SE (DNP)

1977 Dodge Tradesman Street Van (DNP)

1977 Dodge Sportsman Passenger Van (JAG)

1977 Dodge Royal Sportsman Van (DNP)

ENGINE (Optional 440 V-8: B200-300, D150-300, W100-300, AW100): 90-degree, overhead valve. V-8. Cast iron block. Bore & stroke: 4.32 x 3.75 in. Displacement: 439.9 cu. in. Compression ratio: 8.2:1. Brake horsepower: 220 at 4000 R.P.M. Taxable horsepower: 58.55. Torque: 320 lbs.-ft. at 2400 R.P.M. Five main bearings. Hydraulic valve lifters.

CHASSIS Same as 1976; see previous specifications.

TECHNICAL: Same as 1975-76; see previous specifications.

OPTIONS (Factory-Installed): (B Series Vans) Same as 1976 (see 1972-76 lists) except for the following: Convenience package. Custom exterior package. Custom interior package. Easy-order package. Insulation package. Lock package. School bus package (B300 only). Sound control package. Street van package (B100-200). Trailer-assist package. Heavy-duty trailer-assist package (except B100). 4-speed manual overdrive transmission A833 (B100). Wide sport wheels, 15 x 7.00, chrome or painted (B100-200). AM/FM/Stereo Radio, with or without 8-track tape player. (D100-300, W100-300) Same as 1976, except for the following: Fuel Pacer. Tachometer. Vacuum gauge/voltmeter. Easy-order package. Protection package. Sound control package. Two-tone paint (procedure 4), except D/W300. SkyLite sun roof. (Ramcharger) Same as 1976, except for the following: Fuel Pacer. 63 or 117-amp alternator. Vacuum gauge/Voltmeter. Electric tachometer. Speedometer. (km/miles) and odometer (km). Easy-order package. Luxury package. Upper side molding package (for SE). Heavy-duty GVW package (5200, 5600, or 6100 lbs.). Snow plow package. Deluxe vinyl interior trim. Cloth/vinyl trim. Styled road wheels. Wide sport wheels (painted spokes) Chrome disc wheels.

1977 Dodge Tradesman Custom Sport Van (DNP)

HISTORICAL: Introduced: August, 1976 (Heavy ½-ton models in mid-year). Calendar year production: 474,001. Model year sales: 463,218. Model year production: 623,460. Innovations: Warlock factory-custom street truck. Fuel Pacer system. Historical notes: Pickups and vans achieved unpredicted social acceptability in 1977. 4wd trucks boomed in popularity — both sports-utility types like Ramcharger, and 4wd pickups. Total industry 4wd production was 762,356 units, a 24 percent jump over 1976. In fact, the 4wd market grew 84 percent between 1975 and '77. Trucks accounted for nearly one-fourth of the total motor vehicle production this year, and light-duty trucks made up over 89 percent of total truck production. Dodge set a new truck production record, and sales gained 14.5 percent. Vans were Dodge's hottest seller, gaining 22.5 percent over 1976. Model year truck sales consisted of 215,409 light conventional models, 226,066 vans, 14,796 Ramchargers, and 5,926 Trail Dusters. Dodge dropped out of the medium-duty truck business this year. The factory at Windsor, Ontario was converted to build light-duty trucks. A Canadian-American Automotive Trade Treaty allowed Dodge to build light-duty trucks in Canada, for sale in the U.S., without paying duties. Output from the Canadian plant was needed to keep up with demand.

Pricing

1977	5	4	3	2	1
Ramcharger — (½-Ton) — (106 in. w.b.)					
AD100 2wd	750	1500	2500	3500	5000
AW100 4wd	840	1680	2800	3900	5600
B100 Series Tradesman Van — (½-Ton) — (109 or 127 in. w.b.)					
Van (109)	530	1050	1750	2450	3500
Van (127)	560	1100	1850	2600	3700
B200 Series Tradesman Van — (¾-Ton) — (109 or 127 in. w.b.)					
Van (109)	480	975	1600	2250	3200
Van (127)	520	1020	1700	2400	3400
Maxivan	540	1080	1800	2500	3600
B300 Series Tradesman Van — (1-Ton) — (109 or 127 in. w.b.)					
Van (109)	450	900	1500	2100	3000
Van (127)	480	975	1600	2250	3200
Maxivan	520	1020	1700	2400	3400
CB300 Series Kary Van — (1-Ton) — (127 or 145 in. w.b.)					
10-ft. Body	500	1000	1650	2300	3300
12-ft. Body	520	1020	1700	2400	3400
D100 Series Pickup — (½-Ton) — (115 or 131 in. w.b.)					
Utiline (115)	740	1470	2450	3350	4900
Sweptline (115)	750	1500	2500	3500	5000
Utiline (131)	750	1500	2500	3500	5000
Sweptline (131)	770	1550	2550	3600	5100
D100 Club Cab Pickup — (½-Ton) — (133 or 149 in. w.b.)					
Sweptline (133)	720	1450	2400	3300	4800
Sweptline (149)	740	1470	2450	3350	4900
D150 Series Pickup — (H-D ½-Ton) — (115 or 131 in. w.b.)					
Utiline (115)	680	1350	2250	3150	4500
Sweptline (115)	690	1380	2300	3200	4600
Utiline (131)	700	1400	2350	3250	4700
Sweptline (131)	720	1450	2400	3300	4800
D150 Club Cab Pickup — (½-Ton) — (133 or 149 in. w.b.)					
Sweptline (133)	750	1500	2500	3500	5000
Sweptline (149)	700	1400	2350	3250	4700
D200 Series Pickup — (¾-Ton) — (131 in. w.b.)					
Utiline	740	1470	2450	3350	4900
Sweptline	750	1500	2500	3500	5000
D200 Club or Crew Cab Pickup — (¾-Ton) — (149 or 165 in. w.b.)					
Utiline Club	680	1350	2250	3150	4500
Sweptline Crew	690	1380	2300	3200	4600
Sweptline Crew	660	1320	2200	3100	4400
Util. Crew (165)	600	1200	2000	2800	4000
Swept. Crew (165)	620	1230	2050	2900	4100
D300 Series Pickup — (1-Ton) — (131 or 149 in. w.b.)					
Sweptline (131)	570	1140	1900	2650	3800
Swept. Line (149)	590	1170	1950	2700	3900
W100 Series 4x4 Pickup — (½-Ton) — (115 or 131 in. w.b.)					
Utiline (115)	800	1600	2650	3700	5300
Sweptline (115)	830	1650	2750	3850	5500
Utiline (131)	810	1620	2700	3800	5400
Sweptline (131)	840	1680	2800	3700	5600
W100 Series Club Cab 4x4 Pickup — (½-Ton) — (133 or 149 in. w.b.)					
Sweptline (133)	740	1470	2450	3350	4900
Sweptline (149)	720	1450	2400	3300	4800
W150 Series 4x4 Pickup — (½-Ton) — (115 or 131 in. w.b.)					
Utiline (115)	700	1400	2350	3250	4700
Sweptline (115)	720	1450	2400	3300	4800
Utiline (131)	720	1450	2400	3300	4800
Sweptline (131)	740	1470	2450	3350	4900
W150 Club Cab 4x4 Pickup — (½-Ton) — (133 or 149 in. w.b.)					
Sweptline (133)	690	1380	2300	3200	4600
Sweptline (149)	740	1470	2450	3150	4500
W200 Series 4x4 Pickup — (¾-Ton) — (131 in. w.b.)					
Utiline	720	1450	2400	3300	4800
Sweptline	740	1470	2450	3350	4900
W200 Club or Crew Cab 4x4 Pickup — (¾-Ton) — (149 in. w.b.)					
Sweptline Club	750	1500	2500	3500	5000
Utiline Crew	720	1450	2400	3300	4800
Sweptline Crew	740	1470	2450	3350	4900

NOTE: Add 10 percent for V-8 engine.

1978 DODGE

½-TON VAN — B100 SERIES — SIX-CYLINDER and V-8 / ¾-TON VAN — B200 SERIES — SIX-CYLINDER and V-8 / 1-TON VAN — B300 SERIES — SIX-CYLINDER and V-8 / 1-TON KARY VAN — CB300 SERIES — SIX-CYLINDER and V-8: — Vans received their first significant exterior and interior changes since 1971, starting with a lowered beltline, which allowed deeper side windows. Side doors on 127 in. wheelbase models moved ahead 16 in., as windows were repositioned. A redesigned roof allowed installation of vents and a sun roof option. Two-tone bodies and six paint colors were new. Van rears gained a new look through new vertical taillights and body line moldings. Inside sat a new instrument panel and redesigned steering wheel. Engine covers looked less utilitarian than before. Interior trim panels and other appointments were more attractive; seats were more comfortable. The Maxivan was stretched 8 in., to 220 in. overall, providing seating space for 15 people. The Maxiwagon version could now be equipped with wraparound rear quarter windows for greatly improved visibility. The Maxi was the largest van in the industry. Radio equipment options for pickups were also available for vans. Continued for another year was the popular Street Van package, for do-it-yourself van customizers. Engine and transmission options remained the same as 1977.

1978 Dodge Power Wagon Utiline Pickup (DNP)

½-TON PICKUP — D100 SERIES — SIX-CYLINDER and V-8 / HEAVY ½-TON PICKUP — D200 SERIES — SIX-CYLINDER and V-8 / ¾-TON PICKUP — D200 SERIES — SIX-CYLINDER and V-8 / 1-TON PICKUP — D300 SERIES — SIX-CYLINDER and V-8 / ½-TON 4x4 — W150 SERIES — SIX-CYLINDER and V-8 / ¾-TON 4x4 — W200 SERIES — SIX-CYLINDER and V-8 / 1-TON 4x4 — W300 SERIES — SIX-CYLINDER and V-8: — Heavy ½-ton models D150 and W150, introduced in mid-year 1977, had Gross Vehicle Weight ratings (GVWR) above 6,000 pounds. That was the cutoff point for the most restrictive U.S. exhaust emission regulations for light-duty trucks. Trucks rated higher had to meet only the more liberal exhaust rules, which applied to heavy models. For the first time, Dodge installed a diesel engine in light-duty trucks. An inline six of 243 cu. in. displacement, it developed 103 horsepower at 3700 R.P.M. Diesels required two 12-volt batteries and were offered only in D/W150 and D/W200 model pickups. New this year was a D300 1-ton dual wheel Crew Cab Sweptline pickup. Appearance changes through the lineup were minimal — little more than six new body colors and a new tilt-column steering wheel. A factory-installed trailer towing hitch was now optional. Other options included a sporty three-spoke steering wheel with satin chrome spokes and black rim; bucket seats in Club Cab models; Adventurer SE trim on all models; and six radio options. That entertainment list included an AM radio with 40-channel CB, and AM/FM/Stereo radio with CB or 8-track tape player (or alone), as well as standard AM and FM models. A new 4wd transfer case shifter included a positive range detent to prevent accidental partial engagement. Sweptline pickup beds were redesigned to sit level on the chassis. All 225 cu. in. slant six engines now had two-barrel carburetors. Dodge carried forward its line of "adult toys" which included the Street Van, Warlock, Macho Power Wagon, and 4x4 Dodge Macho Ramcharger. One more was introduced at mid-year (late March 1978): the most famous "toy" of all, the D150 Li'l Red Truck. Built on the 115 in. wheelbase Utiline ½-ton, the Li'l Red Truck was powered by a high-output 360 cu. in. four-barrel V-8, through a 3.55:1 rear axle. It came from the factory with chrome-plated valve covers, air cleaner, and vertical stacks. Body paint was Canyon Red, with accent stripes, genuine oak side boards, and Adventurer trim. Interiors were black or red, with either bench or bucket seats. This limited-production vehicle was designed to be a conversation-starter and traffic builder on the sales floor. Utiline models now had rectangular stop/turn/backup lights.

1978 Dodge 4x4 Ramcharger (DNP)

½-TON RAMCHARGER 2WD — AD100 SERIES — SIX-CYLINDER and V-8 / ½-TON RAMCHARGER 4x4 — AW100 SERIES — SIX-CYLINDER and V-8: — Ramcharger continued with no appearance changes. As before, engine choices included the 225 cu. in. six as well as 318, 360, 400 and 440 cu. in. V-8s. Two 4-speed manual transmissions and an automatic were available. Bucket front seats were new, as was a front bench seat for six-passenger seating. Other new options included sunscreen glass for rear quarters and tailgate, 6 new body colors, and heavy-duty shock absorbers. The Ramcharger Macho 4x4 continued. A Hurst shift lever and knob were standard.

228

1978 Dodge Power Wgn. "Macho" Sweptline P.U. (DNP)

I.D. DATA: A serial number Vehicle Identification Number (VIN) plate was on the driver's door latch post. The 7-element number contained 13 alpha-numeric characters. The first two characters gave Model Designation. Next came a Body Code digit. Next, a letter indicating GVW class (A = 6000 lbs. or less; B = 6001 to 10,000 lbs.; etc.). The next letter showed Engine Type. Next came the final digit in the year of manufacture ("8" for 1978). The next letter indicated assembly plant, followed by a 6-digit sequence number. Model Designation index: A1 (AW100); B1 (B100); B2 (B200); B3 (B300); C3 (CB300); D1 (D100/150); D2 (D200); R2 (RD200); D3 (D300); E1 (AD100); W1 (W150); W2 (W200); W3 (W300). Body Type index: 0 (forward control, motor home chassis, Kary Van or sport-utility); 1 (Tradesman van, conventional cab/chassis); 2 (Sportsman, Crew Cab/chassis); 3 (Utiline conventional cab); 4 (Sweptline conventional cab); 5 (Maxivan, Utiline Crew Cab); 6 (Sportsman Maxiwagon, Sweptline Crew Cab); 7 (flat face cowl, Sweptline Club Cab); 8 (cowl/windshield, Club Cab); 9 (Utiline Club Cab). Engine Type index: A (440-3); B (225-1); C (225-2); D (440-1); E (318-1); F (360-1); G (318-3); H (400-1); K (360-3); H (243 diesel); X (special six); V (special V-8). Assembly Plant index: J = Tecumseh Road; K = Pillette Road; N = Burt Road (KDX); S = Warren No. 1; T = Warren No. 2; X = Missouri; V = Warren No. 3 (compact). Engine numbers were in the same locations as 1975-77.

1978 Dodge Tradesman Panel Delivery Van (DNP)

Model	Body Type	Price	Weight	Prod. Total
AD100/AW100 Ramcharger Sport — (½-Ton) — (106 in. w.b.)				
AD100	2wd — no top	4687	3560	2481
AW100	4wd — no top	5746	4075	19,123
B100-300 Series Tradesman Van — (½-Ton) — (109 in. w.b.)				
B100	Van	4612	3435	16,915
(127 in. w.b.)				
B100	Van	4769	3550	8586
(¾-Ton) — (109 in. w.b.)				
B200	Van	4752	3585	17,619
(127 in. w.b.)				
B200	Van	4909	3710	42,111
B200	Maxivan	5153	—	19,406
(1-Ton) — (109 in. w.b.)				
B300	Van	4926	3675	193
(127 in. w.b.)				
B300	Van	5052	3805	4569
B300	Maxivan	5379	4000	9893
CB300 Series Kary Van — (1-Ton) — (127 in. w.b.)				
CB300	10-ft. Body	6548	4660	—
(145 in. w.b.)				
CB300	12-ft. Body	7749	5210	—
D100 Series — (½-Ton) — (115 in. w.b.)				
D100	Utiline Pickup	4171	3490	Note 1
D100	Sweptline Pickup	4171	3515	Note 1
(131 in. w.b.)				
D100	Utiline Pickup	4313	3490	Note 1
D100	Sweptline Pickup	4313	3620	Note 1

NOTE 1: Total model year production: (115 in.) 47,971; (131 in.) 64,968.

1978 Dodge Club Cab Sweptline Pickup (DNP)

Model	Body Type	Price	Weight	Prod. Total
D100 Series Club Cab — (½-Ton) — (133 in. w.b.)				
D100	Sweptline Pickup	4462	3730	3253
(149 in. w.b.)				
D100	Sweptline Pickup	4604	3870	8428
D150 Series (H-D ½-Ton) — (115 in. w.b.)				
D150	Chassis & Cab	4230	3165	—
D150	Utiline Pickup	4452	3555	—
D150	Sweptline Pickup	4452	3580	—
(131 in. w.b.)				
D150	Chassis & Cab	4303	3190	—
D150	Utiline Pickup	4525	3665	—
D150	Sweptline Pickup	4525	3695	—
(133 in. w.b.)				
D150	Club — Sweptline	4743	3795	—
(149 in. w.b.)				
D150	Club — Sweptline	4816	3960	—
D200 Series — (¾-Ton) — (131 in. w.b.)				
D200	Chassis & Cab	4571	3325	Note 2
D200	Utiline Pickup	4792	3755	Note 2
D200	Sweptline Pickup	4792	3785	Note 2

NOTE 2: Total model year production: 19,387.

Model	Body Type	Price	Weight	Prod. Total
D200 Series Club Cab — (¾-Ton) — (149 in. w.b.)				
D200	Sweptline Pickup	5074	3955	Note 3
D200 Series Crew Cab — (¾-Ton) — (149 in. w.b.)				
D200	Chassis & Cab	5354	3725	Note 3
D200	Utiline (V-8)	6945	4195	Note 3
D200	Sweptline (six)	5576	4095	Note 3
(165 in. w.b.)				
D200	Chassis & Cab	5532	4095	Note 3
D200	Sweptline	5754	4555	Note 3

NOTE 3: Total model year production: (149 in.) 7567; (165 in.) 1604.

NOTE 4: Models equipped with 318 cu. in. V-8 were part of RD200 series.

Model	Body Type	Price	Weight	Prod. Total
D300 Series — (1-Ton) — (131 in. w.b.)				
D300	Sweptline Pickup	5513	4300	774
(135 in. w.b.)				
D300	Chassis & Cab	4875	3735	11,408
(149 in. w.b.)				
D300	Chassis & Cab	5405	—	Note 5
D300	Sweptline Pickup	5804	—	Note 5
(159 in. w.b.)				
D300	Chassis & Cab	4949	3880	2648
(165 in. w.b.)				
D300	Crew — Chassis/Cab	5955	—	Note 5
D300	Crew — Sweptline	6438	—	Note 5

NOTE 5: Total model year production: (149 in.) 1195; (165 in.) 501.

Model	Body Type	Price	Weight	Prod. Total
W150 Series 4x4 — (½-Ton) — (115 in. w.b.)				
W150	Chassis & Cab	5292	3780	Note 6
W150	Utiline Pickup	5514	4125	Note 6
W150	Sweptline Pickup	5514	4150	Note 6
(131 in. w.b.)				
W150	Chassis & Cab	5366	3790	Note 6
W150	Utiline Pickup	5587	4220	Note 6
W150	Sweptline Pickup	5587	4250	Note 6

NOTE 6: Total model year production: (115 in.) 24,921; (131 in.) 20,418.

1978 Dodge Adventurer Sweptline Pickup (DNP)

Model	Body Type	Price	Weight	Prod. Total
W150 Series Club Cab 4x4 — (½-Ton) — (133 in. w.b.)				
W150	Sweptline Pickup	5805	4285	2221
(149 in. w.b.)				
W150	Sweptline Pickup	5878	4420	2283
W200 Series 4x4 — (¾-Ton) — (131 in. w.b.)				
W200	Chassis & Cab	5705	3945	Note 7
W200	Utiline Pickup	5927	4375	Note 7
W200	Sweptline Pickup	5927	4405	Note 7
(149 in. w.b.)				
W200	Club — Sweptline	6218	4605	2822
W200 Series Crew Cab 4x4 — (¾-Ton) — (149 in. w.b.)				
W200	Chassis & Cab	6503	4345	Note 7
W200	Sweptline Pickup	6725	4690	Note 7

NOTE 7: Total model year production: (131 in.) 13,413; (149 in. Crew Cab) 1709.

Model	Body Type	Price	Weight	Prod. Total
W300 Series 4x4 — (1-Ton) — (135 in. w.b.)				
W300	Chassis & Cab	6872	4480	1326

NOTE 8: Weights and prices shown are for 6-cyl. models, except where a V-8 was the base engine.

1978 Dodge Royal Sportsman Maxi Van (DNP)

ENGINES (Standard six: all models) Inline. Overhead valve. Slant six. Cast iron block. Bore & stroke: 3.4 in. x 4.125 in. Displacement: 224.8 cu. in. Compression ratio: 8.4:1. Brake horsepower: 110 @ 3600 R.P.M. Taxable horsepower: 27.70. Torque: 175 lbs.-ft. @ 1600 R.P.M. Four main bearings. Solid valve lifters. 2-barrel carb.

ENGINES (Standard V-8: all models) 90-degree, overhead valve V-8. Cast iron block. Bore & stroke 3.91 in. x 3.31 in. Displacement: 318.3 cu. in. Compression ratio: 8.6:1. Brake horsepower: 145 @ 4000 R.P.M. Taxable horsepower: 48.92. Torque: 250 lbs.-ft. @ 2000 R.P.M. Five main bearings. Hydraulic Valve lifters.

ENGINES (Optional 360 V-8: all models) 90-degree, overhead valve V-8. Cast iron block. Bore & stroke: 4.00 in. x 3.58 in. Displacement: 360 cu. in. Compression ratio: 8.5:1. Brake horsepower: 160 @ 4000 R.P.M. Taxable horsepower: 50.2. Torque: 280 lbs.-ft. @ 2000 R.P.M. Five main bearings. Hydraulic valve lifters.

1978 Dodge Crew Cab Sweptline "Dualie" Pickup (DNP)

ENGINES (Optional 400 V-8: all except B100, D100) 90-degree, overhead valve V-8. Cast iron block. Bore & stroke: 4.34 in. x 3.38 in. Displacement: 400 cu. in. Compression ratio: 8.2:1. Brake horsepower: 170 @ 4000 R.P.M. Taxable horsepower: 60.3. Torque: 300 lbs.-ft. @ 2000 R.P.M. Five main bearings. Hydraulic Valve lifters.

ENGINES (Optional 440 V-8: B200-300, D150-300, W150-300, AW100): 90-degree, overhead valve V-8. Cast iron block. Bore & stroke: 4.32 in. x 3.75 in. Displacement: 440 cu. in. Compression ratio: 8.2:1. Brake horsepower: 200 @ 3600 R.P.M. Taxable horsepower: 58.55. Torque: 330 lbs.-ft. @ 2800 R.P.M. Five main bearings. Hydraulic valve lifters.

1978 Dodge Power Wagon Sweptline Pickup (DNP)

ENGINES (Optional diesel: D150-200, W150-200) Inline. 4-cycle. Six-cylinder. Cast iron block. Bore & stroke: 3.62 in. x 3.94 in. Displacement: 243 cu. in. Compression ratio: 20:1. Brake horsepower: 100 @ 3700 R.P.M. Torque: 165 lbs.-ft. @ 2200 R.P.M. Seven main bearings. Mechanical valve lifters. Note: Diesel engine, built for Chrysler by Mitsubishi, was not available in California.

CHASSIS (B100) Wheelbase: 109 or 127 in. Tires: E78 x 15-B four-ply. GVW: 4600 lbs.

CHASSIS (B200) Wheelbase: 109 or 127 in. Tires: G78 x 15-B four-ply. GVW: 5500 lbs.

CHASSIS (B300) Wheelbase: 109 or 127 in. Tires: 8.00 x 16.5-C six-ply. GVW: 6400 lbs.

CHASSIS (CB300) Wheelbase: 127 or 145 in. Tires: 8.75 x 16.5-C ten-ply. GVW: 7700 lbs.

CHASSIS (Ramcharger) Wheelbase: 106 in. Tires: E78 x 15-B four-ply. GVW: 4900 lbs.

CHASSIS (D100/150) Wheelbase: 115 or 131 in. (Club Cab, 133 or 149 in.) Tires: G78 x 15-B four-ply. GVW: 5000 lbs.

1978 Dodge Royal Sportsman SE Van (DNP)

CHASSIS (D200) Wheelbase: 131, 149 (Club Cab, Crew Cab) or 165 in. (Crew Cab). Tires: 8.00 x 16.5-D eight-ply. GVW: 6200 lbs.

CHASSIS (D300) Wheelbase: 131, 135, 149, 159 or 165 in. Tires: 8.00 x 16.5-D eight-ply. GVW: 6600 lbs.

CHASSIS (W150) Wheelbase: 115 or 131 in. (Club Cab, 133 or 149 in.). Tires: H78 x 15-B. GVW: 5400 lbs.

CHASSIS (W200) Wheelbase: 131 or 149 in. Tires: 8.00 x 16.5-D eight-ply. GVW: 6500 lbs.

CHASSIS (W300) Wheelbase: 135 in. Tires: 8.75 x 16.5-E ten-ply. GVW: 8500 lbs.

TECHNICAL: Same as 1975-77; see previous specifications.

OPTIONS: Same as 1977, but add the following: (Vans) SkyLite sun roof. Trip computer. Unibelt restraint system. Spare tire cover. AM Radio/CB Transceiver. AM/FM/Stereo Radio with CB Transceiver. (Pickups) 4-speed overdrive transmission (floor shift) A833. Tilt steering column. AM/CB radio. AM/FM/Stereo radio. (Ramcharger) Low-back bucket seat. High-back command bucket seat. Tilt-steering column. AM/CB radio. AM/FM/Stereo/CB radio. AM/FM/Stereo radio with 8-track stereo player.

HISTORICAL: Introduced: August 1977. (Vans, January 1978). Calendar year sales (U.S.): 489,134. Model year sales: 480,035 (including Plymouth Trail Duster). Calendar year production: 489,074. Model year production: 383,167. Innovations: Maxivan stretched to become the largest van in the industry. Diesel engine.

HISTORY: A strike at the van assembly plant late in 1977 delayed introduction of the 1978 vans, as old parts on hand had to be used up before production began on new models. Because the light-duty market continued to shift away from commercial applications to a personal-use market, Dodge continued to focus on those buyers with its "Adult Toys" collection. One specialized truck was sold only in the West: a 4x4 replica of Rod Hall's race truck, called "The Force." The Force Power Wagon featured Mickey Thompson shocks, extra-leaf front springs, Hickey rollbar and grille guard,

Hella driving lights, Sears Adventurer tires, Superior wheels, front and rear axle trusses, floor mats, and special paint and stripes. It sold for $1400 more than the base price of the short-box ½-ton 4x4. This was another good year for the Dodge truck division, as production topped the record set in 1977. Canadian production fell 35 percent, due to factory changeover. Calendar year U.S. retail sales also set a record. For the model year, 235,160 conventional models were sold; 220,315 Tradesman vans; 17,283 Ramchargers; and 6,934 Plymouth Trail Dusters. A total of 7,717 Plymouth Voyager and 23,989 Dodge Sportsman wagons were counted in station wagon sales. The diesel engine option lasted only this one year, selling only 2,587 units. The Tradesman was the industry's most popular van, and Dodge's leading truck model. Sales of the Li'l Red Trucks came to 2,188.

1978 Dodge Tradesman Street Van (DNP)

Pricing

1978	5	4	3	2	1
Ramcharger — (½-Ton) — (106 in. w.b.)					
AD100 2wd	750	1500	2500	3500	5000
AW100 4wd	840	1680	2800	3900	5600
B100 Series Tradesman Van — (½-Ton) — (109 or 127 in. w.b.)					
Van (109)	530	1050	1750	2450	3500
Van (127)	560	1100	1850	2600	3700
B200 Series Tradesman Van — (¾-Ton) — (109 or 127 in. w.b.)					
Van (109)	480	975	1600	2250	3200
Van (127)	520	1020	1700	2400	3400
Maxivan	540	1080	1800	2500	3600
B300 Series Tradesman Van — (1-Ton) — (109 or 127 in. w.b.)					
Van (109)	450	900	1500	2100	3000
Van (127)	480	975	1600	2250	3200
Maxivan	520	1020	1700	2400	3400
CB300 Series Kary Van — (1-Ton) — (127 or 145 in. w.b.)					
10-ft. Body	500	1000	1650	2300	3300
12-ft. Body	520	1020	1700	2400	3400
D100 Series Pickup — (½-Ton) — (115 or 131 in. w.b.)					
Utiline (115)	740	1470	2450	3350	4900
Sweptline (115)	750	1500	2500	3500	5000
Utiline (131)	750	1500	2500	3500	5000
Sweptline (131)	770	1540	2550	3600	5100
D100 Club Cab Pickup — (½-Ton) — (133 or 149 in. w.b.)					
Sweptline (133)	720	1450	2400	3300	4800
Sweptline (149)	740	1470	2450	3350	4900
D150 Series Pickup — (H-D ½-Ton) — (115 or 131 in. w.b.)					
Utiline (115)	680	1350	2250	3150	4500
Sweptline (115)	690	1380	2300	3200	4600
Utiline (131)	700	1400	2350	3250	4700
Sweptline (131)	720	1450	2400	3300	4800
D150 Club Cab Pickup — (½-Ton) — (133 or 149 in. w.b.)					
Sweptline (133)	750	1500	2500	3500	5000
Sweptline (149)	700	1400	2350	3250	4700
D200 Series Pickup — (¾-Ton) — (131 in. w.b.)					
Utiline	740	1470	2450	3350	4900
Sweptline	750	1500	2500	3500	5000
D200 Club or Crew Cab Pickup — (¾-Ton) — (149 or 165 in. w.b.)					
Utiline Club	680	1350	2250	3150	4500
Utiline Crew	690	1380	2300	3200	4600
Sweptline Crew	660	1320	2200	3100	4400
Util. Crew (165)	600	1200	2000	2800	4000
Swept. Crew (165)	620	1230	2050	2900	4100
D300 Series Pickup — (1-Ton) — (131, 149 or 165 in. w.b.)					
Sweptline (131)	570	1140	1900	2650	3800
Swept. Club (149)	590	1170	1950	2700	3900
Crew Sweptline	560	1100	1850	2600	3700
W150 Series 4x4 Pickup — (½-Ton) — (115 or 131 in. w.b.)					
Utiline (115)	800	1600	2650	3700	5300
Sweptline (115)	830	1650	2750	3850	5500
Utiline (131)	810	1620	2700	3800	5400
Sweptline (131)	840	1680	2800	3700	5600
W150 Club Cab 4x4 Pickup — (133 or 149 in. w.b.)					
Sweptline (133)	780	1560	2600	3600	5200
Sweptline (149)	750	1500	2500	3500	5000
W200 Series 4x4 Pickup — (¾-Ton) — (131 in. w.b.)					
Utiline	720	1450	2400	3300	4800
Sweptline	740	1470	2450	3350	4900
W200 Club or Crew Cab 4x4 Pickup — (¾-Ton) — (149 in. w.b.)					
Club Sweptline	750	1500	2500	3500	5000
Crew Sweptline	720	1450	2400	3300	4800

NOTE: Add 10 percent for V-8 engine.

1979 DODGE

1979 Dodge Power Wagon Sweptline Pickup (DNP)

1979 Dodge Power Wagon Sweptline Pickup (DNP)

½-TON VAN — B100 SERIES — SIX-CYLINDER and V-8 / ¾-TON VAN — B200 SERIES — V-8 / 1-TON VAN — B300 SERIES — V-8 / 1-TON KARY VAN — V-8: — Vans gained a front end restyle this year, following the new side and rear appearance of 1978. This van was all new from the windshield pillar forward. Overall length added 3 in. and the hood opening was made longer and wider. Larger bushings and softer spring rates in the front suspension achieved a 10 percent improvement in ride and handling. The new front styling also contributed to lowered wind resistance, for better fuel mileage. A new grille with stacked rectangular quad headlamps, standard on top-of-the-line models, gave a fresh new appearance. An energy-absorbing steering column was added. Heating and air conditioning were improved. B100 models could have the 225 cu. in. slant six or 318 cu. in. V-8, but larger vans now came with a V-8 only. All other basic specifications were as before. New options included a tilt steering wheel, electric door locks, and rear window defroster (on single rear door models). Tilt steering was available only with power steering and automatic transmission. The Street Van continued with the same appearance changes as standard models.

½-TON PICKUP — D100 SERIES — SIX-CYLINDER and V-8 / HEAVY ½-TON PICKUP — D150 SERIES — SIX-CYLINDER and V-8 / ¾-TON PICKUP — D200 SERIES — SIX-CYLINDER and V-8 / 1-TON PICKUP — D300 SERIES — V-8 / ½-TON 4x4 — W150 SERIES — SIX-CYLINDER and V-8 / ¾-TON 4x4 — W200 SERIES — V-8 / 1-TON 4x4 — W300 SERIES — V-8: — Full-size pickups gained a new front end appearance which included a new hood, cowl top panel, grille and headlight treatment. Quad rectangular headlamps became standard on top-of-the-line models, while single round headlamps remained on base models. Chassis lubrication intervals were extended to two years or 22,500 miles for trucks with less than 8,500 pound GVW ratings. Galvanized steel saw use on the inside panel of Sweptline tailgates, and on cowl side outer panels of all models. An engine coolant reserve system was added. Club Cab models got rear quarter windows that opened. Other improvements included upgraded interiors for conventional and Club Cab Adventurer SE models, two new optional tape stripe packages, optional electric door locks, and air conditioning on 6-cyl. models. Due to stricter federal fuel efficiency standards, the 400 and 440 cu. in. V-8s were dropped. The D100 was now subject to federal fuel mileage standards, so its standard gear included a 225 cu. in. six with single-barrel carburetor, radial tires, and a torque converter lockup. Dodge's popular "Adult Toys" line continued. All were based on conventional models, and given the same improvements as the standard line. Paint and striping on the Macho Power Wagon and Warlock II were updated, and the Li'l Red Truck carried over for its second (and final) year.

1979 Dodge D-50 Sport Mini-Pickup (DNP)

MINI PICKUP — D50 SERIES — FOUR: — The only all-new vehicle for 1979 was a mini pickup designed and built for Dodge by Mitsubishi (Chrysler's Japanese partner). Setting on a 109.4 in. w.b. chassis, the D50 had a 6½-ft. cargo box and carried a payload of 1400 pounds. It came in two trim levels: Standard and Sport. Engine choices were a 2-liter (122 cu. in.) or 2.6-liter (156 cu. in.) four. The littlest Dodge truck gave a smooth, passenger car-like ride with its very good A-arm front suspension, solid rear axle and leaf spring layout. Styling was quite attractive too, and interior trim on the Sport model was quite pleasant, with bucket seats and carpeting on the floor. The Standard model used a 4-speed transmission, but the Sport carried a 5-speed. Automatic was optional on both.

1979 Dodge Adventurer Club Cab Sweptline Pickup (DNP)

½-TON RAMCHARGER 2WD — AD100 SERIES — SIX-CYLINDER and V-8 / ½-TON RAMCHARGER 4x4 — AW100 SERIES — V-8: — Ramchargers received the same new front end treatment as the pickup models. An optional sound insulation package delivered a quieter ride. Roofs were now made of galvanized steel, and more comprehensive primer protection was applied to bodyside panels. Added to the option list were electric door locks, a tilt steering wheel, and new tape stripe packages. 2wd Ramchargers could have the 225 cu. in. six, or 318 or 360 cu. in. V-8. 4wd models were V-8 only. The Macho Ramcharger gained new tape striping and special tailgate designation.

I.D. DATA: Serial and engine numbers were in the same locations, with the same coding, as in 1978.

1979 Dodge D-50 Mini-Pickup (DNP)

1979 Dodge Adventurer SE Sweptline Pickup (DNP)

1979 Dodge Custom Utiline Pickup (DNP)

1979 Dodge Adventurer Club Cab Sweptline Pickup (DNP)

ENGINES (Standard six: B100, D100-200, W150, AD100): Inline. Overhead valve. Slant six. Cast iron block. Bore & stroke: 3.4 x 4.125 in. Displacement: 224.8 cu. in. Compression ratio: 8.4:1. Brake horsepower: 110 at 3600 R.P.M. Taxable horsepower: 27.70. Torque: 175 lbs.-ft. at 1600 R.P.M. Four main bearings. Solid valve lifters.

ENGINE (Standard V-8: B100-300, D100-200, W150-200, AD100, AW100): 90-degree, overhead valve. V-8. Cast iron block. Bore & stroke: 3.91 x 3.31 in. Displacement: 318.3 cu. in. Compression ratio: 8.6:1. Brake horsepower: 145 at 4000 R.P.M. Taxable horsepower: 48.92. Torque: 250 lbs.-ft. at 2000 R.P.M. Five main bearings. Hydraulic valve lifters.

ENGINE (Optional 360 V-8: B200-300, D150-200, W150-300, AD100, AW100; standard on D300): 90-degree, overhead valve. V-8. Cast iron block. Bore & stroke: 4.00 x 3.58 in. Displacement: 360 cu. in. Compression ratio: 8.5:1. Brake horsepower: 160 at 4000 R.P.M. Taxable horsepower: 50.2. Torque: 280 lbs.-ft. at 2000 R.P.M. Five main bearings. Hydraulic valve lifters.

Model	Body Type	Price	Weight	Prod. Total
D50 Series Mini Pickup — (¼-Ton) — (109.4 in. w.b.)				
D50	Sweptline	4819	2410	—
D50	Sport	5608	2410	—
AD100/AW100 Ramcharger — (½-Ton) — (106 in. w.b.)				
AD100	2wd — no top	5483	3660	—
AW100	4wd — no top	6998	4175	—
B100-300 Series Tradesman Vans — (½-Ton) — (109 in. w.b.)				
B100	Van	4992	3435	—
(127 in. w.b.)				
B100	Van	5160	3550	—
(¾-Ton) — (109 in. w.b.)				
B200	Van	5326	3585	—
(127 in. w.b.)				
B200	Van	5468	3710	—
B200	Maxivan	5855	—	—
(1-Ton) — (109 in. w.b.)				
B300	Van	5523	3675	—
(127 in. w.b.)				
B300	Van	5608	3805	—
B300	Maxivan	6008	4000	—
CB300 Series Kary Van — (V-8 only) — (1-Ton) — (127 in. w.b.)				
CB300	10-ft. Body	7124	4760	—
(145 in. w.b.)				
CB300	12-ft. Body	8411	5210	—
D100 Series — (½-Ton) — (115 in. w.b.)				
D100	Utiline Pickup	4499	3490	—
D100	Sweptline Pickup	4499	3515	—
(131 in. w.b.)				
D100	Utiline Pickup	4651	3490	—
D100	Sweptline Pickup	4651	3620	—
D150 Series — (H-D ½-Ton) — (115 in. w.b.)				
D150	Utiline Pickup	5115	3620	—
D150	Sweptline Pickup	5115	3645	—
(131 in. w.b.)				
D150	Utiline Pickup	5194	3730	—
D150	Sweptline Pickup	5194	3760	—
(133 in. w.b.)				
D150	Club — Sweptline	5146	3795	—
(149 in. w.b.)				
D150	Club — Sweptline	5223	3950	—
D200 Series — (¾-Ton) — (131 in. w.b.)				
D200	Utiline Pickup	5125	3755	—
D200	Sweptline Pickup	5125	3785	—
(149 in. w.b.)				
D200	Club — Sweptline	5427	3955	—
D200 Series Crew Cab — (V-8 only) — (¾-Ton) — (149 in. w.b.)				
D200	Sweptline Pickup	6142	4625	—
(165 in. w.b.)				
D200	Sweptline Pickup	6331	4655	—
D300 Series — (1-Ton) — (131 in. w.b.)				
D300	Sweptline Pickup	5737	4300	—
(135 in. w.b.)				
D300	Chassis & Cab	5936	3735	—
(149 in. w.b.)				
D300	Chassis & Cab	6322	—	—
D300	Sweptline Pickup	6046	—	—
(159 in. w.b.)				
D300	Chassis & Cab	6014	3880	—
(165 in. w.b.)				
D300	Crew — Sweptline	6565	—	—
W150 Series 4x4 — (½-Ton) — (115 in. w.b.)				
W150	Utiline Pickup	5897	4125	—
W150	Sweptline Pickup	5897	4150	—
(131 in. w.b.)				
W150	Utiline Pickup	5902	4220	—
W150	Sweptline Pickup	5902	4250	—
W150 Series Club Cab 4x4 — (V-8 only) — (½-Ton) — (133 in. w.b.)				
W150	Sweptline Pickup	6416	4360	—
(149 in. w.b.)				
W150	Sweptline Pickup	6567	4495	—
W200 Series 4x4 — (V-8 only) — (¾-Ton) — (131 in. w.b.)				
W200	Utiline Pickup	6565	4365	—
W200	Sweptline Pickup	6565	4395	—
(149 in. w.b.)				
W200	Club — Sweptline	6876	4620	—
W200 Series Crew Cab 4x4 — (V-8 only) — (¾-Ton) — (149 in. w.b.)				
W200	Sweptline Pickup	8235	4785	—
W300 Series 4x4 — (360 cu. in. V-8) — (1-Ton) — (135 in. w.b.)				
W300	Chassis & Cab	8237	4525	—

NOTE 1: Weights and prices shown are for 6-cyl. models, except where a 318 or 360 cu. in. V-8 was the base engine.

232

1979 Dodge 4x4 Ramcharger (DNP)

ENGINE (D50): Inline. Overhead cam. Four-cylinder. Cast iron block. Bore & stroke: 84.0mm x 90.0mm. Displacement: 2000 cc (122 cu. in.). Compression ratio: 8.5:1. Brake horsepower: 93 at 5200 R.P.M. Torque: 108 lbs.-ft. at 3000 R.P.M.

ENGINE (D50 Sport): Inline. Overhead cam. Four-cylinder. Cast iron block. Bore & stroke: 91.1mm x 98.0mm. Displacement: 2555 cc (156 cu. in.). Compression ratio: 8.2:1. Brake horsepower: 105 at 5000 R.P.M. Torque: 139 lbs.-ft. at 2500 R.P.M.

CHASSIS Same as 1978, except: (D50) Wheelbase: 109.4 in.

TECHNICAL: Same as 1975-78; see previous specifications.

1979 Dodge 4x4 Ramcharger SE (DNP)

1979 Dodge Royal Sportsman Maxi Van (DNP)

OPTIONS: Same as 1978, but add the following: (Vans) Quad rectangular headlamps. (Standard Pickups) Quad rectangular headlamps. "Tuff" type steering wheel (three-spoke). AM/FM Stereo radio with either 8-track tape player or CB transceiver. (Ramcharger) Tape stripe package. Lockable console. Quad rectangular headlamps. Skylite sun roof. "Tuff" type three-spoke steering wheel. AM/FM/Stereo radio with either 8-track tape player or CB transceiver. AM/CB radio/transceiver.

HISTORICAL: Introduced: August, 1978. Model year sales: 391,396 (177,937 conventional; 151,070 Tradesman vans; 15,754 Ramchargers; 6114 Traildusters; 27,517 D50 pickups; and 13,004 Arrow pickups) Calendar year sales: 352,292. Calendar year production (U.S.): 303,075. Innovations: Mini pickup. Galvanized steel in certain panels. Historical notes: Gasoline shortages and higher prices caused a softening in the truck market. After a record year in 1978, total U.S. industry shipments declined 18.1 percent. Dodge's van sales were down 48 percent, pickups 30 percent, and sport-utility vehicles off 21 percent. Diminished production caused Dodge to drop to number four in the industry, behind GMC. Dodge's role as a major supplier of RV chassis proved nearly a disaster, as that business almost entirely dried up. In June, 1979, Dodge closed its RV lines. Due to more stringent corporate average fuel economy (CAFE) goals for vans and trucks in the 1980s, Dodge passenger vans were reclassified as trucks beginning on October 1, 1979. Ford and GM followed suit as of January, 1980. Production of the Li'l Red Truck in this, its final year, totalled 5,118 units.

1979 Dodge Royal Sportsman SE Van (DNP)

1979 Dodge Tradesman Custom Van (DNP)

1979	5	4	3	2	1
D50 Series Mini Pickup — (¼-Ton) — (109.4 in. w.b.)					
Sweptline	630	1250	2100	3000	4200
Sport	680	1350	2250	3150	4500
Ramcharger — (½-Ton) — (106 in. w.b.)					
AD100 2wd	750	1500	2500	3500	5000
AW100 4wd	840	1680	2800	3900	5600
B100 Series Tradesman Van — (½-Ton) — (109 or 127 in. w.b.)					
Van (109)	530	1050	1750	2450	3500
Van (127)	560	1100	1850	2600	3700
B200 Series Tradesman Van — (¾-Ton) — (109 or 127 in. w.b.)					
Van (109)	480	975	1600	2250	3200
Van (127)	520	1020	1700	2400	3400
Maxivan	540	1080	1800	2500	3600
B300 Series Tradesman Van — (1-Ton) — (109 or 127 in. w.b.)					
Van (109)	450	900	1500	2100	3000
Van (127)	480	975	1600	2250	3200
Maxivan	520	1020	1700	2400	3400
CB300 Series Kary Van — (1-Ton) — (127 or 145 in. w.b.)					
10-ft. Body	500	1000	1650	2300	3300
12-ft. Body	520	1020	1700	2400	3400
D100 Series Pickup — (½-Ton) — (115 or 131 in. w.b.)					
Utiline (115)	740	1470	2450	3350	4900
Sweptline (115)	750	1500	2500	3500	5000
Utiline (131)	750	1500	2500	3500	5000
Sweptline (131)	770	1550	2550	3600	5100
D100 Club Cab Pickup — (½-Ton) — (133 or 149 in. w.b.)					
Sweptline (133)	720	1450	2400	3300	4800
Sweptline (149)	740	1470	2450	3350	4900
D150 Series Pickup — (H-D ½-Ton) — (115 or 131 in. w.b.)					
Utiline (115)	680	1350	2250	3150	4500
Sweptline (115)	690	1380	2300	3200	4600
Utiline (131)	700	1400	2350	3250	4700
Sweptline (131)	720	1450	2400	3300	4800
D150 Club Cab Pickup — (½-Ton) — (133 or 149 in. w.b.)					
Sweptline (133)	750	1500	2500	3500	5000
Sweptline (149)	700	1400	2350	3250	4700
D200 Series Pickup — (¾-Ton) — (131 in. w.b.)					
Utiline	740	1470	2450	3350	4900
Sweptline	750	1500	2500	3500	5000
D200 Club or Crew Cab Pickup — (¾-Ton) — (149 or 165 in. w.b.)					
Sweptline Club	680	1350	2250	3150	4500
Utiline Crew	690	1380	2300	3200	4600
Sweptline Crew	660	1320	2200	3100	4400
Util. Crew (165)	600	1200	2000	2800	4000
Swept. Crew (165)	620	1230	2050	2900	4100
D300 Series Pickup — (1-Ton) — (131, 149 or 165 in. w.b.)					
Sweptline (131)	570	1140	1900	2650	3800
Swept. Club (149)	590	1170	1950	2700	3900
Crew Sweptline	560	1100	1850	2600	3700
W150 Series 4x4 Pickup — (½-Ton) — (115 or 131 in. w.b.)					
Utiline (115)	800	1600	2650	3700	5300
Sweptline (115)	830	1650	2750	3850	5500
Utiline (131)	810	1620	2700	3800	5400
Sweptline (131)	840	1680	9800	3900	5600
W150 Club Cab 4x4 Pickup — (133 or 149 in. w.b.)					
Sweptline (133)	780	1560	2600	3600	5200
Sweptline (149)	750	1500	2500	3500	5000
W200 Series 4x4 Pickup — (¾-Ton) — (131 in. w.b.)					
Utiline	720	1450	2400	3300	4800
Sweptline	740	1470	2450	3350	4900
W200 Club or Crew Cab 4x4 Pickup — (¾-Ton) — (149 in. w.b.)					
Club Sweptline	750	1500	2500	3500	5000
Crew Sweptline	720	1450	2400	3300	4800

NOTE: Add 10 percent for V-8 engine.

1980 DODGE

1980 Dodge D50 Mini-Pickup (RPZ)

1980 Dodge D50 "Sport" Mini-Pickup (RPZ)

¼-TON MINI PICKUP — D50 SERIES - FOUR-CYLINDER: — This popular subcompact from Mitsubishi entered its second year with very minimal change. A lockable, sliding glass rear cab window was a new option. One paint color was added to the standard model, another to the Sport model. Color choices on the standard were Warm White, Light Tan and Black; but Spitfire Orange, Yellow, and Bright Metallic Blue on the Sport. The Sport model also gained a macho look with black base color and wide multi-color side stripe that had colors radiating from the wheel openings.

1980 Dodge B200 Forward Control Panel Van (RPZ)

½-TON VAN — B100 SERIES — SIX-CYLINDER and V-8 / ¾-TON VAN — B200 SERIES — SIX-CYLINDER and V-8 / 1-TON VAN — B300 SERIES — V-8: — For the first time in their long history, passenger vans (Sportsman wagons) were counted as trucks rather than cars. Changes for 1980 were slight. Four-speed overdrive manual transmission became standard on ½ and ¾-ton models; TorqueFlite 3-speed automatic on the 1-ton B300. Large vented windows replaced dual vented windows in the sliding side cargo door, with dual vented windows on the left side. A vented window for the single rear door became optional. Other options included power front door windows, an electronic travel computer, wide-pad brake pedal (on models with automatic transmission), lighted vanity mirror in the right sun visor, reading lamp in the headliner, bright finish hitch-type towing bumper with wide center strap, and halogen headlamps for better visibility. Two new entertainment packages were offered: an AM/FM/Stereo computerized radio with Search Tune, and an AM/FM/Stereo with cassette tape player and Dolby Noise Reduction System. Standard van equipment included painted bumpers and grille, dual cargo doors, chrome hubcaps, driver's sun visor, power steering (on B300), and 225 cu. in. slant six engine (318 V-8 on the B300).

1980 Dodge D150 Adventurer SE Sweptline Pickup (RPZ)

½-TON PICKUP — D150 SERIES - SIX-CYLINDER and V-8 / ¾-TON PICKUP — D200 SERIES — SIX-CYLINDER and V-8 / 1-TON PICKUP — D300 SERIES - V-8 / ½-TON 4x4 — W150 SERIES — SIX-CYLINDER and V-8 / ¾-TON 4x4 — W200 SERIES — V-8 / 1-TON 4x4 — W300 SERIES — V-8: — Full-size conventional trucks received only a minor facelift this year. Grille openings were painted black to achieve a new frontal look, but this was the only appearance change. After 23 consecutive years, the D100 model was dropped, making the D150 the lightest full-size model. D-Series improvements included a switch to 4-speed manual overdrive transmission on the D150 for added fuel economy; optional power front door windows; a styled, bright finished, hitch-type towing bumper with

wide center step; halogen headlamps (on dual headlight system); and a suspended accelerator pedal. Due to pressure from higher fuel prices, triggered by OPEC, W-Series 4x4 models changed to part time 4wd. This improved fuel economy and front axle serviceability, while reducing weight and drive line noise. Dodge trucks used two part-time transfer cases made by Chrysler's New Process Division: NP208 on ½ and ¾-ton models, and NP205 on the 1-ton and ¾-ton Crew Cab models. Standard transmission on all 4x4 models became the 4-speed manual NP435, replacing the former 3-speed. The popular Macho Power-Wagon, with its distinctive two-tone color scheme and large graphics, continued for 1980. Standard equipment on D/W models included chrome front bumper and grille, chrome hubcaps (D only), power brakes, 5x7 inch mirrors, bench seat, dome and courtesy lights, front/rear shocks (front only on 1-ton models), and an axle jack.

1980 Dodge Ramcharger SE "Macho" Wagon (RPZ)

½-TON RAMCHARGER 2WD — AD100 SERIES — SIX-CYLINDER and V-8 / ½-TON RAMCHARGER 4x4 — AW100 SERIES — V-8: — Part time 4wd was the big change for 1980 Ramchargers, which continued to be offered in standard or premium price class. Automatic transmission was standard on 2wd models, but the NP435 manual 4-speed and automatic were offered on 4wd models. Fifteen body paint colors (including nine new ones) were available. Other appearance items included all-new wheel covers and hubcaps, a chrome step-type towing bumper, and aluminum road wheels. Ramchargers also offered the same new options as pickups and vans — power front windows, two new entertainment systems, and halogen headlamps. New on Ramchargers only was an optional fold-up rear bench seat. A rear compartment mat, formerly optional, was now standard. So were rear courtesy lamps and a suspended gas pedal, plus power steering on 4wd models. Manual front locking hubs had to be turned by hand for 4wd in the part-time system, which used the NP208 transfer case. The 318 cu. in. V-8 now ran with a four-barrel carburetor for better performance. Ramcharger standard equipment included power brakes, chrome bumpers front and rear, chrome grille and hubcaps, map/courtesy light, rear compartment light, chrome outside mirrors, front and rear shock absorbers, and an axle jack.

1980 Dodge W150 Club Cab Power Wagon (RPZ)

I.D. DATA: (D50 Imported Pickups) The 13-character VIN was stamped on a plate on the left top side of the instrument panel, visible through the windshield. The first digit showed the truck line (9 = Dodge D50; 0 = Plymouth Arrow). Second digit indicated GVW and number of driving wheels (J = 2wd, less than 6000 lbs.). Third digit was the price class (L = low line; P = premium). Fourth digit showed body type (4 = conventional cab with Sweptline box). Fifth letter gave engine displacement (U = 2-liter; W = 2.6 liter). Sixth letter gave model year (A = 1980). Seventh came the transmission code (1 = 4-speed manual, U.S.; 2 = 4-speed, Calif.; 3 = 4-speed, Canada; 4 = 5-speed, U.S.; 5 = 5-speed, Calif.; 6 = 5-speed, Canada; 7 = automatic, U.S.; 8 = automatic, Calif.; 9 = automatic, Canada). Trim code was denoted by the eighth digit (1 = low line; 3 = high 1; 5 = high 2; 6 = premium). The last 5 digits formed the sequence number, starting with 00001. (Other models) The 13-character VIN was on an identification plate on the driver's door or "B" post. The first two characters designated Model. The next digit showed Body Type. Next came a letter for GVW Class. Next, a letter indicating Engine Type. The sixth letter indicated model year (A = 1980). The next letter was Assembly Plant. Finally came a 6-digit sequence number, which began with 100001 for Warren Truck Plant No. 1, Missouri Truck and Jefferson Truck; with 300001 for the Windsor Pillette plant; with 500001 at Warren Truck No. 2, and 700001 at Warren Truck Plant No. 3. Model index: B1 (B100); B2 (B200); B3 (B300); C3 (CB300); D1 (D150); D2 (D200); R2 (RD200); D3 (D300); W1 (W150); W2 (W200); W3 (W300); A1 (AW100); E1 (AD100). Body Type index: 0 (Ramcharger sport-utility, forward control, motor home chassis or incomplete chassis; 1 (Dodge Van, conventional cab & chassis, CB300); 2 (Sportsman, crew cab & chassis, CB300 without body); 3 (Utiline conventional cab); 4 (Sweptline conventional cab); 5 (Maxivan, Utiline crew cab); 6 (Sportsman Maxiwagon or Sweptline crew cab); 7 (cowl & windshield, club cab and chassis); 9 (Utiline club cab). GVW Class index: A (6000 lbs. or less); B (6001 to 8500 lbs.); K (8501 to 10,000 lbs.); etc. Engine Type index: B (225-1-2V); C (225-2-1V); E (318-1-2V); F (360-1-2V); G (318-2-2V); K (360-3-2V); N (225-1-1V); P (318-1-4V); S (360-HP-4V); T (360-1-4V); V (special V-8); X (special six). Assembly Plant index: C (Jefferson Ave.); K (Windsor, Pillette Road); N (Burt Road, KDX); S (Warren Truck No. 1); T (Warren Truck No. 3); V (Warren Truck No. 3); X (Missouri). Example: B12ABAK300001 designated a Sportsman B100, rated 6000 lbs. GVW or less, with 225 cu. in. slant six engine and two-barrel carburetor, 1980 model, built at Windsor with serial number 300001.

Model	Body Type	Price	Weight	Prod. Total
D50 Series Mini Pickup — (¼-Ton) — (109.4 in. w.b.)				
D50	Sweptline	4870	2573	—
D50	Sport	5683	2648	—
AD100/AW100 Ramcharger — (½-Ton) — (106 in. w.b.)				
AD100	2wd — hardtop	6793	3660	—
AW100	4wd — hardtop	8298	4150	—
B100-300 Series Sportsman Wagons — (½-Ton) — (109.6 in. w.b.)				
B100	Wagon	6564	3444	—
(127.6 in. w.b.)				
B100	Wagon	6736	3595	—
(¾-Ton) — (109.6 in. w.b.)				
B200	Wagon	6876	3460	—
(127.6 in. w.b.)				
B200	Wagon	7051	3584	—
B200	Maxiwagon	8152	4009	—
(1-Ton) — (127.6 in. w.b.)				
B300	Wagon	8300	4121	—
B300	Maxiwagon	8659	4325	—
B100-300 Series Tradesman Van — (½-Ton) — (109.6 in. w.b.)				
B100	Van	5470	3232	—
(127.6 in. w.b.)				
B100	Van	5645	3351	—
(¾-Ton) (109.6 in. w.b.)				
B200	Van	5795	3237	—
(127.6 in. w.b.)				
B200	Van	5969	3349	—
B200	Maxivan	6369	3607	—
(1-Ton) — (127.6 in. w.b.)				
B300	Van	7289	3800	—
B300	Maxivan	7686	4066	—
D150 Series — (½-Ton) — (115 in. w.b.)				
D150	Utiline Pickup	5275	3288	—
D150	Sweptline Pickup	5275	3323	—
131 in. w.b.)				
D150	Utiline Pickup	5360	3402	—
D150	Sweptline Pickup	5360	3437	—
(133 in. w.b.)				
D150	Club — Sweptline	6503	3666	—
(149 in. w.b.)				
D150	Club — Sweptline	6588	3796	—
D200 Series — (¾-Ton) — (131 in. w.b.)				
D200	Utiline Pickup	6052	3736	—
D200	Sweptline Pickup	6052	3771	—
(149 in. w.b.)				
D200	Club — Sweptline	7010	3969	—
D200 Series Crew Cab — (¾-Ton) — (149 in. w.b.)				
D200	Sweptline Pickup	7555	4212	—
(165 in. w.b.)				
D200	Sweptline Pickup	7647	4502	—
D300 Series — (1-Ton) — (131 in. w.b.)				
D300	Sweptline Pickup	6577	4573	—
(149 in. w.b.)				
D300	Club — Sweptline	7130	4383	—
D300 Series Crew Cab — (1-Ton) — (165 in. w.b.)				
D300	Sweptline Pickup	8461	4793	—
W150 Series 4x4 — (½-Ton) — (115 in. w.b.)				
W150	Utiline Pickup	7181	3797	—
W150	Sweptline Pickup	7181	3832	—
131 in. w.b.)				
W150	Utiline Pickup	7266	3912	—
W150	Sweptline Pickup	7266	3947	—
(133 in. w.b.)				
W150	Club — Sweptline	7837	4090	—
(149 in. w.b.)				
W150	Club — Sweptline	7990	4235	—
W200 Series 4x4 — (¾-Ton) — (131 in. w.b.)				
W200	Utiline Pickup	7853	4120	—
W200	Sweptline Pickup	7853	4155	—
(149 in. w.b.)				
W200	Club — Sweptline	8503	4544	—
W200 Crew Cab 4x4 — (¾-Ton) — (149 in. w.b.)				
W200	Sweptline Pickup	9512	4842	—
W300 Series 4x4 — (1-Ton) — (135 in. w.b.)				
W300	Chassis & Cab	8869	4806	—

ENGINES: Same as 1979 except: (225 cu. in. slant six) Standard on D150, W150, B100, B200 and AD100. (318 cu. in. V-8) Standard on D150, D200, W150, W200, B100-300, AD100 and AW100.
CHASSIS (D50) Wheelbase: 109.4 in. Tires: 6.00 x 14-C. GVW: 4045-4120 lbs.

1980 Dodge B200 Sportsman Maxiwagon (RPZ)

CHASSIS (B100) Wheelbase: 109.6 or 127.6 in. Tires: P205/75R15-B. GVW: 4700-5100 lbs. Axle Capacity: (front) 3300 lbs.; (rear) 3550 lbs.

CHASSIS (B200) Wheelbase: 109.6 or 127.6 in. Tires: P22/75R15-B. GVW: 6050 lbs. Axle Capacity: (front) 3300 lbs.; (rear) 3550 lbs.

CHASSIS (B300) Wheelbase: 127.6 in. Tires: 8.00 x 16.5-E. GVW: 7000-7200 lbs. Axle Capacity: (front) 3600 lbs.; (rear) 5500 lbs.

CHASSIS (D150) Wheelbase: 115 or 131 in. (Club Cab, 133 or 149 in.). Tires: P195/75R-15B. GVW: 4800 lbs. (Club, 6050). Axle Capacity: (front) 3300 lbs.; (rear) 3400 lbs.

CHASSIS (D200) Wheelbase: 131, 149 (Club Cab) or 165 in. (Club/Crew Cab). Tires: 8.00 x 16.5-D. GVW: 6500 lbs. (Club, 7500; Crew, 8550). Axle Capacity: (front) 3700 lbs.; (rear) 5500 lbs.

CHASSIS (D300) Wheelbase: 149 in. or 165 in. (Crew Cab). Tires: 9.50 x 16.5-E. GVW: 9000 lbs. (Crew, 10,000). Axle Capacity: (front) 4000 lbs.; (rear) 6200 lbs.

CHASSIS (W150) Wheelbase: 115 or 131 in. (Club Cab, 133 or 149 in.). GVW: 6050 lbs. Axle Capacity: (front) 3500 lbs.; (rear) 3600 lbs.

CHASSIS (W200) Wheelbase: 131 or 149 in. GVW: 6900 lbs. Axle Capacity: (front) 3500 lbs.; (rear) 5500 lbs. (Club/Crew, 8550).

CHASSIS (W300) Wheelbase: 135 in. GVW: 10,000 lbs. Axle Capacity: (front) 4500 lbs.; (rear) 7500 lbs.

CHASSIS (Ramcharger) Wheelbase: 106 in. Tires: P225/75R15-B. GVW: 5300-6050 lbs.

TECHNICAL: Selective sliding gear transmission. Speeds: (B100-200, D150) 4-speed overdrive; (B300) 3-speed automatic; (D200-300, W150-300) 4-speed manual. 4wd transfer case: part time. Clutch: (B100-200, D150-300 with 115/131 in. w.b.) 10 in.; (others) 11 in. Hydraulic brakes: front disc, rear drum. Electronic ignition system. 48-amp alternator. Fuel tank: (D/W) 18-gallon; (vans) 22-gallon; (Ramcharger) 24-gallon.

1980 Dodge Ramcharger SE Utlity Wagon (RPZ)

OPTIONS (Factory-Installed): (B Vans) Chrome bumpers (front/rear). Bumper guards (front/rear). Chrome bumper hitch. Single rear door. Sliding side door. Door check arms. Door edge protectors. Tinted glass. Sunscreen. Banded glass. Chrome grille. Skylite sun roof. Color-keyed spare tire cover. Painted spoke white wheels (15x7.00). Chrome disc five-slot wheels. Aluminum ribbed wheels. Deluxe chrome or premium wheel covers. Window retention. Upper, lower, upper/lower, or wheel lip molding package. Dual outside mirors: 5x7 in. chrome, 6x9 in. painted, or 6x9 in. chrome lo-mount. Lighted vanity mirror. Dual horns. Interior reading light. Hood release lock. Rubber floor mats. Deluxe heater. Auxiliary rear heater. Cargo area headliner. Dual quad headlights. Speedometer (km/mph) and trip odometer (km). Oil pressure gauge. Cigar lighter. Digital clock. Electric rear window defroster. Air conditioning. Power brakes. Power steering. Power windows. Power door locks (front or all). Radios: AM; AM/FM; AM/FM/Stereo with search; AM/FM/Stereo with 8-track or cassette tape player; AM/FM/Stereo with CB. Rear speaker. Cruise control. Tilt steering column. Dome light switch. Unibelt restraint system (color-keyed). Deluxe windshield wipers. Front stabilizer bar. Heavy-duty shocks (rear, or front/rear). 63 or 117-amp alternator. Maximum cooling system. Auxiliary transmission cooler. 36-gallon fuel tank. Engine block heater. (D/W models) Chrome rear bumper (D100-200, W150). Painted bumper (front or rear). Rear step bumper. Tinted glass. Quad rectangular headlights. Marker lights. In-cab hood release. Dual mirrors: 6x9 in. lo-

235

mount; 7½x10½ lo-mount; or 7x10 West Coast. Upper, lower, or upper/lower body molding package. Dual horns. Skylite sun mount. Inside tire carrier (D/W150-200). Underslung tire carrier (D/W200). White spoke wheels (D150). Chrome disc wheels (D150). Aluminum ribbed wheels (D150). Chrome deluxe wheels covers (D150-200, W150). Premium wheels (D/W150). Flip-out rear quarter window (D/W150-200 Club Cab). Sliding rear window. Camper package: 7500, 9000 or 10,000 lbs. (D/W200-300). Big Horn package (D/W150-200). Protective package. Sound control package. Tape stripe package (except W300). Trailer-towing package. Stake body: 8-ft. (D200-300, W200); 9½-ft. (D/W300); 12½-ft. (D/W300). Skid plates, transfer case (W models). Front stabilizer bar (D/W300). Flip-type hinged Club Cab seats (D/W150-200). Cruise control. Tilt steering. Sport steering wheel (except W200-300). Hand throttle. Unibelt restraint. Floor mats. Headliner: Oil pressure gauge. Speedometer (km/mi). Odometer (km). Cigar lighter. Clock. Air conditioning. Power brakes. Power steering. Power windows. Power door locks. Deluxe heater. Radios: AM; AM/FM; AM/FM/Stereo; AM/FM/Stereo with search, 8-track player, cassette player, or CB. Engine block heater. 63 or 117-amp alternator. Maximum cooling system. Auxiliary transmission cooler. 21-gallon fuel tank. Heavy-duty shocks: front or rear (D/W300); front and rear (all). (Ramcharger) Step rear bumper. Tinted glass. Privacy sun screen. Quad rectangular headlamps. Dual horns. Inside hood release. Chrome lo-mount mirrors (6x9 or 7½x10½). Upper, lower or upper/lower body molding package. Roll bar. Skid plates (fuel tank or transfer case). Skylite sun roof. Outside tire carrier. White spoke wheels. Chrome disc five-slot wheels. Aluminum ribbed wheels. Chrome deluxe or premium wheel covers. SE package. Heavy-duty GVW package (5300, 5850, 6010 or 6050 lbs.). Convenience package. Insulation package. Macho 4wd package. Protection package. Sound control package. Sno-Commander package. Tape stripe (Graduated Sport) package. Trailer-towing package. Rear bench seat (3-passenger). Tilt steering column. Cruise control. Front stabilizer bar (standard or heavy-duty). Cigar lighter. Clock. Lockable console. Shoulder belts. Speedometer (km/mi) and odometer (km). Oil pressure gauge. Deluxe heater. Radios (same as D/W models). Power steering. Power windows. Power door locks. Heavy-duty shocks (front/rear). Color-keyed rubber floor mats. Air conditioning. 63 or 117-amp alternator. Maximum cooling system. Auxiliary transmission cooler. 35-gallon fuel tank. Engine block heater.

HISTORICAL: Introduced: August 1979. Calendar year sales: 228,500. Model year sales: 251,442 (96,468 light-duty conventional; 80,183 Tradesman vans; 22,840 Sportsman wagons; 9411 Ramchargers; and 42,540 D50 mini pickups). Calendar year production: 119,232. Historical notes: The U.S. truck industry took a severe beating in 1980, as total shipments plunged 45 percent — the lowest figure since 1967. Light-duty trucks did worse yet, dropping 47 percent. Dodge production took it on the chin as well, plummeting 60.6 percent to just 119,232 trucks. Sales dropped over 35 percent, due largely to high interest rates that resulted from the Federal Reserve Board's attempt to control inflation. The sole bright spot for Chrysler was its captive import mini-trucks. Sales of these subcompact Dodge and Plymouth models jumped to 63,056. In March, the plant at Fenton, Missouri was shut down. Van production from that plant was consolidated in Windsor, Ontario. Chrysler also closed its RV chassis production facility at Warren, Michigan early in 1980, bowing out of the Class A motor home business. The Jefferson Avenue pickup plant was converted at the end of the 1980 model year to production of the new K-cars for 1981.

Pricing

	5	4	3	2	1
1980					
D50 Series Mini Pickup — (¼-Ton) — (109.4 in. w.b.)					
Sweptline	620	1300	2150	3050	4300
Sport	690	1380	2300	3200	4600
Ramcharger Hardtop — (1-Ton) — (106 in. w.b.)					
AD100 2wd	780	1560	2600	3600	5200
AW100 4wd	870	1750	2900	4100	5800
B100 Series Van/Sportsman — (½-Ton) — (109 or 127.6 in. w.b.)					
Van (109)	540	1080	1800	2500	3600
Van (127)	560	1100	1850	2600	3700
Wagon (109)	590	1170	1950	2700	3900
Wagon (127)	620	1230	2050	2900	4100
B200 Series Van/Sportsman — (¾-Ton) — (109.6 or 127.6 in. w.b.)					
Van (109)	520	1020	1700	2400	3400
Van (127)	530	1050	1750	2450	3500
Wagon (109)	560	1100	1850	2600	3700
Wagon (127)	590	1170	1950	2700	3900
Maxivan	570	1140	1900	2650	3800
Maxiwagon	620	1230	2050	2900	4100
B300 Series Van/Sportsman — (1-Ton) — (127.6 in. w.b.)					
Van	500	1000	1650	2300	3300
Maxivan	520	1020	1700	2400	3400
Wagon	530	1050	1750	2450	3500
Maxiwagon	540	1080	1800	2500	3600
D150 Series Pickup — (½-Ton) — (115 or 131 in. w.b.)					
Utiline (115)	690	1380	2300	3200	4600
Sweptline (115)	700	1400	2350	3250	4700
Utiline (131)	700	1400	2350	3250	4700
Sweptline (131)	720	1450	2400	3300	4800
D150 Club Cab Pickup — (½-Ton) — (133 or 149 in. w.b.)					
Sweptline (133)	750	1500	2500	3500	5000
Sweptline (149)	740	1470	2450	3350	4900
D200 Series Pickup — (¾-Ton) — (131 in. w.b.)					
Utiline	740	1470	2450	3350	4900
Sweptline	750	1500	2500	3500	5000
D200 Club Cab Pickup — (¾-Ton) — (149 in. w.b.)					
Sweptline	700	1400	2350	3250	4700
D200 Crew Cab Pickup — (¾-Ton) — (149 or 165 in. w.b.)					
Sweptline (149)	630	1250	2100	3000	4200
Sweptline (165)	600	1200	2000	2800	4000

	5	4	3	2	1
D300 Series Pickup — (1-Ton) — (131 or 149 in. w.b.)					
Sweptline	600	1200	2000	2800	4000
Sweptline Club Cab	620	1230	2050	2900	4100
D300 Series Crew Cab Pickup — (1-Ton) — (165 in. w.b.)					
Sweptline	690	1380	2300	3200	4600
W150 Series 4x4 Pickup — (½-Ton) — (115 or 131 in. w.b.)					
Utiline (115)	810	1620	2700	3800	5400
Sweptline (115)	840	1680	2800	3900	5600
Utiline (131)	830	1650	2750	3850	5500
Sweptline (131)	870	1750	2900	4100	5800
W150 Series Club Cab 4x4 Pickup — (½-Ton) — (133 or 149 in. w.b.)					
Sweptline (133)	850	1700	2850	4000	5700
Sweptline (149)	840	1680	2800	3900	5600
W200 Series 4x4 Pickup — (¾-Ton) — (131 in. w.b.)					
Utiline	830	1650	2750	3850	5500
Sweptline	850	1700	2850	4000	5700
W200 Club Cab 4x4 Pickup — (¾-Ton) — (149 in. w.b.)					
Sweptline	750	1500	2500	3500	5000
W200 Crew Cab 4x4 Pickup — (¾-Ton) — (149 in. w.b.)					
Sweptline	720	1450	2400	3300	4800

NOTE: Deduct 10% for six-cylinder engine.

1981 DODGE

1981 Dodge Ram Mini-Pickup (DNP)

RAM 50 CUSTOM PICKUP: — Styling was carried over for '81. Among standard features were: Cargo lamp, Cigarette lighter. Dome light with driver and passenger side door switches. Emergency flashers. A 15.1-gallon fuel tank. Color-keyed headliner. Inside hood release. Interior rearview mirror. Dual exterior rearview mirrors. Adjustable steering column with lock. Dual sun visors. AM radio. Tinted glass. Trip odometer. Two-speed windshield wipers with washers. Four-speed manual transmission.

RAM 50 ROYAL PICKUP: — This was a new series for 1981. It came with most of the same standard features as the Custom plus a higher level of trim, inside and out.

RAM 50 SPORT PICKUP: — The Sport was the flashiest Ram 50 pickup. It had high-back bucket seats, center console, oil pressure gauge, ammeter, body side tape stripes, spoke road wheels, and a five speed manual transmission.

I.D. DATA (Ram 50): See D150 I.D.

Model	Body Type	Price	Weight	Prod. Total
9JL4	Pickup (Custom)	6145	2537	—
9JH4	Pickup (Royal)	6550	—	—
9JH4	Pickup (Sport)	7022	2648	—

ENGINE (Ram 50): 2.0L (122 cu.in.) OHC. Four-cylinder. Brake horsepower: 90 at 5000 R.P.M. Bore & stroke: 3.30 x 3.54 in. Compression ratio: 8.5:1. Carburetor: 2-bbl.

ENGINE (Royal, Sport): 2.6L (156 cu. in.). Four-cylinder. Brake horsepower: 105 at 5000 R.P.M. Bore & stroke: 3.59 x 3.86 in. Compression ratio: 8.2:1. Carburetor: 2-bbl.

CHASSIS Wheelbase: 109.4 in. Overall length: 184.6 in. Overall height: 60.6 in. (Custom). 59.8 in. (Royal, Sport). Overall width: 65 in. GVW. 4045-4120 lbs. Tires: 6.00 x 14C (Custom), 185SR14 SBR (Royal, Sport).

POWERTRAIN OPTION: Three-speed automatic transmission.

CONVENIENCE OPTIONS: Air conditioning. Chrome rear step bumper. Low-luster Black rear step bumper. Front bumper guards. Electronic digital clock. Front floor mats. 18-gallon fuel tank. Front grille guard. Low-mount chrome exterior mirrors. Vinyl bodyside molding. Vinyl pickup box top edge molding. Mud guards. Power steering. Sliding rear window. Sun roof. Bodyside tape stripe. Wheel trim rings.

1981 Dodge 4x4 Ramcharger (DNP)

RAMCHARGER SPORT UTILITY VEHICLE: — The 1981 Ramcharger shared front end and taillight styling with "D" series pickups. Wraparound rear quarter windows were integrated into the integral steel roof. The newly designed rear liftgate was made of light-weight fiberglass and had two pneumatic-assist cylinders. The Ramcharger was offered in 2wd (AD150) and part-time 4wd (AW150). Among standard features were: Dry type air cleaner. 48-amp alternator. Ashtray. Bright front and rear bumpers. Automatic choke. Cleaner Air System. Coolant reserve system. Insulated dash liner. Color-keyed door trim panels and armrests. Electronic ignition system. Black floor mat. 35-gallon fuel tank. Tinted glass. Glove box. Aluminum grille with painted plastic insert and headlamp doors. Fresh air heater with defrosters. Single electric horn. Bright hubcaps. Front wheel locking hubs (4wd). Combination map/courtesy light on instrument panel. Dual bright finish 5 in. by 7 in. short arm exterior mirrors. 10 in. inside rearview mirror. Power front disc brakes. Power steering (4wd). Deluxe vinyl low-back bucket seats. Inside spare tire mounting. Rear roof vent. AM radio. Front stabilizer bar (4wd). Sun visors. Two-speed NP208 transfer case (4wd). Dual jet windshield washers. Two-speed windshield wipers. Three-speed automatic transmission (2wd). Four-speed manual (4wd). Brake system warning light. Dual braking system with separate brake fluid reservoirs in the master cylinder.

I.D. DATA (Ramcharger): See D150 I.D.

Model	Body Type	Price	Weight	Prod. Total
AD150	Utility	8257	—	—
AW150	Utility (4wd)	9466	4174	—

ENGINES (Ramcharger): 5.2-liter (318 cu. in.) V-8. Brake horsepower: 120 at 3600 R.P.M. Bore & stroke: 3.91 x 3.315 in. Compression ratio: 8.5:1. Carburetor: 2-bbl.

CHASSIS FEATURES Wheelbase 106 in. Overall length: 184.6 in. (without bumper guards). 186.1 in. (with bumper guards). Overall width: 79.5 in. GVW. 5300 lbs. (2wd), 5850 lbs. (4wd). Tires: P235/75R15 BSW GBR.

POWERTRAIN OPTIONS: 5.2L (318 cu. in.) Carburetor: 4-bbl. V-8 (4wd), 5.9L (360 cu. in.) Carburetor: 4-bbl. V-8 (4wd). Three-speed TorqueFlite automatic transmission (4wd).

OPTION PACKAGES (Ramcharger Royal S.E.): Bright windshield and drip rail molding; bright taillamp housing; power steering; Ram's head hood ornament; Leaping Ram with "150 Royal S.E." plaque on front fender; bright aluminum grille with chromed plastic insert and headlamp doors; tailgate upper and lower moldings with bright applique panel; woodgrain applique on interior of door with assist strap and carpeting on lower door panel; color-keyed driver and front passenger high-back Command bucket seats with cloth and vinyl trim (included inboard fold-down armrests on seats and locable console with removable styrofoam beverage chest); color-keyed folding rear bench seat with cloth and vinyl trim; color-keyed carpeting; color-keyed rear side and liftgate inner trim panels; woodtone instrument cluster faceplate; instrument panel plaque; black leather wrapped steering wheel with black horn pad and woodtone insert; color-keyed spare tire cover (n.a. with 10R15LT tires); cigar lighter; dual horns; bright front door sill scuff plate; insulation under hood panel; oil pressure and engine temperature gauges; color-keyed cowl side trim panels; trip odometer.

MACHO RAMCHARGER: Royal S.E. trim; special two-tone exterior paint; macho tape stripe; high gloss black front and rear bumpers; five outline White lettered SBR tires; four radial-ribbed aluminum wheels on 2wd (steel-spoke orange wheels with black accent on 4wd); sport bar.

RAMCHARGER BIG HORN: Ram's head hood ornament; Big Horn side nameplates; Gold filigree pinstriping; Ram's hide vinyl and simulated lambs wool trim high-back bucket seats with matching rear bench seat and a center console; convenience package; electronic digital clock.

CONVENIENCE PACKAGE: Day/night 10 in. interior rearview mirror; glove box with lock and light; ash receiver light; in-cab actuated hood lock release; two-speed windshield wipers with intermittent wipe.

PROTECTION PACKAGE: Door edge protectors; bright front bumper with guards and nerf strips; bright rear bumper with nerf strips.

TRAILER TOWING PACKAGES: Light-duty; heavy-duty (4wd only):

SNO-COMMANDER PACKAGE: (4wd only) snow removal equipment.

CONVENIENCE OPTIONS: Air conditioning. Heavy-duty alternators and batteries. Painted rear step type bumper. Cigar lighter. Electronic digital clock. Lockable console. Auxiliary transmission oil to air cooler. Maximum cooling. Oil pressure, engine temperature, and trip odometer gauges; bright insert grille and bright headlamp doors; halogen headlamps; Deluxe bi-level heater; engine block heater; in cab-actuated hood lock release; dual electric horns; color-keyed rubber (accessory type) mats for driver's compartment; dual low-mount bright 6 in. x 9 in. mirrors; dual low-mount extended bright 7½ in. x 10½ in. mirrors; lower molding; upper molding; power door locks; power steering; power windows; Radios: AM/FM, AM/FM stereo, AM/FM stereo/cassette tape player, AM/FM stereo with 8-track tape player, AM/FM stereo with 40-channel CB, AM/FM stereo with Search-Tune; heavy-duty shocks; fuel tank skid plate; transfer case skid plate (4wd); automatic speed control; sport bar; front stabilizer bar; heavy-duty front stabilizer bar (4wd); tilt steering column; Sky Lite sun roof; privacy glass sun screen; deluxe color-keyed unibelt restraint system; bright wheel covers; premium wheel covers (n.a. with 4wd); Wheels: aluminum radial ribbed, five slot chrome disc, white painted steel spoke; two-speed windshield wipers with intermittent wipe.

NOTE: Ramcharger exterior colors for 1981 included: Bright Silver Metallic, Medium Seaspray Green Metallic, Impact Orange, Daystar Blue Metallic, Cashmere, Impact Red, Nightwatch Blue, Ginger, Medium Crimson Red, Impact Blue, Coffee Brown Metallic, Black, Light Seaspray Green Metallic, Graphic Yellow, Pearl White.

1981 Dodge Ram Royal SE Maxi-Wagon Van (DNP)

B150 VAN: — Basic styling was unchanged for 1981. Among the standard features were: Dry type air cleaner. 48-amp alternator. Driver and front passenger armrests. Ashtray. 325-amp battery. Power front disc brakes (except 109.6 in. and 127.6 in. w.b's with 4700 lb. GVW). Painted front and rear bumpers. Double hinged right ride and rear cargo doors. Electronic ignition system. Driver's compartment floor mat. 22-gallon fuel tank. Glove box. Argent finish grille. Color-keyed hardboard headliner in driver's compartment. Single electric horn. Color-keyed horn pad. Bright finish hubcaps. Ammeter, fuel gauge, odometer, oil pressure indicator light, speedometer, and temperature gauge. Duel 5" x 7" painted exterior mirrors. AM radio. Low-back bucket seat with vinyl trim for driver. Driver side sun visor. Spare tire carrier. Traffic Hazard warning switch. Two-speed windshield wipers with washers. Brake system warning light. Energy absorbing steering column. Ignition and steering column lock. Dual braking system. The B150 Long Range Van had special trim and higher capacity.

B150 WAGON: — The E150 Wagon had most of the same standard features as the van plus (or in place of): Windows all around. Black full width floor mat. Fresh air heater with defroster. 10 in. inside rearview mirror. Two color-keyed padded sun visors. Driver and front passenger low back vinyl bucket seats. Three-passenger quick-release vinyl rear bench seat including three seat belts.

1981 Dodge Ram Mini-Van (DNP)

B150 MINI-RAM WAGON: — The new Mini-Ram van came on a 109.6 in. w.b. and had many interior and exterior refinements such as: Bright grille. Bright front and rear bumpers. Wheel covers. Bright 5 in. x 7 in. outside rearview mirrors. 36-gallon fuel tank. Custom S.E. Decor Package. Door-operated light switches. Convenience Package.

I.D. DATA (B150): See D150 I.D.

Model	Body Type	Price	Weight	Prod. Total
B150 Series — Van — (109.6 in. w.b.)				
B150	Van	6418	3274	—
(127.6 in. w.b.)				
B150	Van	—	—	—
B150	Long Range Van	6330	—	—
(109.6 in. w.b.)				
B150	Wagon	7477	3493	—
(127.6 in. w.b.)				
B150	Wagon	—	—	—
B150	Mini Ram Wagon	7705	—	—

ENGINE (B150): — 3.7-liter (225 cu. in.). Slant six-cylinder. Brake horsepower: 95 at 3600 R.P.M. Bore & stroke: 3.40 x 4.12 in. Carburetor: 1-bbl.

B250 VAN: — The B250 shared most of the same standard features offered on the B150. However, it was a bit more heavy-duty and could be ordered the extra long "Maxi" body.

B250 WAGON: — The ¾-ton B250 wagon had most of the same features as the B150. It was offered in regular or extended ("Maxi") bodies. Maxi-wagons came with an automatic transmission.

B250 MINI-RAM WAGON: — This was a slightly more heavy-duty version of the B150 Mini-Ram Wagon. It came with the same standard features.

I.D. DATA (B250): See D150 I.D.

Model	Body Type	Price	Weight	Prod. Total
B250 Series (109.6 in. w.b.)				
B250	Van	6883	3383	—
(127.6 in. w.b.)				
B250	Van	—	—	—
(109.6 in. w.b.)				
B250	Wagon	7902	3646	—
(127.6 in. w.b.)				
B150	Wagon	—	—	—
B250	Mini-Ram Wagon	8297	—	—

ENGINE (B250): Same as B150.

B350 VAN: The 1-ton B350 had most of the same standard features as the B150 plus (or in place of): Larger brakes. Higher capacity rear springs. Power steeing. Automatic transmission. Both regular, and extended "Maxi Van" bodies were offered.

B350 WAGON: This was Dodge's heftiest people hauler. It was available in regular or Maxi bodies.

I.D. DATA (B350): See D150 I.D.

Model	Body Type	Price	Weight	Prod. Total
B350	Van	8709	3931	—
B350	Wagon	9467	4234	—

ENGINE (350): 5.2L (318 cu. in.) V-8. Brake horsepower: 140 at 3600 R.P.M. Bore & stroke: 3.91 x 3.31. Compression ratio: 8.5:1. Carburetor: 2-bbl.

CB350 KARY VAN: The CB350 Kary Van was offered in three sizes and three w.b. Automatic transmission was standard.

I.D. DATA (CB350): See D150 I.D.

Model	Body Type	Price	Weight	Prod. Total
CB350	Van (10-ft. body)	—	—	—
CB350	Van (12-ft. body)	—	—	—
CB350	Van (15-ft. body)	—	—	—

ENGINE (CB350): 5.2-liter (318 cu. in.) V-8. Brake horsepower: 170 at 4000 R.P.M. Bore & stroke: 3.91 x 3.31 in. Compression ratio: 8.5:1. Carburetor: 4-bbl.

ENGINE: (127.6 in. w.b.) 5.9-liter (360 cu. in.) V-8. Brake horsepower: 180 at 3600 R.P.M. Bore & stroke: 4.00 x 3.58. Compression ratio: 8.6:1. Carburetor: 4-bbl.

CHASSIS FEATURES: Wheelbase: 109.6 in. (B150, B250), Wheelbase: 127.6 in. (B350). Wheelbase: 163.6 in. (CB350). Overall length: 178.9 in. (109.6 in. w.b.), 196.9 in. (127.6 in. w.b.), 222.9 in. (Maxi van/wagon). Overall width: 79.8 in. Overall height: 79.6 in. (109.6 in. w.b.), 80.6 in. (Maxi van/wagon), 80.9 in. (127.6 in. w.b.). GVW: 4700-5300 lbs. (B150), 6010-6400 lbs. (B250), 7000-9000 lbs. (B350), 7500-10,000 lbs. (Kary Van). Tires: P195/75R x 15 (B150), P225/75R x 15 (B250), 8.00 x 16.5E (B350 Maxi van/wagon), 8.75 x 16.5E (Kary Van).

POWERTRAIN OPTIONS: 5.2L Carburetor: 2-bbl. V-8, 5.2L Carburetor: 4-bbl. V-8, 5.9L Carburetor 4-bbl. V-8, (B250, B350). Three-speed automatic transmission.

VAN OPTION PACKAGES: TRAILER TOWING PACKAGES CONVENIENCE PACKAGE: Cigar lighter; glove box lock; in cab actuated hood lock release; two-speed windshield wipers with intermittent wipe. ROYAL EXTERIOR PACKAGE: bright grille, front and rear bumpers, taillamp bezels, windshield molding; dual 5 in. x 7 in. exterior mirrors; dual vertically stacked quad rectangular headlamps with halogen high beam lamps. ROYAL INTERIOR PACKAGE: color-keyed bucket seat floor risers; cigar lighter; electronic digital clock; color-keyed carpeting in driver's compartment, horn pad with woodtone applique insert; vinyl front door trim panels with woodtone applique; deluxe vinyl trimmed low-back driver's seat; garnish trim over front pillars, front door headers and around windshield; insulated dash liner; insulated headliner in drivers compartment; instrument panel nameplate; scuff pads; unibelt restraint system.

238

VAN and WAGON CONVENIENCE OPTIONS: Air conditioning (integral front or rear auxiliary). Heavy-duty alternators and batteries. Bright hitch type rear bumper. Bright front and rear bumpers. Front and rear bumper guards and Nerf strips. Cigar lighter. Electronic digital clock. Auxiliary transmission oil to air cooling. Maximum engine cooling. Electric rear window defroster. Dual rear doors with fixed or vented glass. Single rear door with vented glass. Sliding passenger side door. 36-gallon fuel tank. Oil pressure gauge. Trip odometer. Sun screen privacy glass. Tinted windows. Bright grille (included dual quad rectangular headlamps, vertically stacked with halogen high beams. Passenger compartment headliner. Rear auxiliary heater. Deluxe front heater. Dual electric horns. Interior reading lamp in driver's compartment. In-cab actuated hood release lock. Two color-keyed accessory type rubber mats for driver's compartment. Dual low-mount 6 in. x 9 in. bright or painted mirrors. Dual short arm bright 5 in. x 7 in. exterior mirrors. Illuminated vanity. Interior day/night rearview mirror. Lower, side and rear moldings. Upper, side and rear moldings and bright taillamp bezels. Upper and lower moldings. Power door locks. Power steering. Power front door windows. RADIOS: AM/FM, AM/FM stereo, AM/FM stereo with cassette tape player and Dolby Noise Reduction System, AM/FM stereo with 8-track tape player, AM/FM stereo with Search-Tune, AM/FM stereo with 40-channel CB transceiver. Rear speaker (for AM or AM/FM radios only). Heavy-duty front and rear shock absorbers. Color-keyed spare tire carrier. Automatic speed control. Front stabilizer bar. Tilt type steering column. Leather wrapped steering wheel. Sky Lite sun roof. Door operated dome light switch. WHEELS: Radial ribbed aluminum, 5-slot chrome disc, white painted spoke. Bright wheel covers. Premium wheel covers. Deluxe windshield wipers. Vinyl low-back front bucket seats (Van). Driver deluxe vinyl trim low-back bucket seat (Van). Driver and passenger deluxe vinyl trim low-back bucket seats (Van). Cloth and vinyl trim driver and passenger high-back. Command bucket seats, non-swivel base (Van). Deluxe driver and passenger high-back Command reclining bucket seats (Van). Wheel lip moldings (Van). Metal door check arms (Van).

WAGON OPTION PACKAGES: CUSTOM S.E. PACKAGE: Custom nameplates; bright molding around windshield, side and rear windows (except driver and passenger door windows); bright taillamp bezels; dual vertically stacked quad rectangular headlamps with halogen high beams; instrument panel lower skirts (left and right side); cigar lighter; headliner in driver and passenger compartments; vinyl door and side trim panels with plaid insert; color-keyed carpeting; dash liner insultion; garnish trim over front doors, compartment windows and headers around rear. ROYAL PACKAGE: (included items in Custom S.E. Package plus) Royal nameplates; bright lower side and rear molding; dual vertically stacked quad rectangular headlamps with halogen high beams and bright grille; bright front and rear bumpers; dual 5 in. x 7 in. bright exterior mirrors; woodtone applique on lower face of instrument panel; horn pad with woodtone insert; spare tire cover; vinyl door and side trim panels with woodtone trim; door operated dome light switches on all doors; garnish trim over front doors, compartment windows, headers around rear compartment windows and front pillar and windshield; dual electric horns; U-belt restraint system; driver and front passenger low-back bucket seats and bench seat in deluxe vinyl trim (blue or cashmere); driver and passenger compartment soft-cloth covered headliner with insulation; accessory floor mats in driver's compartment; electronic digital clock. ROYAL S.E. PACKAGE: Royal S.E. nameplates; bright upper side and rear moldings; bright bumper guards with nerf strips; body side and rear woodtone tape applique with dual gold accent stripes; vinyl door and side trim panels with woodtone trim and front door applique pull strap; color-keyed carpeted engine housing cover; oil pressure gauge and trip odometer; power steering; leather-wrapped steering wheel; 10 in. day/night interior rearview mirror; glove box lock and light; deluxe two-speed with intermittent wipe windshield wipers; in cab actuated hood release lock; ignition and headlight switch with time delay; cigar lighter light; courtesy step well lamp (front and side doors); color-keyed driver and front passenger high-back reclining command bucket seats and a three-passenger bench seat with cloth and vinyl trim in blue, cashmere or red. HEAVY-DUTY INSULATION PACKAGE: included with integral front mounted air conditioning. For Royal and Royal S.E. wagons: interior lower fiberglass insulation panels (not offered on standard single rear door or optional sliding side door); insulation under floor covering. For Custom S.E. wagons: includes for Royal and Royal S.E. plus: full length headling with insulation. For Custom wagons: included items for Custom S.E. plus: interior lower trip panels in passenger compartment (in blue or cashmere); color-keyed garnish trim over front door headers and around headliner and rear compartment window; dash liner insulation; sliding door track cover. EIGHT-PASSENGER SEATING PACKAGE: (B250, B350 Wagon and Maxi-wagon models) included one additional quick release three-passenger bench seat with three seat belts. QUAD SEATING PACKAGE. EIGHT-PASSENGER TRAVEL SEATING PACKAGE. FIVE, SEVEN OR EIGHT-PASSENGER CONVERT-A-BED SEATING PACKAGES. TWELVE-PASSENGER SEATING PACKAGE: 127.6 in. w.b. Maxiwagons only (required window retention and rear door(s) with optional vented glass at extra cost) included three additional bench seats: 2nd (3-pass.), 3rd (3-pass.), 4th (4-pass.); tire carrier relocated under 4th bench seat; 8510 lb. GVW package. CONVENIENCE PACKAGE: cigar lighter; glove box lock. 10 in. day/night rearview mirror; cigar lighter light; automatic door switches for interior dome lights; courtesy step well lamp (front and side doors). LIGHT-DUTY TRAILER TOWING PACKAGE: (required automatic transmission and 36-gallon fuel tank) maximum cooling; heavy-duty variable load flasher; seven wire harness; bright hitch type rear bumper; Class I ball hitch. HEAVY-DUTY TRAILER TOWING PACKAGE: (B250, B350) (required automatic transmission, V-8 engine, transmission auxiliary air cooler and 36-gallon fuel tank) maximum cooling; 100-amp alternator; 430 amp Cold Crank battery; seven-wire harness; Class IV tow bar hitch (load equalizing); heavy-duty variable load flasher; heavy-duty front and rear shocks.

NOTE: 1981 Dodge Van exterior color included: Cashmere, Graphic Yellow, Impact Orange, Impact Red, Medium Crimson Red, Coffee Brown Metallic, Impact Blue, Nightwatch Blue, Light Seaspray Green Metallic, Medium Seaspray Green Metallic, Daystar Blue Metallic, Bright Silver Metallic, Pearl White, Black. 1981 Dodge Wagon exterior color choices were: Cashmere, Graphic Yellow (n.a. on Royal or Royal S.E.), Impact Red, Medium Crimson Red, Ginger (n.a. on Royal or Royal S.E.),

Coffee Brown Metallic, Impact Blue (n.a. on Royal or Royal S.E.), Nightwatch Blue, Medium Seaspray Green Metallic (n.a. on Royal or Royal S.E.), Bright Silver Metallic, Daystar Blue Metallic, Pearl White, Black.

1981 Dodge Power Ram Sweptline Pickup (DNP)

D150 SERIES — CUSTOM PICKUP: — Full-size Dodge pickups received an attractive new look for 1981. The exterior featured new aerodynamic styling. The grille had a rectangular sections theme and was bordered on each end by a slightly recessed single rectangular headlight. Amber parking lights were beneath each headlight. "Dodge" was spelled in block letters on the center face of the hood. Side marker lights were located on the lower section of the front fender, between the bumper and wheel well opening. The redesigned tailgate had caliper latches to make it easier to open and close. The instrument panel was also new. Among standard features were: All-vinyl bench seat in black, blue, cashmere, or red. Glove box. Built in dash map light. Independent front suspension. 20-gallon fuel tank. Energy absorbing steering column. Front disc brakes. Bright front bumper (painted on cab and chassis models). Cleaner air system. Coolant reserve system. Insulated dash liner. Color-keyed door interior trim panels and armrests. Black floor mat with padding. Fresh air heater with defrosters. Single electric horn. Bright hub caps. Padded instrument panel. Dual bright finish short-arm outside rearview mirrors. 10 in. inside rearview mirror. AM radio. Color-keyed sun visors. Traffic hazard warning switch. Dual jet windshield washers. Two-speed windshield wipers. The D150 Custom pickup was offered in four w.b. and with "smooth side" Sweptline or "rear fendered" Utiline pickup boxes. Buyers had their choice of conventional or club cabs. The Club Cab had 34 cu. ft. of in cab storage space behind the front seat.

I.D. DATA (D150): There were 17 symbols in the V.I.N. The first three identified the manufacturer, make and type of vehicle. Next was the letter which represented the GVW range. After that came three characters which identified series and body style. After that was the character that identified the engine. It was followed by a check digit, which in turn was followed by a letter representing the model year and a character which identified the assembly plant. The last six digits were sequential production numbers.

Model	Body Type	Price	Weight	Prod. Total
D150	Pickup (6½-ft. Utiline)	5997	3259	—
D150	Pickup (6½-ft. Sweptline)	5997	3239	—
D150	Pickup (8-ft. Utiline)	6085	3369	—
D150	Pickup (8-ft. Sweptline)	6085	3339	—
D150	Pickup (6½-ft. Club Cab)	7232	3657	—
D150	Pickup (8-ft. Club Cab)	7328	3786	—

ENGINE (D150): 3.7L (225 cu. in.) Slant six-cylinder. Brake horsepower: 95 at 3600 R.P.M. Bore & stroke: 3.40 x 4.12 in. Compression ratio: 8.4:1. Carburetor: 1-bbl. (Conventional Cab).

ENGINE: 5.2L (318 cu. in.) V-8. Brake horsepower: 135 at 4000 R.P.M. Bore & stroke: 3.91 x 3.31. Compression ratio: 8.5:1. Carburetor: 2-bbl. (Club Cab). N.A. in CA.

D250 CUSTOM PICKUP: The D250 was basically a ¾-ton version of the ½-ton D150. It came with most of the same standard features, but could haul heavier loads. It was offered in three w.b. and with conventional, club or 6-passenger crew cabs. The 149 in. w.b. Crew Cab had a 6½-ft. box. The 165 in. w.b. Crew Cab had an 8-ft. box.

I.D. DATA (D250 Custom): See D150 I.D.

Model	Body Type	Price	Weight	Prod. Total
D250	Chassis w/cab	7079	3485	—
D250	Pickup (8-ft. Utiline)	6744	3756	—
D2500	Pickup (8-ft. Sweptline)	6744	3726	—
D250	Pickup (8-ft. Club Cab)	7753	3966	—
D250	Pickup (6½-ft. Crew Cab)	8421	4232	—
D250	Pickup (8-ft. Crew Cab)	8500	4490	—

ENGINE (D250 Custom): Same as D150.

D350 CUSTOM PICKUP: The husky 1-ton D350 had most of the same standard features as the other series. In addition it had a heavier duty front axle, and rear springs. It was available in three w.b. and with conventional, club or crew cabs. The Crew Cab had dual rear wheels.

I.D. DATA (D350 Custom): See D150 I.D.

Model	Body Type	Price	Weight	Prod. Total
D350 Series — (131 in. w.b.)				
D350	Chassis w/cab	6862	3688	—
(135 in. w.b.)				
D350	Chassis w/cab	7503	4002	—
D350	Pickup (8-ft. Sweptline)	7301	4002	—
D350	Pickup (8-ft. Club Cab)	7867	4371	—
(159 in. w.b.)				
D350	Chassis w/cab	7588	3876	—
D350	Pickup (Crew Cab)	9367	4781	—

ENGINE (D350 Custom): 5.2L (318 cu. in.) V-8. Brake horsepower: 160 at 4000 R.P.M. Bore & stroke: 3.91 x 3.31. Compression ratio: 8.0:1. Carburetor: 4-bbl.

D450 CUSTOM CHASSIS & CAB: The D450 was only available with a conventional cab. It came with most of the same standard features offered on the D350, but had a higher maximum payload capacity. Dual rear wheels were standard.

I.D. DATA (D450 Custom): See D150.

Model	Body Type	Price	Weight	Prod. Total
D450 Series — (135 in. w.b.)				
D450	Chassis w/cab	9057	3861	—
(159 in. w.b.)				
D450	Chassis w/cab	9114	3870	—

ENGINE (D450 Custom): 5.9L (360 cu. in.) V-8. Brake horsepower: 175 at 4000 R.P.M. Bore & stroke: 4.0 x 3.58 in. Compression ratio: 8.0:1. Carburetor: 4-bbl.

CHASSIS FEATURES: Wheelbase 115 in. (D150), 131 in. (D150, D250, D350), 133 in. (D150 Club Cab), 135 in. (D450), 149 in. (D150, D250, D350), 159 in. (D450), 165 in. (D250 & D350 Crew Cab). Overall width: 79.5 in. (94.2 in. models with dual rear wheels). Overall length: 190.78 in. (D150 Conv Cab 115 in. w.b.), 210.78 in. (131 in. w.b. Conv Cab), 208.78 in. (133 in. w.b. Club Cab), 228.81 in. (149 in. Club Cab) 224.78 in. (149 in. w.b. Crew Cab), 244.78 in. (165 in. w.b. Crew Cab). GVW: 4800-6010 lbs. (D150), 6050 lbs. (W150), 6500-8550 lbs. (D250), 6900-8550 lbs. (W250), 9000-10,000 lbs. (D350), 10,000 (W350 Chas. w/cab), 10,500 lbs. (D450), 11,000 lbs. (W450). Tires: P195/75R x 15 (D150 Conv Cab), P235/75R x 15 (D150 Club Cab), 8.00 x 16.5D (D250 Conv Cab, D350 Crew Cab), 8.75 x 16.5E (D250 Club Cab), 9.50 x 16.5E (D250 Crew Cab), 9.50 x 16.5E (D350), 8.00 x 16E (D450).

POWERTRAIN OPTIONS: 5.2L (318 cu. in.) Carburetor: 2-bbl. V-8 (D150, D250, W150), 5.2L (318 cu. in.) Carburetor: 4-bbl. V-8 (D150, D250, W150, W250), 5.9L (360 cu. in.) Carburetor: 4-bbl. V-8 (D150, D250, D350, W150, W250). 4-speed manual NP435 (D150 Conventional Cab, 4-speed manual with overdrive was standard), 3-speed automatic.

OPTION PACKAGES: FOUR-WHEEL DRIVE: (Pickups: W150, W250. Chassis w/cab: W250, W350, W450. Called "Power Rams". Had most of the features found on the 2wd models plus (or in place of): Power steering, part-time 4wd, 2-speed transfer case, front wheel locking hubs, leaf spring front suspension. STAKE BODY: An 8 ft. stake body was available on D250, D350 and W250; a 9½-ft. body was available on D350, D450, W350, and W450; a 12½-ft. stake body was available on D350 and D450. SNO-COMMANDER PACKAGE: factory installed snow removal package with power angling blade with positive instrument panel mounted fingertip controls; seven way control valve, power lift, and plow lights. RETRIEVER WRECKER: complete wrecker with 5-ton capacity winch, rapid-shift winch control, tow bar with sling and towing chains, large-capacity deck-mounted tool box, sentry signal switch panel, and power take off assembly. D350 DYNA-TRAC: dual rear wheels, a 6900 lb. rear axle and a GVW rating of 10,000 lbs. CUSTOM S.E. PACKAGE: (n.a. on Club or Crew cabs) bright windshield, backlight, drip rail, and taillamp trim; plaque on front fender with "leaping Ram" and "Custom S.E."; bench seat color-keyed with hinged seat back and cloth and vinyl trim; nameplate on instrument panel; bright seatback hinge cover; front door bright trim applique and pull strap; carpeting with underlayment; cigar lighter. ROYAL PACKAGE: (in addition to or in place of items in Custom S.E. Package) upper and lower tailgate molding (Sweptlines); deluxe vinyl trimmed bench seat; two jump seats (Club Cab), bright seat back hinge cover for rear seat of Crew Cabs; carpeting on lower portion of door; woodgrain instrument cluster faceplate; black steering wheel horn pad with woodgrain insert; bright door sill scuff plates (front door only); color-keyed soft headliner (n.a. Crew Cabs); garnish trim over windshield, front pillar, door header, quarter trim panel upper and over backlight (n.a. Crew Cab); cowl side trim panels; dome lamp mounted center of roof (Club Cabs); insulation under hood panel. ROYAL S.E. PACKAGE: (in addition to or in place of items in Royal Package) Ram's head hood ornament; "Dodge Ram" nameplate on Sweptline pickup tailgate; flipout quarter window with banded glass (Club Cab pickups); dual horns; bright aluminum grille with chrome plastic insert and headlamp doors; power steering; bright tailgate applique panel (Sweptlines); deluxe cloth and vinyl trimmed bench seat; front door woodgrain trim applique, assist strap and carpeting on lower portion; Black leather wrapped steering wheel; oil pressure and engine temperature gauges; trip odometer. MACHO PACKAGE: two-tone paint scheme, bold body striping, orange painted spoke road wheels, raised outline white letter steel-belted radial tires, roll bar, black front and rear bumpers.

CONVENIENCE OPTIONS: Air conditioning. Heavy-duty alternators and batteries. Painted or bright bumpers. Rear hitch type bumper. Rear step type bumper. Cigar lighter. Electric clock. Maximum cooling. Auxiliary cooling. 30-gallon fuel tank. Oil pressure, engine temperature, and trip odometer gauges. Tinted glass. Halogen headlights. Headliner. Deluxe heater. Engine block heater. Dual electric horns. Front clearance and identification lights. In cab hood release. Dual low mount and low mount extended mirrors. Upper, lower or upper and lower moldings. Electric door locks. Power steering. Power windows. RADIOS: AM/FM, AM/FM stereo, AM/FM stereo w/8-Track, AM/FM stereo with CB, AM/FM stereo with

Search-Tune. Flip type seats (with Club Cab models). Heavy-duty shocks. Sky Lite sun roof. Spare tire carrier. Speed control. Sport bar. Stabilizer bar. Tilt steering column. Sport steering wheel. Unibelt restraint system (color-keyed). Road type wheels. Aluminum radial ribbed wheels. Chrome disc (5-slot) wheels. Painted steel spoke (white) wheels. Wheel covers. Sliding rear window. Rear quarter flip-out window (Club Cabs). Two-speed windshield wipers with intermittent wipe. Skid plate.

NOTE: Exterior colors for full-size 1981 Dodge trucks were: Cashmere, Graphic Yellow, Impact Orange, Impact Red, Medium Crimson Red, Ginger, Coffee Brown Metallic, Daystar Blue Metallic, Impact Blue, Night watch Blue, Light Seaspray Green Metallic, Medium Seaspray Green Metallic, Bright Silver Metallic, Pearl White, Black.

1982 DODGE

RAMPAGE HIGH-LINE PICKUP: — The new Rampage was the first front-wheel drive pickup to be offered by one of the Big Three auto-makers. It combined the comfort and conveniences of a passenger car with the utility of a pickup. It shared front end styling with the Dodge Charger. Sloping hood, deeply recessed rectangular headlights, bumper integrated rectangular slots theme grille, "smooth side" Sweptline box, and large rectangular taillights were styling highlights. Among standard features on the Rampage High-Line were: Four-speed transaxle with 3.13 O.T.G. ratio. McPherson-type Iso-strut front suspension with linkless sway bar. Mini-module fan assembly. Power disc brakes. Tinted glass. Bright sill, wheel lip and belt moldings. Left hand remote control mirror. Color-keyed spot steering wheel. Dual horns. Front and rear bumper rub strips. AM ratio. Rallye wheel dressup. Day/night inside mirror. Glove box lock. Cigar lighter. Inside hood release. Black belt, windshield, and backlight moldings. Key-in-ignition buzzer. Dome lamp. Black door handle inserts. All vinyl custom level high-back bucket seats and all vinyl Custom door trim. Uni-body construction.

1982 Dodge Rampage Sport Mini-Pickup (DNP)

RAMPAGE SPORT PICKUP: — The Sport came with many of the same features as the High-Line plus (or in place of): Two-tone paint and tape treatment. Lower sill blackout. 14 in. color-keyed rallye wheels. Black letter tires. Cargo box flange trim molding. Contoured cloth covered sport bucket seats with adjustable seat backs. Sport door trim. Shift lever console. Rallye cluster with tach, clock, odometer.

I.D. DATA (Rampage): See D150 I.D.

Model	Body Type	Price	Weight	Prod. Total
ZH28	Pickup	6698	2246	—
ZS28	PU (Sport)	7204	2293	—

ENGINE (Rampage): 2.2L (135 cu. in.) Four-cylinder. Brake horsepower: 84 at 4800 R.P.M. Bore & stroke: 3.44 x 3.62. Compression ratio: 8.5:1. Carburetor: 2-bbl.

CHASSIS FEATURES Wheelbase: 104.2 in. Overall length: 183.6 in. Overall width: 66.8 in. Overal height: 51.8 in. GVW: 3450 lbs. Tires: P175/75 R13 (High-Line), P195/60 R14 (Sport).

POWERTRAIN OPTIONS: TorqueFlite automatic.

CONVENIENCE OPTIONS: Air conditioning. Intermittent wipers. Heavy-duty battery. Tonneau cover. Power steering. Clock (High-Line). Heavy-duty cooling. Undercoating. Automatic speed control. Engine block heater. Rally cluster (High-Line). 14 in. road wheels. Cloth and vinyl bucket seats (High-Line). Light package. Cargo box side rails. Dual remote control mirrors. Popular equipment package. Console (High-Line). Radios: AM/FM Stereo, AM/FM Stereo with cassette player, AM/FM Stereo with 8-track tape player.

NOTE: Rampage High-Line exterior colors for 1982 included: Graphic Red, Spice Tan, Manila Cream, Black, Burnished Silver, and Charcoal Gray. Sport models were offered in: Graphic Red, Black, Silver, and Charcoal Gray; and two-tone combinations of Graphic Red upper with a Spitfire Orange lower and accent tape, and Black upper with Silver lower with a Black tape.

240

RAM 50 CUSTOM PICKUP: — While basic styling was unchanged, the 1982 Ram 50 did receive a new, blacked out grille and headlamp trim. Also, the "Ram" name on the front fenders was now placed ahead of side badge. Among standard features were: Argent painted front bumper with black rubber ends. Cargo lamp. Cigarette lighter. Dome light with driver and passenger side door switches. Emergency flashers. 18-gallon fuel tank. Tinted glass. Color-keyed headliner. Inside hood release. Bright hub caps. Left and right sides black sport type exterior mirrors. Bright windshield molding. AM radio. Adjustable angle steering column. Dual sun visors. Trip odometer. Two-speed windshield wipers with washers. Four-speed manual transmission. This year for the first time, the Ram 50 Custom was available with 4wd drive. The 4 x 4 version had most of the same standard features as the 2wd version plus all-terrain tires and power steering.

RAM 50 ROYAL PICKUP: — The Royal had more deluxe interior and exterior trim than the Custom. White sidewall tires, chrome front bumper, and carpeting were just a few of its luxury touches. It also came with a 5-speed manual transmission.

RAM 50 SPORT PICKUP: — The Sport had the most flair of any Ram 50 pickup. In addition to many of the items standard on the Custom, it also had: Center console with oil pressure gauge, ammeter and (5-speed manual) transmission shift lever. AM/FM Stereo radio. Wide spoke road wheels. Tape stripe. Bucket seats. Like the Custom, it was also available with 4wd.

Model	Body Type	Price	Weight	Prod. Total
9JL4	Pickup (Custom)	6408	2573	—
9JL4	Pickup (Custom 4wd)	8361	—	—
9JH4	Pickup (Royal)	6892	—	—
9JP4	Pickup (Sport)	7474	2648	—
9JP4	Pickup (Sport 4wd)	9245	—	—

ENGINE (Ram 50): 2.0L (122 cu. in.) OHC four-cylinder. Brake horsepower: 90 at 5000 R.P.M. Bore & stroke: 3.30 x 3.54. Compression ratio: 8.5:1. Carburetor: 2-bbl. (Custom). 2.6L (156 cu. in.) four-cylinder. Brake horsepower: 105 at 5000 R.P.M.. Bore & stroke: 3.59 x 3.86. Compression ratio: 8.2:1. Carburetor: 2-bbl. (Royal, Sport).

CHASSIS FEATURES Wheelbase: 109.4 (2wd), 109.8 in. (4wd). Overall length: 184.6 in. Overall height: 60.6 in. (Custom), 59.8 in. (Royal, Sport). Overall width: 65 in. GVW: 4045-4120 lbs. Tires: 6.00 x 14C (Custom), 185SR14 SBR (Royal, Sport).

POWERTRAIN OPTIONS: Three-speed automatic transmission. 5-speed manual transmission (Custom).

CONVENIENCE OPTIONS: 4wd: (Custom, Sport) power steering, aluminum transfer case, Power Ram emblems. Air conditioning. Chrome rear step bumper. Low-luster black rear step bumper. Electronic digital clock. Front floor mats. Grille guard. Bright low-mount exterior mirrors. Vinyl body side molding. Front and rear wheel openings moldings. Mud guards. Power steering. Sliding rear window. Automatic speed control. Sport bar. Sun roof. Pickup bed liner. Body side tape stripe.

NOTE: The Power Ram 50 4wd pickup was named "Four-Wheeler of the Year" by *Four Wheeler* and *Off Road* magazine.

1982 Dodge 4x4 Ramcharger Royal SE (DNP)

RAMCHARGER SPORT UTILITY VEHICLE: — Styling was carried over from 1981. As before, both 2wd (AD150) and part-time 4wd (AW150) were offered. With its transfer case shift selector in the "two-wheel high" mode, the 4wd could drive with rear power only. When the system was in 2wd, the front axle was disconnected and not in operation. Among standard Ramcharger features were: Dry type air cleaner. Ash tray. Bright front and rear bumpers. Automatic choke. Cigar lighter. Insulated dash liner. Cleaner air system. Coolant reserve system. Color-keyed inner door trim panels and arm rests. Electronic ignition system. Black floor mat. 35-gallon fuel tank. Tinted glass (all windows). Glove box. Aluminum grille surround molding with painted plastic insert and headlamp doors. Fresh air heater with defrosters. Insulated hood pad. In cab hood release. Dual electric horns. Bright hubcaps. Front wheel automatic-locking type hubs (4wd). Speedometer, odometer, ammeter, fuel gauge, oil pressure and engine temperature indicator lights. Dual bright finish short arm 5" x 7" exterior mirrors. 10" day/night interior rearview mirror. Bright quarter side window and windshield moldings. Power front disc brakes. Power steering. AM radio. Rear roof vent. Deluxe vinyl low-back front bucket seats. Inside spare tire mounting. Front stabilizer bar (4wd). Sun visors. Dual jet windshield washers. Two-speed windshield wipers. Three-speed automatic transmission (2wd). 4-speed manual (4wd).

Model	Body Type	Price	Weight	Prod. Total
AD150	Utility	8989	—	—
AW150	Utility (4wd)	10,095	4163	—

ENGINE (Ramcharger): 5.2 liter (318 cu. in.) V-8. Brake horsepower: 120 at 3600 R.P.M. Bore & stroke: 3.91 x 3.31. Compression ratio: 8.5:1. Carburetor: 2-bbl. (This engine was not available in 4wd Ramchargers.)

CHASSIS FEATURES Wheelbase: 106 in. Overall length: 184.6 in. (without bumper guards), 186.1 in. (with bumper guards). Overall width: 79.5 in. GVW 5300 lbs. (2wd), 5850 lbs. (4wd). Tires: P235/75R15 BSW GBR.

POWERTRAIN OPTIONS: 5.2L (318 cu. in.) 4-bbl. V-8 (4wd). Three-speed TorqueFlite automatic (4wd).

OPTION PACKAGES: SNO-COMMANDER PACKAGE: (4wd only) power angling blade with blade markers; hydro/electric controls; powerlift; plow lights; 114-amp alternator; 500-amp maintenance free battery; maximum engine cooling; Sno-Commander decal; transmission oil temperature light with automatic transmission. SNO-PREPARATION PACKAGE: (4wd only) 114-amp alternator; 500-amp maintenance free battery; maximum engine cooling. CONVENIENCE PACKAGE: Halogen headlamps; glove box lock and light; ash receiver light; two-speed windshield wipers with intermittent wipe. RAMCHARGER ROYAL S.E.: bright drip rail molding; bright taillamp housing; Ram's head hood ornament; Leaping Ram with "150 Royal S.E." plaque on front fender; bright aluminum grille surrounded with chromed plastic insert and bright headlamp doors; liftgate upper and lower moldings with brushed finish applique panel; woodgrain interior door trim applique, assist straps, carpeting on lower door panel; driver and front passenger high-back Command bucket seats with cloth and vinyl trim (included inboard fold-down arm rests on seats, and lockable console with removable styrofoam beverage chest); folding rear bench seat with cloth and vinyl trim; color-keyed carpeting with underlayment; color-keyed cowl side trim panels; color keyed rear side and liftgate inner trim panels; woodtone instrument cluster faceplate; nameplate on instrument panel; luxury steering wheel with woodtone insert around rim; color-keyed spare tire cover (n.a. with 10R15LT tires); bright front door sill scuff plate; oil pressure and engine temperature gauges; trip odometer. FILIGREE STRIPE PACKAGE: included bodyside, wheel lip and hood stripes; light-reflective stripe decal with Dodge Ram on liftgate. HEAVY-DUTY TRAILER TOWING PACKAGE: (4wd only) maximum cooling; 60-amp alternator; 430-amp maintenance free battery; seven wire harness; class IV tow bar hitch; heavy-duty variable load turn signal flasher; heavy-duty front and rear shocks; heavy-duty front stabilizer bar.

CONVENIENCE OPTIONS: Air conditioning. Heavy-duty alternators and batteries. Painted step type rear bumper. Front bumper and guards with rub strips and rear bumper with rub strips. Electronic digital clock. Auxiliary transmission oil to air cooler. Maximum cooling. Oil pressure and engine temperature gauges. Trip odometer. Bright grille insert and bright headlamp doors (included Rams head hood ornament). Deluxe bi-level heater. Engine block heater. Dual bright 6 x 9 in. low mount mirrors. Dual bright 7½ x 10½ in. low mount extended mirrors. Bright lower molding with black vinyl insert and integral wheel lip moldings. Lower and upper moldings. Bright upper moldings. Power door locks. Power windows. AM/FM Stereo Radios: with cassette tape player and deleting, with 8-track tape player, with Search-Tune and electronic tuning, with 40-channel CB transceiver. Heavy-duty front and rear shocks. Fuel tank shield. Transfer case skid plate (4wd). Automatic speed control. Sport bar. Front stabilizer bar. Heavy-duty front stabilizer bar (4wd). Tilt steering column (automatic transmission required). Luxury steering wheel. Privacy glass sun screen. Various tires. Deluxe bright wheel covers. Wheels: aluminum radial ribbed; 5-slot chrome disc (n.a. on 4wd); white painted steel spoke (n.a. on 2wd). Two-speed windshield wipers with intermittent wipe. Deluxe split-back front bench seat in red, cashmere or blue.

NOTE: Exterior colors available on 1982 Ramchargers included: Burnished Silver Metallic, Medium Seaspray Green Metallic, Daystar Blue Metallic, Cashmere, Pear White, Impact Red, Ginger, Morocco Red, Black, Charcoal Grey Metallic, Dark Blue Metallic, Manila Cream, Spice Tan Metallic.

B150 VAN: — Basic styling was unchanged for 1982. Among standard features were: brake system warning light. Dual braking system with separate brake fluid reservoirs in the master cylinder. Dry type air cleaner. 53-amp alternator. Driver and front passenger arm rests. Ashtray. 325-amp battery. Power front disc brakes (except 109.6 in. w.b. and 127.6 in. w.b. with 4700 lb. GVW). Painted front and rear bumpers. Double hinged type cargo doors on right side and rear (no glass). Cigar lighter. Electronic ignition system. Driver's compartment floor mat. 22-gallon fuel tank. Glove box. Argent finish grille. 7 in. round headlights. Hardboard headliner in driver's compartment (white). In-cab actuated hood release. Color-keyed horn pad. Dual electric horns. Bright finish hub caps. Ammeter, fuel gauge, oil pressure indicator light, speedometer, temperature gauge. Dual bright 5 x 7 in. exterior mirrors. AM radio. Drivers low-back bucket seat with vinyl trim. Driver's side sun visor. Spare tire carrier. Traffic hazard warning switch. Two-speed non-intermittent wet arm windshield wipers with washers. The Long Range Ram Van came with most of the same features plus (or in place of): 36-gallon fuel tank. Bright front and rear bumpers. Bright wheelcovers, windshield molding, taillamp bezels and grille with quad headlamps. 109.6 in. w.b.

B150 WAGON: — Last year's attractive styling was retained for the new 1982 B150 Wagons. It came with most of the same standard features as the B150 van plus (or in place of): Air vent doors. Right side double doors with vented glass. Single rear door with fixed glass and inside door handle and lock button. Black full width floor mat. Color-keyed driver's compartment headliner. Fresh air heater with defroster. 10 in. day/night inside rearview mirror. Power steering. Driver and front passenger low-back vinyl bucket seats in blue or cashmere. Three-passenger matching rear bench seat. Two sun visors. Glass all around. 4-speed manual with overdrive transmission.

1982 Dodge Mini Ram Van (DNP)

B150 MINI-RAM WAGON: — The unchanged Mini-Ram Wagon came with such features as: Five passenger seating. Bright grille. Bright front and rear bumpers. Bright wheel covers body side windows and rear window moldings. 36-gallon fuel tank. Interior lower vinyl trim panels. Convenience Package. Intermittent type windshield wipers. Full length color-keyed headliner. 109.6 in. w.b.

I.D. DATA (B150): See D150 I.D.

Model	Body Type	Price	Weight	Prod. Total
B150	Van (109.6 in. w.b.)	7046	3286	—
B150	Van (127.6 in. w.b.)	—	—	—
B150	Long Range Van	6928	—	—
B150	Wagon (109.6 in. w.b.)	8482	3604	—
B150	Wagon (109.6 in. w.b.)	—	—	—
B150	Wagon (127.6 in. w.b.)	—	—	—

ENGINE (B150): 3.7-liter (225 cu. in.) Six-cylinder. Brake horsepower: 95 at 3600 R.P.M. Bore & stroke: 3.40 x 4.12. Compression ratio: 8.4:1. Carburetor: 1-bbl.

ENGINE (B250 Van): The B250 shared most of the same standard features offered on the B150 (plus power steering). It was a bit more heavy-duty and could be ordered with the extra long "Maxi" body.

ENGINE (B250 Wagon): The ¾-ton B250 wagon had most of the same standard features as the B150. It was offered in regular or extra long Maxi bodies. Maxiwagons came with a three-speed TorqueFlite automatic transmission.

ENGINE (B250 Mini-Ram Wagon): This was a slightly heavier-duty version of the B150 Mini-Ram Wagon. It came with the same standard features plus 8-passenger seating.

I.D. DATA (B250): See D150 I.D.

Model	Body Type	Price	Weight	Prod. Total
B250	Van (109.6 in. w.b.)	7578	3447	—
B250	Van (127.6 in. w.b.)	—	—	—
B250	Maxivan	—	—	—
B250	Wagon (109.6 in. w.b.)	8482	3769	—
B250	Wagon (127.6 in. w.b.)	—	—	—
B250	Maxiwagon	—	—	—
B250	Mini-Ram Van	9046	—	—

ENGINE (B250): Same as B150.

ENGINE (Van): The 1-ton B350 had most of the same standard features as the B150 plus (or in place of): Larger brakes. Power steering. Axle type jack. Three-speed automatic transmission. Both regular and extended Maxivan bodies were offered.

ENGINE (B350 Wagon): This was Dodge's most heavy-duty people hauler. Most standard features echoed those of the B150 wagons. It was available in regular or Maxiwagon bodies.

I.D. DATA (B350): See D150 I.D.

Model	Body Type	Price	Weight	Prod. Total
B350	Van	8929	3891	—
B350	Maxivan	—	—	—
B350	Wagon	10,159	4249	—
B350	Maxiwagon	—	—	—

ENGINE (B350): 5.2-liter (318 cu. in.) V-8, Brake horsepower: 135 at 4000 R.P.M. Compression ratio: 8.5:1. Bore & stroke: 3.91 x 3.31. Carburetor: 2-bbl. (n.a. in compression ratio).

CHASSIS FEATURES Wheelbase: 109.6 in. (B150, B250), 127.6 in. Overall length: 178.9 in. (109.6 in. w.b.), 196.9 in. (127.6 in. w.b.), 222.9 in. (Maxivan/wagon). Overall width: 79.8 in. Overall height: 79.6 in. (109.6 in. w.b.), 80.6 in. (Maxivan/wagon), 80.9 in. (127.6 in. w.b.). GVW: 4700-5300 lbs. (B150), 6010-6400 lbs. (B250), 7500-9000 lbs. (B350). Tires: P195/75R15 or P205/75R15 (B150), P225/65R15 or P235/75R15 (B250), P235/75R15XL (B250 Maxivan/wagon), 8.00-16.5E or 8.75-16.5E (B350).

POWERTRAIN OPTIONS: 5.2L (318 cu. in.) 2-bbl. V-8 (B150, B250), 5.2L 4-bbl. V-8, 5.9L (360 cu. in.) 4-bbl. V-8 (B350). Three-speed automatic transmission (B150, B250).

VAN OPTION PACKAGES: CONVENIENCE PACKAGE: cigar lighter light; courtesy step well lamp for front and side doors (for use with Royal interior package only); glove box lock and light; ignition and headlight switch with time delay (n.a. with tilt steering column); two-speed windshield wipers with intermittent wipe. EXTERIOR APPEARANCE PACKAGE: bright grille; dual vertically stacked quad rectangular headlamps with Halogen highbeams; bright front and rear bumpers; bright taillamp bezels; bright body-side and rear window molding for Van Window Packages; bright windshield molding. ROYAL INTERIOR PACKAGE: bucket seat floor risers; electronic digital clock; color-keyed carpeting in driver's compartment; color-keyed instrument panel with woodtone applique; instrument panel lower skirts (left and right sides); color-keyed vinyl front door trim panels with woodtone applique and chrome-trimmed arm rest base; deluxe vinyl-trimmed low-back driver's seat; instrument panel nameplate; insulated dash liner; insulated headliner in driver's compartment; luxury steering wheel with woodtone insert around rim; moldings over front pillars, front door headers and around windshield; power steering (on B150 models); scuff pads. HEAVY-DUTY TRAILER TOWING PACKAGE: (B250, B350) (required at extra cost: 318 4-bbl. V-8, or 360 4-bbl. V-8, automatic transmission, transmission auxiliary oil cooler and 36-gallon fuel tank) 60-amp alternator; 430-amp battery; maximum engine cooling; seven-wire harness; heavy-duty front and rear shocks; tow bar hitch; heavy-duty variable load flasher. LOCK PACKAGE: two keys: one operated ignition and front doors; one operated side and rear doors. WAGON OPTION PACKAGES: ROYAL PACKAGE: (n.a. on Mini-Ram Wagon) Royal nameplates; bright lower side and rear moldings; dual vertically stacked quad rectangular headlamps with Halogen high beams and bright grille; bright front and rear bumpers; bright molding around windshield, side and rear windows (except driver and passenger door windows); bright taillamp bezels; woodtone applique on lower face of instrument panel; color-keyed spare tire cover; vinyl door and side trim panels with woodtone trim; garnish moldings over front doors, passenger compartment windows, headers around rear compartment windows and front pillar and windshield; driver and front passenger low-back bucket seats and bench seat in deluxe vinyl trim (blue, cashmere, or red); soft cloth-covered headliner with insulation; accessory floor mats in driver's compartments; electronic digital clock; instrument panel lower skirts; color-keyed garnish; dash liner insulation; luxury steering wheel with woodtone trim. ROYAL S.E. PACKAGE: (n.a. Mini-Ram Wagon) included items listed for Royal Package plus: Royal S.E. nameplates; bright upper side and rear moldings; bright bumper guards with rub strips, front and rear, body side and rear woodtone tape applique with dual gold accent strips; vinyl door and side trim panels with woodtone trim and front door applique pull straps; carpeted engine housing cover (color-keyed); oil pressure gauge and trip odometer; glove box lock and light; deluxe two-speed windshield wipers with intermittent wipe; ignition and headlight switch with time delay; cigar lighter light; courtesy step well lamp (front and side doors); driver and front passenger color-keyed high-back reclining Command bucket seats and a three-passenger bench seat with plaid cloth and vinyl trim (blue, cashmere, red or silver). EXTERIOR APPEARANCE PACKAGE: bright grille; bright front and rear bumpers; bright taillamp bezels; bright windshield molding; dual vertically stacked quad rectangular headlamps with Halogen high beams; bright side and rear window moldings (except driver and front passenger door windows). INSULATION PACKAGE: Royal and Royal S.E. Wagons: interior lower fiberglass insulation panels (not on standard single rear door or optional sliding side door); insulation under floor covering. Custom Wagons: included items in Royal and Royal S.E. insulation package plus interior lower trim panels in passenger compartment (in blue or cashmere); color-keyed garnish moldings over front door headers and around headliner and rear compartment window; dash liner insulation; sliding side door track cover; white hardboard headliner in passenger compartment. EIGHT-PASSENGER SEATING PACKAGE: (B250, B350 Wagon and Maxiwagon) included one additional quick-release three-passenger bench seat with three seat belts; not available on B350 Maxiwagons with 8,510 lb. GVW Package. QUAD COMMAND SEATING PACKAGES. FIVE OR EIGHT-PASSENGER CONVERT-A-BED SEATING PACKAGES. EIGHT-PASSENGER TRAVEL SEATING PACKAGE. TWELVE PASSENGER SEATING PACKAGE: (B350) (required window retention and rear door(s) with optional vented glass at extra cost) included two additional bench seats; 2nd (3-pass.); 3rd (4-pass.); spare tire carrier relocated under 3rd bench seat; n.a. on B350 Maxiwagon models with 8,510 lb. GVW Package. FIFTEEN-PASSENGER SEATING PACKAGE: (B350 Maxiwagons only) (required 8,510 lb. GVW Package, window retention and rear door(s) with optional vented glass at extra cost) included three additional bench seats; 2nd (3-pass.); 3rd (3-pass.); 4th (4-pass.); tire carrier relocated under 4th bench seat. HEAVY-DUTY TRAILER TOWING PACKAGE: (B250, B350) (n.a. Mini-Ram Wagon) (required automatic transmission on B250 models, 318 cu. in. 4-bbl. or 360 cu. in. V-8 engine, transmission auxiliary oil cooler and 36-gallon fuel tank) maximum cooling; 60-amp alternator; 430-amp battery; seven wire harness; Class IV tow bar hitch; heavy-duty variable load turn signal flasher; heavy-duty front and rear shock absorbers. CONVENIENCE PACKAGE: cigar lighter; glove box lock and light; ignition and headlight switch with time delay (n.a. with tilt steering column); two-speed windshield wipers with intermittent wipe; courtesy step well lamp for front and side doors (for use with Royal Package only).

VAN AND WAGON CONVENIENCE OPTIONS: Air conditioning. Heavy-duty alternators and batteries. Bright front and rear bumpers. Bright front and rear bumper guards and rub strips. Electronic digital clock. Auxiliary transmission oil to air cooling. Maximum engine cooling. Rear window defroster. Sliding passenger side door. Dual rear door with vented glass. Single rear door with vented glass. 36-gallon fuel tank. Oil pressure and trip odometer gauges. Sun screen privacy glass (wagon). Banded glass front door and vent window (Van). Tinted glass (all windows). Bright grille (included dual quad rectangular headlamps; vertically stacked, with Halogen high beams). Deluxe front heater. Auxiliary rear heater. Engine block heater. Two color-keyed accessory type rubber floor mats in drivers compartment. Dual bright low-mount 6 x 9 in. exterior mirrors. Lower molding (included side, rear and bright taillamp bezels). Upper moldings (included side, rear and bright taillamp bezels). Upper and lower moldings with bright taillamp bezels. Electronic monitor display warning indicator for engine oil level, transmission oil level, radiator coolant level, and transmission oil temperature. Power front door locks. Power front door windows.

Radios: AM/FM Stereo; AM/FM Stereo electronically tuned with cassette tape player and Dolby noise reduction system; AM/FM Stereo with Search-Tune and electronic tuning; AM/FM Stereo with eight track tape player; AM/FM Stereo with 40-channel CB transceiver. Heavy-duty shocks. Automatic speed control. Front stabilizer bar. Tilt steering column. Luxury type steering wheel. Radial ribbed aluminum wheels. Five-slot chrome disc wheels. Deluxe bright wheel covers. Deluxe two-speed windshield wipers with intermittent wipe.

NOTE: Dodge Van and Wagon exterior colors for 1982 were: Cashmere, Manila Cream, Charcoal Grey Metallic, Impact Red, Ginger, Morocco Red, Spice Tan Metallic, Dark Blue Metallic, Medium Seaspray Green Metallic, Daystar Blue Metallic, Burnished Silver Metallic, Pearl White, Black.

1982 Dodge D150 Custom Ram Sweptline Pickup (OCW)

D150 CUSTOM PICKUP: — Basic styling was unchanged for 1982. Standard features included: Independent front suspension. Energy absorbing steering column. Dry type air cleaner. Ashtray. Bright front bumper. Automatic choke. Cigar lighter. Cleaner air system. Coat hooks. Coolant reserve system. Dash and plenum liner. Door inner trim panels with pull straps and arm rests. Electronic ignition system. Black floor mat with padding (color-keyed carpeting on Miser models). 20-gallon fuel tank. Glove box. Aluminum grille with painted plastic insert and headlight doors. Fresh air heater with defrosters. In cab hood release. Dual electric horns. Bright hub caps. Padded instrument panel. Dual bright finish mirrors. 10 in. day/night interior rearview mirror. Bright windshield molding. Power front disc brakes (except D150 115 in. and 131 in. wheelbases with 4,800 lb. GVW). AM radio. All-vinyl bench seat in black, blue or cashmere (conventional Cab). Sun visors. Traffic hazard warning switch. Two-speed windshield wipers. Dual jet windshield washers. As before, D150 buyers could choose from Sweptline or Utiline boxes. And conventional or Club cabs. (Club cabs were only available with Sweptline boxes. Flip-out side windows and flip-down rear seats were now standard in Club Cabs. A special Miser model was offered. It had most of the same standard features found in the base D150 pickup plus: bright finish grille; bright wheel covers; Ram's head hood ornament, gold body-side tape stripes, deluxe pleated vinyl seat, woodtoned instrument panel, and color keyed carpeting.

I.D. DATA (D150): See 1981 D150 I.D.

1982 Dodge Ram Club Cab Sweptline Pickup (DNP)

Model	Body Type	Price	Weight	Prod. Total
D150	Pickup (6½' Utiline)	6847	3288	—
D150	Pickup (½' Sweptline)	6721	3268	—
D150	Pickup (8' Utiline)	6997	3398	—
D150	Pickup (8' Sweptline)	6871	3368	—
D150	Pickup (6½' Miser)	5899	3239	—
D150	Pickup (8' Miser)	5999	—	—
D150	Pickup (8' Club Cab)	8381	3927	—

ENGINE (D150 Custom): 3.7L (225 cu. in.) slant six-cylinder. Brake horsepower: 95 at 3600 R.P.M. Bore & stroke: 3.40 x 4.12. Compression ratio: 8.4:1. Carburetor: 1-bbl.

1982 Dodge Ram Sweptline Pickup (DNP)

ENGINE (Conventional Cab): 5.2L (318 cu. in.) V-8, Brake horsepower: 135 at 4000 R.P.M. Bore & stroke: 3.91 x 3.3a. Compression ratio: 8.5:1. Carburetor: 2-bbl.

ENGINE (Club Cab): 5.2L 2-bbl. V-8 (n.a. in Calif.)

ENGINE (D250 Custom Pickup): The ¾-ton D250 shared most standard features with the D150. It too was offered with conventional or Club cabs.

I.D. DATA (D250): See D150 I.D.

Model	Body Type	Price	Weight	Prod. Total
D250	Chas. w/cab	7860	3521	—
D250	Pickup (8' Utiline)	7754	3773	—
D250	Pickup (8' Sweptline)	7629	3743	—
D250	Pickup (8' Club Cab)	8859	4124	—

ENGINE (D250 Custom): Same as D150, except in Calif. There the 3.7L six-cylinder had 90 horsepower, and the 5.2L V-8 had 4-bbl. carburetor and 160 horsepower.

ENGINE (D350 Custom Pickup): The 1-ton D350 could be had with conventional, Club, or Crew cabs. The Crew Cab had four doors and could seat six passengers. The "smooth side" Sweptline was the only box available on D350's. Standard equipment echoed that on the D150. Although Crew Cabs (like Club Cabs) had deluxe vinyl split-back bench seats in blue, cashmere, red, or silver.

I.D. DATA (D350): See D150 I.D.

Model	Body Type	Price	Weight	Prod. Total
D350	Chas. w/cab (131" w.b.)	8234	3563	—
D350	Pickup (8' Swept)	8661	3958	—
D350	Chas. w/cab (135" w.b.)	8664	3865	—
D350	Pickup (Club Cab 149" w.b.)	9125	4181	—
D350	Pickup (Crew Cab 149" w.b.)	9435	4458	—
D350	Chas. w/cab (159" w.b.)	8743	3934	—
D350	Pickup (Crew Cab 165" w.b.)	9550	4592	—

ENGINE (D350 Custom): 5.2L (318 cu. in.) V-8. Brake horsepower: 160 at 4000 R.P.M. Bore & stroke: 3.91 x 3.31. Compression ratio: 8.0:1. Carburetor: 4-bbl.

CHASSIS FEATURES Wheelbase: 115 in. (D150 Conv Cab), 131 in. (D150, D250, D350 Conv Cab), 149 in. (Club Cab, D350 Crew Cab), 165 in. (D350 Crew Cab). Overall width: 79.5 in. (94.2 in. with dual rear wheels). Overall length: 190.78 in. (D150 Conv Cab), 210.78 in. (Conv Cab), 228.81 in. (Club Cab), 224.78 in. (D350 Crew Cab), 244.78 in. (D350 Crew Cab 165 in. w.b.). GVW: 4800-5850 lbs. (D150), 6010 lbs. (W150), 6400-7500 lbs. (D250), 6900-7500 lbs. (W250), 8510-10,000 lbs. (D350), 8510 lbs. (W350). Tires: P195/75R15 (D150 Conv Cab), P235/75R15 (D150 Club Cab), 8.00-16.5D (D250 Conv Cab), 8.75-16.5E (D250 Club Cab), 9.50-16.5E (D350).

POWERTRAIN OPTIONS: 5.2L 2-bbl. V-8 (D150, D250 Conv Cab), 5.2L 4-bbl. V-8 (D150, D250), 5.9L (360 cu. in.) 4-bbl. V-8 (D350, W150, W250, W350). 3-speed automatic transmission.

1982 Dodge Power Ram 4x4 Pickup (DNP)

OPTION PACKAGES: FOUR-WHEEL DRIVE: (Pickups: W150, W250, W350, Chas. w/cab: W350) Called "Power Rams" had most of the features found on 2wd models plus (or in place of): power steering, part-time 4wd, 2-speed transfer case, front wheel locking hubs, leaf spring front suspension. STAKE BODY: An 8 ft. stake body was available on the D250 and D350; a 9½ ft. body was available on the D350 and W350; a 12½ ft. stake body was available on the D350. KARY VAN: this body was offered on D350's with 159 in. w.b. and 10,000 lbs. GVW. RETRIEVER WRECKER: complete wrecker with 5-ton capacity winch, rapid-shift winch control, tow bar with sling and towing chains, large-capacity deck-mounted tool box, and a sentry signal switch panel with a four-bulb flashing light bar. SNO-COMMANDER PACKAGE: (W150, W250, W350 131 in. w.b. Conv Cabs and 149 in. w.b. Club Cab 4wd pickups) includes a power angling blade with positive instrument-panel-mounted fingertip controls that easily raised and lowered the plow blade and angled it to discharge snow left or right; seven-way control valve; power lift; and plow lights. (A heavy-duty version of this package was available on the W350 131 in. w.b. Conv Cab Pickup). D350 Dyna-Trac: dual rear wheels, a 6900 lb. rear axle, and a GVW rating of 10,000 lbs. TRAILER TOWING PACKAGE. ROYAL PACKAGE: (n.a. on Club Cab, Crew Cab, or Miser) bright backlight and drip rail molding; plaque on front fender with "leaping Ram" and "Royal" name, bright taillamp bezels (Sweptline) upper and lower tailgate moldings (Sweptline); color-keyed cloth and vinyl trim bench seat in blue, cashmere, or red; nameplate on instrument panel; front door bright trim applique and pull straps; woodtone instrument panel applique; carpeting with underlayment; insulation under hood panel; color-keyed hardboard headliner. ROYAL S.E. PACKAGE: (n.a. on Miser, in addition to or in place of Royal Package features) Ram's Head hood ornament; "Dodge Ram" nameplate on Sweptline Pickup tailgate; bright aluminum grille with chrome plastic insert and headlamp doors; power steering; bright tailgate applique (Sweptline); premium color-keyed, cloth and vinyl trim bench seat in blue, cashmere, red, or silver; front door woodgrain trim applique, assist strap and carpeting on lower portion; luxury steering wheel with woodtone insert around rim; oil pressure and engine temperature gauges; trip odometer; bright door sill scuff plates; color-keyed soft headliner (n.a. Crew Cab); garnish molding over windshield, front pillar, door header, quarter trim panel upper and over backlight (n.a. Crew Cab); cowl side trim panels; dome lamp mounted center of roof (Club Cab); a rear side and back trim panels (Club Cab). LIGHT PACKAGE: Halogen headlights, ash receiver light, glove box lock & light, exterior cargo light, map light.

CONVENIENCE OPTIONS: Air conditioning. Heavy-duty alternators and batteries. Rear step type bumper. Electric digital clock. Auxiliary transmission oil to air cooler. Maximum cooling. 30-gallon fuel tank. Oil pressure and engine temp gauges. Trip odometer. Tinted glass. Bright insert grille (includes Ram's head hood ornament). Deluxe bi-level heater. Engine block heater. Dual exterior low mount or low mount extended bright mirrors. Upper moldings. Lower moldings. Upper and lower moldings. Power door locks. Power steering. Power windows. Radios: AM/FM Stereo, AM/FM Stereo with electronic tuning and cassette tape player, AM/FM Stereo with 8-track tape player, AM/FM Stereo with Search-Tune and electronic tuning, AM/FM Stereo with 40-channel CB. Heavy-duty shocks. Spare tire carrier inside body. Automatic speed control. Front stabilizer bar. Tilt steering column. Luxury steering wheel. Transfer case skid plate. Bright wheel covers. Wheels: aluminum radial ribbed; chrome disc (5-slot); painted steel wheel spoke (White). Sliding rear window. Two-speed windshield wipers with intermittent wipe.

NOTE: D series colors for 1982 included: Cashmere, Spice Tan Metallic, Charcoal Gray Metallic, Medium Seaspray Green Metallic, Ginger, Daystar Blue Metallic, Manila Cream, Dark Blue Metallic, Impact Red, Morocco Red, Burnished Silver Metallic, Pearl White, Black.

1983 DODGE

1983 Dodge Rampage 2.2 Sport Mini-Pickup (DNP)

RAMPAGE PICKUP: — Styling of the front wheel drive Rampage mini-pickup was unchanged for 1983. Standard features included: Iso-Strut front suspension with coil springs. Linkless-type front sway bar. Load sensing brake system. Unibody construction. Double-wall pickup box. One piece tailgate with center release lever and covered support cables that were concealed when the tailgate was up. Power front disc brakes. Ashtray. 335-amp maintenance free battery. Flexible body color front bumper integral with front end panel, backed by steel bumper bar mounted to

1983 Dodge Rampage Mini-Pickup (DNP)

energy absorbers. Black styled end caps on rear bumper. Front and rear bumper protective rub strip. Color-keyed carpeting. Cigarette lighter. Cleaner Air System. Quartz clock with trip odometer. Directional signals with lane-change feature. 13-gallon fuel tank. Halogen headlamps. Heater and defroster. Inside hood release. Hood silencer pad. Dual horns. Electronic ignition and voltage regulator. Dome light. Glove box lock. LH remote rearview mirror (black). Day/night interior mirror. Visor vanity mirror. Black belt molding. Cargo box flange trim. Bright sill molding and wheel lip. Black windshield and rear window molding. Package tray. Leaf springs rear suspension. Body side and rear tape stripe. Four-speed manual with overdrive transmission. Lower cab back trim panel. 13 in. rallye wheels. Electric windshield washers. Deluxe windshield wipers with intermittent wipe. Payload capacity 1145 lbs. All vinyl low-back bucket seats in brown/beige, black or red.

1983 Dodge Rampage 2.2 Sport Mini-Pickup (DNP)

RAMPAGE 2.2 PICKUP: — The 2.2 came with most of the same features as the base Rampage pickup plus (or in place of): Cloth and vinyl high-back bucket seats with integral head restraints and reclining seat backs in red/black. Applied hood scoop. Body side and rear tape stripe with 2.2 graphics. Five speed manual transmission with overdrive. Rallye instrument cluster (included tachometer, analog clock, and trip odometer). Console shift lever. AM radio. 14 in. rallye wheels.

I.D. DATA (Rampage): See D150 I.D.

Model	Body Type	Price	Weight	Prod. Total
ZH28	Pickup	6683	2245	—
ZS28	Pickup 2.2	7255	2311	—

ENGINE (Rampage): 2.2L (135 cu. in.) Transmission-4. Brake horsepower: 84 at 4800 R.P.M. Bore & stroke: 3.44 x 3.62. Compression ratio: 8.5:1. Carburetor: 2-bbl.

CHASSIS FEATURES Wheelbase: 104.2 in. Overall length: 183.6 in. Overall width: 66.8 in. Overall height: 51.8 in. GVW: 3450 lbs. Tires: P175/75R x 13 SBR black sidewall (Rampage), P195/60R x 14 SBR RBL (2.2).

POWERTRAIN OPTION: Five-speed manual with overdrive (Rampage). Three-speed TorqueFlite automatic transmission.

OPTION PACKAGES: LIGHT PACKAGE: ash receiver light (std on 2.2), glove box light, headlamps-on warning buzzer, ignition switch light with time delay, and map/courtesy light. PROTECTION PACKAGE: vinyl lower body side corrosion protection, undercoating, floor mats. COLD WEATHER PACKAGE: 430-amp maintenance-free battery, engine block heater.

CONVENIENCE OPTIONS: Air conditioning. Front license plate bracket. Rallye cluster. Center console with storage area. High capacity engine cooling system. High-altitude emission control system. RH remote control mirror (painted). Power steering. RADIOS: AM, AM/FM stereo (electronically tuned), AM/FM stereo, AM/FM stereo with cassette player (electronically tuned). Glove box side rails. Automatic speed control. Tonneau cover. 14 in. cast aluminum wheels. 13 in. Rallye wheels. 14 in. Rallye wheels. Cloth and vinyl low-back bucket seats with adjustable head restraints and reclining seatbacks (in brown/beige or red) (Rampage). All-vinyl high-back bucket seats with integral head restraints and reclining seatbacks (black) (no-cost option for 2.2).

NOTE: Rampage exterior colors for 1983 were: Sable Brown (Rampage), Charcoal Gray Metallic (Rampage), Bright Silver Crystal Coat, Beige Crystal Coat (Rampage), Graphic Red, Pearl White, Black. Two-Tone combinations were: Graphic Red/Flat Black, Black/Burnished Silver Metallic, Bright Silver Crystal Coat/Flat Black, Pearl White/Flat Black.

1983 Dodge Ram 50 Mini-Pickup (DNP)

RAM 50 CUSTOM PICKUP: — Basic styling was carried over for 1983. Sales literature claimed Ram 50's were "among the finest, most technically advanced anywhere in the world." They were gaining a reputation as being one of the best compact pickups on the market. Among standard features were: Argent painted front bumper with Black rubber ends. Cargo lamp. Cigarette lighter. Dome light with driver and passenger side door switches. Emergency flashers. 18-gallon fuel tank. Tinted glass. Color-keyed headliner. Inside hood release. Bright hup caps. Left and right sides black sport type exterior mirrors. Bright windshield molding. AM radio. Adjustable angle steering column. Dual sun visors. Trip odometer. Two-speed windshield wipers with washers. Four-speed manual transmission. This year, as in 1982, the Ram 50 Custom was available with 4wd. The 4x4 version had most of the same standard features as the 2wd version plus all-terrain tires and power steering.

RAM 50 ROYAL PICKUP: — The Royal had more deluxe interior and exterior trim than the Custom. White sidewall tires, chrome front bumper, and carpeting were just a few of its luxury touches. It also came with a 5 speed manual transmission.

RAM 50 SPORT PICKUP: — The Sport had the most flair of any Ram 50 pickup. In addition to many of the items standard on the Custom, it also had: Center console with oil pressure gauge, ammeter and (5-speed manual) transmission shift lever. AM/FM stereo radio. Wide spoke road wheels. Tape stripe. Bucket seats. Like the Custom, it was also available with 4wd.

I.D. DATA (Ram 50): See D150 I.D.

Model	Body Type	Price	Weight	Prod. Total
9JL4	Pickup (Custom)	6266	2345	—
9JL4	Pickup (Custom 4wd)	—	—	—
9JH4	Pickup (Royal)	7135	2510	—
9JP4	Pickup (Sport)	7732	2530	—
9JP4	Pickup (Sport 4wd)	—	—	—

ENGINE (Ram 50): 2.0L (122 cu. in.) OHC. Four-cylinder. Brake horsepower: 90 at 5000 R.P.M. Bore & stroke: 3.30 x 3.54 in. Compression ratio: 8.5:1. Carburetor: 2-bbl. (Custom).

ENGINE (Ram 50): 2.6L (156 cu. in.) Four-cylinder. Brake horsepower: 105 at 5000 R.P.M. Bore & stroke: 3.59 x 3.86 in. Compression ratio: 8.2:1. Carburetor: 2-bbl. (Royal, Sport).

CHASSIS FEATURES: Wheelbase: 109.4 in. (2wd), 109.8 in. (4wd). Overall length: 184.6 in. Overall height: 60.6 in. (Custom). 59.8 in. (Royal, Sport). Overall width: 65 in. GVW. 4045-4120 lbs. Tires: 6.00 x 14C (Custom), 185SR x 14 SBR (Royal, Sport).

POWERTRAIN OPTIONS: Three-speed automatic transmission. 5-speed manual transmission (Custom). 2.3L (140 cu. in.) Turbo Diesel OHC Four-cylinder.

CONVENIENCE OPTIONS: FOUR-WHEEL DRIVE: (Custom, Sport) power steering, aluminum transfer case, Power Ram emblems. Air conditioning. Chrome rear step bumper. Low-luster black rear step bumper. Electronic digital clock. Front floor mats. Grille guard. Bright low-mount exterior mirrors. Vinyl body side molding. Front and rear wheel openings moldings. Mud guards. Power steering. Sliding rear window. Automatic speed control. Sport bar. Sun roof. Pickup bed liner. Body side tape stripe.

1983 Dodge Power Ram 4x4 Mini-Pickup (DNP)

1983 Dodge 4x4 Ramcharger (DNP)

RAMCHARGER SPORT UTILITY VEHICLE: — Styling was unchanged for 1983. As before, both 2wd (AD150) and part-time 4wd (AW150) were offered. With its transfer case shift selector in the "two-wheel high" mode, the 4wd could drive with rear power only. When the system was in 2wd, the front axle was disconnected and not in operation. Among standard Ramcharger features were: Dry type air cleaner. Ashtray. Bright front and rear bumpers. Automatic choke. Cigar lighter. Insulated dash liner. Cleaner air system. Coolant reserve system. Color-keyed inner door trim panels and armrests. Electronic ignition system. Black floor mat. 35-gallon fuel tank. Tinted glass (all windows). Glove box. Aluminum grille with painted plastic insert and headlamp doors. Fresh air heater with defrosters. Insulated hood inner panel. In cab hood release. Dual electric horns. Bright hubcaps. Front wheel automatic-locking type hubs (4wd). Speedometer, odometer, ammeter, fuel gauge, oil pressure and engine temperature indicator lights. Dual bright finish short arm 5 in. x 7 in. exterior mirrors. 10 in. day/night interior rearview mirror. Bright quarter side window and windshield moldings. Power front disc brakes. Power steering. AM radio. Rear roof vent. Deluxe vinyl high-back front bucket seats. Inside spare tire mounting. Front stabilizer bar (4wd). Sun visors. Dual jet windshield washers. Two-speed windshield wipers. Three-speed automatic transmission.

I.D. DATA (Ramcharger): See 1981 D150 I.D.

Model	Body Type	Price	Weight	Prod. Total
AD150	Utility	9494	—	—
AW150	Utility (4wd)	11,039	4065	—

ENGINES (Ramcharger): 5.2-liter (318 cu. in.) V-8. Brake horsepower: 120 at 3600 R.P.M. Bore & stroke: 3.91 x 3.31 in. Compression ratio: 8.5:1. Carburetor: 2-bbl.

CHASSIS FEATURES Wheelbase 106 in. Overall length: 184.6 in. (without bumper guards). 186.1 in. (with bumper guards). Overall width: 79.5 in. GVW. 5300 lbs. (2wd), 5850 lbs. (4wd). Tires: P235/75R x 15 BSW GBR.

POWERTRAIN OPTIONS: 5.2L (318 cu. in.) Carburetor 4-bbl. V-8 (4wd). Four-speed manual (4wd).

OPTION PACKAGES: SNO-COMMANDER PACKAGE: (4wd only) power angling blade with blade markers; hydro/electric controls; powerlift; plow lights; 114-amp alternator; 500-amp maintenance free battery; maximum engine cooling; Sno-Commander decal; transmission oil temperature light with automatic transmission. SNO-PREPARATION PACKAGE: (4wd only) 114-amp alternator; 500-amp maintenance free battery; maximum engine cooling; transmission oil temperature light with automatic transmission. CONVENIENCE PACKAGE: Halogen headlamps; glove box lock and light; ash recever light; two-speed windshield wipers with intermittent wipe. RAMCHARGER ROYAL S.E.: bright drip rail molding; bright taillamp housing; Ram's head hood ornament; Leaping Ram with "150 Royal S.E." plaque on front fender; bright aluminum grille with chromed plastic insert and bright headlamp doors; liftgate upper and lower moldings with bright applique panel; woodtone interior door trim applique, assist straps, carpeting on lower door panel; driver and front passenger high-back Command bucket seats with cloth and vinyl trim (included inboard fold-down arm rests on seats, and lockable console); folding rear bench seat with cloth and vinyl trim; color-keyed carpeting with underlayment; color-keyed rear side and liftgate inner trim panels; woodtone instrument cluster faceplate; nameplate on instrument panel; sport steering wheel; color-keyed spare tire cover (n.a. with 10R x 15LT tires); bright front door sill scuff plate; oil pressure and engine temperature gauges; trip odometer; color-keyed cowl inner trim panels. FILIGREE STRIPE PACKAGE: included bodyside, wheel lip and hood stripes; plus tape stripe decal with "Dodge Ram" on liftgate. TRAILER PREPARATION PACKAGE: (4wd only) maximum cooling; 500-amp maintenance free heavy-duty battery; heavy-duty variable load flasher; heavy-duty front and rear shocks; heavy-duty front stabilizer bar.

CONVENIENCE OPTIONS: Air conditioning. Heavy-duty alternators and batteries. Painted step type rear bumper. Front bumper guards. Electronic digital clock. Auxiliary transmission oil to air cooler. Maximum cooling. Oil pressure and engine temperature gauges. Trip odometer. Bright grille insert and bright headlamp doors (included Ram's head hood ornament). Engine block heater. Dual bright 6 in. x 9 in. mount mirrors. Lower molding. Lower and upper moldings. Bright upper moldings. Power door locks. Power windows. AM/FM stereo RADIOS. with cassette tape player and electronic tuning, with electronic tuning. Heavy-duty front and rear shocks. Fuel tank shield. Transfer case skid plate (4wd). Automatic speed control. Sport bar. Front stabilizer bar. Heavy-duty front stabilizer bar

(4wd). Tilt steering column (automatic transmission required). Sport steering wheel. Privacy glass sun screen. Various tires. Bright wheel covers. Aluminum radial ribbed wheels. Two-speed windshield wipers with intermittent wipe.

NOTE: Ramcharger exterior colors for 1983 included: Burnished Silver Metallic, Beige Sand, Light Blue Metallic, Pearl White, Graphic Red, Crimson Red, Black, Charcoal Grey Metallic, Nightwatch Blue, Sable Brown, Spice Metallic.

1983 Dodge Ram Maxi-Wagon Passenger Van (DNP)

B150 VAN: — Once again, styling was unchanged for the new model year. Standard features included: Brake system warning light. Dual braking system with separate brake fluid reservoirs in the master cylinder. Dry type air cleaner. 60-amp alternator. 370-amp battery. Painted front and rear bumpers. Power brakes. Cigar lighter. Electronic ignition system. Floor mat. 22-gallon fuel tank. Glove box. In-cab actuated hood release. Bright hubcaps. Bumper type jack. Dual bright exterior mirrors. Double hinged type cargo doors right side and rear (no glass). Door locks. Argent grille. 7 in. round headlights. Deluxe front heater. Hardboard headliner in driver's compartment. Driver's side sun visor. Traffic warning switch. Two-speed windshield wipers with washers. Driver arm rest. All vinyl low-back driver's bucket seat in black, blue, or beige. A Long Range Ram Van was once again offered. It came with a 36-gallon fuel tank; bright front and rear bumpers; bright windshield molding, wheel covers, taillamp bezels, and grille with quad headlights. Four-speed manual with overdrive.

B150 WAGON: Sales literature promoted the new Dodge Wagon as a "sensible and modern people mover that's right for the times." It came with many of the same features found on the B150 Van plus (or in place of): Driver and front passenger arm rests. Hinged type right side double doors with vented glass. Single rear door with fixed glass and inside door handle and lock button. Full width black floor mat. Deluxe fresh air heater with defroster. Interior 10 in. day/night mirror. Power sterring. AM radio. Driver and passenger deluxe vinyl Command bucket seats with Unibelt system and 3-pass. rear bench seat in matching trim (blue or beige). Two color-keyed sun visors. Glass all around.

B150 MINI RAM WAGON: — The Mini Ram Wagon had standard seating for five. It could reportedly carry twice as much cargo as America's largest car-type station wagon. Standard features included: Bright grille. Bright front and rear bumpers, wheel covers, and side and rear window moldings. 36-gallon fuel tank. Interior lower vinyl trim panels. Carpeting. Dual quad stacked headlights.

I.D. DATA (B150): See D150 I.D.

Model	Body Type	Price	Weight	Prod. Total
B150 Series — (109.6 in. w.b.)				
B150	Van	7339	3299	—
(127.6 in. w.b.)				
B150	Van	—	—	—
(109.6 in. w.b.)				
B150	Wagon	9068	3585	—
(127.6 in. w.b.)				
B150	Wagon	—	—	—
B150	Long Range Ram Van	7367	—	—
B150	Mini Ram Wagon	9154	—	—

ENGINE (B150): 3.7L (225 cu. in.) Six-cylinder. Brake horsepower: 95 at 3600 R.P.M. Bore & stroke: 3.40 x 4.12 in. Compression ratio: 8.4:1. Carburetor: 1-bbl.

ENGINE (B250 VAN): The B250 shared most of the same standard features offered on the B150 (plus power steering). It was a bit heavier-duty and could be ordered with the 26 in. longer Maxi body. The B250 Maxi wagon had a payload capacity of 2650 lbs.

ENGINE (B250 WAGON): The B250 Wagon had most of the same standard features as the B150. It was offered in regular or extra long Maxi bodies. Maxiwagons came with a three-speed automatic transmission.

I.D. DATA (B250): See D150 I.D.

Model	Body Type	Price	Weight	Prod. Total
B250 Series — (109.6 in. w.b.)				
B250	Van	8409	3473	—
(127.6 in. w.b.)				
B250	Van	—	—	—
B250	Maxivan	—	—	—
(109.6 in. w.b.)				
B250	Wagon	—	—	—

Model	Body Type	Price	Weight	Prod. Total
(127.6 in. w.b.				
B250	Wagon	10,011	3913	—
B250	Maxiwagon	—	—	—

ENGINE (B250): Same as B150, except 5.2L. Carburetor: 2-bbl. V-8 was standard on Maxiwagon.

ENGINE (B350 VAN): The 1-ton B350 had most of the same standard features as the B150 plus (or in place of): Larger brakes. Power steering. Axle type jack. Three-speed automatic transmission. Both regular and extended Maxivan bodies were offered.

ENGINE (B350 WAGON): This continued to be Dodges most heavy-duty people hauler. It was equipped with most of the same items found on the B150. Buyers had their choice of regular or extended (Maxi) bodies.

I.D. DATA (B350): See D150 I.D.

Model	Body Type	Price	Weight	Prod. Total
B350	Van	9703	3981	—
B350	Maxivan	—	—	—
B350	Wagon	11,233	4309	—
B350	Maxiwagon	—	—	—

ENGINE (B350): 5.2-liter (318 cu. in.) V-8, Brake horsepower: 135 at 4000 R.P.M. Bore & stroke: 3.91 x 3.31 in. Compression ratio: 8.5:1. Carburetor: 2-bbl. Maxiwagon came with 5.2L. Carburetor: 4-bbl. V-8.

CHASSIS FEATURES: Wheelbase: 109.6 in. (B150, B250), 127.6 in. Overall length: 178.9 in. (109.6 in. w.b.), 196.9 in. (127.6 in. w.b.), 222.9 in. (Maxi van/wagon). Overall width: 79.8 in. Overall height: 79.6 in. (109.6 in. w.b.), 80.6 in. (Maxi van/wagon), 80.9 in. (127.6 in. w.b.) GVW: 4700-6010 lbs. (B150), 6010-6400 lbs. (B250), 7500-9000 lbs. (B350). Tires: P195/75R x 15 (109.6 in. w.b B150), P205/75R x 15 (127.6 in. w.b. B150), P225/75R x 15 (B250), 8.75 x 16.5E (B350).

POWERTRAIN OPTIONS: 5.2L, Carburetor: 2-bbl. V-8 (B150, B250), 5.2L, Carburetor: 4-bbl. V-8 (B150, B250, B350), 5.9L (360 cu. in.) V-8 (B350). Three speed automatic transmission.

VAN OPTION PACKAGES: CONVENIENCE PACKAGE: Cigar lighter light; courtesy step well lamp for front and side doors (for use with Royal Interior Package only); glove box lock and light; ignition and headlight switch with time delay (n.a. with tilt steering column); two-speed windshield wipers with intermittent wipe. **EXTERIOR APPEARANCE PACKAGE:** bright grille; dual vertically stacked quad rectangular headlamps with Halogen high beams; bright front and rear bumpers; bright taillamp bezels; bright rear bodyside molding for van window package; bright windshield molding. **ROYAL INTERIOR PACKAGE:** color-keyed bucket seat floor risers; electronic digital clock; color-keyed carpeting in driver's compartment; color-keyed instrument panel with woodtone applique; instrument panel lower skirts (right and left sides); color-keyed vinyl front door trim panels with woodtone applique and chrome trimmed arm rest base; deluxe vinyl trimmed high-back Command driver and passenger seats (blue, beige or red); color-keyed garnish moldings over front pillars and front door headers and around windshield; instrument panel nameplate; insulated dash liner; insulated headliner in driver's compartment; luxury steering wheel with woodtone insert around rim; power steering on B150 models; scuff pads. **TRAILER TOWING PREPARATION PACKAGE:** (B250, B350) (required equipment at extra cost: 318 4-bbl. carburetor or 360 4-bbl. carburetor V-8, automatic transmission, transmission auxiliary oil cooler, and certain selected axle ratios) 500-amp maintenance-free heavy-duty battery; maximum engine cooling; heavy-duty shocks; heavy-duty variable load flasher; front stabilizer bar. **LOCK PACKAGE:** two keys (one operated ignition and front doors; the other operated side and rear doors).

WAGON OPTION PACKAGES: ROYAL PACKAGE: Royal nameplates; bright lower side and rear moldings; bright grille and dual vertically stacked quad rectangular headlamps with Halogen high beams; bright front and rear bumpers; bright molding around windshield, and side and rear fixed windows (except driver and passenger door windows); bright taillamp bezels; woodtone applique on lower face of instrument panel; spare tire cover; vinyl door and side trim panels with woodtone trim; garnish trim over front doors and passenger compartment windows, the headers around rear compartment windows, front pillars and windshield; driver and front passenger high-back Command bucket seats, and three-passenger bench seat in cloth and vinyl trim (blue, beige, silver, or red); soft cloth covered headliner with insulation; accessory floor mats in driver's compartment; electronic digital clock; instrument panel lower skirts; color-keyed carpeting; dash liner insulation; luxury steering wheel with woodtone rim insert. **ROYAL S.E. PACKAGE:** included items in Royal Package plus: Royal S.E. nameplates; bright upper side and rear moldings; bright bumper guards with rub strips; vinyl door and side trim panels with woodtone trim; front door applique pull strap; carpeted engine housing cover; oil pressure gauge and trip odometer; glove box lock and light; deluxe two-speed windshield wipers with intermittent wipe; ignition and headlight switch with time delay; cigar lighter light; courtesy step well lamp (front and side doors); driver and front passenger reclining high-back Command bucket seats and a three-passenger bench seat with deluxe cloth and vinyl trim. **EXTERIOR APPEARANCE PACKAGE:** Bright grille; bright front and rear bumpers; bright taillamp bezels and windshield molding; dual vertically stacked quad rectangular headlamps with Halogen high beams; bright side and rear fixed window moldings (except driver and front passenger door windows). **INSULATION PACKAGE:** for Royal and Royal S.E. Wagons: interior lower fiberglass insulation panels (n.a. on standard single rear door or optional sliding side door); insulation under floor covering. For Customs Wagons: included Royal and Royal S.E. items plus interior lower left trim panels in passenger compartment (blue or beige); color-keyed garnish moldings over windshield and front door headers, and around headliner and rear compartment window; dash liner insulation; sliding side door track cover; white hardboard headliner in passenger compartment; insula-

246

tion under headliner. **EIGHT-PASSENGER SEATING PACKAGE:** (B150 109.6 in. w.b. models with 6010 lb. GVW Package and all B250 and B350 Wagon and Maxiwagons) included one additional quick-release three-passenger bench seat with three seat belts. **EIGHT-PASSENGER TRAVEL SEATING PACKAGE. TWELVE-PASSENGER SEATING PACKAGE:** (B350) (required rear door(s) with optional vented glass at extra cost) included two additional bench seats; 2nd (3-pass.); 3rd (4-pass.); window retention; spare tire carrier loaded under 3rd bench seat. **FIFTEEN-PASSENGER SEATING PACKAGE:** (B350 Maxiwagon) (required 8510 lb. GVW Package, and rear door(s) with optional vented glass at extra cost) included three additional bench seats; 2nd (3-pass.); 3rd (3-pass.); 4th (4-pass.); window retention; spare tire carrier relocated under 4th bench seat. **TRAILER TOWING PREPARATION PACKAGE:** (B250, B350) (required automatic transmission on B250 models, 318 cu. in. 4-bbl. carburetor. (Carburetor: 2-bbl. in CA) or 360 cu. in. V-8, transmission auxiliary oil cooler, and specified rear axle ratio) included maximum cooling; 500-amp maintenance free heavy-duty battery; heavy-duty variable load turn signal flasher; heavy-duty shocks; front stabilizer bar. **CONVENIENCE PACKAGE:** cigar lighter light; glove box lock and light; ignition and headlight switch with time delay (n.a. with tilt steering column); two-speed windshield wipers with intermittent wipe; courtesy step well lamp for front and side doors (for use with Royal Package only).

VAN and WAGON CONVENIENCE OPTIONS: Air conditioning. Heavy-duty alternator battery. Bright front and rear bumpers. Bright front and rear bumper guards and rub strips. Electronic digital clock. Transmission auxiliary oil cooler. Maximum engine cooling. Rear window defroster. Dual rear doors with vented and banded glass (Wagon). Single rear door with vented and banded glass. Sliding passenger side door with no glass (Van), fixed glass, or with vented and banded glass (Wagon). 36-gallon fuel tank. Oil pressure and trip odometer gauges. Sun screen privacy glass (Wagon). Banded front door glass and vent window (Van). Bright finish grille (included dual quad rectangular headlamps, vertically stacked, with Halogen high beams). Cargo compartment white hardboard headliner (Van). Power steering (B150 Van). Auxiliary rear heater. Engine block heater. Scuff pads. **RADIOS:** AM (Van); AM/FM/MX stereo, electronically tuned, with cassette tape player and Dolby Noise Reduction System; AM/FM stereo electronically tuned; AM/FM/MX stereo manually tuned. Heavy-duty shocks. Power door locks. Power windows (front doors). **SEATS:** (Van) deluxe vinyl trim high-back Command driver's bucket; driver and passenger high-back Command buckets in cloth and vinyl trim (Royal interior trim required); driver and passenger high-back Command buckets in deluxe vinyl trim; driver and passenger low-back buckets in deluxe vinyl trim. Heavy-duty shocks. Automatic speed control. Front stabilizer bar. Tilt type steering column. Luxury type steering wheel. Sun screen privacy glass. Tape stripes. Deluxe wheel covers. Aluminum ribbed wheels. Intermittent type windshield wipers. Lower moldings (included side, rear and bright taillamp bezels). Upper moldings (included side, rear and bright taillamp bezels). Upper and lower moldings (included side, rear and bright taillamp bezels).

NOTE: Exterior colors for 1983 Dodge Vans and Wagons were: Beige Sand, Sable Brown, Charcoal Gray Metallic, Graphic Red, Crimson Red, Spice Metallic, Nightwatch Blue, Light Blue Metallic, Burnished Silver Metallic, Pearl White, Black.

1983 Dodge Ram "Miser" Sweptline Pickup (DNP)

D150 CUSTOM PICKUP: — Basic styling was unchanged for 1983. Standard features included: Independent front suspension. Energy absorbing steering column. Dry type air cleaner. Ashtray. Bright front bumper. Automatic choke. Cigar lighter. Cleaner air system. Coat hooks. Coolant reserve system. Dash and plenum liner. Door inner trim panels with straps and arm rests. Electronic ignition system. Black floor mat with padding (color-keyed carpeting on Miser models). 20-gallon fuel tank. Glove box. Aluminum grille with painted plastic insert and headlight doors. Fresh air heater with defrosters. In cab hood release. Dual electric horns. Bright hub caps. Padded instrument panel. Dual bright finish mirrors. 10 in. day/night interior rearview mirror. Bright windshield molding. Power front disc brakes (except D150 115 in. and 131 in. w.b. with 4800 lb. GVW). 4-speed manual with overdrive. All-vinyl bench seat in black, blue or cashmere. Sun visors. Traffic hazard warning switch. Two-speed windshield wipers. Dual jet windshield washers. All D150 pickups had the conventional (3-passenger) cab. Buyers could choose from Sweptline (with smooth sides) or Utiline (with rear fenders) boxes.

A special Miser model was offered. It had most of the same standard features found in the base D150 pickup plus: bright finish grille; bright wheel covers; Ram's head hood ornament; gold body-side tape stripes; deluxe pleated vinyl seat; woodtoned instrument panel; and color-keyed carpeting.

I.D. DATA (D150): See 1981 D150 I.D.

1983 Dodge Royal Ram Sweptline Pickup (DNP)

Model	Body Type	Price	Weight	Prod. Total
D150	Pickup (6½-ft. Utiline)	6915	—	—
D150	Pickup (6½-ft. Sweptline)	6787	3244	—
D150	Pickup (8-ft. Utiline)	7069	3368	—
D150	Pickup (8-ft. Sweptline)	6941	3338	—
D150	Pickup (6½-ft. Miser)	5989	—	—
D150	Pickup (8-ft. Miser)	6184	—	—

ENGINE (D150 Custom): 3.7L (225 cu. in.) Slant six-cylinder. Brake horsepower: 95 at 3600 R.P.M. Bore & stroke: 3.40 x 4.12 in. Compression ratio: 8.4:1. Carburetor: 1-bbl.

ENGINE (D250 CUSTOM PICKUP): The ¾-ton D250 shared most standard features with the D150. It was available with either Sweptline or Utiline boxes and a conventional (3-passenger) cab.

I.D. DATA (D250): See D150 I.D.

Model	Body Type	Price	Weight	Prod. Total
D250	Chassis w/cab	8387	3561	—
D250	Pickup (8-ft. Utiline)	7816	3764	—
D250	Pickup (8-ft. Sweptline)	7688	3734	—

ENGINE (D250 Custom): Same as D150, except in Calif. There the 3.7L, Six-cylinder had 84 brake horsepower.

ENGINE (D350 CUSTOM PICKUP): The 1-ton D350 could be had with conventional, or Crew Cabs. The Crew Cab had four doors and could seat six-passengers. The "smooth side" Sweptline was the only box available on D350s. Standard equipment echoes that on the D150 except automatic transmission was standard. Although Crew Cabs had deluxe vinyl split-back bench seats in blue, beige, or red.

I.D. DATA (D350): See D150 I.D.

Model	Body Type	Price	Weight	Prod. Total
D350 Series — (131 in. w.b.)				
D350	Chassis w/cab	8553	3601	—
D350	Pickup (8-ft. Sweptline)	8856	3879	—
(135 in. w.b.)				
D350	Chassis w/cab	—	—	—
(149 in. w.b.)				
D350	Pickup (Crew Cab)	10,010	4379	—
(159 in. w.b.)				
D350	Chassis w/cab	—	—	—
(165 in. w.b.)				
D350	Pickup (Crew Cab)	10,128	4513	—

ENGINE (D350 Custom): 5.2L (318 cu. in.) V-8. Brake horsepower: 160 at 4000 R.P.M. Bore & stroke: 3.91 x 3.31 in. Compression ratio: 8.0:1. Carburetor: 4-bbl.

1983 Dodge Power Ram "Miser" Sweptline Pickup (DNP)

CHASSIS FEATURES: Wheelbase: 115 in. (D150 Conv Cab), 131 in. (D150, D250, D350 Conv Cab), 149 in. (D350 Crew Cab), 165 in. (D350 Crew Cab). Overall width: 79.5 in. (94.2 in. with dual rear wheels). Overall length: 190.78 in. (D150 Conv Cab), 210.78 in. (Conv Cab), 224.78 in. (D350 Crew Cab), 244.78 in. (D350 Crew Cab 165 in. w.b.). GVW: 4800-5850 lbs. (D150), 6010 lbs. (W150), 6400-7500 lbs. (D250), 6900-7500 lbs. (W250), 8510-10,000 lbs. (D350), 8510 lbs. (W350). Tires: P195/75R x 15 (D150), 8.00 x 16.5D (D250), 9.50 x 16.5E (D350).

POWERTRAIN OPTIONS: 5.2L Carburetor 2-bbl. V-8 (D150, D250), 5.2L Carburetor 4-bbl. V-8 (D150, D250), 5.9L (360 cu. in.) Carburetor 4-bbl. V-8 (D350, W150, W250, W350). 3-speed automatic transmission. (D150, D250), 4-speed manual NP435 (D150, D350).

OPTION PACKAGES: FOUR-WHEEL DRIVE: (Pickups: W150, W250, W350. Chas. w/cab: W350) Called "Power Rams" had most of the features found on 2wd models plus (or in place of): power steering, part-time 4wd, 2-speed transfer case, automatic locking hubs, leaf spring front suspension. STAKE BODY: An 8-ft. stake body was available on the D250, D350 and W350. A 9½-ft. body was available on the D350 and W350; a 12½-ft. stake body was available on the D350. DUMP TRUCK: (D350, W350) 135 in. w.b. 10,000 lb GVW. KARY VAN: this body was offered on D350's with 159 in. w.b. and 10,000 lbs. GVW. RETRIEVER WRECKER: complete wrecker with 5-ton capacity winch, rapid-shift winch control, tow bar with sling and towing chains, large-capacity deck-mounted tool box, a sentry signal switch panel and dual combination roof light bar. SNO-COMMANDER PACKAGE: (W150, W250, W350) (131 in. w.b. only on W350) includes a power angling blade with positive instrument-panel-mounted fingertip controls that easily raised and lowered the plow blade and angled it to discharge snow left or right; seven-way control valve; power lift; and plow lights. (A heavy-duty version of this package was available on the W350 131 in. w.b. Conv Cab Pickup). D350 Dyna-Trac: dual rear wheels, a 7500 lb. rear axle, and a GVW rating of 10,000 lbs. TRAILER TOWING PACKAGE. ROYAL PACKAGE: (n.a. on Crew Cab), bright backlight and drip rail molding; plaque on front fender with "Leaping Ram" and "Royal" name; bright taillamp bezels (Sweptline) upper and lower tailgate moldings (Sweptline); color-keyed cloth and vinyl trim bench seat in blue, beige, or red; nameplate on instrument panel; front door bright trim applique and pull straps; woodtone instrument panel applique; carpeting with underlayment; insulation under hood panel; color-keyed hardboard headliner. ROYAL S.E. PACKAGE: (in addition to or in place of Royal Package features) Ram's Head hood ornament; "Dodge Ram" nameplate on Sweptline Pickup tailgate; bright aluminum grille with chrome plastic insert and headlamp doors; power steering; bright tailgate applique panel (Sweptline); deluxe color-keyed, cloth and vinyl trim bench seat in blue, beige, red, or silver; front door woodtone trim applique, assist strap and carpeting on lower portion; black four-spoke sport steering wheel; oil pressure and engine temperature gauges; trip odometer; bright door sill scuff plates; color-keyed soft headliner (n.a. Crew Cab); garnish molding over windshield, front pillar, door header, quarter trim panel upper and over backlight (n.a. Crew Cab); cowl side trim panels. LIGHT PACKAGE: Halogen headlamps, ash receiver light, glove box lock and light, exterior cargo light, map light.

CONVENIENCE OPTIONS: Air conditioning. Heavy-duty alternators and batteries. Rear step type bumper. Electric digital clock. Auxiliary transmission oil to air cooler. Maximum cooling. 30-gallon fuel tank. Oil pressure and engine temperature gauges. Trip odometer. Tinted glass. Bright insert grille (includes Ram's head hood ornament. Engine block heater. Dual exterior low mount 6 in. x 9 in. bright mirrors. Upper moldings. Lower moldings. Upper and lower moldings. Power door locks. Power steering. Power windows. Radios: AM, AM/FM stereo, AM/FM stereo with electronic tuning and cassette tape player, AM/FM stereo with electronic tuning. Heavy-duty shocks. Spare tire carrier inside body. Automatic speed control. Front stabilizer bar. Tilt steering column. Sport steering wheel. Transfer case skid plate. Bright wheel covers. Wheels: aluminum radial ribbed; chrome disc (5-slot); painted steel spoke (white). Sliding rear window. Two-speed windshield wipers with intermittent wipe.

NOTE: D series exterior colors for 1983 included: Beige Sand, Sable Brown (n.a. on Miser), Charcoal Gray Metallic (n.a. on Miser), Graphic Red, Crimson Red, Spice Metallic, Nightwatch Blue, Light Blue Metallic (n.a. on Miser), Burnished Silver Metallic (n.a. on Miser), Pearl White. Two two-tone paint procedures and filigree pin tape stripes were optional.

1984 DODGE

RAMPAGE PICKUP: — Sales literature described Rampage as "America's only front-wheel drive sport pickup." A new two rectangular slots grille made it look even sportier than before. That coupled with the four rectangular Halogen headlamps, new fascia with integral rub strip and new hood treatment, combined to create a more "up scale" appearance. Among standard features were: 60-amp alternator. Instrument panel ashtray. 335-amp maintenance free battery. Front disc brakes. Iso-Strut front suspension with coil springs. Load sensing brake system. Unibody construction. Carpeting. Cigarette lighter. Directional signals with lane change feature. Electronic fluid control system. 13-gallon fuel tank. Tinted glass. Cloth covered headliner. Heater and defroster. Inside hood release. Hood silencer pad. Dual horns. Electronic ignition and voltage regulator. Parking brake warning light. Glove box. Black left and right remote exterior mirrors. Day/night inside rearview mirror. Black belt molding. Cargo box flange trim molding. Black windshield and rear window molding. Bright wheel lip molding. Package trays. Rack and pinion steering gear. Four-spoke type steering wheel. Leaf springs rear suspension. Black tape insert tailgate lift handle. Body side and rear tape stripe. Four-speed manual with overdrive. Lower cab back trim panel. Electric windshield washers. Deluxe windshield wipers with intermittent wipe. All vinyl low-back bucket seats with adjustable head restraints and reclining seatbacks in Brown/Saddle, Charcoal/Silver, or Red.

RAMPAGE 2.2 PICKUP: The 2.2 came with most of the same features as the base Rampage pickup plus (or in place of): Cloth and vinyl high-back bucket seats with integral head restraints and reclining seatbacks in Brown/Saddle, Charcoal/Silver, or Red. Rallye instrumentation (included tach, oil pressure gauge, trip odometer, temperature gauge). Electronically tuned AM radio. 14 in. Rallye wheels. Five-speed manual with overdrive. 2.2 tape stripe graphics.

I.D. DATA (Rampage): See D150 I.D.

Model	Body Type	Price	Weight	Prod. Total
ZH28	Pickup	6786	2293	—
ZS28	Pickup (2.2)	7315	2357	—

ENGINE (Rampage): 2.2L (135 cu. in.). Transmission-4. Brake horsepower: 84 at 4800 R.P.M. Bore & stroke: 3.44 x 3.62 in. Compression ratio: 8.5:1. Carburetor: 2-bbl.

CHASSIS FEATURES: Wheelbase: 104.2 in. Overall length: 183.6 in. Overall width: 66.8 in. Overall height: 51.8 in. GVW. 3450 lbs. Tires: P175/75R x 13 SBR BSW (Rampage), P195/60R x 14 SBR RBL (2.2).

POWERTRAIN OPTION: Five-speed manual with overdrive (Rampage). Three-speed TorqueFlite automatic transmission.

OPTION PACKAGES: PROSPECTOR PACKAGE: (Rampage) Light Package, RBL tires and 14 in. wheels; console; power steering; electronically tuned AM radio with integral digital clock; cargo box side rails; Prospector decals. (2.2) Two-Tone Paint Package; Light package; air conditioning; power steering; electronically tuned AM/FM stereo radio with integral digital clock; tonneau cover; Prospector decals. LIGHT PACKAGE: ash receiver light; glove box light; headlamps on warning buzzer; ignition switch light with time delay; map/courtesy light. PROTECTION PACKAGE: undercoating; floor mats. COLD WEATHER PACKAGE: 430-amp maintenance free battery; engine block heater.

CONVENIENCE OPTIONS: Air conditioning. Front license plate bracket. Rallye cluster (included tach, oil pressure and temperature gauges, trip odometer). Console. Engine cooling. Power steering. AM radio electronically tuned with integral digital clock. Electronically tuned AM/FM stereo radio with cassette tape player and integral digital clock. Cargo box side rails. Automatic speed control. Tonneau cover. 14 in. Rallye wheels. Cast aluminum 14 in. road wheels. Cloth and vinyl low-back bucket seats (Rampage).

NOTE: Rampage color choices for 1984 included: Charcoal Gray Metallic (Rampage), Garnet Red Pearl Coat (Rampage), Beige Crystal Coat (Rampage), Silver Radiant Crystal Coat, Graphic Red, Black (Rampage), Pearl White (Rampage), Brown Spice Metallic. Two-Tone combinations. Graphic Red/Black (2.2), Brown Spice Metallic/Black (2.2), Beige Crystal Coat/Brown Spice Metallic (Rampage), Garnet Red Pearl Coat/Black (Rampage), Silver Radiant Crystal Coat/Charcoal Grey Metallic.

1984 Dodge Ram Royal SE Sweptline Pickup (JAG)

RAM 50 CUSTOM: — Except for the standard argent painted grille, basic styling was unchanged for 1984. Other standard features included: Argent painted front bumpers with black rubber ends. Dome light with driver and passenger side door switches. Emergency flashers. 15-gallon fuel tank. Color-keyed headliner. Inside hood release. Argent hubcaps. Black left side swingaway exterior mirror. Interior rearview mirror. Adjustable angle steering column. Dual sun visors. Cargo tie-down bars (tubular low-mount on both sides of pickup box interior). Trip odometer. Door ajar, key in ignition warning buzzer. Vinyl bench seat available in beige or gray. Two-speed windshield wipers with washers. The Power Ram 50 Custom 4x4 came with most of the same standard features plus the added pulling power of 4wd. This year automatic locking front hubs were standard. Shifting from the 4wd mode to the 2wd mode and back again was accomplished by a flick of the shift lever.

RAM 50 ROYAL PICKUP: — The Royal came with most of the same features as the Custom plus (or in place of): Cloth and vinyl bench seat (in Beige or Gray). Chrome front bumper with black rubber ends. Double wall cargo box. Cargo lamp. Cigarette lighter. 18-gallon fuel tank. Chrome grille. Bright hubcaps. Black right and left swingaway exterior mirrors. Bright drip rail and windshield molding. AM radio. Tinted glass. Conventional spare tire. Two-tone tape treatment. Wheel trim rings. The Power Ram 50 Royal 4x4 came with most of the same standard features.

1984 Dodge Ram 50 Mini-Pickup (DNP)

RAM 50 SPORT PICKUP: "One of the most complete pickups for the money" is how sales literature described the Sport. It came with most of the same items found on the Royal plus (or in place of): Center console with oil pressure gauge, ammeter, and transmission shift lever. Wide spoke road wheels. Body side tape stripe. Variable speed windshield wipers. Sport steering wheel. High-back velour cloth bucket seats (gray) with matching door trim panels. The Power Ram 50 Sport had 4wd.

I.D DATA (Rampage 50): See D100 I.D.

Model	Body Type	Price	Weight	Prod. Total
4JL61	Pickup (Custom)	5684	2425	—
4JL61	Pickup (Custom 4wd)	—	—	—
4JH61	Pickup (Royal)	6290	2447	—
4JH61	Pickup (Royal 4wd)	—	—	—
4JP61	Pickup (Sport)	7018	2617	—
4JP61	Pickup (Sport 4wd)	—	—	—

ENGINE (Ram 50): 2.0L (122 cu. in.) OHC. Four-cylinder. Brake horsepower: 90 at 5000 R.P.M. Bore & stroke: 3.30 x 3.54 in. Compression ratio: 8.5:1. Carburetor: 2-bbl. (Custom Royal). 2.6L (156 cu. in.) OHC. Four-cylinder. Brake horsepower: 108 at 5000 R.P.M. Bore & stroke: 3.59 x 3.86 in. Compression ratio: 8.7:1. Carburetor: 2-bbl. (Royal 4wd, Sport).

CHASSIS FEATURES: Wheelbase: 109.4 in. (2wd), 109.8 in. (4wd). Overall length: 184.6 in. Overall width: 65 in. Overall height: 60.6 in. (Custom). 59.8" (Royal, Sport), 63.4 in. (Power Rams). GVW. 4045-4520 lbs. Tires: 6.00 x 14 BSW (Custom), 185SR x 14 SBR (Royal, Sport), G78 x 15 (Power Rams).

POWERTRAIN OPTION: 2.6L OHC. Four-cylinder (Royal), 2.3L (140 cu. in.) OHC. Turbo Diesel. Four-cylinder (Royal, Sport). Five-speed manual with overdrive (Custom) three-speed automatic transmission.

1984 Dodge Power Ram 50 4x4 Mini-Pickup (DNP)

CONVENIENCE OPTIONS: Air conditioning. Chrome rear step bumper (n.a. Custom). Electronic digital clock (n.a. Custom). California emissions package. High altitude emissions package. Chrome low mount exterior mirrors. Black left and right side swingaway exterior mirrors (Custom). Power steering. AM radio (Custom). Sliding rear window. Automatic speed control (n.a. Custom). Body side tape stripe (Custom, n.a. Sport). Tinted glass (n.a. Custom). Wheel trim rings (Custom, n.a. Sport). FOUR-WHEEL DRIVE: mud guards; engine splash pan, front suspension, transfer case skid plates; front tow hook; automatic locking front hubs.

NOTE: Dodge Ram 50 exterior colors for 1984 included: Custom: Polar White, Safari Red, Beige Metallic, Light Blue Metallic. Royal: Beige Metallic/Cream, Safari Red/White, Light Blue Metallic/Medium Blue, Silver Metallic/Charcoal, Polar White/Beige. Sport: Charcoal Metallic, Silver Metallic, Velvet Black, Safari Red, Polar White, Atlantic Blue Metallic.

RAMCHARGER SPORT UTILITY VEHICLE: — Styling was unchanged for 1984. As before, both 2wd (AD150) and part-time 4wd (AW150) were offered. With its transfer case shift selector in the "two-wheel high" mode, the 4wd could drive with rear power only. When the system was in 2wd, the front axle was disconnected and not in operation. Among standard Ramcharger features were: Dry type air cleaner. Ashtray. Bright front and

1984 Dodge 4x4 Ramcharger (DNP)

rear bumpers. Automatic choke. Cigar lighter. Insulated dash liner. Cleaner air system. Coolant reserve system. Color-keyed inner door trim panels and armrests. Electronic ignition system. Black floor mat. 35-gallon fuel tank. Tinted glass (all windows). Glove box. Aluminum grille surround molding with painted plastic insert and headlamp doors. Fresh air heater with defrosters. Insulated hood pad. In cab hood release. Dual electric horns. Bright hubcaps. Front wheel automatic-locking type hubs (4wd). Speedometer, odometer, ammeter, fuel gauge, oil pressure and engine temperature indicator lights. Dual bright finish short arm 5 in. x 7 in. exterior mirrors. 10 in. day/night interior rearview mirror. Bright quarter side window and windshield moldings. Power front disc brakes. Power steering. AM radio. Rear roof vent. Deluxe vinyl low-back front bucket seats. Inside spare tire mounting. Front stabilizer bar (4wd). Sun visors. Dual jet windshield washers. Two-speed windshield wipers. Three-speed automatic transmission (2wd). Four-speed manual (4wd).

I.D. DATA (Ramcharger): See 1981 D150 I.D.

Model	Body Type	Price	Weight	Prod. Total
AD150	Utility	—	—	—
AW150	Utility (4wd)	10,945	4381	—

ENGINE (Ramcharger): 5.2-liter (318 cu. in.) V-8. Brake horsepower: 120 at 3600 R.P.M. Bore & stroke: 3.91 x 3.31 in. Compression ratio: 8.5:1. Carburetor: 2-bbl. (This engine was not available in Calif. in 4wd Ramchargers.)

CHASSIS FEATURES: Wheelbase: 106 in. Overall length: 184.6 in. (without bumper guards). 186.1 in. (with bumper guards). Overall width: 79.5 in. GVW: 5300 lbs. (2wd). 5850 lbs. (4wd). Tires: P235/75R x 15 BSW GBR.

POWERTRAIN OPTION: 5.2L (318 cu. in.) Carburetor: 4-bbl. V-8 (4wd). Three-speed TorqueFlite automatic (4wd).

OPTION PACKAGES: SNO-COMMANDER PACKAGE: (4wd only) power angling blade with blade markers; hydro/electric controls; powerlift; plow lights; 114-amp alternator; 500-amp maintenance free battery; maximum engine cooling; Sno-Commander decal; transmission oil temperature light with automatic transmission. SNO-PREPARATION PACKAGE: (4wd only) 114-amp alternator; 500-amp maintenance free battery; maximum engine cooling. CONVENIENCE PACKAGE: Halogen headlamps; glove box lock and light; ash receiver light; two-speed windshield wipers with intermittent wipe. RAMCHARGER ROYAL S.E.: bright drip rail molding; bright taillamp housing; Ram's head hood ornament; Leaping Ram with "Royal S.E." plaque on front fender; bright aluminum grille with chromed plastic insert and bright headlamp doors; liftgate upper and lower moldings with applique panel; woodtone interior door trim applique, assist straps, carpeting on lower door panel; driver and front passenger high-back Command bucket seats with cloth and vinyl trim (included inboard fold-down armrests on seats, and lockable console with removable styrofoam beverage chest); folding rear bench seat with cloth and vinyl trim; color-keyed carpeting with underlayment; color-keyed cowl side trim panels; color-keyed rear side and liftgate inner trim panels; woodtone instrument cluster faceplate; nameplate on instrument panel; luxury steering wheel with woodtone insert around rim; color-keyed spare tire cover (n.a. with 10R x 15LT tires); bright front door sill scuff plate; oil pressure and engine temperature gauges; trip odometer. FILIGREE STRIPE PACKAGE: included bodyside, wheel lip and hood stripes; light-reflective stripe decal with Dodge Ram on liftgate. HEAVY-DUTY TRAILER TOWING PACKAGE: (4wd only) maximum cooling; 60-amp alternator; 430-amp maintenance free battery; seven wire harness; class IV tow bar hitch; heavy-duty variable load turn signal flasher; heavy-duty front and rear shocks; heavy-duty front stabilizer bar. PROSPECTOR PACKAGES.

CONVENIENCE OPTIONS: Air conditioning. Heavy-duty alternators and batteries. Painted step type rear bumper. Front bumper and guards with rub strips and rear bumper with rub strips. Electronic digital clock. Auxiliary transmission oil to air cooler. Maximum cooling. Oil pressure and engine temperature gauges. Trip odometer. Bright grille insert and bright headlamp doors (included Ram's head hood ornament). Deluxe bi-level heater. Engine block heater. Dual bright 6 in. x 9 in. low mount mirrors. Dual bright 7½ in. x 10½ in. low mount extended mirrors. Bright lower molding with Black vinyl insert and integral wheel lip moldings. Lower and upper moldings. Bright upper moldings. Power door locks. Power windows. AM/FM stereo RADIOS: with cassette tape player and electronic tuning, with Search-Tune and electronic tuning, with 40-channel CB transceiver. Heavy-duty front and rear shocks. Fuel tank shield. Transfer case skid plate (4wd). Automatic speed control. Sport bar. Front stabilizer bar. Heavy-duty front stabilizer bar (4wd). Tilt steering column (automatic

transmission required). Sport steering wheel. Privacy glass sun screen. Various tires. Deluxe bright wheel covers. WHEELS: aluminum radial ribbed; 5-slot chrome disc (n.a. on 4wd); White painted steel spoke (n.a. on 2wd). Two-speed windshield wipers with intermittent wipe.

MINI RAM VAN: — The compact, front wheel drive Mini Ram Van shared most standard features with the Caravan. A right side, sliding cargo door without glass, and no rear seats were a couple exceptions. Its cargo compartment width between wheelhousings was 49.2 in. Maximum interior height was 48.8 in. Maximum interior width was 64.3 in. And total cargo volume was 133 cu. ft.

MINI RAM VAN ROYAL: The Royal was a step up in trim. It came with such "extras" as: Body color front and rear bumper end caps. Front and rear bumper protective rub strips. Cloth covered front compartment headliner. Dual note horn. Luxury steering wheel. Right side sun visor. Five-speed manual with overdrive.

I.D. DATA (Mini Ram Van): See D100 I.D.

Model	Body Type	Price	Weight	Prod. Total
SKE35	Mini Van	7586	2679	—
SKS35	Mini Van (Royal)	8345	2772	—

ENGINE (Mini Ram Van): Same as Caravan.

CHASSIS FEATURES: Wheelbase: 112 in. Overall length: 175.9 in. Overall width: 69.6 in. Overall height: 64.2 in. GVW. 3900-4400 lbs. Tires: P185/75R x 14.

POWERTRAIN OPTION: 2.6L (156 cu. in.) OHC. Four-cylinder. Three-speed automatic transmission.

CONVENIENCE OPTIONS: Most of the same items offered on the Caravan plus the following packages: Van Conversion; Basic Group; Light; and Maximum GVW.

CARAVAN: — The new trendsetting front-wheel-drive Caravan was part car, part station wagon, part van. It was a true multi-purpose vehicle. According to sales literature it "might be the most exciting vehicle to hit the streets since the horseless carriage." The Caravan looked like a downsized '84 Dodge Van. It had a sloping hood with Chrysler Star ornament on it, a multi-rectangular sections grille (divided horizontally at the center), quad stacked rectangular headlights, and large wraparound taillights. The tailgate lifted up. And there was a sliding door on the right side in addition to the two front doors. Standard features included: Unibody construction. 60-amp alternator. 335-amp maintenance free battery. Power front disc brakes with load sensing proportioning valve. Color-keyed front and rear bumper end caps. Bright front and rear bumpers. Carpeting. Cigarette lighter. Coolant overflow reservoir. Rear compartment sliding door with vented glass. Remote release fuel filler door. 15-gallon fuel tank. Halogen headlights. Cloth covered driver and passenger compartment headliner. Heater with upper level ventilation. Inside hood release. Single horn. Odometer. Day/night inside rearview mirror. Driver and passenger compartments dome lights. Black left outside, remote control-mirror. Black rear window and windshield molding. Clear coat paint. Lower bodyside protective coating. Electronically tuned AM radio with integral digital clock. Low back front bucket seats. Three passenger rear bench seat. Rack-and-pinion power steering. Vinyl-covered two-spoke steering wheel. Underslung tire carrier. Five-speed manual transmission. Two-speed windshield wipers with wet arm washers. Deluxe wheel covers. Cloth low-back front bucket seats in Beige, Red, Silver/Charcoal. A 3-pass. rear bench seat in matching trim was included.

CARAVAN S.E.: The S.E. (Special Edition) came with most of the same standard features as the base Caravan plus (or in place of): Premium wheel covers. Deluxe cloth low-back front bucket seats in Beige, Red, Blue, Silver/Charcoal, Saddle/Brown. A three-passenger bench seat in matching trim.

CARAVAN L.E.: The L.E. (Limited Edition) had most of the same standard features as the S.E. plus (or in place of): Dual horns. RH remote control outside rearview mirror. Luxury steering wheel. Luxury cloth high-back front bucket seats in beige, red, blue silver/charcoal, saddle/brown. A 3-passenger bench seat in matching trim was included.

I.D. DATA (Caravan): See D100 I.D.

Model	Body Type	Price	Weight	Prod. Total
SKL36	Mini-Van	8280	2937	—
SKH36	Mini-Van (S.E.)	8517	2984	—
SKP36	Mini-Van (L.E.)	9105	3030	—

ENGINES (Caravan): 2.2L (135 cu. in.) OHC transverse. Four-cylinder. Brake horsepower: 101 at 5600 R.P.M. Bore & stroke: 3.44 x 3.62 in. Compression ratio: 9.0:1. Carburetor: 2-bbl.

CHASSIS FEATURES Wheelbase 112 in. Overall length: 175.9 in. Overall width: 69.6 in. Overall height: 64.2 in. GVW: 4250-4600 lbs. Tires: P185/75R x 14.

POWERTRAIN OPTIONS: 2.6L (156 cu. in.) OHC. Four-cylinder. Three-speed automatic transmission.

OPTION PACKAGES: GAUGE ALERT PACKAGE: engine temperature gauge with high temperature warning light; oil pressure gauge with low pressure warning light; low voltage warning light; trip odometer with pushbutton reset. LIGHT PACKAGE: ash receiver light; front map/reading light (two); headlamp switch callout light; ignition switch light with time delay; instrument panel door ajar light; instrument panel low fuel warning light; instrument panel low washer fluid light; liftgate-mounted dual floodlights; underhood compartment light. DELUXE SOUND INSULATION PACKAGE:

(standard on L.E.) door to sill seals; liftgate, passenger and cargo floor, underhood, under instrument panel, wheel housing silencers. SEVEN-PASSENGER SEATING PACKAGE: (S.E. and L.E.) included 2nd seat (two-passenger bench with fixed back, side armrests and quick-release attachments); 3rd (3-passenger bench with folding back, side armrests, adjustable feature, slid front to rear on tracks, and quick release attachments); three storage bins (under 2nd seat right riser cover); ash receiver in C-pillar; upgraded brakes and suspension; P195/75R x 14 SBR BSW tires.

CONVENIENCE OPTIONS: Air conditioning. 500-amp maintenance free battery. Electrically heated liftgate window defroster. 20-gallon fuel tank. Sun screen glass (all windows except windshield and front doors). Roof luggage rack. Color-keyed front and rear floor accessory mats. RH remote control exterior mirror. Power door locks. Power liftgate release. Power driver's bucket seat. Power front door windows (n.a. on base Caravan). RADIOS: AM/FM stereo with integral digital clock and cassette tape player and four speakers; AM/FM stereo with integral digital clock and four speakers. (Both radios were electronically tuned.) Automatic speed control. Tilt steering column. TIRES: P195/75R x 14 SBR BSW, P205/70R x 14 SBR RBI Eagle GT, P205/70R x 14 SBR WSW. Rear cargo compartment tonneau cover (5-pass. models only). Rear quarter windows remote control vent. Wire wheel covers. Cast aluminum road wheels. Styled steel road wheels with bright centers and trim rings. Deluxe intermittent wipe windshield wipers. Liftgate wiper/washer.

NOTE: Caravan exterior colors for 1984 included: Beige Crystal Coat, Black, Mink Brown Pearl Coat, Saddle Brown Crystal Coat, Gunmetal Blue Pearl Coat, Charcoal Crystal Coat, Garnet Red Pearl Coat, Radiant Silver Crystal Coat, White, Glacier Blue Crystal Coat (available on S.E. and L.E. only). Two-Tone combinations included: Beige Crystal Coat/Mink Brown Pearl Coat, White/Glacier Blue Crystal Coat, Saddle Brown Crystal Coat/Black, Garnet Red Pearl Coat/Black, Mint Brown Pearl Coat/Black, White/Saddle Brown Crystal Coat, Radiant Silver Crystal Coat/Gunmetal Blue Pearl Coat, Charcoal Crystal Coat/Black, White/Charcoal Crystal Coat. Two-tones were only available on S.E. and L.E.

B150 VAN: — Styling was unchanged for 1984. Some standard features were: Independent front suspension. Computer selected front springs. Brake system warning light. Energy absorbing steering column. 60-amp alternator. Driver armrest. Ashtray. 370-amp battery. Power front disc brakes. Painted front and rear bumpers. Key-in-ignition, headlamps on, and fasten seat belts warning buzzer. Double hinged type right side and rear cargo doors (no glass). Cigar lighter. Door locks. Electronic ignition system. Driver's compartment floor mat. 22-gallon fuel tank. Tinted glass. Glove box. Argent finish grille. 7 in. round headlamps. Hardboard headliner in driver's compartment. Deluxe front heater. In-cab actuated hood release. Dual electric horns. Bright hub caps. Dual 5 in. by 7 in. bright exterior mirrors. Low-back driver's bucket seat with deluxe vinyl trim in Black or Beige. Driver side sun visor. Spare tire carrier. Two-speed windshield wipers with washers. Four-speed manual transmission with overdrive.

B150 LONG RANGE RAM VAN: — The Long Range Ram Van had bright bumpers; 36-gallon fuel tank; bright grille; quad rectangular headlights; wheel covers. It was available in 109.6 in. and 127.6 in. w.b.

B150 WAGON: — The attractive B150 Wagon came with most of the same standard features found on the B150 Van plus (or in place of): Driver and front passenger armrests. Cleaner air system. Right side double doors with vented glass. Single rear door with fixed glass, inside door handle and lock button. Full width Black floor mat. Tinted glass (all windows). Full length headliner. Deluxe fresh air heater with defroster. 10 in. interior rearview mirror. Two color-keyed sun visors.

B150 RAM VALUE WAGON: — The Ram Value Wagon came with: Bright front and rear bumpers. 36-gallon fuel tank. Oil pressure and trip odometer gauges. Bright grille (included dual quad rectangular headlamps, vertically stacked, with Halogen high beams). Deluxe bright wheel covers. Color-keyed full length carpeting. Intermittent type windshield wipers.

I.D. DATA (B150): See D100 I.D.

Model	Body Type	Price	Weight	Prod. Total
B150 Series — (109.6 in. w.b.)				
B150	Van	7712	3440	—
(127.6 in. w.b.)				
B150	Van	—	—	—
B150	Long Range Ram Van	7812	—	—
(109.6 in. w.b.)				
B150	Wagon	9559	3805	—
(127.6 in. w.b.)				
B150	Wagon	—	—	—
B150	Ram Value Wagon	9659	—	—

ENGINE (B150): 3.7 liter (225 cu. in.) Six-cylinder. Brake horsepower: 95 at 3600 R.P.M. Bore & stroke: 3.40 x 4.12 in. Compression ratio: 8.4:1. Carburetor: 1-bbl.

ENGINE (B250 Van): The B250 Van shared most of the same standard features offered on the B150 (plus power steering). It was a bit more heavy-duty and could be ordered with the 26 in. longer Maxi body (on 127.6 in. w.b.)

ENGINE (B250 Wagon): The B250 Wagon had most of the same standard features as the B150. It was offered in regular or extra long Maxi bodies. Maxiwagons had a three-speed automatic transmission.

I.D. DATA (B250): See D100 I.D.

Model	Body Type	Price	Weight	Prod. Total
B250 Series — (109.6 in. w.b.)				
B250	Van	8351	3490	—
(127.6 in. w.b.)				
B250	Van	—	—	—
B250	Maxivan	—	—	—
(109.6 in. w.b.)				
B250	Wagon	—	—	—
(127.6 in. w.b.)				
B250	Wagon	9987	4030	—
B250	Maxiwagon	—	—	—

ENGINE (B250): Same as B150 except 5.2L, Carburetor: 2-bbl. V-8 was standard on Maxiwagon.

B350 VAN: The 1-ton B350 had most of the same standard features as the B150 plus (or in place of): Larger brakes. Higher capacity front axle. Three-speed automatic transmission. Axle type jack. Both regular and extended Maxivan bodies were offered.

B350 WAGON: The husky B350 wagon was equipped with most of the same items found on the B150. Buyers could choose from regular or extended Maxiwagon bodies.

I.D. DATA (B350): See D100 I.D.

Model	Body Type	Price	Weight	Prod. Total
B350	Van	9650	3990	—
B350	Maxivan	—	—	—
B350	Wagon	11,278	4420	—
B350	Maxiwagon	—	—	—

ENGINE (B350): 5.2L (318 cu. in.) V-8. Brake horsepower: 135 at 4000 R.P.M. Bore & stroke: 3.91 x 3.31 in. Compression ratio: 8.5:1. Carburetor: 2-bbl. Maxiwagon came with 5.9L (360 cu. in.) Carburetor: 4-bbl. V-8.

CHASSIS FEATURES: Wheelbase: 109.6 in. (B150, B250), 127.6 in. Overall length: 178.9 in. (109.6 in. w.b.), 196.9 in. (127.6 in. w.b.), 222.9 in. (Maxi van/wagon). Overall width: 79.8 in. Overall height: 79.6 in. (109.6 in. w.b.), 80.6 in. (Maxi van/wagon), 80.9 in. (127.6 in. w.b.). GVW: 4700-6010 lbs. (B150), 6010-6400 lbs. (B250), 7500-8510 lbs. (B350). Tires: P195/75R x 15 (4700 lb. GVW B150), P205/75R x 15 (B150), P225/75R x 15 (B250), P235/75R x 15XL (B250 Maxi), 8.00 x 16.5E (B350), 8.75 x 16.5E (B350 Maxi).

POWERTRAIN OPTION: 5.2L (318 cu. in.) Carburetor: 2-bbl. V-8 (B150, B250), 5.9L (360 cu. in.) Carburetor: 4-bbl. V-8 (B250, B350). Three-speed automatic transmission.

VAN OPTION PACKAGES: CONVENIENCE PACKAGE: low washer fluid level warning light; glove box lock and light; ignition and headlight switch with time delay (n.a. with tilt steering column); 2-speed windshield wipers with intermittent wipe. PROSPECTOR PACKAGES: Package 1: vinyl high-back Command driver and passenger bucket seats in blue, beige or red; Convenience Package; bright grille; dual vertically stacked quad headlights with Halogen high beams; bright front and rear bumpers; 36-gallon fuel tank; oil pressure gauge and trip odometer; bright wheel covers; bright low-mount 6 in. x 9 in. mirrors; Prospector nameplates. Package 2: all items in Package 1 plus: Exterior Appearance Package; electronically tuned AM radio with digital clock. Package 1 for Van Conversions: Van Conversion Appearance Package; Convenience Package; 36-gallon fuel tank; oil pressure gauge and trip odometer; bright low-mount mirrors; power door locks; scuff pads; speed control; Prospector nameplates. Package 2 for Van Conversions: all items in Package 1 plus: bright bumpers, guards and nerf strips; automatic transmission; front air conditioning; dual rear cargo doors with vented glass; power windows; tilt steering column. Package 1 for Long Range Ram Van: vinyl high-back Command driver and passenger bucket seats; Convenience Package; oil pressure gauge and trip odometer; bright low-mount mirrors; electronically tuned AM radio with digital clock; scuff pads; Prospector nameplates. EXTERIOR APPEARANCE PACKAGE: bright grille; dual vertically stacked quad rectangular headlamps with Halogen high beams; bright front and rear bumpers; bright taillamp bezels; bright rear body side fixed window molding with Vision Van Window Package; bright windshield molding. TRAILER TOWING PREPARATION PACKAGE: (B250, B350) (required equipment at extra cost: 318 Carburetor 2-bbl. or 360 Carburetor 4-bbl. V-8, automatic transmission auxiliary cooling, and certain selected axle ratios) 500-amp heavy-duty battery; maximum engine cooling; heavy-duty shocks; heavy-duty variable load flasher; front stabilizer bar. LOCK PACKAGE: two keys; one operated ignition and front doors; one key operated side and rear cargo doors. VAN CONVERSION APPEARANCE PACKAGE: exterior Appearance Package; garnish trim over front door headers, A-pillar, around windshield; woodgrained applique instrument panel with color-keyed left and right lower skirts.

WAGON OPTION PACKAGES: ROYAL S.E. PACKAGE: bright front and rear bumpers; bright grille and vertically stacked quad rectangular headlamps with Halogen high beams; bright moldings around windshield, and side and rear fixed windows (except driver and passenger door windows), lower body side, and Leading Ram plaque on front door; bright taillamp bezels; deluxe two-speed windshield wipers with intermittent wipe; carpeting on floor around engine housing cover; cigar lighter light; courtesy step well lamp (front and side doors); dash liner insulation; front door trim panel with assist strap; glove box lock and light; soft cloth covered headliner with insulation; ignition and headlamp switch with time of delay (n.a. with optional tilt steering column); instrument panel lower side skirts; dome/reading lamps (two); oil pressure gauge and trip odometer; driver and front passenger reclining high-back Command bucket seats and rear bench seat(s) in deluxe cloth and vinyl trim (in blue, beige or red); color-keyed spare tire cover; low washer fluid warning light; woodtone applique on lower face of instrument panel. EXTERIOR APPEARANCE PACKAGE: Bright grille; bright front and rear bumpers; bright taillamp bezels; bright windshield moldings; dual vertically stacked quad rectangular headlamps with Halogen high beams; bright side and rear fixed window moldings (except driver and front passenger door windows). EIGHT-PASSENGER SEATING PACKAGE: included one additional quick-release three-passenger bench seat with three seat belts. TWELVE-PASSENGER SEATING PACKAGE: (all B350 models) (rear door(s) with optional vented glass required at extra cost) included two additional bench seats; 2nd (3-pass.); 3rd (4-pass.); spare tire carrier relocated under 3rd bench seat. FIFTEEN-PASSENGER SEATING PACKAGE: (B350 Maxiwagon) (8510 lb. GVW Package, and rear door(s) with optional vented glass required at extra cost) included three additional bench seats; 2nd (3-pass.); 3rd (3-pass.); 4th (4-pass.); tire carrier relocated under 4th bench seat. TRAILER TOWING PREPARATION PACKAGE: (B250, B350) (V-8 engine and transmission oil to air auxiliary cooling required) included maximum engine cooling; 500-amp maintenance free heavy-duty battery; heavy-duty variable load turn signal flasher; heavy-duty front and rear shock absorbers; front stabilizer bar.

CONVENIENCE PACKAGE: same as Vans. PROSPECTOR PACKAGES: Package 1: Convenience Package; bright front and rear bumpers; 36-gallon fuel tank; oil pressure gauge and trip odometer; bright grille with quad headlamps and Halogen high beams; bright low-mount mirrors and wheel covers; Prospector nameplates. Package 2: all items in Package 1 plus: Royal S.E. Decor Package; bright bumpers, guards and nerf strips. Package 3: all items in Package 2 plus: two-tone paint procedure APC; air conditioning (front); power door locks; power windows; tilt steering column (when automatic transmission was ordered). Package 1 for Ram Value Wagon: bright bumpers, guards and nerf strips; sun screen glass; bright low-mount mirrors; Prospector nameplates.

VAN and WAGON CONVENIENCE OPTIONS: Air conditioning. Heavy-duty alternator and battery. Bright front and rear bumpers. Bright front and rear bumper guards and nerf strips. Transmission oil-to-air auxiliary cooling. Rear window defroster. Dual rear doors with vented glass (Van). Single rear door with fixed or vented glass (Van). Single rear door with vented glass (Wagon). Sliding passenger side door with no glass (Van); fixed glass (Van), or vented glass (Wagon). Oil pressure gauge. Trip odometer. Sun screen glass (Wagon). Banded front door glass and vent window (Van). Bright grille (included dual quad rectangular headlamps, vertically stacked, with Halogen high beams). Rear auxiliary heater (Wagon). Engine block heater. Color-keyed accessory type rubber mats in driver's compartment (Wagon). Dual low-mount bright 6 in. x 9 in. exterior mirrors. Lower molding (included side and rear). Upper molding (included side, rear, and bright taillamp bezels). Heavy-duty shock absorbers. Power door locks. Power windows (front doors only). Automatic speed control. Tilt steering column. Front stabilizer bar. Luxury type steering wheel. Deluxe wheel covers. RADIOS: (electronically tuned) AM (Van), AM/FM/MX stereo, AM/FM/MX stereo with cassette tape player. Ribbed aluminum wheels. Argent painted 5-slot disc wheels with bright trim ring. Intermittent type windshield wipers. SEATS: (Van) driver high-back Command buckets in deluxe vinyl trim; driver and passenger low-back buckets in deluxe vinyl trim.

NOTE: Dodge Van and Wagon exterior colors for 1984 included: Beige Sand, Charcoal Metallic, Crimson Red, Spice Metallic, Navy Blue Metallic, Light Blue Metallic, Silver Metallic, Pearl White, Black, Canyon Red (available only with Prospector Package with two-tone paint procedure).

1984 Dodge Ram Sweptline Pickup (DNP)

D100 PICKUP: — The new D100 shared styling with last year's full size Dodge pickups. Among the many standard features were: Dry type air cleaner. Double-walled construction pickup box. Ashtray. Bright front bumper. Automatic choke. Cigar lighter. Clean air system. Coat hooks. Coolant reserve system. Insulated dash and plenum liner. Door inner trim panels with pull straps and armrests. Electronic ignition system. Exhaust emissions control system. Carpeting. 20-gallon fuel tank. Glove box. Aluminum grille with painted plastic insert and headlamp doors. Two rectangular headlamps. Heater with defrosters. In cab hood release. Dual electric horns. Bright hub caps. Black instrument cluster face plate with storage box and bright trim. Padded instrument panel. Dual bright finish short arm 5 in. x 7 in. exterior mirrors. 10 in. day/night interior rearview mirror. Bright windshield molding. Power front disc brakes. All vinyl bench seat. Two sun visors. Key in ignition, headlamps on, fasten seat belts warning buzzer. Dual jet windshield wipers. Two-speed windshield wipers. Brake system warning light. Dual braking system with separate brake fluid reservoirs in the master cylinder. Recessed inside door release. The D100 was only available with the smooth sided Sweptline box in 6½-ft. and 8-ft. lengths.

I.D. DATA (D100): See 1981 D150 I.D.

Model	Body Type	Price	Weight	Prod. Total
D100	Pickup (6½-ft.)	6393	3380	—
D100	Pickup (8-ft.)	6601	—	—

ENGINE (D100): 3.7 liter (225 cu. in.) Six-cylinder. Brake horsepower: 95 at 3600 R.P.M. Bore & stroke: 3.40 x 4.12 in. Compression ratio: 8.4:1. Carburetor: 1-bbl.

ENGINE (D150 Pickup): The ½-ton D150 could haul almost 1000 lbs. more in payload than the D100. It was offered in 6½-ft. and 8-ft. Utiline and Sweptline boxes. Most standard features were the same as those offered on the D100.

I.D. DATA (D150): See D100 I.D.

Model	Body Type	Price	Weight	Prod. Total
D150	Pickup (6½-ft. Utiline)	7226	—	—
D150	Pickup (6½-ft. Sweptline)	7094	3805	—
D150	Pickup (8-ft. Utiline)	7383	—	—
D150	Pickup (8-ft. Sweptline)	7251	3480	—

I.A. DATA (D150 Engine): Same as D100.

D250 PICKUP: The ¾-ton D250 came with larger brakes, different four-speed manual transmission (no overdrive), higher capacity rear axle and front and rear springs, and greater maximum payload capacity than either the D100 or D150. It was available with Utiline or Sweptline boxes.

I.A. DATA (D250): See D100 I.D.

Model	Body Type	Price	Weight	Prod. Total
D250	Chassis w/cab	—	3645	—
D250	Pickup (8-ft. Utiline)	8132	—	—
D250	Pickup (8-ft. Sweptline)	8001	3825	—

ENGINE (D250): Same as D100 for pickups (except in Calif.) Chassis with cab had 5.9L (360 cu. in.) V-8. Brake horsepower: 185 at 4000 R.P.M. Bore & stroke: 4.00 x 3.58 in. Compression ratio: 8.0:1. Carburetor: 4-bbl.

D350 PICKUP: Dodge's most heaviest-duty pickup in 1984 was the 1-ton D350. It was offered in three w.b. A conventional cab was standard on the 131 in. w.b. The 149 in. and 165 in. w.b. D350s came with 4-door, six-passenger Crew Cabs. Most standard features were the same as those on the other series. D350 pickups were only offered with the smooth side Sweptline box.

I.A. DATA (D350): See D100 I.D.

Model	Body Type	Price	Weight	Prod. Total
D350 Series — (131 in. w.b.)				
D350	Chassis w/cab	—	—	—
(135 in. w.b.)				
D350	Chassis w/cab	—	—	—
(159 in. w.b.)				
D350	Chassis w/cab	—	—	—
D350	Pickup (8-ft.)	8990	4045	—
D350	Pickup (6½-ft. Crew Cab)	10,172	4550	—
D350	Pickup (8-ft. Crew Cab)	10,264	4685	—

ENGINE (D350): 5.9L (360 cu. in.) V-8. Brake horsepower: 180 at 3600 R.P.M. Bore & stroke: 4.00 x 3.58 in. Compression ratio: 8.0:1. Carburetor: 4-bbl.

CHASSIS FEATURES: Wheelbase: 115 in. (D100, D150), 131 in., 149 in. (D350), 165 in. (D350), 135 in. (D350 Chas. w/cab), 159 in. (D350 Chas. w/cab). Overall width: 79.5 in. Overall length: (without rear bumpers) 190.78 in. (115 in. w.b.), 210.78 in. (131 in. w.b.), 224.24 in. (149 in. w.b.), 244.24 in. (165 in. w.b.). GVW: 4800 lbs. (D100), 4800-5850 lbs. (D150), 6400-7500 lbs. (D250), 8510-10,100 lbs. (D350). Tires: P195/75R x 15 (D100, D150), 8.00 x 16.5D (D250), 9.50 x 16.5E (D350).

POWERTRAIN OPTION: 5.2L (318 cu. in.) Carburetor: 2-bbl. V-8 (D100, D150, D250), 5.9L Carburetor: 4-bbl. V-8 (D100, D150, D250). Three-speed automatic transmission.

OPTION PACKAGES: FOUR-WHEEL DRIVE: (called Power Ram) power steering; two-speed transfer case; leaf spring front suspension; automatic locking hubs; Power Ram nameplates. ROYAL S.E. PACKAGE: bright rear window and drip rail molding; plaque on front fender with leaping ram and Royal S.E. name; Ram's head hood ornament; Dodge Ram nameplate on tailgate; bright taillamp housing (Sweptline); bright aluminum grille with chrome plastic insert and headlamp doors; power steering; bright tailgate applique panel (Sweptline); deluxe cloth and vinyl bench seat in red, beige, silver or blue; nameplate on instrument panel; woodtone instrument panel applique and bright trim; front door woodtone trim applique, with assist strap and carpeting on lower portions; Black two-spoke 15 in. diameter steering wheel; color-keyed carpeting with underlayment; oil pressure and engine temperature gauges; trip odometer; color-keyed soft headliner (n.a. on Crew Cab); garnish trim over windshield, front pillar, door header, quarter trim panel upper, and over backlight (n.a. Crew Cab); insulation under hood panel; cowl side trim panels. PROSPECTOR RAM PICKUPS: (2wd, 4wd D150, D250, D350, W150, W250, W350) Package 1: bright low-mount mirrors, rear bumper, wheel covers; 30-gallon fuel tank; intermittent wipers; Light Package; oil pressure and temperature gauges; trip odometer; Prospector nameplates; Ram's Head hood ornament; tinted glass. Package 2: all items in Package 1 plus: Royal S.E. Decor Package. Package 3: all items in Package 2 plus: air conditioning; electronically tuned AM radio with integral digital clock; Two-Tone Paint Procedure APC. CREW CAB RAM SWEPTLINE PICKUPS: (2wd, 4wd, D350, W350) Package 1: bright low-mount mirrors, rear bumper, wheel covers; cloth and vinyl bench seats; intermittent wipers; Light Package; oil pressure and temperature gauges; trip odometer; Prospector nameplates; Ram's head hood ornament; 30-gallon fuel tank; tinted glass. Package 2: all items in Package 1 plus: electronically tuned AM radio with integral digital clock; Royal S.E. Decor Package. PROSPECTOR RAM SWEPTLINE PICKUPS: (2wd and 4wd D100, W100) Package 1: bright low-mount mirrors, rear bumper; intermittent wipers; Light Package; oil pressure and temperature gauges; trip odometer; Prospector nameplates; 30-gallon fuel tank; tinted glass; sliding rear window. LIGHT PACKAGE: Halogen headlamps; ash receiver light; glove box lock and light; exterior cargo light; map light on instrument panel. TRAILER TOWING PREPARATION PACKAGE: (required various extra cost items) 500-amp maintenance free battery; maximum engine cooling; heavy-duty variable load flasher; front stabilizer bar; heavy-duty front and rear shock absorbers.

CONVENIENCE OPTIONS: Air conditioning. 114-amp alternator. 500-amp battery. White painted front and/or rear bumpers. Bright rear bumper. Step type rear bumper. Transmission oil to air auxiliary cooler. 30-gallon fuel tank. Oil pressure gauge. Engine temperature gauge. Trip odometer. Tinted glass. Bright grille insert (included Ram's head hood ornament). Engine block heater. Dual bright 6 in. x 9 in. exterior mirrors. Upper moldings. Lower moldings with partial wheel lip. Power steering. Power door locks. Electronically tuned AM radio. AM/FM stereo radio with cassette tape player. Heavy-duty shocks. Inside body spare tire carrier. Automatic speed control. Front stabilizer bar. Tilt type steering column. Sport type steering wheel. Transfer case skid plate. Bright wheel covers. Aluminum radial ribbed wheels. Painted 5-slot disc wheels. Painted spoke wheels. Sliding rear window. Two-speed windshield wipers with intermittent wipe.

NOTE: Exterior colors for 1984 Dodge Ram pickups included: Beige Sand, Black, Charcoal Metallic, Light Blue Metallic, Graphic Red, Navy Blue Metallic, Pearl White, Silver Metallic, Spice Metallic, Canyon Red (available only with Prospector Package with two-tone paint procedure).

1985 DODGE

RAM 50 CUSTOM: — The Ram 50 received a facelift for 1985. "Dodge" was printed in big letters on the wide top segment of the new thin rectangular slots theme grille. As before the four rectangular headlamps were slightly recessed in the grille. Among standard features were: Black front bumper with black rubber ends. Double wall cargo box. Cargo lamp. Cigarette lighter. Dome light with driver and passenger side door switches. Emergency flashers. 18-gallon fuel tank. Argent painted grille. Color-keyed headline. Inside hood release. Argent hubcaps. Day/night interior rearview mirror. Black left and right swingaway exterior mirrors. AM radio. Adjustable angle steering column. Dual sun visors. Cargo tie-down bars. Tinted glass. Conventional spare tire. Trip odometer. Door ajar, key in ignition warning buzzer. Two-speed windshield wipers with washers. The Power Ram 50 Custom had many of the same standard features plus 4wd.

RAM 50 ROYAL: The Royal came with most of the same items as the Custom plus (or in place of): Chrome front bumper with black rubber ends. Carpeting. Black grille with bright accents. Bright hubcaps. Bright drip rail and windshield molding. Two tone treatment. The Power Ram 50 Royal had 4wd.

1985 Dodge Ram 50 Mini-Pickup (DNP)

RAM 50 SPORT: The Sport had most of the same features as the Custom plus special interior and exterior trim. The Power Ram 50 Sport had 4wd.

I.D. DATA (Ram 50): See D100 I.D.

Model	Body Type	Price	Weight	Prod. Total
4JL61	Pickup (Custom)	5684	—	—
4JL61	Pickup (Custom 4wd)	—	—	—
4JL61	Pickup (Royal)	6290	—	—
4JL61	Pickup (Royal 4wd)	—	—	—
4JP61	Pickup (Sport)	7018	—	—
4JL61	Pickup (Sport 4wd)	—	—	—

ENGINE (Ram 50): 2.0L (122 cu. in.) OHC. Four-cylinder. Brake horsepower: 90 at 5000 R.P.M. Bore & stroke: 3.30 x 3.54 in. Compression ratio: 8.5:1. Carburetor: 2-bbl. (Custom). 2.6L (156 cu. in.) OHC. Four-cylinder. Brake horsepower: 104 at 4800 R.P.M. Compression ratio: 8.7:1. Carburetor: 2-bbl. (Royal, Sport).

CHASSIS FEATURES: Wheelbase: 109.4 in. (2wd), 109.8 in. (4wd). Overall length: 184.6 in. Overall width: 65 in. Overall height: 60.6 in. (Custom), 59.8 in. (Royal, Sport), 63.4 in. (4wd). GVW. 4045-4520 lbs. Tires: 185SR x 14 SBR BSW (2wd), GR78 x 15 SBR BSW (4wd).

POWERTRAIN OPTION: 2.3L (143 cu. in.) OHC. Turbo Diesel. Four-cylinder (Royal). Three-speed automatic transmission.

OPTION PACKAGES: FOUR-WHEEL DRIVE. EASY ORDER PACKAGE: (Power Ram 50 Custom) double wall pickup box; cigar lighter; AM radio; cargo light; tinted glass; day/night mirror. PREMIUM PACKAGE: (Royal) tachometer; console with gauges; full trim cab; bucket seats with deluxe cloth trim; sport steering wheel; variable intermittent wiper; AM/FM/MPX radio; power steering (2wd); tape stripes; silver painted wide spoke wheels. ROAD WHEEL PACKAGE: (available with Premium Package only) chrome wide spoke wheels with bright center cap; 185SR x 14 SBR RWL tires (2w); GR78 x 15 SBR RWL tires (4wd).

CONVENIENCE OPTIONS: Air conditioning. Chrome rear step bumper (Royal). Black rear step bumper (Custom). Electronic digital clock (Royal). California emissions package. High altitude emissions package. Chrome low mount exterior mirrors. Vinyl bodyside molding (Custom). Power steering. Sliding rear window. AM/FM stereo radio (Royal). Bodyside tape stripe (Custom). Wheel trim rings (Custom).

NOTE: Ram 50 exterior colors for 1985 were: Custom: Beige Metallic, Atlantic Blue Metallic, Safari Red, Polar White, Bright Silver. Royal: Beige Metallic/Tan, Atlantic Blue Metallic/White, Medium Red/White, Charcoal/White, Polar White/Tan. Royals with Premium Package: Medium Red, Atlantic Blue Metallic, Charcoal Metallic, Beige Metallic, Polar White.

1985 Dodge 4x4 Ramcharger Prospector (DNP)

RAMCHARGER SPORT UTILITY VEHICLE: — Styling was basically unchanged for 1985. However, on the AW150 4wd version, drivers were now able to shift on the go, into 4wd and back into 2wd at speeds up to 55 mph. There was no longer any need to stop the vehicle and get out to unlock the front hubs. Among standard features on the 2wd (AD150) and 4wd Ramchargers were: Dry type air cleaner. Ashtray. Bright front and rear bumpers. Key-in-Ignition, headlamps-on, and fasten-seat belts warning buzzer. Automatic choke. Cigar lighter. Cleaner air system. Coolant reserve system. Insulated dash liner. Inner door trim panels with arm rests and pull straps. Electronic ignition system. Black floor mat with padding (padding not available in rear compartment). 35-gallon fuel tank. Tinted glass (all windows). Glove box. Aluminum grille with painted plastic insert and headlamp doors. Color-keyed soft cloth headliner. Fresh air heater with defrosters. Hood inner panel insulation. In cab hood release. Dual electric horns. Bright hubcaps. Map/courtesy light on instrument panel. Rear compartment courtesy lights. Dual bright finish short arm exterior mirrors. 10 in. day/night inside rearview mirror. Bright quarter side window and windshield moldings. Power front disc brakes. Power steering. Electronically tuned AM radio with digital clock. Rear roof vent. Deluxe vinyl high-back bucket seats in red, blue or tan. Inside spare tire mounting. Front stabilizer bar (4wd). Sun visors. Dual jet windshield washers. Two-speed windshield wipers. Independent front suspension (2wd). Front leaf springs (4wd). Three speed automatic transmission (2wd). NP435 4-speed manual (4wd).

I.D DATA (Ramcharger): See D100 I.D.

Model	Body Type	Price	Weight	Prod. Total
AD150	Utility	10,471	—	—
AW150	Utility (4wd)	11,581	4315	—

ENGINE (Ramcharger): 5.2L (318 cu. in.) V-8. Brake horsepower: 120 at 3600 R.P.M. Bore & stroke: 3.91 x 3.31 in. Compression ratio: 8.5:1. Carburetor: 2-bbl.

CHASSIS FEATURES: Wheelbase: 106 in. Overall length: 184.6 in. (without bumper guards), 186.1 in. (with bumper guards). Overall width: 79.5 in. GVW: 5300 lbs. (2wd), 5850 lbs. (4wd). Tires: P235/75R x 15XL steel belted radial.

POWERTRAIN OPTION: 5.9L (360 cu. in.). Carburetor: 4-bbl. V-8. (n.a. in Calif.) Three-speed TorqueFlite automatic transmission (4wd).

OPTION PACKAGES: RAMCHARGER ROYAL SE PACKAGE: bright aluminum grille with chromed plastic insert, headlamp doors, and Halogen headlamps; bright drip rail molding; Ram hood ornament; Royal SE plaque on front fender; liftgate upper and lower moldings with bright applique panel; bright taillamp housing; color-keyed driver and front passenger high-back Command bucket seats with cloth trim (inboard fold down arm rests and lockable console was included); color-keyed folding rear bench seat with cloth trim; color-keyed carpeting with underlayment throughout; bright scuff plates; woodtone door trim applique, assist strap, and carpeting on lower door panel; color-keyed rear side and lifegate inner trim panels; woodtone instrument cluster faceplate and bright trim; color-keyed spare tire cover (n.a. on 10R x 15LT tires); bright front door sill scuff plate; oil pressure and engine temperature gauges; trip odometer; sport steering wheel cover; color-keyed cowl inner trim panels. PROSPECTOR PACKAGE 1: convenience package; oil pressure and temperature gauges; trip odometer; sun screen privacy glass; bright grille with headlamp doors, Halogen headlamps, and Ram's head hood ornament; bright front bumper guards; bright low-mount mirrors; deluxe wheel covers; Prospector nameplates. PROSPECTOR PACKAGE 2: all items in Package 1 plus: AM/FM stereo radio (electronically tuned); Royal SE Decor package; power door locks. PROSPECTOR PACKAGE 3: Royal SE Decor package; two-tone paint procedure; convenience package; air conditioning; front bumper guards (2wd only); sun screen glass; dual low-mount mirrors (2wd); power door locks (2wd); power windows; speed control; argent painted spoke road wheels with bright trim; P235/75R x 15XL SBR WLT (2wd); 10R x 15LT-B SBR WLT (4wd); Prospector nameplates. CONVENIENCE PACKAGE: ash receiver light; glove box light and lock; two-speed windshield wipers with intermittent wipe. FILIGREE TAPE STRIPE PACKAGE: bodyside, wheel lip, and hood, gold pin tape stripes; plus tape stripe decal with "Dodge Ram" on liftgate. SNO-COMMANDER PACKAGE: (4wd only) power angling blade with blade markers; hydro/electric controls; power lift; plow lights; 114-amp alternator; 500-amp maintenance-free heavy-duty battery; maximum engine cooling; Sno-Commander decal; transmission oil temperature light with automatic transmission. SNO-PREPARATION PACKAGE: (4wd only) 114-amp alternator; 500-amp maintenance free heavy-duty battery; maximum engine cooling; transmission oil temperature light with automatic transmission. TRAILER TOWING PREPARATION PACKAGE: maximum engine cooling; 500-amp maintenance-free heavy-duty battery; heavy-duty variable load flasher; heavy-duty front and rear shocks; front stabilizer bar on 2wd models; heavy-duty front stabilizer bar on 4wd models.

CONVENIENCE OPTIONS: Air conditioning. 114-amp alternator. 500-amp heavy-duty maintenance free battery. Painted step type rear bumper. Front bumper guards. Auxiliary transmission oil to air cooler. Maximum cooling. Oil pressure and engine temperature gauges. Trip odometer. Sun screen privacy glass (rear quarter and liftgate only). Bright grille insert and bright headlamp doors. Halogen headlamps. Ram's head hood ornament. Engine block heater. Dual bright low-mount mirrors. Lower side and partial wheel lip molding. Bright upper side and rear molding. Power door locks. Power windows. AM/FM stereo radio (electronically tuned) with integral digital clock. AM stereo/FM stereo electronically tuned radio with Seek-and-Scan, cassette player with automatic reverse, four speakers, and integral digital clock. Fuel tank shield. Transfer case shield (4wd). Heavy-duty shocks. Automatic speed control. Sport bar. Front stabilizer bar. Heavy-duty front stabilizer bar (4wd). Tilt steering column. Sport steering wheel. Deluxe wheel covers. Aluminum radial ribbed wheels. Argent painted steel spoke wheels with bright trim ring. Two-speed windshield wipers with intermittent wipe. Deluxe split-back front bench seat in red, blue, or tan (this was a no-charge option).

NOTE: Ramcharger exterior colors for 1985 included: Black, Light Blue Metallic, Navy Blue Metallic, Charcoal Metallic, Cream, Forest Green Metallic, Canyon Red Metallic, Golden Brown Metallic (available with Prospector package with two-tone paint procedure only), Graphic Red, Silver Metallic, White.

1985 Dodge Mini Ram Van (DNP)

MINI RAM VAN: — The compact, front wheel drive Mini Ram Van shared most standard features with the Caravan. A right side, sliding cargo door without glass, and no rear seats were a couple exceptions. Its cargo compartment width between wheelhousings was 49.2 in. Maximum interior height was 48.8 in. Maximum interior width was 64.3 in. And total cargo volume was 133 cu. ft.

MINI RAM VAN ROYAL: The Royal was a step up in trim. It came with such "extras" as: Body color front and rear bumper end caps. Front and rear bumper protective rub strips. Cloth covered front compartment headliner. Chrome grille. Dual note horn. Luxury steering wheel. Right side sun visor. Five-speed manual with overdrive.

I.D. DATA (Mini Ram Van): See D100 I.D.

Model	Body Type	Price	Weight	Prod. Total
SKE35	Mini Van	7972	—	—
SKS35	Mini Van (Royal)	8760	—	—

ENGINE (Mini Ram Van): Same as Caravan.

CHASSIS FEATURES: Wheelbase: 112 in. Overall length: 175.9 in. Overall width: 69.6 in. Overall height: 64.2 in. GVW: 3900-4400 lbs. Tires: P185/75R x 14.

POWERTRAIN OPTION: 2.6L (156 cu. in.) OHC. Carburetor: 4-bbl. Three-speed automatic transmission.

CONVENIENCE OPTIONS: Most of the same items offered on the Caravan (plus dual black oversized foldaway exterior mirrors; Trenton cloth low-back bucket seat(s); Tribune cloth high-back bucket seats with lockable storage drawer under passenger seat; saddle grain vinyl high-back passenger bucket seat with lockable storage drawer underneath).

OPTION PACKAGES: BASIC GROUP PACKAGE: 500-amp battery; color-keyed driver and cargo compartment carpeting; remote control fuel filler door release; 20-gallon fuel tank; gauge with gauge alert package; maximum GVW package; full length cloth covered headliner; light package; sliding side door exterior lock; right side illuminated vanity mirror; dual black remote control exterior mirrors; power liftgate release; power steering; automatic speed control; tilt steering column; deluxe windshield wipers with intermittent wipe; rear window wiper/washer. GAUGE WITH GAUGE ALERT, LIGHT, and SPORT ROAD WHEEL (Royal only) packages same as Caravan. MAXIMUM GVW PACKAGE: heavy-duty rear brakes; heavy-duty suspension; P195/75R x 14 SBR BSE tires. VAN CONVERSION PACKAGE: (4520 lb. GVW package required at extra cost) black front and rear bumper nerf stripes; bright bumpers with color-keyed end caps; remote release fuel filler door; gauge with gauge alert package; chrome/argent finish grille; padded instrument panel with woodtone trim bezels; light package; bright trim around lights; exterior sliding side door lock; dual black remote control mirrors; power steering; driver and passenger seating package; two-spoke luxury steering wheel; underslung tire carrier.

NOTE: Exterior colors for 1985 Dodge Mini Ram Vans included: Cream Crystal Coat, Black Crystal Coat, Mink Brown Pearl Coat, Gold Dust Crystal Coat, Gunmetal Blue Pearl Coat (extra cost), Crimson Red Crystal Coat, Garnet Red Pearl Coat (extra cost), Radiant Silver Crystal Coat, White Crystal Coat.

CARAVAN: — Styling was unchanged for 1985. Dodge continued to promote the front wheel drive Caravan as a "transportation revolution." Standard features included: 60-amp alternator. 335-amp maintenance free battery. Power brakes (front disc, rear drum) with load sensing proportioning valve. Color-keyed front and rear bumper end caps. Front and rear bright bumpers with rub strips. Carpeting. Keys-in-ignition, fasten seat belts, headlamps on warning chimes. Cigarette lighter. Coolant overflow reservoir. Front door demisters. Sliding cargo compartment door with vented glass. Electronic ignition and voltage regulator. Remote fuel filler door release. 15-gallon fuel tank. Tinted glass (all windows). Bright grille. Cloth covered driver and passenger compartment headliner. Bi-level ventilation heater. Inside hood release. Single note horn. Driver and passenger compartments dome light. Day/night inside rearview mirror. Black LH remote control exterior mirror. Black rear window and windshield molding. AM radio with electronic tuning and integral digital clock. Rack and pinion power steering. Two-spoke vinyl steering wheel. Compact spare tire. Five-speed manual transmission with overdrive. Deluxe wheel covers. Two speed windshield wipers with wet arm washers. Liftgate wiper/washer. Cloth low-back front bucket seats in tan, red, silver/charcoal. A matching three-passenger bench seat was included.

CARAVAN SE: The SE came with most of the same standard features as the base Caravan, plus (or in place of): Styled road type wheels with bright trim ring, hub center and nut covers. Deluxe cloth low-back front seats in tan, red, blue, silver/charcoal. A three-pass. bench seat in matching trim. Bright upper bodyside and liftgate.

CARAVAN LE: The LE came with most of the same standard features as the SE plus (or in addition to): Dual black remote control exterior mirrors. Bodyside and liftgate woodtone. Luxury steering wheel. Luxury cloth high-back front bucket seats with integral headrests, arm rests, seatback storage pockets, and driver and passenger recliners. The seats were offered in tan, red, silver/charcoal. A three-passenger bench seat in matching trim was included.

I.D. DATA (Caravan): See D100 I.D.

Model	Body Type	Price	Weight	Prod. Total
SKL36	Wagon	9147	—	—
SKH36	Wagon (SE)	9393	—	—
SKP36	Wagon (LE)	10,005	—	—

ENGINE (Caravan): 2.2L (135 cu. in.) OHC. Transverse. Four-cylinder. Brake horsepower: 101 at 5600 R.P.M. Bore & stroke: 3.44 x 3.62 in. Compression ratio: 9.0:1. Carburetor: 2-bbl.

CHASSIS FEATURES: Wheelbase: 112 in. Overall length: 175.9 in. Overall width: 69.6 in. Overall height: 64.2 in. GVW: 4600 lbs. Tires: P185/75R x 14. SBR BSW.

POWERTRAIN OPTION: 2.6L (156 cu. in.) OHC. Four-cylinder. Three-speed automatic transmission.

CONVENIENCE OPTIONS: Most of the same items offered on the Caravan plus the following package: Van Conversion; Basic Group; Light; and Maximum GVW.

OPTION PACKAGES: BASIC GROUP: (Caravan) light package; deluxe intermittent windshield wipers; dual note horns; power liftgate release; 500-amp battery; dual remote mirrors; deluxe sound insulation. POPULAR EQUIPMENT DISCOUNT PACKAGE: (SE, LE) light package; gauge with gauge alert package; deluxe windshield wipers; AM/FM stereo radio with clock; dual note horns; automatic speed control; power liftgate release; dual remote mirrors; deluxe sound insulation (std on LE); luxury steering wheel; illuminated visor vanity mirror; overhead console (LE only). LUXURY EQUIPMENT DISCOUNT PACKAGE: (LE) popular equipment package; tilt steering column; dual power mirrors; power front door windows; power door locks; power driver's seat. TRAVEL EQUIPMENT DISCOUNT PACK-

AGE: (SE, LE) 2.6L. 4-cyl. with automatic transmission; seven passenger seating package; sun screen glass; remote control rear vent windows; 20-gallon fuel tank; 500-amp battery. **GAUGE ALERT PACKAGE:** engine coolant temperature gauge with high temperature warning light; oil pressure gauge with low pressure warning light; low voltage warning light; trip odometer with pushbutton reset. **LIGHT PACKAGE:** Ash receiver light; front map/reading light (two); headlamp switch time delay call-out light; ignition switch light with time delay; instrument panel door-ajar light; instrument panel low fuel warning light; instrument panel low washer fluid light; underhood compartment light; liftgate mounted dual floodlights. **DELUXE SOUND INSULATION PACKAGE:** door to sill seals; liftgate, passenger floor, under hood, under instrument panel, wheelhousing silencers. **SEVEN PASSENGER SEATING PACKAGE:** (SE, LE) included second seat (two-passenger bench with fixed back, side arm rests, and quick-release attachments); third seat (three-passenger bench with folding back, side arm rests, adjustable feature, and quick release attachments); three storage bins (in third seat arm rests and right rear trim panel); ash receiver in C-pillar (below belt); heavy-duty suspension; heavy-duty rear brakes; P195/75R x 14 SBR BSW tires. **SPORT ROAD WHEEL PACKAGE:** P205/70R x 14 SBR RWL tires; cast aluminum wheels.

CONVENIENCE OPTIONS: Air conditioning. 500-amp battery. Black front and rear bumper guards. Forward storage console. Converta-bed rear seating (Caravan and SE). Electrically head liftgate defroster. Accessory type floor mats. 20-gallon fuel tank. Sunscreen glass. Roof mounted luggage rack. Dual exterior remote control mirrors. Dual power remote control exterior mirrors. Bodyside vinyl molding. Power door locks. Power liftgate release. Power driver's seat. Power front door windows (SE, LE). **RADIOS:** AM/FM with electronic tuning, four speakers, integral digital clock; AM stereo/FM stereo with electronic tuning, Seek-and-Scan, cassette player with automatic reverse, four speakers, integral digital clock; AM stereo/FM stereo 36-watt Ultimate Sound System, electronic tuning, memory scan, up-and-down scan, cassette player with automatic reverse, metal tape capability, five channel graphic equalizer, joystick balance/fader control, four speakers, ambient sound control, integral digital clock. Automatic speed control. Tilt steering column. Heavy-duty suspension (P195/75R x 14 tires included). Conventional spare tire. P195/75R x 14 SBR BSW tires. P205/70R x 14 SBR RWL or WSW tires. Rear cargo comparment tonneau cover (five-passenger models only). Remote control rear quarter vent windows. Sport wheel covers (SE, LE). Wire wheel covers (SE, LE). Styled road-type wheels with bright trim ring, hub center and nut cover (Caravan). Omission of woodgrain applique when monotone paint was ordered (no-cost option only available on LE). Vinyl low-back front bucket seats (no-cost option on base Caravan). Vinyl high-back front bucket seats with integral headrest, armrest, and driver and passenger recliners (SE, LE).

NOTE: Caravan exterior colors for 1985 included: Cream Crystal Coat, Black Crystal Coat, Mink Brown Pearl Coat, Crimson Red Crystal Coat, Gunmetal Blue Pearl Coat (extra cost), Gold Dust Crystal Coat, Garnet Red Pearl Coat (extra cost), Radiant Silver Crystal Coat, White Crystal Coat, Glacier Blue Crystal Coat (S.E., L.E.). Two-Tone Colors: Cream Crystal Coat/Gold Dust Crystal Coat, Garnet Red Pearl Coat/Black Crystal Coat, Radiant Silver Crystal Coat/Gunmetal Blue Pearl Coat, White Crystal Coat/Gold Dust Crystal Coat, Mink Brown Pearl Coat/Black Crystal Coat, Glacier Blue Crystal Coat/Black Crystal Coat. (All two-tones were only available on SE and LE models).

1985 Dodge Ram Window Van (DNP)

B150 VAN: — Styling was unchanged for 1985. Standard features included: Brake warning system light. Padded instrument panel and sun visor. Ashtray. Power front disc brakes. Painted front and rear bumpers. Key in ignition, headlamps on, fasten seat belts warning buzzer. Cigar lighter. Cleaner Air System. Double hinged type right side cargo and rear doors with no glass. Electronic ignition system. Floor mat (black) for drivers side of compartment. 22-gallon fuel tank. Tinted glass. Glove box. Argent finish grille. 7 in. round headlamps. Driver's compartment headliner. Deluxe fresh air heater with defroster. In-cab activated hood release. Dual electric horns. Bright hubcaps. Dual bright 5 in. x 7 in. exterior mirrors. Nameplate on front doors. Power steering. Color-keyed steering wheel. Driver's side sun visor. Inside mounted spare tire carrier. Wiper arm mounted electric windshield washers. Two-speed windshield wipers. Four-speed manual with overdrive.

B150 LONG RANGE RAM VAN: — The 1985 Long Range Ram Van came with such "extras" as: Bright front and rear bumpers. 35-gallon fuel tank. Bright finish grille. Wheel covers. Quad rectangular headlamps.

B150 WAGON: — The B150 Wagon kept its attractive styling for another year. It came with most of the same standard features found on the B150 Van plus (or in place of): Driver and front passenger armrests. Right side double door with vented glass. Rear single door with fixed glass and inside door handle and lock button. Full-width black floor mat. Full length headliner. Five-passenger seating. Interior day/night rearview mirror. Electronically tuned AM radio with digital clock. Two sun visors.

B150 RAM VALUE WAGON: — The Ram Value Wagon was only available on a 109.6 in. w.b. It came with: Bright front and rear bumpers. Oil pressure gauge. Trip odometer. Bright grille (included quad rectangular headlamps, vertically stacked, with Halogen high beams). Deluxe bright wheel covers. Full length color-keyed carpeting. Intermittent type windshield wipers.

I.D. DATA (B150): See D100 I.D.

Model	Body Type	Price	Weight	Prod. Total
B150 Series —	**(109.6 in. w.b.)**			
B150	Van	8432	3440	—
B150	Long Range Ram Van	8522	—	—
B150	Wagon	10,118	3805	—
(127.6 in. w.b.)				
B150	Van	—	—	—
B150	Long Range Ram Van	—	—	—
B150	Wagon	—	—	—
B150	Value Wagon	10,169	—	—

ENGINE (B150): 3.7 liter (225 cu. in.) Six-cylinder. Brake horsepower: 95 at 3600 R.P.M. Bore & stroke: 3.40 x 4.12 in. Compression ratio: 8.4:1. Carburetor: 1-bbl.

ENGINE (B250 Van): The B250 Van shared most of the same standard features offered on the B150. It was a bit heavier-duty and could be ordered with the 26 in. longer Maxi body (on 127.6 in. w.b.).

ENGINE (B250 Wagon): The B250 Wagon had most of the same standard features as the B150. It was offered in regular or extra long Maxi bodies. Maxiwagons had a three-speed automatic transmission.

I.D. DATA (B250): See D100 I.D.

Model	Body Type	Price	Weight	Prod. Total
B250 Series —	**(109.6 in. w.b.)**			
B250	Van	8824	3490	—
B250	Wagon	—	—	—
(127.6 in. w.b.)				
B250	Van	—	—	—
B250	Maxivan	—	—	—
B250	Wagon	10,641	3805	—
B250	Maxiwagon	—	—	—

ENGINE (B250): Same as B150 except 5.2L, Carburetor: 2-bbl. V-8 was standard on Maxiwagon.

B350 VAN: This was Dodge's top light-duty van. It had more of the same standard features as the B150 plus (or in place of): Larger brakes. Higher capacity front axle. Three-speed automatic transmission. Axle type jack. Both regular and extended Maxivan bodies were offered.

B350 WAGON: The ultimate Dodge people hauler was the B350 Maxiwagon. It could be ordered with seats for up to 15 passengers (at extra cost). The regular B150 Wagon also had a lot of carrying capacity.

I.D. DATA (B350): See D100 I.D.

Model	Body Type	Price	Weight	Prod. Total
B350	Van	9929	3490	—
B350	Maxivan	—	—	—
B350	Wagon	11,705	4420	—
B350	Maxiwagon	—	—	—

ENGINE (B350): 5.2L (318 cu. in.) V-8. Brake horsepower: 135 at 4000 R.P.M. Bore & stroke: 3.91 x 3.31 in. Compression ratio: 8.5:1. Carburetor: 2-bbl. Vans and Maxivans with GVW ratings over 7500 lbs. came with 5.9L (360 cu. in.) Carburetor: 4-bbl. V-8.

CHASSIS FEATURES: Wheelbase: 109.6 in. (B150, B250), 127.6 in. (B350). Overall length: 178.9 in. (109.6 in. w.b.), 196.9 in. (127.6 in. w.b.), 222.9 in. (Maxi). Overall width: 79.8 in. Overall height: 79.6 in. (109.6 in. w.b.), 80.9 in. (127.6 in. w.b.), 80.6 in. (Maxi). GVW: 4300-6010 lbs. (B150), 6010-6400 lbs. (B250), 7500-8510 lbs. (B350). Tires: P195/75R x 15 (B150's with 4700 lb. GVW), P205/75R x 15 (B150), P225/75R x 15 (B250), P235/75R x 15XL (B250), 8.00 x 16.5E (B350), 8.75 x 16.5E (B350 Maxi).

POWERTRAIN OPTION: 5.2L Carburetor: 2-bbl. V-8 (B150, B250), 5.9L Carburetor: 4-bbl. V-8 (B250, B350). Three-speed automatic transmission.

VAN OPTION PACKAGES: **EXTERIOR APPEARANCE PACKAGE:** bright taillamp bezels; front front and rear bumpers; bright grille; dual vertically stacked rectangular headlamps with Halogen high beams; rear bodyside fixed window with Vision Van Window Package and vented glass only, bright molding; bright windshield molding. **CONVENIENCE PACKAGE:** cigar lighter light; low washer fluid level warning light; ignition and headlight switches lights with time delay (n.a. with tilt steering column); glove box lock and light; deluxe two-speed windshield wipers with intermittent wipe. **LOCK PACKAGE:** two keys: one operated ignition and front doors, the other operated side and rear cargo doors. **TRAILER TOWING PREPARATION PACKAGE:** (B250, B350) (required equipment at extra cost: 318 2-bbl V-8 or 360 4-bbl. V-8 engine, automatic transmission, auxiliary cooling and certain selected axle ratios) 500-amp battery; maximum engine cooling; heavy-duty shocks; front stabilizer bar; heavy-duty variable load flasher. SCHOOL BUS PACKAGE: (B350) (with Solid Side Panel Van or Vision Van) (with Solid Side Panel Van or Vision Van; required equipment at extra cost: Van Window Package for Solid Side Panel Van or Vision Van; vented glass with Van Window Package; 360 V-8; 8510 lb. GVW Package) Banded front door main glass and vent wings; school bus yellow paint; parking brake switch. VAN CONVERSION APPEARANCE PACKAGE: Exterior Appearance package; woodtone applique on instrument panel with color-keyed left and right lower skirts; garnish trim over front door headers, A-pillar, and around windshield. PROSPECTOR VAN CONVERSION PACKAGE: front air conditioning; bright front and rear bumpers, guards and nerf strips; Convenience Package; power door locks; 35-gallon fuel tank; dual low-mount exterior mirrors; oil pressure gauge; Prospector nameplates; rubber scuff pads; automatic speed control; tilt steering column; automatic transmission; trip odometer; Van Conversion Appearance Package; power front door windows.

WAGON OPTION PACKAGES: ROYAL SE PACKAGE: bright front and rear bumpers; bright grille and vertically stacked quad rectangular headlamps with Halogen high beams; bright moldings around windshield and side and rear fixed windows (except driver and passenger door windows), lower bodyside and rear; Leaping Ram plaque with 150, 250 and 350 Royal SE on front door; deluxe two-speed windshield wipers with intermittent wipe; color-keyed carpeting around engine housing cover and over fuel filler cover, cigar lighter light; courtesy step well lamp (front and side doors); dash liner insulation; front door trim panel applique with assist strap; glove box lock and light; soft cloth covered headliner with insulation; ignition and headlamp switch with time delay (n.a. with tilt steering column); color-keyed instrument panel lower skirts; dome/reading lamps (two); nameplates on instrument panel; oil pressure gauge and trip odometer; driver and front passenger reclining high-back Command bucket seats and rear bench seat(s) in deluxe Kincaid cloth and Saddle Grain vinyl trim; color-keyed spare tire cover; luxury steering wheel; low washer fluid warning light; woodtone applique on lower face of instrument panel. EXTERIOR APPEARANCE PACKAGE: bright grille, front and rear bumpers, taillamp bezels, windshield molding; dual vertically stacked quad rectangular headlamps with Halogen high beams; bright side and rear fixed window moldings (except driver and front passenger windows). EIGHT-PASSENGER SEATING PACKAGE: (B150 109.6 in. w.b. with 6010 lb. GVW Package and all B250 and B350 models) included one additional quick release three-passenger bench seat. TWELVE-PASSENGER SEATING PACKAGE: (B350) (rear door(s) with optional vented glass required at extra cost) included two additional bench seats; 2nd (3-pass.); 3rd (4-pass.); spare tire carrier relocated under 3rd bench seat. FIFTEEN-PASSENGER SEATING PACKAGE: (B350 Maxiwagon) (8510 lb. GVW Package and rear door(s) with optional vented glass required at extra cost) included three additional bench seats; 2nd (3-pass.); 3rd (3-pass.); 4th (4-pass.); tire carrier relocated under 4th seat. TRAILER TOWING PREPARATION PACKAGE, and CONVENIENCE PACKAGE same as Van. PROSPECTOR PACKAGES: (n.a. Ram Value Wagon) Package 1: Convenience Package; bright front and rear bumpers; 35-gallon fuel tank; oil pressure gauge and trip odometer; bright grille with quad headlamps and Halogen high beams; dual low-mount mirrors and wheel covers; Prospector nameplates. Package 2: all items in Package 1 plus: Royal SE Decor Package; bright front and rear bumpers, guards and nerf strips. Package 3: all items in Package 2 plus: two-tone paint procedure; front air conditioning; power door locks; power windows; tilt steering column (when automatic transmission was ordered).

1985 Dodge Ram Panel Delivery Van (DNP)

VAN and WAGON CONVENIENCE OPTIONS: Front integral air conditioning. Rear auxiliary air conditioning. Heavy-duty alternator. Heavy-duty battery. Bright front and rear bumpers. Bright front and rear bumpers, guards and nerf strips. Transmission oil to air auxiliary cooling. Maximum engine cooling. Rear window defroster. Dual rear doors with vented glass. Single rear door with vented glass. Passenger side sliding door with vented glass. 35-gallon fuel tank. Oil pressure gauge. Trip odometer. Sun screen glass. Bright grille (included quad rectangular headlamps, vertically stacked, with Halogen high beams). Engine block heater. Dual bright low-mount exterior mirrors. Lower moldings (included side and rear). Upper moldings (included side, rear, and bright taillamp bezels). Power door locks. Power windows (front doors only). RADIOS: AM/FM stereo, electronic tuning, integral digital clock; AM stereo/FM stereo with electronic tuning, Seek and Scan, cassette player with automatic reverse, Dynamic Noise Reduction, four speakers, integral digital clock; AM stereo/FM stereo 36-watt Ultimate Sound System with electronic tuning, memory scan, up and down scan, cassette player with automatic reverse, metal tape capability, Dynamic Noise Reduction, 5-channel graphic equalizer, joy-stick balance/fader control, ambient sound control, four speakers, integral digital clock. Heavy-duty shocks. Automatic speed control. Front stabilizer bar. Tilt type steering column. Luxury steering wheel. Bright wheel covers. 15 in. aluminum road wheels. 15 in. argent painted spoked road wheels with bright trim ring. Deluxe windshield wipers with intermittent wipe.

1985 Dodge Ram Sweptline Pickup (DNP)

D100 PICKUP: — Styling was carried over from the previous year. The D100 was offered with 6½-ft. and 8-ft. Sweptline boxes. Standard features included: Brake system warning light. Dual braking system with separate brake fluid reservoirs in the master cylinder. Dry type air cleaner. 60-amp alternator. Ashtray. Maintenance-free battery. Bright finish front bumpers. Automatic choke. Cigar lighter. Cleaner air system. Corrosion protection (extensive use of galvanized steel). Insulated dash and plenum liner. Color-keyed door inner trim panels with pull straps and armrests. Electronic ignition system. Carpeting. 20-gallon fuel tank. Glove box. Aluminum grille with painted plastic insert and headlamp doors. Fresh air heater with defrosters. In-cab hood release. Dual electric horns. Black instrument cluster faceplate with storage box. Padded instrument panel. Interior dome light. Dual bright finish short arm exterior mirrors. 10 in. day/night inside rearview mirror. Bright windshield molding. Power front disc brakes. All vinyl, color-keyed bench seat. Sun visors. Traffic hazard warning switch. Key-in-ignition, headlamps-on, and fasten seat belts warning buzzer. Dual jet windshield wipers. Two-speed windshield wipers. 4-speed manual with overdrive.

I.D. DATA (D100): See 1981 D150 I.D.

Model	Body Type	Price	Weight	Prod. Total
D100	Pickup (6½-ft.)	6775	3380	—
D100	Pickup (8-ft.)	6991	—	—

ENGINE (D100): 3.7L (225 cu. in.) Slant Six-cylinder. Brake horsepower: 95 at 3600 R.P.M. Bore & stroke: 3.40 x 4.12 in. Compression ratio: 8.4:1. Carburetor: 1-bbl.

ENGINE (D150 Pickup): The D150 Pickup had an approximately 1000 lb. greater payload capacity than the D100. It was offered in 6½-ft. and 8-ft. Utiline and Sweptline boxes. Most standard features were the same as that on the D100.

I.D. DATA (D150): See D100 I.D.

1985 Dodge Power Ram Sweptline Pickup (DNP)

Model	Body Type	Price	Weight	Prod. Total
D150	Pickup (6½-ft. Utiline)	7589	3405	—
D150	Pickup (6½-ft. Sweptline)	7456	3385	—
D150	Pickup (8-ft. Utiline)	7755	3510	—
D150	Pickup (8-ft. Sweptline)	7622	3480	—

ENGINE (D150): Same as D100.

ENGINE (D250 Pickup): The ¾-ton D250 came with larger (12.82 x 1.19 in. front, 12 x 2.5 in. rear) brakes, different four-speed manual (NP435), higher capacity rear axle and front and rear springs, and 9.0 dual diaphram vacuum booster. It was available with Utiline or Sweptline boxes.

I.A. DATA (D250): See D100 I.D.

Model	Body Type	Price	Weight	Prod. Total
D250	Chassis w/cab	9018	3645	—
D250	Pickup (8-ft. Utiline)	8522	3855	—
D250	Pickup (8-ft. Sweptline)	8389	3825	—

ENGINE (D150): Same as D100 for pickups. Chassis with cab had 5.9L (360 cu. in.) V-8. Brake horsepower: 185 at 4000 R.P.M. Bore & stroke: 4.00 x 3.58 in. Compression ratio: 8.0:1. Carburetor: 4-bbl.

ENGINE (350 Pickup): The 1-ton D350 was offered in three w.b. A conventional cab was standard on the 131 in. w.b. The 149 in. and 165 in. w.b. D350's came with 4-door, six-passenger Crew Cabs. Most standard features were the same as those on the other series. D350 pickups were only offered with the "smooth side" Sweptline box.

I.A. DATA (D350): See D100 I.D.

Model	Body Type	Price	Weight	Prod. Total
D350	Chassis w/cab	10,012	3665	—
D350	Pickup (8-ft.)	9331	4045	—
D350 Series — (135 in. w.b.)				
D350	Chassis w/cab	10,340	3940	—
D350	Pickup (6½-ft. Crew Cab)	10,535	4550	—
(159 in. w.b.)				
D350	Chassis w/cab	10,423	4010	—
D350	Pickup (8-ft. Crew Cab)	10,629	4685	—

ENGINE (D350): 5.9L (360 cu. in.) V-8. Brake horsepower: 185 at 4000 R.P.M. Bore & stroke: 4.00 x 3.58 in. Compression ratio: 8.0:1. Carburetor: 4-bbl.

CHASSIS FEATURES: Wheelbase: 115 in. (D100, D150), 131 in., 149 in. (D350), 165 in. (D350), 135 in. (D350 Chas. w/cab), 159 in. (D350 Chas. w/cab). Overall width: 79.5 in. Overall length: 190.78 in. (115 in. w.b.), 210.78 in. (131 in. w.b.), 224.24 in. (149 in. w.b. Crew Cab), 244.24 in. (165 in. w.b. Crew Cab). GVW: 4800 lbs. (D100), 4800-5850 lbs. (D150), 6010 lbs. (W100, W150), 6400-7500 lbs. (D250), 6900-7500 lbs. (W250), 8510 lbs. (W350). 8510-10,100 lbs. (D350). Tires: P195/75R x 15 (D100, D150), 8.00 x 16.5D (D250), 9.50 x 16.5E (D350).

POWERTRAIN OPTION: 5.2-liter (318 cu. in.) Carburetor: 2-bbl. V-8 (n.a. D350), 5.9L (360 cu. in.) Carburetor: 4-bbl. V-8 4-speed manual NP435 (D100, D150), 3-speed automatic transmission.

OPTION PACKAGES: FOUR-WHEEL DRIVE: (W100, W150, W250, W350) in addition to or in place of D series features: 2-speed transfer case, the driver could shift from 2wd to 4wd and back while the vehicle was in motion at speeds up to 55 mph. Power steering. "Power Ram" emblem on front fenders. ROYAL SE PACKAGE: bright aluminum grille with chrome plastic insert, headlamp doors and Halogen headlamps; bright drip rail and rear window molding; bright tailgate applique panel (Sweptline); bright tail-lamp housings (Sweptline); Dodge Ram nameplate on Sweptline pickup tailgate applique panel; plaque on front fender with "leaping ram" and Royal SE name; Ram's head hood ornament; color-keyed carpeting with underlayment (rubber floor mat was a no-charge option); color-keyed cowl side trim panels; color-keyed garnish trim over windshield, front pillar, door header, quarter trim panel upper, and over backlight (n.a. Crew Cab); color-keyed soft headliner (n.a. Crew Cab); deluxe Tribune cloth bench seat (all-vinyl was a no-charge option); front door woodtone trim applique with assist strip and carpeting on lower portion; bright sill scuff plates; insulation under hood panel; oil pressure and engine temperature gauges; trip odometer; woodtone instrument panel applique and bright trim. LIGHT PACKAGE: ash receiver light, exterior cargo light, glove box lock and light on instrument panel. TRAILER TOWING PREPARATION PACKAGE: (n.a. with Six, 4-speed manual overdrive, or 2.94 axle ratio on D150) 500-amp maintenance free-battery; front stabilizer bar, heavy-duty front and rear shock absorbers, heavy-duty load flasher, maximum engine cooling. JOB RATED PACKAGE: (D250 and W250 only) 114-amp alternator, 500-amp maintenance free battery, argent painted rear step type bumper, maximum engine cooling, 7500 lb. GVW package, 30-gallon fuel tank (W250), skid plate (W250), front stabilizer bar, heavy-duty shocks (D250). PROSPECTOR PACKAGES: (D150, D250, D350, W150, W250, W350 conventional cab Sweptline pickups) Package 1: bright front bumper guards, bright low-mount mirrors, bright wheel covers, intermittent wipers, light package, oil pressure and temperature gauges, trip odometer, Prospector nameplates, Ram's head hood ornament, 30-gallon fuel tank, tinted glass. Package 2: all the items in Package 1 plus Royal SE Decor Package. Package 3: all the items in package 2 plus: air conditioning, AM radio (electronically tuned, with integral digital clock), power door locks, two-tone paint procedure APC. (2wd and 4wd D350, W350 Crew Cab pickups): Package 1: bright front bumper guards, low-mount mirrors, wheel covers; intermittent wipers; light package; oil pressure and temperature gauges; trip odometer; Prospector nameplates; Ram's head hood ornament; Tempo cloth bench seats; 30-gallon fuel tank; tinted glass. Package 2: all items in Package 1 plus: electronically tuned AM radio with integral digital clock; Royal SE Decor Package. (D100, W100 conventional cab pickups): Package 1: same as first Package 1 except it had sliding rear window and did NOT have Ram's head hood ornament. SNO-COMMANDER PACKAGES: (specific GVW packages, 5.2L or 5.9L V-8 engines and transmission auxiliary oil cooler with automatic transmission were required at extra cost) 500-amp maintenance-free battery, front clearance and identification lights, Hydro/electric controls, maximum engine cooling, 114-amp alternator, plow lights, power angling blade with blade markers, power lift, Sno-Commander decal, transmission oil temperature light with automatic transmission. SNO-PREPARATION PACKAGE: (specific GVW packages, 5.2L or 5.9L V-8 engines and transmission auxiliary oil cooler with automatic transmission were required at extra cost) 114-amp alternator, 500-amp maintenance free battery, maximum engine cooling, transmission oil temperature light with automatic transmission.

256

CONVENIENCE OPTIONS: Air conditioning with bi-level ventilation. 114-amp alternator. 500-amp maintenance free battery. Front bumper guards. Rear step bumper. Auxiliary transmission oil to air cooler. 30-gallon fuel tank. Oil pressure, engine coolant temperature gauges. Trip odometer. Tinted glass. Bright insert grille, included Halogen headlamps, bright headlamp doors, and Ram's head hood ornament. Engine block heater. Dual low-mount exterior mirrors. Upper moldings. Lower moldings with partial wheel lip. Power door locks. Power steering. Power windows. Radios: AM, AM/FM stereo, AM stereo/FM stereo with cassette player. Heavy-duty shock absorbers. Spare tire carrier inside body. Automatic speed control. Front stabilizer bar. Tilt steering column. Spot type steering wheel. Transfer case skid plate. Bright wheel covers. Aluminum radial ribbed wheels. Painted spoke wheels. Sliding rear window. Deluxe two-speed windshield wipers with intermittent wipe.

NOTE: D series exterior colors for 1985 included: Black, Light Blue Metallic, Navy Blue Metallic, Charcoal Metallic, Cream, Forest Green Metallic, Canyon Red Metallic, Golden Brown Metallic (available with Prospector Package with two-tone paint procedure only), Graphic Red, Silver Metallic, White.

1986 DODGE

RAM 50 PICKUP: — The Ram 50 received a minor facelift. The grille now had a narrower upper section with "Dodge" printed in smaller letters than in 1985. The grille "slots" were a bit larger and extended to underneath the four recessed rectangular headlights. Among standard features were: Color-keyed short arm rests. Cigar lighter. Rubber mat floor covering. Inside hood release. Dome light. Day/night rearview mirror. AM radio. All vinyl bench seat. Adjustable steering column. Two-spoke plastic steering wheel. Trip odometer. Skid plates (4wd). Torsion bar front, leaf rear suspension (4wd). 45-amp alternator. Power front disc brakes. Electronic ignition. Black front bumper. Double wall cargo box. Corrosion protection. 18-gallon fuel tank. Tinted glass (all windows). Argent grille. Argent hubcaps. Cargo box light. Black left and right swingaway outside mirrors. Two-speed windshield wipers. Five-speed manual transmission. The Power Ram 50 had most of the same features plus 4wd, an aluminum transfer case with chain belt drive, and automatic locking hubs.

1986 Dodge Ram 50 Mini-Pickup (DNP)

RAM 50 SPORT: The Sport lived up to its name in looks and performance. It came with many of the same standard features as the Ram 50 plus (or in place of): Long color-keyed arm rests. Electronic digital clock. Carpeting. Cloth and vinyl bench seat (high-back cloth and vinyl buckets on the 4wd). Soft-feel two-spoke steering wheel. Color-keyed scuff plate. Power steering. Chrome front bumper. Chrome/black grille. Bright drip rail and windshield moldings. Vinyl bodyside moldings. 14 in. painted wide spoke wheels (15 in. on 4wd). The Power Ram 50 Sport shared most of these features plus 4wd.

I.D. DATA (Ram 50): See D100 I.D.

Model	Body Type	Price	Weight	Prod. Total
P24	Pickup (Ram 50)	5788	2566	—
P24	Pickup (Ram 50 4wd)	—	—	—
P44	Pickup (Sport)	6712	2568	—
P44	Pickup (Sport 4wd)	—	—	—

ENGINE (Ram 50): 2.0L (122 cu. in.) OHC. Four-cylinder. Brake horsepower: 90 at 5000 R.P.M. Bore & stroke: 3.30 x 3.54 in. Compression ratio: 8.5:1. Carburetor: 2-bbl. (Ram 50 2wd). 2.6L (156 cu. in.) OHC. Four-cylinder. Brake horsepower: 104 at 4800 R.P.M. Compression ratio: 8.7:1. Carburetor: 2-bbl. (Ram 50 4wd, Sport).

CHASSIS FEATURES: Wheelbase: 109.4 in. (2wd), 109.8 in. (4wd). Overall length: 184.4 in. Overall width: 65 in. Overall height: 57.5 in. (2wd), 61.6 in. (4wd). Box length (inside at floor): 81.5 in. Box width (inside at floor): 60 in. GVW. 4045-4475 lbs. Tires: 185SR x 14 BSW (2wd), GR78 x 15 BSW (4wd).

1986 Dodge Ram 50 Sport Mini-Pickup (DNP)

POWERTRAIN OPTION: Three-speed automatic transmission.

OPTION PACKAGES: 4wd. PREMIUM PACKAGE: (Sport only) tachometer; console with oil pressure gauge and ammeter; high back premium cloth bucket seats; variable intermittent windshield wipers; AM/FM stereo radio; power steering (2wd, std. on 4wd); chrome wide spoke wheels; RWL tires. Air conditioning. Power steering. Black rear step bumper (Ram 50). Chrome rear step bumper (Sport). Chrome low-mount exterior mirrors. Vinyl bodyside molding (Ram 50). Bodyside and tailgate tape stripes (Ram 50). Wheel trim rings (Ram 50). Sliding rear window.

1986 Dodge Power Ram 50 Sport Mini-Pickup (DNP)

NOTE: Exterior Ram 50, and Ram 50 Sport colors for 1986 were: Medium Blue, Charcoal, Bright Red, Bright Silver, Black, Gold, White. The last two colors had Brown/Beige interiors. The others had Gray interiors.

NOTE: Ram 50 and Power Ram 50 "Spring Specials" were offered in early 1986. They features: Cut-pile carpeting. Cloth and vinyl bench seat. Color coordinated carpeted door panel inserts. Deluxe sport steering wheel. Chromed front bumper. Tape stripes. The Ram 50 2wd was offered in four two-tone paint treatments with painted wide spoke wheels, or seven monotone exterior colors with chromed wheels. The Power Ram 50 had chrome wheels and a choice of seven monotone paint treatments.

1986 Dodge 4x4 Ramcharger Royal SE (DNP)

RAMCHARGER SPORT UTILITY VEHICLE: — The 1986 Ramcharger shared the "D" series pickups attractive facelift. There was 106 cu. ft. of cargo room (with the standard rear seat removed). Both 2wd (AD150) and part time 4wd (AW150) were offered. As in '85, the 4wd Ramcharger could be shifted on the run into 4wd or back into 2wd at speeds up to 55 mph.

Among standard features were: Dry type air cleaner. 60-amp alternator. Ashtray. 400-amp maintenance free battery. Power front disc brakes. Bright front and rear bumpers. Fasten seat belts, headlights on, key in ignition warning buzzers. Cigar lighter. Coolant reserve system. Corrosion protection. Insulated dash liner. Color-keyed door inner trim panels, armrests and pull straps. Electronic ignition with voltage regulation system. Black floor mats. 35-gallon fuel tank. Tinted glass (all windows). Glove box. Aluminum grille with painted plastic insert and headlamp bezels. Color-keyed soft cloth headliner. Fresh air heater with defrosters. Hood inner panel insulation. Dual note electric horns. Bright hub caps. 10 in. day/night rearview mirror. Dual bright short arm 5 in. x 7 in. exterior mirrors. Quarter side window, rear window, and windshield bright moldings. Power steering. Deluxe vinyl high-back front bucket seats. Rear roof vent. Three-passenger rear bench seat. Inside spare tire mounting. Sun visors. Dual jet windshield washers. Two-speed windshield wipers. Three speed automatic (2wd). 4-speed manual (4wd).

I.D DATA (Ramcharger): See D100 I.D.

1986 Dodge 4x4 Ramcharger Royal SE (DNP)

Model	Body Type	Price	Weight	Prod. Total
AD150	Utility	11,534	—	—
AW150	Utility (4wd)	12,763	4549	—

ENGINE (Ramcharger): 5.2L (318 cu. in.) V-8. Brake horsepower: 120 at 3600 R.P.M. Bore & stroke: 3.91 x 3.31 in. Compression ratio: 8.5:1. Carburetor: 2-bbl.

CHASSIS FEATURES: Wheelbase: 106 in. Overall length: 184.6 in. (without bumper guards). Overall width: 79.5 in. GVW: 5600 lbs. (2wd), 6000-6400 lbs. (4wd). Tires: P235/75R x 15XL SBR.

POWERTRAIN OPTION: 5.9L (360 cu. in.). Carburetor: 4-bbl. V-8 (n.a. in CA). Three-speed automatic transmission (4wd).

OPTION PACKAGES: ROYAL SE PACKAGE: bright drip rail molding; bright grille with bright insert and bright headlight bezels; Halogen headlights; bright liftgate applique, upper and lower moldings, taillight housing; front fender Leaping Ram plaque "150 Royal SE"; Ram's head hood ornament; bright door sill scuff plate; center console; color-keyed carpeting throughout with underlayment; color-keyed cowl side trim panels; color-keyed rear side and liftgate inner trim panels with woodtone applique; color-keyed spare tire cover; vinyl door trim panels with woodtone trim, assist strap, arm rest, and carpeting on lower door; deluxe cloth and vinyl trim high-back bucket seats; Euro-sport steering wheel (black); folding rear bench seat in cloth with vinyl trim; nameplate on instrument panel; woodtone applique on instrument panel. HEAVY DUTY PACKAGE: front stabilizer bar on 2wd; heavy-duty front stabilizer bar on 4wd; heavy-duty front and rear shocks. POWER CONVENIENCE PACKAGE: power door locks; power windows. CONVENIENCE PACKAGE: ash receiver light; glove box lock and light; intermittent windshield wipers. TWO-TONE PAINT PACKAGE: lower bodyside moldings with black vinyl insert and bright partial wheel lip moldings; two-tone paint; upper side and rear exterior moldings. PROSPECTOR PACKAGES: Package 1: convenience package; deluxe wheel covers; grille with bright insert, headlight bezels, Halogen headlights and Ram's head hood ornament; power convenience package; sunscreen glass (rear quarter and liftgate windows only). Package 2: all items in package 1 except sunscreen glass, plus: dual 6 in. by 9 in. low-mount mirrors; front bumper guards; Royal SE Decor Package. Package 3: air conditioning; aluminum ribbed road wheels; AM stereo/FM stereo radio (electronically tuned) with integral clock; convenience package; dual low-mount 6 in. by 9 in. mirrors (2wd); P235/75R x 5XL RWL tires; power convenience package; Royal SE Decor Package; speed control; sunscreen glass (rear quarter and liftgate windows only); two-tone paint package.

CONVENIENCE OPTIONS: Air conditioning. Heavy-duty alternator. Anti-spin rear axle. Heavy-duty battery. Painted step type rear bumper. Front bumper guards. Auxiliary transmission oil to air cooling. Maximum engine cooling. Sunscreen privacy glass (rear quarter windows and liftgate only). Engine block heater. Dual bright low-mount exterior mirrors. Bright lower bodyside moldings with black vinyl insert and partial wheel lip. AM stereo/FM stereo (electronically tuned) with integral digital clock. AM stereo/FM stereo (electronically tuned) with seek-and-scan, cassette player with automatic reverse, integral digital clock. Automatic speed control. Sport bar. Tilt steering column. Argent painted steel spoke wheels with bright trim ring and hub center. Radial ribbed aluminum wheels. Two-speed windshield wipers with intermittent wipe.

NOTE: Ramcharger exterior colors for 1986 included: Light Cream, Golden Bronze Pearl Coat, Twilight Blue Pearl Coat, Graphic Red, Gold Dust, Radiant Silver, Ice Blue, White, Black, Charcoal Pearl Coat.

1986 Dodge Mini Ram Van (DNP)

MINI RAM VAN: — The compact, front wheel drive Mini Ram Van shared most standard features with the Caravan. A right side, sliding cargo door without glass, and no rear seats were a couple exceptions. Its cargo compartment width between wheelhousings was 49.2 in. Maximum interior height was 48.8 in. Maximum interior width was 64.3 in. And total cargo volume was 133 cu. ft.

1986 Dodge Mini Ram Van Royal (DNP)

MINI RAM VAN ROYAL: The Royal was a step up in trim. It came with such "extras" as: Body color front and rear bumper end caps. Front and rear bumper protective rub strips. Cloth covered front compartment headliner. Dual note horn. Luxury steering wheel. Right side sun visor. Five-speed manual with overdrive. Styled road type wheels with bright trim ring, hub cover and nut cover.

I.D. DATA (Mini Ram Van): See D100 I.D.

Model	Body Type	Price	Weight	Prod. Total
K13	Mini Van	8308	2754	—
K63	Mini Van (Royal)	9128	2828	—

ENGINE (Mini Ram Van): Same as Caravan.

CHASSIS FEATURES: Wheelbase: 112 in. Overall length: 175.9 in. Overall width: 69.6 in. Overall height: 64.2 in. GVW: 3900-4400 lbs. Tires: P185/75R x 14.

POWERTRAIN OPTIONS: 2.6L (156 cu. in.) OHC. Four-cylinder. Three-speed automatic transmission.

CONVENIENCE OPTIONS: Most of the same items offered on the Carvan (plus lockable storage drawer under passenger bucket seat; dual fold away type exterior mirrors.

OPTION PACKAGES: VAN CONVERSION PACKAGE: accessory wire harness; black front and rear rub strips; bright bumpers with color-keyed end caps; driver and passenger seating package; gauge with gauge alert package; chrome/argent finish grille; 4500 lb. package; light package; bright trim on front park/side marker/turn, rear backup/side marker/stop/tail/turn lights; power steering; luxury two-spoke steering wheel. BASIC GROUP PACKAGE: 500-amp battery; remote release fuel filler door; 20-gallon fuel tank; gauge with gauge alert package; light package; sliding side door outside lock; maximum GVW package; power liftgate release; power steering; electronic speed control; tilt steering column; deluxe windshield wipers with intermittent wipe; rear window wiper/washer with fixed intermittent wipe. MAXIMUM 4810 lb. GVW PACKAGE: Heavy-duty brakes; heavy-duty suspension; LT195/75R x 14 SBR BSW tires. SPORT ROAD WHEEL PACKAGE: (Mini Ram Van Royal only, n.a. with 4810 lb. GVW package) cast aluminum 14 in. wheels; P195/75R x 14 SBR BSW tires with 2.2L engine; P205/70R x 14 SBR BSW tires with 2.6L engine. GAUGE WITH GAUGE ALERT and LIGHT packages same as Caravan.

NOTE: Mini Ram Van colors for 1986 included: Light Cream, Black Golden Bronze Pearl Coat, Dark Cordovan Pearl Coat, Gunmetal Blue Pearl Coat (extra cost), Gold Dust, Garnet Red Pearl Coat (extra cost), Radiant Silver, White, Ice Blue.

CARAVAN: — Styling was carried over from the previous year. Among the changes made for 1986 were: New brake proportioning valve, integrated wraparound front air dam, outside lock on sliding door, and improved manual transmission. Standard features included: 60-amp alternator. 335-amp maintenance free battery. Power brakes (front disc, rear drum) with load sensing proportioning valve. Color-keyed front and rear bumper end caps. Rear passenger assist strap. Front wheel drive. Front and rear bright bumpers with rub strips. Carpeting. Keys-in-ignition, fasten seat belts, headlamps on warning chimes. Cigarette lighter. Coolant overflow reservoir. Front door demisters. Sliding cargo compartment door with vented glass. Electronic ignition and voltage regulator. Remote fuel filler door release. 15-gallon fuel tank. Tinted glass (all windows). Bright grille. Cloth covered headliner. Bi-level ventilation heater. Inside hood release. Single note horn. Driver and passenger compartments dome light. Day/night inside rearview mirror. Black LH remote control exterior mirror. Black rear window and windshield molding. AM radio with electronic tuning and integral digital clock. Rack and pinion power steering. Deluxe two-spoke vinyl steering wheel. Compact spare tire. Five-speed manual transmission with overdrive. Deluxe wheel covers. Two speed windshield wipers with wet arm washers. Liftgate wiper/washer. Cloth with vinyl trim low back front bucket seats in cordovan, almond, silver/charcoal. A matching three-passenger bench seat was included.

CARAVAN SE: The SE (Special Edition) came with most of the same standard features as the base Caravan, plus (or in place of): Bright upper bodyside and liftgate moldings. Styled road type wheels with bright trim ring, hub center and nut covers. Deluxe cloth and vinyl trim. Low-back front bucket seats in cordovan, almond, blue, silver/charcoal and 3-passenger bench seat in matching trim. Dual note horn. Front folding arm rests.

CARAVAN LE: The LE (Luxury Edition) came with most of the same standard features as the SE plus (or in place of): Dual black remote control exterior rearview mirrors. Forward storage console. High-back reclining front bucket seats in luxury cloth with vinyl trim in cordovan, almond, silver/charcoal (blue was available with the optional vinyl upholstery). A three-passenger bench seat with matching trim. Deluxe sound insulation. Woodgrain center bodyside and liftgate applique. Ash receiver light. Luxury steering wheel.

I.D. DATA (Caravan): See D100 I.D.

Model	Body Type	Price	Weight	Prod. Total
K21	Mini-Van	9506	3005	—
K41	Mini-Van (SE)	9785	3046	—
K51	Mini-Van (LE)	10,528	3071	—

ENGINE (Caravan): 2.2L (135 cu. in.) OHC. Transverse. Four-cylinder. Brake horsepower: 101 at 5600 R.P.M. Compression ratio: 9.0:1. Carburetor: 2-bbl.

CHASSIS FEATURES: Wheelbase: 112 in. Overall length: 175.9 in. Overall width: 69.6 in. Overall height: 64.2 in. GVW: 4450-4600 lbs. Tires: P185/75R x 14 SBR.

POWERTRAIN OPTIONS: 2.6L (156 cu. in.) OHC. Four-cylinder. Three-speed automatic.

OPTION PACKAGES: BASIC GROUP: (Caravan) black front and rear bumper guards; 500-amp maintenance-free battery; deluxe intermittent windshield wipers; dual-note horns; dual remote control mirrors; light package; sliding side door with outside key lock. POPULAR EQUIPMENT DISCOUNT PACKAGE: (SE, LE) accessory carpeted floor mats front and rear; AM stereo/FM stereo radio with integral clock; 500-amp maintenance-free battery; deluxe sound insulation; deluxe intermittent windshield wipers; dual non-power remote control mirrors (SE); dual-note horns; electronic speed control; forward storage console; gauge with gauge alert package; illuminated visor vanity mirrors; light package; luxury steering wheel; overhead console (LE); power liftgate release; remote control rear quarter vent windows; sliding side door outside key lock. LUXURY EQUIPMENT DISCOUNT PACKAGE: (LE) popular equipment package; power door locks; power driver's bucket seat; power front doors windows; tilt steering column. TRAVEL EQUIPMENT DISCOUNT PACKAGE: (SE, LE) exterior right remote control mirror (SE); 500-amp maintenance free battery; dual-note horns (LE); 20-gallon fuel tank; 2.6L OHC. Four with automatic transmission; remote control rear quarter vent windows; seven passenger seating package; sliding side door outside key lock; sun screen glass. GAUGE ALERT PACKAGE: engine coolant temperature gauge with high temperature warning light; low voltage warning light; oil pressure gauge and low pressure warning light; trip odometer with pushbutton reset. LIGHT PACKAGE: (500-amp battery required on LE); ash receiver light; front map/reading lights (two); headlight switch callout light with time delay; ignition switch light with time delay; instrument panel door-ajar; low fuel warning and low washer fluid lights; liftgate mounted dual floodlights; underhood light. SEVEN-PASSENGER SEATING: (SE, LE) included second rear seat (two-passenger bench with fixed back, side arm rests and quick-release attachments); third seat (three-passenger bench with folding back, side arm rests, adjustable feature and quick-release attachments); ash receiver in right C-pillar, below belt, heavy-duty rear brakes; P195/75R x 14 SBR BSW tires; dual rear storage bins with arm rest covers incorporated into wheelwells. EIGHT-PASSENGER SEATING PACKAGE: (SE) included three-passenger front 40/60 bench seat in cloth vinyl trim; second seat and third seats like those in the 7-passenger seating package; heavy-duty rear brakes; heavy-duty suspension; P195/75R x 14 SBR BSW tires; dual rear storage bins with arm rests covers incorporated into wheelwells. SPORT WHEEL PACKAGE: 14 in. cast aluminum wheels; P195/75R x 14 SBR BSW tires (with 2.2L engine); P205/70R x 14 SBR WLT tires with 2.6L engine.

CONVENIENCE OPTIONS: Air conditioning. 500-amp maintenance free battery. Converta-bed rear seating (n.a. LE). Electric liftgate window defroster. 20-gallon fuel tank. Sunscreen glass. Roof mounted luggage rack. Dual remote control exterior mirrors (Caravan & SE). Color-keyed vinyl bodyside molding (standard woodtone applique omitted on LE models). Power door locks. Power liftgate release. Power release. Power driver's bucket seat. RADIOS: AM stereo/FM stereo with electronic tuning and four speakers; premium AM stereo/FM stereo with electronic tuning, seek-and-scan, Dynamic Noise Reduction, cassette tape player with automatic reverse, four speakers, AM stereo/FM stereo 36-watt Ultimate Sound System with electronic tuning, memory scan, up and down scan, Dynamic Noise Reduction, cassette tape player with automatic reverse, metal tape capability, five band graphic equalizer, joystick balance/fader control, ambience sound control, four speakers. Electronic speed control. Tilt steering column. Heavy-suspension (P195/75R x 14 tires included). Conventional spare tire. TIRES: P195/75R x 14 SBR BSW, P205/70R x 14 SBR WSW, P205/70R x 14 SBR black letter. Rear cargo compartment tonneau cover (5 or 6-pass. models only, n.a. with Converta-Bed). Wire wheel covers (SE, LE). Deluxes intermittent wipe windshield wipers with wet-arm washers.

NOTE: Caravan exterior monotone colors for 1986 included: Light Cream Black, Golden Bronze Pearl Coat, Dark Cordovan Pearl Coat, Gunmetal Blue Pearl Coat (extra cost), Gold Dust, Garnet Red Pearl Coat (extra cost), Radiant Silver, White, Ice Blue. Two-tone color combinations were: Gold Dust/Golden Bronze Pearl Coat, Garnet Red Pearl Coat/Black, Radiant Silver/Black, Light Cream/Golden Bronze Pearl Coat, Gunmetal Blue Pearl Coat/Black, Ice Blue/Gunmetal Blue Pearl Coat.

1986 Dodge Ram Passenger Van (JAG)

B150 VAN: — Dodge Ram Vans received an attractive, though minor, facelift for 1986. The Dodge name was now centered on the face of the downward sloping hood. Directly below it was the new, large rectangular slots theme grille with two rectangular headlamps integrated into it. The front bumper was also revised to include an indentation for a license plate in its center. Among standard features were: 60-amp alternator. Ashtray. 400-amp battery. Power front disc braks. Fasten seat belts, headlights on, the key in ignition warning buzzer. Cigar lighter. Corrosion protection. Right side and rear cargo doors (with no glass). Electronic ignition and voltage regulation system. Black floor mat on drivers side. Tinted front door windows and windshield. Glove box. Argent finished grille. Deluxe fresh air heater with defroster. In cab actuated hood release. Dual note electric horns. Bright hub caps. Bright 5 in. by 7 in. exterior mirrors. Nameplates on front doors, hood, and rear doors. Deluxe vinyl trim low-back drivers bucket seat. Front stabilizer bar. Drivers side sun visor. Electric windshield washers. Two-speed windshield wipers. 4-speed manual with overdrive.

B150 LONG RANGE RAM VAN: — The 1986 Long Range Ram Van came with such "extras" as: Bright front and rear bumpers. 35-gallon fuel tank. Bright finish grille. Rectangular Halogen headlights. Deluxe wheel covers.

1986 Dodge Ram Royal SE Passenger Van (DNP)

B150 WAGON: — The B150 Ram Wagon came with most of the same standard features found on the van plus (or in place of); Electronically tuned AM radio with integral digital clock. Right side and single rear doors. Black full length floor mat. All windows tinted. Rectangular Halogen headlights. Full length white hardboard headliner. Deluxe heater. 10 in. day/night inside rearview mirror. Front and rear doors side step sill scuff pads. Driver and passenger side sun visors.

B150 RAM VALUE WAGON: — The Ram Value Wagon was only available on a 109.6 in. w.b. Among its "extra" standard features were: Bright front and rear bumpers. Color-keyed full length carpeting. Insulated dash liner. Glove box with lock and light. Bright finish grille. Pecan woodtone instrument panel applique. Color-keyed instrument panel lower skirts. Cigar lighter, ignition and headlight symbol with time delay, and low washer fluid lights. Bright side and rear windows, taillight bezels, and windshield moldings. Inside mounted spare tire cover. Deluxe wheel covers. Two-speed intermittent type windshield wipers.

I.D. DATA (B150): See D100 I.D.

Model	Body Type	Price	Weight	Prod. Total
B150 Series — (109.6 in. w.b.)				
B13	Van	9040	3581	—
B13	Long Range Ram Van	9109	—	—
B11	Wagon	10,987	3966	—
(127.6 in. w.b.)				
B13	Van	—	—	—
B13	Long Range Ram Van	—	—	—
B11	Wagon	—	—	—
B11	Value Wagon	10,947	—	—

ENGINE (B150): 3.7L (225 cu. in.) Six-cylinder. Brake horsepower: 95 at 3600 R.P.M. Bore & stroke: 3.40 x 4.12 in. Compression ratio: 8.4:1. Carburetor: 1-bbl.

ENGINE (B250 Van): The handsome ¾-ton B250 Ram Van shared most of the same standard features offered on the ½-ton B150. However, it could be ordered with the 26 in. longer Maxi body (on 127.6 in. w.b.) Maxivan cargo area capacity was an impressive 304.5 cu. ft.

ENGINE (B250 Wagon): The B250 Ram Wagon had most of the same standard features as the B150 version. In addition to being heavier-duty, it could be had in regular or extra long Maxi bodies. Maxiwagons came with a payload capacity of 2545 lbs. and automatic transmission.

I.D. DATA (B250): See D100 I.D.

1986 Dodge Ram Royal Passenger Van (DNP)

Model	Body Type	Price	Weight	Prod. Total
B250 Series — (109.6 in. w.b.)				
B23	Van	9489	3539	—
B21	Wagon	—	—	—
(127.6 in. w.b.)				
B23	Van	—	—	—
B23	Maxivan	—	—	—
B21	Wagon	11,535	4135	—
B21	Maxiwagon	—	—	—

ENGINE (B250): Same as B150 except 5.2L, Carburetor: 2-bbl. V-8 was standard on Maxiwagon.

ENGINE (B350 Van): The top Dodge Ram Van for 1986 remained the B350. It came with most of the same standard features as the B150 plus (or in place of): Larger front and rear brakes. Three-speed automatic transmission. Axle type jack. It was offered with the regular or extended Maxivan bodies. Both were on the 127.6 in. w.b.

ENGINE (B350 Wagon): The heftiest Ram Wagon was the 1-ton B350. It could be ordered with seats for up to 12 people (regular wagon) or up to 15-passengers in the Maxiwagon.

I.D. DATA (B350): See D100 I.D.

Model	Body Type	Price	Weight	Prod. Total
B350 Series				
B33	Van	10,716	4037	—
B33	Maxivan	—	—	—
B31	Wagon	12,650	4475	—
B31	Maxiwagon	—	—	—

1986 Dodge Custom Ram Van (DNP)

ENGINE (B350): 5.2L (318 cu. in.) V-8. Brake horsepower: 135 at 4000 R.P.M. Bore & stroke: 3.91 x 3.31 in. Compression ratio: 8.5:1. Carburetor: 2-bbl. Maxiwagons and Vans and Maxivans with GVW ratings over 7500 lbs. came with 5.9L (360 cu. in.) Carburetor: 4-bbl. V-8.

CHASSIS FEATURES: Wheelbase: 109.6 in. (B150, B250), 127.6 in. Overall length: 178.9 in. (109.6 in. w.b.), 196.9 in. (127.6 in. w.b.), 222.9 in. (Maxi). Overall width: 79.8 in. Overall height: 79.6 in. (109.6 in. w.b.), 80.9 in. (127.9 in. w.b.), 80.6 in. (Maxi). GVW: 5000-6010 lbs. (B150), 6010-6400 lbs. (B250), 7500-9000 lbs. (B350). Tires: P195/75R x 15 (B150's with 5000 lb. GVW rating), P205/75R x 15 (B150), P225/75R x 15 or P235/75R x 15XL (B250), 8.00 x 16.5E (B350), 8.75 x 16.5E (B350 Maxi).

POWERTRAIN OPTIONS: 5.2L Carburetor: 2-bbl. V-8 (B150, B250), 5.9L Carburetor: 4-bbl. V-8 (B250, B350). Three-speed automatic transmission.

VAN OPTION PACKAGES: CONVENIENCE PACKAGE: power door locks (all doors); deluxe two-speed windshield wipers with intermittent wipe; glove box lock and light; ignition switch light and headlight symbol light with time delay (n.a. with tilt steering column); low washer fluid warning light. EXTERIOR APPEARANCE PACKAGE: bright front and rear bumpers, grille, side and rear fixed window moldings (with Vision Van Window Package and vented side glass), single rear door window surround molding; taillight bezels, windshield molding; rectangular Halogen headlights. LOCK PACKAGE: two keys; one operated ignition and front doors, the other operated side and rear cargo doors. POWER CONVENIENCE PACKAGE: power door locks; power windows (driver and front passenger doors only, front door lower trim panels included). SCHOOL BUS PACKAGE: (B350 Van with Solid Side Panel Van or Vision Van only) banded glass in front doors and vent wings; parking brake switch; school bus yellow paint. VAN CONVERSION APPEARANCE PACKAGE: accessory wiring harness, 500-amp maintenance free battery; Exterior Appearance Package garnish trim over front door headers; A-pillar, and around windshield; luxury steering wheel; woodtone applique instrument panel with color-keyed left and right lower skirts. PROSPECTOR VAN CONVERSION PACKAGE: front air conditioning; automatic speed control; automatic transmission; bright bumper guards and black protective rub strips; Convenience Package; dual low-mount exterior mirrors; dual rear cargo doors with vented glass; 35-gallon fuel tank; oil pressure gauge; Power Convenience Package; rubber scuff pads; tilt steering column; trip odometer; Van Conversion Appearance Package.

WAGON OPTION PACKAGES: EIGHT-PASSENGER SEATING PACKAGE: (B150 109.6 in. w.b. with 6010 lb. GVW package, all B250, B350 Wagon and Maxiwagon models) included one additional quick-release 3-pass. rear bench seat. TWELVE-PASSENGER SEATING PACKAGE: (B350) (rear door(s) with optional vented glass required at extra cost) included two additional rear bench seats: 2nd (3-pass.); 3rd (4-pass.); spare tire carrier relocated under third bench seat. FIFTEEN-PASSENGER SEATING PACKAGE: (B350 Maxiwagon with 8510 lb. GVW package and rear door(s) with vented glass) included three additional rear bench seats: 2nd (3-pass.); 3rd (4-pass.); 4th (4-pass.); spare tire carrier relocated under fourth bench seat. PROSPECTOR PACKAGES: (n.a. Ram Value Wagon) Package 1: automatic speed control; bright deluxe wheel covers, front and rear bumpers, grille, 6 in. x 9 in. low-mount mirrors; 35-gallon fuel tank; Convenience Package. Package 2: all items in Package 1 plus: bright bumper guards and black rub strips; Royal SE Decor Package. Package 3: all items in Package 2 plus: front air conditioning; Power Convenience Package; tilt steering column (when ordered with automatic transmission); two-tone paint package. CONVENIENCE PACKAGE and POWER CONVENIENCE PACKAGE: same as Vans. TWO-TONE PAINT PACKAGE: bright taillight bezels; lower side and rear moldings; two-tone paint; upper side and rear moldings; the main color was used above the upper molding and below the lower molding, with the secondary color running in a wide band between the moldings. ROYAL SE PACKAGE: (n.a. Ram Value Wagon) bright bumpers, grille, moldings on lower bodyside and rear and around windshield and side and rear fixed windows (except driver and passenger door windows); bright taillight bezels; deluxe two-speed windshield wipers with intermittent wipe; Leaping Ram plaque on front door; cigar lighter light; color-keyed accessory type rubber floor mats on drivers compartment floor; color-keyed carpeting on floor, around engine housing cover and over fuel filler cover; color-keyed instrument panel lower side skirts; luxury steering wheel; spare tire cover; courtesy step well light (front and side doors); dash liner insulation; dome/reading lamps; driver and front passenger reclining high-back Command bucket seats and rear bench seat(s) in color-keyed deluxe Kincaid cloth with Saddle Grain vinyl trim; front door arm rests with bright trim; front door trim panel applique with pull strap; garnish trim for sliding side door track cover; glove box lock and light; ignition switch light and headlight symbol light with time delay (n.a. with tilt steering column); low washer fluid warning light; nameplate on instrument panel; soft cloth covered headliner with insulation; woodtone applique on lower face of instrument panel.

VAN and WAGON CONVENIENCE OPTIONS: Front air conditioning. Rear auxiliary air conditioning. 114-amp alternator. 500-amp battery. Bumper guards with black protective strips. Transmission oil to air auxiliary cooling. Maximum engine cooling. Rear window defroster. Single rear door with vented glass. Dual rear doors with vented glass. Engine block heater. 35-gallon fuel tank. Sun screen privacy glass. Rear auxiliary heater. Dual bright low-mount exterior mirrors. Lower bodyside and rear moldings. Electronically tuned AM stereo/FM stereo radio with four speakers. Electronically tuned AM stereo/FM stereo with seek and scan, Dynamic Noise Reduction, cassette tape player with automatic reverse, and four speakers. Heavy-duty shocks. Automatic speed control. Tilt steering column. Deluxe wheel covers. Argent painted steel spoke road type wheels with bright hub and trim rings. Deluxe windshield wipers with intermittent wipe.

NOTE: Ram Van and Wagon exterior colors for 1986 were: Light Ivory Cream, Light Blue Metallic, Forest Green Metallic, Burnished Silver Metallic, Charcoal Gray Metallic, Medium Tan Metallic, Walnut Brown Metallic, Black, Medium Blue Metallic, White, Crimson Red.

1986 Dodge Custom Ram Sweptline Pickup (DNP)

D100 PICKUP: — Dodge "D" series pickups received an attractive facelift for 1986. The new grille consisted of four large "slots." The headlight doors were of matching height, which made them appear to be part of the grille. The front bumper was also revised. D100 buyers had their choice of 6½-ft. and 8-ft. Sweptline boxes. Among standard features were: Dry type air cleaners. 60-amp alternator. Ashtray. 400-amp maintenance-free battery. Power front disc brakes. Bright front bumper. Fasten seat belts, headlights-on, key-in-ignition warning buzzer. Cigar lighter. Coolant overflow reservoir. Corrosion protection. Insulated dash liner. Color-keyed arm rest, inner trim panels, and door pull straps. Electronic ignition and voltage regulation system. Carpeting. 20-gallon fuel tank. Tinted glass. Glove box. Fresh air heater with defrosters. In cab hood release. Dual note electric horns. Wheel covers. 10 in. day/night inside rearview mirror. Dual short-arm exterior rearview mirrors. Bright windshield molding. Color-keyed all-vinyl bench seat. Sun visors. Dual jet windshield washers. Two-speed windshield wipers. Four-speed manual with overdrive.

I.D. DATA (D100): See 1981 D150 I.D.

1986 Dodge Ram Sweptline Pickup (JAG)

Model	Body Type	Price	Weight	Prod. Total
D100	Pickup (6½-ft.)	7291	3451	—
D100	Pickup (8-ft.)	7515	3545	—

ENGINE (D100): 3.7L (225 cu. in.) Six-cylinder. Brake horsepower: 95 at 3600 R.P.M. Bore & stroke: 3.40 x 4.12 in. Compression ratio: 8.4:1. Carburetor: 1-bbl.

ENGINE (D150 Pickup): The D150 had most of the same features as the D100, but it could haul up to 1000 lbs. more payload.

I.D. DATA (D150): See D100 I.D.

Model	Body Type	Price	Weight	Prod. Total
D150	Pickup (6½-ft.)	8010	3456	—
D150	Pickup (6½-ft.)	8184	3550	—

ENGINE (D150): Same as D100.

ENGINE (D250 Pickup): The ¾-ton D250 had most of the same features as the D100 plus (or in place of): Larger brakes. Higher capacity rear axle, front and rear springs. A different (NP435) 4-speed manual transmission. And a 9.0 dual diaphragm vacuum booster.

1986 Dodge Ram Royal SE Sweptline Pickup (DNP)

I.A. DATA (D250): See D100 I.D.

Model	Body Type	Price	Weight	Prod. Total
D250	Chas.w/cab	10,479	3631	—
D250	Pickup (8-ft.)	9333	3851	—

ENGINE (D250): Same as D100.

ENGINE (D350 Pickup): The 1-ton D350 pickup shared most standard features with the D250. However, it had a greater payload capacity.

I.D. DATA (D350): See D100 I.D.

Model	Body Type	Price	Weight	Prod. Total
D350 Series — (131 in. w.b.)				
D350	Chas. w/cab	10,976	3762	—
D350	Pickup (8-ft.)	11,311	4093	—
(135 in. w.b.)				
D350	Chas. w/cab	11,256	4072	—
(159 in. w.b.)				
D350	Chas. w/cab	11,343	4142	—

1986 Dodge Power Ram Royal SE Sweptline Pickup (DNP)

ENGINE (D350): 5.9L (360 cu. in.) V-8. Brake horsepower: 185 at 4000 R.P.M. Bore & stroke: 4.00 x 3.58 in. Compression ratio: 8.0:1. Carburetor: 4-bbl.

CHASSIS FEATURES: Wheelbase: 115 in. (D100, D150), 131 in., 135 in. (D350), 159 in. (D350), GVW: 4950-5000 (D100), 4950-6050 (D150), 6300-6400 (W100, W150), 6600-8510 (D250), 6900-8510 (W250), 8700-10,500 (D350), 10,100-11,000 (W350). Tires: P195/75R x 15 (D100, D150), LT215/85R x 16C (D250), LT235/85R x 16E (D350).

POWERTRAIN OPTIONS: 5.2L (318 cu. in.) Carburetor: 2-bbl. V-8 (D100, D150, D250), 5.9L (360 cu. in.) Carburetor: 4-bbl. V-8. 4-speed automatic transmission.

OPTION PACKAGES: FOUR-WHEEL DRIVE: (W100, W150, W250 pickups, W250, W230 Chas. w/cab): Ram Trac parttime 4wd system (let drivers shift from 2wd to 4wd while traveling at up to 55 mph); power steering; two speed transfer case; Power Ram fender emblems. HEAVY-DUTY

1986 Dodge Ram Royal SE Sweptline Pickup (DNP)

PACKAGE: front stabilizer bar, heavy-duty shocks. POWER CONVENIENCE PACKAGE: power door locks, power front door windows. LIGHT PACKAGE: ash receiver light, exterior cargo light, glove box lock and light, map light. TWO-TONE PAINT PACKAGE: (n.a. on Chas. w/cab models) lower body-side moldings with black vinyl insert and bright partial wheel lip moldings; two-tone paint; upper side and rear exterior moldings. JOB-RATED PACKAGE: (n.a. with Six or on Chas. w/cab models) D250 and W250 only: 114-amp alternator, 500-amp maintenance-free battery, front stabilizer bar, 30-gallon fuel tank (W250), heavy-duty shocks, maximum engine cooling, 7500 lb. GVW, argent painted rear step bumper, transfer case skid plate (W250). PROSPECTOR PACKAGES: (Ram Sweptline pickups; D150, D250, D350, W150, W250) Package 1: electronic tuning AM radio with integral digital clock; bright front bumper guards with black insert; bright deluxe wheel covers; dual low-mount 6 in. x 9 in. mirrors; engine coolant temperature and oil pressure gauges; trip odometer; intermittent windshield wipers; light package; Ram's head hood ornament. Package 2: all items in package 1 plus: power convenience package, Royal SE Decor package. Package 3: all items in package 2 plus: air conditioning, two-tone paint package. SNO-COMMANDER PACKAGE LIGHT-DUTY: (W150 and W250) front clearance and identification lights; hydroelectric controls; plow lights; power angling blade with blade markers; power lift with seven-way control valve; Sno-Commander decal on pickups; spare tire and wheel with 7500 lb. GVW package (W250 pickup only); transmission oil temperature light with automatic transmission. SNO-COMMANDER PACKAGE HEAVY DUTY: (W250 and W350 models only) front clearance and identification lights; hydro-electric controls, plow lights; 96 in. long power angling blade with blade markers; power lift with seven way control valve; Sno-Commander decal on pickups; transmission oil temperature light with automatic transmission. ROYAL SE PACKAGE: (n.a. on D100 or W100, power steering required on D150 and D250 models) bright drip rail and rear window molding; bright grille with bright insert and headlight bezels; bright tailgate applique panel with Dodge Ram nameplate; bright taillight housing; bright tailgate upper and lower moldings; front fender leaping Ram plaque "Royal SE"; Halogen headlights; Ram's head hood ornament; bright door sill scuff plate; color-keyed carpeting with undelayment; color-keyed cowl side trim panels, soft cloth headliner, upper greenhouse garnish, vinyl door trim panels with woodtone stripe, assists strap with bright trim, arm rest, and carpeting on lower door; deluxe cloth with vinyl trim bench seats; electronically tuned AM radio with integral digital clock; Euro-sport steering wheel (black); hood inner panel insulation; nameplate on instrument panel; oil pressure and engine coolant temperature gauges; trip odometer; woodtone applique and bright trim on instrument panel.

CONVENIENCE OPTIONS: Air conditioning. 114-amp alternator. Antispin rear axle. Bright rear bumper. Step type rear bumper. Front bumper guards with black rub strip insert. Electronic digital clock integral with radio. Auxiliary transmission oil to air cooler. Maximum engine cooling. 30-gallon fuel tank. Engine block heater. Gauges for engine coolant temperature, fuel level, and oil pressure; ammeter; odometer; trip odometer; speedometer. Dual low-mount exterior mirrors. Lower body side and partial wheel lip moldings. Electronic tuning AM radio with integral digital clock. AM stereo/FM stereo radio with integral digital clock. Automatic speed control. Power steering. Tilt steering column. Deluxe wheel covers. Aluminum radial ribbed wheels (D150, W150 only). Argent painted steel spoke wheels with bright trim ring and hub center (D150, W150 only). Lockable sliding rear window. Two-speed windshield wipers with intermittent wipe.

NOTE: D series exterior colors for 1986 included: Black, Navy Blue Metallic, Cream, Medium Tan Metallic, Burnished Silver Metallic, Light Blue Metallic, Charcoal Gray Metallic, Canyon Red Metallic, Graphic Red, White.

DURANT FAMILY

By Jeff Gillis

Barely a month after his departure from the presidency of General Motors, flamboyant Billy Durant was in the automotive business again. This time the company bore *his* name. With the enthusiasm of a teenager, the 60-year-old restructured his organization for direct competition with GM.

For one thing, Durant's new line of vehicles was aimed at a similar price spectrum. Recognizing the value of a light-duty commercial line, Durant targeted his new Star for this category.

1920 Star Delivery Van (JG/DFR)

With introduction of the low-priced Star, in the summer of 1922, Durant had a sturdy, economical chassis for a light-duty truck. Powered by a four-cylinder, Continental flathead engine, the 1923 Model C Star featured the Durant tubular backbone and a flat frame which, like that of the Ford Model T, allowed many body styles to be fitted.

Labeled a Model CC, the Star truck had bodies sourced primarily from Martin-Parry Co. in York, Pa. and Indianapolis, Ind. They included an Open Delivery Wagon, Closed Panel Van and the industry's first regular-production station wagon. Prices for Star commercials ranged from $445 to $844.

For 1924, the CC line continued unchanged. It would not be until late spring that the trucks followed the change of passenger cars to a Model F series. This permitted the factory to phase-out inventories of parts. Prices were lowered, putting the little Star in solid competition with the Ford Model T.

Following introduction of a Model F commercial chassis, production continued, unchanged, until late 1925. At some time during the year, the station wagon disappeared from sales catalogs. Other commercial deletions followed. However, even without being promoted heavily, commercial vehicle sales continued at a reasonable pace.

Advertising of the commercial line remained a low-key effort during 1926, even though a new chassis design and advanced body styling were seen. The straight frame gave way to a conventional rear kick-up type and the tubular backbone was gone, too. New body styles included roadsters equipped with pickup or closed commercial boxes in place of luggage or rumbleseat compartments. In addition, the company offered a handsome, factory-built dealer service truck.

The year 1927 saw little change in the light-duty truckline. However, a new "big brother" appeared in the form of a one-ton series offering both four- and six-cylinder engines. By late in the season, the output of Star trucks was falling. However, the line was continued for 1928 nearly unchanged.

By January, 1928, the Star Six passenger car was replaced by the Durant Model 55. The four-cylinder Star was now known as Model M-2, but would be dropped before the summer. The four-cylinder model then became the Durant M-2, which was used as the basis for a light-duty commercial car chassis. Things were much the same except for slightly higher ($25 for the chassis) prices and a new model called the Convertible Business Roadster. It featured a trunk lid that was readily removable, to allow installation of a slip-in pickup box. Also added to the Durant truck-line was a Closed Cab Pickup.

By April, 1928, name changes were again in the offing. When the Star was exported, the name "Rugby" was used. So, the Rugby name was gradually applied to the domestic trucks. At first, the four-cylinder line retained the Durant name, while the six-cylinder series used Rugby. However, in a few months, even the fours had the Rugby name.

Durant Motors also marketed a ¾-ton truck based on its Model 65 six-cylinder passenger car chassis. This was the "Fast Mail," a *Speedwagon* type of truck sold in 1928 and 1929. A one-ton series was also available in both four- and six-cylinder versions. It appeared about March, 1928 and continued through 1929.

Little change was witnessed in the Rugby commercial line through 1929, but the major change was one that revealed what was transpiring in sales. In January, 1930, an "entirely new line" was announced by Durant Motors. It had restyled bodies and updated components and the truck line was no exception. But, drastic cuts in availability revealed Durant's inability to impact the market with its Rugby nameplate.

The Rugby ½-ton commercial chassis, for 1930, was available with just two body types. There was the Commercial Panel and a Commercial Canopy truck. Both featured a new six-cylinder Continental engine identical to that of Model 6-14 autos. Trucks and cars shared the 6-14 designation. Sales were disappointing. By mid-1930, production of 6-14 trucks ceased, though sales of leftover units continued. Also dribbling out of Durant agencies were the larger one-tonners, which were sold into 1931. No longer available, after 1929, was the ¾-ton truck.

By April 1931, Durant Motors was financially unstable. Commercial vehicle production had stopped entirely; auto production was grinding to a halt. The doors of the Lansing factory were closed on January 30, 1932. Production in Toronto, Canada continued for a short time under direction of Dominion Motors, which soon replaced the Durant with its own Frontenac.

1923 DURANT FAMILY

1923 Star Panel Delivery (JG/DFR)

COMMERCIAL — MODEL CC SERIES — FOUR-CYLINDER: — Almost from the beginning, the Star line offered a commercial series. Available on the same 102 in. w.b. and powered by the same 4-cyl. engine, the commercial line offered a first in the introduction of the station wagon body style. While this body was available for attachment to a variety of chassis, Durant Motors was the first manufacturer to offer the body as a "factory" item. It was not a special body, a way all other manufacturers handled such demand. Despite the fact that this was a passenger body, it was classed as a commercial vehicle by Durant. The body was built by Martin-Parry and was almost identical to the body fitted to the competing Model T Ford. A bare commercial chassis was available, as well as open and closed delivery versions. Capacity of the commercial line was between ¼- and ½-ton, depending on body style. Electric starting was standard equipment on the commercial line.

I.D. DATA: Serial number located on right side front of dash. Prefix identifies manufacturing plant as follows: "C" is Oakland, Calif.,; "L" is Lansing, Mich.; "T" is Toronto, Canada; "E" is Elizabeth, N.J. and "N" is Long Island City, N.Y. Starting: C-1; E-1; L-1; N-8; T-1. Ending: C-18,389; E-119,987; L-44,255; N-3,850; T-17412. Serial number spans include both cars and trucks. Engine numbers located on left-hand side of crankcase at upper corner. (Branhams calls this "right side" of crankcase, meaning right side of crankcase when looking only at left side of block.)

1923 Star Huckster Express (DFW/RVH)

Model	Body Type	Price	Weight	Prod. Total
Model CC	**— (¼-Ton to ½-Ton) —**	**(4-cyl.)**		
CC	Chassis	380	—	—
CC	Station Wagon	610	—	—
CC	Open Dely. Wagon	610	—	—
CC	Closed Dely. Wagon	645	—	—

ENGINE: Vertical. Cast en bloc. Four-cylinder. Cast en bloc. Bore & stroke: 3⅜ in. x 4¼ in. Displacement: 103.4 cu. in. Brake horsepower: 35. Net horsepower: 15.63. Three main bearings. Solid valve lifters. Carburetor one-barrel.

1923 Star Canopy Top Express (JG/DFR)

CHASSIS: Wheelbase: 102 in. Tires: 30 x 3½ in.

TECHNICAL: Selective sliding transmission. Speeds: 3F/1R. Floor-mounted gearshift lever. Single plate clutch. Sprial Bevel drive. Semi-floating rear axle. Rear wheel brakes: (foot) contracting; (hand) expanding. Wood-spoke wheels.

OPTIONS: Front bumper. Outside rearview mirror. Runningboard step plates. Motometer. Side curtains. Special equipment package including nickel trim and disc-wheels. Special colors.

HISTORICAL: Introduced: Jan. 1923. Calendar year registrations: Stars totaled 105,288 registrations in 1923, including both passenger cars and trucks.

Innovations: First factory built station wagon was made by Star. All new commercial vehicle series.

Notes: William C. Durant founded Durant Motors, with corporate headquarters in New York City. "For your all-wealther car get a sedan Star" was a company advertising slogan. The Star's 2.2-litre engine was built by Continental Motors Co. The 1-ton Mason truck was also built by a Durant owned company. Star sold many commercial vehicles in the export market.

Pricing

	5	4	3	2	1
1923					
Model CC Series					
Station Wagon	1650	3300	5500	7700	11,000
Open Delivery Wagon	1200	2460	4100	5700	8200
Closed Delivery Wagon	1300	2550	4250	5900	8500

1924 DURANT FAMILY

1924 Star Panel Delivery (JG/DFR)

1924 Star Depot Hack (JG/HFM)

COMMERCIAL — MODEL F SERIES — FOUR-CYLINDER: — For 1924, styling changes represented the major alterations in the line for both passenger and commercial vehicles. Body choices on the commercial line matched those of the previous year, with the exception of a fully-enclosed cab on the panel delivery. This model was not available in 1923. Prices rose slightly. The bodies, unchanged from 1923, were supplied by Martin-Parry.

I.D. DATA: Serial number located: Same as 1923; same codes. (Model C) Starting: C-18,390; E-119,989; L-44,255; T-17,413. (Model C) Ending: C-22,000; E-180,000; L-55,000; T-19,900. (Model F) Starting: C-200,000; E-200,000; L-200,000; T-200,000. (Model F) Ending: C-214,191; E-260,016; L-230,712; T-206,108.

1924 Star Canopy Top Express (JG/DFR)

Model	Body Type	Price	Weight	Prod. Total
Model F	**— (¼-Ton to ½-Ton) — (4-cyl.)**			
F	Chassis	405	1105	—
F	Station Wagon	635	(2400)	—
F	Open Dely. Wagon	565	(1800)	—
F	O.F. Closed Dely. Wag.	585	(2120)	—
F	C.F. Closed Dely. Wag.	610	(2155)	—

NOTE: Weights in brackets are estimates based on comparable vehicles.

ENGINE: Vertical. Cast en bloc. Four-cylinder. Cast en bloc. Bore & stroke: 3⅜ in. x 4¼ in. Displacement: 130.4 cu. in. Brake horsepower: 35. Net horsepower: 15.63. Three main bearings. Solid valve lifters. Carburetor one-barrel.

CHASSIS (Model F): Wheelbase: 102-109 in.* Tires: 30 x 3½ in.

* NOTE: The 1924 Star Delivery Wagon with Panel Top and Vestibule front had a 109 in. w.b.

TECHNICAL: Selective sliding transmission. Speeds: 3F/1R. Floor-mounted gearshift lever. Single plate clutch. Sprial bevel drive. Semi-floating rear axle. Rear wheel brakes: (foot) contracting; (hand) expanding. Wood-spoke wheels.

OPTIONS: Front bumper. Outside rearview mirror. Runningboard step plates. Motometer. Side curtains (specific models). Special equipment package including nickel trim and disc-wheels. Special colors. Aftermarket bodies for chassis-only.

1924 Star Panel Side - Closed Front Delivery (JG/DFR)

HISTORICAL: Introduced: Jan. 1924. Calendar year registrations: (cars and trucks) 72,020.

Innovations: New fully-enclosed cab for panel delivery truck.

Pricing

1924 **Model F**	5	4	3	2	1
Station Wagon	1650	3300	5500	7700	11,000
Open Delivery Wagon	1200	2460	4100	5700	8200
Open Vestibule Closed Delivery Wagon	1300	2550	4250	5900	8500
Closed Vestibule Closed Delivery Wagon	1250	2500	4150	5800	8300

1925 DURANT FAMILY

1925 Star Enclosed Cab Pickup (DFW/RCK)

COMMERCIAL — SERIES F-25 — FOUR-CYLINDER: — Model year 1925 was a repeat of 1924 with no change to the line other than the lack of mention of the station wagon body style. Production of this body style, in 1924, dropped sharply. This was probably the reason for it being dropped in 1925. Sales remained constant on the remainder of the commercial line. Through this period, heavier trucks were built (over 1-ton capacity) under the name Mason Roadking, which became the Flint Roadking in 1925. Star prices included tools, jack, speedometer, electric horn, ignition theft lock, demountable rims, spare tire carrier and headlight dimmer.

I.D. DATA: Serial number located: Same as 1923; same codes. Starting: C-214,192; E-260.017; L-230,713; T-206,109. Ending: C-280,631; E-289,986; L-298,294; T-277,533. Engine numbers located: same as 1923.

1925 Star Enclosed Cab Pickup (DFW/RCK)

Model	Body Type	Price	Weight	Prod. Total
F-25	Chassis	445	1105	—
F-25	Open Dely. Wag.	540	(1800)	—
F-25	Open Front Panel Dely. Wag.	600	(2120)	—
F-25	Closed Panel Dely. Wag.	635	(2155)	—

NOTE: Weights in brackets are estimates based on comparable models.

ENGINE: Vertical. Cast en bloc. Four-cylinder. Bore & stroke: 3⅜ in. x 4¼ in. Displacement: 130.4 cu. in. Brake horsepower: 35. Net horsepower: 15.63. Three main bearings. Solid valve lifters. Carburetor one-barrel.

CHASSIS (Series F-25): Wheelbase: 102-109 in. Tires: 30 x 3½ in.

1925 Star Depot Hack (DFW/BAC)

TECHNICAL: Selective sliding transmission. Speeds: 3F/1R. Floor-mounted gearshift lever. Single plate clutch. Sprial bevel drive. Semi-floating rear axle. Brakes: Service contracting on rear wheels; emergency expanding on rear wheels. Wood spoke wheels.

OPTIONS: Front bumper. OSRV mirror. Runningboard step plates. Moto-meter. Side curtains (specific models). Special equipment package. Non-factory colors. Aftermarket bodies for chassis-only.

HISTORICAL: Introduced: Jan. 1925. Calendar year registrations: (cars and trucks) 74,543.

Innovations: Station wagon deleted. Durant-built Mason "Road King" renamed a Flint model. (Flint was another company in W.C. Durant's second automotive empire.)

NOTES: Stars were built by Durant Motors, Inc. of New Jersey. Other features included a cellular radiator, force feed and splash lubrication, two-unit starting system and vacuum gasoline feed. "Low cost transporation" was the company slogan this year.

Pricing

	5	4	3	2	1
1925					
Series F-25					
Open Delivery Wagon	1200	2460	4100	5700	8200
Open Vestibule Closed Delivery Wagon	1300	2550	4250	5900	8500
Closed Vestibule Closed Delivery	1250	2500	4150	5800	8300

1926 DURANT FAMILY

1926 Star Roadster w/Panel Box (JG/DFR)

COMMERCIAL — MODEL M SERIES/MODEL R SERIES — FOUR-CYLINDER/SIX-CYLINDER: — With the announcement of the six-cylinder line for 1926, new styling and changes in the commercial line were evident. Gone was the station wagon, but a roadster had been added. It was available with either pickup box or closed commercial box. Even a dealer service truck was shown in the 1926 sales folders. Larger tires and an improved four-cylinder engine completed the styling changes. Prices edged upwards again and the light commercial line met with moderate sales success. Standard equipment was the same as in 1925. In both 1926 and 1927, Star produced a line of one-ton trucks with both four- and six-cylinder power. The four would replace the Flint Road King of 1925, and the six would go under the title Star compound "Fleetruck.

I.D. DATA: Serial number located: Same as 1923; same coding. Model F starting: C-280,632; E-289,987; L-298,295; T-227,534. Model F ending: C-325,000; E-325,000; L-325,000; T-325,000. Model M starting: 350,000; Model M ending: 379,999; Model R starting: 1,000. Model R ending: 15,999. Engine numbers located: same as 1923.

1926 Star Convertible Roadster w/Commercial Box (JG)

Model	Body Type	Price	Weight	Prod. Total
M	Chassis	425	—	—
M	Rds. Pickup	525	—	—
M	Closed Box Rds. Pickup	540	—	—
M	Open Cab Canopy	565	—	—
M	Closed Cab Canopy	590	—	—
M	Steel Panel Dely.	670	—	—
M	Service Truck	1000	—	—
Road King — (1-Ton) — (4-cyl.)				
M	Chassis	—	—	—
Fleetruck — (1-Ton) — (6-cyl.)				
R	Chassis	975	—	—

ENGINE (4-cyl.): Vertical. Cast en block. Four-cylinder. Cast iron. Bore & stroke: 3⅜ in. x 4¼ in. Displacement: 152.1 cu. in. Brake horsepower: 30 at 2200 R.P.M. Net horsepower: 18.23. Three main bearings. Solid valve lifters. Carburetor one-barrel.

ENGINE (6-cyl.): Vertical. Cast en block. Six-cylinder. Cast iron. Bore & stroke: 2¾ in. x 4¾ in. Displacement: 169.2 cu. in. Brake horsepower: 40 at 2400 R.P.M. Net horsepower: 18.15. Four main bearings. Solid valve lifters. Carburetor one-barrel.

CHASSIS (Model M): Wheelbase: 103 in. Tires: 29 x 4.40 in. (balloon).

1926 Star Closed Front With Cowl Steel Panel (JG/DFR)

CHASSIS (Model R): Wheelbase: 107 in. Tires: 29 x 4.40 in. (balloon).

NOTE: Chassis specifications for 1-ton models not available. The wheelbase given above is for six-cylinder passenger cars. A 1-ton truck would probably be larger.

TECHNICAL: Selective sliding transmission. Speeds: 3F/1R (*). Floor-mounted gearshift lever. Single-plate, dry disc clutch. Semi-floating rear axle. Brakes: (foot) contracting on rear wheels; (hand) expanding on rear wheels. Wood spoke wheels.

NOTE (*): The Fleetruck advertised a four-speed transmission as ''the greatest single step forward in a quarter century of motor transportation.''

OPTIONS: Front bumper. OSRV mirror. Step plates. Motometer. Delixe equipment. Special paint. Aftermarket bodies for chassis-only.

HISTORICAL: Introduced: Jan. 1926. Calendar year registrations: (cars and trucks) 79,309.

Innovations: New 6-cyl. series. 1 in. longer for 4-cyl. w.b. Sixes have new 107 in. w.b. New body styles include open and closed box roadster pickups, closed cab canopy, steel panel delivery and service truck.

NOTES: The Fleetruck's 4-spd. transmission was said to reduce fuel costs by 20 percent. It's official name was ''Star Six Compound Fleetruck.'' New 2.8-litre six also built by Continental Motors Co. The new 152.1 cu. in. four was Continental's Model 14L powerplant.

Pricing

1926	5	4	3	2	1
Model M Series					
Rds. Pickup	1350	2650	4400	6150	8800
Closed Box Pickup	1300	2550	4250	5900	8500
Open Cab Canopy Delivery	1200	2400	4000	5600	8000
Closed Cab Canopy Delivery	1200	2460	4100	5700	8200
Steel Panel Delivery	1300	2550	4250	5900	8500
Service Truck	1250	2500	4150	5800	8300
Road King					
1-Ton Express	830	1650	2750	3850	5500
Fleetruck					
1-Ton Express	830	1650	2750	3850	5500

1927-1928 DURANT

COMMERCIAL — MODEL M — FOUR-CYLINDER: — For 1927, the commercial line was being slowly phased out. The models of the previous year were continued. By mid-year, production of the four-cylinder light commercial line had been terminated. It would seem, however, that sales may have continued into 1928, because the National Automobile Dealer's Association (NADA) lists the 1928 Star Model M in its *Official used Car Guide* from the summer of 1934.

I.D. DATA: Serial number located: Same as 1923. Model M starting: 380,000. Model M ending: 414,999. Model R starting: 16,000. Model R ending: 32,999. Engine numbers located same as 1923.

Model	Body Type	Price	Weight	Prod. Total
Model M Series — (¼- to ½-Ton) — (4-cyl.)				
M	Chassis	470	1550	—
M	Rds. Pickup	545	—	—
M	Closed Box Rds. Pickup	570	—	—
M	Open Cab Canopy	585	—	—

Model	Body Type	Price	Weight	Prod. Total
M	Closed Cab Canopy	610	—	—
M	Steel Panel Dely.	710	—	—
M	Service Truck	712	—	—
Road King — (1-Ton) — (4-cyl.)				
M	Chassis		—	—
Fleetruck — (1-Ton) — (6-cyl.)				
R	Chassis	1025	—	—

1927 Star Deluxe Service and Supply Car (JG/DFR)

ENGINE (Model M): Inline. L-head. Four-cylinder. Cast iron. Bore & stroke: 3⅜ in. x 4¼ in. Displacement: 152.1 cu. in. Brake horsepower: 30 at 2200 R.P.M. Net horsepower: 18.23. Three main bearings. Solid valve lifters. Carburetor one-barrel.

ENGINE (Model R): Inline. L-head. Six-cylinder. Cast iron block. Bore & stroke: 2¾ in. x 4¾ in. Displacement: 169.2 cu. in. Brake horsepower: 40 at 2400 R.P.M. Net horsepower: 18.15. Four main bearings. Solid valve lifters. Carburetor one-barrel.

CHASSIS: Same as 1926.

TECHNICAL: Same as 1926.

OPTIONS: Same as 1926.

1927 Star Canopy Top Open Cab Express (JG/DFR)

1927 Star Canopy Top w/Closed Cab and Cowl (JG/DFR)

Pricing

1928 DURANT FAMILY

1928 Rugby Light Four Delivery Roadster (JG/DFR)

DURANT — MODEL M-2 SERIES — FOUR-CYLINDER: — In January 1928, Durant Motors announced a restyled line of cars. The Star name would remain on the four-cylinder model, and the Durant name, which had been discontinued in mid-1926, would appear again on the three six-cylinder models. At the Toronto factory, in Canada, the commercial line would be revived using the Durant name and featuring a variety of body styles similar to those available on the Star chassis in 1926-1927. Production at the Elizabeth, N.J. factory listed only the bare chassis and the convertible roadster under the Durant name on the price list, but it is believed the complete line was also available from the Elizabeth factory. The models shown below are those listed in a 1934 NADA *used Car Guide.* The small, ½-ton, commercial line was powered by the same Continental four-cylinder engine used in the Star. It featured only updated styling and paint schemes as the change for 1928. A second line of trucks, this a three-quarter ton series built on the model 65 Durant chassis, would be produced only in the Lansing plant. These would bear the Rugby name, not Durant. This series had only six-cylinder models. Having started in late March 1928, production of trucks under the Durant name continued for only a few months and by summer, all commercial production would change to the Rugby name. Prior to this, the Rugby name had been used on Star cars that were made for export sale. However, the NADA continued to list these Series M-2 Durant trucks in 1929. This was probably because sales of trucks remaining in inventory continued into calendar 1929.

I.D. DATA: Serial number located on dash under hood. Starting: 1001. Ending: 34,999. Engine numbers located on left side of cylinder block. Numbers not available.

NOTE: The serial number span indicates trucks and cars built in mixed production.

Model	Body Type	Price	Weight	Prod. Total
Durant Series M-2 — (½-Ton) — (4-cyl.)				
M-2	Conv. Rds. w/Open Box	—	—	Note 1
M-2	Conv. Rds. w/Closed Box	—	—	Note 1
M-2	Closed Cab Express	—	—	Note 1
M-2	Canopy Express	—	—	Note 1
M-2	Straight Side Express	—	—	Note 1
M-2	Panel Body	—	—	Note 1
M-2	Chassis	495	1605	Note 1

NOTE 1: Production figures for Durant and Rugby trucks for 1928 totaled about 900 vehicles.

NOTE 2: The NADA listed this as the "M-2" series in its used car guides.

ENGINE (Durant M-2): Inline. L-head. (Continental W5). Four-cylinder. Cast iron block. Bore & stroke: 3⅜ in. x 4¼ in. Displacement: 152.1 cu. in. Compression ratio: 4.20:1. Brake horsepower: 36 at 2400 R.P.M. Net horsepower: 18.2. Three main bearings. Solid valve lifters. Tillotson model one-barrel (one-inch).

$495
nsing, Mich.

1928 Rugby Light Four Chassis and Cowl (JG/DFR)

RUGBY — SERIES T/S-2/L-8 — (ALL ENGINES): —Apparently, three lines of Rugby trucks (a name formerly used on cars exported to British Commonwealth countries) were produced by Durant in 1928. The S-2 was the Durant M-2 with another name. It was identical in specifications and also its half-ton rating. There was also a ¾-ton Model T series, which seems to have been released in April of the year. It was based on the six-cylinder Durant 65 and shared that passenger car's 110 in. w.b. Using the same engine, but with a 128 in. w.b., was the 1-ton Rugby "Fast Mail." Designated the L-2 series, this truck featured a four-speed transmission and a hand-brake that worked on all four wheels. An interesting new model was a commercial-chassis station wagon named the Suburban.

I.D. DATA: Serial number located: Same as Durant. Starting: (Model T) 1001; (others) N/A. Ending: (Model T) 1199; (others) N/A. Engine numbers located: Same as Durant. Numbers unavailable.

Model	Body Type	Price	Weight	Prod. Total
Rugby S-2 — (½-Ton) — (4-cyl.)				
S-2	Chassis	495	1605	Note 1
S-2	Conv. Rds. w/o Box	580	—	Note 1
S-2	Open Express	—	—	Note 1
S-2	Canopy Express	—	—	Note 1
S-2	Suburban (Sta. Wag.)	—	—	Note 1
S-2	Panel	775	—	Note 1
Rugby "T" — (¾-Ton) — (6-cyl.)				
T	Chassis	725	1780	Note 2
T	Pickup	—	—	Note 2
T	Canopy Express	—	—	Note 2
T	Screen Delivery	—	—	Note 2
T	Panel	—	—	Note 2
T	Sedan Delivery	—	—	Note 2
Rugby "Fast Mail" — (1-Ton) — (6-cyl.)				
L-2	Chassis	725	—	Note 1
L-2	Open Express	—	—	Note 1
L-2	Canopy Express	—	—	Note 1
L-2	Screenside Express	—	—	Note 1
L-2	Suburban (Sta. Wag.)	—	—	Note 1
L-2	Panel Body	975	—	Note 1

NOTE 1: Production of Durant and Rugby trucks totaled about 900 vehicles.

NOTE 2: Serial numbers suggest production of 198 Model T Rugbys.

ENGINE (Series S-2): Same as Durant M-2 engine.

ENGINE: Inline. L-head. Continental Model T. Six-cylinder. Cast iron. Bore & stroke: 2⅞ in. x 4¾ in. Displacement: 185 cu. in. Compression ratio: 4.79:1. Brake horsepower: 47 at 2800 R.P.M. Net horsepower: 19.84. Four main bearings. Solid valve lifters. Carburetor: Tillotson model one-inch, one-barrel.

CHASSIS (Durant M-2 Series): Wheelbase: 107 in. Tires: 29 x 4.40 in. (Fisk).

CHASSIS (Rugby S-2 Series): Wheelbase: 107 in. Tires: 29 x 4.40 in.

CHASSIS (Rugby T Series): Wheelbase: 110 in. Tires: 29 x 5.00 in. (Fisk).

CHASSIS (Rugby L-2 Series): Wheelbase: 128 in.

1928 Rugby Model X 1-Ton Chassis and Cowl (JG/DFR)

267

1928 Durant Convertible With Open Box (JG/DFR)

1928 Durant Closed Cab Panel Delivery (JG/DFR)

1928 Durant Canopy Top Express (JG/DFR)

1928 Durant Conv. Roadster w/Panel Box (JG/DFR)

1928 Durant Special Straight Side Express (JG/DFR)

1928 Rugby Light Four Suburban (JG/DFR)

1928 Durant Half-Ton Truck, Front View (JG/DFR)

268

1928 Rugby Light Four Canopy Top Express (JG/DFR)

HISTORICAL: Introduced: January. Calendar year registrations: (1927 cars and trucks) 55,039. Calendar year registrations: (1928 cars & trucks) 71,368.

Innovations: In 1928, there was a new Durant Model M-2 commercial vehicle series which used a Continental Special (36 horsepower) instead of Continental 14L (30 horsepower) version of the 152.1 cu. in. four. It had a w.b. of 4 in. longer than the Star Model M.

TECHNICAL: Selective sliding transmission. Speeds: 3F/1R (4F/1R on 1-ton "Fast-Mail.") Floor-mounted gearshift lever. Dry disc type clutch. Asbestos lining. Semi-floating rear axle. Spiral bevel gear. Overall ratio: (S-2s) 4.87:1; (L-2) 4.79:1. Four-wheel mechanical brakes. Wood spoke wheels.

OPTIONS: Clock. Spotlight. Backing light. Windshield Wings. Heater. Bumper. Spring covers. Speedometer (on S-2). Gasoline gauge (S-2). Thermometer (S-2). Stoplight (S-2). Shock absorbers (S-2). Spare tire. Tire cover. Tire lock. Power trie pump. Special paint. Aftermarket bodies.

HISTORICAL: Introduced: Jan. 1928. Calendar year registrations: (cars and trucks) 71,368. Calendar year production: (trucks) approximately 900.

Innovations: Star commercial line adopts Durant name. Durant commercial line becomes Rugby truck. New Rugby six-cylinder was introduced.

NOTES: Rugby "Fast Mail" 1-ton express with 6-cyl. engine and 128 in. w.b. also available in 1928. Durant and Rugby trucks had Autolite ignition and Bendix brakes. The Rugby name was previously used on Stars sold in the British Commonwealth countries.

Pricing

	5	4	3	2	1
1928					
Durant Series M-2					
Conv. Rds. w/o Open Box	1350	2650	4400	6150	8800
Conv. Rds. w/Closed Box	1300	2550	4250	5900	8500
Closed Cab Express	1200	2400	4000	5600	8000
Canopy Express	1200	2460	4100	5700	8200
Straight Side Express	1200	2400	4000	5600	8000
Panel Body	1300	2550	4250	5900	8500
Rugby Series S-2					
Conv. Rds. w/Open Box	1350	2650	4400	6150	8800
Open Express	1200	2400	4000	5600	8000
Canopy Express	1200	2460	4100	5700	8200
Station Wagon	1850	3750	6250	8750	12,500
Panel	1300	2550	4250	5900	8500
Rugby Model T					
Pickup	1130	2250	3750	5250	7500
Canopy	1150	2310	3850	5400	7700
Screen	1150	2310	3850	5400	7700
Panel	1200	2400	4000	5600	8000
Sedan Delivery	1250	2500	4150	5800	8300
Rugby "Fast Mail"					
Express	1100	2200	3650	5100	7300
Canopy	1130	2250	3750	5250	7500
Screen	1130	2250	3750	5250	7500
Station Wagon	1650	3300	5500	7700	11,000
Panel	1170	2340	3900	5450	7800

1929 DURANT FAMILY

1929 Rugby Cab with Open Express Body (JG/DFR)

DURANT — MODEL S-2 SERIES — FOUR-CYLINDER: — According to *USED CAR VALUE GUIDES* published by the National Automobile Dealers Association (NADA), Durant trucks continued to be sold in 1929. Factory records suggest, however, that none were produced. Since the NADA guides are generally a reliable source of information, we can guess that trucks sold in 1929 were leftover 1928 models. This would be consistent with NADA listings indicating no change in model nomenclature, prices or specifications. In fact, these guides indicate that trucks made or sold after August 1928 were considered "1929." (This was in the period when most manufacturers released several series each year; the summer

line being sold as next year's model.) This could mean that all of the trucks were sold in 1928 (remember that production supposedly ceased in March of that year) although some may have been titled as 1929 models. In any case, the main difference in a 1929 Durant truck would be a serial number above 35001.

1929 Rugby Model X One-Ton Canopy Express (JG/DFR)

1929 Rugby Model X One-Ton Grain Body (JG/DFR)

I.D. DATA: Serial number located on dash under hood. Starting: 35001. Ending: 42000. Engine numbers located on left side of cylinder block. Numbers not available.

NOTE: The serial number span indicates trucks and cars built in mixed production.

Model	Body Type	Price	Weight	Prod. Total
Durant Series S-2 — (½-Ton) — (4-cyl.)				
S-2	Chassis	495	1605	Note 1
S-2	Conv. Rds. w/Open Box	—	—	Note 1
S-2	Conv. Rds. w/Closed Box	—	—	Note 1
S-2	Closed Cab Express	—	—	Note 1
S-2	Canopy Express	—	—	Note 1
S-2	Straight Side Express	—	—	Note 1
S-2	Panel Body	—	—	Note 1

NOTE 1: Apparently, no Durant trucks were produced in 1929.

1929 Rugby Model X One-Ton Stake Body (JG/DFR)

1929 Rugby Model X One-Ton Express (JG/DFR)

1929 Rugby One-Ton Chassis and Cowl (JG/DFR)

1929 Rugby One-Ton Panel Delivery Body (JG/DFR)

1929 Rugby Fast Mail Chassis and Cowl (JG/DFR)

1929 Rugby Fast Mail Canopy Express (JG/DFR)

1929 Rugby One-Ton Express Chassis and Cab (JG/DFR)

1929 Rugby Fast Mail Screenside Express (JG/DFR)

ENGINE (Durant S-2): Inline. L-head. (Continental W5). Four-cylinder. Cast iron block. Bore & stroke: 3⅜ in. x 4¼ in. Displacement: 152.1 cu. in. Compression ratio: 4.20:1. Brake horsepower: 36 at 2400 R.P.M. Net horsepower: 18.2. Three main bearings. Solid valve lifters. Carburetor: Tillotson model one-inch, one-barrel

RUGBY — SERIES S-4/T/L-2 — (ALL ENGINES):—For 1929, the S-2 became the S-4. There were no changes in the specifications for this 4-cyl. powered ½-tonner. It remained on the 107 in. w.b. formerly used by the Star car. The ¾-ton Model T was also carried over. It again used the Durant 65 passenger car's 110 in. w.b. and 6-cyl. engine. Standard equipment on this truck, which cost extra on other models, included a speedometer, gasoline gauge, thermometer, stoplight and shock absorbers. The 'Fast Mail' also returned. It had acquired — temporarily — a 3x2 transmission in place of its former four-speed.

I.D. DATA: Serial number located: Same as Durant. Starting: (S-4) 1001; (T) 1201; (L-2) N/A. Ending: (S-4) 1226; (T) 2000; (L-2) N/A.

Model	Body Type	Price	Weight	Prod. Total
Rugby S-4 — (½-Ton) — (4-cyl.)				
S-4	Chassis	495	1605	Note 1
S-4	Pickup	580	—	Note 1
S-4	Canopy Express	—	—	Note 1
S-4	Screen Delivery	—	—	Note 1
S-4	Sedan Delivery	—	—	Note 1
S-4	Panel	775	—	Note 1
Rugby "T" — (¾-Ton) — (6-cyl.)				
T	Chassis	725	1780	Note 2
T	Pickup	—	—	Note 2
T	Canopy Express	—	—	Note 2
T	Screen Delivery	—	—	Note 2
T	Panel	—	—	Note 2
T	Sedan Delivery	—	—	Note 2
Rugby 'Fast Mail' — (1-Ton) — (6-cyl.)				
L-2	Chassis	725	—	Note 3
L-2	Open Express	—	—	Note 3
L-2	Canopy Express	—	—	Note 3
L-2	Screen Delivery	—	—	Note 3
L-2	Suburban (Sta. Wag.)	—	—	Note 3
L-2	Panel	—	—	Note 3

NOTE 1: Serial number span suggests production of 225 Series S-4 Rugbys.

NOTE 2: Serial number span suggests production of 799 Model T Rugbys.

1929 Rugby Fast Mail Suburban (JG/DFR)

NOTE 3: Total production known to be about 1,300 units, for **all** Rugbys. Considering Notes 1 and 2, this suggests production of about 276 'Fast Mails.'

ENGINE (Series S-4): Same as Durant M-2 engine.

ENGINE: Inline. L-head. (Continental). Six-cylinder. Cast iron. Bore & stroke: 2⅞ in. x 4¾ in. Displacement: 185 cu. in. Compression ratio: 4.79:1. Brake horsepower: 47 at 2800 R.P.M. Net horsepower: 19.84. Four main bearings. Solid valve lifters. Carburetor: Tillotson model one-inch, one-barrel.

CHASSIS (Durant M-2): Wheelbase: 107 in. Tires: 29 x 4.40 in. (Fisk).

CHASSIS (Rugby S-4): Wheelbase: 107 in. Tires: 29 x 4.40 in. (Fisk).

CHASSIS (Rugby T Series): Wheelbase: 110 in. Tires: 29 x 5.00 in. (Fisk).

1929 Rugby Fast Mail Panel Delivery (JG/DFR)

1929 Rugby One-Ton Three-Panel Grain Body (JG/DFR)

1929 Rugby Model X One-Ton Panel Delivery (JG/DFR)

1929 Rugby One-Ton Two-Unit Stake Body (JG/DFR)

1929 Rugby Model X One-Ton Panel Delivery (JG/DFR)

1929 Rugby Two-Unit Wide Express (JG/DFR)

1929 Rugby Two-Unit Express Body w/Cab (JG/DFR)

1929 Rugby One-Ton Canopy Top Express (JG/DFR)

1929 Rugby Fast Mail Open Express w/Cab (JG/DFR)

1929 Rugby Model X One-Ton Dump Truck (JG/DFR)

1929 Rugby Model X 1-Ton 2-Unit Wide Exp. (JG/DFR)

CHASSIS (Rugby L-2 Series): Wheelbase: 128 in.

TECHNICAL: Selective sliding transmission. Speeds: 3F/1R (3x2 transmission on 'Fast-Mail'). Floor-mounted gearshift lever. Dry disc type clutch. Asbestos lining. Spiral Bevel gear, semi-floating rear axle. Overall ratio: (S-4) 4.87:1; (T) 4.79:1; (L-2) N/A. Four-wheel mechanical brakes. Wood spoke wheels.

OPTIONS: Clock. Spotlight. Backing light. Windshield wings. Heater. Bumper. Spring covers. Speedometer (on S-4). Gasoline gauge (on S-4). Thermometer (on S-4). Stoplight (on S-4). Shock absorbers (on S-4). Spare tire. Tire cover. Tire lock. Power tire pump. Special paint. Aftermarket truck bodies.

HISTORICAL: Introduced: Jan. 1929. Calendar year registrations: (cars and trucks) 47,716. Calendar year production: About 1,300 Rugby trucks.

Innovations: New 3x2 transmission for 'Fast Mail' truck. Last season for sales of Durant commercial vehicles.

NOTES: Durant's Elizabeth, N.J. factory was sold in 1929. Production of most commercial vehicles was moved to the company's Lansing, Mich. plant. Only a handful of trucks were sourced from Toronto, Canada after 1929 and all of these were 1-tonners.

1929 Rugby One-Ton Hand Hoist Dump Body (JG/DFR)

Pricing

1929

	5	4	3	2	1
Durant Series S-2					
Conv. Rds. w/Open Box	1350	2650	4400	6150	8800
Conv. Rds. w/Closed Box	1300	2550	4250	5900	8500
Express	1200	2400	4000	5600	8000
Canopy	1200	2460	4100	5700	8200
Straight Side Express	1200	2400	4000	5600	8000
Panel	1300	2550	4250	5900	8500
Rugby Series S-4					
Pickup	1200	2400	4000	5600	8000
Canopy	1200	2460	4100	5700	8200
Screen	1200	2460	4100	5700	8200
Sedan Delivery	1300	2650	4350	6050	8700
Panel	1300	2550	4250	5900	8500
Rugby Model T					
Pickup	1130	2250	3750	5250	7500
Canopy	1150	2310	3850	5400	7700
Screen	1150	2310	3850	5400	7700
Panel	1200	2400	4000	5600	8000
Sedan Delivery	1250	2500	4150	5800	8300
Rugby "Fast Mail"					
Express	1100	2200	3650	5100	7300
Canopy	1130	2250	3750	5250	7500
Screen	1130	2250	3750	5250	7500
Station Wagon	1650	3300	5500	7700	11,000
Panel	1170	2340	3900	5450	7800

ED BUSINESS

1930 Rugby Model 6-15 Panel Delivery Body (JG/DFR)

RUGBY — SERIES S-4/SERIES 6-14 — FOUR-CYLINDER/SIX-CYLINDER: — Information about light-duty Rugby trucks made after 1929 is slightly contradictory. An *NADA USED CAR GUIDE* published in 1934 indicates that both the S-4 and 6-14 lines were marked in 1930. The first was a four-cylinder truck in the 107 in. w.b., while the other was a 6-cyl. with a new 199 cu. in. displacement and longer 112 in. w.b. According to Jeff Gillis, of the Durant Family Registry, production of the "S" models actually ended in 1929 and only sixes was built thereafter. In Gillis' own words, "In 1930, the Model 6-14 6-cyl. light truck would be offered in only two versions, a panel and open delivery with canopy. Production of this model would cease, sometime in 1930, again due to poor sales. The 4-cyl. Model X and 6-cyl. 'Express,' both 1-ton vehicles, were in production through most of 1928-1929. They were replaced by only a 6-cyl. Model 615, for 1930, which became the Model 616 shortly before production was ended." Since the NADA's data was the most complete at press time, we are using it, with the realization that future research may turn up additional facts about these model years. Hopefully, future editions of this catalog will clear up any discrepancies.

1930 Rugby Commercial Panel Delivery (JG/DFR)

I.D. DATA: Serial number located on name plate attached to right side of dash under hood. Starting: (Model S-4) 1227; (Model 6-14) 1001. Ending: (Model S-4) 1500; (Model 6-14(1098. Engine numbers located on name plate attached to left side of motor. Engine numbers are not available.

Model Series	Body Type	Price	Weight	Prod. Total
S-4 — (½-Ton) — (4-cyl.)				
S-4	Chassis	495	1605	Note 1
S-4	Pickup	—	—	Note 1
S-4	Canopy or Screen Dely.	—	—	Note 1
S-4	Panel	—	—	Note 1
S-4	Sedan Dely.	—	—	Note 1
Series 6-14 — (½-Ton) — (6-cyl.)				
6-14	Chassis	655	2035	Note 2
6-14	Pickup	—	—	Note 2
6-14	Canopy or Screen Dely.	—	—	Note 2
6-14	Panel	885	—	Note 2
6-14	Sedan Dely.	—	—	Note 2

NOTE 1: Serial number span suggests production of 273 units.

NOTE 2: Serial number span suggests production of 97 units.

ENGINE (Series S-4): Inline. L-head. (Continental). Four-cylinder. Cast iron block. Bore & stroke: 3⅜ in. x 4¼ in. Displacement: 152 cu. in. Compression ratio: 4.20:1. Brake horsepower: 36 at 2400 R.P.M. Net horsepower: 18.15. Three main bearings. Solid valve lifters. Carburetor: Tillotson model one-inch, one-barrel.

ENGINE (Series 6-14): Inline. L-head. (Continental). Six-cylinder. Cast iron. Bore & stroke: 3¼ in. x 4 in. Displacement: 199 cu. in. Compression ratio: 5.32:1. Brake horsepower: 58 at 3100 R.P.M. Net horsepower: 25.14. Four main bearings. Solid valve lifters. Carburetor: Stromberg model one-barrel, 1¼ in.

1930 Rugby Commercial Canopy Express (JG/DFR)

1930 Rugby Model 6-15 Screen Side Express (JG/DFR)

NOTE: Same engine as 1930 Durant 6-14 passenger car.

CHASSIS (Series S-4): Wheelbase: 107 in. Tires: 29 x 4.40 in. (Fisk).

CHASSIS (Series 6-14): Height: 70 in. Tires: 5.00 x 19 in.

TECHNICAL: Selective sliding transmission. Speeds: 3F/1R. Floor-mounted gearshift lever. Dry disc type clutch. Asbestos lining. Spiral bevel gear, semi-floating rear axle. Overall ratio: (S-4) 4.87:1; (6-14) 4.44:1. Four-wheel mechanical brakes. Wood spoke wheels.

OPTIONS: Clock. Spotlight. Heater. Bumper. Spring covers. Speedometer (on S-4). Shatter-proof glass. Windshield wings, roadster. Power tire pump. Gasoline gauge (on S-4). Thermometer (on S-4). Stoplight (on S-4). Spare tire. Tire cover. Tire lock. Special paint. Aftermarket truck bodies. Disk or wire wheels.

HISTORICAL: Introduced: January 1929. Calendar year registrations: (cars and trucks) 21,440. Calendar year production: According to Durant historian Jeff Gillis, of Green Bay Wis., "Sales dropped slightly, to around 400 (commercial) vehicles in 1930." This is consistent with the total of 370 production units indicated by serial number span.

Innovations: New 6-14 6-cyl. series. Longer wheelbase.

NOTES: Some 1-ton Rugby "Fast Mail" express trucks with the 3x2 transmission may have also been built this year. According to Jeff Gillis, after 1929 a "handful" of these were built in the Toronto, Canada factory. The Lansing, Mich. factory continued to make the ½-ton trucks.

1930 Rugby Mod. 6-15 Hand Hoist Dump Body (JG/DFR)

1930 Rugby Model 6-15 Stake Body (JG/DFR)

1930 Rugby Model 6-15 Grain Body (JG/DFR)

1930 Rugby Model 6-15 Open Express Body (JG/DFR)

Pricing

	5	4	3	2	1
1930					
Rugby Series S-4					
Pickup	1200	2400	4000	5600	8000
Canopy	1200	2460	4100	5700	8200
Screen	1200	2460	4100	5700	8200
Panel	1300	2550	4250	5900	8500
Sedan Delivery	1300	2650	4350	6050	8700
Rugby Series 6-14					
Pickup	1130	2250	3750	5250	7500
Canopy	1150	2310	3850	5400	7700
Screen	1150	2310	3850	5400	7700
Panel	1200	2400	4000	5600	8000
Sedan Delivery	1250	2500	4150	5800	8300

1931-1932 DURANT

1931 Rugby One-Ton Panel Delivery (OCW)

RUGBY — SERIES 6-15 — SIX-CYLINDER: — According to 6-15 Durant sales literature, the Rugby Model 6-15 was produced in 1931. Trucks made between January and July were considered 1931 models. Trucks made from August on, were considered 1932 models. This change took place at about serial number L1154. The 1932 models had the same Continental 22A 6-cyl. engine, but were rated at significantly higher horse-power (although compression, displacement and torque out-put did not change.) The later version of the powerplant switch from a Stromberg to Tillotson carburetor, although both had a 1¼ in. venturi opening. The later Rugbys also had smaller tires and a numerically lower gear ratio.

I.D. DATA: Serial number located on name plate attached to right side of dash under hood. Serial numbers: (1931) L1099 to L1154; (1932) L1155 and up. Engine numbers located on name plate on left side of engine. Engine numbers are not available.

Model 1931	Body Type	Price	Weight	Prod. Total
Rugby Series 6-15 — (½-Ton) — (6-cyl.)				
6-15	Chassis	655	2045	Note 1
6-15	Pickup	—	—	Note 1
6-15	Canopy	—	—	Note 1
6-15	Screen	—	—	Note 1
6-15	Panel	885	—	Note 1
6-15	Sedan Delivery	—	—	Note 1
1932				
Rugby Series 6-15 — (½-Ton) — (6-cyl.)				
6-15	Chassis	655	2045	Note 2
6-15	Pickup	—	—	Note 2
6-15	Canopy	—	—	Note 2
6-15	Screen	—	—	Note 2
6-15	Panel	885	—	Note 2
6-15	Sedan Delivery	—	—	Note 2

NOTE 1: Serial number span indicates 55 units built.

NOTE 2: Production unknown; cannot be estimated.

ENGINE (1931): Inline. L-head. (Continental). Six-cylinder. Cast iron block. Bore & stroke: 3¼ in. x 4 in. Displacement: 199 cu. in. Compression ratio: 5.32:1. Brake horsepower: 58 at 3100 R.P.M. Net horsepower: 25.4. Torque: 99 lbs.-ft. at 1200 R.P.M. Four main bearings. Solid valve lifters. Carburetor: Stromberg model 1¼-inch, one-barrel

ENGINE (1932): Inline. L-head. (Continental). Six-cylinder. Cast iron block. Bore & stroke: 3¼ in. x 4 in. Displacement: 199 cu. in. Compression ratio: 5.32:1. Brake horsepower: 71 at 3300 R.P.M. Net horsepower: 25.4. Torque: 99 lbs.-ft. at 1200 R.P.M. Four main bearings. Solid valve lifters. Carburetor: Tillotson model J5B 1¼-inch, one-barrel.

NOTE: This was the same version of the Continental 22 engine used in Durant 6-19 passenger cars.

CHASSIS (Series 6-15): Wheelbase: 112 in. Height: 70 in. Tires: (1931) 5.00 x 19 in.; (1932) 4.75 x 19 in.

TECHNICAL: Selective sliding transmission. Speeds: 3F/1R. Floor-mounted gearshift lever. Dry disc type clutch. Asbestos lining. Spiral bevel gear, semi-floating rear axle. Overall ratio: (1931) 4.4:1; (1932) 3.90:1. Bendix four-wheel mechanical brakes. Wood spoke wheels.

OPTIONS: Clock. Spotlight. Heater. Bumper. Spring covers. Shatter-proof glass. Power tire pump. Spare tire. Tire cover. Tire lock. Special paint. Aftermarket truck bodies. Disk or wire wheels.

HISTORICAL: Introduced: (1931) Jan. 1931; (1932) Aug. 1931. Calendar year registrations: (1931) 7,229; (1932) 1,135. Includes cars and trucks.

Innovations: Higher horsepower rating in 1932. Changed to smaller tires in 1932. Tillotson carb adopted for new series. New 6-15 series designation indicator higher horsepower models.

NOTES: Last year for Rugby light-duty trucks was 1931-1932.

Pricing

1931-1932 Rugby Series 6-15	5	4	3	2	1
Pickup	1130	2250	3750	5250	7500
Canopy	1150	2310	3850	5400	7700
Screen	1150	2310	3850	5400	7700
Panel	1200	2400	4000	5600	8000
Sedan Delivery	1250	2500	4150	5800	8300

FARGO

By Jim Benjaminson
Additional Research: By R. Perry Zavitz

The Fargo line of commercial vehicles from Chrysler Corporation has had a long and varied history. Its origins began in the early days of the company, yet the Fargo name is barely known in the country of its origin. The name is nearly a household word elsewhere in the world.

Early in his plans for the Chrysler Corporation, Walter P. Chrysler knew he had to fill all segments of the marketplace for his firm to survive. Using the popular, mid-priced Chrysler car as his base, Chrysler branched out in all directions. He entered the low-priced field with the Plymouth; the lower-medium-price range with the DeSoto and the luxury market with the Imperial. For the commercial buyer, he decided to organize a new and separate company. It was known as Fargo Motor Corporation.

Fargo was not an automatic offering to other Chrysler franchise holders. In a bulletin issued July 9, 1928, J.E. Fields (Chrysler vice-president in charge of sales) stated "only where local conditions warrant, where finances are adequate and where a commercial car activity will not detract from passenger car operations, will the Fargo franchise be offered to Chrysler distributors and dealers." The Fargo franchise was next offered to DeSoto dealers and, then, to dealers outside the Chrysler organization.

1947 Fargo 1-Ton Military Type 4x4 Power Wagon (RPZ)

The Fargo line initially consisted of ½-ton and ¾-ton chassis, with a choice of bodies including a Panel Delivery and sedan body with windows. Further expansion of the initial line included plans for trucks up to two-tons, but only a one-ton would eventually see the light of day.

Chrysler Corporation was, by the end of July, able to purchase the huge Dodge Brothers' holdings. These included not only Dodge trucks, but Graham Brothers trucks as well (Graham was the line's medium-and heavy-duty offering). This resulted in a "new ball game" as Chrysler found itself literally swimming in truck lines.

The depression of late 1929 brought a need to rationalize the lineup. It was easy to drop the Graham Brothers name (the Grahams had already resigned to begin production of an automobile under their own name). By 1930, the original Fargo would be gone as well, yet the name was destined to live for another 42 years!

Following the shut down of Fargo production lines, the Fargo Motor Corporation became Chrysler's national fleet sales organization. In 1931, it absorbed the National Fleet Sales Divisions of Dodge Brothers and Chrysler Corporation. Fargo's new function was to further sales of Chrysler-built cars and trucks to national fleet users, fed-

eral and state governments and certain larger counties and cities by making vehicles meeting specified customer requirements. Although the Fargo Corporation was to handle fleet sales of *all* Chrysler-built products, it wasn't long before a need began to appear for the re-emergence of the Fargo truck line.

From 1933-1935, over 3,500 Fargo 1½-ton trucks were built in Detroit and exported around the world. Then came 1936 and Canada, where the Fargo name got a new, long-term lease on life.

1954 Fargo Town Panel Delivery (RPZ)

Because of its size, Chrysler-Canada's method of dualing its dealers was significantly different than in the United States. Chrysler and Plymouth were paired in one division, with DeSoto-Dodge paired in the other. (In the United States, each division was individually structured.) Because of the pairings in Canada, Chrysler-Plymouth was "out in the cold" as far as truck sales were concerned. So, for 1936, the Fargo truck line made its debut in the Dominion and was added to the Chrysler division.

The first Fargo pickups, of 1936, were little more than Plymouth passenger cars with Dodge pickup cabs. The hood, fenders, headlamps, running boards were pure Plymouth, yet the vehicle was fitted with a unique grille insert and radiator ornament. Fargo even shared Dodge's new truck assembly plant on Tecumseh Road.

For 1937, the Fargo was based solely on Dodge sheetmetal (as was the Plymouth Commercial Car line here). But, there was a difference; while the Plymouth Commercial Car was offered only in half-ton configurations, the Fargo lineup included models up to three-tons. The Plymouth Commercial Car lasted only through 1941, but Fargo remained a Canadian offering through 1972.

While those in the know tend to think of the Fargo as a purely Canadian truck from this point on, production actually took place (with the exception of World War II) in Detroit as well as Canada. However, the trucks were sold only in Canada and other export markets.

As the years passed, Fargos differed less and less from Dodges on which they were based. By the end, the nameplates read "Fargo" while the hubcaps read "Dodge." By 1972, the need to rationalize once again came to Chrysler Corporation. As the model year ended, so, too, came the end of the line for the once proud Fargo name.

(To muddy the waters a little further, it should be mentioned in passing that some export commercial vehicles were sold under the DeSoto nameplate long after the passenger car by the same name had passed from the scene. The DeSoto truck, like the Fargo, was merely a Dodge under its skin).

1928-1929 FARGO

1929 Fargo Clipper station wagon (CHC)

PACKET — SERIES EE — FOUR-CYLINDER: — Fargo Motor Corp. was essentially a fleet sales branch of Chrysler Corp. After 1932, Fargo sold various Chrysler products — mainly Dodge trucks — with Fargo nameplates. From 1935 on, the Fargo name was used mainly on Canadian and export market vehicles. However, the pre-1932 models had no exact equivalents among other Chrysler products and were included in American automobile reference books. The smaller Packet series used many of the same components as Chrysler "65", DeSoto and Plymouth passenger cars, although the bodies were truck bodies. A chassis and cowl, plus four basic body styles were offered. The open delivery truck body could be ordered in either canopy or screenside form, apparently at the same price. Some special-order bodies were also constructed on an aftermarket basis. Plymouth components included fenders, lamps, bumpers and the four-cylinder Model Q engine, as well as chassis, frame, transmission, springs and brakes. A DeSoto rear axle was used. Standard equipment included a single driver's seat, Delco-Remy ignition, wood spoke wheels and roll-up door windows. Packets were rated for a payload of ½-ton. The panel delivery is believed to have been the most common model in both Fargo lines. The "sedan delivery" was actually more like a modern suburban. It had two side doors and nine-passenger seating. Pickup trucks were listed in factory literature without prices or weights. It's possible that none were over built.

1929 Fargo Clipper canopy delivery (CHC)

1929 Fargo Deluxe Panel Delivery (CHC)

276

I.D. DATA: Serial number located on instrument panel. Starting: (Detroit, Mich.) EE-000P; (Windsor, Ont.) EE-902S. Ending: (Detroit, Mich.) EE-102R; (Windsor, Ont.) EE-906R. Engine numbers located on the left side of motor. Starting: 175000 and up.

Model	Body Type	Price	Weight	Prod. Total
Packer Series — (4-cyl.) — (½-Ton)				
EE	Chassis & Cowl	545	1825	Note 1
EE	Panel	795	2730	Note 1
EE	Canopy Dely.	895	2725	Note 1
EE	Screen Dely.	895	2725	Note 1
EE	Pickup	—	—	Note 1
EE	Sedan Dely.	895	3050	Note 1

NOTE 1: Series production was 1,063 units for the model year.

1929 Fargo Clipper Panel Delivery (RPZ)

1929 Fargo Clipper Deluxe Panel Delivery (CHC)

1929 Fargo Clipper Long Wheelbase Panel Delivery

ENGINE: Inline. L-head. Four-cylinder. Cast iron block. Bore & stroke: 3⅝ in. x 4⅛ in. Displacement: 170.3 cu. in. Compression ratio: 4.6:1. Brake horsepower: 45 at 2800 R.P.M. Net horsepower: 21.03. Three main bearings. Carburetor: Carter.

CLIPPER — SERIES ED — SIX-CYLINDER: — The Clipper was another Fargo truck model that was approximately 10 in. longer than the Packet. Many of its components were shared with the Chrysler 65 passenger car, although the bodies were actually the same used on Packet models. The two lines also shared the same radiator shell and hood designs. The engine was the Chrysler "Silver Dome" six-cylinder powerplant. Other Chrysler parts included wheels, optional bumpers and Lovejoy shock absorbers. Clippers had a ¾-ton payload rating.

I.D. DATA: Serial number located on instrument panel. Starting: (Detroit) ED-000P; (Detroit) ED-901C. Ending: (Detroit) ED-142P; (Detroit) ED-901R.

1929 Fargo Clipper Screenside Delivery (CHC)

1929 Fargo Clipper Panel Truck (CHC)

Model	Body Type	Price	Weight	Prod. Total
Clipper Series — (6-cyl.) — (¾-Ton)				
ED	Chassis & Cowl	725	2325	Note 1
ED	Panel	975	3175	Note 1
ED	Canopy Dely.	1075	3215	Note 1
ED	Screen Dely.	1075	3215	Note 1
ED	Pickup	—	—	Note 2
ED	Sedan Dely.	1075	3475	Note 1

NOTE 1: Series production was 1,424 units for the model year.

ENGINE: Inline. L-head. Six-cylinder. Cast iron block. Bore & stroke: 3⅛ in. x 4¼ in. Displacement: 195.6 cu. in. Compression ratio: 5.2:1. Brake horsepower: 65 at 3200 R.P.M. Net horsepower: 23.43. Seven main bearings. Carburetor: Stromberg.

1929 Fargo Clipper High-Headroom Studio Truck (CHC)

CHASSIS (Packet): Wheelbase: 109¾ in. Length: 169 in. Front tread: 56 in. Rear tread: 56 in. Tires: 4.75 x 20 (six-ply).

CHASSIS (Clipper): Wheelbase: 113 in. Length: 179 in. Tires: 5.50 x 18 (six-ply).

NOTE: Cargo carrying area of the Clipper sedan delivery was 72¾ in. long x 49 in. wide and 47¼ in. high.

TECHNICAL: Manual transmission. Speeds: 3F/1R. Floor-mounted gearshift lever. Dry disc type clutch. Semi-floating rear axle. Overall ratio: 4.7:1 (Packet). Four-wheel hydraulic brakes. Wood-spoke wheels.

OPTIONS: Front and rear bumpers, on Packet ($15); on Clipper ($20). Single sidemount. Dual sidemount. Leatherette sidemount cover(s). Rearview outside mirror(s). Wire spoke wheels. Chrome wheel trim rings. Spare tire locks. Dual taillights. Panel body in prime coat, both series ($250). Glass side body in prime coat, both series ($350). Paint, any Plymouth, DeSoto, Chrysler "65" color ($25). Special body colors ($50). Full-width seat for sedan type body, both series ($37.50).

1929 Fargo 9-Passenger Suburban Sedan (CHC)

1929 Fargo Clipper 9-Passenger Suburban Sedan (CHC)

1929 Fargo Commercial Display Van (RPZ)

HISTORICAL: Introduced: Mid-1928 (as 1929 models). Model year production: 2,487 (both series).

Two new Chrysler Corp. truck lines introduced under Fargo name. Production of Packets began Sept. 1928; ended March 1929. Production of Clippers began Aug. 1928; ended March 1930. Packets built in both United States and Canada; Clippers in U.S.A. only. Disney Film Recording Corp. used a Fargo Clipper with custom-made "high-head-room" panel Delivery body. Some say the Fargo name was taken from Wells Fargo. Others say a Chrysler executive from Fargo, N.D. coined the name.

Pricing

1928-192	5	4	3	2	1
Packet Series					
Panel	900	1800	3000	4200	6000
Canopy Dely.	780	1560	2600	3600	5200
Screen Dely.	780	1560	2600	3600	5200
Sedan Dely.	750	1500	2500	3500	5000
Pickup	830	1650	2750	3850	5500
Clipper Series					
Panel	1130	2250	3750	5250	7500
Canopy Dely.	950	1900	3150	4400	6300
Screen Dely.	980	1950	3250	4550	6500
Sedan Dely.	930	1860	3100	4350	6200
Pickup	980	1950	3250	4550	6500

1930 FARGO

1930 Fargo Packet Ambulance (OCW)

PACKET — SERIES EE — SIX-CYLINDER: — In 1930, the Packet became a six-cylinder model. There were actually two separate 1930 series. Both had the same "EE" serial number prefix, similar wheelbases, nearly identical styling and common technical features, except engines. The Packets produced from August 1929 to May 1930 used the DeSoto "K" engine. Packets built after May 1930, switched to a larger-bore, slightly more powerful DeSoto "CK" engine. In the Fargo trucks, a Carter carburetor was used on this engine, instead of the Stromberg carb used with DeSoto passenger cars.

I.D. DATA: Serial number located on instrument panel. Starting: (K engine) EE188D and up; (CK engine) EE300R to EE3055. Engine numbers located on the left side of motor. Starting: (K engine) 83164 and up; (CK engine) DD28656 to DD29759.

Model	Body Type	Price	Weight	Prod. Total
Packer Series — ("K" 6-cyl.) — (½-Ton)				
EE (K)	Chassis & Cowl	595	1935	Note 1
EE (K)	Panel	845	2825	Note 1
EE (K)	Canopy Dely.	945	2845	Note 1
EE (K)	Screen Dely.	945	2845	Note 1
EE (K)	Pickup	—	—	Note 1
EE (K)	Suburban (Sed. Dely.)	—	—	Note 1
Packet Series — ("CK" 6-cyl.) — (½-Ton)				
EE (CK)	Chassis & Cowl	595	1935	Note 2
EE (CK)	Panel	845	2825	Note 2
EE (CK)	Canopy Dely.	945	2845	Note 2
EE (CK)	Screen Dely.	945	2845	Note 2
EE (CK)	Pickup	—	—	Note 2
EE (CK)	Suburban (Sed. Dely.)	—	—	Note 2

NOTE 1: Series production was 2,059 units.
NOTE 2: Series production was 110 units.

ENGINE (K engine): Inline. L-head. Six-cylinder. Cast iron block. Bore & stroke: 3 in. x 4⅛ in. Displacement: 174.9 cu. in. Compression ratio: 5.2:1. Brake horsepower: 57 at 3400 R.P.M. Net horsepower: 21.6. Four main bearings. Solid valve lifters. Carburetor: Stromberg 1V.

ENGINE (CK engine): Inline. L-head. Six-cylinder. Cast iron block. Bore & stroke: 3⅛ in. x 4⅛ in. Displacement: 189.8 cu. in. Compression ratio: 5.2:1. Brake horsepower: 60 at 3400 R.P.M. Net horsepower: 23.4. Four main bearings. Solid valve lifters. Carburetor: Carter 1V.

1930 Fargo Clipper Special Town Car Delivery (CHC)

278

1930 Fargo Clipper Panel Delivery Van (CHC)

CLIPPER — SERIES ED — SIX-CYLINDER: — The 1928-1929 Clippers had looked somewhat unusual because they used identical bodies as the Packets, on a longer wheelbase. For model year 1930, this was "corrected" by giving the Clipper the same wheelbase as the Packet. This meant that the main difference between the two lines was a heavier-duty Clipper chassis (¾-ton rating) and larger (Chrysler "CJ" type) Clipper engine.

I.D. DATA: Serial number located on instrument panel. Starting: ED131 and up. Engine numbers located on left side of motor. Starting: 241281 and up.

1930 Fargo Clipper Commercial Display Van (CHC)

1930 Fargo Clipper 9-Passenger Suburban Sedan (CHC)

Model	Body Type	Price	Weight	Prod. Total
Clipper Series — (6-cyl.) — (¾-Ton)				
ED	Chassis & Cowl	725	2340	Note 1
ED	Panel	975	3195	Note 1
ED	Canopy Dely.	1075	3230	Note 1
ED	Screen Dely.	1075	3230	Note 1
ED	Pickup	—	—	Note 1
ED	Suburban (Sed. Dely.)	—	—	Note 1

NOTE 1: See 1928-1929 Clipper production total. Historians believe this total includes all Clippers produced.

ENGINE: Inline. L-head. Six-cylinder. Cast iron block. Bore & stroke: 3⅛ in. x 4¼ in. Displacement: 195.6 cu. in. Compression ratio: 5.2:1. Brake horsepower: 62 at 3200 R.P.M. Net horsepower: 23.44. Four main bearings. Solid valve lifters. Carburetor: Carter 1V.

FREIGHTER — SERIES C — SIX-CYLINDER: — Continuing with the Plymouth-like use of ship names, Fargo's new-for-1930 1-ton line was called the Freighter series. These trucks had a nearly 2 ft. longer w.b. than the other lines, with correspondingly larger bodies. The engines for Freighters were the same ones used in Packets. Styling differences included distinctive fenders, double belt moldings, larger window areas (some models had additional window openings) and squarer-cornered bodies.

1930 Fargo Freighter Chassis & Cab (CHC)

1930 Fargo Freighter Panel Delivery Truck (OCW)

1930 Fargo Freighter Screenside Delivery Truck (CHC)

1930 Fargo Freighter Panel Delivery (CHC)

1930 Fargo Freighter Special Deluxe Express (RPZ)

I.D. DATA: Serial number located on instrument panel. Starting: not available. Engine numbers located on left side of motor. Starting: not available

Model Series	Body Type Freighter Series — (6-cyl.) — (1-Ton)	Price	Weight	Prod. Total
C	Chassis and Cowl	795	2725	—
C	Gravity Dumper	—	—	—
C	Screen Dely.	1055	3660	—
C	Panel	1145	3820	—
C	Suburban (Sed. Dely.)	—	—	—
C	Express	1010	3590	—
C	Grain Body	1045	3715	—
C	Stake Bed (weather proof)	1045	3790	—
C	Farm Truck	1045	3815	—
C	DeLuxe Pickup	—	—	—
C	Tractor Truck Cab	—	—	—
C	Flatbed	—	—	—
C	Fire Truck	—	—	—
C	Hoist Body	—	—	—

ENGINES: See Packet engines specifications above.

1930 Fargo Freighter 9-Passenger Suburban Sedan

CHASSIS (Packet Series): Wheelbase: 109¾ in. Length: 169 in. Tires: (early) 4.75 x 20 in.; (late) 5.00 x 19 in.

CHASSIS (Clipper Series): Wheelbase: 109¾ in. Length: 169 in. Tires: 5.50 x 18 (six-ply).

CHASSIS (Freighter Series): Wheelbase: 133 in. Length: (approx.) 202 in.

NOTE: Freighters had 1¾ in. wide 14 in. diameter front brake drums and 2 in. wide-15 in. diameter rear brake drums.

1930 Fargo Freighter Platform with Stake Body (CHC)

TECHNICAL: Manual transmission. Speeds: 3F/1R. Floor-mounted gearshift lever. Dry disc type clutch. Semi-floating rear axle. Overall ratio: (Freighter) 5.7:1. Lockheed four-wheel hydraulic brakes. Wood-spoke wheels.

NOTE: It's likely that a four-speed transmission was either standard or optional in Freighters.

OPTIONS: Front and rear bumpers ($15). Single sidemount. Dual sidemounts. Leatherette sidemount cover(s). Panel body in prime ($250). glass side body in prime ($350). Paint, standard Plymouth, DeSoto, Chrysler colors ($25). Paint, special colors ($50). Extra bucket seats ($22.50 each). Full-width seat for sedan body ($37.50). Wire spoke wheels. Chrome-plated dc wheels. Chrome-plated headlight buckets. Wraparound bumpers. Spare tire locks. Outside rearview mirror.

HISTORICAL: Introduced: (K Packet) August 1929; (CK Packet) May 1930; (Clipper) Aug. 1929; (Freighter) June 1929.
Packet six-cylinder line introduced. New "CK" engine for Packets in Spring 1930. Clipper had new, smaller wheelbase. All-new Freighter 1-ton model released.
Don Butler's book *The Plymouth-Desoto Story* pictures a super-deluxe Clipper with open chauffer's compartment, high-head room panel delivery body, wraparound bumpers. Chrome-plated disc wheels and chrome headlight buckets. Don also pictures an ambulance on the Packet chassis. Fargo truck production was low in this era, explaining the many special bodies, done to pick up extra sales.

1930 Fargo Freighter 1-Ton Cattle Truck (CHC)

1930 Fargo Freighter Enclosed Cab Express (CHC)

1930 Fargo Freighter Model I Gravity Dump Body (CHC)

Pricing

	5	4	3	2	1
1930					
Packet Series					
Panel	950	1900	3150	4400	6300
Canopy Dely.	840	1680	2800	3900	5600
Screen Dely.	870	1750	2900	4100	5800
Pickup	810	1620	2700	3800	5400
Suburban Sed.	890	1770	2950	3850	5900

NOTE: Add 5 percent for "CK" engine; Packets only.

	5	4	3	2	1
Clipper Series					
Panel	930	1860	3100	4350	6200
Canopy Dely.	830	1650	2750	3850	5500
Screen Dely.	850	1700	2850	4000	5700
Pickup	800	1600	2650	3700	5300
Suburban Sed.	870	1750	2900	4100	5800
Freighter Series					
Dumper	750	1500	2500	3500	5000
Screen Dely.	720	1450	2400	3300	4800
Panel	740	1470	2450	3350	4900
Suburban Sed.	680	1350	2250	3150	4500
Express	600	1200	2000	2800	4000
Grain Body	600	1200	2000	2800	4000
Stake	600	1200	2000	2800	4000
Farm Truck	600	1200	2000	2800	4000
DeL. Pickup	1350	2700	4500	6300	9000
Fire Truck	750	1500	2500	3500	5000
Flatbed	600	1200	2000	2800	4000
Hoist Body	600	1200	2000	2800	4000

1931 FARGO

PACKET — SERIES EE — SIX-CYLINDER: — According to contemporary reference sources, such as the 1934 "N.A.D.A. Official Used Car Guide," Fargo Packets produced after Sept. 1930 were sold as 1931 models. This series was a carryover of the late 1930 models with the DeSoto CK engine. It would include Packets with serial numbers above EE3055 and engine numbers above DD29760. There were no product changes. Prices and weights and all specifications are identical to the late 1930 trucks. Refer to the 1930 section of this catalog for additional information.

1933-1935 FARGO

FARGO — 1933-1935 — SIX-CYLINDER: — With the Fargo production lines shutdown (see introductory text), emphasis was switched to selling badge-engineered 1½-ton "Dodge" models in various export markets. These trucks are beyond the scope of this catalog, as are the Dodge buses, with Fargo nameplates, that were sold in this period.

1936 FARGO

1936 Fargo Model FD-1 ½-Ton Pickup (C. Parker/JB)

HALF-TON — SERIES FD-1 — SIX-CYLINDER: — With Plymouth's entry into the commercial vehicle field, Chrysler switched to using the Fargo name on two types of vehicles: American style trucks and foreign-built trucks. As this catalog covers only North American products, we'll be concerned only with the American style light-duty models. These were sourced from both the Detroit, Mich. and Windsor, Ontario factories. Sales, however, were carried out exclusively in the Canadian market. The lineup included ½-ton, 1½-ton and two-ton models made in the U.S. and Canada and 3-tonners made only in Canada. The ½-ton models, alone, fall within the scope of this catalog. These trucks looked identical to 1936 Plymouth "P1" models, without Plymouth name badges. A different type hood ornament and hub caps were used. Also, the body-color panel that ran vertically down the center of the Plymouth grille was removed, exposing the bars underneath. "Veed" horizontal bands of bright metal crossed the center section of the grille at the top, at hood louver height, at fender catwalk height and above the bumper.

I.D. DATA: Serial number located on dash. Starting: (Windsor) 9551001; (Detroit) 8823101. Ending: (Windsor) 9551424; (Detroit) 8823882. Engine numbers located on the left side of motor, in front, near hose connection. Engine code T-24. Starting: FD1-1001 and up.

Model Series FD-1 — (6-cyl.) — (½-Ton)	Body Type	Price	Weight	Prod. Total
FD-1	Pickup	737	2660	1204

ENGINE (K engine): Inline. L-head. Six-cylinder. Cast iron block. Bore & stroke: 3⅛ in. x 4⅜ in. Displacement: 201.3 cu. in. Compression ratio: 6.7:1. Brake horsepower: 82 at 3600 R.P.M. Net horsepower: 23.44. Four main bearings. Solid valve lifters. Carburetor: Carter 1V.

CHASSIS (Series FD-1): Wheelbase: 116 in. Tires: 6.00 x 16 (six-ply).

TECHNICAL: Manual transmission. Speeds: 3F/1R. Floor-mounted gearshift lever. Dry disc type clutch. Semi-floating rear axle. Four-wheel hydraulic brakes.

OPTIONS: See 1936 Plymouth options.

HISTORICAL: Introduced: Fall 1935. Model year production: (Canada) 423; (USA) 781.
New light-duty Fargo truck line introduced for sale in Canada.

Pricing

1936	5	4	3	2	1
Pickup	750	1500	2500	3500	5000

1937 FARGO

1937 Fargo ½-Ton Pickup (C.D. Clayton)

HALF-TON/¾-TON — FE SERIES — SIX-CYLINDER: — The 1937 Canadian Fargo was pure Dodge, with slightly different hubcaps and trim. It corresponded to the contemporary Model MC Dodge truck in all other regards. It appears that an attractive medium-blue was the standard factory paint finish color. The half-tonners were designated FE-1 models; the ¾-tonners were called FE-2 models.

I.D. DATA: Serial number located on dash under hood. On front end of left frame member to rear of front spring hanger or just above rear front spring hanger. Starting: (Windsor) 9551451; (Detroit) 8824001. Ending: (Windsor) 9552257; (Detroit) 8824950. (Serial numbers for FE-2 models, at Windsor, were 9565001 and up.) Engine numbers located on plate on side of motor. Engine code T-39.

Model Series FE-1 — (6-cyl.) — (½-Ton)	Body Type	Price	Weight	Prod. Total
FE-1	Pickup	777	2700	—
FE-1	Panel	944	2955	—
FE-1	Sedan Delivery	977	2845	—
FE-1	Chassis	721	2350	—
Series FE-2 — (6 cyl.) — (¾-Ton)				
FE-2	Chassis	845	3200	—

NOTE: Production, (Canada) 807; (U.S.A.) 949.

ENGINE: Inline. L-head. Six-cylinder. Cast iron block. Bore & stroke: 3.375 x 4.062 in. Displacement: 218.1 cu. in. Compression ratio: 6.5:1. Brake horsepower: 87 at 3600 R.P.M. Net horsepower: 25.35. Four main bearings. Solid valve lifters. Carburetor: Stromberg 1V model EXV-2.

CHASSIS: (Series FE-1). Wheelbase: 116 in. Tires: 6.00 x 16 four-ply.

CHASSIS: (Series FE-2). Wheelbase: 120 in. Tires: TA-15 six-ply.

TECHNICAL: Manual transmission. Speeds: 3F/1R. Floor-mounted gearshift lever. Dry disc type clutch. Semi-floating rear axle. Four-wheel hydraulic brakes. Steel disc wheels.

OPTIONS: See 1937 Dodge truck section.

HISTORICAL: Introduced: Fall 1936. Model year production: (Canada) 807; (United States) 949. Innovations: Fargo adapts Dodge chassis and sheet metal in 1937. One-Ton, 1½-ton, two-ton and three-ton Fargo trucks were also built in both the United States and Canada in 1937.

Pricing

1937	5	4	3	2	1
Series FE-1 — (½-Ton)					
Pickup	750	1500	2500	3500	5000
Panel	670	1350	2250	3150	4500
Sedan Delivery	720	1450	2400	3300	4800
Series FE-2 — (¾-Ton)					
Pickup	590	1170	1950	2700	3900
Panel	530	1050	1750	2450	3500

1938 FARGO

1938 Fargo Commercial Station Wagon (OCW)

½-TON/¾-TON — FG SERIES — SIX-CYLINDER: — The 1938 Fargos seen in Canada looked similar to the Series RC and Series RD Dodge light-duties seen in the United States. Only the nameplates and hub caps were slightly different. ½-ton models were known as FG-1's, while ¾-ton trucks were listed as FG-2's. A new 136 in. w.b. option was available in the ¾-ton chassis.

I.D. DATA: Serial number in same location as 1937. (FG-1 Series) — Windsor: 9552301 to 9553075; Detroit: 8862001 to 8862703. (FG-2 Series) — Windsor: 9565201 and up. Engine numbers located in same locations as 1937. Engine code T59.

Model Series FG-1 — (6-cyl.) — (½-Ton)	Body Type	Price	Weight	Prod. Total
FG-1	Chassis	725	1975	Note 1
FG-1	Pickup	774	2700	Note 1
FG-1	Panel	925	2955	Note 1
FG-1	Sedan Delivery	944	2845	Note 1
Series FG-2 — (6 cyl.) — (¾-Ton)				
FG-2	Chassis	858	2375	Note 1
FG-2	Pickup	915	3150	Note 1

NOTE 1: Total production, was 1477 (all models).

ENGINE: Same as 1937.

CHASSIS: Same as 1937, plus 136 in. w.b. option for FG-2.

TECHNICAL: Same as 1937.

OPTIONS: See 1938 Dodge truck section.

HISTORICAL: Introduced: Fall 1938. Model year production: (Canada) 775; (United States) 702. Historical notes: Fargo trucks of 1-, 1½-, 2- and 3-ton payload capacity were again produced in both Detroit and Windsor.

Pricing

1938	5	4	3	2	1
Series FG-1 — (½-Ton)					
Pickup	750	1500	2500	3500	5000
Panel	670	1350	2250	3150	4500
Sedan Delivery	720	1450	2400	3300	4800
Series FG-2 — (¾-Ton)					
Pickup	590	1170	1950	2700	3900
Panel	530	1050	1750	2450	3500

1939 FARGO

1939 Fargo ½-Ton Pickup (RPZ)

½-TON/¾-TON — FH SERIES — SIX-CYLINDER: — Dodge trucks had a new appearance for 1939. The 25th. "Silver Anniversary" trucks had a rounded hood with horizontal grille bars in the nose near the top center and two separate grilles — also with horizontal bars — in the splash pans of the fenders. They were divided by a V-shaped chrome piece extending to the hood sides. Headlamps were mounted on pedestals attached to the front fenders. The side hood panels had four chrome trimmed horizontal louvers. Canada's Fargo trucks adopted the same appearance, but with their own nameplates and hubcaps. Different six-cylinder engines were now used in ½-ton and ¾-ton models.

1939 Fargo Panel Delivery (RPZ)

I.D. DATA: Serial number located on dash under hood. On front end of frame member to rear of front spring hanger, or just above rear front spring hanger. (FH-1 Series) — Windsor: 9553101 to 9553927; Detroit: 8862801 to 8863132. (FH-2 Series) — Detroit: 8756501 to 8756527. Engine numbers located on plate on side of motor. Engine codes (FH-1) T69; (FH-2) T71.

Model	Body Type	Price	Weight	Prod. Total
Series FH-1 — (6-cyl.) — (½-Ton)				
FH-1	Chassis	690	2175	Note 1
FH-1	Pickup	735	2925	Note 1
FH-1	Panel	855	3025	Note 1
Series FH-2 — (6-cyl.) — (¾-Ton)				
FH-2	Chassis	830	2350	Note 2
FH-2	Express	880	3150	Note 2

NOTE 1: Production total: 1158.
NOTE 2: Production total: 27.

1939 Fargo Commercial Station Wagon (RPZ)

282

ENGINE (FH-1): Inline. L-head. Six-cylinder. Cast iron block. Bore & stroke: 3⅜ x 3¾ in. Displacement: 201.3 cu. in. Compression ratio: 6.7. Brake horsepower: 82 at 3600 R.P.M. Four main bearings. Solid valve lifters. Carburetor: Carter 1V model B6H1 or C6J1.

NOTE: While having the same displacement as 1939 Plymouth (United States) engines, this Canadian power plant had a different bore & stroke configuration.

ENGINE (FH-2): Inline. L-head. Six-cylinder. Cast iron block. Bore & stroke: 3⅜ x 4 1/16 in. Displacement: 218.1 cu. in. Compression ratio: 6.5:1. Brake horsepower: 84 at 3600 R.P.M. Net horsepower: 23.44. Four main bearings. Solid valve lifters. Carburetor: Stromberg 1V.

CHASSIS: (Series FH-1). Wheelbase: 116 in. Tires: 6.00 x 16 four-ply.

CHASSIS: (Series FH-2). Wheelbase: 120 in. Tires: TA-15-15 six-ply.

TECHNICAL: Selective synchromesh transmission. Speeds: 3F/1R. Floor-mounted gearshift lever. Single dry disc clutch. Semi-floating rear axle. Four-wheel hydraulic brakes. Steel disc wheels.

OPTIONS: Same as 1939 Dodge truck options.

1939 Fargo 1-Ton H-D Railway Express Van (RPZ)

HISTORICAL: Introduced: Fall 1938. Model year production: FH-1: (Detroit) 331; (Windsor) 827; FH-2: (Detroit) 27. Historical notes: Fargos continued to be available in heavier payload ratings in both the United States and Canada.

Pricing

1939	5	4	3	2	1
Series FH-1 — (½-Ton)					
Pickup	800	1600	2650	3700	5300
Panel	720	1450	2400	3300	4800
Series FH-2 — (¾-Ton)					
Express	620	1230	2050	2900	4100

1940 FARGO

½-TON/¾-TON — FJ SERIES — SIX-CYLINDER: — For 1940, the V-shaped chrome on the Fargo (and Dodge) grille was changed to a piece of chrome with an "upside-down" T-shape that ran vertically over the upper section of the rounded nose. Below it, the horizontal bars were decorated with chrome pieces of diminishing size and a triangle of chrome, at bottom center, ran vertically up the middle. This rather ornate arrangment looked quite nice. Sales of both ½-ton and ¾-ton Fargos picked up a bit, making them a little more common than the comparable 1939 models.

I.D. DATA: Serial and engine numbers in same locations. Serial numbers: (FJ-1) — Windsor: 9553951 to 9555134; Detroit: 8863201 to 8864593. (FJ-2) — Windsor: 9565901 to 9566468; Detroit: 8756551 to 8756583. Engine codes: (FJ-1) T93; (FJ-2) T95.

Model	Body Type	Price	Weight	Prod. Total
Series FJ-1 — (6-cyl.) — (½-Ton)				
FJ-1	Chassis	690	2200	Note 1
FJ-1	Pickup	735	2950	Note 1
FJ-1	Panel	855	3050	Note 1
Series FJ-2 — (6-cyl.) — (¾-Ton)				
FJ-2	Chassis	830	2325	Note 2
FJ-2	Express	880	3025	Note 2

NOTE 1: Production — (Canada) 1184; (U.S.) 1392.
NOTE 2: Production — (Canada) 568; (U.S.) 32.

ENGINES: FJ-1 models used the same engine as the FH-1 models of 1939. FJ-2 models used the same engine as the FH-2 models of 1939.

CHASSIS: See 1939 section.

TECHNICAL: See 1939 section.

OPTIONS: See 1940 Dodge truck options.

HISTORICAL: Introduced: Sept. 1939. Model year production: 3176. Innovations: New grille styling. Historical notes: In the heavy-duty truck line, new 1½-ton and 2-ton Cab-Over-Engine (COE) Fargo models were introduced this year. Also newly available, from the Canadian factory, was a 4-ton line.

Pricing

1940	5	4	3	2	1
Series FJ-1 — (½-Ton)					
Pickup	780	1560	2600	3600	5200
Panel	700	1400	2350	3250	4700
Series FJ-2 — (¾-Ton)					
Express	600	1200	2000	2800	4000

1941 FARGO

1941 Fargo ½-Ton Pickup (B. Roycroft/JB)

½-TON/¾-TON — FK SERIES — SIX-CYLINDER: — The 1941 Fargo grille treatment was rather handsome. Five heavy horizontal chrome bars separated the body-color bars in the lower grilles on each fender "catwalk". The main grilles, also using horizontal bars, looked like stylized butterfly wings. A slim, "golf tee" shaped opening down the center had three horizontal chrome pieces (of descending sizes) at the top of a Chrome Fargo nameplate. There were also three (smaller) horizontal chrome bars just below the nameplate and chrome beltline moldings going from the grille to the rear of the cab. Four chrome horizontal louvers also decorated the hood sides.

I.D. DATA: Serial numbers and engine numbers in same locations. Serial numbers: (FK-1) — Windsor: 9555151 to 9556640; Detroit: 8864601 to 8865401. (FK-2) — Detroit: 8756601 to 8756653. Engine Codes: (FK-1) T113; (FK-2) T115.

Model Series FK-1 — (6-cyl.) — (½-Ton)	Body Type	Price	Weight	Prod. Total
FK-1	Chassis & Cab	730	2775	Note 1
FK-1	Pickup	775	2975	Note 1
FK-1	Panel	895	3175	Note 1
Series FK-2 — (6 cyl.) — (¾-Ton)				
FK-2	Chassis & Cab	870	2925	Note 2

NOTE 1: Production — (Canada) 1490; (U.S.) 800.
NOTE 2: Production — (U.S.) 52.

ENGINES: (FK-1) See 1939 Fargo 218.1 cu. in. engine specifications. (FK-2) Engine data not available.

CHASSIS: See 1940 Fargo section.

TECHNICAL: See 1940 Fargo section.

OPTIONS: See 1941 Dodge truck options.

HISTORICAL: Introduced: September 1940. Model year production: 2342. Innovations: FK-2 ¾-ton series produced in U.S. only. New grille styling. Historical Notes: Fargos were sold through Canadian Plymouth dealers. Heavy trucks of 1-ton, 1½-ton and 2-ton capacity were sourced from factories in both the U.S. and Canada. In addition, a 4-tonner was produced in Detroit while 2½-ton and 3-ton models were built in Windsor.

Pricing

1941	5	4	3	2	1
Series FK-1 — (½-Ton)					
Pickup	780	1560	2600	3600	5200
Panel	700	1400	2350	3250	4700
Series FK-2 — (¾-Ton)					
Express	600	1200	2000	2800	4000

1942-1945 FARGO

1942 Fargo Commercial-Body Station Wagon (RPZ)

½-TON/¾-TON — FK/FL SERIES — SIX-CYLINDER: — According to Canadian references sources, Fargos produced in 1942 and 1943 belonged to a "combined" series, which included ½-ton (Series FL-1-16) and ¾-ton (Series FL-2-20) models. However, other sources indicate that 1943 production was limited to Canada, where only a 2½-ton line was built. The 1942 (or 1942-1943) ½-tonner continued to use the code T113 six-cylinder engine (218.1 cu. in.). These trucks had Windsor serial numbers 9556641 to 9557582, indicating production of 942 units. The 1942 (or 1942-1943) ¾-tonner used a larger six-cylinder engine with bore and stroke of 3⅜ x 4¼ in. It displaced 228.1 cu. in. and developed 105 h.p. at 3600 R.P.M. Windsor serial numbers for the FL-2-20 started at 9567123. Ending numbers or production totals are not available. W.B. were again 116 in. for the ½-ton and 120 in. for the ¾-ton. In 1944, the only trucks available in the light-duty category were ½-tons in the FL-1S Series. These had Windsor serial numbers 90022001 to 90023500 and also used the 218.1 cu. in. Six-cylinder. Production totaled 1500 units. This series was carried over for 1945, along with the FK-1 which was last seen in 1941. These were again built both in Windsor and Detroit. The 1945 serial numbers were: Windsor 90030023 to 90030220 for FL-1S trucks (197 built) and Detroit 8866001 to 8869368 for FK-1 trucks (3367 built). During these years, large 2-tonners were also made in both nations, while a 2½-tonner was built only in Canada.

1946-1947 FARGO

1947 Fargo 1-Ton Military Type 4x4 Power Wagon (RPZ)

½-TON/¾-TON — FL SERIES — SIX-CYLINDER: — Styling of the postwar Fargos had the same characteristics as the prewar trucks. The ½-ton line continued to use the 116 in. w.b. and the 218.1 cu. in. six-cylinder. Features of ¾-ton models included a longer w.b. and larger displacement engine. Our Canadian reference sources indicate that nothing changed between model years 1946 and 1947; even the prices for both years are the same. The serial number sequence even continued unbroken, with trucks above number 90039753 representing the 1947 series.

1947 Fargo 1-Ton H-D Grain Box Body (JB/POC)

I.D. DATA: Serial numbers were located on a dash plate below the hood; on a plate on the footboard and on the frame in back of the left front spring shackle. (FL-1) — Windsor: (1946) 90037929 to 90039753; (1947) 90039754 to 90043030. (FL-2) — Windsor: (1946) 90050429 and up. (1947) Same starting number. Engine numbers located: on left side of motor below cylinder head; on front right side of motor and (on heavy-duties) on chain case at front end of motor. Engine codes: (FL-1) T113; (FL-2) T117.

Model	Body Type	Price	Weight	Prod. Total
Series FL-1 — (6-cyl.) — (½-Ton)				
FL-1	Chassis & Cab	978	2550	Note 1
FL-1	Pickup	1044	2775	Note 1
FL-1	Panel	1205	3025	Note 1
Series FL-2 — (6 cyl.) — (¾-Ton)				
FL-2	Chassis & Cab	1204	2750	Note 2
FL-2	Express	1270	3000	Note 2

NOTE 1: Production — (1946) 1825; (1947) 3277.
NOTE 2: Production — (1946-1947) not available.

ENGINE (FL-1 Series): Inline. L-head. Six-cylinder. Cast iron block. Bore & stroke: 3⅜ x 4 1/16 in. Displacement: 218.1 cu. in. Compression ratio: 6.7:1. Brake horsepower: 95 at 3600 R.P.M. Net horsepower: 25.35. Four main bearings. Solid valve lifters. Carburetor: Ball & Ball 1V.

ENGINE (FL-2 Series): Inline. L-head. Six-cylinder. Cast iron block. Bore & stroke: 3⅜ x 4¼ in. Displacement: 228.1 cu. in. Compression ratio: 6.0:1. Brake horsepower: 105 at 3600 R.P.M. Net horsepower: 25.35. Four main bearings. Solid valve lifters. Carburetor: Ball & Ball 1V.

CHASSIS: (Series FL-1). Wheelbase: 116 in. Tires: 6.00 x 16 four-ply.

CHASSIS: (Series FL-2). Wheelbase: 120 in. Tires: TA-15 six-ply.

TECHNICAL: Selective synchromesh transmission. Speeds: 3F/1R. Column-mounted gearshift. Single dry disc clutch. Semi-floating rear axle. Four-wheel hydraulic brakes. Steel disc wheels.

OPTIONS: See 1946-1947 Dodge truck options.

HISTORICAL: Introduced: December 1945. Model year production: (FL-1) 5102, both years combined. Historical notes: Also built in the United States was a 1-ton Fargo featuring a 4x4 drive system. These trucks used the same model number, engine and serial numbers used on 1-ton models.

Pricing

1946-47	5	4	3	2	1
Series FL-1 — (½-Ton)					
Pickup	770	1550	2550	3600	5100
Panel	690	1380	2300	3200	3900
Series FL-2 — (¾-Ton)					
Express	590	1170	1950	2700	3900
Series FL-3 — (4x4) — (1-Ton)					
Express	630	1260	2100	3000	4200

1948-1949 FARGO

½-TON — "F" SERIES — SIX-CYLINDER: — Dodge announced new truck styling for model-year 1948. Fargos got the same appearance updates. They included a flat front end; squared-off fenders with integrated head-

1948 Fargo Cab and Front End Styling (RPZ)

lights; lower, wider "Alligator-Jaw" type hood and squarer cab with much larger glass area. The grille had 10 slots (five on each side of center) which were separated by three wide chrome moldings running across the front. The bottom molding was the widest and the others got a little shorter. The Fargo name appeared, in block letters, above the shortest (uppermost) grille molding. Then came another band of chrome along the edges of the nose, which was decorated with a large chrome mascot at the top. Light-duty models were virtually all ½-tonners (a 1-ton line, including the 4x4, was available). One line, the F-1-B, was merchandised as a combined 1948-1949 Series. Another line, the FM-1, was also the same through both model-years, although a serial number cut-off (for 1948) is listed. Larger trucks sold with Fargo name badges included 1-ton, 1½-ton, 2-ton and 2½-ton models made in both countries, plus a 3-ton line produced only in the Windsor, Canada factory.

I.D. DATA: Serial and engine numbers in the same locations. Serial numbers: (FM-1) — Windsor (1948) 9050000 to 90505203; (1949) 90503204 to 90505700 and 90505701 to 90506287. (F-1-B) — Detroit (1948-1949) 82044001 to 82127008. Engine codes: (1948/FM-1) T143; (1949/FM-1) T143 and T173; (1948-1949/F-1-B) T142.

1948 Fargo Cargo Delivery Van (RPZ)

Model	Body Type	Price	Weight	Prod. Total
Series FM-1 — (6-cyl.) — (½-Ton)				
FM-1	Chassis & Cab	1382	2825	Note 1
FM-1	Pickup	1480	3125	Note 1
FM-1	Panel	1712	3225	Note 1
Series F-1-B — (6 cyl.) — (½-Ton)				
F-1-B	Chassis & Cab	—	2925	Note 2
F-1-B	Express	—	3300	Note 2

NOTE 1: Production — (1948) 5203; (1949) 2497 with T143 engine and 587 with T173 engine.
NOTE 2: Production — (1948-1949) 83,007.

ENGINE (FM-1): Inline. L-head. Six-cylinder. Cast iron block. Bore & stroke: 3⅜ x 4 1/16 in. Displacement: 218.1 cu. in. Compression ratio: (1948) 6.5:1; (1949) 6.7:1. Brake horsepower: (1948) 95 at 3600 R.P.M.; (1949) 97 at 3600 R.P.M. Net horsepower: 27.34. Four main bearings. Solid valve lifters. Carburetor: Ball & Ball 1V.

NOTES: The 95 h.p. engine has code T143. The 97 h.p. engine has code T-173. Data on the F-1-B engine not available at press time.

CHASSIS: (Series FM-1). Wheelbase: 108 in. Tires: 6.00 x 16 four-ply.

CHASSIS: (Series F-1-B). Wheelbase: 108 in. Tires: 6.00 x 16 four-ply.

1949 Fargo Platform With Stake Body (RPZ)

TECHNICAL: Selective synchromesh. Speeds: 3F/1R. Floor-mounted gearshift. Single dry disc clutch. Semi-floating rear axle. Four-wheel hydraulic brakes. Steel disc wheels.

OPTIONS: See 1948 or 1949 Dodge section.

HISTORICAL: Introduced: December 1947 (F-1-B). Model year production: 91,294. Innovations: All-new styling. Shorter w.b. Historical notes: Strong postwar demand for cars and trucks pushed Fargo production to all-time record levels. Full-line of Fargo trucks duplicated that offered by Dodge in the U.S.

Pricing

1948-49	5	4	3	2	1
Series FM-1 — (½-Ton)					
Pickup	720	1450	2400	3300	4800
Panel	670	1350	2250	3150	4500
Series F-1-B — (½-Ton)					
Express	750	1500	2500	3500	5000

1950 FARGO

1950 Fargo ½-Ton Pickup (Mantobia Archives via DFW)

½-TON — "F" SERIES — SIX-CYLINDER: — Styling of the 1950 Fargos was unchanged. The grille again had three thick bars over slotted openings. The top bar was shortest; the others each a bit longer. The hood lip was trimmed with a bright metal piece. The Fargo name appeared in block letters above the top grille bar. It was also stamped on the hood side badges. The hood ornament had a round piece at its front.

I.D. DATA: Serial and engine numbers in the same locations (see 1946-1947). (FN-1) — Windsor: 90506288 to 90512524. (F-2-B) — Detroit: 82140001 to 82212862. Engine codes: (FN-1) T173; (F-2-B) T172.

Model	Body Type	Price	Weight	Prod. Total
Series FN-1 — (6-cyl.) — (½-Ton)				
FN-1	Pickup	1480	3150	Note 1
FN-1	Panel	1712	3250	Note 1
Series F-2-B — (6 cyl.) — (½-Ton)				
F-2-B	Express	—	3150	Note 2

NOTE 1: Production 6237.
NOTE 2: Production 72,861.

ENGINE (FN-1): Inline. L-head. Six-cylinder. Cast iron block. Bore & stroke: 3⅜ x 4 1/16 in. Displacement: 218.1 cu. in. Compression ratio: 6.7:1. Brake horsepower: 97 at 3600 R.P.M. Net horsepower: 25.35. Four main bearings. Solid valve lifters. Carburetor: Carter 1V.

NOTE: Engine data for F-2-B Series not available.

CHASSIS: (Series FN-1). Wheelbase: 108 in. Tires: 6.00 x 16 four-ply.

CHASSIS: (Series F-2-B). Wheelbase: 108 in. Tires: 6.00 x 16 four-ply.

TECHNICAL: Selective synchromesh transmission. Speeds: 3F/1R. Floor-mounted gearshift. Single dry disc clutch. Semi-floating rear axle. Four-wheel hydraulic brakes. Steel disc wheels. Drivetrain options: Remote (column-mounted) gearshift selector.

OPTIONS: See 1950 Dodge truck options.

1950 Fargo Platform With Stake Body (RPZ)

HISTORICAL: Introduced: October 1949. Model year production: 79,098. Innovations: changes to grille styling. Historical notes: A full-range of larger Fargo trucks, from 1-ton to 4-ton, were produced in both the U.S. and Canada. Some used a 236 cu. in. Six-cylinder engine that produced 109 h.p. at 3600 R.P.M. Identical trucks (except for trim and name badges) were sold under the DeSoto nameplate in some export markets.

Pricing

1950	5	4	3	2	1
Series FN-1 — (½-Ton)					
Pickup	720	1450	2400	3300	4800
Panel	670	1350	2250	3150	4500
Series F-2-B — (½-Ton)					
Express	750	1500	2500	3500	5000

1951-1952 FARGO

½-TON/¾-TON — "F" SERIES — SIX-CYLINDER: — A modest restyling brought a new front end with a round-cornered, rectangle-shaped grille opening. Two thick body-color bars ran across it, linked by ribbed and center-indented chrome ornament. At its outer ends, the lower bar incorporated round parking lights. Also new were rear quarter windows as a pickup truck cab option. Reappearing this season was a ¾-ton series using the 228.1 cu. in. engine as base power plant. It offered a choice of short and long w.b. These trucks were introduced for model-year 1951 and carried over for the 1952 sales season without changes.

I.D. DATA: Serial and engine numbers in same location (see 1946-1947). **1951 Serial numbers**/(FO-1) — Windsor: 90512551 to 90517404. (F-3-B) — Detroit: 82215001 to 82256916. (FO-2) — Windsor: 91506451 & up. Engine codes: (FO-1) T307; (F-3-B) T306 and (FO-2) unavailable. **1952 Serial numbers**/(FO-1) — Windsor: 90517405 to 90522063. (F-3-B) — Detroit: 82257601 to 82302000. (FO-2) — Windsor; 91508066 & up. Engine codes: same as 1951.

1951 Fargo ¾-Ton Cab and Express (RPZ)

Model	Body Type	Price	Weight	Prod. Total
Series FO-1 — (6-cyl.) — (½-Ton)				
FO-1	Chassis & Cab	1541	2275	Note 1
FO-1	Pickup	1642	—	Note 1
FO-1	Panel	1886	—	Note 1
Series F-3-B — (6 cyl.) — (½-Ton)				
F-3-B	Express	—	—	Note 2
Series FO-2 — (6 cyl.) — (¾-Ton) — (116 in. w.b.)				
FO-2	Chassis & Cab	1831	2700	Note 3
FO-2	Express	1927	—	Note 3
(126 in. w.b.)				
FO-2	Chassis & Cab	1882	2725	Note 3
FO-2	Express	2017	—	Note 3

NOTE 1: Production (1951) 4854; (1952) 4658.
NOTE 2: Production (1951) 41,915; (1952) 44,399.
NOTE 3: Production unavailable for both years.
NOTE 4: Prices above are 1951 prices. For 1952: (FO-1 Series) Pickup/$1745; Chassis/$1643; Panel/$2009. (FO-2 Series) 126 in. w.b. Chassis/$1960; 126 in. w.b. Express/$2115 (others) not available.

1951 Fargo Town Panel Delivery (RPZ)

ENGINE (FO-1): Inline. L-head. Six-cylinder. Cast iron block. Bore & stroke: 3⅜ x 4 1/16 in. Displacement: 218.1 cu. in. Compression ratio: 6.7:1. Brake horsepower: 97 at 3600 R.P.M. Net horsepower: 25.35. Four main bearings. Solid valve lifters. Carburetor: Carter.

NOTE: Data on F-3-B engine not available at presstime.

ENGINE (FO-2): Inline. L-head. Six-cylinder. Cast iron block. Bore & stroke: 3⅜ x 4¼ in. Displacement: 228.1 cu. in. Compression ratio: 6.0:1. Brake horsepower: 105 at 3600 R.P.M. Net horsepower: 28.45. Four main bearings. Solid valve lifters. Carburetor: Carter.

1952 Fargo Cab And Front End Styling (RPZ)

1952 Fargo ½-Ton Pickup (L. Knutsen/J. Benjaminson)

1952 Fargo ½-Ton Pickup (L. Knutson/J. Benjaminson)

CHASSIS: (Series F-3-B). Wheelbase: 108 in. Tires: 6.70 x 15.

CHASSIS: (Series FO-2). Wheelbase: 116/126 in. Tires: 7 x 17.5 six-ply.

TECHNICAL: Same as 1950.

OPTIONS: See 1951-1952 Dodge truck options.

HISTORICAL: Introduced: January 1, 1951; January 1, 1952. Model year production: (½-Ton) 1951/46,769; 1952/49,058. Innovations: New styling. Revised grille design. New ¾-ton series. Rear quarter windows for pickups. New 116 and 126 in. w.b. available on ¾-ton models. Historical notes: Other payload capacities offerd by Fargo in 1951 included (U.S.A.) 1-ton; 1½-ton; 2-ton; 2½-ton; 2¾-ton and 3-ton. (Canada) 1½-ton, 2-ton and 3-ton. A 1-ton 4x4 model was also built in both nations.

Pricing

1951-52	5	4	3	2	1
Series FO-1 — (½-Ton)					
Pickup	720	1450	2400	3300	4800
Panel	670	1350	2250	3150	4500
Series FO-2 — (¾-Ton) (116 in. w.b.)					
Pickup	630	1260	2100	3000	4200
Express	600	1200	2000	2800	4000
(126 in. w.b.)					
Pickup	620	1230	2050	2900	4100
Panel	590	1170	1950	2700	3900
Series F-3-B — (½-Ton)					
Express	750	1500	2500	3500	5000

1953 FARGO

½-TON/¾-TON — "F" SERIES — SIX-CYLINDER: — Styling for the 1953 Fargo light-duty trucks was unchanged. Pickups now came in solid colors (earlier models had the cargo box finished in black). Running boards were still painted black. ¾-tonners now used the 126 in. w.b. only.

I.D. DATA: Serial and engine numbers in same locations. Serial numbers: (FP-1) — Windsor: 90522101 to 90525323. (FP-2) — Windsor: 91509601 and up. (F-4-B) Detroit: 82302001 to 82335036. Engine Codes: (FP-1) T307; (FP-2) not available; (F-4-B) T306.

Model	Body Type	Price	Weight	Prod. Total
Series FP-1 — (6-cyl.) — (½-Ton)				
FP-1	Chassis & Cowl	1400	2275	Note 1
FP-1	Chassis & Cab	1643	—	Note 1
FP-1	Pickup	1763	—	Note 1
FP-1	Panel	2009	—	Note 1
Series FP-2 — (6 cyl.) — (¾-Ton)				
FP-2	Chassis & Cowl	1731	2650	Note 2
FP-2	Chassis & Cab	1960	—	Note 2
FP-2	Express	2115	—	Note 2
Series F-4-B — (6-cyl.) — (½-Ton)				
F-4-B	Chassis	—	2400	Note 3

NOTE 1: Production — 3223.
NOTE 2: Not available.
NOTE 3: Production — 33,035.

ENGINE: Same as 1951-1952 engines.

CHASSIS: (Series FP-1). Wheelbase: 108 in. Tires: 6.70 x 15 four-ply.

CHASSIS: (Series FP-2). Wheelbase: 126 in. Tires: 7.00 x 17.5 six-ply.

CHASSIS: (Series F-4-B). Wheelbase: 108 in. Tires: 6.70 x 15 four-ply.

TECHNICAL: Selective synchromesh transmission. Speeds: 3F/1R. Floor-mounted gearshift. Single dry disc clutch. Semi-floating rear axle. Four-wheel hydraulic brakes. Steel disc wheels.

OPTIONS: Chrome front bumpers. Dual OSRV mirrors. Dual windshield wipers. Dual taillights. Oversize tires. Wheel trim rings. Cab with rear quarter windows. Deluxe cab equipment. Remote (column) gearshift controls. Fog lights. Spot lights.

HISTORICAL: Introduced: Fall 1952. Model year production: (½-ton) 36,258. Innovations: Grille styling revisions. All ¾-ton models now on 126 in. w.b. Historical notes: Other 1953 Fargos were available in the following ton ratings: (U.S.) 1-ton, 1½-ton, 2-ton, 2½-ton, 3-ton, 3½-ton and 4-ton. (Canada) 1-ton, 2-ton, 2½-ton, 3-ton and 3½-ton. A 1-ton 4x4 was built only in the United States this year.

Pricing

1953	5	4	3	2	1
Series FP-1 — (½-Ton)					
Pickup	680	1350	2250	3150	4500
Panel	660	1320	2200	3100	4400
Series FP-2 — (¾-Ton)					
Express	590	1170	1950	2700	3900
Series F-4-B — (½-Ton)					
Pickup	740	1470	2450	3350	4900
Panel	700	1400	2350	3250	4700

1954 FARGO

1954 Fargo Town Panel Delivery (RPZ)

½-TON/¾-TON — FC SERIES — SIX-CYLINDER/V-8: — For 1954, the grille was slightly changed again. There were now separate, ribbed chrome ornaments at the center of each of the thick horizontal bars and the bars themselves no longer extended past the grille opening. This opening now had a traphazoid shape, (instead of retangular shape with rounded corners. The front fender feature line also extended to the rear of the cab, instead of blending into the doors. Round parking lamps were mounted directly below the round headlamps. Turn signal lights, when optionally ordered, were small squares directly under the headlights. The Fargo name appeared on the nose, trailing edge of the front fender sides and the hubcaps. The higher front fenders made the hood look lower. A new V-8 engine option was available on both ½-ton and ¾-ton trucks. A 116 in. w.b. was used for the larger series. A choice of 108 or 116 in. w.b. was offered to ½-ton buyers.

I.D. DATA: Serial and engine numbers located: See 1946-1947 Section (FC-1-B). Windsor: 90525351 to 90528406 — Engine code T335. Detroit: 82338001 to 82372344 — Engine code T334. Detroit: 85328001 to 85330985 — Engine code T334. Detroit: 84250001 to 84262923 — Engine code VT334. Detroit: 86100001 to 86100446 — Engine code VT334 (FC-1-C). Detroit: 83398001 to 83404307 — Engine code T336. Detroit: 85517001 to 85517631 — Engine code T336. Detroit: 84650001 to 84652998 — Engine code T336. Detroit: 86300001 to 86300105 — Engine code VT336.

NOTE: "T" engine is 6-cyl. "VT" engine is V-8.

Model	Body Type	Price	Weight	Prod. Total
Series FC-1-B — (6-cyl.) — (½-Ton) — (108 in. w.b.)				
FC-1-B	Cowl & Chassis	1400	2200	Note 1
FC-1-B	Cab & Chassis	1669	2675	Note 1
FC-1-B	Pickup	1790	2975	Note 1
FC-1-B	Panel	2990	3150	Note 1
Series FC-1-C — (6-cyl.) — (¾-Ton) — (116 in. w.b.)				
FC-1-C	Chassis & Cowl	—	2325	Note 2
FC-1-C	Chassis & Cab	—	2800	Note 2
FC-1-C	Express	—	3175	Note 2

NOTE 1: Production — (T335 engine) 3056; (T334 engine) 37,327; (VT334 engine) 13,367.
NOTE 2: Production — (T336 engine) 6936; (VT336 engine) 3101.
NOTE 3: Factory Prices: add for FC-1-B with 116 in. w.b.; add for optional V-8 engine.

ENGINE (FC-1-B, standard): Inline. L-head. Six-cylinder. Cast iron block. Bore & stroke: 3⅜ x 4.25 in. Displacement: 228.1 cu. in. Compression ratio: 7.25:1. Brake horsepower: 108 at 3600 R.P.M. Carburetor: Carter 1V model D6S1.

ENGINE (FC-1-B, optional): Vee-block. OHV. Eight-cylinder. Cast iron block. Bore & stroke: 3.438 x 3.25 in. Displacement: 241.3 cu. in. Compression ratio: 7.50:1. Brake horsepower: 150 at 4400 R.P.M. Carburetor: Carter 2V.

NOTE: FC-1-C engine specification not available. In the U.S., the ½-ton and ¾-ton Dodge trucks shared the same engines and it is likely this was also the case with Fargos. If so, the above specifications would apply to both series, even though different engine code numbers were used.

CHASSIS: (Series FC-1-B, standard). Wheelbase: 108 in. GVW: 5100 lbs. Tires: 6.70 x 15 four-ply.

CHASSIS: (Series FC-1-B, optional). Wheelbase: 116 in. GVW: 5100 lbs. Tires: 6.70 x 15 four-ply.

CHASSIS: (Series FC-1-C, standard). Wheelbase: 116 in. GVW: 5800 lbs. Tires: 7.00 x 17.5 six-ply.

TECHNICAL: Selective synchromesh transmission. Speeds: 3F/1R. Floor-mounted gearshift. Single plate dry disc clutch. Semi-floating rear axle. Four-wheel hydraulic brakes. Steel disc wheels.

OPTIONS: Chrome front bumper. Rear bumper. Rear step bumper. Right-hand OSRV mirror. Oversize tires. Wheel trim rings. Radio and antenna. Heater. Remote (column) gearshift controls. Cigar lighter. Fog lights. Special paint colors. Seat covers. Deluxe cab equipment. Cab rear quarter windows. Bumper guards. Spot light.

HISTORICAL: Introduced: November 1953. Model year production: (½-ton) 53,750; (¾-ton) 10,037. Innovations: Higher, more slab-sided front fender styling. New traphazoid-shape grille with shorter bars. Optional V-8 engine available. Two w.b. for ½-ton models. Historical notes: Production of ½-ton and ¾-ton models included 47,319 six-cylinder trucks and 16,468 with optional V-8 engine. 1954 Fargos were also available in the following ton ratings: (U.S.) 1-ton, 1½-ton, 2-ton, 2½-ton, 3-ton and 4-ton. (Canada) 1-ton, 1½-ton, 2-ton, 3-ton, and 3½-ton.

Pricing

1954	5	4	3	2	1
Series FC-1-B — (½-Ton) — (108 in. w.b.)					
Pickup (6-cyl.)	700	1400	2350	3250	4700
Panel (6-cyl.)	690	1380	2300	3200	4600
Pickup (V-8)	750	1500	2500	3500	5000
Panel (V-8)	740	1470	2450	3350	4900
Series FC-1-B — (½-Ton) — (116 in. w.b.)					
Pickup (6-cyl.)	680	1350	2250	3150	4500
Panel (6-cyl.)	660	1320	2200	3100	4400
Pickup (V-8)	720	1450	2400	3300	4800
Panel (V-8)	700	1400	2350	3250	4700
Series FC-1-C — (¾-Ton) — (116 in. w.b.)					
Express (6-cyl.)	650	1300	2150	3050	4300
Express (V-8)	630	1250	2100	3000	4200

1955 FARGO

½-TON/¾-TON — SERIES FC — SIX-CYLINDER/V-8: — A new, wrap-around windshield characterized the modest styling changes for 1955 Fargo light-duty trucks. Two even wider horizontal bars crossed the trapazoid-shaped radiator grille opening. On pickups, the standard cab had a single-piece rear window. Glass curving around the rear quarters of the cab was optional. Also available this year was a choice between "lowside" and "highside" cargo boxes. Model I.D. badges were also restyled.

I.D. DATA: Serial number located: See 1946-47 Section. (FC-3-B) Windsor: 90528451 to 90531257 — Engine code: T335 — (108 in. w.b.) — Production: 2,806 (Canada). Detroit: 82373001 to 82397181 — Engine code: T334 — (108/116 in. w.b.) — Production: 24,180 (US) Detroit: 84265001 to 84284000 — Engine code: VT334 — (108/116 in. w.b.) — Production: 18,999 (US). (FC-3-C) Detroit: 83405001 to 83409905 — Engine code: T336 — Production: 4,904. Detroit: 80200101 to 80200199 — Engine code: T361 — Production: 198. Detroit: 84654001 to 84658200 — Engine code: VT336 — Production: 4,199. Detroit: 84803001 to 84806500 — Engine code: VT338 — Production: 3,499.

Model	Body Type	Price	Weight	Prod. Total
Series FC-3-B —	**(½-Ton) — (108/116 in. w.b.)**			
FC-3-B	Chassis & Cowl	—	2200	Note 1
FC-3-B	Chassis & Cab	—	2675	Note 1
FC-3-B	Pickup	—	2975	Note 1
FC-3-B	Panel	—	3150	Note 1
Series FC-3-C —	**(¾-Ton) — (116 in. w.b.)**			
FC-3-C	Chassis & Cowl	—	2325	Note 1

NOTE 1: See I.D. Data (above) for production totals.

ENGINE (6-Cyl.) Inline: L-head. Six-cylinder. Cast iron block. Bore & stroke: 3.44 x 4.5 in. Displacement: 250.6 cu. in. Compression ratio: 7.5:1. Brake horsepower: 125 at 3600 R.P.M. Carburetor: Carter 1V model 2192.

ENGINE (V-8) Vee-block. OHV. Eight-cylinder. Cast iron block. Bore & stroke: 3.438 x 3.25 in. Displacement: 241.3 cu. in. Compression ratio: 7.6:1. Brake horsepower: 157 at 4400 R.P.M. Carburetor: Carter two-barrel.

CHASSIS: See 1954 Fargo section.

TECHNICAL: See 1954 Fargo section.

OPTIONS: See 1955 Dodge truck section.

HISTORICAL: Introduced: Fall 1954. Model year production: (½-Ton) 45,985; (¾-Ton) 12,800. (Total) 58,785. Innovations: New "high-sides" cargo bed available. Wraparound windshields introduced. Historical notes: Fargo produced a total of 45,985 six-cylinder and 18,999 V-8 powered trucks in the ½-Ton and ¾-Ton 1955 series.

Pricing

1955	5	4	3	2	1
Series FC-3-B — (½-Ton) — (108 in. w.b.)					
Pickup (6-cyl.)	700	1400	2350	3250	4700
Pickup (V-8)	750	1500	2500	3500	5000
Panel (6-cyl.)	690	1380	2300	3200	4600
Panel (V-8)	740	1470	2450	3350	4900
(116 in. w.b.)					
Pickup (6-cyl.)	680	1350	2250	3150	4500
Pickup (V-8)	720	1450	2400	3300	4800
Panel (6-cyl.)	660	1320	2200	3100	4400
Panel (V-8)	700	1400	2350	3250	4700
Series FC-3-C — (¾-Ton) — (116 in. w.b.)					
Express (6-cyl.)	650	1300	2150	3050	4300
Express (V-8)	630	1250	2100	3000	4200

1956 FARGO

½-TON/¾-TON — FC SERIES — SIX-CYLINDER/V-8: — Like the Dodge trucks sold in the United States, the 1956 Fargo models looked virtually identical to the previous year's offerings. a 250 cu. in. six was the standard engine. Optionally available was a V-8 power plant. Other extra-cost items included chrome bumpers, grilles and hubcaps and rear quarter windows for pick-up truck cabs. In addition to the ½-ton and ¾-ton models covered here, larger Fargo trucks were available. They included 1-ton, ½-ton, 2-ton, 2½-ton, 3-ton and 4-ton vehicles sourced from the U.S. factory in Detroit, plus 1-ton, 2-ton, 3-ton and 3½-ton models sourced from the Canadian plant at Windsor, Ontario. All were produced for marketing through Plymouth dealers in Canada.

I.D. DATA: Serial Number Located: Same as previous. (FC-4-B) Windsor: 90531301 to 90532955 — Engine code T435 — (6-cyl.) — Production: 1,654. Detroit: 82398001 to 82407868 — Engine code T434 — (6-cyl.) — Production: 9,867. Detroit: 84284001 to 84287960 — Engine code VT434 — (V-8) — Production: 3,959. (FC-4-C) Detroit: 83411001 to 83413368 — Engine code T436 — (6-cyl.) — Production: 2,367. Detroit: 84660001 to 84661053 — Engine code VT436 - (V-8) — Production: 1,052.

Model	Body Type	Price	Weight	Prod. Total
Series FC-4-B —	**(6-cyl.) — (½-Ton) — (108 in. w.b.)**			
FC-4-B	Chassis & Cowl	—	2200	—
FC-4-B	Chassis & Cab	2770	2675	—
FC-4-B	Pickup	3095	2975	—
FC-4-B	Panel	3260	3150	—
(116 in. w.b.)				
FC-4-B	Chassis & Cowl	2800	2225	—
FC-4-B	Chassis & Cab	2800	2700	—
FC-4-B	Pickup	3195	3025	—
Series FC-4-C —	**(6 cyl.) — (¾-Ton) — (116 in. w.b.)**			
FC-4-C	Chassis & Cowl	—	2625	—
FC-4-C	Chassis & Cab	—	3100	—
FC-4-C	Express	—	3475	—

NOTE: See I.D. Data section, above, for available production totals.

ENGINE (Base) Inline. L-head. Six-cylinder. Cast iron block. Bore & stroke: 3.438 x 4.50 in. Displacement: 250.6 cu. in. Compression ratio: 7.5:1. Brake horsepower: 125 at 3600 R.P.M. Taxable horsepower: 25.4. Solid valve lifters. Carburetor: Carter 1V Model 2296.

ENGINE (Optional) Vee-block. OHV. Eight-cylinder. Cast iron block. Bore & stroke: 3.625 x 3.256 in. Displacement: 268.8 cu. in. Compression ratio: 8.0:1. Brake horsepower: 180 at 4400 R.P.M. Hydraulic valve lifters. Carburetor: Carter 2V.

CHASSIS (Series FC-4-B) Wheelbase: 108 in. Tires: 6.70 x 15 four-ply.

CHASSIS (Series FC-4-B) Wheelbase: 116 in. Tires: 6.70 x 15 four-ply.

CHASSIS (Series FC-4-C) Wheelbase: 116 in. Tires: 7 x 17.5 six-ply.

TECHNICAL: Selective synchromesh transmission. Speeds: 3F/1R. Floor shift. Single plate dry disc clutch. Shaft drive. Semi-floating rear axle. Four-wheel hydraulic brakes. Steel disc wheels.

OPTIONS: Chrome front bumper. Rear bumper. Rear step bumper. Deluxe cab option. Deluxe interior package. Two-tone paint. Bumper guards. Single or dual OSRV mirrors. Radio and antenna. Heater. Fog lights. Wheel trim rings. Oversize tires. Whitewall tires. Seat covers. Spotlight. Right-hand interior sun visor. Right-hand taillight. Directional signals.

HISTORICAL: Introduced: October 7, 1955. Calendar year production: (Light-duty) 18,899. Innovations: Larger, more powerful six-cylinder and V-8 engines.

Pricing

1956	5	4	3	2	1
Series FC-4-B — (6-cyl.) — (½-Ton) — (108 in. w.b.)					
Pickup	700	1400	2350	3250	4700
Panel	690	1380	2300	3200	4600
(116 in. w.b.)					
Pickup	680	1350	2250	3150	4500
Series FC-4-C — (6-cyl.) — (¾-Ton) (116 in. w.b.)					
Express	650	1300	2150	3050	4300

NOTE: Add 5 percent for V-8 engine.

1957 FARGO

1957 Fargo Deluxe ½-Ton Utiline Pickup (CHC/JB)

FARGO D100/D110 — FK SERIES — SIX-CYLINDER/V-8: — Styling changes for 1957 Fargos were identical to those for 1957 Dodge trucks. They included hooded front fenders (shrouding the single headlights) with bright metal panels around the headlight lenses. A large, horizontal air intake slot was above the grille ensemble, which consisted of another long horizontal slot decorated with a long horizontal bar and short vertical center piece. A painted trim panel surrounded the grille and extended out to the edges of the body. It housed a round parking lamp at each end, just beyond the main grille bar. Another horizontal chromed molding stretched the full width of the front, between the air slot (on top) and grille (on bottom). The sheet metal above the center of this molding had six square indentations. Ornamentation included Fargo chrome block lettering above the air slot and jet-like fenderside decorations with I.D. badges behind them. Trucks with V-8s had a large, chrome "V" on their nose. On standard models the bumpers were painted and the trim panel surrounding the grille was body-color. Deluxe models had chrome bumpers and white-painted grille surrounds. Two-tone paint treatments used the main color on the cab roof and lower body and rear fenders, with the secondary color on the hood, upper cowl, doors above featureline and the entire cargo box. Wheels were done in the secondary color.

I.D. DATA: Location of Serial Number: on left or right door pillar post; on dash under hood and on front frame rail in vicinity of spring hanger. All 1957 models sourced from Windsor factory. Starting Number: (6-cyl.) 90533051; (V-8) 90700001. Engine Number Location: on left side of motor, below cylinder head or on front right of motor; also on timing gear cover.

1957 Fargo ½-Ton Utiline Pickup (D. Pollack/JB)

Model	Body Type	Price	Weight	Prod. Total
Series FK6 — (6-cyl.) — (½-Ton) — (108 in. w.b.)				
D100	Chassis & Cab	2875	2675	—
D100	Pickup	3225	2975	—
D100	Panel	3350	3150	—
(116 in. w.b.)				
D110	Chassis & Cab	2900	2700	—
D110	Pickup	3275	3000	—
Series FK8 — (V-8) — (½-Ton) — (108 in. w.b.)				
D100	Chassis & Cab	2975	2750	—
D100	Pickup	3325	3050	—
D100	Panel	3450	3225	—
(116 in. w.b.)				
D110	Chassis & Cab	3000	2775	—
D110	Pickup	3375	3075	—

NOTE: Production totals not available.

ENGINE (Base) Inline. L-head. Six-cylinder. Cast iron block. Bore & stroke: 3.438 x 4.50 in. Displacement: 250.6 cu. in. Compression ratio: 7.5:1. Brake horsepower: 125 at 3600 R.P.M. Taxable horsepower: 25.4. Solid valve lifters. Carburetor: Carter 1V Model 2296.

ENGINE (Optional) Vee-block. OHV. Eight-cylinder. Cast iron block. Bore & stroke: 3.812 x 3.312 in. Displacement: 302.5 cu. in. Compression ratio: 8.0:1. Brake horsepower: 200 at 4400 R.P.M. Hydraulic valve lifters. Carburetor: Carter 2V Model 2299.

CHASSIS (Series D100) Wheelbase: 108 in. Tires: 6.70 x 15 four-ply.

CHASSIS (Series D110) Wheelbase: 116 in. Tires: 6.70 x 15 four-ply.

TECHNICAL: Selective synchromesh transmission. Speeds: 3F/1R. Floor shift. Single plate dry disc clutch. Shaft drive. Semi-floating rear axle. Four-wheel hydraulic brakes. Steel disc wheels.

OPTIONS: Chrome front bumper. Rear bumper. Rear step bumper. Deluxe cab option. Deluxe interior package. Two-tone paint. Bumper guards. Single or dual OSRV mirror(s). Radio and antenna. Heater. Fog lights. Wheel trim rings. Oversize tires. Whitewall tires. Seat covers. Spotlight. Right-hand interior sun visor. Right-hand taillight. Directional signals. Power Steering. Overdrive transmission. Loadflite push-button automatic transmission.

HISTORICAL: Introduced: October 15, 1956. Innovations: New front end styling. Larger, more powerful V-8 engines. All new K Series. ¾-ton line discontinued. Historical notes: Town Wagons, imported from the U.S., were also sold by Fargo dealers in Canada this year. Larger Fargos available included 1-ton, 2-ton, 3-ton and 3½-ton models.

Pricing

	5	4	3	2	1
1957					
(108 in. w.b.)					
Pickup	750	1500	2500	3500	5000
Panel	720	1450	2400	3300	4800
(116 in. w.b.)					
Pickup	690	1380	2300	3200	4600

NOTE: Add 5 percent for V-8.

1958 FARGO

FARGO D100/D110 — FL SERIES — SIX-CYLINDER/V-8: — The 1958 Fargos had a lower, flatter hood atop a flat, shelf-like upper fender and front panel arrangement. A sculptured feature line ran from the bottom of the fender crowns back to the doors. Quad headlamps were set side-by-side in protruding housings which flanked either side of a grille with three thick horizontal bars. An air slot below the grille had another horizontal bar through it. Round parking lamps were centered below the headlamps. The Fargo name, in chrome block letters, was on the front right above the grille. A new wraparound bumper was used. Other nameplates were on the sides of the hood and fenders.

I.D. DATA: Location of Serial Number: Same as 1957. Starting Number: (6-cyl.) FL6D1W1001; (V-8) FL8D1W1001. First two symbols indicated series. Third symbol indicated engine type. Fourth and fifth symbols indicate D100 line. "W" indicated Windsor factory. Remaining digits represent sequential production number. Engine Number Location: Same as 1957.

Model	Body Type	Price	Weight	Prod. Total
Series D100 — (6-cyl.) — (½-Ton) — (108 in. w.b.)				
FL6	Chassis	2122	2200	—
FL6	Pickup	2251	2975	—
FL6	Panel	2595	3150	—
Series D110 — (6-cyl.) — (½-Ton) — (116 in. w.b.)				
FL6	Chassis	2141	2225	—
FL6	Pickup	2277	3025	—
Series D100 — (V-8) — (½-Ton) — (108 in. w.b.)				
FL8	Chassis	2246	2300	—
FL8	Pickup	2379	3075	—
FL8	Panel	2719	3250	—
Series D110 — (V-8) — (½-Ton) — (116 in. w.b.)				
FL8	Chassis	2265	2325	—
FL8	Pickup	2401	3125	—

NOTE: Production totals not available.

ENGINE (6-cyl.): Same as 1957.

ENGINE (V-8): Vee-block. OHV. Eight-cylinder. Cast iron block. Bore & stroke: 3.875 x 3.312 in. Displacement: 312.5 cu. in. Compression ratio: 8.5:1. Brake horsepower: 220 at 4400 R.P.M. Overhead valves. Carburetor: Carter 2V Model 2299.

CHASSIS (Series D100) Wheelbase: 108 in. Tires: 6.70 x 15 four-ply.

CHASSIS (Series D110) Wheelbase: 116 in. Tires: 6.70 x 15 four-ply.

TECHNICAL: Selective synchromesh transmission. Speeds: 3F/1R. Floor shift. Single plate dry disc clutch. Shaft drive. Semi-floating rear axle. Four-wheel hydraulic brakes. Steel disc wheels.

OPTIONS: Chrome bumpers. Chrome hubcaps. Painted rear bumper. Rear step bumper. Deluxe cab option. Deluxe interior. Heater. Two-tone. Bumper guards. Single or dual OSRV mirror(s). Radio and antenna. Fog lights. Wheel trim rings. Oversize tires. Whitewall tires. Seat covers. Spotlight. Directional signals. Power steering. Power brakes. Overdrive. Load flite. Clearance marker lights for cab roof. Long-arm rearview mirrors.

HISTORICAL: Introduced: November, 1957. Innovations: Dual headlights. Larger displacement higher horsepower V-8 engine. Historical notes: Town Wagons were imported from the United States again this year. Available again, in larger tonnage classes, were 1-ton, 2-ton, 3-ton and 3½-ton Fargo trucks.

Pricing

	5	4	3	2	1
1958					
Series D100 — (108 in. w.b.)					
Pickup	690	1380	2300	3200	4600
Panel	680	1350	2250	3150	4500
(116 in. w.b.)					
Pickup	650	1300	2150	3050	4300

289

1959-1965 FARGO

1959 Fargo Town Panel Delivery (CHC/JB)

FARGO — LIGHT TRUCK SERIES — SIX-CYLINDER/V-8: — Styling features of 1959-1964 Fargo trucks are shown in the accompanying photos. Design changes paralleled those for Dodge models during the same period. The only differences were in nameplates, minor trim items and types of engines used.

Since we have no (Canadian) Sanford Evans Truck Data Book covering these years, it's impossible to provide serial numbers, prices, weights, specifications or model listings for these models.

Dodge passenger car engines used in Canada during this time span included the 250 cu. in. six, 313 cu. in. V-8 and a 361 cu. in. V-8 in 1959. In 1960, only the two V-8s were offered. The smaller V-8 was the sole power plant from 1961-1964. For 1965, new engines — a 225 cu. in. six and 317 cu. in. V-8 were available. It seems likely that these were the primary engines used in Fargo trucks. Specifications for those Canadian engines not previously covered are listed below.

1960 Fargo FW100 Power Wagon 4x4 Town Wagon (RPZ)

1961 Fargo PLatform With Stake Body (CHC/JB)

290

1962 Fargo F100 Sweptline Pickup (RPZ)

ENGINE (6-cyl.): Inline. OHV. Six-cylinder. Cast iron block. Bore & stroke: 3.40 x 4.125 in. Displacement: 224.7 cu. in. Compression ratio: 8.4:1. Brake horsepower: 145 at 4000 R.P.M. Hydraulic valve lifters. Carburetor: Carter 1V model 3999.

ENGINE: Vee-block. OHV. Eight-cylinder. Cast iron block. Bore & stroke: 4.125 x 3.375 in. Displacement: 360.8 cu. in. Compression ratio: 10.0:1. Brake horsepower: 295 at 4400 R.P.M. Hydraulic valve lifters. Carburetor: Carter 4V model 3104.

1963 Fargo P200/P300 Door-To-Door Utilivan (RPZ)

1964 Fargo A100 Traniline Van and Pickup (RPZ)

ENGINE (V-8): Vee-block. OHV. Eight-cylinder. Cast iron block. Bore & stroke: 3.906 x 3.312 in. Displacement: 317.3 cu. in. Compression ratio: 9.0:1. Brake horsepower: 230 at 4400 R.P.M. Hydraulic valve lifters. Carburetor: Carter 2V model 4011.

ENGINE (V-8): Vee-block. OHV. Eight-cylinder. Cast iron block. Bore & stroke: 3.875 x 3.312 in. Displacement: 312.5 cu. in. Compression ratio: 9.0:1. Brake horsepower: 225 at 4400 R.P.M. Hydraulic valve lifters. Carburetor: Carter 2V model 2991.

1966 FARGO

½-TON/¾-TON — D/W/P/A SERIES — SIX-CYLINDER/V-8: — The 1966 Fargo model lineup included conventional light-duty trucks (D Series), 4x4 trucks (W Series), parcel delivery vans (P Series) and forward control vans (A Series). ½-tonners were coded as "100" models, while a "200" designation was used to identify ¾-tonners. Styling wise, these had the same general appearance of Dodges of the same year. The pickups, panels and "carryall" type Town Wagons featured a squarish looking body with large, single round headlights and a grille having three horizontal and three vertical cross members. The "W" trucks were similar, but had a 4x4 drivetrain. The "P" models were walk-in delivery type trucks, also with squarish bodies. The vans featured a slanting two-piece windshield, two large round headlights and a simple grille with one horizontal and one vertical member. Pickups came in Utiline (pontoon rear fenders) and Sweptline (slab rear fenders) styles. Offered in the van series was a wagon model (with windows), a closed panel body for commercial use and a pickup with no upper rear body sheet metal.

I.D. DATA: Serial numbers were located on left-hand door hinge pillar post. Six-cylinder starting numbers began with four symbols which varied as follows: "FD1A" for D100 with 114 in. w.b. "FD1B" for D100 with 128 in. w.b. "FD2A" for D200 with 128 in. w.b. "FD2B" for D200 with 146 in. w.b. "FW1A" for W100. "FW2A" for W200 with standard cab. "FP1A" for P100. "FP3A" for P300. "FA1A" for A100. V-8 starting numbers began with four symbols which varied as follows: "FD1J" for D100 with 114 in. w.b. "FD1K" for D100 with 128 in. w.b. "FD2J" for D200 with 128 in. w.b. "FD2K" for D200 with 146 in. w.b. "FW1J" for W100. "FW2J" for W200 with standard cab. "FW2K" for W200 with Crew Cab. The last seven digits, in all cases, were: 2945001. Ending numbers are unavailable.

Model Series D100 — (6-cyl.) — (½-Ton) — (114 in. w.b.)	Body Type	Price	Weight	Prod. Total
FD1A	Chassis & Cab	—	2945	—
FD1A	Utiline Pickup	—	3305	—
FD1A	Sweptline Pickup	—	3355	—
FD1A	Town Panel	—	3415	—
FD1A	Town Wagon	—	3645	—

NOTE: with available V-8 engines the fourth symbol in model number changes to "J" and prices and weights are higher.

Model Series D110 — (6 cyl.) — (½-Ton) — (128 in. w.b.)	Body Type	Price	Weight	Prod. Total
FD1B	Chassis & Cab	—	—	—
FD1B	Utiline Pickup	—	—	—
FD1B	Sweptline Pickup	—	—	—
FD1B	Town Panel	—	—	—
FD1B	Town Wagon	—	—	—

NOTE: with available V-8s the fourth symbol in model number changes to "K" and prices and weights are higher.

Model Series D200 — (6-cyl.) — (¾-Ton) — (128 in. w.b.)	Body Type	Price	Weight	Prod. Total
FD2A	Chassis & F.F. Cowl	—	—	—
FD2A	Chassis & Cab	—	3500	—
FD2A	Utiline Pickup	—	3940	—
FD2A	Sweptline Pickup	—	4000	—
FD2A	Town Panel	—	—	—
FD2A	Town Wagon	—	—	—

NOTE: with available V-8s the fourth symbol in model number changes to "J" and prices and weights increase.

Model Series D210 — (6-cyl.) — (¾-Ton) — (146 in. w.b.)	Body Type	Price	Weight	Prod. Total
FD2B	Chassis & Cab	—	—	—
FD2B	Utiline Pickup	—	—	—
FD2B	Sweptline Pickup	—	—	—

NOTE: with available V-8 engines the fourth symbol in model number changes to "K" and prices and weights increase.

Model Series W100 — 4x4 — (6 cyl.) — (½-Ton) — (114 in. w.b.)	Body Type	Price	Weight	Prod. Total
FW1A	Cab & Chassis	—	3750	—
FW1A	Utiline Pickup	—	4110	—
FW1A	Sweptline Pickup	—	4160	—
FW1A	Town Wagon	—	4220	—

NOTE: These are 4x4s. With available V-8s the fourth symbol in model number changes to "J" and prices and weights increase.

Model Series W200 — (4x4) — (6-cyl.) — (¾-Ton) — (128 in. w.b.)	Body Type	Price	Weight	Prod. Total
FW2A	Chassis & Cab	—	3945	—
FW2A	Utiline Pickup	—	4385	—
FW2A	Sweptline Pickup	—	4445	—
FW2A	Town Wagon	—	—	—

NOTE: These are 4x4s. With 6-cyl. Crew Cab the fourth symbol in model number changes to "B" and w.b. is 146 in. With V-8 Crew Cab the fourth symbol in model number changes to "K" and w.b. is 146 in. With V-8 and standard cab fourth symbol in model numbers changes to "J". All add to prices/weights.

Model Series P100 — (6-cyl.) — (½-Ton) — (104 in. w.b.)	Body Type	Price	Weight	Prod. Total
FP1A	Stripped Chassis	—	—	—
FP1A	Utilivan	—	—	—

NOTE: Walk-in Parcel Delivery Series; 6-cyl. engines only; forward control.

Model Series P300 — (6-cyl.) — (¾-Ton) — (125/137 in. w.b.)	Body Type	Price	Weight	Prod. Total
FP3A	Stripped Chassis (125 in.)	—	—	—
FP3A	Stripped Chassis (137 in.)	—	—	—

NOTE: Walk-in Parcel Delivery Series; 6-cyl. engines only; forward control.

Model Series A100 — (6-cyl.) — (½-Ton) — (90 in. w.b.)	Body Type	Price	Weight	Prod. Total
FA1A	Pickup	—	2770	—
FA1A	Van	—	2137	—
FA1A	Wagon	—	3175	—

NOTE: Compact forward-control vans; 6-cyl. engines only; "van" has solid panel sides; "wagon" has windows/passenger seating.

ENGINE (6-cyl.): Inline. OHV. Six-cylinder. Cast iron block. Bore & stroke: 3.40 x 4.125 in. Displacement: 224.7 cu. in. Compression ratio: 8.4:1. Brake horsepower: 145 at 4000 R.P.M. Taxable horsepower: 27.7. Hydraulic valve lifters. Carburetor: Carter 4V model 4111. Torque: 215 lbs.-ft. at 1600 R.P.M.

ENGINE (V-8): Vee-block. OHV. Eight-cylinder. Cast iron block. Bore & stroke: 3.906 x 3.312 in. Displacement: 318.14 cu. in. Compression ratio: 9.0:1. Brake horsepower: 230 at 4400 R.P.M. Hydraulic valve lifters. Carburetor: Carter 2V model 4123.

CHASSIS: (Series D100. Wheelbase: 114 in. Tires: 6.70 x 15.

CHASSIS: (Series D110). Wheelbase: 128 in. Tires: 6.70 x 15.

CHASSIS: (Series D200). Wheelbase: 128 in. Tires: 6.50 x 16.

CHASSIS: (Series D210). Wheelbase: 146 in. Overall length: 223 15/16 in. Tires: 6.50 x 16.

CHASSIS: (Series W100). Wheelbase: 114 in. Tires: 6.50 x 16.

CHASSIS: (Series W200). Wheelbase: 128 in. Tires 7.00 x 17.5.

CHASSIS: (Series P100). Wheelbase: 104 in. Overall length: 181 13/16 in. Tires: 7.00 x 17.5 6PR.

CHASSIS: (Series P300). Wheelbase: 125 in. Overall length: 205⅜ in. Tires: 7.00 x 17.5 6PR.

CHASSIS: (Series P310). Wheelbase: 137 in. Overall length: 217⅜ in. Tires: 7.00 x 17.5 6PR.

CHASSIS: (Series A100). Wheelbase: 90 in. Tires: 6.50 x 13.

TECHNICAL: Selective synchromesh transmission. Speeds: 3F/1R. Column shift. Single dry disc clutch. Shaft drive. Semi-floating rear axle. Four-wheel hydraulic brakes. Steel disc wheels.

OPTIONS: Custom cab equipment. Chrome bumpers. Rear bumper. Push-button Loadflite automatic transmission. Four-speed manual transmission. Power steering. Power brakes. Dual OSRV mirrors. Long-arm OSRV mirrors. Two-tone paint. Radio and antenna. Heater. Whitewall tires. Oversize tires. Front locking hubs (4x4).

HISTORICAL: Introduced: Fall 1965.

Pricing

1966	5	4	3	2	1
Series D100 — (6-cyl.) — (½-Ton)					
Utiline Pickup (SWB)	600	1200	2000	2800	4000
Sweptline Pickup (SWB)	650	1300	2150	3050	4300
Town Panel (SWB)	680	1350	2250	3150	4500
Town Wagon (SWB)	740	1470	2450	3350	4900
Utiline Pickup (LWB)	570	1140	1900	2650	3800
Sweptline Pickup (LWB)	620	1230	2050	2900	4100
Town Panel (LWB)	650	1300	2150	3050	4300
Town Wagon (LWB)	700	1400	2350	3250	4700
Series D200 — (6-cyl.) — (¾-Ton)					
Utiline Pickup (SWB)	590	1170	1950	2700	3900
Sweptline Pickup (SWB)	630	1250	2100	3000	4200
Town Panel	660	1320	2200	3100	4400
Town Wagon	720	1450	2400	3300	4800
Utiline Pickup (LWB)	560	1100	1850	2600	3700
Sweptline Pickup (LWB)	600	1200	2000	3000	4000
PARCEL DELIVERY VANS — (6-cyl. only) — (104 in. w.b.)					
Walk-in Van	480	975	1600	2250	3200
(125 in. w.b.)					
Walk-in Van	500	1000	1650	2300	3300
(137 in. w.b.)					
Walk-in Van	520	1020	1700	2400	3400
Series A100 — (6-cyl. only)					
Pickup	560	1100	1850	2600	3700
Panel Van	530	1050	1750	2450	3500
Passenger Wagon	570	1140	1900	2650	3800

NOTE: Add five percent for V-8; add five percent for 4x4.

1967-1968 FARGO

1968 Fargo F100 Utiline Pickup (RPZ)

½-TON/¾-TON — D/W/P/A SERIES — SIX-CYLINDER/V-8: — Fargos produced for the Canadian market had the same general appearance as Dodge trucks made for sale in the U.S. as 1967 and 1968 models. (See the Dodge section for representative photos and imagine Fargo nameplates on the front.)

On pickups the grille had a broad horizontal bar, with three large "teeth", going horizontally down the center. The single, round taillights were surrounded by bright metal trim panels, extending from the grille, which also housed upright parking lamps.

A 170 cu. in. six-cylinder engine was standard in the A100/A108 vans. Other trucks used the 225 cu. in. six (optional in the vans) as base power plant. A 318 cu. in. V-8 was optional in all Fargo trucks, except the "P" Series walk-in Utilivans. This series did have something new, however. It was the ¾-ton P200 line offering 104 and 122 in. wheelbases.

Also new, for the compact van series, was a pair of "King-Size" models on a 108 in. wheelbase. They were called A108s, but did not include the pickup version. Only commercial and passenger vans were included.

Several models listed for 1967 were not listed for 1968 (and vice versa). Otherwise the trucks of the two years were virtually identical.

I.D. DATA: Location of serial numbers: Same as 1966. All carryover models had the same first four symbols in their serial numbers. A new P200 series had "FP2A" and "FP2B" as the first four symbols for 104 in. wheelbase and 122 in. wheelbase models, respectively. Also new for the A100 Series was a V-8 option ("FA1J") plus 108 in. wheelbase models with both six-cylinder ("FA1B") and V-8 ("FA1K") engines. The last seven symbols used in all starting serial numbers changed annually. For 1967, they were 2945118. For 1968, they were 2J10001.

Model	Body Type	Price	Weight	Prod. Total
Series D100 — (6-cyl.) — (½-Ton) — (114 in. w.b.)				
FD1A	Chassis & Cab	—	3030	—
FD1A	Utiline Pickup	—	3390	—
FD1A	Sweptline Pickup	—	3440	—
FD1A	Town Panel (1967)	—	—	—
FD1A	Town Wagon (1967)	—	—	—

NOTE: With V-8 fourth symbol in model number becomes "J" and prices/weights are higher. Town Panel and Town Wagon not available in 1968.

Model	Body Type	Price	Weight	Prod. Total
Series D110 — (6-cyl.) — (½-Ton) — (128 in. w.b.)				
FD1B	Chassis & Cab	—	3500	—
FD1B	Utiline Pickup	—	3940	—
FD1B	Sweptline Pickup	—	4000	—

NOTE: With V-8 fourth symbol in model number becomes "K" and prices/weights are higher.

Model	Body Type	Price	Weight	Prod. Total
Series D200 — (6-cyl.) — (¾-Ton) — (128 in. w.b.)				
FD2A	Flat-face Cowl	—	3585	—
FD2A	Chassis & Cab	—	3500	—
FD2A	Utiline Pickup	—	4025	—
FD2A	Sweptline Pickup	—	4085	—
FD2A	Town Panel (1967)	—	—	—
FD2A	Town Wagon (1967)	—	—	—

NOTE: With V-8 fourth symbol in model number becomes "J" and prices/weights are higher. Town Panel and Town Wagon not available in 1968.

Model	Body Type	Price	Weight	Prod. Total
Series D210 — (6-cyl.) — (¾-Ton) — (146 in. w.b.)				
FD2B	Chassis & Cab	—	—	—
FD2B	Utiline Pickup	—	—	—
FD2B	Sweptline Pickup	—	—	—

NOTE: With V-8 fourth symbol in model number becomes "K" and prices/weights are higher.

Model	Body Type	Price	Weight	Prod. Total
Series W100 — (6-cyl.) — (½-Ton) (4x4) — (114 in. w.b.)				
FW1A	Chassis & Cab (1968)	—	3750	—
FW1A	Utiline Pickup	—	4110	—
FW1A	Sweptline Pickup	—	4160	—
FW1A	Town Wagon (1967)	—	—	—

NOTE: With V-8 fourth symbol in model number becomes "J" and prices/weights are higher. Chassis & Cab listed for 1968 only. Town Wagon listed 1967 only.

Model	Body Type	Price	Weight	Prod. Total
Series W200 — (6-cyl.) — (¾-Ton) (4x4)				
FW2A	Chassis & Cab (1968)	—	3945	—
FW2A	Utiline Pickup	—	4385	—
FW2A	Sweptline Pickup	—	4445	—
FW2B	Crew Cab Utiline	—	4745	—
FW2B	Crew Cab Sweptline	—	4795	—
FW2B	Crew Cab Chassis (1968)	—	4385	—

NOTE: With V-8 the fourth symbol in model number becomes "J" ("K" with Crew Cab) and prices/weights are higher. Crew Cabs use 146 in. wheelbase. Others use 128 in. wheelbase.

Model	Body Type	Price	Weight	Prod. Total
Series P100 — (6-cyl.) — (½-Ton) - (104 in. w.b.)				
FP1A	Parcel Van Chassis	—	—	—
Series P200 — (6-cyl.) — (¾-Ton) — (104/122 in. w.b.)				
FP2A	Parcel Van Chassis (SWB)	—	—	—
FP2B	Parcel Van Chassis (LWB)	—	—	—
Series P300 — (6-cyl.) — (¾-Ton) — (125/137 in. w.b.)				
FP3A	Parcel Van Chassis (SWB)	—	—	—
FP3B	Parcel Van Chassis (LWB)	—	—	—

NOTE: Six-cylinder only. "SWB" means shortest wheelbase shown above listing; "LWB" means longest wheelbase shown above listing.

Model	Body Type	Price	Weight	Prod. Total
Series A100 — (6-cyl.) — (½-Ton) — (90 in. w.b.)				
FA1A	Pickup	—	2770	—
FA1A	Commercial Van	—	2800	—
FA1A	Passenger Wagon	—	3035	—

NOTE: With V-8 the fourth symbol in model number becomes "J" and prices/weights are higher.

Model	Body Type	Price	Weight	Prod. Total
Series A108 — (6-cyl.) — (½-Ton) — (108 in. w.b.)				
FA1B	Commercial Van	—	—	—
FA1B	Passenger Wagon	—	—	—

NOTE: With V-8 the fourth symbol in model number becomes "K" and prices/weights are higher.

ENGINE: Same as 1966, plus (6-cyl.). Inline. OHV. Six-cylinder. Cast iron block. Bore & stroke: 3.40 x 3.125 in. Displacement: 170.2 cu. in. Brake horsepower: 101 at 4000 R.P.M. Taxable horsepower: 27.70. Hydraulic valve lifters. Carburetor: Carter 1V. Torque (Compression): 145 lbs.-ft. at 1600 R.P.M.

ENGINE (Optional V-8) Vee-block. OHV. Eight-cylinder. Cast iron block. Bore & stroke: 4.25 x 3.38 in. Displacement: 383 cu. in. Brake horsepower: 258 at 4400 R.P.M. Hydraulic valve lifters. Carburetor: 2-bbl. Torque (Compression): 375 lbs.-ft. at 2800 R.P.M.

CHASSIS Same as 1966, plus: (Series P200) Wheelbase: 104 in. Tires: 7 x 17.5 six-ply.

CHASSIS (Series P200) Wheelbase: 122 in. Tires: 7 x 17.5 six-ply.

CHASSIS (Series A108) Wheelbase: 108 in. Tires: 6.50 x 13 four-ply.

TECHNICAL: Same as 1966.

OPTIONS: Same as 1966, plus new 383 cu. in. V-8 engine.

HISTORICAL: Introduced: Fall 1966; Fall 1967. Innovations: New P200 Utilivan series. Commercial vans and passenger vans (wagons) available with new 108 in. wheelbase. New V-8 engine option for all A100/A108 models. Front end restyled for 1967. Historical notes: The Town Panel and Town Wagon were not produced under the Fargo name after 1967. In the U.S., Dodge did not offer these models in either 1967 or 1968.

Pricing

	5	4	3	2	1
1967-1968					
Series D100 — (6-cyl.) — (½-Ton))					
Utiline Pickup (SWB)	600	1200	2000	2800	4000
Sweptline Pickup (SWB)	650	1300	2150	3050	4300
Town Panel (1967)	680	1350	2250	3150	4500
Town Wagon (1967)	740	1470	2450	3350	4900
Utiline Pickup (LWB)	570	1140	1900	2650	3800
Sweptline Pickup (LWB)	620	1230	2050	2900	4100
Series D200 — (6-cyl.) — (¾-Ton)					
Utiline Pickup (SWB)	590	1170	1950	2700	3900
Sweptline Pickup (SWB)	630	1250	2100	3000	4200
Town Panel (1967)	660	1320	2200	3100	4400
Town Wagon (1967)	720	1450	2400	3300	4800
Utiline Pickup (LWB)	560	1100	1850	2600	3700
Sweptline Pickup (LWB)	600	1200	2000	3000	4000

Parcel Delivery Vans — (6-cyl. only) — (½-Ton) — (104 in. w.b.)	5	4	3	2	1
Walk-in Van (¾-Ton) — (102 in. w.b.)	480	975	1600	2250	3200
Walk-in Van (122 in. w.b.)	480	975	1600	2250	3200
Walk-in Van (125 in. w.b.)	500	1000	1650	2300	3300
Walk-in Van (137 in. w.b.)	500	1000	1650	2300	3300
Walk-in Van	520	1020	1700	2400	3400
Series A100 Vans					
Pickup	560	1100	1850	2600	3700
Commercial Panel Van	530	1050	1750	2450	3500
Passenger Wagon	570	1140	1900	2650	3800
Series A108 Vans					
Commercial Panel Van	560	1100	1850	2600	3700
Passenger Wagon	600	1200	2000	3000	4000

NOTE: Add 5 percent for V-8.
Add 5 percent for 4x4 ("W" prefix on 4x4s)
Town Panel and Town Wagon available in 1967 only.
All prices based on top-of-line models.

1969 FARGO

1969 Fargo FW100 4x4 Utiline Power Wagon (RPZ)

½-TON/¾-TON — D/W/P/A SERIES — SIX-CYLINDER/V-8: As illustrated in the accompanying photo, Fargo trucks continued to look like their Dodge counterparts sold in the United States. Styling was much like the 1967-1968 models, with the addition of round side-marker lights and new trim for the hood and fendersides. There were few changes in the model line-up or powertrain offerings. The Fargo name appeared on the hood and the tailgate.

I.D. DATA: Location of serial number: same as 1966. The first four symbols of serial number are the same as model number (see list below). The last seven symbols for A100 Series were 2S85001. The last seven symbols for all other series were 2J25001.

Model	Body Type	Price	Weight	Prod. Total
Series D100 — (6-cyl.) — (½-Ton) — (114 in. w.b.)				
FD1A	Chassis & Cab	2688	—	—
FD1A	Utiline Pickup	2805	—	—
FD1A	Sweptline Pickup	2844	—	—
(V-8)				
FD1J	Chassis & Cab	2843	3045	—
FD1J	Utiline Pickup	2960	3405	—
FD1J	Sweptline Pickup	3000	3455	—
Series D110 — (6 cyl.) — (½-Ton) — (128 in. w.b.)				
FD1B	Chassis & Cab	2732	3085	—
FD1B	Utiline Pickup	2850	3445	—
FD1B	Sweptline Pickup	2889	3495	—
(V-8)				
FD1K	Chassis & Cab	2888	—	—
FD1K	Utiline Pickup	3005	3535	—
FD1K	Sweptline Pickup	3044	3595	—
Series D200 — (6-cyl.) — (¾-Ton) — (128 in. w.b.)				
FD2A	Chassis & Cab	2982	3370	—
FD2A	Utiline Pickup	3099	—	—
FD2A	Sweptline Pickup	3139	—	—
(V-8)				
FD2J	Chassis & Cab	3137	—	—
FD2J	Utiline Pickup	3255	3810	—
FD2J	Sweptline Pickup	3294	3870	—
Series D210 — (6-cyl.) — (¾-Ton) — (146 in. w.b.)				
FD2B	Chassis & Cab	3843	3775	—
FD2B	Utiline Pickup	3941	4135	—
FD2B	Sweptline Pickup	4000	4185	—
(V-8)				
FD2K	Chassis & Cab	3990	3840	—
FD2K	Utiline Pickup	4107	4270	—
FD2K	Sweptline Pickup	4146	4330	—

Model	Body Type	Price	Weight	Prod. Total
Series W100 — (6-cyl.) — (½-Ton) (4x4) — (114 in. w.b.)				
FW1A	Utiline Pickup	3479	4020	—
FW1A	Sweptline Pickup	3518	4070	—
(V-8)				
FW1B	Utiline Pickup	3628	—	—
FW1B	Sweptline Pickup	3664	—	—
Series W110 — (6-cyl.) — (½-Ton) (4x4) — (128 in. w.b.)				
FW1J	Utiline Pickup	3524	—	—
FW1J	Sweptline Pickup	3563	—	—
(V-8)				
FW1K	Utiline Pickup	3664	—	—
FW1K	Sweptline Pickup	3703	—	—
Series W200 — (6-cyl.) — (¾-Ton) (4x4) — (128 in. w.b.)				
FW2A	Cab & Chassis	3764	3785	—
FW2A	Utiline Pickup	3882	4225	—
FW2A	Sweptline Pickup	3921	4285	—
Series W200 Crew Cab — (6-cyl.) — (¾-Ton) (4x4) — (146 in. w.b.)				
FW2B	Crew Cab Utiline	4927	4620	—
FW2B	Crew Cab Sweptline	4966	4670	—
Series W200 — (V-8) — (¾-Ton) (4x4) — (128 in. w.b.)				
FW2J	Chassis & Cab	3904	—	—
FW2J	Utiline Pickup	4021	—	—
FW2J	Sweptline Pickup	4061	—	—
Series W200 Crew Cab — (V-8) — (¾-Ton) (4x4) — (146 in. w.b.)				
FW2K	Crew Cab Utiline	5066	—	—
FW2K	Crew Cab Sweptline	5106	—	—
Series P100 Parcel Van — (6-cyl.) — (½-Ton) — (104 in. w.b.)				
FP1A	Chassis	1914	—	—
(6-cyl.) — (¾-Ton) — (104/122 in. w.b.)				
FP2A	Chassis (104 in.)	2210	2380	—
FP2B	Chassis (122 in.)	2256	—	—
Series P300 Parcel Van — (6-cyl.) — (¾-Ton) — (125/137 in. w.b.)				
FP3A	Chassis (125 in.)	2498	2095	—
FP3B	Chassis (137 in.)	2538	—	—
Series A100 Van — (6-cyl.) — (½-Ton) — (90 in. w.b.)				
FA1A	Pickup	2562	2895	—
FA1A	Commercial Van	2795	2895	—
FA1A	Passenger-Wagon	3073	3125	—
(V-8)				
FA1J	Pickup	2748	—	—
FA1J	Commercial Van	2981	2925	—
FA1J	Passenger Wagon	3260	3202	—
Series A110 Van — (6-cyl.) — (½-Ton) — (108 in. w.b.)				
FA1B	Commercial Van	2942	2585	—
FA1B	Passenger Wagon	3221	2955	—
(V-8)				
FA1K	Commercial Van	3128	3150	—
FA1K	Passenger Wagon	3407	3300	—

ENGINES: (See previous specifications).

ENGINES (Std. A100) 170 cu. in. six-cylinder.

ENGINES (Std. D/W/P Series) 225 cu. in. six-cylinder.

ENGINES (Std. V-8, all except "P" Series) 318 cu. in. V-8.

ENGINES (Optional V-8, all except "P" Series) 383 cu. in. V-8.

CHASSIS (Series D100) Wheelbase: 114/128 in. GVW: 4300 to 5200 lbs. Tires: 8.15 x 15.

CHASSIS (Series W100) Wheelbase: 114/128 in. GVW: 5100-6000 lbs. Tires: 6.50 x 16.

CHASSIS (Series D200) Wheelbase: 128/146 in. GVW: 5200 to 7500 lbs. Tires: 6.50 x 16.

CHASSIS (Series W200) Wheelbase: 128/146 in. GVW: 6000 to 8000 lbs. Tires: 7.17 x 15.

CHASSIS (Series P100/P200) Wheelbase: 104/122 in. GVW: 5400 to 7500 lbs. Tires: 6.50 x 16.

CHASSIS (Series P300) Wheelbase: 125/137 in. GVW: 6000 to 10,000 lbs. Tires: 7.15 x 15.

CHASSIS (Series A100) Wheelbase: 90/108 in. GVW: 3800 to 5200 lbs. Tires: 6.95 x 14.

TECHNICAL: Selective synchromesh transmission. Speeds: 3F/1R. Column shift. Single plate dry disc clutch. Shaft drive. Semi-floating rear axle. Four-wheel hydraulic brakes. Steel disc wheels.

OPTIONS: Custom Cab package. Custom interior trim. Chrome rear bumper. Painted rear bumper. Chrome front bumper. Two-tone paint. Radio. Tinted glass. 318 cu. in. V-8 engine. 383 cu. in. V-8 engine. 225 cu. in. slant-six engine (in A100s). Four-speed manual transmission. Automatic transmission. No spin rear axle. Power steering. Power brakes. OSRV mirror(s). Long-arm OSRV mirror(s). Whitewall tires. Full wheel discs. Body-side moldings. Two-speed windshield washer/wipers. Heavy-duty shocks. Heavy-duty springs. Heavy-duty battery. Heavy-duty clutch.

HISTORICAL: Introduced: Fall 1968. Innovations: Larger tires for A100/A108 vans. Side marker safety lamps added to front fenders. 4x4 models now avaiable on long and short wheelbases. Historical notes: In addition to its light-duty lines, Fargo continued to offer large over-the-road type trucks.

Pricing

1969

	5	4	3	2	1
Series D100 — (6-cyl.) — (½-Ton)					
Utiline Pickup (SWB)	600	1200	2000	2800	4000
Sweptline Pickup (SWB)	650	1300	2150	3050	4300
Utiline Pickup (LWB)	570	1140	1900	2650	3800
Sweptline Pickup (LWB)	620	1230	2050	2900	4100
Series D200 — (6-cyl.) — (¾-Ton)					
Utiline Pickup (SWB)	590	1170	1950	2700	3900
Sweptline Pickup (SWB)	630	1250	2100	3000	4200
Utiline Pickup (LWB)	560	1100	1850	2600	3700
Sweptline Pickup (LWB)	600	1200	2000	3000	4000
Parcel Delivery Vans — (6-cyl. only)					
½-Ton Utilivan (104 in.)	480	975	1600	2250	3200
¾-Ton Utilivan (104 in.)	480	975	1600	2250	3200
¾-Ton Utilivan (122 in.)	500	1000	1650	2300	3300
¾-Ton Utilivan (125 in.)	500	1000	1650	2300	3300
¾-Ton Utilivan (137 in.)	520	1020	1700	2400	3400
Series A100 Vans					
Pickup	560	1100	1850	2600	3700
Commercial Panel Van	530	1050	1750	2450	3500
Passenger Wagon	570	1140	1900	2650	3800
Series A108 Vans					
Commercial Panel Van	560	1100	1850	2600	3700
Passenger Wagon	600	1200	2000	3000	4000

NOTE: Add 5 percent for V-8. Add 5 percent for 4x4.
All prices based on top-of-the-line trimmed models.

1970 FARGO

1970 Fargo A100 Sportsman Forward Control Van (RPZ)

½-TON/¾-TON — D/W/P/A SERIES — SIX-CYLINDER/V-8: — Like its U.S. cousin, Dodge, the Canadian Fargo received a new grille for 1970. It had four horizontal slots stamped through the panel which crossed the front end and also housed the single round headlamps. This gave a cross-bar appearance. The parking lamps were set in the outer corners of the lower slots. Everything else was much the same as before, although there were new decal packages to dress-up what was basically a ten year old body.

The vans also looked like the contemporary Dodge models, but you could not miss the Fargo name on the hood. It was spelled out in large block letters.

I.D. DATA: Location of Serial Number: Same as previous. The numbers now had 14 symbols. The first symbol was an "F" for all models. The next five symbols corresponded to the "model numbers" shown on the chart below. The last eight symbols were OT100001 (starting number) for all series. Ending numbers are not available.

Model	Body Type	Price	Weight	Prod. Total
Series D100 — (6-cyl.) — (½-Ton) — (114 in. w.b.)				
D17AB	F.F. Cowl	—	—	—
D11AB	Chassis & Cab	2808	3075	—
D13AB	Utiline	2909	2510	—
D14AB	Sweptline	2948	2550	—
Series D100 — (V-8) — (½-Ton) — (114 in. w.b.)				
D17AE	F.F. Cowl	—	—	—
D11AE	Chassis & Cab	2946	3095	—
D13AE	Utiline	3047	3436	—
D14AE	Sweptline	3086	3485	—
Series D110 — (6-cyl.) — (½-Ton) — (128 in. w.b.)				
D17AB	F.F. Cowl	—	—	—
D11AB	Chassis & Cab	2853	—	—
D13AB	Utiline	2954	—	—
D14AB	Sweptline	2993	—	—

Model	Body Type	Price	Weight	Prod. Total
Series D110 — (V-8) — (½-Ton) — (128 in. w.b.)				
D17AE	F.F. Cowl	—	—	—
D11AE	Chassis & Cab	2991	—	—
D13AE	Utiline	3092	3565	—
D14AE	Sweptline	3131	3625	—
Series D200 — (6-cyl.) — (¾-Ton) — (128 in. w.b.)				
D27BB	F.F. Cowl	—	—	—
D21BB	Chassis & Cab	3054	3430	—
D23BB	Utiline	3154	3870	—
D24BB	Sweptline	3194	3930	—
Series D200 — (V-8) — (¾-Ton) — (128 in. w.b.)				
D27BE	F.F. Cowl	—	—	—
D21BE	Chassis & Cab	3210	3455	—
D23BE	Utiline	3310	3895	—
D24BE	Sweptline	3350	3955	—
Series D200 — (6-cyl.) — (Crew Cab) — (¾-Ton) — (146 in. w.b.)				
D22BB	Chassis & Cab	3886	3845	—
D25BB	Utiline	4032	4205	—
D26BB	Sweptline	4075	4255	—
Series D200 — (V-8) — (Crew Cab) — (¾-Ton) — (146 in. w.b.)				
D22BE	Chassis & Cab	4041	3870	—
D25BE	Utiline	4187	4230	—
D26BE	Sweptline	4254	4280	—
Series D200 — (6-cyl.) — (Crew Cab) — (¾-Ton) — (160 in. w.b.)				
D22BB	Chassis & Cab	4062	—	—
D25BB	Utiline	4211	—	—
D26BB	Sweptline	4254	—	—
Series D200 — (V-8) — (Crew Cab) — (¾-Ton) — (160 in. w.b.)				
D22BE	Chassis & Cab	4218	—	—
D25BE	Utiline	4366	—	—
D26BE	Sweptline	4409	—	—
Series W100 (4x4) — (6-cyl.) — (½-Ton) — (114 in. w.b.)				
E11AB	Chassis & Cab	3475	3555	—
E13AB	Utiline	3573	3915	—
E14AB	Sweptline	3613	3965	—
Series W100 — (4x4) — (V-8) — (½-Ton) — (114 in. w.b.)				
E11AE	Chassis & Cab	3622	—	—
E13AE	Utiline	3722	—	—
E14AE	Sweptline	3762	—	—
Series W100 — (4x4) — (6-cyl.) — (½-Ton) — (128 in. w.b.)				
E11AB	Chassis & Cab	3518	—	—
E13AB	Utiline	3618	—	—
E14AB	Sweptline	3658	—	—
Series W100 — (4x4) — (V-8) — (½-Ton) — (128 in. w.b.)				
E11AE	Chassis & Cab	3667	—	—
E13AE	Utiline	3766	—	—
E14AE	Sweptline	3806	—	—
Series W200 — (4x4) — (6-cyl.) — (¾-Ton) — (128 in. w.b.)				
E21BB	Cab & Chassis	3814	3785	—
E23BB	Utiline	3915	4225	—
E24BB	Sweptline	3954	4285	—
Series W200 — (4x4) — (V-8) — (¾-Ton) — (128 in. w.b.)				
E21BE	Cab & Chassis	3962	—	—
E23BE	Utiline	4063	—	—
E24BE	Sweptline	4102	—	—
Series W200 — (4x4) — (6-cyl.) — (Crew Cab) — (¾-Ton) — (146 in. w.b.)				
E21BB	Cab & Chassis	4936	4260	—
E23BB	Utiline	5081	4620	—
E24BB	Sweptline	5125	4670	—
Series W200 — (4x4) — (V-8) — (Crew Cab) — (¾-Ton) — (146 in. w.b.)				
E21BE	Cab & Chassis	5084	—	—
E23BE	Utiline	5230	—	—
E24BE	Sweptline	5273	—	—
Series P200 — (6-cyl.) — (¾-Ton) — (104/122 in. w.b.)				
F21BB	Parcel Chassis (SWB)	2317	2380	—
F21BB	Parcel Chassis (LWB)	2336	—	—
Series P300 — (6-cyl.) — (¾-Ton) — (104 in. w.b.)				
F31BB	Parcel Chassis	2569	2805	—
(125 in. w.b.)				
F31BB	Parcel Chassis	2604	—	—
(137 in. w.b.)				
F31BB	Parcel Chassis	2640	—	—
Series A100 — (6-cyl.) — (½-Ton) — (90 in. w.b.)				
A11AA	Pickup	2672	1990	—
A12AA	Tradesman Van	2871	2920	—
A13AA	Sportsman Van	3297	3230	—
A14AA	Custom Sportsman	3699	3290	—
Series A100 — (V-8) — (½-Ton) — (90 in. w.b.)				
A11AE	Pickup	2871	2928	—
A12AE	Tradesman Van	3070	2958	—
A13AE	Sportsman Van	3496	3268	—
A14AE	Custom Sportsman	3898	3328	—
Series A108 — (6-cyl.) — (½-Ton) — (108 in. w.b.)				
A12AA	Tradesman Van	3020	3130	—
A13AA	Sportsman Van	3472	3360	—
A14AA	Custom Sportsman	3877	3420	—
Series A108 — (V-8) — (½-Ton) — (108 in. w.b.)				
A12AE	Tradesman Van	3219	3168	—
A13AE	Sportsman Van	3672	3398	—
A14AE	Custom Sportsman	4076	3458	—

ENGINE (Standard A100/A108): Inline. OHV. Six-cylinder. Cast iron block. Bore & stroke: 3.4 x 3.64 in. Displacement: 198 cu. in. Brake horsepower: 120 at 4000 R.P.M. Taxable horsepower: 27.7. Hydraulic valve lifters. Carburetor: Carter 1V. Torque: 182 lbs.-ft. at 1600 R.P.M.

ENGINE (Optional A100/A108; Standard all others): Inline. OHV. Six-cylinder. Cast iron block. Bore & stroke: 3.4 x 4.125. Displacement: 225 cu. in. Brake horsepower: 140 at 3900 R.P.M. Taxable horsepower: 27.7. Hydraulic valve lifters. Carburetor: Carter 1V. Torque 215 lbs.-ft. at 1600 R.P.M.

ENGINE (Base V-8): Vee-block. OHV. Eight-cylinder. Cast iron block. Bore & stroke: 3.91 x 3.31 in. Displacement: 318 cu. in. Brake horsepower: 210-212 at 4000 R.P.M. Taxable horsepower: 48.92. Hydraulic valve lifters. Carburetor: Carter 2V. Torque: 318-322 lbs.-ft. at 2800 R.P.M.

ENGINE (Optional V-8): Vee-block. OHV. Eight-cylinder. Cast iron block. Bore & stroke: 4.25 x 3.38 in. Displacement: 383 cu. in. Brake horsepower: 258 at 4400 R.P.M. Taxable horsepower: 57.8. Hydraulic valve lifters. Carburetor: Carter 2V. Torque: 375 lbs.-ft. at 2800 R.P.M.

CHASSIS: (Series D100). Wheelbase: 114/128 in. GVW: 4300-5200 lbs. Tires: G78 x 15B.

CHASSIS: (Series D200). Wheelbase: 128/146 in. GVW: 6100-7500 lbs. Tires: 8.00 x 16.5.

CHASSIS: (Series W100). Wheelbase: 114/128 in. GVW: 5100-5600 lbs. Tires: G78 x 15B.

CHASSIS: (Series W200). Wheelbase: 128/146 in. GVW: 6500-8000 lbs. Tires: 8.00 x 16.

CHASSIS: (Series P200). Wheelbase: 104/122 in. GVW: 5400-7500 lbs. Tires: 6.50 x 16.

CHASSIS: (Series P300). Wheelbase: 104/125/137 in. GVW: 7000-10,000 lbs. Tires: 8.00 x 16.5E.

CHASSIS: (Series A100/A108). Wheelbase: 90/108 in. GVW: 3800-5400 lbs. Tires: E78 x 14B.

TECHNICAL: Selective synchromesh transmission. Speeds: 3F/1R. Controls located: steering column. Single-plate dry disc clutch. Shaft drive. Semi-floating rear axle. Four-wheel hydraulic brakes. Steel disc wheels.

OPTIONS: Chrome front bumper. Rear bumper. Two-tone paint. Sport decal package. Custom cab package. OSRV mirrors. Bumper guards. Radio. Heater. Clock. Cigar lighter. Radio antenna. Seat covers. Snow plow. Adventurer camper package. Custom wheel discs. Whitewall tires. Cab clearance marker lamps. Loadflite automatic transmission. Anti-spin axle. Four-speed transmission. Heavy-duty three-speed transmission. Power steering (V-8 only). Power brakes. Chrome grille.

HISTORICAL: Introduced: Fall 1969. Innovations: Pickup grille redesigned. New 160 in. ¾-ton w.b. Sport decal packages introduced.

Pricing

1970

	5	4	3	2	1
Series D100 — (6-cyl.) — (½-Ton)					
Utiline Pickup (SWB)	600	1200	2000	2800	4000
Sweptline Pickup (SWB)	650	1300	2150	3050	4300
Utiline Pickup (LWB)	570	1140	1900	2650	3800
Sweptline Pickup (LWB)	620	1230	2050	2900	4100
Series D200 — (6 cyl.) — (¾-Ton)					
Utiline Pickup (SWB)	590	1170	1950	2700	3900
Sweptline Pickup (SWB)	630	1250	2100	3000	4200
Crew Cab Utiline Pickup	600	1200	2000	3000	4000
Crew Cab Sweptline Pickup	650	1300	2150	3050	4300
Series P Parcel Vans — (6 cyl.)					
½-Ton Utilivan	480	975	1600	2250	3200
¾-Ton Utilivan	520	1020	1700	2400	3400
Series A100 Vans — (6 cyl.)					
Pickup	560	1100	1850	2600	3700
Sportsman	570	1140	1900	2650	3800
Tradesman	530	1050	1750	2450	3500
Custom Sportsman	620	1230	2050	2900	4100
Series A108 Vans — (6 cyl.)					
Tradesman	560	1100	1850	2600	3700
Sportsman	600	1200	2000	3000	4000
Custom Sportsman	650	1300	2150	3050	4300

NOTE: Add five percent for V-8.
Add five percent for 4x4.
All prices based on high-trim level trucks.

1971 FARGO

½-TON/¾-TON — D/F/W/P/B SERIES — SIX-CYLINDER/V-8: — Dodge (U.S.) and Fargo (Canada) got one last year out of their pickup truck body first introduced in 1961. There were no basic styling changes from the previous season, although a new "SE" trim package was released as a top-of-the-line option.

An all-new "B" Series of vans was introduced, with modernized styling including a forward slanting hoodline and "electric shaver" grille with an oblong opening across its center. This "slot" held the parking lamps at each corner and had the Fargo name in its center. The bumper was center-slotted, too. And the windshield was a one-piece, slanted design. Wheelbases were considerably lengthened to 109 in. for the standard models and 127 in. for the "maxi-van" styles. The new hood gave easier outside engine access, a change that mechanics appreciated.

The Utilivan chassis, designed for door-to-door delivery van bodies manufactured by outside suppliers, continued to come in a wide range of wheelbase sizes. These trucks could still be had only with six-cylinder engines.

I.D. DATA: Serial Number in same location. The numbers consisted of 14 symbols. The first symbol for all series was an "F" for Fargo. The next five symbols corresponded to the "model numbers" on the chart below. The last eight symbols indicated additional codes and sequential production numbers. Starting numbers for all "B" Series vans were 1V300001. Starting numbers for all other Series were 1S300001. Example: D100 Utiline Pickup had starting serial number FD13AB1S300001.

Model	Body Type	Price	Weight	Prod. Total
Series D100 — (6-cyl.) — (½-Ton) — (114 in. w.b.)				
D11AB	Chassis & Cab	2949	—	—
D13AB	Utiline Pickup	3132	—	—
D14AB	Sweptline Pickup	3132	—	—
(V-8)				
D11AE	Chassis & Cab	3103	3075	—
D13AE	Utiline Pickup	3286	3435	—
D14AE	Sweptline Pickup	3286	3485	—
Series D110 — (6-cyl.) — (½-Ton) — (128 in. w.b.)				
D11AB	Chassis & Cab	2996	3095	—
D13AB	Utiline Pickup	3179	3450	—
D14AB	Sweptline Pickup	3179	3505	—
(V-8)				
D11AE	Chassis & Cab	3149	3080	—
D13AE	Utiline Pickup	3332	3465	—
D14AE	Sweptline Pickup	3332	3525	—
Series D200 — (6-cyl.) — (¾-Ton) — (128 in. w.b.)				
D21BB	Chassis & Cab	3247	3430	—
D23BB	Utiline Pickup	3414	3870	—
D24BB	Sweptline Pickup	3414	3930	—
(V-8)				
D21BE	Chassis & Cab	3442	3455	—
D23BE	Utiline Pickup	3609	3895	—
D24BE	Sweptline Pickup	3609	3955	—
Series D210 — (6-cyl.) — (¾-Ton) — (Crew Cab) — (146 in. w.b.)				
D22BB	Chassis & Cab	4081	3845	—
D25BB	Utiline Pickup	4276	4205	—
D26BB	Sweptline Pickup	4276	4255	—
(V-8)				
D22BE	Chassis & Cab	4276	3870	—
D25BE	Utiline Pickup	4471	4230	—
D26BE	Sweptline Pickup	4471	4280	—
(6-cyl.) — (160 in. w.b.)				
D22BB	Chassis & Cab	4258	—	—
D25BB	Utiline Pickup	4456	—	—
D26BB	Sweptline Pickup	4456	—	—
(V-8)				
D22BE	Chassis & Cab	4453	—	—
D25BE	Utiline Pickup	4651	—	—
D26BE	Sweptline Pickup	4651	—	—
Series W100 — (6-cyl.) — (½-Ton) (4x4) — (114 in. w.b.)				
E11AB	Chassis & Cab	3631	3555	—
E13AB	Utiline Pickup	3782	3915	—
E14AB	Sweptline Pickup	3782	3965	—
(V-8)				
E11AE	Chassis & Cab	3853	3575	—
E13AE	Utiline Pickup	4004	3935	—
E14AE	Sweptline Pickup	4004	3985	—
Series W110 — (6-cyl.) — (½-Ton) (4x4) — (128 in. w.b.)				
E11AB	Chassis & Cab	3677	—	—
E13AB	Utiline Pickup	3828	—	—
E14AB	Sweptline Pickup	3828	—	—
(V-8)				
E11AE	Chassis & Cab	3900	—	—
E13AE	Utiline Pickup	4051	—	—
E14AE	Sweptline Pickup	4051	—	—
Series W200 — (6-cyl.) — (¾-Ton) (4x4) — (128 in. w.b.)				
E21BB	Chassis & Cab	4063	3785	—
E23BB	Utiline Pickup	4214	4225	—
E24BB	Sweptline Pickup	4214	4285	—
(V-8)				
E21BE	Chassis & Cab	4286	4015	—
E23BE	Utiline Pickup	4437	4455	—
E24BE	Sweptline Pickup	4437	4515	—
Series W200 — (6-cyl.) — (¾-Ton) (4x4 Crew Cab) — (146 in. w.b.)				
E22BB	Chassis & Cab	5193	4260	—
E25BB	Utiline Pickup	5385	4620	—
E26BB	Sweptline Pickup	5385	4670	—
(V-8)				
E22BE	Chassis & Cab	5416	4280	—
E25BE	Utiline Pickup	5608	4640	—
E26BE	Sweptline Pickup	5608	4690	—
Series P200 — (6-cyl.) — (¾-Ton) — (104/122 w.b.)				
F21BB	Utilivan (104 in. w.b.)	2431	2380	—
F21BB	Utilivan (122 in. w.b.)	2452	—	—
Series P300 — (6-cyl.) — (¾-Ton) — (104/125/137 w.b.)				
F31BB	Utilivan (104 in. w.b.)	2674	2805	—
F31BB	Utilivan (125 in. w.b.)	2709	—	—
F31BB	Utilivan (137 in. w.b.)	2745	—	—
Series B100 — (6-cyl.) — (½-Ton) — (109 in. w.b.)				
B12AA	Tradesman Van	3161	3218	—
B13AB	Sportsman Wagon	3620	3465	—
B15AB	Custom Sportsman	3864	3610	—
B14AB	Royal Sportsman	4067	3655	—
(V-8)				
B12AE	Tradesman Van	3324	3343	—
B13AE	Sportsman Wagon	3754	3590	—
B15AE	Custom Sportsman	3998	3735	—
B14AE	Royal Sportsman	4201	3780	—

Model (6-cyl.) — (127 in. w.b.)	Body Type	Price	Weight	Prod. Total
B12AA	Tradesman Van	3317	3313	—
B13AB	Sportsman Wagon	3776	3560	—
B15AB	Custom Sportsman	4020	3705	—
B14AB	Royal Sportsman	4221	3750	—
(V-8)				
B12AE	Tradesman Van	3479	3438	—
B13AE	Sportsman Wagon	3910	3685	—
B15AE	Custom Sportsman	4154	3830	—
B14AE	Royal Sportsman	4355	3875	—
Series B200 — (6-cyl.) — (¾-Ton) — (109 in. w.b.)				
B22AA	Tradesman Van	3272	—	—
B23AB	Sportsman Van	3703	3565	—
B25AB	Custom Sportsman	3946	—	—
B24AB	Royal Sportsman	4148	—	—
(V-8)				
B22AE	Tradesman Van	3434	—	—
B23AE	Sportsman Van	3837	—	—
B25AE	Custom Sportsman	4080	—	—
B24AE	Royal Sportsman	4282	—	—
(6-cyl.) — (127 in. w.b.)				
B22AA	Tradesman Van	3427	—	—
B23AB	Sportsman Van	3857	3660	—
B25AB	Custom Sportsman	4100	—	—
B24AB	Royal Sportsman	4303	—	—
(V-8)				
B22AE	Tradesman Van	3590	—	—
B23AE	Sportsman Van	3991	—	—
B25AE	Custom Sportsman	4234	—	—
B24AE	Royal Sportsman	4437	—	—
Series B300 — (6-cyl.) — (¾-Ton) — (109 in. w.b.)				
B32BB	Tradesman Van	3437	—	—
B33BB	Sportsman Wagon	3882	3800	—
B35BB	Custom Sportsman	4134	—	—
B34BB	Royal Sportsman	4329	—	—
(V-8)				
B32BE	Tradesman Van	3571	—	—
B33BE	Sportsman Wagon	4016	—	—
B35BE	Custom Sportsman	4268	—	—
B34BE	Royal Sportsman	4463	—	—
(6-cyl.) — (127 in. w.b.)				
B32BB	Tradesman Van	3592	—	—
B33BB	Sportsman Wagon	4037	3890	—
B35BB	Custom Sportsman	4289	—	—
B34BB	Royal Sportsman	4483	—	—
(V-8)				
B32BE	Tradesman Van	3726	—	—
B33BE	Sportsman Wagon	4170	—	—
B35BE	Custom Sportsman	4423	—	—
B34BE	Royal Sportsman	4617	—	—

NOTE: Apparently the "300" trucks, which Dodge merchandised in the U.S. as 1-tonners, were considered heavy-duty ¾-tonners in Canada where they were marketed under the Fargo name.

ENGINES: Same as 1970 for comparable models. The B100 vans used the same base and optional engines as the A100 vans had previously used.

CHASSIS (Series D100) Wheelbase: 114/128 in. GVW: 4300-5200 lbs. Tires: G78 x 15B.

CHASSIS (Series F100) Wheelbase: 114/128 in. GVW: 5500-5600 lbs. Tires: 8.25 x 15B.

CHASSIS (Series D200) Wheelbase: 128/160 in. GVW: 6100-7500 lbs. Tires: 8.00 x 16.5D.

CHASSIS (Series W200) Wheelbase: 128/160 in. GVW: 6500-8000 lbs. Tires: 8.00 x 16.

CHASSIS (Series P200) Wheelbase: 104/122 in. GVW: 5400-7500 lbs. Tires: 6.50 x 16.

CHASSIS (Series P300) Wheelbase: 104/125/137 in. GVW: 7000-10,000 lbs.

CHASSIS (Series B100) Wheelbase: 109/127 in. Length: 176/194 in. Height: 80.8 in. GVW: 4200-4700/4300-4800 lbs. Tires: E78 x 14B.

CHASSIS (Series B200) Wheelbase: 109/127 in. Length: 176/194 in. Height: 80.8 in. GVW: 5200-5400/5300-5500 lbs. Tires: G78 x 15B.

CHASSIS (Series B300) Wheelbase: 109/127 in. Length: 176/194 in. Height: 80.8 in. GVW: 6100-7500/6200-7700 lbs. Tires: 8.00 x 16.5C.

TECHNICAL: Selective synchromesh transmission. Speeds: 3F/1R. Column gearshift control. Single plate dry disc clutch. Shaft drive. Semi-floating rear axle. Four-wheel hydraulic brakes. Steel disc wheels.

OPTIONS: Chrome front bumper. Rear bumper, painted or chrome. Custom trim package. Adventurer trim package. Adventurer Sport package. Adventurer "SE" package. Bumper guards. Radio. Heater. Clock. Cigar lighter. Radio antenna. Seat covers. Camper Special package. Whitewall tires. OSRV dual mirrors, regular or "long-arm" type. Air conditioning. Two-tone paint. Bucket seats. Oversize tires. "383" V-8 engine. "225" slant six engine (vans). Power steering. Automatic transmission. Four-speed transmission. Heavy-duty three-speed transmission. No spin rear axle. Power brakes. Tinted glass. Chrome wheel covers. Auxiliary seats (vans). School Bus van package. Heavy-duty springs. Heavy-duty shocks. Chrome grille.

HISTORICAL: Introduced: Fall 1970. Innovations: All-new van styling and new B100 Series of vans, with modernized styling and longer wheelbase. New trim packages and decal options for pickups. Historical notes: "Fargo" continued to appear on the front of additional heavy-duty trucks available for the Canadian market this season.

Pricing

1971	5	4	3	2	1
Series D100 — (6-cyl.) — (½-Ton)					
Utiline Pickup (SWB)	600	1200	2000	2800	4000
Sweptline Pickup (SWB)	650	1300	2150	3050	4300
Utiline Pickup (LWB)	570	1140	1900	2650	3800
Sweptline Pickup (LWB)	620	1230	2050	2900	4100
Series D200 — (6-cyl.) — (¾-Ton)					
Utiline Pickup (SWB)	590	1170	1950	2700	3900
Sweptline Pickup (SWB)	630	1250	2100	3000	4200
Crew Cab Utiline (LWB)	600	1200	2000	2800	4000
Crew Cab Sweptline (LWB)	650	1300	2150	3050	4300
Maxi Crew Cab Utiline (160 in.)	620	1230	2050	2900	4100
Maxi Crew Cab Sweptline (160 in.)	630	1250	2100	3000	4200
Parcel Delivery Vans — (6-cyl.)					
½-Ton Utilivan (104 in.)	480	975	1600	2250	3200
¾-Ton Utilivan (104 in.)	480	975	1600	2250	3200
¾-Ton Utilivan (122 in.)	500	1000	1650	2300	3300
¾-Ton Utilivan (125 in.)	500	1000	1650	2300	3300
¾-Ton Utilivan (137 in.)	520	1020	1700	2400	3400
Series B100 — (6-cyl.) — (½-Ton)					
Tradesman Van	590	1170	1950	2700	3900
Sportsman Van	620	1230	2050	2900	4100
Custom Sportsman	680	1350	2250	3150	4500
Royal Sportsman	700	1400	2350	3290	4700
Series B200 — (6-cyl.) — (¾-Ton)					
Tradesman Van	600	1200	2000	2800	4000
Sportsman Wagon	630	1250	2100	3000	4200
Custom Sportsman	690	1380	2300	3200	4600
Royal Sportsman	720	1450	2400	3300	4800
Series B300 — (6-cyl.) — (¾-Ton)					
Tradesman Van	630	1250	2100	3000	4200
Sportsman Wagon	660	1320	2200	3100	4400
Custom Sportsman	720	1450	2400	3300	4800
Royal Sportsman	750	1500	2500	3500	5000

NOTE: Add 5 percent for V-8.
Add 5 percent for 4x4.
Add 5 percent for B100/B200/B300 maxi-van.
Add 10 percent for SE package.
Add 5 percent for Sport package
Prices based on high-trim levels, excluding above.

1972 FARGO

1972 Fargo B300 Tradesman Commercial Van (RPZ)

½-TON/¾-TON — D/W SERIES — SIX-CYLINDER/V-8: This year, it was the Fargo pickups turn to be redesigned. The trucks had overall rounder lines and a 1 in. longer wheelbase. Headlamps appeared in squarish bright metal housings. The grille had four slots (two on each side of center) housed in a slightly protruding surround. Fargo I.D. appeared on the hood lip and tailgate.

The only models available were pickups. They came in fenderside (Utiline) or smooth-side (Sweptline) choices. Both ½-tons and ¾-tons came with sixes and V-8s and on 115 or 131 in. wheelbases. The ¾-tonners were also available on two longer wheelbases with Crew Cab features. This was the last year for the Fargo nameplate in Canada and the line was trimmed down accordingly.

I.D. DATA: Serial numbers in same locations. The serial numbers had 14 or 15 characters. They began with F or FF. The next five characters were those shown in the model numbers below. Then came the symbols "2S". The last six (digits) were 500001 for all series.

1972 Fargo F-100 Sweptline Pickup (RPZ)

1972 Fargo Sweptline Pickup Truck (J. Benjaminson)

Model	Body Type	Price	Weight	Prod. Total
Series D100 — (6-cyl.) — (½-Ton) — (115 in. w.b.)				
D11AB	Chassis & Cab	3157	3095	—
D13AB	Utiline Pickup	3319	3450	—
D14AB	Sweptline Pickup	3319	3505	—
(V-8)				
D11AE	Chassis & Cab	3309	3075	—
D13AE	Utiline Pickup	3470	3435	—
D14AE	Sweptline Pickup	3470	3485	—
Series D110 — (6-cyl.) — (½-Ton) — (131 in w.b.)				
D11AB	Chassis & Cab	3203	—	—
D13AB	Utiline Pickup	3363	—	—
D14AB	Sweptline Pickup	3363	—	—
(V-8)				
D11AE	Chassis & Cab	3355	—	—
D13AE	Utiline Pickup	3515	3565	—
D14AE	Sweptline Pickup	3515	3525	—
Series D200 — (6-cyl.) — (¾-Ton) — (131 in. w.b.)				
D21BB	Chassis & Cab	3441	3430	—
D23BB	Utiline Pickup	3603	3870	—
D24BB	Sweptline Pickup	3603	3930	—
(V-8)				
D21BE	Chassis & Cab	3650	3666	—
D23BE	Utiline Pickup	3811	4095	—
D24BE	Sweptline Pickup	3811	4124	—
Series D200 — (6-cyl.) — (¾-Ton) — (Crew Cab) — (149 in. w.b.)				
D21BB	Chassis & Cab	4308	3845	—
D23BB	Utiline Pickup	4538	4205	—
D24BB	Sweptline Pickup	4538	4255	—
(V-8)				
D21BE	Chassis & Cab	4517	—	—
D23BE	Utiline Pickup	4747	—	—
D24BE	Sweptline Pickup	4747	—	—
(6-cyl.) — (165 in. w.b.)				
D21BB	Chassis & Cab	4672	—	—
D23BB	Utiline Pickup	4905	4420	—
D24BB	Sweptline Pickup	4905	4449	—
(V-8)				
D21BE	Chassis & Cab	4881	3991	—
D23BE	Utiline Pickup	5113	4469	—
D24BE	Sweptline Pickup	5113	—	—

Model	Body Type	Price	Weight	Prod. Total
Series W100 — (6-cyl.) — (½-Ton) (4x4) — (115 in. w.b.)				
FW11AB	Chassis & Cab	3812	3555	—
FW13AB	Utiline Pickup	3977	3915	—
FW14AB	Sweptline Pickup	3977	3965	—
Series W100 — (V-8) — (½-Ton) (4x4) — (115 in. w.b.)				
FW11AE	Chassis & Cab	4041	—	—
FW13AE	Utiline Pickup	4205	—	—
FW14AE	Sweptline Pickup	4251	—	—
(6-cyl.) — (131 in. w.b.)				
FW11AB	Chassis & Cab	3859	—	—
FW13AB	Utiline Pickup	4023	—	—
FW14AB	Sweptline Pickup	4023	—	—
(V-8)				
FW11AE	Chassis & Cab	4087	—	—
FW13AE	Utiline Pickup	4205	—	—
FW14AE	Sweptline Pickup	4251	—	—
Series W200 — (6-cyl.) — (¾-Ton) (4x4) — (131 in. w.b.)				
W21BB	Chassis & Cab	4368	3785	—
W23BB	Utiline Pickup	4531	4225	—
W24BB	Sweptline Pickup	4531	4285	—
(V-8)				
W21BE	Chassis & Cab	4596	—	—
W23BE	Utiline Pickup	4760	—	—
W24BE	Sweptline Pickup	4760	—	—
(6-cyl.) — (149 in. w.b.)				
W21BB	Chassis & Cab	5539	4260	—
W23BB	Utiline Pickup	5745	4620	—
W24BB	Sweptline Pickup	5745	4670	—
(V-8)				
W21BE	Chassis & Cab	5768	—	—
W23BE	Utiline Pickup	5973	—	—
W24BE	Sweptline Pickup	5973	—	—

ENGINES: Same as 1970 for comparable models.

CHASSIS: See information in chart above.

TECHNICAL: Same as 1970 for comparable models.

OPTIONS: Same as 1971.

HISTORICAL: Introduced: Fall 1972. New styling and grille. Longer wheelbases. Historical notes: Last year for Fargo nameplate in Canada.

Pricing

1972	5	4	3	2	1
Series D100 — (6-cyl.) — (½-Ton)					
Utiline Pickup (SWB)	620	1230	2050	2900	4100
Sweptline Pickup (SWB)	680	1350	2250	3150	4500
Utiline Pickup (LWB)	600	1200	2000	2800	4000
Sweptline Pickup (LWB)	650	1300	2150	3050	4300
Series D200 — (6-cyl.) — (½-Ton)					
Utiline Pickup (SWB)	600	1200	2000	2800	4000
Sweptline Pickup (SWB)	650	1300	2150	3050	4300
Utiline Pickup (LWB)	630	1250	2100	3000	4200
Sweptline Pickup (LWB)	680	1350	2250	3130	4500
Crew Cabs — (6-cyl.) — (¾-Ton)					
Utiline Pickup (SWB)	700	1400	2350	3290	4700
Sweptline Pickup (SWB)	720	1450	2400	3300	4800
Utiline Pickup (LWB)	740	1470	2450	3350	4900
Sweptline Pickup (LWB)	750	1500	2500	3500	5000

By Charles Webb

The first Ford commercial vehicle was the 1905 Delivery Car. It was essentially just a Model C automobile with a delivery top. This 10 horsepower vehicle cost nearly $1,000 and was discontinued at the end of the model year. From 1906 through 1911, people who wanted a Ford truck had to make it themselves. Many did. Thousands of Model C, N, and T autos were converted, by their owners, into commercial vehicles.

1905 Ford Delivery Van (JAW)

After two years of testing by John Wanamaker stores in New York and Bell Telephone Company branches all over the country, the Delivery Car was reintroduced in 1912. This time it was on a Model T chassis. Sales literature proclaimed it "The car that delivers the goods. Tougher than an army mule and cheaper than a team of horses."

The one-ton Model TT (Model T Ton) made its debut in 1917. However, aftermarket sources had been making such vehicles out of Model Ts earlier.

The first factory produced Ford pickup arrived in the spring of 1925. It was basically a Model T Runabout with optional pickup box.

1943 Ford Model GC 4x4 Military Cargo Express (OCW)

1951 Ford F-1 Pickup (R. Foerster)

The light-duty Ford truck line expanded, in 1928, when the Model A debuted. Added to the catalog was a Delivery Car and Ford's first Panel truck. Also introduced was the Model AA 1½-ton series.

1952 Ford F-1 Pickup (JAW)

1955 Ford One-Ton Parcel Van (S. Morgan/DB)

A couple years later, in 1930, one of the rarest Fords ever appeared. This Town Car Delivery had an all-aluminum body and Deluxe trim. Its Town Car inspired styling made it an ideal choice for exclusive shops or any business with snob appeal. Unfortunately, it was snubbed by the market and few were sold.

1956 Ford F-100 Pickup (K. Leitgabel)

Big news for 1932 wasn't a new model, but the debut of a soon to be legendary power plant; the Ford flathead V8. However, it wasn't available on commercial vehicles until late in the model year. So, most 1932 Ford trucks had the four-cylinder engine.

1956 Ford F-100 Pickup (JAW)

Ford reintroduced an old idea in 1937. It was the Standard Coupe with Pickup Body and was offered in response to Chevrolet, who came out with a similar vehicle the previous year. Sales were poor and it was discontinued at the end of the model year. Chevrolet kept building their model until 1942, despite low demand.

1957 Ford Panel Delivery (R. Warner)

In 1938, a series of one-ton trucks joined the Ford light-duty truck line. A ¾-ton series was added in late 1939. Ford made one of the best-looking ½-ton pickups of all time in 1940. Its front end styling was similar to, but *not* interchangeable with, the attractive passenger car-line. Even the cab was improved to give it a more "car-like" appearance.

1959 Ford Ranchero Custom Pickup (DFW/GC)

In 1948 the F-1 was Ford's first truly new postwar vehicle. Handsome styling made it a standout from the start. In 1953, Ford stylists topped themselves with the beautiful F-100 series. Here was a truck anyone would be proud to park in front of their house. The 1953-'56 Ford F-100s are among the most desirable pickups ever produced.

1964 Ford Falcon Club Wagon (JAW)

1967 Ford Econoline Panel Van (JAW)

In 1957, F-100 styling changed. The new models were attractive, but some said they lacked the classic beauty of their predecessors. Good news for the year was introduction of Ranchero. This unique vehicle was like nothing else on the road. It combined passenger car styling and interior appointments with pickup truck practicality. It would be two years before Chevrolet could catch up and offer a competitive model.

Year 1961 saw the introduction of the Econoline Van. This was one of the most significant vehicles of the postwar era. Not only did it have 39 percent more load space than a typical ½-ton panel truck, but it was also easier to maneuver and could go almost twice as far on a gallon of gasoline. This was truly one of Ford's "better ideas."

1967 Ford Econline Pickup (JAW)

Chevrolet came out with a Corvair-based van, in 1961, but it was the Econoline that set the standards in vans that other truck-makers (including Chevrolet) would copy.

1969 Ford Bronco Utility (CW)

By the 1970s, vans evolved from work vehicles to play machines for the young. Ford was first to offer a van especially for this market. In 1976, the Cruising Van came ''customized'' from the factory.

1971 Ford F-250 Sport Custom Pickup (JAW)

1975 Ford Ranchero 500 Sport Pickup (CW)

Another Ford truck, introduced in the 1960s, gained popularity in the 1970s. It was the Bronco 4x4 utility vehicle. The first 1966 models were rather spartan, even when fully-optioned. However, they became more luxurious as the years passed.

1976 Ford F-100 Ranger XLT Pickup (JAW)

During the same period, pickups also evolved from being primarily work vehicles to, in some cases, replacements for the family car. It was not unusual, in the 1970s and 1980s, to see pickups that were flashier and more pampered by their owners than passenger cars.

1977 Ford F-150 Ranger XLT Pickup (JAW)

Ford entered the compact truck market, in 1972, with the Mazda-built Courier. A decade later, it came out with a domestic-built small truck; the Ranger. The down-sized Bronco II was added to the light-duty truck line in 1984.

1984 Ford F-150 XLT Styleside Pickup (JAG)

Ford's most radically new truck, in the 1980s, was the Aerostar. It was introduced in mid-1985 to compete with Chrysler's hot Caravan/Voyager mini-van. The Aerostar's distinctive areodynamic styling set it apart from other Ford light-duty trucks. Although it got off to a slow start, you can be sure the Aerostar will not only catch the competition, but maybe even surpass it.

1905 FORD

1905 Ford Model C Delivery Van (OCW)

FORD DELIVERY CAR: — This vehicle shared most of its components with Ford's Model C passenger car. It came with, a Dodge two-speed forward, one reverse, transmission with floor controls, cone clutch and drum brakes on the rear wheels. A nine gallon fuel tank was provided. Chains drove the rear axle. The body was 42 inches long, 49 inches high and 40 inches wide. The Model E Delivery Car was only offered in 1905.

I.D. DATA: Serial numbers were mounted on the dash, next to the steering column.

Model	Body Type	Price	Weight	Prod. Total
E	Delivery Car	950	1350	10

ENGINE (Delivery Car): 120.5 cu. in. Two-cylinder. 10 horsepower. Bore & stroke: 4.25 in. x 4.5 in. Holley carburetor.

CHASSIS: Wheelbase: 78 in. Payload: 600-800 lbs. Tires: 2.5 in. wide.

OPTIONS: Lights.

Pricing

	5	4	3	2	1
1905					
Model E — (78 in. w.b.)					
Delivery Car	3900	7800	13,000	18,200	26,000

1906-1908 FORD

MODEL N RUNABOUT: — Buyers who wanted a Ford commercial vehicle in 1906 thru 1908, had to build one themselves. The Model N Runabout was a popular choice for light truck conversions. A distinctive feature of this vehicle was its ''plowshare'' front fenders. An item introduced in 1907 was the tub and fin radiator. Transmission was of the two-speed planetary type.

I.D. DATA: Serial numbers were mounted on the dash, next to the steering wheel.

Model	Body Type	Price	Weight	Prod. Total
N	Runabout	600	1050	—

ENGINE (Model N Runabout): 149 cu. in. Inline four-cylinder. 15 to 18 horsepower. Bore & stroke: 3.75 in. x 3⅜ in. Holley carburetor.

CHASSIS: Wheelbase: 84 in. Tires: 30 in.

OPTIONS: Three-inch wheels. Bulb horn. Cowl lamps.

Pricing

	5	4	3	2	1
1906					
Model T — (84 in. w.b.)					
Runabout	2100	4200	7000	9800	14,000
1907					
Model T — (84 in. w.b.)					
Runabout	2100	4200	7000	9800	14,000
1908					
Model T — (84 in. w.b.)					
Runabout	2100	4200	7000	9800	14,000

1909-1910 FORD

1910 Ford Model T Commercial Roadster (OCW)

MODEL T CHASSIS: — Once again, if you wanted a Ford ''truck'' you had to make it yourself. A Model T chassis was a good place to start. It featured front and rear transverse springs. One-piece steel engine pan. Non-tapered rear axles. ''I'' beam front axle. Brass radiator and lamps. Early 1909 Model Ts had square-tipped front fenders, built-in water pumps, two foot-pedals and two control levers. Later that year, rounded fenders with small ''bills'' were used. Also, the water pump was eliminated and three foot-pedals and one lever were used. The 1910 version was pretty much the same as late 1909 models, except for some changes in the rear axle.

I.D. DATA: Serial numbers for 1909 ranged from 1 to 11,145 (the early 1909 vehicles went up to 2,500). For 1910 the range was 11,146 to 31,532.

Model	Body Type	Price	Weight	Prod. Total
T	Chassis	—	900	—

1910 Ford Model T ''Wanamaker'' Canopy Express (OCW)

ENGINE (Model T): (Early 1909 to serial #2500) 176.7 cu. in. L-Head Four-cylinder. 22 horsepower at 1600 R.P.M. Bore & stroke: 3.75 in. x 4 in. Compression ratio: 4.5:1. Kingston 5-ball, Buffalo carburetor. (Late 1909 and 1910: the same basic engine, but cooled by thermo-syphon action.)

CHASSIS: Wheelbase: 100 in. Length: 134.5 in. Tires: 30 x 3 in. front, 30 x 3.5 in. rear.

OPTIONS: Windshield. Top. Gas headlights. Bumpers. Speedometer. Auto chimes. Prestolite tanks.

Pricing

	5	4	3	2	1
1909					
Model T — (100 in. w.b.)					
Chassis	1130	2250	3750	5250	7500
1910					
Model T — (100 in. w.b.)					
Chassis	1130	2250	3750	5250	7500

1911 FORD

1911 Ford Model T C-Cab Delivery Van (OCW)

MODEL T CHASSIS: — If you wanted a Ford truck in 1911, you again had to make it yourself. The Model T chassis featured new wheels, fenders, radiator and front and rear axles.

I.D. DATA: Serial numbers began at approximately 31,533 and ran to about 70,749.

Model	Body Type	Price	Weight	Prod. Total
T	Chassis	—	940	248

ENGINE (Model T): 176.7 cu. in. L-Head Four-cylinder. 22 horsepower at 1600 R.P.M. Bore & stroke: 3.75 in. x 4 in. Compression ratio: 4.5:1. Kingston 5-ball, Holley 4500, Holley H-14550 carburetor.

CHASSIS: Wheelbase: 100 in. Length: 128 in. Tires: 30 x 3 in. front, 30 x 3.5 in. rear.

Pricing

	5	4	3	2	1
1911					
Model T — (100 in. w.b.)					
Chassis	1130	2250	3750	5250	7500

302

1912 FORD

1912 Ford Model T C-Cab Delivery Van (DFW/PTC)

MODEL T COMMERCIAL ROADSTER: — This model debuted (and died) in 1912. It featured a removable rumble seat, curved rear fenders, and front fenders in lipped or plain styles. It also had a one-piece dashboard.

MODEL T DELIVERY CAR: — Also new this year was the Delivery Car. It had a wooden body and twin rear doors. Other standard items included: Speedometer. Brass windshield frame. Tool kit. Three oil lamps. Two six inch gas lamps. Horn. Gas generator. Two-piece dashboard.

I.D. DATA (Model T): Serial numbers ran from about 70,750 to approximately 157,424.

Model	Body Type	Price	Weight	Prod. Total
T	Chassis	—	940	2133
T	Comm. Rdstr.	590		13,376
	(This includes the Torpedo Roadster)			
T	Delivery Car	700	—	1845

ENGINE (Model T): 176.7 cu. in. L-Head Four-cylinder. 22 horsepower at 1600 R.P.M. Bore & stroke: 3.75 in. x 4 in. Compression ratio: 4.5:1. Holley H-1 4550 carburetor.

CHASSIS: Wheelbase: 100 in. Length: 128 in. (chassis) 134.5 in. (Roadster, Delivery Car). Tires: 30 x 3 in. front, 30 x 3.5 in. rear.

1912 Ford Model T C-Cab Window Van (G. Teters)

1912	5	4	3	2	1
Model T — (100 in. w.b.)					
Chassis	1130	2250	3750	5250	7500
Comm. Rdstr.	1950	3900	6500	9100	13,000
Dely. Car	1500	3000	5000	7000	10,000

1913-1916 FORD

1914 Ford Model T Panel Delivery Van (OCW)

1913 Ford Model T Depot Hack (OCW)

1914 Ford Model T Fixed-Top Express (DFW/PTC)

1913 Ford Model T Panel Delivery Van (OCW)

1915 Ford Model T Panel Side Delivery Van (OCW)

MODEL T DELIVERY CAR: — This vehicle was withdrawn from the market early in the 1913 model year.

MODEL T CHASSIS: — Ford went out of the truck business in 1913 and stayed out officially until 1917. However, that didn't stop customers from making their own trucks based on the Model T chassis (even though doing so voided their warranty). In fact, many aftermarket component suppliers produced form-a-truck kits specifically for the Model T Ford. Few changes were made to the Model T chassis during this period. Perhaps the most were made for 1915 models. These included: A different differential housing. New coils and coil box. Lower louvered hood. Ribbed transmission pedals. Hand operated Klaxon horn. Round lensed tail and cowl lights. Lipped front fenders. In 1916, a steel hood replaced the aluminum one and the transmission cover was made of cast iron. Brass trim was replaced with less expensive materials. And metal, rather than wooden seat frames were used.

1915 Ford Model T Closed Cab Express (DFW/BWW)

1915 Ford Model T Fixed-Top Express (DFW/HC)

I.D. DATA: The serial numbers for 1913 models began at approximately 157,425 and ended at 248,735. For 1914 models the range was approximately 320,000 to 670,000. For 1915 models, about 670000 to 856,513. For 1916, 856,514 to 1,362,989.

Model	Body Type	Price	Weight	Prod. Total
1913				
T	Delivery Car	625	—	513
T	Chassis	—	940	8438
1914				
T		—	960	119
1915				
T		410	980	13,459
1916				
T		360	1060	11,742

1915 Ford Model T Panel Delivery Van (DFW/GFC)

1916 Ford Model T w/Columbia Swell-side Panel Body

ENGINE (Model T): 176.7 cu. in. L-Head four-cylinder. 22 horsepower at 1600 R.P.M. Bore & stroke: 3.75 in. x 4 in. Compression ratio: 4.0:1. Holley S, Kingston Y carburetor (Holley G in 1914-1916).

CHASSIS: Wheelbase: 100 in. Length: 128 in. Tires: 30 x 3 in. front, 30 x 3.5 in. rear.

1916 Ford Model T Open Express (DFW/RLC)

Pricing

	5	4	3	2	1
1913					
Model T — (100 in. w.b.)					
Chassis	1130	2250	3750	5250	7500
Dely. Car	1500	3000	5000	7000	10,000
1914					
Model T — (100 in. w.b.)					
Chassis	1130	2250	3750	5250	7500
Dely. Car	1500	3000	5000	7000	10,000
1915					
Model T — (100 in. w.b.)					
Chassis	1130	2250	3750	5250	7500
Dely. Car	1500	3000	5000	7000	10,000
1916					
Model T — (100 in. w.b.)					
Chassis	1130	2250	3750	5250	7500
Dely. Car	1500	3000	5000	7000	10,000

1917-1919 FORD

1917 Ford Model T Panel Delivery Van (DFW/OHS)

MODEL T CHASSIS: — One of the most noticable changes for 1917 was the discontinuance of the brass radiator. Other changes included: Revised windshield mounting base. Nickel plated hub caps, and steering gear box. Black radiator shell. New hood. Curved fenders. For 1919 models, the cover on the engine timing gear was changed, as were the front radius rod and rear axle.

1917 Ford Model T Roadster Pickup (OCW)

I.D. DATA: For 1917 models, serial numbers ranged from 1,362,990 to 2,113,501. For 1918: 2,113,502 to 2,756,251. For 1919: 2,756,252 to 3,277,851.

Model 1917	Body Type	Price	Weight	Prod. Total
T	Chassis	325	1060	41,165
1918				
T	Chassis	325	1060	37,648
1919				
T	Chassis	475	1060	47,125

1918 Ford Model T Mifflinburg Model 200A Panel (OCW)

1918 Ford Model T Express (ATC/HE)

ENGINE (Model T): 176.7 cu. in. L-Head four-cylinder. 20 horsepower at 1600 R.P.M. Bore & stroke: 3.75 in. x 4 in. Compression ratio: 4.0:1. Kingston L2, Holley G carburetor (1917-18) Kingston L4, Holley NH (1919).

MODEL TT CHASSIS: Production of the new one-ton chassis began on July 27, 1917. It was essentially a modified and beefed-up version of the Model T chassis. Standard features included: A 10-gallon gas tank. Worm drive rear axle. Solid rubber tires. Dual brake system. Cowl lamps. In mid-model year 1919, cowl lamps became optional. Also that year, Ford produced its 100,000th one-ton chassis.

I.D. DATA: See Model T.

1919 Ford Model T Roadster Pickup (OCW)

Model 1917	Body Type	Price	Weight	Prod. Total
TT	Chassis	600	1450	3
1918				
TT	Chassis	600	1450	41,105
1919				
TT	Chassis	550	1477	70,816

ENGINE (Model TT): Same as Model T.

CHASSIS: Wheelbase: (Model T) 100 in. (Model TT) 124 in. Length: (Model T) 128 in. Tires: 30 x 3 front, 30 x 3.5 rear.

OPTIONS: Pneumatic tires (1919).

Pricing

	5	4	3	2	1
1917					
Model T — (100 in. w.b.)					
Chassis	1050	2100	3500	4900	7000
Model TT — (124 in. w.b.)					
Chassis	900	1800	3000	4550	6500
1918					
Model T — (100 in. w.b.)					
Chassis	1050	2100	3500	4900	7000
Model TT — (124 in. w.b.)					
Chassis	900	1800	3000	4550	6500
1919					
Model T — (100 in. w.b.)					
Chassis	1050	2100	3500	4900	7000
Model TT — (124 in. w.b.)					
Chassis	900	1800	3000	4550	6500

1920 FORD

MODEL T CHASSIS: — The Model T Chassis was basically the same as last year's version. However, some changes were made. Among them were a new 16 inch hard rubber steering wheel, lighter connecting rods and a stamped fan.

I.D. DATA (Model T): Serial numbers ran from 3,277,852 to 4,233,351.

Model	Body Type	Price	Weight	Prod. Total
T	Chassis	525	1060	35,092

ENGINE (Model T): 176.7 cu. in. L-Head four-cylinder. 20 horsepower at 1600 R.P.M. Bore & stroke: 3.75 in. x 4 in. Compression ratio: 4.0:1. Kingston L4, Holley NH carburetor.

1920 Ford Model T Open Express (DFW/CL)

MODEL TT CHASSIS: — Aside from a revised driveshaft coupling sleeve, the new Model TT chassis was pretty much left unchanged for 1920. As before, several aftermarket sources offered a wide variety of bodies for the Model TT (and Model T) chassis. This was the last year for the plain glass headlamp lenses.

I.D. DATA (Model TT): See Model T I.D.

Model	Body Type	Price	Weight	Prod. Total
TT	Chassis	660	1477	135,002

NOTE: For August 1, 1919 to July 30, 1920.

ENGINE (Model TT): Same as Model T.

CHASSIS: Wheelbase: (Model T) 100 in. (Model TT) 124 in. Length: (Model T) 128 in. Tires: (Model T) 30 x 3 in. front, 30 x 3.5 in. rear. (Model TT) 30 x 3 in. front, 32 x 3.5 in. rear.

OPTIONS: Starter. Demountable rims. Pneumatic rear tires. Speedometer.

1920 Ford Model T Closed Cab Express (OCW)

Pricing

	5	4	3	2	1
1920					
Model T — (100 in. w.b.)					
Chassis	1050	2100	3500	4900	7000
Model TT — (124 in. w.b.)					
Chassis	900	1800	3000	4550	6500

1921-1922 FORD

1921 Ford Model T Atlas 10-pass. Bus Body (OCW)

MODEL T CHASSIS: — Changes for 1921 included a slightly modified frame and different headlight lenses. Among the standard features on the Model T chassis were: Running boards with aprons. A taillight. Front fenders. Two headlights. A horn. A hood. And a tool kit. In 1922, the rear axle was improved and a four-pinion differential replaced the two-pinion one.

I.D. DATA (Model T): For 1921 the serial numbers ran from 4,233,352 to 5,223,135. For 1922 they were: 5,223,136 to 6,543,606.

Model	Body Type	Price	Weight	Prod. Total
1921				
T	Chassis	345	1060	36,792
1922				
T	Chassis	295	1060	38,541

NOTE: The 1922 production # includes worldwide production.

ENGINE (Model T): 176.7 cu. in. L-Head four-cylinder. 20 horsepower at 1600 R.P.M. Bore & stroke: 3.75 in. x 4 in. Compression ratio: 3.98:1. Kingston L4 or Holley NH carburetor.

MODEL TT CHASSIS: — A feature introduced on the 1921 Model TT (and T) chassis were "green visor" headlight lenses. A large chunk of the upper headlight lense was tinted green as a safety precaution, to cut glare.

I.D. DATA (Model TT): See Model T.

1922 Ford Model T Roadster Pickup (OCW)

Model	Body Type	Price	Weight	Prod. Total
1921				
TT	Chassis	360	1477	42,860
1922				
TT	Chassis	390	1477	154,039

NOTE: Production figures for 1921 refer to domestic production from Aug. 1, 1920 to Dec. 31, 1921. The 1922 figure represents worldwide calender year production.

ENGINE (Model TT): Same as Model T.

CHASSIS: Wheelbase: (Model T) 100 in. (Model TT) 124 in. Length: (Model T) 128 in. Tires: (Model T) 30 x 3 in. front, 30 x 3.5 in. rear. (Model TT) 30 x 3 in. front, 32 x 3.5 in. rear.

OPTIONS: Starter. Demountable rims. 10 inch pinion rear axle.

Pricing

1921	5	4	3	2	1
Model T — (100 in. w.b.)					
Chassis	1050	2100	3500	4900	7000
Model TT — (124 in. w.b.)					
Chassis	900	1800	3000	4550	6500
1922					
Model T — (100 in. w.b.)					
Chassis	1050	2100	3500	4900	7000
Model TT — (124 in. w.b.)					
Chassis	900	1800	3000	4550	6500

1923-1924 FORD

1923 Ford Model T Roadster Pickup (MTFCA)

MODEL T CHASSIS: — Magneto headlamps and oil taillamps were a couple of standard features on the Model T chassis. In 1924, Ford began making its own truck bodies. These were dealer installed. Late in the year, the engine was improved via use of lighter pistons. A distinguishing feature of 1924 Model Ts was their higher radiator and hood.

I.D. DATA (Model T): For 1923 numbers ranged from 6,543,607 to 7,927,374. For 1924: 7,927,375 to 10,266,471.

Model	Body Type	Price	Weight	Prod. Total
1923				
T	Chassis	235	1060	52,317
1924				
T	Chassis	230	1060	47,901

NOTE: Production figures are worldwide calender year production.

1923 Ford Model T Police Paddy Wagon (JL)

ENGINE (Model T): 176.7 cu. in. L-Head four-cylinder. 20 horsepower at 1600 R.P.M. Bore & stroke: 3.75 in. x 4 in. Compression ratio: 4.0:1. Kingston L4, Holley NH carburetor.

MODEL TT CHASSIS: — Late 1923 Model TTs had an apron under the radiator. Among the Ford built bodies available in 1924 were: Express (pickup) and canopy top trucks. Canopy models came either open, screened-side or curtained. (Early 1924 canopies were one-piece but, later in the year, they were replaced by a two-piece design.) Also available were open cab and closed cab models. The latter featured a sloping windshield and "half moon" shaped side openings which could be fitted with curtains.

I.D. DATA (Model TT): See Model T.

1923 Ford Model T Panel Delivery Van (DFW/TDB)

Model	Body Type	Price	Weight	Prod. Total
1923				
TT	Chassis	380	1477	261,661
1924				
TT	Chassis	370	1477	204,851

NOTE: Figures for 1924 represent worldwide calendar year production.

ENGINE (Model TT): Same as Model T engine.

1924 Ford Model T Panel Delivery Van (OCW)

CHASSIS: Wheelbase: (Model T) 100 in. (Model TT) 124 in. Length: (Model T) 128 in. Tires: (Model T) 30 x 3 in. front, 30 x 3.5 in. rear. (Model TT) 32 x 4.5 in. rear.

OPTIONS: 30 x 5 eight-ply rear tires. 32 x 3.5 solid rubber tires. Battery. Starter. Generator. Demountable wheels. Truck rear bed.

Pricing

1923	5	4	3	2	1
Model T — (100 in. w.b.)					
Chassis	1050	2100	3500	4900	7000
Model TT — (124 in. w.b.)					
Chassis	900	1800	3000	4550	6500

	5	4	3	2	1
1924					
Model T — (100 in. w.b.)					
Chassis	1050	2100	3500	4900	7000
Model TT — (124 in. w.b.)					
Chassis	900	1800	3000	4550	6500

1925 FORD

1925 Ford Model T Express (OCW)

MODEL T RUNABOUT WITH PICKUP BODY: — The first factory produced Ford pickup truck was made April 15, 1925. Actually, the pickup box was an option for the Runabout. It had an adjustable tailgate, four stake pockets, heavy-duty rear springs and eight-inch diameter by 1.19 inch wide rear brake drums.

I.D. DATA (Model T): Started at 10,266,472. Ended at 12,218,728.

Model	Body Type	Price	Weight	Prod. Total
T	Chassis	225	1060	6,523
T	Pickup	281	1471	33,795

NOTE: The chassis production figures represent worldwide calendar year production.

ENGINE (Model T): 176.7 cu. in. L-Head four-cylinder. 20 horsepower at 1600 R.P.M. Bore & stroke: 3.75 in. x 4 in. Compression ratio: 3.98:1. Kingston L4, Holley NH carburetor.

MODEL TT TRUCK CHASSIS: — Available, optionally, for the first time was a Ford produced closed cab and a hand-operated windshield wiper. Like the Model T, the Model TT had an improved lubrication system and a 5-to-1 steering ratio. This steering ratio was, at first, an option. It was later made standard. The Model TT had 12 inch by two inch wide rear brake drums.

I.D. DATA (Model TT): See Model T.

Model	Body Type	Price	Weight	Prod. Total
TT	Chassis	365	1477	249,406

NOTE: The production figures refer to worldwide calendar year production.

ENGINE (Model TT): Same as Model T.

CHASSIS: Wheelbase: (Model T) 100 in. (Model TT) 124 in. Tires: 30 x 3 in. front, 30 x 3.5 in. rear.

OPTIONS: 30 x 5 rear tires. Battery headlamps. Starter. Demountable wheels. Oil lamp. Open cab. Express body. Canopy. Curtained canopy. Closed cab. Screened canopy. Stake body. Grain side. Windshield wiper. Open Cab pickup body for Runabout. Truck rear bed.

Pricing

	5	4	3	2	1
1925					
Model T — (100 in. w.b.)					
Pickup	980	1950	3250	4550	6500
Model TT — (124 in. w.b.)					
Pickup	900	1800	3000	4200	6000

1926-1927 FORD

1926 Ford Model T Closed Cab Express (DFW/MQ)

MODEL T RUNABOUT WITH PICKUP BODY: — The new Runabout was introduced in July of 1925. It had: Wider runningboards. Nickle-plated headlight rims. Eleven-inch rear brake drums. An 1½ inch lower chassis. Revised fenders. Modified springs and front spindles. More louvers on the sides of the hood. Vented cowl. A higher radiator. A slightly different box (changed so a canopy could be added). When purchased separately, the box was painted black. However, factory assembled models were Commercial Green. In March of 1927, buyers were given three new colors to chose from: black, blue or brown.

I.D. DATA (Model T): For "1926" models serial numbers started at 12,218,729 and ended at 14,049,029. For "1927" Model Ts the range was 14,049,030 to 15,006,625.

Model	Body Type	Price	Weight	Prod. Total
1926				
T	Chassis	290	1250	—
1927				
T	Chassis	300	1250	—
1926				
T	Pickup	366	1745	75,406
1927				
T	Pickup	381	1745	28,142

1926 Ford Model T C-Cab Delivery Van (DFW)

ENGINE (Model T): 176.7 cu. in. L-Head four-cylinder. 22 horsepower at 1600 R.P.M. Bore & stroke: 3.75 in. x 4 in. Compression ratio: 3.98:1. Kingston L4, Holley NH, Holley Vaporizer, Kingston Regenerator carburetor.

1926 Ford Model T Roadster Pickup (OCW)

CHASSIS (Model TT): As before, the Model TT one-ton truck chassis was available with several optional bodies. Balloon front and rear tires became standard in mid-1926.

I.D. DATA (Model TT): See Model T.

Model 1926	Body Type	Price	Weight	Prod. Total
TT	Chassis	365	1477	228,496
1927				
TT	Chassis	325	1477	83,202

ENGINE (Model TT): Same as Model T.

1927 Ford Model T Roadster Pickup (OCW)

CHASSIS: Wheelbase: (Model T) 100 in. (Model TT) 124 in. Tires: 30 x 3.5 in. (early 1926). 29 x 4.40 balloon (later).

OPTIONS: Pickup body. Windshield wiper. Front and rear bumpers. Rear-view mirror. 29 x 4.40 balloon tires (early 1926). Closed cab. Open cab. Platform body. Express body. Curtained canopy. Oversized rear tires. Starter. Oil cowl lamp. Stake body.

Pricing

	5	4	3	2	1
1926					
Model T — (100 in. w.b.)					
Pickup	980	1950	3250	4550	6500
Model TT — (124 in. w.b.)					
Express	900	1800	3000	4200	6000
1927					
Model T — (100 in. w.b.)					
Pickup	980	1950	3250	4550	6500
Model TT — (124 in. w.b.)					
Express	900	1800	3000	4200	6000

1928 FORD

1928 Ford Model A Roadster Pickup (HACJ)

MODEL A PICKUP: — Essentially, this was a Model A chassis with a Model T runabout pickup body added. Only the open cab was offered, until August 1928, when a closed cab was made available. In mid-year, the service brakes were separated from the parking brakes and the taillight was relocated. The Model A pickup had a red phenolic steering wheel and in the center of the radiator was the new Ford script in oval emblem. Those made later in the year had higher hood louvers than early 1928 models. The interior trim was brown. The wood floors were made of beech, birch, maple, pine or oak. Like the metal skid strips, they were painted body color.

DELUXE DELIVERY CAR: — Basically, this was a Model A Tudor Sedan with blanked-out rear side windows, a single rear door and two folding seats. It was offered in the same colors available on regular passenger cars. The spare tire was mounted in the left front fender well. A battery and ignition system replaced the Model Ts magneto ignition. The Deluxe Delivery Car (or Sedan Delivery) had to be special ordered.

1928 Ford Model A Produce Truck (OCW)

MODEL A PANEL: — This was Ford's first panel truck. It wasn't introduced until late in the year. It had two rear doors and two folding seats. The body was made of steel with a wood frame. The cargo area was 46.5 inches high, 57 inches long and 50 inches wide. A fifth wheel, rear view mirror and hand operated windshield wiper were standard.

I.D. DATA (Model A): Engine numbers, Oct. 20, 1927 to Dec. 1928: 1-810,122.

Model	Body Type	Price	Weight	Prod. Total
A	Chassis	—	—	—
A	Open Cab Pickup	395	—	—
A	Closed Cab Pickup	445	2073	26,179
A	Sedan Delivery	595	—	—
A	Panel	575	—	3,744

ENGINE (Model A): 200.5 cu. in. L-Head four-cylinder. 40 horsepower at 2200 R.P.M. Bore & stroke: 3⅞ in. x 4¼ in. Compression ratio: 4.22:1. Double Venturi carburetor.

CHASSIS: Wheelbase: 103.5 in. Tires: 4.75 x 19 in. balloon.

1928 Ford Model AA Platform Stake Bed (IMSC)

1928 Ford Model A Enclosed Cab Pickup (OCW)

1928 Ford Model A Deluxe Delivery Car (DFW/LS)

OPTIONS: Pin stripes. Special paint. A screened partition (Delivery Car). Tire cover.

NOTE: Exterior colors for 1928 Ford Commercial vehicles were Black or Ross Moss Green

1928 Ford Model A Closed Cab Pickup (OCW)

Pricing

1928	5	4	3	2	1
Model A — (103 in. w.b.)					
Sed. Dely.	1800	3600	6000	8400	12,000
Open Cab Pickup	1650	3300	5500	7700	11,000
Closed Cab Pickup	980	1950	3250	4550	6500
Panel	930	1860	3100	4350	6200

1929 FORD

1929 Ford Model A U.S. Mail Van (CE)

1929 Ford Model A Deluxe Sedan Delivery (OCW)

DELUXE DELIVERY CAR: — According to sales literature, the new Deluxe Delivery Car was "designed for use by exclusive shops and for speedy, safe deliveries of fragile merchandise." It closely followed the lines of the Ford sedan. The body was all steel and the front end trim was nickel plated. There were two folding seats in the driver's compartment. They were upholstered in brown cross cobra grain artificial leather. The large rear door had a window in it to aid visability. The cargo area was lined with cardboard. The Deluxe Delivery Car was available in three exterior colors. The roof covering was made of imitation black leather. There was a dome light on the windshield header.

1929 Ford Model A Closed Cab Pickup (BS/IM)

1929 Ford Model A Closed Cab Express (M. Quesques)

1929 Ford Model A Ford Closed Cab Pickup (GCC)

1929 Ford Model AA Roadster Pickup (JCL)

MODEL A PICKUP: — About the only difference in the 1929 pickup was a new black steering wheel. The body, tailgate and enclosed cab were made of steel. The open cab version had an easy to remove top and side curtains. Its doors were similar to those used on the roadster. The one-piece windshield was made of shatter-proof glass and could be tilted in or out for ventilation. The heavy floor boards had steel batten-strips to withstand wear. The radiator shell was black. The bumper was nickel plated.

1929 Ford Model A Roadster Pickup (OCW)

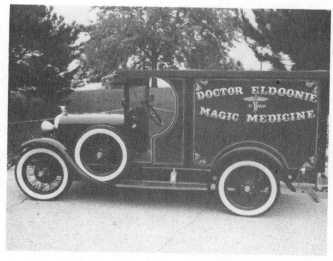

1929 Ford Model A C-Cab Panel Delivery Van (DE)

1929 Ford Model A Panel Delivery (George Davis)

MODEL A PANEL DELIVERY: — You'd have to look under the hood to find much of anything new on the 1929 Panel. Like the passenger cars, it had a larger, three-brush generator. The Panel Delivery was built of steel with the roof covered with bright, black, heavy coated rubber material. Double doors at the rear gave a wide opening for loading. And the small window in each door aided in visability. There were two folding seats in the driver's compartment. A dome light was standard. The radiator shell and headlights were black.

I.D. DATA (Model A): Engine numbers (Jan. 1929 to Dec. 1929): 810,123 to 2,742,695.

1929 Ford Model AA Panel Delivery Van (OCW)

Model	Body Type	Price	Weight	Prod. Total
A	Chassis	—	—	—
130A	Sedan Delivery	595	—	—
A	Open Cab Pickup	430	—	—
78A	Closed Cab Pickup	445	—	77,917
79A	Panel	575	2,500	—

NOTE: Prices fluctuated during the model year.

1929 Ford Model A Station Wagon (OCW)

312

ENGINE (Model A): 200.5 cu. in. L-Head four-cylinder. 40 horsepower at 2200 R.P.M. Bore & stroke: 3⅞ in. x 4¼ in. Compression ratio: 4.22:1. Double Venturi carburetor.

CHASSIS: Wheelbase: 103.5 in. Tires: 4.75 x 19 in. balloon.

OPTIONS: Rearview mirror. Removable tray (Delivery Car). Pinstripes. Special paint. Screened partition (Delivery Car).

NOTE: Exterior colors for 1929 Ford commercial vehicles were: Black, Commercial Drab, L'Anse Dark Green, Gunmetal Blue, Rock Moss Green.

Pricing

	5	**4**	**3**	**2**	**1**
1929					
Model A — (103 in. w.b.)					
Sed. Dely.	1800	3600	6000	8400	12,000
Open Cab Pickup	1650	3300	5500	7700	11,000
Closed Cab Pickup	980	1950	3250	4550	6500
Panel	930	1860	3100	4350	6200

1930 FORD

1930 Ford Model A Open Cab Pickup (OCW)

MODEL A PICKUP: — Early 1930 pickups were just leftover 1929 models. It wasn't until mid-year that a new truck-line was really introduced. Styling resembled the previous year's models. However, the 1930 version had roadster type doors, wider fenders and a one-piece, flat-folding windshield. The radiator shell and headlight pods were black. Early models had black cowl strips. On later models the cowl stripes were painted body color. The spare tire was carried in a front fender well. The runningboards had an embrossed, non-skid surface. The pickup box was carried over from 1929. Its hardwood floors were painted body color. The top was covered with rubber covered fabric. Upholstery was black Cobra cross grain imitation leather. The headlining was also black. Both open and closed cabs were available.

TOWN CAR DELIVERY: — This is one of the rarest production Fords ever made. It looked like a Town Car with blanked-out rear quarter windows. It had a convertible top over the driver's section, carriage lights on the side, cowl lamps and stainless steel trim on the front end. The top was covered with black artificial leather. The wheels were painted the same color as the paint stripe. A unique feature of this vehicle was its all-aluminum body.

DELUXE DELIVERY CAR: — The Delivery Car was at least more than a "customized" Tudor Sedan with no rear quarter windows. It had its own distinctive body that could hold longer and wider loads. The Deluxe Delivery Car could be ordered in the same colors offered on passenger cars. The cowl molding, headlight pods and radiator shell were stainless steel. Masonite and steel paneling was used in the interior. Also inside were two seats with a tool box under them and a dome light behind.

PANEL: — The new Model A Panel featured: A black enamelled radiator shell and headlight pods. Nearly foot-high steel plates inside with wood slats above to protect the interior from the cargo. Two folding front seats. An outside sunvisor. Dome light. Fender well spare tire carrier. And a spacious cargo area that was 46.4 inches wide and over 59 inches long. It also had a two-bar, chrome plated bumper until August 1930, when it was replaced by a single-bar one painted black. The taillight was located on the side of the body until the fall of 1930.

I.D. DATA (Model A): Engine numbers from Jan. 1930 to Dec. 1930: 2,742,696 to 4,237,500.

1930 Ford Model A Mail Truck (OCW)

1930 Model A Ford Sedan Delivery (OCW)

Model	Body Type	Price	Weight	Prod. Total
A	Chassis	345	—	—
295A	Town Car Delivery	—	—	3
130B	Deluxe DeliveryCar	—	2282	4629
78A	Open Cab Pickup	—	2073	3429
82B	Closed Cab Pickup	435	2215	86,383
79B	Panel Delivery	590	2416	—

ENGINE (Model A): 200.5 cu. in. L-Head four-cylinder. 40 horsepower at 2200 R.P.M. Bore & stroke: 3⅞ in. x 4¼ in. Compression ratio: 4.22:1. Double Venturi carburetor.

CHASSIS: Wheelbase: 103.5 in. Tires: 4.75 x 19 balloon.

1930 Ford Model A Canopy Express (MES/DFW)

OPTIONS: Rearview mirror. Removable tray (Delivery Car). Special paint. Screen partition (Delivery Car).

NOTE: Ford trucks in 1930 were offered in Black, Blue Rock Green, Menelas Orange, Phoenix Brown, Pegex Orange, Rock Moss Green and Rubellite Red.

Pricing

1930 Model A — (103 in. w.b.)	5	4	3	2	1
Town Car Delivery	3400	6900	11,500	16,100	23,000
Deluxe Delivery	3000	6000	10,000	14,000	20,000
Open Cab Pickup	1600	3150	5250	7300	10,500
Closed Cab Pickup	1050	2100	3500	4900	7000
Panel Delivery	980	1950	3250	4550	6500

1931 FORD

1931 Ford Model A Sedan Delivery (OCW)

DELUXE DELIVERY: — Although the Deluxe Delivery had a distinctive body, it used passenger car stainless steel trim on the cowl molding, radiator shell and headlamps. A new rear door lock was introduced early in the model year. A formerly optional partition and shelfing unit became standard. A drop floor version of this vehicle was added later in the year, but proved unpopular. It had a door-mounted taillight, headlining and no rear bumpers.

1931 Ford Model AA Panel Delivery (OCW)

313

TOWN CAR DELIVERY: — The most prestigious Ford commercial vehicle was the aluminum bodied Town Car Delivery. It had a canopy roof over the driver's compartment, new sloping windshield, carriage lamps, stainless steel front end trim, cowl lamps, bright metal spare tire cover bands, two dome lights, two black leather upholstered seats with a sliding door behind them and twin fender wells. The first 50 Town Car Deliveries came with brown carpeting. Customers could chose from 40 exterior colors.

SPECIAL DELIVERY: — This was essentially a Ford station wagon with blanked-out rear windows and two doors instead of four. The body was made of maple and birch, with basswood roof slats. On the inside were imitation leather seats. The hood, cowl and windshield frame were painted Manilla Brown. There was a partition behind the front seats and fixed glass in the rear windows. This vehicle has also been called the Natural Wood Panel Delivery.

1931 Ford Model 66-A Deluxe Pickup (F.S. Soden)

1931 Ford Model 66-A Deluxe Pickup, rear (F.S. Soden)

DELUXE PICKUP: — A distinctive feature of this model was its integral-style, wood lined cargo box with chrome plated brass rails on the upper part of the sides. The standard cowl lamps also gave it a refined touch. Most of these trucks were built for the Refrigeration Division of General Electric. It was only offered with closed cab.

1931 Ford Model A Closed Cab Pickup (CE)

314

MODEL A PICKUP: — The type 78B pickup body debuted in mid model year. It had nearly five more cubic feet of cargo space than the 1930 version. The 16-gauge steel floor had a sub-floor of hardwood. New for 1931 were the fenders and one-piece splash guard shields.

DROP FLOOR PANEL: — This was a new model for 1931. It was designed for customers who wanted more interior height. A section of the floor was dropped to about the center of the axle. The rear door panels were lined with masonite until October 1931, when they were replaced with steel panels.

PANEL: — These were unchanged from last year.

I.D. DATA: Engine numbers ran from 4,237,501 to 4,826,746.

1931 Ford Model A Fire Squad Truck (OCW)

Model	Body Type	Price	Weight	Prod. Total
A	Chassis	340	—	—
295A	Town Car Delivery	1150	—	196
255A	Special Delivery	615	—	900 (Note 1)
66A	Deluxe Pickup	—	—	293
78B	Pickup	—	—	98,166 (Note 2)
225A	Drop Floor Panel	560	—	1954
79B	Panel	—	—	8282
130B	Deluxe Delivery	540	—	9606 (Note 3)

NOTE 1: Of these, 19 were made in Dec. 1930, 841 in 1931 and 40 in 1932.

NOTE 2: 2,637 had open cabs.

NOTE 3: 77 were drop floor versions.

ENGINE (Model A): 200.5 cu. in. L-Head four-cylinder. 40 horsepower at 2200 R.P.M. Bore & stroke: 3⅞ in. x 4¼ in. Compression ratio: 4.22:1. Double venturi carburetor.

CHASSIS: Wheelbase: 103.5 in. Payload: (Pickup) 750 lbs. Tires: 5.00 x 19 in.

OPTIONS: Canopy top with side curtains (this top was modified when the new, larger pickup box was introduced in May of 1931). Spare tire (the spare wheel was standard). Special paint. Rear view mirror.

NOTE: 1931 Ford trucks were offered in 38 colors, including Yukon yellow, Menelous orange and Rubellite red.

Pricing

1931 Model A — (103 in. w.b.)	5	4	3	2	1
Town Car Delivery	3400	6900	11,500	16,100	23,000
Deluxe Delivery	3000	6000	10,000	14,000	20,000
Open Cab Pickup	1600	3150	5250	7300	10,500
Closed Cab Pickup	1050	2100	3500	4900	7000
Drop Floor Panel	1000	2000	3300	4600	6600
Panel	980	1950	3250	4550	6500
Deluxe Panel	1020	2050	3400	4800	6800

1932 FORD

1932 Ford V-8 Panel Delivery (J. Neal East)

SEDAN DELIVERY CAR: — This was essentially what its name implied, a sedan converted into a delivery car. It featured a Deluxe Tudor sedan body shell with blanked-out rear quarter windows and a 36 inch wide, 34 inch high rear door. The spare tire was carried in a front fender well. Early models had a hood with 20 louvers. Later 1932 model hoods had 25. This was done to improve engine cooling, a problem fairly common to models equipped with the new flathead V-8. However, a majority of 1932 Sedan Deliveries were powered by the four-cylinder engine.

I.D. DATA (Sedan Delivery): Starting engine numbers: 5,000,005 and up.

Model	Body Type	Price	Weight	Prod. Total
B410	Sedan Delivery	520	—	401
4/V-8	Sedan Delivery	570	—	401

ENGINE: 200.5 cu. in. L-Head four-cylinder. 50 horsepower at 2800 R.P.M. Bore & stroke: 3⅞ in. x 4¼ in. Compression ratio: 4.6:1. Zenith or Holley double venturi carburetor.

ENGINE: 221 cu. in. L-Head. V-8. 65 horsepower at 3400 R.P.M. Bore & stroke: 3-1/16 x 3¾ in. Compression ratio: 5.5:1. One-barrel carburetor.

MODEL B PICKUP: — Big news for 1932 was the introduction of Ford's V-8. However, it wasn't made available for commercial vehicles until late in the model year. So, most 1932 Ford pickups were powered by the four-cylinder. Styling refinements were similar to those on the passenger car line, although the body was lengthened by almost 10 inches. The spare tire was mounted in the front fender well. The grille and headlight pods were black. Buyers could chose from either open or closed cab versions. A three-speed manual transmission was standard.

1932 Ford United Parcel Service Van (DFW/UPS)

MODEL B STANDARD PANEL DELIVERY: — The new Panel Delivery was more than a foot longer than the previous year's model. It was also nearly two inches wider, but just a fraction of an inch higher on the inside. It had all-steel construction, a 17-gallon fuel tank and a sloping windshield. Unlike the pickup, it no longer had an outside windshield visor. The vast majority were powered by the four-cylinder engine.

DELUXE PANEL DELIVERY: — This was Ford's fanciest light-duty panel. It had the same features as the standard version plus: Stainless steel cowl lights and headlights. Bright trimmed grille. High polish exterior paint. Chrome plated front bumper, windshield wiper and rearview mirror. Masonite lined interior.

I.D. DATA (Model B): See Sedan Delivery.

Model	Body Type	Price	Weight	Prod. Total
B18	Chassis	—	—	
B76	Open Cab Pickup	—	—	593
B82	Closed Cab Pickup	435	—	
B79	Standard Panel	520	—	
B79	Deluxe Panel	540	—	392

ENGINE: See Sedan Delivery.

CHASSIS: Wheelbase: 106 in. Tires: 5.25 x 18 in.

OPTIONS: Spare tire. Spare tire cover. Outside rearview mirror. Special paint.

Pricing

1932 (106 in. w.b.)	5	4	3	2	1
Sedan Delivery	2700	5400	9000	12,600	18,000
Open Cab Pickup	1650	3300	5500	7700	11,000
Closed Cab Pickup	1010	2030	3350	4700	6700
Panel	1020	2050	3400	4800	6800
Deluxe Panel	1050	2100	3500	4900	7000

1933 FORD

1933 Ford V-8 Sedan Delivery (LS/DFW)

SEDAN DELIVERY: — The Sedan Delivery had a distinctive body of its own in 1933. However, it still shared the passenger car's styling, which included: A new slanted radiator with vertical bars, acorn-shaped headlight shells, a one-piece bumper with a center "dip" and rear-slanting hood louvers. The instrument panel, with a round 90 m.p.h. speedometer, was mounted directly in front of the steering wheel. The driver's bucket seat was fully adjustable and upholstered to match all other interior trim. The insulating board side panels and durable imitation leather headlining were finished in dark brown. The rear door glass could be lowered. A floor-shifted three-speed manual transmission was standard.

I.D. DATA (Sedan Delivery): Beginning engine numbers: Model C four-cylinder 5,185,849. Model 40 V-8 18-2031127.

Model	Body Type	Price	Weight	Prod. Total
850	Sedan Delivery (4-cyl.)	520	—	

ENGINE (Sedan Delivery): Displacement: 200.5 cu. in. L-Head four-cylinder. 50 horsepower at 2800 R.P.M. Bore & stroke: 3⅞ in. x 4¼ in. Compression ratio: 4.6:1. Zenith or Holley double venturi carburetor.

ENGINE (Sedan Delivery): Displacement: 221 cu. in. L-Head. V-8. 75 horsepower at 3800 R.P.M. Bore & stroke: 3-1/16 x 3¾ in. Compression ratio: 6.3:1. one-barrel carburetor.

1933 Ford V-8 Closed Cab Pickup (OCW)

1933 Ford V-8 Roadster Pickup (OCW)

PICKUP: — The 1933 Ford pickup resembled the previous year's model, although it did have a longer wheelbase. It could be had in either closed or open cab. Close fitting side curtains were available for the open cab. The floor was made of steel with pressed in skid strips. There was a wood underfloor. The steel tailgate had three hinges. Sturdy corner braces supported the sides and flareboards. A floor-shifted three-speed manual transmission was standard. The front bumper was black.

1933 Ford V-8 Sedan Delivery (OCW)

STANDARD PANEL DELIVERY: — The 1933 Panel Delivery had less rear overhang than the 1932 version. The quarter panels were also revised a bit and the radiator was slanted back. There was a right-hand fender well for the spare tire. The interior featured a hardwood floor interlocked with metal skid strips. There were steel panels on the lower portion of the sides and hardwood slats on the remaining area. A one-piece welded frame held the two steel rear doors. The body had a glossy satin finish.

316

DELUXE PANEL DELIVERY: — Some items that set the Deluxe models apart from standard versions were: Cowl lamps. Side panel moldings. Highly polished finish. Chrome plated rear view mirror, windshield wiper and front bumper. Masonite interior side panels. Insulated roof lined with artificial leather.

I.D. DATA (Model 46): See Sedan Delivery.

1933 Ford One-Ton Bakery Truck (OCW)

Model	Body Type	Price	Weight	Prod. Total
46	(810) Chassis w/cab	—	—	—
46	(820) Panel	510	—	—
46	(820) Deluxe Panel	530	—	—
46	(830) Pickup	—	—	—

ENGINE (Model 46): See Sedan Delivery.

CHASSIS: Wheelbase: 112 in. Length: 176 in. (Sedan Delivery). Width: 57⅜ in. (Sedan Delivery). Height: 68 in. (Sedan Delivery). Tires: 5.50 x 17 in.

OPTIONS: Greyhound radiator ornament. Closed face metal tire cover. Bumper guards. Dual horns. Dual windshield wipers. Spotlight. 14 inch steel spoked wheels. Special paint.

Pricing

	5	4	3	2	1
1933					
(112 in. w.b.)					
Sedan Delivery	2100	4200	7000	9800	14,000
Closed Cab Pickup	930	1860	3100	4350	6200
Panel	1050	2100	3500	4900	7000
Deluxe Panel	1130	2250	3750	5250	7500

NOTE: Add 45 percent to the closed cab pickup prices for an open cab version.

1934 FORD

SEDAN DELIVERY: — The 1934 Sedan Delivery had a slightly changed grille with fewer vertical bars, but looked basically the same as last year. The biggest change came in the V-8 engine. It received a new fuel induction system, a fully counter-balanced cast alloy steel crankshaft, open skirt pistons, waterline thermostats, improved fuel pump and unitized valve assemblies. The cargo area was 59 inches long and 45.75 inches wide. It had insulating board side panels. A single bucket seat, one sunvisor and a three-speed floor-shifted manual transmission were standard.

I.D. DATA (Sedan Delivery): — The starting engine number for 1934 was 18-451,478.

Model	Body Type	Price	Weight	Prod. Total
46	(850) Sedan Dely.	—	—	9021

ENGINE (Sedan Delivery): 221 cu. in. L-Head. V-8. 90 horsepower at 3800 R.P.M. Bore & stroke: 3-1/16 in. x 3¾ in. Compression ratio: 6.3:1. Two-barrel. Downdraft carburetor.

NOTE: A total of 281 of the 1934 Sedan Deliveries were powered by last year's four-cylinder engine.

PICKUP: The Ford script, in a blue oval on the side of the hood, was one of the major styling changes made for 1934 on the 112 inch wheelbase pickup. The box was 69.75 inches long and 44 inches wide. It had a heavy steel floor panel with pressed-in skid strips and a seasoned wood underfloor. Sockets at the end of the flare boards could be used for small stake racks, advertising panels, or special tops. The pickup was available with either open or closed cab. Just 347 open cab Ford Pickups were built in 1934 and this style cab was discontinued.

1934 Ford V-8 Panel Delivery (OCW)

1934 Ford V-8 Panel Delivery (OCW)

PANEL DELIVERY: — The 112 inch wheelbase Panel was basically the same vehicle as the 1933, except for some minor trim changes. It had a hardwood floor with metal skid strips. There were steel panels along the sides to the top of the wheel housings and hardwood slats to the ceiling to protect the body from loads. Insulating board was placed over heavy wood bows in the top. The twin steel rear doors were hung in a one-piece welded steel frame that was "thoroughly dust-proofed." Heavy forged hinges permitted opening the doors 180 degrees. The body had a glossy satin finish.

DELUXE PANEL DELIVERY: — The 112 inch wheelbase Deluxe had the same features as the standard Panel plus: A highly polished finish, "Rustless" steel cowl lights and chrome plated rearview mirror, windshield wiper and front bumper. The side panels were framed by moldings. The interior side panels were made of masonite. The insulated roof was lined with artificial leather and had a dome light.

1934 Ford One-Ton Police Paddy Wagon (OCW)

I.D. DATA (Model 46): See Sedan Delivery.

Model	Body Type	Price	Weight	Prod. Total
46	(810) Chassis w/Cab	445	—	—
46	(820) Panel	550	—	—
46	(820) Deluxe Panel	565	—	—
46	(830) Pickup	470 (*)	2514	—

(*): Closed cab.

ENGINE (Model 46): See Sedan Delivery.

CHASSIS: Wheelbase: 112 in. Length: (Pickup) 179.5 in. (Sedan Delivery) 176 in. (Panel) 180.75. Width: (Sedan Delivery) 57⅜ in. (Panel) 66-5/16 in. (Pickup) 66.25 in. Tires: 5.50 x 17. in.

OPTIONS: Low compression cylinder heads. Spare tire cover. Dual windshield wipers. Spare tire. Outside rearview mirror. Passenger seat (Panel). Special paint.

Pricing

1934 (112 in. w.b.)	5	4	3	2	1
Sedan Delivery	2200	4350	7250	10,150	14,500
Closed Cab Pickup	980	1950	3250	4550	6500
Panel	1050	2100	3500	4900	7000
Deluxe Panel	1130	2250	3750	5250	7500

NOTE: Add 50 percent to closed cab price for the rare 1934 open cab pickup.

1935 FORD

1935 Ford V-8 Sedan Delivery (R.M. Bowman)

1935 Ford Special Delivery (FMCC/DFW)

SEDAN DELIVERY: — It is little wonder Fords were the best-selling trucks (and cars) in 1935. They were attractively restyled. The new, narrower grille, with its four horizontal bars crossing the vertical ones, helped give it a more streamlined appearance. So did the longer hood. The new, more rounded fenders also enhanced that image. The single rear door opened up to a cargo area that was a roomy 65 inches long, 44 inches high and 46.8 inches wide. The radiator grille and windshield frame were painted body color. A floor-shift three-speed manual was standard.

I.D. DATA (Sedan Delivery): — Engine numbers started at 18-1,234,357.

Model	Body Type	Price	Weight	Prod. Total
48	(780) Sedan Delivery	586	—	—

ENGINE (Sedan Delivery): 221 cu. in. L-head. V-8. 85 horsepower at 3800 R.P.M. Bore & stroke: 3-1/16 in. x 3¾ in. Compression ratio: 6.3:1. two-barrel carburetor.

1935 Ford V-8 Pickup Truck (OCW)

PICKUP: The ½-ton pickup body was basically the same as the one introduced three years earlier. However, now it was all-steel and a panel was added, between the runningboards and box, to give it a more "one-piece" look. The graceful new fenders and slooping radiator also enhanced the truck's appearance. The front bumper had dual pin stripes. The grille added two horizontal pieces. The engine was mounted over eight inches further forward. More of the payload weight was now placed on the front wheels, so some of the rear overhang could be eliminated.

PANEL DELIVERY: — Among the features of the new ½-ton Panel were: Steel-and-board interbody paneling; hardwood plank flooring; a dome light; longer front and rear springs and revised parking brake control.

DELUXE PANEL DELIVERY: — Some of the things that set the Deluxe Panel apart from the Standard were: An aluminum painted grille; color-keyed wheels; chrome-plated twin horns; a lined interior; chrome-plated windshield wiper(s) and chromed rear view mirror.

I.D. DATA (Model 50): See Sedan Delivery.

1935 Ford Stretch-bodied Limousine (BLHU/DFW)

Model	Body Type	Price	Weight	Prod. Total
50	(810) Chassis w/Cab	—	—	—
50	(820) Panel	565	—	—
50	(820) Deluxe Panel	580	—	4946
50	(830) Pickup	480	—	—

ENGINE (Model 50): See Sedan Delivery.

CHASSIS: Wheelbase: 112 in. Length: 182¾ in. (Sedan Dely.) Height: 64⅝ in. (Sedan Dely.) Tires: 6.00 x 16 in.

OPTIONS: Passenger seat (Panel, Sedan Delivery). Roll-down rear window (Panel, Sedan Delivery). Heater. Radio. Spare tire. Bumpers. Spare tire cover. Chrome plated outside rear view mirror. Dual windshield wipers. Cigarette lighter. Two taillights (Sedan Delivery). Bumper guards. Special paint.

Pricing

1935 (112 in. w.b.)	5	4	3	2	1
Sedan Delivery	1850	3750	6250	8750	12,500
Pickup	900	1800	3000	4200	6000
Panel	870	1750	2900	4100	5800
Deluxe Panel	900	1800	3000	4200	6000

318

1936 FORD

1936 Ford V-8 Sedan Delivery (OCW)

SEDAN DELIVERY: — The most noticable styling changes for 1936 were the wraparound grille with vertical bars and new rear fenders. The hoodside louvers now had just one horizontal trim piece running through their center. Among the less obvious changes were: A larger capacity radiator; helical-type gears for first and second; new "short spoke" steel wheels and the fact that the center of the rear bumper pulled inward, rather than dipped forward, as did the front bumper. The interior featured insulating board side panels and a wood floor. A single driver's seat was standard. A small number of 1936 Sedan Deliveries had glass windows instead of the traditional steel panels. This made them look very much like two-door sedans.

I.D. DATA (Sedan Delivery): — Engine numbers began at 18-2,207,111.

Model	Body Type	Price	Weight	Prod. Total
68	(780) Sedan Delivery	—	3002	7500

ENGINE (Sedan Delivery): — 221 cu. in. L-Head. V-8. 85 horsepower at 3800 R.P.M. Bore & stroke: 3-1/16 in. x 3¾ in. Compression ratio: 6.3:1. Two-barrel downdraft carburetor.

1936 Ford V-8 Pickup (D. Whiting)

1936 Ford Pickup Truck (DFW)

1936 Ford V-8 Pickup Truck (OCW)

PICKUP: — The slightly revised radiator shell and wheels were about the only changes made to the 1936 ½-ton pickup. The box had a heavy steel floor panel with pressed-in skid strips. The tailgate was also all-steel.

1936 Ford V-8 Light-Duty Panel Delivery (OCW)

1936 Ford V-8 One-Ton Panel Delivery (OCW)

PANEL: — The new ½-ton panel looked pretty much the same as the 1935 model. The wood floors had metal skid strips. The rear doors were hung in a one-piece steel frame. Boards and steel panels on the inner walls provided extra protection. Panels could be made into "Station Wagons" (by adding rear quarter glass windows) on a special order basis.

DELUXE PANEL: — The Deluxe Panels shared the same features as the standard models plus: An insulated interior; body-color wheels and bright-finished twin horns, windshield wipers and outside rearview mirror. There was also an aluminum finish grille. This model was discontinued during the model year.

I.D. DATA (½-Ton): See Sedan Delivery.

Model	Body Type	Price	Weight	Prod. Total
67/68	(810) Chassis w/Cab	—	—	—
67/68	(820) Panel	—	3188	—
67/68	(820) Deluxe Panel	—	8225	—
67/68	(830) Pickup	—	2852	—
67/68	(840) Driveway Chassis	—	—	—

NOTE: Model # format 60 horsepower V8/85 horsepower V8.

ENGINE (½-Ton): Same as Sedan Delvery.

ENGINE (Optional): 136 cu. in. L-head. V-8. 60 horsepower at 3600 R.P.M. Bore & stroke: 2-3/5 in. x 3-1/5 in. Compression ratio: 6.6:1. Two-barrel downdraft carburetor.

CHASSIS: Wheelbase: 112 in. Tires: 6.00 x 16 in.

OPTIONS: Passenger seat (Panel, Sedan Delivery). Spare tire cover. Left-hand spare (Pickup). Canopy Top (Pickup). Spotlight. Outside rearview mirror. Dual windshield wipers. Stainless steel hub caps. Wheel trim rings. Radio. Heater. Locking gas cap. White sidewall (WSW) tires. **Deluxe Equipment Package, Sedan Delivery:** Dual windshield wipers. Two sun visors. Bright finish radiator grille, windshield frame, outside rearview mirror, horn grilles and windshield wipers. Two-tone paint.

Pricing

1936 (112 in. w.b.)	5	4	3	2	1
SedanDelivery	1850	3750	6250	8750	12,500
Pickup	900	1800	3000	4200	6000
Panel	870	1750	2900	4100	5800
Deluxe Panel	900	1800	3000	4200	6000

1937 FORD

1937 Ford V-8 Business Coupe with Tailbox (LS/DFW)

STANDARD COUPE WITH PICKUP BODY: — This was a new model that would only last a year. As its name implies, this was basically a stock 1937 Ford coupe with a down-sized ½-ton pickup box incorporated into the trunk. The box was 33 inches wide, 64 inches long and a foot high.

1937 Ford V-8 Deluxe Sedan Delivery (LS/DFW)

1937 Ford V-8 Standard Sedan Delivery (OCW)

SEDAN DELIVERY: — Although the body shell was basically the same as the one introduced in 1935, the front end of the Sedan Delivery was attractively restyled for 1937. The most noticeable change was the fender integrated headlights. The "V" like wraparound grille had horizontal bars and a vertical bar down its center. The sleek hoodside vents echoed the look of the grille. The windshield was now of two-piece design. The Sedan Delivery had a wide, single rear door and an all-steel top. The wood floor planking was interlocked by steel skid strips. Insulation board sidepanels were used. A single driver's seat, front bumper guards, a lined interior, one sun visor and a three-speed manual transmission were among the standard features.

I.D. DATA: Serial numbers ranged from 18-3,331,857 thru 18-4,186,446.

1937 Ford V-8 Standard Delivery (J. Griscon)

Model	Body Type	Price	Weight	Prod. Total
78	(770-A) Coupe w/Pickup body	—	—	—
74/78	(780) Sedan Delivery	585/595	2765/2991	7841

NOTE: Model number format: 60 horsepower V8/85 horsepower V8.

ENGINE: Displacement: 136 cu. in. L-Head. V-8. 60 horsepower at 3500 R.P.M. Bore & stroke: 2-3/5 in. x 3-1/5 in. Compression ratio: 6.6:1. Two-barrel downdraft carburetor.

ENGINE (Optional): Displacement: 221 cu. in. L-Head. V8. 85 horsepower at 3800 R.P.M. Bore & stroke: 3-1/16 in. x 3¾ in. Compression ratio: 6.3:1. Two-barrel downdraft carburetor.

1937 Ford V-8 Pickup (OCW)

320

PICKUP: — Styling changes on the ½-ton pickup were less dramatic than those on the Sedan Delivery. The revised grille now featured horizontal, rather than vertical, bars. The windshield was two-piece. The hood louvers were shorter. The cargo box was enlarged a bit to increase load length by 4 inches. It had a steel floor panel with pressed-in skid strips and a wood sub-floor. There was a new, rod-style tailgate hinge. The tailgate itself was embossed to read "Ford V-8".

1937 Ford V-8 Panel Delivery (B. Glade)

PANEL: — This model shared its looks with the pickup. A new feature was an all-steel roof. A dome light, wood floors with interlocking steel skid plates, spare tire cover and steel dual rear doors were among the standard features. Panels could be made into "station wagons" on a special order basis.

1937 Ford V-8 Light-Duty Stake Bed (LS/DFW)

1937 Ford V-8 Light-Duty Flatbed (OCW)

PLATFORM/STAKE: — The frame of the Platform/Stake was built up in order for the platform to conform to normal loading dock heights. The racks were 29.5 inches high and featured steel side panels in their forward area. The hardwood floor was interlocked by steel skid strips. A single windshield wiper and front and rear bumpers were standard.

I.D. DATA (112 in. w.b.): See Sedan Delivery.

Model	Body Type	Price	Weight	Prod. Total
73/77	(800) Platform	485	2700	—
73/77	(805) Stake	550	2870	—
73/77	(810) Chassis w/Cab	360	2012	—
73/77	(820) Panel	570	3226	—
73/77	(830) Pickup	470	2625	—
73/77	(840) Chassis w/open Driveway front end	370	2238	—

NOTE: Model number format: 60 horsepower V8/85 horsepower V8.

1937 Ford One-Ton Armored Car (NSPC/JE)

1937 Ford One-Ton Armored Car, rear view (NSPC/JE)

1937 Ford 3/4-Ton Cabinet Body Utility (NSPC/JE)

CHASSIS: Wheelbase: 112 in. Length: 186.76 in. (Pickup). 189.63 in. (Platform/Stake). 195.09 in. (Panel) 178.67 in. (Sedan Delivery) 179.5 in. Tires: (Coupe w/Pickup body) 5.50 x 16; (Sedan Delivery) 6.00 x 16 in.

POWERTRAIN OPTIONS: Transmission with lower ratio gears. Four-speed manual.

CONVENIENCE OPTIONS: Lined interior (Pickup). Radio. Heater. Stainless steel "spider" wheel covers. Passenger side windshield wiper. Right-hand sun visor. Windshield defroster. Spotlight. Outside rear view mirror. Deluxe Equipment group: Dual horns. Twin windshield wipers. Two sun visors. Chrome plated grille. Outside rear view mirror. Wipers. Windshield frame. Twin horns and hood louver moldings. Special paint. Two-tone paint.

1937	5	4	3	2	1
(112 in. w.b.)					
Sedan Delivery	1650	3300	5500	7700	11,000
Pickup	870	1750	2900	4100	5800
Panel	840	1680	2800	3900	5600
(122 in. w.b.)					
Stake	830	1650	2750	3850	5500
Platform	780	1560	2600	3600	5200

1938 FORD

1938 Ford V-8 Deluxe Station Wagon (OCW)

SEDAN DELIVERY: — The new sedan delivery shared its looks with the Ford Standard passenger car line. Most striking was its curved, horizontal-bar grille that wrapped around the hoodsides. The front fenders resembled the previous year's model, but were new. However, the rear fenders were the same as those used in 1937. The body shell was virtually the same as the one introduced in 1935. Its styling was jazzed up a bit, early in the model year. Extra grille moldings, a bright windshield frame and stainless steel belt molding were added. The Sedan Delivery had a hardwood floor with steel skid strips. It had a load width of 52 inches and a load height of 44.75 inches. A driver's seat and single windshield wiper were standard.

I.D. DATA (Sedan Delivery): Serial numbers; 81A: 18-4,186,447 to 18-4,661,100. 82A: 54-358,335 & up.

1938 Ford Commercial Depot Hack (OCW)

Model	Body Type	Price	Weight	Prod. Total
82A/81A	780 Sedan Delivery	690/700	2677/2858	3986

NOTE: Model number format: 60 horsepower V8/85 horsepower V8.

ENGINE (Sedan Dely.): 136 cu. in. L-Head. V-8. 60 horsepower at 3500 R.P.M. Bore & stroke: 2-3/5 in. x 3-1/5 in. Compression ratio: 6.6:1. two-barrel carburetor.

ENGINE (Optional): Displacement: 221 cu. in. L-Head. V8. 85 horsepower at 3800 R.P.M. Bore & stroke: 3-1/16 in. x 3¾ in. Compression ratio: 6.12:1. Two-barrel downdraft carburetor.

1938 Ford V-8 Pickup Truck (LOC/DFW)

1938 Ford V-8 1/2 Ton Pickup (Bill Ballas photo)

112 INCH PICKUP: — The new ½-ton pickup featured attractive styling. The refined, curved, almost egg-shaped grille had numerous horizontal bars with a trim piece dividing the grille vertically. The hood louvers also had a horizontal theme. The fenders resembled those on the passenger car-line. The headlights were encased in new teardrop-shaped pods. Skid strips were stamped in the steel floor. A wood sub-floor gave extra support. Drop chain locking links clamped body sides to the tailgate, when in the closed position. The load length was 77.75 inches.

112 INCH PANEL: — The ½-ton Panel received a new body to go with its new looks. Load length was now 87.78 inches at the floor. The rear door opening was 46.2 inches wide and 44 inches high. The sides of the all-steel body were double-sealed at the floor, with rubber and felt to help keep out dust and moisture. The floors were made of hardwood. The spare tire carrier was located on the right-hand side of the vehicle, between the passenger side door and rear fender. A new option offered this year was fender skirts.

112 INCH PLATFORM/STAKE: — A couple new features offered on the ½-ton Platform/Stake truck this year were a left rear fender mounted fuel filler pipe and bright-center hub caps. The stake sides were hinged and removable for easier loading. On each forward stake section was a large metal advertising panel. The hardwood floor planking was locked together and protected by steel skid strips. Load length was 80 inches. The stake sections were 29.5 inches high. A three-speed manual transmission was standard.

I.D. DATA (112 Inch): See Sedan Delivery.

Model	Body Type	Price	Weight	Prod. Total
82C/81C (800) Platform		610	2614/2812	96
82C/81C (805) Stake		625	2767/2954	2500
82C/81C (810) Chassis w/Cab		560	2302/2528	389
82C/81C (820) Panel		685	2895/3012	6447
82C/81C (830) Pickup		590	2633/2791	30,943
82C/81C (840) Chassis w/open Driveaway front end		465	1896/2092	1718
82C/81C (850) Chassis w/closed Driveaway front end		485	1922/2119	158

NOTE: Model number format: 60 horsepower V8/85 horsepower V8. Prices are for 60 horsepower V8.

ENGINE (112 Inch): See Sedan Delivery.

122 INCH EXPRESS: — This one-ton pickup was new for 1938. Styling resembled that of the ½-ton. However, it had a stronger chassis and larger body. Load length was 96 inches. The hardwood floor planks were protected and interlocked by steel skid strips. The front and side panels were reinforced and sockets were provided in the flare boards for side boards. An 18-gallon fuel tank, chrome plated front bumper and three-speed manual transmission were among the standard features. The fuel filler pipe was located on the right-hand side of the cab, between the door and pickup box.

122 INCH PANEL: — Basically, this looked like (and was) a larger capacity version of the ½-ton panel. It featured a welded, all-steel body. The panel sides were double-sealed at the floor with felt and rubber. A welded, reinforced channel steel frame helped to maintain the alignment of the rubber-sealed rear doors. Load length was 107.25 inches at the floor. The rear opening was 46.2 inches wide by 46.5 inches high.

122 INCH PLATFORM/STAKE: — The one-ton Platform/Stake had hardwood floor planking bolted to bridge-type steel framework. The stake rack was built of hardwood with sturdy stakes. The forward section on each side was hinged to swing out for easy loading. A 28 inch wide by 34.88 inch tall metal panel on the rack could be used for advertising purposes. The cargo area was 90.4 inches long and 74 inches wide.

I.D. DATA (122 Inch): See Sedan Delivery.

Model	Body Type	Price	Weight	Prod. Total
82Y/81Y (800) Platform		725	—	—
82Y/81Y (805) Stake		745	—	—
82Y/81Y (810) Chassis w/Cab		670	—	—
82Y/81Y (820) Panel		850	—	—
82Y/81Y (830) Pickup		730	—	—
82Y/81Y (840) Chassis w/Open Driveaway front end		465	—	—
82Y/81Y (850) Chassis w/Closed Driveaway front end		560	—	—

NOTE: Model number format: 60 horsepower V8/85 horsepower V8. Prices are for 85 horsepower V8. The 60 horsepower versions were $10 cheaper.

CHASSIS (112 Inch Series and Sedan Delivery): Wheelbase: 112 in. Length: 178.67 in. (Sedan Delivery). 183.74 in. (Pickup). 195.09 in. (Panel). 189.6 in. (Platform/Sedan). Width: 72.14 in. Height: 69.67 in. (Panel). 66.67 in. (Sedan Delivery). 71.45 in. (Pickup). Tires: 6.00 x 16 in. 122 Inch Series: Wheelbase: 122 in. Length: 199.89 in. (Platform/Stake). 217.39 in. (Pickup). 209.39 in. (Panel). Width: 73.62 in. (Pickup, Panel). 79.24 in. (Platform/Stake). Height: 85.64 in. (Panel). 79.44 in. (Pickup, Platform/Stake). Tires: 6.00 x 17 six-ply (front); 7.00 x 17 six-ply (rear).

POWERTRAIN OPTIONS: Four-speed manual.

1938 Ford V-8 Pickup Truck (OCW)

1938 Ford V-8 3/4 Ton Pickup (DFW)

CONVENIENCE OPTIONS: Outside mounted spare tire. Spotlight. Grille guard. Passenger side windshield wiper. Fog lights (Sedan Delivery). "Spider" wheel covers (Sedan Delivery). Radio. Wheel trim rings. Heater. Locking gas cap. License plate frame. Cigar lighter (Sedan Delivery). 6.50 x 16 six-ply tires (112 in. Series). Fender skirts (Panel). Masonite lined interior (Panel). Colored wheels. WSW tires. Oversized tires (122 in. series). Deluxe Equipment Package: Deluxe passenger car hub caps; chrome-plated radiator grille, outside rear view mirror and windshield frame.

Pricing

	5	4	3	2	1
1938					
(112 in. w.b.)					
Sedan Delivery	1650	3300	5500	7700	11,000
Platform	800	1600	2650	3700	5300
Stake	840	1680	2800	3900	5600
Panel	870	1750	2900	4100	5800
Pickup	870	1750	2900	4100	5800
(122 in. w.b.)					
Platform	780	1560	2600	3600	5200
Stake	830	1650	2750	3850	5500
Panel	840	1680	2800	3900	5600
Pickup	850	1700	2850	4000	5700

1939 FORD

1939 Ford V-8 Sedan Delivery (LS/DFW)

SEDAN DELIVERY: — The Sedan Delivery received a very minor facelift for 1939. Loop-style hood side moldings, a different hood ornament and bright wraparound horizontal trim strips on the grille, were the most noticeable changes. Among the standard features were: Dual windshield wipers; an outside rear view mirror; hardwood floors (protected by steel skid strips); friction-type door checks (to hold all doors when in open position); spare wheel mounted inside body; a fully lined and insulated interior and driver's seat.

I.D. DATA (Sedan Delivery): Serial numbers began at 54-506,501.

Model	Body Type	Price	Weight	Prod. Total
82A/81A	(780) Sedan Delivery	685	2677/2858	—

NOTE: Price is for 85 horsepower version.

ENGINE (Sedan Delivery): 136 cu. in. L-Head. V-8. 60 horsepower at 3500 R.P.M. Bore & stroke: 2-3/5 in. x 3-1/5 in. Compression ratio: 6.6:1. Two-barrel carburetor.

ENGINE (Optional): 221 cu. in. L-Head. V8. 85 horsepower at 3800 R.P.M. Bore & stroke: 3-1/16 in. x 3¾ in. Compression ratio: 6.12:1. Two-barrel carburetor.

112 INCH PICKUP: — Elimination of the V8 emblem on the grille, a sleeker hood ornament/latch handle and passenger car hub caps were the biggest styling changes for 1939. The 112 inch Pickup had a wood sub-floor. Skid strips were stamped in the steel floor. Drop chain locking links clamped body sides to the tailgate, when in the closed position. The box had a load width of 53.6 inches and a load height of 77.7 inches.

112 INCH PANEL: — If you liked the 112 inch Panel of 1938, you'd like the 1939 version. They were virtually identical, although the new one had hydraulic brakes. The sides of the all-steel body were double-sealed at the floor with rubber and felt. The floors were made of hardwood. The spare tire carrier was located on the right-hand side of the vehicle, between the passenger side door and rear fender. The rear door opening was 46.2 inches wide and 44 inches high.

112 INCH PLATFORM/STAKE: — The stake sides were hinged and removable for easier loading. On each forward stake section was a large metal advertising panel. The hardwood planking was locked together and protected by steel skid strips. Load length was 80 inches. The hardwood stake sections were 29.5 inches high. A three-speed manual transmission was standard.

I.D. DATA (112 Inch): See Sedan Delivery.

1939 Ford V-8 Business Coupe with Tailbox (OCW)

Model	Body Type	Price	Weight	Prod. Total
92D/91D	(80) Platform	605	—	—
92D/91D	(81) Chassis w/ Cab	555	—	—
92D/91D	(82) Panel	670	—	—
92D/91D	(83) Pickup	NA	—	—
92D/91D	(84) Chassis w/Cowl	480	—	—
92D/91D	(85) Chassis w/cowl & windshield	500	—	—
92D/91D	(86) Stake	625	—	—

NOTE: Model number format: 60 horsepower V8/85 horsepower V8.

112 INCH ENGINE: See Sedan Delivery.

122 INCH ¾-TON EXPRESS: This series was introduced in mid-model year. It shared its wheelbase, driveline, frame and suspension with the one-ton. However it had the ½-ton's 12 inch brakes. Its cargo box was 96 inches long, 54 inches wide and 21.5 inches to the top of flare boards. Sockets were provided in flare boards for side boards or top. Section corner posts were rounded. There were rolled edges on the flare boards and tailgate. The front and side panels were reinforced. The hardwood floor planks were protected and interlocked by steel skid strips.

122 INCH ¾-TON PANEL: Sales literature bragged the 122 inch ¾-ton Panel featured "smart styling that brings prestige to its owner." It had a welded all-steel body. Panel sides were double-sealed at the floor with felt and rubber. Welded, reinforced channel steel frame helped maintain the alignment of the rubber sealed doors. Its rear opening was 46.2 inches wide and 46.5 inches high.

122 INCH ¾-TON PLATFORM/STAKE: The ¾-ton Platform/Stake was especially designed for bulky loads. It had a sturdy steel bridge-type platform frame, hardwood floor and smooth-surfaced rack boards with rounded corners. There was a large metal advertising panel on each forward stake section. The platform sides and end were protected by the steel frame rail. The ends of the body sills had strong steel caps riveted to the frame rail and bolted to the sills. The stake sockets were doubly reinforced, welded to the inside of the frame rail and riveted to the outside. Large steel interlocking plates were bolted to the corners of top rack boards, tying them rigidly together to prevent "fanning". The three person, waterproof seat could be adjusted to three positions.

122 INCH ¾-TON I.D.: See Sedan Delivery.

Model	Body Type	Price	Weight	Prod. Total
92D/91D	(80) Platform	—	—	—
92D/91D	(81) Chas. w/Cab	—	—	—
92D/91D	(82) Panel	—	—	—
92D/91D	(83) Pickup	—	—	—
92D/91D	(84) Chassis w/Cowl	—	—	—
92D/91D	(85) Chassis w/Cowl & Windshield	—	—	—
92D/91D	(86) Stake	—	—	—

NOTE: Format: 60 horsepower V8/85 horsepower V8.

ENGINE (112 Inch ¾-Ton): Same as 112 in. series.

122 INCH ONE-TON EXPRESS: — This model was virtually identical to the ¾-ton series, except for its brakes, wheels and tires. The one-ton pickup had extra large load capacity. The cargo box featured a hardwood floor with steel skid strips. The front and side panels were reinforced. And the flareboards and tailgate had rolled edges. The spare wheel and fuel inlet were located on the right-hand side of the vehicle.

122 INCH ONE-TON PANEL: — The One-Ton Panel was very similar to the ¾-ton version. Its dual rear doors were hung in a welded, one-piece channel steel frame. Panel sides were double-sealed at the floor with felt and rubber. Load length was 107.25 inches at the floor. Width was 55.25 inches and height 55 inches.

122 INCH ONE-TON PLATFORM/STAKE: — The One-Ton Platform/Stake shared its body with the ¾-ton version, but it could haul heavier loads. Its wheels were equipped with full, truck type, flat-base rims. The hardwood floors were interlocked with steel skid strips. The stake pockets were doubly reinforced. The stakes themselves were made of straight-grain hardwood. The rack boards were smooth surfaced with rounded corners and edges. They had large steel interlocking plates bolted to their corners.

122 INCH ONE-TON I.D.: — See Sedan Delivery.

Model	Body Type	Price	Weight	Prod. Total
92Y/91Y	(80) Platform	—	—	—
92Y/91Y	(81) Chassis w/Cab	—	—	—
92Y/91Y	(82) Panel	—	—	—
92Y/91Y	(83) Pickup	—	—	—
92Y/91Y	(84) Chassis w/Cowl	—	—	—
92Y/91Y	(85) Chassis w/Windshield	—	—	—
92Y/91Y	(86) Stake	—	—	—

ENGINE (122 Inch One-Ton): Same as 112 in. series.

CHASSIS (112 in. Series and Sedan Delivery): Wheelbase: 112 in. Length: 178.67 in. (Sedan Delivery). 183.74 in. (Pickup). 195.09 in. (Panel). 189.6 in. (Platform/Stake). Width: 72.14 in. Height: 69.67 in. (Panel). 66.67 in. (Sedan Delivery). 71.45 in. (Pickup). GVW: 4300. Tires: 6.00 x 16 in. 122 Inch ¾-Ton and One-Ton: Wheelbase: 122 in. Length: 199.89 in. (Platform/Stake). 217.39 in. (Pickup). 209.39 in. (Panel). Width: 73.62 in. (Pickup, Panel). 79.24 in. (Platform/Stake). Height: 85.64 in. (Panel). 79.44 in. (Pickup, Platform/Stake). GVW: 5400 lbs. (¾-ton). 6400 lbs. (one-ton) Tires: 6.50 x 16 six-ply front; 7.00 x 16 six-ply rear (¾-ton). 6.00 x 17 six-ply front; 7.00 x 17 six-ply rear (one-ton).

POWERTRAIN OPTIONS: 95 horsepower 239 cu. in. V8. Four-speed manual.

CONVENIENCE OPTIONS: Plated rear bumper. Passenger seat (Panel). Outside mounted spare tire. Spotlight. Grille guard. Passenger side windshield wiper. Fog lights (Sedan Dely.) Radio. Wheel trim rings. Heater. Locking gas cap. Cigar lighter (Sedan Dely.) WSW tires. Fender skirts. Right-hand sun visor.

Pricing

1939	5	4	3	2	1
(112 in. w.b.) — (½-Ton)					
Sedan Delivery	1800	3600	6000	8400	12,000
Pickup	870	1750	2900	4100	5800
Panel	870	1750	2900	4100	5800
Stake	830	1650	2750	3850	5500
(122 in. w.b.) — (¾-Ton and 1-Ton)					
Pickup	830	1650	2750	3850	5500
Panel	830	1650	2750	3850	5500
Stake	780	1560	2600	3600	5200

1940 FORD

1940 Ford V-8 Light-Duty Panel Delivery (OCW)

SEDAN DELIVERY: — The attractive new Sedan Delivery styling was based on the 1940 Deluxe passenger car-line. Its hardbound floor was protected by steel skid strips. The interior was fully lined and insulated. The windshield opened. There were friction-type door checks to hold all doors when in open position. The spare tire was mounted inside, under the floor. The Sedan Delivery had a single rear door and longer and wider cargo area than the previous year's model. Standard features included: Driver's seat; dual wipers; two sun visors; two ash trays; a clock; plastic gauge panel and three-speed manual transmission.

I.D. DATA (Sedan Delivery): VINs began at BB54-506501 (60 horsepower V8) or 18-5210701 (85 horsepower V8).

Model	Body Type	Price	Weight	Prod. Total
022A-01C	(78) Sedan Delivery	690/705	2638/2844	5325 note

NOTE: Format: 60 horsepower/85 horsepower. A total of 4,451 had 85 horsepower V8s; 758 had the 60 horsepower V8 and 116 had the 95 horsepower V8.

1940 Ford V-8 Light-Duty Panel Delivery (OCW)

1940 Ford V-8 Light-Duty Panel Delivery (OCW)

ENGINE (Sedan Delivery): 136 cu. in. L-Head. V8. 60 horsepower at 3500 R.P.M. Bore & stroke: 2-3/5 in. x 3-1/5 in. Compression ratio: 6.6:1. 2-bbl. carburetor.

ENGINE (Optional): 221 cu. in. L-Head. V8. 85 horsepower at 3800 R.P.M. Bore & stroke: 3-1/16 in. x 3¾ in. Compression ratio: 6.12:1. 2-bbl. carburetor.

1940 Ford V-8 Pickup (OCW)

112 INCH PICKUP: — Many people believe this is one of the best looking pickups ever made. It featured passenger car front end styling. Fender intergrated headlights with egg-shaped rims and vertical-bar grille. The cab was strengthened and altered slightly to give it a more "car-like" appearance. On the inside, the seats were built with new interlaced mattress-type coil springs. The spare tire was mounted on the right-hand side of the truck, between the cab and rear fender. Load length was 77.7 inches. Load width was 60.34 inches.

112 INCH PANEL: — In addition to attractive styling, the 112 inch wheelbase Panel featured new tongue and groove flooring and double bodysides at the floor. An interior fully lined with fiberboard was available at extra cost. The spare tire was located on the right-hand side, between the passenger door and the rear fender. The 112 inch Panel had a load width of 55 inches, load length of 87.78 inches and load height of 78.87 inches. The twin rear doors could be held open in two positions.

112 INCH PLATFORM/STAKE: — The new cargo body had single-piece side rack sections that were made from hardwood boards with smooth surfaces and rounded corners. The loading height was lowered 3 inches. The frame featured steel side rails riveted to heavy-gauge steel cross girders. The spare wheel carrier was mounted under the body at the rear. A new feature was splash shield type rear fenders. Load area was 80 inches long and 67 inches wide. The stakes were 29.5 inches high.

I.D. DATA (112 Inch): See Sedan Delivery.

1940 Ford V-8 Pickup (OCW)

Model	Body Type	Price	Weight	Prod. Total
02C/01C	(81) Chassis w/Cab	555/570	2119/2319	—
02C/01C	(80) Platform	610/625	2428/2622	—
02C/01C	Panel	675/690	2706/2906	—
02C/01C	(83) Pickup	580/595	2450/2645	—
02C/01C	(84) Chassis w/Cowl	465/480	1786/1986	—
02C/01C	(85) Chassis w/Cowl & windshield	485/500	1905/2013	—
02C/01C	(86) Stake	630/645	2568/2764	—

NOTE: Format: 60 horsepower V8/85 horsepower V8.

112 INCH ENGINE: See Sedan Delivery.

122 INCH ¾-TON EXPRESS: — A flatter-faced hood with taller vertical bar grille and fender-mounted, pod-type headlights quickly set the ¾-ton pickup apart from the ½-ton. It had a steel interlocked wood floor and a load capacity of 59.1 cubic feet. New features included: Sealed beam headlights; higher power generator and battery; 36 x 1.75 inch longitudinal springs and a different axle design. There were three stake sockets in each flareboard for rack or side boards. The tailgate could be lowered flush with the floor or swung all the way down.

122 INCH ¾-TON PANEL: — Like the ¾-ton Express, the ¾-ton Panel had a more truck-like appearance than the ½-ton version. However, interior features were similar. The floors were of the tongue and groove variety and the twin rear doors had two-position checks. The spare tire was located on the right-hand side between the passenger door and the rear fender. The roof rail, top and body sides were welded together for greater rigidity and strength. The driver's seat was upholstered in durable, waterproof-coated fabric.

122 INCH ¾-TON PLATFORM/STAKE: — The ¾-ton Platform/Stake was especially designed for bulky loads. It had a sturdy steel bridge-type platform frame, hardwood floor and smooth-surfaced rack boards with rounded corners. There was a large metal advertising panel on each forward stake section. The platform sides and end were protected by the steel frame rail. The ends of the body sills had strong steel caps riveted to the frame rail and bolted to the sills. The stake sockets were doubly reinforced, welded to the inside of the frame rail and riveted to the outside. Large steel interlocking plates were bolted to the corners of top rack boards, tying them rigidly together to prevent "fanning". The three person's waterproof seat could be adjusted to three positions.

I.D. DATA (122 Inch ¾-Ton): See Sedan Delivery.

Model	Body Type	Price	Weight	Prod. Total
02D/01D	(81) Chassis w/Cab	615/630	2391/2577	—
02D/01D	(80) Platform	670/685	2903/3089	—
02D/01D	(82) Panel	785/800	3256/3442	—
02D/01D	(83) Pickup	680/695	2960/3146	—
02D/01D	(84) Chassis w/Cowl	525/540	2061/2247	—
02D/01D	(85) Chassis w/Cowl & windshield	545/560	2088/2274	—
02D/01D	(86) Stake	695/710	3156/3342	—

NOTE: Format: 60 horsepower V8/85 horsepower V8.

ENGINE (122 Inch ¾-Ton): Same as 112 in. series.

122 INCH ONE-TON EXPRESS: — This model was virtually identical to the ¾-ton series, except for its brakes, wheels and tires. The one-ton pickup had extra large load capacity. The cargo box featured a hardwood floor with steel skid strips. The front and side panels were reinforced and the flareboards and tailgate had rolled edges. The spare wheel and fuel inlet were located on the right-hand side of the vehicle.

122 INCH ONE-TON PANEL: — The one-ton Panel was very similar to the ¾-ton version. Its dual rear doors were hung in a welded, one-piece channel steel frame. Panel sides were double-sealed at the floor with felt and rubber. Load length was 107.25 inches at the floor. Width was 55.25 inches and height 56 inches.

122 INCH ONE-TON PLATFORM/STAKE: — The one-ton Platform/Stake shared its body with the ¾-ton version, but it could haul heavier loads. Its wheels were equipped with full truck type, flat base rims. The hardwood floors were interlocked with steel skid strips. The stake pockets were doubly reinforced. The stakes themselves were made of straight-grain hardwood. The rack boards were smooth surfaced with rounded corners and edges. They had large steel interlocking plates bolted to their corners.

I.D. DATA (122 Inch 1-Tonner): See Sedan Delivery.

Model	Body Type	Price	Weight	Prod. Total
92Y/91Y	(80) Platform	705/720	3021/3207	—
92Y/91Y	(81) Chassis w/Cab	650/665	2578/2764	—
92Y/91Y	(82) Panel	820/835	3328/3514	—
92Y/91Y	(83) Pickup	715/730	3103/3289	—
92Y/91Y	(84) Chassis w/Cowl	560/575	2230/2416	—
92Y/91Y	(85) Chassis w/windshield	560	2274	—
92Y/91Y	(86) Stake	730/745	3274/3460	—

NOTE: Format: 60 horsepower/85 horsepower.

ENGINE (122 Inch One-Ton): Same as 112 inch wheelbase series.

CHASSIS (112 In. Series and Sedan Delivery): Wheelbase: 112 in. Length: 178.67 in. (Sedan Delivery). 183.74 in. (Pickup). 195.45 in. (Panel). 189.6 in. (Platform/Stake). Width: 72.14 in. Height: 75.85 in. (Panel). 71.45 in. (Platform/Stake, Pickup). GVW: 4300 lbs. Tires: 6.00 x 16 in. **122 Inch ¾-Ton and One-Ton:** Wheelbase: 122 in. Length: 201.84 in. (Platform/Stake). 203.34 in. (Pickup). 215.57 in. (Panel). Width: 73.62 in. (Pickup, Panel). 79.24 in. (Platform/Stake). Height: 82.64 in. (Panel). 76.2 in. (Pickup, Platform/Stake). GVW: 5400 lbs. (¾-ton); 6400 lbs. (one-ton). Tires: 6.50 x 16 six-ply front; 7.00 x 16 six-ply rear (¾-ton). 6.00 x 17 six-ply front; 7.00 x 17 six-ply rear (one-ton).

POWERTRAIN OPTIONS: 95 horsepower 239 cu. in. V8. Four-speed manual transmission.

1940 Ford V-8 Pickup (DFW)

CONVENIENCE OPTIONS: Plated rear bumper. Passenger seat (Panel). Outside mounted spare tire. Spotlight. Grille guard. Passenger side windshield wiper. Fog lights (Sedan Dely.) Radio. Wheel trim rings. Heater. Locking gas cap. Cigar lighter (Sedan Dely.) WSW tires. Fender skirts. Right-hand sun visor. 7.00 x 17 or 7.50 x 17 eight-ply tires (one-ton). Two-piece sliding rear window (Pickup, Platform/Stake). A specially formed, thick cushioned seat of fully aerated foam rubber, covered with duck. Heavy-duty 11 inch clutch.

Pricing

1940	5	4	3	2	1
(112 in. w.b.) — (½-Ton)					
Sedan Delivery	2100	4200	7000	9800	14,000
Pickup	980	1950	3250	4550	6500
Panel	980	1950	3250	4550	6500
Stake	930	1860	3100	4350	6200
(122 in. w.b.) — (¾-Ton)					
Pickup	900	1800	3000	4200	6000
Panel	900	1800	3000	4200	6000
Stake	850	1700	2850	4000	5700
(122 in. w.b.) — (1-Ton)					
Pickup	870	1750	2900	4100	5800
Panel	870	1750	2900	4100	5800
Stake	830	1650	2750	3850	5500

1941 FORD

1941 Ford V-8 Business Coupe with Tailbox (ABE/DFW)

SEDAN DELIVERY: — Rather than sharing its looks with the passenger cars, the new 1941 Sedan Delivery used slightly modified styling from the previous year. In fact, it went from being based on the 1940 Deluxe series to the Standard. It came with the commercial car parking lamps and vertical bar grille. The fuel filler cap was recessed. There were new, Ford script hub caps and different (optional) bumper guards. The hardwood floor had steel skid plates. A door check could hold the large rear door open. The spare tire was located under the floor and could not be removed if the back door was locked. The load length was 74.6 inches. A driver's seat and a three-speed manual were a couple of the standard features.

I.D. DATA (Sedan Delivery): The VIN range for V-8 models ran from 18-5896295 through 18-6769035. Four-cylinder models went from 9A-38 through 9C-13200. And six-cylinder powered vehicles, 1GC-1 through 1GC-34800.

Model	Body Type	Price	Weight	Prod. Total
1NC	(78) Sedan Delivery	730	2593	6881
1GC	(78) Sedan Delivery	730	2738	6881
11C	(78) Sedan Delivery	730	2763	6881

NOTE: Format:4/6/V8. Price listed is for V8 models. Deduct $15 for six, $20 for four.

ENGINE (Sedan Delivery): Displacement: 119.7 cu. in. L-head. Four-cylinder. 30 horsepower at 2800 R.P.M. Bore & stroke: 3.19 in. x 3.75 in. Compression ratio: 6.0:1. One-barrel updraft carburetor.

ENGINE (Optional): Displacement: 225.8 cu. in. L-Head. Six-cylinder. 90 horsepower at 3300 R.P.M. Bore & stroke: 3.3 in. x 4.4 in. Compression ratio: 6.7:1. One-barrel carburetor.

ENGINE (Optional): Displacement: 221 cu. in. L-Head. V8. 90 horsepower at 3800 R.P.M. Bore & stroke: 3.19 in. x 3.75 in. Compression ratio: 6.2:1. Two-barrel carburetor. (At the beginning of the model year, the V8 was rated at 85 horsepower.)

1941 Ford V-8 Pickup (Lou Harrison/DFW)

112 INCH PICKUP: — Styling changes were rather mild for 1941. Among them were: Different parking lamp lenses; wider hood nose moldings and rectangular nameplates on the side of the hood. The instrument cluster graphics were revised. The "V8" logo was removed from the tailgate. And the hub caps had the Ford script on them. The seat had mattress type coil springs. There were 40.25 x 2 inch front springs and the rear springs of the pickup were slightly longer. As before, the spare tire was placed on the right-hand side, between the cab and rear fender. Four-cylinder models came with a four-speed manual transmission. A three-speed manual was standard with the Six and V8.

112 INCH PLATFORM/STAKE: — The 112 inch Platform/Stake shared the pickups' changes. The platform frame had steel side rails riveted to heavy gauge steel cross girders. The side rack sections were made from hardwood boards with smoothed surfaces and rounded corners. The spare tire was mounted under the platform, at the rear.

112 INCH PANEL: — The 112 inch Panel lost none of its good looks in 1941. In fact, some think the minor styling changes made added to its charm. It came with tongue and groove hardwood flooring. The bodysides were double sealed at the floor. Strip felt was compressed between the outer side panel and the floor plank, then sheet rubber was cemented to the top of the floor plank and the inside of the side panel. The rear doors were rubber-sealed all around. An interior light, facing the load area, was standard.

I.D. DATA (112 Inch): See Sedan Delivery.

Model	Body Type	Price	Weight	Prod. Total
1NC	(80) Platform	640	2460	207
1GC	(80) Platform	640	2613	207
11C	(80) Platform	640	2630	207
1NC	(81) Chassis w/Cab	580	2146	5129
1GC	(81) Chassis w/Cab	580	2303	5129
11C	(81) Chassis w/Cab	580	2316	5129
1NC	(82) Panel	700	2738	11,183
1GC	(82) Panel	700	2871	11,183
11C	(82) Panel	700	2909	11,183
1NC	(83) Pickup	605	2483	70,190
1GC	(83) Pickup	605	2640	70,190
11C	(83) Pickup	605	2653	70,190
1NC	(84) Chassis w/Cowl	490	1813	876
1GC	(84) Chassis w/Cowl	490	1968	876
11C	(84) Chassis w/Cowl	490	1983	876
1NC	(85) Chassis w/Windshield	510	1840	280
1GC	(85) Chassis w/Windshield	510	1997	280
11C	(85) Chassis w/Windshield	510	2010	280
1NC	(86) Stake	660	2602	1529
1GC	(86) Stake	660	2758	1529
11C	(86) Stake	660	2772	1529

NOTE: Format: 4/6/V8. Price listed is for V8 models. Deduct $15 for Six, $20 for Four. Similar production totals indicate series total, not individual model output.

112 INCH ENGINE: See Sedan Delivery.

122 INCH ¾-TON EXPRESS: — Mild styling changes were made to the ¾-ton pickup. Among them were: Hub caps had the Ford name on them (this change was made during the model year, so some came with the old "V8" emblem); accent moldings placed around the hoodside louvers and the Ford nameplate placed slightly off-center on the louvers. Wider trim was used on the hood nose with the Ford name spelled out vertically on it. The wood floor was protected and interlocked by steel skid strips. The tailgate had truss-type rolled edge. The bodyside panels had smaller panels to increase rigidity. There were three stake pockets in each flare board.

122 INCH ¾-TON PANEL: — The ¾-ton Panel had tongue and groove hardwood flooring. The body sides were double sealed at the floor with felt and rubber. The roof rail, top and bodysides were welded together for greater rigidity and strength.

122 INCH ¾-TON PLATFORM/STAKE: — The ¾-ton Platform/Stake had a "bridge-like" platform frame. The floors were made of hardwood and were interlocked to the frame by steel skid strips. Platform sides and end were protected by the steel frame rail. The stake sockets were doubly reinforced. The stakes themselves were made of straight-grained hardwood. The rack boards were smoothly surfaced with rounded corners and edges.

I.D. DATA (¾-Ton): Same as Sedan Delivery except the letter code "Y" replaced "A" and "C".

Model	Body Type	Price	Weight	Prod. Total
1ND	(80) Platform	700	3087	274
1GD	(80) Platform	700	3087	274
11D	(80) Platform	700	3087	274
1ND	(81) Chassis w/Cab	645	2575	—
1GD	(81) Chassis w/Cab	645	2575	—
11D	(81) Chassis w/Cab	645	2575	—
1ND	(82) Panel	815	3364	1591
1GD	(82) Panel	815	3364	1591
11D	(82) Panel	815	3364	1591
1ND	(83) Pickup	710	3144	5084
1GD	(83) Pickup	710	3144	5084
11D	(83) Pickup	710	3144	5084
1ND	(84) Chassis w/Cowl	555	2245	—
1GD	(84) Chassis w/Cowl	555	2245	—
11D	(84) Chassis w/Cowl	555	2245	—
1ND	(85) Chassis w/Windshield	575	2272	—
1GD	(85) Chassis w/Windshield	575	2272	—
11D	(85) Chassis w/Windshield	575	2272	—
1ND	(86) Stake	725	3340	—
1GD	(86) Stake	725	3340	—
11D	(86) Stake	725	3340	—

NOTE: Format: 4/6/V8. Weight and price listed are for V8 model. Deduct $15 for Six, $6 for Four. Similar production totals indicate series total, not individual model output.

122 INCH ¾-TON ENGINE: See Sedan Delivery.

122 INCH 1-TON EXPRESS: Light-duty pickup truck buyers who wanted extra payload capacity choose the one-ton over the similar ¾-ton model. The floor planking was made of hardwood and interlocked by steel skid strips. The narrow wheel housings helped to maximize load width. The two-position tailgate had truss-type rolled edge. The bodyside panels had smaller panels to increase rigidity. There were three stake pockets in each flareboard. The seat was adjustable to three positions. It featured interlaced mattress-type springs and was upholstered with a durable, waterproof fabric.

122 INCH ONE-TON PANEL: Steel panels and hardwood boards protected the bodysides. The seasoned hardwood floor had evenly spaced steel skid strips. Side panels were double sealed at the floor with rubber and felt to exclude moisture and dust. The twin rear doors were hung in a rigid one-piece channel steel frame. They were rubber-sealed all around. An interior light was standard.

122 INCH ONE-TON PLATFORM/STAKE: The 1941 one-ton Platform/Stake resembled the previous year's model. But it came with an extended substructure and minus the sign panels. The wheels were equipped with full truck-type flat base rims. Steel skid strips were bolted to the cross girders of the platform frame. They interlocked the hardwood floor planking. Large pressed steel gussets were used to attach the platform frame to the bodysills. The ends of the bodysills were protected by strong steel caps, which were riveted to the frame rail and bolted to the sills. The stakes were made of straight-grained hardwood. The rack boards were smooth surfaced with rounded corners and edges.

I.D. DATA (122 Inch 1-Ton): See ¾-ton I.D.

1941 Ford V-8 Pickup (Dennis S. Olsen)

Model	Body Type	Price	Weight	Prod. Total
1NY	(80) Platform	735	3224	528
1GY	(80) Platform	735	3224	528
11Y	(80) Platform	735	3224	528
1NY	(81) Chassis w/Cab	680	2829	—
1GY	(81) Chassis w/Cab	680	2829	—
11Y	(81) Chassis w/Cab	680	2829	—
1NY	(82) Panel	850	3527	1222
1GY	(82) Panel	850	3527	1222
11Y	(82) Panel	850	3527	1222
1NY	(83) Pickup	745	3288	5317
1GY	(83) Pickup	745	3288	5317
11Y	(83) Pickup	745	3288	5317
1NY	(84) Chassis w/Cowl	590	2481	—
1GY	(84) Chassis w/Cowl	590	2481	—
11Y	(84) Chassis w/Cowl	590	2481	—
1NY	(85) Chassis w/Windshield	610	2526	—
1GY	(85) Chassis w/Windshield	610	2526	—
11Y	(85) Chassis w/Windshield	610	2526	—
1NY	(86) Stake	760	3477	1500
1GY	(86) Stake	760	3477	1500
11Y	(86) Stake	760	3477	1500

NOTE: Format: 4/6/V8. Weight and price for V8. Deduct $15 for Six, $6 for four. Similar production total indicates series total, not individual model output.

ENGINE (122 Inch One-Ton): See Sedan Delivery.

CHASSIS: (112 Inch Series and Sedan Delivery): Wheelbase: 112 in. Length: 178.67 in. (Sedan Delivery). 183.74 in. (Pickup). 195.45 in. (Panel). 189.6 in. (Platform/Stake). Width: 72.14 in. Height: 75.85 in. (Panel). 71.45 in. (Platform/Stake, Pickup). GVW: 4300. Tires: 6.00 x 16 in.

(122 Inch ¾ & One-Ton): Wheelbase: 122 in. Length: 201.84 in. (Platform/Stake). 203.34 in. (Pickup). 215.57 in. (Panel). Width: 73.62 in. (Panel, Pickup). 79.24 in. (Platform/Stake). Height: 82.64 in. (Panel). 76.2 in. (Pickup, Platform/Stake). GVW: 5400 lbs. (¾-ton). 6400 lbs. (one-ton). Tires: 6.00 x 17 six-ply front; 7.00 x 16 six-ply rear (¾-ton). 6.00 x 17 six-ply front; 7.00 x 17 six-ply rear (one-ton).

1941 Ford V-8 Pickup (OCW)

POWERTRAIN OPTIONS: 239 cu. in V-8. Heavy-duty four-speed manual transmission.

CONVENIENCE OPTIONS: Plated rear bumper. Passenger seat (Panel). Grille guard. Passenger side windshield wiper. Outside mounted spare tire. Spotlight. Fog lights (Sedan Delivery). Radio. Wheel trim rings. Heater. Locking gas cap. Cigar lighter (Sedan Delivery). WSW tires. Fender skirts. Right-hand sun visor. 7.00 x 17 or 7.50 x 17 eight-ply tires (one-ton). Two-piece sliding rear window (Pickup, Platform/Stake). Heavy-duty 11 inch clutch.

Pricing

	5	**4**	**3**	**2**	**1**
1941					
(112 in. w.b.) — (½-Ton)					
Sedan Delivery	2100	4200	7000	9800	14,000
Pickup	980	1950	3250	4550	6500
Panel	980	1950	3250	4550	6500
Stake	930	1860	3100	4350	6200
(122 in. w.b.) — (¾-Ton)					
Pickup	900	1800	3000	4200	6000
Panel	900	1800	3000	4200	6000
Stake	850	1700	2850	4000	5700
(122 in. w.b.) — (1-Ton)					
Pickup	870	1750	2900	4100	5800
Panel	870	1750	2900	4100	5800
Stake	830	1650	2750	3850	5500

1942 FORD

1942 Ford V-8 Deluxe Sedan Delivery (OCW)

SEDAN DELIVERY: — The Sedan Delivery was restyled for 1942. It had concealed runningboards. 1941 style front fenders. The grille had a narrow center section with vertical bars on either side. The parking lights were located above the painted grille frame. Super Deluxe models had a front bumper. A 120-amp hour battery. The Sedan Delivery could hold up to 92.5 cubic feet of cargo. The hardwood floor was protected by steel skid strips. The interior was fully lined and insulated. Trucks powered by a six had a 10 inch clutch. Those with V8s had a nine inch clutch.

I.D. DATA (Sedan Delivery): The VINs for 90 horsepower V-8 models ranged from 18-67969036 thru 18-6925898; for the 100 horsepower V8 models, 99A-46670 thru 99A-583000. Six-cylinder VINs were 1GC-34801 thru 1GC-227523.

Model	Body Type	Price	Weight	Prod. Total
2GA	(78) Sedan Dely.	825	3075	1316
21A	(78) Sedan Dely.	825	3075	1316
29A	(78) Sedan Dely.	825	3075	1316

NOTE: Model # format, 6/90 horsepower V8/100 horsepower V8. Weight and price for V8. Similar production totals indicate series total, not individual model output.

ENGINE (Sedan Delivery): Displacement: 225.8 cu. in. Six-cylinder. 90 horsepower at 3300 R.P.M. Bore & stroke: 3.3 in. x 4.4 in. Compression ratio: 6.7:1. 1-bbl. updraft carburetor. Or 221 cu. in. flathead V8, 90 horsepower at 3800 R.P.M. Bore & stroke: 3.19 in. x 3.75 in. Compression ratio: 6.2:1. 2-bbl. carburetor.

114 INCH PICKUP: — The '42 Ford ½-ton pickup featured new styling that was instantly recognizable. The front end now had a slightly protruding flat faced panel. It incorporated the headlights and the "waterfall" painted vertical bars grille. The Ford name was printed in molding on the face of the hood just above the grille. The parking lights were fender mounted near the headlights. There were louvers on the side of the hood. The Ford script on the hub caps was stylized a bit to give a "winged" effect. The spare tire was moved to the left-hand side of the truck. The gas filler pipe was in the tire's old position. The rectangular Shiftoguide speedometer indicated when to shift gears for greatest pulling ability and best economy. On the left of the speedometer were the fuel and temperature gauges; on the right, the oil pressure gauge and ammeter. The floor of the welded pickup body was steel, with strips stamped in. But there was a hardwood floor beneath. The pickup also had a new truck type chassis.

114 INCH PANEL: The restyled ½-ton panel had a lower floor, which gave it three inches more interior height than the '41 version. It had a new "straight rail" frame and truck type front suspension. Gas tank capacity was reduced from 19 gallons to 17 and the filler pipe was relocated to the left-hand side of the vehicle. Steel panels and hardwood boards were used on the interior to protect body sides. Steel skid strips were placed in the hardwood floors. The rear doors were rubber sealed all around.

112 INCH PLATFORM/STAKE: — As before, the ½-ton Platform/Stake had a hardwood platform with steel skid strips bolted to a frame girder. This helped keep the planks from spreading or warping. The one-piece side rack sections featured straight grained hardwood stakes and smooth surfaced rackboards. Steel interlocking plates held the racks together. Some new items included: Heavy-duty shock absorbers. Different runningboards. Rubber-cushioned rear engine mounts. A transverse steering tie rod and drag link.

I.D. DATA (114 Inch): Same as Sedan Delivery, plus four-cylinder VINs ranged from 9C-13201 on up.

1942 Ford V-8 Panel Delivery (OCW)

Model	Body Type	Price	Weight	Prod. Total
2NC	(80) Platform	720	2788	—
2GC	(80) Platform	7203	2788	—
21C	(80) Platform	720	2788	—
29C	(80) Platform	720	2788	—
2NC	(81) Chas. w/Cab	645	2455	—
2GC	(81) Chas. w/Cab	645	2455	—
21C	(81) Chas. w/Cab	645	2455	—
29C	(81) Chas. w/Cab	645	2455	—
2NC	(82) Panel	770	2999	—
2GC	(82) Panel	770	2999	—
21C	(82) Panel	770	2999	—
29C	(82) Panel	770	2999	—
2NC	(83) Pickup	675	2728	—
2GC	(83) Pickup	675	2728	—
21C	(83) Pickup	675	2728	—
29C	(83) Pickup	675	2728	—
2NC	(84) Chas. w/Cowl	555	2078	—
2GC	(84) Chas. w/Cowl	555	2078	—
21C	(84) Chas. w/Cowl	555	2078	—
29C	(84) Chas. w/Cowl	555	2078	—
2NC	(85) Chas. w/Windshield	740	2102	—
2GC	(85) Chas. w/Windshield	740	2101	—
21C	(85) Chas. w/Windshield	740	2102	—
29C	(85) Chas. w/Windshield	740	2101	—
2NC	(86) Stake	740	2923	—
2GC	(86) Stake	740	2923	—
21C	(86) Stake	740	2923	—
29C	(86) Stake	740	2923	—

NOTE: Model # format, 4/6/9 horsepower V8/10 horsepower V8. Weight & price for V8.

328

1942 Ford V-8 Stake Body Truck (DFW)

ENGINE (114 Inch): Same as Sedan Delivery plus: Displacement: 119.7 cu. in. L-Head Four. 30 horsepower at 2800 R.P.M. Bore & stroke: 3.19 in. x 3.75 in. Compression ratio: 6.0:1. Carburetor: one-barrel.

122 INCH ¾-TON EXPRESS: — The ¾-ton now shared basic styling with the ½-ton series. Aside from looks, it was pretty much the same as 1st year, altough it was about 3 in. wider. The floor planking was made of hardwood and interlocked by steel skid strips. The tailgate could be lowered flush with the floor, or swung all the way down. There were stake pockets in the flareboards for rack or side boards.

122 INCH ¾-TON PANEL: — From the drivers seat, the '42 ¾-ton Panel didn't seem all that much different from the '4a. The seat was a bit more comfortable, the interior was 2.5 in. wider, and the truck was about 2 in. longer. A three-speed manual was standard, except on 4-cyl. models. They cme with a four-speed manual. The hardwood floor had steel skid strips. The side panels were double sealed at the floor with felt and rubber. The rear doors were rubber sealed all around. The joints were waterproofed by sealing with a caulking compound.

122 INCH ¾-TON PLATFORM/STAKE: — The ¾-ton Platform/Stake had double insulated stake sockets welded to the inside of the frame rail and riveted to the outside. This helped to keep the rack sided from spreading when loads pressed against them. The stakes were made of straight-grained hardwood. The rackboards were smoothly surfaced with rounded corners and edges. Large steel interlocking plates were bolted to the corners of top rack boards.

I.D. DATA (112 Inch ¾-Ton): Same as the Sedan Delivery except the letter "Y" replaced letters "A" and "C".

Model	Body Type	Price	Weight	Prod. Total
2ND	(80) Platform	765	3114	119
2GD	(80) Platform	765	3114	119
21D	(80) Platform	765	3114	119
29D	(80) Platform	765	3114	119
2ND	(81) Chassis w/Cab	715	2656	—
2GD	(81) Chassis w/Cab	715	2656	—
21D	(81) Chas. w/Cab	715	2656	—
29D	(81) Chas. w/Cab	715	2656	—
2ND	(82) Panel	885	3403	2881
2GD	(82) Panel	885	3403	288
21D	(82) Panel	885	3403	288
29D	(82) Panel	885	3403	288
2ND	(83) Pickup	770	3209	1345
2GD	(83) Pickup	770	3209	1345
21D	(83) Pickup	770	3209	1345
29D	(83) Pickup	770	3209	1345
2ND	(84) Chas. w/Cowl	620	2279	—
2GD	(84) Chas. w/Cowl	620	2279	—
21D	(84) Chas. w/Cowl	620	2279	—
29D	(84) Chas. w/Cowl	620	2279	—
2ND	(85) Chas. w/Windshield	640	2302	—
2GD	(85) Chas. w/Windshield	640	2302	—
21D	(85) Chas. w/Windshield	640	2302	—
29D	(85) Chas. w/Windshield	640	2302	—
2ND	(86) Stake	790	3367	312
2GD	(86) Stake	790	3367	312
21D	(86) Stake	790	3367	312
29D	(86) Stake	790	3367	312

NOTE: Model # format, 4/6/90 horsepower V-8/100 horsepower V-8. Weight and price for V-8. Similar production totals indicate series total, not individual model output.

122 INCH ¾-TON ENGINE: See 112 Inch Series.

122 INCH 1-TON EXPRESS: The 1942 1-ton pickup came with a 19 gallon fuel tank (located under the seat), a rubber-cushioned rear engine mount, and a 10 in. clutch. It also had almost 2 in. more front overhang than the '41. The truss-type rolled edge tailgate could be lowered flush with the floor or placed fully down. The body side panels were stamped with smaller panels to increase rigidity. There were stake pockets in each flare-board for rack or side boards.

122 INCH 1-TON PANEL: The new 1-ton Panel was slightly bigger than last yearst model. Its twin rear doors were hung in a welded one-piece channel steel frame and rubber sealed all around. The drip mold was extended and welded to the roof rail. This assembly was then welded to the body side panel. The joints were waterproofed by sealing with a caulking compound. Steel skid strips were evenly spaced in the hardwood floors. The interior body sides were protected by steel panels and hardwood boards.

122 INCH 1-TON PLATFORM/STAKE: The 1-ton Platform/Stake body was identical to that of the ¾-ton Platform/Stake. However, its chassis was built to handle heavier loads. To make them easier to handle and reduce splintering, the rack boards were smooth surfaced and had rounded edges and corners. The hardwood floor planking was interlocked with steel skid strips. Pressed steel gussets were used to attach the platform frame to the body sills.

I.D. DATA (122 Inch 1-Ton): See ¾-ton.

1942 Ford V-8 Pickup (WAD/DFW)

Model	Body Type	Price	Weight	Prod. Total
2NY	(80) Platform	815	3246	50
2GY	(80) Platform	815	3246	50
21Y	(80) Platform	815	3246	50
29Y	(80) Platform	815	3246	50
2NY	(81) Chassis w/Cab	760	2897	—
2GY	(81) Chassis w/Cab	760	2897	—
21Y	(81) Chassis w/Cab	760	2897	—
29Y	(81) Chassis w/Cab	760	2897	—
2NY	(82) Panel	930	3561	385
2GY	(82) Panel	930	3561	385
21Y	(82) Panel	930	3561	385
29Y	(82) Panel	930	3561	385
2NY	(83) Pickup	815	3367	1574
2GY	(83) Pickup	815	3367	1574
21Y	(83) Pickup	815	3367	1574
29Y	(83) Pickup	815	3367	1574
2NY	(84) Chas. w/Cowl	665	2510	—
2GY	(84) Chas. w/Cowl	665	2510	—
21Y	(84) Chas. w/Cowl	665	2510	—
29Y	(84) Chas. w/Cowl	665	2510	—
2NY	(85) Chas. w/Windshield	685	2543	—
2GY	Chassis. w/Windshield	685	2543	—
21Y	(85) Chas. w/Windshield	685	2543	—
29Y	(85) Chas. w/Windshield	685	2543	—
2NY	(86) Stake	840	3499	378
2GY	(86) Stake	840	3499	378
21Y	(86) Stake	840	3499	378
29Y	(86) Stake	840	3499	378

NOTE: Model # format, 4/6/90 horsepower V8/100 horsepower V-8. Weight and price for V8. Similar production totals indicate series total, not individual model output.

CHASSIS (114 Inch Series and Sedan Delivery): Wheelbase: 122 in. Overall length: 194.3 in. (Sedan Delivery), Overall width: 72.14 in. (Pickup, Panel), 60.2 in. (Sedan Delivery). Overall height: 68.15 in. (Sedan Delivery), 71.45 in. (Pickup, Platform/Stake), 75.85 in. (Panel). GVW: 4300. Tirs: 6.00 x 16 in. 4-ply.

(122 Inch ¾- & 1-Ton): Wheelbase: 122 in. Overall width: 79.24 in. (Panel, Sedan), 73.62 in. (Pickup, Panel). GVW: 5400 (¾-ton), 6400 (1-ton). Tires: 6.00 x 16 6-ply.

1942 Ford V-8 Pickup (OCW)

POWERTRAIN OPTIONS: 100 horsepower 239 V-8. Four-speed manual. Heavy-duty 3-speed manual.

CONVENIENCE OPTIONS: Hot water heater. Rear shock absorbers. Plated rear bumper. Passenger seat (Panel). Grille guard. Passenger side windshield wiper. Outside mounted spare tire. Spotlight. Fog lights (Sedan Delivery). Radio. Locking gas cap. Cigar lighter (Sedan Delivery). WSW tires. RH sunvisor. Heavy-duty clutch.

Pricing

	5	4	3	2	1
1942					
(114 in. w.b.) — (½-Ton)					
Sedan Delivery	1950	3900	6500	9100	13,000
Pickup	980	1950	3250	4550	6500
Panel	950	1900	3150	4400	6300
Stake	870	1750	2900	4100	5800
(122 in. w.b.) — (¾-Ton)					
Pickup	900	1800	3000	4200	6000
Panel	870	1750	2900	4100	5800
Stake	840	1680	2800	3900	5600

1944 FORD

Pricing

	5	4	3	2	1
1944					
(114 in. w.b.) — (½-Ton)					
Pickup	980	1950	3250	4550	6500
Panel	950	1900	3150	4400	6300
Stake	870	1750	2900	4100	5800
(122 in. w.b.) — (¾-Ton)					
Pickup	900	1800	3000	4200	6000
Panel	870	1750	2900	4100	5800
Stake	840	1680	2800	3900	5600

1945 FORD

LIGHT-DUTY PICKUP: — The "waterfall" grille found on prewar Ford pickups was carried over on the new 1945 models. The biggest styling changes were: application of an accent color to the lamp bezels, grille and door handles; elimination of the contrasting paint from the nameplate on the hood's face and a larger outside rearview mirror. Some improvements were made to the chassis. Among them were a better steering gear mounting, universal joint grease fittings and wider frame rails. Because of the rubber shortage, a spare tire was not offered. However, if a buyer was lucky enough to find one, he or she mounted it on the side of the box between the cab and rear fender.

LIGHT-DUTY STAKE: — This model was not offered until later in the year. It shared the same styling and improvements as the pickup. The stakes and floors were made of hardwood. All light-duty Ford trucks were powered by the improved 100 horsepower flathead V-8.

1945 Ford Pickup (OCW)

I.D. DATA (Light-Duty): VIN began at 99C-623330.

Model	Body Type	Price	Weight	Prod. Total
59C	(83) Pickup	918	2865	19,706
59C	(81) Chassis w/Cab	888	2592	564
59C	(84) Chassis w/Cowl	—	—	—
59C	(85) Chasssis w/Wind-shield	—	—	—
59C	(86) Stake	—	3135	1442

ENGINE (Light-Duty): Displacement: 225.8 cu. in. L-Head V-8, 100 horse-power at 3800 R.P.M. Bore & stroke: 3-3/16 in. x 3¾ in. Compression ratio: 6.75:1. Two-barrel carburetor.

TONNER OPEN EXPRESS: — This light-duty pickup may have looked the same as the ½-ton, but it could haul a much bigger payload. Among the new standard equipment were a four-speed manual transmission and an 11 inch clutch.

TONNER STAKE: — Hardwood floors and stakes from Ford's own forests were used on these trucks. As on all Ford trucks of this vintage, the cab was very spratan. The 60 m.p.h. speedometer occupied the bulk of the rectangular instrument panel pod that included a fuel, temperature and oil gauges and an ammeter.

I.D. DATA: See Light-Duty.

Model	Body Type	Price	Weight	Prod. Total
59Y	(83) Pickup	—	—	—
5GY	(83) Pickup	—	—	—
59Y	(81) Chassis w/Cab	—	—	—
5GY	(81) Chassis w/Cab	—	—	—
59Y	(86) Stake	—	—	—
5GY	(86) Stake	—	—	—

NOTE: Model # format, V-8/6. A six was not even offered until late in the model year.

ENGINE (Tonner): Same as light-duty.

CHASSIS (Light-Duty): Wheelbase: 114 in. Overall width: 72.14 in. Overall height: 71.45 in. GVW: 4700. Tires: 6.50 x 16 six-ply.

CHASSIS (Tonner): Wheelbase: 122 in. Overall width: 73.62 in. (Pickup); 79.24 in. (Sedan Delivery). Overall height: 76.2 in. GVW: 6600. Tires: 7.00 x 17 six-ply front; 7.50 x 17 eight-ply rear.

POWERTRAIN OPTIONS: 226 cu. in. Six.

CONVENIENCE OPTIONS: Passenger side sunvisor. Heavy-duty battery. Heavy-duty generator. AM radio. Heater-defroster. Right-hand windshield wiper. Seat covers. Right-hand taillight.

NOTE: A 1945 Light-duty ½-ton pickup had the honor of being the 31,000,000th Ford built.

1946 Ford Sedan Delivery (DFW/J. Barton)

6½ FT. SEDAN DELIVERY: — This vehicle featured Deluxe passenger car styling. The two headlights were fender mounted. The grille consisted of three horizontal bars (with red indentations) protruding from the rectangular opening. The small rectangular parking lights were on the face of the hood. The instrument panel, hub caps, bumpers and front end ornamentation were also the same as the car's. Among the mechanical improvements for '46 were: self-centering brakes; improved springs and shocks; different transmission rear mount and heavy-duty voltage regulator.

½-TON/6½ FT. PICKUP: — If you liked the 1945 Ford ½-ton pickup, you'd like the '46. For all practical purposes they were almost identical. About the only changes were new (passenger car) hub caps and self-centering brakes. Late in the model year, its name was changed to 6½ ft. Pickup. The cab door molding grooves were painted cream. Aluminum pistons were used in the V8.

½-TON/6½ FT. STAKE: — This was basically the same truck offered in 1945. However, it and the other Ford trucks were now available in five colors: black, Greenfield green, light Moonstone gray, Modern blue and Vermilion. All were trimmed in Tacoma cream.

½-TON/7½ FT. PANEL: — Material shortages limited production of the ½-ton Panel. Unlike the Sedan Delivery, it shared styling and mechanical features with the rest of the truck line. Its hardwood floors had steel skid strips to make loading and unloading easier.

I.D. DATA (½-Ton): The VIN range on V-8 powered models was: 699C-62330 thru 699C-1343165. On six-cylinder models it was: 1GC-227524 thru 1GC-314949.

Model	Body Type	Price	Weight	Prod. Total
69C	(78) Sedan Delivery	1186	2978	3187
6GC	(78) Sedan Delivery	1186	2978	3187
69C	(80) Platform	—	—	—
6GC	(80) Platform	—	—	—
69C	(81) Chassis w/Cab	984	2626	4239
6GC	(81) Chassis w/Cab	984	2626	4239
69C	(82) Panel	1189	3238	5539
6GC	(82) Panel	1189	3238	5539
69C	(83) Pickup	1022	2966	75,088
6GC	(83) Pickup	1022	2966	75,088
69C	(84) Chassis w/Cowl	852	2276	1258
6GC	(84) Chassisw/Cowl	852	2276	1258
69C	(85) Chassisw/Windshield	883	2306	932
6GC	(85) Chassisw/Windshield	883	2306	932
69C	(86) Stake	1105	3086	2310
6GC	(86) Stake	1105	3086	2310

NOTE: Model # format, V-8/6-cyl. Weights and prices for V-8 models.

1946 Ford Pickup (DFW)

Pricing

	5	4	3	2	1
1945					
(114 in. w.b.) — (½-Ton)					
Pickup	980	1950	3250	4550	6500
Panel	950	1900	3150	4400	6300
Stake	870	1750	2900	4100	5800
(122 in. w.b.) — (¾-Ton)					
Pickup	900	1800	3000	4200	6000
Panel	870	1750	2900	4100	5800
Stake	840	1680	2800	3900	5600

1946 Ford Deluxe Pickup (R.S. Pasquerella)

ENGINE (½-Ton): Displacement: 239.4 cu. in. L-Head V-8. 100 horsepower at 3800 R.P.M. Bore & stroke: 3-3/16 in. x 3¾ in. Compression ratio: 6.75:1. 2-bbl. carburetor. Or 226 cu. in. L-Head Six. 95 horsepower at 3300 R.P.M. Bore & stroke: 3.3 in. x 3.4 in. Compression ratio: 6.2:1. 1-bbl. Holley carburetor.

TONNER/8 FT. EXPRESS: — The oversized wheel and tires of the 1945 "Tonner" (one-t on) were now optional. Otherwise, Ford's top light-duty pickup was basically unchanged for 1946.

TONNER/7½ FT. PLATFORM/STAKE: — This was essentially a carryover from the previous year. The main difference was that buyers now had a wider choice of exterior colors. The wheels and runningboards were black. The platform was made of hardwood.

TONNER/9 FT. PANEL: — The new Tonner Panel was the largest such vehicle offered by Ford in 1946. The hardwood floors had metal skid strips. A single driver's seat was standard.

I.D. DATA (Tonner): Same as on ½-ton except substitute the letter "Y" for "C".

Model	Body Type	Price	Weight	Prod. Total
69Y	(80) Platform	—	—	—
6GY	(80) Platform	—	—	—
69Y	(81) Chassis w/Cab	1150	3136	—
6GY	(81) Chassis w/Cab	1150	3136	—
69Y	(82) Panel	1248	3848	—
6GY	(82) Panel	1248	3848	—
69Y	(83) Pickup	1248	3606	—
6GY	(83) Pickup	1248	3606	—
69Y	(84) Chassis w/Cowl	1013	2776	—
6GY	(84) Chassis w/Cowl	1013	2776	—
69Y	(85) Chassis w/Windshield	—	—	—
6GY	(85) Chassis w/Windshield	—	—	—
69Y	(86) Stake	1270	3751	—
6GY	(86) Stake	1270	3751	—

NOTE: Format: 4/6/V8. Weight and price for V8. Deduct $15 for Six, $6 for four. Similar production total indicates series total, not individual model output.

ENGINE (Tonner): Same as ½-Ton.

CHASSIS (½-Ton): Wheelbase: 114 in. Overall width: 72.14 in. Overall height: 71.45 in. GVW: 4700. Tires: 6.50 x 16 (V-8); 6.00 x 16 in. front and 6.50 x 16 in. rear (6-cyl.).

CHASSIS (Tonner): Wheelbase: 122 in. GVW: 6600. Tires: 7.00 x 17 in. front, 7.50 x 17 in. rear.

CONVENIENCE OPTIONS: Passenger seat (Panel). Heavy-duty battery. Heavy-duty generator. AM radio. Right-hand windshield wiper. Heater-defroster. Seat covers. Right-hand taillight.

Pricing

	5	4	3	2	1
1946					
(114 in. w.b.) — (½-Ton)					
Sedan Delivery	1950	3900	6500	9100	13,000
Pickup	980	1950	3250	4550	6500
Panel	950	1900	3150	4400	6300
Stake	870	1750	2900	4100	5800
(122 in. w.b.) — (¾-Ton)					
Pickup	900	1800	3000	4200	6000
Panel	870	1750	2900	4100	5800
Stake	840	1680	2800	3900	5600

1947 Ford Pickup (A&A)

6½ FT. SEDAN DELIVERY: — The Sedan Delivery was the only 1947 Ford light-duty commercial vehicle to receive a facelift. It came in mid-model year and was rather mild. New, round parking lamps were located below the headlights. A medallion, on the face of the hood, identified whether the truck was powered by a six-cylinder or V8 engine. The grille bars were now smooth and most of the vertical identations on the trim piece above them were removed. The lines under the Ford nameplate ran horizontally, rather than vertically as before.

6½ FT. PICKUP: — The Ford ½-ton pickup was unchanged for 1947. Late in the model year, an all new six-cylinder engine was made available. However, according to Ford truck expert James Wagner, "it is doubtful that any trucks were built during 1947 incorporating it."

7½ FT. PANEL: — Although unchanged for 1947, the 7½-foot Panel was more popular than before. The main reason was increased availability of parts. This meant more could be produced for the truck-hungry postwar market.

6½ FT. PLATFORM/STAKE: — Hardwood floors and stakes were used on the unchanged 1947 Platform/Stake with 6½-foot bed. Black running-boards and wheels were standard.

I.D. DATA (6½ Ft.): V-8 engine VIN ranged from 799C-715264 thru 799C-2148508. 6-cyl. powered vehicles; 71GC-230698 thru 71GC-410109.

Model	Body Type	Price	Weight	Prod. Total
79C	(78) Sedan Delivery	1302	3164	3484
7GC	(78) Sedan Delivery	1302	3164	3484
79C	(80) Platform	—	—	Note
7GC	(80) Platform	—	—	Note
79C	(81) Chassis w/Cab	1098	2571	Note
7GC	(81) Chassis w/Cab	1098	2571	Note
79C	(82) Panel	1300	3183	Note
7GC	(82) Panel	1300	3183	Note
79C	(83) Pickup	1143	2921	Note
7GC	(83) Pickup	1143	2921	Note
79C	(84) Chassis w/Cowl	937	2221	Note
7GC	(84) Chassis w/Cowl	937	2221	Note
79C	(85) Chassis w/Windshield	—	—	Note
7GC	(85) Chassis w/Windshield	—	—	Note
79C	(86) Stake	1223	3021	Note
6GC	(86) Stake	1223	3021	Note

NOTE: Format, V8/6. Weight and prices for V8. Total ½-ton production for 1947 (*not* including Sedan Delivery) 62,072.

ENGINE (6½-Ton): Displacement: 239.4 cu. in. L-Head V-8. 100 horsepower at 3800 R.P.M. Bore & stroke: 3-3/16 in. x 3¾ in. Compression ratio: 6.2:1. Two-barrel carburetor. Or 226 cu. in. L-Head Six. 95 horsepower at 3300 R.P.M. Bore & stroke: 3.3 in. x 3.4 in. Compression ratio: 6.2:1. One-barrel carburetor.

8 FT. EXPRESS: — The 1947 8-Foot Express pickup was virtually the same as the '46. It was even offered in the same five colors: black, Greenfield green, light Moonstone gray, moden blue and vermilion. All were trimmed in Tacoma Cream.

9 FT. PANEL: — The hardwood floors of the one-ton Panel had metal skid strips. A single driver's seat was standard. Styling and other features were carried over from the previous model year.

7½ FT. PLATFORM/STAKE: — There was virtually no difference between the 1947 and 1946 one-ton 7½-foot Platform/Stake.

I.D. DATA (1-Ton): Same as on ½-ton, except substitute the letter "Y" for "C".

Model	Body Type	Price	Weight	Prod. Total
79Y	(80) Platform	—	—	Note
7GY	(80) Platform	—	—	Note
79Y	(81) Chassis w/Cab	1291	3148	Note
7GY	(81) Chassis w/Cab	1291	3148	Note
79Y	(82) Panel	1545	3848	Note
7GY	(82) Panel	1545	3848	Note
79Y	(83) Pickup	1390	3648	Note
7GY	(83) Pickup	1390	3648	Note
79Y	(84) Chassis w/Cowl	1130	2765	Note
7GY	(84) Chassis w/Cowl	1130	2765	Note
79Y	(85) Chassis w/Windshield	—		Note
7GY	(85) Chassis w/Windshield	—		Note
79Y	(86) Stake	1421	3748	Note
6GY	(86) Stake	1421	3748	Note

NOTE: Prices and weights for V8. Total one-ton production in 1947 was, 29,343.

ENGINE (1-Ton): Same as ½-ton.

CHASSIS (½-Ton): Wheelbase: 114 in. GVW: 4700. Tires: 6.00 x 16, four-ply; (Sedan Delivery) 6.50 x 16, six-ply.

CHASSIS (1-Ton): Wheelbase: 122 in. GVW: 6600. Tires: 7.00 x 17 six-ply front; 7.50 x 17 eight-ply rear.

CONVENIENCE OPTIONS: Passenger seat (Panel). Heavy-duty battery. Heavy-duty generator. AM radio. Right-hand windshield wiper. Heater-defroster. Seat covers.

Pricing

1947	5	4	3	2	1
(114 in. w.b.) — (½-Ton)					
Sedan Delivery	1950	3900	6500	9100	13,000
Pickup	980	1950	3250	4550	6500
Panel	950	1900	3150	4400	6300
Stake	870	1750	2900	4100	5800
(122 in. w.b.) — (¾-Ton)					
Pickup	900	1800	3000	4200	6000
Panel	870	1750	2900	4100	5800
Stake	840	1680	2800	3900	5600

1948 FORD

1948 Ford Deluxe Pickup (OCW)

F-1 PICKUP: — This was Ford's first really new postwar vehicle. The headlights were in the recessed, horizontal-bar pattern grille. The squared-off fenders and hood and new one-piece windshield contributed to a crisp, modern look. The spare tire was relocated to underneath the box. The new, all-steel "million dollar" cab was wider, longer and taller than before. It was also insulated from vibration and noise via a new cab suspension system. Rubber pads and rubber insulated bolts were used at the front corners and Lever Action links in torsion type rubber bushings were placed at each rear corner. Among the standard features were: extra large rear cab window; ash tray; glove compartment; cowl ventilator; air-wing ventilators; three-spoke 18-inch diameter steering wheel; Synchro-Silent three-speed manual transmission and black wheels and runningboards.

F-1 8 FT. PANEL: — The F-1 Panel shared the same attractive styling as the rest of the '48 truck-line. It had a larger load area than the Panel it replaced. The floors were solid plywood, with steel skid strips. To help keep out dust, fumes and moisture, weather sealing strips joined the floor to the side panel. The driver sat on a "Spiralounge" seat. It floated on variable-rate spiral coil springs adjustable to the driver's weight. An hydraulic shock absorber controlled movement of the seat and back. Two-position door checks held the twin, weather-sealed rear doors to either full or 90-degree opening. The runningboards were the same color as the body. A rear bumper was standard.

F-1 PLATFORM/STAKE: — The F-1 Platform/Stake had hardwood floors that were rabbeted and firmly interlocked. There were long-wearing steel skid strips. The stake racks were also made of hardwood. They had steel interlocking plates bolted on them to hold stake sections firmly. The frame, bumper and runningboards were black.

I.D. DATA (F-1): The VIN range for 6-cyl. models: 87HC-6911 thru 87HC-166979. For V-8 models: 88RC-101 thru 88RC-139262.

1948 Ford Panel Delivery (DFW/LS)

Model	Body Type	Price	Weight	Prod. Total
8HC	(80) Platform	1238	2986	Note
8RC	(80) Platform	1238	2986	Note
8HC	(81) Chassis w/Cab	1161	2680	Note
8RC	(81) Chassis w/Cab	1161	2680	Note
8HC	(82) Panel	1412	3256	Note
8RC	(82) Panel	1412	3256	Note
8HC	(83) Pickup	1232	3061	Note
8RC	(83) Pickup	1232	3061	Note
8HC	(84) Chassis w/Cowl	969	2251	Note
8RC	(84) Chassis w/Cowl	969	2251	Note
8HC	(85) Chassis w/Windshield	1000	2283	Note
8RC	(85) Chassis w/Windshield	1000	2283	Note
8HC	(86) Stake	1275	3126	Note
8RC	(86) Stake	1275	3126	Note

NOTE: Model # format, 6-cyl./V8. Weight and prices for V-8. Total 1948 F-1 production was 108,006.

ENGINE (F-1): Displacement: 2264 cu. in. L-Head Six. 95 horsepower at 3300 R.P.M. Bore & stroke: 3.3 in. x 3.4 in. Compression ratio: 6.2:1. 1-bbl. carburetor. Or 239.4 cu. in. L-Head V-8. 100 horsepower at 3800 R.P.M. Bore & stroke: 3-3/16 in. x 3¾ in. Compression ratio: 6.2:1. 2-bbl. carburetor.

F-2 8 FT. EXPRESS: — This was Ford's first ¾-ton since World War II. Larger tires, a 4.86:1 rear axle ratio, four-speed manual transmission, and rubber encased center bearing were a few things that set the F-2 apart from the ½-ton F-1. Like all '48 Ford light-duty trucks, toward the end of the model year, the chrome-plated grille bars were replaced with painted ones. Also, the bright finish vent window division bar was phased-out, for black painted ones, as the 1949 model year approached.

F-2 PLATFORM/STAKE: — The F-2 Platform/Stake could reportedly pull a 9.5 percent concrete grade in high gear and better than a 30 percent grade in first gear. Engine speed at 35 m.p.h. was 1,910 R.P.M. It had a load length of 90.3 in. and a load width of 74 in. The runningboards and bumper were black.

I.D. DATA (F-2): Same as F-1 except replace the letter "C" with "Y".

Model	Body Type	Price	Weight	Prod. Total
8HD	(80) Platform	1344	3493	Note
8RD	(80) Platform	1344	3493	Note
8HD	(81) Chassis w/Cab	1251	3099	Note
8RD	(81) Chassis w/Cab	1251	3099	Note
8HD	(83) Pickup	1362	3587	Note
8RD	(83) Pickup	1362	3587	Note
8HD	(84) Chassis w/Cowl	1059	2670	Note
8RD	(84) Chassis w/Cowl	1059	2670	Note
8HD	(85) Chassis w/Windshield	—		Note
8RD	(85) Chassis w/Windshield	—		Note
8HD	(86) Stake	1391	3683	Note
8RD	(86) Stake	1391	3683	Note

NOTE: Model # format, 6-cyl./V8. Prices for 6-cyl. (add $21 for V8). Weights for V8. Total F-2 production in 1948 was, 13,255.

ENGINE (F-2): Same as F-1.

F-3 EXPRESS: — Although called a "one-ton," the actural payload capacity of the F-3 pickup was nearer to 1½-tons. Typical equipment on this model included: three-spoke, 18 inch diameter steering wheel; double-acting shock absorbers on the front; cowl ventilation; 20-gallon fuel tank; spare wheel and tire; channel front bumper and jack and tool kit. The frame, wheels and runningboard were black.

F-3 PLATFORM/STAKE: — This model had hardwood floors rabbeted and firmly interlocked with steel skid strips. The stakes were also made of hardwood.

I.D. DATA (F-3): Same as F-2.

Model	Body Type	Price	Weight	Prod. Total
8HY	(80) Platform	1432	3706	Note
8RY	(80) Platform	1432	3706	Note
8HY	(81) Chassis w/Cab	1340	3310	Note
8RY	(81) Chassis w/Cab	1340	3310	Note
8HY	(83) Pickup	1451	3816	Note
8RY	(83) Pickup	1451	3816	Note
8HY	(84) Chassis w/Cowl	1158	2881	Note
8RY	(84) Chassis w/Cowl	1158	2881	Note
8HY	(85) Chassis w/Windshield	—	—	Note
8RY	(85) Chassis w/Windshield	—	—	Note
8HY	(86) Stake	1480	3926	Note
8RY	(86) Stake	1480	3926	Note

NOTE: Model # format, 6-cyl./V8. Prices and weights for V8. Total F-3 production in 1948 was 22,069.

ENGINE (F-3): Same as F-1.

CHASSIS (F-1): Wheelbase: 114 in. Overall length: 188.78 in. (Pickup); 202.13 in. (Panel); 195.96 in. (Platform/Stake). Overall width: 75.94 in. (Pickup); 75.62 in. (Panel); 71.28 in. (Platform/Stake). Overall height: 75.64 in. (Pickup, Platform/Stake); 79.18 in. (Panel). GVW: 4700. Tires: 6.00 x 16, four-ply.

CHASSIS (F-2 & F-3): Wheelbase: 122 in. Overall length: 206.96 in. (Pickup); 206.52 in. (Platform/Stake). Overall width: 75.94 in. (Pickup); 79.24 in. (Platform/Stake). Overall height: 76.52 in. (F-2), 77.42 in. (F-3). GVW: 5700 (F-2), 6800 (F-3). Tires: 6.50 x 16, six-ply. (F-2); 7.00 x 17 six-ply. (F-3).

POWERTRAIN OPTIONS: Heavy-duty three-speed transmission. Heavy-duty four-speed manual transmissions. 4.27:1 rear axle ratio.

CONVENIENCE OPTIONS: 11 in. clutch. Spiralounge bucket seat. Heavy-duty radiator. Magic Air heater-defroster. Recirculating heater-defroster. Automatic push-button tuning radio. 13 oz. nylon duck or a strong water-proofed fiber seat covers. Twin hi-way horns. Sealed beam spotlight. Sealed beam road lamps. Fire extinguisher. Reflector flare set. Grille guards. Automatic windshield washer (vacuum operated by touch of button). "See Clear" windshield washer (operated by foot plunger). Extension arm mirror. Front tow hooks. Illuminated cigar lighter. Leather door arm rest. Gas tank locking cap. Radiator over flow tank. Passenger side sunvisor. Right-hand windshield wiper. 7.00 x 16 in. and 7.5- x 16 in. tires (F-2). 7.50 x 17 in. tires (F-3).

Pricing

	5	4	3	2	1
1948					
F-1 — (½-Ton)					
Pickup	1000	2000	3300	4600	6600
Panel	980	1950	3250	4550	6500
Stake	900	1800	3000	4200	6000
F-2 — (¾-Ton)					
Pickup	900	1800	3000	4200	6000
Panel	890	1770	2950	4150	5900
Stake	810	1620	2700	3800	5400
F-3 — (1-Ton)					
Pickup	870	1750	2900	4100	5800
Panel	850	1700	2850	4000	5700
Stake	780	1560	2600	3600	5200

1949 FORD

F-1 6½ FT. PICKUP: — Body color-coordinated wheels and elimination of the red stripe on the grille bars were the two most noticeable styling changes for 1949. The interior featured an adjustable seat with thick rubberized hair padding, individually pocketed coil springs and scientifically designed cushion contours. A sun visor, glove compartment and ash tray were standard in, what sales literature called, Ford's "million dollar" truck cab. Level-Action cab suspension insulated the cab from frame weave, vibration and noise. The tailgate was strengthened with a tapered, truss-type rolled edge. Anti-rattle drop chains held the tailgate flush with the floor or let it drop all the way down. The "no-catch," rolled-edge flare boards strengthened the body and offered better sliding surface for objects loaded from the side. Stake pockets permitted mounting of uprights for special sides and tops. The runningboards and bumpers were painted black.

F-1 8 FT. PANEL: — The new F-1 Panel had solid plywood floors with steel skid strips. Weather-sealing strips joined the floor to the side panel. They helped keep out dust, fumes and moisture. The adjustable "Spiralounge" bucket driver's seat floated on a variable-rate, spiral coil spring, which was adjustable to the driver's weight. The weather-sealed rear doors were

hinged to a rugged, one-piece steel door frame. Two-position door checks held rear doors to either full or a 90 degree opening. The F-1 had a total capacity of 160.3 cubic feet. The runningboards were the same color as the truck.

F-1 6½ FT. PLATFORM/STAKE: — "The thrifty answer to loads that need headroom." So claimed sales literature for the '49 Ford F-1 Platform/Stake truck. This was especially true of those powered by the standard 95 horsepower six-cylinder engine. The F-1 Platform/Stake could carry a payload up to 1370 pounds. The floors and stake racks were made of select hardwood from Ford's own hardwood forests. The floors were rabbeted and firmly interlocked with steel skid strips. The frame, bumper and runningboards were painted black.

I.D. DATA (F-1): The VIN range for 6-cyl. models was 97HC-92251 and up. For V-8 models: 98RC-73088 and up.

1949 Ford Pickup (OCW)

Model	Body Type	Price	Weight	Prod. Total
9HC	(80) Platform	1338	2946	Note
9RC	(80) Platform	1338	2946	Note
9HC	(81) Chassis w/Cab	1224	2634	Note
9RC	(81) Chassis w/Cab	1224	2634	Note
9HC	(82) Panel	1504	3216	Note
9RC	(82) Panel	1504	3216	Note
9HC	(83) Pickup	1302	2998	Note
9RC	(83) Pickup	1302	2998	Note
9HC	(84) Chassis w/Cowl	1001	2205	Note
9RC	(84) Chassis w/Cowl	1001	2205	Note
9HC	(85) Chassis w/Windshield	1038	2237	Note
9RC	(85) Chassis w/Windshield	1038	2237	Note
9HC	(86) Stake	1375	3086	Note
9RC	(86) Stake	1375	3086	Note

NOTE: Model # format, 6-cyl./V8. Prices and weights for 6-cyl. Total F-1 production in 1949 was 104,803.

ENGINE (F-1): Displacement: 226 cu. in. L-Head Six. 95 horsepower at 3300 R.P.M. Bore & stroke: 3.3 in. x 3.4 in. Compression ratio: 6.8:1. 1-bbl. carburetor. Or 239.4 cu. in. L-Head V-8. 100 horsepower at 3800 R.P.M. Bore & stroke: 3-3/16 in. x 3¾ in. Compression ratio: 6.2:1. 2-bbl. carburetor.

F-2 8 FT. EXPRESS: — the F-2 ¾-ton pickup had a roomy, 96.05 inch long, 54 inch wide cargo box. It's payload capacity was 1,910 pounds (on 7.50 x 16, six-ply tires). The standard rear axle ratio was 4.86:1. A four-speed manual transmission was also standard. The front springs were shackled at the forward end for more stable steering. A U-type support helped relieve the radiator of road strains. The straight-through type muffler increased engine performance. The tire carrier was rear-mounted, under the frame. Rubber axle bumpers minimized shock of spring bottoming.

F-2 7½ FT. PLATFORM/STAKE: — Because of its slightly heavier body, the F-2 Platform/Stake had a payload capacity about 120 pounds less than the F-2 pickup. However, like the pickup, its frame, wheels bumper and runningboards were black. The hardwood floors were interlocked with steel skid strips.

1949 Ford F-1 Pickup (JLC)

Model	Body Type	Price	Weight	Prod. Total
9HD	(80) Platform	1461	3453	Note
9RD	(80) Platform	1461	3453	Note
9HD	(81) Chassis w/Cab	1345	3053	Note
9RD	(81) Chassis w/Cab	1345	3053	Note
9HD	(83) Pickup	1466	3555	Note
9RD	(83) Pickup	1466	3555	Note
9HD	(84) Chassis w/Cowl	1122	2624	Note
9RD	(84) Chassis w/Cowl	1122	2624	Note
9HD	(85) Chassis w/Windshield	1158	2656	Note
9RD	(85) Chassis w/Windshield	1158	2656	Note
9HD	(86) Stake	1507	3643	Note
9RD	(86) Stake	1507	3643	Note

NOTE: Model # format, 6-cyl./V8. Prices and weights for 6-cyl. Total F-2 production for 1949 was, 12,006.

ENGINE (F-2): Same as F-1.

F-3 8 FT. EXPRESS: — Standard features on the hefty F-3 one-ton pickup included: four-speed manual transmission; full-floating rear axle; double anchor type "feather foot" brakes; 20-gallon fuel tank; airplane type shock absorbers on the front axle; 17-inch disc wheels; 11-inch Gyro-Grip clutch; straight-through muffler. The frame, wheels, bumper and running-boards were black.

1949 Ford F-3 Platform Stake (DFW/ATHS)

F-3 7½ FT. PLATFORM/STAKE: — The F-3 Platform/Stake had a load capacity of about 2,700 pounds. That was just slightly less than the F-3 Express. Its hardwood floors were rabbeted and firmly interlocked with long wearing steel skid strips. The stakes were also made of hardwood.

F-3 PARCEL DELIVERY: — This new model was available in either 104 inch or 122 inch wheelbases. It was adaptable to many body styles. It had a large glass area which improved visiblity. The gearshift was column-mounted to maximize floor space. The low floor-to-ground height made it easier to load (and unload). The forepart of the engine was readily access-ible by removing the grille. The bulk of the engine was hidden under a hinged cover in the cab. A heavy-duty three-speed manual transmission was standard. The frame, wheels and bumper were black. The F-3 Parcel Delivery had bright metal grille bars. The headlights, parking lamps and nameplate had a bright finish. The adjustable, tilt-forward-type driver's seat had a folding back.

I.D. DATA (F-3): Same as F-2.

Model	Body Type	Price	Weight	Prod. Total
9HY	(80) Platform	1540	3706	Note
9RY	(80) Platform	1540	3706	Note
9HY	(81) Chassis w/Cab	1424	3260	Note
9RY	(81) Chassis w/Cab	1424	3260	Note
9HY	(83) Pickup	1545	3751	Note
9RY	(83) Pickup	1545	3751	Note
9HY	(86) Stake	1587	3896	Note
9RY	(86) Stake	1587	3896	Note
9HY	(84) Chassis w/Cowl	1201	2831	Note
9RY	(84) Chassis w/Cowl	1201	2831	Note
9HY	(85) Chassis w/Windshield	1238	2863	Note
9RY	(85) Chassis w/Windshield	1238	2863	Note
9HJ	(85) Chassis w/Front End	1120	2990	—
9H2J	Chassis w/Front End	1132	3060	—

NOTE: Prices and weight for 6-cyl. Total F-3 production for 1949 was 21,200.

CHASSIS (F-1): Wheelbase: 114 in. Overall length: 188.78 in. (Pickup); 202.13 in. (Panel) 195.96 in. (Platform/Stake). Overall width: 75.94 in. (Pickup); 75.62 in. (Panel); 71.28 in. (Platform/Stake). Overall height: 75.64 in. (Pickup, Platform/Stake); 79.18 in. (Panel). GVW: 4700. Tires: 6.00 x 16 four-ply.

CHASSIS (F-2 & F-3): Wheelbase: 122 in. or 104 in. (Panel Delivery). Overall length: 206.96 in. (Pickup); 206.52 in. (Platform/Stake). Overall width: 75.94 in. (Pickup); 79.24 in. (Platform/Stake). Overall height: 76.52 in. (F-2); 77.42 in. (F-3). GVW: 5700 (F-2); 6800 (F-3). Tires: 6.50 x 16 six-ply. (F-2); 7.00 x 17 six-ply. (F-3).

POWERTRAIN OPTIONS: Heavy-duty three-speed transmission. Heavy-duty four-speed manual transmission. 4.27:1 rear axle ratio.

CONVENIENCE OPTIONS: 11 in. clutch. Spiralounge bucket seat. Heavy-duty radiator. Magic Air heater-defroster. Recirculating heater-defroster. Automatic push-button tuning radio. 13 oz. nylon duck or strong water-proofed fiber seat covers. Twin hi-way horns. Sealed beam spot light. Sealed beam road lamps. Fire extinguisher. Reflector flare set. Grille guards. Automatic windshield washer (vacuum operated by touch of but-ton). "See Clear" windshield washer (operated by foot plunger). Extension arm mirror. Front tow hooks Illuminated cigar lighter. Leather door arm rest. Gas tank locking cap. Radiator over flow tank. Passenger side sunvi-sor. Right-hand windshield wiper. 7.00 x 16 in. and 7.50 x 16 in. tires (F-2). 7.50 x 17 in. tires (F-3).

Pricing

	5	4	3	2	1
1949					
F-1 — (½-Ton)					
Pickup	1000	2000	3300	4600	6600
Panel	980	1950	3250	4550	6500
Stake	900	1800	3000	4200	6000
F-2 — (¾-Ton)					
Pickup	900	1800	3000	4200	6000
Panel	890	1770	2950	4150	5900
Stake	810	1620	2700	3800	5400
F-3 — (1-Ton)					
Pickup	870	1750	2900	4100	5800
Panel	850	1700	2850	4000	5700
Stake	780	1560	2600	3600	5200

1950 FORD

1950 Ford F-1 Deluxe Pickup (OCW)

F-1 6½ FT. PICKUP: — This was a carbon copy of the previous year's model, although minor modifications were made to the engine. Late in the year, the shift lever for the standard three-speed manual transmission was moved from the floor to the column. Among standard features were: "No-Catch" rolled edge flareboards on the 45 cubic foot box; removable brake drums; two-position tailgate; semi-floating hypoid rear axle; all-steel floor with hardwood sub-floor to minimize denting; "Fingertip" control adjust-able seat with thick rubberized hair padding; twenty gallon fuel tank; sunvi-sor; extra large rear cab window; ashtray; glove compartment; black run-ningboards; three-spoke, 18 inch diameter steering wheel and straight through type muffler.

F-1 8 FT. PANEL: — The unchanged 8-foot Panel featured the following: Solid plywood floor with steel skid strips; sealed-tight joining of floor to side panels (with weather sealing strips to help exclude dust, fumes, mois-ture); bucket type driver's seat which floated on a variable rate spiral coil spring adjustable to the driver's weight (An hydraulic shock absorber con-troled movement of seat and back) and two-position door checks to hold the twin, weather-sealed rear doors to either full or 90 degree opening. The all-steel welded body featured heavy-gauge side and roof panels and a sturdy steel frame with reinforcing brackets. The runningboards were the same color as the truck.

F-1 6½ FT. PLATFORM/STAKE: — The F-1 Platform/Stake was carried over from the previous year. Its hardwood floors were rabbeted and firmly interlocked with long wearing steel skid strips. Floors and stake racks fea-tured select hardwood from Ford's own forests. Steel interlocking plates, bolted to hardwood rack boards, held stake sections firmly. The loading height was a low 32 inches from ground to floor (with 6.50 x 16 inch tires). An adjustable bench seat was standard, but the Spiralounge bucket seat was available. The runningboards were black.

1950 Ford F-2 Pickup (OCW)

I.D. DATA (F-1): The 1950 VIN range continued from 1949.

Model	Body Type	Price	Weight	Prod. Total
9HC	(80) Platform	1302	2975	127
9RC	(80) Platform	1302	2975	127
9HC	(81) Chassis w/Cab	1188	2645	3935
9RC	(81) Chassis w/Cab	1188	2645	3935
9HC	(82) Panel	1458	3195	22,421
9RC	(82) Panel	1458	3195	22,421
9HC	(83) Pickup	1256	3025	148,956
9RC	(83) Pickup	1256	3025	148,956
9HC	(84) Chassis w/Cowl	965	2145	652
9RC	(84) Chassis w/Cowl	965	2145	652
9HC	(85) Chassis w/Windshield	1002	2237	1343
9RC	(85) Chassis w/Windshield	1002	2237	1343
9HC	(86) Stake	1338	3095	2259
9RC	(86) Stake	1338	3095	2259

NOTE: Format: 4/6/V8. Weight and price for V8. Deduct $15 for Six, $6 for four. Similar production total indicates series total, not individual model output.

ENGINE (F-1): See 1949 F-1 engine.

F-2 8 FT. EXPRESS: — Like the F-1, the F-2 was the same as last year. It came with a four-speed manual transmission; Gyro-Grip 11-inch clutch and full-floating rear axle. The pickup box was 96.05 inches long, 54 inches wide, 21.7 inches high and had a two-position tailgate. It was just over 25 inches from the floor to the ground. This made loading (and unloading) easier. The cab came with the same features as the F-1 including the standard 60 m.p.h. speedometer and oil, fuel, temperature and battery gauges.

F-2 7½ FT. PLATFORM/STAKE: — The F-2 Platform/Stake could carry over 500 pounds more payload than the F-1. And its standard four-speed manual offered extra pulling power in first gear. It had hardwood floors and stakes. The F-2's ground to floor height was 35.14 inches. The runningboards and bumper were black. The spare tire carrier was rear mounted under the frame.

I.D. DATA (F-2): See F-1.

Model	Body Type	Price	Weight	Prod. Total
9HD	(80) Platform	1398	3450	105
9RD	(80) Platform	1398	3450	105
9HD	(81) Chassis w/Cab	1293	3040	2207
9RD	(81) Chassis w/Cab	1293	3040	2207
9HD	(83) Pickup	1383	3520	21,464
9RD	(83) Pickup	1383	3520	21,464
9HD	(84) Chassis w/Cowl	1070	2550	138
9RD	(84) Chassis w/Cowl	1070	2550	138
9HD	(85) Chassis w/Windshield	—	2572	112
9RD	(85) Chassis w/Windshield	—	2572	112
9HD	(86) Stake	1455	3640	1545
9RD	(86) Stake	1455	3640	1545

NOTE: Format: 4/6/V8. Weight and price for V8. Deduct $15 for Six, $6 for four. Similar production total indicates series total, not individual model output.

ENGINE (F-2): Same as F-1.

F-3 8 FT. EXPRESS: — This was, indeed, the "light-duty truck for big truckloads." It could carry a payload almost twice that of the F-1. Among the standard features were: four-speed manual transmission; 10-inch clutch; extra-large 14 x 2 inch rear brakes; full floating rear axle with load free axle shafts; 17 inch disc wheels with advanced two-piece, wide-base rims; I-beam axle designed for fore and aft steering and telescopic shock absorbers. A channel bumper was attached directly to the extended frame. Other features included a rubber encased center bearing; needle bearing universal joints; Loadomatic ignition with full-automatic vacuum controlled distributor; 20-gallon fuel tank and three-spoke, 18 inch diameter steering wheel.

F-3 7½ FT. PLATFORM/STAKE: — The F-3 Platform/Stake was also capable of fairly heavy-duty chores. In high gear, the F-3 equipped with a 4.86:1 axle pulled its GVW up a seven percent smooth concrete grade. In first gear, a grade well over 30 percent could be handled. Engine speed, at 35 m.p.h., was an economical 1770 R.P.M. (with standard 4.86 axle). Its hardwood floors were rabbeted and firmly interlocked with long wearing steel skid strips. The stakes were also made of select hardwoods. The frame, wheels, bumper and runningboards were black.

F-3 PARCEL DELIVERY: — A column-shifted, heavy-duty three-speed manual transmission, 17 gallon fuel tank, bright grille bars and a six-cylinder engine were standard in the 1950 Parcel Delivery. The adjustable, tilt-forward type driver's seat had a folding back. The engine was "hidden" under a hinged cover in the cab. As in 1949, it was offered in two wheelbases, 104 or 122 inches.

I.D. DATA (F-3): See F-1 I.D.

Model	Body Type	Price	Weight	Prod. Total
9HY	(80) Platform	1488	3680	131
9RY	(80) Platform	1488	3680	131
9HY	(81) Chassis w/Cab	1382	3270	3028
9RY	(81) Chassis w/Cab	1382	3270	3028
9HY	(83) Pickup	1472	3770	20,446
9RY	(83) Pickup	1472	3770	20,446
9HY	(84) Chassis w/Cowl	1159	2780	2917
9RY	(84) Chassis w/Cowl	1159	2780	2917
9HY	(85) Chassis w/Windshield	1196	2812	568
9RY	(85) Chassis w/Windshield	1196	2812	568
9HY	(86) Stake	1545	3870	1992
9RY	(86) Stake	1545	3870	1992

NOTE: Format: 4/6/V8. Weight and price for V8. Deduct $15 for Six, $6 for four. Similar production total indicates series total, not individual model output.

1950 Ford Ranger 4x4 Carryall (FMC)

ENGINE (F-3): Same as F-1.

CHASSIS (F-1): Wheelbase: 114 in. Overall length: 188.78 in. (Pickup); 202.13 in. (Panel); 195.96 in. (Platform/Stake). Overall width: 75.94 in. (Pickup); 75.62 in. (Panel); 71.28 in. (Platform/Stake). Overall height: 75.64 in. (Pickup, Platform/Stake); 79.18 in. (Panel). GVW: 4700. Tires: 6.00 x 16, four-ply.

CHASSIS (F-2 & F-3): Wheelbase: 122 in. Overall length: 206.96 in. (Pickup); 206.52 in. (Platform/Stake). Overall width: 75.94 in. (Pickup); 79.24 in. (Platform/Stake). Overall height: 76.52 in. (F-2); 77.42 in. (F-3). GVW: 5700 (F-2); 6800 (F-3). Tires: 6.50 x 16, six-ply (F-2); 7.00 x 17, six-ply. (F-3).

POWERTRAIN OPTIONS: Heavy-duty three-speed/heavy-duty four-speed manual transmissions. 4.27:1 rear axle ratio.

CONVENIENCE OPTIONS: 11 inch clutch. Spiralounge bucket seat. Heavy-duty radiator. Magic Air heater-defroster. Recirculating heater-defroster. Automatic push button tuning radio. 13 oz. nylon duck or a strong waterproofed fiber seat covers. Twin hi-way horns. Sealed beam spot light. Sealed beam road lamps. Fire extinguisher. Reflector flare set. Grille guards. Automatic windshield washer (vacuum operated by touch of button). "See Clear" windshield washer (operated by foot plunger). Extension arm mirror. Front tow hooks Illuminated cigar lighter. Leather door arm rest. Gas tank locking cap. Radiator over flow tank. Passenger side sunvisor. Right-hand windshield wiper. 7.00 x 16 and 7.50 x 16 tires (F-2). 7.50 x 17 tires (F-3).

NOTE: Color choices for 1950 included: Black, Meadow Green, Palisade Green, Sheridan Blue, Silvertone Gray, Vermilion.

Pricing

	5	4	3	2	1
1950					
F-1 — (½-Ton)					
Pickup	1000	2000	3300	4600	6600
Panel	980	1950	3250	4550	6500
Stake	900	1800	3000	4200	6000
F-2 — (¾-Ton)					
Pickup	900	1800	3000	4200	6000
Panel	890	1770	2950	4150	5900
Stake	810	1620	2700	3800	5400
F-3 — (1-Ton)					
Pickup	870	1750	2900	4100	5800
Panel	850	1700	2850	4000	5700
Stake	780	1560	2600	3600	5200

1951 FORD

1951 Ford F-1 Pickup (OCW)

F-1 6½ FT. PICKUP: — Ford restyled its light-duty trucks for 1951. They now had a wider, single bar grille with headlight pods at each end. A "Dagmar" was located at the grille's center and to each side. At the upper border of the grille were three rectangular open slots. This theme was echoed on the face of the hood, just below the Ford name. Spear shaped trim was placed on the sides of the hood. There was also a new, ribbed bumper. Among standard features were: an improved, column mounted three-speed manual transmission; larger rear window; dual windshield wipers; a new box (with straight sided corner pillars); a steel floor and level opening tailgate and a 3.92:1 base rear axle gear ratio. There was 45 cubic foot load capacity in the box.

F-1 8 FT. PANEL: — The new F-1 Panel shared many of the same features as the pickup, including a new instrument panel. A single bucket type driver' seat and twin rear doors were standard. The floor was solid plywood with steel skid strips. It could haul payloads up to 1330 pounds.

F-1 8 FT. DELUXE PANEL: — Panel buyers who wanted something with a little fancier, could order the new Deluxe model. It had a full length glass wool headliner and the interior walls were lined with Masonite. Plus it came with most of the other "Five Star Extra" cab features. This included distinctive "missle" style ornaments on the sides of the hood.

F-1 6½ FT. PLATFORM/STAKE: — As before, the Platform/Stake had hardwood floors with steel skid strips. The removable stake racks were made of straight grained wood. There was a steel rub rail around the platform, with steel caps on the ends of the body sills. Pockets were flush with the floor, welded to the inside of the frame rail and riveted to the outside. Load space was 84.3 inches long (80 inches with stakes) and 71.28 inches wide (67 inches with stakes). The stakes were 29.54 inches high.

I.D. DATA (F-1): VIN range was, Six: F1H1 (2-letter plant code) 10,001 and up. V-8: F1R1 (2-letter plant code) 10,001 and up. The plant codes were: AT = Atlanta. BF = Buffalo. CH = Chicago. CS = Chester (PA). DL = Dallas. EG = Edgewater (NJ). HM = Highland Park (MI). KC = Kansas City (MO). LB = Long Beach. LU = Louisville. MP = Memphis. NR = Norfolk. RH = Richmond (CA). SP = St. Paul (MN). SR = Somerville (MA).

Model	Body Type	Price	Weight	Prod. Total
1HC	(80) Platform	—	2975	85
1RC	(80) Platform	—	2975	85
1HC	(81) Chassis w/Cab	—	2645	4083
1RC	(81) Chassis w/Cab	—	2645	4083
1HC	(82) Panel	—	3195	14,940
1RC	(82) Panel	—	3195	14,940
1HC	(82B) Panel	—	—	2326
1RC	(82B) Panel	—	—	2326
1HC	(83) Pickup	—	3025	117,414
1RC	(83) Pickup	—	3025	117,414
1HC	(84) Chassis w/Cowl	—	2145	371
1RC	(84) Chassis w/Cowl	—	2145	371
1HC	(85) Chassis w/Windshield	—	—	1007
1RC	(86) Chassis w/Windshield	—	3095	1442

NOTE: Format: 4/6/V8. Weight and price for V8. Deduct $15 for Six, $6 for four. Similar production total indicates series total, not individual model output.

ENGINE (F-1): See 1949 F-1 engine.

F-2 8 FT. EXPRESS: — A couple new features added during the model run on F-2 trucks were: 12 x 2 inch self-energizing front and rear brakes and a drum-type, driveshaft-mounted parking brake. Like the F-1, the F-2 pickup had a new box with straight sided corner pillars. Dual windshield wipers were now standard.

F-2 7½ FT. PLATFORM/STAKE: — The power plants of F-2 Platform/Stake were improved for the new model year, although their horsepower rating remained the same. The six-cylinder had a new water pump, level mounted manifold, heavier walled main bearings, aluminum timing gear, revised camshaft and a new torsional damper. The V-8 had a new camshaft, water pump and offset piston pins.

I.D. DATA (F-2): Same as F-1 except the first two characters are "F2".

Model	Body Type	Price	Weight	Prod. Total
1HD	(80) Platform	—	3450	78
1RD	(80) Platform	—	3450	78
1HD	(81) Chassis w/Cab	—	3040	1494
1RD	(81) Chassis w/Cab	—	3040	1494
1HD	(83) Pickup	—	3520	17,485
1RD	(83) Pickup	—	3520	17,485
1HD	(84) Chassis w/Cowl	—	2550	157
1RD	(84) Chassis w/Cowl	—	2550	157
1HD	(85) Chassis w/Windshield	—	—	216
1RD	(85) Chassis w/Windshield	—	—	216
1HD	(86) Stake	—	3640	1039
1RD	(86) Stake	—	3640	1039

NOTE: Format: 4/6/V8. Weight and price for V8. Deduct $15 for Six, $6 for four. Similar production total indicates series total, not individual model output.

ENGINE (F-2): See F-1.

F-3 8 FT. EXPRESS: — The F-3 remained the biggest pickup in Ford's light-duty truck line up. It shared styling with the others and like the F-2, received new front and rear brakes and a driveshaft-mounted parking brake, during the model year. Those equipped with a V-8 engine had a V-8 emblem above the grille.

F-3 7½ FT. PLATFORM/STAKE: — Ford's most popular light-duty stake truck in 1951 was the F-3. The increased fuel economy of available engines added to the appeal of this sturdy vehicle. As before, the wood stake sides could be snuggley locked to hold the racks firmly in place.

F-3 PARCEL DELIVERY: — The '51 Parcel Delivery had round parking lamps and a new grille that was very similar to that used on other light-duty Ford trucks.

I.D. DATA (F-3): Same as F-1 except the first two character were "F3".

Model	Body Type	Price	Weight	Prod. Total
1HY	(80) Platform	—	3680	96
1RY	(80) Platform	—	3680	96
1HY	(81) Chassis w/Cab	—	3270	2949
1RY	(81) Chassis w/Cab	—	3270	2949
1HY	(83) Pickup	—	3770	19,848
1RY	(83) Pickup	—	3770	19,848
1HY	(84) Chassis w/Cowl	—	2780	932
1RY	(84) Chassis w/Cowl	—	2780	932
1HY	(85) Chassis w/Windshield	—	—	454
1RY	(86) Chassis w/Windshield	—	3870	1667

NOTE: Format: 4/6/V8. Weight and price for V8. Deduct $15 for Six, $6 for four. Similar production total indicates series total, not individual model output.

ENGINE (F-3): See F-1.

CHASSIS: Same as 1950.

POWERTRAIN OPTIONS: Heavy-duty three-speed/heavy-duty four-speed manual transmissions. 4.27:1 and 4.09:1 rear axle ratios.

CONVENIENCE OPTIONS: Spiralounge bucket seat. Heavy-duty radiator. Magic Air heater-defroster. Radio. Seat covers. Twin horns. Sealed beam spot light. Fire extinguisher. Grille guards. Windshield washer. Gas tank locking cap. 11 in. clutch. Heavy-duty fan. Right-hand rear taillight. Rear bumper. Electric windshield wipers.

FIVE STAR EXTRA PACKAGE: Dome light with door switches. Deluxe door trim. Chromed windshield molding. Dual horns. Foam rubber seat padding. Vinyl and mohair seat upholstery. Extra sound insulation. Cigarette lighter. (On panel this package included: an auxiliary seat with two-tone upholstery, plus heavy masonite lining above and perforated headlining on roof panel, backed by thick glass wool insulating pad.)

NOTE: Colors offered for 1951 were: Alpine Blue, Black, Meadow Green, Sea Island Green, Sheridan Blue, Silvertone Gray and Vermilion.

Pricing

1951	5	4	3	2	1
F-1 — (½-Ton)					
Pickup	1010	2030	3350	4700	6700
Panel	1000	2000	3300	4600	6600
Stake	920	1850	3050	4300	6100
F-2 — (¾-Ton)					
Pickup	920	1850	3050	4300	6100
Panel	900	1800	3000	4200	6000
Stake	830	1650	2750	3850	5500
F-3 — (1-Ton)					
Pickup	890	1770	2950	4150	5900
Panel	870	1750	2900	4400	5800
Stake	800	1600	2650	3700	5300

1952 FORD

COURIER CUSTOM SEDAN DELIVERY: — The new Courier Sedan Delivery was based on the Ford Ranch Wagon. It shared its attractive exterior styling with the passenger car line. The grille had a three-bladed round spinner in its center. The circular, fender-mounted parking lights were located under the recessed style headlights. The Ford emblem was centered on the face of the hood. There were simulated scoops on the rear quarter panels. Tube-like round taillights protruded from the rear fenders. The interior featured a headlining, foam padded vinyl covered driver's seat and gray masonite interior wall liners. Buyers had their choice of 10 colors.

I.D. DATA (Courier): VIN began at A2 (Plant Code) 100,001 and up. V-8 powered models started with "B2" instead of "A2".

Model	Body Type	Price	Weight	Prod. Total
—	Sedan Delivery	1539	3109	—

ENGINE (Courier): Displacement: 215 cu. in. OHV Six-cylinder, 101 horsepower at 3500 R.P.M. Compression ratio: 7.0:1. One-barrel carburetor. Or 239 cu. in. L-Head V-8, 110 horsepower at 3800 R.P.M. Bore & stroke: 3.19 in. x 3.75 in. Compression ratio: 7.2:1. Two-barrel carburetor.

F-1 6½ FT. PICKUP: — Ford trucks received a minor facelift for '52. The molding on the face of the hood was now painted. The word Ford was spelled out above the grille opening panel. The grille was now painted white. The hood side "spears" were altered. They now featured a small circular emblem toward the tip which included the F-1 insignia in red. The front fender braces, used for the last 10 years, were eliminated. Among standard equipment was: Column mounted three-speed manual transmission; dual windshield wipers; steel-floored box with level opening tailgate and 90 Amp-hour battery.

F-1 8 FT. PANEL: — The F-1 Panel's floor was made of solid plywood with steel skid strips. A single bucket type driver's seat and twin rear doors were standard. The bezel on the taillight lenses was eliminated in midyear.

1952 Ford F-1 Deluxe Pickup (OCW)

F-1 8 FT. DELUXE PANEL: — In addition to the styling changes found on all Ford trucks, the Deluxe Panel came with features found in the "Five Star Extra" option. One such item was chrome extentions on the side of the hood, from the F-1 insignia toward the cab.

F-1 6½ FT. PLATFORM/STAKE: — Aside from the mild facelift, there was little difference between this year's model and last. The wood side racks were removable. The platform was made of hardwood with a steel skid strips.

I.D. DATA (F-1): See 1951 F-1 I.D. For '52, the first four characters are Six: F2D2. V-8: F2R2.

Model	Body Type	Price	Weight	Prod. Total
F-1	(80) Platform	1465	2940	19
F-1	(81) Chassis w/Cab	1339	2610	2844
F-1	(82) Panel	1647	3160	6565
F-1	(82B) Panel	—	—	1611
F-1	(83) Pickup	1425	2990	81,537
F-1	(84) Chassis w/Cowl	1088	2110	287
F-1	(85) Chassis w/Windshield	—	—	252
F-1	(86) Stake	1505	3060	1033

NOTE: Prices and weights for 6-cyl.

ENGINE (F-1): six, same as Courier. V-8 had 106 horsepower at 3500 R.P.M. Compression ratio: 6.8:1.

F-2 8 FT. EXPRESS: — The F-2 pickup shared the minor styling changes found on the F-1. It, too, was basically the same as the 1951 model.

F-2 7½ FT. PLATFORM/STAKE: — As before, this model was a slightly heavier-duty version of its F-1 counterpart.

I.D. DATA (F-2): See F-1 I.D.

Model	Body Type	Price	Weight	Prod. Total
F-2	(80) Platform	1610	3400	28
F-2	(81) Chassis w/Cab	1487	2990	1121
F-2	(83) Pickup	1594	3470	15,136
F-2	(84) Chassis w/Cowl	1234	2500	276
F-2	(85) Chassis w/Windshield	—	—	233
F-2	(86) Stake	1668	3590	785

NOTE: Prices and weights are for 6-cyl.

ENGINE (F-2): See F-1.

F-3 8 FT. EXPRESS: — This pickup was built for maximum light-duty hauling. It had a GVW rating over 2000 pounds greater than the F-1.

F-3 7½ FT. PLATFORM/STAKE: — Except for a minor facelift, the F-3 was the same as last year.

I.D. DATA (F-3): See F-1 I.D.

Model	Body Type	Price	Weight	Prod. Total
F-3	(80) Platform	1714	3645	37
F-3	(81) Chassis w/Cab	1584	3225	1731
F-3	(83) Pickup	1702	3725	15,771
F-3	(84) Chassis w/Cowl	1329	2735	590
F-3	(85) Chassis w/Windshield	—	—	204
F-3	(86) Stake	1766	3825	1658

NOTE: Prices and weight are for 6-cyl.

ENGINE (F-3): Same as F-1.

CHASSIS: Same as 1951. Sedan Delivery wheelbase: 115 in. Overall length: 197.8 in. Overall width: 73.2 in. Tires: 6.00 x 16 in.

POWERTRAIN OPTIONS: Three-speed manual with overdrive/heavy-duty three-speed manual or heavy-duty four-speed manual transmissions.

CONVENIENCE OPTIONS: Grille guard. Windshield washer. Heater-defroster. Heavy-duty battery. Rear bumper. Radio. Right-hand sunvisor. Turn signals. Seat covers. Fire extinguisher.

FIVE STAR EXTRA CAB: Dome light. Glove box lock. Locks for both doors. Deluxe door trim. Chrome windshield molding. Two-tone upholstery. Foam rubber seat padding. Right-hand and left-hand sunvisors.

NOTE: Color choices for 1952 included: Black, Glen Mist Green, Meadow Green, Sheridan Blue, Sandpiper Tan, Vermilion and Woodsmoke Gray.

Pricing

	5	4	3	2	1
1952					
Courier					
Sedan Delivery	1050	2100	3500	4900	7000
F-2 — (½-Ton)					
Pickup	1010	2030	3350	4700	6700
Panel	1000	2000	3300	4600	6600
Stake	920	1850	3050	4300	6100
F-2 — (¾-Ton)					
Pickup	920	1850	3050	4300	6100
Panel	900	1800	3000	4200	6000
Stake	830	1650	2750	3850	5500
F-3 — (1-Ton)					
Pickup	890	1770	2950	4150	5900
Panel	870	1750	2900	4400	5800
Stake	800	1600	2650	3700	5300

1953 FORD

COURIER CUSTOM SEDAN DELIVERY: — The Courier received a minor facelift for 1953. Rectangular parking lights were seen between the front bumper and wraparound center grille bar. A spinner was located in the middle of the bar with vertical stripes on either side of it. There was also a new hood ornament and improved front suspension. The cooling system capacity of V-8 powered models was increased. The interior featured a headliner, foam padded vinyl covered driver's seat, Golden Anniversary horn button, and masonite interior wall liners. A three-speed manual transmission was standard.

I.D. DATA (Courier): Same as 1952 except for the first two characters. They were now, for 6-cyl.: A3. V-8: B3.

Model	Body Type	Price	Weight	Prod. Total
—	Sedan Delivery	1515	3109	—

1953 Ford Courier Anniversary Sedan Delivery

ENGINE (Courier): Same as 1952.

1953 Ford F-100 Anniversary Pickup (OCW)

F-100 6½ FT. PICKUP: — The F-100 was introduced on March 13, 1953. It had a sleeker, more modern look than last year's model. The Ford emblem was on the face of the wider hood. Chrome trimmed headlight pods were recessed and connected to the new two-bar grille. The grille had a section in the center for the engine emblem and (on Deluxe models) three vertical chrome "teeth" on either side. The wider seat had "Counter Shock seat snubbers" that absorbed road shocks for a softer, smoother ride. (Both seat and seatback were independently adjustable.) Other new features included: overlapping windshield wipers; sound deadener on doors; restyled "Driverized" cab with push-button door handles; deeper "arm rest" windows; five percent bigger, one-piece curved glass windshield; the new bolted box had a stronger tailgate and toggle-type latches. A three-speed manual transmission was among the standard features.

F-100 6½ FT. PLATFORM/STAKE: — The Platform/Stake shared the styling changes of the F-100 pickup. The stake racks were held firmly at the top with interlocking steel plates which were bolted to rack boards for extra strength. The stake and rack boards were made of straight grained seasoned wood. The stake pockets were flush with the floor for unobstructed, open platform use. Heavy, steel rub rail and steel caps, on the body ends, protected the platform.

F-100 8 FT. PANEL: — In addition to the other previously mentioned F-100 changes for 1953, the 8-Ft. Panel had beefed-up rear doors, steel slats above the interior body side panels, different runningboards and a rectangular dome light. It had a 155.8 cubic foot cargo area. The rear door opening was 50.8 inches wide and 45.4 inches high.

F-100 8 FT. DELUXE PANEL: — This was basically just a dolled-up version of the standard Panel. It came with most of the features found on the Driverized Deluxe Cab package.

1953 Ford F-100 Anniversary Pickup (IOA)

338

I.D. DATA (F-1-00): See 1952 F-1 I.D. In 1953, the first four characters for 6-cyl. were: "F10D3", for V-8: "F10R3". A one character plant code was used.)

Model	Body Type	Price	Weight	Prod. Total
F-100	(80) Platform	1367	—	64
F-100	(81) Chassis w/Cab	1259	2747	3061
F-100	(82A) Panel	1540	3392	9951
F-100	(82B) Panel (Deluxe)	—	—	2000
F-100	(83) Pickup	1330	3102	116,437
F-100	(84) Chassis w/Cowl	1012	2202	361
F-100	(85) Chassis w/Windshield	—	—	48
F-100	(86) Stake	1405	3217	1517

NOTE: Prices and weights are for 6-cyl.

1953 Ford F-100 Anniversary Pickup (J. Scray)

ENGINE (F-100): Same as 1952.

F-250 8 FT. EXPRESS: — The new F-250 pickup was not only a couple feet longer than the F-100; it could also haul heavier cargo. Some of its standard features were: Heavy-duty three-speed column shift transmission, parking brake control on dash, 10 inch clutch, 2600-lb. capacity front axle, Timken-Detroit hypoid rear axle and new bolt-construction box.

F-250 7½ FT. PLATFORM/STAKE: — The F-250 Platform/Stake had most of the same features as its F-100 counterpart. However it was capable of hauling heavier loads.

I.D. DATA (F-250): Same as F-100 except first five characters were, 6-cyl.: F25D3. V-8: F25R3.

Model	Body Type	Price	Weight	Prod. Total
F-250	(80) Platform	1465	—	81
F-250	(81) Chassis w/Cab	1359	3092	2534
F-250	(83) Pickup	1450	3482	23,363
F-250	(84) Chassis w/Cowl	1111	2537	489
F-250	(85) Chassis w/Windshield	—	—	137
F-250	(86) Stake	1519	3667	1995

NOTE: Prices and weights are for 6-cyl.

ENGINE (F-250): Same as F-100.

F-350 9 FT. EXPRESS: — Ford's biggest light-duty pickup, in 1953, was the new 9 ft. Express. Like the F-250, it came with a heavy-duty, column-shifted, three-speed manual transmission. However, it had heftier front and rear axles, large 13 x 2.5 in. rear brakes and higher capacity front springs.

F-350 9 FT. PLATFORM/STAKE: — These replaced the F-4 series of previous years. They shared most of the same standard features as the F-350 pickup.

I.D. DATA (F-350): Same as F-100 except first five characters were, 6-cyl.: F35D3. V-8: F35R3.

Model	Body Type	Price	Weight	Prod. Total
F-350	(80) Platform	1645	—	86
F-350	(81) Chassis w/Cab	1498	3406	5152
F-350	(83) Pickup	1608	3906	7757
F-350	(84) Chassis w/Cowl	1259	2851	375
F-350	(85) Chassis w/Windshield	—	—	201
F-350	(86) Stake	1695	4326	2202

NOTE: Prices and weight are for Six.

ENGINE (F-350): Same as F-100.

CHASSIS (Courier Sedan Delivery): Wheelbase: 115 in. Overall length: 197.8 in. Overall width: 74.3 in. Tires: 7.10 x 15.

(F-100): Wheelbase: 110 in. Overall length: 194.3 in. (Platform/Stake); 189.1 in. (Pickup); 201.8 in. (Panel). Overall width: 71.3 in. (Platform/Stake); 75.6 in. (Panel); 75.7 in. (Pickup). GVW: 4800. Tires: 6.00 x 16.

(F-250): Wheelbase: 118 in. GVW: 6900. Tires: 6.50 x 16.

(F-350): Wheelbase: 130 in. Overall length: 108 in. (Pickup). Overall width: 54 in. (Pickup). GVW: 9500. Tires: 8 x 17.5.

1953 Ford F-500 Anniversary Wrecker (M. Carbonella)

POWERTRAIN OPTIONS: Heavy-duty three-speed manual/three-speed with overdrive or four-speed manual transmissions. Ford-O-matic automatic.

CONVENIENCE OPTIONS: Heavy-duty battery. Rear bumper (Pickup). Right-hand sunvisor. Radio. Tinted glass. Grille guard. Seat covers. Heavy-duty fan. Windshield washers. Tow hooks. Various rear axle ratios. Deluxe cab, includes: Twin electric horns; two-tone seat upholstery; foam rubber seat padding; customized door and body trim; perforated therm-acoustic headlining backed by glass-wool insulation; sound deadener on floor and rear cab panels; grip type arm rests on both doors; large dome light with automatic door switches; two sunvisors; illuminated cigar lighter; lock on dispatch box and distinctive chrome or bright metal hardware and exterior trim.

NOTE: The Ford truck crest debuted this year. It featured "Ford" in writing above a gear crossed by a lightning bolt.

Pricing

1953	5	4	3	2	1
Courier					
Sedan Delivery	1050	2100	3500	4900	7000
F-100 — (½-Ton)					
Pickup	1010	2030	3350	4700	6700
Panel	1000	2000	3300	4600	6600
Stake	920	1850	3050	4300	6100
F-250 — (¾-Ton)					
Pickup	920	1850	3050	4300	6100
Stake	830	1650	2750	3850	5500
F-350 — (1-Ton)					
Pickup	890	1770	2950	4150	5900
Stake	800	1600	2650	3700	5300

1954 FORD

COURIER CUSTOM DELIVERY: — A slightly revised grille had round parking lights at each end of the main bar and a spinner in the center. There was also new taillight trim among the most noticeable styling changes for '54. The interior featured a new "Astra Dial" speedometer, idiot lights for the oil and generator (instead of gauges) and a new steering wheel and horn button. A lot of improvements were hidden. These included: Ball joint front suspension; chassis modifications; three-piece front stabilizer bar; new shock absorbers and a heavier-duty rear axle.

I.D. DATA (Courier): Began with "A4" (for six-cylinder models) or "U4" (for V-8s). That was followed by the plant code, body type code and production sequence number, according to final assembly location.

Model	Body Type	Price	Weight	Prod. Total
—	Sedan Delivery	1515	3109	—

ENGINE (Courier): Displacement: 223 cu. in. OHV Six, 115 horsepower at 3900 R.P.M. Bore & stroke: 3.62 in. x 3.60 in. Compression ratio: 7.2:1. Holley one-barrel carburetor. Or displacement: 239 cu. in. OHV V-8, 130 horsepower at 4200 R.P.M. Bore & stroke: 3.50 in. x 3.10 in. Compression ratio: 7.2:1. Holley two-barrel carburetor.

1954 Ford F-100 Pickup (A&A)

F-100 6½ FT. PICKUP: — Styling changes were limited primarily to the grille. On the upper section of the center bar, above the three rectangular slots, was an emblem indicating which engine powered the vehicle. An "8" inside a "V" indicated V-8 power. A four-pointed star, with three bright strips at an angle on each side, let people know a six-cylinder engine was under the hood. The F-100 had a 45 cubic foot payload capacity. That made it one of the biggest pickup boxes in the half-ton field. The box had heavy gauge steel side panels with roll-top steel flare boards. The seasoned wood floorboards were interlocked with durable steel skid strips extending the full length of the floor. Rubber cushion strips, on the sides of the tailgate, helped eliminate rattles. There were four stake pockets, in corner posts, to permit mounting of uprights for special tops. The cab featured a one-piece curved windshield, rearview mirror, four foot wide rear window, weather sealing around doors and body joints (to keep out dust, fumes and moisture) and new upholstery of full-breathing, woven vinyl.

1954 Ford F-100 Panel Delivery (H. Brandt)

F-100 8 FT. PANEL: — The 1954 F-100 Panel had a 155.8 cubic foot load capacity. Standard features included: Integral rear fenders; two heavy-steel rear doors that opened fully or held firmly at 90 degrees; steel side paneling; solid plywood floors with steel skid strips; fully weatherized driver's compartment; driver's seat; two taillights; heavy-gauge steel curved channel rear bumper; center cowl ventilator; water, temperature and fuel gauges; ash receptacle; dispatch box; dual windshield wipers; right and rear door lock; left-hand outside rearview mirror and bright hub caps.

F-100 8 FT. DELUXE PANEL: — The Deluxe Panel had most of the same features as the standard version plus: Two-tone upholstered driver's seat with foam rubber padding; harmonizing door panel trim; full-length glass-wool insulated headliner; sound deadener on driver's compartment floor; heavy masonite lining on panel sides; distinctive hood trim; bright metal drip molding, air wing frames and chevrons on grille; matched door locks on all doors; grip-type arm rest on each front door; illuminated cigar lighter; dispatch box lock; dome light with automatic door switches and twin, matched-tone electric horns.

F-100 6½ FT. PLATFORM/STAKE: — The F-100 Platform/Stake came with a frame of heavy-gauge steel side rails riveted to steel cross girders. Heavy steel brackets were riveted to girders and bolted to the sills for greater durability. All corners were reinforced with large, steel gusset plates. The stake and rack boards were straight-grained seasoned wood. The stake racks were held firmly at the top with interlocking steel plates. These were bolted to the rack boards for added strength. The stake pockets were flush with the floor, for unobstructed open platform use. Heavy steel rub rails and steel caps on body ends protected the platform. Splash guards and a long arm left-hand OSRV mirror were a couple of the standard features. The spare tire carrier was located under the floor.

1954 Ford F-100 Pickup (J. Charter)

I.D. DATA (F-100): The VIN range for six-cylinder models began at F10D4 ( ) 10001. For V-8, F10V4 ( ) 10001. In the blank space was the one character plant code.

Model	Body Type	Price	Weight	Prod. Total
F-100	(80) Platform	1355	—	49
F-100	(81) Chassis w/Cab	1247	—	5930
F-100	(82A) Panel	1528	—	8078
F-100	(82B) Panel (Deluxe)	—	—	1015
F-100	(83) Pickup	1318	—	101,202
F-100	(84) Chassis w/Cowl	1000	—	275
F-100	(85) Chassis w/Windshield	—	—	66
F-100	(86) Stake	1393	—	972

NOTE: Prices and weights are for 6-cyl. The V-8 cost $71 more.

ENGINE (F-100): Same as Courier.

NOTE: The engines were called the "Cost-Chipper Six" and the "Power King V-8."

F-250 8 FT. EXPRESS: — A step up from the F-100 was the lookalike F-250 pickup. It was more heavy-duty and had a larger load capacity. It came equipped with the same standard features as the F-100. The frame, runningboards and bumper were painted black.

F-250 7½ FT. PLATFORM/STAKE: — Among standard items on the F-250 Platform/Stake were: a curved instrument panel; charge indicator; under the floor tire carrier; right door lock; Air Wing ventilating windows in doors; left side sunvisor; single electric horn; speedometer; water, oil pressure and fuel gauges and outside rearview mirror. The frame, runningboards and bumper were painted black.

I.D. DATA (F-250): Same as F-100 except first five characters were, for Six-cylinder models: F25D4. V-8s: F25V4.

Model	Body Type	Price	Weight	Prod. Total
F-250	(80) Platform	1465	—	100
F-250	(81) Chassis w/Cab	1359	—	2547
F-250	(83) Pickup	1450	—	20,669
F-250	(84) Chassis w/Cowl	1111	—	376
F-250	(85) Chassis w/Windshield	—	—	170
F-250	(86) Stake	1519	—	1780

NOTE: Prices are for 6-cyl. Add $71 for V-8.

ENGINE (F-250): See F-100.

F-350 9 FT. EXPRESS: — With a maximum GVW rating of 7,100 pounds, the F-350 pickup was certainly capable of hauling some heavy loads. Its standard features echoed those of the F-100. Ford-O-Matic Drive was made available, as an extra-cost option on the F-350, for the first time this year.

F-350 9 FT. PLATFORM/STAKE: — Standard equipment on the F-350 Platform/Stake included a heavy-duty three-speed manual transmission; high capacity front springs; parking brake control mounted on the instrument panel and six-stud ventilated disc wheels.

I.D. DATA (F-350): Same as F-100 except the first five characters for the 6-cyl. were: F35D4. For the V-8: F35V4.

Model	Body Type	Price	Weight	Prod. Total
F-350	(80) Platform	1609	—	217
F-350	(81) Chassis w/Cab	1462	—	5642
F-350	(83) Pickup	1572	—	4482
F-350	(84) Chassis w/Cowl	1223	—	546
F-350	(85) Chassis w/Windshield	—	—	242
F-350	(86) Stake	1659	—	2758

NOTE: Prices and weight are for 6-cyl.

ENGINE (F-350): See F-100.

CHASSIS (Courier Sedan Delivery): Wheelbase: 115 in. Overall length: 197.8 in. Overall width: 74.3 in. Tires: 7.10 x 15.

(F-100): Wheelbase: 110 in. Overall length: 194.3 in. (Platform/Stake); 189.1 in. (Pickup); 201.8 in. (Panel). Overall width: 71.3 in. (Platform/Stake); 75.6 in. (Panel); 75.7 in. (Pickup). GVW: 4800. Tires: 6.00 x 16.

(F-250): Wheelbase: 118 in. Overall length: 108 in. (Pickup). GVW: 6900. Tires: 6.50 x 16.

(F-350): Wheelbase: 130 in. Overall length: 108 in. (Pickup). Overall width: 54 in. (Pickup). Overall height: 22.2 in. (Pickup). GVW: 9500. Tires: 8 x 17.5.

POWERTRAIN OPTIONS: Heavy-duty three-speed manual/three-speed with overdrive/ or four-speed manual transmissions. Ford-O-matic transmission.

CONVENIENCE OPTIONS: Heavy-duty battery. Vacuum booster brakes. Rear bumper (Pickup). Side mounted spare tire carrier (Pickup). Road lamps. Stop light. Right-hand sunvisor. Radio. Tinted glass. Grille guard. Seat covers. Hand brake signal. Spotlight. Right-hand taillight. Heater-defroster (Magic Aire or recirculating). Heavy-duty fan. Windshield washers. Tow hooks. Various rear axle ratios. Deluxe cab includes: Streamlined spear ornament on sides. Bright metal chevrons on grille. Bright metal frames around air wing vents. Bright finish drip molding cap. Twin electric horns. Two-tone seat upholstery. Foam rubber seat padding. Customized door and body trim. Perforated thermacoustic headlining backed by glass wool insulation. Sound deadener on floor and rear cab panels. Grip type arm rests on both doors. Large dome light with automatic door switches. Two sunvisors. Illuminated cigar lighter. Lock on dispatch box.

NOTE: Colors for 1954 included: Raven Black, Sheridan Blue, Meadow Green, Vermilion, Dovetone Gray, Glacier Blue, Light Green, Goldenrod Yellow. The last color replaced Dovetone Gray in mid-year.

Pricing

1954	5	4	3	2	1
Courier					
Sedan Delivery	1070	2150	3550	5000	7100
F-100 — (½-Ton)					
Pickup	1020	2050	3400	4800	6800
Panel	1010	2030	3350	4700	6700
Stake	930	1860	3100	4350	6200
F-250 — (¾-Ton)					
Pickup	930	1860	3100	4350	6200
Stake	840	1680	2800	3900	5600
F-350 — (1-Ton)					
Pickup	900	1800	3000	4200	6000
Stake	810	1620	2700	3800	5400

1955 FORD

COURIER CUSTOM DELIVERY: — The Courier Sedan Delivery was attractively restyled for 1955. It was longer, lower and wider than the 1954 model. Large round, spinner-style signal lights were placed under the hooded headlights in the concave, grid pattern grille. The sides featured some moderate body sculpturing that resulted in a modest tailfin under which the circular taillights slightly protruded. The stiffer frame had a lower profile and improvements were made to the brakes, suspension and shock absorbers. The interior was upholstered in a copper-tone vinyl. The Courier had a wraparound windshield.

I.D. DATA (Courier): Same as 1954 except the first two characters were: 6-cyl.: "A5". V-8: "U5".

Model	Body Type	Price	Weight	Prod. Total
—	Sedan Delivery	1725	3141	—

ENGINE (Courier): Displacement: 223 cu. in. OHV Six, 120 horsepower at 4000 R.P.M. Bore & stroke: 3.62 in. x 3.60 in. Compression ratio: 7.5:1. Holley one-barrel carburetor. Or displacement: 272 cu. in. OHV V-8, 162 horsepower at 4400 R.P.M. Bore & stroke: 3.62 in. x 3.30 in. Compression ratio: 7.6:1. Holley two-barrel carburetor.

F-100 6½ FT. PICKUP: — A winged, "V" styled, two-bar grille quickly set the '55 F-100 apart from the '54. Which emblem appeared in the center of the "V" depended on the power plant. "V-8" meant V-8 engine. A four pointed star indicated the truck had a six-cylinder engine. The hood side medallion was changed to the Ford name in script connected to the F-100 designation circled. Exclusive seat shock snubbers were built into the standard seat. They helped absorb jars and jolts to give a smoother, more comfortable ride. The seat was covered in non-sticking, easy to clean, cool woven plastic. The F-100 came with a 45 cubic foot pickup box with slanting flareboards, double walled steel doors, a curved one-piece windshield and a four-foot wide rear window. The wheels were white.

F-100 6½ FT. PLATFORM/STAKE: — A new feature the Platform/Stake shared with the pickup was 52 inch rear springs. Television commercials of the day bragged about the '55 Ford truck's short stroke engine. This was one of the factors in Ford truck claims of "triple economy." The other two were convenience of the "Driverized" cabs and bigger payload capacities. The F-100 Platform/Stake had straight-grained wood stakes.

F-100 8 FT. PANEL: — The Panel had a 155.8 cubic foot load capacity. It had a plywood floor with close-spaced skid strips. It was dust-sealed at body side panels by a special compound. The big rear door had two-position door checks.

F-100 8 FT. CUSTOM PANEL: — The nameplate under the door windows let everyone know this was the Custom Panel. It came with such "customized extras" as: a fully-lined interior; glass-wool roof insulation and foam-rubber seat padding.

I.D. DATA (F-100): Same as 1954 except for the first five characters which now read: Six: F10D5. V-8: F10V5.

Model	Body Type	Price	Weight	Prod. Total
F-100	(80) Platform	1498	3040	69
F-100	(81) Chassis w/Cab	1383	2730	6477
F-100	(82A) Panel	1681	3245	11,198
F-100	(82B) Panel (Custom)	—		1076
F-100	(83) Pickup	1460	3080	124,842
F-100	(84) Chassis w/Cowl	1122	2230	482
F-100	(85) Chassis w/Windshield	—	—	21
F-100	(86) Stake	1538	3165	997

NOTE: Weight and prices are for 6-cyl.

ENGINE (F-100): Same as 1954 except the compression ratio on the six-cylinder and V-8 was 7.5:1.

F-250 8 FT. EXPRESS: — Except for the mild styling changes noted for the F-100, the F-250 remained pretty much the same as the previous year's model. A couple of new options were available at extra cost. These were 11-leaf rear springs and power brakes. Standard features included: Direct, double-acting telescopic shocks (front and rear); 90 amp-hr battery; 10 inch clutch; hydraulic brakes; 5000-lb. capacity rear axle; heavy-duty oil bath air cleaner; 17-gallon fuel tank; dispatch box; water temperature, oil pressure, and fuel gauges; dual windshield wipers; inside rearview mirror; right-hand door lock and spare tire carrier under the frame.

F-250 7½ FT. PLATFORM/STAKE: — The F-250 Platform/Stake was 74 inches wide with 32 inch high stakes. The seat was covered with dool woven plastic upholstery. A left-hand outside rearview mirror was standard. The spare tire carrier was located under the floor.

I.D. DATA (F-250): Same as F-100 except the first five characters were, 6-cyl.: F25D5. V-8: F25V5.

Model	Body Type	Price	Weight	Prod. Total
F-250	(80) Platform	1617	3465	143
F-250	(81) Chassis w/Cab	1503	3075	3229
F-250	(83) Pickup	1602	3510	23,505
F-250	(84) Chassis w/Cowl	1240	2570	299
F-250	(85) Chassis w/Windshield	—	—	195
F-250	(86) Stake	1674	3650	1803

NOTE: Prices and weights are for Six.

ENGINE (F-250): Same as F-100.

F-350 9 FT. EXPRESS: — This was the ultimate light-duty Ford pickup for 1955. It had a big 74 cubic foot load capacity body. The box had slanting flareboards and eight deep stake pockets. The rigid tailgate had toggle-type latches.

F-350 9 FT. PLATFORM/STAKE: — A distinguishing feature of the F-350 was its ventilated disc wheels. It had a one-piece curved windshield, four-foot wide rear window, cool woven plastic upholstery, double-wall steel doors and steel rub rails.

I.D. DATA (F-350): Same as F-100 except the first five characters were: 6-cyl.: F35D5. V-8: F35V5.

Model	Body Type	Price	Weight	Prod. Total
F-350	(80) Platform	1771	4090	272
F-350	(81) Chassis w/Cab	1614	3520	7114
F-350	(83) Pickup	1732	3990	5450
F-350	(84) Chassis w/Cowl	1359	3015	883
F-350	(85) Chassis w/Windshield	—	—	284
F-350	(86) Stake	1824	4375	3504

NOTE: Prices and weights for 6-cyl.

ENGINE (F-350): Same as F-100.

CHASSIS (Courier Sedan Delivery): Wheelbase: 115.5 in. Overall length: 197.6 in. Overall width: 75.9 in. Tires: 7.10 x 15 in.

(F-100): Wheelbase: 110 in. Overall length: 189.1 in. (Pickup). Overall height: 75.5 in. (Pickup). Overall width: 75.7 in. (Pickup). GVW: 4000-5000 in. Tires: 6.00 x 16 in.

(F-250): Wheelbase: 118 in. Overall length: 203.2 in. (Cw/c). GVW: 7400. Tires: 6.50 x 16 in.

(F-350): Wheelbase: 130 in. GVW: 9800. Tires: 8 x 17.5 in.

1955 Ford F-100 Pickup w/Sidemount (OCW)

POWERTRAIN OPTIONS: Medium-duty three-speed manual (F-100); four-speed manual or 3-speed manual with overdrive transmissions. Ford-O-matic drive.

CONVENIENCE OPTIONS: Various rear axle ratios. Heavy-duty two-stage rear springs. Outside rearview mirror (left or right). Heavy-duty radiator. Heavy-duty radiator grille guard. Electric windshield wipers. 7.50 x 17 in. tires. 7.00 x 16 tires. Dual rear wheels (F-350 Platform/Stake). Hand brake signal. Oil filter. Radio. Magicaire heater-defroster. Recirculating heater-defroster. Seat cover. Windshield washer. Front tow hooks. Dual air horns. Tinted glass. Argent paiant finish hub caps. Tachometer. Heavy-duty generator. Gas tank locking cap. Governors. Spare tire lock and chain. Rear bumper (Pickup). Right-hand taillight. Custom cab, includes: arm rests; color keyed two-tone upholstery; dual horns; light gray sunvisors; seat side bolsters; kick and door panels; headliner; five inch thick, full foam-rubber cushioning in the seat; bright "Custom Cab" nameplate (below the window on the doors) and bright grille trim.

NOTE: Colors for 1955 included: Raven Black, Aquatone Blue, Banner Blue, Waterfall Blue, Meadow Green, Goldenrod Yellow, Sea Sprite Green, Snowshoe White and Torch Red. Two-tone paint treatments were available with white and any of the other colors.

PRODUCTION NOTE: Ford had a 30 percent share of the truck market in 1955.

Pricing

1955	5	4	3	2	1
Courier					
Sedan Delivery	1100	2200	3650	5100	7300
F-100 — (½-Ton)					
Pickup	1020	2050	3400	4800	6800
Panel	1010	2030	3350	4700	6700
Stake	930	1860	3100	4350	6200
F-250 — (¾-Ton)					
Pickup	930	1860	3100	4350	6200
Stake	840	1680	2800	3900	5600
F-350 — (1-Ton)					
Pickup	900	1800	3000	4200	6000
Stake	810	1620	2700	3800	5400

1956 FORD

COURIER CUSTOM DELIVERY: — "The perfect combination of distinction and utility." Some feel it's hard to disagree with that Ford advertising claim. As before, Courier styling was based on the passenger car-line. The Courier name was written in chrome on the front fenders. The side hinged rear door could open to reveal a 6½-feet long, over five-feet wide cargo area. The grille resembled last year's, but was different. So were the parking lights, which were now rectangular. A driver's bucket seat was standard, but a full width bench seat was available at extra cost. Buyers had their choice of 10 exterior colors.

I.D. DATA (Courier): Same as last year except the first two characters: 6-cyl.: "A6". V-8: "U6".

Model	Body Type	Price	Weight	Prod. Total
—	Sedan Delivery	1738		

1956 Ford Courier Sedan Delivery (DFW)

ENGINE (Courier): Displacement: 223 cu. in. OHV Six, 137 horsepower at 4200 R.P.M. Bore & stroke: 3.62 in. x 3.60 in. Compression ratio: 8.0:1. Holley one-barrel carburetor. Or displacement: 272 cu. in. OHV V-8, 173 horsepower at 4400 R.P.M. (176 horsepower with automatic). Bore & stroke: 3.62 in. x 3.30 in. Compression ratio: 8.0:1. Holley two-barrel carburetor.

1956 Ford F-100 6½-Ft. Pickup (OCW)

F-100 6½ FT. PICKUP: — The new Ford trucks for '56 debuted Sept. 23, 1955. Sales literature boosted of ''new styling'', but aside from a ''full wrap'' windshield and a slightly different grille, they looked basically the same as the previous model-year. The standard ''Driverized'' cab had free-breathing woven plastic upholstery; seat shock snubbers; independent seat and seat back adjustment; ''High-Dial'' instrumentation with a shielded, indirectly-lighted instrument cluster; push-button door handles; ''Lifeguard'' door latches; double-wall safety doors; ''Lifeguard'' deep-dish steering wheel; king-size door openings; complete weather-sealing; direct line accelerator linkage; level-action cab suspension; air wing vents; full-scoop cowl ventilator; left-hand sunvisor; rearview mirror; ashtray; dispatch box and a right-hand door key lock. A new standard feature on all Ford light-duty trucks were tubeless tires. And a new 10½ inch clutch was standard on F-100s with V-8 engines.

F-100 8 FT. EXPRESS: — This new model used the F-250's frame. It had a roomy 65.4 cubic foot cargo area. Like all Ford light-duty trucks, it had a grille with a heavy, forward slanting upper bar and thinner lower bar. The upper bar dipped in the center and provided space for engine identification. Hooded headlights, with parking lights directly underneath, were integrated into the ends of the grille.

F-100 6½ FT. PLATFORM/STAKE: — The F-100 Platform/Stake had over 40 square feet of platform area, straight grained wood stakes and could haul payloads up to 1,615 pounds. According to sales literature, it had the highest capacity frame and axles in the ½-ton field.

F-100 8 FT. PANEL: — This was one of the most attractive panel trucks on the road in 1956. Like other F-100s, it had a new wraparound windshield, facelifted grille, deep dish steering wheel and Lifeguard door latches. The right-hand rearview mirror was now mounted on the upper corner of the door.

F-100 8 FT. CUSTOM PANEL: — Inside or out, it was easy to identify the Custom Panel. Distinctive exterior features included: a chrome-plated grille and gas filler cap and a Custom Cab nameplate under the door windows. The interior was fully lined, had glass wool roof insulation and foam rubber seat padding.

I.D. DATA (F-100): The VIN began: 6-cyl.: F10D ( ) 10,001 and up. V-8: F10V ( ) 10,001 and up. The one-character plant code went in the blank spot. F-11 code used for low-GVW models.

1956 Ford F-100 Pickup w/Sidemount Option (D.Hoy)

1956 Ford F-100 Deluxe Custom Cab Pickup (OCW)

Model	Body Type	Price	Weight	Prod. Total
F-100	(80) Platform	1613	3030	74
F-100	(81) 110 in. Chassis & Cab	1485	2720	9251
F-100	(81) 118 in. Chassis & Cab	1519	—	Note
F-100	(82A) Panel	1857	3245	14,023
F-100	(82B) Panel (Custom)	—	—	1190
F-100	(83) Pickup (6½ ft.)	1577	3070	137,581
F-100	(83) Pickup (8 ft.)	1611	3325	25,122
F-100	(84) Chassis w/Cowl	1239	2200	599
F-100	(85) Chassis w/Windshield	—	—	12
F-100	(86) Stake	1673	3155	984

NOTE: Weights and prices are for 6-cyl. Production # for chassis w/Cab includes 110 inches and 118 inches.

ENGINE (F-100): Displacement: 223 cu. in. OHV Six, 133 horsepower at 4000 R.P.M. Bore & stroke: 3.62 in. x 3.60 in. Compression ratio: 7.8:1. one-barrel carburetor. Or displacement: 272 cu. in. OHV V-8, 167 horsepower at 4400 R.P.M. Bore & stroke: 3.62 in. x 3.30 in. Compression ratio: 7.8:1. two-barrel carburetor.

F-250 8 FT. EXPRESS: — A sales catalog proclaimed the F-250 the ''first choice truck where toughness counts.'' Its maximum payload capacity was increased by 522 pounds this year. Other new features were tubeless tires, standard medium-duty three-speed manual transmission, thicker brake linings and (on V-8 models) a 10½ inch clutch. The F-250 pickup had an all bolted 65.4 cubic foot cargo area with exclusive clamp-tight tailgate and six stake pockets. The cab had the same features as the F-100.

F-250 7½ FT. PLATFORM/STAKE: — The F-250 Platform/Stake had a platform area of over 50 square feet and could haul a payload of up to 3,395 pounds. The straight-grained wood stakes fit into steel lined stake pockets and were easy to remove for loading. It had a heavy gauge ''bridge type'' steel frame and steel rub rail. Tubeless tires and medium-duty three-speed manual transmission were just a couple standard features.

I.D. DATA (F-250): Same as F-100 except the first four characters were: 6-cyl.: F25D. V-8: F25V. F26 code used for low GVW models.

Model	Body Type	Price	Weight	Prod. Total
F-250	(80) Platform	1752	3460	206
F-250	(81) Chassisw/Cab	1624	3040	5028
F-250	(83) Pickup	1726	3505	28,341
F-250	(84) Chassis w/Cowl	1378	2545	436
F-250	(85) Chassis w/Windshield	—	—	205
F-250	(86) Stake	1812	3645	2173

NOTE: Prices and weights are for 6-cyl.

1956 Ford F-100 Pickup (K. Leitgabel)

F-250 ENGINE: See F-100 engine.

F-350 9 FT. EXPRESS: — The 1956 Ford F-350 had up to 1,200 pounds more GVW than other one-ton trucks. Its GVW rating increased 300 pounds this year, thanks mainly to the use of higher capacity tubeless tires. Also new was a stronger banjo-type rear axle housing and thicker brake linings. The F-350 pickup featured an extra large 74 cubic foot express body, with slanting flareboards to further increase effective load capacity. There were eight deep stake pockets and a rigid tailgate with exclusive toggle-type latches. This was the only Ford one-ton to come solely with single rear tires.

F-350 9 FT. PLATFORM/STAKE: — The F-350 Platform/Stake was indeed a "big payloader at light-duty cost." Its maximum payload (with dual rear wheels) was 5,120 pounds. It had steel stake sides and steel lined stake pockets with a swing-open center rack section for greater loading convenience. Like the F-350 pickup, it came equipped with a heavy-duty three-speed manual transmission.

I.D. DATA (F-350): Same as F-100 except the first four characters were: 6-cyl.: F35D. V-8: F35V. F36 code used for low-GVW models.

Model	Body Type	Price	Weight	Prod. Total
F-350	(80) Platform	1909	4010	387
F-350	(81) Chassis w/Cab	1761	3440	11,482
F-350	(83) Pickup	1887	3910	6226
F-350	(84) Chassis w/Cowl	1514	2910	1226
F-350	(85) Chassis w/Windshield	1983	4295	5019
F-350	(86) Stake	1983	4295	5019

NOTE: Prices and weights are for 6-cyl.

ENGINE (F-350): Same as F-100.

CHASSIS (Courier Sedan Delivery): Wheelbase: 115.5 in. Overall length: 197.6 in. Overall width: 75.9 in. Tires: 7.10 x 15.

(F-100): Wheelbase: 110 in. Overall length: 189.1 in. (Pickup). Overall height: 75.5 in. (Pickup). Overall width: 75.7 in. (Pickup). GVW: 4000-5000. Tires: 6.00 x 16.

(F-250): Wheelbase: 118 in. Overall length: 203.2 in. (Cw/c). GVW: 7400. Tires: 6.50 x 16.

(F-350): Wheelbase: 130 in. GVW: 9800. Tires: 8 x 17.5.

POWERTRAIN OPTIONS: Medium-duty three-speed manual (F-100); four-speed manual or three-speed manual with overdrive transmissions. Ford-O-Matic drive.

1956 Ford Special Delivery Van Body (DFW/HBC)

CONVENIENCE OPTIONS: Various rear axle ratios. Heavy-duty two-stage rear springs. Outside rearview mirror (left or right). Heavy-duty radiator. Heavy-duty radiator grille guard. Electric windshield wipers. 7.50 x 17 in. tires. 7.00 x 16 tires. Dual rear wheels (F-350 Platform/Stake). Hand brake signal. Oil filter. Radio. Magicaire heater-defroster. Recirculating heater-defroster. Seat cover. Windshield washer. Front tow hooks. Dual air horns. Tinted glass. Argent paiant finish hub caps. Tachometer. Heavy-duty generator. Gas tank locking cap. Governors. Spare tire lock and chain. Rear bumper (Pickup). Right-hand taillight. Full wrap rear window. Seat belts. Power steering. Custom Cab, includes: armrests; color-keyed two-tone upholstery; dual horns; light gray sunvisors; seat side bolsters; kick and door panels; headliner; five inch thick, full foam-rubber cushioning in the seat; bright "Custom Cab" nameplate below the window on the doors and bright grille trim.

NOTE: Colors for 1956 included: Raven Black, Nocturn Blue, Diamond Blue, Meadow Green, Meadowmist Green, Goldenrod Yellow, Platinum Gray, Colonial White, Vermilion. Any of those colors could be combined with Colonial White for a two-tone effect.

PRODUCTION NOTE: Ford's share of new truck registrations dropped slightly to 29 percent of the total U.S. market.

Pricing

1956	5	4	3	2	1
Courier					
Sedan Delivery	1110	2220	3700	5200	7400
F-100 — (½-Ton)					
Pickup	1040	2070	3450	4850	6900
Panel	1020	2050	3400	4800	6800
Stake	950	1900	3150	4400	6300
F-250 — (¾-Ton)					
Pickup	950	1900	3150	4400	6300
Stake	850	1700	2850	4000	5700
F-350 — (1-Ton)					
Pickup	920	1850	3050	4300	6100
Stake	830	1650	2750	3850	5500

1957 FORD

RANCHERO PICKUP: — The new Ranchero made its debut on December 8, 1957, at the National Automobile Show in New York. This handsome sedan-pickup was basically just what it looked like; a standard Ranch Wagon (station wagon) converted into a pickup. Although sales literature proclaimed it "a new idea in motor vehicles," it wasn't. Ford of Australia had first built the roadster-pickup "Ute" in 1934. Its success inspired the development of a car based truck for the American market. The spare tire was stored behind the passenger seat. However, since the Ranchero's box was bolted over the same rear section used in the station wagon, some owners made a hinge and used the wagon's spare tire well. Standard features included: bright-metal windshield, back window and vent wing moldings; bright-metal grille and front and rear bumpers; choice of tan-and-brown woven plastic with tan vinyl bolster or blue vinyl with white bolster upholstery and three-speed manual transmission.

1957 Ford Ranchero Custom Pickup (OCW)

CUSTOM RANCHERO: — People who wanted a little more flash, could opt for the Custom Ranchero. It had distinctive bright-metal full length side moldings. A Bright metal cap molding surrounded the top of body and rear of the cab. It was offered in either single-tone or "Style-Tone" exterior colors. The latter consisted of Colonial white above the side moldings, with any of 10 other colors below the side moldings and on the cab roof. Four combinations of upholstery were offered with white vinyl facings and bolsters. These were: tan-and-brown or white-and-blue woven plastic or all-red or all-green vinyl.

1957 Ford Ranchero Custom Pickup (T. Lerdaar)

I.D. DATA (Ranchero): The first letter indicated engine ("A" = six, "C" = V-8). It was followed by a single digit indicating the model year. Next was the assembly plant code, the body type code, then the sequential production numbers.

Model	Body Type	Price	Weight	Prod. Total
66A	Pickup	2098	3251	6428
66B	Custom Pickup	2149	3276	15,277

ENGINE (Ranchero): Displacement: 223 cu. in. OHV Six, 144 horsepower at 4200 R.P.M. Bore & stroke: 3.62 in. x 3.60 in. Compression ratio: 8.6:1. Holley one-bbl. carburetor.

ENGINE (Custom Ranchero): Displacement: 272 cu. in. OHV V-8, 190 horsepower at 4500 R.P.M. Bore & stroke: 3.62 in. x 3.30 in. Compression ratio: 8.6:1. Holley 2-bbl. carburetor.

CHASSIS: Wheelbase: 116 in. Overall length: 202 in. Overall width: 77 in. Overall height: 57.2 in. GVW: 4600. Tires: 8.00 x 14 in.

POWERTRAIN OPTIONS: Ford-O-Matic automatic or Overdrive transmissions. 190 horsepower 272 cu. in. V-8 (Ranchero), 212 horsepower 292 cu. in. V-8 (Custom Ranchero).

1957 Ford Ranchero Custom Pickup (OCW)

CONVENIENCE OPTIONS: Power steering. Power brakes. Power seat. Power windows. Full-flow oil filter. Heavy-duty Super-filter air cleaner. MagicAire system. Signal seeking radio. Self-regulating electric clock. Sunburst wheel covers. Aquamatic windshield washer-wiper. Lifeguard padded instrument panel and cushioned sunvisors. Seat belts. Tinted safety glass. Air conditioner (for models with V-8 engine). Whitewall tires. Special fuel and vacuum pump unit. Outside rearview mirror.

NOTE: The following exterior colors were offered: Raven black. Dresden blue. Starmist blue. Colonial white. Cumberland green. Willow green. Silver mocha. Doeskin tan. Woodsmoke gray. Gunmetal gray. Flame red.

COURIER SEDAN DELIVERY: — The Courier was all new for 1957. Hooded headlights; a full-width horizontal bar grille (with rectangular parking lights intergrated into it); canted fins above the large, round taillights; a rear opening hood and rear sloping windshield posts were some of the most noticeable changes. The Courier had a one-piece, lift-up tailgate with divided glass rear window. There were under-floor storage compartments behind the front seat. The interior also featured new "safety-curved" instrument panel with recessed controls restyled Lifeguard steering wheel and a safety-swivel rearview mirror. The cargo area was insulated and fully lined. A three-speed manual transmission was standard.

I.D. DATA (Courier): VIN began with engine designation code. Next was the assembly plant code, body type code and then sequential production numbers (starting at 100,001).

Model	Body Type	Price	Weight	Prod. Total
—	(78A) Sedan Delivery	1989	3234	6178

ENGINE (Courier): Displacement: 223 cu. in. OHV Six, 144 horsepower at 4200 R.P.M. Bore & stroke: 3.62 in. x 3.60 in. Compression ratio: 8.6:1. Holley 1-bbl. carburetor.

F-100 PICKUP: — "A completely new concept in pickup design with a functional purpose" claimed sales literature. The F-100 was extensively restyled for '57. The single bar (with slots in its lower half) grille had hooded headlights at either end. The flat, wrapover hood had ribs in its center section. The flush fenders added to a more "modern" look. This was especially noticeable on pickups, with the flush "Style side" box. The '57 F-100 was also two inches wider, and 3½ inches lower than the '56. In addition it had: longer and wider springs with fewer leaves (for less inter-leaf friction), suspended pedals; a two inch wider, wraparound windshield; hydraulic actuated clutch; new king pins and a large diameter spindle, for greater durability and steering ease. Buyers had their choice of four F-100 pickups: 6½ Ft. Styleside with steel floor; 6½ Ft. Flareside with wood floor; 8 Ft. Styleside with steel floor or 8 ft. Flareside with wood floor.

F-100 PLATFORM/STAKE: — The new F-100 Platform/Stake shared most standard features with the F-100 pickup. However, it had a wood platform bed with removable rack sections. The side boards and uprights were made of straight grained wood. Body sills were protected by steel end caps.

F-100 PANEL: — Like the pickup, the '57 F-100 Panel had new modern styling. Flush, sculptured bodysides, ribs on the flat hood, elimination of the runningboards and wraparound taillights added to the vehicle's sleek appearance. It had 158 cubic feet of cargo capacity.

I.D. DATA (F-100): The VIN consisted of series code, engine code, assembly plant code and sequential production numbers (starting at 100,001).

Model	Body Type	Price	Weight	Prod. Total
F-100	(80) Platform	1818	3065	Note 2
F-100	(81) Chassis w/Cab	1671	2760	Note 2
F-100	(81) Chassis w/Cab 118"	1708	2850	Note 2
F-100	(82) Panel	2082	3330	Note 2
F-100	(83) Pickup	1789	3110	Note 2
F-100	(83) 118 in. w.b. Pickup	1828	3285	Note 2
F-100	(84) Chassis	1419	2206	Note 2
F-100	(86) Stake	1889	3200	Note 2

NOTE 1: The price was the same for the Flareside and Styleside pickups.

NOTE 2: Ford records show the following F-100 production breakouts: (cowl) 97; (windshield) 200; (cab) 6086; (cab stake) 269; (cab pickup) 13,122; (cab pickup, flush) 64,050; (cab express) 2,319; (cab express flush) 20,114; (panel standard) 6,654 and (panel deluxe) 711. Similar production totals indicate series total, not individual model output.

ENGINE (F-100): Same as Courier except 139 horsepower at 4200 R.P.M and 8.3:1 compression ratio.

F-250 EXPRESS: — The F-250 pickup was all new for '57. Not only in styling, but the king pins, parking brake location, hub caps, dash, rear springs, and fuel filler location. Even the rear window was larger. The F-250 was available in Flareside (with wood floor and a runningboard between the rear fender and back of cab) or flush Styleside. The latter's steel floor box measured 94.4 by 73.2 inches. Its tailgate was 50.2 inches wide and the taillight lenses were built into the rear section on either side of the tailgate. Only the left-hand lens had a bulb behind it, unless the extra-cost turn signal option was ordered.

F-250 PLATFORM/STAKE: — The F-250 Platform/Stake may have had a restyled cab, but its cargo body was virtually the same as that used for the last 19 years. Steel skid strips protected the floor. The side boards and stakes were made of strong, straight-grained wood. Body sills were protected by steel end caps. An all steel rub rail protected the body.

I.D. DATA (F-250): See F-100 I.D.

Model	Body Type	Price	Weight	Prod. Total
F-250	(80) Platform	1973	3475	Note 1
F-250	(81) Chassis w/Cab	1827	3100	Note 1
F-250	(83) Pickup	1955	3535	Note 1
F-250	(84) Chassis	1575	2597	Note 1
F-250	(84) Chassis	1575	2597	Note 1
F-250	(86) Stake	2044	3650	Note 1

NOTE 1: Ford records show the following F-250 production breakouts: (cowl) 188; (windshield) (43); (cab) 3017; (cab stake) 1,119; (cab express) 4,321 and (cab express flush) 10,936.

ENGINE (F-250): Same as F-100.

F-350 EXPRESS: — The F-350 was the top of the line light-duty Ford pickup. It shared the new "modern" styling features with the F-100 and F-250. It also had a beefed-up chassis featuring: 2000 pound rear springs; heavier king pins and a 3800 pound front axle. The round taillights on the Styleside models were flush-mounted on either side of the 50.2 inch wide tailgate. The Flareside box was also available. A four-speed manual was standard.

F-350 PLATFORM/STAKE: — Loadspace on the hefty F-350 Platform/Stake was 106 inches long, 82 inches wide and 31.2 inches to the top of the racks. The center sections of the removable racks swung open for faster side loading. It had steel channel uprights and an all-steel rub rail.

I.D. DATA (F-350): See F-100 I.D.

Model	Body Type	Price	Weight	Prod. Total
F-350	(80) Platform	2172	3965	Note 1
F-350	(81) Chassis w/Cab	1987	3470	Note 1
F-250	(83) Pickup	2135	3875	Note 1
F-250	(84) Chassis	1736	2916	Note 1
F-350	(86) Stake	2247	4325	Note 1

NOTE 1: Ford records show the following F-350 production breakouts: (cowl) 688; (windshield) 207; (cab) 7,339; (cab stake) 2,746; (cab platform) 1,370 and (cab express flush) 1,869.

ENGINE (F-350): Same as F-100.

CHASSIS (Courier Sedan Delivery): Wheelbase: 116 in. Overall length: 203.5 in. GVW: 4600. Tires: 7.50 x 14, four-ply.

(F-100): Wheelbase: 110 in. and 118 in. GVW: 4000 to 5000. Tires: 6.70 x 15, four-ply.

(F-250): Wheelbase: 118 in. GVW: 4900 to 7400. Tires: 6.50 x 16, six-ply.

(F-350): Wheelbase: 130 in. GVW: 7600 to 9800. Tires: 8 x 17.5, six-ply.

POWERTRAIN OPTIONS: 171 horsepower 272 V-8. 190 horsepower 272 V-8 (Courier). Medium-duty three-speed transmission(F-100, F-250). Heavy-duty three-speed transmission (F-350). Four-speed manual transmission. Three-speed w/overdrive Ford-O-Matic transmission.

1957 Ford Ranchero Custom Pickup (DFW/DPL)

CONVENIENCE OPTIONS: Transistor powered truck radio. Signal seeking radio (Courier). MagicAire heater-defroster. Windshield washers. Power brakes. Outside rearview mirror (bright metal on Pickup, painted on others). Heavy-duty grille guard. Turn signals. Sealed beam spotlight. Seat covers. Heavy-duty rear springs. Recirculating heater-defroster. Heavy-duty radiator. Dual electric windshield wipers. Side mounted tire carrier (Pickup). Spare tire. Safety package, includes: padded instrument panel and cushioned sunvisors; tinted glass; full wrap rear window; rear bumper (Pickup); front and rear chrome bumper (Styleside Pickup); chrome front bumper; right-hand arm rest; outside left or right telescopic mirror for cabs; outside non-telescopic mirror; tow hooks; seat belts; fire extinguishers (1½ qt. or 4-lb. dry chemical); cigar lighter; dome light; splash guards; locking gas tank cap; Deluxe heater (Courier); bumper guards (Courier); Deluxe wheel covers (Courier) and under-dash light (Courier). Custom Cab, includes: two-tone seat upholstery; foam-rubber padding in seat cushion and back; Thermacoustic headlining backed by ½ inch of glass wool insulation; sound deadener on floor and rear cab panel; insulation on front cowl wall in cab; hardboard door and cowl side trim panels; arm rest on left door; dome light with manual switch; right-hand sunvisor; illuminated cigar lighter; bright metal grille; headlight assembly; windshield reveal molding; parking light rims; "Custom Cab" emblem on each door; matched locks on both doors.

NOTE: The 1957 Ford truck line was introduced on Feb. 1, 1957.

Pricing

1957	5	4	3	2	1
Courier					
Sedan Delivery	980	1950	3250	4550	6500
Ranchero					
Pickup	1050	2100	3500	4900	7000
Custom Pickup	1100	2200	3650	5100	7300
F-100 — (½-Ton)					
Flareside Pickup	890	1770	2950	4150	5900
Styleside Pickup	930	1860	3100	4350	6200
Panel	850	1700	2850	4000	5700
Stake	830	1650	2750	3850	5500
F-250 — (¾-Ton)					
Flareside Pickup	750	1500	2500	3500	5000
Styleside Pickup	780	1560	2600	3600	5200
Stake	780	1560	2600	3600	5200
F-350 — (1-Ton)					
Flareside Pickup	740	1470	2450	3350	4900
Styleside Pickup	770	1550	2550	3600	5100
Stake	750	1500	2500	3500	5000

1958 FORD

1958 Ford Ranchero Custom Pickup (OCW)

RANCHERO PICKUP: — The Ranchero received a T-Bird inspired facelift for '58. Among new styling features were: quad headlights, a fake air scoop on the hood and a bumper-integrated honeycomb-pattern grille. The instrument panel was also changed. However, the taillights and tailgate were carried over from 1957. Some changes were made to the chassis. These included a three-piece stablizier bar, different shock absorbers and the upper suspension arm bushings were permanently lubricated. Standard features included: Bright-metal windshield, back window, vent wing and side moldings; bright-metal grille and front and rear bumpers; light-and medium-blue vinyl or light brown vinyl and medium brown woven plastic upholstery. Three-speed manual transmission.

CUSTOM 300 RANCHERO PICKUP: — This model was a step up from the standard Ranchero. It was instantly recognized by its distinctive exterior side moldings with gold anodized aluminum inserts. The interior featured foam rubber in the seat cushions; arm rests on both doors; a sun visor on the right side; horn ring and cigarette lighter. The upholstery could be had in light blue vinyl and medium blue woven plastic; light brown vinyl and medium brown woven plastic; white and red vinyl and light and medium green vinyl. The Custom Ranchero was available in single or 11 Style-Tone color combinations. (Colonial white in combination with any of the other standard colors plus Sun Gold and Palomino Tan.)

I.D. DATA (Ranchero): See 1957 Ranchero I.D.

Model	Body Type	Price	Weight	Prod. Total
66A	Pickup	2170	3265	1471
66B	Custom Pickup	2236	3275	8479

ENGINE (Ranchero): Displacement: 223 cu. in. OHV Six, 145 horsepower at 4200 R.P.M. Bore & stroke: 3.62 in. x 3.60 in. Compression ratio: 8.6:1. Holley one-bbl. carburetor.

CHASSIS: Wheelbase: 116 in. Overall length: 202.9 in. Overall width: 77 in. Overall height: 57.5 in. GVW: 4600. Tires: 7.50 x 14, four-ply.

POWERTRAIN OPTIONS: 205 horsepower 292 cu. in. V-8, 300 horsepower 352 cu. in. V-8, Ford-O-Matic automatic, Cruise-O-Matic automatic (available with the 352 cu. in. V-8) and overdrive.

CONVENIENCE OPTIONS: Power steering. Power brakes. Power seat. Power windows. 8.00 x 14, six-ply tires. Whitewall tires. Full-flow oil filter (six-cylinder only). Heavy-duty Super-filter air cleaner. MagicAire system. Console Range or Signal-Seek radio. Electric clock. Fashion-Ray wheel covers. Aquamatic windshield washer-wiper. Padded instrument panel and sun visors. Seat belts. I-Rest tinted safety glass. SelectAire (V-8 only) or PolarAire conditioner. Vacuum booster windshield wipers. Outside rearview mirror.

NOTE: Colors offered on the 1958 Ranchero include: Azure blue; Silvertone blue; Seaspray green; Silvertone green; Desert beige; Bali bronze; Gunmetal gray; Torch red; Raven black and Colonial white.

1958 Ford Courier Sedan Delivery (OCW)

COURIER SEDAN DELIVERY: — The new Courier featured a restyled hood and front end. Four headlights, a Thunderbird inspired "honeycomb" bumper-intergrated grille (with "Ford" printed above it) and a fake hood scoop were among the most noticeable changes. The cargo area was lined and insulated. There was storage space behind the seats. A three-speed manual transmission was standard.

I.D. DATA (Courier): See 1957 Courier I.D.

Model	Body Type	Price	Weight	Prod. Total
—	(78A) Sedan Delivery	2062	3303	3352

ENGINE (Courier): Same as 1957.

F-100 PICKUP: — The new thin horizontal and vertical bar grille was bordered at each side by two encased headlights. The circular parking lamps were located under the headlights. The F-100 pickup was offered in two sizes (6½ and 8 feet) and with two styles of boxes: the traditional Flareside, with wooden floorboards and rear fenders and the "smooth side" Styleside which had an all-steel box. Among the standard features were: a "Lifeguard" steering wheel; safety double-grip door locks; sound deadener on doors; left-hand sunvisor; Hi-Dri all-weather ventilation; ash receptacle; dispatch box; 12-volt electrical system; 10 inch clutch; 18-gallon fuel tank; front and rear double acting telescopic shock absorbers and three-speed manual transmission.

F-100 7½ FT. PANEL: — The facelifted F-100 Panel had a cargo area 91.6 inches long and 51.6 inches wide. The plywood floor was chemically treated for longer life and supported by steel cross sills. Side joints were sealed for dust-tight load protection. Among the standard features were: a white bumper; wraparound taillights (they only worked on Custom models); right and rear door lock; hub caps; dome light; left-hand outside rearview mirror; single electric horn; under-frame spare tire carrier and left-hand sunvisor.

F-100 PLATFORM/STAKE: — Except for a facelift, the new F-100 Platform/Stake was basically unchanged for 1958. However, there were several new options available on it. The Platform's loadspace was 84.3 inches long, 71.3 inches wide and had a payload rating of 1720 pounds. The Stake's loadspace was 80 inches long, 67 inches wide and it had stakes 24.7 inches high. Sideboards and uprights were made of straight-grained wood. Body sills were protected by steel end caps.

I.D. DATA (F-100): See 1957 F-100 I.D.

Model	Body Type	Price	Weight	Prod. Total
F-100	(80) Platform	—	3065	Note 1
F-100	(81) Chassis w/Cab	1758	2760	Note 1
F-100	Styleside Pickup	1874	3110	Note 1
F-100	Flareside Pickup	—	3096	Note 1
F-100	Styleside Pickup 118"	1913	3285	Note 1
F-100	Flareside Pickup 118"	—	3529	Note 1
F-100	Chassis w/cab 118"	1793	2850	Note 1
F-100	(82) Panel	2167	3300	Note 1
F-100	Chassis	1504	2200	Note 1
F-100	(86) Stake	1974	3470	Note 1

NOTE 1: Ford records show the following F-100 production breakouts: (cowl) 84; (windshield) 30; (cab) 6,084; (cab platform and rack) 198; (Flareside pickup) 11,818; (Styleside pickup) 56,454; (Flareside express) 1,833; (Styleside express) 20,928; (Standard Panel) 6,560 and (Custom Panel) 592.

ENGINE (F-100): Same as 1957.

F-250 PICKUP: — The ¾-ton F-250 was available in Styleside or Flareside versions. It came with most of the same standard features as the F-100 plus larger brakes, a higher capacity rear axle and front and rear springs.

F-250 PLATFORM/STAKE: — Except for the facelift, the new F-250 Platform/Stake was essentially the same as last year's model. The sideboards and uprights were made of straight-grained wood. Body sills were protected by steel end caps. The all-steel rub rail protected the body from excessive wear. Stake loadspace was 90 inches long, 74 inches wide and 28.3 inches to the top of the racks. Platform loadspace was 93.4 inches long and 79.3 inches wide.

I.D. DATA (F-250): See 1957 F-100 I.D.

Model	Body Type	Price	Weight	Prod. Total
F-250	(80) Platform	—	3475	Note 1
F-250	(81) Chassis w/cab	1912	3100	Note 1
F-250	Pickup (Styleside)	2040	3535	Note 1
F-250	Pickup (Flareside)	—	3529	Note 1
F-250	(84) Chassis	1660	2545	Note 1
F-250	(86) Stake	2129	3650	Note 1

NOTE 1: Ford records show the following F-250 production break-outs: (cowl) 176; (windshield) 55; (cab) 2,637; (cab platform and rack) 826; (cab Flareside express) 3,155; (cab Styleside express) 10,555.

F-250 ENGINE: — Same as F-100.

346

F-350 PICKUP: — This was Ford's heftiest light-duty pickup. The Styleside version had a cargo area that was 106.44 inches long and 73.04 inches wide. Its payload capacity was 3360 pounds. The Flareside's cargo area was 108 inches long and 54 inches wide. It had a payload capacity of 3470 pounds. A four-speed manual transmission was standard.

F-350 PLATFORM/STAKE: — The F-350 may have had a new face for '58, but underneath it was pretty much the same as last years model. Buyers could order dual wheels at extra cost. The F-350 Platform/Stake had steel uprights and center rack sections that swung open for faster side loading. A four-speed manual transmission was standard.

F-350 I.D.: — See F-100.

Model	Body Type	Price	Weight	Prod. Total
F-350	(80) Platform	—	3965	Note 1
F-350	(81) Chassis w/cab	2072	3470	Note 1
F-350	Pickup (Styleside)	2220	3950	Note 1
F-350	Pickup (Flareside)	—	3944	Note 1
F-350	(84) Chassis	1821	2910	Note 1
F-350	(86) Stake	2332	4325	Note 1

NOTE 1: Ford records show the following F-350 production break-outs: (cowl) 598; windshield (60); (cab) 7,150; (cab, platform and rack) 2,548; (cab Flareside express (994) and (cab Styleside express) 1,974.

F-350 ENGINE: — Same as F-100.

CHASSIS (Courier Sedan Delivery): Wheelbase: 116 in. Overall length: 203.5 in. GVW: 4600. Tires: 7.50 x 14, four-ply.

(F-100): Wheelbase: 110 in. and 118 in. GVW: 4000 to 5000. Tires: 6.70 x 15, four-ply.

(F-250): GVW: 4900 to 7400. Tires: 6.50 x 16, six-ply.

(F-350): Wheelbase: 130 in. GVW: 7600 to 9800. Tires: 8 x 17.5, six -ply.

POWERTRAIN OPTIONS: 171 horsepower 272 V8. 190 horsepower 272 V8 (Courier). Medium-duty three-speed transmission (F-100, F-250). Heavy-duty three-speed transmission. (F-350). Four-speed manual transmission. Three-speed transmission with overdrive. Ford-O-Matic.

CONVENIENCE OPTIONS: Transistor powered truck radio. Signal seeking radio (Courier). MagicAire heater-defroster. Windshield washers. Power brakes. Dual rear tires (not available on Pickup). Whitewall tires. Outside rearview mirror (bright metal on Pickup, painted on others). Heavy-duty grille guard; turn signals; sealed-beam spotlight; seat covers; heavy-duty rear springs; recirculating heater-defroster; heavy-duty radiator; dual electric windshield wipers; side-mounted tire carrier (Pickup); spare tire; Safety Package, includes: padded instrument panel and cushioned sunvisors; tinted glass; full wrap rear window (Pickup); rear bumper (Pickup); front and rear chrome bumper (Styleside Pickup); chrome front bumper; right-hand arm rest; outside left or right telescopic mirror for cabs; outside non-telescopic mirror; tow hooks; seat belts; fire extinguishers (1½ qt. or 4 lb. dry chemical); cigar lighter; dome light; splash guards; locking gas tank cap; Deluxe heater (Courier); bumper guards (Courier); Deluxe wheel covers (Courier) and under-dash light (Courier). Custom Cab, includes: two-tone brown and white woven nylon-saran seat upholstery in a hound's tooth pattern; foam-rubber padding in seat cushion and back; thermacoustic headlining backed by ½ in. of glass wool insulation; sound deadener on floor and rear cab panel; insulation on front cowl wall in cab; hardboard door and cowl side trim panels; arm rest on left door; dome light with manual switch; right-hand sunvisor; illuminated cigar lighter; bright metal grille, headlight assembly, windshield reveal molding, parking light rims; "Custom Cab" emblem on each door; matched locks on both doors.

NOTE: Standard Ford truck colors for 1958 were: Vermilion (red), Midnight Blue, Azure Blue, Gunmetal Gray, Raven Black, Colonial White, Meadow Green, Seaspray Green, Goldenrod Yellow, or Prime. Any of the standard colors listed could be combined with Colonial White for a Two-Tone effect.

Pricing

	5	4	3	2	1
1958					
Courier					
Sedan Delivery	980	1950	3250	4550	6500
Ranchero					
Pickup	1050	2100	3500	4900	7000
Custom Pickup	1100	2200	3650	5100	7300
F-100 — (½-Ton)					
Flareside Pickup	890	1770	2950	4150	5900
Styleside Pickup	930	1860	3100	4350	6200
Panel	850	1700	2850	4000	5700
Stake	830	1650	2750	3850	5500
F-250 — (¾-Ton)					
Flareside Pickup	750	1500	2500	3500	5000
Styleside Pickup	780	1560	2600	3600	5200
Stake	780	1560	2600	3600	5200
F-350 — (1-Ton)					
Flareside Pickup	740	1470	2450	3350	4900
Styleside Pickup	770	1550	2550	3600	5100
Stake	750	1500	2500	3500	5000

1959 FORD

CUSTOM RANCHERO: — The base Ranchero was discontinued for 1959. The only model offered was the former top-of-the-line Custom. In addition to a two inch longer wheelbase, the load area was lengthened by seven inches. The Ranchero's boxy styling mirrored that of 1959 Ford passenger cars. It had a star-pattern aluminum grille. The circular front signal lights were integrated into the bumper. "Ford" was spelled out on the face of the hood. A larger, compound-curved windshield was used. It provided 20 percent more visibility. The larger round taillights were placed lower than the previous year's model. Its interior was based on that offered on the Country Sedan wagon. The Ranchero's split seat backs tilted forward for easy access to storage space behind driver's seat or spare tire behind passenger's seat. A three-speed manual transmission was standard.

I.D. DATA (Ranchero): See 1957 Ranchero I.D.

Model	Body Type	Price	Weight	Prod. Total
66C	Pickup	2313	—	14,169

ENGINE (Ranchero): Displacement: 223 cu. in. Six, 145 horsepower at 4200 R.P.M. Bore & stroke: 3.62 in. x 3.60 in. Compression ratio: 8.4:1. One-bbl. carburetor.

CHASSIS: Wheelbase: 118 in. Overall length: 208 in. Overall width: 76.6 in. Overall height: 58 in. Tires: 7.50 x 14 4-ply.

POWERTRAIN OPTIONS: Ford-O-Matic and Cruise-O-Matic automatics. Overdrive. Equa-lock limited slip differential. 200 horsepower 292 V-8, 300 horsepower Interceptor 352 special V-8.

NOTE: The Cruise-O-Matic was only available with the optional 300 horsepower 352 cu. in. V-8.

CONVENIENCE OPTIONS: Power steering. Power brakes. Power windows. MagicAire or recirculating-type heater system. Console Range or Signal-Seek radio. Electric clock. Bright-metal wheel covers. Aquamatic windshield washer-wiper. Padded instrument panel and sunvisors. Seat belts. I-Rest tinted safety glass. PolarAire Conditioner (V-8 only). Dual electric windshield wipers. Outside rearview mirror. 8.00 x 14 4- or 6-ply tubeless tires. WSW tires.

NOTE: Colors offered on '59 Rancheros were: Raven black. Gunsmoke gray. Colonial white. Surf blue. Wedgewood blue. Sherwood green. April green. Torch red. Tahitian bronze. Fawn tan. Inca Gold. In addition, Colonial white could be combined with any color listed. And Surf blue combined with Wedgewood blue, April green with Sherwood green or Fawn Tan with Tahitian bronze to create "Style Tone" color combinations.

COURIER SEDAN DELIVERY: — The Courier was restyled for 1959. Hooded, T-Bird inspired quad headlights were placed above the full width, star pattern aluminum grille. Circular parking lights were recessed in the bumper. The Courier nameplate was on the rear quarter panel. Glass side windows replaced the previous blanked out area. This, and the new two-piece tailgate made Courier look like a standard two-door Ford station wagon. However, unlike the wagons, it came with just the driver's seat. A three-speed manual transmission was standard.

I.D. DATA (Courier): See 1957 Courier.

Model	Body Type	Price	Weight	Prod. Total
—	Sedan Dely.	2424	—	5141

ENGINE (Courier): Displacement: 223 cu. in. OHV Six, 145 horsepower at 4000 R.P.M. Bore & stroke: 3.62 in. x 3.60 in. Compression ratio: 8.6:1. Holley 1-bbl. carburetor.

1959 Ford F-100 Styleside Pickup (C. Webb)

F-100 PICKUP: — The F-100 received a mild, but very attractive facelift for 1959. The new hood featured the Ford name on its face in big block letters. The grille had a thick horizontal bars theme. Parking lamps were in the same location, although now they were rectangular, not round. The front bumper was raised slightly (on Custom Cab models) and featured an indentation to the center for the license plate. A different Ford F-100 nameplate, with the Ford truck crest, was used on the front fenders. A new option was four-wheel-drive. The F-100 was offered in 6½ ft. and 8 ft. sizes and with the Styleside (flush side) welded all metal body, or Flareside with runningboard between rear fender and back of cab and wooden floor with steel skid strips. Among the standard features were: Hi-Dri ventilation. Nylon-polyethylene-saran seat upholstery. Toggle-type tailgate latches. Double acting front and rear shock absorbers. Three-speed manual transmission.

F-100 PLATFORM/STAKE: — The F-100 Platform/Stake shared the same styling changes as the pickup. Steel skid strips protected the seasoned wood floor boards and made it easier to slide heavy cargo in or out. Sideboards and stakes were made of straight-grained wood. Bolted steel plates held sideboards firmly together at the top. Heavy gauge steel stake pockets were set flush with the floor. Body sills were protected by steel end caps. An all-steel rub rail protected the body. Stake loadspace was 80 in. long, 67 in. wide, and 24.8 in. to top of racks. Platform loadspace was 84.3 in. long, 71.3 in. wide.

F-100 7½ FT. PANEL: — Standard features on the 1959 F-100 Panel included: White contour front and rear bumpers. Right and rear door lock. Dual vacuum booster windshield wipers. Hub caps. Dome light. Chrome LH rearview mirror. Single electric horn. Under frame spare tire carrier. LH sunvisor. Taillight-stoplight-license plate light on left rear door. The plywood floor was supported on steel cross sills.

I.D. DATA (F-100): See 1957 F-100 I.D.

1959 Ford F-100 Styleside Custom Cab Pickup (OCW)

Model	Body Type	Price	Weight	Prod. Total
F-100	(80) Platform	—	3053	Note 1
F-100	(81) Chas. w/Cab	1814	2748	Note 1
F-100	118 in. w.b. Chas. w/Cab	1852	2838	Note 1
F-100	Pickup (Flareside)	1932	3084	Note 1
F-100	(118 in. w.b.) Pickup (Flareside)	1971	3262	Note 1
F-100	Pickup (Styleside)	1948	3098	Note 1
F-100	(118 in. w.b.) Pickup (Styleside)	1987	3273	Note 1
F-100	(82) Panel	2230	3318	Note 1
F-100	(84) Chassis	1558	2194	Note 1
F-100	(86) Stake	2024	3458	Note 1

NOTE 1: Ford records show the following F-100 production break-outs: (cowl) 173; (windshield) 4; (cab) 8942; (platform and rack) 301; (Flareside pickup) 26,616; (Styleside pickup) 112,082; (standard Panel) 7,963 and (Custom Panel) 982.

ENGINE (F-100): Same as Courier except 139 horsepower at 4200 R.P.M and 8.3:1 compression ratio.

F-250 PICKUP: — Like the F-100, the F-250 received an attractive facelift for 1959. Buyers had their choice of Flareside or Styleside boxes, and four-wheel-drive (at extra cost). Most standard features were the same as those found on the F-100.

F-250 PLATFORM/STAKE: — The F-250 Platform/Stake had most of the same features as its F-100 counterpart. However, it could haul heavier loads. Stake loadspace was 90 in. long, 74 in. wide and 28.3 in. to top of racks. Platform loadspace was 93.4 in. long, 79.3 in. wide.

I.D. DATA (F-250): See F-100.

Model	Body Type	Price	Weight	Prod. Total
F-250	(80) Platform	—	3463	Note 1
F-250	(81) Chas. w/Cab	1971	3088	Note 1
F-250	Pickup (Flareside)	2090	3513	Note 1
F-250	Pickup (Styleside)	2106	3523	Note 1
F-250	(84) Chassis	1704	2539	Note 1
F-250	(86) Stake	2181	3638	Note 1

NOTE 1: Ford records show the following F-250 production break-outs: (cowl) 195; (windshield) 139; (cab) 4,016; (platform and rack) 1,093; (Flareside pickup) 4,827 and (Styleside pickup) 16,491.

ENGINE (F-250): Same as F-100.

F-350 PICKUP: — The F-350 shared styling changes and most standard features with the F-250. But it was capable of hauling much heavier loads. It was available in Styleside or Flareside versions. The Flareside had wood floors protected by full length skid strips. A four-speed manual transmission, front only shock absorbers, and drum and band type parking brakes were standard.

F-350 PLATFORM/STAKE: — This was the longest light-duty Ford truck of its type in '59. It had rugged steel channel stakes for greater rigidity. Stake loadspace was 106 in. long, 82 in. wide, and 31.2 in. to top of racks. Platform loadspace was 109.4 in. long, and 87.3 in. wide.

I.D. DATA (F-350): See F-100.

Model	Body Type	Price	Weight	Prod. Total
F-350	(80) Platform	—	3953	Note 1
F-350	(81) Chassis w/Cab	2130	3458	Note 1
F-350	Pickup (Flareside)	2269	3932	Note 1
F-350	Pickup (Styleside)	2285	3938	Note 1
F-350	(84) Chassis	1863	2904	Note 1
F-350	(86) Stake	2381	4313	Note 1

NOTE 1: Ford records show the following F-350 production break-outs: (cowl) 749; (windshield) 150; (cab) 12,896; (platform and rack) 1093; (Flareside pickup) 4827 and (Styleside pickup) 16,491.

ENGINE (F-350): Same as F-100.

CHASSIS (Courier Sedan Delivery): Wheelbase: 118 in. Overall length: 208 in. Overall width: 76.6 in. GVW: 4600. Tires: 7.50 x 14 4-ply.

(F-100): Wheelbase: 110 in. and 118 in. GVW: 4000 to 5000. Tires: 6.70 x 15 4-ply.

(F-250): Wheelbase: 118 in. GVW: 4900 to 7400. Tires: 6.50 x 16 6-ply.

(F-350): Wheelbase: 130 in. GVW: 7700 to 9800. Tires: 8 x 17.5 6-ply.

POWERTRAIN OPTIONS: 186 horsepower 292 V-8. 200 horsepower 292 V-8 (Courier). Medium-duty 3-speed (F-100, F-250). Heavy-duty (F-100, Courier) 3-speed transmission (F-350). 4-speed manual transmission. 3-speed w/overdrive (F-100) Ford-O-Matic automatic. Cruise-O-Matic automatic (Courier). Heavy-duty Cruise O-Matic (F-250, F-350).

CONVENIENCE OPTIONS: Transistor powered truck radio. Signal seeking radio (Courier). MagicAire heater-defroster. Windshield washers. Power steering. Power brakes. ICC clearance lights. 16 x 15K heavy-duty wheels (F-100). Outside rearview mirror (bright metal on Pickup, painted on others). Heavy-duty grille guard. Turn signals. Sealed beam spotlight. Seat covers. Four-wheel-drive. Heavy-duty rear springs. Recirculating heater-defroster. Heavy-duty radiator. Dual electric windshield wipers. Side mounted tire carrier (Pickup). Spare tire. **Safety Package:** Padded instrument panel and cushioned sunvisors. Tinted glass. Full wrap rear window. Rear bumper (Pickup). Front and rear chrome bumper (Styleside Pickup). Chrome front bumper. RH arm rest. Outside left or right telescopic mirror for cabs. Outside non telescopic mirror. Tow hooks. Seat belts. Fire extinguishers (1½ qt. or 4 lb. dry chemical). Cigar lighter. Dome light. Splash guards. Locking gas tank cap. Deluxe heater (Courier). Bumper guards (Courier). Deluxe wheelcovers (Courier). Underdash light (Courier). **Custom Cab:** Woven nylon-saran seat upholstery in a Candy-striped pattern with vinyl bolster and seat facing; foam-rubber padding in seat cushion and back; white fleck pattern hardboard on headlining and sides of load compartment (on Panel); sound deadener on floor and rear cab panel; insulation on front cowl wall in cab; two-tone paint on doors and instrument panel; arm rest on left door; white steering wheel with chrome horn ring; RH sunvisor; illuminated cigar lighter; bright metal grille, headlight assembly, windshield reveal molding, parking light rims; "Custom Cab" emblem on each door, matched locks on both doors.

NOTE: Colors available on 1959 Ford light-duty trucks included: Academy Blue, Goldenrod Yellow, Vermilion, April Green, Meadow Green, Indian Turquoise, Wedgewood Blue, Colonial White, Raven Black or Prime.
Any standard color listed could be combined with Colonial White for a two-tone effect.

PRODUCTION NOTE: Ford captured 31.09 percent of all new truck registrations in 1959.

Pricing

	5	4	3	2	1
1959					
Courier					
Sedan Dely.	530	1050	1750	2450	3500
Ranchero					
Pickup	1050	2100	3500	4900	7000
Custom Pickup	1100	2200	3650	5100	7300
F-100 — (½-Ton)					
Flareside Pickup	890	1770	2950	4150	5900
Styleside Pickup	930	1860	3100	4350	6200
Panel	850	1700	2850	4000	5700
Stake	830	1650	2750	3850	5500

	5	4	3	2	1
F-250 — (¾-Ton)					
Flareside Pickup	750	1500	2500	3500	5000
Styleside Pickup	780	1560	2600	3600	5200
Stake	780	1560	2600	3600	5200
F-350 — (1-Ton)					
Flareside Pickup	740	1470	2450	3350	4900
Styleside Pickup	770	1550	2550	3600	5100
Stake	750	1500	2500	3500	5000

NOTE: Add 5 percent for 4wd.

1960 FORD

1960 Ford Falcon Ranchero Pickup (K. Buttolph)

FALCON RANCHERO: — The Ranchero was now in the compact Falcon series. Sales literature proclaimed it "America's lowest priced pickup" and boasted of mileage up to 30 m.p.g. Its styling was plain yet attractive. The two headlights were nestled in the grille cavity. The concave aluminum grille had a pattern of horizontal and vertical lines. The slab sides had mild body sculpturing. Two large round taillights were used. Other features included: single unit-body construction (with bolt on fenders); independent front suspension; variable-rate rear left springs; duo-servo hydraulic brakes; compound curved windshield and a sloping hood. There was 31.6 cubic feet of loadspace in the six-foot box, which featured an "instant-lock" tailgate. Standard equipment included: bright metal windshield and drip moldings; front and rear bumpers; arm rests; dome light; spare tire and wheel (behind seat); sunvisors; dispatch box; ash tray; double-grip door locks; "Lifeguard" steering wheel; foam rubber seat cushion padding; light brown, western motif, vinyl seat covering with beige vinyl bolsters and seat facings and three-speed manual transmission.

1960 Ford Falcon Ranchero Pickup (OCW)

I.D. DATA (Falcon Ranchero): The first digit represents the model year. It is followed by a letter that represents the assembly plant. The next two digits identify the product line and body style. The next letter designates the engine. The last six digits are sequential numbers.

Model	Body Type	Price	Weight	Prod. Total
—	Pickup	1882	2435	21,027

ENGINE (Falcon Ranchero): Displacement: 144 cu. in. OHV Six, 90 horsepower at 4200 R.P.M. Bore & stroke: 3.5 in. x 2.5 in. Compression ratio: 8.7:1. Holley one-barrel carburetor.

CHASSIS: Wheelbase: 109.9 in. Overall length: 189 in. Overall width: 70 in. Overall height: 54.5 in. Payload: 800 lbs. Tires: 6.50 x 13.

POWERTRAIN OPTIONS: Ford-O-Matic transmission.

CONVENIENCE OPTIONS: Heavy-duty battery. Heavy-duty generator. Deluxe Trim Package, includes: bright metal exterior moldings; taillight ornaments; white steering wheel with chrome horn ring; cigar lighter; dome light door switch; Deluxe seat trim; wheel covers; windshield washers; dual electric windshield wipers and whitewall tires.

NOTE: Solid colors available were: Platinum. Monte Carlo red. Skymist blue. Adriaic green. Corinthian white, Meadow green. Beachwood brown. Belmont blue. Raven black. Turquoise. Two tone combinations were: black and platinum, Skymist and Belmont blue, Adriatic and Meadow green, Corinthian white with any other solid color.

COURIER SEDAN DELIVERY: — Once again, the Courier looked like a Ford two-door Ranch wagon with just a driver's seat. It was completely restyled for 1960. The new Courier was wider, longer and lower than the '59. It was also sleeker. The four bright trimmed headlights were tucked into the recessed, mesh-style grille. The Ford name was printed on the face of the sloping hood. A chrome strip ran from the top of the front bumper to the length of the small horizontal tailfin. Under the fin was a semi-circular taillight. The 1960 Courier had a spacious 97.4 cubic foot cargo area. This was the last year for the Courier sedan delivery.

I.D. DATA (Courier): See 1957 Courier I.D.

Model	Body Type	Price	Weight	Prod. Total
—	(69) Sedan Delivery	2456	—	2,374

ENGINE (Courier): Same as 1959.

1960 Ford F-100 Styleside Custom Cab Pickup (S. Soloy)

F-100 PICKUP: — In contrast to last year's clean look, the 1960 F-100 was jazzed up considerably. The Ford truck badge emblem was centered on the face of the hood, between two vent slots. The new rectangular pattern grille extended down to include the parking lights. A thick bar at its top connected the larger, inward slanting headlight pods. This gave the truck a "bug-eyed" appearance. The hoodside ornament was changed to that of a stylized "rocket" or arrow (depending on your point of view). Improvements were made to the springs, door seals, electrical and exhaust systems. The F-100 pickup could be ordered in 110 inch and 118 inch wheelbases and with either Flareside or Styleside boxes. Among the standard features were: "Lifeguard" steering wheel; safety double-grip door locks; plain nylon-rayon-saran seat upholstery with gray vinyl bolster and seat facings; dome light; left-hand sunvisor; ash receptacle; dispatch box; coat hook; white instrument cluster cover plate; Hi-Dri all-weather ventilation and three-speed manual transmission. Four-wheel-drive was available, at extra cost, along with many other options.

F-100 PANEL: — The 1960 F-100 Panel had a facelift and a beefed-up frame. The brakes were also improved. Among the standard features were: bright-color plaid nylon-rayon-saran seat upholstery with vinyl bolster and seat facing; white contour front and rear bumpers; right and rear door lock; dual vacuum booster windshield wipers; "Lifeguard" steering wheel; large dome light; chrome left-hand outside rearview mirror; single electric horn; under-frame type spare tire carrier; left-hand sunvisor; tail-light-stoplight-license plate light on left rear door; plywood floor (chemically treated for longer life and supported on steel cross sills); sealed side joints; twin rear doors hinged to one-piece channel steel door frame and two-position door checks. The cargo area was 91.6 inches long, 51.6 inches high and 51.6 inches wide (at floor). There was a total of 158 cubic feet of cargo area. The sides of body, from floor to top of wheelhouses, were protected by steel paneling. Smooth steel slats protected the load above these panels. This was the last, conventional, full-size Ford panel truck.

F-100 PLATFORM/STAKE: — The F-100 Platform/Stake received the same facelift as the F-100 pickup. Steel skid strips protected the floor and made it easier to slide cargo in or out. Heavy gauge steel stake pockets were set flush with the floor. Sideboards and stakes were made of straight-grained wood. Bolted steel plates held side boards firmly together at the top yet permitted quick, easy removal of stake sections. Body sills were protected by steel end caps. An all-steel rub rail protected the load. Stake loadspace was 80 inches long, 67 inches wide and 24.8 inches to top of racks. Platform loadspace was 84.3 inches long and 71.3 inches wide.

I.D. DATA (F-100): See 1957 F-100 I.D.

Model	Body Type	Price	Weight	Prod. Total
F-100	(80) Platform	—	3053	—
F-100	(81) Chassis w/Cab	1839	2748	—
F-100	(118 in.) Chassis w/Cab	1897	2828	—
F-100	Flareside Pickup	1956	3088	—
F-100	(118 in.) Flareside Pickup	1994	3253	—
F-100	Styleside Pickup	1972	3105	—
F-100	(118 in.) Styleside Pickup	2010	3263	—
F-100	Panel	2268	3248	—
F-100	(84) Chassis	1580	2184	—
F-100	(86) Stake	2049	3178	—

NOTE 1: Ford records show the following F-100 production break-outs: (cowl) 121; (cab) 17,159; (Platform and rack) 245; (Flareside pickup) 27,383; (Styleside pickup) 113,875; (Standard Panel) 8,543; (Custom Panel) 947; (4x4 Cab) 442; (4x4 Flareside pickup) 964 and (4x4 Styleside pickup) 4,334.

ENGINE (F-100): Same as 1959.

F-250 PICKUP: — The F-250 pickup was offered in Flareside and Styleside versions. It could also be ordered with four-wheel-drive (at extra cost). New standard features on that option were 1,200-lb. front and 1,950-lb. rear springs. Nominal payload of F-250 pickups was 3550-pounds.

F-250 PLATFORM/STAKE: — These were also available with four-wheel-drive. Nominal payload capacity on the Stake was 3500-lbs. On the Platform it was 3700-lbs. The F-250 Stake with 7½-foot body had two-piece side and tail racks for greater loading convenience. The side boards and stakes were made of straight grained wood. Steel skid strips protected the floor.

I.D. DATA (F-250): See 1957 F-100 I.D.

Model	Body Type	Price	Weight	Prod. Total
F-250	(80) Platform	—	—	—
F-250	(81) Chassis w/Cab	1998	2998	—
F-250	Flareside Pickup	2115	3423	—
F-250	Stylkeside Pickup	2131	3433	—
F-250	(84) Chassis	1729	2444	—
F-250	(86) Stake	2208	3498	—

NOTE 1: Ford records show the following F-250 production break-outs: (cowl) 125; (windshield) 21; (cab) 4,811; (platform and rack) 1,017; (Flareside pickup) 6,356; (Styleside pickup) 15,518; (4x4 cab) 411; (4x4 platform and rack) 98; (4x4 Flareside pickup) 828 and (4x4 Styleside pickup) 1,806.

F-250 ENGINE: Same as F-100.

F-350 PICKUP: — The big light-duty Ford pickup in 1960 was the F-350. It was offered in Flareside or Styleside versions. Among standard features were: four-speed manual transmission; six-hole disc wheels; drum and band parking brakes; 3800-pound capacity front axle; 7200-pound rear axle. Single- stage rear springs and front-only shock absorbers.

F-350 PLATFORM/STAKE: — Although it had most of the same standard features as the F-100 and F-250 versions, the F-350 Platform/Stake was capable of hauling heavier loads. Its payload capacity was rated at 5075 -pounds (Stake) or 5450-pounds (Platform). The F-350 Stake had three-section sides, a swing-open center rack and steel stakes. A four-speed manual gear box was standard.

I.D. DATA (F-350): See F-100 I.D.

Model	Body Type	Price	Weight	Prod. Total
F-350	(80) Platform	—	3953	—
F-350	(81) Chassis w/Cab	2155	3458	—
F-350	Flareside Pickup	2296	3938	—
F-350	Styleside Pickup	2312	3938	—
F-350	(84) Chassis	1885	2904	—
F-350	(86) Stake	2407	4313	—

NOTE 1: Ford records show the following F-350 production break-outs: (cowl) 945; (windshield) 175; (cab) 12,761; (cab, platform and rack) 4,129; (Flareside pickup) 1,213 and (Styleside pickup) 2,140.

F-350 ENGINE: Same as F-100.

CHASSIS (Courier Sedan Delivery): Wheelbase: 119 in. Overall length: 213.7 in. Overall width: 81.5 in. GVW: 4600. Tires: 7.50 x 14, four -ply.

(F-100): Wheelbase: 110 in. and 118 in. GVW: 4000 to 5000 lbs. Tires: 6.70 x 15, four-ply.

(F-250): Wheelbase: 118 in. GVW: 4900 to 7400 lbs. Tires: 6.50 x 16, six-ply.

(F-350): Wheelbase: 130 in. GVW: 7700 to 9800 lbs. Tires: 8 x 17.5, six-ply.

POWERTRAIN OPTIONS: 171 horsepower 292 V8. 185 horsepower 292 V8 (Courier). Medium-duty three-speed (F-100, F-250), heavy-duty three-speed (F-350) or four-speed manual transmission. Three-speed w/over-drive transmission (F-100, Courier); Ford-O-Matic transmission (F-100, Courier); Heavy-duty Cruise-O-Matic (F-250, F-350) or Cruise-O-Matic (Courier) ransmissions.

CONVENIENCE OPTIONS: Transistor powered truck radio. Signal-seeking radio (Courier). MagicAire heater-defroster. Windshield washers. Power steering. Power brakes. Four-wheel-drive. Rear shocks (F-350). Outside rearview mirror (bright metal on Pickup, painted on others). Heavy-duty grille guard. Turn signals. Sealed beam spotlight. Seat covers. Auxliary seat (Panel). ICC lights. ICC reflectors. Heavy-duty rear springs. Recirculating heater-defroster. Heavy-duty radiator. Dual electric windshield wipers. Side mounted tire carrier (Pickup). Spare tire. Safety package, includes: padded instrument panel and cushioned sunvisors; tinted glass; full-wrap rear window; rear bumper (Pickup); front and rear chrome bumper (Styleside Pickup); chrome front bumper; right-hand arm rest; outside left or right telescopic mirror for cabs; outside non-telescopic mirror; two hooks; seat belts; fire extinguishers (1½-qt. or 4-lb. dry chemical); cigar lighter; dome light; splash guards; locking gas tank cap; Deluxe heater (Courier); bumper guards (Courier); Deluxe wheel covers (Courier) and under-dash light (Courier). Custom Cab, includes: multi-colored woven nylon-saran seat upholstery (in striped pattern with vinyl bolster and seat facing foam-rubber padding in seat cushion and back); white

349

splatter-pattern hardboard on headlining and sides of load compartment on panel truck; sound deadener on floor of driver's compartment; insulation on firewall; two-tone paint on doors and instrument panel; arm rest on left door; white steering wheel with chrome ring; chrome-trimmed instrument cluster; bright metal grille and headlight assembly; bright metal windshield reveal molding; "Custom Cab" emblems on side doors; matched locks on all doors and dual wrap-around taillights at belt line.

NOTE: 1960 Ford "Diamond Lustre" standard colors were: Monte Carlo Red, Goldenrod Yellow, Academy Blue, Skymist Blue, Caribbean Turquoise, Adriatic Green, Holly Green, Corinthian White, Raven Black. Any standard color could be combined with Corinthian White for two-tone effect.

HISTORICAL: Total light-duty truck production (including P-100; P-350 and P-400 Series models) was 255,538. Ford was America's number two truck-maker in terms of output. Ford installed and tested a gas engine in a prototype truck this year.

Pricing

1956	5	4	3	2	1
Courier					
Sedan Delivery	520	1020	1700	2400	3400
Ranchero (Falcon)					
Pickup	680	1350	2250	3150	4500
F-100 — (½-Ton)					
Flareside Pickup	890	1770	2950	4150	5900
Styleside Pickup	930	1860	3100	4350	6200
Panel	850	1700	2850	4000	5700
Stake	830	1650	2750	3850	5500
F-250 — (¾-Ton)					
Flareside Pickup	750	1500	2500	3500	5000
Styleside Pickup	780	1560	2600	3600	5200
Stake	780	1560	2600	3600	5200
F-350 — (1-Ton)					
Flareside Pickup	740	1470	2450	3350	4900
Styleside Pickup	770	1550	2550	3600	5100
Stake	750	1500	2500	3500	5000

Price estimates (1955-up) based on top-of-the-line models.
Add five percent for 4x4.

1961 FORD

1961 Ford Falcon Ranchero Pickup (DFW)

FALCON RANCHERO PICKUP: — A new convex grille, with many thin vertical and horizontal pieces, was the most noticeable change for 1961. The spring rates were lowered and the rubber upper A-arm bushings were replaced with treaded metal ones. On the inside, the dome light was moved to the ceiling. The rocker panels and all main underbody structural members were heavily zinc-coated to protect against rust and corrosion. The six-foot pickup box provided over 31.5 cubic feet of usable loadspace. There was over 42 inches of flat floor width between the wheelhousings. The seat was covered with brown "western motif" vinyl with beige vinyl bolsters and seat facings. Other standard features included: chrome front and rear bumpers; bright-metal windshield reveal moldings; two arm rests; dome light; rearview mirror; spare tire and wheel (behind seat); two sunvisors; dispatch box; ash tray; Double-Grip door locks; "Lifeguard" steering wheel and three-speed manual transmission.

FALCON SEDAN DELIVERY: — The New Falcon Sedan Delivery shared its good looks with the Ranchero. It resembled a regular Falcon wagon. However, the side windows were blanked-out from the front doors back. It had the wagon's tailgate with roll-down window. The three-passenger seat was covered in vinyl. The plywood floor was rubber-coated.

I.D. DATA (Falcon Ranchero/Sedan Delivery): See 1960 Ranchero I.D.

1961 Ford Falcon Ranchero Pickup (OCW)

Model	Body Type	Price	Weight	Prod. Total
66A	Pickup	1887	2338	20,937
—	Sedan Delivery	2109	2463	1,988

ENGINE (Falcon Ranchero/Sedan Delivery): Displacement: 144 cu. in. Six-cylinder. 85 horsepower at 4200 R.P.M. Bore & stroke: 3.50 in. x 2.50 in. Compression ratio: 8.7:1. One-barrel carburetor.

CHASSIS: Wheelbase: 109.9 in. Overall length: 189 in. Overall width: 70 in. Overall height: 54.5 in. Payload: 800 lbs. Tires: 6.50 x 13-4PR on 13 x 4½ J safety-type wheels.

POWERTRAIN OPTIONS: Ford-O-Matic Drive automatic. 101 horsepower 170 cu. in. Six.

CONVENIENCE OPTIONS: Heavy-duty battery. Heater and defroster. Hydro-carbon emission control device. Radio and front mounted antenna. Safety Package "A" included: padded instrument panel and sunvisors; seat belts; white sidewall tires; 6.50 x 13-6PR tires; bright metal wheel covers; tinted windshield; windshield washers; electric windshield wipers; cigarette lighter; white steering wheel with chrome horn ring and backup lights. Deluxe Trim Package, includes: bright-metal molding around box and cab back; bright-metal taillight trim rings; bright metal door window moldings; white steering wheel with horn ring; cigarette lighter; dome light door switch; plus black and white or red and white vinyl upholstery.

NOTE: Colors offered on 1961 Rancheros were: Raven black. Montecarlo red, Silver gray, Chesapeake blue, Cambridge blue, Starlight blue, Laurel green, Mint green, Algiers bronze, Garden turquoise, Aquamarine, and Corinthian white. Optional two-tone combinations: Cambridge blue and Starlight blue, Laurel green and Mint green, plus Corinthian white and any solid color.

ECONOLINE PICKUP: — This looked like an Econoline van that had been customized and turned into a pickup. "Ford" was printed in block letters on the front face of the vehicle. On either side of the name were the two headlights. They were set in large, rectangular pods which came to a point at their inner ends. The small wraparound parking lights were located just above the front bumper. "Econoline" was written, in chrome, a bit below the vent windows of both doors. Cargo area was 85.9 inches long and 63 inches wide. The sides were 22.4 inches high. The cab featured: vinyl upholstery; three-speed manual transmission and an insulated engine cover between the driver and passenger seats.

1961 Ford Falcon Van (OCW)

ECONOLINE VAN: — The new Econoline van had 39 percent more loadspace than a typical half-ton panel truck. The large interior load area was over 54 inches high and 65 inches wide. Total loadspace was 204.4 cubic feet. The Econoline got better gas mileage (up to 30 m.p.g.) than standard pickups and was easier to maneuver. Among the standard features were: double side and rear doors; electric windshield wipers; outside rearview mirror; front and rear bumpers; dome light; single electric horn; turn signals and I-Beam front axle.

1961 Ford Econoline 8-Pass. Station Bus (OCW)

ECONOLINE STATION BUS: — "Announcing a new kind of station wagon" proclaimed sales literature. The station bus was essentially an Econoline van with a view. It had windows all around. There were two front doors, a pair of rear doors and two side doors (in the center on the passenger side). Standard features included: electric windshield wipers; rearview mirror; dome light; hubcaps; electric horn; turn signals; tire carrier; mechanical jack; contour front and rear bumpers and three-speed manual transmission.

I.D. DATA (Econoline): VIN # began at E105 (A) 100001.

Model	Body Type	Price	Weight	Prod. Total
E-103	Pickup	1880	2555	—
E-104	Van	1981	2588	—
E-113	Station Bus	2092	2778	—

NOTE 1: Ford records show the following Econoline production break-outs: (89B Standard Econoline bus) 8,511; (89B Custom Econoline bus) 6,571; (87A Standard Pickup) 11,893; (87A Custom Pickup) 3,000; (89A Standard Van) 28,932 and (89A Custom Van) 2,228.

ENGINE (Econoline): Displacement: 144 cu. in. Six-cylinder. 85 horsepower at 4200 R.P.M. Bore & stroke: 3.50 in. x 2.50 in. Compression ratio: 8.7:1. One-barrel carburetor.

CHASSIS: Wheelbase: 90 in. Overall length: 168.4 in. Overall width: 65 in. GVW: 3300 lbs. Tires: 7.00 x 13, six-ply.

POWERTRAIN OPTIONS: None.

1961 Ford Econoline Pickup w/Sports Body (JAG)

CONVENIENCE OPTIONS: AM radio. Fresh air heater/defroster. Windshield washers. Auxiliary gas heater. Auxiliary step. Safety Package "A," includes: padded instrument panels and sunvisors; rear door glass (van); flip or stationary seat (van); arm rests; right-hand sun visor; interior rearview mirror; cigar lighter; horn ring; ICC four-lamp flasher; dual horns; left-hand door lock; tinted windshield; bright-metal wheel covers; front and rear chrome bumpers; cargo area dome light (van) and positive crankcase ventilation. Tires: 6.50 x 13-4PR whitewall. 7.00 x 13-6PR black- or whitewall. Custom Equipment Package, includes: (on van) right-hand air duct; arm rests; cigar lighter; cargo area dome light; driver's side door lock; windows in rear doors; chrome horn ring; dual electric horns; bright-metal hubcaps; foam seat padding; passenger stationary seat; twill stripe woven plastic seat upholstery; right-hand sunvisor. (on Station Bus) twill-stripe woven plastic upholstery; hardboard sides and door trim; black vinyl arm rests; right-hand air duct; coat hooks; passenger area dome light; driver's side door lock; cigar lighter; right-hand sun visor; full-length floor mat; fiberglass interior window molding; full-length headliner; dual electric horn; chrome horn ring; bright-metal hubcaps; chrome window latches; plastic foam padding for right passenger seat; second rear passenger seat

(wagon); second and third rear passenger seats (includes heavy-duty front and rear springs and 7.00 x 13 6-PR tires (wagon). Living Quarters Interior, includes: (wagon) four-passenger sleeping capacity kit with cushions and window screens and heavy-duty battery.

NOTE: Color choices for the 1961 Econoline van were: Montecarlo Red, Raven Black, Academy Blue, Starlight Blue, Mint green, Holly Green, Goldenrod Yellow, Caribbean Turquoise, Corinthian White. Two-tone paint scheme: any standard color combined with Corinthian White.

F-100 PICKUP: — Ford's light-duty trucks were restyled this year from the frame up. They were wider and lower than last year's models. The grille consisted of two horizontal bars with a single headlight at both ends. The rectangular parking lamps were between the bars, next to the headlights. The Ford name, in block letters, was centered between the upper and lower grille pieces. This entire unit was framed with a molding. Above it were four rectangular slots and, centered on the face of the hood, the Ford truck badge. A "rocket" style emblem, carried the Ford and F-100 names. The larger windshield was of the non-wraparound variety and came with new "center sweep" wipers. The rear cab window was 28 percent larger. Vertical rectangular taillights were used as was a 64.5 inch wide, "grain tite" tailgate. Buyers had their choice of two boxes: the Flareside had rolled edge flaresides and runningboards between the cab and rear fender. The Styleside was smooth-sided. Stylesides now had a one-piece cab-and-box, which helped make them appear a bit sleeker than before. Four-wheel-drive was only available (at extra cost) on Flareside pickups. Both 6½ foot and 8 foot versions of these boxes were offered. Standard features included: Instant-Action tailgate with rattleproof hinged support arms, instead of chains, on Styleside; brown basket weave vinyl seat upholstery with dark brown moroco-grained vinyl bolster and seat facings; perforated, insulated headlining (Styleside); "Lifeguard" steering wheel; safety double-grip door latches; dome light; left-hand sunvisor; ash receptacle; dispatch box; dual electric windshield wipers; theft-retardant ignition switch; rearview mirror; All-Weather venilation; concentric steering column. Three-speed manual transmission.

F-100 PLATFORM/STAKE: — These shared the same styling and most other features found on F-100. Steel skid strips protected the floor and made it easier to slide cargo in or out. Heavy gauge steel stake pockets were set flush with the floor. Side boards and stakes were made of straight-grained wood. Bolted steel plates held the removable side boards firmly together at the top. Body sills were protected by steel end caps. An all-steel rub rail protected the body.

I.D. DATA (F-100): See 1957 F-100.

Model	Body Type	Price	Weight	Prod. Total
F-100	(80) Platform	—	3142	—
F-100	(81) Chassis w/Cab	1851	2827	—
F-100	Chassis w/cab (122 in. w.b.)	1882	2881	—
F-100	Flareside Pickup	1966	3167	—
F-100	Flareside Pickup (118 in. w.b.)	2001	3306	—
F-100	Styleside Pickup	1981	3129	—
F-100	Styleside Pickup (118 in. w.b.)	2017	3440	—
F-100	(84) Chassis	1597	2319	—
F-100	(86) Stake	2057	3267	—

NOTE 1: Ford records show the following F-100 production break-outs: (cowl) 46; (windshield) 17; (cab chassis) 12,544; (cab integral pickup) 62,410; (cab, platform and rack) 152; (Flareside pickup) 21,474; (4x4 cab) 180; (Flareside pickup) 3,361; (4x4 Flareside pickup) 2,468 and (4x4 Styleside pickup) 255.

ENGINE (F-100): Displacement: 223 cu. in. Six-cylinder. 135 horsepower at 4000 R.P.M. Bore & stroke: 3.62 in. x 3.60 in. Compression ratio: 8.4:1. One-barrel carburetor.

F-250 PICKUP: — The F-250 was a slightly more heavy-duty version of the F-100. It had larger brakes and higher capacity rear axle and rear springs. Buyers could choose from 8-foot Flareside or Styleside versions. Four-wheel-drive was only available (at extra cost) on the Flareside. Eight-hole disc wheels were standard.

F-250 PLATFORM/STAKE: — The F-250 Platform/Stake was longer and had a higher payload capacity than the F-100. Stake loadspace was 90 inches long, 74 inches wide and 28.3 inches to the top of the racks. Platform loadspace was 93.4 inches long and 79.3 inches wide. Sideboards and stakes were made of straight-grained wood.

I.D. DATA (F-250): See F-100.

Model	Body Type	Price	Weight	Prod. Total
F-250	(80) Platform	—	3409	—
F-250	(81) Chassis w/Cab	2005	3069	—
F-250	Flareside Pickup	2120	3494	—
F-250	Styleside Pickup	2134	3499	—
F-250	(84) Chassis	1741	2561	—
F-250	(86) Stake	2211	3594	—

NOTE 1: Ford records show the following F-250 production break-outs: (cowl) 108; (windshield) 27; (cab chassis) 3,557; (4x4 cab) 359; (cab-integral pickup) 10,008; (4x4 Styleside pickup) 149; (cab, platform and rack) 701; (4x4 cab, platform and rack) 78; (Flareside pickup) 4,426 and (4x4 Flareside pickup) 1,671.

ENGINE (F-250): See F-100.

F-350 PICKUP: — Although it shared "F" series styling changes for 1961, underneath the F-350 was pretty much the same as the previous year's model. However, its wheelbase was stretched to 132 inches. Both Flareside and Styleside version were offered. The Flareside had rolled edge flareboards and runningboards between the cab and rear fender. The Styleside had a one-piece integral pickup body with smooth sides. In addition to most of the same standard features found on the F-100, the F-350 had larger brakes, a heavier-duty clutch, front-only shock absorbers and a four-speed-manual transmission.

F-350 PLATFORM/STAKE: — This continued to be the heftiest light-duty Platform/Stake Ford offered. It had steel stakes. The three-section stakes sides and swing open center rack proved easier loading and unloading. Stake loadspace was 105.9 inches long, 82 inches wide and 31.2 inches to the top of the racks. Platform loadspace was 109.4 inches long and 87.3 inches wide.

I.D. DATA (F-350): See F-100.

Model	Body Type	Price	Weight	Prod. Total
F-350	(80) Platform		4017	—
F-350	(81) Chassis w/Cab	2171	3357	—
F-350	Flareside Pickup	2305	3849	—
F-350	Styleside Pickup	2321	3849	—
F-350	(84) Chassis	1906	2849	—
F-350	(86) Stake	2418	4317	—

NOTE 1: Ford records show the folliwing F-350 production break-outs: (cowl) 666; (windshield) 72; (cab chassis) 10,750; (cab, platform and rack) 2,821; (Flareside pickup) 947 and (Styleside pickup) 1,191.

ENGINE (F-350): See F-100.

CHASSIS: Wheelbase: 114 in. (F-100); 122 in. (F-100, F-250); 132 in. (F-350); 120 in. (4x4). GVW: F-100: 4000 to 5000 lbs. (5600-lbs. for 4x4). F-250: 4900 to 7400 lbs. F-350: 7600 to 9600 lbs. Tires: 6.70 x 15 four-ply (F-100); 6.50 x 16, six-ply (F-250); 8 x 17.5, six-ply (F-350).

POWERTRAIN OPTIONS: Three-speed w/overdrive (F-100), medium-duty three-speed (F-100, F-250), heavy-duty three-speed (F-350) or four-speed (F-100, F-250, 4x4) manual transmissions. Ford-O-matic transmission (F-100). Heavy-duty Cruise-O-Matic transmission (F-250, F-350). 160 horse-power 292 V-8.

CONVENIENCE OPTIONS: Four-wheel-drive (F-100/F-250 Flareside). 3500-lb. capacity rear axle (F-250 4x4). Radio. Left-hand armrest. Right-hand armrest. Fresh air heater.Recirculating heater. Painted rear bumper. Chrome front and rear bumpers (Styleside). Side mount spare wheel carrier. Heavy-duty clutch (F-100/F-250). Tinted windshield. Left and/or right outside rearview mirrors. Extra cooling radiator. Heavy-duty front springs (F-100, F-250). Heavy-duty two-stage rear springs (F-100, F-250). Heavy-duty rear springs (F-100, F-250). Larger tires. Whitewall tires. Woven plastic trim for std. cab. Turn signals. Windshield washer. Rear wraparound window (Styleside). Right-hand sunvisor. Custom Cab, includes: twill stripe woven plastic upholstery with brown woven-in bolster and brown morocco-grained vinyl facings; chrome trimmed instrument cluster; white steering wheel with chrome horn ring; foam rubber in seat (five-inches in cushion and 1¾ inches in seatback); cigar lighter; left-hand armrest; right-hand sunvisor; insulation on cowl wall in cab (F-350; standard on F-100/F-250); bright metal grille and headlight assembly; bright metal windshield reveal molding; matched locks on both doors; two-tone interior; coat hook.

NOTE: Standard Ford F series colors for 1961 were: Montecarlo Red, Goldenrod Yellow, Raven Black, Mint Green, Holly Green, Caribbean Turquoise, Academy Blue, Starlight Blue, and Corinthian White. A two tone effect was available by combining any standard color with Corinthian White (F-100 and F-250 Styleside pickups only).

HISTORICAL: Total light truck production was 213,345 units for the model-year. This included all Rancheros, Couriers and Econolines, as well as P-100 parcel delivery trucks and P-350/P-400 chassis models.

Pricing

1961	5	4	3	2	1
Falcon					
Sedan Delivery	700	1400	2350	3250	4700
Ranchero	740	1470	2450	3350	4900
Econoline					
Pickup	520	1020	1700	2400	3400
Van	420	840	1400	1950	2800
Station Bus	480	975	1600	2250	3200
F-100 — (½-Ton)					
Flareside Pickup	890	1770	2950	4150	5900
Styleside Pickup	930	1860	3100	4350	6200
Panel	850	1700	2850	4000	5700
Stake	830	1650	2750	3850	5500
F-250 — (¾-Ton)					
Flareside Pickup	750	1500	2500	3500	5000
Styleside Pickup	780	1560	2600	3600	5200
Stake	780	1560	2600	3600	5200
F-350 — (1-Ton)					
Flareside Pickup	740	1470	2450	3350	4900
Styleside Pickup	770	1550	2550	3600	5100
Stake	750	1500	2500	3500	5000

NOTE: Price estimates, 1955-up, based on top-of-the-line models. Add five percent for 4x4.

1962 FORD

1962 Ford Falcon Ranchero Pickup (OCW)

FALCON RANCHERO PICKUP: — The Ranchero featured a new squared-off grille with all vertical pieces. Parking lights were now integrated into the new front bumper. The hood was modified to give a hood scoop effect. The taillights were also revised. Other less visable changes for '62 included: increased brake lining; a pump-mounted in-line fuel filter; a clutch interlock (this became optional later in the model year); a fully aluminized muffler; improved carburetor and choke controls; white-lettered hub caps and narrower (one inch) whitewall tires (on vehicles so equipped). A three-speed manual transmission was standard.

FALCON SEDAN DELIVERY: — As before, this vehicle looked like a two-door Falcon wagon with blanked-out rear side windows. It even had the wagon's tailgate, with roll-down rear window. The tailgate opening was nearly four feet wide at the floor. The Sedan Delivery had a 76.2 cubic foot load capacity with 87 inches of loadspace length. The driver's compartment featured a three-passenger seat covered with long-wearing vinyl in a brown or beige color scheme.

I.D. DATA (Falcon Ranchero/Sedan Delivery): See 1960 Ranchero.

Model	Body Type	Price	Weight	Prod. Total
27	Pickup	1889	2348	20,842
—	Sedan Delivery	2111	2463	1,568

ENGINE (Falcon Ranchero/Sedan Delivery): Displacement: 144 cu. in. Six-cylinder. 85 horsepower at 4200 R.P.M. Bore & stroke: 3.50 in. x 2.50 in. Compression ratio: 8.7:1. One-barrel carburetor.

CHASSIS: Wheelbase: 109.5 in. Overall length: 189 in. Overall width: 70 in. Overall height: 54.5 in. GVW: 3250 lbs. Tires: 6.50 x 13, four-ply.

POWERTRAIN OPTIONS: Ford-O-Matic Drive. 101 horsepower 170 cu. in. six-cylinder. Four-speed manual transmission.

CONVENIENCE OPTIONS: Whitewall tires. AM radio. Heater and defroster. Bright metal wheel covers. Tinted windshield. Cigarette lighter. Backup lights. Electric windshield wipers (two-speed). Safety Package A, includes: padded instrument panel and sun visors. Sedan Delivery Deluxe Package, includes : bright-metal exterior moldings; tail lamp ring ornament; white steering wheel with chrome horn ring; cigarette lighter; dome light door switch; sun visor on right side; arm rests; deluxe brown nylon and vinyl or red and white all-vinyl upholstery. Ranchero Deluxe Trim Package, includes: bright-metal molding around box and cab back; bright metal tail-light trim rings; bright-metal door window moldings; white steering wheel with horn ring; cigarette lighter; dome light door switch; black and white or red and white vinyl upholstery.

1962 Ford Deluxe Econoline Pickup (OCW)

1962 Ford F-100 Frontal Styling (JAG)

ECONOLINE PICKUP: — Apparently, Ford didn't want to mess with a good thing. Styling was carried over to the new model year. However, Econolines now had larger wheelbearings. Standard features included: vinyl upholstery; three-speed manual transmission and an insulated engine cover.

1962 Ford Econoline Delivery Van (JAG)

ECONOLINE VAN: — Standard items on the 1962 Econoline Van included: double side and rear doors; electric windshield wipers; outside rear view mirror; front and rear bumpers; dome light; single electric horn; turn signals; I-Beam front axle; direct-acting, telescopic shock absorbers (front and rear); Soft-Action rear suspension with variable-rate and semi-elliptic leaf springs.

I.D. DATA (Econoline): V.I.D. numbers began at E-105 (A) 205000.

Model	Body Type	Price	Weight	Prod. Total
E-103	Custom Pickup	1881	2533	8140
E-104	Econovan	2070	2568	50,645

ENGINE (Econoline): Displacement: 144 cu. in. Six-cylinder. 85 horsepower at 4200 R.P.M. Bore & stroke: 3.50 in. x 2.50 in. Compression ratio: 8.7:1, one-barrel carburetor.

CHASSIS: Wheelbase: 90 in. Overall length: 168.4 in. Overall width: 65 in. GVW: 3300. Tires: 7.00 x 13.

POWERTRAIN OPTIONS: None.

CONVENIENCE OPTIONS: AM radio. Fresh air heater/defroster. Auxiliary step. Padded instrument panels and sun visors. Rear door glass (van). Flip-up or stationary seat (van). Arm rests. Right-hand sun visor. Cigar lighter. Horn ring. ICC four lamp flasher. Dual horns. Left-hand door lock. Tinted windshield. Bright-metal wheel covers. Front and rear chrome bumpers. Cargo area domelight (van). Positive crankcase ventilation. Tires: 6.50 x 13-4PR whitewall; 7.00 x 13-6PR black- or whitewall. Custom Equipment Package, includes: (Van) Right-hand air duct; arm rests; cigar lighter; cargo area dome light; driver's side door lock; windows in rear doors; chrome horn ring; dual electric horns; bright-metal hub caps; foam seat padding; passenger stationary seat; twill stripe woven plastic seat upholstery; right-hand sun visor. (Pickup) Woven plastic upholstery; right-hand arm rests; right-hand sun visor; cigar lighter; chrome horn ring; dual horns; cab rear wrap-around quarter windows; glove compartment door with cylinder lock; bright metal hub caps; coat hook; front body interior insulation; foam padding in passenger seat cushion and back; left-hand side-mounted cargo doors and 4350-pound GVW package.

FALCON STATION BUS: — The station bus was now considered part of the Falcon line. Standard equipment included: vinyl upholstery; two-speed electric windshield wipers; foam-cushioned adjustable driver's seat; front passenger seat; front arm rests; ash tray; dual horns and dome lights; left-hand air inlet; left-hand sun visor; inside rearview mirror and retractable side step.

FALCON CLUB WAGON: — Standard features on the Club Wagon included: woven plastic upholstery; full-length floor mat and headlining; foam-cushioned front passenger seat; painted left-hand outside mirror; windshield washers; cigarette lighter; dual sun visors; four coat hooks and right-hand air inlet.

1962 Ford Falcon Deluxe Club Wagon (OCW)

FALCON DELUXE CLUB WAGON: — This was the top-of-the-line model. It featured (in addition to, or in place of, items on the base club wagon): padded instrument panel; all-vinyl pleated upholstery; Deluxe steering wheel; padded sun visors; bright left-hand outside mirror; bright-finished bumpers; bright body side moldings; bright hub caps and a spare tire cover.

I.D. DATA (Falcon): The first digit indicated the year. The second (letter) designated the assembly plant. The third digit identified the line. The fourth the body style. The fifth (letter) represented the engine. The last six digits were the sequential production numbers.

Model	Body Type	Price	Weight	Prod. Total
E-11	Station Bus	2287	2712	Note 1
E-12	Club Wagon	2436	2770	Note 1
E-13	Club Wagon (Deluxe)	2673	2796	Note 1

NOTE 1: Ford Falcon production records list the Model 89B "Business Club Wagon" with a production total of 18,153 units. There are no separate breakouts for the three models/trim levels.

ENGINE (Falcon): Station Bus and Club Wagon, same as Econoline. Deluxe Club Wagon: Displacement: 170 cu. in. Six-cylinder. 101 horsepower at 4400 R.P.M. Bore & Stroke: 3.50 in. x 2.94 in. Compression Ratio: 8.7:1, one-barrel carburetor.

CHASSIS: Wheelbase: 90 in. Overall length: 168.3 in. Overall width: 75 in. Overall height: 76.9 in. Tires: 6.50 x 13.

POWERTRAIN OPTIONS: 170 cu. in. six-cylinder.

CONVENIENCE OPTIONS: Arm rests (for second/third seats). Cigarette lighter. Full wheel covers. Gas-fired recirculating heater. Non-glare inside mirror. Outside rearview mirrors. Padded instrument panel and sun visors. AM radio. Second or second and third row three-passenger seats. Seat belts. Spare tire cover lock. Spotlight. Right-hand sun visor. Tinted windshield. Windshield washers.

1962 Ford F-100 Styleside Pickup (JAG)

F-100 PICKUP: — The F-100 received a very minor facelift for 1962. The Ford name was now printed in smaller block letters just above the grille frame. A thin horizontal bar, divided at the center by a thin vertical bar, ran between the two larger ones. The hub caps were also changed to solid argent silver finish. Buyers could choose from 6½-foot and 8-foot Flareside and Styleside models. Two versions of the Styleside were offered, the intergal "one-piece" type, introduced in 1961, and the "two-piece" type used on 1957-60 models. Four-wheel-drive (4x4) models were not available with integral Styline bodies. Standard equipment included: left-hand sun visor; dome light; oil filter; painted front bumper; electric windshield wipers; dispatch box and rear view mirror.

F-100 PLATFORM/STAKE: — Except for the minor styling changes noted on the pickup, the 1962 F-100 platform/stake was basically the same as last year's model. Its side boards and stakes were made of wood. Bolted steel plates held side boards firmly together at top, yet permitted quick, easy removal of stake sections. Body sills were protected by steel end caps.

I.D. DATA (F-100): See 1957 F-100 I.D.

Model	Body Type	Price	Weight	Prod. Total
F-100	(80) Platform	—	3142	Note 1
F-100	(81) Chassis w/Cab	1864	2827	Note 1
F-100	(122") Chassis w/cab	1901	2939	Note 1
F-100	Flareside Pickup	1979	3194	Note 1
F-100	(118") Flareside Pickup	2015	3384	Note 1
F-100	Styleside P.U. (integral)	1995	3244	Note 1
F-100	Styleside P.U. (separate)	2006	—	Note 1
F-100	(118") Styleside P.U.	2031	3409	Note 1
F-100	(118") Styleside (seperate)	2042	—	Note 1
F-100	(84) Chassis	1610	2319	Note 1
F-100	(86) Stake	2070	3267	Note 1

NOTE 1: Ford records show the following F-100 production break-outs: (cowl) 16; (windshield) 11; (cab) 9,456; (integral-body pickup) 68,983; (cab, platform and rack) 175; (Flareside cab-pickup) 29,934 and (Styleside cab-pickup) 24,610.

ENGINE (F-100): Same as 1961.

F-250 PICKUP: — Three styles of F-250 pickups were offered in 1962: Flareside, integral Styleside, and "two-piece" Styleside. Four-wheel-drive was available at extra cost.

F-250 PLATFORM/STAKE: — The F-350 Stake had a loadspace 90 inches long, 74 inches wide and 28.3 inches to the top of the racks. The Platform had a loadspace 93.4 inches long and 79.3 inches wide. Steel skid strips protected the floor and made it easier to slide cargo in or out. The side boards and stakes were made of straight-grained wood. An all-steel rub rail protected the body.

I.D. DATA (F-250): See F-100 I.D.

Model	Body Type	Price	Weight	Prod. Total
F-250	(80) Platform	3409	—	—
F-250	(81) Chassis w/Cab	2005	3069	—
F-250	Pickup (Flareside)	2120	3494	—
F-250	Pickup (Styleside)	2134	3499	—
F-250	(84) Chassis	1741	2561	—
F-250	(86) Stake	2211	3594	—

Note 1: Ford records show the following F-250 production break-outs: (cowl) 94; (windshield) 130; (cab) 4,483; (integral-body pickup) 10,703; (cab, platform and rack) 867; (Flareside cab-pickup) 7,247 and (Styleside cab-pickup) 6,002.

ENGINE (F-250): See F-100.

F-350 PICKUP: — The rear axle capacity of the husky F-350 pickup was more than double that of the F-100. It also had a much roomier cargo area. The F-350 was available with 9 foot. Flareside and Styleside boxes. Four-speed manual transmission was standard.

F-350 PLATFORM/STAKE: — The F-350 Platform/Stake had a 9 foot body with steel stakes. Body sills were protected by steel end caps. Heavy-gauge steel stake pockets were set flush with the floor, which had steel skid strips. The spare tire carrier was located under the frame. A four-speed manual transmission was standard.

I.D. DATA (F-350): See F-100 I.D.

Model	Body Type	Price	Weight	Prod. Total
F-350	(80) Platform	—	4017	—
F-350	(81) Chas. w/Cab	2171	3357	—
F-350	Pickup (Flareside)	2305	3849	—
F-350	Pickup (Styleside)	2321	3849	—
F-350	(84) Chassis	1906	2849	—
F-350	(86) Stake	2419	4317	—

NOTE 1: Ford records show the following F-350 production break-outs: (cowl) 794; (windshield) 102; (cab) 12,483; (cab, platform and rack) 4,229; (Flareside cab-pickup) 1,216 and (Stleside cab-pickup) 1,503.

ENGINE (F-350): See F-100.

CHASSIS: Wheelbase: 114 in. (F-100); 122 in. (F-100, F-250); 132 in. (F-350); 120 in. (4x4). GVW: F-100: 4000 to 5000-lbs. (5600 4x4). F-250: 4900 to 7400-lbs. F-350: 7600 to 9600-lbs. Tires: 6.70 x 15, four-ply (F-100); 6.50 x16, six-ply (F-250); 8 x 17.5, six-ply (F-350).

POWERTRAIN OPTIONS: Three-speed with overdrive (F-100)/ medium-duty three-speed (F-100, F-250)/ heavy-duty three-speed (F-350)/ four-speed (F-100, F-250, 4wd)/ Ford-O-Matic (F-100) or heavy-duty Cruise-O-Matic (F-250, F-350) transmissions. 160 horsepower 292 V-8.

CONVENIENCE OPTIONS: Four-wheel-drive (F-100, F-250 Flaresides). 3500-lb. capacity rear axle (F-250 4x4). Radio. Left-hand armrest. Right-hand armrest. Painted rear bumper. Chrome front and rear bumpers (Styleside). Fresh air heater. Recirculating heater. Laminated glass. Side mount spare wheel carrier. Heavy-duty clutch (F-100, F-250). Tinted windshield. Left and/or right outside rearview mirrors. Extra cooling radiator. Heavy-duty front springs (F-100, F-250). Heavy-duty two-stage rear springs (F-100, F-250). Heavy-duty rear springs (F-100, F-250). Larger tires. WSW tires. Woven plastic trim for standard cab. Turn signals. Windshield washer. Rear wrap around window (Styleside). Right-hand sunvisor.

Custom Cab, includes: woven plastic upholstery with bolster and vinyl facings; chrome-trimmed instrument cluster; white steering wheel with chrome horn ring; foam rubber in seat (five inches in cushion and 1¾ inches in seatback); cigar lighter; left-hand armrest; right-hand sunvisor; insulation on cowl wall in F-350 cab (standard in F-100/F-250); bright metal grille and headlight assembly; bright metal windshield reveal molding; matched locks on both doors; two-tone interior and coat hook.

HISTORICAL: Introduced: Fall 1961. Model-year production: (light-duty total) 267,878; includes "P" series parcel vans as follows: P-100/227 units; P-200/2,269 units and P-400/1,149 units. This total *does not* include the 18,153 Falcon "Business Club Wagons," which Ford lumped-in with passenger cars. Innovations: New grille with Ford name above it. Tapered seat spark plugs introduced. Ford adopted air-cooled ignition contact points for trucks. The design of multiple electrical connectors was simplified. Over 600 different truck-model variations were available this year.

Pricing

	5	4	3	2	1
1962					
Falcon					
Sedan Delivery	700	1400	2350	3250	4700
Ranchero	740	1470	2450	3350	4900
Econoline					
Pickup	520	1020	1700	2400	3400
Van	420	840	1400	1950	2800
Station Bus	480	975	1600	2250	3200
F-100 — (½-Ton)					
Flareside Pickup	890	1770	2950	4150	5900
Styleside Pickup	930	1860	3100	4350	6200
Panel	850	1700	2850	4000	5700
Stake	830	1650	2750	3850	5500
F-250 — (¾-Ton)					
Flareside Pickup	750	1500	2500	3500	5000
Styleside Pickup	780	1560	2600	3600	5200
Stake	780	1560	2600	3600	5200
F-350 — (1-Ton)					
Flareside Pickup	740	1470	2450	3350	4900
Styleside Pickup	770	1550	2550	3600	5100
Stake	750	1500	2500	3500	5000

NOTE: Add five percent for 4x4.
1955-up prices based on top-of-line models.

1963 FORD

1963 Ford Falcon Rancero Pickup (OCW)

FALCON RANCHERO PICKUP: — The most noticeable change for '63 was the Ranchero's new convex horizontal grid grille. The taillights were also revised. The parking lights had amber lenses. The Ford name was printed in black on the hub caps. Other new features included: self adjusting brakes; an aluminized tailpipe; electric windshield wipers; hydraulic valve lifters (for the six); a fully-synchronized three-speed manual transmission and a larger front stabilizer strut. As before, the six-foot long, 4½-foot wide and 15½ inch deep pickup box provided a total of 31½ cubic feet of usable loadspace. The integral cab and pickup box were made of heavy-gauge steel. The spare tire was still located in the cab, behind the seat, for easy roll-out acessibility. The upholstery had a "western motif" (steer's head pattern) imprinted on beige vinyl with lighter beige vinyl bolsters and seat facings.

FALCON SEDAN DELIVERY: — According to sales literature, the 1963 Falcon Sedan Delivery was "designed to haul small loads which require protection from the weather." Its seven-foot floor was constructed of steel and weather-sealed plywood with longitudinal steel strips to provide easier loading. The tailgate could be opened with a single center latch and its rear window could be manually lowered. Standard equipment included: bright-metal drip moldings; dome light; spare tire and wheel; left side sunvisor; dispatch box; ash try; Double-Grip door locks; Lifeguard steering wheel and dual single-speed electric windshield wipers.

I.D. DATA (Falcon Ranchero/Sedan Delivery): — See 1960 Ranchero.

Model	Body Type	Price	Weight	Prod. Total
27	Pickup	1898	2348	18,533*
—	Sedan Delivery	2111	2463	1,038

NOTE: A total of 6,315 of the pickups were equipped with the Deluxe option. A total of 113 Sedan Deliveries were Deluxe versions, too.

ENGINE (Falcon Ranchero/Sedan Delivery): Displacement: 144 cu. in. Six-cylinder. 85 horsepower at 4200 R.P.M. Bore & stroke: 3.50 x 2.50 in. Compression ratio: 8.7:1. One-barrel carburetor.

CHASSIS: Wheelbase: 109.5 in. Overall length: 189 in. Overall width: 70 in. Overall height: 54.5 in. Payload Capacity: 800 lbs. Tires: 6.50 x 13-4PR on 13x4½ J safety-type wheels.

POWERTRAIN OPTIONS: 101 horsepower 170 cu. in. six-cylinder. 164 horsepower 260 cu. in. V-8. Four-speed manual or Ford-O-Matic transmission.

NOTE: The V-8 was introduced in mid-model year. Vehicles so-equipped had 7.00 x 13 tires, a larger rear axle and special underbody reinforcements.

CONVENIENCE OPTIONS: Power steering (only with V-8). Heavy-duty battery. Whitewall tires. 6.50 x 13 6-PR tires. Heater and defroster. Air conditioner. Push-button radio and front mounted antenna. Seat belts. Power-operated tailgate window (Sedan Delivery). Bright metal wheel covers. Tinted glass. Windshield washers. Two-speed electric windshield wipers. Cigarette lighter. Backup lights. Safety Package "A" with padded instrument panel and sunvisors. Deluxe Trim Package, includes: (Sedan Delivery) bright-metal moldings on door window frames and tailgate window opening; arm rests; right-hand sunvisor. (Ranchero): bright-metal moldings around top of box and cab back, plus frames on door window. (Both): a black or red steering wheel with horn ring; cigarette lighter; dome light door switch and black or red vinyl upholstery.

NOTE: Solid colors available in '63 were: Raven black, Rangoon red, Viking blue, Oxford blue, Silver moss, Ming green, Champagne, Glacier blue, Heritage burgundy, Sandshell beige, and Corinthian white. Optional two-tone combinations were: Glacier blue and Viking blue, Black and Champagne, and Corinthian white with any solid color.

ECONOLINE PICKUP: — Although the styling was untouched, changes were· made to the Econoline for 1963. Among them were gray-toned upholstery and five-leaf rear springs. The standard features included: vinyl upholstery; three-speed manual transmission; insulated engine cover and amber parking lights lenses.

1963 Ford Econoline Deluxe 8-Pass. Station Bus

ECONOLINE VAN: — Standard items on the 1963 Econoline Van included: double side and rear doors; electric windshield wipers; outside rear view mirror; front and rear bumpers; dome light; single electric horn; turn signals; I-Beam front axle; direct-acting, telescopic shock absorbers (front and rear) and Soft-Action rear suspension with variable-rate, semi-elliptic leaf springs.

I.D. DATE (Econoline): — See F-100 I.D.

Model	Body Type	Price	Weight	Prod. Total
E103	Pickup	1890	2533	Note 1
E104	Van	2069	2568	Note 1

NOTE 1: Ford records show Econoline production break-outs as follows: **Pickup:** (standard) 10,372; (Custom) 1,022. **Regular van:** (standard) 47,119; (Custom) 1,501. **Display van:** (standard) 3,359; (Custom) 98; **Window van:** (standard) 5,376; (Custom 332) and **Cargo van:** (standard) 1,153; (Custom) 88.

ENGINE (Econoline): Displacement: 144 cu. in. OHV. Six-cylinder. 85 horsepower at 4200 R.P.M. Bore & stroke: 3.50 in. x 2.50 in. Compression ratio: 8.7:1. one-barrel carburetor.

CHASSIS: Wheelbase: 90 in. Overall Length: 168.4 in. Overall Width: 65 in. GVW: 3,300. Tires: 6.50 x 13.

POWERTRAIN OPTIONS: None

CONVENIENCE OPTIONS: AM radio. Fresh air heater/defroster. Auxiliary step. Padded instrument panels and sunvisors. Rear door glass (van). Flip or stationary seat (van). Arm rests. Right-hand sunvisor. Cigar lighter. Horn ring. ICC four lamp flasher. Dual horns. Left-hand door lock. Tinted windshield. Bright-metal wheel covers. Cargo area domelight (van). Positive crankcase ventilation. Tires: 6.50 x 13 in. 4-PR whitewall. 7.00 x 13 in. 6-PR blackwall or whitewall. Custom Equipment Package, includes: (Van) Right-hand air duct; arm rests; cigar lighter; cargo area dome light; driver's side door lock; windows in rear doors; chrome horn ring; dual electric horns; bright metal hub caps; foam seat padding; passenger stationary seat; twill stripe woven plastic seat upholstery; right-hand sunvisor. (Pickup) Woven plastic upholstery; right-hand air rests. Arm rests. Right-hand sunvisor. Cigar lighter. Chrome horn ring. Dual horns. Cab rear wrap-around quarter windows. Glove compartment door with cylinder lock. Bright metal hub caps. Coat hook. Front body interior insulation. Foam padding in passenger seat cushion and back. One-Ton payload package. Left-hand side mounted cargo doors. 4,350 pound GVW package.

FALCON STATION BUS: — The unchanged station bus had a 204 cubic foot load capacity. Standard equipment included: gray vinyl upholstery; two-speed electric windshield wipers; foam-cushioned adjustable driver's seat; front passenger seat; front arm rests; ash tray; dual horns and dome lights; left-hand air inlet; left-hand sunvisor; inside rearview mirror and retractable side step.

FALCON CLUB WAGON: — Standard features on the Club Wagon included: woven plastic upholstery; full-length floor mat and headlining; foam-cushioned front passenger seat; painted left-hand outside mirror; windshield washers; cigarette lighter; dual sunvisors; four coat hooks and right-hand air inlet.

FALCON DELUXE CLUB WAGON: — This was the top-of-the-line model. It featured (in addition to, or in place of, items on the base club wagon): padded instrument panel; all-vinyl pleated upholstery; Deluxe steering wheel; padded sunvisors; bright left-hand outside mirror; bright finish bumpers; bright bodyside moldings; bright hub caps and a spare tire cover.

I.D. DATA (Falcon): See 1962 Falcon I.D.

Model	Body Type	Price	Weight	Prod. Total
E11	Station Bus	2287	2712	Note 1
E12	Club Wagon	2436	2770	Note 1
E13	Club Wagon (Deluxe)	2673	2796	Note 1

NOTE 1: Ford records show the following production break-outs: (standard Station Bus) 10,332; (Custom Station Bus) 4,378 and (Club Wagon) 2,923.

ENGINE: (Falcon): Station bus and Club wagon, same as Econoline. Deluxe Club Wagon: Displacement: 170 cu. in. Six-cylinder. 101 horsepower at 4400 R.P.M. Bore & Stroke: 3.50 x 2.94 in. Compression Ratio: 8.7:1. one-barrel carburetor.

CHASSIS: Wheelbase: 90 in. Overall Length: 168.3 in. Overall Width: 75 in. Overall Height: 76.9 in. Tires: 6.50 x 13.

POWERTRAIN OPTIONS: 170 cu. in. six.

CONVENIENCE OPTIONS: Arm rests (for second/third seats). Cigarette lighter. Full wheel covers. Gas-fired recirculating heater. Non-glare inside mirror. Outside rearview mirrors. Padded instrument panel and sun visors. AM radio. Second or second and third row three-passenger seats. Seat belts. Spare tire cover lock. Spotlight. Right-hand sunvisor. Tinted windshield. Windshield washers.

1963 Ford F-100 Styleside Custom Cab Pickup (CW)

F-100 PICKUP: — According to sales literature, the new 1963 F-100 pickup was "built for rough loading and hard use." The copy said, " It's designed to keep going no matter what, to stay out of trouble and hold down your repair bills." Like big, 20-ton trucks, the F-100 had an I-beam front axle; parallel-rail frame; variable-rate rear springs and a straddle-mounted rear axle drive pinion. A new grille with small, stacked horizontal pieces was the main styling change for the year. The pedals' position was now closer to the floor. A three-spoke steering wheel was used. Standard transmission was a new, fully-synchronized three-speed manual unit. There were locks on both doors. The seats had new synthetic foam cushions. Plus, there was a 20x12x2½ inch storage compartment, with zippered vinyl cover, optional at extra-cost. Buyers could choose from three body styles: Flareside (with wood floor and running board between rear fender and back of cab); integral one-piece cab and Styleside box (with steel floor); or two-piece cab-pickup with Styleside box.

F-100 PLATFORM/STAKE: — The new F-100 Platform/Stake shared most of the same features as the pickup. Steel skid strips protected its floor. Heavy gauge steel stake pockets were set flush with the floor. Side boards and stakes were made of straight-grained wood. Body sills were protected by steel end caps.

I.D. DATA (F-100): The first letter and two digits represented the series. Next was the letter code for the engine, letter code for assembly plant, then six digits which indicated sequential production numbers.

1963 Ford F-100 Styleside Custom Cab Pickup (JAG)

Model	Body Type	Price	Weight	Prod. Total
F-100	(80) Platform	2052	3152	Note 1
F-100	(81) Chassis w/Cab	1888	2837	Note 1
F-100	Flareside Pickup	2002	3204	Note 1
F-100	(118") Flareside Pickup	2038	3409	Note 1
F-100	Styleside Pickup	2030	3254	Note 1
F-100	(118") Styleside Pickup	2066	3389	Note 1
F-100	Styleside P.U. (integral)	2019	3254	Note 1
F-100	(118") Styleside Pickup	2055	3417	Note 1
F-100	(86) Stake	2094	3277	Note 1

Note 1: Ford records show the following F-100 production breakouts: (cowl) 20; (windshield) 19; (cab) 6,686; (4x4 cab) 179; (integral pickup) 40,535; (cab, platform and rack) 190; (Flareside cab-pickup) 35,963; (Styleside cab-pickup) 76,728; (4x4 Flareside cab-pickup) 967 and (4x4 Styleside cab-pickup) 2,809.

ENGINE (F-100): Same as 1962.

F-250 PICKUP: — The ¾-ton F-250 pickup came with most of the same features as the F-100. It was available in 8-ft. Flareside and (one- or two-piece) Styleside versions. Four-wheel-drive (4x4) was an extra-cost option.

F-250 PLATFORM/STAKE: — Like all light duty Ford trucks in '63, the F-250 Platform/Stake had 22 pounds of sound deadening insulation. That was about eight pounds more than Chevrolet's extra-cost cab. Loadspace on the 7½-ft. Stake bed was 90 x 74 inches with 28.3 inches height to top of racks. An all-steel rub rail protected the body. Bolted steel plates held side boards firmly together at top, yet permitted quick, easy removal of stake sections.

I.D. DATA (F-250): See F-100.

Model	Body Type	Price	Weight	Prod. Total
F-250	(80) Platform	2206	3459	Note 1
F-250	(81) Chassis w/Cab	2042	3119	Note 1
F-250	Flareside Pickup	2157	3569	Note 1
F-250	Styleside Pickup	2183	3564	Note 1
F-250	Styleside P.U. (integral)	2172	3590	Note 1
F-250	(86) Stake	2247	3644	Note 1

Note 1: Ford records show the following F-250 production break-outs: (cowl) 63; (windshield) 72; (cab) 4,273; (4x4 cab) 348; (integral pickup) 5,456; (platform) 795; (4x4 platform) 89; (Flareside pickup) 6,673; (Styleside pickup) 14,159; (4x4 Flareside pickup) 865 and (4x4 Styleside pickup) 1,835.

ENGINE (F-250): See F-100.

F-350 PICKUP: The biggest Ford pickup in 1963 was the one-ton F-350. It was available with 9-ft. Flareside (with wood floors and running boards from rear fender to back of cab) or smooth-side two-piece Styleside. It came with a four-speed manual transmission as standard equipment.

F-350 PLATFORM/STAKE: — The 9-ft. F-350 Platform/Stake was more than adequate to handle payloads too bulky or heavy for its F-100 or F-250 counterparts. It had steel stakes and an all-steel rub rail.

I.D. DATA (F-350): See F-100.

Model	Body Type	Price	Weight	Prod. Total
F-350	(80) Platform	2410	4147	Note 1
F-350	(81) Chassis w/Cab	2212	3487	Note 1
F-350	Pickup	2345	3989	Note 1
F-350	Pickup	2362	3977	Note 1
F-350	(86) Stake	2459	4427	Note 1

356

Note 1: Ford records show the following F-350 production break-outs: (cowl) 676; (windshield) 120; (cab) 15,127; (platform) 3,808; (Flareside) 1,240 and (Styleside) 1,470.

ENGINE (F-350): See F-100.

CHASSIS: Wheelbase: 114 in. (F-100); 122 in. (F-100, F-250); 132 in. (F-350); 120 in. (4x4). GVW: **(F-100):** 4000- to 5000-lbs. (5600-lbs. 4x4). **(F-250):** 4900- to 7400-lbs. **(F-350):** 7600- to 9600-lbs. Tires: 6.70 x 15, four-ply (F-100); 6.50 x 16, six-ply (F-250); 8 x 17.5, six-ply (F-350)

POWERTRAIN OPTIONS: Three-speed with overdrive (F-100); medium-duty three -speed (F-100/F-250); heavy-duty three-speed (F-350); four-speed (F-100/F-250/4x4); Ford-O-Matic (F-100); heavy-duty Cruise-O-Matic (F-250/F-350) transmissions. 160 horsepower 292 V8.

CONVENIENCE OPTIONS: Four-wheel-drive (F-100/F-250 Flaresides). 3500-lb. capacity rear axle (F-250 4x4). Radio. Left-hand armrest. Right-hand armrest. Heater-defroster. 42-and 60-ampere alternators. Painted rear bumper. Chrome front and rear bumpers (Styleside). Side mount spare wheel carrier. Heavy-duty clutch (F-100, F-250). Tinted windshield. Left and/or right outside rearview mirrors. Extra cooling radiator. Heavy-duty front springs (F-100), F-250. Heavy-duty two-stage rear springs (F-100, F-250). Heavy-duty rear springs (F-100, F-250). Larger tires. White-wall tires. Woven plastic trim for standard cab. Turn signals. Windshield washer. Rear wrap around window (Styleside). Right-hand sunvisor. Custom Cab, includes: woven plastic upholstery with bolster and vinyl facings; chrome trimmed instrument cluster; white steering wheel with chrome horn ring; foam rubber in seat (five inches in cushion); cigar lighter; left-hand armrest; right-hand sunvisor; insulation on cowl wall in F-350 cab (standard in F-100/F-250); bright metal grille and headlight assembly; bright metal windshield reveal molding; matched locks on both doors; two-tone interior and coat hook.

HISTORICAL: Introduced: Fall 1961. Model Year Production: (All light-duty trucks) 315,274. This total includes: (P-100 chassis) 421; (P-350 chassis and windshield) 461; (P-350 stripped chassis) 1,791; (P-400 stripped chassis) 1,234 and (P-400 chassis and windshield) 207 trucks in the parcel delivery series. This total does not include Falcon Station Buses. Innovations: Redisgned pickup grille. Diesel engine introduced for some larger "F" series trucks.

Pricing

1963	5	4	3	2	1
Falcon					
Sedan Delivery	700	1400	2350	3250	4700
Ranchero	720	1470	2450	3350	4900
Econoline					
Pickup	520	1020	1700	2400	3400
Van	420	840	1400	1950	2800
Station Bus	480	975	1600	2250	3200
F-100 — (½-Ton)					
Flareside Pickup	890	1770	2950	4150	5900
Styleside Pickup	930	1860	3100	4350	6200
Panel	850	1700	2850	4000	5700
Stake	830	1650	2750	3850	5500
F-250 — (¾-Ton)					
Flareside Pickup	750	1500	2500	3500	5000
Styleside Pickup	780	1560	2600	3600	5200
Stake	780	1560	2600	3600	5200
F-350 — (1-Ton)					
Flareside Pickup	740	1470	2450	3350	4900
Styleside Pickup	770	1550	2500	3600	5100
Stake	750	1500	2500	3500	5000

Add five percent for 4x4.
1955-up prices based pon top-of-the-line models.

1964 FORD

1964 Ford Falcon Ranchero Pickup (OCW)

FALCON RANCHERO PICKUP: — The Ranchero was restyled for '64. Although it bore a strong resemblance to the previous model, it was different. This truck was longer, wider and heftier. It had new bumpers, a new hood, bodyside sculpturing and trim, taillights and a forward slanting grille. The interior had a new dash and shallow-dish, color-keyed steering wheel. The Ranchero standard cab's vinyl upholstery had a steer's head imprint on the seat cushion and seat back, with color-matching bolsters around the sides, top and bottom. The improved chassis had larger rear springs and better front suspension lower arm bushings. The 6 x 4½ foot x 14.5 inch deep box provided 30 cubic feet of usable loadspace. The tailgate was only 28 inches above the ground. Side loading height was just 39.5 inches. Standard equipment included: chrome front and rear bumpers; dual electric windshield wipers; dual electric horns; bright metal windshield reveal moldings, taillight trim rings and hub caps; arm rests; dome light; rearview mirror; sunvisors; dispatch box; ash tray; spare tire and spare wheel.

FALCON SEDAN DELIVERY: — The Falcon Sedan Delivery shared styling and mechanical features with the Ranchero. The tailgate opening was 45.5 inches wide and 27 inches high. It had a 78 cubic foot cargo area. Its seven foot long floor was made of steel and weather-sealed plywood with longitudinal steel strips. All main underbody structural members were heavily galvanized for protection against rust and corrosion. Standard items included: bright metal drip moldings; left side sunvisor and most features found on the Ranchero.

I.D. DATA (Falcon Ranchero/Sedan Delivery): See 1960 Ranchero I.D.

Model	Body Type	Price	Weight	Prod. Total
66A	Pickup	2047	2748	9,916
78A	Sedan Delivery	2260	2858	776

ADDITIONAL PRODUCTION: In addition to the production figures given above, for the standard models, Ford records show the following production break-outs: (Model 66B Deluxe Ranchero) 7,165; (Model 66H Deluxe Ranchero w/bucket seats) 235 and (Model 78B) Deluxe Sedan Delivery) 98.

ENGINE (Falcon Ranchero/Sedan Delivery): Displacement: 144 cu. in. OHV Six. 85 horsepower at 4200 R.P.M. Bore & stroke: 3.50 in. x 2.50 in. Compression ratio: 8.7:1. One-barrel carburetor.

CHASSIS: Wheelbase: 109.5 in. Overall length: 189.5 in. Overall width: 71.6 in. GVW: 3340. Tires: 6.50 x 13 6-PR (Six-cylinder); 7.00 x 13 4-PR (V-8).

POWERTRAIN OPTIONS: Four-speed manual or Ford-O-Matic transmissions. 101 horsepower 170 cu. in. six-cylinder. 116 horsepower 200 cu. in. six-cylinder (w/automatic only). 164 horsepower 260 cu. in. V-8.

CONVENIENCE OPTIONS: Power steering. Heavy-duty battery. Heater and defroster. Air conditioner. Push-button radio and front-mounted antenna. White sidewall tires. Bright metal wheel covers. Tinted glass. Two speed electric windshield wipers with windshield washers. Bucket seats. Cigarette lighter. Backup lights. Bodyside moldings (Ranchero). Safety belts. Power-operated tailgate window (Sedan Delivery). **Safety Package:** padded instrument panel and sunvisors. **Deluxe Trim Package:** (Sedan Delivery) bright metal moldings on door window frames and tailgate window opening, arm rests and right-hand sunvisor; (Ranchero) bright metal moldings around top of box and cab back, plus frames on door windows; (Both models) a black or red steering wheel with horn ring, cigarette lighter, dome light door switch and black or red pleated vinyl upholstery.

NOTE: 7,400 Rancheros had the Deluxe package. Of these, 235 were equipped with bucket seats.

NOTE: Solid colors available on the 1964 Ranchero/Sedan Delivery were: Raven black, Rangoon red, Guardsman blue, Skylight blue, Silversmoke gray, Dynasty green, Vintage burgundy, Chantilly beige and Wimbledon white. Optional two-tone combinations were: Guardsman blue with Skylight blue; Skylight blue with Guardsman blue or Wimbledon white for upper body color, with any of the above colors for the lower part of the body.

ECONOLINE PICKUP: — You'd have to go inside to find much difference from last year's model. Among the new features were: cab headliner, color-keyed upholstery and a locking glove compartment. Other standard features included: a spare tire; vinyl upholstery; three-speed manual transmission; insulated engine cover; left-hand sunvisor and single horn.

ECONOLINE VAN: — An 8½-inch heavy-duty clutch and self-adjusting brakes were a couple standard items on the new Econoline Van. Other standard features were: color-keyed vinyl upholstery; left-hand fresh air inlet; dual electric windshield wipers; painted front and rear bumpers and hub caps; dome lights; ash tray; matched locks for all doors; coat hook; headlining in driver's area and arm rests.

ECONOLINE PANEL VAN: — This new model was basically just an Econoline van without side cargo doors.

I.D. DATA: See F-100 I.D.

Model	Body Type	Price	Weight	Prod. Total
87A	Standard Pickup	1885	2530	4,196
89A	Standard Van	2091	2565	44,059
89A	Standard Panel Van	2037	2565	1,770

ADDITIONAL PRODUCTION: In addition to the figures given above, Ford records show the following production break-outs: (87B Custom Econoline Pickup) 988; (89E Standard Display Van) 3,621; (89F Standard Window Van) 6,289; (89G Standard Cargo Van) 1,495; (89A Custom Panel Van) 90; (89A Custom Regular Van) 2,741; (89E Custom Display Van) 138; (89F Custom Window Van) 812 and (89G Custom Cargo Van) 215.

ENGINE (Econoline): Displacement: 114 cu. in. OHV six-cylinder. 85 horsepower at 4200 R.P.M. Bore & stroke: 3.50 x 2.50 in. Compression Ratio: 8.7:1. One-barrel carbureator.

CHASSIS: — Wheebase: 90 in. Overall Length: 168.4 in. Overall Width: 65 in. GVW: 3,600-4,850 pounds. Tires: 6.50 x 13.

POWERTRAIN OPTIONS: — 170 cu. in. six-cylinder. Four-speed manual or three-speed automatic transmissions.

CONVENIENCE OPTIONS: AM radio. Fresh air heater/defroster. Padded instrument panel and sunvisors. Flip-Swing or stationary passenger seat. Seat belts. Interior rearview mirror. ICC emergency lamp flasher. Tinted windshield. Windshield washer. Two-speed electric windshield wipers. Front and rear chrome bumpers. Whitewall tires. **Display Van Option:** fixed windows in the right side of the cargo area. **Window Van Option:** fixed windows all around. **Custom Package:** color-keyed woven plastic upholstery; right-hand fresh-air inlet and sunvisor; cigar lighter; dual horns; bright metal hub caps; chrome horn ring; cowl-wall trim panels; insulation on cowl wall; headlining on cargo area; windows in rear doors; foam padding and optional passenger seat; (Custom Pickup also has) woven plastic upholstery; right-hand air duct; arm rests; right-hand sunvisor; cigar lighter; chrome horn ring; dual horns; Cab rear wrap-around quarter windows; glove compartment door with cylinder lock; bright metal hub caps; coat hook; front body interior insulation; foam padding in passenger seat cushion and back. **One-Ton Payload Package:** left-hand side-mounted cargo doors and 4,350 or 4,850-pound GVW Packages.

NOTE: Econoline color choices for '64 were: Rangoon Red, Bengal Tan, Raven Black, Pagoda Green, Holly Green, Caribbean Turquoise, Academy blue, Skylight Blue, Wimbledon White, Chrome Yellow, Pure White. A two-tone effect was available with Wimbledon White combined with any standard color except Chrome Yellow or Pure White.

FALCON STATION BUS: The unchanged station bus had a 204 cu. ft. load capacity. Standard equipment included: gray vinyl upholstery; two-speed electric windshield wipers; foam-cushioned adjustable driver's seat; front passenger seat; front arm rests; ash tray; dual horns and dome lights; left-hand air inlet and sunvisor; inside rearview mirror and retractable side step.

FALCON CLUB WAGON: — Standard features on the Club Wagon included: woven plastic upholstery; full-length floor mat and headlining; foam-cushioned front passenger seat; painted left-hand outside mirror; windshield washers; cigarette lighter; dual sunvisors; four coat hooks and right-hand air inlet.

1964 Ford Falcon Deluxe Club Wagon (JAG)

FALCON DELUXE CLUB WAGON: — This was the top-of-the-line model. It featured (in addition to, or in place of, items on the base club wagon): padded instrument panel; all-vinyl pleated upholstery; Deluxe steering wheel; padded sunvisors; bright left-hand outside mirror; bright-finish bumpers, bodyside moldings and hub caps; and a spare tire cover.

I.D. DATA (Falcon): See 1962 Falcon I.D.

Model	Body Type	Price	Weight	Prod. Total
E-11	(89B) Standard Station Bus	2318	2712	9,249
E-12	(89D) Club Wagon	2467	2770	Note 1
E-13	(89D) Deluxe Club Wagon	2684	2796	Note 1

NOTE 1: Total production of both "Club Wagon" models was 2,687. Also listed in Ford records is the production of 4,729 Model 89C Custom Station Buses.

ENGINE (Falcon): Station bus and Club wagon, same as Econoline. Deluxe Club Wagon: Displacement: 170 cu. in. OHV six-cylinder. 101 horsepower at 4400 R.P.M. Bore & stroke: 3.50 in. x 2.94 in. Compression ratio: 8.7:1. One-barrel carburetor.

CHASSIS: Wheelbase: 90 in. Overall Length: 168.3 in. Overall Width: 75 in. Overall Height: 76.9 in. GVW: Tires: 6.50 x 13 in.

POWERTRAIN OPTIONS: 170 cu. in. Six-cylinder.

CONVENIENCE OPTIONS: Arm rests (for second and third seats). Cigarette lighter. Full wheel covers. Gas-fired recirculating heater. Non-glare inside mirror. Outside rearview mirrors. Padded instrument panel and sunvisors. AM radio. Second or second and third row three-passenger seats. Seat belts. Spare tire cover lock. Spotlight. Right-hand sunvisor. Tinted windshield. Windshield washers.

1964 Ford F-100 Styleside Custom Cab Pickup (OCW)

F-100 PICKUP: — Ford light-duty trucks received a new grille for 1964. It featured eight open rectangular stampings. Also, the Ford block letters above the grille were spaced a bit further apart. The cab roof was an inch higher. The three-spoke steering wheel was color-keyed. More padding was used in the seatback. And four more pounds of insulation were added. Buyers could choose from the wood floor Flareside or steel floor, two-piece Styleside. The latter had double-walled construction and a single, center-latched tailgate that could easily be operated with one hand. The Flareside and Styleside were offered in 6½ foot and 8 foot versions. The new 128 inch wheelbase Styleside was designed in particular for pickup camper applications.

F-100 PLATFORM/STAKE: — These were handy for bulky, odd-shaped cargo. The platform was made of hardwood interlocked with steel skid strips. Body sills were protected by steel end caps. Side boards and stakes were made of wood. Styling and cab features were the same as those found on F-100 pickups.

I.D. DATA (F-100): See 1963 F-100 I.D.

Model	Body Type	Price	Weight	Prod. Total
F-100	(80) Platform	2000	3180	Note 1
F-100	(81) Chassis w/Cab	1848	2855	Note 1
F-100	Flareside Pickup	1964	3220	Note 1
F-100	Flareside Pickup (118")	2000	3430	Note 1
F-100	Styleside Pickup	1979	3220	Note 1
F-100	Styleside Pickup (118" w.b.)	2016	3425	Note 1
F-100	(86) Stake	2055	3295	Note 1

NOTE 1: Ford records show the following F-100 production break-outs: (cowl) 13; (cab) 15,845; (cab, platform & rack) 175; (platform) 20; (Flareside pickup) 28,876; (Styleside pickup) 152,272; (4x4 cab) 330; (4x4 Flareside pickup) 802; (4x4 Styleside pickup) 2,922.

ENGINE (F-100): Same as 1963.

F-250 PICKUP: — The F-250 pickup shared most of the same features as the F-100, but was capable of hauling heavier loads. It too was offered in Flareside and two-piece Styleside versions. Both boxes were 8-feet long.

F-250 PLATFORM/STAKE: — F-250 Platform loadspace was 93.4 inches long and 79.3 inches wide. F-250 Stake loadspace was 90 inches long, 74 inches wide and 28.3 inches to the top of the racks. Bolted steel plates held side boards firmly together at top, yet allowed fast removal of stake sections when so desired. An all-steel rub rail protected the body.

I.D. DATA (F-250): See F-100.

Model	Body Type	Price	Weight	Prod. Total
F-250	(80) Platform	2162	3500	Note 1
F-250	(81) Chassis w/Cab	2011	3155	Note 1
F-250	Flareside Pickup	2123	3610	Note 1
F-250	Styleside Pickup	2140	3620	Note 1
F-250	(86) Stake	2217	3690	Note 1

NOTE 1: Ford records show the following F-250 production break-outs: (cowl) 66; (windshield) 29; (cab) 5,149; (4x4 cab) 410; (cab, platform & rack) 662; (platform) 83; (4x4 cab, platform & rack) 68; (4x4 platform) 29; (Flareside pickup) 7,621; (Styleside pickup) 28,104; (4x4 Flareside pickup) 1,028 and (4x4 Styleside pickup) 2,232.

ENGINE (F-250): See F-100.

F-350 PICKUP: — The one-ton F-350 pickup was available in two 9-foot box versions: Flareside (with wood floor and runningboard from rear fender to back of cab) and two-piece Styleside (with steel floor and "smooth" sides). A four-speed manual transmission was standard.

F-350 PLATFORM/STAKE: — This was Ford's largest light-duty Platform/Stake. Its cargo area was nearly two-feet longer than its F-250 counterpart. And its payload capacity was greater. It had steel stakes for greater rigidity. Heavy gauge steel stake pockets were set flush with the floor, which contained steel skid strips.

I.D. DATA (F-350): See F-100.

Model	Body Type	Price	Weight	Prod. Total
F-350	(80) Platform	2369	4140	Note 1
F-350	(81) Chassis w/Cab	2176	3480	Note 1
F-350	Flareside Pickup	2311	3980	Note 1
F-350	Styleside Pickup	2322	3970	Note 1
F-350	(86) Stake	2423	2423	Note 1

NOTE 1: Ford records show the following F-350 production break-outs: (cowl) 648; (windshield) 82; (cab) 17,686; (cab, platform & rack) 3,684; (platform) 404; (Flareside pickup) 1,388 and (Styleside pickup) 1,714.

ENGINE (F-350): See F-100.

CHASSIS: Wheelbase: 114 in. (F-100); 128 in. (F-100, F-250); 132 in. (F-350). GVW: 4200-5000 (F-100); 4900-5600 (F-100 4x4); 4800-7500 (F-250); 4900-7700 (F-250 4x4); 8000-10,000 (F-350). Tires: 6.70 x 15 (F-100); 6.50 x 16 (F-250); 8 x 17.5 (F-350).

POWERTRAIN OPTIONS: 292 V8. Cruise-O-Matic; heavy-duty three-speed manual; overdrive; or four-speed manual transmissions.

CONVENIENCE OPTIONS: Four-wheel-drive. Right-hand sunvisor. Left- or Right-hand storage compartment. Windshield washer. Two-speed electric windshield wipers. Seat belts. Radio. Safety package (padded dash and visors). Fresh air heater. Grille guard. Heavy-duty radiator. Rear shock absorbers (F-350). ICC clearance and marker lights. Bright metal bodyside molding (Styleside). Full foam cushion seat. Outside rearview mirrors. Heavy-duty rear springs. **Custom Cab,** includes: Striped upholstery with bolster and vinyl facings; chrome horn ring; cigar lighter; left-hand arm rest; right-hand sunvisor; extra insulation; bright metal grille and headlight assembly; bright metal windshield reveal molding; matched locks on both doors and two-tone interior.

Pricing

1964	5	4	3	2	1
Falcon					
Sedan Delivery	660	1320	2200	3100	4400
Ranchero	690	1380	2300	3200	4600
Econoline					
Pickup	520	1020	1700	2400	3400
Van	420	840	1400	1950	2800
Station Bus	480	975	1600	2250	3200
F-100 — (½-Ton)					
Flareside Pickup	890	1770	2950	4150	5900
Styleside Pickup	930	1860	3100	4350	6200
Panel	850	1700	2850	4000	5700
Stake	830	1650	2750	3850	5500
F-250 — (¾-Ton)					
Flareside Pickup	750	1500	2500	3500	5000
Styleside Pickup	780	1560	2600	3600	5200
Stake	780	1560	2600	3600	5200
F-350 — (1-Ton)					
Flareside Pickup	740	1470	2450	3350	4900
Styleside Pickup	770	1550	2550	3600	5100
Stake	750	1500	2500	3500	5000

NOTE: Add five percent for 4x4.

1965 FORD

1965 Ford Falcon Ranchero Pickup (Tom Kelley)

FALCON RANCHERO PICKUP: — Compared to last year, styling changes were mild for '65. The Ranchero received a new grille that featured horizontal bars divided in the center by a thin vertical bar. An ornament was added to its hood. Some improvements were made to the chassis, but most attention was placed on the power plants. Standard equipment included: chrome front and rear bumpers; dual electric windshield wipers; dual electric horns; tailgate steer head ornament; bright metal windshield molding, roof drip moldings, taillight trim rings and hub caps; "Palomino" vinyl interior trim with arm rests, door panels, cowl sides and steering wheel in matching color; dome light; dispatch box; ash tray; "Double-Grip" door locks; "Lifeguard" steering wheel; bright-metal horn ring and three-speed manual transmission.

FALCON SEDAN DELIVERY: — This was the last year for this vehicle. The sedan delivery body type was rapidly losing popularity. It, and many panel trucks, were being replaced by vans. Payloads as heavy as 6900-pounds could be held in the spacious 78 cubic foot cargo area. A single center tailgate latch lowered the tailgate. The floor was constructed of steel and weather-sealed plywood with longitudinal steel skid strips that eased the sliding of heavy packages in and out. Standard features included most of the same items on the Ranchero. However, the Sedan Delivery only had one arm rest and one sunvisor.

I.D. DATA (Falcon Ranchero/Sedan Delivery): See 1960 Ranchero.

1965 Ford Falcon Ranchero Pickup (DFW)

Model	Body Type	Price	Weight	Prod. Total
66A	Pickup	2095	2713	10,539
78A	Sedan Delivery	2309	2798	649

ADDITIONAL PRODUCTION: In addition to the figures given above, Ford records show the following production break-outs: (66G Standard Ranchero w/bucket seats) 16; (66B Deluxe Ranchero) 7,734; (66H Deluxe Ranchero w/bucket seats) 990 and (78B Deluxe Sedan Delivery) 112.

ENGINE (Falcon Ranchero/Sedan Delivery): Displacement: 170 cu. in. six-cylinder. 105 horsepower at 4400 R.P.M. Bore & stroke: 3.50 in. x 2.94 in. Compression ratio: 9.1:1. Holley one-barrel carburetor.

CHASSIS: Wheelbase: 109.5 in. Overall length: 190 in. Overall width: 71.6 in. GVW: 3340-3640. Tires: 6.95 x 14 4-PR.

POWERTRAIN OPTIONS: 120 horsepower 200 cu. in. six-cylinder. 200 horsepower 289 cu. in. V-8. 225 horsepower 289 cu. in. V-8. Four-speed manual (with V-8) or three-speed, dual-range Cruise-O-Matic transmissions.

1965 Ford Falcon Deluxe Ranchero Pickup (OCW)

CONVENIENCE OPTIONS: Power steering. Heavy-duty battery. Fresh air heater and defroster. Air conditioner. Seat belts. Power-operated tailgate window (Sedan Delivery). Whitewall tires. Three types of bright metal wheel covers. Tinted glass. Two-speed electric windshield wipers with windshield washers. Outside mirror. Push-button radio. 42-ampere-hour alternator. ICC emergency light flasher. Cigarette lighter. Bucket seats with carpeting (available with Ranchero standard interior). Bucket seats with or without console, special door trim panels, arm rests and carpeting (availabile with Rancheros having deluxe interiors.) **Safety Package,** includes: padded dash or dash and sunvisors. **Courtesy Light Package,** includes: ash tray; dispatch box; map; backup and door courtesy lights, plus cargo area light for Sedan Delivery. **Deluxe Trim Package,** includes: (Sedan Delivery) arm rest on right side, sunvisor on right side, black or red color-keyed steering wheel and black or red pleated vinyl upholstery; (Ranchero): bright metal moldings around top of box and cab back on bodysides and on rocker panels, cab front floor carpeting, added sound deadener, cab front floor carpeting, deluxe instrument panel and ''Palomino'' blue, black or red pleated vinyl seat trim with color-keyed steering wheel; (Both Models) bright metal moldings on side door window frames, dome light door switches and cigarette lighter.

NOTE: A total of 16 standard and 990 (of the 7,734) Deluxe Rancheros had bucket seats.

NOTE: Solid colors available were: Raven black, Wimbledon white, Rangoon red, Vintage burgundy, Caspian blue, Silver blue, Champagne beige, Prairie bronze, Dynasty green, Ivy green, Phoenician yellow and Twilight gray. In addition, Tropical turquoise, Honey gold and Silversmoke gray were available with the Deluxe trim package. A special two-tone option had side moldings with Wimbledon white paint between the moldings and on the cab roof. Red was used only when the main body color was white. This option was available with any of the above colors except Silversmoke gray.

ECONOLINE PICKUP: — Heavier bumpers and new hub caps were the biggest styling changes for 1965. Also new were a lower seat, revised heater, different steering column bracket and license plate bracket and lamp on the rear left cargo door. Standard features included: Spare tire; vinyl upholstery; three-speed manual transmission; insulated engine cover; left-hand sunvisor and single horn.

ECONOLINE VAN: — The Econoline Van had 204 cubic feet of loadspace. It had a loading height of just 22.5 inches. Among the standard features were: color-keyed vinyl upholstery; left-hand fresh air inlet; dual electric windshield wipers; left-hand sunvisor; painted front and rear bumpers and hub caps; dome lights; ash tray; matched locks for all doors; coat hook; headlining in driver's area and arm rests.

ECONOLINE PANEL VAN: — This new model was basically just an Econoline van with no side cargo doors.

I.D. DATA (Econoline): See F-100 I.D.

1965 Ford Econoline Deluxe Pickup (OCW)

Model	Body Type	Price	Weight	Prod. Total
E-100	Pickup	1901	2585	Note 1
E-100	Van	2108	2595	Note 1
E-100	Panel Van	2054	2595	Note 1

NOTE 1: Ford records show the following Econoline production breakouts: **Pickups:** (87A standard) 4,340; (87B Custom) 3,065. **Econo Vans:** (89H panel) 967; (89A regular) 35,972; (89E display) 2,381; (89F window) 5,156; (89G cargo) 1,136. **Extended Van:** (89S panel) 229; (89J regular) 7,924; (89M display) 129; (89N window) 1,358 and (89R cargo) 449.

ENGINE (Econoline): Displacement: 170 cu. in. six-cylinder. 105 horsepower at 4400 R.P.M. Bore & stroke: 3.50 in. x 2.94 in. Compression Ratio: 9.1:1. One-barrel carburetor.

CHASSIS: Wheelbase: 90 in. Overall length: 168.4 in. Overall width: 65 in. GVW: 3600-4850. Tires: 6.95 x 14.

POWERTRAIN OPTIONS: Four-speed manual and three-speed automatic transmissions.

CONVENIENCE OPTIONS: AM radio. Fresh air heater/defroster. **Super Van:** an 18-inch extension to the van, with heavy-duty underbody components. Padded instrument panel and sunvisors. Flip-Swing or stationary passenger seat. Seat belts. Interior rearview mirror. ICC emergency lamp flasher. Tinted glass. Windshield washer. Two-speed electric windshield wipers. Front and rear chrome bumpers. Whitewall tires. **Display Van option:** fixed windows in the right side of the cargo area. **Window Van option:** fixed windows all around. **Custom package,** includes: color-keyed woven plastic upholstery; right-hand fresh-air inlet; right-hand sunvisor; cigar lighter; dual horns; bright metal hub caps; chrome horn ring; cowl-wall trim panels; insulation on cowl wall; headlining on cargo area; windows in rear doors; foam padding and optional passenger seat, plus (Pickup) woven plastic upholstery; right-hand air duct; arm rests; right-hand sunvisor; cigar lighter; chrome horn ring; dual horns; cab rear wrap-around quarter windows; glove compartment door with cylinder lock; bright metal hub caps; coat hook; front body interior insulation; and foam padding in passenger seat cushion and back. **One-Ton Payload Package:** left-hand side-mounted cargo doors and 4350 or 4850 pound GVW packages.

FALCON STATION BUS: Station Bus changes for 1965 echoed those on the Econoline. Among the standard featues were: vinyl upholstery; two-speed electric windshield wipers; foam-cushioned adjustable driver's seat; front passenger seat; front arm rests; ash tray; dual horns and dome lights; left-hand air inlet and sunvisor; inside rearview mirror and retractable side step.

FALCON CLUB WAGON: — Standard features on the Club Wagon included: woven plastic upholstery; full-length floor mat and headlining; foam-cushioned front passenger seat; painted left-hand outside mirror; windshield washers; cigarette lighter; dual sunvisors; four coat hooks and right-hand air inlet.

FALCON DELUXE CLUB WAGON: — This was the top-of-the-line model. It featured (in addition to, or in place of, items on the base Club Wagon): padded instrument panel; all-vinyl pleated upholstery; Deluxe steering wheel; padded sunvisors; bright left-hand outside mirror; bright finish bumpers; bright bodyside moldings; bright hub caps and a spare tire cover.

I.D. DATA (Falcon): See 1962 Falcon I.D.

Model	Body Type	Price	Weight	Prod. Total
E-11	Station Bus	2293	2778	Note 1
E-12	Club Wagon	2438	2878	Note 1
E-13	Deluxe Club Wagon	2635	2918	Note 1

NOTE 1: Ford records show the following Econo Bus production break-outs: (89B standard) 7,116; (89K standard extended) 573; (89C Custom) 3,813 and (89D Club Wagon) 2,259.

ENGINE (Falcon): Same as Econoline.

CHASSIS: Wheelbase: 90 in. Overall length: 168.3 in. Overall width: 75 in. Overall height: 76.9 in. GVW: Tires: 6.50 x 13.

POWERTRAIN OPTIONS: 240 cu. in. six-cylinder. Automatic transmission.

CONVENIENCE OPTIONS: Arm rests (for second and third seats). Cigarette lighter. Full wheel covers. Gas-fired recirculating heater. Non-glare inside mirror. Outside rearview mirrors. Padded instrument panel and sunvisors. AM radio. Second or second and third row three-passenger seats. Seat belts. Spare tire cover lock. Spotlight. Right-hand sunvisor. Tinted windshield. Windshield washers.

1965 Ford F-100 Styleside Pickup (OCW)

F-100 PICKUP: — Changes for 1965 included a new grille with 18 rectangular openings. The parking lamps were relocated to above the headlights with "Ford" spelled out in block letters in the space between them. Series I.D. emblems were moved to the front fenders. Also new was Twin I-Beam independent front suspension, Haltenberger steering linkage and a different instrument panel. Buyers were offered 6½-foot and 8-foot versions of Flareside or Styleside boxes. Four-wheel-drive could be ordered at extra cost.

F-100 PLATFORM/STAKE: — The F-100 Platform/Stake had most of the same features as the F-100 pickup. It could haul bulky and awkward shaped loads that might not fit properly in a pickup. The hardwood floor boards were interlocked with steel skid strips. A steel rub rail protected the body.

1965 Ford F-100 Del. Styleside Custom Cab Pickup (JAG)

360

I.D. DATA (F-100): See 1963 F-100 I.D.

Model	Body Type	Price	Weight	Prod. Total
F-100	(80) Platform	2002	3290	Note 1
F-100	(81) Chassis w/Cab	1852	2850	Note 1
F-100	Flareside Pickup	1966	3170	Note 1
F-100	Flareside Pickup (118" w.b.)	2002	3325	Note 1
F-100	Styleside Pickup	1981	3225	Note 1
F-100	Styleside Pickup (118" w.b.)	2018	3360	Note 1
F-100	(86) Stake	2057	3165	Note 1

NOTE 1: Ford records show the following F-100 production break-outs: (windshield) 1; (cab) 7,367; (cab, platform and rack) 148; (cab platform) 25; (Flareside) 34,184 and (Styleside) 178,581.

1965 Ford F-100 Deluxe Styleside Pickup (JAG)

ENGINE (F-100): Displacement: 240 cu. in. six-cylinder. 150 horsepower at 4000 R.P.M. Bore & stroke: 4.00 in. x 3.18 in. Compression ratio: 9.2:1. One-barrel carburetor.

F-250 PICKUP: — In addition to changes made on the F-100, F-250s also had a 4.56:1 rear axle ratio and a 3000-pound capacity front suspension. Eight foot Flareside and Styleside boxes were offered. Four-wheel-drive could be had at extra cost.

F-250 PLATFORM/STAKE: — The ¾-ton F-250 Platform/Stake had hardwood floors with steel skid strips. Body sills were protected by steel end caps. This was the only light-duty Ford Platform/Stake available with four-wheel-drive (at extra cost).

I.D. DATA (F-250): See F-100.

Model	Body Type	Price	Weight	Prod. Total
F-250	(80) Platform	2164	3465	Note 1
F-250	(81) Chassis w/Cab	2013	3110	Note 1
F-250	Crew Cab Chassis (147")	—		Note 1
F-250	Flareside Pickup	2123	3530	Note 1
F-250	Styleside Pickup	2141	3570	Note 1
F-250	Crew Cab Pickup (147")	—		Note 1
F-250	(86) Stake	2218	3645	Note 1

NOTE 1: Ford records show the following F-250 production break-outs: (windshield) 166; (cab) 5,995; (platform and rack) 874; (platform) 150; (Flareside) 7,500 and (Styleside) 42,044.

ENGINE (F-250): See F-100.

F-350 PICKUP: — Big, nine foot Flareside and Styleside pickup boxes were offered to buyers of Ford's heftiest light-duty truck. Unlike the F-100 and F-250, Twin-I-Beam front suspension was *not* standard on the F-350.

F-350 PLATFORM/STAKE: — The F-350 Platform/Stake was capable of hauling substantially heavier loads than either F-100 or F-250 versions. Steel stakes were used for greater rigidity. A four-speed manual was standard.

I.D. DATA (F-350): See F-100.

Model	Body Type	Price	Weight	Prod. Total
F-350	(80) Platform	2370	4015	Note 1
F-350	(81) Chassis w/Cab	2177	3425	Note 1
F-350	Crew Cab Chassis (152")	—		Note 1
F-350	Flareside Pickup	2313	3890	Note 1
F-350	Styleside Pickup	2370	3920	Note 1
F-350	Crew Cab Pickup (152")	—		Note 1
F-350	(86) Stake	2425	4255	Note 1

NOTE 1: Ford records show the following F-350 production break-outs: (cowl) 759; (windshield) 118; (cab) 17,063; (cab, platform and rack) 3,996; (platform) 424; (Flareside) 2,085 and (Styleside) 1,934.

ENGINE (F-350): See F-100.

CHASSIS: Wheelbase: 115 in. (F-100); 129 in. (F-100, F-250); 132 in. (F-350); 147 in. (F-350 Crew Cab); 152 in. (F-350 Crew Cab). GVW: 4200-5000 lbs. (F-100); 4600-5600 lbs. (F-100 4x4); 4800-7500 lbs. (F-250); 4900-7700 lbs. (F-350); 6000-10,000 lbs. (F-350). Tires: 7.15 x 15 (F-100); 6.50 x 16 (F-250); 8 x 17.5 (F-350).

POWERTRAIN OPTIONS: 352 V-8. 300 cu. in. heavy-duty six-cylinder. Cruise-O-Matic automatic, heavy-duty three-speed manual, overdrive and four-speed manual transmissions.

CONVENIENCE OPTIONS: Four-wheel-drive. Right-hand sunvisor. Left- or Right-hand storage compartment. Windshield washer. Two-speed electric windshield wiper rearview mirrors. Heavy-duty rear springs. Bucket seats. **Custom Cab,** includes: upholstery with bolster and vinyl facings; chrome horn ring; cigar lighter; left-hand arm rest; right-hand sunvisor; extra insulation; bright metal grille and headlight assembly; bright metal windshield reveal molding and matched locks on both doors. **Camper Special,** includes: dual Western mirrors; unique fender emblem; extra cooling radiator; ammeter; oil pressure gauge; a 300 cu. in. six-cylinder or 352 cu. in. V-8; Cruise-O-Matic automatic or four-speed manual transmissions; extended tailpipe and 70 amp./hr. battery.

HISTORICAL NOTES: Introduced: October 1964. Model Year Production: 391,524 including Ranchero/Sedan Delivery/Econoline Bus/F-100/F-250/F-350 and "P" Series. Model year output of "P" Series trucks included: (P-100 parcel stripped) 205; (P-350 parcel stripped) 2,988 and (P-400 parcel stripped) 1,771. Ford dealers sold a record 489,510 trucks in calendar year 1965, with most gains being registered in the heavy-duty market. However, sales of conventional light-duties were up 22 percent. Philip Caldwell was Truck Operations Manager.

Pricing

1965	5	4	3	2	1
Falcon					
Sedan Delivery	660	1320	2200	3100	4400
Ranchero	690	1380	2300	3200	4600
Econoline					
Pickup	520	1020	1700	2400	3400
Van	420	840	1400	1950	2800
Station Bus	480	975	1600	2250	3200
F-100 — (½-Ton)					
Flareside Pickup	890	1770	2950	4150	5900
Styleside Pickup	930	1860	3100	4350	6200
Panel	850	1700	2850	4000	5700
Stake	830	1650	2750	3850	5500
F-250 — (¾-Ton)					
Flareside Pickup	750	1500	2500	3500	5000
Styleside Pickup	780	1560	2600	3600	5200
Stake	780	1560	2600	3600	5200
F-350 — (1-Ton)					
Flareside Pickup	740	1470	2450	3350	4900
Styleside Pickup	770	1550	2550	3600	5100
Stake	750	1500	2500	3500	5000

NOTE: Add five percent for 4x4.

1966 FORD

1966 Ford Falcon Ranchero Pickup (OCW)

RANCHERO PICKUP: — The Ranchero may have dropped the "Falcon" from its name, but its heritage was in no doubt. However, in addition to Falcon, it shared many components with Fairlane. The taillights were vertical and the grille had horizontal bars with slightly recessed headlights integrated into it. Parking lights remained in the bumper. The rear window was slightly recessed. The standard version had no side trim. Its vinyl upholstery was available in black or parchment. The Ranchero's new suspension featured front coil springs and five-leaf rear springs. There was

39.1 cubic feet of cargo space. Standard payload capacity was 850-pounds. Standard equipment included: Fresh air heater and defroster; bright horn ring; padded dash and sunvisors; seat belts; inside rearview mirror; spare tire behind seat; windshield washers; ICC emergency light flasher; cigarette emblem on glove box door; courtesy and dome lights; arm rests; left-hand OSRV mirror; backup lights; non-glare wiper arms; chrome bumpers; bright windshield and backlight moldings; "Ranchero" script on front fenders; bright drip rail moldings; bright taillight bezels; bright pickup box moldings; "Ranchero" tailgate emblem and bright hub caps.

RANCHERO CUSTOM PICKUP: — Buyers who wanted their Ranchero with a little more flash, opted for the Custom version. It had most of the same features as the standard model, plus a "Ranchero" emblem on the rear roof pillars; bright door window frames; bright wheel cutout moldings; bright rocker panel moldings; bodyside contour line paint stripes; full color-keyed carpeting; Deluxe instrument panel ornamentation; Deluxe door trim panels and retainers and rear vinyl-covered trim panel. Its vinyl upholstery had a crinkle-grained pattern.

I.D. DATA (Ranchero): See 1960 Ranchero I.D.

Model	Body Type	Price	Weight	Prod. Total
66A	Pickup	2330	—	9480
66B	Deluxe Pickup	2411	—	11,038

ADDITIONAL PRODUCTION: Ford also built 1,242 Model 66D Deluxe Rancheros w/ bucket seats.

ENGINE (Ranchero): Displacement: 200 cu. in. Six-cylinder. 120 horse-power at 4400 R.P.M. Bore & stroke: 3.68 in. x 3.13 in. Compression ratio: 9.2:1. Holley one-barrel carburetor.

CHASSIS: Wheelbase: 113 in. Overall length: 197.5 in. Overall width: 74.7 in. GVW: 3775-4400 lbs. Tires: 7.35 x 14.

POWERTRAIN OPTIONS: 200 horsepower 289 cu. in. V-8. 225 horsepower 289 cu. in. V-8. Four-speed manual transmission (with V-8 only). Cruise-O-Matic automatic. Limited-slip differential.

CONVENIENCE OPTIONS: Heavy-duty shock absorbers. Wheel covers. Power steering. Heavy-duty battery. Push-button radio. SelectAire air conditioner. Tinted glass. ICC reflectors. Two-speed electric windshield wipers. Deluxe seat belts with retractors and warning light. 7.75 x 14 4-PR tires. Whitewall tires. Higher capacity rear suspension. **Visibility Package:** includes, two-speed electric windshield wipers, inside non-glare mirror, outside remote-control mirror. **Courtesy Light Package:** includes, ash tray, glove box, and map light. **Seat Packages:** (available on Custom only) includes, bucket seats alone or bucket seats with console.

NOTE: A total of 1,242 of the 1966 Rancheros had bucket seats.

NOTE: Two interior vinyl colors were available on standard models: black and parchment. Four interior vinyl colors are available on Custom models: red, blue, black and parchment. Exterior colors were: Raven black, Wimbledon white, Candyapple red, Vintage burgundy, Silver Frost, Nightmist blue, Silver blue, Arcadian blue, Tahoe turquoise, Ivy green, Sauterne gold, Springtime yellow, Antique bronze, Sahara beige and Emberglo. Body side contour line paint stripes for the Custom model were Raven black, Wimbledon white or Rangoon red.

BRONCO ROADSTER: — A TV commercial called the Bronco "a stablemate of Mustang." The roadster was the base model of this new four-wheel-drive vehicle and it looked it. It didn't have a roof or doors. Styling was neat, but boxy. The Ford name was printed on the center bar of the grille. Parking lights were at each end of the bar. The rectangular taillights were mounted vertically on the rear of the vehicle. "Ford" was printed on the far right center of the tailgate. The license plate bracket was on the opposite end. Among standard features were: a three-speed fully synchronized transmission; "Mono-Beam" front suspension; through-drive two-speed transfer case; 11 x 2 inch front brakes and a folding windshield.

BRONCO SPORTS UTILITY: — This looked like a mini, mini-pickup. It had an all-steel, bolted-on, removable roof over the front seat. The side doors had roll-up windows. The compact rear cargo area could hold up to 32.1 cubic feet of whatever one wanted to haul.

BRONCO WAGON: — This was the most luxurious Bronco. It had a full length roof and large quarter windows.

I.D. DATA (Bronco): See F-100 I.D.

Model	Body Type	Price	Weight	Prod. Total
U-130	Roadster	2404	2750	4090
U-140	Sports Utility	2480	2955	6930
U-150	Wagon	2625	3025	12,756

ENGINE (Bronco): Displacement: 170 cu. in. six-cylinder. 105 horsepower at 4400 R.P.M. Bore & stroke: 3.50 in. x 2.94 in. Compression ratio: 9.1:1. One-barrel carburetor.

CHASSIS: Wheelbase: 90 in. Overall length: 152.1 in. Overall width: 68.8 in. GVW: 3900-4700 lbs. Tires: 7.35 x 15.

POWERTRAIN OPTIONS: 289 cu. in. V-8.

CONVENIENCE OPTIONS: Bucket seats. Cigarette lighter. Cab doors. Closed crankcase emmissions (required in California). Heavy-duty clutch (with six-cylinder). Tailgate mounted spare tire carrier. Rear seat. Heavy-duty battery. Front bumper guards. Heavy-duty alternator. Cooling package. GVW package. Arm rests. Limited-slip front axle. Limited-slip rear axle. Chrome front and rear bumpers.

ECONOLINE PICKUP: — Styling was virtually untouched for 1966. However, some changes were made. These included: non-glare windshield wiper arms, new seat belts and a padded dash. Some standard features were: Seven-foot long cargo box; spare tire; vinyl upholstery; three-speed manual transmission; insulated engine cover; left-hand sunvisor and single horn.

ECONOLINE VAN: — The Econoline Van had 204 cubic feet of loadspace. It had a loading height of just 22.5 inches. Among the standard features were: color-keyed vinyl upholstery; left-hand fresh air inlet; dual electric windshield wipers; left-hand sunvisor; painted front and rear bumpers and hub caps; dome lights; ash tray; matched locks for all doors; coat hook; headlining in driver area and armrests.

ECONOLINE PANEL VAN: — This new model was basically just an Econoline van with no side cargo doors.

I.D. DATA (Econoline): See F-100 I.D.

Model	Body Type	Price	Weight	Prod. Total
E-100	(87A) Standard Pickup	1897	2610	2578
E-100	(89A) Standard Van	2194	2670	23,861
E-100	(89H) Standard PanelVan	2139	2645	669

ADDITIONAL PRODUCTION: In addition to the above figures, Ford records show the following Econoline production break-outs: (87B Custom pickup) 512; (89E Std. display van) 2,488; (89F std. window van) 4,250; (89G std. cargo van) 537; (89J std. regular Super Van) 27,393; (89M display Super Van) 381; (89N window Super Van) 3,437; (89R cargo Super Van) 934; (89S panel Super Van) 558; (89A Deluxe regular van) 563; (89E Deluxe display van) 119; (89F Deluxe window van) 252; (89G Deluxe cargo van) 88; (89H Deluxe panel van) 23; (89J Deluxe regular Super Van) 1,660; (89M Deluxe display Super Van) 44; (89N Deluxe window Super Van) 740; (89R Deluxe cargo Super Van) 132 and (89S Deluxe cargo Super Van) 41.

ENGINE (Econoline): Displacement: 170 cu. in. six-cylinder. 105 horsepower at 4400 R.P.M. Bore & stroke: 3.50 in. x 2.94 in. Compression Ratio: 9.1:1. One-barrel carburetor.

CHASSIS: Wheebase: 90 in. Overall length: 168.4 in. Overall width: 65 in. GVW: 3600-4930 lbs. Tires: 6.95 x 14.

POWERTRAIN OPTIONS: Three-speed automatic.

CONVENIENCE OPTIONS: AM radio. Fresh air heater/defroster. **Super Van:** 18-inch extension to the vans with heavy-duty underbody; padded instrument panel and sunvisors; "Flip-Swing" or stationary passenger seat; seat belts; interior rearview mirror; ICC emergency lamp flasher; tinted windshield; windshield washer; two-speed electric windshield wipers; front and rear chrome bumpers and whitewall tires. **Display Van Option:** fixed windows in the right side of the cargo area. **Window Van Option:** fixed windows all around. **Custom Package:** color-keyed woven plastic upholstery; right-hand fresh-air inlet; right-hand sunvisor; cigar lighter; dual horns; bright metal hub caps; chrome horn ring; cowl-wall trim panels; insulation on cowl wall; headlining on cargo area; windows in rear doors; foam padding and optional passenger seat; plus (Pickup) woven plastic upholstery; right-hand air duct; right-hand visor; cigar lighter; chrome horn ring; dual horns; cab rear wraparound quarter windows; glove compartment door with cylinder lock; bright metal hub caps; coat hook; front body interior insulation and foam padding in passenger seat cushion and back. **One-Ton Payload Package,** includes left side-mounted cargo doors, 4350 or 4850 lb. GVW.

FALCON CLUB WAGON: Club Wagon changes for 1966 echoed those on the Econoline. Among the standard features were: vinyl upholstery; two-speed electric windshield wipers; foam-cushioned adjustable driver's seat; front passsenger seat; front arm rests; ash tray; dual horns and dome lights; left air inlet and sunvisor; inside rearview mirror and retractable side step.

FALCON CUSTOM CLUB WAGON: — Standard features on the Club Wagon included: Woven plastic upholstery; full-length floor mat and headlining; foam-cushioned front passenger seat; painted left-hand outside mirror; windshield washers; cigarette lighter; dual sunvisors; four coat hooks and right-hand air inlet.

FALCON DELUXE CLUB WAGON: — This was the top-of-the-line model. It featured (in addition to, or in place of, items on the base Club Wagon): padded instrument panel; all-vinyl pleated upholstery; Deluxe steering wheel; padded sunvisors; bright left-hand OSRV mirror; bright-finish bumpers; bright bodyside moldings; bright hub caps and spare tire cover.

I.D. DATA (Falcon): See 1962 Falcon I.D.

Model	Body Type	Price	Weight	Prod. Total
E-11	Club Wagon	2462	3053	Note 1
E-12	Custom Club Wagon	2591	3163	Note 1
E-13	Deluxe Club Wagon	2779	3183	Note 1

NOTE 1: Ford records show the following Bus and Club Wagon production break-outs: (89B standard bus) 4,382; (89K standard Super bus) 2,468; (89C Club Wagon) 2,087; (89T Super Club Wagon) 1,788; (89D Deluxe Club Wagon) 1,007 and (89L Deluxe Super Club Wagon) 1,188.

ENGINE (Falcon): Same as Econoline.

CHASSIS: Wheelbase: 90 in. Overall length: 168.3 in. Overall width: 75 in. Overall height: 76.9 in. Tires: 6.50 x 13.

POWERTRAIN OPTIONS: Three-speed automatic transmission. 240 cu. in. six-cylinder.

CONVENIENCE OPTIONS: Arm rests (for second and third seats). Cigarette lighter. Full wheel covers. Gas-fired recirculating heater. Non-glare inside mirror. OSRV mirrors. Padded instrument panel and sun visors. AM radio. Second or second and third row three-passenger seats. Seat belts. Spare tire cover lock. Spotlight. Right-hand sun visor. Tinted windshield. Windshield washers.

F-100 PICKUP: — Except for a slightly modified series emblem and new grille with two long rectangular slots over 18 small ones, the F-100 was about the same as last year's model. Buyers could choose from 6½-foot and 8-foot box Flaresides and Stylesides. The 4x4 option could now be had on either F-100 wheelbase (at extra cost). Among standard features were: Argent painted hub caps; Twin-I-Beam independent front suspension; fresh air heater/defroster; padded dash; windshield washers and emergency flashers.

F-100 PLATFORM/STAKE: — The F-100 Platform/Stake had hardwood floorboards that were interlocked with steel skid strips. Floor corners were reinforced with steel angle brackets. Standard features echoed those on the F-100 pickup.

I.D. DATA (F-100): See 1963 F-100 I.D.

Model	Body Type	Price	Weight	Prod. Total
F-100	(80) Platform	2101	3095	Note 1
F-100	(81) Chassis w/Cab	1951	2850	Note 1
F-100	Flareside Pickup	2069	3145	Note 1
F-100	Flareside Pickup (118")	2105	3295	Note 1
F-100	Styleside Pickup	2085	3210	Note 1
F-100	Styleside Pickup (118")	2121	3310	Note 1
F-100	(86) Stake	2156	3220	Note 1

NOTE 1: Ford records show the following F-100 production break-outs; **4x2 Trucks:** (windshield) 1; (cab) 4,274; (cab, platform and rack) 120; (cab platform) 13; (Flareside pickup) 26,491 and (Styleside pickup) 224,497. **4x4 Trucks:** (cab) 145; (Flareside pickup) 839 and (Styleside pickup) 4,493.

ENGINE (F-100): Same as 1965.

F-250 PICKUP: — Buyers of a ¾-ton F-250 had their choice of Flareside or Styleside pickup boxes. They could also order a six-passenger Crew Cab model. It had four doors, two bench seats and a 6½-foot pickup box (it could be ordered without the box). The interior was either beige, blue, green or red.

F-250 PLATFORM/STAKE: — F-250 Platform/Stake styling underwent the same minor changes as its F-100 counterpart. It also had seasoned hardwood floors with interlocking steel skid strips.

I.D. DATA (F-250): See F-100.

Model	Body Type	Price	Weight	Prod. Total
F-250	(80) Platform	2263	3540	Note 1
F-250	(81) Chassis w/Cab	2113	3135	Note 1
F-250	Flareside Pickup	2226	3530	Note 1
F-250	Styleside Pickup	2244	3545	Note 1
F-250	Crew Cab Pickup (147")	—	—	Note 1
F-250	Crew Cab Chassis (147")	—	—	Note 1
F-250	(86) Stake	2317	3720	Note 1

NOTE 1: Ford records show the following F-250 production break-outs; **4x2 Trucks:** (windshield) 142; (cab) 6,187; (cab, platform and rack) 1,747; (cab platform) 129; (Flareside pickup) 6,699 and (Styleside pickup) 58,489. **4x4 Trucks:** (cab) 644; (cab, platform and rack) 125; (cab platform) 29; (Flareside pickup) 1,595 and (Styleside pickup) 3,559.

ENGINE (F-250): See F-100.

F-350 PICKUP: — The one-ton F-350 came with most of the same standard features as the F-100, except for Twin-I-Beam front suspension. Both Flareside (with wood floors and runningboard from rear fender to back or cab) and Styleside (smooth side) boxes were offered. Also available was a six-passenger crew cab with (or without) an 8-ft. pickup box.

F-350 PLATFORM/STAKE: — The hardwood floorboards of the F-350 Platform/Stake could haul heavier (and bulkier) payloads than the other light-duty Ford Platform/Stakes. A four-speed manual transmission was standard.

I.D. DATA (F-350): See F-100.

Model	Body Type	Price	Weight	Prod. Total
F-350	(80) Platform	2469	4080	Note 1
F-350	(81) Chassis & Cab	2276	3505	Note 1
F-350	Chassis $ Crew Cab (152")	—	—	Note 1
F-350	Flareside Pickup	2416	3895	Note 1
F-350	Styleside Pickup	2425	3920	Note 1
F-350	Crew Cab Pickup (152")	—	—	Note 1
F-350	(86) Stake	2524	4320	Note 1

NOTE 1: Ford records show the following F-350 production break-outs; (cowl) 782; (windshield) 184; (cab) 19,716; (cab, platform and rack) 4,596; (cab platform) 729; (Flareside pickup) 3,928 and (Styleside pickup) 2,605.

ENGINE (F-350): See F-100.

CHASSIS: Wheelbase: 115 in. (F-100); 129 in. (F-100/F-250); 132 in. (F-350); 147 in. (F-250 Crew Cab); 152 in. (F-350 Crew Cab). GVW: 4200-5000 lbs. (F-100); 4600-5600 lbs. (F-100 4x4); 4800-7500 lbs. (F-250); 4900-7700 lbs. (F-250 4x4); 6000-10,000 lbs. (F-350). Tires: 7.75 x 15 (F-100); 6.50 x 16 (F-250); 8 x 17.5 (F-350).

POWERTRAIN OPTIONS: 300 cu. in. six-cylinder. 352 V-8. Cruise-O-Matic automatic/heavy-duty three-speed manual/overdrive and four-speed manual transmissions.

CONVENIENCE OPTIONS: Four-wheel-drive. Right-hand sunvisor. Left- or right-hand storage compartments. Bucket seats. Radio. Fresh air heater. Grille guard. Heavy-duty radiator. Rear shock absorbers (F-350). Power steering. ICC clearance and marker lights. Bright metal body side molding (Styleside). Full foam cushion seat. Outside rearview mirrors. Heavy-duty rear springs. **Custom Cab,** includes: striped upholstery with bolster and vinyl facings; chrome horn ring; cigar lighter; left-hand arm rest; right-hand sunvisor; extra insulation; bright metal grille and headlight assembly; bright metal windshield reveal molding; matched locks on both doors; "Custom Cab" plaques and bright hub caps. **Camper Special Package,** includes: dual Western mirrors; unique fender emblem; extra cooling radiator; ammeter; oil pressure gauge; a 300 cu. in. six-cylinder or 352 cu. in. V-8 engine; Cruise-O-Matic or four-speed manual transmissions; extended tailpipe; 70 amp.-hr. battery and 55-ampere alternator.

HISTORICAL: Introduced: Oct. 1, 1965. Model year production (light-duty trucks including 171 P-100; 2,945 P-350 and 2,239 P-400 parcel delivery truck chassis) was 494,909 units. Calendar year registrations included 331,498 truck in the 6000-lb. or less category and 98,490 trucks between 6001 and 10,000-lbs. Ford was America's number 2 truck-maker in 1966, which was an all-time record sales season. Calendar year sales were pegged at 536,427 units. Innovations: Ranchero redesigned. Ford Bronco introduced. Ranchero has optional 289 cu. in. V-8.

Pricing

1966	5	4	3	2	1
Ranchero					
Pickup	680	1350	2250	3150	4500
Custom Pickup	700	1400	2350	3250	4700
Bronco					
Roadster	850	1700	2850	4000	5700
Sports Utility	900	1800	3000	4200	6000
Wagon	900	1800	3000	4200	6000
Econoline					
Pickup	520	1020	1700	2400	3400
Van	440	870	1450	2050	2900
Panel Van	420	840	1400	1950	2800
Club Wagon	480	975	1600	2250	3200
Custom Club Wagon	520	1020	1700	2400	3400
Deluxe Club Wagon	540	1080	1800	2500	3600
F-100 — (½-Ton)					
Flareside Pickup	890	1770	2950	4150	5900
Styleside Pickup	930	1860	3100	4350	6200
Panel	850	1700	2850	4000	5700
Stake	830	1650	2750	3850	5500
F-250 — (¾-Ton)					
Flareside Pickup	750	1500	2500	3500	5000
Styleside Pickup	780	1560	2600	3600	5200
Stake	780	1560	2600	3600	5200
F-350 — (1-Ton)					
Flareside Pickup	740	1470	2450	3350	4900
Styleside Pickup	770	1550	2550	3600	5100
Stake	750	1500	2500	3500	5000

NOTE: Add five percent for 4x4.

1967 FORD

1967 Ford Fairlane Ranchero Pickup (OCW)

FAIRLANE RANCHERO PICKUP: — After a year of transition, the Ranchero was now clearly a Fairlane based vehicle. Design features included: Quad stacked headlights and a one-piece aluminum grille (its fine gridwork was accented by a wider, full-length horizontal bar in the center and three vertical bars). The rectangular taillights were divided in the center by backup lights. There were also bright metal moldings on the windshield, hood, drip rail, back of the cab and cargo box; two-speed windshield wipers; windshield washers; a padded dash and sunvisors; dome light; ICC emergency flasher; horn ring; heater; cigarette lighter; left-hand remote control rearview mirror; seat belts; energy-absorbing steering wheel; color-keyed floor mat; arm rests; ash tray; courtesy light door switches and three-speed manual transmission.

FAIRLANE 500 RANCHERO PICKUP: — The new mid-level Ranchero had most features of the standard version, plus: deep-pile, color-keyed wall-to-wall carpeting; instrument panel applique; electric clock; trim panel for rear of cab; bright metal wheel lip moldings and lower bodyside moldings; bright door window frames; bodyside paint stripes and bright wheel covers. The full-width seat was upholstered in red, blue, parchment or ivy gold pleated vinly trim color-keyed to 13 exterior colors.

FAIRLANE 500 XL RANCHERO PICKUP: — A unique medallion in the center of the grille let everyone know you were driving the new top-of-the-line Ranchero. In addition to items offered on the 500, the 500 XL had: bucket seats; center console and special trim items.

I.D. DATA (Ranchero): See 1960 Ranchero I.D.

Model	Body Type	Price	Weight	Prod. Total
66A	Pickup	2514	3010	5858
66B	"500" Pickup	2611	3020	9504
66D	"500 XL" Pickup	2768	3050	1881

ENGINE (Ranchero): Displacement: 200 cu. in. Six-cylinder. 120 horsepower at 4400 R.P.M. Bore & stroke: 3.68 in. x 3.13 in. Compression ratio: 9.2:1. Holley one-barrel carburetor.

CHASSIS: Wheelbase: 113 in. Overall length: 199.9 in. Overall width: 74.7 in. GVW: 3850-4750 lbs. Tires: 7.35 x 14 4-PR.

POWERTRAIN OPTIONS: 200 horsepower "289" V-8. 225 horsepower "289" V-8 (discontinued during the model year). 270 horsepower "390" V-8. 315 horsepower "390" V-8. 320 horsepower "390 GT" V-8 (mid-model year replacement for the 390/315 V-8). Four-speed manual or SelectShift Cruise-O-Matic transmissions. Limited-slip rear axle.

CONVENIENCE OPTIONS: 42 or 55 Ampere alternator. Heavy-duty battery. A 7½-inch diameter vacuum booster or front disc brakes including vacuum booster. Electric clock (Ranchero). Extra-cooling fan and radiator (included with air conditioner). **Heavy-Duty Suspension Package,** includes: heavy-duty shock absorbers; 1,165-lb. rear springs. Linkage-type power steering. Push-button radio and antenna. Stereo-Sonic tape system (not with four-speed transmission and air conditioner). Deluxe woodgrain steering wheel. SelectAire conditioner. Shoulder harness for driver and passenger. Tinted glass (windshield or all-around). Wheel covers (Ranchero). Deluxe wheel covers. Styled steel wheels. 7.75 x 14 4-PR and 8-PR tires. Whitewall tires.

NOTE: Interior colors: Parchment, red or blue interior vinyl colors were available on Ranchero. Parchment, red, blue or ivy gold interior vinyl colors were available on the Ranchero 500. Parchment, red, blue or black interior vinyl colors were available on the Ranchero 500 XL. Exterior colors: Raven black, Wimbledon white, Candyapple red, Silver Frost, Nightmist blue, Sauterne gold (500 and 500 XL), Springtime yellow, Clearwater Aqua (500 and 500 XL), Dark Moss green, Vintage burgundy, Brittany blue, Frost turquoise (500 XL), Beige Mist, Pebble beige and Burnt Amber. Bodyside contour line paint stripes for 500 and 500XL were white, black or red. (Red stripes with red interior, black stripes with black interior.)

BRONCO ROADSTER: — The new '67 Bronco looked about the same as last year's model. However, a few changes were made. Among them were: variable speed windshield wipers; padded sunvisors; dual master cylinder; self-adjusting brakes and backup lights. As before, the 4x4 Bronco roadster had no doors or roof. Its rectangular taillights were mounted vertically on the rear of the vehicle. "Ford" was printed on the far right-center of the tailgate. The license plate bracket was on the opposite end. Among standard features were: a three-speed fully synchronized transmission; "Mono-Beam" front suspension; a through-drive two-speed transfer case; 11 x 2 inch front brakes and a folding windshield.

BRONCO PICKUP: — Last year's Sports Utility was now a "pickup". It had an all-steel, bolted-on, removable roof over the front seat. The side doors had roll-up windows. The compact rear cargo area could hold up to 32.1 cubic feet of whatever one wanted to haul.

BRONCO WAGON: — This was the most luxurious Bronco. It had a full length roof and large quarter windows.

I.D. DATA (Bronco): See F-100 I.D.

Model	Body Type	Price	Weight	Prod. Total
U-130	Roadster	2417	2775	698
U-140	Pickup	2546	2995	2602
U-150	Wagon	2633	3095	10,930

ENGINE (Bronco): Displacement: 170 cu. in. Six-cylinder. 105 horsepower at 4400 R.P.M. Bore & stroke: 3.50 in. x 2.94 in. Compression ratio: 9.1:1. One-barrel carburetor.

CHASSIS: Wheelbase: 90 in. Overall length: 152.1 in. Overall width: 68.8 in. GVW: 3850-4700 lbs. Tires: 7.35 x 15.

POWERTRAIN OPTIONS: 289 V-8.

CONVENIENCE OPTIONS: Bucket seats. Cigarette lighter. Cab doors. Closed crankcase emmission (required by California Air Resources Board). Heavy-duty clutch (with six-cylinder). Tailgate mounted spare tire carrier. Rear seat. Heavy-duty battery. Front bumper guards. Heavy-duty alternator. Cooling package. GVW package. Arm rests. Limited-slip front axle. Limited-slip rear axle. Chrome front and rear bumpers. Auxiliary fuel tank with skid plate (11.5 gallon capacity). Wheelcovers. Tailgate moldings. Bodyside moldings. **SPORT PACKAGE,** includes: (Wagon and Pickup) bright horn ring, headlight bezels, taillight bezels, tailgate handle, windshield rails, instrument panel trim, side window frames and grille (with "Ford" in red applique on it); chrome-plated bumpers with front bumper guards; dual arm rests; trimmed headboard headliner; wheelcovers; vinyl floor mat (wagon) and cigar lighter.

ECONOLINE PICKUP: — This would be the last year for the Econoline pickup. Once again, it received only minor changes from the previous year's model. Perhaps the most important of these was the dual brake master cylinder. Among the standard features were: 7-foot long, 5-ft. wide and nearly 2-ft. deep dispatch box with reinforced stake pockets; vinyl seats; fresh air heater/defroster; two-speed windshield wipers; seat belts; spare tire; left-hand outside mirror; painted front bumper and hub caps; ash tray; ICC emergency lamp flasher; coat hook; windshield washers and mechanical jack.

ECONOLINE VAN: — This van had right side and rear cargo doors (left-hand side doors were available). Vent type or fixed windows could be had on all right side and rear cargo doors. The Econoline Van came with most of the same standard features as the Pickup plus: dual OSRV mirrors; painted rear bumper and armrest for driver.

ECONOLINE PANEL VAN: — This vehicle did not have side cargo doors. Fixed or vent type rear door windows were optional. Most standard features were the same as those on the Econoline Van.

I.D. DATA (Econoline): See F-100 I.D.

Model	Body Type	Price	Weight	Prod. Total
E-100	Pickup	2111	2625	Note 1
E-100	Van	2308	2715	Note 1
E-150	Panel Van	2254	2690	Note 1

NOTE 1: Production By Body Type Number: (87A-Std.) 1,697; (87B) 318; (89A) 21,107; (89E-Std.) 3,249; (89F-Std.) 3,752; (89G-Std.) 492; (89H-Std.) 618; (89J-Std.) 23,009; (89M-Std.) 357; (89N-Std.) 3,434; (89R-Std.) 821; (89S) 431; (89A-Cust.) 327; (89E-Cust.) 299; (89F-Cust.) 268; (89G-Cust.) 23; (89H-Cust.) 24; (89J-Custom) 1,027; (89M-Cust.) 41; (89N-Cust.) 563 and (89R-Cust.) 100.

ENGINE (Econoline): Displacement: 170 cu. in. Six-cylinder. 105 horsepower at 4400 R.P.M. Bore & stroke: 3.50 in. x 2.94 in. Compression Ratio: 9.1:1. One-barrel carburetor.

CHASSIS: Wheebase: 90 in. Overall length: 168.4 in. Overall width: 65 in. GVW: 4350-4930 lbs. Tires: 6.95 x 14.

POWERTRAIN OPTIONS: 240 cu. in. six-cylinder. Three-speed automatic transmission.

CONVENIENCE OPTIONS: AM radio. Auxiliary gas or hot water heaters. Super Van: 18 in. extension to the vans with heavy-duty underbody. Ammeter and oil pressure gauge. Western-type rearview mirrors. Flip-Swing passenger seat. Tinted glass all around (pickup and window vans). Tinted windshield. Front and rear chrome bumpers. Folding driver's seat. Stationary passenger seat for vans. Cargo door positioners. Whitewall tires. **Display Van Option,** includes: fixed windows in the right side of the cargo area. **Window Van Option,** includes: fixed windows all around. **Custom Package,** includes: color-keyed woven plastic upholstery; right-hand arm rest (vans); right- and left-hand arm rest (pickup); lighter; dual horns; bright metal hubcaps; chrome horn ring; cowl-wall trim panels; insulation on cowl wall; headlining on cargo area; window in rear van doors; foam padding in passenger seat (with optional seat on vans); rear quarter windows (pickup); bright body moldings; heavy-duty front and rear shocks; heavy-duty front and rear springs and safety shoulder harness. **GVW Packages:** 4750 lb. and 4930 lb.

NOTE: Econoline color choices for 1967 were: Rangoon red, Pebble beige, Raven black, Springtime yellow, Holly green, Lunar green, Frost turquoise, Harbor blue, Wimbledon white, Chrome yellow and Pure white. A two-tone paint effect was available with Wimbledon white combined with any other standard color except Chrome yellow or Pure white.

FALCON CLUB WAGON: Club Wagon changes for 1967 echoed those on the Econoline. Among the standard features were: vinyl upholstery; two-speed electric windshield wipers; foam-cushioned adjustable driver's seat; front passsenger seat; front arm rests; ashtray; dual horns and dome lights; left air inlet and sunvisor; inside OSRV mirror; retractable side step; backup lights; left OSRV mirror; windshield washer and stablilizer bar.

FALCON CUSTOM CLUB WAGON: — Standard features included most of what was on the Club Wagon plus: cigar lighter; dome light in rear compartment; left outside door lock; second seat; horn ring and emergency flashers.

FALCON DELUXE CLUB WAGON: — This was the top-of-the-line model. It featured (in addition to, or in place of, items on the base Club Wagon): cigar lighter; chrome front and rear bumpers; chrome left OSRV mirror.

I.D. DATA (Falcon): See 1962 Falcon I.D.

Model	Body Type	Price	Weight	Prod. Total
89B	Club Wagon	2532	2985	4,233
89C	Custom Club Wagon	2668	3095	1,538
89D	DeLuxe Club Wagon	2841	3115	741

ADDITIONAL PRODUCTION: Also produced were 2,248 Model 98K Club Wagon ELS models; 2,063 Model 89T Custom Club Wagon ELS models and 1,261 Model 89L DeLuxe Club Wagon ELS models.

ENGINE (Falcon): Same as Econoline.

CHASSIS: Wheelbase: 90 in. Overall length: 168.3 in. Overall width: 75 in.

POWERTRAIN OPTIONS: Three-speed automatic transmission.

CONVENIENCE OPTIONS: Arm rests (for second and third seats). Cigarette lighter. Full wheel covers. Gas-fired recirculating heater. Non-glare inside mirror. Outside rearview mirrors. Padded instrument panel and sunvisors. AM radio. Second or second and third row three-passenger seats. Seat belts. Spare tire cover lock. Spotlight. Right-hand sunvisor. Tinted windshield. Windshield washers.

F-100 PICKUP: — Ford light-duty trucks were restyled for 1967. Headlights were integrated into a rectangular slots grille. Parking lights were now located directly below the headlights. "Ford" was placed in block letters on the face of the hood. Like Styleside side panels, the hood was double-walled. Both hood and tailgate had one-hand operation. Running-boards on Flaresides were a wide, ribbed-steel step between the cab and rear fender. They facilitated easy loading from either side. The forward-slanting series I.D. emblem was moved to the side of the hood. The cabs were improved. There was nearly four more inches of shoulder room. Seats were three inches wider and "deep-cushioned." A new "swept-away" instrument panel provided extra space. The overall effect gave the cab a more car-like look and feel. Two cargo boxes were offered in 6½-ft. and 8-ft. sizes. They were the wood-floored Flareside and the steel-floored Styleside. Among standard features were: Color-keyed padded dash; foot-operated parking brake; molded fiberboard glove box with push-button latch; bright aluminum door scuff plates; slide-action air vents; one-piece hardboard headlining; full-width red, blue, green or beige vinyl-trimmed seats (color-keyed to cab paint); seat belts for driver and passenger; seat belt anchorage for center passenger; padded dash and sunvisors; emergency lamp flasher; backup lights; dual safety hydraulic brake system with warning light; windshield washers; dual electrical two-speed windshield wipers (with non-glare wiper arms); interior and left OSRV mirrors and three-speed fully-synchronized manual transmission.

F-100 PLATFORM/STAKE: — The good-looking '67 F-100 Platform/Stake could haul most lightweight, bulky loads with ease. Its seasoned hardwood floorboards were interlocked with steel skid strips. Floor corners were reinforced with steel angle brackets. It came with most of the same standard features as the F-100 pickup, plus right and left outside rearview mirrors.

I.D. DATA (F-100): See 1963 F-100 I.D.

Model	Body Type	Price	Weight	Prod. Total
F-100	(80) Platform and Rack	2224	3190	Note 1
F-100	(81) Chassis w/Cab	2072	2945	Note 1
F-100	Flareside Pickup	2198	3265	Note 1
F-100	Flareside Pickup 118" w.b.	2237	—	Note 1
F-100	Styleside Pickup	2237	—	Note 1
F-100	Styleside Pickup 118" w.b.	2273	—	Note 1
F-100	(86) Stake	2278	3315	Note 1

NOTE 1: Ford records show the following F-100 production break-outs: **4x2 Trucks:** (chassis & cowl) 1; (chassis & windshield) 1; (chassis & cab) 2,905; (cab, platform and rack) 80; (cab and platform) 17; (Flareside pickups) 18,307; (Styleside pickups) 204,710. **4x4 Trucks:** (chassis & cab) 135; (Flareside pickups) 481 and (Styleside pickups) 3,455.

ENGINE (F-100): Displacement: 240 cu. in. Six-cylinder. 150 horsepower at 4000 R.P.M. Bore & stroke: 4.0 in. x 3.18 in. Compression ratio: 9.2:1. One-barrel carburetor.

1967 Ford F-250 "Camper Special" Pickup (JAG)

F-250 PICKUP: — The F-250 shared most of the same styling and other features of the F-100. However, it was a bit more heavy-duty. Its front axle had a 400-pound greater capacity than the F-100; its rear axle almost 2000-pounds more. In addition, it had larger (12⅛ x 2 inch) brakes. A new item exclusive on the F-250 for '67 was 3.89 inch frame section modules. Both Styleside and Flareside boxes were offered. The six-passenger Crew Cab was available with or without a 6½-ft. pickup box.

NOTE: Travel Industries designed a sleek camper specifically for the Ford F-250 ¾-ton pickup. It was available through many Ford dealers. The camper was made of strong, lightweight plastic. It was 33 percent larger inside and 40 percent lighter than similar size units. Prices for the 10½-ft. camper ranged from $1,995 to $2,895.

F-250 PLATFORM/STAKE: — The F-250 ¾-ton Platform/Stake had ample cargo room. Inside length was 90 inches (Stake); 93.4 inches (Platform). Rear opening was 73.7 inches (Stake); 79.3 inches (Platform). The stake height was 28.3 inches. Like the F-100, it had seasoned hardwood floorboards.

I.D. DATA (F-250): See F-100.

Model	Body Type	Price	Weight	Prod. Total
F-250	(80) Platform	2443	3190	Note 1
F-250	(81) Chassis w/Cab	2282	2945	Note 1
F-250	Crew Cab Chassis (149'')	—	—	Note 1
F-250	Flareside Pickup	2409	3660	Note 1
F-250	Styleside Pickup	2446	3675	Note 1
F-250	Crew Cab Pickup (149'')	—	—	Note 1
F-250	(86) Stake	2498	3835	Note 1

NOTE 1: Ford records show the following F-250 production break-outs: **4x2 Trucks:** (cowl) 5; (windshield) 197; (chassis & cab) 4,316; (cab, platform & rack) 438; (cab & platform) 76; (Flareside pickup) 4,412; (Styleside pickup) 58,506. **4x4 Trucks:** (chassis & cab) 426; (cab, platform & rack) 89; (cab & platform) 25; (Flareside pickup) 915 and (Styleside pickup) 3,836.

ENGINE (F-250): See F-100.

F-350 PICKUP: — Only the Flareside pickup was offered this year in the one-ton F-350 series. It had a new 135 inch wheelbase. There were runningboards between the cab and rear fenders; seasoned hardwood floors with steel skid strips to help when sliding cargo into place; rubber covered, forged steel chains to support the tailgate and steel side panels (with rolled edges) to provide extra strength and ridigity. It had a cargo capacity of 74 cubic feet. The F-350 now had Twin-I-Beam front suspension. A four-speed manual transmission was standard. A six-passenger crew cab, with or without a pickup box, was available.

F-350 PLATFORM/STAKE: — Buyers had their choice of 9-foot or 12-foot Platform/Stakes this year. Both had seasoned hardwood floors with steel skid strips. The floor corners were reinforced with steel angle brackets. A four-speed manual transmission and two outside rearview mirrors were standard.

I.D. DATA (F-350): See F-100.

Model	Body Type	Price	Weight	Prod. Total
F-350	(80) 9 ft.Platform	2606	4285	Note 1
F-350	(80) 12 ft. Platform	—	—	Note 1
F-350	(81) Chassis w/Cab	2401	2401	Note 1
F-350	Crew Cab Chassis (159'')	—	—	Note 1
F-350	Flareside Pickup	2550	—	Note 1
F-350	Crew Cab Pickup (159'')	—	—	Note 1
F-350	(86) Stake	2606	4285	Note 1
F-350	(86) 12 ft. Stake	—	—	Note 1

NOTE 1: Ford records show the following F-350 production break-outs: (cowl) 320; (windshield) 84; (chassis and cab) 16,738; (cab, platform and rack) 2,574; (cab platform) 273 and (Flareside pickup) 1,411.

ENGINE (F-350): See F-100.

CHASSIS: Wheelbase: 115 in. (F-100); 131 in. (F-100, F-250); 135 in. (F-350); 149 in. (F-250 Crew Cab); 159 in. (F-350); 164.5 in. (F-350 Crew Cab). GVW: 4200-5000 lbs. (F-100); 4900-5600 lbs. (F-100 4x4); 4800-7500 lbs. (F-250); 6800-7700 lbs. (F-250 4x4); 6800-10,000 lbs. (F-350). Tires: 8.15 x 15 (F-100); 8.00 x 16.5 (F-250/F-350).

POWERTRAIN OPTIONS: 170 horsepower 300 cu. in. Six-cylinder. 208 horsepower 352 cu. in. V-8. Three-speed w/overdrive transmission (F-100). Four-speed manual transmission. Cruise-O-Matic.

CONVENIENCE OPTIONS: Dual rear wheels (F-350). Bucket seats. Power steering. 25-gallon under cab fuel tank with stone shield (with or without standard tank). Heavy-duty black vinyl seat trim. Deluxe fresh air heater-defroster. Radio and antenna. Dual electric horns. Shoulder safety harness. Orschein parking brake lever (F-250, F-350). Air conditioner. Limited-slip differential. **Camper Special Package:** includes: 70 amp.-hr. battery; oil presure gauge; ammeter; deluxe fresh air heater; dual electric horns; dual chrome 6 in. x 10 in. western type mirrors; extra-cooling radiator; extended tailpipe; camper wiring harness; rear shock absorbers (F-350) and "Camper Special" emblem. **Custom Cab:** includes, woven-plastic seat trim in red, blue, green or beige color keyed to exterior paint; deep foam-cushioned full-width seat; arm rests; rubber floor mat; cigar lighter; bright finish horn ring; headlining retainer molding; instrument cluster; padded dash; bright metal grille and headlight assembly; windshield reveal molding and "Custom Cab" plaques. **Ranger Package:** includes, full-width deep-cushioned seat upholstered in vinyl with a soft cloth appearance; vinyl door trim panels and nylon carpeting trimmed with bright metal moldings; color-keyed arm rests; bright-finished horn ring, instrument

cluster, headlining and instrument padding moldings; bright-finished front bumper, grille and headlight assembly, hub caps, wheel lip and rocker panel moldings.

NOTE: Standard colors for 1967 were: Rangoon red, Pebble beige, Raven black, Springtime yellow, Holly green, Lunar green, Frost turquoise, Harbor blue, Wimbledon white, Chrome yellow and Pure white. Regular two-tone paint option included Wimbledon white applied to entire cab roof (including drip rails and entire back panel above beltline molding and extending around cab corners to door openings). Deluxe two-tone paint option was available with F-100/F-250 Styleside pickups. It included Wimbledon white applied to the sheetmetal below the side molding and lower tailgate section. All other sheet metal was painted the basic color selected. This package included bright bodyside moldings, lower tailgate molding and taillight bezels and was also offered in combination with the regular two-tone paint options.

Pricing

1967	5	4	3	2	1
Ranchero					
Fairlane 500 Pickup	680	1350	2250	3150	4500
Fairlane 500 XL Pickup	700	1400	2350	3250	4700
Bronco					
Roadster	850	1700	2850	4000	5700
Sports Utility	900	1800	3000	4200	6000
Panel Van	420	840	1400	1950	2800
Club Wagon	480	975	1600	2250	3200
Custom Club Wagon	520	1020	1700	2400	3400
Deluxe Club Wagon	540	1080	1800	2500	3600
F-100 — (½-Ton)					
Flareside Pickup	890	1770	2950	4150	5900
Styleside Pickup	930	1860	3100	4350	6200
Panel	850	1700	2850	4000	5700
Stake	830	1650	2750	3850	5500
F-250 — (¾-Ton)					
Flareside Pickup	750	1500	2500	3500	5000
Styleside Pickup	780	1560	2600	3600	5200
Stake	780	1560	2600	3600	5200
F-350 — (1-Ton)					
Flareside Pickup	740	1470	2450	3350	4900
Styleside Pickup	770	1550	2550	3600	5100
Stake	750	1500	2500	3500	5000

NOTE: Add 5 percent for 4wd.

1968 FORD

1968 Ford Fairlane Ranchero Pickup (OCW)

RANCHERO PICKUP: — Once again the Ranchero was on its own. Although it still was obviously derived from the Fairlane. The quad headlights were now mounted horizontally and integrated into the horizontal theme, recessed grille. Small, wraparound corner lights were on the fenders, just above the front bumper. The taillights were vertical. "Ford" was printed on the tailgate. Under it, in a corner, was the Ranchero signature. Side vent windows were eliminated. There was a new, curved lower control arm in the front suspension. The color-coordinated interior was available in black, blue or parchment. The 6½-foot pickup box had 39.1 cubic feet of cargo space. Sides were double-walled and the tailgate opened with one hand. A three speed manual transmission was standard.

RANCHERO 500 PICKUP: — The mid-level Ranchero was the 500. Like the lower- and higher-priced versions, it had flow-through ventilation and an improved chassis. Its interior featured deep-pile carpeting, distinctive instrument panel trim, electric clock and four upholstery color choices. On the outside were high-style wheel covers and special bodyside molding.

RANCHERO GT PICKUP: — This was the ultimate Ranchero for '68. Sales literature called it "Excitingly elegant." It was easily distinguished from the others by the bold color-keyed "C" strips on its sides. It had a GT emblem in the center of the radiator, GT hub caps and 12-slot styled steel wheels, GT dash plate, deluxe interior featuring pleated vinyl bucket seats and deep-pile carpeting.

I.D. DATA (Ranchero): See 1960 Ranchero.

Model	Body Type	Price	Weight	Prod. Total
66A	Pickup	2632	3135	5014
66B	Pickup (500)	2731	3140	10,029
66D	Pickup (GT)	2964	3150	1669

ENGINE (Ranchero): Displacement: 200 cu. in. Six-cylinder. 115 horsepower at 3800 R.P.M. Bore & stroke: 3.68 in. x 3.13 in. Compression ratio: 8.8:1. Holley one-barrel carburetor.

ENGINE (Ranchero/Ranchero 500): Displacement: 289 cu. in. V-8. 195 horsepower at 4600 R.P.M. Bore & stroke: 4.00 in. x 2.87 in. Compression ratio: 8.7:1. Holley two-barrel carburetor (Ranchero GT).

CHASSIS: Wheelbase: 116 in. GVW: 3900-4800. Tires: 7.35 x 14.

POWERTRAIN OPTIONS: 195 horsepower "289" V-8 (Ranchero, 500). 210 horsepower "302" V-8. 265 horsepower "390" V-8. 280 horsepower "390" V-8. 315 horsepower "390" V-8. 335 horsepower "428-CJ" V-8. Four-speed manual transmission. SelectShift Cruise-O-Matic transmission. Limited-slip rear axle.

CONVENIENCE OPTIONS: Power steering. Tinted glass (windshield or all around). Wheel covers. Slotted steel wheels. Courtesy lights. Electric clock (Ranchero). 55-Ampere alternator. Bodyside molding (Ranchero). Power front disc brakes. Vinyl roof. Tachometer (with V-8 engines). SelectAire conditioner. Console (with bucket-seats in 500 or GT). AM/FM stereo radio. Heavy-duty battery. Bucket seats. Heavy-Duty Suspension Package: includes, heavy-duty front and rear shocks and 1280-lb. rear springs.

BRONCO ROADSTER: — the most noticeable change to the four-wheel-drive Bronco for '68 was the addition of side-marker lights on the front fenders, and reflectors on the lower rear quarter panels. Minor revisions were made to the inteior, in particular the armrest, window crank knobs and door handles. A heater and defroster were now standard. Free-running front hubs and a dry type air cleaner were also new. Among the other standard features were: three-speed fully-synchronized transmission; Mono-Beam front suspension; through-drive two-speed transfer case; 11 x 2 in. front brakes and folding windshield.

BRONCO PICKUP: — This cute vehicle was also little changed. It had an all-steel, bolt-on, removable roof over the front seat. The side doors had roll-up windows. The compact rear cargo area could hold up to 32.1 cubic feet of whatever one wanted to haul.

BRONCO WAGON: — This was the most luxurious Bronco. It had a full length roof and large quarter windows.

I.D. DATA (Bronco): See F-100 I.D.

Model	Body Type	Price	Weight	Prod. Total
U-130	Roadster	2638	2815	—
U-140	Pickup	2741	2995	—
U-150	Wagon	2851	3095	—

ENGINE (Bronco): Displacement: 170 cu. in. Six-cylinder. 105 horsepower at 4400 R.P.M. Bore & stroke: 3.50 in. x 2.94 in. Compression ratio: 9.1:1. one-barrel carburetor.

CHASSIS: Wheelbase: 90 in. Overall length: 152.1 in. Overall width: 68.8 in. GVW: 3850-4700. Tires: 7.35 x 15.

POWERTRAIN OPTIONS: "289" V-8.

CONVENIENCE OPTIONS: Bucket seats. Cigarette lighter. Cab doors. Closed crankcase emmission (required in Calif.). Heavy-duty clutch (with Six). Tailgate mounted spare tire carrier. Rear seat. Heavy-duty battery. Front bumper guards. Heavy-duty alternator. Cooling package. GVW package. Arm rests. Limited slip front axle. Limited slip rear axle. Chrome front and rear bumpers. Auxiliary fuel tank with skid plate (11.5 gallon capacity). Wheelcovers. Tailgate moldings. Bodyside moldings. **Sport Package,** includes: (Wagon and Pickup) frosted horn ring; headlight bezels; taillight bezels; tailgate handle; chrome windshield drip moldings, instrument panel trim and side window frames and grille (with "Ford" in red appliqued to it); chrome plated bumpers with front bumper guards; dual armrests; trimmed hardboard headliner; wheelcovers; vinyl floor mat (wagon) and cigar lighter.

FALCON CLUB WAGON/ECONOLINE VANS: Due to a United Auto Worker (UAW) strike, the 1967 vans were carried over until early 1968. At that point, a new line of "1969" vans was marketed. (See "historical notes" below for production data.

F-100 PICKUP: — The most noticeable change to Ford light-duty trucks, in 1968, was their new grille.It was split in the center by a thick horizontal bar and had thinner, shorter horizontal bars "floating" above and below it. Also new were the side-marker lights which were integrated into the series identification emblem on the sides of the hood. The interior was color-coordinated with exterior paint. It included a chair-height seat; "swept-away" instrument panel; padded sunvisors; armrests with paddle-type door latch handles; dome light; double-grip door locks; deluxe fresh air heater with three-speed fan and illuminated controls; hardboard headlining; seat belts with push-button buckles; floor mat and vinyl seat trim in red, blue, black or beige. F-100 buyers could choose from 6½-foot or 8-foot cargo boxes, in either Flareside or Styleside versions. A three-speed fully-synchronized transmission was standard.

1968½ Ford Chateau 12-passenger Club Wagon (JAG)

F-100 PLATFORM/STAKE: — The F-100 Platform/Stake was ideal for hauling bulky or odd shaped items. Its seasoned hardwood floor boards were interlocked with steel skid strips. Floor corners were reinforced with steel angle brackets. It also had side-marker lights on the front fenders and reflectors on sides and back of platform. Like the pickup, it came with Twin-I-Beam front suspension.

I.D. DATA (F-100): See 1963 F-100 I.D.

Model	Body Type	Price	Weight	Prod. Total
F-100	(80) Platform	2343	3280	Note 1
F-100	(81) Chassisw/Cab	2193	3035	Note 1
F-100	Flareside Pickup	2318	3355	Note 1
F-100	Flareside Pickup (LWB)	2357	3490	Note 1
F-100	Styleside Pickup	2357	3400	Note 1
F-100	Styleside Pickup (LWB)	2393	3505	Note 1
F-100	(86) Stake	2398	3405	Note 1

NOTE 1: Ford records show the following F-100 production break-outs: (chassis & cab) 2,616; (cab, platform and rack) 98; (cab and platform) 16; (Flareside Pickup) 16,686 and (Styleside) 285,015.

ENGINE (F-100): Same as 1967.

F-250 PICKUP: — The F-250 shared most features of The F-100. In addition, it came with Flex-O-Matic rear suspension, which combined longer springs with a unique device that automatically adjusted spring length for varying load conditions. Two 8-foot cargo boxes were offered. The Styleside had sleek styling and bodyside panels extended forward to hug the contour of rear cab corners. It had double-wall side panels and tailgate, plus an all-steel floor. The Flareside came with runningboards between cab and rear fenders, seasoned hardwood floorboards with steel skid strips, rubber covered forged steel chains to support tailgate and steel side panels with rolled edges to provide extra strength and rigidity.

F-250 PLATFORM/STAKE: — The F-250 Platform/Stake could haul larger and heavier loads on its hardwood platform than the F-100. It had 10 inches more inside length and nearly four inch higher stakes. Unlike the F-100, it was available with four-wheel-drive (at extra cost).

I.D. DATA (F-250): See F-100.

Model	Body Type	Price	Weight	Prod. Total
F-250	(80) Platform	2576	—	Note 1
F-250	Flareside Pickup	2542	3695	Note 1
F-250	Styleside Pickup	2579	3710	Note 1
F-250	Pickup w/Crew Cab	—	—	Note 1
F-250	(81) Chassis w/Cab	2415	3275	Note 1
F-250	Chassis w/Crew (149") Cab	—	—	Note 1
F-250	(86) Stake	2631	3870	Note 1

Note 1: Ford records show the following F-250 production break-outs: (cowl) 7; (windshield) 108; (cab chassis) 5,762; (cab platform and rack) 621; (cab platform) 150; (Flareside pickup) 5,298; (Styleside pickup) 90,170.

ENGINE (F-250): See F-100.

F-350 PICKUP: — Like other '68 light-duty Ford trucks, the 1-ton F-350 came with many safety features. Among them were: dual hydraulic brake system with warning light; seat belts; energy absorbing instrument panel with padding; double-yoke safety door latches and safety hinges; positive door lock buttons; windshield washers; two-speed windshield wipers; padded safety sunvisors; double-thick laminate safety glass windshield; inside day/night rearview mirror; backup lights; side-marker lights or reflectors; four-way emergency flashers; energy-absorbing arm rests and safety-designed door handles; glare-reduced windshield wiper arms and blades and horn button. The F-350 was only offered with the Flareside cargo box. A four-speed manual transmission was standard.

F-350 PLATFORM/STAKE: — This was the largest light-duty Platform/Stake available from Ford in 1968. Dual rear wheels could be ordered for even greater payload capacity. Seasoned hardwood floors were interlocked with steel skid strips. Floor corners were reinforced with steel angle brackets. A four-speed manual transmission was standard.

I.D. DATA (F-350): See F-100.

Model	Body Type	Price	Weight	Prod. Total
F-350	(80) 9 ft. Platform	2829	4305	Note 1
F-350	(80) 12 ft. Platform	2868	4580	Note 1
F-350	(81) Chas. w/Cab	2526	3710	Note 1
F-350	Flareside Pickup	2675	4170	Note 1
F-350	Crew Cab Pickup (164.5")	—	—	Note 1
F-350	Chassis/Crew Cab (164.5")	—	—	Note 1
F-350	(86) 9 ft. Stake	2883	4545	Note 1
F-350	(86) 12 ft. Stake	2922	4925	Note 1

NOTE 1: Ford records show the following F-350 production break-outs: (cowl) 388; (windshield) 99; (cab chassis) 22,389; (cab, platform and rack) 4,451; (cab platform) 487; (Flareside pickup) 1,612.

ENGINE (F-350): See F-100.

CHASSIS: Wheelbase: 115 in. (F-100); 131 in. (F-100/F-250); 135 in. (F-350); 149 in. (F-250 Crew Cab); 159 in. (F-350); 164.5 in. (F-350 Crew Cab). GVW: 4200-5000 lbs. (F-100); 4600-5600 lbs. (F-100 4x4); 6100-7500 lbs. (F-250); 6300-7700 lbs. (F-250 4x4); 6600-10,000 lbs. (F-350). Tires: 8.15 x 15 (F-100); 8.00 x 16.5 (F-250/F-350).

POWERTRAIN OPTIONS: 165 horsepower 300 cu. in. Six. 215 horsepower 360 cu. in. V8. 255 horsepower 390 cu. in. V-8. Three-speed overdrive (F-100); four-speed manual and Cruise-O-Matic transmissions.

CONVENIENCE OPTIONS: Dual rear wheels (F-350). Bucket seats. Power steering. Power front disc brakes (F-250, F-350). Convenience lighting package. 25-gallon under cab fuel tank with stone shield (with or without standard tank). Tinted glass. Heavy-duty black vinyl seat trim. Deluxe fresh air heater-defroster. Radio and antenna (push-button or manual). Dual electric horns. Shoulder safety harness. Heavy-duty rear springs with Flex-O-Matic suspension (F-100). Orschein parking brake lever (F-250, F-350). Air conditioner. Limited-slip differential. **Camper Special Package:** includes, 70 amp.-hr. battery; oil pressure gauge; ammeter; dual electric horns; dual chrome 6 in. x 10 in. western type mirrors; extra-cooling radiator; extended tailpipe; camper wiring harness; rear shock absorbers (F-350); "Camper Special" emblem. **Custom Cab Package:** includes, woven-plastic seat trim on a deep foam-cushioned full width seat; color-coordinated floor mat; horn ring; headlining retainer molding; custom instrument cluster; bright metal grille and headlight assembly; windshield reveal molding; "Custom Cab" plaques. **Ranger Package:** includes, full-width deep-cushioned seat upholstered in vinyl with a soft cloth appearance; door trim panels and carpeting trimmed with bright metal moldings; bright finished horn ring, instrument cluster; bright-finished front bumper, grille and headlight assembly, wheel lip and rocker panel moldings. Explorer Special Package.

NOTE: Standard colors for 1968 were: Rangoon Red, Pebble Beige, Raven Black, Meadowlark Yellow, Holly Green, Lunar Green, Sky View Blue, Harbor Blue, Wimbledon White, Chrome Yellow, Pure White. Regular two-tone paint option: Wimbledon White applied to entire cab roof including drip rails and back panel above belt-line molding and extending around cab corners to door openings. Deluxe two-tone paint: (F-100/F-250 Stylesides) Wimbledon White applied to the sheetmetal below the side molding and lower tailgate section. All other sheetmetal was painted to basic color selected. This package included bright body side molding, lower tailgate molding and taillight bezels. Combination two-tone paint option: was available combining the regular and deluxe two-tone paint options.

HISTORICAL: Introduced: Fall 1967. Total light-duty truck production, including Bronco/Ranchero/Econoline/Pickups/P-350/P-400: 414,968. Innovations: New Flex-O-Matic rear suspension standard on F-250 and optional on F-100. Ranchero is five inches long and has new vinyl top option. Bronco receives safety improvements and swing-away spare tire carrier. Historical notes: Due to a UAW strike, Econoline vans and Club Wagons were carried over, from 1967, until early 1968, when they were released as "1969" models. In spite of this, Ford records do show production break-outs, for model year 1968, as follows: **Econoline:** (89A std. cargo van) 31,983; (89C std. display van) 2,207; (89E std. window van) 5,933; (89B custom cargo van) 1,929; (89D custom display van) 111; (89F custom window van) 800. **Falcon:** (82A Club Wagon) 5,648; (82B Custom Club Wagon) 3,292 and (82C Deluxe Club Wagon) 2,297.

Pricing

1968	5	4	3	2	1
Ranchero					
Fairlane Pickup	680	1350	2250	3150	4500
Fairlane GT Pickup	700	1400	2350	3250	4700
Bronco					
Roadster	850	1700	2850	4000	5700
Sports Utility	900	1800	3000	4200	6000
Wagon	900	1800	3000	4200	6000
Econoline					
Van	440	870	1450	2050	2900
Panel Van	420	840	1400	1950	2800
Club Wagon	480	975	1600	2250	3200
Custom Club Wagon	520	1020	1700	2400	3400
Deluxe Club Wagon	540	1080	1800	2500	3600

	5	4	3	2	1
F-100 — (½-Ton)					
Flareside Pickup	890	1770	2950	4150	5900
Styleside Pickup	930	1860	3100	4350	6200
Panel	850	1700	2850	4000	5700
Stake	830	1650	2750	3850	5500
F-250 — (¾-Ton)					
Flareside Pickup	750	1500	2500	3500	5000
Styleside Pickup	780	1560	2600	3600	5200
Stake	780	1560	2600	3600	5200
F-350 — (1-Ton)					
Flareside Pickup	740	1470	2450	3350	4900
Styleside Pickup	770	1550	2550	3600	5100
Stake	750	1500	2500	3500	5000

NOTE: Add 5 percent for 4wd.

1969 FORD

1969 Ford Ranchero Pickup (OCW)

RANCHERO PICKUP: — The most striking styling change for '69 was the Ranchero's new hood scoop. Aside from that, and a slightly revised grille, things looked pretty much the same as last year. Rear side marker lights replaced the refectors used in '68. The suspension system and brake linings were also modified. On the inside, instrument dial faces were now silver and a different design was used on the three-passenger seat. It was upholstered in all-vinyl (black, blue or Nugget gold) and color-coordinated with vinyl trim panels and interior paint. Other standard features included: Deluxe seat belts with outboard retractors; vinyl-coated rubber floor mat; vinyl headlining; ventless side windows; door-operated courtesy light switches; fresh air heater/defroster with sliding controls; satin-finished horn ring; day/night inside rearview mirror; spare tire and tool storage compartments behind the split seat back and three-speed manual transmission.

RANCHERO 500 PICKUP: — In addition to, or in place of, Ranchero features, the 500 had: deep-pile wall-to-wall carpeting (color-coordinated with the black, red, blue, or Nugget gold pleated upholstery); Deluxe door trim panels and moldings; electric clock; spare tire cover; bright metal wheel covers; bright metal bodyside and wheel opening moldings.

RANCHERO GT PICKUP: — The GT emblem was moved from the center of the grille to the lower left-hand corner, next to the headlights. The upper part of the bodyside "C" stripe was lowered. Special features of the GT included: a uniquely detailed grille; Sport hood scoop; Deluxe wheel covers; whitewall tires and distinctive GT body stripe in black, white, red or gold, color-coordinated with body and interior color schemes.

I.D. DATA (Ranchero): See 1960 Ranchero.

1969 Ford Ranchero Sport Pickup (DFW/DPL)

Model	Body Type	Price	Weight	Prod. Total
66A	Pickup	2623	3185	5856
66B	Pickup (500)	2740	3190	11,214
66C	Pickup (GT)	2954	3200	1658

ENGINE (Ranchero): Displacement: 250 cu. in. Six-cylinder. 155 horsepower at 4000 R.P.M. Bore & stroke: 3.68 in. x 3.91 in. Compression ratio: 9.0:1. One-barrel carburetor.

1969 Ford Ranchero Pickup (DFW)

ENGINE (Ranchero 500): Displacement: 302 cu. in. V-8. 220 horsepower at 4600 R.P.M. Bore & stroke: 4.00 in. x 3.00 in. Compression ratio: 9.5:1. Two-barrel carburetor (GT).

CHASSIS: Wheelbase: 116 in. GVW: 4000-4950. Tires: 7.35 x 14B.

POWERTRAIN OPTIONS: 220 horsepower "302" V-8. 250 horsepower "351" V-8. 290 horsepower "351" V-8. 320 horsepower "390" V-8. 335 horsepower "428" V-8. 335 horsepower "428 Cobra Jet" V-8. Four-speed manual transmission. SelectShift Cruise-O-Matic transmission.

NOTE: The "428" engine package included: performance/handling suspension; extra cooling radiator; 80-amp-hour battery, cast aluminum rocker covers; bright radiator cap, dipstick, oil filler cap and air-cleaner top; and "428" emblem. In addition, the "428 Ram-Air Cobra Jet" V-8 included a special induction system that forced cool outside air directly to the carburetor through a hood air scoop for peak power.

1969 Ford Ranchero Pickup w/428 Cobra Jet V-8 (JAG)

CONVENIENCE OPTIONS: 7.75 x 14B and D or F70 x 14B tires. Power front disc brakes. Tachometer (for V-8s). Bodyside moldings (Ranchero, 500). SelectAire conditioner. AM/FM stereo radio. Deluxe steering wheel. Intermittent windshield wipers. Vinyl roof. Electric clock (Ranchero). Power steering. Forced ventilation system. Tinted glass (all around). Wheel covers. Styled steel wheels. Heavy-duty suspension package. Courtesy light group. Bucket seats.

NOTE: In addition to the production figures given, 727 Rancheros came with bucket seats.

NOTE: Exterior colors offered on 1969 Rancheros were: Raven black; Wimbledon white; Candy Apple red; Royal maroon; Dresden blue; Brittany blue metallic; Presidential blue metallic; Aztec aqua; Gulfstream aqua metallic; New lime; Lime gold metallic; Meadowlark yellow; Black Jade metallic; Champagne gold metallic and Indian Fire metallic. Two-tone combinations were available with Wimbledon white roofs and all other body colors or Raven black roofs with all colors except Dresden, Brittany and Presidential blues or Black Jade.

BRONCO PICKUP: — The 4x4 Bronco looked about the same as it always had. However, there were some changes. For example, the windshield no longer folded down. Also, the side marker light pads on the lower forward section of the front fenders had a lighter color. There was a black steering wheel grommet. The cowl area was improved to reduce road noise. The insulation was improved. The doors were changed. During the model year, two-speed electric windshield wipers became standard.

BRONCO WAGON: — The wagon's body was beefed up a bit, particularly the door frames, rocker panels and roof. The roof was no longer detachable. There were fixed windows in the rear liftgate and on each side of the rear compartment.

1969 Ford Bronco 4x4 Utility (DFW/DPL)

1969 Ford Bronco Deluxe 4x4 Utility (JAG)

1969 Ford Bronco 4x4 Utility (JAG)

I.D. DATA (Bronco): See F-100 I.D.

Model	Body Type	Price	Weight	Prod. Total
U-140	Pickup	2834	2990	2317
U-150	Wagon	2945	3090	18,639

ENGINE (Bronco): Displacement: 170 cu. in. Six-cylinder. 105 horsepower at 4400 R.P.M. Bore & stroke: 3.50 in. x 2.94 in. Compression ratio: 9.1:1. one-barrel carburetor.

CHASSIS: Wheelbase: 90 in. Overall length: 152.1 in. Overall width: 68.8 in. GVW: 3850-4700. Tires: 7.35 x 15.

POWERTRAIN OPTIONS: "289" V-8.

CONVENIENCE OPTIONS: Bucket seats. Cigarette lighter. Closed crankcase emmission (required in California). Heavy-duty clutch (with six-cylinder engine). Tailgate mounted spare tire carrier. Rear seat. Heavy-duty battery. Front bumper guards. Heavy-duty alternator. Cooling package. GVW package. Arm rests. Limited-slip front axle. Limited-slip rear axle. Chrome front and rear bumpers. Auxiliary fuel tank with skid plate (11.5 gallon capacity). Wheelcovers. Tailgate moldings. Bodyside moldings. **Sport Package:** (Wagon and Pickup), includes: frosted horn ring, headlight bezels, taillight bezels, tailgate handle, windshield drip, instrument panel trim, side window frames and grille (with red Ford appliques); chrome-plated bumpers with front bumper guards; dual arm rests; trimmed hardboard headliner; wheel covers; vinyl floor mat (wagon); cigar lighter; pleated parchment interior and aluminum door trim appliques.

ECONOLINE E-100 CARGO VAN: — Although introduced in February 1968, these were considered 1969 models. (There were no "1968" Econolines.) Styling was dramatically changed. The horizontal bars theme grille was enlarged and had the Ford name in block letters on its upper portion. Trim rings made the two round headlights seem larger than before. Above the headlights and grille was the sloping hood. It could be opened for checking fluid levels in the radiator, battery, brake master cylinder and windshield washer reservoir. Complete access to the engine could be attained by removing the cover within the vehicle. Since the engine had been pushed forward a bit, it was now possible to swing the driver's seat into the cargo area. Vertical, rectangular taillights were used on the rear. The right-hand cargo doors had push-button handles and all doors had "slam type" latches. Standard features included: Vinyl color-coordinated upholstery; painted front and rear bumpers and hub caps; left-hand fresh air inlet; dome lights in driver's compartment and cargo area; ash tray; single electric horn; coat hook; mechanical jack; double-grip door locks on all doors with reversible keys; push-pull interior door locks (except rear doors); metal door checks; individual driver's seat; headlining in driver and passenger area; fresh air heater and defroster and double cargo doors at right and rear.

ECONOLINE E-100 WINDOW VAN: — As the name suggests, the window van had glass all around. On it (and other E-100s) the cargo area was 11½ feet long and 53.5 inches wide. It shared most standard features with the Cargo Van.

ECONOLINE E-100 DISPLAY VAN: — This model had windows at the rear and on the right-hand side. It came with the same standard features as the Cargo Van.

I.D. DATA (Econoline E-100): See F-100 I.D.

Model	Body Type	Price	Weight	Prod. Total
E-140	Cargo Van	2489	3040	Note 1
E-150	Window Van	2567	3115	Note 1
E-160	Display Van	2522	3085	Note 1

NOTE 1: Available production break-outs are given at the end of the Econoline section.

ENGINE (Econoline E-100): Displacement: 170 cu. in. Six-cylinder. 105 horsepower at 4400 R.P.M. Bore & stroke: 3.50 in. x 2.94 in. Compression ratio: 9.1:1. One-barrel carburetor.

ECONOLINE E-200 CARGO VAN: — For heavier loads, buyers could move up to the E-200 series. Its front axle had a capacity of 2750-lbs.; the rear axle 3300-lbs. It also had larger (11 x 3 in. front / 11 x 2¼ in. rear) brakes. Standard features echoed those of the E-100 Cargo Van.

ECONOLINE E-200 WINDOW VAN: — This vehicle shared styling with the E-100 window van and load capacity with other E-200 vans.

ECONOLINE E-200 DISPLAY VAN: — This vehicle shared styling with the E-100 Display Vans and load capacity with other E-200 vans.

I.D. DATA (Econoline E-200): See E-100.

Model	Body Type	Price	Weight	Prod. Total
E-240	Cargo Van	2592	3165	Note 1
E-250	Window Van	2670	3240	Note 1
E-260	Display Van	2625	3210	Note 1

NOTE 1: Available production break-outs are given at the end of the Econoline section.

ENGINE (Econoline E-200): Same as E-100.

ECONOLINE E-300 CARGO VAN: — For really big loads, it was hard to beat the E-300 Cargo Van. Its front axle capacity was rated at 3300-lbs.; rear axle 4800-lbs. The front brakes were 12 x 3 in.; the rears 12 x 12½ in. A 10 inch clutch was standard. Its front and rear springs were also heavy-duty.

ECONOLINE E-300 WINDOW VAN: — Same features as the Cargo Van, plus windows all around.

ECONOLINE E-300 DISPLAY VAN: — Had same features as the Cargo Van, plus windows on the right hand side.

I.D. DATA (Econoline E-300): See F-100 I.D.

Model	Body Type	Price	Weight	Prod. Total
E-340	Cargo Van	2745	3880	Note 1
E-350	Window Van	2825	3820	Note 1
E-360	Display Van	2780	3790	Note 1

NOTE 1: Ford records show the following 1969 Econoline production break-outs: (89A Standard Cargo Van) 69,806; (89C Standard display van) 6,337; (89E Standard Window Van) 14,383; (89B Custom Cargo Van) 4,665; (89D Custom Display Van) 1,077 and (89F Custom Window Van) 1,774.

ENGINE (Econoline E-300): Displacement: 240 cu. in. Six-cylinder. 150 horsepower at 4000 R.P.M. Bore & stroke: 4.00 in. x 3.18 in. Compression ratio: 9.2:1. One-barrel carburetor.

CHASSIS: Wheelbase: 105.5 in. (123.5 in. Super Van). Tires: (E-100) E78-14B; (E-200) G78-15B; (E-300) 8.00 x 16.5.

POWERTRAIN OPTIONS: "240" six-cylinder engine. "302" V-8 engine. Select Shift Cruise-O-Matic transmission.

CONVENIENCE OPTIONS: Push-button radio. Stationary or flip-fold passenger seat. High output heater and defroster. Auxiliary hot water heater. Air conditioner. Insulation package. Insulated floor mats. Inside body rub rails. Inside or western-type rearview mirrors. Deluxe driver and/or stationary passenger seats with color-coordinated floor mats. Auxiliary step for right-side cargo doors. Dual electric horns. Courtesy light switches for front or all doors. Padded instrument panel. Shoulder harness. Stationary glass or vents in rear and/or right side cargo doors. Tinted glass. Inside

rear door latch and lock. Scuff pads at front door wells. School bus package for E-200 and E-300 Window Vans with 123.5 inch wheelbase. **Custom Equipment Package:** (in addition to or in place of standard items): deluxe pleated vinyl seat trim; bright metal front and rear bumpers and hub caps; horn ring; cigarette lighter; color-coordinated floor mat on left side; glove box door with lock and bright metal grille, taillight bezels, vent window and windshield moldings.

1969 Ford 12-Passenger Club Wagon (JAG)

CLUB WAGON: — Club wagons were basically Econolines made for hauling people. The base model held five passengers. Among standard features were: Twin-I-Beam independent front suspension; vinyl seat trim; arm rests on front doors and at right side of 3+passenger seats; ash trays, front and rear; black floor mats; coat hook; two dome lights; dual sunvisors; instrument panel padded on right side; bright instrument cluster trim; glove box door with lock; headlining in front compartment; dual outside rearview mirrors; backup lights; inside rearview mirror; emergency lamp flasher; retracting step for double side doors; rear reflectors and side marker lights at front and rear.

CUSTOM CLUB WAGON: — This was a step up from the base model. Both shared many of the same features. However, the Custom also had: pleated vinyl seat trim; interior vinyl side and floor trim panels; arm rests for all seats; color-cordinated front and rear floor mats; four coat hooks; full-length headlining; window trim moldings; cigarette lighter; scuff pads at front door wells; spare tire cover; horn ring; bright metal grille; instrument panel padded full width; custom ornaments; bright metal bodyside moldings, taillight bezels and hub caps, plus added insulation.

CHATEAU CLUB WAGON: — At the top-of-the-line was the Chateau. It had, in addition to or in place of Custom Club Wagon features: pleated DeLuxe cloth seat trim with vinyl bolsters; similar trim on interior door and side panels with simulated woodgrain bands; full-length color coordinated carpeting with dash insulator; chrome front and rear bumpers; bright metal dual outside mirrors; bright metal moldings around windshield, side and rear windows; bright metal rear body molding and Chateau ornaments.

I.D. DATA (Club Wagon): See F-100.

Model	Body Type	Price	Weight	Prod. Total
E-110	Club Wagon	2897	3425	10,956
E-120	Club Wagon (Custom)	3121	3600	11,725
E-130	Club Wagon (Chateau)	3025	3630	9702

ENGINE (Club Wagon): Same as E-300.

CHASSIS: Wheelbase: 105.5 in. or 123.5 in. (optional). Tires: E78-14B.

POWERTRAIN OPTIONS: "302" V-8 engine. Select Shift Cruise-O-Matic transmission.

CONVENIENCE OPTIONS: Power steering. Ammeter and oil pressure gauge. Heavy-duty battery. Heavy-duty shocks. Whitewall tires. Chrome front and rear bumpers. Cigarette lighter. Courtesy light switches for all doors. Door positioners for all door. Air conditioner. Insulation package. Inside body rub rails. High-output heater/defroster. Auxiliary hot water heater for passenger compartment. Tinted glass. AM radio.

F-100 PICKUP: — The new light-duty Ford trucks had a revised grille. It featured two thin horizontal bars, crossed by three vertical ones, above and below a thicker horizontal center bar. Aside from that, styling was basically carried over from the previous year. Among the standard features were: three-speed fully synchronized manual transmission; color coordinated interior; dome light; Hi-Dri all-weather ventilation; Deluxe fresh air heater with three-speed fan; ash tray; glove compartment; energy absorbing arm rests with paddle-type door latch handles; seat belts; hardboard headlining; black floor mat; vinyl seat trim in black, blue, red or parachment and padded instrument panel. Both Styleside and Flareside versions were offered in either 6½-foot or 8-foot cargo box lengths.

I.D. DATA (F-100): See 1963 F-100.

1969 Ford F-100 Deluxe Styleside Long-Bed Pickup (JAG)

1969 Ford F-100 Deluxe Styleside Pickup (JAG)

Model	Body Type	Price	Weight	Prod. Total
F-100	(81) Chassis w/Cab	2230	3060	Note 1
F-100	6½ ft. Flareside Pickup	2354	3380	Note 1
F-100	6½ ft. Styleside Pickup	2393	3440	Note 1
F-100	8 ft. Flareside Pickup	2393	3490	Note 1
F-100	8 ft. Styleside Pickup	2430	3505	Note 1

NOTE 1: Ford records show the following F-100 production break-outs: (4x2 chassis & cab) 3,058; (4x2 Flareside pickups) 16,248; (4x2 Styleside pickups) 315,979; (4x4 chassis & cab) 56; (4x4 Flareside pickup) 465 and (4x4 Styleside pickup) 7,940. **Note:** Break-outs by cargo box length not available.

ENGINE (F-100): Same as 1968.

1969 Ford F-250 Deluxe Styleside Pickup (JAG)

F-250 PICKUP: — The F-250 Pickup had most of the same features as the F-100. Plus, it came with Flex-O-Matic rear suspension. The Styleside had double-wall side panels and tailgate; flat-top wheelhousings; stake pockets and an all-steel floor. A single center latch mechanism opened the tailgate. Steel support straps held the tailgate in open position. The Flareside had running boards between the cab and rear fenders. It came with seasoned hardwood floorboards, with steel skid strips to help slide cargo into place. Rubber-covered, forged steel chains supported the tailgate when open. Toggle-type latches maintained a tight seal when the tailgate was closed. Heavy gauge steel side panels with flared sides had rolled edges for extra strength and rigidity.

F-250 PLATFORM/STAKE: — Floor frames of the F-250 Platform/Stake were made of steel cross sills riveted to steel siderails. Floor boards were interlocked with steel skid strips and corners were reinforced with steel brackets. Formed steel caps over the ends of the body sills acted as bumpers for loading docks. Sideboards and stakes were straight-grained hardwood.

I.D. DATA (F-250): See F-100.

Model	Body Type	Price	Weight	Prod. Total
F-250	(81) Chassis w/Cab	2461	3290	Note 1
F-250	Flareside Pickup	2588	3710	Note 1
F-250	Styleside Pickup	2624	3725	Note 1
F-250	(80) Platform	2621	3705	—
F-250	(86) Stake	2677	3885	Note 1
F-250	Crew Cab Pickup 147" w.b.	—	—	Note 1
F-250	Crew Cab Pickup 147" w.b.	—	—	Note 1

NOTE 1: Ford records show the following F-250 production break-outs: (4x2 chassis and windshield) 242; (4x2 chassis and cab) 6,093; (4x2 Platform and Rack) 586; (4x2 Platform) 73; (4x2 Flareside pickups) 3,827; (4x2 Styleside pickups) 101,603; (4x4 chassis and cab) 641; (4x4 Platform and Rack) 102; (4x4 Platform) 30; (4x4 Flareside pickups) 973 and (4x4 Styleside pickups) 10,286. **Note:** Separate break-outs by cargo box length or Crew Cabs are not available.

ENGINE (F-250): Same as F-100.

F-350 PICKUP: — F-350 buyers had to settle for the Flareside cargo box. It had a cargo capacity of 74 cubic feet. That was almost 10 more than the comparable F-250 Flareside. Plus, it could haul heavier payloads. A four-speed manual transmission was standard.

F-350 PLATFORM/STAKE: — The F-350 Platform/Stake had most of the same features as the F-250 version. However, rather than wood, it used reinforced steel stakes. Also, it was available with dual rear wheels (at extra cost). A four-speed manual transmission was standard.

I.D. DATA (F-350): See F-100.

Model	Body Type	Price	Weight	Prod. Total
F-350	(81) Chassis w/Cab	2579	3615	Note 1
F-350	Chassis w/Cab (LWB)	—	—	Note 1
F-350	Flareside Pickup	2727	4075	Note 1
F-350	Crew Cab Pickup (LWB)	—	—	Note 1
F-350	(80) 9 ft. Platform	2881	4200	Note 1
F-350	(80) 12 ft. Platform	2920	4600	Note 1
F-350	(86) 9 ft. Stake	2935	4440	Note 1
F-350	(86) 12 ft. Stake	2975	4945	Note 1

NOTE 1: Ford records show the following F-350 (all 4x2) production break-outs: (cowl) 331; (windshield) 206; (chassis & cab) 27,817; (platform and rack) 5,335; (cab and platform) 613 and Flareside pickup (1,829).

ENGINE (F-350): See F-100.

CHASSIS: Wheelbase: 115 in. (F-100); 131 in. (F-100/F-250); 135 in. (F-350); 149 in. (F-250 Crew Cab); 159 in. (F-350); 164.5 in. (F-350 Crew Cab). GVW: 4200-5000 lbs. (F-100); 4600-5600 lbs. (F-100 4x4); 6100-7500 lbs. (F-250); 6300-7700 lbs. (F-250 4x4); 6600-10,000 lbs. (F-350). Tires: 8.25 x 15 (F-100); 8.00 x 16.5 (F-250/F-350).

POWERTRAIN OPTIONS: 300 cu. in. Six, 360 V-8, 390 V-8. 3-speed w/overdrive (F-100). 4-speed manual. Cruise-O-Matic automatic.

CONVENIENCE OPTIONS: Four-wheel-drive. F-100 4x4s had Mono-Beam front suspension with coil springs and forged radius rods and a single-speed transfer case coupled to a four-speed transmission. The F-250 4x4 front suspension consisted of resilient long leaf springs with lubrication free shackles (They also had a standard two-speed transfer case and three-speed manual transmission). Electric power pack (underhood 2500-watt generator). Frame mounted 25-gallon fuel tank. **Convenience Group**; included cargo area light; courtesy light door switches; day/night mirror and engine compartment light. Tool towage box (8-ft. Styleside). Bright bodyside moldings (Styleside). Western type mirrors (fixed or swing-lock). Spare tire carrier (inside box on Styleside, ahead of left rear fender on Flareside). Bright finish grille. Rear step bumper (Styleside). Bright hub caps. Bright or "Mag" wheel covers for 15 inch wheels. Extra cooling equipment. Chrome contour front bumpers. Chrome or painted contour rear bumpers for Stylesides. Painted channel rear bumper for Flaresides. Brush-type grille guard. Free-running front hubs for 4x4s. Oil-bath engine air cleaner. Velocity-type engine governor. Vacuum brake booster. Power disc front brakes (F-250/F-350). Power steering (F-100/F-250). Flex-O-Matic rear suspension (F-100). Heavy-duty shocks. Heavy-duty front springs. Heavy-duty alternator. Heavy-duty battery. SelectAire conditioner (includes standard fresh air heater in an integral unit). Push-button radio. Manual radio. Ammeter and oil pressure gauge. Bucket seats color-coordinated to exterior paint. Lockable cab storage compartment behind the seat. Remote-control outside mirror. Tinted windshield. Tinted glass all around. Cab market and identification lights. Shoulder harnesses. Dual electric horns. Heavy-duty black vinyl seat trim. Full-width Custom Cab seat. **Custom Cab Equipment:** includes, deep-foam seat cushion and foam padding in seat back; woven plastic seat trim; color-coordinated floor mat; custom instrument cluster; horn ring; cigarette lighter; bright metal head-lining retainer and door cover plate moldings; bright metal front bumper, grille, windshield moldings and taillamp bezels. **Ranger package:** includes, color-coordinated pleated vinyl upholstery with a clothlike pattern; wood-grain inserts in instrument cluster; bright metal instrument panel molding; pleated vinyl door trim with simulated woodgrain insert and bright molding; door courtesy light switches; wall-to-wall carpeting; distinctive grille; bright metal hub caps and trim on rocker panels, front wheel opening lips, roof drip rails and around rear window; Ranger emblem; cargo area light; bright metal tailgate release handle, rocker panel extension, rear wheel opening lip and tailgate moldings. **Camper Special Package:** includes, 70 ampere-hour battery; oil pressure gauge; ammeter; extra-cooling radiator; dual bright metal 6 x 10 in. Western type mirrors; extended tailpipe; front side marker lights; camper wiring harness; rear shock absorbers (F-350) and "Camper Special" emblem. **Farm & Ranch Special:** includes, (F-100/F-250 Stylesides) heavy-duty Twin-I-Beam front suspension; heavy-duty Flex-O-Matic rear suspension; front and nine inch high side cargo boards painted body-color; rear step bumper with provision for trailer hitch; chrome western swing-lock mirrors; heavy-duty battery; heavy-duty alternator; bright-metal bodyside moldings and "Farm & Ranch Special" insignia on cowl. **Contractor Special:** includes, (for 8-ft. Styleside) heavy-duty Package 1 with heavy-duty front and rear springs; rear step bumper; convenience group; dual chrome western swing-lock mirrors; contractor box on both sides with key-lockable fold-down doors and "Contractor Special" insignia on cowlsides. (Package 2: everything on package 1 plus underhood electric power pack.)

NOTE: Standard colors for 1969 were: Raven black; Wimbledon white; Norway green; New lime; Boxwood green; Candy Apple red; Royal maroon; Pebble beige; Cordova copper; Empire yellow; Lunar green; Reef aqua; Sky View blue; Harbor blue; Chrome yellow and Pure white. With regular two-tones the accent color was applied to the roof and upper back panel with a belt line molding from door to door, around back of the cab. Deluxe two-tones (Styleside only) had accent color applied to the area below the bodyside and lower tailgate moldings, which were included in this option. Combination two-tones (Stylesides only) featured the regular and deluxe two-tone options combined with the accent color applied as specified for these options.

HISTORICAL: Introductory dates: (Vans) Spring 1968; (Others) Fall 1968. Calendar year production: 639,948. Industry share: 32.60 percent. Calendar year registrations by weight class: (6000-lbs. or under) 399,285; (6000-10,000 pounds) 179,082. Model year production of light-duty trucks including Ranchero, Bronco and Econoline 647,948 (This includes 2,780 P-350 parcel vans and 2,382 P-400 parcel vans). Innovations: Completely redesigned and reengineered Econoline van introduced in Feb. 1968 as a 1969 model. The Econoline boasted more cargo space and passenger carrying room than any similar competing model. It featured Twin I-Beam front suspension; V-8 options and two wheelbase choices. Historical notes: P. Caldwell was V.P. and general manager of the Ford Truck Division of Ford Motor Co. This was a record year for sales, with 713,699 deliveris made for the Jan. thru Jan. period. A total of 13,915 Ford trucks (of all sizes) were made with diesel engines. Other engine installations included 158,521 sixes and 467,512 V-8s.

Pricing

1969	5	4	3	2	1
Ranchero					
Fairlane Pickup	680	1350	2250	3150	4500
Fairlane GT Pickup	700	1400	2350	3250	4700
Bronco					
Pickup	850	1700	2850	4000	5700
Wagon	900	1800	3000	4200	6000
Econoline					
Van	440	870	1450	2050	2900
Panel Van	420	840	1400	1950	2800
Club Wagon	480	975	1600	2250	3200
Custom Club Wagon	520	1020	1700	2400	3400
Deluxe Club Wagon	540	1080	1800	2500	3600
F-100 — (½-Ton)					
Flareside Pickup	890	1770	2950	4150	5900
Styleside Pickup	930	1860	3100	4350	6200
F-250 — (¾-Ton)					
Flareside Pickup	750	1500	2500	3500	5000
Styleside Pickup	780	1560	2600	3600	5200
Stake	780	1560	2600	3600	5200
F-350 — (1-Ton)					
Flareside Pickup	740	1470	2450	3350	4900
Styleside Pickup	770	1550	2550	3600	5100
Stake	750	1500	2500	3500	5000

NOTE: Add 5 percent for 4x4.

1970 FORD

1970 Ford Ranchero Squire Sport Pickup (OCW)

RANCHERO PICKUP: — The 1970 Ranchero was sleek and stylish. It had rounded fender contours, a slightly sloping hood, hidden windshield wipers and a criss-cross pattern full-width grille with four headlights recessed in it. Standard features included: bright left-hand remote control outside mirror; bright windshield, rear window, drip rail and top of cargo box moldings; bright taillight bezels; bright hub caps; full-width seat upholstered in black, blue or gold vinyl with pleated seatback; color-keyed vinyl door trim panels with bright frames; color-keyed rubber floor covering; Flow-through ventilation; ventless side windows; locking steering column; fresh air heater/defroster; trim panel behind the split seatback (with spare tire and tool compartment cover); Deluxe seat belts with outboard retractors and shoulder harnesses (also center passenger seat belts); armrests with integral, squeeze-type door handles; vinyl-framed day/night mirror; cigarette lighter and emergency lamp flasher.

RANCERHO 500 PICKUP — This was the most popular Ranchero in 1970. In addition to, or in place of, standard Ranchero features, the 500 had: pleated, all-vinyl seat upholstery in black, red, blue, white or ginger; deep pile, wall-to-wall carpeting; woodtone inlay in padded steering wheel hub; electric clock; arm rests with bright base; Deluxe grille with center crest; bright metal wheel covers; bright metal side moldings with vinyl insert; bright metal wheel lip moldings and bright metal hidden wiper lip molding.

RANCHERO GT PICKUP: — The GT had, in addition to or in place of all the standard Ranchero features, a Deluxe grille with center GT crest; colorful laser stripe (red, brown, green or blue color-keyed with exterior) on sides and tailgate; GT letters and chevrons on sides; Sport-scoop hood; Deluxe wheel covers; fiberglass-belted whitewall tires; bright metal wheel lip and hidden wiper lip moldings; pleated, all-vinyl seat upholstery in black, red, blue, white or ginger; deep-pile, wall-to-wall carpeting; woodtone inlay panel in padded steering wheel hub; electric clock and black lower instrument panel.

RANCHERO SQUIRE PICKUP: — Sales literature called this the "New ultimate in personal pickup luxury." The Squire had (in addition to or in place of all the standard Ranchero features): color-coordinated, deep-pile wall-to-wall carpeting; woodtone panel under instruments; woodtone inlay in padded steering wheel hub; electric clock; Deluxe grille with center crest; woodtone panels on sides and tailgate; fiberglass belted whitewall tires; Deluxe wheel covers; bright metal hidden wiper lip molding and Ranchero Squire script on front fenders.

I.D. DATA (Ranchero): See 1960 Ranchero I.D.

Model	Body Type	Price	Weight	Prod. Total
661	Pickup	2646	3285	4816
66B	Pickup (500)	2860	3295	8976
66C	Pickup (GT)	3010	3445	3905
66D	Pickup (Squire)	2965	3330	3943

ENGINE (Ranchero): Displacement: 250 cu. in. OHV six-cylinder. 155 horsepower at 4000 R.P.M. Bore & stroke: 3.68 x 3.91 in. Compression ratio: 9.0:1. One-barrel carburetor (Ranchero 500/Squire). Displacement: 302 cu. in. V8. 220 horsepower at 4600 R.P.M. Bore & stroke: 4 x 3 in. Compression ratio: 9.5:1. two-barrel carburetor (GT).

CHASSIS: Wheelbase: 117 in. Overall length: 206.2 in. Tires: E78-14 4PR.

POWERTRAIN OPTIONS: 220 horsepower "302" V8. 250 horsepower "351" V8. 300 horsepower "351" V8. 360 horsepower "429 Thunder-Jet" V8. 370 horsepower "429 Cobra" V8. 370 horsepower "429 Cobra Jet" V8. Four-speed manual transmission with Hurst shifter. Select Shift Cruise-O-Matic transmission.

NOTE: The Cobra V8 includes performance handling package; 80-amp. hr. battery;, 55-amp. alternator; dual exhausts and appearance package with bright cast aluminum rocker covers. The Cobra Jet V8 had all this, plus Ram-Air induction system with pop through "shaker" hood air scoop for peak performance.

CONVENIENCE OPTIONS: Rim-blow sport steering wheel (allowed one to blow the horn by squeezing the rim). AM/FM stereo radio. SelectAire conditioner with hi-level outlets. Hidden headlamps (Squire/GT/500). Vinyl roof in black or white. Intermittent windshield wipers. AM push-button radio. Electric clock (Ranchero). Power steering. Tinted glass. Deluxe wheel covers. Sport-styled wheel covers. Styled steel wheels. **Visibility Group:** includes, ash tray, map, glove compartment and underhood lights; warning lights for seat belts and parking brake and "headlight-on" reminder buzzer. Tachometer (V8s only). High-back bucket seats in black or white knitted vinyl (Squire/GT/500). Power front disc brakes. Racing-type mirrors painted body-color (left-hand mirror includes remote control). Shaker hood scoop with Ram-air induction system (included with optional 429 Cobra Jet V8). Flat black paint on hood and scoop of Ranchero GT. Heavy-duty suspension package. Heavy-duty battery. Extra-cooling radiator. **Class II Trailer Towing Package:** includes: front power disc brakes; heavy-duty suspension; cooling package; heavy-duty alternator and battery; F78-14 4PR or E70-14 4PR or F70-14 4PR whitewall tires.

NOTE: Ranchero colors for 1970 were: Raven black; Wimbledon white; Candy apple red; Calypso coral; Dark maroon; Dark blue; Medium blue metallic; Platinum; Medium and Dark Ivy green metallic; New lime; Champagne gold; Morning gold; Carmel bronze metallic and Bright yellow. Two-tone combinations were available with Wimbledon white roofs and all other body colors except Platinum. Raven black roofs were available with all colors except Dark blue, Medium blue and Dark Ivy green.

BRONCO PICKUP: — Styling changes were minor for the four-wheel-drive Bronco in 1970. The front side marker light and rear quarter panel reflector were now flush-mounted and higher than before. Standard features included: all-vinyl, full-width seat; fresh air heater and defroster; lockable glove compartment; padded instrument panel; energy-absorbing sunvisors; vinyl-coated floor mat; floor-mounted T-bar transfer case control; Mono-Beam suspension; self-adjusting brakes and fully-synchronized three-speed manual transmission.

BRONCO WAGON: — The Bronco wagon shared the features of the pickup, but had a full-length roof. The roof had fixed windows in the rear liftgate and on each side of the rear compartment.

I.D. DATA (Bronco): See F-100 I.D.

Model	Body Type	Price	Weight	Prod. Total
U140	Pickup	3035	2990	1700
U150	Wagon	3149	3090	16,750

ENGINE (Bronco): Displacement 170 cu. in. OHV six-cylinder. 105 horsepower at 4400 R.P.M. Bore & stroke: 3.50 x 2.94 in. Compression ratio: 9.1:1. One-barrel carburetor.

CHASSIS: Wheelbase: 90 in. Overall length: 152.1 in. Overall width: 68.8 in. GVW: 3850-4700 lbs.. Tires: 7.35 x 15.

POWERTRAIN OPTIONS: 302 cu. in. V8.

CONVENIENCE OPTIONS: Convenience Group: includes, cigarette lighter; map light (inside 10 inch day/night mirror); horn ring; one-pint oil bath air cleaner (302 V8); right-hand chrome rearview mirror; bucket seats; shoulder harness; rear seat (wagon w/bucket seat option); chrome bumpers; skid plates for standard fuel tank and transfer case; inside tailgate mounted spare tire carrier (included with rear seat option); exterior rear-mounted swing-away tire carrier; bright metal wheel covers; high-flotation tires; auxiliary 11.5 gallon fuel tank (with skid plate); manual radio and antenna; bright bodyside and tailgate moldings; bright metal rocker panel moldings; Dana free-running front hubs; hand-operated throttle and heavy-duty front axle carrier assembly (special order). **Sport Package:**, includes: bright metal "Sport Bronco" emblem; pleated parchment vinyl front seat; vinyl door trim panels with bright metal moldings; hardboard headlining with bright metal retainer moldings (Wagon); parchment vinyl simulated-carpet front floor mat with bright metal retainers (rear floor mat included with optional rear seat); cigarette lighter; satin-finish horn ring; bright metal drip rail moldings; bright metal windshield and window frames; bright metal grille molding and tailgate release handle; bright headlight, side light, reflector and taillight bezels; Argent silver-painted grille with bright Ford letters; chrome bumpers front and rear; chrome front bumper guards; bright metal wheel covers (w/15 inch wheels only) and 6.50 x 16-6PR TT tires. **Dealer-installed accessories:** Power-take-off (front-mounted). Warn free-running front hubs (manual or automatic). Snow plows. Snow plow angling kits. Front auxiliary air springs. Front-mounted winch. Trailer hitch. Trailer towing mirror. Locking gas cap. Front tow hooks. Compass. Fire extinguisher. Tachometer. Two-way radio.

NOTE: Bronco color choices for 1970 were: Raven black; Wimbledon white; Candy Apple red; Royal maroon; Sky View blue; Harbor blue; Diamond blue; Acapulco blue; Reef aqua; Norway green; Boxwood green; Mojave tan; Chrome yellow; Pinto yellow; Carmel bronze metallic; New lime and Yucatan gold. Bronco roofs were painted Wimbledon white.

ECONOLINE E-100 CARGO VAN: — Except for a slight revision to the side marker lamps and reflectors (the rear ones were now at the same level as the front ones), the Econoline was basically unchanged for 1970. Standard features included: vinyl color-coordinated upholstery; painted front and rear bumpers and hub caps; left-hand fresh air inlet; dome lights in driver's compartment and cargo area; ash tray; single electric horn; coat hook; mechanical jack; Double-grip door locks on all doors (with reversible keys); Push-pull interior door locks (except rear doors); metal door checks; individual driver's seat; headlining in driver and passenger area; fresh air heater and defroster and double cargo doors at right and rear.

ECONOLINE E-100 WINDOW VAN: — As the name suggests, the window van had glass all around. Like other E-100s, its cargo area was 11½-feet long and 53.5-inches wide. It shared most standard features with the Cargo Van.

ECONOLINE E-100 DISPLAY VAN: — This model had windows at the rear and on the right-hand side. It came with the same standard features as the Cargo Van.

I.D. DATA (Econoline): See F-100 I.D.

Model	Body Type	Price	Weight	Prod. Total
E-140	Cargo Van	2673	3265	Note 1
E-150	Window Van	2751	3340	Note 1
E-160	Display Van	2706	3310	Note 1

NOTE 1: For production break-outs see end of Econoline listings.

ENGINE (Econoline E-100): Displacement: 170 cu. in. OHV six-cylinder. 105 horsepower at 4400 R.P.M. Bore & stroke: 3.50 x 2.94 in. Compression ratio: 9.1:1. One-barrel carburetor.

ECONOLINE E-200 CARGO VAN: — For heavier loads, buyers could move up to the E-200 series. Its front axle had a capacity of 2750-lbs. The rear axle capacity was 3300-lbs. It also had larger (11 x 3 in. front/11 x 2¼ in. rear) brakes. Standard features echoed those of the E-100 Cargo Van.

ECONOLINE E-200 WINDOW VAN: — This vehicle shared styling with the E-100 Window Van and load capacity with other E-200 vans.

ECONOLINE E-200 DISPLAY VAN: — This vehicle shared styling with the E-100 Display Van and load capacity with other E-200 vans.

I.D. DATA (Econoline E-200): See E-100.

Model	Body Type	Price	Weight	Prod. Total
E-240	Cargo Van	2776	3385	Note 1
E-250	Window Van	2854	3460	Note 1
E-260	Display Van	2809	3430	Note 1

NOTE 1: For production break-outs see end of Econoline listings.

ENGINE (Econoline E-200): Same as E-100.

ECONOLINE E-300 CARGO VAN: — For really big loads, it was hard to beat the E-300 Cargo Van. Its front axle capacity was rated at 3300-lbs. Rear axle was 4800-lbs. The front brakes were 12 x 3 inches, the rears 12 x 12½ inches. A 10 inch clutch was standard. Its front and rear springs were also heavy-duty.

ECONOLINE E-300 WINDOW VAN: — Had same features as the Cargo Van, plus windows all around.

ECONOLINE E-300 DISPLAY VAN: — Had the same features as the Cargo Van, plus windows on the right-hand side.

I.D. DATA (Econoline E-300): See F-100 I.D.

Model	Body Type	Price	Weight	Prod. Total
E-340	Cargo Van	2865	3790	Note 1
E-350	Window Van	3009	3920	Note 1
E-360	Display Van	2964	3890	Note 1

NOTE 1: Ford records show the following Econoline production break-outs: (89A Standard Cargo Van) 75,179; (89C Standard Display Van) 8,471; (89E Standard Window Van) 16,192; (89B Custom Cargo Van) 6,533; (89D Custom Display Van) 846 and (89F Custom Window Van) 1,884.

ENGINE (Econoline E-300): Displacement: 240 cu. in. Six-cylinder. 150 horsepower at 4000 R.P.M. Bore & stroke: 4.00 x 3.18 in. Compression ratio: 9.2:1. One-barrel carburetor.

CHASSIS: Wheelbase: 105.5 in. (123.5 in. SuperVan) Tires: E78-14B (E-100); G78-15B (E-200); 8.00 x 16.5 in. (E-300).

POWERTRAIN OPTIONS: "240" six-cylinder engine. "302" V8 engine. SelectShift Cruise-O-Matic transmission.

CONVENIENCE OPTIONS: Push-button radio. Stationary or flip-fold passenger seat. High output heater and defroster. Auxiliary hot water heater. Air conditioner. Insulation package. Insulated floor mats. Inside body rub rails. Inside or Western-type OSRV mirrors. Deluxe driver and/or stationary passenger seats with color-coordinated floor mats. Auxiliary step for right-side cargo doors. Dual electric horns. Courtesy light switches for front or all doors. Padded instrument panel. Shoulder harness. Stationary glass or vents in rear and/or side cargo doors. Tinted glass. Inside rear door latch and lock. Scuff pads at front door wells. School bus package for E-200 and E-300 Window Vans with 123.5 inch wheelbase. **Custom Equipment Package:** (in addition to or in place of standard items) Deluxe pleated vinyl seat trim; bright metal front and rear bumpers and hub caps; horn ring; cigarette lighter; color-coordinated floor mat on left side; glove box door with lock and bright metal grille, taillight bezels, vent window and windshield moldings.

NOTE: Econoline colors for 1970 were: Sky View blue; Harbor Blue; Reef aqua; Cactus green; Crystal green; Tampico yellow; Pinto yellow; Chrome yellow; Baja beige; Candy Apple red and Wimbledon white. Two-tone paint combinations were available.

CLUB WAGON: — Club wagons were basically Econolines made for hauling people. The base model held five passengers. Among standard features were: Twin-I-Beam independent front suspension; vinyl seat trim; arm rests on front doors and at right side of 3+passenger seats; ash trays front and rear; black floor mats; coat hook; two dome lights; dual sunvisors; instruments panel (padded on right side); bright instrument cluster trim; glove box door with lock; headlining in front compartment; dual outside rear view mirrors; backup lights; inside rearview mirror; emergency lamp flasher; retracting step for double side doors; rear reflectors and side marker lights at front and rear.

CUSTOM CLUB WAGON: — This was a step up from the base model. Both shared many of the same features. The Custom, however, also had: pleated vinyl seat trim; interior vinyl side and door trim panels; arm rests for all seats; color-coordinated front and rear floor mats; four coat hooks; full-length headlining; window trim moldings; cigarette lighter; scuff pads at front door wells; spare tire cover; horn ring; bright-metal grille; full-width padded instrument panel; Custom ornaments; bright metal bodyside moldings, taillight bezels and hub caps and added insulation.

CHATEAU CLUB WAGON: — At the top-of-the-line was the Chateau. It had, in addition to or in place of Custom Club Wagon features: pleated deluxe cloth seat trim with vinyl bolsters; similar trim on interior door and side panels (with simulated woodgrain bands); full-length color-coordinated carpeting with dash insulator; chrome front and rear bumpers; bright metal dual outside mirrors; bright metal molding around windshield, side and rear windows; bright-metal rear body molding and Chateau ornaments.

I.D. DATA (Club Wagon): See F-100.

Model	Body Type	Price	Weight	Prod. Total
E-110	Club Wagon	3109	3595	Note 1
E-120	Custom Club Wagon	3334	3710	—
E-130	Chateau Club Wagon	3483	4180	—

ENGINE (Club Wagon): Same as E-300.

CHASSIS: Wheelbase: 105.5 in. (123.5 in. optional) Tires: E78-14B.

POWERTRAIN OPTIONS: "302" V8. Select Shift Cruise-O-Matic transmission.

CONVENIENCE OPTIONS: Power steering. Ammeter and oil pressure gauge. Heavy-duty battery. Heavy-duty shocks. Whitewall tires. Chrome front and rear bumpers. Cigarette lighter. Courtesy light switches for all doors. Door positioners for all doors. Air conditioner. Insulation package. Inside body rub rails. High-output heater/defroster. Auxiliary hot water heater for passenger compartment. Tinted glass. AM radio.

F-100 CUSTOM PICKUP: — The 1970 Ford light-duty trucks had a new grille. It featured a grid-pattern divided at the center by a vertical bar. The parking lamps were slightly lower and of the wraparound variety. The rear side marker lamps were now at the end of bodyside spear sculpturing. Standard features included: three-speed manual transmission; color-coordinated interior; door courtesy light switches; Hi-Dri all-weather ventilation; Deluxe fresh air heater with three-speed fan; ash tray; glove compartment; aluminum scuff plates; Deluxe instrument cluster bezel; seat belts; hardboard headlining; black floor mats with heel pads; vinyl seat trim with embossed patterned rib inserts in black, blue, red, parchment or green; bright grille and chrome front bumper. Both Styleside and Flareside versions were offered in either 6½-foot or 8-foot cargo box lengths.

I.D. DATA (F-100): See 1963 F-100.

1970 Ford F-100 Ranger Styleside Pickup (JAG)

Model	Body Type	Price	Weight	Prod. Total
F-100	(81) Chassis w/Cab	2384	3160	Note 1
F-100	6½-ft. Flareside Pickup	2510	3475	Note 1
F-100	6½-ft. Styleside Pickup	2550	3540	Note 1
F-100	8-ft. Flareside Pickup	2610	3690	Note 1
F-100	8-ft. Styleside Pickup	2650	3705	Note 1

NOTE 1: Ford records show the following F-100 production figure break-outs: (Chassis and cab) 2,688; (Flareside pickup) 13,551 and (Styleside pickup). **Note:** No additional break-outs are given.

ENGINE (F-100): Same as 1968.

F-250 CUSTOM PICKUP: — The F-250 pickup had most of the same features as the F-100. It also had Flex-O-Matic rear suspension. The Styleside had double-wall side panels and tailgate, flat-top wheel housings, stake pockets and an all-steel floor. A single center latch mechanism opened the tailgate. Steel support straps held the tailgate in open position. The Flareside had running boards between the cab and rear fenders. It came with seasoned hardwood floorboards with steel skid strips to help slide cargo into place. Rubber-covered forged steel chains supported the tailgate when open. Toggle-type latches maintained a tight seal when tailgate was closed. Heavy gauge steel side panels, with flared sides, had rolled edges for extra strength and rigidity.

F-250 PLATFORM/STAKE: — Floor frames of the F-250 Platform/Stake were made of steel cross-sills riveted to steel side rails. Floorboards were interlocked with steel skid strips and the corners were reinforced with steel brackets. Formed steel caps, over the ends of the body sills, acted as bumpers for loading docks. Sideboards and stakes were straight-grained hardwood.

I.D. DATA (F-250): See F-100.

Model	Body Type	Price	Weight	Prod. Total
F-250	(81) Chassis w/Cab	2615	3370	Note 1
F-250	Flareside Pickup	2740	3790	Note 1
F-250	Styleside Pickup	2780	3805	Note 1
F-250	(80) Platform	2775	3705	Note 1
F-250	(86) Stake	2830	3885	Note 1
F-250	Crew Cab Pickup (LWB)	—	—	Note 1
F-250	Crew Cab Chassis (LWB)	—	—	Note 1

NOTE 1: Ford records show the following F-250 production break-outs: (windshield) 131; (cab chassis) 6,366; (cab, platform and rack) 650; (cab platform) 130; (Flareside pickup) 4,683 and (Styleside pickup) 121,265. **Note:** No additional break-outs are available.

ENGINE (F-250): Same as F-100.

F-350 CUSTOM PICKUP: — F-350 buyers had to settle for the Flareside cargo box. It had a cargo capacity of 74 cubic-feet. That was almost 10 more than the comparable F-250 Flareside. It could also haul heavier payloads. A four-speed manual transmission was standard.

F-350 PLATFORM/STAKE: — The F-350 Platform/Stake had most of the same features as the F-250 version. However, rather than wood, it used reinforced steel stakes. Also, it was available with dual rear wheels (at extra cost). A four-speed manual transmission was standard.

I.D. DATA (F-350): See F-100.

Model	Body Type	Price	Weight	Prod. Total
F-350	(81) Chassis w/Cab	2720	3725	Note 1
F-350	(LWB) Chassis w/Cab	2770	3835	Note 1
F-350	Flareside Pickup	3505	4290	Note 1
F-350	Crew Cab Pickup (LWB)	—	—	Note 1
F-350	(80) 9-ft. Platform	2880	4310	Note 1
F-350	(80) 12-ft. Platform	—	4600	Note 1
F-350	9-ft. Stake	2935	4550	Note 1
F-350	(86) 12-ft. Stake	—	4945	Note 1

NOTE 1: Ford records show the following F-350 production break-outs: (cowl) 149; (windshield) 152; (chassis & cab) 27,511; (cab, platform & rack) 5,341; (cab platform) 609 and (Flareside pickups) 1,570. **Note:** No additional break-outs are available.

ENGINE (F-350): See F-100.

CHASSIS: Wheelbase: 115 in. (F-100); 131 in. (F-100/F-250); 135 in. (F-350); 149 in. (F-250 Crew Cab); 159 in. (F-350); 164.5 in. (F-350 Crew Cab). GVW: 4200-5000 lbs. (F-100); 4600-5600 lbs. (F-100 4x4); 6100-7500 lbs. (F-250); 6300-7700 lbs. (F-250 4x4); 6600-10,000 lbs. (F-350). Tires: G78 x 15 (F-100); 8.00 x 16.5 (F-250/F-350).

POWERTRAIN OPTIONS: 300 cu. in. six-cylinder engine. "302" V8 (F-100). "360" V8; "390" V8. Four-speed manual transmission. Select Shift Cruise-O-Matic transmission.

CONVENIENCE OPTIONS: Four-wheel-drive. F-100 model 4x4s had Mono-Beam front suspension with coil springs, steering linkage shock absorber and forged radius rods. The F-100 single-speed transfer case was coupled to a four-speed transmission. The F-250 model 4x4 front suspension consisted of resilient long leaf springs with lubrication-free shackles; standard two-speed transfer case and three-speed transmission. Electric power pack (underhood 2500 watt generator). Frame mounted 25-gallon fuel tank. **Convenience Group:** includes, cargo area light; courtesy light door switches; day/night mirror and engine compartment light. Tool storage box for eight-foot Styleside. Bright bodyside moldings (Styleside). Western type mirrors (fixed or swing-lock). Spare tire carrier (inside box on Styleside, ahead of left rear fender on Flareside). Black-textured painted floor. Rear step bumper (Styleside). Bright hub caps. Bright or "Mag" wheel covers for 15 inch wheels. Extra-cooling equipment. Chrome contour rear bumpers for Stylesides. Painted channel rear bumpers for Flaresides. Brush-type grille guard. Free-running front hubs for 4x4s. Oil bath engine air cleaner. Sliding rear window (standard on F-250 "Camper Special"). Velocity-type engine governor. Vacuum brake booster. Power disc front brakes (F-250/F-350). Power steering (F-100/F-250). Flex-O-Matic rear suspension (F-100). Heavy-duty shocks. Heavy-duty front springs. Heavy-duty alternator. Heavy-duty battery. Select Aire air conditioner (includes standard fresh air heater in an integral unit). Push-button radio. Manual radio. Ammeter and oil pressure gauge. Bucket seats color coordinated to exterior paint. Lockable cab stowage compartment behind the seat. Remote-control outside mirror. Tinted windshield. Tinted glass all around. Cab marker and identification lights. Shoulder harnesses. Dual electric horns. Heavy-duty black vinyl seat trim. Full width Custom Cab seat. **Sport Custom Cab:** includes, deep-foam seat cushion and foam padding in seatback; pleated basket weave vinyl seat trim inserts; grained vinyl bolsters; color-coordinated floor mat; horn ring; cigarette lighter; bright rocker panel, wheel lip, windshield molding and taillamp bezels (Stylesides have tailgate applique). **Ranger Package:** includes, woodgrain inserts in instrument cluster; pleated vinyl door trim with simulated woodgrain insert and bright molding; bright seat-pivot arm covers; glove box plaque; bright metal hub caps, roof drip rails and moldings around rear window; Ranger emblem and bright metal tailgate release handle. **Camper Special Package:** 70 ampere-hour battery; oil pressure gauge; ammeter; extra-cooling radiator; sliding rear window (F-250); dual bright metal 6 x 10 in. Western type mirrors; camper wiring harness; rear shock absorbers (F-350); "Camper Special" emblem. **Farm & Ranch Special:** (F-100/F-250 Stylesides), includes: front and nine inch high side cargo boards painted body-color; rear step bumper; bright Western swing-lock mirrors and "Farm & Ranch Special" insignia. **Contractor Special:** (for eight-foot Styleside) includes, rear step bumper; dual bright Western long arm mirrors; contractor box on both sides with key-lock fold down doors and "Contractor Special" insignia. **Ranger XLT Package:** (Styleside and Chassis w/Cab), includes: — in addition to, or in place of Ranger equipment — pleated cloth and vinyl seat upholstery; color-keyed carpeting; special insulation; convenience group; sound-absorbing perforated headlining; bright instrument panel molding on right side; heater modesty panel with woodtone inserts; bright rocker panel and wheel lip moldings and woodtone tailgate panel. **Heavy-duty Special:** (for eight-foot Styleside), includes heavy-duty front springs; battery; alternator; ammeter; oil pressure gauge; rear step bumper; dual bright western swing-lock mirrors and "Heavy Duty Special" insignia.

NOTE: Standard colors for 1970 were: Raven black; Wimbledon white; New lime; Boxwood green; Candy Apple red; Royal maroon; Mojave tan; Yucatan gold; Pinto yellow; Diamond blue; Reef aqua; Sky View blue; Harbor blue; Chrome yellow and Pure white. Regular two-tones: accent color was applied to roof and upper back panel with a beltline molding from door-to-door around back of cab. Deluxe two-tone: (Styleside only) accent color applied to area below bodyside and lower tailgate moldings, which were included with this option. Combination two-tone: (Styleside only) regular and deluxe two-tone options combined with accent color applied as specified for these two options.

HISTORICAL: Introduced: September 19, 1969. Calendar year production: 626,585. Market penetration: 36.50 percent of total industry. New truck registrations by weight class, for calendar year: (6000-pounds and under) 399,285; (6001-10,000 pounds) 179,082. Model year production (light-duty including Bronco/Ranchero/Econoline): 659,722 units including 2,359 of the P-350 parcel delivery vans and 2,074 of Ford's P-400 parcel delivery vans. Calendar year retail deliveries: 682,789. Calendar year North American sales: 730,268. Engine production, by calendar year: (V-8) 478,821; (six-cylinder) 132,016; (diesel) 15,748. Innovations: New "Explorer Special" option introduced featuring Shetland plaid upholstery. Automatic choke standard on light-duty trucks. F-100s used fiberglass-belted tires as a regular feature. Other new features for F-100s included a simulated vinyl cab roof and optional sliding rear cab window. Historical notes: Calendar year 1970 was the second best sales season in Ford truck history up to that point. The company offered over 1,300 separate models (including medium- and heavy-duty trucks. J.B. Naughton became V.P. and General Manager of Ford Truck Division.

	5	4	3	2	1
1970					
Ranchero					
Pickup	750	1500	2500	3500	5000
GT Pickup	800	1600	2650	3700	5300
500 Pickup	840	1680	2800	3900	5600
Squire Pickup	890	1770	2950	4150	5900
Bronco					
Pickup	850	1700	2850	4000	5700
Wagon	900	1800	3000	4200	6000
Econoline E-100					
Cargo Van	440	870	1450	2050	2900
Window Van	470	950	1550	2200	3100
Display Van	500	1000	1650	2300	3300
Custom Wagon	570	1140	1900	2650	3800
Chateau Wagon	600	1200	2000	2800	4000
Econoline E-200					
Cargo Van	400	800	1350	1900	2700
Window Van	440	870	1450	2050	2900
Display Van	470	950	1550	2200	3100
Econoline E-300					
Cargo Van	390	780	1300	1800	2600
Window Van	420	840	1400	1950	2800
Display Van	450	900	1500	2100	3000
F-100 — (½-Ton)					
Flareside Pickup	930	1860	3100	4350	6200
Styleside Pickup	980	1950	3250	4550	6500
F-250 — (¾-Ton)					
Flareside Pickup	890	1770	2950	4150	5900
Styleside Pickup	920	1850	3050	4300	6100
Stake	830	1650	2750	3850	5500
Crew Cab Pickup	830	1650	2750	3850	5500
F-350 — (1-Ton)					
Flareside Pickup	800	1600	2650	3700	5300
Stake	780	1560	2600	3600	5200
Crew Cab Pickup	780	1560	2600	3600	5200

1971 FORD

1971 Ford Torino Ranchero 500 Sport Pickup (OCW)

RANCHERO PICKUP: — The new Ranchero looked pretty much the same as last year's model. That wasn't bad. It had a thin horizontal bars grille, with a larger bar in the center connecting the headlights. This grille was exclusive to the standard Ranchero. All 1971 Rancheros had flared and finned brake drums, higher rate front springs and a new throttle control mechanism. Other standard features included: Full-width seat upholstered in black, blue or gold vinyl with pleated seatback; color-keyed vinyl door trim panels with bright moldings; color-keyed rubber floor covering; Flow-through ventilation; ventless side windows; locking steering column; fresh air heater/defroster; trim panel behind the split seat back (with spare tire and tool compartment cover); Deluxe seat belts with outboard retractors and shoulder harnesses (also center passenger seat belts); armrests with integral, squeeze-type door handles; vinyl-framed day/night mirror; cigarette lighter; emergency lamp flasher; bright left-hand remote-control mirror; hidden windshield wipers; bright windshield, rear window, drip rail and top of cargo box moldings; bright taillight bezels and hub caps and fiberglass-belted tires.

RANCHERO 500 PICKUP: — The major styling change was to the grille. The basic theme remained the same as in 1970, but it was now divided into two sections. Sandwiched in the center of the division was an oblong emblem. The 500 had, in addition to or in place of standard Ranchero features: pleated, all-vinyl seat upholstery in black, green, blue, vermilion or ginger; deep-pile wall-to-wall carpeting; woodtone inlay around padded steering wheel horn bar; electric clock; armrests with bright base; Deluxe grille with center crest; bright metal wheel covers and rocker panel moldings; bright metal bodyside molding and bright wheel lip and hidden wiper lip moldings.

RANCHERO GT PICKUP: — The GT had (in addition to or in place of all the standard Ranchero features): Deluxe grille with center GT crest; ribbed argent rocker panel molding with GT letters; Sport-scoop hood; sporty wheel covers; fiberglass-belted whitewall tires; bright metal wheel lip and hidden wiper lip moldings; pleated, all-vinyl seat upholstery in black, green, blue, vermilion or ginger; deep-pile, wall-to-wall carpeting; woodtone inlay panel around padded steering wheel horn bar; electric clock and black lower instrument panel.

RANCHERO SQUIRE PICKUP: — The Squire had (in addition to or in place of all the standard Ranchero features): Color-coordinated deep-pile, wall-to wall-carpeting; woodtone panel under instruments; woodtone inlay around padded steering wheel horn bar; electric clock; Deluxe grille with center crest; woodtone panels on sides and tailgate; fiberglass-belted whitewall tires; Deluxe wheel covers; bright metal hidden wiper lip molding; Ranchero Squire script on front fenders and a knit-vinyl seat in black, vermilion, blue, green or ginger.

I.D. DATA (Ranchero): See 1960 Ranchero I.D.

Model	Body Type	Price	Weight	Prod. Total
66A	Pickup	2851	3285	6041
66B	Pickup (500)	2983	3295	12,678
66C	Pickup (GT)	3273	3445	3632
66E	Pickup (Squire)	3192	3330	2595

ENGINE (Ranchero): Displacement: 250 cu. in. OHV. Six-cylinder. 145 horsepower at 4000 R.P.M. Bore & stroke: 3.68 x 3.91 in. Compression ratio: 9.0:1. one-barrel carburetor (Ranchero/500/Squire). Displacement: 302 cu. in. OHV. V8. 210 horsepower. Bore & stroke: 4 x 3 in. Compression ratio: 9.0:1. Two-barrel carburetor (GT).

CHASSIS: Wheebase: 117 in. Overall length: 206.2 in. GVW: Tires: E78-14 4PR.

POWERTRAIN OPTIONS: 210 horsepower "302" V8. 240 horsepower "351" V8. 285 horsepower "351" V8. 360 horsepower "429 Thunder Jet" V8. 370 horsepower "429 Cobra Jet" V8. 370 horsepower "429 CJ-R" V8. Four-speed manual transmission with Hurst shifter. SelectShift Cruise-O-Matic transmission.

NOTE: The 429 CJ V8 came with a 80-amp.-hour battery, 55-amp. alternator, dual exhaust and appearance package with bright cast aluminum rocker covers. The 429 CJ-R V8 had all the CJ equipment, plus Ram-Air induction system with pop-through "shaker" hood air scoop and special performance handling package.

CONVENIENCE OPTIONS: Rim-blow sport steering wheel. AM/FM stereo radio. Select Aire air conditioner. Hidden headlamps (Squire/GT/500). Vinyl roof in black or white. Power full-width seat with four-way adjustment. Intermittent windshield wipers. AM push-button radio. Electric clock (Ranchero). Power steering. Tinted glass. Deluxe wheel covers. Sporty wheel covers. Hub caps and trim rings. Front bumper guards. Styled steel wheels. **Visibility Group:** includes, ash tray, map, glove compartment and underhood lights; warning lights for seat belts and parking brake; and headlight-on warning buzzer and light. Tachometer (V8s only). High-back bucket seats in green, ginger, black or white knit-vinyl (Squire/GT/500). Power front disc brakes. Racing-type mirrors painted body color (left-hand mirror includes remote control). Shaker hood scoop with Ram-Air induction system (included with optional 429 CJ-R V8 and available for 351-4V V8). Flat back paint on hood and scoop of Ranchero GT. Heavy-duty suspension. Heavy-duty battery. Extra cooling radiator. **Class II (2000-3500-lb.) Trailer Towing Package:** includes front power disc brakes; heavy-duty suspension; cooling package; heavy-duty alternator and battery with 351 V8s. **Ranchero Special Package:** includes, choice of eight chromatic exterior colors and four unique matching interior trims; distinctive black, non-reflective painted hood; black vinyl roof; special accent black-painted box interior; unique bodyside stripe; twin racing mirrors (painted body color); bright hub caps and trim rings.

NOTE: 1971 Ranchero colors: White; Bright red; maroon metallic; Dark blue metallic; Medium blue metallic; Grabber blue; Pastel blue; Light Pewter metallic; Dark green metallic; Medium green metallic; Grabber green metallic; Light green; Gray gold metallic; Light gold; Medium yellow gold; Grabber yellow. Black painted roofs were available with all colors except Dark blue metallic.

1971 Ford Bronco 4x4 Utility Wagon (FMC)

BRONCO PICKUP: — Styling changes were minor for the four-wheel-drive Bronco in 1971. About the biggest change was a new 12.7 gallon fuel tank and a heavy-duty front driving axle. The standard features included: all-vinyl, full-width seat; fresh air heater and defroster; lockable glove compartment; padded instrument panel; energy-absorbing sunvisors; vinyl-coated rubber floor mat; floor-mounted T-bar transfer case control; Mono-Beam front suspension; self-adjusting brakes and fully-synchronized three-speed manual transmission.

BRONCO WAGON: — The Bronco wagon shared the features of the pickup, but had a full length roof. The roof had fixed windows in the rear liftgate and on each side of the rear compartment.

I.D. DATA (Bronco): See F-100 I.D.

Model	Body Type	Price	Weight	Prod. Total
U-140	Pickup	3466	2990	1503
U-150	Wagon	3570	3090	18,281

ENGINE (Bronco): Displacement: 170 cu. in. OHV. Six-cylinder. 105 horsepower at 4400 R.P.M. Bore & stroke: 3.50 x 2.94 in. Compression ratio: 9.1:1. One-barrel carburetor.

CHASSIS: Wheelbase: 90 in. Overall length: 152.1 in. Overall width: 68.8 in. GVW: 3850-4700 lbs. Tires: 7.35 x 15.

POWERTRAIN OPTIONS: "302" V8.

CONVENIENCE OPTIONS: Extra-cooling V8 radiator. Left-hand remote-control outside mirror. Hardboard headlining (Pickup). G78-15 tires (4700 lb. GVW package). **Convenience Group:** includes, cigarette lighter; map light; inside 10 inch day/night mirror and horn ring. One-pint oil bath air cleaner ("302" V8). Right-hand chrome rearview mirror. Bucket seats. Shoulder harness. Rear seat (Wagon w/bucket seat option). Chrome bumpers. Skid plates for standard fuel tank and transfer case. Inside tailgate mounted spare tire carrier (included with rear seat option). Exterior rear-mounted swing-away tire carrier. Bright metal wheel covers. High-floatation tires. Auxiliary 11.5 gallon fuel tank with skid plate. Manual radio and antenna. Bright bodyside and tailgate moldings. Bright metal rocker panel molding. Dana free-running front hubs. Hand-operated throttle. Heavy-duty front axle carrier assembly (special order). **Sport Package:** includes, bright metal "Sport Bronco" emblem; pleated parchment vinyl front seat; vinyl door trim panels with bright metal moldings; hardboard headlining with bright metal retainer moldings (Wagon); parchment vinyl simulated-carpet front floor mat with bright metal retainers; rear floor mat (with optional rear seat); cigarette lighter; satin-finish horn ring; bright metal drip rail moldings. Bright metal windshield and window frames. Bright metal grille molding and tailgate release handle; bright headlight, side light, reflector and taillight bezels; Argent-painted grille with bright F-O-R-D letters; chrome bumpers, front and rear; chrome front bumper guards; bright metal wheel covers (with 15 inch wheels only) and 6.50 x 16-6PR TT tires. **Dealer-installed Accessories:** Power-take-off (front-mounted). Warn free-running front hubs (manual or automatic). Snow plows. Snow plow angling kits. Front auxiliary air springs. Front-mounted winch. Trailer hitch. Trailer towing mirror. Locking gas cap. Front tow hooks. Compass. Fire extinguisher. Tachometer. Two-way radio.

NOTE: A special customized Baja Bronco, based on the wagon, was available from Bill Stroppe & Associates.

ECONOLINE E-100 CARGO VAN: — Econolines receive a new grille for 1971. It now appeared to be divided into two sections. The half below the headlights used the same horizontal and vertical bars theme as before. The upper part featured a "black out" section with the word "Ford" proportionally printed in chrome letters. There was also new interior trim and bright signal and axle levers. In addition, the fuel tank capacity dropped from 24 to 21 gallons and the front springs rates rose from 915- to 1040-pounds. Standard features included: Vinyl color-coordinated upholstery; painted front and rear bumpers and hub caps; left-hand fresh air inlet; dome lights in driver's compartment and cargo area; ash tray; single electric horn; coat hook; mechanical jack; double-grip door locks on all doors (with reversible keys); push-pull interior door locks (except rear doors); metal door checks; individual driver's seat; headlining in driver and passenger area; fresh air heater and defroster and double cargo doors at right and rear.

ECONOLINE E-100 WINDOW VAN: — As the name suggests, the window van had glass all around. On it (and other E-100s) the cargo area was 11½ feet long and 53.5 inches wide. It shared most standard features with the Cargo Van.

ECONOLINE E-100 DISPLAY VAN: — This model had windows at the rear and on the right-hand side. It came with the same standard features as the Cargo Van.

I.D. DATA (Econoline E-100): See F-100 I.D.

Model	Body Type	Price	Weight	Prod. Total
E-140	Cargo Van	2983	3260	Note 1
E-150	Window Van	3061	3335	Note 1
E-160	Display Van	3106	3305	Note 1

NOTE 1: See production total notes at end of Econoline section.

ENGINE (Econoline E-100): Displacement: 170 cu. in. OHV. Six-cylinder. 105 horsepower at 4400 R.P.M. Bore & stroke: 3.50 x 2.94 in. Compression ratio: 9.1:1. One-barrel carburetor.

ECONOLINE E-200 CARGO VAN: — For heavier loads, buyers could move up to the E-200 series. Its front axle had a capacity of 2750 lbs. The rear axle capacity was 3300 lbs. It also had larger (11 x 3 in. front/11 x 2¼ in. rear) brakes. Standard features echoed those of the E-100 Cargo Van.

ECONOLINE E-200 WINDOW VAN: — This vehicle shared styling with the E-100 window van and load capacity with other E-200 vans.

ECONOLINE E-200 DISPLAY VAN: — This vehicle shared styling with the E-100 Display Van and load capacity with other E-200 vans.

I.D. DATA (Econoline E-200): See E-100.

Model	Body Type	Price	Weight	Prod. Total
E-240	Cargo Van	3072	3350	Note 1
E-250	Window Van	3150	3395	Note 1
E-260	Display Van	3106	3425	Note 1

NOTE 1: See production total note at end of Econoline data.

ENGINE (Econoline E-200): Same as E-100.

ECONOLINE E-300 CARGO VAN: — For really big loads, it was hard to beat the E-300 Cargo Van. Its front axle capacity was rated at 3300 lbs, rear axle at 4800 lbs. The front brakes were 12 x 3 in., the rear 12 x 12½ in. A 10 in. clutch was standard. Its front and rear springs were also heavy duty.

ECONOLINE E-300 WINDOW VAN: — Had same features as the Cargo Van plus windows all around.

ECONOLINE E-300 DISPLAY VAN: — Had same features as the Cargo Van plus windows on the right hand side.

I.D. DATA (Econoline E-300): See F-100 I.D.

Model	Body Type	Price	Weight	Prod. Total
E-340	Cargo Van	3094	3790	Note 1
E-350	Window Van	3172	3440	Note 1
E-360	Display Van	3108	3425	Note 1

NOTE 1: Production: (89A standard Cargo Van) 58,995; (89B standard Cargo Custom) 4,470; (89C standard Display Van) 5,265; (89D Custom Display Van) 410; (89E standard Window Wagon) 13,101 and (89F Custom Window Van).

ENGINE (Econoline E-300): Displacement: 240 cu. in. OHV. Six-cylinder. 150 horsepower at 4000 R.P.M. Bore & stroke: 4.00 x 3.18 in. Compression ratio: 9.2:1. One-barrel carburetor.

CHASSIS: Wheelbase: 105.5 in. (123.5 in. SuperVan) Tires: E78-14B (E-100); G78-15B (E-200); 8.00 x 16.5 (E-300).

POWERTRAIN OPTIONS: "240" six-cylinder engine. "302" V8. Select Shift Cruise-O-Matic transmission.

CONVENIENCE OPTIONS: Push-button radio. Stationary or flip-fold passenger seat. High output heater and defroster. Auxiliary hot water heater. Air conditioner. Insulation package. Insulated floor mats. Inside body rub rails. Inside or western-type rearview mirrors. Deluxe driver and/or stationary passenger seats with color-coordinated floor mats. Auxiliary step for right-side cargo doors. Dual electric horns. Courtesy light switches for front or all doors. Padded instrument panel. Shoulder harness. Stationary glass or vents in rear and/or right-side cargo doors. Tinted glass. Inside rear door latch and lock. Scuff pads at front door wells. School bus package for E-200 and E-300 Window Vans with 123.5 inch wheelbase. **Custom Equipment Package:** includes (in addition to or in place of standard items): deluxe pleated vinyl seat trim; bright metal front and rear bumpers, hub caps and horn ring; cigarette lighter; color-coordinated floor mat on left side; glove box door with lock and bright metal grille, taillight bezels, vent window and windshield moldings.

NOTE: Econoline colors for 1971 were: Sky View blue; Harbor blue; Diamond blue; Reef aqua; Seafoam green; Boxwood green; Fiesta tan; Chrome yellow; Baja beige; Candy Apple red and Wimbledon white. Two-tone paint combinations were also available.

1971 Ford Forward Control Club Wagon (JAG)

CLUB WAGON: — Club wagons were basically Econolines made for hauling people. The base model held five passengers. Among standard features were: Twin-I-Beam independent front suspension; vinyl seat trim; arm rests on front doors and at right side of 3+passenger seats; ash trays, front and rear; black floor mats; coat hook; two dome lights; dual sunvisors; instrument panel padded on right side; bright instrument cluster trim; glove box door with lock; headlining in front compartment; dual outside rear view mirrors; backup lights; inside rearview mirror; emergency lamp flasher; retracting step for double side doors; rear reflectors and side marker lights at front and rear.

CUSTOM CLUB WAGON: — This was a step up from the base model. Both shared many of the same features. However, the Custom also had: pleated vinyl seat trim; interior vinyl side and door trim panels; arm rests for all seats; color-coordinated front and rear floor mats; four coat hooks; full-length headlining; window trim moldings; cigarette lighter; scuff pads at front door wells; spare tire cover; horn ring; bright metal grille; instrument panel padded full-width; Custom ornaments; bright metal bodyside moldings; taillight bezels and hub caps and added insulation.

CHATEAU CLUB WAGON: — At the top-of-the-line was the Chateau. It had, in addition to or in place of Custom Club Wagon features: pleated Deluxe cloth seat trim with vinyl bolsters; similar trim on interior door and side panels (with simulated woodgrain bands); full-length, color-coordinated carpeting (with dash insulator); chrome front and rear bumpers; bright metal dual outside mirrors; bright metal molding around windshield, side and rear windows; bright-metal rear body molding and Chateau ornaments.

I.D. DATA (Club Wagon): — See F-100.

Model	Body Type	Price	Weight	Prod. Total
E-110	Club Wagon	3453	3595	6801
E-120	Club Wagon (Custom)	3678	3710	8817
E-130	Club Wagon (Chateau)	3827	4180	5438

ENGINE (Club Wagon): Same as E-300.

CHASSIS: Wheelbase: 105.5 in. (123.5 in. optional) Tires: E78-14B.

POWERTRAIN OPTIONS: "302" V8. SelectShift Cruise-O-Matic transmission.

CONVENIENCE OPTIONS: Power steering. Ammeter and oil pressure gauge. Heavy-duty battery. Heavy-duty shocks. Whitewall tires. Chrome front and rear bumpers. Cigarette lighter. Courtesy light switches for all doors. Door positioners for all doors. Air conditioner. Insulation package. Inside body rub rails. Highoutput heater/defroster. Auxiliary hot water heater for passenger compartment. Tinted glass. AM radio.

NOTE: Club Wagon colors for 1971 were: Wimbledon white; Sky View blue; Diamond blue; Harbor blue; Reef aqua; Seafoam green; Boxwood green; Fiesta tan; Chrome yellow; Baja beige and Candyapple red. Custom and Chateau Club Wagons: Winter blue metallic; Scandia green metallic; Fiesta tan; Chrome yellow; Saddletan metallic and Wimbledon white. Two-tone paint combinations were available using selected accent colors. Regular: the accent color on the roof. Deluxe: accent color on roof and below the side and rear body moldings (included with this option) and grille area, when painted grille is used.

F-100 CUSTOM PICKUP: — The grille was modified on Ford light-duty trucks for 1971. As before, it had a two-piece look. However, there was now a horizontal bar in the center of each section, above and below which were three rectangular slots. Among the standard features were: Deluxe fresh air heater with three-speed fan; Hi-Dri ventilation; door courtesy light switches; ash tray; right-hand coat hook; Wedge-type vent window handles; Glove compartment with push-button catch; hardboard headlining; black floor mats with heel pads; aluminum scuff plates; Deluxe instrument cluster bezel; color-keyed steel door trim panels and black, blue, red, parchment or green vinyl seat trim with chevron pattern vinyl inserts. Both 6½-foot and eight-foot Styleside and Flareside cargo boxes were offered.

I.D. DATA (F-100): See 1963 F-100.

Model	Body Type	Price	Weight	Prod. Total
F-100	(81) Chassis w/Cab	2647	3160	Note 1
F-100	Flareside Pickup 6½'	2810	3475	Note 1
F-100	Styleside Pickup 6½'	2810	3540	Note 1
F-100	Flareside Pickup 8'	2928	3675	Note 1
F-100	Styleside Pickup 8'	2928	3740	Note 1

NOTE 1: Ford records show the following F-100 production break-outs: **4x2 Models:** (cab chassis) 2,580; (Flareside pickup) 10,106; (styleside pickup) 332,131; **4x4 Models:** (cab chassis) 96; (Flareside pickup) 591 and (Styleside pickup) 12,870.

ENGINE (F-100): Displacement: 240 cu. in. OHV. Six-cylinder. 140 horsepower at 4000 R.P.M. Bore & stroke: 4.0 x 3.18 in. Compression ratio: 8.9:1. one-barrel carburetor.

F-250 PICKUP: — The F-250 pickup had most of the same features as the F-100. In addition, it came with power brakes and Flex-O-Matic rear suspension. The Styleside had double-wall side panels and tailgate, flat-top wheelhousings, stake pockets and an all-steel floor. A single center latch mechanism opened the tailgate. Steel support straps held the tailgate in open position. The Flareside had runningboards between the cab and rear fenders. It had seasoned hardwood floorboards with steel skid strips to help slide cargo into place. Rubber-covered forged steel chains supported the tailgate when open. Toggle-type latches maintained tight seal when the tailgate was closed. Heavy-gauge steel side panels, with flared sides, had rolled edges for extra strength and rigidity.

F-250 PLATFORM/STAKE: — Floor frames of the F-250 Platform/Stake were made of steel cross sills riveted to steel side rails. Floorboards were interlocked with steel skid strips and corners were reinforced with steel brackets. Formed steel caps over the ends of the body sills acted as bumpers for loading docks. Sideboards and stakes were straight-grained hardwood.

I.D. DATA (F-250): See F-100.

Model	Body Type	Price	Weight	Prod. Total
F-250	(81) Chassis w/Cab	2979	3370	Note 1
F-250	Flareside Pickup	3145	3790	Note 1
F-250	Styleside Pickup	3145	3805	Note 1
F-250	(80)Platform	3255	3780	Note 1
F-250	(86)Stake	3288	3885	Note 1
F-250	Crew Cab Pickup (LWB)	—	—	Note 1
F-250	Crew Cab Chassis (LWB)	—	—	Note 1

NOTE 1: Ford records show the following F-250 production break-outs: **4x2 Models:** (chassis & windshield) 43; (chassis & cab) 5,467; (cab, platform & rack) 398; (platform & cab) 40; (Flareside pickup) 2,684; (Styleside pickup) 117,820; **4x4 Models:** (chassis & cab) 649; (cab, platform & rack) 87; (cab and platform) 23; (Flareside pickup) 635 and (Styleside pickup) 16,164.

ENGINE (F-250): Same as F-100.

F-350 PICKUP: — F-350 buyers had to settle for the Flareside cargo box. It had a cargo capacity of 74 cubic feet. That was almost 10 more than comparable F-250 Flareside. Plus, it could haul heavier payloads. A four-speed manual transmission was standard.

F-350 PLATFORM/STAKE: — The F-350 Platform/Stake had most of the same features as the F-250 version. However, rather than wood, it used reinforced steel stakes. Also, it was available with dual rear wheels (at extra cost). A four-speed manual transmission was standard.

I.D. DATA (F-350): See F-100.

Model	Body Type	Price	Weight	Prod. Total
F-350	(81) Chassis w/Cab	3104	3615	Note 1
F-350	Chassis w/Cab (LWB)	—	—	Note 1
F-350	Flareside Pickup	3253	4185	Note 1
F-350	Crew Cab Pickup (LWB)	—	—	Note 1
F-350	(80) 9' Platform	3470	4310	Note 1
F-350	(80) 12' Platform	3530	4600	Note 1
F-350	(86) 9' Stake	3508	4550	Note 1
F-350	(86) 12' Stake	3568	4945	Note 1

NOTE 1: Ford records show the following F-350 production totals: (chassis & cowl) 150; (chassis & windshield) 143; (chassis & cab) 28,432; (cab, platform & rack) 5,087; (cab, platform) 412 and (Flareside pickup) 1,349.

ENGINE (F-350): See F-100.

CHASSIS: Wheelbase: 115 in. (F-100); 131 in. (F-100/F-250); 135 in. (F-350); 149 in. (F-250 crew cab); 159 in. (F-350); 164.5 in. (F-350 crew cab). GVW: 4500-5000 lbs. (F-100); 4600-5600 lbs. (F-100 4x4); 6100-7500 lbs. (F-250); 6300-7700 lbs. (F-250 4x4); 6600-10,000 lbs. (F-350). Tires: 8.25 x 15 (F-100); 8.00 x 16.5 (F-250/F-350).

POWERTRAIN OPTIONS: "300" Six. "302" V8 (F-100). "360" V8. "390" V8. Four-speed manual transmission. SelectShift Cruise-O-Matic transmission.

NOTE: Most 1971 light duty Ford Trucks (86%) had V8s and 43.7% had automatic transmission.

CONVENIENCE OPTIONS: Four-wheel-drive (F-100 4x4s had Mono-Beam front suspension with coil springs, steering linkage shock absorber and forged radius rods, plus a single-speed transfer case coupled to a four-speed transmission.) F-250 4x4 had a front suspension consisting of resilient long leaf springs with lubrication-free shackles. They also had a standard two-speed transfer case and three-speed transmission. Electric power pack (underhood 2500 watt generator). Frame-mounted 25-gallon fuel tank. **Convenience Group:**, includes cargo area light; courtesy light door switches; day/night mirror and engine compartment light. Tool storage box (8-ft. Styleside). Bright bodyside moldings (Styleside). Western type mirrors (fixed or swing-lock). Spare tire carrier (inside box on Styleside/ahead of left rear fender on Flareside). Black-textured painted roof. Rear step bumper (Styleside). Bright hub caps. Bright or "Mag" wheel covers for 15 inch wheels. Extra-cooling equipment. Chrome contour rear bumpers for Stylesides. Painted channel rear bumper for Flaresides. Brush-type grille guard. Free-running front hubs for 4x4s. Oil-bath engine air cleaner. Sliding rear window. Velocity-type engine governor. Vacuum brake booster. Power disc front brakes (F-250/F-350). Power steering (not w/4x4). Flex-O-Matic rear suspension (F-100). Heavy-duty front springs. Heavy-duty alternator. Heavy-duty battery. SelectAire air conditioner (includes standard fresh air heater in an integral unit). Push-button radio. Manual radio. Ammeter and oil pressure gauge. Bucket seats color-coordinated to exterior paint. Lockable cab stowage compartment behind the seat. Remote-control outside mirror. Tinted windshield. Tinted glass all around. Cab marker and identification lights. Shoulder harnesses. Dual electric horns. Heavy-duty black vinyl seat trim. Full-width Custom Cab seat. **Sport Custom Cab:** including deep-foam seat cushion and foam padding in seatback; pleated, basketweave vinyl seat trim inserts with grained vinyl bolsters; color-coordinated floor mats and horn ring; cigarette lighter; bright rocker panel, wheel lip, windshield molding and taillamp bezels; black tailgate applique (on Stylesides). **Ranger Package:** includes, color-coordinated pleated cloth-with-vinyl seat trim upholstery; wood tone instrument panel and horn bar; vinyl door panels; heater panel with wood tone insert; bright headlining molding; bright seat pivot covers; bright hub caps, roof drip rails and around rear window; Ranger emblem; stylesides included bright bodyside moldings and argent tailgate panel; rocker panel and wheel lip moldings were optional. **Camper Special Package:** including, 70 amp.-hr. battery; oil pressure gauge; ammeter; extra-cooling radiator; sliding rear cab window (F-250); dual bright metal 6 x 10 in. Western long-arm mirrors; camper wiring harness; rear shock absorbers (F-350) and "Camper Special" emblem. **Ranger XLT Package:** (for Stylesides and chassis & cabs) includes, in addition to, or in place of Ranger equipment: pleated cloth and vinyl seat upholstery; color-keyed carpeting; special insulation; convenience group; perforated headlining; color-keyed pleated vinyl door panels with woodtone applique; Styleside decor including bright bodyside moldings with woodgrain accents, bright rocker panel, wheel lip moldings and woodtone tailgate applique. **Heavy-Duty Special:** (for 8-ft. Styleside), includes Heavy-duty front springs and battery; altenator; ammeter; oil pressure gauge; rear step bumper; dual bright western swing-lock mirrors and "Heavy-Duty Special" insignia. **Explorer Package "A":** includes, Medium blue, Lime gold or Saddletan metallic paint; special random striped cloth seat trim in unique sew-style (blue, green or ginger); full-foam seat; bright front bumper guards, drip moldings and hub caps and Explorer glove box ornament. **Package "B":** includes package A, plus bright box rails (F-100, 131 inch wheelbase only); bright spear molding; swing lock mirrors and mag-type wheel covers (F-100 only). **Package "C"** includes A and B, plus Cruise-O-Matic transmission and power steering. **Package "D"** includes A, B and C, plus air conditioning and tinted glass.

NOTE: Most 1971 light duty Ford trucks (57.6 percent) came with an AM radio. 35.3 percent had power steering; 25.6 percent tinted glass; 42.4 percent power brakes and 9.7 percent air conditioning.

NOTE: Standard colors for 1971 were: Raven black; Wimbledon white; Mallard green; Boxwood green; Seafoam green; Calypso coral; Candy Apple red; Regis red; Mojave tan; Prairie yellow; Diamond blue; Swiss aqua; Sky View blue; Bahama blue; Chrome yellow and Pure white. Two-Tones, Regular: accent color was applied to roof and upper back panel with a belt line molding from door to door around back of cab; Deluxe: (Stylesides only) accent color was applied to area below the bodyside and lower tailgate moldings, which were included in this option. Combination: (Stylesides only) regular and deluxe two-tone options were combined with accent color applied as specified for these two options.

HISTORICAL: Introduced Oct. 30, 1970. Calendar year production: 628,126. Calendar year factory shipments by weight class: (up to 6000 lbs.) 381,900; (6001 to 10,000 lbs.) 166,500. Calendar year registrations by weight class: (up to 6000 lbs.) 424,280; (6001 to 10,000 lbs.) 188,325. Calendar year engine production: (4-cyl.) none; (6-cyl.) 104,587; (V-8) 506,518; (diesel) 17,021; (Total all Ford trucks) 628,126. Model year production: (light-duty) 671,053 — including 2,642 of the P-350 parcel delivery van chassis and 2,330 of the P-400 parcel delivery van chassis. Innovations: Econoline and Club Wagon models receive new front end treatments. Introduced on both series were new options including power steering and high-capacity air conditioner. Rancheros received a new frontal treatment and throttle response mechanism improvements. Historical: J. B. Naughton was again V.P. and General Manager of Ford's truck arm. Ford dealers delivered a record 735,370 trucks to customers in 1971. Domestic sales increased eight percent. Ford was America's number two truck-maker in 1971.

Pricing

1971	5	4	3	2	1
Ranchero					
Pickup	750	1500	2500	3500	5000
GT Pickup	800	1600	2650	3700	5300
500 Pickup	840	1680	2800	3900	5600
Squire Pickup	890	1770	2950	4150	5900
Bronco					
Pickup	850	1700	2850	4000	5700
Wagon	900	1800	3000	4200	6000
Econoline E-100					
Cargo Van	440	870	1450	2050	2900
Window Van	470	950	1550	2200	3100
Display Van	500	1000	1650	2300	3300
Custom Wagon	570	1140	1900	2650	3800
Chateau Wagon	600	1200	2000	2800	4000
Econoline E-200					
Cargo Van	400	800	1350	1900	2700
Window Van	440	870	1450	2050	2900
Display Van	470	950	1550	2200	3100
Econoline E-300					
Cargo Van	390	780	1300	1800	2600
Window Van	420	840	1400	1950	2800
Display Van	450	900	1500	2100	3000
F-100 — (½-Ton)					
Flareside Pickup	930	1860	3100	4350	6200
Styleside Pickup	980	1950	3250	4550	6500
F-250 — (¾-Ton)					
Flareside Pickup	890	1770	2950	4150	5900
Styleside Pickup	920	1850	3050	4300	6100
Stake	830	1650	2750	3850	5500
Crew Cab Pickup	830	1650	2750	3850	5500
F-350 — (1-Ton)					
Flareside Pickup	800	1600	2650	3700	5300
Stake	780	1560	2600	3600	5200
Crew Cab Pickup	780	1560	2600	3600	5200

NOTE: Add five percent for 4x4.

1972 Ford Ranchero Squire Sport Pickup (OCW)

RANCHERO PICKUP: — A separate body-frame, as opposed to the previous unit-body, was now used to make the Ranchero. It was bigger and bolder looking than ever in '72. Styling was highlighted by a large, new, squared-oval, slightly protruding grille. Upper bodyside sculpturing began beneath the new recessed door handles and ran to the taillights. New link-coil rear suspension made for better roadability. Four convenient tie-down bars were located in the walls of the 6½-foot cargo body. With the standard model discontinued, the 500 was now the base Ranchero. Among standard features were: a highback, full-width seat upholstered in black, blue, ginger, green or white vinyl; color-keyed vinyl door trim panels with bright trim; deep-pile wall-to-wall carpeting; Hi-level, flow-through ventilation; ventless door windows; Impact-absorbing steering column; padded steering wheel hub; lockable glove box; locking steering column; fresh-air heater/defroster; trim panel behind the split-back seat; vinyl headliner; seat belts with outboard retractors and shoulder harnesses (also center passenger seat belts); armrests with recessed squeeze-type door handles; vinyl-framed day/night mirror; cigarette lighter; padded, color-keyed instrument panel; emergency lamp flasher; Deluxe grille with moldings; chrome bumpers; bright left-hand mirror with remote control; hidden windshield wipers; bright metal windshield, rear window, drip rail and top of cargo box moldings; belted tires; bright metal hub caps and bright taillight bezels.

RANCHERO GT PICKUP: — The GT had (in addition to or in place of all of the standard Ranchero 500 features): Two-tone argent grille. Color-keyed body side stripe. Hood with twin-air-scoop design. Racing mirrors painted body colors (left side remote control). Hub caps with trim rings. WSW belted tires. Unique door trim panels formed of resilient plastic with long, molded armrests. Spare tire and tool compartment cover. Ranchero GT instrument panel plaque. High-back bench seat with horizontal pleats in its vinyl upholstery to give a bucket seat appearance.

1972 Ford Ranchero Squire Sport Pickup (OCW)

RANCHERO SQUIRE PICKUP: — The Squire had (in addition to or in place of the standard Ranchero 500 features): Deluxe chrome wheel covers; woodtone panels on sides and tailgate; Ranchero Squire script on front fenders; Squire crest on grille; woodtone panel around instruments; electric clock; bright armrest bases; Spare tire and tool compartment cover and Squire instrument panel plaque.

I.D. DATA (Ranchero): See 1960 Ranchero I.D.

Model	Body Type	Price	Weight	Prod. Total
97D	Pickup (500)	2850	3295	23,431
97R	Pickup (GT)	3201	3445	12,620
97K	Pickup (Squire)	3088	3330	4283

ENGINE (Ranchero): Displacement: 250 cu. in. Six-cylinder. 98 net horsepower at 3400 R.P.M. Bore & stroke: 3.68 in. x 3.91 in. Compression ratio: 8.0:1. one-barrel carburetor (500/Squire). Displacement: 302 cu. in. V-8. Bore & stroke: 4 in. x 3 in. 140 net horsepower at 4000 R.P.M. Compression ratio: 8.5:1. two-barrel carburetor (GT).

CHASSIS: Wheelbase: 118 in. Overall length: 216 in. GVW: Tires: E78-14B (E70-14B whitewall on GT).

POWERTRAIN OPTIONS: "302" V8 (2V); "351" V8 (2V); "351" V8 (4V); "400" V8 (2V); "429" V8 (4V). Four-speed manual transmission with Hurst floor shifter. SelectShift Cruise-O-Matic transmission.

NOTE: Ram-Air induction system with functional hood air scoop was available for "351" (4V) and "429" V8 engines in Ranchero 500 and GT.

CONVENIENCE OPTIONS: SelectAire conditioner. Power steering. **Protection Group:** includes, (500) chrome bumper guards; vinyl insert bodyside moldings and door edge guards and Flight-bench seat (500/Squire). Cloth upholstery for the standard seat and Sport cloth seat. **Instrumentation Group:**, includes, (V8s) tachometer; trip odometer; clock; ammeter; water temperature and oil pressure gauges. Highback bucket seats in knitted vinyl. Vinyl roof in black or white. Power front disc brakes. AM/FM stereo radio. AM radio. 15 inch wheels. Full wheel covers. Deluxe wheel covers. Hub caps with trim rings. Mag-style wheels. Tinted glass. Color glow paints (Ivy or Gold Glow). Class II 2000-3500 lbs./Class III 3500-6000 lbs. trailer towing packages. Rim-blow sport steering wheel. Electric clock. Racing type mirrors painted body-color. Black painted hood. **Visibility Group:** includes, ash tray, under hood and glove box lights; parking brake light and seat belt warning lights. **Performance/Handling Package:** (offered with "351" (4V) and "429" V8s) includes, high-rate rear springs; heavy-duty front and rear shock absorbers; rear stabilizer bar and heavy-duty front stabilizer bar. **Ranchero Special Package:** includes, choice of Ivy Glow or Gold Glow paint; green vinyl roof or Ivy Glow brown vinyl roof with Gold glow; bright front bumper guards; bright wheel lip moldings; black Sport cloth interior with Ivy Glow or Ginger Sport cloth interior with Gold Glow (both with matching vinyl trim); twin color-keyed racing mirrors; bright hub caps and bright trim rings.

NOTE: The colors available on the 1972 Rancheros were: White; Bright red; maroon; Dark blue metallic; Medium blue metallic; Light blue; Light pewter metallic; Dark green metallic; Medium green metallic; Bright green; gold metallic; Ginger metallic; medium Goldenrod; medium Bright yellow; gray-gold metallic. (Ivy Glow; Gold Glow, Black or white vinyl roofs were offered).

BRONCO PICKUP: — Styling of the 4x4 Bronco was basically the same as last year. Some changes were made to the standard equipment. It now included bucket seats and a 3.50:1 rear axle (on V8 powered units). Also standard were: pleated vinyl seats; floor-mounted T-bar transfer case control; suspended foot pedals; fresh air heater and defroster; lockable glove compartment; padded instrument panel; two-speed electric windshield wipers; sunvisors; vinyl-coated rubber floor mat and fully-synchronized three-speed manual transmission.

BRONCO WAGON: — The Bronco wagon shared the features of the pickup, but had a full-length roof. The roof had fixed windows in the rear liftgate and on each side of the rear compartment.

I.D. DATA (Bronco): See F-100 I.D.

Model	Body Type	Price	Weight	Prod. Total
U-140	Pickup	3414	2990	Note 1
U-150	Wagon	3588	3090	Note 1

NOTE 1: Ford records show total Bronco production of 21,894 units with no break-outs by body style.

ENGINE (Bronco): Displacement: 170 cu. in. Six-cylinder. 105 horsepower at 4400 R.P.M. Bore & stroke: 3.50 in. x 2.94 in. Compression ratio: 9.1:1. One-barrel carburetor. (not available in California).

CHASSIS: Wheelbase: 92 in. Overall length: 152.1 in. Overall width: 68.8 in. GVW: 4300-4900 lbs. Tires: E78 x 15.

POWERTRAIN OPTIONS: "302" V8.

CONVENIENCE OPTIONS: Extra-cooling V8 radiator. Left-hand remote control outside mirror. Hardboard headlining (Pickup). **Convenience Group:** cigarette lighter; map light and inside 10 inch day/night mirror. Horn ring. Right-hand chrome rearview mirror. Bucket seats. Shoulder harness and rear seat (Wagon). Chrome bumpers. Skid plates for standard fuel tank and transfer case. Inside tailgate mounted spare tire carrier (incl. with wagon). Exterior rear-mounted swing+away tire carrier. Bright metal wheel covers. High-flotation tires. Auxiliary 7.5 gallon fuel tank with skid plate. Manual radio and antenna. Bright bodyside and tailgate moldings. Bright metal rocker panel molding. Hand-operated throttle. **Sport Package:** includes, bright metal "Sport Bronco" emblem; pleated parchment vinyl front seat; vinyl door trim panels with bright metal moldings; hardboard headlining with bright metal retainer moldings (Wagon); parchment vinyl front floor mat (included with optional rear seat); cigarette lighter; horn ring; bright metal drip rail moldings; bright metal windshield and window frames; bright metal grille molding and tailgate release handle; bright headlight, side light, reflector and taillight bezels; Argent-painted grille with bright F-O-R-D letters; chrome bumpers, front and rear; chrome front bumper guards; bright metal wheel covers (w/15 inch wheels only) and 7.00 x 15-C 'TT' tires. **Dealer-Installed Accessories:** Power-take-off (front-mounted). Warn free-running front hubs (manual or automatic). Snow plows. Snow plow angling kits. Front auxiliary air springs. Front-mounted winch. Trailer hitch. Trailer towing mirror. Locking gas cap. Front tow hooks. Compass. Fire extinguisher. Transmission oil cooler. Tachometer. **4500 lb. GVW Package:** includes, 2780 lb. rear axle; front springs rated at 1000 lbs.; rear springs rated at 1475 lbs. and G78-15B tires. **4900 lb. GVW Package:** includes, 3300 lbs. Traction-Lok rear axle plus H-D front and rear spring ratings and tires same as 4500 lb. package. **Ranger Package:** includes, argent grille; bucket seats; lower bodyside stripes; fiberboard headliner; cut-pile carpeting front and rear; wheel covers; white power dome and white spare tire carrier.

NOTE: Bronco color choices for 1972 were: Wimbledon white; Candy Apple red; Royal maroon; Wind blue; Bahama blue; Bay roc blue metallic; Seapine green metallic; Swiss aqua; Winter green; Chelsea green metallic; Mallard green; Sequoia brown metallic; Hot ginger metallic; Prairie yellow; Calypso coral; Tampico yellow and Chrome yellow. Bronco roofs were painted Wimbledon white when two-toning was ordered.

1972 Ford Econoline Cargo Van (OCW)

ECONOLINE E-100 CARGO VAN: — Biggest news for '72 was the availability of a sliding, side cargo door. This was especially useful for cargo handling in cramped alleys and beside loading docks. Three separate tracks, at top, bottom and center, gave bridge-like support for smooth one-handed operation. Aside from that, a smaller (20.3 gallon) fuel tank and larger (11 inch) clutch, were about the only other changes made for the new model year. Standard features included: vinyl color-coordinated upholstery; painted front and rear bumpers and hub caps; left-hand fresh air inlet; dome lights in driver's compartment and cargo area; ash tray; single electric horn; coat hook; mechanical jack; double-grip door locks on all doors (with reversible keys); push-pull interior door locks (except rear doors); metal door checks; individual driver's seat; headlining in driver and passenger area; fresh air heater and defroster and double cargo doors at right and rear.

ECONOLINE E-100 WINDOW VAN: — As the name suggests, the window van had glass all around. Like other E-100s, its cargo area was 11½ feet long and 53.5 inches wide. It shared most standard features with the Cargo Van.

ECONOLINE E-100 DISPLAY VAN: — This model had windows at the rear and on the right-hand side. It came with the same standard features as the Cargo Van.

I.D. DATA (Econoline E-100): See F-100 I.D.

Model	Body Type	Price	Weight	Prod. Total
E-140	Cargo Van	2757	3275	Note 1
E-150	Window Van	2829	3350	Note 1
E-160	Display Van	2787	3320	Note 1

NOTE 1: See production data at end of Econoline section.

ENGINE (Econoline E-100): Displacement: 170 cu. in. Six-cylinder. 105 horsepower at 4400 R.P.M. Bore & stroke: 3.50 in. x 2.94 in. Compression ratio: 9.1:1. One-barrel carburetor.

ECONOLINE E-200 CARGO VAN: — For heavier loads, buyers could move up to the E-200 series. Its front axle had a capacity of 2750 lbs. The rear axle was rated for 3300 lbs. It also had larger (11 x 3 in. front/11 x 2¼ in. rear) brakes. Standard features echoed those of the E-100 Cargo Van.

ECONOLINE E-200 WINDOW VAN: — This vehicle shared styling with the E-100 window van and load capacity with other E-200 vans.

ECONOLINE E-200 DISPLAY VAN: — This vehicle shared styling with the E-100 Display Van and load capacity with other E-200 vans.

I.D. DATA (Econoline E-200): See E-100.

Model	Body Type	Price	Weight	Prod. Total
E-240	Cargo Van	2844	3345	Note 1
E-250	Window Van	2916	3420	Note 1
E-260	Display Van	2874	3390	Note 1

NOTE 1: See production data at end of Econoline section.

ENGINE (Econoline E-200): Same as E-100.

ECONOLINE E-300 CARGO VAN: — For really big loads, it was hard to beat the E-300 Cargo Van. Its front axle capacity was 3300 lbs. and rear axles were rated at 4800 lbs. The bigger brakes were 12 x 3 inches up front/12 x 12½ inches at the rear. Its front and rear springs were also heavy-duty.

ECONOLINE E-300 WINDOW VAN: — Had same features as the Cargo Van, plus windows all around.

ECONOLINE E-300 DISPLAY VAN: — Had same features as the Cargo Van, plus windows on the right-hand side.

I.D. DATA (Econoline E-300): See F-100 I.D.

Model	Body Type	Price	Weight	Prod. Total
E-340	Cargo Van	3304	3450	Note 1
E-350	Window Van	3376	3525	Note 1
E-360	Display Van	3334	3495	Note 1

NOTE 1: Ford records show the following Econoline production break-outs: (89A standard cargo van) 60,509; (89C standard display van) 7,198; (89E standard window van) 13,382; (89B Custom cargo van) 5,123; (89D Custom display van) 94; (89F Custom window van) 1,828 and (33A cut-away van) 850.

ENGINE (Econoline E-300): Displacement: 240 cu. in. Six-cylinder. 150 horsepower at 4000 R.P.M. Bore & stroke: 4.00 in. x 3.18 in. Compression ratio: 9.2:1. One-barrel carburetor.

CHASSIS: Wheelbase: 105.5 in. (123.5 in. SuperVan). Tires: E78-14B (E-100); G78-15B (E-200); 8.00 x 16.5 in. (E-300). GVW: 4800 lbs. (E-100); 6000 lbs. (E-200); 8300 lbs. (E-300).

POWERTRAIN OPTIONS: "240" Six. "302" V8. SelectShift Cruise-O-Matic transmission.

CONVENIENCE OPTIONS: Push-button radio. Stationary or flip-fold passenger seat. High-output heater and defroster. Auxiliary hot water heater. Air conditioner. Insulation package. Insulated floor mats. Inside body rub rails. Inside or western-type rearview mirrors. Deluxe driver and/or stationary passenger seats with color-coordinated floor mats. Auxiliary step for right-side cargo doors. Dual electric horns. Courtesy light switches for front or all doors. Padded instrument panel. Shoulder harness. Stationary glass or vents in rear and/or right-side cargo doors. Tinted glass. Inside rear door latch and lock. Scuff pads at front door wells. School bus package for E-200 and E-300 Window Vans with 123.5 inch wheelbase. **Custom Equipment Package:** includes, (in addition to or in place of standard items): Deluxe pleated vinyl seat trim; bright metal front and rear bumpers and hub caps; horn ring; cigarette lighter; color-coordinated floor mat on left-hand side; glove box door with lock; bright metal grille, taillight bezels, vent window and windshield moldings.

CLUB WAGON: — Club wagons were basically Econolines made for hauling people. The base model held five passengers. Among standard features were: Twin-I-Beam independent front suspension; vinyl seat trim; arm rests on front doors and at right side of 3+passenger seats; ash trays, front and rear; black floor mats; coat hook; two dome lights; dual sunvisors; instrument panel padded on right side; bright instrument cluster trim; glove box door with lock; headlining in front compartment; dual outside rear view mirrors; backup lights; inside rearview mirror; emergency lamp flasher; retracting step for double side doors; rear reflectors and side marker lights at front and rear.

CUSTOM CLUB WAGON: — This was a step up from the base model. Both shared many of the same features. However, the Custom also had: pleated vinyl seat trim; interior side and door trim panels; arm rests for all seats; color-coordinated front and rear floor mats; four coat hooks; full-length headlining; window trim moldings; cigarette lighter; scuff pads at front door wells; spare tire cover; horn ring; bright metal grille; instrument panel padded full width; Custom ornaments; bright metal bodyside moldings, taillight bezels and hub caps and added insulation.

CHATEAU CLUB WAGON: — At the top-of-the-line was the Chateau. It had, in addition to or in place of Custom Club Wagon features: pleated Deluxe cloth seat trim with vinyl bolsters. Similar trim on interior door and die panels with simulated woodgrain bands. Full-length color coordinated carpeting with dash insulator. A bright metal rear body molding and Chateau ornaments.

I.D. DATA (Club Wagon): See F-100.

Model	Body Type	Price	Weight	Prod. Total
E-110	Club Wagon	3309	3595	5833
E-120	Club Wagon (Custom)	3647	3710	6608
E-130	Club Wagon (Chateau)	3791	4180	4955

ENGINE (Club Wagon): Same as E-300.

CHASSIS: Wheelbase: 105.5 in. or 123.5 in. (optional) Tires: E78-14B.

POWERTRAIN OPTIONS: "302" V8. SelectShift Cruise-O-Matic transmission.

CONVENIENCE OPTIONS: Power steering. Ammeter and oil pressure gauge. Heavy-duty battery. Heavy-duty shocks. Whitewall tires. Chrome front and rear bumpers. Cigarette lighter. Courtesy light switches for all doors. Door positioners for all door. Air conditioner. Insulation package. Inside body rub rails. High-output heater/defroster. Auxiliary hot water heater for passenger compartment. Tinted glass. AM radio. Heavy-duty Package. Seating Packages: 8-passenger/12-passenger.

NOTE: Paint colors for standard 1972 Club Wagon were: Wind blue; Diamond blue; Harbor blue; Tidewater aqua; Mill Valley green; Boxwood green; Fiesta tan; Baja beige; Candy Apple red; Wimbledon white; Chrome yellow. Custom and Chateau Club Wagons also came in: Brook blue metallic; Scandia green metallic; Fiesta tan; Saddletan metallic; Wimbledon white and Chrome yellow. Two-tone paint combinations were available using selected accent colors. Regular: accent color on roof. Deluxe: accent color on roof and below the side and rear body moldings included with this option and grille area (when not bright metal).

COURIER PICKUP: — This was Ford's entry into the mini-pickup market. According to Ford's marketing division, the typical Courier buyer was expected to be slightly younger than the average domestic pickup buyer. "About one-third will be under 35 years old," they said. " The buyer also will be more likely to have a high school education or beyond. The Courier was made in Japan by Mazda, but had its own distinctive front end

styling. The bright metal and plastic grille ran full-width and encased the two round headlights. The parking lights were integrated into the wraparound front bumper. The front hinged hood was released from inside the cab and was counter-balanced to stay open. The full-width tailgate featured raised "Courier" letters painted a contrasting color. Among standard equipment was: 11 tie-down hooks around the box and tailgate for securing cargo or a tarpaulin; rear mud flaps; bright hubcaps; white sidewall tires; vinyl upholstery, headliner and door panels; padded armrests; padded sunvisors; tool set emergency flashers; outside rearview mirror; axle type jack with crank and four-speed manual transmission.

Model	Body Type	Price	Weight	Prod. Total
—	Pickup	2222	2420	(*)26,958

(*) Courier sales total for calendar year 1972.

ENGINE (Courier): Displacement: 109.5 cu. in. Inline. 4-cyl. Net horsepower 74 at 5000 R.P.M. (67 horsepower at 5000 R.P.M. in CA.) Bore & stroke: 3.07 in. x 3.70 in. Compression ratio: 8.6:1. Zenith Stromberg two-barrel carburetor.

CHASSIS: Wheelbase: 104.3 in. Overall length: 172 in. Overall width: 61.6 in. GVW Rating: 3910 lbs. Tires: 6.00 x 14.

Options: AM radio. Rear step bumper.

F-100 CUSTOM PICKUP: — Styling changes for 1972 were limited to a modified, rectangular slot grille. Standard features included: Deluxe fresh air heater; door courtesy light switches; ash tray; coat hook; vent window handles; glove compartment; hardboard headlining; floor mats; Deluxe instrument cluster bezel; color-keyed door trim panels; three-speed manual transmission; black, blue, parchment or green vinyl seat trim with vinyl inserts; aluminum scuff plates; windshield washers; left-hand interior mirror; day/night mirror; two-speed windshield wipers; backup lights; sunvisors; arm rests; seat belts; double-walled tailgate and side panels; power brakes (on F-100s over 5500 lb. GVW) and Twin-I-Beam front suspension. Once again, 6½-foot and 8-foot Styleside and Flareside models were available.

I.D. DATA (F-100): See 1963 I.D.

Model	Body Type	Price	Weight	Prod. Total
F-100	(81) Chassis w/Cab	2550	3160	Note 1
F-100	Flareside Pickup 6½'	2703	3475	Note 1
F-100	Styleside Pickup 6½'	2703	3540	Note 1
F-100	Flareside Pickup 8'	2739	—	Note 1
F-100	Styleside Pickup 8'	2739	—	Note 1

NOTE 1: Ford records show the following F-100 production break-outs: (chassis & cab) 2,461; (Flareside pickup) 3,034 and (Styleside pickup) 457,746.

ENGINE (F-100): See 1971 F-100 Engine.

1972 Ford F250 Ranger XLT Camper Special (OCW)

F-250 CUSTOM PICKUP: — The F-250 pickup had most of the same features as the F-100. However, it also came with power brakes and the Flex-O-Matic rear suspension, which automatically adjusted spring stiffness for varying loads. The Styleside had sleek body panels extending all the way forward to hug the rear cab corners. Its pickup box featured strong, double-wall side panel construction, a sturdy tailgate that could support a ton, wide apart flat-top wheelhousings, deep stake pockets and an all-steel floor. The Flareside had runningboards between cab and rear fenders for easy side loading. Its seasoned hardwood floorboards had interlocked steel skid strips. Rubber-covered forged steel chains supported the tailgate when open. Toggle type latches maintained tight seal when tailgate was closed.

I.D. DATA (F-250): See F-100.

Model	Body Type	Price	Weight	Prod. Total
F-250	(81) Chassis w/Cab	2870	3370	Note 1
F-250	Crew Cab & Chassis (LWB)	3368	—	Note 1
F-250	Flareside Pickup	3020	3790	Note 1
F-250	Styleside Pickup	3020	3805	Note 1
F-250	Crew Cab Pickup (LWB)	3518	—	Note 1

NOTE 1: Ford records show the following F-250 production break-outs: (chassis & cab) 7,674; (Flareside pickup) 3,004; (Styleside Pickup) 187,348.

ENGINE (F-250): Displacement: 300 cu. in. Six-cylinder. 165 horsepower at 3600 R.P.M. Bore & stroke: 4.0 in. x 3.98 in. Compression ratio: 8.6:1. One-barrel carburetor.

F-350 CUSTOM PICKUP: — The F-350 came in one pickup box style, the Flareside. Its "desired" payload, including driver and passenger was, 2440 lbs. That was more than double the payload of the F-100, which it shared most other features with. A four-speed manual transmission was standard.

F-350 PLATFORM/STAKE: — This model was offered in two sizes, 9-foot and 12 foot. Both had floor frames formed of steel cross sills riveted to steel side rails. The floorboards were interlocked with steel skid strips. The corners were reinforced with steel brackets. Formed steel caps over the ends of the body sills acted as bumpers against loading docks. Side boards were straight-grained hardwood. Stakes were steel. A four-speed manual transmission was standard.

I.D. DATA (F-350): See 1963 F-100 I.D.

Model	Body Type	Price	Weight	Prod. Total
F-350	(81) Chassis w/Cab	2985	3725	Note 1
F-350	Chas. w/Crew Cab	—	—	Note 1
F-350	Flareside Pickup	3120	4185	Note 1
F-350	Crew Cab Pickup	—	—	Note 1
F-350	(80) 9-ft. Platform	3335	4310	Note 1
F-350	(80) 12-ft. Platform	3393	—	Note 1
F-350	(86) 9-ft. Stake	3375	4550	Note 1
F-350	(86) 12-ft. Stake	3433	—	Note 1

NOTE 1: Ford records show the following F-350 production break-outs: (chassis & cowl) 80; (chassis & cab) 42,084; (cab, platform & rack) 6,656; (cab, platform) 749 and (Styleside) 11,889. **PARCEL VAN PRODUCTION:** (P-350) 1,054; (P-400) 6,251.

ENGINE (F-350): See F-250.

CHASSIS: Wheelbase: 115 in. (F-100); 131 in. (F-100/F-250); 135 in. (F-350); 149 in. (F-250 Crew Cab); 159 in. (F-350); 164.5 in. (F-350 Crew Cab). GVW: 4450-5500 lbs. (F-100); 6200-8100 lbs. (F-250); 6600-10,000 lbs. Tires: G78 x 15 (F-100); 8.00 x 16.5D (F-250/F-350).

POWERTRAIN OPTIONS: "302" V8 (F-100). "360" V8. "390" V8. Four-speed manual transmission. SelectShift Cruise-O-Matic transmission.

1972 Ford Econoline Cimarron 185 Camper (OCW)

CONVENIENCE OPTIONS: Air conditioner. Rear step bumper (Styleside). Spare tire carrier. Convenience Group (cargo light; inside 12 inch day/night mirror; glove box door lock and engine compartment light). Remote control mirror for driver's door. Western mirrors. Tool box with door lock (Styleside). Auxiliary fuel tank. AM/FM stereo radio. AM radio. Full wheel covers or mag-style wheel covers. Black textured roof with bright belt and drip moldings. Electric Power Pak (2500-watt underhood generator). Sliding rear window. Power steering (not w/4x4). Power brakes (F-100); std. F-250/F-350. Ammeter and oil pressure gauge. Styleside body moldings. Bright hub caps. Chrome contour rear bumper for Stylesides. Painted channel rear bumper for Flaresides. Tinted glass all around. Shoulder harness. Dual electric horns. Heavy-duty black vinyl seat trim. Free-running front hubs for F-100 4x4s (std. F-250). Oil bath engine air cleaner. **Four-Wheel-Drive:** includes, (F-100) Mono-Beam front suspension with full-floating axle; coil springs; forged radius rods and track bar; power brakes; steering linkage shock absorber and a single-speed transfer case with four-speed manual transmission; (F-250) Heavy-duty front sus-

pension with long, resilient leaf springs and lube-free shackles; power brakes; free-running hubs; two-speed transfer case and four-speed manual transmission. **Northland Special Package:** includes, engine block heater; heavy-duty battery and alternator; 50 percent (-35 degrees F) antifreeze and Traction-Lok rear axle. **Sport Custom Package:** includes, (in addition to or in place of Custom items) extra deep-foam seat cushion; pleated vinyl seat trim inserts with grained vinyl bolsters; color-keyed vinyl door panels with bright moldings; color-keyed floor mats; cigarette lighter; bright windshield, rocker panel and wheel lip moldings. **Ranger Package:** includes, (in addition to or in place of Sport Custom features) color-keyed, pleated cloth with vinyl trim seat upholstery; woodtone instrument panel and horn bar; heater panel with woodtone insert; bright headlining molding; color-keyed vinyl door panels; bright seat pivot covers; bright rear window and roof drip moldings and hub caps (Stylesides include bright bodyside moldings and argent tailgate panel). Rocker panel and wheel lip moldings optional. **Ranger XLT Package:** includes, (in addition to or in place of Ranger items) Deluxe pleated cloth with vinyl trim seat uphol-stery; color-keyed pleated vinyl door panels with woodtone applique; color-keyed wall-to-wall carpeting and additional insulation. **Convenience Group:** (w/Styleside Decor) includes bright bodyside moldings with wood-grain accents; bright rocker panel and wheel lip moldings and woodtone tailgate panel. **Camper Special Package:** Heavy-duty battery and alternator; ammeter, oil pressure gauge; bright Western long-arm mirrors; extra cooling package camper wiring harness; dual electric horns; rear shocks (F-350) and emblem.

PRODUCTION NOTE: Most 1972 Ford light-duty trucks (62.3 percent) had an AM radio; 1.6 percent had AM/FM radio; 45.7 percent used power steering; 12.6 percent featured air conditioning; 88.9 percent had V8s. 49.9 percent used automatic transmission and 28.5 percent wore tinted glass.

NOTE: Standard colors for 1972 were: Wimbledon white; Mallard green; Seapine green metallic; Winter green; Calypso coral; Candy Apple red; Royal maroon; Prairie yellow; Tampico yellow; Swiss aqua; Wind blue; Bahama blue; Bay Roc blue metallic; Sequoia brown metallic; Chrome yel-low and Pure white. Two-tones: (Regular) accent color was applied to roof and upper back panel with a beltline molding from door-to-door around back of cab. (Deluxe) for Styleside only, had accent color applied to area below the bodyside and lower tailgate moldings, which were included in this option. (Combination) for Styleside only, had regular and deluxe two-tone options combined with accent color applied as specified for these two options.

HISTORICAL: Introduced: Sept. 24, 1971. Calendar year production: 795,987 (or 32.20 percent of industry.) Calendar year registrations by weight class: (up to 6000 lbs.) 502,219; (6001 to 10,000 lbs.) 225,399. Dealer deliveries, in calendar year: 735,370. Model year production (light-duty only): 886,649. Innovations: All-new Ranchero Deluxe pickup introduced. Econolines featured new, optional sliding door and power brakes. Pickup truck grilles restyled. Historical notes: Ford's North American truck sales topped the previous high (786,444) by a wide margin, totaling 795,987 units for a new all-time record. D.E. Petersen was V.P. and General Manager of Truck Operations. Ford leaped ahead of Chevrolet in calendar year production for 1972, by building 795,987 trucks to Chevy's 770,773 (Chevy dropped to a 31.10 percent market share.)

Pricing

1972	5	4	3	2	1
Courier					
Pickup	450	900	1500	2100	3000
Ranchero					
GT Pickup	800	1600	2650	3700	5300
500 Pickup	840	1680	2800	3900	5600
Squire Pickup	890	1770	2950	4150	5900
Bronco					
Pickup	850	1700	2850	4000	5700
Wagon	900	1800	3000	4200	6000
Econoline E-100					
Cargo Van	440	870	1450	2050	2900
Window Van	470	950	1550	2200	3100
Display Van	500	1000	1650	2300	3300
Custom Wagon	570	1140	1900	2650	3800
Chateau Wagon	600	1200	2000	2800	4000
Econoline E-200					
Cargo Van	400	800	1350	1900	2700
Window Van	440	870	1450	2050	2900
Display Van	470	950	1550	2200	3100
Econoline E-300					
Cargo Van	390	780	1300	1800	2600
Window Van	420	840	1400	1950	2800
Display Van	450	900	1500	2100	3000
F-100 — (½-Ton)					
Flareside Pickup	930	1860	3100	4350	6200
Styleside Pickup	980	1950	3250	4550	6500
F-250 — (¾-Ton)					
Flareside Pickup	890	1770	2950	4150	5900
Styleside Pickup	920	1850	3050	4300	6100
Stake	830	1650	2750	3850	5500
Crew Cab Pickup	830	1650	2750	3850	5500
F-350 — (1-Ton)					
Flareside Pickup	800	1600	2650	3700	5300
Stake	780	1560	2600	3600	5200
Crew Cab Pickup	780	1560	2600	3600	5200

NOTE: Add five percent for 4x4

1973 FORD

RANCHERO 500 PICKUP: — The Ranchero received a toned down front end for 1973. The grille was smaller, flatter and contained the parking lights in its criss-cross pattern. The new straight front bumper was energy-absorbing. The front fenders were more rounded and didn't come to a point as in previous years. Also new for '73 was an inside hood release and improved rear brakes. Among the standard features were: Four cargo tie downs. Full-width seat upholstered in black, blue, ginger, green or beige vinyl. Color-keyed vinyl door trim panels with bright trim. Deep-pile wall to wall carpeting. Hi-level, flow-through ventilation. Ventless door windows. Impact absorbing steering column. Padded steering wheel hub. Lockable glove box. Locking steering column. Fresh-air heater/defroster. Trim panel behind the split-back seat. Vinyl headliner. Seat belts with outboard retractors and shoulder harnesses (also center passenger belts). Armrests with recessed door handles. Vinyl framed day/night rearview mirror. Cigarette lighter. Padded, color-keyed instrument panel. Emergency lamp flasher. Deluxe grille with moldings. Chrome bumpers. Bright L-H mirror with remote control. Hidden windshield wipers. Bright-metal windshield, rear window, drip rail and top of cargo body moldings. Belted tires. Bright-metal hub caps. Bright taillight bezels.

RANCHERO GT PICKUP: — The GT had (in addition to or in place of all of the Standard Ranchero 500 features): Color-keyed body sidestripe and racing mirrors painted body colors (left-side remote control). Black hub caps with bright trim rings. White-lettered tires. GT grille in resilient plastic with long, molded armrests. Spare tire and tool compartment cover. Ranchero GT instrument panel plaque. High-back seats.

1973 Ford Ranchero Squire Sport Pickup (OCW)

RANCHERO SQUIRE PICKUP: — The Squire had (in addition to or in place of all the standard Ranchero features): Deluxe chrome wheel covers. Woodtone panels on sides and tailgate. Ranchero Squire script on front fenders. Squire crest on grille. Woodtone panel around instruments. Electric clock. Bright armrest bases. Squire tire and tool compartment cover. Squire instrument panel plaque. Bright trim on pedals.

I.D. DATA (Ranchero): See 1960 Ranchero I.D.

Model	Body Type	Price	Weight	Prod. Total
97D	Pickup(500)	2904	—	25,634
97R	Pickup	2323	—	4787
97K	Pickup Squire	3142	—	15,320

ENGINE (Ranchero): Displacement: 250 cu. in. OHV. Six. 98 net horsepower at 3400 R.P.M. Bore & stroke: 3.68 x 3.91 in. Compression ratio: 8.0:1. 1-bbl. carburetor (500/Squire). Displacement: 302 cu. in. V8. Bore & stroke: 4 x 3 in. 140 net horsepower at 4000 R.P.M. Compression ratio: 8.5:1. 2-bbl. carburetor (GT).

CHASSIS: Wheelbase: 118 in. Overall length: 216 in. GVW: Tires: E78-14B (E70B white-lettered on GT).

POWERTRAIN OPTIONS: 302 V8 (2V). 351 V8 (2V). 351 V8 (4V). 400 V8 (2V). 429 V8 (4V). Four-speed manual transmission with Hurst floor shifter.

CONVENIENCE OPTIONS: SelectAire air conditioner. Power steering. **Protection Group:** includes, (500) door edge and bumper guards; vinyl insert bodyside moldings and front bumper rubber inserts. (500 Squire) Flight-bench seat. Cloth upholstery for standard seat in 500. Sport cloth seat high-back vinyl bucket seats. Vinyl roof in black or white. Power front disc brakes. AM/FM stereo radio. AM radio. 15 inch wheels. Full wheel covers. Deluxe wheel covers. Hub caps with trim rings. Mag-style wheels. Tinted glass. Class II (2000-3500 lb.) and Class III. 3500-6000 lb. trailer towing packages. Rim-blow sport steering wheel. Electric clock. Racing type mirrors painted body-color. **Visibility Group:** includes, illuminated light switch; ashtray, underhood and courtesy lights; parking brake and seat belt warning lights. **Peformance/Handling Package:**(offered with 351 (4V) and 429 V8s) includes, high-rate rear springs, heavy-duty front and rear shock absorbers, rear stabilizer bar and heavy-duty front stabilizer bar. **Heavy-duty Suspension Package:** includes, heavy-duty shock absorbers and rear springs. **Instrument Group:** includes, (V8): tach, trip odometer, clock, ammeter, water temperature and oil pressure gauges.

NOTE: Colors offered on 1973 Rancheros were: White; Bright red; Medium blue metallic; Light blue; Light pewter metallic; Dark green metallic; Light green; Medium brown metallic; tan; Medium copper metallic; Medium Bright yellow. Color Glow paints were: Blue Glow, Ivy Glow and Gold Glow (optional). Black or white vinyl roofs were available.

NOTE: According to a *Popular Mechanics* poll of owners, the four things Ranchero owners liked best about their vehicles were: handling, styling, comfort and ride. By far the biggest complaint was poor gas mileage, although many blamed this on the anti-pollution equipment. The majority were pleased with the Ranchero. In fact, 83.5 percent said they would buy another. When asked the same question, only 77.2 percent of El Camino said they would purchase another.

BRONCO WAGON: — The pickup was discontinued, so the four-wheel-drive wagon was the only Bronco model available in 1973. Styling was basically the same as last year. Among the standard features were: Bucket vinyl seats. A floor-mounted T-bar transfer case control. Suspended foot pedals. Fresh air heater and defroster. Lockable glove compartment. Padded instrument panel. Two-speed electric windshield wipers. Sunvisors. Vinyl-coated rubber floor mat. Fully synchronized three-speed manual transmission. Full length roof with fixed windows in the rear liftgate and on each side of the rear compartment.

I.D. DATA (Bronco): See F-100 I.D.

Model	Body Type	Price	Weight	Prod. Total
U-100	Wagon	3636	3090	21,894

ENGINE (Bronco): Displacement: 200 cu. in. OHV Six, 84 net horsepower at 3800 R.P.M. Bore & stroke: 3.68 x 3.13 in. Compression ratio: 8.3:1. 1-bbl. carburetor.

CHASSIS: Wheelbase: 92 in. Overall length: 152.1 in. Overall width: 68.8 in. GVW: 4300-4900 lbs. Tires: E78-15.

POWERTRAIN OPTIONS: 302 V8. Cruise-O-Matic automatic.

CONVENIENCE OPTIONS: Extra-cooling V8 radiator. L-H remote control outside mirror. Power steering (with V8). **Convenience Group:** cigarette lighter, map light, inside 10 inch day/night rear view mirror. R-H chrome rearview mirror. Shoulder harness. Rear seat. Chrome bumper Skid plates for standard fuel tank and transfer case. Inside tailgate mounted spare tire carrier (incl. with rear seat option). Exterior rear-mounted swing-away tire carrier. Bright metal wheel covers. High-flotation tires. Auxiliary 7.5 gallon fuel tank with skid plate. Manual radio and antenna. Bright bodyside and tailgate moldings. Bright metal rocker panel molding. Hand-operated throttle.

SPORT BRONCO PACKAGE: — Bright metal "Sport Bronco" emblem. Pleated parchment vinyl front seat. Vinyl door trim panels with bright metal moldings. Hardboard headlining with bright metal retainer moldings. Parchment vinyl front floor mat with bright metal retainers. Rear floor mat included with optional rear seat. Cigarette lighter. Horn ring. Bright metal drip rail moldings. Bright metal windshield and window frames. Bright metal grille molding and tailgate release handle. Bright headlight, side light, reflector and taillight bezels. Argent-painted grille with bright F-O-R-D letters. Chrome bumpers front and rear. Chrome front bumper guard. Bright metal wheel covers w/15 in. wheels only). 6.50 x 16 6PR TT tires. **Dealer-Installed Accessories:** Power-take-off (front-mounted). Warn free-running front hubs (manual or automatic). Snow plows. Snow plow angling kits. Front auxiliary air springs. Front-mounted winch. Trailer hitch. Trailer towing mirror. Locking gas cap. Front tow hooks. Compass. Fire extinguisher, transmission oil cooler. Tach. **4500 lb. GVW Package:** 2780 lb. rear axle, front springs rated at 1000 lbs., rear springs rated at 1475 lbs, G78-15B tires. **4900 lb. GVW Package:** 3300 lb. Traction-Lok rear axle, H-D front and rear springs rating, tires same as 4500 lb. package. **Ranger Package:** argent grille, bucket seats, lower bodyside strips, fiberboard headliner, cut-pile carpeting front and rear, wheel covers, white power dome, white spare tire carrier.

ECONOLINE E-100 CARGO VAN: — The Econoline was little changed for the new year. However, the front axle capacity was increased 50 pounds. And the optional air conditioning evaporator was now located under the floor. Some standard features included: Vinyl color-coordinated upholstery. Painted front and rear bumpers and hub caps. L-H fresh air inlet. Dome lights in driver's compartment and cargo area. Ash tray. Single electric horn. Coat hook. Mechanical jack. Double-grip door locks on all doors with reversible keys. Push-pull interior door locks (except rear doors). Metal door checks. Individual driver's seat. Headlining in driver and passenger area. Fresh air heater and defroster. Double cargo doors at right and rear.

ECONOLINE E-100 WINDOW VAN: — As the name suggests, the window van had glass all around. Like other E-100s, its cargo area was 11½ ft. long and 53.5 in. wide. It shared most standard features with the Cargo Van.

ECONOLINE E-100 DISPLAY VAN: — This model had windows at the rear and on the right-hand side. It came with the same standard features as the Cargo Van.

I.D. DATA (Econoline E-100): See F-100 I.D.

Model	Body Type	Price	Weight	Prod. Total
E-140	Cargo Van	2738	3240	Note 1
E-150	Window Van	2808	3285	Note 1
E-160	Display Van	2880	3240	Note 1

NOTE 1: See production data at end of Econoline section.

ENGINE (Econoline E-100): Displacement: 170 cu. in. OHV. Six. 105 horsepower at 4400 R.P.M. Bore & stroke: 3.50 x 2.94 in. Compression ratio: 9.1:1. One-bbl. carburetor.

ECONOLINE E-200 CARGO VAN: — For heavier loads, buyers could move up to the E-200 series. Its front axle had a capacity of 2750 lbs. The rear axle had a 3300 lb. rating. It also had larger (11 x 3 in. front / 11 x 2¼ in. rear) brakes. Standard features echoed those of the E-100 Cargo Van.

ECONOLINE E-200 WINDOW VAN: — This vehicle shared styling with the E-100 window van and load capacity with other E-200 vans.

ECONOLINE E-200 DISPLAY VAN: — This vehicle shared styling with the E-100 Display Van and load capacity with other E-200 vans.

I.D. DATA (Econoline E-200): See E-100.

Model	Body Type	Price	Weight	Prod. Total
E-240	Cargo Van	2873	3290	Note 1
E-250	Window Van	2945	3365	Note 1
E-260	Display Van	2903	3335	Note 1

NOTE 1: See production data at end of Econoline section.

ENGINE (Econoline E-200): Same as E-100.

ECONOLINE E-300 CARGO VAN: — For really big loads, it was hard to beat the E-300 Cargo Van. Its front axle capacity was rated at 3300 lbs. Its rear axle was rated at 4800 lbs. The front brakes were 12 x 3 in., the rears 12 x 12½ in. Its front and rear springs were also heavy-duty.

ECONOLINE E-300 WINDOW VAN: — Had same features as the Cargo Van, plus windows all around.

ECONOLINE E-300 DISPLAY VAN: — Had some features as the Cargo Van, plus windows on the right-hand side.

I.D. DATA (Econoline E-300): See F-100 I.D.

Model	Body Type	Price	Weight	Prod. Total
E-340	Cargo Van	—	—	Note 1
E-350	Window Van	—	—	Note 1
E-360	Display Van	—	—	Note 1

NOTE 1: Ford records show the following Econoline production breakouts: (89A standard cargo van) 60,509; (89B Custom cargo van) 5,123; (89C standard display van) 7,198; (89D Custom display van) 94; (89E standard window van) 13,382; (89F Custom window van) 1,828; (33A cutaway camper special) 850.

ENGINE (Econoline E-300): Displacement: 240 cu. in. OHV. Six. 150 horsepower at 4000 R.P.M. Bore & stroke: 4.00 x 3.18 in. Compression ratio: 9.2:1. One-bbl. carburetor.

CHASSIS: Wheelbase: 105.5. in. (123.5 in. SuperVan). Tires: E78-14B (E-100); G78-15B (E-200); 8.00 x 16.5 (E-300). GVW: 4800 lbs. (E-100); 6000 lbs. (E-200); 8300 lbs. (E-300).

POWERTRAIN OPTIONS: 240 Six. 302 V8. SelectShift Cruise-O-Matic automatic transmission.

CONVENIENCE OPTIONS: Push-button radio. Stationary or flip-fold passenger seat. High output heater and defroster. Auxiliary hot water heater. Air conditioner. Insulation package. Insulated floor mats. Inside body rub rails. Inside or Western-type rearview mirrors. Low-mount rearview mirrors. Wheel cover adapters. Wheel covers. Deluxe driver and/or stationary passenger seats with color-coordinated floor mats. Auxiliary step for right-side cargo doors. Dual electric horns. Courtesy light switches for front or all doors. Padded instrument panel. Shoulder harness. Stationary glass or vents in rear and/or right-side cargo doors. Tinted glass. Inside rear door latch and lock. Scuff pads at front door wells. School bus package for E-200 and E-300 Window Vans with 123.5 inch wheelbase. **Custom Equipment Package:** includes (in addition to or in place of standard items), Deluxe pleated vinyl seat trim, bright metal front and rear bumpers and hub caps, horn ring, cigarette lighter, color-coordinated floor mat on L-H side, glove box door with lock, bright metal grille, taillight bezels, vent window and windshield moldings.

CLUB WAGON: — Club Wagons were basically Econolines made for hauling people. The base model held five passengers. Among standard features were: Twin-I-Beam independent front suspension. Vinyl seat trim. Arm rests on front doors and at right side of three-passenger seats. Ash trays, front and rear. Black floor mats. Coat hook. Two dome lights. Dual sunvisors. Instrument panel padded on right side. Bright instrument cluster trim. Glove box door with lock. Headlining in front compartment. Dual outside rear view mirrors. Backup lights. Inside rearview mirror. Emergency lamp flasher. Retracting step for double side doors. Rear reflectors. Side marker lights at front and rear.

CUSTOM CLUB WAGON: — This was a step up from the base model. Both shared many of the same features, however, the Custom also had: Pleated vinyl seat trim. Interior vinyl side and door trim panels. Arm rests for all seats. Color-coordinated front and rear floor mats. Four coat hooks. Full-length headlining. Window trim moldings. Cigarette lighter. Scuff pads at front door wells. Spare tire cover. Horn ring. Bright metal grille. Full-width, padded instrument panel. Custom ornaments. Bright metal bodyside moldings, taillight bezels and hub caps. Added insulation.

CHATEAU CLUB WAGON: — At the top-of-the-line was the Chateau. It had, in addition to or in place of Custom Club Wagon features,: Pleated deluxe cloth seat trim with vinyl bolsters. Similar trim on interior door and die panels with simulated woodgrain bands. Full-length color coordinated carpeting with dash insulator. Chrome front and rear bumpers. Bright metal dual outside mirrors. Bright metal molding around windshield, side and rear windows. Bright metal rear body molding. Chateau ornaments.

I.D. DATA (Club Wagon): See F-100.

Model	Body Type	Price	Weight	Prod. Total
E-110	Club Wagon	3140	—	5,833
E-120	Club Wagon (Custom)	3748	—	6,608
E-130	Club Wagon (Chateau)	3892	—	4,955

ENGINE (Club Wagon): Same as E-300.

CHASSIS: Wheelbase: 105.5 in. (123.5 in. optional) Tires: E78-14B.

POWERTRAIN OPTIONS: 302 V8. SelectShift Cruise-O-Matic automatic transmission.

CONVENIENCE OPTIONS: Power steering. Ammeter and oil pressure gauge. Heavy-duty battery. Heavy-duty shocks. Whitewall tires. Chrome front and rear bumpers. Cigarette lighter. Courtesy light switches for all doors. Door positioners for all door. Air conditioner. Insulation package. Inside body rub rails. High-output heater / defroster. Auxiliary hot water heater for passenger compartment. Tinted glass. AM radio.

COURIER PICKUP: — Early '73 Couriers were identical to the '72s. In mid-model year, the Courier name was removed from the hood and replaced with the Ford name (in block letters). The Ford nameplate was also put on the tailgate. Among the standard equipment was: 11 tie-down hooks around the box and tailgate for securing cargo or a tarpaulin. Rear mud flaps. Bright hubcaps. Whiteside wall tires. Vinyl upholstery, headliner and door panels. Padded armrests. Padded sunvisors. Tool set emergency flashers. Outside rearview mirror. Axle type jack with crank. Four-speed manual transmission.

I.D. DATA (Courier):

Model	Body Type	Price	Weight	Prod. Total
—	Pickup	2508	2515	—

ENGINE (Courier): Displacement: 109.5 cu. in. Inline 4-cyl.. Net horsepower 74 at 5000 R.P.M. (67 horsepower at 5000 R.P.M. in California). Bore & stroke: 3.07 x 3.70 in. Compression ratio: 8.6:1. Zenith Stromberg 2-bbl. carburetor.

CHASSIS: Wheelbase: 104.3 in. Overall length: 172 in. Overall width: 61.6 in. GVW Rating: 3910 lbs. Tires: 6.00 x 14.

POWERTRAIN OPTIONS: Jatco automatic transmission.

CONVENIENCE OPTIONS: AM radio. Rear step bumper. Six by nine inch swing-lok mirrors. Tinted glass. Full wheel covers. Air conditioning. **Dress Up Package:** Backlite, windshield, drip and bodyside moldings; front bumper guards.

1973 Ford F-100 Styleside Pickup w/Camper (DFW)

F-100 CUSTOM PICKUP: — Although it bore a strong resemblance to last year's model, many changes were made for 1973. Parking lights were moved to above the headlights. In the slot between them, "Ford" was spelled out in block letters. The rectangular slots grille was divided at the center by a vertical bar. The former convex bodyside "spear" was replaced by a concave groove that ran almost the full length of the vehicle (on Styleside models) from the parking lights back. Side marker lights were placed in the groove. A series I.D. emblem was placed slightly below the groove between the door and front tire opening. The new hood had a flatter face. The cab was longer and had behind the seat storage area. Ford Custom pickups had a standard 7 in. full-foam cushioned seat. The seat back also tilted back more than last year's, for car-like comfort. Some other standard features were: Deluxe fresh air heater / defroster. Seat belts, windshield washers. Two-speed windshield wipers. Dome light with door courtesy switch. Ash tray. Glove compartment with push-button latch. Rubber floor mat. Day/night rearview mirror. Bright L-H and R-H exterior mirrors. Hub caps. Three-speed manual transmission. Color-keyed padded instrument panel. Chrome front bumper. Frame mounted fuel tank. Front disc brakes. Long 2½ in. wide rear leaf springs. Twin-I-Beam independent front suspension. New simplified box construction utilizing a single strong sheet of steel making the inside panel, wheelhouse and part of the floor one solid piece. A new frame with six crossmembers (four placed at the rear half of the frame to provide extra strength under the pickup box for carrying heavy loads).

1973 Ford F-100 Ranger XLT Styleside Pickup (OCW)

I.D. DATA (F-100): See 1971 F-100 I.D.

Model	Body Type	Price	Weight	Prod. Total
F-100	(81) Chassis w/Cab	—	—	Note 1
F-100	Flareside (SWB)	—	—	Note 1
F-100	Styleside (SWB)	—	—	Note 1
F-100	Flareside (LWB)	2889	3495	Note 1
F-100	Styleside (LWB)	2925	3590	Note 1

NOTE 1: Ford records show the following F-100 production break-outs: (chassis & cab) 2,461; (Flareside) 3,034 and (Styleside) 457,746.

ENGINE (F-100): See 1972 F-100 engine.

F-250 CUSTOM PICKUP: — The F-250 had most of the same standard features as the F-100, plus power brakes. The Styleside had sleek body panels extending all the way forward to hug the rear cab corners. Its pickup box featured strong, double-walled side panel construction. Each inner and outer panel was one solid piece. The tailgate was also double-walled. Flareside pickups had running boards between cab and fenders for easy side loading. The seasoned hardwood floor boards had interlocking steel skid strips. Rubber-covered forged-steel chains supported the tailgate when open, toggle-type latches maintained tight seal when tailgate was closed.

I.D. DATA (F-250): See F-100 I.D.

Model	Body Type	Price	Weight	Prod. Total
F-250	Chassis w/Cab	—	—	Note 1
F-250	Chassis w/crew cab	—	—	Note 1
F-250	Flareside Pickup	—	—	Note 1
F-250	Styleside Pickup	3183	3925	Note 1
F-250	Pickup w/crew cab	—	—	Note 1

NOTE 1: Ford records show the following F-250 production break-outs: (chassis & cab) 7,674; (Flareside) 3,004; (Styleside) 187,348.

ENGINE (F-250): See 1972 F-250 Engine.

F-350 CUSTOM PICKUP: — The F-350 pickup was now only available with the Styleside box. It was similar in construction to F-250 Stylesides except it was more heavy-duty and had the spare tire location built into the outer right side. A four-speed manual transmission was standard.

F-350 PLATFORM/STAKE: — This model was offered in two sizes: 9 ft. and 12 ft. Both had floor frames formed of steel cross sills riveted to steel side rails. Floorboards were interlocked with steel skid strips and corners were reinforced with steel brackets. Formed steel caps covered the ends of body sills. Sideboards were made of hardwood and stakes were steel.

I.D. DATA (F-350): See F-100 I.D.

1973 Ford F-350 Styleside Pickup w/Super Cab (OCW)

Model	Body Type	Price	Weight	Prod. Total
F-350	(81)Chassis w/cab	—	—	Note 1
F-350	Chassis w/crew cab	—	—	Note 1
F-350	Styleside Pickup	—	—	Note 1
F-350	Pickup w/crew cab	—	—	Note 1
F-350	Pickup/super camper spl.	—	—	Note 1
F-250	(80) 9-ft. Platform	—	—	Note 1
F-350	(80) 12-ft. Platform	—	—	Note 1
F-350	(86) 9-ft. Stake	—	—	Note 1
F-350	(86) 12-ft. Stake	—	—	Note 1

NOTE 1: Ford records show the following F-350 production break-outs: (chassis & cowl) 80; (chassis & cab) 42,084; (cab, platform & rack) 6,656; (cab, platform) 749 and (Styleside) 11,889. **PARCEL VANS:** (P-350) 1,054; (P-400) 6,251.

ENGINE (F-350): Platform/Stake and Chassis w/cab same as F-250. Styleside Pickup: 360 cu. in. V8.

CHASSIS: Wheelbase: 117 in. (F-100); 133 in. (F-100/F-250); 140 in. (F-350); 137 in. (F-350 Chassis/Stake); 161 in. (F-350 Platform/Stake). GVW: 4600-5500 (F-100), 6200-8100 (F-250), 8350-10,000 (F-350). Tires: G78-15B (F-100), 8.00 x 16.5D (F-250), 8.75 x 16.5E (F-350).

POWERTRAIN OPTIONS: 300 Six (F-100), 302 V8 (F-100), 360 V8, 390 V8, 460 V8. 4-speed manual, Cruise-O-Matic automatic.

1973 Ford F-100 Styleside Pickup (JAG)

CONVENIENCE OPTIONS: Four-wheel drive. Pickup box cover (standard: fiberglass construction, tinted side and rear windows, T-handle locking rear lift gate, rubber cushioned tie-downs. Deluxe: sliding side windows with screens, bright side and rear window moldings, roof vent, interior dome light, color-keyed body strip in a choice of five colors). Knitted vinyl seat trim. Heavy-duty black vinyl seat trim. Vinyl insert bodyside molding. AM/FM stereo radio. AM radio. Intermittent windshield wipers. **Super Camper Special:** front and rear stablizier bars; heavy-duty frame; automatic transmission; extra-cooling; 360 V8; power front disc brakes; 55 amp. alternator; 70 amp.-hr. battery; oil pressure gauge and ammeter; bright Western mirrors; dual horns; heavy-duty shocks; camper wiring harness. Rear step bumper. Western style mirrors. Sliding rear cab window. Concealed spare tire and wheel. Auxiliary 12 volt 70 amp-hr battery. Air conditioner. Black or white texture painted roof (included bright drip rail molding). Full wheel covers. Mag style covers. 22.5-gallon auxiliary fuel tank (20.2 gal. F-100). Dual tape stripes. Bright tie-down hooks. Super cooling package. Slide out spare tire carrier. Tool stowage box with locking door. **Convenience Group:** cargo, engine, glove compartment and ash tray lights; glove compartment door lock, door map pockets and 12 in. day/night mirror. **Northland Special Package:** engine block heater, 50 percent (-30 degree F antifreeze, 70 amp-hr battery, 55 amp alternator and limited slip rear axle. Power steering. Power front disc brakes (4x2's). High output heater. Trailer towing packages. Ammeter and oil pressure gauge. Bright hub caps. Bright contour rear bumper for Stylesides. Painted channel rear bumper for Flaresides. Tinted glass all around. Shoulder harness. Oil-bath engine air cleaner. Frame-anchored camper tie-down system. Heavy-duty 50-amp camper wiring harness. **Ranger Package:** (in addition to or in place of Custom features) color-keyed pleated cloth seat upholstery with metallic vinyl bolsters; instrument panel molding with black accent; color-keyed door panels with bright moldings; additional insulation; perforated headlining (insulated) with bright molding; color-keyed vinyl coated floor mat with heel pads; cigarette lighter; brighter windshield, rear window and roof drip moldings; bright rocker panel and wheel lip moldings; bright hub caps (except 4x4 option and dual rear wheel units); Styleside pickups included bright tailgate moldings (top and bottom), taillight bezels; bright recessed tailgate handle. **Ranger XLT Package:** (in addition to or in place of Ranger items) deluxe color-keyed, long wearing cloth with vinyl trim seat upholstery; color-keyed pleated vinyl upper door panel with simulated woodgrain accented moldings and map pocket lower panels color-keyed wall to wall nylon carpeting; black steering wheel with simulated woodgrain insert; bright seat-pivot covers; additional insulation and double-wrapped muffler; convenience group; color-keyed vinyl headlining (with special insulation) and sunvisors; Styleside pickup included bright bodyside moldings with vinyl insert; upper tailgate applique panel and molding; aluminum tailgate applique panel.

HISTORICAL: Introduced: December 1972. Model year production (light-duty trucks only, including parcel vans) 886,649.

1973 Ford F-100 Ranger XLT Styleside Pickup (OCW)

Pricing

	5	4	3	2	1
1973					
Courier					
Pickup	450	900	1500	2100	3000
Ranchero					
GT Pickup	840	1600	2650	3700	5300
500 Pickup	840	1680	2800	3900	5600
Squire Pickup	890	1770	2950	4150	5900
Bronco					
Pickup	850	1700	2850	4000	5700
Wagon	900	1800	3000	4200	6000
Econoline E-100					
Cargo Van	440	870	1450	2050	2900
Window Van	470	950	1550	2200	3100
Display Van	500	1000	1650	2300	3300
Custom Wagon	570	1140	1900	2650	3800
Chateau Wagon	600	1200	2000	2800	4000
Econoline E-200					
Cargo Van	400	800	1350	1900	2700
Window Van	440	870	1450	2050	2900
Display Van	470	950	1550	2200	3100
Econoline E-300					
Cargo Van	390	780	1300	1800	2600
Window Van	420	840	1400	1950	2800
Display Van	450	900	1500	2100	3000
F-100 — (½-Ton)					
Flareside Pickup	930	1860	3100	4350	6200
Styleside Pickup	980	1950	3250	4550	6500
F-250 — (¾-Ton)					
Flareside Pickup	890	1770	2950	4150	5900
Styleside Pickup	920	1850	3050	4300	6100
Stake	830	1650	2750	3850	5500
Crew Cab Pickup	830	1650	2750	3850	5500
F-350 — (1-Ton)					
Flareside Pickup	800	1600	2650	3700	5300
Stake	780	1560	2600	3600	5200
Crew Cab Pickup	780	1560	2600	3600	5200

1974 FORD

1974 Ford Ranchero 500 Sport Pickup (OCW)

RANCHERO 500 PICKUP: — The Ranchero received a very mild facelift for '74. The grille design was squared off a bit. It was divided into eight rectangular sections containing a criss-cross pattern. The parking lights were hidden in the grille. The front bumper now had a slight dip under the grille. Standard features included: Black saddle, blue, tan, or green upholstery. Color-keyed vinyl door trim panels with bright trim. Color-keyed

steering wheel and column. Deep pile carpeting. Hi-level, flow-through ventilation. Ventless door windows. Energy-absorbing steering column. Padded steering wheel hub. Lockable glove box. Locking steering column. Fresh-air heater defroster. Trim panel behind the split-back seat. Vinyl headliner. Color-keyed seat belts with out-board retractors and shoulder harnesses (also center passenger seat belts). Armrests with recessed door handles. Vinyl-framed day/night mirror. Cigarette lighter. Padded, color-keyed instrument panel. Emergency lamp flasher. Spare tire and tool compartment. Deluxe grille with moldings. Bright energy absorbing front bumper. Bright left hand mirror with remote control. Hidden windshield wipers. Bright metal windshield, rear window, drip rail and top of cargo body moldings. Bright metal hub caps. Four cargo tie-downs.

RANCHERO GT PICKUP: — The GT had (in addition to or in place of the Ranchero 500 features): Color-keyed body side stripe. Sport style mirrors painted body-color (both with remote controls). Black hub caps with bright trim rings. White-lettered belted tires. GT grille crest. Spare tire and tool compartment cover. Bright trim on pedals. GT instrument panel plaque.

RANCHERO SQUIRE PICKUP: — The Squire had (in addition to or in place of Ranchero 500 features): Deluxe bright wheel covers. Simulated wood-grain panels on sides and tailgate. Ranchero Squire script on front fenders. Squire crest on grille. Woodtone panel around instruments. Electric clock. Spare tire and tool compartment cover. Bright trim on pedals. Squire instrument panel plaque.

I.D. DATA (Ranchero): See 1960 Ranchero I.D.

Model	Body Type	Price	Weight	Prod. Total
97D	Pickup (500)	3258	3915	18,447
97R	Pickup (GT)	3555	3980	11,328
97K	Pickup (Squire)	3575	3940	3150

ENGINE (Ranchero): Displacement: 302 cu. in. V8. 140 net horsepower at 3800 R.P.M. Bore & stroke: 4 in. x 3 in. Compression ratio: 8.0:1. 2-bbl. carburetor.

CHASSIS: Wheelbase: 118 in. Overall length: 218.3 in. GVW: 5480-5950. Tires: F78-14B (F70-14B white-lettered on GT).

POWERTRAIN OPTIONS: 250 cu. in. Six-cylinder (this engine was discontinued, then reinstated later in the model year). "351" V8 (2V). "351" V8 (4V). "400" V8. "460" V8. SelectShift Cruise-O-Matic transmission (required with optional engines).

CONVENIENCE OPTIONS: Performance Cluster: includes, tachometer, trip odometer, clock, ammeter, water temperature and oil pressure gauges (also includes heavy-duty battery). SelectAire Conditioner with automatic temperature control. SelectAire conditioner. Power steering. **ProtectionGroup (Bumpers):** inludes, front and rear bumper guards and front bumper rubber inserts. **Protection Group (Appearance):** includes, spare tire lock, floor mats, license plate frame and door edge guards. Vinyl insert bodyside molding. Anti-theft alarm system. Power side windows. Tilt steering wheel. Cruise control. **Convenience Group:** includes, right and left remote control mirrors, interval windshield wipers, vanity mirror. Restraint system. Sport flight bench seat with vinyl trim. **Brougham Decor Group:** includes, split bench seat with super-soft vinyl or knit cloth upholstery for the standard seat in Ranchero 500 and Squire. Bucket seats. Vinyl roof. Power brakes. AM radio. 15-inch wheels. Luxury wheel covers. Hub caps with trim rings. Magstyle wheels. Tinted glass. Electric clock. Dual sport style mirrors. **Light Group:** includes, ash tray, underhood and glove box lights, parking brake warning light, lights-on warning buzzer and illuminated light switch. Class II (2000-3500 lb.) or Class III (3500-6000 lb.) trailer towing package. **Handling Suspension Package:** includes, heavy-duty shock absorbers, rear springs and heavy-duty rear stabilizer bar.

NOTE: Colors offered on 1974 Rancheros were: White; Bright red; Medium blue metallic; Pastel blue; Bright dark blue metallic; Dark green metallic; Pastel lime; Saddle bronze metallic; Medium copper metallic; Bright green-gold metallic; Medium dark gold metallic; Medium ivy-bronze metallic and maize yellow. Optional "Color Glow" finishes were: Green Glow; Ginger Glow; Tan Glow and Gold Glow. Black, white, blue, green, brown, tan or gold vinyl roofs were available.

BRONCO WAGON: — Bronco styling was carried over for 1974. A few minor changes were made to this four-wheel-drive vehicle. Among them: the automatic gear selector dial had a light, a different steering gear was used and a dome light replaced the map light as standard equipment. Other standard features included: Vinyl bucket seats. Floor mounted T-bar transfer case control. Suspended foot pedals. Fresh air heater and defroster. Lockable glove compartment. Padded instrument panel. Two-speed electric windshield wipers. Sunvisors. Vinyl-coated rubber floor mat. Fully synchronized three-speed manual transmission. Full-length roof with fixed windows in the rear liftgate and on each side of the rear compartment.

I.D. DATA (Bronco): See F-100 I.D.

Model	Body Type	Price	Weight	Prod. Total
U-100	Wagon	4182	3420	18,786

ENGINE (Bronco): Displacement: 200 cu. in. Six-cylinder. 84 net horsepower at 3800 R.P.M. Bore & stroke: 3.68 in. x 3.13 in. Compression ratio: 8.3:1. 1-bbl. carburetor.

CHASSIS: Wheelbase: 92 in. Overall length: 152.1 in. Overall width: 68.8 in. GVW: 4300-4900 lbs.. Tires: E78 x 15 in.

POWERTRAIN OPTIONS: 302 cu. in. V8. Cruise-O-Matic transmission.

CONVENIENCE OPTIONS: Extra-cooling V8 radiator. L-H remote control outside mirror. Knitted vinyl upholstery. Power steering. **Convenience Group:** includes, cigarette lighter, map light, 10 inch inside day/night mirror. Shoulder harness. Rear seat. Chrome bumper. Skid plates for standard fuel tank and transfer case (incl. with rear seat option). Inside tailgate mounted spare tire carrier (incl. with rear seat option). Exterior rear-mounted swing-away tire carrier. Bright metal wheel covers. High-flotation tires. Auxiliary 7.5 gallon fuel tank with skid plate. Manual radio and antenna. Bright bodyside and tailgate moldings. Bright metal rocker panel molding. Hand-operated throttle. **Sport Bronco Package:** includes: Bright metal "Sport Bronco" emblem. Pleated parchment vinyl front seat. Vinyl door trim panels with bright metal moldings. Hardboard headlining with bright metal retainer moldings. Parchment vinyl front floor mat with bright metal retainers. Rear floor mat included with optional rear seat. Cigarette lighter. Horn ring. Bright metal drip rail moldings. Bright metal windshield and window frames. Bright metalgrille molding and tailgate release handle. Bright headlight, side light, reflector and taillight bezels. Argent-painted grille with bright F-O-R-D letters. Chrome bumpers, front and rear. Chrome front bumper guards. Bright metal wheel covers (w/15 inch wheels only). 6.50 x 16-6PR TT tires. **Dealer-installed Accessories:** Power-take-off (front-mounted). Warn free-running front hubs (manual or automatic). Snow plows. Snow plow angling kits. Front auxiliary air springs. Front-mounted winch. Trailer hitch. Trailer towing mirror. Locking gas cap. Front tow hooks. Compass. Fire extinguisher. Transmission oil cooler. Tachometer. **4500 lb. GVW Package:** includes, 2780 lb. rear axle, front springs rated at 1000 lbs., rear springs rated at 1475 lbs. and G78-15B tires. **4900 lb. GVW Package:** includes, 3300 lb. Traction-Lok rear axle (front and rear spring ratings and tires same as 4500 lb. package.) **Ranger Package:** includes, argent grille, bucket seats, lower bodyside stripes, fiberboard headliner, cut-pile carpeting front and rear, wheel covers, white power dome and white spare tire carrier.

1974 Ford Econoline Custom Cargo Van (OCW)

ECONOLINE E-100 CARGO VAN: — The step wells were now stamped and covered with rubber mats. Aside from that, the new Econoline was pretty much unchanged for 1974. Standard features included: Vinyl color-coordinated upholstery. Painted front and rear bumpers and hub caps. L-H fresh air inlet. Dome light in driver's compartment and cargo area. Ash tray. Single electric horn. Coat hook. Mechanical jack. Double-grip door locks on all doors with reversible keys. Push-pull interior door locks (except rear doors). Metal door checks. Individual driver's seat. Headlining in driver and passenger area. Fresh air heater and defroster. Double cargo doors at right and rear.

ECONOLINE E-100 WINDOW VAN: — As the name suggests, the window van had glass all around. On it and other E-100s the cargo area was 11½ feet long and 53.5 inches wide. It shared most standard features with the Cargo Van.

ECONOLINE E-100 DISPLAY VAN: — This model had windows at the rear and on the right-hand side. It came with the same standard features as the Cargo Van.

I.D. DATA (Econoline E-100): See F-100 I.D.

Model	Body Type	Price	Weight	Prod. Total
E-140	Cargo Van	3176	3240	Note 1
E-150	Window Van	3248	3320	Note 1
E-160	Display Van	3206	3285	Note 1

NOTE 1: Available production totals listed under E-300 chart below.

ENGINE (Econoline E-100): Displacement: 170 cu. in. Six-cylinder. 105 horsepower at 4400 R.P.M. Bore & stroke: 3.50 in. x 2.94 in. Compression ratio: 9.1:1. One-bbl. carburetor. Displacement: 300 cu. in. Six-cylinder engine standard in California.

ECONOLINE E-200 CARGO VAN: — For heavier loads, buyers could move up to the E-200 series. Its front axle had a capacity of 2750 lbs. The rear axle was rated for 3300 lbs. It also had larger (11 x 3 in. front/11 x 2¼ in. rear) brakes. Standard features echoed those of the E-100 Cargo Van.

ECONOLINE E-200 WINDOW VAN: — This vehicle shared styling with the E-100 window van and load capacity with other E-200 vans.

ECONOLINE E-200 DISPLAY VAN: — This vehicle shared styling with the E-100 Display Van and load capacity with other E-200 vans.

I.D. DATA (Econoline E-200): See E-100.

Model	Body Type	Price	Weight	Prod. Total
E-240	Cargo Van	3241	3290	Note 1
E-250	Window Van	3313	3370	Note 1
E-260	Display Van	3271	3335	Note 1

NOTE 1: Available production totals listed under E-300 chart below.

ENGINE (Econoline E-200): Same as E-100.

ECONOLINE E-300 CARGO VAN: — For really big loads, it was hard to beat the E-300 Cargo Van. Its front axle capacity was rated at 3300 lbs. and its rear axle at 4800 lbs. The front brakes were 12 x 3 in., the rears 12 x 12½ in. A 10-inch clutch was standard. The front and rear springs were also heavy-duty.

ECONOLINE E-300 WINDOW VAN: — This truck had the same features as the Cargo Van, plus windows all around.

ECONOLINE E-300 DISPLAY VAN: — This truck had the same features as the Cargo Van, plus windows on the right-hand side.

I.D. DATA (Econoline E-300): See F-100 I.D.

Model	Body Type	Price	Weight	Prod. Total
E-340	Cargo Van	3523	3670	Note 1
E-350	Window Van	3595	3750	Note 1
E-360	Display Van	3553	3715	Note 1

ENGINE (Econoline E-300): Displacement: 240 cu. in. Six-cylinder. 150 horsepower at 4000 R.P.M. Bore & stroke: 4.00 in. x 3.18 in. Compression ratio: 9.2:1. One-bbl. carburetor. Displacement: 300 cu. in. Six-cylinder standard in California.

CHASSIS: Wheelbase: 105.5 in. (123.5 in. SuperVan) Tires: E78-14B (E-100); G78-15B (E-200); 8.00 x 16.5 in. (E-300). GVW: (in pounds) 4800 (E-100); 6000 (E-200); 8300 (E-300).

POWERTRAIN OPTIONS: "240" Six. "300" Six. "302" V8. SelectShift Cruise-O-Matic transmission.

CONVENIENCE OPTIONS: Push-button radio. Stationary or flip-fold passenger seat. High-output heater and defroster. Auxiliary hot water heater. Air conditioner. Insulation package. Insulated floor mats. Inside body rub rails. Inside or Western-type rearview mirrors. Low-mount rearview mirrors. Wheel cover adapters. Wheel covers. Deluxe driver and/or stationary passenger seats with color-coordinated floor mats. Auxiliary step for right-side cargo doors. Dual electric horns. Courtesy light switches for front or all doors. Padded instrument panel. Shoulder harness. Stationary glass or vents in rear and/or right-side cargo doors. Tinted glass. Inside rear door latch and lock. Scuff pads at front door wells. School bus package for E-200 and E-300 Window Vans with 123.5 inch wheelbase. **Custom Equipment Package:** includes, (in addition to or in place of standard items): Deluxe pleated vinyl seat trim, bright metal front and rear bumpers and hub caps, horn ring, cigarette lighter, color-coordinated floor mat on L-H side, glove box door with lock, bright metal grille, taillight bezels, vent window and windshield moldings.

CLUB WAGON: — Club wagons were basically Econolines made for hauling people. The base model held five passengers. Among standard features were: Twin-I-Beam independent front suspension. Vinyl seat trim. Arm rests on front doors and at right side of 3+passenger seats. Ash trays, front and rear. Black floor mats. Coat hook. Two dome lights. Dual sunvisors. Instrument panel padded on right side. Bright instrument cluster trim. Glove box door with lock. Headlining in front compartment. Dual outside rear view mirrors. Backup lights. Inside rearview mirror. Emergency lamp flasher. Retracting step for double side doors. Rear reflectors. Side marker lights at front and rear.

CUSTOM CLUB WAGON: — This was a step up from the base model. Both shared many of the same features, however, the Custom also had: Pleated vinyl seat trim. Interior vinyl side and door trim panels. Arm rests for all seats. Color-coordinated front and rear floor mats. Four coat hooks. Full-length headlining. Window trim moldings. Cigarette lighter. Scuff pads at front door wells. Spare tire cover. Horn ring. Bright metal grille. Instrument panel padded full width. Custom ornaments. Bright metal bodyside moldings, taillight bezels and hub caps. Added insulation.

CHATEAU CLUB WAGON: — At the top-of-the-line was the Chateau. It had, in addition to or in place of Custom Club Wagon features: Pleated Deluxe cloth seat trim with vinyl bolsters. Similar trim on interior door and die panels with simulated woodgrain bands. Full-length color coordinated carpeting with dash insulator. Chrome front and rear bumpers. Bright metal dual outside mirrors. Bright metal molding around windshield, side and rear windows. Bright metal rear body molding. Chateau ornaments.

I.D. DATA (Club Wagon): See F-100.

Model	Body Type	Price	Weight	Prod. Total
E-100	Club Wagon	3869	3550	11,331
E-200	Club Wagon (Custom)	3943	3650	12,038
E-300	Club Wagon (Chateau)	4176	4060	7,459

ENGINE (Club Wagon): Same as E-300.

CHASSIS: Wheelbase: 105.5 in. (123.5 in. optional). Tires: E78-14B.

POWERTRAIN OPTIONS: 302 V8. SelectShift Cruise-O-Matic transmission.

CONVENIENCE OPTIONS: Power steering. Ammeter and oil pressure gauge. Heavy-duty battery. Heavy-duty shocks. Whitewall tires. Chrome front and rear bumpers. Cigarette lighter. Courtesy light switches for all doors. Door positioners for all door. Air conditioner. Insulation package. Inside body rub rails. High-output heater/defroster. Auxiliary hot water heater for passenger compartment. Tinted glass. AM radio.

COURIER PICKUP: — The Courier was unchanged in 1974. Among the standard equipment were: 11 tie-down hooks around the box and tailgate for securing cargo or a tarpaulin. Rear mud flaps. Bright hubcaps. White-side wall tires. Vinyl upholstery, headliner and door panels. Padded armrests. Padded sunvisors. Tool set emergency flashers. Outside rearview mirror. Axle type jack with crank. Four-speed manual transmission.

Model	Body Type	Price	Weight	Prod. Total
—	Pickup	2969	2510	(*)44,491

(*) Courier calendar year sales total.

ENGINE (Courier): Displacement: 109.5 cu. in. Inline 4-cyl. Net horsepower 74 at 5000 R.P.M. (67 horsepower at 5000 R.P.M. in Calif.) Bore & stroke: 3.07 in. x 3.70 in. Compression ratio: 8.6:1. Zenith Stromberg 2-bbl. carburetor.

CHASSIS: Wheelbase: 104.3 in. Overall length: 172 in. Overall width: 61.6 in. GVW Rating: 3910 lbs. Tires: 6.00 x 14.

POWERTRAIN OPTION: Jatco automatic transmission.

CONVENIENCE OPTIONS: AM radio. Rear step bumper. Six by nine inch Swing-Lok mirrors. Tinted glass. Full wheel covers. Air conditioning. **Dress-Up Package:** includes, backlite, windshield, drip and bodyside moldings and front bumper guards.

NOTE: According to a *Popular Mechanics* survey, the majority of Courier buyers (68.6 percent) used it as a second ''car.'' The main reason most purchased one was for economy, although handling tied with economy as the best liked feature.

F-100 CUSTOM PICKUP: — Styling was unchanged for 1974. However, a new extended cab model was made available in June of '74. The ''Super Cab'' was offered with either a full-width rear foam seat or two facing jump seats that folded out of the way when not in use. In all, it provided 44 cubic feet of extra load space. The Super Cab had a stiffer frame. It was available with 6¾-foot or 8-foot Styleside boxes. Both sizes of Styleside and Flareside boxes were offered on the regular (three-passenger) F-100 pickups as well. Standard F-100 features included: Deluxe fresh air heater/defroster. Energy-absorbing sunvisors and instrument panel padding. Instrument cluster with green backlighting. Keyless locking doors. Color-keyed molded door panels with integral armrests and paddle-type door handles. Seat belts. Windshield washers. Two-speed windshield wipers. Dome light with door courtesy light switches. Ash tray. Large glove compartment with push-button latch. Sponge-grain headlining. Black rubber floor mat. Door scuff plates. Black, red, blue or green vinyl seat trim. 10 inch day/night rearview mirror. Left- and right-hand bright metal exterior mirrors. Taillights with integral stop, turn, backup lights and reflector. Hub caps (except 4x4). Bright tailgate handle depression (Styleside). Three-speed manual transmission.

I.D. DATA (F-100): See 1971 F-100 I.D.

Model	Body Type	Price	Weight	Prod. Total
F-100	(81) Chassis w/Cab	3092	3125	Note 1
F-100	6¾-ft. Flareside Pickup	3246	3480	Note 1
F-100	8-ft. Flareside Pickup	3282	3570	Note 1
F-100	6¾-ft. Styleside Pickup	3246	3480	Note 1
F-100	8-ft. Styleside Pickup	3282	3570	Note 1
F-100	6¾-ft. Supercab Pickup	4185	3820	Note 1
F-100	8-ft. Supercab Pickup	4221	3930	Note 1

NOTE 1: Ford records show the following F-100 production break-outs: **(4x2)** (chassis & cab) 2,241; (Flareside pickup) 2,517; (Styleside pickup) 389,407; (Supercab pickup) 17,537. **(4x4)** (chassis & cab) 2,547; (Flareside pickup) 176 and (Styleside pickup) 26,788.

ENGINE (F-100): Same as 1973 for regular cab models. Super Cabs came with a big V8 engine: Displacement: 360 cu. in. V8. Bore & stroke: 4.05 in. x 3.50 in. 2-bbl. carburetor.

F-250 CUSTOM PICKUP: — The F-250 had most of the same features as the F-100. It too was offered with regular or Super cabs and with Flareside or Styleside boxes. Power brakes and a three-speed manual transmission were standard.

I.D. DATA (F-250): See F-100 I.D.

Model	Body Type	Price	Weight	Prod. Total
F-250	(81) Chassis w/Cab	3410	3480	Note 1
F-250	Chassis w/Crew Cab	4229	4100	Note 1
F-250	Flareside Pickup	3564	3900	Note 1
F-250	Styleside Pickup	3564	3900	Note 1
F-250	Supercab Pickup	4473	4015	Note 1
F-250	Crew Cab Pickup	4371	4455	Note 1

NOTE 1: Ford records show the following F-250 production break-outs: **(4x2)** (chassis & cab) 5,616; (Flareside pickup) 1,787; (Styleside pickup) 123,711; (Supercab) 10,852. **(4x4)** (chassis & cab) 1,137; (Flareside pickup) 645 and (Styleside pickup) 34,618.

ENGINE (F-250): Displacement: 300 cu. in. Six-cylinder. 120 net horsepower at 3400 R.P.M. Bore & stroke: 4.00 in. x 3.98 in. Compression ratio: 8.0:1. One-bbl. carburetor. Super Cab had ''360'' V8.

F-350 CUSTOM PICKUP: — The F-350 pickup was only offered with the Styleside box. However, there were three choices of cabs: regular, Super, or Crew. Standard features included: front shocks, (front and rear) heavy-duty power front disc brakes.

F-350 PLATFORM/STAKE: — Two lengths of one-ton F-350 Platform/Stakes were available: 9 foot and 12 foot. Floor frames of the Platform/Stake were made of steel cross sills riveted to steel side rails. Floorboards were interlocked with steel brackets. Formed steel caps covered ends of body sills. Side boards were hardwood and stakes were steel. A four-speed manual transmission was standard.

I.D. DATA (F-350): See F-100 I.D.

Model	Body Type	Price	Weight	Prod. Total
F-350	(81) Chassis w/Cab	3510	3795	Note 1
F-350	Styleside Pickup	3958	4345	Note 1
F-350	Super Cab Pickup	5070	4570	Note 1
F-350	(80) 9-ft. Platform	3873	4375	Note 1
F-350	Crew Cab Pickupm	4514	4730	Note 1
F-350	(80) 12-ft. Platform	4875	—	Note 1
F-350	Chassis w/Crew Cab	4363	4290	Note 1
F-350	(86) 9-ft. Stake	3912	4615	Note 1
F-350	(86) 12- ft. Stake	5115	—	Note 1

NOTE 1: Ford records show the following F-350 production break-outs: **All 4x2** (cowl & cab) 144; (chassis & cab) 48,812; (cab, platform & rack) 7,546; (cab, platform) 786; (Supercab) 1340 and (Styleside cab) 9,929.

ENGINE (F-350): See F-250 for Platform/Stake & Chasis w/Cab. Pickups used the ''360'' V8.

CHASSIS: Wheelbase: 117 in. (F-100); 133 in. (F-100/F-250); 139 in. (F-100/F-250 Super Cab); 140 in. (F-350); 137 in. (F-350 Platform/Stake); 155 in. (Super Cab); 161 in. (F-350 Platform/Stake). GVW (in pounds): 4600-5500 (F-100); 6200-8100 (F-250); 8350-10,000 (F-350). Tires: G78 x 15B (F-100); 8.00 x 16.5D (F-250) and 8.75 x 16.5E (F-350).

POWERTRAIN OPTIONS: 300 Six-cylinder engine (F-100). ''302'' V8 (F-100). ''360'' V8. ''390'' V8. ''460'' V8. Four-speed manual or Cruise-O-Matic transmissions.

CONVENIENCE OPTIONS: Four-wheel-drive (F-100/F-250). **Pickup box cover:** (Standard) has fiberglass construction; tinted side and rear windows; T-handle locking rear liftgate and rubber cushioned tie-downs. (Deluxe) has sliding side windows with screens; bright side and rear window moldings; roof vent; interior dome light and color-keyed body strip (in a choice of five colors). Knitted vinyl seat trim. Folding bench or jump seats (Super Cab). Heavy-duty black vinyl seat trim. Vinyl insert bodyside molding. AM/FM stereo radio. AM radio. Intermittent windshield wipers. **Super Camper Special:** front and rear stablizer bars; heavy-duty frame; automatic transmission; extra-cooling system; ''360'' V8; power front disc brakes; 55 amp. alternator; 70 amp.-hr. battery; oil pressure gauge and ammeter; bright Western mirrors; dual horns; heavy-duty shocks and camper wiring harness. Rear step bumper. Western style mirrors. Sliding rear cab window. Concealed spare tire and wheel. Auxiliary 12 volt 70 amp.-hr. battery. Air conditioner. Black or white texture painted roof (includes bright drip rail moldings). Full wheel covers. Mag style wheel covers. 22.5-gallon auxiliary fuel tank (20.2 gal. F-100). Dual tape stripes. Bright tie-down hooks. Super-cooling package. Slide-out spare tire carrier. Tool stowage box with locking door. **Convenience Group:** includes, cargo, engine, glove compartment and ash tray lights; glove compartment door lock, door map pockets and 12 inch day/night mirror. **Northland Special Package:** includes, engine block heater, 50 percent (-30 degrees F) anti-freeze, 70 amp.-hr. battery, 55 amp. alternator and limited-slip rear axle. Power steering. Power front disc brakes (4x2s). High-output heater. Trailer towing packages. Ammeter and oil pressure gauge. Bright hub caps. Bright contour rear bumper for Stylesides. Painted channel rear bumper for Flaresides. Tinted glass all around. Shoulder harness. Oil-bath engine air cleaner. Frame-anchored camper tie-down system. Heavy-duty 50-amp. camper wiring harness. **Ranger Package:** includes, (in addition to or in place of Custom features) color-keyed pleated cloth seat upholstery with metallic vinyl bolsters; instrument panel molding with black accent; color-keyed door panels with bright moldings; additional insulation; perforated headlining (insulated) with bright molding; color-keyed vinyl coated floor mat with heel pads; cigarette lighter; bright windshield, rear window and roof drip moldings; bright rocker panel and wheel lip moldings and bright hub caps (except 4x4 option and dual rear wheel units). Styleside pickups also included bright tailgate moldings (top and bottom), taillight bezels and bright recessed tailgate handle. **Ranger XLT Package:** includes, (in addition to or in place of Ranger items) Deluxe color-keyed, long wearing cloth with vinyl trim seat upholstery; color-keyed pleated vinyl upper door panel with simulated woodgrain accented moldings and map pocket lower panels, color-keyed wall-to-wall nylon carpeting; black steering wheel with simulated woodgrain insert; bright seat-pivot covers; additional insulation and double-wrapped muffler; convenience group; color-keyed vinyl headlining (with special insulation) and sunvisors. Styleside pickup included bright bodyside moldings with vinyl insert; upper tailgate applique panel and molding; aluminum tailgate applique panel.

NOTE: Standard colors for 1974 were: Wimbledon white; Samoa lime; Pastel lime; Limestone green metallic; Village green; Candy Apple red; Sandpiper yellow; Burnt orange; Raven black; Wind blue; Light Grabber blue; Midnight blue metallic; Sequoia brown metallic and Chrome yellow. New Ivy Glow and Gold Glow colors were optional. Different two-tones could be obtained by using all standard colors, except Chrome Yellow. Wimbledon white could be used as the accent color for any other color.

HISTORICAL: Introduced: Sept. 21, 1973. Calendar year production (all Ford trucks): 1,028,507 or 36.10 percent of industry. Model year production: (light-duty) 928,882; (medium-duty) 44,452; (heavy-duty) 80,238; (all) 1,053,572. Calendar year sales, by line: (Ranchero) 26,731; (Bronco) 18,786; (Courier) 44,491; (Econoline) 122,623; (other light-duty) 561,108; (medium- and heavy-duty) 84,185 and (extra-heavy-duty) 28,784; (Total) 886,708. Calendar year registrations by weight class: (up to 6000 lbs.) 513,367; (6001-10,000 lbs.) 246,989. Innovations: Ranchero facelifted. Improved Bronco steering. Super Cab pickup introduced. This was the third best truck sales year in Ford's history. The company retained its number one position in calendar year production. Its sales total of 886,708 units compared favorably to Chevrolet's 885,362, allowing Ford to regain the lead in the domestic industry. Donald E. Peterson was V.P. and General Manager of Ford Motor Company Truck Operations.

Pricing

1974	5	4	3	2	1
Courier					
Pickup	450	900	1500	2100	3000
Ranchero					
500 Pickup	830	1650	2750	3850	5500
GT Pickup	850	1700	2850	4000	5700
Squire Pickup	890	1770	2950	4150	5900
Bronco					
Wagon	850	1700	2850	4000	5700
Econoline E-100					
Cargo Van	440	870	1450	2050	2900
Window Van	470	950	1550	2200	3100
Display Van	500	1000	1650	2300	3300
Club Wagon	570	1140	1900	2650	3800
Custom Club Wagon	600	1200	2000	2800	4000
Chateau Club Wagon	630	1250	2100	3000	4200
Econoline E-200					
Cargo Van	400	800	1350	1900	2700
Window Van	440	870	1450	2050	2900
Display Van	470	950	1550	2200	3100
Econoline E-300					
Cargo Van	390	780	1300	1800	2600
Window Van	420	840	1400	1950	2800
Display Van	450	900	1500	2100	3000
F-100 — (½-Ton)					
Flareside Pickup	720	1450	2400	3300	4800
Styleside Pickup	740	1470	2450	3350	4900
Super Cab Pickup	750	1500	2500	3500	5000
F-250 — (¾-Ton)					
Flareside Pickup	690	1380	2300	3200	4600
Styleside Pickup	700	1400	2350	3250	4700
Super Cab	720	1450	2400	3300	4800
F-350 — (1-Ton)					
Pickup	690	1380	2300	3200	4600
Crew Cab Pickup	660	1320	2200	3100	4400
Stake	630	1250	2100	3000	4200

NOTE: Add five percent for 4x4.

1975 FORD

1975 Ford Econoline 500 Chateau Van (OCW)

RANCHERO 500 PICKUP: — Styling was unchanged for 1975, except for a new steering wheel and different filler neck to comply with no-lead gasoline requirements. Standard features included: Vinyl upholstery and door trim. Panels with bright trim. Color-keyed steering wheel and column. Deep-pile carpeting. Hi-level, flow-through ventilation. Ventless door windows. Energy-absorbing steering column. Padded steering wheel hub. Lockable glove box. Locking steering column. Fresh-air heater defroster. Trim panel behind the split-back seat. Vinyl headliner. Color-keyed day/night mirror. Cigarette lighter. Padded, color-keyed instrument panel. Emergency lamp flasher. Spare tire and tool compartment. Deluxe grille with moldings. Bright energy absorbing front bumper. Bright left-hand mirror with remote control. Hidden windshield wipers. Bright metal windshield, rear window, drip rail and top of cargo body moldings. Bright metal hub caps. Power steering. Power brakes. Cruise-O-Matic automatic.

RANCHERO GT PICKUP: — The GT had (in addition to or in place of the Ranchero 500 features): Color-keyed bodyside stripe. Sport style mirrors painted body colors, both with remote controls. Black hub caps with bright trim rings. Lettered belted tires. GT grille crest. Spare tire and tool compartment cover. Bright trim on pedals. GT instrument panel plaque.

RANCHERO SQUIRE PICKUP: — The Squire had (in addition to or in place of Ranchero 500 features): Deluxe bright wheel covers. Simulated woodgrain panels on sides and tailgate. Ranchero Squire script on front fenders. Squire crest on grille. Woodtone panel around instruments. Electric clock. Spare tire and tool compartment cover. Bright trim on pedals. Squire instrument panel plaque.

I.D. DATA (Ranchero): See 1960 Ranchero I.D.

Model	Body Type	Price	Weight	Prod. Total
97D	Pickup (500)	4049	3915	8778
97R	Pickup (GT)	4381	3980	6114
97K	Pickup (Squire)	4407	3940	1549

ENGINE (Ranchero): Displacement: 351 M (modified). V8. 148 net horsepower at 3800 R.P.M. Bore & stroke: 4 in. x 3.5 in. Compression ratio: 8.0:1. 2-bbl. carburetor.

CHASSIS: Wheebase: 118 in. Overall length: 218.3 in. GVW: 5480-5950. Tires: G78-14B (G70-14B white-letter on GT).

POWERTRAIN OPTIONS: "351" V8. "400" V8. "460" V8.

CONVENIENCE OPTIONS: Performance Cluster: includes, tachometer, trip odometer, clock, ammeter, water temperature and oil pressure gauges (also includes heavy-duty battery). SelectAire air conditioner with automatic temperature control. SelectAire air conditioner. Power steering. **Protection Group, bumpers:** includes front and rear bumper guards, front bumper rubber inserts. **Protection Group, Appearance:** includes, spare tire lock, floor mats, license plate frame and door edge guards. Vinyl insert bodyside molding. Anti-theft alarm system. Power side windows. Tilt steering wheel. Cruise control. **Convenience Group:** includes, right- and left-hand remote control mirrors, interval windshield wipers, vanity mirror. Restraint system. Sport flight bench seat with vinyl trim. **Brougham Decor Group:** includes, split bench seat with super-soft vinyl or knit cloth upholstery, Brougham door trim panels, cut-pile carpeting. Bucket seats. Vinyl roof. Power brakes. AM radio. 15-inch wheels. Luxury wheel covers. Hub caps with trim rings. Mag style wheels. Tinted glass. Electric clock. Dual sport style mirrors. **Light Group:** includes, ash tray, underhood and glove box lights, parking brake warning light, lights-on warning buzzer and illuminated light switch. Class II (1000-3500 lb.) or Class III (3500-6000 lb.) trailer towing package. **Handling Suspension Package:**, includes, heavy-duty shock absorbers, rear springs and heavy-duty rear stabilizer bar. Fuel guard warning light. Power door locks. Heavy-duty electrical system. H78-14B/G70-14B/H70-14B tires. (white sidewall tires available).

NOTE: Colors offered on 1975 Rancheros were: White; Bright red; Dark red; black; Pastel blue; Bright Dark blue metallic; Light green-gold metallic; Light green; Saddle bronze metallic; Dark copper metallic; Dark yellow-green metallic; Medium Dark gold metallic and Pastel yellow. Color Glow paints were: green glow, ginger glow, tan glow and silver-blue glow were optional. Black, white, blue, green, brown or tan vinyl roofs were available.

BRONCO WAGON: — A heftier rear axle, revised exhaust system and fuel filler, higher riding height, and — late in the year — front disc brakes, were among "major" changes made on the 1975 Bronco 4x4. Other standard features included: Vinyl bucket seats. Floor-mounted T-bar transfer case control. Suspended foot pedals. Fresh air heater and defroster. Lockable glove compartment. Padded instrument panel. Two-speed electric windshield wipers. Sun visors. Vinyl-coated rubber floor mat. Fully-synchronized three-speed manual transmission. Full-length roof with fixed windows in the rear liftgate and on each side of the rear compartment.

I.D. DATA (Bronco): See F-100 I.D.

Model	Body Type	Price	Weight	Prod. Total
U-100	Wagon	4979	3490	11,273

ENGINE (Bronco): Displacement: 200 cu. in. Six-cylinder. 84 net horsepower at 3800 R.P.M. Bore & stroke: 3.68 in. x 3.13 in. Compression ratio: 8.3:1. 1-bbl. carburetor.

CHASSIS: Wheebase: 92 in. Overall length: 152.1 in. Overall width: 69.1 in. Overall height: 70.1 in. GVW: 4400-4900. Tires: E78 x 15.

POWERTRAIN OPTIONS: "302" V8. Cruise-O-Matic transmission.

CONVENIENCE OPTIONS: Extra-cooling V8 radiator. L-H remote control outside mirror. Knitted vinyl upholstery. Power steering. **Convenience Group:** includes, cigarette lighter, map light, inside 10 inch day/night rearview mirror and R-H chrome rearview mirror. Shoulder harness. Rear seat. Chrome bumper. Skid plates for standard fuel tank and transfer case. Inside tailgate mounted spare tire carrier (included with rear seat option). Exterior rear-mounted swing-away tire carrier. Bright metal wheel covers. High-flotation tires. Auxiliary 7.5 gallon fuel tank with skid plate. Manual radio and antenna. Bright bodyside and tailgate moldings. Bright metal rocker panel molding. Hand-operated throttle. **Sport Bronco Package:** includes, bright metal "Sport Bronco" emblem. Pleated parchment vinyl front seat. Vinyl door trim panels with bright metal moldings. Hardboard headlining with bright metal retainer moldings. Parchment vinyl front floor mat with bright metal retainers. Rear floor mat included with optional rear seat. Cigarette lighter. Horn ring. Bright metal drip rail moldings. Bright metal windshield and window frames. Bright metal grille molding and tailgate release handle. Bright headlight, side light, reflector and taillight bezels. Argent-painted grille with bright F-O-R-D letters. Chrome bumpers, front and rear. Chrome front bumper guards. Bright metal wheel covers (w/15 inch wheels only). 6.50 x 16-6PR "TT" tires. **Dealer-**

installed Accessories: Power-take-off (front-mounted). Warn free-running front hubs (manual or automatic). Snow plows. Snow plow angling kits. Front auxiliary air springs. Front-mounted winch. Trailer hitch. Trailer towing mirror. Locking gas cap. Front tow hooks. Compass. Fire extinguisher. Transmission oil cooler. Tach. 4600 lb. and 4900 lb. GVW packages. **Ranger Package:** includes, Argent silver grille, bucket seats, lower body-side stripes, fiberboard headliner, cut-pile carpeting front and rear, wheel covers, white power dome and white spare tire carrier. Reduced External Sound Package. **Northland Special option:** includes, single element 600 watt engine block heater, 50 percent (-30 degrees F) antifreeze, 70 amp.-hr. battery, 60-amp alternator and limited-slip rear axle.

ECONOLINE E-100 CARGO VAN: — These were the first of the "third generation" Econolines. The Ford name was now printed, in smaller letters, on the face of the longer hood. The higher, rectangular theme split level grille was bordered by slightly recessed round headlights on either end. The entire grille and headlight section was framed by bright trim. Parking lights were located directly above the bumper, under the headlights. The side marker lights were in the full-length concave bodyside "grooves". The 1975 Econolines also featured bodyon-frame construction, improved Twin-I-Beam front suspension, an 18 percent larger windshield, computer-selected front coil springs, wiper arm mounted windshield washer jets, molded and heavily insulated engine cover console and bolt-on front fenders. Among the standard features were: Full-foam driver's bucket seat. Color-keyed vinyl seat trim in black, blue, green or tan. Color-keyed seat belt. Color-keyed windshield trim moldings. Color-keyed engine cover with clipboard flashlight pocket and removable ash tray designed into console. Fresh air heater defroster. Fresh air vents with blend-air control. Two-speed electric windshield wipers. Energy-absorbing sun visor on driver's side. Front and cargo area dome lights. Front compartment hardboard headlining and insulated floor mat with scuff plates. Push-pull door lock buttons. Arm rest. Coat hook. Electric horn. Door checks. Latch release handles on side cargo doors. Argent bumpers. Argent hub caps. Bright windshield molding and mirrors.

ECONOLINE E-100 WINDOW VAN: — As the name suggests, the window van had glass all around. It shared standard features with the Cargo Van.

ECONOLINE E-100 DISPLAY VAN: — This model had windows at the rear and on the right-hand side. It came with the same standard features as the Cargo Van.

I.D. DATA (Econoline E-100): See F-100.

Model	Body Type	Price	Weight	Prod. Total
—	Cargo Van	3683	3940	Note 1
	Window Van	3769	3970	Note 1
	Display Van	3722	3955	Note 1

NOTE 1: See production data at end of E-350 model listing.
NOTE 2: Total Ford Van sales in the 1975 model year were 113,715.

ENGINE (Econoline E-100): Displacement: 300 cu. in. Six, 120 horsepower at 3400 R.P.M. Bore & stroke: 4.00 in. x 3.98 in. Compression ratio: 8.0:1. 1-bbl. carburetor.

ECONOLINE E-150 CARGO VAN: — This was the first year for this series. It had a slightly higher GVW rating than the E-100. Unlike the E-100, it could be operated on either leaded or unleaded gasoline. Standard features echoed those on the E-100.

ECONOLINE E-150 DISPLAY VAN: — This van shared styling with the E-100 Display Van, but had greater load capacity.

ECONOLINE E-150 WINDOW VAN: — This van shared styling with the E-100 Window Van, but had greater load capacity.

I.D. DATA (Econoline E-150): See F-100.

Model	Body Type	Price	Weight	Prod. Total
E-140	Cargo Van	3903	3945	Note 1
E-160	Display Van	3942	3960	Note1
E-150	Window Van	3989	3975	Note 1

NOTE 1: See production data at end of E-350 model listing.

ENGINE (Econoline E-150): Same as E-100.

ECONOLINE E-250 CARGO VAN: — The new E-250 had a higher GVW rating and heavier-duty front and rear axles than the E-150. It also came with eight-hole, rather than five-hole, wheels. Standard features were the same as those on the E-100.

ECONOLINE E-250 DISPLAY VAN: — This vehicle shared styling and features with the E-100, but had greater load capacity.

ECONOLINE E-250 WINDOW VAN: — This vehicle shared styling and features with the E-100 Display Van, but had greater load capacity.

ECONOLINE E-250 CUTAWAY VAN: — This van with Camper Special Packages was designed to readily accommodate custom motor homes.

ECONOLINE E-250 PARCEL DELIVERY: — This vehicle looked more like a typical delivery truck than a van. It was basically a cutaway chassis with a large cargo body added.

I.D. DATA (Econoline E-250): See F-100.

Model	Body Type	Price	Weight	Prod. Total
E-240	Cargo Van	4204	4340	Note 1
E-260	Display Van	4244	4355	Note 1
E-250	Window Van	4291	4370	Note 1
E-270	Cutaway Van	4294	3790	Note 1
E-280	Parcel Delivery	6265	5735	Note 1

NOTE: See production data at end of E-350 model listing.

ENGINE (Econoline E-250): Same as E-100.

ECONOLINE E-350 CARGO VAN: — This was the top-of-the-line Econoline. It had heavy-duty front and rear shocks and a greater load capacity than the other series. Standard features were the same as those on the E-100, plus automatic transmission.

ECONOLINE E-350 DISPLAY VAN: — See E-250 Display Van.

ECONOLINE E-350 WINDOW VAN: — See E-250 Window Van.

ECONOLINE E-350 CUTAWAY VAN: — See E-250 Cutaway Van.

ECONOLINE E-350 PARCEL DELIVERY: — See E-250 Parcel Delivery.

I.D. DATA (Econoline E-350): See F-100.

Model	Body Type	Price	Weight	Prod. Total
E-340	Cargo Van	4444	4520	Note 1
E-360	Display Van	4484	4535	Note 1
E-350	Window Van	4531	4550	Note 1
E-370	Cutaway Van	4400	3875	Note 1
E-380	Parcel Delivery	6265	5735	Note 1

NOTE: Ford records show the following production break-outs for 1975 Econolines: (89A-B Cargo Vans) 51,710; (89C-D Display Vans) 1,758; (89E-F Window Vans) 12,269; (Econoline type Cutaway/less Parcel Vans) 3,528; (Parcel Delivery Vans) 1,646. Ford also continued to produce the "P" series (Walk-in type) Parcel Delivery vans and built 467 of the P-350 model and 1,245 of the P-400 model during the 1975 model year.

ENGINE (Econoline E-350): Same as E-100.

CHASSIS: Wheelbase: 124 in. or 138 in. (158 in. available on Cutaway and Parcel Delivery) Overall width: 70.3 in. Overall length: 186.8 in. (with 124 inch wheelbase); or 206.8 in. (with 138 inch wheelbase). GVW: 5100-10,725 lbs. Tires: F78-15B PT (E-100); H78-15D (E-150); 8.00 x 16.5D TT (E-250); 8.75 x 16.5EC on Econoline Parcel Delivery. 9.50 x 16.5D TT (E-350); 8.00 x 16.5D dual rear on Econoline parcel delivery.

POWERTRAIN OPTIONS: Cruise-O-Matic transmission. "351" V8. "460" V8 (E-250/E-350).

CONVENIENCE OPTIONS: Custom Van: (in addition to or place of standard) color-keyed padded full-length instrument panel with wood grained vinyl applique; color-keyed seat pedestal, cowl-side trim panels, vinyl front door trim panels; insulated floor mats, roof rail garnish moldings, bright hub caps, taillight bezels, vent and rear window frames. **Chateau Van:** (has, in addition to or in place of Custom) Super Soft vinyl seat trim, color-keyed cut-pile carpeting on front floor and lower section of engine cover, padded vinyl front door trim panels with wood grained vinyl applique in center and carpeted lower panel, wood grained vinyl horn bar insert in steering wheel. Bright grille, bright bumpers, bright bodyside and rear moldings. Wheel covers. R-H sliding cargo door. Adjustable or flip-fold passenger seat. High output heater and defroster. Auxiliary hot water heater. Bright grille and/or front and rear bumpers. Full-length, insulated carpet or mat (138 inch wheelbase only). Courtesy light switches on front, or all, doors. Two-stage door positioners for hinged cargo doors. **Northland Special Package:** (includes engine block heater, -35 F antifreeze, 77 amp. hr. battery, 60 amp. alternator and high-output heater). Engine block heater. Locking fuel cap. Tinted glass. Full-length hardboard headlining. Dual electric horns. Insulation Package. Protection Group (front door edge guards and front and side sliding door stepwell pads). Interior rub rails (138 inch only). School Bus Package for 138 inch wheelbase Window Van. Cloth insert seat trim. Shoulder belts. Spare tire and wheel. Spare tire cover. Bright hub caps. Trailer Towing Package (for Class I, II, III and IV trailers). Front stabilizer bar. Captain's chair. Air conditioning. Power steering. Auxiliary fuel tank. Interval windshield wipers. Swing-out recreation mirrors. Swing-Lok low mount Western mirrors. AM radio. AM/FM stereo. AM/FM stereo with tape player. Door windows for rear and/or side cargo doors. One way glass in rear side windows and rear door. Flip-open windows for cargo doors. Job-engineered interior packages. **Low-Line Camper Package:** includes: 60 amp. alternator, 77 amp.-hr. battery, auxiliary 81 amp.-hr. battery, heavy-duty shocks (with E-250), Custom trim package, camper wiring harness, "Camper Special" emblem and extra-cooling package. **High-Line Camper Special Package:** includes: (basic package plus/or) 90 amp. alternator, adjustable passenger seat, external auxiliary oil cooler, fuel monitor warning light and ammeter and oil pressure gauge, front stabilizer bar, dual horns, 351 cubic inch V8, Chateau trim package, high-output heater, power steering, tinted windshield and glass.

NOTE: Econoline colors for 1975 included: Wimbledon white; Candy Apple red; Brook blue Metallic; Wind blue; Hatteras green Metallic; Baytree green; Glen green; Hot Ginger Metallic; Vineyard gold; Parrot orange; Autumn tan and Chrome yellow. Medium Green Glow and Medium Ginger Glow were optional. Five separate and distinctive Tu-Tone paint schemes were available.

E-100 CLUB WAGON: — The new E-100 Club wagon shared the Econoline Vans' styling and other changes. It was offered in five- or eight-passenger versions. Among the standard features were: Full foam front bucket seats. Color-keyed patterned vinyl seat trim in black, blue, green or tan. Seat belts. Color-keyed windshield trim moldings. Fresh air heater/defroster. Fresh air vents with blend-air control. Two-speed electric windshield wipers. Wiper arm mounted washer jets. Sun visors. Rearview mirror. Dome lights. Front compartment hardboard headlining and insulated floor mat with scuff plates. Push-pull door lock buttons. Arm rests. Coat hook. Electric horns. Door checks. Flip-open windows in sliding door and opposite windows. Argent bumpers and hub caps. Bright windshield moldings. Outside rearview mirrors.

E-150 CLUB WAGON: — This was a slightly heavier-duty version of the E-100. It had a longer (138 inch) wheelbase and was also offered in five- and eight-passenger versions. Standard features were same as those on the E-100.

E-250 CLUB WAGON: — The E-250 Club Wagon could be had with five-, eight-, or twelve-passenger capacity packages. It had most of the same features as the E-100.

I.D. DATA (Club Wagon): See F-100.

Model	Body Type	Price	Weight	Prod. Total
E-100	Club Wagon	4446	4225	Note 1
E-150	Club Wagon	4340	4340	Note 1
E-250	Club Wagon	5004	4690	Note 1

NOTE 1: Ford records show the following production break-outs for 1975 Econoline Club Wagons: (82A Standard) 3,656; (82B Custom) 4,767 and (82C Chateau) 9,008.

ENGINE (Club Wagon): Same as E-100 Econoline (E-100 and E-150). Displacement: 351 cu. in. V8. Net horsepower 143 at 3600 R.P.M. Bore & Stroke: 4.00 in. x 3.50 in. Compression ratio: 8.2:1. 2-bbl carburetor (E-250).

CHASSIS: Wheelbase: 124 in. (E-100); 138 in. (E-150/E-250). Overall width: 70.3 in. Overall length: See Econoline. GVW: 5600-5900 lbs. (E-100); 6050-6300 lbs. (E-150); 7100-8550 lbs. (E-250). Tires: G78-15B (E-100); G78-15D (E-150); 8.00 x 16.5D (E-250).

POWERTRAIN OPTIONS: "351" V8. "460" V8. SelectShift Cruise-O-Matic automatic transmission.

CONVENIENCE OPTIONS: Auxiliary fuel tank. Speed control. Power steering. Captain's chair. AM radio. AM/FM stereo radio. AM/FM stereo with tape player. High-capacity air conditioner. One-way glass. Wheel covers. Swing-Lok western mirrors. Swing-Lok low-mount western mirrors. Bright non-telescopic mirrors. Swing-out recreation mirrors. High-output heater/defroster. Auxiliary hot water heater. Bright grille and/or bumpers. Full-length insulated floor mat. Courtesy light switches for all doors. Hinged side doors in place of sliding door. Two-stage door positioners for all hinged double doors. Locking gas cap. Intermittent two-speed windshield wipers. **Instrument Package:** includes, fuel monitor warning light, ammeter and oil pressure gauge. Northland Special Package. Engine block heater. Tinted glass. Full-length hardboard headlining. Insulation package. **Protection Group:** includes, front door edge guards and front and side sliding door step well pads). Shoulder harness. Spare tire cover. Bright hub caps. Low-Line Camper Package. High-Line Camper Special Package. Light-, heavy- and extra-heavy-duty trailer Towing packages. **Custom Package:** includes, (in addition to or in place of standard) color-keyed, padded, full-length instrument panel with wood grained vinyl applique; color-keyed seat pedestal, cowl trim panels and padded vinyl door trim panels; cigarette lighter. Insulated full-length floor mats. Window garnish moldings, color-keyed armrests on three- and four-passenger seats, three coat hooks, aluminum scuff plates on side and rear doors, bright hub caps, taillight bezels and window frames. **Chateau Package:** has (in addition to or in place of Custom) Super Soft vinyl seat trim, color-keyed cut-pile carpeting on full-length of floor, lower section of engine cover and rear wheel wells; vinyl door trim panels with wood grained vinyl applique in center and carpeted lower section, color-keyed vinyl headlining (insulated), wood-grained vinyl horn bar insert, color-keyed vinyl spare tire cover; bright grille, bumpers, lower bodyside and rear moldings.

NOTE: Standard Club Wagon colors for 1975 were: Wimbledon white; Candy Apple red; Brook blue Metallic; Wind blue; Hatteras green metallic; Baytree green; Glen green; Hot Ginger metallic; Vineyard gold; Parrot orange; Autumn tan and Chrome yellow. Custom and Chateau colors were: Brook blue metallic; Hatteras green metallic; Autumn tan; Chrome yellow and Wimbledon white. Medium Green Glow and Medium Ginger Glow were optional on Standard, Custom and Chateau Club Wagons. Five Tu-Tone paint schemes were available.

COURIER PICKUP: — Styling was unchanged for 1975. Standard features included: Biscuit-pattern, full-width vinyl upholstered seat (in black or light beige). Padded instrument panel with ammeter, fuel and temperature gauges and oil pressure warning light. Cigarette lighter. Inside hood release. Tool kit. Beige vinyl headliner. Armrests. Six-leaf rear springs. Cylindrical double-acting shock absorbers. Independent front suspension.

I.D. DATA (Courier): —

Model	Body Type	Price	Weight	Prod. Total
—	Pickup	3146	2510	56,073

ENGINE (Courier): Displacement: 110 cu. in. OHC. Four-cylinder.

CHASSIS: Wheelbase: 104.3 in. Overall length: 172 in. Overall height: 61.6 in. Overall width: 61.6 in. GVW Rating: 3,955 lbs. Tires: 6.00 x 14.

POWERTRAIN OPTIONS: Automatic tranmission with floor-mounted T-bar handle.

CONVENIENCE OPTIONS: Push-button AM radio. Pickup box cover. Deluxe pickup box cover (includes dome light, tinted side windows and wood grain side stripe). Full wheel covers. Bright-framed 6x9 in. swing-lock western mirrors. Argent painted rear step bumper. Tinted glass. Dress-up Package: bright bodyside protective molding with black vinyl insert, bright front bumper guards with rubber inserts, bright molding around windshield and back window and bright drip molding. Air conditioner.

NOTE: The 1975 Courier was available in six exterior colors: red, blue, green, yellow, white and tan.

F-100 CUSTOM PICKUP: — Exterior styling remained unchanged for 1975. Once again, buyers had their choice of Flareside or Styleside boxes. Regular or Super cabs were available. The latter made for 44 cubic feet of cargo space behind the front seat. Standard F-100 features included: Deluxe fresh air heater/defroster (high-output heater with Super Cab). Energy-absorbing sunvisors and instrument panel padding. Instrument cluster with green backlighting. Keyless locking doors. Color-keyed molded door panels with integral armrests and paddle-type door handles. Seat belts. Windshield washers. Two-speed electric windshield wipers. Dome light with door courtesy light switches. Ash tray. Large glove compartment with push-button latch. Sponge-grain headlining. Black rubber floor mat. Door scuff plates. Black, red, blue or green vinyl seat trim. 10 inch day/night rearview mirror. L-H and R-H bright metal exterior mirrors. Taillights with integral stop, turn, backup lights and reflector. Hub caps (except 4x4s without full-time drive). Three-speed manual transmission.

I.D. DATA (F-100): See 1971 F-100 I.D.

Model	Body Type	Price	Weight	Prod. Total
F-100	(81) Chassis w/Cab	3487	3135	Note 1
F-100	Chassis w/Super Cab	4079	3505	Note 1
F-100	Flareside Pickup 6¾'	3640	3490	Note 1
F-100	Styleside Pickup 6¾'	3640	3490	Note 1
F-100	Flareside Pickup 8'	3676	3570	Note 1
F-100	Styleside Pickup 8'	3676	3570	Note 1
F-100	SuperCab Pickup 6¾'	4233	3860	Note 1
F-100	SuperCab Pickup 8'	4229	3765	Note 1

NOTE 1: Ford records show the following F-100 production break-outs: **4x2** (Cab Pickup) 173,965; (Supercab Pickup) 16,792. **4x4** (Cab Pickup) 37,297.

ENGINE (F-100): Displacement: 300 cu. in. Six-cylinder. 120 horsepower at 3400 R.P.M. Bore & stroke: 4.00 x 3.98 in. Compression ratio: 8.0:1. One-barrel carburetor.

F-150 CUSTOM PICKUP: — This new series was basically just a slightly heavier-duty version of the F-100. It came with heftier front axle and rear springs. Regular cab models were only available on the 133 inch wheelbase and could carry a payload of 2275 lbs. Super Cab versions were offered on 139/155 inch wheelbases. Standard features were the same as those on the F-100, plus power brakes. Both Flareside and Styleside boxes were available.

I.D. DATA (F-150): See F-100 I.D.

Model	Body Type	Price	Weight	Prod. Total
F-150	(81) Chassis w/Cab	3849	3350	Note 1
F-150	Flareside Pickup	4002	3770	Note 1
F-150	Styleside Pickup	4002	3770	Note 1
F-150	SuperCab Pickup 133"	4541	3925	Note 1
F-150	SuperCab Pickup 155"	4644	4005	Note 1
F-150	Chassis & SuperCab	4387	3570	Note 1

NOTE 1: Ford records show the following F-150 production breakouts: (Cab Pickup) 80,917; (Supercab Pickup) 20,958. These records do not indicate any 4x4 production of F-150s.

ENGINE (F-150): See F-100.

F-250 CUSTOM PICKUP: — The F-250 had most of the same features as the F-100. It, too, was offered with regular or Super cabs and with Flareside or Styleside boxes. Power brakes and a three-speed manual transmission were standard.

I.D. DATA (F-250): See F-100 I.D.

Model	Body Type	Price	Weight	Prod. Total
F-250	(81) Chassis w/Cab	3946	3495	Note 1
F-250	Flareside Pickup	4099	3915	Note 1
F-250	Styleside Pickup	4099	3915	Note 1
F-250	SuperCab Pickup	4603	4035	Note 1
F-250	SuperCab Chassis	4449	3680	Note 1

NOTE 1: Ford records show the following F-250 production break-outs: **4x2** (Cab Pickup) 86,106; (SuperCab Pickup) 29,622. **4x4** (Cab Pickup) 47,226.

ENGINE (F-250): Displacement: 300 cu. in. Six-cylinder. 120 net horsepower at 3400 R.P.M. Bore & stroke: 4.00 x 3.98 in. Compression ratio: 8.0:1. One-barrel carburetor. Super Cab had "360" V8.

F-350 CUSTOM PICKUP: The F-350 pickup was only offered with the Styleside box. However, there were three choices of cabs: regular, Super, or Crew. Front only shocks, (front and rear with Super Cab) a four-speed manual transmission and power brakes were standard.

F-350 PLATFORM/STAKE: — Two lengths of one ton F-350 Platform/stakes were available: nine-foot and 12-foot. Floor frames of the Platform/Stake were made of steel cross sills riveted to steel side rails. Floorboards were interlocked with steel brackets. Formed steel caps covered ends of body sills. Side boards were hardwood and stakes were steel. A four-speed manual tranmission was standard.

I.D. DATA (F-350): See F-100 I.D.

Model	Body Type	Price	Weight	Prod. Total
F-350	(81) Chassis w/Cab	4089	3795	Note 1
F-350	Styleside Pickup	4519	4535	Note 1
F-350	SuperCab Pickup	4997	4525	Note 1
F-350	(80) 9-ft. Stake	—	4620	Note 1
F-350	Crew Cab Pickup	5063	4730	Note 1
F-350	(80) 12-ft. Stake	—	—	Note 1
F-350	Chassis w/Crew	4902	4290	Note 1
F-350	(86) 9-ft. Platform	—	4380	Note 1
F-350	(86) 12-ft. Platform	—	—	Note 1

NOTE 1: Ford records show the following F-350 production break-outs: (Cab Pickup) 41,616; (SuperCab Pickup) 2,816.

ENGINE (F-350): Same as F-250 for Platform, Stake and Chassis-Cab. Pickups had the 360 cubic inch V8 as standard equipment.

CHASSIS: Wheelbase: 117 in. (F-100); 133 in. (F-100/F-250); 139 in. (F-100/F-250 SuperCab); 140 in. (F-350); 137 in. (F-350 Platform/Stake); 155 in. (SuperCab); 161 in. (F-350 Platform/Stake). GVW (in pounds): 4650-5500 (F-100); 6050 (F-150); 6200-8100 (F-250); 8350-10,000 (F-350). Tires: G78-15B (F-100); L78-15D (F-150); 8.00 x 16.5D (F-250); 8.75 x 16.5E (F-350).

POWERTRAIN OPTIONS: V8 engines: (F-100) ''302'' (Others) ''360/390/460'' V8. Four-speed manual Cruise-O-Matic transmissions.

CONVENIENCE OPTIONS: Four-wheel-drive (F-100/F-250). Pickup box cover: (standard) has fiberglass construction, tinted side and rear windows, roof vent, T-handle locking rear liftgate and rubber cushioned tie-downs; (Deluxe) has sliding side windows with screens, bright side and rear window moldings, interior dome light, color-keyed two-tone paint. Knitted vinyl seat trim. Heavy-duty black vinyl seat trim. Speed control. Vinyl insert bodyside molding. Folding bench or jump seats (Super Cab). AM/FM stereo radio. AM radio. Intermittent windshield wipers. **Camper Special:** includes, front and rear stabilizer bars; automatic transmission; extra-cooling package; low fuel economy warning light; power front disc brakes; 55 amp. alternator; 70 amp.-hr. battery; oil pressure gauge and ammeter; bright western mirrors; dual horns; heavy-duty rear shocks; camper wiring harness. Rear step bumper. Western style mirrors. Sliding rear cab window. Concealed spare tire and wheel. Auxiliary 12-volt 70 amp.-hr. battery. Air conditioner. Flip open rear side window (Super Cab). Black or white texture painted roof (included bright drip rail molding). Full wheel covers. Mag style covers. Dual tape stripes. Bright tie-down hooks. Super-cooling package. Slide-out spare tire carrier. Tool stowage box with locking door. **Convenience Group:** includes, cargo, engine, glove compartment, two courtesy and ash tray lights; glove compartment door lock. Door map pockets and 12 inch day/night mirror. **Northland Special Package:** includes, engine block heater, 50 percent (-30 degree F) antifreeze; 70 amp.-hr. battery, 55 amp. alternator and limited-slip rear axle. Power steering. Power front disc brakes (4x2s). High output heater. Trailer towing packages. Ammeter and oil pressure gauge. Bright hub caps. Bright contour rear bumper for Stylesides. Painted channel rear bumper for Flaresides. Tinted glass all around. Frame-anchored camper tie-down system. Heavy-duty 50-amp camper wiring harness. **Ranger Package:** includes, (in addition to or in place of Custom features) color-keyed super soft vinyl seat upholstery in black, red (not w/Super Cab), blue, green or ginger; instrument panel molding with black accent; shoulder-high vinyl bolster around rear area (Super Cab); color-keyed door panels with bright moldings; additional insulation; perforated headlining (insulated) with bright molding; color-keyed vinyl nylon carpeting; two courtesy lights; cigarette lighter; bright windshield, rear window and roof drip moldings; bright rocker panel and wheel lip moldings; bright hub caps (except 4x4 option and dual rear wheel units); Styleside pickups included bright side body moldings with vinyl insert, tailgate moldings (top and bottom), tail-light bezels. (Note: Ranger trim not available on Crew Cab). **Ranger XLT:** (in addition to or in place of Ranger items) deluxe color-keyed, long wearing cloth with vinyl trim seat upholstery; color-keyed pleated vinyl upper door panel with simulated woodgrain accented moldings and map pocket, lower panels color-keyed wall to wall cut-pile nylon carpeting; bright instrument panel molding with simulated woodgrain insert; bright seat-pivot covers; additional insulation; bright wheel covers convenience group; color-keyed vinyl headlining (with special insulation) and sunvisors. On Styleside pickups included bright tailgate applique panel and molding. Aluminum tailgate applique panel.

CUSTOM DECOR GROUP: — (For Regular and Super Cab pickups), includes: knitted vinyl seat trim in black, red, blue, green or ginger; color-keyed floor mats with insulation; bright moldings around windshield and rear window; bright drip rail moldings and bright hub caps (except F-100 4x4s).

NOTE: Standard colors for 1975 included: Wimbledon white; Vineyard gold; Viking red; Baytree green; Hatteras green metallic; Glen green; Candy Apple red; Parrot orange; Raven black; Wind blue; Bahama blue; Midnight blue metallic; Sequoia brown metallic and Chrome yellow. New Ginger Glow and Medium Green Glow colors were optional. Different two-tones could be obtained by using all the standard colors except Chrome Yellow. Wimbledon White could be used as the accent color for any color. TWO-TONES: Regular: accent color was applied to the roof and upper back panel with a belt line molding around back of cab. Deluxe; (Stylesides only) accent color was applied to the area below the bodyside and lower tailgate moldings which were included in this option. Combination: (Stylesides only) regular and deluxe two-tone options were combined with the accent color applied as specified for these two options. White Bodyside Accent Panel: (Stylesides only) with all body colors except White on Ranger and Ranger XLT, and with regular two-tone White accent.

390

PRODUCTION NOTE: 1975 model year Ford light conventional truck sales totaled 448,081.

Pricing

1975	5	4	3	2	1
Courier					
Pickup	450	900	1500	2100	3000
Ranchero					
500 Pickup	830	1650	2750	3850	5500
GT pickup	850	1700	2850	4000	5700
Squire Pickup	890	1770	2950	4150	5900
Bronco					
Wagon	850	1700	2850	4000	5700
Econoline E-100					
Cargo Van	440	870	1450	2050	2900
Window Van	470	950	1550	2200	3100
Display Van	500	1000	1650	2300	3300
Club Wagon	570	1140	1900	2650	3800
Custom Club Wagon	600	1200	2000	2800	4000
Chateau Club Wagon	630	1250	2100	3000	4200
Econoline E-200					
Cargo Van	400	800	1350	1900	2700
Window Van	440	870	1450	2050	2900
Display Van	470	950	1550	2200	3100
Econoline E-300					
Cargo Van	390	780	1300	1800	2600
Window Van	420	840	1400	1950	2800
Display Van	450	900	1500	2100	3000
F-100 — (½-Ton)					
Flareside Pickup	720	1450	2400	3300	4800
Styleside Pickup	740	1470	2450	3350	4900
Super Cab Pickup	750	1500	2500	3500	5000
F-250 — (¾-Ton)					
Flareside Pickup	690	1380	2300	3200	4600
Styleside Pickup	700	1400	2350	3250	4700
Super Cab	720	1450	2400	3300	4800
F-350 — (1-Ton)					
Pickup	690	1380	2300	3200	4600
Crew Cab Pickup	660	1320	2200	3100	4400
Stake	630	1250	2100	3000	4200

1976 FORD

1976 Ford Ranchero Sport Pickup (JAG)

RANCHERO 500 PICKUP: — Aside from modifications to the engines (to improve fuel economy), and some different upholstery, the '76 Ranchero was pretty much the same as the previous year's model. Standard features included: Vinyl upholstery and door trim. Panels with bright trim. Color keyed steering wheel and column. Deep-pile carpeting. Hi-level, flow-through ventilation. Ventless door windows. Energy-absorbing steering column. Padded steering wheel hub. Lockable glove box. Locking steering column. Fresh-air heater defroster. Trim panel behind the split-back seat. Vinyl headliner. Color-keyed seat belts with outboard retractors and shoulder harnesses (also center passenger seat belts). Armrests with recessed door handles. Vinyl-framed day/night mirror. Cigarette lighter. Padded, color-keyed instrument panel. Emergency lamp flasher. Spare tire and tool compartment. Bright grille with moldings. Bright energy absorbing front bumper. Bright left-hand mirror with remote control. Hidden windshield wipers. Bright metal windshield, rear window, drip rail and top of cargo body moldings. Bright metal hub caps. Power steering. Power brakes. Cruise-O-Matic automatic.

RANCHERO GT PICKUP: — The GT had (in addition to or in place of the Ranchero 500 features): Color-keyed bodyside stripe. Sport style mirrors painted body colors both with remote controls. Black hub caps with bright trim rings. Lettered belted tires. GT grille crest. Spare tire and tool compartment cover. Bright trim on pedals. GT instrument panel plaque.

RANCHERO SQUIRE PICKUP: — The Squire had (in addition to or in place of Ranchero 500 features): Deluxe bright wheel covers. Simulated woodgrain panels on sides and tailgate. Ranchero Squire script on front fenders. Squire crest on grille. Woodtone panel around instruments. Electric clock. Spare tire and tool compartment cover. Bright trim on pedals. Squire instrument panel plaque.

I.D. DATA (Ranchero): See 1960 Ranchero I.D.

Model	Body Type	Price	Weight	Prod. Total
97D	Pickup (500)	4315	3915	9958
97R	Pickup (GT)	4649	3980	4942
97K	Pickup (Squire)	4668	3940	1172

ENGINE (Ranchero): 351 M (modified) V8, 148 net horsepower at 3800 R.P.M. Bore & stroke: 4 x 3.5 in. Compression ratio: 8.0:1. 2-bbl. carburetor.

CHASSIS: Wheelbase: 118 in. Overall length: 218.3 in. GVW: 5,480-5,950. Tires HR78-14B steel belted radial ply (G70-14B white-lettered on GT).

POWERTRAIN OPTIONS: ''351'' V8. ''400'' V8. ''460'' V8.

CONVENIENCE OPTIONS: Performance Cluster: tachometer, trip odometer, clock, ammeter, water temperature and oil pressure gauges (also includes heavy-duty battery). SelectAire Conditioner with automatic temperature control. SelectAire conditioner. Power steering. **Protection Group (Bumpers):** front and rear bumper guards, front bumper rubber inserts. **Protection Group (Appearance):** spare tire lock, floor mats, license plate frame and door edge guards. Vinyl insert bodyside molding. Anti-theft alarm system. Power side windows. Tilt steering wheel. Cruise control. **Convenience Group:** right and left remote control mirrors, interval windshield wipers, automatic parking brake release, vanity mirror. Restraint system. **Brougham Decor Group:** split bench seat with supersoft vinyl or knit cloth upholstery for the standard seat in Ranchero 500 and Squire. Bucket seats. Vinyl roof. Power brakes. AM radio. 15-inch wheels. Luxury wheel covers. Hub caps with trim rings. Mag style wheels. Tinted glass. Electric clock. Dual sport style mirrors. **Light Group:** ash tray, underhood and glove box lights: parking brake warning light lights-on warning buzzer: illuminated light switch. Class II (2000-3500 lb) or Class III (3500-6000 lb) trailer towing package. **Handling Suspension Package:** Heavy-duty shock absorbers, rear springs and heavy-duty rear stabilizer bar. Fuel guard warning light. Power door locks. Heavy-duty electrical system. H78-14B, G70-14B, H70-14B tires. WSW available. Power seat. **Explorer Package:** broadcloth interior (vinyl optional), sports wheel covers, vinyl roof, WSW tires, white side stripe, and hood ornament.

NOTE: Colors offered on 1976 Rancheros were: White, bright red, dark red, black, light blue, bright dark blue metallic, silver metallic, light green, saddle bronze metallic, dark brown metallic, dark yellow-green metallic, tan, pastel yellow. Color glow paints; green glow, tan glow and silver-blue glow were optional. Black, white, blue, green, brown or tan vinyl roofs were available.

BRONCO WAGON: — Standard features on the four-wheel-drive 1976 Bronco included: Mono-Beam front suspension. Solid state ignition. Front disc brakes. Variable ratio parking brake control. Vinyl bucket seat (driver's only). Floor mounted T-bar transfer case control. Suspended foot pedals. Double-acting shock absorbers. Fresh air heater and defroster. Lockable glove compartment. Padded instrument panel. Two-speed electric windshield wipers. Sunvisors. Vinyl-coated rubber floor mat. Fully synchronized three-speed manual. Full-length roof with fixed windows in the rear liftgate and on each side of the rear compartment. Dome light. Painted channel-type steel bumpers.

I.D. DATA (Bronco): See F-100 I.D.

Model	Body Type	Price	Weight	Prod. Total
U-100	Wagon	5078	3490	13,625

ENGINE (Bronco): Displacement: 200 cu. in. Six, 84 net horsepower at 3800 R.P.M. Bore & stroke: 3.68 x 3.13. Compression ratio: 8.3:1. 1-bbl. carburetor.

CHASSIS: Wheelbase: 92 in. Overall length: 152.1 in. Overall width: 69.1 in. Overall height: 70.1 in. GVW: 4400-4900. Tires: E78-15.

POWERTRAIN OPTIONS: ''302'' V8. Cruise-O-Matic automatic transmission.

CONVENIENCE OPTIONS: Extra cooling V8 radiator. LH remote control outside mirror. Passenger front bucket seat. Heavy-duty shocks. Power steering. **Convenience Group:** cigarette lighter, map light, inside 10 inch day/night rear view mirror. RH chrome rearview mirror. Shoulder harness. Rear seat. Chrome bumper with chrome front guards. Skid plates for fuel tank and transfer case, 600 watt single element engine block heater. Dual horns. Exterior rear-mounted swing+away tire carrier. Bright metal wheel covers. High-flotation tires. Auxiliary 7.5 gallon fuel tank with skid plate. Manual radio and antenna. Bright bodyside and tailgate moldings. Bright metal rocker panel molding. Hand operated throttle.

SPORT BRONCO PACKAGE: — Right-hand front seat and sunvisor. Vinyl door trim panels with bright metal moldings. Hardboard headlining with bright metal retainer moldings. Steering wheel with woodtone horn pad. Vinyl front and rear floor mats with bright metal retainers. Cigarette lighter. Horn ring. Bright metal drip rail moldings. Bright metal windshield and window frames. Bright metal grille molding and tailgate release handle. Bright headlight, side light, reflector and taillight bezels. Argent-painted grille with bright F-O-R-D letters. Chrome bumpers, front and rear. Chrome front bumper guards. Bright metal wheel covers.

DEALER INSTALLED ACCESSORIES: — Power take-off (front mounted). Warn free-running front hubs (manual or automatic). Snowplows. Snowplow angling kits. Front auxiliary air springs. Front mounted winch. Trailer hitch. Trailer towing mirror. Locking gas cap. Front tow hooks. Compass. Fire extinguisher. Transmission oil cooler. Tach. 4600 lb. GVW Package: rear springs rated at 1240 lbs., E78-15B tires (requires rear bench seat and RH front seat). **4900 GVW Package:** rear springs rated at 1475 lbs., G78-15 B tires. Reduced External Sound Package: **Northland Special:** single element 600 watt engine block heater, 50 percent (-30 degrees F)

antifreeze, 70 amp hr battery, 60-amp alternator and limited-slip rear axle.
Ranger Package: Color-keyed full carpeting (including tailgate and wheel-housings). Color-keyed vinyl door trim panels with burl woodtone accept. Color-keyed vinyl trim with insulation on rear quarter panels. Cloth and vinyl seat trim in tan, blue or green. Color-keyed instrument panel paint. Hood and lower bodyside tape stripes, white stripe with orange accent. Swing-away spare tire carrier. Spare tire cover, white vinyl with orange accent and Bronco insignia. Coat hook. **Special Decor Group:** (available on standard and Sport Bronco) Black grille. Solid exterior colors (white roof is available). Color-keyed tape stripe across hood and along upper body sides. Bright wheel covers. Bright windshield and window frames.

NOTE: Bronco color choices in 1976 were: Wimbledon white, castillo red, candyapple red, midnight blue metallic, bahama blue, bali blue, hatteras green metallic, glen green, dark jade metallic, silver metallic, indio tan, copper metallic, mecca gold, cayan red, raven black, chrome yellow. Glamour color paints: Ginger glow and medium green glow were optional. Bronco roofs were painted Wimbledon white when a two-tone was desired.

ECONOLINE E-100 CARGO VAN: — Econolines were basically unchanged for 1976. Power brakes and a three-speed manual transmission were standard. Other standard features were: Full-foam driver's bucket seat. Color-keyed vinyl seat trim in black, blue, green or tan. Color-keyed seat belt. Color-keyed windshield trim moldings. Color-keyed engine cover with clipboard flashlight pocket and removable ash tray designed into console. Fresh air heater defroster. Fresh air vents with blend air control. Two-speed electric windshield wipers. Energy absorbing sunvisor on driver's side. Front and cargo area dome lights. Front compartment hardboard headlining and insulated floor mat with scuff plates. Push-pull door lock buttons. Armrest. Coat hook. Electric horn. Door checks. Latch release handles on side cargo doors. Argent bumpers. Argent hub caps. Bright windshield molding and mirrors.

ECONOLINE E-100 WINDOW VAN: — As the name suggests, the window van had glass all around. It shared standard features with the cargo van.

ECONOLINE E-100 DISPLAY VAN: — This model had windows at the rear and on the right hand side. It came with the same standard features as Cargo Van.

I.D. DATA (Econoline E-100): See F-100.

Model	Body Type	Price	Weight	Prod. Total
E-040	Cargo Van	3882	3890	Note
E-050	Window Van	3968	3915	Note
E-060	Display Van	3921	3905	Note

NOTE: Total Ford van sales in the 1976 model year was 179,820.

ENGINE (Econoline E-100): Displacement: 300 cu. in. Six, 120 horsepower at 3400 R.P.M. Bore & stroke: 4.00 x 3.98. Compression ratio: 8.0:1. 1-bbl. carburetor.

ECONOLINE E-150 CARGO VAN: — This was the second year for this series. It had a slightly higher GVW rating than the E-100. Unlike the E-100, it could be operated on either leaded or unleaded gasoline. Standard features echoed those on the E-100.

ECONOLINE E-150 DISPLAY VAN: — This van shared styling with the E-100 Display Van but had greater load capacity.

ECONOLINE E-150 WINDOW VAN: — This van shared styling with the E-100 Window Van, but had greater load capacity.

I.D. DATA (Econoline E-150): See F-100.

Model	Body Type	Price	Weight	Prod. Total
E-140	Cargo Van	4064	3850	Note
E-160	Display Van	4103	3865	Note
E-150	Window Van	4150	3875	Note

NOTE: See E-100.

ENGINE (Econoline E-150): Same as E-100.

ECONOLINE E-250 CARGO VAN: — The new E-250 had a higher GVW rating and more heavy duty front and rear axles, than the E-150. It also came with eight, rather than five, hole wheels. Standard features were the same as those on the E-100.

ECONOLINE E-250 DISPLAY VAN: — This vehicle shared styling and features with the E-100, but had greater load capacity.

ECONOLINE E-250 WINDOW VAN: — This vehicle shared styling and features with the E-100 Window Van, but had greater load capacity.

ECONOLINE E-250 CUTAWAY VAN: — This van with Camper Special Packages was designed to readily accommodate custom motor homes.

ECONOLINE E-250 PARCEL DELIVERY: — This vehicle looked more like a typical delivery truck than a van. It was basically a cutaway chassis with a large cargo body added.

I.D. DATA (Econoline E-250): See F-100.

Model	Body Type	Price	Weight	Prod. Total
E-240	Cargo Van	4360	4380	Note
E-260	Display Van	4400	4395	Note
E-250	Window Van	4447	4410	Note
E-270	Cutaway Van	4154	3950	Note
E-280	Parcel Delivery	6129	5405	Note

NOTE: See E-100.

ENGINE (Econoline E-250): Same as E-100.

ECONOLINE E-350 CARGO VAN: — This was the Top of the line Econoline. It had heavy-duty front and rear shocks and a greater load capacity than the other series. Standard features were the same as those on the E-100.

ECONOLINE E-350 DISPLAY VAN: — See E-250 Display Van.

ECONOLINE E-350 WINDOW VAN: — See E-250 Window Van.

ECONOLINE E-350 CUTAWAY VAN: — See E-250 Cutaway Van.

ECONOLINE F-350 PARCEL DELIVERY: — See E-250 Parcel Delivery.

I.D. DATA (Econoline E-350): See F-100.

Model	Body Type	Price	Weight	Prod. Total
E-340	Cargo Van	4543	4545	Note
E-360	Display Van	4583	4560	Note
E-350	Window Van	4630	4575	Note
E-370	Cutaway Van	4259	3995	Note
E-380	Parcel Delivery	6538	5715	Note

NOTE: See E-100.

ENGINE: (Econoline E-350): Same as E-100.

CHASSIS: Wheelbase: 124 in. or 138 in. (158 in. available on Cutaway and Parcel Delivery) Overall Width: 70.3 in. Overall length: 186.8 in. (124 in. wb), 206.8 in. (138 in. wb), GVW: 5100-10,725. Tires: F78-15B PT (E-100) H78-15D PT (E-150) 8.00 x 16.5D TT (E-250, 8.75 x 16.5E C on PDV) 9.50 x 16.5D TT (E-350, 8.00 x 16.5D dual rear on PDV)

POWERTRAIN OPTIONS: Cruise-O-Matic automatic. 351 V8, 460 V8 (E-250, E-350).

CONVENIENCE OPTIONS: Custom Van: (in addition to or in place of standard) color-keyed padded full-length instrument panel with wood grained vinyl applique; color-keyed seat pedestal, cowl-side trim panels, vinyl front door trim panels; insulated floor mats, roof rail garnish moldings, bright hub caps, taillight bezels, vent and rear window frames. **Chateau Van:** (in addition to or in place of Custom) Super Soft finyl seat trim, color-keyed cut pile carpeting on front floor and lower section of engine cover, padded vinyl front door trim panels with woodgrained vinyl applique in center and carpeted lower panel, woodgrained vinyl horn bar insert in steering wheel. Bright grille, bright bumpers, bright bodyside and rear moldings. Wheel covers. RH sliding cargo door. Adjustable or flip-fold passenger seat. High output heater and defroster. Auxiliary hot water heater. Bright grille and/or front and rear bumpers. Full length, insulated carpet or mat (138 in. wb only). Courtesy light switches, front or all doors. Two stage door positioners for hinged cargo doors. Northland Special Package (includes engine block heater -35 F anti-freeze, 77 amp hr battery, 60 amp alternator and high output heater). Engine block heater. Locking fuel cap. Tinted glass. Full length hardboard headlining. Dual electric horns. Insulation Package. Protection Group (front door edge guards and front and side sliding door stepwell pads). Interior rub rails (138 in. only). School Bus Package for 138 in. wb Window Van. Cloth insert seat trim. Shoulder harness. Spare tire and wheel. Spare tire cover. Bright hub caps. Trailer Towing Package (for Class I, II, III and IV trailers). Front stabilizer bar. Captains chair. Air conditioning. Power steering. Auxiliary fuel tank. Interval windshield wipers. Swing lok western mirrors. Swingout recreation mirrors. Swing-Lok low mount Western mirrors. AM radio. AM/FM stereo. AM/FM stereo with tape player. Door windows for rear and/or side cargo doors. One way glass in side windows and rear door. Flip-open windows for cargo doors. Job-engineered interior packages. **Low Line Camper Package:** 60 amp alternator, 77 amp-hr battery, auxiliary 81 amp-hr battery, heavy-duty shocks (with E-250), Custom trim package, camper wiring harness, ''Camper Special'' emblem, extra cooling package. **High Line Camper Special Package:** (basic package plus/or) 90 amp alternator, adjustable passenger seat, external auxiliary oil cooler, fuel monitor warning light and ammeter and oil pressure gauge, front stablizier bar, dual horns, 351 V8, Chateau trim package, high output heater, power steering, tinted windshield and glass.

NOTE: Econoline colors for 1976 included: Wimbledon White, Candyapple Red, Brook Blue Metallic, Bali Blue, Hatteras Green Metallic, Silver Metallic, Glen Green, Copper Metallic, Peppertree Red, Harness Tan, Indio Tan and Chrome Yellow. Medium Green Glow and Medium Ginger Glow were optional. Five separate and distinctive Tu-Tone paint schemes were available.

NOTE: According to a *Popular Mechanics* survey, most 1976 Ford van buyers (53.9 percent) used their vehicle for recreation. The four features they liked best about it were: handling, ride, comfort, and styling. Also, these owners reported having fewer mechanical problems than owners of comparable Chevy and Dodge vans. Not surprisingly, 88.2 percent said they would buy another Ford van.

E-100 CLUB WAGON: — The new E-100 Club wagon shared the Econoline Van's styling and other changes. It was offered in five or eight passenger versions. Among the standard features were: Full foam front bucket seats. Color-keyed patterened trim panels. Seat belts. Color-keyed windshield trim moldings. Fresh air heater/defroster. Fresh air vents with blend air control. Two-speed electric windshield wipers. Wiper arm mounted washer jets. Sunvisors. Rearview mirror. Dome lights. Front compartment hardboard headlining and insulated floor mat with scuff plates. Push-pull door lock buttons. Armrests. Coat hook. Electric horns. Door checks. Flip-open windows in sliding door and opposite windows. Argent bumpers and hub caps. Bright windshield moldings. Painted outside rearview mirrors.

E-150 CLUB WAGON: — This was a slightly more heavy-duty version of the E-100. It could be had in 124 in. or 138 in. wb and was also offered in five and eight passenger versions. Standard features were same as those on the E-100.

E-250 CLUB WAGON: — The E-250 Club Wagon could be had with five, eight, or twelve passenger capacity. It had most of the same features as the E-100.

I.D. DATA (Club Wagon): See F-100.

1976 Ford Club Wagon Passenger Van (JAG)

Model	Body Type	Price	Weight	Prod. Total
E-100	Club Wagon	5018	—	—
E-150	Club Wagon	5248	—	—
E-250	Club Wagon	5461	—	—

ENGINE (Club Wagon): Same as E-100 Econoline (E-100 and E-150). Displacement: 351 cu. in. V8, 143 net horsepower at 3600 R.P.M. Bore & stroke: 4.00 x 3.50 in. Compression ratio: 8.2:1. 2-bbl. carburetor (E-250).

CHASSIS: Wheelbase: 124 in. (E-100), 138 in. (E-150, E-250). Overall length: See Econoline. GVW: 5600-5900 (E-100), 6010-6300 (E-150), 7000-8450 (E-250), 5-passenger. Tires: G78-15B (E-100), G78-15D (E-150), 8.00 x 16.5D (E-250).

POWERTRAIN OPTIONS: 351 V8, 460 V8. SelectShift Cruise-O-Matic automatic.

CONVENIENCE OPTIONS: Auxiliary fuel tank. Speed control. Power steering. Captain's chair. AM radio. AM/FM stereo radio. AM/FM stereo with tape player. High-capacity air conditioner. One way glass. Wheel covers. Swing-Lok western mirrors. Swing-Lok low-mount western mirrors. Bright non telescopic mirrors. Swing-out recreation mirrors. High-output heater/defroster. Auxiliary hot water heater. Bright grille and/or bumpers. Full-length insulated floor mat. Courtesy light switches for all doors. Hinged side doors in place of sliding door. Two-stage door positioners for all hinged double doors. Locking gas cap. Intermittent two-speed windshield wipers. **Instrument Package:** fuel monitor warning light, ammeter and oil pressure gauge. Northland Special Package. Engine block heater. Tinted glass. Full length hardboard headlining. Insulation package. Protection Group (front door edge guards and front and side sliding door step well pads). Shoulder harness. Spare tire cover. Bright hub caps. Low Line Camper Package. High Line Camper Special Package. Trailer Towing Packages (LD, HD, Extra heavy-duty). **Custom Package:** (in addition to or in place of standard) color-keyed padded full-length instrument panel with woodgrained vinyl applique; color-keyed seat pedestal, cowl trim panels, padded vinyl door trim panels; cigarette lighter, insulated full-length floor mats. Window garnish moldings, color-keyed armrests on three and four passenger seats, three coat hooks, aluminum scuff plates on side and rear doors, bright hub caps, taillight bezels and window frames. **Chateau Package:** (in addition to or in place of Custom) Super Soft vinyl seat trim, color-keyed cut pile carpeting full-length of floor, lower section of engine cover and rear wheel wells; vinyl door trim panels with woodgrained vinyl applique in center and carpeted lower panel, color-keyed vinyl headlining (insulated), woodgrained vinyl horn bar insert, color-keyed vinyl spare tire cover; bright grille, bumpers, lower bodyside and rear moldings. **Convenience Group:** courtesy light door switches, day/night mirror, 2-speed windshield wipers.

NOTE: Standard Club Wagon colors for 1976 were: Wimbledon White, Silver Metallic, Candyapple Red, Brook Blue Metallic, Bali Blue, Hatteras Green Metallic, Glen Green, Copper Metallic, Peppertree Red, Harness Tan, Indio Tan and Chrome Yellow. Custom and Chateau colors were: Silver Metallic, Brook Blue Metallic, Hatteras Green Metallic, Indio Tan, Chrome Yellow and Wimbledon White. Medium Green Glow and Ginger Glow were optional on Standard, Custom and Chateau Club Wagons. Five Tu-Tone paint schemes were available.

COURIER PICKUP: — The Courier received a new grille for '76. It resembled previous ones except it had a horizontal bars theme. The cab was three inches longer. Standard features included: Biscuit-pattern, full-width vinyl upholstered seat (in red, blue, tan or black). Padded instrument panel. Six leaf rear springs. Double-acting shocks front and rear. Independent front suspension.

I.D. DATA (Courier): There were 11 symbols in the V.I.N. The first six were letters. They represented: Manufacturer, assembly plant, series, engine, model year, and production month. The last five digits were the sequential production numbers.

Model	Body Type	Price	Weight	Prod. Total
—	Pickup	—	2605	51,408

ENGINE (Courier): Displacement: 110 cu. in. OHC four-cylinder.

1976 Ford Courier Mini-pickup (JAG)

CHASSIS: Wheelbase: 104.3 in. Overall length: 171.5 in. Overall width: 63 in. Overall height: 61.5 in. GVW: 4,005 lbs. Tires: 6.00 x 14 6PR WSW.

POWERTRAIN OPTIONS: Automatic transmission with floor mounted T-bar handle. Five-speed overdrive manual transmission.

CONVENIENCE OPTIONS: Pickup box cover. Deluxe pickup box cover (includes tinted side windows, woodgrain vinyl side stripe and a dome light). Air conditioner. AM or AM/FM monaural radio with pushbutton tuning. Tinted glass all around. Bright-framed western mirrors. Convenience/Decor Group: Interior: cut-pile carpet; day/night mirror; lights in glove box, ash tray and engine compartment; deluxe steering wheel; woodgrain vinyl instrument panel applique and manual transmission shift knob; glove box door lock; courtesy light switch. Exterior: bodyside molding with black vinyl insert (N.A. with tape stripe); chromed front bumper guards with rubber inserts; bright windshield, drip rail and back-light moldings; full wheel covers. COLD Weather Group: electric rear window defroster, heavy-duty battery and high-output heater.
Argent painted rear step bumper. Dual-accent tape stripe color-keyed to exterior paint. Concorde silver metallic paint.

NOTE: The 1976 Courier was available in seven exterior colors.

1976 Ford F-100 Styleside 4x4 Pickup (JAG)

F-100 CUSTOM PICKUP: — Ford light-duty trucks received a mild facelift for 1976. The two headlights were each recessed in a blacked-out "square" at each end of the vertically split, rectangular openings grille. A new cargo body was offered; the 6½ ft. Flareside. It had seasoned hardwood floorboards. Early models had 40 percent flareboards. Later in the model year, 90 percent flareboards were used. In addition to these "shorties," 8 ft. Flaresides and 6¾ ft. and 8 ft. Styleside cargo boxes were also available. The Stylesides could be ordered in regular or Super Cab versions. The later had a 44 cu. ft. cargo space behind the front seat (rear bench or jump seats were extra cost options). Among standard F-100 features for 1976 were: Bright grille. Chromed front bumper. Twin-I-Beam front suspension. Deluxe fresh air heater/defroster (high output heater with SuperCab). Energy absorbing sunvisors and instrument panel padding. Instrument cluster with green back lighting. Keyless locking doors. Color-keyed molded door panels with integral armrests and paddle-type door handles. 3-point restraint system. Windshield washers. Two-speed windshield wipers. Dome light with door courtesy light switches. Ash tray. Large glove compartment with push button latch. Sponge-grain headlining. Black rubber floor mat. Door scuff plates. Black, tan, red, blue or green vinyl seat trim coordinated with exterior paint colors. 10 in. rearview mirror. LH and RH bright-metal exterior mirrors. Taillights with integral stop, turn, backup lights and reflector. Hub caps (except 4x4s and dual rear wheel units). Three-speed manual transmission.

I.D. DATA (F-100): See 1971 F-100 I.D.

Model	Body Type	Price	Weight	Prod. Total
F-100	(81) Chas. w/Cab	3655	3145	—
F-100	Chas. w/SuperCab	4229	3765	—
F-100	(6½ ft.) Pickup (Flare)	3827	3495	—
F-100	(6¾ ft.) Pickup (Style)	3827	3495	—
F-100	(8 ft.) Pickup (Flare)	3873	3595	—
F-100	(8 ft.) Pickup (Style)	3873	3595	—
F-100	(6¾ ft.) Pickup (Supercab)	4229	3765	—
F-100	(8 ft.) Pickup (SuperCab)	—	—	—

1976 Ford F-100 Ranger XLT Styleside Pickup (OCW)

ENGINE (F-100): See 1975 F-100 Engine.

F-150 CUSTOM PICKUP: — Sales literature called this the "heavy duty" ½ ton. Like the F-100, it had Mono-Beam front suspension with full floating front axle, coil springs, forged-steel radius rods and track bar for ruggedness and ride. Power disc/drum brakes and a steering linkage shock absorber were also standard. Along with most of features listed for the F-100. Buyers could choose from Flareside (6½ ft. "Shortie," or 8 ft.), Styleside (8 ft.) and regular or Super cabs.

I.D. DATA (F-150): See F-100.

1976 Ford F-150 4x4 Ranger XLT Styleside Pickup

Model	Body Type	Price	Weight	Prod. Total
F-150	(81)Chas. w/Cab	4062	3430	—
F-150	Chas. w/SuperCab	4471	3655	—
F-150	(81) (6½ ft.) Pickup (Flare)	—	—	—
F-150	(8 ft.) Pickup (Flare)	4235	3850	—
F-150	(8 ft.) Pickup (Style)	4235	3850	—
F-150	Pickup (Super Cab)	4644	4005	—

ENGINE (F-150): See F-100.

F-250 CUSTOM PICKUP: — The F-250 had most of the same features as the F-100. It too was offered with regular or Super cabs and with Flareside or Styleside boxes. Power brakes and a three-speed manual transmission were standard.

I.D. DATA (F-250): See F-100 I.D.

1976 Ford F-250 Styleside Pickup w/ Camper Shell

Model	Body Type	Price	Weight	Prod. Total
F-250	(81) Chas. w/Cab	4141	3535	—
F-250	Pickup (Flare)	4313	3955	—
F-250	Pickup (Style)	4313	3955	—
F-250	Pickup (Super Cab)	4721	4110	—
F-250	Chas. w/Super Cab	4471	3655	—

ENGINE (F-250): Displacement: 300 cu. in. Six, 120 net horsepower at 3400 R.P.M. Bore & stroke: 4.00 x 3.98. Compression ratio: 8.0:1. 1-bbl. carburetor. Super cab had 360 V8.

F-350 CUSTOM PICKUP: — The F-350 pickup was only offered with the Styleside box. However, there were three choices of cabs: Regular, Super, or Crew. Front only shocks, front and rear with Super Cab) a four-speed manual transmission, and power brakes were standard.

F-350 PLATFORM/STAKE: — Two lengths of one ton F-350 Platform/Stakes were available. 9 ft. and 12 ft. Floor frames of the Platform/Stake were made of steel cross sills riveted to steel siderails. Floorboards were interlocked with steel brackets. Formed steel caps covered ends of body sills. Side boards were hardwood and stakes were steel. A four-speed manual transmission was standard.

I.D. DATA (F-350): See F-100 I.D.

Model	Body Type	Price	Weight	Prod. Total
F-350	(81) Chassis w/Cab	4289	3845	—
F-350	Chassis w/Super Cab	4924	4185	—
F-350	Pickup (Style)	4664	4415	—
F-350	Pickup (Super Cab)	5097	4545	—
F-350	(80) (9 ft.) Platform	4806	4425	—
F-350	Pickup (Crew Cab)	5291	4785	—
F-350	(80) (12 ft.) Platform	—	—	—
F-350	Chassis w/Crew Cab	5131	4345	—
(86)	(9 ft.) Stake	4847	4665	—
(86)	(12 ft.) Stake	—	—	—

ENGINE (F-350): Same as F-250 for Platform/Stake and Chassis w/Cab. Pickup had 360 V8.

CHASSIS: Wheelbase: 117 in. (F-100), 133 in. (F-100, F-250), 139 in. (F-100, F-250 Super Cab), 140 in. (F-350), 137 in. (F-350 Platform/Stake), 155 in. (Super Cab), 161 in. (F-350 Platform/Stake). GVW: 4600-5700 (F-100), 6050-6400 (F-150), 6200-8100 (F-250), 6650-10,000 (F-350). Tires: G78-15B (F-100), L78-15D 8.00 x 16.5D (F-250, F-350).

POWERTRAIN OPTIONS: "302" V8 (F-100). "360" V8. "390" V8. "460" V8. 4-speed manual, Cruise-O-Matic automatic. Four-speed manual or Cruise-O-Matic transmissions.

CONVENIENCE OPTIONS: Pickup box cover (standard: fiberglass construction, tinted side and rear windows, roof vent, T-handle locking rear lift gate. Deluxe: sliding side windows with screens, bright side and rear window moldings, interior dome light, Tu-Tone paint color keyed to the most popular truck colors. Knitted vinyl seat trim. Bright metal bodyside molding with vinyl insert. Speed control. AM/FM stereo radio. AM radio. Folding bench or jump seats (Super Cab). Intermittent windshield wipers. **Super Camper Special:** front and rear stabilizer bars; heavy-duty frame; automatic transmission; extra cooling; 360 V8; power front disc brakes; 55 amp. alternator; 70 amp-hr battery; oil pressure gauge and ammeter; bright western mirrors; dual horns; heavy-duty shocks; camper wiring harness. Rear step bumper. Western style mirrors. Sliding rear cab window. Concealed spare tire and wheel. Auxiliary 12 volt 70 amp-hr battery. Air conditioner. Black or white texture painted roof (included bright drip rail molding). Full wheel covers. Mag style covers. Dual tape stripes. Bright tie-down hooks. Super cooling package. Slide out spare tire carrier. Tool stowage box with locking door. **Visibility Group:** cargo, engine, glove compartment and ash tray lights. **Convenience Group:** glove compartment door lock, intermittent windshield wipers and 12 in. day/night mirror. **Northland Special Package:** engine block heater, 50 percent (-35 degree F) antifreeze, 70 amp-hr battery, 60 amp alternator and limited slip rear axle. Power steering. Power front disc brakes (4x2's). High output heater. Trailer towing packages. Ammeter and oil pressure gauge. Bright hub caps. Bright contour rear bumper for Stylesides. Painted channel rear bumper for Flaresides. Tinted glass all around. Frame-anchored camper tie-down system. Heavy-duty 50 amp camper wiring harness. **Ranger:** (in addition to or in place of Custom features) color-keyed super soft vinyl seat upholstery; instrument panel molding with black accent; color-keyed door panels with bright moldings; shoulder high vinyl bolster around rear area (Super Cab); additional insulation; perforated headlining (insulated) with bright molding; color-keyed wall to wall carpeting; black steering wheel with woodgrain insert; cigarette lighter; bright windshield, rear window, rear quarter window (Super Cab), and roof drip moldings; bright hub caps (except 4x4, option and dual rear wheel units). Styleside pickups included bright bodyside moldings with vinyl insert, tailgate moldings (top and bottom), taillight bezels. **Ranger XLT:** (in addition to or in place of Ranger items) deluxe color-keyed, long wearing cloth with vinyl (or Super Soft vinyl) trim seat upholstery; color-keyed pleated padded upper door panel with simulated woodgrain applique; color-keyed wall to wall cut-pile nylon carpeting; bright seat-pivot covers; additional insulation; convenience group; color-keyed vinyl headlining (with special insulation) and sunvisors; bright rocker panel molding, bright wheel covers, Styleside pickup included; upper tailgate applique panel and molding; aluminum tailgate applique panel.

CUSTOM DECOR GROUP: — (available for Custom pickups, regular or Super Cab) knitted vinyl seat trim; color-keyed floor mats with insulation; bright moldings around windshield and rear window; bright drip rail moldings; bright hub caps (except 4x4's, bright hub caps included on F-250 4x4 with full time drive, but not other 4x4's). **XLT Luxury Group:** (Texas Ranger in Texas) unique trim from color-keyed wheel covers to special headlining; available only with regular cab Styleside pickups (4x2). Four-wheel drive (F-100, F-150, F-250).

NOTE: Standard colors for 1976 were: Wimbledon White, Mecca Gold, Indio Tan, Castillo Red, Copper Metallic, Hatteras Green Metallic, Glen Green, Candyapple Red, Raven Black, Bali Blue, Bahama Blue, Midnight Blue Metallic, Silver Metallic, Chrome Yellow. Ginger Glow and Medium Green Glow colors were optional. Different Tu-Tones could be obtained by using all the standard colors except Chrome Yellow. Wimbledon White could be used as the accent color for any color. The various Tu-Tone applications were the same as they were in 1975.

PRODUCTION NOTE: 1976 model year Ford light conventional truck sales totaled 663,537.

Pricing

1976	5	4	3	2	1
Courier					
Pickup	450	900	1500	2100	3000
Ranchero					
500 Pickup	830	1650	2750	3850	5500
GT Pickup	850	1700	2850	4000	5700
Squire Pickup	890	1770	2950	4150	5900
Bronco					
Wagon	850	1700	2850	4000	5700
Econoline E-100					
Cargo Van	440	870	1450	2050	2900
Window Van	470	950	1550	2200	3100
Display Van	500	1000	1650	2300	3300
Club Wagon	570	1140	1900	2650	3800
Custom Club Wagon	600	1200	2000	2800	4000
Chateau Club Wagon	630	1250	2100	3000	4200
Econoline E-200					
Cargo Van	400	800	1350	1900	2700
Window Van	440	870	1450	2050	2900
Display Van	470	950	1550	2200	3100
Econoline E-300					
Cargo Van	390	780	1300	1800	2600
Window Van	420	840	1400	1950	2800
Display Van	450	900	1500	2100	3000
F-100 — (½-Ton)					
Flareside Pickup	720	1450	2400	3300	4800
Styleside Pickup	740	1470	2450	3350	4900
Super Cab Pickup	750	1500	2500	3500	5000
F-250 — (¾-Ton)					
Flareside Pickup	690	1380	2300	3200	4600
Styleside Pickup	700	1400	2350	3250	4700
Super Cab	720	1450	2400	3300	4800
F-350 — (1-Ton)					
Pickup	690	1380	2300	3200	4600
Crew Cab Pickup	660	1320	2200	3100	4400
Stake	630	1250	2100	3000	4200

1977 FORD

1977 Ford Ranchero GT Sport Pickup (OCW)

RANCHERO 500 PICKUP: — The Ranchero received its first styling change in years. It had rectangular, stacked headlights, criss cross pattern rectangular grille and fender integral wraparound parking lights. It also had new doors and revised quarter panels. Standard features included: Select-Shift Cruise-O-Matic automatic. Power brakes and steering. Wiper-mounted windshield washer jets. Bright hub caps. Bright windshield, drip rail and cargo body moldings. Carpeting. Vinyl door trim. Spare tire compartment. Vinyl covered bench seat (in blue, red, gray, jade, chamois or saddle).

RANCHERO GT PICKUP: — In addition to most items on the 500, the GT had: GT strip in black, orange, silver, white or brown. Dual racing mirrors. Bright hub caps with trim rings. Flight bench seat covered in fine grain Mateao vinyl. Sports instrument panel. Luxury steering wheel.

RANCHERO SQUIRE PICKUP: — In addition to most items on the 500, the Squire had: Simulated woodgrain paneling on sides and tailgate. Deluxe wheel covers.

I.D. DATA (Ranchero): See 1960 Ranchero.

Model	Body Type	Price	Weight	Prod. Total
97D	Pickup (500)	4618	3915	9453
97R	Pickup (GT)	4984	3940	12,462
97K	Pickup (Squire)	4971	3980	1126

ENGINE (Ranchero): Displacement: 302 cu. in. V8, 130 net horsepower at 3800 R.P.M. Bore & stroke: 4 in. x 3 in. Compression ratio: 8.0:1. 2-bbl. carburetor.

CHASSIS: Wheebase: 118 in. Overall length: 220.1 in. Overall height: 53.5 in. GVW: 5452-5904. Tires: G78-14B (G70-14B on GT).

POWERTRAIN OPTIONS: 351 cu. in V8. 400 cu. in. V8.

CONVENIENCE OPTIONS: Altitude-compesating carburetor. **Appearance Protection Group:** door edge guards, floor mat and license plate frame. **Brougham Decor Group:** split bench seat in cloth and vinyl trim or Mateao vinyl upholstery; seats adjust individually. Bucket seats (include matching door trim panels and cut-pile carpet.) **Bumper Protection Group:** front and rear bumper guards and front bumper rub strips. **Convenience Group:** intermittent wipers and automatic parking brake release (also for 500 and Squire, RH remote control mirror and trip odometer). Engine block heater. **Handling Suspension Package:** 1250 lb. payload, heavy-duty rear springs and rear stabilizer bar. Heavy-duty alternator. Heavy-duty battery. Illuminated entry system. **Light Group:** underhood, glove box and ashtray light, "headlights-on" warning buzzer, and "door ajar" light. Power door windows. Power flight bench seat covered in fine grain Mateao vinyl or optional cloth and vinyl. Racing mirror (dual, color-keyed). Leather wrapped sport steering wheel. Tinted glass all around. **Trailer Towing Package:** Class II (2000-3500 lb.) includes heavy-duty handling suspension package, extra cooling package, 3.00 rear axle ratio and wiring harness; requires either 351 V8 or 400 V8. Class III (3500-6000 lb.) includes everything in Class II package plus 60-amp alternator; requires 400 V8. Vinyl roof in red, black, silver, brown or white (n.a. with Tu-Tone). Wheel lip moldings. Deluxe wheel covers. Hub caps with trim rings. Luxury wheel covers. **Sports Instrument Panel:** tach, trip odometer, ammeter, temperature and oil gauges, electric clock and luxury steering wheel. Fingertip speed control. AM/FM stereo with search. AM/FM monaural. AM radio. SelectAire conditioner (also available with automatic temperature control). Tilting steering wheel. Front cornering lamps. Mag 500 chrome wheels. Day/date digital clock. Wire wheel covers.

NOTE: Colors offered on 1977 Rancheros were: Black, Silver Metallic, Dark Red, Dark Blue Metallic, Bali Blue, Dark Jade Metallic, Bright Saddle Metallic, Champagne, Dark Brown Metallic, Cream, White. Optional Color Glow Paints: Bright Blue Glow, Light Jade Glow, Chamois Glow.

BRONCO WAGON: — Standard features on the four-wheel drive 1977 Bronco included: Mono-Beam front suspension. Solid state ignition. Front disc brakes. Variable ratio parking brake control. Vinyl bucket seat (driver's only). Floor mounted T-bar transfer case control. Suspended foot pedals. Double acting shock absorbers. Fresh air heater and defroster. Lockable glove compartment. Two-speed electric windshield wipers. 41-amp-hr battery. Sunvisors. Vinyl-coated rubber floor mat. Fully synchronized three-speed manual. Full length roof with fixed windows in the rear liftgate and on each side of the rear compartment. Dome light. Painted channel-type steel bumpers.

I.D. DATA (Bronco): See F-100 I.D.

Model	Body Type	Price	Weight	Prod. Total
U-100	Wagon	5260	3490	13,335

ENGINE (Bronco): Displacement: 200 cu. in. Six, 84 net horsepower at 3800 R.P.M. Bore & stroke: 3.68 in. x 3.13 in. Compression ratio: 8.3:1. 1-bbl. carburetor.

CHASSIS: Wheelbase: 92 in. Overall length: 152.1 in. Overall width: 69.1 in. Overall height: 70.1 in. GVW: 4400-4900. Tires: E78 x 15 in.

POWERTRAIN OPTIONS: 302 V8. Cruise-O-Matic automatic.

CONVENIENCE OPTIONS: Extra cooling V8 radiator. LH remote control outside mirror. Free running hubs. Passenger front bucket seat. Heavy-duty shocks. 53- and 68-amp-hr batteries. Power steering. **Convenience Group:** cigarette lighter, map light, inside 10 in. day/night rearview mirror. RH chrome rearview mirror. Shoulder harness. Rear seat. Chrome bumper with chrome front guards. Skid plates for fuel tank and transfer case 600 watt single element engine block heater. Dual horns. Exterior rear-mounted swing+away tire carrier. Bright metal wheel covers. High-flotation tires. Auxiliary 7.5 gallon fuel tank with skid plate. Manual radio and antenna. Bright bodyside and tailgate moldings. Bright metal rocker panel molding. Hand-operated throttle. **Sport Bronco Package:** Right hand front seat and sunvisor. Vinyl door trim panels with bright metal moldings. Hardboard headlining with bright metal retainer moldings. Steering wheel with woodtone horn pad. Vinyl front and rear floor mats with bright metal retainers. Cigarette lighter. Horn ring. Passengers seat. Bright metal drip rail moldings. Bright metal windshield and window frames. Bright metal grille molding and tailgate release handle. Bright headlight, side light, reflector and taillight bezels. Argent-painted grille with bright F-O-R-D letters. Chrome bumpers, front and rear. Chrome front bumper guards. Bright metal wheel covers. **Dealer Installed Accessories:** Power take-off (front mounted). Warn free-running front hubs (manual or automatic). Snowplows. Snowplow angling kits. Front auxiliary air springs. Front mounted winch. Trailer hitch. Trailer towing mirror. Locking gas cap. Front tow hooks. Compass. Fire extinguisher. Transmission oil cooler. Tach. 4600 lb. GVW Package rear springs rated at 1240 lbs., E78-15B tires (requires rear bench seat and RH front seat.) 4900 **GVW Package:** rear springs rated at 1475 lbs., G78-15 B tires. Reduced External Sound Package. **Northland Special:** single element 600 watt engine block heater, 50 percent (-30 degress F) antifreeze, 70 amp hr battery, 60-amp alternator.

and limited-slip rear axle. **Ranger Package:** Color-keyed full carpeting (including tailgate and wheelhousings.) Passenger's seat. Color-keyed vinyl door trim panels with burl woodtone accent. Color-keyed vinyl trim with insulation on rear quarter panels. Cloth and vinyl seat trim in tan, blue or green. Color-keyed padded instrument panel paint. Hood and lower bodyside tape stripes, white stripe with orange accent. Swing-away spare tire carrier. White vinyl with orange accent and Bronco insignia. Coat hook. **Special Decor Group:** (available on standard and Sport Bronco) Black grille. Solid exterior colors (white roof is available). Color-keyed tape stripe across hood and along upper bodysides. Bright wheel covers. Bright windshield and window frames.

ECONOLINE E-100 CARGO VAN: — The growing popularity of vans among the youth market was apparent on the cover of the '77 Econoline sales catalog. It featured the photo of an Econoline with a trick paint job and fancy wheels. For the second year in a row, Ford continued to offer "custom" look vans straight from the factory. The rear spring rating was dropped slightly, but aside from that, the 1977 Econoline was basically the same as the 1976 version. Among the standard features were: Full-foam driver's bucket seat. Color-keyed vinyl seat trim in black, blue, jade or tan. Color-keyed seat belt. Color-keyed windshield trim moldings. Color-keyed engine cover with clipboard flashlight pocket and removable ash tray designed into console. Fresh air heater defroster. Fresh air vents with blend air control. Two-speed electric windshield wipers. Wiper-arm mounted washer jets. Front and cargo area dome lights. Front compartment hardboard headlining and insulated floor mat with scuff plates. Push-pull door lock buttons. Armrest. Coat hook. Electric horn. Door checks. Latch release handles on side cargo doors. Argent bumpers. Argent hub caps. Bright windshield molding. Painted mirrors.

ECONOLINE E-100 WINDOW VAN: — As the name suggests, the window van had glass all around. It shared most standard features with the Cargo Van.

ECONOLINE E-100 DISPLAY VAN: — This model had windows at the rear and on the right-hand side. It came with the same standard features as the Cargo Van.

I.D. DATA (Econoline E-100): See F-100.

Model	Body Type	Price	Weight	Prod. Total
E-040	Cargo Van	4245	3875	Note
E-050	Window Van	4350	3900	Note
E-600	Display Van	4314	3890	Note

NOTE: Total Ford Van sales in the 1977 model year were 138,064.

ENGINE (Econoline E-100): Displacement: 300 cu. in. Six, 120 horsepower at 3400 R.P.M. Bore & stroke: 4.00 in. x 3.98 in. Compression ratio: 8.0:1. One-bbl. carburetor.

ECONOLINE E-150 CARGO VAN: — The E-150 could run on leaded or unleaded gas. It had a slightly higher GVW rating than the E-100. Unlike the E-100, it could be operated on either leaded or unleaded gasoline. Standard features echoed those on the E-100.

ECONOLINE E-150 DISPLAY VAN: — This van shared styling with the E-100 Display Van but had greater load capacity.

ECONOLINE E-150 WINDOW VAN: — This van shared styling with the E-100 Window Van, but had greater load capacity.

I.D. DATA (Econoline E-150): See F-100.

Model	Body Type	Price	Weight	Prod. Total
E-140	Cargo Van	4465	3833	Note
E-160	Display Van	4535	3850	Note
E-150	Window Van	4570	3860	Note

NOTE: See E-100.

ENGINE (Econoline E-150): Same as E-100.

ECONOLINE E-250 CARGO VAN: — The new E-250 had a higher GVW rating and more heavy-duty front and rear axles, than the E-150. It also came with eight, rather than five, hole wheels. Standard features were the same as those on the E-100.

ECONOLINE E-250 DISPLAY VAN: — This vehicle shared styling and features with the E-100, but had greater load capacity.

ECONOLINE E-250 WINDOW VAN: — This vehicle shared styling and features with the E-100 Window Van, but had greater load capacity.

ECONOLINE E-250 CUTAWAY VAN: — This van with Camper Special Packages was designed to readily accommodate custom motor homes.

ECONOLINE E-250 PARCEL DELIVERY: — The E-250 Parcel Delivery van was capable of hauling a payload up to 2,340 lbs. Its cargo area was 149.9 in. long and 74.3 in. high. The rear door opening was 84.7 in. wide.

I.D. DATA (Econoline E-250): See F-100.

Model	Body Type	Price	Weight	Prod. Total
E-240	Cargo Van	4780	4365	Note
E-260	Display Van	4850	4380	Note
E-250	Window Van	4886	4395	Note
E-270	Cutaway Van	4622	3935	Note
E-280	Parcel Delivery	6220	5390	Note

NOTE: See E-100.

ENGINE (Econoline E-250): Same as E-100.

ECONOLINE E-350 CARGO VAN: — This was the Top of the line Econoline. It had heavy-duty front and rear shocks and a greater load capacity than the other series. Standard features were the same as those on the E-100.

ECONOLINE E-350 DISPLAY VAN: — See E-250 Display Van.

ECONOLINE E-350 WINDOW VAN: — See E-250 Window Van.

ECONOLINE E-350 CUTAWAY VAN: — See E-250 Cutaway Van.

ECONOLINE E-350 PARCEL DELIVERY: — This heavy-duty van came in two wheelbases. Styling and features were the same as those offered on the E-250.

I.D. DATA (Econoline E-350): See F-100.

Model	Body Type	Price	Weight	Prod. Total
E-340	Cargo Van	4962	4530	Note
E-360	Display Van	5033	4545	Note
E-350	Window Van	5068	4560	Note
E-370	Cutaway Van	4718	3980	Note
E-380	Parcel Delivery	6654	5700	Note

NOTE: See E-100.

ENGINE (Econoline E-350): Same as E-100.

CHASSIS: Wheelbase: 124 in. 138 in. (158 in. available on Cutaway and Parcel Delivery). Overall width: 70.3 in. Overall length: 186.8 in. (124 in. w.b.), 206.8 in. (138 in. w.b.) GVW: 5150-11,000. Tires: F78-15B. (E-100) H78-15D PT (E-150), 8.00 x 16.5D TT (E-250), 8.75 x 16.5E C on PDV) 9.50 x 16.5D TT (E-350, 8.00 x 16.5D dual rear on PDV).

POWERTRAIN OPTIONS: Cruise-O-Matic automatic. "351" V8. "460" V8 (E-250, E-350).

CONVENIENCE OPTIONS: CUSTOM VAN: (in addition to or place of standard) color-keyed padded full-length instrument panel with wood grained vinyl applique; color-keyed seat pedestal, cowl-side trim panels, vinyl front door trim panels; insulated floor mats, roof rail garnish moldings, bright hub caps, taillight bezels and vent and rear window frames. **Chateau Van:** (in addition to or in place of Custom) Super Soft vinyl seat trim, color-keyed cut pile carpeting on front floor and lower section of engine cover, padded vinyl front door trim panels with woodgrained vinyl applique in center and carpeted lower panel, wood grained vinyl horn bar insert in steering wheel. Bright grille, bright bumpers, bright bodyside and rear moldings. Wheel covers. R-H sliding cargo door. Adjustable or flip-fold passenger seat. High output heater and defroster. Auxiliary hot water heater. Cruising Van Interior (full carpeting and insulation, captain's chairs). Bright grille and/or front and rear bumpers. Full length, insulated carpet or mat (138 in. w.b. only). Courtesy light switches, front or all doors. Two stage door positioners for hinged cargo doors. Northland Special Package (includes engine block heater -35 F anti-freeze, 77 amp hr battery, 60 amp alternator and high output heater). Engine block heater. Locking fuel can. Tinted glass. Full length hardboard headlining. Insulation Package. Protection Group (front door edge guards and front and side sliding door stepwell pads). Interior rub rails (138 in. only). School Bus Package for 138 in. w.b. Window Van. Argyle cloth insert seat trim. Spare tire and wheel. Spare tire cover. Bright hub caps. Trailer Towing Package (for Class I, II, III and IV trailers). Front stabilizer bar. Captain's chair. Air conditioning. Power steering. Auxiliary fuel tank. Interval windshield wipers. Swing lok western mirrors. Swing-out recreation mirrors. Swing-Lok low mount Western mirrors. AM radio. AM/FM monaural. AM/FM stereo. AM/FM stereo with tape player. Door windows for rear and/or side cargo doors. One way glass in rear side windows and rear door. Flip-open windows for cargo doors. Job-engineered interior packages. **Low Line Camper Package:** 60 amp alternator, 77 amp-hr battery, auxiliary 81 amp-hr battery, heavy-duty shocks (with E-250), Custom trim package, camper wiring harness, "Camper Special" emblem, extra cooling package. **High Line Camper Special Package:** (basic package plus/or) 90 amp alternator, adjustable passenger seat, external auxiliary oil cooler, fuel monitor warning light and ammeter and oil pressure gauge, front stabilizer bar, dual horns, 351 V8, Chateau trim package, high output heater, power steering, tinted windshield and glass.

NOTE: Econoline colors for 1977 included: Wimbledon White, Candyapple Red, Brook Blue Metallic, Light Blue, Silver Metallic, Light Jade, Dark Brown Metallic, Indio Tan, Tangerine, Midnight Blue Metallic, Raven Black, Chrome Yellow, Dark Jade Metallic are standard. Jade Glow and Cinnamon Glow were optional. Five Tu-Tone paint schemes were available.

E-100 CLUB WAGON: — Rerated rear springs and new wheelcovers were the "major" changes for 1977. The E-100 was offered in five- and eight-passenger versions. Among the standard features were: Full foam front bucket seats. Color-keyed patterned vinyl seat trim in black, blue, jade or tan. Seat belts. Two-speed electric windshield wipers. Wiper arm mounted washer jets. 10 in. rearview mirror. Dome lights. Insulated floor mat with scuff plates. Three armrests. Dual horns. Flip-open windows in sliding door and opposite windows. Painted bumpers, 5 in. x 8 in. mirrors and hub caps. Bright windshield molding.

E-150 CLUB WAGON: — This was a slightly more heavy-duty version of the E-100. It could be had in 124 in. or 138 in. w.b. and was also offered in five- and eight-passenger versions. Standard features were same as those on the E-100.

E-250 CLUB WAGON: — The E-250 Club Wagon could be had with five-, eight-, or twelve-passenger capacity. It had most of the same features as the E-100.

I.D. DATA (Club Wagon): See F-100.

Model	Body Type	Price	Weight	Prod. Total
E-100	Club Wagon	5485	4090	—
E-150	Club Wagon	5680	4225	—
E-250	Club Wagon	5921	4735	—

ENGINE (Club Wagon): Same as Econoline E-100.

CHASSIS: Wheelbase: 124 in. (E-100), 138 in. (E-150, E-250). Overall length: See Econoline. GVW: 5600-5900 (E-100), 6010-6300 (E-150), 7000-8450 (E-250), 5-passenger. Tires: G78 x 15B (E-100), H78 x 15D (E-150), 8.00 x 16D (E-250).

POWERTRAIN OPTIONS: "351" V8. "460" V8. SelectShift Cruise-O-Matic automatic transmission.

CONVENIENCE OPTIONS: Auxiliary fuel tank. Speed control. Power steering. Captain's chair. AM radio. AM/FM stereo radio. AM/FM stereo w/tape player. High-capacity or front only air conditioner. Privacy glass. Wheel covers. Swing-Lok western mirrors. Swing-Lok low-mount western mirrors. Bright non telescopic mirrors. Swing-out recreation mirrors. High-output heater. Roof luggage carrier. Spare tire lock. Low-mount Swing-Lok bright mirrors. AM/FM monaural radio. Bright grille and/or bumpers. Full-length insulated floor mat. **Free Wheeling Option:** black rocker panel paint accent, painted bumpers, grille and mirrors; forged aluminum wheels and RWL tires. Courtesy light switches for all doors. Hinged side doors in place of sliding door. Two-stage door positioners for all hinged double doors. Locking gas cap. Intermittent two-speed windshield wipers. **Instrument Package:** fuel monitor warning light, ammeter and oil pressure gauge. Northland Special Package. Engine block heater. Tinted glass. Full length hardboard headlining. Insulation package. Protection Group (front door edge guards and front and side sliding door step well pads). Shoulder harness. Spare tire cover. Bright hub caps. Low Line Camper Package. High Line Camper Special Package. Trailer Towing Packages (LD, HD, Extra HD). **Custom Package:** (in addition to or in place of standard) color-keyed full-length instrument panel with woodgrained vinyl applique; padded vinyl door trim panels; cigarette lighter, insulated full-length floor mats. Window garnish moldings, color-keyed armrests on three and four passenger seats, three coat hooks, aluminum scuff plates on side and rear doors, bright hub caps, taillight bezels and window frames. **Chateau Package:** (in addition to or in place of Custom) Super Soft vinyl seat trim, color-keyed cut pile carpeting full-length of floor, lower section of engine cover and rear wheel wells; vinyl door trim panels with woodgrained vinyl applique in center and carpeted lower panel, color-keyed vinyl headlining (insulated), woodgrained vinyl horn bar insert, color-keyed vinyl spare tire cover; bright grille, bumpers, lower body side and rear moldings. **Convenience Group:** courtesy light door switches, day/night mirror, 2-speed windshield wipers.

NOTE: Standard Club Wagon colors for 1977 were: Wimbledon White, Candyapple Red, Brook Blue Metallic, Light Blue, Silver Metallic, Light Jade, Dark Brown Metallic, Indio Tan, Tangerine, Midnight Blue Metallic, Raven Black, Chrome Yellow, Dark Jade Metallic. Optional were: Jade and Cinnamon Glow. Five Tu-Tone paint schemes were offered.

1977 Ford Courier Mini-Pickup (OCW)

COURIER PICKUP: — The restyled Courier was introduced in the spring of 1977. Between the recessed headlights was the two level, horizontal bars theme grille. New, wraparound taillights highlighted the rear end treatment. Standard items included: Vinyl headliner. Inside hood release. Full width vinyl upholstered seat. Hinged seat back for easy access to stowage area. Independent front suspension. Six leaf rear springs. Double-acting shocks front and rear.

I.D. DATA (Courier): See 1976 Courier I.D.

Model	Body Type	Price	Weight	Prod. Total
—	Pickup	—	2675	13,167

ENGINE (Courier): Displacement: 110 cu. in. OHC 4-cylinder.

CHASSIS: Wheelbase: 106.9 in. (6 ft. box), 112.8 in. (7 ft. box). Overall length: 177.9 in. (6 ft. box), 189.4 in. (7 ft. box). Overall width: 63 in. Overall height: 61.5 in. GVW: 3965 lbs. Tires: 6.00 x 14 in.

POWERTRAIN OPTIONS: Automatic transmission. Five-speed manual transmission.

CONVENIENCE OPTIONS: AM or AM/FM monaural radios. Air conditioning. Tinted glass all around. Western rearview mirrors. Rear step bumper. **Cold Weather Group:** electric rear window defroster, heavy-duty battery, and high-output heater. Radial tires. Cast aluminum wheels. Free wheeling Packages A and B.

1977 Ford F-250 Ranger 4x4 Styleside Pickup (OCW)

F-100 CUSTOM PICKUP: — Styling was unchanged for 1977. Among standard features were: Fresh air heater/defroster (high output heater with Super Cab). Energy-absorbing instrument panel padding. Instrument cluster with green backlighting. Behind-seat storage. Molded door panels with integral armrests and paddle-type door handles. Two-speed windshield wipers. Dome light with door courtesy light switches. Ashtray. Glove compartment. Headlining. Black floor mat. Door scuff plates. Full-foam seat (7 in. of foam in seat and 5 in. in back). Black, red, tan or jade green vinyl seat trim. Twin-I-Beam front suspension. No-rust fender liners. F-100 buyers had their choice of the 6¾ ft. and 8 ft. Styleside, 6½ ft. and 8 ft. Flareside, or 6¾ ft. and 8 ft. (Styleside) Super Cab. The later featured an extended cab with room for an (optional) folding rear seat (or two jump seats) behind the front seat.

I.D. DATA (F-100): See 1971 F-100 I.D.

1977 Ford F-250 Ranger 4x4 Styleside Pickup (JAG)

Model	Body Type	Price	Weight	Prod. Total
F-100	(81) Chassis w/Cab	3846	3145	—
F-100	Chassis w/Super Cab	4372	3550	—
F-100	(6½ ft.) Pickup (Flare)	4076	3495	—
F-100	(6¾ ft.) Pickup (Style)	4076	3495	—
F-100	(8 ft.) Pickup (Flare)	3897	3595	—
F-100	(8 ft.) Pickup (Style)	3897	3595	—
F-100	Pickup (Super Cab)	4602	3905	—

ENGINE (F-100): Same as 1976, except Compression ration was 8.9:1.

F-150 CUSTOM PICKUP: — Once again, the F-150 was Ford's "heavy-duty" ½-ton. Its payload ranged from 605 lbs. to 930 lbs. greater than F-100's. However, it shared most standard feature with that series, with the addition of power brakes.

I.D. DATA (F-150): See F-100.

Model	Body Type	Price	Weight	Prod. Total
F-150	(81) Chassis w/Cab	4332	3435	—
F-150	Chassis w/Super Cab	4683	3660	—
F-150	(8 ft.) Pickup (Flare)	4561	3855	—
F-150	(8 ft.) Pickup (Style)	4561	3855	—
F-150	Pickup (Super Cab)	4913	4010	—

NOTE: The Super Cab was offered with either 6¾ ft. or 8 ft. Styleside boxes.

ENGINE (F-150): Same as F-100.

F-250 CUSTOM PICKUP: — The F-250 had most of the same features as the F-100. It too was offered with regular or Super cabs and with Flareside or Styleside boxes. Power brakes and a three-speed manual transmission were standard.

I.D. DATA (F-250): See F-100 I.D.

Model	Body Type	Price	Weight	Prod. Total
F-250	(81) Chassis w/Cab	4438	3540	—
F-250	Chassis w/Crew Cab	5183	4180	—
F-250	(8 ft.) Pickup (Flare)	4667	3960	—
F-250	(8 ft.) Pickup (Style)	4667	3960	—
F-250	Pickup (Super Cab)	5013	4115	—
F-250	(6¾ ft.) Pickup (Crew Cab)	5414	4535	—
F-250	Chassis w/Super Cab	4783	3760	—

NOTE: Super Cab was available with 6¾ ft. and 8 ft. styleside boxes.

ENGINE (F-250): Displacement: 300 cu. in. Six, 120 net horsepower at 3400 R.P.M. Bore & stroke: 4.00 in. x 3.98 in. Compression ratio: 8.0:1. 1-bbl. carburetor. Super Cab had 360 V8.

F-350 CUSTOM PICKUP: — The F-350 pickup was only offered with the Styleside box. However, there were three choices of cabs: regular, Super, or Crew. Front only shocks, (front and rear with Super Cab) a four-speed manual transmission, and power brakes were standard.

F-350 PLATFORM/STAKE: — Two lengths of 1-ton F-350 Platform/Stake's were available: 9 ft. and 12 ft. Floor frames of the Platform/Stake were made of steel cross sills riveted to steel siderails. Floorboards were interlocked with steel brackets. Formed steel caps covered ends of body sills. Side boards were hardwood and stakes were steel. A four-speed manual transmission was standard.

I.D. DATA (F-350): See F-100 I.D.

Model	Body Type	Price	Weight	Prod. Total
F-350	(81) Chassis w/Cab	4639	3850	—
F-350	(80) (9 ft.) Platform	5187	4430	—
F-350	Styleside Pickup 140''	5016	4415	—
F-350	(86) (9 ft.) Stake	5230	4670	—
F-350	Pickup (Super Cab)m	5414	4545	—
F-350	Pickup (Crew Cab)	5615	4790	—
F-350	Crew Cab Chassis 167''	5455	4350	—
F-350	SuperCab Chassis 185''	5184	4185	—

ENGINE (F-350): Same as F-250 for Platform/Stake & Chassis w/Cab. Pickup had "351" V8.

CHASSIS: Wheelbase: 117 in. (F-100), 133 in. (F-100, F-150, F-250), 139 in. (F-100, F-150, F-250 Super Cab), 155 in. (Super Cab), 137 in. (F-350 Platform/Stake), 140 in. (F-350), 161 in. (F-350 Platform/Stake), 150 in. (F-250 Crew Cab), 166.5 in. (F-350 Crew Cab). GVW: 4700-5650 (F-100), 6050-6200 (F-150), 6200-8100 (F-250), 8300-10,000 (F-350). Tires: G78-15B (F-100), L78-15D (F-150), 8.00 x 16.5D (F-250, F-350).

POWERTRAIN OPTIONS: "302" V8 (F-100 Reg. Cab). "351" V8. "400" V8. "460" V8 (F-150, F-250, F-350). Four-speed manual transmission. Cruise-O-Matic automatic transmission.

CONVENIENCE OPTIONS: Air conditioner. Breathable knitted vinyl seat trim. Speed control. Flip-open windows on Super Cabs (plain or tinted glass). Dual tape paint strips for Stylesides (available in five paint-keyed colors). Bright metal bodyside moldings with vinyl insert (std. Ranger, Ranger XLT). Rear step bumper for Stylesides. Bright contour rear bumper. Painted channel-type bumper for Flaresides. AM radio. AM/FM radio. AM/FM stereo radio (with speaker in each door). Black or white texture painted roof with bright drip and back of cab moldings. Tool stowage box with locking door (located in curbside of pickup box skirt on 8 ft. Stylesides). Fixed Western-type 6½ ft. by 9½ ft. painted mirrors. Recreation swing-out bright mirrors. Low-profile bright mirrors. Non-telescopic painted mirrors. Box cover for 8 ft. Stylesides (tinted side and rear windows, roof vent, and liftgate, Deluxe models had sliding side windows with screens, dome light, Tu-Tone, sliding front box cover window available with white cover). Super cooling package (available with 351 and bigger V8s). Spare tire lock. Sliding rear window. Bright tie down hooks for Stylesides (three on each side and two on tailgate). Concealed spare tire (in right side of F-350 Styleside and Camper Special). Mag style wheel covers for 15 in. wheels. Full wheel covers on pickups with 15 in. and 16.5 in. wheels. Slide-out spare tire carrier. Auxiliary 12-volt 68 amp-hr battery with dual circuit charging system for campers. Full width foam rear seat that folds flat when not in use (Super Cab). Two jump seats with foam padded cushion and back that fold out of the way when not in use (Super Cab). **Convenience Package:** intermittent wipers, glove box lock, 12 in. day/night rearview mirror. Electric block heater. Electric rear window defroster. Flareside special trim package. Color-keyed rubber floor mats. Auxiliary fuel tank. Locking fuel cap. Dual electric horns. Bright hub caps. 5 amber clearance lights. **Visibility Light Group:** cargo body, glove box, ashtray, engine compartment and under instrument panel lights. **Northland Special:** engine block heater, 50 percent (-35 degrees F) antifreeze, 68 amp-hr battery, 60 amp alternator, limited slip rear axle. **Protection Package:** bright door edge guards, front bumper guards and front bumper rub strip. Heavy-duty black vinyl seat upholstery. Tinted glass (windshield or all around.) Trailer towing packages (up to 10,000 lbs.) F-250/350 **Camper Special Package:** (std. on F-350 140 in. w.b. Camper Special) 60 amp alternator, 68 amp-hr battery (77 amp hr with 460 V8), oil pressure gauge, ammeter, dual electric horns, bright 6¾ in. x 9½ in. swing-out recreation mirrors, front and rear stabilizer bars, extra cooling package, Camper wiring harness, heavy-duty shocks (front and rear), "Camper Special" emblem, heavy-duty in-tank oil cooler with Cruise-O-Matic. **Pinstripe Accent Package:** (6½ ft. Flareside) black channel rear bumper, tape pinstriping and blackout painted grille insert. Four-wheel drive (F-150, F-250). **Custom Decor Group:** knitted vinyl seat trim, color-keyed floor mats with insulation, bright moldings around windshield and rear window, bright drip rail moldings, bright hub caps. **Ranger:** bright moldings on windshield, rear window, rear quarter windows (Super Cab) and drip rails; plus bright hub caps (single rears); nylon carpeting; instrument panel molding with black accent; door panels with bright moldings; shoulder high vinyl bolster around rear area (Super Cab); seat back cover; additional cab insulation; perforated, insulated headlining; two courtesy lights (Super Cab); Stylesides also include bright side moldings with vinyl insert and bright tailgate moldings. **Ranger XLT:** Stylesides had new upper and lower bodyside molding combination; bright wheel covers; wall to wall cut pile carpeting covered floor insulation; vinyl headlining with sound absorbing backing; cloth and vinyl or Super Soft vinyl seat upholstery; vinyl door trim panels with insulation; convenience group; instrument panel with simulated woodgrained applique within bright surround moldings. **XLT Luxury Group:** plush cloth and super-soft vinyl upholstery; padded design headlining plus color-keyed wheel covers and carpeted floor and back panel up to rear window of behind the seat storage area.

NOTE: Standard F-series colors for 1977 included: Raven Black, Wimbledon White, Candyapple Red, Castilo Red, Silver Metallic, Midnight Blue Metallic, Light Blue, Bahama Blue, Light Jade, Dark Jade Metallic, Chrome Yellow, Indio Tan, Medium Copper, Copper Metallic. New Jade Glow and Dark Cinnamon Glow were optional. Wimbledon White could be used as the accent color for any exterior color except Silver Metallic. TWO-TONE APPLICATIONS: Regular: accent on roof and upper back panel. Deluxe: (Stylesides only) accent color inside molding. Combination: (Stylesides only) combines regular and deluxe.

PRODUCTION NOTE: 1977 model year Ford light conventional truck sales totaled 723,925.

Pricing

	5	4	3	2	1
1977					
Courier					
Pickup	450	900	1500	2100	3000
Ranchero					
500 Pickup	830	1650	2750	3850	5500
GT Pickup	850	1700	2850	4000	5700
Squire Pickup	890	1770	2950	4150	5900
Bronco					
Wagon	850	1700	2850	4000	5700
Econoline E-100					
Cargo Van	440	870	1450	2050	2900
Window Van	470	950	1550	2200	3100
Display Van	500	1000	1650	2300	3300
Club Wagon	570	1140	1900	2650	3800
Custom Club Wagon	600	1200	2000	2800	4000
Chateau Club Wagon	630	1250	2100	3000	4200
Econoline E-200					
Cargo Van	400	800	1350	1900	2700
Window Van	440	870	1450	2050	2900
Display Van	470	950	1550	2200	3100
Econoline E-300					
Cargo Van	390	780	1300	1800	2600
Window Van	420	840	1400	1950	2800
Display Van	450	900	1500	2100	3000
F-100 — (½-Ton)					
Flareside Pickup	720	1450	2400	3300	4800
Styleside Pickup	740	1470	2450	3350	4900
Super Cab Pickup	750	1500	2500	3500	5000
F-250 — (¾-Ton)					
Flareside Pickup	690	1380	2300	3200	4600
Styleside Pickup	700	1400	2350	3250	4700
Super Cab	720	1450	2400	3300	4800
F-350 — (1-Ton)					
Pickup	690	1380	2300	3200	4600
Crew Cab Pickup	660	1320	2200	3100	4400
Stake	630	1250	2100	3000	4200

1978 FORD

RANCHERO 500 PICKUP: — Styling was unchanged for 1978. Standard features included: SelectShift Cruise-O-Matic. Power steering and brakes. Bright hub caps. Vinyl door trim and spare tire compartment. Carpeting. Vinyl-covered bench seat in blue, russet, grey, jade, chamois or saddle.

RANCHERO GT PICKUP: — The GT was once again the most popular Ranchero. It had most of the same items as the 500 plus: Flight bench seat in Mateao vinyl or optional cloth and vinyl. Cut-pile carpeting. GT stripe. Dual sport mirrors. Bright hub caps with trim rings.

RANCHERO SQUIRE PICKUP: — In addition to most of the items on the 500, the Squire had: Simulated woodgrain paneling on sides and tailgate. Deluxe wheel covers.

I.D. DATA (Rancher): See 1960 Ranchero I.D.

Model	Body Type	Price	Weight	Prod. Total
97D	Pickup (500)	5179	3698	9911
97R	Pickup (GT)	5400	3716	12,469
97K	Pickup (Squire)	5532	3728	907

NOTE: A limited number of Shelby GT Rancheros were made for Ford Motor Company. These had a 400 cu. in. V8, electronic ignition, Twin comfort lounge seats, T-Bird door panels, and gray dashboard with full instrumentation.

ENGINE (Ranchero): Displacement 302 cu. in. V8, 130 net horsepower at 3800 R.P.M. Bore & stroke: 4 x 3 in. Compression ratio: 8.0:1. 2-bbl. carburetor.

398

CHASSIS: Wheelbase: 118 in. Overall length: 220.1 in. Overall height: 53.5 in. GVW: 4725-5685. Tires: G78-14B (G70-14B on GT).

POWERTRAIN OPTIONS: 351 V8, 400 V8.

NOTE: Most 1978 Rancheros, 76 percent, came with one of the optional engines.

CONVENIENCE OTPIONS: Dual sport mirrors. Wire wheelcovers. Magnum 500 chrome wheels. SelectAire conditioner (available with manual or automatic temperature control. AM/FM stereo with 8-track tape. AM/FM stereo with cassette tape player. AM/FM stereo with search feature. AM/FM stereo. AM/FM monaural. AM radio. Day/date clock. **Sports Instrumentation Group:** woodtone applique around instrument cluster pods; tach, temperature and oil pressure gauges, trip odometer, ammeter, electric clock and luxury steering wheel. Tilt steering wheel. Cornering lamps. Six-way power flight bench or split bench seat. **Appearance Protection Group:** door edge guards, floor mat and license plate frames. Deluxe wheel covers. Wheel trim rings. Vinyl roof in black, white, red, blue and cordovan (not available with GT or Tu-Tones). Wheel lip moldings. **Convenience Group:** intermittent windshield wipers, automatic parking brake release, RH remote control mirror, trip odometer, and passenger visor vanity mirror. Fingertip speed control. Illuminated entry system. **Light Group:** engine compartment, glove box and ashtray lights; plus "door ajar" warning light and "headlights on" warning buzzer. Power door windows. Tinted glass all around. Engine block heater. Heavy-duty. **Handling Suspension:** Heavy-duty rear springs, and rear stablizer bar. Heavy-duty alternator. Heavy-duty battery. Medium-duty trailer towing package. Traction-lok differential (N.A. in CA). **Bumper Protection Group:** front and rear bumper guards and front bumper rub strips. Bodyside protection molding with vinyl insert for 500 (N.A. with Tu-Tone). Lower bodyside protection (application of vinyl along the lower sides to help protect against stone pecking. **Brougham Decor Group:** split bench seat in cloth and vinyl trim or Maeao vinyl upholstery. Bucket seats. H78-14B, HR78-14B, G70-14B and H70-14B tires.

NOTE: Colors offered on 1978 Rancheros were: Russet Metallic, Dove Grey, Dark Midnight Blue, Creme, Light Chamois, Black, Polar White, Silver Metallic, Light Blue, Dark Jade Metallic, Dark Brown Metallic, Bright Blue Glow, Light Jade Glow, Champagne Metallic. Tu-Tone option (500 only): accent color was applied on roof, hood and lower bodyside.

1978 Ford Bronco Ranger XLT Utility Wagon (JAG)

BRONCO CUSTOM: — The 4-wheel-drive Bronco was completely restyled for 1978. As sales literature stated, it was "all new, top to bottom, front to rear." Front end design echoed that used on the full-size truck. The honeycomb theme grille and two recessed, rectangular headlights, were surrounded by bright molding. The amber wraparound parking lights were beneath the headlights. "Ford" was printed in block letters on the face of the hood. The rectangular side marker lights were located in the bodyside sculpturing which ran straight from the upper part of the headlight level almost the entire length of the truck. Standard features included: Deep foam bucket seats. Color-keyed instrument and door trim panel in red, black, blue, green or tan. Steering wheel and hornpad were black, sunvisors were white. Bright hub caps. Bright door-mounted mirrors on both sides. Black painted front and rear bumpers. Power brakes. Twenty-five gallon fuel tank. Four-speed manual.

I.D. DATA (Bronco): See F-100 I.D.

Model	Body Type	Price	Weight	Prod. Total
U-150	Wagon	6543	4509	70,546

ENGINE (Bronco): Displacement: 351 cu. in. V8, 2-bbl. carburetor.

CHASSIS: Wheelbase: 104 in. Overall length: 180.3 in. Overall width: 79.3 in. Overall height: 75.5 in. Tires: L78 x 15B.

POWERTRAIN OPTIONS: Cruise-O-Matic automatic. Displacement: 400 cu. in. V8.

NOTE: Most 1978 Broncos, 78.9 percent, came with an automatic.

CONVENIENCE OPTIONS: Bright wheel lip moldings. Inside spare tire cover. Mag style wheel covers. Narrow bodyside paint stripe. ComfortVent heater. Console (with front bucket seats). **Convenience Group:** intermittent wipers, gathered map pockets and 12 in. day/night mirror. Heavy-duty scissor-type jack. Insulation package. Lighted visor vanity mirror. Rear floor mat. Front bench seat. Folding rear bench seat (includes rear floor mat). Tinted glass all around. **Visibility Group:** lights in glove box,

1978 Ford Bronco Ranger XLT Utility Wagon (OCW)

ashtray and underhood: instrument panel courtesy lights and dome light with integral map light (not included with front bench seat). **Handling Package:** rear stablizer bar, quad front and heavy-duty rear shocks. **Northland Special Package:** 68-amp-hr. battery, 60 amp alternator, dual 600 watt engine block heater and limited slip rearaxle. Rear stablizer bar. Skid plates for standard fuel tank and transfer case. Trailer towing packages (light and heavy duty). 32-gallon fuel tank in lieu of standard (includes skid plate. Inside locking hood release. **Protection Group:** bright door edge guards, front bumper guards and front bumper rub strip. **Security Group:** locking gas cap, inside hood release lock, spare tire lock and locking glove box. **Free Wheeling Package:** tricolor striping, black bumpers, dual black low-mount mirrors, sport steering wheel, black glove box applique, and five 15 x 6 styled steel wheels with raised white letter tires (15 x 8 styled steel wheels available after 11-7-77). **Ranger XLT:** rectangular headlamps, bright front and rear bumpers, bright molding around front windshield, rear side windows, wheel lips and lower section of tailgate, body side molding with black vinyl insert and bright taillight bezels; cut-pile carpeting, door trim panels with woodgrain accent, seat covering in vinyl or vinyl and cloth, spare tire cover, woodtone dash with bright moldings, and "Ranger XLT" plaque on the glove box. Tilt steering wheel. Privacy glass. Low-mount Western mirrors. Air conditioning. AM digital clock radio. AM/FM stereo. Quad front shock absorbers. Recreation swing-out mirrors. Sliding side windows. GT bar. Sport steering wheel. 5-slot forged aluminum 15 in. wheels. Maintenance-free battery. Speed control. Swing away spare tire carrier. 40-channel CB radio. Front tow hooks. Front and rear contour bumpers. 10-hole forged aluminum 15 in. wheels. Painted styled steel white 15 x 6 wheels. Part-time 4x4 (with automatic).

NOTE: A total of 68.7 percent of 1979 Broncos had bucket seats, 63 percent tinted glass, 32.4 percent an AM radio, and 53.3 percent air conditioning.

NOTE: Bronco color choices for 1979 were: Raven Black, Wimbledon White, Candyapple Red, Castillo Red, Medium Copper, Silver Metallic, Midnight Blue Metallic, Light Blue, Bahama Blue, Dark Jade Metallic, Light Jade, Chrome Yellow, Tan, Cream, Dark Brown Metallic, Jade Glow, Dark Cinnamon Glow, Bright Emerald, Bright Yellow. Choice of black or white fiberglass rear roof section to go with any exterior color. Tu-Tone choices: Special hood and roof Tu-Tone: black or white only to match black or white fiberglass roof, available with all solid exterior colors. Combination Tu-Tone: hood/roof/bodyside in black or white only to match black or white roof, includes special hood/roof and Deluxe Tu-Tone with moldings. Deluxe Tu-Tone: accent color applied within bodyside molding and upper and lower tailgate, bodyside molding included.

ECONOLINE E-100 CARGO VAN: — Econolines received a minor facelift for 1978. The very similar, but revised grille, had less bright work, which gave it a semi "blacked out" appearance. Different paint treatment of two-tone vans added to the "new" look. The speedometer now had kilometer per hour reading beneath the miles per hour markings. Standard features were: Full-foam driver's bucket seat. Color-keyed vinyl seat trim in black, blue, jade green or tan. Turn indicators with lane change feature. Padded full width instrument panels. Brake warning light. Two-speed electric windshield wipers. Wiper arm mounted washer jets. Dome lights. Front compartment headlining and insulated floor mat with scuff plates. Electric horn. Door checks. Argent painted bumpers and hub caps. Bright windshield molding. Painted 5 in. x 8 in. mirrors. Hinged side cargo doors (sliding door available at no extra cost). Power steering. Three-speed manual. Twin-I-Beam front suspension.

ECONOLINE E-100 WINDOW VAN: — As the name suggests, the window van had glass all around. It shared standard features with the cargo van.

ECONOLINE E-100 DISPLAY VAN: — This model had windows at the rear and on the right hand side. It came with the same standard features as Cargo Van.

I.D. DATA (Econoline E-100): See F-100.

Model	Body Type	Price	Weight	Prod. Total
E-040	Cargo Van	4840	3810	Note
E-040	Window Van	4965	3837	Note
E-040	Display Van	4927	3824	Note

NOTE: Total Ford van sales in the 1978 model year was 228,849.

ENGINE (Econoline E-100): Displacement: 300 cu. in. Six, 120 horsepower at 3400 R.P.M. Bore & stroke: 4.00 x 3.98. Compression ratio: 8.0:1. 1-bbl. carburetor.

ECONOLINE E-150 CARGO VAN: — The E-150 could run on leaded or unleaded gas. It had a slightly higher GVW rating than the E-100. Unlike the E-100, it could be operated on either leaded or unleaded gasoline. Standard features echoed those on the E-100.

ECONOLINE E-150 SUPER CARGO VAN: — This van was introduced in January 1978. It had a 20 in. extended rear overhang. That allowed owners to carry longer loads. Standard features were same as on E-100.

ECONOLINE E-150 DISPLAY VAN: — The van shared styling with the E-100 Display Van but had greater load capacity.

ECONOLINE E-150 SUPER DISPLAY VAN: — See E-150 Super Cargo Van.

ECONOLINE E-150 WINDOW VAN: — This van shared styling with the E-100 Window Van, but had greater load capacity.

ECONOLINE E-150 SUPER WINDOW VAN: — See E-150 Super Cargo Van.

I.D. DATA (Econoline E-150): See F-100.

Model	Body Type	Price	Weight	Prod. Total
E-140	Cargo Van	5008	3741	Note
E-140	Super Cargo Van	5232	—	Note
E-160	Display Van	5095	3755	Note
E-160	Super Display Van	5319	—	Note
E-150	Window Van	5133	3768	Note
E-150	Super Window Van	5319	—	Note

NOTE: See E-100.

ENGINE (Econoline E-150): Same as E-100.

ECONOLINE E-250 CARGO VAN: — The new E-250 had a higher GVW rating and more heavy duty front and rear axles, than the E-150. It also came with eight, rather than five, hole wheels. Standard features were the same as those on the E-100.

ECONOLINE E-250 SUPER CARGO VAN: — See E-150 Super Cargo Van.

ECONOLINE E-250 DISPLAY VAN: — This vehicle shared styling and features with the E-100, but had greater load capacity.

ECONOLINE E-250 SUPER DISPLAY VAN: — See E-150 Super Cargo Van.

ECONOLINE E-250 WINDOW VAN: — This vehicle shared styling and features with the E-100 Window Van, but had greater load capacity.

ECONOLINE E-250 SUPER WINDOW VAN: — See E-150 Super Cargo Van.

ECONOLINE E-250 CUTAWAY VAN: — This van with Camper Special Packages was designed to readily accommodate custom motor homes.

ECONOLINE E-250 PARCEL DELIVERY: — The E-250 Parcel Delivery van was capable of hauling a payload up to 2,340 lbs. Its cargo area was 149.9 in. long and 74.3 in. high. The rear door opening was 84.7 in. wide.

I.D. DATA (Econoline E-250): See F-100.

Model	Body Type	Price	Weight	Prod. Total
E-240	Cargo Van	5356	4217	Note
—	Super Cargo Van	5437	—	Note
E-260	Display Van	5444	4232	Note
—	Super Display Van	5525	—	Note
E-250	Window Van	5482	4245	Note
—	Super Window Van	5563	—	Note
E-270	Cutaway Van	5237	—	Note
E-280	Parcel Delivery	6553	5294	Note

NOTE: See E-100.

ENGINE (Econoline E-250): Same as E-100.

ECONOLINE E-350 CARGO VAN: — This was the Top of the line Econoline. It had heavy-duty front and rear shocks and a greater load capacity than the other series. Standard features were the same as those on the E-100.

ECONOLINE E-350 SUPER CARGO VAN: — See E-150 Super Cargo Van.

ECONOLINE E-350 DISPLAY VAN: — See E-250 Display Van.

ECONOLINE E-350 SUPER DISPLAY VAN: — See E-150 Super Cargo Van.

ECONOLINE E-350 WINDOW VAN: — See E-250 Window Van.

ECONOLINE E-350 SUPER WINDOW VAN: — See E-150 Super Cargo Van.

ECONOLINE E-350 CUTAWAY VAN: — See E-250 Cutaway Van.

ECONOLINE E-350 PARCEL DELIVERY: — This heavy-duty van came in two wheelbases. Styling and features were the same as those offered on the E-250.

I.D. DATA (Econoline E-350): See F-100.

Model	Body Type	Price	Weight	Prod. Total
E-340	Cargo Van	5538	4376	Note
—	Super Cargo Van	—	—	Note
E-360	Display Van	5627	4395	Note
—	Super Display Van	—	—	Note
E-350	Window Van	5665	4385	Note
—	Super Window Van	—	—	Note
E-370	Cutaway Van	5354	—	Note
E-380	Parcel Delivery	7318	5648	Note

NOTE: See E-100.

ENGINE (Econoline E-350): Same as E-100.

CHASSIS: Wheelbase: 124 in. and 138 in. Overall length: 186 in. (E-100, E-150 124 in. wb), 206.8 in. (138 in. wb), 226.8 in. (Super Vans). Overall height: 79.6 in. (E-100), 81 in. (E-150, 124 in. wb), 81.2 in. (E-150 138 in. wb), 82.6 in. (E-250), 84.5 in. (E-350). Tires: GVW: 5750-11,000. Tires: F78-15B PT (E-100), L78-15B PT (E-150), 8.00 x 16.5D TT (E-250, 8.75 x 16.5E C PDV), 9.50 x 16.5D TT (E-350, 8.00 x 16.5D PDV).

POWERTRAIN OPTIONS: Cruise-O-Matic automatic. 351 V8, 460 V8 (E-250, E-350). Four-speed manual with overdrive.

CONVENIENCE OPTIONS: Custom Van: (in addition to or in place of standard) color-keyed padded full-length instrument panel with wood grained vinyl applique; front side and door trim panels; insulated front floor mats, roof rail garnish moldings, bright hub caps, taillight bezels, vent and rear window frames. **Chateau Van:** (in addition to or in place of Custom) Super Soft Ruffino vinyl seat trim, color-keyed cut pile carpeting on front floor, padded vinyl front door trim panels with woodgrained vinyl applique in center and carpeting lower panel, woodgrained vinyl horn bar insert in steering wheel, courtesy lights for all doors. Bright grille, bright bumpers, bright bodyside and rear moldings. Wheel covers. RH sliding cargo door. Adjustable or flip-fold passenger seat. High output heater and defroster. Auxiliary hot water heater. **Cruising Van:** captain's chairs, full length carpeting, deluxe insulation package with woodgrain vinyl paneling and sport steering wheel. **Free Wheeling:** (interior) full length carpeting, front door trim panels and deluxe insulation package. (exterior) 5-slot forged aluminum wheels, RWL tires, black bumpers, grille, stripe, and mirrors. Bright grille and/or front and rear bumpers. Full length, insulated carpet or mat (138 in. WB only). Courtesy light switches, front or all doors. Two stage door positioners for hinged cargo doors. Northland Special Package (includes engine block heater -35 F anti-freeze, 68 amp hr battery, 60 amp alternator and high output heater). Engine block heater. Locking fuel cap. Tinted glass. Full length hardboard headlining. Bodyside tape stripe (black, tan, white or gold). Bright grille surround molding. Black push bar. Fog lights. Ten inch portholes with privacy glass. Sport rails. Tilt steering. Speed control. Dual electric horns. Insulation Package. Protection Group (front door edge guards and front and side sliding door stepwell pads and front bumper guards). Huntsman cloth seat trim. Spare tire and wheel. Spare tire cover. Bright hub caps. Handling Package (front stablizer bar, heavy-duty shocks and heavy-duty front springs). Captains chair. Air conditioning. Power steering. Auxiliary fuel tank. Trailer towing packages. Swingout recreation mirrors. Low mount Western mirrors. AM radio. AM/FM stereo. AM/FM stereo with tape player. Door windows for rear and/or side cargo doors. One way glass in rear side windows and rear door. Flip-open windows for cargo doors. Simulated leather wrapped steering wheel. Mag style wheel covers. Painted styled steel wheels. 10-hole forged aluminum wheels. 5-slot forged aluminum wheels. Step bumper. Sport steering wheel. ComfortVent heater (N.A. with A.C.).

NOTE: Econoline colors for 1978 included: Wimbledon White, Candyapple Red, Light Blue, Silver Metallic, Light Jade, Dark Brown Metallic, Indio Tan Coral, Midnight Blue Metallic, Raven Black, Chrome Yellow, Dark Jade Metallic were standard. Blue Glow, Jade Glow, and Cinnamon Glow were optional. Four Tu-Tone paint schemes were offered. Tu-Tone paint schemes were available.

1978 Ford Club Wagon Chateau Passenger Van (OCW)

E-100 CLUB WAGON: — The new Club Wagon shared the mild styling changes found on the Econoline. E-100 was offered in 5 and 8 passenger versions. Among the standard features were: Full foam front bucket seats. Color-keyed patterned vinyl seat trim. Seat belts. Color-Two-speed electric windshield wipers. Wiper arm mounted washer jets. 10 in. rearview mirror. Dome lights. Insulated floor mat with scuff plates. Three armrests. Dual horns. Flip-open windows in sliding door and opposite windows. Painted bumpers, 5 in. x 8 in. mirrors and hub caps. Bright windshield molding.

E-150 CLUB WAGON: — This was a slightly more heavy-duty version of the E-100. It could be had in 124 in. or 138 in. wb and was also offered in five and eight passenger versions. Standard features were same as those on the E-100.

E-150 SUPER WAGON: — This was basically the same as the 138 in. wb E-150 but had an 20 in. extended rear overhang.

E-250 CLUB WAGON: — The E250 Club Wagon could be had with five, eight, or twelve passenger capacity. It had most of the same features as the E-100.

E-250 SUPER WAGON: — This was basically an E-250 with a 20 in. rear overhang.

I.D. DATA (Club Wagon): See F-100.

Model	Body Type	Price	Weight	Prod. Total
E-100	Club Wagon	5485	4090	—
E-150	Club Wagon	5680	4225	—
E-150	Super Wagon	6194	—	—
E-250	Club Wagon	5921	4735	—
E-250	Super Wagon	6506	—	—

ENGINE (Club Wagon): Same as Econoline E-100.

CHASSIS: Wheelbase: 124 in. (E-100), 138 in. (E-150, E-250). Overall length: See Econoline. GVW: 5600-5900 (E-100), 6010-6300 (E-150), 7000-8450 (E-250), 5-passenger. Tires: G78 x 15B (E-100), H78 x 15D (E-150), 8.00 x 16D (E-250).

POWERTRAIN OPTIONS: 351 V8, 460 V8. SelectShift Cruise-O-Matic automatic.

CONVENIENCE OPTIONS: Auxiliary fuel tank. Speed control. Power steering. Captain's chair. AM radio. AM/FM stereo radio. AM/FM stereo w/tape player. High-capacity or front only air conditioner. Privacy glass. Wheel covers. Swing-Lok Western mirrors. Swing-Lok low-mount Western mirrors. Bright non telescopic mirrors. Swing-out recreation mirrors. High-output heater. Roof luggage carrier. Spare tire lock. Low-mount Swing-Lok bright mirrors. AM/FM monaural radio. Bright grille and/or bumpers. Full-length insulated floor mat. **Free Wheeling Option:** black rocker panel paint accent, painted bumpers, grille and mirrors; forged aluminum wheels and RWL tires. Courtesy light switches for all doors. Hinged side doors in place of sliding door. Two-stage door positioners for all hinged double doors. Locking gas cap. Intermittent two-speed windshield wipers. **Instrument Package:** fuel monitor warning light, ammeter and oil pressure gauge. Northland Special Package. Engine block heater. Tinted glass. Full length hardbound headlining. Insulation package. Protection Group (front door edge guards and front and side sliding door step well pads). Shoulder harness. Spare tire cover. Bright hub caps. Low Line Camper Package. High Line Camper Special Package. Trailer Towing Packages (LD, HD, Extra HD). **Custom Package:** (in addition to or in place of standard) color-keyed padded full-length instrument panel with wood-grained vinyl applique; color-keyed seat pedestal, cowl trim panels, padded vinyl door trim panels; cigarette lighter, insulated full-length floor mats, window garnish moldings, color-keyed armrests on three and four passenger seats, three coat hooks, aluminum scuff plates on side and rear doors, bright hub caps, taillight bezels and window frames. **Chateau Package:** (in addition to or in place of Custom) Super Soft vinyl seat trim, color-keyed cut pile carpeting full-length of floor, lower section of engine cover and rear wheel wells; vinyl door trim panels with woodgrained vinyl applique in center and carpeted lower panel, color-keyed vinyl headlining (insulated), woodgrained vinyl horn bar insert, color-keyed vinyl spare tire cover; bright grille, bumpers, lower bodyside and rear moldings. **Convenience Group:** courtesy light door switches, day/night mirror, 2-speed windshield wipers.

COURIER PICKUP: — The biggest styling change for 1978 was moving the parking lamps from the bumper to the grille. Standard features included: Vinyl headliner. Inside hood release. Full width vinyl upholstered seat. Hinged seat back for easy access to stowage area. Independent front suspension. Six-leaf rear springs. Double-acting shocks front and rear.

I.D. DATA (Courier): See 1976 Courier I.D.

Model	Body Type	Price	Weight	Prod. Total
—	Pickup	3895	2675	70,546

ENGINE (Courier): Displacement: 110 cu. in. OHC four-cylinder.

CHASSIS: Wheelbase: 106.9 in. (6 ft. box), 112.8 in. (7 ft. box). Overall length: 177.9 in. (6 ft. box), 189.4 in. (7 ft. box). Overall width: 63 in. Overall height: 61.5 in. GVW: 3.965 lbs. Tires: 6.00 x 14 in.

POWERTRAIN OPTIONS: Floor shifted automatic or five-speed manual (with overdrive).

CONVENIENCE OPTIONS: AM or AM/FM monaural radios. Air conditioning. Tinted glass all around. Western rearview mirrors. Rear step bumper. Radial tires. Cast aluminum wheels. COLD Weather Group: electric rear window defroster, heavy-duty battery, and high-output heater. Free Wheeling Packages A and B.

F-100 CUSTOM PICKUP: — Ford light duty trucks had new styling for 1978. The Ford name was now spelled in block letters on the face of the hood. Wraparound amber parking lights were located below each of the headlights. The higher grille had a rectangular slots theme and was rounded slightly at the sides. Headlights and grille were encased in a thick bright trim frame (with optional chrome grille). The revised front bumper had a heftier appearance. Among standard features were: Chromed contour front bumper. Argent grille. Turn signal lever with lane change feature. Behind-seat storage area (regular cabs). Full-width, energy absorbing instrument panel. Molded door trim panels with armrests. Large glove box with push button latch and woodgrain vinyl applique on door. Argent hub caps. Black carpet grain floor mat. Headlining. Door scuff plates. Mohave embossed vinyl seat trim. Twin-I-Beam front suspension. No rust front fender liners. Three-speed manual transmission. F-100 buyers could choose from all-steel, welded construction Styleside or seasoned hardwood floor Flareside boxes in either long or short wheelbases. Super Cab models were only offered in the Styleside.

I.D. DATA (F-100): See 1971 F-100 I.D.

Model	Body Type	Price	Weight	Prod. Total
F-100	(81) Chassis w/Cab	4168	3099	—
F-100	Chassis w/Super Cab	4726	3589	—
F-100	(6½ ft.) Pickup (Flare)	4399	3453	—
F-100	(6¾ ft.) Pickup (Style)	4399	3453	—
F-100	(8 ft.) Pickup (Flare)	4475	3518	—
F-100	(8 ft.) Pickup (Style)	4475	3518	—
F-100	Pickup (Super Cab)	4957	3493	—

ENGINE (F-100): Same as 1977 but 132 horsepower at 3600 R.P.M.

F-150 CUSTOM PICKUP: — The F-150 was a bit more heavy duty than the F-100. Its payload capacity was several hundred pounds greater. However, it came with most of the same standard features, plus power brakes. The Super Cab (with area behind the front seat for an optional folding rear seat or two jump seats) was offered with the 6¾ in. and 8 ft. Styleside box. The regular cab was only available in the 8 ft. Styleside or Flareside box.

I.D. DATA (F-150): See F-100 I.D.

Model	Body Type	Price	Weight	Prod. Total
F-150	(81) Chassis w/Cab	4548	3190	—
F-150	Chassis w/Super Cab	5030	3609	—
F-150	(8 ft.) Pickup (Flare)	4779	3579	—
F-150	(8 ft.) Pickup (Style)	4779	3579	—
F-150	Pickup (Super Cab)	5262	3963	—

ENGINE (F-150): Same as F-100.

1978 Ford F-250 Ranger XLT Styleside Pickup (JAG)

F-250 CUSTOM PICKUP: — The F-250 had most of the same features as the F-100. It too was offered with regular or Super cabs and with Flareside or Styleside boxes. Power brakes and a three-speed manual transmission were standard.

I.D. DATA (F-250): See F-100 I.D.

Model	Body Type	Price	Weight	Prod. Total
F-250	(81) Chassis w/Cab	4856	3488	—
F-250	Chassis w/Crew Cab	5634	4100	—
F-250	Pickup (Flare)	5087	3877	—
F-250	Pickup (Style)	5087	3877	—
F-250	Pickup (Super Cab)	5433	4088	—
F-250	Pickup (Crew Ca)	5866	4455	—
F-250	Chas. w/Super Cab	5201	3734	—

ENGINE (F-250): Same as F-100.

F-350 CUSTOM PICKUP: — The F-350 pickup was only offered with the Styleside box. However, there were three choices of cabs: Regular, Super, or Crew. Front only shocks, (rear with Super Cab) a four-speed manual transmission, and power front brakes were standard.

F-350 PLATFORM/STAKE: — Two lengths of one ton F-350 Platform/Stake's were available: 9 ft. and 12 ft. Floor frames of the Platform/Stake were made of steel cross sills riveted to steel siderails. Floorboards were interlocked with steel brackets. Formed steel caps covered ends of body sills. Side boards were hardwood and stakes were steel. A four-speed manual transmission was standard.

I.D. DATA (F-350): See F-100 I.D.

Model	Body Type	Price	Weight	Prod. Total
F-350	(81)Chassis w/cab 137"	5187	3783	—
F-350	(155 in. wb) SuperCab Chassis 155"	5943	4285	—
F-350	(140 in. wb) Pickup (Style)	5776	4462	—
F-350	(80) (9 ft.) Platform	5768	4385	—
F-350	Pickup (Super Cab)	6174	4674	—
F-350	(86) (9 ft.) Stake	5814	4625	—
F-350	Pickup (Crew Cab)	6160	4748	—
F-350	(167 in. wb) Crew Cab Chassis 167"	5941	4307	—

ENGINE (F-350): Same as F-250 for Platform/Stake & Chas. w/Cab. Pickup had 351 V8.

CHASSIS: Wheelbase: 117 in. (F-100), 133 in. (F-100, F-150, F-250), 140 in. (F-350), 139 in. (F-100, F-150, F-250 SC), 155 in. (SC), 150 in. (F-250 CC), 166.5 in. (F-350 CC), 137 in. (F-350 Platform/Stake), 161 in. (F-350 Platform/Stake). Overall length: 195.1 in. (F-100 6¾ ft. Style), 211.3 in. (F-100, F-150, F-250 8 ft. Style), 217.3 in. (F-100, F-150, F-250 6¾ in. SC), 233.5 in. (8 ft. SC), 192.2 in. (F-100 6½ ft. Flare), 208.4 in. (8 ft. Flareside), 221.8 in. (9 ft. Platform/Stake), 259.3 in. (12 in. Platform/Stake). GVW: 4900-5800 (F-100), 6050-6400 (F-150), 6200-7800 (F-250), 8300-10,000 (F-350). Tires: F78 x 15B PT (F-100), L78 x 15B PT (F-150), 8.00 x 16.5D TT (F-250, F-350).

POWERTRAIN OPTIONS: 4-speed manual, 4-speed manual with overdrive, Cruise-O-Matic automatic. 302 V8 (F-100, F-150), 351 V8, 400 V8, 460 V8 (N.A. F-100).

CONVENIENCE OPTIONS: Bright box rails for 8 ft. Stylesides. Bright body side molding with black vinyl insert (for Custom and Ranger Stylesides and Chassis Cabs). Bright rocker panel molding (N.A. with Lariat, Crew Cab, Flareside, or Deluxe Tu-Tones). Bright wheel lip molding (Custom only). Narrow bodyside molding (for Custom Stylesides and Chassis Cabs). Tape/paint stripe dual narrow extending the full length of Styleside pickups, available in five colors with solid exterior paint or regular Tu-Tone only. Pickup box cover (textured white fiberglass and lined side and rear windows, adjustable roof vent and liftgate). Deluxe box cover (sliding side windows with screens, bright side and rear window moldings, dome light, Tu-Tone paint). Sliding front window available on white box cover. High output heater. ComfortVent heater. Rear bench or jump seats (Super Cab). **Convenience Package:** intermittent wipers, 12 in. day/night mirror, and door map pockets. **Visibility/Light Group:** glove box, ashtray, under instrument panel, engine compartment, and cargo box lights. Electric rear window defroster. Breathable knitted vinyl seat upholstery. Duraweave polyknit seat upholstery. Heavy-duty black vinyl seat upholstery. Rainbow tape stripe (Stylesides). GT bar (Stylesides). Forged aluminum wheels (5-slot brushed or 10-hole polished). Styled steel wheels. Step bumper. **Free Wheeling Styleside:** "A": interior in silver and black with red accents, rainbow bodyside tape stripe, blackout grille and black front bumper (an optional black rear contour or step bumper was required). "B": black GT bar, painted styled steel wheels in white or yellow, and a spare tire lock. **Free Wheeling Flareside:** distinctive pinstriping (black, white or gold), blackout grille plus black front and rear bumpers. Four-wheel drive (now available on Super Cab, in addition to regular and Crew Cabs). Tilt steering wheel. CB radio. Engine block heater. Super cooling package. Trailer towing packages. **Northland Special:** engine block heater, -35 degrees F antifreeze, 68 amp-hr battery, 60 amp alternator, and limited slip rear axle. **Handling Package:** (F-100, F-150) front stablizier bar, heavy-duty front and rear shocks, and heavy-duty front springs (radial tires were recommended). Amber cab clearance lights (five). Locking inside hood release. 8 chromed tie-down hooks. **Protection Package:** bright door edge guards, front bumper guards and rub strip. **Security Group:** locking gas cap(s), glove box door, inside hood release and spare tire (regular carrier only). Recreation swing-out mirrors (6¾ in. x 9½ in.). Low-mount western 9 in. x 6 in. mirrors. Digital AM clock radio (displayed time and radio frequency). AM, AM/FM, and AM/FM stereo radios. Air conditioning. Illuminated vanity mirror. Speed control. Sliding rear window. Tool stowage box with locking door in curbside of pickup box skirt on 8 ft. Stylesides. Sport steering wheel with brushed spokes and simulated leather wrapped padded rim. Simulated leather wrapped steering wheel (included woodgrain vinyl horn pad with Custom and Ranger). Maintenance-free battery. Chromed or black contour rear bumpers (Styleside), black channel (Flareside). Painted styled steel 15 in. wheels. Slide-out spare tire carrier. Chrome grille and bright headlight surround (grille only with Custom). Mag-style wheel covers for 15 in. wheels. Full wheel covers for pickups with 15 in. or 16.5 in. wheels. Flip open rear side windows on Super Cabs (plain or tinted glass) with bright moldings and window latch. **Ranger:** (in addition to or in place of Custom items) rectangular headlights, bright moldings on roof drip rail and all windows, bright narrow bodyside moldings (all cabs and Stylesides), bright hub caps (except dual rears), bright upper and lower tailgate moldings and bright taillight bezels, Chain Mail vinyl seat upholstery with color-keyed seat back cover (regular cabs), floor covering, sun visors and headliner with bright moldings, added sound insulation, (Skanda cloth upholstery optional at no extra charge). **Ranger XLT:** bright aluminum bodyside molding with black vinyl insert, and bright moldings on roof drip rail, windshield, rear window, rear side windows (Super Cabs and Crew Cab); Westminster cloth seat upholstery with vinyl trim; (Chain Mail vinyl was a no-cost option), wall to wall cut-pile carpeting covered floor insulation; vinyl headlining had sound absorbing backing; door trim panels had woodgrain vinyl insert and bright trim moldings; steering wheel horn bar had woodgrain vinyl surround; Stylesides had special tailgate applique with bright backup light and wheel lip moldings. **Ranger Lariat:** (Styleside) deluxe tu-tone paint treatment with "race track" molding; special Ranger Lariat emblems, black tailgate applique (solid exterior paint colors were available); Picton cloth seat upholstery trimmed with super-soft vinyl; deluxe seat belts; color-keyed vinyl headlining with special sound absorbing padding and button quilted design; door trim panels with padded inserts above and map pockets in the lower door; wall to wall plus side cowl carpeting. Camper Special Package.

NOTE: F-series colors for 1978 were: Raven Black, Wimbledon White, Candyapple Red, Castillo Red, Silver Metallic, Midnight Blue Metallic, Light Blue, Bahama Blue, Light Jade, Dark Jade Metallic, Chrome Yellow Tan, Medium Copper, Dark Brown Metallic, Dark Cinnamon Glow, Cream, Jade Glow. Maroon, Bright Yellow and Tangerine were available on special order at extra cost. Wimbledon White could be used as the accent color for any exterior color except Silver Metallic and Cream. Regular, Deluxe and combination Tu-Tones were available. Interior colors were: black, blue, red, jade green or saddle.

PRODUCTION NOTE: 1978 model year Ford light conventional truck sales totaled 875,153.

Pricing

	5	4	3	2	1
1978					
Courier					
Pickup	450	900	1500	2100	3000
Ranchero					
500 Pickup	830	1650	2750	3850	5500
GT Pickup	850	1700	2850	4000	5700
Squire Pickup	890	1770	2950	4150	5900
Bronco					
Wagon	890	1770	2950	4150	5900
Econoline E-100					
Cargo Van	440	870	1450	2050	2900
Window Van	470	950	1550	2200	3100
Display Van	500	1000	1650	2300	3300
Club Wagon	570	1140	1900	2650	3800
Custom Club Wagon	600	1200	2000	2800	4000
Chateau Club Wagon	630	1250	2100	3000	4200
Econoline E-200					
Cargo Van	400	800	1350	1900	2700
Window Van	440	870	1450	2050	2900
Display Van	470	950	1550	2200	3100
Econoline E300					
Cargo Van	390	780	1300	1800	2600
Window Van	420	840	1400	1950	2800
Display Van	450	900	1500	2100	3000
F-100 — (½-Ton)					
Flareside Pickup	740	1470	2450	3350	4900
Styleside Pickup	750	1500	2500	3500	5000
Super Cab Pickup	—	—	—	—	5100
F-250 — (¾-Ton)					
Flareside Pickup	700	1400	2350	3250	4700
Styleside Pickup	720	1450	2400	3300	4800
Super Cab	740	1470	2450	3350	4900
F-350 — (1-Ton)					
Pickup	690	1380	2300	3200	4600
Crew Cab Pickup	660	1320	2200	3100	4400
Stake	630	1250	2100	3000	4200

1979 FORD

1979 Ford Ranchero GT Sport Pickup (OCW)

RANCHERO 500 PICKUP: — Styling was unchanged for 1979. Standard features include: SelectShift automatic transmission. Power steering and brakes. Bright hub caps. Vinyl door trim and spare tire compartment. Carpeting. Cloth/vinyl combination trimmed bench seat.

RANCHERO GT PICKUP: — The GT was once again the most popular Ranchero. It had most of the same items as the 500 plus: Flight bench seat in cloth and vinyl with matching door trim panels and cut-pile carpet. GT stripe. Dual sport mirrors. Bright hub caps with trim rings. Sports instrumentation group with engine turned cluster applique.

RANCHERO SQUIRE PICKUP: — In addition to most of the items on the 500, the Squire had: Simulated woodgrain paneling on sides and tailgate. Deluxe wheel covers.

I.D. DATA (Ranchero): See 1960 Ranchero I.D.

Model	Body Type	Price	Weight	Prod. Total
97D	Pickup (500)	5866	3698	12,093
97R	Pickup (GT)	6289	3716	12,159
97K	Pickup (Squire)	6014	3728	758

ENGINE (Ranchero): Displacement: 302 cu. in. V8, 130 net horsepower at 3800 R.P.M. Bore & stroke: 4 in. x 3 in. Compression ratio: 8.0:1. 2-bbl. carburetor.

CHASSIS: Wheebase: 118 in. Overall length: 220.1 in. Overall height: 53.5 in. GVW: 4725-5685. Tires: HR78-14B (RWL on GT).

POWERTRAIN OPTIONS: 351 V8.

NOTE: Most 1979 Rancheros, 67.9 percent, came with the 351 V8.

CONVENIENCE OPTIONS: Dual sport mirrors. Wire wheelcovers. Magnum 500 chrome wheels. SelectAire conditioner available with manual or automatic temperature control. AM/FM stereo with 8-track tape. AM/FM stereo with cassette tape player. AM/FM stereo with search feature. AM/FM stereo. AM/FM monaural. AM radio. Day/date clock. **Sports Instrumentation Group:** woodtone applique around instrument cluster pods; tach, temperature and oil pressure gauges, trip odometer, ammeter, electric clock and luxury steering wheel. Tilt steering wheel. Cornering lamps. Six-way power flight bench or split bench seat. **Appearance Protection Group:** door edge guards, floor mat and license plate frames. Deluxe wheel covers. Wheel trim rings. Vinyl roof in black, white, red, blue and cordovan (not available with GT or Tu-Tones). Wheel lip moldings. **Convenience Group:** intermittent windshield wipers, automatic parking brake release, RH remote control mirror, trip odometer, and passenger visor vanity mirror. Fingertip speed control. Illuminated entry system. **Light Group:** engine compartment, glove box and ashtray lights; plus "door ajar" warning light and "headlights on" warning buzzer. Power door windows. Tinted glass all around. Engine block heater. **Heavy-Duty Handling Suspension:** Heavy-duty rear springs, and rear stabilizer bar. Heavy-duty alternator. Heavy-duty battery. Medium-duty trailer towing package. Traction-lok differential (n.a. in California). **Bumper Protection Group:** front and rear bumper guards and front bumper rub strips. Bodyside protection molding with vinyl insert for 500 (n.a. with Tu-Tone). Lower bodyside protection (application of vinyl along the lower sides to help protect against stone pecking.) **Brougham Decor Group:** split bench seat in cloth and vinyl trim or Maeao vinyl upholstery. Bucket seats. **Limited Production Ranchero:** leather seat, steering wheel and dash pad; T-Bird (or Cougar) inner door panels, wide wheel opening moldings WSW tires, and wire wheel covers.

NOTE: Colors offered on 1979 Rancheros were: Dark Red, Dove Grey, Midnight Blue Metallic, Pastel Chamois, Light Chamois, Black, Polar White, Silver Metallic, Light Medium Blue, Dark Jade Metallic, Dark Cordovan Metallic. Optional glamour colors: burnt orange glow, light jade glow, medium blue glow. Tu-Tone option (500 only): accent color was applied on roof, hood and lower bodyside.

NOTE: Just over 30 percent of 1979 Rancheros had steel styled wheels, 29.2 percent wheel covers, 7.6 percent trailer towing equipment, 3.7 percent bucket seats, 88.9 percent air conditioing and 94 percent tinted glass.

1979 Ford Bronco Custom Ranger XLT Utility Wagon

BRONCO CUSTOM: — After last year's dramatic styling changes, the four-wheel-drive Bronco was left pretty much alone for 1979. As before, the front end design echoed that used on the full-size pickups. The honeycomb theme grille and two recessed, rectangular headlights, were surrounded by bright molding. The amber wraparound parking lights were beneath the headlights. "Ford" was printed in block letters on the face of the hood. The rectangular side marker lights were located in the bodyside sculpturing which ran straight from the upper part of the headlight level almost the entire length of the truck. Standard features included: Deep foam bucket seats. Color-keyed instrument and door trim panel in red, black, blue, jade or sand tan. Steering wheel and horn pad were black, sunvisors were white. Bright hub caps. Bright door-mounted mirrors on both sides. Black painted front and rear bumpers. Power brakes. Twenty-five gallon fuel tank. Four-speed manual. Hardboard rear quarter panels.

I.D. DATA (Bronco): See F-100 I.D.

Model	Body Type	Price	Weight	Prod. Total
U-150	Wagon	7733	4569	75,761

ENGINE (Bronco): Displacement: 351 cu. in. V8, 2-bbl. carburetor.

CHASSIS: Wheelbase: 104 in. Overall length: 180.3 in. Overall width: 79.3 in. Overall height: 75.5 in. Tires: L78 x 15B in.

POWERTRAIN OPTIONS: Cruise-O-Matic automatic. 400 cu. in. V8.

NOTE: Most 1979 Broncos, 78.8 percent, came with an automatic.

1979 Ford Bronco Ranger XLT Utility Wagon (JAG)

CONVENIENCE OPTIONS: Bright wheel lip moldings. Chrome bumpers. Tri-color or Chromatic tape stripe. Narrow bodyside paint stripe. Comfort-Vent heater. Console (with front bucket seats). **Convenience Group:** intermittent wipers, gathered map pockets and 12 in. day/night mirror. Heavy-duty scissor-type jack. Insulation package. Lighted visor vanity mirror. Rear floor mat. Front bench seat. Folding rear bench seat (includes rear floor mat). Tinted glass all around. **Visibility Group:** lights in glove box, ashtray and underhood: instrument panel courtesy lights and dome light with integral map light (not included with front bench seat). **Handling Package:** rear stablizer bar, quad front and heavy-duty rear shocks. Captains chairs with fold down arm rests. Part time 4-wheel-drive (with automatic). Trailer towing packages; light (up to 2000 lbs.), heavy-duty (over 2000 lbs.). Thirty-two gallon fuel tank in lieu of standard (includes skid plate. Inside locking hood release. **Protection Group:** bright door edge guards, front bumper guards and front bumper rub strip. **Security Group:** locking gas cap, inside hood release lock, spare tire lock and locking glove box. **Free Wheeling Package:** tri-color or chromatic tape stripe striping, black bumpers, dual black low-mount mirrors, sport steering wheel, black glove box applique, and five 15 x 6 styled steel wheels in white or chrome yellow, with raised white letter L78 x 15C tires. **Ranger XLT:** insulation package, rectangular headlamps, bright front and rear bumpers, bright molding around front windshield, rear side windows, wheel lips and lower section of tailgate, bodyside molding with black vinyl insert and bright taillight bezels; cut-pile carpeting, door trim panels with woodgrain accent, seat covering in vinyl or vinyl and cloth, spare tire cover, woodtone dash with bright moldings, and "Ranger XLT" plaque on the glove box. Tilt steering wheel. Privacy glass. Low-mount western mirrors. Air conditioning. AM digital clock radio. AM/FM stereo. Quad front shock absorbers. Recreation swing-out mirrors. Sliding side windows. GT bar. Sport steering wheel. 5-slot forged aluminum 15 in. wheels. Maintenance-free battery. Speed control. Swing away spare tire carrier. 40-channel CB radio. Front tow hooks. Front and rear contour bumpers. 10-hole forged aluminum 15 in. wheels. Painted styled steel white 15 x 6 wheels 5-slot forged aluminum 15 x6 wheels. AM radio. AM/FM monaural radio.

NOTE: A total of 62.2 percent of '79 Broncos had air conditioning, 29.9 percent had cruise control, and 33.5 percent had tilt steering.

NOTE: Bronco color choices for 1979 were: Raven Black, Wimbledon White, Candyapple Red, Maroon Metallic, Coral, Silver Metallic, Dark Blue Metallic, Light Medium Blue, Bright Emerald, Dark Jade Metallic, Light Jade, Midnight Jade, Gold Metallic, Light Sand, Dark Brown Metallic, Medium Copper Metallic, Bright Yellow, Medium Blue Glow, Walnut Glow. Standard Bronco paint scheme: solid exterior body color with rear fiberglass roof in Black, Sand, or White.

1979 Ford Econoline 100 Chateau Window Van (OCW)

ECONOLINE E-100 CARGO VAN: — The Econoline received a new criss-cross pattern grille for 1979. New, slightly recessed rectangular headlights were on each side of the grille. Rectangular parking lights were directly below the headlights. Among the standard features were: Full-foam driver's bucket seat. Vinyl seat trim in black, blue, Jade or Sand. Padded full-width instrument panel. Brake warning light. Two-speed electric windshield wipers. Wiper-arm-mounted washer jets. Dome lights. Front com-

partment headlining and insulated floor mat with scuff plates. Door checks. Argent-painted bumpers and hub caps. Bright windshield molding. Painted mirrors. Hinged side cargo doors (sliding door available at no extra cost).

ECONOLINE E-100 DISPLAY VAN: — This model had windows at the rear and on the right hand side. It came with the same standard features as the Cargo Van.

ECONOLINE E-100 WINDOW VAN: — The Window Van had glass all around. It shared features with the Cargo Van.

I.D. DATA (Econoline): See F-100.

Model	Body Type	Price	Weight	Prod. Total
E-040	Cargo Van	5441	3659	Note
E-050	Window Van	5578	3686	Note
E-600	Display Van	5532	3673	Note

NOTE: Total Econoline model year sales in 1979 were 184,722.

ENGINE (Econoline E-100): Displacement: 300 cu. in. Six, 120 horse-power at 3400 R.P.M. Bore & stroke: 4.00 in. x 3.98 in. Compression ratio: 8.0:1. One-bbl. carburetor.

ECONOLINE E-150 CARGO VAN: — The slightly more heavy-duty E-150 had most of the same standard features as the E-100. Four-hole wheels were a distinctive item found only on this series.

ECONOLINE E-150 SUPER CARGO VAN: — This van had the same features as the E-150 Cargo Van plus a 20 in. extended rear overhang. This allowed carrying of longer loads. The maximum cargo length (right side, without passenger's seat) was 14 feet.

ECONOLINE E-150 DISPLAY VAN: — This van shared styling with the E-100 but had greater load capacity.

ECONOLINE E-150 WINDOW VAN: — This van shared styling with the E-100 Window Van, but had greater load capacity.

ECONOLINE E-150 SUPER WINDOW VAN: — See E-150 Super Cargo Van.

I.D. DATA (Econoline E-150): See F-100.

1979 Ford Cruising Van (OCW)

Model	Body Type	Price	Weight	Prod. Total
E-140	Cargo Van	5722	3822	Note
E-150	Window Van	5860	3851	Note
E-160	Display Van	5814	3876	Note
S-140	Super Cargo Van	6078	3960	Note
S-150	Super Window Van	6217	3975	Note
S-160	Super Display Van	6171	3989	Note

NOTE: See E-100.

ENGINE (Econoline E-150): Same as E-100.

ECONOLINE E-250 CARGO VAN: — The new E-250 had a higher GVW rating and more heavy-duty front and rear axles, than the E-150. It also came with eight-hole wheels. Standard features were the same as those on the E-100 except the three-speed manual was not available in California.

ECONOLINE E-250 SUPER CARGO VAN: — See E-150 Cargo Van.

ECONOLINE E-250 DISPLAY VAN: — This vehicle shared styling and features with the E-100, but had greater load capacity.

ECONOLINE E-250 SUPER DISPLAY VAN: — See E-150 Super Cargo Van.

ECONOLINE E-250 WINDOW VAN: — This vehicle shared styling and features with the E-100 Window Van, but had greater load capacity.

ECONOLINE E-250 SUPER WINDOW VAN: — See E-150 Super Cargo Van.

ECONOLINE E-250 CUTAWAY VAN: — This van with Camper Special Packages, was designed to readily accommodate custom motor homes.

ECONOLINE E-250 PARCEL DELIVERY: — The E-250 Parcel Delivery van was 149.9 in. long and 74.3 in. high in its cargo area. The rear door opening was 84.7 in. wide.

Model	Body Type	Price	Weight	Prod. Total
E-240	Cargo Van	5994	4144	Note
E-250	Window Van	6133	4173	Note
E-260	Display Van	6087	4159	Note
E-240	Super Cargo Van	6535	4349	Note
E-250	Super Window Van	6674	4364	Note
E-260	Super Display Van	6628	4378	Note

NOTE: See E-100.

ENGINE (Econoline E-250): Same as E-100.

ECONOLINE E-350 CARGO VAN: — This was the top-of-the-line Econoline Van. It had heavy-duty front and rear shocks and a greater load capacity than the other series. Standard features were the same as the E-100.

ECONOLINE E-350 SUPER CARGO VAN: — See E-150 Super Cargo Van.

ECONOLINE E-350 DISPLAY VAN: — See E-250 Display Van.

ECONOLINE E-350 SUPER DISPLAY VAN: — See E-150 Super Cargo Van.

ECONOLINE E-350 WINDOW VAN: — See E-250 Window Van.

ECONOLINE E-350 SUPER WINDOW VAN: — See E-150 Super Cargo Van.

ECONOLINE E-350 CUTAWAY VAN: — See E-250 Cutaway Van.

ECONOLINE E-350 PARCEL DELIVERY: — See E-250 Parcel Delivery.

I.D. DATA (Econoline E-350): See F-100.

Model	Body Type	Price	Weight	Prod. Total
E-340	Cargo Van	6387	4323	Note
E-350	Window Van	6526	4352	Note
E-360	Display Van	6480	4338	Note
S-340	Super Cargo Van	7249	4449	Note
S-350	Super Window Van	7387	4464	Note
S-360	Super Display Van	7341	4478	Note
E-37W	Cutaway	6188	3917	Note
E-383	Parcel Delivery	8187	5279	Note

NOTE: See E-100.

ENGINE (Econoline E-350): Same as E-100.

CHASSIS: Wheelbase: 124 in. (E-100, E-150) 138 in. Overall length: 186.8 in. (124 in. w.b.), 206.8 in. (138 in. w.b.), 226.8 in. (138 in Super Van). GVW: 5050-5650 (E-100), 6050-6300 (E-150), 6500-8250 (E-250), 8550-9800 (E-350). Tires: F78 15B PT (E-100), L78 x 15B PT (E-150), 8.00 x 16.5D TT (E-250), 9.50 x 16.5D TT (E-350).

POWERTRAIN OPTIONS: 302 V-8. 351 V-8. 460 V-8 (E-250, E-350). 300 heavy-duty Six (E-350). Four-speed manual with overdrive. Select Shift automatic.

CONVENIENCE OPTIONS: Custom Van: (in addition to or in place of standard) woodtone applique on instrument panel, front side cowl and door trim panels, cigarette lighter, front compartment headlining, insulated front floor mats, front roof rail garnish moldings, bright hub caps, bright taillight bezels, bright window frames with optional rear windows. **Chateau:** (in addition to or in place of Custom features) super soft vinyl or cloth and vinyl seat trim, cutpile carpeting in front and courtesy light switches for all doors, chrome front and rear bumpers, bright grille surround molding, bright lower bodyside character line molding, bright mirrors. Sports rails. Bodyside accent tape stripe. Three-color "Cruising Van" theme tape stripe. Porthole in right and left side. Moldings: bright grille surround, deluxe accent with bright drip rail moldings plus center bodyside and lower character line moldings, bright lower character line, bright drip rails, bright window moldings. Audio: AM radio, AM/FM monaural, AM/FM stereo, AM/digital clock radio, AM/FM stereo with tape deck or cassette player. 40-channel CB. Rear speakers. Premium Sound System. Air conditioning front or high capacity. Heaters: high out-put, ComfortVent, or auxiliary for cargo area. Roof/floor insulation package. Deluxe insulation package. Convenience group (with intermittent wipers, dome light switches in all doors and day/night mirror). Dome light courtesy switches for all doors. Western low-mount mirrors. Swing-out recreation mirrors. Sport steering wheel with simulated leather wrapping. Simulated leather wrapped steering wheel. Tilt steering. Speed control. Tinted glass all around. Privacy glass. Flip-open or fixed windows were available in all cargo doors. Single sliding side cargo door in lieu of double doors. Combination 3-passenger rear seat that converts into a bed. Dual or quad Captain's Chairs (reclining and swivel or reclining only). Passenger's seat. Flip-fold passengers seat. Cloth and vinyl trim for bucket and Captain's chairs. **Free Wheeling Packages:** Full-length carpeting, front door trim panels and the deluxe insulation package were part of the interior package. The Free Wheeling exterior package included 5-slot matte finish aluminum wheels, RWL tires, blackout grille, black painted bumpers and mirrors, and a black lower bodyside panel bordered by a half in. black stripe. Trailer Towing Packages: 5-Slot or 10-hole forged aluminum wheels. **Cruising Van:** Three color tape stripes, 10-hole polished-finish forged aluminum wheels, portholes, blackout grille, black mirrors and bumpers, Chateau front door trim panels, woodtone vinyl applique with bright surround on instrument panel, courtesy dome light switches on all doors, deluxe insulation package, full-length carpeting, Sport steering wheel, two reclining Captain's Chairs. Heavy-duty shocks. Front stabilizer bar. Engine block heater. Oil pressure gauge and ammeter. Cooling Packages: (super and extra). Push bar plus fog lights and covers. **Protection Group:** front and sliding door black step-well pads, front door edge guards, and front bumper guards (require chrome bumpers). **Security Group:** Locking gas cap, inside locking hood release and spare tire lock. Inside locking hood release. Chrome or painted argent step bumper. Chrome contour bumpers. Deluxe wheel covers.

1979 Ford Club Wagon Chateau Passenger Van (OCW)

E-100 CLUB WAGON: — A new, quick release feature was on all three-passenger bench seats. This allowed for faster adjustment of cargo and/or seating capacity. The E-100 was offered in 5 an 8 passenger versions. Among the standard features were: Front bucket and rear bench seats. Color-keyed patterned vinyl seat trim. Seat belts. Two-speed electric windshield wipers. Wiper arm mounted washer jets. 10 in. rearview mirror. Dome lights. Insulated floor mat with scuff plates. Three armrests. Dual horns. Flip-open windows in sliding door and opposite windows. Painted bumpers, 5 in. x 8 in. mirrors and hub caps. Bright windshield molding.

E-150 CLUB WAGON: — This was a slightly more heavy-duty version of the E-100. It could be had in 124 in. or 138 in. w.b. and was also offered in five and eight passenger versions. Standard features were same as those on the E-100.

E-150 SUPER WAGON: — This was basically the same as the 138 in. w.b. E-150 but had an 20 in. extended rear overhang.

E-250 CLUB WAGON: — The E-250 Club Wagon could be had with five, eight, or twelve passenger capacity. It had most of the same features as the E-100.

E-250 SUPER WAGON: — This was basically an E-250 with a 20 in. rear overhang.

E-350 SUPER WAGON: — The heavy-duty E-350 provided 20 in. more inside length than regular 138 in. wheelbase Club Wagons. Heavy-duty shocks were standard.

I.D. DATA (Club Wagon): See F-100.

Model	Body Type	Price	Weight	Prod. Total
E-100	Club Wagon	6307	3933	—
E-150	Club Wagon	6410	4005	—
E-150	Super Wagon	6951	4254	—
E-250	Club Wagon	6877	4443	—
E-250	Super Wagon	7513	4570	—
E-350	Super Wagon	8084	4815	—

ENGINE (Club Wagon): Same as Econoline E-100. (302 V-8 required on E-100 in California, 351 V-8 required on E-350 Super Wagon in California.)

CHASSIS: Wheelbase: 124 in. (E-100), 138 in. (E-150, E-250, E-350). Overall length: See Econoline. GVW: 5400-9000. Tires: G78 x 15B (E-100), H78 x 15D (E-150), 8.00 x 16D (E-250), 9.50 x 16.5D (E-350).

POWERTRAIN OPTIONS: 302 V-8, 351 V-8, 460 V-8. SelectShift Cruise-O-Matic automatic. Four-speed manual w/overdrive.

CONVENIENCE OPTIONS: Most of the same items available on the Econoline plus 4-passenger rear bench seat. Snack-game table.

NOTE: Econoline and Club Wagon colors for 1979 were: Wimbledon White, Candyapple Red, Light Medium Blue, Silver Metallic, Light Medium Pine, Dark Brown Metallic, Light Sand, Coral, Dark Blue Metallic, Raven Black, Bright Yellow, Dark Jade Metallic, Maroon. Optional Glow colors: Medium blue, Camel, Walnut. Bodyside accent tape stripe was available in Raven Black, Dark Blue Metallic, Dark Brown Metallic, Coral, Camel Glow, Walnut Glow, Light Sand, Wimbledon White or Bright Yellow. Four two-tone paint schemes were available.

COURIER PICKUP: — "Tough as all outdoors." That's what sales literature said of the new 1979 Courier. Styling remained the same as last year, but changes were made under the hood. A 2.0 litre engine was now standard. Other standard features included: Bright hub caps. Color-keyed vinyl headlining, seat and door trim panels. Instrument lighting intensity control. Cigarette lighter. Brake warning light. New dome light. Door vent windows with wedge-type handles. Padded instrument panel. Hinged seat back for easy access to storage area. Inside hood release. WSW tires. Cargo tie-down hooks. Bright front bumper. One-hand tailgate operation. Four-speed manual transmission.

I.D. DATA (Courier): See 1976 Courier I.D.

Model	Body Type	Price	Weight	Prod. Total
—	Chassis & Cab	4711	2430	Note
—	Pickup	4861	2680	Note

1979 Ford Courier Pickup w/Sport Group Package (OCW)

NOTE: Total Courier sales for model year 1979 was 76,883.

ENGINE (Courier): 2.0-Litre. OHC. Four-cylinder.

CHASSIS: Wheelbase: 106.9 in. (6 ft. box), 112.8 in. (7 ft. box). Overall length: 177.9 in. (6 ft. box), 189.4 in. (7 ft. box). Overall width: 63 in. Overall height: 61.5 in. GVW: 4100 lbs. Tires: 6.00 x 14C WSW.

POWERTRAIN OPTIONS: Floor shifted automatic or five-speed manual transmission (with overdrive).

CONVENIENCE OPTIONS: AM or AM/FM monaural pushbutton radios. Air conditioning. Low-mounted western mirrors. Tinted glass all around. Radial tires. Cast aluminum wheels. **Soft Ride Package:** 3,600 lb. GVWR, 5-leaf progressive-rate rear springs, and 2,010 lb. rated rear axle. Rear step bumper. **Free Wheeling Packages:** "A" includes: black painted GT bar and push bar. "B" includes: "A" plus cast aluminum wheels, RWL 70 series tires (5), and three color accent tape stripe. **XLT Package:** Interior: Soft, supple vinyl seat and door trim. Woodtone upper door trim panel and transmission shift knob. Cut-pile carpeting. Day/night mirror. Ashtray, under hood and glove box lights. Glove box lock. Sport steering wheel. Temperature gauge and ammeter. Exterior: Bright grille. Bright windshield, rear window, drip rail, wheel lip and taillight surround moldings. Deluxe wheelcovers. Dual accent pin stripes. **Sports Group:** Black sport steering wheel, bucket seats trimmed in black vinyl with black and white plaid fabric inserts, black carpet and interior trim, woodtone applique on instrument cluster mask, temperature gauge, and ammeter.

NOTE: The 1979 Courier was available in seven exterior colors: Red, white, light blue, silver metallic, dark brown, black, or yellow.

F-100 CUSTOM PICKUP: — The biggest styling change for 1979 was rectangular headlights were now standard. Other standard features included: Full foam seat. Chrome contour front bumper. Vent window handle. Argent grille. Behind seat storage area (regular cabs). Full-width, energy absorbing instrument panel. Molded door trim panels with armrests. Large glove box with pushbutton latch and woodtone applique on door. Dome lamp. Argent hub caps. Black carpet-grain floor mat. Headlining. Door scuff plates. Embossed vinyl seat trim. Special floor, door trim panel with headliner insulation. Three-speed manual transmission (Super Cab had automatic). Buyers could choose from 6½ ft. and 8 ft. Flaresides with regular cab, or 6¾ ft. or 8 ft. Stylesides in regular or Super Cabs.

I.D. DATA (F-100): See 1971 F-100 I.D.

Model	Body Type	Price	Weight	Prod. Total
F-100	(81) Chassis w/Cab	4878	3094	—
F-100	SuperCab Chassis	5875	3576	—
F-100	(6½ ft.) Pickup (Flare)	5085	3448	—
F-100	(6¾ ft.) Pickup (Style)	5085	3448	—
F-100	(8 ft.) Pickup (Flare)	5179	3513	—
F-100	(8 ft.) Pickup (Style)	5179	3513	—
F-100	Pickup (Super Cab)	6255	3930	—

ENGINE (F-100): Displacement: 300 cu. in. Six-cylinder. Brake horsepower: 117 at 3000 R.P.M. Bore & stroke: 4.00 x 3.98 in. Compression ratio: 8.9:1. Carburetor: One-bbl. This engine was not available in California.

F-150 CUSTOM PICKUP: — Ford's "heavy"duty" ½-ton could haul several hundred pounds more payload than the F-100. It came with most of the same standard features plus power brakes. The regular cab was available with 8-ft. all steel Styleside or wood floorboard Flareside boxes. The Super Cab, with space behind the front seat for an optional rear seat or jump seats, came with 6¾-ft. or 8-ft. Styleside boxes.

I.D. DATA (F-150): See F-100.

Model	Body Type	Price	Weight	Prod. Total
F-150	(81) Chassis w/Cab	5018	3221	—
F-150	SuperCab Chassis	6075	3655	—
F-150	Pickup (Flare)	5489	3605	—
F-150	Pickup (Style)	5489	3605	—
F-150	Pickup (Super Cab)	6302	4009	—

ENGINE (F-150): Same as F-100.

F-250 CUSTOM PICKUP: — The F-250 had most of the same features as the F-100. It too was offered with regular or Super cabs and with Flareside or Styleside boxes. Power brakes and a three-speed manual transmission were standard.

1979 Ford F-250 Ranger XLT Styleside Pickup (OCW)

I.D. DATA (F-250): See F-100 I.D.

Model	Body Type	Price	Weight	Prod. Total
F-250	(81) Chassis w/Cab	5525	3479	—
F-250	Chassis w/Crew Cab	6361	4025	—
F-250	Pickup (Flare)	5822	3868	—
F-250	Pickup (Style)	5822	3868	—
F-250	Pickup (Super Cab)	6301	4081	—
F-250	Pickup (Crew Cab)	6657	4380	—
F-250	Chassis w/Super Cab	6074	3727	—

ENGINE (F-250): Same as F-100. Super and Crew Cab required a V-8 in California.

1979 Ford F-350 Ranger XLT Styleside Pickup (OCW)

F-350 CUSTOM PICKUP: — The F-350 pickup was only offered with the Styleside box. However, there were three choices of cabs: regular, Super, or Crew. Front only shocks, a four-speed manual transmission and heavy-duty power front disc brakes were standard.

F-350 PLATFORM/STAKE: — Two lengths of 1-ton F-350 Platform/Stakes were available: 9-ft. and 12-ft. Floor frames of the Platform/Stake were made of steel cross sills riveted to steel siderails. Floorboards were interlocked with steel brackets. Formed steel caps covered ends of body sills. Side boards were hardwood and stakes were steel. A four-speed manual transmission was standard.

I.D. DATA (F-350): See F-100 I.D.

Model	Body Type	Price	Weight	Prod. Total
F-350	(81) Chassis w/Cab 137"	6141	3905	—
F-350	SuperCab Chassis 155"	6908	4121	—
F-350	(140 in. w.b.) Styleside Pickup 140"	6739	4341	—
F-350	Pickup (Super Cab)	7318	4510	—
F-350	(80) 9-ft. Platform	7132	4507	—
F-350	Pickup (Crew Cab)	7233	4766	—
F-350	(86) 9-ft. Stake	7181	4747	—
F-350	Chassis w/Crew Cab	7233	4766	—

ENGINE (F-350): Same as F-250 for Platform/Stake and Chassis w/Cab except 8.0:1 compression ratio. Pickup had 351 V-8.

CHASSIS: Wheelbase: 117 in. (F-100), 133 in. (F-100, F-150, F-250), 140 in. (F-350), 139 in. (F-100, F-150, F-250 Super Cab), 155 in. (Super Cab), 150 in. (F-350 Crew Cab), 165.5 in. (F-350 Crew Cab), 137 in. (F-350 Platform/Stake), 161 in. (F-350 Platform/Stake). Overall length: 195.1 in. (F-100 6¾-ft. Style), 211.3 in. (F-100, F-150, F-250 8-ft. Style), 140 in. (F-350 Style), 217.4 in. (F-100, F-150, F-250 6¾-ft. Super Cab), 233.6 in. (8-ft. Super Cab), 192.2 in. (F-100 6½-ft. Flare), 208.4 in. (8-ft. Flareside), 221.9 in. (9-ft. Platform-Stake), 259.5 in. (12-ft. Platform-Stake). GVW: 4800-5800 (F-100), 6050-6400 (F-150), 6200-7900 (F-250), 8900-10,000 (F-350). Tires: F78 x 15B PT (F-100), L78 x 15B PT (F-150), 8.00 x 16.5D TT (F-250), 9.50 x 16.3E TT (F-350).

POWERTRAIN OPTIONS: Four-speed manual. Four-speed manual with overdrive. Select Shift automatic 300 heavy-duty Six (F-350), 302 V-8 (F-100, F-150), 351 V-8, 400 V-8, 460 V-8 (n.a. F-100).

1979 Ford Ranger XLT "Indy 500" Pickup (IMSC/JLM)

CONVENIENCE OPTIONS: Bright box rails for 8-ft. Stylesides. Bright body side molding with black vinyl insert. Bright rocker panel molding (Stylesides only). Bright wheel lip molding (Custom stylesides only). Narrow bright bodyside molding (for Custom Stylesides). Tape/stripe dual narrow extending the full length of Styleside pickups, available with solid exterior paint or regular Tu-Tone only. Pickup box cover (textured white or Sand, fiberglass and tinted side and rear windows, adjustable roof vent and lift-gate). Deluxe box cover (sliding side windows with screens, bright side and rear window moldings, dome light.) Sliding front window available for standard or deluxe box cover. High output heater. ComfortVent heater. Rear bench or jump seats (Super Cab). **Convenience Group:** intermittent wipers, 12 in. day/night mirror, and map pockets. **Light Group:** glove box, ashtray, under instrument panel, engine compartment, and cargo box lights. Breathable knitted vinyl seat upholstery. Chain mail pattern vinyl seat upholstery. Duraweave polyknit seat upholstery. Heavy-duty black vinyl seat upholstery. Multistripe cloth inserts for Ranger regular and Super Cabs. Rainbow tape stripe Stylesides. GT bar (Stylesides). Forged aluminum wheels (5-slot brushed for 10-hole polished). Styled steel wheels. Rear step bumper. **Free Wheeling Styleside:** "A": interior in silver and black with red accents, multi-color bodyside tape stripe (Chromatic tape stripe optional), blackout grille and black front bumper (an optional black rear contour or step bumper was required). "B": black GT bar, painted styled steel wheels in white or yellow, and a spare tire lock. **Free Wheeling Flareside:** distinctive pinstriping (black, white or orange), blackout grille plus black front and rear bumpers. Four-wheel-drive (now available on F-350 series). Tilt steering wheel. CB radio. Engine block heater. Super cooling package. Trailer towing packages. High altitude emission system. **Handling Package:** (F-100, F-150) front stabilizer bar, heavy-duty gas-filled front and rear shocks, and heavy-duty front springs (radial tires were recommended). Roof clearance lights (five). Push bar. Locking inside hood release. Fog lamps. 8 chromed tie-down hooks. Front tow hook. **Protection Package:** bright door edge guards, front bumper guards and front bumper rub strip. **Security Group:** locking gas cap, glove box door, inside hood release and spare tire. Recreation swing-out mirrors (6¾ in. x 9½ in.). (N.A. with F-100). Low-mount western 9 in. x 6 in. mirrors, bright or black. Digitial AM clock radio. AM, AM/FM, and AM/FM stereo radios. Air conditioning. Illuminated vanity mirror. Speed control. Sliding rear window. Tool storage box with locking door in curbside of pickup box skirt on 8-ft. Stylesides. Sport steering wheel with simulated leather wrapped padded rim. Simulated leather wrapped steering wheel. Chromed or painted argent step bumper for Styleside. Chromed or black contour rear bumpers (Styleside), black channel (Flareside). White painted styled steel 15 in. wheels. Slide-out spare tire carrier. Chrome grille insert with bright headlight doors. Chromatic tape stripe. (Stylesides). Mag-style wheel covers for 15 in. wheels. Full wheel covers for pickups. **Ranger:** (in addition to or in place of Custom items) bright moldings, on roof drip rail, windshield, backlight and rear side windows (Super Cab); bright narrow bodyside moldings (all cabs and Stylesides), bright hub caps (except dual rears), bright upper and lower Styleside tailgate moldings and bright taillight bezels, bright wheel lip moldings, Chain Mail vinyl or multi-stripe cloth seat upholstery with color-keyed floor covering, sunvisors and white headliner, added sound insulation. **Ranger XLT:** bright aluminum bodyside molding with black vinyl insert, cloth seat upholstery with vinyl trim; (Chain Mail vinyl was a no-cost option), wall to wall cut-pile carpeting covered floor insulation; door trim panels had woodgrain vinyl insert and bright trim moldings; aluminum tailgate applique with black "Ford" letters and bright moldings. **Ranger Lariat:** (Styleside) deluxe tu-tone paint treatment with "race track" molding; special Ranger Lariat emblems, black tailgate applique (solid exterior paint exterior paint colors were available); cloth seat upholstery trimmed with super-soft vinyl (Duraweave polyknit, knitted vinyl or all-vinyl optional at no cost) color-keyed vinyl headlining with special sound absorbing padding and button quilted design; door trim panels with padded inserts above and map pockets in the lower door; wall to wall plus side cowl carpeting. F-250/350 Camper Special Package.

NOTE: Standard F-series colors for 1979 were: Raven Black, Wimbledon White, Candyapple Red, Maroon Metallic, Silver Metallic, Dark Blue Metallic, Light Medium Blue, Light Jade, Dark Jade Metallic, Bright Yellow, Gold Metallic, Medium Copper Metallic, Dark Brown Metallic, Light Sand, Coral. Optional Glow Colors: Medium Blue and Walnut. TU-TONE CHOICES: Regular: accent color was applied on roof and upper back panel; included a belt-line molding around back of cab; available with all type cabs and optional dual tape stripes. Accent: combined regular tu-tone with color-keyed dual tape stripes and had special tailgate applique. Deluxe: accent color was applied inside upper and lower tailgate molding; standard on Ranger Lariat; on other trim levels the tu-tone option included bright molding additions or deletions as needed to complement tu-tone scheme. Combination: regular and deluxe tu-tone combined.

406

PRODUCTION NOTE: Ford sold a total of 742,761 1979 light conventional trucks.

Pricing

1979	5	4	3	2	1
Courier					
Pickup	450	900	1500	2100	3000
Ranchero					
500 Pickup	830	1650	2750	3850	5500
GT Pickup	850	1700	2850	4000	5700
Squire Pickup	890	1770	2950	4150	5900
Bronco					
Wagon	890	1770	2950	4150	5900
Econoline E-100					
Cargo Van	440	870	1450	2050	2900
Window Van	470	950	1550	2200	3100
Display Van	500	1000	1650	2300	3300
Club Wagon	570	1140	1900	2650	3800
Custom Club Wagon	600	1200	2000	2800	4000
Chateau Club Wagon	630	1250	2100	3000	4200
Econoline E-200					
Cargo Van	400	800	1350	1900	2700
Window Van	440	870	1450	2050	2900
Display Van	470	950	1550	2200	3100
Econoline E-300					
Cargo Van	390	780	1300	1800	2600
Window Van	420	840	1400	1950	2800
Display Van	450	900	1500	2100	3000
F-100 — (½-Ton)					
Flareside Pickup	740	1470	2450	3350	4900
Styleside Pickup	750	1500	2500	3500	5000
Super Cab Pickup	—	—	—	—	5100
F-250 — (¾-Ton)					
Flareside Pickup	700	1400	2350	3250	4700
Styleside Pickup	720	1450	2400	3300	4800
Super Cab	740	1470	2450	3350	4900
F-350 — (1-Ton)					
Pickup	690	1380	2300	3200	4600
Crew Cab Pickup	660	1320	2200	3100	4400
Stake	630	1250	2100	3000	4200

1980 FORD

1980 Ford Bronco Custom Sport Utlity Wagon (JAG)

BRONCO CUSTOM: — The 4x4 Bronco trimmed down a bit for 1980. Although the front end treatment resembled that used on 1978-79 models it was different. The grille was revised and the parking lights were now recessed directly beneath the headlights. New, wraparound taillights were used. Also new was twin beam independent front suspension. And an improved four-wheel drive transfer case. In addition, the selector lever was relocated. Standard features included: Bucket seats. Vinyl sun visors. Padded instrument panel. Armrests. Dome lamp. Windshield header and "A" pillar moldings. Locking steering column. Antitheft sliding door lock buttons. Inside hood release. Cowl side trim. Rubber floor mats. Black front and rear bumpers. Bright hub caps and door mounted mirrors. Swingdown tailgate with power window. Power brakes and steering. Four-speed manual transmission.

I.D. DATA (Bronco): See F-100 I.D.

Model	Body Type	Price	Weight	Prod. Total
U-150	Wagon	8392	4083	48,837

ENGINE (Bronco): 300 cu. in. Six-cylinder. Displacement: 302 cu. in. V-8 (standard in California).

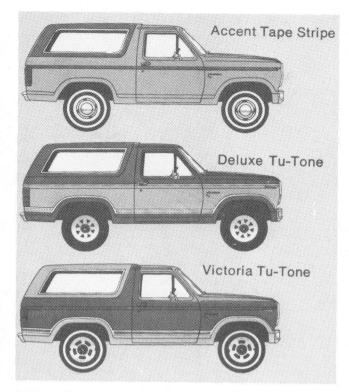

1980 Ford Bronco Exterior Trim Packages (JAG)

CHASSIS: Wheebase: 104.7 in. Overall length: 117.6 in. Overall height: 74.3 in. Tires: L78 x 15B in.

POWERTRAIN OPTIONS: SelectShift automatic. 302 V-8, 351 V-8.

NOTE: Most 1980 Broncos, 42.2 percent, came with the 302 V-8, 41 percent had the 351 V-8, and 71.2 percent the automatic.

1980 Ford Bronco Utility w/Freewheeling Package (JAG)

CONVENIENCE OPTIONS: Bright wheel lip moldings. Chrome bumpers. Tri-color tape stripe on hood and sides. Padded black GT bar. Chrome grille. ComfortVent, high output, or auxiliary heaters. Console. **Convenience Group:** intermittent wipers, map box in doors, headlamp-on warning buzzer, RH door courtesy light switch, 12 in. mirror. Front bench seat. Flip/fold rear bench seat. Tinted glass all around. Privacy glass in quarter windows. **Light Group:** lights in glove box, ashtray and underhood: instrument panel courtesy lights, dome light with map light, RH door courtesy light, headlamp-on warning buzzer (the underhood light had a 20-ft. cord). **Handling Package:** front stabilizer bar, quad heavy-duty hydraulic front and rear shocks. Captain's chairs. Tool storage box. Part time four-wheel-drive (with optional automatic transmission). Trailer towing packages; light (up to 2000 lbs.) heavy-duty (over 2000 lbs.). Thirty-two gallon fuel tank in lieu of standard (includes skid plate.) Inside locking hood release. **Protection Group:** bright door edge guards, front bumper guards and front bumper rub strip. **Security Group:** locking gas cap, inside hood release lock, spare tire lock and locking glove box. **Free Wheeling Package:** "A": pinstripes along bodyside, hood, tailgate and around door windows: sport wheel covers, bright bumpers. "B": sports instrumentation, simulated leather wrapped steering wheel, fog lamps, bumper guards, handling package, GT bar, white styled steel wheels. **Ranger XLT:** brushed aluminum tailgate applique with bright letters, chrome bumpers, bright rear side window moldings, bright lower bodyside molding with black vinyl insert, Ranger XLT plaque, cloth trim or patterned vinyl interior, cut-pile carpeting, bright accents on door trims panels with lower area carpeted, rear quarter trim panels with integral armrests, storage bin and cargo lamp: front vinyl headliner on foam padding, deluxe seat belts, black vinyl spare tire cover, courtesy lighting, simulated leather wrapped steering

wheel, cigar lighter, woodtone accent around horn pad, polished woodtone applique on instrument panel with bright molding around instruments. Heavy-duty air cleaner. Heavy-duty shocks. Auxiliary transmission cooling package. White styled steel wheels. Chrome rear step bumper. Argent rear step bumper. Speed control. Swing away spare tire carrier. 40-channel CB radio. Front tow hooks. Front and rear contour bumpers. 10-hole forged aluminum wheels with plastic coating. Sport wheelcovers. 5-slot forged aluminum 15 x 6 wheels. AM radio. AM/FM monaural radio.

NOTE: A total of 76.4 percent of 1980 Broncos had bucket seats, 61.6 percent tinted glass, 42.7 percent styled steel wheels, 59.9 percent air conditioning, 23.9 percent stereo, and 20.2 percent AM/FM radio.

1980 Ford Bronco Sport Utility Wagon (OCW)

NOTE: Bronco color choices for 1980 were: Raven Black, Wimbledon White, Candyapple Red, Silver Metallic, Light Sand, Maroon, Dark Chamois Metallic, Midnight Blue Metallic, Medium Blue, Light Caramel, Dark Pine Metallic, Medium Grey Metallic, Dark Silver Blue Metallic, Light Medium Pine, Chamois Glow, Walnut Glow, Sand Glow, Medium Copper, Bright Yellow. Tu-Tone effect with exterior color accented with roof available in six different colors. Accent Tape Stripe available with solid color or Victoria Tu-Tone. Deluxe Tu-Tone accent color covers center bodyside panel, lower molding is brushed aluminum on Custom. Victoria Tu-Tone accent color is on the front of roof, hood and around door window, accent also covers lower bodyside.

1980 Ford Econoline 100 Chateau Passenger Van (JAG)

ECONOLINE E-100 CARGO VAN: — The new Econoline Vans styling was unchanged for 1980. Among the standard features were: Full-foam driver's bucket seat. Vinyl seat trim in black, Medium Wedgewood Blue, Red or Sand. Padded full-width instrument panel. Brake warning light. Two-speed electric windshield wipers. Wiper-arm-mounted washer jets. Dome lights. Front compartment handling and insulated floor mat with scuff plates. Door checks. Argent-painted bumpers and hub caps. Bright windshield molding. Painted mirrors. Hinged side cargo doors (sliding door available at no extra cost).

ECONOLINE E-100 DISPLAY VAN: — This model had windows at the rear and on the right hand side. It came with the same standard features as the Cargo Van.

ECONOLINE E-100 WINDOW VAN: — The Window Van had glass all around. It shared standard features with the Cargo Van.

I.D. DATA (Econoline): See F-100.

Model	Body Type	Price	Weight	Prod. Total
E-040	Cargo Van	5714	3680	Note
E-050	Window Van	5867	3813	Note
E-060	Display Van	5812	3802	Note

NOTE: Total model year production for 1980 Econolines was 114,645.

ENGINE (Econoline E-100): Displacement: 300 cu. in. Six-cylinder. Brake horsepower: 120 at 3400 R.P.M. Bore & stroke: 4.00 in. x 3.98 in. Compression ratio: 8.0:1. One-bbl. carburetor.

ECONOLINE E-150 CARGO VAN: — The slightyly more heavy-duty E-150 had most of the same standard features as the E-100.

ECONOLINE E-150 SUPER CARGO VAN: — This van had the same features as the E-150 Cargo Van plus a 20 in. extended rear overhang. This allowed carrying of longer loads. The maximum cargo length (right side, without passenger's seat) was 14 feet.

ECONOLINE E-150 DISPLAY VAN: — This van shared styling with the E-100 but had greater load capacity.

ECONOLINE E-150 WINDOW VAN: — This van shared styling with the E-100 Window Van, but had greater load capacity.

ECONOLINE E-150 SUPER WINDOW VAN: — See E-150 Super Cargo Van.

I.D. DATA (Econoline E-150): See F-100.

Model	Body Type	Price	Weight	Prod. Total
E-140	Cargo Van	6597	4160	Note
E-150	Window Van	6750	4317	Note
E-160	Display Van	6695	4306	Note
S-140	Super Cargo Van	7115	4349	Note
S-150	Super Window Van	7268	4506	Note
S-160	Super Display Van	7213	4495	Note

NOTE: See E-100.

ENGINE (Econoline E-150): Same as E-100.

ECONOLINE E-250 CARGO VAN: — The new E-250 had a higher GVW rating and more heavy-duty front and rear axles, than the E-150. It also came with eight-hole wheels. Standard features were the same as those on the E-100 except the three-speed manual was not available in California.

ECONOLINE E-250 SUPER CARGO VAN: — See E-150 Cargo Van.

ECONOLINE E-250 DISPLAY VAN: — This vehicle shared styling and features with the E-100, but had greater load capacity.

ECONOLINE E-250 SUPER DISPLAY VAN: — See E-150 Super Cargo Van.

ECONOLINE E-250 WINDOW VAN: — This vehicle shared styling and features with the E-100 Window Van, but had greater load capacity.

ECONOLINE E-250 SUPER WINDOW VAN: — See E-150 Super Cargo Van.

ECONOLINE E-250 CUTAWAY VAN: — This van with Camper Special Packages, was designed to readily accommodate custom motor homes.

ECONOLINE E-250 PARCEL DELIVERY: — The E-250 Parcel Delivery van was 149.9 in. long and 74.3 in. high in its cargo area. The rear door opening was 84.7 in. wide.

I.D. DATA (Econoline E-250): See F-100.

Model	Body Type	Price	Weight	Prod. Total
E-240	Cargo Van	6597	4160	Note
E-250	Window Van	6750	4317	Note
E-260	Display Van	6695	4306	Note
S-240	Super Cargo Van	7115	4349	Note
S-250	Super Window Van	7268	4506	Note
S-260	Super Display Van	7213	4495	Note

NOTE: See E-100.

ENGINE (Econoline E-250): Same as E-100.

ECONOLINE E-350 CARGO VAN: — This was the top-of-the-line Econoline Van. It had heavy-duty front and rear shocks and a greater load capacity than the other series. Standard features were the same as the E-100.

ECONOLINE E-350 SUPER CARGO VAN: — See E-150 Super Cargo Van.

ECONOLINE E-350 DISPLAY VAN: — See E-250 Display Van.

ECONOLINE E-350 SUPER DISPLAY VAN: — See E-150 Super Cargo Van.

ECONOLINE E-350 WINDOW VAN: — See E-250 Window Van.

ECONOLINE E-350 SUPER WINDOW VAN: — See E-150 Super Cargo Van.

ECONOLINE E-350 CUTAWAY VAN: — See E-250 Cutaway Van.

ECONOLINE E-350 PARCEL DELIVERY: — See E-250 Parcel Delivery.

I.D. DATA (Econoline E-350): See F-100.

Model	Body Type	Price	Weight	Prod. Total
E-340	Cargo Van	6972	4352	Note
E-350	Window Van	7124	4509	Note
E-360	Display Van	7069	4498	Note
S-340	Super Cargo Van	7784	4466	Note
S-350	Super Window Van	7937	4623	Note
S-360	Super Display Van	7882	4600	Note
E-37W	Cutaway	6731	3840	—
E-383	Parcel Delivery	9077	5338	Note

NOTE: See E-100.

ENGINE (Econoline E-350): Same as E-100.

CHASSIS: Wheelbase: 124 in. (E-100, E-150) 138 in. Overall length: 186.8 in. (124 in. w.b.), 206.8 in. (138 in. w.b.), 226.8 in. (138 in Super Van). GVW: 5050-5650 (E-100), 6050-6300 (E-150), 6500-8250 (E-250), 8550-9800 (E-350). Tires: F78 x 15B PT (E-100), L78 x 15B PT (E-150), 8.00 x 16.5D TT (E-250), 9.50 x 16.5D TT (E-350).

POWERTRAIN OPTIONS: 302 V-8. 351 V-8. 460 V-8 (E-250, E-350). 300 heavy-duty Six (E-350). Four-speed manual with overdrive. Select Shift automatic.

CONVENIENCE OPTIONS: Custom Van: (in addition to or in place of standard) woodtone applique on instrument panel, front side cowl and door trim panels, cigarette lighter, front compartment headlining, insulated front floor mats, front roof rail garnish moldings, bright hub caps, bright taillight bezels, bright window frames with optional rear windows. **Chateau:** (in addition to or in place of Custom features) super soft vinyl or cloth and vinyl seat trim, cutpile carpeting in front and courtesy light switches for all doors, chrome front and rear bumpers, bright grille surround molding, bright lower bodyside character line molding, bright mirrors. Sports rails. Bodyside accent tape stripe. Three-color "Cruising Van" theme tape stripe. Porthole in right and left side. Moldings: bright grille surround, deluxe accent with bright drip rail moldings plus center bodyside and lower character line moldings, bright lower character line, bright drip rails, bright window moldings. Audio: AM radio, AM/FM monaural, AM/FM stereo, AM/digital clock radio, AM/FM stereo with tape deck or cassette player. 40-channel CB. Rear speakers. Premium Sound System. Air conditioning front or high capacity. Heaters: high out-put, or auxiliary for cargo area. Roof/floor insulation package. Deluxe insulation package. Convenience group (with intermittent wipers, dome light switches in all doors and day/night mirror). Dome light courtesy switches for all doors. Western low-mount mirrors (bright or black). Swing-out recreation mirrors (E-350). Sport steering wheel. Simulated leather wrapped steering wheel. Tilt steering. Speed control. Tinted glass all around. Privacy glass. Flip-open or fixed windows were available in all cargo doors. Single sliding side cargo door in lieu of double doors. Combination 3-passenger rear seat that converts into a bed. Dual or quad Captain's Chairs (reclining and swivel or reclining only). Passenger's seat. Flip-fold passengers seat. Cloth and vinyl trim for bucket and Captain's chairs. **Free Wheeling Packages:** Full-length carpeting, front door trim panels and the deluxe insulation package were part of the interior package. The Free Wheeling exterior package included 5-slot matte finish aluminum wheels, blackout grille, black painted bumpers and mirrors, and a black lower bodyside panel bordered by a half inch black stripe. Trailer Towing Packages: 5-Slot or 10-hole forged aluminum wheels. **Cruising Van:** Three color tape stripes, 10-hole polished-finish forged aluminum wheels, portholes, blackout grille, black mirrors and bumpers, Chateau front door trim panels, woodtone vinyl applique with bright surround on instrument panel, courtesy dome light switches on all doors, deluxe insulation package, full-length carpeting, Sport steering wheel, two reclining Captain's Chairs. Heavy-duty shocks. Front stabilizer bar. Engine block heater. Oil pressure gauge and ammeter. Cooling Packages: (super and extra). Push bar plus fog lights and covers. **Protection Group:** front and sliding door black stepwell pads, front door edge guards, and front bumper guards (require chrome bumpers). **Security Group:** Locking gas cap, inside locking hood release and spare tire lock. Inside locking hood release. Chrome or painted argent step bumper. Chrome contour bumpers. Deluxe wheel covers.

1980 Ford Club Wagon Chateau w/Deluxe Accent 2-Tone

E-100 CLUB WAGON: — Styling was carried over from the previous year. The E-100 Club Wagon was available in five or eight passenger versions. Among the standard features were: Front bucket and rear bench seats. Color-keyed patterned vinyl seat trim. Seat belts. Two-speed electric windshield wipers. Wiper arm mounted washer jets. 10 in. rearview mirror. Dome lights. Insulated floor mat with scuff plates. Three armrests. Dual horns. Flip-open windows in sliding door and opposite windows. Painted bumpers, 5 in. x 8 in. mirrors and hub caps. Bright windshield molding.

E-150 CLUB WAGON: — This was a slightly more heavy-duty version of the E-100. It could be had in 124 in. or 138 in. w.b. and was also offered in five and eight passenger versions. Standard features were same as those on the E-100.

E-150 SUPER WAGON: — This was basically the same as the 138 in. w.b. E-150 but had an 20 in. extended rear overhang.

E-250 CLUB WAGON: — The E-250 Club Wagon could be had with five, eight, or twelve passenger capacity. It had most of the same features as the E-100.

E-250 SUPER WAGON: — This was basically an E-250 with a 20 in. rear overhang.

E-350 SUPER WAGON: — The heavy-duty E-350 provided 20 in. more inside length than regular 138 in. w.b. Club Wagons. Heavy-duty shocks were standard.

I.D. DATA (Club Wagon): See F-100.

Model	Body Type	Price	Weight	Prod. Total
E-100	Club Wagon	6862	3988	—
E-150	Club Wagon	7078	4039	—
E-150	Super Wagon	7831	4336	—
E-250	Club Wagon	7538	4450	—
E-250	Super Wagon	8165	4625	—
E-350	Super Wagon	8758	4901	—

NOTE: Total 1980 Club Wagon model year production was 26,498.

ENGINE (Club Wagon): Same as Econoline E-100. (302 V-8 required on E-100 in California, 351 V-8 required on E-350 Super Wagon in California.)

CHASSIS: Wheelbase: 124 in. (E-100), 138 in. (E-150, E-250, E-350). Overall length: See Econoline. GVW: 5400-9400. Tires: G78 x 15B (E-100), H78 x 15D (E-150), 8.00 x 16D (E-250), 9.50 x 16.5D (E-350).

POWERTRAIN OPTIONS: 302 V-8, 351 V-8, 400 V-8, 460 V-8. SelectShift automatic. Four-speed manual w/overdrive.

CONVENIENCE OPTIONS: Most of the same items available on the Econoline plus 4-passenger rear bench seat. Snack-game table.

NOTE: Econoline and Club Wagon colors for 1980 were: Wimbledon White, Candyapple Red, Light Medium Blue, Silver Metallic, Dark Pine Metallic, Dark Brown Metallic, Light Sand, Dark Silver Blue Metallic, Raven Black, Bright Yellow, Maroon. Optional Glow colors: Sand, Walnut. Bodyside accent tape stripe was available in Raven Black, Midnight Blue Metallic, Dark Brown Metallic, Sand Glow, Light Sand, Wimbledon White or Gold Yellow. Four two-tone paint schemes were available.

1980 Ford Courier XLT Mini-Pickup (JAG)

COURIER PICKUP: — If you liked the '79 Courier, you'd like the 1980. For all practical purposes, they were the same. Buyers could still choose from a six or seven foot box. Among the standard features were: Color-keyed vinyl headlining, seat and door trim panels. Instrument lighting intensity control. Cigarette lighter. Brake warning light. New dome light. Door vent windows with wedge-type handles. Padded instrument panel. Hinged seat back for easy access to stowage area. Inside hood release. WSW tires. Cargo tie-down hooks. Bright front bumper. One-hand tailgate operation. Four-speed manual transmission.

I.D. DATA (Courier): See 1976 Courier I.D.

Model	Body Type	Price	Weight	Prod. Total
—	Chassis & Cab	4712	2430	Note
—	Pickup	4859	2680	Note

NOTE: Total Courier sales for model year 1980 was 78,401.

ENGINE (Courier): 2.0-Litre. OHC. Four-cylinder.

CHASSIS: Wheelbase: 106.9 in. (6 ft. box), 112.8 in. (7 ft. box). Overall length: 177.9 in. (6 ft. box), 189.4 in. (7 ft. box). Overall width: 63 in. Overall height: 61.5 in. GVW: 4100 lbs. Tires: 6.00 x 14C WSW.

POWERTRAIN OPTIONS: Floor shifted automatic or five-speed manual transmission (with overdrive).

CONVENIENCE OPTIONS: AM or AM/FM monaural pushbutton radios. Air conditioning. Low-mounted western mirrors. Tinted glass all around. Radial tires. Cast aluminum wheels. **Soft Ride Package:** 3,600 lb. GVWR, 5-leaf progressive-rate rear springs, and 2,010 lb. rated rear axle. Rear step bumper. **Free Wheeling Packages:** "A" includes: black painted GT bar and push bar. "B" includes: "A" plus cast aluminum wheels, RWL 70 series tires (5), and three color accent stripe. **XLT Package:** Interior: Soft, supple vinyl seat and door trim. Woodtone upper door trim panel and transmission shift knob. Cut-pile carpeting. Day/night mirror. Ashtray, under hood and glove box lights. Glove box lock. Sport steering wheel. Temperature gauge and ammeter. Exterior: Bright grille. Bright windshield, rear window, drip rail, wheel lip and taillight surround moldings.

Deluxe wheelcovers. Dual accent pin stripes. **Sports Group:** Black sport steering wheel, bucket seats trimmed in black vinyl with black and white plaid fabric inserts, black carpet and interior trim, woodtone applique on instrument cluster mask, temperature gauge, and ammeter.

1980 Ford F-100 Ranger Styleside 4x4 Pickup (JAG)

F-100 CUSTOM PICKUP: — The "first new truck of the '80s." That's what Ford advertising claimed of its new light-duty trucks. They featured a new vertical and horizontal bars theme grille. Rectangular parking lights were recessed below each rectangular headlight, which were also recessed. The "Ford" letters on the face of the hood were slanted back. Rectangular slots were located between the grille and new, larger front bumper. Styleside models now had wraparound taillights. And the Super Cab featured a distinctive "Twin window" treatment. The interiors were also redesigned. New seats gave passengers approximately 10 percent more legroom. New transfer case shift pattern (had "2H" located up out of the way (4x4). Standard features included: Bright front bumper, grille surround, windshield molding, LH and RH door mounted mirrors. Argent hub caps. Pushbutton door handles. All-vinyl seat trim. Instrument panel with cluster trim applique and full-width pad. Glove box with latch. LH door courtesy light switch. Temperature gauge. Color-keyed windshield pillar, header, cowl side trim panels and door trim panels with foam-padded armrests. Scuff plates. Coat hook. Dome light. Floor insulation and carpet-texture rubber mat. Easily removable tailgate (Styleside). Radial ply tires. Maintenance-free battery. Long windshield wiper blades with dual port washer spray nozzles. Coolant recovery system. Rubber-isolated front coil springs. Lower overall steering ratio. Locking steering column. Horizontal sliding door lock buttons. Entry shield on door latch. Door vent windows with steel pushbutton lock. Aerodynamic design (reportedly this reduced air drag at highway speeds as much as 13 percent). Twin-I-Beam independent front suspension. Three speed manual transmission. The F-100 pickup could be ordered with 6½-ft. Flareside, or 6¾-ft. or 8-ft. Styleside boxes. Only the regular cab was available.

I.D. DATA (F-100): See 1971 F-100 I.D.

Model	Body Type	Price	Weight	Prod. Total
F-10	Pickup (Flare)	5549	—	—
F-10	(6¾-ft.) Pickup (Style)	5549	3324	—
F-10	(8-ft.) Pickup (Style)	5633	3391	—

ENGINE (F-100): Same as 1979 except: Brake horsepower: 119 at 3200 R.P.M.

NOTE: Most 1980 F-100's (73 percent) came with this (300 Six) engine.

1980 Ford F-150 Custom Flareside 4x4 Pickup (JAG)

F-150 CUSTOM PICKUP: — The 150 was Ford's heavy-duty ½-ton. It had most of the same features as the F-100, plus power brakes. Both Flareside and Styleside boxes were available. Stylesides could be had in regular or Super cabs. The latter provided space behind the front seat for an optional rear bench seat or two jump seats. The F-150 4x4 like all F-Series with optional 4x4, had new Twin-Traction Beam Independent Suspension.

I.D. DATA (F-150): See F-100.

Model	Body Type	Price	Weight	Prod. Total
F-15	(6½-ft.) Pickup (Flare)	5697	—	—
F-15	(6¾-ft.) Pickup (Style)	5697	3388	—
F-15	(8-ft.) Pickup (Style)	5782	3457	—
X-15	Pickup (Super Cab)	6400	3691	—

1980 Ford F-150 Ranger Styleside 4x4 Pickup (JAG)

ENGINE (F-150): See F-100.

NOTE: A total of 41.7 percent of the F150s built in 1980 came with the 300 cu. in. six-cylinder engine.

F-250 CUSTOM PICKUP: — The ¾-ton F-250 was offered in regular or Super Cabs. However, the only box available was the Styleside. Standard features echoed those of the F-100 with the addition of power brakes.

I.D. DATA (F-250): See F-100 I.D.

Model	Body Type	Price	Weight	Prod. Total
—	Chassis w/Cab	6515	—	—
F-25	(8-ft.) Pickup (Style)	6234	3636	—
X-25	Pickup (Super Cab)	6741	3815	—

ENGINE (F-250): Same as F-100.

NOTE: This engine (300 Six) was in 22.3 percent of 1980 F-250s. Most (58.5 percent) had the optional 351 V-8.

1980 Ford F-350 Ranger XLT Super Cab Pickup (JAG)

F-350 CUSTOM PICKUP: — The 1-ton F-350 was offered in regular and Super Cab versions. Both featured the "smooth side" all steel Styleside box. New for 1980 was a dual rear wheel Styleside Pickup. Except for having a four-speed manual transmission and power brakes, most F-350 features were the same as those on the F-100.

I.D. DATA (F-350): See F-100 I.D.

Model	Body Type	Price	Weight	Prod. Total
F-37	Chassis w/Cab	6457	3805	—
F-35	Pickup (Style)	6769	4080	—
X-35	Pickup (Super Cab)	7362	4338	—

ENGINE (F-350): Same as F-100 but Compression ratio: 8.0:1.

NOTE: Only 10 percent of the F-350s built in 1980 came with the 300 cu. in. six-cylinder engine. A total of 56.6 percent had the optional 400 cu. in. V8.

1980 Ford F-350 Ranger XLT Styleside 4x4 Pickup (JAG)

CHASSIS: Wheelbase: 116.8 in. (F-100, F-150), 133 in. (all), 138.8 in. (F-150, F-250 Super Cab), 155 in. (F-150, F-250, F-350 Super Cab). Overall length: 187.8 in. (F-100, F-150 Flare), 192.1 in. (F-100, F-150 Style), 208.3 in. (Style), 214.1 in. (F-150, F-250 Super Cab), 230.3 in. (F-350 Super Cab). GVW: 4700-5150 (F-100), 5250-6000 (F-150), 6350-8200 (F-250), 8650-10,000 (F-350). Tires: P195/75R x 15SL (F-100), P215/75R x 15SL (F-150), P225/75R x 15SL (F-150 Super Cab), 8.00 x 16.5D (F-250), 9.50 x 16.5E (F-350).

POWERTRAIN OPTIONS: 302 V-8 (F-100, F-150, F-250), 351 V-8 (F-150, F-250, F-350), 400 V-8 (F-350). Four-speed manual, four-speed manual with overdrive, SelectShift automatic.

NOTE: Most 1980 F-350s (67.7 percent) had the four-speed manual. However, an automatic was the choice in 43 percent of F-100s, 55.5 percent of F-150s and 51 percent of F-250s.

1980 Ford F-350 Ranger XLT 4x4 Camper Special (JAG)

CONVENIENCE OPTIONS: Chrome grille. Accent tape stripe (for SRW Stylesides). Lower bodyside molding with black vinyl insert (for SRW Stylesides). Bright wheel lip moldings (for SRW Custom Stylesides). Bright box rails for 8-ft. Styleside Pickups. GT bar with three equipment mounting tabs on top. AM, AM/FM monaural, AM/FM stereo (speakers mounted in door panels), AM/FM stereo with 8-track tape player, AM/FM stereo with cassette tape player, 40-channel CB radio. Air conditioning. High output or ComfortVent heaters. **Convenience Group:** intermittent wipers, 12 in. day/night mirror, map box on doors, headlamp on warning buzzer, and courtesy light switch on RH door with Custom. Electronic digital clock. Fingertip speed control. **Light Group:** lights in glove box, ashtray, under instrument panel, dome lamp with map light, cargo box light, headlamp-on warning buzzer, and courtesy light switch on RH door with Custom, plus new movable underhood worklight with 20-ft. retractable cord. Bright low-mount western mirrors. Bright low-mount recreation mirrors. Power steering. Power brakes (F-100). Simulated leather-wrapped steering wheel. Tinted sliding rear window. Tilt steering wheel. Tinted glass all around. Tool storage box located under the hood (includes movable underhood worklight with 20-ft. retractable cord and inside locking hood release). Slide-out spare tire carrier. Spare tire carrier side mounted inside Styleside box. Center console (SCs with Captain's Chairs). Reclining Captain's Chairs (SC). Forward facing, folding rear seat (SC). Center facing folding rear seats (SC). Heavy-duty black vinyl, knitted vinyl or all-vinyl seat trim. Cloth and vinyl inserts (Ranger). Folding seat back (Customs). Auxiliary fuel tank. Heavy-duty front and rear shocks. Oil pressure and ammeter gauges. **Handling Package:** Front and rear stabilizer bars, heavy-duty front and rear shocks and heavy-duty front springs. Front and rear stabilizer bars. Engine block heater. Extra cooling engine package. Engine cooling engine package. Special altitude performance package. Camper special package. Trailer towing packages. Dual horns. Fog lamps (included plastic covers and bright front bumper guards). Inside locking hood release. Five roof clearance lights. **Exterior Protection Group:** bright door edge guards, front bumper guards and front bumper rub strip. **Security Lock Group:** locking gas cap, inside hood release and glove box, also spare tire lock. Sports instrumentation. Eight chromed tie-down hooks (Styleside). Argent step (Styleside), chrome step (SRW Styleside), chrome channel (Flareside) or chrome contour (SRW Styleside) rear bumpers. Deluxe wheel covers. White painted styled steel wheels. 10-hole polished forged aluminum wheels with clear plastic coating. Sport wheel covers. 5-slot brushed forged aluminum wheels with clear plastic coating. **Free Wheeling:** "A": pinstriping, blackout grille and headlamp doors, and sport wheel covers. "B": includes "A" plus fog lamps and bumper guards, handling package, bright rear contour bumper (Styleside), bright channel bumper (Flareside), 10-hole aluminum wheels (in place of wheel covers), simulated leather-wrapped steering wheel plus sports instrumentation package (tach, trip odometer, ammeter and oil pressure gauge), GT bar and styled steel wheels (Styleside 4x4). **Ranger:** (in addition to or in place of all Custom features) brushed aluminum lower bodyside molding, black insert around the back window, bright hub caps (except with dual rears), all-vinyl or cloth and vinyl seat trim, courtesy lighting with passenger side door switch as well as driver's, bright accents on door trim panels, cigarette lighter, woodtone accent around steering wheel horn pad, polished woodtone applique on instrument panel, color-keyed seat belts, folding seat back, color-keyed floor mat. **Ranger XLT:** (in addition to or in place of Ranger features) brushed aluminum tailgate applique with bright letters (Styleside), XLT emblem on sides and tailgate, Flareside tailgate trim had raised FORD letters in contrasting color and a dual-colored tap strip setting off those letters, Flaresides and dual rear wheel Stylesides included dual-colored narrow upper and lower bodyside tape stripes, grained-vinyl with cloth inserts seat trim (all-vinyl was a no-charge option), color-keyed cut-pile carpeting covered floor insulation padding, carpeted storage area behind seat, carpeted lower door trim panels, vinyl headliner on foam padding, bright Ranger XLT on instrument panel, bright aluminum door scuff plates, full color-keyed moldings. **Ranger Lariat:** brushed aluminum lower bodyside molding with black vinyl insert, brushed aluminum tailgate with black out area that carried the black insert theme around the pickup, tape stripe running on top of the front fender up the "B" pillar, unique seat trim sew style in cloth and vinyl or all-vinyl, Lariat instrument panel with polished woodtone applique and bright "Ranger Lariat" script, map box on lower door covered with carpeting, "B" pillars and rear window molding, thick cut-pile carpeting, luxury type steering wheel, color-keyed cloth headlining backed with foam insulation, Lariat plaque on each side and tailgate. Four-wheel-drive (F-150, F-250, F-350). Snow plow preparation package (4x4). Automatic locking front hubs (4x4).

NOTE: Colors for 1980 were: Raven Black, Wimbledon White, Candyapple Red, Silver Metallic, Light Sand, Maroon, Dark Chamois Metallic, Midnight Blue Metallic, Medium Blue, Light Caramel, Dark Pine Metallic, Medium Gray Metallic, Dark Silver Blue Metallic, Light Medium Pine, and optional glamour colors: Chamois Glow, Walnut Glow, Sand Glow. Accent tape stripe: bodyside tape runs from front marker lamp to taillamp. Available separately or with regular or Victoria tu-tone. TU-TONES: Regular: accent color covered roof and upper back panel, included dual tape stripe to divide colors. Deluxe: accent color on center bodyside area and on tailgate below upper molding. Combination: regular and deluxe tu-tone combined. Victoria: accent color applied to hood, upper fender, around door window, and the lower bodyside.

PRODUCTION NOTE: Model year 1980 Ford light conventional truck sales totaled 537,476.

Pricing

1980	5	4	3	2	1
Courier					
Pickup	450	900	1500	2100	3000
Ranchero					
500 Pickup	830	1650	2750	3850	5500
GT Pickup	850	1700	2850	4000	5700
Squire Pickup	890	1770	2950	4150	5900
Bronco					
Wagon	890	1770	2950	4150	5900
Econoline E-100					
Cargo Van	440	870	1450	2050	2900
Window Van	470	950	1550	2200	3100
Display Van	500	1000	1650	2300	3300
Club Wagon	570	1140	1900	2650	3800
Custom Club Wagon	600	1200	2000	2800	4000
Chateau Club Wagon	630	1250	2100	3000	4200
Econoline E-200					
Cargo Van	400	800	1350	1900	2700
Window Van	440	870	1450	2050	2900
Display Van	470	950	1550	2200	3100
Econoline E-300					
Cargo Van	390	780	1300	1800	2600
Window Van	420	840	1400	1950	2800
Display Van	450	900	1500	2100	3000
F-100 — (½-Ton)					
Flareside Pickup	740	1470	2450	3350	4900
Styleside Pickup	750	1500	2500	3500	5000
Super Cab Pickup	—	—	—	—	5100
F-250 — (¾-Ton)					
Flareside Pickup	700	1400	2350	3250	4700
Styleside Pickup	720	1450	2400	3300	4800
Super Cab	740	1470	2450	3350	4900
F-350 — (1-Ton)					
Pickup	690	1380	2300	3200	4600
Crew Cab Pickup	660	1320	2200	3100	4400
Stake	630	1250	2100	3000	4200

1981 FORD

BRONCO CUSTOM: — Styling of the four-wheel drive Bronco was unchanged for 1981. Interior colors offered were: Black, Red, Medium Blue, Fawn, Nutmeg and Spruce. Standard features included: Bucket seats; vinyl sun visors; padded instrument panel; armrests; dome lamp; windshield header and "A" pillar moldings; locking steering column; anti-theft sliding door lock buttons; inside hood release; cowlside trim; rubber floor mats; black front and rear bumpers; bright hub caps and door-mounted mirrors; swing-down tailgate with power window; power brakes and steering and four-speed manual transmission.

I.D. DATA (Bronco): See F-100 I.D.

Model	Body Type	Price	Weight	Prod. Total
U-150	Wagon	9085	4038	37,396

ENGINE (Bronco): 300 cu. in. Six-cylinder. Displacement: 302 cu. in. V-8 (standard in Calif.)

1981 Ford Bronco XLT 4x4 Utility Wagon (OCW)

CHASSIS: Wheelbase: 104.7 in. Overall length: 177.6 in. Overall height: 73.2 in. Tires: P215/75R-15 SL.

POWERTRAIN OPTIONS: SelectShift automatic transmission. "302" V-8. "351" V-8. Four-speed manual transmission with overdrive.

NOTE: Most 1981 Broncos, 66 percent, came with automatic transmission and 37 percent had the "302" V-8, while 38.3 percent had the "351" V-8.

CONVENIENCE OPTIONS: Bright wheel lip moldings. Chrome bumpers. Tri-color tape stripe. Chromatic tape. Padded black GT bar. Chrome grille. High-output or auxiliary heaters. Console. Rear window defroster. Soft wrap steering wheel. AM/FM stereo w/eight-track player. **Convenience Group:** includes, intermittent wipers; map box in doors; headlamp-on warning buzzer; R-H door courtesy light switch; 12-inch mirror and visor vanity mirror; front bench seat; flip/fold rear bench seat; power windows; tinted glass all around and privacy glass in quarter windows. **Light Group:** includes, lights in glove box, ashtray and underhood; instrument panel courtesy lights; dome light with map light; R-H door courtesy light and headlamp-on warning buzzer (the underhood light had a 20 foot cord). **Handling Package:** includes, front stabilizer bar and quad heavy-duty hydraulic front and dual heavy-duty rear shocks. Captain's chair. Underhood tool box. Part time four-wheel-drive (with optional automatic transmission). **Sports Instrumentation option:** includes, tachometer; ammeter; oil pressure gauge and trip odometer. **Trailer Towing Packages:** light-duty (up to 2000 lbs.) and heavy-duty (over 2000 lbs.) 32-gallon fuel tank in lieu of standard (includes skid plate). Inside locking hood release. **Protection Group:** includes, bright door edge guards; front bumper guards and front bumper rub strip. **Security Group:** includes, locking gas cap; inside hood release lock; spare tire lock and locking glove box. **Free-Wheeling Packages:** "A" includes, pinstripes along bodyside, hood, tailgate and around door windows, sport wheel covers and bright bumpers. "B" includes sports instrumentation, soft-wrap steering wheel, fog lamps with covers, bumper guards, handling package, GT bar and white styled steel wheels. **Ranger XLT:** includes, brushed aluminum tailgate applique with bright letters; chrome bumpers; bright rear side window moldings; bright lower bodyside molding with black vinyl insert; Ranger XLT plaque; cloth trim on interior; full cut-pile carpeting; bright and woodtone accents on door trim panels with lower area carpeted; rear quarter trim panels with integral armrests; storage bin and cargo lamp; front vinyl headliner on foam padding; deluxe seat belts; black vinyl spare tire cover; courtesy lighting; soft-wrap steering wheel; visor vanity mirror; cigar lighter; woodtone accent around horn pad and polished woodtone applique on instrument panel with bright molding around instruments. Heavy-duty air cleaner. Heavy-duty shocks. Auxiliary transmission cooling package. White styled steel wheels. Chrome rear step bumper. Argent rear step bumper. Speed control. Swing-away spare tire carrier. 40-channel CB radio. Front tow hooks. Front and rear contour bumpers. 10-hole forged aluminum wheels with plastic coating. Sport wheelcovers. Five-slot forged aluminum 15 x 6 inch wheels. AM radio. AM/FM monaural radio. Snow plow preparation package. Special high-altitude performance package.

NOTE: A total of 78.5 percent of 1981 Broncos had bucket seats and 54.8 percent came with the Ranger XLT package.

NOTE: Bronco color choices for 1981 were: Raven Black, Wimbledon White, Silver Metallic, Medium Grey Metallic, Candyapple Red, Maroon, Medium Blue, Midnight Blue Metallic, Dark Spruce Metallic, Fawn, Dark Cocoa Metallic, Dark Chamois Metallic, Medium Caramel Metallic, Light Caramel, Tan, Bittersweet Glow, Medium Blue Glow, Medium Spruce Glow, Fawn Glow. Tu-Tone effect: exterior body color accented by roof available in six different colors. Accent Tape Stripe available with solid exterior color, Tu-Tone effect and Victoria Tu-Tone. Deluxe Tu-Tone: accent color covers center bodyside panel (includes lower bodyside protection molding with black vinyl insert.) Victoria Tu-Tone: accent color is on the front roof, hood and lower bodyside (includes lower bodyside protection molding with black vinyl insert).

ECONOLINE E-100 CARGO VAN: — If you liked the '80 Econoline, you'd probably like the '81. It looked the same on the outside. However, changes were made to the standard and optional upholstery. Among the standard features were: Full-foam driver's bucket seat; ribbed vinyl seat trim in black, Medium blue, Red, Fawn or Nutmeg; padded full-width instrument panel; brake warning light; two-speed electric windshield wipers; wiper-arm-mounted washer jets; dome lights; front compartment headlining; column-mounted ignition switch; door checks; Argent-painted bumpers and hub caps; bright windshield molding; painted mirrors; hinged side cargo doors (sliding door available at no extra cost) and halogen headlights.

ECONOLINE E-100 DISPLAY VAN: — This model had windows at the rear and on the right-hand side. It came with the same standard features as the Cargo Van.

ECONOLINE E-100 WINDOW VAN: — The Window Van had glass all around. It shared features with the Cargo Van.

I.D. DATA (Econoline): See F-100.

Model	Body Type	Price	Weight	Prod. Total
E-040	Cargo Van	6420	3650	Note
E-050	Window Van	6575	3677	Note
E-060	Display Van	6522	3664	Note

NOTE: Total model year production for 1981 Econolines was 108,599.

ECONOLINE E-100: 300 cu. in. Six-cylinder. 120 horsepower at 3400 R.P.M. Bore & stroke: 4.00 in. x 3.98 in. One-barrel carb.

ECONOLINE E-150 CARGO VAN: — The slightyly heavier-duty E-150 had most of the same standard features as the E-100.

ECONOLINE E-150 SUPER CARGO VAN: — This van had the same features as the E-150 Cargo Van, plus a 20 inch extended rear overhang. This allowed carrying of longer loads. The maximum cargo length (right side, without passengers' seat) was 14 feet.

ECONOLINE E-150 DISPLAY VAN: — This van shared styling with the E-100, but had greater load capacity.

ECONOLINE E-150 WINDOW VAN: — This van shared styling with the E-100 Window Van, but had greater load capacity.

ECONOLINE E-150 SUPER WINDOW VAN: — See E-150 Super Cargo Van.

I.D. DATA (Econoline E-150): See F-100.

Model	Body Type	Price	Weight	Prod. Total
E-140	Cargo Van	6597	4160	Note
E-150	Window Van	6750	4317	Note
E-160	Display Van	6695	4306	Note
S-140	Super Cargo Van	7115	4349	Note
S-150	Super Window Van	7268	4506	Note
S-160	Super Display Van	7213	4495	Note

NOTE: See E-100.

ENGINE (Econoline E-150): Same as E-100.

ECONOLINE E-250 CARGO VAN: — The new E-250 had a higher GVW rating and heavier-duty front and rear axles than the E-150. It also came with eight-hole wheels. Standard features were the same as those on the E-100, but three-speed manual transmission was not available in California.

ECONOLINE E-250 SUPER CARGO VAN: — See E-150 Cargo Van.

ECONOLINE E-250 DISPLAY VAN: — This vehicle shared styling and features with the E-100, but had greater load capacity.

ECONOLINE E-250 SUPER DISPLAY VAN: — See E-150 Super Cargo Van.

ECONOLINE E-250 WINDOW VAN: — This vehicle shared styling and features with the E-100 Window Van, but had greater load capacity.

ECONOLINE E-250 SUPER WINDOW VAN: — See E-150 Super Cargo Van.

ECONOLINE E-250 CUTAWAY VAN: — This van, with "Camper Special" packages, was designed to readily accommodate custom motor homes.

ECONOLINE E-250 PARCEL DELIVERY: — The E-250 Parcel Delivery Van was 149.9 inches long and 74.3 inches high in its cargo area. The rear door opening was 84.7 inches wide.

I.D. DATA (Econoline E-250): See F-100.

Model	Body Type	Price	Weight	Prod. Total
E-240	Cargo Van	7299	4090	Note
E-250	Window Van	7454	4119	Note
E-260	Display Van	7400	4105	Note
S-240	Super Cargo Van	7646	4203	Note
S-250	Super Window Van	7801	4232	Note
S-260	Super Display Van	7748	4218	Note

NOTE: See E-100.

ENGINE (Econoline E-250): Same as E-100.

ECONOLINE E-350 CARGO VAN: — This was the top-of-the-line Econoline Van. It had heavy-duty front and rear shocks and a greater load capacity than vans in the other series. Standard features were the same as the E-100.

ECONOLINE E-350 SUPER CARGO VAN: — See E-150 Super Cargo Van.

ECONOLINE E-350 DISPLAY VAN: — See E-250 Display Van.

ECONOLINE E-350 SUPER DISPLAY VAN: — See E-150 Super Cargo Van.

ECONOLINE E-350 WINDOW VAN: — See E-250 Window Van.

ECONOLINE E-350 SUPER WINDOW VAN: — See E-150 Super Cargo Van.

ECONOLINE E-350 CUTAWAY VAN: — See E-250 Cutaway Van.

ECONOLINE E-350 PARCEL DELIVERY: — See E-250 Parcel Delivery.

I.D. DATA (Econoline E-350): See F-100.

Model	Body Type	Price	Weight	Prod. Total
E-340	Cargo Van	7539	4263	Note
E-350	Window Van	7693	4292	Note
E-360	Display Van	7640	4278	Note
S-340	Super Cargo Van	8340	4428	Note
S-350	Super Window Van	8495	4457	Note
S-360	Super Display Van	8441	4443	Note
E-37B	Cutaway	6822	3635	Note
E-380	Parcel Delivery	9803	5198	Note

NOTE: See E-100.

ENGINE (Econoline E-350): Same as E-100.

CHASSIS: Wheelbase: 124 in. (E-100/E-150); 138 in. (E-250/E-350). Overall length: 186.8 in. (w/124 in. w.b.), 206.8 in. (w/138 in. w.b.); 226.8 in. (w/138 in. w.b. Super Van). GVW (in pounds): 5200-5600 (E-100); 5850-6300 (E-150); 6500-8250 (E-250); 8550-9750 (E-350). Tires: P205/75R15SL (E-100); P225/75R15SL (E-150); 8.00 x 16.5D (E-250); 9.50 x 16.5E (E-350).

POWERTRAIN OPTIONS: "302" V-8. "351" V-8. "400" V-8 (E350). "460" V-8 (E-350). Four-speed manual w/overdrive or Select Shift transmissions.

CONVENIENCE OPTIONS: Custom Van: includes, (in addition to or in place of standard van): woodtone applique on instrument panel, front side cowl and door trim panels; cigarette lighter; front compartment headlining; insulated front floor mats; front roof rail garnish moldings; bright hubcaps; bright taillight bezels and bright window frames with optional rear windows. **Chateau Package:** includes, (in addition to, or in place of, Custom features) super-soft vinyl or cloth and vinyl seat trim, cut-pile carpeting in front and courtesy light switches for all doors, chrome front and rear bumpers, bright grille surround molding, bright lower bodyside character line molding and bright mirrors. Sports rails. Bodyside accent tape stripe. Pinstripe tape in black, white or gold. Chrome grille. **Deluxe Accent Molding package:** includes, bright drip rail, center bodyside and lower character line moldings. Bright drip rails. Bright window moldings. Console. R-H visor mirror. Power door locks. AM radio. AM/FM monaural radio. AM/FM stereo radio. AM/digital clock radio. AM/FM stereo radio with tape deck or cassette player. 40-channel CB. Rear speakers. Premium Sound System. Air conditioning front or high capacity. Heaters: High-Output, ComfortVent or Auxiliary (for cargo area). Roof/floor insulation package. Deluxe insulation package. Convenience group (with intermittent wipers, dome light switches in all doors and day/night mirror). Dome light courtesy switches for all doors. Western low-mount mirrors. Swing-out recreation mirrors (E-350). Tilt steering. Speed control. Tinted glass all around. Privacy Glass. Flip-open or fixed windows available in all cargo doors. Single sliding side cargo door in lieu of double doors. Combination three-passenger rear seat that converts into a bed. Dual or quad Captain's chairs (reclining and swivel or reclining only). Passengers' seat. Flip-fold passengers' seat. Cloth and vinyl trim for bucket and Captain's chairs. **Light Group:** includes, dual beam dome light, headlamps on buzzer, underhood light and dome light switches on all doors. Chrome or Argent silver step bumper. 18-gallon auxiliary fuel tank (138 inch wheelbase req.) Trailer towing packages. Five-slot or 10-hole forged aluminum wheels. Heavy-duty shocks. Handling Package. Power steering. Front stabilizer bar. Engine block heater. Oil pressure gauge and ammeter. Cooling Packages: (super and extra). Push bar plus fog lights and covers. **Protection Group:** includes, front and sliding door, black stepwell pads, front door edge guards and front bumper guards (chrome bumpers req.) **Security Group:** includes, locking gas cap, inside locking hood release and spare tire lock. Inside locking hood release. Chrome or painted argent step bumper. Chrome contour bumpers. Deluxe wheel covers.

1981 Ford Club Wagon Chateau Passenger Van (OCW)

E-100 CLUB WAGON: — Exterior styling features were carried over from 1980. However, different style upholstery was used. Among the standard features were: Front bucket seats and a rear bench seats. Color-keyed patterned vinyl seat trim. Seat belts. Two-speed electric windshield wipers. Wiper arm mounted washer jets. 10 inch rear view mirror. Dome lights. Insulated floor mat with scuff plates. Three armrests. Dual horns. Flip-open windows in sliding door and opposite windows. Painted bumpers, 5x8 inch mirrors and hubcaps. Bright windshield molding.

E-150 CLUB WAGON: — This was a slightly heavier-duty version of the E-100. It could be had in 124 or 138 inch wheelbases and in five- and eight-passenger versions. Standard features were same as those on the E-100.

E-150 SUPER WAGON: — This was basically the same as the 138 inch wheelbase E-150, but had a 20 inch extended rear overhang.

E-250 CLUB WAGON: — This was available in 11- and 12-passenger versions only. An eight-passenger version was available with quad Captain's Chairs and a four-passenger bench seat.

E-350 SUPER WAGON: — The heavy-duty E-350 provided 20 inches more inside length than regular 138 inch wheelbase Club Wagons. Heavy-duty shocks were standard.

I.D. DATA (Club Wagon): See F-100.

Model	Body Type	Price	Weight	Prod. Total
E-100	Club Wagon	7591	3848	Note
E-150	Club Wagon	7851	3869	Note
E-150	Super Wagon	8495	4284	Note
E-250	Club Wagon	10,082	4858	Note
E-350	Super Wagon	9568	4821	Note

NOTE: Total 1981 Club Wagon model year production was 25,051.

ENGINE: Same as Econoline E-100. ("302" V-8 required on E-100 in Calif. "351" V-8 required on E-350 Super Wagon in Calif.)

CHASSIS: Wheelbase: 124 in. (E-100); 138 in. (E-150/E-250/E-350). Overall length: See Econoline. GVW: 5400-9400 lbs. Tires: G78 x 15B (E-100); H78 x 15D (E-150); 8.00 x 16D (E-250); 9.50 x 16.5D (E-350).

POWERTRAIN OPTIONS: 302 V-8. 351 V-8. 400 V-8. 460 V-8. Select Shift automatic or four-speed manual w/overdrive transmissions.

CONVENIENCE OPTIONS: Same as for Econoline, plus four-passenger rear bench seat. Snack-game table.

NOTE: Econoline and Club Wagon colors for 1981 were: Wimbledon White, Candyapple Red, Antique Cream, Silver Metallic, Dark Pine Metallic, Raven Black, Medium Caramel Metallic, Dark Silver Blue Metallic, Black, Dark Cocoa, Dark Chamois Metallic, Maroon. Optional Glow colors: Medium Blue, Fawn, Light Fawn. Three Tu-Tone combinations were available.

1981 Ford Courier Mini-Pickup (OCW)

COURIER PICKUP: — Once again, stylists left the Courier alone. About the only way to tell it from last year's model was: new lap belt for center passenger position, a visible vehicle identification number mounted on the dash and bright argent instrument panal appliques. Standard features included: Four-speed manual transmission; power front disc brakes; independent front suspension; one-hand tailgate operation; bright front bumper; bright hubcaps; whitewall tires; seats and door panels trimmed in pleated vinyl; seatback hinged for easy access to behind-seat storage area; inside hood release; door vent windows; dome light and cigarette lighter.

I.D. DATA (Courier): See F-100 I.D.

Model	Body Type	Price	Weight	Prod. Total
—	Chassis & Cab	6198	2430	Note
—	Pickup	6404	2680	Note

NOTE: Total Courier sales for model year 1981 were 66,155.

CHASSIS: Wheelbase: 106.9 in. (6-ft. box); 112.8 in. (7-ft. box). Overall length: 177.9 in. (6-ft. box); 189.4 in. (7-ft. box). Overall width: 63 in. Overall height: 61.5 in. GVW: 4100 lbs. Tires: 6.00 x 14C WSW.

COURIER ENGINE: 2.0-litre OHC four-cylinder.

POWERTRAIN OPTIONS: 2.3-litre engine. Automatic and five-speed manual transmissions (with overdrive).

CONVENIENCE OPTIONS: AM monaural radio. AM/FM monaural radios. Air conditioning. All tinted glass. Argent rear bumper. **Cold Weather Group:** includes, electric rear window defroster, H-D battery and high-output heater. Low-mount Western mirrors. **Soft-Ride package:** includes, 3600-lb. GVWR and five-leaf progressive-rate rear springs. **Exterior Decor Group:** (not available with XLT/chassis-cab/ or tri-color accent stripe), includes, bright drip rail and wheel lip moldings and bright bodyside moldings with black vinyl inserts. Tri-color accent tape stripe (n/a with Exterior Decor

Group; replaces bodyside molding with XLT. **XLT Package:** includes, exterior bright grille surround; bright moldings on windshield, rear window, drip rails, wheel lips and taillight surround; bright bodyside moldings with black vinyl inserts; bright Red XLT fender placques and Deluxe wheel covers. Interior: Herringbone cloth seat trim in three color choices (Tan, Red and Blue); contrasting accent stripe on seat back and door trim; color-keyed cut-pile carpeting; cowl trim panels; instrument panel; headlining; seats; heater shroud; ashtray; sun visors and shift boot. Woodtone upper door trim panel with contrasting accent stripe and floorshift knob. Day/night mirror. Ashtray, underhood and glove box lights. Glove box lock. Sport steering wheel with black spokes. Temperature gauge and ammeter. **Free-Wheeling Package:** includes, black-painted GT bar; pushbar; tri-color accent tape stripe and Deluxe wheel covers. **Sports Group:** includes, Sport steering wheel with bright argent spokes; temperature gauge and ammeter; individually adjustable bucket seats trimmed in black vinyl (with black-and-white plaid fabric inserts); soft black shift lever knob; bright argent instrument panel appliques; black carpeting and interior trim and radial tires.

F-100 CUSTOM PICKUP: — The handsome aerodynamic styling was carriedover for 1981. Standard features included: Bright front bumper, grille surround and windshield molding; left- and right-hand door-mounted mirrors; Argent hubcaps; pushbutton door handles; all-vinyl seat trim; instrument panel with cluster trim applique and full-width pad; behind-seat storage (on Customs built after 10/6/'80); glovebox with latch; L-H door courtesy light switch; temperature gauge; color-keyed windshield pillar, header and cowlside trim panels and door trim panels with foam-padded armrests; scuff plates; coat hook; dome light; floor insulation and carpet-texture rubber mat; easily removable tailgate (Styleside); radial-ply tires; maintenance-free battery; long windshield wiper blades with dual-port washer spray nozzles; coolant recovery system; rubber-isolated front coil springs; locking steering column; horizontal sliding door lock buttons; entry shield on door latch; door vent windows with steel pushbutton lock; Twin-I-Beam independent front suspension and three-speed manual transmission. The F-100 pickup could be ordered with 6½-foot Flareside or 6¾- and 8-foot Styleside boxes. Only the regular cab was available.

I.D. DATA (F-100): The first three symbols identified the manufacturer, make and type of vehicle. Fourth (letter) identified the brake system and GVWR class. The next three identified line, series, chassis, cab and/or body type. The eighth identified the engine. Ninth is the check digit. Tenth represents model year, followed by character identifying assembly plant and sequential production.

Model	Body Type	Price	Weight	Prod. Total
F-10	Flareside Pickup	6026	—	—
F-10	6¾-ft. Styleside Pickup	6026	3264	—
F-10	8-ft. Styleside Pickup	6112	3349	—

I.D. DATA (F-100): Same as 1980.

1981 Ford F-150 Ranger XLT Styleside 4x4 Pickup (OCW)

F-150 CUSTOM PICKUP: — The F-150 was Ford's heavy-duty ½-ton. It had most of the same features as the F-100, plus power brakes. Both Flareside and Styleside boxes were available. Stylesides could he had in regular or Super cabs. The latter provided space behind the front seat for an optional rear bench seat or two jump seats.

I.D. DATA (F-150): See F-100 I.D.

Model	Body Type	Price	Weight	Prod. Total
F-15	6½-ft. Flareside Pickup	6300	—	—
F-15	6¾-ft. Styleside Pickup	6300	3315	—
F-15	8-ft. Styleside Pickup	6387	3404	—
X-15	SuperCab Pickup	7197	3614	—

F-250 CUSTOM PICKUP: — The ¾-Ton F-250 was offered in regular or Super cabs. However, the only box available was the Styleside. Standard features echoed those of the F-100, with the addition of power brakes.

I.D. DATA (F-250): See F-100 I.D.

Model	Body Type	Price	Weight	Prod. Total
—	Chassis w/Cab	7182	3467	—
F-25	8-ft. Styleside Pickup	6772	3565	—
X-25	SuperCab Pickup	7424	3849	—

ENGINE (F-250): Same as F-100.

F-350 CUSTOM PICKUP: — The 1-Ton F-350 was only offered in regular cab version. It featured the "smoothside" all-steel Styleside box. Except for having a four-speed manual transmission and power brakes. Most F-350 features were the same as those on the F-100. However, the F-350 was the only F-Series Styleside to offer dual rear wheels.

I.D. DATA (F-350): See F-100 I.D.

Model	Body Type	Price	Weight	Prod. Total
F-37	Chassis w/Cab	7527	3759	—
F-35	Styleside Pickup	7750	4299	—

ENGINE (F-350): 351 cu. in. V-8. Brake horsepower: 156 horsepower at 4000 R.P.M. Bore & stroke: 4.00 x 3.50. Carburetor: two-barrel.

CHASSIS: Wheelbase: 116.8 in. (F-100/F-150); 133 in. (all); 138.8 in. (F-100/F-250 SC); 155 in. (F-150/F-250/F-350 SC). Overall length: 187.8 in. (F-100/F-150 Flareside); 192.1 in. (F-100/F-150 Styleside); 208.3 in. (Styleside); 214.1 in. (F-150/F-250 SC); 230.3 in. (F-350 SC). GVW in pounds: 4700-5150 (F-100); 5250-6000 (F-150); 6350-8200 (F-250); 8650-10,000 (F-350). Tires: P195/75R 15SL (F-100); P215/75R 15SL (F-150); P225/75R 15SL (F-150 SC); 8.00 x 16.5D (F-250) and 9.50 x 16.5E (F-350).

POWERTRAIN OPTIONS: 255 V-8 (F-100). 302 V-8 (F-100/F-150/F-250). 351 V-8 (F-150/F-250/F-350). 400 V-8 (F-350). Four-speed manual, four-speed manual with overdrive or Select Shift automatic transmissions.

1981 Ford F-150 Ranger Styleside Pickup (OCW)

CONVENIENCE OPTIONS: Accent tape stripe. Chrome grille. Tri-color tape stripe (for regular cab Styleside). Upper bodyside protection molding. Lower bodyside molding with black vinyl insert (for Styleside). Heavy-duty air cleaner (4x4). Bright wheel lip moldings (for Custom and Ranger Styleside). Bright box rails for 8-ft. Styleside Pickups. Upper bodyside tape stripe (Styleside). Quad heavy-duty front shocks and heavy-duty rear shocks (4x4). AM radio. AM/FM monaural radio. AM/FM stereo radio. AM/FM stereo radio with 8-track tape player. AM/FM stereo radio with cassette tape player. Air conditioning. High-output heaters. **Convenience Group:** includes, intermittent wipers, 12 inch day/night mirror, molded bin on lower doors, headlamps on warning buzzer and courtesy light switch on R-H door (with Custom0. Electronic digital clock. Fingertip speed control. **Light Group:** includes, light in glove box, ashtray and under instrument panel; dome lamp with map light; cargo box light; headlamp-on warning buzzer; courtesy light switch on R-H door with Custom, plus movable underhood worklight with 20-foot retractable cord. Bright low-mount swing-away Western mirrors. Remote-control low-mount Western mirrors. Bright low-mount recreation mirrors. Power steering. Soft-wrapped steering wheel. Tinted sliding rear window. Tilt steering wheel. Tinted glass all around. Tool storage box located under the hood (includes movable underhood worklight with 20-foot retractable cord and inside locking hood release). Slide-out spare tire carrier. Spare tire carrier side-mounted inside Styleside box. Center console (SCs with Captains chairs). Reclining Captain's chairs (SC). Forward-facing, folding rear seat (SC). Center-facing folding rear seats (SC). Heavy-duty black vinyl, knitted vinyl or all-vinyl seat trim. Cloth and vinyl inserts (Ranger, Custom). Auxiliary transmission cooler. Heavy-duty front and rear shocks. Quad heavy-duty front shocks and heavy-duty rear shocks (F-150 w/4x4). Auxiliary fuel tank. **Handling Package:** includes, front and rear stabilizer bars, heavy-duty front and rear shocks and heavy-duty front springs. Oil pressure and ammeter gauges. Engine block heater. Extra-cooling engine package. Super-cooling engine package. Front and rear stabilizer bars. "Camper Special" package. Trailer towing packages. Dual note horns. Fog lamps (includes plastic covers and bright front bumper guards. Power door locks. Inside locking hood release. Five roof clearance lights. **Exterior Protection Group:** includes, bright door edge guards, front bumper guards and front bumper rub strip. **Security Lock Group:** includes, locking gas cap, inside hood release and glove box and spare tire lock. Bright instrumentation. Eight (SRW Styleside) or six (DRW Styleside) chrome tie-down hooks. Argent step (Styleside). Chrome step (SRW Styleside). Chrome channel (Flareside). Chrome contour (SRW Styleside) rear bumpers. Deluxe wheel covers. White painted styled steel wheels. 10-hole polished forged aluminum wheels with clear plastic coating. Sport wheel covers. Five-slot brushed forged-aluminum wheels with clear plastic coating. **Free-Wheeling Packages:** "A" includes, pinstriping (or tri-color tape stripe on Styleside/Deluxe tu-tone on Flareside); blackout grille and headlamp doors and sport wheel covers. "B" includes, all in "A," plus fog lamps and bumper guards; handling package; bright rear contour bumper (Styleside); bright channel bumper (Flareside); white styled-steel wheels (in place of wheel covers); soft-

wrapped steering wheel and Sports Instrumentation package (w/tachometer, trip odometer, ammeter and oil pressure gauge). **Ranger Package:** includes, (in addition to or in place of Custom features) brushed aluminum upper bodyside and tailgate moldings; bright insert around the back window; bright hubcaps (except with dual rear wheels); all-vinyl or cloth and vinyl seat trim; courtesy lighting with passenger side door switch as well as driver's; bright accents on door trim panels, cigarette lighter and ashtray light; woodtone accent around steering wheel horn pad; polished woodtone applique on instrument panel; color-keyed seat belts and color-keyed floor mat. **Ranger XLT Package:** includes, (in addition to or in place of Ranger features), brushed aluminum tailgate applique with bright letters and black tape stripe at bottom (Styleside) and XLT emblems. Flareside tailgate trim had raised Ford letters that matched the contrasting color in the surrounding dual-colored tape stripe. Flareside and DRW Stylesides included dual-colored narrow upper and lower bodyside tape stripes; grained-vinyl w/cloth seat trim inserts (all-vinyl was a no-cost option); color-keyed cut-pile carpeting covering floor insulation padding and lower door trim panels; carpeted storage area behind seat; cloth headliner on foam padding; new style special color keyed moldings and bright aluminum door scuff plates. **Ranger Lariat Package:** includes, brushed aluminum lower bodyside molding with black vinyl insert; tailgate applique; dual narrow tape stripe; special "cushioned" seat trim; new style special cloth with vinyl bolsters trim; "Ranger Lariat" script on woodtone appliqued instrument panel; woodtone applique on door panels; map boxes on doors covered with carpeting, thick cut-pile carpeting and luxury steering wheel. **4x4 Option:** includes, (F-150/250/350) P-metric steel-belted radial tires (F-150); ladder-type frame; integral front axle skid plate; 4x4 indicator light on instrument panel; four-speed manual transmission; free-running front hubs. Snow preparation package (4x4). Automatic locking front hubs (4x4).

PRODUCTION NOTE: Model year 1981 Ford light conventional truck sales totaled 470,756.

NOTE: Interior colors for 1981 were: Fawn, Medium Blue, Red, Black, Nutmeg or Spruce (except SuperCab). Exterior colors included: Raven Black, Wimbledon White, Silver Metallic, Medium Grey Metallic, Candyapple Red, Maroon, Midnight Blue Metallic, Medium Blue, Dark Spruce Metallic, Fawn, Dark Chamois Metallic, Medium Caramel Metallic, Light Caramel, Tan and optional "glamour" colors: Medium Blue Glow, Medium Spruce Glow and Fawn Glow. Tu-tones: (Regular) accent color covered the roof and upper back panel; dual tape stripe included to divide colors. (Deluxe) accent color on center bodyside area and on tailgate below upper molding; moldings were included as needed. (Combination) regular and deluxe tu-tones combined. (Victoria) Accent color applied to hood, upper fender, around door window, and lower bodyside. Tape stripes: Accent; (SRW Styleside only) bodyside tape ran from the front marker lamp to the taillamp; available separately or with regular or Victoria tu-tone. Tri-color: (SRW Styleside only) as name implies. Upper Bodyside: (available on regular and Super Cab) highlights upper portion of SRW Styleside pickup; available separately or with regular tu-tone.

1982 FORD

1982 Ford Bronco XLT Lariet 4x4 Utility Wagon (JAG)

BRONCO: — The 4x4 Bronco received a mild facelift for 1982. The revised grille had only three vertical bars and the Ford script in an oval emblem in its center. This emblem was also placed on the lower left corner of the tailgate. Standard features included: bucket seats; vinyl sunvisors; padded instrument panel; armrests; dome lamp; windshield header and "A" pillar moldings; AM radio (could be deleted for credit); inside hood release; cowlside trim panels; rubber floor mats; black front and rear bumpers; bright hub caps and door-mounted mirrors; swingdown tailgate with power window; power brakes and steering; four-speed manual transmission and black grille.

I.D. DATA (Bronco): See F-100 I.D.

Model	Body Type	Price	Weight	Prod. Total
U-150	Wagon	9899	4079	—

ENGINE (Bronco): 300 cu. in. Six-cylinder. Displacement: 302 cu. in. V-8 (standard in Calif.).

CHASSIS: Wheelbase: 104.7 in. Overall length: 177.6 in. Overall height: 73.2 in. Overall width: 77.2 in. Tires: P215/75R x 15 SL.

POWERTRAIN OPTIONS: SelectShift automatic transmission. "302" V-8. "351" V-8. Four-speed manual transmission with overdrive.

CONVENIENCE OPTIONS: Bright wheel lip moldings. Chrome bumpers. Tri-color tape stripe. Accent tape stripe. Black GT bar. Chrome grille. Upper bodyside tape stripe. Lower bodyside molding. High output or auxiliary heaters. Console. Rear window defroster. Soft wrap steering wheel. **Convenience Group:** includes, intermittent wipers; map box in doors; headlamp-on warning buzzer; R-H door courtesy light switch; 12 in. mirror; visor vanity mirror; front bench seat; flip/fold rear bench seat; power windows. tinted glass all around and privacy glass in quarter windows. **Light Group:** includes, lights in glove box, ashtray and underhood; instrument panel courtesy lights; dome light with map light; R-H door courtesy light and headlamp-on warning buzzer (the underhood light had a 20-ft. cord). **Handling Package:** includes, front stabilizer bar, quad heavy-duty hydraulic front shocks and dual heavy-duty rear shocks. Captain's chairs. Underhood tool box. Part time 4x4 (with optional automatic transmission). **Sports Instrumentation:** includes, tachometer; ammeter; oil pressure gauge and trip odometer. Heavy-duty trailer towing package. Heavy-duty battery. Ampere and oil pressure gauges. Thirty-two gallon fuel tank in lieu of standard (includes skid plate). Inside locking hood release. **Protection Group:** includes, bright door edge guards; front bumper guards and front bumper rub strip. **Security Group:** includes, locking gas cap; inside hood release lock; spare tire lock and locking glove box. Super engine cooling package. Extra engine cooling package. Fog lamps. Exterior sound package. Cigarette lighter. Power door locks. **XLT Lariat:** includes, bright front and rear bumpers; black grille; bright hub caps, windshield, quarter window and upper bodyside (with vinyl insert) protection moldings; bright wheel lip moldings; bodyside molding accent tape stripe; brushed aluminum tailgate applique; dome lamp; left- and right-hand courtesy light switches; color-keyed carpeting; left-hand rear quarter trim panel cargo lamp; door trim panel with bright surround molding; woodtone panel with full length storage bins; color-keyed vinyl headliner; simulated woodtone applique and bright moldings instrument panel; bright scuff plates; deluxe seat belts; cloth and vinyl seat trim; soft-wrap steering wheel with woodtone insert; molded rear quarter trim panels with armrests; speaker grilles; storage bin and light; spare tire cover; cigarette lighter and added insulation. **XLS Package:** has most of the features of the XLT, plus: black gloss on front and rear bumpers; black gloss grille; argent styled steel wheels with black hub; black gloss windshield molding; black treatment on headlamp doors and around window, door handles, locks, mirrors and tailgate lock; "XLS" tape; door trim panel with bright surround; brushed aluminum applique and steering wheel trim. Speed control. Swing-Away spare tire carrier. 40-channel CB. Front tow hooks. Cast aluminum wheels. Styled steel painted (white) wheels. Sport wheel covers. Deluxe argent styled steel wheels. AM/FM monaural, AM/FM stereo, AM/FM stereo with cassette or 8-track player. Snow plow packages. High-altitude emissions system. Heavy-duty auxiliary battery.

NOTE: Bronco color choices for 1982 were: Raven black, Wimbledon white, silver metallic, Medium grey metallic, Candyapple red, Midnight blue metallic, Medium blue metallic, Bright blue, Dark Spruce Metallic, Light Spruce, maroon, Dark Fawn Metallic, Fawn, Medium Caramel Metallic, tan, Dark brown Metallic, Medium yellow, Light Spruce Glow and Bittersweet Glow.

ECONOLINE E-100 CARGO VAN: — Styling was unchanged for the new model year. Among the standard features were: Full-foam driver's bucket seat; vinyl seat trim; padded full-width instrument panel; brake warning light; two-speed electric windshield wipers; wiper-arm-mounted washer jets; dome lights; front compartment headlining; column-mounted ignition switch scuff plates; door checks; Argent-painted bumpers and hub caps; bright windshield molding; painted mirrors and hinged side cargo doors (sliding door available at no extra cost).

ECONOLINE E-100 DISPLAY VAN: — This model had windows at the rear and on the right-hand side. It came with the same standard features as the Cargo Van.

ECONOLINE E-100 WINDOW VAN: — The Window Van had glass all around. It shared standard features with the Cargo Van.

I.D. DATA (Econoline): See F-100.

Model	Body Type	Price	Weight	Prod. Total
E-040	Cargo Van	7056	3664	—
E-050	Window Van	7237	3691	—
E-060	Display Van	7172	3678	—

ENGINE (Econoline E-100): Displacement: 300 cu. in. Six-cylinder. Brake horsepower: 120 at 3400 R.P.M. Bore & stroke: 4.00 in. x 3.98 in. Compression ratio: 8.0:1. One-barrel carburetor.

ECONOLINE E-150 CARGO VAN: — The slightly heavier-duty E-150 had most of the same standard features as the E-100.

ECONOLINE E-150 SUPER CARGO VAN: — This van had the same features as the E-150 Cargo Van plus a 20 inch extended rear overhang. This allowed carrying of longer loads. The maximum cargo length (right side, without passenger seat) was 14 feet.

ECONOLINE E-150 DISPLAY VAN: — This van shared styling with the E-100, but had greater load capacity.

ECONOLINE E-150 WINDOW VAN: — This van shared styling with the E-100 Window Van, but had greater load capacity.

ECONOLINE E-150 SUPER WINDOW VAN: — See E-150 Super Cargo Van.

I.D. DATA (Econoline E-150): See F-100.

Model	Body Type	Price	Weight	Prod. Total
E-140	Cargo Van	7303	3617	—
E-150	Window Van	7485	3644	—
E-160	Display Van	7419	3631	—
S-140	Super Cargo Van	7963	3923	—
S-150	Super Window Van	8145	3952	—
S-160	Super Display Van	8079	3938	—

ENGINE (Econoline E-150): Same as E-100.

ECONOLINE E-250 CARGO VAN: — The new E-250 had a higher GVW rating and more heavy-duty front and rear axles, than the E-150. It also came with eight-hole wheels. Standard features were the same as those on the E-100 except the three-speed manual was not available in Calif.

ECONOLINE E-250 SUPER CARGO VAN: — See E-150 Cargo Van.

ECONOLINE E-250 DISPLAY VAN: — This vehicle shared styling and features with the E-100, but had greater load capacity.

ECONOLINE E-250 SUPER DISPLAY VAN: — See E-150 Super Cargo Van.

ECONOLINE E-250 WINDOW VAN: — This vehicle shared styling and features with the E-100 Window Van, but had greater load capacity.

ECONOLINE E-250 SUPER WINDOW VAN: — See E-150 Super Cargo Van.

ECONOLINE E-250 CUTAWAY VAN: — This van with Camper Special Packages, was designed to readily accommodate custom motor homes.

ECONOLINE E-250 PARCEL DELIVERY: — The E-250 Parcel Delivery van was 149.9 inches long and 74.3 inches high in its cargo area. The rear door opening was 84.7 inches wide.

I.D. DATA (Econoline E-250): See F-100.

Model	Body Type	Price	Weight	Prod. Total
E-240	Cargo Van	8199	4132	—
E-250	Window Van	8381	4161	—
E-260	Display Van	8315	4147	—
S-240	Super Cargo Van	8573	4245	—
S-250	Super Window Van	8755	4274	—
S-260	Super Display Van	8689	4260	—

ENGINE (Econoline E-250): Same as E-100.

ECONOLINE E-350 CARGO VAN: — This was the top-of-the-line Econoline Van. It had heavy-duty front and rear shocks and a greater load capacity than the other series. Standard features were the same as the E-100.

ECONOLINE E-350 SUPER CARGO VAN: — See E-150 Super Cargo Van.

ECONOLINE E-350 DISPLAY VAN: — See E-250 Display Van.

ECONOLINE E-350 SUPER DISPLAY VAN: — See E-150 Super Cargo Van.

ECONOLINE E-350 WINDOW VAN: — See E-250 Window Van.

ECONOLINE E-350 SUPER WINDOW VAN: — See E-150 Super Cargo Van.

ECONOLINE E-350 CUTAWAY VAN: — See E-250 Cutaway Van.

ECONOLINE E-350 PARCEL DELIVERY: — See E-250 Parcel Delivery.

I.D. DATA (Econoline E-350): See F-100.

Model	Body Type	Price	Weight	Prod. Total
E-340	Cargo Van	8424	4305	—
E-350	Window Van	8606	4334	—
E-360	Display Van	8540	4320	—
S-340	Super Cargo Van	9404	4470	—
S-350	Super Window Van	9585	4499	—
S-360	Super Display Van	9520	4485	—
E-37B	Cutaway	—	3677	—
E-380	Parcel Delivery	—	5240	—

ENGINE (Econoline E-350): Same as E-100.

CHASSIS: Wheelbase: 124 in.; (E-100/E-150) 138 in. Overall length: 186.8 in. (124 in. w.b.); 206.8 in. (138 in. w.b.); 226.8 in. (138 in Super Van). GVW: (in pounds) 5200-5600 (E-100); 5800-6300 (E-150); 6500-7900 (E-250); 8550-9750 (E-350). Tires: P205/75R x 15 SL (E-100); P225/75R x 15 SL (E-150); 8.00 x 16.5D TT (E-250); 9.50 x 16.5E (E-350).

POWERTRAIN OPTIONS: "302" V-8. "351" V-8. "400" V-8 (E-350). "460" V-8 (E-350) Four-speed manual w/overdrive or SelectShift automatic transmissions.

CONVENIENCE OPTIONS: Custom Van: includes, (in addition to or in place of standard) woodtone applique on instrument panel, front side cowl and door trim panels; cigarette lighter; front compartment headlining; insulated front floor mats; front roof rail garnish moldings; bright hub caps; bright taillight bezels and bright window frames with optional rear windows. **Chateau:** includes, (in addition to or in place of Custom features) super soft vinyl or cloth and vinyl seat trim; cutpile carpeting in front; courtesy light switches for all doors; chrome front and rear bumpers; bright grille surround molding; bright lower bodyside character line moldings and bright mirrors. Sports rails. Bodyside accent tape stripe. Pinstripe tape in black, white or gold. Chrome grille. Deluxe Accent Moldings (bright drip rail, center bodyside and lower character line moldings). Bright drip rails. Bright window moldings. Console. Right-hand visor mirror. Power door locks. **Audio Options:** AM radio. AM/FM monaural radio. AM/FM stereo. AM/digital clock radio. AM/FM stereo with tape deck or cassette player. 40-channel tape player. 40-channel CB. Rear speakers. Premium Sound System. Air conditioning front or high-capacity. Heaters: high output or auxiliary (for cargo area) types. Roof/floor insulation package. Deluxe insulation package. Convenience group (with intermittent wipers, dome light switches in all doors and day/night mirror). Dome light courtesy switches for all doors. Western low-mount mirrors. Swing-out recreation mirrors. Tilt steering. Speed control. Tinted glass all around. Privacy glass. Flip-open or fixed windows (available in all cargo doors). Single sliding side cargo door in lieu of double doors. Combination three-passenger rear seat that converts into a bed. Dual or quad Captain's Chairs (reclining and swivel or reclining only). Passengers' seat. Flip-fold passengers' seat. Cloth and vinyl trim for bucket seat and Captain's chairs. **Light Group:** dual beam dome light; headlamps on buzzer; underhood light and dome light switches on all doors. Chrome or argent step bumper. 18-gallon auxiliary fuel tank (138 inch wheelbase). Trailer Towing Packages. Five-slot or 10-hole forged aluminum wheels. Heavy-duty shocks. Handling Package. Power steering. Front stabilizer bar. Engine block heater. Oil pressure gauge and ammeter. Cooling Packages: (super and extra). Push bar plus fog lights and covers. **Protection Group:** front and sliding door black step-well pads, front door edge guards and front bumper guards (require chrome bumpers). **Security Group:** Locking gas cap; inside locking hood release and spare tire lock and inside locking hood release. Chrome or painted argent step bumper. Chrome contour bumpers. Deluxe wheel covers.

E-100 CLUB WAGON: — The new E-100 Club Wagon looked the same as last year's model. That wasn't bad! Among the standard features were: front bucket seats and rear bench seats; color-keyed patterned vinyl seat trim; seat belts; two-speed electric windshield wipers; wiper arm mounted washer jets; 10 inch rearview mirror; dome lights; insulated floor mat with scuff plates; three armrests; dual horns; flip-open windows in sliding door and opposite windows; painted bumpers; 5 x 8 in. mirrors and hub caps and bright windshield molding.

E-150 CLUB WAGON: — This was a slightly heavier-duty version of the E-100. It could be had in 124 or 138 inch wheelbases and was also offered in five- and eight-passenger versions. Standard features were same as those on the E-100.

E-150 SUPER WAGON: — This was basically the same as the 138 inch wheelbase E-150, but it had a 20 inch extended rear overhang.

E-250 CLUB WAGON: — This was available in 11- and 12-passenger versions. Also, an eight-passenger version was available with quad Captain's Chairs and a four-passenger bench seat.

E-350 SUPER WAGON: — The heavy-duty E-350 provided 20 inches more inside length than regular 138 inch wheelbased Club Wagons. Heavy-duty shocks were standard.

I.D. DATA (Club Wagon): See F-100.

Model	Body Type	Price	Weight	Prod. Total
E-100	Club Wagon	8501	3889	—
E-150	Club Wagon	8794	3896	—
E-150	Super Wagon	9480	4216	—
E-250	Club Wagon	11,058	4838	—
E-350	Super Wagon	10,785	4751	—

ENGINE (Club Wagon): Same as Econoline.

CHASSIS: Wheelbase: 124 in. (E-100); 138 in. (E-150/E-250/E-350). Overall width: 79.7 in. GVW: 5400-9400 lbs. Tires: P205/75R x 15 SL.

POWERTRAIN OPTIONS: "302" V-8. "351" V-8. "400" V-8. "460" V-8. SelectShift automatic or four-speed manual w/overdrive transmissions.

CONVENIENCE OPTIONS: Most of the same items available on the Econoline, plus four-passenger rear bench seat. Snack-game table.

COURIER PICKUP: — This was the last year for the Courier. It received new (padded) steering and column with stalk-mounted gear-shift controls. Other standard features included: four-speed manual transmission; power front disc brakes; independent front suspension; one-hand tailgate operation; bright front bumper; bright hubcaps and whitewall tires. The seats and door panels were trimmed in pleated vinyl. The seatback was hinged for easy access to behind-seat stowage area. Also included were an inside hood release; door vent windows; dome light and cigarette lighter.

I.D. DATA (Courier): See F-100 I.D.

Model	Body Type	Price	Weight	Prod. Total
—	Chassis & Cab	—	2430	—
—	Pickup	S6.614	2680	—

NOTE: Total Courier sales for model year 1982 were 66,155.

CHASSIS: Wheelbase: 106.9 in. (6 ft. box); 112.8 in. (7 ft. box). Overall length: 177.9 in. (6 ft. box); 189.4 in. (7 ft. box). Overall width: 63 in. Overall height: 61.5 in. GVW: 4100 lbs. Tires: 6.00 x 14C WSW.

ENGINE (Courier): 2.0 liter OHC four-cylinder.

POWERTRAIN OPTIONS: 2.3 liter engine. Automatic and five-speed manual transmission (with overdrive).

CONVENIENCE OPTIONS: AM or AM/FM monaural radios. Air conditioning. Tinted glass all around. Argent rear bumper. **Cold Weather Group:** includes, electric rear window defroster; heavy-duty battery and high-output heater; and low-mount Western mirrors. **Soft Ride Package:** 3600 lbs. GVWR and 5-leaf progressive-rate rear springs. **Exterior Decor Group:** (not

available with XLT, chassis-cab or tri-color accent tape stripe), includes bright drip rail and wheel lip molding; bright bodyside moldings with black vinyl inserts; tri-color accent tape stripe (not available with Exterior Decor Group and replaces bodyside molding with XLT). **XLT Package:** includes, bright moldings on windshield, rear window, drip rails, wheel lips and taillight surround; bright bodyside moldings with black vinyl inserts; bright red XLT fender plaques and deluxe wheel covers. **Free Wheeling Package:** includes, black-painted GT bar; push bar; tri-color accent ape stripe and deluxe wheel covers. **Sport Group:** includes, sport steering wheel with bright argent spokes; temperature gauge and ammeter; individually adjustable bucket seats (trimmed in black vinyl with black and white plaid fabric inserts); black soft shift lever knob; bright argent instrument panel appliques; black carpeting and black interior trim. Radial tires. **XLT Interior:** includes, Herringbone cloth seat trim in three color choices (tan, red and blue); contrasting accent stripe on seatback and door trim; color-keyed cut-pile carpeting; cowl trim panels; instrument panel; headlining; seats; heater shroud; ashtray; sunvisors and shift boot; woodtone upper door trim panel with contrasting accent stripe and floorshift knob; day/night mirror; ashtray, underhood and glove box lights; glove box lock; Sport steering wheel with black spokes; temperature gauge and ammeter.

1982 Ford F-100 XLT Lariat Styleside Pickup (JAG)

F-100 PICKUP: — The most noticeable styling change for 1982 was the removal of the Ford name, in block letters, from the face of the hood. It was replaced by the Ford oval in the center of the revised, rectangular slots theme grille. Also new were lubed-for-life ball joints and adjustable camber. Among standard features were: chrome front bumper; bright grille surround, windshield molding and door-mount mirrors; Argent hub caps; all-vinyl seat trim; full-foam seat over springs; folding seatback access to behind seat storage area; glove box; left door courtesy light switch; temperature gauge; color-keyed windshield pillar, header and cowl side trim panels and door trim panels (with foam padded armrests); floor insulation and carpet-texture rubber mat; inside hood release; black applique instrument panel; black steering wheel; vinyl headlining (SuperCab) and three-speed manual transmission. The F-100 was available with 6½-ft. Flareside and 6¾-ft. or 8-ft. Styleside versions.

I.D. DATA (F-100): See 1981 F-100 I.D.

Model	Body Type	Price	Weight	Prod. Total
F-10	Flareside Pickup 6½'	6840	—	—
F-10	Styleside Pickup 6¾'	6713	3080	—
F-10	Styleside Pickup 8'	6863	3152	—

ENGINE (F-100): 232 cu. in. V-6. Brake horsepower: 112 at 4000 R.P.M. Bore & stroke: 3.81 x 3.39 in. Compression ratio: 8.6:1. Carburetor: One-barrel. (A "300" six-cylinder or "302" V-8 was required in Calif.)

1982 Ford F-150 Ranger XLS Styleside 4x4 Pickup (JAG)

F-150 PICKUP: — The F-150 was Ford's heavy-duty ½-ton. It had most of the same features as the F-100, plus power brakes. Both Flareside and Styleside boxes were available. Stylesides could be had in regular or Super cabs. The latter provided space behind the front seat for an optional bench seat or two jump seats.

I.D. DATA (F-150): See F-100.

Model	Body Type	Price	Weight	Prod. Total
F-15	Flareside Pickup 6½'	7094	—	—
F-15	Styleside Pickup 6¾'	6969	3303	—
F-15	Styleside Pickup 8'	7119	3404	—
X-15	SuperCab Pickup	8010	3635	—

1982 Ford Ranger XLS Styleside Pickup (JAG)

ENGINE (F-150): 300 cu. in. Six-cylinder. Brake horsepower: 119 at 3200 R.P.M. Bore & stroke: 4 x 3.98 in. Compression ratio: 8.9:1. Carburetor: One-barrel.

F-250 PICKUP: — The regular cab F-250 was only offered with the 8-foot Styleside box. SuperCab models came with either the 6¾- or 8-foot box. Standard features were similar to those on the F-100, with the addition of power brakes. Heavy-duty F-250s also had four-speed manual transmission.

I.D. DATA (F-250): See F-100 I.D.

Model	Body Type	Price	Weight	Prod. Total
—	Chassis w/Cab	7527	3481	—
F-25	Styleside Pickup	7568	3579	—
X-25	SuperCab Pickup	8227	3906	—

ENGINE (F-250): Same as F-150.

1982 Ford Ranger Styleside Pickup (JAG)

F-350 PICKUP: — The F-350 was only offered in regular cab and with "smoothside" Styleside box. The F-350 pickup could also be had with dual rear wheels. Such models had Flareside-like rear fenders, but otherwise looked like Stylesides. Except for having power brakes, power steering and a four-speed manual transmission, most F-350 standard features were the same as those on F-100s.

I.D. DATA (F-350): See F-100 I.D.

Model	Body Type	Price	Weight	Prod. Total
F-37	Chassis w/Cab	8648	3717	—
F-35	Styleside Pickup	8901	3961	—
X-35	Super Cab Pickup	—	—	—

ENGINE (F-350): 351 cu. in. V-8. Bore & stroke: 4.00 x 3.50 in. Carburetor: Two-barrel.

CHASSIS: Wheelbase: 116.8 in. (F-100/F-150); 133 in. (all); 138.8 in. (F-150/F-250 Super Cab); 155 in. (F-150/F-250 SuperCab). Overall length: 189.3 in. (Flareside); 192.1 in. (F-100/F-150 Styleside); 208.3 in. (Style); 214.1 in. (F-150/F-250 Super Cab); 230.3 in. (F-150/F-250 Super Cab). GVW (in pounds): 4650-5050 (F-100); 5250-6450 (F-150); 6500-9200 (F-250); 8900-11,000 (F-350). Tires: P215/75R x 15SL (F-100/F-150); 8.00 x 16.5 (F-250); 9.50 x 16.5E (F-350).

POWERTRAIN OPTIONS: "255" V-8 (F-100). "302" V-8 (F-100/F-150/F-250). "351" V-8 (F-150/F-250/F-350). "400" V-8 (F-250 H-D/F-350). Four-speed manual; four-speed manual with overdrive (F-100/F-150/F-250); SelectShift automatic or automatic overdrive transmissions.

CONVENIENCE OPTIONS: Four-wheel-drive (F-150/F-250/F-350). Chrome grille. Chromatic tape stripe. Tri-colored tape strip. Accent tape stripe. Lower bodyside molding with black vinyl insert. Bright box rails for 8-foot Styleside. Wheel lip moldings. Radios: AM; AM/FM monaural; AM/FM stereo (speakers mounted in door panels); AM/FM stereo with cassette player and AM/FM stereo radio with 8-track tape player. Air conditioning. High-output heater. **Convenience Group:** includes, interval wipers; 12 inch day/night mirror; R-H visor vanity mirror; molded bin on lower doors; headlamps on warning buzzer and courtesy light switch on R-H door. Electronic digital clock. Fingertip speed control. Vinyl headliner.

1982 Ford Ranger Styleside Pickup (JAG)

Light Group: includes, movable underhood worklight with 20 ft. retractable cord, plus lights in glove box; ashtray and under instrument panel; dome lamp with map lights; cargo box light; headlamps-on warning buzzer and courtesy light switch on R-H door. Power door locks. Power steering. Power windows. Tinted sliding rear window. Tilt steering wheel. Tinted glass all around. Tool storage box located under the hood (included movable underhood worklight with 20-ft. retractable cord and inside locking hood release). Slide-out spare tire carrier. Spare tire carrier side-mounted inside Styleside box. Center console (SC with Captain's Chairs). Electric remote control swing-away mirrors. Black low-mount western swing-away mirrors. Bright low-mount western swing-away mirrors. Bright low-mount recreational mirrors. Bright swingaway recreational mirrors. Reclining Captain's Chairs. Forward facing rear seat (folds down to form flat floor (SC). Center-facing folding rear seats (SC). Heavy-duty black vinyl. Knitted vinyl. Auxiliary fuel tank. **Handling Package:** includes, front and rear stabilizer bars; heavy-duty front and rear shocks and heavy-duty front springs. Heavy-duty shock absorbers. Oil pressure and ammeter gauges. Front and rear stabilizer bars. Engine block heater. Extra engine cooling package. Super engine cooling package. Camper special package. Trailer towing packages. Heavy-duty air cleaner. Dual note horns. Color-keyed floor mats in lieu of standard carpeting with XLS. Five roof clearance lights. **Exterior Protection Group:** includes, bright door edge guards, front bumper guards and front bumper rub strip. **Security Lock Group:** includes, locking gas cap; inside hood release and glove box; also spare tire lock (with under frame and in-box carrier). Sports instrumentation (tach, ammeter, oil pressure gauge and trip odometer). **Rear Bumpers:** black step (XLS Style); argent step (Styleside); chrome step (SRW Styleside); chrome channel (Flareside) and chrome contour (SRW Styleside). Deluxe wheel covers. White styled steel wheels. Deluxe argent styled steel wheels. Spot wheel covers. Cast aluminum wheels. **XLS:** includes, "XLS" tape stripe; argent styled steel wheels with black hubs; black front and rear bumpers; black-out treatment on grille and headlamp doors; black side window surround; black door handles and locks, windshield molding, mirrors and tailgate handle (Styleside); cigarette lighter; left- and right-hand courtesy light switches; bright surround door trim panel moldings; color-keyed carpeting; brushed aluminum applique instrument panel; folding fully covered seat back; cloth and vinyl seat trim; aluminum scuff plates; brushed aluminum trim steering wheel.**XL:** includes, bright hub caps; bright upper body moldings, windshield, rear window; tape letters on tailgate; cigarette lighter; left- and right-hand courtesy light switches; day/night mirror; bright surround door trim panel moldings; color-keyed mat; woodtone applique instrument panel; fully-covered folding seat back; cloth and vinyl seat trim; aluminum scuff plates; vinyl headlining and trim panel moldings above belt line. **XLT Lariat:** includes, (in addition to or in place of items on XL or XLS) upper bodyside protection with vinyl; tape stripe; bright windshield, rear window, wheel lip; brushed aluminum tailgate applique; bright door trim panel moldings with woodtone applique; color-keyed carpeting; woodtone applique instrument panel, deluxe steering wheel with woodtone insert, moldings/trim panels above belt line (and below in SC). Explorer package.

NOTE: Interior F-series colors in 1982 were: Fawn, Dark Blue, Red, Black, Nutmeg or Spruce (except SC). Exterior colors included: Raven Black, Wimbledon White, Silver Metallic, Medium Grey Metallic, Candyapple Red, Midnight Blue Metallic, Medium Blue Metallic, Bright Blue, Dark Spruce Metallic, Light Spruce, Dark Fawn Metallic, Fawn, Medium Carmel Metallic, Tan, Dark Brown Metallic, Maroon, Light Spruce Glow (optional). TU-TONE: regular: accent color covered roof and upper back panel; dual-color tape strip divided colors. Deluxe: accent color on center bodyside area and tailgate; moldings or tapes included as needed. Combination: regular and deluxe tu-tones combined. Victoria: accent color applied to hood, upper fender, around door window, and the lower bodyside; tape and moldings included as needed.

1983 FORD

BRONCO CUSTOM: — Styling of the 4wd Bronco was carried over from the previous year. Standard features included: Bucket seats. Vinyl sun visors. Padded instrument panel. Armrests. Dome lamp. Windshield header and "A" pillar moldings. AM radio (could be deleted for credit). Flip/fold rear bench seat. Halogen headlights. Full instrumentation. Black front and rear bumpers. Bright hub caps. Black scuff plate. Twin Traction Beam independent front suspension. Power brakes and steering. Four-speed manual transmission. Black grille.

1983 Ford Bronco XLS Sport Utility Wagon w/4x4 (JAG)

I.D. DATA (Bronco): See F-100 I.D.

Model	Body Type	Price	Weight	Prod. Total
U-150	Wagon	10,858	4079	—

ENGINE (Bronco): Displacement: 300 cu. in. Six-cylinder. 302 cu. in. V-8 (standard in CA).

CHASSIS: Wheebase: 104.7 in. Overall length: 177.6 in. Overall height: 73.2 in. Overall width: 77.2 in. Tires: P215/75R x 15 SL.

POWERTRAIN OPTIONS: Select Shift automatic. 302 V-8. 351 V-8. 4-speed manual with overdrive. Limited slip front axle.

CONVENIENCE OPTIONS: Chrome front, or front and rear bumpers. Tri-color tape stripe. Accent tape stripe. Black GT bar. Chrome grille. Upper bodyside tape stripe. Lower bodyside molding. High output heater. Center console. Electric rear window defroster. Electric remote control swing-gaway rearview mirrors. **Convenience Group:** intemittent wipers, map box in doors, headlamp-on warning buzzer, RH door courtesy light switch, 12 in. mirror, visor vanity mirror. Front bench seat. Rear bench seat delete. Power windows. Tinted glass all around. Privacy glass in quarter windows. **Light Group:** lights in glove box, ashtray and underhood: instrument panel courtesy lights, dome light with map light, RH door courtesy light, headlamp-on warning buzzer (the underhood light had a 20 ft. cord). **Handling Package:** front & rear stablizier bars, quad heavy-duty front and dual heavy-duty rear shocks. Captains chairs. Underhood tool box. Automatic locking hubs. Traction-Lok front and/or rear axle. **Sports Instrumentation:** tach & odometer. Recreational mirrors. Bright low-mount western mirrors. Heavy-duty trailer towing package. Thirty-two gallon fuel tank in lieu of standard includes skid plate. Sliding rear quarter windows. **Protection Group:** bright door edge guards, front bumper guards and front bumper rub strip. **Security Group:** locking gas cap, inside hood release lock, spare tire lock and locking glove box.
Super engine cooling package. Extra cooling package. Fog lamps. Exterior sound package. Cigarette lighter. Power door locks. XLT: bright front & rear bumpers, Black grille, bright hub caps, windshield, quarter window; lower bodyside protection molding with vinyl insert, brushed aluminum tailgate applique, dome lamp, LH & RH courtesy light switches, color-keyed carpeting, LH rear quarter trim panel cargo lamp, door trim panel with bright surround molding, woodtone panel with full length storage bins, color-keyed vinyl headliner, simulated woodtone applique and bright moldings instrument panel, bright scuff plates, deluxe seat belts, cloth and vinyl seat, trim soft-wrap steering wheel with woodtone insert, molded rear quarter trim panels with armrests, speaker grilles, storage bin and light, spare tire cover, cigarette lighter, added insulation. **XLS Package:** has most of the features of the XLT plus: Black gloss on front and rear bumpers, Black gloss grille, argent styled steel wheels with Black hub, Black gloss windshield molding, treatment on headlamp doors and around window, door handles, locks, mirrors and tailgate lock, "XLS" tape, door trim panel with bright surround, brushed aluminum applique and steering wheel trim. Speed control. Swing away spare tire carrier. 40-channel CB. Front tow hooks. Cast aluminum wheels. Styled steel painted (White) wheels. Sport wheel covers. Deluxe argent styled steel wheels. AM/FM monaural, AM/FM stereo, AM/FM stereo with cassette or 8-track player. Snow plow packages. High altitude emmissions system. Heavy-duty auxiliary battery.

NOTE: Bronco color choices for 1983 were: Raven Black, Wimbledon White, Candyapple Red, Dark Red Metallic, Midnight Blue Metallic, Bright Blue, Walnut Metallic, Copper, Desert Tan, Light Desert Tan, Light Charcoal Metallic, Dark Charcoal Metallic, Blue Glow, Light Teal Glow. Fiberglass roof colors were: Black, Midnight Blue, Candyapple Red, Desert Tan, White.

ECONOLINE E-100 CARGO VAN: — Econoline styling was unchanged for 1983. Among the standard features were: Full-foam driver's bucket seat. Vinyl seat trim. Padded full-width instrument panel. Brake warning light. Two-speed electric windshield wipers. Wiper-arm-mounted washer jets. Dome lights. Front compartment headlining. Column mounted ignition switch scuff plates. Door checks. Argent-painted bumpers and hub caps. Bright windshield molding. Painted mirrors. Hinged side cargo doors (sliding door available at no extra cost).

ECONOLINE E-100 DISPLAY VAN: — This model had windows at the rear and on the right hand side. It came with the same standard features as the Cargo Van.

ECONOLINE E-100 WINDOW VAN: — The Window Van had glass all around. It shared standard features with the Cargo Van.

I.D. DATA (Econoline): See F-100 I.D.

Model	Body Type	Price	Weight	Prod. Total
E-04	Cargo Van	7310	3763	—
E-05	Window Van	7498	3802	—
E-06	Display Van	7432	3797	

ENGINE (Econoline E-100): Displacement: 300 cu. in. Six-cylinder. 120 horsepower at 3400 R.P.M. Bore & stroke: 4.00 in. x 3.98 in. Compression ratio: 8.0:1. One-bbl. carburetor.

ECONOLINE E-150 CARGO VAN: — The slightyly more heavy-duty E-150 had most of the same standard features as the E-100.

ECONOLINE E-150 SUPER CARGO VAN: — This van had the same features as the E-150 Cargo Van plus a 20 in. extended rear overhang. This allowed carrying of longer loads. The maximum cargo length (right side, without passengers seat) was 14 feet.

ECONOLINE E-150 DISPLAY VAN: — This van shared styling with the E-100 but had greater load capacity.

ECONOLINE E-150 SUPER DISPLAY VAN: — See E-150 Super Cargo Van.

ECONOLINE E-150 WINDOW VAN: — This van shared styling with the E-100 Window Van, but had greater load capacity.

ECONOLINE E-150 SUPER WINDOW VAN: — See E-150 Super Cargo Van.

I.D. DATA (Econoline E-150): See F-100 I.D.

Model	Body Type	Price	Weight	Prod. Total
E-14	Cargo Van	7566	3736	—
E-15	Window Van	7754	3775	—
E-16	Display Van	7688	3770	—
S-14	Super Cargo Van	8388	4134	—
S-15	Super Window Van	8576	4173	—
S-16	Super Display Van	8510	4168	—

ENGINE (Econoline E-150): Same as E-100.

Model	Body Type	Price	Weight	Prod. Total
S-260	Super Display Van	9615	4517	—

ENGINE (Econoline E-250): Same as E-100.

ECONOLINE E-350 CARGO VAN: This was the top-of-the-line Econoline Van. It had heavy-duty front and rear shocks and a greater load capacity than the other series. Standard features were the same as the E-100.

ECONOLINE E-350 SUPER CARGO VAN: — See E-150 Super Cargo Van.

ECONOLINE E-350 DISPLAY VAN: — See E-250 Display Van.

ECONOLINE E-350 SUPER DISPLAY VAN: See E-150 Super Cargo Van.

ECONOLINE E-350 WINDOW VAN: — See E-250 Window Van.

ECONOLINE E-350 SUPER WINDOW VAN: — See E-150 Super Cargo Van.

ECONOLINE E-350 CUTAWAY VAN: — See E-250 Cutaway Van.

ECONOLINE E-350 PARCEL DELIVERY: — See E-250 Parcel Delivery.

I.D. DATA (Econoline E-350): See F-100 I.D.

Model	Body Type	Price	Weight	Prod. Total
E-34	Cargo Van	8668	4460	—
E-35	Window Van	8856	4513	—
E-36	Display Van	8790	4494	—
S-34	Super Cargo Van	9632	4608	—
S-35	Super Window Van	9820	4661	—
S-36	Super Display Van	9754	4642	—
E-37B	Cutaway	8835	3815	—

ECONOLINE E-250 CARGO VAN: — The new E-250 had a higher GVW rating and more heavy-duty front and rear axles, than the E-150. It also came with eight-hole wheels. Standard features were the same as those on the E-100 except the three-speed manual was not available in CA.

ECONOLINE E-250 SUPER CARGO VAN: — See E-150 Cargo Van.

ECONOLINE E-250 DISPLAY VAN: — This vehicle shared styling and features with the E-100, but had greater load capacity.

ECONOLINE E-250 SUPER DISPLAY VAN: — See E-150 Super Cargo Van.

ECONOLINE E-250 WINDOW VAN: — This vehicle shared styling and features with the E-100 Window Van, but had greater load capacity.

ECONOLINE E-250 SUPER WINDOW VAN: — See E-150 Super Cargo Van.

ECONOLINE E-250 CUTAWAY VAN: — This van with Camper Special Packages, was designed to readily accommodate custom motor homes.

ECONOLINE E-250 PARCEL DELIVERY: — See E-250 Parcel Delivery Van was 149.9 in. long and 73.3 in. high in its cargo area. The rear door opening was 84.7 in. wide.

I.D. DATA (Econoline E-250): See F-100 I.D.

Model	Body Type	Price	Weight	Prod. Total
E-240	Cargo Van	8815	4146	—
E-250	Window Van	9002	4212	—
E-260	Display Van	8937	4189	—
S-240	Super Cargo Van	9493	4474	—
S-250	Super Window Van	9680	4540	—
E-380	Parcel Delivery	—	5240	—

ENGINE (Econoline E-350): Same as E-100.

CHASSIS: Wheelbase: 124 in. (E-100, E-150) 138 in. Overall length: 186.8 in. (124 in. w.b.), 206.8 in. (138 in. w.b.), 226.8 in. (138 in. Super Van). GVW: 5200 (E-100), 5850-6350 (E-150), 6750-7900 (E-250), 8750-11,000 (E-350). Tires: P205/75R x 15SL (E-100), P225/75R x 15SL (E-150), 8.00 x 16.5D (E-250), 9.50 x 16.5E (E-350).

POWERTRAIN OPTIONS: 5.0L V-8. 5.8L V-8. 6.9L Diesel V-8. 7.5L V-8 (E-350). Four-speed manual with overdrive. Select Shift automatic.

CONVENIENCE OPTIONS: XL PACKAGE: vinyl bucket seats, front compartment carpeting, color-keyed door trim panels, leather tone inserts on instrument panel, courtesy lights, interval wipers; bright grille, front and rear bumpers, and low-mount swingaway mirrors. Cloth and vinyl Captain's chairs. Air conditioning. High-capacity air conditioner and auxiliary heater. Heavy-duty battery. Chrome rear step bumper. Chrome bumpers. Super engine cooling. Auxiliary fuel tank. Ammeter and oil pressure gauges. Privacy Glass. Swing-out rear door and/or cargo door glass. Tinted glass. Handling package. Deluxe Insulation Package. Light and Convenience group. Bright low-mount swingaway mirrors. Bright swing-out recreation mirrors. Deluxe two-tone paint. Power door locks. Speed control. Tilt steering wheel. Heavy-duty front & rear springs. Trailer Towing Packages. Wheel covers. AM/FM monaural, AM/FM stereo, AM/digital clock radio, AM/FM stereo with cassette player. Hinged side cargo door.

E-100 CLUB WAGON: — The new E-100 Club Wagon looked the same as last years model. But that wasn't bad. Among the standard features were: Front bucket seats and a rear bench seat. Color-keyed patterned vinyl seat trim. Seat belts. Two-speed electric windshield wipers. Wiper arm mounted washer jets. 10 in. rearview mirror. Dome lights. Insulated floor mat with scuff plates. Three armrests. Dual horns. Flip-open windows in sliding door and opposite windows. Painted bumpers, 5 in. x 8 in. mirrors and hub caps. Bright windshield molding. This was the last year for the E-100 Club Wagon series.

E-150 CLUB WAGON: — This was a slightly more heavy-duty version of the E-100. It could be had in 124 in. or 138 in. w.b. and was also offered in five and eight passenger versions. Standard features were same as those on the E-100.

E-150 SUPER WAGON: — This was basically the same as the 138 in. w.b. E-150 but had a 20 in. extended rear overhang.

E-250 CLUB WAGON: — This was available in 11-, 12-passenger versions only. Also 8-passenger version available with quad Captains Chairs and a 4-passenger bench seat.

E-350 SUPER WAGON: — The heavy-duty E-350 provided 20 in. more inside length than regular 138 in. w.b. Club Wagons. Heavy-duty shocks were standard.

I.D. DATA (Club Wagon): See F-100.

Model	Body Type	Price	Weight	Prod. Total
E-100	Club Wagon	8501	3889	—
E-150	Club Wagon	8794	3896	—
E-150	Super Wagon	9480	4216	—
E-250	Club Wagon	11,058	4838	—
E-350	Super Wagon	10,785	4751	—

ENGINE (Club Wagon): Same as Econoline.

CHASSIS: Wheelbase: 124 in. (E-100), 138 in. (E-150, E-250, E-350). Overall width: 79.7 in. Overall length: 186.8 in. (124 in. w.b.) 206.8 in. (138 in. w.b.) 226.8 in. (138 in. w.b. Super Wagon). GVW: 6000-9400. Tires: P225/75R x 15SL, 8.75 x 16.5E.

POWERTRAIN OPTIONS: 5.0L V-8, 5.8L V-8, 6.9L Diesel V-8, 7.5L V-8. Select Shift automatic. Four-speed manual w/overdrive.

CONVENIENCE OPTIONS: Most of the same items available on the Econoline plus 4-passenger rear bench seat. Snack-game table.

RANGER PICKUP: — The new Ranger was introduced in early 1982 as a 1983 model. It looked like a down sized F-100. The grille featured a rectangular sections theme with the Ford script in an oval emblem in the left corner, and a rectangular headlight on each end. This entire sectioned was framed in bright molding. Rectangular parking lights were directly below the headlights. The rectangular side marker lights were placed vertically on the front fenders. The Ranger nameplate was also on the front fenders. Taillights were of the wrap around variety. The double walled box was 85 in. long and 54.3 in. wide (40.4 in. at the wheelhouse), and had a quick release tailgate. Standard features included: Halogen headlights. 4-speed manual. Floor mat. Vinyl bench seat with folding backrest. Two outside rearview mirrors. Styled steel wheels.

I.D. DATA (Ranger): See F-100 I.D.

1983 Ford Ranger XLT 4x4 Pickup (OCW)

Model	Body Type	Price	Weight	Prod. Total
R-10	107.9 in. w.b. Pickup (Style)	6289	2526	—
R-10	113.9 in. w.b. Pickup (Style)	6446	—	—

ENGINE (Ranger): 2.0L (121 cu. in.) Four-cylinder. Brake horsepower: 80 horsepower at 4800 R.P.M. Bore & stroke: 3.15 x 3.85.

CHASSIS: Wheebase: 107.9 in., 113.9 in. Overall length: 175.6 in. (107.9 in. w.b.), 187.6 in. (113.9 in. w.b.). Overall width: 66.9 in. Overall height: 64 in. (67.1 in. 4x4). GVW: 3740-4220. Tires: P185/75R x 14.

POWERTRAIN OPTIONS: 2.3L Four. 2.2L Diesel Four. 2.8L V-6. 5-speed manual with overdrive. Automatic.

CONVENIENCE OPTIONS: Four-Wheel-Drive: Twin-Traction Beam front axle, 2700 lb. rear axle, power brakes, 2.3L Four, 2-speed part-time transfer case. Headliner. 4x4 tape stripe. **Radios:** AM/FM monaural, AM/FM stereo, AM/FM stereo with cassette tape player. Air conditioning. Black rear step bumper. **Convenience Group:** duel electric horns (except with 2.2L diesel), interval windshield wipers, passengers visor vanity mirror, drivers sun visor band, cigarette lighter. Tinted glass all around. **Light Group:** ashtray, cargo box, glove box lights; passenger door courtesy light switch, headlights-on warning buzzer. Floor console (for bucket seats). Bright low-mount western swingaway mirrors. Power steering. Power brakes. Tilt steering wheel. Sliding rear window. Eight cargo tie-down hooks. Pivoting vent windows. Fingertip speed control. Reclining bucket seats. Knitted vinyl contoured bench seat. Cloth and vinyl bench seat. Payload packages up to 1770 lb. Heavy-duty air cleaner. Heavy-duty battery. Camper package. Extra cooling. Auxiliary 13-gallon fuel tank. **Gauge Package:** ammeter, oil pressure gauge, temperature gauge, and trip odometer. Engine block heater. Heavy-duty shocks. Tow hooks. Snow plow special package. Automatic locking hubs (4x4). Heavy-duty front suspension (4x4). Traction lok rear axle. Limited slip front axle (4x4). **Handling Package:** Heavy-duty front and rear shock absorbers and front and rear stabilizer bars (rear only with 4x4). Skid plates (4x4). Calif. emissions system. High altitude emissions system. **Security Lock Group:** glove box lock, locking gas cap, and underbody spare tire carrier lock. **Exterior Protection Group:** chrome front bumper with end caps, black front bumper guards and black upper bodyside molding with dual red accent stripes. Chrome front bumper. Cast aluminum wheels. White spot wheels. Deluxe wheel trim. Cast aluminum spare wheel (4x4). **XL:** (in addition to or in place of standard features) bright rear window insert molding, deluxe wheel trim and chrome front bumper; woodtone instrument cluster applique, color-keyed headliner, contoured knitted vinyl bench seat, color keyed seat belts with tension eliminator, color-keyed steering wheel and floor mats, passenger door courtesy light switch, aluminum scuff plates. **XLS:** (in addition to or in place of XL features) blackout trim components and special "XLS" tape stripe, bucket seats, color-keyed deluxe steering wheel, gauge package, brushed pewter-tone cluster applique on instrument panel, color-keyed cloth door trim with carpeted map pocket, black scuff plates. **XLT:** (in addition to or in place of XLS features) chrome front bumper with black end caps, full length lower bodyside molding, accent bodyside paint stripes, deluxe wheel trim and brushed aluminum tailgate applique; full cloth door trim with color keyed molding and bright insert, carpeted lower portion and map pockets; cloth seat trim, carpeting, color-keyed deluxe steering wheel, wood tone cluster applique on instrument panel.

F-100 PICKUP: — Styling was carried over from the previous year. As a means of saving horsepower and fuel, Ford light-duty trucks came with a viscous type fan clutch. It engaged the fan only as needed. The fan did not run constantly. Standard F-100 features included: Chrome front bumper. Light argent grille with bright surround. Bright windshield molding. Argent hub caps. Bright door-mounted mirrors. Rectangular halogen headlights. Wraparound taillights. Easily removable tailgate (Styleside). Rope tie holes in corner stake pockets (Styleside). AM radio. All-vinyl seat trim. Full-foam seat over springs. Folding seat back access to behind seat storage area. Pivoting vent windows. Glove box. LH door courtesy light switch and dome lamp. Temperature gauge. Color-keyed windshield pillar, header and cowl side trim panels. Color-keyed door trim panels with foam-padded armrests. Coat hook. Floor insulation and carpet-texture rubber mat. Rearview mirror. Inside hood release. Black scuff plates. Black steering wheel. Power brakes. Three-speed manual transmission. Buyers could choose from 6½ ft. Flareside and 6¾ ft. or 8 ft. Styleside boxes.

I.D. DATA (F-100): See 1981 F-100 I.D.

419

Model	Body Type	Price	Weight	Prod. Total
F-10	(6½-ft) Pickup (Flare)	7068	3266	—
F-10	(6¾-ft.) Pickup (Style)	6909	3240	—
F-10	(8-ft.) Pickup (Style)	7063	3326	—

ENGINE (F-100): Same as 1982.

F-150 PICKUP: — The "heavy-duty" ½-ton F-150 had most of the same standard features as the F-100. It was available with the 6½' Flareside and 6¾ ft. or 8 ft. Styleside boxes. Regular and Super cabs were offered (the later only with Styleside box).

I.D. DATA (F-150): See F-100 I.D.

Model	Body Type	Price	Weight	Prod. Total
F-15	(6½-ft) Pickup (Flare)	7327	3418	—
F-15	(6¾-ft.) Pickup (Style)	7169	3391	—
F-15	(8-ft.) Pickup (Style)	7322	3507	—
X-15	Pickup (Super Cab)	8232	3752	—

ENGINE (F-150): Same as 1982.

F-150 PICKUP: — F-250 pickups came with a 8 ft. Styleside box and either regular or Super cabs. They shared most of the same standard features as found on F-100's. However, the F-250 heavy-duty models had power steering, a 4-speed manual, and an 11 in. clutch.

I.D. DATA (F-150): See F-100 I.D.

Model	Body Type	Price	Weight	Prod. Total
—	Chas. w/Cab	7869	3472	—
F-25	Pickup (Style)	7803	3695	—
X-25	Pickup (Super Cab)	9028	4127	—

ENGINE (F-250): Same as F-150.

F-350 PICKUP: — The husky F-350 was offered in regular and 6-pass. Crew cabs. All had the 8 ft. Styleside box. Standard features included most of those found on the F-100 plus power steering, an 11 in. clutch, and 4-speed manual transmission. A regular cab F-350 was available with dual rear wheels.

I.D. DATA (F-350): See F-100 I.D.

Model	Body Type	Price	Weight	Prod. Total
F37	Chassis w/Cab	8953	3794	—
F-35	Pickup (Style)	9212	4071	—
W-35	Pickup (Crew Cab)	10,131	4553	—
—	6-wheel Pickup (Style)	—	—	—

ENGINE (F-350): 5.8L (351 cu. in.) V-8. Compression ratio: 8.3:1. Carburator: 2-bbl. (n.a. in CA). Crew Cab had 4.9L (300 cu. in.) Six-cylinder.

CHASSIS: Wheebase: 116.8 in. (F-100, F-150) 133 in. (all), 138.8 in. (F-150, F-250 SC), 155 in. (F-150, F-250, SC), 168.4 in. (F-350 CC). Overall length: 192.1 in. (F-100, F-150 Style), 189.3 in. (Flare), 208.3 in. (Style), 214.1 in. (F-150 SC), 230.3 in. (F-150, F-250 SC), 237.6 in. (F-350 CC). GVW: 4700 (F-100), 5250-6450 (F-150), 6300-9000 (F-250), 8700-11,000 (F-350). Tires: P195/75R x 15SL (F-100), P215/75R x 15SL (F-150), LT215/85R x 16C (F-250), LT235/85R x 16E (F-350).

POWERTRAIN OPTIONS: 4.9L (300 cu. in.) Six (F-100), 5.0L (302) V-8 (F-100, F-150, F-250), 5.8L (351) V-8 (F-250, F-250 heavy-duty, F-350), 7.5L V-8 (F-250 heavy-duty, F-350), 6.9L (420) Diesel V-8 (F-250 heavy-duty, F-350). 4-speed manual (F-150, F-250), 4-speed manual with overdrive (F-100, F-150, F-250), SelectShift automatic, automatic overdrive (F-100, F-150, F-250).

CONVENIENCE OPTIONS: Four-Wheel-Drive. Chrome grille. Tri-colored tape stripe. Accent tape stripe (Style). Lower bodyside molding with Black vinyl insert for SRW Stylesides with standard or XL trim. Wheel lip moldings. **Radios:** AM/FM monaural (single speaker), AM/FM stereo (speakers mounted in door panels), AM/FM stereo with cassette tape player. Air conditioning. High output heater. Cigarette lighter. **Convenience Group:** interval wipers, 12 in. day/night mirror, RH visor vanity mirror, molded bin on lower doors, headlights-on warning buzzer, and courtesy light switch on RH door with standard trim. **Deluxe Insulation Package:** color-keyed headliner and moldings (door upper, "B" pillar and rear window) plus aluminum door scuff plates with standard regular cab; also includes Black fully insulated floor mat with standard trim and covered back panel. Electronic digital clock (included date/time/elapsed time display with new stopwatch feature). Fingertip speed control. **Light Group:** movable under hood worklights with 20 ft. retractable cord plus lights in glove box, ashtray, under instrument panel, dual beam dome/map light, cargo box light, headlights-on warning buzzer, and courtesy light switch for RH door. Power door locks. Power steering. Power windows. Tinted sliding rear window. Tilt steering wheel. Tinted glass. Tool storage box located under the hood. In-box spare tire carrier side mounted inside Styleside box. Center console (SC's with Captain's Chairs). Electric remote control swingaway mirrors. Bright low-mount swingaway western mirrors. Bright swing-out recreational mirrors. Cloth and vinyl seat trim. Heavy-duty black vinyl, or knitted vinyl seat trim. Folding rear bench seat (SC). Two center facing jump seats that fold out of the way (SC). Auxiliary fuel tank. 20-gallon outside of frame fuel tank (DRW Chas. w/cab) in lieu of standard. Auxiliary transmission oil cooler. **Handling Package:** front and rear stabilizer bars, heavy-duty front and rear shock absorbers and heavy-duty front springs. Heavy-duty shock absorbers. Oil pressure and ammeter gauges. Engine oil cooler for 7.5L (460) V-8. Front and rear stabilizer bars. Engine block heater. Extra engine cooling package. Super engine cooling package. Trailer towing package. Camper package. Limited slip/traction - lok rear axle. Heavy-duty air cleaner. Dual note horns. 5 roof clearance lights. **Exterior Protection Group:** bright door edge guards, front bumper guards and front bumper rub strip. **Security Lock Group:** locking gas cap, inside hood

release and glove box; also spare tire lock (with under-frame and in-box carrier). **Sports Instrumentation:** tach, ammeter, oil pressure gauge and trip odometer. **Rear Bumpers:** argent step (Style), chrome step (SRW Style), chrome channel (Flare), and chrome contour (SRW Style). Cast aluminum wheels. White styled steel wheels. Sport wheel covers. Deluxe argent styled steel wheels. Deluxe wheels covers. **XL:** (in addition to or in place of standard features) LH & RH courtesy light switch, day/night mirror, bright surround door trim panel moldings, color-keyed floor mat, woodtone applique on instrument panel, folding fully covered seat back, deluxe seat belts, cloth and vinyl seat trim, aluminum scuff plates, sun visors, headlining, moldings/trim panels above belt line; bright upper bodyside and tailgate moldings on SRW Stylesides, bodyside surround tape strip and tailgate tape letters on Flareside and DRW pickups; bright hub caps (except on DRW) and bright rear window molding. **XLS:** (in addition to or in place of items on the XL) color-keyed carpeting, brushed aluminum applique on instrument panel, brushed aluminum trim steering wheel; two-color "XLS" tape stripe, argent styled steel wheels with Black hubs, Black front and rear bumpers, blackout treatment on grille and headlamp doors; Black door handles, windshield molding, low-mount western swingaway mirrors.

XLT: (in addition to or in place of items on the XL) door trim panel moldings with bright surround with woodtone applique and map box, color-keyed carpeting, deluxe steering wheel, moldings/trim panels above belt line (and below on SC), full length lower bodyside molding, with protective Black vinyl insert and distinctive brushed aluminum tailgate applique.

NOTE: F-series colors for 1983 included: Raven Black, Candyapple Red, Dark Red Metallic, Midnight Blue Metallic, Bright Blue, Dark Teal Metallic, Copper, Wimbledon White, Desert Tan, Light Charcoal Metallic, Light Desert Tan, Dark Charcoal Metallic, Walnut Metallic, Blue Glow and Light Teal Glow were optional "glamour" colors. TU-TONES: Regular: accent color covered roof and upper back panel; dual color tape stripe divided colors. Deluxe: accent color on center bodyside area and tailgate; molding or tapes included as needed. Combination: regular and deluxe tu-tones combines. Victoria: accent color applied to hood, upper fender, around door window, and lower bodyside; tape and moldings included as needed.

1984 FORD

1984 Ford "Eddie Bauer" Bronco II Utility Wagon (JAG)

BRONCO II: — This was the full-size Bronco's little 4x4 brother. It was meant to compete with Chevrolet's S-10 Blazer. Basic styling resembled that of the big Bronco, but there were some differences. Most noticeably, the Bronco II had a shorter grille with more vertical bars. The Ford emblem was placed in the lower left-hand area of the grille. The grille and headlights were framed by bright trim. Parking lights were beneath the headlights. Rectangular side marker lights were placed vertically on the front fenders. A distinctive feature was the wraparound rear quarter windows. Among the standard features were: Twin-Traction Beam front axle; power brakes and steering; front and rear stabilizer bars; four-speed manual transmission; reclining front seats; split fold-down rear bench seat; halogen headlights; dual, outside foldaway rearview mirrors; bright front and rear contour bumpers; sport wheel covers; color-keyed carpeting; full-length cloth headliner and sunvisors.

I.D. DATA (Bronco II): See F-150 I.D.

Model	Body Type	Price	Weight	Prod. Total
U-14	Wagon	9998	3237	—

ENGINE (Bronco II): 171 cu. in. V-6. Brake horsepower: 115 at 4600 R.P.M. Bore & stroke: 3.66 x 2.70 in. Compression ratio: 8.6:1. Carburetor: Two-barrel.

CHASSIS: Wheelbase: 94 in. Overall length: 158.4 in. Overall width: 68 in. Overall height: 68.2 in. Tires: P195/75R x 15 SL.

POWERTRAIN OPTIONS: Three-speed automatic or five-speed manual transmission.

CONVENIENCE OPTIONS: Chrome grille. Tu-Tone paints. Sport tape stripe. **Eddie Bauer Bronco II package:** includes, special Tu-Tone paint treatment; "Eddie Bauer" emblem; XLT level trim inside and out; cast aluminum wheels; all-terrain tires with raised white letters; ammeter, oil pressure and temperature gauges; trip odometer; dual Captain's chairs; AM/FM stereo radio; tilt steering wheel; floor console; dual electric horns;

interval windshield wipers; passenger visor vanity mirror; driver's sunvisor band; ashtray and glove box lights; headlamps-on warning buzzer; Eddie Bauer field bag and map holder. AM/FM monaural radio. AM/FM stereo. AM/FM stereo radio with cassette tape player. Dual or quad Captain's chairs (include power lumbar support and zippered map pocket on seat back). Air conditioning. Tinted glass. **Convenience Group:** includes, interval windshield wipers; visor vanity mirror; cigarette lighter; dual electric horns and driver's sunvisor band. **Light Group:** includes, glove box; ashtray and cargo area light; passenger door and liftgate courtesy light switches and "headlights on" warning buzzer. Fingertip speed control. Tilt steering wheel. Rear window wiper/defroster. Flip-open liftgate window. Flip-up, open air roof. Flip-open removable quarter windows (gray tinted). Pivoting front vent windows. Privacy glass. **Floor Console:** includes, gauge package; trash bin; cassette tape tray; coin tray; two cup depressions and electronic graphic warning display module. **Overhead Console:** includes, digital clock and pivoting map light; bright; low-mount western swingaway mirrors and outside swingaway spare tire carrier. Roof rack. Rear seat delete. Carpet delete. Automatic locking hubs. Engine block heater. Super engine cooling. Heavy-duty maintenance-free battery. Heavy-duty air cleaner. **Gauge Package:** includes, ammeter; temperature and oil pressure gauges, plus resettable trip odometer. Heavy-duty shocks. Snow plow special package. Trailer towing package. Tow hooks. Limited slip front axle. Traction-lok axle. California emissions system. High-altitude emissions system. **Exterior Protection Group:** includes, bright front and rear bumpers with black end caps; black front bumper guards and black upper bodyside molding with two red accent strips. Transfer case skid plate. Front license plate bracket. Cast aluminum wheels. White sport styled steel wheels. Deluxe wheel trim (includes argent styled steel wheel with bright trim ring, lug nuts and black hub cover). **XLT Package:** chrome grille bodyside accent stripe, pivoting front vent windows, tinted glass, deluxe wheel trim, cloth and vinyl seat trim with full cloth door trim panels with a map pocket, carpet insert and bright headlights; color-keyed instrument panel and deluxe steering wheel; woodtone applique on instrument cluster; color-keyed deluxe seat belts; courtesy light switches; liftgate operated cargo area light; rear quarter trim panels included integral padded armrests, speaker grilles and storage compartments. **XLS Package:** "XLS" tape striping in three colors on the lower bodysides, rocker panel molding spats; blacked out grille surround, bumpers and bumper end caps; deluxe wheel trim; cloth door trim panels had carpet insert and map pocket; deluxe steering wheel, color-keyed instrument panel (with storage bin); full instrumentation.

NOTE: BRONCO II color choices for 1984 were: Raven Black, Polar White, Light Charcoal Metallic, Dark Canyon Red, Light Blue, Medium Blue Metallic, Midnight Blue Metallic, Medium Desert Tan, Walnut Metallic, Light Desert Tan, Bright Bittersweet, Bright Copper Glow. Interior trim colors were: Dark Blue, Canyon Red, Tan.

BRONCO: — Styling of the 4wd Bronco was carried over from the previous year. Standard features included: Bucket seats. Vinyl sunvisors. Padded instrument panel. Armrests. Dome lamp. Windshield header and "A" pillar moldings. AM radio (could be deleted for credit). Flip/fold rear bench seat. Halogen headlights. Full instrumentation. Black front and rear bumpers. Bright hub caps. Black scuff plate. Twin Traction Beam independent front suspension. Power brakes and steering. Four-speed transmission.
Fold-down tailgate with power window.

I.D. DATA (Bronco): See F-150 I.D.

Model	Body Type	Price	Weight	Prod. Total
U-150	Wagon	10,858	4079	—

ENGINE (Bronco): Displacement: 300 cu. in. Six-cylinder. 302 cu. in. V-8 (standard in Calif.)

CHASSIS: Wheelbase: 104.7 in. Overall length: 177.6 in. Overall height: 73.2 in. Overall width: 77.2 in. Tires: P215/75R x 15 SL.

POWERTRAIN OPTIONS: SelectShift automatic. 302 V-8, 351 V-8, 351 HO V-8. Four-speed transmission with overdrive. Limited slip front axle.

CONVENIENCE OPTIONS: Chrome front, or front and rear bumpers. Tri-color tape stripe. Accent tape stripe. Black GT bar. Chrome grille. Upper bodyside tape stripe. Lower bodyside molding. High output heater. Center console. Electric rear window defroster. Electric remote control swing-gaway rearview mirrors. **Convenience Group:** intermittent wipers, map box in doors, headlamp-on warning buzzer, RH door courtesy light switch, 12 in. mirror, visor vanity mirror. Front bench seat. Power windows. Tinted glass all around. Privacy glass in quarter windows. **Light Group:** lights in glove box, ashtray and underhood: instrument panel courtesy lights, dome light with map light, RH door courtesy light, headlamp-on warning buzzer (the underhood light had a 20-ft. cord). **Handling Package:** front and rear stabilizer bars, quad heavy-duty front and dual heavy-duty rear shocks. Captains chairs. Underhood tool box. Automatic locking hubs. Traction-Lok front and/or rear axle. **Sports Instrumentation:** tachometer and odometer. Recreational mirrors. Bright low-mount western mirrors. Heavy-duty trailer towing package. Thirty-two gallon fuel tank in lieu of standard (includes skid plate). Sliding rear quarter windows. **Protection Group:** bright door edge guards, front bumper guards and front bumper rub strip. **Security Group:** locking gas cap, inside hood release lock, spare tire lock and locking glove box. Super engine cooling package. Extra engine cooling package. Fog lamps. Exterior sound package. Cigarette lighter. Power door locks. XLT: bright front and rear bumpers, black grille, bright hub caps, windshield, quarter window; lower bodyside protection molding with vinyl insert, brushed aluminum tailgate applique, dome lamp, LH and RH courtesy light switches, color-keyed carpeting, LH rear quarter trim panel cargo lamp, door trim panel with bright surround molding, woodtone panel with full length storage bins, color-keyed vinyl headliner, simulated woodtone applique and bright moldings instrument panel, bright scuff plates, deluxe seat belts, cloth and vinyl seat trim, soft-wrap steering wheel with woodtone insert, molded rear quarter trim panels with armrests, speaker grilles, storage bin and light, spare tire cover, cigarette

lighter, added insulation. **XLS Package:** has most of the features of the XLT plus: black gloss on front and rear bumpers, black gloss grille, argent styled steel wheels with black hub, black gloss windshield molding, treatment on headlamp doors and around window, door handles, locks, mirrors and tailgate lock, "XLS" tape, door trim panel with bright surround, brushed aluminum applique and steering wheel trim. Speed control. Swing away spare tire carrier. 40-channel CB. Front tow hooks. Cast aluminum wheels. Styled steel painted (white) wheels. Sport wheel covers. Deluxe argent styled steel wheels. AM/FM monaural, AM/FM stereo, AM/FM stereo with cassette or 8-track player. Snow plow packages. High altitude emissions system. Heavy-duty auxiliary battery.

ECONOLINE E-150 CARGO VAN: — The most noticeable styling change for '84 was the Ford name in script in an oval, on the center of the grille. Also, the bright outer trim that surround the grille was eliminated. Among the standard features were: Power brakes. Halogen headlights. AM radio. Bright hub caps. Three-speed manual transmission.

ECONOLINE E-150 SUPER CARGO VAN: — This van had the same features as the E-150 Cargo Van plus a 20 in. extended rear overhang. This was especially useful for hauling longer loads.

ECONOLINE E-150 DISPLAY VAN: — This van had windows at the rear and on the right-hand side. It came with the same standard features as the Cargo Van.

ECONOLINE E-150 SUPER DISPLAY VAN: — See E-150 Super Cargo Van.

ECONOLINE E-150 WINDOW VAN: — This window van had glass all around. It shared standard features with the Cargo Van.

ECONOLINE E-150 SUPER WINDOW VAN: — See E-150 Super Cargo Van.

I.D. DATA (Econoline E-150): See F-100 I.D.

Model	Body Type	Price	Weight	Prod. Total
E-150	Cargo Van	7759	3720	—
E-150	Window Van	7946	3786	—
E-150	Display Van	7880	3763	—
E-150	Super Cargo Van	8893	4039	—
E-150	Super Window Van	9080	4105	—
E-150	Super Display Van	9015	4082	—

ENGINE (Econoline E-150): 300 cu. in. Six-cylinder. Brake horsepower: 120 at 3400 R.P.M. Bore & stroke: 4.00 x 3.98 in. Compression ratio: 8.0:1. Carburetor: One-bbl.

ECONOLINE E-250 CARGO VAN: — The new E-250 had a higher GVW rating and more heavy-duty front and rear axles, than the E-150. It also came with eight-hole wheels. Standard features were the same as those on the E-100 except the three-speed transmission was not available in Calif.

ECONOLINE E-250 SUPER CARGO VAN: — See E-150 Cargo Van.

ECONOLINE E-250 DISPLAY VAN: — This vehicle shared styling and features with the E-100, but had greater load capacity.

ECONOLINE E-250 SUPER DISPLAY VAN: — See E-150 Super Cargo Van.

ECONOLINE E-250 WINDOW VAN: — This vehicle shared styling and features with the E-100 Window Van, but had greater load capacity.

ECONOLINE E-250 SUPER WINDOW VAN: — See E-150 Super Cargo Van.

ECONOLINE E-250 CUTAWAY VAN: — This van with Camper Special Packages, was designed to readily accommodate custom motor homes.

ECONOLINE E-250 PARCEL DELIVERY: — The E-250 Parcel Delivery van was 149.9 in. long and 74.3 in. high in its cargo area. The rear door opening was 84.7 in. wide.

I.D. DATA (Econoline E-250): See F-100 I.D.

Model	Body Type	Price	Weight	Prod. Total
E-240	Cargo Van	8815	4146	—
E-250	Window Van	9002	4212	—
E-260	Display Van	8937	4189	—
S-240	Super Cargo Van	9493	4474	—
S-250	Super Window Van	9680	4540	—
S-260	Super Display Van	9615	4517	—

ENGINE (Econoline E-250): Same as E-100.

ECONOLINE E-350 CARGO VAN: — This was the top-of-the-line Econoline Van. It had heavy-duty front and rear shocks and a greater load capacity than the other series. Standard features were the same as the E-100.

ECONOLINE E-350 SUPER CARGO VAN: — See E-150 Super Cargo Van.

ECONOLINE E-350 DISPLAY VAN: — See E-250 Display Van.

ECONOLINE E-350 SUPER DISPLAY VAN: — See E-150 Super Cargo Van.

ECONOLINE E-350 WINDOW VAN: — See E-250 Window Van.

ECONOLINE E-350 SUPER WINDOW VAN: — See E-150 Super Cargo Van.

ECONOLINE E-350 CUTAWAY VAN: — See E-250 Cutaway Van.

ECONOLINE E-350 PARCEL DELIVERY: — See E-250 Parcel Delivery.

I.D. DATA (Econoline E-350): See F-100 I.D.

Model	Body Type	Price	Weight	Prod. Total
E-340	Cargo Van	9043	4442	—
E-350	Window Van	9231	4508	—
E-360	Display Van	9165	4485	—
S-340	Super Cargo Van	10,511	4613	—
S-350	Super Window Van	10,699	4679	—
S-360	Super Display Van	10,633	4656	—
E-37B	Cutaway	—	3992	—
E-380	Parcel Delivery	—	5395	—

ENGINE (Econoline E-350): Same as E-100.

CHASSIS: Wheelbase: 124 in. (E-100, E-150) 138 in. Overall length: 186.8 in. (124 in. w.b.), 206.8 in. (138 in. w.b.), 226.8 in. (138 in Super Van). GVW: 5250-6350 (E-150), 6800-7900 (E-250), 8750-11,000 (E-350). Tires: P225/75R x 15 SL (E-150), 8.00 x 16.5D (E-250), 9.50 x 16.5E (E-350).

POWERTRAIN OPTIONS: 5.0L V-8. 5.8L V-8. 6.5L Diesel V-8. 7.5L V-8. Four-speed transmission with overdrive. Select Shift automatic.

CONVENIENCE OPTIONS: XL Package: vinyl bucket seats, front compartment carpeting, color-keyed door trim panels, leather tone inserts on instrument panel, courtesy lights, interval wipers; bright grille, front and rear bumpers, and low-mount swingaway mirrors. Cloth and vinyl Captain's Chairs. Air conditioning. High-capacity air conditioner and auxiliary heater. Heavy-duty battery. Chrome rear step bumper. Chrome bumpers. Super engine cooling. Auxiliary fuel tank. Ammeter and oil pressure gauges. Privacy glass. Swing-out rear door and/or cargo door glass. Tinted glass. Handling package. Deluxe insulation package. Light and Convenience group. Bright low-mount swingaway mirrors. Bright swing-out recreation mirrors. Deluxe two-tone paint. Power door locks. Speed control. Tilt steering wheel. Heavy-duty front and rear springs. Trailer Towing Packages. Wheel covers. Radios: AM/FM monaural, AM/FM stereo, AM/digital clock radio, AM/FM stereo with cassette player. Hinged side cargo door.

1984 Ford Club Wagon Chateau Passenger Van (JAG)

E-150 CLUB WAGON: — Like the Econoline, the 1984 Club Wagon received a minor facelift. Standard features included: Four-speed transmission with overdrive. Eighteen gallon fuel tank. Argent bumpers, grille, and mirrors. Color-keyed vinyl seat trim. Power steering and brakes. Halogen headlights. AM radio. Sliding side doors with swing-out windows. Full-length floor mat. Bright hub caps. Hardboard headliner (front only). Padded sunvisors. Color-keyed instrument panel.

E-250 CLUB WAGON: — The E-250 had most of the same standard features as the E-150, with a few exceptions: SelectShift automatic. 22.1 gallon fuel tank. Heavier-duty battery.

E-250 CLUB WAGON: — This was basically the same as the 138 in. w.b. E-250, but had an 20 in. extended rear overhang.

E-350 SUPER WAGON: — This heavy-duty wagon provided 20 in. more inside space than regular 138 in. Club Wagons. It could hold up to 15 passengers (with optional seating package).

I.D. DATA (Club Wagon): See F-100 I.D.

Model	Body Type	Price	Weight	Prod. Total
E-150	Club Wagon	9527	3947	—
E-250	Club Wagon	11,388	4873	—
E-250	Super Wagon	11,825	4852	—
E-350	Super Wagon	11,498	4923	—

ENGINE (Club Wagon): Same as E-150 Econoline.

CHASSIS: See Econoline.

POWERTRAIN OPTIONS: See Econoline.

CONVENIENCE OPTIONS: Most of the same items and packages that were offered on the Econoline plus: 4-, 7-, 8-, 11- and 12-passenger seating packages. **Club Wagon XL:** bright bumpers, taillight bezels, low-mount western swing-away mirrors; color-keyed front, side and rear door trim panels with leather-tone inserts, color-keyed carpeting front to rear, door trim panels map pockets, full-length white hardboard headliner with insulation, instrument panel appliques and vinyl steering wheel pad with look of leather. **Club Wagon XLT:** chrome grille, bright window moldings, lower bodyside moldings and lower bodyside accent paint in addition to Club Wagon XL features; front bucket seats upholstered in color-keyed cloth and vinyl (premium vinyl available at no extra cost), headliner was color-keyed vinyl (full length in long w.b. model and Super Wagon, color-keyed sunvisors (LWB) and spare tire cover with storage pocket; RH visor vanity mirror, step well pads for the front and sliding side doors; courtesy light

switch on every door and a 3-way switch for the rear dome lamp. Available on all Club Wagons was a three-passenger rear seat that could convert into a bed.

NOTE: Econoline and Club Wagon colors for 1984 were: Raven Black, Polar White, Light Charcoal Metallic, Dark Canyon Red, Midnight Canyon, Red Metallic, Light Blue, Midnight Blue Metallic, Light Desert Tan, Medium Desert Tan, Walnut Metallic, Medium Copper Metallic, Bright Copper Glow.

1984 Ford Ranger Long Bed Mini-Pickup (JAG)

RANGER PICKUP: — Ranger styling was unchanged for 1984. Like full size Ford pickups, it had double-wall construction in hood, roof, doors, pickup box sides and tailgate. The box was all-welded with integral floor skid strips, stake pockets and rope tie holds. The Ranger had Twin-I-Beam independent front suspension with lubed for life ball joints. Inside, the full foam bench seat had a Flex-O-lator spring design for added comfort. There was 39.2 in. of headroom and 42.4 in. of legroom. Among standard features were: Black front bumper. Dual mirrors. Chrome grille and windshield moldings. Argent styled steel wheels with black hub covers. Tethered gas cap. Vinyl bench seat with folding, covered seat back. Instrument panel storage bin and glove box. Inside hood release. Day/night rearview mirror. AM radio. Courtesy light switch for drivers door. Dome lamp. Black floor mat.

RANGER "S" PICKUP: — This was a "no Frills" version of the base Ranger pickup, with fewer standard features.

I.D. DATA (Ranger): See F-100 I.D.

Model	Body Type	Price	Weight	Prod. Total
(107.9 in. w.b.)				
R-10	Pickup (Style)	6462	2544	—
R-10	Pickup (Style)	5993	—	—
(113.9 in. w.b.)				
R-10	Pickup (Style)	6620	2576	—
R-10	Pickup (Style)	6146	—	—

ENGINE (Ranger): 2.0L (121 cu. in.) Four-cylinder. (2.3L I-4 standard on 4x4s, and 4x2s in Calif.)

CHASSIS: Wheelbase: 107.9 in, 113.9 in. Overall length: 175.6 in. (107.9 in. w.b.), 187.6 in. (113.9 in. w.b.). Overall width: 66.9 in. Overall height: 64 in. (67.1 in. 4x4). GVW: 3780-4500. Tires: P185/75R x 14.

POWERTRAIN OPTIONS: 2.3L Four. 2.2L Diesel Four. 2.8L V-6. Five-speed manual with overdrive. Automatic.

CONVENIENCE OPTIONS: Four-Wheel-Drive: Twin-Traction Beam front axle, 2,700 lb. rear axle, power brakes, 2.3L Four, 2-speed part-time transfer case. Headliner. Tri-color sport tape stripe. 4x4 tape stripe. **Radios:** AM/FM monaural, AM/FM stero, AM/FM stereo with cassette tape player. Air conditioning. Black rear step bumper. **Convenience Group:** dual electric horns (except with 2.2L diesel), interval windshield wipers, passengers visor vanity mirror, driver's sunvisor band, cigarette lighter. Tinted glass all around. **Light Group:** ashtray, cargo box, glove box lights; passenger door courtesy light switch, headlights-on warning buzzer. Floor console (for bucket seats). Overhead console (included pivoting map light and electronic digital clock). Bright low-mount western swingaway mirrors. Power steering. Power brakes. Tilt steering wheel. Sliding rear window. Eight cargo tie-down hooks. Pivoting vent windows. Fingertip speed control. Reclining bucket seats. Knitted vinyl contoured bench seat. Cloth and vinyl bench seat. Cloth contoured bench seat. Cloth contoured bench seat. Payload packages up to 1,770 lb. Heavy-duty air cleaner. Heavy-duty battery. Camper package. Super engine cooling. Auxiliary 13-gallon fuel tank. **Gauge Package:** ammeter, oil pressure gauge, temperature gauge, and trip odometer. Engine block heater. Heavy-duty shocks. Tow hooks. Snow plow special package. Automatic locking hubs (4x4). Heavy-duty front suspension. Traction lok rear axle. Limited slip front axle (4x4). **Handling Package:** Heavy-duty front and rear shock absorbers and front and rear stabilizer bars (rear only with 4x4). Skid plates (4x4). California emissions system. High altitude emissions system. **Security Lock Group:** glove box lock, locking gas cap, and underbody spare tire carrier lock. **Exterior Protection Group:** chrome front bumper with end caps, black front bumper guards and black upper bodyside molding with dual red accent stripes. Chrome front bumper. Cast aluminum wheels. White sport wheels. Deluxe wheel trim. Cast aluminum spare wheel (4x4). **XL:** (in addition to or in place of standard features) bright wheel lip moldings, bright rear window insert molding, deluxe wheel trim and chrome front bumper; woodtone instrument cluster applique, color-keyed cloth headliner, contoured knitted vinyl bench seat, color-keyed seat belts with tension eliminator, color-keyed steering wheel and floor mats, passenger door courtesy light switch, aluminum scuff plates. **XLS:** (in addition to or in place of XL features) blackout trim components and special "XLS" three-color tape stripe, reclining cloth and vinyl bucket seats, color-keyed deluxe steering wheel, gauge package, brushed pewter-tone cluster applique on instrument panel, color-keyed cloth door trim with carpeted map pocket, black scuff plates. XLT: (in addition to or in place of XLS features) chrome front bumper with black end caps, full length black lower bodyside molding with bright accent, dual accent bodyside paint stripes, deluxe wheel trim and brushed aluminum tailgate applique; full cloth door trim with color-keyed molding and bright insert, carpeted lower portion and map pockets; cloth seat trim, full color-keyed carpeting, color-keyed deluxe steering wheel, wood tone cluster applique on instrument panel.

NOTE: Ranger interior colors for 1984 were: Dark Blue, Canyon Red, Tan. Exterior colors were: Raven Black, Polar White, Light Charcoal Metallic, Dark Canyon Red, Light Blue, Medium Blue Metallic, Midnight Blue Metallic, Medium Desert Tan, Walnut Metallic, Light Desert Tan, Bright Bittersweet, Bright Copper Glow (optional). TU-TONES: Regular: accent color was applied to lower bodyside/tailgate; included two-color tape stripe. Deluxe: accent color was applied to mid-bodyside/tailgate; included upper and lower two-color tape stripes. (Regular and Deluxe n.a. on XLS.) Special: accent color was applied to mid-bodyside, inside pickup box, rear of roof and B-pillar, back of cab and tailgate; included upper and lower two-color tape strips; lower two-color tape stripe and rocker panel paint was replaced by XLS tape stripe when ordered with XLS trim.

1984 Ford F-150 XLT Styleside 4x4 Pickup (JAG)

F-150 PICKUP: — The F-150 was now Ford's base light-duty truck. Styling was carried over from last year. Among standard features were: Chrome front bumper. Light argent grille with bright surround. New bright hub caps. Bright door-mounted mirrors. Rectangular halogen headlights. All vinyl seat trim. AM radio. Pivoting vent windows. Glove box. Temperature gauge. Color-keyed windshield pillar, header and cowl-side trim panels. New textured steel roof, cloth headliner with Super Cab. Color-keyed door trim panels with foam-padded armrests. Floor insulation and carpet-texture rubber mat. Day/night rearview mirror. Inside hood release. Key in ignition warning buzzer. Parking brake engaged warning light. Coat hook. LH courtesy light. Argent instrument panel applique (woodtone with diesel). Folding seat back. Black steering wheel. Three speed manual transmission. The F-150 was available with 6½-ft. Flareside, and 6¾-ft. and 8-ft. Styleside boxes. In addition to the regular one, the Styleside could also be had with the Super Cab.

1984 Ford F-150 XLT Styleside Pickup (JAG)

I.D. DATA (F-150): See F-100 I.D.

Model	Body Type	Price	Weight	Prod. Total
F-15	(6½-ft.) Flareside Pickup	7381	3400	—
F-15	(6¾-ft.) Styleside Pickup	7219	3390	—
F-15	(8-ft.) Styleside Pickup	7376	3501	—
X-15	(6¾-ft.) Super Cab Pickup	8690	3765	—
X-15	(8-ft.) Super Cab Pickup	8847	3871	—

ENGINE (F-150): 4.9L (300 cu. in.) Six-cylinder. Brake horsepower: 120 at 3000 R.P.M. Bore & stroke: 4 x 3.98 in. Compression ratio: 8.5:1. Carburetor: One-bbl.

F-250 PICKUP: — The F-250 was only available with the 8-ft. Styleside box. But it could be had in regular or (F-250 Heavy-duty) Super Cab. The Super Cab had room behind the front seat for an optional rear seat which could fold down flat. Two center facing jump seats were standard. They too could fold out of the way to make room for cargo. Most standard F-250 features were the same as those offered on the on the F-150 plus a 4-speed manual transmission and, on F-250 Heavy Dutys, an 11 in. clutch.

I.D. DATA (F-250): See F-150 I.D.

Model	Body Type	Price	Weight	Prod. Total
—	Chassis w/Cab	8314	3426	—
F-25	Styleside Pickup	8146	3666	—
X-25	Super Cab Pickup	9826	4279	—

ENGINE (F-250): See F-150. (F-250 Heavy-duty 4x4's had 5.8L V-8, except in CA.)

F-350 PICKUP: — The F-350 was offered in regular and 6-passenger Crew Cabs. Both had 8-ft. Styleside boxes. It had most of the same standard features as the F-150 plus power steering.

I.D. DATA (F-350): See F-150 I.D.

Model	Body Type	Price	Weight	Prod. Total
F-37	Chassis w/Cab	9403	3927	—
F-35	Styleside Pickup	9666	4030	—
W-35	Crew Cab Pickup	10,547	4948	—

ENGINE (F-350): Same as F-150. (F-350s with 4wd had 5.8L V-8, except in Calif.)

CHASSIS: Wheelbase: 116.8 in. (F-150), 133 in. (Styleside), 138.8 in. (F-150 Super Cab), 155 in. (F-150, F-250 Heavy-duty Super Cab), 168.4 in. (F-350 Crew Cab). Overall length: 189.3 in. (Flareside), 192.1 in. (F-150 Styleside), 208.3 in. (Styleside), 214.1 in. (F-150 Super Cab), 230.3 in. (F-150, F-250 Super Cab), 243.6 in. (F-350 Crew Cab). GVW: 5250-6450 (F-150), 6300-9000 (F-250), 8700-11,000 (F-350). Tires: P195/75R x 15SL (F-150), LT215/85R x 16C (F-250), LT235/85R x 16E (F-250 Heavy-duty, F-350), LT215/85R x 16D (F-350 dual rear wheels/regular cab).

POWERTRAIN OPTIONS: 5.0L V-8 (F-150, F-250), 5.8L V-8, 5.8L HO (high output) V-8 (F-150, F-250), 7.5L V-8 (F-250 Heavy-duty, F-350), 6.9L Diesel V-8 (F-250 Heavy-duty, F-350), 4-speed manual (F-150, F-250), 4-speed manual with overdrive (F-150, F-250), Automatic overdrive (F-150, F-250), SelectShift automatic.

1984 Ford F-150 XLT Styleside Pickup (JAG)

CONVENIENCE OPTIONS: Four-Wheel-Drive: power brakes, manual locking free running hubs, power steering, 2-spd. transfer case, and 4-spd. manual. Automatic locking hubs (4x4). Chrome grille. Accent tape stripe (Styleside). Lower bodyside molding with black vinyl insert (Styleside). Bright wheel lip moldings (Style). **Radios:** AM/FM monaural (single speaker), AM/FM stereo (speakers mounted in door panels), AM/FM stereo with cassette tape player, and radio credit option (deleted standard AM radio for credit). Air conditioning. High output heater (std. with Crew Cab). **Convenience Group:** interval wipers, 12 in. day/night mirror, RH visor vanity mirror, molded bin on lower doors, headlights-on warning buzzer, and courtesy light switch on RH door. **Deluxe Insulation Package:** color-keyed cloth headliner, floor mats with full insulation (carpet on Crew Cab), back panel cover, and moldings (headliner, "B" pillar and back panel), plus aluminum door scuff plates. Electronic Digitial Clock. Fingertip speed control (with resume feature). **Light Group:** movable underhood worklight with 20 ft. retractable cord plus lights in glove box, under instrument panel, dual beam dome/map light, cargo box light, headlights-on warning buzzer, and ashtray light and courtesy light switch on RH door. Power door locks/windows (n.a. with Crew Cab). Power steering (4x2). Tinted sliding rear window. Tilt steering wheel. Tinted glass. Tool storage box (located under the hood). Spare tire carrier, in box side mounted (Style). Center console (SC with Captain's Chairs). Bright low-mount swing away western mirrors. Bright swing out recreation mirrors. Reclining Captain's Chairs (SC). Folding forward facing rear seat (SC). Cloth and vinyl seat trim. Heavy-duty charcoal vinyl or knitted vinyl seat trim. Special cloth and vinyl seat trim (for XLT). Auxiliary fuel tank. Auxiliary transmission oil cooler. **Handling Package:** front and rear stabilizer bars, heavy-duty front and rear shocks (quad front on F-150 regular cab 4x4), and heavy-duty front springs. Heavy-duty shocks. **Heavy-Duty Front Suspension Package:** (133 in. w.b. F-150 4x4). Heavy-duty 3,800 lb. rated front axle and springs, 3.54 axle ratio and heavy-duty front and rear shock absorbers. (A version of this package was also offered for F-250, F-350 4x4s.) Oil pressure and ammeter gauges. Front and rear stabilizer bars. Engine block heater. Extra engine cooling package. Super engine cooling package. Trailer towing package. Camper package. Heavy-duty air cleaner. Dual electric horns. 5 roof clearance lights. **Exterior Protection Group:** front bumper guards and front bumper rub strip. **Security Lock Group:** locking gasp cap, inside hood release and glove box; also spare tire lock. **Sports Instrumentation:** tach, ammeter, oil pressure gauge and trip odometer. Skid plates (4x4s) include transfer and fuel tank protective plates. **Rear Bumpers:** argent step (Styleside), chrome step (Styleside), chrome channel (Flareside) and chrome contour (Styleside). Deluxe wheel covers (n.a. with 4x4s or DRW). White styled steel wheels (F-150). Sport wheel covers (F-150). Cast aluminum wheels (F-150). **XL:** (in addition to or in place of items on standard model) bright wheel lip moldings and new two-color dual bodyside accent side paint stripes on SRW Stylesides (bodyside surround tape stripe and tailgate tape letters on Flareside and DRW trucks); bright insert on rear window weatherstrip; cigarette lighter, LH and RH courtesy light switch, 12 in. day/night mirror, bright surround door trim panel moldings, color-keyed floor mat, woodtone applique instrument panel, folding fully covered seat back (fixed front on CC and folding rear), deluxe seat belts, cloth and vinyl seat trim, aluminum scuff plates, cloth headlining, moldings/trim panels above beltline. **XLT:** (in addition to or in place of items on the XL) full-length lower bodyside molding with protective black vinyl insert and distinctive brushed aluminum Styleside tailgate applique; wall to wall cut-pile carpeting, Door trim panels with bright surround and woodtone applique and storage bin, woodtone insert steering wheel, moldings/trim panels above beltline (also below beltline with SC).

NOTE: Interior colors for 1984 were: Charcoal, Dark Blue, Canyon Red, Tan. Exterior colors were: Raven Black, Polar White, Light Charcoal Metallic, Bright Canyon Red, Light Blue, Medium Blue Metallic, Midnight Blue Metallic, Medium Desert Tan, Walnut Metallic, Light Desert Tan, Medium Copper Metallic, Bright Copper Glow (optional). **TU-TONE: Regular:** accent color covers the roof and upper back panel. **Deluxe:** accent color on center bodyside area and tailgate; moldings or tapes included as needed. **Combination:** regular and deluxe tu-tones combined. **Victoria:** accent color applied to hood, upper fender, around door window, and the lower bodyside; tape and moldings were included as needed.

1985 FORD

1985 Ford Bronco II XLT Utility Wagon (JAG)

BRONCO II: — Styling on the compact 4wd Bronco II was carried over from last year. Standard features included: Tinted glass. Full instrumentation. Transfer case skid plate. Power brakes and steering. Front and rear stabilizer bars. Five-speed transmission. Reclining front seats. Split fold down rear bench seat. Halogen headlights. Dual outside foldaway rear view mirrors. Bright front and rear contour bumpers. Sport wheel covers. Color-keyed carpeting. Full-length cloth headliner. Sun visors.

I.D. DATA (Bronco II): See F-150 I.D.

Model	Body Type	Price	Weight	Prod. Total
U-14	Wagon	10,889	3227	—

ENGINE (Bronco II): 171 cu. in. V-6. Brake horsepower: 115 net horsepower at 4600 R.P.M. Bore & stroke: 3.66 x 2.70. Compression ratio: 8.6:1. Carburetor: 2-bbl.

CHASSIS FEATURES: Wheebase: 94 in. Overall length: 158.4 in. Overall width: 68 in. Overall height: 68.2 in. Tires: P195/75R x 15SL.

POWERTRAIN OPTIONS: 3-speed automatic. Automatic transmission with overdrive.

CONVENIENCE OPTIONS: Chrome grille. Tu-Tone paints. Sport tape stripe. **Eddie Bauer Bronco II:** special Tu-Tone paint treatment, "Eddie Bauer" emblem, XLT-level trim inside and out, cast aluminum wheels, all

424

1985 Ford Bronco II XLT Utility Wagon (JAG)

terrain tires with raised White letters, ammeter, oil pressure and temperature gauges, trip odometer, dual Captain's chairs, AM/FM stereo radio, tilt steering wheel, floor console, dual electric horns, interval windshield wipers, passenger visor vanity mirror, dark tinted Privacy glass, driver's sun visor band, ashtray and glove box lights, headlamps-on warning buzzer, Eddie Bauer field bag and map folder. AM/FM monaural radio. AM/FM stereo. AM/FM stereo radio with cassette tape player. Dual or quad Captain's chairs (include power lumbar support and zippered map pocket on seat back). Air conditioning. Tinted glass. **Convenience Group:** internval windshield wipers, visor vanity mirror, cigarette lighter, dual electric horns, driver's sun visor band. **Light Group:** glove box, ashtray and cargo area lights; passenger door and liftgate courtesy light switches, and "headlights on" warning buzzer. Fingertip speed control. Tilt steering wheel. Rear window wiper/defroster. Flip-open liftgate window. Flip-up, open air roof. Flip-open removable quarter windows (gray tinted). Pivoting front vent windows. Privacy glass. **Floor Console:** includes gauge package, trash bin, cassette tape tray, coin tray, two cup depressions, and electronic graphic warning display module. **Overhead Console:** includes digital clock and pivoting map light. Bright, low-mount western swingaway mirrors. Outside swingaway spare tire carrier. Roof rack. Rear seat delete. Carpet delete. Automatic locking hubs. Engine block heater. Super engine cooling. Heavy-duty maintenance-free battery. Heavy-duty air cleaner. Electronically tuned stereo and cassette player. Premium sound system. Odometer. Heavy-duty shocks. Snow plow special package. Trailer towing package. Tow hooks. Limited slip front axle. Traction-lok axle. California emissions system. High altitude emissions system. **Exterior Protection Group:** bright front and rear bumpers with Black end caps, Black front bumper guards, Black upper bodyside molding with two Red accent stripes. Transfer case skid plate. Front license plate bracket. Cast aluminum wheels. White sport styled steel wheels Deluxe wheel trim (includes argent styled steel wheel with bright trim ring, lug nuts and black hub cover). **XLT Package:** chrome grille bodyside accent stripe, pivoting front vent windows, tinted glass, deluxe wheel trim, cloth and vinyl seat trim with full cloth door trim panels with a map pocket, carpet insert and bright headlights; color-keyed instrument panel and deluxe steering wheel; woodtone applique on instrument cluster; color-keyed deluxe seat belts; courtesy light switches; liftgate operated cargo area light; rear quarter trim panels included integral padded armrests, speaker grilles and storage compartments. **XLS Package:** "XLS" tape striping in three colors on the lower bodysides, rocker panel molding spats; blacked out grille surround, bumpers and bumper end caps; deluxe wheel trim; cloth door trim panels had carpet insert and map pocket; sport steering wheel, color-keyed instrument panel (with storage bin); full instrumentation.

BRONCO: Outside of some new options, the four-wheel-drive Bronco was unchanged for 1985. Standard features included: 4-speed transmission. Intermittent wipers. Vinyl front bucket seats. Flip/fold rear bench seat. Power steering and brakes. Power tailgate window. AM radio. Twin-Traction Beam independent front suspension. Manual locking front hubs. Heavy-duty front shock absorbers. Padded instrument panel. Seat belts cigar lighter. Front and rear floor mats. Scuff plates. Dual low-mount mirrors. Day/night rearview mirror.

I.D. DATA (Bronco): See F-150 I.D.

Model	Body Type	Price	Weight	Prod. Total
U-150	Wagon	11,993	4373	—

ENGINE (Bronco): 300 cu. in. Six-cylinder. Brake horsepower: 120 net horsepower. Compression ratio: 8.5:1. One-bbl. Displacement: 302 cu. in. V-8. (standard in Calif.)

CHASSIS FEATURES: Wheelbase: 104.7 in. Overall length: 177.6 in. Overall height: 72.9 in. Overall width: 77.2 in. Tires P215/75R x 15SL.

POWERTRAIN OPTIONS: 3-speed automatic, four-speed automatic with overdrive transmission. 302 V-8, 351 V-8, 351 HO V-8. Four-speed transmission with overdrive. Limited slip front axle.

CONVENIENCE OPTIONS: White styled steel wheels. Deluxe argent styled steel wheels. Cloth and vinyl bucket and/or bench seats. High output heater. Center console. Electric rear window defroster. Front bench seat. Rear bench seat delete. Power windows. Tinted glass all around. Privacy glass in quarter windows. **Light Group:** lights in glove box, ashtray and underhood: instrument panel courtesy lights, dome light with map light, RH door courtesy light, headlamp-on warning buzzer (the underhood light had a 20 ft. cord). Power door locks. Captain's chair. Underhood tool box. Automatic locking hubs. Traction-Lok front and/or rear axle. **Sports Instrumentation:** tach and odometer. Recreational mirrors. **Trailer Tow-**

ing Package: 7-wire trailer wiring harness, 71-amp hr battery, super engine cooling, auxiliary transmission oil cooler, heavy-duty flasher, handling package (automatic transmission required). **Security Group:** locking gas cap, inside hood release lock, spare tire lock and locking glove box. Super engine cooling package. Extra engine cooling package. Fog lamps. Exterior sound package. Cigarette lighter. Power door locks. **XLT:** Cloth and vinyl bucket seats. Tach and trip odometer, sun visors color-keyed carpeting, color-keyed vinyl front headlines, courtesy lights, visor vanity mirror, soft-wrapped steering wheel, bodyside protection molding with vinyl insert, dome light, rear door panel armrests, storage bin. **Eddie Bauer Package:** air conditioning, cruise control, tilt steering wheel, fuel-injected V-8. Captains chairs full carpeting, light group, AM/FM radio, center console, Privacy glass, heavy-duty battery, special exterior trim. Cruise control. Deluxe two-tone paint. Victoria paint treatment. Heavy-duty rear shocks. Skid plate. Cast aluminum sheets. AM/FM stereo. AM/FM stereo with cassette player. Snow plow package. California emissions system.

ECONOLINE E-150 CARGO VAN: — Exterior styling was left untouched for 1985. Power steering was now standard on E-150 Econolines. Among the other standard features were: Power brakes. Halogen headlights. AM radio. Bright hub caps. Three-speed manual transmission.

ECONOLINE E-150 SUPER CARGO VAN: — This van had the same features as the E-150 Cargo Van plus a 20 in. extended rear overhang. This was especially useful for hauling longer loads.

ECONOLINE E-150 DISPLAY VAN: — This van had windows at the rear and on the right-hand side. It came with the same standard features as the Cargo Van.

ECONOLINE E-150 WINDOW VAN: The window van had glass all around. It shared standard features with the Cargo Van.

ECONOLINE E-150 SUPER WINDOW VAN: See E-150 Super Cargo Van.

I.D. DATA (Econoline): See F-100.

Model	Body Type	Price	Weight	Prod. Total
E-150	Cargo Van	8561	3755	—
E-150	Window Van	8755	3807	—
E-150	Display Van	8688	3786	—
E-150	Super Cargo Van	9688	4154	—
E-150	Super Window Van	9844	4220	—

ENGINE (Econoline E-100): 300 cu. in. Six-cylinder. Brake horsepower: 120 at 3400 R.P.M. Bore & stroke: 4.00 in. x 3.98 in. Compression ratio: 8.0:1. Carburetor: one-bbl.

ENGINE E-250 Econoline: Same as E-100.

ECONOLINE E-350 CARGO VAN: — This was the top-of-the-line Econoline Van. It had heavy-duty front and rear shocks and a greater load capacity than the other series. Standard features were the same as the E-100.

ECONOLINE E-350 SUPER CARGO VAN: — See E-150 Super Cargo Van.

ECONOLINE E-350 DISPLAY VAN: — See E-250 Display Van.

ECONOLINE E-350 WINDOW VAN: — See E-250 Window Van.

ECONOLINE E-350 SUPER WINDOW VAN: — See E-150 Super Cargo Van.

ECONOLINE E-350 CUTAWAY VAN: See E-250 Cutaway Van.

ECONOLINE E-350 PARCEL DELIVERY: See E-250 Parcel Delivery.

I.D. DATA (Econoline E-350): See F-100.

Model	Body Type	Price	Weight	Prod. Total
E-340	Cargo Van	9949	4464	—
E-350	Window Van	10,143	4530	—
E-360	Display Van	10,076	4507	—
S-340	Super Cargo Van	10,948	4646	—
S-350	Super Window Van	11,142	4712	—
E-37B	Cutaway	—	3840	—

ECONOLINE E-250 CARGO VAN: The new E-250 had a higher GVW rating and more heavy-duty front and rear axles, than the E-150. It also came with eight-hole wheels. Standard features were the same as those on the E-100 except the three-speed manual was not available in Calif.

ECONOLINE E-250 SUPER CARGO VAN: See E-150 Cargo Van.

ECONOLINE E-250 DISPLAY VAN: This vehicle shared styling and features with the E-100, but had greater load capacity.

ECONOLINE E-250 WINDOW VAN: This vehicle shared styling and features with the E-100 Window van, but had greater load capacity.

ECONOLINE E-250 SUPER WINDOW VAN: See E-150 Super Cargo Van.

ECONOLINE E-250 CUTAWAY VAN: This van with Camper Special Packages, was designed to readily accommodate custom motor homes.

ECONOLINE E-250 PARCEL DELIVERY: The E-250 Parcel Delivery van was 149.9 in. long and 74.3 in. high in its cargo area. The rear door opening was 84.7 in. wide.

ENGINE (Econoline E-250): Same as F-100.

Model	Body Type	Price	Weight	Prod. Total
E-240	Cargo Van	9817	4251	—
E-250	Window Van	10,011	4294	—
E-260	Display Van	9944	4317	—
S-240	Super Cargo Van	10,447	4500	—
S-250	Super Window Van	10,641	4566	—

ENGINE (Econoline E-350): Same as E-100.

CHASSIS: Wheelbase: 124 in. (E-150) 138 in. Overall length: 186.8 in. (124 in. w.b.), 206.8 in. (138 in. w.b.), 226.8 in. (138 in. Super Van). GVW: 5250-6300 (E-150), 6800-7900 (E-250), 8900-10,900 (E-350). Tires: P235/75R x 15 (E-150), LT215/85R x 16D (E-250), LT235/85R x 16E (E-350).

POWERTRAIN OPTIONS: 5.0L V-8. 5.8L V-8. 6.9L Diesel V-8. 7.5L V-8. Four-speed manual with overdrive. Select Shift automatic transmission.

CONVENIENCE OPTIONS: XL Package: vinyl bucket seats, front compartment carpeting, color-keyed door trim panels, leather tone inserts on instrument panel, courtesy lights, interval wipers; bright grille, front and rear bumpers, and low-mount swingaway mirrors. Cloth and vinyl Captain's Chairs. Air conditioning. High capacity air conditioner and auxiliary heater. Heavy-duty battery. Chrome rear step bumper. Chrome bumpers. Super engine cooling. Auxiliary fuel tank. Ammeter and oil pressure gauges. Privacy Glass. Swing-out rear door and/or cargo doorglass. Tinted glass. Handling package. Deluxe insulation Package. Light and Convenience group. Bright low-mount swingaway mirrors. Bright swing-out recreation mirrors. Deluxe two-tone paint. Power door locks. Speed control. Tilt steering wheel. Heavy-duty front and rear springs. Trailer Towing Packages. Wheel covers. Radios: AM/FM monaural, AM/FM stereo, AM/digital clock radio, AM/FM stereo with cassette player. Hinged side cargo door.

E-150 CLUB WAGON: — Like the Econoline, Club Wagon styling was unchanged for 1985. Among the standard features were: Four-speed manual with overdrive transmission. Eighteen gallon fuel tank. Argent bumpers, grille, and mirrors. Color-keyed vinyl seat trim. Power steering and brakes. Halogen headlights. AM radio. Sliding side doors with swing-out windows. Full-length floor mat. Bright hub caps. Hardboard headliner (front only). Padded sun visors. Color-keyed instrument panel 138 in. w.b.).

E-250 CLUB WAGON: — The E-250 had most of the same standard features as the E-150, with a couple exceptions: Select Shift automatic. Heavier duty battery. (with Diesel)

E-350 SUPER WAGON: — This heavy-duty wagon provided 20 in. more inside space than regular 138 in. Club Wagons. It could hold up to 15 passengers (with optional seating package).

I.D. DATA (Club Wagon): See F-100.

Model	Body Type	Price	Weight	Prod. Total
E-150	Club Wagon	—	—	—
E-250	Club Wagon	—	—	—
E-350	Super Wagon	—	—	—

ENGINE (Club Wagon): Same as E-150 Econoline.

CHASSIS FEATURES: See Econoline.

POWERTRAIN OPTIONS: See Econoline.

CONVENIENCE OPTIONS: Most of the same items and packages that were offered on the Econoline plus: 7-, 8-, 11-, 12- and 15-passenger seating packages. Club Wagon XL: bright bumpers, taillight bezels, low-mount western swing-away mirrors; color-keyed front, side and rear door trim panels with leather-tone inserts, color-keyed carpeting front to rear, door trim panels map pockets, full-length White hardboard headliner with insulation, instrument panel appliques and vinyl steering wheel pad with look of leather. Club Wagon XLT: chrome grille, bright window moldings, lower bodyside moldings and lower bodyside accent paint in addition to Club Wagon XL features; front bucket seats upholstered in color-keyed cloth and vinyl (premium vinyl available at no extra cost), headliner was color-keyed. Color-keyed sun visors and spare tire cover with storage pocket; RH visor vanity mirror, step well pads for the front and sliding side doors; courtesy light switch on every door and a 3-way switch for the rear dome lamp.

1985 Ford Ranger 4x4 Sport Mini-Pickup (JAG)

RANGER Pickup: — Sales literature bragged of the many features the compact Ranger shared with full size Ford trucks: A rugged ladder type frame, double-walled construction, Twin-I-Beam independent front suspension, and a high payload capacity. Steps were taken in construction of Rangers to help prevent corrosion. These included use of aluminized wax, plastic parts, urethane anti-corrosion spray, galvanized metal and zinc-coated metal. Other standard features included: Black front bumper. Dual fold-away mirrors. Chrome grille and windshield moldings. Argent styled steel wheels with bright aluminum hub covers. Vinyl bench seat with folding, covered seat back. Soft-feel steering wheel. Instrument panel storage bin and glove box. Inside hood release. Day/night rearview mirror. AM radio dome lamp. Driver's door courtesy light switch. RH passenger assist handle. Black vinyl coated rubber floor mat. Black scuff plates. Vinyl door trim. 5-speed manual with overdrive transmission.

RANGER "S" Pickup: This was a "no frills" version of the base Ranger pickup with fewer standard features.

I.D. DATA (Ranger): See F-100 I.D.

Model	Body Type	Price	Weight	Prod. Total
(107.9 in. w.b.)				
R-10	Styleside Pickup	6675	2585	—
R-10	Styleside Pickup "S"	5993	—	—
(113.9 in. w.b.)				
R-10	Styleside Pickup	6829	2614	—

ENGINE (Ranger): 2.3L I-4 EFO (Electronic Fuel Injection). 2.0L I-4 was subject to restricted availabilty.

CHASSIS FEATURES: Wheebase: 107.9 in., 113.9 in. Overall length: 175.6 in. (107.9 w.b.), 187.6 in. (113.9 w.b.). Overall width: 66.9 in. Overall height: 64 in. (67.1 in. 4x4). GVW: 3800-4500. Tires: P185/75R x 14 SL.

POWERTRAIN OPTIONS: 2.8L V-6. Automatic overdrive transmission.

CONVENIENCE OPTIONS: Four-Wheel-Drive. Headliner. Sport Tape stripe (tri-color). **4x4 tape stripe. Radios:** AM/FM stereo, AM/FM stereo with cassette tape player, electronic AM/FM stereo with cassette tape player and two rear speakers, premium sound system (included power amplifier and dual rear speakers. Air conditioning. Black rear step bumper. Chrome rear step bumper with black end caps. **Convenience Group:** dual electric horns, interval windshield wipers, passengers visor vanity mirror and a driver's sun visor band plus a cigarette lighter. Tinted glass all around. **Light Group:** ashtray, cargo box, glove box, engine compartment lights; headlights on warning buzzer and a passenger door courtesy light switch. Floor console (included gauge package, graphic display module, cassette tape tray, coin holder, storage bin. Overhead console (included pivoting map light and electronic digital clock). Bright low-mount western swing-gaway mirrors. Power steering. Power brakes. Power window/lock group. Tilt steering wheel. Speed control. Tinted sliding rear window. Cargo tie-down hooks. Pivoting vent windows. Tilt-up/open air roof (glass could be opened or completely removed). Reclining cloth and vinyl bucket seats. Knitted vinyl contoured bench seat. Cloth and vinyl bench seat. Cloth contoured bench seat. Payload packages up to 1,765 lbs. Heavy-duty air cleaner. Heavy-duty battery. Camper package. Super engine cooling (included in towing package). Auxiliary fuel tank. **Gauge Package:** ammeter, oil pressure gauge, temperature gauge and trip odometer. Engine block heater. Heavy-duty shocks. Tow hooks. Trailer towing package. Snow Plow special package (4x4). Automatic locking hubs (4x4). Traction-Lok rear axle. Limited slip front axle (4x4). Heavy-duty front suspension (4x4). **Handling Package:** Heavy-duty front and rear shocks and front and rear stabilizer bars (rear only with 4x4s). Skid plates (4x4). High-altitude emissions system. **Security Lock Group:** glove box lock, locking gas cap and underbody spare tire carrier lock. **Exterior Protection Group:** chrome front bumper with end caps, black front bumper guards and black upper bodyside molding with dual Red accent stripes. Chrome front bumper without end caps. Cast aluminum wheels. White sport wheels. Deluxe wheel trim. **XL:** (in addition to or in place of standard features) bright wheel lip moldings, rear window insert molding, deluxe wheel trim and chrome front bumper; woodtone instrument cluster applique, color-keyed cloth headliner, contoured knitted vinyl bench seat, color-keyed seat belts with tension eliminator feature, color-keyed floor mat, passenger door courtesy light switch, aluminum scuff plates, bright bezel dome light. **XLS:** (in addition to or in place of feature on the XL) blackout exterior trim and distinctive "XLS" three-color tape stripe, reclining cloth and vinyl bucket seats, leather wrapped "A-frame" steering wheel, gauge package full color keyed door trim with cloth and carpet insert and map pocket, full carpeting. **XLT:** (in addition to or in place of features on XL) chrome front bumper with black end caps, full length black lower bodyside molding with bright accent, dual accent bodyside paint stripes and brushed aluminum tail gate applique, full cloth door trim with color-keyed molding and bright insert, carpeted lower portion and map pocket, contoured bench seat with cloth seat trim, full color-keyed carpeting, leather wrapped "A-frame" steering wheel with center horn blow, vent windows with tinted side windows.

NOTE: Ranger interior color choices for 1985 were: Regatta Blue, Canyon Red, Tan. Exterior paint colors included: Raven Black, Silver Metallic, Light Canyon Red, Midnight Blue Metallic, Light Regatta Blue, Dark Canyon Red, Bright Regatta Blue Metallic, Wimbledon White, Light Desert Tan, Dark Charcoal Metallic, Walnut Metallic, Dark Spruce Metallic. TU-TONE: Regular: accent color was applied to lower bodyside/tailgate; included two-color tape stripe. (N.A. with XLS.) Deluxe: accent color was applied to mid-bodyside/tailgate; included upper and lower two-color tape stripes. (N.A. with XLS.) Special: accent color was applied to mid-bodyside, inside pickup box, rear of roof and B-pillar, back of cab and tailgate; included upper and lower two-color tape stripes; lower two-color tape stripe and rocker panel paint was replaced by XLS tape stripe when ordered with XLS trim.

1985 Ford F-150 Sport Flareside 4x4 Pickup (JAG)

F-150 PICKUP: — Basic styling was unchanged for 1985, although optional side body molding now started below the front side marker lights. Standard features included: Twin-I-Beam independent front suspension (4x4s had Twin-Traction Beam Independent front suspension). Chrome front bumper. Light argent grille with bright surround molding. Bright hub caps. Black foldaway door mounted mirrors. Rectangular halogen headlights. Rope tie down holes (Styleside). New all-vinyl seat trim. Pivoting vent windows. Glove box. Temperature gauge. Lighted ash tray. Argent instrument panel appliques (woodtone with 6.9L diesel) and black control knobs. Color-keyed door trim panels with foam-padded armrests. Floor insulation and rubber mat. 9⅝ in. day/night rearview mirror. Inside hood release. Dome light. Reversible keys. AM radio. Coat hook. LH courtesy light switch. Black steering wheel. Vinyl sunvisors. Power brakes. Power steering. 10 in. clutch. Three-speed manual. Flareside and Styleside (with regular or Super Cab) were offered.

I.D. DATA (F-150): See 1981 F-100 I.D.

1985 Ford F-150 XLT Styleside 4x4 Pickup (JAG)

Model	Body Type	Price	Weight	Prod. Total
F-15	(6½-ft.) Flareside Pickup	7962	3412	—
F-15	(6¾-ft.) Styleside Pickup	7799	3402	—
F-15	(8-ft.) Styleside Pickup	7965	3513	—
X-15	(6¾-ft.) Super Cab Pickup	9134	3756	—
X-15	(8-ft.) Super Cab Pickup	9300	3962	—

ENGINE (F-150): 4.9L (300 cu. in.) Six-cylinder. Brake horsepower: 120 at 3000 R.P.M. Bore & stroke: 4 x 3.98 in. Compression ratio: 8.5:1. Carburetor: One-bbl.

F-250 PICKUP: — The F-250 was only offered with the 8-ft. Styleside box, but it could be had in regular or (F-250HD) Super Cab. The Super Cab had room behind the front seat for an optional forward facing rear seat which could fold down flat. Two center facing jump seats were standard. When folded out of the way, there was an extra 29.8 cu. ft. of interior loadspace for cargo. Most standard F-250 features were the same as those offered on the F-150 plus a four-speed manual and, on F-250HDs, an 11 in. clutch.

I.D. DATA (F-250): See F-150 I.D.

Model	Body Type	Price	Weight	Prod. Total
—	Chassis w/Cab	9138	3732	—
F-25	(8-ft.) Styleside Pickup	8951	3785	—
X-25	(8-ft.) Super Cab Pickup	10,250	4305	—

ENGINE (F-250): Same as F-150 but n.a. in CA in F-250HD.

1985 Ford F-250 XLT Styleside 4x4 Pickup (JAG)

F-350 PICKUP: — The F-350 was offered in 8-ft. Styleside boxes with regular or Crew Cabs. The latter featured four doors and two full width bench seats. Both Regular and Crew Cab models could be ordered with dual rear wheels. An 11 in. clutch and four-speed manual were standard on all F-350s.

I.D. DATA (F-350): See F-150.

Model	Body Type	Price	Weight	Prod. Total
F-37	Chassis w/Cab	9138	3732	—
F-37	(161 in. w.b.) Chas. w/Cab	9234	3861	—
F-35	Styleside Pickup	10,437	4004	—
W-35	Crew Cab Pickup	10,993	4713	—

ENGINE (F-350): Same as F-150. 4wd F-350s and those with dual rear wheels, came with 5.8L V-8, except in Calif.

CHASSIS: Wheelbase: 116.8 in. (F-150), 133 in. (Styleside), 138.8 in. (F-150 Super Cab), 155 in. (F-150, F-250HD Super Cab), 168.4 in. (F-350 Crew Cab). Overall length: 189.3 in. (Flareside), 192.1 in. (F-150 Styleside), 208.3 in. (Styleside), 214.1 in. (F-150 Super Cab), 230.3 in. (F-150, F-250 Super Cab), 243.7 in. (F-350 Crew Cab). GVW: 5250-6450 (F-150), 6300-9000 (F-250), 8700-11,000 (F-350). Tires: P195/75R x 15SL (F-150), LT215/85R x 16C (F-250), LT235/85R x 16E (F-250HD, F-350), LT215/85R x 16D dual rear wheels/regular cab).

POWERTRAIN OPTIONS: 5.0L V-8 (F-150, F-250, 5.0L V-8 EFI) (Electronic Fuel Injection) (F-150, F-250), 5.8L V-8, 5.8L HO (high output) V-8 (F-150, F-250), 7.5L V-8 (F-250HD, F-350), 6.9L Diesel V-8 (F-250HD, F-350). 4-speed manual (F-150), 4-speed manual with overdrive (F-150, F-250), Automatic overdrive (F-150, F-250), SelectShift automatic.

CONVENIENCE OPTIONS: Four-Wheel-Drive: power brakes, manual locking free running hubs, power steering, two-speed transfer case, and four-speed manual. Automatic locking hubs (4x4). Chrome grille. Bodyside protection molding with black vinyl insert (Style). Bright wheel lip moldings (Style). **Radios:** Electronic AM/FM stereo with search and cassette tape player, AM/FM stereo (speakers mounted in door panels), AM/FM stereo with cassette tape player, and radio credit option (deleted standard AM radio for credit). Air conditioning. High output heater (std. with Crew Cab). **Convenience Group:** interval wipers, 12 in. day/night mirror, RH visor vanity mirror, carpeted map pocket on lower doors, headlights-on warning buzzer, and courtesy light switch on RH door. **Headliner and Deluxe Insulation Package:** color-keyed cloth headliner, black floor mats with full insulation (carpet on Crew Cab), back panel cover, and moldings (door upper, "B" pillar and rear window), plus aluminum door scuff plates. Electronic digital clock. Speed control (with resume feature). **Light Group:** movable under-hood worklight with 20-ft. retractable cord plus lights in glove box, under instrument panel, dual beam dome/map light, cargo box light, headlights-on warning buzzer, and courtesy light switch on RH door. Power door locks/windows (n.a. with Crew Cab). Manual steering (F-150 regular cab). Tinted sliding rear window. Tilt steering wheel. Tinted glass. Spare tire carrier, in box side mounted (Style). Center console (SC with Captain's Chairs). Bright low-mount swing away western mirrors. Bright swing-out recreation mirrors. Reclining Captain's Chairs (SC). Folding, forward facing rear seat (SC). Cloth and vinyl seat trim. Knitted vinyl seat trim. Auxiliary fuel tank. Auxiliary transmission oil cooler. **Handling Package:** front and rear stabilizer bars, heavy-duty front and rear shocks (quad front on F-150 regular cab 4x4), and heavy-duty front springs. Heavy-duty shocks. **Heavy-Duty Front Suspension Package:** (133 in. w.b. F-150 4x4) Heavy-duty 3800-lb. reated front axle and springs, 3.54 axle ratio and heavy-duty front and rear shock absorbers. (A version of this package was also offered for F-250, F-350 4x4s) Oil pressure and ammeter gauges. Front and rear stabilizer bars. Engine block heater. Extra engine cooling package. Super engine cooling package. Trailer towing package. Camper package. Heavy-duty air cleaner. Dual electric horns. 5-roof clearance lights. **Exterior Protection Group:** front bumper guards and front bumper rub strip. **Security Lock Group:** locking: gas cap, inside hood release and glove box; also spare tire lock. **Sports Instrumentation:** tach, ammeter, oil pressure gauge and trip odometer. Skid plates (4x4s) include transfer and fuel tank protective plates. **Rear Bumpers:** argent step (Styleside), chrome step (Styleside), and chrome channel (Flareside). Deluxe wheel covers (n.a. with 4x4s or DRW). White styled steel wheels (F-150). Sport wheel

covers (F-150). **XL:** (in addition to or in place of items on standard model) bright wheel lip moldings and two-color full length side paint stripes on SRW Stylesides (bodyside surround tape stripe and tailgate surround tape stripe on Flareside and DRW trucks); bright insert on rear window weatherstrip' cigarette lighter, LH & RH courtesy light switch, 12 in. day/night mirror, bright dome light bezel, bright surround door trim panel moldings, color-keyed floor mat, woodtone applique instrument panel, folding fully covered seat back (fixed front and folding rear on CC), deluxe seat belts, cloth and vinyl seat trim, aluminum scuff plates, cloth headlining, moldings/trim panels above belt line. **XLT Lariat:** (in addition to or in place of items on the XL) full-length black bodyside molding with bright insert, wheel lip moldings, distinctive brushed aluminum Styleside tailgate applique with red reflective lower portion; wall to wall carpeting, Door trim panels with bright surround, cloth insert, and carpeted lower area and map pocket. Soft wrapped with woodtone insert moldings/trim panels above belt line.

NOTE: Interior colors for 1985 were: Charcoal, Regatta Blue, Canyon Red, Tan. Exterior colors were: Raven Black, Silver Metallic, Bright Canyon Red, Midnight Blue Metallic, Light Regatta Blue, Dark Canyon Red, Dark Teal Metallic, Dark Charcoal Metallic, Desert Tan Metallic, Wimbledon White, Light Desert Tan, Bright Regatta Blue Metallic. TU-TONES: Regular: accent color covered roof and upper cab back panel. Deluxe: accent color covered center bodyside area and tailgate; moldings or tape were included or deleted as needed. Combination: regular and deluxe tu-tone combined. Victoria: accent color was applied to hood, upper fender, around window and lower bodyside; tape was included and moldings were deleted as required.

1986 FORD

1986 Ford Aerostar XL Passenger Van (FMC)

AEROSTAR: — After some delays, the Aerostar was introduced in the summer of '85 as an '86 model. This compact van's aerodynamic styling seemed more akin to Ford's autombile than truck line. Aerostar's front end steeply sloped to the blunt, four horizontal bars grille, which was sandwiched between the two rectangular headlights and wraparound parking lights. It had a one-piece liftgate and a sliding door on the passenger's side. The Aerostar's instrument panel was computer designed and featured a backlit speedometer and lighted speedometer needle for good legibility at night. Standard features included: Front bucket seats (wagon also had rear seats). Twin-tube low pressure gas shock absorbers. Five-speed manual with overdrive. Manual rack and pinion steering. Argent styled steel wheels with bright hub caps. Full wrapover, color-keyed door panels. Color-keyed soft vinyl steering wheel. AM radio. White fiberboard front compartment headliner. Dual aero foldaway mirrors. Front compartment carpeting (a rubber mat replaced the carpet if it was deleted).

I.D. DATA (Aerostar): See F-150 I.D.

Model	Body Type	Price	Weight	Prod. Total
A-140	Cargo Van	8774	2755	—
A-110	Wagon	9398	3123	—
A-150	Window Van	9764	2893	—

ENGINE (Aerostar): 2.3 liter 4-cylinder.

CHASSIS: Wheelbase: 118.9 in. Overall length: 174.9 in. Overall width: 71.7 in. Overall height: 72.6 in. Tires: P185/75R x 14SL.

POWERTRAIN OPTIONS: Automatic with overdrive. 2.8 liter V-6.

CONVENIENCE OPTIONS: Power rack and pinion steering. **Payload Packages:** 1,600 lb. and 2,000 lb. (both include power steering). Cloth seat trim. Air conditioning. Supercool radiator cooling. Rear window defroster and wiper/washer. AM/FM stereo radio. AM/FM stereo radio with cassette. Bright outside swingaway mirrors. Side door fixed window. Polished aluminum wheels. Speed control and tilt steering wheel. Engine block heater. California emissions system. High altitude emissions system. **XL Van:** AM/FM stereo radio, interval wipers, tinted glass, courtesy lamp switches for all doors, cargo lamps instrument panel glove box and vanity panel, two-tone rocker panel accent treatment, painted bodyside pinstripes, bright grille, bright full aluminum wheel covers, deluxe high-impact color-coordinated plastic bumpers, dual reclining cloth Captain's chairs

427

with inboard armrests, 16 oz. full-length carpeting. Bright argent grille. Sliding bodyside windows. Argent styled steel wheels with bright hub caps. Tinted glass. Interval wipers. Electronic digital clock. **Convenience Group:** courtesy light switches (all doors), cargo lamps, instrument panel glove box and vanity panel. **Light Group:** underhood, glove box, front reading, ashtray and under instrument panel lamps and headlamp on alert.

NOTE: Aerostar color choices for 1986 were: Silver Clearcoat Metallic, Bright Canyon Red, Dark Grey Clearcoat Metallic, Desert Tan, Dark Canyon Red Clearcoat Metallic, Bright Copper Clearcoat Metallic, Bright Regatta Blue Clearcoat Metallic, Light Chestnut Clearcoat Metallic, Midnight Regatta Blue, Dark Walnut Clearcoat Metallic, Light Regatta Blue, Colonial White. Two-tone paint: lower accent treatment.

BRONCO II: — Styling on the compact 4wd Bronco II was carried over from last year. A new feature was the tip-and slide front passenger seat which provided more convenient access to the rear passenger area. With four passengers seated, the Bronco provided 21.1 in. of load floor length and 25.6 cu. ft. of cargo volume. With rear seat backs down, the load floor length increased to 52.5 in. and cargo volume to 64.9 cu. ft. Among the many standard features were: Tinted glass. Full instrumentation. Transfer case skid plate. Power brakes and steering. Front and rear stabilizer bars. Five-speed manual. Reclining front seats. Split fold down rear bench seat. Halogen headlights. Dual outside foldaway rearview mirrors. Bright front and rear contour bumpers. Sport wheel covers. Color-keyed carpeting. Full-length cloth headliner. Sunvisors.

NOTE: A 4x2 Bronco II was reportedly offered for a short time, then discontinued.

I.D. DATA (Bronco II): See F-150 I.D.

Model	Body Type	Price	Weight	Prod. Total
U-14	Wagon	11,501	3072	—

ENGINE (Bronco II): 2.9L V-6 EFI (electronic fuel injection).

CHASSIS: Wheelbase: 94 in. Overall length: 158.2 in. Overall width: 68 in. Overall height: 68.4 in. Tires: P195/75R x 15 SL.

POWERTRAIN OPTIONS: Four-speed automatic with overdrive transmission.

CONVENIENCE OPTIONS: Touch-Drive electric shift transfer case. **Eddie Bauer Bronco II:** Special Tu-Tone paint treatment, "Eddie Bauer" emblem, XLT-level trim inside and out, cast aluminum wheels, all terrain tires with raised white letters, ammeter, oil pressure and temperature gauges, trip odometer, dual Captain's chairs, AM/FM stereo radio, tilt steering wheel, floor console, dual electric horns, interval windshield wipers, passenger visor vanity mirror, dark tinted Privacy glass, driver's sunvisor band, ashtray and glove box lights, headlamps-on warning buzzer, Eddie Bauer garment and tote bags. AM/FM stereo radio with cassette tape player. Dual Captains chairs. Cloth/vinyl 60/40 split bench seat. Air conditioning. Tinted glass. Luggage rack. Cloth/vinyl reclining bucket seats. **Light Group:** glove box, ashtray and cargo area light; passenger door and liftgate courtesy light switches, and "headlights on" warning buzzer. Fingertip speed control. Tilt steering wheel. Rear window wiper/defroster. Flip-open liftgate window. Flip-up, open air roof. Flip-open removable quarter windows. Pivoting front vent windows. Privacy glass. **Floor Console:** includes gauge package, trash bin, cassette tape tray, coin tray, two cup depressions, and electronic graphic warning display module. **Overhead Console:** includes digital clock and pivoting map light. Bright, low-mount western swingaway mirrors. Outside swingaway spare tire carrier. Rear seat delete. Carpet delete. Automatic locking hubs. Engine block heater. Super engine cooling. Heavy-duty shocks. Snow plow special package. Trailer towing package. Tow hooks. Limited slip front axle. California emissions system. High altitude emissions system. Plate bracket. Cast aluminum wheels. White sport styled steel wheels. Deluxe wheel trim (includes argent styled steel wheel with bright trim ring, lug nuts and black hub cover). **XLT Package:** chrome grille bodyside accent stripe, pivoting front vent windows, tinted glass, deluxe wheel trim, cloth and vinyl seat trim with full cloth door trim panels with a map pocket, carpet insert and bright headlights; courtesy light switches; liftgate operated cargo area light; rear quarter trim panels.

NOTE: BRONCO II color choices for 1986 were: Dark Grey Metallic, Raven Black, Medium Silver Metallic, Bright Canyon Red, Dark Canyon Red, Light Regatta Blue, Dark Shadow Blue Metallic, Colonial White, Dark Walnut Metallic, Light Desert Tan, Desert Tan Metallic, Dark Spruce Metallic (Eddie Bauer only). Deluxe two-tone paint: accent color was applied to mid-bodyside/liftgate below the chamfer and above the rocker area; included two-color tape stripe at the two-tone break.

BRONCO: — The attractive 4wd Bronco was basically unchanged for 1986. Standard features included: Twin-Traction Beam independent front suspension. Power steering and brakes. A 32-gallon fuel tank. Front vinyl bucket seats. Color-keyed floor mat. Flip/fold back seat. Power tailgate window. Interval wipers. AM radio. Tinted glass. Pivoting front bent windows. Chrome front and rear contour bumpers. Bright swing away mirrors. Sport wheel covers. Four-speed manual.

I.D. DATA (Bronco): See F-150 I.D.

Model	Body Type	Price	Weight	Prod. Total
U-150	Wagon	12,782	4267	—

ENGINE (Bronco): 300 cu. in. Six-cylinder. Net horsepower: 120. Compression ratio: 8.5:1. Carburetor: One-bbl.

CHASSIS: Wheelbase: 104.7 in. Overall length: 177.7 in. Overall height: 74 in. Overall width: 77.2 in. Tires: P235/75R x 15 SL BSW.

POWERTRAIN OPTIONS: 5.0L EFI, 5.8L HO. Four-speed manual with overdrive Automatic. Automatic with overdrive transmission.

CONVENIENCE OPTIONS: California emissions system. High altitude system. P235/75R x 15XL BSW or RWL all terrain tires. 31 x 10.5R x 15C RWL all terrain tires. Cloth and vinyl bucket seats. Cloth and vinyl bench seat. Cloth Captain's chairs. Air conditioner. Heavy-duty battery. Chrome rearstep bumper. Floor console. Super engine cooling. Rear window defroster. Privacy glass. Handling package. Engine block heater. Automatic locking hubs. **Light Group:** glove box and underhood light, dual beam map/dome light, under instrument panel courtesy lights, passenger side door courtesy light switch, headlights "On" warning buzzer. Transfer case skid plate. Outside swingaway spare tire carrier. Speed control/tilt steering wheel. Heavy-duty front suspension/snow plow package. **Trailer Towing Package:** 7-wire trailer wiring harness, 71-amp hour battery, super engine cooling, auxiliary transmission oil cooler, heavy-duty flasher, handling package. Deluxe two-tone paint. Victoria two-tone paint. Deluxe argent styled steel wheels. White styled steel wheels. AM/FM stereo. AM/FM stereo with cassette player. Power door locks/power windows. **Exterior Protection Group:** includes front bumper guards and front bumper rub strips. **Eddie Bauer Bronco:** two-tone paint, dual bodyside paint stripes, privacy glass, all-terrain RWL tires, deluxe argent styled steel wheels, Captain's chairs in special cloth trim with fold-down armrests, fully carpeted interior, center floor console, air conditioning, speed control/tilt steering wheel, light group, AM/FM stereo radio, heavy-duty battery, Eddie Bauer garment and equipment bags. **XLT:** chrome grille insert, chrome front and rear bumpers, lower bodyside protection molding, rear fold down tailgate with brushed aluminum applique, bright moldings on rear quarter windows, cloth and vinyl front bucket seats, 16-oz. color-keyed cut-pile carpeting, center console with a covered storage compartment plus depressions for beverage cups, door trim panels included a padded cloth insert on the upper half and a carpeted lower insert with map pocket, soft wrapped steering wheel, AM/FM stereo radio.

NOTE: Bronco colors for 1986 were: Raven Black, Dark Canyon Red, Colonial White, Light Regatta blue, Medium Silver Metallic, Dark Shadow Blue Metallic, Dark Grey Metallic, Light Desert Tan, Bright Canyon Red, Desert Tan Metallic. Bronco roof colors: Black, Dark Shadow Blue, Light Desert Tan, White. Two-tone effect: exterior color accented by rear fiberglass roof. Deluxe Two-Tone: includes accent color on center bodyside area and on tailgate between tape stripe below the mid-bodyside depression upper and lower bodyside protection molding. Victoria Two-Tone: includes accent color on hood, upper fender, around door window and on lower bodyside below the lower bodyside protection molding.

1986 Ford E-150 Econoline XL Cargo Van (FMC)

ECONOLINE E-150 CARGO VAN: — Exterior styling was left untouched for 1986. Among the standard features were: Power steering. Adjustable passenger seat (could be deleted). Color-keyed continuous loop seat belts. Inside hood release. Front door courtesy light switch (both doors). Step-well pads for the front doors and side cargo door. Day/night rearview mirror. Rear door latch and lock. Rear door positioners. Cigarette lighter. Bright hub caps. Bright windshield moldings.

ECONOLINE E-150 SUPER CARGO VAN: — This van had the same features as the E-150 Cargo Van plus a 20 in. extended rear overhang. This was especially useful for hauling longer loads.

ECONOLINE E-150 WINDOW VAN: — This window van had glass all around. It shared standard features with the Cargo Van.

ECONOLINE E-150 SUPER WINDOW VAN: — See E-150 Super Cargo Van.

I.D. DATA (Econoline E-150): See F-100.

Model	Body Type	Price	Weight	Prod. Total
E-150	Cargo Van	9439	3764	—
E-150	Window Van	9710	3791	—
E-150	Super Cargo Van	10,593	—	—
E-150	Super Window Van	10,863	—	—

ENGINE (Econoline E-150): 300 cu. in. Six-cylinder. Brake horsepower: 120 at 3400 R.P.M. Bore & stroke: 4.00 x 3.98 in. Compression ratio: 8.0:1. Carburetor: One-bbl.

ECONOLINE E-250 CARGO VAN: — The new E-250 had a higher GVW rating and more heavy-duty front and rear axles, than the E-150. It also came with eight-hole wheels. Standard features were the same as those on the E-100 except the three-speed manual was not available in Calif.

ECONOLINE E-250 SUPER CARGO VAN: — See E-150 Cargo Van.

ECONOLINE E-250 WINDOW VAN: — This vehicle shared styling and features with the E-100 Window Van, but had greater load capacity.

ECONOLINE E-250 SUPER WINDOW VAN: — See E-150 Super Cargo Van.

ECONOLINE E-250 CUTAWAY VAN: — This van with Camper Special Packages, was designed to readily accommodate custom motor homes.

ECONOLINE E-250 PARCEL DELIVERY: — The E-250 Parcel Delivery van was 149.9 in. long and 74.3 in. high in its cargo area. The rear door opening was 84.7 in. wide.

I.D. DATA (Econoline E-250): See F-150.

Model	Body Type	Price	Weight	Prod. Total
E-240	Cargo Van	10,561	4278	—
E-250	Window Van	10,831	4307	—
S-240	Super Cargo Van	11,222	—	—
S-250	Super Window Van	—	—	—

ENGINE (Econoline E-250): Same as E-100.

ECONOLINE E-350 CARGO VAN: — This was the top-of-the-line Econoline Van. It had heavy-duty front and rear shocks and a greater load capacity than the other series. Standard features were the same as the E-100.

ECONOLINE E-350 SUPER CARGO VAN: — See E-150 Super Cargo Van.

ECONOLINE E-350 WINDOW VAN: — See E-250 Window Van.

ECONOLINE E-350 SUPER WINDOW VAN: — See E-150 Super Cargo Van.

ECONOLINE E-350 CUTAWAY VAN: — See E-250 Cutaway Van.

ECONOLINE E-350 PARCEL DELIVERY: — See E-250 Parcel Delivery.

I.D. DATA (Econoline E-350): See F-150.

Model	Body Type	Price	Weight	Prod. Total
E-340	Cargo Van	11,264	4411	—
E-350	Window Van	11,534	4440	—
S-340	Super Cargo Van	12,322	—	—
S-350	Super Window Van	12,593	—	—
E-37B	Cutaway	11,940	4138	—
E-380	Parcel Delivery	—	—	—

ENGINE (Econoline E-350): Same as E-150.

CHASSIS: Wheelbase: 124 in. (E-150) 138 in. Overall length: 186.8 in. (124 in. w.b.), 206.8 in. (138 in. w.b.), 226.8 in. (138 in. Super Van). GVW: 5250-6300 (E-150), 6800-7900 (E-250), 8900-10,900 (E-350). Tires: P205/75R x 15 XL (E-150), LT215/85R x 16D (E-250), LT235/85R x 16E (E-350).

POWERTRAIN OPTIONS: 5.0L EFI V-8. 5.8L HO V-8. 6.9L Diesel V-8, 7.5L V-8. Four-speed manual with overdrive transmission. Select Shift automatic. Automatic overdrive.

CONVENIENCE OPTIONS: XL Package: vinyl bucket seats, front compartment carpeting, color-keyed door trim panels, leather tone inserts on instrument panel, courtesy lights, interval wipers; bright grille, front and rear bumpers, and low-mount swingaway mirrors. Cloth and vinyl Captain's Chairs. Air conditioning. High-capacity air conditioner and auxiliary heater. Heavy-duty battery. Chrome rear step bumper. Chrome bumpers. Super engine cooling. Auxiliary fuel tank. Ammeter and oil pressure gauges. Privacy glass. Swing-out rear door and/or cargo door glass. Tinted glass. Handling package. Deluxe insulation package. Light and Convenience group. Bright low-mount swingaway mirrors. Bright swing-out recreation mirrors. Deluxe two-tone paint. Power door locks. Speed control. Tilt steering wheel. Heavy-duty front and rear springs. Trailer Towing Packages. Wheel covers. AM/FM monaural, AM/FM stereo, AM/digital clock radio, AM/FM stereo with cassette player. Hinged side cargo door.

E-150 CLUB WAGON: — Club Wagon styling was unchanged for 1986. Among the standard features were: Bucket front seats and rear bench seat with "quick release" feature. Low angle steering wheel with full-width horn pad on the spokes. Front door vent windows. Ashtray and pockets molded into the engine cover. Power steering and brakes. 23.4 gallon fuel tank. Four-speed manual with overdrive transmission. Gas pressurized shock absorbers. Body on frame construction. Twin-I-Beam independent front suspension.

E-250 CLUB WAGON: — The slightly more heavy-duty E-250 came with most of the same features as the E-150, with the exception of SelectShift automatic transmission.

E-350 SUPER WAGON: — This heavy-duty wagon provided 20 in. more inside space than regular Club Wagons. It could hold up to 15 passengers (with optional seating package).

I.D. DATA (Club Wagon): See F-100.

Model	Body Type	Price	Weight	Prod. Total
E-150	Club Wagon	12,274	4326	—
E-250	Club Wagon	13,838	4931	—
E-350	Super Wagon	14,849	5238	—

ENGINE (Club Wagon): Same as Econoline.

CHASSIS: Same as Econoline.

POWERTRAIN OPTIONS: Same as Econoline.

CONVENIENCE OPTIONS: Most of the same items and packages that were offered on the Econoline plus: 7-, 8-, 11-, 12- and 15-passenger seating packages. **Club Wagon XL:** AM radio, interval windshield wipers, cour-

tesy light switches on all doors (a 3-way switch on the rear dome lamp), tinted glass, inside hood release, ammeter and oil pressure gauges, a high-output heater, rear door positioners, premium vinyl seat trim, stepwell pads on the front doors and sliding side door, seat belt reminder chime, bright low-mount swingaway mirrors, bright bumpers and window moldings; color-keyed front, side and rear door trim panels; color-keyed carpeting, front door map pockets. (The Trim Credit Options deleted the front door trim panels, the side and rear trim panels and garnish moldings, and included a black insulated floor mat and argent bumpers.) **Club Wagon XLT:** chrome grille, chrome bumpers with black rub strip, deluxe wheel covers, lower bodyside moldings and lower body side accent paint; reclining front Captain's Chairs and rear bench seat upholstered in cloth and vinyl; full-length cloth headliners, electronic digital clock, headlights-on alert chime, dual beam/dome map light and underhood light, RH visor mirror. (A combination rear seat/bed option, was available in the E150 XLT. It could be used as either a 3-passenger bench seat or a larger 62 in. x 72 in. bed.)

NOTE: Econoline and Club Wagon colors for 1986 were: Dark Grey Metallic, Dark Walnut Metallic, Medium Silver Metallic, Dark Shadow Blue Metallic, Medium Canyon Red Metallic, Light Desert Tan, Light Regatta Blue Metallic, Desert Tan Metallic, Light Regatta Blue, Colonial White.

1986 Ford Ranger STX (4x4) Super Cab Pickup (FMC)

RANGER PICKUP: — Styling was essentially unchanged for 1986. Among standard features were: Power brakes. Ammeter, temperature and oil gauges. Trip odometer. Interval wipers. Instrument panel storage bin. Lockable glove box. Inside hood release. Day/night rearview mirror. Color-keyed seat belts with comfort regulator feature. Halogen headlights. Bright grille and windshield moldings. Black foldaway mirrors. 5-speed manual with overdrive. Ranger buyers in 1986 now had their choice of two cabs, regular or Super. The Super Cab provided nearly 17 in. of additional cargo length behind the front seat. Optional rear vinyl jump seats were available at extra cost. The Super Cab came only with a 6-ft. box. But the regular cab Ranger could be had in 6-ft. or 7-ft. box.

RANGER "S" PICKUP: — The "S" was more basic than the base model. It had fewer frills. Low price and top economy was its main selling feature. It was only offered with the regular cab.

I.D. DATA (Ranger): See F-100 I.D.

Model	Body Type	Price	Weight	Prod. Total
R-10	Styleside Pickup	5993	—	—
R-10	(107.9 in. w.b.) Pickup	6834	2507	—
R-10	(113.9 in. w.b.) Pickup	6991	2545	—
R-14	Super Cab Pickup	7822	2671	—

ENGINE (Ranger): 2.3L I-4 EFI (Electronic Fuel Injection). The "S" came with 2.0L I-4 (except in Calif. and high altitude areas).

CHASSIS: Wheelbase: 107.9 in, 113.9 in, 125 in. (SC). Overall length: 175.6 in. (107.9 in. w.b.), 187.6 in. (113.9 in. w.b.), 192.7 in. (SC). Overall width: 66.9 in. Overall height: 64 in. (4x2), 64.1 in. (4x2 SC), 66.7 in. (4x4). GVW: 3820-4740. Tires: P195/75R x 14SL, P185/75R x 14SL ("S"), P195/75R x 15SL (4x4).

POWERTRAIN OPTIONS: 2.3L Turbo Diesel, 2.9L V-6 EFI. Automatic with overdrive transmission.

CONVENIENCE OPTIONS: Four-Wheel Drive: manual locking free running hubs, Twin-Traction Beam independent front suspension, front stabilizer bar, 2-speed manual shift transfer case, power steering. Air conditioning. "Touch-Drive" electric shift (4x4). Power steering. Speed control/tilt steering wheel. Cloth contoured bench seat. Cloth 60/40 split bench seat. Sport cloth bucket seats. Overhead console/digital clock. Cloth headliner. Tach. **Radios:** AM/FM stereo, AM/FM stereo with cassette player, electronic AM/FM stereo with cassette tape player. Power windows and door locks. Bright low-mount swingaway mirrors. Tinted glass. Black rear step bumper. Chrome rear step bumper. **Chrome Package:** bright bumpers, low-mount swingaway mirrors, and special tailgate applique. Sliding rear window. Handling package. Heavy-duty front suspension package (4x4). Camper package. Auxiliary fuel tank. Super engine cooling. Payload packages. Rear axle. Limited slip rear axle. Cast aluminum wheels (4x4). WSW all season, BSW all terrain, WSW all season, BSW all season, and RWL off road tires. California emissions system. High altitude emissions system. Cargo cover (SC). Dual Captian's chairs (SC). Rear vinyl jump seat (SC). Pivoting quarter windows

(SC). **XL:** (regular cab only; in addition to or in place of standard features) 2.9L V-6, knitted vinyl contoured bench seat; color-keyed floor mat, cloth headliner and moldings; interval windshield wipers, power steering, bright front bumper with black rub strip, bright wheel lip moldings and rear window trim, and deluxe wheel trim; tinted glass. **STX:** (in addition to or in place of items on XL; available on reg. or Super Cabs) gas-pressurized shocks, front stabilizer bar, P205/70R x 14SL RWL tires (4x2); power steering, two-tone paint, black grille, black bumpers, reclining bucket seats (Captain's chairs in SC), AM/FM stereo, skid plates (4x4), P215/75R x 15SL (4x4). **XLT:** (Super Cab only; in addition to or in place of items on STX) cloth upholstery on 3-pass. 60/40 front split bench seat, cloth door trim panels with map pockets and carpeted lower sections, tinted pivoting vent windows, 16-oz. color-keyed carpeting, color-keyed leather wrapped A-frame steering wheel, inside cargo cover.

NOTE: Exterior colors for 1986 Rangers included: Dark Canyon Red, Medium Silver Metallic, Raven Black, Colonial White, Desert Tan, Light Regatta Blue, Dark Grey Metallic, Dark Spruce Metallic, Silver Clearcoat Metallic, Dark Canyon Red Metallic, Dark Shadow Blue Metallic, Desert Tan Metallic, Bright Regatta Blue Clearcoat Metallic, Light Chestnut Clearcoat Metallic, Dark Walnut Metallic, Bright Canyon Red. Deluxe Two-Tone: Accent color was applied to mid-bodyside/tailgate. Included bright upper and lower bodyside molding paint breaks.

1986 Ford F-150 Lariat XLT Styleside Pickup (FMC)

F-150 PICKUP: — Basic styling remained unchanged for 1986. Standard features included: Twin-I-Beam independent front suspension (4x4s had Twin-Traction Beam Independent front suspension). Chrome front bumper. Light argent grille with bright surround molding. Bright windshield molding. Black foldaway door mounted mirrors. Rectangular Halogen headlights. Bright hub caps and tailgate handle. Rope tie down holes (Styleside). All-vinyl seat trim. Pivoting vent windows. Locking glove box. Ammeter, oil pressure, fuel and temperature gauges. Lighted ash tray. Cigarette lighter. Argent instrument panel appliques (woodtone with 6.9L Diesel). Color-keyed door trim panels with foam-padded armrests. Black rubber mat floor covering. 12 in. day/night rearview mirror. Inside hood release. Black dome light bezel (bright with SC). AM radio. Coat hook. LH courtesy light switch. Black steering wheel. Vinyl sunvisors. Power brakes. Power steering. 10 in. clutch. Three-speed manual. Flareside and Styleside (with regular or Super Cab) were offered.

I.D. DATA (F-150): See 1981 F-100 I.D.

Model	Body Type	Price	Weight	Prod. Total
F-15	(6½-ft.) Flareside Pickup	8625	3412	—
F-15	(6¾-ft.) Styleside Pickup	8373	3315	—
F-15	(8-ft.) Styleside Pickup	8548	3411	—
X-15	(6¾-ft.) Super Cab Pickup	10,272	3883	—
X-15	(8-ft.) Super Cab Pickup	10,446	3974	—

ENGINE (F-150): 4.9L (300 cu. in.) Six-cylinder. Net horsepower: 120 at 3000 R.P.M. Bore & stroke: 4 x 3.98 in. Compression ratio: 8.5:1. Carburetor: One-bbl.

F-250 PICKUP: — The F-250 was only offered with the 8-ft. Styleside box. But it could be had in regular or (F-250HD) Super Cab. The Super Cab had room behind the front seat for a forward facing rear seat which folded down flat. Two center facing jump seats were optional. When folded out of the way, there was an extra 29.8 cu. ft. of interior loadspace for cargo. Most standard F-250 features were the same as those offered on the F-150 plus a four-speed manual transmission and, on F-250HDs, an 11 in. clutch.

I.D. DATA (F-250): See F-150 I.D.

Model	Body Type	Price	Weight	Prod. Total
F-25	(8-ft.) Styleside Pickup	9646	3708	—
X-25	(8-ft.) Super Cab Pickup	11,645	4465	—

ENGINE (F-250): Same as F-150 but n.a. in Calif. in F-250HD.

F-350 PICKUP: — The F-350 was offered in 8-ft. Styleside boxes with regular or Crew Cabs. The latter featured four doors and two full bench seats. The regular Cab F-350 had dual rear wheels (DRW), Crew Cab models could be ordered with DRW or single rear wheels (SRW). An 11 in. clutch and four-speed manual were standard on all F-350s.

I.D. DATA (F-350): See F-150.

Model	Body Type	Price	Weight	Prod. Total
F-37	(133 in. w.b.) Chassis w/Cab	10,117	3574	—
F-37	(137 in. w.b.) Chassis w/Cab	10,429	3930	—
F-37	(161 in. w.b.) Chassis w/Cab	10,515	4059	—
F-35	Styleside Pickup	12,228	4332	—
W-35	Crew Cab Pickup	13,171	4809	—

ENGINE (F-350): Same as F-150. 4wd F-350s and those with dual rear wheels, came with 5.8L V-8, except in Calif.

CHASSIS: Wheelbase: 116.8 in. (F-150), 133 in. (Styleside), 138.8 in. (F-150 Super Cab), 155 in. (F-150, F-250HD Super Cab), 168.4 in. (F-350 Crew Cab). Overall length: 189.3 in. (Flare), 192.1 in. (F-150 Styleside), 208.3 in. (Styleside), 214.1 in. (F-150 Super Cab), 230.3 in. (F-150, F-250 Super Cab), 243.7 in. (F-350 Crew Cab). GVW: 4800-6250 (F-150), 6300-8800 (F-250), 8800-11,000 (F-350). Tires: P195/75R x 15SL (F-150), LT215/85R x 16C (F-250), LT235/85R x 16E (F-250HD, F-350).

POWERTRAIN OPTIONS: 5.0L EFI (Electronic Fuel Injection) V-8 (F-150, F-250), 5.8L HO (high output) V-8 (F-250HD, F-350), 7.5L V-8 (F-250HD, F-350), 6.9L Diesel V-8 (F-250HD, F-350). Four-speed manual transmission (F-150, F-250), 4-speed manual with overdrive (F-150, F-250), Automatic overdrive (F-150, F-250), SelectShift automatic.

CONVENIENCE OPTIONS: Four-Wheel-Drive: power brakes, manual locking free running hubs, power steering, 2-spd. transfer case, and 4-spd. manual. Automatic locking hubs (F-150 4x4). Chrome grille. Black vinyl bodyside molding with bright insert (Style). Bright wheel lip molding (Styleside). **Radios:** Electronic AM/FM stereo with cassette player, AM/FM stereo (speakers mounted in door panels), AM/FM stereo with cassette tape player, and radio credit option (deleted standard AM radio for credit). Air conditioning. High output heater (std.with 6.9L Diesel). **Convenience Group:** interval wipers, 12 in. day/night mirror, RH visor vanity mirror, carpeted map pocket on lower doors, headlights-on audible warning, and courtesy light switch on RH door. Headliner and deluxe insulation package. Electronic digital clock. Speed control (with resume feature). **Light Group:** underhood worklight plus lights in glove box, under instrument panel, dual beam dome/map light, cargo box light, headlights-on audible warning, and courtesy light switch on RH door. Power door locks/windows (n.a. with Crew Cab). Manual steering (F-150 4x2). Tinted sliding rear window. Tilt steering wheel. Tinted glass. Bright low-mount swing away 8 in. x 5 in. mirrors (RH convex glass). Bright swing out recreational mirrors (6¾ in. x 9½ in). Reclining Captain's Chairs with console (SC). Folding center facing jump seat (SC). Auxiliary fuel tank. **Handling Package:** front and rear stabilizer bars, heavy-duty rear springs on 4x4 w/6.9L Diesel, heavy-duty front and rear shocks (quad front on F-150 reg. cab 4x4), and heavy-duty front springs. Engine block heater. Super engine cooling package. Trailer towing package. Camper package. Heavy-duty battery. Tach with trip odometer. Roof clearance lights. **Exterior Protection Group:** front bumper guards and front bumper rub strip. Skid plates (4x4s). **Rear Bumpers:** argent step (Styleside), chrome step (Styleside), Deluxe wheel covers. Sport wheel covers (F-150). **XL:** (in addition to or in place of items on standard model) bright wheel lip moldings and rear window molding insert, dual bodyside accent paint stripes on SRW Stylesides. LH & RH courtesy light switch, bright dome light bezel, bright surround door trim panel moldings, color-keyed floor mat, woodtone applique instrument panel, folding fully covered seat back (fixed front and folding rear on CC), deluxe seat belts, cloth and vinyl seat trim, aluminum scuff plates, cloth headlining, black steering wheel. **XLT:** (in addition to or in place of items on the XL) Lower bodyside molding with protective black vinyl insert and distinctive aluminum Styleside tailgate applique with red reflective lower; color-keyed carpeting, Door trim panels with bright molding, cloth inert, carpeted lower and map pocket, soft wrapped steering wheel with woodtone insert.

NOTE: Interior colors for 1986 were: Canyon Red, Chestnut, Regatta Blue, Medium Gray (n.a. on XLT Lariat, Super Cab and Crew Cab). Exterior colors included: Raven Black, Dark Canyon Red, Colonial White, Light Regatta Blue, Medium Silver Metallic, Dark Shadow Blue Metallic, Dark Grey Metallic, Light Desert Tan, Bright Canyon Red, Desert Tan Metallic, Dark Spruce Metallic. TU-TONES: Deluxe: accent color covered center bodyside area and tailgate; included mid-bodyside tape strip and lower bodyside protection molding on SRW reg. cab and SC Stylesides, mid and lower bodyside tape on other models. Combination: included accent color applied to roof and deluxe tu-tone as described, no tape or molding paint break was utilized on the roof. Victoria: accent color was applied to hood, upper fenders, around windows and lower bodyside; included lower bodyside protection molding and tape upper paint break.

GMC

By Robert C. Ackerson

Early GMC light-duty trucks, like their larger capacity counterparts, enjoyed a solid reputation for reliability and rugged construction. During World War I, the Model 16 one-ton truck was used extensively, by the U.S. Army, as an ambulance. After the war, it became the basis for the K-Series trucks.

1912 GMC Reliance 'H' Stake Bed (Steve Schmidt)

1914 GMC Covered Flare Board (OCW)

1915 GMC Model 15 Express Truck (OCW)

During the twenties, GMC turned to several manufacturers for its truck engines. In 1927, the GMC one-ton models used a six-cylinder Buick power plant. A year later, in 1928, the T-19 one-tonner was powered by a Pontiac engine.

The introduction of the T-19, whose combined 1928 and 1929 sales exceeded 20,000 units, marked a major advance in truck styling at GMC. Its headlights were relo-

1917 GMC Model 16 3/4-Ton Stake (CPC/W. Wedekind)

1918 GMC Half-Ton Military Ambulance (CMW/CE)

1918 GMC Model 16 One-Ton Flatbed (CPC/P. Reynolds)

cated next to the radiator. The fenders were more deeply crowned and the radiators were chrome plated.

The GMC-Buick connection lead, in 1931, to the manufacturing of GMC's own "Buick" engines. This development brought an extensive series of GMC engines based on the Buick design. These power plants were produced in various displacements. They were used in GMC trucks with a wide variety of load capacities and remained in production even after optional V-8s were released in 1955. In fact, they survived until the V-6 engine appeared in 1963.

During the mid-thirties, GMC trucks gradually shed many styling items associated with the previous decade,

431

such as exterior-mounted windshield visors and highly visible hood louvers. As a result, appearances became more streamlined and attractive. By 1937, the design format that survived many years — it was essentially unchanged until the late forties — was well established.

1919 GMC Screenside Delivery Truck (DFW/MPB)

1937 GMC ½-Ton Pickup (S. Glesbrenner)

The light-duty models had V-angled windshields, bullet-shaped headlights, rounded fenders and prominent GMC identification on each side of the hood. The 1941 models — with a new 228 cubic inch overhead valve six-cylinder engine, had fender-mounted headlights and a grille consisting of a broad base and a narrower top section, both of which had wide, horizontal bars.

1959 GMC ½-Ton Wide-Side Pickup (S. Soloy)

This appearance was continued after the war. It lasted until new models were ready for introduction in the summer of 1947. These were modern-looking vehicles with headlights mounted low in the fenders, a simple grille arrangement (with four, fluted-horizontal bars) and a body whose extremities were round and smooth. This general styling format remained virtually unchanged until 1954, but numerous technical changes were incorporated to avoid any suggestion of obsolesence. Most noteworthy, was the availability of dual-range Hydra-Matic transmission beginning in 1953.

The following year, GMC light-duty trucks were given several major styling revisions, including a one-piece curved windshield, a much broader grille and rectangular parking lamps (positioned at the outer limits of the grille.)

1960 GMC 4x4 Carryall Suburban (GMC)

1968 GMC ½-Ton Wide-Side Pickup (C. Webb)

These developments did not, however, change the basic character of GMC trucks. Radical change would have to wait for model-year 1955. That year marked the introduction of new models with styling that possessed strong influences from the General Motors auto divisions. Leading the list of new styling schemes was a panoramic windshield. Not far behind was a grille/bumper arrangement that, at least in theme, resembled others seen earlier on Oldsmobiles.

Even Cadillac, it seemed, had a role in the styling of the latest GMC trucks, as evidenced by the visors installed over the headlights. Paralleling Chevrolet's introduction of its Cameo Carrier, GMC released a comparable model called the Suburban Pickup. (Ed. Note: This may actually have been a case of adopting generic corporate terminology, as some used car guides contemporary to this period also list the Chevrolet product as a "suburban pickup.") Both of these models were advanced guard units, foretelling the coming of the fenderless GMC "Wide-Side" models in 1958.

1970 GMC ¾-Ton Wide-Side Pickup (D. Monetti)

1972 GMC ¾-Ton Wide-Side Camper Special (GMC)

Eventually, the influence of automotive styling upon GMC truck design faded. Before it had run its course, a new line of 1960-1961 models appeared with futuristic front ends. By 1964, these developments had run their natural course and GMC trucks returned to front ends that were characterized by simple, horizontal forms and windshields that no longer had "dog leg" corner posts. New to the GMC line, that year, were the Handi-Van models on a trim 90 inch wheelbase. They were available with either four- or six-cylinder engines.

1976 GMC "Jimmy" 4x4 Utlity Wagon (GMC)

In 1967, GMC pickups were totally restyled. The main bodyside creases were lowered. Instead of being just below the beltline, they were now on the feature line that bisected the fender cutouts into equal semicircles. This style was popular. Three years later, when the first 4x4 "Jimmy" model was introduced, it still had a similar appearance.

Introduction of the Jimmy widened GMC's role in the growing RV market and was followed, in 1971, with release of the "Sprint." This was GMC's version of Chevrolet's El Camino. At the same time, GMC vans were redesigned along more contemporary lines.

When it came time to update GMC pickups, in 1973, the company pulled out all stops. It extended the line to include 3+3 type models with six doors and six-passenger accomodations. By 1978, GMC pickups — like those from Chevrolet — were available with diesel engines. That year, the Sprint name was replaced with "Caballero."

1984 GMC S-15 "Indy Hauler" Pickup (IMSC/JLM)

Significant styling changes were made to GMC full-size pickups in 1981. They were intended to improve aerodynamics and, thus, have a positive effect on fuel efficiency. The following year, the company entered the mini-truck market with its S-15 model line. This move was followed by the introduction of the Safari mini-vans, as 1985 models.

1920-1926 GMC

1920 GMC Model 16 3/4- to 1-Ton Canopy (D. Sagvold)

1921 GMC Model 16 Panel Delivery (Dennis Sagvold)

1922 GM K-16 One-Ton Express (Ben Ostergen)

SERIES 16 — ¾-TON: — The Series 16 truck was fitted with an open canopy body. No changes: 1920-1926.

Model Series 16	Body Type	Price	Weight	Prod. Total
16	¾-Ton	—	—	—

ENGINE: L-head, inline. Four-cylinder. Cast iron block. Brake horsepower: 37 at 1810 R.P.M.

CHASSIS (Series 16): Wheelbase: 132 in.

TECHNICAL: Manual transmission. Speeds: 3F/1R. Floor mounted gear shift lever.

1923 GMC One-Ton Canopy Express (Dennis Sagvold)

Pricing

1920-1926	5	4	3	2	1
Canopy	980	1950	3250	4550	6500

1927 GMC

There's two ways to look at 1927 GMC light-duty history: 1) there were *no* GMC light-duties, or, 2) the GMC light-duty was a *Pontiac.* Historians have stated views on this both ways. Pontiac was a brand new lower-medium priced car. This hot-selling GM nameplate was introduced January 3, 1926. By October, a Deluxe Delivery built on Pontiac running gear was introduced (See separate Pontiac section). In 1928, this same truck — unchanged, except for radiator shell detailing — was marketed as the GMC T-11. According to records in Pontiac Motor Division's historical files, this change took place late in the summer of 1927, at which point the "second series" (a.k.a. "1928 Series") of cars and trucks was in the showrooms. So, trucks with GMC badges were built only as 1928s, although it's possible that some states registered them as 1927s.

1928 GMC

1928 GMC Panel Delivery Truck (DFW/BCA)

SERIES T-11 — ½-TON: — In late 1927 GMC re-entered the light duty truck field with its new T-11 series. These trucks were identical to the 1927 Pontiac models except for having a GMC radiator shield.

An addition to the instrument panel was the gasoline gauge which, on the 1927 Pontiac models, was located on the fuel tank.

Model Series T-11	Body Type	Price	Weight	Prod. Total
T-11	½-Ton Chassis	—	—	—

1928 GMC Screenside Express (OCW)

1928 GMC Panel Delivery (OCW)

ENGINE: L-head, inline. Six-cylinder. Cast iron block. Bore & stroke: 3.25 in. x 3.75 in. Displacement: 186.5 cu. in. Compression ratio: 4.9:1. Brake horsepower: 48 at 2850 R.P.M. Mechanical valve lifters. Carburetor: Carter 1-barrel.

CHASSIS (Series T-11): Wheelbase: 110 in. Tires: 4.75 x 20 in.

TECHNICAL: Manual transmission. Speeds: 3F/1R. Floor mounted gear shift lever. Overall ratio: 4.18:1. Four-wheel, mechanical brakes.

OPTIONS: Disc wheels.

HISTORICAL: Calendar year registrations: (all models) 17,568.
Engine now used convex rather than concave interior cylinder walls. First year for fuel pump rather than vacuum feed. Also introduced was a new clutch and transmission.

Pricing

1928 Light Duty	5	4	3	2	1
Pickup	980	1950	3250	4550	6500
Panel	930	1860	3100	4350	6200

1929 GMC

1929 GMC "Fifth Avenue" Panel Delivery (DFW/DPL)

SERIES T-11 — 6-CYLINDER: — No change in exterior appearance from 1928. Mechanical alterations were extensive. The six-cylinder engine's displacement was boosted to 200.4 cu. in. The torque tube drive used previously was replaced by a Hotchkiss system.

I.D. DATA: Serial number located on left side of frame below front fender. Starting: 410202 and up. Engine numbers located on left side of cylinder block behind oil filter.

Model Series T-11	Body Type	Price	Weight	Prod. Total
T-11	Chassis	625	2135	—

ENGINE: L-head, inline (Pontiac manufacture). Six-cylinder. Cast iron block. Bore & stroke: 3.31 in. x 3.88 in. Displacement: 200.4 cu. in. Compression ratio: 4.9:1. Brake horsepower: 60 at 3000 R.P.M. Mechanical valve lifters. Carburetor: Marvel 1-barrel.

CHASSIS (Series T-11): Wheelbase: 109.625 in. Tires: 5.00 x 19 in.

TECHNICAL: Manual, sliding gear transmission. Speeds: 3F/1R. Floor mounted gear shift lever. Overall ratio: 4.36:1. Mechanical brakes. 4 pressed steel wheels.

HISTORICAL: Calendar year registrations: (all models) 14,300.

Pricing

1929 Light Duty	5	4	3	2	1
Pickup	980	1950	3250	4550	6500
Panel	930	1860	3100	4350	6200

1930 GMC

SERIES T-11/T-15 — 6-CYLINDER: — No changes for 1930 except that all GMC trucks used six-cylinder engines.

I.D. DATA: Serial number located on left side of frame below front fender. Starting: (T-11) 591519 and up, (T-15) 101 and up. Engine numbers located on left side of cylinder block behind oil filter.

Model Series T-11	Body Type	Price	Weight	Prod. Total
T-11	Chassis	625	1980	—
Series T-15				
T-15	Chassis	695	2500	—

ENGINE: L-head, inline (Pontiac manufacture). Six-cylinder. Cast iron block. Overall length: 167.73 in. Bore & stroke: 3.31 in. at 3.88 in. Displacement: 200.4 cu. in. Compression ratio: 4.9:1. Brake horsepower: 60 at 3000 R.P.M. Mechanical valve lifters. Carburetor: Marvel 1-barrel.

CHASSIS (Series T-11): Wheelbase: 109.625 in. Length: 167.63 in.

CHASSIS (Series T-15): Wheelbase: 130 in.

TECHNICAL: Manual transmission. Speeds: 3F/1R. Column mounted gear shift lever. Single dry plate clutch. Hypoid, semi-floating rear axle. Mechanical, four-wheel brakes. Pressed steel wheels.

OPTIONS: Front bumper. Rear bumper.

HISTORICAL: Calendar year registrations: (all models) 9,004.

Pricing

1930 Light Duty	5	4	3	2	1
Pickup	1000	2000	3300	4600	6600
Panel	980	1950	3250	4550	6500
Stake	900	1800	3000	4200	6000

1931 GMC

SERIES T-11/T-15 — 6-CYLINDER: — No appearance changes for 1931.

I.D. DATA: Serial number located (T-11): on left side of frame below front fender. (T-15): on right side of frame below front fender. Starting: (T-11) 591519 and up, (T-15) 101 and up. Engine numbers located on left side of cylinder block behind oil filter.

1931 GMC Police Paddy Wagon (ATC)

Model	Body Type	Price	Weight	Prod. Total
Series T-11				
T-11	½-Ton Chassis	625	1885	—
Series T-15				
T-15	¾-Ton Chassis	695	2500	—

ENGINE: L-head, inline (Pontiac manufacture). Six-cylinder. Cast iron block. Bore & stroke: 3.31 in. x 3.88 in. Displacement: 200.4 cu. in. Compression ratio: 4.9:1. Brake horsepower: 60 at 3000 R.P.M. Mechanical valve lifters. Carburetor: Marvel 1-barrel.

1931 GMC One-Ton Stake (MSC/Jack L. Martin)

CHASSIS (Series T-11): Wheelbase: 109.625 in. Overall length: 167.63 in.

CHASSIS (Series T-15): Wheelbase: 130 in.

1931 GMC Police Paddy Wagon (OCW)

436

TECHNICAL: Manual transmission. Speeds: 3F/1R. Column mounted gear shift lever. Single dry plate clutch. Hypoid, semi-floating rear axle. Mechanical, four-wheel brakes. Pressed steel wheels.

OPTIONS: Front bumper. Rear bumper.

HISTORICAL: Calendar year registrations: (all models) 6,919.

Pricing

1931 Light Duty	5	4	3	2	1
Pickup	1000	2000	3300	4600	6600
Panel	980	1950	3250	4550	6500
Stake	900	1800	3000	4200	6000

1932 GMC

1932 GMC Pickup Express Truck (DFW/SI)

SERIES T-11/T-15 — 6-CYLINDER: — No appearance changes for 1932. GMC replaced the Pontiac engine with one of its own manufacture.

I.D. DATA: Serial number located (T-11): on left side of frame below front fender. (T-15): on right side of frame below front fender. Starting: Serial numbers were included on 1931 range. Serial numbers found on right frame side rail at front and on caution plate mounted on instrument panel. Engine numbers located on left lower front end.

Model	Body Type	Price	Weight	Prod. Total
Series T-11				
T-11	½-Ton Chassis	625	1885	—
Series T-15				
T-15	1-Ton Chassis	645	2300	—

ENGINE: Inline, OHV. Six-cylinder. Cast iron block. Bore & stroke: 3.312 in. x 3.875 in. Displacement: 221.4 cu. in. Brake horsepower: 69 at 2800 R.P.M. Mechanical valve lifters. Carburetor: 1-barrel.

CHASSIS (Series T-11): Wheelbase: 109.625 in. Overall length: 167.63 in.

CHASSIS (Series T-15): Wheelbase: 121 in.

TECHNICAL: Manual transmission. Speeds: 3F/1R. Floor mounted gear shift lever. Single, dry-disc clutch. Hypoid, semi-floating rear axle. Mechanical, four-wheel brakes. Pressed steel wheels.

OPTIONS: Front bumper. Rear bumper.

HISTORICAL: Calendar year registrations: (all models) 6,359.

Pricing

1932 Light Duty	5	4	3	2	1
Pickup	1000	2000	3300	4600	6600
Panel	980	1950	3250	4550	6500
Stake	900	1800	3000	4200	6000

1933-1934 GMC

In 1933 and 1934, GMC did not produce light-duty trucks. The lowest rating available on GMC products in these years was 1½-tons.

1935 GMC

SERIES T-16L — 6-CYLINDER: — GMC returned to light-duty truck manufacture with the T-16L model.

I.D. DATA: Serial number located on right frame side rail at front and on caution plate on instrument panel. Starting: T-16L - 4001 and up. Engine numbers located on left lower front end of cylinder block.

Model Series T-16L	Body Type	Price	Weight	Prod. Total
T-16L	¾-Ton Chassis	595	2945	—

ENGINE: Inline, L-head. Six-cylinder. Cast iron block. Bore & stroke: 3.3125 in. x 4.125 in. Displacement: 213 cu. in. Mechanical valve lifters. Carburetor: 1-barrel.

CHASSIS (Series T-16L): Wheelbase: 131 in.

TECHNICAL: Manual transmission. Speeds (T-14): 3F/1R, all others four-speed. Floor mounted gear shift lever. Single, dry-disc clutch. (T-14): Hypoid, semi-floating rear axle, all others full-floating. Mechanical, four-wheel brakes. Pressed steel wheels.

OPTIONS: Front bumper. Rear bumper. Heater.

HISTORICAL: Calendar year registrations: (all models) 11,442.

Pricing

1935 Light Duty	5	4	3	2	1
Pickup	780	1560	2600	3600	5200
Panel	750	1500	2500	3500	5000

1936 GMC

1936 GMC Panel Delivery Truck (DFW/MVMA)

SERIES T-14/T-16L — 6-CYLINDER: — The latest GMC light-duty models featured enclosed front and rear fenders and a rounder grille with prominent vertical bars. A long and narrow engine vent panel was located directly below the "General Motors Truck" plaque on the hood sides. Early production models had a "blister" type roof visor.

I.D. DATA: Serial number located on right hand frame side rail at front and on caution plate on instrument panel. Starting: T-14: T14-001 to 11251. Ending: T-16L: T-16L-9051 to 18801. Engine numbers located on left lower front of cylinder block.

Model Series T-14	Body Type	Price	Weight	Prod. Total
T-14	½-Ton Chassis	425	2210	—
T-14	Pickup Body	41	—	—
T-14	Cab*	100	—	—
Series T-16L				
T-16L	¾-Ton Chassis	525		

Note: With shatter-proof glass.

ENGINE: Inline, L-head. Six-cylinder. Cast iron block. Bore & stroke: 3.3125 in. x 4.125 in. Displacement: 213 cu. in. Mechanical valve lifters. Carburetor: 1-barrel.

CHASSIS (Series T-14): Wheelbase: 126 in. Tires: 6:00 x 16 four-ply in early 1936 only. (Later became an $8 option).

CHASSIS (Series T-16L): Wheelbase: 131 in.

TECHNICAL: Manual, synchromesh transmission. Speeds (T-14): 3F/1R; (All others) four-speed. Floor-mounted gear shift lever. Single, dry plate clutch. Axle: (T-14) Hypoid, semi-floating rear; (All others) full-floating.

OPTIONS: Front bumper. Rear bumper. Heater. Accessory Group #1 ($23.50). Heavy-duty shocks ($10.20). 6.50 x 16 six-ply tires ($20).

HISTORICAL: Calendar year registrations: (all models) 26,980.

1936 GMC Stake Bed (CPC/Lindon's Sales & Service)

1936 GMC Walk-in Milk Delivery Van (DFW/MPC)

Pricing

1936 Light Duty	5	4	3	2	1
Pickup	830	1650	2750	3850	5500
Panel	780	1560	2600	3600	5200

1937 GMC

1937 GMC Pickup Truck (DFW/BLHU)

SERIES T-14/T-16L/F-16L — 6-CYLINDER: — Identifying the 1937 GMC trucks was a revamped front end design with headlights set in the fender valleys, new "Dual Tone" color designs and a grille combining three sections of horizontal bars with a broad center portion of horizontal fins. A series of Model F walk-in vans were introduced. The L-head engine used for the GMC light-duty models was enlarged to displace 230 cubic inches.

I.D. DATA: Serial number located on right hand frame side rail at front and on caution plate on instrument panel. Starting: T-14: T-14-11252 to 34527. T-16L: T-16L-18802 and up. F-16L: F-16L-001 and up. Engine numbers located on left lower front of cylinder block.

Model	Body Type	Price	Weight	Prod. Total
Series T-14A				
T-14A	½-Ton Chassis	425	2195	—
T-14A	Pickup Body	43	—	—
T-14A	Cab	102	—	—
Series T-14B				
T-14B	½-Ton Chassis	395	N/A	—
T-14B	Pickup body	31	—	—
T-14B	Cab	102	—	—
Series T-16L				
T-16L	¾-Ton Chassis	535	3155	—
F-16L				
F-16L	¾-Ton Chassis	645	3230	—

1937 GMC Pickup Truck (DFW/BLHU)

ENGINE: Inline, L-head. Six-cylinder. Cast iron block. Bore & stroke: 3.4375 in. x 4.125 in. Displacement: 230 cu. in. Mechanical valve lifters. Carburetor: 1-barrel.

CHASSIS (Series T-14A, T-14B): Wheelbase: 112 in. Tires: 6.00 x 16 four-ply.

CHASSIS (Series T-16L): Wheelbase: 131.5 in.

CHASSIS (Series F-16L): Wheelbase: 108 in.

1937 GMC Half-Ton Pickup (Hoosier Auto Show)

TECHNICAL: Manual, synchromesh transmission. Speeds: (T-14) 3F/1R; (all others) 4F/1R. Floor-mounted gear shift lever. Single, dry plate clutch. Axle: (T-14) Hypoid, semi-floating; (all others) full-floating. Hydraulic four-wheel brakes. Pressed steel wheels. Heavy duty shocks ($10.20). 6.50 x 16.6 ply tires, T-14B ($20); 6.00 x 16 six-ply ($8). four-speed transmission ($15.25). Shatter-proof glass ($12.50).

438

1937 GMC Half-Ton Pickup (CPC/Robert Cloud)

OPTIONS: Front bumper ($6.50). Rear bumper. Heater. Seat covers. Tire carrier, T-14B ($3.50). Tire carrier, T-14A ($10.20). Accessory Group #1 for T-14B ($29.40). Accessory Group #1 for T-14A ($26).

HISTORICAL: Calendar year registrations: (all models) 43,522.

1937 GMC Carryall Suburban (GMC)

Pricing

1937 Light Duty	5	4	3	2	1
Pickup	830	1650	2750	3850	5500
Panel	780	1560	2600	3600	5200

1938 GMC

1938 GMC One-Ton Pickup Truck (OCW)

SERIES T-14A/T-14B/T-145/T-15/T-155 — 6-CYLINDER — The latest GMC trucks featured hood-mounted headlights and grilles with added brightwork. No hood louvers were installed. This was the last year the light-duty models used single-piece windshields.

I.D. DATA: Serial number located on right-hand frame side rail at front and on caution plate on firewall. Starting: T-14A: T-14A-11252 to 34527. T-14B: T-14B-34528 and up. T-145: T-145-001 and up. T-15: T-15-5001 and up. T-155: T-155-001 and up. Engine numbers located right side of crankcase.

Model	Body Type	Price	Weight	Prod. Total
Series T-14A				
T-14A	½-Ton Chassis	410	2195	—
Series T-14B				
T-14B	½-Ton Chassis	445	2300	—
Series T-145				
T-145	¾-Ton Chassis	515	2470	—
Series T-15				
T-15	¾-Ton Chassis	545	2655	—
Series T-155				
T-155	¾-Ton Chassis	565	2795	—

1938 GMC Pickup Truck (OCW)

ENGINE: Inline. L-head. Six-cylinder. Cast iron block. Bore & stroke: 3.4375 in. x 4.125 in. Displacement: 230 cu. in. Brake H.P.: 86 at 3600 R.P.M. Four main bearings. Mechanical valve lifters. Carburetor: Zenith one-barrel.

CHASSIS (Series T-14): Wheelbase: 112 in. Tires: 6.00 x 16 in.

CHASSIS (Series T-14A): Wheelbase: 126 in.

CHASSIS (Series T-15): Wheelbase: 131.5 in.

CHASSIS (Series T-145): Wheelbase: 126 in.

CHASSIS (Series T-155): Wheelbase: 131.5 in.

TECHNICAL: Manual, synchromesh transmission. Speeds: (T-14) 3F/1R; (all others) 4F/1R. Floor-mounted gear shift lever. Single, dry plate clutch. Rear axle: Hypoid, semi-floating. Overall ratio: (T-14) 4.11:1. Hydraulic, four-wheel brakes. Pressed steel wheels. Heavy-duty shocks. Various tire sizes. Four-speed transmission.

OPTIONS: Front bumper. Rear bumper. Radio. Heater. Clock. Cigar lighter. Radio antenna. Seat covers. Tire carriers.

HISTORICAL: Calendar year registrations: (all models) 20,152.

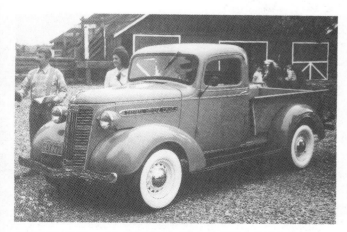

1938 GMC Standard Half-Ton Pickup (CPC/L. Yunker)

Pricing

1938	5	4	3	2	1
Light-Duty					
½-Ton Pickup	840	1680	2800	3900	5600
½-Ton Panel	810	1620	2700	3800	5400
Medium-Duty					
¾-Ton Pickup	830	1650	2750	3850	5500
¾-Ton Panel	780	1560	2600	3600	5200
1-Ton Pickup	740	1470	2450	3350	4900
1-Ton Panel	690	1380	2300	3200	4600
Dely. Van	630	1250	2100	3000	4200

1939 GMC

1939 GMC ¾-Ton Armored Car (NSPC/JE)

SERIES AC-100/AC-150/AC-250 — 6-CYLINDER: — The 1939 pickups had V-shaped, two-piece windshields and 228 cubic inch overhead valve six-cylinder engines as well as the revised styling of other GMC trucks. The grille remained high and narrow. But, it had a more massive appearance, thanks to the thick and sharply-angled horizontal bars attached to a center vertical bar. The design seemed to be patterned after a fish skelton. The uppermost bar carried the GMC logo. As in earlier years, the side hood bar read "GENERAL MOTORS TRUCK," but its leading edge was more blunt than in 1938.

I.D. DATA: Serial number located on right-hand frame side rail at front and on caution plate on firewall. Starting: AC-100: AC-101-001 and up. AC-100 (123.25 inch wheelbase) AC-102-001 and up. AC-150: AC-152-001 and up. AC-250: AC-252-001 and up. Engine numbers located right side of crankcase.

1939 GMC Utility Body Truck (DFW/MVMA)

1939 GMC Panel Delivery Truck (DFW/BLHU)

Model	Body Type	Price	Weight	Prod. Total
Series AC-100				
AC-100	½-Ton Chassis 113.5 in. w.b.	460	2230	—
AC-100	½-Ton Chassis Cab 113.5 in. w.b.	557	2620	—
AC-100	½-Ton Pickup 113.5 in. w.b.	593	2855	—
AC-100	½-Ton Panel 113.5 in. w.b	669	3495	—
AC-100	½-Ton Chassis 123.75 in. w.b.	490	2290	—
	Cab 123.75 in. w.b.	97	—	—
	Pickup Body 123.75 in. w.b.	46	—	—
Series AC-150				
AC-150	¾-Ton Chassis	535	2470	—
AC-150	¾-Ton Chassis Cab	632	2860	—
AC-150	¾-Ton Pickup	678	3135	—
AC-150	¾-Ton Stake	703	3480	—
AC-150	¾-Ton Panel	775	3800	—
Series AC-250				
AC-250	1-Ton Chassis	555	2660	—
AC-250	1-Ton Chassis Cab	652	3050	—
AC-250	1-Ton Platform	708	3565	—
AC-250	1-Ton Pickup	728	3360	—
AC-250	1-Ton Stake	734	3855	—
AC-250	1-Ton Panel	825	4060	—

1939 GMC Suburban Carryall (OCW)

ENGINE: Inline. OHV. Six-cylinder. Cast iron block. Bore & stroke: 3.5625 in. x 3.8125 in. Displacement: 228 cu. in. Brake H.P.: 80 at 3000 R.P.M. Four main bearings. Hydraulic valve lifters. Carburetor: one-barrel.

CHASSIS (Series AC-100): Wheelbase: 113.5/123.75 in. Tires: 6.50 x 16 in. Wheels: 16 x 4.50 in.

CHASSIS (Series AC-150): Wheelbase: 123.75 in.

CHASSIS (Series AC-250): Wheelbase: 133 in.

TECHNICAL: Manual, synchromesh transmission. Speeds: 3F/1R. Floor-mounted gear shift lever. Single plate, dry-disc clutch. Hypoid, semi-floating rear axle. Overall ratio: (AC-100): 4.11:1. Hydraulic, four-wheel brakes. Pressed steel wheels, (AC-100) 16 x 4.50 in. Heavy-duty shocks. Larger tires. Four-speed transmission ($15.40 for AC-100).

OPTIONS: Front bumper. Rear bumper. Heater ($23.50). Clock. Cigar lighter. Seat covers. Tire carriers. Deluxe Chassis Group. Accessory Group. Chrome headlights ($3.50).

HISTORICAL: Calendar year registrations: (all models) 34,908.

Pricing

	5	4	3	2	1
1939					
Light-Duty					
½-Ton Pickup	840	1680	2800	3900	5600
½-Ton Panel	810	1620	2700	3800	5400
Medium-Duty					
¾-Ton Pickup	830	1650	2750	3850	5500
¾-Ton Panel	780	1560	2600	3600	5200
1-Ton Pickup	740	1470	2450	3350	4900
1-Ton Panel	690	1380	2300	3200	4600
Dely. Van	630	1250	2100	3000	4200

1940 GMC

1940 GMC Pickup Truck (DFW)

SERIES AC-100/AC-150/AC-250/AC-300 — 6-CYLINDER: — New for 1940 was a revised "Quick-Vision" instrument panel, sealed beam headlights and front fender mounted parking lights.

I.D. DATA: Serial number located on right-hand frame side rail at front and on right side of firewall. Starting: AC-100 (113.5 in. w.b.): AC-101-001 and up. AC-150 (123.75 in. w.b.) AC-150: AC-102-001 and up. AC-250: AC-252-001 and up. Engine numbers located crankcase side.

Model	Body Type	Price	Weight	Prod. Total
Series AC-100				
AC-100	½-Ton Chassis 113.5 in. w.b.	460	2285	—
AC-100	½-Ton Chassis Cab 113.5 in. w.b.	557	2675	—
AC-100	½-Ton Pickup 113.5 in. w.b.	590	2910	—
AC-100	½-Ton Panel 113.5 in. w.b.	669	3140	—
AC-100	½-Ton Canopy 113.5 in. w.b.	705	3140	—
AC-100	½-Ton Screen 113.5 in. w.b.	723	3205	—
AC-100	½-Ton Suburban 113.5 in. w.b.	810	3275	—
AC-100	½-Ton Chassis 123.75 in. w.b.	475	2315	—
AC-100	½-Ton Chassis Cab 123.75 in. w.b.	572	2705	—
AC-100	½-Ton Pickup 123.75 in. w.b.	618	2975	—
AC-100	½-Ton Stake 123.75 in. w.b.	643	3255	—
AC-100	½-Ton Panel 123.75 in. w.b.	715	3200	—
Series AC-150				
AC-150	¾-Ton Chassis	535	2515	—
AC-150	¾-Ton Chassis Cab	632	2905	—
AC-150	¾-Ton Pickup	678	3175	—
AC-150	¾-Ton Stake	703	3455	—
AC-150	¾-Ton Panel	775	3400	—
Series AC-250				
AC-250	1-Ton Chassis	555	2760	—
AC-250	1-Ton Chassis Cab	652	3150	—
AC-250	1-Ton Platform	708	3740	—
AC-250	1-Ton Pickup	729	3465	—
AC-250	1-Ton Stake	734	3970	—
AC-250	1-Ton Panel	825	3780	—
AC-250	1-Ton Canopy	866	3740	—
AC-250	1-Ton Screen	886	3825	—

Model	Body Type	Price	Weight	Prod. Total
Series AC-300				
AC-300	1-Ton Chassis	575	3035	—
AC-300	1-Ton Chassis Cab	672	3425	—
AC-300	1-Ton Platform	728	3995	—
AC-300	1-Ton Pickup	753	3740	—
AC-300	1-Ton Stake	754	4245	—
AC-300	1-Ton Panel	845	4055	—
AC-300	1-Ton Canopy	886	4015	—
AC-300	1-Ton Screen	906	4100	—

ENGINE: Inline, OHV. Six-cylinder. Cast iron block. Bore & stroke: 3.5625 in. x 3.8125 in. Displacement: 228 cu. in. Brake H.P.: 80 at 3000 R.P.M. Four main bearings. Hydraulic valve lifters. Carburetor: 1-barrel.

CHASSIS (Series AC-100): Wheelbase: 123.75 in. Tires: 6.50 x 16 in. Wheels: 16 x 4.50 in.

CHASSIS (Series AC-100): Wheelbase: 113.5 in. Tires: 6.00 x 16 in.

CHASSIS (Series AC-150): Wheelbase: 123.75 in.

CHASSIS (Series AC-250/AC-300): Wheelbase: 133 in.

1940 GMC Walk-in Bread Delivery Van (OCW)

1940 GMC Model AC101 ½-ton Pickup Truck (OCW)

1940 GMC Panel Delivery Truck (DFW/LOC)

TECHNICAL: Manual, transmission. Speeds: 3F/1R. Floor mounted gear shift lever. Single dry-disc clutch. Hypoid, semi-floating rear axle. Overall ratio: (AC-100): 4.11:1. Hydraulic, 4-wheel brakes. Pressed steel wheels. 4-speed transmission ($15.40). Right-side wiper ($5.50).

OPTIONS: Front bumper. Rear bumper. Radio. Heater. Clock. Cigar lighter. Radio antenna. Seat covers. Air cleaner ($3.05). Oil filter ($4). Single action shocks ($10.20). Chrome head lamps ($3). Chrome park lamps ($9). DS Guard ($6.50). **Deluxe Chassis Group.** Tire carrier. Available colors: Brewster green, Narva, Ferrara Blue.

HISTORICAL: Calendar year registrations: (all models) 38,841.

Pricing

1940	5	4	3	2	1
Light Duty — (113.5 in. w.b.)					
½-Ton Pickup	840	1680	2800	3900	5600
½-Ton Panel	810	1620	2700	3800	5400
½-Ton Canopy Dely.	830	1650	2750	3850	5500
½-Ton Screen Side Dely.	830	1650	2750	3850	5500
½-Ton Suburban	840	1680	2800	3900	5600
Medium Duty — (123.75 in. w.b.)					
½-Ton Pickup	830	1650	2750	3850	5500
½-Ton Panel	780	1560	2600	3600	5200
½-Ton Stake	720	1450	2400	3300	4800
¾-Ton Pickup	750	1500	2500	3500	5000
¾-Ton Panel	700	1400	2350	3250	4700
¾-Ton Stake	650	1300	2150	3050	4300
Medium Duty — (133 in. w.b.)					
1-Ton Pickup	750	1500	2500	3500	5000
1-Ton Panel	720	1450	2400	3300	4800
1-Ton Canopy Dely.	740	1470	2450	3350	4900
1-Ton Screen Side Dely.	740	1470	2450	3350	4900
1-Ton Stake	620	1230	2050	2900	4100

1941 GMC

1941 GMC Pickup With Stake Sides (DFW/NA)

SERIES CC-100/CC-150/CC-250/CC-260/CC-300 — 6-CYLINDER: — The headlights were moved out onto the fenders for 1941 and now carried the parking lights. Also adopted was a new two-tier grille arrangement highlighted by horizontal bars.

I.D. DATA: Serial number located on right-hand frame side rail at front and on right side of firewall. Starting: CC-100: CC-101-001 and up. CC-100 (125.25 inch wheelbase): CC-102-001 and up. CC-150: CC-152-001 and up. CC-250 (115 inch wheelbase): CCX-250-001 and up. CC-250 (134.50 inch wheelbase) CC-252-001 and up. CC-260: CC-262-001 and up. CC-300: CC-302-001 and up. Engine numbers located crankcase side. Starting: CC-100: A22800001 and up. CC-150: B22800001 and up.

Model	Body Type	Price	Weight	Prod. Total
Series CC-100				
CC-100	½-Ton Chassis	515	2340	—
CC-100	½-Ton Chassis Cab	615	2730	—
CC-100	½-Ton Pickup	648	2965	—
CC-100	½-Ton Pickup Stake	666	3030	—
CC-100	½-Ton Panel	730	3195	—
CC-100	½-Ton Canopy Exppress	765	3195	—
CC-100	½-Ton Screen	790	3260	—
CC-100	½-Ton Suburban	875	3330	—
CC-100	½-Ton Chassis 125.25 in. w.b.	530	2395	—
CC-100	½-Ton Chassis Cab 125.25 in. w.b.	630	2785	—
CC-100	½-Ton Pickup 125.25. in. w.b.	675	3055	—
CC-100	½-Ton Pickup Stake 125.25. in. w.b.	695	3130	—
CC-100	½-Ton Stake 125.25. in. w.b.	700	3335	—
CC-100	½-Ton Panel 125.25. in. w.b.	775	3280	—

Model	Body Type	Price	Weight	Prod. Total
Series CC-150				
CC-150	¾-Ton Chassis	595	2455	—
CC-150	¾-Ton Chassis Cab	695	2845	—
CC-150	¾-Ton Pickup	740	3115	—
CC-150	¾-Ton Pickup Stake	760	3190	—
CC-150	¾-Ton Stake	765	3395	—
CC-150	¾-Ton Panel	840	3340	—
Series CC-250				
CC-250	1-Ton Chassis 115 in. w.b.	620	N/A	—
CC-250	1-Ton Chassis 125.25 in. w.b.	620	N/A	—
CC-250	1-Ton Chassis 134.50 in. w.b.	620	2665	—
CC-250	1-Ton Chassis Cab 134.50 in. w.b.	720	3055	—
CC-250	1-Ton Platform 134.50 in. w.b.	775	3625	—
CC-250	1-Ton Pickup 134.50 in. w.b.	795	3370	—
CC-250	1-Ton Pickup Stake 134.50 in. w.b.	817	3460	—
CC-250	1-Ton Stake 134.50 in. w.b.	800	3875	—
CC-250	1-Ton Panel 134.50 in. w.b.	895	3685	—
CC-250	1-Ton Canopy Express 134.50 in. w.b.	935	3645	—
CC-250	1-Ton Canopy Screen 134.50 in. w.b.	963	3730	—
Series CC-260				
CC-260	1-Ton Chassis	635	2955	—
CC-260	1-Ton Chassis Cab	735	3345	—
CC-260	1-Ton Platform	790	3915	—
CC-260	1-Ton Stake	815	4165	—
CC-260	1-Ton Pickup	810	3660	—
CC-260	1-Ton Pickup Stake	832	3750	—
CC-260	1-Ton Panel	915	3975	—
CC-260	1-Ton Canopy Exp.	955	3935	—
CC-260	1-Ton Canopy Screen	982	4020	—
Series CC-300				
CC-300	1-Ton Chassis	645	3075	—
CC-300	1-Ton Chassis Cab	745	3465	—
CC-300	1-Ton Platform	800	4035	—
CC-300	1-Ton Stake	825	4285	—
CC-300	1-Ton Pickup	820	3780	—
CC-300	1-Ton Pickup Stake	842	3870	—
CC-300	1-Ton Panel	925	4095	—
CC-300	1-Ton Canopy Exp.	965	4055	—
CC-300	1-Ton Canopy Screen	992	4140	—

ENGINE: Inline. OHV. Six-cylinder. Cast iron block. Bore & stroke: 3.5625 in. x 3.8125 in. Displacement: 228 cu. in. Brake H.P.: 80 at 3000 R.P.M. (93 H.P. at 3200 R.P.M. after June 1941.) Four main bearings. Hydraulic valve lifters. Carburetor: one-barrel.

CHASSIS (Series CC-150): Wheelbase: 125.25 in. Tires: 7.00 x 15 in. Wheels: 15 x 5.50 in.

CHASSIS (Series CC-100): Wheelbase: 125.25 in. Tires: 6.50 x 16 in. Wheels: 16 x 4.50 in.

CHASSIS (Series CC-100): Wheelbase: 115 in.

CHASSIS (Series CC-260): Wheelbase: 134.50 in.

CHASSIS (Series CC-250): Wheelbase: 115/125.25/134.5 in.

CHASSIS (Series CC-300): Wheelbase: 134.50 in.

TECHNICAL: Manual transmission. Speeds: 3F/1R. Floor mounted gear shift lever. Single dry-disc clutch. Hypoid, semi-floating rear axle. Overall ratio: (CC-100): 4.11:1, (CC-150): 4.55:1. Hydraulic brakes. Pressed steel wheels. Four-speed transmission ($15.40). Economy engine ($10).

OPTIONS: Front bumper. Rear bumper. Radio. Master heater ($11.55). Clock. Cigar lighter. Radio antenna. Seat covers ($2.50). Air cleaner ($3.10). Oil filter ($4). Defroster ($6.25). Whipcord upholstery ($9.25). Heater and defroster ($17.80). Available colors: Permanent red, Pimpernal, Ferrara blue.

HISTORICAL: Calendar year registrations: (all models) 45,703.

Pricing

1941	5	4	3	2	1
Light-Duty — (115 in. w.b.)					
½-Ton Pickup	870	1750	2900	4100	5800
½-Ton Panel	840	1680	2800	3900	5600
½-Ton Canopy Dely.	850	1700	2850	4000	5700
½-Ton Screenside Dely.	850	1700	2850	4000	5700
½-Ton Suburban	870	1750	2900	4100	5800
½-Ton Stake	750	1500	2500	3500	5000
Light-Duty — (125 in. w.b.)					
½-Ton Pickup	850	1700	2850	4000	5700
½-Ton Panel	830	1650	2750	3850	5500
½-Ton Stake	740	1470	2450	3350	4900

	5	4	3	2	1
Medium-Duty — (125 in. w.b.)					
¾-Ton Pickup	780	1560	2600	3600	5200
¾-Ton Panel	750	1500	2500	3500	5000
¾-Ton Stake	660	1320	2200	3100	4400
Medium-Duty (134 in. w.b.)					
1-Ton Pickup	700	1400	2350	3250	4700
1-Ton Panel	680	1350	2250	3150	4500
1-Ton Canopy Dely.	690	1380	2300	3200	4600
1-Ton Screenside Dely.	690	1380	2300	3200	4600
1-Ton Stake	600	1200	2000	2800	4000

1942 GMC

SERIES CC-100/CC-150/CC-250/CC-260/CC-300 — 6-CYLINDER: — No changes for 1942.

I.D. DATA: Serial number located on right-hand frame side rail at front and on right side of firewall. Starting: CC-100: CC-101-001 and up. CC-100 (125.25 in. w.b.): CC-102-001 and up. CC-150: CC-152-001 and up. CC-250 (115 in. w.b.): CC-251-001 and up. CC-250 (125.25 in. w.b.): CC-252-001 and up CC-250: (134.50 in. w.b.): CC-252-001. CC-260: CC-262-001 and up. CC-300: CC-302-001 and up. Engine numbers located crankcase side.

Model	Body Type	Price	Weight	Prod. Total
Series CC-100				
CC-100	½-Ton Chassis	515	2340	—
CC-100	½-Ton Chassis Cab	615	2730	—
CC-100	½-Ton Pickup	648	2965	—
CC-100	½-Ton Pickup Stake	666	3030	—
CC-100	½-Ton Panel	730	3195	—
CC-100	½-Ton Canopy Exp.	765	3195	—
CC-100	½-Ton Screen	790	3260	—
CC-100	½-Ton Suburban	875	3330	—
CC-100	½-Ton Chassis (125.25 in. w.b.)	530	2395	—
CC-100	½-Ton Chassis Cab (125.25 in. w.b.)	630	2785	—
CC-100	½-Ton Pickup (125.25 in. w.b.)	675	3055	—
CC-100	½-Ton Pickup Stake (125.25 in. w.b.)	695	3130	—
CC-100	½-Ton Stake (125.25 in. w.b.)	700	3335	—
CC-100	½-Ton Panel 125.25 in. w.b.)	775	3280	—
Series CC-150				
CC-150	¾-Ton Chassis	595	2455	—
CC-150	¾-Ton Chassis Cab	695	2845	—
CC-150	¾-Ton Pickup	740	3115	—
CC-150	¾-Ton Pickup Stake	760	3190	—
CC-150	¾-Ton Stake	765	3395	—
CC-150	¾-Ton Panel	840	3340	—
Series CC-250				
CC-250	1-Ton Chassis (115 in. w.b.)	620	2588	—
CC-250	1-Ton Chassis 125.25 in. w.b.	620	2613	—
CC-250	1-Ton Chassis	620	2665	—
CC-250	1-Ton Chassis Cab	720	3055	—
CC-250	1-Ton Platform	775	3625	—
CC-250	1-Ton Pickup	795	3370	—
CC-250	1-Ton Pickup Stake	817	3460	—
CC-250	1-Ton Stake	800	3875	—
CC-250	1-Ton Panel	895	3685	—
CC-250	1-Ton Canopy Exp.	935	3645	—
CC-250	1-Ton Canopy Screen	963	3730	—
Series CC-260				
CC-260	1-Ton Chassis	635	2955	—
CC-260	1-Ton Chassis Cab	735	3345	—
CC-260	1-Ton Platform	790	3915	—
CC-260	1-Ton Stake	815	4165	—
CC-260	1-Ton Pickup	810	3660	—
CC-260	1-Ton Pickup Stake	832	3750	—
CC-260	1-Ton Panel	915	3975	—
CC-260	1-Ton Canopy Exp.	955	3935	—
CC-260	1-Ton Canopy Screen	982	4020	—
Series CC-300				
CC-300	1-Ton Chassis	645	3075	—
CC-300	1-Ton Chassis Cab	745	3465	—
CC-300	1-Ton Platform	800	4035	—
CC-300	1-Ton Stake	825	4285	—
CC-300	1-Ton Pickup	820	3780	—
CC-300	1-Ton Pickup Stake	842	3870	—
CC-300	1-Ton Panel	925	4095	—
CC-300	1-Ton Canopy Exp.	965	4055	—
CC-300	1-Ton Canopy Screen	992	4140	—

ENGINE: Inline, OHV. Six-cylinder. Cast iron block. Bore & stroke: 3.5625 in. x 3.8125 in. Displacement: 228 cu. in. Brake H.P.: 93 at 3200 R.P.M. Four main bearings. Hydraulic valve lifters. Carburetor: 1-barrel.

CHASSIS (Series CC-100): Wheelbase: 115/125.25 in.

CHASSIS (Series CC-150): Wheelbase: 125.25 in.

CHASSIS (Series CC-250): Wheelbase: 115/125.25/134.50 in.

CHASSIS (Series CC-260): Wheelbase: 134.50 in.

CHASSIS (Series CC-300): Wheelbase: 134.50 in.

TECHNICAL: Manual transmission. Speeds: 3F/1R. Floor mounted gear shift lever. Single dry-disc clutch. Hypoid, semi-floating rear axle. Overall ratio: (CC-100): 4.11:1, (CC-150): 4.55:1. Hydraulic, 4 wheel brakes. Pressed steel wheels. 4-speed transmission.

OPTIONS: Front bumper. Rear bumper. Radio. Heater. Clock. Cigar lighter. Radio antenna. Seat covers. Air cleaner. Oil filter. Defroster. Whipcord upholstery.

Pricing

	5	4	3	2	1
1942					
Light Duty					
(115 in. w.b.)					
½-Ton Pickup	870	1750	2900	4100	5800
½-Ton Panel	840	1680	2800	3900	5600
½-Ton Canopy Dely.	850	1700	2850	4000	5700
½-Ton Screenside Dely.	850	1700	2850	4000	5700
½-Ton Suburban	870	1750	2900	4100	5800
½-Ton Stake	750	1500	2500	3500	5000
(125 in. w.b.)					
½-Ton Pickup	850	1700	2850	4000	5700
½-Ton Panel	830	1650	2750	3850	5500
½-Ton Stake	740	1470	2450	3350	4900
Medium Duty					
(125 in. w.b.)					
¾-Ton Pickup	780	1560	2600	3600	5200
¾-Ton Panel	750	1500	2500	3500	5000
¾-Ton Stake	660	1320	2200	3100	4400
(134 in. w.b.)					
1-Ton Pickup	700	1400	2350	3250	4700
1-Ton Panel	680	1350	2250	3150	4500
1-Ton Canopy Dely.	690	1380	2300	3200	4600
1-Ton Screenside Dely.	690	1380	2300	3200	4600
1-Ton Stake	600	1200	2000	2800	4000

1945-1946 GMC

1946 GMC Deluxe Pickup (DSO)

GMC — LIGHT-DUTY — (ALL ENGINES): — GMC resumed production with the light-duty trucks virtually identical to their prewar counterparts. The front grille was characterized by a horizontal bar scheme with the GMC logo prominently displayed on the uppermost section. The headlights extended forward from the fenders and were crowned by torpedo-shaped parking lights. The side hood section carried a long chrome spear bearing "General Motors Truck" lettering.

I.D. DATA: Serial numbers placed on front section of right side frame rail and on engine firewall. Starting: Model CC-101 — CC-101-16726 and up. Model CC-102 — CC-102-16726 and up. Engine numbers located on left side of cylinders block behind oil filler.

Model	Body Type	Price	Weight	Prod. Total
Series CC-101				
CC-101	½-Ton Chassis	651	2340	—
CC-101	½-Ton Chassis & Cab	761	2730	—
CC-101	½-Ton Pickup	805	2965	—
CC-101	½-Ton Panel	887	3195	—
Series CC-102				
CC-102	½-Ton Chassis	666	2395	—
CC-102	½-Ton Chassis & Cab	776	2785	—
CC-102	½-Ton Pickup	832	3055	—

ENGINE: Inline. OHV. Six-cylinder. Cast iron block. Bore & stroke: 3.5625 in. x 3.8125 in. Displacement: 228 cu. in. Brake horsepower: 93. Mechanical valve lifters. Carburetor: 1-barrel.

CHASSIS (Series CC-101): Wheelbase: 115 in. Tires: 15 in. 6-ply.

CHASSIS (Series CC-102): Wheelbase: 125.25 in. Tires: 15 in. 6-ply.

TECHNICAL: Manual synchromesh transmission. Speeds: 3F/1R. Floor mounted gear shift. Single plate, dry disc clutch. Semi-floating rear axle. Hydraulic, 4 wheel brakes. Pressed steel wheels. 4-speed manual transmission ($15).

OPTIONS: Rear bumper. Bumper guards. Radio. Heater. Clock. Cigar lighter. Radio antenna. Seat covers. Spotlight.

HISTORICAL: Calendar year registrations: 25,645 (all series).

Pricing

	5	4	3	2	1
1946					
Light Duty					
(115 in. w.b.)					
½-Ton Pickup	870	1750	2900	4100	5800
½-Ton Panel	840	1680	2800	3900	5600
½-Ton Canopy Dly.	850	1700	2850	4000	5700
½-Ton Screenside Dly.	850	1700	2850	4000	5700
½-Ton Suburban	870	1750	2900	4100	5800
½-Ton Stake	750	1500	2500	3500	5000
(125 in. w.b.)					
½-Ton Pickup	850	1700	2850	4000	5700
½-Ton Panel	830	1650	2750	3850	5500
½-Ton Stake	740	1470	2450	3350	4900
Medium Duty					
(125 in. w.b.)					
¾-Ton Pickup	780	1560	2600	3600	5200
¾-Ton Panel	750	1500	2500	3500	5000
¾-Ton Stake	660	1320	2200	3100	4400
(134 in. w.b.)					
1-Ton Pickup	700	1400	2350	3250	4700
1-Ton Panel	680	1350	2250	3150	4500
1-Ton Canopy Dly.	690	1380	2300	3200	4600
1-Ton Screenside Dly.	690	1380	2300	3200	4600
1-Ton Stake	600	1200	2000	2800	4000

1947 GMC

GMC — LIGHT-DUTY — (ALL ENGINES): — GMC trucks were unchanged from 1946.

I.D. DATA: Unchanged from 1946. Starting: (FC-101) FC-101-001 and up; (FC-102) FC-102-001 and up; (FC-152) FC-152-001 and up; (FC-151) FC-151-001 and up; (FC-252) FC-252-001 and up; (FC-281) FC-281-001 and up; (FC-283) FC-283-001 and up; (CC-101) CC-101-18832 and up; (CC-102) CC-102-18832 and up; (EC-101) EC-101-001 and up; (EC-102) EC-102-001 and up; (EC-152) EC-152-001 and up; (EF-241) EF-241-001 and up; (EF-242) EF-242-001 and up; (EFP-241) EFP-241-001 and up; (EFP-242) EFP-242-001 and up; (EC-251) EC-251-001 and up; (ECX-252) ECX-252-001 and up; (EC-252) EC-252-001 and up; (EC-283) EC-283-001 and up. Engine numbers located: Unchanged from 1946.

Model	Body Type	Price	Weight	Prod. Total
Series FC-101				
FC-101	½-Ton Chassis	845	2580	—
FC-101	½-Ton Chassis Cab	1030	3075	—
FC-101	½-Ton Pickup	1085	3310	—
FC-101	½-Ton Panel	1410	4010	—
FC-101	½-Ton Canopy Exp.	1460	3990	—
FC-101	½-Ton Suburban	1445	—	—
Series FC-102				
FC-102	½-Ton Chassis	865	2560	—
FC-102	½-Ton Chassis Cab	1050	3055	—
FC-102	½-Ton Pickup	1120	3325	—
FC-102	½-Ton Platform	1175	3605	—
Series FC-152				
FC-152	¾-Ton Chassis	940	2820	—
FC-152	¾-Ton Chassis Cab	1125	3315	—
FC-152	¾-Ton Pickup	1195	3585	—
FC-152	¾-Ton Platform	1250	3865	—

Model	Body Type	Price	Weight	Prod. Total
Series FC-251				
FC-251	1-Ton Chassis 116 in. w.b.	985	3165	—
Series FC-252				
FC-252	1-Ton Chassis	1005	3195	—
FC-252	1-Ton Chassis Cab	1190	3690	—
Series FC-253				
FC-253	1-Ton Chassis	1020	3240	—
FC-253	1-Ton Chassis Cab	1205	3735	—
FC-253	1-Ton Pickup	1305	4050	—
FC-253	1-Ton Panel	1645	4835	—
FC-253	1-Ton Platform Stake	1385	4563	—
FC-253	1-Ton Platform	1320	4313	—
FC-253	1-Ton Canopy	1720	4775	—
Series FC-281				
FC-281	1-Ton Chassis	1115	3710	—
FC-281	1-Ton Chassic Cab	1300	4205	—
FC-281	1-Ton Platform Stake	1480	5033	—
FC-281	1-Ton Platform	1415	4783	—
Series FC-283				
FC-283	1-Ton Chassis	1145	3885	—
FC-283	1-Ton Chassis Cab	1330	4380	—
FC-283	1-Ton Platform Stake	1545	5424	—
FC-283	1-Ton Platform	1465	5129	—
FC-283	1-Ton Platform Express	1550	5510	—
Series CC-101				
CC-101	½-Ton Chassis	721	2390	—
CC-101	½-Ton Chassis & Cab	848	2780	—
CC-101	½-Ton Pickup	891	3015	—
CC-101	½-Ton Panel	990	3325	—
Series CC-102				
CC-102	½-Ton Chassis	741	2440	—
CC-102	½-Ton Chassis & Cab	868	2830	—
CC-102	½-Ton Pickup	927	3100	—
Series EC-101				
EC-101	½-Ton Chassis	758	2390	—
EC-101	½-Ton Chassis & Cab	885	2780	—
EC-101	½-Ton Pickup	928	3015	—
EC-101	½-Ton Panel	1029	3325	—
EC-101	½-Ton Canopy Express	1076	3305	—
EC-101	½-Ton Suburban	1219	—	—
Series EC—102				
EC-102	½-Ton Chassis	778	2440	—
EC-102	½-Ton Chassis & Cab	905	2830	—
EC-102	½-Ton Pickup	964	3100	—
EC-102	½-Ton Panel	1089	3405	—
EC-102	½-Ton Stake	1012	3380	—
Series EC-152				
EC-152	¾-Ton Chassis	881	2485	—
EC-152	¾-Ton Chassis & Cab	1008	2875	—
EC-152	¾-Ton Pickup	1067	3145	—
EC-152	¾-Ton Panel	1192	3450	—
EC-152	¾-Ton Stake	1115	3425	—
Series EF-241				
EF-241	1-Ton Parcel Delivery	1995	3120	—
Series EFP-241				
EFP-241	1-Ton Bakers Delivery	2560	3310	—
Series EC-251				
EC-251	1-Ton Chassis	953	3060	—
EC-251	1-Ton Chassis & Cab	1080	3450	—
Series ECX-252				
ECX-252	1-Ton Chassis	953	3100	—
EXC-252	1-Ton Chassis & Cab	1080	3490	—
Series EC-252				
EC-252	1-Ton Chassis	953	3120	—
EC-252	1-Ton Chassis & Cab	1080	3510	—
EC-252	1-Ton Pickup	1179	3825	—
EC-252	1-Ton Panel	1312	4220	—
EC-252	1-Ton Stake	1203	4338	—
EC-252	1-Ton Platform	1170	4088	—
EC-252	1-Ton Canopy Express	1363	4160	—
Series EC-282				
EC-282	1¼-Ton Chassis	935	3510	—
EC-282	1¼-Ton Chassis & Cab	1062	3900	—
EC-282	1¼-Ton Pickup	1161	4215	—
EC-282	1¼-Ton Panel	1294	4610	—
EC-282	1¼-Ton Stake	1185	4728	—
EC-282	1¼-Ton Platform	1152	4478	—
EC-282	1¼-Ton Canopy Express	1345	4550	—
Series EC-283				
EC-283	1¼-Ton Chassis	974	3575	—
EC-283	1¼-Ton Chassis Cab	1101	3965	—
EC-283	1¼-Ton Platform	1215	4714	—
EC-283	1¼-Ton Platform Stake	1268	5009	—
EC-283	1¼-Ton Platform Express	1288	5095	—

ENGINE: Unchanged from 1945-46.

CHASSIS (Series CC-101): Wheelbase: 115 in. Tires: 15, 6-ply.

CHASSIS (Series CC-102): Wheelbase: 125.25 in. Tires: 15, 6-ply.

CHASSIS (Series EC-101): Wheelbase: 115 in. Tires: 15, 6-ply.

CHASSIS (Series EC-102): Wheelbase: 125.25 in. Overall length: 206 in. Tires: 15, 6-ply.

CHASSIS (Series EC-152): Wheelbase: 125.25 in. Overall length: 206 in. Tires: 7.00 x 15.

CHASSIS (Series EF-241): Wheelbase: 102 in. Tires: 7.00 x 16, 6-ply.

CHASSIS (Series EFP-241): Wheelbase: 102 in. Tires: 7.00 x 16, 6-ply.

444

CHASSIS (Series EC-251): Wheelbase: 115 in. Tires: 7.00 x 16, 6-ply.

CHASSIS (Series ECX-252): Wheelbase: 125.50 in. Tires: 7.00 x 16, 6-ply.

CHASSIS (Series EF-242): Wheelbase: 132 in.

CHASSIS (Series EC-282): Wheelbase: 134.25 in.

CHASSIS (Series EC-283): Wheelbase: 160 in.

CHASSIS (Series EC-252): Wheelbase: 134.50 in. Tires: 7.00 x 16, 6-ply.

CHASSIS (Series EC-282): Wheelbase: 134.50 in. Tires: 6.00 x 20, 6-ply.

CHASSIS (Series FC-101): Wheelbase: 116 in. Overall length: 196.575 in.

CHASSIS (Series FC-102): Wheelbase: 125.25 in. Overall length: 206 in.

CHASSIS (Series FC-152): Wheelbase: 125.25 in. Overall length: 206 in.

CHASSIS (Series FC-251): Wheelbase: 116 in. Overall length: 196.575 in.

CHASSIS (Series FC-152): Wheelbase: 125.25 in. Overall length: 206 in.

CHASSIS (Series FC-251): Wheelbase: 116 in. Overall length: 196.575 in.

CHASSIS (Series FC-252): Wheelbase: 125.25 in. Overall length: 206 in.

CHASSIS (Series FC-253): Wheelbase: 137 in. Overall length: 223.875 in.

CHASSIS (Series FC-281): Wheelbase: 137 in. Overall length: 223.875 in.

CHASSIS (Series FC-283): Wheelbase: 161 in. Overall length: 265 in.

TECHNICAL: Unchanged from 1945-46.

OPTIONS: Front bumper. Rear bumper. Bumper guards. Radio. Heater. Clock. Cigar lighter. Radio antenna. Seat covers. Spotlight.

HISTORICAL: Calendar year registrations: 49,187 (all series).

Pricing

1947	5	4	3	2	1
Light Duty					
(115 in. w.b.)					
½-Ton Pickup	870	1750	2900	4100	5800
½-Ton Panel	840	1680	2800	3900	5600
½-Ton Canopy Dely.	850	1700	2850	4000	5700
½-Ton Screenside Dely.	850	1700	2850	4000	5700
½-Ton Suburban	870	1750	2900	4100	5800
½-Ton Stake	750	1500	2500	3500	5000
(125 in. w.b.)					
½-Ton Pickup	850	1700	2850	4000	5700
½-Ton Panel	830	1650	2750	3850	5500
½-Ton Stake	740	1470	2450	3350	4900
Medium Duty					
(125 in. w.b.)					
¾-Ton Pickup	780	1560	2600	3600	5200
¾-Ton Panel	750	1500	2500	3500	5000
¾-Ton Stake	660	1320	2200	3100	4400
(134 in. w.b.)					
1-Ton Pickup	700	1400	2350	3250	4700
1-Ton Panel	680	1350	2250	3150	4500
1-Ton Canopy Dely.	690	1380	2300	3200	4600
1-Ton Screenside Dely.	690	1380	2300	3200	4600
1-Ton Stake	600	1200	2000	2800	4000

1948 GMC

1948 GMC Cantrell Station Wagon (OCW)

GMC — LIGHT-DUTY — (ALL ENGINES): — Mid-way through 1947 GMC introduced totally restyled light-duty trucks. The appearance of these models was attractive, devoid of excess trim, smooth and streamlined. Large GMC lettering was mounted at the top of a simple multi-tiered grille with broad horizontal bars. The headlights were mounted totally within the front fenders and small, circular parking lights were positioned directly below the headlights. Drivers were quick to appreciate the GMC's improved cab ventilation, improved visibility and revamped front suspension system.

I.D. DATA: Serial number located stamped on plate positioned on left door hinge pillar. Starting: (EF-241) EF-241-1559 and up; (EFP-241) EFP-241-1559 and up; (EF-242) EF-242-1559 and up; (EFP-242) EFP242-1559 and up; (FC-101) FC-101-2430 and up; (FC-102) FC-102-2430 and up; (FC-152) FC-152-601 and up; (FC-251) FC-251-517 and up; (FC-252) FC-252-517 and up; (FC-253) FC-253-517 and up. Engine numbers located on left-side of cylinder block behind oil filter. Starting: A24869253, C24875484, B270745183.

1948 GMC Suburban Carryall (OCW)

Model	Body Type	Price	Weight	Prod. Total
Series FC-101				
FC-101	½-Ton Chassis	915	2580	—
FC-101	½-Ton Chassis & Cab	1135	3065	—
FC-101	½-Ton Pickup	1200	3330	—
FC-101	½-Ton Panel	1385	3500	—
FC-101	½-Ton Canopy Express	1435	3500	—
FC-101	½-Ton Suburban	1015	—	—
Series FC-102				
FC-102	½-Ton Chassis	935	2560	—
FC-102	½-Ton Chassis & Cab	1155	3045	—
FC-102	½-Ton Pickup	1240	3335	—
FC-102	½-Ton Stake	1300	3660	—
Series FC-152				
FC-152	¾-Ton Chassis	1025	2820	—
FC-152	¾-Ton Chassis & Cab	1245	3305	—
FC-152	¾-Ton Pickup	1330	3595	—
FC-152	¾-Ton Stake	1390	3910	—
Series EF-241				
EF-241	1-Ton Package Delivery	2595	3120	—
Series EF-242				
EF-242	1¼-Ton Package Delivery	2870	3330	—
Series EFP-241				
EFP-241	1-Ton Package Delivery	2760	3310	—
Series FC-251				
FC-251	1-Ton Chassis	1095	3165	—
Series FC-252				
FC-252	1-Ton Chassis	1115	3195	—
FC-252	1-Ton Chassis & Cab	1335	3680	—
Series FC-253				
FC253	1-Ton Chassis	1130	3240	—
FC-253	1-Ton Chassis & Cab	1350	3725	—
FC-253	1-Ton Pickup	1460	4055	—
FC-253	1-Ton Platform	1475	4260	—
FC-253	1-Ton Stake	1550	4510	—
FC-253	1-Ton Panel	1620	4335	—
FC-253	1-Ton Canopy Express	1695	4340	—

ENGINE: Inline, OHV. 6-cylinder. Cast iron block. Bore & stroke: 3.5625 x 3.8125 in. Displacement: 228 cu. in. Brake horsepower: 93. Mechanical valve lifters. Carburetor: Carter 1-barrel.

CHASSIS (Series FC-101): Wheelbase: 116 in. Overall length: 196.575 in. Tires: 6.00 x 16, 6-ply.

CHASSIS (Series FC-102): Wheelbase: 125.25 in. Overall length: 206 in. Tires: 6.00 x 16, 6-ply.

CHASSIS (Series FC-152): Wheelbase: 125.25 in. Overall length: 206 in. Tires: 15, 6-ply.

CHASSIS (Series EF-241): Wheelbase: 102 in. Tires: 7.00 x 16, 6-ply.

CHASSIS (Series EF-242): Wheelbase: 132 in. Tires: 8.25 x 16, 10-ply.

CHASSIS (Series EFP-241): Wheelbase: 102 in. Tires: 7.00 x 16, 6-ply.

1948 GMC EC-102 ½-Ton Pickup (LS)

CHASSIS (Series FC-251): Wheelbase: 116 in. Overall length: 196.575 in. Tires: 7.00 x 17, 6-ply.

CHASSIS (Series FC-252): Wheelbase: 125.25 in. Overall length: 206 in. Tires: 7.00 x 17, 6-ply.

CHASSIS (Series FC-253): Wheelbase: 137 in. Overall length: 224.125 in. Tires: 7.00 x 17, 6-ply.

TECHNICAL: Manual, synchromesh. Speeds: 3F/1R. Floor-mounted gearshift. Clutch: Single disc, diaphragm spring. Semi-floating (½-ton), full-floating (all others) rear axle. Overall ratio: 4.11.1 (FC-101). Hydraulic, 4-wheel brakes. Pressed steel wheels.

DRIVETRAIN OPTIONS: 4-speed manual transmission ($50). Oil bath air filter ($3.50). AC oil filter ($10). Vacuum pump on fuel pump ($8). Double action front shock absorbers ($10). Double action rear shock absorbers ($10).

OPTIONS: Rear bumper. Bumper guards. Radio. Heater. Clock. Cigar lighter. Radio antenna. Seat covers. Chrome radiator grille ($10).

HISTORICAL: Introduced: Summer, 1947. Calendar year registrations: 74,857 (all series).

1948 GMC Panel Delivery (DSO)

Pricing

1948	5	4	3	2	1
Series FC-101					
Pickup	1080	2160	3600	5050	7200
Panel	1000	2000	3300	4600	6600
Canopy Express	1010	2030	3350	4700	6700
Suburban	1020	2050	3400	4800	6800
Series FC-102)					
Pickup	1020	2050	3400	4800	6800
Stake	900	1800	3000	4200	6000
Series FC-152					
Pickup	980	1950	3250	4550	6500
Stake	920	1850	3050	4300	6100
Series EF-214					
Package Delivery	900	1800	3000	4200	6000
Series EF-242					
Package Delivery	870	1750	2900	4100	5800
Series EFP-241					
Package Delivery	840	1680	2800	3900	5600
Series FC-253					
Pickup	930	1860	3100	4350	6200
Platform	870	1750	2900	4100	5800
Stake	890	1770	2950	4150	5900
Panel	900	1800	3000	4200	6000
Canopy Express	920	1850	3050	4300	6100

445

1949 GMC

GMC — LIGHT-DUTY — (ALL ENGINES): — GMC trucks were unchanged from 1948.

I.D. DATA: Serial number located unchanged from 1948. Starting: FC-152-181-314, Oakland 601-605. EF-241 and EFP-241-3983 and up. FC-101-25887-64000. FC-102-25887-64000. FC-152-6885-20200. FC-251-8076-19101. FC-252-8076-19101. FC-253-8076-19101. Engine number location unchanged from 1948.

Model	Body Type	Price	Weight	Prod. Total
Series FC-101				
FC-101	½-Ton Chassis	985	2580	—
FC-101	½-Ton Chassis & Cab	1210	3065	—
FC-101	½-Ton Pickup	1275	3330	—
FC-101	½-Ton Panel	1455	3985	—
FC-101	½-Ton Canopy Express	1505	3985	—
FC-101	½-Ton Suburban	1685	—	—
Series FC-102				
FC-102	½-Ton Chassis	1005	2560	—
FC-102	½-Ton Chassis & Cab	1230	3045	—
FC-102	½-Ton Pickup	1315	3335	—
FC-102	½-Ton Stake	1375	3660	—
Series FC-152				
FC-152	¾-Ton Chassis	1080	2820	—
FC-152	¾-Ton Chassis & Cab	1305	3305	—
FC-152	¾-Ton Pickup	1390	3595	—
FC-152	¾-Ton Stake	1450	3910	—
Series FP-152				
FP-152	1-Ton Chassis Delivery	1095	2575	—
Series EF-241				
EF-241	1-Ton Delivery	2840	3120	—
Series EF-242				
EF-242	1¼-Ton Delivery	3115	3330	—
Series EFP-241				
EFP-241	1-Ton Delivery	—	3310	—
Series EFP-242				
EFP-242	1¼-Ton Delivery	—	3450	—
Series FC-251				
FC-251	1-Ton Chassis	1150	3165	—
Series FC-252				
FC-252	1-Ton Chassis	1150	3195	—
FC-252	1-Ton Chassis & Cab	1375	3680	—
Series FC-253				
FC-253	1-Ton Chassis	1150	3240	—
FC-253	1-Ton Chassis & Cab	1375	3725	—
FC-253	1-Ton Pickup	1485	4055	—
FC-253	1-Ton Panel	1665	4820	—
FC-253	1-Ton Stake	1575	4510	—
FC-253	1-Ton Platform	1500	4260	—
FC-253	1-Ton Canopy Express	1740	4825	—

ENGINE: Unchanged from 1948.

CHASSIS: Unchanged from 1948.

TECHNICAL: Unchanged from 1948.

OPTIONS: Rear bumper. Bumper guards. Radio. Heater. Clock. Cigar lighter. Radio antenna. Seat covers. Chromed bumper.

HISTORICAL: Calendar year registrations: 80,407 (all series).

Pricing

	5	4	3	2	1
1949					
Series FC-101					
Pickup	1080	2160	3600	5050	7200
Panel	1000	2000	3300	4600	6600
Canopy Express	1010	2030	3350	4700	6700
Suburban	1020	2050	3400	4800	6800
Series FC-102					
Pickup	1020	2050	3400	4800	6800
Stake	900	1800	3000	4200	6000
Series FC-152					
Pickup	980	1950	3250	4550	6500
Stake	920	1850	3050	4300	6100
Series EF-214					
Package Delivery	900	1800	3000	4200	6000
Series EF-242					
Package Delivery	870	1750	2900	4100	5800
Series EFP-241					
Package Delivery	840	1680	2800	3900	5600
Series FC-253					
Pickup	930	1860	3100	4350	6200
Platform	870	1750	2900	4100	5800
Stake	890	1770	2950	4150	5900
Panel	900	1800	3000	4200	6000
Canopy Express	920	1850	3050	4300	6100

1950 GMC

1950 GMC Pickup (DFW)

GMC — LIGHT-DUTY — (ALL ENGINES): — No physical changes were made in the GMC light-truck line for 1950. However, the 228 cu. in. six-cylinder engine was increased in horsepower to 96.

I.D. DATA: Serial number location unchanged from 1949. Engine numbers location unchanged from 1949.

Model	Body Type	Price	Weight	Prod. Total
Series FC-101				
FC-101	½-Ton Chassis	975	2550	—
FC-101	½-Ton Chassis & Cab	1200	2980	—
FC-101	½-Ton Pickup	1265	—	—
FC-101	½-Ton Panel	1445	—	—
FC-101	½-Ton Canopy Express	1495	—	—
FC-101	½-Ton Suburban	1675	—	—
Series FC-102				
FC-102	½-Ton Chassis	995	2540	—
FC-102	½-Ton Chassis & Cab	1220	2970	—
FC-102	½-Ton Pickup	1305	—	—
FC-102	½-Ton Stake	1365	—	—
Series FC-152				
FC-152	¾-Ton Chassis	1070	2775	—
FC-152	¾-Ton Chassis & Cab	1295	3225	—
FC-152	¾-Ton Pickup	1380	—	—
FC-152	¾-Ton Stake	1440	—	—
Series FP-152				
FP-152	¾-Ton Chassis Delivery	—	2515	—
Series FC-251				
FC-251	1-Ton Chassis	—	3000	—
Series FC-252				
FC-252	1-Ton Chassis	—	3040	—
FC-252	1-Ton Chassis & Cab	—	3490	—
Series FC-253				
FC-253	1-Ton Chassis	—	3084	—
FC-253	1-Ton Chassis & Cab	—	3535	—
Series FC-281				
FC-281	1-Ton Chassis	1210	3460	—
FC-281	1-Ton Chassis & Cab	1435	3905	—
FC-281	1-Ton Platform	1560	—	—
FC-281	1-Ton Stake	1635	—	—

ENGINE: Inline. OHV. 6-cylinder. Cast iron block. Bore & stroke: 3.5625 x 3.8125 in. Displacement: 228 cu. in. Brake horsepower: 96 at 3200 R.P.M. Mechanical valve lifters. Carburetor: Carter 1-barrel.

1950 GMC Forward Control Step-Van (RPZ)

1950 GMC Panel Delivery (DFW/ATA)

CHASSIS (Series FC-101): Wheelbase: 116 in. Overall length: 196.575 in. Tires: 6.00 x 16, 6-ply.

CHASSIS (Series FC-102): Wheelbase: 125.25 in. Overall length: 206 in. Tires: 6.00 x 16, 6-ply.

CHASSIS (Series FC-152): Wheelbase: 125.25 in. Overall length: 206 in. Tires: 15, 6-ply.

CHASSIS (Series FC-152): Wheelbase: 125.25 in. Overall length: 206 in. Tires: 15, 6-ply.

CHASSIS (Series FC-250): Wheelbase: 116/125.25/137 in. Overall length: 196.575-206 x 223.875 in. Tires: 7.00 x 17, 6-ply.

CHASSIS (Series FC-281): Wheelbase: 137 in. Overall length: 223.875 in. Tires: 7.00 x 20, 8-ply.

TECHNICAL: Manual, synchromesh. Speeds: 3F/1R. Floor-mounted gearshift. Single disc, diaphragm spring clutch. Semi-floating (½-ton), full-floating (all others) rear axle. Hydraulic, 4-wheel brakes. Pressed steel wheels.

DRIVETRAIN OPTIONS: 4-speed manual transmission. Oil bath. Oil filter. AC oil filter. Vacuum pump on fuel pump. Double action front and rear shock absorbers.

OPTIONS: Rear bumper. Bumper guards. Radio. Heater. Clock. Cigar lighter. Radio antenna. Seat covers. Chrome radiator grille.

HISTORICAL: Calendar year registrations: 97,200 (all series). Innovations: more powerful six-cylinder engine introduced.

1950 GMC Stand-up Milk Delivery Van (DFW/GHB)

Pricing

	5	4	3	2	1
1950					
Series FC-101					
Pickup	1080	2160	3600	5050	7200
Panel	1000	2000	3300	4600	6600
Canopy Express	1010	2030	3350	4700	6700
Suburban	1020	2050	3400	4800	6800
Series FC-102					
Pickup	1020	2050	3400	4800	6800
Stake	900	1800	3000	4200	6000
Series FC-152					
Pickup	980	1950	3250	4550	6500
Stake	920	1850	3050	4300	6100
Series EF-214					
Pkg Delivery	900	1800	3000	4200	6000
Series EF-242					
Pkg Delivery	870	1750	2900	4100	5800
Series EFP-241					
Pkg Delivery	840	1680	2800	3900	5600
Series FC-253					
Pickup	930	1860	3100	4350	6200
Platform	870	1750	2900	4100	5800
Stake	890	1770	2950	4150	5900
Panel	900	1800	3000	4200	6000
Canopy Express	920	1850	3050	4300	6100

1951 GMC Panel Delivery (OCW)

GMC — LIGHT-DUTY — (ALL ENGINES): — Unchanged from 1950.

I.D. DATA: Serial number location unchanged from 1950. Engine number location unchanged from 1950.

Model	Body Type	Price	Weight	Prod. Total
Series 100-22				
101-22	½-Ton Chassis	1025	2615	—
101-22	½-Ton Chassis & Cab	1265	3045	—
101-22	½-Ton Pickup	1330	3275	—
101-22	½-Ton Panel	1510	3575	—
101-22	½-Ton Canopy Express	1560	3540	—
101-22	½-Ton Suburban	1702	3860	—
102-22	½-Ton Chassis	1045	2610	—
102-22	½-Ton Chassis & Cab	1285	3040	—
102-22	½-Ton Pickup	1370	3365	—
102-22	½-Ton Stake Rack	1435	3655	—
152-22	¾-Ton Chassis	1150	2870	—
152-22	¾-Ton Chassis & Cab	1390	3320	—
152-22	¾-Ton Pickup	1475	3640	—
152-22	¾-Ton Stake Rack	1540	3925	—
P152-22	¾-Ton Chassis Delivery	1170	2550	—
Series 250-22				
252-22	1-Ton Chassis	1222	3130	—
252-22	1-Ton Chassis & Cab	1462	3580	—
253-22	1-Ton Chassis	1222	3170	—
253-22	1-Ton Chassis & Cab	1462	3620	—
253-22	1-Ton Panel	1762	4385	—
253-22	1-Ton Pickup	1572	4105	—
253-22	1-Ton Platform	1587	4165	—
253-22	1-Ton Stake Rack	1652	4395	—
253-22	1-Ton Canopy Express	1837	4410	—

ENGINE: Inline. OHV. 6-cylinder. Cast iron block. Bore & stroke: 3.5625 x 3.8125 in. Displacement: 228 cu. in. Brake horsepower: 100 at 3400 R.P.M.

CHASSIS (Series 100-22): Wheelbase: 116/125.25 in. Overall length: 197/206 in. Tires: 6.00 x 16, 6-ply.

1951 GMC Forward Control Step-Van (RPZ)

447

CHASSIS (Series 250-22): Wheelbase: 125.25/137 in. Overall length: 206/224 in. Tires: 7.00 x 17, 6-ply.

TECHNICAL: Manual synchromesh transmission. Speeds: 3F/1R. Floor mount gearshift. Single disc, diaphragm spring clutch. Semi-floating (½-Ton), full-floating (all others) rear axles. Hydraulic, four-wheel brakes. Pressed steel wheels.

DRIVETRAIN OPTIONS: Option list unchanged from 1950.

OPTIONS: Rear bumper. Bumper guards. Radio. Heater. Clock. Cigar lighter. Radio antenna. Seat covers. Chrome grille.

HISTORICAL: Calendar year registrations: 100,285 (all series). Innovations: horsepower of the GMC 228 cu. in. engine increased to 100.

Pricing

	5	4	3	2	1
1951					
Series 100-22					
½-Ton Pickup	1080	2160	3600	5050	7200
½-Ton Panel	1000	2000	3300	4600	6600
½-Ton Canopy Express	1010	2030	3350	4700	6700
½-Ton Suburban	1020	2050	3400	4800	6800
Series 150-22					
¾-Ton Pickup	1020	2050	3400	4800	6800
¾-Ton Stake	900	1800	3000	4200	6000
1-Ton Pickup	980	1950	3250	4550	6500
1-Ton Stake	920	1850	3050	4300	6100
½-Ton Package Delivery	900	1800	3000	4200	6000
¾-Ton Package Delivery	870	1750	2900	4100	5800
1-Ton Package Delivery	840	1680	2800	3900	5600
1-Ton Pickup	930	1860	3100	4350	6200
1-Ton Platform	870	1750	2900	4100	5800
1-Ton Stake	890	1770	2950	4150	5900
1-Ton Panel	900	1800	3000	4200	6000
1-Ton Canopy Express	920	1850	3050	4300	6100

1952 GMC

1952 GMC Model 100 Deluxe ½-Ton Pickup (GMC)

GMC — LIGHT-DUTY — (ALL ENGINES): — Unchanged from 1951.

I.D. DATA: Serial number stamped on plate located on left door hinge pillar. Engine number located on left side of cylinder block behind oil filler.

1952 GMC "Big Window" Deluxe Cab Pickup (DFW)

448

1952 GMC Deluxe ½-Ton Pickup (RPZ)

Model	Body Type	Price	Weight	Prod. Total
Series FC-100-22				
101-22	½-Ton Chassis	1073	2640	—
101-22	½-Ton Chassis & Cab	1317	3105	—
101-22	½-Ton Pickup	1385	3365	—
101-22	½-Ton Panel	1566	3575	—
101-22	½-Ton Canopy Express	1617	3555	—
101-22	½-Ton Suburban	1826	3890	—
Series 102-22				
102-22	½-Ton Chassis	1094	2635	—
102-22	½-Ton Chassis & Cab	1338	3100	—
102-22	½-Ton Pickup	1427	3465	—
102-22	½-Ton Stake Rack	1496	3705	—
Series P152-22				
P152-22	¾-Ton Chassis	1204	2845	—
P152-22	¾-Ton Chassis & Cab	1448	3330	—
P152-22	¾-Ton Pickup	1537	3095	—
P152-22	¾-Ton Stake Rack	1606	3915	—
P152-22	¾-Ton Chassis Delivery .	1225	—	—
Series PM-152-22				
PM152-22	¾-Ton Chassis Delivery	1380	2695	—
Series 250-22				
252-22	1-Ton Chassis (125.25 in. w.b.)	1282	3110	—
252-22	1-Ton Chassis & Cab	1526	3595	—
Series 253-22				
253-22	1-Ton Chassis (137 in. w.b.)	1282	3135	—
253-22	1-Ton Chassis & Cab (137 in. w.b.)	1526	3620	—
253-22	1-Ton Panel	1641	4355	—
253-22	1-Ton Pickup	1657	4130	—
253-22	1-Ton Platform	1725	4170	—
253-22	1-Ton Stake Rack	1831	4405	—
253-22	1-Ton Canopy Express	1907	4300	—

ENGINE: Unchanged from 1957.

CHASSIS (Series 100-22): Wheelbase: 116/125.25 in. Overall length: 196.575 x 206 in. Tires: 6.00 x 16, 6-ply.

CHASSIS (Series 250-22): Wheelbase: 125.25/137 in. Overall length: 206 x 223.875 in. Tires: 7.00 x 17, 6-ply.

TECHNICAL: Unchanged from 1951.

OPTIONS: Rear bumper. Bumper guards. Radio. Heater. Clock. Cigar lighter. Radio antenna. Seat covers. Chrome grille.

HISTORICAL: Calendar year registrations: 79,612 (all series).

1952 GMC Model 101-22 ½-Ton Pickup (RLH)

Pricing

1952	5	4	3	2	1
Series 100-22					
½-Ton Pickup	1080	2160	3600	5050	7200
½-Ton Panel	1000	2000	3300	4600	6600
½-Ton Canopy Express	1010	2030	3350	4700	6700
½-Ton Suburban	1020	2050	3400	4800	6800
Series 150-22					
¾-Ton Pickup	1020	2050	3400	4800	6800
¾-Ton Stake	900	1800	3000	4200	6000
1-Ton Pickup	980	1950	3250	4550	6500
1-Ton Stake	920	1850	3050	4300	6100
½-Ton Package Delivery	900	1800	3000	4200	6000
¾-Ton Package Delivery	870	1750	2900	4100	5800
1-Ton Package Delivery	840	1680	2800	3900	5600
1-Ton Pickup	930	1860	3100	4350	6200
1-Ton Platform	870	1750	2900	4100	5800
1-Ton Stake	890	1770	2950	4150	5900
1-Ton Panel	900	1800	3000	4200	6000
1-Ton Canopy Express	920	1850	3050	4300	6100

1953 GMC

1953 GMC Pickup (CW)

GMC — LIGHT-DUTY — (ALL ENGINES): — The GMC light-duty trucks would be extensively restyled in 1954. But the big news for 1953 was the availability of a 4-speed Hydra-Matic transmission option. This transmission, which was available on all ½-Ton to 1½-Ton models was standard on the GMC Package Delivery model.
   Models with automatic transmission carried Hydra-Matic identification plates on their side hood panels.

I.D. DATA: Vehicle Serial number is found on a plate positioned on left door hinge pillars. Engine number located on left side of cylinder block behind oil filler.

1953 GMC Navy Survey Panel (D. Russel/CPC)

Model	Body Type	Price	Weight	Prod. Total
Series 100-22				
101-22	½-Ton Chassis & Cowl	1073	2615	—
101-22	½-Ton Chassis & Cab	1317	3080	—
101-22	½-Ton Pickup	1385	3340	—
101-22	½-Ton Panel	1566	3550	—
101-22	½-Ton Canopy Express	1617	3530	—
101-22	½-Ton Suburban	1834	3865	—
102-22	½-Ton Chassis & Cowl	1094	2610	—
102-22	½-Ton Chassis & Cab	1338	3075	—
102-22	½-Ton Pickup	1427	3440	—
102-22	½-Ton Stake Rack	1496	3680	—
Series 150-22				
152-22	¾-Ton Chassis & Cowl	1204	2825	—
152-22	¾-Ton Chassis & Cab	1448	3310	—
152-22	¾-Ton Pickup	1537	3675	—
152-22	¾-Ton Stake Rack	1606	3895	—
Series PM-150-22				
152-22	¾-Ton Chassis Package Delivery	1380	2080	—
Series 250-22				
252-22	1-Ton Chassis & Cowl	1282	3090	—
252-22	1-Ton Chassis & Cab	1526	3575	—
253-22	1-Ton Chassis & Cowl	1282	3115	—
253-22	1-Ton Chassis & Cab	1526	3600	—
253-22	1-Ton Pickup	1641	4110	—
253-22	1-Ton Platform	1657	4150	—
253-22	1-Ton Stake Rack	1725	4385	—
253-22	1-Ton Panel	1831	4335	—
253-22	1-Ton Canopy Express	1907	4260	—

ENGINE: Unchanged from 1952.

CHASSIS Unchanged from 1952.

TECHNICAL: Unchanged from 1952 except for availability of Hydra-Matic.

DRIVETRAIN OPTIONS: Dual Range Hydra-Matic (standard Model PM-152-22) transmission.

OPTIONS: Rear bumper. Bumper guards. Radio. Heater. Clock. Cigar lighter. Radio antenna. Seat covers. Chrome grille.

HISTORICAL: Calendar year registrations: 82,296 (all series).

1953 GMC Pickup w/modern wheels and tires (DFW)

Pricing

1953	5	4	3	2	1
Series 100-22					
½-Ton Pickup	1080	2160	3600	5050	7200
½-Ton Panel	1000	2000	3300	4600	6600
½-Ton Canopy Express	1010	2030	3350	4700	6700
½-Ton Suburban	1020	2050	3400	4800	6800
Series 150-22					
¾-Ton Pickup	1020	2050	3400	4800	6800
¾-Ton Stake	900	1800	3000	4200	6000
1-Ton Pickup	980	1950	3250	4550	6500
1-Ton Stake	920	1850	3050	4300	6100
½-Ton Package Delivery	900	1800	3000	4200	6000
¾-Ton Package Delivery	870	1750	2900	4100	5800
1-Ton Package Delivery	840	1680	2800	3900	5600
1-Ton Pickup	930	1860	3100	4350	6200
1-Ton Platform	870	1750	2900	4100	5800
1-Ton Stake	890	1770	2950	4150	5900
1-Ton Panel	900	1800	3000	4200	6000
1-Ton Canopy Express	920	1850	3050	4300	6100

1954 GMC "Big Window" Deluxe Cab Pickup (OCW)

GMC — LIGHT-DUTY — (ALL ENGINES): — GMC trucks were given their most extensive styling revision since 1948. The familiar GMC grille format was continued, but it was much broader and included rectangular parking lights in its design. Also found on the 1954 model was a one-piece windshield.

The power rating of the 248.5 cu. in. six was increased to 125 horsepower and was the new standard engine for the light-duty GMC models.

I.D. DATA: Serial number location unchanged from 1943. Engine number location unchanged from 1953.

Model	Body Type	Price	Weight	Prod. Total
Series 100-24 — 116/125.25 in. w.b.				
101-24	½-Ton Chassis Cowl (SWB)	—	—	—
101-24	½-Ton Chassis Cab (SWB)	1317	3085	—
101-24	½-Ton Pickup (SWB)	1385	3355	—
101-24	½-Ton Pickup (SWB)	1385	3355	—
101-24	½-Ton Panel (SWB)	1566	3535	—
101-24	½-Ton Canopy (SWB)	1617	3485	—
101-24	½-Ton Suburban (LWB)	1890	3820	—
102-24	½-Ton Chassis Cowl (LWB)	—	—	—
102-24	½-Ton Chassis Cab (LWB)	1338	3080	—
102-24	½-Ton Pickup (LWB)	1427	3370	—
102-24	½-Ton Stake Rack (LWB)	—	—	—
Series 150-24				
152-24	¾-Ton Chassis Cowl	—	—	—
152-24	¾-Ton Chassis Cab	1448	3370	—
152-24	¾-Ton Pickup	1537	3720	—
152-24	¾-Ton Stake Rack	1606	4010	—
Series PM-150-24				
PM-152 -24	¾-Ton Chassis Package Delivery	1380	2665	—
Series 250-24				
252-24	1-Ton Chassis Cowl	—	—	—
252-24	1-Ton Chassis Cab	1526	3660	—
252-24	1-Ton Chassis Cowl	—	—	—
253-24	1-Ton Platform	1657	4260	—
253-24	1-Ton Stake Rack	1725	4530	—
253-24	1-Ton Panel	1831	4325	—
253-24	1-Ton Canopy Express	1907	4270	—

Note 1: A Deluxe ½-Ton Panel was available for $1,615. A Deluxe one-ton panel was also available for $1,831.

1954 GMC ½-Ton Pickup (GMC)

1954 GMC Deluxe ½-Ton Pickup (Rick Schissler)

ENGINE: Inline. OHV. 6-cylinder. Cast iron block. Bore & stroke: 3.718 x 3.08 in. Displacement: 248.5 cu. in. Brake horsepower: 125. Hydraulic valve lifters. Carburetor: 1-barrel.

CHASSIS Unchanged from 1953.

TECHNICAL: Unchanged from 1953.

OPTIONS: Rear bumper. Bumper guards. Radio. Heater. Clock. Cigar lighter. Radio antenna. Seat covers. External sun shade. Spotlight. Chrome grille.

HISTORICAL: Calendar year registrations: 66,644 (all series).

Pricing

	5	4	3	2	1
1954					
Series 100-22					
Pickup	1140	2280	3800	5300	7600
Panel	1020	2050	3400	4800	6800
Canopy Delivery	1040	2070	3450	4850	6900
Suburban	1050	2100	3500	4900	7000
Pickup (LWB)	1110	2220	3700	5200	7400
Stake Rack	1000	2000	3300	4600	6600
Series 150-22					
Pickup	1020	2050	3400	4800	6800
Stake Rack	950	1900	3150	4400	6300
Series 250-22					
Pickup	980	1950	3250	4550	6500
Platform	900	1800	3000	4200	6000
Stake Rack	920	1850	3050	4300	6000
Panel	950	1900	3150	4400	6300
Canopy Express	960	1920	3200	4500	6400

1955 GMC

1955 GMC ½-Ton Custom Cab Stepside Pickup (GMC)

GMC — LIGHT-DUTY — (ALL ENGINES): — GMC introduced both new styling and a new V-8 engine (actually a Pontiac V-8) in 1955. The first significant change since 1947 was dramatic. The front end featured a two-bar grille format suggesting that of the 1954 Oldsmobile. Hooded headlights and a bumper with protruding circular guards reflected styling themes that had earlier been associated with Cadillac. No hood ornament was fitted. Following tradition, GMC lettering, more stylized than ever, was mounted on the lower hood surface. For 1955 it was positioned in an oblong cove with a gridwork background. The use of a panoramic windshield and backlight substantially increased the glass area of the GMC pickups. The higher front fender line extended back through the full length of the cab. Joining the GMC truck line was the Suburban, GMC's version of the Chevrolet Cameo pickup.

I.D. DATA: Serial number located inside cab or on truck firewall. Stamped on this "GMC Service Parts Identification" plate was the model of the engine, transmission, service brake and axle. Engine numbers located: 6-cylinder: on leftside of cylinder block behind oil filler.

Model	Body Type	Price	Weight	Prod. Total
Series 100 — (114 in. w.b.)				
101	½-Ton Chassis Cab	1398	3025	—
101	½-Ton Pickup	1488	3375	—
101	½-Ton Panel	1753	3605	—
101	½-Ton Delivery Panel	1823	3605	—
101	½-Ton Suburban Pickup	1923	3535	—
101	½-Ton Suburban	2076	3830	—
Series 102 — (123.25 in. w.b.)				
102	½-Ton Chassis Cab	1419	3070	—
102	½-Ton Pickup	1519	3450	—
102	½-Ton Stake Rack	1604	3665	—
Series 100-8 — (114 in. w.b.)				
101-8	½-Ton Chassis Cab	1498	3135	—
101-8	½-Ton Chassis Cab	1498	3135	—
101-8	½-Ton Pickup	1588	3485	—
101-8	½-Ton Panel	1853	3715	—
101-8	½-Ton Delivery Panel	1923	3715	—
101-8	½-Ton Suburban	2176	3940	—
101-8	½-Ton Suburban Pickup	2023	3645	—
Series 102-8 (123.25 in. w.b.)				
102-8	½-Ton Chassis Cab	1519	3180	—
102-8	½-Ton Pickup	1619	3560	—
102-8	½-Ton Stake Rack	1704	3775	—
Series 150				
152	¾-Ton Chassis Cab	1549	3370	—
152	¾-Ton Pickup	1649	3750	—
152	¾-Ton Stake Rack	1734	3965	—
Series 150-8				
152-8	¾-Ton Chassis Cab	1649	3480	—
152-8	¾-Ton Pickup	1749	3860	—
152-8	¾-Ton Stake Rack	1834	4075	—
Series PM-150				
PM-151	¾-Ton Chassis (104 in. w.b.)	1499	2865	—
PM-152	¾-Ton Chassis (125 in. w.b.)	1499	2925	—
PM-153	¾-Ton Chassis (137 in. w.b.)	1499	2945	—
Series 250				
251	1-Ton Chassis Cab (114 in. w.b.)	1653	3605	—
252	1-Ton Chassis & Cab (123.25 in. w.b.)	1653	3630	—
253	1-Ton Chassis & Cab (135 in. w.b.)	1653	3670	—
253	1-Ton Pickup	1778	4120	—
253	1-Ton Platform	1793	4235	—
253	1-Ton Stake Rack	1873	4510	—
253	1-Ton Panel	2053	4355	—
253	1-Ton Delivery Panel	2123	4355	—
Series 250-8				
251	1-Ton Chassis Cab (114 in. w.b.)	1753	3715	—
252	1-Ton Chassis Cab (123.25 in. w.b.)	1753	3740	—
253	1-Ton Chassis Cab (135 in. w.b.)	1753	3780	—
253	1-Ton Pickup (135 in. w.b.)	1878	4230	—
253	1-Ton Platform	1893	4345	—
253	1-Ton Stake Rack	1973	4620	—
253	1-Ton Panel	2153	4465	—
253	1-Ton Delivery Panel	2223	4465	—
Series PM-250 (Forward Control)				
PM-251	¾-Ton Chassis (104 in. w.b.)	1601	2935	—
PM-252	¾-Ton Chassis (125 in. w.b.)	1601	3000	—
PM-253	¾-Ton Chassis (137 in. w.b.)	1601	3015	—

ENGINE (Standard: Series 100, 150, PM-150, 250, PM-250): Inline. OHV. 6-cylinder. Cast iron block. Bore & stroke: 3.71875 x 3.8125 in. Displacement: 248 cu. in. Compression: 7.5:1. Brake horsepower: 125 at 3600 R.P.M. Max torque: 214 lb.-ft. at 1550 R.P.M. Carburetor: Holley 1-barrel model 1904.

ENGINE (Standard: Series 100-8, 150-8, 250-8): V-type. OHV. 8-cylinder. Cast iron block. Bore & stroke: 3.75 x 3.25 in. Displacement: 287.2 cu. in. Compression ratio: 7.4:1. Brake horsepower: 155 at 3600 R.P.M. Max torque: 246 lb.-ft. at 2200-2600 R.P.M. 5 main bearings. Hydraulic valve lifters. Carburetor: Carter or Rochester model 2-barrel.

CHASSIS (Series 100): (Model 101), 100-8 (Model 101-8), 250 (Model 251), 250-8 (Model 251-8). Wheelbase: 114 in. Overall length: 193.56 (Pickup Suburban), 185.687 (all others). Overall height: 74 in. Front/Rear Tread: 61/61 in. Tires: 6.70 x 15, 9-ply (½-Ton).

1955 GMC Suburban Pickup (Ted Stevens/CPC)

CHASSIS (Series 100): (Model 102), 100-8 (Model 102-8), 150 (Model 152), Series 150-8 (Model 152-8), 250 (Model 252), 250-8 (Model 252-8). Wheelbase: 123.25 in. Overall length: 205.5625 in. Front/Rear Tread: 61/61 in. Tires: 6.70 x 15, 4-ply (½-Ton), 7.00 x 17.5, 6-ply (¾-Ton), 8.00 x 17.5, 6-ply (1-Ton).

CHASSIS (Series PM-150): (Model PM-151), PM-250 (Model 251). Wheelbase: 104 in. Tires: 8.00 x 19.5, 6-ply.

CHASSIS (Series PM-150): (Model PM-152). Wheelbase: 125 in.

CHASSIS (Series PM-150): (Model 153). Wheelbase: 137 in.

CHASSIS (Series 250): (Model 253), 250-8 (Model 253-8). Wheelbase: 135 in. Overall length: 215.8125 in. Front/Rear Tread: 61/61 in.

CHASSIS (Series PM-250): (Model PM-252). Wheelbase: 125 in.

CHASSIS (Series PM-250): (Model PM-253). Wheelbase: 137 in.

TECHNICAL: Manual, synchromesh. Speeds: 3F/1R (4F/1R 1-Ton models). Column (floor 4-speed) mounted gearshift. Diaphragm spring clutch, 10.0 in. dia, (10.5 in. dia ¾-Ton, 1-Ton models). Semi-floating rear axle-½-Ton models, full-floating rear axle-¾-Ton, 1-Ton models. Hydraulic brakes. 4-wheel, 11 x 2 in. front, 11 x 1.75 in. rear-½-Ton, 12 x 2 in. front, 14 x 2.5 in. rear-1-ton models. Pressed steel wheels.

DRIVETRAIN OPTIONS: 4-speed Hydra-Matic. (½-Ton models only). 4-speed manual transmission. Power steering. Oil bath. Air cleaner. 55-amp generator. Heavy-duty suspension.

OPTIONS: Rear bumper. Bumper guards. Radio. Heater. Clock. Cigar lighter. Radio antenna. Seat covers. External sun shade. Spotlight. White sidewall tires. Day/night mirror. Windshield washer. Dual arm rests. Backup lights. Emergency brake alert light.

HISTORICAL: Calendar year registrations: 84,877 (all series). Innovations: Introduction of V-8 engines for light-duty trucks. First year for 12-volt electrical system. Suburban Pickup also referred to as "Town and Country" model.

Pricing

1955	5	4	3	2	1
Series 100-22					
Pickup	1140	2280	3800	5300	7600
Panel	1020	2050	3400	4800	6800
Canopy Express	1040	2070	3450	4850	6900
Suburban	1050	2100	3500	4900	7000
Pickup (LWB)	1110	2220	3700	5200	7400
Stake Rack	1000	2000	3300	4600	6600
Series 150-22					
Pickup	1020	2050	3400	4800	6800
Stake Rack	950	1900	3150	4400	6300
Series 250-22					
Pickup	980	1950	3250	4550	6500
Platform	900	1800	3000	4200	6000
Stake Rack	920	1850	3050	4300	6100
Panel	950	1900	3150	4400	6300
Canopy Express	960	1920	3200	4500	6400
Series 100					
Pickup	1110	2220	3700	5200	7400
Panel	1150	2310	3850	5400	7700
Delivery Panel	1180	2370	3950	5500	7900
Suburban Pickup	1800	3600	6000	8400	12,000
Suburban	1200	2400	4000	5600	8000
Series 150					
Pickup	930	1860	3100	4350	6200
Stake Rack	800	1600	2650	3700	5300
Series 250					
Pickup	840	1680	2800	3900	5600
Platform	650	1300	2150	3050	4300
Stake Rack	660	1320	2200	3100	4400
Panel	950	1900	3150	4400	6300
Delivery Panel	980	1950	3250	4550	6500

1956 GMC

1956 GMC Cantrell Wood-bodied Carryall (OCW)

GMC — LIGHT-DUTY — (ALL ENGINES): — After the dramatic changes of 1955 the latest GMC trucks were virtually unchanged in appearance. Mechanical revisions were highlighted by larger six-cylinder and V-8 engines now displacing 269.5 and 316.6 cu. in. respectively.

I.D. DATA: The GMC Service Parts Identification Plate is located inside the cab or on the truck firewall. Stamped on the plate is the model of engine, transmission, service brakes and front and rear axles. Location of engine numbers unchanged from 1955.

Model	Body Type	Price	Weight	Prod. Total
Series 100				
101	½-Ton Chassis & Cab	1629	3060	—
101	½-Ton Panel	2028	3640	—
101	½-Ton Panel Deluxe	2120	3640	—
101	½-Ton Pickup	1732	3410	—
101	½-Ton Canopy Express	—	3570	—
101	½-Ton Suburban	2422	3865	—
102	½-Ton Chassis & Cab	1651	3130	—
102	½-Ton Pickup	1765	3510	—
102	½-Ton Stake Rack	—	3725	—
Series 150				
152	¾-Ton Chassis & Cab	1808	3425	—
152	¾-Ton Pickup 7.5 ft.	1922	3805	—
152	¾-Ton Stake Rack 7.5 ft.	2013	4020	—
Series PM150 Fwd				
151	¾-Ton Chassis	1756	2900	—
Series 250				
251	1-Ton Chassis & Cab (114 in. w.b.)	1920	3615	—
252	1-Ton Chassis & Cab (123.25 in. w.b.)	1920	3635	—
253	1-Ton Chassis & Cab (135 in. w.b.)	1920	3660	—
253	1-Ton Panel 9 ft.	2373	4345	—
253	1-Ton Panel Deluxe 9 ft.	2465	4345	—
253	1-Ton Pickup 9 ft.	2055	4110	—
253	1-Ton Platform	—	4225	—
253	1-Ton Stake Rack	2168	4500	—
Series PM250 Fwd				
251	1-Ton Chassis	1866	3030	—

ENGINE: Inline. OHV. 6-cylinder. Cast iron block. Bore & stroke: 3.78 x 4.0 in. Displacement: 269.5 cu. in. Compression ratio: 7.5:1. Brake horsepower: 130 at 3600 R.P.M. Max. Torque: 238 lb.-ft. @ 1400. Carburetor: Holley 1-barrel Model 1904.

ENGINE (Optional Series 100, 150, 250): V-Type, OHV. 8-cylinder. Cast iron block. Bore & stroke: 3.937 x 3.25 in. Displacement: 316.6 cu. in. Compression ratio: 7.8:1. Brake horsepower: 180 at 4400 R.P.M. Max. Torque: 276 lb.-ft. @ 2200 R.P.M. Five main bearings. Hydraulic valve lifters. Carburetor: Rochester 2-barrel.

CHASSIS (Series 100): Wheelbase: 114/123.25 in. Overall length: 194 (Pickup, Suburban)/186 in. Frt/Rear Tread: 61/61. Tires: 6.70 x 15, 4-ply.

CHASSIS (Series 150): Wheelbase: 123.25 in. Overall length: 206 in. Frt/Rear Tread: 61/61. Tires: 7 x 17.5, 4-ply.

CHASSIS (Series PM150): Wheelbase: 104/125/137 in. Tires: 8 x 19.5, 6-ply.

CHASIS (Series 250): Wheelbase: 114/123.25/135 in. Overall length: 186/206/216 in. Tires: 8 x 17.5, 6-ply.

TECHNICAL: Unchanged from 1955.

OPTIONS: Rear bumper. Bumper guards. Radio. Heater. Clock. Cigar lighter. Radio antenna. Seat covers. External Sun Shade, Spotlight. See 1955 section for additional listings.

452

HISTORICAL: Calendar year registrations: 82,266 (all series).

Pricing

	5	4	3	2	1
1956					
Series 100					
Pickup	1110	2220	3700	5200	7400
Panel	1150	2310	3850	5400	7700
Delivery Panel	1180	2370	3950	5500	7900
Suburban Pickup	1800	3600	6000	8400	12,000
Suburban	1200	2400	4000	5600	8000
Series 150					
Pickup	930	1860	3100	4350	6200
Stake Rack	800	1600	2650	3700	5300
Series 250					
Pickup	840	1680	2800	3900	5600
Platform	650	1300	2150	3050	4300
Stake Rack	660	1320	2200	3100	4400
Panel	950	1900	3150	4400	6300
Delivery Panel	980	1950	3250	4550	6500

1957 GMC

1957 GMC Suburban Carryall (DFW)

GMC — LIGHT-DUTY — (ALL ENGINES): — GMC trucks for 1957 featured a new grille design. Replacing the twin-bar arrangement was an insert with a center divider and horizontal bars. A model designation plaque was placed in the left section. The secondary grille mesh which served as a backdrop for the GMC logo on the 1955 and 1956 models was eliminated.

I.D. DATA: Serial number location unchanged from 1956. Engine number location unchanged from 1956.

Model	Body Type	Price	Weight	Prod. Total
Series 100				
101	½-Ton Chassis & Cab	1743	3040	—
101	½-Ton Panel	2147	3620	—
101	½-Ton Panel (Deluxe)	2239	3620	—
101	½-Ton Pickup	1846	3390	—
101	½-Ton Canopy Express	—	3550	—
101	½-Ton Suburban	2498	3845	—
102	½-Ton Chassis & Cab	1782	3110	—
102	½-Ton Pickup	1896	3490	—
Series 150				
152	¾-Ton Chassis & Cab	1928	3435	—
152	¾-Ton Pickup 7.5 ft.	2042	3815	—
152	¾-Ton Stake Rack, 7.5 ft.	2133	—	—
Series PM150				
151	¾-Ton Chassis (104 in. w.b.)	1839	2915	—
152	¾-Ton Chassis (125 in. w.b.)	1877	2970	—
153	¾-Ton Chassis (137 in w.b.)	1909	2995	—
Series 250				
251	1-Ton Chassis & Cab (114 in. w.b.)	2056	3635	—
252	1-Ton Chassis & Cab (123/25 in. w.b.)	2056	3655	—
253	1-Ton Chassis & Cab (135 in. w.b.)	2056	3680	—
253	1-Ton Panel 9 ft.	2519	4365	—
253	1-Ton Panel Deluxe 9 ft.	2572	4365	—
253	1-Ton Pickup 9 ft.	2191	4130	—
253	1-Ton Stake Rack	2304	4520	—

NOTE: 4wd. Models available in Series 100, 150, 250.

ENGINE (Standard Series 100, 150, 250, PM150): Inline. OHV. 6-cylinder. Cast iron block. Bore & stroke: 3.78 x 4.0 in. Displacement: 269.5 cu. in. Compression ratio: 7.5:1. Brake horsepower: 130 at 3600 R.P.M. Carburetor: Holley 1-barrel model 1904.

ENGINE (Optional: Series 100, 150, 250): V-type, OHV. 8-cylinder. Cast iron block. Bore & stroke: 3.94 x 3.56 in. Displacement: 347 cu. in. Brake horsepower: 206 at 4400 R.P.M. Max torque: 317 lbs.-ft. at 2000-2200 R.P.M. 5 main bearings. Hydraulic valve lifters. Carburetor: 2-barrel.

CHASSIS (Series 100): Wheelbase: 114/123.25 in. Overall length: 194 (Pickup, Suburban)/186/206 in. Frt./Rear Tread: 61/61 in. Tires: 6.70 x 15, 4-ply.

CHASSIS (Series 150): Wheelbase: 123.25 in. Overall length: 206 in. Frt./Rear Tread: 61/61 in. Tires: 7.00 x 17.5, 6-ply.

CHASSIS (Series PM150): Wheelbase: 104/125/137 in. Tires: 8.00 x 19.5, 6-ply.

CHASSIS (Series 250): Wheelbase: 114/123.25/135 in. Overall length: 186/206/216 in. Tires: 8.00 x 17.5, 6-ply.

CHASSIS (Series PM250): Wheelbase: 104/125/137 in. Tires: 8.00 x 19.5, 6-ply.

TECHNICAL: Unchanged from 1956.

OPTIONS: Rear bumper. Bumper guards. Radio. Heater. Clock. Cigar lighter. Radio antenna. Seat covers. Custom interior, Chrome exterior trim. White sidewall tires, Day/Night mirror. Dual arm rests. Backup lights.

HISTORICAL: Calendar year registrations: 62,165 (all series).

Pricing

	5	4	3	2	1
1957					
Series 100					
Pickup	1110	2220	3700	5200	7400
Panel	1150	2310	3850	5400	7700
Delivery Panel	1180	2370	3950	5500	7900
Suburban Pickup	1800	3600	6000	8400	12,000
Suburban	1200	2400	4000	5600	8000
Series 150					
Pickup	930	1860	3100	4350	6200
Stake Rack	800	1600	2650	3700	5300
Series 250					
Pickup	840	1680	2800	3900	5600
Platform	650	1300	2150	3050	4300
Stake Rack	660	1320	2200	3100	4400
Panel	950	1900	3150	4400	6300
Delivery Panel	980	1950	3250	4550	6500

1958 GMC

1958 GMC Suburban Carryall (DFW/GHB)

GMC — LIGHT-DUTY — (ALL ENGINES): — A new wide-side pickup body feature, dual headlights and a restyled grille highlighted the appearance of the 1958 GMC trucks. A broad crease on the wide-side models was suggestive of a similar style used by Cadillac in 1956. The front hood GMC logo was slimmed down and series numeral identification was placed in the center of the grille. Also found on the 1958 models were new hubcaps less ornate than those used from 1955 through 1957.

I.D. DATA: Serial number located: A GMC Service Parts Identification Plate was installed inside the cab or on the firewall. Engine numbers located: 6-cylinder: located on leftside of cylinder block behind oil filler.

1958 GMC Model 100 Pickup (GMC)

Model	Body Type	Price	Weight	Prod. Total
Series 100				
101	½-Ton Chassis & Cab	1815	3050	—
101	½-Ton Panel 7 ft.	2230	3650	—
101	½-Ton Panel Deluxe 7 ft.	2322	3655	—
101	½-Ton Pickup 6.5 ft.	1929	3400	—
101	½-Ton Pickup 6.5 ft. (WS)	1950	3450	—
101	½-Ton Suburban	2581	3990	—
102	½-Ton Chassis & Cab (123.25 in. w.b.)	1864	3120	—
102	½-Ton Pickup	1978	3540	—
102	½-Ton Pickup (WS)	1999	3590	—
Series 150				
152	¾-Ton Chassis & Cab	2000	3400	—
152	¾-Ton Pickup	2114	3820	—
152	¾-Ton Pickup (WS)	2135	3870	—
152	¾-Ton Stake Rack	2205	4020	—
Series PM150				
151	¾-Ton Chassis (104 in. w.b.)	1855	2760	—
151	¾-Ton Panel 8 ft.	3322	—	—
152	¾-Ton Chassis (125 in. w.b.)	1893	2815	—
152	¾-Ton Panel 10 ft.	3409	—	—
153	¾-Ton Chassis (137 in. w.b.)	1925	2860	—
153	¾-Ton Panel 12 ft.	3524	—	—
Series 250				
251	1-Ton Chassis & Cab (114 in. w.b.)	2128	3635	—
252	1-Ton Chassis & Cab (123.25 in. w.b.)	2128	3655	—
253	1-Ton Chassis & Cab (135 in. w.b.)	2128	3680	—
253	1-Ton Panel 9 ft.	2591	4450	—
253	1-Ton Panel Deluxe 9 ft.	2683	4455	—
253	1-Ton Pickup	2263	4130	—
253	1-Ton Stake Rack	2376	4520	—
Series PM250				
251	1-Ton Chassis (104 in. w.b.)	2021	3005	—
251	1-Ton Panel 8 ft. (104 in. w.b.)	3488	—	—
252	1-Ton Chassis (125 in. w.b.)	2058	3080	—
252	1-Ton Panel 10 ft. (125 in. w.b.)	3574	—	—
253	1-Ton Chassis (137 in. w.b.)	2091	3125	—
253	1-Ton Panel (137 in. w.b.)	3090	—	—

Note: Series 100, 150, 250 available in 4wd models.

ENGINE (Standard: Series 100, 150, 250, PM150, PM250): Inline. OHV. 6-cylinder. Cast iron block. Bore & stroke: 3.78 x 4.0 in. Displacement: 269.5 cu. in. Compression ratio: 7.5:1. Brake horsepower: 130 at 3600 R.P.M. Carburetor: Holly 1-barrel model 1904.

ENGINE (Optional: Series 100, 150, 250): V-type, OHV. 8-cylinder. Cast iron block. Bore & stroke: 3.875 x 3.5625 in. Displacement: 336.1 cu. in. Brake horsepower: 200 at 4400 R.P.M. Max torque: 307 lbs.-ft. at 2000-2400 R.P.M.

CHASSIS unchanged from 1957.

453

TECHNICAL: unchanged from 1957.

OPTIONS: Rear bumper. Bumper guards. Radio. Heater. Clock. Cigar lighter. Radio antenna. Seat covers. Spotlight. White sidewall tires. Exterior mirror. Custom Cab. Custom exterior trim.

HISTORICAL: Calendar year registrations: 55,950 (all series). Model year production: 64,216 (all series). Innovations: New, larger displacement V-8 introduced.

Pricing

1958	5	4	3	2	1
Series 100					
Pickup	1140	2280	3800	5300	7600
Pickup (WS)	1150	2310	3850	5400	7700
Pickup (LWB)	1100	2200	3650	5100	7300
Pickup (WS, LWB)	1110	2220	3700	5200	7400
Panel	1130	2250	3750	5250	7500
Panel Deluxe	1150	2310	3850	5400	7700
Suburban	1170	2340	3900	5450	7800
Series 150					
Pickup	900	1800	3000	4200	6000
Pickup (WS)	930	1860	3100	4350	6200
Stake Rack	750	1500	2500	3500	5000
Series PM150					
Panel 8 ft.	950	1900	3150	4400	6300
Panel 10 ft.	920	1850	3050	4300	6100
Panel 12 ft.	890	1770	2950	4150	5900
Series 250					
Pickup	920	1850	3050	4300	6100
Panel	830	1650	2750	3850	5500
Panel Deluxe	840	1680	2800	3900	5600
Stake Rack	720	1450	2400	3300	4800
Series PM250					
Panel 8 ft.	920	1850	3050	4300	6100
Panel 10 ft.	900	1800	3000	4200	6000

1959 GMC

1959 GMC 1-Ton Platform Stake Bed (S. Soloy)

GMC — LIGHT-DUTY — (ALL ENGINES): — Not found on the 1959 GMC models was the pseudo-automotive front bumper with its twin pod-like bumper guards. Instead a more functional straight-line bumper was used.

I.D. DATA: Serial number location unchanged from 1958. Engine number location unchanged from 1958.

Model	Body Type	Price	Weight	Prod. Total
Series 100				
101	½-Ton Chassis & Cab	1880	3050	—
101	½-Ton Panel	2295	3650	—
101	½-Ton Panel Deluxe	2387	3655	—
101	½-Ton Pickup 6.5 ft.	1994	3400	—
101	½-Ton Pickup 6.5 ft. (WS)	2015	3450	—
101	½-Ton Suburban	2678	3990	—
102	½-Ton Chassis & Cab (123.25 in. w.b.)	1929	3120	—
102	½-Ton Pickup 8 ft.	2043	3540	—
102	½-Ton Pickup 8 ft. (WS)	2064	3590	—

Model	Body Type	Price	Weight	Prod. Total
Series 150				
152	¾-Ton Chassis & Cab	2064	3400	—
152	¾-Ton Pickup	2178	3820	—
152	¾-Ton Pickup (WS)	2199	3870	—
152	¾-Ton Stake Rack	2209	4020	—
Series PM-150				
151	¾-Ton Chassis (104 in. w.b.)	1919	2760	—
151	¾-Ton Panel 8 ft. (104 in. w.b.)	3386	—	—
152	¾-Ton Chassis (125 in. w.b.)	1957	2815	—
152	¾-Ton Panel 10 ft. (125 in. w.b.)	3473	—	—
153	¾-Ton Chassis (137 in. w.b.)	1989	2860	—
Series 250				
251	1-Ton Chassis & Cab (114 in. w.b.)	2192	3635	—
252	1-Ton Chassis & Cab (123.25 in. w.b.)	2192	3655	—
253	1-Ton Chassis & Cab (135 in. w.b.)	2192	3680	—
253	1-Ton Panel 10 ft. (135 in. w.b.)	2655	—	—
253	1-Ton Panel Deluxe 10 ft. (135 in. w.b.)	2747	—	—
253	1-Ton Pickup	2327	4130	—
253	1-Ton Stake Rack	2440	4520	—
Series PM-250				
251	1-Ton Chassis (104 in. w.b.)	2085	3005	—
251	1-Ton Panel (104 in. w.b.)	3553	—	—
252	1-Ton Chassis (125 in. w.b.)	2123	3080	—
252	1-Ton Panel (125 in. w.b.)	3639	—	—
253	1-Ton Chassis (137 in. w.b.)	2155	3125	—
253	1-Ton Panel (137 in. w.b.)	3754	—	—

ENGINE: unchanged from 1958.

CHASSIS: unchanged from 1958.

TECHNICAL: unchanged from 1958.

OPTIONS: Rear bumper. Bumper guards. Radio. Heater. Clock. Cigar lighter. Radio antenna. Seat covers. Spotlight. Chrome bumpers. Custom interior package. Custom exterior trim. White sidewall tires. Exterior mirrors.

HISTORICAL: Calendar year registrations: 69,509 (all series). Model year production: 77,473 (all series).

Pricing

1959	5	4	3	2	1
Series 100					
Pickup	1140	2280	3800	5300	7600
Pickup (WS)	1150	2310	3850	5400	7700
Pickup (LWB)	1100	2200	3650	5100	7300
Pickup (WS, LWB)	1110	2220	3700	5200	7400
Panel	1130	2250	3750	5250	7500
Panel Deluxe	1150	2310	3850	5400	7700
Suburban	1170	2340	3900	5450	7800
Series 150					
Pickup	900	1800	3000	4200	6000
Pickup (WS)	930	1860	3100	4350	6200
Stake Rack	750	1500	2500	3500	5000
Series PM-150					
Panel 8 ft.	950	1900	3150	4400	6300
Panel 10 ft.	920	1850	3050	4300	6100
Panel 12 ft.	890	1770	2950	4150	5900
Series 250					
Pickup	920	1850	3050	4300	6100
Panel	830	1650	2750	3850	5500
Panel Deluxe	840	1680	2800	3900	5600
Stake Rack	720	1450	2400	3300	4800
Series PM-250					
Panel 8 ft.	920	1850	3050	4300	6100
Panel 10 ft.	900	1800	3000	4200	6000

1960 GMC

GMC — LIGHT-DUTY — (ALL ENGINES): — From any viewpoint this was a year equal in significance to 1948 and 1955 in GMC history. A drastic restyling resulted in a very futuristic front end appearance for the GMC dominated by high mounted parking lights set in large grid works. Along with a new suspension system the GMC light-duty trucks had stronger yet lighter frames.

As an option to the standard 6-cylinder engines the GMC trucks were available with a new V-6 engine displacing 305 cu. in.

I.D. DATA: The serial number is stamped on the identification plate mounted on the cowl left side panel inside the cab or on the left door hinge pillar. Data on the plate includes truck model number, chassis serial number, certified gross and maximum gross vehicle weight and net horsepower. Engine numbers located 6-cylinder: located on left side of cylinder block behind oil filler. 8-cylinder: stamped on top of cylinder block ahead of right-bank cylinder head.

1960 GMC ½-Ton Wide-Side Pickup (GMC)

Model	Body Type	Price	Weight	Prod. Total
Series 1000				
1001	½-Ton Delivery Van (98 in. w.b.)	2658	3900	—
1001	½-Ton Chassis & Cab (115 in. w.b.)	1958	3415	—
1001	½-Ton Panel (7.5-ft.) (115 in. w.b.)	2389	3970	—
1001	½-Ton Panel Custom (7.5-ft.) (115 in. w.b.)	2486	3985	—
1001	½-Ton Pickup (6.5-ft.) (WS) (115 in. w.b.)	2093	3835	—
1001	½-Ton Pickup (6.5-ft.) (FS) (115 in. w.b.)	2072	3785	—
1001	½-Ton Suburban (115 in. w.b.)	2821	4300	—
1002	½-Ton Chassis & Cab (127 in. w.b.)	2008	3485	—
1002	½-Ton Pickup 8-ft. (WS) (115 in. w.b.)	2143	3955	—
1002	½-Ton Pickup 8-ft. (FS) (115 in. w.b.)	2122	3905	—
Series 1500				
1502	¾-Ton Chassis & Cab (127 in. w.b.)	2142	3720	—
1502	¾-Ton Pickup, 8-ft. (WS) (127 in. w.b.)	2277	4190	—
1502	¾-Ton Pickup, 8-ft. (FS) (127 in. w.b.)	2256	4140	—
1502	¾-Ton Stake, 8-ft. (127 in. w.b.)	2347	4380	—
Series P-1500 Forward Control Models				
P-1501	¾-Ton Chassis (104 in. w.b.)	1676	2635	—
P-1502	¾-Ton Chassis (125 in. w.b.)	1714	2685	—
P1503	¾-Ton Chassis (137 in. w.b.)	1746	2720	—
Series 2500				
2502	1-Ton Chassis & Cab (127 in. w.b.)	2281	3955	—
2503	1-Ton Chassis & Cab (133 in. w.b.)	2281	3970	—
2503	1-Ton Panel, 10.5-ft. (133 in. w.b.)	2841	4687	—
2503	1-Ton Panel, Custom, 10.5-ft. (133 in. w.b.)	2938	4700	—
2503	1-Ton Pickup (133 in. w.b.)	2416	4415	—
2503	1-Ton Stake (133 in. w.b.)	2529	4810	—

1960 GMC One-Ton Platform Stake (GMC)

Model	Body Type	Price	Weight	Prod. Total
Series P-2500 Forward Control Models				
P-2502	1-Ton Chassis (125 in. w.b.)	1904	3035	—
P-2503	1-Ton Chassis (137 in. w.b.)	1937	3070	—

NOTE: Series 1000, 1500 available in 4wd models.

ENGINE (Standard: P-1500, P-2500, Van Model 1001): Inline. OHV. 6-cylinder. Cast iron block. Bore & stroke: 3.78 x 4.0 in. Displacement: 269.5 cu. in. Compression ratio: 7.5:1. Brake horsepower: 133 at 3600 R.P.M. Max torque: 244 lb.-ft. at 1300-2000 R.P.M. Carburetor: 1-barrel.

ENGINE (Standard: Series 1000, 1500, 2500): V-type. OHV. "305 A". 6-cylinder. Cast iron block. Bore & stroke: 4.25 x 3.58. Displacement: 304.7 cu. in. Compression ratio: 7.75:1. Brake horsepower: 142 at 3800 R.P.M. Max torque: 260 lb.-ft. at 1600 R.P.M. Four main bearings. Carburetor: Holley 1-barrel, model 1904.

1960 GMC Crew Cab Pickup/Track Cleaner (GMC)

CHASSIS (Series 1000): Wheelbase: 98/115/127 in. Overall length: 186.75 x 206.25. Tires: 7.10 x 15, 4-ply.

CHASSIS (Series 1500): Wheelbase: 127 in. Overall length: 206.25 in. Tires: 7.00 x 17.5, 6-ply.

CHASSIS (Series P-1500): Wheelbase: 104/125/137 in. Tires: 7.00 x 15.5, 6-ply.

CHASSIS (Series 2500): Wheelbase: 127/133 in. Overall length: 206.25 x 216.25 in. Tires: 8.00 x 17.5, 6-ply.

CHASSIS (Series P-2500): Wheelbase: 125/137 in. Tires: 8.00 x 19.5, 6-ply.

TECHNICAL: Manual, synchromesh. Speeds: 3F/1R (4R/1R-Series 2500). Column (floor-Series 2500) mounted gearshift. Semi-floating (½-Ton), Full-floating (all others) rear axle. Hydraulic, 4-wheel brakes. Pressed steel wheels.

DRIVETRAIN OPTIONS: Hydro-matic. Auxiliary rear springs (½-Ton, ¾-Ton models). Slip-limited differential. Full-lock differential.

OPTIONS: Bumper front chrome. Rear bumper. Bumper guards. Radio. Heater. Clock. Cigar lighter. Radio antenna. Seat covers. Exterior mirrors. White sidewall mirror. Mud flaps. Safety light markers. Windshield washer. Seat belts.

HISTORICAL: Calendar year registrations: 82,546 (all series). Model year production: 104,310 (all series). Innovations: Introduction of V-6 engine.

Pricing

1960 Light Duty	5	4	3	2	1
(115 in. w.b.)					
½-Ton Fender-Side Pickup	600	1200	2000	2800	4000
½-Ton Wide-Side Pickup	680	1350	2250	3150	4500
(127 in. w.b.)					
½-Ton Fender-Side Pickup	600	1200	2000	2800	4000
½-Ton Wide-Side Pickup	680	1350	2250	3150	4500
Panel	540	1080	1800	2500	3600
Suburban	570	1140	1900	2650	3800
¾-Ton Fender-Side Pickup	540	1080	1800	2500	3600
¾-Ton Wide-Side Pickup	560	1100	1850	2600	3700
Stake	530	1050	1750	2450	3500
(1-Ton) — (121 in. w.b. & 133 in. w.b.)					
Pickup	520	1020	1700	2400	3400
Panel	480	975	1600	2250	3200
Stake	470	950	1550	2200	3100
(95 in. w.b.)					
Delivery Van	520	1020	1700	2400	3400

1961 GMC

1961 GMC Deluxe Carryall Suburban (GMC)

SERIES 1000, K-1000, 1500, K-1500, 2500, V-3000, V-3500 — SIX-CYLINDERS — GMC trucks were carred over unchanged into the 1961 model year.

I.D. DATA: Serial number located stamped on identification plate mounted on cowl left side panel inside the cab or on left door hinge pillar - includes truck model number, Chassis serial number, certified gross and maximum gross vehicle weight and net horsepower. Engine numbers located L-6 - stamped on a boss on crank case adjacent to the distributor; V-6 - stamped on top of cylinder block ahead of right - bank cylinder head. 305 engine for Series 1000 and 1500 have a C prefix for identification purposes.

Model	Body Type	Price	Weight	Prod. Total
Series 1000				
1001	½-Ton Dely. Van Jr. (98 in. w.b.)	2701	3900	—
1001	½-Ton Chassis and Cab, (115 in. w.b.*)	1958	3400	—
1001	½-Ton Pickup (WS) (115 in. w.b.*)	2093	3795	—
1001	½-Ton Pickup (FS) (115 in. w.b.*)	2072	3760	—
1001	½-Ton Panel (7.5 ft.)	2389	4050	—
1001	½-Ton Panel (7.5 ft.)	2486	4060	—
1001	½-Ton Suburban	2821	4385	—

* 127" w.b. available
(4wd models: Add $693 to factory price. Identified as Series K1000)

Series 1500				
1502	¾-Ton Chassis and Cab	2142	3740	—
1502	¾-Ton Pickup (8 ft.) (WS)	2277	4210	—
1502	¾-Ton Pickup (8 ft.) (FS)	2256	4160	—
1502	¾-T Stake (8 ft.)	2347	4400	—

(4wd models: Add $710 to factory prices. Identified as Series K1500)

Series 2500				
2502	1-Ton Chassis and Cab (121 in. w.b. B)*	2281	4045	—
2503	1-Ton Pickup	2416	4620	—
2503	1-Ton Panel (12.5 ft.)	2841	4845	—
2503	1-Ton Panel (10.5 ft.) Cust.	2938	4860	—
2503	1-Ton Stake	2529	4885	—

* B - 133 in. w.b. available

ENGINE (Standard: Series 1000, 1500, 2500 except Van Model 1001): V-type. Ohv. Six-cylinder. Cast iron block. Bore & stroke: 4.25 in. x 3.58 in. Displacement: 304.7 cu. in. Compression ratio: 7.75:1. Brake horsepower: 142 at 3800 R.P.M. Max. Torque: 260 lb.-ft. at 1600 R.P.M. Four main bearings. Hydraulic valve lifters. Carburetor: Holley 1-Bbl. owned raft model 1904.

ENGINE (Standard: Van Model 1001, Series P1500, P2500): Inline. Ohv. Six-cylinder. Cast iron block. Bore & stroke: 3.78 in. x 4 in. Displacement: 269.5 cu. in. Compression ratio: 7.75:1. Brake horsepower: 133 at 3600 R.P.M. Max. Torque: 260 lb.-ft. at 1600-2000 R.P.M. Hydraulic valve lifters. Carburetor Holley model 1904 FS.

CHASSIS (Series Dely. Van Jr. Model 1000): Wheelbase: 98 in. Tires: 7.10-15 in.

CHASSIS (Series 1000): Wheelbase: 115-127 in. Length: 206 (115" w.b.). Front tread: 63.1 in. Rear tread: 61 in. Tires: 7.10-15 in.

CHASSIS (Series 1500): Wheelbase: 127 in. Front tread: 63.1 in. Rear tread: 61.1 in. Tires: 7-17.5 in.

CHASSIS (Series 2500): Wheelbase: 121-133 in. Tires: 8-17.5 in.

TECHNICAL: Manual transmission. Speeds: 3 F/1R. Column-mounted gearshift. Borg & Beck 10½'', single-plate dry disc-std clutch: Series 1000, 1500 Borg & Beck 11'', single plate dry disc-std. K models optional. Series 1000 hypoid, semi-floating rear axle. Overall ratio: (Series 1000) 3.38 or 3.07, (K-1000, K-1500) 3.54, (1500) 4.56. Optional ratios: (Series 1500) 4.10, (2500) 4.57, 5.14. Hydraulic, four-wheel brakes. Steel, disc wheels. Technical options: Automatic transmission: Hydra-Matic (Series 1000, 1500, 2500) $253. Four-speed transmission. Model SM420 (Std. on 2500, optional on 1000, K100, K1500, 1500). Power steering.

OPTIONS: Rear bumper. Radio. Heater. Clock. Cigar lighter. Radio antenna. Seat covers. Custom rear bumper. Outside mirror.

HISTORICAL: Calendar year production: 74,996.

Pricing

1961	5	4	3	2	1
(95 in. w.b.)					
Dely. Van	520	1020	1700	2400	3400
(115 in. w.b.)					
½-Ton Fender-SidePickup	600	1200	2000	2800	4000
½-Ton Wide-Side Pickup	680	1350	2250	3150	4500
(127 in. w.b.)					
½-Ton Fender-Side Pickup	600	1200	2000	2800	4000
½-Ton Wide-Side Pickup	680	1350	2250	3150	4500
Panel	540	1080	1800	2500	3600
Suburban	570	1140	1900	2650	3800
¾-Ton Fender-Side Pickup	540	1080	1800	2500	3600
¾-Ton Wide-Side Pickup	560	1100	1850	2600	3700
Stake	530	1050	1750	2450	3500
(121 & 133 in. w.b.)					
1-Ton Pickup	520	1020	1700	2400	3400
1-Ton Panel	480	975	1600	2250	3200
1-Ton Stake	470	950	1550	2200	3100

1962 GMC

1962 GMC Wide-Side Pickup (GMC)

SERIES 1000, K-1000, 1500, K-1500, 2500, V-3000, V-3500 — SIX-CYLINDERS — The simple expedient of smoothing out the GMC's hood line and installing parking/directional lights in a hood-wide cove dramatically altered the 1962 pickup's appearance. Instead of the extreme shape of the front air intake used in 1960-61, the latest models use a simpler, long and narrow opening to achieve the same purpose.

I.D. DATA: Serial number located stamped on identification plate mounted on cowl left side panel inside the cab or on left door hinge pillar - includes truck model number, Chassis serial number, certified gross and maximum gross vehicle weight and net horse power. Engine numbers located L-6 stamped on a boss or crank case adjacent to the distributor; V-6 stamped on top of cylinder block ahead of right-bank cylinder head. 305 engines for 1000, 1500 have a C for identification purpose. Example: 305C 137 786 (D-heavy duty).

Model	Body Type	Price	Weight	Prod. Total
Series 1000				
1001	½-Ton, Dely. Van Jr. (98 in. w.b.)	2752	3900	—
1001	½-Ton Chassis and Cab, (115 in. w.b.)	2009	3400	—
1001	½-Ton Pickup (WS) (115 in. w.b.)	2144	3795	—
1001	½-Ton Pickup (FS) (115 in. w.b.)	2123	3760	—
1001	½-Ton Panel (7.5 ft.)	2440	4050	—
1001	½-Ton Panel Custom (7.5 ft.)	2537	4060	—
1001	½-Ton Suburban	2882	4385	—

(4wd models: Add $665 to factory price, Identified as Series K1000).

Model	Body Type	Price	Weight	Prod. Total
Series 1500				
1502	¾-Ton Chassis and Cab	2194	3740	—
1502	¾-Ton Pickup (8 ft.) (WS)	2329	4210	—
1502	¾-Ton Pickup (8 ft.) (FS)	2308	4160	—
1502	¾-Ton Stake (8 ft.)	2399	4400	—

(4wd models: Add $693 to factory prices, Identified as Series K1500)

Model	Body Type	Price	Weight	Prod. Total
Series 2500				
2502	1-Ton Chassis and Cab (121 in. w.b.)	2336	4045	—
2503	1-Ton Pickup	2471	4620	—
2503	1-Ton Panel (10.5 ft.)	2896	4845	—
2503	1-Ton Panel (10.5 ft.) Cust.	2993	4860	—
2503	1-Ton Stake	2584	4885	—

ENGINE (Standard: Series 1000, 1500, 2500): 60°, V-type, Ohv. Six-cylinder. Cast iron block. Bore & stroke: 4.25 in. x 3.58 in. Displacement: 304.7 cu. in. Compression ratio: 7.75:1. Brake horsepower: 142 at 3800 R.P.M. Max. Torque: 260 lb.-ft. at 1600 R.P.M. Four main bearings. Hydraulic valve lifters. Carburetor: Bendix-Stromberg model WW 381031.

ENGINE (Standard: Dely. Van Junior): Inline. Ohv. Six-cylinder. Cast iron block. Bore & stroke: 3.78 in. x 4 in. Displacement: 269.5 cu. in. Compression ratio: 7.75:1. Brake horsepower: 133 at 3600 R.P.M. Max. Torque: 260 lb.-ft. at 1600 R.P.M. Hydraulic valve lifters. Carburetor: Holley model 1904 FS.

CHASSIS (Series 1000, Dely. Van Junior): Tires: 7.10-15 in.

CHASSIS (Series 1000): Wheelbase: 115-127 in. Overall length: 206 (115 in. w.b.) in. Front tread: 63.1 in. Rear tread: 61.0 in. Tires: 7.10-15 in.

CHASSIS (Series 1500): Wheelbase: 127 in. Front tread: 63.1 in. Rear tread: 61.0 in. Tires: 7-17.5 in.

CHASSIS (Series 2500): Wheelbase: 121-133 in. Tires: 8-17.5 in.

TECHNICAL: Manual transmission. Speeds: 3F/1R. Column-mounted gearshift. Clutch: Borg & Beck 10½'' std., single-plate, dry disc, Series 1000-1500, 11'' std. K-models, opt. 1000-1500. 1000 hypoid, semi-floating rear axle. Overall ratio: (1000) 3.38.1 or 3.07, (K1000, K1500) 3.54:1, (1500) 4.56:1 (opt. 4.10:1/2500 4.57:1 or 5.10:1). Steel disc wheels. Hydra-Matic transmission (on Series 1000, 1500, 2500). Power-Lok differential. Model SM420 4-spd. (std. on 2500), opt. on 1000, K1000, K1500, 1502 - $153. Auxiliary rear spring. Choice of rear axle ratio. Power steering.

OPTIONS: Rear bumper. Bumper guards. Radio. Heater. Clock. Cigar lighter. Radio antenna. Seat covers. Custom rear bumper. Outside mirror.

HISTORICAL: Calendar year production: 89,789.

1962 GMC Wide-Side Pickup w/Camper Unit (DFW)

Pricing

1962 Light Duty	5	4	3	2	1
(98 in. w.b.)					
Dely. Van	520	1020	1700	2400	3400
(115 in. w.b.)					
½-Ton Fender-Side Pickup	620	1230	2050	2900	4100
½-Ton Wide-Side Pickup	690	1380	2300	3200	4600
(127 in. w.b.)					
½-Ton Fender-Side Pickup	620	1230	2050	2900	4100
½-Ton Wide-Side Pickup	690	1380	2300	3200	4600
½-Ton Panel	560	1100	1850	2600	3700
½-Ton Suburban	590	1170	1950	2700	3900
¾-Ton Fender-Side Pickup	560	1100	1850	2600	3700
¾-Ton Wide-Side Pickup	570	1140	1900	2650	3800
Stake	530	1050	1750	2450	3500

(121 & 133 in. w.b.)	5	4	3	2	1
1-Ton Pickup	520	1020	1700	2400	3400
1-Ton Panel	480	975	1600	2250	3200
1-Ton Stake	470	950	1550	2200	3100

1963 GMC

GMC Forward Control Handi-Van (GMC)

SERIES 1000, K-1000, 1500, K-1500, 2500, 3500 — SIX-CYLINDER — No changes were made in the GMC truck line for 1963.

I.D. DATA: Serial number located on plate mounted on left cab door hinge pillar. Consists of a four digit vehicle code prefix followed by a five digit serial number. Starting: 10001 and up. GMC did not produce vehicles on the basis of annual model change. No yearly serial number ranges are available. Engine numbers located: (V-6): stamped on top of the cylinder head ahead of the right-cylinder head. It consists of an engine number prefix, (ex: TDGOC) followed by a five digit serial number identified to the vehicle serial number. If undersized main and connecting rod bearings are used, an ''A'' suffix added. A ''B'' suffix is used for oversized pistons. ''AB'' means a combination of ''A'' and ''B''. A plate indicating the vehicle's trim and paint numbers is located on engine side of firewall in back of hood hinge on the right side of the body. Production of 1964 model Handi-Vans began late in calendar year 1963.

Model	Body Type	Price	Weight	Prod. Total
Series 1000				
1001	½-Ton Chassis and Cab (115 in. w.b.)	2007	3340	—
1001	½-Ton Pickup (WS) (115 in. w.b.)	2142	3735	—
1001	½-Ton Pickup (FS) (115 in. w.b.)	2121	3700	—
1001	½-Ton Panel (7.5 ft.)	2438	3980	—
1001	½-Ton Panel Custom (7.5 ft.)	2535	3990	—
1001	½-Ton Suburban	2824	4230	—

(4wd models: Add $665 to factory price. Identified as Series K1000).

Model	Body Type	Price	Weight	Prod. Total
Series PB-1000				
PB-1001	½-Ton FWD Utility	2535	3540	—
Series 1500				
1502	¾-Ton Chassis and Cab	2193	3760	—
1502	¾-Ton Pickup (8 ft.) (WS)	2328	4230	—
1502	¾-Ton Pickup (8 ft.) (FS)	2307	4200	—
1502	¾-Ton Stake (8 ft.)	2398	4395	—

(4wd models: Add $693 to factory prices. Identified as Series K1500)

Model	Body Type	Price	Weight	Prod. Total
Series PB-1500 and PB-2500				
PB-1501	¾-Ton Utility FWD (104 in. w.b.)	3153	4545	—
PB-2501	1-Ton Utility FWD (104 in. w.b.)	3345	4855	—
Series 2500				
2502	1-Ton Chassis and Cab (121 in. w.b.)	2352	3900	—
2503	1-Ton Panel (10.5 ft.)	2912	4785	—
2503	1-Ton Panel Cust. (10.5 ft.)	3009	4800	—
2503	1-Ton Pickup (9 ft.)	2487	4385	—
2503	1-Ton Stake	2600	4755	—

ENGINE (Standard: Series 1000, 1500, 2500): V-type, Ohv. Six-cylinder. Cast iron block. Bore & stroke: 4.25 in. x 3.58 in. Displacement: 304.7 cu. in. Compression ratio: 7.75:1. Brake horsepower: 142 at 3800 R.P.M. Max. Torque: 260 lb. ft. at 1600 R.P.M. Four main bearings. Hydraulic valve lifters. Carburetor: Stromberg model WW 23-151.

ENGINE (Standard: Series P-1000, PB-1000): Inline. Ohv. Four-cylinder. Cast iron block. Bore & stroke: 3.875 in. x 3.25 in. Displacement: 153 cu. in. Compression ratio: 8.5. Brake horsepower: 90 at 4000 R.P.M. Max. Torque: 152 lb. ft. at 2400 R.P.M. Five main bearings. Hydraulic valve lifters. Carburetor: Rochester 1-bbl. 7020103.

ENGINE (Standard: Series PB-1500 and PB-2500): Inline, OHV. Six-cylinder. Cast iron block. Bore & stroke: 3.875 in. x 3.25 in. Displacement: 230 cu. in. Compression ratio: 8.5:1. Brake horsepower: 140 at 4400 R.P.M. Max. Torque: 220 lb. ft. at 1600 R.P.M. Five main bearings. Hydraulic valve lifters. Carburetor: Rochester 7023003.

CHASSIS (Series 1000): Wheelbase: 115-127 in. Overall length: 206 (115 in. w.b.) in. Front tread: 63.1 in. Rear tread: 61.0 in. Tires: 7.10 x 15 in.

CHASSIS (Series PB-1000): Wheelbase: 102 in. Tires: 6.70 x 15 in.

CHASSIS (Series 1500): Wheelbase: 127 in. Tires: 7 x 17.5 in.

CHASSIS (Series PB-1500): Wheelbase: 104-137 in. Tires: 7 x 17.5 in.

CHASSIS (Series 2500): Wheelbase: 121-133 in (Chassis and Cab), all other 133 in. Tires: 8 x 17.5 in.

CHASSIS (Series PB-2500): Wheelbase: 104-137 in. Tires: 7 x 17.5 in.

TECHNICAL: Manual transmission, General Motors SM318. Speeds: 3F/1R. Column-mounted gearshift. Clutch: Borg & Beck, 10½" disc, single-plate, dry disc. Series 1000: semi-floating, hypoid gear rear axle. Overall ratio: (1000): 3.07:1 (opt. 3.54:1), (1500): 4.10:1 (opt. 4.56:1), (K1500): 4.56:1. Hydraulic, 4 wheel brakes. Steel disc wheels. Power-Lok differential. New process Model 745-G, heavy duty 3-spd. GM model SM424 - 4-spd. Model AT-218, Pow-R-Flo automatic trans. Hydra-Matic automatic trans. Power steering: $135.

OPTIONS: Rear bumper. Bumper guards. Radio. Heater. Clock. Cigar lighter. Radio antenna. Seat covers. Custom rear bumper. Outside mirror.

HISTORICAL: Calendar year production: 101,234

Pricing

	5	4	3	2	1
1963					
Light Duty					
(98 in. w.b.)					
Dely. Van	520	1020	1700	2400	3400
(115 in. w.b.)					
½-Ton Fender-Side Pickup	620	1230	2050	2900	4100
½-Ton Wide-Side Pickup	690	1380	2300	3200	4600
(127 in. w.b.)					
½-Ton Fender-Side Pickup	620	1230	2050	2900	4100
½-Ton Wide-Side Pickup	690	1380	2300	3200	4600
½-Ton Panel	560	1100	1850	2600	3700
½-Ton Suburban	590	1170	1950	2700	3900
¾-Ton Fender-Side Pickup	560	1100	1850	2600	3700
¾-Ton Wide-Side Pickup	570	1140	1900	2650	3800
Stake	530	1050	1750	2450	3500
(121 & 133 in. w.b.)					
1-Ton Pickup	520	1020	1700	2400	3400
1-Ton Panel	480	975	1600	2250	3200
1-Ton Stake	470	950	1550	2200	3100
FWD					
½-Ton 4x4 Utility	570	1140	1900	2650	3800
¾-Ton 4x4 Utility	540	1080	1800	2500	3600
1-Ton 4x4 Utility	520	1020	1700	2400	3400

1964 GMC

1964 GMC Carryall Suburban (GMC)

458

SERIES 1000, I-1000, K-1000, 1500, I-1500, K-1500, 2500, I-2500, 3500 IN LINE SIX — SIX-CYLINDER — GMC pickup bodies were identical to those of 1964 with one important exception: the old "dog leg" windshield was replaced by single curved glass section. An important new model, the Handi-Van marked GMC's entry into the light van market.

I.D. DATA: Serial number located on plate mounted on left cab door hinge pillar. Engine numbers located: V-6 engine: stamped on top of the cylinder block ahead of the right cylinder head. Serial numbers are not used on in-line engines. Numbers appearing on crankcase boss at rear of distributor are building date code.

Model	Body Type	Price	Weight	Prod. Total
Series G-1000				
G-1001	½-Ton Handi Van	2042	2820	—
Series I-1000				
I-1001	½-Ton Chassis and Cab (115 in. w.b.)	1890	2910	—
I-1001	½-Ton Pickup (WS) (115 in. w.b.)	2025	3305	—
I-1001	½-Ton Pickup (FS) (115 in. w.b.)	2004	3255	—
I-1001	½-Ton Panel (7.5 ft.) Dlx.	2321	3490	—
I-1001	½-Ton Panel (7.5 ft.) Cust.	2418	3490	—
I-1001	½-Ton Suburban	2719	3745	—
Series 1000				
1001	½-Ton Chassis and Cab (115 in. w.b.)	2006	3340	—
1001	½-Ton Pickup (WS) (115 in. w.b.)	2141	3735	—
1001	½-Ton Pickup (FS) (115 in. w.b.)	2130	3685	—
1001	½-Ton Panel (7.5 ft.) Cust.	2437	3920	—
1001	½-Ton Suburban	2834	4175	—
(4wd models: Add $676 to factory price. Identified as Series K-1000)				
Series PB1000				
PB1001	½-Ton FWD Van (7 ft.)	2537	3520	—
Series I-1500				
I-1500	¾-Ton Chassis and Cab	2075	3330	—
I-1500	¾-Ton Pickup (8 ft.) (WS)	2210	3810	—
I-1500	¾-Ton Pickup (8 ft.) (FS)	2189	3770	—
I-1500	¾-Ton Stake (8 ft.)	2397	4395	—
Series 1500				
1502	¾-Ton Chassis and Cab	2192	3760	—
1502	¾-Ton Pickup (8 ft.) (WS)	2327	4240	—
1502	¾-Ton Pickup (8 ft.) (FS)	2306	4200	—
1503	¾-Ton Stake (8 ft.)	2397	4395	—
(4wd models: Add $676 to factory price. Identified as Series K-1500)				
Series PB1500 and PB2500				
PB-1502	¾-Ton FWD Van (125 in. w.b.)	3244	5050	—
PB-1503	¾-Ton FWD Van (137 in. w.b.)	—	—	—
PB-2502	1-Ton FWD Van (125 in. w.b.)	3436	5270	—
PB-2503	1-Ton FWD Van (137 in. w.b.)	3436	5270	—
Series I-2500				
I-2502	1-Ton Chassis and Cab (121 in. w.b.)	2231	3495	—
I-2503	1-Ton Panel (10.5 ft.) Dlx.	2791	4330	—
I-2503	1-Ton Panel (10.5 ft.) Cust.	2888	4330	—
I-2503	1-Ton Pickup (9 ft.) (FS)	2366	3990	—
I-2503	1-Ton Stake (9 ft.)	2479	4350	—
Series 2500				
2502	1-Ton Chassis and Cab	2351	3925	—
2503	1-Ton Panel (10.5 ft.) Dlx.	2911	4760	—
2503	1-Ton Panel (10.5 ft.) Cust.	3008	4760	—
2503	1-Ton Pickup (9 ft.)	2486	4420	—
2503	1-Ton Stake	2599	4780	—

ENGINE (Standard: I-1000, I-1500): Inline. OHV. Six-cylinder. Cast iron block. Bore & stroke: 3.875 in. x 3.25 in. Displacement: 230 cu. in. Compression ratio: 8.5:1. Net horsepower: 120 at 3600 R.P.M. Max. Torque: 220 lbs. ft. at 1600. Four main bearings. Hydraulic valve lifters. Carburetor: Rochester down draft model B10Z3011 or 7024009.

ENGINE (Standard: 1000, 1500, K-1000, K-1500): V-type. OHV. Six-cylinder. Cast iron block. Bore & stroke: 4.25 in. x 3.58 in. Displacement: 304.7 cu. in. Compression ratio: 7.75:1. Brake horsepower: 465 at 3800 R.P.M. Max. Torque: 280 lb. ft. at 1600 R.P.M. Net horsepower: 142 at 3800 R.P.M. Four main bearings. Hydraulic valve lifters. Carburetor: Bendix-Stromberg down draft, 2-Bbl. model WW381094 (early), WW 381123 (late).

ENGINE (Standard: Series P-1000 and PB-1000): Inline. OHV. Four-cylinder. Cast iron block. Bore & stroke: 3.875 in. x 3.25 in. Displacement: 153 cu. in. Brake horsepower: 90 at 4000 R.P.M. Max. Torque: 152 lb. ft. at 2400 R.P.M. Five main bearings. Hydraulic valve lifters. Carburetor: Rochester 1-Bbl. model 7020103.

CHASSIS (Series G-1000): Wheelbase: 90 in. Tires: 6.50 x 13 in.

CHASSIS (Series I-1000): Wheelbase: 115-127 in. Overall length: 206 (115 in. w.b.) in. Height: 71 in. Front tread: 63.1 in. Rear tread: 61.1 in. Tires: 6.70 x 15 in.

CHASSIS (Series 1000): Wheelbase: 115-127 in. Overall length: 206 (115 in. w.b.) in. Height: 71 in. Front tread: 63.1 in. Rear tread: 61.1 in. Tires: 7.10 x 15 in.

CHASSIS (Series I-1500): Wheelbase: 127 in. Front tread: 63.1 in. Rear tread: 61.1 in. Tires: 7 x 17.5 in.

CHASSIS (Series 1500): Wheelbase: 127 in. Height: 71 in. Front tread: 63.1 in. Rear tread: 61.1 in. Tires: 7 x 17.5 in.

CHASSIS (Series PB-1500): Wheelbase: 125-137 in. Tires: 7 x 17.5 in.

CHASSIS (Series PB-2500): Wheelbase: 125-137 in. Tires: 8 x 19.5 in.

CHASSIS (Series I-2500): Wheelbase: 121-157 (Chassis and Cab) 133 in. (all others). Tires: 8 x 17.5 in.

CHASSIS (Series 2500): Wheelbase: 121-157 (Chassis and Cab), 133 in. (all others). Tires: 8 x 17.5 in.

TECHNICAL: Manual transmission. General Motors SM318 (Series: 1000, K-1000, I-1000, 1500, K-1500, I-1500). Speeds: 3F/1R. Column-mounted gear shift lever. Single plate dry-disc clutch. "GM-10" std. I-1000, I-1500, 11" opt. I-100, I-1500 Borg & Beck - 10½ 1000, 11" all K models, 11" opt. - Series 1000/1500. Hypoid, semi-floating rear axle. Overall ratio (1000): 3.07:1 (opt. 3.54:1), (I-1000): 3.54:1 (opt. 3.09, 3.92:1). Hydraulic, 4 wheel - I-1500, 1500, K-1500: 4.56:1 brakes (opt. 4.10). Steel disc wheels. Power steering - $135. Power-lock differential. Hydra-Matic Transmission - $188. New Process Model 745-G, heavy duty 3-spd. GM Model SM424 - 4 spd. Model AT-218. Pow-R-Flo automatic (Series 1000, I-1000, I-1000, 1500, I-1500).

OPTIONS: Rear bumper. Bumper guards. Radio. Heater. Clock. Cigar lighter. Radio antenna. Seat covers. Custom rear bumper. Outside mirror. Gauge package. Air conditioning. Spare tire side carrier. Full view rear cab window. Soft-ray tinted glass. Padded instrument panel. Seat belts.

HISTORICAL: Calendar year production: 110,521.

Pricing

1964	5	4	3	2	1
Light Duty					
(98 in. w.b.)					
Dely. Van	520	1020	1700	2400	3400
(115 in. w.b.)					
½-Ton Fender-Side Pickup	620	1230	2050	2900	4100
½-Ton Wide-Side Pickup	690	1380	2300	3200	4600
(127 in. w.b.)					
½-Ton Fender-Side Pickup	620	1230	2050	2900	4100
½-Ton Wide-Side Pickup	690	1380	2300	3200	4600
½-Ton Panel	560	1100	1850	2600	3700
½-Ton Suburban	590	1170	1950	2700	3900
¾-Ton Fender-Side Pickup	560	1100	1850	2600	3700
¾-Ton Wide-Side Pickup	570	1140	1900	2650	3800
Stake	530	1050	1750	2450	3500
(121 & 133 in. w.b.)					
1-Ton Pickup	520	1020	1700	2400	3400
1-Ton Panel	480	975	1600	2250	3200
1-Ton Stake	470	950	1550	2200	3100
FWD					
½-Ton 4x4	540	1080	1800	2500	3600
¾-Ton 4x4	520	1020	1700	2400	3400
1-Ton 4x4	480	975	1600	2250	3200

1965 GMC

1965 GMC Deluxe Cab Wide-Side Pickup (GMC)

SERIES G-1000, I-1000, PB-1000, I-1500, 1500, PB-1500, PB-2500, I-2500, 2500 — SIX-CYLINDER — No design changes for 1965.

I.D. DATA: Serial number located on plate mounted on left cab door hinge pillar. Engine numbers located: (V-6): stamped on top of the cylinder block ahead of the right-cylinder head. Serial numbers not used on inline engines. Numbers appearing on crankcase boss at rear of distributor are building date codes.

What's new?

1965 GMC Panel Delivery Van (JAG)

Model	Body Type	Price	Weight	Prod. Total
Series G-1000				
G-1001	½-Ton Handi Van	2080	2825	—
G-1101	½-Ton Handi Van	2330	3040	—
Series I-1000				
I-1001	½-Ton Chassis and Cab (115 in. w.b)	1890	2910	—
I-1001	½-Ton Pickup (WS) (115 in. w.b.)	2025	3305	—
I-1001	½-Ton Pickup (FS) (115 in. w.b.)	2004	3255	—
I-1001	½-Ton Panel (7.5 ft.) Deluxe	2321	3490	—
I-1001	½-Ton Panel (7.5 ft.) Cust.	2418	3490	—
I-1001	½-Ton Suburban	2718	3745	—
Series 1000				
1001	½-Ton Chassis and Cab (115 in. w.b)	2006	3340	—
1001	½-Ton Pickup (WS) (115 in. w.b.)	2141	3735	—
1001	½-Ton Pickup (FS) (115 in. w.b.)	2120	3685	—
1001	½-Ton Panel (7.5 ft.) Dlx.	2437	3920	—
1001	½-Ton Panel (7.5 ft.) Cust.	2534	3920	—
1001	½-Ton Suburban	2834	4175	—
(4wd models: Add $665 to factory price. Identified as Series K-1000)				
Series PB-1000				
PB-1001	½-Ton FWD Van	2534	3520	—
Series I-1500				
I-1502	¾-Ton Chassis and Cab	2075	3330	—
I-1502	¾-Ton Pickup (8 ft.) (WS)	2210	3810	—
I-1502	¾-Ton Pickup (8 ft.) (FS)	2189	3770	—
I-1502	¾-Ton Stake Rack (8 ft.)	2280	3965	—
Series 1500				
1502	¾-Ton Chassis and Cab	2193	3760	—
1502	¾-Ton Pickup (8 ft.) (WS)	2328	4240	—
1502	¾-Ton Pickup (8 ft.) (FS)	2307	4200	—
1502	¾-Ton Stake Rack (8 ft.)	2398	4395	—
(4wd models: Add $692 to factory price, identified as Series K1500)				
Series PB-1500 and PB-2500				
PB-1502	¾-Ton Van (125 in. w.b.)	3238	5050	—
PB-2502	1-Ton Van (125 in. w.b.)	3434	5270	—
Series I-2500				
I-2502	1-Ton Chassis and Cab (121 in. w.b.)	2232	3495	—
I-2503	1-Ton Panel (10.5 ft.) Dlx.	2792	4330	—
I-2503	1-Ton Panel Cust. (10.5 ft.)	2889	4330	—
I-2503	1-Ton Pickup (9 ft.) (FS)	2367	3994	—
I-2503	1-Ton Stake Rack (9 ft.)	2480	4350	—
Series 2500				
2502	1-Ton Chassis and Cab (121 in. w.b.)	2351	3925	—
2503	1-Ton Panel (10.5 ft.) Dlx.	2911	4760	—
2503	1-Ton Panel (10.5 ft.) Cust.	3008	4760	—
2503	1-Ton Pickup (9 ft.) (FS)	2486	4420	—
2503	1-Ton Stake Rack (9 ft.)	2599	4780	—

ENGINE (Standard: Series 1000, K-1000, 1500, K-1500, 2500, 3500): V-type, overhead valve. Six-cylinder. Cast iron block. Bore & stroke: 4.25 in. x 3.58 in. Displacement: 304.7 cu. in. Compression ratio: 7.75:1. Brake horsepower: 165 at 3800 R.P.M. Max. Torque: 280 lb. ft. at 1000 R.P.M. Net horsepower: 142 at 3800 R.P.M. Four main bearings. Hydraulic valve lifters. Carburetor: Stromberg 2-bbl. model WW 23-153A.

ENGINE (Standard: Series I-1000, I-1500, I-2500; Optional: G-1000 ($27), PB-1000 ($65): Inline, overhead valve. Six-cylinder. Cast iron block. Bore & stroke: 3.87 in. x 3.25 in. Displacement: 230 cu. in. Compression ratio: 8.5:1. Brake horsepower: 140 at 4400 R.P.M. Max. Torque: 220 lb. ft. at 1600 R.P.M. Seven main bearings. Hydraulic valve lifters. Carburetor: Rochester single barrel model B.

ENGINE (Standard: Series G-1000): Inline, OHV. Six-cylinder. Cast iron block. Bore & stroke: 3.56 in. x 3.25 in. Displacement: 194 cu. in. Brake horsepower: 120 at 4400 R.P.M. Max. Torque: 177 lb. ft. at 2400 R.P.M. Seven main bearings. Hydraulic valve lifters. Carburetor: Rochester 1-bbl.

ENGINE (Standard: Series PB-1000): Inline, OHV. Four-cylinder. Cast iron block. Bore & stroke: 3.875 in. x 3.25 in. Displacement: 153 cu. in. Brake horsepower: 90 at 4000 R.P.M. Max. Torque: 152 lb. ft. at 2400 R.P.M. Five main bearings. Hydraulic valve lifters. Carburetor: Rochester 1-bbl. model 7020103.

CHASSIS (Series G-1000): Wheelbase: 90 in. Tires: 6.50 x 13 in.

CHASSIS (Series I-1000): Wheelbase: 115-127 in. Length: 206 (115 in. w.b.) in. Height: 71 in. Front tread: 63.1 in. Rear tread: 61.1 in. Tires: 7.75 x 15 in. (8.15 x 15 available)

CHASSIS (Series 1000): Wheelbase: 115-127 in. Length: 206 (115 in. w.b.) in. Height: 71 in. Tires: 8.15 x 15 in.

CHASSIS (Series PB-1000): Wheelbase: 102 in. Tires: 7.75 x 15 in.

CHASSIS (Series I-1500): Wheelbase: 127 in. Height: 71 in. Front tread: 63.1 in. Rear tread: 61.1. in. Tires: 7.17 x 5 in.

CHASSIS (Series 1500): Wheelbase: 125-137 in. Tires: 7 x 17.5 in.

CHASSIS (Series PB-1500): Wheelbase: 125-137 in. Tires: 7 x 17.5 in.

CHASSIS (Series PB-2500): Wheelbase: 125-137 in. Tires: 8x 19.5 in.

CHASSIS (Series I-2500): Wheelbase: 121-133 in. Tires: 8 x 17.5 in.

CHASSIS (Series 2500): Wheelbase: 121-133 in. Tires: 8 x 17.5 in.

TECHNICAL: Manual transmission, General Motors SM318. Speeds: 3F/1R. Column mounted gearshift. Clutch: Single-plate, dry disc; 10'' dia. (I-1000, I-1500) Borg and Beck, 10½'' diam. — 1000, 11'' dia. — all "K" models. Semi-floating, hypoid gear rear axle. Overall ratio: (1000): 3.07:1 (opt. 3.54:1). (I-1000): 3.5:1 (opt. 3.09, 3.92:1). (I-1500, 1500, K-1500): 4.56:1 (opt. 4.10, 4.56:1). Hydraulic, 4 wheel brakes. Steel disc wheels. Heavy-duty, 70 amp battery. Overdrive. Free wheeling hubs (4wd).

OPTIONS: Rear bumper. Bumper guards. Radio. Heater. Clock. Cigar lighter. Radio antenna. Seat covers. Custom rear bumper. Outside mirror. Gauge package. Air conditioning. Spare tire side carrier. Full view rear cab window. Soft-Ray tinted glass. Padded instrument panel. Seat belts.

HISTORICAL: Calendar year production: 136,705

Pricing

1965 Light Duty	5	4	3	2	1
(98 in. w.b.)					
Dely. Van	520	1020	1700	2400	3400
(115 in. w.b.)					
½-Ton Fender-Side Pickup	620	1230	2050	2900	4100
½-Ton Wide-Side Pickup	690	1380	2300	3200	4600
(127 in. w.b.)					
½-Ton Fender-Side Pickup	620	1230	2050	2900	4100
½-Ton Wide-Side Pickup	690	1380	2300	3200	4600
½-Ton Panel	560	1100	1850	2600	3700
½-Ton Suburban	590	1170	1950	2700	3900
¾-Ton Fender-Side Pickup	560	1100	1850	2600	3700
¾-Ton Wide-Side Pickup	570	1140	1900	2650	3800
Stake	530	1050	1750	2450	3500
(121 & 133 in. w.b.)					
1-Ton Pickup	520	1020	1700	2400	3400
1-Ton Panel	480	975	1600	2250	3200
1-Ton Stake	470	950	1550	2200	3100
FWD					
½-Ton 4x4	540	1080	1800	2500	3600
¾-Ton 4x4	520	1020	1700	2400	3400
1-Ton 4x4	480	975	1600	2250	3200

1966 GMC

No design changes were made in the GMC truck design for 1966. The horsepower rating for the six-cylinder engine was increased to 155 horsepower. The Handi-Van engines were rated at 120 and 140 horsepower.

I.D. DATA: Serial number located on plate mounted on left cab door hinge pillar. Starting: GMC trucks were not formally produced on a year-to-year model change. Engine numbers located: V-6 engines: Stamped on top of the cylinder block ahead of the right cylinder head. Serial numbers not used on in-line engines. Numbers appearing on crankcase boss at rear of distributor are building date codes.

1966 GMC ½-Ton Short Box Wide-Side Pickup (G. Clarey)

Model	Body Type	Price	Weight	Prod. Total
Series G-1000				
G-1001	½-Ton Handi Van	2116	2690	—
G-1011	½-Ton Handi Bus	2363	3040	—
G-1021	¾-Ton Handi Bus	2496	3135	—
G-1031	1-Ton Handi Bus	2722	3195	—
Series I-1000				
I-1001	½-Ton Chassis and Cab (115 in. w.b.*)	1927	2910	—
I-1001	½-Ton Pickup (WS) (115 in. w.b.*)	2071	3305	—
I-1001	½-Ton Pickup (FS) (115 in. w.b.*)	2050	3255	—
I-1001	½-Ton Panel (7.5 ft.) Dlx. (115 in. w.b.)	2361	3490	—
I-1001	½-Ton Panel (7.5 ft.) Cust. (115 in. w.b.)	2458	3490	—
I-1001	½-Ton Suburban (115 in. w.b.)	2706	3745	—
Series 1000				
1001	½-Ton Chassis and Cab (115 in. w.b.*)	2054	3340	—
1001	½-Ton Pickup (WS) (115 in. w.b.*)	2199	3735	—
1001	½-Ton Pickup (FS) (115 in. w.b.*)	2177	3685	—
1001	½-Ton Panel (7.5 ft.) Dlx. (115 in. w.b.)	2488	3920	—
1001	½-Ton Panel (7.5 ft.) Cust. (115 in. w.b.)	2585	3920	—
1001	½-Ton Suburban (115 in. w.b.)	2830	4175	—

(4wd models: Add $665 to factory price. Identified as Series K100)

NOTE: WS = Wide Side — FS = Fleet Side
* 127 in. w.b. available

Model	Body Type	Price	Weight	Prod. Total
Series PB-1000				
PB-1000	½-To FWD Van	2618	3520	
Series I-1500				
I-502	¾-Ton Chassis and Cab	2111	3330	—
I-1502	¾-Ton Pickup (8 ft.) (WS)	2255	3810	—
I-1502	¾-Ton Pickup (8 ft.) (FS)	2234	3770	—
I-1502	¾-Ton Stake Rack (8 ft.)	2327	3965	—
Series 1500				
1502	¾-Ton Chassis and Cab	2240	3760	—
1502	¾-Ton Pickup (8 ft.) (WS)	2385	4240	—
1502	¾-Ton Pickup (8 ft.) (FS)	2363	4200	—
1502	¾-Ton Stack Rack (8 ft.)	2456	4395	—

(4wd models: Add $693 to factory price. Identified as Series K-1500)

Model	Body Type	Price	Weight	Prod. Total
Series PB-1500				
PB-1502	¾-Ton Van (125 in. w.b.)	3284	5070	
Series PB-2500				
PB-2502	1-Ton Van (125 in. w.b.)	3480	5295	
Series I-2500				
I-2502	1-Ton Chassis and Cab (121 in. w.b.)	2268	3495	—
I-2503	1-Ton Panel (10.5 ft.) Dlx.	2831	4330	—
I-2503	1-Ton Panel (10.5 ft.) Cust.	2928	4330	—
I-2503	1-Ton Pickup (9 ft.) (FS)	2413	3990	—
I-2503	1-Ton Stack Rack (9 ft.)	2527	4350	—
Series 2500				
2502	1-Ton Chassis and Cab (121 in. w.b.)	2399	3925	—
2503	1-Ton Panel (10.5 ft.) Dlx.	2926	4760	—
2503	1-Ton Panel (10.5 ft.) Cust.	3059	4760	—
2503	1-Ton Pickup (9 ft.) (FS)	2544	4420	—
2503	1-Ton Stake Rack (9 ft.)	2658	4780	—

1966 GMC C910 ½-Ton Fender-Side Pickup (RPZ)

ENGINE (Series 305E. Standard: 1000, 1500, 2500, K-1000, K-1500): V-type, OHV. Model 305E. Six-cylinder. Cast iron block. Bore & stroke: 4.25 in. x 3.58 in. Displacemet: 304.7 cu. in. Compression ratio: 7.75:1. Brake horsepower: 170 at 4000 R.P.M. Max. Torque: 277 lb. ft. at 1600 R.P.M. Four main bearings. Hydraulic valve lifters. Carburetor: Stromberg 2-bbl.model WW23-161.

ENGINE (Standard: I-1000, I-1500, I-2500): Inline, OHV. Model 250-6. Six-cylinder. Cast iron block. Bore & stroke: 3.87 in. x 3.53 in. Displacement: 250 cu. in. Compression ratio: 8.5:1. Brake horsepower: 150 at 4200 R.P.M. Max. Torque: 235 lb. ft. at 1600 R.P.M. Seven main bearings. Hydraulic valve lifters. Carburetor: Rochester 1-Bbl. model B.

1966 GMC C910 ½-Ton Panel Delivery (RPZ)

ENGINE (Standard: Series PB-1000): Inline. OHV. Four-cylinder. Cast iron block. Bore & stroke: 3⅞ in. x 3¼ in. Displacement: 153 cu. in. Brake horsepower: 90 at 4000 R.P.M. Max. Torque: 152 lb. ft. at 2400 R.P.M. Five main bearings. Hydraulic valve lifters. Carburetor: Rochester 1-Bbl. model 7020103.

CHASSIS (Series G-1000): Wheelbase: 90 in. Tires: 6.50 x 13 in.

1966 GMC C930 1-Ton Carryall Suburban (RPZ)

ENGINE (Standard: Series G-1000, except Model G-1031): Inline. OHV. Six-cylinder. Cast iron block. Bore & stroke: 3.56 in. x. 3.25 in. Displacement: 194 cu. in. Brake horsepower: 120 at 4400 R.P.M. Max. Torque: 177 lb. ft. at 2400 R.P.M. Seven main bearings. Hydraulic valve lifters. Carburetor: Rochester 1-Bbl. model.

ENGINE (Standard: Model G-1031, Optional Series G-1000 and PB-1000): Inline. OHV. Six-cylinder. Cast iron block. Bore & stroke: 3.875 in. x 3.25 in. Displacement: 230 cu. in. Compression ratio: 8.5:1. Brake horsepower: 140 at 4400 R.P.M. Max. Torque: 220 lb. ft. at 1600 R.P.M. Seven main bearings. Hydraulic valve lifters. Carburetor: Rochester 1-Bbl. model B.

1966 GMC Forward Control Handi-Van (RPZ)

CHASSIS (Series 1000): Wheelbase: 115-127 in. Length: 206 (115 in. w.b.) in. Height: 71 in. Front tread: 63.1 in. Rear tread: 61.1 in. Tires: 8.15 x 15 in.

CHASSIS (Series I-1500): Wheelbase: 127 in. Tires: 7 x 17.5 in.

CHASSIS (Series Model PB-1500): Wheelbase: 125-137 in. Tires: 7 x 17.5 in.

CHASSIS (Series I-1000): Wheelbase: 115-127 in. Length: 206 (115 in. w.b.) in. Height: 71 in. Front tread: 63.1 in. Rear tread: 61.1 in. Tires: 7.75 x 15 in. (8.15 x 15 available)

CHASSIS (Series PB-1000): Wheelbase: 102 in. Tires: 7.75 x 15 in.

1966 GMC Forward Control Value Van (RPZ)

1966 GMC Forward Control Handi-Bus (RPZ)

1966 GMC Forward Control Utility Van (RPZ)

CHASSIS (Series 1500): Wheelbase: 127 in. Height: 71 in. Tires: 7 x 17.5 in.

CHASSIS (Series Model PB-2500): Wheelbase: 125-137 in. Tires: 8 x 19.5 in.

CHASSIS (Series I-2500): Wheelbase: 121-133 in. Tires: 8 x 17.5 in.

CHASSIS (Series 2500): Wheelbase: 121-133 in. Tires: 8 x 17.5 in.

TECHNICAL: Manual transmission. General Motors SM318. Speeds: 3F/1R. Column-mounted gear shift lever. Single plate, dry-disc clutch. 10 in. dia. (I-1000 - 1-1500), Borg and Beck, 10½ in. dia. - 1000, 11" dia. - all "K" models. Semi-floating, hypoid gear rear axle. Overall ratio: (1000): 3.07:1, (opt. 3.54:1), (I-1000): 3.5:1 (opt. 3.09, 3.92:1), (I-1500, 1500, K-1500): 4.56:1 (opt. 4.10, 4.56:1). Hydraulic, 4 wheel brakes. Steel disc wheels. Hydra-matic overdrive. 4-speed manual, GM Model SM424. 11 in. dia. clutch (Series 1000, 1500). New Process, heavy-duty 3 spd. Model 745-G. Model AT-218, Pow-R-Flo automatic (Series 1000, I-100, 1500, I-1500). Power steering ($135).

OPTIONS: Rear bumper. Bumper guards. Radio. Heater. Clock. Cigar lighter. Radio antenna. Seat covers. Custom rear bumper. Outside mirror. Gauge package. Air conditioning. Spare tire side carrier. Full view rear cab window. Soft-ray tinted glass. Padded instrument panel. Seat belts.

HISTORICAL: Calendar year production: 127,294.

Pricing

1966 Light Duty	5	4	3	2	1
(90 in. w.b.)					
Window Van	560	1100	1850	2600	3700
Dely. Van	520	1020	1700	2400	3400
(115 in. w.b.)					
½-Ton Fender-Side Pickup	620	1230	2050	2900	4100
½-Ton Wide-Side Pickup	690	1380	2300	3200	4600
(127 in. w.b.)					
½-Ton Fender-Side Pickup	620	1230	2050	2900	4100
½-Ton Wide-Side Pickup	690	1380	2300	3200	4600
½-Ton Panel	560	1100	1850	2600	3700
½-Ton Suburban	590	1170	1950	2700	3900
¾-Ton Fender-Side Pickup	560	1100	1850	2600	3700
¾-Ton Wide-Side Pickup	570	1140	1900	2650	3800
Stake	530	1050	1750	2450	3500
(121 & 131 in. w.b.)					
1-Ton Pickup	520	1020	1700	2400	3400
1-Ton Panel	480	975	1600	2250	3200
1-Ton Stake	470	950	1550	2200	3100
FWD					
½-Ton 4x4	540	1080	1800	2500	3600
¾-Ton 4x4	520	1020	1700	2400	3400
1-Ton 4x4	480	975	1600	2250	3200

1967 GMC

New styling and numerous technical refinements made 1967 a banner year for GMC. Replacing the angular-shaped bodies used since 1960 were units with rounded edges, smooth surfaces and lower body areas/chrome accents. The GMC's grillework was very neat, consisting of a wide center

bar bearing GMC lettering, a center divider and encompassing the dual headlight system.

Numerous standard safety features were standard on the 1967 models. Among these was an energy-absorbing instrument panel and steering column, dual braking system, seat belts and four-way hazard flashing lights.

I.D. DATA: Serial number located on plate mounted on left cab door hinge pillar. Starting: GMC trucks were not formally produced on a year-to-year model change. Engine numbers located: (V-6): stamped on top of the cylinder block ahead of the right-cylinder head. Serial numbers not used on inline engines. Numbers appearing on crankcase boss at rear of distributor are building date codes.

Model Body Type	Price	Weight	Prod. Total
Series G-1500			
GS-1600G ½-Ton Handi Van	2252	2900	—
GS-1600K ½-Ton Handi Bus	2430	3095	—
GS-1600W ½-Ton Handi Bus Cust.	2565	3190	—
GS-1600X ½-Ton Handi Bus Dlx.	2754	3225	—
Series G-2500			
GS-2630G ¾-Ton Handi Van	2585	3140	—
GS-2630K ¾-Ton Handi Bus	2708	3285	—
GS-2630W ¾-Ton Handi Bus Cust.	2843	3385	—
GS-2630X ¾-Ton Handi Bus Dlx.	3032	3435	—
Series P-1500, 2500, 3500			
PS-1600H ½-Ton Van	2746	3650	—
PS-2590J ¾-Ton Van Round	3292	4715	—
PS-2630H ¾-Ton Van Square	3380	5025	—
PS-3590J 1-Ton Van Round	3489	4940	—
PS-3630H 1-Ton Van Square	3576	5250	—
PT-2590J ¾-Ton Van Round (Diesel)	5234	5435	—
PT-2630H ¾-Ton Van Square (Diesel)	5321	5745	—
PT-3590J 1-Ton Van Round (Diesel)	5339	5590	—
PT-3630H 1-Ton Van Square (Diesel)	5426	5905	—
Series C-1500			
CS-1570V ½-Ton Chassis and Cab	2057	2975	—
CS-1570C ½-Ton Pickup (FS) (6.5 ft.)	2182	3320	—
CS-1570D ½-Ton Pickup (WS) (6.5 ft.)	2225	3385	—
CS-1590C ½-Ton Pickup (FS) (8 ft.)	2232	3400	—
CS-1590D ½-Ton Pickup (WS) (8 ft.)	2275	3490	—
CS-1590G ½-Ton Panel	2948	3760	—
CS-1590K ½-Ton Suburban	2979	3980	—

(Some models available in Series CM-1500 with 305 cid V-6 engine)
(4wd models: identified as Series K-1500)

Series C-2500			
CS-2590V ¾-Ton Chassis and Cab	2233	3415	—
CS-2590C ¾-Ton Pickup (FS)	2359	3815	—
CS-2590D ¾-Ton Pickup (WS)	2402	3905	—
CS-2590F ¾-Ton Stake	2448	4040	—
CS-2590K ¾-Ton Panel	2739	4165	—
CS-2590K ¾-Ton Suburban	2969	4385	—

(Same models available in Series CM-2500 with 305 cid V-6 engine)
(4wd models: identified as Series K-2500)

Series C-3500			
CS-3600V 1-Ton Chassis and Cab	2389	3600	—
CS-3600C 1-Ton Pickup	2536	4030	—
CS-3600F 1-Ton Stake Rack	2647	4430	—

(Same models available in Series CM-3500 with 305 cid V-6 engine)

1967 GMC Pickup w/modern camper and wheels (JLC)

ENGINE (Standard: Series G-1500, G-2500, P-1500): Inline, OHV. Six-cylinder. Cast iron block. Bore & stroke: 3.875 in. x 3.25 in. Displacement: 230 cu. in. Compression ratio: 8.5:1. Brake horsepower: 140 at 4400 R.P.M. Max. Torque: 220 lb. ft. at 1600 R.P.M. Net horsepower: 120 at 3600 R.P.M. Seven main bearings. Hydraulic valve lifters. Carburetor: Rochester 1-bbl. model M 7028006/7028010.

ENGINE (Standard: Series P-2500, P-3500, C-1500, C-2500, C-3500): Inline, OHV. Six-cylinder. Cast iron block. Bore & stroke: 3.875 in. x 3.53 in. Displacement: 250 cu. in. Compression ratio: 8.5:1. Brake horsepower: 155 at 4200 R.P.M. Seven main bearings. Hydraulic valve lifters. Carburetor: Carter downdraft 1-bbl. model 3891593.

1967 GMC Deluxe Carryall Suburban (OCW)

ENGINE (Standard: Series CM-1500, CM-2500, CM-3500): V-type, OHV. Six-cylinder. Cast iron block. Bore & stroke: 4.25 in. x 3.58 in. Displacement: 304.7 cu. in. Compression ratio: 7.75:1. Brake horsepower: 170 at 4000 R.P.M. Max. Torque: 277 lb. ft. at 1600 R.P.M. Four main bearings. Hydraulic valve lifters. Carburetor: Stromberg 2-bbl. model WW 23-161.

ENGINE (Standard: Diesel P-2500, P-3500): Inline, OHV, diesel. Three-cylinder. Cast iron block. Bore & stroke: 3.875 in. x 4.5 in. Displacement: 159 cu. in. Brake horsepower: 82 at 2500 R.P.M.

ENGINE (Optional: G Models): V-type, OHV. Eight-cylinder. Cast iron block. Bore & stroke: 3.875 in. x 3.0 in. Displacement: 283 cu. in. Brake horsepower: 175 at 4400 R.P.M. Max. Torque: 275 lb. ft. at 2400 R.P.M. Five main bearings. Hydraulic valve lifters.

ENGINE (Optional: Series P-1500, P-2500, P-3500, C-1500, C-2500, C-3500): Inline, OHV. Six-cylinder. Cast iron block. Bore & stroke: 3.875 in. x 4.5 in. Displacement: 292 cu. in. Compression ratio: 8.1:1. Brake horsepower: 170 at 4000 R.P.M. Max. Torque: 275 lb. ft. at 1600 R.P.M. Seven main bearings. Hydraulic valve lifters. Carburetor: Rochester 1-bbl. model 7028012/7028013.

CHASSIS (Series G-1500): Wheelbase: 90-108 in. Tires: 6.95 x 14 in.

CHASSIS (Series P-1500): Wheelbase: 102 in. Tires: 8.15 x 15 in.

CHASSIS (Series P-3500): Wheelbase: 104-137 in. Tires: 8 x 19.5 in.

CHASSIS (Series C-2500/CM-2500): Wheelbase: 127 in. Length: 200.5 in. Height: 74.5 in. Tires: 7 x 17.5 in.

CHASSIS (Series G-2500): Wheelbase: 108 in. Tires: 7.75 x 15 in.

CHASSIS (Series P-2500): Wheelbase: 104-137 in. Tires: 7 x 17.5 in.

CHASSIS (Series C-1500/CM-1500): Wheelbase: 115-127 in. Length: 200.5 in. Height: 74.5 in. Tires: 7.75 x 15 in.

CHASSIS (Series C-3500): Wheelbase: 133-157 in. Tires: 8 x 17.5 in.

TECHNICAL: Three-speed, synchromesh transmission. Speeds: 3F/1R. Column-mounted gearshift. Clutch: Single-plate, dry disc. (230 & 250 cu. in. engines), coil spring single dry plate (292, 283 cu. in. engine); semi-floating (½-ton), full-floating (¾-ton & 1-ton) rear axle. Hydraulic, 4 wheel brakes. Kelsey-Hayes pressed steel wheels. Turbo-Hydra-Matic automatic transmission. 4-spd. manual trans. Auxiliary rear springs. No-Spin Differential. Heavy-duty suspension. Camper-Cruiser Package.

OPTIONS: Rear bumper. Radio. Heater. Clock. Cigar lighter. Radio antenna. Seat covers. Super Custom Package. Spare tire carrier. Gauge package. Air conditioning. Dual side mirrors. Seat belts. Bucket seats.

HISTORICAL: Calendar year production: 130,659

Pricing

	5	4	3	2	1
1967					
(90 in. w.b.)					
½-Ton Handi Van	570	1140	1900	2650	3800
½-Ton Handi Bus Dlx.	600	1200	2000	2800	4000
(102 in. w.b.)					
½-Ton Van	540	1080	1800	2500	3600
(115 in. w.b.)					
Fender-Side ½-Ton Pickup	1050	2100	3500	4900	7000
Wide-Side ½-Ton Pickup	1130	2250	3750	5250	7500
(127 in. w.b.)					
Fender-Side ½-Ton Pickup	1050	2100	3500	4900	7000
Wide-Side ½-Ton Pickup	1130	2250	3750	5250	7500
½-Ton Panel	600	1200	2000	2800	4000
½-Ton Suburban	680	1350	2250	3150	4500
Fender-Side ¾-Ton Pickup	900	1800	3000	4200	6000
Wide-Side ¾-Ton Pickup	980	1950	3250	4550	6500
¾-Ton Panel	530	1050	1750	2450	3500
¾-Ton Suburban	600	1200	2000	2800	4000
¾-Ton Stake	520	1020	1700	2400	3400
(133 in. w.b.)					
1-Ton Pickup	870	1750	2900	4100	5800
1-Ton Stake Rack	830	1650	2750	3850	5500

1968 GMC Wide-Side Pickup w/later camper unit (DFW)

No changes were made in the GMC truck design for 1968.

I.D. DATA: Serial number located on plate mounted on left cab door hinge pillar. Starting: GMC trucks were not formally produced on a year-to-year model change. Engine numbers located: V-6 engines: stamped on top of the cylinder block ahead of the right cylinder head. Serial numbers not used on in-line engines. Numbers appearing on crank case boss at rear of distributor are building date codes.

Model Body Type	Price	Weight	Prod. Total
Series G-1500			
GS-1600G ½-Ton Handi Van (90 in. w.b.)	2306	2900	—
GS-1600K ½-Ton Handi Bus (90 in. w.b.)	2546	3095	—
GS-1600W ½-Ton Handi Bus Cust. (90 in. w.b.)	2674	3190	—
GS-1600X ½-Ton Handi Bus Cust. Dlx. (90 in. w.b.)	2865	3225	—
Series G-2500			
GE-2630G ¾-Ton Handi Van (307 cid V-8)	2712	3290	—
GE-2630K ¾-Ton Handi Bus (307 cid V-8)	2942	3435	—
GE-2630W ¾-Ton Handi Bus Cust. (307 cid V-8)	3069	3535	—
GE-2630X ¾-Ton Handi Bus C. Dlx. (307 cid V-8)	3260	3585	—
Series P-1500-2500-3500			
PS-1550H ½-Ton Van	2824	3710	—
PS-2580H ¾-Ton Steel Van	3586	5180	—
PS-3580H 1-Ton Steel Van	3766	5395	—
PT-2580H ¾-Ton Steel Van (125 in. w.b.) (Diesel)	5528	6070	—
PT-3580H 1-Ton Steel Van (125 in. w.b.) (Diesel)	5608	6170	—
Series C-1500			
CS-1570V ½-Ton Chassis and Cab (115 in. w.b.)	2210	2975	—
CS-1570C ½-Ton Pickup (FS) (6.5 ft.)	2319	3320	—
CS-1570D ½-Ton Pickup (WS) (6.5 ft.)	2362	3385	—
CS-1590C ½-Ton Pickup (FS) (8 ft.)	2369	3400	—
CS-1590D ½-Ton Pickup (WS) (8 ft.)	2412	3490	—
CS-1590G ½-Ton Panel	2689	3760	—
CS-1590K ½-Ton Suburban	2934	3980	—
(Same models available as Series CM-1500 with 305 cid V-6)			
(4wd models: CK prefix)			
Series C-2500			
CS-2590V 1-Ton Chassis and Cab	2389	3415	—
CS-2590C 1-Ton Pickup (FS) (8 ft.)	2498	3815	—
CS-2590D 1-Ton Pickup (WS) (8 ft.)	2541	3905	—
CS-2590F 1-Ton Stake (8 ft.)	2591	4040	—
CS-2590G 1-Ton Panel	2831	4165	—
CS-2590K 1-Ton Suburban	3188	4385	—
(Same models available as Series CM-2500 with 305 cid V-6)			
(4wd models: CK prefix)			

ENGINE (Standard: G-1500, G-2500, P-1500): Inline. OHV. Six-cylinder. Cast iron block. Bore & stroke: 3.875 in. x 3.25 in. Displacement: 230 cu. in. Compression ratio: 8.5:1. Brake horsepower: 140 at 4400 R.P.M. Seven main bearings. Hydraulic valve lifters. Carburetor: Rochester 1-Bbl. model 7028017.

ENGINE (Standard: C-1500, C-2500, C-3500, P-2500, P-3500): Inline. OHV. Six-cylinder. Cast iron block. Bore & stroke: 3.875 in. x 3.53 in. Displacement: 250 cu. in. Compression ratio: 8.5:1. Brake horsepower: 155 at 4200 R.P.M. Seven main bearings. Hydraulic valve lifters. Carburetor: Carter downdraft 1-Bbl. model 3891593.

ENGINE (Standard: CM-1500, CM-2500, CM-3500): V-type. OHV. Six-cylinder. Cast iron block. Bore & stroke: 4.25 in. x 3. 58 in. Displacement: 304.7 cu. in. Compression ratio: 7.75:1. Brake horsepower: 170 at 4000 R.P.M. Max. Torque: 277 lb. ft. at 1600 R.P.M. Four main bearings. Hydraulic valve lifters. Carburetor: Stromberg 2-Bbl. model WW23-161.

ENGINE (Standard: Diesel P-2500, P-3500): Inline. OHV. Diesel. Three-cylinder. Cast iron block. Bore & stroke: 3.875 in. x 4.5 in. Displacement: 159 cu. in. Brake horsepower: 82 at 2500 R.P.M.

ENGINE (Optional: G-1500, G-2500): V-type. OHV. Eight-cylinder. Bore & stroke: 3.875 in. x 3.25 in. displacement: 307 cu. in. Compression ratio: 9.0:1. Brake horsepower: 200 at 4600 R.P.M. Five main bearings. Hydraulic valve lifters. Carburetor: Rochester 2-Bbl.

ENGINE (Optional: C-1500, C-2500, C-3500): V-type. OHV. Eight-cylinder. Cast iron block. Bore & stroke: 4.09 in. x 3.76 in. Displacement: 396 cu. in. Compression ratio: 9.0:1. Brake horsepower: 310 at 4800 R.P.M. Max. Torque: 400 lb. ft. at 3200 R.P.M. Five main bearings. Hydraulic valve lifters. Carburetor: Rochester model 4MV7028211.

ENGINE (Optional: P-1500, P-2500, P-3500, C-1500, C-2500, C-3500, 4wd models): Inline. OHV. Six-cylinder. Cast iron block. Bore & stroke: 3.875 in. x 4.12 in. Displacement: 292 cu. in. Compression ratio: 8.1:1. Brake horsepower: 170 at 4000 R.P.M. Max. Torque: 275 lb. ft. at 1600 R.P.M. Seven main bearings. Hydraulic valve lifters. Carburetor: Rochester 1-Bbl. model M7028021/7028013.

CHASSIS (Series G-1500): Wheelbase: 90-108 in. Tires: 6.95 x 14 in.

CHASSIS (Series G-2500): Wheelbase: 108 in. Tires: 7.75 x 15 in.

CHASSIS (Series P-1500): Wheelbase: 102 in. Tires: 8.15 x 15 in.

CHASSIS (Series C-2500): Wheelbase: 127 in. Tires: 7 x 17.5 in.

CHASSIS (Series P-2500): Wheelbase: 125-133 in. Tires: 8 x 17.5 in.

CHASSIS (Series P-3500): Wheelbase: 125-157 in. Tires: 8 x 17.5 in.

CHASSIS (Series C-1500): Wheelbase: 115-127 in. Tires: 8.15 x 15 in.

CHASSIS (Series C-3500): Wheelbase: 133-157 in. Tires: 8 x 17.5 in.

TECHNICAL: Manual, synchromesh transmission. Speeds: 3F/1R. Column-mounted gear shift lever. Single plate, dry-disc clutch. (230 and 250 cu. in engines), coil spring single plate (292, 307, 396 cu. in. engines). Semi-floating (½-Ton), full-floating (¾-Ton and 1-Ton) rear axle. Hydraulic, 4 wheel brakes. Kelsey-Hayes, pressed steel wheels. Overdrive (C-1500 only). Power steering. Turbo Hydra-Matic. 4-speed manual transmission. Camper package ($71): C-2500, C-3500. Auxliary rear spring. No-spin differential. Heavy duty suspension. Power brakes. Heavy-duty clutch.

OPTIONS: Rear bumper. Radio. Heater. Clock. Cigar lighter. Radio antenna. Seat covers. Air conditioning. Tinted glass. Spare tire carrier.

HISTORICAL: Calendar year production: 148,479.

Pricing

1968	5	4	3	2	1
(90 in. w.b.)					
½-Ton Handi Van	570	1140	1900	2650	3800
½-Ton Handi Bus Dlx.	600	1200	2000	2800	4000
(102 in. w.b.)					
½-Ton Van	540	1080	1800	2500	3600
(115 in. w.b.)					
Fender-Side ½-Ton Pickup	1050	2100	3500	4900	7000
Wide-Side ½-Ton Pickup	1130	2250	3750	5250	7500
(127 in. w.b.)					
Fender-Side ½-Ton Pickup	1050	2100	3500	4900	7000
Wide-Side ½-Ton Pickup	1130	2250	3750	5250	7500
½-Ton Panel	600	1200	2000	2800	4000
½-Ton Suburban	680	1350	2250	3150	4500
Fender-Side ¾-Ton Pickup	900	1800	3000	4200	6000
Wide-Side ¾-Ton Pickup	980	1950	3250	4550	6500
¾-Ton Panel	530	1050	1750	2450	3500
¾-Ton Suburban	600	1200	2000	2800	4000
¾-Ton Stake	520	1020	1700	2400	3400
(133 in. w.b.)					
1-Ton Pickup	870	1750	2900	4100	5800
1-Ton Stake Rack	830	1650	2750	3850	5500

1969 GMC

1969 GMC Wide-Side Pickup (RPZ)

Making external identification of 1969 model GMC trucks easy was the relocation of their GMC letters from the center of the grille to the forward hood surface.

I.D. DATA: Serial number located on plate mounted on left cab door hinge pillar. Starting: GMC trucks were not formally produced on a year-to-year model change. Engine numbers located: V-6 engines: stamped on top of the cylinder block ahead of the right cylinder head. Serial numbers not used on in-line engines. Numbers appearing on crank case boss at rear of distributor are building date codes.

Model	Body Type	Price	Weight	Prod. Total
Series G-1500				
GS-1600G	½-Ton Handi Van	2387	2900	—
GS-1600K	½-Ton Handi Bus	2654	3095	—
GS-1600W	½-Ton Handi Bus Custom	2781	3190	—
GS-1600X	½-Ton Handi Bus C. Dlx.	2972	3225	—
Series G-2500				
GE-2630G	¾-Ton Handi-Van	2764	3290	—
GE-2630K	¾-Ton Handi Bus	3021	3435	—
GE-2630W	¾-Ton Handi Bus Custom	3149	3535	—
GE-2630X	¾-Ton Handi Bus C. Dlx.	3340	3585	—
Series P-1500, 2500, 3500				
PS-1550H	½-Ton Van	2904	3710	—
PS-2580H	¾-Ton Steel Van	3682	5180	—
PS-2580S	¾-Ton Alum. Van	4470	—	—
PS-3580H	1-Ton Steel Van	3858	5395	—
PS-3580S	1-Ton Alum Van	4646	—	—
Series C-1500				
CS-1570V	½-Ton Chassis and Cab	2260	2990	—
CS-1570C	½-Ton Pickup (FS) (6.5 ft.)	2370	3335	—
CS-1570D	½-Ton Pickup (WS) (6.5 ft.)	2413	3400	—
CS-1590C	½-Ton Pickup (FS) (8 ft.)	2420	3415	—
CS-1590D	½-Ton Pickup (WS) (8 ft.)	2463	3505	—
CS-1590G	½-Ton Panel	2823	3775	—
CS-1590K	½-Ton Surburban	3059	3750	—

(Same models available as Series CM-1500 - 305 cid V-8)
(4wd models: KS prefix)

Series C-2500				
CS-2590V	¾-Ton Chassis and Cab	2491	3430	—
CS-2590C	¾-Ton Pickup (FS) (8 ft.)	2601	3830	—
CS-2590D	¾-Ton Pickup (WS) (8 ft.)	2644	3920	—
CS-2600D	¾-Ton Pickup (WS) (8.5 ft.)	2707	3980	—
CS-2590G	¾-Ton Panel	3035	3660	—
CS-2590K	¾-Ton Surburban	3312	4140	—

(Same models available in Series CM-2500 with 305 cid V-6 engine)
(4wd models: KS prefix)

Series C-3500				
CS-3600V	1-Ton Chassis and Cab	2626	3615	—
CS-3600C	1-Ton Pickup (FS) (9 ft.)	2759	4045	—
CS-3600D	1-Ton Pickup (WS) (8.5 ft.)	2821	4105	—

(Same models available as Series CM-3500 with 305 cid V-6 engine)

ENGINE: (Standard: G-1500, G-2500, P-1500): Inline. OHV. Six-cylinder. Cast iron block. Bore & stroke: 3.875 in. x 3.25 in. Displacement: 230 cu. in. Compression ratio: 8.5:1. Brake horsepower: 140 at 4400 R.P.M. Seven main bearings. Hydraulic valve lifters. Carburetor: Rochester 1-Bbl. model 7028017.

1969 GMC C2500 Panel Delivery (RPZ)

ENGINE (Standard: P-2500, P-3500, C-1500, C-2500, C-3500): Inline. OHV. Six-cylinder. Cast iron block. Bore & stroke: 3.875 in. x 3.53 in. Displacement: 250 cu. in. Compression ratio: 8.5:1. Brake horsepower: 155 at 4200 R.P.M. Seven main bearings. Hydraulic valve lifters. Carburetor: Carter downdraft 1-Bbl. model 3891593.

ENGINE (Standard CM-1500, CM-2500, CM-3500): V-type. OHV. Six-cylinder. Cast iron block. Bore & stroke: 4.25 in. x 3.58 in. Displacement: 304.7 cu. in. Compression ratio: 7.75:1. Brake horsepower: 170 at 4600 R.P.M. Max. Torque: 277 lb. ft. at 1600 R.P.M. Four main bearings. Hydraulic valve lifters. Carburetor: Stromberg 2-Bbl. model WW23-161.

1969 GMC C1500 Suburban Carryall (RPZ)

ENGINE (Optional: G-1500, G-2500): V-type. OHV. Eight-cylinder. Cast iron block. Bore & stroke: 3.875 in. x 3.25 in. Displacement: 307 cu. in. Compression ratio: 9.0:1. Brake horsepower: 200 at 4600 R.P.M. Five main bearings. Hydraulic valve lifters. Carburetor: Rochester 2-Bbl.

ENGINE (Optional: P-1500, P-2500, P-3500, C-1500, C-2500, C-3500): Inline. OHV. Six-cylinder. Cast iron block. Bore & stroke: 3.875 in. x 4.12 in. Displacement: 292 cu. in. Compression ratio: 8.1:1. Brake horsepower: 170 at 4000 R.P.M. Max. Torque: 275 lb. ft. at 1600 R.P.M. Seven main bearings. Hydraulic valve lifters. Carburetor: Rochester 1-Bbl. model M7028021/7028013.

ENGINE (Optional: C-1500, C-2500, C-3500): V-type. OHV. Eight-cylinder. Cast iron block. Bore & stroke: 4.09 in. x 3.76 in. Displacement: 396 cu. in. Compression ratio: 9.0:1. Brake horsepower: 310 at 4800 R.P.M. Max. Torque: 400 lb. ft. at 3200 R.P.M. Five main bearings. Hydraulic valve lifters. Carburetor: Rochester model 4MV7028211.

CHASSIS (Series G-1500): Wheelbase: 90-108 in. Tires: 6.95 x 14 in.

1969 GMC K910 (4x4) Wide-Side Pickup (RPZ)

CHASSIS (Series G-2500): Wheelbase: 108 in. Tires: 7.15 x 15 in.

CHASSIS (Series P-1500): Wheelbase: 102 in. Tires: 8.25 x 15 in.

CHASSIS (Series C-2500): Wheelbase: 127-133 in. Length: 200.5 in. Height: 74.5 in. Tires: 8 x 16.5 in.

CHASSIS (Series P-2500): Wheelbase: 125-133 in. Tires: 8 x 16.5 in.

CHASSIS (Series P-3500): Wheelbase: 125-157 in. Tires: 8 x 16.5 in.

CHASSIS (Series C-1500): Wheelbase: 115-127 in. Length: 200.5 in. Height: 74.5 in. Tires: 8.25 x 15 in.

CHASSIS (Series C-3500): Wheelbase: 133-157 in. Height: 74.5 in. Tires: 8 x 16.5 in.

1969 GMC LWB Forward Control Handi-Van (RPZ)

TECHNICAL: Manual, synchromesh transmission. Speeds: 3F/1R. Column-mounted gear shift lever. Single plate, dry-disc clutch (230 and 250 cu. in. engines), coil spring single dry plate (292, 307, 396 cu. in. engines). Semi-floating (½-Ton), full-floating (¾-Ton and 1-Ton) rear axle. Hydraulic, 19 wheel brakes. Kelsey-Hayes pressed steel wheels. Overdrive (C-1500 only). Turbo Hydra Matic. 4-speed manual transmission. Auxliary rear spring. Camper package. No-spin differential. Power steering. Heavy-duty suspension. Heavy-duty 3-speed manual.

OPTIONS: Rear bumper. Radio AM push button, AM/FM push button. Heater. Clock. Cigar lighter. Radio antenna. Seat covers. Super custom package. Air conditioning. Tinted glass. Tachometer.

HISTORICAL: Calendar year production: 150,180.

Pricing

1969	5	4	3	2	1
(90 in. w.b.)					
½-Ton Handi Van	570	1140	1900	2650	3800
½-Ton Handi Bus Dlx.	600	1200	2000	2800	4000
(102 in. w.b.)					
½-Ton Van	540	1080	1800	2500	3600
(115 in. w.b.)					
Fender-Side ½-Ton Pickup	1080	2160	3600	5050	7200
Wide-Side ½-Ton Pickup	1150	2310	3850	5400	7700
(127 in. w.b.)					
Fender-Side ½-Ton Pickup	1080	2160	3600	5050	7200
Wide-Side ½-Ton Pickup	1150	2310	3850	5400	7700
½-Ton Panel	600	1200	2000	2800	4000
½-Ton Suburban	690	1380	2300	3200	4600
Fender-Side ¾-Ton Pickup	900	1800	3000	4200	6000
Wide-Side ¾-Ton Pickup	980	1950	3250	4550	6500
¾-Ton Panel	530	1050	1750	2450	3500
¾-Ton Suburban	620	1230	2050	2900	4100
¾-Ton Stake	520	1020	1700	2400	3400
(133 in. w.b.)					
1-Ton Pickup	870	1750	2900	4100	5800
1-Ton Stake Rack	830	1650	2750	3850	5500

1970 GMC

Joining the GMC line in 1970 was the Jimmy model. Available in either two- or four-wheel drive and with a removable hardtop the Jimmy was GMC's entry into the expanding off-road recreational vehicle market. With a standard 6-cylinder engine and two-wheel drive, its starting price was $2,377.

1970 GMC C910 "Long Box" Wide-Side Pickup (RPZ)

I.D. DATA: Serial number located on plate mounted on left cab door hinge pillar. Starting: GMC trucks were not formally produced on a year-to-year model change. Engine numbers located: (V-6): stamped on top of the cylinder block ahead of the right-cylinder head. Serial numbers not used on inline engines. Numbers appearing on crankcase boss at rear of distributor are building date codes.

Model	Body Type	Price	Weight	Prod. Total
Series Jimmy K-1550				
KS-15514	½-Ton 4wd Util. Open	2947	3595	—
(2wd version: CS prefix)				
Series G-1500				
GS-1600G	½-Ton Handi Van	2464	2975	—
GS-1600K	½-Ton Handi Bus	2758	3165	—
GS-1600W	½-Ton Handi Bus Cust.	2886	3275	—
GS-1600X	½-Ton Handi Bus Cust. Dlx.	3077	3310	—
Series G-2500				
GE-2630G	¾-Ton Handi Van (307 cid V-8)	2840	3370	—
GE-2630K	¾-Ton Handi Bus (307 cid V-8)	3126	3510	—
GE-2630W	¾-Ton Handi Bus Cust. (307 cid V-8)	3253	3640	—
GE-2630X	¾-Ton Handi Bus Cust. Dlx. (307 cid V-8)	3444	3690	—
Series P-1500, 2500, 3500				
PS-15535	½-Ton Van	3099	3715	—
PS-25835	¾-Ton Steel Van	3864	5085	—
PS-25885	¾-Ton Alum. Van	4652	—	—
PS-35835	1-Ton Steel Van	4038	5255	—
PS-35855	1-Ton Alum. Van	4826	—	—
Series C-1500				
CS-15703	½-Ton Chassis and Cab	2381	3025	—
CS-15704	½-Ton Pickup (FS) (6.5 ft.)	2496	3365	—
CS-15734	½-Ton Pickup (WS) (6.5 ft.)	2534	3440	—
CS-15904	½-Ton Pickup (FS) (8 ft.)	2534	3445	—
CS-15934	½-Ton Pickup (WS) (8 ft.)	2571	3540	—
CS-15905	½-Ton Panel	3047	3650	—
CS-15916	½-Ton Suburban	3287	3790	—
(4wd models: KS prefix)				
Series C-2500				
CS-25903	¾-Ton Chassis and Cab	2628	3430	—
CS-25904	¾-Ton Pickup (FS) (8 ft.)	2728	3830	—
CS-25934	¾-Ton Pickup (WS) (8 ft.)	2766	3925	—
CS-26034	¾-Ton Pickup (WS) (8.5 ft.)	2830	3965	—
CS-25905	¾-Ton Panel	3245	4040	—
CS-25906	¾-Ton Suburban	3417	4165	—
(4wd models: KS prefix)				
Series C-3500				
CS-36003	1-Ton Chassis and Cab	2712	3575	—
CS-36004	1-Ton Pickup (FS) (9 ft.)	2850	4005	—
CS-36034	1-Ton Pickup (WS) (8.5 ft.)	2911	4090	—

ENGINE (Standard: all Models): Inline, OHV. Six-cylinder. Cast iron block. Bore & stroke: 3.875 in. x 3.53 in. Displacement: 250 cu. in. Compression ratio: 8.5:1. Brake horsepower: 155 at 4200 R.P.M. Seven main bearings. Hydraulic valve lifters. Carburetor: Carter downdraft 1-bbl. model 3891593.

ENGINE (Optional: all Models): V-type, OHV. Eight-cylinder. Cast iron block. Bore & stroke: 3.875 in. x 3.25 in. Displacement: 307 cu. in. Compression ratio: 9.0:1. Brake horsepower: 200 at 4600 R.P.M. Five main bearings. Hydraulic valve lifters. Carburetor: Rochester 2-bbl.

ENGINE (Optional: Series P-1500, P-2500, P-3500, C-1500, C-2500, C-3500): Inline, OHV. Six-cylinder. Cast iron block. Bore & stroke: 3.875 in. x 4.12 in. Displacement: 292 cu. in. Compression ratio: 8.1:1. Brake horsepower: 170 at 4000 R.P.M. Max. Torque: 275 lb. ft. at 1600 R.P.M. Seven main bearings. Hydraulic valve lifters. Carburetor: Rochester 1-bbl. model M7028012/7028013.

ENGINE (Optional: C-1500, C-2500, C-3500): V-type, OHV. Eight-cylinder. Cast iron block. Bore & stroke: 4.0 in. x 3.48 in. Displacement: 350 cu. in. Compression ratio: 9.0:1. Brake horsepower: 225 at 4800 R.P.M. Max. Torque: 365 lb. ft. at 3200 R.P.M. Five main bearings. Hydraulic valve lifters. Carburetor: Rochester 2-bbl.

ENGINE (Optional: C-1500, C-2500, C-3500): V-type, OHV. Eight-cylinder. Cast iron block. Bore & stroke: 4.09 in. x 3.76 in. Displacement: 396 cu. in. Compression ratio: 9.0:1. Brake horsepower: 310 at 4800 R.P.M. Max. Torque: 400 lb. ft. at 3200 R.P.M. Five main bearings. Hydraulic valve lifters. Carburetor: Rochester model 4MV7028211.

CHASSIS (Series Jimmy K-1550): Wheelbase: 104 in. Length: 177.5 in. Height: 68.7 in. Front tread: 60.4 in. Rear tread: 60.4 in. Tires: E78 x 15 in.

CHASSIS (Series G-1500): Wheelbase: 90-108 in. Tires: 6.95 x 14 in.

CHASSIS (Series G-2500): Wheelbase: 108 in. Tires: 7.75 x 15 in.

CHASSIS (Series C-1500): Wheelbase: 115-127 in. Tires: G78 x 15 in.

CHASSIS (Series P-1500): Wheelbase: 102 in. Tires: G78 x 15 in.

CHASSIS (Series P-2500): Wheelbase: 125-133 in. Tires: 8.75 x 16.5 in.

CHASSIS (Series P-3500): Wheelbase: 125-151 in. Tires: 8.75 x 16.5 in.

CHASSIS (Series C-2500): Wheelbase: 127-133 in. Tires: 8.75 x 16.5 in.

CHASSIS (Series C-3500): Wheelbase: 133-157 in. Tires: 8.75 x 16.5 in.

TECHNICAL: Manual, synchromesh transmission. Speeds: 3F/1R. Column mounted gearshift. Clutch: Single-plate, dry disc. (250 cid engine), all others: coil spring dry plate. Semi-floating (½-ton), full-floating (¾-ton & 1-ton) rear axle. Hydraulic, 4 wheel brakes. Kelsey-Hayes pressed steel wheels. Turbo-Hydra-Matic automatic transmission (350 and 400). Camper Package (C-2500, C-3500). Wide ratio Muncie 3-speed manual. Free-wheeling hubs (4wd). No spin differential. Power steering. Front stabilizer bar. Rear leaf springs. 42 amp generator. Heavy-duty battery. Heavy-duty rear spring. Heavy-duty front shocks. Auxiliary full tank.

OPTIONS: Rear bumper. Radio AM, AM/FM push-button. Heater. Clock. Cigar lighter. Radio antenna. Seat covers. Super Custom Package (Jimmy C-1500, C-2500, C-3500). Marker lights. Air conditioning. Gauge package. Tilt steering wheel. Shoulder belts. Tinted glass. Dual outside mirror. Dome light switch. Side wheel carrier. Full foam seat. Sierra Grande package.

HISTORICAL: Calendar year production: 121,833. First year for Jimmy model.

Pricing

1970	5	4	3	2	1
(90 in. w.b.)					
½-Ton Handi Van	570	1140	1900	2650	3800
½-Ton Handi Bus Dlx.	600	1200	2000	2800	4000
(102 in. w.b.)					
½-Ton Van	540	1080	1800	2500	3600
(115 in. w.b.)					
Fender-Side ½-Ton Pickup	1080	2160	3600	5050	7200
Wide-Side ½-Ton Pickup	1150	2310	3850	5400	7700
(127 in. w.b.)					
Fender-Side ½-Ton Pickup	1080	2160	3600	5050	7200
Wide-Side ½-Ton Pickup	1150	2310	3850	5400	7700
½-Ton Panel	600	1200	2000	2800	4000
½-Ton Suburban	690	1380	2300	3200	4600
Fender-Side ¾-Ton Pickup	900	1800	3000	4200	6000
Wide-Side ¾-Ton Pickup	980	1950	3250	4550	6500
¾-Ton Panel	530	1050	1750	2450	3500
¾-Ton Suburban	620	1230	2050	2900	4100
¾-Ton Stake	520	1020	1700	2400	3400
(133 in. w.b.)					
1-Ton Pickup	870	1750	2900	4100	5800
1-Ton Stake Rack	830	1650	2750	3850	5500
FWD					
(104 in. w.b.)					
FWD Jimmy	1050	2100	3500	4900	7000
2wd Jimmy	980	1950	3250	4550	6500

1971 GMC

No appearance changes were introduced on the 1971 models. These were highlighted by the use of blacked-out grille sections and a new two-tone color scheme for Wide-Side bodied pickups.

Added to the GMC lineup were new vans with extended hoods for easier services and sliding side doors. They were equipped with single headlamps and grilles with narrow horizontal bars.

I.D. DATA: Serial number combination GVW and serial number plate located on left door hinge pillar. Example: Starting: (pickup) CE-140( )100001 and up. Engine number indicates manufacturing plant, month, and day of manufacture and transmission type. 6-cyl: located on pad at right hand of cylinder block at rear of distributor. 8-cyl: located on pad at front, right hand of cylinder block.

Model	Body Type	Price	Weight	Prod. Total
Series C-1500				
CE-15703	½-Ton Chassis and Cab	2786	3160	—
CE-15704	½-Ton Pickup (FS) (6.5 ft.)	2946	3500	—
CE-15734	½-Ton Pickup (FS) (6.5 ft.)	2946	3575	—
CE-15904	½-Ton Pickup (FS) (8 ft.)	2983	3575	—
CE-15934	½-Ton Pickup (WS) (8 ft.)	2983	3665	—
CE-15916	½-Ton Suburban	3757	3910	—
(4wd models: KE prefix)				
Series C-2500				
CE-25903	¾-Ton Chassis and Cab	3027	3570	—
CE-25904	¾-Ton Pickup (FS) (8 ft.)	3188	3970	—
CE-25934	¾-Ton Pickup (WS) (8 ft.)	3188	4055	—
CE-26034	¾-Ton Pickup (WS) (8.5 ft.)	3252	4100	—
CE-25906	¾-Ton Suburban	3886	4295	—
(4wd models: KE prefix)				
Series C-3500				
CE-36003	1-Ton Chassis and Cab	3118	3695	—
CE-36004	1-Ton Pickup (FS) (9 ft.)	3171	4125	—
CE-36034	1-Ton Pickup (WS) (8.5 ft.)	3332	4215	—
Series Sprint				
53480	½-Ton Pickup Sedan (307 cid V-8)	2988	3418	—
53680	½-Ton Pickup Sedan Cust. (307 cid V-8)	3074	3442	—
Series Jimmy K-1550				
KE-15514	½-Ton 4wd Util. Open	3374	3730	—
Series G-1500				
GE-16005	½-Ton Vandura (110 in. w.b.) (307 cid V-8)	3053	3445	—
GE-16006	½-Ton Rally (110 in. w.b.) (307 cid V-8)	3503	3750	—
GE-16036	½-Ton Rally STX (110 in. w.b.) (307 cid V-8)	3790	3420	—
Series G-2500				
GE-26005	¾-Ton Vandura (110 in. w.b.) (307 cid V-8)	3196	3625	—
GE-26006	¾-Ton Rally (110 in. w.b.) (307 cid V-8)	3581	3900	—
GE-26036	¾-Ton Rally STX (110 in. w.b.) (307 cid V-8)	3808	4010	—
Series G-3500				
GE-36005	1-Ton Vandura (110 in. w.b.) (307 cid V-8)	3307	3695	—
GE-36306	1-Ton Rally (100 in. w.b.) (307 cid V-8)	3824	4280	—
GE-36336	1-Ton Rally STX (110 in. w.b.) (307 cid V-8)	4111	4505	—
Series P-1500, 2500, 3500				
PS-15535	½-Ton Van	2415	3740	—
PE-25835	¾-Ton Van	4312	5200	—
PE-35835	1-Ton Van	4486	5375	—

ENGINE (Standard: All models): Inline. OHV. Six-cylinder. Cast iron block. Bore 3.875 in. x 3.53 in. Displacement: 250 cu. in. Compression ratio: 8.5:1. Brake horsepower: 145 at 4200 R.P.M. Seven main bearings. Hydraulic valve lifters. Carburetor: Rochester 1-Bbl.

ENGINE (Optional: All models): V-type. OHV. Eight-cylinder. Cast iron block. Bore & stroke: 3.875 in. x 3.25 in. Displacement: 307 cu. in. Compression ratio: 8.5:1. Brake horsepower: 200 at 4600 R.P.M. Five main bearings. Hydraulic valve lifters. Carburetor: Rochester 2-Bbl.

ENGINE (Optional: P-1500, P-2500, P-3500, C-1500, C-2500, C-3500): Inline. OHV. Six-cylinder. Cast iron block. Bore & stroke: 3.875 in. x 4.12 in. Displacement: 292 cu. in. Compression ratio: 8.0:1. Brake horsepower: 165 at 4000 R.P.M. Max. Torque: 270 lb. ft. at 1600 R.P.M. Net horsepower: 125 at 3600 R.P.M. Seven main bearings. Hydraulic valve lifters. Carburetor: Rochester 1-Bbl.

ENGINE (Optional: K-1550, C-1500, C-2500, C-3500): V-type. OHV. Eight-cylinder. Cast iron block. Bore & stroke: 4.0 in. x 3.5 in. Displacement: 350 cu. in. Compression ratio: 8.5:1. Brake horsepower: 250 at 4600 R.P.M. Max Torque: 350 lb. ft at 3000 R.P.M. Net horsepower: 170 at 3600 R.P.M. Five main bearings. Hydraulic valve lifters. Carburetor: Rochester 2-Bbl.

ENGINE (Optional C-1500, C-2500, C-3500): V-type. OHV. Eight-cylinder. Cast iron block. Bore & stroke: 4.125 in. x 3.75 in. Displacement: 402 cu. in. Compression ratio: 8.5:1. Brake horsepower: 300 at 4800 R.P.M. Net horsepower: 240 at 4400 R.P.M. Five main bearings. Hydraulic valve lifters. Carburetor: Rochester 4-Bbl.

CHASSIS (Sprint Series): Wheelbase: 116 in. Overall length: 206.8 in. Height: 544 in. Front tread: 60.2 in. Rear tread: 59.2 in. Tires: E78-14B.

CHASSIS (Jimmy Series): Wheelbase: 104 in. Overall length: 177.5 in. Height: 68.7 in. Front tread: 60.4 in. Rear tread 60.4 in. Tires: E78-15B.

CHASSIS (Series G-1500): Wheelbase: 110-125 in. Overall length: 178 x 202.2 in. Height: 80 in. Tires: F78 x 14B in.

CHASSIS (Series G-2500): Wheelbase: 110-125 in. Overall length: 178 x 202.2 in. Height: 80 in. Tires: G78 x 15B in.

CHASSIS (Series G-3500): Wheelbase: 110-125 in. Overall length: 178 x 202.2 in. Height: 80 in. Tires: 8 x 16.5C in.

CHASSIS (Series P-1500): Wheelbase: 102 in. Height: 75 in. Tires: G78 x 15B in.

CHASSIS (Series P-2500, P-3500): Wheelbase: 125-133 in. Overall length: 220.75 x 244.75 in. Tires: 8.75 x 16.5C in.

CHASSIS (Series C-1500): Wheelbase: 115-127 in. Tires: G78 x 15B in.

CHASSIS (Series C-2500): Wheelbase: 127-133 in. Tires: 8.75 x 16.5C in.

CHASSIS (Series C-3500): Wheelbase: 133-157 in. Overall length: 244.75 x 265.75 in. Tires: 8.75 x 16C in.

TECHNICAL: Manual, Saginaw, fully-synchronized transmission. Speeds: 3F/1R. Column-mounted gear shift lever. Single dry, plate-disc clutch (250 cid engine) coil spring single dry plate all others. Semi-floating (½-ton) full floating (¾-ton and 1-ton) rear axle. Hydraulic, 4-wheel brakes. Kelsey-Hayes pressed steel wheels. Turbo Hydra-matic automatic transmission 350 and 400 (258.25). Wide ratio Muncie 3-speed manual. 4-speed, floor-mounted shifter trans. Free wheeling hubs (4wd). No-spin axle. Camper package. Power brakes. Power steering. Front stablizer bar. Rear leaf spring. 42-amp generator. 9.50 x 16.5 tires. Heavy-duty battery. Heavy-duty rear springs. Heavy-duty front shocks. Various axle ratios. Auxiliary fuel tank.

OPTIONS: Rear bumper. Radio. Clock. Radio antenna. Seat covers. SP Package (Spring) $365. Super custom package (Jimmy). Sierra package (C-1500, C-2500, C-3500). Extra wheel. Deluxe heater. Gauge package. Tilt steering wheel. Shoulder belts. Tinted glass. Dual exterior mirrors. Dome light switch. Side wheel carrier. Full-foam seat.

HISTORICAL: First year for Sprint model.

Pricing

	5	4	3	2	1
1971					
(90 in. w.b.)					
½-Ton Handi Van	570	1140	1900	2650	3800
½-Ton Handi Bus Dlx.	600	1200	2000	2800	4000
(102 in. w.b.)					
½-Ton Van	540	1080	1800	2500	3600
(115 in. w.b.)					
Fender-Side ½-Ton Pickup	1110	2220	3700	5200	7400
Wide-Side ½-Ton Pickup	1140	2280	3800	5300	7600
(127 in. w.b.)					
Fender-Side ½-Ton Pickup	1110	2220	3700	5200	7400
Wide-Side ½-Ton Pickup	1140	2280	3800	5300	7600
½-Ton Panel	650	1300	2150	3050	4300
½-Ton Suburban	740	1470	2450	3350	4900
Fender-Side ¾-Ton Pickup	930	1860	3100	4350	6200
Wide-Side ¾-Ton Pickup	1000	2000	3300	4600	6600
¾-Ton Panel	630	1250	2100	3000	4200
¾-Ton Suburban	660	1320	2200	3100	4400
¾-Ton Stake	540	1080	1800	2500	3600
(133 in. w.b.)					
1-Ton Pickup	870	1750	2900	4100	5800
1-Ton Stake Rack	830	1650	2750	3850	5500
FWD					
(104 in. w.b.)					
4x4 Jimmy	1070	2150	3550	5000	7100
4x2 Jimmy	1000	2000	3300	4600	6600

1972 GMC

1972 GMC Sprint Pickup (GMC)

Joining the GMC light-duty line in 1972 was GMC's version of the Chevrolet El Camino, the Sprint. It was distinguished from the El Camino by its GMC side body trim and GMC grille lettering.

Replacing the old Handi Van models were Vandura versions based upon the Van platform introduced a year earlier.

I.D. DATA: Serial number vehicle identification located on top of instrument panel, left front. Body numbers, trim and paint plate-left upper portion of horizontal surface of shroud under hood (see bottom for sample).* Starting: 50001. Engine numbers located (6-cyl.): on pad at right-hand side of cylinder block at rear of distributor. (8-cyl.): on pad at front, right-hand side of cylinder block, on boss above filler plug.

Model	Vin
53380	5C80D2B500001
53480	5C80H2B500001
53680	5D80H2B500001

* Example
5: Signifies GMC
C: regular Sprint, Pickup
D: Custom Sprint
80: Body Style
D: LF-250
F: 32748
H: 350-V-8-2-bbl.
J: V-8 350-4-bbl.
U: 402 V-8 4-bbl.
W: V-8 454 4-bbl.
2: Model Year Code
Assembly Plant Location:
B-Baltimore
K-Leeds
L-Van Nuys
Last 5 didigts — sequential production number

Model	Body Type	Price	Weight	Prod. Total
Sprint Series				
53680	½-Ton Pickup Sedan (307 cid V-8)	2881	3418	—
53680	½-Ton Pickup Sedan, Custom (307 cid V-8)	2960	3442	—
Jimmy Series K-1550				
KE-15514	½-Ton 4wd Utility (2wd model: CE-15514)	3266	3830	—
Series G-1500				
GE-16005	½-Ton Vandura (110 in. w.b.) (307 cid V-8)	2897	3580	—
GE-16006	½-Ton Rally (110 in. w.b.) (307 cid V-8)	3405	3890	—
GE-16036	½-Ton Rally STX (110 in. w.b.) (307 cid V-8)	3684	4055	—
Series G-2500				
GE-26005	¾-Ton Vandura (110 in. w.b.) (350 cid V-8)	3034	3770	—
GE-26006	¾-Ton Rally (110 in. w.b.) (350 cid V-8)	3759	4130	—
Series G-3500				
GE-36005	1-Ton Vandura (110 in. w.b.) (350 cid V-8)	3142	3950	—
GE-36306	1-Ton Rally (110 in. w.b.) (350 cid V-8)	3718	4390	—
GE-36336	1-Ton Rally STX (110 in. w.b.) (350 cid V-8)	3997	4610	—
Series P-1500, 2500, 3500				
PS-15535	½-Ton Van	3259	3810	—
PE-25835	¾-Ton Van (125 in. w.b.)	4113	5280	—
PE-35835	1-Ton Van (125 in. w.b.)	4279	5445	—
Series C-1500				
CE-15703	½-Ton Chassis and Cab (115 in. w.b.)	2660	3280	—
CE-15704	½-Ton Pickup (FS) (6.5 ft.)	2804	3620	—
CE-15734	½-Ton Pickup (WS) (6.5 ft.)	2804	3690	—
CE-15904	½-Ton Pickup (FS) (8 ft.)	2840	3695	—
CE-15934	½-Ton Pickup (WS) (8 ft.)	2840	3775	—
CE-15916	½-Ton Suburban	3655	4090	—
(4wd models: KE prefix)				
Series C-2500				
CE-25903	¾-Ton Chassis and Cab (127 in. w.b.)	2890	3585	—
CE-25904	¾-Ton Pickup (FS) (8 ft.)	3035	3990	—
CE-25934	¾-Ton Pickup (WS) (8 ft.)	3035	4070	—
CE-26034	¾-Ton Pickup (WS) (8.5 ft.)	3096	4125	—
CE-25906	¾-Ton Suburban	3782	4510	—
(4wd models: KE prefix)				
Series C-3500				
CE-36003	1-Ton Chassis and Cab (133 in. w.b.)	2977	3705	—
CE-36004	1-Ton Pickup (FS) (9 ft.)	3113	4135	—
CE-36034	1-Ton Pickup (WS) (8.5 ft.)	3172	4215	—

ENGINE (Standard: all Models): Inline, OHV. Six-cylinder. Cast iron block. Bore & stroke: 3.9 in. x 4.5 in. Displacement: 250 cu. in. Compression ratio: 8.5:1. Brake horsepower: 145 at 4200 R.P.M. Max. Torque: 230 lb. ft. at 1600 R.P.M. Net horsepower: 110 at 4000 R.P.M. Seven main bearings. Hydraulic valve lifters. Carburetor: Rochester 1-bbl.

ENGINE (Standard: Series P-1500, Optional: C Series): Inline, OHV. Six-cylinder. Cast iron block. Bore & stroke: 3.875 in. x 4.125 in. Displacement: 292 cu. in. Compression ratio: 8.0:1. Brake horsepower: 165 at 4000 R.P.M. Max. Torque: 270 lb. ft. at 1600 R.P.M. Net horsepower: 125 at 3600 R.P.M. Seven main bearings. Hydraulic valve lifters. Carburetor: Rochester 1-bbl.

ENGINE: V-type, OHV. Eight-cylinder. Cast iron block. Bore & stroke: 3.875 in. x 3.25 in. Displacement: 307 cu. in. Compression ratio: 8.5:1. Brake horsepower: 200 at 4600 R.P.M. Max. Torque: 300 lb. ft. at 2400 R.P.M. Net horsepower: 135 at 4000 R.P.M. Five main bearings. Hydraulic valve lifters. Carburetor: Rochester 2-bbl.

ENGINE: V-type, OHV. Eight-cylinder. Cast iron block. Bore & stroke: 4.125 in. x 3.75 in. Displacement: 402 cu. in. Compression ratio: 8.5:1. Brake horsepower: 300 at 4800 R.P.M. Net horsepower: 240 at 4400 R.P.M. Five main bearings. Hydraulic valve lifters. Carburetor: Rochester 4-bbl.

ENGINE (Optional: Sprint): V-type, OHV. Eight-cylinder. Cast iron block. Bore & stroke: 4.251 in. x 4.0 in. Displacement: 454 cu. in. Compression ratio: 8.5:1. Net horsepower: 270 at 4000 R.P.M. Max. Torque: 390 lb. ft. at 3200 R.P.M. Five main bearings. Hydraulic valve lifters. Carburetor: Rochester 4-bbl.

ENGINE: V-type, OHV. Eight-cylinder. Cast iron block. Bore & stroke: 4.0 in. x 3.5 in. Displacement: 350 cu. in. Compression ratio: 8.5:1. Brake horsepower: 250 at 4600 R.P.M. Max. Torque: 350 lb. ft. at 3000 R.P.M. Five main bearings. Hydraulic valve lifters. Carburetor: Rochester 2-bbl.

CHASSIS (Sprint Series): Wheelbase: 116 in. Overall length: 206.8 in. Height: 54.4 in. Front tread: 60.2 in. Rear tread: 59.2 in. Tires: E78 x 14B in.

CHASSIS (Jimmy Series): Wheelbase: 104 in. Length: 177.5 in. Height: 68.7 in. Front tread: 60.4 in. Rear tread: 60.4 in. 4wd. Tires: E78 x 15B in.

CHASSIS (Series G-1500): Wheelbase: 110-125 in. Overall length: 178 x 202.2 in. Height: 80 in. Tires: E78 x 14B in.

CHASSIS (Series G-2500): Wheelbase: 110-125 in. Overall length: 178 x 202.5 in. Height: 80 in. Tires: E78 x 15B in.

CHASSIS (Series G-3500): Wheelbase: 110-125 in. Overall length: 178 x 202.5 in. Height: 80 in. Tires: 8 x 16.5 in.

CHASSIS (Series P-1500): Wheelbase: 102 in. Tires: G78 x 15B in.

CHASSIS (Series P-2500): Wheelbase: 125-133 in. Tires: 8.75 x 16.5 in.

CHASSIS (Series P-3500): Wheelbase: 125-157 in. Tires: 8.75 x 16.5 in.

CHASSIS (Series C-1500): Wheelbase: 115-127 in. Overall length: 200.5 in. Height: 74.5 in. Tires: G78 x 15B in.

CHASSIS (Series C-2500): Wheelbase: 127-133 in. Overall length: 200.5 in. Height: 76.5 in. Tires: 8.75 x 16.5C in.

CHASSIS (Series C-3500): Wheelbase: 133-157 in. Tires: 8.75 x 16.5C in.

TECHNICAL: Manual, all synchromesh transmission. Speeds: 3F/1R. Column-mounted gearshift. Clutch: Single-plate, dry disc. (250 cid engine), all others: coil spring dry plate. Semi-floating (½-ton), full-floating (¾-ton & 1-ton) rear axle. Hydraulic, 4 wheel brakes. Kelsey-Hayes pressed steel wheels. Turbo-Hydra-Matic automatic transmission. Camper Package. Dual rear wheels (C-3500). 4-speed close-ratio manual transmission (Sprint). Auxiliary rear springs. No-spin differential. Power steering. Heavy-duty suspension. Heavy-duty 3-spd. manual transmission.

OPTIONS: Rear bumper. Radio AM, AM/FM. Heater. Clock. Cigar lighter. Radio antenna. Seat covers. SP Package (Sprint) ($350). Super Custom Package (Jimmy C-Series) ($365). Sierra Grande Package (C-Series). Air conditioning. Auxiliary lighting. Sprint optional equipment. Custom interior. Power door locks. Operating convenience group. Vinyl roof cover. Cruise-Master speed control. Bucket seats. Sport steering wheel. Confor-tilt steering wheel. Wheel covers. Rally wheels.

HISTORICAL: Calendar year production: 132,243.

Pricing

	5	4	3	2	1
1972					
(90 in. w.b.)					
½-Ton Handi Van	570	1140	1900	2650	3800
½-Ton Handi Bus Dlx.	600	1200	2000	2800	4000
(102 in. w.b.)					
½-Ton Van	540	1080	1800	2500	3600
(115 in. w.b.)					
Fender-Side ½-Ton Pickup	1110	2220	3700	5200	7400
Wide-Side ½-Ton Pickup	1140	2280	3800	5300	7600
(127 in. w.b.)					
Fender-Side ½-Ton Pickup	1110	2220	3700	5200	7400
Wide-Side ½-Ton Pickup	1140	2280	3800	5300	7600
½-Ton Panel	650	1300	2150	3050	4300
½-Ton Suburban	740	1470	2450	3350	4900
Fender-Side ¾-Ton Pickup	930	1860	3100	4350	6200
Wide-Side ¾-Ton Pickup	1000	2000	3300	4600	6600
¾-Ton Panel	630	1250	2100	3000	4200
¾-Ton Suburban	660	1320	2200	3100	4400
¾-Ton Stake	540	1080	1800	2500	3600
(133 in. w.b.)					
1-Ton Pickup	870	1750	2900	4100	5800
1-Ton Stake Rack	830	1650	2750	3850	5500
FWD					
(104 in. w.b.)					
4x4 Jimmy	1070	2150	3550	5000	7100
4x2 Jimmy	1000	2000	3300	4600	6600

1973 GMC

1973 GMC Sprint "High Sierra" Pickup (DFW)

All new models destined for a long production life debuted in 1973. Styling was extremely attractive. Single lamp head lights were featured and a grille consisting of three sections with black inserts was used. Engine size plaques were installed in the right side section. A mid-body trim arrangement allowed the installation of either two-tone color schemes or a wood-grain insert.

For multi-purpose use a 3 + 3 model with four-doors and six passenger capacity was now available. The GMC Suburban joined in the restyling process and proved extremely popular with customers interested in a vehicle for towing travel trailers while also possessing room for six-passengers and their luggage.

Joining the restyling bandwagon was the Sprint, which like the Chevrolet El Camino, was styled along the lines of the latest Chevelle automobile.

I.D. DATA: Serial number combination VIN and rating plate located on left door pillar. Third letter identifies engines: Q: 250 cu. in. L-6, T:292 cu. in. L-6, X:307 cu. in. V-8, Y:350 cu. in. V-8, Z:454 cu. in. V-8. Starting: GMC trucks not produced on a yearly model change basis - no serial numbers are available. Engine numbers 6-cyl: located on pad at right side of cylinder block at rear of distributor. 8-cyl: located on pad at front right side of cylinder block.

Model	Body Type	Price	Weight	Prod. Total
Sprint Series				
5AC80	½-Ton Sedan Pickup	2976	3625	—
5AD80	½-Ton Sedan Pickup Cust.	3038	3635	—
Jimmy Series				
TK-10514	½-Ton 4wd Utility	3319	3757	—
TC-10514	½-Ton 2wd Utility	—	—	—
Series G-1500				
TG-11005	½-Ton Vandura (110 in. w.b.) (307 cid V-8)	2942	3518	—
TG-11006	½-Ton Rally (110 in. w.b.) (307 cid V-8)	3455	3822	—
TG-11006	½-Ton Rally (110 in. w.b.) (307 cid V-8)	3785	3985	—
Series G-2500				
TG-21005	¾-Ton Vandura (110 in. w.b.) (350 cid V-8)	3079	3658	—
TG-21006	¾-Ton Rally (110 in. w.b.) (350 cid V-8)	3531	3901	—
TG-21006	¾-Ton Rally STX (125 in. w.b.) (350 cid V-8)	3831	4064	—
Series G-3500				
TG-31005	1-Ton Vandura (110 in. w.b.) (350 cid V-8)	3188	3962	—
TG-31306	1-Ton Rally (110 in. w.b.) (350 cid V-8)	3772	4358	—
TG-31306	1-Ton Rally STX (125 in. w.b.) (350 cid V-8)	4102	4478	—
Series P-1500, 2500, 3500				
TP-10542	½-Ton Van (7 ft.)	3453	4040	—
TP-20842	¾-Ton Van (10 ft.)	4234	5278	—
TP-30842	1-Ton Van (10 ft.)	4402	5548	—
Series C-1500				
TC-10703	½-Ton Chassis and Cab (307 cid V-8)	2695	3296	—
TC-10703	½-Ton Pickup (FS) (6.5 ft.) (307 cid V-8)	2882	3622	—
TX-10703	½-Ton Pickup (WS) (6.5 ft.) (307 cid V-8)	2882	3741	—
TC-10903	½-Ton Pickup (FS) 8 ft. (307 cid V-8)	2918	3718	—
TC-10903	½-Ton Pickup (WS) (8 ft.) (307 cid V-8)	2918	3843	—
TC-10906	½-Ton Suburban (129.5 in. w.b.) (307 cid V-8)	3710	4136	—
(4wd models: KC prefix)				

Model	Body Type	Price	Weight	Prod. Total
Series C-2500				
TC-20903	¾-Ton Chassis and Cab (131.5 in. w.b.) (307 cid V-8)	2934	3650	—
TC-20903	¾-Ton Pickup (FS) (8 ft.) (307 cid V-8)	3119	4045	—
TC-20903	¾-Ton Pickup (WS) (8 ft.) (307 cid V-8)	3119	4170	—
TC-20963	¾-Ton Pickup Crew Cab (8 ft.) (307 cid V-8)	4152	4423	—
TC20906	¾-Ton Suburban (129.5 in. w.b.) (307 cid V-8)	4040	4624	—
(4wd models: KC prefix)				
Series C-3500				
TC-30903	1-Ton Chassis and Cab (135.1 in. w.b.) (307 cid V-8)	3023	3810	—
TC-30903	1-Ton Pickup (FS) (8 ft.) (307 cid V-8)	3207	4236	—
TC-30903	1-Ton Pickup (WS) (8 ft.)	3207	4326	—
TC-30963	1-Ton Pickup crew cab 8 ft. (307 cid V-8)	4226	4424	—

ENGINE (Standard: All models except Sprint): Inline. OHV. Six-cylinder. Cast iron block. Bore & stroke: 3⅞ in. x 3½ in. Displacement: 250 cu. in. Compression ratio: 8.25:1. Net horsepower: 100 at 3600 R.P.M. Net Torque: 175 lb. ft. at 2000 R.P.M. Seven main bearings. Hydraulic valve lifters. Carburetor: Rochester 1-Bbl.

ENGINE (Standard: Sprint, optional: C-1500, C-2500, C-3500): V-type. OHV. Eight-cylinder. Cast iron block. Bore & stroke: 3⅞ in. x 3¼ in. Displacement: 307 cu. in. Compression ratio: 8.5:1. Net horsepower: 115 at 3600 R.P.M. Net Torque: 205 lb. ft. at 2000 R.P.M. Five main bearings. Hydraulic valve lifters. Carburetor: 2-Bbl.

ENGINE (Optional: C-1500, C-2500, C-3500, P-1500, P-2500, P-3500): Inline. OHV. Six-cylinder. Cast iron block. Bore & stroke: 3⅞ in. x 4⅛ in. Displacement: 292 cu. in. Compression ratio: 8.0:1. Net horsepower: 120 at 3600 R.P.M. Net Torque: 225 lb. ft. at 2000 R.P.M. Seven main bearings. Hydraulic valve lifters. Carburetor: 1-Bbl.

ENGINE (Optional: Spring, Jimmy, G Series, P. Series): V-type. OHV. Eight-cylinder. Cast iron block. Bore & stroke: 4 in. x 3.48 in. Displacement: 350 cu. in. Compression ratio: 8.5:1. Net horsepower: 155 at 4000 R.P.M. Net Torque: 255 lb. ft. at 2400 R.P.M. Five main bearings. Hydraulic valve lifters. Carburetor: 2-Bbl.

CHASSIS (Sprint Series): Wheelbase: 116 in. Overall length: 201.6 in. Height: 53.8 in. Front tread: 58.5 in. Rear tread: 57.8 in. Tires: G78 x 14B in.

CHASSIS (Jimmy Series): Wheelbase: 106.5 in. Overall length: 184.5 in. Height: 67.5 w/o top, 69.5 w/top - 2wd, 69.5 w/o top, 71.5 w/top - 4wd. Tires: E78 x 15B in.

CHASSIS (Series G-1500): Wheelbase: 110-125 in. Overall length: 178 x 202.2 in. Tires: G78 x 14B in.

CHASSIS (Series G-2500): Wheelbase: 110-125 in. Overall length: 178 x 202.2 in. Tires: G78 x 15B in.

CHASSIS (Series G3500): Wheelbase: 110-125 in. Overall length: 178 x 202.2 in. Tires: 8.00 x 16.5C in.

CHASSIS (Series P-1500): Wheelbase: 102 in. Height: 75 in. Tires: G78 x 15B in.

CHASSIS (Series P-2500): Wheelbase: 125-135 in. Tires: 8.75 x 16.5C in.

CHASSIS (Series P-3500): Wheelbase: 125-157 in. Overall length: 220.75 x 265.75 in. Tires: 9.50 x 16.5D in.

CHASSIS (Series C-1500): Wheelbase: 117.5-131.5 in. Overall length: 191-212 in. Height: 69.8 in. Front tread: 65.8 in. Rear tread: 62.7 in. Tires: G78 x 15B in.

CHASSIS (Series C-3500): Wheelbase: 131.5-164.5 in. Overall length: 2112 x 244.43 in. Height: 71.8 in. Front tread: 65.8 in. Rear tread: 62.7 in. Tires: 8.75 x 16.5C in.

TECHNICAL: Manual synchromesh transmission. Speeds: 3F/1R. Column mounted gearshift. Camper package. Dual rear wheels (C-3500). Turbo Hydra-Matic 350, 400/475. Various clutches and rear axle ratios. 4-speed manual transmission. Front stablizier bar (2wd).

OPTIONS: Chrome bumpers. Radio AM, AM/FM. SP Package (Sprint). High Sierra Package (Sprint Custom). Sierra Package (Jimmy, C-series). Sierra Grande Package (C-Series). Power steering. Below-eye-line mirrors. Drip moldings. Sliding rear window. Cargo lamp. Gauge package. Air conditioning. Tachometer. Comfortilt steering wheel. Exterior tool and storage compartment. Wheel covers. Whitewall tires. Special trim molding. Woodgrain exterior trim. Rear step bumper. Glide-out spare tire carrier.

HISTORICAL: Calendar year production: 166,733.

1973 GMC High Sierra Custom Pickup (JAG)

Pricing

	5	4	3	2	1
1973					
(116 in. w.b.)					
½-Ton Sprint Cus.	830	1650	2750	3850	5500
(106 in. w.b.)					
FWD ½-Ton Jimmy	980	1950	3250	4550	6500
2wd ½-Ton Jimmy	830	1650	2750	3850	5500
(110 in. w.b.)					
½-Ton Rally Van	780	1560	2600	3600	5200
(117 in. w.b.)					
Fender-Side ½-Ton Pickup	810	1620	2700	3800	5400
Wide-Side ½-Ton Pickup	840	1680	2800	3900	5600
(125 in. w.b.)					
Fender-Side ½-Ton Pickup	830	1650	2750	3850	5500
Wide-Side ½-Ton Pickup	850	1700	2850	4000	5700
½-Ton Suburban	830	1650	2750	3850	5500
Fender-Side ¾-Ton Pickup	750	1500	2500	3500	5000
Wide-Side ¾-Ton Pickup	780	1560	2600	3600	5200
¾-Ton Suburban	770	1550	2550	3600	5100
¾-Ton Rally Van	750	1500	2500	3500	5000
(125 & 135 in. w.b.)					
1-Ton Pickup	750	1500	2500	3500	5000
1-Ton Crew Cab Pickup	700	1400	2350	3250	4700

1974 GMC

1974 GMC High Sierra Wide-Side Pickup w/camper (JAG)

470

GMC pickups and Suburbans now used grilles with GMC letterings in the center section. The Sprint grille carried similarly styled lettering in its grille's center portion, which also features two prominent horizontal bars and a center divider mounted ahead of a black gridwork.

I.D. DATA: Serial number located: A combination VIN and rating plate located on left door pillar: The VIN consists of thirteen symbols. The first two (letter) indicate division and chassis type. The third (letter) identifies engine as follows: Q-250 cu. in. Starting: 10001 and up. Engine numbers (6-cyl.): located on pad at right hand side of cylinder block at rear of distributor. (8-cyl.): located on pad at front, right side of cylinder block. Starting: 10001 and up (coincide with serial number). Serial number located L-6, T: 292 cu. in. L-6, Y:350 cu. in. V-6, 2:454 cu. in.V-8, the fourth (digit) identifies series. The fifth (digit) indicates body type. The sixth (letter) is the model year.

Model	Body Type	Price	Weight	Prod. Total
Sprint Series				
5AC80	½-Ton Sedan Pickup (350 cid V-8)	3119	3817	—
5AD80	½-Ton Sedan Pickup Classic (350 cid V-8)	3277	3832	—
Jimmy Series				
TK-10514	½-Ton 4wd Utility (350 cid V-8)	3798	3796	—
TC-10514	½-Ton 2wd Utility	—	—	—
Series G-1500				
TG-11005	½-Ton Vandura (110 in. w.b.) (350 cid V-8)	3238	3250	—
TG-11006	½-Ton Rally (110 in. w.b.) (350 cid V-8)	3867	3837	—
TG-11006	½-Ton Rally STX (125 in. w.b.)	4232	4000	—
Series G-2500				
TG-21005	¾-Ton Vandura (110 in. w.b.) (350 cid V-8)	3377	3615	—
TG-21006	¾-Ton Rally (110 in. w.b.) (350 cid V-8)	3965	3891	—
TG-21006	¾-Ton Rally STX (125 in. w.b.) (350 cid V-8)	4330	4054	—
Series G-3500				
TG-31005	1-Ton Vandura (110 in. w.b.) (350 cid V-8)	3495	3904	—
TG-31303	1-Ton Rally Camper Spl (125 in. w.b.) (350 cid V-8)	4161	3662	—
TG-31303	1-Ton Magna Van (10 ft.) (350 cid V-8)	4643	4833	—
TG-31306	1-Ton Rally (110 in. w.b.) (350 cid V-8)	4200	4364	—
TG-31306	1-Ton Rally STX (110 in. w.b.) (350 cid V-8)	4565	4577	—
Series P-1500, 2500, 3500				
TP-10542	½-Ton Van (7 ft.)	3763	4064	—
TP-20842	¾-Ton Van (10 ft.)	4634	5306	—
TP-30842	1-Ton Van (10 ft.)	4842	5485	—
Series C-1500				
TC-10703	½-Ton Pickup (FS) (6.5 ft.) (350 cid V-8)	3117	3653	—
TC-10703	½-Ton Pickup (WS) (6.5 ft.) (350 cid V-8)	3117	3757	—
TC-10903	½-Ton Pickup (FS) (8 ft.) (350 cid V-8)	3153	3761	—
TC-10903	½-Ton Pickup (WS) (8 ft.) (350 cid V-8)	3153	3871	—
TC-10906	½-Ton Suburban (129.5 in. w.b.) (350 cid V-8)	4026	4211	—
(4wd models: TK prefix)				
Series C-2500				
TC-20903	¾-Ton Chassis and Cab (131.5 in. w.b.) (350 cid V-8)	3267	3714	—
TC-20903	¾-Ton Pickup (FS) (8 ft.) (350 cid V-8)	3434	4109	—
TC-20903	¾-Ton Pickup (WS) (8 ft.) (350 cid V-8)	3434	4219	—
TC-20963	¾-Ton Pickup Crew Cab (350 cid V-8)	4544	4458	—
	¾-Ton Stake (8 ft.) (350 cid V-8)	3580	4342	—
	¾-Ton Stake (12 ft.) (350 cid V-8)	3695	4554	—
TC-20906	¾-Ton Suburban (129.5 in. w.b.) (350 cid V-8)	4933	4946	—
(4 wd models: TK prefix)				
Series C-3500				
TC-30903	1-Ton Chassis and Cab (131.5 in. w.b.) (350 cid V-8)	3364	3878	—
TC-30903	1-Ton Pickup (FS) (8 ft.) (350 cid V-8)	3531	4304	—
TC-30903	1-Ton Pickup (WS) (8 ft.) (350 cid V-8)	3531	4379	—
	1-Ton Stake (8 ft.) (350 cid V-8)	3677	4506	—
	1-Ton Stake (9 ft.) (350 cid V-8)	3792	4728	—
TC-30913	1-Ton Pickup Crew Cab (350 cid V-8)	4626	5002	—

1974 GMC Sprint High Sierra Pickup (DFW/DPL)

ENGINE (Standard: all Models except Sprint): Inline, OHV. Six-cylinder. Cast iron block. Bore & stroke: 3⅞ in. x 3½. Displacement: 250 cu. in. Compression ratio: 8.25:1. Net horsepower: 100 at 3600 R.P.M. Torque: 175 lb. ft. at 1800 R.P.M. Seven main bearings. Hydraulic valve lifters. Carburetor: 1-bbl.

ENGINE (Optional: Series C-2500, C-3500; Standard: G-2500, G-3500): Inline, OHV. Six-cylinder. Cast iron block. Bore & stroke: 3⅞ in. x 4.12 in. Displacement: 292 cu. in. Compression ratio: 8.0. Net horsepower: 120 at 3000 R.P.M. Torque: 215 lbs. ft. at 2000 R.P.M. Seven main bearings. Hydraulic valve lifters. Carburetor: 1-bbl.

ENGINE (Optional: C-1500, G-1500; Standard: Sprint): Inline, OHV. Eight-cylinder. Cast iron block. Bore & stroke: 4 in. x 3.48 in. Displacement: 350 cu. in. Compression ratio: 8.5. Brake horsepower: 5. Net horsepower: 145 at 3600 R.P.M. Torque: T-250 at 2200 R.P.M. Five main bearings. Hydraulic valve lifters. Carburetor: 2-bbl.

ENGINE (Optional: C-Series, G-Series, Sprint): Inline, OHV. Eight-cylinder. Cast iron block. Bore & stroke: 4 in. x 3.48 in. Displacement: 350 cu. in. Compression ratio: 8.5. Brake horsepower: 5. Net horsepower: 160 at 3800 R.P.M. Torque: 255 at 2400 R.P.M. Five main bearings. Hydraulic valve lifters. Carburetor: Rochester 4-bbl.

ENGINE (Optional: C-Series, Sprint): Inline, OHV. Eight-cylinder. Cast iron block. Bore & stroke: 4¼ in. x 4 in. Displacement: 454 cu. in. Compression ratio: 8.5. Brake horsepower: 5. Net horsepower: 245 at 4000 R.P.M. Torque: 365 at 2800 R.P.M. Five main bearings. Hydraulic valve lifters. Carburetor: Rochester Quadra Jet 4-bbl.

CHASSIS (Sprint): Wheelbase: 116 in. Length: 201.6 in. Height: 53.8 in. Front tread: 58.5 in. Rear tread: 57.8 in. Tires: G78 x 14B in.

CHASSIS (Series Jimmy): Wheelbase: 106.5 in. Length: 184.5 in. Height: 67.5 in. (w/o top), 6.95 in. (w/top) — 2wd. 69.5 in. (w/top), 71.5 in. (w/top) - 4wd. Front tread: 64.5 in. — 2wd. 65.75 in. — 4wd. Rear tread: 63.0 in. — 2 wd. 62.74 in. — 4wd. Tires: E78 x 15B in.

CHASSIS (Series G-3500): Wheelbase: 110-125 in. Length: 178 x 202.2 in. Tires: 8 x 16.5C in.

CHASSIS (Series P-2500): Wheelbase: 125-133 in. Length: 220.75 x 244.75 in. Tires: 8.75 x 16.5C in.

CHASSIS (Series G-2500): Wheelbase: 110-125 in. Length: 178 x 202.2 in. Tires: G78 x 15B in.

CHASSIS (Series G-1500): Wheelbase: 110-125 in. Length: 178 x 202.2 in. Tires: E78 x 14B in.

CHASSIS (Series P-1500): Wheelbase: 102 in. Height: 75 in. Tires: G78 x 15B in.

CHASSIS (Series P-3500): Wheelbase: 125-157 in. Length: 220.75 x 265.75 in. Tires: 8.75 x 16.5C in.

1974 GMC Sprint Sport Pickup (OCW)

CHASSIS (Series C-1500): Wheelbase: 117.5-131.5 in. Overall length: 191.5 x 211.25 in. Height: 69.8 in. Front tread: 65.8 in. Rear tread: 62.7 in. Tires: G78 x 15B in.

CHASSIS (Series C-2500): Wheelbase: 131.5-164.5 in. Overall length: 212-244.43 in. Height: 69.8 in. Front tread: 65.8 in. Rear tread: 62.7 in. Tires: 8.75 x 16.5C in.

CHASSIS (Series C-3500): Wheelbase: 131.5-164.5 in. Overall length: 212 x 244.43 in. Height: 71.8 in. Front tread: 65.8 in. Rear tread: 62.7 in. Tires: 8.75 x 16.5C in.

TECHNICAL: Manual, all synchromesh transmission. Manual all synchromesh transmission. Speeds: 3F/1R. Column mounted gearshift. Turbo-Hydra-Matic 350, 400/475 automatic transmission. Camper package. Dual rear wheels (C-3500). Various clutches, rear axle ratios. 4-speed manual transmission. Front stablizer bar.

OPTIONS: Chromed front bumper. Chromed rear bumper. Radio AM, AM/FM. SP Package (Sprint) ($250). High Sierra Package (Sprint Custom) ($131). Sierra Package (Jimmy, C-Series). Super Custom (CC-Series) Sierra Grande Package. Power steering. Below-Eye-Line Mirrors. Drip moldings. Sliding rear window. Cargo lamp. Gauge package. Air conditioning. Tachometer. Comfortilt steering wheel. Wood-grain exterior trim. Rear step bumper. Glide out spare tire carrier. Chromed front bumper with rubber. Impact strip. Exterior tool & storage compartment. Wheel covers. White wall tires.

HISTORICAL: Calendar year sales: 142,055.

Pricing

1974	5	4	3	2	1
(116 in. w.b.)					
½-Ton Sprint Cus.	830	1650	2750	3850	5500
(106 in. w.b.)					
4x4 ½-Ton Jimmy	980	1950	3250	4550	6500
4x2 ½-Ton Jimmy	830	1650	2750	3850	5500
(110 in. w.b.)					
½-Ton Rally Van	780	1560	2600	3600	5200
(117 in. w.b.)					
Fender-Side ½-Ton Pickup	810	1620	2700	3800	5400
Wide-Side ½-Ton Pickup	840	1680	2800	3900	5600
(125 in. w.b.)					
Fender-Side ½-Ton Pickup	830	1650	2750	3850	5500
Wide-Side ½-Ton Pickup	850	1700	2850	4000	5700
½-Ton Suburban	830	1650	2750	3850	5500
Fender-Side ¾-Ton Pickup	750	1500	2500	3500	5000
Wide-Side ¾-Ton Pickup	780	1560	2600	3600	5200
¾-Ton Suburban	770	1550	2550	3600	5100
¾-Ton Rally Van	750	1500	2500	3500	5000
(125 & 135 in. w.b.)					
1-Ton Pickup	750	1500	2500	3500	5000
1-Ton Crew Cab Pickup	700	1400	2350	3250	4700

1975 GMC

1975 GMC Sierra Classic Crew Cab Pickup (RPZ)

Once again, a revamped grille was the prime visual indentification of the new GMC pickups. Its format for 1975 moved the GMC lettering into a center location where it was mounted on the single horizontal divider which in turn was intersected by two vertical bars.

I.D. DATA: Serial number combination VIN and rating plate located on left door panel. The VIN consists of thirteen symbols. The first two (letters) indicate division and classic type. The third (letter) identifies engine as follows: Q-250 cu. in. L-6, T: 292 cu. in. L-6, Y: 350 cu. in. (V-8), Z: 454 cu. in. V-8. Starting: Pickup: TC (Q) 145 (F) 50001 and up. Vandura: TG (Q) 155 (F) 50001 and up. Engine numbers located: (6-cyl.) on pad at right side of cylinder block at rear of distributor. (8-cyl.) located on pad at front, right side of cylinder block. Starting: same as VIN.

Model	Body Type	Price	Weight	Prod. Total
Sprint Series				
5AC80	½-Ton Sedan Pickup (350 cid V-8)	3828	3706	—
5AD80	½-Ton Sedan Pickup Classic (350 cid V-8)	3966	3748	—
Jimmy Series				
TK-10514	½-Ton 4wd Utility Open	4569	4026	—
TK-10516	½-Ton 4wd Utility Open w/top	4998	4272	—
CK-10514	½-Ton 2wd Utility Open	—	—	—
CK-10516	½-Ton 2wd Utility Open	—	—	—
Series G-1500				
TG-11005	½-Ton Vandura (110 in. w.b.) (350 cid V-8)	3443	3584	—
TG-11006	½-Ton Rally (110 in. w.b.) (350 cid V-8)	4103	3935	—
TG-11006	½-Ton Rally STX (110 in. w.b.) (350 cid V-8)	4506	4098	—
Series G-2500				
TG-21005	¾-Ton Vandura (110 in. w.b.) (350 cid V-8)	3653	3625	—
TG-21006	¾-Ton Rally (110 in. w.b.) (350 cid V-8)	4275	3910	—
TG-21006	¾-Ton Rally STX (125 in. w.b.) (350 cid V-8)	4678	4073	—
Series G-3500				
TG-31005	1-Ton Vandura (110 in. w.b.) (350 cid V-8)	3743	3917	—
TG-31303	1-Ton Vandura Special (110 in. w.b.) (350 cid V-8)	4167	—	—
TG-31303	1-Ton Camper Special (125 in. w.b.) (350 cid V-8)	4377	—	—
TG-31303	1-Ton Magna Van (10 ft.) (350 cid V-8)	4970	4998	—
TG-31306	1-Ton Rally (110 in. w.b.) (350 cid V-8)	4477	4369	—
TG-31306	1-Ton STX (110 in. w.b.) (350 cid V-8)	4880	4583	—
Series P-1500, 2500, 3500				
TP-10542	½-Ton Van (7 ft.)	4532	—	—
TP-20842	¾-Ton Van (10 ft.) (350 cid V-8)	5242	5382	—
TP-30842	1-Ton Van (10 ft.) (350 cid V-8)	5499	5588	—
Series C-1500				
TC-10703	½-Ton Chassis and Cab (117.5 in. w.b.) (350 cid V-8)	3676	—	—
TC-10703	½-Ton Pickup (FS) (6.5 ft.) (350 cid V-6)	3609	3783	—
TC-10703	½-Ton Pickup (WS) (6.5 ft.) (350 cid V-6)	3609	3796	—
TC-10903	½-Ton Pickup (FS) (8 ft.) (350 cid V-8)	3652	3774	—
TC-10903	½-Ton Pickup (WS) (8 ft.) (350 cid V-8)	3652	3844	—
TC-10906	½-Ton Suburban (350 cid V-8)	4707	4336	—
(4wd models: TK prefix)				
Series C-2500				
TC-20903	¾-Ton Chassis and Cab (131.5 in. w.b.) (cid V-8)	3863	3737	—
TC-20903	¾-Ton Pickup (FS) (8 ft.) (350 cid V-8)	4030	4137	—
TC-20903	¾-Ton Pickup (WS) (8 ft.) (350 cid V-8)	4030	4207	—
TC-20943	¾-Ton Pickup Bonus Cab (350 cid V-8)	4613	—	—
TC-20963	¾-Ton Pickup Crew Cab (350 cid V-8)	5002	4935	—
	¾-Ton Stake (8 ft.) (350 cid V-8)	4246	4365	—
TC-20906	¾-Ton Suburban (350 cid V-8)	5045	4664	—
(4wd models: TK prefix)				
Series C-3500				
TC-30903	1-Ton Chassis and Cab (131.5 in. w.b.) (350 cid V-8)	3996	3913	—
TC-30903	1-Ton Pickup (FS) (8 ft.) (350 cid V-8)	4163	4344	—
TC-30903	1-Ton Pickup (WS) (8 ft.) (350 cid V-8)	4163	4379	—
TC-30963	1-Ton Pickup Crew Cab (350 cid V-8)	5155	4987	—
	1-Ton Stake (9 ft.) (350 cid V-8)	4498	4761	—

1975 GMC Sierra Classic Suburban Carryall (OCW)

ENGINE (Optional: all Models): V-type, gasoline. Eight-cylinder. Cast iron block. Bore & stroke: 4 in. x 3½ in. Displacement: 350 cu. in. Net horsepower: 160 at 3800 R.P.M. Net Torque: 250 lb. ft. at 2400 R.P.M. Five main bearings. Hydraulic valve lifters. Carburetor: 4-bbl.

ENGINE (Standard: Series C-2500, C-3500, P-1500, P-2500, P-3500, G-2500, G-3500): Inline, OHV. Six-cylinder. Cast iron block. Bore & stroke: 3⅞ in. x 4⅛ in. Displacement: 292 cu. in. Compression ratio: 8.0:1. Net horsepower: 120 at 3600 R.P.M. Net Torque: 215 lb. ft. at 2000 R.P.M. Seven main bearings. Hydraulic valve lifters. Carburetor: 1-bbl.

ENGINE (Optional: Sprint 4wd ½-Ton, ¾-Ton Pickup): V-type, OHV. Eight-cylinder. Cast iron block. Bore & stroke: 4⅛ in. x 4 in. Displacement: 400 cu. in. Compression ratio: 8.5:1. Net horsepower: 175 at 3600 R.P.M. Five main bearings. Hydraulic valve lifters. Carburetor: 4-bbl.

ENGINE (Optional: Series C-1500, C-2500, C-3500, Sprint ($340): V-type, OHV. Eight-cylinder. Cast iron block. Bore & stroke: 4⅛ in. x 4 in. Displacement: 454 cu. in. Compression ratio: 8.25:1. Brake horsepower: 5. Net horsepower: 245 at 4000 R.P.M. Net. Torque: 355 lb. ft. at 3000 R.P.M. Five main bearings. Hydraulic valve lifters. Carburetor: Rochester Quadra-Jet 4-bbl.

CHASSIS (Sprint): Wheelbase: 116 in. Length: 201.6 in. Height: 53.8 in. Front tread: 58.5 in. Rear tread: 57.8 in. Tires: GR78 x 15B in.

CHASSIS (Jimmy): Wheelbase: 106.5 in. Length: 184.5 in. Height: 66.75 in. w/o top, 68.75 in. w/top — 2wd; 69 in. w/o top, 71 in. w/top — 4wd. Front tread: 64.5 in. 2wd, 65.75 in. 4wd. Rear tread: 63 in. 2wd., 62.75 4wd. Tires: H78 x 15B in.

CHASSIS (Series G-1500): Wheelbase: 110-125 in. Length: 178 x 202.2 in. Height: 78.8 x 81.2 in. Tires: E78 x 15B in.

CHASSIS (Series P-2500): Wheelbase: 125-133 in. Length: 220.75 x 244.75 in. Tires: 8.75 x 16.5C in.

CHASSIS (Series G-2500): Wheelbase: 110-125 in. Length: 178 x 202.2 in. Height: 78.8 x 81. 2 in. Tires: J78 x 15B in.

CHASSIS (Series G-3500): Wheelbase: 110-146 in. Tires: 8.00 x 16.5C in.

CHASSIS (Series P-1500): Wheelbase: 102 in. Height: 75 in. Tires: L78 x 15B. in.

CHASSIS (Series P-3500): Wheelbase: 125-151 in. Length: 220.75 x 268.75 in. Tires: 8.75 x 16.5C in.

CHASSIS (Series C-1500): Wheelbase: 117.5-131.5 in. Length: (WS) 191¼ in. x 211¼ in. (FS) 190¼ in. x 210¼ in. Tires: G78 x 15B in.

CHΛSSIS (Series C-2500): Wheelbase: 131.5-164.5 in. Length: (WS) 191¼ in. x 211¼ in. x 244¼ in. (FS) 210¼ in. x 244¼ in. Tires: 8.75 x 16.5C in.

CHASSIS (Series C-3500): Wheelbase: 131.5-164.5 in. Length: (WS) 211¼ in. x 244¼ in. (FS) 210¼ in. x 244¼ in. Tires: 8.75 x 16.5C in.

ENGINE (Standard: Series C-1500, Jimmy, Sprint, G-1500): Inline, gasoline. Six-cylinder. Cast iron block. Bore & stroke: 3⅞ in. x 3½ in. Displacement: 250 cu. in. Compression ratio: 8.25:1. Net horsepower: 105 at 3800 R.P.M. Net Torque: 185 lb. ft. at 1200 R.P.M. Seven main bearings. Hydraulic valve lifters. Carburetor: 1-bbl.

ENGINE (Optional: Series C-1500, Sprint): V-type, gasoline. Eight-cylinder. Cast iron block. Bore & stroke: 4 in. x 3½ in. Displacement: 350 cu. in. Compression ratio: 8.5:1. Net horsepower: 145 at 3800 R.P.M. Net Torque: 250 lb. ft. at 2200 R.P.M. Five main bearings. Hydraulic valve lifters. Carburetor: 2-bbl.

1975 GMC Sprint Pickup w/Sport Trim (DFW)

1975 GMC Jimmy 4x4 Utility With Wagon Shell (OCW)

TECHNICAL: Manual, all synchromesh transmission. Speeds: 3F/1R. Column mounted gear shift lever. Clutch: (C-1500) 11 in. dia. (6 and 8-cyl.), (C-2500, C-3500): 11 in. dia. (6-cyl.), 12 in. dia. (V-8) 6-cyl. — engines use single disc with either diaphragm or coil springs, V-8's have single disc with coil spring pressure plate. Semi-floating (½-ton), full-floating (¾-ton and 1-ton) rear axle. Overall ratio: (C-1500): 3.73 (6-cyl.), 3.40 (V-8), (C-2500): 4.56 (6-cyl.), 3.73 (V-8), 4.10 (Crew Cab), (C-3500) 4.10:1. Pressed steel brakes: (Series 1500) 7/16 in., ½ in. bolts, (Series 2500, 3500) 9/16 in. bolts. Turbo-Hydra-Matic automatic transmission. Camper Package. Dual rear wheels (C-3500). 4-speed manual transmission. Heavy-duty radiator. Heavy-duty generator. Heavy-duty battery.

OPTIONS: Chromed front bumper. Chromed rear bumper. Radio AM, AM/FM, windshield embedded antenna. Clock. Cigar Lighter. SP Package (Sprint) ($215). High Sierra Package (Sprint Classic) ($113). High Sierra Package (Jimmy, Series C). Sierra Classic Package (Series C). Sierra Grande Package (Series C). Gauge Package. Tachometer. Drip moldings. Exterior tool and storage compartment. Air conditioning. White sidewall tires (C-1500 only). Below-Eyeline mirrors. Comfortilt steering wheel. Rear step bumper. Chrome front bumper with rubber impact strips. Wood-grain exterior trim (WS only). Sliding rear window. Cargo area lamp. Box-mounted spare tire. Glide-out spare tire carrier.

HISTORICAL: Calendar year sales: 140,423.

Pricing

	5	4	3	2	1
1975					
(116 in. w.b.)					
½-Ton Sprint Cus.	830	1650	2750	3850	5500
(106 in. w.b.)					
4x4 ½-Ton Jimmy	980	1950	3250	4550	6500
4x2 ½-Ton Jimmy	830	1650	2750	3850	5500
(110 in. w.b.)					
½-Ton Rally Van	780	1560	2600	3600	5200
(117 in. w.b.)					
Fender-Side ½-Ton Pickup	810	1620	2700	3800	5400
Wide-Side ½-Ton Pickup	840	1680	2800	3900	5600
(125 in. w.b.)					
Fender-Side ½-Ton Pickup	830	1650	2750	3850	5500
Wide-Side ½-Ton Pickup	850	1700	2850	4000	5700
½-Ton Suburban	830	1650	2750	3850	5500
Fender-Side ¾-Ton Pickup	750	1500	2500	3500	5000
Wide-Side ¾-Ton Pickup	780	1560	2600	3600	5200
¾-Ton Suburban	770	1550	2550	3600	5100
¾-Ton Rally Van	750	1500	2500	3500	5000
(125 & 135 in. w.b.)					
1-Ton Pickup	750	1500	2500	3500	5000
1-Ton Crew Cab Pickup	700	1400	2350	3250	4700

1976 GMC

No changes were made in GMC trucks for 1976.

I.D. DATA: Serial number a combination VIN and rating plate is located on the left door lock pillar. The components of the VIN are identical as those of 1975. The sequential production number begins after the assembly plant code. Pickup: TC (V) 146 (F) 500001 and up, Vandura: TG (D) 156 (F) 500001 and up. Ending: Same as 1975. Engine numbers located the third symbol of the VIN is the engine code: D-250 cid L-6, T-292 cid L-6, Q-305 cid 2-bbl. V-8, V-350 cid, 2-bbl. V-8, L-350 cid, 4-bbl. V-8, U-400 cid, 4-bbl. V-8, S¹-454 cid, 4-bbl. V-8, Y²-454 cid 4-bbl. V-8.

1 — 6000 lbs. and under GVMR.
2 — over 6001 lbs. GVMR.

1976 GMC Sprint Pickup (DFW)

1976 GMC Sierra Classic 25 Indy 500 Pickup (IMSC/JLM)

Model	Body Type	Price	Weight	Prod. Total
Sprint Series				
5AC80	½-Ton Sedan Pickup (305 cid V-8)	4333	3791	—
5AD80	½-Ton Sedan Pickup Classic (305 cid V-8)	4468	3821	—
Jimmy Series				
TK-10516	½-Ton 4wd Utility (350 cid V-8)	5364	4496	—
TC-10516	½-Ton 2wd Utility (350 cid V-8)	—	—	—
Series G-1500				
TG-11005	½-Ton Vandura (110 in. w.b.) (350 cid V-8)	3811	3703	—
TG-11006	½-Ton Rally (110 in. w.b.) (350 cid V-8)	4509	4027	—
TG-11306	½-Ton Rally STX (110 in. w.b.) (350 cid V-8)	5102	4403	—
Series G-2500				
TG-21005	¾-Ton Vandura (110 in. w.b.) (350 cid V-8)	4022	3730	—
TG-21006	¾-Ton Rally (110 in. w.b.) (350 cid V-8)	4682	4013	—
TG-21306	¾-Ton Rally STX (125 in. w.b.)	5220	4369	—

1976 GMC Wide-Side Pickup (JAG)

Model	Body Type	Price	Weight	Prod. Total
Series G-3500				
TG-31005	1-Ton Vandura (110 in. w.b.) (350 cid V-8)	4143	3971	—
TG-31303	1-Ton Vandura Special (110 in. w.b.) (350 cid V-8)	4533	3698	—
TG-31303	1-Ton Camper Special (125 in. w.b.) (350 cid V-8)	4731	3767	—
TG-31303	1-Ton Magna Van (350 cid V-8)	5405	5100	—
TG-31306	1-Ton Rally (125 in. w.b.) (350 cid V-8)	4915	4431	—
TG-31306	1-Ton Rally STX (125 in. w.b.) (350 cid V-8)	5318	4618	—
Series P-1500, 2500, 3500				
TP-10542	½-Ton Van (7 ft.)	4855	4311	—
TP-20842	¾-Ton Van (10 ft.) (125 in. w.b.) (350 cid V-8)	5563	5465	—
TP-30842	1-Ton Van (10 ft.) (125 in. w.b.) (350 cid V-8)	5864	5671	—
Series C-1500				
TC-10703	½-Ton Chassis and Cab (117.5 in. w.b.) (350 cid V-8)	3957	3532	—
TC-10703	½-Ton Pickup (FS) (6.5 ft.) (117.5 in. w.b.) (350 cid V-6)	3863	3863	—
TC-10703	½-Ton Pickup (WS) (6.5 ft.) (117.5 in. w.b.) (350 cid V-8)	3863	3931	—
TC-10903	½-Ton Pickup (FS) (8 ft.) (117.5 in. w.b.) (350 cid V-8)	3908	3987	—
TC-10903	½-Ton Pickup (WS) (8 ft.) (117.5 in. w.b.) (350 cid V-8)	3908	4063	—
TC-10906	½-Ton Suburban (129.5 in. w.b.) (350 cid V-8)	5087	4469	—
(4wd models: TK prefix)				
Series C-2500				
TC-20903	¾-Ton Chassis and Cab (131.5 in. w.b.) (350 cid V-8)	4139	3840	—
TC-20903	¾-Ton Pickup (FS) (8 ft.) (131.5 in. w.b.) (350 cid V-8)	4306	4238	—
TC-20903	¾-Ton Pickup (WS) (8 ft.) (131.5 in. w.b.) (350 cid V-8)	4306	4314	—
TC-20943	¾-Ton Chassis and Bonus Cab (350 cid V-8)	4786	4308	—
TC-20943	¾-Ton Pickup Bonus Cab (350 cid V-8)	4953	4786	—
TC-20963	¾-Ton Chassis and Crew Cab (350 cid V-8)	5160	4551	—
TC-20963	¾-Ton Pickup Crew Cab (350 cid V-8)	5327	5029	—
	¾-Ton Stake (8 ft.) (350 cid V-8)	4734	4468	—
TC-20906	¾-Ton Suburban (350 cid V-8)	5375	4851	—
(4wd models: TK prefix)				
Series C-3500				
TC-30903	1-Ton Chassis and Cab (131.5 in. w.b.) (350 cid V-8)	4279	3997	—
TC-30903	1-Ton Pickup (FS) (8 ft.) (350 cid V-8)	4446	4426	—
TC-30903	1-Ton Pickup (WS) (8 ft.) (350 cid V-8)	4446	4467	—
TC-30943	1-Ton Chassis and Bonus Cab (350 cid V-8)	5210	4530	—
TC-30943	1-Ton Pickup (WS) Bonus Cab (350 cid V-8)	5377	5004	—
TC-30963	1-Ton Chassis and Crew Cab (350 cid V-8)	5320	4607	—
TC-30963	1-Ton Pickup (WS) Crew Cab (350 cid V-8)	5487	5081	—
TC-31003	1-Ton Stake (9 ft.) (350 cid V-8)	4939	4845	—

ENGINE (Standard: Series C-1500, Sprint, Blazer, Series-G): Inline, OHV. Six-cylinder. Cast iron block. Bore & stroke: 3⅞ in. x 3½ in. Displacement: 250 cu. in. Compression ratio: 8.25:1. Net horsepower: 100 at 3600 R.P.M. Net Torque: 175 lb. ft. at 1800 R.P.M. Seven main bearings. Hydraulic valve lifters. Carburetor: 1-bbl.

ENGINE (Standard: Series C-2500, C-3500, P-Series): Inline, OHV. Six-cylinder. Cast iron block. Bore & stroke: 3⅞ in. x 4⅛ in. Displacement: 292 cu. in. Compression ratio: 8.0:1. Net horsepower: 120 at 3600 R.P.M. Net Torque: 275 lb. ft. at 2000 R.P.M. Seven main bearings. Hydraulic valve lifters. Carburetor: 1-bbl.

ENGINE (Optional: all Models): V-type, OHV. Eight-cylinder. Cast iron block. Bore & stroke: 4 in. x 3½ in. Displacement: 350 cu. in. Compression ratio: 8.5:1. Net horsepower: 165 at 3800 R.P.M. Net Torque: 255 lb. ft. at 2800 R.P.M. Five main bearings. Hydraulic valve lifters. Carburetor: 4-bbl., Mod-Quad.

ENGINE (Optional: Series C-1500): V-type, OHV. Eight-cylinder. Cast iron block. Bore & stroke: 4 in. x 3½ in. Displacement: 350 cu. in. Compression ratio: 8.5:1. Net horsepower: 145 at 3800 R.P.M. Net Torque: 250 lb. ft. at 2200 R.P.M. Five main bearings. Hydraulic valve lifters. Carburetor: 2-bbl.

ENGINE (Optional: ½-Ton, ¾-Ton — 4wd, Series G, Jimmy, Sprint ($148): V-type, OHV. Eight-cylinder. Cast iron block. Bore & stroke: 4⅛ in. x 4 in. Displacement: 400 cu. in. Compression ratio: 8.5:1. Net horsepower: 175 at 3600 R.P.M. Net Torque: 290 lb. ft. at 2800 R.P.M. Five main bearings. Hydraulic valve lifters. Carburetor: 4-bbl., Mod-Quad.

ENGINE (Optional: Series C-1500, C-2500, C-3500): V-type, OHV. Eight-cylinder. Cast iron block. Bore & stroke: 4¼ in. x 4 in. Displacement: 454 cu. in. Compression ratio: 8.25:1. Net horsepower: 240 at 3800 R.P.M. Max. Torque: 370 lb. ft. at 2800 R.P.M. Five main bearings. Hydraulic valve lifters. Carburetor: Rochester Mod Quad. 4-bbl.

CHASSIS (Sprint): Wheelbase: 116 in. Length: 201.6 in. Height: 53.8 in. Front tread: 58.5 in. Rear tread: 57.8 in. Tires: GR78 x 15B in.

CHASSIS (Jimmy): Wheelbase: 106.5 in. Length: 184.5 in. Height: 66.75 in. w/o top, 68.75 in. w/top — 2wd; 69 in. w/o top, 71 in. w/top — 4wd. Front tread: 64.5 in. 2wd, 65.75 in. 4wd. Rear tread: 63 in. 2wd., 62.75 4wd. Tires: H78 x 15B in.

CHASSIS (Series G-1500): Wheelbase: 110-125 in. Length: 178 x 202.2 in. Height: 78.8 x 81. 2 in. Tires: E78 x 15B in.

CHASSIS (Series G-2500): Wheelbase: 110-125 in. Length: 178 x 202.2 in. Height: 78.8 x 81. 2 in. Tires: J78 x 15B in.

CHASSIS (Series G-3500): Wheelbase: 110-146 in. Tires: 8.00 x 16.5C in.

CHASSIS (Series P-1500): Wheelbase: 102 in. Height: 75 in. Tires: L78 x 15B. in.

CHASSIS (Series P-2500): Wheelbase: 125-133 in. Length: 220.75 x 244.75 in. Tires: 8.75 x 16.5C in.

CHASSIS (Series P-3500): Wheelbase: 125-157 in. Length: 220.75 x 268.75 in. Tires: 8.75 x 16.5C in.

CHASSIS (Series C-1500): Wheelbase: 117.5-131.5 in. Length: (WS) 191¼ in. x 211¼ in. (FS) 190¼ in. x 210¼ in. Height: 69.8 in. Front tread: 65.8 in. Rear tread: 62.7 in. Tires: G78 x 15B in.

CHASSIS (Series C-2500): Wheelbase: 131.5-164.5 in. Length: (WS) 211¼ in. x 244¼ in. (FS) 210¼ in. x 244¼ in. Height: 69.8 in. Front tread: 65.8 in. Rear tread: 62.7 in. Tires: 8.75 x 16.5C in.

CHASSIS (Series C-3500): Wheelbase: 131.5-164.5 in. Length: (WS) 211¼ in. x 244¼ in. (FS) 210¼ in. x 244¼ in. Height: 71.8 in. Front tread: 65.8 in. Rear tread: 62.7 in. Tires: 8.75 x 16.5C in.

TECHNICAL: Manual, synchromesh: all gears transmission. Speeds: 3F/1R (all 1500 and 2500 series except 2500 Series Crew Cab. 4-spd. manual with floor-mounted shifter std. on all Series 2500 and 3500 Crew Cab. Column mounted gear shift lever. Clutch: 11 in. dia. (250, 292 cu. in 6-cyl. and V-8's with 2-Bbl. carb., 12 in. dia. (all V-8's with 4-bbl. carburetion). Salisbury semi-floating (C-1500), full-floating (C-2500, C-3500) rear axle. Hydraulic, four-wheel brakes (front disc, rear-air-finned cast iron drums.) Steel disc wheels. Turbo-Hydra-Matic automatic transmission. Heavy-duty suspension. Heavy-duty 3-speed manual transmission. Four-speed manual transmission. Dual rear wheels (C-3500, 1-ton wide-side, Bonus & Crew Cab model). Camper Package. Heavy-duty chassis (C-1500). Front stablizier bar. Delco freedom battery. Locking differential.

OPTIONS: Radio AM, AM/FM, AM/FM/8-track tape. Clock. Bucket seats (2-door models only). Sierra Classic Package (YE9), (2-doors models only). Sierra Grande Package (262) (2-door models only). High Sierra (Z84) not available for Crew & Bonus Cab). Gauge package, tachometer. Headlamp warning system. Air conditioning. Full wheel covers (15, 16, 16.5'' wheels). Comfortilt steering wheel. Full-width rear step bumper. Swing-out camper mirrors (painted or stainless steel). Rally wheel. Sliding rear window. Swing-out spare tire carrier. SP Package (Sprint) ($226). Sierra Madre Del Sur (Sprint) ($128). Two-tone paint. Special two-tone with secondary. Neutral or contrasting color. Delux two-tone contrasting or complementary secondary color on roof and sides. Special and deluxe two-tones have upper and lower body side moldings.

HISTORICAL: Calendar year production: 223,805.

Pricing

	5	4	3	2	1
1976					
(116 in. w.b.)					
½-Ton Sprint Cus.	830	1650	2750	3850	5500
(106 in. w.b.)					
4x4 ½-Ton Jimmy	980	1950	3250	4550	6500
4x2 ½-Ton Jimmy	830	1650	2750	3850	5500
(110 in. w.b.)					
½-Ton Rally Van	780	1560	2600	3600	5200
(117 in. w.b.)					
Fender-Side ½-Ton Pickup	810	1620	2700	3800	5400
Wide-Side ½-Ton Pickup	840	1680	2800	3900	5600
(125 in. w.b.)					
Fender-Side ½-Ton Pickup	830	1650	2750	3850	5500
Wide-Side ½-Ton Pickup	850	1700	2850	4000	5700
½-Ton Suburban	830	1650	2750	3850	5500
Fender-Side ¾-Ton Pickup	750	1500	2500	3500	5000
Wide-Side ¾-Ton Pickup	780	1560	2600	3600	5200
¾-Ton Suburban	770	1550	2550	3600	5100
¾-Ton Rally Van	750	1500	2500	3500	5000
(125 & 135 in. w.b.)					
1-Ton Pickup	750	1500	2500	3500	5000
1-Ton Crew Cab Pickup	700	1400	2350	3250	4700

1977 GMC

1977 GMC Sierra Classic Wide-Side Pickup (OCW)

GMC — LIGHT-DUTY — (ALL ENGINES): — Truck spotters identified the newest GMC light-duty models by the shape of their grille which now had 4 vertical dividers and a broad horizontal bar with centered GMC lettering.

I.D. DATA: A VIN and rating plate is located on the left door lock pillar. Starting: 500001 and up. Engine no. location: 6-cylinder. Located on pad at the right side of cylinder block at the rear of the distributor. 8-cylinder: Located on pad at front right side of cylinder block. Starting engine no. same as VIN.

Model	Body Type	Price	Weight	Prod. Total
Series SAC80				
SAC80	½-Ton Pickup Sedan	4268	3791	—
SAC80	½-Ton Pickup Sedan Classic	4403	3821	—
Series TK10516 — Jimmy — V-8 — (305 cu. in.)				
TK10516	½-Ton 4wd Utility Hardtop	5603	3914	—
TK10516	½-Ton 4wd Utility Convertible	5503	3864	—

NOTE: 2wd versions have TC prefix

Model	Body Type	Price	Weight	Prod. Total
Series G1500 — V-8 — (305 cu. in.)				
TC11005	½-Ton Vandura (110 in. w.b.)	4112	3586	—
TG11006	½-Ton Rally (110 in. w.b.)	4885	3913	—
TG11306	½-Ton Rally STX (125 in. w.b.)	5634	4314	—
Series G2500 — V-8 — (350 cu. in.)				
TG21005	¾-Ton Vandura (110 in. w.b.)	4375	3607	—
TG21006	¾-Ton Rally (110 in. w.b.)	5110	3890	—
TG21306	¾-Ton Rally STX (125 in. w.b.)	5773	4267	—
Series G3500 — V-8 — (350 cu. in.)				
TG31005	1-Ton Vandura (110 in. w.b.)	4496	3840	—
TG31603	1-Ton Vandura Spl. (110 in. w.b.)	4950	3557	—
TG31303	1-Ton Rally Camper Spl. (110 in. w.b.)	4991	3629	—
TG31303	1-Ton Magna Van (110 in. w.b.)	6275	4981	—
TG31306	1-Ton Rally (110 in. w.b.)	5368	4300	—
TG31306	1-Ton Rally STX (110 in. w.b.)	5871	4508	—
Series P1500/2500/3500				
TP10542	½-Ton Van, 7-ft.	5391	4176	—
TP20842	¾-Ton Van, 10-ft.	6287	5273	—
TP30842	1-Ton Van, 10-ft.	6603	5493	—
Series C1500				
TC10703	½-Ton Chassis and Cab (350 cu. in. V-8)	4206	3383	—
TC10703	½-Ton Pickup (FS) 6.5-ft. (305 cu. in. V-8)	4122	3585	—
TC10703	½-Ton Pickup (WS) 6-ft. (305 cu. in. V-8)	4122	3645	—
TC10903	½-Ton Pickup (FS), 8-ft.	4172	3700	—
TC10903	½-Ton Pickup (WS), 8-ft.	4172	3791	—
TC10906	½-Ton Suburban	5279	4315	—

NOTE: 4wd models have TK prefix. Add $1100 to factory price.

1977 GMC Sierra Classic Wide-Side Pickup (JAG)

Model	Body Type	Price	Weight	Prod. Total
Series C2500				
TC20903	¾-Ton Chassis and Cab (350 cu. in. V-8)	4399	3662	—
TC20903	¾-Ton Pickup (FS), 8-ft. (350 cu. in. V-8)	4624	4051	—
TC20903	¾-Ton Pickup (WS), 8-ft. (350 cu. in. V-8)	4624	4142	—
TC20943	¾-Ton Chassis and Bonus Cab (350 cu. in. V-8)	5046	4164	—
TC20943	¾-Ton Pickup (WS), Bonus Cab (350 cu. in. V-8)	5271	4644	—
TC20943	¾-Ton Pickup (WS), Crew Cab (350 cu. in. V-8)	5645	—	—
TC20943	¾-Ton Platform and Stake, 8-ft. (350 cu. in. V-8)	5039	4296	—
TC20906	¾-Ton Suburban (350 cu. in. V-8)	5725	4649	—

NOTE: 4wd models have TK prefix. Add $1076 to factory price.

Model	Body Type	Price	Weight	Prod. Total
Series C3500 — V-8 — (350 cu. in.)				
TC30903	1-Ton Chassis and Cab (131.5 in. w.b.)	4539	3803	—
TC30903	1-Ton Pickup (FS), 8-ft.	4764	4238	—
TC30903	1-Ton Pickup (WS), 8-ft.	4764	4283	—
TC30943	1-Ton Chassis and Bonus Cab	5470	4444	—
TC30943	1-Ton Pickup (WS) Bonus Cab	5695	4924	—
TC30943	1-Ton Chassis and Crew Cab	5580	—	—
TC30943	1-Ton Pickup (WS) Crew Cab	5805	—	—
TC31003	1-Ton Platform and Stake, 9-ft.	5223	4650	—

NOTE: 4wd models have TK prefix. Add $248 to factory price.

ENGINE (Standard C2500, C3500): Inline. OHV. 6-cylinder. Cast iron block. Bore & stroke: 3.87 x 4.12 in. Displacement: 292 cu. in. Compression ratio: 8.0:1. Net horsepower: 120 at 3600 R.P.M. Net torque: 215 lb.-ft. at 2000 R.P.M. Seven main bearings. Hydraulic valve lifters. Carburetor: 1-barrel.

ENGINE (Standard C1500, C1500/F44): Inline. OHV. 6-cylinder. Cast iron block. Bore & stroke: 3.87 x 3.53 in. Displacement: 250 cu. in. Compression ratio: 8.23:1. Net horsepower: 110 at 3800 R.P.M. Net torque: 195 lb.-ft. at 1600 R.P.M. Seven main bearings. Hydraulic valve lifters. Carburetor: 1-barrel.

ENGINE (Optional: C1500): (Not available for California delivery). V-type. OHV. 8-cylinder. Cast iron block. Bore & stroke: 3.74 x 3.48 in. Displacement: 305 cu. in. Compression ratio: 8.5:1. Net horsepower: 145 at 3800 R.P.M. Net torque: 245 lb.-ft. at 2400 R.P.M. Five main bearings. Hydraulic valve lifters. Carburetor: 2-barrel.

1977 GMC Sprint Pickup (DFW)

1977 GMC Sierra Classic 25 Indy 500 Pickup (IMSC/JLM)

ENGINE (Optional: C1500, C1500/F44, C2500, C3500): V-type. OHV. 8-cylinder. Cast iron block. Bore & stroke: 4.00 x 3.48 in. Displacement: 350 cu. in. Compression ratio: 8.5:1. Net horsepower: 165 at 3800 R.P.M. Net torque: 260 lb.-ft. at 2400 R.P.M. (255 at 2800 R.P.M. for 6001 GVW lbs. and above). Five main bearings. Hydraulic valve lifters. Carburetor: 4-barrel.

ENGINE (Optional: C1500, C1500/F44, C2500, C3500): V-type. OHV. 8-cylinder. Cast iron block. Bore & stroke: 4.25 x 4.00 in. Displacement: 454 cu. in. Compression ratio: 8.25:1. Net horsepower: 245 at 3800 R.P.M. Net torque: 365 lb.-ft. at 2800 R.P.M. Five main bearings. Hydraulic valve lifters. Carburetor: 4-barrel. 6001 lbs. and above GVW ratings: Brake horsepower: 240 at 3800 R.P.M. Net torque: 370 lb.-ft at 2800 R.P.M. California ratings: Brake horsepower: 250 at 3800 R.P.M. Net torque: 385 lb.-ft. at 2800 R.P.M.

ENGINE: Available for 4wd trucks with 6001 lbs. and above GVW only. V-type. OHV. 8-cylinder. Cast iron block. Bore & stroke: 4.13 x 3.75 in. Displacement: 400 cu. in. Compression ratio: 8.5:1. Net horsepower: 175 at 3600 R.P.M. Net torque: 290 lb.-ft. at 2800 R.P.M. Five main bearings. Hydraulic valve lifters. Carburetor: 4-barrel.

CHASSIS (Series Sprint): Wheelbase: 116 in. Overall length: 213.3 in. Overall height: 53.8 in. Front/Rear Tread: 58.5/57.8 in. Tires: GR78 x 15B.

CHASSIS (Series Jimmy): Wheelbase: 106.5 in. Overall length: 184.4 in. Overall height: 69.8 in. Front/Rear Tread: 66.7/63.7 in. Tires H78 x 15B.

CHASSIS (Series G1500): Wheelbase: 110/125 in. Overall length: 178/202.2 in. Overall height: 78.8 x 81.2 in. Tires: E or F78 x 15B.

CHASSIS (Series G2500): Wheelbase: 110/125 in. Overall length: 178/202.2 in. Overall height: 78.8 x 81.2 in. Tires: J78 x 15B.

CHASSIS (Series G3500): Wheelbase: 110/146 in. Tires: 8.00 x 16.5C (8.75 x 16.5D — Camper and Magna Van).

CHASSIS (Series P1500): Wheelbase: 102 in. Overall length: 175 in. Tires: L78 x 15B.

CHASSIS (Series P2500): Wheelbase: 125/133 in. Overall length: 220.75/244.75 in. Tires: 8.75 x 16.5C.

CHASSIS (Series P3500): Wheelbase: 125/157 in. Overall length: 220.75/268.75 in. Tires: 8.75 x 16.5C.

CHASSIS (Series C1500): Wheelbase: 117.5/131.5 in. Overall length: 191.3/212 in. Overall height: 69.8 in. Front/Rear Tread: 65.8/62.7 in. Tires: G78 x 15B.

CHASSIS (Series C2500): Wheelbase: 117.5/131.5/164.5 in. Overall length: 191.3/212/244.43 in. Overall height: 69.8 in. Front/Rear Tread: 65.8/62.7 in. Tires: 8.75 x 16.5C, Bonus Cab 8.75 x 16.5 (Front-C, Rear-D) Crew Cab 9.50 x 16.5D).

CHASSIS (Series C3500): Wheelbase: 131.5/164.5 in. Overall length: 212/244.43 in. Overall height: 71.8 in. Front/Rear Tread: 65.8/62.7 in. Tires: 8.75 x 16.5C, Bonus/Crew Cab 9.50 x 16.5E.

TECHNICAL: Manual, synchromesh. Speeds: 3F/1R (C3500 has 4-speed manual). Column (Floor on C3500) mounted gearshift. Clutch: 11 in. all full size Pickups, 12 in. diameter optional, 6-cylinder single disc with diaphragm or coil springs. V-8 models have single disc with coil springs. Semi-floating (½-Ton models), Full-floating (all others) rear axle. Overall ratio: C1500 3.40:1, C2500, C3500 4.10. Front disc, rear drum, hydraulic brakes. Pressed steel wheels.

DRIVETRAIN OPTIONS: Automatic transmission: Turbo-Hydra-Matic. 4-speed manual. Larger size tires (tube-style and tubeless). Power steering. Power brakes (C1500). Engine oil cooler. 61 amp generator. Heavy-duty shocks. Heavy-duty springs. Heavy-duty battery. Trailering package. Camper package. Dual rear wheels (C3500).

OPTIONS: Chrome front bumper. Chrome rear bumper. AM, AM/FM, AM/FM 8-track CB radio. Electric clock. Floor mats. Two-tone exterior paint. Intermittent windshield wipers. Interior hood release. Power windows. Power door locks. White sidewall tires. Pickup box side rails. Rear step bumper. Below eyeline mirrors. Rear step bumper. Cargo area lamp. Sliding rear window. Gauge package. Tachometer. Speed and cruise control. Air conditioning. Tilt steering wheel. 15, 16, 16.5 in. styled wheel. White letter tires. PA6 spoke wheel (C, K1500). Swing-out spare tire carrier.

HISTORICAL: Calendar year sales: 234,992 (all series).

476

Pricing

	5	4	3	2	1
1977					
Series Sprint — V-8 — (116 in. w.b.)					
Sprint Pickup	750	1500	2500	3500	5000
Sprint Classic Pickup	830	1650	2750	3850	5500
Series Jimmy — V-8 — (106 in. w.b.)					
4x4 Jimmy	1000	2000	3300	4600	6600
Series G1500 — Van — (½-Ton)					
Vandura	600	1200	2000	2800	4000
Rally	740	1470	2450	3350	4900
Rally STX	770	1550	2550	3600	5100
P1500 Van	530	1050	1750	2450	3500
Series G2500 — Van — (¾-Ton)					
Vandura	590	1170	1950	2700	3900
Rally	720	1450	2400	3300	4800
Rally STX	750	1500	2500	3500	5000
P2500 Van	520	1020	1700	2400	3400
Series G3500 — Van — (1-Ton)					
Vandura	570	1140	1900	2650	3800
Vandura Special	590	1170	1950	2700	3900
Rally Camper Special	620	1230	2050	2900	4100
Magna	540	1080	1800	2500	3600
Rally	570	1140	1900	2650	3800
Rally STX	590	1170	1950	2700	3900
P3500 Van	520	1000	1650	2300	3300
Series C1500 — Pickup — (½-Ton)					
Fender-Side Short Box					
Pickup	810	1620	2700	3800	5400
Wide-Side Short Box Pickup	830	1650	2750	3850	5500
Fender-Side Long Box Pickup	830	1650	2750	3850	5500
Wide-Side Long Box Pickup	840	1680	2800	3900	5600
Suburban	850	1700	2850	4000	5700
Series C2500 — Pickup — (¾-Ton)					
Fender-Side Pickup	770	1550	2550	3600	5100
Wide-Side Pickup	800	1600	2650	3700	5300
Bonus Cab Pickup	780	1560	2600	3600	5200
Crew Cab Pickup	770	1550	2550	3600	5100
Stake	720	1450	2400	3300	4800
Suburban	800	1600	2650	3700	5300
Series C3500 — Pickup — (1-Ton)					
Fender-Side Pickup	740	1470	2450	3350	4900
Wide-Side Pickup	770	1550	2550	3600	5100
Bonus Cab Pickup	750	1500	2500	3500	5000
Crew Cab Pickup	740	1470	2450	3350	4900
Stake	700	1400	2350	3250	4700

NOTE: Prices are top of the line models. Add 5 percent for 4wd.

1978 GMC

1978 GMC Sierra Classic Wide-Side Diesel Pickup (OCW)

GMC — LIGHT-DUTY — (ALL ENGINES): — The most important news from GMC was the new Caballero which replaced the Sprint as GMC's entry in the sports-pickup field. The Caballero was nearly a foot shorter in overall length and nearly 600 lbs. lighter than the former model but possessed equal cargo carrying capacity. The Caballero also had a new V-6 engine as its base powerplant.

Its new styling included a completely new roofline, small side quarter windows and a wraparound rear window. The front featured single rectangular headlights. The spare tire was carried under the pickup box floor and was accessible from the vehicle's interior. Although the Caballero was shorter on the outside it had greater interior roominess in all length and height dimensions. The pickup box length at the floor was virtually the same as before and longer at the top of the box.

I.D. DATA: Serial number location same as 1977. Starting: 50001 and up. Engine numbers located same as 1977.

1978 GMC Caballero "Diablo" Pickup (OCW)

Model	Body Type	Price	Weight	Prod. Total
Series Caballero — (V-8) — (305 cu. in.)				
SAW80	½-Ton Pickup Sedan	4774	3184	—
SAW80 /YE7	½-Ton Pickup Sedan Diablo	4953	3184	—
Series Jimmy — (V-8) — (305 cu. in.)				
TK10516	½-Ton Utility with hardtop	6378	4280	—
TK10516	½-Ton Utility with convertible top	6278	4132	—

NOTE: 2wd versions have TC prefix.

Model	Body Type	Price	Weight	Prod. Total
Series G1500				
TG11005	½-Ton Vandura (110 in. w.b.) (305 cu. in. V-8)	4609	3652	—
TG11006	½-Ton Rally (110 w.b.) (305 cu. in. V-8)	5468	3956	—
TG11306	½-Ton Rally STX (110 in. w.b.) (305 cu. in. V-8)	6181	4323	—
Series G2500				
TG21005	¾-Ton Vandura (110 in. w.b.) (350 cu. in. V-8)	4905	3661	—
TG21006	¾-Ton Rally (110 in. w.b.) (350 cu. in. V-8)	5726	3944	—
TG21306	¾-Ton Rally STX (125 in. w.b.) (350 cu. in. V-8)	6439	4282	—
Series G3500				
TG31005	1-Ton Vandura (110 in. w.b.) (350 cu. in. V-8)	5055	3896	—
TG31603	1-Ton Vandura Special (110 in. w.b.) (350 cu. in. V-8)	5599	3944	—
TG31303	1-Ton Rally Camper Special (125 in. w.b.) (350 cu. in. V-8)	5482	3639	—
TG31503	1-Ton Magna Van STX (125 in. w.b.) (350 cu. in. V-8)	6857	5047	—
TG31306	1-Ton Rally (125 in. w.b.) (350 cu. in. V-8)	6037	4357	—
TG31306	1-Ton Rally STX (125 in. w.b.) (350 cu. in. V-8)	6590	4530	—
Series P1500, P2500, P3500				
TP10542	½-Ton Van, 7-ft.	5771	4172	—
TP20842	¾-Ton Van, 10-ft., (125 in. w.b.) (350 cu. in. V-8)	6753	5283	—
TP30842	1-Ton Van, 10-ft., (125 in. w.b.) (350 cu. in. V-8)	6978	5503	—
Series C1500				
TC10703	½-Ton Chassis & Cab (350 cu. in. V-8)	4543	3570	—
TC10703	½-Ton Pickup (FS), 6.5-ft. (305 cu. in. V-8)	4418	3579	—
TC10703	½-Ton Pickup (WS), 6.5-ft. (305 cu. in. V-8)	4418	3639	—
TC10903	½-Ton Pickup (FS), 8-ft. (305 cu. in. V-8)	4493	3694	—
TC10903	½-Ton Pickup (WS), 8-ft. (305 cu. in. V-8)	4493	3775	—
TC10906	½-Ton Suburban Endgt, 8-ft. (305 cu. in. V-8)	5800	4257	—

NOTE: 4wd models have K prefix.

Model	Body Type	Price	Weight	Prod. Total
Series C2500				
TC20903	¾-Ton Chassis & Cab (131.5 in. w.b.) (350 cu. in. V-8)	4813	3665	—
TC20903	¾-Ton Pickup (FS), 8-ft. (131.5 in. w.b.) (350 cu. in. V-8)	5038	4054	—
TC20903	¾-Ton Pickup (WS), 8-ft. (131.5 in. w.b.) (350 cu. in. V-8)	5038	4135	—
TC20943	¾-Ton Chassis & Bonus Cab (350 cu. in. V-8)	5512	4176	—
TC20943	¾-Ton Pickup (WS) Bonus Cab (350 cu. in. V-8)	5737	4646	—

Model	Body Type	Price	Weight	Prod. Total
TC20943	¾-Ton Chassis & Crew Cab (350 cu. in. V-8)	5886	—	—
TC20943	¾-Ton Pickup (WS) Crew Cab (350 cu. in. V-8)	6111	—	—
TC20943	¾-Ton Platform & Stake, 8-ft. (350 cu. in. V-8)	5541	4299	—
TC20906	¾-Ton Suburban Endgt. (350 cu. in. V-8)	6381	4620	—

NOTE: 4wd models have K prefix.

Model	Body Type	Price	Weight	Prod. Total
Series C3500				
TC30903	1-Ton Chassis & Cab (131.5 in. w.b.) (350 cu. in. V-8)	5055	3792	—
TC30903	1-Ton Pickup (FS), 8-ft. (131.5 in. w.b.) (350 cu. in. V-8)	5280	4181	—
TC30903	1-Ton Pickup (WS), 8-ft. (131.5 in. w.b.) (350 cu. in. V-8)	5280	4262	—
TC30943	1-Ton Chassis & Bonus Cab (350 cu. in. V-8)	5937	4439	—
TC30943	1-Ton Pickup (WS) Bonus Cab (350 cu. in. V-8)	6162	4909	—
TC30943	1-Ton Chassis & Bonus Cab (350 cu. in. V-8)	6047	—	—
TC30943	1-Ton Pickup (WS) Crew Cab (350 cu. in. V-8)	6272	—	—
TC31003	1-Ton Platform & Stake, 9-ft. (350 cu. in. V-8)	5886	4655	—

NOTE: 4wd models have K prefix.

ENGINE (Standard C1500): Inline. OHV. 6-cylinder. Cast iron block. Bore & stroke: 3.876 x 3.530 in. Compression ratio: 8.25:1. Net horsepower: 115 at 3800 R.P.M. Net torque: 195 lb.-ft. at 1800 R.P.M. (above 6001 lb. GVW). Net horsepower 100 at 3600 R.P.M., Net torque: 175 lb.-ft. at 1800 R.P.M. Seven main bearings. Hydraulic valve lifters. Carburetor: Mono-Jet model 1ME.

ENGINE (Standard C2500, C3500): Inline. OHV. 6-cylinder. Cast iron block. Bore & stroke: 3.8764 x 4.120 in. Displacement: 292 cu. in. Compression ratio: 8.0:1. Net horsepower: 120 at 3600 R.P.M. Net torque: 215 lb.-ft. at 2000 R.P.M. Seven main bearings. Hydraulic valve lifters. Carburetor: 1-barrel.

ENGINE (Optional C1500, Caballero): V-type. OHV. 8-cylinder. Cast iron block. Bore & stroke: 3.736 x 3.480 in. Displacement: 305 cu. in. Compression ratio: 8.5:1. Net horsepower: 145 at 3800 R.P.M. Net torque: 245 lb.-ft. at 2400 R.P.M. Five main bearings. Hydraulic valve lifters. Carburetor: 2-barrel model 2GC.

ENGINE (Optional: all models): V-type. OHV. 8-cylinder. Cast iron block. Bore & stroke: 4.0 x 3.480 in. Displacement: 350 cu. in. Compression ratio: 8.5:1. Net horsepower: 165 at 3800 R.P.M. Net torque: 260 lb.-ft. at 2400 R.P.M. Five main bearings. Hydraulic valve lifters. Carburetor: 4-barrel model M4MC/MV.

ENGINE (Optional K1500, K2500, K3500): V-type. OHV. 8-cylinder. Cast iron block. Bore & stroke: 4.125 x 3.750 in. Displacement: 400 cu. in. Compression ratio: 8.5:1. Net horsepower: 175 at 3600 R.P.M. Net torque: 290 lb.-ft. at 2800 R.P.M. Five main bearings. Hydraulic valve lifters. Carburetor: 4-barrel model M4MC/MV.

ENGINE (Optional C1500, C2500, C3500, K1500, K2500, K3500): V-type. OHV. 8-cylinder. Cast iron block. Bore & stroke: 4.250 x 4.0 in. Displacement: 454 cu. in. Compression ratio: 8.5:1. Net horsepower: 205 at 3600 R.P.M. Net torque: 355 lb.-ft. at 2800 R.P.M. Five main bearings. Hydraulic valve lifters. Carburetor: 4-barrel model M4MC/MV.

ENGINE (Optional C1500): V-type. Diesel. 8-cylinder. Cast iron block. Bore & stroke: 4.057 x 3.385 in. Displacement: 350 cu. in. Compression ratio: 20.5:1. Net horsepower: 120 at 3600 R.P.M. Net torque: 222 lb.-ft. at 1900 R.P.M. Five main bearings. Hydraulic valve lifters.

ENGINE (Standard Caballero): V-type. OHV. 6-cylinder. Cast iron block. Bore & stroke: 3.50 x 3.48 in. Displacement: 200 cu. in. Compression ratio: 8.2:1. Net horsepower: 95 at 3800 R.P.M. Net torque: 160 lb.-ft. at 2000 R.P.M. Carburetor: Rochester 2-barrel.

ENGINE (Optional Caballero): (available with automatic transmission only). Standard engine for California delivery. V-6. OHV. 6-cylinder. Cast iron block. Bore & stroke: 3.80 x 3.40 in. Displacement: 235 cu. in. Compression ratio: 8.0:1. Net horsepower: 105 at 3400 R.P.M. Net torque: 185 lb.-ft. at 2000 R.P.M. Hydraulic valve lifters. Carburetor: Rochester 2-barrel.

CHASSIS Unchanged except for new Caballero Series. Wheelbase: 117.1 in. Overall length: 201.6 in. Overall height: 53.8 in. Front/Rear Tread: 58.5/57.8 in. Tires: P205 x 75R14.

TECHNICAL: Manual, synchromesh. Speeds: 3F/1R (4-speed standard C3500, models 7C20943 Crew & Bonus Cabs). Column (floor 4-speed) mounted gearshift. 11 in. dia; 12 in. dia with 350,400, 454 cu. in. V-8s with 4-barrel carburetor clutch. Semi-floating (½-Ton), Full-floating (¾-Ton and 1-Ton) rear axle. Overall ratio: C1500-3.07:1, C1500 Diesel-2.76:1, C2500, C3500-4.10:1, K2500-4.10:1, K1500-4.56:1. Front disc, rear drum hydraulic (all power except C1500) brakes. Pressed steel wheels.

DRIVETRAIN OPTIONS: Automatic transmission. CBC-350 3-speed automatic torque converter. 4-speed manual, model CH-465. Power steering. Power brakes (C1500). Trailering package. Camper special package. Heavy-duty generator. Engine oil cooler. Heavy-duty shock absorber. Heavy-duty front and rear springs. Heavy-duty Freedom battery. Dual rear wheels (C3500, K3500, 8-ft. box wideside only). Front stabilizer bar.

OPTIONS: Chrome front bumper. Chrome rear bumper. AM, AM/FM, AM/FM 8-track, CB radio. Front bumper guards. Rear step bumper. Tilt steering wheel. Swing-out camper mirrors. Sliding rear window. White stripe tires. White letter tires. Spoke wheels. Wheel covers (15, 16, 16.5 in.) Swing-out spare tire carrier. Sierra Classic package (C-series). Gypsy package (G-series) ($1050). 8-passenger package (G-series) ($180). 12-passenger package (G-series) ($380). Street Coupe equipment (C1500). High Sierra package (Jimmy and C-Series) ($781). Bucket seats. Cargo area lamp. Power windows. Power door locks. Pickup box side rails. Speed and cruise controls. Garage package. Air conditioning. Tachometer. Below eye-line mirrors. Auxiliary fuel tank. Color-keyed floor mats. Intermittent windshield wipers. Soft-ray tinted glass. Two-tone exterior paint combinations.

HISTORICAL: Model year sales: 283,540 (all series). Innovations: New Caballero introduced.

Pricing

1978	5	4	3	2	1
Series Caballero — (V-8) — (116 in. w.b.)					
Caballero Pickup	750	1500	2500	3500	5000
Diablo Pickup	830	1650	2750	3850	5500
Series Jimmy — (V-8) — (106 in. w.b.)					
4x4 Jimmy	1000	2000	3300	4600	6600
Series G1500 — (Van) — (½-Ton)					
Vandura	600	1200	2000	2800	4000
Rally	740	1470	2450	3350	4900
Rally STX	770	1550	2550	3600	5100
P1500 Van	530	1050	1750	2450	3500
Series G2500 — (Van) — (¾-Ton)					
Vandura	590	1170	1950	2700	3900
Rally	720	1450	2400	3300	4800
Rally STX	750	1500	2500	3500	5000
P2500 Van	520	1020	1700	2400	3400
Series G3500 — (Van) — (1-Ton)					
Vandura	570	1140	1900	2650	3800
Vandura Special	590	1170	1950	2700	3900
Rally Camper Special	620	1230	2050	2900	4100
Magna	540	1080	1800	2500	3600
Rally	570	1140	1900	2650	3800
Rally STX	590	1170	1950	2700	3900
P3500 Van	520	1040	1650	2300	3300
Series C1500 — (Pickup) — (½-Ton)					
Fender-Side Short Box Pickup	810	1620	2700	3800	5400
Wide-Side Short Box Pickup	830	1650	2750	3850	5500
Fender-Side Long Box Pickup	830	1650	2750	3850	5500
Wide-Side Long Box Pickup	840	1680	2800	3900	5600
Suburban	850	1700	2850	4000	5700
Series C2500 — (Pickup) — (¾-Ton)					
Fender-Side Pickup	770	1550	2550	3600	5100
Wide-Side Pickup	800	1600	2650	3700	5300
Bonus Cab Pickup	780	1560	2600	3600	5200
Crew Cab Pickup	770	1550	2550	3600	5100
Stake	720	1450	2400	3300	4800
Suburban	800	1600	2650	3700	5300
Series C3500 — (Pickup) — (1-Ton)					
Fender-Side Pickup	740	1470	2450	3350	4900
Wide-Side Pickup	770	1550	2550	3600	5100
Bonus Cab Pickup	750	1500	2500	3500	5000
Crew Cab Pickup	740	1470	2450	3350	4900
Stake	700	1400	2350	3250	4700

NOTE: Prices are top of the line models. Add 5 percent for 4wd.

1979 GMC

GMC — LIGHT-DUTY — (ALL ENGINES): — Styling refinements for 1979 included bright trim added to the lower grille portion and a black-colored mesh back-drop for the main grille section. The Caballero also received a new grille with a prominent horizontal emphasis.

Pickup interiors had a new standard vinyl seat trim. All models except Caballero and P-series had a wider vent window post for added theft protection.

I.D. DATA: Unchanged from 1978. Starting: 500001 and up. Engine number location unchanged from 1978. Starting: 500001 and up.

Model	Body Type	Price	Weight	Prod. Total
Series Caballero — (V-8) — (305 cu. in.)				
1AW80	½-Ton Sedan Pickup	5378	3188	—
1AW80 /YE7	½-Ton Sedan Pickup Diablo	5580	3328	—

478

Model	Body Type	Price	Weight	Prod. Total
Series Jimmy — (V-8) — (305 cu. in.)				
TK10516	½-Ton Utility Hardtop	7373	4371	—
TK10516	½-Ton Utility Convertible	7273	4457	—

NOTE: 2wd models have TC prefix.

Model	Body Type	Price	Weight	Prod. Total
Series G1500 — (V-8) — (305 cu. in.)				
TG11005	½-Ton Vandura (110 in. w.b.)	5312	3093	—
TG11006	½-Ton Rally (110 in. w.b.)	6229	3998	—
TG11306	½-Ton Rally STX (125 in. w.b.)	7030	4349	—
Series G2500 — (V-8) — (350 cu. in.)				
TG21005	¾-Ton Vandura (110 in. w.b.)	5606	3689	—
TG21006	¾-Ton Rally (110 in. w.b.)	6397	3970	—
TG21306	¾-Ton Rally, STX (125 in. w.b.)	7186	4318	—
Series G3500 — (V-8) — (350 cu. in.)				
TG31005	1-Ton Vandura (110 in. w.b.)	5822	3914	—
TG31303	1-Ton Vandura Special (110 in. w.b.)	5383	3547	—
TG31332	1-Ton Rally Camper Special (110 in. w.b.)	6293	3688	—
TG31303	1-Ton Magna Van (110 in. w.b.)	7032	—	—
TG31306	1-Ton Rally (110 in. w.b.)	6774	4378	—
TG31306	1-Ton Rally STX (125 in. w.b.)	7410	4556	—
Series C1500 — (V-8) — (305 cu. in.)				
TC10703	½-Ton Chassis & Cab (117.5 in. w.b.)	4943	3406	—
TC10703	½-Ton Pickup (FS), 6.5-ft.	5091	3570	—
TC10703	½-Ton Pickup (WS), 6.5-ft.	5091	3628	—
TC10903	½-Ton Chassis & Cab (131.5 in. w.b.)	5023	3467	—
TC10903	½-Ton Pickup (FS), 8-ft.	5171	3693	—
TC10903	½-Ton Pickup (WS), 8-ft.	5171	3767	—
TC10906	½-Ton Suburban (Endgt)	6614	4285	—

NOTE: 4wd versions have TK prefix.

Model	Body Type	Price	Weight	Prod. Total
Series C2500 — (V-8) — (350 cu. in.)				
TC20903	¾-Ton Chassis & Cab (131.5 in. w.b.)	5481	3676	—
TC20903	¾-Ton Pickup (FS), 8-ft.	5742	4061	—
TC20903	¾-Ton Pickup (WS), 8-ft.	5742	4135	—
TC20943	¾-Ton Chassis & Bonus Cab	6233	4224	—
TC20943	¾-Ton Pickup (WS) Bonus Cab	6516	4682	—
TC20943	¾-Ton Chassis & Crew Cab	6634	—	—
TC20943	¾-Ton Pickup (WS) Crew Cab	6918	—	—
TC20906	¾-Ton Platform & Stake, 8-ft.	6239	4209	—
TC21003	¾-Ton Suburban, (Endgt)	7075	4556	—
Series C3500 — (V-8) — (350 cu. in.)				
TC30903	1-Ton Chassis & Cab (131.5 in. w.b.)	5941	3899	—
TC30903	1-Ton Pickup (FS), 8-ft.	6237	4284	—
TC30903	1-Ton Pickup (WS), 8-ft.	6237	4358	—
TC30943	1-Ton Chassis & Bonus Cab	6740	4453	—
TC30943	1-Ton Pickup (WS) Bonus Cab	7023	4912	—
TC30943	1-Ton Chassis & Crew Cab	6900	—	—
TC30943	1-Ton Pickup (WS) Crew Cab	7183	—	—
TC31003	1-Ton Platform & Stake, 9-ft.	6856	4671	—

1979 GMC Sierra Classic Wide-Side Pickup (JAG)

ENGINE: Unchanged from 1978 except for L39 engine option for Caballero. V-type. OHV. 8-cylinder. Cast iron block. Bore & stroke: 3.5 x 3.48 in. Displacement: 267 cu. in. Net horsepower: 125. Hydraulic valve lifters. Carburetor: Rochester 2-barrel.

CHASSIS Unchanged from 1978.

TECHNICAL: Unchanged from 1978.

OPTIONS: Laredo package (Caballero) ($155). High Sierra package (Caballero, C1500) ($748). Gypsy package (G-series). 8-passenger package (G-series) ($191). 12-passenger package (G-series) ($403). Sierra Grande package (C-series). Sierra Classic package (C-series). Street Coupe equipment (C1500). Bucket seats. N67 Rally wheels. PA6 styled wheels. PH7 styled aluminum wheels (Street Coupe models only).

HISTORICAL: Calendar year sales: Vandura/Rally 41,587, Suburban 6984, Jimmy 11,804, P-Series 5045, Caballero 6412, C, K-Series 106,504.

Pricing

1979	5	4	3	2	1
Series Caballero — (V-8) — (116 in. w.b.)					
Caballero Pickup	750	1500	2500	3500	5000
Diablo Pickup	830	1650	2750	3850	5500
Series Jimmy — (V-8) — (106 in. w.b.)					
4x4 Jimmy	1000	2000	3300	4600	6600
Series G1500 — (Van) — (½-Ton)					
Vandura	600	1200	2000	2800	4000
Rally	740	1470	2450	3350	4900
Rally STX	770	1550	2550	3600	5100
P1500 Van	530	1050	1750	2450	3500
Series G2500 — (Van) — (¾-Ton)					
Vandura	590	1170	1950	2700	3900
Rally	720	1450	2400	3300	4800
Rally STX	750	1500	2500	3500	5000
P2500 Van	520	1020	1700	2400	3400
Series G3500 — (Van) — (1-Ton)					
Vandura	570	1140	1900	2650	3800
Vandura Special	590	1170	1950	2700	3900
Rally Camper Special	620	1230	2050	2900	4100
Magna	540	1080	1800	2500	3600
Rally	570	1140	1900	2650	3800
Rally STX	590	1170	1950	2700	3900
P3500 Van	520	1000	1650	2300	3300
Series C1500 — (Pickup) — (½-Ton)					
Fender-Side Short Box					
Pickup	810	1620	2700	3800	5400
Wide-Side Short Box Pickup	830	1650	2750	3850	5500
Fender-Side Long Box Pickup	830	1650	2750	3850	5500
Wide-Side Long Box Pickup	840	1680	2800	3900	5600
Suburban	850	1700	2850	4000	5700
Series C2500 — (Pickup) — (¾-Ton)					
Fender-Side Pickup	770	1550	2550	3600	5100
Wide-Side Pickup	800	1600	2650	3700	5300
Bonus Cab Pickup	780	1560	2600	3600	5200
Crew Cab Pickup	770	1550	2550	3600	5100
Stake	720	1450	2400	3300	4800
Suburban	800	1600	2650	3700	5300
Series C3500 — (Pickup) — (1-Ton)					
Fender-Side Pickup	740	1470	2450	3350	4900
Wide-Side Pickup	770	1550	2550	3600	5100
Bonus Cab Pickup	750	1500	2500	3500	5000
Crew Cab Pickup	740	1470	2450	3350	4900
Stake	700	1400	2350	3250	4700

NOTE: Prices are top of the line models. Add 5 percent for 4wd.

1980 GMC

1980 GMC Caballero Pickup (DFW)

GMC — LIGHT-DUTY — (ALL ENGINES): — Changes for 1980 were essentially cosmetic in nature. The Caballero's grille was fitted with vertical bars while the center grille bar on other light-duty GMC trucks was now painted to match the body color.

I.D. DATA: Unchanged from 1979. Starting: 100001 and up. Engine numbers location unchanged from 1979.

1980 GMC Sierra Classic "Indy Hauler" Pickup (DFW)

Model	Body Type	Price	Weight	Prod. Total
Series Caballero — (V-8) — (305 cu. in.)				
1AW80	½-Ton Sedan Pickup	5911	3098	—
1AW80 /YE7	½-Ton Sedan Pickup Diablo	6129	—	—
Series Jimmy — (V-8) — (305 cu. in.)				
TK10516	½-Ton 4wd Utility Hardtop	8078	4418	—
TK10516	½-Ton 4wd Utility Convertible top	7975	—	—

NOTE: 2wd versions have TC prefix.

1980 GMC Sierra Classic "Indy Hauler" Pickup (OCW)

Series G1500 — (V-8) — (305 cu. in.)			
TG11005	½-Ton Vandura (110 in. w.b.)	5748	3652	—
TG11006	½-Ton Rally (110 in. w.b.)	6747	3971	—
TG11306	½-Ton Rally (125 in. w.b.)	7699	4153	—
Series G2500 — (V-8) — (350 cu. in.)			
TG21005	¾-Ton Vandura (110 in. w.b.)	6183	3756	—
TG21006	¾-Ton Rally (110 in. w.b.)	7023	4012	—
TG11306	¾-Ton Rally STX (125 in. w.b.)	7975	4202	—

1980 GMC Rally STX Passenger Van (OCW)

Model	Body Type	Price	Weight	Prod. Total
Series G3500 — (V-8) — (350 cu. in.)				
TG31305	1-Ton Vandura (125 in. w.b.)	7060	4154	—
TG31303	1-Ton Vandura Spl (125 in. w.b.)	5860	3524	—
TG31332	1-Ton Rally Camper Spl (125 in. w.b.)	6808	3736	—
TG31303	1-Magna Van (125 in. w.b.)	7785	—	—
TG31306	1-Ton Rally (125 in. w.b.)	7901	4450	—
TG31306	1-Ton Rally STX (125 in. w.b.)	8680	—	—
Series P1500, P2500, P3500				
TP10542	½-Ton Van, 7-ft.	6785	4332	—
TP20842	¾-Ton Van, 10-ft. (125 in. w.b.) (350 cu. in. V-8)	8139	5425	—
TP30842	1-Ton Van, 10-ft. (125 in. w.b.) (350 cu. in. V-8)	8409	5599	—
Series G1500				
TC10703	½-Ton Chassis & Cab (117.5 in. w.b.) (305 cu. in. V-8)	5785	3243	—
TC10703	½-Ton Pickup (FS), 6.5-ft.	5505	3612	—
TC10703	½-Ton Pickup (WS), 6.5-ft.	5505	3609	—
TC10903	½-Ton Chassis & Cab (131.5 in. w.b.) (350 cu. in. V-8)	5870	3317	—
TC10903	½-Ton Pickup (FS), 8-ft. (305 cu. in. V-8)	5590	3692	—
TC10903	½-Ton Pickup (WS), 8-ft. (305 cu. in. V-8)	5590	3767	—
TC10906	½-Ton Suburban Endgt. (305 cu. in. V-8)	7456	4208	—

NOTE: 4wd versions have TK prefix.

Model	Body Type	Price	Weight	Prod. Total
Series C2500				
TC20903	¾-Ton Chassis & Cab (131.5 in. w.b.) (350 cu. in. V-8)	6216	3625	—
TC20903	¾-Ton Pickup (FS), 8-ft. (350 cu. in. V-8)	6326	4009	—
TC20903	¾-Ton Pickup (WS), 8-ft. (350 cu. in. V-8)	6326	4084	—
TC20943	¾-Ton Chassis & Bonus Cab (350 cu. in. V-8)	6904	4330	—
TC20943	¾-Ton Pickup (WS) Bonus Cab (350 cu. in. V-8)	7241	—	—
TC20943	¾-Ton Chassis & Crew Cab	7218	—	—
TC20943	¾-Ton Pickup (WS) Crew Cab (350 cu. in. V-8)	7495	—	—
TC20906	¾-Ton Suburban (350 cu. in. V-8)	7923	4504	—

NOTE: 4wd versions have TK prefix.

Model	Body Type	Price	Weight	Prod. Total
Series C3500				
TC30903	1-Ton Chassis & Cab (131.5 in. w.b.) (350 cu. in. V-8)	6399	3848	—
TC30903	1-Ton Pickup (FS), 8-ft. (350 cu. in. V-8)	6687	4232	—
TC30903	1-Ton Pickup (WS), 8-ft. (350 cu. in. V-8)	6687	4307	—
TC30943	1-Ton Chassis & Bonus Cab (350 cu. in. V-8)	7120	4364	—
TC30943	1-Ton Pickup (WS) Bonus Cab (350 cu. in. V-8)	7397	4823	—
TC30943	1-Ton Chassis & Crew Cab (350 cu. in. V-8)	7374	—	—
TC30943	1-Ton Pickup (WS) Crew Cab (350 cu. in. V-8)	7651	—	—
TC31003	1-Ton Platform & Stake (350 cu. in. V-8)	7481	4708	—

ENGINE: Unchanged from 1979.

CHASSIS Unchanged from 1979.

1980 GMC Cutaway Van w/Mini-Motorhome (OCW)

480

TECHNICAL: Manual, synchromesh. Speeds: 3F/1R (4-speed C3500). Column (floor-4-speed) mounted gearshift. 11 in. dia, 12 in. dia with 350, 400, 454 cu. in. engines with 4-barrel carburetor clutch. Semi-floating (½-Ton models), Full-floating (all others) rear axle. Overall ratio: C1500 3.07:1, C1500 diesel 2.76:1, C2500, C3500 4.11:1. Front disc, rear drum, hydraulic, power assisted except brakes for C1500. Pressed steel wheels. Automatic transmission CBC-350, 3-speed automatic. 4-speed manual model CH-465. Power steering. Power brakes (C1500). Trailering package. Camper package. Heavy-duty generator. Engine oil cooler. Heavy-duty shock absorbers. Heavy-duty springs. Heavy-duty Freedom battery. Dual rear wheels. Front stabilizer bar. F-44 package.

OPTIONS: Chrome front bumper. Rear bumper. AM, AM/FM radio. Electric clock. Air conditioning. Color-keyed floor mats. Tinted glass. Chrome grille. Tilt steering wheel. Intermittent wipers. Sliding rear windows. Loredo package (Caballero) ($165). Gypsy package (G-series). 8-passenger package (G-series) ($225). 12-passenger package (G-series) ($480). High Sierra package (C-series). Sierra classic package (Jimmy C-series) ($895). Sierra Grande package (C-series). Street Coupe equipment (C1500) and more.

HISTORICAL: Calendar year sales: 141,030: divided as follows: Pickups 102,130. Vandura/Rally 21,007. Suburban 4210. Jimmy 5608. P-models 3612. Caballero 4463.

Pricing

	5	4	3	2	1
1980					
Series Caballero — (V-8) — (116 in. w.b.)					
Caballero Pickup	750	1500	2500	3500	5000
Diablo Pickup	830	1650	2750	3850	5500
Series Jimmy — (V-8) — (106 in. w.b.)					
4x4 Jimmy	1000	2000	3300	4600	6600
Series G1500 — (Van) — (½-Ton)					
Vandura	600	1200	2000	2800	4000
Rally	740	1470	2450	3350	4900
Rally STX	770	1550	2550	3600	5100
P1500 Van	530	1050	1750	2450	3500
Series G2500 — (Van) — (¾-Ton)					
Vandura	590	1170	1950	2700	3900
Rally	720	1450	2400	3300	4800
Rally STX	750	1500	2500	3500	5000
P2500 Van	520	1020	1700	2400	3400
Series G3500 — (Van) — (1-Ton)					
Vandura	570	1140	1900	2650	3800
Vandura Special	590	1170	1950	2700	3900
Rally Camper Special	620	1230	2050	2900	4100
Magna	540	1080	1800	2500	3600
Rally	570	1140	1900	2650	3800
Rally STX	590	1170	1950	2700	3900
P3500 Van	520	1000	1650	2300	3300
Series C1500 — (Pickup) — (½-Ton)					
Fender-Side Short Box Pickup	810	1620	2700	3800	5400
Wide-Side Short Box Pickup	830	1650	2750	3850	5500
Fender-Side Long Box Pickup	830	1650	2750	3850	5500
Wide-Side Long Box Pickup	840	1680	2800	3900	5600
Suburban	850	1700	2850	4000	5700
Series C2500 — (Pickup) — (¾-Ton)					
Fender-Side Pickup	770	1550	2550	3600	5100
Wide-Side Pickup	800	1600	2650	3700	5300
Bonus Cab Pickup	780	1560	2600	3600	5200
Crew Cab Pickup	770	1550	2550	3600	5100
Stake	720	1450	2400	3300	4800
Suburban	800	1600	2650	3700	5300
Series C3500 — (Pickup) — (1-Ton)					
Fender-Side Pickup	740	1470	2450	3350	4900
Wide-Side Pickup	770	1550	2550	3600	5100
Bonus Cab Pickup	750	1500	2500	3500	5000
Crew Cab Pickup	740	1470	2450	3350	4900
Stake	700	1400	2350	3250	4700

NOTE: Prices are top of the line models. Add 5 percent for 4wd.

1981 GMC

GMC — LIGHT TRUCK — (ALL SERIES) — SIX-CYLINDER/V-8: — There were many important changes made in the latest GMC trucks that made them far more fuel efficient than in years past. New aerodynamically designed front sheet metal was both attractive and a contributor to less wind drag. Overall, the GMC pickups weighed less in 1980 but there was no reduction in their payload capacities. The front disc brakes on the C1500, C2500 and their 4wd counterparts were of a low-drag design. Also introduced were rear springs on the 2 and 4wd ½-ton and ¾-ton models that were shot-peened for added strength. Most GMC trucks with the optional automatic transmission had re-engineered clutch plates for quieter operation.

Interior changes included a higher grade standard interior with full foam seat cushions and a more attractive vinyl upholstery. The instrument panel now had a foam-padded pad with a GMC nameplate.

Helping identify the 1981 GMC was a new grille format with rectangular headlights (single on base models) and new side marker lights.

1981 GMC Caballero Pickup (DFW/GMC)

I.D. DATA: The vehicle identification number is stamped on a plate attached to the left top of the instrument panel on C, K and G-series. On P-series the plate is attached to the front of the dash and toe panel to the left of the steering column. Starting: 100001 and up. Engine numbers located: 6-cyl.-located on pad found at right handside of cylinder block at rear of distributor. 8-cyl.-located on pad at front right side of cylinder block.

Model	Body Type	Price	Weight	Prod. Total
Series Caballero				
1AW80	½-Ton Sedan Pickup	6988	3181	—
1AW80 /YE7	½-Ton Sedan Pickup Diablo	7217	—	—
Series Jimmy				
TK10516	½-Ton 4wd Utility Hardtop	8856	4087	—
TK10516	½-Ton 4wd Utility Convertible top	8750	—	—

NOTE: 2wd versions have TC prefix.

Model	Body Type	Price	Weight	Prod. Total
Series G1500				
TG11005	½-Ton Vandura (110 in. w.b.)	6434	3577	—
TG11006	½-Ton Rally (110 in. w.b.)	7465	3907	—
TG11306	½-Ton Rally Custom (125 in. w.b.)	8304	4602	—
TG11306	½-Ton Rally STX (125 in. w.b.)	8515	4602	—
Series G2500				
TG21005	¾-Ton Vandura (110 in. w.b.)	6756	3631	—
TG21006	¾-Ton Rally (110 in. w.b.)	7617	3928	—
TG21306	¾-Ton Rally Custom (125 in. w.b.)	8456	4096	—
TG21306	¾-Ton Rally STX (125 in. w.b.)	8667	4096	—
Series G3500 — (V-8) — (350 cu. in.)				
TG31305	1-Ton Vandura (125 in. w.b.)	8056	4285	—
TG31303	1-Ton Vandura Special (125 in. w.b.)	6764	3578	—
TG31332	1-Ton Rally Camper Special (125 in. w.b.)	7765	3746	—
TG31303	1-Ton Magna Van, 10-ft.	9053	—	—
TG31306	1-Ton Rally (125 in. w.b.)	8997	4602	—
TG31306	1-Ton Rally Custom (125 in. w.b.)	9653	4602	—
TG31306	1-Ton Rally STX (125 in. w.b.)	9863	4602	—
Series P2500, P3500				
TP20842	¾-Ton Van, 10-ft.	9711	5479	—
TP30842	1-Ton Van, 10-ft.	9959	5671	—
Series C1500				
TC10703	½-Ton Pickup (FS), 6.5-ft.	6012	3348	—
TC10703	½-Ton Pickup (WS), 6.5-ft.	6012	3391	—
TC10903	½-Ton Pickup (FS), 8-ft.	6099	3457	—
TC10903	½-Ton Pickup (WS), 8-ft.	6099	3518	—
TC10906	½-Ton Suburban (305 cu. in. V-8)	8517	4246	—

NOTE: 4wd versions have TK prefix.

Model	Body Type	Price	Weight	Prod. Total
Series C2500				
TC20903	¾-Ton Chassis & Cab (131.5 in. w.b.)	6780	3326	—
TC20903	¾-Ton Pickup (FS), 8-ft.	6757	3710	—
TC20903	¾-Ton Pickup (WS), 8-ft.	6757	3771	—
TC20943	¾-Ton Chassis & Bonus Cab	7622	4246	—
TC20943	¾-Ton Pickup (WS) Bonus Cab	7935	—	—
TC20943	¾-Ton Chassis & Crew Cab	7912	—	—
TC20943	¾-Ton Pickup (WS) Crew Cab	8225	—	—
TC20906	¾-Ton Suburban (350 cu. in. V-8)	8771	4566	—

NOTE: 4wd versions have TK prefix.

Model	Body Type	Price	Weight	Prod. Total
Series C3500				
TC30903	1-Ton Chassis & Cab (131.5 in. w.b.)	6895	3893	—
TC30903	1-Ton Pickup (FS), 8-ft.	7214	4249	—
TC30903	1-Ton Pickup (WS), 8-ft.	7214	4310	—
TC30943	1-Ton Chassis & Bonus Cab	7800	4327	—
TC30943	1-Ton Pickup (WS) Bonus Cab	8114	4744	—
TC30943	1-Ton Chassis & Crew Cab	8090	—	—
TC30943	1-Ton Pickup (WS) Crew Cab	8404	—	—
TC31003	1-Ton Platform	7951	4757	—

ENGINE: Except for the following dimensions of GMC light-duty trucks were unchanged from 1980.

CHASSIS (Series Jimmy): Tires: P225 x 75R15.

CHASSIS (Series C1500): Tires: FR78 x 15B.

1981 GMC ¾-Ton Indy 500 Wrecker (IMSC/JLM)

TECHNICAL: Transmission: Manual, synchromesh. Speeds: 3F/1R (C2500 Bonus/Crew, C3500, K3500 4F/1R). Column (floor-4-speed) mounted gearshift. Clutch: 11 in. dia, 12 in. dia optional Semi-floating C1500, C2500, K1500, K2500, Full-floating C3500, K2500, heavy-duty K3500 rear axle. Overall ratio: C1500 2.73:1, C2500, K2500 3.42:1, K3500 Bonus/Crew 4.56:1, all others 4.10:1. Hydraulic, 4-wheel, front disc, rear drum, (power-assisted except for C1500) brakes. Kelsey-Hayes pressed steel wheels.

DRIVETRAIN OPTIONS: Auxiliary fuel tank. Auxiliary battery. Locking differential. Automatic transmission. Turbo-hydro-matic. Front dual shocks (K1500, K2500). Cold climate package. Engine oil cooler. SC, 63 amp generator. Heavy-duty automatic transmission cooler. Heavy-duty battery. Heavy-duty front and rear shocks. Heavy-duty radiator. Trailering package. Heavy-duty power brakes. Dual exhausts. Dual rear wheels (C3500). Front stabilizer bar. Fuel tank stone shield. Heavy-duty front stabilizer bar. Heavy-duty front springs. Extra capacity rear springs. Extra-high capacity rear springs. Basic camper equipment package. Deluxe camper equipment package.

OPTIONS: Front bumper chromed. Rear bumper chromed. Chromed rear step bumper. Cargo area lamp. Front bumper guards. Cigar lighter. Dome lamp. Deluxe instrument panel. Color-keyed floor mats. Cruise control. High-back bucket seats. Halogen hi-beam headlamps (requires deluxe appearance package). Sliding rear window. Power door locks. Power windows. Cast aluminum wheels. Painted West Coast mirrors. Rally wheels. Styled wheels. Intermittent windshield wipers. Windshield antenna. Gage package. Glide-out spare tire carrier. Tinted glass. Radio AM/FM/CB, with cassette or 8-track tape. Roof marker lights. Exterior decor package. Deluxe two-tone exterior paint. Wheel opening moldings. Door edge guards. Stainless steel below eye-line mirror. Painted below eye-line mirror. Bright body molding. Black body molding. Amarillo package (Caballero) ($161). 8-passenger package (G-series) ($219). 12-passenger package (G-series) ($467). Street Sedan equipment (G-series). High Sierra package (C-series). Sierra Grande package (C-series). Sierra Classic package (Jimmy, C-series) ($881). Street Coupe equipment (C1500). Deluxe appearance package and more.

HISTORICAL: Calendar year sales: 141,335 distributed as follows: Pickups 97,599. Vandura/Rally 22,982. Suburban 4349. Jimmy 4689. P-Series 3454. Caballero 3994.

1982 GMC

GMC — LIGHT TRUCK — (ALL SERIES) — SIX-CYLINDER/V-8: — Leading the 1982 GMC truck lineup were the new S15 models. Work on these trucks began in October, 1978 and they were regarded as General Motors' response to the increasing popularity of imported light trucks. Compared to the Chevrolet LUV Series 11 model the S15 and the Chevrolet S10, which except for minor details were comparable to the S15, was 2 in. lower, and has a w.b. just 0.4 in. longer.

481

1982 GMC "Jimmy" Sport Utility w/Diesel (OCW)

Most mechanical components for the S15 came from General Motors' G-cars which included the Chevrolet Monte Carlo and Pontiac Grand Prix. Its base engine and transmission was supplied by Isuzu.

Other changes for 1982 included a 90-degree diesel engine which had as its standard transmission the same New Process four-speed transmission that was introduced during 1981 for the GMC Special Economy truck. Also available on some GMC models was a new four-speed automatic transmission, the THG-700R4, which had a lock-up torque converter that engaged in second, third and overdrive.

No longer offered was the 305 cu. in. LG9 V-8.

The latest Caballero had new front end styling with a cross-hatched grille design and dual rectangular headlights. A total of five new exterior colors were offered along with new two-tone combinations. Technical refinements included dual cowl-mounted "fluidic" windshield washers and a fender-mounted fixed mast radio antenna. A three-speed automatic transmission was standard on all 1982 Caballeros.

I.D. DATA: Unchanged from 1981. Engine numbers location unchanged from 1981.

Model	Body Type	Price	Weight	Prod. Total
Series Caballero				
1GW80	½-Ton Sedan Pickup	7995	3294	—
1GW80 /YE7	½-Ton Sedan Pickup Diablo	8244	3300	—
Series Jimmy				
TK10516	½-Ton 4wd Hardtop Utility	9874	4294	—

NOTE: 2wd versions have TC prefix.

Model	Body Type	Price	Weight	Prod. Total
Series G1500				
TG11005	½-Ton Vandura (110 in. w.b.)	6908	3708	—
TG11006	½-Ton Rally (110 in. w.b.)	8122	4015	—
TG11306	½-Ton Rally Custon (110 in. w.b.)	9040	4273	—
TG11306	½-Ton Rally STX (110 in. w.b.)	9268	4313	—
Series G2500				
TG21005	¾-Ton Vandura (110 in. w.b.)	7256	3782	—
TG21306	¾-Ton Rally (110 in. w.b.)	8486	4207	—
TG21306	¾-Ton Rally Custom (125 in. w.b.)	9204	4294	—
TG21306	¾-Ton Rally STX (125 in. w.b.)	9432	4334	—
Series G3500 — (V-8) — (350 cu. in.)				
TG31305	1-Ton Vandura (125 in. w.b.)	8494	4251	—
TG31305	1-Ton Vandura Special (125 in. w.b.)	7361	3739	—
TG31332	1-Ton Rally Camper Special (125 in. w.b.)	8452	3951	—
TG31303	1-Magna Van, 10-ft.	10,141	5515	—
TG31306	1-Ton Rally (125 in. w.b.)	10,228	4595	—
TG31306	1-Ton Rally STX (125 in. w.b.)	11,174	4854	—
Series P2500, P3500				
TP20842	¾-Ton Value Van, 10-ft.	11,744	5774	—
TP30842	1-Ton Value Van, 10-ft.	11,820	5939	—
Series S15				
TS10603	½-Ton Pickup (WS) 6-ft.	6600	2509	—
TS10803	½-Ton Pickup (WS), 7.5-ft.	6750	2584	—
Series C1500				
TC10703	½-Ton Pickup (FS), 6.5-ft.	6689	3418	—
TC10703	½-Ton Pickup (WS), 6.5-ft.	6564	3461	—
TC10903	½-Ton Pickup (WS), 8-ft.	6714	3613	—
TC10906	½-Ton Suburban (350 cu. in. V-8)	9744	4295	—

NOTE: 4wd versions have TK prefix.

Model	Body Type	Price	Weight	Prod. Total
Series C2500				
TC20903	¾-Ton Chassis & Cab (131.5 in. w.b.)	7865	3661	—
TC20903	¾-Ton Pickup (FS), 8-ft.	7857	3956	—
TC20903	¾-Ton Pickup (WS), 8-ft.	7732	3999	—
TC20943	¾-Ton Pickup (WS) Bonus Cab	9123	4748	—
TC20943	¾-Ton Pickup (WS) Crew Cab	9439	4809	—
TC20906	¾-Ton Suburban (350 cu. in. V-8)	9978	4677	—

NOTE: 4wd versions have TK prefix.

Model	Body Type	Price	Weight	Prod. Total
Series C3500				
TC30903	1-Ton Chassis & Cab (131.5 in. w.b.)	7990	3973	—
TC30903	1-Ton Pickup (FS), 8-ft.	8474	4323	—
TC30903	1-Ton Pickup (WS), 8-ft.	8349	4394	—
TC30943	1-Ton Chassis & Bonus Cab	8943	4400	—
TC30943	1-Ton Pickup (WS) Bonus Cab	9286	4817	—
TC30943	1-Ton Chassis & Crew Cab	9259	4626	—
TC30943	1-Ton Pickup (WS) Crew Cab	9602	4878	—
TC31003	1-Ton Platform	9191	5293	—

1982 GMC Sierra Classic Wide-Side Pickup (OCW)

ENGINE (Standard: C1500, C2500, K1500, G-Series): Inline. OHV. 6-cylinder. Cast iron block. Bore & stroke: 3.9 x 4.5 in. Displacement: 250 cu. in. Compression ratio: 8.3:1. Net horsepower: 110 at 3600 R.P.M. Max torque: 195 lb.-ft. at 2000 R.P.M. CC1500 Brake horsepower: 120 at 3800 R.P.M. Max torque: 200 lb.-ft. at 2000 R.P.M. Seven main bearings. Hydraulic valve lifters. Carburetor: Rochester Staged model 2-barrel.

ENGINE (Optional: C1500, C2500, K1500: (Not available in California). V-type. OHV. 8-cylinder. Cast iron block. Bore & stroke: 3.736 x 3.480 in. Displacement: 305 cu. in. Compression ratio: 9.2:1. Net horsepower: 160 at 4400 R.P.M. Max torque: 235 lb.-ft. at 2000 R.P.M. C1500 Brake horsepower: 165 at 4400 R.P.M. Max torque: 240 lb.-ft. at 2000 R.P.M. Five main bearings. Hydraulic valve lifters. Carburetor: Rochester Staged model 4-barrel, Electronic Spark Control.

ENGINE (Optional C2500, C2500/F44, C-3500, K2500/F44, K3500, P2500, P3500, G1500, G2500): (Not available in California). V-type. 8-cylinder. Cast iron block. Bore & stroke: 4.0 x 3.5 in. Displacement: 350 cu. in. Compression ratio: 8.2:1. Net horsepower: 165 at 3800 R.P.M. Max torque: 275 lb.-ft at 1600 R.P.M. Five main bearings. Hydraulic valve lifters. Carburetor: Rochester 4-barrel.

ENGINE: V-type. OHV. Diesel. 8-cylinder. Cast iron block. Bore & stroke: 3.98 x 3.80 in. Displacement: 379 cu. in. Compression ratio: 21.5:1. Net horsepower: 130 at 3600 R.P.M. Max torque: 240 lb.-ft. at 2000 R.P.M. Hydraulic valve lifters.

1982 GMC Caballero Pickup (OCW)

1982 GMC Vandura Passenger Van (OCW)

ENGINE (Standard: C2500/F44, C2500, C3500, K2500, K3500, P2500, P3500): Inline. OHV. 6-cylinder. Cast iron block. Bore & stroke: 3.876 x 4.12 in. Displacement: 292 cu. in. Compression ratio: 7.8:1. Net horsepower: 115 at 3400 R.P.M. Max torque: 215 lb.-ft. at 1000 R.P.M. Seven main bearings. Hydraulic valve lifters. Carburetor: Rochester 1-barrel.

ENGINE (Optional: C2500/F44, C2500, C3500, K3500, Suburban (C2500): V-type. OHV. Cast iron block. Bore & stroke: 4.54 x 4.0 in. Displacement: 454 cu. in. Compression ratio: 7.9:1. Net horsepower: 210 at 3800 R.P.M. Max torque: 340 lb.-ft. at 2800 R.P.M. Five main bearings. Hydraulic valve lifters. Carburetor: Rochester 4-barrel.

ENGINE (Standard: Caballero): (except California). V-type. OHV. 6-cylinder. Cast iron block. Bore & stroke: 3.7 x 3.48 in. Displacement: 229 cu. in. Compression ratio: 8.6:1. Net horsepower: 110 at 4200 R.P.M. Max torque: 170 lb.-ft. at 2000 R.P.M. Four main bearings. Hydraulic valve lifters. Carburetor: Rochester 2-barrel.

ENGINE (Optional: Caballero): V-type. OHV. 8-cylinder. Cast iron block. Bore & stroke: 3.7 x 3.48 in. Displacement: 305 cu. in. Compression ratio: 8.6:1. Net horsepower: 150 at 3800 R.P.M. Max torque: 240 lb.-ft. at 2400 R.P.M. Five main bearings. Hydraulic valve lifters. Carburetor: Rochester Staged 4-barrel.

ENGINE (Optional: Caballero): (except California). V-type. OHV. 8-cylinder. Cast iron block. Bore & stroke: 3.5 x 3.48 in. Displacement: 267 cu. in. Compression ratio: 8.3:1. Net horsepower: 115 at 4000 R.P.M. Max torque: 200 lb.-ft. at 2400 R.P.M. Five main bearings. Hydraulic valve lifters. Carburetor: Rochester Staged 2-barrel.

ENGINE (Optional: Caballero): (except California). V-type. OHV. 6-cylinder. Cast iron block. Bore & stroke: 3.8 x 3.4 in. Displacement: 231 cu. in. Compression ratio: 8.0:1. Net horsepower: 110 at 3800 R.P.M. Max torque: 190 lb.-ft. at 1600 R.P.M. Five main bearings. Hydraulic valve lifters. Carburetor: Rochester 2-barrel.

ENGINE (Standard S15): Inline. OHV. OHC. 4-cylinder. Cast iron block. Bore & stroke: 3.42 x 3.23 in. Displacement: 119 cu. in. Compression ratio: 8.4:1. Net horsepower: 82 at 4600 R.P.M. Max torque: 101 lb.-ft. at 3000 R.P.M. Hydraulic valve lifters.

ENGINE (Optional S15): V-type. OHV. 6-cylinder. Cast iron block. Bore & stroke: 3.50 x 2.99 in. Displacement: 173 cu. in. Compression ratio: 8.5:1. Net horsepower: 110 at 4800 R.P.M. Max torque: 148 lb.-ft. at 2000 R.P.M. Hydraulic valve lifters.

1982 GMC Vandura Panel Delivery Van (OCW)

CHASSIS Unchanged except for addition of Series S15 Series: Wheelbase: 108.3 x 117.9 in. Overall length: 178.2 x 194.1 in. Overall heigth: 59 in. Front/Rear Tread: 64.7 x 64.7 in. Tires: P195 x 75R14, fiberglass-belted. Optional: P195 x 75R14, steel-belted P205 x 75R14, P205 x 70R14.

TECHNICAL: Manual, synchromesh. Speeds: 3F/1R (S15 4F/1R, C2500, C3500, all 4wd 4F/1R). Column (4-speed floor) mounted gearshift. 11 in. dia, all full-sized models, 12 in. dia optional clutch. Semi-floating G1500, C1500, K1500, C2500, K2500, Full-floating all others full-sized models rear axle. Overall ratio: C1500 2.73:1, C2500, K2500 3.42:1, K3500 Bonus/Crew 4.56:1. All other full-sized models 4.10:1, S15 2.56, 2.73, 3.08, 3.42, 3.73:1, depending R.P.M. engine and transmission. Hydraulic, 4-wheel, front disc, rear drum brakes. Kelsey-Hayes pressed steel wheels.

DRIVETRAIN OPTIONS: 3-speed automatic. 4-speed manual overdrive. 4-speed manual. 4-speed automatic with overdrive. Auxiliary fuel tank. Pre-cleaned air cleaner. Locking differential. Cold climate package. Engine oil cooler. Fuel tank shield. 63-amp generator (standard on K3500). Heavy-duty automatic transmission cooler. Heavy-duty battery. Heavy-duty front and rear shock absorbers. Heavy-duty radiator. Heavy-duty power brakes. Auxiliary battery. Dual exhausts. Dual rear wheels. Front tow hooks. Front quad shock absorbers. Front stabilizer bar. Heavy-duty front springs. Extra capacity rear springs. Heavy-duty rear springs. Camper chassis equipment — basic and deluxe. S15 options: Heavy-duty payload equipment. Heavy-duty trailering package. 20-gallon fuel tank. 5-speed manual transmission (V-8 only).

OPTIONS: Rear bumper. Chromed, chromed or painted rear step. AM, AM/FM, AM/FM stereo CB radio. Electric clock. Cigar lighter. Amarillo package (Caballero) ($183). Sierra Classic package (Jimmy). 8-passenger package (G-series) ($250). 12-passenger package (G-series) ($533). High Sierra equipment (S15) ($325). Sierra Classic equipment (S15) ($550). Gypsy equipment (S15) ($775). High Sierra package (C-series). Sierra Classic package (C-series). Intermittent windshield wipers. Painted or stainless steel below eye-line mirrors. Stainless steel camper mirror. Bright or black body side molding. Deluxe bright molding package. Door edge guards. Two-tone paint. Deluxe two-tone paint. Exterior decor package. Special two-tone paint. Sliding rear window. Glide-out or side mounted spare tire carrier. Tinted glass. Rally wheels. Styled wheels. Power door locks. Power windows. Roof marker lights. Air conditioning. Chromed front bumper guards. Cargo area lamp. Color-keyed floor mats. Comfort tilt steering wheel. Deluxe front appearance package. Dome light. Gauge package. Halogen headlamps.

HISTORICAL: Calendar year sales: 200,214 divided as follows: Full-size Pickups 109,762. S15 39,359. Vandura/Rally 27,661. Suburban 9490. Jimmy 6574. Jimmys 1228. P-Series 3765. Caballero 2573.

1983 GMC

1983 GMC High Sierra Wide-Side Pickup (OCW)

GMC — LIGHT-TRUCK — (ALL SERIES) — FOUR-CYLINDER/SIX-CYLINDER/V-8: — The full size GMC models were, except for revised parking light placement and grille format, unchanged from 1982. Improving their resistance to corrosion was added use of galvanized steel in the pickup box front panel plus a Zincrometal inner hood liner.

The G2500 and G3500 Vans and Sport Vans were now offered with the 6.2 liter diesel engine as well as the four-speed overdrive automatic transmission. Numerous refinements were also part of the 1983 GMC van scene. These included a revised steering wheel angle that was close to that used on pickup models and a floor-mounted manual transmission lever. Also installed on the vans were "wet arms" windshield washers with wiper arm located nozzles, a new rear door hinge pivot, new rear latch and floating roller mechanism for the sliding door and an interior hood release. All vans with manual transmission could be ordered with a tilt steering wheel. Anti-chip coating was installed along the lower body from the front wheel wheels to the rear doors of all vans.

Added to the S15 line were 4wd and extended cab models as well as a 2.0 liter 38 horsepower L-4. Vying for the attention of down-sized truck buyers was the S15 Jimmy which was 15.3 in. shorter and 14.8 in narrower than the full-sized Jimmy.

1983 GMC S-15 Mini-Pickup (OCW)

I.D. DATA: The VIN is found on a plate attached to the top left of the instrument panel. Engine numbers located: 6-cyl.-located on a pad found on right hand side of cylinder block at rear of distributor. 8-cyl.-located on a pad located at front right side of cylinder block.

1983 GMC Sierra Classic Indy Hauler Pickup (IMSC/JLM)

Model	Body Type	Price	Weight	Prod. Total
Series Caballero				
1GW80	½-Ton Sedan Pickup	8191	3372	—
1GW80 /YE7	½-Ton Diablo Pickup	8445	3337	—
Series K1500 Jimmy				
TK10516	½-Ton 4wd Hardtop Utility	10,287	4426	—

NOTE: 2wd versions have TC prefix.

1983 GMC "Jimmy" Sport Utility (OCW)

Model	Body Type	Price	Weight	Prod. Total
Series S15 Jimmy				
TT10516	½-Ton 4wd Hardtop Utility	9433	3106	—

NOTE: 2wd versions have TC prefix.

Model	Body Type	Price	Weight	Prod. Total
Series G1500				
TG11005	½-Ton Vandura (110 in. w.b.)	7101	3711	—
TG11006	½-Ton Rally (110 in. w.b.)	8597	4039	—
TG11306	½-Ton Rally Custom (125 in. w.b.)	9533	—	—
TG11306	½-Ton Rally STX (125 in. w.b.)	9789	—	—
Series G2500				
TG21005	¾-Ton Vandura (110 in. w.b.)	7714	3812	—
TG21306	¾-Ton Rally (125 in. w.b.)	8968	4278	—
TG21306	¾-Ton Rally Custom (125 in. w.b)	9701	—	—
TG21306	¾-Ton Rally STX (125 in. w.b.)	9957	—	—

1983 GMC "Jimmy" Sport Utility (OCW)

Model	Body Type	Price	Weight	Prod. Total
Series G3500				
TG31305	1-Ton Vandura	8718	4399	—
TG31306	1-Ton Rally (350 cu. in. V-8)	11,371	4719	—
TG31306	1-Ton Rally Custom (350 cu. in. V-8)	12,104	—	—
TG31306	1-Ton Rally STX (350 cu. in. V-8)	12,306	—	—
Series P2500, P3500				
TP20842	¾-Ton Value Van, 10.5-ft.	12,031	5801	—
TP30842	1-Ton Value Van, 10-5 ft.	12,107	5946	—
Series S15				
TS10603	½-Ton Pickup (WS), 6-ft.	6343	2537	—
TS10803	½-Ton Pickup (WS), 7.5-ft.	6496	2618	—
TS10653	½-Ton Pickup Ext. Cab	6725	2647	—
Series C1500				
TC10703	½-Ton Pickup (FS), 6.5-ft.	6835	3408	—
TC10703	½-Ton Pickup (WS), 6.5-ft.	6707	3471	—
TC10903	½-Ton Pickup (WS), 8-ft.	6860	3633	—
TC10906	½-Ton Suburban (305 cu. in. V-8)	9951	4293	—

NOTE: 4wd versions have TK prefix.

Model	Body Type	Price	Weight	Prod. Total
Series C2500				
TC20903	¾-Ton Chassis & Cab	8032	3614	—
TC20903	¾-Ton Pickup (FS), 8-ft.	8525	3964	—
TC20903	¾-Ton Pickup (WS), 8-ft.	8397	4025	—
TC20943	¾-Ton Pickup Crew Cab	9637	4806	—
TC20906	¾-Ton Suburban (350 cu. in. V-8)	10,187	4697	—

NOTE: 4wd versions have TK prefix.

Model	Body Type	Price	Weight	Prod. Total
Series C3500				
TC30903	1-Ton Chassis & Cab	8160	3965	—
TC30903	1-Ton Pickup (FS), 8-ft.	8654	4319	—
TC30903	1-Ton Pickup (WS), 8-ft.	8526	4380	—
TC30943	1-Ton Chassis & Bonus Cab	9131	4406	—
TC30943	1-Ton Pickup Bonus Cab	9481	4815	—
TC30943	1-Ton Chassis & Crew Cab	9453	4467	—
TC30943	1-Ton Pickup Crew Cab	9803	4878	—

ENGINE: (GMC engines were unchanged except for the following new or revised engines). **(Standard: C1500, C2500, K1500, G-Series):** Inline. OHV. 6-cylinder. Cast iron block. Bore & stroke: 3.9 x 4.5 in. Displacement: 250 cu. in. Compression ratio: 8.3:1. Net horsepower: C1500: 120 at 4000 R.P.M., Max torque: 205 lb.-ft. at 2000 R.P.M. All others: 115 at 3600 R.P.M. Max torque: 200 lb.-ft at 1600 R.P.M. Seven main bearings. Hydraulic valve lifters. Carburetor: Rochester 2-barrel.

1983 GMC Caballero Pickup w/diesel (OCW)

1983 GMC Rally Van Passenger Van (OCW)

ENGINE (Optional C2500/F44, C2500, C3500, K3500, C2500 Suburban): V-type. OHV. 8-cylinder. Cast iron block. Bore & stroke: 4.3 x 4.0 in. Displacement: 454 cu. in. Compression ratio: 7.9:1. Net horsepower: 230 at 3800 R.P.M. Max torque: 360 lb.-ft. at 2800 R.P.M. Five main bearings. Hydraulic valve lifters. Carburetor: Rochester 4-barrel.

1983 GMC Suburban Carryall (OCW)

ENGINE (Optional Caballero): (207 cu. in. V-8 not offered). V-type. OHV. Diesel. 8-cylinder. Cast iron block. Bore & stroke: 3.736 x 3.48 in. 350 cu. in. New horsepower: 105. Five main bearings. Hydraulic valve lifters. Fuel injection.

ENGINE (Standard S15 Blazer, Extended Cab models): Inline. OHV. 4-cylinder. Cast iron block. Bore & stroke: 3.50 x 3.15 in. Displacement: 121 cu. in. Compression ratio: 9.3:1. Net horsepower: 83 at 4600 R.P.M. Max torque: 108 lb.-ft. at 2400 R.P.M. Hydraulic valve lifters. Carburetor: Rochester 2-barrel.

CHASSIS Dimensions unchanged from 1982 except as follows: (Series K15 Jimmy). Wheelbase: 100.5 in. Overall length: 170.3 in. Overall height: 65 in. Front/Rear Tread: 55.6/55.1 in. Tires: P195 x 75R15.

CHASSIS (Series S15 Extended Cab): Wheelbase: 122.9 in. Overall height: 59.4 in. Front/Rear Tread: 64.7/64.7 in. Tires: P195 x 75R14.

TECHNICAL: Unchanged from 1982.

OPTIONS: Amarillo package (Caballero) ($189). Sierra Classic package (K1500 Jimmy) ($983). Sierra Classic package (S15 Jimmy) ($576). Gypsy package (S15 Jimmy). 8-passenger package (G-series) ($264), 12-passenger package (G-series) ($552). High Sierra equipment (S15, C-series). Sierra classic equipment (S15, C-series). Gypsy equipment (S15). For additional options refer to 1982 GMC section.

HISTORICAL: Calendar year sales: 238,411 divided as follows: Full-sized pickups 105,741. S15 40,491. Vandura/Rally 45,535. Suburban 11,292. Jimmy 7361, S-Jimmy 21,760. P-Series 4071. Caballero 2160.

1984 GMC

GMC — LIGHT-TRUCK — (ALL SERIES) — FOUR-CYLINDER/SIX-CYLINDER/V-8 — S-15 Regular Cab models with 2wd were now offered with a new Sport Suspension Package that included quick-ratio power steering gear, special front stabilizer bar and larger-than-standard shock absorbers.

1984 GMC Sierra Classic Wide-Side Pickup (OCW)

Introduced on the full-size models were two-sided galvanized steel interior door panels. Also installed were semi-metallic front brake linings on C1500, K1500 and C2500 and K2500 models. Most of these GMC trucks also had new Non-asbestos rear brake linings. All C/K pickups and Chassis-Cabs had new plastic fuel tank stone shields.

I.D. DATA: Unchanged from 1983. Engine numbers location unchanged from 1983.

Model	Body Type	Price	Weight	Prod. Total
Series Caballero				
1GW80	½-Ton Sedan Pickup	8522	3298	—
1GW80	½-Ton SS Diablo	8781	3305	—
Series Jimmy				
TK10516	½-Ton 4wd Utility	10,819	4409	—
Series S15 Jimmy				
TT10516	½-Ton 4wd Utility	9685	3146	—
Series G1500 — (Van)				
G11005	½-Ton Vandura (110 in. w.b.)	7541	3732	—
G11006	½-Ton Rally (110 in. w.b.)	9089	4085	—
G11306	¾-Ton Rally Custom (125 in. w.b.)	10,062	—	—
G11306	½-Ton Rally STX (125 in. w.b.)	10,327	—	—
Series G2500 — (Van)				
G21005	¾-Ton Vandura (110 in. w.b.)	8176	3813	—
G21306	¾-Ton Rally (125 in. w.b.)	9477	4276	—
G21306	¾-Ton Rally Custom (125 in. w.b.)	10,238	—	—
G21306	¾-Ton Rally STX (125 in. w.b.)	10,503	—	—
Series G3500 — (Van)				
G31305	1-Ton Vandura (125 in. w.b.)	9212	4305	—
G31306	1-Ton Rally (125 in. w.b.)	11,964	4984	—
G31306	1-Ton Rally Custom (125 in. w.b.)	12,724	—	—
G31306	1-Ton Rally STX (125 in. w.b.)	12,990	—	—
Series G3500 — (Hi-Cube Van)				
G31303	1-Ton Hi-Cube, 10-ft.	11,624	5423	—
G31603	1-Ton Hi-Cube, 12-ft.	12,894	5891	—
Series P2500, P3500 — (Step Van)				
CP20842	¾-Ton Value Van, 10.5-ft.	12,588	5860	—
CP30842	1-Ton Value Van, 10.5-ft.	12,666	5998	—
Series S15				
S10603	½-Ton Pickup (WS), 6-ft.	6398	2574	—
S10803	½-Ton Pickup (WS), 7.5-ft.	6551	2649	—
S10653	½-Ton Ext. Cab Pickup (WS)	6924	2705	—
Series C1500				
C10703	½-Ton Pickup (FS), 6.5-ft.	7101	3434	—
C10703	½-Ton Pickup (WS), 6.5-ft.	6970	3481	—
C10903	½-Ton Pickup (WS), 8-ft.	7127	3644	—
C10906	½-Ton Suburban (305 cu. in. V-8)	10,368	4310	—
Series C2500				
C20903	¾-Ton Chassis & Cab	8342	3617	—
C20903	¾-Ton Pickup (FS), 8-ft.	8319	3977	—
C20903	¾-Ton Pickup (WS), 8-ft.	8188	4039	—
C20943	¾-Ton Pickup Bonus Cab	9645	4742	—
C20943	¾-Ton Pickup Crew Cab	9975	4803	—
C20906	¾-Ton Suburban (350 cu. in. V-8)	10,599	4098	—
Series C3500				
C30903	1-Ton Chassis & Cab	8474	3990	—
C30903	1-Ton Pickup (FS), 8-ft.	8966	4342	—
C30903	1-Ton Pickup (WS)	8834	4404	—
C30943	1-Ton Chassis & Bonus Cab	9471	4412	—
C30943	1-Ton Pickup Bonus Cab	9815	4822	—
C30943	1-Ton Chassis & Crew Cab	10,146	4883	—

NOTE: 4wd GMC trucks have "K" prefix in model number. S15 Series: 6-ft. box = 108.3 in. w.b.; 7.5-ft. box = 122.9 in. w.b. Full size pickups: 6.5-ft. box = 117.5 in. w.b.; 8-ft. box = 131.5 in. w.b.

ENGINE: All GMC engines from 1983 were carried unchanged into 1984. They only change was the adoption of identical power ratings for all applications of the 250 and 305 cu. in. engines.

485

1984 GMC "Jimmy" Club Coupe (ext. cab) Pickup (OCW)

1984 GMC S-15 Mini-Pickup (OCW)

1984 GMC S-15 "Indy Hauler" Pickup (IMSC/JLM)

1984 GMC S-15 High Sierra Mini-Pickup (JAG)

CHASSIS All GMC dimensions were unchanged for 1984.

TECHNICAL: No changes from 1983 data.

486

1984 GMC "S-15 Jimmy" Mini-Sport Utility (OCW)

1984 GMC Sierra Classic Suburban Carryall (OCW)

1984 GMC Rally STX Passenger Van (OCW)

OPTIONS: Cargo area lamp. Color-keyed floor mats. Comfortilt steering wheel. Deluxe front appearance package. Dome light. Gauge package. Halogen headlights. Intermittent windshield wipers. Painted and stainless steel below eyeline mirrors. Stainless steel camper mirrors. Black and bright body molding. Door edge guards. Special two-tone paint. Sliding rear window. Tinted glass. Rally wheels. Styled wheels. Electronic cruise control. Reclining bucket seats (Suburban). Rear heater (Suburban). Electric window tailgate (Suburban), (and more). Chromed front bumper guards. Chromed or painted rear step bumper. Radio AM, AM/FM stereo with cassette player, Seek and Scan. Quartz electric clock. Cigar lighter. Amarillo package (Caballero) ($189). Sierra Classic equipment (Jimmy) ($983). Sierra Classic equipment (S15 Jimmy) ($576). Gypsy equipment (S15 Jimmy, C-series, S-series). 8-passenger package (G-series) ($270). High Sierra equipment (S-series, C-series). Sierra Classic equipment (S-series, C-series).

HISTORICAL: Calendar year sales: 280,531 divided as follows: Safari (introduced as 1985 model) 217. Full-sized pickups 121,704. S-15 43,742. Vandura/Rally 45,991. Suburban 16,132. Jimmy 8488. S-Jimmy 34,519. P-Series 7036. Caballero 2702.

1985 GMC

1985 GMC Sierra Classic 10 Wide-Side Pickup (F.T. Taber)

GMC — LIGHT-TRUCK — (ALL SERIES) — FOUR-CYLINDER/SIX-CYLINDER/V-8: — The 1985 full-sized GMC models were identified by their new front end appearance featuring stacked rectangular headlights, a bold three-section grille format with blacked-out gridwork and red-letter GMC identification.

Wide-Side models with single rear wheels were offered with a new optional custom two-tone color scheme. All models had wet-arm-type windshield washers. Both 2 and 4wd models could be fitted with front tow hooks.

Interior changes included a new seat cushion contour and seat back angle for the standard bench seat. Both the optional custom vinyl and custom cloth fabrics were new for 1985.

A major technical development was the use of a 4.3 liter, 262 cu. in. "Vortex" V-6 as the base engine for the C/K1500 and light-duty-emission C2500 pickups.

Numerous changes were also made in the S15 line for 1985. Like its larger counterparts the S15 had a black chrome insert for its partitioned front grille. The Custom Two-Tone paint option included "Sunshine" body striping. All models had restyled fender nameplates and a new paint scheme for the optional styled wheels.

New optional custom vinyl and custom cloth seats trim was offered in any of four colors.

Standard on all models except the 2wd short w.b. conventional cab pickup was the new 2.5 liter Tech IV engine with electronic fuel injection.

Additional refinements included use of a partitioned fuse panel, two-side-galvanized steel for the hood inner panel and fender skirts, welded-on bumper brackets, adjust-on-release rear brake adjusters, new valving for the shock absorbers, new controls for the optional intermittent wipers and a new variable-ratio manual steering gear.

The Caballero also used the 4.3 "Vortex" V-6 as its standard engine. The optional 305 cu. in. V-8 now had a 9.5:1 compression ratio and an electronic spark control. A 65-amp generator was standard on Caballeros with air conditioning.

New standard stainless steel full wheel covers with a brushed-finish center with GMC lettering were standard. A total of nine new exterior colors were offered. The Caballero's standard velour cloth interior was also new for 1985.

GMC's entry into the so-called mini-van market, the Safari, featured an integral body-frame design on a 11 in. w.b. Its standard powerplant was the 151 cu. in. L-four with the "Vortex" V-6 optional. A wide variety of exterior color and trim levels were offered. The Safari had a maximum capacity of 151.8 cu. ft. with the second and available rear seats removed. With room for five passengers load capacity was 86.2 ft.

1985 GMC S-15 High Sierra Mini-Pickup (JAG)

I.D. DATA: Serial number location unchanged from 1984. Engine numbers location unchanged from 1984.

Model	Body Type	Price	Weight	Prod. Total
Series Caballero				
W80	½-Ton Sedan Pickup	8933	3252	—
W80	½-Ton Sedan SS Diablo	9198	3263	—
Series K1500 Jimmy				
K10	½-Ton 4wd Utility	11,223	4462	—
Series S15 Jimmy				
T10	½-Ton 4wd Tailgate Utility	9994	3156	—
Series Safari				
M10	½-Ton Safari Cargo Van	7821	3048	—
M10	½-Ton Safari SL	8195	3277	—
M10	½-Ton Safari SLX	8623	—	—
M10	½-Ton Safari SLE	9359	—	—
Series G1500				
G11	½-Ton Vandura (110 in. w.b.)	7987	3668	—
G11	½-Ton Rally (110 in. w.b.)	9517	4037	—
G11	½-Ton Rally Custom (125 in. w.b.)	10,514	—	—
G11	½-Ton Rally STX (125 in. w.b.)	10,827	—	—
Series G2500				
G21	¾-Ton Vandura (110 in. w.b.)	8581	3811	—
G21	¾-Ton Rally (125 in. w.b.)	9915	4277	—
G21	¾-Ton Rally Custom (125 in. w.b.)	10,695	—	—
G21	¾-Ton Rally STX (125 in. w.b.)	11,007	—	—
Series G3500				
G31	1-Ton Vandura (125 in. w.b.)	10,342	4402	—
G31	1-Ton Rally (125 in. w.b.)	12,291	4988	—
G31	1-Ton Rally Custom (125 in. w.b.)	13,071	—	—
G31	1-Ton Rally STX (125 in. w.b.)	13,383	—	—
G31	1-Ton Cutaway (125 in. w.b.)	8950	3731	—
Series G3500 — (Magnavan)				
G31	1-Ton Magnavan, 10-ft.	12,097	5054	—
G31	1-Ton Magnavan, 12-ft.	13,351	5891	—
Series P2500/P3500				
P20	¾-Ton Value Van	13,038	5860	—
P30	1-Ton Value Van	13,119	5998	—
Series S15				
S10	½-Ton Pickup (WS), 6-ft.	5990	2567	—
S10	½-Ton Pickup (WS), 7.5-ft.	6702	2656	—
S10	½-Ton Pickup (WS) Ext. Cab	7167	2711	—
Series C1500				
C10	½-Ton Pickup (FS), 6.5-ft.	7428	3439	—
C10	½-Ton Pickup (WS), 6.5-ft.	7295	3486	—
C10	½-Ton Pickup (WS), 8-ft.	7461	3048	—
C10	½-Ton Suburban (305 cu. in. V-8)	10,700	4311	—
Series C2500				
C20	¾-Ton Chassis & Cab	8516	3626	—
C20	¾-Ton Pickup (FS), 8-ft.	8677	3986	—
C20	¾-Ton Pickup (WS), 8-ft.	8543	4048	—
C20	¾-Ton Pickup (WS) Bonus Cab	9902	4747	—
C20	¾-Ton Pickup (WS) Crew Cab	10,238	4808	—
C20	¾-Ton Suburban (350 cu. in. V-8)	10,953	4705	—
Series C3500				
C30	1-Ton Chassis & Cab	8650	3994	—
C30	1-Ton Pickup (FS), 8-ft.	9167	4347	—
C30	1-Ton Pickup (WS), 8-ft.	9033	4409	—
C30	1-Ton Chassis & Bonus Cab	9667	4418	—
C30	1-Ton Pickup (WS) Bonus Cab	10,033	4829	—
C30	1-Ton Chassis & Crew Cab	10,005	4479	—
C30	1-Ton Pickup (WS) Crew Cab	10,371	4890	—

ENGINE (Standard: C/K1500 and C2500 Pickups): V-type. OHV. 6-cylinder. Cast iron block. Bore & stroke: 4.00 x 3.48 in. Displacement: 262 cu. in. Compression ratio: 9.3:1. Net horsepower: 155 at 4000 R.P.M. Net torque: 230 lb.-ft. at 2400 R.P.M. Carburetor: Rochester Quadrajet, Electronic Spark Control.

ENGINE (Optional: C/K1500): V-type. OHV. 8-cylinder. Cast iron block. Bore & stroke: 3.74 x 3.48 in. Displacement: 305 cu. in. Compression ratio: 9.2:1. Net horsepower: 160 at 4400 R.P.M. Net torque: 235 lb.-ft. at 2000 R.P.M. Five main bearings. Hydraulic valve lifters. Carburetor: Rochester 4-barrel, Electronic Spark Control.

ENGINE (Optional: C2500, K1500, K2500): V-type. OHV. 8-cylinder. Cast iron block. Bore & stroke: 4.0 x 3.48 in. Displacement: 350 cu. in. Compression ratio: 8.2:1. Net horsepower: 165 at 3800 R.P.M. Net torque: 275 lb.-ft. at 1600 R.P.M. Five main bearings. Hydraulic valve lifters. Carburetor: Rochester 4-barrel.

ENGINE (Optional: C2500, C3500, K3500): V-type. OHV. 8-cylinder. Cast iron block. Bore & stroke: 4.25 x 4.0 in. Displacement: 454 cu. in. Compression ratio: 7.9:1. Net horsepower: 230 at 3800 R.P.M. Net torque: 360 lb.-ft. at 2800 R.P.M. Five main bearings. Hydraulic valve lifters. Carburetor: Rochester 4-barrel.

ENGINE (Optional: All C1500, K1500, C2500, K2500, C3500, K3500): V-type. OHV. 8-cylinder. Cast iron block. Bore & stroke: 3.98 x 3.80 in. Displacement: 379 cu. in. Compression ratio: 21.3:1. Net horsepower: 130 at 3000 R.P.M. Net torque 240 lb.-ft. at 2000 R.P.M. Hydraulic valve lifters. Carburetor: fuel injection.

CHASSIS Unchanged from 1984 except for addition of Safari. Safari Series: Wheelbase: 111 in. Overall length: 176.8 in. Overall height: 71.7 in. Tires: P195 x 75R15.

TECHNICAL: Standard all full-size models except C1500, K1500. Manual, synchromesh transmission. Speeds: 4F/1R. Floor-mounted gearshift. Semi-floating (½-Ton), Full-floating (all others) rear axle. Overall ratio: 2.73:1, 3.42:1, 4.10:1, 4.56:1, 3.73:1, 3.08:1 depending upon model, engine, transmission selection. Hydraulic, front disc, rear drum brakes. Kelsey-Hayes pressed steel wheels.

TECHNICAL: Optional C1500, standard on selected models with V-6 and diesel engines. Manual, synchromesh transmission. Speeds: 4F/1R (overdrive). Floor-mounted gearshift.

TECHNICAL: Standard C1500. Manual, synchromesh transmission. Speeds: 3F/1R. Column-mounted gearshift.

TECHNICAL: Optional (depending on model/engine/transmission choice). Automatic transmission. Speeds: 3F/1R. Column-mounted gearshift.

TECHNICAL: Optional (depending on model/engine/transmission choice). Automatic transmission. Speeds: 4F/1R (with overdrive). Column-mounted gearshift.

OPTIONS: Rear bumper chromed. Radio: AM, AM/FM, AM/FM stereo, AM/FM stereo with cassette. Electric clock. Cigar lighter. Air conditioning. Cast aluminum wheels (C/K1500). Bright wheel covers. Styled wheels (C/K1500). Sierra Classic trim package. High Sierra trim package. Deluxe front end appearance package (includes dual headlights). Color-keyed floor mats. Black and bright bodyside moldings. Custom and deluxe molding packages. Chromed front bumper guards. Door edge guards. Rally wheels (C/K1500). Amarillo package (Caballero) ($195). Intermittent wipers. Gauge package. Power door locks. Power windows. Tinted glass. Dome light. Camper mirrors. West Coast mirrors. Halogen hi-beam headlamps. Roof marker lamps. Cargo area lamp. Comfortilt steering wheel. Sliding rear window. Various exterior two-tone paint schemes. Gypsy sport package (S15). K1500 Jimmy Silverado package ($1015). S15 Jimmy Sierra Classic package ($595).

HISTORICAL: Calendar year production: 316,533 divided as follows: Vandura/Rally Vans 22,805. S15 57,740. S15 Jimmy 51,582. Jimmy 11,525. Safari 34,181. Caballero 3057. Suburban 23,850. Full-Size Pickups 105,651. P-Series 5842.

1986 GMC

1986 GMC Vandura w/Rank & Son Conversion (RSB)

GMC — LIGHT-TRUCK — (1986 SERIES) — ALL-ENGINES: — The GMC Caballero offered a four-speed overdrive automatic transmission with the standard V-6 engine in 1986. Other changes were minor.

Full-size K-1500 Jimmys had new molded front-bucket seats with folding seatbacks. The cloth seat-trim option included a reclining seatback feature and the passenger seat included the slide-forward, easy-entry feature which had been standard on the smaller S-15 series. Black and white tops were available with solid colors, while a new steel-gray top was available to match a similar exterior color.

New for the "S" series Jimmy was a revamped instrument cluster with warning lights on either side of the combination fuel/speedometer gauge. Added to the 1986 option list was a 2.8-liter V-6 with TBI. Technical changes were the same as for comparable Chevrolets, including a new Delcotron generator, lighter pistons, 30-degree exhaust valve seats, low-pressure gas shocks, new paint and trim options and a hinged rear-mounted spare tire carrier.

The Safari mini-van, introduced six months earlier, was unchanged, except for use of the new Delcotron. Without optional passenger seats, the Safari had 189.9 cu. ft. of payload space. Even with the seat, storage room was a respectable 83.7 cu. ft. A second optional passenger bench seat could also be ordered. Three trim levels: SL, SLX and SLE were available for passenger models.

GMC vans, (and other big trucks) used a new five-ribbed poly-vee generator accessory belt. Both the Rally Wagon and Vandura had modest refinements. The conventional sliding side door could be replaced, at no extra cost, with 60/40 swing-out doors incorporating a new sliding 90-degree door check system. This prevented fouling between the right front side door and forward side swing-out door.

S-15 pickups had the same new IP treatment as the "S" Series Blazer. It also included a new package tray and trim plates. The Insta-Trac 4x4 option provided off-road capability with a shift that could be switched from 4x2 to 4x4 at any speed. Engine improvements were also new.

Full-size GMC pickups featured GM's 4.3-liter Vortec Six (V-6) as standard equipment. A 50,000-mile warranty was offered for Diesel-engined trucks. The GMC Suburban had new bucket seats with outboard armrests as a 1986 extra.

An interesting item to collectors was the method used to promote GMC's 1986 models as the "ultimate upscale" trucks. The company contacted the Classic Car Club of America to arrange an advertising photograph that featured an S-15 pickup truck towing an L-29 Cord to a stately looking mansion. Parked in the mansions four-car garage were a 1937 Bugatti, 1930s Buick, and a 1957 Cushman Eagle Indian motorcycle.

The Cord in the photo was borrowed from the well-known collection of the late Barney Pollard. The Bugatti was once one of Ettore Bugatti's personal cars which were scheduled to be shown at Pebble Beach. The Buick was a "resto-rod," refurbished with modern appointments. Credit for this idea, which used the slogan "The Classic No Enthusiast Should Be Without" went to McCann-Erickson, a Detroit advertising agency.

Additional models covered in this section include the GMC Magnavan (King-size van) and the GMC Value Van (Step-Van type truck), which were both little changed from 1985.

I.D. DATA: The V.I.N. had 17 symbols. The first three identified country, manufacturer and type vehicle. The fourth, a letter, designated GVW range. The next three identified series, nominal payload and body style. The eighth character indicated the engine. Next came a check digit. The tenth symbol, a letter, indicated model year. The eleventh designated assembly plant. The last six symbols were the production sequence numbers.

Model	Body Type	Price	Weight	Prod. Total
Caballero — (½-Ton) — (117.1 in. w.b.) — (V-6)				
W80	Sport Pickup	9623	3234	—
W80	Diablo Pickup	9936	3239	—
K1500 Jimmy — (½-Ton) — (4x4) — (106.5 in. w.b.) — (V-8)				
K18	Utility Wagon	12,085	4444	—
S15 Jimmy — (½-Ton) — (4x4) — (100.5 in. w.b.) — (V-6)				
T18	Utility Wagon (Gate)	10,745	3152	—
Safari — (½-Ton) — (111 in. w.b.) — (V-6)				
M10	Cargo Van	8945	3258	—
M10	SL Pass. Van	9086	3434	—
M10	SLX Pass. Van	9541	3509	—
M10	SLE Pass. Van	10,265	3569	—
G1500 Van — (½-Ton) — (110/125 in. w.b.) — (V-6)				
G15	Vandura (SWB)	8677	3700	—
G15	Rally (SWB)	10,283	4052	—
G15	Custom Rally (SWB)	11,341	4153	—
G15	Rally STX (SWB)	11,673	4196	—
G2500 Van — (¾-Ton) — (110/125 in. w.b.) — (V-6)				
G25	Vandura (SWB)	9308	3786	—
G25	Rally (SWB)	10,706	4244	—
G25	Custom Rally (SWB)	11,533	4345	—
G25	Rally STX (SWB)	11,864	4388	—
G3500 Van — (1-Ton) — (125 in. w.b.) — (V-8)				
G35	Vandura	11,129	4526	—
G35	Rally	13,173	4526	—
G35	Custom Rally	14,001	5117	—
G35	Rally STX	14,331	5261	—
Magnavan — (1-Ton) — (125/146 in. w.b.) — (V-8)				
G31	10-ft. Van (SWB)	13,492	5209	—
G31	12-ft. Van (LWB)	14,803	5886	—
Value Van — (125/133/178 in. w.b.) — (6-cyl.)				
P22	¾-Ton Panel (10½-ft.)	14,338	5869	—
P32	1-Ton Panel (10½-ft.)	14,422	6022	—
S10 Pickup — (½-Ton) — (108.3/122.9 in. w.b.) — (V-6)				
S14	6-ft. Wideside Spec.	5990	2574	—
S14	6-ft. Wideside	7046	2574	—
S14	7½-ft. Wideside	7281	2645	—
S14	6-ft. Bonus Cab	7733	2713	—

Model	Body Type	Price	Weight	Prod. Total
C1500 Pickup — (½-Ton) — (117.5/131.5 in. w.b.) — (V-6)				
C14	6½-ft. Fenderside (SWB)	7955	3385	—
C14	6½-ft. Wideside (SWB)	7815	3432	—
C14	8-ft. Wideside (SWB)	7989	3595	—
C14	Suburban V-8 (LWB)	11,528	4279	—
C2500 Pickup — (¾-Ton) — (131.5 in. w.b.) — (V-6)				
C24	Chassis & Cab	9667	3607	—
C24	8-ft. Fenderside	9304	3930	—
C24	8-ft. Wideside	9164	3992	—
C23	8-ft. Bonus Cab Wide	11,154	4773	—
C23	8-ft. Crew Cab Wide	11,502	4834	—
C26	Suburban (V-8)	12,349	4771	—
C3500 Pickup — (1-Ton) — (134.5/164.5) — (6-cyl.)				
C34	Chassis & Cab (SWB)	9843	4011	—
C34	Fenderside (SWB)	10,381	4426	—
C34	Wideside (SWB)	10,242	4426	—
C33	Bonus Cab Chassis (LWB)	10,901	4451	—
C33	Bonus Cab Wide (LWB)	11,282	4862	—
C33	Crew Cab Chassis (LWB)	11,253	4512	—
C33	Crew Cab Wide (LWB)	11,633	4923	—

NOTE 1: S-10 Jimmy also available w/4x2.

NOTE 2: All Pickups also available w/4x4.

NOTE 3: "SWB" indicates shortest wheelbase shown above each series listing. "LWB" indicates longest wheelbase shown above each series listing.

NOTE 4: All 1-ton pickups listed above are models with 8-ft. long pickup boxes.

ENGINE (Std.:S-14/T-18/M10): Inline. OHV. Four-cylinder. Cast iron block. Bore & stroke: 4.0 x 3.0 in. Displacement: 151 cu. in. (2.5-liter). Brake horsepower: 92 at 4400 R.P.M. Taxable horsepower: 25.6. Hydraulic valve lifters. Electronic Fuel Injection. Torque (Compression): 134 lbs.-ft. at 2800 R.P.M.

ENGINE (Std.:C33/C34/P22/P32/C14 Bonus/C14 Crew; Opt.: C24/C23): Inline. OHV. Six-cylinder. Cast iron block. Bore & stroke: 3.88 x 4.12 in. Displacement: 292 cu. in. (4.8-liter). Brake horsepower: 115 at 4000 R.P.M. Taxable horsepower: 36.13. Hydraulic valve lifters. Carburetor: One-barrel. Torque (Compression): 210 lbs.-ft. at 800 R.P.M.

ENGINE (Std.: W80; Opt.: M10): Vee-block. OHV. Six-cylinder. Cast iron block. Bore & stroke: 4.0 x 3.48 in. Displacement: 262 cu. in. (4.3-liter). Brake horsepower: 140 at 4000 R.P.M. Taxable horsepower: 38.4. Hydraulic valve lifters. Electronic Fuel Injection. Torque (Compression): 225 lbs.-ft. at 2000 R.P.M.

ENGINE (Std.: C14/C24/G15/G25): Vee-block. OHV. Six-cylinder. Cast iron block. Bore & stroke: 4.0 x 3.48 in. Displacement: 262 cu. in. (4.3-liter). Brake horsepower: 155 at 4000 R.P.M. Taxable horsepower: 38.4. Hydraulic valve lifters. Carburetor: Four-barrel. Torque (Compression): 230 lbs.-ft. at 2400 R.P.M.

ENGINE (Std.: K18/Suburban; Opt.: C14/C23/C24/G14): Vee-block. OHV. Eight-cylinder. Cast iron block. Bore & stroke: 3.74 x 3.48 in. Displacement: 305 cu. in. (5.0-liter). Brake horsepower: 160 at 4400 R.P.M. Taxable horsepower: 44.76. Hydraulic valve lifters. Carburetor: Four-barrel. Torque (Compression): 235 lbs.-ft. at 2000 R.P.M.

ENGINE (Opt.: C23/C24/C33/C34/Suburban; Std.: G35): Vee-block. OHV. Eight-cylinder. Cast iron block. Bore & stroke: 4.0 x 3.48 in. Displacement: 350 cu. in. (5.7-liter). Brake horsepower: 161 at 3800 R.P.M. Taxable horsepower: 51.2. Hydraulic valve lifters. Carburetor: Four-barrel. Torque (Compression): 275 lbs.-ft. at 2400 R.P.M.

ENGINE (Opt.:C14/C22/C23/T18/C14 Suburban/C26 Suburban): Vee-block. OHV. Eight-cylinder. Cast iron block. Bore & stroke: 3.98 x 3.82 in. Displacement: 379 cu. in. (6.2-liter). Brake horsepower: 130 at 3600 R.P.M. Taxable horsepower: 50.69. Hydraulic valve lifters. Carburetor: Diesel induction system. Torque (Compression): 240 lbs.-ft. at 2000 R.P.M.

CHASSIS (Caballero): Wheelbase: 117.1 in. Overall length: 201.6 in. Height: 53.8 in. Tires: P205/75R14 in.

CHASSIS (S-15 Pickup): Wheelbase: 108.3/122.9 in. Overall length: 178.2/194.2 in. Height: 61.3 in. Tires: P195/75R14 in.

CHASSIS (S-15 Jimmy): Wheelbase: 100.5 in. Overall length: 170.3 in. Height: 64.7 in. Tires: P195/75R15 in.

CHASSIS (C1500 Pickup): Wheelbase: 117.5/131.5 in. Overall length: 193.5/213.4 in. Height: 69.2 in. Tires: P195/75R15 in.

CHASSIS (C2500 Pickup): Wheelbase: 131.5 in. Overall length: 213.4 in. Height: 72.2 in. Tires: LT215/85R16 in.

CHASSIS (C3500 Pickup): Wheelbase: 131.5 in. Overall length: 213.4 in. Height: 73.6 in. Tires: LT235/85R16D-E in.

CHASSIS (T18 Jimmy 4x4): Wheelbase: 106.5 in. Overall length: 184.8 in. Height: 73.8 in. Tires: P215/75R15 in.

CHASSIS (C1500 Suburban): Wheelbase: 129.5 in. Overall length: 219.1 in. Height: 72.0 in. Tires: P235/75R15 in.

CHASSIS (G1500 Van): Wheelbase: 110/125 in. Overall length: 178.2/202.2 in. Height: 79.4 in. Tires: P205/75R15 in.

CHASSIS (Safari): Wheelbase: 111 in. Overall length: 176.8 in. Height: 71.7 in. Tires: P195/75R15 in.

NOTE: Selected specifications.

TECHNICAL: Manual synchromesh transmission. Speeds: 3F/1R or 5F/1R. Column or floor-mounted gearshift. Hypoid rear axle. Front disc/rear drum brakes. Steel disc wheels.

NOTE: Exact specifications vary per series.

TECHNICAL: Automatic transmission. Speeds: 3F/1R and 4F/1R. Column or floor-mounted gearshift. Hypoid rear axle. Front disc/rear drum brakes. Steel disc wheels.

NOTE: Exact specifications vary per series.

SELECTED OPTIONS: (Caballero): Amarillo package ($225). V-8 engine. **(K18 Jimmy)** Silverado package ($1015). 6.2L diesel engine. **(S15 Jimmy)** Sierra Classic package ($595). Gypsy package. **(Safari)** Tilt steering ($115). Cruise control ($195). **(Vans)** V-8 engine. Diesel engine. 12-passenger package. **(Value Vans)** 11,000-pound rear axle. 5.7L V-8 engine. Diesel engine. **(S10 Pickup)** High Sierra package. Sierra Classic package. Gypsy package. **(Pickup/Suburban)** High Sierra package. Sierra Classic package. V-8 engine (except Suburbans). Diesel engine.

NOTE: Also see 1986 Chevrolet option data.

HISTORICAL: Introduced: Oct., 1985. Model year sales: (Vans) 39,099; (Safari) 29,743; (S15 Pickup) 49,139; (S15 Jimmy) 43,710; (Jimmy) 9686; (Caballero) 2795; (Suburban) 19,287; (Pickups) 114,115; (Value Vans) 4158. (Total, through Sept., 1986) 311,732.

Redesigned "S" Series instrument panel. Lighter weight alloy pistons in 2.8-liter V-6. Throttle-body fuel injection used on 2.8-liter V-6. Full-size light-duty trucks have new type generator belt. Vortec six standard for full-size pickups.

GMC's model year sales (through Sept., 1986) were almost 7000 units higher than the all-time record set in 1985. During 1986, GMC announced that a new line of smaller conventional pickups would be introduced in May, 1987.

HUDSON MOTOR CAR CO.

By John A. Gunnell

Hudson Motor Car Co. was incorporated on Feb. 24, 1909, the name coming from J.L. Hudson, a department store owner and investor in the new automobile company. The Detroit-based firm did not introduce series production of light-duty trucks until 1929, but many car-to-truck conversions were made from at least 1913 on.

1913 Hudson Super Six Dealer Service Truck (OCW)

Commonly seen in the pre-World War I era, and later, were service cars that Hudson dealers used as pickups, tow vehicles and to aid stranded motorists. There are photos of so many of these that one would suppose Hudson encouraged their construction and use.

1917 Hudson Military Ambulance (OCW)

The Hudson service cars are quite handsome trucks with several common features like high-side cargo boxes with bright-metal railings, platform type rear extensions (probably made of diamond plate) and oversized rear tires. Roadster conversions were prevalent in the teens, with panel body types also appearing from 1919 on. By the 1920s, the Essex roadster became a popular base vehicle for the service cars. At least one such vehicle, with disc wheels, was employed at the Detroit factory in 1921.

1917 Hudson Military Transport Wagon (OCW)

By 1914, ambulances on the Hudson chassis — with large panel bodies — began to appear. During World War I, many of these were built for U.S. Army use. Carved-side hearses were also seen as early as 1915. In the same period, some dealer service cars were handed down to volunteer fire departments for hose wagon and rescue squad work. Hudson's high-speed "Super Six" engine helped when it came to quick response to emergencies.

1919 Hudson Super Six Dealer Service Van (OCW)

Hudson's first line of commercial vehicles offered to the public was provdied in 1929 under the Dover nameplate. These were essentially Essex trucks, introduced on July 1 of that year. Five three-quarter ton rated models comprised the line. Interestingly, Pontiac — arch rival of Essex — had introduced a light truck in 1927. These Dovers — like their competition — were equipped with deluxe-level features like sidemounts, chrome-rimmed headlights and double belt moldings.

In 1930, Essex passenger cars grew bigger, but a line of trucks made under this name were actually 1929 Dovers with new I.D. badges. Apparently, Dover sales had not matched factory production schedules and trucks leftover from inventory were simply sold as the "new" Essex. The ploy didn't help much during the Depression, as 1930 serial numbers indicate slightly *decreased* production.

Hudson historian Don Butler says the commercial car line was "faltering badly as a salable product'' by 1931. There were 10 models which, again, were mostly a continuation of the 1929 Dovers on a shorter wheelbase than the then-current Essex cars.

Factory shipments for 1932 totaled 412 Essex commercial vehicles — probably leftover 1931 models. At least, no trucks are believed to have been merchandised in 1932's model lineup. They returned on April 1 of the following year as Essex-Terraplanes. There were numerous models including specially designed postal delivery vans with sliding side doors, high-headroom styling and fancy-edged body paneling. There was also a short-coupled sedan delivery.

1922 Essex Factory Service Express (OCW)

Terraplane's streamlined approach to styling, in 1934, was carried over to the commercial vehicle lineup. This resulted in trucks with a most distinctive appearance that look almost toy-like in catalog artwork. These models were truly half-car and half-truck a theme that would soon become characteristic of the Hudson coupe-express.

1922 Essex Dealer Service Pickup (OCW)

For 1935, the Terraplane Six trucks were slightly more modernized in appearance — particularly the front end sheet metal. The year's cab-pickup express was the first to use this name and had features, like removable tool lockers, which survived throughout postwar times. By this time, there was also a "commercial car line" of sedans, coupes, taxis (and aftermarket station wagons) produced on a heavier-duty car chassis and having such features as removable or folding leatherette seats for cargo-carrying conversions.

Styling for 1936 was more "art deco" looking and more streamlined. The woodie wagon became a more or less "factory" model in the truck line, although its body was still outside-souced. Half-ton commercial cars were also continued. In 1937, the utility coupe pickup joined this sub-series. It featured a telescoping cargo box that slid in and out of the five-window coupe body like a dresser drawer. An innovation of this year was the "Big Boy" series, which included trucks having the same body and cargo area dimensions as the regular trucks, but using a longer wheelbase.

According to Hudson, relocating the back wheels seven inches rearward allowed heavy loads to be balanced better on the chassis and created less of an adverse effect on road handling when such loads were cornered. 1938 brought the name Hudson-Terraplane into official usage, while the compact new Hudson 112 line was also provided with light-duty commercial models. Considering that just over 800 units were shipped by the factory, Hudson's line of 19 models in three series was somewhat incredible.

1923 Essex Cotton-Beverly Station Wagon (OCW)

In 1939, the line was reduced to 14 models in three series with the new three-quarter ton Pacemaker having a single panel on an 118-inch wheelbase. Gone was the Terraplane name. Remaining were the half-ton Hudson 112 on a 112-inch wheelbase and the three-quarter ton "Big Boys" on a 119-inch wheelbase. The following year, the half-tons gained one inch of wheelspan and the "Big Boys" grew to 125 inches, these being the only changed offerings in a total of 10 models. A cleaner "ship's prow" front end was adapted.

Both series grew three inches in wheelbase for 1941 and the commercial coupe adapted a stationary cargo box. Styling was modestly changed. Station wagons moved to the car-lines, reducing the trucks and utility cars to eight models. This total was cut in half for 1942, when the only true trucks were the half-ton pickup and three-quarter ton "Big Boy" with a larger Hudson badge on its nose. This was continued into 1947, virtually without change, then dropped. At this juncture, Hudson light-duty truck history came to a close.

491

1929 HUDSON

1929 Dover High-headroom Screenside Express (OCW)

LIGHT-TRUCK — DOVER SERIES — SIX-CYLINDER: — The Dover was the first Hudson-built commercial vehicle offered to the public. It used parts from different Hudson products with commercial bodies. Taken from the small Essex passenger car (a companion make to Hudson) was the hood, cowl, windshield, fenders, runningboards and headlamps, plus the engine. Axles, springs and other chassis components were beefed-up from passenger car specifications. For example, the frame was a bridge type, eight inches deep with six crossmembers. Standard equipment included four-wheel Bendix brakes, hexagonal hub caps, electric gas gauge, automatic spark advance, Alemite lubrication, flat radiator cap, doors with weather-proofing rubber cloth covered cardboard and a single side mounted spare. Hudson even supplied stencils to help buyers letter their company names on the trucks. The Dover had the same wheelbase and general size of the year's Essex and was rated at ¾-ton. Styling features included double rows of short horizontal hood louvers, flat radiators, torpedo headlights, double belt moldings, full-crown fenders and name badges with the winged horse, Pegasus, of Greek mythology. While the Dover engine had the same displacement as a 1929 Essex engine, it, too, was beefed-up to give slightly more horsepower. All models had front opening, rear-hinged doors.

I.D. DATA: Serial number located on top of right rear frame crossmember. Starting: 10,001. Ending: 12,204. Engine numbers located on left side of motor just ahead of water inlet. Motor numbers not available.

Model	Body Type	Price	Weight	Prod. Total
Dover Series — (6-cyl.) — (¾-Ton)				
Dover	Chassis and Cab	595	1930	Note 1
Dover	Panel	895	2910	Note 1
Dover	Screen/Canopy Exp.(*)	885	2865	Note 1
Dover	Pickup	835	2715	Note 1
Dover	Sedan Delivery	—	—	Note 1
Dover	Mail Delivery Panel	—	—	Note 1

NOTE 1: Production for calendar year was 2,203 units.
NOTE 2: Hudson shipment records showed 2,130 commercial vehicle shipments in 1929. This could indicate that some trucks were picked up by customers, at the factory, eliminating shipping.
(*) The canopy express sold for $870.

1929 Dover Closed-Cab w/Open Express Body(OCW)

ENGINE: Inline. L-head. Six-cylinder. Cast iron block. Bore & stroke: 2¾ in. x 4½ in. Displacement: 160.4 cu. in. Compression ratio: 5.8:1. Brake horsepower: 55 at 3600 R.P.M. Net horsepower: 18.2. Three main bearings. Solid valve lifters. Carburetor: Marvel model 5.

CHASSIS (Dover Series): Wheelbase: 110½ in. Overall length: 156.5 in. (approx.). Front tread: 56 in. Rear tread: 56 in. Tires: (front) 30 x 5.00 in.; (rear) 31 x 5.50 in.

NOTE: Pickup box measurements were 71 inches long by 42¼ inches wide and 18½ inches high on sides. The ''high head room'' style canopy express measured 50½ inches from box floor to top.

TECHNICAL: Sliding gear manual transmission. Speeds: 3F/1R. Floor mounted gearshift lever. Single, plate type clutch w/cork inserts running in oil. Semi-floating rear axle. Overall ratio: 5.6:1. Bendix four-wheel mechanical brakes. Wood-spoke wheels.

OPTIONS: Front bumper. Deluxe equipment package. Single sidemount (standard). Side curtains (canopy express). Leatherette sidemount cover. Outside rearview mirror. Overdrive. Special paint. Pickup bed rails. Low rear step plate. Aftermarket bodies.

1929 Dover DeLuxe Panel Delivery (RAW)

HISTORICAL: Introduced: July 1929, according to N.A.D.A. Calendar year registrations: 401 units. Calendar year shipments: 2,130. Calendar year production: 2,203. Innovations: First commercial vehicle released by Hudson for sale to the public. Distinctive radiator shell with horizontal shutters on Dover. New English-sounding brand name was used only one year. Later models had higher arched rooflines. Historical note: The president of Essex was William J. McAneeny. Dealers, as in the past, got factory encouragement to use Hudson-built trucks as service vehicles. A factory bulletin advised about how to convert the express-pickup into a service vehicle by removing flareboards and adding tubular side rails and lower rear step plates. Canopy express model could also convert into a pickup truck. Dover bodies were probably built by Hercules Products, Inc., of Evansville, Ind. According to Hudson historian Alex Burr, there is a story that Dover mail trucks were used by the Post Office until 1945 and then sold for $50. The only known suvivor of this postal fleet was once part of Harrah's Automobile Collection in Reno, Nevada.

NOTE: NADA production date disagrees with factory weight sheet dates. First weight sheet, dated May 3, 1929, shows weight of 3193 pounds for pickup with wood slat flareboards. Second sheet dated May 10, 1929 shows weight of 3095 pounds for same truck with Masonite flareboards.

Pricing

1929	5	4	3	2	1
Dover Series					
Panel Delivery	1350	2700	4500	6300	9000
Screenside Delivery	1300	2550	4250	5900	8500
Canopy Express	1200	2460	4100	5700	8800
Flareboard Pickup	1450	2850	4750	6650	9500
Bed Rail Pickup	1800	3600	6000	8400	12,000
Sedan Delivery	1500	3000	5000	7000	10,000
Mail Truck w/sliding doors	3000	6000	10,000	14,000	20,000

EDITOR'S NOTE: The Dover mail truck in Harrah's 1986 auction sold for $26,000, but the Harrah's sales tended to inflate values based on the fact that William F. Harrah owned the vehicles.

1930 HUDSON

COMMERCIAL CAR — ESSEX SERIES — SIX-CYLINDER: — Dover light trucks became Essex commercial cars in model-year 1930. These did not follow the wheelbase and size increase of new Essex passenger cars. Instead, they were virtually identical to 1929 Dovers. Even the serial number sequence continued unbroken. So this was, essentially, a name change only. Production simply continued, after Jan. 1930, under the Essex name. Some minor new features included a redesigned dashboard, scroll-marked fenders and radiator, larger size tires, double cowl ventilators and toggle lever operated windshield. Some standard features of Dover and Essex trucks not previously noted were revolving window lifts for door glass, shatter-proof windshield, adjustable steering wheel, electric gas/oil gauge(s), courtesy light for reading delivery slips at night and leather upholstered adjustable seats.

I.D. DATA: Serial number located on top of right rear frame crossmember. Starting: 12,205. Ending: 14,035. Engine numbers located on left side of motor just ahead of water inlet. Motor numbers unavailable.

Model	Body Type	Price	Weight	Prod. Total
Essex Series — (6-cyl.) — (¾-Ton)				
ECC	Chassis and Cab	595	1970	Note 1
ECC	Panel	895	2910	Note 1
ECC	Pickup	835	2715	Note 1
ECC	Screen	885	2865	Note 1
ECC	Sedan Delivery	—	—	Note 1
ECC	Canopy Express	870	2865	Note 1

NOTE 1: Production for calendar year (based serial numbers) was 1,830 units.
NOTE 2: "ECC" means "Essex Commercial Car." This is our code; not a factory code.

1930 Essex Panel Delivery (DFW/MM)

ENGINE: Inline. L-head. Six-cylinder. Cast iron block. Bore & stroke: 2¾ in. x 4½ in. Displacement: 160 cu. in. Compression ratio: 5.8:1. Brake horsepower: 58 at 3300 R.P.M. Net horsepower: 18.2. Three main bearings. Solid valve lifters. Carburetor: Marvel model 5.

CHASSIS (Essex Series): Wheelbase: 110½ in. Overall length: 156.5 in. (approx.). Front tread: 56 in. Rear tread: 56 in. Tires: 19 x 5.00 in.

TECHNICAL: Sliding gear manual transmission. Speeds: 3F/1R. Floor mounted gearshift lever. Single, plate type clutch w/cork inserts running in oil. Semi-floating rear axle. Overall ratio: 5.6:1. Bendix four-wheel mechanical brakes. Wood-spoke wheels.

OPTIONS: Front bumper. Deluxe equipment package. Single sidemount (standard). Side curtains (canopy express). Sidemount cover. OSRV mirror. Overdrive. Special paint. Pickup bed rails. Low step plate. Custom bodies.

HISTORICAL: Introduced: Jan. 1930. Calendar year registrations: 589 units. Calendar year shipments: 1,066. Calendar year production, by serial numbers: 1,830 units. Innovations: Trucks adopt Essex name. Improved combustion chamber and manifold design for more horsepower. New dash. Larger tires. New automatic choke. Marvel carb had new accelerator pump. Historical notes: Some Essex station wagons were built, probably by Hercules. These were on the commercial car chassis.

1930 Essex Panel Delivery (DFW/MM)

Pricing

1930	5	4	3	2	1
Essex Commercial Car Series					
Panel Delivery	1850	2700	4500	6300	9000
Pickup	1450	2850	4750	6650	9500
Screenside Express	1300	2550	4250	5900	8500
Canopy Express	1200	2460	4100	5700	8200
Sedan Delivery	1500	3000	5000	7000	10,000

NOTE: Add 30 percent for original dealer side rail (service truck) pickup conversions.

1931 HUDSON

COMMERCIAL CAR — ESSEX SERIES — SIX-CYLINDER: — Hudson historians vary on information about 1931 Essex commercial cars. Alex Burr, writing some years ago in *Old Cars Weekly*, said Hudson records showed 720 commercial vehicle shipments for 1931, although factory weight sheets, parts books and interchange books list no such model. Burr mentions, also, that no registrations are listed in other reference sources. Historian Don Butler in *The History of Hudson*, says, "The Essex commercial car line, faltering badly as a salable product, continued as offered for 1930. Serial numbers ranged upward from 14036." One of our contemporary reference sources, the *N.A.D.A. Official Used Car Guide*, (effective July 16, 1934 to Aug. 20, 1934 inclusive) lists a 1930 Essex commercial series with absolutely no changes in models, weights or specifications, but with substantially lowered factory prices. It also gives the starting number that Don Butler mentions. Since the Essex passenger car of this season had a 113 inch wheelbase, as opposed to the commercial car's 110½ inches, it would be best to assume that the trucks did not have the same changes as passenger models. In other words, it's most likely that the 1931 Essex commercial car was the same as the 1930 counterpart model, which was the same as the 1929 Dover light-duty truck. Continuance of the same serial number sequence lends support to this view. The inference is that sales continued in 1931, perhaps marketing leftover 1929-1930 vehicles until inventories were deleted.

I.D. DATA: Serial number located on top of right rear frame crossmember. Starting: 14,036 and up. Although no ending numbers are available, the number of shipments mentioned in the introductory text (720) seems believable and would hint of an ending serial number in the "ballpark" of 14,756. Engine numbers located on left side of motor just ahead of water inlet. Motor numbers unavailable.

Model	Body Type	Price	Weight	Prod. Total
Essex Series — (6-cyl.) — (¾-Ton)				
ECC	Chassis and Cab	435	1970	Note 1
ECC	Panel	735	2910	Note 1
ECC	Screen Delivery	725	2865	Note 1
ECC	Canopy Dely.	710	2865	Note 1
ECC	Pickup-Express	675	2715	Note 1
ECC	Sedan Delivery	—	—	Note 1

NOTE 1: Hudson recorded 720 commercial car shipments in 1931.
NOTE 2: Chassis price is according to 1934 NADA guidebook. Prices for other models are extrapolations.
NOTE 3: "ECC" is our designation for Essex commercial car.

ENGINE: Inline. L-head. Six-cylinder. Cast iron block. Bore & stroke: 2¾ in. x 4½ in. Displacement: 160 cu. in. Compression ratio: 5.8:1. Brake horsepower: 58 at 3300 R.P.M. Net horsepower: 18.2. Three main bearings. Solid valve lifters. Carburetor: Marvel model 5.

CHASSIS (Essex Series): Wheelbase: 110½ in. Overall length: 156.5 in. (approximate). Front tread: 56 in. Rear tread: 56 in. Tires: 19 x 5.00 in.

TECHNICAL: Sliding gear manual transmission. Speeds: 3F/1R. Floor mounted gearshift lever. Single, plate type clutch w/cork inserts running in oil. Semi-floating rear axle. Overall ratio: 5.6:1. Bendix four-wheel mechanical brakes. Wood-spoke wheels.

OPTIONS: Front bumper. Deluxe equipment package. Single sidemount (standard). Side curtains (canopy express). Sidemount cover. OSRV mirror. Overdrive. Special paint. Pickup bed rails. Low step plate. Custom bodies.

HISTORICAL: Introduced: November 1930. Calendar year shipments: 720. Historical notes: Most likely, 1931 was a year in which excess inventory was carried over from 1930. According to historian Alex Burr, writing in *Old Cars Weekly*, there are no references in factory parts books to 1931 models. Weight sheets do not list 1931 models. Burr adds that the *Automotive News Almanac* of 1968 also shows a lack of Hudson truck output in calendar year 1931. However, 1931 models were listed in the *1934 NADA Used Car Guide* and factory records show 720 shipments.

Pricing

	5	4	3	2	1
1931					
Essex Commercial Car Series					
Panel Delivery	1850	2700	4500	6300	9000
Pickup	1450	2850	4750	6650	9500
Screenside Express	1300	2550	4250	5900	8500
Canopy Express	1200	2460	4100	5700	8200
Sedan Delivery	1500	3000	5000	7000	10,000

NOTE: Add 30 percent for original dealer side rail (service truck) pickup conversions.

1932 HUDSON

ESSEX-TERRAPLANE — SERIES K — SIX-CYLINDER: — The Essex Terraplane passenger cars were introduced in July 1932. There was no corresponding commercial vehicle line. In all sources previously noted, there was no mention of commercial car production in calendar 1932. There are also, no factory weight sheets or shipment records for commercial vehicles. According to Hudson historian Alex Burr, there are unconfirmed rumors of a corporate power struggle, in 1932, between Hudson and Essex management. This may have caused inner unrest, that delayed plans to market an Essex-Terraplane truck line.

1933 HUDSON

1933 Essex-Terraplane Pickup (DFW/MVMA)

ESSEX-TERRAPLANE — SERIES K — SIX-CYLINDER: — The Terraplane line, introduced as an Essex sub-series in the 1932 passenger car offerings, gained a number of commercial vehicles for 1933. All of these models used the Essex-Terraplane Six's 106 inch wheelbase chassis. Also used was the Terraplane Six's lower body, skirted fenders, slanting windshield, V-type slanting radiator, bullet headlamps and winged hood ornament. Once again, two long rows of short vertical louvers decorated the hood sides. The trucks also used the cars' V-type front bumper, but lacked fender top parking lamps. Doors opened front-to-rear. However, one factory model — the standard panel delivery — had a van-like body with a high roof and sliding front doors. (*) Something else found on trucks — except the car-like sedan delivery — was outside windshield sun visors and standard side mounted spares. Interestingly, 1930-1939 Hudson parts books list four models, factory weight sheets showed only two and the NADA listed six (two without prices or weights.) In his Crestline book, Don Butler pictures four models. All have wire-spoke wheels. Name badges on the trucks said "Terraplane." Due to the smaller wheelbase, they were down-rated to ½-ton.

(*) In all likelihood, the standard panel van was a variation of, or the same body as, the 1929 Dover mail truck. This body was probably built by York-Hoover body company.

I.D. DATA: Serial number located on top of right rear frame crossmember. Starting: 364,125 and up. (Note: Estimated ending number based on 1933 shipments.) Engine numbers located on left side of motor just ahead of water inlet. Motor numbers unavailable.

Model Series K	Body Type — (½-Ton) — (6-cyl.)	Price	Weight	Prod. Total
K	Chassis and Cab	375	1865	Note 1
K	Sedan Delivery	545	2395	Note 1
K	Panel Delivery	530	2610	Note 1
K	Pickup	440	2350	Note 1
K	Screenside Delivery	—	—	Note 1
K	Canopied Delivery	—	—	Note 1
K	Mail Delivery	—	—	Note 1

NOTE 1: Calendar year shipments totaled 430 units.

494

1933 Essex-Terraplane Panel Delivery (DFW/MVMA)

ENGINE: Inline. L-head. Six-cylinder. Cast iron block. Bore & stroke: 2-15/16 in. x 4¾ in. Displacement: 193.1 cu. in. Compression ratio: 5.8:1. Brake horsepower: 70 at 3200 R.P.M. Net horsepower: 20.7. Three main bearings. Solid valve lifters. Carburetor: Carter model 267S.

CHASSIS (Essex Series): Wheelbase: 106 in. Front tread: 56 in. Rear tread: 56 in. Tires: 17 x 5.25 in.

TECHNICAL: Sliding gear manual transmission. Speeds: 3F/1R. Floor mounted gearshift lever. Single, plate type clutch w/cork inserts running in oil. Semi-floating rear axle. Overall ratio: 4.11, 4.56, 3.8. Bendix four-wheel mechanical brakes. Wire-spoke wheels.

OPTIONS: Front bumper. Deluxe equipment package. Single sidemount. Canvas side mount cover. Dual windshield wipers. Dual taillights. Rear bumper (sedan delivery). Two tone paint. Special colors. Side curtains (canopy and screenside deliveries). Right-hand passenger seat in sedan or panel delivery trucks. OSRV mirror. White sidewall tires. Wheel trim rings. License frames. Oil bath air cleaner.

1933 Essex-Terraplane Sedan Delivery (DFW/MVMA)

HISTORICAL: Introduced: April 1933. Calendar year shipments: 430. Innovations: New Essex-Terraplane name and more streamlined styling. Shorter wheelbase chassis. Larger, more powerful six-cylinder engine. Wire spoke wheels. Historical notes: Roy O. Chapin took over as president of Essex-Terraplane in May, 1933. Terraplane name believed to be derived from a sports car that Harry Miller designed. Hudson operated in "red ink" during these bleak depression years.

1933 Essex-Terraplane Special Mail Truck (DFW)

Pricing

	5	4	3	2	1
1933					
Essex-Terraplane Series					
Sedan Delivery	1350	2700	4500	6300	9000
Panel Delivery	1250	2500	4150	5800	8300
Deluxe Panel Delivery	1300	2550	4250	5900	8500
Pickup-Express	1200	2460	4100	5700	8200
Screenside Delivery	1200	2400	4000	5600	8000
Canopied Delivery	1150	2310	3850	5400	7700
Mail Delivery Van	2250	4500	7500	10,500	15,000

1934 HUDSON

1934 Terraplane Commercial Coach (OCW)

TERRAPLANE — SERIES K — SIX-CYLINDER: — The Terraplane changed from a sub-series to a separate marque in 1934. Essex was gone forever. Styling was completely new, highlighted by a broad grille with thin, converging bars, heavily streamlined valanced front and rear fenders, heavily veed front bumpers and long, low hoods. There were seven vertical tapered hood louvers, hidden on the curb-side by the truck's standard sidemount spare. The chassis and cab looked strangely attractive with the sweeping rear fenders swooping out towards the rear. And sedan deliveries had a curved, wraparound rear with double center-opening doors. On this and a new utility coach, passenger seats were removable. A four-door taxicab, with "suicide doors" front and rear, utilized the heavy-duty commercial underpinnings. Wood-bodied wagons were made by at least two aftermarket firms: J.T. Cantrell & Co. of Huntington, N.Y. and Colton Body Co. of Concord, N.H. Both used commercial chassis supplied by local dealers and built the woodies as a private venture. The utility coach was a two-door sedan with bolt-in passenger seats front and rear, snap-on covers to protect the upholstery and blanked-out rear quarter windows. Equipment features included winged radiator caps, wire spoke wheels, torpedo headlamps and larger chrome hub caps. Deluxe models came with dual horns, dual visors and twin-taillights and front fender lamps. A longer wheelbase increased payload capacity to ¾-ton.

I.D. DATA: Serial number located on dash under hood inside right-hand door hinge pillar, just above upper hinge. Also right side of frame, just ahead of front spring hanger. Starting: 373,000 and up. Engine numbers located on left side of cylinder block ahead of water inlet. Motor numbers not available.

1934 Terraplane Chassis and Cab (OCW)

Model	Body Type	Price	Weight	Prod. Total
Terraplane Series K — (¾-Ton) — (6-cyl.)				
K	Chassis and Cab	480	2250	Note 1
K	Chassis only	405	1950	Note 1
K	Cab Pickup	515	2675	Note 1
K	Utility Coach	530	2560	Note 1
K	Sedan Delivery	595	2680	Note 1
K	Taxicab	Note 3	Note 3	Note 1
K	Cantrell Station Wagon	Note 2	Note 2	Note 1
K	Cotton Station Wagon	Note 2	Note 2	Note 1

NOTE 1: Factory shipments totaled 1,901 units.
NOTE 2: Station wagons were built on the chassis-only.
NOTE 3: The Taxicab was based on compartment sedan which sold for $780 and weighed 2,805 pounds.

ENGINE: Inline. L-head. Six-cylinder. Chrome alloy block. Bore & stroke: 3 in. x 5 in. Displacement: 212 cu. in. Compression ratio: 5.8:1. Brake horsepower: 80 at 3600 R.P.M. Net horsepower: 21.6. Three main bearings. Solid valve lifters. Carburetor: Carter.

CHASSIS (Terraplane Series): Wheelbase: 112 in. Overall length: 190 in. (approx.). Front tread: 56 in. Rear tread: 56 in. Tires: 17 x 5.50 in.

NOTE: Pickup cargo box was 70½ in. long by 45½ in. wide and 16½ in. deep. Bottom of box sat 24 in. off road. Sedan delivery had 36 in. high, 38 in. wide double-door opening; cargo area measuring 93 in. long, 43 in. high and 50 in. wide.

1934 Terraplane Cab Pickup Express (DFW)

TECHNICAL: Sliding gear manual transmission. Speeds: 3F/1R. Floor mounted gearshift lever. Single plate type clutch w/cork inserts running in oil. Semi-floating rear axle. Overall ratio: 4.1:1. Bendix four-wheel mechanical brakes. 17 in. wire-spoke wheels were standard. 16 inch wire or steel disc wheels (with 16 x 6.00 tires) were optional.

OPTIONS: Front bumper. Rear bumper. Deluxe equipment. Single sidemount. Metal sidemount covers. Steel disc wheels. Special paint. Station wagon bodies. Aftermarket bodies. OSRV mirror. License plate holder. Removable front seats. Dual windshield wipers. Radio. Antenna. Wheel trim rings. White sidewall tires. Dual taillights. Heater. Axleflex front suspension. Hill-Hold device.

HISTORICAL: Introduced: Jan. 1934. Calendar year registrations: 517. Calendar year shipments: 1,901. Innovations: New longer wheelbase. Axleflex front suspension introduced. Adopted Lovejoy shock absorbers. New Hill-Hold option. Historical notes: Roy Chapin relinquished his presidency of Hudson-Essex to A. Edward Barit.

Pricing

1934 Terraplane Series	5	4	3	2	1
Cab Pickup	1300	2550	4250	5900	8500
Utility Coach	900	1800	3000	4200	6000
Sedan Delivery	1350	2700	4500	6300	9000
Compartment Sedan Taxicab	1050	2100	3500	4900	7000
Cantrell Station Wagon	1950	3900	6500	9100	13,000
Cotton Station Wagon	1800	3600	6000	8400	12,000

1935 HUDSON

1935 Terraplane Panel Delivery (DFW/MVMA)

TERRAPLANE — SERIES GU — SIX-CYLINDER: — There were minor styling changes for 1935. A new grille featured six thin horizontal bars, a thick vertical center spine and narrower vanes that angled outward from the grille base. Hood louvers were slightly tilted towards the rear and decorated with three horizontal chrome strips. Truck bodies went back to the practice of being sourced from outside suppliers, in this case Detweiler for cab type models and York-Hoover for panel deliveries. The Detweiler pickups could be had with removable inner side-storage lockers that hid the wheelhousings. Payload ratings were again ¾-ton. Steel disc wheels were most commonly used on trucks, which still had single, curb-side sidemounted spares.

I.D. DATA: Serial number located on dash under hood inside right-hand door hinge pillar, just above upper hinge. Also right side of frame, just ahead of front spring hanger. Starting: 51-101 and up. The serial number consisted of the first two numbers which were the series code designation, followed by production sequence numbers starting at 101 and up. Engine numbers located on left side of cylinder block ahead of water inlet. Engine numbers unavailable.

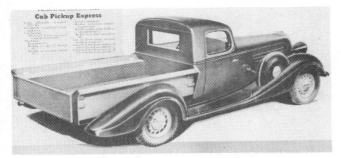

1935 Terraplane Cab Pickup Express (DFW/WRHS)

Model	Body Type	Price	Weight	Prod. Total
Terraplane Series — (¾-Ton) — (6-cyl.)				
51	Chassis	430	1950	Note 1
51	Chassis & Cab	515	2305	Note 1
51	Cab Pickup	545	2605	Note 1
51	Utility Coach	565	2535	Note 1
51	Sedan Delivery	675	2770	Note 1

NOTE 1: Factory shipments 1,281 trucks.

ENGINE: Inline. L-head. Six-cylinder. Chrome alloy block. Bore & stroke: 3 in. x 5 in. Displacement: 212 cu. in. Compression ratio: 6.0:1. Brake horsepower: 88 at 3800 R.P.M. Net horsepower: 21.6. Three main bearings. Solid valve lifters. Carburetor: Carter.

NOTE: It is not clear if the optional 100 horsepower engine was offered in Terraplane trucks this year. It was offered in 1936 and specifications are included in that section.

CHASSIS: Wheelbase: 112 in. Overall length: 190 in. Front tread: 56 in. Rear tread: 56 in. Tires: 16 x 6.00 in. Steel spoke wheel discs.

TECHNICAL: Sliding gear manual transmission. Speeds: 3F/1R. Floor mounted gearshift lever. Single plate type clutch w/cork inserts running in oil. Semi-floating rear axle. Overall ratio: 4.11:1. Bendix four-wheel mechanical brakes. Steel-spoke wheel discs.

OPTIONS: Radio ($51.81). Seat covers ($7.50). High compression cylinder head, if available in trucks ($8.50). Zenith radio ($44). Twin air horns ($11.50). Dual step lamps. Single side mount. Metal sidemount covers. Wire wheels. Wheel trim rings. Utility boxes. OSRV mirror. Whitewall tires. License holder. Fog lights. Grille guard.

HISTORICAL: Introduced: Nov. 21, 1934. Calendar year registrations: 638. Calendar year shipments: 1,281. Innovations: One-year return to complete outside sourcing of truck bodies. Mechanical brakes improved.

Pricing

1935	5	4	3	2	1
Terraplane Series GU					
Cab Pickup	1300	2550	4250	5900	8500
Utility Coach	900	1800	3000	4200	6000
Sedan Delivery	1350	2700	4500	6300	9000
Commercial Station Wagon	1950	3900	6500	9100	13,000
Taxicab	1050	2100	3500	4900	7000

1936 HUDSON

1936 Terraplane Custom Panel Delivery (DFW)

496

TERRAPLANE — SERIES 61 — SIX-CYLINDER: — This year brought the famous teardrop-shaped grille that characterized the Terraplane's best remembered image. Nine chevron type moldings ran down the face of the grille. The series 61 Deluxe line lacked external horns and had single taillights. Passenger cars in the series 62 Custom line were fancier looking and fuller equipped, but this line was devoid of trucks, which were all Deluxes. A station wagon was added to the line. It rode the commercial chassis. The woodies were bodied by Baker-Rauling. Factory-sourced bodies were now used on all trucks, but panels, which York-Hoover continued to make. Hudson also brought out a pickup conversion kit. Wheelbase increased to 115 inches. Payload was again ¾-ton. A new safety feature was hydraulic brakes. Two engines were available — both sixes — with 88 and 100 horsepower ratings. Sidemount spares were no longer standard.

I.D. DATA: Serial number located on dash under hood inside right-hand door hinge pillar, just above upper hinge. Also right side of frame, just ahead of front spring hanger. Starting: 61-101. Explanation: "61" equals series code; "101" is sequential starting number. Engine numbers located on left side of cylinder block ahead of water inlet. Starting: 15,700 and up.

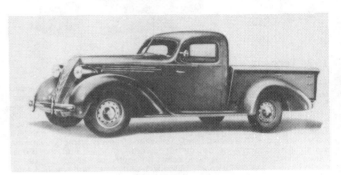

1936 Terraplane Cab Pickup Express (OCW)

Model	Body Type	Price	Weight	Prod. Total
Terraplane Series — (¾-Ton) — (6-cyl.)				
61	Chassis	445	2045	Note 1
61	Chassis & Cab	530	2390	Note 1
61	Cab Pickup	560	2790	Note 1
61	Utility Coach	580	2625	Note 1
61	Custom Panel Delivery	685	2960	Note 1
61	Custom Station Wagon	750	2995	Note 1

NOTE 1: Factory shipments 4,548 trucks.

ENGINE: Inline. L-head. Six-cylinder. Chrome alloy block. Bore & stroke: 3 in. x 5 in. Displacement: 212 cu. in. Compression ratio: 6.0:1. Brake horsepower: 88 at 3800 R.P.M. Net horsepower: 21.6. Three main bearings. Solid valve lifters. Carburetor: Carter model 331S.

ENGINE: Inline. L-head. Six-cylinder. Chrome alloy block. Bore & stroke: 3 in. x 5 in. Displacement: 212 cu. in. Compression ratio: 7.0:1. Brake horsepower: 100 at 3800 R.P.M. Net horsepower: 21.6. Three main bearings. Solid valve lifters. Carburetor: Carter model 331S.

CHASSIS: Wheelbase: 115 in. Overall length: 195 in. Tires: 16 x 6.00 in.

TECHNICAL: Sliding gear manual transmission. Speeds: 3F/1R. Floor mounted gearshift lever. Single plate type clutch w/cork inserts running in oil. Semi-floating rear axle. Bendix four-wheel hydraulic brakes. Steel-spoke wheel discs.

OPTIONS: Radio. Seat covers. High-compression cylinder head. Twin air horns. Dual step lamps. OSRV mirror. Wheel trim rings. Bed utility box. Whitewall tires. License holder. Fog lights. Grille guard.

HISTORICAL: Introduced: Oct. 1935. Calendar year registrations: 1,905. Calendar year shipments: 4,548. Innovations: Longer new wheelbase. Totally revamped styling. "Factory" woodie wagon (Baker-Rauling bodies) introduced; merchandised as a car according to a "Red Book." Historical notes: Hudson historian Alex Burr believes that the factory treated the station wagons as part of commercial vehicle line. Knightstown Body Co. did ambulance conversions on 1936 Terraplane commercial chassis.

Pricing

1936	5	4	3	2	1
Terraplane Series 61					
Cab Pickup	1200	2400	4000	5600	8000
Utility Coach	830	1650	2750	3850	5500
Custom Panel Delivery	1300	2550	4250	5900	8500
Custom Station Wagon	1800	3600	6000	8400	12,000
Taxicab	900	1800	3000	4200	6000

1937 HUDSON

1937 Terraplane Utility Coupe (DFW/BLHU)

TERRAPLANE — SERIES 70 — SIX-CYLINDER: — Terraplane's mesh teardrop grille was replaced by one that looked more conventional. It had a tapering band of chrome blades running vertically downwards and two lower side grilles with horizontal bars. Wheelbase was up two inches and headlamps were now mounted on the radiator shell. A new model was the utility coupe pickup. It was essentially the regular Terraplane business coupe with a slip-in pickup box that "telescoped" into the trunk. Taxicabs and station wagons were again available and usually registered as commercial vehicles. It's most likely that taxi production was included in Hudson's passenger car totals. In this series, the "Utility" models were ½-ton rated, while regular trucks were rated ¾-tons. Standard equipment included front bumpers; one spare wheel; spare tire and tube; bumper guards; special radiator ornament; double windshield wipers; heavy-duty stabilizer and safety glass.

1937 Terraplane Series 70 Custom Panel Delivery

I.D. DATA: Serial number located on dash under hood; right door pillar; right side of frame ahead of front spring hanger. Starting: 70-1001. Ending: 70-8001. Explanation: "70" is series code; followed by sequential production numbers. Engine numbers located on left side of cylinder block. Starting: 250,000. Ending: 352,074.

1937 Terraplane Series 70 Cab Pickup Express

Model Series 70	Body Type — (6-cyl.) — (½-Ton)	Price	Weight	Prod. Total
70	Utility Coach	725	2685	Note 1
70	Utility Coupe Pickup	750	2855	Note 1
(¾-Ton)				
70	Chassis only	570	2080	Note 1
70	Chassis & Cab	670	2445	Note 1
70	Cab Pickup	700	2980	Note 1
70	Panel Delivery	830	3150	Note 1
70	Station Wagon	905	3060	Note 1

NOTE 1: A total of 8,085 commercial vehicles were shipped by Hudson in calendar 1937. This total also includes trucks in the "Big Boy" series. From serial numbers, it can be estimated that 950 "Big Boy" trucks were made. Such an estimate suggests that about 7,108 of the vehicles shipped were 70 Series models. Serial numbers for this series suggest production of 7,000 units, which appears to be in the right "ballpark."

1937 Terraplane Funeral Van (OCW)

ENGINE: Inline. L-head. Six-cylinder. Iron alloy block. Bore & stroke: 3 in. x 5 in. Displacement: 212 cu. in. Compression ratio: 6.0:1. Brake horsepower: 88 at 3800 R.P.M. Net horsepower: 21.6. Three main bearings. Solid valve lifters. Carburetor: Carter.

NOTE: Terraplane passenger cars in "71" series came with 6.25:1 compression and 96 horsepower (standard) or 7.0:1 compression and 102 horsepower (optional), while those in Super Terraplane "72" series offered 6.25:1 compression two-barrel engines with 101 horsepower (standard) or 7.0:1 compression two-barrel engines with 107 horsepower (optional). Some of these engines may have been available for trucks at extra-cost.

1937 Terraplane "Big Boy" Cab Pickup Express

TERRAPLANE "BIG BOY" — SERIES 78 — SIX-CYLINDER: — Having its own chassis, not shared with Terraplane or Hudson passenger cars, was the "Big Boy" commercial vehicle line with a 124 inch wheelbase. Strangely enough, the name of the series gave a slightly improper impression, because these trucks had the *same* body dimensions and payload ratings as the 70 series models. The real difference was relocation of the rear wheels seven inches rearward. Hudson claimed, in advertising, that this improved handling with heavy loads. Standard equipment included front bumpers; one spare wheel, tire and tube; bumper guards; special radiator ornament; double windshield wipers; heavy-duty stabilizer; safety glass; spring covers; twin horns and custom steering wheel.

I.D. DATA: Serial number located: same as above. Starting: 78-101. Ending: 78-1051. Explanation: Same as above; "78" is series code. Engine numbers located: Same as above. Starting: 250,000. Ending: 352,074.

1937 Hudson "Big Boy" Taxicab (DFW)

497

Model	Body Type	Price	Weight	Prod. Total
Series 78 "Big Boy" — (6-cyl.) — (¾-Ton)				
78	Chassis only	600	2170	Note 1
78	Chassis & Cab	700	2540	Note 1
78	Cab Pickup	740	3080	Note 1
78	Custom Panel Delivery	880	3210	Note 1

NOTE 1: See note above under 70 series. Available records suggest 950 "Big Boy" commercial vehicles were produced in calendar 1937.

ENGINE: See Series 70 engine specifications above.

CHASSIS (Series 70): Wheelbase: 117 in. Front tread: 56 in. Rear tread: 56 in. Tires: 16 x 6.00 in.

CHASSIS (Series 72): Wheelbase: 124 in. Front tread: 56 in. Rear tread: 56 in. Tires: 16 x 6.00 in.

TECHNICAL: Sliding gear manual transmission. Speeds: 3F/1R. Floor mounted gearshift lever. Single disc type clutch w/cork inserts running in oil. Semi-floating rear axle. Overall ratio: 4.11:1. Four-wheel hydraulic brakes. Steel-disc wheels. Automatic clutch. "Electric Hand" gearshifting device.

OPTIONS: Front bumper. Bumper guards. Sidemount spare tire. Sidemount cover (metal). Radio. Antenna. Fender skirts. OSRV mirror. External sunvisor. Fog lights. Grille guard. Wheel trim rings. Right-hand taillight. Custom steering wheel. License plate fromes. Pickup bed cargo lockes. Heater.

HISTORICAL: Introduced: Oct. 1936. Calendar year registrations: 4,823. Innovations:Longer wheelbases. New extra-long wheelbase "Big Boy" series for "balanced weight distribution." Higher horsepower engine options released. Radial Safety Control suspension introduced. Axleflex discontinued. New hydraulic brakes. Historical notes: Roy D. Chapin died of pnuemonia, at age 56, on Feb. 16, 1936. A. Edward Barit became president of Hudson Motor Car Co. Panel delivery bodies were made by York-Hoover, as were bodies for the utility coach, utility coupe and cabs and cab pickups. This was the highest year for commercial vehicle production, by Hudson since it began.

Pricing

	5	4	3	2	1
1937					
Terraplane Series 70 — (½-Ton)					
Utility Coach	810	1620	2700	3800	5400
Utility Coupe Pickup	1150	2310	3850	5400	7700
Terraplane Series 70 — (¾-Ton)					
Cab Pickup	1130	2250	3780	5250	7500
Panel Delivery	1170	2340	3900	5450	7800
Station Wagon	1700	3450	5750	8050	11,500
"Big Boy" Series 78 — (¾-Ton)					
Cab Pickup	1050	2100	3500	4900	7000
Custom Panel Delivery	1130	2250	3750	5250	7500
Big Boy Taxicab	900	1800	3000	4200	6000

1938 HUDSON

1938 Hudson-Terraplane 3/4-ton Pickup (OCW)

TERRAPLANE — SERIES 80 — SIX-CYLINDER: — Terraplane became a Hudson Series, instead of being merchandised as an individual marque. There was new front end styling with a longer hood that opened above the bead line and had removable side panels. The radiator grille was more vertical. It had a slightly modified V-shaped chrome center panel extending from the top to around the "bell" visible below the bumper line. Wide horizontal bars characterized the grille design. The 117 inch wheelbase was used and all models were rated for ¾-ton payloads. According to Alex Burr, the 1938 panel delivery bodies were sourced from Checker Cab Co. Burr also speaks of Terraplane 80 and Hudson 112 utility and station wagon models as "commercial vehicles," although "Red Book" listed them with passenger car-lines. Since they are not in our other catalogs, we'll also cover them here. These models all had Hudson-built bodies, except the woodie wagons. They were made by U.S. Body & Forging Co. of Frankfort, Ind.

I.D. DATA: Serial number located on top of block between first two exhaust flanges. Starting: 80-101. Ending: 80-56040. Explanation: It appears similar numbering sequence was used on both cars and trucks this year. Serial numbers suggest mixed production. Engine numbers located on boss near top and left side of block. Starting: 360,000 and up. (First Series).

NOTE: On first 1938 Hudsons, engine number differs from serial number and is stamped on a boss near top and left side of cylinder block. In later production, the engine number corresponds with serial number and is in the same location as serial numbers above.

Model	Body Type	Price	Weight	Prod. Total
Series 80 - (¾-Ton) — (6-cyl.)				
80	Chassis only	597	2105	Note 1
80	Chassis & Cab	704	2540	Note 1
80	Cab Pickup	734	2985	Note 1
80	Custom Panel Delivery	900	3135	Note 1
Utility Series - (6-cyl.)				
80	Utility Coupe	789	2840	Note 1
80	Utility Coach	779	2835	Note 1
80	Utility Touring Coach	799	2840	Note 1
80	Station Wagon	965	3055	Note 1

NOTE 1: Shipments of commercial vehicles in 1938 were just 808 units for all three series.

ENGINE: Inline. L-head. Six-cylinder. Chrome alloy block. Bore & stroke: 3 in. x 5 in. Displacement: 212 cu. in. Compression ratio: 6.0:1. Brake horsepower: 96 at 3900 R.P.M. Net horsepower: 21.6. Three main bearings. Solid valve lifters. Carburetor: Carter model.

NOTE: High-compression (7.0:1) engine with 102 horsepower at 3900 R.P.M. was optional.

1938 Hudson-Terraplane "Big Boy" Cab Pickup (OCW)

HUDSON-TERRAPLANE — SERIES 88 — SIX-CYLINDER: — The "Big Boy" series was continued and promoted for better balanced load handling. Styling was the same as on Series 80 models, as were body dimensions. The main difference, again, was rearward positioning of the back axle. Both series were passenger-car-like in many regards, although the frames and chassis components were of heavy-duty design for increased load carrying ability.

I.D. DATA: Serial number located: Same as above. Starting: 88-101. Ending: 88-56040. Engine numbers location: Same as above. Starting: 36,000 and up.

Important: See note above concerning corresponding serial and engine numbers in late 1938 production.

Model	Body Type	Price	Weight	Prod. Total
Series 88 — (¾-Ton) — (6-cyl.)				
88	Chassis only	627	2210	Note 1
88	Chassis & Cab	734	2645	Note 1
88	Cab Pickup	775	3020	Note 1
88	Custom Panel Delivery	951	3195	Note 1

NOTE 1: Shipments totaled 808 units for all three series with no breakouts available.

ENGINE: Same as Series 80 engine.

1938 Hudson-Terraplane Custom Panel Delivery (OCW)

HUDSON 112 — SERIES 89 — SIX-CYLINDER: — The Hudson 112 had the same general styling as Terraplanes, but a different hood treatment. The hood side panels were plain, except for latch handles. A smaller wheelbase was used and body components were corresponding proportioned. A smaller, less powerful six-cylinder engine was employed for trucks in this line. Some sources say these were ½-ton models, but the "Red Books" of the day list them in the ¾-ton payload class. They were definitely down-rated to ½-tonners in 1939, without changing basic specifications. So, it seems the discrepancy is in what they were called — not what they were.

I.D. DATA: Serial number location: Same as above. Starting: 89-101. Ending: 89-56040. Engine numbers location: Same as above. Numbers not available.

Important: See note above concerning corresponding serial and engine numbers in late 1938 production.

Model Series 89	Body Type (¾-ton) (6-cyl.)	Price	Weight	Prod. Total
89	Chassis only	532	—	
89	Chassis & Cab	638	2375	Note 1
89	Cab Pickup	671	2750	Note 1
89	Panel Delivery	822	2975	Note 1
Utility Series — (6-cyl.)				
89	Utility Coupe	724	2660	Note 1
89	Utility Coach	697	2600	Note 1
89	Utility Touring Coach	716	2605	Note 1

NOTE 1: Shipments totaled 808 units for all three series with no breakouts available.

ENGINE: Inline. L-head. Six-cylinder. Chrome alloy block. Bore & stroke: 3 in. x 4⅛ in. Displacement: 175 cu. in. Compression ratio: 6.5:1. Brake horsepower: 83 at 4000 R.P.M. Net horsepower: 21.6. Three main bearings. Solid valve lifters. Carburetor: Carter.

NOTE: Pistons from this engine fit both the 212 cu. in. six and 254 cu. in. Hudson Eight, while connecting rods interchanged between the "212" and the "254" engines.

CHASSIS (Series 80): Wheelbase: 117 in. Front Tread: 56 in. Rear Tread: 56 in. Tires: 16 x 6.00 (four-ply).

CHASSIS (Series 88): Wheelbase: 124 in. Front Tread: 56 in. Rear Tread: 56 in. Tires: 16 x 6.00 (four-ply).

CHASSIS (Series 89): Wheelbase: 112 in. Front Tread: 56 in. Rear Tread: 56 in. Tires: 16 x 5.50 (four-ply).

NOTE: Tire options were 16 x 6.00 in. (six-ply); 16 x 6.50 in. (six-ply) and 15 x 7.00 (six-ply).

TECHNICAL: Sliding gear manual transmission. Speeds: 3F/1R. Floor mounted gearshift lever. Single plate type clutch w/cork inserts running in oil. Semi-floating rear axle. Overall ratio: (std.) 5⅛:1, (opt.) 4-5/9:1. Four-wheel hydraulic brakes. Steel disc wheels. Selective Automatic shift transmission.

OPTIONS: Same as 1937.

HISTORICAL: Introduced: Oct., 1937. Calendar year registrations: 719. Calendar year shipments: (all series) 808. Innovations: Terraplanes become Hudson model. Checker Cab builds some Hudson truck bodies. New Hudson 112 commercial vehicle line intended to return company to low-price field. Historical notes: Hudson Motor Car Co. spent $11,000,000 to introduce and promote the new Hudson 112 series. Last season for Terraplane name was 1938. A.E. Barit continued as Hudson president. The company lost $4,670,004 by year's end, due to recession.

Pricing

	5	4	3	2	1
1938					
Hudson-Terraplane Series 80					
Cab Pickup	980	1950	3250	4550	6500
Custom Panel Delivery	1130	2250	3750	5250	7500
Utility Coupe	720	1450	2400	3300	4800
Utility Coach	810	1620	2700	3800	5400
Utility Touring Coach	680	1350	2250	3150	4500
Station Wagon	1700	3450	5750	8050	11,500
Hudson "Big Boy" Series 88					
Cab Pickup	1050	2100	3500	4900	7000
Custom Panel Delivery	1130	2250	3750	5250	7500
Hudson 112 Series 89					
Cab Pickup	980	1950	3250	4550	6500
Panel Delivery	1050	2100	3500	4900	7000
Utility Coupe	680	1350	2250	3150	4500
Utility Coach	750	1500	2500	3500	5000
Utility Touring Coach	810	1620	2700	3800	5400

1939 HUDSON

HUDSON 112 — SERIES 90 — SIX-CYLINDER: — All 1939 Hudsons had a new front end, plus redesigned fenders that harmonized with the body styling. The grille was made up of right and left sections shaped somewhat like a harp. It had horizontal bars and did not go up as high on the nose of the trucks as it had in the past. The Hudson 112 models had torpedo headlights on the sides of the hood. Smoother and rounder front fenders were decorated with arrowhead-shaped ornaments on front. Ornamental grilles were added to the "catwalk" area of the fenders before production start up, but do not appear in preliminary sales literature. The trucks had alligator hoods controlled by an under-dash opening mechanism. Horizontal moldings decorated the hoodsides. Included in the 112 series were pickup and panels, as well as the bare chassis and chassis with cab (for aftermarket bodies), plus the "business car" models. In the latter group was the utility coach (with removable seats), utility coupe (with pull-out 3-position pickup box) and the station wagon (by U.S. Body & Forging Co.). In some used car guides, these are listed as passenger cars, but it seems that the factory thought of them as commercial vehicles. Both the trucks and the business cars were rated for ½-ton payloads.

I.D. DATA: Serial number located on top of cylinder block between number one and two exhaust manifold flanges. Serial and engine numbers are now the same. Starting: 90-101. Ending: 90-54902. Explanation: First two symbols indicate model year and series. The following symbols indicate sequential production number. Passenger cars and commercial vehicles made in mixed production.

IMPORTANT NOTE: On 1930 and later Hudson passenger cars, in addition to the above serial number location, the serial number was also stamped on the right frame on side rail above rear of front spring. Also, on inside right-hand door hinge pillar, just above hinge. Also, on right-hand side of frame ahead of front spring hanger. Truck sections in our reference sources do not list these additional serial number locations, although it is likely they were used on trucks, too. If this is true, from late-1938 on, the numbers stamped on the frame and door hinge pillar should match the numbers stamped on the original, factory-installed engine.

Model Hudson 112 Series (Trucks)	Body Type (½-Ton) (6-cyl.)	Price	Weight	Prod. Total
90	Chassis only	553	2025	Note 1
90	Chassis & Cab	654	2369	Note 1
90	Pickup	691	2770	Note 1
90	Custom Panel	850	2922	Note 1
(Business Cars)				
90	Utility Coach	725	2634	Note 1
90	Utility Coupe	750	2714	Note 1
90	Station Wagon	931	2880	Note 1

NOTE 1: Hudson shipped only 640 commercial vehicles (all series) in calendar 1939.

ENGINE: Inline. L-head. Six-cylinder. Chrome alloy block. Bore & stroke: 3 in. x 4⅛ in. Displacement: 175 cu. in. Compression ratio: 6.7:1. Brake horsepower: 86 at 4000 R.P.M. Net horsepower: 21.6. Three main bearings. Solid valve lifters. Carburetor: Carter model W1-438S.

1939 Hudson "Big Boy" Cab Pickup Express (OCW)

HUDSON "BIG BOY" — SERIES 98 — SIX-CYLINDER: — Hudson "Big Boy" trucks had the styling of the Hudson 112 models with a longer wheelbase. This year, the span between the front and rear wheels was even greater, growing two additional inches. Putting the wheels right under the center of the cargo area was said to provide better balanced load handling. Like Hudson 112 pickups, the "Big Boy" version carried its spare behind the cab and came with removable tool lockers on the inner sides of the box. Panel deliveries had a very streamlined appearance, especially when the rear quarter panels (which swept down at the rear) were finished in contrasting color. They had double rear doors, 151 cubic feet of load space and carried their spares inside, upright against a wall. All "Big Boy" models again had a ¾-ton payload rating. The larger 212 cu. in. six was optional in the larger trucks.

I.D. DATA: Serial number location: same as above. Starting: 98-101. Ending: 98-54902.

Model	Body Type	Price	Weight	Prod. Total
Hudson "Big Boy" Series — (¾-Ton) — (6-cyl.)				
98	Chassis only	592	2155	Note 1
98	Chassis & Cab	699	2556	Note 1
98	Pickup	743	2940	Note 1
98	Custom Panel	914	3072	Note 1
98	Taxicab (86 h.p.)	909	2912	Note 1
98	7P Taxi w/Partition (96 h.p.)	1139	3032	Note 1

NOTE 1: Hudson shipped only 640 commercial vehicles (all series) in calendar 1939.

ENGINE: Base engine was the 86 horsepower job described above under Hudson 112 engines.

ENGINE: (Big Boy Series, optional) Inline. L-head. Six-cylinder. Chrome alloy block. Bore & stroke: 3 in. x 5 in. Displacement: 212 cu. in. Compression ratio: 6.2:1. Brake horsepower: 96 at 3900 R.P.M. Net horsepower: 21.6. Three main bearings. Solid valve lifters. Carburetor: Carter model W1-438S.

HUDSON PACEMAKER — SERIES 91 — SIX-CYLINDER: — Hudson's Pacemaker 91 series gained some commercial vehicles in mid-1939. These trucks had one big styling difference from the more familiar models — their headlights were flush-mounted in the front fenders and somewhat teardrop-shaped. Only a panel delivery was offered to the public, although at least one pickup was built around the Hudson factory. Pacemaker panels had a 118 inch wheelbase. They were rated for ¾-ton and used the 212 cu. in. engine. Pacemakers were equipped with Auto-Poise Control. This consisted of a bar attached to the frame across the front of the chassis. Its ends were angled backward to form arms that attached to the front wheel spindles. The result was a torsional effect that pulled the wheels back to a center location whenever they moved away from a straight-ahead position. Checker Motors supplied the Pacemaker Panel body, which was the only model to still offer sidemounted spare tire location.

I.D. DATA: Serial number location: same as above. Starting: 91-101 and up.

Model	Body Type	Price	Weight	Prod. Total
Hudson Pacemaker Series — (¾-Ton) — (6-cyl.)				
91	Custom Panel	880	3037	Note 1

NOTE 1: Hudson shipped only 640 commercial vehicles (all series) in calendar 1939.

ENGINE: Base engine was the 96 horsepower job described above as a "Big Boy" option.

CHASSIS (Hudson 112): Wheelbase: 112 in. Overall length: 187⅞ in. Front tread: 56 in. Rear tread: 59.5 in. Tires: (std.) 16 x 6.00 in.; (opt.) 16 x 6.50 in. and 15 x7.00 in.

CHASSIS (Hudson "Big Boy"): Wheelbase: 119 in. Front tread: 56 in. Rear tread: 59.5 in. Tires: (std.) 16 x 6.00 in.; (opt.) 16 x 6.50 in. and 15 x7.00 in.

CHASSIS (Hudson Pacemaker): Wheelbase: 118 in. Overall length: 193-7/16 in. Front tread: 56 in. Rear tread: 59.5 in. Tires: 16 x 6.00 in. (other sizes may have been optional).

NOTE 1: The 15 x 7.00 tire option required special wheels.
NOTE 2: Standard tire size for "business cars" in the Hudson 112 series was 16 x 5.50.

TECHNICAL: Sliding gear transmission. Speeds: 3F/1R. Floor mounted gearshift lever. Single plate, type clutch w/cork inserts running in oil. Semi-floating rear axle. Overall ratio: 4.1:1. Four-wheel hydraulic brakes. Steel-disc wheels. Drivetrain options: Column gearshift control.

OPTIONS: Front bumper. Single sidemount (Pacemakers). Bumper guards. Removable tool lockers. Wheel trim rings. License plate holder. Radio. Antenna. OSRV mirror. Column gearshift control. Special paint. Two-tone paint. External sunvisor. Right-hand taillight. Deluxe equipment package. Dual windshield wipers. Dual sunvisor. Spotlight. Fog lamps. Grille guard. Whitewall tires. Oversize tires. Special 15 inch wheels. Heaters (custom and deluxe). Air electric horns. Seat covers.

HISTORICAL: Introduced: (Pacemaker) March 1939; (others) October 1938. Calendar year registrations: 409. Calendar year shipments: 640. Innovations: Flush-mounted headlights on Pacemaker. Column gearshift control available. Auto-Poise Control system. Two-inch longer wheelbase for "Big Boy" models. Catwalk grilles added for decoration. Historical notes: All panel delivery bodies were again built by Checker Motor Co. Utility coupes also offered in Hudson Six (Series 92), Country Club Six (Series 93) and Country Club Eight (Series 95) passenger car-lines.

Pricing

	5	4	3	2	1
1939					
Hudson 112 Series					
(Trucks)					
Pickup	980	1950	3250	4550	6500
Custom Panel	1050	2100	3500	4900	7000

500

	5	4	3	2	1
(Business Cars)					
Utility Coach	750	1500	2500	3500	5000
Utility Coupe	830	1650	2750	3850	5500
Station Wagon	1950	3900	6500	9100	13,000
Hudson "Big Boy" Series					
Pickup	1050	2100	3500	4900	7000
Custom Panel	1130	2250	3750	5250	7500
Taxicab (86 h.p.)	750	1500	2500	3500	5000
7P Partition Taxicab	830	1650	2750	3850	5500
Hudson Pacemaker Series					
Custom Panel	1170	2340	3900	5450	7800

1940 HUDSON

1940 Hudson Six Panel Delivery (DFW/MVMA)

HUDSON SIX — SERIES 40-C/40-T — SIX-CYLINDER: — For 1940, Hudsons adopted a ship's prow nose treatment. The grille consisted of seven more massive moldings running horizontally across the fender catwalks on either side. Fenders were flattened up a bit on the sides and more drastically arched at the top. Round sealed-beam headlights were set into teardrop-shaped chrome housings, with parking lamps directly below. Hood side trim was again horizontal. The chassis-only was dropped. There were "business cars" in the base Series 40 lineup again. "Red Books" do not show a station wagon, for this, or any, series. However, Hudson historian Alex Burr says that factory weight sheets list such a model, as well as a taxicab. While wheelbases increased by one inch, the ½-ton rating was continued. The trucks were known as Hudson Six models, Series 40-C. The business cars were known as Travelers, Series 40-T.

I.D. DATA: Serial number located in same location as 1939. Serial and engine numbers are the same. Starting: 40-101. Ending: 40-89192.

Model	Body Type	Price	Weight	Prod. Total
Hudson 6 Series — (½-Ton) — (6-cyl.)				
(Trucks)				
40-C	Chassis & Cab	654	2575	Note 1
40-C	Pickup	691	2945	Note 1
40-C	Panel Delivery	850	3225	Note 1
(Traveler Models)				
40-T	½-Ton Coach	719	2855	Note 1
40-T	½-Ton Coupe	672	2890	Note 1
40-T	Station Wagon	—	—	Note 1
40-T	Taxi	—	—	Note 1

NOTE 1: Shipment from factory totaled 1,035 for all series in calendar year.

ENGINE: Inline. L-head. Six-cylinder. Chrome alloy. Bore & stroke: 3.00 x 4.125 in. Displacement: 174.9 cu. in. Compression ratio: 6.5:1. Brake horsepower: 92 at 4000 R.P.M. Net horsepower: 21.6. Three main bearings. Solid valve lifters. Carburetor: Carter model WDO-454S two-barrel.

HUDSON "BIG BOY" — SERIES 48 — SIX-CYLINDER: — Hudson "Big Boy" commercial vehicles could be identified by their longer wheelbase. In addition, the hood side trim had three extra short horizontal moldings and the upper molding had a V-shaped piece hanging down like an icicle. The line included trucks, a carry-all for passengers (actually a large sedan) and a seven passenger sedan. The carry-all was actually a taxicab with changeable interior. By folding the three-passenger center seat forward, removing the rear seat cushion, raising the seat back and moving around the trunk shelf and spare tire, a six-foot long cargo area with level load floor was provided. Upholstery in this model was of durable, tan imitation leather. All "Big Boy" models were rated to carry ¾-ton payloads. In this series, the chassis and cab was not offered, but a bare chassis was. This could be used for aftermarket bodies of various design. A new 125 inch wheelbase was used.

I.D. DATA: Serial number location: Same as 1939. Starting: 48-101. Ending: 48-89192. Engine number location: Same as 1939.

Model "Big Boy" (Trucks)	Body Type Series — (¾-Ton) — (6-cyl.)	Price	Weight	Prod. Total
48-C	Chassis only	699	2675	Note 1
48-C	Pickup	743	3045	Note 1
48-C	Panel Delivery	914	3310	Note 1
(Business Cars)				
48-P	9P Carry-All Sedan	989	3245	Note 1
48-P	7P Sedan	1095	3140	Note 1

NOTE 1: Factory shipments totaled 1,035 for all series in calendar 1939.

ENGINE: Inline. L-head. Six-cylinder. Chrome alloy block. Bore & stroke: 3 in. x 5 in. Displacement: 212 cu. in. Compression ratio: 6.5:1. Brake horsepower: 98 at 4000 R.P.M. Net horsepower: 21.6. Three main bearings. Solid valve lifters. Carburetor: Carter model WDO-454S two-barrel.

CHASSIS (Traveler): Wheelbase: 113 in. Overall length: 190⅜ in. Height: 70.5 in. Front tread: 56¼ in. Rear tread: 59½ in. Tires: (std.) 16 x 6.00 in.; (opt.) 16 x 6.50 in. and 18 x6.00 in.

CHASSIS ("Big Boy"): Wheelbase: 125 in. Overall length: 202⅜ in. Height: 70.5 in. Front tread: 56¼ in. Rear tread: 59½ in. Tires: (std.) 16 x 6.00 in.; (opt.) 16 x 6.50 in.; 18 x6.00 in.; 15 x 7.00 in.

NOTE 1: 15 in. and 18 in. tires require special wheels.
NOTE 2: Pickup box lengths varied: by series as follows: (Traveler) 80 in.; ("Big Boy") 90 in.

TECHNICAL: Sliding gear transmission. Speeds: 3F/1R. Column mounted gearshift lever. Single plate, type clutch w/cork inserts running in oil. Semi-floating rear axle. Overall ratio: (Series 40) 4.555:1; (Series 48) 4.1:1. Four-wheel hydraulic brakes. Steel-disc wheels. Drivetrain options: overdrive.

OPTIONS: Turn signals ("Big Boy"). Air foam seat cushions. Weather master fresh air and heat control. Deluxe equipment package. Whitewall tires. Special paint. Two-tone paint. Over or undersize tires. Wheel trim rings. Radio and antenna. Seat covers. OSRV mirror. Tool lockers. Bumper guards. Grille guard. Fender skirts. Dual wipers. Right-hand taillight.

HISTORICAL: Introduced: Jan. 1940. Calendar year registrations: 760. Calendar year shipments: 1,035. Innovations: Sealed-beam headlights. Optional turn signals. Longer wheelbase for both series. New Carry-All sedan. Distributor relocated to rear of engine. Independent front coil spring suspension introduced. Larger rear leaf springs. Historical notes: Hudson dropped to tenth rank in auto industry. "Red ink" for the year totaled $1,507,780.

Pricing

1939	5	4	3	2	1
Hudson Six Series					
Pickup	980	1950	3250	4550	6500
Panel Delivery	1050	2100	3500	4900	7000
Traveler Line					
Utility Coach	750	1500	2500	3500	5000
Utility Coupe	830	1650	2750	3850	5500
Station Wagon	1950	3900	6500	9100	13,000
Taxi	750	1500	2500	3500	5000
"Big Boy" Series					
Pickup	1050	2100	3500	4900	7000
Panel Delivery	1130	2250	3750	5250	7500
9P Carry-All Sedan	830	1650	2750	3850	5500
7P Sedan	750	1500	2500	3500	5000

1941 HUDSON

1941 Hudson All-Purpose Delivery Van (OCW)

HUDSON SIX — SERIES C-10 — SIX-CYLINDER: — Up front, the '41 Hudsons looked like 1940 models. Wheelbases increased three inches. Hood side trim was revised and had a kind of "hockey stick" look. The grille gained two horizontal bars, for a total of nine. Commercial vehicles in the Hudson Six lineup included a pickup, all-purpose delivery and two Traveler utility models — the coach and the coupe. This year's station wagon was officially a passenger car in the C-11 Super Six series on a 121 inch wheelbase. (See the *Standard Catalog of American Cars 1805-1942* for information on this wagon.) The new All-Purpose Delivery truck was not a panel truck. It had a body made by Divco and was a walk-in type delivery van similar to a Divco milk truck or IHC Metro. However, the Hudson product was highly streamlined. There was also a change in the Traveler Utility Coupe. It no longer had the telescoping type slide-in pickup box. Instead, a cargo box was built into the trunk. It had a level plywood floor and hinged "tailgate."

I.D. DATA: Serial number located on top of cylinder block between number one and two exhaust manifold flanges. Serial and engine numbers are the same. Starting: C-1101 and up.

Model Hudson Six Series (Trucks)	Body Type — (½-Ton) — (6-cyl.)	Price	Weight	Prod. Total
C-10	Chassis & Cab	746	2575	Note 1
C-10	Pickup	782	2935	Note 1
C-10	All-Purpose Delivery	1176	3120	Note 1
(Travelers)				
C-10	Utility Coach	840	2900	Note 1
C-10	Utility Coupe	780	2890	Note 1

NOTE 1: Factory shipments totaled 812 units for all series in calendar 1941.

ENGINE: Inline. L-head. Six-cylinder. Chrome alloy block. Bore & stroke: 3.00 in. x 4.125 in. Displacement: 174.9 cu. in. Compression ratio: 7.25:1. Brake horsepower: 92 at 4000 R.P.M. Net horsepower: 21.6. Three main bearings. Solid valve lifters. Carburetor: Carter model WA1-454S one-barrel.

NOTE: The 212 cu. in., 98 horsepower engine was optional in the C-10 models. See "Big Boy" engine specifications below.

1941 Hudson "Big Boy" Cab Pickup Express (OCW)

"BIG BOY" — SERIES C-18 — SIX-CYLINDER: — "Big Boy" models now had a three inch longer wheelbase. Their slightly more elaborate hood side trim had one extra lower horizontal molding. A bigger 98 horsepower 6-cylinder engine was standard. The chassis-and-cab returned to the lineup, but the panel truck was gone. The Carry-All sedan and pickup were carried over on the new, longer wheelbase. There was also a "Big Boy" taxi cab.

I.D. DATA: Serial number location: Same as above. Starting: C-18-101 and up.

Model "Big Boy" Series (Trucks)	Body Type — (¾-Ton) — (6-cyl.)	Price	Weight	Prod. Total
C-18	Chassis & Cab	795	2670	Note 1
C-18	Pickup	834	3040	Note 1
C-18	9P Carry-All	1094	3200	Note 1
C-18	Taxicab			Note 1

NOTE 1: Factory shipments totaled 812 units for all series in calendar year.

ENGINE: Inline. L-head. Six-cylinder. Chrome alloy block. Bore & stroke: 3.00 in. x 5.00 in. Displacement: 212 cu. in. Compression ratio: 6.5:1. Brake horsepower: 98 at 4000 R.P.M. Net horsepower: 21.6. Three main bearings. Solid valve lifters. Carburetor: Carter model WDO-501S two-barrel.

CHASSIS (Series C-10): Wheelbase: 116 in. Overall length: 195¼ in. Height: 68 in. Front tread: 56¼ in. Rear tread: 59½ in. Tires: 16 x 6.00 in.

CHASSIS (Series C-18): Wheelbase: 128 in. Overall length: 216½ in. Height: 68¾ in. Front tread: 56¼ in. Rear tread: 59½ in. Tires: 15 x 7.00 in.

TECHNICAL: Sliding gear transmission. Speeds: 3F/1R. Column mounted gearshift lever. Single plate, type clutch w/cork inserts running in oil. Semi-floating rear axle. Overall ratio: (C-10) 4.5:1; (C-18) 4.1:1. Four-wheel hydraulic brakes. Steel-disc wheels. Drivetrain options: Vacumotive drive.

OPTIONS: Deluxe radio ($49.75). Custom heater/defroster ($26). Clock ($13.50). Spotlight ($17). Junior radio ($29.50). Custom radio ($67.50). Power radio antenna ($6.75). Weathermaster heater/defroster ($36). Directional signals ($17.50 or $19.50). Seat cover ($7.25). Large hub caps ($6.75). Air foam seats. Twin horn. Overdrive. Vacumotive drive. OSRV mirror. Special paint. Two-tone paint. Oversize tires. Wheel trim rings. License plate frame. Whitewall tires.

HISTORICAL: Introduced: Aug. 1, 1940. Calendar year registrations: 736. Calendar year shipments: 812. Innovations: Three inch longer wheelbases for all models. New Vacumotive drive option. All-Purpose delivery van introduced. Hudson promoted "symphonic" styling of interior color schemes. Historical notes: Hudson fell to 13th rank in the industry with 1941 business down by 9.5 percent from the year before. Hudson won *Safety Engineering* magazine's annual safety engineering awards. Taxi-cabs and station wagons were also made in the Country Club Eight series this year.

Pricing

	5	4	3	2	1
1941					
Hudson Six Series					
Pickup	980	1950	3250	4550	6500
All-Purpose Delivery	1200	2400	4000	5600	8000
Traveler Line					
Utility Coupe	830	1650	2750	3850	5500
Utility Coach	750	1500	2500	3500	5000
"Big Boy" Series					
Pickup	1050	2100	3500	4900	7000
9P Carry-All Sedan	830	1650	2750	3850	5500
Taxicab	750	1500	2500	3500	5000

1942 HUDSON

HUDSON - TRAVELER — SERIES T-20 — SIX-CYLINDER: — Hudsons had a longer, lower body appearance and lower height in 1942. The grille sported a wider horizontal bar treatment with the bottom three rows extending the full width of the trucks. The Traveler series consisted of the coach and coupe utility models; the last "commercial cars" Hudson was ever to build. Both, of course, looked outwardly like passenger cars. They even had the new "speedline" moldings on the front fender sides. Run-ningboards disappeared on both models. Both were shown with white sidewall tires in catalog artwork. The coach had the front window treat-ment of the Hudson DeLuxe six, but a plainer-looking type bumper. A utility box inside its trunk was a feature of the coupe. As in 1941, this was sta-tionary and did not slide out like a drawer. Hudson historian Alex Burr in an article in *Old Cars Weekly* noted that a factory AEB memo dated March 18, 1942 mentions a Model 28 commercial station wagon. How-ever, the only station wagon that contemporary reference sources give specifications for is the Model 21 Super Six version, which was officially a passenger car. This wagon is covered in the *Standard Catalog of American Cars 1805-1942* by Krause Publications.

I.D. DATA: Serial number located on top of cylinder block between number one and two exhaust manifold flanges. Serial and engine numbers are the same. Starting: T-20-101. Ending: T-20-41232.

Model	Body Type	Price	Weight	Prod. Total
Traveler Series — (½-Ton) — (6-cyl.)				
T-20	Utility Coupe	829	2900	Note 1
T-20	Utility Coach	867	2905	Note 1

NOTE 1: Factory shipments (all series) for calendar year were 67 units.

ENGINES: See specifications for "A" and "C" engines below.

ENGINE A: Inline. L-head. Six-cylinder. Chrome alloy block. Bore & stroke: 3.00 in. x 4.125 in. Displacement: 174.9 cu. in. Compression ratio: 7.25:1. Brake horsepower: 92 at 4000 R.P.M. Net horsepower: 21.6. Three main bearings. Solid valve lifters. Carburetor: Carter model WDO-501S two-bar-rel.

NOTE: This engine was standard equipment in all T-20 and C-20 models. The 102 horsepower six of 212 cu. in. was optional in T-20 models. The 98 horsepower version of the same engine was optional in C-20s.

ENGINE B: Inline. L-head. Six-cylinder. Chrome alloy block. Bore & stroke: 3.00 in. x 5.00 in. Displacement: 212 cu. in. Compression ratio: 6.5:1. Brake horsepower: 98 at 4000 R.P.M. Net horsepower: 21.6. Three main bearings. Solid valve lifters. Carburetor: Carter model WDO-501S two-bar-rel.

NOTE: This engine was optional in C-20s and standard in C-28s.

ENGINE C: Inline. L-head. Six-cylinder. Chrome alloy block. Bore & stroke: 3.00 in. x 5.00 in. Displacement: 212 cu. in. Compression ratio: 6.5:1. Brake horsepower: 102 at 4000 R.P.M. Net horsepower: 21.6. Three main bearings. Solid valve lifters. Carburetor: Carter model WDO-501S two-bar-rel.

NOTE: This engine was available, as an option, only in T-20 utility models.

HUDSON — SERIES C-20 — SIX-CYLINDER: — The Hudson Six commer-cial series was comparable to the Series 20P Deluxe Six Hudson passenger cars. The "C" prefix indicated commercial vehicle. There was only one model, the 116 inch wheelbase ½-ton pickup. New features included the 1942 grille and "draft-free" door glass system. The hood saw slight revision, too, but the trucks did not have all the up-dates that Hudson lavished on passenger cars such as speedboards in place of running-boards. This also meant they did not have the lower body perimeter mold-ings, which Hudson added to cars to hide a joint line caused by the elimi-nation of runningboards.

I.D. DATA: Serial number location: Same as above. Starting: C-22-101 and up. Engine number location: Same as above; unavailable.

Model	Body Type	Price	Weight	Prod. Total
Hudson Six Series — (½-Ton) — (6-cyl.)				
C-20	Pickup	907	2910	Note 1

NOTE 1: Factory shipments (all series) for calendar year were 67 units.

ENGINE: See specifications for engines "A" and "B" above.

HUDSON BIG BOY — SERIES C-28 — SIX-CYLINDER: — Another one-model series was the 1942 "Big Boy" line. This ¾-ton pickup was on a long 128 inch wheelbase. This gave a stance, similar to that of 1941 models, where the rear wheels were actually further back than the center of the cargo box. (Too bad they didn't have pickup models like Chevrolet's "Big Dooley" back in 1942, since Hudson's "Big Boy" would have made a great "country Cadillac"). We have already mentioned the fact that Hudson his-torian Alex Burr found factory references to a model 28 "Big Boy" station wagon dated in March 1942. "Whether any of these were actually built is not known," said Burr. "But, it is doubtful, as production of Hudson vehi-cles ceased for the duration of the war (on) about this date."

I.D. DATA: Serial number location: Same as above. Starting: C-28-101 and up. Engine number location: Same as above; unavailable.

Model	Body Type	Price	Weight	Prod. Total
Hudson "Big Boy" Series — (¾-Ton) — (6-cyl.)				
C-28	Pickup	961	3040	Note 1

NOTE 1: Factory shipments (all series) for calendar year were 67 units.

ENGINE: See specifications for engine "B" above.

CHASSIS (Series T-20): Wheelbase: 116 in. Overall length: 195¼ in. Height: 66½ in. Front tread: 56¼ in. Rear tread: 59½ in. Tires: 16 x 6.00 in.

CHASSIS (Series C-20): Wheelbase: 116 in. Overall length: 195¼ in. Height: 66½ in. Front tread: 56¼ in. Rear tread: 59½ in. Tires: 16 x 6.00 in.

CHASSIS (Series C-28): Wheelbase: 128 in. Overall length: 216½ in. Height: (loaded) 66½ in. Front tread: 56¼ in. Rear tread: 59½ in. Tires: 15 x 7.00 in.

TECHNICAL: Sliding gear manual transmission. Speeds: 3F/1R. Column mounted gearshift lever. Single plate, type clutch w/cork inserts running in oil. Semi-floating rear axle. Overall ratio: (C-20) 4.5:1; (C-28) 4.1:1. Four-wheel hydraulic brakes. Steel-disc wheels. Drivetrain options: Over-drive transmission. Drive-Master gearshifting. Vacumotive drive.

OPTIONS: Option availability and costs were nearly the same as 1941, with some indications that prices may have been lowered slightly. There was only one new radio option. It featured an auxiliary foot control but-ton, variable tone control and automatic volume control. Hudson claimed it was so advanced that car buyers wouldn't want another type. Vacumo-tive drive and overdrive were again offered. A new option was Drive-Mas-ter, an automatic clutch with vacuum power unit. The operation of this system is fully explained in Don Butler's book *The History of Hudson* by Crestline Publishing Co. of Sarasota, Fla.

HISTORICAL: Introduced: Aug. 23, 1941. Calendar year shipments: 67. Innovations: Runningboards eliminated on "business car" models. New Drivemaster system. Rear springs re-worked for 1½ in. height reduction. Trucks receive "draft free" side windows. Historical notes: World War II's outbreak brought an end to regular production on Feb. 5, 1942. Hudson had assets of $15,354,342 in 1942, against liabilities of $4,715,580. The company reported $10,638,762 in working capitol. Book value of its stock (1941 annual report) was $15.89. 1941 earnings per share were $2.36. Hudson began producing 1942 models on July 21, 1941. On Sept. 8, 1941, the company shipped the first Wright airplane engine parts it was produc-ing for the Allied war effort. An order to stop truck-making was issued, to all manufacturers, by the War Production Board, on March 4, 1942. Five days later, truck rationing began.

Pricing

	5	4	3	2	1
1942					
Traveler Series					
Utility Coupe	830	1650	2750	3850	5500
Utility Coach	750	1500	2500	3500	5000
Hudson Six Series					
Pickup	980	1950	3250	4550	6500
Hudson "Big Boy" Series					
Pickup	1050	2100	3500	4900	7000

1946 HUDSON

1946 Hudson Coupe Express Pickup (L. Capp)

CAB PICKUP — SERIES 58 — SIX-CYLINDER: — The only Hudson commercial vehicle to return after the war was the Cab Pickup (or Pick-up, as Hudson wrote it). This model had the wheelbase of the prewar "Big Boy" and a similar ¾-ton rating, but used a more powerful Super Six engine. It was separately merchandised as the Series 58 Pick-up. Styling changes from 1942 were very minor. The nose no longer had an ornament and vertical molding. A new hood mascot was positioned further back on the hood. The hood side molding lost the "icicle" that hung down from it in 1942. A more massive upper molding sat above a full-width grille that tucked-in at its center. A new center grille emblem was indirectly lighted and a more massive bumper protected the front end. Standard equipment included twin windshield wipers; 30-hour clock; single vibrator horn; rear vision mirror; speedometer; water temperature indicator; fuel gauge; Tele-flash signals for oil pressure and charge rate; complete lock equipment for all doors; ash receiver in instrument panel; package compartment with lock; Hi-Test safety glass; front bumper guards; cowl ventilator screen and water separator; choice of body colors; double lubrication system; vacuum automatic spark ignition system; 17-plate, 96-ampere-hour battery; extra-capacity ventilated generator with full voltage regulator; Finger-touch starting system; 16½ gallon fuel tank; large constant pressure fuel pump; 13-quart cooling system; independent front suspension with coil springs; semi-elliptic "splayed" rear springs; hydraulic shock absorbers and six-ply tires. The pickup cab came with a three-man front seat upholstered in durable leatheroid material. Features of the interior included latch type wing windows, "Handy Shift" column controls, a large rear window and big "Full-Vision" windshield. The Armored X-type frame with extra-deep, box-section side rails was reinforced with four crossmembers. "True Center-Point" steering (described previously) was featured. The pickup box had sturdy steel sides and a heavy-gauge reinforced steel floor. It measured 93 inches long, 48⅜ inches wide and 18-5/16 inches high. This provided 48 cubic feet of cargo carrying space. Loading height, floor to ground, was 26⅜ inches loaded and 30 inches unloaded. Exterior dimensions included a 64¾ inch cab width and 57 inch load box width.

1946 Hudson Coupe Express Pickup (OCW)

I.D. DATA: Serial number located on a boss near top and left side of cylinder block. Also on cylinder block between number one and number two exhaust manifold. Also on front door hinge post. Starting: 38-101. Ending: 38-91194. Engine numbers and serial numbers were the same.

Model Series	Body Type 58 — (¾-Ton) — (6-cyl.)	Price	Weight	Prod. Total
58	Cab Pickup	1154	3080	3104

ENGINE: Inline. L-head. Six-cylinder. Chrome alloy block. Bore & stroke: 3.00 in. x 5.00 in. Displacement: 212 cu. in. Compression ratio: 6.50:1. Brake horsepower: 102 at 4000 R.P.M. Net horsepower: 21.6. Three main bearings. Solid valve lifters. Carburetor: Carter model WDO-501S two-barrel.

CHASSIS (Series 58): Wheelbase: 128 in. Overall length: 216½ in. Height: (unloaded) 67⅝ in., (loaded) 66½ in. Front tread: 56¼ in. Rear tread: 59½ in. Tires: 16 x 6.50 (six-ply).

TECHNICAL: Sliding gear manual transmission. Speeds: 3F/1R. Column mounted gearshift lever. Single plate, type clutch w/cork inserts running in oil. Semi-floating rear axle. Overall ratio: 4-5/9:1. Double-Safe four-wheel hydraulic brakes. Steel-disc wheels. Drivetrain options: Handi-shift. Overdrive. Vacumotive drive. Drive-Master.

OPTIONS: White sidewall tires (not available until 1947). Directional signals ($26). Weather-Master heater. Radio ($77). Vacumotive drive ($40). Drive-Master, includes Vacumotive Drive ($98). Overdrive ($88). OSRV mirror. Wheel trim rings ($13). Commodore bumper bar extensions ($10). Commodore electric clock ($14). Large hub caps ($9). Oil bath air cleaner ($3). Combination fuel and vacuum pump ($7). Cream wheel color (no cost). Commodore fender lamps ($16). Commodore horn ring with standard steering wheel ($6). Custom 18 inch steering wheel with horn ring ($19).

HISTORICAL: Introduced: Oct. 1, 1945. Calendar year shipments: 3,104. Innovations: Super-Six engine made standard in pickup trucks. New grille styling. Latest type sealed-beam headlights used. Historical notes: Production of postwar Hudsons began on Aug 30, 1945. The company displayed a 1909 Hudson at the Automotive Golden Jubilee in Detroit, Mich. Production of pickup trucks leaped 282.3 percent from 1941 totals. Hudson, however, built fewer passenger cars than 1941.

Pricing

1946 Cab Pick-Up Series	5	4	3	2	1
Cab Pickup	1050	2100	3500	4900	7000

1947 HUDSON

1947 Hudson Coupe Express Pickup (OCW)

CAB PICKUP — SERIES 178 — SIX-CYLINDER: — Styling was very modestly altered for 1947. In fact, the main change was a larger company emblem above the grille. It was set in a redesigned die-casting with flared edges. The front bumper guards of cars were more widely spaced apart and key locks were used on the driver's door. However, the bumper guards used on trucks were the same found on 1942 "Big Boy" models. Thus, the minor grille and door lock changes are the main changes between 1946 and 1947 pickups. The pickups, again unlike cars, still had runningboards. Standard equipment details were the same as listed for 1946 pickups in the previous entry. The trucks were now designated part of the "178" Hudson series and were, indeed, the only model in this line. They were, again, ¾-ton rated. GVW ratings were 4,810 pounds; the same as 1946 models.

1947 Hudson Coupe Express Pickup (OCW)

I.D. DATA: Serial number locations: Same as 1946. Starting: 178-101. Ending: 178-88724. Engine number locations: Same as 1946. Serial numbers and engine numbers were the same.

Model Series 178 — (¾-Ton) — (6-cyl.)	Body Type	Price	Weight	Prod. Total
178	Cab Pickup	1522	3110	2917

1947 Hudson Coupe Express Pickup (OCW)

ENGINE: Inline. L-head. Six-cylinder. Cast alloy block. Bore & stroke: 3.00 in. x 5.00 in. Displacement: 212 cu. in. Compression ratio: 6.50:1. Brake horsepower: 102 at 4000 R.P.M. Net horsepower: 21.6. Three main bearings. Solid valve lifters. Carburetor: Carter model WDO-151S two-barrel.

CHASSIS (Series 178): Wheelbase: 128 in. Overall length: 216½ in. Height: (unloaded) 67⅝ in., (loaded) 66½ in. Front tread: 56¼ in. Rear tread: 59½ in. Tires: 16 x 6.50 (six-ply).

TECHNICAL: Sliding gear manual transmission. Speeds: 3F/1R. Column mounted gearshift lever. Fluid-cushioned, triple-sealed single-plate type clutch w/cork inserts running in oil. Semi-floating rear axle. Overall ratio: 4-5/9:1. Double-Safe four-wheel hydraulic brakes. Steel-disc wheels. Drivetrain options: Handi-shift. Overdrive. Vacumotive drive. Drive-Master.

OPTIONS: Vacumotive drive ($40). Drive-Master, includes Vacumotive Drive ($98). Oil bath air cleaner ($3). Overdrive transmission ($88). Combination fuel and vacuum pump ($7). Rear axle with 4-1/9:1 gear ratio (no cost). Air foam seat cushion ($9). Front bumper bar extension ($10). Electric clock ($14). Fender top lamps ($16). Horn ring with standard 17 in.

steering wheel ($19). Right side inside sunvisor ($3). Large hub caps ($9). Custom 18 in. steering wheel with horn ring ($19). Oversize tires with large hub caps ($28). Turn signals ($26). Radio ($77). Weather-Master heater ($50). Chrome wheel rings ($13). Two-tone finish ($18). 6.50 x 15 or 7.00 x 15 in. tires. White sidewall tires (available late 1947).

1947 Hudson Coupe Express (EK/VVV)

HISTORICAL: Introduced: Dec. 1946 (sales began). Calendar year shipments: 2,917. Innovations: New grille emblem. Whitewall tires returned as optional equipment late in 1947 model-year. Redesigned door handles. Historical notes: Six prototype wood-bodied station wagons were built and used around the Hudson factory. Discounting AMC as a continuation of Hudson, this was the company's last year of commercial vehicle production. Historian Donald F. Butler, who worked for Hudson at this time as a designer, sketched a pickup version of the soon-to-be-released Hudson "Step-Down" models. It appears on page 282 of his book *The History of Hudson* (Crestline Publishing). According to Butler, Hudson also built a prototype Step-Down pickup with a 1949 serial number during 1948.

1947 Hudson Coupe Express Pickup (OCW)

Pricing

1947 Series 178	5	4	3	2	1
Pickup	1050	2100	3500	4900	7000

IHC

By John Gunnell

The history of International Harvester Co. traces back to the invention of the McCormick reaper, in 1831. This researcher's grandfather sold such farm machines, for Cyrus McCormick, in the 1880s. It was in 1902, that the IHC merger took place.

1907 IHC Auto Wagon Delivery Van (OCW)

1905 IHC Auto Wagon (Mike Carbonella Photo)

1913 IHC Model MW Flareboard Express (R. Theimer)

1907 IHC Auto Wagon Delivery Van (J. Small)

By 1907, series production of the IHC high-wheel Auto-Buggy began. Almost immediately, grain box models were offered. These were called Auto-Wagons and were actually light-duty trucks. Van, buses and more substantial express wagons were on the road by 1912. A year later, the company decided that its motor vehicle operations should be concentrated on the manufacture of trucks.

1915 IHC Model AW Flare Board Express (D. Christie)

In 1915, a new line of four-cylinder trucks with a "shovel-nose" hood — like Renaults of the day — was brought out. These had payloads ranging upwards from 3/4-ton. A unique feature was placement of the radiator *behind* the engine.

1922 IHC Model S "Red Baby" (Hope Emerich)

A line of famous IHC models, new for 1921, was designated the "S" series. These trucks became popularly known as "Red Babies," due to their small size and bright red finish. They were marketed through IHC farm equipment dealers and caught on with American farmers. The "S" stood for speed-truck and they could zip along at up to 30 m.p.h. A popular configuration was the 1/2-ton pickup.

Production of 50,000 units, in 1929, put IHC in the big leagues. With 170 sales branches, the company blanketed the country and ranked high against major competitors. In fact, for a while, only Chevy and Ford outdid IHC in truck business. It would be years before Dodge and GMC overtook International.

1935 IHC Screenside Delivery (D.H. Landis)

Through the 1930s, IHC adopted alphabetical designations, producing the A- (1930-1932), B- (1933-1934) and C- (1934-1936) series. By this time, there were 217 agencies nationwide.

The "C" series trucks are famous for being the first IHCs to sport car-like styling. They had a v-type aluminum grille and slanted windshield.

A significant light-duty model evolved for 1937. It brought a more modern, streamlined appearance to the line, with its fat-fendered look and turret top styling. Handsome pickups and panel trucks were joined by a wood-bodied station wagon that received lots of promotional attention.

1938 IHC Model D-2 Station Wagon (OCW)

Introduced in 1940, the graceful-looking "K" series carried IHC through the World War II era in grand style. It survived, with just modest changes, through 1949. Also notable was a 1938 innovation, the Metro-bodied multi-stop delivery van. This small businessman's dream truck would soon be available in bakery truck, milk truck and mini-bus styles.

Postwar buyers were treated to a new "KB" model in 1949. It had a steering column mounted gearshift and 82 h.p. "Green Diamond" six. It was also about this time that the Travelall, a station wagon-like panel truck, debuted.

1951 IHC Pickup (J.R. Faureau)

During the early 1950s, handsomely styled "R" and "S" series trucks were produced. They pioneered such features as one-piece wraparound windshields, two-tone paint jobs and 12-volt electrical systems. Continuing to do yoeman's duties were a wide variety of Metros, with styling much like that of prewar times.

IHC went back to the "A" designation in 1957-1958. This time the letter stood for "anniversary," as this was considered the company's 50th anniversary of truck-making. New for 1959, were "C" models with quad headlights, V-8 engines and optional "Bonus Load" styling. These trucks had slab-sided rear quarters, instead of pontoon fenders. IHC advertised "the box is as wide as the cab" and "25 percent more cargo room."

(Continued to page 571)

1909 IHC

1909 IHC Auto Wagon Express (OCW)

AUTO WAGON — MODEL A — TWO-CYLINDER: — International Harvester Company was formed in 1907. The company's first light-duty truck was the Auto Wagon, a commercial version of the Auto Buggy passenger car. Both vehicles were high-wheeler types using a 20 h.p. air-cooled two-cylinder engine. The Auto Wagons had a wagon-like express body mounted on the steel frame behind a high platform on which the two-passenger seat was placed. Most of the body work was of wood. While early Auto Buggies employed a tiller steering system, a steering wheel seems to have been standardized with the appearance of the 1908 sales catalog. Thus, all of these "trucks" probably had steering wheels. Speeds up to 20 m.p.h. were possible, although 10-12 m.p.h. was the regular cruising speed range. Accessory rear seats were available to change the Auto Wagon into a part-time passenger car.

I.D. DATA: Serial number located on manufacturer's plate. Auto Buggy and Auto Wagon serial numbers were in the same sequence. Serial numbers appear to be consecutive and carried over from year-to-year through 1912. An Auto Wagon belonging to the Indianapolis Motor Speedway "Hall of Fame" museum bears serial number 2551. This corresponds with information that 2,700 IHCs were built between Oct. 1907 and March 1910. Specific starting and ending numbers, by year, are not available.

Model	Body Type	Price	Weight	Prod. Total
A	Auto Wagon - 2P	600	1600	Note 1

NOTE 1: See serial number data.

ENGINE: Horizontal-opposed. Four-cycle. Air-cooled. Two-cylinder. Cast iron block. Displacement: 196.25 cu. in. Bore & stroke: 5 in. x 5 in. ALAM horsepower: 14-20 h.p. Cooling: Double fan system. Ignition: Via six battery cells. Carburetor: Described as "reliable and simple." Induction system ued a "reliable" carburetor.

CHASSIS: Wheelbase: 84 in. Front tread: 56 in. Rear tread: 56 in. Tires: Various sizes up to 44 in. diameter.

TECHNICAL: Planetary transmission. Speeds: 2F/1R. Outboard-mounted gear shift lever. Positive type clutch. Chain-drive. Rear wheel brakes. Wood spoke wheels.

OPTIONS: Single front-mounted acetylene gas headlamp. Front-mounted gas tank. Rear passenger seat. Front seat cushions.

HISTORICAL: Introduced during 1909. First IHC commercial vehicle. The Auto Wagon is said to be the first IHC automobile to carry a model designation. It was not considered a "motor truck" until 1912. IHC specifications and serial numbers were not listed with the Association of Licensed Automobile Manufacturers indicating that the firm was not a member of ALAM. This "truck" was designed by Mr. E.A. Johnson.

Pricing

	5	4	3	2	1
1909 **Model A Series** Auto Wagon	2650	5250	8750	12,250	17,500

1910 IHC

1910 IHC Auto Wagon Express (OCW)

AUTO WAGON — MODEL A — TWO-CYLINDER: — The Model "A" IHC Auto Wagon was carried into 1910 without major changes. In 1910, model numbers were begun as a means of parts identification, but not to designate particular models. There was a special "wide track" model-option featuring 60 in. wide front and rear treads which were better-suited for use on roads in southern states.

I.D. DATA: Serial number located on manufacturer's plate. Serial numbers above 2700 appeared after March 1910. Starting and ending numbers, by year, are not available.

Model	Body Type	Price	Weight	Prod. Total
A	Auto Wagon - 2P	800	1600	Note 1

NOTE 1: Total production of IHC high-wheelers between 1907 and 1912 was approximately 4,500. This includes both Auto Buggies and Auto Wagons. Production included 2,700 built through March 1910 and about 1,800 built thereafter.

ENGINE: Horizontal-opposed. Four-cycle. Air-cooled. Two-cylinder. Cast iron block. Displacement: 196.5 cu. in. Bore & stroke: 5 in. x 5 in. ALAM horsepower: 14-20 h.p. Cooling: Double fan system. Ignition: Via six battery cells. Carburetor: Described as "reliable and simple."

CHASSIS: Wheelbase: 84 in. Front tread: 56 in. Rear tread: 56 in. Tires: Various sizes up to 44 in. diameter.

TECHNICAL: Planetary transmission. Speeds: 1F/2R. Outboard-mounted gear shift lever. Positive type clutch. Chain-drive. Rear wheel brakes. Wood spoke wheels.

OPTIONS: Single center front acetylene gas headlamp. Front-mounted gas tank. Rear passenger seat. Front seat cushion.

HISTORICAL: The initials IHC came into widespread use for these vehicles during 1910. The company built some four-cylinder passenger cars this year. After 1911, the IHC automobile department was shut down.

Pricing

	5	4	3	2	1
1910 **Model A Series** Auto Wagon	2650	5250	8750	12,250	17,500

1911 IHC

AUTO WAGON — MODEL A — TWO-CYLINDER: — The Model A IHC Auto Wagon entered its final year of production in 1911. By this time, dual brass headlamps and even cowl lamps were showing up on these primitive trucks. Although the name Auto Wagon would be replaced by the designation Motor Truck, and some refinements would occur, the IHC high-wheel commercial vehicles did not disappear.

1911 IHC Auto Wagon Utility Express (MVMA/DFW)

I.D. DATA: Serial number located on manufacturer's plate. All 1911 serial numbers were above 2,700. Number 4,500 was the approximate ending number for the series, as far as can be determined.

Model	Body Type	Price	Weight	Prod. Total
A	Auto Wagon - 2P	800	1600	Note 1

NOTE 1: It appears that approximately 1,800 vehicles were built in the 1911 series.

ENGINE: Horizontal-opposed. Four-cycle. Air-cooled. Two-cylinder. Cast iron block. Displacement: 196.5 cu. in. Bore & stroke: 5 in. x 5 in. ALAM horsepower: 14-20 h.p. Cooling: Double fan system. Ignition: Six battery cells.

CHASSIS: Wheelbase: 84 in. Front tread: 56 in. Rear tread: 56 in. Tires: Various sizes up to 44 in. diameter.

TECHNICAL: Planetary transmission. Speeds: 2F/1R. Outboard-mounted gear shift lever. Positive type clutch. Chain-drive. Rear wheel brakes. Wood spoke wheels.

OPTIONS: Single center-mounted front acetylene headlamp. Dual side-mounted acetylene headlamps. Rear passenger seat ("Sunday Go To Meeting" seat). Front seat cushions.

HISTORICAL: Final year for IHC automobile production.

Pricing

1911 Model A Series	5	4	3	2	1
Auto Wagon	2650	5250	8750	12,250	17,500

1912 IHC

MOTOR TRUCK — AW/MW — TWO-CYLINDER: — In its 1912 *Directory of Automobiles* the motoring publication *Automobile Trade Journal* referenced some new models bearing the familiar IHC logo. "The International Harvester Co., Harvester Building, Chicago, Ill. is exhibiting at the Chicago Show its 1000 lb. delivery wagon, with open panel express body," the report began, going on to describe a larger, more powerful high-wheel commercial vehicle that replaced the original Auto Wagon. The 1912 line actually consisted of "AW" and "MW" series and several new body types. An IHC-built air-cooled engine was used in the AW series. The MW models, at first, utilized a British-American-built water-cooled powerplant. This year, in addition to the open delivery, there were panel trucks, hucksters, canopy wagons, mail trucks and auto-buses. The high-wheelers were now called "Motor Trucks" and featured a short hood in the front, dual acetylene headlamps, cowl lamps and a horn. Many models were also fitted with full or partial side curtains, upholstered seats, fenders, folding windshields, tool boxes and auxiliary seats.

I.D. DATA: Serial number located on manufacturer's plate.

1912 IHC Motor Truck Delivery Van (HAC/DFW)

Model	Body Type	Price	Weight	Prod. Total
AA	½-Ton Dely. Wag. - 2P2P	800	2500	—
AW	½-Ton Panel Exp. - 2P	900	2540	—
MW	½-Ton Panel Exp. - 2P	950	2695	—
MW	½-Ton Can. Exp. - 9P	1050	2600	—
MA	½-Ton Dely. Wag. - 2P	850	2610	—

ENGINE (AW): Horizontal-opposed. Four-cycle. Air-cooled. Two-cylinder. Cast iron block. Displacement: 196.5 cu. in. Bore & stroke: 5 in. x 5 in. ALAM horsepower: 18-20 h.p. Ignition: Bosch magneto. Lubrication: Mechanical oiler system.

ENGINE (MW): Horizontal-opposed. Water-cooled. Two-cylinder. Cast iron alloy. Displacement: 196.5 cu. in. Bore & Stroke: 5 in. x 5 in. ALAM Horsepower: 15 h.p.

1912 IHC Motor Truck Express Wagon (OCW)

CHASSIS: Wheelbase: 90 in. Overall Length: 96 in. Height: 48 in. Front tread: 56 in. Rear tread: 56 in. Tires: Various sizes up to 44 in. diameter.

TECHNICAL: Individual clutch type transmission. Speeds: 2F/1R. Outboard-mounted gear shift lever. Positive type clutch. Chain-drive rear axle. Expanding/contracting rear wheel brakes. Wood spoke wheels.

OPTIONS: Dual acetylene headlamps. Cowl lamps. Side curtains. Upholstered seat. Auxiliary seats. 60 inch southern tread. Leather fenders. Acetylene tank. Tool box. Folding windshield. Tool boxes. Express box tarpauline. Canopy style top.

HISTORICAL: First true IHC trucks this year. New water cooled engine available. Last year for right-hand drive only. Some Auto Wagons still made (through 1916).

Pricing

1912	5	4	3	2	1
Series AA					
Dely. Wag.	2700	5400	9000	12,600	18,000
Series MW					
Dely. Wag.	2700	5400	9000	12,600	18,000
Panel Exp.	2800	5600	9350	13,100	18,700
Series AW					
Panel Exp.	2800	5600	9350	13,100	18,700

1913-1914 IHC

1913 IHC Motor Wagon Panel Express Wagon (OCW)

MOTOR TRUCK — AW/MW — TWO-CYLINDER: — There were four Motor Trucks offered by International Harvester Co. for the 1913 and 1914 model years. All were listed in used car reference books as Panel Express vehicles. At least some left-hand drive units appeared in 1913. Photos from the period suggest that many purpose-built bodies appeared and that open delivery wagons were still available.

I.D. DATA: Serial number located on manufacturer's plate.

1914 IHC Motor Wagon Canopy Delivery (OCW)

Model	Body Type	Price	Weight	Prod. Total
AA	½-Ton Panel Express - 2P	800	2500	—
AW	½-Ton Panel Express - 2P	900	2695	—
MA	½-Ton Panel Express - 3P	850	2610	—
MW	½-Ton Panel Express - 2P	950	2695	—

NOTE 1: Models AA and AW were rated for 800 lb. capacity
NOTE 2: Models MA and MW were rated for 1000 lb. capacity.
NOTE 3: Gross vehicle weights were as follows: (Model AA) 3300 lbs.; (Model AW) 3340 lbs.; (Model MA) 3610 lbs. and (Model MW) 3695 lbs.

ENGINE: Horizontal-opposed. Four-cycle. Air-cooled. Two-cylinder. Cast iron block. Displacement: 196.5 cu. in. Bore & stroke: 5 in. x 5 in. ALAM horsepower: 18-20 h.p. Ignition: Bosch magneto. Lubrication: Mechanical oiler system.

NOTE: The "M" engine had similar specifications, but featured water-cooling.

1914 IHC Model MW Flare Board Express (OCW)

CHASSIS: Wheelbase: 90 in. Overall Length: 96 in. Height: 48 in. Front tread: 56 in. Rear tread: 56 in. Tires: Sizes up to 44 in. diameter.

TECHNICAL: Individual clutch type transmission. Speeds: 2F/1R. Outboard-mounted gear shift lever. Positive type clutch. Chain-drive to rear axle. Expanding/contracting rear wheel brakes. Wood spoke wheels.

OPTIONS: Acetylene tank. Acetylene headlamps. Cowl lamps. Kerosene taillamp. Upholstered seat. Auxiliary seats. 60 inch souther tread. Leather fenders. Tool box. Two-piece folding windshield. Side curtains. Tool box. Express box tarpaulin. Canopy style top.

1914 IHC Model MA Flare Board Express (OCW)

HISTORICAL: First appearance of left-hand steering. Final full production year for air-cooled models as a "contemporary" product. (Some Model A's built through 1916). In 1914, the name International began to appear on the company's trucks, replacing the initials IHC.

Pricing

1913-1914	5	4	3	2	1
Series AA					
Panel Exp.	2700	5400	9000	12,600	18,000
Series AW					
Panel Exp.	2700	5400	9000	12,600	18,000
Series MA					
Panel Exp.	2800	5600	9350	13,100	18,700
Series MW					
Panel Exp.	2800	5600	9350	13,100	18,700

1915 IHC

MOTOR TRUCK — MODEL E/F — TWO-CYLINDER: — Different reference sources list different trucks in the IHC product line for 1915. There is a Model M ½-ton listed in one used car price book, along with the ¾-ton Model E. A vehicle weight guide from the State of Wisconsin shows only the ¾-ton Model E and one-ton Model F. And a *Branham Automobile Reference Book* shows only the one-ton Model F. The Model M was a carryover of the 1913-1914 Model MW. The Model E was probably a transitional model. However, the Model F was more revolutionary. It was an all-new, larger vehicle that was only nominally a light-duty truck. In most body configurations, it was clearly intended for heavy-duty usage. Among its innovations were a unique sloping hood, rear-mounted (behind engine) radiator, artillery wheels with hard rubber tires and built-in fenders. Also, below the hood was a new four-cylinder power plant.

I.D. DATA: Serial number located on manufacturer's plate on dashboard. Model F (only): Starting number 501. Ending number: 600.

Model	Body Type	Price	Weight	Prod. Total
M	½-Ton Chassis - 2P	750	2700	—
E	¾-Ton Chassis - 2P	1000	3300	—
F	1-Ton Chassis - 2P	1500	3950	99

NOTE 1: Branham's lists serial numbers 501 to 600 for the 1915 Model F, suggesting production of 99 units for the year.

NOTE 2: Capacity Ratings: (Model E) 1500 lbs.; (Model F) 2000 lbs.

NOTE 3: Gross Pounds: (Model E) 4800 lbs.; (Model F) 5950 lbs.

ENGINE: Inline. Cast en block. Four-cylinder. Cast iron block. Bore & stroke: 3½ in. x 5¼ in. ALAM horsepower: 19.60 h.p. Bosch or Dixie magneto ignition.

NOTE: The Model M used the same two-cylinder water-cooled engine of 1913-1914.

CHASSIS (Model F): Wheelbase: 128 in. Front tread: 56 in. Rear tread: 56 in. Tires: 36 in. diameter. See previous sections for specifications pertaining to other models.

TECHNICAL: Selective sliding transmission. Speeds: 3F/1R. Floor-mounted gear shift lever. Internal gear rear axle. Overall ratios: (Model F) 7.91:1. Expanding and contracting rear wheel brakes. Artillery spoke wheels.

OPTIONS: Headlamps. Cowl lamps. Taillights. Pneumatic tires ($55). Windshield. Side curtains. Electric lighting ($75).

HISTORICAL: The new-for-1915 four-cylinder engine had the same bore and stroke measurements as the Model 8-16 International farm tractor engine. The ¾-ton Model F found favor with many fire apparatus builders as the basis of a light-duty fire truck combining faster road speeds with rugged and durable construction. IHC held approximately four percent of the total domestic truck market in these years, which was considered a very strong showing.

Pricing

1915	5	4	3	2	1
Model M					
½-Ton Chassis	1500	3000	5000	7000	10,000
Model E					
¾-Ton Chassis	1425	2850	4750	6650	9500
Model F					
1-Ton Chassis	1500	2950	4950	6900	9900

1916-1920 IHC

MOTOR TRUCK — MODEL H/F — FOUR-CYLINDER: — International Harvester Co. was primarily involved in the heavy-duty truck building market through 1920. Models between one-ton and 3-½-tons represented the mainstay products during this period. Nevertheless, there were two offerings — the one-ton Model F and the ¾-ton Model H, that *some* light commercial vehicle fans will insist should be covered here. The Model F specifications (presented in the previous section) remained unchanged during this time span. Refer back to 1915 for these. The Model H was a similar looking vehicle, but on a slightly smaller scale. It also featured the sloping, Renault-like hood, behind-the-engine radiator and the 20 h.p. four-cylinder engine. After its introduction in 1916, this ¾-tonner was carried over, through 1920, with the main change each season being the manufacturer's suggested retail price.

I.D. DATA: Serial number located on manufacturer's plate on the dashboard. Annual starting and ending numbers are as follows:

	MODEL F	MODEL H
(1916)	601-1417	501-1096
(1917)	1418-3956	1097-3300
(1918)	3957-7385	3301-5304
(1919)	7386-8976	5305-5999
(1920)	8977-& up	6000-& up

Model 1916	Body Type	Price	Weight	Prod. Total
F	1-Ton Express	1550	3950	816
H	¾-Ton Express	1250	3650	595
1917				
F	1-Ton Chassis	1500	3950	2538
H	¾-Ton Chassis	1225	3650	2203
1918				
F	1-Ton Chassis	1750	3950	3428
H	¾-Ton Chassis	1450	3650	2200
1919				
F	1-Ton Chassis	1750	3950	1590
H	¾-Ton Chassis	1450	3650	694

Model 1920	Body Type	Price	Weight	Prod. Total
F	1-Ton Chassis	—	3950	—
H	¾-Ton Chassis	—	3650	—

NOTE 1: Production estimates above based on serial numbers. Increased production consistent with World War I demand for trucks.

NOTE 2: GVW Ratings: (Model F) 5950 lbs.; (Model H) 5150 lbs.

ENGINE: Inline. Cast en block. Four-cylinder. Cast iron block. Bore & stroke: 3½ in. x 5¼ in. ALAM horsepower: 19.60 h.p. Holley carburetor. Magneto ignition by Bosch or Dixie.

CHASSIS (Model F): Wheelbase: 128 in. Front tread: 56 in. Rear tread: 56 in. Tires: 36 in. diameter.

CHASSIS (Model H): Wheelbase: 115 in. Front tread: 56 in. Rear tread: 56 in.

TECHNICAL: Selective sliding transmission. Speeds: 3F/1R. Floor-mounted gear shift lever. Internal gear rear axle. Overall ratio: (Model F) 7.91:1; (Model H) 6.8:1. Expanding and contracting rear wheel brakes. Artillery spoke wheels.

OPTIONS: Headlamps. Cowl lamps. Taillights. Pneumatic tires ($55). Windshield. Side curtains. Electric lighting ($75).

HISTORICAL: Like other U.S. truck manufacturers, IHC made a formidable effort to support the Allied Operations in Europe during World War I. On June 14, 1916, an IHC Model F became the first truck to climb Pike's Peak in Colorado. The last of the original Auto Wagons left the IHC Akron works in Akron, Ohio in 1916. In 1919, IHC purchased the Parlin & Orendorff Co. of Canton, Ill., a major farm equipment manufacturer, thereby strengthening the entire company.

Pricing

1916-1920 Model F	5	4	3	2	1
1-Ton Chassis	1500	2950	4950	6900	9900
Model H					
¾-Ton Chassis	1500	3000	5000	7000	10,000

1921 IHC

1921 IHC Model S "Red Baby" Pickup Truck

MOTOR TRUCK — MODELS S AND 21 — FOUR-CYLINDER: — Like other truck manufacturer's, International Harvester Co. introduced a line of smaller, faster "speed" trucks in 1921. The new Model S was one of these. It was rated for ¾-ton and featured a conventional style hood, flat radiator and pneumatic tires. The engine used was a Lycoming KB four-cylinder with the radiator in front. Standard features included electric starting and lighting, a storage battery, power tire pump and electric horn. These trucks were painted bright red at the factory and they became known as "Red Babies." Their scaled-down size and lighter weight made road speeds of 25 to 30 m.p.h. possible. A one-ton Model 21 truck was also offered to replace the earlier and similar Model H. This truck retained the sloping hood and rear-of-engine radiator mounting. It was not a true light-duty truck in today's meaning of the term, but some light commercial vehicle buffs do collect such rigs that fall into the borderline one-ton class.

I.D. DATA: Serial number located on manufacturer's plate on dash. (Model S) Serial numbers 101 through 2600 were used in 1921. (Model 21) Serial numbers through 567 were used in 1921, but beginning number is unavailable. Engine numbers located on left-hand side at base of engine block.

Model 1921	Body Type	Price	Weight	Prod. Total
Model S Series				
S	¾-Ton Chassis	—	2600	2499
Model 21 Series				
21	1-Ton Chassis	—	3030	566

NOTE 1: Production totals are estimates based on serial number references.

NOTE 2: Prices were listed as "available upon application" since dealer discounts were common.

NOTE 3: (Model S) Net Wt. = 3511 lbs.; Load Capacity = 1500 lbs.; GVW = 5011 lbs. (Model 21) Net Wt. = 3980 lbs.; Load Capacity = 2000 lbs.; GVW = 5980 lbs. (Data from Wisconsin state weight guide.)

ENGINE: Inline. L-head. Four-cylinder. Cast iron block. Bore & stroke: 3½ in. x 5¼ in. Displacement: 192.4 cu. in. Brake horsepower: 35 at 2100 R.P.M. Net horsepower: 19.60 (ALAM). Main bearings: Two. Valve lifters: Solid. Carburetor: Ensign model.

CHASSIS (Model S): Wheelbase: 115 in. Front tread: 56 in. Rear tread: 56 in. Tires: 30 x 5.25 pnuematic.

NOTE: A 124 inch wheelbase appears to have been optional.

CHASSIS (Model 21): Wheelbase: 115 in. Front tread: 56 in. Rear tread: 56 in. Tires: 30 x 5.25 pnuematic.

TECHNICAL (Model S): Selective sliding transmission. Speeds: 3F/1R. Floor-mounted gearshift. Clutch: Multiple disc type. Semi-floating rear axle. Overall ratio: 6.3:1. Rear wheel brakes. Artillery spoke wheels.

NOTE: Technical data for the Model 21 is similar to the 1916-1920 Model H. Exception: 6.8:1 final gear ratio.

OPTIONS: Full-length running boards. Speedometer. Variety of cabs and bodies. Wire spoke wheels. Taillight.

HISTORICAL: Production: Over 33,000 IHC Model S trucks were built between 1921 and 1926. Innovations: During this period, IHC had a large force of field representatives to maintain contact with its farm implement dealers and agents nationwide. They were called blockmen and drove red Model S pickups as service trucks. Before long, these "Red Babies" seemed as common in rural areas as Model T Fords. A cast iron promotional model toy version was made. In addition, the Buddy L toy company also sold a toy version of the Model S. Both of these toys are collectible items now. During 1921, IHC Model S truck manufacturing moved to the Springfield Works, Springfield, Ohio.

Pricing

1921	5	4	3	2	1
Model S Series — (¾-Ton)					
Chassis	1050	2100	3500	4900	7000
Pickup	1450	2850	4750	6650	9500
Express	1350	2700	4500	6300	9000
Stake	1350	2700	4500	6300	9000
Ambulance	1450	2850	4750	6650	9500
Panel	1450	2850	4750	6650	9500
Model 21 Series — (1-Ton)					
Chassis	980	1950	3250	4550	6500
Express	1200	2400	4000	5600	8000
Panel	1300	2550	4250	5900	8500
Stake	1200	2400	4000	5600	8000
Dump	1300	2550	4250	5900	8500
-Tank	1350	2700	4500	6300	9000

1922 IHC

MOTOR TRUCK — MODELS S AND 21 — FOUR-CYLINDER: — Both the Model S and Model 21 were carried over, basically unchanged, for model year 1922. The weights of both saw a slight increase, suggesting the inclusion of more standard equipment. An "Inspection Service Policy" was offered to buyers this season.

I.D. DATA: Serial number located on manufacturer's plate on dash. Serial numbers 2601 to 9900 were used on 1922 Model S trucks. Serial numbers 568 to 787 were used on 1922 Model 21 trucks. Engine numbers located on left side of motor at base.

Model	Body Type	Price	Weight	Prod. Total
Model S Series				
S	¾-Ton Chassis	—	2761	7299
Model 21 Series				
21	1-Ton Chassis	—	3030	219
21	1-Ton Chassis	—	3160	219

1922 IHC Model S "Red Baby" Pickup (John Scott)

NOTE 1: Production totals are estimates based on serial number references.

NOTE 2: Prices listed "available upon application" due to dealer discount programs.

NOTE 3: (Model S) Net. Wt. = 3661 lbs.; Load Capacity = 2000 lbs.; GVW = 5661 lbs. (Model 21) Net. Wt. = 4030 lbs.; Load Capacity = 2000 lbs.; GVW = 6030 lbs. (Data from Wisconsin state weight guide.)

ENGINE: Inline. L-head. Four-cylinder. Cast iron block. Bore & stroke: 3½ in. x 5¼ in. Displacement: 192.4 cu. in. Brake horsepower: 35 at 2100 R.P.M. ALAM horsepower: 19.60 h.p. Two main bearings. Solid valve lifters. Ensign carburetor.

CHASSIS (Model S): Wheelbase: 115/124⅛ in. Front tread: 56 in. Rear tread: 56 in. Tires: 30 x 5.25 pnuematic.

CHASSIS (Model 21): Wheelbase: 115 in. Front tread: 56 in. Rear tread: 56 in. Tires: 30 x 5.25 pneumatic.

TECHNICAL (Model S): Selective sliding transmission. Speeds: 3F/1R. Floor-mounted gear shift lever. Multiple disc type clutch. Semi-floating rear axle. Overall ratio: 6.3:1. Rear wheel brakes. Artillery spoke wheels.

NOTE: Technical data for Model 21 similar to 1916-1920 Model H. Final gear ratio changed to 7.0:1 this year.

OPTIONS: Full-length running boards. Speedometer. Variety of cabs and bodies. Wire spoke wheels. Front bumper. Taillight.

HISTORICAL: Approximately 7,500 of the ¾-ton and one-ton trucks were made this year. Free inspection service policy was offered this year.

Pricing

1922	5	4	3	2	1
Model S Series — (¾-Ton)					
Chassis	1050	2100	3500	4900	7000
Pickup	1450	2850	4750	6650	9500
Express	1350	2700	4500	6300	9000
Stake	1350	2700	4500	6300	9000
Ambulance	1450	2850	4750	6650	9500
Panel	1450	2850	4750	6650	9500
Model 21 Series — (1-Ton)					
Chassis	980	1950	3250	4550	6500
Express	1200	2400	4000	5600	8000
Panel	1300	2550	4250	5900	8500
Stake	1200	2400	4000	5600	8000
Dump	1300	2550	4250	5900	8500
Tank	1350	2700	4500	6300	9000

1923 IHC

MOTOR TRUCK — MODEL S AND MODEL 21 — FOUR-CYLINDER: — The Model S had a slightly lower shipping weight, but higher hood and load capacity this season. It was up-rated to a one-tonner. There was no basic change in design, however. The Model 21 was carried over from 1922 with unchanged specifications. Serial and motor number locations changed this year.

1923 IHC Panel Delivery (Giant Mfg. Co./DFW)

I.D. DATA: Serial number located on floorboard in right side of driving compartment. Serial numbers 9901 to 20644 were used on 1923 Model S trucks. Serial numbers for the Model 21 started at 787, with ending number not available. Engine numbers located on left-hand side of crankcase.

Model	Body Type	Price	Weight	Prod. Total
Model S Series				
S	1-Ton Chassis	—	2700	10,743
Model 21 Series				
21	1-Ton Chassis	—	3030	—

NOTE 1: Model S production total is an estimate based on serial number references.

NOTE 2: Prices listed "available upon application" due to dealer discount program.

NOTE 3: (Model S) Net Wt. = 3650 lbs.; Load Capacity = 2000 lbs.; GVW = 5650 lbs. (Model 21) Net Wt. = 3980 lbs.; Load Capacity = 2000 lbs.; GVW = 5980 lbs. (Data from Wisconsin State weight guide).

ENGINE: Inline. L-head. Four-cylinder. Cast iron block. Bore & stroke: 3½ in. x 5¼ in. Displacement: 192.4 cu. in. Brake horsepower: 35 at 2100 R.P.M. Net horsepower: 19.60 (ALAM). Main bearings: Two. Valve lifters: Solid. Carburetor: Ensign.

CHASSIS (Model S): Wheelbase: 115/128 in. Front tread: 56 in. Rear tread: 56 in. Tires: 30 x 5.25 pneumatic.

CHASSIS (Model 21): Wheelbase: 115/128 in. Front tread: 56 in. Rear tread: 56 in. Tires: 30 x 5.25 pneumatic.

TECHNICAL (Model S): Selective sliding transmission. Speeds: 3F/1R. Floor-mounted gearshift. Clutch: Multiple disc type. Semi-floating rear axle. Overall ratio: 6.3:1. Rear wheel brakes. Artillery spoke wheels.

NOTE: Technical data for Model 21 similar to 1916-1920 Model H.

OPTIONS: Full-length running boards. Speedometer. Variety of cabs and bodies. Wire spoke wheels. Front bumper. Taillight.

HISTORICAL: During 1923, a brand new IHC factory was built in Fort Wayne, Ind. This was the final season for production of the Model 21.

Pricing

	5	4	3	2	1
1923					
Model S Series (1-Ton)					
Chassis	1050	2100	3500	4900	7000
Pickup	1450	2850	4750	6650	9500
Express	1350	2700	4500	6300	9000
Stake	1350	2700	4500	6300	9000
Ambulance	1450	2850	4750	6650	9500
Panel	1450	2850	4750	6650	9500
Model 21 Series (1-Ton)					
Chassis	980	1950	3250	4550	6500
Express	1200	2400	4000	5600	8000
Panel	1300	2550	4250	5900	8500
Stake	1200	2400	4000	5600	8000
Dump	1300	2550	4250	5900	8500
Tank	1350	2700	4500	6300	9000

1924 IHC

1924 IHC Panel Delivery Van (OCW)

MOTOR TRUCK — MODEL S SPEED TRUCK — FOUR-CYLINDER: — The International (IHC identification was no longer used on the vehicles, although it was still the corporate abbreviation) Model S Speed Truck was carried over from 1923 without change. Please refer to the 1923 section for information about this model. The Model 21 was no longer available. Gone from all International trucks this season were sloped, French-style hoods and behind-the-engine radiators. The company, by now, had a total of 102 factory branches and 1,500 dealers. An industrial tractor was introduced by IHC this year under its McCormick-Deering farm equipment nameplate. Serial numbers 15800 to 20645 were found on 1924 Model S trucks, suggesting production of some 4,845 units. This brought total production of this truck, over four years, to more than 25,000 units.

1925 IHC

1925 IHC Huckster Express (Mike Carbonella Photo)

MOTOR TRUCK — SPECIAL DELIVERY — FOUR-CYLINDER: — A new ¾-ton Special Delivery model was introduced under the International truck nameplate this year. It had a 116 in. wheelbase and was powered by a four-cylinder Waukesha engine. This model carried the International name on the sides of its butterfly hood above eight vertical louvers, whereas the Model S had the name on the body sill behind the cab doors. Standard Special Delivery features included pneumatic tires, air cleaner, electric lights, electric starter and speedometer. Among a long list of extra-cost options were full-length running boards, water pump and deluxe nickle-plated radiator shell. This model should not be confused with the SD, an updated version of the Model S one-ton.

MOTOR TRUCK — MODELS S, SD AND SL — FOUR-CYLINDER: — The Model S continued to be available for one-ton truck buyers in 1925. It was joined by two new variations, the SD and SL, which were produced in relatively small numbers. All of these continued to use the 20 h.p. (ALAM) Lycoming Model K engine. This was the only year that the SD and SL were rated at one ton. Both were uprated to 1-½-tons for 1926 when they became the basis for IHC's first tractor-trailer truck series, with a 110 inch wheelbase. Also, the company started manufacturing buses this season and made at least several Lang-bodied buses on the Model S running gear, probably with an extended wheelbase.

I.D. DATA: Serial number located on floor board in right side of driving compartment. Serial numbers 501 and up were used on Special Delivery trucks. Serial numbers 20645 and up were used on Model S trucks. Serial numbers 501 and up were used on both Model SD and SL trucks. Engine numbers located on left side of crankcase.

Model	Body Type	Price	Weight	Prod. Total
Special Delivery Series — (¾-Ton)				
—	Spec. Dely.	—	1850	—
Model S Series (1-Ton)				
S	Chassis	—	2700	—
SD	Chassis	—	2855	—
SL	Chassis	—	3156	—

NOTE 1: Prices upon application due to dealer discount program.

NOTE 2: (Model S) Net. Wt. = 3650 lbs. w/pnuematic tires; Load Capacity = 2000 lbs.; GVW = 5650 lbs. (Model SD) Net Wt. = 3720 lbs.; Load Capacity = 2000 lbs.; GVW = 5720 lbs. (Data from Wisconsin state weight guide.)

ENGINE (Special Delivery): Inline. L-head. Waukesha four-cylinder. Cast iron block. Bore & stroke: 3¼ in. x 4½ in. Displacement: 149.3 cu. in. Net horsepower: 16.90. Solid valve lifters. Carburetor: Own.

ENGINE (Model S, SD and SL): Inline. L-head. Lycoming four-cylinder. Cast iron block. Bore & stroke: 3½ in. x 5¼ in. Displacement: 192.4 cu. in. Brake horsepower: 35 at 2100 R.P.M. Net horsepower: 19.60 (ALAM) Two main bearings. Solid valve lifters. Ensign carburetor.

CHASSIS (Special Delivery): Wheelbase: 116 in. Front tread: 56 in. Rear tread: 56 in. Tires: 30 x 5.25 pnuematic.

CHASSIS (Model S): Wheelbase: 115/124 in. Front tread: 56 in. Rear tread: 56 in. Tires: 30 x 5.25 pneumatic.

TECHNICAL (Model S): Selective sliding transmission. Speeds: 3F/1R. Floor-mounted gear shift lever. Multiple disc type clutch. Semi-floating rear axle. Rear wheel brakes. Artillery spoke wheels.

OPTIONS: Front bumper. Pneumatic tires. Full-length running boards. Nickel plated radiator (Special Delivery). Water pump (Special Delivery). Variety of bodies and cabs. Speedometer (std. on Special Delivery). Wire spoke wheels. Dual taillights.

HISTORICAL: IHC began manufacturing buses in 1925.

Pricing

	5	4	3	2	1
1925					
Special Delivery Series — (¾-Ton)					
Chassis	1200	2400	4000	5600	8000
Panel Dely.	1350	2700	4500	6300	9000
Model S Series — (1-Ton)					
Chassis	1050	2100	3500	4900	7000
Pickup	1350	2700	4500	6300	9000
Express	1300	2550	4250	5900	8500
Stake	1300	2550	4250	5900	8500
Ambulance	1350	2700	4500	6300	9000
Panel	1350	2700	4500	6300	9000
Lang Bus	980	1950	3250	4550	6500
Model SD Series — (1-Ton)					
Chassis	980	1950	3250	4550	6500
Model SL Series — (1-Ton)					
Chassis	980	1950	3250	4560	6500

1926 IHC

MOTOR TRUCK — MODEL S — FOUR-CYLINDER: — The nearest thing to a light-duty International truck in 1926 was the one-ton Model S speed chassis. A new shipping weight of 2670 lbs. was given for this model, which continued to use the four-cylinder Lycoming engine. Annual serial numbers, still found in the same locations, began with 27238-C. Little else about the truck seems to have changed. Consult the 1925 section of this catalog for additional information. The models SD and SL were up-rated to 1-½-tons and available as tractor-trailer trucks. The 1925 type Special Delivery model was no longer available, although a different truck using the same designation would be introduced in the spring of 1927 as the Series S Special Delivery. In general terms, this was the season that enclosed cabs began to appear in greater evidence on all IHC trucks.

1926 IHC Huckster Express (NI/DFW)

1927-1928 IHC

1927 IHC Light-Duty Stake Bed (OCW)

SPECIAL DELIVERY — SERIES S — FOUR-CYLINDER: — Featuring up-to-date, passenger car-like styling that set it apart from earlier IHC products, the second type of Special Delivery from International bowed in the spring of 1927. This ¾-ton C-cab panel delivery was characterized by a longer, lower hood, wider and flatter cowl, crisper body sills with full-length running boards, full crown fenders, drum headlights, a nickle-plated radiator shell, multiple vertical hood louvers and a lower overall body height. The engine was a 20 h.p. Waukesha four-cylinder. A 116 inch wheelbase was featured in 1927, growing to 124 inches for 1928. Factory-crafted bodies were fitted.

I.D. DATA: Serial number located on plate on dash; also on right side of floorboard. Production started, each year, with number 501, with a suffix used to indicate series production. Motor numbers on left side of crankcase.

Model Series S	Body Type	Price	Weight	Prod. Total
Spl. Dely.	¾-Ton Panel Dely.	720	2188	—
Spl. Dely.	¾-Ton Pickup	—	—	—
Spl. Dely.	¾-Ton Canopy Dely.	—	—	—
Spl. Dely.	¾-Ton Screen Dely.	—	—	—
Spl. Dely.	¾-Ton Sed. Dely.	—	—	—

1928 IHC Armored Car (Commercial Chassis)

513

ENGINE: Inline. L-head. Four-cylinder. Cast iron block. Bore & stroke: 3½ in. x 4½ in. Displacement: 173 cu. in. Brake horsepower: 30 at 2700 R.P.M. Net horsepower: 19.60 (NACC). Valve lifters: Solid. Carburetor: Zenith.

CHASSIS: Wheelbase: (1927) 116 in.; (1928) 124 in. Front tread: 56 in. Rear tread: 56 in. Tires: 30 x 5 in.

TECHNICAL: Selective sliding transmission. Speeds: 3F/1R. Floor-mounted gearshift. Clutch: Multiple disc. Semi-floating rear axle. Rear wheel brakes. Artillery spoke wheels.

OPTIONS: Front bumper. Special paint. Sidemount spare tire. Dual tail-lamps. Auxiliary passenger seat.

1928 IHC Six Speed Special Depot Wagon (OCW)

HISTORICAL: Introduced: Spring 1927. Calendar year sales: (1927) 16,356 for all trucks. Calendar year production: A total of 25,000 IHC trucks were built in 1927, including all models from ¾ ton up to five tons. Innovations: "Six-Speed Special" introduced in heavy truck lineup and new generation of light-duty Special Delivery models appeared at mid-year 1927. In December, 1927 a Special Delivery made a 6,618 mile trip from Nairobi to Algiers, in Africa, via the Sahara Desert. The truck averaged 15 m.p.g. of gasoline for the 16 day journey.

Pricing

1927-1928 Series "S" (¾-Ton)	5	4	3	2	1
Panel Dely.	1450	2850	4700	6600	9400
Pickup	1350	2700	4500	6300	9000
Canopy Dely.	1300	2600	4300	6000	8600
Screen Dely.	1200	2460	4100	5700	8200
Sedan Dely.	1500	2950	4950	6900	9900

1929 IHC

1929 IHC Light-Duty Stake Bed (Mike Carbonella photo)
514

SPECIAL DELIVERY — SERIES S — FOUR-CYLINDER: — The Series "S" Special Delivery continued to be offered on the ¾-ton chassis. There were no changes to speak of. This was a record season for International truck sales in all weight classes and categories. There were still several one ton series available. However, this was also the period in which organizations like the National Automobile Dealers Association (NADA), officially began listing light commercial vehicles, up to and including ¾-ton capacity, in their automobile price guides. Since these are basic reference sources for a catalog of this type, we will use the same system as the contemporary organizations did.

I.D. DATA: Serial number located on plate on dash; also on right side of floorboard. Production started each year with number 501, with a suffix used to indicate series production. Motor numbers on left side of block.

Model Series S	Body Type	Price	Weight	Prod. Total
Spl. Dely.	¾-Ton Panel Dely.	720	2188	—
Spl. Dely.	¾-Ton Pickup	—	—	—
Spl. Dely.	¾-Ton Canopy Dely.	—	—	—
Spl. Dely.	¾-Ton Screen Dely.	—	—	—
Spl. Dely.	¾-Ton Sedan Dely.	—	—	—

ENGINE: Inline. L-head. Four-cylinder. Cast iron block. Bore & stroke: 3½ in. x 4½ in. Displacement: 173 cu. in. Brake horsepower: 30 at 2700 R.P.M. Net horsepower: 19.60 (NACC). Valve lifters: Solid. Carburetor: Zenith.

CHASSIS: Wheelbase: 124 in. Front tread: 56 in. Rear tread: 56 in. Tires: 30 x 5 in.

TECHNICAL: Selective sliding transmission. Speeds: 3F/1R. Floor-mounted gearshift. Clutch: Multiple disc. Semi-floating rear axle. Rear wheel brakes. Artillery spoke wheels.

OPTIONS: Front bumper. Special paint. Sidemount spare tire. Dual tail-lamps. Auxilliary passenger seat.

HISTORICAL: Introduced: December 1928. Calendar year sales: (All IHC trucks) 31,434. Calendar year production: (All IHC trucks) Over 50,000 units. By 1929, International Harvester had expanded to 170 branches nationwide. Total production of all IHC trucks surpassed 50,000 units.

Pricing

1929 Series "S" (¾-Ton)	5	4	3	2	1
Panel Dely.	1450	2850	4700	6600	9400
Pickup	1350	2700	4500	6300	9000
Canopy Dely.	1300	2600	4300	6000	8600
Screen Dely.	1200	2460	4100	5700	8200
Sedan Dely.	1500	2950	4950	6900	9900

1930 IHC

1930 IHC Model A2 Panel Delivery (OCW)

LIGHT TRUCK — SERIES AW-1 — FOUR-CYLINDER: — International trucks, large and small, came in a brand new "A" series this year. They were, indeed, handsome vehicles with plated radiator shells of a squarer design, torpedo headlights, more rounded full-crown fenders, squarer hoods, diamond pattern running boards of wider design, cowl vents and cowl lamps and distinctive wraparound belt moldings. These were again ¾-ton models using the same Waukesha engine. A choice of 124 or 136 inch wheelbase was available.

I.D. DATA: Serial number located on plate on dash; also on right side of floor board. Production started with number 501. Motor numbers on left side of block.

Model	Body Type	Price	Weight	Prod. Total
Series AW-1				
AW-1	¾-Ton Chassis	720	2622	—
AW-1	¾-Ton Panel Dely.	720	2188	—
AW-1	¾-Ton Pickup	—	—	—
AW-1	¾-Ton Canopy Dely.	—	—	—
AW-1	¾-Ton Screen Dely.	—	—	—
AW-1	¾-Ton Sed. Dely.	—	—	—

ENGINE: Inline. L-head. Four-cylinder. Cast iron block. Bore & stroke: 3½ in. x 4½ in. Displacement: 173 cu. in. Brake horsepower: 30 at 2700 R.P.M. Net horsepower: 19.60 (NACC) Solid valve lifters. Carburetor: Zenith.

CHASSIS: Wheelbase: 124/136 in. Front tread: 56 in. Rear tread: 56 in. Tires: 30 x 5 in.

TECHNICAL (Model S): Selective sliding transmission. Speeds: 3F/1R. Floor-mounted gear shift lever. Multiple disc type clutch. Semi-floating rear axle. Rear wheel brakes. Artillery spoke wheels.

OPTIONS: Sidemounted spare. Special paint. Front bumper. Dual tail-lights. Cowl lamps. Deluxe trim package. Bed rails.

HISTORICAL: Introduced Mid-1930. Calendar year sales: (all trucks) 23,703 units. After 1929, the economic depression sent IHC sales tumbling down to below the levels of the late 1920s. During this period, IHC was third in total U.S. truck sales. Most years, behind Ford and Chevrolet, but usually out-selling Dodge. Its rating in the light truck field, however, was much lower and management became interested in marketing a ½-ton model.

Pricing

1930	5	4	3	2	1
Series AW-1 — (¾-Ton) — (124 in. w.b.)					
Chassis	1200	2400	4000	5600	8000
Panel Dely.	1450	2850	4750	6650	9500
Pickup	1450	2850	4700	6600	9400
Canopy Dely.	1350	2650	4400	6150	8800
Screen Dely.	1300	2550	4250	5900	8500
Sedan Dely.	1500	3000	5000	7000	10,000
Series AW-1 — (¾-Ton) — (136 in. w.b.)					
Chassis	1050	2100	3500	4900	7000
Panel Dely.	1350	2700	4500	6300	9000
Pickup	1300	2600	4300	6000	8600
Canopy Dely.	1200	2460	4100	5700	8200
Screen Dely.	1170	2340	3900	5450	7800
Sedan Dely.	1450	2850	4750	6650	9500

1931 IHC

LIGHT TRUCK — SERIES AW-1/SERIES A-1 — FOUR-CYLINDER: — For 1931, IHC offered ¾-ton trucks in two series. Both looked the same, being similar in appearance and style to last season's AW-1. They both used a Waukesha four-cylinder engine and 136 in. w.b. However, the new A-1 Series ¾-ton was slightly larger overall, more expensive and a bit pricier. The engine used in the smaller line was Waukesha's "XA" model, while the larger truck had an "XAH" engine with a larger bore, but the same stroke, for nine additional brake horsepower. Styling features included chrome radiator shells, torpedo headlights, vertical louver hoods, cadet sun visors, "spider" style spoke steel wheels and full running boards. Tools, jack, tool box, ammeter, electric head and taillamps, radiator guard, front fenders and horn. The A-1 model still used a vacuum tank fuel system. It had its light switch on the steering column. A mechanical split-type universal joint was used. The transmission was a four-speed manual unit. Line-bored main bearings and poured rods were used.

I.D. DATA: Serial number located on plate on dash and on floor board at right side. Numbers 501 and up (both series). Motor number on left side of crankcase.

Model	Body Type	Price	Weight	Prod. Total
Series AW-1 Special Delivery				
AW-1	¾-Ton Chassis	650	2620	—
AW-1	¾-Ton Pickup	882	3542	—
AW-1	¾-Ton Canopy Dely.	900	3827	—
AW-1	¾-Ton Screen Dely.	900	3827	—
AW-1	¾-Ton Panel	1006	3910	—
AW-1	¾-Ton Sedan Dely.	1070	3781	—
Series A-1				
A-1	¾-Ton Chassis	675	2740	—

NOTE 1: Prices for truck bodies were available upon application at IHC dealers.

ENGINE (Series AW-1): Inline. L-head. Four-cylinder. Cast iron block. Bore & stroke: 3½ in. x 4½ in. Displacement: 173 cu. in. Brake horsepower: 30 at 2700 R.P.M. Net horsepower: 19.6 (NACC). Line bored main bearings and rods. Solid valve lifters. Carburetor: Zenith.

ENGINE (Series A-1): Inline. L-head. Four-cylinder. Cast iron block. Bore & stroke: 3⅝ in. x 4½ in. Displacement: 185.8 cu. in. Brake horsepower: 39 at 2400 R.P.M. Net horsepower: 21.03 (NACC). Line bored main bearings. Poured rods. Solid valve lifters. Carburetor: Zenith.

CHASSIS (Series AW-1): Wheelbase: 136 in. Front tread: 56 in. Rear tread: 56 in. Tires: 30 x 5 in.

CHASSIS (Series A-1): Wheelbase: 136 in. Front tread: 56 in. Rear tread: 56 in. Tires: 30 x 5 in.

TECHNICAL: Selective sliding transmission. Speeds: 3F/1R. Floor-mounted gear shift lever. Multiple disc type clutch. Semi-floating rear axle. Bendix rear wheel brakes. Steel spoke wheels.

NOTE: The A-1 models had a four-speed manual transmission.

OPTIONS: Rearview mirror. Cowl lamps. Sidemounted spare. Front bumper. Rear bumper. Various cabs and bodies. Windshield wiper. Special paint. Dual taillights.

HISTORICAL: Introduced December 1930. Calendar year registrations: (all IHC trucks) 21,073. The new Model A-1 Series was introduced in 1931. A total of 109,220 trucks of ¾-ton or less capacity were produced by all companies in the United States and Canada this year. IHC trucks held 24 percent of the domestic truck market. Production was low due to the depression. IHC was the third-ranked truck maker in the country, but no production breakouts are available. However, experts believe that the majority of sales went to smaller ¾-tonners.

Pricing

1931	5	4	3	2	1
Series AW-1 (¾-Ton)					
Chassis	1200	2400	4000	5600	8000
Pickup	1450	2850	4750	6650	9500
Canopy Dely.	1450	2850	4700	6600	9400
Screen Dely.	1350	2650	4400	6150	8800
Panel	1300	2550	4250	5900	8500
Sedan Dely.	1500	3000	5000	7000	10,000
Series A-1 (¾-Ton)					
Chassis	1110	2250	3750	5250	7500

1932 IHC

1932 IHC Model A1 Panel Delivery (OCW)

LIGHT TRUCK — SERIES AW-1/A-1/M-2 — FOUR-CYLINDER: — The AW-1 and A-1 lines continued to be offered as ¾-ton trucks for 1932. There was little or no change in both products. A new model was the one ton M-2. It used the "XAH" Waukesha four-cylinder engine. Smaller International trucks used a windshield with an arched lower edge, while larger capacity models had rectangular windshields.

I.D. DATA: Serial number located on plate on dash and on floor board at right side. (Both Series) Numbers 501 and up. Motor numbers on left side of crankcase.

Model	Body Type	Price	Weight	Prod. Total
Series AW-1 Special Delivery				
AW-1	¾-Ton Chassis	600	2620	—
AW-1	¾-Ton Pickup	852	3542	—
AW-1	¾-Ton Canopy Dely.	870	3827	—
AW-1	¾-Ton Screen Dely.	870	3827	—
AW-1	¾-Ton Panel	956	3910	—
AW-1	¾-Ton Sedan Dely.	1020	3781	—

Model	Body Type	Price	Weight	Prod. Total
Series A-1				
A-1	¾-Ton Chassis	615	2740	—
A-1	¾-Ton Pickup	867	3562	—
A-1	¾-Ton Canopy Dely.	885	3947	—
A-1	¾-Ton Screen Dely.	885	3947	—
A-1	¾-Ton Panel	971	4030	—
A-1	¾-Ton Sedan Dely.	1035	3901	—
Series M-2				
M-2	One-Ton Chassis	850	3081	—

NOTE 1: Truck body prices available upon application.

ENGINE (Series AW-1): Inline. L-head. Four-cylinder. Cast iron block. Bore & stroke: 3½ in. x 4½ in. Displacement: 173 cu. in. Brake horsepower: 30 at 2700 R.P.M. Net horsepower: 19.6 (NACC). Line bored main bearings and rods. Solid valve lifters. Carburetor: Zenith.

ENGINE (Series A-1 and M-2): Inline. L-head. Four-cylinder. Cast iron block. Bore & stroke: 3⅝ in. x 4½ in. Displacement: 185.8 cu. in. Brake horsepower: 39 at 2400 R.P.M. Net horsepower: 21.03 (NACC). Line bored main bearings and poured rods. Solid valve lifters. Carburetor: Zenith.

CHASSIS (Series AW-1): Wheelbase: 136 in. Front tread: 56 in. Rear tread: 56 in. Tires: 30 x 5 in.

CHASSIS (Series A-1): Wheelbase: 136 in. Front tread: 56 in. Rear tread: 56 in. Tires: 30 x 5 in.

CHASSIS (Series M-2): Wheelbase: 118 in. Front tread: 60 in. Rear tread: 60 in.

TECHNICAL (Series AW-1): Selective sliding transmission. Speeds: 3F/1R. Floor-mounted gear shift lever. Multiple disc type clutch. Semi-floating rear axle. Bendix rear wheel brakes. Steel spoke wheels.

TECHNICAL (Series A-1, M-2): Selective sliding transmission. Speeds: 3F/1R. Floor-mounted gear shift lever. Multiple disc type clutch. Semi-floating rear axle. Bendix rear wheel brakes. Steel spoke wheels.

OPTIONS: Rearview mirror. Cowl lamps. Side mount spare tire. Front bumper. Rear bumper. Various cabs and bodies. Windshield wiper. Special paint. Dual taillights.

HISTORICAL: Introduced December 1931. Calendar year registrations: (all IHC trucks) 15,752. New M-2 Series introduced. Truck-makers in the U.S. and Canada produced only 79,127 units of ¾-ton and under capacity and only 1,618 units of one ton or 1-½-ton capacity. It was obvious that the continuing depression was having a negative effect on the industry. IHC was still the nation's third largest seller of all kinds of trucks, but the lack of a ½-ton model was costing the loss of sales to firms like Ford and Chevrolet.

Pricing

	5	4	3	2	1
1932					
Series AW-1 (¾-Ton)					
Chassis	1200	2400	4000	5600	8000
Pickup	1450	2850	4750	6650	9500
Canopy Dely.	1450	2850	4700	6600	9400
Screen Dely.	1350	2650	4400	6150	8800
Panel	1300	2550	4250	5900	8500
Sedan Dely.	1500	3000	5000	7000	10,000
Series A-1 (¾-Ton)					
Chassis	1110	2250	3750	5250	7500
Pickup	1200	2400	4000	5600	8000
Canopy Dely.	1180	2370	3950	5500	7900
Screen Dely.	1100	2200	3650	5100	7300
Panel	1050	2100	3500	4900	7000
Sedan Dely.	1300	2550	4250	5900	8500
Series M-2 (One-Ton)					
Chassis	1020	2500	3400	4800	6800

1933 IHC

LIGHT TRUCK — SERIES D-1/A-1/M-2 — (ALL ENGINES): — International needed a low-priced ½-ton truck to compete with Ford and Chevrolet during the Great Depression. The company did not have such a model or a factory setup to produce one. Willys-Overland had introduced the Model C-113 in this market during 1931, before entering receivership. So IHC made a deal to market a modified version of this ½-ton through International dealers for 1933. It was called the D-1 series and used the same 113 in. w.b. as the Willys model with a slightly larger version of the same six-cylinder engine. Manufacturing was sourced from the Willys-Overland factory in Toledo, Ohio, but the trucks carried International nameplates. Styling was characterized by single-bar bumpers, more rounded rooflines and a visorless windshield. Although the prices were very low for these models, they included wire wheels and a sidemounted spare tire as standard equipment. The ¾-ton A-1 series continued to be available. Also carried over was the M-2 one-ton series. Both of the larger lines had little change from last season.

516

1933 IHC Pickup (OCW)

I.D. DATA: Serial number located on plate on dash and also on the right side of the floor board. Serial numbers began at number 501 for all series. Ending numbers are not available. Engine numbers located on the left side of crankcase.

Model	Body Type	Price	Weight	Prod. Total
Series D-1				
D-1	½-Ton Chassis	360	2100	—
D-1	½-Ton Pickup	475	2698	—
D-1	¾-Ton Canopy Dely.	550	2775	—
D-1	½-Ton Screen Dely.	550	2775	—
D-1	¾-Ton Panel	565	2882	—
D-1	¾-Ton Sedan Dely.	630	2725	—
Series A-1				
A-1	¾-Ton Chassis	615	2812	—
A-1	¾-Ton Pickup	867	3562	—
A-1	¾-Ton Screen Dely.	885	3947	—
A-1	¾-Ton Canopy Dely.	885	3947	—
A-1	¾-Ton Panel	971	4030	—
A-1	¾-Ton Sedan Dely.	1035	3901	—
Series M-2				
M-2	One-Ton Chassis	850	3081	—

NOTE 1: By early 1934, Willys-Overland reported that 17,000 series D-1 trucks had been built for International Harvester Corp.

1933 IHC Pickup (OCW)

ENGINE (Series D-1): Inline. L-head. Six-cylinder. Cast iron block. Bore & stroke: 3-5/16 in. x 4-1/8 in. Displacement: 213 cu. in. Brake horsepower: 70 at 3400 R.P.M. Net horsepower: 26.33 (NACC). Slip-in main bearings and rod bearings. Solid valve lifters.

ENGINE (Series A-1 and M-2): Inline. L-head. Four-cylinder. Cast iron block. Bore & stroke: 3⅝ in. x 4½ in. Displacement: 185.8 cu. in. Brake horsepower: 39 at 2400 R.P.M. Net horsepower: 21.03 (NACC). Line bored main bearings and rod bearings. Solid valve lifters. Carburetor: Zenith.

CHASSIS (Series D-1): Wheelbase: 113 in. Front tread: 56 in. Rear tread: 56 in. Tires: 5.25 x 18 in.

CHASSIS (Series A-1): Wheelbase: 136 in. Front tread: 56 in. Rear tread: 56 in. Tires: 30 x 5.00 in.

CHASSIS (Series M-2): Wheelbase: 118 in. Front tread: 60 in. Rear tread: 60 in.

TECHNICAL (Series D-1): Synchromesh transmission. Speeds: 3F/1R. Floor-mounted gear shift lever. Multiple disc clutch. Semi-floating rear axle. Overall ratio: 4.18:1. Two-shoe Bendix brakes. Wire spoke wheels.

1933 IHC Canopy Delivery Truck (OCW)

TECHNICAL (Series A-1, M-2): Selective sliding transmission. Speeds: 4F/1R. Floor-mounted gear shift lever. Multiple disc type clutch. Semi-floating rear axle. Overall ratio: 4.18:1. Bendix rear wheel brakes. Steel spoke wheels.

OPTIONS: Front bumper (std. on D-1). Rear bumper (std. on D-1). Single sidemount. Rearview mirror. Various cabs and bodies. Windshield wiper. Bumper guards. Shock absorbers (std. on D-1). Special paint. Dual taillights. Wire wheels. Various axle ratios. Seat covers. Pedestal mirror (for sidemount). Spotlight. Cowl lamps.

1933 IHC Model Panel Delivery Truck (OCW)

HISTORICAL: Introduced January 1933. Calendar year registrations: (All IHC trucks) 26,658. Calendar year production: Approximately 17,000 D-1 models. No breakouts for other models. New ½-ton series. Synchromesh manual tranmission. Production of 100 Series D-1 trucks per day was originally scheduled, but Willys-Overland's financial instability created problems. Ultimately, the ½-ton trucks were built in batches of 2,500 or 5,000 units at a time. Due to the extremely low prices, profits from this model were very low or non-existant.

1933 IHC Model Pickup (OCW)

Pricing

1933	5	4	3	2	1
Series D-1 (½-Ton)					
Chassis	1140	2280	3800	5300	7600
Pickup	1200	2480	4050	5650	8100
Canopy Dely.	1200	2400	4000	5600	8000
Screen Dely.	1110	2220	3700	5200	7400
Panel	1070	2150	3550	5000	7100
Sedan Dely.	1300	2600	4300	6000	8600
Series A-1 (¾-Ton)					
Chassis	1110	2250	3750	5250	7500
Pickup	1200	2400	4000	5600	8000
Canopy Dely.	1180	2370	3950	5500	7900
Screen Dely.	1100	2200	3650	5100	7300
Panel	1050	2100	3500	4900	7000
Sedan Dely.	1300	2550	4250	5900	8500
Series M-2 (One-Ton)					
Chassis	1020	2500	3400	4800	6800

1934 IHC

1934 IHC Pickup (OCW)

LIGHT TRUCK — SERIES C-1/D-1/A-1/M-2 — (ALL ENGINES): — Willys-Overland continued to produce the ½-ton D-1 series for International Harvester in early 1934. It was joined by an all-new ½-ton C-1 Series, built in IHC's factory. This model featured a raked V-type radiator, deluxe style sidemount spare skirted fenders and more streamlined cowl, cab and hood. Like the D-1, the new model had IHC's model "Heavy Duty" six-cylinder engine of 213 cu. in. displacement. However, it was tuned to give more horsepower and a higher R.P.M. peak. The standard wheelbase was 113 in., but a 125 in. stance was optional. Other features included slip-in mains and rods, sparkplug cables in conduits, two-shoe Bendix brakes, and three-speed conventional transmission. Also carriedover, with only minor alterations, were the ¾-ton A-1 and the one-ton M-2 lines.

I.D. DATA: Serial number located on a plate on dash and also on right side of the floor board. Serial numbers began at number 501 for all series. Ending numbers are not available. Engine numbers located on left side of crankcase.

1934 IHC Pickup (OCW)

Model	Body Type	Price	Weight	Prod. Total
Series D-1				
D-1	½-Ton Chassis	360	2100	—
D-1	½-Ton Pickup	475	2698	—
D-1	½-Ton Canopy Dely.	550	2775	—
D-1	½-Ton Screen Dely.	550	2775	—
D-1	½-Ton Panel	565	2882	—
D-1	½-Ton Sedan Dely.	630	2725	—
Series C-1				
C-1	½-Ton Chassis (L.W.B.)	470	2330	—
C-1	½-Ton Chassis (S.W.B.)	445	2320	—
C-1	½-Ton Pickup (S.W.B.)	545	3005	—
Series A-1				
A-1	¾-Ton Chassis	615	2812	—
A-1	¾-Ton Pickup	867	3562	—
A-1	¾-Ton Screen Dely.	885	3947	—
A-1	¾-Ton Canopy Dely.	885	3947	—
A-1	¾-Ton Panel	971	4030	—
A-1	¾-Ton Sedan Dely.	1035	3081	—
Series M-2				
M-2	One-Ton Chassis	850	3081	—

ENGINE (Series D-1/C-1): Inline. L-head. Six-cylinder. Cast iron block. Bore & stroke: 3-5/16 in. x 4⅛ in. Displacement: 213 cu. in. Brake horsepower: (D-1) 70 at 3400 R.P.M. (C-1) 78 at 3600 R.P.M. Net horsepower: (D-1) 16.33; (C-1) 26.3 (NACC). Slip-in main bearings and rod bearings. Solid valve lifters.

1934 IHC Model C-1 Station Wagon (OCW)

ENGINE (Series A-1/M-2): Inline. L-head. Four-cylinder. Cast iron block. Bore & stroke: 3⅜ in. x 4½ in. Displacement: 185.8 cu. in. Brake horsepower: 39 at 2400 R.P.M. Net horsepower: 21.03 (NACC). Line bored main bearings and poured rod bearings. Solid valve lifters. Carburetor: Zenith.

CHASSIS (Series D-1): Wheelbase: 113 in. or 125 in. Front tread: 56 in. Rear tread: 56 in. Tires: 5.25 x 18 in.

CHASSIS (Series C-1): Wheelbase: 113 in. Front tread: 56 in. Rear tread: 56 in. Tires: 5.25 x 18 in.

CHASSIS (Series A-1): Wheelbase: 136 in. Front tread: 56 in. Rear tread: 56 in. Tires: 30 x 5.00 in.

CHASSIS (Series M-2): Wheelbase: 118 in. Front tread: 61 in. Rear tread: 61 in.

TECHNICAL (Series C-1/D-1): Synchromesh transmission. Speeds: 3F/1R. Floor-mounted gear shift lever. Multiple disc type clutch. Semi-floating rear axle. Overall ratio: 4.18:1. Two-shoe Bendix brakes. Wire spoke wheels.

TECHNICAL (Series A-1/M-2): Selective sliding transmission. Speeds: 4F/1R. Floor-mounted gear shift lever. Multiple disc type clutch. Semi-floating rear axle. Overall ratio: 4.18:1. Two-shoe Bendix brakes. Steel spoke wheels.

1934 IHC Panel Delivery Truck (NI/DFW)

OPTIONS: Front bumper (std. on D-1). Rear bumper (std. on D-1). Single sidemount. Rearview mirror. Various cabs and bodies. Windshield wiper. Bumper guards. Shock absorbers (std. on D-1). Special paint. Dual tail-lights. Wire wheels (std. on D-1). Various axle ratios. Seat covers. Pedestal mirror (for sidemount). Spotlight. Cowl lamps.

NOTE: Bumpers and shock absorbers were $25 extra on the new C-1.

HISTORICAL: Introduced: (C-1) April, 1934; (others) December, 1933. Calendar year registrations: (All IHC trucks) 31,555.

NOTE: The C-1 line had a total production run of 75,000 units from 1934 to 1937. Breakouts for other models not available.

New C-1 ½-ton series built by IHC. Improved six-cylinder engine. Improved ignition wiring system. New streamlined styling on C-1 models. The D-1/C-1 six-cylinder engine was a product of the Wilson Foundry & Machine Co. of Pontiac, Mich. The popular C-1 was well accepted by IHC buyers and led to a large increase in sales and production. International was again the nation's third-ranked truck builder.

Pricing

	5	4	3	2	1
1934					
Series D-1 (½-Ton)					
Chassis	1140	2280	3800	5300	7600
Pickup	1200	2450	4050	5650	8100
Canopy Dely.	1200	2400	4000	5600	8000
Screen Dely.	1110	2220	3700	5200	7400
Panel	1070	2150	3550	5000	7100
Sedan Dely.	1300	2600	4300	6000	8600
Series C-1 (½-Ton)					
Chassis 125 in. w.b.	1150	2310	3850	5400	7700
Chassis 113 in. w.b.	1170	2340	3900	5450	7800
Pickup 113 in. w.b.	1300	2550	4250	5900	8500
Series A-1 (¾-Ton)					
Chassis	1110	2250	3750	5250	7500
Pickup	1200	2400	4000	5600	8000
Screen Dely.	1100	2200	3650	5100	7300
Canopy Dely.	1180	2370	3950	5500	7900
Panel	1050	2100	3500	4900	7000
Sedan Dely.	1300	2550	4250	5900	8500
Series M-2 (One-Ton)					
Chassis	1020	2500	3400	4800	6800

1935 IHC

1935 IHC Pickup (NI/DFW)

LIGHT TRUCK — SERIES C-1/C-10/C-20/M-3 — (ALL ENGINES): — This was a year for expansion of the famous "C" Series trucks from IHC. The C-1 models were carried over as a ½-ton line. These had two chassis with 113- and 125-in. w.b. They were six-cylinder models. Also available were ¾-ton C-10 models with a four-cylinder power plant. These trucks had a 133 in. wheelbase. The C-20 models were actually large trucks with a 157 in. wheelbase and four-cylinder engines. They had a maximum 1-½-ton capacity, although they were nominally rated for one-ton payloads. The M-2 became the M-3 with a 133 in. w.b. and the four-cylinder engine. The larger trucks had a "V" dip in the front bumper, while the smaller ones again had straight bumpers.

I.D. DATA: Serial number located on a plate on dash and also on right side of the floor board. Serial numbers began at number 501 for all series. Ending numbers are not available. Engine numbers located on left side of crankcase.

1935 IHC Model C-1 Station Wagon (OCW)

Model	Body Type	Price	Weight	Prod. Total
Series C-1				
C-1	½-Ton Chassis (S.W.B.)	400	2050	—
C-1	½-Ton Chassis (L.W.B.)	425	2095	—
Series C-10				
C-10	¾-Ton Chassis	575	2870	—
C-10	¾-Ton Chassis	590	2867	—
Series C-20				
C-20	1-1½-Ton Chassis (S.W.B.)	575	2919	—
C-20	1-1½-Ton Chassis (L.W.B.)	590	2867	—
Series M-3				
M-3	One-Ton Chassis	850	3081	—

ENGINE (Series C-1): Inline. L-head. Six-cylinder. Cast iron block. Bore & stroke: 3-5/16 in. x 4⅛ in. Displacement: 213 cu. in. Brake horsepower: 78 at 3600 R.P.M. Net horsepower: 26.3 (NACC). Slip-in main bearings and rod bearings. Solid valve lifters.

ENGINE (Series C-10/C-20/M-3): Inline. L-head. Four-cylinder. Cast iron block. Bore & stroke: 3⅝ in. x 4½ in. Displacement: 185.8 cu. in. Brake horsepower: 39 at 2400 R.P.M. Net horsepower: 21.03 (NACC). Line bored main bearings and poured rod bearings. Solid valve lifters. Carburetor: Zenith.

CHASSIS (Series C-1): Wheelbase: 113 in. or 125 in. Front tread: 56 in. Rear tread: 56 in. Tires: 5.25 x 18 in.

CHASSIS (Series C-10): Wheelbase: 133 in.

CHASSIS (Series C-20): Wheelbase: 133 in. or 157 in.

CHASSIS (Series M-3): Wheelbase: 133 in.

TECHNICAL: Conventional transmission. Speeds: 3-4F/1R (*). Floor-mounted gear shift lever. Multiple disc type clutch. Semi-floating rear axle. Overall ratio: 4.18:1. Two-shoe Bendix brakes. Wire spoke wheels or steel spoke wheels.

(*) Four-speed transmission in C-10 and C-20 model.

OPTIONS: Front bumper. Rear bumper. Single sidemount. Rearview mirror. Various cabs and bodies. Windshield wiper. Bumper guards. Shock absorbers. Special paint. Dual taillights. Wire wheels. Various axle ratios. Seat covers. Pedestal mirrors. Spotlight. Cowl lamps.

HISTORICAL: Introduced: January 1934. Calendar year registrations: (All IHC trucks) 53,471. During 1936, a total of 316,208 (38.6 percent) of the trucks made by U.S. and Canadian Manufacturers were ¾-ton or less in payload capacity. Another 9,686 trucks were made in the one-ton to under 1-½-ton class. This amounted to 1.1 percent of the North American total.

Pricing

	5	4	3	2	1
1935					
Series C-1 (½-Ton)					
Chassis 113 in. w.b.	1170	2340	3900	5450	7800
Chassis 125 in. w.b.	1170	2310	3850	5400	7700
Series C-10 (¾-Ton)					
Chassis	1110	2220	3700	5200	7400
Chassis	1110	2250	3750	5250	7500
Series C-20 (1-to 1-½-Ton)					
Chassis 133 in. w.b.	980	1950	3250	4550	6500
Chassis 157 in. w.b.	900	1800	3000	4200	6000
Series M-3 (One-Ton)					
Chassis	1020	2500	3400	4800	6800

1936 IHC

1936 IHC Model C-1 Station Wagon (OCW)

LIGHT TRUCK — SERIES C-5/C-1/C-10/CS-20/M-3/C-12 — (ALL ENGINES): — International Harvester again expanded its line of ½-ton to one-ton trucks. There were seven different series within the range. Styling was carried over from 1935. The smaller trucks had skirted fenders and straight front bumpers while larger models had unskirted clamshell fenders and "veed" front bumpers. Four-cylinder Waukesha power plants were used in the C-5, C-10, CS-20 and M-3 series. Other models employed IHC-built six-cylinder engines. The C-1 had its own "Heavy-Duty" 213 cu. in. six rated at 79 h.p. The C-5 used a new "FK" engine with removable valve lifter clusters and a fuel pump in the valve door. It had Bendix hydraulic brakes and a three-speed synchromesh transmission. The C-10 and CS-20 models employed the "XAH" engine. Both had hydraulic brakes and four-speed transmissions. The C-15 used an "Heavy-Duty 2" engine and had hydraulic brakes and a three-speed transmission. The M-3 shared many features of the CS-20 line. A six-cylinder "Heavy-Duty 3" power plant was used in the ¾-ton C-12 which also had hydraulic braking and a four-speed transmission.

I.D. DATA: Serial number located on plate on dash. Also, on right side of the floorboard. Engine numbers located on left side of crankcase. Serial and engine numbers unavailable.

1936 IHC Model C30 Stake Bed (OCW)

Model	Body Type	Price	Weight	Prod. Total
Series C-5				
C-5	½-Ton Chassis (S.W.B.)	415	1981	—
C-5	½-Ton Chassis (L.W.B.)	440	2026	—
Series C-1				
C-1	½-Ton Chassis (S.W.B.)	415	2078	—
C-1	½-Ton Chassis (L.W.B.)	440	2123	—
Series C-10				
C-10	¾-Ton Chassis	590	3089	—
Series C-15				
C-15	¾-1-Ton Chassis	545	2619	—
Series M-3				
M-3	One-Ton Chassis	850	3163	—
Series CS-20				
CS-20	1-1½-Ton Chassis	685	3000	—
Series C-12				
C-12	¾-Ton Chassis	616	3003	—

ENGINE (Series C-5): Inline. L-head. Four-cylinder. Cast iron block. Bore & stroke: 3¼ in. x 4 in. Displacement: 132.7 cu. in. Brake horsepower: 33 at 2800 R.P.M. Net horsepower: 16.9 (NACC). Slip-in main bearings and rod bearings. Solid valve lifters in crankcase.

ENGINE (Series C-1/C-15/C-12): Inline. L-head. Six-cylinder. Cast iron block. Bore & stroke: 3-5/16 in. x 4⅛ in. Displacement: 213 cu. in. Compression ratio: 6.3:1. Brake horsepower: 78 at 3400 R.P.M. Net horsepower: 26.3 (NACC). Four main bearings (insert type). Solid valve lifters. Carburetor: Single downdraft.

ENGINE (Series C-10/CS-20/M-3): Inline. L-head. Four-cylinder. Cast iron block. Bore & stroke: 3⅝ in. x 4½ in. Displacement: 185.8 cu. in. Net horsepower: 21.03 (NACC). Solid valve lifters.

CHASSIS (Series C-5/C-1): Wheelbase: (S.W.B.) 113 in.; (L.W.B.) 125 in. Tires: 5.25 x 18 in.

CHASSIS (Series C-10/C-12): Wheelbase: 133 in.

CHASSIS (Series M-3/CS-20): Wheelbase: 118 in.

CHASSIS (Series C-15): Wheelbase: 136 in.

TECHNICAL (Series C-1/C-5/C-15): Manual transmission. Speeds: 3F/1R. Floor-mounted gear shift lever. Multiple disc type clutch. Semi-floating rear axle. Overall ratio: 4.18 to 8.5. Bendix hydraulic brakes. Wire or steel spoke wheels.

NOTE: Synchromesh three-speed transmission in C-5 models.

TECHNICAL (Series C-10/C-20/C-12/M-3): Manual transmission. Speeds: 4F/1R. Floor-mounted gear shift lever. Multiple disc type clutch. Semi-floating rear axle. Overall ratio: 4.18 to 8.5. Bendix hydraulic brakes. Steel spoke wheels.

OPTIONS: Front bumper. Rear bumper. Single sidemount. Rearview mirror. Pedestal mirror for sidemount. Wire spoke wheels. Bumper guards. Windshield wipers (dual). Special paint. Various bodies. Wheel trim rings. Dual taillights. Seat covers. Oversized (20 in.) tires. Spotlight. License plate frames.

HISTORICAL: Introduced: January 1936. Calendar year registrations: (all IHC trucks) 71,958. Calendar year production: (all IHC trucks) 86,563. Hydraulic brakes standardized for light-duty International trucks. IHC was once again America's third-ranked truck manufacturer and held 11.03 percent of the total market. The sales slump caused by the Great Depression was coming to an end.

Pricing

	5	4	3	2	1
1936					
Series C-5 (½-Ton)					
S.W.B. Chassis	1130	2250	3750	5250	7500
L.W.B. Series	1110	2220	3700	5200	7400
Series C-1 (½-Ton)					
S.W.B. Chassis	1170	2340	3900	5450	7800
L.W.B. Chassis	1170	2310	3850	5400	7700
Series C-10 (¾-Ton)					
Chassis	1110	2220	3700	5200	7400
Series C-15 (¾-One-Ton)					
Chassis	1100	2200	3650	5100	7300
Series M-3 (One-Ton)					
Chassis	1020	2500	3400	4800	5800
Series CS-20 (One-1-½ Ton)					
Chassis	830	1650	2750	3850	5500
Series C-12 (¾-Ton)					
Chassis	1100	2200	3650	5100	7300

NOTE: The value estimates above are for Express (pickup) trucks. Check 1939 price guide for relative prices on other body styles.

1937 IHC

LIGHT TRUCK — SERIES C-5/C-1/C-15//M-3 — (ALL ENGINES): — In early 1937, four series of IHC trucks rated for one ton or lower capacities were carried over, virtually without change. The C-5 was now available only with the shorter 113 in. wheelbase. The same was true of the C-1. Both of these ½-tons used the same engines as last year. As in 1936, the C-15 was classified as a ¾-ton to one-ton model. It, too, was unaltered in any important sense. The M-3 was, likewise, unchanged as far as the basics went. All of these models were cataloged at the same prices in effect during 1936. However, all scaled-in at heavier shipping weights, suggesting some changes in standard equipment. The weight increases ranged from a modest two pound jump on the C-5 to a 127 pound increase for the C-1 and C-15 models. The M-3 gained 117 pounds. Refer to the 1936 section of this catalog for additional specifications for these trucks. Current values for these models are also about the same for both years.

1937-1938 IHC

1937 IHC Mail Delivery Truck (OCW)

LIGHT TRUCK — SERIES D-5/D-2/D-15/ — (ALL ENGINES): — A new Series "D" line of trucks was introduced in the spring of 1937. They featured all-steel cabs with "turret top" styling, the "fat fender" look and split windshields. The grille consisted of five groups of curved horizontal bars separated by bright metal moldings. Each group was wider than the one below it. The trim moldings above and below the top group extended back along the hood sides. Long horizontal hood louvers were between them, with an "International" nameplate in the center. The nose above the grille was flat, rounded and finished in body color. An I-H emblem decorated the nose. Larger, torpedo-shaped headlamp buckets were attacked to the "catwalk" area on pedestals. There were short running boards extending only to the rear of the cab. Single-bar front bumpers were used on all models and spare tires were hung on the passenger side of the body or box, behind the doors. The larger D-15 pickups had horizontal ribs on the box sides. Steel spoke wheels were used on all models. A new station wagon with wood body construction appeared. The D-2 used a "Heavy Duty 213" engine; the D-5 had an "FC" engine and the D-15 employed the "Heavy Duty 213A" engine. All had slip-in mains and rods, Bendix hydraulic brakes and three-speed synchromesh transmission. The D-2 and D-15 had a hand-brake operating on the rear wheels.

I.D. DATA: Serial number located on plate on dash. Also on right floorboard. Engine numbers located on left side of crankcase. Serial and engine numbers unavailable.

1937 IHC Panel Delivery Truck (NI/DFW)

Model	Body Type	Price	Weight	Prod. Total
Series D-5				
D-5	½-Ton Chassis	470	2170	—
Series D-2				
D-2	½-Ton Chassis	455	2290	—
Series D-15				
D-15	¾-One-Ton Chassis	570	2770	—

NOTE 1: Refer to 1936 for "C" and "M" Series data.

NOTE 2: 1938 chassis prices were: (D-5) $490; (D-2) $475 and (D-15) $605.

NOTE 3: Shipping weights for 1938 were unchanged.

1937 IHC Model D-2 Station Wagon (OCW)

ENGINE (Series D-5): Inline. L-head. Four-cylinder. Cast iron block. Bore & stroke: 3¼ in. x 4 in. Displacement: 132.7 cu. in. Brake horsepower: 33 at 2800 R.P.M. Net horsepower: 16.9 (NACC). Slip-in main bearings and rod bearings. Solid valve lifters.

ENGINE (Series D-2/D-15): Inline. L-head. Six-cylinder. Cast iron block. Bore & stroke: 3-5/16 in. x 4⅛ in. Displacement: 213 cu. in. Compression ratio: 6.3:1. Brake horsepower: 78 at 3400 R.P.M. Net horsepower: 26.3 (NACC). Four main bearings (insert type). Solid valve lifters. Carburetor: Single downdraft.

1937 IHC Model D-5 One-Ton Soda Delivery Truck (OCW)

CHASSIS (Series D-5): Wheelbase: 113/125 in.

CHASSIS (Series D-2): Wheelbase: 113 in.

CHASSIS (Series D-15): Wheelbase: 130 in.

TECHNICAL: Manual transmission. Speeds: 3F/1R. Floor-mounted gear shift lever. Multiple dry disc type clutch. Semi-floating rear axle. Bendix hydraulic brakes. Steel spoke wheels.

OPTIONS: Front bumper. Rear bumper. Single sidemount (body side). Rearview mirror. Dual windshield wipers. Special paint. Bumper guards. Wheel trim rings. Dual taillights. Various bodies. Oversized tires. Spotlight. Windshield visor. License frames.

1938 IHC One-Ton Flatbed Truck (OCW)

1937 IHC Deluxe Panel Delivery Truck (J.H. Archives)

1938 IHC Station Wagon (OCW)

HISTORICAL (Series D): Introduced: March 1937. Calendar year registrations: (All IHC trucks) 76,174. Calendar year production: (All IHC trucks) 100,700. All-new "D" series introduced. Turret top cab styling with all-steel construction. Modernized design for D-series. During 1937, IHC increased its lead on Dodge in the U.S. truck market. The company now held 30.22 percent of total American truck output and broke the 100,000 units per year level for the first time. It was again the third largest maker of all types of trucks. For 1938, calendar year registrations for all IHC trucks dropped to 55,836 and calendar year production fell to 51,593 units. That gave IHC a 10.24 percent market share and, once again, third rank in the industry.

1938 IHC Model D-2 Station Wagon (OCW)

Pricing

	5	4	3	2	1
1937-1938					
Series D-5 (½-Ton)					
Chassis	1100	2200	3650	5100	7300
Series D-2 (½-Ton)					
Chassis	1140	2280	3800	5300	7600
Series D-15 (¾-One-Ton)					
Chassis	1050	2100	3500	4900	7000

NOTE 1: See 1936 for 1937 "C" and "M" Series values.

NOTE 2: The value estimates above are for Express (pickup) trucks. Check 1939 price guide for relative prices on other body styles.

1939 IHC

1939 IHC Model D-15 Station Wagon (OCW)

HALF-TON TRUCK — SERIES D-2 — SIX-CYLINDER: — More emphasis was placed on marketing IHC trucks with factory-built bodies starting in 1939. The products in the light-duty truck lines were still the "D" series models and there were no significant changes in styling or engineering. These trucks were promoted with the sales slogan "Beauty Plus Dependability." The ½-ton D-2 models were still available with a choice of two wheelbases. The design features were the same as described in the 1937-1938 section of this catalog.

I.D. DATA (Series D-2/D-5/D-15): Serial number located on plate on dash. Also on floorboard on right side. Numbers for each series prefix began at 501. Engine numbers located on left side of crankcase. Starting numbers unavailable.

Model	Body Type	Price	Weight	Prod. Total
Series D-2 (113 in. w.b.)				
D-2	½-Ton Chassis	475	2290	—
D-2	½-Ton Chassis HE Cab.	583	2725	—
D-2	½-Ton Express	620	3565	—
D-2	½-Ton Canopy Top Express	775	3565	—
D-2	½-Ton Panel	713	3210	—
D-2	½-Ton DM Body	860	3295	—
D-2	½-Ton DB Body	860	3295	—
D-2	½-Ton Sta. Wag.	930	3590	—
D-2	½-Ton Metro Body	1200	—	—
Series D-2 (125 in. w.b.)				
D-2	½-Ton Chassis	500	2315	—
D-2	½-Ton Chassis HE Cab.	608	2750	—
D-2	½-Ton Express	640	3590	—
D-2	½-Ton Stake	668	3625	—
D-2	½-Ton Canopy Top Express	810	3590	—
D-2	½-Ton Panel	750	3315	—

NOTES: "DM Body" is a milk delivery truck.
"DB Body" is a bakery delivery truck.

ENGINE (Series D-2): Inline. L-head. Six-cylinder. Cast iron block. Bore & stroke: 3-5/16 in. x 4⅛ in. Displacement: 213 cu. in. Compression ratio: 6.3:1. Brake horsepower: 78 at 3400 R.P.M. Net horsepower: 26.3 (NACC). Four main bearings (insert type). Solid valve lifters. Carburetor: Single downdraft.

CHASSIS (Series D-2): Wheelbase: 113/125 in.

HALF-TON TRUCK — SERIES D-5 — FOUR-CYLINDER: — International's D-5 series line was carried over without any important changes for model year 1939. This was the four-cylinder version of IHC's smallest truck. Several models such as the station wagon and Metro (bus) were not available with the smaller engine.

Series D-5 (113 in. w.b.)				
D-5	½-Ton Chassis	450	2170	—
D-5	½-Ton Chassis HE Cab.	557	2605	—
D-5	½-Ton Express	595	3445	—
D-5	½-Ton Canopy Top Express	750	3445	—
D-5	½-Ton Panel	688	3090	—
D-5	½-Ton DM Body	835	3175	—
D-5	½-Ton DB Body	835	3175	—
Series D-5 (125 in. w.b.)				
D-5	½-Ton Chassis	475	2195	—
D-5	½-Ton Chassis HE Cab.	583	2630	—
D-5	½-Ton Express	635	3470	—
D-5	½-Ton Stake	643	3505	—
D-5	½-Ton Canopy Top Express	785	3470	—
D-5	½-Ton Panel	725	3195	—

ENGINE (Series D-5): Inline. L-head. Four-cylinder. Cast iron block. Bore & stroke: 3¼ in. x 4 in. Displacement: 132.7 cu. in. Brake horsepower: 33 at 2800 R.P.M. Net horsepower: 16.9 (NACC). Slip-in main bearings. Solid valve lifters.

CHASSIS (Series D-5): Wheelbase: 113/125 in.

¾ to ONE-TON — SERIES D-15 — SIX-CYLINDER: — IHC's larger D-15 light-duty truck was also carried over. There were no more than minor detail changes from previous D-15 models. Two wheelbases were also offered in this range: 113 in. and 130 in.

Series D-15 (113 in. w.b.)				
D-15	¾-One Ton Chassis	605	2770	—
D-15	¾-One Ton Chassis HE Cab.	713	3205	—
D-15	¾-One Ton Express	750	4140	—
D-15	¾-One Ton DM Body	1000	3775	—
D-15	¾-One Ton DB Body	1000	3775	—
D-15	¾-One Ton Stordor	1330	—	—
Series D-15 (130 in. w.b.)				
D-15	¾-One Ton Chassis	605	2800	—
D-15	¾-One Ton Chassis HE Cab.	713	3235	—
D-15	¾-One Ton Express	785	4170	—
D-15	¾-One Ton Stake	788	4110	—
D-15	¾-One Ton Canopy Express	930	4170	—
D-15	¾-One Ton Panel	873	4000	—

1939 IHC Model D-2 Station Wagon (OCW)

ENGINE (Series D-15): Inline. L-head. Six-cylinder. Cast iron block. Bore & stroke: 3-5/16 in. x 4⅛ in. Displacement: 213 cu. in. Compression ratio: 6.3:1. Brake horsepower: 78 at 3400 R.P.M. Net horsepower: 26.3 (NACC). Four main bearings (insert type). Solid valve lifters. Carburetor: Single downdraft.

CHASSIS (Series D-15): Wheelbase: 113/130 in.

TECHNICAL: Synchromesh transmission. Speeds: 3F/1R. Floor-mounted gear shift lever. Multiple dry disc type clutch. Hypoid rear axle. Bendix hydraulic brakes. Steel spoke wheels.

OPTIONS: Front bumper. Rear bumper. Single sidemount (body side). Rearview mirror. Dual windshield wipers. Special paint. Bumper guards. Wheel trim rings. Dual taillights. Oversized tires. Spotlight. Windshield visor. License frames.

HISTORICAL (Series D): Introduced: January 1939. Calendar year registrations: (All IHC trucks) 66,048. Calendar year production: (All IHC trucks) 81,960. IHC continued as America's number three truck maker. It had 11.38 percent of the total U.S. market. Commander Attilio Gatti used a fleet of IHC trucks on his 10th African expedition in 1938-1939. Five of these covered a combined total of 66,000 miles with repair costs totaling just $38. The explorer used several IHC station wagons. A full article on these woodie wagons was printed in the April 1984 issue of *Cars & Parts* magazine.

Pricing

1939	5	4	3	2	1
Series D-2 (½-Ton) — (113 in. w.b.) — (6-cyl.)					
Express	1250	2500	4150	5800	8300
Canopy Express	1250	2520	4200	5850	8400
Panel	1300	2550	4250	5900	8500
DM Body	1170	2340	3900	5450	7800
DB Body	1170	2340	3900	5450	7800
Sta. Wag.	1350	2700	4500	6300	9000
Metro	750	1500	2500	3500	5000
Series D-2 (½-Ton) — (125 in. w.b.) — (6-cyl.)					
Express	1200	2450	4050	5650	8100
Stake	1170	2310	3850	5400	7700
Canopy Exp.	1200	2460	4100	5700	8200
Panel	1250	2500	4150	5800	8300

Series		5	4	3	2	1
Series D-5 (½-Ton) — (113 in. w.b.) — (4-cyl.)						
Express		1170	2340	3900	5450	7800
Canopy Exp.		1180	2370	3950	5500	7900
Panel		1200	2400	4000	5600	8000
DM Body		1100	2200	3650	5100	7300
DB Body		1100	2200	3650	5100	7300
Series D-5 (½-Ton) — (125 in. w.b.) — (4-cyl.)						
Express		1170	2310	3850	5400	7700
Stake		1100	2200	3650	5100	7300
Canopy Exp.		1170	2340	3900	5450	7800
Panel		1180	2370	3950	5500	7900
Series D-15 (¾-One-Ton) — (113 in. w.b.) — (6-cyl.)						
Express		1130	2250	3750	5250	7500
DM Body		1070	2150	3550	5000	7100
DB Body		1070	2150	3550	5000	7100
Stordor		1170	2310	3850	5400	7700
Series D-15 (¾-One-Ton) — (130 in. w.b.) — (6-cyl.)						
Express		1110	2220	3700	5200	7400
Stake		1050	2100	3500	4900	7000
Canopy Exp.		1130	2250	3750	5250	7500
Panel		1140	2280	3800	5300	7600

1940 IHC

1940 IHC Model D-15 Station Wagon (OCW)

HALF-TON TRUCK — SERIES D-2/D-2H/D-2M — SIX-CYLINDER: —
Starting in Oct. 1939, International Harvester Co.'s "D" Series trucks were marketed as 1940 models. They came in capacities of ½-Ton to six-tons. There were three ½-ton truck-lines using the IHC-built six-cylinder engine; the D-2, D-2H and D-2M. The D-2 lineup was on the 113 in. wheelbase. It was down to seven models, with the bakery truck and Metro van bodies deleted. Even prices for remaining models were unchanged, although shipping weights were listed as about 100 pounds lighter. There were no major alterations from 1939 models. A D-2H designation was used for long (125 in.) wheelbase models. These came in the same models as last year, although the Express was now called the "pickup." The Metro delivery van was listed as a separate D-2M Series. It came with either a 102- or 113 in. wheelbase. General styling was continued from the 1937-1938 models.

HALF-TON TRUCK — SERIES D-5 — FOUR—CYLINDER: — Except for slightly increased prices, the D-5 series was carried over, without change, as an early 1940 offering. It came in both 113- and 125 in. wheelbase lines. The bakery truck, on the shorter wheelbase, was no longer cataloged. The four-cylinder Waukesha power plant was again found under the hoods of these trucks.

¾-TON — SERIES D-15L/D-15LL/D-15ML/D29 — SIX-CYLINDER: —
There were four separate ¾-ton series for 1940. The D-15L offered four models on the 113 in. wheelbase with the 78 h.p. six-cylinder engine. The D-15LL offered six additional 130 in. wheelbase trucks with the same engine. The D-15ML was the ¾-ton version of the metro delivery van with 102 or 113 in. wheelbases available. These three series were also offered as one-tons with heavier-duty chassis equipment. Also available, as a ¾-ton only line, was the D-29 series. The D-29s had larger tires, a more powerful six-cylinder engine with longer stroke and came on three wheelbases: 128-, 155- or 173 inches.

ONE-TON TRUCK — SERIES D-15/D-15H/D-15M — SIX-CYLINDER: —
One-ton versions of the "D-15" models were available in three series. These were basically the ¾-tonners with heavier-duty chassis equipment, but the same engines and tires. However, there was no one-ton version of the D-29.

I.D. DATA (Series D-2/D-2H/D-2M): Serial number located on plate on dash. Also on floorboard on right side of driving compartment. Also on left front end of frame, left front spring hanger or front end of right running board shield. Starting: (Series D-2): 80169; (Series D-2H) 80169; (Series D-2M) 501. Ending numbers not available. Engine numbers located on left side of crankcase.

I.D. DATA (Series D-5): Serial number and engine number located in same places. Starting: 3852. Ending: not available.

I.D. DATA (Series D-15L/D-15LL/D-15ML/D-29): Serial number and engine number located in the same places. Starting: (Series D-15): 26800; (Series D-15M): 501; (Series D-29) 688. Ending: (Series D-15M): 688; (other series) not available.

I.D. DATA (Series D-15/D-15H/D-15M): Serial number and engine number located in the same places. The starting numbers were the same as for the comparable ¾-ton trucks in the same lines.

Model	Body Type	Price	Weight	Prod. Total
Series D-2 (113 in. w.b.)				
D-2	½-Ton Chassis & Cowl	475	2187	—
D-2	½-Ton Chassis & Cab.	583	2622	—
D-2	½-Ton Pickup	620	2900	—
D-2	½-Ton Canopy	775	3462	—
D-2	½-Ton Panel	713	3107	—
D-2	½-Ton DM (Milk)	860	3192	—
D-2	½-Ton Stake	930	3487	—
Series D-2H (125 in. w.b.)				
D-2H	½-Ton Chassis & Cowl	500	2212	—
D-2H	½-Ton Chassis & Cab	608	2647	—
D-2H	½-Ton Pickup	660	2925	—
D-2H	½-Ton Canopy	810	3487	—
D-2H	½-Ton Panel	750	3132	—
D-2H	½-Ton Stake	668	3178	—
Series D-2M (Metro Delivery)				
D-2M	½-Ton Panel (S.W.B.)	1100	1942	—
D-2M	½-Ton Panel (L.W.B.)	1170	1952	—
Series D-5 (113 in. w.b.)				
D-5	½-Ton Chassis & Cowl	490	2067	—
D-5	½-Ton Chassis & Cab	598	2502	—
D-5	½-Ton Pickup	635	2780	—
D-5	½-Ton Canopy	790	3342	—
D-5	½-Ton Panel	728	2987	—
D-5	½-Ton DM (Milk)	875	3072	—
Series D-5 (125 in. w.b.)				
D-5	½-Ton Chassis & Cowl	515	2092	—
D-5	½-Ton Chassis & Cab	623	2527	—
D-5	½-Ton Pickup	675	2805	—
D-5	½-Ton Canopy	825	3367	—
D-5	½-Ton Panel	765	3012	—
D-5	½-Ton Stake	683	3058	—
Series D-15L (113 in. w.b.)				
D-15L	¾-Ton Chassis & Cowl	605	2667	—
D-15L	¾-Ton Chassis & Cab	712	3102	—
D-15L	¾-Ton Pickup	750	3380	—
D-15L	¾-Ton DM (Milk)	1000	3672	—
Series D-15LL (130 in. w.b.)				
D-15LL	¾-Ton Chassis & Cowl	605	2697	—
D-15LL	¾-Ton Chassis & Cab	713	3132	—
D-15LL	¾-Ton Pickup	785	3410	—
D-15LL	¾-Ton Canopy	930	3972	—
D-15LL	¾-Ton Panel	873	3617	—
D-15LL	¾-Ton Stake	788	3663	—
Series D-15M (Metro Delivery)				
D-15M	¾-Ton Panel (102 in. w.b.)	1240	2222	—
D-15M	¾-Ton Panel (113 in. w.b.)	1310	2321	—
Series D-29				
D-29	¾-Ton Chassis & Cowl (128 in. w.b.)	650	3553	—
D-29	¾-Ton Chassis & Cab (128 in. w.b.)	758	3788	—
D-29	¾-Ton Chassis & Cowl (155 in. w.b.)	685	3398	—
D-29	¾-Ton Chassis & Cab (155 in. w.b.)	793	—	—
D-29	¾-Ton Chassis & Cowl (173 in. w.b.)	710	3528	—
D-29	¾-Ton Chassis & Cab (173 in. w.b.)	818	—	—
Series D-15 (113 in. w.b.)				
D-15	One-Ton Chassis & Cowl	605	2667	—
D-15	One-Ton Chassis & Cowl	712	3102	—
D-15	One-Ton Pickup	750	3380	—
D-15	One-Ton DM (Milk)	1000	3672	—
Series D-15H (130 in. w.b.)				
D-15H	One-Ton Chassis & Cowl	605	2697	—
D-15H	One-Ton Chassis & Cab	713	3132	—
D-15H	One-Ton Pickup	785	3410	—
D-15H	One-Ton Canopy	930	3972	—
D-15H	One-Ton Panel	873	3617	—
D-15H	One-Ton Stake	788	3663	—
Series D-15M (Metro Delivery)				
D-15M	One-Ton Panel (102 in. w.b.)	1240	2222	—
D-15M	One-Ton Panel (113 in. w.b.)	1310	2321	—

ENGINE (Series D-2/D-2H/D-2M): Inline. L-head. Six-cylinder. Cast iron block. Bore & stroke: 3-5/16 in. x 4⅛ in. Displacement: 213 cu. in. Compression ratio: 6.3:1. Brake horsepower: 78 at 3400 R.P.M. Net horsepower: 26.3 (NACC). Four main bearings. Solid valve lifters. Carburetor: Single downdraft.

ENGINE (Series D-5): Inline. L-head. Four-cylinder. Cast iron block. Bore & stroke: 3¼ in. x 4 in. Displacement: 132.7 cu. in. Brake horsepower: 33 at 2800 R.P.M. Net horsepower: 16.9 (NACC). Slip-in main bearings. Solid valve lifters.

ENGINE (Series D-29): Inline. L-head. Six-cylinder. Cast iron block. Bore & stroke: 3-5/16 in. x 4½ in. Displacement: 232 cu. in. Brake horsepower: 81 at 3200 R.P.M. Net horsepower: 26.3 (NACC). Solid valve lifters.

NOTE: The 81 h.p. engine was used only in the D-29 Series. The D-15L, D-15LL and D-15M trucks used the same 78 h.p. six-cylinder engine as the D-2, D-2H and D-2M ½-ton models. See speficiation above for this engine.

CHASSIS (Series D-2): Wheelbase: 113 in. Tires: 6.00 x 16 (four-ply).

CHASSIS (Series D-2H): Wheelbase: 125 in. Tires: 6.00 x 16 (four-ply).

CHASSIS (Series D-5 [S.W.B.]): Wheelbase: 113 in. Tires: 6.00 x 16 (six-ply).

CHASSIS (Series D-5 [L.W.B.]): Wheelbase: 125 in. Tires: 6.00 x 16 (six-ply).

CHASSIS (Series D-2M): Wheelbase: 102 in. Tires: 6.00 x 16 (four-ply).

CHASSIS (Series D-2M): Wheelbase: 113 in. Tires: 6.00 x 16 (four-ply).

CHASSIS (Series D-15/D-15L): Wheelbase: 113 in. Tires: 7.00 x 16 (six-ply).

CHASSIS (Series D-15LL/D-15H): Wheelbase: 130 in. Tires: 7.00 x 16 (six-ply).

CHASSIS (Series D-15M): Wheelbase: 102 in. Tires: 7.00 x 16 (six-ply).

CHASSIS (Series D-15M): Wheelbase: 113 in. Tires: 7.00 x 16 (six-ply).

CHASSIS (Series D-29): Wheelbase: 128 in. Tires: (Front) 30 x 5 in.; (Rear) 32 x 6 in.

CHASSIS (Series D-29): Wheelbase: 155 in. Tires: (Front) 30 x 5 in.; (Rear) 32 x 6 in.

CHASSIS (Series D-29): Wheelbase: 173 in. Tires: (Front) 30 x 5 in.; (Rear) 32 x 6 in.

1940 International Panel Delivery (OCW)

TECHNICAL: Synchromesh transmission. Speeds: 3F/1R. Floor-mounted gear shift lever. Multiple dry disc type clutch. Hypoid rear axle. Bendix hydraulic brakes. Steel spoke wheels.

OPTIONS: Front bumper. Rear bumper. Single sidemount (body side). Rearview mirror. Dual windshield wipers. Special paint. Bumper guards. Radio. Heater. Wheel trim rings. Dual taillights. Radio antenna. Seat covers. Oversized tires. Spotlight. Windshield visor. License frames. Cab clearance lights. Turn signals.

HISTORICAL: Introduced: Oct. 1939. Calendar year registrations: (All IHC trucks) 76,833. Calendar year production: (All IHC trucks) 81,753. Model year production: (All IHC trucks) 80,810. Industrywide truck production, by capacities, for 1940 was as follows: (¾-Ton or less) 37.2 percent; (One-Ton) 4.9 percent. International Harvester Co. slipped behind Dodge in truck production this year. Dodge had 12.39 percent of the total truck market to gain third rank. IHC had 10.41 percent and was the fourth largest producer. The company was now being threatened by GMC as well.

Pricing

1940	5	4	3	2	1
Series D-2 (½-Ton) — (113 in. w.b.) — (6-cyl.)					
Pickup	1250	2500	4150	5800	8300
Canopy	1250	2520	4200	5850	8400
Panel	1300	2550	4250	5900	8500
Milk Dely.	1170	2340	3900	5450	7800
Stake	1170	2310	3850	5400	7700

	5	4	3	2	1
Series D-2H (½-Ton) — (125 in. w.b.) — (6-cyl.)					
Pickups	1200	2450	4050	5650	8100
Canopy	1200	2460	4100	5700	8200
Panel	1250	2500	4150	5800	8300
Stake	1170	2310	3850	5400	7700
Series D-2M (½-Ton) — (102 or 113 in. w.b.) — (6-cyl.)					
Metro Panel (S.W.B.)	1020	2050	3400	4800	6800
Metro Panel (L.W.B.)	1020	2050	3400	4800	6800
Series D-5 (½-Ton) — (113 in. w.b.) — (4-cyl.)					
Pickup	1170	2340	3900	5450	7800
Canopy	1180	2370	3950	5500	9900
Panel	1200	2400	4000	5600	8000
Milk Dely.	1100	2200	3650	5100	7300
Series D-5 (½-Ton) — (125 in. w.b.) — (4-cyl.)					
Pickup	1170	2310	3850	5400	7700
Canopy	1170	2340	3900	5450	7800
Panel	1180	2370	3950	5500	7900
Stake	1100	2200	3650	5100	7300
Series D-15L (¾-Ton) — (113 in. w.b.) — (6-cyl.)					
Pickup	1130	2250	3750	5250	7500
Milk Dely.	1070	2150	3550	5000	7100
Series D-15LL (¾-Ton) — (130 in. w.b.) — (6-cyl.)					
Pickup	1110	2220	3700	5200	7400
Canopy	1130	2250	3750	5250	7500
Panel	1140	2280	3800	5300	7600
Stake	1050	2100	3500	4900	7000
Series D-15M (¾-Ton) — (102 or 113 in. w.b.) — (6-cyl.)					
Panel (S.W.B.)	980	1950	3250	4550	6500
Panel (L.W.B.)	980	1950	3250	4550	6500
Series D-29 (¾-Ton) — (128, 155 or 173 in. w.b.) — (6-cyl.)					
Chassis & Cowl (128 in. w.b.)	980	1950	3250	4550	6500
Chassis & Cab (128 in. w.b.)	1000	2000	3300	4600	6600
Chassis & Cowl (155 in. w.b.)	930	1860	3100	4350	6200
Chassis & Cab (155 in. w.b.)	950	1900	3150	4400	6300
Chassis & Cowl (173 in. w.b.)	890	1770	2950	4150	5900
Chassis & Cab (173 in. w.b.)	900	1800	3000	4200	6000
Series D-15 (One-Ton) — (113 in. w.b.) — (6-cyl.)					
Pickup	980	1950	3250	4550	6500
Milk Dely.	890	1770	2950	4150	5900
Series D-15H (One-Ton) — (130 in. w.b.) — (6-cyl.)					
Pickup	950	1900	3150	4400	6300
Canopy	950	1900	3150	4400	6300
Panel	980	1950	3250	4550	6500
Stake	900	1800	3000	4200	6000
Series 15M (One-Ton) — (102 or 113 in. w.b.) — (6-cyl.)					
Panel (S.W.B.)	900	1800	3000	4200	6000
Panel (L.W.B.)	900	1800	3000	4200	6000

1940½ IHC

MODEL K TRUCK — SERIES K-1 — SIX-CYLINDER: — An all-new Model K truck was introduced by IHC during model year 1940. The K1 was the ½-ton model having a gross vehicle weight (GVW) rating of 4400 pounds. There was also a K-1H variation or option listed as a ¾-ton. (The "H" suffix apparently meant "heavy-duty.") All model Ks had modernized styling with wider front fenders and flush headlamps. A tall, straight, vertical grille featured bright, horizontal curved bars on either side of a vertical center divider. Rectangular parking lamps were incorporated into the upper corner of the grille. The single-bar bumper ran straight across the front and wider, half-length running boards were seen. The front of the hood arched over to the grille to form a flat, rounded nose which was decorated with an International emblem. The badge had the company name running across three diamonds. Sculpturing appeared on the sides of the hood with an International name at the rear corner. The 213 cu. in. six was promoted as a "Green Diamond" engine.

MODEL K TRUCK — SERIES K-2 — SIX-CYLINDER: — The K-2 Series was the ¾-ton version of the newly restyled International truck. Models in this line had a 5200 pound GVW rating. The NADA actually listed the K-2 as a ½-ton in 1940, but it was uprated to ¾-ton from 1941 on, which appears more correct. Styling characteristics for all model Ks were similar. There were two variations or options for K-2 trucks. The K-2L was a ½-ton and the K-2H was a one ton. (Apparently, the suffix "L" indicated light-duty and the suffix "H" indicated heavy-duty).

MODEL K TRUCK — SERIES K-3 — SIX-CYLINDER: — The new Model K styling was also seen on the one ton K-3 series. These trucks came with a standard 113 in. wheelbase or special 130 in. wheelbase. They had a 6650 pound GVW rating. Two variations or options (K-3L at ½-ton or K-3H at 1¼-tons) were available.

NOTE: Two of the heavier-duty Model Ks offered ¾-ton options with an "L" suffix. These were the K-4L (a variation of the 1¼-ton K-4) and the K-5L (a variation of the 1½-ton K-5). These trucks had respective GVW ratings of 10,000 pounds and 13,500 pounds and could hardly be considered "Light-duty" models regardless of factory nomenclature.

I.D. DATA (Series K-1): Serial number stamped on a plate on dash. Also on floorboard on right side of driving compartment. Also on left front end of frame, left front spring hanger or front end of right running board shield. Starting: 501. Ending: 5468. Engine numbers located on left side of crankcase. Starting and ending numbers not available.

I.D. DATA (Series K-2): Serial number in same locations. Starting: 501. Ending: 3091. Engine numbers in same locations.

I.D. DATA (Series K-3): Serial number in same locations. Starting: 501. Ending: 2308. Engine numbers in same locations.

Model	Body Type	Price	Weight	Prod. Total
Model K-1 — (K-1H — ¾-Ton) — (113 in. w.b.)				
K-1	½-Ton Chassis & Cowl	490	2250	—
K-1	½-Ton Chassis & Cab	598	2645	—
K-1	½-Ton Pickup	640	2923	—
K-1	½-Ton Panel	733	3170	—
K-1	½-Ton Sta. Wag.	1000	3350	—
Model K-1 — (K-1H — ¾-Ton) — (125 in. w.b.)				
K-1	½-Ton Chassis & Cowl	510	2275	—
K-1	½-Ton Chassis & Cab	618	2670	—
K-1	½-Ton Pickup	675	2978	—
K-1	½-Ton Panel	765	3275	—
K-1	½-Ton Sta. Wag.	678	3201	—

NOTE: Serial numbers indicate 4,967 trucks made in this series.

Model	Body Type	Price	Weight	Prod. Total
Model K-2 — (K-2L — ½-Ton) — (K-2H — One-Ton) — (125 in. w.b.)				
K-2	¾-Ton Chassis & Cowl	520	2285	—
K-2	¾-Ton Chassis & Cab	628	2680	—
K-2	¾-Ton Pickup	685	2988	—
K-2	¾-Ton Panel	775	3285	—
K-2	¾-Ton Stake	688	3211	—

NOTE 1: Serial numbers indicate 2,590 trucks made in this series.

Model	Body Type	Price	Weight	Prod. Total
Model K-3 — (K-3L — ½-Ton) — (113 in. w.b.)				
K-3	One-Ton Chassis & Cowl	620	3000	—
K-3	One-Ton Chassis & Cab	728	3395	—
K-3	One-Ton Pickup	770	3673	—
Model K-3 — (K-3L — ½-Ton) — (130 in. w.b.)				
K-3	One-Ton Chassis & Cowl	620	3030	—
K-3	One-Ton Chassis & Cab	728	3425	—
K-3	One-Ton Pickup	805	3796	—
K-3	One-Ton Panel	893	4230	—
K-3	One-Ton Stake	803	4039	—

NOTE 1: Serial numbers indicate 1,807 truck made in this series.

ENGINE (Series K-1): Inline. L-head. Six-cylinder. Cast iron block. Bore & stroke: 3-5/16 in. x 4⅛ in. Displacement: 213 cu. in. Compression ratio: 6.3:1. Brake horsepower: 78 at 3400 R.P.M. Net horsepower: 26.3 (NACC). Four main bearings. Solid valve lifters. Carburetor: Single downdraft.

ENGINE (Series K-2): See Series K-1 engine data above.

ENGINE (Series K-3): See Series K-1 engine date above.

CHASSIS (Series K-1): Wheelbase: 113/125 in. Tires: 6.00 x 16 in.

CHASSIS (Series K-2): Wheelbase: 125 in. Tires: 6.00 x 16 in.

CHASSIS (Series K-3): Wheelbase: 113/130 in. Tires: 6.00 x 16 in.

TECHNICAL: Synchromesh transmission. Speeds: 3F/1R. Floor-mounted gear shift lever. Multiple dry disc type clutch. Hypoid rear axle. Overall ratio: (½-ton) 4.18:1; (¾-one ton) 4.875:1 to 6.5:1. Bendix hydraulic brakes. Steel disc wheels.

OPTIONS: Front bumper. Rear bumper. Bumper guards. Radio. Heater. Clock. Cigar lighter. Radio antenna. Seat covers. External sun shade. Spotlight.

HISTORICAL: See 1940 historical notes.

Pricing

	5	4	3	2	1
1940					
Series K-1/K-1H — (½-Ton-¾-Ton) — (113 in. w.b.)					
Pickup	1300	2550	4250	5900	8500
Panel	1300	2600	4300	6000	8600
Sta. Wag.	1450	2850	4750	6650	9500
Series K-1/K-1H — (½-Ton-¾-Ton) — (125 in. w.b.)					
Pickup	1250	2500	4150	5800	8300
Panel	1250	2520	4200	5850	8400
Stake	1180	2370	3950	5500	7900
Series K-2L/K-2H — (½-Ton-One-Ton) — (125 in. w.b.)					
Pickup	1200	2460	4100	5700	8200
Panel	1250	2500	4150	5800	8300
Stake	1180	2370	3950	5500	7900
Series K-3/K-3L — (½-Ton-One-Ton) — (113 in. w.b.)					
Pickup	1300	2600	4300	6000	8600
Series K-3/K-3L — (½-Ton-One-Ton) — (130 in. w.b.)					
Pickup	1300	2550	4250	5900	8500
Panel	1300	2600	4300	6000	8600
Stake	1140	2280	3800	5300	7600

1941 IHC Model K-5 Station Wagon (OCW)

MODEL K — SERIES K-1 — SIX-CYLINDER: — Running production changes of a minor nature were the only updates for IHC's 1941 Model K trucks. The ½-ton line was again designated the K-1 Series. NADA truck reference books continued to show that a K—1H option, rated at ¾-ton, could be had. This series continued to offer 113 and 125 inch wheelbases. The "Green Diamond" six-cylinder engine was used. One thing that changed from the 1940½ introductory lineup was pricing, which increased $40 to $60 per model. Also new were several additional model offerings; the canopy delivery and KM milk truck on the 113 in. wheelbase and the canopy delivery and KB bakery truck on the 125 in. wheelbase. The entire series was carried over into 1942, basically without change. However, some late-1942 models were built with a minimum of chrome plated parts due to wartime material restrictions.

I.D. DATA: Serial number located on plate on dash. Also on floorboard on right side of driving compartment. Also on left front end of frame, left front spring hanger or right running board shield at front end. Starting: (1941) 5469. (1942) 26491. Ending: (1941) 26490. (1942) 28601. Engine numbers located on left side of crankcase. Engine numbers not available.

Model	Body Type	Price	Weight	Prod. Total
Model K-1 — (½-Ton) — (K-1H — ¾-Ton) — (113 in. w.b.)				
K-1	Chassis & Cowl	550	2250	—
K-1	Chassis & Cab	663	2630	—
K-1	Pickup	710	2908	—
K-1	Canopy	900	3525	—
K-1	Panel	815	3170	—
K-1	KM (Milk)	970	3255	—
K-1	Station Wagon	1140	3250	—
Model K-1 — (½-Ton) — (K-1H — ¾-Ton) — (125 in. w.b.)				
K-1	Chassis & Cowl	570	2275	—
K-1	Chassis & Cab	683	2655	—
K-1	Pickup	745	2963	—
K-1	Canopy	930	3550	—
K-1	Panel	850	3275	—
K-1	Stake	753	3186	—
K-1	KB (Bakery)	1015	3271	—

NOTE 1: Serial numbering indicates 21,021 trucks built in the 1941 series and 2,110 trucks built in the 1942 series.

NOTE 2: In 1942, the same models were marketed at the same prices. However, the weights were reduced by some 45-60 pounds per model.

ENGINE (Series K-1): Inline. L-head. Six-cylinder. Cast iron block. Bore & stroke: 3-5/16 in. x 4⅛ in. Displacement: 213 cu. in. Compression ratio: 6.3:1. Brake horsepower: 82 at 3400 R.P.M. Net horsepower: 26.3 (NACC). Four main bearings of insert type. Solid valve lifters. Carburetor: Single downdraft. Crankcase capacity: 6½ quarts. (Full-pressure type.) Cooling system capacity: 14¾ quarts. Electrical system: six volts. Oil bath air cleaner.

MODEL K — SERIES K-2 — SIX-CYLINDER: — The trucks in the K-2 Series were also little changed. This was again a ¾-ton range having ½-ton (K-2L) and one-ton (K-2H) variations. A canopy delivery truck and KB bakery truck were new models. All of the K-2s used the 125 in. w.b. and the 82 h.p. "Green Diamond" six-cylinder engine. The same models were carried over for 1942 at the same prices and with slightly lower shipping weights. Some late '42s had wartime "blackout" trim.

I.D. DATA: Serial numbers in the same locations. Starting: (1941) 3092. (1942) 13907. Ending: (1941) 13906. (1942) 14455. Engine numbers in the same locations. Starting and ending numbers not available.

1942 IHC Model K-2 Station Wagon (OCW)

Model	Body Type	Price	Weight	Prod. Total
Model K-2 — (¾-Ton) — (K-2L — ½-Ton/K-2H — One-Ton) — (125 in. w.b.)				
K-2	Chassis & Cowl	580	2285	—
K-2	Chassis & Cab	693	2665	—
K-2	Pickup	755	2973	—
K-2	Canopy	940	3560	—
K-2	Panel	860	3285	—
K-2	Stake	763	3196	—
K-2	KB (Bakery)	1025	3370	—

NOTE 1: Serial numbers indicate 10,814 trucks built in the 1941 Series and 548 trucks built in the 1942 series.

NOTE 2: The base shipping weights for 1942 were 2235 pounds for the chassis and cowl and 2630 pounds for the chassis and cab. Weights for other 1942 models not available.

ENGINE (Series K-2): Same as K-1 engine.

MODEL K — SERIES K-3 — SIX-CYLINDER: — The K-3 trucks were in the one ton series. There was a ½-ton K-3L option. Few changes from the 1940½ versions were seen. Two wheelbases, 113 in. and 130 in., were available again. A Model KM milk truck was a new model on the smaller wheelbase. It was offered for 1941 and 1942. New 1941 models for the 130 in. wheelbase included a canopy delivery and station wagon. Both were carried over for 1942. The '42s again had the same prices and slightly lower shipping weights.

I.D. DATA: Serial numbers in same locations. Starting: (1941) 2309. (1942) 12618. Ending: (1941) 12617. (1942) 13605. Engine numbers in same locations. Starting and ending numbers not available.

Model	Body Type	Price	Weight	Prod. Total
Model K-3 — (One-Ton) — (K-3L — ½-Ton) — (113 in. w.b.)				
K-3	Chassis & Cowl	680	3000	—
K-3	Chassis & Cab	793	3380	—
K-3	Pickup	840	3658	—
K-3	KM (Milk Truck)	1110	4005	—
Model K-3 — (One-Ton) — (K-3L — ½-Ton) — (130 in. w.b.)				
K-3	Chassis & Cowl	680	3030	—
K-3	Chassis & Cab	793	3410	—
K-3	Pickup	875	3781	—
K-3	Canopy	1060	4750	—
K-3	Panel	980	4230	—
K-3	Stake	873	4034	—
K-3	Sta. Wag.	1520	4330	—

NOTE 1: Serial numbers indicate 10,308 trucks built in the 1941 series and 987 trucks built in the 1942 series.

NOTE 2: Some 1942 weights were: Chassis & Cowl with 113 in. w.b. (2,667 pounds); Chassis & Cab with 113 in. w.b. (3,062 pounds); Chassis & Cowl with 130 in. w.b. (2,697 pounds); Chassis & Cab with 130 in. w.b. (3,092 pounds).

ENGINE (Series K-3): Same as K-1 engine.

METRO DELIVERY — SERIES D-2M/K-1M/D-15M/K-3M — SIX-CYLIN-DER: — Introduced in 1938, the Metro Delivery was a multi-stop truck featuring a body by Metro Body Co. (This firm later became an IHC subsidiary). These van-like vehicles came in four series. The D-2M had a ½-ton rating and 4600 pound GVW. The K-1M had a ½-ton rating and 4600 pound GVW. The D-15M had a ¾-one ton rating and 7000 pound GVW. The K-3M was a one-ton with 7000 pound GVW. All series offered 102 and 113 in. wheelbases and had "Green Diamond" power plants. In Atlantic City, N.J., a fleet of Metro Delivery vans served many years as "jitney" buses. For 1942, only the K-1M (½-ton) and K-3M (one-ton) series were available.

I.D. DATA: Serial numbers in the same locations. Starting: 1941: (D-2M) 1592 and up. (K-1M) 501 to 1959. (D-15M) 2076 and up. (K-3M) 501 to 2520. 1942: (K-1M) 1960 to 2008. (K-3M) 2521 to 2650. Engine numbers in same locations. Starting and ending numbers not available.

Model	Body Type	Price	Weight	Prod. Total
1941 Metro Delivery Series				
D-2M	½-Ton Panel (102 in. w.b.)	1100	1942	—
D-2M	½-Ton Panel (113 in. w.b.)	1170	1952	—
K-1M	½-Ton Chassis (102 in. w.b.)	560	—	—
K-1M	½-Ton Panel (102 in. w.b.)	1170	—	—
K-1M	½-Ton Chassis (113 in. w.b.)	560	—	—
K-1M	½-Ton Panel (113 in. w.b.)	1215	—	—
D-15M	¾-Ton Panel (102 in. w.b.)	1240	—	—
D-15M	¾-Ton Panel (113 in. w.b.)	1310	—	—
K-3M	One-Ton Chassis (102 in. w.b.)	670	—	—
K-3M	One-Ton Panel (102 in. w.b.)	1280	—	—
K-3M	One Ton Chassis (113 in. w.b.)	670	—	—
K-3M	One-Ton Panel (113 in. w.b.)	1325	—	—
1942 Metro Delivery Van Series				
K-1M	½-Ton Chassis (102 in. w.b.)	560	2025	—
K-1M	½-Ton Panel (102 in. w.b.)	1170	—	—
K-1M	½-Ton Chassis (113 in. w.b.)	560	2035	—
K-3M	One-Ton Chassis (102 in. w.b.)	670	2460	—
K-3M	One-Ton Panel (102 in. w.b.)	1280	—	—
K-3M	One-Ton Chassis (113 in. w.b.)	670	2560	—
K-3M	One-Ton Panel (113 in. w.b.)	1325	—	—

ENGINE (Metro Delivery): Same as K-1 engine.

CHASSIS (Series K-1): Wheelbase: 113/125 in. Front tread: 58-9/32 in. Rear tread: 58-13/16 in. Tires: 6.00 x 16 in.

CHASSIS (Series K-2): Wheelbase: 125 in. Front tread: 58-9/32 in. Rear tread: 58-13/16 in. Tires: 6.00 x 16 in.

CHASSIS (Series K-3): Wheelbase: 113/130 in. Front tread: 58-9/32 in. Rear tread: 58-13/16 in. Tires: 6.00 x 16 in.

CHASSIS (½-Ton Metro Delivery): Wheelbase: 102/113 in. Front tread: 58-9/32 in. Rear tread: 58-13/16 in. Tires: 6.00 x 16 (four-ply).

CHASSIS (¾-Ton-One-Ton Metro Delivery): Wheelbase: 102/113 in. Front tread: 58-9/32 in. Rear tread: 58-13/16 in. Tires: 7.00 x 16 (six-ply).

TECHNICAL: Synchromesh transmission. Speeds: 3F/1R. Floor-mounted gear shift lever. 10 inch diameter single dry-plate clutch. Semi-floating rear axle. Overall ratio: 4.18:1. Four-wheel hydraulic internal expanding brakes. Steel disc wheels. Optional: Four-speed selective, with straight cut gears.

OPTIONS: Front bumper. Rear bumper. Rearview mirror. Wheel trim rings. Spotlight. Dual taillights. Bumper guards. Radio. Heater. Special paint. Oversize tires. Radio antenna. Seat covers. External sun shade. Spotlight. License plate bracket. Side mounted spare (bodyside on station wagon). Dual windshield wiper. Fog lamps.

HISTORICAL: Introduced: (1941) Nov. 1940. (1942) Oct. 1941. Calendar year registrations — All IHC trucks: (1941) 92,482; (1942) unavailable. Calendar year production — All IHC trucks: (1941) 120,843. (1942) 42,126. Model year production — All IHC trucks: (1941) 115,283. With 11.05 percent of the overall truck market, IHC was the fourth-largest truck-maker in calendar 1941. In calendar year 1942, the company's market pentration fell to 4.80 percent and its sales ranking dropped to seventh.

Pricing

1941-1942	5	4	3	2	1
Series K-1 — (½-Ton) — (113 in. w.b.)					
Pickup	1300	2550	4250	5900	8500
Canopy	1300	2650	4350	6050	8700
Panel	1300	2600	4300	6000	8600
Milk Dely.	1110	2220	3700	5250	7500
Sta. Wag.	1450	2850	4750	6650	9500
Series K-1 — (½-Ton) — (125 in. w.b.)					
Pickup	1250	2500	4150	5800	8300
Canopy	1300	2550	4250	5900	8500
Panel	1250	2520	4200	5850	8400
Stake	1180	2370	3950	5500	7900
Bakery Dely.	1100	2200	3650	5100	7300
Series K-2 — (¾-Ton) — (125 in. w.b.)					
Pickup	1200	2460	4100	5700	8200
Canopy	1250	2520	4200	5850	8400
Panel	1250	2500	4150	5800	8300
Stake	1180	2370	3950	5500	7900
Bakery Dely.	1080	2160	3600	5050	7200
Series K-3 — (One-Ton) — (113 in. w.b.)					
Pickup	1200	2400	4000	5600	8000
Milk Dely.	1050	2100	3500	4900	7000

Series K-3 — (One-Ton) — (130 in. w.b.)	5	4	3	2	1
Pickup	1170	2340	3900	5450	7800
Canopy	1200	2460	4100	5700	8200
Panel	1200	2400	4000	5600	8000
Stake	1140	2280	3800	5300	7600
Sta. Wag.	1350	2700	4500	6300	9000
Metro Delivery — (102 in. w.b.)					
D-2M Panel	600	1200	2000	2800	4000
K-1M Panel	590	1170	1950	2700	3900
D-15M Panel	560	1100	1850	2600	3700
K-3M Panel	530	1050	1750	2450	3500
(113 in. w.b.)					
D-2M Panel	620	1230	2050	2900	4100
K-1M Panel	600	1200	2000	2800	4000
D-M15 Panel	570	1140	1900	2650	3800
K-3M Panel	540	1080	1800	2500	3600
Series K-1 — (½-Ton) — (113 in. w.b.)					
Pickup	960	1920	3200	4500	6400
Canopy	980	1950	3250	4550	6500
Panel	930	1860	3100	4350	6200
Milk Dely.	560	1100	1850	2600	3700
Sta. Wag.	1350	2700	4500	6300	9000
Series K-1 — (½-Ton) — (125 in. w.b.)					
Pickup	950	1900	3150	4400	6300
Canopy	960	1920	3200	4500	6400
Panel	920	1850	3050	4300	6100
Stake	930	1860	3100	4350	6200
Bakery Dely.	560	1100	1850	2600	3700
Series K-2 — (¾-Ton) — (125 in. w.b.)					
Pickup	900	1800	3000	4200	6000
Canopy	930	1860	3100	4350	6200
Panel	870	1750	2900	4100	5800
Stake	890	1770	2950	4150	5900
Bakery Dely.	530	1050	1750	2450	3500
Series K-3 — (One-Ton) — (113 in. w.b.)					
Pickup	850	1700	2850	4000	5700
Milk Dely.	500	1000	1650	2300	3300
Series K-3 — (One-Ton) — (130 in. w.b.)					
Pickup	840	1680	2800	3900	5600
Canopy	900	1800	3000	4200	6000
Panel	830	1650	2750	3850	5500
Stake	850	1700	2850	4000	5700
Sta. Wag.	1300	2550	4250	5900	8500
Metro Delivery Series — (102 in. w.b.)					
D-2M Panel	450	900	1500	2100	3000
K-1M Panel	450	900	1500	2100	3000
K-15M Panel	440	870	1450	2050	2900
K-3M Panel	440	870	1450	2050	2900
(113 in. w.b.)					
D-2M Panel	470	950	1550	2200	3100
K-1M Panel	470	950	1550	2200	3100
D-M15 Panel	450	900	1500	2100	3000
K-3M Panel	450	900	1500	2100	3000

1946 IHC

MODEL K — K-1 SERIES — SIX-CYLINDER: — The Model K line of IHC light-duty trucks was carried over for its final year in 1946. Styling was again unchanged. Characteristic appearance features included a "domed" cab roofline, long, pointed hood, flush headlights and a tall, barrel-shaped grille with curved horizontal bars and a vertical center divider. The International nameplate appeared at the lower rear edge of the hood. Decorating the nose was a badge having the company name across three diamonds. "I-H Red" was the company's traditional color for these trucks, but dark green, maroon and black finish was also available. The "Green Diamond" six-cylinder engine was used again. A heavy-duty suspension option coded as K-1H was available and uprated the trucks to ¾-ton, although K-1s are generally considered ½-tonners. They were again available on two different wheelbases. A new ½-ton K-1M was also available on a 102 inch wheelbase. Due to the unstable postwar market, IHCs were sold as chassis or chassis-and-cabs with body work optional. GVW ratings were 4400 pounds for the K-1 and 4600 pounds for the K-1M.

I.D. DATA: Serial number located: See 1945 IHC. Starting: (K-1) 28611. (K-1M) 2009. Ending: (K-1) 49308. (K-1M) 4251. Engine numbers located: See 1945 IHC.

Model	Body Type	Price	Weight	Prod. Total
Series K-1 — (½-Ton) — (113 in. w.b.)				
K-1	Chassis & Cab	883	2645	—
K-1	Chassis	763	2250	—
Series K-1 — (½-Ton) — (125 in. w.b.)				
K-1	Chassis & Cab	—	2760	—
K-1	Chassis	—83	2375	—
Series K-1M — (½-Ton) — (102 in. w.b.)				
K-1M	Chassis	773	2150	—

NOTE: Serial numbers indicate 20,697 trucks built in the K-1 series and 2,242 trucks built in the K-1M series.

1946 International Metro Delivery Van (OCW)

ENGINE (Series K-1): Inline. L-head. Six-cylinder. Cast iron block. Bore & stroke: 3-5/16 in. x 4⅛-in. Displacement: 213 cu. in. Compression ratio: 6.3:1. Brake horsepower: 82 at 3400 R.P.M. Net horsepower: 26.3 (NACC). Max. Torque: 160 lbs.-ft. at 1200 R.P.M. Four main bearings. Solid valve lifters. Carburetor: Zenith.

MODEL K — K-2 SERIES — SIX-CYLINDER: — The K-2 Series continued to be available for ¾-ton truck buyers in 1946. It could be had with light-duty K-2L (½-ton) and heavy-duty K-2H (one-ton) suspension options. The 125 inch wheelbase chassis was used for all models. Under the hood was the "Green Diamond" six-cylinder flathead engine. A heavy-duty Knox pickup box was used. Styling was similar to that of the K-1 trucks. The GVW rating was 5200 pounds.

I.D. DATA: Serial number located: See 1945 IHC. Starting: 17101. Ending: 28480. Engine numbers located: See 1945 IHC.

Model	Body Type	Price	Weight	Prod. Total
Series K-2 — (¾-Ton) — (125 in. w.b.)				
K-2	Chassis	768	2285	—
K-2	Chassis & Cab	888	2680	—
K-2	Express	958	3020	—

NOTE: Serial numbers indicate 11,379 trucks built in the K-2 Series.

ENGINE: See 1946 K-1 engine data.

MODEL K — SERIES K-3 — SIX-CYLINDER: — IHC one-ton trucks were again designated K-3s. A light-duty K-3L suspension option (½-ton rated) was cataloged. These trucks came with 113 or 130 inch wheelbases and "Green Diamond" engines. Styling was similar to other models in larger proportion. A 6650 pound GVW rating applied. There was also a new, 102 inch wheelbase K-3M model, with a 7,000 pound GVW rating.

I.D. DATA: Serial number located: See 1945 IHC. Starting: 19567. Ending 31108. Engine numbers located: See 1945 IHC.

1946 International Pickup Truck (OCW)

Model	Body Type	Price	Weight	Prod. Total
Series K-3 — (One-Ton) — (113 in. w.b.)				
K-3	Chassis	891	3000	—
K-3	Chassis & Cab	1011	3395	—
Series K-3 — (One-Ton) — (130 in. w.b.)				
K-3	Express	1102	3739	—
K-3	Stake	1099	4049	—
Series K-3M — (One-Ton) — (102 in. w.b.)				
K-3M	Chassis	—	2585	—

NOTE: Serial numbers indicate 11,541 trucks built in this series.

ENGINE: See 1946 K-1 engine data.

CHASSIS (Series K-1/K-1M*): Wheelbase: 113/125/102(*) in. Height: 49 in. Front tread: 58-9/32 in. Rear tread: 58-13/16 in. Tires: 6.00 x 16 in.

CHASSIS (Series K-2): Wheelbase: 125 in. Front tread: 58-9/32 in. Rear tread: 58-13/16 in. Tires: 6.00 x 16 in.

CHASSIS (Series K-3/K-3M*): Wheelbase: 113/130/102(*) in. Tires: 7.00 x 16 in.

TECHNICAL: Synchromesh transmission. Speeds: 3F/1R. Floor-mounted gear shift lever. Single-plate dry disc clutch; 10 inch diameter, semi-floating rear axle. Overall ratio: 4.88:1. Four-wheel hydraulic internal expanding brakes. Steel disc wheels. Four-speed manual transmission, with straight cut gears. Rear axle ratios: 3.72:1 through 5.11:1.

OPTIONS: Dual wipers. Rear bumper (station wagon). Single sidemount (station wagon). Dual cab sunvisors. Electric wipers. Knox heavy-duty grain box. Bumper guards. Radio. Heater. Clock. Cigar lighters. Radio antenna. Seat covers. External sun shade. Spotlight. Wheel trim rings. License plate bracket. Turn signals. Dual taillights. Special paint. Oversized tires.

HISTORICAL: Introduced: January 1946. Calendar year registrations: (All IHC trucks) 78,392. Calendar year production: (All IHC trucks) 113,546. IHC became America's fourth largest truck-maker again in 1946, with a 12.05 percent share of the total market. Chevrolet, Ford and Dodge, in order, were the only companies to sell more commercial vehicles.

Pricing

	5	4	3	2	1
1946					
Series K-1 — (½-Ton) — (113 in. w.b.)					
Pickup	920	1850	3050	4300	6100
Panel	690	1380	2300	3200	4600
Series K-1 — (½-Ton) — (125 in. w.b.)					
Pickup	900	1800	3000	4200	6000
Panel	680	1350	2250	3150	4500
Series K-1M — (½-Ton) — (102 in. w.b.)					
Metro Van	480	975	1600	2250	3200
Series K-2 — (¾-Ton) — (125 in. w.b.)					
Pickup	870	1750	2900	4100	5800
Panel	620	1230	2050	2900	4100
Series K-3 — (One-Ton) — (113 in. w.b.)					
Pickup	830	1650	2750	3850	5500
Milk Dely.	480	975	1600	2250	3200
Series K-3 — (One-Ton) — (130 in. w.b.)					
Pickup	800	1600	2650	3700	5300
Stake	590	1170	1950	2700	3900
Series K-3M — (One-Ton) — (102 in. w.b.)					
Metro Van	450	900	1500	2100	3000
Station Wagon					
Sta. Wag.	1200	2460	4100	5700	8200

1947-1949 IHC

1947 International Pickup Truck (DSO)

528

MODEL KB — SERIES KB-1/KB-1M — SIX-CYLINDER: — International introduced a new KB Series in January 1947. It remained in production, with no more than minor changes, through the close of the 1949 model year. Prices increased a bit each year and a few models had shipping weight changes. The KB was mainly an evolutionary series and brought no major alterations to the basically prewar design. The flush headlamps, domed cab roofs, and long, pointed hoods continued to characterize the "IHC look." There was even a crank hole, at the bottom of the grille, through which a manual engine crank could be inserted. The grille was still tall and barrel-shaped, but wing-like side grille extensions were added. They brought the bottom seven grille members out towards the headlights, right over the fender sheet metal. The badge on the nose of the trucks was made larger and now attached to the upper grille bars. In its center was a depression containing a smaller emblem with the International name across-three diamonds. A chrome molding was added on the top of the nose of the hood and model "call-outs" were plated below the International name on the rear lower edge of the hood. Standard equipment included an adjustable bench seat, 80 m.p.h. speedometer, ammeter, water temperature gauge, glove box, Lovejoy refillable shock absorbers, solid front axle, solid rear axle, semi-elliptic rear leaf springs, single interior sun visor and single vacuum-operated windshield wiper. The "Green Diamond" six-cylinder engine was used again. The KB-1 was the ½-ton model on 113 or 125 inch wheelbases. There was also a KB-1M ½-ton on a 102 inch wheelbase. GVW ratings for the two series were 4200 and 4600 pounds, respectively.

I.D. DATA: Serial number located: See 1945 IHC. 1947 starting/ending numbers: (KB-1) 49309/70792. (KB-1M) 4252/6706. (KB-2) 28481/49056. (KB-3) 31109/41078. (KB-3M) 6235/10749. 1948 starting/ending numbers: (KB-1) 70793/93351. (KB-1M) 6707/10633. (KB-2) 49057/74329. (KB-3) 41079/51781. (KB-3M) 10750/16634. 1949 starting numbers: (KB-1) 93352-up. (KB-1M) 10634-up. (KB-2) 74330-up. (KB-3) 51782-up. (KB-3M) 16635-up. Ending numbers for 1949 not available. Engine numbers located: See 1945 IHC. Engine numbers not available.

Model	Body Type	Price	Weight	Prod. Total
1947				
Series KB-1 — (½-Ton) — (113 in. w.b.)				
KB-1	Chassis	874	2350	—
KB-1	Chassis & Cowl	1030	2645	—
KB-1	Express (Pickup)	1098	2959	—
KB-1	Panel	1238	3150	—
KB-1	KBM (Bakery/Milk)	1477	3650	—
Series KB-1 — (½-Ton) — (125 in. w.b.)				
KB-1	Chassis	900	2375	—
KB-1	Chassis & Cowl	1056	2670	—
KB-1	Express (Pickup)	1139	2984	—
KB-1	Panel	1290	3175	—
KB-1	Stake	1145	3201	—
Series KB-1M — (½-Ton) — (102 in. w.b.)				
KB-1M	Chassis	827	2150	—

NOTE: Serial numbers indicate 21,483 trucks built in 1947 Series KB-1 and 2,484 trucks built in 1947 Series KB-1M.

1948 International Pickup Truck (OCW)

1948				
Series KB-1 — (½-Ton) — (113 in. w.b.)				
KB-1	Chassis	890	2250	—
KB-1	Chassis & Cowl	1098	2645	—
KB-1	Express (Pickup)	1186	2959	—
KB-1	Panel	1347	3545	—
KB-1	KBM (Bakery/Milk)	1560	3650	—
Series KB-1 — (½-Ton) — (125 in. w.b.)				
KB-1	Chassis	1066	2375	—
KB-1	Chassis & Cowl	1263	2670	—
KB-1	Express (Pickup)	1368	2984	—
KB-1	Panel	1581	3175	—
KB-1	Stake	1378	3201	—
Series KB-1M — (½-Ton) — (102 in. w.b.)				
KB-1M	Chassis	843	2150	—
KB-1M	Metro	1810	3955	—

NOTE: Serial numbers indicate 22,558 trucks built in 1948 Series KB-1 and 3,926 trucks built in 1948 Series KB-M1.

Model	Body Type	Price	Weight	Prod. Total
Series KB-1 — (½-Ton) — (113 in. w.b.)				
KB-1	Chassis	1045	2250	—
KB-1	Chassis & Cowl	1235	2645	—
KB-1	Express (Pickup)	1331	2959	—
KB-1	Panel	1534	3545	—
Series KB-1 — (½-Ton) — (125 in. w.b.)				
KB-1	Chassis	1071	2375	—
KB-1	Chassis & Cowl	1269	2670	—
KB-1	Express (Pickup)	1373	2984	—
KB-1	Panel	1586	3175	—
KB-1	Stake	1383	3201	—
Series KB-1M — (½-Ton) — (102 in. w.b.)				
KB-1M	Chassis	957	2150	—
KB-1M	Metro	2082	3955	—

NOTE: Production of 1949 models cannot be determined since ending serial numbers are not available.

ENGINE (All 1947-1949 Series): Inline. L-head. Six-cylinder. Cast iron block. Bore & stroke: 3-5/16 in. x 4⅛ in. Displacement: 213 cu. in. Compression ratio: 6.3:1. Brake horsepower: 82 at 3400 R.P.M. Net horsepower: 26.3 (NACC). Max. Torque: 160 lbs. ft. at 1200 R.P.M. Four main bearings. Solid valve lifters. Carburetor: Single downdraft, (model) Zenith.

MODEL KB — SERIES KB-2 — SIX-CYLINDER: — The KB-2 was the ¾-ton version of the updated IHC truck. It was styled and equipped similar to the KB-1. Only the 125 in. wheelbase was available for this series. A popular option for the ¾-ton series was a heavy-duty grain box with checkerplate bed surface promoted as the "Knox Box" after its manufacturer's name (which appeared on the tailgate). Like the KB-1, the KB-2 came in IHC red, dark green, maroon or black finish. These ¾-tonners had a 5200 pound GVW rating.

I.D. DATA: See KB-1 I.D. Data above.

Model 1947	Body Type	Price	Weight	Prod. Total
Series KB-2 — (¾-Ton) — (125 in. w.b.)				
KB-2	Chassis	916	2285	—
KB-2	Chassis & Cab	1066	2680	—
KB-2	Express (Pickup)	1155	3020	—
KB-2	Panel	1306	3245	—
KB-2	Stake	1160	3211	—

NOTE: Serial numbers indicate 20,575 trucks built in 1947 Series KB-2.

1948 International Station Wagon (OCW)

1948	Body Type	Price	Weight	Prod. Total
Series KB-2 — (¾-Ton) — (125 in. w.b.)				
KB-2	Chassis	931	2285	—
KB-2	Chassis & Cab	1139	2680	—
KB-2	Express (Pickup)	1243	3020	—
KB-2	Panel	1415	3640	—
KB-2	Stake	1254	3211	—

NOTE: Serial numbers indicate 25,272 trucks built in 1947 Series KB-2.

1949	Body Type	Price	Weight	Prod. Total
Series KB-2 — (¾-Ton) — (125 in. w.b.)				
KB-2	Chassis	1097	2285	—
KB-2	Chassis & Cab	1295	2680	—
KB-2	Express (Pickup)	1399	3020	—
KB-2	Panel	1612	3640	—
KB-2	Stake	1409	3211	—

NOTE: Production of 1949 models cannot be determined since ending serial numbers are not available.

ENGINE: See KB-1 engine data above.

MODEL KB — SERIES KB-3/KB-3M — SIX-CYLINDER: — The KB-3 was the one-ton version of the updated IHC truck. It was styled and equipped similar to other light-duty 1947-1949 models, except for larger tires and a heavier-duty running gear. The KB-3M was a shorter wheelbase version. GVW ratings for these two lines were 5200 and 6650 pounds, respectively. Power came from the same "Green Diamond" engine used in other small IHC trucks. The KB-3M, like the KB-1M, came only in chassis form in 1947 and gained a Metro walk-in van body for 1948 and 1949.

I.D. DATA: See KB-1 I.D. Data above.

1949 International Panel Truck (B. Heller)

Model 1947	Body Type	Price	Weight	Prod. Total
Series KB-3 — (One-Ton) - (113 in. w.b.)				
KB-3	Chassis	1067	3000	—
KB-3	Chassis & Cowl	1217	3395	—
KB-3	Express (Pickup)	1291	3709	—
KB-3	KM (Milk)	1671	4005	—
Series KB-3 — (One-Ton) — (130 in. w.b.)				
KB-3	Chassis	1067	3130	—
KB-3	Chassis & Cowl	1223	3425	—
KB-3	Express (Pickup)	1334	3739	—
KB-3	Panel	1483	4090	—
KB-3	Stake	1322	4049	—
Series KB-3M — (One-Ton) — (102 in. w.b.)				
KB-3M	Chassis	990	2585	—

NOTE: Serial numbers indicate 9,969 trucks built in 1947 Series KB-3 and 4,514 trucks built in 1947 Series KB-3M.

1948	Body Type	Price	Weight	Prod. Total
Series KB-3 — (One-Ton) — (113 in. w.b.)				
KB-3	Chassis	1093	3000	—
KB-3	Chassis & Cowl	1301	3395	—
KB-3	Express (Pickup)	1390	3709	—
KB-3	KM (Milk)	1764	4005	—
Series KB-3 — (One-Ton) — (130 in. w.b.)				
KB-3	Chassis	1244	3130	—
KB-3	Chassis & Cowl	1442	3425	—
KB-3	Express (Pickup)	1572	3739	—
KB-3	Panel	1785	4090	—
KB-3	Stake	1572	4049	—
Series KB-3M — (One-Ton) — (102 in. w.b.)				
KB-3M	Chassis	1016	2585	—
KB-3M	Metro	1982	4390	—

NOTE: Serial numbers indicate 11,702 trucks built in 1948 Series KB-3 and 5,884 trucks built in 1948 Series KB-3M.

1949	Body Type	Price	Weight	Prod. Total
Series KB-3 — (One-Ton) — (113 in. w.b.)				
KB-3	Chassis	1249	3000	—
KB-3	Chassis & Cowl	1447	3395	—
KB-3	Express (Pickup)	1525	3709	—
KB-3	KBM (Bake/Milk)	2017	4400	—
Series KB-3 — (One-Ton) — (130 in. w.b.)				
KB-3	Chassis	1249	3130	—
KB-3	Chassis & Cowl	1446	3425	—
KB-3	Express (Pickup)	1576	3815	—
KB-3	Panel	1790	4090	—
KB-3	Stake	1576	4049	—
Series KB-3M — (One-Ton) — (102 in. w.b.)				
KB-3M	Chassis	1145	2585	—
KB-3M	Metro	2270	4390	—

NOTE: Production of 1949 models cannot be determined since ending serial numbers are not available.

ENGINE: See KB-1 engine data above.

CHASSIS (Series KB-1/KB-1M*): Wheelbase: 113/125/102(*) in. Height: 49 in. Front tread: 58-9/32 in. Rear tread: 58-13/16 in. Tires: 6.00 x 16 in.

CHASSIS (Series KB-2): Wheelbase: 125 in. Front tread: 58-9/32 in. Rear tread: 58-13/16 in. Tires: 6.00 x 16 in.

CHASSIS (Series KB-3/KB-3M*): Wheelbase: 113/130/102(*) in. Tires: 7.00 x 16 in.

TECHNICAL: Synchromesh transmission. Speeds: 3F/1R. Floor-mounted gear shift lever. Single-plate dry disc clutch; 10 inch diameter, semi-floating rear axle. Overall ratio: 3.72:1 to 5.11:1. Four-wheel hydraulic internal expanding brakes. Steel spoke wheels. Four-speed manual transmission, with straight cut gears.

OPTIONS: Front bumper. Rear bumper. Single sidemount (station wagons). Dual cab interior sun visors. Dual electric wipers. Knox box. Bumper guards. Radio. Heater. Clock. Cigar lighters. Radio antenna. Seat covers. External sun shade. Spotlight. Wheel trim rings. License plate frame. Turn signals. Dual taillights. Special paint. Oversized tires. Deluxe panel body. Station wagon body. Metro bus interior. Deluxe trim package.

HISTORICAL: Introduced: (1947) Jan. 1947; (1948) Jan. 1, 1948; (1949) Jan.1949. Calendar year production: All IHC products: (1947) 153,009; (1948) 166,784; (1949) 110,558. Model year production: Same as above calendar year totals. New KB series introduced in 1947. IHC industry ranking (and market share) for the three years was as follows: 1947 — ranked fourth (12.37 percent); 1948 — ranked fourth (12.18 percent); 1949 — ranked fourth (9.77 percent). Mr. J.L. McCaffrey was president of IHC. W.V. Reese was engineering manager. W.K. Perkins was manager of sales. All-time record truck sales were recorded in 1948. IHC had about 15,000 truck division employees. The company was headquartered in Chicago, Ill. IHC trucks were nicknamed "corn-binders."

Pricing

	5	4	3	2	1
1947-1949					
Series KB-1 — (½-Ton) — (113 in. w.b.)					
Express (Pickup)	920	1850	3050	4300	6100
Panel	690	1380	2300	3200	4600
KBM (Bake/Milk)	540	1080	1800	2500	3600
Series KB-1 — (½-Ton) — (125 in. w.b.)					
Express (Pickup)	900	1800	3000	4200	6000
Panel	680	1350	2250	3150	4500
Stake	630	1250	2100	3000	4200
Series KB-1M — (½-Ton) — (102 in. w.b.)					
Metro Van	480	975	1600	2250	3200
Series KB-2 — (¾-Ton) — (125 in. w.b.)					
Express (Pickup)	870	1750	2900	4100	5800
Panel	620	1230	2050	2900	4100
Stake	600	1200	2000	2800	4000
Series KB-3 — (One-Ton) — (113 in. w.b.)					
Express (Pickup)	830	1650	2750	3850	5500
KM (Milk)	480	975	1600	2250	3200
Series KB-3 — (One-Ton) — (130 in. w.b.)					
Express (Pickup)	800	1600	2650	3700	5300
Panel	600	1200	2000	2800	4000
Stake	590	1170	1950	2700	3900
Series KB-3M — (One-Ton) — (102 in. w.b.)					
Metro Van	450	900	1500	2100	3000
Station Wagons (Custom Body)					
Sta. Wag. (all)	1200	2400	4000	5600	8000

1950-1952 IHC

1950 International Panel Truck (DSO)

MODEL L — ALL SERIES — SIX-CYLINDER: — An all-new L Series line of trucks was introduced by IHC in January 1950. They were totally restyled and re-engineered. Styling characteristics included a one-piece windshield, two-section rear cab window, broad flat fenders and a wide and flat front end cap. Single headlamps were flush-mounted into keyhole-shaped recesses with rectangular parking lamps below. The new grille consisted of three horizontal bars, with the lowest stretching under the parking lamps, with 19 vertical "blades" above. The three outermost vertical blades on each side were shorter. A bright metal strip ran across the lower edge of the nose, which had an IHC shield on it, plus a chrome molding. A painted, wraparound bumper protected the front. Under the hood was a new overhead valve inline six-cylinder engine. These models were first merchandised mainly as chassis and cab trucks. More information about body styles was released in 1952. A station wagon with wood-body construction could be ordered for just about any chassis. Metro vans, milk trucks, bakery trucks and small school buses were available, too. (Note: Factory prices for 1950-1951 bodies can be estimated by comparing comparable chassis & cab prices for the three years included in this section).

I.D. DATA: Serial number located: See 1945 ID data. These trucks were not produced on a yearly model basis. Year model determined by date of original sale to operator. Starting serial numbers were 501 up. Engine numbers located: See 1945 I.D. Data. Engine numbers not available.

Model	Body Type	Price	Weight	Prod. Total
1950				
Series L-110/L-111/L-112				
L-11	Chassis & Cab	1304	2965	—
Series L-120/L-121/L-122				
L-12	Chassis & Cab	1439	3230	—
Series LM-120/LM-121/LM-122				
LM-12	Chassis (for Metro)	1183	2370	—
Series L-150				
L-15	Chassis & Cab	1600	3880	—
Series L-153				
L-153	1-Ton School Bus	1468	3540	—
Series LM-150				
LM-15	Chassis (for H-D Metro)	1354	2970	—
1951				
Series L-110/L-111/L-112				
L-11	Chassis & Cab	1350	2965	—
Series L-120/L-121/L-122				
L-12	Chassis & Cab	1490	3230	—
Series LM-120/LM-121/LM-122				
LM-12	Chassis (for Metro)	1175	2370	—
Series LB-140 Metro				
LB-14	½-Ton Milk Truck	1980	3015	—
Series L-150/L-151				
L-15	Chassis & Cab	1657	3880	—
Series L-153				
L-153	1-Ton School Bus	1535	3540	—
Series LM-150				
LM-15	Chassis (for H-D Metro)	1350	2970	—
1952				
Series L-110/L-111/L-112				
L-11	Chassis & Cab	1375	2965	—
L-11	Pickup	1468	—	—
L-11	Panel	1658	—	—
Series L-120/L-121/L-122				
L-12	Chassis & Cab	1505	3230	—
L-12	Pickup	1598	—	—
L-12	Panel	1788	—	—
Series LM-120/LM-121/LM-122				
LM-12	½-Ton Metro (102 in w.b.)	2289	—	—
LM-12	¾-Ton Metro (115 in. w.b.)	2344	—	—
LM-12	1-Ton Metro (122 in. w.b.)	2506	—	—
Series LB-140				
LB-14	Milk Truck	2750	3015	—
Series L-150/L-151				
L-15	Chassis & Cab	1699	3880	—
Series L-153				
L-15	1-Ton School Bus (130 in. w.b.)	1510	3540	—
Series LM-150/LM-151				
LM-15	¾-Ton Heavy-Duty Metro (115 in. w.b.)	2519	—	—
LM-15	1-Ton Heavy-Duty Metro (122 in. w.b.)	2681	—	—

1951 IHC Pickup (J.R. Faureau)

ENGINE (All Series): Inline. Overhead valve. Six-cylinder. Cast iron block. Bore & stroke: 3-9/16 in. x 3-11/16 in. Displacement: 220 cu. in. Brake horsepower: 101. Net horsepower: 30.4 (NACC).

CHASSIS (Series L-110/L-111): Wheelbase: 115/127 in.

CHASSIS (Series L-112/L-120 Heavy-Duty): Wheelbase: 127 in.

CHASSIS (Series L-130): Wheelbase: 134 in.

CHASSIS (Metro Van): Wheelbase: 102/115 in.

TECHNICAL: Synchromesh transmission. Speeds: 3F/1R. Column or floor-mounted gear shift lever. Single-plate dry disc clutch; 10 in. diam. Semi-floating rear axle. Four-wheel hydraulic brakes. Steel disc wheels. Four-speed transmission.

1952 International Pickup Truck (OCW)

Cab and Truck Body Prices
(Cab Price)
Series L-110 .... $230
Series L-120 .... $230
Series L-130 .... $230
Series L-150 .... $239
(Pickup Body)
Series L-110/115 in. w.b./6½ ft. box $93
Series L-120/115 in. w.b./6½ ft. box $93
Series L-110/127 in. w.b./8 ft. box $108
Series L-120/127 in. w.b./8 ft. box $108
Series L-130/134 in. w.b./9 ft. box $127
(Panel Body)
Series L-110/115 in. w.b./7½ ft. cargo $513
Series L-120/115 in. w.b./7½ ft. cargo $513
(Metro Van Body)
Series LM-120/102 in. w.b. w/std. body $2289
Series LM-120/115 in. w.b. w/std. body $2344
Series LM-120/122 in. w.b. w/std. body $2506
Series LM-150/115 in. w.b. w/std. body $2519
Series LM-150/122 in. w.b. w/std. body $2681
Series LM-150/134 in. w.b. w/std. body $2788

OPTIONS: Front bumper. Rear bumper. Dual interior sun visors. Dual electric wipers. Turn signals. Fender skirts. Bumper guards. Radio. Heater. Clock. Cigar lighter. Radio antenna. Seat covers. External sun shade. Spotlight. Wheel trim rings. License plate frame. Special paint. Oversized tires. Deluxe trim packages. Station wagon body.

HISTORICAL: Introduced: Jan. 1950. Calendar year registrations: all IHC: (1950) 97,818; (1951) 95,184. Calendar year production: IHC, 5000 lbs. and less: (1949) 18,368; (1950) 26,350; (1951) 31,588. IHC, 5001 to 10,000 lbs.: (1949) 38,306; (1950) 27,330; (1951) 28,996. (Tabulated by GVW) Model year production: all IHC: (1950) 106,418; (1951) 151,439. New L Series styling with modernized features. All-new overhead valve six-cylinder. First column shift availability.

IHC held its fourth rank in the truck industry. The company's second best year in history was recorded in 1951. The company produced 5-ton trucks for the military this season. A new motor truck engineering lab was opened at Ft. Wayne, Ind. in 1951. In 1951, the company announced that one million trucks it had produced were still in service.

1952 International Travelall (OCW)

Pricing

1950-1952	5	4	3	2	1
Series L-110/L-111					
½-Ton Pickup (6½ ft.)	850	1700	2850	4000	5700
½-Ton Pickup (8 ft.)	840	1680	2800	3900	5600
½-Ton Panel (7½ ft.)	660	1320	2200	3100	4400
Series L-112					
¾-Ton Pickup (6½ ft.)	840	1680	2800	3900	5600
¾-Ton Pickup (8 ft.)	830	1650	2750	3850	5500
¾-Ton Panel (7½ ft.)	650	1300	2150	3050	4300
Series L-120					
¾-Ton Pickup (6½ ft.)	750	1500	2500	3500	5000
¾-Ton Pickup (8 ft.)	740	1470	2450	3350	4900
¾-Ton Panel (7½ ft.)	590	1170	1950	2700	3900
Series LM-120/LM-150/LM-151					
½-Ton Metro	450	900	1500	2100	3000
¾-Ton Metro	450	900	1500	2100	3000
1-Ton Metro	440	870	1450	2050	2700
Series L-130					
1-Ton Pickup (9 ft.)	470	950	1550	2200	3100
Series L-153					
1-Ton School Bus	380	750	1250	1750	2500
Series LB-140					
Milk Truck	420	840	1400	1950	2800
Station Wagons					
½-Ton (Wood)	980	1950	3250	4550	6500
¾-Ton (Wood)	900	1800	3000	4200	6000
1-Ton (Wood)	830	1650	2750	3850	5500

1953-1955 IHC

1953 International Pickup (HAS)

MODEL R — ½-TON — SIX-CYLINDER: — IHC R Series trucks were introduced in 1953. Light-duty models were marketed through 1955. Stylingwise, they looked like a modernized L Series with sculpturing removed from fender and hood sides. Front end panels were now slightly concave with an oval grille opening. A hefty single grille bar, with "I-H" in its center, spanned the opening horizontally. Single, round headlamp housings protruded slightly and had rectangular parking lamps underneath. An air slot was cut into the lower front edge of the hood. Trim consisted of a bright metal hood molding, side hood ornaments and International nameplates (at the rear of the hood). Two-tone finish was optional. Half-ton lines were the light-duty R-100 (115 in. w.b.) and heavier-duty R-110 (115 or 127 in. w.b.) The R-100 had a 4200 pound GVW rating, but could be ordered with an R-102 option that increased the GVW to 4600 pounds. The R-110 also had a 4200 pound GVW and two options; the R-111 (4800 pound GVW) and R-112 (5400 pound GVW). Standard equipment included gauges, a single interior sun visor, bench seat, small hub caps, black sidewall tires and tire changing tools. The overhead valve "Silver Diamond" six-cylinder engine was carried over from 1952 for the new trucks. For 1953 and 1954 these trucks were identical in features, models, prices and weights. In 1955, a chassis without cab was added and prices increased slightly, although weights were unchanged.

I.D. DATA: Serial number located on the left side frame rail behind front spring hanger. Also stamped on capacity plate attached to the left door pillar. Starting: Numbers began at 501 up for each series. Ending: Not available. Engine numbers located: Stamped on boss on left-hand upper-front side of crankcase. Engine numbers not available.

1953 International Cantrell Station Wagon (OCW)

NOTE: International trucks were not produced on a yearly model basis change. Year model was determined by the date of original sale to operator, as shown by bill of sale or title. Serial numbers were continued from 1953.

Model	Body Type	Price	Weight	Prod. Total
1953-154				
Series R-100/R-102 — (½-Ton) — (115 in. w.b.)				
R-100	Chassis & Cab	1230	2980	—
R-100	Pickup	1324	3310	—
Series R-110/R-111/R-112 — (½-Ton) — (115 in. w.b.)				
R-110	Chassis & Cab	1290	3115	—
R-110	Pickup	1384	3445	—
R-110	Panel	1576	3720	—
Series R-110/R-111/R-112 — (½-Ton) — (127 in. w.b.)				
R-110	Chassis & Cab	1315	3200	—
R-110	Pickup	1424	3585	—
R-110	Stake	1502	—	—
1955				
Series R-100/R-102 — (½-Ton) — (115 in. w.b.)				
R-100	Chassis & Cowl	1063	2490	—
R-100	Chassis & Cab	1305	2980	—
R-100	Pickup	1399	3310	—
Series R-110/R-111/R-112 — (½-Ton) — (115 in. w.b.)				
R-110	Chassis & Cowl	1123	2625	—
R-110	Chassis & Cab	1365	3115	—
R-110	Pickup	1459	3445	—
R-110	Stake	1552	—	—
R-110	Panel	1656	3720	—
Series R-110/R-111/R-112 (½-Ton) — (127 in. w.b.)				
R-110	Chassis & Cowl	1148	2710	—
R-110	Chassis & Cab	1390	3200	—
R-110	Pickup	1484	3585	—
R-110	Stake	1577	—	—

ENGINE: Inline. Overhead valve. Six-cylinder. Cast iron block. Bore & stroke: 3-9/16 in. x 3-11/16 in. Displacement: 220.5 cu. in. Compression ratio: 6.5:1 (7.01 after 1954). Brake horsepower: 100 at 3600 R.P.M. (104 at 3600 after 1954). Net horsepower: 30.4 (NACC). Max. Torque: 173.5 lbs. ft. at 1200 R.P.M. Four main bearings. Solid valve lifters.

NOTE: The "Silver Diamond" six-cylinder engine featured rifle-drilled connecting rods, full-pressure lubrication and heat-treated aluminum alloy pistons with four piston rings.

1953 International Travelall (DFW)

532

MODEL R — ¾-TON — SIX-CYLINDER: The R-120 was the basic ¾-ton series offered by IHC from 1953 to 1955. It had a 5400 pound GVW rating. Also available were the R-121 (5900 pound GVW) and R-122 (6500 pound GVW) chassis options. The R-120/R-122 trucks could be had on either the 115 or 127 in. w.b. Styling and equipment features were similar to those of the ½-tonners. Hydra-matic automatic transmission was a new-for-1955 option for all light-duty IHC trucks. An identifying series designation appeared on the side of the hoods at the cowl. For 1953 and 1954, these trucks were identical in features, models, prices and weights. In 1955, a chassis & cowl only configuration was added and prices went up slightly, although weights were unchanged. Also available on the ¾-ton chassis was the Metro Delivery van, with a choice of 102, 115 or 122 in. w.b. The "Silver Diamond" six was used in all of these trucks.

I.D. DATA: See ½-ton series I.D. Data above.

1953 International Pickup (OCW)

Model	Body Type	Price	Weight	Prod. Total
1953-1954				
Series R-120/R-121/R-122 — (¾-Ton) — (115 in. w.b.)				
R-120	Chassis & Cab	1372	3380	—
R-120	Pickup	1466	3710	—
R-120	Panel	1658	3985	—
Series R-120/R-121/R-122 — (¾-Ton) — (127 in. w.b.)				
R-120	Chassis & Cab	1397	3410	—
R-120	Pickup	1506	3795	—
R-120	Stake	1584	—	—
Series RA-120/RA-121/RA-122 — (¾-Ton) — (115 in. w.b.)				
RA-120	Metroette Chassis	2175	3158	—
Series RM-120/RM-121/RM-122 — (¾-Ton) — (102 in. w.b.)				
RM-120	Metro (std. body)	2314	—	—
RM-120	Metro Flat Back	2374	—	—
Series RM-120/RM-121/RM-122 — (¾-Ton) — (115 in. w.b.)				
RM-120	Metro (std. body)	2369	—	—
RM-120	Metro Flat Back	2429	—	—
RM-120	School Bus	3319	—	—
Series RM-120/RM-121/RM-122 — (¾-Ton) — (122 in. w.b.)				
RM-120	Metro (std. body)	2531	—	—
RM-120	Metro Flat Back	2591	—	—
1955				
Series R-120/R-121/R-122 — (¾-Ton) — (115 in. w.b.)				
R-120	Chassis & Cowl	1205	2890	—
R-120	Chassis & Cab	1447	3380	—
R-120	Pickup	1556	3710	—
R-120	Panel	1738	3985	—
Series R-120/R-121/R-122 — (¾-Ton) — (127 in w.b.)				
R-120	Chassis & Cowl	1230	2920	—
R-120	Chassis & Cab	1472	3410	—
R-120	Pickup	1581	3740	—
R-120	Stake	1659	—	—
Series RA-120/RA-121/RA-122 — (¾-Ton) — (115 in. w.b.)				
RA-120	Chassis (Metroette)	2225	3158	—
Series RM-120/RM-121/RM-122 — (¾-Ton) — (102 in. w.b.)				
RM-120	Metro Chassis	1230	2520	—
RM-120	Metro Body	2364	—	—
Series RM-120/RM-121/RM-122 — (¾-Ton) — (115 in. w.b.)				
RM-120	Metro Chassis	1230	2650	—
RM-120	Metro Body	2419	—	—
RM-120	Metro Flat Back	2479	—	—
RM-120	Metro-Lite Body	2990	—	—
RM-120	School Bus (forward seat)	3369	—	—
RM-120	School Bus (full seat)	3369	—	—
Series RM-120/RM-121/RM-122 — (¾-Ton) — (122 in. w.b.)				
RM-120	Metro Chassis	1255	2740	—
RM-120	Metro Flat Back	2641	—	—
RM-120	Metro-Lite Body	3040	—	—

NOTE: GVW rating for the Metroette was 9000 pounds. GVW ratings for Metros were as follows: (RM-120) 5400 pounds, (RM-121) 6000 pounds, (RM-122) 6600 pounds.

ENGINE: "Silver Diamond" engine in all models. See specifications above.

1954 International Pickup (IOA)

MODEL R — 1-TON — SIX-CYLINDER: The R-130 was the basic 1-ton series offered by IHC from 1953-1955. It had a 6800 pounds GVW rating. Also available were the R-131 (7700 pound GVW) and R-132 (8600 pound GVW) chassis options. The R-130/R-131/R-132 trucks could be had on either a 115, 122 or 134 in. w.b. Styling and equipment features were similar to those of other models. A four-speed transmission was, however, standard with the 1-tonners. These trucks had series identification on the sides of the hood near the cowl, below the "International" name.

1954 International 4x4 Pickup (OCW)

I.D. DATA: See ½-ton series I.D. Data above.

Model	Body Type	Price	Weight	Prod. Total
1953-1954				
Series R-130/R-131/R-132 — (1-Ton) — (115 in. w.b.)				
R-130	Chassis & Cab	1474	3610	—
R-130	Pickup	1700	—	—
R-130	Stake	1700	—	—
Series R-130/R-131/R-132 — (1-Ton) — (134 in. w.b.)				
R-130	Chassis & Cab	1489	3650	—
R-130	Pickup	1617	4060	—
R-130	Stake	1715	—	—
1955				
Series R-130/R-131/R-132 — (1-Ton) — (122 in. w.b.)				
R-130	Chassis & Cowl	1322	3130	—
R-130	Chassis & Cab	1564	3620	—
R-130	Stake	1790	—	—
Series R-131/R-131/R-132 — (1-Ton) — (134 in. w.b.)				
R-130	Chassis & Cowl	1322	3160	—
R-130	Chassis & Cab	1564	3650	—
R-130	Pickup	1692	4060	—
R-130	Stake	1790	—	—

1954 International Pickup (S. Soloy)

ENGINE: "Silver Diamond" engine in all series. See speficiation above.

CHASSIS (½-Ton Series): Wheelbase: 115/127 in. Height: 51-5/16 in. Front tread: 58-9/32 in. Rear tread: 58-13/16 in. Tires: 6.00 x 16 in.

CHASSIS (¾-Ton Series): Wheelbase: 102/115/122/127 in. Tires: 6.50 x 16 six-ply.

CHASSIS (1-Ton Series): Wheelbase: 115/122/134 in. Tires: 7.50 x 16 in.

TECHNICAL (½-Ton and ¾-Ton Series): Synchromesh transmission. Speeds: 3F/1R. Floor mounted gear shift lever. Single-plate dry disc clutch; 11 in. diam. Hotchkiss type full-floating hypoid rear axle. Overall ratio: 4.1:1. Pres-stop twin-shoe drum brakes. Steel disc wheels. Heavy-duty three-speed transmission (all models). Hydra-Matic transmission (1955 only).

1955 International Travelall (RPZ)

TECHNICAL (1-Ton Series): Sliding gear transmission with "carburized" gears. Speeds: 4F/1R. Floor mounted gear shift lever. Single-plate dry disc clutch; 11 in. diam. Hotchkiss type full-floating hypoid rear axle. Overall ratio: 6.616:1. Pres-stop twin-shoe drum brakes. Steel disc wheels. Hydra-Matic transmission (1955 only).

1955 International Pickup (S. Soloy)

OPTIONS: Chrome front bumper. Rear bumper. Dual sidemount (body side). Full foam rubber seat padding. Dome light. Bumper guards. Radio (AM). Heater (fresh air or recirculating models). Clock. Cigar lighter. Radio antenna. Seat covers. External sun shade. Spotlight. Right-hand sunvisor. Door arm rests. Electric windshield wipers. Lockable glove compartment. Special paint. Wheel trim rings. Turn signals. White sidewall tires. Pickup box side panels. OSRV mirror. Deluxe equipment package. Deluxe cab interior.

HISTORICAL: Introduced Jan. 1953. Calendar year registrations: 95,404 (all 1953 models). 84,222 (all 1954 models). 100,441 (all 1955 models). Calendar year registration weight class: (1953) 39,507 in 5000 lb. or less category and 21,083 in 5001 to 10,000 lb. class. Total for all 1953 models 121,522. (1954) 29,322 in 5000 lb. or less category and 12,945 in 5001 to 10,000 lb. class. (1955) 35,330 in 5000 or less category and 20,843 in 5001 to 10,000 lbs. Updated styling. Hydra-Matic transmission available in 1955 models. New Metroette and Metro-Lite models.

J.L. McCaffrey was IHC president in 1953 when the R-100 series debuted. IHC was third-ranked in United States truck production for 1953, despite a Borg-Warner transmission plant strike that cost the company about 15,000 assemblies. During 1953 IHC introduced two "R" model 4x4 trucks, LP gas attachments for certain R trucks and the Travelall station wagon. McCaffrey continued to head the company in 1954, when sales of all models slipped 20.9 percent. Three-speed fully automatic transmissions were made a late 1954 option for light duty models and tubeless tires become standard equipment. IHC's output rose 37 percent in 1955, despite a 26 day factory strike. The company retained number three position in truck production.

Pricing

	5	4	3	2	1
1953-1955					
Series R-100 Light-Duty — (½-Ton) — (115 in. w.b.)					
Pickup (6½ ft.)	850	1700	2850	4000	5700
Series R-110 Heavy-Duty — (½-Ton) — (115/127 in. w.b.)					
Pickup (6½ ft.)	840	1680	2800	3900	5600
Panel (7½ ft.)	660	1320	2200	3100	4400
Pickup (8 ft.)	830	1650	2750	3850	5500
Stake	810	1620	2700	3800	5400
Series R-120 — (¾-Ton) — (115/127 in. w.b.)					
Pickup (6½ ft.)	830	1650	2750	3850	5500
Panel (7½ ft.)	650	1300	2150	3050	4300
Pickup (8 ft.)	810	1620	2700	3800	5400
Stake	800	1600	2650	3700	5300
Series RA-120 — (¾-Ton) — (115 in. w.b.)					
Metroette	400	800	1350	1900	2700
Series RM-120 — (¾-Ton) — (102/115/122 in. w.b.)					
Metro Dely. (102 in. w.b.)	450	900	1500	2100	3000
Metro Flat Back (102 in. w.b.)	440	870	1450	2050	2900
Metro Dely. (115 in. w.b.)	450	900	1500	2100	3000
Metro Flat Back (115 in. w.b.)	440	870	1450	2050	2900
Metro Bus (115 in. w.b.)	440	870	1450	2050	2900
Metro Dely. (122 in. w.b.)	440	870	1450	2050	2900
Metro Flat Back (122 in. w.b.)	420	840	1400	1950	2800
Metro-Lite (115 in. w.b.)	400	800	1350	1900	2700
Metro-Lite (122 in. w.b.)	400	800	1350	1900	2700
Series R-130 — (1-Ton) — (115/122/134 in. w.b.)					
Pickup (6½ ft.)	480	975	1600	2250	3200
Stake (6½ ft.)	450	900	1500	2100	3000
Pickup (9 ft.)	470	950	1550	2200	3100
Stake (8 ft.)	440	870	1450	2050	2900
Stake (9 ft.)	420	840	1400	1950	2800

1956-1957 IHC

1956 International Travelall (DFW/MVMA)

MODEL S — ½-TON — SIX-CYLINDER: — A new S Series was brought out by IHC late in 1955 and continued through mid-1957. Since IHC trucks were not sold on a model year basis, some of these may have been registered as 1955 models, although they are usually thought of as 1956-1957 vehicles. They had a somewhat squarer, more sculptured look with their headlights mounted high on the fenders inside chrome rings. An opening at the front center edge of the wider, flatter hood formed a wide air scoop. The grille insert was somewhat traphazoid shaped and painted, rather than plated. It had a similarly shaped, but narrower, opening flanked by two rather large, round parking lights. A winged "IH" badge was on the nose and the hoodsides, near the cowl, carried the International name and a series designation. A new windshield permitted more visibility comparable to then popular wraparound windshields. Regular and Deluxe cab interiors were available. The standard trim was in gray vinyl coordinated with a gray interior color combination. These trucks still had separate "pontoon" rear fenders and full runningboards. Half-tonners came in the lighter-duty (4200 pound GVW) S-100/Series and the heavier-duty (also 4200 pound GVW) S-110 series. The S-100 line had an S-102 option (5000 pound GVW) and the S-110 had an S-112 option (5400 pound GVW). There were two wheelbases for the S-110s and a new Travel-all model that resembled a suburban (station wagon). The 1957 model had slightly increased prices and the same models.

I.D. DATA: Serial number located on left side of frame rail behind front spring hanger. Also stamped on capacity plate attached to left door pillar. Serial numbers were continued from 1953. Numbers are not available. Engine numbers located stamped on boss on left-hand upper front side of crankcase. Engine numbers not available.

NOTE: IHC trucks were not produced on a yearly model basis change. Year model was determined by date of original sale to operator, as shown

1956 International Panel Delivery (OCW)

by bill of sale or title. Because of different state laws, 1955, 1956 and 1957 Model S titles can be found, although this series was built less than two years.

Model	Body Type	Price	Weight	Prod. Total
Series S-100/S-102 — (½-Ton) — (115 in. w.b.)				
S-100	Chassis & Cab	1370	2980	—
S-100	Pickup	1471	3310	—
Series S-110/S-112 — (½-Ton) — (115 in. w.b.)				
S-110	Chassis & Cab	1465	3115	—
S-110	Pickup	1566	3445	—
S-110	Panel	1793	3720	—
S-110	Travel-all	2066	4000	—
Series S-110/S-112 — (½-Ton) — (127 in. w.b.)				
S-110	Chassis & Cab	1490	3200	—
S-110	Pickup	1607	3530	—
S-110	Stake	1681	3585	—
S-110	Platform	1628		—

NOTE: In 1957, the ½-ton trucks were $60 more expensive and had identical shipping weights as compared to the 1956 introductory prices above.

1956 International Travelall (OCW)

ENGINE (Series S-100/S-102): Inline. Overhead valve. Six-cylinder. Cast iron block. Bore & stroke: 3-9/16 in. x 3-11/16 in. Displacement: 220.5 cu. in. Compression ratio: 6.5:1. Brake horsepower: 100 at 3600 R.P.M. Net horsepower: 30.4 (NACC). Max. Torque: 173.5 lbs. ft. at 1200 R.P.M. Four main bearings. Solid valve lifters.

NOTE: "Silver Diamond" engine.

ENGINE (Series S-110/S-112): Inline. Overhead valve. Six-cylinder. Cast iron block. Bore & stroke: 3-9/16 in. x 4.018 in. Displacement: 240 cu. in. Brake horsepower: 140.8 at 3800 R.P.M. Net horsepower: 30.4 (NACC). Max. Torque: 223.5 lbs. ft. at 2000 R.P.M. Four main bearings. Solid valve lifters.

NOTE: This new powerplant was known as the "240 Black Diamond" engine.

1956 International Pickup (OCW)

1956 International Pickup (DFW)

MODEL S — ¾-TON — SIX-CYLINDER: — The S-120 was the basic ¾-ton series offered by IHC in 1956-1957. It had a 5400 pound GVW rating. Also available was an S-122 (6900 pound GVW) chassis option. These trucks came on either the 115 in. or 127 in. w.b., when equipped with conventional rear wheel drive. In addition, there was a four-wheel-drive (4x4) chassis option for ¾-ton trucks on four different wheelbases: 115, 122, 127 or 134 inches. Also available on a ¾-ton chassis, were Metro van-type trucks. Here, the base series was coded SM-120 and the heavier-duty chassis option was the SM-122. The Metros came on 102, 115 and 122 in. w.b. with standard, flatback or Metrolite bodies. Gross vehicle weight ratings were 5400 pounds for the SM-120 and 6600 pounds for the SM-122. IHC also continued to market ¾-ton milk/bakery delivery vans on the 115 in. w.b. These were in the SA-120 Series and had a 6500 pound GVW rating. All of these trucks used the "240 Black Diamond" engine. They were sold from late 1955 to mid-1957.

I.D. DATA: See ½-Ton Series I.D. Data above.

Model	Body Type	Price	Weight	Prod. Total
Series S-120/S-122 — (¾-Ton) — (115 in. w.b.)				
S-120	Chassis & Cab	1547	3380	—
S-120	Pickup	1647	3710	—
S-120	Panel	1857	3985	—
S-120	Travel-all	2148	4265	—
Series S-120/S-122 — (¾-Ton) — (127 in. w.b.)				
S-120	Chassis & Cab	1572	3410	—
S-120	Pickup	1689	3795	—
S-120	Stake	1763	3869	—
S-120	Platform	1710	—	—
Series S-120 — (¾-Ton) — (4x4) — (115 in. w.b.)				
S-120	Chassis & Cab	2027	3880	—
S-120	Pickup	2128	4210	—
S-120	Panel	2355	4485	—
S-120	Travel-all	2628	4765	—
Series S-120 — (¾-Ton) — (4x4) — (122 in. w.b.)				
S-120	Chassis & Cab	2037	3908	—
Series S-120 — (¾-Ton) — (4x4) — (127 in. w.b.)				
S-120	Chassis & Cab	2047	3922	—
S-120	Platform	2185	—	—
S-120	Stake	2238	4527	—
S-120	Pickup	2164	4307	—
Series S-120 — (¾-Ton) — (4x4) — (134 in. w.b.)				
S-120	Chassis & Cab	2057	3938	—
S-120	Platform	2216	—	—
S-120	Stake	2294	4628	—
S-120	Pickup	2194	4348	—
Series SA-120/SA-122 — (¾-Ton) — (115 in. w.b.)				
SA-120	Milk Dely.	2490	2675	—
SA-120	Dely. Body	2490	2675	—
Series SM-120/SM-122 — (¾-Ton) — (102 in. w.b.)				
SM-120	Chassis	1298	2650	—
SM-120	Std. Metro Body	2523	3705	—
Series SM-120/SM-122 — (¾-Ton) — (115 in. w.b.)				
SM-120	Chassis	1298	2650	—
SM-120	Std. Metro Body	2582	4570	—
SM-120	Flat Back Metro	2647	4650	—
SM-120	Metro-lite	3199	—	—
Series SM-120/SM-122 — (¾-Ton) — (122 in. w.b.)				
SM-120	Chassis	1323	2740	—
SM-120	Flat Back Metro	2820	4900	—
SM-120	Metro-Lite	3251	—	—

NOTE: Prices increased for 1957 ¾-ton models as follows: Conventional S-120/S-122 ($70); 4x4 S-120/S-122 ($150); SA-120 ($115); SM-120/SM-122 w/102 in. w.b. ($118); SM-120/SM-122 w/115 in. w.b. ($121) and SM-120/SM-122 w/122 in. w.b. ($133). Shipping weights were unchanged from 1956.

ENGINE: The "Silver Diamond" engine was used in ¾-ton milk delivery, Metro van and Metro-lite trucks. (SA/SM models). The "240 Black Diamond" engine was used in other ¾-ton trucks with conventional or four-wheel-drive running gear.

MODEL S — 1-TON — SIX-CYLINDER: — S-130 was IHC's designation for the 7000 pound GVW, 1-ton models that it produced from late 1955 to mid-1957. There was an S-132 chassis option to raise GVW ratings to a hefty 8800 pounds. A 122 in. w.b. chassis was marketed, plus a chassis and three factory bodies on a longer 134 in. w.b. One-ton versions of the Metro Delivery models were also offered. There was the basic 7000 pound GVW lighter-duty version, plus an SM-132 option with a 9000 pound GVW rating.

I.D. DATA: See ½-Ton Series I.D. Data above.

Model	Body Type	Price	Weight	Prod. Total
Series S-130/S-132 — (1-Ton) — (122 in. w.b.)				
S-130	Chassis & Cab	1664	3620	—
Series S-130/S-132 — (1-Ton) — (134 in. w.b.)				
S-130	Chassis & Cab	1664	3650	—
S-130	Pickup	1801	4060	—
S-130	Platform	1823	—	—
S-130	Stake	1901	—	—
Series SM-130/SM-132 — (1-Ton) — (122 in. w.b.)				
S-130	Chassis	1495	2940	—
SM-130	Flat Back Steel Body	2992	5100	—
SM-130	Metro-Lite Body	3423	4210	—
Series SM-130/SM-132 — (1-Ton) — (134 in. w.b.)				
SM-130	Chassis	1495	2980	—
SM-130	Flat Back Steel Body	3107	5390	—
SM-130	Metro-Lite Body	3623	4480	—

ENGINE: The "Silver Diamond" engine was used in the SM-130/SM-132 Metro vans. The "240 Black Diamond" engine was used in other models.

CHASSIS (½-Ton Series): Wheelbase: 115/127 in. Front tread: 58-9/32 in. Rear tread: 58-13/16 in. Tires: 6.00 x 16 in.

CHASSIS (¾-Ton Series): Wheelbase: 102/115/122/127 in. Tires: 6.50 x 16 six-ply.

CHASSIS (1-Ton Series): Wheelbase: 122/134 in. Tires: 7.50 x 16 in.

TECHNICAL: Same as comparable 1955 models.

OPTIONS: Chrome front bumper. Rear bumper. Single sidemount (body-side mounting). Deluxe cab interior. Foam rubber seats. Dome light. Bumper guards. Radio (AM). Heater. Clock. Cigar lighter. Radio antenna. Seat covers. External sun shade. Spotlight. Right-hand sun visor. Door arm rests. Electric wipers. Lockable glove compartment. Special paint. Two-tone paint. Wheel trim rings. Turn signals. White sidewall tires. Pickup box side panels. OSRV mirror. Deluxe equipment package.

1957 International Metro Jitney Bus (OCW)

HISTORICAL: Introduced mid to late 1955 through mid-1957. Calendar year registrations, all models: (1956) 108,014. (1957) 96,956. Calendar year production: (1956) 137,839 all IHC models. (1957) 121,775 all IHC models. Calendar year registrations by weight class: (1956) 20,696 in 5000 lb. or less category and 23,830 in 5001 to 10,000 lb. class. (1957) 33,572 in 6000 lb. or less category and 18,296 in 6001 to 10,000 lb. class. Four-wheel-drive introduced in ¾-ton series. The Travel-all became a standard factory model.

IHC production for 1956 was up 5.7 percent over 1955. In 1956, V-8 engines were introduced for heavy-duty models. The company began celebrating its 50th year of truck production in 1957. From 1907 through 1956 IHC built more than 2.6 million trucks. They claimed that 1.1 million were still in use in 1957. An "A" for "Anniversary" series was introduced, in mid-1957, to commemorate the occasion. J.L. McCaffrey became chairman of the board and P.V. Moulder was president. The company retained number three position in the truck industry.

Pricing

1956-1957	5	4	3	2	1
Series S-100 — (½-Ton) — (115 in. w.b.)					
Pickup (6½ ft.)	920	1850	3050	4300	6100
Series S-110 — (Heavy-Duty ½-Ton) — (115/127 in. w.b.)					
Pickup (6½ ft.)	900	1800	3000	4200	6000
Panel	680	1350	2250	3150	4500
Travel-all	830	1650	2750	3850	5500
Pickup (8 ft.)	890	1770	2950	4150	5900
Stake	830	1650	2750	3850	5500
Platform	810	1620	2700	3800	5400
Series S-120 — (¾-Ton) — (115/127 in. w.b.)					
Pickup (6½ ft.)	830	1650	2750	3850	5500
Panel	600	1200	2000	2800	4000
Travel-all	750	1500	2500	3500	5000
Pickup (8 ft.)	810	1620	2700	3800	5400
Stake	750	1500	2500	3500	5000
Platform	740	1470	2450	3350	4900

NOTE: Add 5 percent for 4x4 models.

	5	4	3	2	1
SA Milk Truck	420	840	1400	1950	2800
Metro Body (102 in. w.b.)	450	900	1500	2100	3000
Metro Dely. (115 in. w.b.)	450	900	1500	2100	3000
Metro Flat Back (115 in. w.b.)	440	870	1450	2050	2900
Metro-Lite (115 in. w.b.)	420	840	1400	1950	2800
Metro Flat Back (122 in. w.b.)	400	800	1350	1900	2700
Metro-Lite (122 in. w.b.)	420	840	1400	1950	2800
Series S-130 — (1-Ton) — (122 in. w.b.)					
Chassis & Cab	450	900	1500	2100	3000
Series S-130 — (1-Ton) — (122/134 in. w.b.)					
Pickup (9 ft.)	500	1000	1650	2300	3300
Platform (9 ft.)	470	950	1550	2200	3100
Stake (9 ft.)	480	975	1600	2250	3200
Metro Flat Back (122 in. w.b.)	400	800	1350	1900	2700
Metro-Lite (122 in. w.b.)	420	840	1400	1950	2800
Metro Flat Back (134 in. w.b.)	390	780	1300	1800	2600
Metro-Lite (134 in. w.b.)	400	800	1350	1900	2700

1958 IHC

1958 International A-100 Anniversary pickup (OCW)

MODEL A — ½-TON — SIX-CYLINDER: — IHC introduced its modernized Model A Series in mid-1957. Styling revisions included a full wraparound windshield, flatter roof, flatter hood, slab-sided bodies with sculptured front and rear fenders and squarer front fenders with parking lamps above the single round headlamps inside the fender nacelles. The hood had a wider air scoop up front, with a larger winged "IH" emblem below it. The grille was a refined version of the previous one without parking lights. Custom trim versions of the pickup were added to the lineup. They had "lightening bolt" side spears and, often, two-tone finish. An International name appeared on the trailing edge of upper front fenders. Series designations were moved to the front fendersides, behind the headlights. A "220 Black Diamond" engine was used in A-100 models (also with A-102 chassis option) and the "240 Black Diamond" powerplant was used in other half-tonners. A new model was a Utility pickup with "crew" type cab.

I.D. DATA: Refer to 1956-1957 section.

1958 IHC Model A-100 Custom Pickup (S. Soloy)

Model	Body Type	Price	Weight	Prod. Total
Series A-100/A-102 — (½-Ton) — (110 in. w.b.)				
A-100	Chassis & Cab	1785	3120	—
Series A-100/A-102 — (½-Ton) — (114 in. w.b.)				
A-100	Chassis & Cab	1785	3130	—
A-100	Pickup (7 ft.)	1905	3460	—
A-100	Cust. Pickup (7 ft.)	2212	3460	—
A-100	Panel (7 ft.)	2198	3735	—
A-100	Travelall (7 ft.)	2517	4015	—
Series A-110/A-112 — (½-Ton) — (110 in. w.b.)				
A-110	Chassis & Cab	1887	3140	—
Series A-110/A-112 — (½-Ton) — (114 in. w.b.)				
A-110	Chassis & Cab	1887	3150	—
A-110	Pickup (7 ft.)	2008	3480	—
A-110	Cust. Pickup (7 ft.)	2314	3480	—
A-110	Panel (7 ft.)	2300	3735	—
A-110	Travelall	2619	4035	—
Series A-110/A-112 — (½-Ton) — (126 in. w.b.)				
A-110	Chassis & Cab	1914	3170	—
A-110	Pickup (8½ ft.)	2052	3555	—
Series A-110/A-112 — (½-Ton) — (129 in. w.b.)				
A-110	Utl. Chassis & Cab	3006	3634	—
A-110	Utl. Chassis & Cust. Cab	3114	—	—
A-110	Utl. Pickup (6 ft.)	3135	—	—
A-110	Cust. Utl. Pickup (6 ft.)	3297	—	—

ENGINE (Series A-100/A-102): "220 Black Diamond". Inline. Overhead valve. Six-cylinder. Cast iron block. Bore & stroke: 3-9/16 in. x 3-11/16 in. Displacement: 220.5 cu. in. Brake horsepower: 112.5 at 3800 R.P.M. Net horsepower: 30.4 (NACC). Max. Torque: 194.4 lbs. ft. at 1600-2000 R.P.M. Four main bearings. Solid valve lifters.

NOTE 1: This engine was also standard in AB-120, AM-120 and AM-130 models.

NOTE 2: The A-100 could be optioned with a "240 Black Diamond" or "264 Black Diamond" engines.

ENGINE (Series A-110/A-112): "240 Black Diamond". Inline. Overhead valve. Six-cylinder. Cast iron block. Bore & stroke: 3-9/16 in. x 4.018 in. Displacement: 240.3 cu. in. Brake horsepower: 140.8 at 3800 R.P.M. Net horsepower: 30.4 (NACC). Max. Torque: 223.5 lbs. ft. at 2000 R.P.M. Four main bearings. Solid valve lifters.

NOTE 1: This engine was standard in A-110, A-120 and A-130 models. It was available as an option for AM-120, AM-130 and A-100 models.

NOTE 2: A "264 Black Diamond" engine was optional.

MODEL A — ¾-TON — SIX-CYLINDER: — The A-120/A-122 Series offered one dozen conventional trucks on four different wheelbases. Styling changes were in the same mold as those on the ½-tons, except that proportions were somewhat larger. New models were crew-cab-like utility pickups. A new technical feature for all light-duty IHC trucks was a 12-volt electrical system. Also available on the ¾-ton chassis were "AB" (bakery truck type) panels and "AM" (Metro-type) trucks and coaches. A similarly styled new model was the "AM-80" four-cylinder Metro-Mite mini-van. Although it was not a ¾-ton truck, we're listing the "Mite" with other Metro-type models. It was, a small truck with a 96 in. w.b. and 3800 pound GVW rating. The Metro-lite, an aluminum body version of the full-size Metro, now came in 9 ft. 8 in. and 10 ft. 8 in. ¾-ton models.

I.D. DATA: Refer to 1956-1957 section.

Model	Body Type	Price	Weight	Prod. Total
Series A-120/A-122 — (¾-Ton) — (110 in. w.b.)				
A-120	Chassis & Cab	2002	3555	—
Series A-120/A-122 — (¾-Ton) — (114 in. w.b.)				
A-120	Chassis & Cab	2002	3565	—
A-120	Pickup (7 ft.)	2123	3895	—
A-120	Cust. Pickup (7 ft.)	2424	3895	—
A-120	Panel (7 ft.)	2396	4170	—
A-120	Travelall (7 ft.)	2691	4450	—
Series A-120/A-122 — (¾-Ton) — (126 in. w.b.)				
A-120	Chassis & Cab	2029	3585	—
A-120	Pickup (8½ ft.)	2167	3970	—

Model	Body Type	Price	Weight	Prod. Total
Series A-120/A-122 — (¾-Ton) — (129 in. w.b.)				
A-120	Chassis & Utl. Cab	3125	—	—
A-120	Chassis & Utl. Cab	3232	—	—
A-120	Utl. Pickup (6 ft.)	3254	—	—
A-120	Cust. Utl. Pickup (6 ft.)	3415	—	—

NOTE: These trucks could also be ordered with IHC's four-wheel-drive option. The 4x4 package added $642 to the factory prices and 270 pounds to the shipping weight.

Model	Body Type	Price	Weight	Prod. Total
Series AM-80 Metro-Mite — (½-Ton) — (96 in. w.b.)				
AM-80	Walk-In Panel	2251	2800	×
Series AB-120 Metroette — (¾-Ton) — (115 in. w.b.)				
AB-120	Panel	2891	4755	×
Series AM-120 Metro — (¾-Ton) — (102 in. w.b.)				
AM-120	Chassis & Front Sec.	2075	2520	×
AM-120	Std. Metro (7¾ ft.)	2930	4335	×
Series AM-120 Metro — (¾-Ton) — (115 in. w.b.)				
AM-120	Chassis & Front Sec.	2075	2650	×
AM-120	Std. Metro (9½ ft.)	2996	4570	×
AM-120	Flat Back Metro (9½ ft.)	3070	4650	×
AM-120	Metro-Lite (9¾ ft.)	3694	—	×
AM-120	Metro Coach 8-Pass.	4156	—	×
AM-120	Metro School Bus 12-Pass.	4308	—	×
AM-120	Metro School Bus 16-Pass.	4156	—	×
Series AM-120 Metro — (¾-Ton) — (122 in. w.b.)				
AM-120	Metro-Lite (10¾ ft.)	3747	—	×
AM-120	Flat Back Metro (10½ ft.)	3265	—	×
AM-120	Chassis & Front Sec.	2103	2740	×

ENGINE: The "220 Black Diamond" engine was used in A-100/A-102/AB-120/AM-120 models. Other models (except AM-80) used the "240 Black Diamond" as base engine. A "264 Black Diamond" engine was optional in A-120s.

MODEL A — 1-TON — SIX-CYLINDER: — Two lines of 1-ton models were included in the A Series. The first included the big pickups and utility pickups with crew cabs. These were designated A-130s and an A-132 option was available. Their GVW ratings ranged from 7000 to 8000 pounds and three wheelbases were available. The second line was comprised of various Metro vans which also came with three, but different, wheelbases. Designated AM-130s (or AM-132s with a heavier-duty chassis option), the Metros had GVW ratings between 7000 and 9000 pounds.

I.D. DATA: Refer to 1956-1957 section.

Model	Body Type	Price	Weight	Prod. Total
Series A-130/A-132 — (1-Ton) — (117 in. w.b.)				
A-130	Chassis & Cab	2129	3765	—
Series A-130/A-132 — (1-Ton) — (126 in. w.b.)				
A-130	Chassis & Cab	2140	3785	—
A-130	Chassis & Cab	2277	4195	—
Series A-130/A-132 — (1-Ton) — (129 in. w.b.)				
A-130	Pickup (8½ ft.)	2150	3805	—
A-130	Utility Chassis & Cab	3226	—	—
A-130	Cust. Utility Chassis & Cab	3334	—	—
Series AM-130/AM-132 — (1-Ton) — (115 in. w.b.)				
AM-130	Std. Metro (9½ ft.)	3202	—	—
AM-130	Flat Back Metro (9½ ft.)	3275	—	—
Series AM-130/AM-132 — (1-Ton) — (122 in. w.b.)				
AM-130	Chassis & Frt. Sec.	2309	2940	—
AM-130	Metro Lite (10 ft. 8 in.)	3957	4250	—
AM-130	Flat Back Metro (10½ ft.)	3471	5100	—
Series AM-130/AM-132 — (1-Ton) — (134 in. w.b.)				
AM-130	Chassis & Frt. Sec.	2309	2980	—
AM-130	Flat Back Metro (12 ft. 7 in.)	3601	5390	—
AM-130	Metro Lite (12 ft. 8 in.)	4183	4480	—

ENGINE Series AM-80 "Metro-Mite": Inline. Overhead valve. Four-cylinder. Cast iron block. Bore & stroke: 2⅞ in. x 3½ in. Displacement: 90.884 cu. in. Brake horsepower: 59.6 at 4600-4800 R.P.M. Net horsepower: 13.2 (NACC). Max. Torque: 87.4 lbs. ft. at 1600-2400 R.P.M.

NOTE: This engine was available in the Metro-Mite only.

1958 IHC Travelette Crew Cab Pickup (S.Soloy)

ENGINE: The "220 Black Diamond" engine (see A-100 ½-ton series engine specifications) was base equipment in AM-130 1-ton Metro vans. The "240 Black Diamond" engine (see A-110 ½-ton series engine specifications) could also be installed in these trucks as optional equipment.
The "240 Black Diamond" engine was standard equipment in A-130 trucks. A "264 Black Diamond" engine was optionally available. See specifications below.

OPTIONAL ENGINE (Available in A-100, A-110, A-120 and A-130.) "264 Black Diamond": Inline. Overhead valve. Six-cylinder. Cast iron block. Bore & stroke: 3-11/16 in. x 4⅛ in. Displacement: 264.3 cu. in. Brake horsepower: 153.5 at 3800 R.P.M. Net horsepower: 32.6 (NACC). Max. Torque: 248 lbs. ft. at 2400 R.P.M. Four main bearings. Solid valve lifters.

CHASSIS (½-Ton Series): Wheelbase: 110/114//126/129 in. Tires: (A-100) 6.70 x 15 in.; (A-110) 6.00 x 16 six-ply.

CHASSIS (¾-Ton Series): Wheelbase: 102/114/115/122/126/129 in. Tires: (A-120 and AM-120) 7.00 x 17.5 six-ply; (AB-120) 7.00 x 17.5 six-ply.

CHASSIS (1-Ton Series): Wheelbase: 115/117/122/126/129/134 in. Tires: (All) 8.00 x 17.5 six-ply.

CHASSIS (Metro-Mite Series): Wheelbase: 96 in. Tires: 6.40 x 15 four-ply.

TECHNICAL: Same as comparable 1955 models.

OPTIONS: Chrome front bumper. Rear bumper. Deluxe cab interior. Foam rubber seats. Dome light. Door arm rest. Bumper guards. Radio (AM). Heater (fresh air type or recirculating type). Clock. Cigar lighter. Radio antenna. Seat covers. Custom exterior trim. Spotlight. Right-hand sun visor. Electric wipers. Lockable glove box. Special paint. Two-tone paint. Wheel trim rings. Directional signals. White sidewall tires. Pickup box side panels. OSRV mirror. Right-hand OSRV mirror.

HISTORICAL: Introduced mid-1957. Calendar year registrations by weight class: (1958) 27,721 in 6000 lbs. and less category and 14,270 in 6001 to 10,000 lb. class. Calendar year production: (all 1958 IHC) 81,213. Calendar year registration (all 1958 IHC): 89,721 units. Innovations: The new, light-weight Metro-Mite was introduced as the smallest multi-step vehicle in the United States. "Travel Crew" six-man pickup truck cabs were introduced. A new truck sales processing center was opened in Ft. Wayne. Historical notes: The 1958 IHC products were promoted as "Golden Anniversary" models. The "A" Series prefix indicated anniversary models. F.W. Jenks became president of IHC during 1958. Calendar year production was the lowest total in the postwar era. In April 1958, IHC's Metro Body Co. produced its 150th unit since the firm became an IHC subsidiary in 1948. The company said 10.8 percent of all trucks, on the road were IH models.

Pricing

1957½-1958	5	4	3	2	1
Series A-100 — (½-Ton)					
Pickup (7 ft.)	900	1800	3000	4200	6000
Cust. Pickup (7 ft.)	930	1860	3100	4350	6200
Panel (7 ft.)	690	1380	2300	3200	4600
Travelall (7 ft.)	840	1680	2800	3900	5600
Series A-110 — (Heavy-Duty ½-Ton)					
Pickup (7 ft.)	890	1770	2950	4150	5900
Cust. Pickup (7 ft.)	920	1850	3050	4300	6100
Panel (7 ft.)	680	1350	2250	3150	4500
Travelall	830	1650	2750	3850	5500
Pickup (8½ ft.)	—	—	—	—	5500
Utl. Pickup (6 ft.)	660	1320	2200	3100	4400
Cust. Utl. Pickup (6 ft.)	680	1350	2250	3150	4500
Series A-120 — (¾-Ton)					
Pickup (7 ft.)	830	1650	2750	3850	5500
Cust. Pickup (7 ft.)	—	—	—	—	5600
Panel (7 ft.)	630	1250	2100	3000	4200
Travelall (7 ft.)	750	1500	2500	3500	5000
Pickup (8½ ft.)	—	—	—	—	5300
Utl. Pickup (6 ft.)	620	1230	2050	2900	4100
Cust. Utl. Pickup (6 ft.)	630	1250	2100	3000	4200

NOTE: Add 5 percent for 4x4 models.

	5	4	3	2	1
Metro-Mite					
Walk-In Panel	470	950	1550	2200	3100
Metroette — (¾-Ton)					
Milk/Bakery	450	900	1500	2100	3000
Metro Delivery Vans — (¾-Ton)					
Metro (7¾ ft.)	480	975	1600	2250	3200
Metro (9½ ft.)	470	950	1550	2200	3100
Flat Back (9½ ft.)	420	840	1400	1950	2800
Metro-Lite (9¾ ft.)	400	800	1350	1900	2700
8P Coach	450	900	1500	2100	3000
12P Coach	450	900	1500	2100	3000
16P Coach	450	900	1500	2100	3000
Metro-Lite (10¾ ft.)	390	780	1300	1800	2600
Flat Back (10½ ft.)	400	800	1350	1800	2500
Series A-130 — (1-Ton)					
Pickup (8½ ft.)	680	1350	2250	3150	4500
Utl. Pickup	600	1200	2000	2800	4000
Cust. Utl. Pickup	630	1250	2100	3000	4200
Metro Delivery Vans — (1-Ton)					
Metro (9½ ft.)	450	900	1500	2100	3000
Flat Back (9½ ft.)	400	800	1350	1900	2700
Metro-Lite (10 ft. 8 in.)	390	780	1300	1800	2600
Flat Back (10½ ft.)	420	840	1400	1950	2800
Metro-Lite (12 ft. 8 in.)	440	870	1450	2050	2900
Flat Back (12 ft. 7 in.)	420	840	1400	1950	2800

1959 IHC

1959 International Travelall (OCW)

MODEL B — ½-TON — SIX-CYLINDER: — IHC did a nice job of modernizing its products in 1959. Changes included a new '55 Chevy-like grille and quadruple headlights. These were stacked vertically inside a chrome-rimmed housing. Bright metal windshield moldings appeared. There were bright-rimmed, round parking lights below the headlights, too. The entire image was brighter and more up-to-date. Crew cab utility pickups were now called "Travelettes." Chrome bumpers and whitewalls, once uncommon on IH pickups, were now nearly standard fare. There was even a V-8 engine option released during 1959. Standard ½-ton models were in the B-100 Series, which included the traditional heavy chassis option coded B-102. GVWs ranged from 4200 to 5000 pounds as in 1958. There was again a heavy-duty ½-ton series, coded B-110 and having a B-112 option. These trucks had GVWs between 4200 and 5800 pounds. The Metro-Mite was also still available in the ½-ton range. It was unchanged in any regard and the 1958 section can be referred to for data on this model.

I.D. DATA: Refer to the 1956-1957 section.

Model	Body Type	Price	Weight	Prod. Total
Series B-100/B-102 — (110 in. w.b.)				
B-100	Chassis & Cab	1927	3120	—
(114 in. w.b.)				
B-100	Chassis & Cab	1927	3130	—
B-100	Pickup (7 ft.)	2045	3460	—
B-100	Panel (7 ft.)	2340	3735	—
B-100	Travelall	2659	4015	—
Series B-110/B-112 — (110 in. w.b.)				
B-110	Chassis & Cab	1998	3140	—
(114 in. w.b.)				
B-110	Chassis & Cab	1998	3150	—
B-110	Pickup (7 ft.)	2116	3480	—
B-110	Panel	2411	3755	—
B-110	Travelall	2730	4035	—
(126 in. w.b.)				
B-110	Chassis & Cab	2025	3170	—
B-110	Pickup (8½ ft.)	2154	3555	—
(129 in. w.b.)				
B-110	Travelette Chassis & Cab	3117	3634	—
B-110	Travelette (6 ft.)	3244	—	—

ENGINE: "220 Black Diamond." Inline. Overhead valve. Six-cylinder. Cast iron block. Bore & stroke: 3-9/16 in. x 3-11/16 in. Displacement: 220.5 cu. in. Brake horsepower: 112.5 at 3800 R.P.M. Net horsepower: 30.4 (NACC). Maximum torque: 194.4 lbs.-ft. at 1600-2200 R.P.M.

NOTE: This engine was standard for 1959 in ¾-ton (AM-120) and 1-ton (AM-130) Metro Delivery vans. It was also standard in B-100 models.

ENGINE: "240 Black Diamond." Inline. Overhead valve. Six-cylinder. Cast iron block. Bore & stroke: 3-9/16 in. x 4.018 in. Displacement: 240.3 cu. in. Brake horsepower: 140.8 at 3800 R.P.M. Net horsepower: 30.4 (NACC). Max. Torque: 223.5 lbs. ft. at 2000 R.P.M.

NOTE: This engine was standard for 1959 in the B-110, B-120 and B-130 models. It was optional in Metro Delivery vans in the AM-120 and AM-130 series.

ENGINE: "264 Black Diamond." Inline. Overhead valve. Six-cylinder. Cast iron block. Bore & stroke: 3-11/16 in. x 4⅛ in. Displacement: 264.3 cu. in. Brake horsepower: 153.5 at 3800 R.P.M. Net horsepower: 32.6 (NACC). Max. Torque: 248 lbs. ft. at 2400 R.P.M.

NOTE: This engine was optional for 1959 in B-110, B-120 and B-130 models.

ENGINE: "V-266." Vee-block. Overhead valve. Eight-cylinder. Cast iron block. Bore & stroke: 3⅝ in. x 3-7/32 in. Displacement: 265.761 cu. in. Brake horsepower: 154.8 at 4400 R.P.M. Net horsepower: 42.1 (NACC). Max. Torque: 227.1 lbs. ft. at 2800 R.P.M.

NOTE: This engine was released during the 1959 model year as an option for the B-100, B-110, B-120 and B-130 models.

ADDITIONAL NOTE: The Metro-Mite for 1959 used the same engine as the 1958 Metro-Mite.

1959 IHC Travelette Crew Cab Pickup (S. Soloy)

MODEL B — ¾-TON — SIX-CYLINDER: — The 1959 ¾-ton series was updated similar to the ½-ton models. Series designations corresponded to 1958 with "B" instead of "A" prefixes. The Custom versions of pickups were now an option instead of a separate model. A four-wheel-drive option was again available for ¾-tonners, at a slightly higher price. Metroette panel trucks and Metro vans and coaches were available in ¾-ton "AB" and "AM" series, rather than the new "B" series. This is because they were unchanged from 1958, except for a price increase averaging about $130 per model. Readers interested in these trucks should refer to the 1958 section for weights, specifications and current values.

I.D. DATA: Refer to the 1956-1957 section.

Model	Body Type	Price	Weight	Prod. Total
Series B-120/B-122 — (110 in. w.b.)				
B-120	Chassis & Cab	2152	3555	—
(114 in. w.b.)				
B-120	Chassis & Cab	2152	3565	—
B-120	Pickup (7 ft.)	2270	3895	—
B-120	Panel (7 ft.)	2548	4170	—
B-120	Travelall	2840	4450	—
(126 in. w.b.)				
B-120	Chassis & Cab	2179	3585	—
B-120	Pickup (8½ ft.)	2308	3970	—
(129 in. w.b.)				
B-120	Travelette Chassis & Cab	3274	—	—
B-120	Travelette (6 ft.)	3401	—	—

NOTE 1: Add $765 and 270 pounds for 4x4 trucks.

NOTE 2: Refer to 1958 for Metroette and Metro Delivery Van models. The 1959 Metroette was $3051 and 1959 Metro vans ranged from $2203 to $4367 in price.

1959 IHC Model B-100 Bonus Load Pickup (S. Soloy)

MODEL B — 1-TON — SIX-CYLINDER: — Changes in the Model B 1-tonners were patterned after those for conventional light-duties in the ½- and ¾-ton series. Models, wheelbases and GVW ratings corresponded to those of 1958's A-130 models. The AM-130 Metro vans were carried over without any changes except for higher prices. Readers interested in these trucks should refer to the 1958 section for weights, specifications and current values.

I.D. DATA: Refer to the 1956-1957 section.

Model	Body Type	Price	Weight	Prod. Total
Series B-130/B-132 — (117 in. w.b.)				
B-130	Chassis & Cab	2217	3765	—
(126 in. w.b.)				
B-130	Chassis & Cab	2228	3785	—
B-130	Pickup (8½ ft.)	2357	4195	—
(129 in. w.b.)				
B-130	Chassis & Cab	2239	3805	—
B-130	Travelette Chassis & Cab	3315	—	—

NOTE 1: Refer to 1958 for Metro Delivery van models. Prices for 1959 Metro Vans (1-ton) ranged from $2426 to $4378.

CHASSIS: Same as comparable 1958 models.

TECHNICAL: Same as comparable 1955 models.

OPTIONS: See 1958 options.

HISTORICAL: Calendar year registrations by weight: (1959) 42,963 in the 6000 lbs. and less category and 17,183 in the 6001 to 10,000 lb. class. Calendar year registrations (all IHC models): 108,828. Calendar year production: 143,199 (12.56 percent)

The new "B" series introduced new styling, a "Bonus Load" pickup body, heavier frame construction. In March, a 266 cu. in. V-8 was introduced for the light duty models. By November, the V-8 was made standard in all "B" lines.

IH's share of the total U.S. truck market climbed to 12.74 percent in 1959. F.W. Jenks continued as president. Construction started, early in 1960, on a new 625,000 sq. ft. master motor truck parts depot at Ft. Wayne.

Pricing

1959	5	4	3	2	1
Series B-100/B-102 — (¾-Ton)					
Pickup (7 ft.)	850	1700	2850	4000	5700
Panel (7 ft.)	680	1350	2250	3150	4500
Travelall	830	1650	2750	3850	5500
Series B-110/B-112 — (Heavy-Duty ½-Ton)					
Pickup (7 ft.)	830	1650	2750	3850	5500
Panel	600	1200	2000	2800	4000
Travelall	780	1560	2600	3600	5200
Pickup (8½ ft.)	750	1500	2500	3500	5000
Travelette	700	1400	2350	3250	4700

NOTE: Add 10 percent for Custom trim package.

Series B-120/B-122 — (¾-Ton)					
Pickup (7 ft.)	700	1400	2350	3250	4700
Panel (7 ft.)	570	1140	1900	2650	3800
Travelall	750	1500	2500	3500	5000
Pickup (8½ ft.)	690	1380	2300	3200	4600
Travelette (6 ft.)	680	1350	2250	3150	4500

NOTE: Add 5 percent for 4x4 trucks.

Series B-130/B-132 — (1-Ton)					
Pickup (8½ ft.)	680	1350	2250	3150	4500
Travelette	660	1320	2200	3100	4400

NOTE: Add 5 percent for V-8 engines.

ADDITIONAL NOTE: Refer to 1958 section for Metro-Mite, Metroette and Metro Delivery Van prices.

1960 IHC

1960 International Travelall (DFW)

MODEL B — ½-TON — EIGHT-CYLINDER: — The B Series was carried over for 1960 with one major technical change; the V-266 engine was made standard equipment. Six-cylinder engines became a delete-option. Appearance changes were virtually non-existant, but the front emblem was given a new silver background to help distinguish the 1960 model-year status. The International name appeared below the contour line at the rear front fenders and "V" emblems (with V-8 engines) were on the front sides of the fenders behind the headlights. The Metro-Mite was also still available in the ½-ton range and again unchanged even in price and weight. Refer to the 1958 section for data on this model.

I.D. DATA: Refer to the 1956-1957 section.

Model Series	Body Type	Price	Weight	Prod. Total
B-100 — (B-102) — (110 in. w.b.)				
B-100	Chassis & Cab	2032	3264	—
(114 in. w.b.)				
B-100	Chassis & Cab	2032	3274	—
B-100	Pickup (7 ft.)	2151	3604	—
B-100	Panel (7 ft.)	2425	3879	—
B-100	Travelall	2845	4159	—
Series B-110 — (B-112) — (110 in. w.b.)				
B-110	Chassis & Cab	2089	3262	—
(114 in. w.b.)				
B-110	Chassis & Cab	2089	3272	—
B-110	Pickup (7 ft.)	2208	3602	—
B-110	Panel	2480	3877	—
B-110	Travelall	2890	4155	—
(126 in. w.b.)				
B-110	Chassis & Cab	2116	3292	—
B-110	Pickup (8½ ft.)	2245	3677	—
(129 in. w.b.)				
B-110	Travelette Chassis & Cab	3208	—	—
B-110	Travelette (6 ft.)	3335	—	—

ENGINE: The V-266 engine was standard in B-100, B-110, B-120 and B-130 models. The "220 Black Diamond" engine was standard in AB-120, AM-120 and AM-130 models. The "240 Black Diamond" engine was optional in B-110, B-120 and B-130 models. The "A55" four-cylinder engine was again used in Metro-Mites. Refer to 1959 section for engine specifications.

MODEL B — ¾-TON — EIGHT-CYLINDER: — IHC's ¾-ton trucks had the same basic changes as the ½-ton models. The price of the four-wheel-drive option increased slightly. Metroette panel trucks and Metro vans and coaches were again available as a continuation of the old AB-120 and AM-120 series. These trucks continued to use the 220 cu. in. six as base powerplant. Refer to the 1958 section for data on these models. Prices were the same as in 1959 for the ¾-ton Metros.

I.D. DATA: Refer to the 1956-1957 section.

Model Series	Body Type	Price	Weight	Prod. Total
B-120 — (B-122) — (110 in. w.b.)				
B-120	Chassis & Cab	2241	3677	—
(114 in. w.b.)				
B-120	Chassis & Cab	2241	3687	—
B-120	Pickup (7 ft.)	2359	4017	—
B-120	Panel (7 ft.)	2637	4292	—
B-120	Travelall	3001	4572	—
(126 in. w.b.)				
B-120	Chassis & Cab	2268	3707	—
B-120	Pickup (8½ ft.)	2397	4092	—
(129 in. w.b.)				
B-120	Travelette Chassis & Cab	3359	—	—
B-120	Travelette (6 ft.)	3490	—	—

NOTE 1: Add $783 and 270 pounds for 4x4 trucks.

NOTE 2: Refer to 1958 for Metroette and Metro Delivery Van models. The 1960 Metroette was $3051 and 1960 Metro Vans were priced from $2203 to $4367.

MODEL B — 1-TON — EIGHT-CYLINDER: — Changes for the 1960 Model B 1-tonners followed those for conventional ½-tonners and ¾-tonners. The new V-8 made these trucks modestly pricier than last year. AM-130 Metro Delivery vans were continued from 1958 models and specifications with only the factory prices being changed. These prices were still above 1958 levels but lower than the 1959 prices. This is probably a reflection of production economies realized by manufacturing the same model for several years. IHC was able to pass on its savings using lower prices to buyers to promote extra sales of its basically old-fashioned product. And, of course, the operators of these strictly commercial vehicles were more interested in low prices and reliability, than style. Please refer to the 1958 section for weights, specifications and current values of Metro vans.

I.D. DATA: Refer to the 1956-1957 section.

Model Series	Body Type	Price	Weight	Prod. Total
B-130 — (B-132) — (117 in. w.b.)				
B-130	Chassis & Cab	2284	3887	—
(126 in. w.b.)				
B-130	Chassis & Cab	2295	3907	—
B-130	Pickup (8½ ft.)	2424	4317	—
(129 in. w.b.)				
B-130	Chassis & Cab	2305	3927	—
B-130	Travelette Chassis & Cab	3381	—	—

NOTE 1: Refer to 1958 for Metro Delivery van models. Prices for 1960 1-ton Metro vans ranged from $2421 to $4371.

CHASSIS: Same as comparable 1958 models.

TECHNICAL: Same as comparable 1955 models.

OPTIONS: See 1958 options.

HISTORICAL: Introduced Jan. 1960. Calendar year registrations by weight: 30,666 in 6000 lb. and under category. 16,223 in 6001 to 10,000 lb. class. Calendar year registration (all IHC models): 110,349. Calendar year production: 119,696 (9.99 percent market share).

V-8 engine now standard in conventional light-duty trucks up to 1-ton. Six-cylinder engines continued to be available as optional equipment.

E.W. Jenks continued as company president, S.G. Johnson headed engineering and L.W. Pierson was sales manager.

Pricing

	5	4	3	2	1
1960					
Series B-100/B-102 — (½-Ton)					
Pickup (7 ft.)	890	1770	2950	4150	5900
Panel (7 ft.)	700	1400	2350	3250	4700
Travelall	850	1700	2850	4000	5700
Series B-110/B-112 — (Heavy-Duty ½-Ton)					
Pickup (7 ft.)	850	1700	2850	4000	5700
Panel	630	1250	2100	3000	4200
Travelall	810	1620	2700	3800	5400
Pickup (8½ ft.)	780	1560	2600	3600	5200
Travelette	740	1470	2450	4350	4900

NOTE: Add 10 percent for Custom trim package.

	5	4	3	2	1
Series B-120/B-122 — (¾-Ton)					
Pickup (7 ft.)	740	1470	2450	4350	4900
Panel (7 ft.)	600	1200	2000	2800	4000
Travelall	780	1560	2600	3600	5200
Pickup (8½ ft.)	720	1450	2400	3300	4800
Travelette (6 ft.)	700	1400	2350	3250	4700

NOTE: Add 5 percent for 4x4 trucks.

	5	4	3	2	1
Series B-130/B-132 — (1-Ton)					
Pickup (8½ ft.)	700	1400	2350	3250	4700
Travelette	690	1380	2300	3200	4600

NOTE: Deduct 5 percent for 6-cyl. engines.

ADDITIONAL NOTE: Refer to 1958 section for Metro-Mite, Metroette and Metro Delivery Van prices.

1961 IHC

1961 IHC Scout w/Steel Cab Top (S. Soloy)

MODEL 80 — ¼-TON SCOUT — FOUR-CYLINDER: — In 1961, International Harvester's truck division pioneered the development of the recreational vehicle market with the introduction of the International Scout, a totally new sport utility truck. It had rounded, boxy lines, a three-passenger cab and compact five-foot pickup bed. The grille was a rectangle with a mesh screen insert with "I-H" in the center. It was flanked by round headlamps. A bright metal Scout script was on the front fender sides. The cab-top was removable, as were the doors and the windshield could be lowered flat against the hood. Standard equipment included a front bumper, sealed beam headlights, combination tail and stoplamp, parking lights, electric horn, spare wheel and tire, four-wheel hydraulic brakes, 52-inch adjustable bench seat, side-mounted mirror, 12-volt electrical system and "Comanche" four-cylinder engine. The Scout came in colors of white, tan, metallic blue, red, metallic green or yellow with a black frame. The cab-top or optional Travel-top could be painted white for two-toning at no charge. The Scout was marketed in 4x2 and 4x4 models. Pickup beds were integral with the cab and had full-length, square inner housings, covering the wheels and fuel tank(s), on which four passengers could sit. There was a drop tailgate and simple round taillamps at the rear. The GVW was 3200 pounds (4x2) and 3900 pounds (4x4).

I.D. DATA (all Series): Serial number stamped on a plate on dash and on left front siderail. Numbers were a continuation of previous numbers. Starting and ending numbers are not available. The 1961 models had the suffix "-1" following the serial number for "1961." Engine numbers were stamped on the right side of crankcase at the upper front. International trucks were not produced on a yearly model basis. Model year was determined by date of original sale as shown on Bill of Sale or title.

Model	Body Type	Price	Weight	Prod. Total
Scout Series — (¼-Ton) — (100 in. w.b.)				
80	Utility Pickup (5 ft.)	1771	2800	Note 1
Scout 4x4 Series — (¼-Ton) — (100 in. w.b.)				
80	Utility Pickup (5 ft.)	2139	3000	Note 1

NOTE 1: More than 28,000 Scouts were sold in 1961.

540

1961 IHC Scout w/Vinyl Cab Top (S. Soloy)

ENGINE (Scout 80 Sports Utility): Comanche Four. Inline. OHV. (Single bank of V-8). Four-cylinder. Cast iron block w/aluminum intake manifold. Bore & stroke: 3⅞ in. x 3-7/32 in. Displacement: 151.84 cu. in. Compression ratio: 8.19:1. Brake horsepower: 93.4 at 4400 R.P.M. Net horsepower: 24.1 (NACC). Max. Torque: 135 lbs. ft. at 2400 R.P.M. Solid valve lifters. Carburetor: Downdraft. Features: Fuel pump. Fuel filter. 11-gallon fuel tank (left side of body). Oil bath air cleaner. Full-pressure lubrication. External gear oil pump. Wire mesh floating oil strainer. Deep sump oil pan.

NOTE: This engine was derived from the IH V-304 eight-cylinder engine. It was used only in the Scout.

1961 IHC Scout w/Steel Travel-Top (S. Soloy)

MODEL C — ½-TON — EIGHT-CYLINDER: — The 1961 Model C International trucks had a lower, wider appearance. The front fender line was lowered and, in the front, extended straight across. The hood was widened and lowered accordingly. Its lower lip still formed an air-scoop-like opening and there were scallop-like contours molded into the top surface. A winged "IH" emblem decorated the front of the hood. Dual headlamps now sat side-by-side with each pair housed in bright metal trimmed ovals. Oval shaped parking lights were directly below them. The grille was a wide, concave affair stamped out of anodized aluminum with six "stacks" of six oval shaped openings. There was a new wraparound bumper. A V-8 series designation badge and International chrome script appeared on the rear sides of the hood (except when the optional six-cylinder engine was ordered, of course). Doors and cabs were redesigned too. There was a standard C-100 line and C-102 option with GVW ratings of 4200 to 5000 pounds. The heavier ½-ton series was the C-110 with C-112 chassis option. These trucks had GVW ratings between 4200 and 5800 pounds. Wheelbases of 115, 119, 122, 131 and 140 inches were offered in the two lines, making them longer than previous models. The AM-80 Metro-Mite walk-in panel truck was also available. It was again a direct carryover of the 1958 model. (Refer to 1958 section.)

Model	Body Type	Price	Weight	Prod. Total
Series C-100/C-102 — (119 in. w.b.)				
C-100	Chassis & Cab	2069	3265	—
C-100	Pickup (7 ft.)	2187	3640	—
C-100	Panel (7 ft.)	2502	4095	—
C-100	Travelall	2853	4240	—
C-100	Cust. Travelall	3139	—	—
Series C-110/C-112 — (115 in. w.b.)				
C-110	Chassis & Cab	2092	3290	—
(119 in. w.b.)				
C-110	Chassis & Cab	2092	3295	—
C-110	Pickup (7 ft.)	2210	3670	—
C-110	Panel (7 ft.)	2524	3850	—
C-110	Travelall	2876	3995	—
C-110	Cust. Travelall	3162	—	—
(122 in. w.b.)				
C-110	Chassis & Cab	2108	3301	—
(131 in. w.b.)				
C-110	Chassis & Cab	2118	3325	—
C-110	Pickup (8½ ft.)	2248	3750	—
(140 in. w.b.)				
C-110	Travelette P.U. Chassis & Cab	2699	3829	—
C-110	Travelette P.U. (6 ft.)	2843	—	—

NOTE: For 1961, the AM-80 Metro-Mite was $2251 and 2800 lbs. See 1958 section for other data on this model.

1961 International Travelall (OCW)

ENGINE (all Trucks): A-55 Engine. Inline. Overhead valve. Four-cylinder. Cast iron block. Bore & stroke: 2⅞ in. x 3½ in. Displacement: 90.884 cu. in. Brake horsepower: 59.6 at 4600-4800 R.P.M. Net horsepower: 13.2 (NACC). Max. Torque: 87.4 lbs. ft. at 1600-2400 R.P.M.

NOTE: This engine was used only in the AM-80 Metro-Mite. It was based on the English Austin engine.

ENGINE: V-266 Engine. Overhead valve. Vee-block. Eight-cylinder. Cast iron block. Bore & stroke: 3⅝ in. x 3-7/32 in. Displacement: 154.8 cu. in. Brake horsepower: 154.8 at 4400 R.P.M. Net horsepower: 42.1 (NACC). Max. Torque: 227.1 lbs. ft. at 2800 R.P.M. Solid valve lifters. Carburetor: Downdraft.

NOTE: Standard in C-100, C-110, C-120, C-120 (4x4) and C-130 series.

ENGINE: "220 Black Diamond." Inline. OHV. Six-cylinder. Cast iron block. Bore & stroke: 3⅝ in. x 3-7/32 in. Displacement: 220.5 cu. in. Brake horsepower: 112.5 at 3800 R.P.M. Net horsepower: 30.4. Max. Torque: 194.4 lbs. ft. at 1600-2000 R.P.M. Four main bearings. Solid valve lifters. Carburetor: Downdraft.

NOTE: Standard in Metroette AB-120 and Metro AM-120 and AM-130. Optional: C-100.

ENGINE: "240 Black Diamond." Inline. Overhead valve. Six-cylinder. Cast iron block. Bore & stroke: 3-9/16 in. x 4.02 in. Displacement: 240.3 cu. in. Brake horsepower: 140.8 at 3800 R.P.M. Net horsepower: 30.4 (NACC). Max. Torque: 223.5 lbs. ft. at 2000 R.P.M. Four main bearings. Solid valve lifters. Carburetor: Downdraft.

NOTE: Optional in AB-120 (Metroette), AM-120/AM-130 (Metro), C-100, C-110, C-120 and C-130 series.

MODEL C — ¾-TON — EIGHT-CYLINDER: — Styling changes for the ¾-ton "C" line were similar to those appearing on the ½-ton "C" line. There was a base C-120 series and a C-122 chassis option. Models on the 115, 119, 122, 131 and 140 in. w.b. were offered. GVWs were 5400 to 7000 pounds for conventional drive trucks and 7000 pounds for trucks with the 4x4 option. Again carried over from 1958 were the AB-120 (Metroette) and AM-120 (Metro Delivery) models. These were sold at the same prices as in effect during 1960 and shipping weights were unchanged. Refer to 1958 section for information about models, specifications and current values.

Model	Body Type	Price	Weight	Prod. Total
Series C-120/C-122 — (115 in. w.b.)				
C-120	Chassis & Cab	2247	3476	—
(119 in. w.b.)				
C-120	Chassis & Cab	2247	3480	—
C-120	Pickup (7 ft.)	2365	3855	—
C-120	Panel (7 ft.)	2679	4035	—
C-120	Travelall	2970	4180	—
C-120	Cust. Travelall	3249	—	—
(122 in. w.b.)				
C-120	Chassis & Cab	2263	3486	—
(131 in. w.b.)				
C-120	Chassis & Cab	2273	3604	—
C-120	Pickup (8½ ft.)	2403	4029	—
(140 in. w.b.)				
C-120	Travelette Chassis & Cab	2854	4052	—
C-120	Travelette Pickup (6 ft.)	2998	—	—

NOTE 1: Add $614 and 270 pounds for C-120 models with the 4x4 option.

NOTE 2: For 1961, the AB-120 Metroette was $3056 and 4755 lbs.; the AM-120 Metro Delivery models were the same as 1958 except no standard Metro body was listed on the 102 in. wheelbase. Prices for Metros ranged from $2208 to $4372. Shipping weights, specifications and current values for these models were the same as in 1958. Consult the 1958 section for data.

MODEL C — 1-TON — EIGHT-CYLINDER: — As usual, the one-ton "C" series followed the styling pattern of the lighter-duty conventional trucks. They were built on wheelbases of 122, 131, 134 and 140 inches. There was a C-132 option with heavier-duty suspension system. GVW ratings ranged from 7000 to 8800 pounds. There was also a series of one-ton Metro Delivery van models which were an exact continuation of the 1958 line with 1960 prices. For model listings, specifications and current values on these AM-130 trucks consult the 1958 section of this catalog.

Model	Body Type	Price	Weight	Prod. Total
Series C-130/C-132 — (122 in. w.b.)				
C-130	Chassis & Cab	2346	3630	—
(131 in. w.b.)				
C-130	Chassis & Cab	2357	3655	—
C-130	Pickup (8½ ft.)	3486	4080	—
(134 in. w.b.)				
C-130	Chassis & Cab	2368	3666	—
(140 in. w.b.)				
C-130	Travelette Chassis & Cab	2938	4114	—

NOTE: For 1961, the AM-130 Metro Delivery models were the same as 1958. Prices for one-ton Metros ranged from $2421 to $4209. Shipping weights, specifications and current values for these models were the same as in 1958. Consult the 1958 section for data.

CHASSIS (Scout 80 Series): Wheelbase: 100 in. Overall length: 154 in. Width: 68.6 in. Height: (4x2) 67 in.; (4x4) 68 in. Ground clearance: (Rear) 9.3 in.; (Front) 4x2 — 9 in. 4x4 — 9.3 in. Tires: Four-ply. For 4x2 models — 6.50 x 15 P.C. For 4x4 models — 6.00 x 16 P.C. tube-type, non-directional.

CHASSIS (Series AM-80 Metro-Mite): Wheelbase: 96 in. Tires: 6.50 x 14 four-ply.

CHASSIS (Series C-100/C-102): Wheelbase: 119 in. Tires: 6.70 x 15 four-ply.

CHASSIS (Series C-110/C-112): Wheelbase: 115/119/122/131/140 in. Tires: 7.10 x 15 four-ply.

CHASSIS (Series C-120/C-122): Wheelbase: 115/119/122/131/140 in. Tires: 7.00 x 15.5 six-ply.

CHASSIS (Series C-130/C-132): Wheelbase: 122/131/134/140 in. Tires: 8.00 x 17.5 six-ply.

CHASSIS (Series AB-120 Metroette): Wheelbase: 115 in. Tires: 7.00 x 17.5 six-ply.

CHASSIS (Series AM-120/AM-122 Metro): Wheelbase: 102/115/122 in. Tires: 7.00 x 17 six-ply.

CHASSIS (Series AM-130/AM-132 Metro): Wheelbase: 115/122/134 in. Tires: 8.00 x 17.5 six-ply.

TECHNICAL (Scout Series): Synchromesh transmission. Speeds: 3F/1R. Floor mounted gear shift lever. Clutch: 10 in. diameter, single-plate, 6-spring, coil spring vibration damper. Single reduction hypoid type rear axle (2300 lb. capacity). Overall ratio: 4.27:1. Four wheel hydraulic brakes. Wheels: (4x2) 15 in. disc. 4.50K rim w/hubcaps. (4x4) 16 in. disc, 4.50E rim. Drivetrain options: Optional transfer case on 4x4 models controls engagement of front-wheel-drive and provides extra low gear that multiplies torque power to the wheels. This unit mounted to the transmission and had a multi ratio power divider. Three position shifting — (low) 3.333; (2nd) 1.851 to 1; (high) direct drive. Front axle on 4x4 models was a single-reduction type with 4.27:1 ratio. The 4x2 models had a 2000 lb. capacity I-beam type axle instead. Power-take-off was available at extra cost for 4x4 models. Full torque type with front and rear output shafts mounted on transfer case, left side. Winch drive and mounting parts.

TECHNICAL (other Series): Same as previous model years since 1955.

1961 IHC Scout w/Vinyl Travel-Top (S. Soloy)

OPTIONS (Scout Series): Front axle locking hubs for 4x4 model, manual or automatic. Skidplate. Rear axle, 4.27:1 with Power-Lok differential. Full-length Steel Travel-Top enclosure with lift-gate and windows. Vinyl-coated Sport-Top with snap-on curtains. Cushioned seats and back rests over wheel housings. Sun visors. Arm rests. Safety belts. Fresh air heater/defroster. Radio and aerial. Cigar lighter. Inside mirror. Seat covers. Bucket seats. Floor mat for 4x4 (std. 4x2). 60-amp battery. Directional turn signals. 40-amp alternator. Hand throttle control. Increased capacity cooling. Dual 11-gallon fuel tanks. Front tow hook. Grille guard. Rear bumper. Rear tow hook. Trailer hitch. Under coating. Right-hand drive. Power take-off. Snow plow. Special tires. Ramsey model 200 winch, front mounted w/150 ft. cable and hook.

OPTIONS (Series "C"): Chrome front bumper. Rear bumper. OSRV mirror(s). Undercoating. Trailer hitch. Grille guard. Bumper guards. Radio (AM). Heater (fresh air type or recirculating). Clock. Cigar lighter. Radio antenna. Seat covers. Dual sun visors. Spotlight. Electric wipers. Special paint. Two-tone finish. Custom trim package. Deluxe cab package. Front mounted winch. Directional turn signals. Safety belts. High side pickup box panels. Clearance marker lights. Arm rests. Increased capacity cooling. Heavy-Duty battery. Power-lok differential. Foam seat cushions. Floor mat. 40-amp alternator. Snow plow. Power steering. Power brakes. Automatic transmission.

541

1961 IHC Scout Convertible w/doors (S. Soloy)

HISTORICAL: Introduced Nov. 1, 1960. Calendar year registrations: (all IHC trucks) 116,538. Calendar year registrations (by weight class): 6000 lbs. and under — 48,997. 6001 to 10,000 lbs. — 13,085. Calendar year production: (all models) 142,816. New styling. Independent front suspension. International Scout introduced.

F.W. Jenks continued as IHC president. R.M. Buzard was vice-president of the Motor Truck Division. The company was headquarted in Chicago, Ill. and had plants in Emeryville, Calif., Ft. Wayne, Ind.; Indianapolis, Ind.; Springfield, Ohio and Bridgeport, Conn. IHC increased its market share, although overall truck sales were down.

Pricing

	5	4	3	2	1
1961 **Series Scout 80 — (¼-Ton)**					
Pickup (5 ft.)	830	1650	2750	3850	5500
4x4 Pickup (5 ft.)	870	1750	2900	4100	5800

NOTES: Add 5 percent for vinyl Sport-Top (full-enclosure).
Add 4 percent for steel Travel-Top.

Series C-100 — (½-Ton)					
Pickup (7 ft.)	830	1650	2750	3850	5500
Panel (7 ft.)	680	1350	2250	3150	4500
Travelall	900	1800	3000	4200	6000
Cust. Travelall	980	1950	3250	4550	6500
Series C-110 — (Heavy-Duty ½-Ton)					
Pickup (7 ft.)	840	1680	2800	3900	5600
Panel (7 ft.)	690	1380	2300	3200	4600
Travelall	920	1850	3050	4300	6100
Cust. Travelall	1000	2000	3300	4600	6600
Pickup (8½ ft.)	830	1650	2750	3850	5500
Travelette Pickup	750	1500	2500	3500	5000

NOTE: Deduct 5 percent for six-cylinder engine (all series "C")

Series C-120 — (¾-Ton)					
Pickup (7 ft.)	770	1550	2550	3600	5100
Panel (7 ft.)	620	1230	2050	2900	4100
Travelall	830	1650	2750	3850	5500
Cust. Travelall	890	1770	2950	4150	5900
Pickup (8½ ft.)	750	1500	2500	3500	5000
Travelette Pickup	720	1450	2400	3300	4800

NOTE: Add 5 percent for 4x4 option

NOTE: See 1958 section for Metroette and Metro Delivery prices.

Series C-130 — (1-Ton)					
Pickup (8½ ft.)	700	1400	2350	3250	4700
Travelette Pickup	650	1300	2150	3050	4300

NOTE: See 1958 section for AM-130 Metro Delivery prices.

1962 IHC

MODEL 80 — ¼-TON SCOUT — FOUR-CYLINDER: — The Scout was carried over for 1962 with no major alterations. Roll-up windows became a new option. As in 1961, the standard model came with a Sport-Top, made of vinyl-coated material, which was removable. The doors could also be removed for Jeep-like off-roading with the windshield up or folded flat. The Sport-Top full-body enclosure gave the buyer a full-length vinyl-coated roof covering with snap-on curtains to cover the five-foot pickup box. A full-length steel Travel-Top was the ultimate option. It, too, was removable. Like the original version, the '62 carried its spare tire and wheel mounted vertically at the center of the box wall, behind the driver's seat.

I.D. DATA: Serial numbers located in the same locations. The numbering system was basically the same. The 1962 models had the suffix "-2" following the serial number for "1962."

1962 International Scout Utility (DFW/MVMA)

Model	Body Type	Price	Weight	Prod. Total
Scout Series — (¼-Ton) — (100 in. w.b.)				
80	Utility Pickup (5 ft.)	1754	2800	—
Scout 4x4 Series — (¼-Ton) — (100 in. w.b.)				
80	Utility Pickup (5 ft.)	2132	3000	—

ENGINE: Engine specifications and applications were unchanged. See 1961 engine data for specifications and useage.

MODEL C — ½-TON — EIGHT-CYLINDER: — There were no obvious changes in the "C" series ½-tonners. Styling and engineering was carried over from 1961. Featured in both lines was the "Bonus Load" pickup truck with 7-foot box. This style pickup also came in the C-110 with an 8½ ft. box. The Metro-Mite was droppd in 1962.

Model	Body Type	Price	Weight	Prod. Total
Series C-100/C-102 — (119 in. w.b.)				
C-100	Chassis & Cab	2072	3265	—
C-100	Pickup (7 ft.)	2191	3640	—
C-100	Bonus Load Pickup (7 ft.)	2207	3630	—
C-100	Panel (7 ft.)	2505	4095	—
C-100	Travelall	2795	4240	—
C-100	Cust. Travelall	3075	—	—
Series C-110/C-112 — (115 in. w.b.)				
C-110	Chassis & Cab	2096	3290	—
(119 in. w.b.)				
C-110	Chassis & Cab	2096	3295	—
C-110	Pickup (7 ft.)	2214	3670	—
C-110	Bonus Load Pickup (7 ft.)	2230	3660	—
C-110	Panel (7 ft.)	2528	3850	—
C-110	Travelall	2819	3995	—
C-110	Cust. Travelall	3099	—	—
(122 in. w.b.)				
C-110	Chassis & Cab	2112	3301	—
(131 in. w.b.)				
C-110	Chassis & Cab	2123	3325	—
C-110	Pickup (8½ ft.)	2252	3750	—
C-110	Bonus Load Pickup (8½ ft.)	2268	3740	—
(140 in. w.b.)				
C-110	Travelette Chassis & Cab	2704	3829	—
C-110	Travelette Pickup (6 ft.)	2847	—	—
C-110	Travelette Pickup (6 ft.)	2847	—	—

MODEL C — ¾-TON — EIGHT-CYLINDER: — The "C" series ¾-tonners were also carried over from 1961. "Bonus Load" pickups were available with both the 7-foot and 8½ ft. boxes. The AB-120 Metroette and AM-120 Metros were again offered as a continuation of the series introduced in 1958. (See 1958 for Metroette/Metro data.)

1962 IHC Scout w/Steel Travel-Top (S. Soloy)

Model	Body Type	Price	Weight	Prod. Total
Series C-120/C-122 — (115 in. w.b.)				
C-120	Chassis & Cab	2251	3476	—
(119 in. w.b.)				
C-120	Chassis & Cab	2251	3480	—
C-120	Pickup (7 ft.)	2369	3855	—
C-120	Bonus Load Pickup (7 ft.)	2385	3845	—
C-120	Panel (7 ft.)	2683	4035	—
C-120	Travelall	2974	4180	—
C-120	Cust. Travelall	3254	—	—
(122 in. w.b.)				
C-120	Chassis & Cab	2267	3486	—
(131 in. w.b.)				
C-120	Chassis & Cab	2278	3604	—
C-120	Pickup (8½ ft.)	2407	4029	—
C-120	Bonus Load Pickup (8½ ft.)	2423	4019	—
(140 in. w.b.)				
C-120	Travelette Chassis & Cab	2859	4052	—
C-120	Travelette Pickup (6 ft.)	3002	—	—

NOTE 1: Add $614 and 270 pounds for 4x4.

NOTE 2: For 1962, the AB-120 Metroette and the AM-120 Metro Delivery models had the same prices and weights as 1961.

MODEL C — 1-TON — EIGHT-CYLINDER: — The 1-ton "C" series was another carry over from 1961. It had the 8½-ft. "Bonus Load" pickup included. The 1-ton Metros were also offered as a continuation of the 1958 series. (See 1958 for AM-130 Metro data). Four-wheel-drive (4x4) was made available for the C-130 models this season.

Model	Body Type	Price	Weight	Prod. Total
Series C-130/C-132 — (122 in. w.b.)				
C-130	Chassis & Cab	2350	3630	—
(131 in. w.b.)				
C-130	Chassis & Cab	2361	3655	—
C-130	Pickup (8½ ft.)	2490	4080	—
C-130	Bonus Load Pickup (8½ ft.)	2507	4070	—
(134 in. w.b.)				
C-130	Chassis & Cab	2372	3666	—
(140 in. w.b.)				
C-130	Travelette Chassis & Cab	2942	4114	—

NOTE: Add $1109 and 285 pounds for C-130 4x4 models.

NOTE: For 1962, the AM-130 Metro Delivery models were priced from $2431 to $4220.

CHASSIS (all Series): Same as 1961 except AM-80 discontinued.

TECHNICAL (all Series): Same as 1961.

OPTIONS (all Series): Same as 1961 except new roll-up windows for Scouts.

HISTORICAL: Introduced Nov. 1, 1961. Calendar year registrations: 130,959. Calendar year production: (all IHC models) 147,285 (11.47 percent). Innovations: Scout gets roll-up windows. Metro-Mite dropped temporarily for new design change over. Historical notes: Historically, the company introduced its heavy-duty Load Star line in March of 1962. Also received was a government order for 3224 5-ton 6x6 tactical motor truck to be produced in Ft. Wayne through Sept. 1962. 300 additional workers were hired. On Nov. 8, 1961, 4000 more trucks were added to the order.

Pricing

	5	4	3	2	1
1962					
Scout 80 — (¼-Ton)					
Pickup (5 ft.)	830	1650	2750	3850	5500
4x4 Pickup (5 ft.)	870	1750	2900	4100	5800

NOTE: Add 5 percent for vinyl Sport-Top (full-enclosure).

NOTE: Add 4 percent for steel Travel-Top.

	5	4	3	2	1
Series C-100 — (½-Ton)					
Pickup (7 ft.)	830	1650	2750	3850	5500
Bonus Pickup (7 ft.)	840	1680	2800	3900	5600
Panel (7 ft.)	680	1350	2250	3150	4500
Travelall	900	1800	3000	4200	6000
Cust. Travelall	980	1950	3250	4550	6500
Series C-110 — (Heavy-Duty ½-Ton)					
Pickup (7 ft.)	840	1680	2800	3900	5600
Bonus Pickup (7 ft.)	850	1700	2850	4000	5700
Panel (7 ft.)	690	1380	2300	3200	4600
Travelall	720	1850	3050	4300	6100
Cust. Travelall	1000	2000	3300	4600	6600
Pickup (8½ ft.)	830	1650	2750	3850	5500
Travelette Pickup	750	1500	2500	3500	5000

NOTE: Deduct 5 percent for six-cylinder (all series "C")

	5	4	3	2	1
Series C-120 — (¾-Ton)					
Pickup (7 ft.)	770	1550	2550	3600	5100
Bonus Pickup (7 ft.)	780	1560	2600	3600	5200
Panel (7 ft.)	620	1230	2050	2900	4100
Travelall	830	1650	2750	3850	5500
Cust. Travelall	890	1770	2950	4150	5900
Pickup (8½ ft.)	750	1500	2500	3500	5000
Bonus Pickup (8½ ft.)	—	—	—	—	—
Travelette Pickup	720	1450	2400	3300	4800

NOTE: Add 5 percent for 4x4 option (all series). See 1958 section for Metroette and Metro pricings.

	5	4	3	2	1
Series C-130 — (1-Ton)					
Pickup (8½ ft.)	700	1400	2350	3250	4700
Bonus Pickup (8½ ft.)	720	1450	2400	3300	4800
Travelette Pickup	650	1300	2150	3050	4300

NOTE: See 1958 section for AM-130 Metro prices.

1963 IHC

MODEL 80 — ¼-TON SCOUT — FOUR-CYLINDER: — The Scout for 1963 looked like the Scout for 1962 and had the same engine specifications. The 4x2 version was lower in price, while the 4x4 edition was more expensive.

I.D. DATA: Serial numbers were in the same locations. The 1963 models had the suffix "-3" following the serial number to indicate "1963."

Model	Body Type	Price	Weight	Prod. Total
Scout Series				
80	Pickup (5 ft./4x2)	1701	2800	—
80	Pickup (5 ft./4x4)	2188	3000	—

ENGINE: The 1963 Scouts used the 4-152 engine. See 1961 specifications for "Comanche Four."

MODEL CM — METRO-MITE/METRO — FOUR-CYLINDER: — The Metro-Mite was offered in a new "CM" Series, the base model being the CM-75. A walk-in version was called the CM-80. The main change from the earlier Metro-Mite was a horizontal bar grille without vertical center divider and a new power plant. The Scout's 4-152 engine was used. These trucks had a 4000 pound GVW. Also new was a ½-ton Metro delivery van, the CM-110 (with a CM-112 chassis option). It had the same type of new grille as the "Mite" and shared the 4-152 engine. The wheelbase was 6 inches longer, however, and GVW was 4500 to 5500 pounds. The larger Metros were still "AM" models based on 1958 designs.

Model	Body Type	Price	Weight	Prod. Total
Series CM-75/CM-80 — (¼-Ton)				
CM-75	Metro-Mite Panel (7 ft.)	2345	—	—
CM-80	Metro-Mite Walk-In (7 ft.)	2372	—	—
Series CM-110 — (½-Ton)				
CM-110	Metro-Mite Walk-In (8 ft.)	2675	—	—

ENGINE: The CM-75/CM-80 Metro-Mites used the 4-152 "Comanche Four." See 1961 engine data.

1963 IHC Fenderside Pickup Truck (D. Sagvold)

MODEL C — ½-TON — SIX-CYLINDER: — A new C-1000 style light-duty truck line was introduced in November 1962. The "IH" hood badge lost its wings and single headlamps returned. The grille was now a gridwork of two horizontal bars intersected by nine vertical members with the International name spelled out between the bars at the center. There were twin air slots between the grille and somewhat less chrome trimmings. Six-cylinder engines became standard equipment and a V-8 was optional. Wheelbases and GVWs were the same as comparable 1962 models. The Travelette crew cabs got the "Bonus Load" treatment, too.

Model	Body Type	Price	Weight	Prod. Total
Series C-1000 — (½-Ton) — (119 in. w.b.)				
C-1000	Chassis & Cab	1941	3265	—
C-1000	Pickup (7 ft.)	2061	3640	—
C-1000	Bonus Load Pickup (7 ft.)	2077	3630	—
C-1000	Travelall/Panel (7 ft.)	2373	3820	—

Model	Body Type	Price	Weight	Prod. Total
Series C-1100 — (Heavy-Duty ½-Ton) — (115 in. w.b.)				
C-1100	Chassis & Cab	1965	3290	—
(119 in. w.b.)				
C-1100	Pickup (7 ft.)	2086	3675	—
C-1100	Bonus Load Pickup (7 ft.)	2102	3665	—
C-1100	Travelall/Panel (7 ft.)	2398	3855	—
(131 in. w.b.)				
C-1100	Chassis & Cab	1965	3290	—
C-1100	Pickup (8½ ft.)	2086	3675	—
C-1100	Bonus Load Pickup (8½ ft.)	2102	3665	—
(140 in. w.b.)				
C-1100	Travelette Chassis & Cab	2571	3830	—
C-1100	Travelette Bonus Load Pickup	2714	—	—

ENGINE: The BG-241 engine (formerly called the ''240 Black Diamond'') was standard equipment in C-1000 and C-1110 models. See 1961 engine data.

MODEL C — ¾-TON — SIX-CYLINDER: — The C-1200 was the ¾-ton version of the 1963 IHC light-truck. Here, too, the six-cylinder replaced the V-8 as standard engine. A ''Bonus Load'' version of the Travelette model was new. All else was comparable to 1962 offerings. The AM-120 Metros and AB-120 Metroette continued to be based on the 1958 series. Refer back to the 1958 section for this data. Model offerings were trimmed to the standard 9 ft. 6 in. Metro, Flat Back Metro, Metro Van and Metro Lite on 115 or 122 inch wheelbases with 5400 to 6000 pound GVWs.

Model	Body Type	Price	Weight	Prod. Total
Series C-1200 — (¾-Ton) — (115 in. w.b.-131 in. w.b.)				
1200	Chassis & Cab	2089	3475	—
(119-131 in. w.b.)				
1200	Pickup (7 ft.)	2086	3675	—
1200	Bonus Load Pickup (7 ft.)	2102	3665	—
1200	Panel (7 ft./119 in. w.b.)	2398	3855	—
(140 in. w.b.)				
1200	Travelette Chassis & Cab	2571	3830	—
1200	Bonus Load Travelette Pickup	2714	—	—

NOTE 1: Add $638 for 4x4 models.

NOTE 2: The 1963 Metroette AB-120 was $3105 and 4755 lbs. The 1963 Metro AM-120S were $3072 to $3789 and 4570 to 4650 lbs.

ENGINE: The BG-241 engine (formerly called the ''240 Black Diamond'') was standard equipment in C-1200 models. See 1961 engine data.

MODEL C — 1-TON — SIX-CYLINDER: — The one-tonner had the same basic changes as lighter IHC trucks. The 8½ pickup was issued in ''Bonus Load'' configuration and the six-cylinder became standard. The AM-130 Metro line was a continuation of the 1958 series including the standard Metro on a 115 in. w.b. and the Flat Back, Van and Metro-Lite on 115/122/134 in. w.b. Refer to the 1958 section for basic Metro data.

Model	Body Type	Price	Weight	Prod. Total
Series C-1300 — (1-Ton) — (122-134 in. w.b.)				
C-1300	Chassis & Cab	2190	3630	—
(131 in. w.b.)				
C-1300	Pickup (8½ ft.)	2327	4080	—
C-1300	Bonus Load Pickup (8½ ft.)	2838	—	—

NOTE 1: Add $1147 for 4x4 models.

NOTE 2: The 1963 Metro AM-130s were $3270 to $4048 and 4320 pounds for Metro-Lite.

ENGINE: The BG-241 engine (formerly called the ''240 Black Diamond'') was standard equipment in C-1300 models. See 1961 engine data.

ADDITIONAL ENGINE DATA: A BG-220 engine (formerly called ''220 Black Diamond'') was standard in AB-120, AM-120 and AM-130 and optional in CM-75 and CM-110. The BG-241 engine was also optional in AB-120, AM-120 and AM-130. The V-266 engine was optional in C-1000, C-1200 and C-1300. (See 1961 engine data).

1963 IHC Travelall Station Wagon (D. Sagvold)

544

CHASSIS (Scout Series): See 1961 data.

CHASSIS (Metro-Mite Series): Wheelbase: 96 in. Tires: 6.50 x 15 in.

CHASSIS (Series CM-110 Metro): Wheelbase: 102 in. Tires: 6.70 x 15 in.

CHASSIS (Series AM-120 Metro): Wheelbase: 115/122 in. Tires: 7.00 x 17.5 in.

CHASSIS (Series AM-130 Metro): Wheelbase: 115/122/134 in. Tires: 8.00 x 17.5 in.

CHASSIS (Series AB-120 Metroette): Wheelbase: 115 in. Tires: 7.00 x 17.5 in.

CHASSIS (Series C-1000): Wheelbase: 119 in. Tires: 6.70 x 15 in.

CHASSIS (Series C-1100): Wheelbase: 115/119/131/140 in. Tires: 7.10 x 15 in.

CHASSIS (Series C-1200): Wheelbase: 115/119/131/140 in. Tires: 7.00 x 17.5 in.

CHASSIS (Series C-1300): Wheelbase: 122/131/134 in. Tires: 8.00 x 17.5 in.

TECHNICAL (all Series): Same as 1961.

OPTIONS (all Series): Same as 1961-1962. Power steering was available for $174.

1963 IHC Bonus Load Pickup Truck (D. Sagvold)

HISTORICAL: Introduced November 1, 1962. Calendar year registrations: (All IHC trucks) 145,105. Calendar year registrations by weight class: (up to 6000 lbs.) 57,497; (6001 to 10,000 lbs.) 14,294. Calendar year production: (All IHC models) 168,296 (IHC had an 11.50 percent market share). Innovations: New Metro-Mite series uses four-cylinder Scout engine. Six-cylinder engines become standard equipment in ''C'' series trucks again. ''C'' series has modernized styling.

H.O. Bercher was now president of IHC, while R.M. Buzard remained executive vice-president of the Truck Division. During the summer of 1963 a three-year program for expansion and improvement of the Ft. Wayne works began. This was an all-time record year for the company.

Pricing

	5	4	3	2	1
1963					
Scout Series — (¼-Ton)					
4x2 Pickup	830	1650	2750	3850	5500
4x4 Pickup	870	1750	2900	4100	5800

NOTES: Add 5 percent for vinyl Sport-Top (full-length).
  Add 10 percent for steel Travel-Top.

	5	4	3	2	1
Series CM-75/80 Metro-Mite — (¼-Ton)					
Panel	570	1100	1850	2600	3700
Walk-In Panel	560	1080	1800	2500	3600
Series CM-110 Metro — (½-Ton)					
Walk-In Panel	590	1140	1900	2650	3800
Series C-1000 — (½-Ton)					
Pickup (7 ft.)	810	1620	2700	3800	5400
Bonus Load Pickup (7 ft.)	830	1650	2750	3850	5500
Travelall	850	1700	2850	4000	5700
Panel	800	1400	2350	3250	4700
Series C-1100 — (Heavy-Duty ½-Ton)					
Pickup (7 ft.)	830	1650	2750	3850	5500
Bonus Load Pickup (7 ft.)	840	1680	2800	3900	5600
Travelall	870	1750	2900	4100	5800
Panel	720	1450	2400	3300	4800
Pickup (8 ft.)	810	1620	2700	3800	5400
Bonus Load Pickup (8 ft.)	830	1650	2750	3850	5500
Travelette Pickup	750	1500	2500	3500	5000
Bonus Load Travelette	770	1550	2550	3600	5100

NOTE: Add 5 percent for V-8 (all ''C'' series)

Series C-1200 — (¾-Ton)	5	4	3	2	1
Pickup (7 ft.)	810	1620	2700	3800	5400
Bonus Load Pickup (7 ft.)	830	1650	2750	3850	5500
Travelall	840	1680	2800	3900	5600
Panel	680	1350	2250	3150	4500
Travelette Pickup	800	1400	2350	3250	4700
Bonus Load Travelette Pickup	720	1450	2400	3300	4800

NOTE: Add 5 percent for 4x4 models (C-1200/C-1300)

Series C-1300 — (1-Ton)	5	4	3	2	1
Pickup (8½ ft.)	770	1550	2550	3600	5100
Bonus Load Pickup (8½ ft.)	780	1560	2600	3600	5200

1964 IHC

1964 IHC Travelall Station Wagon (S.Soloy)

Model	Body Type	Price	Weight	Prod. Total
Series CM-75 — (4x2) Metro — (96 in w.b.)				
CM-75	Metro-Mite Body	2345	2955	—
Series CM-80 — (4x2) Metro — (96 in. w.b.)				
CM-80	Metro-Mite Body	2372	2955	—
Series CM-110 — (4x2) Metro — (102 in. w.b.)				
CM-110	Metro-Mite Body	2675	3345	—

ENGINE: See 1963 section, 4-152 engine specifications.

OPTIONS (BG-220): Six-cylinder engine. T-28 Metro-Matic transmission ($250). OSRV mirror. Grille guard. Special paint. Radio. Rear bumper. Heater.

METRO/METROETTE — SERIES "A" — SIX-CYLINDER: — The Metro delivery van series was an important part of IHC truck offerings in payload capacities up to 1-ton. "A" series trucks were, technically, a direct continuation of the 1958 line. There were, of course, some updated features, but they were of a relatively minor nature. The AB-120 Metroette was an old-fashioned looking milk delivery truck with styling that dated back to 1956. The lighter version was considered a medium-duty (¾-ton) truck. It was coded the AB-120, used a 115 inch wheelbase and had a 5400 pound GVW. The regular metros were "AM" models. The "AM-120" was the ¾-ton line and the "AM-130" was the 1-ton. These trucks were available on a variety of wheelbases: 102, 115, 122 and 134 inches. GVWs ranged between 5400 and 6500 pounds for AM-120s and 7000 to 9000 pounds for AM-130s. Base engine was the BG-220; the 220.5 cu. in. six. The BG-241 engine was optionally available.

Model	Body Type	Price	Weight	Prod. Total
Series AB-120 — (4x2) Metro — (115 in. w.b.)				
AB-120	Milk D'ly. Body	3105	4755	—
Series AM-120 — (4x2) Metro				
AM-120	Metro (102-115 in. w.b.)	3072	4570	—
AM-120	Flat Back (115-134 in. w.b.)	3150	4650	—
AM-120	Metro-Van (115-122 in. w.b.)	3276	5080	—
AM-120	Metro-Lite (115-122 in. w.b.)	3789	—	—
AM-120	Metro-Coach (115 in. w.b.)	4440	—	—
Series AM-130 — (4x2) Metro				
AM-130	Metro (115 in. w.b.)	3270	—	—
AM-130	Flat Back (115-134 in. w.b.)	3483	—	—
AM-130	Metro-Van (115-122 in. w.b.)	3475	—	—
AM-130	Metro-Lite (122-134 in. w.b.)	4048	4160	—

ENGINE: See 1963 section, BG-220 engine specifications.

OPTIONS: Power steering ($175). Power brakes ($61). BG-241 engine ($37). T-28 Metro-Matic transmission ($220). OSRV mirrors. Grille guard. Special paint. Rear bumper. Radio. Heater. Oversize tires.

LIGHT-TRUCK — C-900 — FOUR-CYLINDER: — An all-new IHC product for 1964 was the C-900 compact truck. This unique and somewhat advanced vehicle was basically a smaller-than-standard pickup with the Scout's four-cylinder engine, a 107 inch wheelbase and a 6 ft. long pickup box. It had the same general styling as the standard-size "C" series models except it was not a slab-side pickup. Instead, it had rear fenders that protruded from the pickup box like a Ford Flare side or Chevrolet step-side. It was one of the first down-sized pickup trucks. However, buyers could also order a C-900 chassis-and-cab and have aftermarket stake and platform bodies added.

Model	Body Type	Price	Weight	Prod. Total
Series C-900 — (4x2) Truck — (107 in. w.b.)				
C-900	Chassis & Cab	1837	2875	—
C-900	Pickup (6 ft.)	1952	3210	—

ENGINE: See 1963 section, 4-152 engine specifications.

1964 International Metro School Bus (RPZ)

SCOUT — SERIES 80 — FOUR-CYLINDER: — The 1964 International Scout looked the same as the 1963 model. There were no major technical changes. Under the hood, once again, was the Comanche four-cylinder engine. Prices for both the 4x2 and 4x4 models underwent a modest increase.

I.D. DATA: Serial Number located on plate on dash; on right-hand floor board inside cab; on left front frame side rail and on front right-hand running board shield. Numbers for 1964 had a "-4" suffix to indicate model year. Numbers are not available. Engine numbers located on right upper front side of six-cylinder engine crankcase. On left upper front of V-8 engine crankcase. (Diesel engine: plate on left side of engine.) Due to more series being offered, a slightly different data listing format is used here. Factory price includes cab and Federal Excise Tax. Prices listed are for minimum wheelbase. Prices for major items of optional equipment follow each model series and, where applicable, should be added to the base chassis-and-cab price to arrive at "built-up" prices. Specifications apply to basic standard chassis. The buyers' original Bill of Sale again determined model year since IHC trucks were not manufactured on a yearly model basis.

Model	Body Type	Price	Weight	Prod. Total
Series Scout 80 — (4x2) — (100 in. w.b.)				
80	Pickup (5 ft.)	1722	2800	—
Series Scout 80 — (4x4) — (100 in. w.b.)				
80	Pickup (5 ft.)	2210	3000	—

ENGINE: See 1963 section, 4-152 engine specifications.

OPTIONS (Scout): Panel top in lieu of standard cab ($139). R-14 Power-Lok rear axle ($38). R-23 Power-Lock rear axle ($92). See 1961 for additional Scout options.

METRO-MITE — SERIES CM — FOUR-CYLINDER: — The small Metro-Mite delivery vans in the "CM" series were of the more modern, boxy design with full-across horizontal grille bars. The CM-75/CM-80 lines featured a 4000 pound GVW rating and had a 96 inch wheelbase. With a 102 inch wheelbase and 4500 pound GVW, plus larger tires, the CM-110 Metro-Mite was a bit larger rig which shared the modernized styling. All of these models had single front and rear wheels as base equipment.

TRUCKS — SERIES "C" — SIX-CYLINDER: — The "C" series IHC pickups for 1964 looked similar to the redesigned 1963 models. These "corn-binders" came in two ½-ton lines (C-1000 and C-1100) both using the BG-241 six-cylinder engine as standard equipment. All of the C-1000s had a 119 inch wheelbase and GVWs between 3265 and 3965 pounds. The C-1100s came with 115, 119, 131 and 140 inch wheelbases. These ½-tonners had GVW ratings from 3290 to 3845 pounds. The BG-241 engine was standard. Both ½-ton series came with standard conventional drive trains. The ½-ton C-1100 series was also offered with a 4x4 option costing $572. The C-1200 was the ¾-tonner. It came with the same wheelbases. A 4x4 drive train option was $610 extra. For 1-ton buyers, the C-1300 line was available, too. It offered 122, 131 and 134 inch wheelbases, plus wheelbases of 120 and 129 inches with 4x4. The 4x4 option was $1122 extra for C-1300s. They had GVWs ranging as high as 10,000 pounds. The V-266 engine was available, at extra cost, in all series and a larger V-304 engine option was now offered, too.

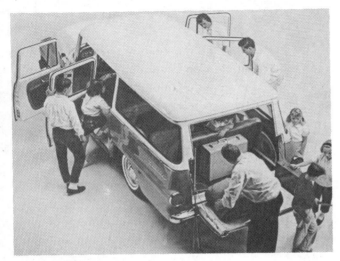

1964 IHC Travelall, rear view (S. Soloy)

Model	Body Type	Price	Weight	Prod. Total
Series C-1000 — (4x2) Truck				
C-1000	Chassis & Cab (119 in. w.b.)	2003	3265	—
C-1000	Pickup (119 in. w.b.)	2124	3640	—
C-1000	B.L. Pickup (119 in. w.b.)	2135	3650	—
C-1000	Panel (119 in. w.b.)	2427	3820	—
C-1000	Travelall (119 in. w.b.)	2631	3965	—
Series C-1100 — (4x2/4x4) Truck				
C-1100	Chassis & Cab (115-131 in. w.b.)	2003	3290	—
C-1100	Pickup (115-131 in. w.b.)	2124	3665	—
C-1100	B.L. Pickup (119-131 in. w.b.)	2135	3655	—
C-1100	Travelette Cab (140 in. w.b.)	2631	3830	—
C-1100	Panel (119 in. w.b.)	2427	3845	—
C-1100	Travelette P.U. (140 in. w.b.)	2770	—	—
C-1100	Cust. Travelall (119 in. w.b.)	2731	3990	—

NOTE: Add $572 for 4x4 option. (C-1100)

Model	Body Type	Price	Weight	Prod. Total
Series C-1200 — (4x2/4x4) Truck				
C-1200	Chassis & Cab (115-131 in. w.b.)	2126	3475	—
C-1200	Pickup (115-131 in. w.b.)	2246	3850	—
C-1200	B.L. Pickup (119-131 in. w.b.)	2258	3840	—
C-1200	Panel (119 in. w.b.)	2550	4035	—
C-1200	Travelette Cab (140 in. w.b.)	2754	4050	—
C-1200	Travelette P.U. (140 in. w.b.)	2893	4797	—
C-1200	Cust. Travelall (119 in. w.b.)	2854	4255	—

NOTE: Add $638 for 4x4 option. (C-1200)

Model	Body Type	Price	Weight	Prod. Total
Series C-1300 — (4x2/4x4) Trucks				
C-1300	Chassis & Cab (122-134 in. w.b.)	2226	3630	—
C-1300	Pickup (131 in. w.b.)	2362	4080	—
C-1300	B.L. Pickup (131 in. w.b.)	2374	4070	—

NOTE: Add $1147 for 4x4 option. (C-1300)

ENGINE (Base): See 1963 section, BG-241 engine specifications.

ENGINE (C-1000/C-1100/C-1200/C-1300): V-304 engine. Vee-block. Overhead valves. Bore & stroke: 3⅞ in. x 3-7/32 in. Displacement: 303.682 cu. in. Brake horsepower: 193.1 at 4400 R.P.M. SAE horsepower: 48.1. Max. Torque: 272.4 lbs. ft. at 2800 R.P.M. Solid valve lifters. Down-draft carburetor.

OPTIONS (C-1000, C-1100, C-1200): Power steering ($174). Power brakes ($51). 8 ft. platform body, except C-1000 ($186). 8 ft. stake body, except C-1000 ($257). V-266 engine ($118). V-304 engine for C-1100 and C-1200 ($179). V-304 LPG engine for C-1100 and C-1200 ($374). T-28 automatic transmission, except 4x4 ($244). T-15 four-speed transmission, except 4x4 ($65). T-16 transmission, C-1200 4x4 ($74). Power-Lok transmission ($60, average). Overdrive ($143). (C-1300) Power brakes ($61). 9 ft. stake body ($319). 9 ft. platform body ($215). V-266 engine ($118). V-304 engine ($179). V-304 LPG engine, with 4x2 only, ($370) and T-28 automatic transmission, C-1300 with 4x2 only, ($220). Plus, options listed for 1963 models.

CHASSIS (Scout Series): Wheelbase: 100 in. Tires: (4x2) 6.50 x 15 in.; (4x4) 6.00 x 16 in.

CHASSIS (Metro-Mite Series): Wheelbase: 96/102 in. Tires: (CM-75/CM-80) 6.50 x 15 in.; (CM-112) 6.70 x 15 in.

CHASSIS (Metro/Metroette Series): Wheelbase: 115/122/134 in. Tires: (AB-AM-120) 7.00 x 17.5 in.; (AM-130) 8.00 x 17.5 in.

CHASSIS (C-900 Compact Truck): Wheelbase: 107 in. Tires: 6.50 x 15 in.

CHASSIS (C-1000): Wheelbase: 119 in. Tires: 6.70 x 15 in.

CHASSIS (C-1100): Wheelbase: 115/119/131/140 in. Tires: 7.10 x 15 in.

CHASSIS (C-1200): Wheelbase: 115/119/131/140 in. Tires: 7.00 x 17.5 in.

CHASSIS (C-1300): Wheelbase: 122/131/134 in. Tires: 8.00 x 17.5 in.

TECHNICAL (C-900): Manual. Synchromesh. Speeds: 3F/1R. Floor-mounted gear shift lever. Single dry disc clutch. Hypoid rear axle. Four-wheel hydraulic brakes. Steel disc wheels.

TECHNICAL: (Except C-900) See specifications for 1963 or previous years.

HISTORICAL: Introduced November, 1963. Calendar year registrations: 148,008 (all IHC truck models). Calendar year registrations by GVW: 6000 lbs. and under — 58,534 units; 6001 to 10,000 lbs. — 15,366 units. Calendar year production: (all IHC trucks) 166,892 (10.69 percent share of market). Innovations: New C-900 compact pickup introduced. Champagne Edition Scout released. The 304 cu. in. V-8 was first made available as an option for trucks under 1-ton this year.

This was the fourth year in a row that IHC truck sales increased. A new 1,400,000 sq. ft. truck plant was under construction in Springfield, Ohio. H.O. Bercher was company president. R.M. Buzard continued to head the Motor Truck Division.

Pricing

	5	4	3	2	1
1964					
Scout Series					
4x2 Pickup	830	1650	2750	3850	5500
4x4 Pickup	870	1750	2900	4100	5800

NOTE: Add 5 percent for full-length vinyl Sport-top. Add 10 percent for steel Travel top. Add 15 percent for "Champagne Edition" Scout.

	5	4	3	2	1
Metro-Mite					
CM-75 Panel	570	1100	1850	2600	3700
CM-80 Walk-in	560	1080	1800	2500	3600
CM-110 Panel	590	1140	1900	2650	3800
Metro/Metroette — (¾-Ton or 1-Ton)					
Milk Dely.	420	840	1400	1950	2800
Metro Body	450	900	1500	2100	3000
Flat Back	440	870	1450	2050	2900
Van	420	840	1400	1950	2800
Metro-Lite	420	840	1400	1950	2800
Metro Coach	470	950	1550	2200	3100
Series C-900 — (Compact)					
Pickup	800	1400	2350	3250	4700
Series C-1000 — (½-Ton)					
Pickup	810	1620	2700	3800	5400
Bonus Load Pickup	830	1650	2750	3850	5500
Panel	800	1400	2350	3250	4700
Travelall	850	1700	2850	4000	5700
Series C-1100 — (Heavy-Duty ½-Ton)					
Pickup	810	1620	2700	3800	5400
Bonus Load Pickup	830	1650	2750	3850	5500
Travelette Pickup	800	1400	2350	3250	4700
Panel	680	1350	2250	3150	4500
Cust. Travelall	850	1700	2850	4000	5700
Series C-1200 — (¾-Ton)					
Pickup	810	1620	2700	3800	5400
Bonus Load Pickup	830	1650	2750	3850	5500
Travelette Camper	810	1620	2700	3800	5400
Panel	680	1350	2250	3150	4500
Travelette Pickup	800	1400	2350	3250	4700
Cust. Travelall	720	1450	2400	3300	4800
Series C-1300 — (1-Ton)					
Pickup	770	1550	2550	3600	5100
Bonus Load Pickup	780	1560	2600	3600	5200

1965 IHC

SCOUT — SERIES 800 — FOUR-CYLINDER — The 1965 Scout 800 had a new, car-like anodized aluminum grille with the word "International" spelled out horizontally along its center. An "I-H" emblem was on the front of the hood. A new, permanently-fixed leak proof windshield made for a tighter interior. Dual variable-speed wipers were now bottom-mounted. Standard equipment included a safety-styled steering wheel, roll-down windows, tension-adjustable vent wings, rotary door locks that could be actuated from inside or outside, pushbutton door handles with separate key locks, suspended pedals, new Vibradamp acoustical headliner (with steel Travel Top) and sound-deadening outer door panel liners. Drip moldings were redesigned to carry water below the windows and there was a new, one-hand tailgate latch release lever. Two-stage support straps were featured on models with tailgate mounted spare tires to prevent full drop from the weight of the tire. Utility models came with hard and soft Cab Tops, Panel top or hard and soft Travel Top. They featured full-width rubber padded seat, all-vinyl Champagne upholstery, ash tray and silver front bumper. Custom models came with hard and soft Cab Tops or hard and soft Travel Top. Deep contoured bucket seats were standard in Travel Top models. Other custom features included all-vinyl champagne upholstery, harmonizing vinyl-covered door panels, dual sunvisors and arm rests, front floor mat, cigar lighter, chrome OSRV mirror, chrome wheel discs and chrome front bumper. There was also a new "Easy View" instrument panel.

I.D. DATA: Serial and engine numbers are in the same location as 1964. Numbers for 1965 had a "-5" suffix to indicate model year. Numbers are not available.

Model	Body Type	Price	Weight	Prod. Total
Scout 800 Series — (4x2)				
800	Pickup (5 ft.)	1720	2800	—
Scout 800 Series — (4x4)				
800	Pickup (5 ft.)	2210	3000	—

ENGINE (Comanche 93): The base engine was the same as 1963. See 1963 section, 4-152 engine specifications.

ENGINE (Turbo III Option): Inline. OHV. Turbo-charged. Four-cylinder. Cast iron block. Bore & stroke: 3⅞x3-7/32 in. Displacement: 151.84 cu. in. Brake horsepower: 111.3 at 4000 R.P.M. Max. Torque: 166.5 lbs. ft. at 3200 R.P.M.

OPTIONS (Scout): Steel Cab Top. Soft Cab Top. Steel Travel Top. Soft Travel Top. Steel Panel Top. (All tops were removable). Heavy-duty rear axle. Oversized tires. Undercoating. Flashing parking and tail lights. Ten-gallon auxiliary gas tank. Windshield washers. Full-width upholstered rear seat. Full transistor push button radio. Fresh air heater and defroster. Four-speed synchromesh transmission. Power take-off. Panel top in lieu of standard Cap top ($140). R-14 "Power-lok" rear axle, all models ($40). R-23 "Power-lok" rear axle, 4x4 models only ($90). Rear compartment seating for custom Travel Top models incuded custom-trim full-width seat with arm rests and rear floor mat. Cushions for benches over wheel housings, all models. Driver's or dual arm rests for utility models. Silver rear bumper for utility models. Chrome rear bumper for custom models. Exterior paint options for 1965 included: (1) Champagne Metallic; (2) Aspen Green; (3) Apache Gold; (4) White; (5) Red; (6) Light Yellow and (7) Moonstone Blue. See 1961 for additional Scout options.

METRO-MITE — "CM" SERIES — FOUR-CYLINDER — The Metro-Mite models were carred over from 1964 more or less intact. Changes, if any, were of a very minor nature.

Model	Body Type	Price	Weight	Prod. Total
Series CM-75 — (4x2) Metro — (96 in. w.b.)				
CM	Metro-Mite Body	2345	2955	—
Series CM-80 — (4x2) Metro — (96 in. w.b.)				
CM	Metro-Mite Body	2370	2995	—
Series CM-110 — (4x2) Metro — (102 in. w.b.)				
CM	Metro-Mite Body	2675	3345	—

ENGINE: See 1963 section, 4-152 engine specifications.

OPTIONS: Power brakes ($60). T-28 Metro-Matic transmission ($250). RA-23 rear axle on CM-75/80 ($80). RA-23 rear axle on CM-110 ($50). OSRV mirror. Grille guard. Special paint. Radio. Rear bumper. Heater.

METRO/METROETTE — SERIES "A" — SIX-CYLINDER — The full-size Metros and the Metroette milk and bakery trucks were carried over from 1964 practically without change.

Model	Body Type	Price	Weight	Prod. Total
Series AB-120 — (4x2) Metroette — (115 in. w.b.)				
AB-120	Milk Dely Body	3105	4755	—
Series AM-120 — (4x2) Metro				
AM-120	Metro (115-122 in. w.b.)	3070	4570	—
AM-120	Flatback (115-122 in. w.b.)	3150	4650	—
AM-120	Metro-Van (115-122 in. w.b.)	3275	5080	—
AM-120	Metro-Lite (115-122 in. w.b.)	3790	—	—
AM-120	Metro Coach (115 in. w.b.)	4440	—	—

Model	Body Type	Price	Weight	Prod. Total
Series AM-130 — (4x2) Metro				
AM-130	Metro (115 in. w.b.)	3270	—	—
AM-130	Flat Back (115-134 in. w.b.)	3345	5050	—
AM-130	Metro-Van (115-122 in. w.b.)	3475	5320	—
AM-130	Metro-Lite (122-134 in. w.b.)	4050	4210	—

ENGINE: See 1963 section, BG-220 engine specifications.

OPTIONS: Power steering ($174). Overdrive ($143). Power brakes ($60). BG-241 engine ($40). BG-265 engine ($60). T-28 Metro-Matic transmission ($220). RA-11 rear axle on AM-120 ($65). OSRV mirror. Special paint. Rear bumper. Radio. Heater. Oversize tires.

LIGHT-TRUCK — D-900 — FOUR-CYLINDER — The compact size International "900" Series pickup was carried over for 1965. This truck, now called a D-900, featured the company's "Bonus Load" (slab-sided) look only. There was little change from last season. Even prices and weights remained the same. These trucks had a tall, flat rear end with round, single taillights mounted high on the fenders and the "International" name lettered across the top of the tailgate.

Model	Body Type	Price	Weight	Prod. Total
Series D-900 — (4x2) — (107 in w.b.)				
D-900	Chassis & Cab	1835	2875	—
D-900	Pickup (6 ft.)	1950	3270	—

ENGINE: See 1963 section, 4-152 engine specifications. Also available was the new Turbo III engine option.

OPTIONS: See 1964 section.

1965 IHC 4x4 Fenderside D-1200 Pickup (G. Gudeman)

TRUCKS — SERIES "D" — SIX-CYLINDER — International's standard ½, ¾ and 1-ton trucks were restyled up front for 1965. They had a new "electric shaver" grille with 31 vertical bars. Running horizontally across the 13 center bars was an "International" nameplate. These trucks came with a choice of conventional styling with flared rear fenders or "Bonus Load" styling with box sides flush with the cab. Except for the new grille, they were virtually unchanged from 1964 appearances.

Model	Body Type	Price	Weight	Prod. Total
Series D-1000 — (4x2) Truck — (119 in w.b.)				
D-1000	Chassis & cab	1975	3265	—
D-1000	Pickup	2100	3640	—
D-1000	Bonus Load Pickup	2110	3630	—
D-1000	Panel	2400	5150	—
D-1000	Travelall	2705	5440	—
Series D-1100 — (4x2/4x4) Truck				
D-1100	Chassis & Cab (115-131 in. w.b.)	2005	3290	—
D-1100	Pickup (119-131 in. w.b.)	2125	3665	—
D-1100	Bonus Load Pickup (119-131 in. w.b.)	2135	3655	—
D-1100	Travelette Cab (140 in. w.b.)	2630	3830	—
D-1100	Panel (119 in. w.b.)	2425	5185	—
D-1100	Travelette Pickup (140 in. w.b.)	2770	—	—
D-1100	Travelall (119 in. w.b.)	2730	5475	—

NOTE: Add $569 and 305 pounds for 4x4 option (D-1100).

Model	Body Type	Price	Weight	Prod. Total
Series D-1200 — (4x2/4x4) Truck				
D-1200	Chassis & Cab (115-131 in. w.b.)	2125	3475	—
D-1200	Pickup (119-131 in. w.b.)	2245	3855	—
D-1200	Bonus Load Pickup (119-131 in. w.b.)	2260	3845	—
D-1200	Panel Body (119 in. w.b.)	2550	5365	—
D-1200	Travelette Cab (140 in. w.b.)	2755	4050	—
D-1200	Travelette Pickup (140 in. w.b.)	2895	—	—
D-1200	Travelall (119 in w.b.)	2855	5655	—

NOTE: Add $609 and 410 pounds for 4x4 (D-1200).

Model	Body Type	Price	Weight	Prod. Total
Series D-1300 — (4x2/4x4) Truck				
D-1300	Chassis & Cab (122-134 in. w.b.)	2225	3660	—
D-1300	Pickup (131 in. w.b.)	2360	4090	—
D-1300	Bonus Load Pickup (131 in. w.b.)	2375	4080	—

NOTE: Add $1123 and 745 pounds for 4x4 (D-1300).

ENGINE: See 1963 section, BG-241 engine specifications.

OPTIONS (D-1000, D-1100, D-1200): Power brakes ($50). V-266 engine ($120). V-304 engine ($180). V-304 LPG engine, in D-1100/1200 except Travelall ($375). BG-241 LPG engine in D-1100 4x2 models ($150). T-28 automatic transmission, except 4x4 models ($245). T-15 four-speed transmission, except 4x4 models ($65). T-16 four-speed transmission, 4x4 models only ($75). T-8 overdrive transmission, D-1000/1100 4x2 models ($145). 8 ft. platform body, except D-1000 ($185). 8 ft. stake body, except D-1000 ($255). (D-1300): Power brakes ($60). V-266 engine ($120). V-304 engine ($180). V-304 LPG engine in D-1300 4x2 models ($370). BG-241 LPG engine, D-1300 4x2 models ($150). T-28 automatic transmission in D-1300 4x2 models. ($220). T-16 four-speed transmission in D-1300 4x4 models ($50). 9 ft. platform body ($215). 9 ft. stake body ($320). Plus options listed for 1963 models.

CHASSIS: See specifications for comparable 1963-1964 models.

TECHNICAL: See specifications for comparable 1963-1964 models.

HISTORICAL: Introduced October 1964. Calendar year registrations by GVW class: (6000 lbs. or less) 58,833); (6001 to 10,000 lbs.) 16,381. Calendar year production: (all IHC truck) 171,638. (9.62 percent). Factory shipments: IHC shipped 64,500 trucks in the under-6000 pounds GVW category and 19,700 trucks in the 6001 to 10,000 pounds GVW category.

Improved Scout 800 models. Scout has new options including four-speed transmission with 4.07:1 rear axle, bucket seats and contoured floor covering. New turbo-charged Comanche four-cylinder engine. Scout available in new Utility and Custom truck lines.

Surveys taken in 1965 showed that nearly 75 percent of all Scouts were purchased primarily for non-business use and that 82 percent of these trucks were ordered with four-wheel-drive. Station wagons and sports cars made up better than one-third of all trade-ins on new Scouts and nearly one-half of Scout buyers had never purchased an International product before. Production for the calendar year was an all-time high record for the Chicago-based truck-maker. Output in calendar 1965 included 26,962 gas powered four-cylinder engines. H.O. Bercher was IHC president and R.M. Buzard continued to head the company's Motor Truck Division as executive vice-president. S.G. Johnson was engineering manager.

Pricing

	5	4	3	2	1
1965					
Scout 800					
4x2 Pickup	870	1750	2900	4100	5800
4x4 Pickup	900	1800	3000	4200	6000

NOTES: Add five percent for full-length Sport Top.
Add seven percent for steel Travel Top.

	5	4	3	2	1
Metro-Mite					
CM-75 Panel	570	1100	1850	2600	3700
CM-80 Walk-In	560	1080	1800	2500	3600
CM-110 Panel	590	1140	1900	2650	3800
Metro/Metroette					
Milk Dely.	560	1080	1800	2500	3600
Metro Body	450	900	1500	2100	3000
Flatback	440	870	1450	2050	2900
Van	450	900	1500	2100	3000
Metro-Lite	420	840	1400	1950	2800
8P Metro Coach	450	900	1500	2100	3000
Series D-900					
Pickup	770	1550	2550	3600	5100
Series D-1000					
Pickup	830	1650	2750	3850	5500
Bonus Load Pickup	840	1680	2800	3900	5600
Panel	720	1450	2400	3300	4800
Travelall	870	1750	2900	4100	5800
Series D-1100					
Pickup	840	1680	2800	3900	5600
Bonus Load Pickup	850	1700	2850	4000	5700
Travelette Pickup	770	1550	2550	3600	5100
Panel	740	1470	2450	3350	4900
Custom Travelall	780	1560	2600	3600	5200
Series D-1200					
Pickup	830	1650	2750	3850	5500
Bonus Load Pickup	840	1680	2800	3900	5600
Travelette Camper	870	1750	2900	4100	5800
Panel	720	1450	2400	3300	4800
Travelette Pickup	720	1450	2400	3300	4800
Custom Travelall	750	1500	2500	3500	5000
Series C-1300					
Pickup	780	1560	2600	3600	5200
Bonus Load Pickup	800	1600	2650	3700	5300

NOTE: Add five percent for 4x4 models (all series).

1966 IHC

SCOUT — SERIES 800 — FOUR-CYLINDER — The Scout Sportop models, introduced in 1966, reflected the trend toward more consumer luxury items. Interior features included bucket seats, matching rear seats, trim panels over the rear wheel housings, a trimmed transmission console and a champagne colored interior. Later that year, a larger four-cylinder engine and a 155 horsepower V-8 were made available. The turbo-charged Comanche III engine was also used in some 1966 models.

I.D. DATA: Serial numbers and engine numbers for all IHC vehicles were in the same locations. Numbers for 1966 had a "-6" suffix to indicate model year. Numbers are not available.

Model	Body Type	Price	Weight	Prod. Total
Scout 800 Series — (4x2)				
800	Utility Roadster	1731	2800	—
800	Utility Traveltop	1904	2900	—
800	Custom Roadster	1858	2800	—
800	Custom Traveltop	2124	2900	—
800	Sportop Soft Top	2442	2800	—
800	Sportop Hardtop	2408	2900	—
800	Utility Pickup	1802	2800	—
800	Custom Pickup	1939	2900	—

NOTE: Add $752 and 200 pounds for 4x4 models.

ENGINE (Commanche 93): Same as 1965.

ENGINE (Turbo III, Optional): Same as 1965.

ENGINE (4-196, optional): Inline. Overhead valve. Four-cylinder. Cast iron block. Bore & stroke: 4⅛ in. x 3-21/32 in. Displacement: 195.44 cu. in. Brake horsepower: 110.8 at 4000 R.P.M. Net horsepower: 27.2. Max. Torque: 180.2 lbs.-ft. at 2000 R.P.M. Carburetor: Single downdraft.

NOTE: The 4-196 engine option was introduced in mid-1966.

ENGINE (V-266, optional): Vee block. Overhead valve. Eight-cylinder. Cast iron block. Bore & stroke: 3⅝ in. x 3-7/32 in. Displacement: 266.76 cu. in. Brake horsepower: 154.8 at 4400 R.P.M. Net horsepower: 42.1. Max. Torque: 227.1 lbs. ft. at 2800 R.P.M.

OPTIONS: Options for 1966 Scouts were similar to those available for 1961-1965 models.

METRO — SERIES "M" — ALL ENGINES — The Metro-Mites and Metros were redesignated "M" models for 1966. The smaller trucks were four-cylinder models and came on two different wheelbases. Those on a 102 inch wheelbase were called M-700s and M-800s. There was also an M-1100 model with a 108 inch wheelbase. Larger Metros used the BG-220 six-cylinder power plant. They were called M-1200s and had wheelbases between 119 and 127 inches. Gross vehicle weights ranged from 4500 to 5500 pounds for M-700/M-800 models and 4500 to 6000 pounds for M-1100s. Also available was the larger M-1200 Metro with wheelbases of 119 to 127 inches. These had GVW ratings in the 8000 to 9000 pound class.

Model	Body Type	Price	Weight	Prod. Total
Series M-700/M-800 — (4x2 Metro-Mite) — (102 in w.b.)				
M-700	Walk-in Panel	2549	3655	—
M-800	Walk-in Panel	2549	3705	—
Series M-1100 — (4x2 Metro) — (108 in. w.b.)				
M-1100	Walk-in Panel	2883	4095	—
Series M-1200 — (4x2 Metro) — (119-127 in w.b.)				
M-1200	Walk-in Panel	3249	4940	—

ENGINES (Standard): M-700/M-800 — 4-152 four-cylinder; M-1100 — 4-152 four-cylinder; M-1200 — BG220 six-cylinder. See 1963 for engine specifications.

OPTIONS: The Turbo III four-cylinder engine was optional in M-700, M-800 and M-1100 models. The BG-220 six-cylinder engine was optional in M-700, and M-800 models. The BG-241 engine was optional in M-1200 models. The V-266 V-8 was optional in M-1200 models. Other Metro options were the same as 1963-1965.

LIGHT-TRUCK — 900A SERIES — FOUR-CYLINDER — The "900" compact pickup was again available in 1966. This was the final season for the small, four-cylinder pickup, which sold for under $2,000. Consequently, there was little change in the product. It's too bad that International didn't keep it going until the early 1970s when the nationwide fuel shortages occured. But, the market for such a truck simply wasn't very large in the mid-1960s. The 900A continued to use a 107 inch wheelbase and had a 4000 pound GVW.

Model	Body Type	Price	Weight	Prod. Total
Series 900A — (4x2) — (107 in. w.b.)				
900A	Chassis & Cab	1865	2875	—
900A	Pickup	1980	3210	—

ENGINE: See 1963 section, 4-152 engine specifications. (The Turbo' 111 four-cylinder was the only possible engine option for the 900A).

OPTIONS: See 1964 section.

1966 International Pickup (OCW)

TRUCKS — SERIES A — SIX-CYLINDER — The standard size pickups for 1966 were characterized by a minor alteration to the grille. A center strip was now used to carry the "International" company name. It ran full-width across the trucks, from headlight to headlight. The upper sides of the box, on pickups, now carried a trim molding on fancier models. Available truck lines included the 1000A and 1100A ½-tonners, the 1200A ¾-ton and the 1300A 1-tonner.

Model	Body Type	Price	Weight	Prod. Total
Series 1000A — (4x2 Truck) — (119 in. w.b.)				
1000A	Chassis & Cab	2005	3130	—
1000A	Pickup (7 ft.)	2126	3500	—
1000A	B.L. Pickup (7 ft.)	2138	—	—
1000A	Panel (7 ft.)	2429	3800	—
Series 1100A — (4x2 Truck) — (115-140 in. w.b.)				
1100A	Chassis & Cab (115-131 in. w.b.)	2035	3180	—
1100A	Pickup (119-131 in w.b.)	2156	3550	—
1100A	B.L. Pickup (119-131 in. w.b.)	2168	—	—
1100A	Panel (7 ft.-119 in. w.b.)	2460	3850	—
1100A	Travelette Cab (140 in. w.b.)	2672	3625	—
1100A	Travelette B.L. Pickup (140 in. w.b.)	2811	3900	—

NOTE: Add $569 for 4x4 option. (1100A models)

Model	Body Type	Price	Weight	Prod. Total
Series 1200A — (4x2 Truck) — (115-140 in. w.b.)				
1200A	Chassis & Cab (115-140 in. w.b.)	2155	3410	—
1200A	Pickup (119-131 in. w.b.)	2275	3780	—
1200A	B.L. Pickup (119-131 in. w.b.)	2287	—	—
1200A	Panel (7 ft.-119 in.w.b.)	2579	4080	—
1200A	Travelette Cab (140 in.w.b.)	2791	3850	—
1200A	B.L. Travelette Pickup (140 in. w.b.)	2930	4185	—

NOTE: Add $609 for 4x4 option (1200A models)

Model	Body Type	Price	Weight	Prod. Total
Series 1300A — (4x2 Truck) — (122-140 in w.b.)				
1300A	Chassis & Cab (122-140 in. w.b.)	2254	3610	—
1300A	Pickup, 8½ ft. (131 in w.b.)	2390	4020	—
1300A	B.L. Pickup, 8½ ft. (131 in. w.b.)	2402	4035	—
1300A	Travelette Cab(140 in w.b.)	2874	4055	—
1300A	B.L. Travelette Pickup (140 in. w.b.)	3016	4390	—

NOTE: Add $1124 for 4x4 option.

ENGINE: See 1963 section, BG-241 engine specifications.

OPTIONS: See 1963 section.

CHASSIS (Series Scout 800): Wheelbase: 100 in. Tires: (4x2) 7.35 x 15 in; (4x4) 6.00 x 16 in.

CHASSIS (Series M-700/M-800): Wheelbase: 102 in. Tires: 7.35 x 15 in.

CHASSIS (Series M-1100): Wheelbase: 108 in. Tires: 7.75 x 15 in.

CHASSIS (Series M-1200): Wheelbase: 119-127 in. Tires 7.00 x 17.5 in.

CHASSIS (Series 900A): Wheelbase: 107 in. Tires: 7.35 x 15 in.

CHASSIS (Series 1000A): Wheelbase: 119 in. Tires: 7.75 x 15 in.

CHASSIS (Series 1100A): Wheelbase: 115 to 140 in. Tires: 8.15 x 15 in.

CHASSIS (Series 1200A): Wheelbase: 115-140 in. Tires: 7.00 x 17.5 in.

CHASSIS (Series 1300A): Wheelbase: 122-140 in. Tires: 8.00 x 17.5 in.

TECHNICAL: Same as comparable models.

HISTORICAL: Introduced: November 1, 1965. Calendar year registrations by GVW class: 6000 pounds or less (62,254); 6001 to 10,000 pounds (15,004). Calendar year production: (all IHC Trucks) 170,385. (9.66 percent share of market).

Scout made available in two new luxury convertible and hardtop models with bucket seats and other passenger car appointments. New 20 percent more powerful "big six" released for Scout 800 models. A new line of pickups with camper conversions introduced. New Metro series truck with aluminum bodies introduced.

Worldwide sales of IHC trucks, service parts and service set a new record in 1966, climbing to $1.2 billion. There was a problem with parts shortages this year, resulting from lack of supplier capacity.

Pricing

1966	5	4	3	2	1
Scout Series 800					
Utility Roadster	870	1750	2900	4100	5800
Utility Traveltop	950	1900	3150	4400	6300
Custom Roadster	890	1770	2950	4150	5900
Custom Traveltop	960	1920	3200	4500	6400
Soft Sportop	980	1950	3250	4550	6500
Hard Sportop	1010	2030	3350	4700	6700
Utility Pickup	890	1770	2950	4150	5900
Custom Pickup	900	1800	3000	4200	6000

NOTES: Add 3 percent for Turbo-charged models.
Add 2 percent for V-8.

	5	4	3	2	1
Series Metro					
M-700 Panel	570	1100	1850	2600	3700
M-800 Panel	560	1080	1800	2500	3600
M-1100 Panel	590	1140	1900	2650	3800
M-1200 Panel	590	1140	1900	2650	3800
Series 900A					
Pickup	770	1550	2550	3600	5100
Series 1000A					
Pickup (7 ft.)	830	1650	2750	3850	5500
Bonus Load Pickup (7 ft.)	840	1680	2800	3900	5600
Panel (7 ft.)	740	1470	2450	3350	4900
Series 1100A					
Pickup	850	1700	2850	4000	5700
Bonus Load Pickup	870	1750	2900	4100	5800
Panel	750	1500	2500	3500	5000
Travelette	780	1560	2600	3600	5200
Bonus Load Travelette	800	1600	2650	3700	5300

Add 5 percent for 4x4 option (all series).

	5	4	3	2	1
Series 1200A					
Pickup	840	1680	2800	3900	5600
Bonus Load Pickup	850	1700	2850	4000	5700
Panel	740	1470	2450	3350	4900
Travelette	740	1470	2450	3350	4900
Bonus Load Travelette	750	1500	2500	3500	5000
Series 1300A					
Pickup (8½ ft.)	800	1600	2650	3700	5300
Bonus Load Pickup (8½ ft.)	810	1620	2700	3800	5400
Travelette	690	1380	2300	3200	4600
Bonus Load Travelette	700	1400	2350	3250	4700

1967 IHC

SCOUT — 800 SERIES — FOUR-CYLINDER — The 1967 Scout was similar to last year's model. It continued to be marketed in three different trim levels: Utility, Custom and Sportop. Utility models had bench seats and silver-gray front bumpers. Custom models had vinyl-covered door panels, dual sunvisors, arm rests, front floor mats, a cigar lighter, chrome OSRV mirror, chrome wheel discs and a chrome front bumper. Deep contoured bucket seats were standard in Customs with soft or all-steel full-length Traveltops. The top series included the slanted-back Sportop (hard or soft), roll-down front windows with chrome moldings, wing-out rear quarter windows with chrome moldings, dual variable-speed wipers, front bucket seats, deluxe front and rear floor mats; chrome outside and inside mirrors, chrome front bumper, chrome rear bumperettes, chrome wheel discs and other luxury appointments. Promotional exphasis was placed on the V-8 model brought out late in calendar year 1966. About 50 pounds of safety equipment was added this season to meet new government regulations. Colors available for 1967 were: Apache gold, Red, Bahama blue, Alpine white, Malibu beige, Tahitian yellow and Aspen green.

I.D. DATA: Serial number located on the left door pillar. The serial number consisted of 13 symbols. The first six identify the serial number. The seventh digit indicates the manufacturing plant. The last six digits are sequential production numbers. Numbers are not available. Engine numbers took the form of a prefix to the engine serial numbers. For example, a V-266 engine serial number would read V-266-000000. Engine numbers are located on machined boss on cylinder block.

1967 International Scout 4x2 Utility (JAG)

Model	Body Type	Price	Weight	Prod. Total
Series Scout 800 — (4x2) — (100 in w.b.)				
800	Utility Roadster	1830	2850	—
800	Utility Traveltop	2043	2950	—
800	Custom Roadster	1998	2850	—
800	Custom Traveltop	2263	2950	—
800	Soft Top (Sportop)	2592	2850	—
800	Hardtop (Sportop)	2558	2950	—
800	Utility Pickup	1945	2850	—
800	Custom Pickup	2082	2950	—
Series Scout 800 — (4x4) — (100 in w.b.)				
800	Utility Roadster	2622	—	—
800	Utility Traveltop	2796	3615	—
800	Custom Roadster	2745	—	—
800	Custom Traveltop	3010	—	—
800	Soft Top (Sportop)	3344	—	—
800	Hardtop (Sportop)	3310	—	—
800	Utility Pickup	2715	3515	—
800	Custom Pickup	2846	—	—

ENGINE (Base 4-152): Inline. OHV. Four-cylinder. Cast iron block. Bore & stroke: 3⅞ in. x 3-7/32 in. Displacement: 151.84 cu. in. Compression ratio: 8.19:1. Brake horsepower: 93 at 4400 R.P.M. Net horsepower: 24.1. Max. Torque: 143 lbs.-ft. at 2400 R.P.M. Hydraulic valve lifters. Carburetor: Holley "1904" model 3479 (single-bore).

ENGINE (Optional/Turbo III): Inline. OHV. Turbo-charged. Four-cylinder. Cast iron block. Bore & stroke: 3⅞ in. x 3-7/32 in. Displacement: 151.84 cu. in. Compression ratio: 8.19:1. Brake horsepower: 111 at 4000 R.P.M. Max. Torque: 166 lbs.-ft. at 3200 R.P.M. Hydraulic valve lifters. Carburetor: Holley "1904" model 3862 (single-bore).

ENGINE (Optional/4-196): Inline. OHV. Four-cylinder. Cast iron block. Bore & stroke: 4⅛ in. x 3-21/32 in. Displacement: 195.44 cu. in. Compression ratio: 8.1:1. Brake horsepower: 111 at 4000 R.P.M. Net horsepower: 27.2. Max. Torque: 180 lbs.-ft. at 2000 R.P.M. Hydraulic valve lifters. Carburetor: Holley 1904 model 3716 (single-bore).

ENGINE (Optional/V-266): Vee block. OHV. Eight-cylinder. Cast iron block. Bore & stroke: 3⅝ in. x 3-7/32 in. Displacement: 266.76 cu. in. Compression ratio: 8.4:1. Brake horsepower: 155 at 4400 R.P.M. Net horsepower: 42.1. Max. Torque: 227.1 lbs.-ft. at 2800 R.P.M. Hydraulic valve lifters. Carburetor: Holley "2300" model 1710 (Two-bore).

OPTIONS (Scout 800 Series): White sidewall tires. Solid state radio. Fresh air heater-defroster. Parking and taillight flasher switch. Ten gallon auxiliary gas tank. Windshield washer. Heavier-duty axles, springs, tires and other special equipment. Rear compartment seating for Travel Top models. Cushions for wheelbase benches. Driver's or dual arm rests for Utility models. Silver gray rear bumper for Utility models. Chrome rear bumper for Custom models. Undercoating.

METRO — SERIES "M" — (ALL ENGINES) — The light-duty IHC Metro vans came in the same series available in 1966. The M-700 and M-800 models were on the 102 inch wheelbase with standard four-cylinder power. M-1100s were on a 108 inch wheelbase with four-cylinder engines as base equipment. The larger M-1200 and MA-1200 models had a choice of wheelbases between 119 and 134 inches. The BG-220 six-cylinder engine was standard in the "1200" series models.

Model	Body Type	Price	Weight	Prod. Total
Series M-700/M-800 — (4x2) Metro — (102 in. w.b.)				
M-700	Walk-In Panel	2549	3655	—
M-800	Walk-In Panel	2549	3705	—
Series M-1100 — (4x2) Metro — (108 in. w.b.)				
M-1100	Walk-In Panel	2883	4095	—
Series M-1200 — (4x2) Metro — (119-127 in. w.b.)				
M-1200	Walk-In Panel	3249	4940	—
Series MA-1200 — (4x2) Metro — (119-134 in. w.b.)				
MA-1200	Walk-In Panel	3907	—	—

ENGINE (Base/4-152): The same engine used as base equipment in the Scout 800 was standard for the M-700, M-800 and M-1100 models. See specifications above.

ENGINE (BG-220): Inline. Overhead Valve. Six-cylinder. Cast iron block. Bore & stroke: 3-9/16 in. x 3-11/16 in. Displacement: 220.5 cu. in. Compression ratio: 7.5:1. Brake horsepower: 112.5 at 3800 R.P.M. Net horsepower: 30.4. Max. Torque: 194.4 lbs.-ft. at 2000 R.P.M. Solid valve lifters (barrel-type). Carburetor: Holley model 1904 (single-bore).

NOTE: The BG-220 engine was standard equipment in M-1200 and MA-1200 models and optional for the M-700, M-800 and M-1100 models.

ENGINE (BG-241): Inline. Overhead valve. Six-cylinder. Cast iron block. Bore & stroke: 3-9/32 in. x 4.018 in. Displacement: 240.3 cu. in. Compression ratio: 7.5:1. Brake horsepower: 140.8 at 3800 R.P.M. Net horsepower: 30.4. Max. Torque: 223.5 lbs.-ft. at 2000 R.P.M. Solid valve lifters (barrel-type). Carburetor: Holley single barrel model 1904.

NOTE 1: The BG-241 engine was optional for M-1200 and MA-1200 Metro models.

NOTE 2: The V-266 engine (see specifications above under Scout engines) was also optional in M-1200 and MA-1200 Metro models.

OPTIONS (Metro Series): Grille guard. Rear bumper. OSRV mirror or mirrors. Radio. Special paint. Oversize tires. Overdrive ($200). Power steering. Automatic transmission. Metro-Matic transmissions ($211). Four-speed transmission.

LIGHT-DUTY — SERIES 900A/908B — ALL-ENGINES — A new, V-8 powered compact pickup series called the 908B joined the IHC truck lineup in 1967. This truck had a slightly larger 115 inch wheelbase and came in two models. The first was a conventional pickup with flared-type rear fenders and a 6-foot 8-inch long pickup box. The second was a slab-sided Bonus Load model with the same box. There seems to be some confusion over the continuation of the 900A series. An N.A.D.A. used car guide of January 1968 shows this model being available as a 1967 truck. However, other reference books indicate the 900A went out of production after the 1966 model year. Possibly, some 1966 versions were carried over and sold as 1967s until the supply was gone.

Model	Body Type	Price	Weight	Prod. Total
Series 900A — (4x2) Truck — (107 in. w.b.)				
900A	Chassic & Cab	1865	2875	—
900A	Pickup (6 ft.)	1980	3210	—
Series 908B — (4x2) Truck — (115 in. w.b.)				
908B	Pickup (6 ft. 8 in.)	2126	3815	—
908B	Bonus Load Pickup (6 ft. 8 in.)	2138	3815	—

ENGINE (4-152): The 900A, if available in 1967, came with the same four-cylinder engine that was standard (base) equipment in the Scout 800. See specifications above. There were no engine options for the 900A models.

ENGINE (V-266): The 908 used the V-266 engine as standard equipment. This was the same V-8 engine that was optional in Scout 800s and "1200" Series Metro vans. See specifications under Scout 800 above. There were no engine options for the 908B models.

OPTIONS (Series 908B): Rear bumper. Radio. Fresh-air heater-defroster. White sidewall tires. OSRV mirror(s). Special paint.

CONVENTIONAL TRUCKS — SERIES "B" — SIX-CYLINDER — A new grille characterized the conventional (standard size) light-duty trucks from IHC for 1967. It featured a segmented bright metal surround over a darker appearing insert. The "International" name was stamped on a horizontal bar that spanned the center of the grille opening. All else was about the same as in 1966. The 1000B series included four models with 4200 to 5000 pound GVW ratings. There were eight models with GVWs of 4700-5800 pounds in the 1100B lineup. Also having eight models was the 1200B series, with GVWs ranging from 5500 to 7300 pounds. There were four more light-duty trucks, with 7000 to 8800 pound GVWs, in the 1300B series. The 1000B and 1100B were lighter - and heavier-duty ½-tonners; the 1200B was the ¾ tonner and the 1300B was a 1-tonner. (IHC usually referred to the various models as "light", "medium" and "heavy" light duty trucks which sounds a little confusing).

Model	Body Type	Price	Weight	Prod. Total
Series 1000B — (4x2) Truck — (119 in. w.b.)				
1000B	Chassis & Cab	2182	3245	—
1000B	Pickup (7 ft.)	2303	3615	—
1000B	Bonus Load Pickup (7 ft.)	2315	3615	—
1000B	Panel (7 ft.)	2623	3915	—
Series 1100B — (4x2) Truck — (115-140 in w.b.)				
1100B	Chassis & Cab	2139	3225	—
1100B	Pickup (6 ft. 8 in.)	2260	3595	—
1100B	Bonus Load Pickup (6 ft. 8 in.)	2272	3595	—
1100B	Pickup (8 ft. ½ in.)	2292	3675	—
1100B	Bonus Load Pickup (8 ft.)	2304	3660	—
1100B	Panel (7 ft.)	2612	3895	—
1100B	Travelette Cab	2846	3670	—
1100B	Travelette Pickup B.L. (6 ft.)	2985	4005	—

NOTE: Add $569 for 4x4 models (Series 1100B).

Model	Body Type	Price	Weight	Prod. Total
Series 1200B — (4x2) Truck — (119-166 in. w.b.)				
1200B	Chassis & Cab	2309	3460	—
1200B	Pickup (7 ft.)	2430	3830	—
1200B	Bonus Load Pickup (7 ft.)	2442	3830	—
1200B	Pickup (8½ ft.)	2462	3900	—
1200B	Bonus Load Pickup (8 ft.)	2474	3885	—
1200B	Panel (7 ft.)	2750	4130	—
1200B	Travelette Cab	2984	3895	—
1200B	Bonus Load Travelette Pickup (6 ft.)	3123	4230	—

NOTE: Add $606 for 4x4 models (Series 1200B).

Series 1300B — (4x2) Truck — (131-156 in. w.b.)

1300B	Chassis & Cab	2419	3671	—
1300B	Pickup (8½ ft.)	2545	4196	—
1300B	Travelette Cab	3066	4196	—
1300B	Bonus Load Travelette Pickup (6 ft.)	3208	4435	—

NOTE: Add $1123 for 4x4 models (Series 1300B).

ENGINE (BG-241): IHC's 240.3 cu. in. six-cylinder engine was standard in all conventional light-duty models. See Metro series engine specifications above. The BG-265 and V-266 power plants were optional for these trucks.

NOTE: Prices given above are for V-8 powered models; trucks with the base six-cylinder engine were $62 less.

OPTIONS: Whitewall tires. Rear Bumper. Power steering. Roof rack (Travelall). Deluxe interior appointments. Custom interior package. Bumper guards. Transistor radio. Fresh-air heater and defroster. Clock. Cigar lighter. Radio antenna. Seat covers. OSRV mirror(s). Custom exterior trim. Wheel trim rings. Two-tone paint. "California" towing mirrors. Oversize tires. Vinyl top (Travelall). Foam rubber seat cushions. Pickup box rails. Automatic transmission. Four-speed transmission.

CHASSIS (Scout 800 Series): Wheelbase: 100 in. Tires 7.35 x 15 in.

CHASSIS (Series M-700/M-800): Wheelbase: 102 in. Tires: 7.35 x 15 in.

CHASSIS (Series M-1100): Wheelbase: 108 in. Tires: 7.75 x 15 in.

CHASSIS (Series M-1200/MA-1200): Wheelbase: 119-134 in. Tires: 7.00 x 17.5 in.

CHASSIS (Series 900A): Wheelbase: 107 in. Tires: 7.35 x 15 in.

CHASSIS (Series 908B): Wheelbase: 115 in. Tires: 7.75 x 15 in.

CHASSIS (Series 1000B): Wheelbase: 119 in. Tires: 8.15 x 15 in.

CHASSIS (Series 1100B): Wheelbase: 115/118/131/140 in. Tires: 8.15 x 15 in.

CHASSIS (Series 1200B): Wheelbase: 115/119/131/140 in. Tires: 7.00 x 17.5 in.

CHASSIS (Series 1300B): Wheelbase: 122/131/140 in. (4x4 wheelbase: 120, 129 and 132 in.) Tires: 8.00 x 17.5 in.

1967 International Scout 4x4 Utility (JAG)

TECHNICAL: Manual (Synchromesh) Transmission. Speeds: 3F/1R or 4F/1R. Floor-mounted gear shift lever. Single-reduction rear axle. Overall ratio: Various. Hydraulic four-wheel brakes. Disc wheels. Drivetrain options: Automatic transmission. Overdrive.

NOTE: Transmissions used in IHC trucks were identified by an "AT" or "T" code listed on the vehicle inspection card attached to left sunvisor. The T-1 and T-2 transmissions were produced by IHC. Models T-4 through T-16 were made by Borg-Warner. The T-17 and T-18 models were by New Process. Models T-30 through T-39 were made by Fuller. For additional applications consult **Motor Truck Repair Manual's** for applicable years.

HISTORICAL: Introduced: November 1, 1966. Calendar year registrations by GWV class: 6,000 pounds or less (62,148); 6001 to 10,000 pounds (13,579). Calendar year production: (all IHC trucks) 167,940 (10.59 percent).

New compact V-8 powered pickup truck line introduced. Revised styling on "B" series conventional trucks. Safety features added to some models to satisfy new government standards.

Worldwide sales by IHC in fiscal-year 1967 topped the $2.5 billion mark for the second year in a row. Truck sales were down five percent from 1966's all-time record. H.O. Bercher continued as company president, while R.O. Musgjerd took over as general manager of the Motor Truck Division.

1967 IHC Scout w/Steel Travel-Top (S. Soloy)

Pricing

1967	5	4	3	2	1
Scout 800 Series					
Utility Roadster	870	1750	2900	4100	5800
Utility Traveltop	950	1900	3150	4400	6300
Custom Roadster	890	1770	2950	4150	5900
Custom Traveltop	960	1920	3200	4500	6400
Soft Top (Sport)	980	1950	3250	4550	6500
Hardtop (Sport)	1010	2030	3350	4700	6700
Utility Pickup	890	1770	2950	4150	5900
Custom Pickup	900	1800	3000	4200	6000

NOTE 1: Add 10 percent for 4x4 model.
Add 5 percent for soft Traveltop.
Add 4 percent for all-steel Traveltop.
Add 2 percent for V-8 model.
Add 3 percent for turbo-charged 4-cyl.

Series Metro	5	4	3	2	1
M-700 Panel	570	1100	1850	2600	3700
M-800 Panel	560	1080	1800	2500	3600
M-1100 Panel	590	1140	1900	2650	3800
M-1200 Panel	590	1140	1900	2650	3800
MA-1200 Panel	600	1200	2000	2800	4000
Series 900A					
Pickup	770	1550	2550	3600	5100
Series 908B					
Pickup	800	1600	2650	3700	5300
Bonus Load Pickup	810	1620	2700	3800	5400
Series 1000B					
Pickup (7 ft.)	830	1650	2750	3850	5500
Bonus Load Pickup (7 ft.)	840	1680	2800	3900	5600
Panel (7 ft.)	740	1470	2450	3350	4900
Series 1100B					
Pickup (6 ft. 8 in.)	850	1700	2850	4000	5700
Bonus Load P.U. (6 ft. 8 in.)	870	1750	2900	4100	5800
Pickup (8½ ft.)	840	1680	2800	3900	5600
Bonus Load P.U. (8 ft.)	850	1700	2850	4000	5700
Panel (7 ft.)	750	1500	2500	3500	5000
Travelette Cab	780	1560	2600	3600	5200
Bonus Load Travelette P.U. (6 ft.)	800	1600	2650	3700	5300
Series 1200B					
Pickup (7 ft.)	840	1680	2800	3900	5600
Bonus Load Pickup (7 ft.)	850	1700	2850	4000	5700
Pickup (8½ ft.)	810	1620	2700	3800	5400
Bonus Load Pickup (8 ft.)	830	1650	2750	3850	5500
Panel (7 ft.)	740	1470	2450	3350	4900
Travelette Pickup	740	1470	2450	3350	4900
Bonus Load Travelette P.U. (6 ft.)	750	1500	2500	3500	5000
Series 1300B					
Pickup (8½ ft.)	800	1600	2650	3700	5300
Travelette	690	1380	2300	3200	4600
Bonus Load Travelette P.U. (6 ft.)	700	1400	2350	3250	4700

NOTE: Add 5 percent for 4x4 (all Series 1100-1300).

1968 IHC

SCOUT — 800 SERIES — FOUR-CYLINDER — Any changes in the 1968 Scout were of a minor nature. The Custom roadster, Sportop hardtop and Custom pickup disappeared as separate models. Engine offerings included the 152 cu. in. four-cylinder as base equipment and the 196 cu. in. four-cylinder, and 266 cu. in. V-8 as options again. The turbo-charged four-cylinder option was discontinued. Standard equipment followed the 1967 pattern.

1968 International Scout 4x4 Utility (DFW)

I.D. DATA: See 1967 section (all models).

Model	Body Type	Price	Weight	Prod. Total
Series Scout 800 — (4x4) — (100 in. w.b.)				
800	Utility Roadster	2875	3465	—
800	Traveltop Utility	3048	3615	—
800	Traveltop Custom	3263	3615	—
800	Softop Sportop	3492	3515	—
800	Utility Pickup	2973	—	—

NOTE 1: Price and weights above are for 4x4 models with the V-8 engine.

ENGINE: See 1967 Scout engine specifications. The turbo-charged four-cylinder engine was dropped.

OPTIONS: See 1967 Scout options.

METRO — SERIES M — ALL ENGINES — Models in the lighter-capacity Metro Series were basically unchanged, but the M-700 model was discontinued. The M-800, M-1100, M-1200 and MA-1200 models continued to be available. The trucks in the "1200" series had a base six-cylinder engine, while the others came standard with the Scout's Comanche "slant four."

Model	Body Type	Price	Weight	Prod. Total
Metro Series M-800 — (4x2) — (102 in. w.b.)				
M-800	Walk-In Panel (7 ft.)	2876	3660	—
Metro Series M-1100 — (4x2) — (108 in. w.b.)				
M-1100	Walk-In Panel (8 ft.)	3271	3830	—
Metro Series M-1200 — (4x2) — (119/134 in. w.b.)				
M-1200	Walk-In Panel (9 ft. 8 in.)	3739	5005	—
MA-1200	Walk-In Panel (9 ft.)	4170	4475	—

NOTE: Prices for M-1200 and MA-1200 include V-8 engine.

ENGINE: See 1967 Metro Series engine specifications.

OPTIONS: See 1967 Metro options.

CONVENTIONAL LIGHT TRUCKS — SERIES C — (ALL ENGINES) — The biggest change in IHC's 1968 conventional light trucks seems to be that the "IH" badge was removed from the hood above the grille center. Travelall models could also be had with a contrast panel on the rear-quarter panels, between the chrome belt moldings and with chrome moldings extending across the doors and front fender sides.

Model	Body Type	Price	Weight	Prod. Total
Series 908C — (4x2) — (115 in. w.b.)				
908C	Pickup (6 ft. 8 in.)	2451	3815	—
908C	Bonus Load Pickup (6 ft. 8 in.)	2463	3815	—
Series 1000C — (4x2) — (119 in. w.b.)				
1000C	Chassis and Cab	2444	3245	—
1000C	Pickup (7 ft.)	2564	3625	—
1000C	Bonus Load Pickup (7 ft.)	2576	3625	—
1000C	Panel (7 ft.)	2968	3915	—
Series 1100C — (4x2) — (115-140 in. w.b.)				
1100C	Chassis and Cab	2398	3225	—
1100C	Pickup (6 ft. 8 in.)	2519	3585	—
1100C	Bonus Load Pickup (6 ft. 8 in.)	2531	3585	—
1100C	Pickup (8 ft. 6 in.)	2651	3675	—
1100C	Bonus Load Pickup (8 ft. 6 in.)	2563	3660	—
1100C	Panel (7 ft.)	2900	3895	—
1100C	Travelette Cab	3105	3670	—
1100C	B.L. Travelette Pickup (6 ft.)	3244	4005	—

NOTE: Add $569 for 4x4 models.

Model	Body Type	Price	Weight	Prod. Total
Series 1200C — (4x2) — (119 to 166 in. w.b.)				
1200C	Chassis and Cab	2531	3460	—
1200C	Pickup (7 ft.)	2651	3830	—
1200C	Bonus Load Pickup (7 ft.)	2663	3830	—
1200C	Pickup (8 ft. 6 in.)	2684	3900	—
1200C	Bonus Load Pickup (8 ft.)	2696	3885	—
1200C	Panel (7 ft.)	3000	4130	—
1200C	Travelette Cab	3205	3895	—
1200C	B.L. Travelette Pickup (6 ft.)	3344	4230	—

NOTE: Add $609 for 4x4 models.

Model	Body Type	Price	Weight	Prod. Total
Series 1300C — (4x2) — (131 to 156 in. w.b.)				
1300C	Chassis and Cab	2613	3675	—
1300C	Pickup (8 ft. 6 in.)	2739	4100	—
1300C	Travelette Cab	3261	4100	—
1300C	B.L. Travelette Pickup (6 ft.)	3403	4435	—

NOTE: Add $1123 for 4x4 models.

ADDITIONAL NOTE: Prices and weights above are for V-8 models.

ENGINE: See 1967 light truck engine specification.

OPTIONS: See 1967 light truck options.

CHASSIS: The 1968 models had the same chassis specifications as comparable 1967 trucks, except for the following change:

(Series M-1100): Tires: 7.00 x 15 in.

TECHNICAL: The 1968 models had the same specifications as comparable 1967 models.

1968 IHC Travelall Station Wagon (S. Soloy)

HISTORICAL: Introduced November 1, 1967. Calendar year registrations by GVW: 6000 pounds or less = 48,200; 6001-10,000 pounds = 20,461. Calendar year production: (all IHC trucks) 145,549.
By 1968, the 200,000th IHC Scout had been built at the Fort Wayne factory. Worldwide sales of trucks in fiscal 1968 were up 2.5 percent from the previous year.

Pricing

	5	4	3	2	1
1968					
Series Scout 800					
Utility Roadster	870	1750	2900	4100	5800
Utility Traveltop	950	1900	3150	4400	6300
Custom Roadster	890	1770	2950	4150	5900
Custom Traveltop	960	1920	3200	4500	6400
Soft Top (Sport)	980	1950	3250	4550	6500
Hardtop (Sport)	1010	2030	3350	4700	6700
Utility Pickup	890	1770	2950	4150	5900
Custom Pickup	900	1800	3000	4200	6000

NOTE 1: Add 10 percent for 4x4 model.
Add 5 percent for soft Traveltop.
Add 4 percent for all-steel Traveltop.
Add 2 percent for V-8 model.
Add 3 percent for turbo-charged 4-cyl.

	5	4	3	2	1
Series Metro					
M-700 Panel	570	1100	1850	2600	3700
M-800 Panel	560	1080	1800	2500	3600
M-1100 Panel	590	1140	1900	2650	3800
M-1200 Panel	590	1140	1900	2650	3800
MA-1200 Panel	600	1200	2000	2800	4000
Series 900A					
Pickup	770	1550	2550	3600	5100
Series 908B					
Pickup	800	1600	2650	3700	5300
Bonus Load Pickup	810	1620	2700	3800	5400

Series 1000B	5	4	3	2	1
Pickup (7 ft.)	830	1650	2750	3850	5500
Bonus Load Pickup (7 ft.)	840	1680	2800	3900	5600
Panel (7 ft.)	740	1470	2450	3350	4900
Series 1100B					
Pickup (6 ft. 8 in.)	850	1700	2850	4000	5700
Bonus Load P.U. (6 ft. 8 in.)	870	1750	2900	4100	5800
Pickup (8½ ft.)	840	1680	2800	3900	5600
Bonus Load P.U. (8 ft.)	850	1700	2850	4000	5700
Panel (7 ft.)	750	1500	2500	3500	5000
Travelette Cab	780	1560	2600	3600	5200
Bonus Load Travelette P.U. (6 ft.)	800	1600	2650	3700	5300
Series 1200B					
Pickup (7 ft.)	840	1680	2800	3900	5600
Bonus Load Pickup (7 ft.)	850	1700	2850	4000	5700
Pickup (8½ ft.)	810	1620	2700	3800	5400
Bonus Load Pickup (8 ft.)	830	1650	2750	3850	5500
Panel (7 ft.)	740	1470	2450	3350	4900
Travelette Pickup	740	1470	2450	3350	4900
Bonus Load Travelette P.U. (6 ft.)	750	1500	2500	3500	5000
Series 1300B					
Pickup (8½ ft.)	800	1600	2650	3700	5300
Travelette	690	1380	2300	3200	4600
Bonus Load Travelette P.U. (6 ft.)	700	1400	2350	3250	4700

NOTE: See 1967 for percent additions for special equipment, optional engines and 4x4 models (all series).

1969-1970 IHC

1969 International Scout 4x4 Utility (JAG)

SCOUT — SERIES 800A — FOUR-CYLINDER: — 1969 was a year for special "limited edition" versions of the Scout. The new Scout Aristocrat featured two-tone metallic paint, wide tires, chrome wheels, a padded and carpeted interior and special "coachman" roof rack. IHC promoted this model as "a classic in its own time." External changes for 1969 models included squarish, chrome trimmed headlight housings. The International nameplate on the mesh grille was smaller in size and moved to the lower left-hand corner. Round side-marker reflectors appeared on the front and rear fender sides. Some other changes included an enlarged window area in steel Traveltops; energy-absorbing steering column; refined steering mechanism; broader power range; new 304 cu. in. V-8 option; aluminized muffler; softer, lower-rate rear springs and factory installed rear step bumper. Standard equipment consisted of padded dash and sun visors; seat belts on all seats; safety door latches; four-way emergency flashers; windshield washer; variable-speed wipers with non-glare arms; fresh air heater and defroster; inside and outside mirrors, backup lights; front and rear side relfectors; dual brake system; self-adjusting brakes with heavy-duty linings and 3,500 pound capacity rear axle. Interior appointments included black vinyl bench seat; insulated rubber floor mat; ash tray and driver's arm rest. A silver-gray front bumper was standard. Colors available included Alpine white, plum metallic, red, medium blue metallic, lime green metallic, copper metallic and gold metallic. These models were carried over, basically without change, for 1970.

Model	Body Type	Price	Weight	Prod. Total
Scout Series 800A — (4x4) — (100 in. w.b.)				
800A	Roadster	3040	3465	—
800A	Pickup	3139	3515	—
800A	Traveltop	3213	3615	—

NOTE 1: Prices and weights are for 1969 four-wheel-drive models with V-8 engine.

NOTE 2: Prices for comparable 1970 models were an average $193 higher. Weights for comparable 1970 models were an average 310 pounds lighter.

ENGINE (Base): The 196 cu. in. four-cylinder engine was standard. See 1967 Scout engine specifications.

ENGINE (Optional): Vee-block, OHV. Eight-cylinder. Cast iron block. Bore & stroke: 3⅞ in. x 3-7/32 in. Displacement: 304 cu. in. Compression ratio: 8.19:1 in. Brake horsepower: 180 at 4400 R.P.M. Net horsepower: 48.1. Max. Torque: 262 lb. ft. at 2400 R.P.M. Hydraulic valve lifters. Carburetor: Holley model 2300G.

NOTE: This was the only optional engine for 1969 Scouts.

OPTIONS (Scout Series): Chrome front bumper. Solid-state push-button radio. Eight-track stereo tape player. Radio antenna package. Dash courtesy lamps. Rear seat for custom Traveltop and Roadster models. Inside or outside spare tire mounting. Wheel well covers/seats (models w/o rear seat). Four-speed transmission. Limited-slip differential. Factory installed integral utility step-bumper and trailer hitch. Dual 10-gallon auxiliary fuel tanks. Increased capacity electrical system. Dual electric horns. Skid plate. Front wheel locking hubs for all-wheel drive. Increased capacity cooling for 4-cylinder engine. Engine governor and hand throttle. Transfer case mounted PTO. Chrome full wheel discs. Silver-gray rear bumper. Front tow hook. Rear tow loop. Various sizes of tires and rims. Custom interior package including: body color interior; bucket seats in black vinyl; matching padded door panels; dual arm rests; textured vinyl front floor mat; cigar lighter and headliner in Traveltop models. Aristocrat trim package (see introductory text).

METRO — SERIES M — FOUR-CYLINDER: — In 1969, the 196 cu. in. four-cylinder engine (4-196) was made standard equipment for all light-duty Metro Vans. Only three models under 1-ton were available. Their GVW ratings were as follows: M-1100 (5500-6000 pounds); M-1200 (8000 pounds) and MA-1200 (9000 pounds). Additional government mandated safety features were made standard equipment. These models were carried over, basically without change, for 1970.

Model	Body Type	Price	Weight	Prod. Total
Metro Series M-1100 — (4x2) — (108 in. w.b.)				
M-1100	Walk-In Panel (8 ft.)	3446	3830	—
Metro Series M-1200 — (4x2) — (119-134 in. w.b.)				
M-1200	Walk-In Panel (9 ft. 8 in.)	3893	5157	—
MA-1200	Walk-In Panel (9 ft.)	4372	4627	—

NOTE 1: Prices and weights given above for the "1200" models include the optional V-304 V-8 engine.

NOTE 2: Prices for 1970 models were around $107 higher and weights for 1970 models were the same as 1969.

ENGINE: The 4-196 engine was standard in all Metro models. See 1967 for engine specifications. Sixes and V-8s were available at extra-cost. They included the BG-265 six-cylinder, V-266 V-8 and V-304 V-8.

OPTIONS: Options available for 1969 Metros were similar to those listed in the 1967 Metro section.

CONVENTIONAL LIGHT TRUCKS — SERIES D — (ALL ENGINES): — All-new styling was seen for conventional light-duty IHC trucks in 1969. The new look was patterned after the design of the Scout with slab-sided fenders, a flat wide hood, Scout-like grille and squarer "green house" area. Other changes included the addition of side safety lights and, usually, the use of contrasting lower body side panels. There were four model lines. The 1000D models had 115 to 131 in. w.b. and 4800-5400 pound GVW ratings. Then came the 1100Ds, with the same wheelbase and GVWs. The 1200D trucks had 115 to 164 in. w.b. and a 6100 to 7500 pound GVW range. Rated for 7000 to 10,000 pounds GVWs; were the 1300Ds on wheelbases of 131 to 156 inches.

Model	Body Type	Price	Weight	Prod. Total
Series 1000D — (4x2) — (115-131 in. w.b.)				
1000D	Chassis & Cab	2524	3417	—
1000D	Pickup (6½ ft.)	2645	3777	—
1000D	Bonus Load Pickup (6½ ft.)	2683	3777	—
1000D	Panel (7 ft.)	3158	4087	—
1000D	Pickup (8 ft.)	2682	3827	—
1000D	Bonus Load Pickup (8 ft.)	2721	3852	—
Series 1100D — (4x2) — (115-131 in. w.b.)				
1100D	Chassis and Cab	2479	3397	—
1100D	Pickup (6½ ft.)	2599	3757	—
1100D	Bonus Load Pickup (6½ ft.)	2638	3757	—
1100D	Panel (7 ft.)	3113	4067	—
1100D	Pickup (8 ft.)	2637	3807	—
1100D	Bonus Load Pickup (8 ft.)	2675	3832	—

NOTE: Add ? percent for 4x4 models.

1969 International Travelall (JAG)

Model	Body Type	Price	Weight	Prod. Total
Series 1200D — (4x2) — (115-164 in. w.b.)				
1200D	Chassis and Cab	2564	3410	—
1200D	Pickup (6½ ft.)	2685	3720	—
1200D	Bonus Load Pickup (6½ ft.)	2724	3720	—
1200D	Panel (7 ft.)	3198	4080	—
1200D	Pickup (8 ft.)	2722	3820	—
1200D	Bonus Load Pickup (8 ft.)	2761	3836	—
1200D	Travelette Cab	3226	3815	—
1200D	Travelette Pickup (6½ ft.)	3394	4025	—
1200D	Bonus Load Travelette Pickup (8 ft.)	3544	4225	—

NOTE: Add for 4x4 models.

Series 1300D — (4x2) — (134-156 in. w.b.)				
1300D	Chassis & Cab	2749	3635	—
1300D	Pickup (9 ft.)	2880	4306	—
1300D	Travelette Cab	3384	4261	—
1300D	Bonus Load Travelette Pickup (6½ ft.)	3544	4621	—

NOTE: Add for 4x4 models.

NOTE 1: Prices given above are for trucks with conventional drive and 304 cu. in. V-8 engines.

NOTE 2: (Series 1000D) Prices for 1970 models were about $142 higher on average. Weights for 1970 models were unchanged. (The panel truck was $209 higher). (Series 1100D) Prices for 1970 models were about $146 higher ($212 for panel truck). Weights for 1970 models were unchanged. (Series 1200D) Prices for 1970 models averaged $160 higher ($228 for panel truck). Weights for 1970 models were slightly different. (Series 1300D) Prices for 1970 models averaged $184 higher. Weights for 1970 models were slightly different.

ENGINE (Series 1000D): Model PT-6-232. Inline, OHV. Six-cylinder. Cast iron block. Bore & stroke: 3¾ in. x 3½ in. Displacement: 232 cu. in. Compression ratio: 8.5:1. Brake horsepower: 145 at 4300 R.P.M. Max. Torque: 215 lb. ft. at 1600 R.P.M. Hydraulic valve lifters. Carburetor: Single Barrel.

NOTE: This new six-cylinder engine was used in 1000D models and 1100D models with four-wheel drive.

ENGINE (Standard Series 1100D): The BG-241 six-cylinder engine was standard in 4x2 models in the 1100D Series. (Standard 1200/1300D Series). The V-266 engine, a V-8, was standard in the 1200D and 1300D models with conventional 4x2 or optional 4x4 drivetrains. See 1967 engine specifications.

1969 International Bonus Load Pickup (JAG)

1970 International Walk-in Panel Delivery (DFW)

ENGINE (Optional): Available options for 1969 IHC trucks included the BG-265 six-cylinder and V-304 V-8. See 1967 engine specificiations.

OPTIONS (Conventional Light Trucks): OSRV mirror(s). Dual "California" trailer mirrors. Custom exterior trim package. Full wheel discs. Camper package ($69). Wheel trim rings. Foam rubber seat cushions. Tinted-glass. Air conditioning. Solid-state push-button radio. Eight-track tape player. Antenna package. Roof rack. High-side pickup box package. Pickup box rails. Rear bumper. Whitewall tires. Power steering. Power brakes. Backup lights. Auxiliary gas tank. Spare tire. Automatic transmission. Four-speed manual transmission.

CHASSIS (Scout Series 800A): Wheelbase: 100 in. Tires: (1969) 7.35 x 15 in.; (1970) E78 x 15 in.

CHASSIS (Series M-1100): Wheelbase: 108 in. Tires: 7.00 x 15 in.

CHASSIS (Series M-1200/MA-1200): Wheelbase: 119 to 134 in. Tires: 7.00 x 17.5 in.

CHASSIS (Series 1000D): Wheelbase: 115-131 in. Tires: (1969) 8.25 x 15 in.; (1970) G78 x 15 in.

CHASSIS (Series 1100D): Wheelbase: 115-131 in. Tires: (1969) 8.25 x 15 in.; (1970) G78 x 15 in.

CHASSIS (Series 1200D): Wheelbase: 115-164 in. Tires: 8.00 x 16.5 in.

CHASSIS (Series 1300D): Wheelbase: 134-156 in. Tires: 8.00 x 16.5 in.

TECHNICAL: See 1967 specifications data.

1970 International Walk-in Panel-interior (DFW)

1970 International Bonus Load Pickup (DFW)

HISTORICAL: Introduced November 1968. Calendar year registrations by GVW Class: (1969) 6000 pounds or less = 41,174; 6001-10,000 pounds = 18,634. (1970) 6000 pounds or less = 44,713; 6001-10,000 pounds = 19,764. Calendar year production: (all IHC trucks) 1969 = 160,255; 1970 = 155,353.

Scout Aristocrat model introduced in the summer of 1969. Scout gets new 304 cu. in. V-8. New three pass muffler gives 10 percent power increase. New "Silent-Bloc" front spring bushings for Scout models. Conventional trucks completely redesigned. New PT-6-232 engine introduced; six-cylinder with hydraulic valve lifters.

By 1969, a number of competitive makes had entered in the sport/utility vehicle class. As a result, Scout sales leveled off at 15,000 to 18,000 units anually. In the IHC Motor Truck Division, J.P. Kaine was Assistant to the vice-president for 1969-1970, with R.L. McCaffre as division sales manager.

Pricing

	5	4	3	2	1
1969-1970					
Scout Series 800A					
Roadster	890	1770	2950	4150	5900
Pickup	960	1920	3200	4500	6400
Traveltop	980	1950	3250	4550	6500
Aristocrat	1050	2100	3500	4900	7000
Metro Series					
M-1100 Panel	590	1140	1900	2650	3800
M-1200 Panel	590	1140	1900	2650	3800
MA-1200 Panel	590	1170	1950	2700	3900
Series 1000D					
Pickup (6½ ft.)	840	1680	2800	3900	5600
B.L. Pickup (6½ ft.)	850	1700	2850	4000	5700
Panel	750	1500	2500	3500	5000
Pickup (8 ft.)	830	1650	2750	3850	5500
B.L. Pickup (8 ft.)	840	1680	2800	3900	5600
Series 1100D					
Pickup (6½ ft.)	870	1750	2900	4100	5800
B.L. Pickup (6½ ft.)	890	1770	2950	4150	5900
Panel	770	1550	2550	3600	5100
Pickup (8 ft.)	800	1600	2650	3700	5300
B.L. Pickup (8 ft.)	810	1620	2700	3800	5400
Series 1200D					
Pickup (6½ ft.)	850	1700	2850	4000	5700
B.L. Pickup (6½ ft.)	870	1750	2900	4100	5800
Panel	750	1500	2500	3500	5000
Pickup (8 ft.)	830	1650	2750	3850	5500
B.L. Pickup (8 ft.)	840	1680	2800	3900	5600
Travelette (6½ ft.)	750	1500	2500	3500	5000
B.L. Travelette (8 ft.)	770	1550	2550	3600	5100
Series 1300D					
Pickup (9 ft.)	810	1620	2700	3800	5400
Travelette	720	1450	2400	3300	4800
B.L. Travelette (6½ ft.)	700	1400	2350	3250	4700

NOTE: See 1967 for percent additions for special equipment, optional engines and 4x4 models (all series).

1971 IHC

SCOUT — SERIES 800B — FOUR-CYLINDER: — The "IH" badge from the nose of the regular Scout was now moved onto the left-hand side of the grille. New special paint and stripping packages were introduced. This was to be the Scout 800's last season.

I.D. DATA: See 1967 section (all models).

Model	Body Type	Price	Weight	Prod. Total
Scout Series 800B — (4x4) — (100 in. w.b.)				
800B	Roadster	3376	—	—
800B	Traveltop	3564	3480	—
800B	Pickup	3483	3380	—

NOTE: Prices and weights are for 4x4 models with V-8 engine.

ENGINE: See 1969-1970 engine specifications data.

OPTIONS: Six-cylinder engine ($87). 304 cu. in V-8 engine ($164). RA-28 rear axle ($61). Custom package, Traveltop ($249). See 1969-1970 section for other optional equipment.

SCOUT — SERIES II: — A new Scout II was introduced in the spring of 1971. The vehicle was completely redesigned and now offered power brakes, power steering, air conditioning, automatic transmission, larger V-8s, a bigger clutch, a wider choice of rear axle ratios, more axle capacity, bigger brakes, automatic or manual locking front hubs for 4x4 models and increased cooling. The body was lower and longer than the Scout 800 with a five cubic foot increase in load space. The rear seat was lowered and increased in width to accomodate three passengers. Sales of the new model exceeded 30,000 units in its first year.

Model	Body Type	Price	Weight	Prod. Total
Scout II Series — (4x4) — (100 in. w.b.)				
S-II	Traveltop	3608	3794	—
S-II	Pickup	3528	3694	—

NOTE 1: Prices and weights are for 4x4 models with V-8 engines.

NOTE 2: Sales were in excess of 30,000 units.

ENGINE: Base engine was the Model 4-196 "slant four" of 196 cu. in. capacity with 111 horsepower. See 1967 specifications.

ENGINE (Optional): The PT-6-232 six-cylinder 135 horsepower engine was available at slight-extra cost. See 1969-1970 specifications.

ENGINE (Optional): The V-304 engine, a 304 cu. in. V-8 of 193 horse-power, was optional. See 1967 specifications.

ENGINE (Optional): Model V-345. Vee-block, OHV. Eight-cylinder. Cast iron block. Bore & stroke: 3⅞ in. x 3-21/32 in. Displacement: 344.96 cu. in. Compression ratio: 8.05:1. Brake horsepower: 196.7 at 4000 R.P.M. Net horsepower: 48.1. Max. Torque: 309 lb. ft. at 2200 R.P.M. Hydraulic valve lifters. Carburetor: Holley model 2300G two-barrel.

NOTE: This was a new option for the Scout II, but was not a new engine. It had been used previously in some other models.

OPTIONS: No specific information. Available options were comparable to those offered for Scout 800 models, plus additions mentioned in text.

METRO — SERIES M — FOUR-CYLINDER: — There were no styling changes, to speak of, in the 1971 Metro models. Everything was about the same as in 1969-1970, except for revised prices and weights and a new base six-cylinder engine in M-1200 and MA-1200 models. These trucks had used the 196 cu. in. four-cyliner power plant as base equipment in 1969 and 1970, but the PT-6-232 six-cylinder engine, which first appeared in 1969, was now standardized.

Model	Body Type	Price	Weight	Prod. Total
Metro Series M-1100 — (4x2) — (108 in. w.b.)				
M-1100	Walk-In Panel (8 ft.)	3794	3830	—
Metro Series M-1200 — (4x2) — (119 in. w.b.)				
M-1200	Walk-In Panel (9 ft. 8 in.)	4744	4410	—
Metro Series MA-1200 — (4x2) — (134 in. w.b.)				
MA-1200	Walk-In Panel (9 ft.)	4820	4485	—

ENGINE: See 1969-1970 engine specifications. The 196 cu. in. four-cylinder was standard in M-1100 Metros. The PT-6-232 six-cylinder engine was standard in M-1200 and MA-1200 Metros.

OPTIONS: Power steering, all models ($258). V-304 eight-cylinder engine ($83). Automatic transmission ($265 average). RA-15 rear axle ($155). RA-126 rear axle ($280). See 1969-1970 section for other optional equipment.

CONVENTIONAL LIGHT TRUCK — SERIES D — SIX-CYLINDER: — "We haven't had a model year since 1907," International Harvester explained in a 1971 advertisement. The ad went on to explain that the company didn't believe in planned obsolescence. However, it also mentioned that the 1971 pickups had a new grille, new hubcaps, different tailgate treatment, new rocker panel trim and several new colors. The grille revision followed the Scout pattern, moving the company's name badge to the left-hand side of the mesh grille insert. At the rear of light-duty models, there were new, vertically-mounted rectangular taillights. Hubcaps were now lacking the small "fins" found on the 1969-1970 style. Model designation badges were also added on the front fender sides, above the side-marker reflectors. Two sets of air vents at the cowl was another minor change. All series used the PT-6-232 engine as standard equipment.

Model	Body Type	Price	Weight	Prod. Total
Series 1000D — (4x2) — (115-131 in. w.b.)				
1010	Chassis and Cab	2815	3417	—
1010	Pickup (6½ ft.)	2962	3777	—
1010	Bonus Load Pickup (6½ ft.)	2974	3777	—
1010	Panel (7 ft.)	3627	4087	—
1010	Travelall	3853	5440	—
1010	Pickup (8 ft.)	3000	3827	—
1010	Bonus Load Pickup (8 ft.)	3012	3827	—

NOTE: Prices are for trucks with V-304 V-8 engine.

1971 IHC Travelall Station Wagon (NI)

Series 1100D — (4x2) — (115-131 in. w.b.)

1110	Chassis & Cab	2795	3397	—
1110	Pickup (6½ ft.)	2941	3757	—
1110	Bonus Load Pickup (6½ ft.)	2953	3757	—
1110	Panel (7 ft.)	3605	4067	—
1110	Travelall	3831	5475	—
1110	Pickup (8 ft.)	2978	3807	—
1110	Bonus Load Pickup (8 ft.)	2990	3807	—

NOTE 1: Prices are for trucks with V-304 V-8 engine.

NOTE 2: Prices for 4x4 models were $613-$705 higher, depending upon body style and wheelbase.

1971 IHC Deluxe Travelall Station Wagon (NI)

Model Series	Body Type	Price	Weight	Prod. Total
Series 1200D — (4x2) — (115-164 in. w.b.)				
1210	Chassis & Cab	2930	3627	—
1210	Pickup (6½ ft.)	3078	3987	—
1210	Bonus Load Pickup (6½ ft.)	3089	3987	—
1210	Panel (7 ft.)	3742	4297	—
1210	Pickup (8 ft.)	3115	4037	—
1210	Bonus Load Pickup (8 ft.)	3127	4037	—
1210	Travelette Cab (6½ ft.)	3592	4067	—
1210	Travelette Pickup (6½ ft.)	3748	4427	—
1210	Bonus Load Travelette Pickup (8 ft.)	3919	4477	—
1210	Travelall	3961	5655	—

NOTE 1: Prices are for trucks with V-304 V-8 engine.

NOTE 2: Prices for 4x4 models were $785 to $973 higher depending upon body style and wheelbase.

SERIES 1300D — (4x2) — (134-156 in. w.b.)

1310	Chassis & Cab	3108	3852	—
1310	Pickup (9 ft.)	3267	4312	—
1310	Travelette Cab	3743	4272	—
1310	Bonus Load Travelette Pickup (6½ ft.)	3903	4632	—

NOTE 1: Prices are for trucks with V-304 V-8 engine.

NOTE 2: The 4x4 option was not available for 1300D trucks in 1971.

ENGINE: The PT-6-232 six-cylinder engine was standard equipment for all 1971 light-duty trucks. See 1969-1970 engine specifications.

OPTIONS: (Series 1010/1110/1210) V-304 engine ($60). V-304 LPG engine, 1110/1210 4x2 models ($195). Five-speed transmission, all 4x2 models ($300). RA-1700 rear axle, all 1210 models ($140). (Series 1310) V-304 engine ($60). V-304 LPG engine, 4x2 models only ($230). T-34 transmission, 4x2 models only ($245). See 1969-1970 section for other optional equipment.

TECHNICAL & CHASSIS: Technical and chassis specfíciations were similar to comparable 1967-1970 models. Refer to these sections for data.

HISTORICAL: Introduced: Fall of 1970. Calendar year registrations by GVW: 6000 pounds or less = 53,077; 6001 to 10,000 pounds = 23,834. Calendar year production: (all IHC trucks) 185,859 (8.97 percent).

All-new Scout II model introduced. Larger V-8 available in Scout II. PT-6-232 engine standard in large Metros and other light-duty trucks. New five-speed transmission in some 4x2 models. Air conditioning, power steering and deluxe interior trim for the Scout II.

Brooks McCormick became president, chief executive officer of IHC this year. K.P. Mazurek was vice president in charge of the Motor Truck Division. Truck sales accounted for $1,522.8 million. V-8 models accounted for 135,269 assemblies out of the calendar year total.

Pricing

	5	4	3	2	1
1971					
Scout Series 800					
Roadster	890	1770	2950	4150	5900
Traveltop	980	1950	3250	4550	6500
Pickup	960	1920	3200	4500	6400
Scout II Series					
Traveltop	1010	2030	3350	4700	6700
Pickup	980	1950	3250	4550	6500

NOTE: Add 5 percent for 4x4 models.
Add 5 percent for Custom trim package.
Add 3 percent for V-8.

	5	4	3	2	1
Metro Series					
M-1100 Panel	590	1140	1900	2650	3800
M-1200 Panel	590	1140	1900	2650	3800
MA-1200 Panel	590	1170	1950	2700	3900
Series 1000D					
Pickup (6½ ft.)	840	1680	2800	3900	5600
B.L. Pickup (6½ ft.)	850	1700	2850	4000	5700
Panel	750	1500	2500	3500	5000
Travelall	840	1680	2800	3900	5600
Pickup (8 ft.)	830	1650	2750	3850	5500
B.L. Pickup (8 ft.)	840	1680	2800	3900	5600

NOTE: Add 3 percent for V-8 engine.
Add 5 percent for Custom trim package.
Add 1 percent for five-speed.

	5	4	3	2	1
Series 1100D					
Pickup (6½ ft.)	870	1750	2900	4100	5800
B.L. Pickup (6½ ft.)	890	1770	2950	4150	5900
Panel	770	1550	2550	3600	5100
Travelall	870	1750	2900	4100	5800
Pickup (8 ft.)	800	1600	2650	3700	5300
B.L. Pickup (8 ft.)	810	1620	2700	3800	5400
Series 1200D					
Panel	750	1500	2500	3500	5000
Pickup (6½ ft.)	850	1700	2850	4000	5700
B.L. Pickup (6½ ft.)	870	1750	2900	4100	5800
Pickup (8 ft.)	830	1650	2750	3850	5500
B.L. Pickup (8 ft.)	840	1680	2800	3900	5600
Travelette Pickup (6½ ft.)	750	1500	2500	3500	5000
B.L. Travelette Pickup (8 ft.)	770	1550	2550	3600	5100

NOTE: Add 5 percent for 4x4 (1100/1200 series only)
Add 3 percent for V-8.
Add 1 percent for five-speed.

	5	4	3	2	1
Series 1300D					
Pickup (9 ft.)	810	1620	2700	3800	5400
Travelette Pickup	720	1450	2400	3300	4800
B.L. Travelette Pickup	700	1400	2350	3250	4700

NOTES: Add 3 percent for V-8.
Add 1 percent for five-speed.

1972 IHC

SCOUT — SERIES II — (ALL ENGINES): — The Scout II was the only Scout available in 1972. Styling characteristics of this model included the longer, lower utility body introduced in mid-1971 and a grille treatment with three horizontal slots stacked on top of each other within a full-width rectangular panel. Round headlights were inside this panel, at the edge of the slots. An International nameplate was placed between the two lower slots at the lower left-hand side. A lower perimeter molding trimmed both sides of the body. There were Traveltop and pickup models, plus a Custom trim package and several decaling options. Base engine was the 196 cu. in. four-cylinder. Options included a 232 cu. in. six and two V-8s. The four-cylinder engine was not available in California.

I.D. DATA: Serial number located on the left front door pillar post. The serial number consists of 13 symbols. The first six identify the serial number. The seventh (digit) designates the manufacturing plant. The last six (digits) are sequential production numbers. Engine model identification takes the form of a prefix to the engine serial number. For example, a V-266 engine serial number would read V-266-000000. Engine numbers are located on a machined boss on the cylinder block. Serial numbers and engine numbers are not available.

Model	Body Type	Price	Weight	Prod. Total
Scout II — (4x2) — (100 in. w.b.)				
S-II	Traveltop	2560	2950	—
S-II	Pickup	2415	2850	—
Scout II — (4x4) — (100 in. w.b.)				
S-II	Traveltop	3340	3050	—
S-II	Pickup	3185	3150	—

ENGINE: Base engine was the model 4-196 "slant four" of 196 cu. in. capacity with 111 horsepower. See 1967 specifications.

ENGINE (Optional): The PT-6-232 six-cylinder 135 horsepower engine was available for $88 extra. See 1969-1970 specifications. (Standard engine in California).

ENGINE (Optional): the V-304 eight-cylinder 193 horsepower engine was available for $161 extra. See 1967 specifications.

ENGINE (Optional): The V-345 eight-cylinder 197 horsepower engine was available for extra cost. See 1971 specifications.

OPTIONS: Power brakes. Power steering. Air conditioning. Custom Traveltop package ($245). RA-28 rear axle ($60). Solid-state push-button radio. Heater and defroster. Single or dual OSRV mirror(s). Roof luggage rack. Tinted windshield. Bucket seats. Radio antenna package. Eight-track tape player. Automatic transmission. Spare tire and carrier. Special paint. Sport decal packages. Full wheel discs. White sidewall tires. Oversize tires. Three-speed manual transmission. Four-speed manual transmission.

METRO — SERIES M — (ALL ENGINES): — A new 258 cu. in. six-cylinder base engine was the big change for 1972 Metro models. It replaced both the M-1100's four-cylinder powerplant and the PT-6-232 engine that came with last season's 1200 series models. The MA-1200 model was no longer being marketed. American Motors was the manufacturer of the new engine.

Model	Body Type	Price	Weight	Prod. Total
Metro Series — (4x2) — (108 in. w.b.)				
M-1100	Walk-In Panel (8 ft.)	3865	3830	—
Metro Series — (4x2) — (119-127 in. w.b.)				
M-1200	Walk-In Panel (9 ft.)	4168	4410	—
M-1200	Walk-In Panel (10 ft.)	4300	4485	—

ENGINE (Metro Series): Model 6-258. Inline, OHV. Six-cylinder. Cast iron block. Bore & stroke: 3.75 in. x 3.9 in. Displacement: 258.1 cu. in. Brake hoserpower: 135 at 3800 R.P.M. Net horsepower: 33.75. Max. Torque: 235 lb. ft. at 2000 R.P.M. Hydraulic valve lifters. Carburetor: Holley model 1940C.

NOTE: AMC engine.

ENGINE (Opt. Metro Series): The V-304 eight-cylinder 193 horsepower engine was available for $35 extra. See 1967 speicifcations.

OPTIONS (Metro Series): Power steering ($258). Automatic transmission ($225 average). RA-15 rear axle, in 1200 series ($75). Radio. Special paint. OSRV mirrors. Oversize tires.

1972 IHC Model 1210 Travelette (Erwin Knapp)

TRAVELALL — SERIES 1010/1110/1210 — (ALL ENGINES): Although we have discussed the Travelall series as a part of the light-duty truck line, it was really quite a unique IHC vehicle. Let's take a closer look at the 1972 model as a representative example. Styling changes for 1972 included a new dashboard and grille design. The grille consisted of five horizontal bars on either side of a vertical center divider. It ran fully across the front of the station wagon like vehicle, with a single round headlight on either end. In Sept. 1971, *Motor Trend* road tested a Travelall and called it "Far and away the best of the real station wagons in design, comfort and quality." Standard equipment included bench seats, seat belts, full instrumentation, safety side markers, front and rear bumpers and a 77 cu. ft. cargo area (124 cu. ft. with seat folded flush to the floor). It came in three series: the 1010 (½-Ton), 1110 (½-Ton) and 1210 (¾-Ton) all on a 119 inch wheelbase. A 4x4 driveline was available.

Model	Body Type	Price	Weight	Prod. Total
Travelall Series — (4x2) — (119 in. w.b.)				
1010	Sta. Wag.	3650	5440	—
1110	Sta. Wag.	3580	5475	—
1210	Sta. Wag.	3705	5655	—
Travelall Series — (4x4) — (119 in. w.b.)				
1110	Sta. Wag. (4x4)	4295	5475	—
1210	Sta. Wag. (4x4)	4515	5990	—

ENGINE (Standard): Base engine was the 6-258 six-cylinder with 135 horsepower. See specifications above.

ENGINE (Optional): The V-304 eight-cylinder 193 horsepower engine was available for $75 extra. See 1967 specifications.

ENGINE (Optional): The V-345 eight-cylinder 197 horsepower engine was available at extra-cost. See 1971 specifications.

ENGINE (Optional): Model V-392. Vee-block. OHV. Eight-cylinder. Cast iron block. Bore & stroke: 4.12 in. x 3.66 in. Displacement: 390.89 cu. in. Brake hoserpower: 253.4 at 4200 R.P.M. Net horsepower: 54.5. Max. Torque: 381.3 lb. ft. at 2800 R.P.M. Hydraulic valve lifters. Carburetor: Two-barrel model Holley 4150.

CHASSIS (Travelall Series): Wheelbase: 119 in. Length: 204 in. Height: 68 in. Front tread: 63 in. Rear tread: 61 in. Tires: G78 x 15 in. Other Travelall chassis features included recirculating ball steering with 17.5: ratio; front torsion bars with shocks and stabilizer bar and rear longitudinal leaf springs with shocks and a 19-gallon fuel tank. (Parallel leaf spring front spension could be substituted for struts and torsion bars).

TECHNICAL (Travelall Series): Manual, synchromesh transmission. Speeds: 3F/1R. Column mounted gear shift lever. Single-plate dry disc clutch. Single reduction rear axle. Overall ratio: 3.73:1. Front and rear drum brakes. Steel disc wheels. Automatic transmission.

CONVENTIONAL LIGHT TRUCKS — SERIES 1110/1210/1310 — (ALL ENGINES): — The same new grille used on the Travelall was found on 1972 International light-duty trucks. There were three series; the 1110 comparing to ½-tonners, the 1210 comparing to conventional ¾-tonners and the 1310 being comparable to a 1-ton line. Various wheelbases were available in each line. For example, in the 1310 series the wheelbase was 131 inches for eight-foot regular or Bonus Load pickup bodies, 134 inches for 9-foot regular pickup, dump, stake or platform bodies and 156 inches for 12-foot stake, dump, platform or van bodies.

As you can tell, the International products were still being merchandised very much like big trucks, rather than like automobiles. That is, the customer purchased the chassis and cab as a unit and ordered the body more-or-less as an option. IHC was a truck-maker's truck-maker, while other companies tended to merchandise light-duty trucks the same way they merchandised cars. Unfortunately, people were starting to buy light-trucks the way they bought cars, which might explain IHC's failure to impact the light-duty market significantly.

Model	Body Type	Price	Weight	Prod. Total
Series 1110 — (4x2) — (115-131 in. w.b.)				
1110	Chassis & Cab	2575	3180	—
1110	Pickup	2715	3555	—
Series 1110 — (4x2) — (115-131 in. w.b.)				
1110	Chassis & Cab	3120	3485	—
1110	Pickup	3265	3860	—
Series 1210 — (4x2) — (115-131 in. w.b.)				
1210	Chassis & Cab	3355	3850	—
1210	Pickup	3510	4215	—
1210	Travelette Cab	3120	3485	—
1210	Travelette Pickup	3265	3860	—
Series 1210 — (4x4) — (115-131 in. w.b.)				
1210	Chassis & Cab	3440	3820	—
1210	Pickup	3580	4195	—
1210	Travelette Cab	4245	4245	—
1210	Travelette Pickup	4410	4635	—
Series 1310 — (4x2) — (131-150 in. w.b.)				
1310	Chassis & Cab	3090	3610	—
1310	Pickup	3100	3630	—
1310	Travelette Cab	3560	3695	—
1310	Travelette Pickup	3715	4045	—

NOTE: Price of a Bonus Load pickup over the standard pickups listed above was $15.

ENGINE: Base and optional engines for conventional light-duty trucks were the same as listed above for Travelalls, plus the V-304 LPG engine was available for 4x2 models in all three series. See option list for prices.

OPTIONS (Conventional Light-Duty Trucks): Chrome front bumper. Rear bumper. Custom trim package. Outside rearview mirror(s). Two-tone paint. Special paint. Bumper guards. Radio. Heater. Clock. Cigar lighter. Radio antenna. Seat covers. Clearance lights. Dual "California" mirrors. Deluxe hub caps. White sidewall tires. Power steering. Power brakes. License plate frames. V-304 engine, all except 1310 ($75). V-304 engine, all 4x2 except 1310 ($240). Five-speed transmission, all 4x2 ($310). RA-17 rear axle, 1200 Series ($140). V-304 engine, 1310 only ($80). V-304 LPG engine, 1300 Series 4x2 ($260). T-34 transmission, 1300 Series 4x2 ($220).

CHASSIS (Scout II Series): Wheelbase: 100 in. Tires: E78 x 15 in.

CHASSIS (Metro Series): Wheelbase: 108/119 in. Tires: (1100 Series) 7.00 x 15 in.; (1200 Series) 7.00 x 17.5 in.

CHASSIS (Travelall Series): Wheelbase: 119 in. Tires: (1010 Series) G78 x 15 in.; (1110 Series) G78 x 15 in.; (1210 Series) 8.00 x 16.5 in.

CHASSIS (Light Trucks, 1110 Series): Wheelbase: 115/131 in. Tires: G78 x 15 in.

CHASSIS (Light Trucks, 1210 Series): Wheelbase: 115/134 in. Tires: 8.00 x 16.5 in.

CHASSIS (Light Trucks, 1310 Series): Wheelbase: 131/150 in. Tires: 8.00 x 16.5 in.

TECHNICAL: Technical specifications for 1972 models were similar to comparable 1967-1970 models. Refer to these sections for data. (Also, see Travelall specifications above).

HISTORICAL: Introduced Fall 1971. Calendar year registrations: 6000 pounds or less = 65,815; 6001-10,000 pounds = 27,110. Calendar year production: (all IHC trucks) 212,654 (8.60 percent). Innovations: New grille styling with horizontal-bar theme for most models. Historical: World-wide sales in fiscal 1972 totaled $3,493,000,000. This was the fifth consecutive year that sales eclipsed a previous record sales year. Plans for increased participation in world markets were announced by IH, which acquired a one-third interest in DAF of Eindhoven, The Netherlands.

1973 IHC Model 1210 Pickup with 4x4 (Erwin Knapp)

Pricing

1972	5	4	3	2	1
Scout II (4x2)					
Traveltop	980	1950	3250	4550	6500
Pickup	960	1920	3200	4500	6400
Scout II (4x4)					
Traveltop	1040	2070	3450	4850	6900
Pickup	1010	2030	3350	4700	6700
Metro Series					
1110 Panel	590	1140	1900	2650	3800
1200 Panel	590	1140	1900	2650	3800
1200 Panel	590	1170	1950	2700	3900
Travelall Series (4x2)					
1010 Sta. Wag.	830	1650	2750	3850	5500
1110 Sta. Wag.	810	1620	2700	3800	5400
1210 Sta. Wag.	800	1600	2650	3700	5300
Travelall Series (4x4)					
1110 Sta. Wag.	870	1750	2900	4100	5800
1210 Sta. Wag.	850	1700	2850	4000	5700
Light Truck — Series 1110 — (4x2)					
Pickup	830	1650	2750	3850	5500
Bonus Load Pickup	840	1680	2800	3900	5600
Light Truck — Series 1110 — (4x4)					
Pickup	850	1700	2850	4000	5700
Bonus Load Pickup	870	1750	2900	4100	5800
Light Truck — Series 1210 — (4x2)					
Pickup	720	1450	2400	3300	4800
Bonus Load Pickup	740	1470	2450	3350	4900
Travelette	700	1400	2350	3250	4700
Light Truck — Series 1210 — (4x4)					
Pickup	740	1470	2450	3350	4900
Bonus Load Pickup	750	1500	2500	3500	5000
Travelette	750	1500	2500	3500	5000
Light Truck — Series 1310 — (4x2)					
Pickup	800	1600	2650	3700	5300
Bonus Load Pickup	700	1400	2350	3250	4700
Travelette	690	1380	2300	3200	4600

NOTES: Add 3 percent for V-8 engine (all series).
Add 1 percent for five-speed transmission.
Add 5 percent for Custom trim packages.

1973 IHC

SCOUT — SERIES II — (ALL ENGINES): — The 1973 Scout II had a new front end treatment. There was still a rectangular front panel with single, round headlamps at each end. Between the headlamps there were now two grilles, one on each side of a narrow, body colored vertical divider. Each grille had a rectangular opening with a chrome surround and six, vertical bars finished in body color. An International nameplate ran horizontally across the lower section of the outer four bars on the left-hand grille. All else was about the same as in 1972.

I.D. DATA: (All Series) See 1972 section.

Model	Body Type	Price	Weight	Prod. Total
Scout II Series — (4x2) — (100 in. w.b.)				
SII	Traveltop	2752	3370	—
SII	Cab Top	2605	3290	—
Scout II Series — (4x4) — (100 in. w.b.)				
SII	Traveltop	3549	3600	—
SII	Cab Top	3394	3500	—

ENGINE: Standard and optional engines were unchanged. See previous sections for specifications. Base equipment was the 6-258 engine introduced in 1972. Options included the V-304 and V-345, which were both available in some IHC trucks from 1967 on. All engines were de-tuned to operate on unleaded gasoline. The 6-258 now gave 115 horsepower at 3800 R.P.M. and developed 199 lbs. ft. of torque at 2000 R.P.M. See footnotes at section end for more details on new power ratings.

OPTIONS: V-304 engine ($85). V-345 engine ($120). RA-28 Trac-Lok rear axle ($60). Custom Traveltop package ($245). Power steering. Power brakes. Air conditioning. Dual OSRV mirrors. Radio. Radio antenna. Roof rack. Deluxe wheels. Sliding side windows. Whitewall tires. Spare tire and carrier. Special paint. Oversize tires. Bucket seats. Console.

METRO — SERIES MS — SIX-CYLINDER: — The Metro van line was designated the MS series this season. There was only 1-ton-or-under model left. This was the MS-1210 chassis. Longer wheelbases ranging from a low of 125 inches to a high of 159 inches were available. Upon ordering a chassis, the buyer could add one of several different sized Walk-In panel bodies.

Model	Body Type	Price	Weight	Prod. Total
Metro Series — (4x2) — (125-159 in. w.b.)				
MS-1210	Chassis	2545	2280	—

ENGINE: The same engines offered in Scout II models were available in the Metro chassis. See Scout II engine section above.

OPTIONS: V-304 engine ($80). V-304 LPG engine ($260). V-345 engine. Dual OSRV mirrors. Automatic transmission. Four-speed transmission. Special paint. Power steering. Power brakes.

1973 International Bonus Load Pickup (JAG)

TRAVELALL — SERIES 1010/1110/1210 — SIX-CYLINDER: — The "big" styling change for 1973 was really pretty small potatoes. It consisted of narrowing the front fender tip badges to put slightly more room between them and the side-markers. There was also a new hub cab design with more pointed center. Standard trim featured a minimum of tinsel with no side moldings. Deluxe trim trucks had a molding along the lower bodyside feature line from behind the front wheel cutout to the rear. Custom trim had a molding around the front wheel cutouts, up the fender and back down the body along the upper beltline. The area inside the moldings was often finished in a contrasting color or with a woodgrain insert on Travel-alls. The taillights were tall, narrow traphazoids positioned base-to-base with the top lens pointing up and the bottom one pointing downwards. A similarly shaped white backup light was incorporated into the bottom lens. The Travelall also featured a drop-down tailgate with lowerable rear window glass. Many units wore vinyl tops and the roof rack was a popular option, too.

Model	Body Type	Price	Weight	Prod. Total
Travelall Series 1010 — (119 in. w.b.)				
1010	Sta. Wag. 4x2	3775	5440	—
Travelall Series 1110 — (119 in. w.b.)				
1110	Sta. Wag. 4x2	3700	5475	—
1110	Sta. Wag. 4x4	4375	5655	—
Travelall Series 1210 — (119 in. w.b.)				
1210	Sta. Wag. 4x2	3820	5475	—
1210	Sta. Wag. 4x4	4600	5990	—

ENGINE: See 1972 Travelall Series engine data.

1973 International Bonus Load Pickup (JAG)

OPTIONS: Power steering, all ($135). V-304 engine, all ($85). V-392 engine ($235). T-34 or T-36 five-speed transmission in all 4x2 models ($310). Automatic transmission, all 4x2 models, average ($240). RA-17 rear axle, all 1200 models ($140). Power brakes. Air conditioning. Roof rack. Vinyl top. Deluxe wheel covers. Custom wheel covers. Wood grain side trim. White sidewall tires. Custom interior package. Dual OSRV mirrors. Towing package. Bumper hitch. "California" trucker mirrors. Over-size tires.

CONVENTIONAL LIGHT TRUCK — SERIES 1010/1110/1210/1310 — SIX-CYLINDER: — The IHC conventional light-duty trucks had the same minor styling changes as Travelalls. They also came with similar levels of trim. There was a handsome new 4x4 hub with turbine type fins around the perimeter.

Model	Body Type	Price	Weight	Prod. Total
Series 1010 — (4x2) — (131 in. w.b.)				
1010	Pickup	2925	3735	—
Series 1110 — (4x2) — (115-131 in. w.b.)				
1110	Chassis & Cab	2710	3180	—
1110	Pickup	2856	3555	—
Series 1110 — (4x4) — (115-131 in. w.b.)				
1110	Chassis & Cab	3269	3485	—
1110	Pickup	3411	3860	—
Series 1210 — (4x2) — (115-149 in. w.b.)				
1210	Chassis & Cab	2831	3410	—
1210	Pickup	2973	3785	—
1210	Travelette Cab	3470	3850	—
1210	Travelette Pickup	3621	4215	—
Series 1210 — (4x4) — (115-149 in. w.b.)				
1210	Chassis & Cab	3544	3820	—
1210	Pickup	3687	4195	—
1210	Travelette Cab	4352	4270	—
1210	Travelette Pickup	4814	4635	—
Series 1310 — (4x2) — (131-150 in. w.b.)				
1310	Chassis & Cab	3155	3610	—
1310	Pickup	3166	3630	—
1310	Travelette Cab	3626	3695	—
1310	Travelette Pickup	3780	4045	—
Series 1310 — (4x4) — (132 in. w.b.)				
1310	Chassis & Cab	4369	4375	—
1310	Pickup (9 ft.)	4522	4375	—

NOTE: Bonus Load pickups were $11 over the cost of standard pickups.

ENGINE: See 1972 conventional light truck engine data.

OPTIONS: V-304 engine, all ($80). V-304 LPG engine, Series 1300, 4x2 only ($260). T-34 transmission, Series 1300 4x2 only ($220). Power steering ($135). Automatic transmission (average $240). Power brakes. Air conditioning. Tinted glass. Deluxe trim package. Custom trim package. White sidewall tires. Dual OSRV mirrors. Dual "California" trucker mirrors. Custom interior package. Cab clearance lights. Tow package. Camper package. V-345 engine. V-392 engine. Oversize tires. Two-tone paint. Special paint. Floor mats. Spare tire and carrier.

CHASSIS (Scout II Series): Wheelbase: 100 in. Tires: E78 x 15 in.

CHASSIS (Series MS-1210): Wheelbase: 125-159 in. Tires: 8.75 x 16 in.

CHASSIS (Series 1010): Wheelbase: 131 in. Tires: G78 x 15 in.

CHASSIS (Series 1110): Wheelbase: 115-131 in. Tires: G78 x 15 in.

CHASSIS (Series 1210): Wheelbase: 115/119/131/149/156 in. Tires: 8.00 x 16.5 in.

CHASSIS (Series 1310): Wheelbase: 131/132/134/149/150 in. Tires: 8.00 x 16.5 in.

1973 International Utility Box Body Pickup (JAG)

TECHNICAL (All Series, 4x2, typical): Manual (synchromesh) transmission. Speeds: 3F/1R. Column mounted gearshift lever. Single plate dry disc clutch. Single reduction rear axle. Overall ratio: 3.31:1; 3.73:1 or 4.27:1. Four-wheel hydraulic brakes. Steel disc wheels. Four-speed transmission. Five-speed transmission. Automatic transmission. Overdrive. Four-wheel-drive running gear.

NOTE: On 4x4 models the front drive axle was full-floating.

HISTORICAL: Introduced Fall 1972. Calendar year registrations: (all IHC trucks) 199,875. Calendar year production: (light-duty trucks): 105,569. Calendar year production: (all IHC trucks): 207,547 (6.91 percent).
New front styling for all models. Engines detoned to operate on low-lead fuel. Optional engine specifications:
V-304 (two-barrel): 147 horsepower at 3900 R.P.M./240 lbs. ft. of torque at 2400 R.P.M.
V-304 (four-barrel): 153 horsepower at 3900 R.P.M./246 lbs. ft. of torque at 2400 R.P.M.
V-345 (two-barrel): 157 horsepower at 3800 R.P.M./266 lbs. ft. of torque at 2400 R.P.M.
V-345 (four-barrel): 163 horsepower at 3800 R.P.M./273 lbs. ft. of torque at 2400 R.P.M.
V-392 (two-barrel): 191 horsepower at 3600 R.P.M./299 lbs. ft. of torque at 2800 R.P.M.
V-392 (four-barrel): 194 horsepower at 3600 R.P.M./308 lbs. ft. of torque at 2800 R.P.M.
IHC was America's fifth largest truck-maker behind Chevrolet, Ford, Dodge and GMC in order. B. McCormick was the company's president and chief executive officer. K.P. Mazurek was president and Corporate VP of the Motor Truck Division.

1973 International Bonus Load Pickup (JAG)

Pricing

1973	5	4	3	2	1
Scout II (4x2)					
Traveltop	980	1950	3250	4550	6500
Cab Top	960	1920	3200	4800	6400
Scout II (4x4)					
Traveltop	1040	2070	3450	4850	6900
Cab Top	1010	2030	3350	4700	6700
Metro Series MS-1210 (4x2)					
Walk-In Panel	590	1170	1950	2700	3900
Travelall Series 1010 (4x2)					
Sta. Wag. (4x2)	830	1650	2750	3850	5500
Travelall Series 1110					
Sta. Wag. (4x2)	810	1620	2700	3800	5400
Sta. Wag. (4x4)	870	1750	2900	4100	5800
Travelall Series 1210					
Sta. Wag. (4x2)	800	1600	2650	3700	5300
Sta. Wag. (4x4)	850	1700	2850	4000	5700
Light Truck Series 1010 (4x2)					
Pickup (6½ ft.)	830	1650	2750	3850	5500
B.L. Pickup (6½ ft.)	840	1680	2800	3900	5600
Pickup (8 ft.)	810	1620	2700	3800	5400
B.L. Pickup (8 ft.)	830	1650	2750	3850	5500
Light Truck Series 1110 (4x2)					
Pickup (6½ ft.)	830	1650	2750	3850	5500
B.L. Pickup (6½ ft.)	840	1680	2800	3900	5600
Pickup (8 ft.)	810	1620	2700	3800	5400
Light Truck Series 1110 (4x4)					
Pickup (6½ ft.)	850	1700	2850	4000	5700
B.L. Pickup (6½ ft.)	870	1750	2900	4100	5800
Pickup (8 ft.)	830	1650	2750	3850	5500
B.L. Pickup (8 ft.)	810	1620	2700	3800	5400
Light Truck Series 1210 (4x2)					
Pickup (6½ ft.)	720	1450	2400	3300	4800
B.L. Pickup (6½ ft.)	740	1470	2450	3350	4900
Pickup (8 ft.)	680	1350	2250	3150	4500
B.L. Pickup (8 ft.)	690	1380	2300	3200	4600
Travelette Pickup (6½ ft.)	690	1380	2300	3200	4600
B.L. Travelette Pickup (6½ ft.)	700	1400	2350	3250	4700
Travelette Pickup (8 ft.)	740	1470	2450	3350	4900
B.L. Travelette Pickup (8 ft.)	750	1500	2500	3500	5000
Light Truck Series 1210 (4x4)					
Pickup (6½ ft.)	740	1470	2450	3350	4900
B.L. Pickup (6½ ft.)	750	1500	2500	3500	5000
Pickup (8 ft.)	690	1380	2300	3200	4600
B.L. Pickup (8 ft.)	700	1400	2350	3250	4700
Travelette Pickup (6½ ft.)	750	1500	2500	3500	5000
B.L. Travelette Pickup (6½ ft.)	770	1550	2550	3600	5100
Travelette Pickup (8 ft.)	750	1500	2500	3500	5000
B.L. Travelette Pickup (8 ft.)	770	1550	2550	3600	5100
Light Truck Series 1310 (4x2)					
Pickup (8 ft.)	800	1600	2650	3700	5300
B.L. Pickup (8 ft.)	810	1620	2700	3800	5400
Pickup (9 ft.)	770	1550	2550	3600	5100
B.L. Travelette Pickup (6½ ft.)	740	1470	2450	3350	4900
Light Truck Series 1310 (4x4)					
Pickup (9 ft.)	720	1450	2400	3300	4800

NOTE: Add three percent for 304 cu. in. V-8.
Add four percent for 345 cu. in. V-8.
Add five percent for 392 cu. in. V-8.
Add five for custom trim package.
Add one percent for five-speed transmission.

1974 IHC

SCOUT — SERIES II — (ALL ENGINES): — There were no changes in the 1974 Scout, but a few more decal options and equipment packages came out. The grille was also slightly revised. It now had an "electric shaver" look with vertical blades all across it.

I.D. DATA (All Series): See 1972 section. Serial numbers for 1974 conventional trucks began with 4 (H) 1 (A) ODHB and up.

Model	Body Type	Price	Weight	Prod. Total
Scout II Series — (100 in. w.b.)				
SII	Traveltop (4x2)	2979	3462	—
SII	Traveltop (4x4)	3943	3717	—
SII	Cab Top (4x2)	2832	3316	—
SII	Cab Top (4x4)	3788	3571	—

NOTE: Above prices include Hydra-Matic and power brakes.

ENGINE: See 1973 Scout II Series engine data.

560

1974 IHC Scout with Travel Top (IHC)

OPTIONS: Automatic transmission ($238 average). Air conditioning ($500 average). AM radio ($70). Deluxe exterior trim package "500" ($69). Deluxe exterior trim package, other models ($120 average). V-304 engine ($100). V-345 engine ($135). Other options similar to 1973.

METRO — SERIES MS — SIX-CYLINDER: — The Metro van line was again carried over as the MS-1210 Series. These trucks were sold as a stripped chassis with hydraulic brakes. Three wheelbases were available. A variety of optional Step-Van bodies could be added, including steel and aluminum versions. The "1200" designation indicated ¾-ton capacity.

Model	Body Type	Price	Weight	Prod. Total
Metro Series				
MS-1210	Step-Van Chassis (125 in.)	2695	3328	—
MS-1210	Step-Van Chassis (137 in.)	2705	3340	—
MS-1210	Step-Van Chassis (159 in.)	2736	3362	—

ENGINE: See 1973 Metro Series engine data.

OPTIONS: Power steering. Power brakes. AM radio ($70). V-304 engine ($100 average). V-345-2 heavy-duty engine ($131). Dual OSRV mirrors. Four-speed transmission. Special paint.

TRAVELALL — SERIES 100/200 — V-8 ENGINE: — Travelalls and conventional light-duty trucks had revised series designations for 1974. Travelalls were available as "100" (½-ton) or "200" (¾-ton) models. There was a new grille with five full-width horizontal bars. Also, the rectangular badges ahead of the front wheel openings were moved down closer to the side-markers. A 345 cu. in. V-8 was now standard equipment in the 4x2 Series 100 Travelall. Other models used the 392 cu. in. V-8 as base engine.

Model	Body Type	Price	Weight	Prod. Total
Travelall Series 100				
100	Sta. Wag. (4x2)	4338	4450	—
100	Sta. Wag. (4x4)	5320	4795	—
Travelall Series 200				
200	Sta. Wag. (4x2)	4798	4696	—
200	Sta. Wag. (4x4)	5498	4899	—

ENGINE: The V-345 eight-cylinder engine was made standard in Series 100 Travelalls with 4x2 running gear. The V-358 eight-cylinder engine was made standard equipment in all other Travelall models. See 1973 engine specifications.

OPTIONS: V-392 engine in "200" Travelall ($185). V-392 engine in "100" Travelall ($255). V-400 engine in "200" Travelall (deduct $55). V-400 engine in "100" Travelall ($131). Power steering. Automatic transmission. Power brakes. Air conditioning. Vinyl top. Deluxe wheel covers. Custom wheel covers. Wood grain side trim. White sidewall tires. Custom interior package. Dual OSRV mirrors. Towing package. Bumper hitch. "California" trucker mirrors. Oversize tires. Tinted glass. Two-tone paint.

CONVENTIONAL LIGHT TRUCKS — SERIES 100/200 — ALL ENGINES: — IHC's light-duty pickup trucks were also available as "100" or "200" series models. They had the new full-width horizontal-bar grille and slightly repositioned side-markers. Series 100 models with 4x4 equipment used the 304 cu. in. V-8 as base engine. The 258 cu. in. six-cylinder was standard in all other models. The regular pickups had the narrower box and flared rear fenders. Bonus Load Pickups had a wider box flush with the sides of the cab. Travelette, crew cab models came both ways. Distinctions of the Deluxe and Custom exterior trim packages were the same as described in the 1973 section.

Model	Body Type	Price	Weight	Prod. Total
Series 100 — (4x2)				
100	Chassis & Cab (115 in. w.b.)	3106	3381	—
100	Chassis & Cab (132 in. w.b.)	3258	3422	—
100	Fender Pickup (115 in. w.b.)	3258	3753	—
100	Fender Pickup (132 in. w.b.)	3294	3842	—
100	Bonus Load Pickup (115 in. w.b.)	3258	3806	—
100	Bonus Load Pickup (132 in. w.b.)	3294	3902	—

Model	Body Type	Price	Weight	Prod. Total
Series 100 — (4x4)				
100	Chassis & Cab (115 in. w.b.)	3877	3571	—
100	Chassis & Cab (132 in. w.b.)	3903	3794	—
100	Fender Pickup (115 in. w.b.)	4031	4143	—
100	Fender Pickup (132 in. w.b.)	4067	4214	—
100	Bonus Load Pickup (115 in. w.b.)	4031	4196	—
100	Bonus Load Pickup (132 in. w.b.)	4067	4274	—
Series 200 — (4x2)				
200	Chassis & Cab (132 in. w.b.)	3362	3745	—
200	Chassis & Cab (149 in. w.b.)	3372	3708	—
200	Chassis & Cab (158 in. w.b.)	3422	3780	—
200	Travelette Chassis & Cab (149 in. w.b.)	4093	4302	—
200	Travelette Chassis & Cab (166 in. w.b.)	4244	4369	—
200	Bonus Load Pickup (132 in. w.b.)	3526	4225	—
200	Fender Pickup (132 in. w.b.)	3526	4165	—
200	Travelette Fender Pickup (149 in. w.b.)	4255	4674	—
200	Travelette Fender Pickup (166 in. w.b.)	4408	4789	—
200	Travelette Bonus Load Pickup (149 in. w.b.)	4255	4727	—
200	Travelette Bonus Load Pickup (166 in. w.b.)	4408	4849	—
Series 200 — (4x4)				
200	Chassis & Cab (132 in. w.b.)	4016	3993	—
200	Fender Pickup (132 in. w.b.)	4181	4413	—
200	Bonus Load Pickup (132 in. w.b.)	4181	4473	—

ENGINE: Four-wheel-drive series 100 models came with the two-barrel 304 cu. in. V-8 as standard equipment. All other models had the 6-258 six-cylinder engine as standard equipment. See 1973 engine specifications.

OPTIONS: 304 cu. in. V-8 in Series 100/4x2 ($100). 304 cu. in. V-8 in series 200 ($100). 345 cu. in V-8 in Series 100 and all-series w/4x4 ($245). 392 cu. in. V-8 in Series 200 ($255). 400 cu. in. V-8, in Series 100 ($255); in Series 100 Travelette ($131). Power steering. Automatic transmission ($238). Power brakes. Air conditioning ($500). Deluxe wheel covers. Custom wheels. Whitewall tires. Dual OSRV mirrors. Towing package ($410). Bumper hitch. "California" trucker mirrors. Clearance marker lights (except ½-ton). Oversize tires. Tinted glass. Two-tone paint. AM radio ($70). Deluxe exterior trim package ($120). Custom exterior trim package ($275). Camper special package w/200 series ($275).

CHASSIS (Scout II Series): Wheelbase: 100 in. Tires: F78 x 15 in.

CHASSIS (Metro Series): Wheelbase: 125-159 in. Tires: 8.75 x 16.5 in.

CHASSIS (Series 100): Wheelbase: 115-132 in. Tires: G78 x 15 in.

CHASSIS (Series 200): Wheelbase: 132-158 in. Tires: 8.00 x 16.5 in.

TECHNICAL (All Series, 4x2, typical): Manual (synchromesh) transmission. Speeds: 3F/1R. Column mounted gearshift lever. Single plate dry disc clutch. Single reduction rear axle. Overall ratio: 3.31:1, 3.73:1 or 4.27:1. Four-wheel hydraulic brakes. Steel disc wheels. Technical options: Four-speed transmission. Five-speed transmission. Automatic transmission. Overdrive. Four-wheel-drive running gear.

NOTE: On 4x4 models the front drive axle was full-floating.

HISTORICAL: Introduced Fall 1973. Calendar year registrations by GVW Class: 6000 lbs. or less = 50,089; 6001 to 10,000 lbs. = 23,567. Calendar year production: (all IHC trucks) 177,915 (6.29 percent). Model year production: (all IHC trucks) 161,375. Model year production: (Scout II) 29,657. Model year production: (Pickups) 36,584.
"Electric Shaver" grilles for Scout II. New series designations for light-duty trucks. V-8 engines become standard equipment in some series.
Although production of light-duty pickups was continued in 1975, this was the last year for IHC as a major light-duty pickup manufacturer. Only 6,329 pickups would be made in 1975, the final year for that series.

OPTION INSTALLATION RATES: The following data indicates percentage of total IHC production having the specified factory options installed.

SERIES 100: Auto. transmission (62.7 percent); power disc brakes (100.0 percent); power steering (70.7 percent); radio AM only (62.7 percent); radio AM/FM stereo (2.4 percent); V-8 engines 350 CID or less (51.7 percent); V-8 engines over 350 CID (51.7 percent); air conditioning (21.9 percent); limited slip differential (19.5 percent); tinted glass (21.9 percent); wheel covers (57.6 percent); interior trim package (43.6 percent); exterior trim package (55.4 percent); four-wheel-drive (25.8 percent) rates based on total output of 20,062.

SERIES 200: Auto. transmission (44.2 percent); power disc brakes (100.0 percent); power steering (70.9 percent); radio AM only (48.3 percent); radio AM/FM stereo (2.1 percent); V-8 engines 350 CID or less (2.1 percent); V-8 engines over 350 CID (20.1 percent); air conditioning (13.6 percent); limited slip differential (17.8 percent); dual rear wheels (18.6 percent); tinted glass (13.6 percent); wheel covers (30.9 percent); interior trim package (29.3 percent); exterior trim package (32.1 percent); four-wheel-drive (39.6 percent) rates based on total output of 21,996.

SCOUT II: Auto. transmission (53.6 percent); power disc brakes (100.0 percent); power steering (61.4 percent); radio AM only (70.8 percent); radio AM/FM stereo (6.7 percent); V-8 engines 350 CID or less (62.7 percent); air conditioning (26.3 percent); limited slip differential (37.2 percent); tinted glass (26.3 percent); wheel covers (64.0 percent); interior trim package (83.5 percent); exterior trim package (82.6 percent); four-wheel-drive (17.1 percent) rates based on total output of 6,714.

TRAVELALL 100: Auto. transmission (95.5 percent); power disc brakes (100.0 percent); power steering (95.4 percent); radio AM (47.3 percent); radio AM/FM stereo (39.9 percent); V-8 engines 350 CID or less (15.1 percent); V-8 engines over 350 CID (84.9 percent); air conditioning (82.8 percent); limited slip differential (20.3 percent); tinted glass (82.8 percent); wheel covers (82.5 percent); interior trim package (72.8 percent); exterior trim package (71.8 percent); four-wheel-drive (40.2 percent) rates based on total output of 1,138.

TRAVELALL 200: Auto. transmission (39.9 percent); power disc brakes (100.0 percent); power steering (51.1 percent); radio AM only (22.4 percent); radio AM/FM stereo (6.1 percent); air conditioning (82.3 percent); limited slip differential (36.1 percent); tinted glass (24.9 percent); wheel covers (22.6 percent); interior trim package (59.7 percent); exterior trim package (53.5 percent); four-wheel-drive (86.1 percent) rates based on total output of 29,238.

Pricing

1974	5	4	3	2	1
Scout II — (4x2)					
Traveltop	980	1950	3250	4550	6500
Cab Top	960	1920	3200	4500	6400
Scout II — (4x4)					
Traveltop	1040	2070	3450	4850	6900
Cab Top	1010	2030	3350	4700	6700
Metro Series — (4x2)					
Step-Van	590	1170	1950	2700	3900
Travelall Series 100					
Sta. Wag. (4x2)	830	1650	2750	3850	5500
Sta. Wag. (4x4)	870	1750	2900	4100	5800
Travelall Series 200					
Sta. Wag. (4x2)	800	1600	2650	3700	5300
Sta. Wag. (4x4)	850	1700	2850	4000	5700
Pickups — Series 100 — (4x2)					
Fender Pickup (115 in. w.b.)	830	1650	2750	3850	5500
Fender Pickup (132 in. w.b.)	810	1620	2700	3800	5400
Bonus Load Pickup (115 in. w.b.)	840	1680	2800	3900	5600
Bonus Load Pickup (132 in. w.b.)	830	1650	2750	3850	5500
Pickups — Series 100 — (4x4)					
Fender Pickup (115 in. w.b.)	830	1700	2850	4000	5700
Fender Pickup (132 in. w.b.)	830	1650	2750	3850	5500
Bonus Load Pickup (115 in. w.b.)	870	1750	2900	4100	5800
Bonus Load Pickup (132 in. w.b.)	840	1680	2800	3900	5600
Pickups — Series 200 — (4x2)					
Fender Travelette (149 in. w.b.)	690	1380	2300	3200	4600
Fender Travelette (166 in. w.b.)	740	1470	2450	3350	4900
Bonus Load (132 in. w.b.)	740	1470	2450	3350	4900
Fender Pickup (132 in. w.b.)	720	1450	2400	3300	4800
Bonus Load Travelette (149 in. w.b.)	700	1400	2350	3250	4700
Bonus Load Travelette (166 in. w.b.)	750	1500	2500	3500	5000
Pickups — Series 200 — (4x4)					
Fender Pickup (132 in. w.b.)	740	1470	2450	3350	4900
Bonus Load Pickup (132 in. w.b.)	750	1500	2500	3500	5000

NOTE: Add 2 percent for Deluxe exterior trim.
Add 5 percent for Custom exterior trim.
Add 4 percent for 345 or 392 cu. in. V-8s.
Add 10 percent for camper special.

1975 IHC

SCOUT XLC — SERIES II — (ALL ENGINES): — The 1975 Scout XLC was basically unchanged from the 1974 model. However, there were a couple of power train changes. The slant-four engine was further detuned and the G-258 engine was dropped. Available options included two V-8s with slightly less horsepower.

1975 IHC Scout with Travel Top (IHC)

I.D. DATA (All Series): See 1972 section.

Model	Body Type	Price	Weight	Prod. Total
Scout II Series XLC — (100 in. w.b.)				
SII	Traveltop (4x2)	3760	3471	—
SII	Traveltop (4x4)	4712	3551	—
SII	Cab Top (4x2)	3285	3376	—
SII	Cab Top (4x4)	4489	3549	—

ENGINE (Scout II Series XLC, Base): Inline, OHV. Four-cylinder. Cast iron block. Bore & stroke: 4⅛. x 3-21/32 in. Displacement: 196 cu. in. Compression ratio: 8.02:1. Brake horsepower: 86 at 3800 R.P.M. Net horsepower: 27.2. Max. Torque: 157 lb. ft. at 2200 R.P.M. Hydraulic valve lifters. Carburetor: Holley model 1920.

ENGINE (Scout II Series XLC, Optional): Vee-block, OHV. Eight-cylinder. Cast iron block. Bore & stroke: 3⅞ in. x 3-7/32 in. Displacement: 304 cu. in. Compression ratio: 8.2:1. Brake horsepower: 140 at 3800 R.P.M. Net horsepower: 48.1. Max. Torque: 243 lb. ft. at 2400 R.P.M. Hydraulic valve lifters. Carburetor: Holley model 2210C.

ENGINE (Scout II Series XLC, Optional): Vee-block, OHV. Eight-cylinder. Cast iron block. Bore & stroke: 3⅞ in. x 3-21/32 in. Displacement: 345 cu. in. Compression ratio: 8.05:1. Brake horsepower: 158 at 3600 R.P.M. Net horsepower: 48.1. Max. Torque: 288 lb. ft. at 2000 R.P.M. Hydraulic valve lifters. Carburetor: Holley two-barrel model 2210.

NOTE: Also available with Holley 2300 four-barrel carb. The four-barrel engine also had 8.05:1 compression. It was rated 168 horsepower at 3800 R.P.M. and developed 288 lbs. ft. of torque at 2000 R.P.M.

METRO — SERIES MS — V-8: This was the last year of production for the IH Metro Vans. As a result, there was no change for the new year, except in base engine. Since the six-cylinder engine was dropped, the 345 cu. in. V-8 became standard equipment.

Model	Body Type	Price	Weight	Prod. Total
Metro Series				
MS-1210	Step-Van Chassis (125 in.)	3452	3328	—
MS-1210	Step-Van Chassis (137 in.)	3462	3340	—
MS-1210	Step-Van Chassis (159 in.)	3493	3362	—

ENGINE: The 345 cu. in./158 horsepower engine was standard equipment. The 345 cu. in. four-barrel engine was optional at a price of $40.

OPTIONS: Same as 1974, except engines. See 1974 section.

TRAVELALL — SERIES 150/200 — V-8: This was also the final season for the famous Travelall. Any changes were of a minor nature. As in 1974, the wheelbase was 120 inches. However, the 304 cu. in V-8 was now standard equipment. Everything else was about the same as in 1974. The 100 Series was redesignated the 150. Two V-8s, the V-345A and V-392 were optional. Standard, Deluxe and Custom trim levels were available again.

1975 IHC Scout Station Wagon (IHC)

Model	Body Type	Price	Weight	Prod. Total
Travelall Series 150				
150	Sta. Wag. (4x2)	4973	4597	—
150	Sta. Wag. (4x4)	5836	4803	—
Travelall Series 200				
200	Sta. Wag. (4x2)	5172	4831	—
200	Sta. Wag. (4x4)	6024	5051	—

ENGINE (Base): The 304 cu. in. V-8 was standard equipment. See Scout II engine specifications above.

ENGINE (Optional): The 345 cu. in. V-8 was optional at a price of $40 extra. See Scout II engine specifications above.

ENGINE (Travelall, Optional): Vee-block, OHV. Eight-cylinder. Cast iron block. Bore & stroke: 4⅛ in. x 3-21/32 in. Displacement: 392 cu. in. Compression ratio: 8.02:1. Brake horsepower: 187 at 3600 R.P.M. Max. Torque: 307 lb. ft. at 2400 R.P.M. Hydraulic valve lifters. Carburetor: Holley four-barrel model 4150.

NOTE: Also available with 8.0:1 compression ratio; 191 horsepower at 3600 R.P.M. and 307 lbs. ft. of torque at 2400 R.P.M.

PICKUP TRUCKS — SERIES 150/200 — V-8: IHC's 1975 Light-duty pickups were similar to 1974 models, except that the ½-ton models were now designated the "150" series. The "200" designation still applied to ¾-ton models. A small V-8 was standard equipment in both lines. These trucks could be optionally equipped with deluxe or custom trim packages. All of the conventional pickups and all of the crew-cab Travelette pickups were now of the "fenderless" Bonus Load style.

Model	Body Type	Price	Weight	Prod. Total
Series 150 — (4x2)				
150	Chassis & Cab (115 in. w.b.)	3800	3624	—
150	Chassis & Cab (132 in. w.b.)	3824	3687	—
150	Bonus Load Pickup (115 in. w.b.)	3952	4029	—
150	Bonus Load Pickup (132 in. w.b.)	3988	4143	—
Series 150 — (4x4)				
150	Chassis & Cab (115 in. w.b.)	4575	3872	—
150	Chassis & Cab (132 in. w.b.)	4601	3938	—
150	Bonus Load Pickup (115 in. w.b.)	4729	4283	—
150	Bonus Load Pickup (132 in. w.b.)	4765	4394	—
Series 200 — (4x2)				
200	Chassis & Cab (132 in. w.b.)	4166	3922	—
200	Chassis & Cab (149 in. w.b.)	4176	3984	—
200	Chassis & Cab (158 in. w.b.)	4226	4024	—
200	Travelette Chassis & Cab (149 in. w.b.)	4897	4377	—
200	Travelette Chassis & Cab (166 in. w.b.)	5048	4435	—
200	Bonus Load Pickup (132 in. w.b.)	4330	4378	—
200	Bonus Load Travelette Pickup (149 in. w.b.)	5059	4788	—
200	Bonus Load Travelette Pickup (166 in. w.b.)	5212	4891	—
Series 200 — (4x4)				
200	Chassis & Cab (132 in. w.b.)	5008	4136	—
200	Bonus Load Pickup (132 in. w.b.)	5173	4592	—

OPTIONS: Chrome front bumper, Series 200. Rear bumper. Air conditioning ($540). Automatic transmission ($287). Power steering ($154). Power brakes. Bumper guards. AM radio ($77). Heater. Clock. Cigar lighter. Radio antenna. Seat covers. Trailer towing package ($451). Deluxe exterior trim package ($144). Custom exterior trim package ($299). Camper Special Package, Series 200 w/4x4 ($302). Tinted glass. V-345 V-8 engine ($40). V-392 V-8 engine ($167). Wheel trim rings. Clearance lamps, Series 200 cab. Dual OSRV mirrors. "California" trucker mirrors. Rear step bumper. Spare tire and carrier. AM/FM radio.

CHASSIS (Scout II Series XLC): Wheelbase: 100 in. Tires: H78 x 15 in.

CHASSIS (Metro Series): Wheelbase: 125-159 in. Tires: 8.75 x 16 in.

CHASSIS (Series 150): Wheelbase: 115-132 in. Tires: H78 x 15 in.

CHASSIS (Series 200): Wheelbase: 132-166 in. Tires: 8.00 x 16.5 in.

TECHNICAL (4x2 Models, Typical): Manual (synchromesh) transmission. Speeds: 3F/1R. Column mounted gearshift lever. Single plate dry disc clutch. Single reduction rear axle. Four-wheel hydraulic brakes. Steel disc wheels. Four-speed transmission. Automatic transmission. Overdrive.

HISTORICAL: Introduced Fall 1974. Calendar year production: (all IHC trucks): 111,352. Model year production (Scout): 25,904. Model year production: (Pickups): 6,329.

New "150" Series replaces "100" Series in ½-ton lineup.

This was the final year of production of IHC Metro vans and conventional light-duty pickups, Travelall and Travelette models.

OPTION INSTALLATION RATES: The following data indicates the percentage of total IHC truck production having the specified options installed. Data is arranged according to series. Percentage figures, in brackets, indicate installation rate. Total series output is given at end of each data block.

SERIES 150: Auto. transmission (64.4 percent); power disc brakes (100.0 percent); power steering (83.9 percent); V-8 engines 350 CID or less (90.3 percent); V-8 engines over 350 CID (9.7 percent); limited slip rear axle (68.3 percent); four-wheel-drive (43.7 percent); interior trim package (12.1 percent); exterior trim package (30.0 percent); AM radio (71.5 percent); AM/FM stereo radio (0.7 percent); tinted glass (22.1 percent); air conditioning (58.6 percent); total output 6,618.

SERIES 200: Auto. transmission (39.1 percent); power disc brakes (100.0 percent); power steering (83.7 percent); V-8 engines 350 CID or less (76.3 percent); V-8 engines over 350 CID (23.7 percent); limited slip rear axle (19.5 percent); dual rear wheels (0.3 percent); four-wheel-drive (46.2 percent); interior trim package (6.6 percent); exterior trim package (12.5 percent); AM radio (57.0 percent); AM/FM stereo radio (0.5 percent); tinted glass (13.3 percent); air conditioning (33.5 percent); total output 10,418.

TRAVELALL 150: Auto. transmission (95.3 percent); power disc brakes (100.0 percent); power steering (93.8 percent); V-8 engines 350 CID or less (36.1 percent); V-8 engines over 350 CID (63.9 percent); limited slip rear axle (18.3 percent); four-wheel-drive (18.3 percent); interior trim package (71.4 percent); exterior trim package (37.4 percent); AM radio (55.6 percent); AM/FM stereo radio (4.6 percent); tinted glass (78.6 percent); air conditioning (86.1 percent); total output 4,224.

TRAVELALL 200: Auto. transmission (22.2 percent); power disc brakes (100.0 percent); power steering (31.0 percent); V-8 engines 350 CID or less (43.3 percent); V-8 engines over 350 CID (56.7 percent); limited slip rear axle (44.8 percent); four-wheel-drive (52.0 percent) interior trim package (11.5 percent); exterior trim package (5.7 percent); AM radio (13.8 percent); AM/FM stereo radio (2.7 percent); tinted glass (26.8 percent); air conditioning (16.9 percent); total output 563.

SCOUT II: Auto. transmission (58.2 percent); power disc brakes (100.0 percent); power steering (79.3 percent); V-8 engines 350 CID or less (82.1 percent); limited slip rear axle (39.2 percent); four-wheel-drive (88.9 percent); steel-belted radial tires (11.2 percent); wheel covers (64.5 percent); interior trim package (61.8 percent); exterior trim package (63.5 percent); AM radio (73.5 percent); AM/FM stereo radio (10.2 percent); tinted glass (38.5 percent); air conditioning (32.3 percent); total output 21,366.

Pricing

1975	5	4	3	2	1
Scout Series XLC — (4x2)					
Traveltop	980	1950	3250	4550	6500
Cab Top	960	1920	3200	4500	6400
Scout Series XLC — (4x4)					
Traveltop	1040	2070	3450	4850	6900
Cab Top	1010	2030	3350	4700	6700
Metro Series					
Step-Van	590	1170	1950	2700	3900
Travelall Series 150					
Sta. Wag. (4x2)	830	1650	2750	3850	5500
Sta. Wag. (4x4)	870	1750	2900	4100	5800
Travelall Series 200					
Sta. Wag. (4x2)	800	1600	2650	3700	5300
Sta. Wag. (4x4)	850	1700	2850	4000	5700
Series 150 Pickup — (4x2)					
Bonus Load Pickup (115 in. w.b.)	840	1680	2800	3900	5600
Bonus Load Pickup (132 in. w.b.)	830	1650	2750	3850	5500
Series 150 Pickup — (4x4)					
Bonus Load Pickup (115 in. w.b.)	870	1750	2900	4100	5800
Bonus Load Pickup (132 in. w.b.)	840	1680	2800	3900	5600
Series 200 Pickup — (4x2)					
Bonus Load Pickup (132 in. w.b.)	740	1470	2450	3350	4900
B.L. Travelette (149 in. w.b.)	700	1400	2350	3250	4700
B.L. Travelette (166 in. w.b.)	750	1500	2500	3500	5000
Series 200 Pickup — (4x4)					
Bonus Load Pickup	750	1500	2500	3500	5000

NOTES: Add 2 percent for Deluxe exterior trim.
Add 5 percent for Custom exterior trim.
Add 4 percent for optional V-8s.
Add 10 percent for Camper Special.

1976 International Scout Terra Pickup (JAG)

SCOUT — SERIES XLC — FOUR-CYLINDER: — International Harvester Company decided to concentrate on its heavy-duty truck line in 1976. As a result, all Step-vans, Travelall station wagons and regular pickups were dropped from production. The only light-duty models available were in the Scout line. Two new Scouts were introduced. They had a longer 118 inch w.b. The hatchback station wagon was called a "Traveler." A pickup truck with a 6-foot box and 11 cu. ft. of behind-the-seat storage was called the "Terra." Also available was the 100 in. w.b. Scout II with its familiar Traveltop "station wagon" configuration. All three Scout models had a restyled grille design. It was divided into three vertical segments, each of which was filled with five horizontal bars. They offered special side appliques. These included white panels, woodgrain with cork finish, a stylized "red feather" design and Rallye racing stripes extending along the sides and up onto the hood. Nine exterior colors now included Winter white, Terra Cotta, Fire orange, Dark brown metallic, Solar yellow, Pewter metallic, Grenoble green, Buckskin, and Glacier blue. Interiors included carpeting, bucket seats and vinyl panels in Ivy green, Wedgewood blue, Parchment, Tanbark and Custom Saddle. Among standard equipment features were power disc brakes, chrome dual mirrors, chrome front and rear bumpers and wheel covers, day/night mirror, increased capacity cooling and undercoating. Four-wheel-drive was available in two versions: a dash-operated single-speed transfer case and a floor-mounted two-speed transfer case. A diesel engine was a new model-option.

I.D. DATA: Serial number located on the left door pillar. The serial number consists of 13 symbols. The first six symbols identify the serial number. The seventh (digit) designates the manufacturing plant. The last six digits are sequential production numbers. Numbers are not available.

Model	Body Type	Price	Weight	Prod. Total
Scout II Series — (4-cyl./Gas) — (100 in. w.b.)				
XLC	Traveltop (4x2)	4793	3746	Note 1
XLC	Traveltop (4x4)	5751	3846	Note 1
Scout II Series — (Diesel) — (100 in. w.b.)				
XLC	Traveltop (4x2)	7381	3983	Note 1
XLC	Traveltop (4x4)	8394	4083	Note 1
Terra Series — (4-cyl./Gas) — (118 in. w.b.)				
XLC	Terra Pickup (4x2)	4612	3761	Note 2
XLC	Terra Pickup (4x4)	5637	3861	Note 2
Terra Series — (Diesel) — (118 in. w.b.)				
XLC	Terra Pickup (4x2)	7200	4026	Note 2
XLC	Terra Pickup (4x4)	8285	4126	Note 2
Traveler Series — (4-cyl./Gas) — (118 in. w.b.)				
XLC	Sta. Wag. (4x2)	5172	4101	Note 3
XLC	Sta. Wag. (4x4)	6122	4201	Note 3
Traveler Series — (Diesel) — (118 in. w.b.)				
XLC	Sta. Wag. (4x2)	7760	4101	Note 3
XLC	Sta. Wag. (4x4)	8770	4202	Note 3

1976 International Scout II (JAG)

NOTE 1: Model year production of Scout II models totaled 17,506 units.

NOTE 2: Model year production of Scout/Terra models totaled 6,496 units.

NOTE 3: Model year production of Scout/Traveler models totaled 7,635 units.

NOTE: A six-cylinder diesel engine was a new power plant option which was merchandised as a model-option.

ENGINE (Base): Inline. OHV. Slanted mounting. Four-cylinder. Cast iron block. Bore & stroke: 4⅛ in. x 3-21/32 in. Displacement: 196 cu. in. Compression ratio: 8.02:1. Brake horsepower: 86 at 3800 R.P.M. Net horsepower: 27.2. Max. Torque: 157 lbs. ft. at 2200 R.P.M. Hydraulic valve lifters. Carburetor: Holley one-barrel model 1904.

ENGINE (Diesel): Inline, OHV. Slant-mounted diesel. Six-cylinder. Cast iron block. Bore & stroke: 3.27 in. x 3.94 in. Displacement: 198 cu. in. Brake horsepower: 92.

NOTE: This engine was built by Nissan of Japan as the "6-33" engine. Diesel-engined IHC trucks were merchandised as a model-option with their own base prices.

ENGINE (Optional): Vee-block. OHV. Eight-cylinder. Cast iron block. Bore & stroke: 3⅜ in. x 3-7/32 in. Displacement: 304 cu. in. Compression ratio: 8.2:1. Brake horsepower: 140 at 3800 R.P.M. Net horsepower: 48.1. Max. Torque: 243 lbs. ft. at 2400 R.P.M. Hydraulic valve lifters. Carburetor: Holley two-barrel model 2210.

NOTE: This engine was merchandised as a separate option at the price of $166 over the base four-cylinder.

ENGINE (Optional): Vee-block. OHV. Eight-cylinder. Cast iron block. Bore & stroke: 3⅜ in. x 3-21/32 in. Displacement: 345 cu. in. Compression ratio: 8.05:1. Brake horsepower 168 at 3800 R.P.M. Max. Torque: 288 lbs. ft. at 2000 R.P.M. Hydraulic valve lifters. Carburetor: Holley four-barrel model 2300.

NOTE: This engine was merchandised as a separate option at a price of $200 over the base four cylinder.

1976 International Scout II (JAG)

CHASSIS (Scout II Series): Wheelbase: 100 in. Overall length: 166.2 in. Height: 65.7 in. Front tread: 58.5 in. Rear tread: 57.62 in. Tires: H78 x 15 LRB.

CHASSIS (Scout Terra Series): Wheelbase: 118 in. Overall length: 184.2 in. Height: 66 in. Front tread: 58.5 in. Rear tread: 57.62 in. Tires: H78 x 15 LRB.

CHASSIS (Scout Traveler Series): Wheelbase: 118 in. Overall length: 184.2 in. Height: 66 in. Front tread: 58.5 in. Rear tread: 57.62 in. Tires: H78 x 15 LRB.
  Other dimensions (all models): Overall width: 70 in. Tailgate opening width: 54.8 in. Tailgate opening height: 40 in. Width between wheel well housings: 42 in. Minimum ground clearance: 7.6 in. The turning diameter was 33 ft. 10 in. for the Scout II and 38 ft. 10 in. for other models.

TECHNICAL: Manual (synchromesh) transmission. Speeds: 3F/1R. Floor mounted gear shift lever. 11-inch angle link, 2000 lb. plate pressure clutch. Dana Model 44 rear axle. Overall ratio: 3.54:1 or 3.73:1. Power front disc/rear drum brakes. Steel disc wheels. Drivetrain options: Trac-Lok limited-slip differential. Heavy-duty clutch. Four-speed transmission. Automatic transmission.

564

1976 International Scout II (JAG)

TECHNICAL (4x4 models): Manual (synchromesh) transmission. Speeds: 3F/1R. Floor mounted gear shift lever. 11-inch angle link, 2000 lb. plate pressure clutch. Dana Model 44, 3500 lb. driving rear axle. Overall ratio: 3.54:1 or 3.73 to 1. Front power disc/rear drum brakes. Five-stud steel disc wheels with 6.00 JK rims. Drivetrain options: Twist-lok manual locking hubs. Automatic locking hubs. Trac-lok limited-slip differential. Heavy-duty clutch. Four-speed transmission. Close-ratio four-speed transmission. Automatic transmission.

OPTIONS: Four-speed transmission ($165). Automatic transmission, except diesel ($306); w/diesel ($141). Two-speed transfer case, 4x4, std. w/diesel ($67). Right-hand drive ($144). Power steering, w/4x2 ($172); w/4x4 ($189). Air conditioning/heater package ($497). Trailering package ($183). Rally package, w/4x2 ($631); w/4x4 ($648). Custom interior trim, w/Traveltop ($221); w/Terra ($198); w/Traveler ($261). Radial tire chrome wheel package ($366). Deluxe exterior trim package ($60). Deluxe interior trim package ($134). Calif. emissions, w/o airpump ($39); w/air pump ($80). AM radio ($83). AM/FM radio ($184). Cruise control ($80). Console, requires bucket seats ($48). Electric clock ($24). Tilt steering wheel, std. w/diesel ($73). Door edge guards ($8). Bumper step w/hitch ball ($37). Body side moldings ($31). Skid plate protector ($39). Automatic front locking hubs w/4x4 ($72). Dual mirrors ($48). Luggage rack, except Terra ($92). Chrome tie-down rails on Terra ($70). G1-amp alternator ($42). Trac-Lok axle ($82). Optional axle ratios ($17). 72-amp battery ($19). Heavy-duty shocks ($13). Heavy-duty front springs & shocks, Traveltop w/4x4 ($17); Terra w/4x4 ($19); Terra & Traveler w/4x2 ($45). Heavy-duty rear springs & shocks, Traveltop w/4x4 ($29). Heavy-duty frt. & rear springs & shocks, Traveler ($38). Modulated fan ($41). Tu Tone paint ($115). Tan vinyl bucket seats ($79); other colors ($101). Rear folding seat, except Terra ($160). Cargo area mat, except Terra ($32). Sliding rear quarter window, Traveltop ($51); Traveler ($66).

HISTORICAL: Introduced Fall 1975. Calendar year registrations (all IHC trucks): 100,657 (3.29 percent). Calendar year registrations by weight class: Under 6000 lbs. = none. 6001 to 1000 lbs. = 34,100. Calendar year production (all IHC trucks): 114,855. Calendar year retail sales (Scout): 30,555. Calendar year production (Scout II): 25,840. Calendar year production (Terra Pickups): 15,732. Innovations: New series of light trucks (Terra) and station wagons (Traveler) introduced. IH became the first American manufacturer to offer diesel power at an option on the Scout II, Traveler and Terra.

1976 International Scout Terra Pickup (JAG)

1976 International Scout Traveler (JAG)

NOTES: B. McCormick continued as IH President and Chief executive officer. J.P. Kaine became, president of the Truck Group. The company operated four U.S. plants in Springfield, Ohio; Fort Wayne, Ind., Indianapolis, Ind. and Shadyside, Ohio during 1976. It had 14,358 employees in these plants. Another 1,482 workers were employed at a fifth plant in Chatham, Ont., Canada. During calendar 1976, IH built 42,683 trucks in Springfield, 72,172 trucks in Ft. Wayne and 13,500 trucks in Canada.

OPTION INSTALLATION RATES: See 1974 for explanation.

TERRA: V-8, 350/Less (60.1 percent); 6-cyl. (5.6 percent**); transmission auto. (41.0 percent); 4-spd. (36.3 percent); brakes pwr. disc. (100.0 percent); power steering (75.9 percent); ltd. slip rear dif. (34.8 percent); 4-whl. drive (54.7 percent); radial tires (4.5 percent); trlr. tow equip. (2.5 percent); rear bumper (100.0 percent); wheels covers (95.7 percent); styled (4.3 percent); trim groups int. (47.0 percent); ext. (47.7 percent); bucket seats (9.9 percent); tint glass (100.0 percent); air cond. (15.9 percent); adj. str. col. (7.2 percent); radios AM (78.9 percent); AM/FM (7.3 percent).

** Standard engine.

SCOUT II: V-8, 350/Less engines (80.6 percent); 6-cyl. engines (1.5 percent**); transmission auto. (61.7 percent); 4-spd. (22.6 percent); brakes pwr. disc (100.0 percent); power steering (86.6 percent); ltd. slip rear dif. (31.8 percent); 4-whl. drive (93.3 percent); radial tires (11.5 percent); trlr. tow equip. (3.4 percent); rear bumper (100.0 percent); wheels covers (92.3 percent); styled (7.7 percent); int. trim groups (74.5 percent); ext. trim groups (66.6 percent); bucket seats (44.1 percent); tint glass (100.0 percent); air cond. (37.3 percent); adj. str. col. (20.1 percent); radios AM (59.5 percent); AM/FM (23.0 percent).

TRAVELER: V-8, 350/Less engines (88.3 percent); 6-cyl. engines (6.1 percent**); transmissions auto. (83.7 percent); 4-spd. (12.0 percent); brakes pwr. disc (100.0 percent); power steering (96.0 percent); ltd.-slip rear dif. (32.5 percent); 4-whl. drive (77.2 percent); radial tires (35.9 percent); trlr. tow equip. (25.8 percent); rear bumper (100.0 percent); wheels covers (84.1 percent); styled (15.9 percent); int. trim groups (90.0 percent); ext. trim groups (86.9 percent); bucket seats (48.2 percent); tint glass (100.0 percent); air cond. (65.9 percent); adj. str. col. (50.7 percent); radios AM (54.2 percent); AM/FM (38.8 percent).

Pricing

1976	5	4	3	2	1
Scout II					
Traveltop (4x2)	900	1800	3000	4200	6000
Traveltop (4x4)	930	1860	3100	4350	6200
Scout II Diesel					
Traveltop (4x2)	850	1700	2850	4000	5700
Traveltop (4x4)	890	1770	2950	4150	5900
Terra					
Pickup (4x2)	870	1750	2900	4100	5800
Pickup (4x4)	900	1800	3000	4200	6000
Terra Diesel					
Pickup (4x2)	820	1650	2750	3850	5500
Pickup (4x4)	850	1700	2850	4000	5700
Traveler					
Sta. Wagon (4x2)	930	1860	3100	4350	6200
Sta. Wag (4x4)	960	1920	3200	4500	6400
Traveler Diesel					
Sta. Wag. (4x2)	890	1770	2950	4150	5900
Sta. Wag. (4x4)	920	1850	3050	4300	6100

NOTES: Add 3 percent for V-8 engines.
Add 3 percent for four-speed transmssion.
Add 6 percent for Rally package.
Add 4 percent for custom trim.
Add 2 percent for deluxe trim.

1977 International Scout Traveler (JAG)

SCOUT — SERIES XLC — 4-CYLINDER GAS/6-CYLINDER DIESEL: — For 1977, the Scout's head lamp buckets were made a bit squarer. A new grille design featured two, thin rectangular "loops" stacked on top of each other with thin vertical blades behind them. The International name plate appeared on the left-hand side between the loops. A new SSII package was introduced and priced at $5,251. Standard equipment included all standard safety, anti-theft, convenience and emission control equipment; 196 cu. in. four-cylinder engine (except diesel models); three-speed manual synchronized floor shift; power front disc and rear drum brakes; H78 x 15 LRB blackwall tires; stainless steel wheels; undercoating; dual chrome door mounted mirrors; tinted glass; dual electric horns; vinyl interior; cigar lighter; manual locking hubs (4x4 models); steel cab w/fiberglass top (Terra) and full-length white top w/integral headliner (Traveler). New options for 1977 models included cruise control and tilt steering.

I.D. DATA: See 1976 section I.D. Data.

Model	Body Type	Price	Weight	Prod. Total
Scout II — (4-cyl.) — (100 in. w.b.)				
XLC	Traveltop (4x2)	4793	3746	Note 1
XLC	Traveltop (4x4)	5751	3846	Note 1
Scout II — Diesel — (100 in. w.b.)				
XLC	Traveltop (4x2)	7381	3983	Note 1
XLC	Traveltop (4x4)	8394	4083	Note 1
Terra — (4-cyl.) — (118 in. w.b.)				
XLC	Pickup (4x2)	4612	3761	Note 2
XLC	Pickup (4x4)	5637	3861	Note 2
Terra — Diesel — (118 in. w.b.)				
XLC	Pickup (4x2)	7200	4026	Note 2
XLC	Pickup (4x4)	8285	4126	Note 2
Traveler — (4-cyl.) — (118 in. w.b.)				
XLC	Sta. Wag. (4x2)	5172	4101	Note 3
XLC	Sta. Wag. (4x4)	6122	4201	Note 3
Traveler — Diesel — (118 in. w.b.)				
XLC	Sta. Wag. (4x2)	7760	4101	Note 3
XLC	Sta. Wag. (4x4)	8770	4201	Note 3

NOTE 1: Model year production of Scout II Models totaled 27,074 units.

NOTE 2: Model year production of Scout/Terra models totaled 2,688 units.

NOTE 3: Model year production of Scout/Traveler models totaled 9,620 units.

1977 IHC Scout II Safari Sport Utility (Dick Bova)

ENGINE: See 1976 engine data.

CHASSIS (Scout II Series): Wheelbase: 100 in. Length: 166.2 in. Height: 65.7 in. Front tread: 58.5 in. Rear tread: 57.62 in. Tires: H78 x 15 LRB.

CHASSIS (Scout Terra Series): Wheelbase: 118 in. Length: 184.2 in. Height: 66 in. Front tread: 58.5 in. Rear tread: 57.62 in. Tires: H78 x 15 LRB.

CHASSIS (Scout Traveler): Wheelbase: 118 in. Length: 184.2 in. Height: 66 in. Front tread: 58.2 in. Rear tread: 57.62 in. Tires: H78 x 15 LRB.

Other dimensions: Same as comparable 1976 models.

TECHNICAL: Same as comparable 1976 models.

OPTIONS: Four-speed transmission ($165). Automatic transmission, except diesel ($306); w/diesel ($141). Two-speed transfer case, 4x4 std. w/diesel ($67). Right-hand drive ($144). Power steering, w/4x2 ($172); w/4x4 ($189). Air conditioning/heater package ($497). Trailering package ($183). Rally package, w/4x2 ($631); w/4x4 ($648). Custom interior trim, w/Traveltop ($221); w/Terra ($198); w/Traveler ($261). Radial tire chrome wheel package ($366). Deluxe exterior trim package ($60). Deluxe interior trim package ($134). Calif. emissions, w/o air pump ($39); w/air pump ($80). AM radio ($83). AM/FM radio ($184). Cruise control ($80). Console, requires bucket seats ($48). Electric clock ($24). Tilt steering wheel, std. w/diesel ($73). Door edge guards ($8). Bumper step w/hitch ball ($37). Body side moldings ($31). Skid plate protector ($39). Automatic front locking hubs w/4x4 ($72). Dual mirrors ($48). Luggage rack, except Terra ($92). Chrome tie-down rails on Terra ($70). 61-amp alternator ($42). Trac-Lok axle ($82). Optional axle ratios ($17). 72-amp battery ($19). Heavy-duty shocks ($13). Heavy-duty front springs & shocks, Traveltop w/4x4 ($17); Terra w/4x4 ($19); Terra & Traveler w/4x2 ($45). Heavy-duty rear springs & shocks, Traveltop w4x4 ($29). Heavy-duty front & rear springs & shocks, Traveler ($38). Modulated fan ($41). Tu-tone paint ($115). Tan vinyl bucket seats ($79); other colors ($101). Rear folding seat, except Terra ($160). Cargo area mat, except Terra ($32). Sliding rear quarter window, Traveltop ($51); Traveler ($66).

1977 International Scout SSII Sport Utility (OCW)

HISTORICAL: Introduced Fall 1976. Calendar year registrations: (all IHC trucks): 107,564. Calendar year retail sales: (Scout II): 32,004. Calendar year production: (all IHC trucks): 110,894 (3.18 percent). Calendar year registrations by weight class: 6000 to 10,000 lbs. = 32,046. Model year production by model: (Terra) 2,688; (Scout II) 27,074 and (Traveler) 9,620: (Total): 39,382. Innovations: New grille. New Scout "SSII" model.

OPTION INSTALLATION RATES: The following data indicates the percentage of factory options installed on 1977 IHC trucks according to series. Percentage figures in brackets indicate installation rate. Series production for model year is given at the end of each data block.

TERRA: V-8 engine (64.2 percent); diesel (14.1 percent); auto transmission (45.6 percent); four-speed trans. (37.6 percent); front disc brakes (100 percent); power steering (82.3 percent); limited-slip (42 percent); four-wheel drive (77.8 percent); styled wheels (10.1 percent); std. wheel covers (89.9 percent); towing package (0.2 percent); rear bumper, std. (32.9 percent); rear bumper, step type (67.1 percent); custom interior trim (47.6 percent); custom exterior trim (46.6 percent); bucket seats (15.1 percent); air conditioning (17.7 percent); tilt steering (11.6 percent); speed control (5.8 percent); AM radio (56.2 percent); AM/FM radio (24.6 percent); radial tires (4.6 percent). Total output: 2,688.

SCOUT II: V-8 engine (87.5 percent); diesel engine (1.7 percent); auto trans. (68.7 percent); four-speed trans. (23.7 percent); front disc brakes (100 percent); power steering (94.3 percent); limited-slip (38.5 percent); four-wheel drive (96.2 percent); styled wheels (37.8 percent); std. wheel covers (56.8 percent); towing package (1.9 percent); rear bumper, std. (48.1 percent); rear bumper, step type (51.4 percent); custom interior trim (61.1 percent); custom exterior trim (58.9 percent); bucket seats (41.4 percent); air conditioning (31.1 percent); tilt steering (20.6 percent); speed control (19.3 percent); AM radio (50.3 percent); AM/FM radio (24.6 percent); radial tires (9.5 percent). Total output: 27,074.

TRAVELER: V-8 engine (93.3 percent); diesel engine (5.2 percent); auto trans (89.3 percent); four speed trans (9.2 percent); front disc brakes (100 percent); power steering (98.1 percent); limited-slip (30.2 percent); four-wheel drive (89.7 percent); styled wheels (30.4 percent); std. wheel cover (69.6 percent); towing package (23.5 percent); rear bumper, std. (71.9 percent); rear bumper, step type (28.1 percent); custom int. trim (94 percent); custom exterior trim (81.8 percent); bucket seats (65.5 percent); air conditioning (68 percent); tilt steering (56.9 percent); speed control (57.5 percent); AM radio (41.1 percent); AM/FM radio (46.6 percent); radial tires (38.1 percent). Total output: 9,620.

Pricing

	5	4	3	2	1
1977					
Scout II					
Traveltop (4x2)	890	1770	2950	4150	5900
Traveltop (4x4)	920	1850	3050	4300	6100
Scout II Diesel					
Traveltop (4x2)	840	1680	2800	3900	5600
Traveltop (4x4)	870	1750	2900	4100	5800
Terra					
Pickup (4x2)	850	1700	2850	4000	5700
Pickup (4x4)	890	1770	2950	4150	5900
Terra Diesel					
Pickup (4x2)	810	1620	2700	3800	5400
Pickup (4x4)	840	1680	2800	3900	5600
Traveler					
Sta. Wag. (4x2)	920	1850	3050	4300	6100
Sta. Wag. (4x4)	950	1900	3150	4400	6300
Traveler Diesel					
Sta. Wag. (4x2)	870	1750	2900	4100	5800
Sta. Wag. (4x4)	900	1800	3000	4200	6000

NOTES: Add 3 percent for V-8 engine.
Add 3 percent for four-speed transmission.
Add 6 percent for Rally package.
Add 8 percent for SSII.
Add 2 percent for deluxe trim.
Add 4 percent for custom trim.

1978 IHC

1978 International Scout Rallye (JAG)

SCOUT — SERIES XLC — (ALL ENGINES): — The Scouts from IHC had a slightly revised grille design for 1978. Basically, the vertical blades were removed from the grille ensemble and the rectangular-shaped bright metal surround was made thicker. Inside the surround were two thin, horizontal "loops" of chrome stacked one on top of the other. The single, round head lamps were housed in large squares on either side of the grille and these were also trimmed with bright metal moldings. The SSII model had its own distinct grille with seven vertical members. Standard equipment included all safety, anti-theft and emissions items required to meet government standards; 196 cu. in. four-cylinder engine; three-speed manual synchronized floor shift; manual steering; power-front disc and rear drum brakes; H78 x 15 LRB blackwall tires; stainless steel wheels; undercoating; dual chrome door mounted mirrors; tinted glass; dual electric horns; vinyl interior; cigar lighter; manual locking hubs (4x4 models); steel cab w/fiber glass top (Terra models) and full-length white top w/integral headliner (Traveler models). The diesel engine was strictly an extra-cost option this year. It had a $2,581 price tag.

I.D. DATA: Serial number located on left door pillar post. The serial number consisted of 13 symbols. The first six symbols identified the serial number. The seventh digit designated the manufacturing plant. The last six digits were sequential production numbers. Numbers are not available.

Model	Body Type	Price	Weight	Prod. Total
Scout Series — V-8 — (4x4)				
XLC	Scout II Traveltop	6329	3846	—
XLC	Scout Terra Pickup	6284	3861	—
XLC	Scout SSII	5563	3455	—
XLC	Traveler Sta. Wag.	6975	4200	—

NOTE: Prices and weights given above are for 4x4 models with the 304 cu. in. V-8 engine. The cost of the 4x4 running gear was around $1,000 and the 304 cu. in. V-8 was about $170 extra.

ENGINE: See 1977 section, engine specifications.

CHASSIS (Scout II Series): Wheelbase: 100 in. Length: 166.2 in. Height: 65.7 in. Front tread: 58.5 in. Rear tread: 57.62 in. Tires: H78 x 15 LRB.

CHASSIS (Scout SSII Series): Wheelbase: 100 in. Length: 166.2 in. Front tread: 58.5 in. Rear tread: 57.62 in. Tires: H78 x 15 LRB.

CHASSIS (Terra/Traveler): Wheelbase: 118 in. Length: 184.2 in. Height: 66.0 in. Front tread: 58.5 in. Rear tread: 57.62 in. Tires: H78 x 15 LRB.

TECHNICAL: Manual (synchromesh) transmission. Speeds: 3F/1R. Floor-mounted gearshift lever. Clutch: 11 in. angle link, 2000 lb. plate pressure. Dana model 44 3500 lb. capacity rear driving axle. Overall ratio: 3.73:1. Front power disc/rear drum brakes. Five-stud disc wheels. Four-speed manual transmission (wide-ratio). Four-speed manual transmission (close-ratio). Three-speed automatic tranmission. Transmission oil cooler. Four-wheel-drive (4x4).

OPTIONS: Optional equipment was similar to 1977 models at similar prices. The 6-33 (Nissan-built) diesel was $2,581 extra. A new Rallyee trim package was $687 extra. The 345 cu. in. V-8 cost $123 over the price of a 304 cu. in. V-8.

HISTORICAL: Introduced Fall 1977. Calendar year registrations by GVW: 6000 to 10,000 pounds = 36,065. Calendar year sales: 35,794 (Scouts). Calendar year production: (all IHC): 123,123 (3.31 percent). Model year production: (Scout II) 26,369 units; (Terra pickup) 2,966 units; (Traveler) 9,856 units; (total) 39,191 units.
New grille design. Diesel engine now merchandised as a separate option instead of a model option.
Brook McCormick was company president. J. Patrick Kaine was president of the truck group. IHC's truck production in calendar 1978 rose to 122,282 units from 1977's 110,894 but was still one of the company's weaker years. Output of the light-duty Scouts saw an increase, however.

OPTION INSTALLATION RATES: See 1974 for explanation.

TERRA: Engines: V-8 under 350 (72.6 percent); diesel (7.4 percent); L-4 (20.0 percent); auto. Trans.: (40.9 percent); 4-spd. (46.1 percent); Disc brakes.: P.Frt. (100.0 percent); power steering (78.5 percent); radial tires (3.3 percent); 4-whl. drive (88.7 percent); ltd. slip rear dif. (38.7 percent); wheels styled (15.8 percent); wheel covers std. (84.2 percent); bumpers reg. (34.0 percent), step (66.0 percent); trlr.tow equip. (2.2 percent); trim groups int. (54.5 percent), ext. (61.8 percent); 2-tone paint (NA); ext. stripes (NA); bucket seats (21.5 percent); tinted glass (100.0 percent); air cond. (18.1 percent); spd. reg. (7.5 percent); adj. str. col. (13.3 percent); audio equipment AM (50.9 percent), AM/FM (11.8 percent); sun roof (1.4 percent). Total output: 2,966.

SCOUT II: Engines: V-8 under 350 (87.7 percent); diesel (2.0 percent); L-4 (10.3 percent); Trans.: auto. (73.0 percent); 4-spd. (20.2 percent); Disc brakes: P.Frt. (100.0 percent); power steering (94.3 percent); radial tires (7.6 percent); 4-whl. drive (97.4 percent); ltd. slip rear dif. (34.8 percent); wheels styled (21.6 percent); wheel covers std. (78.4 percent); bumpers reg. (47.3 percent), step (52.7 percent); trlr.tow equip. (2.7 percent); trim groups int. (76.8 percent), ext. (80.3 percent); 2-tone paint (NA); ext. stripes (NA); bucket seats (63.4 percent); tinted glass (100.0 percent); air cond. (40.3 percent); spd. reg. (26.5 percent); adj. str. col. (31.3 percent); audio equipment AM (44.4 percent), AM/FM (24.9 percent); sun roof (0.6 percent). Total output: 26,369.

TRAVELER: Engines: V-8 under 350 (90.8 percent); diesel (7.6 percent); L-4 (1.6 percent); Trans.: auto. (88.3 percent); 4-spd. (10.6 percent); Disc brakes: P.Frt. (100.0 percent); power steering (93.9 percent); radial tires (52.9 percent); 4-whl. drive (96.4 percent); ltd. slip rear dif. (28.6 percent); wheels styled (22.8 percent); wheel covers std. (77.2 percent); bumpers reg. (75.5 percent), step (24.5 percent); trlr.tow equip. (30.3 percent); trim groups int. (91.3 percent), ext. (91.7 percent); 2-tone paint (NA); ext. stripes (NA); bucket seats (70.9 percent); tinted glass (100.0 percent); air cond. (66.4 percent); spd. reg. (55.0 percent); adj. str. col. (54.2 percent); audio equipment AM (33.7 percent), AM/FM (41.8 percent); sun roof (3.6 percent). Total output: 9,856.

Pricing

1978	5	4	3	2	1
Scout Series (4x2)					
Scout II	850	1700	2850	4000	5700
SSII	900	1770	2950	4150	5900
Terra Pickup	840	1680	2800	3900	5600
Traveler Sta. Wag.	900	1800	3000	4200	6000

NOTES: Add 3 percent for V-8 engine.
Deduct 4 percent for diesel engine.
Add 6 percent for Rallyee package.
Add 4 percent for Custom trim package.
Add 2 percent for 4x4 running gear.

1979 International Scout Terra Suntanner Pickup (OCW)

SCOUT — SERIES XLC — (ALL ENGINES): — The 1979 Scouts had no significant changes from the 1978 models, although various new decal and striping packages were available. Standard equipment was the same as last season.

I.D. DATA: See 1978 section, I.D. data.

Model	Body Type	Price	Weight	Prod. Total
Scout Series — V-8 — (4x4)				
XLC	Scout II Traveltop	7212	3846	—
XLC	Scout Terra Pickup	7263	3861	—
XLC	Scout SSII	6406	3455	—
XLC	Traveler Sta. Wag.	7657	4200	—

NOTE: Prices and weights given above are for 4x4 models with the 304 cu. in. V-8 engine. The cost of the 4x4 running gear was around $1,000 and the 304 cu. in. V-8 was about $170 extra.

1979 International Scout II Rallye (OCW)

ENGINE: See 1977 section, engine specifications.

CHASSIS: See 1978 section, chassis specifications.

TECHNICAL: See 1978 section, technical specifications.

OPTIONS: See 1977 and 1978 section options data. The Rallye package was $732 this year.

HISTORICAL: Introduced Fall 1978. Calendar year registrations by GVW Class: 6000 to 10,000 pounds = 23,464. Calendar year sales: 24,567 (Scouts). Calendar year production (all IHC trucks): 115,453 (3.78 percent). Model year production: (Scout II) 35,286 units; (Terra pickup) 2,437 units; (Traveler) 6,620 units; (total) 44,343 units.
Over 99 percent of all 1979 Scouts had four-wheel-drive (4x4) running gear.

This was the last year for Scout 4x2 models. Company retained its leadership in heavy truck market and took number one spot in medium-duty field away from Ford. A lengthy strike began on Nov. 1 1979 and continued into calendar 1980. It kept production five percent lower than last season. Scout sales also dropped — by nearly one-third for the calendar year. This was attributed to a downturn in the once booming 4x4 truck market.

1979 International Scout Terra Pickup (OCW)

1979 International Scout II Rallye (JAG)

OPTION INSTALLATION RATES: The following data indicates the percentage of factory options installed on 1979 IHC trucks according to series. Percentage figures in brackets indicate installation rate. Model year totals for series production are given at the end of each data block.

TERRA: Engine: V-8 301-349 (81.3 percent); 4-cyl. engines (13.5 percent); diesel engines (5.2 percent); transmissions: auto. (54.9 percent), 4-spd. (40.8 percent); 4x4 drive (100.0 percent); p. frt. disc brakes (100.0 percent); power steering (84.4 percent); steel styled wheels (37.1 percent); wheel covers (62.9 percent); steel radial tires (7.1 percent); trlr. tow equip. (3.3 percent); trim groups int. (62.3 percent), ext. (64.5 percent); bucket seats (30.8 percent); tinted glass (100.0 percent); air cond. (31.3 percent); spd. reg. (12.2 percent); adj. str. col. (20.1 percent); audio equipment AM (41.3 percent), AM/FM (6.8 percent), stereo (8.1 percent), rad./tape (5.4 percent); sun roof (2.6 percent); rear bumper conv. (40.9 percent), step (59.1 percent). Total output: 2,437.

1979 International Scout II Rallye (IHC)

1979 International Scout SSII Sport Utility (OCW)

SCOUT II: Engine: V-8 301-349 (92.1 percent); 4-cyl. engines (6.7 percent); diesel engines (1.2 percent); transmissions auto. (75.3 percent), 4-spd. (19.3 percent); 4x4 drive (99.0 percent); p. frt. disc brakes (100.0 percent); power steering (95.3 percent); steel styled wheels (29.9 percent); wheel covers (70.1 percent); steel radial tires (15.3 percent); trlr. tow equip. (2.7 percent); trim groups int. (79.8 percent), ext. (84.1 percent); bucket seats (65.3 percent); tinted glass (100.0 percent); air. cond. (43.6 percent); spd. reg. (29.8 percent); adj. str. col. (35.1 percent); audio equipment AM (34.7 percent), AM/FM (13.0 percent), stereo (13.0 percent), rad./tape (9.2 percent); sun roof (0.6 percent); rear bumper conv. (52.3 percent), step (47.7 percent). Total output: 35,286.

1979 International Scout Traveler Rallye (OCW)

1979 International Scout II Traveler (OCW)

TRAVELER: Engine: 4-cyl. engines (0.2 percent); diesel engines (3.1 percent); transmissions auto. (89.7 percent), 4-spd. (9.7 percent); 4x4 drive (99.0 percent); p. frt. disc brakes (100.0 percent); power steering (87.3 percent); steel styled wheels (34.3 percent); wheel covers (65.7 percent); steel radial tires (32.9 percent); trlr. tow equip. (27.0 percent); trim groups int. (90.3 percent), ext. (95.7 percent); tinted glass (100.0 percent); air. cond. (66.9 percent); spd. reg. (57.6 percent); adj. str. col. (61.4 percent); bucket seats (72.2 percent); AM/FM (14.8 percent), stereo (14.9 percent), rad./tape (19.6 percent); sun roof (3.8 percent); rear bumper conv. (73.5 percent), step (26.5 percent). Total output: 6,620.

1979 International Scout Terra 4x4 Pickup (OCW)

Pricing

1979 Scout Series (4x2)	5	4	3	2	1
Scout II	840	1680	2800	3900	5600
SS II	870	1750	2900	4100	5800
Terra Pickup	830	1650	2750	3850	5500
Traveler Sta. Wag.	890	1770	2950	4150	5900

NOTES: Add 3 percent for V-8 engine.
Deduct 4 percent for 6-cyl. diesel.
Add 6 percent for Rallyee Package.
Add 4 percent for Custom trim package
Add 2 percent for 4x4 running gear.

1980 IHC

1980 International Scout II (JAG)

SCOUT XLC SERIES — (ALL ENGINES): — A new optional turbocharged diesel engine, extensive new corrosion protection, and a redesigned grille headlined the features of the 1980 International Harvester Scout line of four-wheel-drive sports/utility vehicles. 1980 International Scout models included the Scout II, a 100 in. w.b. vehicle with a full steel top; the Scout Traveler, a 118 in. w.b. hatchback wagon; and the Scout Terra, a 6-foot bed pickup on a 118 in. w.b. Part-time four-wheel-drive was standard on all 1980 Scouts.

International Scout gasoline engine choices included a 196 cu. in. four-cylinder and 304 and 345 cu. in. V8s. Corrosion protection was significantly increased on all 1980 Scout models through the use of zinc-rich primers, zincrometal, galvanized steel, and hot wax applications. **New Appearance.** The front end of the 1980 Scout vehicles had a new look with a black bumper and a restyled black grille with bright trim which incorporated rectangular headlights. A bright grille and chrome bumper was optional. Distinctive new side appliques were available on the Scout models, including ''Spear'', ''See-Thru Flare'', ''Rallye'' stripe patterns and, for Traveler models, Woodgrain trim. Six new exterior colors were also offered: Black Canyon Black; Copper; Dark Brown; Saffron Yellow; Green Metallic; Concord Blue.

Other Scout improvements for 1980 included a redesigned air conditioning unit with improved cooling and quieter operation, power steering as standard on all models, a new 15-inch styled steering wheel, a satin finish dashboard with new graphic identification for gauges, and new optional wheels with turbine-spoke styling.

1980 International Scout II (JAG)

NEW SCOUT FEATURES FOR 1980 — (Drivetrain): — New turbocharged diesel engine option. Four-wheel-drive now standard on all Scout models. Transfer case had new 2.62 low range ratio. Automatic transmission was standard on Traveler models. New axle ratios, 2.72 and 3.31 were offered. Optional air conditioning unit was redesigned for improved cooling, quieter operation, and increased passenger leg room. A 63-amp alternator replaced the previously-available 61-amp alternator. Power steering was standard (except on right-hand drive models). **(Appearance and Convenience):** Grille was redesigned and featured new rectangular headlights. A styled 15-inch diameter steering wheel replaced the previously-standard 17-inch wheel. Side appliques were offered in new designs — Rallye, Spear, and See-Thru Flare, and Woodgrain trim on Traveler models. Standard manual locking hubs were redesigned with larger finger openings and include a Scout logo. New ''Scout'' identification logos were added to the tailgate and rear side panels. Black became the standard color for the grille, bumpers, door glass and vent glass frames, and windshield wiper arms. A new 7 in. turbine spoke design wheel was available with radial tires. A satin finish dashboard included new grahic identification on gauges. Tartan Blue was a new interior color replacing Wedgewood Blue. Six new exterior colors were offered: Black Canyon Black; Copper; Dark Brown; Saffron Yellow; Green Metallic; Concord Blue. **(Design):** Extensive new corrosion protection measures were taken on all models. A new 85 mph/140 kph speedometer head replaced the previous 100 mph/160 kph head.

1980 International Scout II (JAG)

1980 International Scout Terra Pickup (OCW)

1980 SCOUT II, TRAVELER AND TERRA — STANDARD EQUIPMENT —
(Axle, Front): — Dana Model 44, 3,200 lb. capacity driving. Warn manual locking hubs. (Axle, Rear): Dana Model 44, 3,500 lb. capacity, driving. (Brakes, Service): Dual operation hydraulic power brakes, with warning light. Front disc — 11.75 in. rotor with 3.1 in. piston, self adjusting. Total swept area was 226 square inches. Rear drum 11-1/32 x 2¼ DSSA, self adjusting. Total lining area was 101.8 square inches. (Body): All steel welded construction. Steel top with integral headliner and side trim panels (Scout II). Full length white fiberglass top with integral headliner (Traveler). White fiberglass top with integral headliner (Terra). Corrosion protection. Left and right air intake vents. Fresh air heater and defroster. Inside mounted spare tire carrier (bed-mounted on Terra). Windshield-mounted rear view mirror. Two-speed electric windshield wipers and washer. Suspended brake, clutch and accelerator pedals. Padded instrument panel. Padded sun visors. Front floor mat. ⅓-⅔ black vinyl front seat with seat belts. Seat belt retractors. Direct-reading gauges for ammeter, oil, water and fuel. Push-button door locks. Inside hood release. Black steel-framed roll-down windows and vent wings. Push-button locking vent wings. Push-button tailgate with locking latch on lift gate. Push-button tailgate (Terra). Locking, energy-absorbing steering column. Ash tray in instrument panel. Chrome door-mounted mirror (dual chrome mirrors on Traveler models). Two coat hooks (one coat hook on Terra models). Arm rests for driver and passenger doors. (Clutch): 11 inch angle link, 2000 lb. plate pressure. (Cooling System): Radiator frontal area: 477 square inches. Permanent type — 20°F anti-freeze. (Electrical System): 12-volt, 37-amp 10 SI alternator. 12-volt, 40 amp alternator (diesel engines). 300 CCA Battery. 625 CCA battery (diesel engines). Dual stop and taillights. Glow plug indicator (diesel engines). Electric horn. Courtesy lights-dash mounted. "Front axle engaged" indicator light. Parking brake warning light. Dome light with driver and passenger door switches (Two dome lights on Traveler). Cargo light (Terra only). Directional signals. Back-up lights. Traffic hazard flashers. Front and rear side marker lights. (Engine): Scout II and Terra — International 4-196 four-cylinder gasoline engine. Traveler — International V-304 eight-cylinder gasoline engine. Diesels — Nissan 6-33T six-cylinder turbocharged diesel engine. (Transmission): Three-speed synchromesh (gasoline models, N/A Traveler). Four-speed synchromesh (diesel models). Three-speed automatic (Traveler).

Model	Body Type	Price	Weight	Prod. Total
Scout Series — V-8 — (4x4)				
XLC	Scout II Traveltop	8116	3840	—
XLC	Scout Terra Pickup	8017	3864	—
XLC	Traveler Sta. Wag.	8630	4201	—

NOTE: All 1980 Scouts were 4x4 models. The prices and weights above include the 304 cu. in. V-8, which was standard in Travelers and optional in other models.

ENGINE: Scout gasoline engines are manufactured by the International Harvester Components Group in Indianapolis, Ind. The Scout diesel engine is manufactured by the Nissan Motor Corp. in Japan.

ENGINE (4-196): Displacement: 196 cu. in. Bore & stroke: 4⅛ in. x 3-21/32 in. Compression ratio: 8.02 to 1. Net horsepower: 76.5 at 3600 R.P.M. Max. Torque: 153.3 lb. ft. at 2000 R.P.M. Unleaded fuel.

ENGINE (V-304A): Displacement: 304 cu. in. Bore & stroke: 3⅞ in. x 3-7/32 in. Compression ratio: 8.19 to 1. Net horsepower: 122.3 at 3400 R.P.M. Max. Torque: 226.3 lb. ft. at 2000 R.P.M. Unleaded fuel.

ENGINE (V-345A): Displacement: 345 cu. in. Bore & stroke: 3⅞ in. x 3-21/32 in. Compression ratio: 8.05 to 1. Net horsepower: 148 at 3600 R.P.M. Max. Torque: 265 lb. ft. at 2000 R.P.M. Unleaded fuel.

ENGINE (6-33T Diesel): Displacement: 198 cu. in. Bore & stroke: 3.27 in. x 3.94 in. Compression ratio: 22 to 1. Net horsepower: 101 at 3800 R.P.M. Max. Torque: 175 lb. ft. at 2200 R.P.M. Diesel fuel.

CHASSIS (Scout II): Wheelbase: 100 in. Length: 166.2 in. Width: 70 in. Height: 65.7 in. Tailgate opening width: 54.8 in. Tailgate opening height: 40 in. Width between rear wheel housings: 42 in. Front tread: 58.5 in. Rear tread: 57.62 in. Minimum ground clearance: 7.6 in. Turning diameter: (to clear tire) 33 ft. 10 in.; (to clear bumper) 36 ft. 4 in. Cargo capacity: 82 cu. ft. Weight (with standard equipment): (Gasoline) front 2074; rear 1766; total 3840 lbs. (Diesel) front 2286; rear 1797; total 4083 lbs.

CHASSIS (Terra): Wheelbase: 118 in. Length: 184.2 in. Width: 70 in. Height: 66 in. Tailgate opening width: 54.8 in. Width between wheel wells 42 in. Bed length: 72 in. Front tread: 58.5 in. Rear tread: 57.62 in. Minimum ground clearance: 7.6 in. Turning diameter: (to clear tire) 38 ft. 10 in.; (to clear bumper) 40 ft. 5 in. Weight (with standard equipment): (Gasoline) front 2241; rear 1623; total 3864 lbs. (Diesel) front 2470; rear 1647; total 4117 lbs.

CHASSIS (Scout Traveler): Wheelbase: 118 in. Length: 184.2 in. Width: 70 in. Height: 66 in. Tailgate opening width: 54.8 in. Tailgate opening height: 40 in. Width between wheel wells 42 in. Front tread: 58.5 in. Rear tread: 57.62 in. Minimum ground clearance: 7.6 in. Turning diameter: (to clear tire) 38 ft. 10 in.; (to clear bumper) 40 ft. 5 in. Weight (with standard equipment): (Gasoline) front 2437; rear 1764; total 4201 lbs. (Diesel) front 2437; rear 1765; total 4202 lbs.

TECHNICAL:

1980 SCOUT DRIVETRAIN COMBINATIONS

Engine	Transmission	Scout II, Terra Std.	Scout II, Terra Opt.	Traveler Std.	Traveler Opt.
4-196	3-spd. manual (standard)	3.73	none	N/A	
	Wide ratio 4-spd. manual	3.73	*3.54	N/A	
	Close ratio 4-spd. manual	*3.54	3.73	N/A	
6-33T Diesel	Close ratio 4-spd. manual (std.)	3.73	*3.54	3.75	*3.54
	Wide ratio 4-spd. manual	3.73	*3.54	3.73	*3.54
V-304	3-spd. manual (std.)	3.31	3.54	N/A	
	Wide ratio 4-spd. manual	3.31	3.54	N/A	
	Close ratio 4-spd. manual	3.31	3.54	3.31	3.54
	3-spd. automatic	**2.72	3.31	**2.72	3.31
			3.54		3.54
V-345	3-spd. manual (std.)	3.31	3.54	N/A	
	Wide ratio 4-spd. manual	3.31	3.54	N/A	
	Close ratio 4-spd. manual	**2.72	3.54	**2.72	3.54
			***3.73		***3.73
	3-spd. automatic	**2.72	3.31	**2.72	3.31
			3.54		3.54
			***3.73		***3.73

NOTE: All axle ratios available with (rear) Trac-Lok

N/A = Not available

* = 3.54 ratio on 4-196 or 6-33T diesel units is not available with 10-15 LT tires
** = 2.72 ratio on V-304 or V-345 is not available with 10-15 LT tires or tow package.
*** = 3.73 ratio on V-345 requires tow package.

ENGINE RPM AT 55 MPH

Ratio/Tires	H78 x 15	P225/75 R15	10 x 15 LT
2.72	1813	1860	1698
3.31	2197	2263	2066
3.54	2349	2421	2210
3.73	2486	2551	2328

OPTIONAL EQUIPMENT: (Axle, Front): Twist-Lok manual locking hubs. Automatic locking hubs. **(Axle, Rear):** Trac-Lok limited-slip differential. **(Body):** Air conditioning (includes 63 amp alternator and 390 CCA battery on gasoline engines; N/A on 4-196 engine). Bright finish exterior (see "Package Contents"). Cargo area mat (included with rear seat and Deluxe and Custom interiors; N/A on Terra). Chrome tie-down rails (Terra only). Console (bucket seats only). Custom Interior trim (see "Package Contents"). Day/night mirror (included with Custom interior). Deluxe Exterior trim (see "Package Contents"). Deluxe Interior trim (see "Package Contents"). Door edge guards. Dual 7-in. x 10-in. low-profile, mirrors with 4-in. extensions. Folding rear seat (includes cargo area mat; N/A on Terra). Front bucket seats. Luggage rack (N/A on Terra). Sliding rear quarter windows (N/A on Terra). Spare tire lock. Dual chrome door-mounted mirrors. Tinted glass in all windows. Full bright-finish wheel covers. **(Clutch):** Heavy-duty 11-in. angle link, 2,200-lb. plate pressure (required with V-345). **(Electrical):** 63 amp (10 SI) alternator (included with air conditioning and Trailer Towing package). 12 volt 390 CCA battery (included with air conditioning and Trailer Towing package; N/A on diesels). 12 volt 500 CCA maintenance-free battery (N/A on diesels). AM Radio with single speaker. AM-FM radio with single speaker. AM-FM Stereo radio with three speakers. AM-FM Stereo with 8-track tape player, with three speakers. Electric clock. Six-way trailer wiring (included in Trailer Towing package). Cigar lighter. Dual electric horns. **(Engines):** V-304 gasoline engine, two-barrel carburetor, electronic ignition (standard on Traveler). V-345 gasoline engine, four-barrel carburetor, electronic ignition. Automatic cruise control (V-8 engines, automatic transmissions only). California exhaust emission and evaporative system certification (required for Calif. 4-196, V-304 and V-345 gasoline engines and 6-33T diesel engines). Modulated fan (N/A on diesels). **(Finish):** Midnight brown top (Traveler and Terra). "Spear" applique — Green/Blue or Orange/Orange. "Rallye" applique (N/A Scout II) — White / Yellow / Orange or Black / Yellow / Orange. "See Thru Flare" applique (N/A Traveler) — Orange / White or Orange / Black. "Wood Grain" applique (Traveler only). "Gold Rallye" applique (Scout II only). "Silver Rallye" applique (Scout II only). **(Frame):** Heavy-duty rear step bumper. **(Fuel Tank):** Skid plate protector (N/A Traveler). **(Steering):** Sport steering wheel. Tilt steering wheel (standard on diesels). Right-hand drive. **(Suspension):** Heavy-duty front and rear springs with heavy-duty (1-3/16 in. bore) front and rear shock absorbers (N/A Terra). Heavy-duty front and rear shock absorbers (1-2/16 in. bore) (N/A Terra). Heavy-duty front springs with heavy-duty (1-3/16 in. bore) front and rear shock absorbers (Terra only). **(Trailer Towing):** Trailer towing package — includes 63-amp alternator, 390 CCA battery, Class III equalizer hitch, six-way trailer wiring (less connector). Requires V-8 engines. **(Transmissions):** Three-speed automatic (V-8 engines only). Ratios: 1st — 2.45; 2nd — 1.45; 3rd — 1.00; Reverse — 2.20. Wide-ratio four-speed manual. Ratios:

1st — 6.32; 2nd — 3.09; 3rd — 1.68; 4th — 1.00; Reverse — 6.96. Close-ratio four-speed manual. Ratios: 1st — 4.02; 2nd — 2.41; 3rd — 1.41; 4th — 1.00; Reverse — 4.42. Transmission auxiliary oil cooler (automatic transmission only). **(Wheels and Tires):** H78-15, LRB, white sidewall, 6.00 rim, regular tread. H78-15, LRB, 6.00 rim, mud and snow tread. H78-15, LRB, white sidewall, 6.00 rim, mud and snow tread. P225/75 R 15, Goodyear Tiempo radial, white sidewall, 6.00 rim, all-season tread. P225/75 R 15, Goodyear Tiempo radial, white sidewall, 7.00 styled rim, all-season tread. 10-15, LRB, outlined white letters, 8.00 JJ rim with white spoke wheels, on-off highway tread.

OPTION PACKAGE CONTENTS: (Bright Finish Exterior): Silver color grille with bright trim. Chrome front and rear bumpers. Bright vent and side glass frames. Bright windshield moulding. Tinted glass in all windows. **(Deluxe Exterior):** Silver color grille with bright trim. Chrome front and rear bumpers. Bright vent and side glass frames. Bright windshield moulding. Bright/black side trim molding. Tinted glass in all windows. **(Deluxe Interior):** Color-Keyed: Inner door trim panels. Vinyl cargo mat (N/A on Terra). Vinyl floor mats. Vinyl spare tire cover (N/A on Terra or with 10-15 tires). Arm rests. Kick panels. Choice of: Tartan Blue nylon seats with vinyl trim. Russet nylon seats with vinyl trim. Sierra Tan all vinyl seats with pillow effect. Black all vinyl seats with pillow effect. Bright satin finish trim on the instrument panel and transmission shift tower. Cigar lighter. Dual electric horns. **(Custom Interior):** Color-Keyed: Day/night mirror. Inner door trim panels with carpet and map pocket. Vinyl cargo mat (N/A Terra). Vinyl spare tire cover (N/A on Terra or with 10-15 tires). Arm rests. Carpeting on floor in passenger areas. Carpeting on rear inner quarter panels (N/A on Terra). Kick panels. Choice of: Tartan Blue nylon seats with vinyl trim. Russet nylon seats with vinyl trim. Sierra Tan all vinyl seats with pillow effect. Black all vinyl seats with pillow effect. Bright satin finish trim on the instrument panel and transmission shift tower. Cigar lighter. Dual electric horns. **(Styled Wheel Radial Tire Package):** Five 15-in. 7.00 JJ turbine-spoke styled wheels. Five P225/75 R 15 Goodyear Tiempo radial tires. Chrome lug nuts. Black rear axle end plates. **(Off-Road Tire Package):** Five 15-in 8.00 JJ white spoke wheels. Five 10-15 LRB outlined white letter tires, on-off highway tread. Chrome lug nuts. **(Trailer Towing):** N/A 4-196, diesel, 3-speed manual transmission, or 2.72 axle ratio). 63-amp alternator. 390 CCA Battery. Equalizer hitch (Class III). Six-way trailer wiring (less connector).

HISTORICAL: Introduced Fall 1979. Calendar year registrations by GVW Class: 6000-10,000 lbs. = 17,724. Calendar year sales: 18,805 (Scouts). Calendar year production: (all IHC trucks): 67,857 (4.15 percent). Calendar year production: (Scout only): 30,059.

NOTE: Industry reference sources do not record calendar year production totals as IHC refused to provide such figures.

New turbo-charged diesel engine. All Scouts were 4x4 models in 1980. Power steering is standard equipment on regular Scouts. Improved rust protection on all models. Technical refinements to rear axle, transfer case, electrical system and air conditioner.

Final year for light-duty IHC trucks. After 1980, the company concentrated on heavy-duty truck market. There had been plans to bring out a new line of light-duty Scout models for 1982 after IHC's exemption from certain Federal Standards expired at the end of the 1981 model year. Following failure of negotiations to sell both the Scout business and the Ft. Wayne, Ind. factory (where Scouts were built), IHC ended production of the line on Oct. 31, 1980. In mid-1986, International Harvester company's Truck Group adopted the new name Navistar International.

Pricing

1980 Scout Series (4x4)	5	4	3	2	1
Scout II	850	1700	2850	4000	5700
Terra Pickup	840	1680	2800	3900	5600
Traveler Sta. Wag.	900	1800	3000	4200	6000

NOTES: Add 3 percent for V-8 engines.
Add 5 percent for Turbo-Charged diesel engine.
Add 4 percent for Custom Trim package.
Add 6 percent for Rallye Trim.

(Continued from page 506)

1954 International Pickup (OCW)

For 1960, the "B" series moved the quad headlamps sideways, for a lower appearance. Independent front suspension and an hydraulic clutch were technical advances. V-8s became standard for awhile. Before long, the Metro took on a boxier look and a smaller Metro-Mite series bowed.

Making its debut, in 1961, was the Scout. Powered by a slant-mounted half-a-V-8, this Jeep-like utility vehicle started the modern, sporty, four-wheel-drive craze. The

1964 International Travelall (RPZ)

base model was a convertible with removable doors. There were soft-top, hardtop and Traveltop versions, too. Sales leaped off to a strong start.

Booming truck sales, in the '60s, left little time for product development. IHC boasted of not believing in model-year changes for the sake of change. But, by 1970, this philosophy started to whither. The light-duty trucks became more modern and boxier-looking. In addition, a larger, longer, lower and more luxurious Scout II entered the picture in late 1971. It quickly found 30,000 buyers.

1964 International Metro Delivery Van (RPZ)

The energy crunches and economic recessions of the 1970s hurt IHC. By 1975, the company's famous Metro and Travelall models were disappearing — or gone. The Scout seemed to be IHC's best hope. It was treated to countless different decal and trim options. In 1979, IHC introduced the first turbo diesel engine in a 4x4 sports/utility vehicle. It wasn't enough to turn the tide.

In the early 1980s, the company incurred a financial crisis which took it to the brink of bankruptcy in the truck, agricultural and construction equipment markets. To survive the crisis, the Scout was dropped and IHC abandoned the light-duty truck market completely.

In 1986, the company changed its name to Navistar.

KAISER-JEEP

By Robert C. Ackerson

Those who remember James Garner's "Maverick" television series can recall a time when there wasn't a mass-market for 4x4 vehicles. Going "off-road" in those days meant taking a trip to your Kaiser showroom to purchase a Jeep, Jeep wagon or forward-control pickup truck.

Kaiser Industries was the sponsor of Garner's popular T.V. western and the manufacturer of Jeeps from the mid-1950s to late-1960s. In 1953, when the company was still making automobiles, it also made history by purchasing Willys-Overland for $62 million. Edgar F. Kaiser then became president of Willys Motors, a position he held until 1959.

The purchase had its good and bad sides. Pluses included some innovative product developments, a foothold in a growing world vehicle market and the fact that Kaiser kept America's ¼-ton "war hero" alive when it was ailing. On the minus side, there was the sobering fact that the forthcoming boom in off-road and RV interest was a few years too far down the road to benefit Kaiser and make its new venture a total success.

Nevertheless, there was solid reasoning behind Henry J. Kaiser's decision to buy. His former partner, Joe Frazer, had once served (1939-1943) as president of Willys-Overland and used the association to induce the Toledo-based firm to become a supplier of engines for Kaiser cars. Then, too, Kaiser's other businesses — including aluminum and shipbuilding — were worldwide in scope. This fit right in with the Jeep's international popularity. In addition, military Jeep orders, in the Korean War era, provided extra incentive for Kaiser to purchase the ailing Jeep-maker.

At first, Willys was operated as a subsidiary of Kaiser. After the purchase, all production was transferred from Willow Run, Mich. to Toledo. For a while, Kaiser and Henry J autos were built on the same assembly lines as Jeeps.

By 1955, however, several elements faded from the picture. Kaiser stopped building cars, the Korean War ended and civilian demand for 4x4 vehicles was being somewhat substantially filled by cheap, war surplus units. Calendar year registrations of Jeeps were averaging only 24,000 annually throughout the '50s. This eventually warranted a change in direction, with sales promotions and product advances geared to the light-duty truck and family-car markets.

Although Jeep's CJ models were little altered (they still said "Willys" on front), new emphasis began to be placed on expanding the appeal of the overall line to more typical car and truck users. The station wagon models that Willys developed after World War II were dressed-up with Nike missle-shaped side moldings, chrome bumpers, bright hubcaps — even basketweave body textures. Deluxe versions of the conventional pickups were released, in addition to all-new, cab-forward models. Names such as Harlequin, Surrey, Gala and, even Maverick, were applied to fancier models for upscale imaging. Before long, even the CJ was gussied-up with chrome, bright colored paint and a fringed surrey top. A 4x2 version was produced as a mail delivery special and a new line of parcel vans was introduced.

Cruse W. Moss, president of Kaiser-Frazer's automotive division, would later tell historians that the Brooks Steven's designed Jeepster nearly made it back to life in the mid-'50s too. He said the company, aware of the model's popularity, was all set to "green light" its return, but a search failed to turn up the jigs and dies needed to build the Jeepster.

Even without another model, the lineup was full. As the '60s dawned, there were no less than six Universals, 19 pickups and wagons and three "FC" trucks available. By 1961, this climbed to 31 models and, by 1963, there were 49 different varieties of Jeeps including the all-new Gladiator/Wagoneer series.

The change to a more up-to-date appearance theme, in 1963, was accompanied by a corporate realignment. The company was renamed Kaiser-Jeep Corporation. S.A. Girard, who had been president of Willys since 1959, assumed that title at Kaiser-Jeep. Towards the end of the model year, the Kaiser name also began showing up on some of the vehicles.

Kaiser's growing product line did not reflect any major popularity gains for Jeep vehicles. Calendar year registrations averaged 31,500 units per year from 1960-1962 and increased by only an average 12,000, in the 1963-1966 period, on the strength of the Gladiator/Wagoneer.

By the time 1967 rolled around, the tooling for the Jeepster was found. A modernized version, labeled the Jeepster Commando, was released with heavy promotional backing. It was aimed at the same type of weekend off-roaders who had made the International Scout a successful new model. The Commando, however, did not find quite as many buyers waiting as IHC had.

Even with the Commando, Kaiser-Jeep experienced a business downturn. Yearly registrations averaged about 38,100 units between 1967 and 1969. As a result, Kaiser-Jeep Corporation was merged into American Motors during 1970 and put under new AMC management. Formerly a supplier of Kaiser V-8 power plants, AMC took over as parent company of the Jeep vehicle line.

1963 KAISER JEEP

UNIVERSAL/DISPATCHER — SERIES CJ/DJ — FOUR-CYLINDER: — In 1963, Kaiser Industries changed the name of its Willys Motors, Inc. subsidiary. It was now called Kaiser-Jeep Corporation and the Willys name was removed from the vehicles. There were three Jeep 'Universal' models, all rated for one-quarter ton and featuring four-wheel-drive. The CJ-3B was available again. It was characterized by its seven slot grille, slightly raised hood, flat fenders and short hood length. Power came from a 72 horsepower version of the "Hurricane" four-cylinder engine. Larger headlamps, touching the outer grille slots near the top, were one sign of the CJ-5 model. It also had a longer hood, curved fenders and hood, door opening with straighter front edge and sculptured bodysides. Base engine was a 75 horsepower "Hurricane" four-cylinder. The CJ-6 was a stretched version of the CJ-5, with the CJ-3B engine under its hood. Three 4x2 Dispatcher models were also available. They looked similar to CJ-3Bs, but had an I-beam front axle and 60 horsepower "Lightening" L-head four-cylinder engine. Models included the Jeep version with open-side convertible top, the hardtop with a full-enclosure fiberglass top and sliding doors, or the soft top with a full-enclosure fabric top.

I.D. DATA: Serial number located on floor riser. Starting numbers were distinct for each model: (CJ-3B) 57348-59127 and up; (CJ-5) 57548-90027 and up; (CJ-6) 57748--18221 and up; (DJ-3A) 56337-15704 and up. Ending numbers not available. Engine numbers located on right-hand front of block.

Model	Body Type	Price	Weight	Prod. Total
CJ-3B — (4x4) — (80 in. w.b.)				
CJ-3B	¼-Ton Jeep	2015	2132	14,544
CJ-5 — (4x4) — (81 in. w.b.)				
CJ-5		2109	2163	11,304
CJ-6 — (4x4) — (101 in. w.b.)				
CJ-6	¼-Ton Jeep	2204	2225	2108
DJ-3A — (4x2) — (80.1 in. w.b.)				
DJ-3A	¼-Ton Jeep	1492	1709	1552
DJ-3A	¼-Ton Hardtop	1723	2004	Note 2
DJ-3A	¼-Ton Soft Top	1559	1769	Note 2

NOTE 1: Production total estimates determined by subtracting 1963 starting numbers from 1964 starting numbers.
NOTE 2: The production total estimate given above is for all DJ-3A models combined.

ENGINE (CJ-3B/CJ-6): Inline. F-head. Four-cylinder. Cast iron block. Bore & stroke: 3⅛ in. x 4⅜ in. Displacement: 134.2 cu. in. Compression ratio: 6.9:1. Brake horsepower: 72 at 4000 R.P.M. Net horsepower: 15.63. Torque: 114 lbs.-ft. at 2000 R.P.M. Solid valve lifters. Carburetor: Carter.

NOTE: Above engine was optional in CJ-5.

ENGINE (CJ-5): Inline. F-head. Four-cylinder. Cast iron block. Bore & stroke: 3⅛ in. x 4⅜ in. Displacement: 134.2 cu. in. Compression ratio: 7.4:1. Brake horsepower: 75 at 4000 R.P.M. Net horsepower: 15.63. Torque: 114 lbs.-ft. at 2000 R.P.M. Solid valve lifters. Carburetor: Carter.

NOTE: Above engine was optional in CJ-3B and CJ-6.

ENGINE (DJ-3A): Inline. L-head. Four-cylinder. Cast iron block. Bore & stroke: 3⅛ in. x 4⅜ in. Displacement: 134.2 cu. in. Compression ratio: 7.00:1. Brake horsepower: 60 at 4000 R.P.M. Net horsepower: 15.63. Torque: 114 lbs.-ft. at 2000 R.P.M. Solid valve lifters. Carburetor: Carter.

JEEP — SERIES F-134/L6-226/6-230 — (ALL ENGINES): — There were three series of the old-fashioned looking Jeep wagons, pickups and panels available in 1963. Series designations revealed type of engine and displacement. Some sources consider the 4x2 station wagon and 4x4 utility wagon to be passenger cars, but since these are not in our *Standard Catalog of American Cars 1946-1975*, we are covering them here. The pickups and panel deliveries, which are definitely trucks, were in the same series. The trucks were available with the same wheelbase and tonnage ratings as the wagons, or with a longer wheelbase and one-ton rated chassis. Station wagons were offered in standard or custom trim levels. All of these models were basically carryovers from the early 1950s, but now had "Kaiser-Jeep" identification. In the truck lineup, platform stake bed models were available, too. Another choice buyers had was between 4x2 and 4x4 chassis. The grille had nine vertical bars crossed at the top, center and bottom with horizontal chrome moldings and was slightly V-shaped. General body styling was straight from the Jeep "family" look with spare tires carried on the sides of pickups, inside 4x2 wagons and on the roof of 4x4 wagons and vans.

I.D. DATA: Serial number located on door hinge pillar post. Each model had a distinct starting number for 37 variations. These numbers are given in used car guides of the era. The first five digits of the serial numbers, as listed in the chart below, identified the model. These were followed by a hyphen and the sequential number. Engine numbers located on right-hand front of block.

NOTES: The F-134 series designation indicated 134 cu. in. F-head four-cylinder engine. The L6-226 series designation indicated 226 cu. in. L-head six-cylinder engine. The 6-230 series designation indicated 230 cu. in. OHC six-cylinder engine.

Model	Body Type	Price	Weight	Prod. Total
Series F-134 — (½-Ton) — (104.5 in. w.b.)				
58147	Station Wagon (4x2)	2095	2858	566
54347	Traveller (4x2)	2561	3077	Note 2
54147	Utility Wagon (4x2)	2258	2944	Note 3
54148	Utility Wagon (4x4)	2887	3093	448
54247	Panel Delivery (4x2)	2007	2746	224
54248	Panel Delivery (4x4)	2605	2893	606
Series F-134 — (1-Ton) — (118 in. w.b.)				
55248	Pickup (4x4)	2369	3065	937
Series L6-226 — (½-Ton) — (104.5 in. w.b.)				
58167	Station Wagon (4x2)	2344	2971	1053
54167	Utility Wagon (4x2)	2738	3057	Note 2
54367	Traveller (4x2)	2378	2939	Note 2
54168	Utility Wagon (4x4)	3010	3206	7273
54467	Utility Chassis (4x2)	1814	1968	Note 2
54267	Panel Delivery (4x2)	2132	2859	Note 2
55468	Chassis (4x4)	2232	2281	Note 2
54268	Panel Delivery (4x4)	2728	3008	Note 2
54468	Utility Chassis (4x4)	2311	2228	Note 2
Series L6-226 — (1-Ton) — (118 in. w.b.)				
55168	Chassis & Cab (4x4)	2365	2817	Note 2
55268	Pickup (4x4)	2490	3176	1335
55368	Platform Stake (4x4)	2577	3341	Note 2
Series 6-230 — (½-Ton) — (104.5 in. w.b.)				
58177	Station Wagon (4x2)	2450	3047	11
54377	Traveller (4x2)	2792	3240	19
54178	Utility Wagon (4x4)	3117	3307	35
54378	Traveller (4x4)	3389	3410	73
54278	Panel Delivery (4x4)	2835	3561	Note 2
54277	Panel Delivery (4x2)	—	3147	50
Series 6-230 — (1-Ton) — (118 in. w.b.)				
55178	Chassis & Cab (4x4)	2472	2872	1042
55278	Pickup (4x4)	2597	3238	31
55378	Stake (4x4)	2684	3373	45

NOTE 1: Production total estimates determined by subtracting 1963 starting numbers from 1964 starting numbers.
NOTE 2: Model not offered in 1964; production estimate cannot be calculated.
NOTE 3: Starting number for 1964 is identical, which suggests none were built.

ENGINE (F-134): See previous engine specifications for 72-75 horsepower engine.

ENGINE (L6-226): Inline. L-head. Six-cylinder. Cast iron block. Bore & stroke: 3-5/16 in. x 4⅜ in. Displacement: 226.2 cu. in. Compression ratio: 6.86:1 (7.3:1 optional). Brake horsepower: 105 at 3600 R.P.M. Net horsepower: 26.3. Torque: 190 lbs.-ft. at 1400 R.P.M. Solid valve lifters. Carburetor: Carter.

ENGINE (6-230): Overhead Cam. Inline. Six-cylinder. Cast iron block. Bore & stroke: 3.34 in. x 4.38 in. Displacement: 230 cu. in. Compression ratio: 8.5:1. Brake horsepower: 140 at 4000 R.P.M. Net horsepower: 26.77. Torque: 210 lbs.-ft. at 1750 R.P.M. Solid valve lifters. Carburetor: Carter model two-barrel.

FORWARD CONTROL — SERIES FC — (ALL ENGINES): — The Forward-Control Jeep series were carried over for 1963. A four-cylinder engine was standard in the ¾-ton FC-150 line. Other standard equipment included dual wipers, key locks on both doors, dispatch box, color-toned interiors, cool Plasti-Strand upholstery, ash tray, left-hand sunvisor, dome light, rearview mirror and adjustable driver's seat. Deluxe equipment added dual sunvisors, armrests, rear quarter windows, acoustical trim, vinyl windshield trim, chrome safety hand-rail, foam rubber seats, cigarette lighter, and front panel kick pads. The one-ton came standard with the 226 cu. in. "Hurricane" L-head Six. It was designated the FC-170 and, like the FC-150, came in three basic models. Also available was the two FC-170 heavy-duty chassis configurations with dual rear wheels. Customers could have platform, stake or special bodies mounted on this rugged truck chassis. Both cab-overs were 4x4 trucks and four-speed transmission was optional. Standard equipment also included a Safety-View cab, acoustical trim panels on doors and headlining, heavy glass fiber engine cover insulation, console-type instrument panel, vinyl covered dash, Flat-plane steering wheel, feather-light steering, safety door latches, foam rubber seats, suspended pedals and a single-control transfer case lever.

I.D. DATA: Serial number located on door hinge pillar. Unlike other Jeeps, the FC-150 was numbered by series with 65548-20683 the starting number for all models. The FC-170 starting number was 61568-15897. However, the heavy-duty chassis each had distinct starting numbers, 61368-13-10001 for the chassis with windshield and 61568-13-10479 for the chassis and cab. Engine numbers located on front right-hand corner of block.

Model	Body Type	Price	Weight	Prod. Total
Series FC-150 — (¾-Ton) — (4x4) — (81 in. w.b.)				
65548	Chassis & Cab	2507	2764	1091
65548	Pickup	2624	3020	Note 2
65548	Plat. Stake	2725	3187	Note 2
Series FC-170 — (1-Ton) — (4x4) — (103.5 in. w.b.)				
61568	Chassis & Cab	2824	2901	2031
61568	Pickup	2960	3331	Note 2
61568	Platform Stake	3167	3564	Note 2
Series FC-170HD — (1-Ton) — (6x6) — (103.5 in. w.b.)				
61368	Chassis & Windshield	3144	3028	174
61568	Chassis & Cab	3315	3561	Note 2

NOTE 1: Production total estimates determined by subtracting 1963 starting numbers from 1964 starting numbers.
NOTE 2: The production total estimate given directly above is for the entire series.

573

ENGINES: Base engine for FC-150s was the same as CJ-5 engine. Base engine for FC-170s was the same as the L6-226 engine.

1963 Kaiser-Jeep Gladiator Townside Pickup

WAGONEER/GLADIATOR — SERIES J — SIX-CYLINDER: — New for 1963 was a wide range of Jeep carryall-type station wagons and trucks with totally updated styling. The carryalls were called "Wagoneers." The trucks were called "Gladiators" and came in chassis-and-cab, pickup and platform stake models. Pickups were further separated into "Thriftside" (flare fender) and "Townside" (slab fender) model-options. Automatic transmission was available, for the first time with a four-wheel-drive chassis. Two-wheel-drive Wagoneers and Gladiators were also offered. All of these vehicles had more conventional styling than other Jeep products, but the center-grille, with its 12 vertical slots, identified them as "Jeep family" members. Overall styling was boxy, but very crisp and clean. There were nine basic series on three wheelbases: 110, 120 and 126 inches. ½-ton, ¾-ton and one-ton models were offered. Four ½-ton series had GVW ratings of 4200-4500, 4000, 5600 and 5000 pounds. Three ¾-ton series had GVWs of 6600, 6600 or 7600 pounds. Both one-ton series had GVWs of 8600 pounds. The 230 cu. in. overhead cam six-cylinder engine was standard in all lines.

I.D. DATA: Serial number located on left-hand door hinge pillar. The first four digits indicated the truck-line. The fifth symbol was a letter, followed by the sequential number. Starting number for each series was 10001 up. Engine numbers located on right-hand corner of block.

Model	Body Type	Price	Weight	Prod. Total
Series J-100 — (½-Ton) — (4x2) — (110 in. w.b.)				
1314	4-dr. Wagoneer	2589	3480	—
1312	2-dr. Wagoneer	2546	3453	—
1314C	4-dr. Custom Wagoneer	2783	3515	—
1312C	2-dr. Custom Wagoneer	2738	3488	—
1313	Panel Delivery	2438	3253	—
Series J-100 — (½-Ton) — (4x4) — (110 in. w.b.)				
1414	4-dr. Wagoneer	3332	3623	—
1412	2-dr. Wagoneer	3278	3596	—
1414C	4-dr. Custom Wagoneer	3526	3658	—
1412C	2-dr. Custom Wagoneer	3472	3631	—
1413	Panel Delivery	2996	3396	—
Series J-200 — (½-Ton) — (4x2) — (120 in. w.b.)				
2306F	Chassis & Cab	1913	2901	—
2306F	Thriftside Pickup	2014	3196	—
2306F	Townside Pickup	2041	3304	—
Series J-200 — (½-Ton) — (4x4) — (120 in. w.b.)				
2406F	Chassis & Cab	2596	3061	—
2406F	Thriftside Pickup	2696	3361	—
2406F	Townside Pickup	2722	3461	—
Series J-210 — (½-Ton) — (4x2) — (120 in. w.b.)				
2306A	Chassis & Cab	1977	2941	—
2306A	Thriftside Pickup	2078	3236	—
2306A	Townside Pickup	2105	3344	—
Series J-210 — (½-Ton) — (4x4) — (120 in. w.b.)				
2406A	Chassis & Cab	2653	3096	—
2406A	Thriftside Pickup	2734	3396	—
2406A	Townside Pickup	2781	3496	—
Series J-300 — (½-Ton) — (4x2) — (126 in. w.b.)				
3306E	Chassis & Cab	2017	2943	—
3306E	Thriftside Pickup	2133	3263	—
3306E	Townside Pickup	2160	3371	—
Series J-300 — (½-Ton) — (4x4) — (126 in. w.b.)				
3406E	Chassis & Cab	2654	3091	—
3406E	Thriftside Pickup	2769	3441	—
3406E	Townside Pickup	2796	3541	—
Series J-220 — (¾-Ton) — (4x2) — (120 in. w.b.)				
2306B	Chassis & Cab	2062	3024	—
2306B	Thriftside Pickup	2163	3319	—
2306B	Townside Pickup	2189	3427	—
2306B	Platform Stake	2368	3680	—

Model	Body Type	Price	Weight	Prod. Total
Series J-220 — (¾-Ton) — (4x4) — (120 in. w.b.)				
2406B	Chassis & Cab	2753	3214	—
2406B	Thriftside Pickup	2854	3514	—
2406B	Townside Pickup	2881	3614	—
2406B	Platform Stake	3060	3894	—
Series J-310 — (¾-Ton) — (4x2) — (126 in. w.b.)				
3306B	Chassis & Cab	2128	3067	—
3306B	Thriftside Pickup	2243	3387	—
3306B	Townside Pickup	2270	3495	—
3306B	Platform Stake	2468	3771	—
Series J-310 — (¾-Ton) — (4x4) — (126 in. w.b.)				
3406B	Chassis & Cab	2771	3239	—
3406B	Thriftside Pickup	2886	3589	—
3406B	Townside Pickup	2913	3689	—
3406B	Platform Stake	3111	3979	—
Series J-320 — (¾-Ton) — (4x2) — (126 in. w.b.)				
3306C	Chassis & Cab	2283	3168	—
3306C	Thriftside Pickup	2398	3488	—
3306C	Townside Pickup	2425	3596	—
3306C	Platform Stake	2623	3872	—
Series J-320 — (¾-Ton) — (4x4) — (126 in. w.b.)				
3406C	Chassis & Cab	2931	3377	—
3406C	Thriftside Pickup	3046	3727	—
3406C	Townside Pickup	3073	3827	—
3406C	Platform Stake	3271	4117	—
Series J-230 — (1-Ton) — (4x2) — (120 in. w.b.)				
2406D	Chassis & Cab	3578	3874	—
2406D	Platform Stake	3970	4714	—
Series J-330 — (1-Ton) — (4x2) — (126 in. w.b.)				
3406D	Chassis & Cab	3597	3899	—
3406D	Platform Stake	4011	4799	—

NOTE 1: Serial numbers do not carry over consecutively from year-to-year. Production total estimates cannot be made from serial numbers.

NOTE 2: Explanation of "J" series model number suffixes: A = 5600 lb. GVW; B = 6600 lb. GVW; C = 7600 lb. GVW; D = 8600 lb. GVW; E = 5000 lb. GVW; F = 4000 lb. GVW.

ENGINE: The OHC six-cylinder engine described above for 6-230 models was standard equipment in "J"-series models.

CHASSIS: See charts above for wheelbase measurements for each model. Overall length: (CJ-3B) 129.9 in.; (CJ-5) 135.5. in.; (CJ-6) 155.5 in.; (DJ-3A) 125.4 in.; (F-134, L6-226, 6-230) ½-ton 176.2 in.; 1-ton 183.7 in.; (FC-150) 147.3 in.; (FC-170) 181.4 in.; (J-100) 183.66 in. Front tread (CJ-3B) 48.4 in.; (CJ-5) 48.4 in.; (CJ-6) 48.4 in.; (DJ-3A) 48.2 in.; (F-134, L6-226, 6-230) ½-ton: 57 in.; 1-ton: 57 in.; (FC-150) 57 in.; (FC-170) 63.4 in.; (J-100) 57 in. Rear tread: (CJ-3B) 48.4 in.; (CJ-5) 48.4 in.; (CJ-6) 48.4 in.; (DJ-3A) 48.5 in.; (F-134, L6-226, 6-230) ½-Ton: 57 in.; 1-Ton: 63.5 in.; (FC-150) 57 in.; (FC-170) 63.8 in.; (J-100) 57 in. Tires: (CJ-all models) 6.00 x 16 in.; (DJ-3A) 6.50 x 15 in.; (F-134, L6-226, 6-230) ½-Ton 4x2: 6.70 x 15 in.; ½-Ton 4x4: 7.00 x 16 in.; 1-Ton 7.00 x 16 in.; (FC-150) 7.00 x 15 in.; (FC-170) 7.00 x 16 in.; (J-100, J-200) 6.70 x 15 in.; (J-210) 7.60 x 15 in.; (J-300) 7.10 x 15 in.; (J-320) 7.50 x 16 in.; (other models) 7.00 x 16 in.

1963 Kaiser-Jeep 2-Door Wagoneer (KJC)

TECHNICAL: Synchromesh transmission. Speeds: 3F/1R. Floor mounted gearshift lever. Single-plate dry disc clutch. Semi-floating rear axle. Four wheel hydraulic brakes. Steel disc wheels. 4x2 models have I-beam front axle. 4x4 models have hypoid, semi-floating front axle and two-speed transfer case with ratios of 1.00:1 and 2.46:1.

OPTIONS: (CJ & DJ) Convertible top; all-weather canvas top; fiberglass cab top; metal cab top. Four-speed transmission ($194). (All models) Rearview mirror. Radio. Antenna package. Ramsey or Koenig winches for front, rear or bed mount. Warn or Cutlas selective drive hubs. Canfield wrecker for Universals, 4x4 pickup or Forward-Control models. Meyer angle dozers. Jeep-A-Trench. Tailgate loader for 600 lb. or 1000 lb. rated models. Deluxe cab on Forward-Control models. Fresh air heater. Tu-tone paint. Front bumper guards. Directional signals. E-Z Eye glass. Windshield washer. FC-150 front air vent. FC-150 double passenger seat. Oil bath air cleaner. Oil filter. High-altitude cylinder head (no charge). Powr-Lok rear differential. Heavy-duty rear axle. Heavy-duty springs and shock absorbers. Transmission brake. Hot-Climate radiator. Variable and constant-speed governors. Various size and type tires including whitewalls in available sizes. Drawer bar. Stabilizer bar. Rear bumperettes. Automatic transmission in Travelalls and Gladiators. Full wheel disks.

1963 Kaiser-Jeep 4-Door Wagoneer (KJC)

HISTORICAL: Introduced: Fall, 1963. Calendar year production: 110,457 (this included 55,215 four-cylinder and 55,242 six-cylinders). Also included in the total were 12,615 Jeep Universal models and 25,156 Jeep trucks. Innovations: Wagoneer station wagon introduced Gladiator truck series debutes. First automatic transmission and independent front suspension on four-wheel-drive (4x4 vehicles). First OHC engine mass-produced in United States. Historical notes: Sales of Jeeps established all-time records in 1963. Corporate sales achieved record $221,000 (up 42 percent from 1962).

Pricing

	5	4	3	2	1
1963					
Jeep Universal — (4x4)					
CJ-3B Jeep	950	1900	3150	4400	6300
CJ-5 Jeep	980	1950	3250	4550	6500
CJ-6 Jeep	1000	2000	3300	4600	6600
Dispatcher — (4x2)					
Jeep	780	1560	2600	3600	5200
Hardtop	830	1650	2750	3850	5500
Soft Top	810	1620	2700	3800	5400
'Jeep' Wagons and Trucks — (½-Ton)					
Station Wagon	750	1500	2500	3500	5000
Traveller	780	1560	2600	3600	5200
Utility (4x2)	720	1450	2400	3300	4800
Utility (4x4)	800	1600	2650	3700	5300
Panel (4x2)	690	1380	2300	3200	4600
Panel (4x4)	770	1550	2550	3600	5100
(1-Ton)					
Pickup (4x4)	720	1450	2400	3300	4800
Stake (4x4)	680	1350	2250	3150	4500

NOTE: Add three percent for L-head six-cylinder.
Add four percent for OHC six-cylinder.

Forward-Control — (4x4) — (¾-Ton)					
Pickup	700	1400	2350	3250	4700
Stake	660	1320	2200	3100	4400
(1-Ton)					
Pickup	690	1380	2300	3200	4600
Stake	650	1300	2150	3050	4300
Heavy-Duty Pickup	700	1400	2350	3250	4700
Heavy-Duty Stake	660	1320	2200	3100	4400
Fire Truck	830	1650	2750	3850	5500
Gladiator/Wagoneer — (½-Ton)					
4-dr. Wagon	830	1650	2750	3850	5500
2-dr. Wagon	810	1620	2700	3800	5400
4-dr. Custom Wagon	840	1680	2800	3900	5600
2-dr. Custom Wagon	830	1650	2750	3850	5500
Panel Delivery	720	1450	2400	3300	4800

NOTE: Add five percent for 4x4.

Gladiator — (½-Ton) — (120 in. w.b.)					
Thriftside Pickup	750	1500	2500	3500	5000
Townside Pickup	780	1560	2600	3600	5200
(½-Ton) — (126 in. w.b.)					
Thriftside Pickup	720	1450	2400	3300	4800
Townside Pickup	750	1500	2500	3500	5000
(¾-Ton) — (120 in. w.b.)					
Thriftside Pickup	690	1380	2300	3200	4600
Townside Pickup	720	1450	2400	3300	4800
Stake	630	1250	2100	3000	4200
(¾-Ton) — (126 in. w.b.)					
Thriftside Pickup	680	1350	2250	3150	4500
Townside Pickup	700	1400	2350	3250	4700
Stake	620	1230	2050	2900	4100
(1-Ton) — (120 in. w.b.)					
Stake	600	1200	2000	2800	4000
Wrecker	700	1400	2350	3250	4700
Fire Truck	830	1650	2750	3850	5500
(1-Ton) — (126 in. w.b.)					
Stake	600	1200	2000	2800	4000
Wrecker	720	1450	2400	3300	4800
Fire Truck	830	1650	2750	3850	5500

NOTE: Add five percent for 4x4.

UNIVERSAL/DISPATCHER — SERIES CJ/DJ — FOUR-CYLINDER: — Introduced as "the new idea in sports cars," two new models were added to the Jeep "Universal" lineup in 1964. The CJ-5A and CJ-6A "Tuxedo Park" packages were upscale versions of the two base models with features like turbine-style full wheel discs, whitewall tires and spare tire covers. Trim items like windshield hinges, the rearview mirror and bumpers were made of bright metal. Also new for the year (but actually a reincarnation) was the DJ-3A Surrey with stripes and fringe on top and extra chrome goodies. Everything else was much the same as 1963. The 75 horsepower four-cylinder "Hurricane" engine was used in CJs, while Dispatchers had the 60 horsepower "Lightning" L-head four as base equipment. Refer to 1963 for model identification data.

I.D. DATA: Serial number location was the same as 1963. Except for the J-series, early 1964 models used the 1963 numbering system, with the first five digits indicating series and model and the five digits after the hyphen representing the sequential number. Later (and on all 1964 J-series models) the number of digits ahead of the hyphen was reduced to four. Due to space imitations, the later model identifying numbers (with only four digits) are used for most models in the charts below. Remember that it's possible to have 1964 models with five digits ahead of the hyphen. The five digits, in this case, would be the same ones used for the same model in 1963. Engine numbers located on right-hand front of block.

Model	Body Type	Price	Weight	Prod. Total
CJ-3B — (4x4) — (80 in. w.b.)				
CJ-3B	¼-Ton Jeep	2117	2132	—
CJ-5 — (4x4) — (81 in. w.b.)				
CJ-5	¼-Ton Jeep	2211	2163	—
CJ-5A	¼-Ton Jeep Tuxedo	2306	2163	—
CJ-6 — (4x4) — (101 in. w.b.)				
CJ-6	¼-Ton Jeep	2306	2225	—
CJ-6A	¼-Ton Jeep Tuxedo	2401	2225	—
DJ-3A — (4x2) — (80.1 in. w.b.)				
DJ-3A	¼-Ton Jeep	1518	1709	—
DJ-3A	¼-Ton Jeep Hardtop	1747	2004	—
DJ-3A	¼-Ton Jeep Soft Top	1660	1769	—
DJ-3A	¼-Ton Jeep Surrey	—	1819	—

ENGINE: See 1963 engine data for the CJ/DJ series. Except, note that the 72 horsepower engine was no longer used. All CJ models had the 75 horsepower engine. All DJ models had the 60 horsepower engine as standard equipment.

JEEP — SERIES F-134/L6-226/6-230 — (ALL ENGINES): — Jeep station wagons, pickups and panel trucks continued to be sold in 1964. Several models in the L6-226 series were cut, leaving only the standard wheelbase 4x2 station wagon, 4x4 utility wagon and long-wheelbase one-ton pickup truck. The other model lines, as well as the styling of all models, were left unchanged. A lower (133) horsepower version of the overhead cam (OHC) six-cylinder engine was available in 6-230 models, as well as last season's 140 horsepower job.

I.D. DATA: See CJ/DJ serial number information above.

Model	Body Type	Price	Weight	Prod. Total
Series F-134 — (½-Ton) — (104.5 in. w.b.)				
4112	Station Wagon (4x2)	2357	2858	—
54147	Utility Wagon (4x2)	2258	2944	—
4212	Utility Wagon (4x4)	3030	3093	—
4215	Traveller (4x4)	3302	3077	—
4113	Panel Delivery (4x2)	2143	2746	—
4213	Panel Delivery (4x4)	2741	2893	—
Series F-134 — (1-Ton) — (118 in. w.b.)				
4307	Pickup (4x4)	2514	3065	—
Series L6-226 — (½-Ton) — (104.5 in. w.b.)				
58167	Station Wagon (4x2)	2344	2971	—
54168	Utility Wagon (4x4)	3010	3206	—
4113	Panel Delivery (4x2)	2143	2746	—
4213	Panel Delivery (4x4)	2741	2893	—
Series L6-226 — (1-Ton) — (118 in. w.b.)				
4307	Pickup (4x4)	2514	3065	—
Series 6-230 — (½-Ton) — (104.5 in. w.b.)				
6412	Station Wagon (4x2)	2596	2858	—
6415	Utility Traveler (4x2)	2938	3240	—
6512	Utility Wagon (4x4)	3263	3307	—
6515	Utility Traveler (4x4)	3534	3410	—
6513	Panel Delivery (4x4)	2973	3028	—
6413	Panel Delivery (4x2)	2377	3147	—
Series 6-230 — (1-Ton) — (118 in. w.b.)				
6606	Chassis & Cab (4x4)	2619	2872	—
6607	Pickup (4x4)	2744	3238	—
6608	Stake (4x4)	2831	3873	—

ENGINE: Base engines were the same ones offered for the same series in 1963. Refer to the 1963 secton for specifications. There was one new option available in the 6-230 Series, a low-compression version of the 230 cu. in. OHC six-cylinder. Specifications for this engine are given below.

ENGINE (6-230 Series Option): Inline. Overhead camshaft. Six-cylinder. Cast iron block. Bore & stroke: 3.344 in. x 4.375 in. Displacement: 230.5 cu. in. Compression ratio: 7.5:1. Brake horsepower: 133 at 4000 R.P.M. Net horsepower: 26.77. Torque: 199 lbs.-ft. at 2400 R.P.M. Solid valve lifters. Carburetor: Carter model two-barrel.

FORWARD CONTROL/FLEETVAN — SERIES FC/FJ — (ALL ENGINES): — The Forward-Control ¾-ton and one-ton series were carried over for 1963 with one minor "model" change. The FC-170 heavy-duty configuration, with dual rear wheels, was available in chassis-and-cab form only. Standard equipment was similar to that of 1963. Returning this season was the Jeep Fleetvan in FJ-3 and FJ-3A models. Specifically designed for light-duty, multi-stop operation, the Fleetvan was popular with the United States Post Office. Its backbone was the tough Jeep chassis in 4x2 configuration with four-cylinder "Hurricane" engine. With only 81 inches of wheelbase, the boxy little trucks could carry payloads up to 1,000 pounds. It was 64.7 inches wide and 154 inches long. The load space of 87.5 inches supported a cargo capacity of 170 cubic feet. The height of the sliding side doors — one on each side — was 70 inches, for easy walk-through ability. Rear loading height was just 26⅜ inches from the ground, with cargo area access via double rear doors. The engine was located up front and a single seat was provided for the driver. Kaiser advertised that "five Fleetvans take up less garage space than four nationally advertised competitive vehicles."

I.D. DATA: See CJ/DJ serial number information above.

Model	Body Type	Price	Weight	Prod. Total
Series FC-150 — (¾-Ton) — (4x4) — (81 in. w.b.)				
9209	Chassis & Cab	2735	2764	—
9209	Pickup	2853	3020	—
9209	Platform Stake	2954	3187	—
Series FC-170 — (1-Ton) — (4x4) — (103.5 in. w.b.)				
9309	Chassis & Cab	3056	2901	—
9309	Pickup	3192	3331	—
9309	Platform Stake	3399	3564	—
Series FC-170HD — (1-Ton) — (6x6) — (103.5 in. w.b.)				
9325	Chassis & Cab	3547	3561	—
Series FJ-3 Fleetvan — (½-Ton) — (80 in. w.b.)				
62847	Step-in Delivery	2360	2900	—
Series FJ-3A Fleetvan — (½-Ton) — (81 in. w.b.)				
62147	Step-in Delivery	2380	2910	—

ENGINES: Engines for FC-150 and FC-170 models were the same as 1963. The FJ-3 and FJ-3A used the CJ series 75 horsepower four-cylinder F-head engine, as described in the 1963 section of this catalog.

1964 Kaiser-Jeep 2-Door Wagoneer (KJC)

WAGONEER/GLADIATOR — SERIES J — SIX-CYLINDER: — Kaiser's Jeep Wagoneer for 1964 came in two- or four-door wagons and looked just like the original 1963 version. New options included the lower compression 133 horsepower edition of the OHC "Hurricane" six-cylinder engine and air conditioning. Standard drivetrain was the 140 horsepower six linked to a three-speed manual transmission with gearshift lever on the steering column. Optional overdrive and an automatic transmission could be ordered on 4x2 Wagoneers, while only the automatic was optional on 4x4s. A choice of suspension systems was offered on both 4x2 and 4x4 models. Independent front suspension with torsion bar and rear leaf springs was one option. The other was leaf springs all around. Other extras included deluxe trim, power-take-off, power steering, power brakes and a series of dash-mounted lights to indicate whether the Wagoneer was in 4x4 or 4x2 modes. A floor-mounted knob engaged the 4x4 system. Also carried over from 1963 were the Gladiator trucks, which shared basic styling with the Wagoneer. They came in ½-ton, ¾-ton and one-ton configurations. The one-tons were 4x4s only, while the others were available with 4x2 or 4x4 running gear. Wheelbases of 120 or 126 inch were available in all lines. Body styles were the same as 1963.

I.D. DATA: See CJ/DJ serial number information above.

Model	Body Type	Price	Weight	Prod. Total
Series J-100 — (½-Ton) — (4x2) — (110 in. w.b.)				
1314	4-dr. Wagoneer	2673	3480	—
1312	2-dr. Wagoneer	2629	3453	—
1314C	4-dr. Custom Wagoneer	2871	3515	—
1312C	2-dr. Custom Wagoneer	2827	3488	—
1313	Panel Dely.	2511	3253	—
Series J-100 — (½-Ton) — (4x4) — (110 in. w.b.)				
1414	4-dr. Wagoneer	3434	3623	—
1412	2-dr. Wagoneer	3379	3596	—
1414C	4-dr. Custom Wagoneer	3633	3658	—
1412C	2-dr. Custom Wagoneer	3578	3631	—
1413	Panel Dely.	3082	3396	—
Series J-200 — (½-Ton) — (4x2) — (120 in. w.b.)				
2306F	Chassis & Cab	1980	2901	—
2306F	Thriftside Pickup	2081	3196	—
2306F	Townside Pickup	2108	3304	—
Series J-200 — (½-Ton) — (4x4) — (120 in. w.b.)				
2406F	Chassis & Cab	2679	3061	—
2406F	Thriftside Pickup	2779	3361	—
2406F	Townside Pickup	2806	3461	—
Series J-210 — (½-Ton) — (4x2) — (120 in. w.b.)				
2306A	Chassis & Cab	2046	2941	—
2306A	Thriftside Pickup	2147	3236	—
2306A	Townside Pickup	2173	3344	—
Series J-210 — (½-Ton) — (4x4) — (120 in. w.b.)				
2406A	Chassis & Cab	2738	3096	—
2406A	Thriftside Pickup	2839	3396	—
2406A	Townside Pickup	2866	3496	—
Series J-300 — (½-Ton) — (4x2) — (126 in. w.b.)				
3306E	Chassis & Cab	2087	2943	—
3306E	Thriftside Pickup	2202	3263	—
3306E	Townside Pickup	2229	3371	—
Series J-300 — (½-Ton) — (4x4) — (126 in. w.b.)				
3406E	Chassis & Cab	2739	3091	—
3406E	Thriftside Pickup	2854	3441	—
3406E	Townside Pickup	2881	3541	—
Series J-220 — (¾-Ton) — (4x2) — (120 in. w.b.)				
2306B	Chassis & Cab	2132	3024	—
2306B	Thriftside Pickup	2233	3319	—
2306B	Townside Pickup	2260	3427	—
2306B	Plat. Stake	2439	3680	—
Series J-220 — (¾-Ton) — (4x4) — (120 in. w.b.)				
2406B	Chassis & Cab	2841	3214	—
2406B	Thriftside Pickup	2942	3514	—
2406B	Townside Pickup	2969	3614	—
2406B	Platform Stake	3148	3894	—
Series J-310 — (¾-Ton) — (4x2) — (126 in. w.b.)				
3306B	Chassis & Cab	2201	3067	—
3306B	Thriftside Pickup	2316	3387	—
3306B	Townside Pickup	2343	3495	—
3306B	Platform Stake	2541	3771	—
Series J-310 — (¾-Ton) — (4x4) — (126 in. w.b.)				
3406B	Chassis & Cab	2860	3239	—
3406B	Thriftside Pickup	2975	3589	—
3406B	Townside Pickup	3002	3689	—
3406B	Platform Stake	3200	3979	—
Series J-320 — (¾-Ton) — (4x2) — (126 in. w.b.)				
3306C	Chassis & Cab	2359	3168	—
3306C	Thriftside Pickup	2474	3488	—
3306C	Townside Pickup	2501	3596	—
3306C	Platform Stake	2699	3872	—
Series J-320 — (¾-Ton) — (4x4) — (126 in. w.b.)				
3406C	Chassis & Cab	3024	3377	—
3406C	Thriftside Pickup	3139	3727	—
3406C	Townside Pickup	3166	3827	—
3406C	Platform Stake	3364	4117	—
Series J-230 — (1-Ton) — (4x4) — (120 in. w.b.)				
2406D	Chassis & Cab	3687	3874	—
2406D	Platform Stake	4079	4714	—
Series J-330 — (1-Ton) — (4x4) — (126 in. w.b.)				
3406D	Chassis & Cab	3706	3899	—
3406D	Platform Stake	4120	4790	—

NOTE 1: Explanation of "J" series model number suffixes: A = 5600 lb. GVW; B = 6600 lb. GVW; C = 7600 lb. GVW; D = 8600 lb. GVW, E = 5000 lb. GVW; F = 4000 lb. GVW.

ENGINE: Base engine in Wagoneers and Gladiators was the 140 horsepower OHC six-cylinder described in the 1963 section of this catalog. The 133 horsepower OHC six-cylinder engine, described above for the 6-230 series, was also available as an "economy option."

CHASSIS: (All Series except Fleetvan) Same as 1963. (Fleetvan) Wheelbase: See chart. Overall length: 154 in. Tread: 48-9/16 in. Tires: 6.70 x 15 in.

TECHNICAL: Same as 1963.

OPTIONS: (New): Air conditioning. (Others): Same as 1963. (Available prices): Power steering ($81). Overdrive ($126). Four-speed transmission ($109).

HISTORICAL: Introduced: Fall 1963. Calendar year registrations: (Universals) 11,915; (Trucks) 59,180. Calendar year production: 120,830 (This included 58,755 four-cylinders and 62,075 six-cylinders). Innovations: Tuxedo Park IV introduced as a sporty version of the Jeep Universal. Historical notes: Kaiser-Jeep Corp. received an $81 million Army contract for production of trucks and purchased Studebaker's Chippewa plant in South Bend, Inc. Sales again set new records, with $255,582,000 registered for model year 1964. Sales of Jeep "approved" accessories also increased. The number of United States dealers leaped by 15 percent.

1964 Kaiser-Jeep 4-Door Wagoneer (KJC)

Pricing

	5	4	3	2	1
1964					
Jeep Universal — (4x4)					
CJ-3B Jeep	950	1900	3150	4400	6300
CJ-5 Jeep	980	1950	3250	4550	6500
CJ-5A Tuxedo Park	1010	2030	3350	4700	6700
CJ-6 Jeep	1000	2000	3300	4600	6600
CJ-6A Tuxedo Park	1020	2050	3400	4800	6800
Dispatcher — (4x2)					
Jeep	780	1560	2600	3600	5200
Hardtop	830	1650	2750	3850	5500
Soft Top	810	1620	2700	3800	5400
Surrey	840	1680	2800	3900	5600
'Jeep' Wagons and Trucks — (½-Ton)					
Station Wagon	750	1500	2500	3500	5000
Utility (4x2)	720	1450	2400	3300	4800
Utility (4x4)	800	1600	2650	3700	5300
Traveler (4x2)	780	1560	2600	3600	5200
Traveler (4x4)	850	1700	2850	4000	5700
Panel (4x2)	690	1380	2300	3200	4600
Panel (4x4)	770	1550	2550	3600	5100
(1-Ton)					
Pickup (4x4)	720	1450	2400	3300	4800
Stake (4x4)	680	1350	2250	3150	4500

NOTE: Add three percent for L-head six-cylinder.
Add four percent for OHC six-cylinder.

	5	4	3	2	1
Forward-Control — (4x4) — (¾-Ton)					
Pickup	700	1400	2350	3250	4700
Stake	660	1320	2200	3100	4400
(1-Ton)					
Pickup	690	1380	2300	3200	4600
Stake	650	1300	2150	3050	4300
Heavy-Duty Pickup	700	1400	2350	3250	4700
Heavy-Duty Stake	660	1320	2200	3100	4400
Fire Truck	830	1650	2750	3850	5500
Fleetvan — (4x4)					
FJ-3 Step-in Delivery	680	1350	2250	3150	4500
FJ-3A Step-in Delivery	690	1380	2300	3200	4600
Gladiator/Wagoneer — (½-Ton)					
4-dr. Wagon	830	1650	2750	3850	5500
2-dr. Wagon	810	1620	2700	3800	5400
4-dr. Custom Wagon	840	1680	2800	3900	5600
2-dr. Custom Wagon	830	1650	2750	3850	5500
Panel Delivery	720	1450	2400	3300	4800

NOTE: Add five percent for 4x4.

	5	4	3	2	1
Gladiator Pickup/Truck — (½-Ton) — (120 in. w.b.)					
Thriftside Pickup	750	1500	2500	3500	5000
Townside Pickup	780	1560	2600	3600	5200
(½-Ton) — (126 in. w.b.)					
Thriftside Pickup	720	1450	2400	3300	4800
Townside Pickup	750	1500	2500	3500	5000
(¾-Ton) — (120 in. w.b.)					
Thriftside Pickup	690	1380	2300	3200	4600
Townside Pickup	720	1450	2400	3300	4800
Platform Stake	630	1250	2100	3000	4200
(¾-Ton) — (126 in. w.b.)					
Thriftside Pickup	680	1350	2250	3150	4500
Townside Pickup	700	1400	2350	3250	4700
Platform Stake	620	1230	2050	2900	4100
(1-Ton) — (120 in. w.b.)					
Platform Stake	600	1200	2000	2800	4000
Wrecker	700	1400	2350	3250	4700
Fire Truck	830	1650	2750	3850	5500
(1-Ton) — (126 in. w.b.)					
Stake	600	1200	2000	2800	4000
Wrecker	720	1450	2400	3300	4800
Fire Truck	830	1650	2750	3850	5500

NOTE: Add five percent for 4x4.

1965 KAISER JEEP

UNIVERSAL/DISPATCHER — SERIES CJ/DJ — FOUR-CYLINDER: — The name "Kaiser Jeep" was added to the front sides of the hood or fenders of all models this year. On CJ/DJ models, it was accompanied by "Jeep" lettering on the side of the cowl. A new model for 1965 was the DJ-5, which had a lower grille and hood line. Its distinctive, five-slot grille corresponded with the "DJ-5" designation for easy identification. It was a Dispatcher 4x2 type vehicle used primarily for light-duty courier service, mostly by the United States Post Office. A unique accessory was a strangely twisted convex rearview mirror mounted to the left-hand front fender near the front corner of the hood. It had a modified suspension system and, often, came with right-hand drive. There was also a full cab enclosure with sliding side doors and a rear door. A single bucket seat was provided for the operator. Accompanying the new 81 inch wheelbase DJ-5 was a 101 inch wheelbase DJ-6. All other 1964 models in this dual series were carried over, with the exceptions of the DJ-3 soft top and surrey. The "Tuxedo Park" models featured exclusive all-white finish, special rolled-and-pleated upholstery and chrome ornamentation.

I.D. DATA: Serial number located in the same locations. The "new" Gladiators used model numbers identical to those for the "old" Gladiators, except for the alphabetical suffix. Codes for other models were the same as 1964. Engine numbers located in the same places.

Model	Body Type	Price	Weight	Prod. Total
CJ-3B — (4x4) — (80 in. w.b.)				
8105	¼-Ton Jeep	2117	2132	—
CJ-5 — (4x4) — (81 in. w.b.)				
8305	¼-Ton Jeep	2211	2163	—
8322	¼-Ton "Tuxedo Park"	2306	2163	—
CJ-6 — (4x4) — (101 in. w.b.)				
8405	¼-Ton Jeep	2306	2225	—
8422	¼-Ton "Tuxedo Park"	2401	2225	—
DJ-5 — (4x2) — (81 in. w.b.)				
8505	¼-Ton Dispatcher	1744	1823	—
DJ-6 — (4x2) — (101 in. w.b.)				
8605	¼-Ton Dispatcher	1838	1956	—
DJ-3A — (4x2) — (80.1 in. w.b.)				
8201	¼-Ton Jeep	1518	1709	—
8203	¼-Ton Hardtop	1747	2004	—

ENGINES: Refer to 1963 specifications. The DJ-3A used the 60 horsepower engine as standard equipment. All other models used the 75 horsepower engine as standard equipment.

JEEP — SERIES F-134/6-230 — (ALL ENGINES): — The "utility" type Jeep station wagons, panels and pickups also carried "Kaiser Jeep" badges this season. The L6-226 models disappeared and the L-head six-cylinder engine was now used only for the FC-170 trucks. This was the final appearance of the F-134 line.

I.D. DATA: Same as above.

Model	Body Type	Price	Weight	Prod. Total
Series F-134 — (½-Ton) — (104.5 in. w.b.)				
4112	Station Wagon (4x2)	2357	2858	—
4212	Utility Wagon (4x4)	3030	3093	—
4215	Traveller (4x4)	3302	3077	—
4113	Panel Delivery (4x2)	2143	2746	—
4213	Panel Delivery (4x4)	2741	2893	—
Series F-134 — (1-Ton) — (118 in. w.b.)				
4307	Pickup (4x4)	2514	3065	—
Series 6-230 — (½-Ton) — (104.5 in. w.b.)				
6412	Station Wagon (4x2)	2596	3047	—
6512	Utility Wagon (4x4)	3263	3307	—
6513	Panel Delivery (4x4)	2973	3028	—
6413	Panel Delivery (4x2)	2377	3147	—
Series 6-230 — (1-Ton) — (118 in. w.b.)				
6606	Chassis & Cab (4x4)	2619	2872	—
6607	Pickup (4x4)	2744	3238	—
6608	Stake (4x4)	2831	3373	—

ENGINES: Same as 1963-1964, except L-head six-cylinder is not available.

FORWARD CONTROL — SERIES FC — (ALL ENGINES): — There was no Fleetvan series for 1965, but the Forward-Control models remained available in ¾-ton (FC-150) and one-ton (FC-170) configurations. They were very little changed, except for the addition of "Kaiser-Jeep" identification nameplates.

I.D. DATA: Same as above.

Model	Body Type	Price	Weight	Prod. Total
Series FC-150 — (¾-Ton) — (4x4) — (81 in. w.b.)				
9209	Chassis & Cab	2735	2764	—
9209	Pickup	2853	3020	—
9209	Platform Stake	2954	3187	—
Series FC-170 — (1-Ton) — (4x4) — (103.5 in. w.b.)				
9309	Chassis & Cab	3056	2901	—
9309	Pickup	3192	3331	—
9309	Platform Stake	3399	3564	—
Series FC-170HD — (1-Ton) — (6x6) — (103.5 in. w.b.)				
9325	Chassis & Cab	3547	3561	—

ENGINES: Same as 1963-1964.

WAGONEER/GLADIATOR — SERIES J — SIX-CYLINDER: — "Kaiser-Jeep" nameplates replaced the "Jeep" name on the front fendersides of the 1965 Wagoneers and Gladiators. There were actually two separate series of Gladiators this year. The first was comprised of the J-200, J-210, J-300, J-220, J-310, J-320, J-230 and J-330 lines, all of which were carried over from 1964 with no changes in prices, weights or other specifications. For data on these trucks, please refer to the 1964 listings for the same models. The second series of Gladiators was comprised of the J-2500, J-2600, J-3500, J-2700, J-3700, J-2800 and J-3800 lines. These trucks had the same general styling as the early Gladiators and used the same 230 cu. in. OHC six-cylinder engine as standard equipment. A new option was a 327 cu. in. V-8. The GVW ratings for the later series were also slightly higher, in most cases, than the comparable models in the original Gladiator series.

I.D. DATA: Same as above.

1965 Kaiser-Jeep 4-door Wagoneer (KJC)

Model	Body Type	Price	Weight	Prod. Total
Series J-100 — (½-Ton) — (4x2) — (110 in. w.b.)				
1314	4-dr. Wagoneer	2701	3480	—
1312	2-dr. Wagoneer	2658	3453	—
1314C	4-dr. Custom Wagoneer	2896	3515	—
1312C	2-dr. Custom Wagoneer	2853	3488	—
1313	Panel Delivery	2511	3253	—
Series J-100 — (½-Ton) — (4x4) — (110 in. w.b.)				
1414	4-dr. Wagoneer	3449	3623	—
1412	2-dr. Wagoneer	3395	3596	—
1414C	4-dr. Custom Wagoneer	3644	3658	—
1412C	2-dr. Custom Wagoneer	3590	3631	—
1413	Panel Delivery	3082	3396	—
Series J-2500 — (½-Ton) — (4x2) — (120 in. w.b.)				
2306W	Chassis & Cab	2149	2919	—
2306W	Thriftside Pickup	2250	3214	—
2306W	Townside Pickup	2277	3322	—
Series J-2500 — (½-Ton) — (4x4) — (120 in. w.b.)				
2406W	Chassis & Cab	2802	3128	—
2406W	Thriftside Pickup	2903	3423	—
2406W	Townside Pickup	2930	3531	—
Series J-2600 — (½-Ton) — (4x2) — (120 in. w.b.)				
2306X	Chassis & Cab	2263	3060	—
2306X	Thriftside Pickup	2364	3355	—
2306X	Townside Pickup	2390	3463	—
Series J-2600 — (½-Ton) — (4x4) — (120 in. w.b.)				
2406X	Chassis & Cab	2923	3269	—
2406X	Thriftside Pickup	3024	3564	—
2406X	Townside Pickup	3050	3672	—
Series J-3500 — (½-Ton) — (4x2) — (126 in. w.b.)				
3306W	Chassis & Cab	2168	2943	—
3306W	Thriftside Pickup	2282	3263	—
3306W	Townside Pickup	2309	3371	—
Series J-3500 — (½-Ton) — (4x4) — (126 in. w.b.)				
3406W	Chassis & Cab	2821	3152	—
3406W	Thriftside Pickup	2935	3472	—
3406W	Townside Pickup	2962	3580	—
Series J-3600 — (½-Ton) — (4x2) — (126 in. w.b.)				
3306X	Chassis & Cab	2282	3081	—
3306X	Thriftside Pickup	2396	3401	—
3306X	Townside Pickup	2423	3509	—
3306X	Platform Stake	2620	3785	—
Series J-3600 — (½-Ton) — (4x4) — (126 in. w.b.)				
3406X	Chassis & Cab	2942	3081	—
3406X	Thriftside Pickup	3056	3401	—
3406X	Townside Pickup	3083	3509	—
3406X	Platform Stake	3280	3785	—
Series J-2700 — (¾-Ton) — (4x2) — (120 in. w.b.)				
2306Y	Chassis & Cab	2422	3147	—
2306Y	Thriftside Pickup	2523	3442	—
2306Y	Townside Pickup	2549	3550	—
2306Y	Platform Stake	2748	3803	—
Series J-2700 — (¾-Ton) — (4x4) — (120 in. w.b.)				
2406Y	Chassis & Cab	3087	3356	—
2406Y	Thriftside Pickup	3188	3651	—
2406Y	Townside Pickup	3215	3759	—
2406Y	Platform Stake	3393	4012	—
Series J-3700 — (¾-Ton) — (4x2) — (126 in. w.b.)				
3306Y	Chassis & Cab	2441	3168	—
3306Y	Thriftside Pickup	2555	3488	—
3306Y	Townside Pickup	2582	3596	—
3306Y	Platform Stake	2779	3872	—

Model	Body Type	Price	Weight	Prod. Total
Series J-3700 — (¾-Ton) — (4x4) — (126 in. w.b.)				
3406Y	Chassis & Cab	3106	3377	—
3406Y	Thriftside Pickup	3220	3697	—
3406Y	Townside Pickup	3247	3805	—
3406Y	Platform Stake	3444	4081	—
Series J-2800 — (1-Ton) — (4x4) — (120 in. w.b.)				
2406Z	Chassis & Cab	3770	3789	—
2406Z	Platform Stake	4163	4534	—
Series J-3800 — (1-Ton) — (4x4) — (126 in. w.b.)				
3406Z	Chassis & Cab	3788	3822	—
3406Z	Platform Stake	4203	4620	—

NOTE 1: Explanation of "J" series model number suffix: W = 5000 lb. GVW; X = 6000 lb. GVW; Y = 7000 lb. GVW; Z = 8600 lb. GVW.

ENGINES: Base engine was the same as 1963-1964. Specifications for the new V-8 engine option are given below.

ENGINE (Optional): OHV. Vee-block. Eight-cylinder. Cast iron block. Bore & stroke: 4.00 in. x 3.25 in. Displacement: 327 cu. in. Brake horsepower: 250 at 4700 R.P.M. Net horsepower: 51.2. Torque: 340 lbs.-ft. at 2600 R.P.M. Hydraulic valve lifters. Carburetor: Carter.

CHASSIS: Same as 1963-1964.

TECHNICAL: Same as 1963-1964.

OPTIONS: Same as 1963-1964. (Available prices) Power steering ($81). Overdrive ($126). Four-speed transmission ($109).

1965 Kaiser-Jeep 4-Door Super Wagoneer (KJC)

HISTORICAL: Introduced: Fall, 1964. Calendar year production: 108,601 (This included 40,846 four-cylinders and 50,578 six-cylinders, and 17,167 eight-cylinders). Factory shipments totaled 87,900 vehicles 6000 lbs. and under and 5800 vehicles 6001 to 10,000 pounds. Innovations: Fleetvan introduced A new M606 Jeep was produced for foreign markets under foreign aid programs. Eight-cylinder (V-8) engine introduced. Historical notes: Jeep sales to the U.S. Government hit record levels, thanks to the Fleetvan postal trucks.

Pricing

1965

	5	4	3	2	1
Jeep Universal — (4x4)					
CJ-3B Jeep	950	1900	3150	4400	6300
CJ-5 Jeep	980	1950	3250	4550	6500
CJ-5A Tuxedo Park	1010	2030	3350	4700	6700
CJ-6 Jeep	1000	2000	3300	4600	6600
CJ-6A Tuxedo Park	1020	2050	3400	4800	6800
Dispatcher — (4x2)					
DJ-5 Courier	750	1500	2500	3500	5000
DJ-6 Courier	770	1550	2550	3600	5100
DJ-3A Jeep	780	1560	2600	3600	5200
DJ-3A Hardtop	830	1650	2750	3850	5500
'Jeep' Wagons and Trucks — (½-Ton)					
Station Wagon	750	1500	2500	3500	5000
Utility Wagon (4x4)	800	1600	2650	3700	5300
Traveler (4x4)	850	1700	2850	4000	5700
Panel (4x2)	690	1380	2300	3200	4600
Panel (4x4)	770	1550	2550	3600	5100
(1-Ton)					
Pickup (4x4)	720	1450	2400	3300	4800
Stake (4x4)	680	1350	2250	3150	4500

NOTE: Add 3 percent for L-head six-cylinder.

Forward-Control — (4x4) — (¾-Ton)					
Pickup	700	1400	2350	3250	4700
Stake	660	1320	2200	3100	4400
(1-Ton)					
Pickup	690	1380	2300	3200	4600
Stake	650	1300	2150	3050	4300
Heavy-Duty Pickup	700	1400	2350	3250	4700
Heavy-Duty Stake	660	1320	2200	3100	4400
Fire Truck	830	1650	2750	3850	5500

Gladiator/Wagoneer — (½-Ton)	5	4	3	2	1
4-dr. Wagon	830	1650	2750	3850	5500
2-dr. Wagon	810	1620	2700	3800	5400
4-dr. Custom Wagon	840	1680	2800	3900	5600
2-dr. Custom Wagon	830	1650	2750	3850	5500
Panel Delivery	720	1450	2400	3300	4800

NOTE: Add five percent for 4x4.
Add five percent for V-8.

NOTE: For "first series" 1965 Gladiators refer to 1964 prices.

Gladiator Pickup/Truck — (½-Ton) — (120 in. w.b.)	5	4	3	2	1
Thriftside Pickup	750	1500	2500	3500	5000
Townside Pickup	780	1560	2600	3600	5200
Stake	660	1320	2200	3100	4400
(½-Ton) — (126 in. w.b.)					
Thriftside Pickup	720	1450	2400	3300	4800
Townside Pickup	750	1500	2500	3500	5000
Stake	650	1300	2150	3050	4300
(¾-Ton) — (120 in. w.b.)					
Thriftside Pickup	690	1380	2300	3200	4600
Townside Pickup	720	1450	2400	3300	4800
Stake	630	1250	2100	3000	4200
(¾-Ton) — (126 in. w.b.)					
Thriftside Pickup	680	1350	2250	3150	4500
Townside Pickup	700	1400	2350	3250	4700
Stake	620	1230	2050	2900	4100
(1-Ton) — (120 in. w.b.)					
Stake	600	1200	2000	2800	4000
Wrecker	700	1400	2350	3250	4700
Fire Truck	830	1650	2750	3850	5500
(1-Ton) — (126 in. w.b.)					
Stake	600	1200	2000	2800	4000
Wrecker	720	1450	2400	3300	4800
Fire Truck	830	1650	2750	3850	5500

NOTE: Add five percent for 4x4.
Add five percent for V-8.

1966 KAISER JEEP

1966 Kaiser-Jeep Universal CJ-5

UNIVERSAL/DISPATCHER — SERIES CJ/DJ — FOUR-CYLINDER: — As usual, the 1966 Jeeps looked like last year's models. There were no changes in the lineup of CJ 4x4s and DJ 4x2s and the basic specifications were familiar. In the optional equipment department, a V-6 engine was made available for the CJ-5, CJ-6, CJ-5A, CJ-6A, DJ-5 and CJ-6. The four-cylinder base engines were carried over as standard equipment with the 75 horsepower version used in all models except the DJ-3A, which used the 60 horsepower edition. Dropped from production this season were the 'Jeep' wagons and trucks of the early postwar style in the F-134 and 6-230 series. This completed the phaseout of these "old-fashioned" looking models which always seemed to be part truck/part passenger car.

I.D. DATA: Serial number located on left front door hinge pillar post and left firewall. The VIN consists of from nine to 11 symbols. The first five symbols indicate series and body style. The last five or six are sequential production numbers. Engine numbers located on right-hand front of block.

1966 Kaiser-Jeep Universal CJ-5

Model	Body Type	Price	Weight	Prod. Total
CJ-3B — (4x4) — (80 in. w.b.)				
8105	¼-Ton Jeep	2190	2132	—
CJ-5 — (4x4) — (81 in. w.b.)				
8305	¼-Ton Jeep	2284	2163	—
CJ-5A — (4x4) — (81 in. w.b.)				
8322	¼-Ton "Tuxedo Park"	2379	2163	—
CJ-6 — (4x4) — (101 in. w.b.)				
8405	¼-Ton Jeep	2379	2225	—
CJ-6A — (4x4) — (101 in. w.b.)				
8422	¼-Ton "Tuxedo Park"	2475	2225	—
DJ-5 — (4x2) — (81 in. w.b.)				
8505	¼-Ton Dispatcher	1744	1823	—
DJ-6 — (4x2) — (101 in. w.b.)				
8605	¼-Ton Dispatcher	1839	1956	—
DJ-3A — (4x2) — (80.1 in. w.b.)				
8201	¼-Ton Jeep	1519	1709	—
8203	¼-Ton Hardtop	1748	2004	—

1966 Kaiser-Jeep Universal CJ-5

1966 Kaiser-Jeep Universal CJ-5A Hardtop

ENGINE (Same): Same as 1963-1965.

ENGINE (Optional): Vee-block. Overhead valve. Six-cylinder. Bore & stroke: 3.75 in. x 3.40 in. Displacement: 225 cu. in. Compression ratio: 9.0:1. Brake horsepower: 155 at 4400 R.P.M. Net horsepower: 33.75. Torque: 225 lbs.-ft. at 2400 R.P.M. Four main bearings. Hydraulic valve lifters. Carburetor: Carter model two-barrel.

FORWARD CONTROL — SERIES FC — (ALL ENGINES): — Now in their last season, the cute-looking Jeep forward-control models were unchanged in appearance, features or models. The ¾-ton FC-150 continued to be powered by the F-head four-cylinder "Hurricane" engine, while the one-ton FC-170s relied on the L-head six-cylinder "Lightning" engine.

I.D. DATA: Same as above.

Model	Body Type	Price	Weight	Prod. Total
Series FC-150 — (¾-Ton) — (4x4) — (81 in. w.b.)				
9209	Chassis & Cab	2735	2896	—
9209	Pickup	2853	3152	—
9209	Platform Stake	2954	3319	—
Series FC-170 — (1-Ton) — (4x4) — (103.5 in. w.b.)				
9309	Chassis & Cab	3056	2901	—
9309	Pickup	3192	3331	—
9309	Platform Stake	3399	3564	—
Series FC-170HD — (1-Ton) — (6x6) — (103.5 in. w.b.)				
9325	Chassis & Cab	3547	3561	—

ENGINES: Same as 1963-1965.

1966 Kaiser-Jeep 4-Door Super Wagoneer (KJC)

1966 Kaiser-Jeep Super Wagoneer Station Wagon

1966 Kaiser-Jeep Gladiator Townside Pickup

WAGONEER/GLADIATOR — SERIES J — SIX-CYLINDER: — Two "faces" were again seen on Jeep Wagons. Two-door models shared the "Gladiator" look with tall vertical bars in the center only. Four-door Wagoneers had a full-across grille more like a car's than a truck's. It had an "electric shaver" appearance with veed vertical bars. Also, the bodysides were slightly more sculptured and the center bulge hood ended with a dummy air scoop. A new model called the Super Wagoneer came standard with four-wheel-drive, larger tires and V-8 engine. New contrasting side spears, vinyl roofs, mag wheels and roof carriers were optional. Gladiator trucks did not adopt the new frontal treatment and looked much the same as they did when introduced in 1963.

1966 Kaiser-Jeep Wagoneer Panel Ambulance

I.D. DATA: Same as above.

Model	Body Type	Price	Weight	Prod. Total
Series J-100 — (½-Ton) — (4x2) — (110 in. w.b.)				
1314	4-dr. Wagoneer	2838	3480	—
1312	2-dr. Wagoneer	2794	3453	—
1314C	4-dr. Custom Wagoneer	3033	3515	—
1312C	2-dr. Custom Wagoneer	2989	3488	—
1313	Panel Delivery	2650	3253	—
Series J-100 — (½-Ton) — (4x4) — (110 in. w.b.)				
1414	4-dr. Wagoneer	3585	3623	—
1412	2-dr. Wagoneer	3531	3596	—
1414C	4-dr. Custom Wagoneer	3780	3658	—
1412C	2-dr. Custom Wagoneer	3726	3631	—
1413	Panel Delivery	3223	3396	—
1414D	4-dr. Super Wagoneer	5943	4241	—
Series J-2500 — (½-Ton) — (4x2) — (120 in. w.b.)				
2306W	Chassis & Cab	2207	2919	—
2306W	Thriftside Pickup	2308	3214	—
2306W	Townside Pickup	2335	3322	—
Series J-2500 — (½-Ton) — (4x4) — (120 in. w.b.)				
2406W	Chassis & Cab	2861	3128	—
2406W	Thriftside Pickup	2961	3423	—
2406W	Townside Pickup	2988	3531	—
Series J-2600 — (½-Ton) — (4x2) — (120 in. w.b.)				
2306X	Chassis & Cab	2321	3060	—
2306X	Thriftside Pickup	2421	3355	—
2306X	Townside Pickup	2448	3463	—
2306X	Platform Stake	2626	3716	—
Series J-2600 — (½-Ton) — (4x4) — (120 in. w.b.)				
2406X	Chassis & Cab	2981	3269	—
2406X	Thriftside Pickup	3082	3564	—
2406X	Townside Pickup	3109	3672	—
2406X	Platform Stake	3287	3925	—
Series J-3500 — (½-Ton) — (4x2) — (126 in. w.b.)				
3306W	Chassis & Cab	2226	2943	—
3306W	Thriftside Pickup	2340	3263	—
3306W	Townside Pickup	2367	3371	—
Series J-3500 — (½-Ton) — (4x4) — (126 in. w.b.)				
3406W	Chassis & Cab	2879	3152	—
3406W	Thriftside Pickup	2994	3472	—
3406W	Townside Pickup	3021	3580	—
Series J-3600 — (½-Ton) — (4x2) — (126 in. w.b.)				
3306X	Chassis & Cab	2340	3081	—
3306X	Thriftside Pickup	2454	3401	—
3306X	Townside Pickup	2481	3509	—
3306X	Platform Stake	2678	3785	—
Series J-3600 — (½-Ton) — (4x4) — (126 in. w.b.)				
3406X	Chassis & Cab	3000	3290	—
3406X	Thriftside Pickup	3114	3610	—
3406X	Townside Pickup	3141	3718	—
3406X	Platform Stake	3338	3994	—
Series J-2700 — (¾-Ton) — (4x2) — (120 in. w.b.)				
2306Y	Chassis & Cab	2480	3147	—
2306Y	Thriftside Pickup	2580	3442	—
2306Y	Townside Pickup	2607	3550	—
2306Y	Platform Stake	2785	3803	—
Series J-2700 — (¾-Ton) — (4x4) — (120 in. w.b.)				
2406Y	Chassis & Cab	3146	3356	—
2406Y	Thriftside Pickup	3246	3651	—
2406Y	Townside Pickup	3273	3759	—
2406Y	Platform Stake	3451	4012	—
Series J-3700 — (¾-Ton) — (4x2) — (126 in. w.b.)				
3306Y	Chassis & Cab	2498	3168	—
3306Y	Thriftside Pickup	2613	3488	—
3306Y	Townside Pickup	2640	3596	—
3306Y	Platform Stake	2837	3872	—
Series J-3700 — (¾-Ton) — (4x4) — (126 in. w.b.)				
3406Y	Chassis & Cab	3164	3377	—
3406Y	Thriftside Pickup	3279	3697	—
3406Y	Townside Pickup	3305	3805	—
3406Y	Platform Stake	3502	4081	—
Series J-2800 — (1-Ton) — (4x4) — (120 in. w.b.)				
2406Z	Chassis & Cab	3831	3789	—
2406Z	Platform Stake	4223	4534	—
Series J-3800 — (1-Ton) — (4x4) — (126 in. w.b.)				
3406Z	Chassis & Cab	3849	3822	—
3406Z	Platform Stake	4264	4620	—

ENGINES: Same as 1965. The 230 cu. in. inline six-cylinder (140 horsepower) was standard. The 327 cu. in. V-8 (250 horsepower) was standard in the Super Wagoneer and optional in other models.

1966 Kaiser-Jeep Wagoneer Panel Delivery

CHASSIS: Same as 1963-1965 for corresponding models.

TECHNICAL: Same as 1963-1965 for corresponding models.

OPTIONS: Same as 1963-1965 except for new V-6 engine in CJ and DJ models ($191).

HISTORICAL: Introduced: Fall, 1965. Calendar year production: 99,624 (This included 25,400 four-cylinders, 50,578 six-cylinders and 16,800 eight-cylinders). Innovations: New V-6 engine introduced. This was known as the "Dauntless" V-6. Historical notes: The automotive division posted a profit of $7,180,000 before, interest expense. This was up, although model year sales declined 8.3 percent.

Pricing

	5	4	3	2	1
1966					
Jeep Universal — (4x4)					
CJ-3B Jeep	950	1900	3150	4400	6300
CJ-5 Jeep	980	1950	3250	4550	6500
CJ-5A Tuxedo Park	1010	2030	3350	4700	6700
CJ-6 Jeep	1000	2000	3300	4600	6600
CJ-6A Tuxedo Park	1020	2050	3400	4800	6800
Dispatcher — (4x2)					
DJ-5 Courier	750	1500	2500	3500	5000
DJ-6 Courier	770	1550	2550	3600	5100
DJ-3A Jeep	780	1560	2600	3600	5100
DJ-3A Hardtop	830	1650	2750	3850	5500

NOTE: Add three percent for V-6 engine.

	5	4	3	2	1
Forward-Control — (4x4) — (¾-Ton)					
Pickup	700	1400	2350	3250	4700
Stake	660	1320	2200	3100	4400
(1-Ton)					
Pickup	690	1380	2300	3200	4600
Stake	650	1300	2150	3050	4300
Heavy-Duty Pickup	700	1400	2350	3250	4700
Heavy-Duty Stake	660	1320	2200	3100	4400
Fire Truck	830	1650	2750	3850	4500
Wagoneer — (½-Ton)					
4-dr. Wagon	830	1650	2750	3850	5500
2-dr. Wagon	810	1620	2700	3800	5400
4-dr. Custom Station Wagon	840	1680	2800	3900	5600
2-dr. Custom Station Wagon	830	1650	2750	3850	5500
Panel Delivery	720	1450	2400	3300	4800
4-dr. Super Wagon	950	1900	3150	4400	6300

1966 Kaiser-Jeep Gladiator 4x4 Pickup (KJC)

	5	4	3	2	1
Gladiator — (½-Ton) — (120 in. w.b.)					
Thriftside Pickup	750	1500	2500	3500	5000
Townside Pickup	780	1560	2600	3600	5200
Stake	660	1320	2200	3100	4400
(½-Ton) — (126 in. w.b.)					
Thriftside Pickup	720	1450	2400	3300	4800
Townside Pickup	750	1500	2500	3500	5000
Stake	650	1300	2150	3050	4300
(¾-Ton) — (120 in. w.b.)					
Thriftside Pickup	690	1380	2300	3200	4600
Townside Pickup	720	1450	2400	3300	4800
Stake	630	1250	2100	3000	4200
(¾-Ton) — (126 in. w.b.)					
Thriftside Pickup	680	1350	2250	3150	4500
Townside Pickup	700	1400	2350	3250	4700
Stake	620	1230	2050	2900	4100
(1-Ton) — (120 in. w.b.)					
Stake	600	1200	2000	2800	4000
Wrecker	700	1400	2350	3250	4700
Fire Truck	830	1650	2750	3850	5500
(1-Ton) — (126 in. w.b.)					
Stake	600	1200	2000	2800	4000
Wrecker	720	1400	2350	3250	4700
Fire Truck	830	1650	2750	3850	5500
(1-Ton) — (126 in. w.b.)					
Stake	600	1200	2000	2800	4000
Wrecker	720	1450	2400	3300	4800
Fire Truck	830	1650	2750	3850	5500

NOTES: Add five percent for 4x4.
Add five percent for V-8.

1967 KAISER JEEP

1967 Kaiser-Jeep Universal M-715 Military (ATC)

UNIVERSAL/DISPATCHER — SERIES CJ/DJ — FOUR-CYLINDER: — The CJ-3B and both DJ-3A models were discontinued in 1967. The venerable CJ-5, offshoot of the M-38A1 Korean War Army Jeep, was now the mainstay of the ¼-ton utility vehicle lineup. The CJ-5A was again the sportier, more luxurious edition. Basically the same, except for their 20 inch longer wheelbase and stretched bodies, were the CJ-6 and CJ-6A. Also remaining available were the 4x2 Jeeps coded the DJ-5 and DJ-6, which had their characteristic five-slot grilles. Base power plant in all models was the 134.2 cu. in. 75 horsepower F-head four-cylinder engine. Optional in all Jeep Universals was the 225 cu. in. 90-degree V-6, which now cranked-out 160 horsepower.

I.D. DATA: Serial number located on left front door hinge pillar post and left firewall. The VIN consists of from nine to 11 symbols. The first four-or five symbols indicate series and body style. The last five or six are sequential production numbers.

Model	Body Type	Price	Weight	Prod. Total
CJ-5 — (4x4) — (81 in. w.b.)				
8305	Jeep	2361	2163	—
CJ-5A — (4x4) — (81 in. w.b.)				
8322	Jeep	2458	2163	—
CJ-6 — (4x4) — (101 in. w.b.)				
8405	Jeep	2457	2217	—
CJ-6A — (4x4) — (101 in. w.b.)				
8422	Jeep	2553	2217	—
DJ-5 — (4x2) — (81 in. w.b.)				
8505	Dispatcher	1821	1823	—
DJ-6 — (4x2) — (101 in. w.b.)				
8605	Dispatcher	1917	1956	—

ENGINE: Same as 1963-1966 (see text above).

1967 Kaiser-Jeep Jeepster Commando Convertible

1967 Kaiser-Jeep Jeepster Commando Convertible

1967 Kaiser-Jeep Jeepster Commando Hardtop

JEEPSTER COMMANDO — SERIES 8700 — FOUR-CYLINDER: — An all-new line of Jeepster "Commando" models was introduced in January 1967. This was a modernized version of the early postwar Jeepster based on the original Brooks Stevens' design concept with some updating. The hood was widened to overlap the front fenders, which protroded only slightly on the sides and curved downwards, CJ-5-style, at the front. There was a simple, Jeep-like flat front with seven slots, which curved out, over the fenders, at the top. Circular parking lights were mounted outboard of the headlights, over the fenders. There were no actual rear fenders, only a flared contour that ran along the lower edge of the body and over the wheel wells. The horizontally pleated vinyl upholstery covered two bucket seats in front and a small bench seat at the rear. At the angular back of the phaeton-like body was a rear-mounted spare tire and wheel. The Jeepster Commando came in four models: Roadster-coupe; Convertible-phaeton; Station Wagon and Pickup truck. They were rated at ¼-ton and had a 3550 lb. GVW rating (Pickup). All were 4x4 models with the 134.2 cu. in./75 horsepower four-cylinder as base engine. The 225 cu. in./160 horsepower V-6 was optional.

I.D. DATA: Same as above.

1967 Kaiser-Jeep Jeepster Convertible (OCW)

Model	Body Type	Price	Weight	Prod. Total
Jeepster Commando — (4x4) — (101 in. w.b.)				
8701	Convertible	3186	2724	—
8705F	Station Wagon	2749	2673	—
8705	Roadster	2466	2461	—
8705H	Pickup	2548	2610	—

ENGINE: Same as Jeep Universal and Dispatcher.

1967 Kaiser-Jeep 4-Door Super Wagoneer (OCW)

WAGONEER/GLADIATOR — SERIES J — SIX-CYLINDER: — For model-year 1967, there was some paring down of the numerous series and models in the Wagoneer/Gladiator range. This was accomplished by eliminating nearly all 4x2 models, except in the J-100 series. Base engine for all series was the 232 cu. in. OHC six-cylinder with 145 horsepower. The 327 cu. in. V-8 with 250 horsepower was optional once again.

I.D. DATA: Same as above.

Model	Body Type	Price	Weight	Prod. Total
Series J-100 — (½-Ton) — (4x2) — (110 in. w.b.)				
1314	4-dr. Wagoneer	2953	3497	—
1312	2-dr. Wagoneer	2909	3470	—
1314C	4-dr. Custom Wagoneer	3150	3532	—
1312C	2-dr. Custom Wagoneer	3106	3505	—
1313	Panel Dely.	2783	3270	—
Series J-100 — (½-Ton) — (4x4) — (110 in. w.b.)				
1414	4-dr. Wagoneer	3702	3654	—
1412	2-dr. Wagoneer	3648	3627	—
1414C	4-dr. Custom Wagoneer	3898	3689	—
1412C	2-dr. Custom Wagoneer	3844	3662	—
1413	Panel Delivery	3357	3427	—
1414D	Super Wagoneer	6048	4241	—
Series J-2500 — (½-Ton) — (4x4) — (120 in. w.b.)				
2406W	Chassis & Cab	2957	3096	—
2406W	Thriftside Pickup	3058	3391	—
2406W	Townside Pickup	3085	3499	—
Series J-2600 — (½-Ton) — (4x4) — (120 in. w.b.)				
2406X	Chassis & Cab	3078	3237	—
2406X	Thriftside Pickup	3178	3532	—
2406X	Townside Pickup	3205	3640	—
2406X	Platform Stake	3383	3893	—
Series J-2700 — (¾-Ton) — (4x4) — (120 in. w.b.)				
2406Y	Chassis & Cab	3242	3324	—
2406Y	Thriftside Pickup	3343	3619	—
2406Y	Townside Pickup	3369	3727	—
2406Y	Platform Stake	3548	3980	—
Series J-2800 — (1-Ton) — (4x4) — (120 in. w.b.)				
2406Z	Chassis & Cab	3920	3757	—
2406Z	Platform Stake	4312	4502	—
Series J-3500 — (½-Ton) — (4x2) — (126 in. w.b.)				
3406W	Chassis & Cab	2976	3120	—
3406W	Thriftside Pickup	3091	3440	—
3406W	Townside Pickup	3117	3548	—

1967 Kaiser-Jeep 4-Door Wagoneer (OCW)

Model	Body Type	Price	Weight	Prod. Total
Series J-3600 — (½-Ton) — (4x4) — (126 in. w.b.)				
3406X	Chassis & Cab	3096	3258	—
3406X	Thriftside Pickup	3211	3578	—
3406X	Townside Pickup	3238	3686	—
3406X	Platform Stake	3435	3962	—
Series J-2700 — (¾-Ton) — (4x4) — (126 in. w.b.)				
3406Y	Chassis & Cab	3261	3345	—
3406Y	Thriftside Pickup	3375	3665	—
3406Y	Townside Pickup	3402	3773	—
3406Y	Platform Stake	3599	4049	—
Series J-3800 — (1-Ton) — (4x4) — (126 in. w.b.)				
3406Z	Chassis & Cab	3938	3790	—
3406Z	Platform Stake	4353	4588	—

ENGINES: Same as 1963-1966.

1967 Kaiser-Jeep Jeepster Commando Hardtop (JAG)

CHASSIS (Jeepster Commando): Wheelbase: 101 in. Cargo area: 63.8 in. Tires: 7.35 x 15 in. (Other models): Same as 1963-1966.

TECHNICAL (Jeepster Commando): Synchromesh transmission. Speeds: 3F/1R. Floor-mounted gearshift lever. Single-plate dry disc clutch with torsional dampening. Axles: Hypoid gears, full-floating front, semi-floating rear. Overall ratio: 3.54:1. Four-wheel hydraulic brakes. Disc wheels. (Other models): Same as 1963-1966.

OPTIONS: Options available for all models, including Jeepster Commando, were basically the same as 1963-1966 Jeep extra equipment. Jeepster Commando paint options: were: Sprucetrip green; President red; Empire blue; Gold beige; Glacier white and prarie gold.

HISTORICAL: Introduced: Fall 1966. Calendar year production: 116,744 (This included 29,858 'Jeep' vehicles and 86,886 military trucks.) Engine installations broke-out as 28,994 fours, 75,715 sixes and 12,035 V-8s. Innovations: New V-6 engine introduced. This was known as the "Dauntless" V-6. Innovations: Jeepster reintroduced in Jan. 1967. Turbo-Hydramatic transmission available in conjunction with V-6. Historical notes: Kaiser-Jeep's operating profit was $14,530,000; over double that of the previous year. E.F. Kaiser replaced H.J. Kaiser as Chairman of the Board. B.J. Heard was Executive VP and general manager of the Commercial Products Div.

Pricing

1967	5	4	3	2	1
Jeep Universal — (4x4)					
CJ-5 Jeep	930	1860	3100	4350	6200
CJ-5A Jeep	960	1920	3200	4500	6400
CJ-6 Jeep	980	1950	3250	4550	6500
CJ-6A Jeep	1010	2030	3350	4700	6700
Dispatcher — (4x2)					
DJ-5 Courier	740	1470	2450	3350	4900
DJ-6 Courier	750	1500	2500	3500	5000

NOTE: Add four percent for V-6 engine.

Jeepster Commando — (4x4)	5	4	3	2	1
Convertible	840	1680	2800	3900	5600
Station Wagon	810	1620	2700	3800	5400
Coupe-Roadster	870	1750	2900	4100	5800
Pickup	720	1450	2400	3300	4800

NOTE: Add 4 percent for V-6 engine.

Wagoneer					
4-dr. Wagon	830	1650	2750	3850	5500
2-dr. Wagon	810	1620	2700	3800	5400
4-dr. Custom Station Wagon	840	1680	2800	3900	5600
2-dr. Custom Station Wagon	830	1650	2750	3850	5500
Panel Delivery	720	1450	2400	3300	4800
4-dr. Super Wagon	870	1750	2900	4100	5800

NOTES: Add five percent for 4x4.
　　　　Add five percent for V-8 (except Super V-8).

Gladiator — (4x4) — (½-Ton) — (120 in. w.b.)					
Thriftside Pickup	740	1470	2450	3350	4900
Townside Pickup	770	1550	2550	3600	5100
Stake	650	1300	2150	3050	4300
(¾-Ton) — (120 in. w.b.)					
Thriftside Pickup	680	1350	2250	3150	4500
Townside Pickup	690	1380	2300	3200	4600
Stake	600	1200	2000	2800	4000
(1-Ton) — (120 in. w.b.)					
Stake	590	1170	1950	2700	3900
(½-Ton) — (126 in. w.b.)					
Thriftside Pickup	700	1400	2350	3250	4700
Townside Pickup	720	1450	2400	3300	4800
Stake	590	1170	1950	2700	3900
(¾-Ton) — (126 in. w.b.)					
Thriftside Pickup	680	1350	2250	3150	4500
Townside Pickup	690	1380	2300	3200	4600
Stake	590	1170	1950	2700	3900
(1-Ton) — (126 in. w.b.)					
Stake	590	1170	1950	2700	3900

NOTES: Add five percent for V-8.
　　　　Add five percent for 4x2 (Series 2500 only).

1968 KAISER JEEP

1968 Kaiser-Jeep Universal CJ-5 (JAG)

UNIVERSAL/DISPATCHER — SERIES CJ/DJ — FOUR-CYLINDER: — The Universal Jeep continued to resist fadish model year changes for the sake of change. For 1968, the lineup was unaltered and both styling and mechanical features were generally the same as in 1967. However, a new option was a diesel engine. Gas engine selections were unchanged. All models gained a few pounds when government-mandated safety equipment was added to the vehicles, along with emissions control hardware.

I.D. DATA: Serial number located on left front door hinge pillar post and left firewall. The VIN consists of from nine to 11 symbols. The first four or five symbols indicate series and body style. The last five or six are sequential production numbers. Starting serial numbers: (CJ-5) 8305S or 8305015 or 8305C15-228800 and up. (CJ-5A) 8322S-17423 and up. (CJ-6) 8405015 or 8405S-33935 and up. (CJ-6A) 8422S-10462 and up. (DJ-5) 8505015 or 8505S-12261 and up. (DJ-6) 8605015 or 8605S-11461 and up.

1968 Kaiser-Jeep CJ-5 Universal 4x4 w/'Family Camper'

Model	Body Type	Price	Weight	Prod. Total
CJ-5 — (4x4) — (81 in. w.b.)				
8305	Jeep Universal	2683	2212	—
CJ-5A — (4x4) — (81 in. w.b.)				
8322	Jeep Universal	2778	2212	—
CJ-6 — (4x4) — (101 in. w.b.)				
8405	Jeep Universal	2778	2274	—
CJ-6A — (4x4) — (101 in. w.b.)				
8422	Jeep Universal	2875	2274	—
DJ-5 — (4x2) — (81 in. w.b.)				
8505	Jeep Dispatcher	2153	1872	—
DJ-6 — (4x2) — (101 in. w.b.)				
8605	Jeep Dispatcher	2249	2005	—

1968 Kaiser-Jeep CJ-5 Universal 4x4 (KJC)

ENGINES: Same as 1963-1967, plus new diesel option. The diesel was a four-cylinder job with 3.5 x 5 in. bore and stroke. It was rated at 19.6 tax-able horsepower.

1968 Kaiser-Jeep Jeepster Commando Convertible

JEEPSTER COMMANDO — SERIES 8700 — FOUR-CYLINDER: — Changes for the Jeepster Commandos for 1968 included a new top for the convertible, hinged tailgates for better rear seat access, full metal doors with roll-up windows for the convertible and ventipanes on appropriate models. There was also a slight redesign of the name badges on the sides of the hood and newly styled wheel covers. The Jeepster engine options were the same as in 1967. Turbo-Hydramatic transmission was available with the optional V-6.

584

1968 Kaiser-Jeep Jeepster Commando Station Wagon

I.D. DATA: Same as above. Starting serial numbers: (Model) 15-19027 and up. (Convertible) 8701-12215 and up. (Pickup) 8705H15-19027 and up.

1968 Kaiser-Jeep Jeepster Commando Hardtop (JAG)

Model	Body Type	Price	Weight	Prod. Total
Jeepster Commando — (4x4) — (101 in. w.b.)				
8702	2-dr. Convertible	3442	2853	—
8705F	Station Wagon	3005	2722	—
8705	Roadster-Coupe	2730	2510	—
8705H	Pickup Truck	2817	2659	—

ENGINE: Same as 1967.

1968 Kaiser-Jeep 4-Door Wagoneer (KJC)

WAGONEER/GLADIATOR — SERIES J — SIX-CYLINDER/V-8: — The Wagoneers and Gladiators were carried over with some additional cutting of models. Gone from the long-wheelbase series was the flared-rear-fender Thriftside pickup trucks. This reduced the model count to a total of eight Wagoneers and 24 Gladiators. Wagoneers came only in 4x4 form. There was one new Wagoneer, called the Custom V-8, which joined the V8-only Super Wagoneer in a separate sub-series representing the marque's luxury models. Both were priced at above $6,000 in standard form, which included many features that normally sold for extra-cost. A camper package for J-3600 Gladiators was a $267 option.

I.D. DATA: Same system as described above. Starting serial numbers consisted of the series and model code followed by sequential production number. They were: (Wagoneers) 1414017 or 1414S-205868 and up; 1412017 or 1412S-200358 and up; 1414017 or 1414CS-200621 and up; 1412C17 or 1412CS-200015 and up; 1414D19 or 1414DS-101078 and up; 1414X19-30001 and up; 1413S-200583 and up (V-8 100060 and up). (Gladiator) 2406W17 or 2406WS-202456 and up; 2406X1or 2406XS-20257 and up (V-8 101447 and up); 2406Y17 or 2460Y or 2406YS-201297 and up (V8 100235 and up); 2406Z17 or 2406Z or 2406ZS-200020 and up (V-8 100010 and up); 3406W17 or 3406WS-21022 and up (V-8 101794 and up); 3406X17 or 3406XS-200669 and up (V-8 102974 and up); 3406Y17 or 3406Y or 3406YS-200725 up (V-8 100514 and up); 3406Z17 or 3406ZN or 3406ZS-200150 and up (V-8 100139 and up).

Model	Body Type	Price	Weight	Prod. Total
Series J-100 — (½-Ton) — (4x4) — (110 in. w.b.)				
1414S	4-dr. Wagoneer	3869	3710	—
1412S	2-dr. Wagoneer	3815	3683	—
1414CS	4-dr. Custom Wagoneer	4065	3745	—
1412CS	2-dr. Custom Wagoneer	4011	3718	—
1413S	Panel Dely.	3457	3483	—
Series J-100 V-8 — (½-Ton) — (4x4) — (110 in. w.b.)				
1414D	Super Wagoneer	6163	4263	—
1414X	4-dr. Custom Wagoneer	5671	3907	—
Series J-2500 — (½-Ton) — (4x4) — (120 in. w.b.)				
2406W	Chassis & Cab	3119	3152	—
2406W	Thriftside Pickup	3225	3447	—
2406W	Townside Pickup	3253	3555	—
Series J-2600 — (½-Ton) — (4x4) — (120 in. w.b.)				
2406X	Chassis & Cab	3240	3293	—
2406X	Thriftside Pickup	3345	3588	—
2406X	Townside Pickup	3373	3696	—
2406X	Platform Stake	3560	3949	—
Series J-2700 — (¾-Ton) — (4x4) — (120 in. w.b.)				
2406Y	Chassis & Cab	3404	3380	—
2406Y	Thriftside Pickup	3510	3675	—
2406Y	Townside Pickup	3538	3785	—
2406Y	Platform Stake	3725	4036	—
Series J-2800 — (1-Ton) — (4x4) — (120 in. w.b.)				
2406Z	Chassis & Cab	3996	3813	—
2406Z	Platform Stake	4411	4558	—
Series J-3500 — (½-Ton) — (4x4) — (126 in. w.b.)				
3406W	Chassis & Cab	3138	3176	—
3406W	Townside Pickup	3286	3604	—
Series J-3600 — (½-Ton) — (4x4) — (126 in. w.b.)				
3406X	Chassis & Cab	3258	3314	—
3406X	Townside Pickup	3407	3742	—
3406X	Platform Stake	3614	4018	—
Series J-3700 — (¾-Ton) — (4x4) — (126 in. w.b.)				
3406Y	Chassis & Cab	3423	3401	—
3406Y	Townside Pickup	3571	3829	—
3406Y	Platform Stake	3778	4105	—
Series J-3800 — (1-Ton) — (4x4) — (126 in. w.b.)				
3406Z	Chassis & Cab	4015	3846	—
3406Z	Platform Stake	4429	4644	—

ENGINES: Same as 1963-1967.

CHASSIS: Same as 1963-1967 for comparable models.

TECHNICAL: Same as 1963-1967 for comparable models.

OPTIONS: Same as 1963-1967.

HISTORICAL: Introduced: Fall, 1967. Calendar year production: 117,573 (This included a much higher 86,886 'Jeep' vehicles and only 29,858 military trucks). Engine breakouts were: (4-cyl.) 24,458; (6-cyl.) 76,220 and (V-8) 16,895. Innovations: Diesel engine available in some models during 1968 only. Historical notes: New V-6 manufacturing plant opens. A marine version of this engine was also supplied to a major boat engine manufacturer. (Jeeps were built at Toledo and Army trucks at South Bend. The new V-6 manufacturing facility was also in Toledo). J.R. Cody became V.P. and General Manager of the Commercial Division.

Pricing

	5	4	3	2	1
1968					
Jeep Universal — (4x4)					
CJ-5 Jeep	930	1860	3100	4350	6200
CJ-5A Jeep	960	1920	3200	4500	6400
CJ-6 Jeep	980	1950	3250	4550	6500
CJ-6A Jeep	1010	2030	3350	4700	6700
Dispatcher — (4x2)					
DJ-5 Courier	740	1470	2450	3350	4900
DJ-6 Courier	750	1500	2500	3500	5000

NOTE: Add four percent for V-6 engine.
Add five percent for diesel engine.

Jeepster Commando — (4x4)					
Convertible	840	1680	2800	3900	5600
Station Wagon	810	1620	2700	3800	5400
Coupe-Roadster	870	1750	2900	4100	5800
Pickup	720	1450	2400	3300	4800

NOTE: Add four percent for V-6 engine.

	5	4	3	2	1
Wagoneer — (4x4)					
4-dr. Wagon	870	1750	2900	4100	5800
2-dr. Wagon	850	1700	2850	4000	5700
4-dr. Custom Station Wagon	890	1770	2950	4150	5900
2-dr. Custom Station Wagon	870	1750	2900	4100	5800
Panel Delivery	750	1500	2500	3500	5000
4-dr. Super Wagon	920	1850	3050	4300	6100
Custom V-8 Wagon	900	1800	3000	4200	6000

NOTE: Add five percent for V-8 (except Super and Custom V-8).

Gladiator — (4x4) — (½-Ton) — (120 in. w.b.)					
Thriftside Pickup	740	1470	2450	3350	4900
Townside Pickup	770	1550	2550	3600	5100
Stake	650	1300	2150	3050	4300
(¾-Ton) — (120 in. w.b.)					
Thriftside Pickup	680	1350	2250	3150	4500
Townside Pickup	690	1380	2300	3200	4600
Stake	600	1200	2000	2800	4000
(1-Ton) — (120 in. w.b.)					
Stake	590	1170	1950	2700	3900
(½-Ton) — (126 in. w.b.)					
Townside	720	1450	2400	3300	4800
Stake	590	1170	1950	2700	3900
(¾-Ton) — (126 in. w.b.)					
Townside	690	1380	2300	3200	4600
Stake	590	1170	1950	2700	3900
(1-Ton) — (126 in. w.b.)					
Stake	590	1170	1950	2700	3900

NOTES: Add 5 percent for V-8 engine.
Add 10 percent for J-3500 factory Camper Package.

1969 KAISER JEEP

1969 Kaiser-Jeep Universal Model "462"

UNIVERSAL/DISPATCHER — SERIES CJ/DJ — FOUR-CYLINDER: — To conform with federal safety regulations, Jeep products had new side-marker lamps this year. They were mounted to the sides of the hood and rear quarter of the body. The CJ-5A and CJ-6A "Tuxedo Park" models were deleted as was the CJ-6. There was a new, limited-edition "462" model-option including a roll bar, swing-out spare tire carrier, polyglass tubeless tires, skid plate, electric ammeter and oil gauges. It was designed for some serious off-roading. This was the final season for the Kaiser-Jeep name. The company left Kaiser Industries in 1970, becoming Jeep Corporation, a division of American Motors.

I.D. DATA: Serial number located on left front door hinge pillar post and left firewall. The VIN consists of from nine to 11 symbols. The first four to six indicated series and body style. The last five or six are sequential production numbers. Starting serial numbers: (CJ-5) 8305015 or 8305C15-244728 and up. (CJ-6) 8405015-35264 and up. (DJ-5) 8505015-12871 and up.

Model	Body Type	Price	Weight	Prod. Total
CJ-5 — (4x4) — (81 in. w.b.)				
8305	Jeep Universal	2823	2212	—
CJ-6 — (4x4) — (101 in. w.b.)				
8405	Jeep Universal	2918	2274	—
DJ-5 — (4x2) — (81 in. w.b.)				
8505	Jeep Dispatcher	2292	1872	—

ENGINES: Same as 1963-1967, the diesel engine was no longer available.

JEEPSTER COMMANDO — SERIES 8700 — FOUR-CYLINDER: — A more luxurious version of the Jeepser Commando was added to the line in 1969. It was simply called the Jeepster and came only in the convertible body style. New side-marker lights were the main styling change.

I.D. DATA: Same system as above. Starting serial numbers: (Jeepster Conv.) 8701015-12545 and up. (Commandos) [Model] 15-28002 and up; [Conv.] 15-10001 and up; [Pickup] 8705H15-28002 and up.

Model	Body Type	Price	Weight	Prod. Total
Jeepster Commando — (4x4) — (101 in. w.b.)				
8702	2-dr. Convertible	3005	2707	—
8705F	Station Wagon	3113	2722	—
8705	Roadster-Coupe	2824	2510	—
8705H	Pickup	2914	2659	—
Jeepster — (4x4) — (101 in. w.b.)				
8701	2-dr. Convertible	3537	2773	—

ENGINE: Same as 1967-1968.

1969 Kaiser-Jeep Gladiator Townside Pickup

WAGONEER/GLADIATOR — SERIES J — SIX-CYLINDER/V-8: — The Wagoneer and Gladiator models were little-changed for 1969. The Wagoneers were all four-door models. New side-marker lamps were added to the sides of the front and rear fenders. The one-ton trucks on both the 120 and 126 inch wheelbase were dropped. Actually, the J-3800 chassis was still available, but it was down-rated to ¾-tons and an 8000 pounds GVW. It could be equipped with the camper package for $148 extra.

I.D. DATA: Same system as above. Starting serial numbers were (J-2500) 2406W17-202937 and up; (J-2600) 2406X17-202823 and up; (J-2700) 2406Y17-203184 and up; (J-3500) 3406W17-201152 and up; (J-3600) 3406X17-200866 and up; (J-3700) 3406Y17-200848 and up; (J-3800) 3407Z19-300001 and up.

Model	Body Type	Price	Weight	Prod. Total
Series J-100 — (½-Ton) — (4x4) — (110 in. w.b.)				
14140	Wagoneer (6-cyl.)	4145	3710	—
1414C	Custom Wagoneer (6-cyl.)	4342	3745	—
1414X	Wagoneer (V-8)	5671	3907	—
1414D	Custom Wagoneer (V-8)	6163	4263	—
Series J-2500 — (½-Ton) — (4x4) — (120 in. w.b.)				
2406W	Chassis & Cab	3243	3152	—
2406W	Thriftside Pickup	3348	3447	—
2406W	Townside Pickup	3376	3555	—
Series J-2600 — (½-Ton) — (4x4) — (120 in. w.b.)				
2406X	Chassis & Cab	3363	3293	—
2406X	Thriftside Pickup	3469	3588	—
2406X	Townside Pickup	3497	3696	—
2406X	Stake	3684	3949	—
Series J-2700 — (¾-Ton) — (4x4) — (120 in. w.b.)				
2406Y	Chassis & Cab	3528	3380	—
2406Y	Thriftside Pickup	3633	3675	—
2406Y	Townside Pickup	3661	3783	—
2406Y	Stake	3849	4036	—
Series J-3500 — (½-Ton) — (4x4) — (126 in. w.b.)				
3406W	Chassis & Cab	3261	3176	—
3406W	Townside Pickup	3410	3604	—
Series J-3600 — (½-Ton) — (4x4) — (126 in. w.b.)				
3406X	Chassis & Cab	3382	3314	—
3406X	Townside Pickup	3530	3742	—
3406X	Stake	3737	4018	—
Series J-3700 — (¾-Ton) — (4x4) — (126 in. w.b.)				
3406Y	Chassis & Cab	3546	3401	—
3406Y	Townside Pickup	3695	3829	—
3406Y	Stake	3902	4105	—
Series J-3800 — (¾-Ton) — (4x4) — (126 in. w.b.)				
3406Z	Chassis & Cab	4184	3792	—

ENGINES: Same as 1963-1968.

CHASSIS: Same as 1963-1967 for comparable models.

TECHNICAL: Same as 1963-1967 for comparable models.

OPTIONS: Same as 1963-1967.

HISTORICAL: Introduced: Fall, 1968. Calendar year production: 93,160 in the United States and 2,048 in Canada. (This included 61,652 civilian trucks made in Toledo and 29,929 military vehicles built in South Bend.) Innovations: New sporty '462' Jeep model was released. Historical notes: On Feb. 5, 1970 Kaiser-Jeep was purchased for approximately $70 million by AMC.

1969 Kaiser-Jeep Universal CJ-5 (JAG)

Pricing

	5	4	3	2	1
1969					
Jeep					
CJ-5 Jeep	930	1860	3100	4350	6200
CJ-6 Jeep	980	1950	3250	4550	6500
DJ-5 Courier	740	1470	2450	3350	4900

NOTE: Add 4 percent for V-6 engine.

	5	4	3	2	1
Jeepster Commando					
Convertible	840	1680	2800	3900	5600
Station Wagon	810	1620	2700	3800	5400
Coupe-Roadster	870	1750	2900	4100	5800
Pickup	720	1450	2400	3300	4800
Convertible	920	1850	3050	4300	6100

NOTE: Add 4 percent for V-6 engine.

	5	4	3	2	1
Wagoneer					
4-dr. Wagon	870	1750	2900	4100	5800
4-dr. Custom Wagon	890	1770	2950	4150	5900

NOTE: Add five percent for V-8 engine.

	5	4	3	2	1
Gladiator — (½-Ton) — (120 in. w.b.)					
Thriftside Pickup	740	1470	2450	3350	4900
Townside Pickup	770	1550	2550	3600	5100
Stake	650	1300	2150	3050	4300
(¾-Ton) — (120 in. w.b.)					
Thriftside Pickup	680	1350	2250	3150	4500
Townside Pickup	690	1380	2300	3200	4600
Stake	600	1200	2000	2800	4000
(½-Ton) — (126 in. w.b.)					
Townside	720	1450	2400	3300	4800
Stake	590	1170	1950	2700	3900
(¾-Ton) — (126 in. w.b.)					
Townside	690	1380	2300	3200	4600
Stake	590	1170	1950	2700	3900

NOTES: Add 5 percent for V-8 engine.
Add 10 percent for factory Camper Package.

PLYMOUTH

(Prewar) By Jim Benjamison
(Postwar) By Charles Webb

From 1935 to 1942 Commercial versions of Chrysler's low-priced Plymouth were offered, alongside light-duty Dodge trucks, to give holders of joint Chrysler-Plymouth franchises extra sales.

1932 Plymouth Model PB Taxicab (CHC)

1932 Plymouth Model PA Ambulance (CHC)

A "pilot" version Plymouth truck appeared as early as 1930, but failed to see production, probably because Chrysler's non-Dodge outlets had the Fargo truck-line to sell in the United States at this time. However, after 1935, the Fargo became a badge-engineered Dodge marketed exclusively in Canada or as an export to other nations. This created, once more, the need for a non-Dodge commercial vehicle line.

1933 Plymouth Model PC Business Coupe (CHC)

Plymouth tested the waters and, in 1935, began offering a "commercial car" series. It consisted of a modified two-door sedan, converted into a Sedan Delivery type vehicle, which had essentially the same status as a business coupe. Other "business" variations included such models as taxicabs, aftermarket station wagons, ambulances, etc. The true commercial sedan, with blanked-out rear quarters and side-hinged cargo door, earned less than 150 sales. Nevertheless, a Panel Delivery (with a split seatback and inner panels) was added to the commercial car series in 1936.

1934 Plymouth Model PE Westchester Suburban (CHC)

Changing its basic approach in 1937, Plymouth released new models that were built off a real truck platform; one not shared with passenger cars. A Commercial Sedan was marketed, along with an Express — or *Pickup* — Truck. Taxis, ambulances, funeral cars and station wagons were also constructed on chassis-only or chassis-and-cowl versions of the new truck. The prime source of wood station wagon bodies was U.S. Body & Forging Co., of Frankfort, Indiana.

1940 Plymouth "Roadking" Utility Sedan (JAW)

1940 Plymouth ½-Ton Pickup (Ron Barker)

1940 Plymouth ½-Ton Pickup (Ron Barker)

Sales were encouraging enough to continue the truck-line in 1938 and expand it the following season. For 1939, an added series, using the smallest Dodge truck chassis, was released. This "Road King" line included a four-door sedan-ambulance conversion, a coupe with cargo box, a two-door Commercial Sedan and a Sedan Delivery. All had a 114 inch wheelbase. A two-inch longer stance characterized the new P81 Series, which had pickup and chassis-and-cab models.

For 1940, the Plymouth commercial car-line again offered models on two wheelbases. Interestingly, the larger had the car chassis and sheet metal, while the smaller was a true truck carrying over the '39 sheet metal, but with headlights mounted on the fender crease in "bug-eye" fashion.

1941 Plymouth ½-Ton Pickup (Sonny Glesbrenner)

The fact that the real trucks were more compact than the commercial cars seemed illogical. But, perhaps even more surprising, was the continuation of this system in 1941, the final prewar year for dual wheelbases. Again the light-duty trucks had dated styling and a 116 inch wheelbase, while the passenger car-based commercials adopted the year's new sheet metal and rode the 117 inch wheelbase.

1974 Plymouth Trail Duster Utility Wagon (CW)

588

War-shortened model-year 1942 saw both the commercial car-line and light-duty truck series discontinued, although sales of leftover units went on. The small number of units finding buyers were registered (at least in some states) as 1942 models. Some new Commercial Sedans may also have been assembled, probably on a built-to-order basis.

1974 Plymouth Voyager Custom Wagon (CW)

Plymouth trucks did not return immediately following the end of hostilities. In fact, it wasn't until 1974 that the company's name would be appearing on a light-duty (or any other sized) truck. Even at that, the new model's impact on the overall truck market was minor.

1975 Plymouth Trail Duster Open Utility (CW)

1980 Plymouth Trail Duster Utility Wagon (CW)

At first, the entire Plymouth light-duty truck lineup consisted of the Trail Duster 4x4 Sport Utility vehicle and the Voyager (a forward-control passenger van marketed as a "wagon.") The Trail Duster was intended to cash-in on the the booming market for off-road RVs in the seventies. Like

1980 Plymouth Voyager Wagon (CW)

typical Sport Utility trucks, it was pretty spartan in basic form. However, it could be "optioned-out" to almost passenger car luxury. The Voyager Wagon was an attractive people hauler that could carry as many as 15 passengers.

Both Trail Duster and Voyager were made on the same assembly line as nearly identical Dodge versions of the same vehicles. Although as good looking, or better, than most competitors, there was nothing particularly special about them. So, sales were modest.

1983 Plymouth Scamp Mini Sport Pickup (CW)

In 1979, Plymouth expanded its truck offerings by including the Arrow compact pickup. Arrow, like its twin, the Dodge 500, was made by Mitsubishi Motors Corporation in Japan. These trucks soon gained a reputation for being among the best (if not *the* best) compact trucks on the market.

When Chevrolet and Ford phased-out their imported small trucks and replaced them with domestically-produced versions, Plymouth did not follow suit. However, Plymouth did drop the Arrow after the 1982 model year. It was, sort of, replaced by the new Scamp, which was less of a standard type pickup and more like a miniature version of the Ranchero/El Camino genre. Despite its sporty good looks, however, the Scamp lasted only one year.

1982 Plymouth Arrow Mini-Pickup (OCW)

In 1984, Plymouth found a winner in the light-duty truck field. It was the new Voyager; part car, part station wagon and part truck. This new, front-wheel-drive vehicle was unlike anything that Ford or Chevrolet offered. It was also an instant success.

For once, Plymouth was out front! Other truck-makers had to play "catch-up ball."

By 1986, the only light-duty truck offered by Plymouth was the Voyager. Although MoPar truck lovers could still turn to Dodge for a variety of commercial vehicles, Plymouth no longer offered something to fit every light-duty need.

1930-1931 PLYMOUTH

1930 Plymouth 'Pilot Model' Delivery Car (CHC)

COMMERCIAL SEDAN — SERIES 30U — FOUR-CYLINDER: — Plymouth's first entry into the commercial field was a rather half-hearted entry using a passenger car chassis. The Commercial Sedan was a modification of a two-door sedan, with the addition of a door at the rear of the body and the deletion the rear seat. The rear quarter windows were blanked out through the use of removable panels. The idea behind the vehicle was to provide a commercial/passenger vehicle to the small businessman who needed both types of vehicles, but who could afford to purchase only one vehicle. With the rear seat available as an option, it was possible to convert the vehicle into a family car when needed. With the window blanks in place and the rear seat removed, it became the perfect delivery vehicle and its passenger car styling allowed it to go where commercial vehicles were prohibited. At a time when Chrysler Corporation was still building a Fargo commercial car in the same line, as well as a similar vehicle from sister division DeSoto, the Plymouth 30U Commercial Sedan met with little success and the idea was dropped at the end of the year. By then, only 80 vehicles had been sold.

I.D. DATA: Serial number located on right front door post. Starting: Detroit, Mich. — 1,500,001. Ending: Detroit, Mich. — 1,570,188. Engine number located on left front corner of cylinder block, directly above generator mounting. Starting: U200,001. Ending: U277,000.

NOTE: All Plymouth Engine Numbers: The engine number is found on a boss on the left front corner of the cylinder block, usually directly above the generator. The numbers indicate the engine sequential serial number and may also include a series of code letters to advise mechanics that the engine was factory installed with under- or over-sized components. In addition, the model code was stamped into the serial number, indicating the model year of the engine. A typical engine code example is: T50-123456-AB. The letters "T50" indicate the model code (1937 model PT50). The next group (i.e., 123456) is the sequential number. The suffix AB indicates over- and under-size engine components per the following code: A = .020 over-size cylinder bore; B = .010 under-size main and connecting rod bearings; C = .005 over-size rod bearings; AB = .020 over-size cylinders and .010 under-size mains and rods; E = Economy engine with smaller carburetor and intake manifold; X = small bore export engine.

1931 Plymouth 'Red Top' Taxicab (CHC)

Model Series 30U	Body Type	Price	Weight	Prod. Total
30U	Commercial Sedan	750	—	80

590

ENGINE: Inline. L-head. Four-cylinder. Cast iron block. Bore & stroke: 3⅜in. x 4¾ in. Displacement: 196.1 cu. in. Compression ratio: 4.6. Brake horsepower: 48 at 2800 R.P.M. SAE Horsepower: 21.03. Three main bearings. Solid valve lifters. Carburetor: Carter model 130S, Carter model 130SA, Carter model 156-S or Carter model 158-S (Export). Torque: 120 lbs.-ft. at 1200 R.P.M.

CHASSIS (Series 30U): Wheelbase: 109¾ in. Overall length: 169 in. Front tread: 56¼ in. Rear tread: 56⅛ in. Tires: 4.75 x 19 in.

TECHNICAL: (Early models) sliding spur gears; (later models) helical cut gears. Speeds: 3F/1R. Floor shift gearshift lever. Single dry disc clutch. Shaft drive. Semi-floating, spiral bevel. Overall ratio: 4.3 to 1. Four-wheel hydraulic brakes. Wood spoke, (wire optional) wheels. Rim Size: 4.75 x 19 in.

OPTIONS: Front bumper. Rear bumper. Single sidemount. Windshield defroster. Spring covers. Five- or six-bolt lug pattern wire wheels.

HISTORICAL: Production began April 8, 1930; ended June 8, 1931. Model year production: 80 commercial sedans were built. F.L. Rockelman was president of Plymouth in 1930 and 1931.

Pricing

	5	4	3	2	1
1930-1931 Series 30U Commercial Sedan	1350	2700	4500	6300	9000

1935 PLYMOUTH

1935 Plymouth Commercial Sedan (C.Schreckenberg)

COMMERCIAL SEDAN — SERIES PJ — SIX-CYLINDER: — After an absence from the commercial field since 1931, Plymouth re-entered the market with another sedan delivery conversion from a standard passenger car body. Based on the two-door "flatback" sedan, a single rear door was fitted at the rear. Like its 30U counterpart, the PJ's interior was gutted and the rear quarter windows were filled with blanks, which were removable. Like its 30U predecessor, a complete interior was offered, as an option, to convert the vehicle into a standard passenger model. While the 30U version had been the highest priced body style in the vehicle lineup, the PJ version had an asking price of only $100 more than the passenger sedan on which it was based. It was cheaper than sedans in the Deluxe series. This version met with considerably more success than the 30U and 1,142 found buyers.

1935 Plymouth Commercial Station Wagon (CHC)

I.D. DATA: Serial number located on right front door post. Starting: Detroit, Mich.: 1,039,101; Windsor, Ontario: 9,396,076; Los Angeles, Calif.: 3,151,501. Ending: Detroit, Mich.: 1,111,645; Windsor, Ontario: 9,397,345; Los Angeles, Calif.: 3,157,116. Engine number located on left front corner of cylinder block, directly above generator mounting. Starting: PJ-1001. Ending: PJ-359025.

1935 Plymouth High-Speed Safety (Armored) Car (SSP)

Model Series PJ	Body Type	Price	Weight	Prod. Total
651-B	Sedan Delivery	635	2735	1142

ENGINE: Inline. L-head. Six-cylinder. Cast iron block. Bore & stroke: 3⅛in. x 4⅜ in. Displacement: 201.3 cu. in. Compression ratio: 6.7. Brake horsepower: 82 at 3600 R.P.M. SAE Horsepower: 23.44. Four main bearings. Solid valve lifters. Carburetor: Carter model BB439S. Torque: 145 lbs.-ft. at 1200 R.P.M.

CHASSIS: (Series PJ "Business Six"): Wheelbase: 113 in. Overall length: 187⅞ in. Front tread: 56¼ in. Rear tread: 58 in. Tires: 6.00 x 16 in.

1935 Plymouth Commercial Sedan Delivery (CHC)

TECHNICAL: Sliding gear transmission with helical cut gears. Speeds: 3F/1R. Floor shift gearshift lever. Dry, single 9½ in. disc clutch. Shaft drive. Semi-floating, spiral bevel. Overall ratio: 4.125 to 1. Four-wheel hydraulic brakes. Steel spoke "artillery" wheels. Rim Size: 6.00 x 16 in.)

OPTIONS: Front and rear bumper as a package, including spare tire, ($33). Single sidemount (standard). Dual sidemount. Sidemount cover(s). Fender skirts ($9 pair). Bumper guards. Philco Transitone radio ($39.95). Heaters. Glove box door clock ($11.75). Cigar lighter ($1.). Seat covers. Spotlight ($15.95). Clock mirror ($3.95). Locking gas cap ($2.25). Dual air tone external horns ($12.). License plate frames ($2.45). Radiator grille cover ($1.25). Right-hand sun visor ($1.75). Metal spring covers ($6.). Wheel trim rings ($1.35). Right-hand windshield wiper ($4.95). Oil bath air cleaner ($2.50). Sailing ship radiator ornament ($3.50). Duo-Airstream heater ($19.95). Deluxe hot water heater ($15.95). Standard hot water heater ($12.95). 20 inch high-clearance wheels.

HISTORICAL: Production starting date unknown. Production ended August 15, 1935. Model year production: 1,142 Commercial Sedans. Dan S. Eddins was president of Plymouth in 1935.

Pricing

1935 Series PJ	5	4	3	2	1
Sedan Delivery	1300	2550	4250	5900	8500

1936 PLYMOUTH

1936 Plymouth Sedan Delivery (DFW)

COMMERCIAL SEDAN — SERIES P-1 — SIX-CYLINDER: — Again basing its commercial model on the passenger car chassis, Plymouth, for 1936, saw fit to treat the Commercial Sedan to its own body. No longer was the practice of converting a two-door sedan body followed, as it had been previously. Based on the cheaper "Business" chassis, the model's price was reduced $20 from the 1935 version. An improved business climate saw a doubling in sales of this particular body style. For those buyers not wishing to purchase this special body style, Plymouth offered several unique options, on its regular passenger lineup, including special ambulance and hearse conversions for the four-door body and a removable pickup box for use on the business coupe.

I.D. DATA: Serial number located on right front door post. Starting: Detroit, Mich.: 1,111,701; Evansville, Ind.: 9,000,101; Los Angeles, Calif.: 3,157,151; Windsor, Ontario: 9,397,351. Ending: Detroit, Mich.: 1,183,569; Evansville, Ind.: 9,012,724; Los Angeles, Calif.: 3,162,365; Windsor, Ontario: 9,400,000. Engine number located on left front corner of cylinder block, above generator mount. Starting: P2-1001. Ending: P2-532087.

Model Series P-1	Body Type	Price	Weight	Prod. Total
P-1	Commercial Sedan	605	2880	3527

1936 Plymouth Westchester Suburban (CHC)

ENGINE: Inline. Six-cylinder. Cast iron block. Bore & stroke: 3⅛ in. x 4⅜ in. Displacement: 201.3 cu. in. Compression ratio: 6.7. Brake horsepower: 82 at 3600 R.P.M. SAE Horsepower: 23.44. Four main bearings. Solid valve lifters. Carburetor: Carter BB439S; Carter B6F1; Carter C6E1-2. Torque: 145 lbs.-ft. at 1200 R.P.M.

OPTIONAL ENGINE: Economy version with one-inch carburetor and smaller intake manifold developed 65 horsepower at 3000 R.P.M. Identified by engine code P2E. Export versions: 2⅞ in. x 4⅜ in. 170.4 cu. in. Identified by engine code P2X.

CHASSIS: (Series P-1 Business Six): Wheelbase: 113 in. Overall length: 190 in. Front tread: 55⅞ in. Rear tread: 58 in. Tires: 5.25 x 17 in.

TECHNICAL: Sliding gear transmission with helical cut gears. Speeds: 3F/1R. Floor shift gearshift lever. Dry, single 9¼ in. disc clutch. Shaft drive. Semi-floating, spiral bevel. Overall ratio: 4.125 to 1. Steel "artillery" spoke wheels. Rim Size: 6.25 x 17 in.

OPTIONS: Front and rear bumper sold as a package. Single sidemount (standard). Dual sidemount. Fender skirts ($9 pair). Heater (several hot water types available). Spotlight ($15.95). Heavy-duty air cleaner ($2.50). Radiator ornament ($3.50). Metal rear spring covers ($16). Wheels ($15). Deluxe steering wheel ($5). 20 inch high-clearance wheels ($15). Glove box lock ($1). Locking gas cap ($1.50). Deluxe external "Airtone" horns ($12). Right-hand taillamp ($2.85). Right-hand inside sun visor ($1.50). Radiator grill cover ($1.25). Hand brake extension lever ($1.50). Exhaust extension ($1). Chrome wheel discs ($2.30 each). License plate frames ($2.45 pair). Defroster ($1.50). Electric defrost fan ($6.50).

HISTORICAL: Production began September 19 1935; ending August 21, 1936. Model year production: 3,527. Dan S. Eddins was president of Plymouth.

Pricing

1936 Series P-1	5	4	3	2	1
Commercial Sedan	1350	2650	4400	6150	8800

1937 PLYMOUTH

1937 Plymouth Model PT50 Pickup (OCW/IOCS)

COMMERCIAL CAR — SERIES PT-50 — SIX-CYLINDER: — Plymouth entered the commercial field in 1937 with its own truck chassis. It was built on a 116 inch ladder type frame. There was little doubt in anyone's mind that the Plymouth "Commercial Car," as it was called, was a clone of its sister Dodge truck. The reasons for building such a vehicle lied within the corporate structure of Chrysler. Plymouth dealerships were always "dualed" with another corporate offering, either Chrysler, DeSoto or Dodge, giving dealers more than one line to sell. For those dualed with Dodge, there was no need for another commercial vehicle. However, those dealers dualed with DeSoto or Chrysler had no commercial vehicle to sell. In cities where a Plymouth dealership was found on nearly every street corner, the loss of sales did not sit well. In addition, rural areas not served by a Dodge-Plymouth dealership also lost sales to the competition. Offered on the Commercial Car chassis was a sedan delivery, the Express (pickup) and a chassis-and-cab complete with runningboards and rear fenders. For this one year only, the wood-bodied station wagon would ride on the commercial car chassis. (From its inception in 1935, the woodie wagon was considered by the factory to be a "commercial" rather than a

passenger vehicle, but this was the first, last and only station wagon on a commercial chassis). The new pickups were met with a fair amount of enthusiasm. Yet, 1937 would prove to be their best sales year. For the first two years of its existence, the Commercial Car would be built in three factories (Detroit, Evansville and Los Angeles). In its final years, the Evansville plant would discontinue manufacture. Left for the passenger car chassis was the ambulance conversion (the hearse version was discontinued) and a removable pickup box for the business coupe.

1937 Plymouth Sedan Delivery (D.W. Hermany)

I.D. DATA: Serial number located on right front door post. Serial numbers: Detroit, Mich.: 8,850,101 to 8,861,664; Los Angeles, Calif.: 9,206,601 to 9,208,113; Evansville, Ill.: 9,182,701 to 9,185,187. Engine number located on left front corner of block, directly above generator. Starting: T50-1001 on up.

1937 Plymouth Model PT50 Station Wagon (JB)

Model	Body Type	Price	Weight	Prod. Total
Series PT-50				
N.A.	Chassis & Cab	495	2400	158
K-8-2-LR	Pickup	525	3100	10,709
N.A.	Station Wagon	740	2920	602
K-1-3	Sedan Delivery	655	3100	3256

ENGINE: Inline. L-head. Six-cylinder. Cast iron block. Bore & stroke: $3\frac{1}{8}$in. x $4\frac{3}{8}$ in. Displacement: 201.3 cu. in. Compression ratio: 6.7. Brake horsepower: 70 at 3000 R.P.M. SAE Horsepower: 23.44. Four main bearings. Solid valve lifters. Carburetor: Chandler Groves model A2.

1937 Plymouth Sedan Delivery (D. Hermany/DB)

1937 Plymouth Pickup (S.W. Tiernan/DB)

1937 Plymouth Model PT50 Pickup (JB/POC)

CHASSIS (Series PT-50): Wheelbase: 116 in. Tires: 6.00 x 16 in.

TECHNICAL: Sliding gear transmission. Speeds: 3F/1R. Floor shift gearshift lever. Single disc, dry 10 in. plate clutch. Shaft drive. Hypoid, semi-floating rear axle. Overall ratio: 4.1. Four-wheel hydraulic brakes. Steel disc wheels. Rim Size: 6.00 x 16 in.

1937 Plymouth Model PT-50 Chassis-and-Cab (JB)

OPTIONS: Chrome plated rear bumper ($8.50). Single sidemount (standard right side). Dual sidemount: left sidemount optional including tire, tube & tire lock ($10). Bumper guards ($1.50 pair). Chassis accessory group including chrome radiator shell, chrome headlamps and double acting shock absorbers, front and rear ($17). Dual horns ($7.50). Coach lamps for Commercial Sedan ($8.50). Long arm stationary rear view mirror ($1.50). Long arm adjustable rear view mirror ($2.50). Sun visors ($2 each). Metal spare tire cover ($6.50). Chrome windshield frame ($3). Right-hand taillamp ($4). Economy engine package Group 1 ($2.50); same Group 2 ($3). Four-speed transmission ($25). Painted sheet metal including fenders, splash aprons, runningboards ($5). Oil bath air cleaner ($3.75). Vortox air cleaner with standard cap ($17.50); with Vortox cap ($19.50). Governor ($5). Chrome headlamps ($2.75). Oil filter ($3.25). Chrome radiator shell ($6.). Auxiliary seat, Commercial Sedan ($10). Double acting shocks, front ($4.75); rear ($4.75). Right-hand windshield wiper ($4).

1937 Plymouth Seven-Passenger Yellow Taxi Cab (CHC)

HISTORICAL: Production began September 16, 1937; ended August 17, 1938. Model year production: 14,725 Commercial Sedans. Dan S. Eddins was again president of Plymouth.

Pricing

1937 Series PT-50	5	4	3	2	1
Pickup	1350	2700	4500	6300	9000
Sedan Delivery	1400	2800	4650	6500	9300
Station Wagon	1500	3000	5000	7000	10,000

1938 Plymouth P-57 Commercial Sedan Delivery (OCW)

COMMERCIAL CAR — SERIES PT-57 — SIX-CYLINDER: — The Plymouth Commercial Car for 1938 was a slightly restyled version of the 1937 offering. The grille was now squatter, to approximate the styling of the 1938 Plymouth passenger cars. But, that was the only change. Both the 1937 and 1938 Commercial Cars closely resembled the passenger car line, yet there was no interchange of sheetmetal or trim between the two series. Prices were considerably higher for the 1938 models, but the recession of 1938, coupled with the fact that dealers lots were full of trade-ins from the previous record year, spelled disaster as far as production went. Sales dropped to nearly half their 1937 levels. Models offered in the PT57 series included a sedan delivery, the express and the chassis-and-cab. The wood-bodied station wagon once more rode the passenger car chassis. Plymouth continued to offer its ambulance conversion in the regular sedan line, while the removable pickup box was still available for the business coupe.

1938 Plymouth Model PT57 Sedan Delivery (JB/POC)

I.D. DATA: Serial number located on right front door post. Serial numbers: Detroit, Mich.: 8,618,701 to 8,624,135; Los Angeles, Calif.: 9,208,201 to 9,208,797; Evansville, Ind.: 9,185,301 to 9,186,416. Starting: T57-1001 and up.

Model Series PT-57	Body Type	Price	Weight	Prod. Total
N/A	Chassis & Cab	560	1850	95
K-8-2-LR	Pickup (Express)	585	1850	4620
K-1-3	Sedan Dely.	695	1850	1601

ENGINE: Inline. L-head. Six-cylinder. Cast iron block. Bore & stroke: 3⅛ in. x 4⅜ in. Displacement: 201.3 cu. in. Compression ratio: 6.7. Brake horsepower: 70 at 3000 R.P.M. SAE Horsepower: 23.44. Four main bearings. Solid valve lifters. Carburetor: Chandler Groves model A2. Torque: 145 lbs.-ft. at 1200 R.P.M.

1938 Plymouth Model P-5 Business Coupe-Pickup (JB)

593

1938 Plymouth Pickup Truck (D.J. Phillips)

CHASSIS (Series PT-57): Wheelbase: 116 in. Tires: 6.00 x 16 in.

TECHNICAL: Sliding gear transmission. Speeds: (standard) 3F/1R, (optional) 4F/1R with Power-take-off opening. Floor shift gearshift lever. Dry, single 10 inch disc clutch. Shaft drive. Hypoid, semi-floating rear axle. Overall ratio: 4.1. Four-wheel hydraulic brakes. Steel disc wheels. Rim Size: 6.00 x 16 in.

OPTIONS: Chrome plated rear bumper ($8.50). Single sidemount (standard right side only). Dual sidemount: left-hand optional, including tire, tube and tire lock ($10). Bumper guards ($1.50 pair). Chassis accessory group including chrome radiator shell, chrome headlamps and double acting shock absorbers, front and rear ($17). Dual horns ($7.50). Coach lamps for Commercial Sedan ($8.50). Long arm stationary rear view mirror ($1.50). Long arm adjustable rear view mirror ($2.50). Sun visors ($2 each). Metal spare tire cover ($6.50). Chrome windshield frame ($3). Right-hand taillamp ($4). Economy engine package Group 1 ($2.50); same, Group 2 ($3). Four-speed transmission ($25). Painted sheet metal, including fenders, splash aprons, runningboards ($5). Oil bath air cleaner ($3.75). Vortox air cleaner with standard cap ($17.50); with Vortox cap ($19.50). Governor ($5). Chrome headlamps ($2.75). Oil filter ($3.25). Chrome radiator shell ($6.). Auxiliary seat, Commercial Sedan ($10). Double acting shocks, front ($4.75); rear ($4.75). Right-hand windshield wiper ($4).

1938 Plymouth Commercial Station Wagon (CHC)

HISTORICAL: Production began Sept. 16, 1937; ended August 17, 1938. Model year production: 6,316. Dan S. Eddins was again president of Plymouth.

1938 Plymouth Model PT57 Pickup (JB/POC)

594

1939 PLYMOUTH

1939 Plymouth Utility Coupe with Extendable Box (CHC)

ROADKING — SERIES P-7 — SIX-CYLINDER: — For reasons unexplained, Plymouth decided to offer two different lines of commercial vehicles this year. They came on both the passenger car and commercial car chassis. Reverting back to the passenger car line was the Panel Delivery. Made up of its own special body on the P7 Roadking chassis, the panel offered two doors at the rear, while carrying the spare tire in a single sidemounted fender. The interior consisted of a single seat, although a second seat was optional. The rear cargo area was paneled. The windows in both rear doors could also be rolled down if desired. Also offered this year was the familiar commercial sedan, now called a "Utility Sedan." Still based on the two-door passenger car body, this version varied in that it didn't have a regular door at the rear like the previous model. Instead, the opening was through the trunk lid and there was no dividing partition between the trunk area and the rear compartment. The interior was lined and a lockable screen partition could be installed behind the driver's seat. If needed, a full set of seats could be installed to turn the Utility Sedan into a five-passenger vehicle for normal use. Sales of the Panel Delivery were up from 1938, but sales of the Utility Sedan were a disappointing 341 units. The company also continued to offer the ambulance conversion on sedans, as well as the pickup box for the business coupe.

1939 Plymouth Sedan-Ambulance (OCW)

I.D. DATA: Serial number located on right front door post. Serial numbers: Detroit, Mich.: 1,298,001 to 1,377,475; Los Angeles, Calif.: 3,110,001 to 3,114,680; Evansville, Ind.: 9,150,401 to 9,164,593; Windsor, Ontario: 9,603,586 to 9,607,605. Engine number located on left front corner of block, directly above generator. Starting engine number: P8-1001. Ending engine number: P8-411923.

Model Series P-7	Body Type (Roadking)	Price	Weight	Prod. Total
723	Panel Delivery	715	1985	2270
N/A	Utility Sedan	685	2844	341

ENGINE: Inline. L-head. Six-cylinder. Cast iron block. Bore & stroke: 3⅛in. x 4⅜ in. Displacement: 201.3 cu. in. Compression ratio: 6.7:1. Brake horsepower: 82 at 3600 R.P.M. SAE Horsepower: 23.44. Four main bearings. Solid valve lifters. Carburetor: Carter models B6K1, B6M1, DGA1-2 or D6C1-1. Torque: 145 lbs.-ft. at 1200 R.P.M.

1939 Plymouth Sedan Delivery, right view (DFW/MVMA)

OPTIONAL ENGINE: Aluminum hi-compression head gives 7.0 compression ratio and 86 horsepower at 3600 R.P.M. Export engine: Bore & stroke: 2⅞ in. x 4⅜ in. (Engines coded P8X).

1939 Plymouth Roadking Utility Sedan (DFW)

COMMERCIAL CAR — SERIES PT-81 — SIX-CYLINDER: — A completely restyled vehicle was the order of the day for the 1939 Plymouth Commercial Car. Styled to closely match its sister Dodge, the new Plymouth no longer looked like a truck version of a passenger car. It now looked like a big and brawny truck. To some it was not as attractive a vehicle as it had been before. Outside of emblems and hub caps, as well as a three-piece front end ensemble, the Plymouth Commercial Car could easily be mistaken for a Dodge (the Dodge had a two-piece front end) or its Canadian sister, the Fargo (which also had three-piece front end). With the removal of the Sedan Delivery to the passenger car chassis, the PT81 Commercial Car consisted of only the express pickup and the cab and chassis. Prices were lowered slightly and sales increased slightly for the year. The cab of this new vehicle sat several inches farther forward on the chassis. It was advertised as a "real" three-man cab. The pickup box increased in size slightly, as well. Throughout their lifetime, the Plymouth Commercial Cars would all ride a 116 inch wheelbase. Unique to the design of the new cab was a latch located at the top of the door frame. It was claimed this helped to keep the doors from popping open while being operated over rough terrain. Fender mounted spare tires were no longer offered on the commercial vehicles. The spare now rode in a hanger, beneath the pickup box at the rear of the frame rails. However, a few vehicles are known to have had the spare tire mounted forward of the right rear fender, on the runningboard.

I.D. DATA: Serial number located on right front door post. Serial numbers: Detroit, Mich.: 8,624,201 to 8,630,418; Los Angeles, Calif.: 9,208,851 to 9,209,340. Engine number located on left front corner of block, directly above generator. Starting engine number: T81-1001 and up.

Model Series PT-81	Body Type	Price	Weight	Prod. Total
N/A	Chassis & Cab	545	2075	140
N/A	Sedan Delivery	654	2800	13
M-1-2	Pickup	575	2800	6181

ENGINE: Inline. L-head. Six-cylinder. Cast iron block. Bore & stroke: 3⅛in. x 4⅜ in. Displacement: 201.3 cu. in. Compression ratio: 6.7:1. Brake horsepower: 70 at 3000 R.P.M. SAE Horsepower: 23.44. Four main bearings. Solid valve lifters. Torque: 145 lbs.-ft. at 1200 R.P.M.

CHASSIS (Series P-7): Wheelbase: 114 in. Overall length: 182-3/16 in. (without bumpers). Front tread: 56¼ in. Rear tread: 60 in. Tires: 5.50 x 16 in.

CHASSIS (Series PT-81): Wheelbase: 116 in. Overall length: 182. Tires: 6.00 x 16 in.

TECHNICAL (Series P-7): Sliding gear transmission. Speeds: 3F/1R. Floor mounted gearshift lever. Single disc, dry 9¼ in. plate clutch. Shaft drive. Hypoid, semi-floating rear axle. Overall ratio: 3.9:1. Four-wheel hydraulic brakes. Steel disc wheels. Rim Size: 5:50 x 16 in.

TECHNICAL (Series PT-81): Sliding gear transmission: (standard) 3F/1R; (optional) 4F/1R with power-take-off opening. Floor mounted gearshift lever. Dry, single disc clutch. Shaft drive. Hypoid, semi-floating rear axle. Overall ratio: 4.1:1. Four-wheel hydraulic brakes. Four steel disc wheels. Rim Size: 6:00 x 16 in.

1939 Plymouth Half-Ton Pickup (OCW)

OPTIONS (Series P-7): Single sidemount (available only on sedan delivery and utility sedan, standard). Dual sidemount: (Available only on sedan delivery and utility sedan, optional). Fender skirts ($8.25). Bumper guards ($4.50 pair). Electric clock in glove box door ($10). Cigar lighter ($2). Spotlight ($14.50). Chrome wheel discs ($8). Economy engine, group 1 ($2.50). Economy engine, group 2 ($3). Stone deflector, Utility sedan only ($1). Whitewall tires 6.00 x 16 in. ($15.75). 5.50 x 16 in. ($13.75). Heavy-duty air cleaner ($2). 20 in. high-clearance wheels ($18). Glove box lock (75¢). Oil filter ($2.75). Deluxe steering wheel ($5). Rear spring covers ($3). Clock mirror ($3.95). Dual trumpet horns, under hood mount ($8.25). Right-hand inside sun visor ($1.75). License plate frames ($1.75). Fog lamps ($12). Outside rear view mirror ($1.95). Runningboard side mouldings ($1.50). Exhaust extension ($1.). Locking gas cap ($1.50). Heaters: Super Airstream ($24.45); Tri Airstream ($21.45); Deluxe ($18.45); Dual Airstream ($15.45). Defroster ($4.50). Manual radio with Skyway antenna ($41.50); with Roadway antenna, under runningboard mounting ($43.95).

1939 Plymouth Sedan Delivery, left view (DFW/MVMA)

OPTIONS (Series PT-81): Oil bath air cleaner ($3.25). Right-hand taillamp ($4). Chrome headlamps ($2.75). Dual horns ($7.50). Colored sheet metal ($5). Chrome radiator shell ($6). Long arm stationary mirror ($1.50). Long arm adjustable mirror ($2.50). Sun visor ($2). Four-speed transmission ($17.50). Chrome windshield frame ($3). Right-hand windshield wiper ($4). Express type rear bumper ($6). Spare wheel lock ($1.50).

1939 Plymouth PT-81 Chassis With Cargo Body (CHC)

HISTORICAL (Series PT-81): Production began Nov. 1, 1938; ended August 31, 1939. Model year production: 6,321 units. **(Series P-7):** Production began August 18, 1938; ending August 18, 1939. Model year production: 2,270 sedan deliveries and 341 utility sedans were built. Of the 341 Utility Sedans production was broken down as follows: Detroit LHD Domestic market = 308; Detroit LHD Export market = 1; Evansville LHD Domestic = 18; Los Angeles LHD Domestic = 14. Of the 2,270 Panel Delivery's production was broken down as follows: Detroit LHD Domestic Market = 1,779; Detroit LHD Export = 52; Detroit RHD Export = 50; Evansville LHD Domestic = 180; Los Angeles LHD Domestic = 137; Knocked Down Export LHD = 54; Knocked Down Export RHD = 18. In 1939, Dan S. Eddins continued as president of Plymouth.

Pricing

	5	4	3	2	1
1939					
Roadking Series P-7					
Panel Delivery	1350	2650	4400	6150	8800
Utility Sedan	1050	2100	3500	4900	7000
Series PT-81					
Sedan Delivery	1400	2800	4650	6500	9300
Pickup	1350	2700	4500	6300	9000

1940 PLYMOUTH

1940 Plymouth Roadking Utility Sedan (CHC)

ROADKING — SERIES P-9 — SIX-CYLINDER: — The Plymouth passenger car commercial line once again consisted of the Panel Delivery and the Utility Sedan. Both vehicles were restyled to match the normal passenger car line. The only other difference between the 1939 and 1940 models was that the spare tire of the Panel Delivery could no longer be mounted in the fenders. The spare was now carried forward of the right rear fender, in a special indentation in the body. Both body styles offered the same options as the previous year, including the screen partition for the Utility Sedan. The ambulance conversion was offered on either the Deluxe or Roadking chassis. Sales of the Utility Sedan nearly doubled, while sales of the Panel Delivery remained nearly static. While the ambulance conversion of the regular passenger sedan was still offered, it would appear that the removable pickup box for the business coupe was no longer available.

1940 Plymouth Road King Sedan-Ambulance (CHC)

I.D. DATA: Serial number located on right front door post. Serial numbers: Detroit, Mich.: 1,378,001 to 1,454,303; Los Angeles, Calif.: 3,114,801 to 3,121,385; Evansville, Ind.: 9,062,201 to 9,081,375; Windsor, Ontario: 9,368,516 to 9,373,193. Engine number located on left front corner of block, directly above generator. Starting engine number: P9-1001. Ending engine number: P9-415462.

1940 Plymouth Panel Delivery (CHC)

596

Model	Body Type	Price	Weight	Prod. Total
Series P-9 (Roadking)				
N.A.	Utility Sedan	699	2769	589
755	Panel Delivery	720	1941	2889

ENGINE: Inline. L-head. Six-cylinder. Cast iron block. Bore & stroke: 3⅛ in. x 4⅜ in. Displacement: 201.3 cu. in. Compression ratio: 6.7:1. Brake horsepower: 84 at 3600 R.P.M. Horsepower: 23.44. Four main bearings. Solid valve lifters. Carburetor: Carter model D6A1, model D6C1, or model D6P1. Torque: 154 lbs.-ft. at 1200 R.P.M.

OPTIONAL ENGINE: High-compression aluminum head. Compression ratio 7.0 to 1. 87 horsepower at 3600 R.P.M. 158 ft.-lbs. torque at 1200 R.P.M. (Export Engines): Bore & stroke: 2⅞ in. x 4⅜ in., 170.4 cu. in., 70 horsepower.

NOTE: Export engines were code numbered P9X.

1940 Plymouth Model PT105 Pickup (JB/POC)

COMMERCIAL CAR — SERIES PT-105 — SIX-CYLINDER: — Plymouth's truck chassis offering this year was a very slightly updated version of the 1939 model. Visually, the only external changes were the addition of sealed beam headlamps, which resulted in the parking lamps being mounted in small pods atop the headlamp shell. Three horizontal strips of bright trim also adorned the radiator shell, to approximate the grill design of the passenger car line. The line still consisted of only the Express (pickup) and the chassis and cab, still sold with full runningboards and rear fenders. Prices were up $10 over 1939, yet sales were also up slightly.

I.D. DATA: Serial number located on right front door post. Serial numbers: Detroit, Mich.: 8,631,001 to 8,637,730; Los Angeles, Calif.: 9,209,351 to 9,210,053. Engine number located on left front corner of block, directly above generator. Starting engine number: PT105-1001. Ending engine number: PT105-34654.

1940 Plymouth PT-105 Yacht Basin Delivery Truck (CHC)

Model	Body Type	Price	Weight	Prod. Total
Series PT-105				
N.A.	Chassis & Cab	555	2600	174
4012	Pickup (Express)	585	2800	6879

ENGINE: Inline. L-head. Six-cylinder. Cast iron block. Bore & stroke: 3⅛ in. x 4⅜ in. Displacement: 201.3 cu. in. Compression ratio: 6.7:1. Brake horsepower: 79 at 3000 R.P.M. Horsepower: 23.44. Four main bearings. Solid valve lifters. Torque: 154 lbs.-ft. at 1200 R.P.M.

CHASSIS (Series P-9): Wheelbase: 117 in. Front tread: 57 in. Rear tread: 60 in. Tires: 5.50 x 16 in.

CHASSIS (Series PT-105): Wheelbase: 116 in. Overall length: 182 in. Tires: 6.00 x 16 in.

TECHNICAL (Series P-9): Sliding gear transmission. Speeds: 3F/1R. Column mounted gearshift lever. Dry, single 9¼ in. disc clutch. Shaft drive. Hypoid, semi-floating rear axle. Overall ratio: 3.9:1. Four-wheel hydraulic brakes. Steel disc wheels. Rim Size: 5:50 x 16 in.

TECHNICAL (Series PT-105): Sliding gear transmission. Speeds: (std.) 3F/1R; (opt.) 4F/1R with power-take-off opening. Floor mounted gearshift lever. Single, dry 10 in. disc clutch. Shaft drive. Hypoid, semi-floating rear axle. Overall ratio: 4.1:1. Four-wheel hydraulic brakes. Steel disc wheels. Rim Size: 6:00 x 16 in.

OPTIONS (Series P-9): Push-button radio ($47.50). All Weather heater system ($45.50). Electric clock in glove box door ($12). Spotlight, right- or left-hand ($14.50 each). Back-up lamp ($2.95). Exhaust extension ($1). Fender grille guard ($11.20). Fender protectors ($6.25). Fog lamps ($12). Locking gas cap ($1.50). Grille guard ($6.95). Dual trumpet horns (under hood mount) ($8.50). License plate frames ($1.50). Outside rear view mirror ($1.95). Deluxe steering wheel ($8.50). Front center bumper "Superguard" ($1.75). Wheel discs ($1.50) each). Wheel trim rings ($1.50 each). 20 inch high-clearance wheels.

OPTIONS (Series PT-105): Oil bath air cleaner ($2.50). Vortex air cleaner ($17.50 with standard cap or $19.50 w/Vortex cap). Airfoam seat cushions ($10). Right-hand taillamp ($2.50). Domelamp ($3.50). Glove box lock ($1.50). 32 amp generator for slow speed operation ($4). Governor ($5). Chrome headlamps ($3.50). Grille guard ($7.50). Dual horns ($7.50). Heater & defroster ($25). Deluxe Purolator oil filter ($5). Colored sheet metal ($1.50). Long arm stationary mirror ($1.50); same for right-hand side ($3). Sun visor ($2). Inside rear view mirror ($1). Four-speed transmission ($17.50). Chrome windshield frame ($3). RH vacuum windshield wiper ($4). LH electric windshield wiper ($6). Dual electric wipers ($13). Express type rear bumper ($6). Spare wheel lock ($1.50). Economy engine package, group 1 ($2.50), group 2 ($3). Tires: Five 5.25 x 20 four-ply ($18). Five 5.25 x 20 six-ply ($35). Five 6.00 x 16 six-ply ($14.50). Five 6.00 x 18 six-ply (Not listed). Five 6.25 x 16 six-ply ($23.50). Five 6.50 x 16 four-ply ($13.50). Five 6.50 x 16 six-ply ($28.25).

1940 Plymouth Pickup (D. Kostansek/DFW)

HISTORICAL (Series P-9): Production began August 15, 1939; ended July 12, 1940. Model year production: 106,738. Of these, 2,889 were sedan delivery, 589 utility sedans. Of the 589 Utility Sedans, production was broken down as follows: Detroit LHD Domestic market = 502; Detroit LHD Export = 6; Detroit RHD Export = 2; Evansville LHD Domestic = 63; Los Angeles LHD Domestic = 16. Of the 2,889 Panel Delivery's built, production was broken down as follows: Detroit LHD Domestic Market = 2,278; Detroit LHD Export = 39; Detroit RHD Export = 5; Evansville LHD Domestic = 312; Los Angeles LHD Domestic = 255. **(Series PT-105):** Production began Sept. 26, 1939; ended August 20. 1940. Model year production: 7,053. Dan S. Eddins continued as president of Plymouth.

Pricing

	5	4	3	2	1
1940					
Series P-9 Roadking					
Utility Sedan	1050	2100	3500	4900	7000
Panel Delivery	1350	2650	4400	6150	8800
Series PT-105					
Pickup	1350	2700	4500	6300	9000

1941 PLYMOUTH

COMMERCIAL CAR — SERIES PT-125 — SIX-CYLINDER: — 1941 would prove to be the final year for Plymouth's truck chassis "Commercial Car." While the reasons for this have never been fully explained by Chrysler Corporation, it would appear that low sales, plus the demand on the Dodge factories for increased production of military vehicles, worked together to sound the death knoll for the Plymouth "truck." The '41s were slightly restyled to give them a more expensive look. Pricewise, they were more expensive by $35. Production of the Express dipped by 800 units, while the chassis-and-cab found 22 more purchasers than it had in 1940. At the front, the PT-125 series featured an overlay of chrome trim on the same nose piece used since 1939. This resulted in appearance not unlike the 1941 passenger car. The front bumper had a decided "Vee" shape to it and the headlamps were moved outward, to the crown of the fender, resulting in a more 'bug-eyed" appearance. The parking lamps were moved back to the cowl and the familiar Plymouth script moved to the center of the hood panels, from the radiator shell. As the last Plymouth truck rolled off the assembly line, late in 1941, the end of an era in Plymouth truck production had come to a close. It wouldn't be until 1974, that Plymouth would again offer such a vehicle. When it did, it, too, would be based on its sister division, Dodge.

1941 Plymouth Fire & Rescue Squad Pickup (OCW)

I.D. DATA: Serial number located on right front door post. Serial numbers: Detroit, Mich.: 81,000,101 to 81,006,107; Los Angeles, Calif.: 9,210,101 to 9,210,700. Engine number located on left front corner of block, directly above generator. Starting engine number: PT125-1001 and up.

1941 Plymouth P11 Sedan Delivery (JB/POC)

Model Series PT-125	Body Type	Price	Weight	Prod. Total
N.A.	Chassis & Cab	590	2600	196
4112	Pickup	625	2800	6073
N.A.	Panel Delivery	720	2800	—

NOTE: The PT-125 Panel Delivery is listed in contemporary used car price books, although it appears that none may have actually been built.

1941 Plymouth Pickup (Clyde "Buck" Jones)

ENGINE: Inline. L-head. Six-cylinder. Cast iron block. Bore & stroke: 3⅛in. x 4⅜ in. Displacement: 201.3 cu. in. Brake horsepower: 87 at 3800 R.P.M. SAE Net horsepower: 23.44. Four main bearings. Solid valve lifters. Carburetor: Ball & Ball.

1941 Plymouth Pickup Truck (JB)

DELUXE — SERIES P-11/P-11D — SIX-CYLINDER: — Plymouth's passenger car based "commercial" vehicles once again included the Panel Delivery and the Utility Sedan, for the most part based on the P-11 Plymouth chassis. In a rare move, Plymouth offered three passenger car series in 1941, including the P-11 Plymouth, the P-11D Deluxe and the P-12 Special Deluxe. For reasons unknown, while 99.9 percent of the utility sedan and panel delivery production took place on the P-11 chassis, someone with pull at the factory had a single model of each built on the P-11D chassis. In addition, two utility sedans were built on the P-12 Special Deluxe chassis. Outside of restyling to match the regular passenger car line, these "commercial" vehicles did not differ from the previous year's offerings.

I.D. DATA: Serial number located on right front door post. Serial numbers: Detroit, Mich.: 15,000,101 to 15,135,030; Los Angeles, Calif.: 3,121,501 to 3,133,962; Evansville, Ind.: 22,001,001 to 22,036,667; Windsor, Ontario: 9,821,241 to 9,829,853. Engine number located on left front corner of block, directly above generator. Engine numbers: P11-1001 to P11-535085.

1941 Plymouth Sedan Delivery (D.S. Olsen photo)

Model	Body Type	Price	Weight	Prod. Total
Series P-11				
N.A.	Utility Sedan	739	2600	174
820	Sedan Delivery	760	2794	468
Series P-11D				
N.A.	DeL. Utility Sedan	—	—	1
820	DeL. Sedan Delivery	—	—	1
Series P-12				
820	Utility Sedan	—	—	2

ENGINE: See PT-125 engine specifications.

CHASSIS (Series P-11 & P-11D): Wheelbase: 117 in. Overall length: 195 in. Front tread: 57 in. Rear tread: 60 in. Tires: 6:00 x 16 in.

CHASSIS (Series PT-125): Wheelbase: 116 in. Overall length: 182 in. Tires: 6:00 x 16 in.

TECHNICAL (Series PT-125): Sliding gear transmission. Speeds: (std.) 3F/1R; (optional) 4F/1R with power-take-off opening. Floor mounted gearshift lever. Dry, single 10 in. disc clutch. Shaft drive. Hypoid, semi-floating rear axle. Overall ratio: 4.1:1. Four-wheel hydraulic brakes. Steel disc wheels. Rim Size: 6:00 x 16 in.

TECHNICAL (Series P-11/P-12): Sliding gear transmission. Speeds: 3F/1R. Column mounted gearshift lever. Dry, single 9¼ in. disc clutch. Shaft drive. Hypoid, semi-floating rear axle. Overall ratio: 4.1:1. Four-wheel hydraulic brakes. Steel disc wheels. Rim Size: 6:00 x 16 in.

598

OPTIONS (Series PT-125): Oil bath air cleaner ($2.50). Vortex air cleaner with standard cap ($17.50); w/Vortex cap ($19.50). Airfoam seat cushions ($10). Right-hand taillamp ($2.50). Dome lamp ($3.50). Glove box lock ($1.50). 32 amp-generator for slow speed operation ($4). Governor ($5). Chrome headlamps, including cowl lamps ($3.50). Grille guard ($7.50). Dual horns ($7.50). Heater and defroster ($25). Deluxe Purolator oil filter ($5). Colored sheet metal, (no charge). Long arm stationary mirror ($1.50); same for right-hand side ($3). Sunvisor ($2). Inside rearview mirror ($1). Four-speed transmission ($17.50). Chrome windshield frame ($3). Right-hand vacuum windshield wiper ($4). Left-hand electric windshield wiper ($6). Dual electric windshield wipers ($13). Express type rear bumper ($6). Spare wheel lock ($1.50). Economy engine package, group 1 ($4.25); same, group 2 ($3). All tire sets sold in groups of 5: Five 5.25 x 20 four-ply ($18). Five 5.25 x 20 six-ply ($35). Five 6.00 x 16 six-ply ($14.50). Five 6.00 x 18 six-ply (Price not listed). Five 6.25 x 16 six-ply ($23.50). Five 6.50 x 16 four-ply ($13.50). Five 6.50 x 16 six-ply $28.25).

OPTIONS (Series P-11/P-11D): Accessory group B including cigar lighter, glove box lock with steel glove box and stainless steel wheel trim rings ($10). Accessory group C including right-hand windshield wiper and right-hand sunvisor ($5). Bumper fender guards ($8). Bumper center guards ($3). Chrome wheel discs, set of four ($6). Chrome wheel trim rings, set of five ($7.50). Front door armrest ($1.75). Front door vent wings ($12). Glove box lock with steel glove box ($1). Dual horns ($5). Powermatic shifting ($6.50). Eight-tube pushbutton radio ($46.75). Six tube radio ($35.15). Cowl mounted antenna ($6.20). Economy engine, group 1 ($2.50) including small bore carburetor and instake manifold ($3.73). Rear axle ratio ($2.50). Economy engine group 2, same as group 1 except includes throttle stop and heat shields ($3.50). Back-up signal, emergency brake alarm, cigarette lighter, Kool Kushion, exhaust extension, fog lights, six different hot water heaters, cowl mounted outside rearview mirrors, grille guard, insect screen, seat covers, left-hand or right-hand spotlight.

HISTORICAL (Series PT-125): Production began Sept. 18, 1940. End of production not recorded. Model year production: 6,269. **(Series P-11 & Deluxe P-11D):** Production began August 8, 1940; ended July 16, 1941. Model year production: 3,200 P-11s were sedan deliveries, 468 P-11 Utility sedans and one P-11D Utility sedan and one P-11D sedan delivery. Dan S. Eddins was still the president of Plymouth. Of the 468 P-11 Utility Sedans, production was broken down as follows: Detroit LHD Export Market = 1; Detroit RHD Export = 10; Detroit LHD Domestic = 383; Evansville LHD Domestic = 45; Los Angeles LHD Domestic = 29; P-11D Utility Sedan (Detroit) = 1. Of the 3,200 P-11 Panel Delivery's production was broken down as follows: Detroit LHD Domestic Market = 2,537; Detroit LHD Export = 54; Detroit RHD Export = 1; Evansville LHD Domestic = 344; Los Angeles LHD Domestic = 258. Knock Down Export LHD = 6; P-11D Panel Delivery (Detroit) = 1. 2 P-12 Utility Sedans were also Detroit built.

Pricing

1941	5	4	3	2	1
Series PT-125					
Pickup	1400	2750	4550	6350	9100
Panel Delivery	1350	2700	4450	6250	8900
Series P-11					
Utility Sedan	1130	2250	3750	5250	7500
Sedan Delivery	1500	2900	4850	6800	9700
Series P-11D					
DeL. Utility Sedan	Value Inestimable (One Built)				
DeL. Sedan Dely.	Value Inestimable (One Built)				
Series P-12					
Special DeL. Utility Sed.	Value Inestimable (Two Built)				

1942 PLYMOUTH

DELUXE — SERIES P-14S — SIX-CYLINDER: — Plymouth's first entry into the commercial field began in 1930, with the conversion of 80 passenger cars into "Commercial Sedans." Ironically, Plymouth's last prewar entry into the commercial field would also be based on a converted passenger car body style. This time the vehicle was called a "Utility Sedan." The idea behind the two vehicles was the same. Even more ironically, the final production total, 12 years later, would be the same 80 unit figure. Plymouth's passenger car lineup for 1942 consisted of the P-14S Deluxe and the P-14C Special Deluxe. All of the Utility Sedans were based on the Deluxe series. Production of all '42s would be short-lived, as the United States became involved in World War II, yet production of the "commercial" offerings from Plymouth would be completely curtailed. When production resumed, late in 1945, no commercial vehicles would be offered.

I.D. DATA: Serial number located on right front door post. Serial numbers: Detroit, Mich.: 15,135,501 to 15,153,935; Los Angeles, Calif.: 3,134,501 to 3,136,266; Evansville, Ind.: 22,037,001 to 22,041,356; Windsor, Ontario: 9,829,856 to 9,836,986. Engine numbers located on left front corner of block, directly above generator. Starting engine number: P14-1001. Ending engine number: P14-149161.

Model	Body Type	Price	Weight	Prod. Total
Deluxe Series P-14S				
N.A.	Utility Sedan	842	2985	80

ENGINE (Series P-14S): Inline. L-head. Six-cylinder. Cast iron block. Bore & stroke: 3¼in. x 4⅜ in. Displacement: 217.8 cu. in. Compression ratio: 6.8:1. Brake horsepower: 95 at 3400 R.P.M. Horsepower: 25.35. Four main bearings. Solid valve lifters. Carburetor: Carter model B6P1 or B6G1. Torque: 172 lbs.-ft. at 1600 R.P.M.

CHASSIS (Deluxe P-14S): Wheelbase: 117 in. Tires: 16 x 6.00 in.

TECHNICAL (Deluxe P-14S): Sliding gear transmission. Speeds: 3F/1R. Column mounted gearshift lever. Dry, single 9¼ in. plate clutch. Driveshaft. Hypoid, semi-floating rear axle. Overall ratio: 3.9:1 (3.73 with economy engine). Four-wheel hydraulic brakes. Steel disc wheels. Rim Size: 6:00 x 16 in. Power-Matic shifting — vacuum/operated self-shifting ($7.85 option).

OPTIONS: Fender skirts ($12.50). Eight tube pushbutton radio ($54.85). All Weather heating system ($49.20). Electric clock ($9.75). Cigar lighter ($2). Right-hand or left-hand spotlight ($15.80). License plate frames ($2.20). Windshield washer ($3.95). Hand brake alarm ($2.50). Locking gas cap ($1.80). Outside rearview mirror ($2.35). Powermatic shifting ($7.85). Direction signals ($10). Exhaust extension. Wheel trim discs. Wheel trim rings. Buzzer type hand brake alarm. Flashing light type hand brake alarm. Six tube pushbutton radio. Universal mount radio. Skyway external radio antenna. Internal cowl mounted antenna. Crank operated "Cowl Concealed" antenna. Power operated "Cowl Concealed" antenna.

HISTORICAL (Series P-14S): Production began July 25, 1941; ending January 31, 1942. Model year production: 27,645. Of these, 80 were Utility Sedans. Production broke down as follows: Detroit LHD Domestic Market = 63; Detroit LHD Export = 2; Evansville LHD Domestic = 9; Los Angeles LHD Domestic = 6. Dan S. Eddins continued as president of Plymouth.

Pricing

1942 Series P-14S	5	4	3	2	1
Utility Sedan	1150	2310	3850	5400	7700

1974 PLYMOUTH

1974 Plymouth Trail Duster Sport Utility 4x4 (CHC)

TRAIL DUSTER — SERIES PW-100 — (ALL ENGINES): — The new Trail Duster was a handsome sports/utility vehicle. Its two round headlights were slightly recessed into the simple, but appealing, grille (which was outlined in bright trim). The Plymouth name, printed in bright letters, appeared to float in the blacked-out center of the grille. The large, vertical wraparound taillights had backup lights incorporated into their upper section. Standard Trail Duster features included: Full time four-wheel-drive. A single all-vinyl bucket seat with seat belt and retractor. Armrest pads. Color-keyed padded instrument panel. Electronic ignition. Power front disc brakes. Heavy-duty 9¼ in. rear axle. Under-the-hood tool storage. Five shift positions transfer case: 1) Low-lock, for use only on low-traction surfaces such as deep snow, mud or soft sand. 2) Low, for normal operation when additional power is needed on high-traction surfaces. 3) Neutral, with vehicle stopped, both axles are disengaged for power-take-off operation. 4) High, for all normal operation in direct drive on paved or unpaved surfaces. 5) High-lock, for use only on low-traction surfaces such as snow, mud or soft sand. Three-speed manual transmission.

I.D. DATA: A combination of 13 symbols are used. The first seven identify the model, series, G.V.W. Class (A = 6,000 lbs. or less. B = over 6,000 lbs.) engine, model year, and assembly plant. The last six are sequential serial numbers. (They begin each year at 000,001.) The symbols for the engines are A = 440 V-8. B = 225 six. C = 225 six. D = 440 V-8. E = 318 V-8. F = 360 V-8 with 2-bbl. carb. G = 318 V-8. H = 243 Diesel. J = 400 V-8. K = 360 V-8. T = 360 V-8 with 4-bbl. carb. X = Special 6. Y = Special 8.

1974 Plymouth Trail Duster Open Body 4x4 Utility (CHC)

Model	Body Type	Price	Weight	Prod. Total
Trail Duster — (4x4) — (½-Ton)				
PW-100	Topless Utility	3964	3910	5015

ENGINE (Trail Duster PW-100): Displacement: 318 cu. in. V-8. Brake horsepower: 155 at 4000 R.P.M. Bore & stroke: 3.91 in. x 3.31 in. Compression ratio: 8.6:1. Carburetor: 2-bbl.

CHASSIS: Wheelbase: 106 in. Overall length: 184.62 in. Overall width: 79.5 in. Overall height: (with roof): 72 in. Tires: E78-15/B in. GVW rating: 4900 to 6000 lbs.

TECHNICAL: Four-speed manual transmission. TorqueFlite automatic transmission. 360 cu. in. V-8 with 4-bbl. carburetor. 400 cu. in. V-8 with 2-bbl. carb. (not available in California). 440 cu. in. V-8 with 4-bbl. carb.

1974 Plymouth Trail Duster w/Full Vinyl Enclosure

OPTIONS: Sport package: includes deluxe front bucket seats with special trim and a lockable center console with a removable beverage chest; bright front and rear bumper and windshield molding; unique bodyside and tailgate trim; color-keyed door trim panels with map pockets. Inner and outer double-walled steel roof. AM radio. AM/FM radio. Air conditioning. Power steering. Convenience package: glove box lock, glove box light, ash receiver light, inside hood release, and a 12 in. day/night rearview mirror. Tachometer. Bright wheel covers. Trailer towing package: includes light or heavy equipment. Oil pressure gauge. Non-adjustable and forward tilting passenger seat (includes sun visor and seat belt). Deluxe seats (includes console, sun visors and seat belts). Rear bench seat. Outside mounted tire carrier. Vented rear side window. Skid plates (fuel tank shield and transfer case shield). Tinted glass, windshield or all glass. High output heater. Increased cooling. Engine block heater. Hand throttle (not available with TorqueFlite automatic transmission). Step type rear bumper. Front bumper guards. Steel roof (available in body color, vinyl-textured white or black). Two-tone body (include moldings and bright tail lamp bezels). Dual horn. Bright hub caps. Dealer installed soft top. Roll bar.

HISTORICAL: Trail Dusters were built by Dodge. They were offered in the following exterior colors: Light gold. Medium gold. Dark Green metallic. Light blue. Bright red. Light green. Yellow. Avocado metallic. Medium blue metallic. Sunstone. Bronze metallic. Medium gold metallic. White.

VOYAGER — SERIES PB-100 — (ALL ENGINES): — The attractive new Voyager was a van made on the same assembly line as the Dodge Sportsman. It had two round headlights, each encased in a large square shaped piece of bright trim. The blacked-out grille was outlined by bright molding. Four horizontal bright trim pieces ran from headlight to headlight. Sandwiched between them, in the center, was the word "Plymouth." On either side were the rectangular signal lights. The rectangular taillights had backup lights incorporated into them. Standard features included: Forty-one amp alternator. Driver and front passenger armrests. Driver's compartment ash tray. Forty-eight-amp hour battery. Passenger side double doors with vented glass. Electronic ignition. Twenty-three gallon fuel tank. Glove box door with push-button operated latch. Fresh air heater with defrosters. Dual electric horns. Bumper jack. Oil pressure indicator light. Driver and front passenger bucket seats (in blue, green, parchment, or black). Three-passenger bench seat. Two padded sun visors. Spare tire carrier. Traffic hazard warning switch. Two-speed windshield wipers and dual jet washers. Power front disc brakes. Argent and black grille. Front and rear painted bumpers (white). Dual 5 x 7 in. painted exterior mirrors.

1974 Plymouth Voyager Sport Maxi-Wagon (CHC)

Black driver compartment floor mat. Driver compartment headliner. Voyager nameplates. Three-speed manual transmission. Standard sized Voyagers on both short and long wheelbases were promoted as "wagons." Stretched versions, on the long wheelbase only, were "maxi wagons."

I.D. DATA: See Trail Duster.

NOTE: The V.I.N. symbols BA = PB-100, BB = PB-200, BC = PB-300.

1974 Plymouth Model PB100 Voyager Wagon (CHC)

Model	Body Type	Price	Weight	Prod. Total
Voyagers Van — (½-Ton)				
PB-100	Wagon (109 in. w.b.)	3855	3685	Note 1
PB-100	Wagon (127 in. w.b.)	4003	3820	Note 1

NOTE 1: Van production was 11,701 units for all series.

ENGINE: Six-cylinder. Displacement: 225 cu. in. Brake horsepower: 95 at 3600 R.P.M. Bore & stroke: 3.40 in. x 4.12 in. Compression ratio: 8.4:1. Carburetor: 1-bbl. Or Displacement: 318 cu. in. V-8. Brake horsepower: 150 at 4000 R.P.M.. Bore & stroke: 3.91 in. x 3.31 in. Compression ratio: 8.6:1. Carburetor: 2-bbl.

VOYAGER — SERIES PB-200 — (ALL ENGINES): — The PB-200 came in three sizes and could haul heavier payloads than the PB-100. It came equipped with the same standard features.

I.D. DATA: See Trail Duster.

Model	Body Type	Price	Weight	Prod. Total
Voyager Van — (¾-Ton)				
PB-200	Wagon (109 in. w.b.)	3955	3805	Note 1
PB-200	Wagon (127 in. w.b.)	4294	4025	Note 1
PB-200	Maxi-Wagon (127 in. w.b.)	4494	4280	Note 1

NOTE 1: Van production was 11,701 units for all series.

ENGINE: Same as PB-100.

VOYAGER — SERIES PB-300 — (ALL ENGINES): — The PB-300 came in two sizes, both had a 127 inch wheelbase. The ultimate was the extended body version. It could carry more people and heavier loads than any other Voyager. In addition to the standard features found on the PB-100 and PB-200, the PB-300 came with larger brakes and TorqueFlite automatic transmission.

I.D. DATA: See Trail Duster.

Model	Body Type	Price	Weight	Prod. Total
Voyager Van — (1-Ton)				
PB-300	Wagon (127 in. w.b.)	4934	4315	Note 1
PB-300	Maxi-Wagon (127 in. w.b.)	5130	4435	Note 1

NOTE 1: Van production was 11,701 units for all series.

ENGINE: Displacement: 318 cu. in. V-8. (see PB-100).

CHASSIS: Wheelbase (PB-100, PB-200): 109 in.; (PB-100, PB-200, PB-300): 127 in. Overall width: 79.8 in. Overall length: 176 in. (109 in. w.b.), 194 in. (127 in. w.b.), 212 in. (127 in. w.b. extended). Overall height: 77.2 in. (PB-100 109 in. w.b.), 77.3 in. (PB-100 127 in. w.b.), 78.4 (PB-200 109 in. w.b.), 78.6 in. (PB-200 127 in. w.b. and 127 in. w.b. extended body), 79.1 in. (PB-300). Tires (PB-100): E78-15-B, (PB-200) G78-15-B, (PB-300) 8.00-16.5-D.

OPTIONAL PACKAGES: Convenience. Insulation. Trailer towing. Sport: Argent and black grille with bright molding around grille. Dual bright finish 5 x 7 in. exterior mirrors. Bright finish hubcaps. Voyager Sport nameplates. Bright taillamp bezels. Exterior upper front, side, and rear moldings. Sport seat trim (in blue, green, parchment, or black). Vinyl side-trim panels. Armrests at both sides of the rear bench seat. Color-keyed carpeting. Cigarette lighter. Added insulation. Full headliner. Padded instrument panel. Front and rear bright finish bumpers. Fiberglass window trim. Bright finish windshield moldings. Horn bar. Spare tire cover. **Optional Sport interior:** Cloth-and-vinyl front bucket seats with matching rear bench seat and interior trim. **Custom:** Argent and black grille. Front and rear painted bumpers. Exterior dual 5 x 7 in. painted mirrors. Bright-finish hubcaps. Custom nameplates. Bright taillamp bezel. Upper front and side exterior moldings. Color-keyed interior trim. Color-keyed floor mats throughout. Full headliner. Padded instrument panel. Instrument cluster trim dress-up. Horn bar. Cigarette lighter. Fiberglass window trim. Spare tire cover.

CONVENIENCE OPTIONS: Air conditioning (V-8 models only). Automatic speed control (available with V-8 engines and automatic transmission only). Fifty-nine or 70-amp./hr. battery. Front and rear bright-finish bumpers. Cigarette lighter. Heavy-duty clutch (six-cylinder only). Vented glass rear doors. Tinted glass, windshield only or all windows. Passenger compartment headliner. Deluxe heater. Auxiliary heater. Horn bar. Bright finish hubcaps. Padded instrument panel. Interior day/night prismatic mirror. Increased cooling. Oil pressure gauge. Power steering. AM radio. AM/FM radio. Eight-passenger seating (PB-200, PB-300). Twelve-passenger seating (PB-300 w/127 inch wheelbase); 15-passenger seating (PB-300 extended body). Heavy-duty front and rear shock absorbers. Bright-finish wheel covers (except on PB-300). Low-mount exterior mirrors. Inside hood release. Heavy-duty alternator. Sliding side door.

HISTORICAL: Voyager buyers had their choice of 13 exterior colors: Medium blue metallic. Medium gold metallic. Avocado metallic. Turquoise. Medium gold. Bright red. Light green. Light blue. Yellow. Dark green metallic. Light gold. Bronze metallic. White. There were two, two-tone paint options: 1) Main color on top, secondary color on bottom. 2) Main color on top and bottom, secondary color in between.

Pricing

1974	5	4	3	2	1
Trail Duster — (4x4) — (½-Ton)					
Utility	620	1230	2050	2900	4100
PB-100 Voyager Van — (½-Ton) — (109 in. w.b.)					
Wagon	480	975	1600	2250	3200
(127 in. w.b.)					
Wagon	500	1000	1650	2300	3300
PB-200 Voyager Van — (¾-Ton) — (109 in. w.b.)					
Wagon	530	1050	1750	2450	3500
(127 in. w.b.)					
Wagon	540	1080	1800	2500	3600
Maxiwagon	560	1100	1850	2600	3700
PB-300 Voyager Van — (1-Ton) — (127 in. w.b.)					
Wagon	560	1100	1850	2600	3700
Maxiwagon	570	1140	1900	2650	3800

1975 PLYMOUTH

1975 Plymouth Trail Duster w/Fiberglass Top

1975 Plymouth Trail Duster w/Full Vinyl Enclosure

TRAIL DUSTER — PD-100 UTILITY VEHICLE: — Big news for the Trail Duster in 1975 was the addition of a two-wheel-drive model. It looked virtually the same as last year's four-wheel-drive version. But it was 2½ inches lower. It also featured independent front suspension.

I.D. DATA: See 1974 Plymouth Trail Duster.

Model	Body Type	Price	Weight	Prod. Total
Trail Duster — (4x2) — (½-Ton)				
PD-100	Utility	3640	3570	666

ENGINE (Base): Six-cylinder. Displacement: 225 cu. in. Brake horsepower: 105 at 3600 R.P.M. Bore & stroke: 3.40 in. x 4.12 in. Compression ratio: 8.4:1. Carburetor: 1-bbl.

ENGINE (Optional): Displacement: 318 cu. in. V-8. Brake horsepower: 150 at 4000 R.P.M. (155 horsepower in CA). Bore & stroke: 3.91 in. x 3.31 in. Compression ratio: 8.6:1. Carburetor: 2-bbl.

1975 Plymouth Trail Duster w/Fiberglass Top

TRAIL DUSTER PW-100 UTILITY VEHICLE: — To say the four-wheel-drive Trail Duster was little changed for 1975 would be an understatement. The sales catalog used the same cover photo as it had for 1974. Even the new dash looked similar to the "old" one.

Model	Body Type	Price	Weight	Prod. Total
Trail Duster — (4x4) — (½-Ton)				
PW-100	Utility	4546	4085	3877

CHASSIS: Wheelbase: 106 in. Overall length: 184.6 in. Overall width: 79.5 in. Overall height with roof: (PD-100): 70 in.; (PW-100) 72 in. Tires: E78-15/B in. (6-cyl.), E78-15/B (V-8). GVW rating: 4900 to 6000 lbs.

TECHNICAL: Four-speed manual transmission (PW-100). Three-speed TorqueFlite automatic. Two V-8 engines: 360 cu. in. with 2-bbl. carb. and a 440 cu. in. with 4-bbl. carb.

OPTIONS: Sport package: includes unique bodyside and tailgate trim; bright front and rear bumpers, accents and windshield molding; full foam all-vinyl driver and passenger bucket seats; color-keyed door trim panels with map pockets; console and sunvisors. Air conditioning. Power steering. Automatic speed control. Tachometer. Bright wheelcovers. Trailer towing package. Oil pressure gauge. Passenger seat. Deluxe seats including console, sunvisors and seat belts. Rear bench seat. Skid plates. Tinted glass (windshield or all glass). High output heater. Increased cooling. Engine block heater. Hand throttle (not available with TorqueFlite automatic). Step type rear bumper. Front bumper guards. Steel roof (in body color or vinyl textured white or black). Two-tone body (includes moldings and bright taillamp bezels). Dual horn. Bright hubcaps. AM or AM/FM radio. Dealer installed soft top. Thirty-five gallon fuel tank. Front stabilizer bar (PD-100). Heavy-duty shock absorbers. Heavy-duty battery. Heavy-duty alternator. Roll bar. Front passengers seat.

NOTE: The optional soft top had special side windows that could be rolled up. A new body color available on Trail Dusters this year was Silver Cloud Metallic.

VOYAGER — PB-100 WAGON: — Styling was identical to 1974. But that wasn't bad. Standard features included: Electronic ignition, driver and front passenger armrests, power front brakes, argent and black grille, front and rear painted bumpers, white hub caps, dual electric horns, 23-gallon fuel tank, fresh air heater with defrosters, three passenger bench seat, padded sunvisors, spare tire carrier; ashtray, driver compartment headliner, black driver compartment floor mat, Voyager nameplates, and dual painted exterior mirrors.

I.D. DATA: See 1974 Plymouth Voyager.

Model	Body Type	Price	Weight	Prod. Total
Voyagers Van — (½-Ton)				
PB-100	Wagon (109 in. w.b.)	4568	3715	3261
PB-100	Wagon (127 in. w.b.)	4680	3820	1103

ENGINE (Base): Six-cylinder. Displacement: 225 cu. in. Brake horsepower: 95 at 3600 R.P.M. Bore & stroke: 3.40 in. x 4.12 in. Compression ratio: 8.4:1. Carburetor: 1-bbl.

ENGINE (Optional): Displacement: 318 cu. in. V-8. Brake horsepower: 150 at 4000 R.P.M.. Bore & stroke: 3.91 in. x 3.31 in. Compression ratio: 8.6:1. Carburetor: 2-bbl.

VOYAGER — PB-200 WAGON: — The PB-200 came with the same standard features as the PB-100. But buyers had their choice of three sizes. In addition, the payload allowances were much higher.

I.D. DATA: See 1974 Plymouth Voyager.

Model	Body Type	Price	Weight	Prod. Total
Voyager Van — (¾-Ton)				
PB-200	Wagon (109 in. w.b.)	4668	3805	399
PB-200	Wagon (127 in. w.b.)	5102	4025	4237
PB-200	Maxi-Wagon (127 in. w.b.)	5300	4280	1441

ENGINE: Same as PB-100.

1975 Plymouth PB300 Voyager Sport Wagon (CPD)

VOYAGER — PB-300 WAGON: — For maximum load capacities, buyers ordered the PB-300 Voyager. In addition to the standard features found on the PB-100, it came with the axle jack and TorqueFlite automatic transmission.

I.D. DATA: See 1974 Plymouth Voyager.

Model	Body Type	Price	Weight	Prod. Total
Voyager Van — (1-Ton)				
PB-300	Wagon (127 in. w.b.)	5634	4140	802
PB-300	Maxi-Wagon (127 in. w.b.)	5811	4435	3305

ENGINE: Displacement: 318 cu. in. V-8. (see PB-100).

CHASSIS: Wheelbase (PB-100, PB-200): 109 in.; (PB-100, PB-200, PB-300): 127 in. Overall width: 79.8 in. Overall length: (109 in. w.b.) 176 in., (127 in. w.b.) 194 in., (127 in. w.b. extended) 212 in. Overall height: (PB-100/109 in. w.b.) 77.2 in., (PB-100/127 in. w.b.) 77.3 in., (PB-200/109 in. w.b.) 78.4 in., (PB-200/127 in. w.b.) 78.6 in., (PB-300) 79.1 in. Tires: (PB-100/109 in. w.b.): E78-15-B, (PB-100/127 in. w.b.) F78-15-B, (PB-200) G78-15-B, (PB-300) 8.00-16.5-D.

TECHNICAL: TorqueFlite automatic transmission (PB-100, PB-200).

OPTION PACKAGES: Convenience package. Trailer-towing package (two). **Custom Package:** includes Argent and black grille. Front and rear painted bumpers. White painted dual 5 x 7 in. exterior mirrors. Bright finish hubcaps. Voyager Custom nameplates. Bright taillamp bezels. Bright front and side exterior moldings. Color-keyed interior, side trim panels, and floor mats. Full headliner. Padded instrument panel. Instrument cluster trim dress-up. Horn bar. Cigarette lighter. Fiberglass window trim. Spare tire cover. **Sport Package:** includes Argent and black grille with bright molding around grille. Dual bright-finish 5 x 7 in. mirrors. Bright finish hubcaps. Voyager and Sport nameplates. Bright taillamp bezels. Exterior upper front, side and rear moldings. Sport seat trim. Color-keyed carpeting. Full headliner. Padded instrument panel. Bright-finish instrument cluster trim. Padded vinyl trim side panel with woodgrain. Front and rear bright finish bumpers. Fiberglass window trim. Added insulation. Bright-finish windshield trim. Bright-finish side and rear window moldings. Sport spare tire cover. All-vinyl front bucket seats in blue, green, parchment, or black. Optional cloth and vinyl seats in the same colors. **Premium Trim Package:** includes (for Sport) cloth and vinyl seats. Parchment or gold vinyl trim on doors. Carpeted floors, engine housing, seat risers, legs, and more.

601

CONVENIENCE OPTIONS: Single rear door. Left and right-side low mount mirrors. Steel-belted, radial-ply white sidewall tires. Push-button AM/FM radio. Air conditioning (V-8 models only). Automatic Speed Control. (available with V-8 engines and automatic transmission only). Front and rear bright-finish bumpers (standard or Voyager Sport). Heavy-duty clutch (6-cyl. only). Vented glass rear doors. Tinted glass (windshield only or all windows). Passenger compartment headliner. Deluxe heater. Auxiliary heater. Horn bar. Bright-finish hubcaps. Padded instrument panel. Interior day/night prismatic mirror. Increased cooling. Oil pressure gauge. Power steering. AM radio. Eight passenger seating (PB-200, PB-300). Twelve passenger seating (PB-300 127 in. w.b. and extended body models). Fifteen passenger seating (PB-300 extended body). Front and rear heavy-duty shock absorbers. Bright-finish wheel covers (PB-100, PB-200). Inside hood release. Heavy-duty alternator (55-and 72-amp). Sliding side door. Heavy-duty rear leaf springs (PB-100, PB-300). Five-stud disc wheels 15 in. x 6.50 in. (PB-100, PB-200), 16.5 in. x 6.75 in. (PB-300). Two-tone paint (Main color on top, secondary color on bottom. Or, main color on top and bottom, secondary color in between).

Pricing

	5	4	3	2	1
1975					
Trail Duster — (4x2) — (½-Ton)					
Utility	600	1200	2000	2800	4000
Trail Duster — (4x4) — (½-Ton)					
Utility	680	1350	2250	3150	4500
PB-100 Voyager Van — (½-Ton) — (109 in. w.b.)					
Wagon	470	950	1550	2200	3100
(127 in. w.b.)					
Wagon	480	975	1600	2250	3200
PB-200 Voyager Van — (¾-Ton) — (109 in. w.b.)					
Wagon	520	1020	1700	2400	3400
(127 in. w.b.)					
Wagon	530	1050	1750	2450	3500
Maxi-Wagon	540	1080	1800	2500	3600
PB-300 Voyager Van — (1-Ton) — (127 in. w.b.)					
Wagon	540	1080	1800	2500	3600
Maxi-Wagon	560	1100	1850	2600	3700

1976 PLYMOUTH

TRAIL DUSTER — SERIES PD-100 — (ALL ENGINES): — The attractive styling of last year's model was unchanged. In fact, some of the same photos used in the '75 Trail Duster literature showed up in the '76 sales catalog. Standard features included: Full-foam all-vinyl bucket seats. Armrest pads. Color-keyed padded instrument panel. Bright front and rear bumpers. Fuse box located on top of glove box. Three-speed manual transmission. Twenty-four gallon fuel tank.

I.D. DATA: See 1974 Plymouth Trail Duster.

Model	Body Type	Price	Weight	Prod. Total
Trail Duster — (4x2) — (½-Ton)				
PD-100	Utility	3702	3570	4255

NOTE: Production total is for both 4x2 and 4x4 Trail Dusters.

ENGINE (Base): Six-cylinder. Displacement: 225 cu. in. Brake horsepower: 100 at 3600 R.P.M. Bore & stroke: 3.40 in. x 4.12 in. Compression ratio: 8.4:1. Carburetor: 1-bbl.

ENGINE (Optional): Displacement: 318 cu. in. V-8. Brake horsepower: 150 at 4000 R.P.M. (155 horsepower in California). Bore & stroke: 3.91 in. x 3.31 in. Compression ratio: 8.6:1. Carburetor: 2-bbl.

1976 Plymouth Trail Duster SE 4x4 Utility

TRAIL DUSTER — SERIES PW-100 — (ALL ENGINES): — Sales literature called the four-wheel-drive Trail Duster "a pure adventure machine" that could take you "To all those places in this world you haven't been yet." The PW-100 came with the same standard features as the two-wheel-drive PD-100, plus it had a front stabilizer bar and higher capacity front axle. This full-time four-wheel-drive vehicle had five shift positions for on-road cruising and off road use: 1) Low-lock for deep snow, mud, sand. 2) Low for mountainous and hilly terrain. 3) Neutral. 4) High for paved surfaces. 5) High-lock for snow, mud sand.

I.D. DATA: See 1974 Plymouth Trail Duster.

Model	Body Type	Price	Weight	Prod. Total
Trail Duster — (4x4) — (½-Ton)				
PW-100	Utility	4834	3980	Note 1

NOTE 1: See Trail Duster production total above.

CHASSIS: Wheelbase: 106 in. Overall length: 184.6 in. Overall width: 79.5 in. Overall height with roof: 72 in. Tires: E78-15/B. GVW Rating: 4900-6100 lbs.

TECHNICAL: Four-speed manual transmission (PW-100). Three-speed TorqueFlite automatic transmission. Three V-8 engines: 360 cu. in. with 2-bbl. carb. (available in California only). 400 cu. in. with 2-bbl. carburetor. 440 cu. in. with 4-bbl. carburetor.

CONVENIENCE OPTION: Sport package: Deluxe full-foam all vinyl front bucket seats; color-keyed door trim panels with map pockets; center console with removable styrofoam beverage chest; windshield moldings plus unique bodyside, tailgate and interior trim. Air conditioning. Power steering. Automatic speed control. Tachometer. Bright-finish or premium wheel covers. Trailer towing package (52-amp alternator, 70-amp-hour battery, wiring harness, heavy-duty variable load flasher and increased engine cooling system). Sno-Fiter package (PW-100). Convenience package (standard on Sport). Oil pressure gauge. Electric clock. Rear bench seat. Skid plates. Tinted glass (windshield or all glass). High output heater. Increased cooling. Engine block heater. Hand throttle (not available with TorqueFlite automatic). Step type rear bumper. Protection package (includes front bumper guards and door edge protectors). Steel roof (available in body color or vinyl textured white or black). Two-tone body (includes moldings and bright taillamp bezels). Dual horn. Bright hub caps. AM or AM/FM radio. Dealer installed soft top. Thirty-five gallon fuel tank. Heavy-duty shocks. Roll bar. Heavy-duty front stabilizer bar. Low mount mirrors. Cigar lighter. Boca Raton cloth-and-vinyl seats in parchment (hardtops with Sport option only).

1976 Plymouth Voyager Sport Wagon (JAG)

VOYAGER — SERIES PB-100 — (ALL ENGINES): — Voyager styling was carried over from the previous model year. Standard equipment included: Forty-eight-amp alternator. Driver and front passenger armrest. Driver's compartment ash tray. Passenger-side double doors with vented glass. Door locks, all doors. Electronic ignition system. A 22.1 gallon fuel tank. Glove box door with push-button operated latch. Fresh air heater with defrosters. Dual electric horns. Bumper jack. Interior mirror. Oil pressure indicator light. Driver and front passenger bucket seats. Three-passenger rear bench seat. Padded sunvisors. Spare tire carrier. Two-speed windshield wipers with arm-mounted washers. Power front disc brakes. Argent and black grille. Front and rear white painted bumpers. White painted hubcaps. Dual 5 in. x 7 in. painted exterior mirrors. Black driver's compartment floor mat. Driver compartment headliner. Voyager nameplates. Three-speed manual transmission.

I.D. DATA: See 1974 Voyager.

Model	Body Type	Price	Weight	Prod. Total
Voyager Van — (½-Ton)				
PB-100	Wagon (109 in. w.b.)	4768	3715	Note 1
PB-100	Wagon (127 in. w.b.)	4877	3820	Note 1

NOTE 1: Production was 10,819 units for all three Voyager series.
NOTE 2: This includes totals for PB-100, PB-200, and PB-300.

ENGINE: (Base) Six-cylinder. Displacement: 225 cu. in. Brake horsepower: 95 at 3600 R.P.M. Bore & stroke: 3.40 in. x 4.12 in. Compression ratio: 8.4:1. Carburetor: 1-bbl.

ENGINE (Optional): Displacement: 318 cu. in. V-8. Brake horsepower: 150 at 4000 R.P.M. Bore & stroke: 3.91 in. x 3.31 in. Compression ratio: 8.6:1. Carburetor: 2-bbl.

VOYAGER — SERIES PB-200 — (ALL ENGINES): — The allowable driver, passenger, luggage and load weight for the lowest price 109 inch wheelbase PB-200 wagon, was nearly 70 percent greater than that for the equivalent PB-100 Voyager. Buyers had their pick of three sizes of PB-200s. Standard features were the same as those for the PB-100.

I.D. DATA: See 1974 Plymouth Voyager.

Model	Body Type	Price	Weight	Prod. Total
Voyager Van — (¾-Ton)				
PB-200	Wagon (109 in. w.b.)	4863	3805	Note 1
PB-200	Wagon (127 in. w.b.)	4956	4025	Note 1
PB-200	Maxi-Wagon (127 in. w.b.)	5177	4280	Note 1

NOTE 1: Production was 10,819 units for all three Voyager series.

ENGINE: Same as PB-100.

VOYAGER — SERIES PB-300 — (ALL ENGINES): — The PB-300 may have looked like the other series, but it was capable of hauling much heavier loads. TorqueFlite automatic transmission, an axle jack, and larger brakes were standard. In addition to the equipment listed for the PB-100.

I.D. DATA: See 1974 Plymouth Voyager.

Model	Body Type	Price	Weight	Prod. Total
Voyager Van — (1-Ton)				
PB-300	Wagon (127 in. w.b.)	5644	4140	Note 1
PB-300	Maxi-Wagon (127 in. w.b.)	5841	4280	Note 1

NOTE 1: Production was 10,819 units for all three Voyager series.

ENGINE: Displacement: 318 cu. in. V-8. (see PB-100).

CHASSIS: Wheelbase (PB-100, PB-200): 109 in.; (PB-100, PB-200, PB-300): 127 in. Overall width: 79.8 in. Overall length: (109 in. w.b.) 176 in., (127 in. w.b.) 194 in. (127 in. w.b. Maxi-wagon) 212 in. Overall height: 80.8 in. Tires: (PB-100/109 in. w.b.): E78-15-B; (PB-100/127 in. w.b.) F78-15-B; (PB-200/109 in. w.b. and 127 in. w.b.) G78-15-B; (PB-200/127 in. w.b.) H78-15-B; (PB-300) 8.00-16.5-D.

1976 Plymouth Voyager Sport Maxi-Wagon (OCW)

OPTIONAL PACKAGES: Convenience. Insulation. Trailer Towing: Light and heavy-duty. Includes 52-amp alternator, 70 amp-hour battery, increased cooling, heavy-duty variable load flasher and wiring harness. Heavy-duty shock absorbers and 15 in. heavy-duty rims. Eight-passenger seating: (PB-200, PB-300).Twelve-passenger seating: (PB-300). Fifteen-passenger seating: (PB-300). Custom: Argent and black grille. Front and rear white painted bumpers. Dual white painted exterior mirrors (5 in. x 7 in.). Bright-finish hubcaps. Custom nameplates. Bright taillamp bezel. Upper front and side exterior moldings. Color-keyed interi trim. Color-keyed floor mats throughout. Full headliner. Padded instrument panel. Instrument cluster trim dress-up. Horn bar. Cigarette lighter. Fiberglass window trim. Spare tire cover. Low-back front bucket seats in blue, green, parchment or black. Sport Option: Argent and black grille with bright molding around grille. Dual bright finish 5 in. x 7 in. exterior mirrors. Bright finish hubcaps. Voyager Sport nameplates. Bright taillamp bezels. Exterior upper front, side, and rear moldings. Deluxe vinyl seat trim. Color-keyed carpeting. Full headliner. Padded instrument panel with simulated wood-grain insert. Bright finish instrument cluster trim. Padded vinyl trim side panel with wood grain. Front and rear bright finish bumpers. Fiberglass window trim. Added insulation. Bright finish windshield molding. Bright finish side and rear window moldings. Horn bar. Cigarette lighter. Spare tire cover. Sport optional interior: Cloth-and-vinyl high-back front bucket seats with inboard fold-down front armrests in a woven texture available in blue, green or parchment. Matching three-passenger rear bench seat. Color-keyed carpeting, padded side panel and door trim. Premium trim: Bright front and rear bumpers. Dual bright 5 in. x 7 in. exterior mirrors. Bright finish hubcaps. Bright taillamp bezels. Voyager and Sport nameplates. Bright molding around grille, windshield, side and rear windows (except front doors). High-back deluxe cloth-and-vinyl bucket seats with fold down armrests and deluxe cloth-and-vinyl bench seats. Bright instrument cluster trim.

Driver and passenger compartment special door and side panels carpeting. Carpeting on lower engine compartment. Full headliner. Spare tire cover. Additional insulation. Cigarette lighter. Fiberglass window trim.

CONVENIENCE OPTIONS: Air conditioning (front or front and rear, V-8 models only). A 59-amp or 70-amp hour battery. Bright finish front and rear bumpers. Cigarette lighter. Heavy-duty clutch (225 six-cylinder only). Vented glass rear doors. Tinted glass, windshield only or all windows. Passenger compartment headliner. Deluxe heater. Auxiliary rear heater. Horn bar. Bright finish hubcaps. Padded instrument panel. Interior day/night prismatic mirror. Increased cooling. Oil pressure gauge. Power steering. AM or AM/FM radio. Thirty-six gallon gas tank. Front and rear heavy-duty shock absorbers. Two bright finish wheel covers (except on PB-300). Left and right low-mount exterior mirrors. Inside hood release. Heavy-duty alternator (52- and 63-amp). Sliding side door. One piece rear door with fixed glass. Chrome style road wheels (except PB-300). Automatic speed control, available with V-8/automatic transmission models only.

POWERTRAIN OPTIONS: TorqueFlite automatic transmission (PB-100, PB-200). 360 cu. in. V-8. 440 cu. in. V-8 (PB-200, PB-300).

NOTE: The 1976 Plymouth Voyager was available in 14 exterior colors: Bright red. Yellow. Russet. Light blue. Light gold. Bright blue metallic. Medium gold metallic. Light green metallic. Sunstone. Bright green metallic. Bright tan metallic. Dark green metallic. Silver cloud metallic. White. Buyers had their choice of two two-tone paint procedures; 1) Main color on top, seconday color on bottom. 2) Main color on top and bottom, secondary color in between.

Pricing

	5	4	3	2	1
1976					
Trail Duster — (4x2) — (½-Ton)					
Utility	620	1230	2050	2900	4100
Trail Duster — (4x4) — (½-Ton)					
Utility	690	1380	2300	3200	4600
PB-100 Voyager Van — (½-Ton) — (109 in. w.b.)					
Wagon	480	975	1600	2250	3200
(127 in. w.b.)					
Wagon	500	1000	1650	2300	3300
PB-200 Voyager Van — (¾-Ton) — (109 in. w.b.)					
Wagon	530	1050	1750	2450	3500
(127 in. w.b.)					
Wagon	540	1080	1800	2500	3600
Maxi-Wagon	560	1100	1850	2600	3700
PB-300 Voyager Van — (1-Ton) — (127 in. w.b.)					
Wagon	560	1100	1850	2600	3700
Maxi-Wagon	570	1140	1900	2650	3800

1977 PLYMOUTH

TRAIL DUSTER — SERIES PD-100 — (ALL ENGINES): — The Trail Duster received a facelift for 1977. Vertical signal lights were intergrated into the new, horizontal bar grille. The Plymouth nameplate was moved to the face of the hood. A different style of two toning was used. It sandwiched the contrasting color, in a wide band, on the sides and lower grille. Standard features included: low-back front bucket seats, power disc brakes, electronic ignition system, dual outside mirrors, painted hubcaps and three-speed manual transmission.

I.D. DATA: See 1974 Plymouth Trail Duster.

Model	Body Type	Price	Weight	Prod. Total
Trail Duster — (4x2) — (½-Ton)				
PD-100	Utility	4030	3570	—

ENGINE: Six-cylinder. Displacement: 225 cu. in. Brake horsepower: 95 at 3600 R.P.M. Bore & stroke: 3.40 in. x 4.12 in. Compression ratio: 8.4:1. Carburetor: 1-bbl.

TRAIL DUSTER — SERIES PW-100 — (ALL ENGINES): — The four-wheel-drive Trail Duster had the same basic features as the standard version, plus a front stabilizer bar. It was also a couple inches taller.

I.D. DATA: See 1974 Plymouth Trail Duster.

Model	Body Type	Price	Weight	Prod. Total
Trail Duster — (4x4) — (½-Ton)				
PW-100	Utility	5045	3940	—

ENGINE: Same as PD-100 (except in California where standard engine was: 318 cu. in. V-8. Brake horsepower: 150 at 4000 R.P.M. Bore & stroke: 3.91 in. x 3.31 in. Compression ratio: 8.6:1. Carburetor: 2-bbl.

CHASSIS: Wheelbase: 106 in. Overall length: 184.6 in. Overall width: 79.5 in. Overall height: (PD-100): 70 in.; (PW-100): 72 in. Tires: E78-15/B. GVW Rating: 4900 to 6100 lbs.

1977 Plymouth Trail Duster 4x4 Utility (OCW)

TECHNICAL: Four-speed manual transmission with either wide- or close-space ratio (PW-100). Three-speed TorqueFlite automatic transmission. 318 cu. in. V-8 with 2-bbl. carburetor. 360 cu. in. V-8 with 2-bbl. carburetor. 400 cu. in. V-8 with 2-bbl. carburetor and 440 cu. in. V-8 with 4-bbl. carburetor.

1977 Plymouth Trail Duster Sport Utility (CHC)

CONVENIENCE OPTION: Sport interior package (deluxe vinyl bucket seats with matching padded door trim and a console beverage chest with removable insulated liner). High-back Command seats in striped cloth-and-vinyl with matching padded door trim with pull handles and carpeted lower panels, lockable console, inboard fold-down armrests, color-keyed carpeting. Removable steel roof. Soft vinyl roof with roll-up windows. Three-passenger rear bench seat. Sport padded instrument panel with rosewood-grain applique and panel trim molding. Air conditioning. Power steering. Speed control. Sno-plow package (PW-100). Roll bar. Outside spare tire carrier. Eight-spoke white-painted road wheels with raised white lettering on wide tires. Chrome-styled slotted road wheels with raised white lettering on wide all-terrain 10.00-15 LT tires. Trailer-assist package (63-amp alternator, 7-amp-hour battery, wiring harness, heavy-duty variable load flasher and increased engine cooling system). Low-mount mirrors. Convenience package. Oil pressure gauge. Electric clock (not available with tachometer). Fuel tank and transfer case shield. Tinted glass (windshield or all glass). High output heater. Engine block heater. Hand throttle. Step type rear bumper. Protection package (front bumper guards and door edge protectors). Two-tone body with moldings. Dual electric horn. Bright hub caps. AM radio. AM/FM radio. Thirty-five gallon fuel tank. Heavy-duty shock absorbers. Cigar lighter. Heavy-duty front stabilizer bar.

NOTE 1977 Trail Dusters were available in 14 colors: harvest gold, yellow, russet, light green metallic, bright red, medium green sunfire metallic, russet sunfire metallic, bright tan metallic, light tan, silver cloud metallic, white, light blue, black sunfire metallic, medium blue metallic.

1977 Plymouth PB100 Voyager Custom Wagon (CPD)

VOYAGER — SERIES PB-100 — (ALL ENGINES): — The 1977 Voyager looked the same as last year's model. Standard features included: Vinyl interior, driver and front passenger armrests, passenger-side double doors with vented glass, electronic ignition system, 22 gallon fuel tank, dual elec-

tric horns, padded sunvisors, spare tire carrier, two-speed windshield wipers with washers, power front disc brakes, argent and black grille, painted front and read bumpers, dual painted mirrors, painted hubcaps, black driver and passenger compartment floor mat, driver compartment headliner and three-speed manual transmission.

I.D. DATA: See 1974 Plymouth Voyager.

Model	Body Type	Price	Weight	Prod. Total
Voyager Van — (½-Ton)				
PB-100	Wagon (109 in. w.b.)	5198	3715	—
PB-100	Wagon (127 in. w.b.)	5307	3820	—

ENGINE (Base): Six-cylinder. Displacement: 225 cu. in. Brake horsepower: 95 at 3600 R.P.M. Bore & stroke: 3.40 in. x 4.12 in. Compression ratio: 8.4:1. Carburetor: 1-bbl.

ENGINE (Optional): Displacement: 318 cu. in. V-8. Brake horsepower: 150 at 4000 R.P.M.. Bore & stroke: 3.91 in. x 3.31 in. Compression ratio: 8.6:1. Carburetor: 2-bbl.

1977 Plymouth Voyager Sport Wagon (OCW)

VOYAGER — SERIES PB-200 — (ALL ENGINES): — The PB-200 came with many of the same features as the PB-100 Voyager. The maximum weight loads in PB-200 wagons were more than double those in the standard line.

Model	Body Type	Price	Weight	Prod. Total
Voyager Van — (¾-Ton)				
PB-200	Wagon (109 in. w.b.)	5266	3805	—
PB-200	Wagon (127 in. w.b.)	5384	4025	—
PB-200	Maxi-Wagon (127 in. w.b.)	5539	4280	—

ENGINE: Same as PB-100.

VOYAGER — SERIES PB-300 — (ALL ENGINES): — Buyers who wanted maximum load carrying capacity order this series. LoadFlite automatic transmission with fluid level warning light was standard.

I.D. DATA: See 1974 Plymouth Voyager.

Model	Body Type	Price	Weight	Prod. Total
Voyager Van — (1-Ton)				
PB-300	Wagon (127 in. w.b.)	6085	4140	—
PB-300	Maxi-Wagon (127 in. w.b.)	6240	4280	—

ENGINE: Displacement: 318 cu. in. V-8. (See PB-100).

CHASSIS: Wheelbase (PB-100, PB-200): 109 in.; (PB-100, PB-200, PB-300): 127 in. Overall width: 79.8 in. Overall length: (109 in. w.b.) 176 in., (127 in. w.b.) 194 in., (127 in. w.b. extended) 212 in. Overall height: 80.8 in. Tires: (109 in. w.b.) E78-15-B; (PB-100/127 in. w.b.) F78-15-B; (PB-200) H78-15-B; (PB-300) 8.00 x 16.5-D.

TECHNICAL: Four-speed manual, overdrive (PB-100). LoadFlite automatic transmission. 360 cu. in. V-8. 400 cu. in. V-8 (PB-200, PB-300) and 440 cu. in. V-8 (PB-200, PB-300).

OPTIONAL PACKAGES: Convenience. Ignition time delay light. Cigar lighter and light. Courtesy light front door. Glove box light. Ten inch day/night rearview mirror. In cab actuated hood lock release. Premium Trim: (127 in. w.b. V-8 models only) Bright front and rear bumpers. Dual 5 x 7 in. bright mirrors. Bright finish hubcaps and taillamp bezels. Bright molding around grille, windshield, side and rear windows. High-back deluxe cloth and vinyl bucket seats with fold down armrests and matching bench seat. Bright instrument cluster trim. Carpeting. Vinyl covered full headliner. Spare tire cover. Additional insulation. Cigarette lighter. Fiberglass window trim. Exterior upper front, side and rear bright moldings. Padded instrument panel with woodgrain inserts. Horn bar. Voyager Sport optional interior: Woven texture cloth and vinyl high back Command seats with inboard fold down armrests. Three-passenger rear bench seat. Swivel front seats optional. Dual armrest on passenger seat. Color-keyed carpeting, padded side panel trim and door trim. (Available on 127 in. w.b. V-8 models only.) Easy Order Package: Automatic transmission. Convenience package. Dual 5 x 7 in. bright mirrors. Two-tone paint. Power steering. AM radio. Scuff pads. Dome lamp switches, side and rear door operated. Wheel covers. Luxury Package: Automatic transmission. Convenience package. AM/FM radio. Scuff pads. Power steering. Dome lamp switches. Premium wheel covers. Air conditioning. Tinted glass. Speed control. Door edge protection. High back cloth and vinyl Command front bucket seats. Two-tone paint. Sport Interior: (127 in. w.b. V-8 models only) Deluxe pleated all vinyl front bucket seats. A matching three-passenger rear seat. Color-keyed vinyl door trim with padded side panels. Carpeting. Dual bright finish 5 x 7 in. mirrors. Voyager Sport nameplates. Full vinyl covered headliner. Padded instrument panel with simulated woodgrain insert. Bright finish front and rear bumpers. Added insulation. Bright finish windshield, side, and rear window moldings. Cigarette lighter. Spare tire cover. Custom Package: Low-back all vinyl front bucket seat (in blue, green, parchment and black). Padded dash. Horn bar. Cigarette lighter. Bright finish hubcaps. Custom nameplates. Bright taillamp bezel. Upper front and side exterior moldings. Color-keyed floor mats. Full length head-liner. Instrument cluster trim dress up. Fiberglass window trim. Spare tire cover.

CONVENIENCE OPTIONS: Trailer towing (light- or heavy-duty) setup, includes 63-amp alternator, 70-amp hr. battery, increased cooling, heavy-duty variable load flasher and wiring harness. Heavy-duty shock absorbers. Air conditioning (front or front and rear). Automatic speed control (available with V-8 automatic transmission models only). Front and rear bright-finish bumpers. Cigarette lighter. Heavy-duty 11 in. clutch (225 Six only). Vented glass in optional dual rear doors. Tinted glass, windshield only or all windows. Sunscreen glass in rear compartment windows and side door glass (five and eight-passenger wagons only). Passenger com-partemtn headliner. Deluxe heater. Auxiliary rear heater. Horn bar. Bright-finish hubcaps. Padded instrument panel. Interior day/night prismatic 10 inch mirror. Increased cooling. Oil pressure gauge. Tape stripes. Power steering. AM or AM/FM radio. Thirty-six gallon fuel tank. Eight passenger seating (PB-200, PB-300). Twelve passenger seating (PB-300). Fifteen passenger seating (PB-300 Maxi-Wagon). Driver and passenger swivel seats with dual armrests on passenger seat and inboard armrest on driv-er's seat (Sport and Premium Package only). Bright-finish wheel covers. Exterior mirrors, white painted or bright-finish. Inside hood release. Heavy-duty alternator. Sliding side door (127 in. w.b. only). Dual rear door with fixed or vented glass. Chrome-style road wheels (PB-100, PB-200). Wide sport road wheels, chrome disc or white painted spoke (PB-100, PB-200). Fuel pacer system. Front door edge protectors.

Pricing

1977	5	4	3	2	1
Trail Duster — (4x2) — (½-Ton)					
Utility	620	1230	2050	2900	4100
Trail Duster — (4x4) — (½-Ton)					
Utility	690	1380	2300	3200	4600
PB-100 Voyager Van — (½-Ton) — (109 in. w.b.)					
Wagon	480	975	1600	2250	3200
(127 in. w.b.)					
Wagon	500	1000	1650	2300	3300
PB-200 Voyager Van — (¾-Ton) — (109 in. w.b.)					
Wagon	530	1050	1750	2450	3500
(127 in. w.b.)					
Wagon	540	1080	1800	2500	3600
Maxi-Wagon	560	1100	1850	2600	3700
PB-300 Voyager Van — (1-Ton) — (127 in. w.b.)					
Wagon	560	1100	1850	2600	3700
Maxi-Wagon	570	1140	1900	2650	3800

1978 PLYMOUTH

TRAIL DUSTER — SERIES PD-100 — (ALL ENGINES): — After major res-tyling last year, the exterior design was left alone for '78. New optional items included: different seats, sunscreen glass, Hurst transfer case gear selector, three-spoke Tuff steering wheel and tilt steering column, CB radio integrated with an AM/FM stereo and a skylight sun roof. Among the standard equipment was: full-foam deluxe-vinyl bucket seats, armrest pads, padded instrument panel, 10 inch day/night inside rearview mirror, dual 5 x 7 in. bright exterior mirrors and bright front and rear bumpers.

I.D. DATA: See 1974 Plymouth Trail Duster.

Model	Body Type	Price	Weight	Prod. Total
Trail Duster — (4x2) — (½-Ton)				
PD-100	Utility	4647	3570	—

ENGINE: Six-cylinder. Displacement: 225 cu. in. Brake horsepower: 100 at 3600 R.P.M. Bore & stroke: 3.4 in. x 4.12 in. Compression ratio: 8.4:1. Carburetor: 2-bbl.

TRAIL DUSTER — SERIES PW-100 — (ALL ENGINES): — The PW-100 featured full-time four-wheel-drive. It had an inter-axle differential that proportioned power to both the front and rear axles. That allowed the wheels on one axle to travel at a different rate of speed from those on the other axle. This supposedly cut down on tire wear and improved the vehi-cle's handling. A new color offered this year on the PW-100 and PD-100, was "sunrise" orange.

I.D. DATA: See 1974 Plymouth Trail Duster.

Model	Body Type	Price	Weight	Prod. Total
Trail Duster — (4x4) — (½-Ton)				
PW-100	Utility	5684	4085	—

ENGINE: Same as PD-100.

1978 Plymouth Trail Duster 4x4 Utility (OCW)

CHASSIS: Wheelbase: 106 in. Overall length: 184.6 in. Overall width: 79.5 in. Overall height (PW-100): 74.2 in. Tires: H78-15/B (bias polyester). BSW GVW Rating: 6100 lbs.

TECHNICAL: Four-speed manual transmission with either wide or close space ratio. Three-speed LoadFlite automatic transmission. Four V-8 engines: 318 cu. in. with 2-bbl. carburetor; 360 cu. in. with 2-bbl. carbure-tor; 400 cu. in. with 2-bbl. carburetor and 440 cu. in. V-8 with 4-bbl. carburetor.

CONVENIENCE OPTION: Air conditioning. Tinted glass. Sunscreen glass for quarter and rear windows. Step type rear bumper. Cigar lighter. Elec-tric clock. Thirty-five gallon fuel tank. Oil pressure gauge. Deluxe heater. Dual electric horn. Increased cooling. Low mount mirrors (with or without extended arm). Power steering. Radios: AM, AM/FM, AM/FM stereo, AM/FM stereo with 8-track, AM with CB transceiver, AM/FM with CB transceiver. Roll bar. Removable steel hardtop roof. Soft top roof (dealer installed). Skylite sun roof. Three-passenger rear bench seat. Heavy-duty shock absorbers. Skid plate. Automatic speed control. Heavy-duty front stabilizer bar. Tuff steering wheel. Tilt steering column. Tachometer. Hand throttle. Two-tone body. Bright hub caps. Bright finish or premium wheel covers. Chrome slotted or eight-spoke white painted wide sport road wheels. Sport package: Deluxe all-vinyl front bucket seats or cloth and vinyl bucket seats with optional hardtop roof. Color-keyed door trim panels. Lockable console with removable styrofoam beverage chest. Con-venience package. Oil pressure gauge. Cigar lighter. Dual horns. Simulated woodgrain instrument panel faceplate. Bright exterior moldings on the windshield, drip rail, wide body side with black paint fill, and partial front and rear wheel lip. Protection package. Bright hub caps. Sport medallion on front fender. Other packages available on 1978 Trail Dusters were: con-venience, easy order, luxury, protection, Sno-Plow, sound control and light- or heavy-duty trailer towing.

VOYAGER — SERIES PB-100 — (ALL ENGINES): — The new Voyager looked about the same as last year's model from the front. However, changes were made in side and rear body styling. The side marker lights were raised from the lower rear quarter panels to the middle and larger, vertical taillights were used. Five passenger seating, a 22-gallon fuel tank, and a three-speed manual transmission were among the standard fea-tures.

I.D. DATA: See 1974 Plymouth Voyager.

Model	Body Type	Price	Weight	Prod. Total
Voyager Van — (½-Ton)				
PB-100	Wagon (109 in. w.b.)	5302	3715	—
PB-100	Wagon (127 in. w.b.)	5413	3880	—

ENGINE (Base): Six-cylinder. Displacement: 225 cu. in. Brake horsepower: 90 at 3600 R.P.M. Bore & stroke: 3.40 in. x 4.12 in. Compression ratio: 8.4:1. Carburetor: 1-bbl.

ENGINE (Optional): Displacement: 318 cu. in. V-8. Brake horsepower: 140 at 4000 R.P.M.. Bore & stroke: 3.91 in. x 3.31 in. Compression ratio: 8.5:1. Carburetor: 2-bbl.

VOYAGER — SERIES PB-200 — (ALL ENGINES): — Although the wheel-base remained at 127 inches, the largest of the three sizes of PB-200 vans, the Maxi-Wagon, was several inches longer than the 1977 version. It also came with snazzy new wraparound rear quarter windows.

I.D. DATA: See 1974 Plymouth Voyager.

Model	Body Type	Price	Weight	Prod. Total
Voyager Van — (¾-Ton)				
PB-200	Wagon (109 in. w.b.)	5371	3805	—
PB-200	Wagon (127 in. w.b.)	5491	3930	—
PB-200	Maxi-Wagon (127 in. w.b.)	5649	4280	—

ENGINE: Same as PB-100.

1978 Plymouth Voyager Wagon (OCW)

VOYAGER — SERIES PB-300 — (ALL ENGINES): — The PB-300 series was the most practical choice among buyers who hauled heavy loads. As before, it was available in two sizes, big and huge. Fortunately for drivers, power steering was standard, as was a three-speed automatic transmission.

I.D. DATA: See 1974 Plymouth Voyager.

Model	Body Type	Price	Weight	Prod. Total
Voyager Van — (1-Ton)				
PB-300	Wagon (127 in. w.b.)	6569	4140	—
PB-300	Maxi-Wagon (127 in. w.b.)	6893	4280	—

ENGINE: Displacement: 318 cu. in. V-8. (See PB-100).

CHASSIS: Wheelbase (PB-100, PB-200): 109 in.; (PB-100, PB-200, PB-300): 127 in. Overall width: 79.8 in. Overall length: (109 in. w.b.) 179.1 in.; (127 in. w.b.) 197 in.; (Maxi-Wagon) 223.1 in. Overall height: (109 in. w.b.) 79.6 in.; (127 in. w.b.) 80.9 in.; (Maxi-Wagon) 80.6 in. Tires: (PB-100): FR78 x 15B; (PB-200/109 in. w.b.) J78 x 15B; (PB-200/127 in. w.b.) H78 x 15B and (PB-300) 8.00 x 16.5D in.

TECHNICAL: Four-speed manual, overdrive (PB-100). LoadFlite automatic transmission (PB-100, PB-200). 360 cu. in. V-8. 400 cu. in. V-8 (PB-200, PB-300) and 440 cu. in. V-8 (PB-200, PB-300).

OPTIONAL PACKAGES: Convenience. Cigar lighter, glove box light, in-cab-actuated hood lock release, and 10 in. day/night rearview mirror. Custom Package: Custom nameplates. Bright molding around windshield, side and rear windows (except driver and passenger door windws). Color-keyed floor mat. Instrument panel lower skirts. Low-back vinyl bucket seats. Sport Package: Deluxe all vinyl front bucket seats. Matching three passenger rear seat. Color-keyed vinyl door trim with padded side panels. Carpeting. Dual bright finish 5 x 7 in. mirrors. Sport nameplates. Vinyl covered headliner. Spare tire cover. Padded instrument panel with simulated woodgrain insert. Added insulation. Cigar lighter. Bright hub caps. Easy order package: Automatic transmission. Convenience package. Dual 5 x 7 in. bright mirrors. Two-tone paint. Power steering. AM radio. Scuff pads. Dome lamp switches, side and rear door operated. Wheel covers. Luxury package: Automatic transmission. Convenience package. Two-tone paint. AM/FM radio. Power steering. Scuff pads. Bright finish wheel covers. Air conditioning. Tinted glass. Speed control. High-back Command bucket seats. Trailer towing package: Either light or heavy-duty. Premium trim package: (127 in. wheelbase, V-8 models only) Bright front and rear bumpers. High-back deluxe cloth and vinyl bucket seats with matching bench seat. Bright molding around grille. Color-keyed carpeting with floor insulation. Dash liner insulation. Dual electric horns.

CONVENIENCE OPTIONS: Sky Lite sun roof. Air conditioning. Heavy-duty shocks. Automatic speed control. Front and rear bright-finish bumpers. Cigarette lighter. Heavy-duty clutch. Tinted glass, windshield only or all windows. Sunscreen glass in rear compartment windwos and side door glass. Passenger compartment headliner. Deluxe heater. Horn bar. Bright-finish hubcaps. Interior day/night prismatic mirror. Increased cooling. Oil pressure gauge. Power steering. AM or AM/FM radio. Thirty-six gallon fuel tank. Eight passenger seating (PB-200, PB-300). Twelve passenger seating (PB-300). Fifteen passenger seating (PB-300 extended body Maxi-Wagon). Driver and passenger swivel seats. Bright-finish wheel covers. Inside hood release. Heavy-duty alternator. Sliding side door (127 in. wheelbase only). Chrome-style road wheels. Wide sport road wheels, chrome disc or white painted spoke.

Pricing

	5	4	3	2	1
1978					
Trail Duster — (4x2) — (½-Ton)					
Utility	650	1300	2150	3050	4300
Trail Duster — (4x4) — (½-Ton)					
Utility	720	1450	2400	3300	4800
PB-100 Voyager Van — (½-Ton) — (109 in. w.b.)					
Wagon	520	1020	1700	2400	3400
(127 in. w.b.)					
Wagon	500	1000	1650	2300	3300
PB-200 Voyager Van — (¾-Ton) — (109 in. w.b.)					
Wagon	540	1080	1800	2500	3600
(127 in. w.b.)					
Wagon	560	1100	1850	2600	3700
Maxi-Wagon	560	1100	1850	2600	3700
PB-300 Voyager Van — (1-Ton) — (127 in. w.b.)					
Wagon	590	1170	1950	2700	3900
Maxi-Wagon	600	1200	2000	2800	4000

606

1979 PLYMOUTH

1979 Plymouth Arrow Mini-Pickup (OCW)

ARROW PICKUP: — This was the first year for the sporty Arrow pickup. It was made, for Plymouth, by Mitsubishi Motors Corporation in Japan. Styling for this compact truck was clean, yet pretty. The two rectangular headlights were slightly recessed in a ''honeycomb'' rectangular grille. The signal lights were intergrated into the front bumper. The large, vertical wraparound taillamps seemed almost out of proportion to the size of the truck. There was no rear bumper. Standard features included: Tubular cargo tie down bars on the inside of the 81.5 inch long box. Four-speed manual transmission. Power front disc brakes. Adjustable steering column with lock. Vinyl folding bench seat. Color-keyed door trim panels. Dual sunvisors. Cashmere headliner. Padded instrument panel. Black racing type exterior rearview mirror. Argent-painted front bumper with black rubber ends. Upper level vent outlets. Two-speed windshield wipers with washers. Bright hubcaps. Dome light. Electronic ignition system. Two-spoke steering wheel. Tinted glass. Passenger assist grip. AM radio. Cigarette lighter. Cargo lamp. Armrests. Bright windshield molding. Bright drip rail molding. Extra sound insulation.

I.D. DATA: See 1974 Plymouth Trail Duster.

Model	Body Type	Price	Weight	Prod. Total
OJL4	Pickup Sweptline	4819	2410	—

ENGINE: Four-cylinder. Displacement: 122 cu. in. Brake horsepower: 90 at 5000 R.P.M. Bore & stroke: 3.30 in. x 3.54 in. Compression ratio: 8.5:1. Carburetor: 2-bbl.

ARROW SPORT PICKUP: — As good looking as the basic Arrow was, it didn't really seem necessary to offer an even flashier version. But one was available. The Arrow Sport featured: Bodyside tape stripe. Five-speed manual transmission. Vinyl high-back bucket seats. Console. Loop-pile carpet. Tachometer. Oil pressure gauge and ammeter. Three-spoke sport-styled steering wheel. Wide-spoke sport wheels. AM/FM stereo radio.

I.D. DATA: See 1974 Plymouth Trail Duster.

Model	Body Type	Price	Weight	Prod. Total
OJP4	Sport Pickup Sweptline	5608	2410	—

ENGINE: Four-cylinder. Displacement: 156 cu. in. Brake horsepower: 105 at 5000 R.P.M. Bore & stroke: 3.59 in. x 3.86 in. Compression ratio: 8.2:1. Carburetor: 2-bbl.

CHASSIS: Wheelbase: 109.4 in. Overall length: 184.6 in. Overall width: 65 in. Overall height: 60.8 in. Box length: 81.5 in. Box width: 64.2 in. GVW Rating: 3880 lbs. Payload: 1400 lbs. Tires: 6.00 x 14-C in. WSW Bias-Ply (Arrow); 185SR-14 RWL Radial (Arrow Sport).

TECHNICAL: Three-speed automatic transmission.

CONVENIENCE OPTIONS: Step type rear bumper. Grille guard. Roll bar. Sky Lite sun roof. Dual low-mount mirrors. Black racing-type mirror for passenger side.

NOTE: The Arrow pickup was offered in a choice of three exterior colors: Light tan, Canyon red metallic or Warm white. The Arrow Sport could be had in black, Spitfire orange or a two-tone combination of yellow and low-luster black.

TRAIL DUSTER — SERIES PD-100 — (Utility Vehicle): — The rugged Trail Duster received a new, one-piece honeycomb-theme aluminum grille, divided horizontally in the center. Smaller signal lights were now located below the grille, under the headlights. Among standard features were: A three-speed manual transmission. Deluxe vinyl low-back front bucket seats. Color-keyed instrument panel and door trim panels. Black soft-touch vinyl steering wheel and horn pad.

I.D. DATA: See 1974 Plymouth Trail Duster.

Model	Body Type	Price	Weight	Prod. Total
PD-100	Utility Vehicle	5645	3570	—

ENGINE: Six-cylinder. Displacement: 225 cu. in. Brake horsepower: 90 at 3600 R.P.M. Bore & stroke: 3.40 in. x 4.12 in. Compression ratio: 8.4:1. Carburetor: 1-bbl.

NOTE: This engine was not available in California.

1979 Plymouth Trail Duster 4x4 Utility (OCW)

TRAIL DUSTER — SERIES PW-100 — (Utility Vehicle): — The PW-100 had full-time four-wheel-drive. That eliminated the need to shift in or out of four-wheel-drive. Or to lock or unlock the front free-wheeling hubs. It also came with a 3280-lb. capacity front leaf spring suspension, high capacity 3600-lb. rear axle and front stablizer bar.

I.D. DATA: See 1974 Plymouth Trail Duster.

Model	Body Type	Price	Weight	Prod. Total
PW-100	Utility Vehicle	7286	4150	—

ENGINE: Displacement: 318 cu. in. V-8. Brake horsepower: 120 at 3600 R.P.M. Bore & stroke: 3.91 in. x 3.31 in. Compression ratio: 8.5:1. Carburetor: 2-bbl.

CHASSIS: Wheelbase: 106 in. Overall length: 184.6 in. Overall width: 79.5 in. GVW Rating: 4800 to 6050 lbs. (PD-100); 6050 lbs. (PW-100). Tires: FR78-15-B (PD-100); L78-15-B (PW-100).

OPTIONAL PACKAGES: Sno-Commander: (PW-100 only) Power angling blade, power lift, seven-way control valve. Trail Duster Sport: Dual vertically stacked quad rectangular headlights. Bright windshield molding and taillight bezels. Sport nameplates on front fender. Bucket seats. Color-keyed vinyl door trim panels with assist strap. Locking console with removable beverage chest. Woodgrain instrument panel face plate with bright trim.

CONVENIENCE OPTION: Tilt steering column. Sky Lite sun roof. Radios: AM with 40 channel CB; AM/FM/MX stereo with 40-channel CB; AM/FM/MX stereo with eight-track tape. Electric door locks. Five-slot chrome disc wide sport road wheels. White-painted steel spoke wide sport road wheels. Chrome-styled road wheels. Vinyl soft top. Air conditioning. Outside spare tire carrier. Automatic speed control. Power steering. Inside hood lock release. Three-passenger deluxe vinyl split back front bench seat. Low-back cloth and vinyl front bucket seats. Three passenger bench rear seat in matching front seat trim. High-back cloth and vinyl Command front bucket seats (Trail Duster Sport only). Front stabilizer bar (PD-100). Heavy-duty front stabilizer bar (PW-100).

TECHNICAL: 318 cu. in. V-8 (PD-100). 360 cu. in. V-8. Three-speed automatic transmission. NP435 four-speed manual transmission (PW-100). NP445 four-speed manual transmission (PW-100).

NOTE: Trail Duster buyers had their choice of 15 exterior colors in 1979: Formal black, white, cashmere, medium Canyon red, sunburst orange, yellow flame, light silver metallic, cadet blue metallic, ensign blue metallic, teal frost metallic, citron green metallic, medium tan metallic, teal green sunfire metallic, canyon red sunfire metallic, sable brown sunfire metallic.

1979 Plymouth Voyager Maxi-Wagon (OCW)

VOYAGER — SERIES PB-100 — (Wagon): — Styling refinements were made to the Voyager front end in 1979. The new criss-cross theme grille had full length, wraparound signal lights. The Plymouth name was now centered above the grille, rather than to one side (as on last year's model). The front bumper was also new. The overall effect of these changes was to jazz up the Voyager's somewhat plain appearance. And it succeeded. Other less noticeable new features included a coolant reserve system and larger front suspension control arm rubber bushings. Among the standard equipment were: Air vent doors. Driver and front passenger armrests. Ashtray. Painted front and rear bumpers. Automatic choke. Power front disc brakes. Door locks. Twenty-two gallon fuel tank. Argent finish grille with seven inch round headlamps. Hardboard headliner in driver's compartment. Fresh air heater with defrosters. Color-keyed horn pad. Painted hubcaps. Dual painted 5 x 7 in. exterior rearview mirrors. Low-back vinyl front bucket seats and three-passenger bench seat. Two-spoke color-keyed steering wheel. Padded sunvisors. Single rear door with fixed glass. Double hinged passenger side doors with vented glass. Spare tire carrier. Voyager nameplates on both front fenders. Electric wiper arm mounted windshield washers. Two-speed windshield wipers.

I.D. DATA: See 1974 Plymouth Voyager.

Model	Body Type	Price	Weight	Prod. Total
PB-100	Van (109.6 in. w.b.)	5978	3715	—
PB-100	Van (127.6 in. w.b.)	6138	3880	—

ENGINE: Six-cylinder. Displacement: 225 cu. in. Brake horsepower: 90 at 3600 R.P.M. Bore & stroke: 3.40 in. x 4.12 in. Compression ratio: 8.4:1. Carburetor: 1-bbl.

VOYAGER — SERIES PB-200 — (Wagon): — The PB-200 came with most of the same features as the PB-100. However, this more heavy-duty series also offered the spacious, extended body Maxi-Wagon.

I.D. DATA: See 1974 Plymouth Voyager.

Model	Body Type	Price	Weight	Prod. Total
PB-200	Van (109 in. w.b.)	6310	3805	—
PB-200	Van (127 in. w.b.)	6472	3930	—
PB-200	Maxi-Wagon	6870	4280	—

ENGINE: Displacement: 318 cu. in. Brake horsepower: 140 at 4000 R.P.M. Bore & stroke: 3.91 in. x 3.31 in. Compression ratio: 8.6:1. Carburetor: 2-bbl.

VOYAGER — SERIES PB-300 — (Wagon): — The top-of-the-line PB-300 could be ordered in either the standard or extended body (Maxi-Wagon) 127 inch wheelbase versions. Both were made for heavy-duty use. Power steering and automatic transmission were standard.

I.D. DATA: See 1974 Plymouth Voyager.

Model	Body Type	Price	Weight	Prod. Total
PB-300	Van (127.6 in. w.b.)	7641	4140	—
PB-300	Maxi-Wagon (127.6 in. w.b.)	7950	4280	—

ENGINE: Displacement: 318 cu. in. Brake horsepower: 140 at 4000 R.P.M. Bore & stroke: 3.91 in. x 3.31 in. Compression ratio: 8.5:1. Carburetor: 2-bbl.

CHASSIS: Wheelbase (PB-100, PB-200): 109.6 in.; (PB-100, PB-200, PB-300): 127.6 in. Overall width: 79.8 in. Overall length: (109.6 in. w.b.) 179.1 in., (127.6 in. w.b.) 197.1 in., (Maxi-Wagon) 223.1 in. Overall height: (109.6 in. w.b.) 79.6 in., (127.6 in. w.b.) 80.9 in., (Maxi-Wagon) 80.6 in. Tires: (PB-100) ER78 x 15B; (PB-200/109 in. w.b.) J78 x 15B; (PB-200/127.6 in. w.b.) H78 x 15B; (PB-300) 8.00 x 16.5D in. GVW Ratings (lbs.): 4900 to 6000 (PB-100); 6050 to 6400 (PB-200); 6700 to 7800 (PB-300).

TECHNICAL: 318 cu. in. V-8 (PB-100), 360 cu. in. V-8 (PB-200, PB-300). Four-speed manual transmission (PB-100, PB-200). Three-speed automatic transmission (PB-100, PB-200).

OPTIONAL PACKAGES: Custom: Voyager Custom nameplates on front doors. Bright molding around windshield, side and rear windows (except driver and passenger door windows). Bright taillamp bezels. Bright hubcaps. Right and left instrument panel lower skirts. Cigar lighter. White non-vinyl-covered headliner in driver and passenger compartment. Vinyl door and side trim panels with plaid insert. Color-keyed floor mat with floor insulation. Dash liner insulation. Garnish trim over front door headers and around rear compartment windows. Sport: Voyager Sport nameplates on front doors. Bright lower side and rear molding. Bright molding around windshield, side and rear windows (except driver and passenger door windows). Bright finish grille with seven inch round headlamps and grille medallion. Bright taillamp bezels. Bright hubcaps. Bright front and rear bumpers. Dual 5 x 7 in. bright exterior mirrors. Woodgrain applique on lower face of instrument panel. Left and right side instrument panel lower skirts. Cigar lighter. Horn pad with woodgrain insert. Vinyl-covered, color-keyed, insulated headliner in driver and passenger compartments. Color-keyed spare tire cover. Deluxe vinyl seat trim. Vinyl door and side trim panels with woodgrain insert. Color-keyed carpeting with floor insulation. Dash liner insulation. Dome light switches, door operated on all doors. Garnish rim over front door headers, around rear compartment windows and "A" pillar and windshield. Sport Premium Trim: Voyager Sport nameplates on front doors. Bright lower side and rear moldings. Bright molding around windshield, side and rear windows (except driver and passenger door windows). Dual vertically stacked quad rectangular headlamps with bright grille and grille medallion. Bright taillamp bezels. Bright hubcaps. Bright front and rear bumpers. Dual 5 x 7 in. bright exterior mirrors. Woodgrain applique on lower face of instrument panel. Instrument panel lower skirts, left and right. Cigar lighter. Horn pad with woodgrain insert. Vinyl-covered, color-keyed, insulated headliner in driver and passenger compartments. Color-keyed spare tire cover. High-back deluxe cloth-and-vinyl reclining Command bucket seats and deluxe cloth-and-vinyl bench seat. Vinyl door and side trim panels with woodgrain trim and front door applique and pull strap. Color-keyed carpeting with floor insulation. Color-keyed carpeted engine housing cover. Dash liner insulation. Dome light switches, door operated on all doors. Garnish trim over front door headers, around rear compartment windows and "A" pillar and windshield. Dual electric horns. Convenience: Cigar lighter. Glove box lock. Ten inch day/night rearview mirror. In-cab-actuated hood lock release. Light: Ignition switch light with time delay. Glove box light. Cigar lighter light. Automatic door switches for interior dome lights. Courtesy lamps on front and side doors. Luxury: automatic transmission. Convenience package. Two-tone paint. AM/FM radio including front and rear speakers. Power steering. Scuff pads front and side passenger doors. Bright finish wheel covers (PB-300). Premium Class II bright finish wheel covers (PB-100, PB-200). Integral front mounted air conditioning. Automatic speed control. Tinted glass, all windows. Front door edge protectors. High-back cloth-and-vinyl Command bucket seats and cloth-and-vinyl bench seat. Light package. Bumper guards front and rear. Fifteen inch diameter vinyl steering wheel. Easy Order: Automatic transmission. Convenience package. Two-tone paint. AM radio. Bright front and rear bumpers. Bright dual 5 x 7 in. exterior rearview mirrors. Power steering. Scuff pads front and side passenger doors. Wheel covers. Bumper guards front and rear. Fifteen inch diameter vinyl steering wheel. Automatic door switches for interior dome lights. Exterior Molding: Upper side and rear molding. Lower side and rear molding. Upper side and rear and lower side and rear molding.

CONVENIENCE OPTIONS: Bright front and rear bumpers. Bumper guards front and rear. Heavy-duty alternator. Heavy-duty battery. Cigar lighter. Digital clock. Increased cooling. Automatic transmission oil-to-air auxiliary cooler. Rear window electric defroster (for single rear door). Dual rear doors, hinged type. Sliding passenger door. Door metal check arms. Front doors door edge protectors. Rear doors inside handle and lock button. Thirty-six gallon fuel tank. Instrumentation: oil pressure gauge and trip odometer, dual calibrated speedometer and odometer. Tinted glass, windshield or all windows. Sun screen privacy glass. Banded glass, front door glass and vent wings. Bright finish grille with seven inch round headlamps and grille medallion. Dual quad rectangular vertically stacked headlmaps. Passenger compartment headliner. Deluxe high-output heater. Auxiliary heater in passenger compartment. Dual electric horns. In-cab-actuated hood release. Ten inch day/night prismatic type rearview mirror. Dual short-arm 5 x 7 in. bright finish exterior mirrors. Dual low-mount 6 x 9 in. paint finish exterior mirrors. Dual low-mount 6 x 9 in. bright finish exterior mirrors. Wheel lip molding. Choice of three two-tone paint procedures: #1) Upper and lower (50/50 two-tone). #2) Midsection in secondary color, rest of the body in main color. #3) Roof and midsection in secondary color, rest of body in main color. Power steering. Rear radio speaker. Side step sill scuff pads. Heavy-duty shock absorbers, front and rear. Spare tire cover. Dome lamp switches, all doors. Unibelt restraint system. Deluxe windshield wipers, two-speed with intermittent wipe. Wheels: chrome-styled road type, 15 x 6.00 in. wide sport road-type, white-painted steel-spoke 15 x 7.00 in. or five-slot chrome-styled disc, 15 x 7.00 in. Bright hubcaps. Tilt steering column. Radios: AM, AM/FM, AM/FM/MX stereo, AM/FM MX stereo/eight-track tape, AM/40-channel CB transceiver, AM/FM/MX stereo/40-channel CB transceiver. Automatic speed control. Sky Lite sun roofs (available over driver's compartment of five and eight passenger models, and over passenger compartment of 127.6 in. five and eight passenger models). Eight passenger seating (PB-100 with 225 cu. in. six-cylinder, 60000 lb. GVW and LR78 x 15-B tires; PB-200 and PB-300 models). Twelve-passenger seating (127.6 inch wheelbase PB-300, requires optional 7200 lb. GVW package). Fifteen-passenger seating (PB-300 Maxi-Wagon with 7800 lb. GVW package). Air conditioning. Electric door locks. Light- or heavy-duty trailer towing packages.

Pricing

	5	4	3	2	1
1979					
Arrow Series					
Pickup	450	900	1500	2100	3000
Sport Pickup	520	1020	1700	2400	3400
Trail Duster Series PD-100					
Utility	650	1300	2150	3050	4300
Trail Duster Series PW-100 — (4x4)					
Utility	720	1450	2400	3300	4800
Voyager Series					
PB-100 Van	520	1020	1700	2400	3400
PB-200 Van	540	1080	1800	2500	3600
PB-300 Van	590	1170	1950	2700	3900

1980 PLYMOUTH

ARROW PICKUP: — The attractive styling was unchanged for 1980. It still offered the largest payload in the mini-pickup class. That, along with ample legroom, improved steering and good gas mileage, helped make the Arrow an excellent value. Standard features included: power front disc brakes, adjustable steering column, vinyl folding bench seat, dual sunvisors, padded dash, dual racing-type side mirrors, two-speed wipers and washers, tubular cargo tie-down bars in pickup box, electronic ignition,

tinted glass, two-spoke steering wheel, passenger assist grip, AM radio, cigarette lighter cargo lamp, armrests, bright windshield and drip rail moldings and a four-speed manual transmission.

I.D. DATA: See 1974 Plymouth Trail Duster.

1980 Plymouth Arrow Mini-Pickup (CPD)

Model	Body Type	Price	Weight	Prod. Total
OJL4	Pickup Sweptline	4821	2573	—

ENGINE: Four-cylinder. Displacement: 122 cu. in. Brake horsepower: 90 at 5000 R.P.M. Bore & stroke: 3.30 in. x 3.54 in. Compression ratio: 8.5:1. Carburetor: 2-bbl.

ARROW SPORT PICKUP: — A step up from the standard Arrow was the Sport. It came with many of the same features plus: flashy tape striping, low-luster black painted front bumper, raised white-lettered steel-belted radial tires, wide spoke wheels, two-tone high back vinyl bucket seats in cashmere and dark cashmere or black and gray, three-spoke steering wheel, floor console, loop pile carpeting, AM/FM stereo radio, tachometer, oil pressure gauge and ammeter and a five-speed manual transmission with overdrive.

I.D. DATA: See 1974 Plymouth Trail Duster.

1980 Plymouth Arrow Sport Mini-Pickup (CPD)

Model	Body Type	Price	Weight	Prod. Total
OJP4	Sport Pickup Sweptline	5627	2648	—

ENGINE: Four-cylinder. Displacement: 156 cu. in. Brake horsepower: 105 at 5000 R.P.M. Bore & stroke: 3.59 in. x 3.86 in. Compression ratio: 8.2:1. Carburetor: 2-bbl.

CHASSIS: Wheelbase: 109.4 in. Overall length: 184.6 in. Overall width: 65 in. Overall height: 60.6 in. (Arrow); 59.8 in. (Arrow Sport). Tires: 6.00 x 14-C in. (Arrow); 185S x 14 (Arrow Sport). Box length: 81.5 in. Box width: 64.2 in. Maximum payload: 1527 (Arrow); 1557 (Arrow Sport). GVW Rating: 4045 (Arrow); 4120 (Arrow Sport).

TECHNICAL: Automatic transmission.

CONVENIENCE OPTIONS: Sky Lite sun roof, cargo box roll bar, air conditioning, bodyside and tailgate tape stripes (Arrow only), front grille guard, mud guards, low-mount black left and right mirrors, power steering, sliding rear window, low-luster black step-type rear bumper, vinyl bodyside moldings, wheel trim rings (Arrow only).

TRAIL DUSTER — SERIES PD-100: — Two-wheel-drive utility vehicle: Styling was the same as last year and that wasn't bad. Among the standard features were: insulated dash liner, dual exterior mirrors, power front disc brakes, deluxe vinyl low-back bucket seats, two seven inch round headlights, rear compartment floor mat and rear courtesy lamps, independent front coil spring suspension, electronic ignition, 24-gallon fue)l tank, dual jet windshield washers and two-speed windshield wipers and three-speed automatic transmission.

I.D. DATA: See 1974 Plymouth Trail Duster.

Model	Body Type	Price	Weight	Prod. Total
PD-100	Utility Vehicle	6793	3570	—

ENGINE: Six-cylinder. Displacement: 225 cu. in. Brake horsepower: 90 at 3600 R.P.M. Bore & stroke: 3.40 in. x 4.12 in. Compression ratio: 8.4:1. Carburetor: 1-bbl.

1980 Plymouth Trail Duster SE 4x4 Utility Wagon (CPD)

TRAIL DUSTER — SERIES PW-100: Four-wheel- drive utility vehicle: A new part-time four-wheel- drive system replaced the full-time unit. It used a new transfer case design that resulted in less driveline noise, reduced weight and improved fuel economy. Standard features included: leaf spring front suspension, four-speed manual transmission, manual locking hubs, power steering and front stabilizer bar.

I.D. DATA: See 1974 Plymouth Trail Duster.

Model	Body Type	Price	Weight	Prod. Total
PW-100	Utility Vehicle	8298	4150	—

ENGINE: Displacement: 318 cu. in. V-8. Brake horsepower: 120 at 3600 R.P.M. Bore & stroke: 3.91 in. x 3.31 in. Compression ratio: 8.5:1. Carburetor: 2-bbl.

CHASSIS: Wheelbase: 106 in. Overall length: 184.62 in. (without bumper guards); 186.16 in. (with bumper guards). Overall width: 79.5 in. GVW Rating (lbs.): 5300 (PD-100); 5850 (PW-100); 6050 (PW-100 with Sno-Commander Package). Tires: P225/75-R15B glass-belted radials (PD-100); P235/75-15B polyester bias-belted (PW-100).

TECHNICAL: 318 cu. in. V-8 with 2-bbl. carburetor (PD-100). 360 cu. in. V-8 with 4-bbl. carburetor. Three-speed automatic transmission (PW-100).

OPTION PACKAGES: Sno-Commander: (PW-100 only) Power angling blade, power lift, seven-way control valve, plow lights, 35-gallon fuel tank and heavy-duty front leaf springs. Trail Duster Sport: Dual vertically stacked quad rectangular headlamps with halogen high beam lamp, bright windshield, drip rail, quarter side window and liftgate window molding, bright taillamp bezels, sport medallion on front fenders, tailgate surround molding with vinyl tape insert applique, woodtone applique on door trim panels with assist strap and carpeting on lower door panel, cloth and vinyl bucket seats, lockable console with removable styrofoam beverage chest, perforated white hardboard headliner, carpeting, woodtone applique on instrument panel faceplate, Trail Duster Sport nameplate on instrument panel, black horn pad with woodtone applique insert and black two-spoke steering wheel, color-keyed spare tire cover, dual electric horns and bright door sill tread plate. Trail Duster Macho 4x4: (PW-100 only) 15 by 7 inch white painted steel spoke road wheels, "Sport" four-spoke steering wheel, low-luster black painted front and rear bumpers, special low-luster black paint treatment and black/orange tape stripes on lower portion of vehicle, tailgate decals "4WD" and "Plymouth" in black with color accent, limited monotone exterior paint color selection and five 10-15LT outline white-letter tires.

CONVENIENCE OPTIONS: Aluminum radial ribbed road wheels, AM/FM stereo with cassette tape player, AM/FM stereo with search-tune, bright hitch-type rear bumper, tilt steering column, skid plate, fold-up rear bench seat, power windows, deluxe vinyl split-back front bench seat, air conditioning, front stabilizer bar (PD-100), heavy-duty front stabilizer bar (PW-100), aluminum radial ribbed wheels, white painted steel spoke wheels, five-slot chrome disc wheels, step type rear bumper, hitch type rear bumper, electric clock, cigar lighter, lockable console, auxiliary transmission oil to air cooler, 35-gallon fuel tank, oil pressure gauge, tinted glass, quad rectangular dual vertically stacked headlights, engine block heater, deluxe heater, in-cab-actuated hood lock release, dual electric horns, rubber mats, dual low mount mirrors, exterior moldings, power door locks, power steering, AM/FM stereo with 40-channel CB transceiver, roll bar, heavy-duty front and rear shock absorbers, fuel tank shield, transfer case shield, sun roof, speed control, outside mounted swing-out tire carrier, bright wheel covers, premium wheel covers, light and heavy-duty trailer towing packages.

VOYAGER — SERIES PB-100 — (Wagon): Exterior styling was the same as last year's model. However, some changes were made to upholstery designs. Among standard Voyager features were: electronic ignition, seven inch round headlights, color-keyed horn pad, bright hubcaps, padded sunvisors, full width black floor mat, windshield washers, two-speed windshield wipers, low-back vinyl bucket seats up front and a three passenger bench seat in the back, 22 gallon fuel tank, four-speed manual transmission with overdrive, power front disc brakes, argent finish grille and painted front and rear bumpers.

I.D. DATA: See 1974 Plymouth Voyager.

Model	Body Type	Price	Weight	Prod. Total
PB-100	Van (109.6 in. w.b.)	6564	3715	—
PB-100	Van (127.6 in. w.b.)	6736	3880	—

ENGINE: Six-cylinder. Displacement: 225 cu. in. Brake horsepower: 90 at 3600 R.P.M. Bore & stroke: 3.40 in. x 4.12 in. Compression ratio: 8.4:1. Carburetor: 1-bbl.

VOYAGER — SERIES PB-200 — (Wagon): Buyers had their choice of three sizes in this slightly more heavy-duty Voyager series. Top of the line was the spacious Maxi-Wagon. It had over three feet more interior room than the 109.6 inch wheelbase model. Automatic transmission was standard in the Maxi-Wagon.

I.D. DATA: See 1974 Plymouth Voyager.

1980 Plymouth Voyager PB200 Wagon (CPD)

Model	Body Type	Price	Weight	Prod. Total
PB-200	Van (109.6 in. w.b.)	6876	3805	—
PB-200	Van (127.6 in. w.b.)	7051	3930	—
PB-200	Maxi-Wagon	8152	4280	—

ENGINE: (Wagon)Six-cylinder. Displacement: 225 cu. in. Brake horsepower: 90 at 3600 R.P.M. Bore & stroke: 3.40 in. x 4.12 in. Compression ratio: 8.4:1. Carburetor: 1-bbl. (Not available in California).

ENGINE: (Maxi-Wagon) V-8 318 cu. in. Brake horsepower: 120 at 3600 R.P.M. Bore & stroke: 3.91 in. x 3.31 in. Compression ratio: 8.5:1. Carburetor: 2-bbl.

VOYAGER — SERIES PB-300 — (Wagon): Both PB-300 Voyagers had a 127.6 inch wheelbase. They were made for hauling heavy loads. Power steering and a three-speed automatic transmission were standard. The brakes were also bigger on this Voyager series than the other two.

I.D. DATA: See 1974 Plymouth Voyager.

Model	Body Type	Price	Weight	Prod. Total
PB-300	Wagon (127.6 in. w.b.)	8364	4140	—
PB-300	Maxi-Wagon	8664	4280	—

ENGINE: Displacement: 318 cu. in. V-8. Brake horsepower: 120 at 3600 R.P.M. Bore & stroke: 3.91 in. x 3.31 in. Compression ratio: 8.5:1. Carburetor: 2-bbl.

CHASSIS: Wheelbase (Wagon): 109.6 in.; (Wagon and Maxi-Wagon) 127.6 in. Overall length: (Wagon) 178.9 in.; (Wagon) 196.9 in.; (Maxi-Wagon) 222.9 in. Overall width: 79.8 in. Overall height: (109.6 in. w.b.) 79.6 in.; (127.6 in. w.b. Wagon) 80.9 in.; (Maxi-Wagon) 80.6 in. Tires: (PB-100) P195/75R-15B glass-belted radial; (PB-200/109.6 in. w.b. Wagon): P225/75R-15B glass-belted radial; (PB-200/127.6 in. w.b. Wagon): P235/75R-15C glass-belted radial; (PB-300 Wagon): 8.00 x 16.5E polyester bias-belted; (PB-300 Maxi-Wagon): 8.75 x 16.5E polyester bias-belted. GVW Rating (lbs.): (PB-100) 5100; (PB-200 Wagons) 6050; (PB-200 Maxi-Wagon) 6400; (PB-300) 7200.

TECHNICAL: 318 cu. in. V-8 (PB-100 and PB-200 Wagons). 360 cu. in. V-8 (PB-200, PB-300). Three-speed automatic transmission (PB-100 and PB-200 Wagons).

OPTION PACKAGES: Voyager Custom: nameplates, bright molding around windshield, side and rear windows. Bright taillamp bezels. Cigar lighter. Instrument panel lower skirts. Perforated color-keyed hardboard headliner with overprint pattern. Vinyl door and side trim panels with plaid insert. Color-keyed floor mat and floor insulation. Trim over front door headers and around rear compartment window. Plaid vinyl low-back front bucket seats with matching three-passenger rear seat. Voyager Sport: (127.6 inch wheelbase models only) Nameplates. Bright lower side and rear molding. Dual vertically stacked quad rectangular headlamps with halogen high beam and bright grille and grille medallion. Bright front and rear bumpers. Dual bright exterior mirrors. Woodtone applique on lower face of instrument panel. Horn pad with woodtone insert. Spare tire cover. Vinyl door and side trim panels with woodtone trim. Color-keyed carpeting with floor insulation. Dome light switches, door-operated, on all doors. Trim over front door headers, around rear compartment windows and low back front bucket seats. High-back plaid cloth and vinyl front buckets optional. "A" pillar and windshield. Dual electric horns. Voyager Sport with Premium Trim: for PB-100, requires optional 5400 pound GVW. Soft cloth covered headliner over the driver and passenger compartment. Vinyl door and side trim panels with woodtone trim and front door applique pull strap.

Color-keyed carpeted engine housing cover. High-back front bucket seats. Heavy-Duty Insulation: Voyager Sport and Voyager Sport with Premium Trim: Interior lower fiberglass insulation panels. Additional insulation under floor covering. Voyager Custom: The same plus full-length headlining with insulation. Voyager: The same plus Interior lower trim panels in passenger compartment. Color-keyed garnish trim over front door headers and sliding door track and around headliner and rear compartment window. Jute insulation under floor mat. Dashliner insulation. Eight Passenger Seating (PB-200, PB-300 Wagons and Maxi-Wagons): One additional quick-release three-passenger bench seat; eight-passenger Travel Seat. Twelve-Passenger Seating (PB-300 Wagon and Maxi-Wagon): Requires rear door(s) with optional vented glass at extra cost. Includes two additional bench seats; one three-passenger and one four-passenger. Tire carrier relocated under third bench seat. Fifteen-Passenger Seating (PB-300 Maxi-Wagon): Requires optional 8550 pound GVW package and rear door(s) with optional vented glass at extra cost. Includes three additional seats; two three-passenger and one four-passenger. Tire carrier relocated under fourth seat. Light-Duty Trailer Towing: Maximum cooling. Heavy-duty variable load flasher. Seven-wire harness. Bright hitch type rear bumper. Class 1 ball hitch. Heavy-Duty Trailer Towing (PB-200 and PB-300) Maximum cooling. Sixty-three amp alternator. Seventy amp-hr/430 amp Cold Crank battery. Seven-wire harness. Class IV tow bar hitch. Heavy-duty variable load flasher. Heavy-duty front and rear shock absorbers.

CONVENIENCE OPTIONS: Air conditioning (integral front and auxiliary rear). Bright front and rear bumpers. Hitch type rear bumper. Front and rear bumper guards on nerf strips. Cigar lighter. Digital clock. Auxiliary transmission oil to air cooling. Electric rear window defroster. Dual rear doors with fixed or vented glass. Single rear door with vented glass. Sliding door on passenger side. Thirty-six gallon fuel tank. Oil pressure and trip odometer gauges. Tinted glass. Dual quad rectangular headlamps, vertically stacked, with halogen high beams. Bright grille (includes quad headlamps). Passenger compartment headliner. Auxiliary rear heater. Deluxe front heater. Dual electric horns. Interior reading lamp in driver's compartment. In-cab-actuated hood elease lock. Color-keyed rubber floor mats in driver's compartment. Illuminated vanity mirror. Exterior dual low-mount mirrors. Exterior dual short arm mirrors. Wheel lip, lower, and/or upper moldings. Power windows, steering and/or door locks. AM, AM/FM, AM/FM stereo, AM/FM stereo with Search-Tune, AM/FM stereo with eight-track tape player, AM/FM stereo with cassette tape player and Dolby noise reduction system, AM/FM stereo with 40-channel CB transceiver, rear speaker. Heavy-duty shock absorbers. Sky Lite sun roof. Color-keyed spare tire cover. Speed control. Front stabilizer bar. Tilt steering column. Door operated dome light switch. Radial-ribbed aluminum, five-slot chrome disc, or white painted spoke wheels. Bright and premium wheelcovers. Deluxe windshield wipers.

Pricing

	5	4	3	2	1
1980					
Arrow Series					
Pickup	450	900	1500	2100	3000
Sport Pickup	520	1020	1700	2400	3400
Trail Duster Series PD-100					
Utility	650	1300	2150	3050	4300
Trail Duster Series PW-100 — (4x4)					
Utility	720	1450	2400	3300	4800
Voyager Series					
PB-100 Van	520	1020	1700	2400	3400
PB-200 Van	540	1080	1800	2500	3600
PB-300 Van	590	1170	1950	2700	3900

1981 PLYMOUTH

ARROW PICKUP: — The Arrow's good looks weren't tampered with in 1981. Among the standard features were: Argent painted front bumper with black rubber ends. Cargo lamp. Cigarette lighter. Dome light with driver and passenger side door switches. Emergency flashers. A 15.1-gallon fuel tank. Bright argent grille. Color-keyed headliner. Inside hood release. Bright hubcaps. Interior rearview mirror. Dual black racing-type exterior mirrors. Bright drip rail molding. Bright windshield molding. AM radio. Adjustable steering column with lock. Dual sunvisors. Tubular cargo tie down bars on both sides of the interior of the pickup box. Tinted glass. Trip odometer. Two-speed windshield wipers with washers. Four-speed manual transmission. Cashmere interior. Choice of three exterior colors: White, tan or black.

I.D. DATA: There are 17 symbols. The first three indicate the manufacturer, make and type of vehicle. The fourth the G.V.W. range. The next three tell the series and body style. The eighth tells the engine. After that is the check digit and a letter representing the model year. The eleventh symbol identifies the assembly plant. The remaining six digits are the sequential production numbers.

Model	Body Type	Price	Weight	Prod. Total
OJL4	Pickup Sweptline	6202	2520	—

ENGINE: Four-cylinder. Displacement: 122 cu. in. Brake horsepower: 90 at 5000 R.P.M. Bore & stroke: 3.30 in. x 3.54 in. Compression ratio: 8.5:1. Carburetor: 2-bbl.

NOTE: This engine was rated at 88 horsepower in California.

ARROW CUSTOM PICKUP: — This was a new model for '81. It came with many of the same standard features as the basic Arrow plus: Chrome front bumper with black rubber ends. Five-speed manual transmission. Carpeting. Eighteen gallon fuel tank. Vinyl body-side molding. The Custom was offered in three exterior colors: Medium blue metallic, warm white, and black. All had blue interiors.

I.D. DATA: See 1981 Arrow.

Model	Body Type	Price	Weight	Prod. Total
OJH4	Pickup Sweptline	6681	2565	—

ENGINE: Four-cylinder. Displacement: 156 cu. in. Brake horsepower: 105 at 5000 R.P.M. Bore & stroke: 3.59 in. x 3.86 in. Compression ratio: 8.2:1. Carburetor: 2-bbl.

NOTE: This engine was rated at 103 horsepower in California.

ARROW SPORTS PICKUP: — Top of the Arrow line was the Sport. Exclusive to this model were: Center console with oil pressure gauge, ammeter, and transmission shift lever. Gold grille. AM/FM stereo radio. Gold painted wide spoke road wheels. Bodyside tape stripes and a five-speed manual transmission. The Sport was available in two exterior colors, red and Ballast sand metallic. The interior and high-back bucket seats were only available in two-tone cashmere and black.

I.D. DATA: See 1981 Arrow.

Model	Body Type	Price	Weight	Prod. Total
OJP4	Pickup Sweptline	7240	2565	—

ENGINE: Same as Arrow Custom.

CHASSIS: Wheelbase: 109.4 in. Overall length: 184.6 in. Overall width: 65 in. Overall height: 60.6 in. (Arrow); 59.8 in. (Arrow Custom and Arrow Sport). Box length: 81.5 in. Box width: 64.2 in. GVW Rating: 4045 lbs. (Arrow); 4120 lbs. (Arrow Custom and Arrow Sport). Payload (including driver and passengers): 1525 lbs. (Arrow); 1555 lbs. (Arrow Custom and Arrow Sport). Tires: 6.00 x 14C WSW (Arrow); 185SR14 steel-belted radial WSW (Arrow Custom) and 185SR14 steel-belted radial RWL (Arrow Sport).

TECHNICAL: Three-speed automatic transmission.

1981 Plymouth Arrow Mini-Pickup (OCW)

CONVENIENCE OPTIONS: Air conditioning. Chrome rear step bumper. Low-luster black rear step bumper. Front bumper guards (not available with grille guard). Electronic digital clock. Front floor mats (Arrow Custom and Arrow Sport). Eighteen-gallon fuel tank (Arrow). Front grille guard (not available with air conditioning). Low-mount chrome exterior mirrors. Vinyl body-side molding (Arrow). Vinyl pickup box top edge molding. Front and rear wheel openings moldings. Mud guards. Power steering. Sliding rear window. Sport bar in cargo box. Sky Lite sun roof. Bodyside tape stripe (Arrow and Arrow Custom). Wheel trim rings (Arrow and Arrow Custom).

NOTE: Chrysler Corporation was so sure buyers would like the '81 Arrow pickup truck, it offered a money-back guarantee. If you weren't completely satisfied, you could bring it back (in good condition with no metal damage) within 30 days or 1,000 miles, for a refund.

TRAIL DUSTER — SERIES PD-150: — Two-wheel-drive utility vehicle: The Trail Duster received a new look for '81 at its front, rear, and side. It featured a flashier rectangular-section style grille with larger rectangular signal lights directly below the headlights. The backup lights were now on the lower level of the taillights. The two-piece tailgate of previous years was replaced with a one-piece fiberglass liftgate. The new, larger "wrap-around" quarter windows was a real standout feature. Even the instrument panel was changed. Standard equipment included: Bright finish front and rear bumpers. Automatic choke. Cleaner air system. Coolant reserve system. Insulated dash liner. Color-keyed inner door trim panels and armrests. Electronic ignition system. Black front floor mat with padding. Thirty-five gallon fuel tank. Tinted glass, all windows. Aluminum grille with painted plastic insert and headlamp doors. Single rectangular headlamps. Fresh air heater with defrosters. Single electric horn. Bright hubcaps. Padded instrument panel. Combination map/courtesy light on instrument panel. Rear compartment courtesy lights. Dual bright finish short arm 5 x 7 in. exterior mirrors. Power front disc brakes. AM radio. Rear roof vent. Deluxe vinyl low-back bucket seats. Driver and passenger color-keyed sun visors. Bright quarter side window moldings. Dual jet windshield washers. Two-speed windshield wipers. Rear liftgate-open warning light.

I.D. DATA: See 1981 Arrow.

Model	Body Type	Price	Weight	Prod. Total
PD-150	Utility Vehicle	8257	3570	—

ENGINE: Displacement: 318 cu. in. V-8. Brake horsepower: 120 at 3600 R.P.M. Bore & stroke: 3.91 in. x 3.31 in. Compression ratio: 8.5:1. Carburetor: 2-bbl.

TRAIL DUSTER — SERIES PW-150 — (Utility Vehicle): — The part-time four-wheel-drive PW-150, shared most of the same features as the two-wheel-drive PD-150. In addition, it had: Power steering. Front stabilizer bar. Two-speed NP208 transfer case. Locking front wheel hubs. NP435 four-speed manual transmission.

I.D. DATA: See 1981 Arrow.

Model	Body Type	Price	Weight	Prod. Total
PW-150	Utility Vehicle	9508	4126	—

ENGINE: Same as Trail Duster PD-150.

CHASSIS: Wheelbase: 106 in. Overall length: 184.62 in. Overall width: 79.5 in. GVW Rating (lbs.): 5300 (PD-150); 5850 (PW-150). Tires: P235/75R15 BSW GBR (PD-150); P235/75R15B BSW GBR (PW-150).

TECHNICAL: Three-speed automatic transmission. (PW-150). 318 cu. in. V-8 with 4-bbl. carburetor (PW-150). 360 cu. in. V-8 with 4-bbl. carburetor (PW-150).

OPTIONAL PACKAGES: Sno-Commander: Snow removal equipment custom fitted to the vehicle. (PW-150) Convenience: Two-speed intermittent windshield wipers. Day/night interior 10 inch rearview mirror. Glove box lock and light. Ash receiver light. In-cab-actuated hood lock release. Protection: Door edge protectors. Bright front bumper and guards with nerf strips. Bright rear bumper with nerf strips. Sport: Bright windshield and drip rail molding and taillamp bezels. Bright aluminum grille with chrome plastic insert and headlamp doors. Upper and lower liftgate moldings with bright applique panel. Power steering on PD-150 models. Woodtone trim applique on interior doors. Assist straps. Carpeting on lower door panels. Color-keyed driver and front passenger high-back Command bucket seats with cloth-and-vinyl trim. Inboard fold-down armrests on seats. Lockable console with removable styrofoam beverage chest. Color-keyed folding rear bench seat with cloth-and-vinyl trim. Color-keyed soft headliner, carpeting and rear side and liftgate inner trim panels. Woodtone instrument cluster faceplate. Black leather-wrapped steering wheel with black horn pad and woodtone insert. Color-keyed spare tire cover (not available with 10R15 tires). Cigar lighter. Dual horns. Bright front door sill scuff plate. Underhood insulation panel. Oil pressure, engine temperature gauges. Color-keyed cowl side trim panels. Trip odometer. Macho: Sport interior. Special tu-tone exterior paint. Macho tape stripe. High gloss black front and rear bumpers. Five outline white-lettered steel-belted radial tires. Four radial-ribbed aluminum wheels on PD-150. Steel spoke orange wheels and black accent on PW-150. Heavy-duty stabilizer bar (PW-150). Trailer Towing: Light-duty (PD-150, PW-150). Heavy-duty (PW-150).

CONVENIENCE OPTION: Air conditioning. Heavy-duty alternator. Heavy-duty battery. Step type painted rear bumper. Electric digital clock. Lockable console. Auxiliary transmission oil-to-air cooler. Maximum engine cooling. Oil pressure, engine temperature, and trip odometer gauges. Sun screen privacy glass. Bright insert grille and headlamp doors. Halogen headlamps. Deluxe bi-level heater. Engine block heater. In-cab-actuated hood lock release. Two accessory type rubber mats. Dual bright 6 x 9 inch low mount mirrors. Bright 7½ x 10½ inch low mount extended mirrors. Lower exterior moldings. Upper exterior moldings. Power door locks. Power steering. Power windows. Radios: AM/FM. AM/FM stereo. AM/FM stereo/cassette tape player. Dolby noise reduction system. AM/FM stereo/eight-track tape player. AM/FM stereo/electronic search tune. AM/FM stereo with 40-channel CB transceiver. Heavy-duty front and rear shocks. Fuel tank shield. Transfer case shield (not available in PD-150). Automatic speed control. Sport bar. Front stabilizer bar (PW-150). Tilt type steering column. Four-spoke "Sport" steering wheel. Sky Lite sun roof. Bright wheel covers. Premium wheel covers (PD-150). Wheels (15 x 7 in.) Aluminum radial ribbed, five slot chrome disc, white painted steel spoke, road-type spare wheel. Two-speed/intermittent wipe windshield wiper.

NOTE: Trail Duster exterior colors for 1981 were: Bright silver metallic. Coffee brown metallic. Daystar blue metallic. Graphic yellow. Nightwatch blue. Impact orange. Impact blue. Impact red. Light seaspray green metallic. Medium crimson red. Medium seaspray green metallic. Black. Cashmere. Pearl white. Ginger.

VOYAGER — SERIES PB-150 — (Wagon): — The newest thing about the '81 Voyager was a couple of extra-cost seating options: quad Command bucket seats and a convert-a-bed bench seat. Design-wise, it was the same as last year's model. Standard features included: Air vent doors. Driver and front passenger armrests. Driver's compartment ashtray. Front disc brakes. Painted front and rear bumpers. Cleaner air system. Right-side double doors with vented glass. Single rear door with fixed glass and inside door handle and lock button. Electronic ignition system. Black full width floor mat. Twenty-two gallon fuel tank. Argent finish grille. Seven-inch round headlamps. Perforated hardboard headliner with overprint patterin in the drivers compartment. Fresh air heater with defroster. Single electric horn. Color-keyed horn pad. Bright hubcaps. Padded instrument panel and sunvisors. Electric windshield washers and wipers. Brake system warning light. Dual 5 x 7 in. painted exterior mirrors. Nameplate on front doors. AM radio. Driver and front passenger low-back vinyl bucket seats. Three-passenger quick-release vinyl rear bench seat including three seat belts. Spare tire carrier. Color-keyed 16½ inch diameter steering wheel. Four-speed manual transmission.

I.D. DATA: See 1981 Arrow.

Model	Body Type	Price	Weight	Prod. Total
PB-150	Van (109.6 in. w.b.)	7701	3493	—
PB-150	Van (127.6 in. w.b.)	7890	3764	—

ENGINE: Six-cylinder. Displacement: 225 cu. in. Brake horsepower: 90 at 3600 R.P.M. Bore & stroke: 3.40 in. x 4.12 in. Compression ratio: 8.4:1. Carburetor: 1-bbl.

VOYAGER — SERIES PB-250 — (Wagon): — The mid-level Voyager had the same good looks as the basic model, but greater load capacity. This was especially true in the 127.6 inch wheelbase, extended body Maxi-Wagon, which sales literature claimed was "America's roomiest wagon." A three-speed automatic transmission was standard in the Maxi-wagon.

I.D. DATA: See 1981 Arrow.

Model	Body Type	Price	Weight	Prod. Total
PB-250	Van (109.6 in. w.b.)	6579	3805	—
PB-250	Van (127.6 in. w.b.)	6735	3930	—
PB-250	Maxi-Wagon	7696	4280	—

ENGINE: Same as PB-150 for 109.6 in. and standard 127.6 in. wagons. 318 cu. in. V-8. Brake horsepower: 120 at 3600 R.P.M. Bore & stroke: 3.91 in. x 3.31 Compression ratio: 8.5:1. Carburetor: 2-bbl. (Maxi-Wagon).

NOTE: The 318 cu. in. V-8 was not available in California. In that state, a 360 cu. in. V-8 with 4-bbl. carburetor was standard on the Maxi-Wagon.

VOYAGER — SERIES PB-350 — (Wagon): — Power steering and a three-speed automatic transmission were standard on the PB-350. So were a color-keyed 15 inch diameter steering wheel and larger brakes. As before, the PB-350 was for people who had to haul heavy loads on a regular basis.

I.D. DATA: See 1981 Plymouth Arrow.

Model	Body Type	Price	Weight	Prod. Total
PB-350	Wagon	8018	4140	—
PB-350	Maxi-Wagon	8333	4280	—

ENGINE: Same as PB-250 Maxi-Wagon.

CHASSIS: Wheelbase (Wagon): 109.6 in.; (Wagon and Maxi-Wagon) 127.6 in. Overall height: (109.6 in. w.b.) 79.6 in.; (127.6 in. w.b.) 80.9 in.; (Maxi-Wagon) 80.6 in. Overall width: 79.8 in. Overall length: (109.6 in. w.b.) 178.9 in.; (127.6 in. w.b.) 196.9 in.; (Maxi-Wagon) 222.9 in. Tires: (PB-150): P205/75R15 glass-belted radial; (PB-250 109.6 in. w.b.) P225/75R15 glass-belted radial; (PB-250 127.6 in. w.b. Wagon) P235/75R15 glass-belted radial; (PB-250 Maxi-Wagon) P235/75R15XL steel-belted radial; (PB-350 Wagon) 8.00 x 16.5E (10PR) polyester bias-belted. GVW Rating (lbs.): (PB-150) 5300; (PB-250) 5800 to 6400; (PB-350) 7200 to 8510.

TECHNICAL: 318 cu. in. V-8 with 2-bbl. carburetor. (PB-150, PB-250): 318 cu. in. V-8 with 4-bbl. carburetor (PB-150, PB-250, PB-350): 360 cu. in. V-8 with 4-bbl. carb. (PB-250, PB-350).

OPTION PACKAGES: Custom: Voyager nameplates. Bright molding around windshield, side and rear windows (except driver and passenger door windows). Bright taillamp bezels. Quad rectangular headlamps with halogen high beams. Instrument panel lower skirts. Cigar lighter. Color-keyed headliner in driver and passenger compartment. Vinyl door and side trim panels with plaid insert. Color-keyed carpeting. Dash liner insulation. Garnish trim over front door and compartment windows, and headers around rear compartment windows. Sport: Bright lower side and rear molding. Quad rectangular headlamps with halogen high beams and bright grille. Bright front and rear bumpers. Dual 5 x 7 inch bright exterior mirrors. Woodtone applique on lower face of instrument panel. Horn pad with woodtone insert. Spare tire cover. Vinyl door and side trim panels with woodtone trim. Dome light switches, door-operated on all doors. Garnish trim over front doors and compartment windows, headers around rear compartment windows and pillars and windshield. Dual electric horns. Color-keyed unibelt restraint system. Driver and front passenger bucket seats and three-passenger rear bench seat in deluxe vinyl trim. Soft cloth-covered driver and passenger compartment headliner. Accessory floor mats in driver's compartment. Electronic digitial clock. Premier: Bright upper side and rear and lower side and rear moldings. Bright bumpers and bumper guards with nerf strips front and rear. Body-side and rear woodtone tape applique with dual gold accent strips. Vinyl door and side trim panels with woodtone trim and front door applique pull strap. Carpeted engine housing cover. Oil pressure gauge and trip odometer. Power steering. Leather-wrapped steering wheel. Day/night interior mirror. Glove box lock and light. Deluxe windshie wipers (two-speed with intermittent wipe). Inside actuated hood rlease lock. Ignition and headlight switch with time delay. Cigar lighter light. Courtesy step well lamp (front and side doors). Driver and front passenger high-back reclining Command bucket seats and a three-passenger rear bench seat in cloth-and vinyl trim. Heavy-duty Insulation: On Sport and Premier wagons; interior lower fiberglass insulation panels (not offered on standard single rear door or optional sliding side door), insulation under floor covering. On Custom wagons: includes the previous items plus full-length headlining with insulation. Wagons: includes all the previous items, plus interior lower trim panels in passenger compartment (in blue or cashmere), garnish trim over front door headers and around headliner and rear compartment window, dash liner insulation, sliding door track cover. Eight passenger seating: (All PB-250, PB-350 models). One additional quick-release three passenger bench seat with three seat belts (not available with 6100 lbs. GVW package on PB-250 109.6 inch wheelbase model with 6-cyl. engine or on PB-350 Maxi-Wagon with 8510 lbs. GVW package). Quad Command Seating: Four Command high-back bucket seats in blue, cashmere, or red cloth-and-vinyl trim. Eight-passenger Travel Seating. Five-, seven-, or eight-passenger Convert-a-bed seating. Twelve-passenger Seating: (PB-350) Requires window retention and rear door(s) with optional vented glass, includes two additional bench seats (second is three-passenger quick-release, third four-passenger). Tire carrier located under third bench seat (not available on PB-350 Maxi-Wagon with 8510 lbs. GVW package). Fifteen-passenger seating: (PB-350 Maxi-Wagon) Requires window retention and rear door(s) with vented glass. Includes three additional bench seats (second and third are three-passenger, fourth four-passenger). Tire carrier relocated under fourth and fifth bench seat. Convenience: Cigar lighter. Glove box lock. Ten inch day/night rearview mirror. In-cab-actuated hood lock release. Two-speed windshield wipers with intermittent wipe. Light: (Requires cigar lighter at extra cost.) Ignition and headlight switch with time delay (not available with tilt steering column). Glove box light. Cigar lighter light. Automatic door switches for interior dome lights. Courtesy step well lamp for front and side doors. Light-duty trailer towing: (Requires automatic transmission and 36-gallon fuel tank.) Maximum engine cooling. Heavy-duty variable load flasher. Bright hitch-type rear bumper. Class 1 ball hitch (1⅛ inch diameter). Heavy-duty trailer towing: PB-250 and PB-350 models. (Requires automatic transmission and V-8 engine, transmission auxiliary oil cooler and 36-gallon fuel tank.) Maximum cooling. Sixty-three amp. alternator. Seventy amp. hr./430-amp. Cold Crank maintenance-free battery. Seven-wire harness. Class IV tow bar hitch (load equalizing). Heavy-duty variable load flasher. Heavy-duty front and rear shock absorbers.

CONVENIENCE OPTIONS: Air conditioning. Heavy-duty alternator (63-amp. or 117-amp.). Heavy-duty battery (59-amp. hr./375-amp. Cold Crank; 70-amp. hr./430-amp. Cold Crank maintenance-free or 85-amp. hr./500 amp. Cold Crank long life). Hitch type bright rear bumper. Bright front and rear bumper. Bright front and rear bumper with guards and nerf strips. Cigar lighter. Electronic digital clock. Auxiliary transmission oil to air cooling. Maximum engine cooling. Rear window electric defroster for single rear door. Dual rear doors with fixed or vented glass. Single rear door with vented glass. Sliding passenger side door. Thirty-six gallon fuel tank. Oil pressure and trip odometer gauges. Sun screen privacy glass. All windows tinted. Bright grille (includes quad rectangular headlamps with halogen high beams.) Passenger compartment headliner. Auxiliary rear heater. Deluxe front heater. Dual electric horns. Interior reading lamp in driver's compartment. In-cab-actuated hood release. Two color-keyed accessory type rubber mats in driver's compartment. Dual exterior low-mount 6 x 9 in. painted or bright mirrors. Dual exterior short arm 5 x by 7 in. bright mirrors. Illuminated vanity. Interior day/night mirror. Lower molding (includes side and rear). Upper moldings (includes side, rear and bright taillamp bezels). Upper and lower moldings. Electric door locks. Power windows. Electric front doors windows. Radios: AM/FM. AM/FM stereo. AM/FM stereo with cassette tape player and Dolby noise reduction system. AM/FM stereo with eight-track tape player. AM/FM stereo with electronic search-tune. AM/FM stereo with 40-channel CB transceiver. Rear speaker for AM or AM/FM radio only. Heavy-duty front and rear shock absorbers. Color-keyed spare tire cover. Automatic speed control. Front stabilizer bar. Tilt type steering column. Leather-wrapped steering wheel. Sky Lite driver's compartment sun roof. Door operated dome light switch. Color-keyed unibelt restraint system. Wheels: Road-type 15 x 7 in. Radial ribbed aluminum. Five-slot chrome disc. White painted spoke. Road type spare wheel. Bright wheel covers. Premium wheel covers. Deluxe windshield wipers with intermittent wipe.

NOTE: 1981 Voyagers were offered in the following colors: Cashmere. Graphic yellow (not offered on sport or Premier). Impact red. Medium crimson red. Ginger (not offered on Sport or Premier). Coffee brown metallic. Impact blue (not offered on Sport or Premier). Nightwatch blue. Medium seaspray green metallic (not offered on Sport or Premier). Daystar blue metallic. Bright silver metallic. Pearl white. Black. There were two styles of two-toning.

1982 PLYMOUTH

1982 Plymouth Arrow Mini-Pickup (OCW)

ARROW CUSTOM PICKUP: — The Arrow Custom dropped a notch to become the basic pickup in the Arrow line. A blacked-out grille and headlamp trim were the only major styling changes for '82. Standard features included: Argent painted front bumper with black rubber ends. Cargo lamp. Cigarette lighter. Dome light with driver and passenger side door switches. Emergency flashers. 18-gallon fuel tank. Tinted glass. Flat black grille. Color-keyed headliner. Inside hood release. Bright hubcaps. Left and right sides black sport type exterior mirrors. Interior rearview mirror.

Bright drip rail molding. Bright windshield molding. AM radio. Adjustable angle steering column. Dual sunvisors. Tubular low-mount tie-down bars on both sides of the interior of the pickup box. Trip odometer. Two-speed windshield wipers with washers. Four-speed manual transmission. three exterior colors were offered: white, light tan or red.

I.D. DATA: See 1981 Arrow Pickup.

Model	Body Type	Price	Weight	Prod. Total
OJL4	Pickup Sweptline	6408	2540	—

ENGINE: Four-cylinder. Displacement: 122 cu. in. Brake horsepower: 90 at 5000 R.P.M. Bore & stroke: 3.30 in. x 3.54 in. Compression ratio: 8.5:1. Carburetor: 2-bbl.

NOTE: This engine was rated at 88 horsepower in California.

ARROW ROYAL PICKUP: The new Arrow Royal had a slightly higher payload rating than the Custom. It also came with steel-belted radial white sidewall tires, chrome front bumper, vinyl bodyside moldings, carpeting, blue tweed cloth-and-vinyl bench seat and a five-speed manual transmission. Royal buyers had their choice of three exterior colors: Dark blue metallic, white, or medium blue metallic.

I.D. DATA: See 1981 Arrow Pickup.

Model	Body Type	Price	Weight	Prod. Total
OJH4	Pickup Sweptline	6892	2565	—

ENGINE: Four-cylinder. Displacement: 156 cu. in. Brake horsepower: 105 at 5000 R.P.M. Bore & stroke: 3.59 in. x 3.86 in. Compression ratio: 8.2:1. Carburetor: 2-bbl.

NOTE: This engine was rated at 103 horsepower in California.

ARROW SPORT PICKUP: — This was the flashiest and plushest Arrow. In addition to many of the standard features offered on the other two models, it also came with: Center console with oil pressure gauge, ammeter and transmission shift lever. AM/FM stereo radio. Wide spoke color-keyed road wheels. Tape strip on body side, tailgate, wheel lip and air dam. Red/tan two-tone velour cloth bucket seats. Five-speed manual transmission. Two exterior colors were available: Dark red or corsica brown.

I.D. DATA: See 1981 Arrow Pickup.

Model	Body Type	Price	Weight	Prod. Total
OJP4	Pickup Sweptline	7474	2585	—

ENGINE: Same as Arrow Royal.

CHASSIS: Wheelbase: 109.4 in. Overall length: 194.6 in. Overall width: 65 in. Overall height: 60.6 in. (Arrow Custom); 59.8 in. (Arrow Royal and Arrow Sport). Box length: 81.5 in. Box width: 64.2 in. GVW Rating: 4025 lbs. (Arrow Custom with 4-speed manual); 3595 lbs. (Arrow Custom with 5-speed manual); 4120 lbs. (Arrow Royal and Arrow Sport). Payload: 1505 lbs. (Arrow Custom with 4-speed manual); 1055 lbs. (Arrow Custom with 5-speed manual); 1555 lbs. (Arrow Royal); 1535 lbs. (Arrow Sport). Tires: 6.00 x 14C WSW (Arrow Custom with 4-speed manual); 185SR14 steel-belted radial WSW (Arrow Custom with 5-speed manual, Arrow Royal); 185SR14 steel-belted radial RWL (Arrow Sport).

TECHNICAL: Five-speed manual transmission (Arrow Custom). Three-speed automatic transmission (Arrow Royal, Arrow Sport).

CONVENIENCE OPTIONS: Air conditioning (not available with grille guard). Rear step chrome bumper. Rear step low-luster black bumper. Front bumper guards (not available with grille guard). Electronic digital clock. High altitude emmissions package, Arrow Royal, Arrow Sport. Front floor mats, Royal and Sport. Grille guard. Exterior low-mount chrome mirrors. Vinyl bodyside molding on Custom. Vinyl pickup box top edge molding. Front and rear wheel openings moldings on Custom and Royal. Power steering. Sliding rear window. Automatic speed control in Royal and Sport). Sport bar. Skylite sun roof. Bodyside tape stripe on Custom and Royal). Sport tape stripe package on Sport. Wheel trim rings for Custom and Royal. Tonneau cover. Pickup bed liner. Sidewall liners. Runningboards.

1982 Plymouth Voyager Wagon (Family Van)

VOYAGER — SERIES PB-150 — (Wagon): — Voyager styling was carried over from the previous year. Standard features included: Driver and front passenger armrests. Driver's compartment ashtray. Front disc brakes. Painted front and rear bumper. Cigar lighter. Cleaner air system. Right side double doors with vented glass. Single rear door with fixed glass and inside door handle and lock button. Electronic ignition system. Black full width floor mat. Twenty-two gallon fuel tank. Glove box with door. Argent finish grille. Seven-inch round headlamps. Color-keyed driver's compartment headliner. Fresh air heater with defroster. In-cab-activated hood release. Dual electric horns. Bright hubcaps. Driver and passenger compartment lights with door-operated switches. Locks, all doors. Day/night rearview mirror. Dual bright 5 x 7 in. exterior mirrors. Nameplate on front doors. Power steering. AM radio. Driver and front passenger low-back vinyl bucket seats. Three-passenger quick-release vinyl rear bench seat. Color-keyed five inch diameter steering wheel. Padded dash. Brake system warning light. Dual braking system with separate brake fluid reservoirs in the master cylinder. Energy absorbing steering column. Four-speed manual transmission with overdrive.

I.D. DATA: See 1981 Arrow Pickup.

Model	Body Type	Price	Weight	Prod. Total
PB-150	Van (109.6 in. w.b.)	8482	3604	—
PB-150	Van (127.6 in. w.b.)	8682	3604	—

ENGINE: Six-cylinder. Displacement: 225 cu. in. Brake horsepower: 90 at 3600 R.P.M. Bore & stroke: 3.40 in. x 4.12 in. Compression ratio: 8.4:1. Carburetor: 1-bbl.

VOYAGER — SERIES PB-250 — (Wagon): — This was the perfect Voyager for large families or people who did a lot of hauling, yet were concerned with fuel economy. It was the heaviest-duty Voyager available with six-cylinder power. As before, three sizes were offered. The largest was the Maxi-Wagon.

I.D. DATA: See 1981 Arrow Pickup.

Model	Body Type	Price	Weight	Prod. Total
PB-250	Van (109.6 in. w.b.)	8767	3805	—
PB-250	Van (127.6 in. w.b.)	8895	3930	—
PB-250	Maxi-Wagon	9980	4280	—

ENGINE: Same as PB-150 for 109.6 in. and standard 127.6 in. w.b. wagons. 318 cu. in. V-8. Brake horsepower: 120 at 3600 R.P.M. Bore & stroke: 3.91 in. x 3.31 Compression ratio: 8.5:1. Carburetor: 2-bbl. (Maxi-Wagon).

NOTE: The 318 cu. in. V-8 with 2-bbl. carburetor was not available in California.

VOYAGER — SERIES PB-350 — (Wagon): — The ultimate Voyager for big payloads was the PB-350. Larger brakes and a three-speed automatic transmission were standard. The Maxi-Wagon came with heavy-duty shocks.

I.D. DATA: See 1981 Arrow Pickup.

Model	Body Type	Price	Weight	Prod. Total
PB-350	Van (127 in. w.b. wagon)	10,159	4140	—
PB-350	Maxi-Wagon	10,687	4280	—

ENGINE: Same as PB-250 Maxi-Wagon.

CHASSIS: Wheelbase (Wagon): 109.6 in.; (Wagon and Maxi-Wagon) 127.6 in. Overall height: (109.6 in. w.b.) 79.6 in.; (127.6 in. w.b. wagon) 80.9 in.; (Maxi-Wagon) 80.6 in. Overall width: 79.8 in. Overall length: (109.6 in. w.b.) 178.9 in.; (127.6 in. w.b. wagon) 196.9 in.; (Maxi-Wagon) 222.9 in. Tires: (PB-150) P205/75R15 glass-belted radial; (PB-250 127.6 in. w.b. 6010 lbs. GVW) P225/75R15 glass-belted radial; (PB-250 109.6 in. w.b. 6010 lbs. GVW and 127.6 in. w.b. with 6400 lbs GVW) P235/75R15 glass-belted radial; (PB-250 Maxi-Wagon) P235/75R15XL; (PB-350 Wagon 127.6 in. w.b.) 8.00 x 16.5E (10PR) polyester bias-belted; (PB-350 Maxi-Wagon) 8.75 x 16.5E (10PR) polyester bias-belted. GVW Rating: (PB-150) 5300 lbs.; (PB-250/109.6 in. w.b.) 6010 lbs.; (PB-250/127.6 in. w.b.) 6400 lbs.; (PB-250/127.6 in. w.b. Wagon and Maxi-Wagon) 6400 lbs.; (PB-350 127.6 in. w.b. Wagon and Maxi-Wagon) 7500 lbs. and (PB-350 Maxi-Wagon) 8510 lbs.

TECHNICAL: 318 cu. in. V-8 with 2-bbl. carburetor. (PB-150, PB-250). 318 cu. in. V-8 with 4-bbl. carburetor (PB-150, PB-250, PB-350). 360 cu. in. V-8 with 4-bbl. carburetor (PB-350). Three-speed automatic transmission (PB-150, PB-250).

OPTIONAL PACKAGES: Sport: Bright exterior nameplates, lower side and rear moldings. Dual vertically stacked quad rectangular headlamps with halogen high beams and bright grille. Bright front and rear bumpers. Bright molding around windshield, side and rear windows (except driver and passenger door windows). Bright taillamp bezels. Woodtone applique on lower face of instrument panel. Spare tire cover. Vinyl door and side trim panels with woodtone trim. Garnish moldings over front doors and passenger compartment windows, headers around rear compartment windows and front pillar and windshield. Driver and front passenger color-keyed low-back bucket seats and bench seat in deluxe vinyl trim. Soft cloth-covered headliner with insulation in driver and passenger compartment. Accessory floor mats in driver's compartment. Electronic digital clock. Instrument panel lower skirts. Color-keyed carpeting. Dash liner insulation. Luxury steering wheel with woodtone rim insert. Premier: Bright exterior nameplate, upper side and rear moldings. Bright bumper guards with rub strips, front and rear. Bodyside and rear woodtone tape applique with dual gold accent strips. Vinyl door and side trim panels with woodtone trim and front door pull straps. Color-keyed carpeted engine

housing cover. Oil pressure gauge and trip odometer. Glove box lock and light. Deluxe two-speed windshield wipers with intermittent wipe. Ignition and headlight switch with time delay. Cigar lighter light. Courtesy stepwell lamp, front and side doors. Driver and front passenger color-keyed high-back reclining Command bucket seats and a three-passenger bench seat with matching cloth-and-vinyl trim. Exterior appearance package: Bright grille. Bright front and rear bumpers. Bright taillamp bezels. Bright windshield molding. Dual vertically stacked quad rectangular headlamps with halogen high beams. Bright side and rear window moldings (except driver and front passenger door windows). Insulation, Heavy-duty: (For Sport and Premier wagons): includes interior lower fiberglass insulation panels except on standard single rear door or optional sliding side door. Insulation under floor covering. (For Voyager wagons): includes the items listed for Sport and Premier wagons plus: Interior lower trim panels in passenger compartment in blue or cashmere color. Color-keyed garnish moldings over front door headers and around headliner and rear compartment window. Dash liner insulation. Sliding side door track cover. White hardboard headliner in passenger compartment. Quad Command seating: Four high-back Command bucket seats. Five or eight passenger convert-a-bed seating. Eight-passenger travel seating. Eight passenger seating: (all PB-250, PB-350 models) includes one additional quick-release three-passenger bench seat with three seat belts. (Not available on PB-350 Maxi-Wagon with 8510 lbs. GVW package.) Twelve-passenger seating: (all PB-350 models) requires window retention and rear door(s) with optional vented glass. Includes two additional bench seats: The second, a three-passenger quick-release bench seat, the third a four-passenger seat. Spare tire carrier relocated under third bench seat. (Not available on PB-350 Maxi-Wagon with 8510 lb. GVW package.) Fifteen-passenger seating: (PB-350 Maxi-Wagon only.) Requires at extra cost, 8510 lb. GVW package, window retention and rear door(s) with optional vented glass. Includes three additional bench seats: Second and third three-passenger with quick-release. The fourth, four-passenger. Tire carrier relocated under fourth bench seat. Heavy-duty trailer towing: (PB-250 and PB-350 models.) Requires, at extra cost, automatic transmission, 318 cu. in. 4-bbl. or 360 cu. in. 4-bbl. V-8 engine, transmission auxiliary oil cooler and 36-gallon fuel tank. Includes: Maximum cooling. Sixty-amp alternator and 430-amp maintenance-free battery. Seven-wire harness. Class IV tow bar hitch. Heavy-duty variable load flasher. Heavy-duty shocks. Convenience: Cigar lighter light. Glove box lock and light. Ignition and headlight switch with time delay (not available with tilt steering column). Two-speed windshield wipers with intermittent wipe. Courtesy stepwell lamp for front and side doors (for use with Sport package only).

CONVENIENCE OPTIONS: Air conditioning (integral front, auxiliary rear with or without auxiliary heater). Heavy-duty alternators. Heavy-duty batteries. Bright front and rear bumpers, guards and rub strips. Bright front and rear bumpers. Electronic digital clock. Automatic transmission oil to air cooling. Maximum engine cooling. Electric rear window defroster for single rear door. Dual rear doors with vented glass. Single rear door with vented glass. Sliding passenger side door. Thirty-six gallon fuel tank. Oil pressure and trip odometer gauges. Sun screen privacy glass. Tinted glass, all windows. Bright grille with dual quad rectangular headlamps, vertically stacked with halogen high beams. Auxiliary rear heater. Deluxe front heater. Engine block heater. Two color-keyed (accessory type) rubber mats in driver's compartment. Dual low-mount 6 x 9 in. bright exterior mirrors. Lower moldings (includes side, rear and bright taillamp bezels). Upper moldings (includes side, rear and bright taillamp bezels). Upper and lower moldings with bright taillamp bezels. Electronic display warning indicator for engine oil level, transmission oil level, radiator coolant level and transmission oil temperature. Electric door locks. Power front door windows. Radios: AM/FM stereo. AM/FM stereo with cassette tape player, electronic tuning and Dolby noise reduction system. AM/FM stereo with Search-Tune and electronic tuning. AM/FM stereo with eight-track tape player. AM/FM stereo with 40-channel CB transceiver. Heavy-duty shock absorbers. Automatic speed control. Front stabilizer bar. Tilt type steering column. Luxury type steering wheel. Bright deluxe wheel covers. Wheels: (Road type 15 x 7 in.) Aluminum radial ribbed. Five-slot chrome disc. Deluxe two-speed windshield wipers with intermittent wipe.

1983 PLYMOUTH

SCAMP PICKUP: — "The dashing good looks of a sporty car . . . the carry-all utility of a small truck." That's how sales literature described Plymouth's new Scamp. This front-wheel-drive vehicle was more like a mini "El Camino" than a traditional pickup. From the front it looked just like the Plymouth Turismo. The two rectangular headlights were recessed into the front fenders. The aggressive looking "missing teeth" grille and thin front bumper seemed molded into the aerodynamic body. The large, vertical taillights had backup lights in their lower section. Standard equipment included: Cigarette lighter. Cleaner air system. Clock and trip odometer. Coat hooks. Directional signals with lane-change feature. Black exterior door handle inserts. Hazard warning flashers. Electronic fuel control system. Thirteen gallon fuel tank. Tinted glass, all windows. Halogen headlights. Cloth-covered headliner. Heater and defroster. Inside hood release. Hood silencer pad. Dual horns. Electronic ignition and voltage regulator. Instrument panel padding. Glove box lock. Driver's side remote exterior mirror. Interior day/night rearview mirror. Passenger side visor vanity mirror. Cargo box flange trim molding. Bright wheel lip and sill moldings. Black windshield and rear window moldings. Package tray. Rack and pinion steering. Color-keyed four-spoke sport steering wheel. Bodyside and rear stripes. Leaf springs rear suspension. Four-speed manual transmission. Electric windshield washers. Deluxe windshield wipers with intermittent wipe.

I.D. DATA: See 1981 Arrow Pickup.

Model	Body Type	Price	Weight	Prod. Total
MH28	Pickup	6683	2305	—

ENGINE: Four-cylinder. Displacement: 135 cu. in. Brake horsepower: 84 at 4800 R.P.M. Bore & stroke: 3.44 in. x 3.62 in. Compression ratio: 8.5:1. Carburetor: 2-bbl.

SCAMP GT PICKUP: Scamp buyers who wanted something with a bit more flash could step up to the GT. It came with most of the same standard features as the basic model plus: Simulated hood scoop. Rallye instrument cluster that included a tachometer, clock, and trip odometer. AM radio. GT tape graphics stripes. Rallye wheels (14 in. argent steel with trim rings). Five-speed manual transmission. In addition, buyers had a choice of two interiors: Cloth and vinyl high-back bucket seats with integral head restraints and reclining seatbacks, in black with a wide vertical red stripe. Or solid black versions of these seats.

I.D. DATA: See 1981 Arrow Pickup.

Model	Body Type	Price	Weight	Prod. Total
MS28	Pickup	7204	2340	—

ENGINE: Same as Scamp.

CHASSIS: Wheelbase: 104.2 in. Overall length: 183.6 in. Overall width: 66.8 in. Overall height: 51.8 in. Box length: 63.7 in. Payload: 1145 lbs. (Scamp); 1110 lbs. (Scamp GT). Tires: P175/75R13 glass-bleted radio bsw (Scamp); P195/60R14 steel-belted radial BSW with raised black letters (Scamp GT).

TECHNICAL: Five-speed manual tranmission (Scamp). Three-speed automatic transmission.

CONVENIENCE OPTIONS: Light package: ash receiver light, glove box light, headlamps-on warning buzzer, ignition switch light with time delay, map/courtesy light. Protection package: vinyl lower bodyside corrosion protection, undercoating, front floor mats. Cold weather package: 430-amp maintenance-free battery, engine block heater. Air conditioning. Front license plate bracket. Rallye cluster, includes tachometer, clock and trip odometer (Scamp). Console (Scamp). Bright remote control mirror. Power steering. Radios: AM. AM/FM stereo, manually tuned. AM/FM stereo, electronically tuned. AM/FM stereo with cassette tape player and Dolby system, electronically tuned. Cargo box side rails. Automatic speed control. Tonneau cover. Wheels: 14 inch cast aluminum. 13 inch rallye wheels. 14 inch rallye wheels.

VOYAGER — SERIES PB-150 — (Wagon): — Voyager styling was basically unchanged for 1983. However, there was now only one two-tone paint procedure. Standard features included: Brake warning light. Dual braking system with separate brake fluid resevoirs in the master cylinder. Electric windshield washers and wipers. Fade-resistant front disc brakes. Inside hood release. Padded instrument panel and sunvisors. Traffic hazard warning flasher system. Air vent doors. Driver and front passenger armrests. Driver's compartment ashtray. 370-amp maintenance-free battery. Painted front and rear bumper. Cigar lighter. Cleaner air system. Right-side double doors with vented and banded glass. Single rear door with fixed glass and iside door handle and lock button. Electronic ignition system. Full width black floor mat. Twenty-two gallon fuel tank. Tinted glass, all windows. Argent finish grille. Round headlamps. Color-keyed driver's compartment headliner. Deluxe fresh air heater with defroster. In-cab activated hood release. Dual electric horns. Bright hubcaps. Bumper type jack. Interior rearview day/night mirror. Dual bright 5 x 7 in. exterior mirrors. Nameplates on front doors. Power steering. AM radio. Deluxe driver and front passenger high-back vinyl Command bucket seats. Three passenger quick-release deluxe vinyl bench seat with three seat belts. Color-keyed 15 inch diameter steering wheel. Inside mounted spare tire carrier. Four-speed manual transmission with overdrive.

I.D. DATA: See 1981 Arrow Pickup.

Model	Body Type	Price	Weight	Prod. Total
PB-150	Van (109.6 in. w.b.)	8885	3604	—
PB-150	Van (127.6 in. w.b.)	9085	3764	—

ENGINE: Six-cylinder. Displacement: 225 cu. in. Brake horsepower: 90 at 3600 R.P.M. Bore & stroke: 3.40 in. x 4.12 in. Compression ratio: 8.4:1. Carburetor: 1-bbl.

VOYAGER — SERIES PB-250 — (Wagon): — The mid-line PB-250 came with the same standard features as the PB-150, could haul heavier loads. It also offered an additional body size: the 127 inch wheelbase, extended body, Maxi-Wagon. (Maxi-wagons came equipped with automatic transmission.)

I.D. DATA: See 1981 Arrow Pickup.

Model	Body Type	Price	Weight	Prod. Total
PB-250	Van (127.6 in. w.b.)	9486	3930	—
PB-250	Maxi-Wagon (127.6 in. w.b.)	10,030	4280	—

ENGINE: Same as PB-150 for 109.6 in. w.b. and standard 127.6 in. w.b. wagons. 318 cu. in. V-8. Brake horsepower: 120 at 3600 R.P.M. Bore & stroke: 3.91 in. x 3.31 Compression ratio: 8.5:1. Carburetor: 2-bbl. (Maxi-Wagon).

NOTE: The 318 cu. in. V-8 with 2-bbl. carburetor was not available in California.

1983 Plymouth Voyager Wagon (OCW)

VOYAGER — SERIES PB-350 — (Wagon): — The PB-350 was the Voyager for buyers who wanted maximum load capacity. It could be had in a standard 127.6 inch wheelbase version or the extra roomy extended body Maxi-Wagon. Both came equipped with automatic transmission, larger brakes, and axle type jack.

I.D. DATA: See 1981 Arrow Pickup.

Model	Body Type	Price	Weight	Prod. Total
PB-350	Van (127.6 in. w.b. wagon)	10,708	4140	—
PB-350	Maxi-Wagon	11,260	4280	—

ENGINE: Same as PB-250 Maxi-Wagon.

CHASSIS: Wheelbase (Wagon): 109.6 in.; (Wagon and Maxi-Wagon) 127.6 in. Overall height: (109.6 in. w.b.) 79.6 in.; (127.6 in. w.b. wagon) 80.9 in.; (Maxi-Wagon) 80.6 in. Overall width: 79.8 in. Overall length: (109.6 in. w.b.) 178.9 in.; (127.6 in. w.b. wagon) 196.9 in.; (Maxi-Wagon) 222.9 in. Tires: (PB-150): P205/75R15 glass-belted radial; (PB-250/127.6 in. w.b. wagon) P225/75R15 glass-belted radial; (PB-250 Maxi-Wagon) P235/75R15XL steel-belted radial; (PB-350 Wagon) 8.00 x 16.5E polyester bias-belted; (PB-350 Maxi-Wagon) 8.75 x 16.5E polyester bias-belted. GVW Ratings: (PB-150) 5300 to 6010 lbs.; (PB-250) 6010 to 6400 lbs.; (PB-350) 7500 to 8510 lbs.

TECHNICAL: 318 cu. in. V-8 with 2-bbl. carburetor. (PB-150, PB-250). 318 cu. in. V-8 with 4-bbl. carburetor (PB-250, PB-350). 360 cu. in. V-8 with 4-bbl. carburetor (PB-350). Three-speed automatic transmission (PB-150, PB-250 Wagons).

OPTIONAL PACKAGES: Sport: Bright nameplates. Bright lower side and rear moldings. Dual vertically stacked quad rectangular headlamps with halogen high beams and bright grille. Bright front and rear bumpers. Bright molding around windshield and side and rear fixed windows (except driver and passenger door windows). Bright taillamp bezels. Woodtone applique on lower face of instrument panel. Spare tire cover. Vinyl door and side trim panels with woodtone trim. Garnish moldings over front doors and passenger compartment windows, front pillars and windshield. Driver and front passenger color-keyed high-back Command bucket seats and three-passenger bench seat in cloth-and-vinyl trim. Soft cloth-covered headliner with insulation (driver and passenger compartment). Accessory floor mats in driver's compartment. Electronic digitial clock. Instrument panel lower skirts. Color-keyed carpeting. Dash liner insulation. Luxury steering wheel with woodtone rim insert. Premier: Bright exterior nameplate. Bright upper side and rear moldings. Bright bumper guards with rub strips, front and rear. Vinyl door and side trim panels with woodtone trim and front door pull straps. Color-keyed carpeted engine housing cover. Oil pressure gauge and trip odometer. Glove box lock and light. Deluxe two-speed windshield wipers with intermittent wipe. Ignition and headlight switch with time delay. Cigar lighter light. Courtesy step well lamp (front and side doors). Driver and front passenger color-keyed reclining high-back Command bucket seats and a three-passenger bench seat with matching deluxe cloth-and-vinyl trim. Exterior appearance package: Bright grille. Bright front and rear bumpers. Bright taillamp bezels. Bright windshield molding. Dual vertically stacked quad rectangular headlamps with halogen high beams. Bright side and rear fixed window moldings (except driver and front passenger door windows). Heavy-duty insulation package for Sport and Premier: Interior lower fiberglass insulation panels (not on standard single rear door or optional sliding side door). Insulation under floor covering. Insulation package: Includes the items listed in Sport and Premier heavy-duty package, plus the following. Interior lower trim panels in passenger compartment (offered in blue or beige). Color-keyed garnish moldings over windshield and front door headers and around headliner and rear compartment window. Dash liner insulation. Sliding side door track cover. White hardboard headliner in passenger compartment. Insulation under headliner. Eight passenger seating: (PB-150 109.6 in. w.b., models with extra-cost 6010 lbs. GVW package and all PB-250 and PB-350 models.) Includes one additional quick-release three-passenger bench seat with three seat belts. Eight-passenger travel seating. Twelve-passenger seating: (PB-350, requires rear door(s) with optional vented glass at extra cost.). Includes two additional bench seats: Second is a three-passenger quick-release seat. Third is a four-passenger bench seat. Window retention. Spare tire carrier relocated under third bench seat. Fifteen-passenger seating: (PB-350 Maxi-Wagon. Requires 8510 lbs. GVW package and rear door(s) with optional vented glass at extra cost.) Includes three additional bench seats: The second is three-passenger quick-release type.

The third is the same. The fourth is a four-passenger seat with four seat belts. Window retention. Spare tire carrier relocated under fourth bench seat. Trailer towing preparation package: (PB-250, PB-350) Requires automatic transmission, 318 cu. in. V-8 with four-barrel carburetor or 360 cu. in. V-8 with four-barrel carburetor, transmission auxiliary oil cooler and specified rear axle ratio. Includes maximum cooling, 500 amp. maintenance free heavy-duty battery, heavy-duty variable load flasher, heavy-duty front and rear shock absorbers and front stabilizer bar. Convenience: Cigar lighter. Glove box lock and light. Ignition and headlight switch with time delay (not available with tilt steering column). Two-speed windshield wipers with intermittent wipe. Courtesy stepwell lamp for front and side doors (for use with Sport package only).

CONVENIENCE OPTIONS: Air conditioning; integral front, or rear auxiliary (with or without auxiliary heater). A 114-amp. alternator. Heavy-duty 500-amp maintenance-free battery. Bright front and rear bumper guards and rub strips. Bright front and rear bumpers. Electronic digital clock. Auxiliary transmission oil-to-air cooling. Maximum engine cooling. Electric rear window defroster for single rear door. Dual rear doors with vented glass. Single rear door with vented and banded glass. Sliding passenger side door. Thirty-six gallon fuel tank. Oil pressure and trip odometer gauges. Sun screen privacy glass. Bright grille, includes quad rectangular headlamps with halogen high beams. Auxiliary rear heater. Engine block heater. Two color-keyed accessory type rubber mats in driver's compartment. Exterior dual low-mount 6 x 9 in. bright mirrors. Lower moldings, includes side, rear and bright taillamp bezels. Upper moldings, includes side, rear and bright taillamp bezels. Upper and lower moldings, includes side, rear and bright taillamp bezels. Electric door locks. Electric front door windows. Radios: AM/FM stereo electronically tuned. AM/FM stereo, electronically tuned, with cassette tape player and Dolby noise reduction system. AM/FM stereo manually tuned. Heavy-duty shock absorbers. Automatic speed control. Front stabilizer bar. Tilt type steering column. Luxury type steering wheel. Deluxe bright wheel covers. Wheels: (Road type, 15 x 7 in.) Aluminum radial ribbed or five-slot chrome disc. Deluxe two-speed windshield wipers with intermittent wipe.

NOTE: The 1983 Voyager was available in a choice of 13 exterior colors: Graphic red. Beige sand, Crimson red. Spice metallic. Nightwatch blue. Sable brown. Light blue metallic. Charcoal gray metallic. Burnished silver metallic. Pearl white. Black.

1984 PLYMOUTH

1984 Plymouth Voyager Passenger Wagon (CPD)

VOYAGER WAGON: — The Voyager was dramatically changed for 1984. It became less like a traditional van and more like a station wagon. Yet, its exterior resembled the previous year's model from the front. This "shrunken" Voyager had front-wheel-drive. The thin horizontal bars grille had dual, vertically stacked, quad rectangular headlights. Large wraparound signal lights were integrated into it. A "Chrysler star" emblem rose, from above the grille, on the slooping hood. The tall vertical taillights had backup lights built into their lower section. Standard features included: Halogen headlamps. Inside hood release. Five-speed manual transmission with overdrive. Side window de-misters. Tinted glass. Cigarette lighter. Power brakes. Power steering. Electronic digital clock. AM electronic tune radio. Front and rear bumper rub strips. Day/night rearview mirrors. Tethered fuel cap. Headlamps-on chime. Left side remote control exterior mirror. Single note horn. Fifteen-gallon fuel tank. Bright grille. Two-speed windshield wipers with wet arm washers. Color-keyed seat belts with automatic release on front bucket seats.

I.D. DATA: See 1981 Arrow Pickup.

Model	Body Type	Price	Weight	Prod. Total
L36	Mini-Van	8280	2937	—

ENGINE: Four-cylinder. Displacement: 122 cu. in. Brake horsepower: 90 at 5000 R.P.M. Bore & stroke: 3.30 in. x 3.54 in. Compression ratio: 8.5:1. Carburetor: 2-bbl.

1984 Plymouth Voyager Passenger Wagon (CPD)

VOYAGER SE WAGON: The Voyager SE (Special Edition) came with the same standard features as the basic model, plus: Road wheels, a dual note horn, front folding armrests and soft cloth trim panels with carpeted lower insert.

I.D. DATA: See 1981 Arrow Pickup.

Model	Body Type	Price	Weight	Prod. Total
H36	Mini-Van	8517	2984	—

ENGINE: Same as Voyager.

1984 Plymouth Voyager Passenger Wagon (CPD)

VOYAGER LE WAGON: This was the top-of-the-line model most often seen in Voyager "Magic Wagon" advertisements. In addition to the standard features found in the other two versions, the LE (Limited Edition) had: Deluxe sound insulation. High-back front reclining bucket seats. Dual black remote control exterior mirrors. Luxury steering wheel. Center body woodgrain applique. Upper and lower bodyside moldings.

I.D. DATA: See 1981 Arrow Pickup.

Model	Body Type	Price	Weight	Prod. Total
P-36	Mini-Van	9105	3026	—

ENGINE: Same as Voyager.

CHASSIS: Wheelbase: 112 in. Overall length: 175.9 in. Overall width: 69.6 in. Overall height: 64.6 in. Tires: P185/75R14 steel-belted radial black sidewall.

TECHNICAL: Torque-Flite three-speed automatic transmission. Four-cylinder 2.6 liter Mitsubishi built engine.

1984 Plymouth Voyager Passenger Wagon (CPD)

OPTIONAL PACKAGES: Gauge package with gauge alert: Engine coolant temperate gauge with high temperature warning light. Oil pressure gauge with low pressure warning light. Low voltage warning light. Trip odometer with push-button reset. Light package: Ash receiver light. Front map/reading lights. Headlamp switch callout light. Ignition switch light with time delay. Instrument panel door-ajar light, low fuel warning light and low washer fluid light. Underhood compartment light. Liftgate mounted dual floodlights. Basic group: Light package. Deluxe intermittent windshield wiprs. Dual note horns. Power liftgate release. A 500-amp. battery. Dual remote control exterior mirrors. Deluxe sound insulation. Cruise control. Twenty-gallon fuel tank. Sliding door outside lock. Liftgate wiper/washer. Luxury steering wheel. Gauge package with gauge alert. Luxury equipment discount package: Tilt steering column. Power windows. Power front door locks and drivers' seat. Basic group. Travel equipment discount package: (Voyager SE and Voyager LE) Mitsubishi 2.6 liter engine. Seven-passenger seating package. Sun screen glass. Remote control rear vent windows. Twenty-gallon fuel tank. A 500-amp battery. Seven-passenger seating package: (Voyager SE and Voyager LE) Includes second seat (two-passenger bench with fixed back, side armrests and quick-release attachments); third seat (three-passenger bench with folding back, side armrests, adjustable feature and quick-release attachments). Three storage bins (in third seat armrests and right rear trim panel). Ash receiver in C pillar below belt. Heavy-duty suspension and rear brakes. P195/75R14 steel-belted radial black sidewall tires.

CONVENIENCE OPTIONS: Air conditioning. Heavy-duty suspension. A 500-amp. battery. Tonneau cover. Twenty-gallon fuel tank. Sun screen privacy glass. Electric rear window defroster. Power door locks. Luggage rack. Vinyl body side molding. Two-tone paint (Voyager SE). Radios: AM/FM stereo with electronic tuning. AM/FM stereo with electronic tuning and cassette tape player. Cruise control. Dual black remote control exterior mirrors. Tilt steering column. Wire wheel covers (Voyager SE, Voyager LE). Power windows (Voyager SE, Voyager LE). Sport road wheels. Rear quarter vent with remote control. Deluxe windshield wipers. Rear window wiper. High-back bucket seats with vinyl trim (Voyager SE). Power driver's seat.

NOTE: According to a *Popular Mechanics* survey of Plymouth Voyager/Dodge Caravan owners, the SE was the most popular series (60.4 percent). Most buyers (90.3 percent) ordered automatic transmission. The majority of owners (66.3 percent) were age 30 to 49. The three things owners liked best about their vehicle were; handling (52.2 percent), comfort (39.9 percent) and roominess (33.4 percent).

1985 PLYMOUTH

1985 Plymouth Voyager w/Magic Camper Option

VOYAGER WAGON: — After the dramatic changes made in 1984, Voyager styling was basically untouched for the new model year. Standard features included: Front air dam. Sixty-amp. alternator and 335-amp. maintenance-free battery. Power front disc brakes. Color-keyed front and rear bumper end caps. Bright front and rear bumpers with protective rub strips. Carpeting. Warning chimes for key in ignition, "fasten seat belts" and "headlamps on." Cigar lighter. Coolant overflow reservoir. Corrosion protection. Front door windows de-misters. Sliding right side cargo compartment door with vented glass. Electronic ignition and voltage regulator. Remote cable release fuel filler door. Fifteen gallon fuel tank. Tinted glass, all windows. Vented glass body side. Bright grille. Halogen low and high beam headlamps. Cloth-covered driver and passenger compartment headliner. Bi-level ventilation heater. Inside hood release. Single note horn. Liftgate with fixed glass. Driver and passenger compartments dome lights. Day/night rearview mirror. Black left side remote control exterior mirror. Black rear window and windshield molding. AM radio with electronic tuning, digital display, integral digital clock. Color-keyed seat belts with automatic release on front bucket seats. Rack and pinion power steering. Vinyl two-spoke steering wheel. Compact spare tire. Cable winch system underslung tire carrier. Five-speed manual transmission with overdrive. Deluxe wheel covers. Two-speed windshield wipers with wet arm washers. Liftgate wiper/washer. Brake fluid pressure loss warning light. Turn signals with lane-change feature. Dual braking system.

I.D. DATA: See 1981 Arrow Pickup.

Model	Body Type	Price	Weight	Prod. Total
L36	Mini-Van	9147	2911	—

ENGINE: Four-cylinder. Displacement: 122 cu. in. Brake horsepower: 90 at 5000 R.P.M. Bore & stroke: 3.30 in. x 3.54 in. Compression ratio: 8.5:1. Carburetor: 2-bbl.

VOYAGER SE WAGON: The SE was a step up from the standard Voyager. It came with most of the same basic features plus: Deluxe cloth low-back front bucket seats. Bright upper bodyside and lift gate moldings. Luxury wheel covers.

I.D. DATA: See 1981 Arrow Pickup.

Model	Body Type	Price	Weight	Prod. Total
H36	Mini-Van	9393	2984	—

ENGINE: Same as Voyager.

VOYAGER LE WAGON: It was easy to tell which was the top of the line Voyager. The LE came with distinctive woodgrain exterior appliques and surround moldings. The interior featured luxury cloth high-back front bucket sseats with integral headrests, armrests, seatback storage pockets and driver and passenger recliners. It also had a luxury steering wheel.

I.D. DATA: See 1981 Arrow Pickup.

Model	Body Type	Price	Weight	Prod. Total
P-36	Mini-Van	10,005	9105	—

ENGINE: Same as Voyager.

CHASSIS: Wheelbase: 112 in. Overall length: 175.9 in. Overall width: 69.6 in. Overall height: 64.6 in. Tires: P185/75R14 steel-belted radial black sidewwall.

OPTIONAL PACKAGES: Basic group: (Voyager) Light package: Deluxe intermittent winshield wipers. Dual-note horns. Power liftgate release. A 500-amp. battery. Dual remote control mirrors. Deluxe sound insulation package. Popular equipment discount package: (Voyager SE and Voyager LE) Light package. Gauge with gauge alert package. Deluxe intermittent windshield wipers. AM/FM stereo radio with clock. Dual note horns. Automatic speed control. Power liftgate release. Dual remote mirrors. Deluxe sound insulation. Luxury steering wheel. Illuminated visor vanity mirror. Overhead console (for Voyager LE models only). Luxury equipment Discount package: (Voyager LE) Popular equipment package. Tilt steering column. Power mirrors. Power front door windows, door locks, and driver's seat. Travel equipment discount package: (Voyager SE and Voyager LE) Mitsubishi 2.6-liter engine (requires automatic transaxle at extra cost). Seven-passenger seating package. Sun screen glass. Remote control rear vent windows. Twenty-gallon fuel tank. A 500-amp battery. Sport wheel package: P205/70R14 steel-belted radial raised black letter tires. Cast aluminum wheels. Gauge with gauge alert package: Engine coolant temperature gauge with high temperature warning light. Oil pressure gauge with low pressure warning light. Low voltage warning light. Trip odometer with push-button reset. Light package: Ash receiver light. Front map/reading lights. Headlamp switch callout light. Ignition switch light with time delay. Instrument panel door-ajar light, low fuel warning light and low washer fluid light. Underhood compartment light. Liftgate mounted dual floodlights. Deluxe sound insulation package: Door to sill seals. Liftgate, passenger floor, underhood, under instrument panel, and wheelhousing silencers. Seven-passenger seating package: (Voyager SE and Voyager LE) Includes second seat-two-passenger bench with fixed back, side armrests and quick-release attachments; third seat three-passenger bench with folding back, side armrests, adjustable feature (slides front to rear on tracks) and quick-release attachments. Three storage bins (in third seat armrests and right rear trim panel). Ash receiver in C pillar below belt. Heavy-duty suspension, and rear brakes. P195/75R14 steel-belted radial black sidewall tires.

CONVENIENCE OPTIONS: Air conditioning with bi-level ventilation. A 500-amp. maintenance-free heavy-duty battery. Black and front and rear bumper guards. Forward storage console. Converta-Bed rear seating option (Voyager, Voyager SE). Electrically heated liftgate window defroster. Accessory type front and rear floor mats. Twenty-gallon fuel tank. Sun screen glass, all windows except windshield and front doors. Roof mounted luggage rack. Dual black remote control exterior mirrors. Dual back power remote control exterior mirrors. Color-keyed bodyside vinyl molding. Power door locks. Power liftgate release. Power driver's seat. Power windows (Voyager SE, Voyager LE). AM/FM stereo with electronic tuning, digital display, four speakers and integral digital clock. Premium AM stereo/FM stereo radio with electronic tuning, digital display, seek and scan, cassette tape player with automatic reverse, Dynamic Noise Reduction, four speakers and integral digital clock. AM stereo/FM stereo radio with electronic tuning, digital display, 36-watt Ultimate Sound System, memory scan, up-and-down scan, cassette player with automatic reverse and metal tape capability, Dynamic Noise Reduction, five-channel graphic equalizer, joystick balance/fader control, ambience sound control, four speakers and integral digital clock. Automatic speed control. Tilt steering column. Heavy-duty suspension (includes P195/75R14 tires). Conventional spare tire. Tires: P195/75R14 steel-belted radial black sidewall. P205/70R14 steel-belted radial raised black letter. P205/70R14 steel-belted radial white sidewall. Rear cargo compartment tonneau cover. Remote control rear quarter windows vent. Wire wheel covers (Voyager SE, Voyager LE).

TECHNICAL: TorqueFlite three-speed automatic transmission. Four-cylinder 2.6 liter Mitsubishi built engine.

1986 PLYMOUTH

Model	Body Type	Price	Weight	Prod. Total
H21	Mini-Van	9506	3005	—
H41	Mini Van (SE)	9785	3046	—
H51	Mini Van (LE)	10,528	3071	—

ENGINE: Displacement: 2.2L (135 cu. in.) OHC Four. Brake horsepower: 101 at 5600 R.P.M. Compression ratio: 9.0:1. Carburetor: 2-bbl.

CHASSIS: Wheelbase: 112 in. Overall length: 175.9 in. Overall width: 69.6 in. Overall height: 64.2 in. GVW Rating: 4450-4600 lbs. Tires: P185/75R14.

TECHNICAL: 2.6L (156 cu. in.) OHC Four. Three-speed automatic transmission.

1986 Plymouth Voyager Mini-Wagon (CPD)

VOYAGER: — Voyager styling was carried over from 1985. Among changes made for 1986 were: New brake proportioning valve, integrated wraparound front air dam, outside lock on sliding side door and improved manual transmission. Standard features included: Front wheel drive. Maintenance free battery. Power front disc brakes. Carpeting. "Fasten seat belts," "headlights on" and "key in ignition" warning chimes. Electronic digital clock. Cigar lighter. Coolant overflow reservoir. Corrosion protection (extensive use of galvanized steel; urethane protective coating on lower body panels). Front door window de-misters. Sliding right side door with vented glass. Electronic ignition and voltage regulation. Stainless steel exhaust system. Remote release fuel filler door. 15-gallon fuel tank. Tinted glass. Bright grille. Quad halogen headlights. Headliner. Bi-level ventilation heater. Inside hood release. Single note horn. Liftgate with fixed glass. Left remote control exterior mirror. Black rear window and windshield moldings. AM radio with electronic tuning. Rack and pinion power steering. Compact spare tire. Five speed manual with overdrive. Wheel covers. Two-speed windshield wipers with wet arm washers. Liftgate wiper/washer with intermittent wipe.

VOYAGER SE: The SE (Special Edition) came with most of the same items as the base Voyager plus (or in place of): Soft cloth trim panels with carpeted lower insert. Assist strap (on front passenger seat back). Bright upper bodyside and liftgate moldings. Deluxe cloth and vinyl seats with front folding armrests. Styled road wheels with bright trim ring, hub cover and nut covers.

VOYAGER LE: The Voyager LE (Luxury Edition) lived up to its name. It came with most of the same features found on the SE plus (or in place of): Deluxe sound insulation. Dual power remote control exterior rearview mirrors. Dual note horn. Woodtone bodyside and liftgate moldings. Woodtone applique (bodyside applique ommitted when monotone paint was ordered).

I.D. DATA: See 1985 Voyager.

OPTIONAL PACKAGES: Basic group: (Voyager) 20-gallon fuel tank; illuminated vanity mirror; 500-amp maintenance free battery; deluxe intermittent windshield wipers; deluxe sound insulation; dual remote control outside rearview mirrors; sliding side door with outside key lock; Light package; power liftgate release; dual note horns; Gauge Package; cruise control. Popular equipment discount package: (SE, LE) AM stereo/FM stereo radio with integral clock; 500-amp battery; deluxe sound insulation; deluxe intermittent windshield wipers; dual non power remote control mirrors (SE), dual note horns; electronic speed control; gauge and gauge alert package; illuminated visor vanity mirror; light package; luxury steering wheel; overhead console (LE); power liftgate release; remote control rear quarter vent windows; sliding side door outside key lock. Luxury equipment discount package: (LE) popular equipment package; power door locks; power driver's bucket seat; power front door windows; tilt steering column. Travel equipment discount package: (SE, LE) 500-amp. battery; dual note horns; 20-gallon fuel tank; 2.6L engine; automatic transmission; remote control rear quarter vent windows; seven passenger seating package; sliding side door with outside key lock; sunscreen glass. Gauge alert package: engine coolant temperature gauge and high temperature warning light; low voltage warning light; oil pressure gauage and low pressure warning light; trip odometer with push-button reset. Light package: ash receiver light; front map/reading lights (two); headlight switch callout light with time delay; ignition switch light with time delay; instrument panel door ajar, low fuel warning and low washer fluid lights; liftgate mounted dual floodlights; underhood light. Seven passenger seating package: (SE, LE) includes second rear seat (2-passenger bench); third rear seat (3-passenger bench); ash receiver in right C-pillar below belt; heavy-duty rear brakes; heavy-duty suspension; P195/75R14 SBR BSW tires; dual rear storage bins with armrest covers incorporated into wheelwells. Eight passenger seating package: (SE) 3-passenger front bench seat; second seat (2-passenger bench); third seat (3-passenger bench); ash receiver in C-pillar; heavy-duty rear brakes; heavy-duty suspension; P195/75R14 SBR BSW tires; dual rear storage bins with armrest covers incorporated into wheelwells. Sport wheel package: 14 inch cast aluminum wheels; P195/75R14 SBR BSW tires with 2.2L engine; P205/70R14 SBR BLT with 2.6L engine.

CONVENIENCE OPTIONS: Air conditioning. Coverta-bed rear seating. Electric liftgate window defroster. 20-gallon fuel tank. Sunscreen glass. Roof mounted luggage rack. Dual remote control exterior mirrors. Vinyl bodyside molding. Power door locks. Power liftgate release. AM stereo/FM stereo radio. Premium AM stereo/FM stereo radio with cassette tape player. AM stereo/FM stereo with Ultimate Sound System. Electronic speed control. Tilt steering column. Conventional spare tire. Rear cargo compartment tonneau cover. Wire wheel covers (SE, LE). Sport wheel covers (SE, LE). Deluxe windshield wipers with intermittent wipe and wet arm washers.

NOTE: Voyager exterior colors for 1986 included: Light Cream, Black, Golden Bronze Pearl Coat, Dark Cordovan Pearl Coat, Gunmetal Blue Pearl Coat, Gold Dust, Garnet Red Pearl Coat (extra cost) Radiant Silver, White, Ice Blue. Two-Tone Colors were: Gold Dust / Golden Bronze Pearl Coat, Garant Red Pearl Coat / Black, Radiant Silver / Black, Light Cream / Golden Bronze Pearl Coat, Gunmetal Blue Pearl Coat / Black, Ice Blue / Gunmetal Blue Pearl Coat.

PONTIAC MOTOR DIVISION

By John A. Gunnell

Pontiac made light trucks, as well as commercial cars, for both the U.S. and Canadian markets. Less known is the fact that this General Motors company also manufactured GMC buses during World War II and amphibious vehicles during the Korean conflict. The larger vehicles are beyond the scope of our study.

Oakland Motor Car Co. introduced the first Pontiac as a companion make to its Oakland. When the economical little six proved popular, a half-ton Deluxe Delivery van was added. It came out in screen side or panel body models during the new marque's first year.

This 1926 truck was based on the passenger car, sharing its twin-head engine, conventional gear box and wheelbase. Assembly line photos show long rows of these rucks ready for factory shipment, although only two are known to survive today. More than 3,500 units were built.

1935 Pontiac Prototype Panel Delivery (JMS)

In 1928, the Pontiac truck became the GMC Model T-11, which looked identical, except for name badges. It was offered through 1929 and followed by the GMC T-15, which was still Pontiac-powered. Pontiac engines were also used in GMC trucks of the late 1930s and mid-1950s.

1939 Pontiac Prototype Sedan Delivery (PMD)

618

1939 Pontiac Prototype Sedan Delivery (PMD)

Pontiac-based commercial cars, in the form of ambulances and funeral vehicles, became more common in the mid-1930s, although some may have been built earlier. At least one 1930 Oakland combination ambulance and hearse survives in Ohio, so Pontiac conversions may have been built this early as well.

1951 Pontiac Sedan Delivery (PMD)

The company did not supply a special commercial chassis, a practice of some GM divisions, although small numbers of bare chassis were sold to after-market body builders. The Oakland name was dropped in 1931, with leftover cars becoming Pontiac V-8s, a one-year model for 1932. Gardner, of St. Louis, stretched at least one of these into a limousine-funeral car with Gardner name badges.

1951 Pontiac Sedan Delivery (Bill Morton)

1951 Pontiac Sedan Delivery (Jack M. Samples)

By 1935, A.J. Miller Co. and Flxible turned to the Pontiac chassis for hearse and ambulance conversions. From that point on, this became a sizable side-market for Pontiac and lasted into the 1970s.

From 1936-1938, the Pontiac six-cylinder engine was again put in GMC light-duty trucks. Also during these years, badge-engineered panel deliveries were made in Canada. These were promoted as "GMC" products, although the sheet metal, trim and name emblems were Pontiac's. The drive train and running gear came from Chevrolet, however.

1956 Pontiac-Southern Hearse Co. Hearse (EK)

John M. Sawruk, official historian for Pontiac, has turned up photos of a 1935 sedan delivery built completely to U.S. specifications. This prototype precedes another, of 1939 style, of which several photos exist. The '39 has Michigan manufacturer's license plates in the photos, suggesting it was an experimental model. A very important milestone of 1936 was the first line of commercial Pontacs by Superior Body Co., of Lima, Ohio.

Some experts believe that Pontiac trucks continued in the Canadian market in the late 1930s and throughout the 1940s. Historian Bob Lichty has reported seeing a sedan delivery of 1946-1948 style. These would, again, be part Chevrolet/GMC in character. In Australia, many 1941 Pontiac military trucks were produced by Holden. At least some of these were open-cab pickups or "Utes."

1957 Pontiac-Superior Funeral Coach (JAG)

Pontiac station wagons were usually considered part of the passenger car-line. Also available were purpose-built taxicabs, with a heavy-duty, commercial type chassis. Superior-Pontiac hearses and ambulances grew even more common.

During World War II, the Pontiac plant was used for bus construction. Plans for a tank with four straight eight engines were formulated, but it never appeared.

1963 Pontiac-Superior 'Embassy' Limousine (CP/JAG)

Probably the best known of Pontiac's true light-duty trucks are the sedan deliveries of 1949-1953. These were designed as one-step-up delivery vehicles for small businessmen, and, from 1950 on, had the fancy trim level of deluxe passenger cars. Power came from either a straight six or eight, with Hydra-Matic transmission optional, but common.

1964 Pontiac-Superior 8-dr. Airport Limo (D. Barlup)

Once thought to be extremely rare, more of these vehicles seem now to come out of hiding every year. Many are fresh restorations of trucks that led long useful lives before being put out to pasture. In show condition, they seem to generate strong prices in the collector's market.

Calendar year records suggest that under 9,000 Pontiac sedan deliveries were made in the five years. There's probably 400 surviving today. A few experts believe that a couple of 1954 sedan deliveries were produced before the model was dropped. So far, there's no documentation of this viewpoint. Such trucks were also made in Canada (with Chevrolet underpinnings) until about 1958.

1965 Pontiac-Superior Embassy Limousine (CP/JAG)

(Continued to page 629)

1926 PONTIAC

DELUXE SIX — SERIES 6-27 — SIX-CYLINDER: — The ½-ton Pontiac Six delivery car was introduced, in Oct. 1926, as the lowest priced six-cylinder commercial car on the U.S. market. The chassis was the regular passenger car unit with thicker rear springs and heavy-duty commercial balloon tires. Rated payload was 1,000 pounds. Up front, the driver's compartment was nearly identical to that of the Pontiac two-door sedan. Standard Fisher Body parts included seats, a Vision-and-Ventilating (V.V.) windshield, instrument board, cowl, door parts and other fittings. Seats were upholstered in leather-like Fabrikoid. Panel body construction was of the composite type, employing one-piece side panels. "Due to the use of steel braces, mortised joints and the special side panels, the body is unusually soundproof and vibration-free," reported the Oct. 14, 1926 issue of *Automotive Industries*. The body had Duco finish in Balsam blue with a contrasting wide belt of orange extending entirely around the panel body. Standard equipment included rear view mirror, cowl lights, radiator emblem, gasoline gauge, 12-gallon fuel tank, sun visors, plate glass windows with high-speed regulators and nickeled door handles. The roof was covered with a rubberized material supplied by DuPont. A drip molding extended around the entire roof, while lengthwise steel strips protected the hardwood flooring. The body was designed to be exceptionally low at the rear for easy access. Twin, tight-closing doors with rectangular windows were provided at the rear.

I.D. DATA: Serial number located on right side of rear frame crossmember or on frame under left front fender. Starting: 00001-26. Ending: 84261-26. Engine numbers located on left side of crankcase or near left front corner of cylinder block.

Model	Body Type	Price	Weight	Prod. Total
6-27	2-dr. Panel Delivery	770	2470	Note 1

NOTE 1: According to contemporary registration data, a total of 3,611 Pontiac delivery trucks were registered in the United States between 1926 and 1928. This is probably close to total production of this model.

ENGINE: Inline. L-head. Six-cylinder. (Twin head). Cast iron & block. Bore & stroke: 3¼ in. x 3¾ in. Displacement: 186.5 cu. in. Compression ratio: 4.8:1. Brake horsepower: 36 at 2400 R.P.M. Net horsepower: 25.35. Three main bearings. Solid valve lifters. Carburetor: Carter one-barrel.

CHASSIS (6-26): Wheelbase: 110 in. Overall length: 151.25 in. Height: 43 in. Front tread: 56 in. Rear tread: 56 in. Tires: 29 x 4.75 in.

TECHNICAL: Selective sliding transmission. Speeds: 3F/1R. Floor-mounted gearshift lever. Ventilated single disc dry clutch. Shaft drive. Semi-floating rear axle. Overall ratio: 4.18:1. Two-wheel mechanical brakes. Wood-spoke wheels.

OPTIONS: Front bumper. Rear bumper. Single sidemount. Bumper guards. Heater.

HISTORICAL: Introduced October 1926. Calendar year registrations: (Series three-year total) 3,611. Innovations: First Pontiac model year and first Pontiac truck. Lowest cost six-cylinder truck in America. Historical notes: Built as part of Oakland's new "companion car series." The truck's GVW rating was 3,470 pounds. The delivery car was promoted as a truck with the comfort of a passenger car.

Pricing

	5	4	3	2	1
1926					
Pontiac Delivery Car — (6-cyl.)					
Panel Dely.	2100	4200	7000	9000	14,000

1927 PONTIAC

DELUXE DELIVERY — SERIES 6-27 — SIX-CYLINDER: — As the 1926 Pontiac car-line was carried over into 1927 practically unchanged, the company's handsome-looking truck followed suit. The name of the model was changed from "delivery car" to "Deluxe Delivery" and a brand new screenside body type was introduced at the New York Auto Show in Jan. 1927. Instead of a panel body, it had heavy metal screening material on the sides and rear, a drop-down tailgate and rolled leather curtains to cover the screening. The panel truck continued to come with standard Balsam Blue Duco body, black running gear and a wide contrast belt finished in Burning Bush orange. An ad in *Saturday Evening Post*, in the spring of 1927 said, "Only 5 months old and now you see it everywhere" about the Pontiac truck. Indeed, factory photos indicate that a goodly number of the these-trucks were built, although they are rarities today. Standard equipment for 1927 models was as follows: Fisher V.V. one-piece

windshield with automatic cleaner, sun visor, cowl parking lights, individual sedan seats providing passenger car comfort, plate glass windows with high-speed regulators, nickled door handles, 12-gallon gas tank located in the rear for convenience in refueling, special heavy-duty springs and heavy-duty balloon tires. The trucks also had Delco-Remy ignition and rear-wheel mechanical brakes. The trucks featured semi-elliptic leaf springs measuring 29 x 1.75 in. in front and 54 x 1.75 in. at the rear. Tires were of extra-ply, non-skid design.

1927 Pontiac Series 6-27 Screenside Delivery

I.D. DATA: Serial number located on right side of rear frame crossmember or on frame under left front fender. Starting: 145000-27. Ending: 204000-27. Engine numbers located on left side of crankcase or near left front corner of block. Starting: P156250. Ending: P220000 (approximate).

Model	Body Type	Price	Weight	Prod. Total
6-27	2-dr. Panel Delivery	770	2470	Note 1
6-27	2-dr. Screen Delivery	760	2440	Note 1

NOTE 1: A total of 3,611 trucks were registered between 1926 and 1928.

ENGINE: Inline. L-head. Six-cylinder. (Twin head). Cast-iron block. Bore & stroke: 3¼ in. x 3¾ in. Displacement: 186.5 cu. in. Compression ratio: 4.8:1. Brake horsepower: 36 at 2400 R.P.M. Net horsepower: 25.35. Three main bearings. Solid valve lifters. Carburetor: Carter one-barrel.

CHASSIS (6-27): Wheelbase: 110 in. Overall length: 151.25 in. Height: 43 in. Front tread: 56 in. Rear tread: 56 in. Tires: 29 x 4.75 extra-ply.

TECHNICAL: Selective sliding transmission. Speeds: 3F/1R. Floor-mounted gearshift lever. Ventilated single disc dry clutch. Semi-floating rear axle. Overall ratio: 4.18:1. Two-wheel mechanical brakes. Wood-spoke wheels.

OPTIONS: Front bumper. Rear bumper. Single sidemount. Bumper guards. Heater.

HISTORICAL: Introduced Jan. 1927. Calendar year registrations: (three year total) 3,611. Innovations: New screen side delivery introduced. Historical notes: A.R. Glancey was president of Oakland Motor Car Co., which produced Pontiac cars and trucks.

Pricing

	5	4	3	2	1
1927					
Pontiac Deluxe Delivery — (6-cyl.)					
Panel Delivery	1950	3900	6500	9100	13,000
Screen Delivery	1700	3450	5750	8050	11,500

1928 PONTIAC

DELUXE DELIVERY — SERIES 6-27/6-28 — SIX-CYLINDER: — Judging by serial numbers, the Series 6-27 Pontiac truck (like the company's cars) continued into the early part of the 1928 model year. Here, the facts get a little confusing. A period "blue book" shows late-1928 ending serial numbers which would correspond to the new 6-28 series introduced in January 1928. However, no 6-28 series trucks are listed. In reality, cars of both series were quite similar, although 6-28s had four-wheel mechanical brakes; cross-flow radiators; higher-compression cylinder heads; higher, deeper, narrower, radiator shells; manifolding and carburetion improvements; lower body lines; new headlamps and smooth crown fenders with beaded edges. All specifications given in "blue books," except model designations, suggest that 6-28 Series trucks were actually built. If this is true, they were certainly very close in appearance and features to the 6-27 models, except for the changes noted above. Similarities would include the dimensions of the load compartment: 69 inches long, 46 inches high and 43 inches wide. Normal load height of the body was only 25½ inches from the ground. Cargo capacity was 77 cubic feet. Refer to 1926-1927 sections for standard equipment list, upholstery details and finish colors.

One thing for certain is that 1928 was the last year for the Pontiac Deluxe Delivery. In 1929, this vehicle became a GMC truck through the changing of the radiator shell and name badges. But GMC continued to use the Pontiac six-cylinder engine.

I.D. DATA: Serial number located on right side of rear frame crossmember or on frame under left front fender. Starting: 145000-27. Ending: 2040000-28. Engine numbers located on left side of crankcase.

Model	Body Type	Price	Weight	Prod. Total
6-28	Chassis ½-Ton	585	1820	Note 1
6-28	Panel Delivery	770	2455	Note 1
6-28	Canopy Delivery	760	2455	Note 1
6-28	Screen Delivery	760	2465	Note 1
6-28	Pickup	—	—	Note 1
6-28	Sedan Delivery	—	—	Note 1

NOTE 1: A total of 3,611 trucks were registered between 1926 and 1928.

NOTE 2: A pickup and sedan delivery were listed in the N.A.D.A. "blue book" of 1934. These models do not appear in factory literature and were probably listed by N.A.D.A. to cover contemporary pricing of trucks with aftermarket bodies.

1928 Pontiac U.S. Army Scout Car (S. Rawlings)

SCOUT CARS — SERIES 6-28 — SIX-CYLINDER: — Some years ago, Major Stan Rawlings, a Pontiac buff, discovered a series of rare photos taken by the U.S. Army Ordnance Dept. at the Aberdeen (Md.) Proving Grounds. The pictures, dating from 1932, showed several experimental military vehicles based on modified 1928 Series 6-28 Pontiacs. Among them were an armored Scout car and mobile field radio command unit. The Scout car had an armored radiator shell shroud with louvers in front to provide cooling. The windshield was replaced with ¼ inch thick boiler plate with a machine-gun mounted behind it. The body had been removed (or never added). In its place were two bench seats. The running board carried an ammunition canister and tires were floatation type. The radio unit was somewhat similarly modified, but carried communications gear and a map table, instead of weapons. According to Rawlings, the military vehicles were built on brand new 1928 chassis and were updated around 1932. An Indian head hood mascot was retained on both. It protruded right through the armored shroud. Since both of these units were quite heavy and Jeep-like, we felt their inclusion in this catalog was warranted as a side-light to 1928 Pontiac history. Specifications and factory prices for these models are not available.

ENGINE: Inline. L-head. Six-cylinder. Cast iron block. Bore & stroke: 3¼ in. x 3¾ in. Displacement: 186.5 cu. in. Compression ratio: 4.9:1. Brake horsepower: 36 at 2400 R.P.M. Net horsepower: 25.35. Three main bearings. Solid valve lifters. Carburetor: Carter one-barrel.

CHASSIS (6-28): Wheelbase: 110 in. Overall length: 151.25 in. Height: 43 in. Front tread: 56 in. Rear tread: 56 in. Tires: 29 x 4.75 extra-ply.

TECHNICAL: Selective sliding transmission. Speeds: 3F/1R. Floor-mounted gearshift lever. Ventilated single disc dry clutch. Semi-floating rear axle. Overall ratio: 4.18:1. Four-wheel mechanical brakes. Wood-spoke wheels.

1928 Pontiac U.S. Army Scout Car (S. Rawlings)

OPTIONS: Front bumper. Rear bumper. Bumper guards. Heater. Disc wheels.

HISTORICAL: Introduced Jan. 1928. Calendar year registrations: (three year total) 3,611. Innovations: New Oakland type muffler. Improved steering gear. New frame and front axle. New thermostat. New steering wheel. Dash-mounted gasoline gauge. Higher compression GMR cylinder head. Four-wheel brakes. Historical notes: Pontiac opened its new "Daylight Factory" in Pontiac, Mich. during 1928.

Pricing

1928	5	4	3	2	1
6-28 Delivery Car					
Panel Dely.	2100	4200	7000	9000	14,000
Canopy Dely.	1650	3300	5500	7700	11,000
Screen Dely.	1800	3600	6000	8400	12,000
Pickup	1550	3050	5100	7100	10,200
Sedan Dely.	2200	4350	7250	10,150	14,500

1932-1972 PONTIAC

1934 Pontiac Flxible Funeral Coach (CP/JAG)

AMBULANCE/FUNERAL CAR — VARIOUS SERIES — (ALL-ENGINES): — Another interesting side-light to Pontiac's truck-making experience was its ambulance and funeral car business. While some of these vehicles were primarily stretched sedans, many others were as truck-like as the 1926-1928 Deluxe Deliveries and 1949-1953 sedan deliveries.

1935 Pontiac Flxible Funeral Coach (CP/JAG)

1936 Pontiac-Superior Funeral Coach (CP)

The existence of one 1930 Oakland "combination car" (ambulance and hearse) owned by Wayne Weber, of Bryan, Ohio, indicates that Pontiac's parent firm built at least a few "professional vehicles." However, the first documented "Pontiac" funeral car is a 1935 model by Flxible, of Loudonville, Ohio.

1937 Pontiac-Superior 'Graceland' Hearse (CP/JAG)

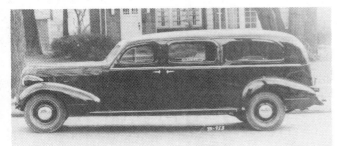

1937 Pontiac Miller Funeral Coach (CP/JAG)

Strangely, there was a 1932 funeral car of Pontiac origin. This was a large sedan made of Pontiac Series 302 V-8 parts, but assembled by Gardner Motor Car Co. of St. Louis and marketed with their name badge. (Historian Elliott Kahn, of Florida, believes that Gardner trucks of this period also used mostly Pontiac parts.)

1937 Pontiac-Superior 'Guardian' Ambulance (DFW/GC)

1937 Pontiac-Superior 'Guardian' Ambulance (CP/JAG)

1937 Pontiac-Superior Rosehill Funeral Coach (CP/JAG)

622

1938 Pontiac-Superior Funeral Coach (CP/JAG)

1940 Pontiac Funeral Coach (CP/JAG)

1941 Pontiac Torpedo Sedan-Taxicab (PMD)

1941 Pontiac-Superior Funeral Coach (CP/JAG)

1946 Pontiac-Superior Ambulance (CP/JAG)

By 1935, Pontiac was seriously involved in the professional car field and this involvement continued at least through the 1970s. Major professional car-makers like Flxible, A.J. Miller and Superior, built their products on new bare chassis and flat-face cowls supplied by Pontiac. These were delivered with assortments of GM and Fisher body and trim parts. The companies stretched the chassis, returned them to Pontiac for engineering approval and completed the bodies in their own factories. After World War II, smaller firms like Acme, Economy Coach and Guy Barnette & Co., made professional cars by modifying production type Pontiac station wagons and sedan deliveries.

1946 Pontiac-Superior Funeral Coach (CP/JAG)

1951 Pontiac-Barnette Funeral Coach (CP/JAG)

1951 Pontiac-Acme Funeral Coach (CP/JAG)

1953 Pontiac-Superior Ambulance (CP/JAG)

1953 Pontiac-Superior Funeral Van (CP/JAG)

1953 Pontiac-Superior Funeral Coach (CP/JAG)

1953 Pontiac-Superior Funeral Coach (CP/JAG)

1954 Pontiac-Superior Funeral Coach (CP/JAG)

1954 Pontiac-Superior Funeral Coach (CP/JAG)

1958 Pontiac-Superior Funeral Coach (CP/JAG)

1963 Pontiac-Superior Combination Car (Joe Stout)

By the late 1950s, Pontiac joined the Amblewagon Automotive Conversion Corp., of Troy, Mich., in promoting two models called the "Ambulette" and "Amblewagon." These were produced on the standard Safari station wagon chassis and intended for use as rescue squad wagons, fire chief cars, police patrol vehicles or industrial ambulances.

1966 Pontiac-Superior High Headroom Ambulance (OCW)

1966 Pontiac-Superior Funeral Coach (CP/JAG)

1967 Pontiac-Superior Funeral Coach (CP/JAG)

1970 Pontiac-Superior Funeral Coach (CP/JAG)

1970 Pontiac-Superior 'Consort' Funeral Coach

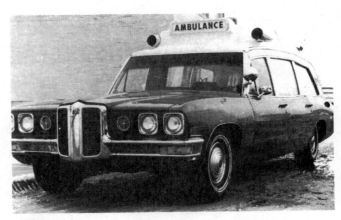

1970 Pontiac-Superior Ambulance (CP/JAG)

1972 Pontiac-Superior Funeral Coach (CP/JAG)

Although it would be beyond the scope of this catalog to cover Pontiac's professional vehicles on a year-by-year basis, the editors felt it would be interesting to show some of the truck-like models of ambulances and funeral cars produced over the years.

1937-1938 PONTIAC

1938 Pontiac-GMC (Canadian) Sedan Delivery (RJ)

GENERAL MOTORS (CANADIAN PONTIAC) TRUCK — SPECIAL SIX SERIES — SIX-CYLINDER: — During the mid-to late-1930s, the light delivery model made under the GMC name by General Motors Products of Canada, was based on that country's Special Six Pontiac car chassis. Built in Oshawa, Ontario, Canada, this truck even had the Pontiac name on the side of its hood. Like other Canadian Pontiacs, it used the same frame and engine as U.S.-built Chevrolets, but the sheet metal and trim were of Pontiac style although the bodies were "Chevrolet" bodies (that is to say that they matched the U.S. domestic Chevy in size and shape). Since these trucks had Indian head ornaments and Pontiac nameplates, we felt it would be interesting to show and discuss them here. The body was of Unisteel construction with floor, cowl, side-panels and roof welded together to form an all-steel body. They had a single, roadside-hinged rear door sealed with sponge rubber and fitted with a lock. Load capacity was 77 cubic feet. A spare wheel was carried below the cargo floor. Standard equipment included Fisher No-Draft ventilation system; Moleskin fabrikoid upholstery; Safety-Shift gear control; AC oil bath air cleaner; automatic choke; Synchromesh transmission; "V" windshield with wiper at bottom; screened cowl ventilator; safety glass throughout; adjustable driver's seat; rearview mirror; safety-tread runningboards; twin-beam headlamps; dome light; hydraulic shock absorbers; ignition lock; package compartment and dashboard provisions for clock, cigar lighter, defroster and radio installaion, plus bumpers and a tool kit.

I.D. DATA: Serial number data not available. Engine number data not available.

Model	Body Type	Price	Weight	Prod. Total
SS	Sedan Delivery (Canada)	650	2970	—

ENGINE: Inline. Overhead valve. Six-cylinder. Cast iron block. Bore & stroke: 3½ in. x 3¾ in. Displacement: 216.5 cu. in. Compression ratio: 6.25:1. Brake horsepower: 85 at 3200 R.P.M. Net horsepower: 29.4. Four main bearings. Solid valve lifters. Carburetor: Carter 1V model W1.

NOTE: Chevrolet-built engine.

CHASSIS (Special Six Series): Wheelbase: 112¼ in. Body length: 66 in. Body width: 54 in. Body height: 41⅛ in. Tires: 6.00 x 16 in.

TECHNICAL: Manual, Synchromesh transmission. Speeds: 3F/1R. Column-mounted gearshift lever. Clutch: Diaphram spring type having cushion mounted disc with braided molded faces. Semi-floating rear axle. Overall gear ratio: 4.22:1. Four-wheel hydraulic brakes. Short-spoke steel disc wheels.

OPTIONS: Front bumper. Rear bumper. Whitewall tires. Right-hand taillight. Fender skirts. Bumper guards. Radio. Heater. Clock. Cigar lighter. Radio antenna. Seat covers. Spotlight. Wheel trim rings. Two-tone finish.

HISTORICAL: Introduced Jan. 1938.
Canadian Pontiac sedan deliveries are believed to have been produced for many years, although no such model was marketed in the United States. Production continued at least through the late-1950s or early 1960s; possibly longer.

Pricing

1937-1939 GMC (Canada) — Pontiac Special Six	5	4	3	2	1
Sedan Delivery	1500	3000	5000	7000	11,000

1949 PONTIAC

1949 Pontiac Sedan Delivery (JMS/PMD)

STREAMLINER — SERIES 25/27 — SIX-CYLINDER/EIGHT-CYLINDER: — Pontiac re-entered the light-truck field, in 1949, with a handsome sedan delivery. It was the first true Pontiac truck produced in the United States since the late 1920s. Although much similar to a station wagon in size and shape, it was a two-door vehicle with a curb-side opening third door (with fixed window) at the rear. Pontiac trimmed it as a "standard" model having black rubber gravel shields and painted headlamp surrounds. It was also cataloged as part of the standard series. However, publicity type photographs of a more deluxe version with bright metal trim and side spears do exist. (This was probably a prototype.) Features of 1949 Pontiacs included wider seats, a horizontal curved windshield, new sealed airplane-type shock absorbers and low-pressure tires. The trucks came with a choice of two flathead engines, a 90 horsepower inline six and 104 horsepower inline eight. The sedan delivery had a 9½ inch step-up in the floor level behind the twin, bucket type seats. The cargo area was 85¾ inches long and the roof was 64¼ inches high. Color choices included all offered for other 1949 Pontiacs, except Blue Lake blue or Coventry gray. The 1949 grille consisted of a full-width center horizontal "wing" with an ornament in a housing at the center. There were short horizonal "teeth" below the bar, but none above it. Rectangular parking lights were mounted at either end, below the single headlamps. "Silver Streak" moldings and an Indian head mascot finished the motif. Upholstery was brown imitation leather.

I.D. DATA: Serial number located on left-hand door pillar. Starting: (Six) P-6R-1001 and up; (Eight) P-8R-1001 and up. Engine numbers located on left side of cylinder block. The engine number is the VIN and should match the number on the door pillar. Starting: (Six) P-6R-1001 and up; (Eight) P-8R-1001 and up.

Model	Body Type	Price	Weight	Prod. Total
Streamliner Series — (6-cyl.)				
6R	Sedan Delivery	1749	3230	Note 1
Streamliner Series — (8-cyl.)				
8R	Sedan Delivery	1817	3295	Note 1

NOTE 1: Calendar year production totaled 2,488 units.

ENGINE: Inline. L-head. Six-cylinder. Cast iron block. Bore & stroke: 3-9/16 in. x 4 in. Displacement: 239.2 cu. in. Compression ratio: (std.) 6.5:1. Brake horsepower: 90 at 3400 R.P.M. Net horsepower: 30.4. Four main bearings. Solid valve lifters. Carburetor: Carter 1V model WAL-537S.

NOTE: Optional 7.5:1 high-compression head used with Hydra-Matic transmission. Hydra-Matic equipped trucks had 93 horsepower at 3400 R.P.M.

ENGINE: Inline. L-head. Eight-cylinder. Cast iron block. Bore & stroke: 4¼ in. x 4¾ in. Displacement: 248.9 cu. in. Compression ratio: (std.) 6.5:1. Brake horsepower: 103 at 3800 R.P.M. Net horsepower: 33.8. Five main bearings. Solid valve lifters. Carburetor: Carter 2V model WCD.

NOTE: Optional 7.5:1 head used with Hydra-Matic transmission. Hydra-Matic equipped trucks had 106 horsepower at 3800 R.P.M.

CHASSIS (Streamliner Series): Wheelbase: 120 in. Overall length: 203.8 in. Height: 64¼ in. Front tread: 58 in. Rear tread: 59 in. Tires: 7.60 x 15 in.

TECHNICAL: Synchromesh transmission. Speeds: 3F/1R. Column-mounted gearshift lever. Single plate dry disc clutch. Semi-floating rear axle. Overall ratio: 4.1:1. Four-wheel hydraulic brakes. Steel disc wheels. Automatic transmission (optional Hydra-Matic Drive).

OPTIONS: Mast antenna. Seven-tube Chieftain radio. No-Blow wind deflectors. Venti-Seat underseat heater. Windshield sunvisor. Traffic light viewer. License frames. Light-up hood ornament. Full wheel discs. Wheel trim rings. White sidewall discs. Deluxe steering wheel. Visor vanity mirror. Directional signals. Compass. Windshield washers. Deluxe electric clock. Glove compartment light. Seat covers. Safti-Jack. OSRV mirror. Back-up lights. Spotlight. Foglights. Bumper guards. Master grille guard. Exhaust deflector. No-Mar gas filler door trim. Underhood trouble lamp. Jack bag. Tool kit.

HISTORICAL: Introduced Jan. 1949. Calendar year production: 2,488. Innovations: First U.S. built Pontiac truck since 1928. New dial cluster dash. New broad rims. New airplane-type shock absorbers. Historical notes: Pontiac sold 21.2 percent of all cars in its price range, but held only .20 percent of the light-duty truck market.

Pricing

1949	5	4	3	2	1
Streamliner Series 6					
Sedan Delivery	1650	3300	5500	7700	11,000
Streamliner Series 8					
Sedan Delivery	1700	3450	5750	8050	11,500

1950 PONTIAC

1950 Pontiac Sedan Delivery (JAG)

STREAMLINER — SERIES 25/27 — SIX-CYLINDER/EIGHT-CYLINDER:
— A sedan delivery truck was again part of Pontiac's Streamliner Six (Series 25) and Streamliner Eight (Series 27) product offerings. The 1950 models were upgraded with additional bright metal trim parts including three-quarter length bodyside moldings, rocker panel moldings, rear gravel shields and headlight rims. New for the year was a radiator grille with five "teeth" spaced across a massive horizontal bar. In the center of this arrangement was a circular red plastic disc bearing an Indian brave's image. Corner bar extensions and parking lamps now curved around the front fenders. The hood ornament was an outward thrusting brave's head in chrome. An illuminated macot was an accessory for the second year in a row. A nameplate below the hood Silver Streaks bore the Pontiac name. A "Silver Streak" script decorated the front fendersides, above the mid-bodyside molding. On eight-cylinder trucks, a number "8" separated the two words. Sedan deliveries were offered in 11 solid colors and five two-tone combinations. Interior trim was now in tan, instead of brown, imitation leather. The 1950 models were slightly heavier and modestly shorter than '49s. Inside panels were brown masonite, painted light gray. A tan imitation leather headliner was fitted. Rubber mats were used on the driving compartment floor and the rear cargo area was covered with linoleum. Standard equipment included a finger-tip starter, low pressure-tires, Tru-Arc steering system, Duflex rear springs, triple-sealed brakes and built-in lifetime oil filter.

1950 Pontiac Sedan Delivery (POCI)

NOTE: Optional 7.5:1 cylinder head with Hydra-Matic gives 113 horsepower at 3600 R.P.M. and 214 lbs.-ft. torque at 2000 R.P.M.

CHASSIS (Streamliner Series): Wheelbase: 120 in. Overall length: 202⅞ in. Height: 62.5 in. Front tread: 58 in. Rear tread: 59 in. Tires: 7.10 x 15 six-ply. (7.60 x 15 four-ply no-cost option)

TECHNICAL: Synchromesh transmission. Speeds: 3F/1R. Column-mounted gearshift lever. Single plate dry disc clutch. Semi-floating rear axle. Overall ratio: 4.1:1. Four-wheel hydraulic brakes. Steel disc wheels. Automatic transmission (Opt.) Hydra-Matic Drive.

OPTIONS: Same as 1949.

HISTORICAL: Introduced Nov. 10, 1949. Calendar year production: 2,158. Innovations:Larger displacement, more powerful straight eight. New model Carter carburetor on eight. Combination fuel pump/vacuum pump added to sixes. New dashboard type heater and carbon core ignition cables. Deluxe trim used on sedan delivery, although it was not part of Pontiac's Deluxe series. Historical notes: Most 1950 Pontiacs were eights and more than half had Hydra-Matic drive. Rio red was a color choice limited to sedan deliveries, station wagons and convertibles.

1950 Pontiac Sedan Delivery (Jack Hughes)

I.D. DATA: Serial number located on left-hand front door pillar; also on lip on front of cylinder block at left side. Starting: (Six) P-6T-1001 and up; (Eight) P-8T-1001 and up. Engine numbers located on lip on front of cylinder block at left side. Engine stamping and door pillar stamping should match.

Model	Body Type	Price	Weight	Prod. Total
Streamliner Series 6				
2571	Sedan Delivery	1733	3309	Note 1
Streamliner Series 8				
2571	Sedan Delivery	1801	3379	Note 1

NOTE 1: A total of 2,158 sedan deliveries were built in calendar year 1950.

ENGINE: Inline. L-head. Six-cylinder. Cast iron block. Bore & stroke: 3-9/16 in. x 4 in. Displacement: 239.2 cu. in. Compression ratio: (std.) 6.5:1. Brake horsepower: 90 at 3400 R.P.M. Net horsepower: 30.4. Torque: 178 lbs.-ft. at 1200 R.P.M. Four main bearings. Solid valve lifters. Carburetor: Carter 1V model WA1-717-S.

NOTE: Optional 7.5:1 cylinder head with Hydra-Matic gives 93 horsepower at 3400 R.P.M. and 183 lbs.-ft. torque at 1200 R.P.M.

ENGINE: Inline. L-head. Eight-cylinder. Cast iron block. Bore & stroke: 3⅜ in. x 3¾ in. Displacement: 268.2 cu. in. Compression ratio: (standard) 6.5:1. Brake horsepower: 108 at 3600 R.P.M. Net horsepower: 36.4. Torque: 208 lbs.-ft. at 1800 R.P.M. Five main bearings. Solid valve lifters. Carburetor: Carter 2V model WCD-719-S.

Pricing

	5	4	3	2	1
1950					
Streamliner Series 6					
Sedan Delivery	1650	3350	5600	7800	11,200
Streamliner Series 8					
Sedan Delivery	1750	3500	5850	8200	11,700

1951 PONTIAC

1950 Pontiac Sedan Delivery (Jack Hughes)

1951 Pontiac Sedan Delivery (Jack M. Samples)

1951 Pontiac Sedan Delivery (Jack M. Samples)

STREAMLINER — SERIES 25/27 — SIX-CYLINDER/EIGHT-CYLINDER:
— New "Silver Anniversary" trim commemorated the Pontiac nameplate's 25th year in 1951. In honor of the occasion the red plastic circular disc in the center of the grille had a gold Indian head and gold band (the same part with silver trim was used other years.) Also changed was the grille ensemble, consisting of two wing-shaped stampings stretching out from a short centerpiece that housed the Indian medallion. There was also a full-width lower bar with two (on each side) shorter vertical bars between it and the "wings." A sure way to identify 1951 models is by the "feather-shaped" tips added to the front of the bodyside moldings. Three stars were embossed on these tips. At the rear, the sedan delivery had a curb-side opening door decorated with a "Pontiac" script above a short Silver Streak molding. Circular taillights were mounted in slightly protruding housings at each rear body corner, inboard of the fenders. There were also Silver Streaks on the hood. The trucks came in any of 12 solid colors or four two-tone combinations. Two-tone choices were Berkshire green over Palmetto green; Saturn gold over Lido beige; Imperial maroon over Sand gray or Palmetto green over Berkshire green. Upholstery was again tan imitation leather. The trucks came with an adjustable driver's seat and folding passenger seat. Bright metal trim was again used on the bodysides, rocker panels, headlights and gravel shields, although the trucks were not listed with other Deluxe models. A solid chrome Indian hood mascot was standard, with the light-up version optional.

1951 Pontiac Sedan Delivery (Bill Morton)

I.D. DATA: Serial number located on left-hand front door pillar. Starting: P-6T-1001 and up. Engine numbers located on lip on front of cylinder block at left side. Engine stamping and door pillar stamping should match.

Model	Body Type	Price	Weight	Prod. Total
Streamliner Series 6				
2571	Sedan Delivery	1811	3403	Note 1
Streamliner Series 8				
2571	Sedan Delivery	1879	3508	Note 1

NOTE 1: Calendar year production was 1,822 units.

ENGINE: Inline. L-head. Six-cylinder. Cast iron block. Bore & stroke: 3-9/16 in. x 4 in. Displacement: 239.2 cu. in. Compression ratio: (standard) 6.5:1. Brake horsepower: 96 at 3400 R.P.M. Net horsepower: 30.4. Torque: 191 lbs.-ft. at 1200 R.P.M. Four main bearings. Solid valve lifters. Carburetor: Rochester 1V model BC.

NOTE: Optional 7.5:1 cylinder head with Hydra-Matic gave 100 horsepower at 3400 R.P.M. and 195 lbs.-ft. torque at 1200 R.P.M.

ENGINE: Inline. L-head. Eight-cylinder. Cast iron block. Bore & stroke: 3⅜ in. x 3¾ in. Displacement: 268.4 cu. in. Compression ratio: (std.) 6.5:1. Brake horsepower: 116 at 3600 R.P.M. Net horsepower: 36.4. Torque: 220 lbs.-ft. at 2000 R.P.M. Five main bearings. Solid valve lifters. Carburetor: Carter 2V model WCD-720S or WCD-720SA.

NOTE: Optional 7.5:1 compression cylinder head with Hydra-Matic gives 120 horsepower at 3600 R.P.M. and 225 lbs.-ft. torque at 2000 R.P.M.

1951 Pontiac Sedan Delivery (PMD)

CHASSIS (Streamliner Series): Overall length: 202.2 in. Height: 63.4 in. Front tread: 58 in. Rear tread: 59 in. Tires: 7.10 x 15 six-ply. (7.60 x 15 four-ply no-cost option)

TECHNICAL: Synchromesh transmission. Speeds: 3F/1R. Column-mounted gearshift lever. Single plate dry disc clutch. Semi-floating rear axle. Overall ratio: 3.6:1; 3.9:1; 4.1:1. Four-wheel hydraulic brakes. Steel disc wheels. Automatic transmission (Optional) Hydra-Matic Drive ($165).

OPTIONS: Same as 1949.

HISTORICAL: Introduced Dec. 11, 1950. Calendar year production: 1,822. Innovations: Stainless steel trim introduced. Increased engine horsepower. New carburetor models. Improved Hydra-Matic with "quick reverse" feature. New 7-pound radiator cap. Six-inch longer rearsprings. Low-gravity type 6-volt battery. Historical notes: Due to Korean War start-up, the National Production Agency put a .20 percent (market share) cap on Pontiac's truck production. Arnold Lenz replaced Harry J. Klinger as Pontiac general manager this year. PMD began production of the "Otter" — a continuous-track military amphibious vehicle — after opening a new plant on April 30, 1951.

Pricing

1951	5	4	3	2	1
Streamliner Series 6					
Sedan Delivery	1700	3450	5750	8050	11,500
Streamliner Series 8					
Sedan Delivery	1800	3600	6000	8400	12,000

1952 PONTIAC

1952 Pontiac (Canadian) Sedan Delivery (OCW)

CHIEFTAIN — SERIES 25/27 — SIX-CYLINDER/EIGHT-CYLINDER: — Characteristics of 1952 Pontiacs included a new front end ensemble. Between the nameplate and the grille molding was a four-vertical sectioned grille. Model designations were eliminated from the bodysides, as were the trim plates extending outboard of the parking lamps. The side moldings had a small, parallel strip on top extending into the front door. Since the Pontiac Streamliner model name was eliminated this year, the Sedan Delivery truck became a Chieftain. It came in both the Chieftain Six (Series 25) and Chieftain Eight (Series 27) product lines. The truck again had Deluxe type trim, but a "standard" model number and small "bottle cap" hub caps. Upholstery was now dark gray imitation leather. As in the

627

past, certain colors (Cherokee red and four two-tone choices) were pretty much exclusive to trucks and station wagons, although the convertible could also be had in the red.

I.D. DATA: Serial number data same as 1949 to 1951. Truck starting numbers were: (6-cyl.) P-6W-1001 and up and (8-cyl.) P-8W-1001 up. "W" code indicated Wilmington, Del. factory, suggesting all trucks were sourced from that plant.

Model	Body Type	Price	Weight	Prod. Total
Chieftain Six				
2571	Sedan Delivery	1850	3308	Note 1
Chieftain Eight				
2571	Sedan Delivery	1920	3413	Note 1

NOTE 1: Calendar year production was 984 units.

ENGINE: Inline. L-head. Six-cylinder. Cast iron block. Bore & stroke: 3-9/16 in. x 4 in. Displacement: 239.2 cu. in. Compression ratio: (std.) 6.8:1. Brake horsepower: 100 at 3400 R.P.M. Net horsepower: 30.4. Torque: 189 lbs.-ft. at 1400 R.P.M. Four main bearings. Solid valve lifters. Carburetor: Rochester 1V model BC.

NOTE: Optional 7.7:1 cylinder head with Hydra-Matic gave 102 horsepower at 3400 R.P.M. and 194 lbs.-ft. torque at 1400 R.P.M.

1952 Pontiac (Canadian) Sedan Delivery (OCW)

ENGINE: Inline. L-head. Eight-cylinder. Cast iron block. Bore & stroke: 3⅜ in. x 3¾ in. Displacement: 268.4 cu. in. Compression ratio: (standard) 6.8:1. Brake horsepower: 118 at 3600 R.P.M. Net horsepower: 36.4. Torque: 222 lbs.-ft. at 2200 R.P.M. Five main bearings. Solid valve lifters. Carburetor: Carter 2V model WCD-720S or WCD-720SA.

NOTE: Optional 7.7:1 cylinder head with Hydra-Matic gave 122 horsepower at 3600 R.P.M. and 227 lbs.-ft. torque at 2200 R.P.M.

CHASSIS (Chieftain Series): Wheelbase: 120 in. Overall length: 202.5 in. Height: 63.1 in. Front tread: 58 in. Rear tread: 59 in. Tires: 7.10 x 15 six-ply. (7.60 x 15 four-ply no-cost option)

TECHNICAL: Synchromesh transmission. Speeds: 3F/1R. Column-mounted gearshift lever. Single plate dry disc clutch. Semi-floating rear axle. Overall ratio: (with Hydra-Matic) 3.63; (with Synchromesh) 4.1:1. Four-wheel hydraulic brakes. Steel disc wheels. Automatic transmission Dual-range Hydra-Matic ($178).

OPTIONS: Same as 1949.

HISTORICAL: Introduced: Nov. 2, 1951. Calendar year production: 984. Innovations: Dual-Range Hydra-Matic Drive. Higher compression cylinder heads. New standard rear axle ratios. Lock ring type pistons. Nylon plastic speedometer gears. Redesigned U-joints. New type brake linings. Fuse and wiring revisions. Extruded generator housing. New Delco 44-5 spark plugs. Recalibrated distributor curve. Historial note: The Office of Price Stability (OPS) was a government agency charged with protecting the economy during the Korean Conflict. The OPS placed a cap of .18 percent on light-truck production by Pontiac. As a result, the company was limited to that share of the overall market in light-duty models. This made the 1952 Pontiac sedan delivery rarer than others. General manager Arnold Lenz was killed in a car-train crash. Robert M. Critchfield was appointed to fill the position.

628

	5	4	3	2	1
1952					
Chieftain Series 6					
Sedan Delivery	1650	3350	5600	7800	11,200
Chieftain Series 8					
Sedan Delivery	1750	3500	5850	8200	11,700

1953 PONTIAC

1953 Pontiac Sedan Delivery (Dick Choler)

CHIEFTAIN — SERIES 25/26 — SIX-CYLINDER/EIGHT-CYLINDER: — New "dual streak" trimmings, all-new body styling, a one-piece curved windshield, twin-feather Indian hood ornament, more massive chrome headlight doors and new front grille (which encircled the parking lights) were characteristics of 1953 Pontiacs. Dual-streak styling referred to arranging the hood Silver Streaks in two thinner bands separated by a wide, body- color panel. While cars had "step-up" design rear fenders, the Sedan Delivery (and station wagon) had fenders extending to the rear in an uninterrupted sweep. Special taillamp assemblies with oval bezels and round lenses were housed in the fenders. The trucks did not have round Indian head medallions on the rear fenders. Also, the bumper guard arrangement on trucks and wagons was unique and similar to that used in 1952. There was no built-in crossbar guard; the license lamp was attached to the rear bumper apron. The license plate was held by a bracket at the center of the panel below the rear door. As previous, the Sedan Delivery — although produced as a "Special" (standard) model — carried Deluxe body moldings and chrome gravel guards (without rear panel extensions). The interior was (Trim Code 83) beige and black imitation leather. A new two-tone Special model steering wheel with finger indentations on the spokes was used in trucks. Inside were an adjustable driver's seat and separate hinged passenger seat, tough ribbed snythetic rubber floor mat, dual sun visors and coated fabric material headliner in lighter beige. The rear compartment had black linoleum floor coverings. Walls were covered with painted masonite panel board, while wheel housings, rear corner panels and the inside of the rear door were painted to match the interior. The trucks' GVW rating, including driver, was 2,320 pounds. It had a 16-gallon gas tank.

I.D. DATA: Serial number located on left-hand door pillar. Starting: (6-cyl.) P-6X-1001; (8-cyl.) P-8X-1001. Engine numbers located on lip on left side of cylinder block. Block stamping and door pillar stamping should match.

Model	Body Type	Price	Weight	Prod. Total
Chieftain Series 6				
2517	Sedan Delivery	1850	3406	Note 1
Chieftain Series 8				
2517	2-dr. Sedan Delivery	1920	3481	Note 1

NOTE 1: Calendar year production was 1,324 units.

ENGINE: Inline. L-head. Six-cylinder. Cast iron block. Bore & stroke: 3-9/16 in. x 4 in. Displacement: 239.2 cu. in. Compression ratio: (std.) 7.0:1. Brake horsepower: 115 at 3800 R.P.M. Net horsepower: 30.4. Torque: 193 lbs.-ft. at 2000 R.P.M. Four main bearings. Solid valve lifters. Carburetor: Carter 2V model WCD-2010-S.

NOTE: Optional 7.7:1 high-compression cylinder head with Hydra-Matic Drive gave 118 horsepower at 3800 R.P.M. and 197 lbs.-ft. of torque at 2000 R.P.M.

ENGINE: Inline. L-head. Eight-cylinder. Cast iron block. Bore & stroke: 3⅜ in. x 3¾ in. Displacement: 268.4 cu. in. Compression ratio: (standard) 6.8:1. Brake horsepower: 118 at 3600 R.P.M. Net horsepower: 36.4. Torque: 222 lbs.-ft. at 2200 R.P.M. Five main bearings. Solid valve lifters. Carburetor: Carter WCD 2V model 719-SA.

1953 Pontiac Sedan Delivery (OCW)

NOTE: Optional 7.7:1 compression cylinder head with Hydra-Matic Drive gave 122 horsepower at 3600 R.P.M. and 227 lbs.-ft. torque at 2200 R.P.M.

CHASSIS (Chieftain Special Series): Wheelbase: 122 in. Overall length: 202.6 in. Height: 65.2 in. Front tread: 58 in. Rear tread: 59.05 in. Tires: 7.10 x 15 six-ply. (front) 28 p.s.i.; (rear) 30 p.s.i. (Special equipment) 7.60 x 15. Other measurements: Overall length with rear door open (229.9 in.); Step-up in floor level back of driver's seat (7.3 in.); Driver's seat to rear door (76 in.); Dash to rear door (135.6 in.); Average height floor to ceiling (41.8 in.); Inside width above wheelhousings (46.5 in.); Top of wheel housings above floor (12 in.).

TECHNICAL: Synchromesh transmission. Speeds: 3F/1R. Column-mounted gearshift lever. Single plate dry disc clutch. Semi-floating rear axle. Overall ratio: (6-cyl./Synchromesh) 4.1:1; (8-cyl./Synchromesh) 3.9:1; (All Hydra-Matic) 3.08:1. Four-wheel mechanical brakes. Steel disc wheels. Automatic transmission Dual-Range Hydra-Matic Drive ($178).

OPTIONS: Power steering ($134). Venti-seat underseat heater/defroster. Chieftain 7-tube radio. Directional signals. Autronic-Eye. Back-up lamps. Non-glare rear view mirror. Rear fender panels (skirts). Exhaust deflector. No-Mar fuel guard door. Deluxe steering wheel. Illuminated hood ornament. Windshield sun visor. Traffic light viewer. Latex foam seat cushions. Windshield washers. OSRV mirror(s). Visor vanity mirror. Glovebox lamp. Underhood lamp. Lighted ash tray. Hand-brake-on signal lamp. Master grille guard. Wing guards. E-Z-Eye glass. Dual fog lamps. Rear speaker. Electric antenna. Safety spot lamp. Chrome trim rings. Safti-jack. Oil bath air cleaner.

DEALER-INSTALLED OPTIONS: Seat covers. Hand spot lamp. Venti-shades. Draft deflectors. Tissue dispenser. Magna tray. Fuel door lock. Simulated wire wheel discs. Illuminated car compass.

HISTORICAL: Introduced Dec. 6, 1952. Calendar year production: 1,324. Innovations: New styling. Longer wheelbase. One-piece windshield. New Uni-steel body. Higher horsepower ratings. Two-barrel carburetor with six. Revised intake manifold. Dip stick relocated. Some Pontiacs made with Chevrolet Powerglide transmissions following Hydra-Matic factory fire. Historical notes: This was the last ''official'' year for Sedan Deliveries, although some truck collectors believe that a 1954 model was planned and, perhaps, built in very small numbers. Pontiac sedan deliveries were built in Canada, at least through 1958. Production of Canadian light-duty trucks totaled 1,407 in 1954; 1,022 in 1955; 1,385 in 1956; 682 in 1957 and 449 in 1958.

Pricing

1953	5	4	3	2	1
Chieftain Series 6					
Sedan Delivery	1900	3850	6400	8900	12,800
Chieftain Series 8					
Sedan Delivery	2050	4050	6750	9450	13,500

(Continued from page 619)

By the mid-1950s, Pontiac had a Special Vehicles Department that was in charge of overseeing production of funeral cars, ambulances and rail-maintenance models. This branch was geared to work chiefly with Superior on factory-approved conversion work. Standard chassis, with flat-face cowls, were shipped to Superior's Mississippi plant to be extended, then re-shipped to Superior's factory for construction of bodies in special jigs, using loose parts supplied by Pontiac and Fisher Body Division.

Firms such as National Body Co., Economy Coach Co., Guy Barnett & Co., Acme and Meteor also made commercial cars on standard or extended chassis Pontiacs, but Superior dominated the field.

Around 1959, Pontiac attempted to impact the emergency vehicle market with its ''Amblewagon,'' a more or less factory-blessed conversion of Amblewagon Automotive Conversion Corp. of Troy, Mich. These were standard-sized wagons with lights, sirens and other rescue vehicle equipment. In the same year, a prototype coupe-pickup — similar to Chevrolet's El Camino — was built on a Catalina chassis. This rare truck still survives today.

Superior was behind the production of Pontiac-based limousines and eight-door airport limos in the 1960s. The stretched sedans — labeled the ''Embassy'' models — had a heavy-duty chassis and were somewhat upgraded to commercial type specifications.

1986 Pontiac Prototype Trans Sport Van (JMS)

In Canada, a panel delivery version of the Pontiac Astre (a badge-engineered Chevy Vega) was available. It was little more than an Astre Safari wagon with sheet metal panels instead of rear sideglass. This did not make the U.S. market when Astres bowed here in 1975.

Other prototype Pontiac trucks have been made in the 1970s and 1980s. They include an El Camino type Grand Am conversion and the futuristic Trans Sport, which made the show circuit in 1986.

1979 LeMans Sport Pickup Truck Prototype (JMS)

STUDEBAKER

By Fred K. Fox

Long before the advent of motorized light-duty trucks, Studebaker was manufacturing horse-drawn commercial vehicles in South Bend, Ind. The H&C Studebaker blacksmith shop was opened in February, 1852. During their first year of business, Henry and Clem Studebaker constructed two wagons which they sold to local farmers. The carrying capacity of these wagons, by today's standards, would classify them as light-duty vehicles, but, of course, the term "light-duty truck" was unknown in 1852.

1914 Studebaker Panel Body Delivery (OCW)

The small blacksmith shop grew quickly from its humble beginnings, and by the time of our country's Centennial in 1876, Studebaker was the largest producer of horse-drawn vehicles in the world. Studebaker experimented with some automobile designs in the late 1890s, and in 1902 they introduced their first car, an electric. In 1904 they brought out a gasoline powered automobile that featured a chassis built by Garford.

1915 Studebaker Model "S" Light Delivery (OCW)

A very limited number of Studebaker Electrics and Garford powered Studebaker gasoline vehicles were sold as commercial units. One of the more interesting models from this period was the Suburban, which was introduced in 1908. The Studebaker Suburban was an open passenger car that could be easily converted to a baggage car by simply removing the rear seat. Studebaker called it "The Adaptable Car."

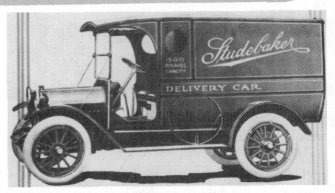

1915 Studebaker Delivery Car - Panel Side Body (ASC)

In late 1908, Studebaker became the sales agent for the new E.M.F. 30 automobile. In 1911, the Studebaker Brothers Manufacturing Company and the E.M.F. Company merged and formed the Studebaker Corporation.

1915 Studebaker Delivery Car - Express Body (ASC)

From late 1911 to early 1913, the new corporation produced a limited number of Flanders 20 half-ton panel deliveries. Selling for $800, the fragile 102 inch wheelbase Flanders deliveries were powered by a 154.8 cubic inch (3⅝ inch bore x 3¾ inch stroke) L-head four-cylinder engine that produced 20 horsepower.

1916 Studebaker 1000lb. Commercial Car - Model SF

Studebaker factories in Detroit used custom built EMF-30 and Flanders-20 pick-ups to transport small parts around the plant. These roadster pick-ups were actually called "pickups" (with no hyphen) in 1913 company literature. This was probably one of the earliest uses of the non-hyphenated pickup name in reference to a motorized light-duty vehicle with a box on the back.

1917 Studebaker Combination Passenger/Express (ASC)

Studebaker formally entered the light-duty vehicle field in 1914 when they introduced their 3/4-ton Model Three Delivery Car. The Delivery Car was available as a closed Panel Side Delivery or open Express Body Delivery. Each was priced at $1,150. Studebaker Delivery Cars were powered by a 192.4 cubic inch (3½ inch bore x 5 inch stroke) L-head four-cylinder engine that produced 30 horsepower. They had a wheelbase of 108½ inches and were fitted with 34 x 4½ tires.

1928 Studebaker Ambulance (WPL)

Studebaker Delivery Cars were available from 1914 to 1917. Prices were lowered to $1,085 in 1915 and in 1916 the Panel Delivery was $875 and the Express Delivery $825. Because of World War I, prices were raised $50 in 1917. The 1915 was a Model Five and the 1916-1917 was a Model SF. In 1916, the wheelbase was increased to 112 inches and the load rating was reduced to 1/2-ton. The same basic engine was used all four years, but for 1916-

1927 Studebaker Panel Express (A&A)

1927 Studebaker "Big Six" Depot Wagon (OCW)

1917 the cylinder bore was increased to 3-7/8 inch. The larger bore increased the displacement to 235.8 cubic inches and the horsepower to 40. Production figures for the 1914-1917 Studebaker Delivery Cars do not exist, but they certainly were not very high. It is unlikely that many have survived.

In 1918, Studebaker discontinued all motorized commercial vehicle production. Larger models were introduced in 1925, but it was not until 1927 that light-duty commercial vehicles returned to Studebaker's lineup.

1928 Studebaker Panel Express (DFW/MVMA)

Between 1927 and 1931, a wide range of Studebaker and Erskine open and closed delivery cars were offered by Studebaker. Most Studebaker versions used Dictator chassis. No pickup-bodied trucks were among the styles offered in 1927-1931. As in 1914-1917, sales of the 1927-1931 light-duty Studebaker commercial cars were not great. In 1932 they again abandoned (except for funeral cars and ambulance chassis) light-duty commercial vehicle production. Experimental vehicles, including even a Rockne pickup, were built in the early 1930s. But, it was not until 1937, that Studebaker again entered the light-duty commercial vehicle field.

1929 Studebaker "Arlington" Funeral Coach (DFW/ASC)

This time, Studebaker wisely decided to produce a pickup style truck. In contrast to earlier ventures, the 1937 undertaking attracted many buyers and established Studebaker as a viable producer of light-duty trucks. Except for 1940 and the World War II period, Studebaker built a continuous line of light-duty trucks right up to the time of the South Bend plant's closing in December 1963.

1930 Studebaker Boulevard Delivery Van (DFW/DPL)

1930 Studebaker Open Express (A&A)

1930 Studebaker 5th-Wheel Trailer Combo (DFW/KCMS)

1931 Studebaker One-Ton Beverage Truck (A&A)

1932 Rockne (By Studebaker) Panel Delivery (A&A)

632

1933 Rockne (By Studebaker) Panel Delivery (A&A)

1933 & 1934 Studebaker Panel Delivery Trucks (A&A)

1934 Studebaker One-Ton Panel Delivery (A&A)

1934 Studebaker One-Ton Panel Delivery (A&A)

Among Studebaker's famous models were the 1937-1939 Coupe-Expresses, the 1941-1948 M series models, the 1949-1954 R series trucks and the 1955-1964 E series models. The last years, 1960 to 1964, of the E series included the popular Lark-bodied Champ models.

As we have shown, Studebaker built some light-duty commercial vehicles prior to 1937, but it was not until the introduction of the Coupe-Express pickup in 1937 that the company gained recognition for being a producer of light-duty trucks. Because of this, my cataloging of Studebaker light-duty trucks will start with the 1937 model year, although you will see earlier models illustrating this introduction.

1937 STUDEBAKER

1938 STUDEBAKER

1937 Studebaker Coupe-Express (A&A)

1938 Studebaker Walk-in Delivery Van (A&A)

MODEL J5 — SIX-CYLINDER: — In 1937, Studebaker introduced its first light-duty pickup, the Coupe-Express. Front end sheet metal, most of the cab, the instrument panel, engine and basic chassis components, came directly from the 1937 Studebaker 5A Dictator passenger car. Since the Coupe-Express was based on a car styling, it had vent windows in the doors, something not offered on most other pickups of the era. It also had dual windshield wipers, dual sun visors, a rear view mirror, dome light and an adjustable seat. The 1937 Coupe-Express was fitted with a double-walled six-foot 16 gauge all-steel pickup box that featured a contoured outer shell that flowed into the rear fenders. The tailgate was smooth and had no name on it. The bed floor was all-steel. The Coupe-Express came with a spare tire mounted in the right front fender well. Front and rear chrome bumpers were also standard. Like the 5A Dictator, the Coupe-Express had an I-beam front axle. The Coupe-Express could be ordered without a pickup box. Another variant was the Suburban Car, a woody station wagon which was based on a J5 windshield cowl chassis. Larger Standard series Studebaker trucks used the same cab as the Coupe-Express. Included in the Standard series was a 1½-ton J15 Express pickup and panel van.

I.D. DATA: The serial number was located on the left side of the frame under the front fender. The engine number was located on the top left side of the cylinder block above the distributor. The beginning serial numbers for the J5 Coupe-Express were J5-001 in South Bend and J5-5,001 in Los Angeles. The beginning engine number was T-701.

Model No. J5 Series Half-Ton	Body Type	Factory Price ($)	Weight	GVW (lbs)	Prod. Total
J5	Pickup	647	3168	4500	3125

ENGINE: Six-cylinder. L-head. Cast iron block. Displacement: 217.8 cu. in. Bore and Stroke: 3¼ in. x 4⅜ in. Compression ratio: 6.01. Brake horsepower: 86 at 3600 R.P.M. Taxable horsepower: 25.38. Maximum Torque: 160 ft. lbs. at 1200 R.P.M. Main bearings: Four. Valve lifters: Solid. Carburetor: Stromberg Model EX-23 one-barrel, Carter Model W1-371S one-barrel or Carter Model WA1-414S one-barrel.

CHASSIS & BODY: Wheelbase: 116 in. Overall length: 193 in. Height: 67 in. Width: 71.75 in. Interior pickup box dimensions: 71.75 in. long x 48.6 in. wide x 14.6 in. high. Front tread: 57.4 in. Rear tread: 60.4 in. Tires: 6.00 x 16.

TECHNICAL: Sliding gear transmission. Speeds: 3F/1R. Synchromesh in second and third. Floor shift control. Single plate dry disc clutch. I-beam front axle. Hypoid semi-floating rear axle. Overall ratio: 4.55:1. Hydraulic brakes. Automatic Hill Holder standard. Steel disc wheels. Two-stage rear springs. Front and rear tubular shocks. Variable ratio steering gear.

OPTIONS: Overdrive transmission. Radio. Heater. Electric clock. Leather upholstery. Cigarette lighter. Rear axle: 4.82:1. Tires: 6.50 x 16. Steel spoke wheels. Cab-high tarpaulin pickup box cover. Locking gas cap. License plate frames. Spotlight. Clear road or amber fog lights. Wig-wag stop light.

HISTORICAL: With sales of over 3,000, the 1937 Coupe-Express was, up to that time, the best selling truck model ever produced by Studebaker. Quite a few 1937 Coupe-Expresses have survived, but there are evidently no surviving J5 Suburban Cars.

Pricing

	5	4	3	2	1
1937 **Model 5A/6A, Dictator Six**					
Cpe Express	1200	2400	4000	5600	8000

MODEL K5 — SIX-CYLINDER: — As in 1937, the 1938 K5 Coupe-Express pickup was based on current year Studebaker car styling. In 1938, Studebaker dropped the Dictator name and returned the Commander model name. The 1938 Coupe-Express front end and cab styling was based on the 1938 Commander Model 7A (identified during the early part of the year as the Studebaker Six). The Commander 7A, in contrast to the State Commander 8A and President 4C, had free-standing headlights instead of the faired-in headlights used on the more expensive models. Raymond Loewy's rakish 1938 car windshield was incorporated into the 1938 Coupe-Express. Restyled front fenders and a shorter front end resulted in the spare wheel and tire sitting much higher than it did in 1937. The rear fenders were unchanged from 1937, but the pickup box was lengthened 5½ inches to make up for the shortened front end. As on the 7A Commander, the K5's front suspension featured Studebaker's independent Planar transverse spring suspension system. This system was first introduced on top line Studebaker cars in 1935. Tubular shocks were replaced by Houdaille lever arm shocks. The six-cylinder engine was bored out an extra 1/16 in. in 1938. The K5's instrument panel was like that used in the 7A Commander. The Suburban Car woody wagon was continued in 1938. A K10 one-ton Fast-Transport with pickup box or panel body was offered in 1938. K10 and larger Standard Series trucks continued with the 1937 cab styling.

1938 Studebaker K-10 Stake Bed (A&A)

I.D. DATA: Serial number location: same as 1937. Engine numbers were located on the top left side rear corner of the cylinder block on early models and on the top left side front corner of the cylinder block on later models. The beginning serial numbers for the K5 Coupe-Express were K5-001 in South Bend and K5-7,501 in Los Angeles. The beginning engine numbers were T-4,301 and H-7,801 (both H and T engines were built in South Bend). Some production figure records indicate that no 1938 K5s were actually produced in Los Angeles.

Model No. K5 Series	Body Type	Factory Price ($)	Weight	GVW (lbs)	Prod. Total
K5	Pickup	850	3250	4500	1000

ENGINE: Six-cylinder. L-head. Cast iron block. Displacement: 226.2 cu. in. Bore and stroke: 3-5/16 in. x 4⅜ in. Compression ratio: 6.0:1. Brake horsepower: 90 at 3400 R.P.M. Taxable horsepower: 26.35. Main bearings: Four. Valve lifters: Solid. Carburetor: Stromberg Model BXO-26 one-barrel.

1938 Studebaker K-10 Pickup (A&A)

1938 Studebaker Furniture Van (A&A)

CHASSIS & BODY: Wheelbase: 116.5 in. Overall length: 193.75 in. Height: 67.75 in. Width: 73 in. Interior pickup box dimensions: 77.25 in. long x 48.6 in. wide x 14.6 in. high. Front tread: 59.4 in. Rear tread: 59.6 in. Tires: 6.00 x 16.

TECHNICAL: Sliding gear transmission. Speeds: 3F/1R. Synchromesh in second and third. Floor shift control. Single plate dry disc clutch. Planar independent front suspension. Hypoid semi-floating rear axle. Overall ratio: 4.55:1. Hydraulic brakes. Steel disc wheels. Two-stage rear springs. Front and rear Houdaille lever arm shocks. Variable ratio steering gear.

1938 Studebaker Specialty Van (A&A)

OPTIONS: Overdrive transmission. Automatic Hill Holder. Radio. Heater. Electric clock. Leather upholstery. Cigarette lighter. Rear axle: 4.82:1. Tires: 6.50 x 16. Cab-high tarpaulin pickup box cover. Locking gas cap. License plate frames. Spotlight. Clear road or amber fog lights. Wig-wag oscillating stop light. Windshield washer. Bumper and grille guards. Fender guide. Fabric radiator cover.

HISTORICAL: In 1938 the K5 used both "T" (truck) prefix engine numbers and regular Commander "H" prefix engine numbers. The recession of 1938 helped cut Coupe-Express sales to one-third of what they were in 1937. No K5 Suburban Car woody wagons are known to have survived.

1938 Studebaker K-10 Fire & Rescue Truck (A&A)

1938 Studebaker Coupe-Express (A&A)

Pricing

Model 7A, Commander Six	5	4	3	2	1
Cpe Express	1200	2400	4000	5600	8000

1939 STUDEBAKER

MODEL L5 — SIX-CYLINDER: — For the second year in a row, the Coupe-Express front sheet metal was restyled to match the current year Studebaker car. As on Commanders and Presidents and, later, Champions, the headlights of the 1939 Coupe-Express were built into the front fenders. The front fenders were an all new design, although the high-mounted spare was retained in the right wheel well. The Commander/President split grille was also adopted on the Coupe-Express. The cab styling, pickup box and instrument panel remained unchanged from 1938 and the original 1937 rear fenders were retained. No significant mechanical changes were made from 1938. The L5 Suburban Car woody wagon and one-ton K10 Fast-Transport were continued. The K10 and larger Standard series trucks continued with the cab style introduced on the 1937 Coupe-Express. Edwards Iron Works, of South Bend, Ind., offered a small pickup box that could fit into the back of a Champion coupe with its trunk lid removed. Unlike the Coupe-Express box, the Edwards box had the "S T U D E B A K E R" name on the tailgate. Edwards called it both the Pick-Up Coupe and the Coupe-Delivery. Rated at only ¼-ton, the Coupe-Delivery did not really fall into the light-duty truck classification.

I.D. DATA: Serial number location: same as 1937-38. Engine number location: same as late 1938. The beginning serial numbers for the L5 Coupe-Express were L5-001 in South Bend and no 1939 Coupe-Express models were assembled in Los Angeles. The beginning engine number was H-42,501.

Model No. L5 Series	Body Type	Factory Price ($)	Weight	GVW (lbs)	Prod. Total
L5	Pickup	850	3250	4500	1200

1939 Studebaker Coupe-Express (A&A)

ENGINE: Six-cylinder. L-head. Cast iron block. Displacement: 226.2 cu. in. Bore and stroke: 3-5/16 in. x 4⅜ in. Compression ratio: 6.0:1. Brake horsepower: 90 at 3400 R.P.M. Taxable horsepower: 26.35. Main bearings: Four. Valve lifters: Solid. Carburetor: Stromberg Model BXO-26 one-barrel.

CHASSIS & BODY: Wheelbase: 116.5 in. Overall length: 195.4 in. Height: 67.75 in. Width: 73 in. Interior pickup box dimensions: 77.25 in. long x 48.6 in. wide x 14.6 in. high. Front tread: 59.4 in. Rear tread: 59.6 in. Tires: 6.00 x 16.

TECHNICAL: Sliding gear transmission. Speeds: 3F/1R. Synchromesh in second and third. Floor or column shift controls. Single plate dry disc clutch. Planar independent front suspension. Hypoid semi-floating rear axle. Overall ratio: 4.55:1. Hydraulic brakes. Steel disc wheels. Two-stage rear springs. Front and rear Houdaille lever arm shocks. Variable ratio steering gear.

OPTIONS: Overdrive transmission. Automatic Hill Holder. Radio. Heater. Electric clock. Leather upholstery. Cigarette lighter. Rear axle: 4.82:1. Tires: 6.50 x 16. Cab-high tarpaulin pickup box cover. Locking gas cap. License plate frames. Spotlight. Clear road or amber fog lights. Wig-wag oscillating stop light. Windshield washer. Bumper and grille guards. Fender guide. Fabric radiator cover.

HISTORICAL: As in 1937 and 1938, no 1939 L5 Suburban Car woody wagons are known to have survived. The Suburban Car production is included in the Coupe-Express production figures and no breakdowns have been discovered. The economy took a definite upturn in 1939, but Coupe-Express sales only increased 20 percent over 1938 and were still way below the 1937 figure.

Pricing

1939	5	4	3	2	1
Model 9A, Commander Six					
Cpe Express	1350	2700	4500	6300	9000

1940 STUDEBAKER

1940 Studebaker Champion Sedan Delivery (A&A)

For the 1940 model year, Studebaker produced no light-duty trucks. The inability of the 1939 Coupe-Express to show a significant sales increase over the 1938 model, convinced Studebaker executives that they were on the wrong track. A pickup with car styling, independent front suspension and a "pretty" pickup box had limited sales appeal in the late thirties. Studebaker was working on a more truck-like light-duty pickup, but it was not ready for the 1940 model year. In the interim, all they could offer was the ¼-ton Champion Coupe-Delivery with the small (68 inch long x 30 inch wide x 18.6 inch high) Edwards Iron Works pickup box in the back and the large (6,750 GVW) one-ton K10 Fast-Transport. The Fast-Transport was available with a panel body or two different 8-foot pickup boxes. The Fast-Transport Custom Express came with a smooth sided box and steel floor, while the cheaper Fast-Transport Standard Express came with a conventional cargo box and a wooden floor. Both of these styles of trucks had "S T U D E B A K E R" on the tailgate. A few Fast-Transports have survived and at least one restored 1940 Champion Coupe-Delivery exists.

1941 STUDEBAKER

1941 Studebaker Deluxe Pickup Truck (FKF)

MODEL M5 — SIX-CYLINDER: — For the 1941 model year, Studebaker introduced a whole new line of commercial vehicles. Called the M series, they all featured the same cab and front end styling. Some of the cab components, including the instrument panel, were borrowed from the 1941 Champion car, but the front end styling was unique to the new truck line. The light-duty pickup version of the M series was the ½-ton M5 Coupe Express (same spelling as the 1937-1939 models, but generally without the hyphen). To save tooling money, the M5 had running boards that were interchangeable from side to side and fenders that were interchangeable, on a given side, from front to rear. The all-steel pickup box was of contemporary design. The Coupe Express was available with or without the box. The name "S T U D E B A K E R" was pressed into the tailgate and on a nameplate on the front of the hood. A left-hand exterior rear view mirror was standard equipment. All M series trucks featured an interior hood release. M5 hubcaps were the same as those used on 1940-1941 Commander cars. The M5 was powered by the same small six-cylinder engine that was used in the Champion car, but it had an I-beam front axle instead of the Champion's Planar independent front suspension. The Standard trim M5 was not nearly as plush as the 1937-1939 Coupe-Express models. It had only one interior sun visor, one windshield wiper, no dome light and no rear bumper. It was also about 10 inches higher than the earlier style. With a base price of $664, it was $186 less than the 1939 Coupe-Express. A Deluxe M5 Coupe Express was offered. A Deluxe version was created by adding a $24.47 Deluxe Equipment Group option to a Standard trim model. The Deluxe Equipment Group included stainless steel grille bar overlays, a hood ornament, bright metal side moldings, chrome exterior rear view mirror, dome light and body color fenders (Standard trim models had black fenders). A one-ton M15 Standard Express with an 8-foot pickup box was also produced.

I.D. DATA: Serial numbers were located on a plate on the left front door hinge pillar or on the left side of the seat riser. Engine numbers were located on the top, left side, front corner of the cylinder block. The beginning serial number for the 1941 M5 Coupe Express was M5-001. The ending serial number was M5-4685. The starting engine number as 1M-001. All domestic M5s were assembled in South Bend, Indiana.

Model No.	Body Type	Factory Price ($)	Weight	GVW (lbs)	Prod. Total
1941 M5 Series					
M5	Pickup	644	2660	4200	4685*

* based on serial number span.

ENGINE: Six-cylinder. L-head. Cast iron block. Displacement: 169.6 cu. in. Bore and stroke: 3 in. x 4 in. Compression ratio: 6.5:1. Brake horsepower: 80 at 4000 R.P.M. Taxable horsepower: 21.6. Maximum torque: 134 ft. lbs. Main bearings: Four. Valve lifters: Solid. Carburetor: Carter Model WA1-496S one-barrel.

1941 Studebaker Pickup Truck (A&A)

CHASSIS & BODY: Wheelbase: 113 in. Overall length: 181.25 in. Height: 77 in. Width: 75.3 in. Interior pickup box dimensions: 78.2 in. long x 48.5 in. wide x 13.4 in. high. Front tread: 59.9 in. Rear tread: 59.6 in. Tires: 6.00 x 16 4-ply.

TECHNICAL: Sliding gear transmission. Speeds: 3F/1R. Synchromesh in second and third. Floor shift control. Single plate dry disc clutch. I-beam front axle. Hypoid semi-floating rear axle. Overall ratio: 4.82:1. Hydraulic brakes. Steel disc wheels. Lever arm shock absorbers. Variable ratio steering gear.

OPTIONS:: Four-speed transmission with floor shift control. Overdrive with three-speed transmission and steering column shift control. Hill Holder. Radio. Heater. Electric clock. Leather upholstery. Door arm rests. Right-hand sun visor. Right-hand windshield wiper. Dome light. Interior rear view mirror. Cigarette lighter. Deluxe steering wheel. Dual horns. Deluxe Equipment Group. Caravan Top. Body color fenders. Chrome rear bumper. Bumper guards. Extra taillight. License plate frames. Locking gas cap. Spotlight. Fog lights. Service light. Windshield washer. Wheel trim rings. Whitewall tires. Six-ply tires. 6.25 x 16, 6.50 x 16 or 7.00 x 16 tires. Two-stage rear springs. 4.55:1 rear axle. Fram oil filter. Oil bath air cleaner.

HISTORICAL: The 1941 M series, with total sales of 8,439 for all models from ½-ton to 1½-tons, set a new high water mark for Studebaker truck production. The M5, with its lower price, I-beam front axle, conventional pickup box and non-car front end, proved to be much more popular than the earlier Coupe-Express. A few M5s were fitted with Montpelier panel bodies or factory stake bodies, but most were sold with pickup boxes. Very few 1941 Deluxe Coupe Express models were sold and they are extremely rare today.

Pricing

1941	5	4	3	2	1
6-cyl., 113" wb					
½ Ton	1050	2100	3500	4900	7000

1941-1945 STUDEBAKER

During World War II, Studebaker assembled 197,678 model US6 2½-ton Hercules-powered 6x6 and 6x4 military trucks. Over 100,000 of these trucks were sent to Russia via Lend-lease. The Studebaker military trucks used a slightly modified M series truck cab. After World War II, the GAZ factory in Gorky, Russia, started production of a series of trucks that were close copies of the Studebaker US6 models. The GAZ cabs were almost identical to the cabs used on the M5 Coupe Express. Many GAZ trucks with M series style cabs are still in use around the world. Studebaker also produced 67,789 Wright Cyclone R-1820 aircraft engines for the Boeing B-17 Flying Fortress and 15,890 tracked Weasel light personnel carriers. 10,647 of the Weasels were the amphibious M-29C version. The Weasel was designed by Studebaker engineers and all were built in Studebaker plants. The Weasel was powered by the same Champion engine that was used in the M5 Coupe Express.

1942 STUDEBAKER

1942 Studebaker Standard Model M5 Pickup (FKF)

MODEL M5 — SIX-CYLINDER: — The basic Coupe Express was continued unchanged in 1942, but the war in Europe, and America's entrance into the war in December 1941, both had their effect on M5 trim and production. The 1942 production started in September 1941 and near that time the Deluxe Equipment Group with its stainless steel grille overlays was discontinued. This was because of the government's need for critical metals for domestic and export military material production. Not long after America's entrance into the war, all chrome plated trim was replaced by painted trim. Cars and trucks with painted trim were called blackout models. All light-duty Studebaker commercial vehicle production was indefinitely suspended on January 31, 1942.

I.D. DATA: Serial number and engine number locations: same as 1941. The starting serial number for the 1942 M5 Coupe Express was M5-4686. The ending serial number was on or before M5-5000. Engine numbers were continuous from 1941 to 1948 and year breaks are not available.

Model No.	Body Type	Factory Price ($)	Weight	GVW (lbs)	Prod. Total
1942 M5 Series					
M5	Pickup	687	2660	4200	315*

* This is the maximum figure possible based on the serial number span.

ENGINE: Six-cyliner. L-head. Cast iron block. Displacement: 169.6 cu. in. Bore and stroke: 3 in. x 4 in. Compression ratio: 6.5:1. Brake horsepower: 80 at 4000 R.P.M. Taxable horsepower: 21.6. Maximum torque: 134 ft. lbs. Main bearings: Four. Valve lifters: Solid. Carburetor: Carter Model WA1-496S one-barrel.

CHASSIS & BODY: Wheelbase: 113 in. Overall length: 181.25 in. Height: 77 in. Width: 75.3 in. Interior pickup box dimensions: 78.2 in. long x 48.5 in. wide x 13.4 in. high. Front tread: 59.9 in. Rear tread: 59.6 in. Tires: 6.00 x 16 4-ply.

TECHNICAL: Sliding gear transmission. Speeds: 3F/1R. Synchromesh in second and third. Floor shift control. Single plate dry disc clutch. I-beam front axle. Hypoid semi-floating rear axle. Overall ratio: 4.82:1. Hydraulic brakes. Steel disc wheels. Lever arm shock absorbers. Variable ratio steering gear.

OPTIONS: Four-speed transmission with floor shift control. Overdrive with three-speed transmission and steering column shift control. Hill Holder. Radio. Heater. Electric clock. Leather upholstery. Door arm rests. Right-hand sun visor. Right-hand windshield wiper. Dome light. Interior rear view mirror. Cigarette lighter. Deluxe steering wheel. Dual horns. Caravan Top. Body color fenders. Chrome rear bumper. Bumper guards. Extra taillight. License plate frames. Locking gas cap. Spotlight. Fog lights. Service light. Windshield washer. Wheel trim rings. Six-ply tires. 6.25 x 16, 6.50 x 16 or 7.00 x 16 tires. Two-stage rear springs. 4.55:1 rear axle. Fram oil filter. Oil bath air cleaner.

HISTORICAL: Because of World War II, very few 1942 M5 Coupe Express pickups were built. Today they are extremely rare, especially the blackout models. Larger model trucks were considered more important to domestic commerce, so Studebaker was allowed to build many more 1942 1½-ton trucks than Coupe Express models.

1942
6-cyl., 113" wb

	5	4	3	2	1
½ Ton	1050	2100	3500	4900	7000

1945 STUDEBAKER

By late 1944, the need for civilian trucks on the home front was very critical. Because of this, the War Production Board authorized some companies to make a limited number of medium-duty trucks. No light-duty models were allowed, but Studebaker, starting in the spring of 1945, produced a few blackout one-ton M15-20 Express models with 8-foot pickup boxes. They were like the prewar M15s, except they used the modified military US6 cab ("C9" cab) that featured a swing windshield and metal door and kick panels. Built in much larger numbers was the M15-28 one-ton truck with dual rear wheels. The 1945 M15s were fitted standard with heavy-duty wheels and springs. They had two windshield wipers, two sun visors, an oil bath air cleaner and an oil filter. The later items were standard on all subsequent M series trucks. Altogether, Studebaker produced 4,000 of the 1945 M15s, but, as mentioned, only a small percentage of those were the Express model with the pickup box. At least two 1945 M15-20 Expresses are known to have survived.

1946 STUDEBAKER

1946 Studebaker Pickup (FKF)

MODEL M5 — SIX-CYLINDER: — After the conclusion of World War II, Studebaker brought back its full line of M series trucks, including the popular ½-ton M5 Coupe Express pickup. Except for a few minor items, the 1946 M5 was identical to the 1941 M5. The Deluxe Equipment Group did not return, but as on 1945 M15s, two windshield wipers, two sun visors, an oil filter and an oil bath air cleaner were made standard on the M5. Also added to the M5 standard list were body color fenders, 6.50 x 16 six-ply tires, two-stage rear springs, a dome light and arm rests. Because of tire shortages, early 1946 models came with a spare wheel, but no spare tire. Early 1946s also had painted hubcaps that were similar in design to those used on 1942 Commander and President cars. The prewar style chrome caps were returned early in the model year. The one-ton pickup, now also called a Coupe Express, was continued from 1945. It, like all 1946 M series models, came with the fixed windshield "C2" cab that had cardboard door and kick panels. The 1946 one-tons were called M15As and they lacked some of the heavy-duty equipment that was standard in 1945.

I.D. DATA: Serial number and engine number locations: Same as 1941-1942. The starting serial number for the 1946 M5 Coupe Express was M5-5001. The ending serial number was on or before M5-19052. Engine numbers were continuous from 1941 to 1948 and year breaks are not available.

Model No.	Body Type	Factory Price ($)	Weight	GVW (lbs)	Prod. Total
1945 M5 Series					
M5	Pickup	929	2710	4500	14,052

NOTE: Because of changing regulations from the Office of Price Administration, M5 prices were raised several times during 1946. They started at $832 in January and were up to $968 by the end of the model year. Production is based on the serial number span.

ENGINE: Six-cylinder. L-head. Cast iron block. Displacement: 169.6 cu. in. Bore and stroke: 3 in. x 4 in. Compression ratio: 6.5:1. Brake horsepower: 80 at 4000 R.P.M. Taxable horsepower: 21.6. Maximum torque: 134 ft. lbs. Main bearings: Four. Valve lifters: Solid. Carburetor: Carter Model WE-532S one-barrel.

CHASSIS & BODY: Wheelbase: 113 in. Overall length: 181.25 in. Height: 77 in. Width: 75.3 in. Interior pickup box dimensions: 78.2 in. long x 48.5 in. wide x 13.4 in. high. Front tread: 59.9 in. Rear tread: 59.6 in. Tires: 6.50 x 16 six-ply.

TECHNICAL: Sliding gear transmission. Speeds: 3F/1R. Synchromesh in second and third. Floor shift control. Single plate dry disc clutch. I-beam front axle. Hypoid semi-floating rear axle. Overall ratio: 4.82:1. Hydraulic brakes. Steel disc wheels. Lever arm shock absorbers. Variable ratio steering gear.

OPTIONS: Four-speed transmission with floor shift control. Overdrive with three-speed transmission and steering column shift control. Hill Holder. Radio. Heater. Electric clock. Interior rear view mirror. Cigarette lighter. Dual horns. Mattex seat covers. Caravan Top. Chrome rear bumper. Heavy-duty bumper. Heavy-duty grille and light guard. Bumper guards. Extra taillight. License plate frames. Locking gas cap. Spotlight. Fog lights. Service light. Hood light. Glove compartment light. Turn signals. Windshield washer. Wheel trim rings. Six blade fan. Extension rear view mirror. Heavy-duty springs. No optional tire sizes were available in 1946.

HISTORICAL: The strong postwar seller's market meant that Studebaker could sell as many M5 pickups as they could build. The larger 6.50 x 16 six-ply tires allowed the GVW to be raised 300 pounds over 1941-42.

1946

	5	4	3	2	1
½ Ton	1050	2100	3500	4900	7000

1947 STUDEBAKER

1947 Studebaker Mail Delivery Truck (A&A)

MODEL M5 — SIX-CYLINDER: — For the 1947 model year, the M5 Coupe Express was little changed from 1946. A few more options were added and a hood ornament, like the prewar Deluxe ornament, was added to all models during mid-year. As with every year, new exterior colors were made available in 1947. Grease fittings were changed from Zerk brand to Alemite brand. M5 windshield cowl chassis with Cantrell woody station wagon bodies were produced for export sales.

I.D. DATA: Serial number and engine number locations: Same as 1941-1946. The starting serial number for the 1947 M5 Coupe Express was M5-19053. The ending serial number was on or before M5-42429. Engine numbers were continuous from 1941 to 1948 and year breaks are not available.

Model No.	Body Type	Factory Price ($)	Weight	GVW (lbs)	Prod. Total
1947 M5 Series					
M5	Pickup	1082	2635	4500	23,377*

* Production is based on serial number span.

1947 Studebaker Cantrell Station Wagon (A&A)

ENGINE: Six-cylinder. L-head. Cast iron block. Displacement: 169.6 cu. in. Bore and stroke: 3 in. x 4 in. Compression ratio: 6.5:1. Brake horsepower: 80 at 4000 R.P.M. Taxable horsepower: 21.6. Maximum torque: 134 ft. lbs. Main bearings: Four. Valve lifters: Solid. Carburetor: Carter Model WE-532S one-barrel or Zenith Model 28BV10 one-barrel.

CHASSIS & BODY: Wheelbase: 113 in. Overall length: 181.25 in. Height: 77 in. Width: 75.3 in. Interior pickup box dimensions: 78.2 in. long x 48.5 in. wide x 13.4 in. high. Front tread: 59.9 in. Rear tread: 59.6 in. Tires: 6.50 x 16 six-ply.

TECHNICAL: Sliding gear transmission. Speeds: 3F/1R. Synchromesh in second and third. Floor shift control. Single plate dry disc clutch. I-beam front axle. Hypoid semi-floating rear axle. Overall ratio: 4.82:1. Hydraulic brakes. Steel disc wheels. Lever arm shock absorbers. Variable ratio steering gear.

1947 Studebaker Pickup (A&A)

OPTIONS: Four-speed transmission with floor shift control. Overdrive with three-speed transmission and steering column shift controls. Hill Holder. Radio. Heater. Electric clock. Interior rear view mirror. Cigarette lighter. Dual horns. Mattex seat covers. Caravan Top. Chrome rear bumper. Heavy-duty bumper. Heavy-duty grille and light guard. Bumper guards. Extra taillight. License plate frames. Locking gas cap. Spotlight. Fog lights. Service light. Hood light. Glove compartment light. Turn signals. Windshield washer. Wheel trim rings. Six blade fan. Extension rear view mirror. Heavy-duty springs. Early cut-in generator. Vacuum booster for windshield wiper. Hood ornament (early). Glare proof interior rear view mirror. Visor vanity mirror. Fire extinguisher. No optional tire sizes were available in 1947.

HISTORICAL: By building large quantities of trucks during World War II, Studebaker gained valuable mass truck production experience. This proved beneficial in the early postwar years. During the 1946 calendar year, Studebaker produced 43,196 commercial vehicles. In 1947 the figure climbed to 67,811. The 1947 figure was greater than the total of all motorized commercial vehicles produced by Studebaker before World War II.

Pricing

1947	5	4	3	2	1
½ Ton	1050	2100	3500	4900	7000

1948 Studebaker Pickup (FKF)

MODEL M5 — SIX-CYLINDER: — M series Studebaker truck production continued into 1948 with few changes from 1947. The standard exterior left-hand mirror was switched from one with fixed length arm to one with an extension arm. Model year production started in the fall of 1947 and ended in March 1948. The early ending date was necessary because of the introduction of the new 1949 series 2R trucks. Besides having new styling, the new models were to be produced in a different plant. This required moving much of the M series production equipment to the new plant. The former M series assembly building was converted into a press shop.

I.D. DATA: Serial number and engine number locations: Same as 1941-1947. The starting serial number for the 1948 M5 Coupe Express was M5-42,430. The ending serial number was on or before M5-52,682. Engine numbers were continuous from 1941 to 1948 and year breaks are not available.

Model No.	Body Type	Factory Price ($)	Weight	GVW (lbs)	Prod. Total
1948 M5 Series					
M5	Pickup	1107	2635	4500	10,253*

* Production is based on serial number span.

1948 Studebaker Pickup (OCW)

ENGINE: Six-cylinder. L-head. Cast iron block. Displacement: 169.6 cu. in. Bore and stroke: 3 in. x 4 in. Compression ratio: 6.5:1. Brake horsepower: 80 at 4000 R.P.M. Taxable horsepower: 21.6. Maximum torque: 134 ft. lbs. Main bearings: Four. Valve lifters: Solid. Carburetor: Zenith Model 2BV10 one-barrel or Carter Model WE-661S one-barrel.

1948 Studebaker Pickup, modified (L. Rowell)

CHASSIS & BODY: Wheelbase: 113 in. Overall length: 181.25 in. Height: 77 in. Width: 75.3 in. Interior pickup box dimensions: 78.2 in. long x 48.5 in. wide x 13.4 in. high. Front tread: 59.9 in. Rear tread: 59.6 in. Tires: 6.50 x 16 six-ply.

TECHNICAL: Sliding gear transmission. Speeds: 3F/1R. Synchromesh in second and third. Floor shift control. Single plate dry disc clutch. I-beam front axle. Hypoid semi-floating rear axle. Overall ratio: 4.82:1. Hydraulic brakes. Steel disc wheels. Lever arm shock absorbers. Variable ratio steering gear.

OPTIONS: Four-speed transmission with floor shift control. Overdrive with three-speed transmission and steering column shift control. Hill Holder. Radio. Heater. Electric clock. Interior rear view mirror. Cigarette lighter. Dual horns. Mattex seat covers. Caravan Top. Chrome rear bumper. Heavy-duty bumper. Heavy-duty grille and light guard. Bumper guards. Extra taillight. License plate frames. Locking gas cap. Spotlight. Fog lights. Service light. Hood light. Glove compartment light. Turn signals. Windshield washer. Wheel trim rings. Six blade fan. Right-hand extension rear view mirror. Heavy-duty springs. Early cut-in generator. Vacuum booster for windshield wiper. Glare proof interior rear view mirror. Visor vanity mirror. Fire extinguisher. No optional tire sizes were available in 1948.

HISTORICAL: Serial numbers indicate a maximum total of 52,682 M5s being built from 1941 to 1948, but a separate factory figure indicates a total of 52,541. This means a few serial numbers in the range were not assigned to any trucks. Most of the missing numbers were probably at the end of the 1942 production run. Prior to the introduction of the 1949 2R series trucks, Studebaker put a lot of effort into a proposed line of R series trucks. The R5 version was to include torsion bar suspension and fenders that blended into the doors like on the new postwar Dodge trucks. The R series trucks were never put into production.

Pricing

1948	5	4	3	2	1
½ Ton	1050	2100	3500	4900	7000

1949 STUDEBAKER

1949 Studebaker Pickup (FKF)

MODELS 2R5 AND 2R10 — SIX-CYLINDER: — For the 1949 model year, Studebaker introduced an all new line of trucks, the 2R series. An R series had been planned, but it never got beyond the prototype stage. The new 2R models were designed by Raymond Loewy's South Bend styling chief, Robert Bourke. Bourke is the same stylist who later created the famous 1953 Studebaker Starliner and Starlight. The new styling was, like the 1947 Studebaker cars, certainly ahead of the competition. It was low and featured no exterior running boards and a smooth double wall pickup box. Unlike earlier Studebaker pickups, it borrowed no sheet metal from any Studebaker cars. The only contemporary car parts it used were Commander hubcaps, inverted Champion headlight rims, and shortly after production started, the Champion hood ornament was adopted. The M series steering wheel, which dated back to the 1941 Champion was retained. The instruments were similar to the ones used in the M series and all 1941 cars, plus 1942 and 1946 Champions. Unlike the M series, the back sides of the instruments were accessible from under the hood instead of from under the instrument panel. Interior door panels were made of steel instead of cardboard. A new addition to the lineup was a ¾-ton 2R10 model. The 2R10 was available with an 8-foot all-steel pickup box and a full-floating rear axle. The larger one-ton model, called the 2R15, was retained. It was also available with an 8-foot pickup box. The ½-ton 2R5 continued with a 6½-foot all-steel pickup box. The "S T U D E B A K E R" name on the pickup boxes was painted the Tusk Ivory accent color. The same accent color was used to highlight the grille and painted bumper. Of course, all could be ordered with no box or a stake bed. Chassis, cowl chassis or windshield cowl chassis configurations were also available for special body applications. The Coupe Express name was discontinued in 1949. Mechanically, the 2R series was little changed from the M series. The standard three-speed transmission on light-duty models now had a steering column shift instead of a floor shift.

1949 Studebaker Stake Bed (A&A)

I.D. DATA: The serial number was located on a plate on the left side of the seat riser. The engine number was located on the top, left side, front corner of the cylinder block. The starting serial number for the 2R5 was R5-001 (HR5-001 in Canada). The starting serial number for the 2R10 was R10-001. The starting engine number for the 2R5 and 2R10 was 1R-001 (H1R-001 for the Canadian 2R5).

Model No.	Body Type	Factory Price ($)	Weight	GVW (lbs)	Prod. Total
1949 2R Series					
½-Ton					
2R5	Pickup	1262	2675	4600	Note 1
¾-Ton					
2R10	Pickup	1367	3040	6100	Note 1

NOTE 1: Exact model year breakdowns of 1949-53 2R series truck production is impossible to give because the model year designation depended on a serial number/date of sale formula. Total domestic production for the five years was very close to the following: 2R5 - 110,500; 2R10 - 37,300.

1949 Studebaker 1/2-ton Pickup (IMSC)

1949 Studebaker Pickup (A&A)

ENGINE: Six-cylinder. L-head. Cast iron block. Displacement: 169.6 cu. in. Bore and stroke: 3 in. x 4 in. Compression ratio: 6.5:1. Brake horsepower: 80 at 4000 R.P.M. Taxable horsepower: 21.6. Maximum torque: 134 ft. lbs. Main bearings: Four. Valve lifters: Solid. Carburetor: Carter Model BBR1-633S one-barrel.

CHASSIS & BODY (2R5): Wheelbase: 112 in. Overall length: 185.6 in. Height: 69.75 in. Width: 75.6 in. Interior pickup box dimensions: 77.8 in. long x 48.5 in. wide x 17.1 in. high. Front tread: 60.8 in. Rear tread: 59.6 in. Tires: 6.00 x 16 four-ply.

CHASSIS & BODY (2R10): Wheelbase: 122 in. Overall length: 203.6 in. Height: 69.9 in. Width: 75.6 in. Interior pickup box dimensions: 95.8 in. long x 48.5 in. wide x 17.1 in. high. Front tread: 60.8 in. Rear tread: 60.4 in. Tires: 6.50 x 16 six-ply.

1949 Studebaker 3/4-ton Pickup (H. Bower)

TECHNICAL: Sliding gear transmission. Speeds: 3F/1R. Synchromesh in second and third. Steering column shift control. Single plate dry disc clutch. I-beam front axle. 2R5 rear axle: Hypoid semi-floating with 4.82:1 overall ratio. 2R10 rear axle: Spiral bevel full-floating with 5.57:1 overall ratio. Hydraulic brakes. Steel disc wheels; slotted on 2R10. Lever arm shock absorbers. Variable ratio steering.

OPTIONS: Four-speed transmission with floor shift control. Overdrive (first only on 2R5, but later on both 2R5 and 2R10). Hill Holder. Radio. Climatizer heater/defroster. Interior rear view mirror. Glare-proof interior rear view mirror. Visor vanity mirror. Cigarette lighter. Dual horns. Caravan Top. Steel stake rack. Chrome front bumper. Chrome or painted rear bumper. Bumper guards. Heavy-duty grille and lamp guard. Extra taillight. License plate frames. Locking gas cap. Right-hand exterior rear view mirror. Spotlight. Fog lights. Turn signals. Exhaust deflector. Windshield washer. Mattex seat covers. Arm rest covers. Hand throttle. Windshield wiper vacuum booster. Fram oil filter. Heavy-duty oil bath air cleaner. Six blade fan. Early cut-in generator. 19 plate battery. Heavy-duty radiator. Two-stage rear springs. Spare tire chain and lock. Optional items specific to the 2R5: Wheel trim rings. 6.00 x 16 six-ply tires. 6.50 x 16 six-ply tires. Optional items specific to the 2R10: 7.00 x 16 six-ply tires. 7.50 x 16 eight-ply tires. Final drive ratio of 4.86:1.

1949 Studebaker Cantrell Station Wagon (A&A)

HISTORICAL: All domestic 2R series trucks were assembled in a giant plant (called the "Chippewa Avenue Plant") outside of South Bend, Ind. Built by the government at the outset of World War II, Studebaker used the plant during the war for assembling 63,789 Wright Cyclone R-1820 aircraft engines. Studebaker purchased the plant after the war and set it up for truck production during early 1948. Model 2R truck production started there in mid-1948. Starting in February 1949 production of 2R5 models was also carried on in Studebaker's Canadian plant in Hamilton, Ontario. A total of 1,498 series 2R5 trucks were built in Canada during the 1949 calendar year. As the seller's market started to fade away, in 1949 and the early 1950s, some Studebaker dealers ended up with more trucks than they could quickly sell. Since the basic styling was unchanged from 1949 to 1953, Studebaker established a year model registration procedure that allowed late 1949 models to be sold as 1950s, late '50 models to be sold as '51s and so on. This is why no definite serial number breaks can be given for 2R series model year. To accurately date a 1949-53 Studebaker truck, the serial number *and* date it was sold to a retail customer needs to be known. Sales in 1949 were very good. Total 2R series (½-ton to 2-ton) sales for the 1949 calendar year were 63,473.

Pricing

1949	5	4	3	2	1
½ Ton	600	1200	2000	2800	4000
¾-Ton	530	1050	1750	2450	3500

1950 STUDEBAKER

1950 Studebaker Pickup (FKF)

MODELS 2R5, 2R6, 2R10 AND 2R11 — SIX-CYLINDER: — The 2R series proved to be a big sales hit in 1949, so no big changes were made in 1950. Early in the model year, a sliding seat mechanism was adopted on all models. A kit allowed this seat to be installed on earlier models. Also, early in the year the horn button medallion was changed from script to block letters. Another early change was the switching of the standard shock absorbers from the lever arm type to the direct action tubular type. The compression ratio was raised from 6.5:1 to 7:1 on the 170 cu. in. engine. This raised the horsepower from 80 to 85. On April 11, 1950, it was announced that the larger 245 cu. in. Commander six-cylinder engine could be ordered in the ½-, ¾- and one-ton models. It was already standard in the larger models. The ½-ton with the "245" was called a 2R6 and the ¾-ton with the "245" was called a 2R11. The 2R6 and 2R11 came standard with heavy-duty front springs. Very few 2R6s or 2R11s were sold during the 1950 model year. As in the past, some new exterior colors were announced each year during 2R series production.

1950 Studebaker Pickup Truck (D.A. Derr)

1950 Studebaker ¾-Ton Utility Truck (A&A)

I.D. DATA: Serial and engine number locations were the same as 1949. Exact serial number breaks between 1949 and 1950 2R5 and 2R10 models were not established. The starting serial number for the 2R6 was R6-101. The starting serial number for the 2R11 was R11-101. The starting engine number for the 2 R6 and 2R11 was 6R-101. The year of a 2R series truck depended on its serial number and when it was first sold to a retail customer.

Model No.	Body Type	Factory Price ($)	Weight	GVW (lbs)	Prod. Total
½-Ton					
2R5	Pickup	1262	2675	4600	Note 1
½-Ton					
2R6	Pickup	1312	2900	4600	Note 1
¾-Ton					
2R10	Pickup	1367	3040	6100	Note 1
2R11	Pickup	1417	3265	6100	Note 1

NOTE 1: Exact model year breakdowns of 1949-53 2R series truck production is impossible to give because the model year designation depended on a serial number/date of sale formula. Total domestic production for the five years was very close to the following: 2R5 - 110,500; 2R6 - 12,150; 2R10 - 37,300; 2R11 - 10,350.

ENGINE: (2R5 and 2R10) Six-cylinder. L-head. Cast iron block. Displacement: 169.6 cu. in. Bore and stroke: 3 in. x 4 in. Compression ratio: 7.0:1. Brake horsepower: 85 at 4000 R.P.M. Taxable horsepower: 21.6. Maximum torque: 138 ft. lbs. Main bearings: Four. Valve lifters: Solid. Carburetor: Carter Model BBR1-633S one-barrel.

ENGINE (Big Six): (2R6 and 2R11) Six-cylinder. L-head. Cast iron block. Displacement: 245.6 cu. in. Bore and stroke: 3-5/16 in. x 4¾ in. Compression ratio: 7.0:1. Brake horsepower: 102 at 3200 R.P.M. Taxable horsepower: 26.3. Maximum torque: 205 ft. lbs. Main bearings: Four. Valve lifters. Solid. Carburetor: Carter Model BBR1-777SA one-barrel.

CHASSIS & BODY (2R5 and 2R6): Wheelbase: 112 in. Overall length: 185.6 in. Height: 69.75 in. Width: 75.6 in. Interior pickup box dimensions: 77.8 in. long x 48.5 in. wide x 17.1 in. high. Front tread: 60.8 in. Rear tread: 59.6 in. Tires: 6.00 x 16 four-ply.

CHASSIS & BODY (2R10 and 2R11): Wheelbase: 122 in. Overall length: 203.6 in. Height: 69.9 in. Width: 75.6 in. Interior pickup box dimensions: 95.8 in. long x 48.5 in. wide x 17.1 in. high. Front tread: 60.8 in. Rear tread: 60.4 in. Tires: 6.50 x 16 six-ply.

TECHNICAL: Sliding gear transmission. Speeds: 3F/1R. Synchromesh in second and third. Steering column shift control. Single plate dry disc clutch. I-beam front axle. 2R5 and 2R6 rear axle: Hypoid semi-floating with 4.82:1 (2R5) and 4.09:1 (2R6) overall ratios. 2R10 and 2R11 rear axle: Spiral bevel full-floating with 5.57:1 (2R10) and 4.86:1 (2R11) overall ratios. Hydraulic brakes. Steel disc wheels; slotted on 2R10 and 2R11. Lever arm or direct acting tubular shock absorbers. Variable ratio steering.

OPTIONS: Four-speed transmission with floor shift control (available on special order only). Overdrive. Hill Holder. Radio. Climatizer heater/defroster. Interior rear view mirror. Glare-proof interior rear view mirror. Visor vanity mirror. Cigarette lighter. Dual horns. Caravan Top. Steel stake rack. Chrome front bumper. Chrome or painted rear bumper. Bumper guards. Heavy-duty grille and lamp guard. Extra taillight. License plate frames. Locking gas cap. Right-hand exterior rear view mirror. Left and right exterior extension rear view mirrors. Spotlight. Fog lights. Turn signals. Underhood light. Service light. Tailgate step. Step for one or both sides of the pickup box. Rear fender gravel shields. Front splash guards. Exhaust deflector. Windshield washer. Mattex seat covers. Arm rest covers. Hand throttle. Windshield wiper vacuum booster. Fram oil filter. Heavy-duty oil bath air cleaner. Six blade fan. Early cut-in generator. 19 plate battery. Heavy-duty radiator. Two-stage rear springs. Heavy-duty rear springs. Spare tire chain and lock. Optional items specific to the 2R5 and 2R6: Wheel trim rings. 6.00 x 16 six-ply tires. 6.50 x 16 six-ply tires. 7.10 x 15 four-ply tires. Optional items specific to the 2R10 and 2R11: 7.00 x 16 six-ply tires. 7.50 x 16 eight-ply tires. Final drive ratio of 4.86:1 (2R10).

HISTORICAL: Total 2R series (½- to 2-ton) production for the 1950 calendar year was 50,323. This was down a little from 1949, which indicated that the strong postwar American demand for commercial vehicles was finally being fulfilled. Studebaker would never again reach the truck production levels it achieved in 1947-1949. The Canadian plant produced 1,823 2R5s during the 1950 calendar year.

Pricing

1950	5	4	3	2	1
½-Ton					
2R5 P.U.	600	1200	2000	2800	4000
2R6 P.U.	620	1230	2050	2900	4100
¾-Ton					
2R10 P.U.	530	1050	1750	2450	3500
2R11 P.U.	540	1080	1800	2500	3600

1951 STUDEBAKER

1951 Studebaker Pickup Truck (DSSC)

MODELS 2R5, 2R6, 2R10 AND 2R11 — SIX-CYLINDER: — Basic ½ and ¾-ton models were continued unchanged from late 1950. A new 2R6 ½-ton off-road Trailblazer was introduced in 1951. The Trailblazer used four or six-ply low pressure 9.00 x 13 tires. The Trailblazer was recommended for use in sand or snow. Various companies, including Montpelier, built panel bodies for light-duty Studebaker trucks. Export woody station wagons were built by the Cantrell Company of Huntington, N.Y. They used ½- or ¾-ton windshield cowl chassis. Because of inflation caused by the Korean War, prices were raised about seven percent. Studebaker introduced a V8 engine for its Commander car models in 1951, but they did not use it in any domestic commercial vehicles.

I.D. DATA: Serial and engine number locations were the same as 1949-50. Exact serial number breaks between 1950 and 1951 models were not established. The year of a 2R series truck depended on its serial number and when it was first sold to a retail customer.

Model No. 1951 2R Series	Body Type	Factory Price ($)	Weight	GVW (lbs)	Prod. Total
½-Ton					
2R5	Pickup	1352	2675	4600	Note 1
2R6	Pickup	1402	2900	4600	Note 1
¾-Ton					
2R10	Pickup	1467	3040	6100	Note 1
2R11	Pickup	1517	3265	6100	Note 1

NOTE 1: Exact model year breakdowns of 1949-53 2R series truck production is impossible to give because the model year designation depended on a serial number/date of sale formula. Total domestic production for the five years was very close to the following: 2R5 - 110,500; 2R6 - 12,150; 2R10 - 37,300; 2R11 - 10,350.

ENGINE (2R5 and 2R10): Six-cylinder. L-head. Cast iron block. Displacement: 169.6 cu. in. Bore and stroke: 3 in. x 4 in. Compression ratio: 7.0:1. Brake horsepower: 85 at 4000 R.P.M. Taxable horsepower: 21.6. Maximum torque: 138 ft. lbs. Main bearings: Four. Valve lifters: Solid. Carburetor: Carter Model BBR1-633S one-barrel.

ENGINE (2R6 and 2R11): Six-cylinder. L-head. Cast iron block. Displacement: 245.6 cu. in. Bore and stroke: 3-5/16 in. x 4¾ in. Compression ratio: 7.0:1. Brake horsepower: 102 at 3200 R.P.M. Taxable horsepower: 26.3. Maximum torque: 205 ft. lbs. Main bearings: Four. Valve lifters. Solid. Carburetor: Carter Model BBR1-777SA one-barrel.

CHASSIS & BODY (2R5 and 2R6): Wheelbase: 112 in. Overall length: 185.6 in. Height: 69.75 in. Width: 75.6 in. Interior pickup box dimensions: 77.8 in. long x 48.5 in. wide x 17.1 in. high. Front tread: 60.8 in. Rear tread: 59.6 in. Tires: 6.00 x 16 four-ply.

CHASSIS & BODY (2R10 and 2R11): Wheelbase: 122 in. Overall length: 203.6 in. Height: 69.9 in. Width: 75.6 in. Interior pickup box dimensions: 95.8 in. long x 48.5 in. wide x 17.1 in. high. Front tread: 60.8 in. Rear tread: 60.4 in. Tires: 6.50 x 16 six-ply.

1951 Studebaker Trailblazer Pickup (FKF)

TECHNICAL: Sliding gear transmission. Speeds: 3F/1R. Synchromesh in second and third. Steering column shift control. Single plate dry disc clutch. I-beam front axle. 2R5 and 2R6 rear axle: Hypoid semi-floating with 4.82:1 (early) or 4.89:1 (late) (2R5) and 4.09:1 (2R6) overall ratios. 2R10 and 2R11 rear axle: Spiral bevel full-floating with 5.57:1 (2R10) and 4.86:1 (2R11) overall ratios. Hydraulic brakes. Steel disc wheels; slotted on 2R10 and 2R11. Direct acting tubular shock absorbers. Variable ratio steering.

OPTIONS: Four-speed transmission with floor shift control (available on special order only). Overdrive. Hill Holder. Radio. Climatizer heater/defroster. Interior rear view mirror. Glare-proof interior rear view mirror. Visor vanity mirror. Cigarette lighter. Dual horns. Caravan Top. Steel stake rack. Chrome front bumper. Chrome or painted rear bumper. Bumper guards. Heavy-duty grille and lamp guard. Extra taillight. License plate frames. Locking gas cap. Right-hand exterior rear view mirror. Left and right exterior extension rear view mirrors. Spotlight. Fog lights. Turn signals. Underhood light. Service light. Tailgate step. Step for one or both sides of the pickup box. Rear fender gravel shields. Front splash guards. Exhaust deflector. Windshield washer. Mattex seat covers. Arm rest covers. Hand throttle. Windshield wiper vacuum booster. Fram oil filter. Heavy-duty oil bath air cleaner. Six blade fan. Early cut-in generator. 19 plate battery. Heavy-duty radiator. Two-stage rear springs. Heavy-duty rear springs. Spare tire chain and lock. Optional items specific to the 2R5 and 2R6: Wheel trim rings. 6.00 x 16 six-ply tires. 6.50 x 16 six-ply tires. 7.10 x 15 four-ply tires. Final drive ratios of 4.55:1 or 4.09:1 (2R5); 4.55:1 or 4.89:1 (2R6). Trailblazer package (2R6 only). Optional items specific to the 2R10 and 2R11: 7.00 x 16 six-ply tires. 7.50 x 16 eight-ply tires. Final drive ratio of 4.86:1 (2R10).

HISTORICAL: Total 2R series (½- to 2-ton) production for the 1951 calendar year was 51,814. The Canadian plant produced 1,546 Model 2R5s during the 1951 calendar year.

Pricing

1951	5	4	3	2	1
½-Ton					
2R5 P.U.	600	1200	2000	2800	4000
2R6 P.U.	620	1230	2050	2900	4100
¾-Ton					
2R10 P.U.	530	1050	1750	2450	3500
2R11 P.U.	540	1080	1800	2500	3600

1952 STUDEBAKER

1952 Studebaker ¾-Ton Pickup (FKF)

MODELS 2R5, 2R6, 2R10 AND 2R11 — SIX-CYLINDER: — The 2R series was continued another year with only minor changes. In January 1952, the interior accent color was changed from Tuscan tan to Pilot gray. At the same time, the seat frame was changed from Tuscan tan to maroon and the interior vinyl covered weather stripping was changed from brown to maroon.

I.D. DATA: Serial and engine number locations were the same as 1949-51. Exact serial number breaks between 1951 and 1952 models were not established. The year of a 2R series truck depended on its serial number and when it was first sold to a retail customer.

Model No. 1952 2R Series	Body Type	Factory Price ($)	Weight	GVW (lbs)	Prod. Total
½-Ton					
2R5	Pickup	1404	2675	4600	Note 1
2R6	Pickup	1454	2900	4600	Note 1
¾-Ton					
2R10	Pickup	1527	3040	6100	Note 1
2R11	Pickup	1574	3265	6100	Note 1

NOTE 1: Exact model year breakdowns of 1949-53 2R series truck production is impossible to give because the model year designation depended on a serial number/date of sale formula. Total domestic production for the five years was very close to the following: 2R5 - 110,500; 2R6 - 12,150; 2R10 - 37,300; 2R11 - 10,350.

ENGINE (2R5 and 2R10): Six-cylinder. L-head. Cast iron block. Displacement: 169.6 cu. in. Bore and stroke: 3 in. x 4 in. Compression ratio: 7.0:1. Brake horsepower: 85 at 4000 R.P.M. Taxable horsepower: 21.6. Maximum torque: 138 ft. lbs. Main bearings: Four. Valve lifters: Solid. Carburetor: Carter Model BBR1-633S one-barrel.

ENGINE (2R6 and 2R11): Six-cylinder. L-head. Cast iron block. Displacement: 245.6 cu. in. Bore and stroke: 3-5/16 in. x 4¾ in. Compression ratio: 7.0:1. Brake horsepower: 102 at 3200 R.P.M. Taxable horsepower: 26.3. Maximum torque: 205 ft. lbs. Main bearings: Four. Valve lifters. Solid. Carburetor: Carter Model BBR1-777SA one-barrel.

CHASSIS & BODY (2R5 and 2R6): Wheelbase: 112 in. Overall length: 185.6 in. Height: 69.75 in. Width: 75.6 in. Interior pickup box dimensions: 77.8 in. long x 48.5 in. wide x 17.1 in. high. Front tread: 60.8 in. Rear tread: 59.6 in. Tires: 6.00 x 16 four-ply.

CHASSIS & BODY (2R10 and 2R11): Wheelbase: 122 in. Overall length: 203.6 in. Height: 69.9 in. Width: 75.6 in. Interior pickup box dimensions: 95.8 in. long x 48.5 in. wide x 17.1 in. high. Front tread: 60.8 in. Rear tread: 60.4 in. Tires: 6.50 x 16 six-ply.

TECHNICAL: Sliding gear transmission. Speeds: 3F/1R. Synchromesh in second and third. Steering column shift control. Single plate dry disc clutch. I-beam front axle. 2R5 and 2R6 rear axle: Hypoid semi-floating with 4.89:1 (2R5) and 4.09:1 (2R6) overall ratios. 2R10 and 2R11 rear axle: Spiral bevel full-floating with 5.57:1 (2R10) and 4.86:1 (2R11) overall ratios. Hydraulic brakes. Steel disc wheels; slotted on 2R10 and 2R11. Direct acting tubular shock absorbers. Variable ratio steering.

OPTIONS: Four-speed transmission with floor shift control (available on special order only). Overdrive. Hill Holder. Radio. Climatizer heater/defroster. Interior rear view mirror. Glare-proof interior rear view mirror. Visor vanity mirror. Cigarette lighter. Dual horns. Caravan Top. Steel stake rack. Chrome front bumper. Chrome or painted rear bumper. Bumper guards. Heavy-duty grille and lamp guard. Extra taillight. License plate frames. Locking gas cap. Right-hand exterior rear view mirror. Left and right exterior extension rear view mirrors. Spotlight. Fog lights. Turn signals. Underhood light. Service light. Tailgate step. Step for one or both sides of the pickup box. Rear fender gravel shields. Front splash guards. Exhaust deflector. Windshield washer. Mattex seat covers. Arm rest covers. Hand throttle. Windshield wiper vacuum booster. Fram oil filter. Heavy-duty oil bath air cleaner. Six blade fan. Early cut-in generator. 19 plate battery. Heavy-duty radiator. Two-stage rear springs. Heavy-duty rear springs. Spare tire chain and lock. Optional items specific to the 2R5 and 2R6: Wheel trim rings. 6.00 x 16 six-ply tires. 6.50 x 16 six-ply tires. 7.10 x 15 four-ply tires. Final drive ratios of 4.55:1 or 4.09:1 (2R5); 4.55:1 or 4.89:1 (2R6). Trailblazer package (2R6 only). Optional items specific to the 2R10 and 2R11: 7.00 x 16 six-ply tires. 7.50 x 16 eight-ply tires. Final drive ratio of 4.86:1 (2R10).

HISTORICAL: Total 2R series (½- to 2-ton) production for the 1952 calendar year was 58,873. The Canadian plant produced 963 Model 2R5s during the 1952 calendar year.

Pricing

1952	5	4	3	2	1
½-Ton					
2R5 P.U.	600	1200	2000	2800	4000
2R6 P.U.	620	1230	2050	2900	4100
¾-Ton					
2R10 P.U.	530	1050	1750	2450	3500
2R11 P.U.	540	1080	1800	2500	3600

1953 STUDEBAKER

1953 Studebaker Pickup with Caravan Top (FKF)

MODELS 2R5, 2R6, 2R10 AND 2R11 — SIX-CYLINDER: — The final year of 2R production again saw few changes from the previous year. Some new exterior colors were introduced and tinted glass was introduced as a new extra cost option.

I.D. DATA: Serial and engine number locations were the same as 1949-52. Exact serial number breaks between 1952 and 1953 models were not established. The year of a 2R series truck depended on its serial number and when it was first sold to a retail customer.

Model No.	Body Type	Factory Price ($)	Weight	GVW (lbs)	Prod. Total
1953 2R Series					
½-Ton					
2R5	Pickup	1404	2675	4600	Note 1
2R6	Pickup	1454	2900	4600	Note 1
¾-Ton					
2R10	Pickup	1527	3040	6100	Note 1
2R11	Pickup	1574	3265	6100	Note 1

NOTE 1: Exact model year breakdowns of 1949-53 2R series truck production is impossible to give because the model year designation depended on a serial number/date of sale formula. Total domestic production for the five years was very close to the following: 2R5 - 110,500; 2R6 - 12,150; 2R10 - 37,300; 2R11 - 10,350.

ENGINE (2R5 and 2R10): Six-cylinder. L-head. Cast iron block. Displacement: 169.6 cu. in. Bore and stroke: 3 in. x 4 in. Compression ratio: 7.0:1. Brake horsepower: 85 at 4000 R.P.M. Taxable horsepower: 21.6. Maximum torque: 138 ft. lbs. Main bearings: Four. Valve lifters: Solid. Carburetor: Carter Model BBR1-633S one-barrel.

ENGINE (2R6 and 2R11): Six-cylinder. L-head. Cast iron block. Displacement: 245.6 cu. in. Bore and stroke: 3-5/16 in. x 4¾ in. Compression ratio: 7.0:1. Brake horsepower: 102 at 3200 R.P.M. Taxable horsepower: 26.3. Maximum torque: 205 ft. lbs. Main bearings: Four. Valve lifters: Solid. Carburetor: Carter Model BBR1-777SA one-barrel.

CHASSIS & BODY (2R5 and 2R6): Wheelbase: 112 in.. Overall length: 185.6 in. Height: 69.75 in. Width: 75.6 in. Interior pickup box dimensions: 77.8 in. long x 48.5 in. wide x 17.1 in. high. Front tread: 60.8 in. Rear tread: 59.6 in. Tires: 6.00 x 16 four-ply.

CHASSIS & BODY (2R10 and 2R11): Wheelbase: 122 in. Overall length: 203.6 in. Height: 69.9 in. Width: 75.6 in. Interior pickup box dimensions: 95.8 in. long x 48.5 in. wide x 17.1 in. high. Front tread: 60.8 in. Rear tread: 60.4 in. Tires: 6.50 x 16 six-ply.

TECHNICAL: Sliding gear transmission. Speeds: 3F/1R. Synchromesh in second and third. Steering column shift control. Single plate dry disc clutch. I-beam front axle. 2R5 and 2R6 rear axle: Hypoid semi-floating with 4.89:1 (2R5) and 4.09:1 (2R6) overall ratios. 2R10 and 2R11 rear axle: Spiral bevel full-floating with 5.57:1 (2R10) and 4.86:1 (2R11) overall ratios. Hydraulic brakes. Steel disc wheels; slotted on 2R10 and 2R11. Direct acting tubular shock absorbers. Variable ratio steering.

OPTIONS: Four-speed transmission with floor shift control (available on special order only). Overdrive. Hill Holder. Radio. Climatizer heater/defroster. Interior rear view mirror. Glare-proof interior rear view mirror. Visor vanity mirror. Cigarette lighter. Dual horns. Caravan Top. Steel stake rack. Chrome front bumper. Chrome or painted rear bumper. Bumper guards. Heavy-duty grille and lamp guard. Extra taillight. License plate frames. Locking gas cap. Right-hand exterior rear view mirror. Left and right exterior extension rear view mirrors. Tinted glass. Spotlight. Fog lights. Turn signals. Underhood light. Service light. Tailgate step. Step for one or both sides of the pickup box. Rear fender gravel shields. Front splash guards. Exhaust deflector. Windshield washer. Mattex seat covers. Arm rest covers. Hand throttle. Windshield wiper vacuum booster. Fram oil filter. Heavy-duty oil bath air cleaner. Six blade fan. Early cut-in generator. 19 plate battery. Heavy-duty radiator. Two-stage rear springs. Heavy-duty rear springs. Spare tire chain and lock. Optional) items specific to the 2R5 and 2R6: Wheel trim rings. 6.00 x 16 six-ply tires. 6.50 x 16 six-ply tires. 7.10 x 15 four-ply tires. Final drive ratios of 4.55:1 or 4.09:1 (2R5); 4.55:1 or 4.89:1 (2R6). Trailblazer package (2R6 only). Optional items specific to the 2R10 and 2R11: 7.00 x 16 six-ply tires. 7.50 x 16 eight-ply tires. Final drive ratio of 4.86:1 (2R10).

HISTORICAL: Total 2R series (½- to 2-ton) production for the 1953 calendar year was 32,012. This was way down from 1952. Many factors caused the decline, including less demand, an old styling, reduced car sales (thus less floor room traffic) and non-competitive pricing because of higher per unit expenses. These problems plagued Studebaker from 1953 on. The Canadian plant produced 772 Model 2R5s in 1953.

Pricing

1953	5	4	3	2	1
½-Ton					
2R5 P.U.	600	1200	2000	2800	4000
2R6 P.U.	620	1230	2050	2900	4100
¾-Ton					
2R10 P.U.	530	1050	1750	2450	3500
2R11 P.U.	540	1080	1800	2500	3600

1954 STUDEBAKER

MODELS 3R5, 3R6, 3R10 AND 3R11 — SIX-CYLINDER: — After five years (1949-1953) of the same styling and trim, Studebaker finally gave their trucks a minor facelift in 1954. The restyled models were called the 3R series and were introduced in March 1954. Except for a new grille with fewer horizontal openings, all the sheet metal was the same as 1949-53. The major changes were in trim and the switch to a curved, one-piece windshield. The headlight rims, side nameplates and hubcaps (3R5 and 3R6) were restyled for 1954. The hood ornament was made an extra cost option and the outside mirror was switched from round to square. The bumper was made solid body color and the grille was painted completely in the accent color. On the inside, the glove box door was restyled and the instruments were rearranged and changed from rectangular to round dials. A V8 engine was introduced in larger models, but the light-duty trucks continued with the same engines that were offered in 1953. The compression ratio of the 170 cubic inch engine was raised from 7:1 to 7.5:1, but no change in horsepower was reported. An electric windshield wiper kit was added to the options list. An adaptor plate allowed this wiper kit to be fitted to 1949-1953 models. Vacuum type wipers continued as standard equipment.

1954 Studebaker Pickup (FKF)

I.D. DATA: Serial and engine number locations were the same as 1949-53. The starting serial number for the 3R5 and R5-111,401 (HR5-6,601 in Canada). The starting serial number for the 3R6 was R6-12,651. The starting serial number for the 3R10 was R10-37,501. The staring serial number for the 3R11 was R11-10,651. The starting engine number for the 3R5 and 3R10 was 1R-149,001. The starting engine number for the 3R6 and 3R11 was 6R-24,701.

Model No. 3R Series	Body Type	Factory Price ($)	Weight	GVW (lbs)	Prod. Total
½-Ton					
3R5	Pickup	1469	2665	4600	Note 1
3R6	Pickup	1522	2890	4800	Note 1
¾-Ton					
3R10	Pickup	1622	3040	6100	Note 1
3R11	Pickup	1675	3265	6300	Note 1

NOTE 1: Production breakdowns are not available. Total production of all 3R models (½-to two-ton) was 12,003.

1954 Studebaker Pickup (DFW/SI)

ENGINE (3R5 and 3R10): Six-cylinder. L-head. Cast iron block. Displacement: 169.6 cu. in. Bore and stroke: 3 in. x 4 in. Compression ratio: 7.5:1. Brake horsepower: 85 at 4000 R.P.M. Taxable horsepower: 21.6. Maximum torque: 138 ft. lbs. Main bearings: Four. Valve lifters: Solid. Carburetor: Carter Model BBR1-633S one-barrel.

ENGINE (3R6 and 3R11): Six-cylinder. L-head. Cast iron block. Displacement: 245.6 cu. in. Bore and stroke: 3-5/16 in. x 4¾ in. Compression ratio: 7.0:1. Brake horsepower: 102 at 3200 R.P.M. Taxable horsepower: 26.3. Maximum torque: 205 ft. lbs. Main bearings: Four. Valve lifters: Solid. Carburetor: Carter Model BBR1-777SA one-barrel.

CHASSIS & BODY (3R5 and 3R6): Wheelbase: 112 in.. Overall length: 185.6 in. Height: 69.75 in. Width: 75.6 in. Interior pickup box dimensions: 77.8 in. long x 48.5 in. wide x 17.1 in. high. Front tread: 60.8 in. Rear tread: 59.6 in. Tires: 6.00 x 16 four-ply.

CHASSIS & BODY (3R10 and 3R11): Wheelbase: 122 in. Overall length: 203.6 in. Height: 69.9 in. Width: 75.6 in. Interior pickup box dimensions: 95.8 in. long x 48.5 in. wide x 17.1 in. high. Front tread: 60.8 in. Rear tread: 60.4 in. Tires: 6.50 x 16 six-ply.

TECHNICAL: Sliding gear transmission. Speeds: 3F/1R. Synchromesh in second and third. Steering column shift control. Single plate dry disc clutch. I-beam front axle. 3R5 and 3R6 rear axle: Hypoid semi-floating with 4.89:1 (3R5) and 4.09:1 (3R6) overall ratios. 3R10 and 3R11 rear axle: Spiral bevel full-floating with 5.57:1 (3R10) and 4.86:1 (3R11) overall ratios. Hydraulic brakes. Steel disc wheels; slotted on 3R10 and 3R11. Direct acting tubular shock absorbers. Variable ratio steering.

OPTIONS: Four-speed synchromesh transmission with floor shift control. Overdrive. Hill Holder. Radio. Climatizer heater/defroster. Interior rear view mirror. Glare-proof interior rear view mirror. Visor vanity mirror. Cigarette lighter. Dual horns. Caravan Top. Chrome front bumper. Chrome or painted rear bumper. Extra taillight. Hood ornament. License plate frames. Locking gas cap. Right-hand exterior rear view mirror. Left and right exterior extension rear view mirrors. Tinted glass. Spotlight. Turn signals. Underhood light. Service light. Tailgate step. Step for one or both sides of the pickup box. Rear fender gravel shields. Front splash guards. Exhaust deflector. Windshield washer. Mattex seat covers. Arm rest covers. Hand throttle. Windshield wiper vacuum booster. Electric windshield wiper kit. Fram oil filter. Heavy-duty oil bath air cleaner. Five or six blade fan. Early cut-in generator. 19 plate battery. Heavy-duty radiator. Two-stage rear springs. Heavy-duty rear springs. 7.5:1 compression ratio ("245" engine). Spare tire chain and lock. Optional items specific to the 3R5 and 3R6: 6.00 x 16 six-ply tires. 6.50 x 16 six-ply tires. 7.10 x 15 four-ply tires. Final drive ratios of 4.55:1 or 4.09:1 (3R5); 4.55:1 or 4.89:1 (3R6). Optional items specific to the 3R10 and 3R11: 7.00 x 16 six-ply tires. 7.50 x 16 eight-ply tires. Final drive ratios of 4.86:1 (3R10) and 4.11:1 (3R11).

HISTORICAL: Studebaker truck sales, like their car sales, continued to decline in 1954. Total 1954 truck (½-ton to two-ton) calendar year production was only 15,608, about one-half of 1953 and one-quarter of 1949. Studebaker joined forces with Packard in October 1954 to form the Studebaker-Packard Corporation, but neither company gained from the consolidation. The Canadian plant produced 263 model 3R5s in 1954.

Pricing

1954	5	4	3	2	1
½-Ton					
3R5 P.U.	600	1200	2000	2800	4000
3R6 P.U.	620	1230	2050	2900	4100
¾-Ton					
3R10 P.U.	530	1050	1750	2450	3500
3R11 P.U.	540	1080	1800	2500	3600

1955 STUDEBAKER

1955 Studebaker Pickup (DS)

MODELS E5, E7, E10 AND E12 — (ALL ENGINES): — Styling changes were limited in 1955, but mechanical changes were the most numerous since 1941. Because of all the mechanical changes, the old R designation was dropped and a new E series introduced. Styling changes included a larger rear window, a larger front name plate and "V8" hood side emblems on models powered by the V8 engine. A new hood ornament had an "8" on V8 engine models and an "S" on six-cylinder engine models. Exterior door visors and a padded dash pad were fitted as standard equipment on all but a few early models. Vinyl and rayon upholstery materials replaced the earlier all vinyl upholstery. The sliding tracks for the seat cushion were discontinued and the 1949 style, with three positioning studs, was returned. The sliding seat was available as an extra cost option. Grille and wheel accent colors were color-keyed to the body colors. In mid-year, a red and white two-tone paint combination was offered on ½-ton models. Exterior door handles were made larger. Mechanical changes included making the V8 engine available in light-duty models, increasing the stroke of the small six and dropping the "245" six from the domestic lineup. The lower end of the small six was also beefed up. The new ½-ton V8 was called the E7 and the new ¾-ton V8 was named the E12. Studebaker's Automatic Drive transmission was made an extra cost option on the E7 and E12. Automatic Drive models were started with a button on the instrument panel, but all others continued with the starter button under the clutch pedal, a method Studebaker had used for many years. Tubeless tires on ½-ton models were introduced during the year. Dry element air cleaners were made standard on all models.

1955 Studebaker 3/4-Ton Pickup (A&A)

I.D. DATA: Serial number and six-cylinder engine number locations were the same as 1949-54. The V8 engine number was located on the top, front end of the cylinder block, next to the oil filler tube. The starting serial number for the E5 was E5-114,001 (HE5-101 in Canada). The starting serial number for the E7 was E7-101. The starting serial number for the E10 was E10-38,001. The starting serial number for the E12 was E12-101. The starting engine number for the E5 and E10 was 1E-101. The starting engine number for the E7 and E12 was 2E-101.

Model No. E Series	Body Type	Factory Price ($)	Weight	GVW (lbs)	Prod. Total
½-Ton					
E5	Pickup	1510	2695	4600	Note 1
E7	Pickup	1595	2970	4800	Note 1
¾-Ton					
E10	Pickup	1690	3070	6100	Note 1
E12	Pickup	1775	3345	6300	Note 1

NOTE 1: Production breakdowns are not available. Total production of all E models (½- to 2-ton) was 27,119. Serial number spans for a particular model give a rough estimate of how many of that model were built in a year.

1955 Studebaker 3/4-Ton Pickup (FKF)

ENGINE (E5 and E10): Six-cylinder. L-head. Cast iron block. Displacement: 185.6 cu. in. Bore and stroke: 3 in. x 4⅜ in. Compression ratio: 7.5:1. Brake horsepower: 92 at 3800 R.P.M. Taxable horsepower: 21.6. Maximum torque: 152 ft. lbs. Main bearings: Four. Valve lifters: Solid. Carburetor: Carter Model BBR1-2125S one-barrel.

ENGINE (E7 and E12): Eight-cylinder. OHV V8. Cast iron block. Displacement: 224.3 cu. in. Bore and stroke: 3-9/16 in. x 2-13/16 in. Compression ratio: 7.5:1. Brake horsepower: 140 at 4500 R.P.M. Taxable horsepower: 40.6. Maximum torque: 202 ft. lbs. Main bearings: Five. Valve lifters: Solid. Carburetor: Stromberg Model WW two-barrel.

CHASSIS & BODY (E5 and E7): Wheelbase: 112 in. Overall length: 185.6 in. Height: 69.75 in. Width: 75.6 in. Interior pickup box dimensions: 77.8 in. long x 48.5 in. wide x 17.1 in. high. Front tread: 60.8 in. Rear tread: 59.6 in. Tires: 6.00 x 16 four-ply.

CHASSIS & BODY (E10 and E12): Wheelbase: 122 in. Overall length: 203.6 in. Height: 69.9 in. Width: 75.6 in. Interior pickup box dimensions: 95.8 in. long x 48.5 in. wide x 17.1 in. high. Front tread: 60.8 in. Rear tread: 60.4 in. Tires: 6.50 x 16 six-ply.

TECHNICAL: Sliding gear transmission. Speeds: 3F/1R. Synchromesh in second and third. Steering column shift control. Single plate dry disc clutch. I-beam front axle. E5 and E7 rear axle: Hypoid semi-floating with 4.09, 4.27 or 4.55:1 (E5) and 3.73, 4.09, 4.27 or 4.55:1 (E7) overall ratios. E10 or E12 rear axle: Spiral bevel full-floating with 4.86 or 5.57:1 (E10) and 4.11 or 4.86:1 (E12) overall ratios. Hydraulic brakes. Steel disc wheels; slotted on E10 and E12. Direct acting tubular shock absorbers. Variable ratio steering.

1955½ Studebaker Two-Toned Pickups (FKF)

OPTIONS: Automatic Drive (E7 and E12 only). Four-speed synchromesh transmission with floor shift control. Overdrive. Hill Holder. Radio. Climatizer heater/defroster. Sliding seat mechanism. Interior rear view mirror. Map light. Accelerator pedal cover. Kleenex dispenser. Cigarette lighter. 3-D Booster horn. Red and white two-tone paint job (mid-year ½-ton only). Caravan Top. Chrome front bumper. Chrome or painted rear bumper. Extra taillight. License plate frames. Locking gas cap. Right-hand exterior rear view mirror. Left and right exterior extension rear view mirrors. Tinted glass. Spotlight. Directional signals. Underhood light. Tailgate step. Step for one or both sides of the pickup box. Rear fender gravel shields. Front splash guards. Exhaust deflector. Windshield washer. Mattex seat covers. Hand throttle. Electric windshield wiper kit. Fram oil filter. Oil bath air cleaner. Five or six blade fan. Headbolt engine heater. Early cut-in generator. 19 plate battery. Heavy-duty radiator. Two-stage rear springs. Heavy-duty springs. Optional tires specific to the E5 and E7: 6.00 x 16 six-ply, 6.50 x 16 six ply and 7.10 x 15 four-ply. Optional tires specific to the E10 and E12: 7.00 x 16 six-ply and 7.50 x 16 eight-ply.

HISTORICAL: Total 1955 truck (½- to 2-ton) calendar year sales climbed to 19,793. The slight improvement can be credited to a good year for the whole industry and the V8 option in light-duty models. The Canadian plant discontinued all truck production after producing 256 Model 1955 E5s.

Pricing

1955	5	4	3	2	1
½-Ton					
E5 P.U.	630	1250	2100	3000	4200
E7 P.U.	650	1300	2150	3050	4300
¾-Ton					
E10 P.U.	570	1140	1900	2650	3800
E12 P.U.	590	1170	1950	2700	3900

1956 STUDEBAKER

1956 Studebaker Transtar Pickup (FKF)

MODELS 2E5, 2E7, AND 2E12 — (ALL ENGINES): — Ever since it was formed in October 1954, the Studebaker-Packard Corporation had been losing money. Because of this, the Studebaker Truck Division was forced to continue with the same basic design. In an effort to attract some new interest, the 1956 2E series trucks were given a slight facelift and all were

645

labeled "Transtars." Transtar nameplates were put on the doors. This was the first time Studebaker attached a model nameplate to the outside of one of its light-duty trucks. Working within their limited budget, the Truck Division actively promoted the Transtar name. It proved to be a popular name, so much so that International picked it up after Studebaker quit the truck business. Design changes included a new, more rounded hood with a large "S T U D E B A K E R" nameplate set in an opening in the front. Large, separate parking lights were added in the front and the pickup box was made three inches wider. The wider box made it necessary to increase the rear tread by three inches. A longer (122-in.) wheelbase option was added to the ½-tons so they could be fitted with an eight-foot pickup box. Full wheel covers were added to the ½-ton option list and whitewall tires were promoted on 2E5s and 2E7s. Two-tones in several different color combinations were offered. The break line between the two colors was relocated from where it was on the 1955-½ two-tones. An optional Deluxe Cab (C4) was introduced, but its introduction was actually a sales ploy, since it had about the same features as the old 2R series cab. The 1956 standard cab was stripped of arm rests, the right sun visor and the ash tray. In 1955 the map light and sliding seat tracks had been dropped from the standard equipment list. The 1956 Deluxe Cab returned all these items except the right arm rest. It also featured a perforated headliner with fiberglass insulation. Both standard and Deluxe cabs continued with the dash pad and door visors. Mechanical options introduced included a four-barrel carburetor for the V8 engine (possibly available on late 1955 models) and a Twin-Traction, limited slip differential for ½-ton models. Studebaker was the first make to offer a limited slip differential on a light-duty truck. The ¾-ton model was switched to a hypoid-type final drive. A one-pint oil bath air cleaner was returned as standard equipment. Early in the model year, the Automatic Drive transmission option was replaced by Flightomatic. Two stage rear springs were made standard equipment. The electrical system was switched from six-volt to twelve-volt and key starting was introduced. The ¾-ton six-cylinder "10" model was dropped from domestic sales. The old "245" six-cylinder engine was available on special order. The "224" V8 was continued on the 2E7 and 2E12, but at least one person special ordered a 2E7 with a "259" V8 and a five-speed transmission. Both of these items were available in larger models. The larger one-ton pickup was continued on a 131 inch wheelbase chassis with a nine-foot pickup box.

I.D. DATA: Serial number and engine number locations were the same as 1955. The starting serial number for the 2E5 was E5-119,501. The starting serial number for the 2E7 was E7-4,601. The starting serial number for the 2E12 was E12-2,101. The starting engine number for the 2E5 was 1E-6,501. The starting engine number for the 2E7 and 2E12 was 2E-7,001.

1956 Studebaker Pickup Truck (DSSC)

Model No. 2E Series ½-Ton	Body Type	Factory Price ($)	Weight	GVW (lbs)	Prod. Total
2E5-112	Pickup	1641	2740	4800	Note 1
2E5-122	Pickup	1677	2880	4800	Note 1
2E7-112	Pickup	1738	3025	5000	Note 1
2E7-122	Pickup	1774	3165	5000	Note 1
¾-Ton					
2E12	Pickup	1915	3410	7000	Note 1

NOTE 1: Production breakdowns are not available. Total production of all 2E models (½- to 2-ton) was 20,218. Serial number spans for a particular model give a rough estimate of how many of that model were built in a year.

ENGINE (2E5): Six-cylinder. L-head. Cast iron block. Displacement: 185.6 cu. in. Bore and stroke: 3 in. x 4⅜ in. Compression ratio: 7.5:1. Brake horsepower: 92 at 3800 R.P.M. Taxable horsepower: 21.6. Maximum torque: 152 ft. lbs. Main bearings: Four. Valve lifters: Solid. Carburetor: Carter Model BBR1-2125S one-barrel.

ENGINE (2E7 and 2E12): Eight-cylinder. OHV V8. Cast iron block. Displacement: 224.3 cu. in. Bore and stroke: 3-9/16 in. x 2-13/16 in. Compression ratio: 7.5:1. Brake horsepower: 140 at 4500 R.P.M. (160 horsepower with optional four-barrel carburetor). Taxable horsepower: 40.6. Maximum torque: 202 ft. lbs. Main bearings: Five. Valve lifters: Solid. Carburetor: Stromberg Model WW two-barrel (optional: Carter Model WCFB four-barrel).

CHASSIS & BODY (2E5-112 and 2E7-112): Wheelbase: 112 in. Overall length: 185.6 in. Height: 69.75 in. Width: 77.5 in. Interior pickup box dimensions: 77.8 in. long x 51.5 in. wide x 17.1 in. high. Front tread: 60.8 in. Rear tread: 62.6 in. Tires: 6.00 x 16 four-ply.

1956 Studebaker 3/4-Ton Transtar Pickup (FKF)

CHASSIS & BODY (2E5-122, 2E7-122 and 2E12): Wheelbase: 122 in. Overall length: 203.6 in. Height: 69.75 in. (69.6 in. for 2E12). Width: 77.5 in. Interior pickup box dimensions: 95.8 in. long x 51.5 in. wide x 17.1 in. high. Front tread: 60.8 in. Rear tread: 62.6 in. (63 in. for 2E12). Tires: 6.00 x 16 four-ply (7.00 x 16 six-ply on 2E12).

TECHNICAL: Sliding gear transmission. Speeds: 3F/1R. Synchromesh in second and third. Steering column shift control. Single plate dry disc clutch. I-beam front axle. 2E5 and 2E7 rear axle: Hypoid semi-floating with 4.27 or 4.55:1 (2E5) and 3.73, 4.09 or 4.27:1 (2E7) overall ratios. 2E12 rear axle: Hypoid full-floating with 4.11 or 4.88:1 overall ratios. Hydraulic brakes. Steel disc wheels; slotted on 2E12. Direct acting tubular shock absorbers. Variable ratio steering.

OPTIONS: Automatic transmission (2E7 and 2E12 only). Four-speed synchromesh transmission with floor shift control. Overdrive. Hill Holder. Twin-Traction (½-ton models only). Deluxe Cab. Radio. Climatizer heater/defroster. Sliding seat mechanism. Interior rear view mirror. Ashtray. Right-hand sun visor. Seat pad. Safety seat belts. Arm rests. Compass. Traffic light viewer. Map light. Accelerator pedal cover. Kleenex dispenser. Cigarette lighter. Dual horns. Two-tone paint. Caravan Top. Painted rear bumper. Extra taillight. Full wheel covers (½-ton only). License plate frames. Locking gas cap. Right-hand exterior rear view mirror. Left and right exterior extension rear view mirrors. Tinted glass. Spotlight. Directional signals. Underhood light. Tailgate step. Step for one or both sides of the pickup box. Rear fender gravel shields. Front splash guards. Exhaust deflector. Windshield washer. Mattex seat covers. Hand throttle. Electric windshield wipers (standard on V8 with automatic transmission). Fram oil filter. One quart oil bath air cleaner. Governor (V8 two-barrel models only). V8 power package (four-barrel carburetor and large air cleaner). Five or six blade fan. Headbolt engine heater. Heavy-duty battery. Heavy-duty radiator. Heavy-duty springs. Heavy-duty shock absorbers. Brake fluid reservoir. Optional tires specific to the 2E5 and 2E7: 6.00 x 16 six-ply, 6.50 x 16 six-ply and 7.10 x 15 four-ply (black or whitewall). Optional tires specific to the 2E12: 7.50 x 16 eight-ply and 7.50 x 17 eight-ply.

HISTORICAL: Production was only a little off of 1955, but way below the record set in 1947-52. Fancy two-tones and numerous options did not help improve sales. The product was good, but prices were not competitive and people were afraid Studebaker-Packard was going out of business. During the year, the Chippewa Avenue plant was leased to Curtiss-Wright and Studebaker truck production was moved back to the main plant.

Pricing

	5	4	3	2	1
1956					
½-Ton					
2E5 (S.W.B.) P.U.	630	1250	2100	3000	4200
2E5 (L.W.B.) P.U.	630	1250	2100	3000	4200
2E7 (S.W.B.) P.U.	700	1400	2350	3250	4700
2E7 (L.W.B.) P.U.	700	1400	2350	3250	4700
¾-Ton					
2E12 P.U.	650	1300	2150	3050	4300

1957 STUDEBAKER

MODELS 3E5, 3E6, 3E7, 3E11 AND 3E12 — (ALL ENGINES): — During the mid-fifties, Studebaker felt it needed annual styling changes for its trucks, so the 1957 Series 3E Transtar models included several changes from 1956, although the basic 1949 body was still being used. A new fiberglass grille with three "buck teeth" and a much larger front bumper gave the light-duty models a new appearance. The parking lights were moved to the top of the front fenders and two-tone models were again given a different separation line. Check mark trim strips were used on the cab to separate the two colors. A safety swing away taillight was made standard equipment. The right-hand taillight was still an extra cost option. On the inside, new instruments, with warning (idiot) lights for oil pressure and charge/discharge, were adopted. The optional Climatizer controls were moved to the center of the dash, thus forcing the optional radio to be hung under the instrument panel. A chrome Transtar dash nameplate, chrome door visors, chrome exterior mirrors and chrome parking lights were added to the Deluxe Cab (C4) package. The hood nameplate was now painted on standard trim models and chrome on Deluxe models. The sliding seat tracks were returned as standard equipment. On V8s, the "224" V8 was replaced by the longer stroke "259" V8. Also, the "245" six was returned as a standard option. Power brakes were added as an option on all models. A heavy-duty engine with chrome top rings, heavy-duty valves, valve rotary caps, etc. was optional on V8 models.

I.D. DATA: Serial number and engine number locations were the same as 1955-56.

starting serial numbers	starting engine numbers
1957 3E5: E5-123,001	1957 3E5: 1E-10,101
1957 3E6: E6-15,501	1957 3E6 & 3E11: 4E-3,401
1957 3E7: E7-7,601	1957 3E7 & 3E12: 3E-2,701*
1957 3E11: E11-12,401	
1957 3E12: E12-3,001	

* Heavy-duty 259 engines had a "5E" engine number prefix.

Model No.	Body Type	Factory Price ($)	Weight	GVW (lbs)	Prod. Total
1957 3E Series					
½-Ton					
3E5-112	Pickup	1722	2745	4800	Note 1
3E5-122	Pickup	1758	2875	4800	Note 1
3E6-112	Pickup	1754	2950	5000	Note 1
3E6-122	Pickup	1789	3075	5000	Note 1
3E7-112	Pickup	1853	3020	5000	Note 1
3E7-122	Pickup	1888	3160	5000	Note 1
¾-Ton					
3E11	Pickup	1911	3310	7000	Note 1
3E12	Pickup	2010	3395	7000	Note 1

NOTE 1: Production breakdowns are not available. Total production of all 1957 3E models (½- to two-ton) was 11,185. Serial number spans for a particular model give a rough estimate of how many of that model were built in a year.

1957 Studebaker Transtar Pickup (A&A)

ENGINE (3E5): Six-cylinder. L-head. Cast iron block. Displacement: 185.6 cu. in. Bore and stroke: 3 in. x 4⅜ in. Compression ratio: 7.5:1. Brake horsepower: 92 at 3800 R.P.M. Taxable horsepower: 21.6. Maximum torque: 152 ft. lbs. Main bearings: Four. Valve lifters: Solid. Carburetor: Carter Model BBR1-2125S one-barrel.

ENGINE (3E6 and 3E11): Six-cylinder. L-head. Cast iron block. Displacement: 245.6 cu. in. Bore and stroke: 3-5/16 in. x 4¾ in. Compression ratio: 7.5:1. Brake horsepower: 106 at 3400 R.P.M. Taxable horsepower: 26.3. Maximum torque: 204 ft. lbs. Main bearings: Four. Valve lifters: Solid. Carburetor: Carter Model BBR1-777SA one-barrel.

ENGINE (3E7 and 3E12): Eight-cylinder. OHV V8. Cast iron block. Displacement: 259.2 cu. in. Bore and stroke: 3-9/16 in. x 3¼ in. Compression ratio: 7.5:1. Brake horsepower: 170 at 4200 R.P.M. (178 horsepower with optional four-barrel carburetor). Taxable horsepower: 40.6. Maximum torque: 250 ft. lbs. Main bearings: Five. Valve lifters: Solid. Carburetor: Stromberg Model WW two-barrel (optional: Carter Model WCFB four-barrel).

CHASSIS & BODY (3E5-112, 3E6-112 and 3E7-112): Wheelbase: 112 in. Overall length: 185.6 in. Height: 69.75 in. Width: 77.5 in. Interior pickup box dimensions: 77.8 in. long x 51.5 in. wide x 17.1 in. high. Front tread: 60.8 in. Rear tread: 62.6 in. Tires: 6.00 x 16 four-ply.

CHASSIS & BODY (3E5-122, 3E6-122, 3E7-122, 3E11 and 3E12): Wheelbase: 122 in. Overall length: 203.6 in. Height: 69.75 in. (69.6 in. for 3E11 and 3E12). Width: 77.5 in. Interior pickup box dimensions: 95.8 in. long x 51.5 in. wide x 17.1 in. high. Front tread: 60.8 in. Rear tread: 62.6 in. (63 in. for 3E11 and 3E12). Tires: 6.00 x 16 four-ply (7.00 x 16 six-ply on 3E11 and 3E12).

1957 Studebaker Walk-in Bakery Delivery (A&A)

TECHNICAL: Sliding gear transmission. Speeds: 3F/1R. Synchromesh in second and third. Steering column shift control. Single plate dry disc clutch. I-beam front axle. 3E5, 3E6 and 3E7 rear axle: Hypoid semi-floating with 4.27 or 4.55:1 (3E5); 4.09 or 4.27:1 (3E6) and 3.73, 4.09 or 4.27:1 (3E7) overall ratios. 3E11 and 3E12 rear axle: Hypoid full-floating with 4.10 or 4.88:1 overall ratios. Hydraulic brakes. Steel disc wheels. Direct acting tubular shock absorbers. Variable ratio steering.

OPTIONS: Flightomatic transmission (3E7 and 3E12 only). Four-speed synchromesh transmission with floor shift control. Overdrive. Hill Holder. Power brakes. Twin-Traction (½-ton models only). Deluxe Cab. Radio. Climatizer heater/defroster. Interior rear view mirror. Ash tray. Right-hand sun visor. Seat pad. Safety seat belts. Arm rests. Compass. Traffic light viewer. Map light. Accelerator pedal cover. Kleenex dispenser. Cigarette lighter. Dual horns. Two-tone paint. Caravan Top. Painted rear bumper. Extra taillight. License plate frames. Locking gas cap. Right-hand exterior rear view mirror. Left and right exterior extension rear view mirrors. Tinted glass. Spotlight. Directional signals. Underhood light. Front splash guards. Fram oil filter. One quart oil bath air cleaner. Governor (V8 two-barrel models only). Heavy-duty engine (V8 models only). V8 power package (four-barrel carburetor and large air cleaner). Five or six blade fan. Headbolt engine heater. Heavy-duty battery. Heavy-duty radiator. Heavy-duty springs. Heavy-duty shock absorbers. Brake fluid reservoir. Optional tires specific to the 3E5, 3E6 and 3E7: 6.00 x 16 six-ply, 6.50 x 16 six-ply and 7.10 x 15 four-ply (black or whitewall). Optional tires specific to the 3E11 and 3E12: 8.00 x 17 eight-ply and 8.00 x 19.5 eight-ply.

HISTORICAL: Sales continued to fall while production costs forced price increases for all models. Studebaker-Packard was close to going out of business in 1957.

Pricing

1957	5	4	3	2	1
½-Ton					
3E5 (S.W.B.) P.U.	630	1250	2100	3000	4200
3E5 (L.W.B.) P.U.	630	1250	2100	3000	4200
3E6 (S.W.B.) P.U.	650	1300	2150	3050	4300
3E6 (L.W.B.) P.U.	650	1300	2150	3050	4300
3E7 (S.W.B.) P.U.	750	1500	2500	3500	5000
3E7 (L.W.B.) P.U.	750	1500	2500	3500	5000
¾-Ton					
3E11 P.U.	570	1140	1900	2650	3800
3E12 P.U.	650	1300	2150	3050	4300

1958 STUDEBAKER

MODELS 3E1, 3E5, 3E6, 3E7, 3E11 AND 3E12 — (ALL ENGINES): — Studebaker-Packard's precarious position forced the Studebaker Truck Division to continue the 3E series into 1958, but this did not stop them from making two major introductions for the 1958 model year. The first was a four-wheel-drive option for ½-, ¾- and one-ton models powered by the "245" six and V8 engines. The four-wheel-drive front axle was manufactured by Napco. Models fitted with four-wheel-drive had a "D" suffix added to their model number. A scalloped right rear fender allowed room for mounting the spare tire on the side of the pickup box on four-wheel-drive models. This type of spare tire mounting was made optional on other models. The four-wheel drive option cost about $1,100, a sizeable sum in 1958. The other introduction was a stripped down ½-ton called the Scotsman. The Scotsman name was first introduced by Studebaker in mid-1957 for their new bare-bones car model. The 1958 Scotsman pickup (3E1) was only available with the "185" six. The Scotsman used a modified 2R series grille, small front bumper and plaid name decals on the hood front, instrument panel and rear apron. The Scotsman came with an inside rear view mirror, but outside ones were extra cost. The Scotsman cab was labeled the "C1" cab. It had no glove box door, a non-sliding seat, painted hubcaps and headlight rims and many other cost cutting features. All the trimming down allowed Studebaker to sell the Scotsman pickup for only $1,595. It was the lowest priced full-sized pickup sold in the U.S. The regular Transtar models remained unchanged from 1957. More effort was made in 1958 to promote sales of non-pickup bodies for their light-duty trucks. Special Powers bodies on 3E6 and 3E11 models were advertised for use by plumbers, contractors and public utility companies.

I.D. DATA: Serial number and engine number locations were the same as 1955-57.

starting serial numbers	starting engine numbers
1958 3E1: E1-101	
1958 3E5: E5-125,401	1958 3E1 & 3E5: 1E-12,601
1958 3E6: E6-16,901	1958 3E6 & 3E11: 4E-5,701
1958 3E7: E7-9,801	1958 3E7 & 3E12: 3E-6,301*
1958 3E11: E11-13,001	
1958 3E12: E12-3,601	

* Heavy-duty 259 engines had a "5E" engine number prefix.

1958 Studebaker 3/4-Ton Transtar 4x4 Pickup (FKF)

Model No.	Body Type	Factory Price ($)	Weight	GVW (lbs)	Prod. Total
1958 3E Series					
½-Ton					
3E1-112	Pickup	1595	2600	4800	Note 1
3E5-112	Pickup	1773	2745	4800	Note 1
3E5-122	Pickup	1808	2875	4800	Note 1
3E6-112	Pickup	1804	2950	5000	Note 1
3E6-122	Pickup	1839	3075	5000	Note 1
3E7-112	Pickup	1903	3020	5000	Note 1
3E7-122	Pickup	1938	3160	5000	Note 1
¾-Ton					
3E11	Pickup	1961	3310	7000	Note 1
3E12	Pickup	2060	3395	7000	Note 1

NOTE 1: Production breakdowns are not available. Total production of all 1958 Series 3E models (½- to two-ton) was 7,085. Serial number spans for a particular model give a rough estimate of how many of that model were built in a year.

ENGINE (3E1 and 3E5): Six-cylinder. L-head. Cast iron block. Displacement: 185.6 cu. in. Bore and stroke: 3 in. x 4⅜ in. Compression ratio: 7.5:1. Brake horsepower: 92 at 3800 R.P.M. Taxable horsepower: 21.6. Maximum torque: 152 ft. lbs. Main bearings: Four. Valve lifters: Solid. Carburetor: Carter Model BBR1-2125S one-barrel.

ENGINE (3E6 and 3E11): Six-cylinder. L-head. Cast iron block. Displacement: 245.6 cu. in. Bore and stroke: 3-5/16 in. x 4¾ in. Compression ratio: 7.5:1. Brake horsepower: 106 at 3400 R.P.M. Taxable horsepower: 26.3. Maximum torque: 204 ft. lbs. Main bearings: Four. Valve lifters: Solid. Carburetor: Carter Model BBR1-777SA one-barrel.

ENGINE (3E7 and 3E12): Eight-cylinder. OHV V8. Cast iron block. Displacement: 259.2 cu. in. Bore and stroke: 3-9/16 in. x 3¼ in. Compression ratio: 7.5:1. Brake horsepower: 170 at 4200 R.P.M. (178 horsepower with optional four-barrel carburetor). Taxable horsepower 40.6. Maximum torque: 250 ft. lbs. Main bearings: Five. Valve lifters: Solid. Carburetor: Stromberg Model WW two-barrel (optional: Carter Model WCFB four-barrel).

CHASSIS & BODY (3E1-112, 3E5-112, 3E6-112 and 3E7-112): Wheelbase: 112 in. Overall length: 185.6 in. Height: 69.75 in. Width: 77.5 in. Interior pickup box dimensions: 77.8 in. long x 51.5 in. wide x 17.1 in. high. Front tread: 60.8 in. Rear tread: 62.6 in. Tires: 6.00 x 16 four-ply.

1958 Studebaker Scotsman Pickup (FKF)

CHASSIS & BODY (3E5-122, 3E6-122, 3E7-122, 3E11 and 3E12): Wheelbase: 122 in. Overall length: 203.6 in. Height: 69.75 in. (69.6 in. for 3E11 and 3E12). Width: 77.5 in. Interior pickup box dimensions: 95.8 in. long x 51.5 in. wide x 17.1 in. high. Front tread: 60.8 in. Rear tread: 62.6 in. (63 in. for 3E11 and 3E12). Tires: 6.00 x 16 four-ply (7.00 x 16 six-ply on 3E11 and 3E12).

TECHNICAL: Sliding gear transmission. Speeds: 3F/1R. Synchromesh in second and third. Steering column shift control. Single plate dry disc clutch. I-beam front axle. 3E1, 3E5, 3E6 and 3E7 rear axle: Hypoid semi-floating with 4.27 or 4.55:1 (3E1 & 3E5); 4.09 or 4.27:1 (3E6) and 3.73, 4.09 or 4.27:1 (3E7) overall ratios. 3E11 and 3E12 rear axle: Hypoid full-floating with 4.10 or 4.88:1 overall ratios. Hydraulic brakes. Steel disc wheels. Direct acting tubular shock absorbers. Variable ratio steering.

OPTIONS: Flightomatic transmission (3E7 and 3E12 only). Four-speed synchromesh transmission with floor shift control. Overdrive. Four-wheel drive (3E6, 3E7, 3E11 & 3E12 models). Hill Holder. Power brakes. Twin-Traction (½-ton models only). Deluxe Cab. Radio. Climatizer heater/defroster. Interior rear view mirror. Ashtray. Right-hand sun visor. Seat pad. Safety seat belts. Arm rests. Compass. Traffic light viewer. Map light. Accelerator pedal cover. Kleenex dispenser. Cigarette lighter. Dual horns. Two-tone paint. (Transtar models only). Caravan Top. Painted rear bumper. Extra taillight. License plate frames. Locking gas cap. Right-hand exterior rear view mirror. Left and right exterior extension rear view mirrors. Tinted glass. Spotlight. Directional signals. Underhood light. Right rear fender kit for spare tire. Front splash guards. Exhaust deflector. Windshield washer. Mattex seat covers. Hand throttle. Electric windshield wipers kit (standard on V8 with automatic transmission). Fram oil filter. One quart oil bath air cleaner. Governor (V8 two-barrel models only). Heavy-duty engine (V8 models only). V8 power package (four-barrel carburetor and large air cleaner). Five or six blade fan. Headbolt engine heater. Heavy-duty battery. Heavy-duty radiator. Heavy-duty springs. Heavy-duty shock absorbers. Brake fluid reservoir. Special options for the Scotsman (3E1): oil bath air cleaner, outside rear view mirror(s), spare tire, two-stage rear springs. Optional tires specific to the 3E1, 3E5, 3E6 and 3E7: 6.00 x 16 six-ply, 6.50 x 16 six-ply and 7.10 x 15 four-ply (black or whitewall). Optional tires specific to the 3E11 and 3E12: 8.00 x 17 eight-ply and 8.00 x 19.5 eight-ply.

HISTORICAL: Nineteen-fifty-eight could very well have been Studebaker-Packard's last year. Car and truck sales for the model year were the lowest since 1945. But, in the fall of 1958, Studebaker introduced its 1959 Lark car and everything turned around. The Lark sold well and the profits began to roll in.

1958 Studebaker Transtar Pickup (DFW)

	5	4	3	2	1
1958					
½-Ton					
3E1 (S.W.B.) P.U.	570	1140	1900	2650	3800
3E5 (S.W.B.) P.U.	630	1250	2100	3000	4200
3E5 (S.W.B.) P.U.	630	1250	2100	3000	4200
3E6 (S.W.B.) P.U.	650	1300	2150	3050	4300
3E6 (L.W.B.) P.U.	650	1300	2150	3050	4300
3E7 (S.W.B.) P.U.	750	1500	2500	3500	5000
3E7 (L.W.B.) P.U.	750	1500	2500	3500	5000
¾-Ton					
3E11 P.U.	570	1140	1900	2650	3800
3E12 P.U.	650	1300	2150	3050	4300

1959 STUDEBAKER

1959 Studebaker Transtar 4x4 Pickup (OCW)

MODELS 4E1, 4E2, 4E3, 4E7, 4E11 AND 4E12 — (ALL ENGINES): — For some odd reason, Studebaker decided not to use the Transtar name in 1959. During 1959, the former Transtar models with the "buck tooth" fiberglass grille were known as the Deluxe series. All domestic Deluxe series models were fitted with a Deluxe Cab (C4). Deluxe models now had key locks on both doors. Deluxe series models had Studebaker door nameplates instead of Transtar names. In contrast to 1957-1958, single-tone Deluxe series models had body color grilles instead of the off-white grilles used the previous two years. Also the parking lights were moved from the top of the fenders down into the grille. The Scotsman series was expanded to include a "245" six model (4E3) and a "259" V8 model (4E2). The plaid name decals were dropped and a simple chrome "-S-" was added to the front of the hood. The Scotsman was also upgraded somewhat. It got a glove compartment door, electric windshield wipers, a spare tire, optional 122-inch wheelbase and a few other extra amenities. Partially because of this, Studebaker raised the price of the Scotsman 185 model ½-ton from $1,595 to $1,791. Studebaker's success with the perky Lark car changed the company's philosophy about developing an austere reputation. Because of the 4E1 and the 4E3 Scotsmans, the six-cylinder engines were not offered as standard power plants for any 1959 domestic ½-ton Deluxe series models. The four-wheel-drive option was continued in 1959. It was available on all ½- to one-ton models powered by the "245" six or V8, including the 4E2 and 4E3 Scotsmans. The standard V8 engine for the 4E7 (½-ton) and 4E12 (¾-ton) V8 Deluxe series models was upgraded to the "289" V8. The old Champion six used in the 4E1 Scotsman was reduced to 169.6 cu. in. All domestic models now came standard with electric windshield wipers.

I.D. DATA: Serial number and engine number locations were the same as 1955-58.

starting serial numbers	starting engine numbers
1959 4E1: E1-1,001	
1959 4E2: E2-101	1959 4E1: 1E-15,001 (170 six)
1959 4E3: E3-101	1959 4E3 & 4E11: 4E-7,301 (245 six)
1959 4E7: E7-11,001	1959 4E2: 3E-8,001 (259 V8)*
1959 4E11: E11-13,501	1959 4E7 & 4E12: 7E-101 (289 V8)**
1959 4E12: E12-3,901	

* Heavy-duty 259 engines had a "5E" engine number prefix.
** Heavy-duty 289 engines had a "6E" engine number prefix.

Model No.	Body Type	Factory Price ($)	Weight	GVW (lbs)	Prod. Total
1959 4E Series					
½-Ton					
4E1-112	Pickup	1791	2660	5000	Note 1
4E1-122	Pickup	1826	2800	5000	Note 1
4E2-112	Pickup	1939	2960	5000	Note 1
4E2-122	Pickup	1974	3150	5000	Note 1
4E3-112	Pickup	1868	2920	5000	Note 1
4E3-122	Pickup	1902	3060	5000	Note 1
4E7-112	Pickup	2071	3000	5200	Note 1
4E7-122	Pickup	2105	3140	5200	Note 1
¾-Ton					
4E11	Pickup	2103	3245	7000	Note 1
4E12	Pickup	2247	3360	7000	Note 1

NOTE 1: Production breakdowns are not available. Total production of all 1959 4E models (½- to two-ton) was 7,737. Serial number spans for a particular model give a rough estimate of how many of that model were built in a year.

ENGINE (4E1): Six-cylinder. L-head. Cast iron block. Displacement: 169.6 cu. in. Bore and stroke: 3 in. x 4 in. Compression ratio: 8.0:1. Brake horsepower: 90 at 4000 R.P.M. Taxable horsepower: 21.6. Maximum torque: 145 ft. lbs. Main bearings: Four. Valve lifters: Solid. Carburetor: Carter Model AS, one-barrel.

1959 Studebaker Deluxe Pickup (FKF)

ENGINE (4E3 and 4E11): Six-cylinder. L-head. Cast iron block. Displacement: 245.6 cu. in. Bore and stroke: 3-5/16 in. x 4¾ in. Compression ratio: 7.5:1. Brake horsepower: 118 at 3400 R.P.M. Taxable horsepower: 26.3. Maximum torque: 204 ft. lbs. Main bearings: Four. Valve lifters: Solid. Carburetor: Carter Model BBR1-777SA one-barrel.

ENGINE (4E2): Eight-cylinder. OHV V8. Cast iron block. Displacement: 259.2 cu. in. Bore and stroke: 3-9/16 in. x 3¼ in. Compression ratio: 7.5:1. Brake horsepower: 180 at 4500 R.P.M. (195 horsepower with optional four-barrel carburetor). Taxable horsepower 40.6. Maximum torque: 260 ft. lbs. Main bearings: Five. Valve lifters: Solid. Carburetor: Stromberg Model WW two-barrel (optional: Carter Model WCFB four-barrel).

ENGINE (4E7 and 4E12): Eight-cylinder. OHV V8. Cast iron block. Displacement: 289 cu. in. Bore and stroke: 3-9/16 in. x 3⅝ in. Compression ratio: 7.5:1. Brake horsepower: 210 at 4500 R.P.M. (225 horsepower with optional four-barrel carburetor). Taxable horsepower 40.6. Maximum torque: 300 ft. lbs. Main bearings: Five. Valve lifters: Solid. Carburetor: Stromberg Model WW two-barrel (optional: Carter Model WCFB four-barrel).

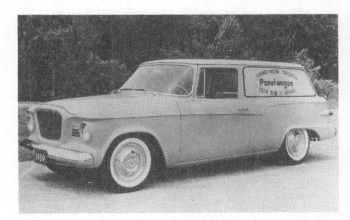

1959 Studebaker Lark Panel Wagon (A&A)

1959 Studebaker Scotsman Pickup (FKF)

CHASSIS & BODY (4E1-112, 4E2-112, 4E3-112 and 4E7-112): Wheelbase: 112 in.. Overall length: 185.6 in. Height: 69.75 in. Width: 77.5 in. Interior pickup box dimensions: 77.8 in. long x 51.5 in. wide x 17.1 in. high. Front tread: 60.8 in. Rear tread: 62.6 in. Tires: 6.00 x 16 four-ply (7.10 x 15 on 4E7).

CHASSIS & BODY (4E1-122, 4E2-122, 4E3-122, 4E7-122, 4E11 and 4E12): Wheelbase: 122 in. Overall length: 203.6 in. Height: 69.75 in. (69.6 in. for 4E11 and 4E12). Width: 77.5 in. Interior pickup box dimensions: 95.8 in. long x 51.5 in. wide x 17.1 in. high. Front tread: 60.8 in. Rear tread: 62.6 in. (63 in. for 4E11 and 4E12). Tires: 6.00 x 16 four-ply (7.10 x 15 on 4E7; 7.00 x 16 six-ply on 4E11 and 4E12).

TECHNICAL: Sliding gear transmission. Speeds: 3F/1R. Synchromesh in second and third. Steering column shift control. Single plate dry disc clutch. I-beam front axle. 4E1, 4E2, 4E3 and 4E7 rear axle: Hypoid semi-floating with 4.27 or 4.55:1 (4E1); 4.09, 4.27 or 4.55:1 (4E2 & 4E3) and 4.09 or 4.27:1 (4E7) overall ratios. 4E11 and 4E12 rear axle: Hypoid full-floating with 4.10 or 4.88:1 overall ratios. Hydraulic brakes. Steel disc wheels. Direct acting tubular shock absorbers. Variable ratio steering.

OPTIONS: Flightomatic transmission (4E2, 4E7 and 4E12 only). Four-speed synchromesh transmission with floor shift control. Overdrive. Four-wheel drive (4E2, 4E3, 4E7, 4E11 & 4E12 models). Hill Holder. Power brakes. Twin-Traction. Radio. Climatizer heater/defroster. Seat pad. Safety seat belts. Compass. Traffic light viewer. Accelerator pedal cover. Kleenex dispenser. Cigarette lighter. Dual horns. Two-tone paint (Deluxe series only). Caravan Top. Painted rear bumper. Extra taillight. License plate frames. Locking gas cap. Right-hand exterior rear view mirror. Left and right exterior extension rear view mirrors. Tinted glass. Spotlight. Directional signals. Underhood light. Right rear fender kit for spare tire. Front splash guards. Exhaust deflector. Windshield washer. Mattex seat covers. Hand throttle. Fram oil filter. One quart oil bath air cleaner. Governor (V8 two-barrel models only). Heavy-duty engine (V8 models only). V8 power package (four-barrel carburetor and large air cleaner). Five or six blade fan. Headbolt engine heater. Heavy-duty battery. Heavy-duty radiator. Heavy-duty springs. Heavy-duty shock absorbers. Brake fluid reservoir. Special options for the Scotsman (4E1, 4E2 and 4E3): outside rear view mirror(s), right hand sun visor, map light, sliding seat, two-stage rear springs. Optional tires specific to the 4E1, 4E2, 4E3 and 4E7: 6.50 x 16 six-ply (also 7.10 x 15 four-ply on Scotsman), whitewalls. Optional tires specific to the 4E11 and 4E12: 7.00 x 17 eight-ply, 7.50 x 17 eight-ply and 8.00 x 17.5 eight-ply.

HISTORICAL: Although Lark sales were good in 1959, Studebaker truck sales made no big improvement over 1958. Many Larks were sold by "Big Three" dealers who had their own trucks to sell. Also, after 11 model years, Studebaker was still marketing the same basic truck body.

Pricing

	5	4	3	2	1
1959					
½-Ton					
4E1 (S.W.B.) P.U.	570	1140	1900	2650	3800
4E1 (L.W.B.) P.U.	570	1140	1900	2650	3800
4E5 (S.W.B.) P.U.	630	1250	2100	3000	4200
4E5 (L.W.B.) P.U.	630	1250	2100	3000	4200
4E6 (S.W.B.) P.U.	650	1300	2150	3050	4300
4E6 (L.W.B.) P.U.	650	1300	2150	3050	4300
4E7 (S.W.B.) P.U.	750	1500	2500	3500	5000
4E7 (L.W.B.) P.U.	750	1500	2500	3500	5000
¾-Ton					
4E11 P.U.	570	1140	1900	2650	3800
4E12 P.U.	650	1300	2150	3050	4300

1960 Studebaker Champ Pickup (FKF)

MODELS 5E5, 5E6, 5E7, 5E11 AND 5E12 — (ALL ENGINES): — Profits from the Lark car finally gave Studebaker's Truck Division a *little* money to work with. One-ton and larger models continued with the old design (again called the Transtar), but light-duty ½- and ¾-ton models finally got a new styling. Borrowing from the concept of the original 1937-39 Coupe-Express, Studebaker took the Lark body and converted it to a truck front end and cab. Except for being chopped off behind the front door and featuring a "brawnier" grille and bumper, the styling, including the instrument panel, was identical to a 1959-1960 Lark four-door sedan. The new cab was called the "T" cab. The old pickup box was continued. Unlike the original Coupe-Express, the new model, called the Champ, used a truck chassis instead of a car chassis. The same wheelbases as offered in 1959 were continued. For 1960, the four-wheel-drive was only offered on the one-ton Transtar ("C" cab) models. One-ton pickups with a nine-foot box were still offered in 1960, but very few were sold. The new Champ was available with a standard T4 cab or a Deluxe T6 cab. The standard cab had painted hubcaps, gas cap, grille, side air intakes and headlight rims. These items were chrome or stainless steel on the Deluxe models. Deluxe models also had side fender moldings, dash pad, sliding rear window, two arm rests, dome light, dual sun visors and bright metal window trim. Studebaker was one of the first companies to offer a pickup with a sliding rear cab window. All ½-ton models had new hubcaps with an "S" in the middle. Hubcaps were optional on ¾-ton models. The Scotsman series was discontinued and the standard engine for the ½- and ¾-ton V8 models was again the 259 cubic inch version. The "259" heavy-duty engine and the "289" engine, standard or heavy-duty, were extra cost options. Dry type air cleaners were standard on all models. The new styling was much lower than older design. Because of this, the Champ had less drag and greater fuel economy. Custom flat front Studebaker delivery vans, with bodies built by an outside firm, but with a Lark grille and a 1955 truck nameplate, were given some promotion during the year. Very few were sold.

I.D. DATA: The 1960 5E T-cab serial number was on a plate mounted on the left door lock pillar post. Engine number locations were the same as 1955-1959.

starting serial numbers	starting engine numbers
1960 5E5: E5-127,301	1960 5E5: 1E-18,301 (170 six)
1960 5E6: E6-18,201	1960 5E6 & 5E11: 4E-9,401 (245 six)
1960 5E7: E7-12,301	1960 5E7 & 5E12: 3E-9,201 (259 V8)*
1960 5E11: E11-13,901	
1960 5E12: E12-4,301	

* Heavy-duty 259 engines had a "5E" engine number prefix; 289 engines had a "7E" engine number prefix; and heavy-duty 289 engines had a "6E" engine number prefix.

1960 Studebaker (modified) Champ 4x4 Pickup (DFW)

1960 Studebaker Transtar 4x4 Pickup (A&A)

Model No.	Body Type	Factory Price ($)	Weight	GVW (lbs)	Prod. Total
1960 5E Series					
½-ton					
5E5-112	Pickup	1875	2775	5000	Note 1
5E5-122	Pickup	1912	2915	5000	Note 1
5E6-112	Pickup	1960	2980	5200	Note 1
5E6-122	Pickup	1996	3120	5200	Note 1
5E7-112	Pickup	2046	3060	5200	Note 1
5E7-122	Pickup	2081	3200	5200	Note 1
¾-Ton					
5E11	Pickup	2108	3340	7000	Note 1
5E12	Pickup	2220	3425	7000	Note 1

NOTE 1: Production breakdowns are not available. Total production of all 1960 5E models (½- to two-ton) was 8,294. Serial number spans for a particular model give a rough estimate of how many of that model were built in a year.

ENGINE (5E5): Six-cylinder. L-head. Cast iron block. Displacement: 169.6 cu. in. Bore and stroke: 3 in. x 4 in. Compression ratio: 8.0:1. Brake horsepower: 90 at 4000 R.P.M. Taxable horsepower: 21.6. Maximum torque: 145 ft. lbs. Main bearings: Four. Valve lifters: Solid. Carburetor: Carter Model AS one-barrel.

ENGINE (5E6 and 5E11): Six-cylinder. L-head. Cast iron block. Displacement: 245.6 cu. in. Bore and stroke: 3-5/16 in. x 4¾ in. Compression ratio: 7.5:1. Brake horsepower: 118 at 3400 R.P.M. Taxable horsepower: 26.3. Maximum torque: 204 ft. lbs. Main bearings: Four. Valve lifters: Solid. Carburetor: Carter Model AS one-barrel.

ENGINE (5E7 and 5E12): Eight-cylinder. OHV V8. Cast iron block. Displacement: 259.2 cu. in. Bore and stroke: 3-9/16 in. x 3¼ in. Compression ratio: 7.5:1. Brake horsepower: 180 at 4500 R.P.M. (195 horsepower with optional four-barrel carburetor). Taxable horsepower 40.6. Maximum torque: 260 ft. lbs. Main bearings: Five. Valve lifters: Solid. Carburetor: Stromberg Model WW two-barrel (optional: Carter Model WCFB four-barrel).

ENGINE (5E7 and 5E12; optional engine): Eight-cylinder. OHV V8. Cast iron block. Displacement: 289 cu. in. Bore and stroke: 3-9/16 in. x 3⅝ in. Compression ratio: 7.5:1. Brake horsepower: 210 at 4500 R.P.M. (225 horsepower with optional four-barrel carburetor). Taxable horsepower 40.6. Maximum torque: 300 ft. lbs. Main bearings: Five. Valve lifters: Solid. Carburetor: Stromberg Model WW two-barrel (optional: Carter Model WCFB four-barrel).

CHASSIS & BODY (5E5-112, 5E6-112 and 5E7-112): Wheelbase: 112 in. Overall length: 179.8 in. Height: 68 in. Width: 77.5 in. Interior pickup box dimensions: 77.8 in. long x 51.5 in. wide x 17.1 in. high. Front tread: 58 in. Rear tread: 62.6 in. Tires: 6.00 x 16 four-ply.

1960 Studebaker Champ Pickup (A&A)

CHASSIS & BODY (5E5-122, 5E6-122, 5E7-122, 5E11 and 5E12): Wheelbase: 122 in. Overall length: 197.8 in. Height: 68 in. (69 in. for 5E11 and 5E12). Width: 77.5 in. Interior pickup box dimensions: 95.8 in. long x 51.5 in. wide x 17.1 in. high. Front tread: 58 in. Rear tread: 62.6 in. (63 in. for 5E11 and 5E12). Tires: 6.00 x 16 four-ply (7.00 x 16 six-ply on 5E11 and 5E12).

TECHNICAL: Sliding gear transmission. Speeds: 3F/1R. Synchromesh in second and third. Steering column shift control. Single plate dry disc clutch. I-beam front axle. 5E5, 5E6 and 5E7 rear axle: Hypoid semi-floating with 4.27 or 4.55:1 (5E5); 3.73, 4.09, 4.27 or 4.55:1 (5E6 & 5E7) overall ratios. 5E11 and 5E12 rear axle: Hypoid full-floating with 4.10 or 4.88:1 overall ratios. Hydraulic brakes. Steel disc wheels. Direct acting tubular shock absorbers. Variable ratio steering.

1960 Studebaker Champ Pickup (OCW)

OPTIONS: Flightomatic transmission (5E7 and 5E12 only). Four-speed synchromesh transmission with floor shift control. Overdrive. Twin-Traction. Hill Holder. Power brakes. Deluxe T6 Cab. Radio. Clock. Climatizer heater/defroster. Safety seat belts. Kleenex dispenser. Cigarette lighter. Dual door locks. Dual horns. Caravan Top. Painted rear bumper. Right-hand taillight. License plate frames. Locking gas cap. Left and right-hand exterior rear view mirrors. Left and right exterior extension rear view mirrors. Tinted glass. Spotlight. Directional signals. Right rear fender kit for spare tire. Inside pickup box tire carrier. Hubcaps (¾-ton models). Front splash guards. Windshield washer. Cushion toppers. Oil filter. One quart oil bath air cleaner. Engine governor. In-line gas filter. 289 or heavy-duty engines (V8 models only). 7.0:1 compression ratio. Four-barrel carburetor (V8s only). Heavy-duty 11 inch clutch (V8 only). Heavy-duty generator. Leece-Neville alternator. Heavy-duty battery. Heavy-duty fan. Heavy-duty radiator. Heavy-duty front springs (5E5). Heavy-duty rear springs. Heavy-duty shock absorbers. Brake fluid reservoir. Items for non-Deluxe Cab: seat pads, padded dash, sliding rear window, right-hand sun visor, arm rests, dome light. Optional tires specific to the 5E5, 5E6 and 5E7: 7.10 x 15 four-ply (black or whitewall), 6.00 x 16 six-ply and 6.50 x 16 six-ply. Optional tires specific to the 5E11 and 5E12: 7.50 x 16 six-ply and 8.00 x 17.5 eight-ply.

HISTORICAL: Production delays and steel strikes held up the introduction of the 5E Champ until the spring of 1960. A short model year kept 5E production from showing any significant increases. No matter what Studebaker did, they had no luck in increasing truck sales. The Champ cab turned out to be poorly designed in regard to rust prevention.

1960 Studebaker Champ Pickup (OCW)

Pricing

1960	5	4	3	2	1
½-Ton					
5E5 (S.W.B.) P.U.	680	1350	2250	3150	4500
5E5 (L.W.B.) P.U.	680	1350	2250	3150	4500
5E6 (S.W.B.) P.U.	690	1380	2300	3200	4600
5E6 (L.W.B.) P.U.	690	1380	2300	3200	4600
5E7 (S.W.B.) P.U.	770	1550	2550	3600	5100
5E7 (L.W.B.) P.U.	770	1550	2550	3600	5100
¾-Ton					
5E11 P.U.	570	1140	1900	2650	3800
5E12 P.U.	650	1300	2150	3050	4300

* Add 10 percent for optional V-8 (210/225 h.p.).

1961 STUDEBAKER

1961 Studebaker Champ Deluxe Pickup (FKF)

MODELS 6E5, 6E7, 6E10 AND 6E12 — (ALL ENGINES): — The big news for 1961 was the introduction of the overhead valve version of the old 170 cubic inch engine. In truck form, the new engine produced 110 h.p.; 20 more than its L-head predecessor. With the introduction of the OHV six, the "245" L-head six was discontinued for the last time. The ¾-ton "10" model returned as the 6E10. As on 1961 Lark cars, the side trim was raised above the contour line on Deluxe Cab (T6) models. The side grilles adjacent to the headlights were switched from a mesh to horizontal bars. The 1961 Champ side grille styling was the same as used on 1959 Lark cars, while the 1960 Champ side grilles were the same design as used on 1960 Lark cars. In January 1961, a new wide Spaceside pickup box was made available. The basic box styling had previously been used by Dodge. Dodge called it the Sweptline box. The dies to manufacture the box were purchased from Dodge and the box was modified to fit the Champ. The front panel next to the cab was redesigned and a tailgate with "S T U D E-B A K E R" on it was added. The older, narrow box with external fenders was retained. The new single wall Spaceside box was identified as the P2 box and the older box, now called the "Double Wall" box, was listed as the P1 box. Fifteen-inch wheels were made standard on ½-ton Champs. A few Champ pickups with Studebaker Cruiser chassis were built for export sales only.

I.D. DATA: The 1961 6E T-cab serial number and engine number locations were the same as 1960.

starting serial numbers	starting engine numbers
1961 6E5: E5-129,601	1961 6E5 & 6E10: 1E-20,601 (170 six)
1961 6E7: E7-13,801	1961 6E7 & 6E12: 3E-11,601 (259 V8)*
1961 6E10: E10-39,001	
1961 6E12: E12-4,701	

* Heavy-duty 259 engines had a "5E" engine number prefix; 289 engines had a "7E" engine number prefix; and heavy-duty 289 engines had a "6E" engine number prefix.

Model No.	Body Type	Factory Price ($)	Weight	GVW (lbs)	Prod. Total
1961 6E Series					
½-ton					
6E5-112	Pickup	1875	2816	5000	Note 1
6E5-122	Pickup	1913	2956	5000	Note 1
6E7-112	Pickup	2050	3080	5200	Note 1
6E7-122	Pickup	2082	3220	5200	Note 1
¾-Ton					
6E10	Pickup	2035	3155	7000	Note 1
6E12	Pickup	2205	3450	7000	Note 1

NOTE 1: Production breakdowns are not available. Total production of all 1961 6E models (½- to two-ton) was 7,641. Serial number spans for a particular model give a rough estimate of how many of that model were built in a year.

ENGINE (6E5 and 6E10): Six-cylinder. OHV in-line six. Cast iron block. Displacement: 169.6 cu. in. Bore and stroke: 3 in. x 4 in. Compression ratio: 8.0:1. Brake horsepower: 110 at 4500 R.P.M. Taxable horsepower: 21.6. Maximum torque: 156 ft. lbs. Main bearings: Four. Valve lifters: Solid. Carburetor: Carter Model AS, one-barrel.

ENGINE (6E7 and 6E12): Eight-cylinder. OHV V8. Cast iron block. Displacement: 259.2 cu. in. Bore and stroke: 3-9/16 in. x 3¼ in. Compression ratio: 7.5:1. Brake horsepower: 180 at 4500 R.P.M. (195 horsepower with optional four-barrel carburetor). Taxable horsepower: 40.6. Maximum torque: 260 ft. lbs. Main bearings: Five. Valve lifters: Solid. Carburetor: Stromberg Model WW two barrel (optional: Carter Model WCFB four-barrel).

ENGINE (6E7 and 6E12; optional engine): Eight-cylinder. OHV V8. Cast iron block. Displacement: 289 cu. in. Bore and stroke: 3-9/16 in. x 3⅝ in. Compression ratio: 7.5:1. Brake horsepower: 210 at 4500 R.P.M. (225 horsepower with optional four-barrel carburetor). Taxable horsepower: 40.6. Maximum torque: 300 ft. lbs. Main bearings: Five. Valve lifters: Solid. Carburetor: Stromberg Model WW two-barrel (optional: Carter Model WCFB four-barrel).

CHASSIS & BODY (6E5-112 and 6E7-112): Wheelbase: 112 in. Overall length: 179.8 in. Height: 65 in. Width: 77.5 in. P1 pickup box interior dimensions: 77.8 in. long x 51.5 in. wide x 17.1 in. high. P2 Spaceside pickup box interior dimensions: 78.75 in. long x 70.75 in. wide x 20 in. high. Front tread: 58 in. Rear tread: 62.6 in. Tires: 6.70 x 15 four-ply.

CHASSIS & BODY (6E5-122, 6E7-122, 6E10 and 6E12): Wheelbase: 122 in. Overall length: 197.8 in. Height: 65 in. (66 in. for 6E11 and 6E12). Width: 77.5 in. P1 pickup box interior dimensions: 95.8 in. long x 51.5 in. wide x 17.1 in. high. P2 Spaceside pickup box interior dimensions: 99 in. long x 70.75 in. wide x 20 in. high. Front tread: 58 in. Rear tread: 62.6 in. (63 in. for 6E11 and 6E12). Tires: 6.70 x 15 four-ply (7.00 x 16 six-ply on 6E11 and 6E12).

TECHNICAL: Sliding gear transmission. Speeds: 3F/1R. Synchromesh in second and third. Steering column shift control. Single plate dry disc clutch. I-beam front axle. 6E5 and 6E7 rear axle: Hypoid semi-floating with 4.09, 4.27 or 4.55:1 (6E5); 3.73, 4.09, 4.27 or 4.55:1 (6E7) overall ratios. 6E10 and 6E12 rear axle: Hypoid full-floating with 4.56 or 4.88:1 (6E10); 4.10, 4.56 or 4.88:1 (6E12) overall ratios. Hydraulic brakes. Steel disc wheels. Direct acting tubular shock absorbers. Variable ratio steering.

OPTIONS: Flightomatic transmission (6E7 and 6E12 only). Four-speed synchromesh transmission with floor shift control. Overdrive. Twin-Traction. Hill Holder. Power brakes. P2 Spaceside pickup box. Deluxe T6 Cab. Radio. Clock. Climatizer heater/defroster. Safety seat belts. Kleenex dispenser. Cigarette lighter. Dual door locks. Dual Horns. Caravan top. Painted rear bumper. Right-hand taillight. License plate frames. Locking gas cap. Left and right-hand exterior rear view mirrors. Left and right exterior extension rear view mirrors. Tinted glass. Spot light. Directional signals. Right rear fender kit for spare tire (P1 box only). Inside pickup box tire carrier. Hubcaps (¾-ton models). Front splash guards. Windshield washer. Cushion toppers. Oil filter. One quart oil bath air cleaner. Engine governor. In-line gas filter. 289 or heavy-duty engines (V8 models only). 7.0:1 compression ratio (V8s only). Positive crankcase ventilation. Four-barrel carburetor (V8s only). Heavy-duty 11" clutch (V8 models only). Heavy-duty generator. Leece-Neville alternator. Heavy-duty battery. Heavy-duty fan. Heavy-duty radiator. Heavy-duty front springs (6E5 & 6E10). Heavy-duty rear springs. Heavy-duty shock absorbers. Brake fluid reservoir. Items for non-Deluxe Cab: seat pads, padded dash, sliding rear window, right-hand sun visor, arm rests, dome light. Optional tires specific to the 6E5 and 6E7: 7.10 x 15 four-ply, 6.00 x 16 four-ply, 6.00 x 16 six-ply, 6.50 x 16 six-ply and whitewalls. Optional tires specific to the 6E10 and 6E12: 7.50 x 16 six-ply.

HISTORICAL: The new OHV six and wide Spaceside box did not help sales. Problems with cracked valve seats on the six-cylinder engine hurt the reputation of the new engine.

Pricing

1961	5	4	3	2	1
½-Ton					
6E5 (S.W.B.) P.U.	680	1350	2250	3150	4500
6E5 (L.W.B.) P.U.	680	1350	2250	3150	4500
6E7 (S.W.B.) P.U.	770	1550	2550	3600	5100
6E7 (S.W.B.) P.U.	770	1550	2550	3600	5100
¾-Ton					
6E10 P.U.	570	1140	1900	2650	3800
6E12 P.U.	650	1300	2150	3050	4300

* Add 10 percent for optional V-8 (210/225 h.p.).

1962 STUDEBAKER

1962 Studebaker Champ Deluxe Pickup (A&A)

MODELS 7E5, 7E7, 7E10 AND 7E12 — (ALL ENGINES): — Although the Lark car front end was restyled in 1961 and again in 1962, the Champ light-duty trucks continued with the 1959-1960 Lark front end styling. Changes for the 1962 model year were minimal. On Deluxe Cab models the side fender trim was again lowered back to the contour line as in 1960. For the first time, the Flightomatic automatic transmission was made an extra cost option on six-cylinder models. The older P1 narrow pickup with the exterior fenders was continued, but the newer Spaceside box was made standard equipment.

I.D. DATA: The 1962 7E T-cab serial number and engine number locations were the same as 1960-61.

starting serial numbers	starting engine numbers
1962 7E5: E5-132,601	1962 7E5 & 7E10: 1E-23,901 (170 six)
1962 7E7: E7-16,201	1962 7E7 & 7E12: 3E-14,801 (259 V8)*
1962 7E10: E10-39,301	
1962 7E12: E12-5,201	

* Heavy-duty "259" engines had a "5E" engine number prefix; "289" engines had a "7E" engine number prefix; and heavy-duty "289" engines had a "6E" engine number prefix.

Model No.	Body Type	Factory Price ($)	Weight	GVW (lbs)	Prod. Total
1962 7E Series					
½-ton					
7E5-112	Pickup	1870	2790	5000	Note 1
7E5-122	Pickup	1915	2930	5000	Note 1
7E7-112	Pickup	2050	3075	5200	Note 1
7E7-122	Pickup	2084	3215	5200	Note 1
¾-Ton					
7E10	Pickup	2035	3355	7000	Note 1
7E12	Pickup	2205	3440	7000	Note 1

NOTE 1: Production breakdowns are not available. Total production of all 1962 Series 7E models (½- to two-ton) was 8,742. Serial number spans for a particular model give a rough estimate of how many of that model were built in a year.

1962 Studebaker Champ Deluxe Pickup (FKF)

ENGINE (7E5 & 7E10): Six-cylinder. OHV in-line six. Cast iron block. Displacement: 169.6 cu. in. Bore and stroke: 3 in. x 4 in. Compression ratio: 8.0:1. Brake horsepower: 110 at 4500 R.P.M. Taxable horsepower: 21.6. Maximum torque: 156 ft. lbs. Main bearings: Four. Valve lifters: Solid. Carburetor: Carter Model AS, one-barrel.

ENGINE (7E7 and 7E12): Eight-cylinder. OHV V8. Cast iron block. Displacement: 259.2 cu. in. Bore and stroke: 3-9/16 in. x 3¼ in. Compression ratio: 7.5:1. Brake horsepower: 180 at 4500 R.P.M. (195 horsepower with optional four-barrel carburetor). Taxable horsepower: 40.6. Maximum torque: 260 ft. lbs. Main bearings: Five. Valve lifters: Solid. Carburetor: Stromberg Model WW two-barrel (optional: Carter Model WCFB four-barrel).

ENGINE (7E7 and 7E12; optional engine): Eight-cylinder. OHV V8. Cast iron block. Displacement: 289 cu. in. Bore and stroke: 3-9/16 in. x 3⅝ in. Compression ratio: 7.5:1. Brake horsepower: 210 at 4500 R.P.M. (225 horsepower with optional four-barrel carburetor). Taxable horsepower 40.6. Maximum torque: 300 ft. lbs. Main bearings: Five. Valve lifters: Solid. Carburetor: Stromberg Model WW two-barrel (optional: Carter Model WCFB four-barrel).

CHASSIS & BODY (7E5-112 and 7E7-112): Wheelbase: 112 in. Overall length: 180.7 in. Height: 65 in. Width: 77.5 in. P1 pickup box interior dimensions: 77.8 in. long x 51.5 in. wide x 17.1 in. high. P2 Spaceside pickup box interior dimensions: 78.75 in. long x 70.75 in. wide x 20 in. high. Front tread: 58 in. Rear tread: 62.6 in. Tires: 6.70 x 15 four-ply.

CHASSIS & BODY (7E5-122, 7E7-122, 7E10 and 7E12): Wheelbase: 122 in. Overall length: 201 in. Height: 65 in. (66 in. for 7E11 and 7E12). Width: 77.5 in. P1 pickup box interior dimensions: 95.8 in. long x 51.5 in. wide x 17.1 in. high. P2 Spaceside pickup box interior dimensions: 99 in. long x 70.75 in. wide x 20 in. high. Front tread: 58 in. Rear tread: 62.6 in. (63 in. for 7E11 and 7E12). Tires: 6.70 x 15 four-ply (7.00 x 16 six-ply on 7E11 and 7E12).

TECHNICAL: Sliding gear transmission. Speeds: 3F/1R. Synchromesh in second and third. Steering column shift control. Single plate dry disc clutch. I-beam front axle. 7E5, and 7E7 rear axle: Hypoid semi-floating with 4.09, 4.27 or 4.55:1 (7E5); 3.73, 4.09, 4.27 or 4.55:1 (7E7) overall ratios. 7E10 and 7E12 rear axle: Hypoid full-floating with 4.56 or 4.88:1 (7E10); 4.10, 4.56, or 4.88:1 (7E12) overall ratios. Hydraulic brakes. Steel disc wheels. Direct acting tubular shock absorbers. Variable ratio steering.

OPTIONS: Flightomatic transmission. Four-speed synchromesh transmission with floor shift control. Overdrive. Twin-Traction. Power brakes. P1 Double Wall pickup box. Deluxe T6 Cab. Radio. Clock. Climatizer heater/defroster. Safety seat belts. Kleenex dispenser. Cigarette lighter. Dual door locks. Dual horns. Caravan Top. Painted rear bumper. Right-hand taillight. License plate frames. Locking gas cap. Left and right-hand exterior rear view mirrors. Left and right exterior extension rear view mirrors. Tinted glass. Spotlight. Directional signals. Rear fender kit for spare tire (P1 box only). Inside pickup box tire carrier. Hubcaps (¾-ton models). Front splash guards. Windshield washer. Cushion toppers. Oil filter. One quart oil bath air cleaner. Engine governor. In-line gas filter. 289 or heavy-duty engines (V8 models only). 7.0:1 compression ratio (V8s only). Positive crankcase ventilation. Four-barrel carburetor (V8s only). Heavy-duty 11 inch clutch (V8 only). Heavy-duty generator. Leece-Neville alternator. Heavy-duty battery. Heavy-duty fan. Heavy-duty radiator. Heavy-duty front springs (7E5 and 7E10). Heavy-duty rear springs. Heavy-duty shock absorbers. Brake fluid reservoir. Items for non-Deluxe Cab: seat pads, padded dash, sliding rear window, right-hand sun visor, arm rests, dome light. Optional tires specific to the 7E5, and 7E7: 7.10 x 15 four-ply, 6.00 x 16 four-ply, 6.00 x 16 six-ply, 6.50 x 16 six-ply and whitewalls. Optional tires specific to the 7E10 and 7E12: 7.50 x 16 six-ply.

HISTORICAL: Sales increased slightly in 1962. Studebaker dealers who were proficient at selling trucks found the Champ an easy pickup to market. With a base price of $1870 for the six-cylinder with the 6½-foot box, the Champ was the lowest priced domestic 5,000 GVW pickup sold in the U.S. in 1962. The problem was that most Studebaker dealers in the early 1960s made little effort to sell trucks.

Pricing

	5	4	3	2	1
1962					
½-Ton					
7E5 (S.W.B.) P.U.	680	1350	2250	3150	4500
7E5 (L.W.B.) P.U.	680	1350	2250	3150	4500
7E7 (S.W.B.) P.U.	770	1550	2550	3600	5100
7E7 (L.W.B.) P.U.	770	1550	2550	3600	5100
¾-Ton					
7E10 P.U.	570	1140	1900	2650	3800
7E12 P.U.	650	1300	2150	3050	4300

* Add 10% for optional V-8 (210/225 h.p.).

1963-1964 STUDEBAKER

MODELS 8E5, 8E7, 8E10 AND 8E12 — (ALL ENGINES): — Studebaker's last trucks were the 8E series models that were produced during the 1963 and shortened 1964 model years. The last Studebaker civilian truck was assembled on December 27, 1963. Although the 8E Champ was the end of the line, it had several improvements over the 1962 7E series. Steering geometry was all new and a new type of constant-ratio steering gear was adopted. Brake and clutch pedals were switched to the swing type. Front shock absorbers were mounted in a new "sea leg" fashion. Wider and longer front springs were adopted. Full-flow oil filters were made standard equipment on all models and the six-cylinder engine was fitted with a new style carburetor. The optional V8 four-barrel carburetor was also changed. The brake master cylinder was moved from the frame to the firewall. Positive crankcase ventilation was made standard equipment. The old narrow P1 "Double Wall" pickup box was discontinued. Air conditioning and a Conestoga camper were added to the option list. During the model year, a five-speed transmission was made an extra cost option. One option never offered on ½-or ¾-ton Studebaker trucks was power steering. During 1963-64, Studebaker assembled an 8E5 forward control van called the Zip-Van. Produced in fairly large quantities, the Zip-Van was built specifically for the U.S. Post Office Department. The Zip-Van had right-hand controls and used Transtar truck instruments. For the 1964 model year, Studebaker introduced the Service Champ. The Service Champ featured fiberglass utility bodies for plumbers, electricians, tire servicemen, etc. Service Champs were available only on 122-inch wheelbase models.

I.D. DATA: The 1963-64 8E T-cab serial number and engine number locations were the same as 1960-62.

starting serial numbers	starting engine numbers
1963-64 8E5: E5-136,001	1963-64 8E5 & 8E10: 1E-27,801 (170 six)
1963-64 8E7: E7-18,901	1963-64 8E7 & 8E12: 3E-18,901 (259 V8)*
1963-64 8E10: E10-39,901	
1963-64 8E12: E12-5,901	

* Heavy-duty 259 engines had a "5E" engine number prefix; 289 engines had a "7E" engine number prefix; and heavy-duty 289 engines had a "6E" engine number prefix.

1963 Studebaker Champ Deluxe Pickup (FKF)

Model No.	Body Type	Factory Price ($)	Weight	GVW (lbs)	Prod. Total
1963-64 8E Series					
½-ton					
8E5-112	Pickup	1915	2790	5000	Note 1
8E5-122	Pickup	1957	2930	5000	Note 1
8E7-112	Pickup	2083	3075	5200	Note 1
8E7-122	Pickup	2120	3215	5200	Note 1
¾-Ton					
8E10	Pickup	2075	3355	7000	Note 1
8E12	Pickup	2244	3440	7000	Note 1

NOTE 1: Production breakdowns are not available. Total 1963 calendar year production of all models (½- to two-ton) was 13,117.

ENGINE (8E5 & 8E10): Six-cylinder. OHV in-line six. Cast iron block. Displacement: 169.6 cu. in. Bore and stroke: 3 in. x 4 in. Compression ratio: 8.0:1. Brake horsepower: 110 at 4500 R.P.M. Taxable horsepower: 21.6. Maximum torque: 156 ft. lbs. Main bearings: Four. Valve lifters: Solid. Carburetor: Carter Model RBS one-barrel.

ENGINE (8E7 and 8E12): Eight-cylinder. OHV V8. Cast iron block. Displacement: 259.2 cu. in. Bore and stroke: 3-9/16 in. x 3¼ in. Compression ratio: 7.5:1. Brake horsepower: 180 at 4500 R.P.M. (195 horsepower with optional four-barrel carburetor). Taxable horsepower: 40.6. Maximum torque: 260 ft. lbs. Main bearings: Five. Valve lifters: Solid. Carburetor: Stromberg Model WW two-barrel (optional: Carter Model AFB four-barrel).

ENGINE (8E7 and 8E12; optional engine): Eight-cylinder. OHV V8. Cast iron block. Displacement: 289 cu. in. Bore and stroke: 3-9/16 in. x 3⅝ in. Compression ratio: 7.5:1. Brake horsepower: 210 at 4500 R.P.M. (225 horsepower with optional four-barrel carburetor). Taxable horsepower 40.6. Maximum torque: 300 ft. lbs. Main bearings: Five. Valve lifters: Solid. Carburetor: Stromberg Model WW two-barrel (optional: Carter Model AFB four-barrel).

CHASSIS & BODY (8E5-112 and 8E7-112): Wheelbase: 112 in. Overall length: 180.7 in. Height: 65 in. Width: 77.5 in. P2 Spaceside pickup box interior dimensions: 78.75 in. long x 70.75 in. wide x 20 in. high. Front tread: 58 in. Rear tread: 62.6 in. Tires: 6.70 x 15 four-ply.

CHASSIS & BODY (8E5-122, 8E7-122, 8E10 and 8E12): Wheelbase: 122 in. Overall length: 201 in. Height: 65 in. (66 in. for 8E11 and 8E12). Width: 77.5 in. P2 Spaceside pickup box interior dimensions: 99 in. long x 70.75 in. wide x 20 in. high. Front tread: 58 in. Rear tread: 62.6 in. (63 in. for 8E11 and 8E12). Tires: 6.70 x 15 four-ply (7.00 x 16 six-ply on 8E11 and 8E12).

TECHNICAL: Sliding gear transmission. Speeds: 3F/1R. Synchromesh in second and third. Steering column shift control. Single plate dry disc clutch. I-beam front axle. 8E5, and 8E7 rear axle: Hypoid semi-floating with 4.09, 4.27 or 4.55:1 (8E5); 3.73, 4.09, 4.27 or 4.55:1 (8E7) overall ratios. 8E10 and 8E12 rear axle: Hypoid full-floating with 4.56 or 4.88:1 (8E10); 4.10, 4.56, or 4.88:1 (8E12) overall ratios. Hydraulic brakes. Steel disc wheels. Direct acting tubular shock absorbers. Constant ratio steering.

1964 Studebaker Postal Zip Van (A&A)

OPTIONS: Flightomatic transmission. Four-speed synchromesh transmission with floor shift control. Five-speed synchromesh transmission with floor shift control. Overdrive. Twin-Traction. Hill Holder. Power brakes. Air conditioning. Deluxe T6 Cab. Radio. Clock. Climatizer heater/defroster. Safety seat belts. Kleenex dispenser. Cigarette lighter. Dual door locks. Dual horns. Standard or Deluxe Conestoga camper. Caravan Top. U2 or U3 Service Champ fiberglass bodies (in 1964, 122-inch wheelbase only). Painted rear bumper. Heavy-duty wraparound cadmium-toned diamond embossed rear step bumper. Right-hand taillight. License plate frames. Locking gas cap. Left and right-hand exterior rear view mirrors. Left and right exterior extension rear view mirrors. Tinted glass. Spotlight. Directional signals. Inside pickup box tire carrier. Hubcaps (¾-ton models). Front splash guards. Windshield washer. Cushion toppers. One quart oil bath air cleaner. Engine governor. In-line gas filter. 289 or heavy-duty engines (V8 models only). 7.0:1 compression ratio (V8s only). Four-barrel carburetor (V8s only). Heavy-duty 11 inch clutch (V8 only). Heavy-duty generator. Alternator. Heavy-duty battery. Heavy-duty fan. Heavy-duty radiator. Heavy-duty front springs (8E5 and 8E10). Heavy-duty rear springs. Heavy-duty shock absorbers. Items for non-Deluxe Cab: seat pads, padded dash, sliding rear window, right-hand sun visor, arm rests, dome light. Optional tires specific to the 8E5 and 8E7: 7.10 x 15 four-ply, 6.00 x 16 four-ply, 6.00 x 16 six-ply, 6.50 x 16 six-ply and whitewalls. Optional tires specific to the 8E10 and 8E12: 7.50 x 16 six-ply.

HISTORICAL: When the Avanti production facilities were sold to Nathan Altman in 1964-1965, he also obtained the Champ and Transtar truck rights, but no trucks were ever produced by the Avanti Motor Corporation. Except for the M and 2R series models, Studebaker light-duty trucks were never produced in large quantities, but hundreds of post-1936 models of all types have been saved by dedicated Studebaker enthusiasts.

Pricing

1963-1964	5	4	3	2	1
½-Ton					
8E5 (S.W.B.) P.U.	680	1350	2250	3150	4500
8E5 (L.W.B.) P.U.	680	1350	2250	3150	4500
8E7 (S.W.B.) P.U.	770	1550	2550	3600	5100
8E7 (L.W.B.) P.U.	770	1550	2550	3600	5100
¾-Ton					
8E10 P.U.	570	1140	1900	2650	3800
8E12 P.U.	650	1300	2150	3050	4300

* Add 10% for optional V-8 (210/225 h.p.).

WILLYS-OVERLAND

By Robert C. Ackerson
Additional research by John A. Gunnell

A fleet of postal delivery wagons, for service in Indianapolis, was built by Overland in 1909. The following March, the Ohio auto-maker expanded operations into the light-duty commercial vehicle field with its Model 37 Covered Delivery Wagon. Some 391 of these passenger car-based trucks were assembled through 1911, the same year a one-ton truck appeared.

John North Willys guided the firm's rising fortunes and, in March 1912, Willys-Overland purchased controlling interest in Gramm Motor Truck Company of Lima, Ohio. In August, Garford Automobile Company, of Elyria, Ohio, was acquired. (Garford also built one-ton trucks, as well as larger models.)

In August, 1912, Willys initiated a court battle against Gramm, charging him with stock manipulation schemes. When the lawsuit was settled, B.A. Gramm — company founder — left to form several other truck firms, such as Gramm-Bernstein, while Willys consumated the purchase of Gramm Motor Truck.

A ¾-ton truck called the Model 65 Willys Utility was introduced by Gramm Motor Truck in January, 1913. Some literature refers to this model as a Willys-Overland product, but the vehicle nameplates were stamped with the Gramm name. Among heavier models, Gramm also offered a one-tonner, while Willys-Overland concurrently marketed an 800-pound Delivery vehicle with open or closed body types.

At the start of calendar 1915, Willys-Overland sold its interest in both Garford and Gramm, although Overland dealers still handled sales of these trucks. In 1916, the Willys Utility was marketed as the Garford Model 64, but it did not return the following season. No longer involved in heavy truck-making, Willys-Overland, nevertheless, remained active in the light-duty field. Its products included the 800-pound Model 83 (1916); the 750-pound Model 75 (1916-1917) and a 1200-pound truck (1916) fittingly called the 1200 model. A light panel and express truck were available, on the Model 90 chassis, for 1918.

Commercial vehicle production ceased during the 1921 recession year. It resumed, in 1922, when the Overland Four chassis was used as the basis for a Light Delivery. These trucks appeared on a list published by *Motor World* on Oct. 25, 1923. They were designated the Overland Model 91ce and had a ½-ton payload rating. A one-ton Garford, the Model 15, was also offered that year.

Willys-Overland continued this line through the 1920s and later — between 1927 and 1931 — resumed active marketing of Gramm-built trucks featuring sleeve-valve engines. When the Whippet was introduced for model year 1927, a light-duty truck version soon followed. These vehicles were stylish performers that came in both four- and six-cylinder versions.

The depression years were rough ones for Willys-Overland and, in spite of the best efforts of its management, the company entered into receivership in early 1933. This took place about the same time that Willys-Overland introduced an important new model. The Willys Series 77 truck, a derivative of a revised passenger car line, was extremely handsome with its sloping front end, flowing fender lines and faired-in headlights.

1909 Overland Screenside Delivery (DFW/DPL)

The original 77 remained in production until 1938. During its tenure, it received numerous styling touches that were, apparently, inspired by developments at both Buick and LaSalle. But, when its replacement — also identified as a "77" — appeared, it was apparent that the Willys-Overland designers had not lost their ability to create fresh new lines that borrowed from no one.

This body style was continued until the end of production in 1942. As the years passed, its appearance became somewhat more conventional. In 1939, the Overland name was temporarily revived. However, of far greater importance was the close association between Willys-Overland's civilian trucks and the early military Jeeps it was building for the United States Army.

During the war years, there was considerable speculation about the direction Willys-Overland would follow when peacetime conditions returned.

When the dust settled, Willys-Overland was in an admirable position. Identified in the public's view as the creator of the Jeep, it quickly moved to begin peacetime production of a civilian version of that remarkable vehicle. Beginning in 1947, Willys-Overland began offering a new series of Brooks Stevens designed trucks that moved the company into the ½-ton and one-ton classes with vehicles that captured the charisma, charm and stamina of the Jeep.

While these trucks enjoyed the benefits of a consistent policy of product improvement, the Jeep models were, by no means, ignored by Willys-Overland or the public. Eager to assure the dominant position in the still embryonic four-wheel-drive market, Willys-Overland went to great lengths to tailor Jeep accessories and options to the needs of its customers.

The CJ-2A was replaced by the CJ-3A model in 1950. The following year a new Farm Jeep model was offered. Two years later, the first of the F-head-engined models, the CJ-3B, was introduced.

Ironically, in 1953, which was Willys-Overland's 50th anniversary, the company was purchased by industrialist Henry J. Kaiser and became part of Kaiser Manufacturing Co. However, the Willys' name remained on some models for years afterwards, although the term 'Jeep' would be slowly phased-in as a replacement. Our catalog coverage of Willys-Overland ends at model year 1962. The 1963-1969 'Jeep' models are covered in the Kaiser-Jeep section and the 1970-1986 models are covered in the AMC-Jeep section.

1911-1912 Overland Mail Delivery Van (DFW/SI)

1913 Willys Utility (by Gramm) 3/4-Ton Truck (OCW)

OVERLAND/GRAMM — MODEL 37/1-TON — FOUR-CYLINDER: — The Overland Model 37 was first listed in 1910 as an 800-pound commercial car. A year later, the Willys-Overland Co. came out with one-ton truck. Willys historian Duane Perrin believes neither was carried over into 1912. John North Willy's company was founded in Detroit. He gained a controlling interest in Gramm, of Ohio, in 1912, although there was no direct association with Willys-Overland Co. A one-ton model was sold as an Overland. It had solid tires and a driver's seat perched in front over the engine. The 37 was a truck-chassis version of the Overland passenger car. Most of these trucks featured panel van type bodies.

I.D. DATA: Serial number located on plate on heel board under left front cushion; on right frame member; on spring hanger, right rear; on right rear frame member and/or under left front fender. Engine numbers located on right front corner of cylinder block and/or left side of engine.
   The 1911 to 1912 serial numbers are not available.

Model	Body Type	Price	Weight	Prod. Total
Overland Model 37				
37	Special Delivery (800 lbs.)	1000	—	—
37	Delivery (800 lbs.)	800	—	—
Overland — 1-Ton				
1T	Truck (2000 lbs.)	1500	—	—
Gramm — 1-Ton				
1T (1911)	Truck (2000 lbs.)	1800	—	—
1T (1912)	Truck (2000 lbs.)	2000	—	—

ENGINE: L-head. Inline. Four-cylinder. Cast iron block. Bore & stroke: 3¾ in. x 4½ in. Displacement: 198.8 cu. in. Net horsepower: 25. Solid valve lifters. Carburetor: one-barrel.

CHASSIS: (Model 37) Wheelbase: 102 in. Tires: 32 x 3½ in. (One-Ton) Wheelbase: 120 in.

TECHNICAL: Selective sliding transmission. Speeds: 3F/1R. Outboard-mounted gearshift lever. Drive system chain. Rear wheel brakes. Wood spoke wheels.

OPTIONS: Bulb horn. Brass sidelights. Headlamps. Taillamps. Special paint. Aftermarket bodies.

HISTORICAL: Driver-over-engine 1-ton truck with solid tires introduced. Overland moved production from Indianapolis, Ind. to Toledo, Ohio. this year. Willys historian Duane Perrin reports that Express Delivery and Panel Delivery versions of the 1912 Overland Model 59 were available. Our research turned up no data on these models.

Pricing

1911-1912	5	4	3	2	1
Overland "37"					
Delivery	1300	2550	4250	5900	8500
Spl. Delivery	1450	2850	4750	6650	9500
Overland					
1-Ton Truck	930	1860	3100	4350	6200
Gramm					
1-Ton Truck	980	1950	3250	4550	6500

WILLYS-OVERLAND — MODEL 69/ONE-TON — FOUR-CYLINDER: — The first appearance of the Willys Utility name on a truck came in 1913. This truck was made by Gramm at Lima, Ohio. Gramm was not officially part of the Willys-Overland Co., although John North Willys controlled both firms, as well as numerous others. A 1½-ton model is beyond the scope of this catalog, but two other 1913 models were one-ton or less. Gramm produced a one-ton truck which is included in this section. Available data is sketchy. Marketed as an Overland gasoline truck was a commercial vehicle of the year's Model 69 four-cylinder passenger car. It came with an open express (large pickup) body or as a full panel van-type truck. The Gramm-built Willys Utility was advertised in the July 1913 *Literary Digest* . It was said to be priced 30-50 percent lower than similar vehicles and described as "practical and up-to-date." It used a 30 horsepower motor governed for a top speed of 18 m.p.h. Pneumatic tires were mounted in front with two inch larger diameter solid tires at the rear. This truck was advertised under the Willys-Overland Co. name and address and used many Model 69 components.

I.D. DATA: Serial number located on plate on heel board under left front cushion; on right frame member; on spring hanger, right rear; on right rear frame member and/or under left front fender. Engine numbers located on right front corner of cylinder block and/or left side of engine.
   Serial numbers for the Overland 69 began at number 1 and ended at 30,026. This series included both passenger cars and trucks.

Model	Body Type	Price	Weight	Prod. Total
Overland Model 69				
69	Open Express	950	—	—
69	Full Panel	1000	—	—
Gramm				
1-Ton	Chassis	1750	—	—
Willys Utility				
¾-Ton	Chassis	1250	—	—

ENGINE (Overland): L-head. Inline. Four-cylinder. Cast iron block. Bore & stroke: 4 in. x 4½ in. Displacement: 226.2 cu. in. Net horsepower: 30.

ENGINE (Willys Utility): Literature mentions a "powerful 30 horsepower motor — controlled by our patented governor. It cannot operate over 18 miles per hour."

CHASSIS (Overland Model 69): Wheelbase: 110 in. Tires: 32 x 3½ in.

CHASSIS (Gramm/Willys Utility): Tires: (front) 34 x 4½ in.; (rear) 36 x 3½ in.

TECHNICAL: An advertisement read: The pressed steel frame is built to stand the most severe strains of heavy loads and the worst possible road conditions. It is thoroughly reinforced. Both the front and rear axles are unusually rugged, and are made in our drop forge plant. It has a three speed transmission — three forward and one reverse. We found that 34 in. x 4½ in. pneumatic tires on the front wheels and 36 in. x 3½ in. solid tires on the rear give the most practical service, so we equipped the truck accordingly. It is a big practical commercial truck — built purely and simply for commercial purposes.

OPTIONS: 60 in. "Southern" gauge. Special paint. Brass side lamps. Bulb horn. Headlamps. Taillamps.

NOTE: In this era many aftermarket accessories were available at dealer agencies.

HISTORICAL: Innovations: New open express available from factory. Three-speed selective transmission replaces two-speed; pedal controlled planetary type. Historical notes: First use of Willys name on a truck occurred this year. Built by Gramm, it followed Overland practice but had side-chain final drive.

Pricing

1913	5	4	3	2	1
Overland					
Open Express	1200	2400	4000	5600	8000
Full Panel	1300	2550	4250	5900	8500
Gramm					
Chassis — 1-Ton	980	1950	3250	4550	6500
Willys					
Chassis — ¾-Ton	1130	2250	3750	5250	7500

1914 WILLYS-OVERLAND

1914 Overland Model 79-DS Panel Delivery (OCW)

OVERLAND — MODEL 79/MODEL-65 — FOUR-CYLINDER: — The Model 79 Overland was a commercial car variation of the Model 79 passenger car. It was cataloged as an 800 lb. commercial chassis. Most likely, buyers would have purpose-built bodies custom made for a chassis. Most were turned out as light vans. Produced only as a commercial vehicle, the Model 65 was a 1500 lb. gasoline truck offered in both 1914 and 1915. It came in "chassis-only" form or with a factory express body. This was the same truck listed by the Association of Licensed Automobile Manufacturers (ALAM) as the "Willys Utility" in the ALAM's 1915 handbook. It was actually made at the Gramm plant in Lima, Ohio.

I.D. DATA: Serial number located on plate on heel board under left front cushion; on right frame member; on spring hanger, right rear; on right rear frame member and/or under left front fender. Engine numbers located on right front corner of cylinder block and/or left side of engine.
  Serial numbers for the Overland 65 are not available. Serial numbers for the Overland 79 began at number 1 and ended at number 45,005. This series included both cars and trucks.

1914 Overland Model 79-DE Flare Board (OCW)

Model	Body Type	Price	Weight	Prod. Total
Overland Model 79				
79	Chassis (800 lbs.)	900	2765	—
Model 65				
65	Willys-Utility Chassis (¾-Ton)	1350	2882	—

ENGINE: Vertical. Four-cylinder. Cast iron block. Bore & stroke: 4⅛ in. x 4½ in. Displacement: 240.5 cu. in. Net horsepower: 27.2 (N.A.C.C.) Solid valve lifters. Carburetor: one-barrel.

CHASSIS (Overland Model 79): Wheelbase: 114 in. Tires: 33 x 4 in.

CHASSIS (Overland Model 65): Wheelbase: 120 in. Front tread: 56 in. Rear tread: 58 in. Tires: (frt.) 34 x 4½ pnuematic; (rear) 36 x 3½ solid.

1914 Willys Utility, Covered Flareboard (OCW)

TECHNICAL: Selective sliding transmission. Speeds: 3F/1R. Outboard-mounted gearshift lever. Cone clutch. Double side chain drive. Contracting and expanding brakes. Wood spoke wheels.

OPTIONS: Bulb horn. Brass sidelights. Headlamps. Taillamps. Special paint. Aftermarket bodies.

HISTORICAL: New Model 79 introduced.
  Willys-Knight was introduced as a new car-line this year. Some Willys-Knight taxicabs and trucks were built later. A Willys-Overland facility became the first auto agency established in Iceland. Trucks sold there could be called "Ice Wagons."

Pricing

1914	5	4	3	2	1
Overland "79"					
Express	1200	2400	4000	5600	8000
Panel	1300	2550	4250	5900	8500
WILLYS UTILITY "65"					
Express	1170	2340	3900	5450	7800
Panel	1250	2500	4150	5800	8300

1915 WILLYS-OVERLAND

WILLYS-OVERLAND — MODEL 65 — FOUR-CYLINDER: — Willys historian Duane Perrin believes that the Willys Utility Model 65 commercial chassis was carried over only in Canada for 1915. There was also a Gramm 65 the same year. The Gramm offered the same two body styles as the Overland (identical prices) plus a more expensive 65A chassis. Based on model similarities and corporate associations, it seems safe to assume this was an instance of "badge-engineering" (selling the same product under two nameplates). The Gramm-made Willys Utility had a four-cylinder engine with separately-cast blocks arranged vertically under its rounded hood. It was water-cooled via a cellular radiator and had jump spark ignition with a magneto and dry batteries as the electric source. The driver sat on the right side and controls were center-mounted. The express model featured a paneled box and long, flat top supported on beams at each corners of the box. The top extended over the driver's compartment.

I.D. DATA: Serial number located on plate on heel board under left front cushion; on right frame member; on spring hanger, right rear; on right rear frame member and/or under left front fender. Engine numbers located on right front corner of cylinder block and/or left side of engine. The Gramm Motor Truck Co., of Lima, Ohio was controlled by John N. Willys at this time and produced a model described as the "Willys Utility 1500 - pound truck." Serial or model numbers for this product are unavailable.

Model	Body Type	Price	Weight	Prod. Total
Willys-Utility — Model 65 (*)				
65	¾-Ton Chassis	1350	2882	—
65	¾-Ton Express	1500	2985	—
65A	¾-Ton Chassis	1800	3000	—

(*) Made by Gramm.

ENGINE: Vertical. Four-cylinder. Cast iron block. Bore & stroke: 4⅛ in. x 4½ in. Displacement: 240.5 cu. in. Net horsepower: 27.2 (N.A.C.C.) Solid valve lifters. Carburetor: one-barrel.

CHASSIS: Wheelbase: 120 in. Front tread: 56 in. Rear tread: 58 in. Tires: (front) 34 x 4½ in., pnewmatic (rear) 36 x 3½ in. solid.

TECHNICAL: Selective sliding transmission. Speeds: 3F/1R. Outboard-mounted gearshift lever. Cone clutch. Drive system: Double side chain. Contracting and expanding rear wheel brakes. Wood spoke wheels.

OPTIONS: 60 in. "Southern" gauge. Bulb horn. Brass sidelights. Brass headlamps. Carbide taillamps. Side curtains. Special paint. Aftermarket bodies.

HISTORICAL: New 65A model introduced. Full electrics also available. There was a 1-ton heavy-duty model, too. Overland introduced left-hand drive this year.

The company had profits of $10 million this year.

Pricing

1915	5	4	3	2	1
Willys Utility					
¾-Ton Express	1170	2340	3900	5450	7800

1916 WILLYS-OVERLAND

1916 Overland Express (DFW/IPC)

WILLYS-OVERLAND — MODEL 83 — FOUR-CYLINDER: — Overland's Model 83 passenger car was the basis for a new commercial vehicle line of 1916. This model had an angular, "cathedral-shaped" radiator, rounded cowl and large sweeping fenders. The body sills were rather high on this model. Also based on a current passenger car, was the Model 75 commercial chassis. The Overland 75 looked like a slightly scaled-down version of the "83." However, it had much lower body sills and a much shorter hood line. Standard equipment for both models included windshield, speedometer, ammeter and demountable rims. The "83" came in two 800 pound models: Express Delivery and Special Delivery, plus as a 1200 pound Open Express truck. The "75" came with a 750 pound payload rating as a Panel Delivery or Screenside Delivery. Standard colors for passenger cars were Brewster green body with fenders and radiator black.

I.D. DATA: Serial number located on plate on heel board under left front cushion; on right frame member; on spring hanger, right rear; on right rear frame member and/or under left front fender. Engine numbers located on right front corner of cylinder block and/or left side of engine.

Serial numbers for the Overland 83 began at number 1 and ended at 102,840. Serial numbers for the Overland 75 began at number 1 and ended at approximately 25,000. There was also a 75B with approximate numbers 25,001 to 65,694. The 75B had 30 horsepower, five more than the 75. Both series included both passenger cars and trucks.

Model	Body Type	Price	Weight	Prod. Total
Overland Model 83				
83	Express Dely. (800 lbs.)	725	2780	—
83	Special Dely. (800 lbs.)	750	2790	—
83B	Open Express (1200 lbs.)	850	3329	—
Overland Model 75				
75LD	Screen Dely. (750 lbs.)	595	3268	—
75PLD	Panel Dely.	625	3268	—

ENGINE (Model 83): Cast en block. Inline. Side-valve (L-head). Four-cylinder. Cast iron block. Bore & stroke: 4⅛ in. x 4½ in. Displacement: 240.5 cu. in. Net horsepower: 27.25 (N.A.C.C.) 5 main bearings. Solid valve lifters. Carburetor: Tillotson.

NOTE: Gravity feed. Splitdorf ignition (single system with two units). 6-Volt. Auto-Lite 6 starter and generator. Willard 80 battery. Helical camshaft drive. Pump cooling. Splash oiling.

658

ENGINE (Model 75): Cylinders cast in blocks of two. Inline. Side-valve. Four-cylinder. Cast iron block. Bore & stroke: 3⅛ in. x 5 in. Displacement: 153.4 cu. in. Net horsepower: 15.63 (N.A.C.C.) Two main bearings. Solid valve lifters. Carburetor: Tillotson.

NOTE: Same as Model 83 except a Gould 80 battery was used and camshaft drive was by chain.

CHASSIS (Overland Model 83): Wheelbase: 106 in. Front and rear tread: 50 or 60 in. Tires: 33 x 4 in.

CHASSIS (Overland Model 75): Wheelbase: 104 in. Front and rear tread: 50 or 60 in. Tires: 31 x 4 in.

TECHNICAL: Selective transmission on axle. Speeds: 3F/1R. Floor-mounted gearshift lever. Cone clutch. (Model 83) ¾-floating; (Model 75) full-floating rear axle. High gear ratio: (Model 83) 3.75:1; (Model 75) 4.00:1. Contracting on jackshaft/expanding rear wheel brakes. Wood spoke wheels.

NOTE: The "83" had semi-elliptic front springs and ¾ elliptic rears. The "75" had semi-elliptic front springs and cantilever rear springs.

OPTIONS: Same as 1915.

HISTORICAL: Innovations: New L-head monobloc engine. Overland "83" commercial vehicles introduced. New "Special Delivery" and screenside delivery bow. Historical notes: Willys-Overland produced 140, 111 passenger vehicles in calendar 1916.

Pricing

1916	5	4	3	2	1
Overland "83"					
Express Dely.	1300	2550	4250	5900	8500
Special Dely.	1450	2850	4750	6650	9500
Open Express	1200	2400	4000	5600	8000
Overland "75"					
Screen	1450	2900	4800	6700	9600
Panel	1500	2900	4850	6800	9700

1917 WILLYS-OVERLAND

WILLYS-OVERLAND — SERIES 90 — FOUR-CYLINDER: — The "90" was produced mainly in Panel Delivery form and remained a staple Willys-Overland product into the early-1920s, when the "Light Four" replaced it. As compared to the previous models, the "90" had a higher, straighter hood and cowl line—both being at the same level on the top surface. However, it resembled the "83" as far as size, sharing the same 106 inch wheelbase. According to Willys historian Duane A. Perrin, a 104 inch wheelbase was available, too. Standard equipment included a Stewart speedometer, Kellogg power tire pump, Willard storage battery, Auto-Lite horn, Stan weld wheel rims, Champion spark plugs and Goodyear or Fisk tires. Perrin adds that the Overland "75" series was carried over for 1917, as well as the Model 83B, a 1,200-pound Express Delivery. Consult our 1916 section for data on these models.

I.D. DATA: Serial number located on plate on heel board under left front cushion; on right frame member; on spring hanger, right rear; on right rear frame member and/or under left front fender. Engine numbers located on right front corner of cylinder block and/or left side of engine. Serial numbers for the 1917 Overland Model 90 began at number 1 and ended at 87,008. This series included both trucks and passenger cars.

Model	Body Type	Price	Weight	Prod. Total
Overland Model 90				
90PLD	Panel Dely. (750 lbs.)	700	2895	—

ENGINE (Series 90): Vertical. Separate cast cylinders. Valves on right side. Four-cylinder. Cast iron block. Bore & stroke: 3⅜ in. x 5 in. Displacement: 178.8 cu. in. Net horsepower: 32 (N.A.C.C.) Two main bearings. Solid valve lifters. Carburetor: Tillotson model V. Other features: Helical drive camshaft. Inlet manifold outside and bolted-on. Iron pistons with three diagonal rings. Thermo-syphon cooling. Circulation splash oiling. Stewart fuel feed. Connecticut ignition. Auto-Lite 6-volt starter.

CHASSIS (Overland Model 90): Wheelbase: 104-106 in. Front and rear tread: (std.) 50 in.; (opt.) 60 in. Tires: 31 x 4 in.

TECHNICAL: Selective sliding transmission. Speeds: 3F/1R. Floor-mounted gearshift lever. Cone type clutch. Three-quarter floating rear axle. High gear ratio: 3.75:1. Rear wheel brakes. Wood spoke wheels.

NOTE: Rear springs of cantilever design.

OPTIONS: 60 in. "Southern" gauge. Special paint. Aftermarket bodies.

Innovations: Series 90 comes out. New, modernized styling. Priced competitively with Model T. Historical notes: The Series 90 engine was the basis for some famous later Willy's power plants. Curtiss Aviation Co. became part of Willys Corp., but was completely separate from Willys-Overland, Co.

Pricing

1917 Overland "90"	5	4	3	2	1
Panel	1350	2700	4500	6300	9000

1918 WILLYS-OVERLAND

WILLYS-OVERLAND — SERIES 90 — FOUR-CYLINDER: — The Overland "90" was carried over into 1918 basically unchanged, except that a heavier duty group of models rated for 1200 pound payloads was added. A new body style, in both weight classes was an open express. Also continuing to be available (see 1916 specifications) was the Model "83" open express.

I.D. DATA: Serial number located on plate on heel board under left front cushion; on right frame member; on spring hanger, right rear; on right rear frame member and/or under left front fender. Engine numbers located on right front corner of cylinder block and/or left side of engine.
  Serial numbers for the 1918 Overland 90/90B were 87,009 to 140,643 passenger cars and trucks inclusive.

Model Overland "90"	Body Type	Price	Weight	Prod. Total
90	Chassis (800 lbs.)	800	2876	—
90	Express	840	2923	—
90	Panel	865	3110	—
90	Chassis (1200 lbs.)	915	3249	—
90	Express	975	3400	—

ENGINE: Vertical. Cylinder cast en bloc. Four-cylinder. Cast iron block. Bore & stroke: 3⅜ in. x 5 in. Displacement: 178.8 cu. in. Net horsepower: 32 (N.A.C.C.) Two main bearings. Solid valve lifters. Carburetor: Tillotson model V.

CHASSIS (Overland "90"): Wheelbase: 106 in. Front and rear tread: (std.) 50 in. (opt.) 60 in. Tires: 31 x 4 in.

TECHNICAL: Selective sliding transmission. Speeds: 3F/1R. Floor-mounted gearshift lever. Cone type clutch. Three-quarter floating rear axle. High gear ratio: 3.75:1. Rear wheel brakes. Wood spoke wheels.

OPTIONS: 60 inch "Southern" gauge. Special paint. Aftermarket bodies.

HISTORICAL: John North Willys had over extended himself in building up his company. This set the stage for a financial reorganization in 1919.

Pricing

1918 Overland "90"	5	4	3	2	1
Express (800 lbs.)	1300	2600	4300	6000	8600
Panel (800 lbs.)	1350	2700	4500	6300	9000
Express (1200 lbs.)	1200	2400	4000	5600	8000

1919 WILLYS-OVERLAND

WILLYS-OVERLAND — SERIES 90 — FOUR-CYLINDER: — The Overland "90" continued to be a staple product for Willys-Overland in 1919. Models were the same offered in 1918. The Model "83B" (see 1916-1918) was also continued until 1920.

I.D. DATA: Serial number located on plate on heel board under left front cushion; on right frame member; on spring hanger, right rear; on right rear frame member and/or under left front fender. Engine numbers located on right front corner of cylinder block and/or left side of engine.
  Serial numbers are not available.

Model Overland "90"	Body Type	Price	Weight	Prod. Total
90CE	Chassis (800 lbs.)	800	2876	—
90CE	Express	840	2923	—
90CE	Panel	865	3110	—
90CE	Chassis (1000 lbs.)	915	3249	—
90CE	Express	975	3400	—

ENGINE: Inline. L-head. Four-cylinder. Cast iron block. Bore & stroke: 3⅜ in. x 5 in. Displacement: 178.9 cu. in. Net horsepower: 32 (N.A.C.C.) Two main bearings. Solid valve lifters. Carburetor: one-barrel.

CHASSIS: See 1918 chassis specifications.

TECHNICAL: See 1918 technical specifications.

OPTIONS: 60 in. "Southern" gauge. Special paint. Aftermarket bodies.

HISTORICAL: The Willys Corporation was organized in 1919. According to historian Duane A. Perrin, it was a holding company for takeovers of firms such as Moline Plow, Tillotson carburetor, Stephens, Curtiss Aeroplane Co. and many others. The Wills Corp. did not include Willys-Overland Co. The company itself, although controlled by John North Willys, was run by a management team picked by Chase National Bank (the note holder). The bank eventually put Walter P. Chrysler in charge of day-to-day operations.

Pricing

1919 Overland Light Four	5	4	3	2	1
Express (800 lbs.)	1300	2600	4300	6000	8600
Panel (800 lbs.)	1350	1700	4500	6300	9000
Express (1000 lbs.)	1200	2400	4000	5600	8000

1920 WILLYS-OVERLAND

OVERLAND — LIGHT-FOUR — FOUR-CYLINDER: — In the Encyclopedia of Commercial Vehicles G.N. Georgaro describes the Overland "Light-Four" as a "Classic" motor truck. This model introduced a dimunitive four-cylinder engine that survived, in some Willys models, until 1963. It was seen mostly in delivery van form. Standard equipment included a Stewart speedometer, Stanweld wheel rims, hand tire pump, Auto-Lite horn, Auto-Lite lamps, Duratex upholstery and four Fisk or Federal Grand tires.

I.D. DATA: Serial number located on plate on heel board under left front cushion; on right frame member; on spring hanger, right rear; on right rear frame member and/or under left front fender. Engine numbers located on right front corner of cylinder block and/or left side of engine.
  Serial numbers are not available.

Model Overland Light-Four	Body Type	Price	Weight	Prod. Total
4	Chassis (800 lbs.)	450	—	—
4	Express	—	—	—
4	Panel	—	—	—
4	Chassis (1000 lbs.)	—	—	—
4	Express	—	—	—

ENGINE: Inline. L-head. Four-cylinder. Cast iron block. Bore & stroke: 3⅜ in. x 4 in. Displacement: 143.1 cu. in. Net horsepower: 27 (N.A.C.C.) Two main bearings. Solid valve lifters. Carburetor: Tillotson one-barrel.
  Features of this engine included: detachable head; cylinders cast en bloc design; cast iron valves; aluminum pistons; diagonally-split piston rings, three per cylinder; splash oiling; gravity fuel feed; Connecticut ignition; 6-volt Auto-Lite ignition.

CHASSIS: Wheelbase: 100 in. Tires: 30 x 3½ in.

TECHNICAL: Selective sliding gear transmission, unit type. Speeds: 3F/1R. Floor-mounted gearshift lever. Plate type clutch. Three-quarter floating rear axle. Overall ratio: 4.50:1. Two wheel rear brakes. Wood spoke wheels.

OPTIONS: Front bumper. Rear bumper. Single sidemount. Special paint. Rearview mirror. Cowl lamps. Side curtains.

HISTORICAL: New Light-Four series introduced.

Pricing

1920 Overland Model 4 ("Light Four")	5	4	3	2	1
Express (800 lb.)	1300	2650	4350	6050	8700
Panel (800 lb.)	1400	2800	4600	6400	9200
Express (1000 lb.)	1200	2450	4050	5650	8100

1921 WILLYS-OVERLAND

OVERLAND — LIGHT-FOUR — FOUR-CYLINDER: — The "Light-Four" continued unchanged from 1920. The commercial car line included the same models; three in the 800-pound payload class and two half-tonners. The one seen most was the panel truck.

I.D. DATA: Serial number located on plate on heel board under left front cushion; on right frame member; on spring hanger, right rear; on right rear frame member and/or under left front fender. Engine numbers located on right front corner of cylinder block and/or left side of engine. Serial numbers are not available.

Model	Body Type	Price	Weight	Prod. Total
Overland Model Four				
4	Chassis (800 lbs.)	450	—	—
4	Express	—	—	—
4	Panel	—	—	—
4	Chassis (1000 lbs.)	—	—	—
4	Express	—	—	—

ENGINE: Inline. L-head. Four-cylinder. Cast iron block. Bore & stroke: 3⅜ in. x 4 in. Displacement: 143.1 cu. in. Net horsepower: 27 (N.A.C.C.) Two main bearings. Solid valve lifters. Carburetor: Tillotson.

CHASSIS: Wheelbase: 100 in. Tires: 30 x 3½ in.

TECHNICAL: Selective sliding gear transmission, unit type. Speeds: 3F/1R. Floor-mounted gearshift lever. Plate type clutch. Three-quarter floating rear axle. Overall ratio: 4.50:1. Rear wheel brakes. Wood spoke wheels.

OPTIONS: Special paint. Rearview mirror. Cowl lamps. Side curtains.

HISTORICAL: Willys-Overland sold less than 50,000 passenger cars (and even fewer trucks) and had an indebtedness of $20 million this year. The future was bright, however. The period from 1921 to 1925 would be turn-around years.

Pricing

1921	5	4	3	2	1
Overland Model Four					
Express (800 lb.)	1300	2650	4350	6050	8700
Panel (800 lb.)	1400	2800	4600	6400	9200
Express (1000 lb.)	1200	2400	4050	5650	8100

1922 WILLYS-OVERLAND

1922 Overland Panel Delivery (Broadway Cleaners)

OVERLAND — LIGHT-FOUR — FOUR-CYLINDER: — The "Light-Four" was virtually the same as the 1921 version this season. This model helped pull Willys-Overland out of receivership.

I.D. DATA: Serial number located on plate on heel board under left front cushion; on right frame member; on spring rear; on right rear frame member and/or under left front fender. Engine numbers located on right front corner of cylinder block and/or left side of engine.
Serial numbers are not available.

Model	Body Type	Price	Weight	Prod. Total
Overland Model Four				
4	Chassis (800 lbs.)	450	—	—
4	Express	—	—	—
4	Panel	—	—	—
4	Chassis (1000 lbs.)	—	—	—
4	Express	—	—	—

ENGINE: Inline. L-head. Four-cylinder. Cast iron block. Bore & stroke: 3⅜ in. x 4 in. Displacement: 143.1 cu. in. Net horsepower: 27 (N.A.C.C.) Two main bearings. Solid valve lifters. Carburetor: Tillotson.

CHASSIS: Wheelbase: 100 in. Tires: 30 x 3½ in.

TECHNICAL: Selective sliding gear transmission. Speeds: 3F/1R. Floor-mounted gearshift lever. Plate type clutch. Three-quarter floating rear axle. Overall ratio: 4.50:1. Rear wheel brakes. Wood spoke wheels.

OPTIONS: Special paint. Spare tire. Rearview mirror. Windshield wiper. Cowl lamps. Side curtains.

Pricing

1922	5	4	3	2	1
Overland Model Four					
Express (800 lb.)	1300	2650	4350	6050	8700
Panel (800 lb.)	1400	2800	4600	6400	9200
Express (1000 lb.)	1200	2400	4050	5650	8100

1923 WILLYS-OVERLAND

OVERLAND — SERIES 91CE — FOUR-CYLINDER: — The 1923 Overland "91CE" model was much similar to the previous Light-Four. The year's main changes included a revamped body style lineup with four ½-ton models: The traditional open express, a new panel, plus canopy and screen-side delivery trucks. The designation Overland "91CE" was used for the commercial vehicles; cars were 91s. Standard equipment included a Stewart speedometer, Duratex upholstery and Trico automatic windshield cleaner. Other features were an Auto-Lite starting and lighting system, Indiana headlamps, Corcolite taillamps, Nagel ammeter and Schwarze horn. A six-volt U.S.L. 80-amp storage battery was used. Average gasoline economy for the Series 91 passenger car was 20 miles per gallon, and it can be assumed the truck version was economical, too.

I.D. DATA: Serial number located on plate on heel board under left front cushion; on right frame member; on spring hanger, right rear; on right rear frame member and/or under left front fender. Engine numbers located on right front corner of cylinder block and/or left side of engine.
Serial numbers for the 1923 Overland 91 began at number 1 and ended at 133,200, passenger cars inclusive.

Model	Body Type	Price	Weight	Prod. Total
Overland Model 91CE				
91CE	½-Ton Chassis	425	2020	—

ENGINE: Vertical. Inline. L-head. Four-cylinder. Cast iron block. Bore & stroke: 3⅜ in. x 4 in. Displacement: 143.1 cu. in. Compression ratio: 4.00:1. Brake horsepower: 27 at 2200 R.P.M. Three main bearings. Solid valve lifters. Carburetor: Tillotson one-barrel.

CHASSIS (Overland Series 91): Wheelbase: 100 in. Tires: 30 x 3½ in.

TECHNICAL: Selective sliding gear transmission. Speeds: 3F/1R. Floor-mounted gearshift lever. Borg & Beck 8-in. disc clutch. Semi-floating "SB" rear axle. Overall ratio: 4.50:1. Rear wheel brakes. Hayes wood spoke wheels.

OPTIONS: 60 in. "Southern" gauge. Special paint. Aftermarket bodies. Rearview mirror(s). Front bumper. Rear fender guards. Side curtains.

HISTORICAL: A 1-ton truck based on the Overland Four car chassis was produced at Willys' Stockport branch in England. It was not offered here.

Pricing

1923	5	4	3	2	1
Overland "91CE"					
Express	1300	2650	4350	6050	8700
Panel	1400	2800	4600	6400	9200
Canopy	1350	2700	4500	6300	9000
Screen	1350	2700	4450	6250	8900

1924 WILLYS-OVERLAND

1924 Overland Screenside Delivery (Linda Clark)

OVERLAND — SERIES 91CE — FOUR-CYLINDER: — The commercial car (light-truck) version of the Overland "91" was again the "91CE". There were only minor changes. A new eight-plate clutch replaced the disc type of 1923. A slight increase in cylinder bore size increased engine displacement to 153.9 cu. in. Horsepower was up to 30. A new Outlook brand windshield cleaner was used.

I.D. DATA: Serial number located on plate on heel board under left front cushion; on right frame member; on spring hanger, right rear; on right rear frame member and/or under left front fender. Engine numbers located on right front corner of cylinder block and/or left side of engine. Serial numbers for the 1924 Overland 91 were 133,201 to 240,271, passenger cars inclusive.

Model	Body Type	Price	Weight	Prod. Total
Overland Model 91CE				
91CE	½-Ton Chassis	395	2040	—

ENGINE: Vertical. Inline. L-head. Four-cylinder. Cast iron block. Bore & stroke: 3½ in. x 4 in. Displacement: 153.9 cu. in. Compression ratio: 4.00:1. Brake horsepower: 30 at 2400 R.P.M. Net horsepower: 19.6 (taxable). Three main bearings. Solid valve lifters. Carburetor: Tillotson one-barrel.

CHASSIS (Overland Series 91CE): Wheelbase: 100 in. Tires: 30 x 3½ in.

TECHNICAL: Selective sliding gear transmission. Speeds: 3F/1R. Floor-mounted gearshift lever. Eight-plate clutch. Semi-floating rear axle. Overall ratio: 4.50:1. Rear wheel brakes. Wood spoke wheels.

OPTIONS: 60 in. "Southern" gauge. Special paint. Aftermarket bodies. Rearview mirror(s). Front bumper. Rear fender guards. Side curtains. Pines tire lock. Spotlight. Crolan gas gauge. Radiator shield. Wind wings. Shock absorbers.

HISTORICAL: Both four-and six-cylinder taxicabs were made available on the Willys-Knight chassis.

Pricing

1924 Overland "91CE"	5	4	3	2	1
Express	1300	2650	4350	6050	8700
Panel	1400	2800	4600	6400	9200
Canopy	1350	2700	4500	6300	9000
Screen	1350	2700	4450	6250	8900

1925 WILLYS-OVERLAND

OVERLAND — SERIES 91CE — FOUR-CYLINDER: — The "91CE" line of trucks was again carried over. There were no major specifications changes.

I.D. DATA: Serial number located on plate on heel board under left front cushion; on right frame member; on spring hanger, right rear; on right rear frame member and/or under left front fender. Engine numbers located on right front corner of cylinder block and/or left side of engine. Serial numbers for the 1925 Overland 91/91A were 240,272 to 339,655, passenger cars inclusive.

Model	Body Type	Price	Weight	Prod. Total
Overland Model 91CE				
91CE	½-Ton Chassis	395	2040	—

ENGINE: Inline. L-head. Four-cylinder. Cast iron block. Bore & stroke: 3½ in. x 4 in. Displacement: 153.9 cu. in. Compression ratio: 4.00:1. Brake horsepower: 30 at 2400 R.P.M. Net horsepower: 19.6. Three main bearings. Solid valve lifters. Carburetor: Tillotson one-barrel.

CHASSIS (Overland Series 91CE): Wheelbase: 100 in. Tires: 30 x 3½ in.

TECHNICAL: Selective sliding gear transmission. Speeds: 3F/1R. Floor-mounted gearshift lever. Eight-plate type clutch. Semi-floating rear axle. Overall ratio: 4.50:1. Rear wheel brakes. Wood spoke wheels.

OPTIONS: 60 in. "Southern" gauge. Special paint. Aftermarket bodies. Rearview mirror(s). Front bumper. Rear fender guards. Side curtains. Pines tire lock. Spotlight. Gas gauge. Radiator shield. Wind wings. Shock absorbers.

HISTORICAL: In contrast to the bleak year of 1921, Willys sold plenty of cars (200,000) and trucks in 1925. Annual profits were nearly as high as the debt of $20 million reported only four years earlier.

Pricing

1925 Overland "91CE"	5	4	3	2	1
Open Express	1300	2650	4350	6050	8700
Canopy	1350	2700	4500	6300	9000
Panel	1400	2800	4600	6400	9200
Screen	1350	2700	4450	6250	8900

NOTE: (with aftermarket bodies).

1926 WILLYS-OVERLAND

OVERLAND — SERIES 91CE — FOUR-CYLINDER: — The Light-Four, Model 91CE was carried over for its final season in 1926. It was still marketed as a half-ton chassis to which customers could add bodies made by aftermarket firms. We have estimated prices for typical body styles of this era in this catalog.

I.D. DATA: Serial number located on plate on heel board under left front cushion; on right frame member; on spring hanger, right rear; on right rear frame member and/or under left front fender. Engine numbers located on right front corner of cylinder block and/or left side of engine. Serial numbers for the 1926 Overland 91/91A were 339,656 to 364,569, passenger cars inclusive.

Model	Body Type	Price	Weight	Prod. Total
Overland Model 91				
91CE	½-Ton Chassis	395	2040	—

ENGINE: Inline. L-head. Four-cylinder. Cast iron block. Bore & stroke: 3½ in. x 4 in. Displacement: 153.9 cu. in. Compression ratio: 4.00:1. Brake horsepower: 30 at 2400 R.P.M. Net horsepower: 19.6. Three main bearings. Solid valve lifters. Carburetor: Tillotson one-barrel.

CHASSIS (Overland Series 91): Wheelbase: 100 in. Tires: 30 x 3½ in.

TECHNICAL: Selective sliding gear transmission. Speeds: 3F/1R. Floor-mounted gearshift lever. Eight-plate type clutch. Semi-floating rear axle. Overall ratio: 4.50:1. Rear wheel brakes. Wood spoke wheels.

OPTIONS: 60 in. "Southern" gauge. Special paint. Aftermarket bodies. Rearview mirror(s). Front bumper. Rear fender guards. Side curtains.

HISTORICAL: Innovations: Whippet replaces the Light-Four effective with 1927 model year (introduced in calendar 1926). Six-cylinder engine optional in Whippet. Historical notes: Last year for Light-Four model.

Pricing

1926	5	4	3	2	1
Overland Model 91					
Open Express	1300	2650	4350	6050	8700
Canopy	1350	2700	4500	6300	9000
Panel	1400	2800	4600	6400	9200
Screen	1350	2700	4450	6250	8900

NOTE: (with aftermarket bodies).

1927 WILLYS-OVERLAND

WHIPPET — SERIES 96 — FOUR-CYLINDER: — The Whippet was America's smallest car when introduced in the fall of 1926, as a '27 model. But it was a fast, strong runner; qualities that made commercial vehicle versions a natural development. It superseded the Overland in Willys-Overland Company's marketing program and is often referred to as the "Willy's Whippet," after 1929. One advanced feature was four-wheel mechanical brakes. The base engine was a 2.2-litre side-valve four. Later, a 2.4-litre six was made an option. A full range of models was available. Styling features included a bright metal rounded radiator shell, vertical hood louvers inside a slightly raised panel and drum type headlights on 1927 models. There was a vacuum feed fuel system and Auto-Lite ignition. The 1927 version had raised panel fenders. The Whippet hood mascot was a racing dog.

NOTE: Whippet trucks with the optional six-cylinder used the engine from theModel 93A passenger car.

I.D. DATA: Serial number located on plate on dash; also on left side of frame member ahead of front spring rear hanger; also on right side of frame at rear end; also under driver's seat cushion. Engine numbers located on either front or rear on upper corner of cylinder block on right side.Serial numbers for 1927 Whippets were number 1 to 110,344 with passenger cars and trucks inclusive.

Model	Body Type	Price	Weight	Prod. Total
Whippet Model 96				
96	½-Ton Chassis	370	1469	—
96	Pickup	—	—	—
96	Canopy Dely.	—	—	—
96	Screen Dely.	—	—	—
96	Panel	—	—	—
96	Sedan Dely.	—	—	—

ENGINE (Base): Inline. L-head. Four-cylinder. Cast iron block. Bore & stroke: 3⅛ in. x 4⅜ in. Displacement: 134.2 cu. in. Brake horsepower: 30 at 2800 R.P.M. Net horsepower: 15.6 (N.A.C.C.) Three main bearings. Solid valve lifters. Carburetor: Tillotson model one-barrel.

ENGINE (Optional): Inline. L-head. Six-cylinder. Cast iron block. Bore & stroke: 3 in. x 4 in. Displacement: 169.6 cu. in. Brake horsepower: 40 at 2800 R.P.M. Net horsepower: 21.6 (N.A.C.C.) Seven main bearings. Solid valve lifters. Carburetor: Tillotson model one-barrel.

CHASSIS (Whippet 96): Wheelbase: 100.25 in. Tires: 28 x 4.75 in.

CHASSIS (Whippet 93A): Wheelbase: 100.25 in. Tires: 29 x 4.75 in.

TECHNICAL: Selective sliding transmission. Speeds: 3F/1R. Floor-mounted gearshift lever. Overall ratio: 4.5:1. Four wheel mechanical brakes. Wood spoke wheels.

OPTIONS: Front bumper. Rear bumper. Single sidemount. Special paint. Rearview mirror.

HISTORICAL: Whippet supersedes the Overland. Whippet features included four-wheel mechanical brakes, European-like styling and full-pressure lubrication. The six-cylinder engine had seven main bearings and invar strut pistons. A Whippet passenger car averaged 52.52 m.p.h. for 24 hours during an endurance run at Indianapolis Motor Speedway.

Pricing

1927	5	4	3	2	1
Whippet Model 96					
Pickup	930	1860	3100	4350	6200
Canopy	950	1900	3150	4400	6300
Screen	960	1920	3200	4500	6400
Panel	1000	2000	3300	4600	6600
Sedan Dely.	1040	2070	3450	4850	6900

NOTE: Add 12 percent for 6-cyl. engine.

1928 WILLYS-OVERLAND

WHIPPET — SERIES 96 — FOUR-CYLINDER: — The 1928 Whippets looked nearly identical to the original, but a plain radiator cap was used. The entire radiator was somewhat higher and narrower, although of similar design. New features included a bango type rear axle, new-sized tires and smoother front fenders without a raised panel. Trucks with the base four-cylinder engine were Model 96s. The optional six-cylinder engine was taken from the Model 6-98 passenger car, which had a 109½ inch wheelbase. Contemporary NADA guides do not list any 109½ inch wheelbase trucks so, apparently, the engine was an option only.

I.D. DATA: Serial number located on plate on dash; also on left side of frame member ahead of front spring rear hanger; also on right side of frame at rear end; also under driver's seat cushion. Engine numbers located on either front or rear on upper corner of cylinder block on right side. Serial numbers for 1928 Whippets were 110,345 to 227,902, passenger cars and trucks inclusive.

Model	Body Type	Price	Weight	Prod. Total
Whippet Model 96				
96	½-Ton Chassis	370	1469	—
96	Pickup	—	—	—
96	Canopy Dely.	—	—	—
96	Screen Dely.	—	—	—
96	Panel	—	—	—
96	Sedan Dely.	—	—	—

ENGINE (Base): Inline. L-head. Four-cylinder. Cast iron block. Bore & stroke: 3⅛ in. x 4⅜ in. Displacement: 134.2 cu. in. Brake horsepower: 32 at 2800 R.P.M. Net horsepower: 15.6 (N.A.C.C.) Three main bearings. Solid valve lifters. Carburetor: Tillotson model one-barrel.

ENGINE (Optional): Inline. L-head. Six-cylinder. Cast iron block. Bore & stroke: 3⅛ in. x 3⅞ in. Displacement: 178.3 cu. in. Brake horsepower: 43 at 2800 R.P.M. Net horsepower: 23.4 (N.A.C.C.) Seven main bearings. Solid valve lifters. Carburetor: Tillotson model one-barrel.

CHASSIS (Whippet Series 96): Wheelbase: 100¼ in. Tires: 28 x 4.75 in.

TECHNICAL: Selective sliding gear transmission. Speeds: 3F/1R. Floor-mounted gearshift lever. Borg & Beck clutch. Bango type rear axle. Overall ratio: 4.5:1. Four wheel mechanical brakes. Wood spoke wheels.

OPTIONS: Same as 1927.

HISTORICAL: Introduced Aug., 1927 (4-cyl.); April, 1928 (6-cyl.) A new plant in Maywood, Calif. was built this year.

Pricing

1928	5	4	3	2	1
Whippet Series 96					
Pickup	930	1860	3100	4350	6200
Canopy	950	1900	3150	4400	6300
Screen	960	1920	3200	4500	6400
Panel	1000	2000	3300	4600	6600
Sedan Dely.	1040	2070	3450	4850	6900

NOTE: Add 12 percent for 6-cylinder. engine.

1929 WILLYS-OVERLAND

WHIPPET — SERIES 96/96A — FOUR-CYLINDER: — The new "Superior" Whippet 96A line was promoted for 1929. This series featured a new radiator that was peaked, instead of rounded, at the top. There was full-crown front fenders and "torpedo" headlights, too. A heavier molding ran down the edge of the hood and cowl sides, curving up across the cowl right at the base of the windshield. There was a longer wheelbase, enlarged standard four-cylinder engine and also a larger optional six. Truck models offered on the Whippet half-ton commercial chassis were the same available in the past. "Fingertip Controls" mounted in a new unit-grouped instrument cluster were another highly-touted 96A feature.

NOTE: Early 1929 models were a carryover of the 1928 series. (See 1928 section for Model 96 data).

I.D. DATA: Serial number located on plate on dash; also on left side of frame member ahead of front spring rear hanger; also on right side of frame at rear end; also under driver's seat cushion. Engine numbers located on either front or rear on upper corner of cylinder block on right side. The 1929 Whippet 96 had serial numbers 227,903 to 321,000. The 1929 Whippet 96A had serial numbers 321,001 to 435,092. Both series included both passenger cars and motor trucks.

Model	Body Type	Price	Weight	Prod. Total
Whippet Model 96				
96	½-Ton Chassis	370	1469	—
96	Pickup	—	—	—
96	Screen Dely.	—	—	—
96	Canopy Dely.	—	—	—
96	Panel	—	—	—
96	Sedan Dely.	—	—	—
Whippet Model 96A				
96A	½-Ton Chassis	405	1691	—
96A	Pickup	—	—	—
96A	Canopy Dely.	—	—	—
96A	Screen Dely.	—	—	—
96A	Panel	—	—	—
96A	Sedan Dely.	—	—	—

ENGINE (Base, Model 96A): Inline. L-head. Four-cylinder. Cast iron block. Bore & stroke: 3⅛ in. x 4¾ in. Displacement: 145.7 cu. in. Compression ratio: 5.4:1. Brake horsepower: 40 at 3200 R.P.M. Net horsepower: 15.6 (N.A.C.C.) Three main bearings. Solid valve lifters. Carburetor: Tillotson model one-barrel.

ENGINE (Optional, Model 98A): Inline. L-head. Six-cylinder. Cast iron block. Bore & stroke: 3⅛ in. x 3⅞ in. Displacement: 178.3 cu. in. Compression ratio: 5.12:1. Brake horsepower: 50 at 3000 R.P.M. Net horsepower: 23.4 (N.A.C.C.) Seven main bearings. Solid valve lifters. Carburetor: Tillotson model one-barrel.

NOTE: This was the engine from the 112½ inch wheelbase Whippet 98A passenger car. The engine was optional in trucks, but no trucks with the 112½ inch wheelbase show up in NADA guides.

CHASSIS (Whippet 96): Wheelbase: 100¼ in. Tires: 28 x 4.75 in.

CHASSIS (Whippet 96A): Wheelbase: 103¼ in. Tires: 28 x 4.75 in. or 4.75 x 19 in.

TECHNICAL: Selective sliding gear transmission. Speeds: 3F/1R. Floor-mounted gearshift lever. Borg & Beck clutch. Semi-floating rear axle. Overall ratio: 4.5:1. Four-wheel mechanical brakes. Wood spoke wheels.

OPTIONS: Front bumper. Sidemounted spare tire. Special paint. Deluxe equipment. Rearview mirror. Side curtains. Auxiliary passenger seat. Aftermarket bodies. Fog lamps.

HISTORICAL: Introduced (Models 96/98) Aug. 1928; (Model 96A) Nov. 1928; (Model 98A) Dec. 1928.

Pricing

1929	5	4	3	2	1
Whippet Series 96 — (100 in. w.b.)					
Pickup	930	1860	3100	4350	6200
Screen	950	1900	3150	4400	6300
Canopy	960	1920	3200	4500	6400
Panel	1000	2000	3300	4600	6600
Sedan Dely.	1040	2070	3450	4850	6900
Whippet Series 96A — (103 in. w.b.)					
Pickup	930	1920	3200	4500	6400
Canopy	980	1950	3250	4550	6500
Screen	1000	2000	3300	4600	6600
Panel	1020	2050	3400	4800	6800
Sedan Dely.	1070	2150	3550	5000	7100

NOTE: Add 12 percent for Whippet six.

1930 WILLYS-OVERLAND

WILLYS-WHIPPET — SERIES 96A/SERIES 98B — (ALL ENGINES): — The Whippet 96A was carried over for 1930 in the same line of six truck models. These were all of the "New Superior" style. A newly-listed feature was a single-lever controlled windshield. A change of this year was a new line of 110 inch wheelbase trucks, merchandised as the "Willy's Six Model 98B." This was technically the Whippet 98 passenger car converted to commercial vehicle form and equipped with a bored-out six-cylinder engine that now displaced 193 cubic inches. Stylingwise, the Willys six looked distinct from the Whippet. It had a taller, more rounded radiator shell, bright metal torpedo headlights, front parking lamps (unusually mounted below the headlights on the tie-bar) and a hood with vertical louvers arranged in three separate groups.

I.D. DATA: Serial number located on plate on dash; also on left side of frame member ahead of front spring rear hanger; also on right side of frame at rear end; also under driver's seat cushion. Engine numbers located on either front or rear on upper corner of cylinder block on right side. The 1930 Whippet had serial numbers 435,093 to 465,000. The 1930 Willys 98B had serial numbers 131,001 to 154,843. Both series included both passenger cars and motor trucks.

Model	Body Type	Price	Weight	Prod. Total
Whippet Model 96A — (4-cyl.)				
96A	½-Ton Chassis	405	1691	—
96A	Pickup	—	—	—
96A	Canopy Dely.	—	—	—
96A	Screen Dely.	—	—	—
96A	Panel	—	—	—
96A	Sedan Dely.	—	—	—
Willys Model 98B — (6-cyl.)				
98B	½-Ton Chassis	525	1903	—
98B	Pickup	—	—	—
98B	Canopy Dely.	—	—	—
98B	Screen Dely.	—	—	—
98B	Panel	—	—	—
98B	Sedan Dely.	—	—	—

ENGINE (Base, Model 96A): Inline. L-head. Four-cylinder. Cast iron block. Bore & stroke: 3⅛ in. x 4¾ in. Displacement: 145.7 cu. in. Compression ratio: 5.4:1. Brake horsepower: 40 at 3200 R.P.M. Net horsepower: 15.6 (N.A.C.C.) Three main bearings. Solid valve lifters. Carburetor: Tillotson model one-barrel.

ENGINE (Optional, Model 96A): Inline. L-head. Six-cylinder. Cast iron block. Bore & stroke: 3.125 in. x 3.875 in. Displacement: 178.3 cu. in. Compression ratio: 5.12:1. Brake horsepower: 50 at 3000 R.P.M. Seven main bearings. Solid valve lifters. Carburetor: Tillotson model one-barrel.

NOTE: This was designated the 98A engine and was still an option for the Whippet 96A, even though the new Willys 98B had a larger six-cylinder engine.

ENGINE (Model 98B): Inline. L-head. Six-cylinder. Cast iron block. Bore & stroke: 3¼ in. x 3⅞ in. Displacement: 192.9 cu. in. Compression ratio: 5.6:1. Brake horsepower: 65 at 3400 R.P.M. Net horsepower: 25.35 (N.A.C.C.) Seven main bearings. Solid valve lifters. Carburetor: Tillotson model J1A.

CHASSIS (Whippet 96A): Wheelbase: 103¼ in. Tires: 4.75 x 19 in.

CHASSIS (Willys 98B): Wheelbase: 110 in. Tires: 5.00 x 19 in.

TECHNICAL: Selective sliding gear transmission. Speeds: 3F/1R. Floor-mounted gearshift lever. Borg & Beck clutch. Semi-floating rear axle. Four-wheel mechanical brakes. Wood spoke or wire spoke wheels.

OPTIONS: Front bumper. Sidemounted spare tire. Special paint. Deluxe equipment. Rearview mirror. Side curtains. Passenger auxiliary seat: Fog lamps. Aftermarket bodies.

HISTORICAL: Introduced: (Whippet) Oct. 1929; (Willys Six) Dec. 1929. Calendar year registrations: 4,264 (all trucks).

John North Willys stepped down from the company presidency this year. Linwood A. Miller, formerly a high-ranking vice president, took over the top spot. In March, Mr. Willys became the first U.S. Ambassador to Poland.

Pricing

1930	5	4	3	2	1
Whippet Series 96A					
Pickup	960	1920	3200	4500	6400
Canopy	980	1950	3250	4550	6500
Screenside	1000	2000	3300	4600	6600
Panel	1020	2050	3400	4800	6800
Sedan Dely.	1070	2150	3550	5000	7100

NOTE: Add 12 percent for Whippet six.

Willys Series 98B	5	4	3	2	1
Pickup	1130	2250	3750	5250	7500
Canopy	1140	2280	3800	5300	7600
Screenside	1170	2340	3900	5450	7800
Panel	1200	2400	4000	5600	8000
Sedan Dely.	1300	2600	4300	6000	8600

1931 WILLYS-OVERLAND

WILLYS-WHIPPET — SERIES 96A/98B/C-113 — (ALL ENGINES): — Still in the 1931 Willys-Overland truck line were the Whippet 96A (or 4-96A) and Willys 98B (or 6-98B) models. These were strictly carryover products;

refer to 1930 for descriptions. Some historical sources do not even list a 1931 Whippet, although NADA guides give a Sept. 1930 starting date for this truck and the Willys Six "98B." In January 1931, a new C-113 model superseded or joined the other series. This new line offered the same truck body styles equipped with the 193 cu. in. six-cylinder engine on a new 113 in. w.b. chassis. Four-wheel mechanical brakes and an Autolite ignition system remained standard equipment. Styling characteristics included a high, narrow radiator with rounded top, torpedo headlights, vertically louvered hood and split windshield.

I.D. DATA: Serial number located on plate on dash; also on left side of frame member ahead of front spring rear hanger; also on right side of frame at rear end; also under driver's seat cushion. Engine numbers located on either front or rear on upper corner of cylinder block on right side.

Serial numbers, passenger cars and trucks: (96A) 465,001 to 470,247; (98B) 154,844 to ending number; (C-113) 1001 to 2399.

NOTE: C-113 is truck only.

Model	Body Type	Price	Weight	Prod. Total
Whippet Model 96A — (4-cyl.)				
96A	½-Ton Chassis	360	1665	—
96A	Pickup	—	—	—
96A	Screen Dely.	—	—	—
96A	Canopy Dely.	—	—	—
96A	Panel	—	—	—
96A	Sedan Dely.	—	—	—
Willys Model 98B — (6-cyl.)				
98B	½-Ton Chassis	525	1905	—
98B	Pickup	—	—	—
98B	Canopy Dely.	—	—	—
98B	Screen Dely.	—	—	—
98B	Panel	—	—	—
98B	Sedan Dely.	—	—	—
Willys Model C-113 — (6-cyl.)				
C-113	½-Ton Chassis	395	1923	—
C-113	Pickup	—	—	—
C-113	Canopy Dely.	—	—	—
C-113	Screen Dely.	—	—	—
C-113	Panel	—	—	—
C-113	Sedan Dely.	—	—	—

ENGINE (Model 96A): Inline. L-head. Four-cylinder. Cast iron block. Bore & stroke: 3⅛ in. x 4¾ in. Displacement: 145.7 cu. in. Compression ratio: 5.4:1. Brake horsepower: 40 at 3200 R.P.M. Net horsepower: 15.6 (N.A.C.C.) Three main bearings. Solid valve lifters. Carburetor: Tillotson model one-barrel.

NOTE: The 50 h.p. six-cylinder engine was optional. See 1930 specifications.

ENGINE (Model 98B): Inline. L-head. Six-cylinder. Cast iron block. Bore & stroke: 3¼ in. x 3⅞ in. Displacement: 192.9 cu. in. Compression ratio: 5.6:1. Brake horsepower: 65 at 3400 R.P.M. Net horsepower: 25.35 (N.A.C.C.) Four main bearings. Solid valve lifters. Carburetor: Tillotson model J1A.

ENGINE (Model C-113): Inline. L-head. Six-cylinder. Cast iron block. Bore & stroke: 3¼ in. x 3⅞ in. Displacement: 192.9 cu. in. Compression ratio: 5.6:1. Brake horsepower: 65 at 3400 R.P.M. Net horsepower: 25.35 (N.A.C.C.) Four main bearings. Solid valve lifters. Carburetor: Tillotson model J1A.

CHASSIS (Whippet 96A): Wheelbase: 103¼ in. Tires: 28 x 4.75 in.

CHASSIS (Willys 98B): Wheelbase: 110 in. Tires: 29 x 5.00 in.

CHASSIS (Willys C-113): Wheelbase: 113 in. Tires: 29 x 5.00 in.

TECHNICAL: Selective sliding gear transmission. Speeds: 3F/1R. Floor-mounted gearshift lever. Borg & Beck clutch. Semi-floating rear axle. Four-wheel mechanical brakes. Wood spoke or wire wheels.

OPTIONS: See 1930.

HISTORICAL: Introduced: (Whippet) Sept. 1930; (Willys Six) Sept. 1930; (C-113) Jan. 1931. Calendar year registrations: 3,131 (all trucks).

The C-113 superseded the Whippet "96A" and Willys six "98B" in Jan. 1931.

Pricing

	5	4	3	2	1
1931					
Whippet Series 96					
Pickup	960	1920	3200	4500	6400
Canopy	980	1950	3250	4550	6500
Screenside	1000	2000	3300	4600	6600
Panel	1020	2050	3400	4800	6800
Sedan Dely.	1070	2150	3550	5000	7100

NOTE: Add 12 percent for Whippet six.

Willys Series 98B					
Pickup	1130	2250	3750	5250	7500
Canopy	1140	2280	3800	5300	7600
Screenside	1170	2340	3900	5450	7800
Panel	1200	2400	4000	5600	8000
Sedan Dely.	1300	2600	4300	6000	8600

	5	4	3	2	1
Willys Series C-113					
Pickup	900	1800	3000	4200	6000
Canopy	920	1850	3050	4300	6100
Screenside	930	1860	3100	4350	6200
Panel	960	1920	3200	4500	6400
Sedan Dely.	1010	2030	3350	4700	6700

1932 WILLYS-OVERLAND

WILLYS — SERIES C-113 — SIX-CYLINDER: — Carried over for 1932 for Willys truck customers wanting light-duty models was the C-113. This ½-tonner again came as a chassis only, or with any of five factory-approved truck bodies. There were the three other models in the "C" series, but the "113" was the only light-duty. The C-101, C-131 and C-157 were rated for 1½-tons.

I.D. DATA: Serial number located on plate on dash; also on left side of frame member ahead of front spring rear hanger; also on right side of frame at rear end; also under driver's seat cushion. Engine numbers located on either front or rear on upper corner of cylinder block on right side.

Serial numbers 2400 to 3893 were used for 1932-1933 models.

Willys Model C-113 — (6-cyl.)				
C-113	½-Ton Chassis	415	1923	—
C-113	Pickup	—	—	—
C-113	Canopy Dely.	—	—	—
C-113	Screen Dely.	—	—	—
C-113	Panel	—	—	—
C-113	Sedan Dely.	—	—	—

ENGINE (Model C-113): Inline. L-head. Six-cylinder. Cast iron block. Bore & stroke: 3¼ in. x 3⅞ in. Displacement: 192.9 cu. in. Compression ratio: 5.26:1. Brake horsepower: 65 at 3400 R.P.M. Net horsepower: 25.35 (N.A.C.C.) Four main bearings. Solid valve lifters. Carburetor: Tillotson model J1A.

CHASSIS (Willys C-113): Wheelbase: 113 in. Tires: 29 x 5.00 in.

TECHNICAL: Selective sliding gear transmission. Speeds: 3F/1R. Floor-mounted gearshift lever. Borg & Beck clutch. Semi-floating rear axle. Four-wheel mechanical brakes. Steel spoke wheels.

OPTIONS: See 1930.

HISTORICAL: Introduced: Jan. 1932. Calendar year registrations: 1,132 (all trucks).

The C-113 was listed by the NADA guide as a "Willys Six." At the request of President Hoover, John North Willys returned to Toledo to manage Willys-Overland, since the Depression had badly hurt the company.

Pricing

	5	4	3	2	1
1932					
Willys Series C-113					
Pickup	900	1800	3000	4200	6000
Canopy	920	1850	3050	4300	6100
Screenside	930	1860	3100	4350	6200
Panel	960	1920	3200	4500	6400
Sedan Dely.	1010	2030	3350	4700	6700

1933 WILLYS-OVERLAND

WILLYS — SERIES 77 — FOUR-CYLINDER: — New from Willys for 1933 was a stylish new "77" light-duty series rated for ½-ton. These trucks had a highly streamlined appearance with a hood that sloped down in the front to meet a new teardrop-shaped veed radiator grille. Four slanted vent doors decorated the rear of the hood sides, near the cowl. Front fenders had skirted valances and faired-in headlights. There was a veed, single-bar front two-piece bumper. Rear fenders were also streamlined and flared outward at the rear. There was a fin-like hood ornament, one-piece windshield and new steel artillery wheels. These were rather small-looking trucks, perched on a short 100 in. w.b. The sole factory model was a panel delivery. The side-opening rear door (it opened towards the street) had a small window and rear-mounted spare tire carrier.

I.D. DATA: Serial number located on plate on dash; also on left side of frame member ahead of front spring rear hanger; also on right side of frame at rear end; also under driver's seat cushion. Engine numbers located on either front or rear on upper corner of cylinder block on right side.

Same serial numbers as 1932.

Model	Body Type	Price	Weight	Prod. Total
Willys Model 77				
77	Panel Dely.	415	—	—

ENGINE: Inline. L-head. Four-cylinder. Cast iron block. Bore & stroke: 3⅛ in. x 4⅜ in. Displacement: 134.2 cu. in. Compression ratio: 5.13:1. Brake horsepower: 48 at 3200 R.P.M. Net horsepower: 15.63 (N.A.C.C.) Three main bearings. Solid valve lifters. Carburetor: Tillotson model one-barrel.

CHASSIS (Willys 77): Wheelbase: 100 in. Tires: 17 x 5.00 in.

TECHNICAL: Selective sliding gear transmission. Speeds: 3F/1R. Floor-mounted gearshift lever. Four-wheel mechanical brakes. Steel artillery wheels.

OPTIONS: See 1930.

HISTORICAL: Introduced: Jan. 1933. Calendar year registrations: 233 (all trucks).

Willys "77" introduced and available in panel delivery form.

Most C-113 models titled in 1933 were built in the 1932 calendar year. Willys trucks built in 1933 are very rare. In 1932, the company was on the verge of receivership and dropped all of its current model lines in place of a new 1933 product called the "Willys 77." In February, 1933, the firm officially entered bank receivership.

Pricing

	5	4	3	2	1
1933					
Willys "77"					
Panel	870	1750	2900	4100	5800

1934 WILLYS-OVERLAND

WILLYS — SERIES 77 — FOUR-CYLINDER: — The Willys "77" was again marketed in 1934. Yearly changes included new wire spoke wheels and redesigned hood louvers. There were four slightly curved, horizontal louvers on the rear sides of the hood. Each was shorter than the one above it. A panel delivery represented the factory's model lineup.

I.D. DATA: Serial number located on left frame ahead of front spring rear hanger; also on tag attached to left front door sill; also on plate on front right-hand side of front frame cross member at center. Starting: 13,821. Ending: 27,005. Engine numbers located on right side, front upper corner of cylinder block.

Model	Body Type	Price	Weight	Prod. Total
Willys Model 77 — (4-cyl.)				
77	Panel Dely. (½-ton)	415	2130	—

ENGINE (Model 77): Inline. L-head. Four-cylinder. Cast iron block. Bore & stroke: 3⅛ in. x 4⅜ in. Displacement: 134.2 cu. in. Compression ratio: 5.13:1. Brake horsepower: 48 at 3200 R.P.M. Net horsepower: 15.63 (N.A.C.C.) Three main bearings. Solid valve lifters. Carburetor: Tillotson model one-barrel.

CHASSIS (Willys 77): Wheelbase: 100 in. Tires: 17 x 5.00 in.

TECHNICAL: Selective sliding gear transmission. Speeds: 3F/1R. Floor-mounted gearshift lever. Four-wheel mechanical brakes. Wire spoke wheels.

HISTORICAL: Calendar year registrations: 25 (all trucks).

Most trucks of the 1934 design were built late in calendar year 1933. These are still quite rare. Total registrations of trucks in the two calendar years came to just 258 vehicles.

Pricing

	5	4	3	2	1
1934					
Willys Model 77					
Panel	870	1750	2900	4100	5800

1935 WILLYS-OVERLAND

WILLYS — SERIES 77 — FOUR-CYLINDER: — For 1935, the Willys "77" truck had a higher, more-conventional veed grille and straighter (non-sloping) hood line. The grille looked somewhat Buick-like. Decorating the sides of the hood were five slanted, oblong "bubbles" for air venting. They looked LaSalle-like. Someone at Willys seemed to appreciate GM design. Parking lights were placed alongside the radiator, under the faired-in headlights. The bumper was again a two-piece affair, veed towards the center. Wire wheels continued. The fenders were done in black; the rest of the truck in body color. A new cab pickup model came out this season.

I.D. DATA: Serial number located on left frame ahead of front spring rear hanger; also on tag attached to left front door sill; also on plate on front right-hand side of front frame cross member at center. Starting: (pickup): 27,001 & up. Starting: (panel): 27,001 & up. Engine numbers located on right side, front upper corner of cylinder block.

Model	Body Type	Price	Weight	Prod. Total
Willys Model 77 — (4-cyl.)				
77	Cab Pickup (½-ton)	475	2040	—
77	Panel Dely. (½-ton)	495	2195	—

ENGINE (Model 77): Inline. L-head. Four-cylinder. Cast iron block. Bore & stroke: 3⅛ in. x 4⅜ in. Displacement: 134.2 cu. in. Compression ratio: 5.23:1. Brake horsepower: 48 at 3200 R.P.M. Net horsepower: 15.63 (N.A.C.C.) Three main bearings. Solid valve lifters. Carburetor: Tillotson model one-barrel.

CHASSIS (Willys 77): Wheelbase: 100 in. Tires: 17 x 5.00 in.

TECHNICAL: Selective sliding gear transmission. Speeds: 3F/1R. Floor-mounted gearshift lever. Overall ratio: 4.3:1. Four-wheel mechanical brakes. Wire spoke wheels.

HISTORICAL: Introduced: Jan. 1, 1935. Calendar year registrations: 2,280 (all trucks).

In January, 1935, John North Willys was again elected as company president, but five months later he suffered a heart attack. He died in August. By December, reorganization of his firm was completed.

Pricing

	5	4	3	2	1
1935					
Willys Model 77					
Pickup	830	1650	2750	3850	5500
Panel	890	1770	2950	4150	5900

1936 WILLYS-OVERLAND

1936 Willys Panel Delivery (DFW/MVMA)

WILLYS — SERIES 77 — FOUR-CYLINDER: — Changes to the 1936 Willys "77" trucks were minor. There was a curvier bumper and artillery style steel spoke wheels made their reappearance. Handles were seen on the sides of the hood underneath the rearmost pair of "bubble" vents. Weights and prices of both models fell a little.

The depression was probably responsible for some reduction in standard equipment that allowed lower prices and resulted in less bulk.

I.D. DATA: Serial number located on left frame ahead of front spring rear hanger; also on tag attached to left front door sill; also on plate on front right-hand side of front frame cross member at center. Starting: (pickup): 37,426 & up. Starting: (delivery): 35,939 & up. Engine numbers located on right side, front upper corner of cylinder block.

Model	Body Type	Price	Weight	Prod. Total
Willys Model 77 — (4-cyl.)				
77	Cab Pickup (½-ton)	395	2000	—
77	Panel Dely. (½-ton)	415	2130	—

ENGINE (Model 77): Inline. L-head. Four-cylinder. Cast iron block. Bore & stroke: 3⅛ in. x 4⅜ in. Displacement: 134.2 cu. in. Compression ratio: 5.7:1. Brake horsepower: 48 at 3200 R.P.M. Net horsepower: 15.63 (N.A.C.C.) Three main bearings. Solid valve lifters. Carburetor: Tillotson model one-barrel.

CHASSIS (Willys 77): Wheelbase: 100 in. Tires: 17 x 5.00 in.

TECHNICAL: Selective sliding gear transmission. Speeds: 3F/1R. Floor-mounted gearshift lever. Overall ratio: 4.3:1. Four-wheel mechanical brakes. Steel artillery spoke wheels.

HISTORICAL: Introduced: Sept. 10, 1935. Calendar year registrations: 2,441 (all trucks). Calendar year production: Willys produced 23,831 vehicles of all types (cars and trucks) in calendar 1936.
Willys-Overland's receivership status ended in February, 1936.

Pricing

	5	4	3	2	1
1936					
Willys Model 77					
Pickup	830	1650	2750	3850	5500
Panel	890	1770	2950	4150	5900

1937 WILLYS-OVERLAND

1937 Willys Half-ton Pickup (DFW/WRHS)

WILLYS — SERIES 77 — FOUR-CYLINDER: — The Willys 77 was completely restyled in 1937. Features included an all-steel body and top; rounded "ship's prow" front having a grille that was integral with the hood and a hood that was hinged at the cowl to open in "alligator" fashion. There were actually two grilles, one on each side of the prow. They consisted of vertical louvers following the rounded hood contour with three louvers near (but below) the top extending back to the cowl. The rounded fenders extended outwards at the top contour to form "beehive" shaped headlight housings which were faired into the fenders and decorated with horizontal ribs on either side. The bumper was a one-piece, single-bar design with guards at each frame horn. These were unusual, but cute-looking trucks. Pickup and panel bodies were again made available.

I.D. DATA: Serial number located on left frame ahead of front spring rear hanger; also on tag attached to left front door sill; also on plate on front right-hand side of front frame cross member at center. Starting: 61,000. Ending: 64,467. Engine numbers located on right side, front upper corner of cylinder block.

Model	Body Type	Price	Weight	Prod. Total
Willys Model 77 — (4-cyl.)				
77	Cab Pickup (½-ton)	395	2000	—
77	Panel Dely. (½-ton)	415	2130	—

ENGINE (Model 77): Inline. L-head. Four-cylinder. Cast iron block. Bore & stroke: 3⅛ in. x 4⅜ in. Displacement: 134.2 cu. in. Compression ratio: 5.7:1. Brake horsepower: 48 at 3200 R.P.M. Net horsepower: 15.63 (N.A.C.C.) Three main bearings. Solid valve lifters. Carburetor: Tillotson model one-barrel.

CHASSIS (Willys 77): Wheelbase: 100 in. Tires: 16 x 5.50 in.

TECHNICAL: Manual transmission. Speeds: 3F/1R. Floor-mounted gearshift lever. Overall ratio: 4.3:1. Four-wheel mechanical brakes. Steel disc wheels.

HISTORICAL: Introduced: Nov. 1936. Calendar year registrations: 1,122 (all trucks). Calendar year production: Willys produced 63,465 vehicles of all types (cars & trucks) in calendar 1937.
Redesigned "77" debuts as a 1937 model.

Pricing

	5	4	3	2	1
1937					
Willys Model 77					
Pickup	770	1550	2550	3600	5100
Panel	840	1680	2800	3900	5600

1938 WILLYS-OVERLAND

1938 Willys Model 77 Pickup

WILLYS — MODEL 38 — FOUR-CYLINDER: — Characteristics of the new 1938 Willys "38" trucks included a newly designed radiator, rain troughs over the doors and a water temperature indicator installed separately from other instruments. The rounded grille and general styling of body and fenders was practically the same as the 1937 model. A new stake truck was cataloged, plus three chassis models. These were: chassis-only; chassis and cowl and chassis cowl and cab. The pickup and panel continued.

I.D. DATA: Serial number located on left frame ahead of front spring rear hanger; also on tag attached to left front door sill; also on plate on front right-hand side of front frame cross member at center. Starting: 65,001. Ending: 89,000. Engine numbers located on right side, front upper corner of cylinder block.

Model	Body Type	Price	Weight	Prod. Total
Willys Model 38 — (4-cyl.)				
38	½-Ton Chassis	330	1285	—
38	½-Ton Chassis & Cowl	400	1677	—
38	½-Ton Chassis & Cab	490	1908	—
38	½-Ton Pickup	530	2226	—
38	½-Ton Stake	545	2220	—
38	½-Ton Panel Dely.	824	2568	—

1938 Willys-Overland Model 77 Pickup (OCW)

ENGINE (Model 38): Inline. L-head. Four-cylinder. Cast iron block. Bore & stroke: 3⅛ in. x 4⅜ in. Displacement: 134.2 cu. in. Brake horsepower: 48 at 3200 R.P.M. Net horsepower: 15.63 (N.A.C.C.) Three main bearings. Solid valve lifters. Carburetor: Tillotson model one-barrel.

CHASSIS (Willys Model 38): Wheelbase: 100 in. Tires: 16 x 5.50 in.

TECHNICAL: Manual transmission. Speeds: 3F/1R. Floor-mounted gearshift lever. Overall ratio: 4.3:1. Four-wheel mechanical brakes. Steel disc wheels.

OPTIONS: Rear bumper. Grille guard. Dual taillamps. Dual windshield wipers. Dual sun visors. Rearview mirror(s). Ash tray (front). Rear fender protection guards. Locking gas cap. Tailpipe extension. Wheel trim rings. Dual horns. License plate frames. Radio antenna. Radio. Radiator cap with blow-off valve. Mirror clock. Glove compartment with door. Grille cover. Seat covers. Aluminum cylinder head. Heater. Heater/defroster. Custom radio with aerial. Windshield wiper vacuum booster pump.

HISTORICAL: Introduced: Sept. 20, 1937. Calendar year registrations: 1,889 (all trucks). Calendar year production: Willys produced 26,286 vehicles of all types (cars and trucks) in calendar 1938.
"Barney" Roos, a former president of the Society of Automotive engineers, came to Willys-Overland this year after a stint with the Rootes automotive companies in England. He assumed the title of Chief Engineer.

Pricing

1938 Willys Model 38	5	4	3	2	1
Pickup	770	1550	2550	3600	5100
Stake	840	1680	2800	3900	5600
Panel	750	1500	2500	3500	5000

1939 WILLYS-OVERLAND

1939 Willys Walk-in Panel Delivery Van (DFW/MVMA)

WILLYS-OVERLAND — SERIES 38/SERIES 48 — FOUR-CYLINDER: — The Overland name was revived for a time in 1939. Later in the year, it was changed to Willys-Overland again. The front end was revamped into a more conventional "ship's prow" design with horizontal louvers from only the middle down. Other louvers were punched into the front fender apron on either side of center. A chrome molding — at beltline height — extended across the sides of the hood and dipped down at the front. The hood ornament looked like a backwards fin. The headlamp housings were thinner and less rounded; the lenses themselves were shield-shaped and rather unusual. The front bumper was a single-bar type without guards. However, guards, dual windshield wipers, dual sun visors and dual taillights were made part of a Deluxe equipment package. Deluxe models were known as "48s." The NADA does not list a "39" truck series although the 61 horsepower engine available in the "39" passenger cars was available in trucks. It was probably an option. A "440" cab-over-engine delivery van is also mentioned in some sources as a 1939 product. It was similar to the model found in our 1941 section (COE Panel delivery).

I.D. DATA: Serial number located on left frame ahead of front spring rear hanger; also on tag attached to left front door sill; also on plate on front right-hand side of front frame cross member at center. Starting: (model 38) 89,001; (model 48) 91,751. Ending: (model 38) 91,750; (model 48) 94,375. Engine numbers located on right side, front upper corner of cylinder block.

1939 Willys Model 38 ½-Ton Pickup (DFW/MVMA)

Model	Body Type	Price	Weight	Prod. Total
Willys Model 38 — (4-cyl.)				
38	½-Ton Chassis	330	1285	—
38	½-Ton Chassis & Cowl	400	1677	—
38	½-Ton Chassis & Cab	490	1908	—
38	½-Ton Pickup	530	2226	—
38	½-Ton Stake	545	2220	—
38	½-Ton Panel Dely.	824	2568	—
Willys Model 48 — (4-cyl.)				
48	½-Ton Pickup	530	2226	—
48	½-Ton Stake	545	2220	—
48	½-Ton Panel	824	2568	—

ENGINE (Both Series): Inline. L-head. Four-cylinder. Cast iron block. Bore & stroke: 3⅛ in. x 4⅜ in. Displacement: 134.2 cu. in. Brake horsepower: 48 at 3200 R.P.M. Net horsepower: 15.6 (N.A.C.C.) Three main bearings. Solid valve lifters. Carburetor: Tillotson model one-barrel.

ENGINE (Optional): Inline. L-head. Four-cylinder. Cast iron block. Bore & stroke: 3⅛ in. x 4⅜ in. Displacement: 134.2 cu. in. Brake horsepower: 61 at 3600 R.P.M. Net horsepower: 15.6 (N.A.C.C.) Three main bearings. Solid valve lifters. Carburetor: Carter model WO-4505.

CHASSIS (Willys Model 38): Wheelbase: 100 in. Tires: 16 x 5.50 in.

CHASSIS (Willys Model 48): Wheelbase: 100 in. Tires: 16 x 5.00 in.

TECHNICAL: Manual transmission. Speeds: 3F/1R. Floor mounted gearshift lever. Overall ratio: (std.) 4.3:1; (opt.) 4.55:1. Four-wheel brakes. Steel disc wheels.

OPTIONS: Rear bumper. Grille guard. Dual taillamps. Dual windshield wipers. Dual sun visors. Rearview mirror(s). Ash tray (front). Rear fender protection guards. Locking gas cap. Tailpipe extension. Wheel trim rings. Dual horns. License plate frames. Radio antenna. Radio. Radiator cap with blow-off valve. Mirror clock. Glove compartment with door. Grille cover. Seat covers. Aluminum cylinder head. Heater. Heater/defroster. Custom radio with aerial. Windshield wiper vacuum booster pump.

HISTORICAL: Introduced: Oct. 1938. Calendar year registrations: 1,634 (all trucks). Calendar year production: Willys produced 18,150 vehicles of all types (cars and trucks) in calendar 1939. Innovations: The Model 77 was given hydraulic brakes. Historical note: The Overland name was temporarily revived, then dropped.

Pricing

1939	5	4	3	2	1
Willys Model 38					
Pickup	750	1500	2500	3500	5000
Stake	830	1650	2750	3850	5500
Panel	740	1470	2450	3350	4900
Willys Model 48					
Pickup	770	1550	2550	3600	5100
Stake	750	1500	2500	3500	5000
Panel	840	1680	2800	3900	5600

1940 WILLYS-OVERLAND

1940 Willys "Quad" Jeep Prototype (OCW)

WILLYS — SERIES 440 — FOUR-CYLINDER: — The 1940 Willys "440" trucks still had a 100 inch wheelbase, although cars in this series were up to a stance of 102 inches. Styling changes included a more vertical nose; the name Willys in capital letters on the upper rear corner of the hood and new teardrop-shaped headlights. Each side of the "prow" was trimmed with four chrome speed lines, largest on top, extending to the cowl and descending in size downward. There were two lower grilles, with horizontal bars and rounded outer edges, on the front below the nose. The hood ornament was round with speed lines emanating back from it. The bumper had two oblong openings punched in it, near the center. Deluxe models had dual windshield wipers, taillights, sun visors and bumper guards. Two four-cylinder engines — 48 horsepower and 58 horsepower — were offered as SC-440 and SCOF-440 economy options. Willys trucks finally got hydraulic brakes.

I.D. DATA: Serial number located on left frame ahead of front spring rear hanger; also on tag attached to left front door sill; also on plate on front right-hand side of front frame cross member at center. Starting: 17,001. Ending: 49,341. Engine numbers located on right side, front upper corner of cylinder block.

Model	Body Type	Price	Weight	Prod. Total
Willys Model 440 — (4-cyl.)				
440	½-Ton Pickup	535	2207	—
440P	½-Ton Panel Dely.	799	2624	—

ENGINE (Model 440): Inline. L-head. Four-cylinder. Cast iron block. Bore & stroke: 3⅛ in. x 4⅜ in. Displacement: 134.2 cu. in. Brake horsepower: 61 at 3600 R.P.M. Net horsepower: 15.6 (N.A.C.C.) Three main bearings. Solid valve lifters. Carburetor: Carter model WO-450S.

CHASSIS (Willys Model 440): Wheelbase: 102 in. Length: 181 in. Front tread: 55 in. Rear tread: 56 in. Tires: 5.50 x 16 in.

TECHNICAL: Manual transmission. Speeds: 3F/1R. Floor-mounted gearshift lever. Single dry disc clutch. Bango rear axle. Overall ratio: (std.) 4.3:1. (opt.) 4.55:1; 4.7:1; 5.11:1. Four-wheel hydraulic brakes. Steel disc wheels.

OPTIONS: Rear bumper. Grille guard. Dual taillamps. Dual windshield wipers. Dual sun visors. Rearview mirror(s). Ash tray (front). Rear fender protection guards. Locking gas cap. Tailpipe extension. Wheel trim rings. Dual horns. License plate frames. Radio antenna. Radio. Radiator cap with blow-off valve. Mirror clock. Glove compartment with door. Grille cover. Seat covers. Aluminum cylinder head. Heater. Heater/defroster. Custom radio with aerial. Windshield wiper vacuum booster pump.

HISTORICAL: Introduced: Oct. 1939. Calendar year registrations: 2,291 (all trucks). Calendar year production: Willys produced 32,930 vehicles of all types (cars, trucks and Jeeps) in calendar 1940.
The American predecessor of the Jeep was assembled in 1940.

Pricing

1940	5	4	3	2	1
Willys Model 440					
Pickup	800	1650	2750	3850	5500
Panel Dely.	890	1770	2950	4150	5900

668

1941 WILLYS-OVERLAND

1941 Willys MA Jeep Universal (OCW)

WILLYS — SERIES 441 — FOUR-CYLINDER: — A new Willys 441 "Americar" series of trucks was introduced Feb. 1, 1941. The Willys-American trade name went along with numerous technical and styling changes. There was a longer 104 inch wheelbase, more powerful engine and new "electric shaver" like one-piece lower grille. There were no longer speed lines on the hoodsides; just a beltline extension molding. The cab-over-engine Step-Van was continued, too. It had "art deco" rounded front fenders, a split windshield, "bug-eye" headlamps and a grille with a "window sash" appearance and the Willys name on top. These vans are supposed to be quite scarce.

I.D. DATA: Serial number located on left frame ahead of front spring rear hanger; also on tag attached to left front door sill; also on plate on front right-hand side of front frame cross member at center. Starting: 50,001. Ending: 80,100. Engine numbers located on right side, front upper corner of cylinder block.

Model	Body Type	Price	Weight	Prod. Total
Willys Model 441 — (4-cyl.)				
441	½-Ton Chassis	360	1285	—
441	½-Ton Chassis & Cowl	442	1677	—
441	½-Ton Chassis & Cab	542	1908	—
441	½-Ton Pickup	587	2207	—
441	½-Ton C.O.E. Panel Dely.	869	2624	—

ENGINE (Series 441): Inline. L-head. Four-cylinder. Cast iron block. Bore & stroke: 3⅛ in. x 4⅜ in. Displacement: 134.2 cu. in. Compression ratio: 6.48:1. Brake horsepower: 63 at 3800 R.P.M. Net horsepower: 15.6 (N.A.C.C.) Three main bearings. Solid valve lifters. Carburetor: Carter model WO-507S.

CHASSIS (Willys Model 441): Wheelbase: 104 in. Length: 181 in. Front tread: 55 in. Rear tread: 56 in. Tires: 5.50 x 16 in.

TECHNICAL: Manual (synchromesh) transmission. Speeds: 3F/1R. Floor-mounted gearshift lever. Single dry disc clutch. Hypoid rear axle. Overall ratio: 4.3:1 and others. Four-wheel hydraulic brakes. Steel disc wheels.

OPTIONS: Rear bumper. Grille guard. Dual taillamps. Dual windshield wipers. Dual sun visors. Rearview mirror(s). Ash tray (front). Rear fender protection guards. Locking gas cap. Tailpipe extension. Wheel trim rings. Dual horns. License plate frames. Radio antenna. Radio. Radiator cap with blow-off valve. Mirror clock. Glove compartment with door. Grille cover. Seat covers. Aluminum cylinder head. Heater. Heater/defroster. Custom radio with aerial. Windshield wiper vacuum booster pump.

HISTORICAL: Introduced: Aug. 28, 1940. Calendar year registrations: 2,031 (all trucks). Calendar year production: Willys produced 28,014 vehicles of all types in calendar 1941. Hypoid rear axle adopted.
Willys-Overland finished its 1941 model run on July 30, 1941. Production of 1942 models commenced on Aug. 2, 1941. Willys-Overland spent $2,170,000 expanding its Toledo factory in 1941. In its 1941 financial statement assets of $7,358,162 was listed against liabilities of $5,551,075. Working capital was $1,807,087. Earnings per common share were .86 and book value of a share of common stock was $3.54. Company officers included Chairman of the Board W.M. Canaday, President J.W. Frazer, Sales Manager G.H. Bell and Chief Engineer D.G. Roos.

1941 Willys Model 441	5	4	3	2	1
Pickup	850	1700	2850	4000	5700
Step-Van	850	1700	2850	4000	5700

1942 WILLYS-OVERLAND

1942 Willys MB Jeep Universal (Stan Brown)

WILLYS — SERIES 442 — FOUR-CYLINDER: — Among characteristics of its 1942 trucks, Willys noted that the four-cylinder "Go-Devil" motor was the same one used in U.S. Army Jeeps. Overdrive was standard on some models this year, but probably just an option for trucks. Styling was identical to 1941, unless some "blackout" models were built late-in-the-year. These would have had painted trim, of course.

I.D. DATA: Serial number located on left frame ahead of front spring rear hanger; also on tag attached to left front door sill; also on plate on front right-hand side of front frame cross member at center. Starting: 80,101. Ending: 92,020. Engine numbers located on right side, front upper corner of cylinder block.

Model	Body Type	Price	Weight	Prod. Total
Willys Model 442 — (4-cyl.)				
442	½-Ton Chassis	410	1272	—
442	½-Ton Chassis & Cowl	525	1670	—
442	½-Ton Chassis & Cab	642	1900	—
442	½-Ton Pickup	732	2238	—
442	½-Ton Panel Dely.	950	2708	—

ENGINE (Series 442): Inline. L-head. Four-cylinder. Cast iron block. Bore & stroke: 3⅛ in. x 4⅜ in. Displacement: 134.2 cu. in. Compression ratio: 6.48:1. Brake horsepower: 63 at 3800 R.P.M. Net horsepower: 15.6 (N.A.C.C.) Three main bearings. Solid valve lifters. Carburetor: Carter model WO-507S.

CHASSIS (Willys Model 442): Wheelbase: 104 in. Length: 181 in. Front tread: 55 in. Rear tread: 58 in. Tires: 5.50 x 16 in.

TECHNICAL: Manual (synchromesh) transmission. Speeds: 3F/1R. Floor-mounted gearshift lever. Single dry disc clutch. Hypoid rear axle. Overall ratio: (std.) 4.3:1. Four-wheel hydraulic brakes. Steel disc wheels. Overdrive.

OPTIONS: Rear bumper. Grille guard. Dual taillamps. Dual windshield wipers. Dual sun visors. Rearview mirror(s). Ash tray (front). Rear fender protection guards. Locking gas cap. Tailpipe extension. Wheel trim rings. Dual horns. License plate frames. Radio antenna. Radio. Radiator cap w/blow-off valve. Mirror clock. Glove compartment with door. Grille cover. Seat covers. Aluminum cylinder head. Heater. Heater/defroster. Custom radio w/aerial. Windshield wiper vacuum booster pump.

HISTORICAL: Introduced: Sept. 1941.
Willys-Overland ended production of 1942 civilian models on Jan. 24, 1942. A truck manufacturing stop order was issued by the War Production Board on March 4. During WWII, together with Ford, the company manufactured the Jeep vehicle originated by American Bantam.

1942 Willys Model 442	5	4	3	2	1
Pickup	850	1700	2850	4000	5700
Panel Dely.	950	1900	3150	4400	6300

1945 WILLYS-OVERLAND

WILLYS — SERIES CJ-2A — FOUR-CYLINDER: — The G.I.'s workhorse, the ¼-ton Jeep utility vehicle (or "reconaissance truck" in U.S. Army lingo), donned civilian garb for the first time in 1945. The civilian Jeep had the same engine as its military counterpart, but the gear ratios in the transmission and axle were changed. A significant change in the civilian Jeep was an available power-take-off attachment. Geared to the Jeep's transmission, it could drive farm equipment, shred corn, fill a silo, operate a winch, etc. There were also better shock absorbers and springs. Other refinements were made in combustion chamber and radiator shrouding designs. Standard equipment included a remote gas filler (military models filled by lifting the driver's seat), seven-inch headlights, an automatic windshield wiper and rear tailgate.

I.D. DATA: Serial number located on plate at left side of driver's seat on floor riser in 1946-1948 model CJ-2A; on right side of dash under hood in 1949-1954 models CJ-2A and CJ-3A/CJ-3B; on left side of dash under hood in 1948-1951 models 2-WD and 4-WD; on left floor riser in back of seat in 1947-1949 models 4-63. Starting: 10001. Ending 11824.
Military Jeeps were produced 1941-1944. No numbers were released for the civilian market in these years.
Engine numbers located on right side of cylinder block; stamped on water pump boss on front of cylinder block.

NOTE: Beginning around 1951 and continuing through at least 1953, each model had a specific serial number prefix such as "451-GC1." The first number indicated the number of cylinders. The second and third numbers indicated model year. The first letter indicated the basic chassis and body type. The second letter indicated model. The fourth number indicated series in any one model year. On most Jeep models the engine and serial numbers were the same.

Model	Body Type	Price	Weight	Prod. Total
Willys Jeep (4-cyl.)				
CJ-2A	2/5 Jeep Utility (4x4)	1090	2037	—

ENGINE (All Series): Inline. L-head. Four-cylinder. Cast iron block. Bore & stroke: 3⅛ in. x 4⅜ in. Displacement: 134.2 cu. in. Compression ratio: 6.5:1. Brake horsepower: 60 at 4000 R.P.M. Net horsepower: 15.63 (N.A.C.C.) Max. Torque: 105 lbs. ft. at 2000 R.P.M. Three main bearings. Solid valve lifters. Carburetor: Carter model WA-1 (613S).

CHASSIS (Jeep CJ-2A): Wheelbase: 80-1/6 in. Length: 129⅞ in. Height: 67¾ in. Front and rear tread: 48-7/16 in. Tires: 6.00 x 16 four-ply.

TECHNICAL: Synchromesh transmission. Speeds: 3F/1R. Transfer case: two-speeds. Floor-mounted gearshift lever. Single, dry plate w/torsional dampening clutch. Hypoid axle, full-floating front, semi-floating rear. Bendix hydraulic brakes. Five disc type 5-stud wheels, size 4.50 x 16 in.

OPTIONS: Power take-off ($96.25). Pulley drive ($57.40). Motor governor ($28.65). Special wheels and 7:00 tires ($4). Front canvas top ($57.80). Hydraulic lift ($225).

HISTORICAL: Introduced: July 1945. Calendar year production: 1,823.
Production of civilian Jeeps started in 1945. Unsold 1941-1942 trucks were made available to "approved" buyers (such as doctors, munitions workers, etc.) during World War II. By Nov. 1945, the Steyr autoplant, in Austria, was building winterized Jeeps — about 25 per day — in Europe. Willys-Overland was always a leader in export marketing and the Jeep was truly a "World Class" type of vehicle.

1945 Jeep Series (4x4)	5	4	3	2	1
CJ-2 Jeep	850	1700	2850	4000	5700

NOTE: All Jeep prices in this catalog are for civilian models unless noted otherwise. Military Jeeps may sell for higher prices.

1946 WILLYS-OVERLAND

1946 Willys-Overland, Jeep Station Wagon 4x4 (DFW)

WILLYS — SERIES CJ-2A — FOUR-CYLINDER: — The 1946 Jeep was part of the same series that first hit the market in 1945. There were no changes. By the end of 1946, over 71,000 examples were built for the civilian market.

I.D. DATA: Serial number located on plate at left side of driver's seat on floor riser in 1946-1948 model CJ-2A; on right side of dash under hood in 1949-1954 models CJ-2A and CJ-3A/CJ-3B; on left side of dash under hood in 1948-1951 models 2-WD and 4-WD; on left floor riser in back of seat in 1947-1949 models 4-63. Starting: 11,825. Ending 83,379.
Engine numbers located on right side of cylinder block; stamped on water pump boss on front of cylinder block.

NOTE: Beginning around 1951 and continuing through at least 1953, each model had a specific serial number prefix such as "451-GC1." The first number indicated the number of cylinders. The second and third numbers indicated model year. The first letter indicated the basic chassis and body type. The second letter indicated model. The fourth number indicated series in any one model year. On most Jeep models the engine and serial numbers were the same.

Model	Body Type	Price	Weight	Prod. Total
Willys Jeep (4-cyl.)				
CJ-2A	2/5-Ton Jeep Utility (4x4)	1146	2074	—

ENGINE (All Series): Inline. L-head. Four-cylinder. Cast iron block. Bore & stroke: 3⅛ in. x 4⅜ in. Displacement: 134.2 cu. in. Compression ratio: 6.5:1. Brake horsepower: 60 at 4000 R.P.M. Net horsepower: 15.63 (N.A.C.C.) Max. Torque: 105 lbs. ft. at 2000 R.P.M. Three main bearings. Solid valve lifters. Carburetor: Carter model WA-1 (613S).

CHASSIS (Jeep CJ-2A): Wheelbase: 80 in. Length: 129⅞ in. Height: 67¾ in. Front tread: 55¼ in. Rear tread: 57 in. Tires: 6.00 x 15 four-ply.

1946 Willys-Overland, Jeep Universal (OCW)

TECHNICAL: Synchromesh transmission. Speeds: 3F/1R. Two-speed transfer case. Floor-mounted gearshift lever. Single dry disc clutch. Hypoid rear axle. Bendix hydraulic brakes. Disc wheels.

OPTIONS: *Power take-off ($96.25). *Pulley drive ($57.40). *Motor governor ($28.65). Special wheels and 7:00 tires ($40). Front canvas top ($57.80). Hydraulic lift ($225). Metal top (Varies).

NOTE: * Applicable also to 473 4-WD Trucks.

HISTORICAL: Introduced: Jan. 1946. Calendar year production: (Sta. Wag.) 6,533. (Jeeps) 71,455; (Trucks) one.
The Willys station wagons and panel delivery trucks bowed this year. Most historians consider the station wagon a car instead of a truck.

Pricing

1946	5	4	3	2	1
Jeep Series (4x4)					
CJ-2 Jeep	850	1700	2850	4000	5700

1947 WILLYS-OVERLAND

1947 Willys-Overland, Jeep Station Wagon 4x2 (OCW)

WILLYS — JEEP SERIES — FOUR-CYLINDER: — New this year was a line of Jeep trucks with a new 63 horsepower engine. There was a pickup and a panel delivery. They had an all-steel cab, split window and full doors with indentation panels. There was a molding down the hood center, chrome bumpers were available — front and rear, and there were even optional chrome hub caps with Willy's "W" symbol in the center. Three decorative, painted moldings trimmed the lower edges of the door, mid-quarter panel and rear quarter panel. Frontal styling followed the theme of the "Universal" Jeep, but the grille was taller and had ten vertical slots compared to seven for the CJ-2A Universal model. The CJ-2A was, once again, basically identical to the previous model.

I.D. DATA: Serial number located on plate at left side of driver's seat on floor riser in 1946-1948 model CJ-2A; on right side of dash under hood in 1949-1954 models CJ-2A and CJ-3A/CJ-3B; on left side of dash under hood in 1948-1951 models 2-WD and 4-WD; on left floor riser in back of seat in 1947-1949 models 4-63. Serial numbers: (Jeep) 83381 to 148459; (Panel) 16535 to H4044; (Trucks) 10001 to 12346.
Engine numbers located on right side of cylinder block; stamped on water pump boss on front of cylinder block.

NOTE: Beginning around 1951 and continuing through at least 1953, each model had a specific serial number prefix such as "451-GC1." The first number indicated the number of cylinders. The second and third numbers indicated model year. The first letter indicated the basic chassis and body type. The second letter indicated model. The fourth number indicated series in any one model year. On most Jeep models the engine and serial numbers were the same.

Model	Body Type	Price	Weight	Prod. Total
Willys Jeep — (4x4) — (4-cyl.)				
CJ-2A	2/5-Ton Jeep Utility (4x4)	1241	2074	—
Willys Truck — (4x2) — (4-cyl.)				
463	½-Ton Panel	1358	2587	—
Willys Truck — (4x4) — (4-cyl.)				
4x4	1-Ton Chassis	1175	1974	—
4x4	1-Ton Chassis & Cab	1529	2809	—
4x4	1-Ton Pickup	1620	3129	—
4x4	1-Ton Platform Stake	1685	3431	—

1947 Willys-Overland, Jeep Universal (OCW)

ENGINE (CJ-2A): Inline. L-head. Four-cylinder. Cast iron block. Bore & stroke: 3⅛ in. x 4⅜ in. Displacement: 134.2 cu. in. Compression ratio: 6.5:1. Brake horsepower: 60 at 4000 R.P.M. Net horsepower: 15.63 (N.A.C.C.) Max. Torque: 105 lbs. ft. at 2000 R.P.M. Three main bearings. Solid valve lifters. Carburetor: Carter model WA-1 (613S).

ENGINE (Model 463): Inline. L-head. Four-cylinder. Cast iron block. Bore & stroke: 3⅛ in. x 4⅜ in. Displacement: 134.2 cu. in. Compression ratio: 6.48:1. Brake horsepower: 63 at 4000 R.P.M. Net horsepower: 15.63 (N.A.C.C.) Max. Torque: 105 lbs. ft. at 2000 R.P.M. Three main bearings. Solid valve lifters. Carburetor: Carter WA-1 model 613S.

CHASSIS (Jeep CJ-2A): Wheelbase: 80 in. Tires: 6.00 x 15 in.

CHASSIS (Model 463): Wheelbase: 104 in. Front tread: 55¼ in. Rear tread: 57 in. Tires: 6.50 x 15 in.

TECHNICAL: Synchromesh transmission. Speeds: 3F/1R. Floor-mounted gearshift lever. Single plate clutch. Hypoid rear axle. Bendix hydraulic brakes. Disc wheels.

OPTIONS: *Power take-off ($96.25). *Pulley drive ($57.40). *Motor governor ($28.65). Special wheels and 7:00 tires ($40). Front canvas top ($57.80). Hydraulic lift ($225). Metal top (Varies).

NOTE: * Applicable also to 473 four-wheel-drive Trucks.

HISTORICAL: Introduced: Jan. 1947. Calendar year production: (Sta. Wag.) 33,214. (Jeeps) 77,958; (Trucks) 8,747.
Two- and four-wheel-drive trucks were introduced by Willys in 1947. Sales were brisk and the company reopened its west coast factory.

Pricing

1947	5	4	3	2	1
Willys Jeep (4x4)					
CJ-2 Jeep	850	1700	2850	4000	5700
Willys Truck (4x2)					
Panel	570	1140	1900	2650	3800
Willys Truck (4x4)					
1-Ton Pickup	530	1050	1750	2450	3500
1-Ton Platform	450	900	1500	2100	3000

1948 WILLYS-OVERLAND

WILLYS — JEEP SERIES — FOUR-CYLINDER: — The CJ-2A Universal Jeep was again carried over as a ¼-ton utility truck available only with 4x4 running gear. There were no big changes. The 4x2 half-ton panel was also available once more. The one-ton 4x4 Jeep truck line included a pickup and platform stake truck.

I.D. DATA: Serial number located on plate at left side of driver's seat on floor riser in 1946-1948 model CJ-2A; on right side of dash under hood in 1949-1954 models CJ-2A and CJ-3A/CJ-3B; on left side of dash under hood in 1948-1951 models 4x2 and 4x4; on left floor riser in back of seat in 1947-1949 models 4-63. Serial numbers: (CJ-2A) 148,459 to 219,588; ("463") 44,045-79,715; (4x2) 12,643-21,010 and (4x4) 12,347-30,575.
Engine numbers located on right side of cylinder block; stamped on water pump boss on front of cylinder block.

Model	Body Type	Price	Weight	Prod. Total
Willys Jeep — (4x4) — (4-cyl.)				
CJ-2A	2/5-Ton Jeep Utility (4x4)	1262	2037	—
Willys Truck — (4x2) — (4-cyl.)				
463	½-Ton Panel	1477	2587	—
Willys Truck — (4x2) — (4-cyl.)				
4x2	Chassis & Cab	1334	2677	—
4x2	Pickup	1427	2995	—
4x2	Platform	1493	3299	—
Willys Truck — (4x4) — (4-cyl.)				
4x4	Chassis & Cab	1652	2809	—
4x4	Pickup	1743	3129	—
4x4	Platform	1807	3431	—

1948 Willys-Overland, Jeep Universal (OCW)

ENGINE (CJ-2A): Inline. L-head. Four-cylinder. Cast iron block. Bore & stroke: 3⅛ in. x 4⅜ in. Displacement: 134.2 cu. in. Compression ratio: 6.5:1. Brake horsepower: 60 at 4000 R.P.M. Net horsepower: 15.63 (N.A.C.C.) Max. Torque: 105 lbs. ft. at 2000 R.P.M. Three main bearings. Solid valve lifters. Carburetor: Carter model WA-1 (613S).

ENGINE (Model 463): Inline. L-head. Four-cylinder. Cast iron block. Bore & stroke: 3⅛ in. x 4⅜ in. Displacement: 134.2 cu. in. Compression ratio: 6.48:1. Brake horsepower: 63 at 4000 R.P.M. Net horsepower: 15.63 (N.A.C.C.) Max. Torque: 105 lbs. ft. at 2000 R.P.M. Three main bearings. Solid valve lifters. Carburetor: Carter WA-1 model 613S.

CHASSIS (Jeep CJ-2A): Wheelbase: 80 in. Front tread: 55¼ in. Rear tread: 57 in. Tires: 6.00 x 15 in.

CHASSIS (Model 463): Wheelbase: 104 in. Front tread: 55¼ in. Rear tread: 57 in. Tires: 6.00 x 15 in.

CHASSIS (Other Models): Wheelbase: 118 in. Front tread: 55¼ in. Rear tread: 57 in. Tires: (4x2) 6.50 x 16 in.; (4x4) 7.00 x 16 in.

TECHNICAL: Synchromesh transmission. Speeds: 3F/1R (4x4 Transfer case: two-speed). Floor-mounted gearshift lever. Single plate clutch. Hypoid rear axle. Hydraulic brakes. Disc wheels.

OPTIONS: *Power take-off ($96.25). *Pulley drive ($57.40). *Motor governor ($28.65). Special wheels and 7:00 tires ($40). Front canvas top ($57.80). Hydraulic lift ($225). Metal top (Varies).

NOTE: * Applicable also to "473" four-wheel-drive trucks.

HISTORICAL: Introduced: Nov. 1947. Calendar year production: (Station Wagon) 22,309; (Jeeps) 63,170; (Trucks) 41,462.
The Willys Jeepster was introduced (see Krause Publication's *Standard Catalog of American Cars 1946-1975* for information about this model.)

Pricing

1948	5	4	3	2	1
Jeep Series (4x4)					
CJ-2 Jeep	850	1700	2850	4000	5700
Willys Truck (4x2)					
Panel	570	1140	1950	2650	3800
Pickup	500	1000	1650	2300	3300
Platform	440	870	1450	2050	2900
Willys Truck (4x4)					
Pickup	530	1050	1750	2450	3500
Platform	450	900	1500	2100	3000

1949 WILLYS-OVERLAND

1949 Willys-Overland, Jeep Panel Delivery (OCW)

WILLYS — JEEP SERIES — FOUR-CYLINDER: — There were no major changes in the 1949 Jeep line. Some trucks formerly available only as 4x4s could now be had as 4x2s.

I.D. DATA: Serial number located on plate at left side of driver's seat on floor riser in 1946-1948 model CJ-2A; on right side of dash under hood in 1949-1954 models CJ-2A and CJ-3A/CJ-3B; on left side of dash under hood in 1948-1951 models 4x2 and 4x4; on left floor riser in back of seat in 1947-1949 models 4-63. Serial numbers: (CJ-2A) 219,589-224,764; (CJ-3A) 10,001 to 35,688; ("463") 79,716-106,503; (4x2) 21,011-26,562 and (4x4) 30,576-43,586.
   Engine numbers located on right side of cylinder block; stamped on water pump boss on front of cylinder block.

NOTE: Beginning around 1951 and continuing through at least 1953, each model had a specific serial number prefix such as "451-GC1." The first number indicated the number of cylinders. The second and third numbers indicated model year. The first letter indicated the basic chassis and body type. The second letter indicated model. The fourth number indicated series in any one model year. On most Jeep models the engine and serial numbers were the same.

Model	Body Type	Price	Weight	Prod. Total
Willys Jeep — (4x4) — (4-cyl.)				
CJ-2A	Jeep Utility	1270	2037	—
CJ-3A	Jeep Utility	1270	2110	—
Willys Truck — (4x2) — (4-cyl.)				
463	½-Ton Panel	1375	2587	—
Willys Truck — (4x2) — (4-cyl.)				
4x2	Chassis & Cab	1282	2677	—
4x2	Pickup	1375	2995	—
4x2	Platform	1442	3299	—
Willys Truck — (4x4) — (4-cyl.)				
4x4	Chassis & Cab	1700	2809	—
4x4	Pickup	1792	3129	—
4x4	Platform Stake	1856	3431	—

ENGINE (CJ-2A/CJ-3A): Inline. L-head. Four-cylinder. Cast iron block. Bore & stroke: 3⅛ in. x 4⅜ in. Displacement: 134.2 cu. in. Compression ratio: 6.5:1. Brake horsepower: 60 at 4000 R.P.M. Net horsepower: 15.63 (N.A.C.C.) Max. Torque: 105 lbs. ft. at 2000 R.P.M. Three main bearings. Solid valve lifters. Carburetor: (CJ models) Carter WA-1 model 613S.

ENGINE (Model 463): Inline. L-head. Four-cylinder. Cast iron block. Bore & stroke: 3⅛ in. x 4⅜ in. Displacement: 134.2 cu. in. Compression ratio: 6.48:1. Brake horsepower: 63 at 4000 R.P.M. Net horsepower: 15.63 (N.A.C.C.) Max. Torque: 105 lbs. ft. at 2000 R.P.M. Three main bearings. Solid valve lifters. Carburetor: (2x2) Carter WA-1 model 613S; (4x4) Carter WO model 596S or 636S.

CHASSIS (Jeep): Wheelbase: 80 in. Front tread: 55¼ in. Rear tread: 57 in. Tires: 6.00 x 15 in.

CHASSIS (Model 463): Wheelbase: 104 in. Front tread: 55¼ in. Rear tread: 57 in. Tires: 6.50 x 16 in.

CHASSIS (Other Models): Wheelbase: 118 in. Front tread: 55¼ in. Rear tread: 57 in. Tires: (4x2) 6.50 x 16 in.; (4x4) 7.00 x 16 in.

TECHNICAL: Synchromesh transmission. Speeds: 3F/1R (4x4's have 2-speed transfer case). Floor-mounted gearshift lever. Single plate clutch. Hypoid rear axle. Four-wheel hydraulic brakes. Disc wheels.

OPTIONS: *Power take-off ($96.25). *Pulley drive ($57.40). *Motor governor ($28.65). Special wheels and 7:00 tires ($40). Front canvas top ($57.80). Hydraulic lift ($225). Metal top (Varies).

NOTE: * Applicable also to 473 four-wheel-drive Trucks.

672

HISTORICAL: Introduced: Nov. 1949. Calendar year production: (Sta. Wag.) 29,290; (Jeeps) 18,342; (Trucks) 18,342.

Pricing

1949	5	4	3	2	1
Jeep Series (4x4)					
CJ-2 Jeep	850	1700	2850	4000	5700
CJ-3 Jeep	850	1700	2850	4000	5700
Willys Truck (4x2)					
Panel	570	1140	1950	2650	3800
Pickup	500	1000	1650	2300	3300
Platform	440	870	1450	2050	2900
Willys Truck (4x4)					
Pickup	530	1050	1750	2450	3500
Platform	450	900	1500	2100	3000

1950 WILLYS-OVERLAND

1950 Willys-Overland, Jeep Pickup (OCW)

WILLYS — JEEP SERIES — FOUR-CYLINDER: — For Jeep, there was a lot new this year. The CJ-3A replaced the CJ-2A as the basic "Universal" Jeep. In the truck (and station wagon) line, there was new front end styling. The fenders had a "peaked," rather than flat flare to them. The grille consisted of five horizontal bright metal moldings running across nine vertical moldings. There was a chrome ornament on the tip of the hood. Two new engines, the "Hurricane" four and the "Lightening" six were offered in wagons, but not (yet) trucks. There was, however a new ½-ton 4x2 truck with the grille revisions.

I.D. DATA: Serial number located on plate at left side of driver's seat on floor riser in 1946-1948 model CJ-2A; on right side of dash under hood in 1949-1954 models CJ-2A and CJ-3A/CJ-3B; on left side of dash under hood in 1948-1951 models 4x2 and 4x4; on left floor riser in back of seat in 1947-1949 models 4-63. Serial numbers: (CJ-3A) 35,689-63,784; ("463") 106,504-112,402; (¾-ton) 26,563-27,787 and (1-ton) 43,587-47,709.
   Engine numbers located on right side of cylinder block; stamped on water pump boss on front of cylinder block.

NOTE: Beginning around 1951 and continuing through at least 1953, each model had a specific serial number prefix such as "451-GC1." The first number indicated the number of cylinders. The second and third numbers indicated model year. The first letter indicated the basic chassis and body type. The second letter indicated model. The fourth number indicated series in any one model year. On most Jeep models the engine and serial numbers were the same.

Model	Body Type	Price	Weight	Prod. Total
Willys Jeep — (4x4) — (4-cyl.)				
CJ-3A	Jeep Utility	1270	2110	—
Willys Truck — (4x2) — (4-cyl.)				
463	½-Ton Panel	1374	2587	—
Willys Truck — (4x2) — (4-cyl.)				
¾-Ton	Chassis & Cab	1282	2677	—
¾-Ton	Pickup	1375	2995	—
¾-Ton	Platform Stake	1441	3299	—
Willys Truck — (4x4) — (4-cyl.)				
1-Ton	Chassis & Cab	1700	2809	—
1-Ton	Pickup	1792	3129	—
1-Ton	Platform Stake	1856	3431	—

1950 Willys-Overland, Jeep Station Wagon 4x4 (OCW)

ENGINE (CJ-3A): Inline. L-head. Four-cylinder. Cast iron block. Bore & stroke: 3⅛ in. x 4⅜ in. Displacement: 134.2 cu. in. Compression ratio: 6.5:1. Brake horsepower: 60 at 4000 R.P.M. Net horsepower: 15.63 (N.A.C.C.) Max. Torque: 105 lbs. ft. at 2000 R.P.M. Three main bearings. Solid valve lifters. Carburetor: (2x2) Carter WA-1 model 613S; (4x4) Carter WO model 596S or 636 S.

ENGINE (Model 463): Inline. L-head. Four-cylinder. Cast iron block. Bore & stroke: 3⅛ in. x 4⅜ in. Displacement: 134.2 cu. in. Compression ratio: 6.48:1. Brake horsepower: 63 at 4000 R.P.M. Net horsepower: 15.63 (N.A.C.C.) Max. Torque: 105 lbs. ft. at 2000 R.P.M. Three main bearings. Solid valve lifters. Carburetor: Carter WA-1 model 613S.

CHASSIS (Jeep): Wheelbase: 80 in. Front tread: 55¼ in. Rear tread: 57 in. Tires: 6.00 x 15 in.

CHASSIS (Model 463): Wheelbase: 104 in. Front tread: 55¼ in. Rear tread: 57 in. Tires: 6.50 x 16 in.

CHASSIS (Model 473): Wheelbase: 118 in. Front tread: 55¼ in. Rear tread: 57 in. Tires: (4x2) 6.50 x 16 in.; (4x4) 7.00 x 16 in.

TECHNICAL: Synchromesh transmission. Speeds: 3F/1R (4x4s have 2-speed transfer case). Floor-mounted gearshift lever. Single dry plate clutch. (Hypoid front axle w/4x4). Hypoid rear axle. Four-wheel hydraulic brakes. Disc wheels.

OPTIONS: *Power take-off ($96.25). *Pulley drive ($57.40). *Motor governor ($28.65). Special wheels and 7:00 tires ($40). Front canvas top ($57.80). Hydraulic lift ($225). Metal top (Varies).

NOTE: * Applicable also to 473 four-wheel-drive Trucks.

HISTORICAL: Introduced: Nov. 1949 and continued. Calendar year production: (Sta. Wag.) 32,218; (Jeeps) 26,624; (Trucks) 22,282. Production of military Jeeps for the Korean War resumed.

Pricing

1950	5	4	3	2	1
Jeep Series (4x4)					
CJ-3 Jeep	850	1700	2850	4000	5700
Willys Truck (4x2)					
Panel	570	1140	1950	2650	3800
Pickup	500	1000	1650	2300	3300
Stake	440	870	1450	2050	2900
Jeep Truck (4x4)					
Pickup	530	1050	1750	2450	3500
Stake	450	900	1500	2100	3000

1951 WILLYS-OVERLAND

WILLYS — JEEP SERIES — FOUR-CYLINDER: — For 1951, Willys continued the 80 inch wheelbase Universal Jeep, Model CJ-3A, which retained the war-proven 134 cubic inch L-head four-cylinder engine. Identifying features included its one-piece windshield design with stamped panels on the lower section of the windshield frame. A military version, the updated M-38, would serve admirably with U.S. Armed Forces in the Korean War. In civilian form, it was made available as a stripped chassis, or with the open utility body, or as a new model called the "Farm Jeep" with a power-take-off (PTO) attachment. Only three stripped chassis and 62 Farm Jeeps were built. This year's Jeep trucks retained the slightly "Veed" egg-crate grille design introduced in 1950. They were all on a 118 inch wheelbase, except the Sedan Delivery, which had a 104 inch wheelbase. The sedan delivery came only as a 4x2 truck. Available on the longer wheelbase, with

either 4x2 or 4x4 running gear, were a stripped chassis, chassis with cab, Pickup and Platform Stake truck. The Sedan Delivery had a 4000 pound GVW rating. All other 4x2 trucks had a 4250 pound GVW and the 4x4s were rated for 5300 pounds. (The CJ-3A had a 3500 pound GVW rating). Power for the trucks was provided by the hotter F-head four-cylinder engine. The 4x4 equipped trucks had "Four-Wheel-Drive" call-outs on the side of the hood.

I.D. DATA: Serial number located on plate at left side of driver's seat on floor riser in 1946-1948 model CJ-2A; on right side of dash under hood in 1949-1954 models CJ-2A and CJ-3A/CJ-3B; on left side of dash under hood in 1948-1951 models 4x2 and 4x4; on left floor riser in back of seat in 1947-1949 models 4-63. Serial numbers: (FJ) 451-GC1 — 10,001 to 10,062; (CJ-3(S) 451-GA1 — 10,001 to 10,003; (CJ-3 (O) 451-GB1 — 10,001 to 54,158; ("473" chassis) CA-1 10,001 to 15,440; ("473" cab) DB1 — 10,001 to 10,530; ("473" Pickup) DC1 — 10,001 to 13,016; ("473" Stake) DD1 — 10,001 to ending; (473E C.C.) — EB1 — 10,001 to 11,894; ("473E" Pickup) — EC1 — 10,001 to 26,029; ("473E" Stake) — ED1 — 10,001 to 10,420.

Engine numbers located on right side of cylinder block; stamped on water pump boss on front of cylinder block.

NOTE: Beginning around 1951 and continuing through at least 1953, each model had a specific serial number prefix such as "451-GC1." The first number indicated the number of cylinders. The second and third numbers indicated model year. The first letter indicated the basic chassis and body type. The second letter indicated model. The fourth number indicated series in any one model year. On most Jeep models the engine and serial numbers were the same.

1951 Willys-Overland, Jeep Rail Utility Truck (OCW)

Model	Body Type	Price	Weight	Prod. Total
Willys Jeep — (4x4) — (4-cyl.)				
FJ	Farm Jeep	1550	2280	—
CJ-3	Jeep (stripped)	1055	1692	—
CJ-3	Jeep (open body)	1290	2110	—
Jeep Trucks — (4x2) — (4-cyl.)				
473-D	Chassis	865	1716	—
473-D	Chassis & Cab	1220	2406	—
473-D	Pickup	1295	2722	—
473-D	Platform Stake	1365	2963	—
Jeep Trucks — (4x4) — (4-cyl.)				
473-E	Chassis	1205	2109	—
473-E	Chassis & Cab	1595	2799	—
473-E	Pickup	1678	3115	—
473-E	Platform Stake	1736	3356	—

ENGINE (CJ-2A): Inline. L-head. Four-cylinder. Cast iron block. Bore & stroke: 3⅛ in. x 4⅜ in. Displacement: 134.2 cu. in. Compression ratio: 6.5:1. Brake horsepower: 60 at 4000 R.P.M. Net horsepower: 15.63 (N.A.C.C.) Max. Torque: 105 lbs. ft. at 2000 R.P.M. Three main bearings. Solid valve lifters. Carburetor: Carter YF model 832S or 832SA.

ENGINE (Model 473): Inline. L-head. Four-cylinder. Cast iron block. Bore & stroke: 3⅛ in. x 4⅜ in. Displacement: 134.2 cu. in. Compression ratio: 7.4:1. Brake horsepower: 72 at 4000 R.P.M. Net horsepower: 15.63 (N.A.C.C.) Max. Torque: 114 lbs. ft. at 2000 R.P.M. Three main bearings. Solid valve lifters. Carburetor: Carter YF model 832S/832SA one-barrel.

CHASSIS (Series FJ/CJ-3A): Wheelbase: 80-1/16 in. Length: 129⅞ in. Height: 67¾ in. (top up). Front and rear tread: 48-7/16 in. Tires: 6.00 x 16 in.

CHASSIS (473 Sedan Delivery): Wheelbase: 104.5 in. Length: 176.25 in. Height: 73.62 in. Front and rear tread: 57 in. Tires: (4x2) 6.70 x 15 in.

CHASSIS (473 Trucks): Wheelbase: 118 in. Length: 183.7 in. Height: 74.3 in. Front and rear tread: 57 in. Tires: (4x2) 6.70 x 15 in.; (4x4) 7.00 x 15 in.

TECHNICAL: Synchromesh transmission. Speeds: 3F/1R (4x4 models have two-speed transfer case). Floor-mounted gearshift lever. Single dry plate clutch. Hypoid rear axle. Overall ratio: 5.38:1. Four-wheel hydraulic brakes. Disc wheels.

NOTE: The 4x4 models had two Hypoid axles with a full-floating type in front; semi-floating rear. Axle capacity (CJ-3A) 2000 pound front; 2500 pound rear.

OPTIONS: *Power take-off ($96.25). *Pulley drive ($57.40). *Motor governor ($28.65). Special wheels and 7:00 tires ($40). Front canvas top ($57.80). Hydraulic lift ($225). Metal top (Varies).

Other options available for Jeep trucks included: Chrome front bumper. Chrome rear bumper. Rearview mirrors. Chrome wheel discs. Bumper guards. Clearance lights.

HISTORICAL: Introduced: (Farm Jeep) July 1951; (Series 451) Nov. 1950. Calendar year registrations: 24,292 (all trucks). Calendar year production: (Jeeps) 76,571; (Station Wagon) 25,316; (Trucks) 20,244.

Military and civilian orders for Willys-Overland vehicles exceeded a quarter-billion dollars in 1951. There was a backlog for Jeep orders that Willys had trouble keeping up with. First half sales figures, of which 90 percent were for the civilian market, set an all-time record and were up 168 percent over the comparable 1950 period.

Pricing

1951	5	4	3	2	1
Jeep Series (4x4)					
Farm Jeep	800	1600	2650	3700	5300
CJ-3 Jeep	850	1700	2850	4000	5700
Jeep Trucks (4x2)					
Chassis & Cab	440	870	1450	2050	2900
Pickup	500	1000	1650	2300	3300
Stake	440	870	1450	2050	2900
Jeep Trucks (4x4)					
Pickup	530	1050	1750	2450	3500
Stake	450	900	1500	2100	3000

1952 WILLYS-OVERLAND

...nce to own at least one of ...hides that will get you ...ers can't.

1952 Willys-Overland, Jeep Pickup (D. Sagvold)

WILLYS — JEEP SERIES — FOUR-CYLINDER: — Willys was producing like crazy to fill military orders for Korean War Jeeps. Civilian models also sold well this year. There wasn't time to worry about changing the products' basic designs. However, all trucks listed in used car guides were 4x4 models. It seems that only the Sedan Delivery was offered with conventional 4x2 running gear. (By the way, a 2000 pound capacity I-beam front axle was used on the 4x2 models.) The 4x4 trucks had "Four Wheel Drive" on the sides of their hoods near the cowl.

I.D. DATA: Serial number located on plate at left side of driver's seat on floor riser in 1946-1948 model CJ-2A; on right side of dash under hood in 1949-1954 models CJ-2A and CJ-3A/CJ-3B; on left side of dash under hood in 1948-1951 models 4x2 and 4x4; on left floor riser in back of seat in 1947-1949 models 4-63. Starting: (CJ-3A) 452-GA1-10,001 to 10,013; (CJ-3A Open) 452-GB1-10,001 to 39,652; ("473-SD") 452-GA1-10,001 to 12,091; ("473" Chassis) 452-FA1-10,001 & up; ("473" Chassis & Cab) 452-EB1-10,001 to 11,085; ("473" Pickup) 452-EC1-10,001 to 23,183; ("473" Stake) 452-ED1-10,001 to 10,358.

Engine numbers located on right side of cylinder block; stamped on water pump boss on front of cylinder block.

NOTE: Beginning around 1951 and continuing through at least 1953, each model had a specific serial number prefix such as "451-GC1." The first number indicated the number of cylinders. The second and third numbers indicated model year. The first letter indicated the basic chassis and body

type. The second letter indicated model. The fourth number indicated series in any one model year. On most Jeep models the engine and serial numbers were the same.

Model	Body Type	Price	Weight	Prod. Total
Willys Jeep — (4x4) — (4-cyl.)				
CJ-3A	Stripped Chassis	1224	1692	—
CJ-3A	Open Body	1352	2108	—
Jeep Trucks — (4x2) — (4-cyl.)				
473-SD	Sedan Dely.	1469	2620	—
Jeep Trucks — (4x4) — (4-cyl.)				
473	Chassis Stripped	1296	2109	—
473	Chassis & Cab	1712	2799	—
473	Pickup	1805	3115	—
473	Platform Stake	1870	3356	—

NOTE: In many cases, accurate estimates of production for individual Jeep models of the early 1950s can be made by subtracting starting from ending serial numbers. We have not made such calculations in this catalog because we have no way of knowing, with absolute certainty, that all numbers within a range were used. However, if you own one of these vehicles and want to get a good "ballpark" production total for your specific model, simply find the correct starting and ending numbers and make the necessary calculations. You'll have a figure very close to, if not exact matching, the correct production break-out.

1952 Willys-Overland, Jeep Station Wagon (OCW)

ENGINE (CJ-2A): Inline. L-head. Four-cylinder. Cast iron block. Bore & stroke: 3⅛ in. x 4⅜ in. Displacement: 134.2 cu. in. Compression ratio: 6.5:1. Brake horsepower: 60 at 4000 R.P.M. Net horsepower: 15.63 (N.A.C.C.) Max. Torque: 105 lbs. ft. at 2000 R.P.M. Three main bearings. Solid valve lifters. Carburetor: Carter YF model 938S or 938SA.

ENGINE (473-SW): Inline. F-head. Four-cylinder. Cast iron block. Bore & stroke: 3⅛ in. x 4⅜ in. Displacement: 134.2 cu. in. Compression ratio: 7.4:1. Brake horsepower: 72 at 4000 R.P.M. Net horsepower: 15.63 (N.A.C.C.) Max. Torque: 114 lbs. ft. at 2000 R.P.M. Three main bearings. Solid valve lifters. Carburetor: Carter YF model 951S.

NOTE: (First series 1951 station wagons were 463 models).

CHASSIS (Series CJ-3A): Wheelbase: 80-1/16 in. Length: 129⅞ in. Height: 67¾ in. (top up). Front and rear tread: 48-7/16 in. Tires: 6.00 x 16 in.

CHASSIS (Sedan Delivery): Wheelbase: 104 in. Length: 176¼ in. Height: 73.62 in. Front and rear tread: 57 in. Tires: (4x2) 6.70 x 15 in.

CHASSIS (Trucks): Wheelbase: 118 in. Length: 183.7 in. Height: 74.3 in. Front and rear tread: 57 in. Tires: (4x4) 7.00 x 15 in.

TECHNICAL: Synchromesh transmission. Speeds: 3F/1R (4x4 models w/two-speed transfer case). Floor-mounted gearshift lever. Single dry plate clutch. Hypoid rear axle. Overall ratio: 5.38:1. Four-wheel hydraulic brakes. Disc wheels.

NOTE: The 4x2 models had a 2000 pounds capacity front I-beam axle. The 4x4 models had a 2000 pound capacity, full-floating type hypoid front axle. A 2500 pound capacity, semi-floating type, hypoid rear axle was used on both 4x2 and 4x4 models.

OPTIONS: (Jeep): Power-take-off ($96.25). Pulley drive ($57.40). Motor governor ($28.65). Special wheels and 7:00 tires ($40). Front canvas top ($57.80). Hydraulic lift ($225). Metal top (various prices). **(4x4 Trucks):** Power-take-off ($96.25). Pulley drive ($57.40). Motor governor ($28.65). Rearview mirror. Sidemount spare on pickups/stakes. Chrome bumper. License frame. **(Sedan Delivery):** Chrome front bumper. Chrome rear bumper. License frame. Chrome wheel disc. Bumperettes. Bumper guards. Wheel trim rings. Whitewall tires. Rearview mirror. Radio and antenna.

HISTORICAL: Introduced: Dec. 10, 1951. Calendar year registrations: 20,356 (all trucks). Calendar year production: (Jeeps) 88,098; (Station Wagons) 12,890; (Trucks) 31,273.

New "Hurricane" F-head engine in Jeeps (late 1952 for 1953 models). Two new 4x2 station wagons and one 4x4 station wagon replaced three discontinued models. Grille styling revised. New M38A1 military jeep introduced. This became the civilian CJ-5.

The one-millionth Jeep was built March 19, 1952. Station wagon output in calendar 1952 included 12,890 two-wheel-drives and 9,713 four-wheel-drives. Defense contracts awarded in 1952 totaled $200,556,116 and included a front-line Jeep ambulance project.

1952	5	4	3	2	1
Jeep Series (4x4)					
CJ-3 Open	850	1700	2850	4000	5700
Jeep Trucks (4x2)					
Sedan Dely.	600	1200	2000	2800	4000
Jeep Trucks (4x4)					
Pickup	540	1080	1800	2900	3600
Stake	450	900	1500	2100	3000

1953 WILLYS-OVERLAND

1953 Willys-Overland, Jeep M38A Universal (OCW)

WILLYS — JEEP SERIES — FOUR-CYLINDER: — The CJ-3B bowed as an added civilian model for 1953. It was basically the same as the carried over CJ-3A but had a higher hood and grille to fit the new 70 horsepower "Hurricane Four" F-head engine. Willys lettering appeared on the front and the raised hoodside panels. The famous Korean War military MD/M38A1 Jeep also entered production late in 1952 as a 1953 model. This would be the basis for the civilian CJ-5 of later years. The CJ-3B used a 70 horsepower version of the truck engine. It had slightly lower compression. Attempts to market a special "Farm Jeep" were revived this season. In the Jeep truck line, the primary change was the addition of a new, 4x4 Sedan Delivery, which joined the 4x2 model. The chassis-only configuration was dropped. Henry J. Kaiser purchased the company, in the spring, changing the name to Willys Motors, Inc.

I.D. DATA: Serial number located on plate at left side of driver's seat on floor riser in 1946-1948 model CJ-2A; on right side of dash under hood in 1949-1954 models CJ-2A and CJ-3A/CJ-3B; on left side of dash under hood in 1948-1951 models 4x2 and 4x4; on left floor riser in back of seat in 1947-1949 models 4-63. Serial numbers: (CJ-3B Open) 453-GB2-10,001 to 37,550; (CJ-3B Farm) 453-GC2-10,001 & up; (CJ-3A) 453-GB1-10,001 & up; (4x2 Sed. Dely.) 453-CA2-10,001 to 12,347; (4x4 Sed. Dely.) 453-RA2-10,001 to 10,992; (4x4 Chassis) 453-EB2-10,001 to 11,516; (4x4 Pickup) 453-EC2-10,001 to 24,128 and (4x4 Stake) 453-ED2-10,001 to 10,694.
　Engine numbers located on right side of cylinder block; stamped on water pump boss on front of cylinder block.

NOTE: Beginning around 1951 and continuing through at least 1953, each model had a specific serial number prefix such as "451-GC1." The first number indicated the number of cylinders. The second and third numbers indicated model year. The first letter indicated the basic chassis and body type. The second letter indicated model. The fourth number indicated series in any one model year. On most Jeep models the engine and serial numbers were the same.

Model	Body Type	Price	Weight	Prod. Total
Willys Jeep — (4x4) — (4-cyl.)				
CJ-3B	Open Body	1377	2098	—
CJ-3B	Farm Open Body	1439	2098	—
CJ-3A	Open Body	1352	2108	—
Jeep Trucks — (4x2) — (4-cyl.)				
475	Sedan Dely.	1469	2620	—
Jeep Trucks — (4x4) — (4-cyl.)				
4x4 75-SD	Sedan Dely.	1920	2976	—
475 4-wd	Chassis & Cab	1712	2799	—
475 -4wd	Pickup	1805	3115	—
475 4-wd	Platform Stake	1870	3356	—

ENGINE (CJ-3A): Inline. L-head. Four-cylinder. Cast iron block. Bore & stroke: 3⅛ in. x 4⅜ in. Displacement: 134.2 cu. in. Compression ratio: 6.48:1. Brake horsepower: 60 at 4000 R.P.M. Net horsepower: 15.63 (N.A.C.C.) Max. Torque: 105 lbs. ft. at 2000 R.P.M. Three main bearings. Solid valve lifters. Carburetor: Carter model YF-938S; YF-938SA.

ENGINE (CJ-3B): Inline. F-head. Four-cylinder. Cast iron block. Bore & stroke: 3⅛ in. x 4⅜ in. Displacement: 134.2 cu. in. Compression ratio: 6.90:1. Brake horsepower: 70 at 4000 R.P.M. Net horsepower: 15.63 (N.A.C.C.) Max. Torque: 114 lbs. ft. at 2000 R.P.M. Three main bearings. Solid valve lifters. Carburetor: Carter model YF-951S.

ENGINE (Series 475): Inline. F-head. Four-cylinder. Cast iron block. Bore & stroke: 3⅛ in. x 4⅜ in. Displacement: 134.2 cu. in. Compression ratio: 7.40:1. Brake horsepower: 72 at 4000 R.P.M. Net horsepower: 15.63. Max. Torque: 114 lbs. ft. at 2000 R.P.M. Three main bearings. Solid valve lifters. Carburetor: Carter model YF-951S.

CHASSIS (CJ-3A/CJ-3B): Wheelbase: 80-1/16 in. Length: 129⅞ in. Height: 67¾ in. Front and rear tread: 48-7/16 in. Tires: 6.00 x 16 in.

CHASSIS (Sedan Delivery 4x2): Wheelbase: 104 in. Length: 176¼ in. Height: 73.62 in. Front and rear tread: 57 in. Tires: (4x2) 6.70 x 15 in.

CHASSIS (Sedan Delivery 4x4): Wheelbase: 104½ in. Length: 176¼ in. Height: 73.62 in. Front and rear tread: 57 in. Tires: (4x4) 7.00 x 15 in.

CHASSIS (Trucks 4x4): Wheelbase: 118 in. Length: 183.7 in. Height: 74.3 in. Front and rear tread: 57 in. Tires: 7.00 x 15 in.

TECHNICAL: Synchromesh transmission. Speeds: 3F/1R (4x4 models with two-speed transfer case). Floor-mounted gearshift lever. Single dry plate clutch. Hypoid rear axle. Overall ratio: 5.38:1. Four-wheel hydraulic brakes. Disc wheels.

NOTE: The 4x2 models have I-beam front axle. The 4x4 models have full-floating hypoid front axle. All models have semi-floating hypoid rear axle.

OPTIONS: (Jeep) Power-take-off ($96.25). Pulley drive ($57.40). Motor governor ($28.65). Special wheels and 7:00 tires ($40). Front canvas top ($57.80). Hydraulic lift ($225). Metal top (various prices). **(4x4 Trucks):** Power-take-off ($96.25). Pulley drive ($57.40). Motor governor ($28.65). Rearview mirror. Sidemount spare on pickups/stakes. Chrome bumper. License frame. **(Sedan Delivery):** Chrome front bumper. Chrome rear bumper. License frame. Chrome wheel disc. Bumperettes. Bumper guards. Wheel trim rings. Whitewall tires. Rearview mirror. Radio and antenna.

HISTORICAL: Introduced: (CJ-3B) Jan. 28, 1953; (others) Oct. 20, 1952. Calendar year registrations: 17,712 (all trucks). Calendar year production: (Trucks) 88,650 Jeeps and Jeep Trucks; (Sta. Wag.) 5,417.
　New CJ-3B features higher hood/grille design to accomodate 71 horsepower "Hurricane Four" F-head engine.
　On April 28, 1953, Kaiser Manufacturing Co. formally purchased Willys-Overland at a cost of $62,381,175. This was Willys-Overland's "Golden Jubilee" year, celebrating the company's 50th anniversary. Production averaged 8,800 trucks monthly. On Sept. 2, 1953 an assembly point in Japan was established. On the same day, Chase Aircraft Co., of Trenton, N.J., became a wholly owned subsidiary of Willys Motors. On Sept. 5, the U.S. Army cut its Jeep orders back by 50 percent. On Sept. 22, vehicle production at a Kaiser plant in the Netherlands was announced.

1953 Willys-Overland, Deluxe Station Wagon (D. Sagvold)

1953	5	4	3	2	1
Jeep Series (4x4)					
CJ-3B Jeep	890	1770	2950	4150	5900
CJ-3B Farm Jeep	850	1700	2850	4000	5700
CJ-3A Jeep	850	1700	2850	4000	5700
Jeep Trucks (4x2)					
Sedan Dely.	600	1200	2000	2800	4000
Jeep Trucks (4x4)					
Sedan Dely.	660	1320	2200	3100	4400
Pickup	560	1100	1850	2600	3700
Stake	450	900	1500	2100	3000

1954 WILLYS-OVERLAND

1954 Willys-Overland, Jeep Station Wagon 4x4 (OCW)

WILLYS — JEEP SERIES — (ALL-ENGINES): — The CJ-3A was dropped for 1954. All three Universal Jeeps offered this season were CJ-3B models. They still said "Willys" above the grille and on the hood sides. The power plant was the F-head four-cylinder. Jeep-truck models had another new grille. It had only three bright metal moldings, running horizontally across the top, middle and bottom. Nine vertical bars, in body color, were behind the bright moldings. All four-cylinder trucks were 4x4s. They were designated "454" models and used the 72 horsepower F-head engine. Three body styles: chassis and cab, pickup and platform stake came in this series. All-new just a 4x2 version of the sedan delivery with a 104½ inch wheelbase used a 90 horsepower F-head six. The second included the 104½ inch wheelbase Sedan Delivery and three 118 inch wheelbase models powered by a 115 horsepower L-head six. This was called a "Super Hurricane" engine.

I.D. DATA: Serial number located on right side of dash under hood; on front frame cross member; on left floor riser in back of driver's seat. Serial numbers: CJ-5 Chassis — 54-10,001 to 12,600 and 454-GA2-10,601 up; CJ-3B-O.B. — 54-10,001 to 12,600 and 454-GB2-12,001 up; 454-GC2-10,001 to 10,012; 454-FA2-10,001 to 13,528; 454-EC2-10,001 to 13,606; 454-ED2-10,001 to 10,185; 454-EB2-10,001 to 10,681; 654-CA2-10,001 to 10,308; 654-EC2-10,001 to 14,927; 654-EB2-10,001 to 10,439; 654-RA2-10,001 to 10,243 and 654-FA2-10,001 to 13,528.
Engine numbers located on right side of cylinder block; stamped on water pump boss on front of cylinder block.

NOTE: On most Jeep models the engine and serial numbers are the same.

Model	Body Type	Price	Weight	Prod. Total
Willys Jeep — (4x4) — (4-cyl.)				
CJ-3B	Stripped Chassis	1145	1718	—
CJ-3B	Open Body	1377	2306	—
CJ-3B	Farm Jeep	1439	2184	—
Jeep Trucks — (4x4) — (4-cyl.)				
454-EB2	Chassis & Cab	1712	2774	—
454-EC2	Pickup	1805	3135	—
454-ED2	Platform Stake	1870	3356	—
Jeep Trucks — (4x2) — (6-cyl.)				
654-CA2	Sedan Dely.	1520	2711	—
Jeep Trucks — (4x4) — (6-cyl.)				
654-RA2	Sedan Dely.	2009	3055	—
654-EB2	Chassis & Cab	1802	2850	—
654-EC2	Pickup	1895	3141	—
654-ED2	Platform Stake	1960	3362	—

ENGINE (CJ-3B): Inline. F-head. Four-cylinder. Cast iron block. Bore & stroke: 3⅛ in. x 4⅜ in. Displacement: 134.2 cu. in. Compression ratio: 6.90:1. Brake horsepower: 70 at 4000 R.P.M. Net horsepower: 15.63. Max. Torque: 114 lbs. ft. at 2000 R.P.M. Three main bearings. Solid valve lifters. Carburetor: Carter YF model 938S or 938SA one-barrel.

ENGINE (Series 454): Inline. F-head. Four-cylinder. Cast iron block. Bore & stroke: 3⅛ in. x 4⅜ in. Displacement: 134.2 cu. in. Compression ratio: 7.40:1. Brake horsepower: 72 at 4000 R.P.M. Net horsepower: 15.63. Max. Torque: 114 lbs. ft. at 2000 R.P.M. Three main bearings. Solid valve lifters. Carburetor: Carter YF model 951S one-barrel.

ENGINE (Model CA — Sed. Dely.): Inline. F-head. Six-cylinder. Cast iron block. Bore & stroke: 3⅛ in. x 3½ in. Displacement: 161.5 cu. in. Compression ratio: 7.6:1. Brake horsepower: 90 at 4200 R.P.M. Net horsepower: 23.44. Max. Torque: 135 lbs. ft. at 2000 R.P.M. Four main bearings. Solid valve lifters. Carburetor: Carter YF model 924S or 2071S one-barrel.

ENGINE (6-226): Inline. L-head. Six-cylinder. Cast iron block. Bore & stroke: 3-5/16 in. x 4⅜ in. Displacement: 226.2 cu. in. Compression ratio: 6.86:1. Brake horsepower: 115 at 3650 R.P.M. Net horsepower: 26.3. Max. Torque: 190 lbs. ft. at 1800 R.P.M. Four main bearings. Solid valve lifters. Carburetor: Carter WDG model 2052S or 2052SA one-barrel.

CHASSIS (CJ-3B): Wheelbase: 80-1/16 in. Length: 129⅞ in. Height: 67¾ in. Front and rear tread: 48-7/16 in. Tires: 6.00 x 16 in.

CHASSIS (Sedan Delivery 4x2): Wheelbase: 104 in. Length: 176¼ in. Height: 73.62 in. Front and rear tread: 57 in. Tires: 6.70 x 15 in.

CHASSIS (Sedan Delivery 4x4): Wheelbase: 104½ in. Length: 176¼ in. Height: 73.62 in. Front and rear tread: 57 in. Tires: 7.00 x 15 in.

CHASSIS (Trucks 4x4): Wheelbase: 118 in. Length: 183.7 in. Height: 74.3 in. Front and rear tread: 57 in. Tires: 7.00 x 15 in.

TECHNICAL: Synchromesh transmission. Speeds: 3F/1R (4x4 models have two-speed transfer case). Floor-mounted gearshift lever. Single dry plate clutch. Hypoid rear axle. Overall ratio: 5.38:1. Four-wheel hydraulic brakes. Disc wheels.

NOTE: The 4x2 models had I-beam front axle. The 4x4 models have full-floating hypoid front axle. All models have semi-floating hypoid rear axle.

OPTIONS: (Jeep): Power-take-off ($96.25). Pulley drive ($57.40). Motor governor ($28.65). Special wheels and 7:00 tires ($40). Front canvas top ($57.80). Hydraulic lift ($225). Metal top (various prices). **(4x4 Trucks):** Power-take-off ($96.25). Pulley drive ($57.40). Motor governor ($28.65). Rearview mirror. Sidemount spare on pickups/stakes. Chrome bumper. License frame. **(Sedan Delivery):** Chrome front bumper. Chrome rear bumper. License frame. Chrome wheel disc. Bumperettes. Bumper guards. Wheel trim rings. Whitewall tires. Rearview mirror. Radio and antenna.

NOTE: The CJ-5 was introduced Nov. 12, 1954.

Late 1954 Willys-Overland, Jeep CJ-5 Universal (OCW)

HISTORICAL: Introduced: (Jeep) Dec. 1, 1953. (Four-cylinder trucks) Feb. 3, 1954. (Six-cylinder trucks) June 30 or May 10, 1954. Calendar year registrations: (Trucks) 9,925; (Jeeps) 7,598. Calendar year production: (commercial vehicles) 75,434. Innovations: New six-cylinder Jeep trucks introduced. The EC, ED and EB models bowed May 10 and the RA, FA models bowed June 30. This was called "Super-Hurricane" engine. Truck grilles redesigned. The CJ-5 was a de-militarized version of the famous M-38 Jeep. Historical Notes: On Feb. 23, 1954 the 500,000th postwar Jeep was built. E.F. Kaiser was president of Willys. C.A. Watson was general sales manager. On July 19, 400 workers were recalled for increased truck programming and car-building assembly lines were temporarily closed for truck erecting. Four days later, Kaiser-Willys announced plans to liquidate surplus facilities and concentrate all car-truck operations in the Toledo area. The Maywood, Calif. factory, opened in 1928, was closed on July 29. It was first converted to a warehouse and, later, sold. On Oct. 5, Kaiser-Willys signed a contract to produce Jeeps in Argentina. Jeep production begins in Brazil, too.

Pricing

1954	5	4	3	2	1
Jeep Series (4x4)					
Open Jeep	890	1770	2950	4150	5900
Farm Jeep	850	1700	2850	4000	5700
Jeep Trucks (4x2)					
Sedan Dely.	600	1200	2000	2800	4000
Jeep Trucks (4x4)					
Pickup	660	1320	2200	3100	4400
Stake	470	950	1550	2200	3100
Sedan Dely.	660	1320	2200	3100	4400
1-Ton Pickup	530	1050	1750	2450	3500
1-Ton Stake	450	900	1500	2100	3000

NOTE: Add 3 percent for 6-cyl. trucks (not avail. in Universal Jeeps).

1955 WILLYS-OVERLAND

1955 Willys-Overland, Jeep CJ-5 Universal (OCW)

WILLYS — JEEP SERIES — (ALL-ENGINES): — The military M38 became the civilian CJ-5 in model-year 1955. It had entirely new bodywork with lower, squarer-cornered door openings, sunk-in headlights, redesigned fenders and an 81-inch (versus CJ-3's 80-inch) w.b. The new front fenders were fuller and had front "flaps" for more protection. A variation from military specifications was a one-piece windshield. Trucks used the grille that came out in 1954. There were four new 4x2 models, two with four-cylinder engines and two with six-cylinder engines. One was the Sedan Delivery and the other was called a Utility Wagon. This was actually the same as the earlier Station Wagon, which was considered a car up to this point. Since Willys had stopped making its conventional passenger cars the Ace, Lark and Bermuda, the company was now intent on being "imaged" as a truck-maker and had the Station Wagon renamed and certified as a truck.

I.D. DATA: Serial number located on right side of dash under hood; on front frame cross member; on left floor riser in back of driver's seat. Serial numbers began with "55" (1955) or "54" (1954 Carryover) followed by three digits designating a specific model. Next came a hyphen and four or five digits indicating production sequence. Starting: (all models) 5001. Ending: numbers are not available. A typical serial number looked like this: 55268-5001. The "55268" designated 1955 Model 6-226 Pickup with 118 in. w.b and the "5001" was the beginning sequential number.
   Engine numbers located on right side of cylinder block; stamped on water pump boss on front of cylinder block.

NOTE: On most Jeep models the engine and serial numbers are the same. Prior to 1955, the "ballpark" production total for each model can be estimated by subtracting the starting sequential number from the ending sequential number. After 1955, ending sequential numbers are not available.

Model	Body Type	Price	Weight	Prod. Total
Willys Jeep — (4x4) — (4-cyl.)				
CJ-3B	Jeep	1411	2134	—
CJ-5	Jeep	1476	2164	—
Jeep Trucks — (4x2) — (4-cyl.)				
475	Sedan Dely.	1494	2786	—
475	Utility Wagon	1748	3009	—
Jeep Trucks — (4x2) — (6-cyl.)				
685	Sedan Dely.	1545	2633	—
Jeep Trucks — (4x4) — (6-cyl.)				
6-226	Sedan Dely. (104.5 in.)	2036	3055	—
6-226	Chassis & Cab (118 in.)	1833	2782	—
6-226	Pickup (118 in.)	1927	3141	—
6-226	Platform Stake (118 in.)	1992	3355	—
Jeep Trucks — (4x2) — (6-cyl.)				
6-226	Sedan Dely.	1584	2890	—
6-226	Utility Wagon	1837	3113	—

ENGINE (CJ-3B/CJ-5): Inline. F-head. Four-cylinder. Cast iron block. Bore & stroke: 3⅛ in. x 4⅜ in. Displacement: 134.2 cu. in. Compression ratio: 6.9:1. Brake horsepower: 70 at 4000 R.P.M. Net horsepower: 15.63. Max. Torque: 114 lbs. ft. at 2000 R.P.M. Three main bearings. Solid valve lifters. Carburetor: Carter YF model 938S or 938SA one-barrel.

ENGINE (Model 475): Inline. F-head. Four-cylinder. Cast iron block. Bore & stroke: 3⅛ in. x 4⅜ in. Displacement: 134.2 cu. in. Compression ratio: 7.4:1. Brake horsepower: 72 at 4000 R.P.M. Net horsepower: 15.63. Max. Torque: 114 lbs. ft. at 2000 R.P.M. Three main bearings. Solid valve lifters. Carburetor: Carter YF model 951S one-barrel.

ENGINE (Model 685): Inline. F-head. Six-cylinder. Cast iron block. Bore & stroke: 3⅛ in. x 3½ in. Displacement: 161.5 cu. in. Compression ratio: 7.6:1. Brake horsepower: 90 at 4200 R.P.M. Net horsepower: 23.4. Max. Torque: 135 lbs. ft. at 2000 R.P.M. Four main bearings. Solid valve lifters. Carburetor: Carter YF model 924S or 2071S one-barrel.

ENGINE (6-226): Inline. Six-cylinder. Cast iron block. Bore & stroke: 3-5/16 in. x 4⅜ in. Displacement: 226.2 cu. in. Compression ratio: 6.86:1. Brake horsepower: 115 at 3650 R.P.M. Net horsepower: 26.3. Max. Torque: 190 lbs. ft. at 1800 R.P.M. Four main bearings. Solid valve lifters. Carburetor: Carter WDG model 2052S or 2052SA one-barrel.

CHASSIS (CJ-5): Wheelbase: 81 in. Length: 135½ in. Height: 69½ in. Front and rear tread: 48-7/16 in. Tires: 6.00 x 16 in.

CHASSIS (Other Models): See 1954 chassis data.

TECHNICAL (CJ-5): Synchromesh transmission. Speeds: 3F/1R (w/two-speed transfer case). Floor-mounted gearshift lever. Single dry plate clutch with torsional dampening, 72 sq. in. area. Full-floating hypoid front axle. Semi-floating hypoid rear axle. Overall ratio: 5.38:1. Bendix hydraulic 9 in. drum brakes. Five 4.50 x 16 five-stud disc wheels.

TECHNICAL (Other Models): See 1954 technical data.

OPTIONS (CJ-5): Five metal and fabric-top options. Ventilating windshield. Power-take-off. Eight body color choices. Approved snow plow. Winch. 36 x 39¾ in. all-steel cargo box.

OPTIONS (Other Models): See previous option data for 1955 and earlier models.

HISTORICAL: Introduced: (CJ-3B/"685") Oct. 11, 1954; (CJ-5) Nov. 12, 1954; ("475") May 26, 1955; (6-226 w/118 inch wheelbase) Oct. 11, 1954; (other 6-226) May 26, 1955. Calendar year registrations: (Trucks) 16,811; (Jeeps) 10,441. Calendar year production: (commercial vehicles) 78,922. This included 47,432 Jeeps. Innovations: Restyled CJ-5, (short wheelbase) and CJ-6 (long wheelbase) Willys Jeeps introduced. Also new 4x2 Dispatcher, a Jeep-like vehicle with the L-head four-cylinder engine, bows Oct. 26, 1955 as a 1956 model. History Notes: Willys withdrew as a U.S. auto-maker in 1955. The Jeep was now the company's mainstay product. In Dec. 1955 the one-millionth Willys commercial vehicle made since World War II was produced. Approximately 46 percent of the company's 1955 commercial units had four-cylinder power plants. Eighty-six percent of Jeep output in calendar 1955 was for the civilian market. Effective with Willy's withdrawal from the passenger car market, sources such as the NADA and National Market Reports began listing Jeep Station Wagons with trucks, sometimes referring to them as "Utility Wagon" models. We will follow this practice in this catalog.

Pricing

	5	4	3	2	1
1955					
Jeep Series (4x4)					
CJ-3B	890	1770	2950	4150	5900
CJ-5	920	1850	3050	4300	6100
Jeep Trucks (4x2)					
Sedan Dely.	620	1230	2050	2900	4100
Utility Wagon	630	1250	2100	3000	4200
Jeep Trucks (4x4)					
Sedan Dely.	680	1350	2250	3150	4500
1-Ton Pickup	540	1080	1800	2500	3600
1-Ton Stake	470	950	1550	2200	3100

NOTE: Add 3 percent for 6-cyl. trucks (not avail. in CJ models).

1956 WILLYS-OVERLAND

WILLYS — JEEP SERIES — (ALL-ENGINES): — The big news from Willys this season was a new 4x4 Jeep called the CJ-6 and a new line of Jeep-like 4x2 models named Dispatchers. The CJ-6 was a stretched version of last year's new CJ-5. Like that model, it had the more aesthetically pleasing curved hood and fenders along with a slightly curved windshield header. There was a 20 inch longer wheelbase. The pickup box was also lengthened — enough to add twin benches along the inner side walls and provide room for up to eight people. The new Dispatcher was designated the DJ-3A model. It had the old-style straight front fenders and seven vertical slots in its grille. The front axle was a solid I-beam type. This was the predecessor of the DJ-5 postal Jeep. It came in open, soft-top and hardtop models. Also new for 1955 was the addition of sedan delivery, utility wagon and pickup models with a four-cylinder engine and 4x4 running gear. By this time, some models were wearing the "Jeep" name instead of the "Willys" name. The CJ-3B said Willys on the grille and hoodsides. The CJ-5, CJ-6 and DJ-3A said Jeep on the sides of the cowl. The trucks with 4x4 running gear said "4-Wheel-Drive" on the side of the hood near the cowl. Four different engines were standard in specific models.

I.D. DATA: Serial number located on right side of dash under hood; on front frame cross member; on left floor riser in back of driver's seat. Engine numbers located on right side of cylinder block; stamped on water pump boss on front of cylinder block.

NOTE: On most Jeep models the engine and serial numbers are the same.

Model	Body Type	Price	Weight	Prod. Total
Willys Jeep — (4x4) — (4-cyl.)				
CJ-3B	Open Body	1615	2134	—
CJ-5	Open Body	1693	2164	—
CJ-6	Open Body	1857	2305	—
Dispatcher — (4x2) — (4-cyl.)				
DJ-3A	Basic	1205	1968	—
DJ-3A	Canvas Top	1261	2016	—
DJ-30A	Hardtop	1397	2205	—
Jeep Trucks — (4x2) — (4-cyl.)				
475	Utility Wagon	2012	2944	—
475	Sedan Dely.	1700	2746	—
Jeep Trucks — (4x2) — (6-cyl.)				
L6-226	Utility Wag.	2118	3057	—
L6-226	Sedan Dely.	2311	2859	—
Jeep Trucks — (4x4) — (4-cyl.)				
475	Sedan Dely.	2114	2951	—
475	Sta. Wag.	2287	3174	—
475	Pickup	1997	3065	—
Jeep Trucks — (4x4) — (6-cyl.)				
L6-226	Sedan Dely.	2176	3055	—
L6-226	Sta. Wag.	2250	3278	—
L6-226	Pickup	2187	3176	—
L6-226	Stake	2118	3341	—

ENGINE (CJ-3B/CJ-5): Inline. F-head. Four-cylinder. Cast iron block. Bore & stroke: 3⅛ in. x 4⅜ in. Displacement: 134.2 cu. in. Compression ratio: 6.9:1. Brake horsepower: 70 at 4000 R.P.M. Net horsepower: 15.63. Max. Torque: 114 lbs. ft. at 2000 R.P.M. Three main bearings. Solid valve lifters. Carburetor: Carter YF model 938S or 938SA one-barrel.

ENGINE (CJ-6/475): Inline. F-head. Four-cylinder. Cast iron block. Bore & stroke: 3⅛ in. x 4⅜ in. Displacement: 134.2 cu. in. Compression ratio: 7.4:1. Brake horsepower: 72 at 4000 R.P.M. Net horsepower: 15.63. Max. Torque: 114 lbs. ft. at 2000 R.P.M. Three main bearings. Solid valve lifters. Carburetor: Carter YF model 938S/938SA one-barrel.

ENGINE (DJ-3): Inline. L-head. Four-cylinder. Cast iron block. Bore & stroke: 3⅛ in. x 4⅜ in. Displacement: 134 cu. in. Compression ratio: 7.4:1. Brake horsepower: 75 at 4000 R.P.M. Net horsepower: 15.63. Max. Torque: 114 lbs. ft. at 2000 R.P.M. Three main bearings. Solid valve lifters. Carburetor: Carter YF model 2392S one-barrel.

ENGINE (6-226): Inline. L-head. Six-cylinder. Cast iron block. Bore & stroke: 3-5/16 in. x 4⅜ in. Displacement: 226.2 cu. in. Compression ratio: 6.86:1. Brake horsepower: 115 at 3650 R.P.M. Net horsepower: 26.3. Max. Torque: 190 lbs. ft. at 1800 R.P.M. Four main bearings. Solid valve lifters. Carburetor: Carter WDG model 2052S or 2052SA one-barrel; Carter WCD model 2204S two-barrel.

CHASSIS (CJ-6): Wheelbase: 101 in. Length: 155½ in. Height: 68¼ in. Front and rear tread: 48-7/16 in. Tires: 6.00 x 16 in. all-service type.

CHASSIS (DJ-3): Wheelbase: 80.09 in. Length: 125.45 in. Height: 62.74 in. (windshield raised). Front and rear tread: 48.25 in. Tires: 6.50 x 15 four-ply tubeless.

CHASSIS (Other Models): See 1954-1955 chassis data for the same models.

TECHNICAL (Basic, all models): Synchromesh transmission. Speeds: 3F/1R. Floor-mounted gearshift lever. Single plate clutch. Hypoid semi-floating rear axle. Overall ratio: 3.54:1, 4.56:1 or 5.38:1. Four-wheel hydraulic brakes. Disc wheels.

NOTES: 4x4 models have two-speed transfer case.
4x2 models have I-beam type front axle.
4x4 models have full-floating hypoid front axle.

OPTIONS (CJ-6): All-weather canvas tops. New body colors. Oversize tires.

OPTIONS (DJ-3A): Convertible top. 40 cu. ft. hardtop with rippled fiberglass roof and 36 in. wide gate opening. Whitewall tires. Chrome wheel discs. Chrome front bumper. Chrome rear bumper. Eight standard body colors. "Law Enforcement" package.

OPTIONS (All Carryover Models): See previous data.

HISTORICAL: Introduced: Aug. 17, 1955 except Dispatcher, which bowed Oct. 26, 1955. Calendar year registrations: 23,488 (all trucks and Jeeps). Innovations: new 1956 Dispatcher model available with canvas top or fiberglass roof with sliding doors, as well as basic open model. History Notes: The 60 horsepower L-head four-cylinder engine was called the "Go-Devil" power plant.

Pricing

	5	4	3	2	1
1956					
Jeep Series (4x4)					
CJ-3B	890	1770	2950	4150	5900
CJ-5	920	1850	3050	4300	6100
CJ-6	830	1650	2750	3850	5500
Dispatcher Series (4x2)					
Open Jeep	800	1600	2650	3700	5300
Canvas Top	830	1650	2750	3850	5500
Hardtop	850	1700	2850	4000	5700
Jeep Trucks (4x2)					
Utility Wagon	650	1300	2150	3050	4300
Sedan Dely.	630	1250	2100	3000	4200

678

	5	4	3	2	1
Jeep Trucks (4x4)					
Sedan Dely.	690	1380	2300	3200	4600
Sta. Wag.	720	1450	2400	3300	4800
Pickup	600	1200	2000	2800	4000
1-Ton Pickup	540	1080	1800	2500	3600
1-Ton Stake	470	950	1550	2200	3100

NOTE: Add 3 percent for 6-cyl. trucks (not avail. in Jeeps).

1957 WILLYS-OVERLAND

1957 Willys-Overland, Jeep FC-150 Universal (SM)

WILLYS — JEEP SERIES — (ALL-ENGINES): — The major innovation of 1957 was the introduction of the Forward Control Jeep, a vehicle that basically resembles the cab of a modern van with a pickup or stake body behind it. This was a cab-over-engine truck. There were actually several passenger-van prototypes done by famed industrial designer Brooks Stevens. One of these is said to survive on the island estate of Henry Kaiser. The production versions came as the FC-150, a ¾-tonner on an 81 inch wheelbase and the FC-170, a one-tonner with 103½ inch wheelbase. The two L-6 engines were used as power plants with 72 h.p. in the FC-150 and 115 h.p. in the FC-170. Jeep type products available this year included the CJ-3B, CJ-5 and CJ-6, none having significant changes, plus the three Dispatcher models. Trucks continued to offer the 1954 style grille. The only really new models were 4x4s in chassis-with-windshield and chassis-with-flat face-cowl configurations. However, the line was greatly expanded through engine, running gear and wheelbase selections, to 13 models with four-wheel-drive (4x4) and four with conventional drive (4x2); a total of 15 models not counting Jeeps or Forward Control models.

I.D. DATA: Serial number located on right side of dash under hood; on front frame cross-member; on left floor riser in back of driver's seat. Engine numbers located on right side of cylinder block; stamped on water pump boss on front of cylinder block.

NOTE: On most Jeep models the engine and serial numbers are the same.

Model	Body Type	Price	Weight	Prod. Total
Willys Jeep — (4x4) — (4-cyl.)				
CJ-3B	Jeep	1799	2132	—
CJ-5	Jeep	1886	2163	—
CJ-6	Jeep	2068	2225	—
Dispatcher — (4x2) — (4-cyl.)				
DJ-3A	Basic	1303	1709	—
DJ-3A	SoftTop	1363	1769	—
DJ-3A	Hardtop	1511	2004	—
Jeep Trucks — (4-cyl.)				
F4-134	Delivery (4x2)	1843	2746	—
F4-134	Utility Wagon (4x2)	2152	2944	—
F4-134	Delivery (4x4)	2391	2895	—
F4-134	Pickup (4x4)	2256	3065	—
Forward Control				
FC-150	Chassis & Cab (4x4)	2217	2764	—
FC-150	Pickup (4x4)	2320	3020	—
FC-150	Stake (4x4)	2410	3187	—
Jeep Trucks — (6-cyl.) — (104.5 in. w.b.)				
L6-226	Chassis (4x4)	1822	1963	—
L6-226	Chassis & F.F. Cowl (4x4)	2122	2140	—
L6-226	Dely. (4x4)	2505	3008	—
L6-226	Utility Wag. (4x4)	2265	3057	—
L6-226	Dely. (4x2)	1958	2859	—
L6-226	Utility Wag. (4x2)	2764	3206	—

Model	Body Type	Price	Weight	Prod. Total
(118 in w.b.)				
L6-226	Chassis (4x4)	1824	2127	—
L6-226	Chassis & F.F. Cowl (4x4)	2124	2237	—
L6-226	Chassis w/W.S. (4x4)	2150	2256	—
L6-226	Chassis & Cab (4x4)	2251	2817	—
L6-226	Pickup (4x4)	2370	3176	—
L6-226	Stake (4x4)	2453	3341	—
Forward-Control				
FC-170	Chassis & Cab (4x4)	2593	2901	—
FC-170	Pickup (4x4)	2713	3331	—
FC-170	Stake (4x4)	2896	3564	—

ENGINE (CJ-3B/CJ-5): Inline. F-head. Four-cylinder. Cast iron block. Bore & stroke: 3⅛ in. x 4⅜ in. Displacement: 134.2 cu. in. Compression ratio: 6.9:1. Brake horsepower: 70 at 4000 R.P.M. Net horsepower: 15.63. Max. Torque: 114 lbs. ft. at 2000 R.P.M. Three main bearings. Solid valve lifters. Carburetor: Carter YF model 938S or 938SA.

ENGINE (CJ6/F4-134): Inline. F-head. Four-cylinder. Cast iron block. Bore & stroke: 3⅛ in. x 4⅜ in. Displacement: 134.2 cu. in. Compression ratio: 7.4:1. Brake horsepower: 72 at 4000 R.P.M. Net horsepower: 15.63. Max. Torque: 114 lbs. ft. at 2000 R.P.M. Three main bearings. Solid valve lifters. Carburetor: Carter YF model 938S/938SA one-barrel.

ENGINE (FC-150): Inline. L-head. Four-cylinder. Cast iron block. Bore & stroke: 3⅛ in. x 4⅜ in. Displacement: 134.2 cu. in. Compression ratio: 7.40:1. Brake horsepower: 72 at 4000 R.P.M. Net horsepower: 15.63. Max. Torque: 114 lbs. ft. at 2000 R.P.M. Three main bearings. Solid valve lifters. Carburetor: Carter YF model 2392S one-barrel.

ENGINE (6-226/FC-170): Inline. L-head. Six-cylinder. Cast iron block. Bore & stroke: 3-5/16 in. x 4⅜ in. Displacement: 226.2 cu. in. Compression ratio: 6.86:1. Brake horsepower: 115 at 3650 R.P.M. Net horsepower: 26.3. Max. Torque: 190 lbs. ft. at 1800 R.P.M. Four main bearings. Solid valve lifters. Carburetor: Carter WDG model 2052S or 2052SA one-barrel; Carter WC model 2204S two-barrel.

CHASSIS (FC-150): Wheelbase: 81 in. Length: 147½ in. Height: 77⅜ in. Front tread: 48¼ in. Rear tread: 48¼ in. Tires: 7.00 x 15 in. four-ply All-Service.

CHASSIS (FC-170): Wheelbase: 103⅝ in. Length: 203 in. Height: 79⅛ in. Front tread: 63½ in. Rear tread: 63½ in. Tires: 7.00 x 16 in. six-ply.

CHASSIS (All Carryover Models): See previous data for comparable models.

TECHNICAL (FC-150/FC-170): Synchromesh transmission. Speeds: 3F/1R (four-speed optional). Floor-mounted gearshift lever. Single dry plate (heavy-duty on FC-170) clutch (FC-150) Semi-floating hypoid. (FC-170) full-floating hypoid rear axle. Overall ratio: (FC-150) 5.38:1. (FC-170) 4.89:1. Four wheel hydraulic (heavy-duty on FC-170) brakes. Disc wheels. (dual rear on FC-170).

TECHNICAL (All Carryover Models): See previous data for comparable models.

OPTIONS (FC-150/FC-170): Fresh air heater. Radio. Tu-tone paint. Front bumper guards. Direction signals. E-Z eye glass. Windshield washer. Front air vent. Double passenger seat. Oil bath air cleaner. Oil filter. High altitude cylinder head (no charge). Four-speed transmission. Power-Lok differential. Heavy-duty rear axle. Heavy-duty springs and shocks. Transmission brake. Hot climate radiator. Power-take-off (center and rear). Governor. Various size/type tires. Draw bar. Stabilizer bar. Rear bumperettes. Selective drive hubs. Bed and/or front mount winch. Snow plow. Dozer blade. Wrecker equipment. Jeep-A-Trench. Service bodies.

OPTIONS (All Carryover Models): See previous data for comparable models.

HISTORICAL: Introduced: (FC-150) Nov. 27, 1956; (FC-170) May 20, 1957; (Others) Aug. 16-17, 1956. Calendar year registrations: 22,005 (all Trucks and Jeeps). Innovations: Forward-control Jeeps (FC-150 and FC-170) introduced. New Continental type L-head six derived from Kaiser passenger car line. History notes: A special Civil Defense rescue truck and Cargo/Personnel Carrier — both with 4x4 running gear — were marketed this year. A military version of the long wheelbase CJ6 was the M-170, a ¼-ton 4x4 front line ambulance.

Pricing

	5	4	3	2	1
1957					
Jeep Series (4x4)					
CJ-3B	890	1770	2950	4150	5900
CJ-5	920	1850	3050	4300	6100
CJ-6	830	1650	2750	3850	5500
Dispatcher Series (4x2)					
Open Jeep	800	1600	2650	3700	5300
Softtop	830	1650	2750	3850	5500
Hardtop	850	1700	2850	4000	5700
Jeep Trucks (4x2)					
Dely.	630	1250	2100	3000	4200
Utility Wagon	650	1300	2150	3050	4300

	5	4	3	2	1
Jeep Trucks (4x4)					
Dely.	690	1380	2300	3200	4600
Pickup	720	1450	2400	3300	4800
Utility Wagon	600	1200	2000	2800	4000
1-Ton Pickup	540	1080	1800	2500	3600
1 Ton Stake	470	950	1550	2200	3100
Forward Control (4x4)					
¾-Ton Pickup	750	1500	2500	3500	5000
¾-Ton Stake	720	1450	2400	3300	4800
1-Ton Pickup	690	1380	2300	3200	4600
1-Ton Stake	660	1320	2200	3100	4400

NOTE: Add 3 percent for 6-cyl. trucks (not avail. in Jeep)

1958 WILLYS-OVERLAND

1958 Willys-Overland, Jeep FC-170 (DFW)

WILLYS — JEEP SERIES — (ALL-ENGINES): — After several years of (for Jeep) major changes, 1958 was the time to settle back and make minor refinements in styling, marketing and pricing. All models, except wagons, deliveries and pickups, now had one-piece windshields. No longer cataloged, except in one one-ton series and the "FC" series, were "chassis" type configurations. The four-cylinder Utility Wagon was made available with 4x4 running gear. In addition, most prices were around $100 to $110 higher.

I.D. DATA: Serial number located on right side of dash under hood; on front frame cross-member; on left floor riser in back of driver's seat. Engine numbers located on right side of cylinder block; stamped on water pump boss on front of cylinder block.

NOTE: On most Jeep models the engine and serial numbers are the same.

Model	Body Type	Price	Weight	Prod. Total
Willys Jeep — (4x4) — (4-cyl.)				
CJ-3B	¼-Ton Jeep	1888	2132	—
CJ-5	¼-Ton Jeep	1979	2163	—
CJ-6	¼-Ton Jeep	2171	2225	—
Dispatcher — (4x2) — (4-cyl.)				
DJ-3A	¼-Ton Basic	1367	1709	—
DJ-3A	¼-Ton Soft Top	1430	1769	—
DJ-3A	¼-Ton Hardtop	1586	2004	—
Jeep Trucks — (4-cyl.)				
FA-134	½-Ton Dely. (4x2)	1934	2746	—
FA-134	½-Ton Utility Wagon (4x2)	2152	2944	—
4F-134	½-Ton Dely. (4x4)	2510	2893	—
4F-134	½-Ton Utility Wagon (4x4)	2654	3093	—
4F-134	1-Ton Pickup (4x4)	2367	3065	—
Forward Control				
FC-150	¾-Ton Chassis (4x4)	2327	2764	—
FC-150	¾-Ton Pickup (4x4)	2444	3020	—
FC-150	¾-Ton Stake (4x4)	2545	3187	—
Jeep Trucks — (6-cyl.) — (104.5 in. w.b.)				
L6-226	½-Ton Dely. (4x2)	2055	2859	—
L6-226	½-Ton Utility Wagon (4x2)	2265	3057	—
L6-226	½-Ton Dely. (4x4)	2630	3008	—
L6-226	½-Ton Utility Wagon (4x4)	2764	3206	—
(118 in. w.b.)				
L6-226	1-Ton Chassis & Cab	2363	2817	—
L6-226	1-Ton Pickup	2488	3176	—
L6-226	1-Ton Stake	2575	3341	—
Forward Control				
FC-170	Chassic & Cab (4x4)	2722	2901	—
FC-170	Pickup (4x4)	2858	3331	—
FC-170	Stake (4x4)	3065	3200	—

ENGINES: Same as comparable 1957 models. See 1957 engine specifications.

CHASSIS (Jeep): Wheelbase: (CJ3) 80 in.; (CJ5) 81 in.; (CJ6) 101 in. Length: (CJ3B) 129⅞ in.; (CJ5) 135½ in.; (CJ6) 155½ in. Height: (CJ3) 67¾ in.; (CJ5) 69½ in.; (CJ6) 68¼ in. Front tread: 48-7/16 in. Rear tread: 48-7/16 in. Tires: 6.00 x 16. four-ply.

CHASSIS (Dispatcher): Wheelbase: 80.09 in. Length: 125.45 in. Height: 62.74 in. Front tread: 55¼ in. Rear tread: 57 in. Tires: 6.40 x 15 in.

CHASSIS (Trucks): Wheelbase: (SWB) 104½ in.; (LWB) 118 in. Length: (SWB) 176.2 in.; (LWB) 183.7 in. Height: (SWB) 72.1 in.; (LWB) 74.3 in. Front tread: (SWB) 57 in.; (LWB) 57 in. (except 1-ton). Rear tread: (SWB) 57 in.; (LWB) 63.5 in. (except one-ton). Tires: 6.70 x 15; 7.00 x 15; 7.00 x 16 (4x4).

CHASSIS (FC-150): Wheelbase: 81 in. Length: 147.3 in. Height: 78 in. Front tread: 57 in. Rear tread: 57 in. Tires: 7.00 x 15 four-ply.

CHASSIS (FC-170): Wheelbase: 103½ in. Length: 181.4 in. Height: 79.4 in. Front tread: 63.4 in. Rear tread: 63.8 in. Tires: 7.00 x 16.

TECHNICAL: (All carryover models) See previous data for comparable 1957 models.

OPTIONS: See previous data for comparable models.

HISTORICAL: Introduced: Aug. 15, 1957. Calendar year registrations: 22,523 (all trucks and Jeeps). Innovations: One-piece windshield on all models. History notes: The JA-3CB was a unique Jeep variant available in Argentina this year. It had built-in step plates, chrome bumpers, chrome "bottle cap" wheel covers, a convertible top and detachable doors. This 4x2 was not marketed in the U.S.

Pricing

1958	5	4	3	2	1
Jeep Series (4x4)					
CJ-3B	890	1770	2950	4150	5900
CJ-5	920	1850	3050	4300	6100
CJ-6	830	1650	2750	3850	5500
Dispatcher Series (4x2)					
Open Jeep	800	1600	2650	3700	5300
Soft Top	830	1650	2750	3850	5500
Hard Top	850	1700	2850	4000	5700
Jeep Trucks (4x2)					
Delivery	630	1250	2100	3000	4200
Utility Wag.	650	1300	2150	3050	4300
Jeep Trucks (4x4)					
Delivery	690	1380	2300	3200	4600
Utility Wag.	600	1200	2000	2800	4000
1-Ton Pickup	540	1080	1800	2500	3600
1-Ton Stake	470	950	1550	2200	3100
Forward Control (4x4)					
¾-Ton Pickup	750	1500	2500	3500	5000
¾-Ton Stake	720	1450	2400	3300	4800
1-Ton Pickup	690	1380	2300	3200	4600
1-Ton Stake	660	1320	2200	3100	4400

NOTE: Add 3 percent for 6-cyl. trucks (not available in Jeeps).

1959 WILLYS-OVERLAND

1959 Willys-Overland, Jeep FC-170 (DFW)

680

WILLYS — JEEP SERIES — (ALL-ENGINES): — New this season was a surrey-top version of the Dispatcher named the Surrey. It was similar to the Jeep Gala, an export model available for rental at beach front resorts. Features included a fringed-and-striped surrey top, chrome bumpers, wheel discs and other bright trim. The striped top came in pink, green or blue contrasted with white. Some model lineups were also shuffled around or trimmed a bit. Along with names like "Surrey" and "Gala," some traditional models got new two-tone trim packages with names. The two-wheel-drive station wagon was called the "Maverick." This was probably related to Kaiser Industries being a sponsor of James Garner's T.V. western series called "Maverick." Jeep stylists also turned out the "Harlequin," an all-steel wagon with special trim including Kaiser's three-diamond logo on the doors. On the Maverick wagon, the main body below the bright metal beltline molding was done in contrasting color. The contrasting section continued onto the front fendersides in the form of a matching inverted triangle, also trimmed with bright moldings. The "greenhouse" was then done in a color that matched the insert panel.

I.D. DATA: Serial number located on right side of dash under hood; on front frame cross- member; on left floor riser in back of driver's seat. Engine numbers located on right side of cylinder block; stamped on water pump boss on front of cylinder block.

NOTE: On most Jeep models the engine and serial numbers are the same.

Model	Body Type	Price	Weight	Prod. Total
Jeep — (4x4) — (4-cyl.)				
CJ-3B	Jeep	1888	2132	—
CJ-5	Jeep	1976	2163	—
CJ-6	Jeep	2171	2225	—
Dispatcher — (4x2) — (4-cyl.)				
DJ-3A	Soft Top	1430	1769	—
DJ-3A	Hardtop	1586	2004	—
Jeep Trucks — (4-cyl.)				
F4-134	Delivery Chassis (4x2)	1582	1855	—
F4-134	Utility Delivery (4x2)	1934	2746	—
F4-134	Utility Delivery (4x4)	2510	2893	—
F4-134	Pickup (4x4)	2368	3065	—
Forward-Control				
FC-150	Chassis & Cab (4x4)	2416	2764	—
FC-150	Pickup (4x4)	2533	3024	—
FC-150	Stake (4x4)	2634	3187	—
Jeep Trucks — (6-cyl.) — (104.5 inch short wheelbase)				
L6-226	Utility Dely. (4x2)	2055	2859	—
L6-226	Utility Wagon (4x2)	2378	3057	—
L6-226	Utility Delivery (4x4)	2630	3008	—
L6-226	Utility Wagon (4x4)	2901	3206	—
(118 inch long wheelbase)				
L6-226	Chassis & Cab (4x4)	2363	2817	—
L6-226	Pickup (4x4)	2488	3176	—
L6-226	Stake (4x4)	2575	3341	—
Forward-Control				
FC-170	Chassis & Cab	2722	2901	—
FC-170	Pickup	2858	3331	—
FC-170	Stake	3065	3564	—

ENGINE: Same as comparable 1957 models. See 1957 engine specifications.

CHASSIS (Jeep Series): Wheelbase: (CJ-3) 80 in.; (CJ-5) 81 in.; (CJ-6) 101 in. Length: (CJ-3) 129⅞ in.; (CJ-5) 135½ in.; (CJ-6) 155½ in. Height: (CJ-3) 67¾ in.; (CJ-5) 69½ in.; (CJ-6) 68¼ in. Front tread: 48-7/16 in. Rear tread: 48-7/16 in. Tires: 6.00 x 16 in.

CHASSIS (Dispatcher Series): Wheelbase: 80.09 in. Length: 125.45 in. Height: 62.74 in. Front tread: 55¼ in. Rear tread: 57 in. Tires: 6.40 x 15 in.

CHASSIS (Jeep-Trucks): Wheelbase: (SWB) 104.5 in.; (LWB) 118 in. Length: (SWB) 176.2 in.; (LWB) 183.7 in. Height: (SWB) 72.1 in.; (LWB) 74.3 in. Front tread: (SWB) 57 in.; (LWB) 57 in. Rear tread: (SWB) 57 in.; (LWB) 63.5 in. (except 1-tons). Tires: 7.00 x 15 in. or others.

CHASSIS (Series FC-150): Wheelbase: 81 in. Length: 147.3 in. Height: 78 in. Front tread: 57 in. Rear tread: 57 in. Tires: 7.00 x 15 in.

CHASSIS (Series FC-170): Wheelbase: 103½ in. Length: 181.4 in. Height: 79.4 in. Front tread: 63.4 in. Rear tread: 63.8 in. Tires: 7.00 x 16 in. (dual rear wheels on heavy-duty models).

TECHNICAL: Same as comparable 1957 models. See 1957 technical specifications.

NEW OPTIONS: Standard and deluxe cab trim. New two-tone paint combinations. Three different color striped tops for Surrey. (Gala) Chrome front bumper. Chrome rear bumper. Chrome bumperettes. Chrome wheel discs.

OLD OPTIONS: See data for previous years. Most options were carried over at slightly higher prices.

HISTORICAL: Introduced: Fall, 1958. Calendar year registrations: (Jeeps) 10,576; (Trucks) 6000 lbs. or less — 11,920; 6001 to 10,000 lbs. — 8,130. Calendar year production: (all models, domestic) 114,881 (10.08 percent market share). Willys, worldwide sales: (Jeeps) 58,238; (Trucks) 56,643. Of this total, 50.7 percent were Jeeps. Innovations: New Surrey model. Maverick version of 4x2 station wagon introduced on May 7, 1959.

It was a dressed-up version of the base model. History notes: A Jeep fleet sales ad of this year printed a list of over 150 companies that used Jeep vehicles and said, "Known by the companies they keep . . . Jeep vehicles." E.F. Kaiser was president of Willys Motors, Inc., a subsidiary of Kaiser Industries, Corp. Willys, on Feb. 26, signed an agreement with its Brazilian affiliate to produce French Renaults in a plant near Sao Paulo. On April 6, Mitsubishi, of Japan, paid $1,790,000 for the rights to build Jeeps there. On Aug. 21, Willys of Canada began production of the CJ-5 at Windsor, Ontario. Jeeps outsold trucks on a worldwide basis this year, but trucks did better in the United States.

Pricing

	5	4	3	2	1
1959					
Jeep Series (4x4)					
CJ-3	900	1800	3000	4200	6000
CJ-5	930	1860	3100	4350	6200
CJ-6	840	1680	2800	3900	5600
Dispatcher Series (4x2)					
Soft Top	810	1620	2700	3800	5400
Hardtop	870	1750	2900	4100	5800
Jeep Trucks (4x2)					
Utility Wagon	660	1320	2200	3100	4400
Delivery	650	1300	2150	3050	4300
Jeep Trucks (4x4)					
Utility Dely.	700	1400	2350	3250	4700
Pickup	600	1200	2000	2800	4000
Utility Wag.	620	1230	2050	2900	4100
1-Ton Pickup	560	1100	1850	2600	3700
1-Ton Stake	480	975	1600	2250	3200
Forward Control (4x4)					
¾-Ton Pickup	770	1550	2550	3600	5100
¾-Ton Stake	740	1470	2450	3350	4900
1-Ton Pickup	700	1400	2350	3250	4700
1-Ton Stake	680	1350	2250	3150	4500

NOTE: Add three percent for six-cylinder trucks (not available for Jeeps). Add five percent for "Maverick."

1960 WILLYS-OVERLAND

1960 Willys-Overland, Jeep Pickup (DFW/RWC)

WILLYS — JEEP SERIES — (ALL-ENGINES): — New/body trim treatments, similar to that introduced on the mid-1959 Maverick, were now available on all Jeep-truck vehicles, except Foward Control models. (The "FC" models had their own Standard and Deluxe treatments for the "Safety-View" cab interior and body exterior). A new "Economy Delivery" truck made its appearance in the 4x2 half-ton lineup. A new Fleetvan was also developed for the U.S. Post Office.

I.D. DATA: Serial number located on right side of dash under hood; on front frame cross-member; on left floor riser in back of driver's seat. Engine numbers located on right side of cylinder block; stamped on water pump boss on front of cylinder block.

NOTE: On most Jeep models the engine and serial numbers are the same.

Model	Body Type	Price	Weight	Prod. Total
Jeep — (4x4) — (4-cyl.)				
CJ-3B	¼-Ton Jeep (80 in. w.b.)	1888	2132	—
CJ-5	¼-Ton Jeep (81 in. w.b.)	1979	2163	—
CJ-6	½-Ton Jeep (101 in. w.b.)	2171	2225	—
Dispatcher — (4x2) — (4-cyl.) — (80 in. w.b.)				
DJ-3A	¼-Ton Soft Top	1430	1769	—
DJ-3A	¼-Ton Hardtop	1586	2004	—
DJ-3A	¼-Ton Surrey	1650	1819	—
Jeep Trucks — (4x2) — (4-cyl.) — (104.5 in. w.b.)				
FA-134	½-Ton Economy Dely.	1582	1855	—
FA-134	½-Ton Sta. Wag.	1995	2858	—
FA-134	½-Ton Utility Wag.	2258	2944	—
FA-134	½-Ton Utility Dely.	1934	2746	—
Jeep Trucks — (4x4) — (4-cyl.) — (104.5 in. w.b.)				
FA-134	½-Ton Utility Wagon	2782	3093	—
FA-134	½-Ton Utility Dely.	2510	2895	—
Jeep Trucks — (4x4) — (4-cyl.) — (118 in. w.b.)				
FA-134	1-Ton Pickup	2368	3065	—
FA-134	1-Ton Stake	2455	3230	—
Forward-Control — (4x4) — (4-cyl.) — (81 in. w.b.)				
FC-150	¾-Ton Chassis & Cab	2416	2896	—
FC-150	¾-Ton Pickup	2533	3152	—
FC-150	¾-Ton Stake	2634	3319	—
Jeep Trucks — (4x2) — (6-cyl.) — (104.5 in. w.b.)				
L6-226	½-Ton Sta. Wagon	2258	2971	—
L6-226	½-Ton Utility Wagon	2378	3057	—
L6-226	½-Ton Utility Dely.	2055	2859	—
Jeep Trucks — (4x4) — (6-cyl.) — (104.5 in. w.b.)				
L6-226	½-Ton Utility Wagon	2901	3206	—
L6-226	½-Ton Utility Dely.	2630	3008	—
Jeep Trucks — (4x4) — (6-cyl.) — (118 in. w.b.)				
L6-226	1-Ton Chassis & Cab	2363	2817	—
L6-226	1-Ton Pickup	2488	3176	—
L6-226	1-Ton Stake	2575	3341	—
Forward-Control — (4x4) — (6-cyl.) — (103.5 in. w.b.)				
FC-170	1-Ton Chassis & Cab	2722	2901	—
FC-170	1-Ton Pickup	2858	3331	—
FC-170	1-Ton Stake	3065	3564	—

ENGINES: Same as comparable 1957 models. See 1957 engine specifications.

CHASSIS (CJ-3-B): Wheelbase: 80 in. Length: 129⅞ in. Height: 67¾ in. Front tread: 48-7/16. Rear tread: 48-7/16 in. Tires: 6.00 x 16 in.

CHASSIS (CJ-5): Wheelbase: 81.09 in. Length: 135.50 in. Height: 69.50 in. Front tread: 48-7/16 in. Rear tread: 48-7/16 in. Tires: 6.00 x 16 in.

CHASSIS (CJ-6): Wheelbase: 101 in. Length: 155½ in. Height: 68¼ in. Front tread: 48-7/16 in. Rear tread: 48-7/16 in. Tires: 6.00 x 16 in.

CHASSIS (DJ-3): Wheelbase: 80.1 in. Length: 125.4 in. Height: 59.8 in. Front tread: 48.2 in. Rear tread: 48.5 in. Tires: 6.50 x 15 in.

CHASSIS (Trucks w/SWB) : Wheelbase: 104.5 in. Length: 176.2 in. Height: 72.1 in. Front tread: 57 in. Rear tread: 57 in. Tires: 7.00 x 15 in. (6.70 x 15 on Station Wagon)

CHASSIS (Trucks, w/LWB): Wheelbase: 118 in. Length: 183.7 in. Height: 74.3 in. Front tread: 57 in. Rear tread: 63.5 in. Tires: 7.00 x 16 in.

CHASSIS (FC-150): Wheelbase: 81 in. Tires: 7.00 x 15 in.

CHASSIS (FC-170): Wheelbase: 103½ in. Tires: 7.00 x 16 in.

TECHNICAL: Same as comparable 1957 models. See 1957 technical specifications.

OPTIONS: See previous data on options for comparable models. Prices increased slightly.

HISTORICAL: Introduced: Fall, 1959. Calendar year registrations: (all trucks and Jeeps) 31,385. Calendar year production: (all models, domestic) 122,446. Of this total, 51.9 percent were Jeeps. Note: 71,159 Willys vehicles made in 1960 were four-cylinder models and 51,287 were six-cylinder vehicles. Innovations: Station wagons, panels get new body trim treatments. History notes: Barney Roos, who is sometimes called "The Father of the Willys Jeep," died of a heart attack in New York City. Sales of Jeep 4x4s reached an all-time high in 1960. In July 1960, Willys was awarded the first of a series of contracts to build Fleetvans for the U.S. Post Office. By Feb. 1961, the number of these units ordered rose to 6,025.

Pricing

	5	4	3	2	1
1960					
Jeep Series (4x4)					
CJ-3	900	1800	3000	4200	6000
CJ-5	930	1860	3100	4350	6200
CJ-6	840	1680	2800	3900	5600
Dispatcher Series (4x2)					
Soft Top	810	1620	2700	3800	5400
Hardtop	870	1750	2900	4100	5800
Surrey	980	1950	3250	4550	6500

	5	4	3	2	1
Jeep Trucks (4x2)					
Economy Dely.	560	1100	1850	2600	3700
Station Wagon	660	1320	2200	3100	4400
Utility Wagon	660	1320	2200	3100	4400
Utility Dely.	650	1300	2150	3050	4300
Jeep Trucks (4x4)					
Utility Wagon	620	1230	2050	2900	4100
Utility Dely.	700	1400	2350	3250	4700
1-Ton Pickup	560	1100	1850	2600	3700
1-Ton Stake	480	975	1600	2250	3200
Forward Control (4x4)					
¾-Ton Pickup	770	1550	2550	3600	5100
¾-Ton Stake	740	1470	2450	3350	4900
1-Ton Pickup	700	1400	2350	3250	4700
1-Ton Stake	680	1350	2250	3150	4500

NOTE: Add three percent for six-cylinder trucks.
Add five percent for custom two-tone trim.

1961 WILLYS-OVERLAND

1961 Willys-Overland, Jeep Station Wagon 4x4 (OCW)

WILLYS — JEEP SERIES — (ALL-ENGINES): — In 1961, Willys introduced the Fleetvan on the commercial vehicle market. It had an 80 inch wheelbase, 133 inch wheelbase overall length and 4x2 running gear. It was well-suited for multi-stop delivery work and featured sit-or-stand driving accomodations. The four-cylinder F-head engine was used. Other changes included deletion of the one-ton 4x4 stake truck with the four-cylinder engine. Also, the Surrey 4x2 Jeep was discontinued temporarily.

I.D. DATA: Serial number located on right side of dash under hood; on front frame cross-member; on left floor riser in back of driver's seat. Engine numbers located on right side of cylinder block; stamped on water pump boss on front of cylinder block.

NOTE: On most Jeep models the engine and serial numbers are the same.

Model	Body Type	Price	Weight	Prod. Total
Jeep — (4x4) — (4-cyl.)				
CJ-3B	¼-Ton Jeep (80 in. w.b.)	1890	2220	—
CJ-5	¼-Ton Jeep (81 in. w.b.)	1980	2251	—
CJ-6	¼-Ton Jeep (101 in. w.b.)	2170	2313	—
Dispatcher — (4x2) — (4-cyl.) — (80.1 in. w.b.)				
DJ-3A	¼-Ton Basic	1365	2797	—
DJ-3A	¼-Ton Soft Top	1430	1857	—
DJ-3A	¼-Ton Hardtop	1585	2092	—
Jeep Trucks — (4x2) — (4-cyl.) — (81 in. w.b.)				
FJ-3A	½-Ton Fleetvan	2380	3045	—
(104.5 in. w.b.)				
F4-134	½-Ton Economy Dely.	1580	1987	—
F4-134	½-Ton Sta. Wag.	1995	2990	—
F4-134	½-Ton Utility Wag.	2260	3076	—
F4-134	½-Ton Utility Dely.	1935	2878	—
Jeep Trucks — (4x4) - (4-cyl.) — (104.5 in. w.b.)				
F4-134	½-Ton Utility Wag.	2780	3225	—
F4-134	½-Ton Utility Dely.	2510	3025	—
(118 in. w.b.)				
F4-134	1-Ton Pickup	2365	3197	—
Forward Control — (4x4) — (4-cyl.) — (81 in. w.b.)				
FC-150	¾-Ton Chassis & Cab	2415	2884	—
FC-150	¾-Ton Pickup	2535	3140	—
FC-150	¾-Ton Platform Stake	2635	3307	—
Jeep Truck — (4x2) — (6-cyl.) — (104.5 in. w.b.)				
L6-226	½-Ton Utility Wag.	2380	3172	—
L6-226	½-Ton Utility Dely.	2055	2974	—
L6-226	½-Ton Sta. Wag.	2260	3103	—
Jeep Truck — (4x4) — (6-cyl.) — (104.5 in. w.b.)				
L6-226	½-Ton Utility Wag.	2900	3321	—
L6-226	½-Ton Utility Dely.	2630	3123	—

Model	Body Type	Price	Weight	Prod. Total
Jeep Truck — (4x4) — (6-cyl.) — (118 in. w.b.)				
L6-226	1-Ton Pickup	2490	3291	—
L6-226	1-Ton Platform Stake	2575	3456	—
L6-226	1-Ton Chassis & Cab	2365	2932	—
Forward-Control — (4x4) — (6-cyl.) — (103.5 in. w.b.)				
FC-170	1-Ton Chassis & Cab	2720	3056	—
FC-170	1-Ton Pickup	2855	3486	—
FC-170	1-Ton Platform Stake	3065	3719	—
FC-170	1-Ton Chassis & Cab (dual rear)	3395	3726	—
FC-170	1-Ton Pickup (dual rear)	3531	4156	—
FC-170	1-Ton Platform Stake (dual rear)	3835	4505	—

ENGINE (Fleetvan): Inline. F-head. Four-cylinder. Cast iron block. Bore & stroke: 3⅛ in. x 4⅜ in. Displacement: 134.2 cu. in. Compression ratio: 7.4:1. Brake horsepower: 75 at 4000 R.P.M. Net horsepower: 15.63. Max. Torque: 115 lbs. ft. at 2000 R.P.M. Three main bearings. Solid valve lifters. Carburetor: Carter model YF.

ENGINE (Carryover Models): Same as comparable 1957 models. See 1957 engine specifications.

CHASSIS (Fleetvan): Wheelbase: 81 in. Length: 154 in. Height: 90.12 in. Front tread: 48-9/16 in. Rear tread: 48-9/16 in. Tires: 6.70 x 15 four-ply tubeless.

CHASSIS (Carryover Models): See previous specifications.

TECHNICAL (Fleetvan): Synchromesh transmission. Speeds: 3F/1R. Floor-mounted gearshift lever. Single plate clutch, 72 sq. in. frictional area. I-beam front axle. Hypoid, semi-floating rear axle. Overall ratio: 4.56:1. Hydraulic 9 in. drum brakes. Four 15 x 5.00 five stud disc wheels.

TECHNICAL (Carryover Models): See previous specifications.

OPTIONS (Fleetvan): Two-tone finish. Ladder racks. Heater. Stake model available. Dual rear wheel platform stake model available in 8000 lb. GVW option.

OPTIONS (Carryover Models): See previous option lists.

HISTORICAL: Introduced: Fall, 1960. Calendar year registrations: 32,644 (all trucks and Jeeps). Calendar year production: (all models, domestic): 123,755 (10.98 percent). This included 68,116 Jeeps (55 percent) and 55,639 (45 percent) Jeep-trucks. The breakout for engine types was 72,913 four-cylinders and 50,842 six-cylinders. Innovations: Four-cylinder Perkins diesel engine made available in Universal Jeep. New "Fleetvan" multi stop delivery truck. History notes: The company set new sales records in 1961. In Canada, Willys underwent expansions including larger production facilities.

Pricing

	5	4	3	2	1
1961					
Jeep Series (4x4)					
CJ-3	920	1850	3050	4300	6100
CJ-5	950	1900	3150	4400	6300
CJ-6	850	1700	2850	4000	5700
Dispatcher Series (4x2)					
Jeep (Open)	800	1600	2650	3700	5300
Soft Top	830	1650	2750	3850	5500
Hardtop	890	1770	2950	4150	5900
Jeep Trucks (4x2)					
Fleetvan	600	1200	2000	2800	4000
Economy Dely.	570	1140	1900	2650	3800
Sta. Wag.	680	1350	2250	3150	4500
Utility Wag.	680	1350	2250	3150	4500
Utility Dely.	660	1320	2200	3100	4400
Jeep Trucks (4x4)					
Utility Wag.	630	1250	2100	3000	4200
Utility Dely.	720	1450	2400	3300	4800
1-Ton Pickup	570	1140	1900	2650	3800
1-Ton Stake	500	1000	1650	2300	3300
Forward Control (4x4)					
¾-Ton Pickup	780	1560	2600	3600	5200
¾-Ton Stake	750	1500	2500	3500	5000
1-Ton Pickup	720	1450	2400	3300	4800
1-Ton Stake	690	1380	2300	3200	4600

NOTE: Add three percent for six-cylinder trucks.

1962 WILLYS-OVERLAND

WILLYS — JEEP SERIES — (ALL-ENGINES): — For 1962, the Surrey returned as part of the Dispatcher 4x2 series. In addition, the FC-170 Series gained pickup and platform-stake models with dual rear wheels. The station wagons with either 4x2 or 4x2 running gear were now described as "Traveller" models. They could be had in solid colors or with two types of two-tone trim. One style was similar to that described for the 1959½ Maverick, except that only the roof was in contrasting color (windshield and door pillars were not). The second treatment is often described as "Rocket" style trim. With this, a contrast panel running the full-length of the bodyside was shaped somewhat like a Nike missile and the roof was finished to match it. Both 4x2 and 4x4 Travellers came with double doors in the rear, plus auxiliary passenger benches hinged to the inner sidewalls. However, the 4x2 had a carpeted cargo floor and spare tire behind the driver's seat. The 4x4 model carried its spare on the roof and had "Jeep 4-wheel Drive" lettering on the right rear door. In May 1962, a new overhead cam six-cylinder engine was introduced for Jeep vehicles. "Who put the big 6 in 62?" asked a sales brochure. The new engine was available in the Jeep Utility Wagon, Station Wagon, Pickup and Panel Delivery trucks only.

1962 Willys-Overland, Jeep CJ-6 Universal (OCW)

I.D. DATA: Serial number located on right side of dash under hood; on front frame cross-member; on left floor riser in back of driver's seat. Engine numbers located on right side of cylinder block; stamped on water pump boss on front of cylinder block.

NOTE: On most Jeep models the engine and serial numbers are the same.

Model	Body Type	Price	Weight	Prod. Total
¼-Ton Jeep — (4x4) — (4-cyl.)				
CJ-3B	Jeep (80 in. w.b.)	1960	2220	—
CJ-5	Jeep (81 in. w.b.)	2055	2251	—
CJ-6	Jeep (101 in. w.b.)	2150	2313	—
¼-Ton Dispatcher — (4x2) — (4-cyl.) — (80 in. w.b.)				
DJ-3A	Basic	1435	1797	—
DJ-3A	Soft Top	1505	1857	—
DJ-3A	Hardtop	1665	2092	—
DJ-3A	Surrey	1775	2007	—
½-Ton Fleetvan — (4x2) — (4-cyl.) — (81 in. w.b.)				
FJ-3A	Fleetvan	2380	3045	—
½-Ton Jeep Trucks — (4x2) — (4-cyl.) — (104.5 in. w.b.)				
F4-134	Economy Dely.	1695	1987	—
F4-134	Station Wagon	2095	2990	—
F4-134	Utility Wagon	N.A.	3076	—
F4-134	Utility Dely.	2005	2878	—
½-Ton Jeep Trucks — (4x4) — (4-cyl.) — (104.5 in. w.b.)				
F4-134	Utility Wagon	2885	3225	—
F4-134	Utility Dely.	2605	3025	—
1-Ton Jeep Truck — (4x4) — (4-cyl.) — (118 in. w.b.)				
F4-134	Pickup	2370	3197	—
Forward Control — (4x4) — (4-cyl.) — (81 in. w.b.)				
FC-150	¾-Ton Chassis & Cab	2505	2884	—
FC-150	¾-Ton Pickup	2625	3140	—
FC-150	¾-Ton Platform Stake	2725	3307	—
½-Ton Jeep Trucks — (4x2) — (6-cyl.) — (104.5 in. w.b.)				
L6-226	Utility Wagon	2345	3172	—
L6-226	Utility Dely.	2130	2974	—
L6-226	Station Wagon	2345	3103	—
½-Ton Jeep Trucks — (4x4) — (6-cyl.) — (104.5 in. w.b.)				
L6-226	Utility Wagon	3010	3321	—
L6-226	Utility Dely.	2730	3123	—
1-Ton Jeep Trucks — (4x4) — (6-cyl.) — (118 in. w.b.)				
L6-226	Pickup	2490	3291	—
L6-226	Platform Stake	2575	3456	—
L6-226	Chassis & Cab	2365	2932	—
Forward Control — (4x4) — (6-cyl.) — (103.5 in. w.b.)				
(single rear wheels)				
FC-170	1-Ton Chassis & Cab	2825	3056	—
FC-170	1-Ton Pickup	2960	3486	—
FC-170	1-Ton Platform Stake	3165	3719	—
(dual rear wheels)				
FC-170	1-Ton Chassis & Cab (*)	3315	3726	—
FC-170	1-Ton Chassis & Cab (**)	3525	3726	—

NOTE: (*) 8000 pounds GVW
(**) 9000 pounds GVW

ENGINE (Tornado 230): Inline. Overhead valve/overhead cam. Six-cylinder. Cast iron with extensive use of aluminum components. Bore & stroke: 3.34 x 4.38 in. Displacement: 230 cu. in. Compression ratio: 8.5:1. Brake horsepower: 140 at 4000 R.P.M. Max. Torque: 210 lbs. ft. and 1750 R.P.M. Overhead valve lifters.

ENGINE (Carryover models): Same as comparable 1957 models. See 1957 engine specifications.

1962 Willys-Overland, Jeep FC-150 Stake Bed (OCW)

1962 Willys-Overland, FC-170 Stake Bed w/dual wheels

CHASSIS: See previous chassis specifications.

TECHNICAL: See previous technical specifications.

OPTIONS: (Carryover): See previous year option lists. Jeep had a wide range of factory options for each separate model. In addition, certain aftermarket items were listed in sales literature as "Jeep Approved Special Equipment and Accessory Options." For 1962, this included steel or canvas tops for Jeep Universals, Ramsey or Koenig winches for all Jeeps, wrecker equipment for Universals, pickups and "FC" models, Meyer angle-dozers, "Jeep-A-Trench" trench-diggers, a tailgate loader for all Jeep-trucks and a convertible top for Universals.

1962 Willys-Overland, Jeep "Gala" Surrey (OCW)

1962 Willys-Overland, Jeep Traveller Station Wagon

683

1962 Willys-Overland, Jeep CJ-3B Universal (OCW)

1962 Willys-Overland, Jeep Panel Delivery (OCW)

1962 Willys-Overland, Jeep 4x4 Pickup (OCW)

1962 Willys-Overland, Jeep Fleetvan (OCW)

684

HISTORICAL: Introduced: Fall, 1961. Calendar year registrations: 30,426 (all trucks and Jeeps). Calendar year production: (All models) 85,623 (6.83 percent). Innovations: Overhead cam six-cylinder engine on May 2, 1962. This was known as the "Tornado OHC" engine. History notes: This was the last year for the Willys-Jeep. After Kaiser's purchase of Willys on April 28, 1953, the products were still called "Willys-Jeep" models. However, by 1957, the name "Jeep" alone was used on the side of the cowl and was gaining in popular useage. Then, in 1963, a running change took place. There was a totally restyled commercial vehicle series known as the "Gladiator." The earliest '63 Gladiators said only "Jeep" on the front fender sides, but before long they read "Kaiser-Jeep." (Note: In this catalog, 1963-1969 Jeeps are listed in the Kaiser section and 1970-1986 Jeeps are found in the AMC section).

1962 Willys-Overland, Jeep FC-150 Stake Bed (OCW)

1963 Willys-Overland, Jeep FC-170 Flatbed (OCW)

Pricing

	5	4	3	2	1
1962					
Jeep Series (4x4)					
CJ-3	920	1850	3050	4300	6100
CJ-5	950	1900	3150	4400	6300
CJ-6	850	1700	2850	4000	5700
Dispatcher Series (4x2)					
Basic Jeep	800	1600	2650	3700	5300
Jeep w/Soft Top	830	1650	2750	3850	5500
Jeep w/Hardtop	890	1770	2950	4150	5900
Surrey	980	1950	3250	4550	6500
Jeep Trucks (4x2)					
Fleetvan	600	1200	2000	2800	4000
Economy Dely.	570	1140	1900	2650	3800
Station Wagon	680	1350	2250	3150	4500
Utility Wagon	680	1350	2250	3150	4500
Utility Dely.	660	1320	2200	3100	4400
Jeep Trucks (4x4)					
Utility Wagon	630	1250	2100	3000	4200
Utility Dely.	720	1450	2400	3300	4800
1-Ton Pickup	570	1140	1900	2650	3800
1-Ton Stake	500	1000	1650	2300	3300
Forward Control (4x4)					
¾-Ton Pickup	780	1560	2600	3600	5200
¾-Ton Stake	750	1500	2500	3500	5000
1-Ton Pickup	720	1450	2400	3300	4800
1-Ton Stake	690	1380	2300	3200	4600

NOTE: Add three percent for 6-cyl. engine trucks.

ILLUSTRATED DIRECTORY TO ADDITIONAL LIGHT-DUTY TRUCK MANUFACTURERS

This section of *The Standard Catalog of American Light-Duty Trucks* is a directory to hundreds of additional companies that built trucks of one-ton and under capacity.

1906 Acme Delivery Wagon (JAW)

The primary list of companies included here was compiled by Professor Donald F. Wood, of the Center For World Business, School of Business, San Francisco State University. Additions were made based on photo contributions from numerous sources and advice from truck historians including: Elliott Kahn, Walter O. MacIlvain, William Pollock, Willard J. Prentice, James J. Schild, Dennis Schrimpf, Donald J. Summar, J.H. Valentine, Raymond A. Wawryzyniak and James A. Wren.

1939 American Bantam Pickup (OCW)

Much information about these makes was discovered in the *Complete Encyclopedia of Commercial Vehicles*, by G.N. Georgano, which Krause Publication's produced in 1979 (this book is currently out of print). Editor John A. Gunnell also referred to many sources contemporary to the vehicles to expand the data on the light-duty models only. Over 500 illustrations were gathered specifically for the directory.

1897 American Electric Vehicle Van (JAW)

1912 Brockway Light Delivery Wagon (JAW)

1898 Brown Touring Cart/Delivery (DPL/NAHC)

No claims are made as to the ''completeness'' of this list at this time. It represents an *extensive* effort to provide light-duty truck enthusiasts with basic information. However, the lack of previous research in this field will surely have an affect on its degree of comprehensiveness.

1901 Clark Steamer Delivery Van (JAW)

Since these "Standard Catalogs" are intended to be collectors' guides, rather than encyclopedias, major emphasis has been placed on making a great deal of information available *as soon as possible*, rather than holding up publication until every "missing link" in the chain of history is clasped. As every vehicle historian knows, tracing missing links can become a never-ending project. We feel that light-duty truck collectors need a reference source right now!

1908 Duplex Power-Wagon Stake Bed (JAW)

1938 Mack Junior Pickup (Sonny Glasbrenner)

The directory that follows is arranged with the brand names of the trucks in alphabetical order. This makes the material self-indexing, so that users can readily find information on a certain make they wish to read about. Photos

are captioned according to either contemporary sources or facts supplied by the contributors. Credits are given in code form, explained elsewhere in this catalog, or in the form of first initial and surname where space permitted.

1937 Mack Junior Cab Express (DFW)

A possibility exists that some trucks shown are models above one-ton capacity. This may occur when we had only one photo of a given make, or where the information provided with a photograph was sketchy. In most cases, the photo of a large truck will be very similar, in appearance, to the same company's one-ton model and possibly even smaller models. Thus, they will still be most useful as an identification aid.

1902 New Era Commercial Runabout (DPL)

We have avoided classifying any makes with terms such as "minor," "obscure," or "miscellaneous." Certainly, some of the makes in Section One may have been produced for a smaller period of time, or in lesser quantities, than other brands included in this section. The determination of which trucks went where was based strictly on the amount of data available (from contributors we worked with) at publication. It is our sincere hope that this catalog will be received well enough to allow future printings in which more makes will be added to both sections.

Note that no attempt has been made to provide current prices for models in the directory. Most trucks found here do not show up frequently in the collector's marketplace, where repeated sales determine "fair market" values. Then, too, research has not been carried far enough to estimate prices based on similarities with other trucks of like rarity, size and body style. Certainly, an honest effort could have been made to appraise *some* of these trucks, but it was decided not to do this on a piecemeal basis.

1900 Riker Delivery Van

1911 Rovan Light Delivery Wagon (JAW)

Another thing that's been avoided is formulating lots of confusing classifications to limit our coverage. The thinking here is that most collectors have a wide span of interests and will consider any "extra" information a bonus. As a result, many types of commercial vehicles — taxis, station wagons, funeral cars, ambulances and utilities — will be discussed. However, we have tried to avoid duplicating coverage of any models listed in our "car catalogs." Checker and Yellow Cab come to mind as examples of makes we have previously researched for the other books and are not included here.

1936 Stewart 1-Ton Panel Delivery (S. Glasbrenner)

1911 Torbenson Auto Delivery Wagon (JAW)

If you find this catalog interesting, please spread the word that a comprehensive guide for light-duty truck collectors has finally arrived. Should you want to know more about trucks, some of the "current works" mentioned in the bibliography may be helpful. We also recommend membership in groups such as the Antique Truck Historical Society, Antique Truck Club of America, Light-Commercial Vehicle Club, Professional Car Society, Society for the Preservation of Antique Motorized Fire Apparatus in America, the Emergency Vehicle Collectors Club or numerous other organizations. For up-to-date information about truck clubs, contact: *Old Cars Weekly*, 700 E. State St., Iola, WI 54990.

(*) With just a few exceptions (necessitated by page layout) the photos shown in this directory follow *after* the text describing their history. In cases where several companies had a common name, the photos after the first listing are of that company's products and so forth.

(**) The term "badge-engineering" applies to cases in which a manufacturer markets two or more basically similar vehicles, with only minor trim changes, under separate nameplates. For example, most Fargo and DeSoto trucks were badge-engineered Dodges.

687

ILLUSTRATED DIRECTORY

A

A.B.C. — **St. Louis, Missouri** — **(1908-1911)** — This auto manufacturer also turned out half-ton delivery vans. They were powered by two-cylinder engines.

ACASON — **Detroit, Michigan** — **(1915-1925)** — This was an assembled truck, made by the Acason Motor Truck Company. Early versions were as light as ½-ton, although the firm soon concentrated on heavier models.

ACME — **Reading, Pennsylvania** — **(1905-1906)** — The Acme Motor Car Co. also built a small delivery truck.

ACME — **Cadillac, Michigan** — **(1915-1931)** — This moderately well-known truck was available in sizes ranging from ¾-ton up to six tons. The manufacturer was named the Cadillac Auto Truck Company; then the Acme Motor Truck Company. In 1918, the firm's ¾-ton model sold for $1,290. It was powered by a Continental motor.

1926 Acme Model 21 One–Ton Flyer Express (OCW)

ACORN — **Cincinnati, Ohio** — **(1910-1912)** — This was a company that produced only light-duty models for just a few years. The Model F was ½-ton delivery with a two-cylinder gasoline engine. It sold for $1,000 in 1910 and $1,150 in 1912. Similarly-sized and engineered, the Model G was $1,200 both years. After 1912, Acorn Motor Car Co. ceased manufacturing trucks.

1925 Acme Laundry Delivery Truck (HACJ/LIAM)

1910 Acorn Commercial Car (OCW)

ADAMS — **Findlay, Ohio** — **(1910-1916)** — In 1911, Adams Bros. Co. brought out a 1500-pound Model B light delivery truck with a two-cylinder gas engine and $1,400 price tag. The one-ton Model A was also marketed through 1916 at $1,850 in chassis form or $1,900 with a delivery van body.

1925 Acme One-Ton Canopy Top w/Curtains (DFW/MG)

1912 Adams One-Ton Truck (RAW)

1914 Adams Model F Dump Truck (OCW)

1915 American Argo Model K-10 Express (OCW)

1914 Adams Model A Covered Flare Board Express (OCW)

1916 American Argo Express (OCW)

AMC/JEEP — Toledo, Ohio — (1970-1986) — Information about this make can be found in the front section of this catalog.

AMERICAN — LaFayette, Indiana — (1918) — Little is known about the firm — the American Motor Vehicle Co. — except that, for a short time, it marketed a ½-ton truck. It also built light vehicles for juveniles.

AMERICAN AUSTIN — Butler, Pennsylvania — (1930-1934) — Based on the English Austin 7, this company's truck line included coupe and panel deliveries through 1933, in which year a Bantam van was added. The panel delivery, a pickup and the ''Pony Express'' were in the 1933 line and 1934's series featured a pickup and panel delivery. All had a 14 horse-power four-cylinder engine and 75 inch wheelbase. Prices were in the $330 to $450 range and weights between 1035 and 1300 pounds were listed. About 8,558 units were built before a bankruptcy that led to reorganization under the name Austin Bantam.

1907 American Juvenile Electric Commercial Car (OCW)

AMERICAN-ARGO — Saginaw, Mich. — (1912-1918) — Also known as Argo Electric. The Argo Electric Vehicle Co. produced electric trucks in 1/2-ton and one-ton series. They were conventional machines with 40-cell batteries, shaft drive and a top speed of 16 miles-per-hour.

1931 American Austin Panel Delivery (DFW/CC)

1931 American Austin Pickup (DFW/MVMA)

1931 American Austin Model 375 Pickup (F. Alduk)

1938 American Bantam Boulevard Delivery (JAW)

1933 American Austin Service Car (OCW)

AMERICAN BANTAM — Butler, Pennsylvania — **(1937-1941)** —
Restyled by Alexis de Sakhnoffski, the Bantam reappeared in 1937. These
mini-trucks retained the Austin wheelbase and engine and came as pickups
and panels. Introductory prices of below $400 began to increase to as high
as $497 for the fancy "Boulevard Delivery" of 1938-1939. A business
coupe was also available in 1938, at $439, as was a chassis-only. The
chassis, pickup and panel survived through 1941, with slightly increased
horsepower the final two years. In 1940, Bantam also developed a quarter-ton light 4x4 for the U.S. Army, which became the prototype for
the World War II Jeep. Bantam built 2,500 military Jeeps in 1941, before
the demand out-paced its production capability. During the war, the company built two-wheel trailers, but motor vehicle manufacturing ceased.

1938 American Bantam Panel Express (WLB)

1939 American Bantam Model 60 Boulevard Delivery

1938 American Bantam Pickup (OCW)

1939 American Bantam Pickup (OCW)

1940 American Bantam Boulevard Delivery (DFW)

1940 American Bantam Boulevard Delivery (OCW)

1940 American Bantam Pickup (B. Johnson/WJP)

1940 American Bantam Pickup (F. Alduk)

ANDERSON — Anderson, Indiana — (1909-1910) — This was a high-wheeler, with chain drive and a two-cylinder engine, built by the Anderson Carriage Manufacturing Co.

1909 Anderson Model B High-Wheel Commercial (WLB)

ANN ARBOR — Ann Arbor, Michigan — (1911-1912) — The Huron River Manufacturing Company built this open delivery van, powered by a two-cylinder engine, and rated at ¾-ton.

ARGO — Saginaw, Michigan — (1911-1915) — The Argo Electric Vehicle Co. built autos and electric trucks in the ½- and one-ton sizes. For more information see the American Argo listing above.

1912 Argo Electric Canopy Top Express Truck (LIAM)

1914 Argo Model L-10 Panel Delivery Body (OCW)

1914 Argo Model K-10 Platform Stake (OCW)

1914 Argo Model K-20 Express (OCW)

ARKLA — Little Rock, Arkansas — (1965) — The Arkansas-Louisiana Gas Co. built 100 light (840-pound capacity) trucks for their own use. Cabs and hoods were made of fiberglass.

ARMLEDER — Cincinnati, Ohio — (1910-1938) — A former wagon-maker, this firm built ¾-ton to 3½-ton trucks through the 1920s and one-ton to 3½-tonner later. Early models were chain-drive fours. Worm drive appeared in 1917 and sixes in 1927. Production was 50-100 units per year. In 1928, Armleder became a division of LeBlond-Schacht.

1914 Armleder Model B Screenside Express (OCW)

ATLANTIC — Newark, N.J. — (1912-1921) — It would appear that the Atlantic Vehicle Co. and the Atlantic Electric Vehicle Co., both of Newark, were related. The second name was, apparently, adopted in 1916. Marketed in 1913 were the Model 10-C ($2,000 the chassis) which was a half-tonner and two one-tonners, the Model 1-C ($2,200 the chassis) and another (priced at $2,400 for a chassis) which had no specific model designation. All three were electric-powered. The smaller model was carried into 1915 as the 10B-10C with a slightly reduced price of $1,960 and the 1-C was sold, that year, at its original price. For 1916, the company name was changed and the product line included a 10-B-C half-ton at $1,800 and 1-A one-ton at $2,200. Insurance booklets stopped listing Atlantics for the 1917 model-year, although other sources indicate that the trucks simply continued without change until 1920. Then, a one-ton electric with chain-drive was available in 1921.

1914 Atlantic Model 10-C Covered Flare Board (OCW)

1914 Atlantic Model 1-C Covered Flare Board (OCW)

ATLAS — York, Pennsylvania — (1916-1923) — The Martin Carriage Works, of York, Pennsylvania, was formed in 1916 and brought out its first truck — a 1500-pound gasoline engined chassis — in the following year. It sold for just $750. The following season, the company name was changed to Martin Truck & Body Corporation, with headquarters remaining in York. A Model 18 ¾-tonner was produced in three chassis configurations: the 106 inch wheelbase chassis sold for $885, while the 118 and 122 inch wheelbase jobs were marketed at $935. These early Atlas trucks had 19.6 horsepower four-cylinder Lycoming engines. By 1919, prices were up to the $1,135 range. A one-tonner with a Buda engine was brought out in 1920. Two years later, the ¾-ton was dropped in favor of heavier trucks. The firm continued to manufacture until 1923 and eventually merged with Selden Motor Truck Co. The Atlas name was then dropped. Catalogs show a full line of available body styles, such as a canopied type furniture truck, vestibuled bakery delivery model and a department store delivery vehicle.

1918 Atlas With No. 938 Furniture Body (DFW/SI)

1918 Atlas 1500-Pound Bakery Delivery (OCW)

1918 Atlas 1500-pound Panel Delivery (OCW)

ATTERBURY — Buffalo, N.Y. — (1910-1935) — Started as the Buffalo truck. By 1911, a one-ton was marketed. Sales were concentrated near Buffalo. Production was low and the one-ton disappeared in the 1920s.

1914 Atterbury Model B Covered Flare Board (OCW)

AUBURN — Auburn, Indiana — (1936) — Near the end of its life, the Auburn Automobile Co., a well-known auto manufacturer built commercial chassis for ambulance and hearse bodies. Few were sold. The firm was also connected with the Stutz Pak-Age Car.

1931 Auburn-Henney Funeral Coach (OCW)

AUGLAIZE - New Bremen, Ohio — (1911-1916) — This company's light-duty trucks included the Model B ½-ton Express wagon with water-cooled two-cylinder engine. It looked like a high-wheeler with small wheels and featured featured double chain-drive and a planetary transmission. Other 1912 Agalize products were the Model C, a 1500-pound Express that sold for $1,650 and the Model D, a one-ton Express with a $2,200 price tag. In 1913, the Model B (which was actually rated for 1200-pounds, rather than an even half-ton) was continued, with the price raised $50 to $1,050. However, the "D" designation was now applied to a 3000-pound truck, rather than a 2000-pounder. In 1914, the company went to the chassis-only configuration with the Model H and Model G. The first was a 1500-pounder with two-cylinder gasoline engine priced at $1,000. The other was a $1,400 one-tonner. In 1915, the price of the Model H was dropped (remember those days?) to $950 for the chassis-only, while an Express body could be had for $990. The Model D was also continued at $1,700 for a chassis and $1,750 for the Express wagon. In Auglaize Motor Car Company's final year of truck-making, the 1916 models were marketed without alphabetical designations. They appear to have been basically the same trucks with new prices; $975 for the ¾-ton and $1,200 for the one-ton. As our photos illustrate, by 1914, some of the Auglaize models were starting to look more like true "automobiles," while others maintained the appearance of powered farm wagons.

1914 Auglaize Model G Flare Board (OCW)

1914 Auglaize Model H Flare Board (OCW)

AVERY — Peoria, Illinois — (1910-1923) — This tractor and farm equipment company built a one-ton with open cab, four-cylinders and chain-drive in 1910-1911. For 1914-1916, there was a gas-powered ¾-ton that listed for $2,000 with enclosed panel or express bodies. In the same years, there was a one-ton Model 41, priced at $1,690 for the chassis. Heavier trucks were built thereafter.

1914 Avery Model C Covered Flare (OCW)

B

BAILEY — Boston, Massachusetts — (1912-1914) — Bailey & Co. built a 300-pound-rated, battery-powered electric van based on its cyclecar. It had a 106 inch wheelbase, pneumatic tires and 20 miles-per-hour top speed. A light-duty service car was also offered.

BAKER-BELL — Philadelphia, Pennsylvania — (1913-1914) — The Baker-Bell Motor Company also built small, closed, delivery vans with capacities between 500- and 1500-pounds.

1914 Bailey Model E Cyclecar Delivery (OCW)

BARKER — Norwalk, Connecticut — (1912-1917) — This firm, the C.L. Barker Company, built larger trucks, but—for a short time—also marketed a model with half-ton capacity.

1914 Barker Model U Flare Board (OCW)

BATTRONIC — Boyertown, Pennsylvania — (1964-1978) — Battronic Truck Corp. built (or builds) step-in type vans and larger buses which are battery powered. The first models represented a joint venture between Exide Battery, Boyertown Auto Body Works and English truck-maker Smith Delivery Vehicles. Since 1969, it has been a subsidiary of Boyertown Auto Body Works, the other firms having withdrawn support. The van has a 2500-pound payload and 25 mile-per-hour top speed.

1975 Battronic Wail-in Delivery Van (OCW)

694

BAUER — Kansas City, Missouri — (1914-1917) — The Bauer Machine Works Company built trucks in the ½- to ¾-ton range. The Bauer Model A, a 1000-pound gas-powered truck, was offered in 1915-1916 as a chassis only. It was priced at $900. In 1916, it also came as a flare board express at $1,050. Added to the product line, in 1916, was the Model B. It was another half-tonner. It was also $1,050 in chassis form and $1,175 in the flare board model.

BAUER — Chicago, Illinois — (1925-1927) — P.E. Hertz, P. Bauer and A.L. Belle Isle formed this taxicab company. The Bauer cabs were very sturdily constructed and advertised as ''wreck-proof'' vehicles. They employed a four-cylinder Buda engine and had a 115 inch wheelbase. An unusual feature was a Westinghouse air-brake system.

1925 Bauer Taxicab (NAHC/DPL)

BEARDSLEY — Los Angeles, California — (1914-1915) — These battery-powered trucks were sold in the ½-ton to one-ton ranges. They were built by the Beardsley Electric Co.

1914 Beardsley Electric Express (JHV)

1914 Beardsley 750-pound Panel Delivery (JHV)

BELL — York, Pennsylvania — (1915-1918) — The Bell Motor Car Co. built both autos and trucks. In 1917, their ½-ton Model 17 sold for $825 as an open delivery and $875 as a closed delivery. It used a gasoline engine.

BERGDOLL — Philadelphia, Pennsylvania — (1910-1913) — The Louis J. Bergdoll Motor Car Company offered delivery vans on their passenger car chassis. A contemporary insurance guide described the company's 1912 model as a 1000- to 1500-pound delivery for $1,500. A truck, of similar capacity with an enclosed body, was offered in 1913. It was then called the Model C and had a $1,600 price tag.

BESSEMER — Grove City, Pennsylvania — (1911-1923) / Plainfield, New Jersey — (1923-1926) — This was primarily a heavy truck, but in some years a ¾-ton model was offered. For example, in 1918, the ¾-ton Bessemer chassis sold for $975. The Bessemer Motor Truck Company was the initial manufacturer. In its later years, the firm went through several mergers.

1914 Bessemer One-Ton Chassis (GEM/DJS)

1914 Bessemer Model C Slat Side Delivery (OCW)

1914 Bessemer Model B Covered Flare Board (OCW)

BEST — Flint, Michigan — (1912-1915) — The Durant-Dort Carriage Company built these small, 76 inch wheelbase, open and closed delivery vans.

1912 Best Panel Delivery Van (HACJ/LIAM)

1914 Best Model A Panel Body Delivery (OCW)

BEYSTER-DETROIT — Detroit, Michigan — (1910-1913) — These were light delivery trucks, mounted on a 105 inch wheelbase. They were built by the Beyster-Detroit Motor Car Co.

1911 Beyster Panel Body Delivery Van (OCW)

BIMEL — Sidney, Ohio — (1916) — A 1,000 pound (half-ton) chassis was cataloged by Bimel Buggy Co. in 1916. It was gasoline-powered and sold for $485. This firm also promoted a six-cylinder automobile which, it appears, was never actually produced. However, the Elco automobile *was* made by the same company between 1915 and 1917.

BINGHAM — Cleveland, Ohio — (1914-1915) — The Bingham Mfg. Co. offered a light-duty truck with 1250-pound capacity. Stake, panel, or open express bodies were available.

BIRCH — Chicago, Illinois — (1916-1923) — Birch Motor College, Inc., had its Model 24 truck on the market just one year — 1918. It was a half-tonner powered by a four-cylinder gas engine. The chassis was $735 and a box body model was $795. This company was connected to a technical school and its cars and trucks were assembled by students. Trucks were not listed until 1918 and may have been offered for one season only.

BLACK CROW — Chicago, Illinois — (1909-1912) / Elkhart, Indiana — (1912) — The Black Manufacturing Co., which moved to Elkhart in 1912, built high-wheeler ½-ton delivery trucks. After the move, the firm's name was Crow Motor Car Co.

BLACKER — Chillicothe, Ohio — (1910-1912) — Blackers came in sizes ranging from ½- to three-tons. They were built by John H. Blacker & Co.

BOARD — Alexandria, Virginia — (1911-1913) — These were "open panel" vehicles, in capacities ranging from 1000- to 6000-pounds, built by the B.F. Board Motor Truck Co.

BORLAND — Chicago, Illinois — (1912-1914) — The Borland-Grannis Company built electric trucks, with ¾-ton capacity.

BOSS — Reading, Pennsylvania — (1905-1906) — Powered by steam, these 1000-pound capacity delivery trucks had wheelbases of 72 inches. They were built by the Boss Knitting Machine Works, which apparently was diversifying.

BOSWORTH — Saugus, Massachusetts — (1903-1904) —Frank C. Bosworth built this 7½ horsepower, steam-powered vehicle that appears to have a large cargo box mounted at the rear. No series production seems to have ensued.

1903 Bosworth With Delivery Box Back (WLB)

BRAMWELL — Springfield, Ohio — (1905) — These were small delivery vans with a 76-inch wheelbase, built by the Springfield Auto Company.

1904 Bramwell Commercial Car Chassis (GR)

BRECHT — St. Louis, Missouri — (1904) — The Brecht Automobile Company made steam-powered automobiles and included a light delivery body in their list of offerings.

BRISCOE — Jackson, Michigan — (1915-1919) — The Briscoe Motor Corp., an auto manufacturer, offered a ½-ton truck on their passenger car chassis.

BROC — Cleveland, Ohio — (1909-1914) — These battery-powered light trucks came with either open or closed bodies. Initially, they were built by the Broc Carriage & Wagon Co. which, after some reorganizations, became the Broc Electric Car Co.

BROCKWAY — Cortland, New York — (1912-1977) — The Brockway Motor Truck Co. was primarily a manufacturer of medium- and heavy-duty trucks. But, at various times, the smallest truck in their offerings qualified for inclusion in this book. For example, in 1916, their ¾-ton chassis, with chain drive and on a 124-inch wheelbase, sold for $1,200. (This price included "Front seat and fenders, two oil dash lamps and oil tail lamp, horn, and set of tools") In the 1930s, Brockway also built a line of electric delivery trucks, ranging in capacity from one to seven tons. There was also a Brockway-Indiana model.

1912 Brockway Commercial Express (OCW)

1914 Brockway Model B Flare Board (OCW)

1914 Brockway Model A Panel Delivery (OCW)

1929 Brockway Type JF Express (DFW/FLP)

1936 Brockway Electric Walk-in Milk Truck (DFW/HAC)

696

1930 Brockway-Indiana Compressor Truck (OCW)

BRODESSER — Milwaukee, Wisconsin — (1910-1911) — This truck was built by a firm named P.H. & Co. Peter H. Brodesser, a German immigrant who made elevators, began building trucks as a sideline. His firm produced models in capacities ranging from one- to three-tons. The 1910 lineup included the Model A one-ton delivery for $1,400. It had a horizontally opposed two-cylinder engine with force-feed lubrication. This truck, with a $100 price increase, was also offered in 1911, when the Model C1 joined it. This was another one-ton with a $1,700 price tag. In 1912, the name "Juno" was adopted. The Juno Motor Truck Co., of Juneau, Wis., later evolved.

1912 Bronx Two-Ton Express Wagon (OCW)

BRONX - Bronx, New York — (1912-1913) — Our photo shows this 800-pound truck parked outside the Bronx Motor Vehicle plant, although most sources give the name Bronx Electric Vehicle Co. The light truck was on a 76 inch wheelbase and could make 14 m.p.h. or 50 miles per charge. A two-tonner was also made.

1914 Bronx Light-Duty Express Wagon (JAW)

BRONX ELECTRIC — Bronx, New York — (1912-1913) — The Bronx Electric Vehicle Company made these electrics, with the smallest having a 76-inch wheelbase and a capacity of 800 lbs.

BROOKS — Saginaw, Michigan — (1911-1913) — These high-wheelers were available with either open or closed bodies. They were powered by an air-cooled engine. During its short production run, the firm had two names. First it was the Brooks Manufacturing Company, then, the Brooks Motor Wagon Company. The latter name was in use by 1912, when an 800-pound-rated two-cylinder model was available. It came as a screenside express, for $500, or a full panel body truck, for $550. By 1912, only the screenside model — now called the "B" and priced at $650 — was marketed.

1912 Brooks Express Wagon (OCW)

BROWN — Peru, Indiana — (1912-1914) — A number of firms built autos and trucks named "Brown." The Brown Commercial Car Company built delivery vans in the ¾-ton to one-ton size range.

1913 Brown Standard Express with Screens (RAW)

1914 Brown Flareboard w/Screens (DFW/MVMA)

1914 Brown Model F Covered Flare Board (OCW)

BROWN — Cincinnati, Ohio — (1916) — Based on their passenger car chassis, the Brown Carriage Company "assembled" this light delivery truck.

BROYHILL — Wayne, Nebraska — (1986?) — Historian Elliott Kahn reports that this articulated (it bends in the middle) cab-over utility is being built by Broyhill Mfg. Co. and features a 4x4 drivetrain. The Park Maintenance Dept. of Clearwater, Florida utilizes one of the trucks.

1986 Broyhill Utility Park Service Truck (EK)

BRUNNER — Buffalo, New York — (1910) — This truck was built by the Brunner Motor Car Co. in a number of sizes, with ½-ton being the smallest.
The manufacturer was Brush Motor Car Co.

1910 Brunner Light Delivery Van (WOM)

BRUSH — Detroit, Michigan — (1908-1913) — A branch of the New York City based United States Motor Co., Brush produced a number of light delivery vans. Offered in 1908 and 1909, at $600, was a 500-pound payload, one-cylinder model. In 1910, there was a Model BC, which was a 600-pound truck at the same price. In 1911-1912, this model continued to

1911 Brush Light Delivery Van (OCW)

698

sell, but at a higher $650. The earliest vans were based on the Brush automobile, which had a six horsepower engine, wooden frame and axles, chain drive, full coil spring suspension and solid tires. In 1912, pneumatic tires were adopted. There was also a light taxi, known as the Titan, which used the same chassis.

BUFFALO — Buffalo, New York — (1912-1916) — These were battery-powered electrics, rated at ¾-ton and one-ton, and built by the Buffalo Electric Vehicle Company. In 1914, the 1500-pound chassis was priced at $2,200, while the one-ton chassis sold for $2,400. In 1915, the Model CCA one-tonner was also sold for $2,400 in chassis-only form. There was also a ½-tonner with its engine under the hood. These trucks had solid rubber tires and double chain drive.

1910 Buffalo Canopy Top Delivery Wagon (JAW)

1910 Buffalo Canopy Top Delivery Wagon (WOM)

1914 Buffalo Closed Body Delivery Van (OCW)

BUICK — **Flint, Michigan** — **(1910-1918/1922-1923)** — This well-known automobile manufacturer built trucks early in its history, utilizing its passenger car chassis. The most common use was for delivery vans. Military ambulances on Buick chassis were common sights during World War I. In 1918, the firm's smallest truck sold for $790, which included the body. Buick also offered trucks during the 1922-1923 model years. Its commercial chassis continued to be used for many years, carrying ambulances, hearses, paddy wagons and, even, fire apparatus.

1914 Buick Model 4 Stake Body Express (OCW)

1911 Buick Express Body Delivery (E. Chatfield/DFW)

1914 Buick Model 3 Panel Body Delivery (OCW)

1913 Buick Telephone Company Express (DFW/IBT)

1915 Buick Two-Cylinder Light Delivery (DFW/MVMA)

1914 Buick Model 4 Covered Flare Board (OCW)

1914 Buick Model 4 Flare Board Express (OCW)

1915 Buick Light Delivery Van (DFW/IBC)

699

1916 Buick Model D-4 One-Ton Flare Board Express

1916 Buick Flare Board Express (VHTM)

1917 Buick Express Truck Conversion (DFW/HEPO)

1928 Buick Panel Delivery (DFW)

1929 Buick Ambulance (OCW)

1934 Buick Ambulance (DFW/MVMA)

1937 Buick Carlsbad Caverns Tour Bus (DFW/CC)

1960 Buick-Superior Hearse (OCW)

BUTLER — Butler, Pennsylvania — (1913-1914) — Built by the Huselton Automobile Company, the truck could carry a ¾-ton load.

C

CADILLAC — Detroit, Michigan — (1904 to date) — This famous GM division marketed light trucks from 1904 through 1909. During its entire history, Cadillac also supplied commercial chassis for ambulances, hearses, flower cars, airport buses, etc. Because of their sturdy construction, many Cadillac passenger cars, late in their lives, were converted into commercial vehicles, with the most typical example being a tow-truck.

1913 Cadillac Screenside Police Patrol Wagon (OCW)

1903 Cadillac Commercial Car (DFW/SBT)

1920 Cadillac Military Searchlight Tender (DFW/ACE)
(A real "light duty" truck!)

1906 Cadillac 9 H.P. Delivery Van (OCW)

1920 Cadillac Extended Chassis Tour Bus (DFW/OHS)

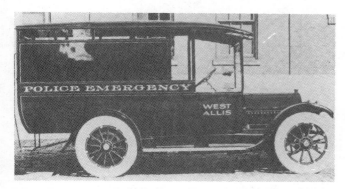

1913 Cadillac Seaman Body Corp. Ambulance (OCW)

1931 Cadillac V-8 Ambulance (CCC)

1940 Cadillac Airport Limousine (DFW/MVMA)

CAPITOL — Washington, D.C. — (1910-1912) — These were chain-driven, battery-powered electric delivery trucks, built by the Washington Motor Vehicle Co.

1910 Capitol Electric Half-Ton Delivery Van (WJP)

CAPITOL — Denver, Colorado — (1914) — These electric delivery vans, built by the Capitol Truck Mfg. Co., were powered by General Electric motors.

1914 Capitol Electric Express Wagon (JAW)

CARTERCAR — Pontiac, Michigan — (1906-1912) — These were light-duty trucks marketed on the Cartercar Company's passenger car chassis. Like the automobiles, these trucks used friction-drive transmissions. This system would ultimately prove unreliable in the commercial vehicle field. The Model C delivery of 1908 was a handsome-looking C-cab van with a $1,400 price tag. The company also produced taxis on the same 96-110 inch wheelbase chassis.

1908 Cartercar Model C Delivery Van (JAW)

1911 Cartercar Bus-back Roadster (OCW)

CASE — New Bremen, Ohio — (1910-1913) — These were 1200-pound capacity delivery vans built by the Case Motor Car Company.

CASS — Port Huron, Michigan — (1910-1915) — The Cass Motor Truck Co. built small trucks, ranging in size from ¾-ton to 1½-ton tons.

1910 Cass Panel Delivery Van (DPL/NAHC)

CAVAC — Plymouth, Michigan — (1910-1911) — These were three-wheel delivery cars built by the Small Motor Co.

702

CECO — Chicago, Illinois — (1914) — These were a van body on a cyclecar. They were built by the Continental Engineering Company.

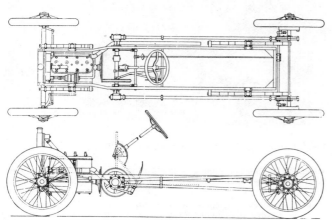

General Chassis Plan and Elevation of Ceco Cyclecar.
This shows the water-cooled motor in place; also the jackshaft differential and tubes for enclosing the driving chains.

1914 Ceco Cyclecar Chassis (OCW)

CHADWICK — Pottstown, Pennsylvania — (1915-1916) — The Chadwick Engineering Works, of Pottstown, Pennsylvania, made this light-duty truck in the mid-Teens. It was rated for a 1000-pound payload capacity. Price for the chassis-only configuration, in 1916, was $620. A delivery body was also offered on this running gear, which was essentially a beefed-up version of the firm's automobile chassis. The engine used was a 16 horsepower LeRoi four-cylinder. This was the company's last shot at manufacturing before its factory was taken over for war work. It had just 13 assemblers.

CHAMPION — Fulton, Illinois — (1913-1917) — Champion Motor Co. produced four versions of its gas-powered 1000-pound Model A truck. The chassis was $725, an Open Express was $750, an Open Express with top was $765 and a Panel was $785. The power team was an L-head four with three-speed transmission attachment.

CHAMPION — Cleveland, Ohio — (1907) — The McCrea Motor Truck Co. built half-ton and two-ton trucks under the Champion name, apparently for just one year. The Model L (which probably stood for ''light truck'') had a delivery type body and sold for $1,850. It was a electric-powered vehicle. The manufacturer may have moved to Chicago, later.

CHAMPION — Milwaukee, Wisconsin — (1912) — Milwaukee Auto Truck Manufacturing Co. was another firm that used the Champion name to designate three models built in 1912. The firm's Model A was a gasoline-engined one-tonner that cost $2,000, while its ''B'' and ''C'' models were rated for two- and three-ton payloads, respectively.

1913 Champion (Milwaukee) Panel Delivery Van (JAW)

CHAMPION — Oswego, New York — (1904-1905) — The Champion Wagon Works also used this popular nameplate on its products. One truck was a battery-powered electric with forward control configuration and double chain drive. It came only as an open-sided van with a top and a one-ton payload rating.

CHASE — Syracuse, New York — (1907-c.1917) — The Chase Motor Truck Co. built trucks in the ¾-ton and up range. In the firm's early years, a business runabout — which could be converted from a four-seat auto to a light-duty truck — was also marketed. In 1916, the firm's ¾-ton model sold for $1,500.

1911 Chase Open Express (VHTM)

1912 Chase Panel Delivery Van (DFW/SI)

1913 Chase Panel Delivery Van (DFW/PTC)

1913 Chase Stakeside Express Wagon (DFW/PTC)

1914 Chase Model D Flare Board (OCW)

1914 Chase Model H Panel Delivery (OCW)

CHAUTAUQUA — Jamestown, New York — (1914) — The Chautauqua Cyclecar Company placed a van body on some of their cyclecars.

CHECKER — Joliet, Illinois — (1920-1923) / Kalamazoo, Michigan — (1923-1984) — This firm — the Checker Cab Mfg. Co. — builds taxicabs, but sometimes their chassis are used for other commercial purposes.

CHEVROLET — Detroit, Michigan — (1918-Present) — Information about this make can be found in the front section of this catalog.

1954 Chevrolet Suburban w/end gate (OCW)

1974 Chevrolet Suburban (JAG)

704

1979 Chevrolet Beauville Sport Van (CMD)

CHICAGO — Chicago, Illinois — (1910-1911) — The Chicago Commercial Car Company built ¾- and one-ton vans.

CHRYSLER — Detroit, Michigan — (1924 to date) — For many years, this well-known auto manufacturer produced commercial chassis. In addition the Fargo, also listed in this catalog, was a Chrysler-made commercial vehicle line produced in the United States through 1932 and as a badge-engineered Canadian and export market line thereafter. (See separate Fargo listing in this catalog.)

1928 Chrysler-Fargo Commercial Car Panel (OCW)

1935 Chrysler-Gillig Ambulance (DFW)

CLARK — Lansing, Michigan — (1910-1912) — These were open express vans built by the Clark Power Wagon Company.

1903 Clark Gas/Electric Commercial Car Express (NAHC)

1910 Clark One-Ton Express Wagon (DFW/SI)

CLARK — Chicago, Illinois — (1910-1914) — The Clark Delivery Wagon Co. built small vans.

1911 Clark Power Wagon (WOM)

1914 Clark Stake Platform Truck (OCW)

1914 Clark Flare Board With Stakes (OCW)

CLEVELAND — Jackson, Michigan — (1913-1914) — This truck was also known as the "New Cleveland." It was a ¾-tonner, of mostly conventional design, which was powered by an unusual four-cylinder engine having an overhead camshaft and overhead valves. The valves were installed at a 45-degree angle. The Cleveland was of delivery wagon style, with a single driver's seat. Other features included pneumatic tires and shaft drive. The company was known as the E.C. Clark Motor Co. and its trade-name was derived by C.D. Paxton, a Cleveland-based marketing firm.

1913 Cleveland Open Express (RAW)

CLIMAX — Sandusky, Ohio — (1907) — The Dunbar Mfg. Co. built a light chassis on which either a passenger car or delivery body could be built.

COLEMAN — Olean, New York — (1910-1915) — Light trucks were made by F. Coleman Carriage & Harness Co. They included 1200-pound vans designated Models A-1 and A-2, which had 20 horsepower, air-cooled two-cylinder engines under the body. There was also a Model B one-ton with 107 inch wheelbase and water-cooled four. In 1914 and 1915, the one-ton Model D was offered, with stake or express bodies, at $1,950 and $2,100, respectively. The small vans had planetary transmissions and double chain-drive.

1914 Coleman Model B Covered Express (OCW)

COLLIER — Cleveland, Ohio — (1917) — The Collier Company built a Light Delivery van in 1917. It was designated the Model M and resembled a passenger car in overall design, although the company did not make autos. This 1500-pound (¾-ton) truck used a four-cylinder gasoline engine and sold for $885 in chassis form. Panel Delivery and Open Express bodies were available. The following season, the firm moved to Bellevue, Ohio.

COLLIER — Bellevue, Ohio — (1918-1922) — After the Collier Company moved to Bellevue, Ohio, the price of its ¾-ton chassis rose by $100 to a total of $985. It was still powered by a gasoline engine of four-cylinder configuration. Models available once again included a Panel Delivery or an Open Express. In 1919, a one-ton truck was added to the line. It featured a Continental Motors power plant and worm drive system. Even larger trucks were brought to market in 1921 and 1922.

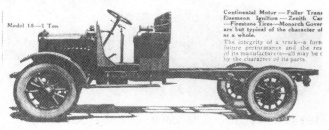

1919 Collier Model 18 One-Ton Chassis (OCW)

COLUMBIA — Hartford, Connecticut — (1899-1907) — This was a very popular make of electric truck, built by the Electric Vehicle Company, which was the successor to the Columbia Automobile Company. Many of their chassis were used for buses. In 1907, the firm concentrated on building gasoline-powered automobiles.

1904 Columbia Electric Panel Delivery (DFW/SI)

COLUMBIA CARRIAGE — Portland, Oregon — (1915) — Columbia Carriage & Auto Works ''GMC Utility Car'' could carry up to 11 passengers or a ton of cargo. It came with four seats, the three rearmost being removable, as was the canopy style top. When thus converted, it became a freight wagon. It had pneumatic tires and could be ordered in any color. The price was $1,400 f.o.b. Portland.

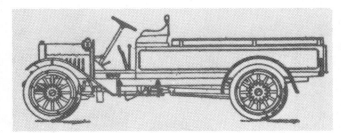

1915 Columbia Carriage GMC 1-Ton Freight Wagon

COMET — Indianapolis, Indiana — (1914) — The Comet Cyclecar Co. attached a delivery box to one of its models.

1914 Comet Cyclecar Model A Delivery Wagon (OCW)

1914 Comet Cyclecar Model B Box Body (OCW)

COMMERCE — Detroit, Michigan — (1911-1926) / Lima, Ohio — (1927-1932) — The Commerce Motor Car Co., of Detroit, built light delivery trucks and canopy express models. They also built bus chassis. In 1927, the firm was acquired by Relay Motors Corp., of Lima, and thus became linked with other moderately well-known makes: Garford, Relay and Service. However, by this time they were no longer marketing ''light-duty'' trucks.

1911 Commerce Light Delivery Van (OCW)

1914 Commerce Model KH Covered Flare Board (OCW)

1914 Commerce Model KC Panel Delivery (OCW)

1914 Commerce Model KA Flare Board (OCW)

1926 Commerce Model 7 Distributor One-Ton Chassis

CORBITT — Henderson, North Carolina — (1913-1958) — Corbitts were a well-known regional truck built until well after the end of World War II. While they were mostly large models, a one-ton Model F ($2,000) appeared as early as 1916. Another four-cylinder job, the Model E, bowed at $1,300 in 1917 and went to $1,800 the next season. It survived until 1925, being joined by the ¾-ton Model H in 1922. The following year, a slightly less powerful ¾-ton Model S was marketed. Also, in 1926, there was the Model 20, with an 18.23 horsepower four-cylinder. One-ton Corbitts were also manufactured in the 1930s.

1914 Corbitt Model F Flare Board (OCW)

COUPLE GEAR — Grand Rapids, Michigan — (1904-1922) — This company specialized in heavy, slow-moving trucks powered by motors in the wheels. In 1908, a one-ton gas/electric model was made. It had drive on the front wheels only and could make nine miles-per-hour. In 1914, another small-sized product was a three-wheel electric contractor's wagon.

1914 Couple Gear 3-Wheel Contractor's Wagon (OCW)

COVERT — Lockport, New York — (1906-1907) — The Covert Motor Vehicle Co. built small delivery trucks with wire-side bodies. Its 1907 two-cylinder, forward-control model was a 1000-pound delivery truck which was priced at $1,000. The body was of the van type with screened side panels. Other features included an 84 inch wheelbase, two-speed gearbox and shaft drive.

C.P.T. — Chicago, Illinois — (1912) — The Chicago Pneumatic Tool Company produced a gasoline powered 1500- to 2000-pound truck chassis for one year. It was marketed at $950. This company also made the Duntley and Giant/Little Giant trucks.

CRANE & BREED — Cincinnati, Ohio — (1909-1924) — Founded in 1850, this former carriage-maker was one of the pioneering firms in the field of purpose-built hearses and ambulances. These were rather heavy vehicles with one-ton or higher payload ratings. In 1915, the least expensive one-tonner sold for $2,000 in chassis form, $3,650 as an ambulance and $3,750 as a hearse. During that same year, there was also the one-ton Model 48. It was $2,850 for the chassis, $4,500 for the ambulance and $5,085 for the top-level of hearse. Pre-1912 models were four-cylinder vehicles with magneto ignition, three-speed gear boxes and chain drive. After 1912, the company concentrated on making only the bodies, which were mounted on a six-cylinder Winton chassis. Such models were produced until 1924.

CRAWFORD — Hagerstown, Maryland — (1911-1917) — The Crawford Automobile Company offered a 1200-pound capacity van on their automobile chassis.

1909 Crawford Commercial Roadster (EK)

CRICKETT — Detroit, Michigan — (1915) — The Cyclecar Company of Detroit produced a gasoline-engined Package Delivery model with a low $345 price tag.

CROCE — Asbury Park, New Jersey — (circa 1918) — The Croce Automobile Company also marketed a line of delivery trucks. Among its models was the ''A,'' which sold for $1,700 in 1914. It was a ¾-ton gasoline-engined truck. For 1915, the Model A came as a $1,650 chassis or $1,800 open or closed cab van. There was also a Model C one-ton chassis ($1,850) in 1914 and an A-1 one-ton chassis ($1,800) in 1915. After skipping one season, Croce returned to the market, in 1917, with three light-duty models.

1914 Croce Panel Body Delivery Car (OCW)

1915 Croce Panel Body Delivery Car (DFW/SI)

1916 Croce Panel Body Delivery Car (DFW/MVMA)

CROFTON — San Diego, California — (1959-1961) — This was a jeep-type vehicle built by the Crofton Marine Engine Co. Additional information about this make can be found in the Crosley section at the front of this catalog. Complete year-by-year coverage is provided in Krause Publications' *Standard Catalog of American Cars 1946-1975.*

1960 Crofton-Bug Utility (Reggie Rapp)

CROSLEY — Cincinnati, Ohio — (1940-1952) — Information about this make can be found in the front section of this catalog.

CROW — Elkhart, Indiana — (1912-1913) — This was a delivery van offered on an auto-maker's chassis. The manufacturer was the Crow Motor Company.

CROWN — Milwaukee, Wisconsin — (1910-1915) — The Crown Commercial Car Co. started out building ½-ton model trucks. It then began building larger capacity models.

CROWTHER-DURYEA — Rochester, New York — (1916) — This light truck was developed by Charles Duryea and built by the Crowther Motor Co.

CROXTON-KEETON — Massilon, Ohio — (1909-1910) — Croxton-Keeton Motor Co. was the parent firm of Croxton Motor Car Co. and also built taxicabs on a beefed-up automobile chassis. These vehicles had sloping hoods, behind-the-engine radiators, 38 h.p. four-cylinder engines, a three-speed selective sliding transmission and shaft drive. The cabs had a 115½ inch wheelbase, 3100-pound curb weight and $3,300 price tag.

CROXTON — Washington, Pennsylvania — (1911-1913) —This company's light-duty commercial vehicles are claimed to all have been taxicabs, but at least one panel body truck was constructed. A characteristic of the make was a sloping hood and behind-the-engine radiator.

1913 Croxton Model A Panel Body Delivery (OCW)

C.T. — Philadelphia, Pennsylvania — (1908-1928) — This company was known as Commercial Truck Co. of America through 1916 and the name C.T. was used for model listings thereafter. Its well-known electric trucks can often be spotted in old photos showing traffic scenes in large Eastern cities. The 1909 line included a ½-ton delivery van priced at $2,200, which was carried over, for 1910, with two more light-duties and various heavier trucks. The smallest was a ¼-ton delivery that sold for $2,000. A one-ton truck was also marketed for $2,800. By 1911, the 500-pounder was lowered in price to $1,900, while the ½-ton increased to $2,250. Price for the one-ton model remained unchanged. In 1912, the three models were $2,000, $2,200 and $2,800 in order. Alphabetical designations were adopted in 1913, the Model A being a 750-pound panel priced at $2,000 and the Model B being a 1500-pound panel for $2,200. The following season the "A" was down-rated to 500-pounds again, and sold for $1,440 in chassis form or $2,000 with the panel body. For 1916, the lightest version was the one-ton Model C at $1,800 for the chassis. The half-ton returned, in 1918, with prices varying from $2,005 to $2,540, depending on the type of battery. This truck could travel 13 m.p.h. In 1925, the C.T. half-ton chassis was $1,900.

1914 C.T. Model 1000 Panel Body Delivery (OCW)

1922 C.T. Electric Flat Front Panel Delivery (DFW/MVMA)

1922 C.T. Electric Panel Delivery (DFW/MVMA)

1925 C.T. Electric Walk-in Delivery (DFW/NA)

CUNNINGHAM — Rochester, New York — (1909-1934) — James Cunningham, Sons, & Co. built some luxury autos, but soon specialized in ambulances and hearses. They were expensive. In the late 1920s, their ambulances and hearses were selling in the $6,300-6,500 price range. A few of their chassis were used for other commercial bodies.

1925 Cunningham Ambulance (DFW/WRHS)

CUSHMAN — Lincoln, Nebraska — (1936 to date) — Cushman Motors, manufacturer of the well-known scooters, outfitted some of their scooters with freight-carrying bodies.

1965 Cushman 3-Wheel Police/Utility Scooter (WJP)

1984 Cushman 3-Wheel "Police Special" Scooter (EK)

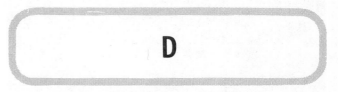

D

DARBY — St. Louis, Missouri — (1910) — This was a small delivery van produced by the Darby Motor Car Company.

DART — Waterloo, Iowa — (1903-date) — This is an old name in the truck business and the manufacturer's name has changed eight times. The firm was in Anderson, Indiana from 1903-1907 and then in Waterloo from 1907-1925. It then moved to Kansas City, Missouri, where it exists today. Presently, it builds mainly large off-highway construction vehicles. At one time, it did build light-duty trucks. In 1916, it sold a Model D with an express body, rated at ¼-ton capacity, for $675. The Model A was rated at ½-ton capacity and the Model BB at ¾-ton capacity.

1914 Dart Model B Flare Board Express (OCW)

1914 Dart Model B Flare Board Express (DFW/HCC)

DAY-ELDER — **Irvington, New Jersey** — **(1919-1937)** — This was a moderately well-known make of truck and bus made by the Day-Elder Motor Truck Company in sizes up to five- or six-tons. From 1916 to 1918, they offered a ¾-ton Day-Elder "Junior," which sold for $950. A one-ton "Senior" model was available concurrently.

1916 Day-Elder One-Ton Stake Body (OCW)

1928 Day-Elder Flare Board Express Wagon (WJP)

1916 Day-Elder Junior 1250-pound Chassis (RAW)

1916 Day-Elder Senior One-Ton Chassis (RAW)

DAYTON — **Joliet, Illinois** — **(1914)** — Like many cyclecar makers, this firm turned out commercial versions of its product for light delivery work. An 18 horsepower four-cylinder engine powered this 105 inch wheelbase machine which, with a delivery box mounted aft, became a light-duty truck. Chicagoan William O. Dayton gave his name to the short-lived venture.

DAYTON — **Dayton, Ohio** — **(1914-1915)** — This company built an electric powered truck with 750-pound payload. It came as a chassis ($1,200) or Closed Panel ($1,600). Dayton Electric Car Company built it.

1914 Dayton Flare Board Express (OCW)

DAY UTILITY - **Detroit, Michigan/Milwaukee, Wisconsin** - **(1912-1914)** — The Day Automobile Co. introduced its ½-ton Special Delivery at a price of $1,150. In 1913, the ½-ton Model C ($1,500) was produced in Michigan, while the ¾-ton Model D was made in both states, but at different prices. The Detroit built version, with a delivery body, was $1,500, while the Milwaukee made Model D (a chassis only) was $1,850. In 1914, the Model D — now called a "convertible," was built in Michigan only, at the $1,500 price.

DECATUR — **Decatur, Indiana** — **(1909-1912) / Grand Rapids, Michigan** — **(1912-1915)** — The Decatur Motor Car Co., and several succeeding firms, built various models of trucks. They included a delivery van designed so that the driver rode in the rear, over the load-carrying body.

1914 Decatur Cyclecar Parcel Post Delivery Wagon

DELCAR — Troy, New York — (1947-1949) — This was a short (60 inch wheelbase) delivery van built by a firm named American Motors, Inc.

DENBY — Detroit, Michigan — (1914-1930) — Usually associated with larger sizes of trucks, the Denby Motor Truck Co. did, in some years of the early 1920s, produce models as small as ¾-ton capacity.

1915 Denby Flare Board Express Wagon (NACH/DPL)

1915 Denby 3/4-Ton Express (OCW)

1916 Denby One-Ton Open Flare Board Express (WOM)

1917 Denby One-Ton With Express Box (Myron Stone)

1916 Denby Type U 3/4-Ton Stake Body (D. Sagvold)

1925 Denby Model 41 One-Ton Chassis (OCW)

DENMO — Cleveland, Ohio — (1916-1918) — The Denneen Motor Co., of Cleveland, announced its first line of trucks late in 1916. A four-cylinder Wisconsin engine powered these conventional models. It was attached to a three-speed tranmission and Torbensen internal gear drive axle. Pneumatic tires were used in front with solid tires at the rear. In 1917 only, the company produced its Model 12, a flare board express with a 1250-pound payload. It sold for $995. By 1918, the firm became Grant Motor Car Corporation and the Grant name was then used on the trucks.

DENNISTON — Buffalo, New York — (1911-1912) — The E.E. Denniston Co. built small delivery vans with a two-cylinder engine.

DeSCHAUM — Buffalo, New York — (1908-1909) — This was a small delivery van, with an 84-inch wheelbase, sold by the DeSchaum Motor Syndicate Co. for a brief period.

DESOTO — Detroit, Michigan — (1930-present) — According to the *Plymouth-DeSoto Story* by Don Butler (Crestline Publishing), the first commercial vehicle made by DeSoto was the rare Model K Commercial Sedan. This ½-ton rated "sedan delivery" had blanked-out rear side windows and a rear access door. Only one was known to exist in 1956! DeSoto components were also used in Chrysler's Fargo truck-line. Depot hacks and taxicabs also rode DeSoto chassis. Starting in 1938, the DeSoto name was used by Chrysler to identify a line of Dodge-like trucks. These were intended to be sold by foreign based dealers of Chrysler products who lacked a Dodge franchise. They were first seen in European countries and spread into the Australian market after World War II. They were virtually identical to the Dodges offered in the same areas, except for nameplates. While use of the name was discontinued in most countries after the demise of DeSoto cars in 1961, certain models assembled in Turkey continued to use this identification.

1958 DeSoto 4x4 Pickup (DFW/DPL)

1958 DeSoto One-Ton Stake Bed (DFW/DPL)

DETROIT — Detroit, Michigan — (1912-1913) — The Detroit Motor Wagon was a model made by Motor Wagon Co. Several light-duty vans of 800- and 1000-pound capacity were offered. The four-cylinder engine sat in a 102 inch wheelbase and was attached to a planetary transmission. Final drive was by chain. The smaller wagon was $610; the larger one $900.

DETROIT — Detroit, Mich. — (1914-1915) — Anderson Electric Car Co. produced a one-ton electric truck under this name in 1914. It was designated the Model 2 and sold for $1,500 in chassis form. This firm also built the Detroit Electric trucks (see next listing) and automobiles.

1914 Detroit Model 2 Truck Chassis (OCW)

1914 Detroit Model 1 Panel Body Delivery (OCW)

DETROIT MOTOR WAGON — Detroit, Michigan — (1913) — The Motor Wagon Company, of Detroit, produced four different 1000-pound (half-ton) models in 1913. The line included an Express Wagon and Stake-bodied truck which both sold for $950 and two panel deliveries. The first panel was $975 and the second — probably a closed cab version — was $985.

DETROIT ELECTRIC — Detroit, Michigan — (1909-1927) — This was a long-lived electric, manufactured at first by the Anderson Carriage Co.; then the Anderson Electric Car Co. and, finally, by the Detroit Electric Car Co. In some years their smaller models were rated at ½-ton capacity.

1910 Detroit Electric 10CWT Delivery Van (OCW)

DeWITT — North Manchester, Indiana — (1984-1986) — This is a replica of the DeWitt auto-buggy, produced in the same town as the original, but many years later. The company tried to generate interest in this beautiful copy of a high-wheeler among car collectors. Though promoted primarily as a passenger vehicle, a cargo box was available for the rear deck.

1984 DeWitt Flare Board Express (EK)

DIAMOND-T — Chicago, Illinois — (1911-1966) — This was a well-known, high quality truck of distinctive appearance, and one which is highly regarded by collectors today. In a few years, they built trucks rated as small as ¾-ton capacity. In 1916, their model JA, rated at ¾-ton, sold for $1,175.

1940 Diamond T One-Ton Pickup (OCW)

1940 Diamond T Light Truck Accessories (OCW)

1948 Diamond T One-Ton Pickup (M. Stowell)

1928 Diamond T One-Ton Dump (Joe Egle)

1935 Diamond T One-Ton Wrecker (Joe Egle)

DISPATCH — Minneapolis, Minnesota — (1910-1919) — The Dispatch Motor Car Co. built both autos and small trucks, styled with Renault-type hoods. In 1918, their ¾-ton truck sold for $1,100.

DIVCO — Detroit, Michigan/ Delaware, Ohio — (1926 to date) — The originator of the Divco milk truck was George Bacon, chief engineer of Detroit Electric Car Co. These stand-up, forward-control vans came in many configurations and sizes. The firm also went through numerous mergers.

1927 Divco Walk-in Milk Delivery Van (OCW)

1947 Divco Van with Charles Wacker Body (DFW/CWC)

1948 Divco Helm's Bakery Delivery Van (OCW)

1948 Divco Walk-in Milk Delivery Van (RAW)

DODGE — Detroit, Michigan — (1918 to date) — Information about this make can be found in the front section of this catalog.

1921 Dodge Brothers Screenside Business Car (OCW)

DORRIS — St. Louis, Missouri — (1912-1925) — The Dorris Motor Car Co. is known mainly for its autos, although it also sold a line of light and medium trucks.

1914 Dorris Newspaper Screenside Delivery (DFW/MPC)

1914 Dorris Panel Body Delivery Van (OCW)

1914 Dorris Platform Stake (OCW)

DORT — Flint, Michigan — (1921-c.1924) — The Dort Motor Car Co. built autos and, in some years, also marketed a panel truck.

714

DOVER — Detroit, Michigan — (1929) — Information about this make can be found in the Hudson listing in the front section of this catalog.

1929 Dover Post Office Special Delivery (DFW/HAC)

1929 Dover Panel Delivery Van (OCW)

1929 Dover Screenside Delivery (DFW/MVMA)

DOWAGIAC — Dowagiac, Michigan — (1909-1912) — This was a light van built by the Dowagiac Motor Car Company.

DOWNING — Detroit, Michigan — (1914) — The Downing Cyclecar Co. built a light van on their cyclecar chassis.

DUDLY — Menominee, Michigan — (1914-1915) — This was a cyclecar with a light van body and known as the "Dudly Bug." It was built by the Dudly Tool Co.

DUER — Chicago, Illinois — (1910) — This was a high-wheeler, steered by a tiller, and made by the Chicago Coach & Carriage Company.

1908 Duer High-Wheel Light Delivery Wagon (JAW)

DUNLAP — Columbus, Ohio — (1914-1915) — The Dunlap Electric Company built a ½-ton capacity, battery-powered truck.

DUNTLEY — (see Little Giant)

DUPLEX — Lansing, Michigan — (1908 to date) — This make of truck has survived for many years, being built by a succession of firms in Charlotte and Lansing, Mich. and then in Winona, Minn. Most of its trucks were very heavy and had all-wheel drive. In their early days a ¾-ton four-wheel drive delivery wagon was built. This two-cylinder vehicle was called the Model A and was a 1500-pound delivery model. It was offered in 1910-1911 for $1,250 as a product of Power Car Co. of Charlotte, Mich. By 1915, the company had become the Duplex Truck Co., of Lansing, Mich.

1914 Duplex Light Express Wagon (DFW/WRHS)

DURANT — Flint, Michigan - (1923-1931) — Information about trucks made by firms that were members of the "Durant Family" companies can be found listed under Durant Family in the front section of this catalog. These firms include Star and Rugby.

1928 Durant Closed Cowl Cab w/Express Body (JG/DFR)

DURYEA — Reading, Pennsylvania — (1899-1917) — There were several firms associated with this famous name. They built some trucks, although not on a regular basis. A pair of two-cylinder models were made under the Chas. E. Duryea Co. name in 1910 and 1911. The 1910 model was a 500-pound delivery selling for $800. A 700-pound delivery, priced at $725, was marketed the next season. Also available, in 1911, was a one-cylinder model called the Tri-Van. It was rated for 400-pounds and sold for $400. After a brief absence from the truck market, a half-ton chassis priced at $600 was offered by Duryea Laboratories in 1916. During 1918, the Duryea Motor Co., of Saginaw, Mich., cataloged four light-duty commercial vehicles, all with 800-pound payload ratings. They included a chassis for $600, the Model A open body express for $625, the Model B convertible body truck for $650 and the Model C panel body delivery for $675. All Duryea trucks were gasoline powered models.

1896 Duryea Military Field Car (DFW/HCHS)

DUTCHER PTV — San Diego, California — (1984) — The Dutcher PTV was a commercial mini-van made by Dutcher Industries, Inc. It had a rear-mounted gasoline engine, automatic transmission and low maintenance, corrosion-resistant chassis structure with replaceable fiberglass body panels and independent suspension system. The truck could accomodate a driver, seven passengers and 20 cubic feet of luggage. It could also be converted to transport two wheelchairs and four passengers.

1984 Dutcher PTV Mini-Van (OCW)

E

EAGLE — St. Louis, Missouri — (1920-1928) — The Eagle Motor Truck Corp. built trucks in a range of sizes, some as small as ½-ton capacity.

ECONOMY — Joliet, Illinois — (1909-1912) — The Economy Motor Car Co. built high-wheel vans with two-cylinder engines. The company's 1910 truck-line was comprised of the Model 1 and the Model 2, both of which used two-cylinder gasoline engines. In chassis only form, the first sold for $850, while the second was $1,200. The designations Model 2 and Model 3 were used in 1911. This Model 2 was a one-ton delivery vehicle with a $1,400 price tag, while the Model 3 was a half-ton delivery selling at $1,150. After reorganizing as the Economy Motor Co. and moving to Tiffin, Ohio, the firm came up with a two truck line for 1918. This included the Model 36-T, a 1200-pound express for $1,095, and the 1-36-T, a one-ton chassis-only priced at $1,295.

1911 Economy 1000-pound Motor Truck (OCW)

ELECTRIC VEHICLE ASSOCIATION — New York City — (c. 1918) — This appears to be a trade organization, rather than a manufacturer. The EVA ran advertisements promoting the sale of electric delivery trucks. A 1918 advertisement told how Mandel Bros., of Chicago, adapted electric delivery wagons which cost only $5.80 per day in total operating costs. The association also had offices in Boston and Chicago.

1918 Panel Delivery from E.V.A. Advertisement

ELLSWORTH — Keokuk, Iowa — (1916-1920) — The Mills-Ellsworth Company built light delivery vans.

ELMIRA — Elmira, New York — (1916-1921) — The Elmira Commercial Motor Car Co. built a ½-ton truck.

ERSKINE — South Bend, Indiana — (1928-1930) — Erskines were a smaller auto built by Studebaker. They offered ½-ton capacity chassis, panels, and screen bodies. In 1929, the six-cylinder chassis sold for $675; the screen body for $860 and the panel body for $875.

1927 Erskine Model 50 Closed Panel Delivery (OCW)

716

1928 Erskine Model 51 Business Coach Sedan (OCW)

ESSEX — Detroit, Michigan — (1919-1933) — Hudson Motor Car Co. offered the Essex as a lower price auto. In some years light trucks were built on their chassis. In 1933, ½-ton Essex trucks, on 106-inch wheelbases, were in the $440-$545 price range. By this time, the trucks were also called Essex-Terraplane. (For additional information, see the Hudson section in front of this catalog.)

F

FALCON — Detroit, Michigan — (1915-1916) — This was a ½-ton truck built by the Falcon Motor Truck Company.

FARGO — Chicago, Illinois — (1913-1921) — The Fargo Motor Car Company built a line of trucks in the ¾-ton to one-ton capacity range.

FARGO - Detroit, Mich — (1930-1972) — Fargo was a name used by Chrysler to sell badge-engineered trucks. The earliest Fargos were sold in the United States. Later, the name was used for trucks sold in Canada and other export markets. For more information see the Fargo section in front of this catalog.)

FAWICK — Sioux Falls, South Dakota — (1913-1916) — Not exactly a household word, this was a make of light truck built by the Fawick Motor Car Co.

FEDERAL — Detroit, Michigan — (1910-1959) — The Federal Motor Truck Company, manufacturer of well-known make of trucks, offered 3/4-ton models in the 1930s. An article in *Special Interest Autos* (1980) indicated questions over actual production. Drawings, but no photos, of these models were thought to exist. Federal also offered a 3/4-tonner in 1949. One-tons were unquestionably produced for many years.

1930 Federal Walk-in Panel (DFW/NAHC)

1939 Federal ¾-Ton Panel (DFW/MVMA)

1939 Federal ¾-Ton Pickup (DFW/MVMA)

1940 Federal Walk-in Package Delivery Van (DFW/SI)

1949 Federal Model 15M Utility Express (DFW/MVMA)

FEDERAL-KNIGHT — Detroit, Michigan — (1924-1928) — In June, 1924, Federal (see above listing) introduced the Willys-Knight sleeve-valve engine to the motor truck industry. A light-duty chassis was engineered to accept this power plant and sell for just $1,095. The Federal-Knight was continued until 1928, at which time Willys-Knight started putting the engine in its own trucks. The model designation "FK" was used to identify those trucks which utilized the Knight "sleeve-valve" engine under license. The power plant was a four-cylinder version with a bore and stroke of 3⅝ x 4 inches and an NACC (National Automobile Chamber of Commerce) horsepower rating of 21.03. The Model FK trucks had a 2300 pound curb weight and one-ton payload rating. The 40 brake-horsepower produced by the novel sleeve-valve engine looked impressive on paper, although its reliability for long term usage was a point of debate among truck fleet operators.

1924 Federal-Knight Panel Delivery (OCW)

1925 Federal-Knight One-Ton Chassis (OCW)

FINDLEY — Geneva, Ohio — (1909-1912) — The Findley Motor Co. was the same as the Ewing Auto Co. and built a number of light-duty trucks and taxis. The Ewing Model C of 1909-1910 was a $3,000 five-passenger taxi. In 1911, Models A and B were made. The "A" was a ½-ton delivery priced at $2,000. The "B" was a two-cylinder delivery rated for 500-pounds and selling for $950. For 1912, the products included express models of "A" and "B" with payload ratings of 750- and 2000-pounds, respectively. The first was still $2,000, but the cheaper truck now had a $1,125 price tag.

FIRESTONE-COLUMBUS — Columbus, Ohio — (1912) — The Columbus Buggy Company built a vehicle which could be converted between being a light van and a passenger car.

FISHER-STANDARD — Detroit, Michigan — (1912-1933) — Built by the Standard Motor Truck Co., whose larger models were called Standards, the Fisher-Standard Junior was a small, ¾-ton to 1½-ton capacity, model offered in the early 1930's.

FLANDERS — Detroit, Michigan — (1912-1913) — Flanders Motor Company, which was to become a part of Studebaker, built autos. However, some of their automobile chassis were outfitted with truck bodies.

1912 Flanders Panel Delivery (OCW)

1912 Flanders Panel Delivery (OCW)

FLINT — Flint, Michigan — (1912-1915) — The Flint was a companion car to the Best. It was built by Durant-Dort Carriage Co. A four was used and the light-duty chassis sold in the $1,285 to $1,375 range.

1914 Flint Model C Panel Body (OCW)

FORD — Detroit, Mich. — (1905 to date) — Information about this make can be found in the front section of this catalog.

1921 Ford Model TT One-Ton Chemical Engine (MBFD)

FRANKLIN — Syracuse, New York — (1902-1935) — The Franklin Automobile Company is known best for its air-cooled autos. Up until 1912, they also marketed a line of light trucks; in addition, some of their later auto chassis were sometimes outfitted with truck and other commercial bodies.

1911 Franklin Commercial Car w/Pneumatics (OCW)

1911 Franklin B.F. Goodrich Express (DFW/SI)

1910 Franklin One-Ton Delivery Van (OCW)

FRAYER-MILLER — Columbus, Ohio — (1906-1910) — This nameplate was a product of Oscar Lear Auto Co. from 1906-1910 and made by Kelly Motor Truck Co. in 1910. A one-ton gasoline truck was a product of 1910. It sold for $2,600 as a chassis.

1907 Frayer-Miller Canopy Stake Bed Express (JAW)

FRITCHLE — Denver, Colorado — (1911-1916) — This was a delivery van version of a battery-powered auto, built by the Fritchle Auto & Battery Company.

1914 Fritchle Panel Body Delivery (OCW)

FRONTMOBILE — Camden, New Jersey — (1918-1919) — The Camden Motors Corporation built both autos and light trucks.

F-S — Milwaukee, Wisconsin — (1912) — The F-S Motors Co. built a short-lived line of trucks, the smallest being rated at ¾-tons.

G

GABRIEL AUTO CO. — Cleveland, Ohio — (1910-1915) — This firm produced many light-duty models in chassis-only form. Its K of 1914-1915 was a 1/2-ton priced at $1,000 and $1,200. The 3/4-ton Model H sold for $1,500 in 1914, $1,600 in 1915-1916. The one-ton model J was $2,000 in both 1914 and 1915. A lower-priced ($1,800) Model O one-tonner bowed in 1916. The firm evolved from the W.H. Gabriel Carriage & Wagon Co. and built cars under that name until 1912. With introduction of a one-ton truck in 1913, the Gabriel Motor Truck Co. was formed. However, it appears that Gabriel Auto Co. continued producing commercial cars and trucks up to two-tons, under the original name, until 1916.

1914 Gabriel Model K Flare Board (OCW)

1914 Gabriel Model H Covered Flare Board (OCW)

1914 Gabriel Model J Covered Flare Board (OCW)

GABRIEL — Cleveland, Ohio — (1913-1920) — Although this company can be dated to 1913 for trucks built under another variation of its name (see previous entry), the name Gabriel Motor Truck Co. was separately attached to several one-ton and under commercial vehicles. The first of these appeared in model year 1917. Available for that season only was the Model B, a gas-powered 1500-pound model priced at a modest $800. It was accompanied by the 2000-pound Model C, another gasoline-engined truck with a price that was twice as high. In 1918, the one-tonner (Model C) was the lightest model, but the price of its chassis-only configuration was raised to $1,750.

GAETH — Cleveland, Ohio — (1906-1910) — The Gaeth Automobile Works also produced some light trucks.

1908 Gaeth One-Ton Delivery Van (OCW)

GALE — Galesburg, Illinois — (1905-1906) — This was a small van, with a 73-inch wheelbase, built by the Western Tool Works.

GALLOWAY — Waterloo, Iowa — (1908-1911) — Agricultural equipment was the first product of this firm organized in 1906. An 18.22 horsepower two-cylinder, solid tire, chain-drive farm wagon type vehicle, which could be fitted with ''Sunday-go-to-meeting'' seats for passenger transport, was introduced in 1908. During the week, this express truck could handle heavy load-carrying chores. It had a load space 78 inches long and 42 inches wide and could carry between 1,000- and 1,500-pounds. Other features included a two-speed planetary transmission and 85 inch wheelbase. The price was $570 or $12 more with the extra seat. One of these rare trucks survives in Bill Pollock's 'Automobile Showcase' in Pottstown, Pa.

1909 Galloway Flare Board (Pollock Auto Showcase)

GARFORD — Lima, Ohio — (1909-1933) — The Garford Motor Truck Co. built a moderately well known large truck; and late in its life became part of a combine which also made Relay, Service, and Commerce trucks. In some years a 3/4-ton capacity Garford was offered. In 1916, the Garford model 64, rated at 3/4-ton capacity, had chain drive, a four-cylinder engine, came with a choice of solid or pneumatic tires, and — as a chassis — sold for $1,350.

1921 Garford 1- to 1½-Ton Livestock Delivery (JAW)

1923 Garford Model 15 Chassis & Cowl (JAW)

1924 Garford Covered Flare Board Express (OCW)

GARY — Gary, Indiana — (1916-1927) — The Gary Motor Truck Co. built trucks ranging in capacity from ¾-ton to five-tons.

1917 Gary Model E ¾-ton Panel Delivery (DFW/SI)

GEM — Grand Rapids, Michigan — (1917-1919) — This was a light delivery van, made by the Gem Motor Car Corporation.

GENERAL — Cleveland, Ohio — (1903) — This was a van version of a runabout, built by the General Automobile & Manufacturing Co.

GENERAL VEHICLE CO. — Long Island City, N.Y. — (1906-1920) — Battery-powered electrics were built by this company under the trade-name "G.V. See listings under that name below.

GENEVA — Geneva, New York — (1912-1919) — The Geneva Wagon Co. produced a line of small trucks. In 1918, their ¾-ton capacity chassis sold for $700, which appeared to be the lowest price of any ¾-ton chassis taken from a list of about 25 makes of that era.

GIANT — Chicago Heights, Illinois — (1911-1923) — Early reference sources, such as the *Manual of Automobile Liability Insurance* listed this truck as the "Little Giant," while later sources, such as *Branham Automobile Reference Book*, called it simply "Giant." The first year for model listings was 1911, although the Imperial Palace Hotel and Casino has a 1909 Giant on display in its Las Vegas Auto Collection. Chicago Pneumatic Tool Co. was actually the manufacturer and *Branham* clearly indicates that Giant Truck Corp. went "out of business" after 1923. The company's first product line consisted of a ¾-ton delivery wagon with a two-cylinder engine and $1,000 price tag. By 1912, a pair of two-cylinder gas-powered models were available. The ¾-ton was the Model C, selling at $1,100 for the chassis. Also offered was a one-ton Model D that came as an open flare board ($1,100), canvas top ($1,150), standard body ($1,150) or full-panel ($1,200). In 1913, there were two ¾-tons, the Models A and B, both at $950, and two one-tons, the Model C ($1,050) and Model D ($1,150).

1918 Giant Express Wagon (DFW/Imperial Palace)

Models available for 1914 were all $1,050 one-tons labeled the D, F and H. The H was carried over for 1915 and 1916 (as the H-3) with a $1,350 price tag. From this point on, mostly 1½ to 5-ton models were marketed, but a ¾-ton called the Model 15 was available until 1918. It used a four-cylinder engine with 3½ x 5 inch bore and stroke that produced 19.60 horsepower. A 3,425 pound curb weight was registered. According to serial numbers, about 800 to 1300 units were produced.

G.J.G. — White Plains, New York — (1912-1913) — The G.J.G. Motor Car Company also built a small van.

GLIDE — Peoria, Illinois — (1911-1912) — The Bartholomew Co. built both autos and small trucks for a short period of time.

GMC — Pontiac, Michigan — (1911 to date) — Information about this make can be found in the front section of this catalog.

1915 GMC Model 15 Canopy Express (OCW)

GRABOWSKY — Detroit, Mich. — (1908-1913) — Max Grabowsky, founder of the Grabowsky Power Wagon Co., was the designer of the Rapid truck. The smallest of his models were one-tonners made in 1910-1911 ($2,300) and 1912-1913 ($2,200). A 22 h.p. two-cylinder engine was used through 1912.

1909 Grabowsky Power Wagon (Pollock Auto Showcase)

GRAHAM BROS. — Evansville, Indiana — (1919-1928) — This firm became associated with Dodge in the 1920s and built light trucks and medium trucks based on the Dodge automobile. Eventually the Graham Brothers truck became the Dodge truck. (See the Dodge section in front of this catalog for additional information and Graham Brothers photos).

1925 Graham Brothers One-Ton Panel Delivery

1925 Graham Brothers United Parcel Truck (DFW/UPS)

1927 Graham Brothers One-Ton Express (OCW)

GRAMM — **Delphos, Ohio** — **(1926-1942)** — The name "Gramm" was associated with several Ohio-built trucks and, in 1915, the Gramm Motor Truck Co. built the first "Willys Utility" model. This company was not a part of Willys-Overland, although John North Willys was, for a time, a majority stockholder in Gramm. The Model 65 Willys Utility was rated at 3/4-ton. In the late 1930s, Gramm Motor Truck Co. had a close relationship with Bickle, of Canada.

1915 Gramm Model 65 1500-Lb. Canopy Express (OCW)

GRAMM-BERNSTEIN — **Lima, Ohio** — **(1912-1930)** — Truck pioneer B.A. Gramm joined with Max Bernstein to start this firm which built mostly large trucks. A one-ton ($1,750); 3/4- to one-ton ($1,350) and one-ton ($1,500) were made in 1914-1915-1916, respectively.

1914 Gramm-Bernstein Model 1 One-Ton Chassis (OCW)

GRANT — **Cleveland, Ohio** — **(1918-1923)** — The Grant Motor Car Corporation built both light-duty and medium-duty trucks. All used four-cylinder Continental engines. The light-duty 3/4-tonner was dropped in 1920.

GRASS-PREMIER — **Sauk City, Wisconsin** — **(1923-1937)** — This was an assembled truck, made by the Grass-Premier Truck Company. They sometimes offered a 3/4-ton capacity model.

GRAY — **Detroit, Michigan** — **(1923-1925)** — The Gray Motor Corp. built autos, and also offered a light van.

1925 Gray One-Ton Chassis (OCW)

GREAT EAGLE — **Columbus, Ohio** — **(1911-1914)** — The United States Carriage Co. built autos and supplied commercial chassis.

1910 Great Eagle Commerical Car Limousine (NAHC)

GRUMMAN — **Garden City, N.Y.** — **(1963 to date)** — Grumman Aerospace company bought the J.B. Olsen Corp., which built aluminum-alloy truck bodies under the "Kurbmaster" trade-name. These trucks use the chassis of other manufacturers with distinctive walk-in van and cube-van type bodies. Smaller models have 102 inch wheelbases.

1983 Grumman-Olson Kubvan Aluminum Minivan (G-O)

G.V. — Long Island City, New York — (1906-1920) — The General Vehicle Co. built a wide range of battery-powered trucks, usually equipped with General Electric motors. As early as 1907, nine different types were offered. They ranged from flatbed trucks to buses and included light-duty models with a payload capacity of 750-pounds. In 1914, the 750-pound chassis sold for $1,370, while a ½-ton chassis was $1,700 and a one-tonner went for $2,100. The following season, the smallest truck was dropped and the two other one-ton-or-under models were joined by a new half-tonner featuring worm drive. Listings for 1915 and 1917 specified "with G.V. batteries," indicating that the firm manufactured its own wet-cell batteries. In other years, however, the brand of batteries was not specified. For 1916, there were two half-ton models, plus a one-ton. The smaller truck could go 12 m.p.h. and had a range of 45 miles. G.V.s came with a "mechanical hand horn, taillamp, hub odometer, kit of tools, charging receptacle and plug with 12 feet of cable." Features of one half-ton included an 88 inch wheelbase and chain drive at a price of $1,700 in 1916. Another one, with a 20 inch longer wheelbase, had worm drive and a $1,950 price tag. The one-ton continued to sell for $2,100. Also marketed in that year were two electric freight trucks, of one-ton capacity, with G.V.X. batteries. The smaller, on a six-foot long chassis, sold for $1,350. The larger, on a 10-foot chassis, was $1,400. Light trucks in the 1918 line included a $1,360 half-ton and the $2,100 one-ton. The company, which started under the name Vehicle Equipment Co., survived only until 1920.

1915 G.V. Panel Body Electric Delivery (RAW)

1914 G.V. 750-Pound Panel Body Electric Delivery (OCW)

1915 G.V. Naval Gun Factory Truck Crane (RAW)

1914 G.V. 1000-Lb. Panel Body Electric Delivery (RAW)

H

HAHN — Hamburg, Pennsylvania — (1907-date) — Now known as a builder of fire apparatus, Hahn Motors, Inc. at one time built a full range of trucks. From time to time, their smallest model would be less than one-ton. In 1916, their ¾-ton chassis was powered by a Continental motor, had a 102-inch wheelbase, worm gear drive, and sold for $1,000. (It also had a Klaxon horn.)

1914 G.V. One-Ton Flare Board Express (OCW)

1917 Hahn One-Ton Model C Canopy Van (JAW)

HANDY WAGON — Auburn, Indiana — (1911-1916) — This was the name of a truck built in Auburn, Ind., best known for its Auburn-Cord-Duesenberg automobiles. Both high-wheeler type Delivery Wagons and conventional ½-tons were produced by the Auburn Motor Chassis Co. The high-wheelers used an air-cooled twin-cylinder engine and chain drive, while the half-tonner was four-cylinder powered.

HARLEY-DAVIDSON - Milwaukee, Wisconsin — (1914-to date) — This well known motorcycle company has made many commercial versions of its products. Most commonly seen are three-wheel delivery vehicles, some with full cab enclosures. These are particularly useful and popular with traffic law enforcement agencies. In the late 1920s — and possibly at other times — Harley-Davidson also produced a motorcycle ambulance.

1927 Harley-Davidson Ambulance (Harley-Davidson)

1914 Harley-Davison Box Body Tricar (OCW)

1972 Harley-Davidson Golf Cart/Utility Scooter (EK)

HART-KRAFT — York, Pennsylvania — (1907-1913) — Early models built by the Hart-Kraft Motor Co. were high-wheelers. Only half-ton delivery wagons were produced through 1910, with trucks and truck chassis leaving the factory thereafter. For 1909, the line consisted of three two-cylinder deliveries, the A1 ($1,100); A2 ($1,175) and A3 ($1,200). In the following year, the B3 ($1,000), B5 ($1,175) and B6 ($1,100) were offered. Only one light truck, the half-ton BX4 ($1,425) was listed for 1911. Then, for the next two years, models included the ½-ton B, ¾-ton BX, ¾-ton G and one-ton E. While prices of $1,800 for the G and $2,000 for the E applied both seasons, the others changed considerably in price. The Model B was $1,175 in 1912 and $825 in 1913, while the BX went from $1,250 to $900. The G and E were part of a new four-cylinder line, introduced in 1911, which took the firm into receivership. Thereafter, Continental engines were used.

1910 Hart-Kraft 1000-Pound Canopy Express (WOM)

1911 Hart-Kraft Light-Duty Bus (JBY/DJS)

HATFIELD — Miamisburg, Ohio — (1907-1908) — Hatfield Motor Vehicle Company built high-wheeler type light Open Delivery vans. They featured a two-cylinder engine, friction transmission and double chain drive. This truck tipped the scales at 1100 pounds and could handle an 800-pound payload.

HATFIELD — Cortland, New York/Cornwall-on-Hudson, New York/Elmira, New York — (1910/1911/1911-1914) — These light-duties were made by Hatfield Motor Vehicle Co. (Hatfield Automobile Truck Co. after 1911). They were small ½- and one-tonners with three-cylinder engines.

1917 Hatfield Model I 1000-Pound Suburban (HAC)

HENDERSON — North Cambridge, Massachusetts — (1916-c. 1926) — Henderson Brothers produced two light-duty models as early as 1916. Both were gas-engined and marketed in chassis-only form. The 1200-pound model was $1,100 and the one-tonner sold for $1,500. One industry trade index indicates that other Henderson chassis in the ¾- to 1½-ton range were available through the middle of the Roaring Twenties.

HENNEGIN — Chicago, Illinois — (1908) — This was a high-wheeler van built by the Commercial Automobile Company. It was listed in the *Manual of Automobile Liability Insurance* for only one model year. Designated the Model A (a designation applied to the initial efforts of many manufacturers), this one was a two-cylinder, gas-fueled delivery rated for a 600-pound payload and selling for $650. The engine was mounted beneath the body and linked to a friction type transmission. Double chain drive carried power to the rear wheels. An 87 inch wheelbase chassis was used.

1908 Hennegin Model F Physician's Car (NAHC)

HERRESHOFF — Detroit, Michigan — (1911-1912) — These were small vans (98-inch wheelbase) made by the Herreshoff Motor Company.

HEWITT — New York City — (1905-1906) — Edward Ringwood Hewitt's first commercial vehicles were light vans on a single-cylinder passenger car chassis. Some sources show this trade name used through 1909, although the *Manual of Automobile Liability Insurance* suggests that the identity Hewitt International (see listing below) had actually been adopted by 1907, which is five years earlier than some secondary references indicate.

HEWITT-INTERNATIONAL — New York City — (1907-1912) — This firm evolved from E.R. Hewitt's original effort (listed above). Its products were primarily heavy trucks, although a one-ton Model 20D was built in 1911 and 1912. It sold for $1,500 in chassis-only form.

HEWITT-LINDSTROM — Chicago, Illinois — (1900-1901) — Financier John Hewitt and engineer Charles A. Lindstrom formed this company to make electric runabouts, town cars, trucks and buses.

1900 Hewitt-Lindstrom Electric Stage Coach (GR)

HEWITT-LUDLOW — San Francisco, California — (c.1912-c.1926) — The Hewitt-Ludlow Auto Company built trucks in the ¾-ton to 3½-ton capacity range. Their 1916 ¾-ton chassis had Buda power, worm drive, a 120-inch wheelbase, and sold for $1,650.

1917 Hewitt-Ludlow 1- to 1½-Ton Gasoline Tanker (JAW)

724

HEWITT-METZGER — New York City — (1913-1914) — When E.R. Hewitt's International Motor Co. (see listing above) merged with Metzger Motor Car Co., a gasoline-engined one-tonner was part of the model lineup. It sold for $1,800. Other models ranged up to 10 tons.

HIGRADE — Grand Rapids, Michigan — (1917-1921) — Highgrade Motors Co. made trucks in the ¾-ton to 1½-ton capacity range.

1918 Higrade A-18 One-Ton Panel Delivery (DFW/SI)

HIND & DAUCH — Sandusky, Ohio — (1907-1908) — Hind & Dauch built a ½-ton capacity delivery van.

HOLSMAN — Chicago, Illinois — (1908-1910) — These were high-wheelers built by the Holsman Automobile Company.

1900 Holsman Telephone Utility Wagon (DFW/WEPS)

HOUGHTON — Marion, Ohio — (1915-1917) — The Houghton Motor Co. assembled light trucks and hearses.

1916 Houghton 1-Ton Panel Delivery (DFW/HAC)

HOWARD — Yonkers, New York — (1903) — The Howard Automobile Company also made a line of trucks, including a half-ton unit with a three-cylinder engine. These trucks were designed by W.S. Howard, who had previously worked for Grant-Ferris Co. Two models were offered; one for carrying passengers and the other for hauling cargo loads up to 1000 pounds. The company also produced a four-ton gas/electric truck, which lies beyond the scope of this catalog.

1895 Howard Canopy Top Suburban (NAHC/OPC)

HOWARD — Boston, Massachusetts — (1915-1916) — The Robert G. Howard Motor Truck Co. built a light, open delivery wagon.

HUDSON — Detroit, Michigan — (1933-1947) — This auto-maker offered pickups and panels these years. See the Hudson chapter in the forward section of this catalog.

HUPMOBILE — Detroit, Michigan — (1912-1925) — Sources differ as to the range of years the Hupp Motor Company also manufactured light-duty trucks and commercial chassis.

1914 Hupmobile Model 32 Panel Body (OCW)

1927 Hupmobile with Station Wagon Body (DFW/CTA)

1925 Hupmobile ''R'' Panel Delivery Van (DFW/OHS)

IDEAL — Fort Wayne, Indiana — (1910-1915) — The Ideal Auto Co. built trucks, ranging in capacity from ¼-ton to 2½-tons.

1914 Ideal Model I Covered One-Ton Flare Board

IMP — Auburn, Indiana — (1913-1915) — This rig was on a cyclecar chassis, and built by the W.H. McIntyre Co.

1914 Imp Light Closed Delivery Car (OCW)

INDEPENDENT — Plano, Illinois — (1911) — The manufacturer of this $750 gasoline-powered Business Model No. 22 was listed as the Harvester Co.

INDEPENDENT — Port Huron, Michigan — (1915-1918) — Independent Motors Co. marketed the 1500- to 2000-pound Model F chassis for four years at a price of $1,285 to $1,385. It was gas-engine powered.

INDEPENDENT — Davenport, Iowa — (1917-1921) — This firm built a one-ton assembled truck with Continental engine, Fuller three-speed gear box and Russel bevel gear rear axle. It had a 135 inch wheelbase.

INDEPENDENT — Youngstown, Ohio — (1918-1923) — A one-tonner was always a part of this company's line. It was another assembled job with a Continental four, three-speed Fuller transmission and worm drive axle.

INDIANA — Marion, Indiana — (1911-1932) / Cleveland, Ohio — (1932-1939) — The Indiana Motors Corporation was absorbed by White. They were a well-known assembler of trucks and, in some years, their lightest model was rated at under one-ton.

1914 Indiana Model B-30 Flare Board Express (OCW)

1932 Indiana 1-to 1½-Ton Dump Truck (NSPC/JE)

1932 Indiana Model 70 1-Ton Milk Van (DFW/VWC)

1937 Indiana Walk-in Milk Delivery (DFW/Volvo-White)
726

1937 Indiana Model 80 Bakery Van (DFW/Volvo-White)

INTERNATIONAL HARVESTER - Chicago, Illinois - (1907-1986) — This firm was known as IHC, International or International Harvester Co. and operates, today, as Navistar International, although light-duty trucks are no longer built. Detailed information about these makes can be found in the forward section of this catalog.

1937 IHC One-Ton Beverage Delivery Truck (OCW)

IROQUOIS — Buffalo, New York — (1906) — The Iroquois Iron Works built two sizes of truck: a four-ton model and a ½-tonner.

J

JACKSON — Jackson, Michigan — (c.1907-1923) — The Jackson Motor Car Company had built passenger cars since 1903, and then began building light trucks. Later, they built heavy trucks.

1908 Jackson Panel Delivery Van (NAHC/DPL)

JAMIESON — Warren, Pennsylvania — (1901-1902) — This was a small delivery truck, and it was made by the Jamieson Automobile Works.

JEFFERY — Kenosha, Wisconsin — (1914-1917) — The Thomas B. Jeffery Company is best-known as the builder of the Jeffery Quad of World War I fame. They also built a lighter, ¾-ton truck, the chassis for which — in 1916 — sold for $900. It rode on 35x4½ inch pneumatic tires and came with an electric starter. In 1917, the Jeffery firm was acquired by Nash.

1914 Jeffery 1500-Pound Flare Board Express (OCW)

1914 Jeffery One-Ton Flare Board with Stakes (OCW)

1915 Jeffery Paddy Wagon (DFW/NAHC)

1916 Jeffery Model 1016 1500-Lb. Panel (DFW/MVMA)

1916 Jeffery 1500-Lb. Flare Board (DFW/MVMA)

JONZ — New Albany, Indiana — (1912-1913) — The American Automobile Manufacturing Company also built a line of trucks, including a ½-ton capacity model.

K

KAISER-JEEP — Toledo, Ohio — (1963-1969) — Information about this make can be found in the front section of this catalog.

1966 Kaiser-Jeep Wagoneer Station Wagon

KANSAS CITY — Kansas City, Missouri — (1905-1917) — These were light vans, sometimes known as the "Kansas City Car," built by the Kansas City Motor Car Company.

KARIVAN — Wheatland, Pennsylvania — (1955) — This was a three-wheeled van, outfitted by Tri-Car, Inc.

KEARNS — Beavertown, Pennsylvania — (1909-1928) — The Kearns Motor Car Company started out building larger trucks, but, just after World War I, it introduced some smaller models including one rated at ½-ton capacity. Prior to this, there was a one-ton Model 35 that sold for $2,950 in 1911, plus a $2,100 one-ton of 1912 and the Model 30, another one-ton of 1914-1915, which retailed for $2,000 to $2,100. Also in 1914, the company sold its Model A, which was a ¾-ton truck. It was priced at $950 for the chassis, $1,000 for a flare board, $1,050 for a stake bed and $1,100 for a panel. In 1916, the name Kearns Motor Truck Co. was used for a small chassis with a 100-pound payload rating which sold for $600. The postwar half-tonner used a Lycoming engine, dry plate clutch and internal gear drive. It was $850.

1914 Kearns Model A Panel Delivery Van (OCW)

1918 Kearns Model DU Covered Flare Board (DFW)

1920 Kearns Flare Board Express (B. Crowley)

KELLAND — Newark, New Jersey — (1922-c. 1926) — The Kelland Motor Car Co. built small, battery-powered vans. Their ½-ton chassis sold for $1,750, and their ¾-ton chassis sold for $1,850.

1920 Kelland Electric Walk-in Delivery Van (DFW/HAC)

KELLEY-SPRINGFIELD — Springfield, Ohio — (1910-1929) — This make suceeded the Frayer-Miller and continued to use air-cooled engines through 1912; water-cooled fours thereafter. Characteristics included sloped hoods, behind-the-engine radiators and a three-speed transmission. One-tons were offered through 1916 as the $2000 Model K-30.

1914 Kelly-Springfield K-30 1-Ton Chassis (OCW)

KENAN — Long Beach, California — (1915) — One of three models produced by Kenan Manufacturing Co. was a 1500-pound (¾-ton) chassis with a gasoline engine and $1,600 price tag.

KENWORTH — Seattle, Washington — (1925 to date) — This firm evolved from Gerlinger Motor Car Co. and took its name from H.W. Kent and E.K. Worthington, who were executives for the predecessor firm which built the Gersix truck. Most Kenworths were in the 1½- to 18-ton range, but one-tons were produced in the middle 1920s.

KEYSTONE — Philadelphia, Pennsylvania — (1919-1923) — This company started as the Commercial Car Unit Co. in Philadelphia and later became Keystone Motor Truck Co. of Oaks, Pa. (Montgomery County). At first, the sole product was a two-tonner. A one-ton model was available in 1920 only. This truck was named the Model 20, which indicated its 2000-pound capacity, rather than model year.

KING — Chicago, Illinois — (1899-1900) — Built by machinist A.W. King, this high-wheel runabout resembled a wagon with flatbed rear deck. It was suitable for light-duty cargo hauling and truck use, as well as passenger carrying.

1896 King High-Wheeler with Platform Deck (NAHC)

KING ZEITLER — Chicago, Illinois — (1919-c. 1929) — The King-Zeitler Company made trucks of between ¾-ton to five-ton capacity.

KISSEL — Hartford, Wisconsin — (1908-1931) — The Kissel Motor Car Company was known for both its autos and trucks, and they are sometimes called "Kissel-Kars." Some of their chassis were used for buses, fire apparatus, and professional cars. In 1916, their ½-ton delivery chassis with a 115-inch wheelbase sold for $950; their next larger chassis was rated at ¾ to one-ton and on a 125-inch wheelbase, and sold for $1,250. Trade directories from the late 1920's show that the smallest, then "Kisselkar" truck was rated at one-ton.

1912 Kissel Kar 1500-Pound Platform (KM/HW)

1913 Kissel Kar 1500-Pound Delivery (DFW/SI)

1914 Kissel Kar One-Ton Platform Stake (OCW)

1912 Kissel Kar 1500-Pound Rack Body (KM/HW)

1914 Kissel Kar 1500-Pound Panel Body Delivery (OCW)

1915 Kissel Kar 1500-Pound Panel Delivery (OCW)

1916 Kissel Kar ¾-to 1-Ton Express w/Stakes (KM/HW)

1922 Kissel 18-Pass. 8-Door Coach Limited (OCW)

1928 Kissel National Hearse (A&A)

1929 Kissel-Bradfield Taxicab (A&A)

KLEIBER — San Francisco, California — (1914-1937) — The Kleiber Motor Truck Company built a full-size range of trucks, although in its later years it was also an important West Coast distributor for Studebaker. For at least two years, 1929 and 1930, their smallest chassis was rated at ¾-ton capacity, and it sold for $1,170.

1930 Kleiber One-Ton Ice Truck (DFW/SI)

KNOX - Springfield, Massachusetts — (1901-1924) — Best-known for its three- and four-wheel tractors, the Knox Automobile Company also made light-duty delivery trucks and ambulances.

1910 Knox ''64'' 1-Ton Holyoke City Ambulance

1902 Knox (Waterless) Light Delivery (JAW)

1904 Knox Canopied Express Delivery (JAW)

1910 Knox Model 64 1-Ton Chicago Ambulance (OCW)

1914 Knox-Martin 3-Wheel Model 31 Tractor (JAW)
(Designed to haul trailers with 3 to 7 ton loads.)

KOEHLER — Newark, N.J. — (1913-1916) — The H.J. Koehler Sporting Goods Co. produced a line of one-tonners under this company name for four years. The 1913-1915 Model A came as a stake-side open flare board truck ($750); an express ($790); a canvas-side ($800) or a panel delivery ($900). The Model K of 1915-1916 was produced in chassis-only form ($895), as well as open-flare ($935) or express ($980). All were powered by four-cylinder, overhead valve gasoline engines. By 1917, the name was changed to H.J. Koehler Motor Corp. and trucks over one-ton were the only products made. Relatives of H.J. Koehler are still active in the truck collecting hobby.

1914 Koehler One-Ton Express Type Wagon (OCW)

KOSMATH — Detroit, Mich. — (1914-1916) — The Kosmath was a continuation of the Miller Car Company's 1914 Model A 1/2-ton panel truck. The first Kosmath was a 1,250-pound gasoline powered truck that sold for $900 with a panel body. In 1915, a 1/2-ton Model 14 was offered in chassis form for $850. This became the Model 15 the following season, which sold for $675 in chassis form and $750 as a panel or express.

1914 Kosmath 1250-Pound Panel Body Ban (OCW)

KREBS — Bellevue, Ohio — (1922-1925) — The Krebs Motor Truck Company built trucks in sizes ranging from ¾ to six-tons. A 1916 trade directory also mentions a Krebs Commercial Car Co., of Clyde, Ohio, which built trucks with Renault-style hoods. Their 1916 ¾-ton chassis on a 120-inch wheelbase with worm drive, pneumatic tires, and a 22.5 hp. engine, sold for $1,600.

1914 Krebs Model BB 1500-Pound Panel Body (OCW)

1915 Krebs Model Light Model F ¾-Ton Express (JAW)

K.R.I.T. — **Detroit, Michigan** — **(1911-1914)** — The Krit Motor Car Company built autos, and also a light delivery body on one of the auto chassis.

1914 K.R.I.T. Model KD ½-Ton Panel (OCW)

L

LAMBERT — **Anderson, Indiana** — **(1912-1917)** — The Buckeye Manufacturing Co. built mainly autos, but also produced some commercial chassis and trucks. The first year for truck production seems to be 1912, when a one-ton express was offered at $1,600. The Model V-3, of 1913-1914, was a one-ton chassis with an $1,800 price tag. For 1915, the line was expanded to include the V-1 with an 800-pound payload rating. It came as a chassis for $900 or a panel at $950. The same year, the V-2 was offered in the 1500-pound class. It sold for $1,125 in chassis form and $1,200 as an express. The V-3 was also carried over at $1,700.

1912 Lambert Panel Delivery (DFW/MVMA)

1914 Lambert Model V-3 Flare Board Express (OCW)

LANDSHAFT — **Chicago, Illinois** — **(1911-1920)** — In its early years, the William Landshaft & Son firm built a ½-ton truck. The company's 1912 line included the Model A, a gas-engined 1000-pound open delivery selling for $950, the Model B, a 1000-pound panel top with a $1,000 price tag, the Model C one-ton open delivery at $1,250 and the Model D panel top for $1,300. All used two-cylinder engines. There were ½-, ¾- and one-tonners in 1913, all being of open express style with prices between $950 and $1,700. For 1914 and 1915, the ¾-ton and one-ton models were continued. By 1916, the smallest Landshaft truck was the one-ton.

1914 Landshaft Model C Flare Board Express (OCW)

LANGE — **Pittsburgh, Pennsylvania** — **(1911-1913)** — In 1913, the Lange Motor Truck Co. produced a one-ton chassis identified as the Model C. It was a gas-engined truck with a $2,250 price tag. The Model C was made through at least 1918. Thereafter, all of the company's products appear to be 1½-tons or heavier.

1914 Lange Model C Flare Board Express (OCW)

LANPHER — **Carthage, Missouri** — **(1910)** — Lanpher Motor Buggy Co. produced the Model L light-delivery for just one season. It was a high-wheel van with a 14 h.p. two-cylinder engine and a $550 price. The truck featured a 76 inch wheelbase, planetary transmission and chain drive.

LANSDEN — **Danbury, Connecticut** — **(1905-1928)** — This is a moderately-well-known battery-powered electric truck, manufactured by the Lansden Company at four successive sites: Newark, Allentown, Brooklyn, and Danbury. Their trucks ranged in capacity from ½-ton to 6-tons. A 1907 listing identifies a 1000-pound payload electric delivery truck selling for $2,350. Other half-tons were made as late as 1915 and sold for $2,535 in express form. In 1918, their ⅓-ton chassis was priced at $1,400 with battery; and $1,150 without. The batteries weighed 1,050 pounds, (more than the truck's payload!). The truck's range (loaded) was 50 miles; unloaded, 60 miles. It could travel at 15 m.p.h.

LARRABEE — Binghamton, New York — (1916-1932) —The Larrabee company was named for H. Chester Larrabee and R.H. Deyo, president. It was one of many companies producing standard asssembled trucks with the general range of one to five tons. Its Model M, of 1917-1918, was a one-ton chassis powered by a four-cylinder gasoline engine. It sold for $1,600 the first year, but was up to $1,950 by 1918. In 1922, the company offered a one-ton "Speed Truck" with a six-cylinder Continental engine and pneumatic tires. The one-ton of 1919 was $1,950. Four-cylinder taxi-cabs were also manufactured in the late 1920s.

LaSALLE — Detroit, Michigan — (1927-1940) — Cadillac's stylish "companion car" became the basis for many commercial car models such as funeral vehicles and ambulances. Companies favoring Cadillac chassis for such conversions included Meteor, of Picqua, Ohio; Eureka, of Rock Falls, Ill.; and Flxible Co., of Loudonville, Ohio. However, very few LaSalle "professional vehicles" appeared prior to 1933, when A.J. Miller Co., of Belle Fontaine, Ohio, turned out a limousine-ambulance for the Stonington Ambulance Corps. on LaSalle running gear. In 1936, a Meteor-LaSalle flower car was built for a funeral parlor. It wasn't until 1937, however, that a new Miller-LaSalle attracted lots of attention at a national funeral director's convention in Louisville, Ken. It was reported to have "out-shone and out-sold the field." Miller sales and production records were broken and LaSalle was, thereafter, assured a strong role in the hearse and ambulance industry. Perhaps that's why Cadillac began offering a factory "stretch" job the same season. Designated the Series 37-50 Commercial Chassis, it featured a 160 inch wheelbase and suitably extended frame. This configuration found 900 buyers in 1938. Buyers totaled 874 the following year and 1,030 in 1940. In 1938, Eureka and Sayers & Scovill, of Cincinnati, began making LaSalle-based flower cars. By 1940, Flxible was also producing such a model. Some unusual LaSalle-based commercial versions included a eight-door wood station wagon of 1940, plus tow truck and fire truck conversions.

1938 LaSalle Funeral Flower Car (DFW/BAC)

LAUTH — Chicago, Illinois — (1907-1910) — This company had English Magnus Hendrickson trucks built expressly for use at its tanning factory. They were light-duty conventionals with gas engines, chain drive, cab roofs and closed delivery bodies. From 1908, cars and trucks were made in limited numbers. Hendrickson designed the first hollow spoke wheel, several transmissions and the first worm drive axle.

LAUTH-JUERGENS — Fremont, Ohio — (1910-1915) —Theodore Juergens joined J. Lauth & Company (See prior listing) in 1908. By 1910, the firm moved to Ohio as the Lauth-Juergens Motor Car Co., which was exclusively a truck-maker. Magnus Hendrickson was chief engineer. The Model K, of 1913-1914, sold for $2,100 in one-ton chassis form. It had a guaranteed-for-life motor. Larger models were built until 1914, when H.G. Burford Co. purchased the firm.

1914 Lauth-Juergens Model K Canopy Express (OCW)

LAVIGNE — Detroit, Michigan — (1914-1915) —The Lavigne Cyclecar Co. offered a delivery model with an eight-foot wheelbase. It was powered by an air-cooled four and had a planetary transmission and shaft drive. The $600 vehicle had a 650 pound GVW.

LAWSON — Pittsburgh, Pennsylvania — (1917-1918) — The Lawson Manufacturing Company built a ½-ton truck.

LEACH — Everitt, Massachusetts — (1899-1900) — This was a steam-powered delivery van on an auto chassis, produced by the Leach Motor Vehicle Company.

LE MOON — Chicago, Illinois — (1910-1939) —Nelson & LeMoon, of Chicago, claimed to have built its first truck in 1906. By 1910, the firm had a one-tonner on the market. Its D1, of 1913, was a one-ton express with a $2,000 asking price. Most of its products were, however, heavier-duties.

LIBERTY — Detroit, Michigan — (1916-1923) — The Liberty Motor Car Company built a six-cylinder automobile and some pictures have been found of a light truck, probably built on a commercial chassis.

1918 Liberty Pickup Truck (DFW/OHS)

LIGHT — New York City — (1914) — This was a three-wheel parcel delivery van built by Light Commercial Car Co. Some sources trace this firm to Marietta, Pa. in 1913. However the *Manual of Automobile Liability Insurance* indicates that 1914 was the only year of production under this corporate name. There were a pair of two-cylinder models having 750-pound payloads. The first was a chassis at $460. A box body model was $15 more.

1914 Light Tri-Car Box Body Delivery (OCW)

LIMA — Lima, Ohio — (1915-1916) — C. E. Miller and F.E. McGraw were the men behind the Lima Light Car Manufacturing Co., of Lima, Ohio. Pooling together $50,000 in capitol stock, the two men launched the firm in April 1915. They dreamed of producing as many as ten cars per day, as well as a line of light-duty trucks. Undoubtedly, these trucks were to be based on the passenger car chassis, which featured an 18 horsepower four-cylinder engine and 100 inch long wheelbase. They were promoted as half-tonners. According to *The Standard Catalog of American Cars 1805-1942*, "Experimental cars were on the road later that month, but whether any production cars followed them is problemmatical. The Lima Light Car Company disappeared from view later that year."

LINCOLN — Chicago, Illinois — (1912-1913) — These were light vans, built by the Lincoln Motor Car Works, a successor to the Sears. For 1912, there were two models, both with 800-pound payloads. The "27" was a closed panel. It sold for $750. The "29" was a $650 express. The two were carried over for 1913, at prices of $685 and $585 respectively. These trucks used a 14 h.p. two-cylinder engine which was air-cooled. They featured a friction type transmission and single chain drive. Solid or pneumatic tires were optional.

LINCOLN — Pontiac, Michigan — (1916) — The only size truck offered by the Lincoln Motor Truck Company was a ¾-ton capacity model. It sold for $925 in chassis form and $985 as an open express. Its features included a four-cylinder OHV engine, three-speed gear box and 122 inch wheelbase. Lincoln absorbed the O.K. Motor Truck Co. in 1916

1930 Lincoln Motion Picture Camera Truck (DFW/CC)

LINCOLN — Dearborn, Michigan — (1920-date) — Henry Ford's luxury car has been used for truck conversions like camping cars (one of which Ford himself used) and the camera truck pictured here.

LINDSLEY — Indianapolis, Indiana — (1908) — This was a high-wheeled, ¾-ton delivery van offered by J. V. Lindsley & Co. It used a two-cylinder gas engine and sold for $500.

LION — New York City — (1920-1921) — The Lion Motor Truck Corp., of New York, N.Y., produced just one model. It was a ¾-ton truck.

LIPPARD-STEWART — Buffalo, New York — (1911-1919) — The Lippard-Stewart Motor Car Company built light trucks, with Renault-style sloped hoods. In 1916, their ½-ton model was on a 106-inch wheelbase and sold for $1,000. Their ¾-ton model sold for $1,600 and was available with three wheelbases: 115-inch, 125-inch and 135-inch. Some individuals associated with this firm left, and formed a new firm which built Stewart trucks, a make which lasted until World War II.

1911 Lippard-Stewart Light Express (OCW)

1914 Lippard-Stewart Model B Panel Delivery (OCW)

LITTLE GIANT — Chicago, Illinois — (1911-1918) — The Chicago Pneumatic Tool Company — a firm which still survives today — made a line of light-duty trucks early in its history. These commercial vehicles were known as Little Giants, which name was also used on the firm's larger (up to 3½-tons) models. The 1911 line included a 1500-lb. Delivery that was powered by a two-cylinder engine and sold for $1,000. In 1912, there were ¾-ton Model C ($1,100 for the chassis) and 1-ton Model D offerings. The

1911 Little Giant Light Express Wagon (OCW)

tonner came in four variations: Open Flare Board ($1,100), Canvas Top Express ($1,150), Standard Body (also $1,150) and Full Panel ($1,200). Two-cylinder gasoline engines were again used in both lines. Model A was the designation for the ¾-ton chassis, which sold for $950 in 1913. This year, both the "C" and "D" were classified as one-tons and, in chassis form, sold for $1,050 and $1,150, respectively. The 1914 line included a trio of one-tons, the Models D, F and H, all priced at $1,050. In 1915, only the "H" (now at $1,350) was back. Light-duties marketed in 1916 were limited to the ¾-ton Model 15 ($1,500) and a one-ton (there was also a 1½-ton version) called the H-3 ($1,350). Later reference sources, contemporary to the 1920s, refer to this company's products simply as "Giants." A 1918, Giant/Little Giant is part of the Imperial Palace Auto Collection.

1911 Little Giant Canopied Delivery (OCW)

1914 Little Giant Model F Platform (OCW)

1914 Little Giant Model H Flare Board (OCW)

1915 Little Giant ¾-Ton Chassis & Cowl (OCW)

1916 Little Giant One-Ton Worm Drive Delivery (OCW)

LITTLEMAC — Muscatine, Iowa - (1929-1935) —According to historian Jeff Gillis, Muscatine Mayor Herbert Thompson and his brother Ralph promoted Clayton Frederick's pint-sized auto in an effort to bring industry to their town. In Nov. 1929, Thompson Motors was incorporated at $1,000,000. The Littlemac rode an 80 inch wheelbase (later increased to 82 inches) and had a Continental four-cylinder engine. Six "truckette" versions of the vehicle were manufactured, including a very boxy panel delivery. They cost about $500. The first was delivered to a local baker in Aug. 1931.

1932 Littlemac Panel Truckette (Jeff Gillis)

1932 Littlemac Panel Truckette (Jeff Gillis)

1932 Littlemac Panel Truckette (Jeff Gillis)

734

LOCOMOBILE — Bridgeport, Connecticut — (1901-1929) — Just after the turn of the Century, the Locomobile Company of America built a ½-ton capacity "Locodelivery" powered by steam, with a 12½-gallon fuel tank, a 50-gallon water tank and 16-inch boiler, and selling for $2,000. They also built heavy trucks just before World War I; in addition, their auto chassis were sometimes outfitted with commercial bodies.

1918 Locomobile Sightseeing Tour Bus (DFW/OHS)

LOGAN — Chillicothe, Ohio — (1907-1908) —This firm was undoubtedly connected to the company in the following listing, although, in this case, the name Logan Construction Co. was used. The 1907 line included the Model N, a 1200-pounder and the 2½-ton Model M. In 1908, there was a one-ton Model T. They used two-cylinder gasoline engines. The "N" sold for $1,000, while the "T" was $2,250.

LOGAN EXPRESS — Chillicothe, Ohio — (1904-1908) —Benjamin A. Gramm started this firm as a part of his Motor Storage & Mfg. Co. It produced two- and four-cylinder cars with both air- and water-cooled engines. The 1905 Logan Express was a commercial version of the two-cylinder Model D touring car. By 1907, trucks became the company's mainstay product. After a 1908 bankruptcy, B.A. Gramm moved to Bowling Green, Ohio, to establish Gramm-Logan Motor Car Co., which built only trucks. The firm then became Gramm-Bernstein and Gramm, both headquartered in Lima, Ohio.

1905 Logan Model E Express Wagon (JAW)

LOOMIS — Westfield, Massachusetts — (1901) — The Loomis Automobile Co. produced light vans, powered by a single-cylinder engine.

LORD BALTIMORE — Baltimore, Maryland — (1911-1914) —This company's first light-duty truck was the half-ton Model D truck chassis of 1913, which sold for $1,300. A one-tonner priced at $2,250 and called the Model C was also a part of the line. For 1914 a one-ton, the Model B, had a $2,000 price tag. While some sources indicate the firm survived until 1916, still building one-tons, contemporary insurance manuals have no listings later than 1914.

1914 Lord Baltimore Model B Covered Express (OCW)

LOYAL — Lancaster, Ohio — (1918-1920) — The Loyal Motor Truck Company built light trucks during its short life. Its 1918 ½-ton model sold for $800, and was on a 110-inch wheelbase. The ¾-ton model was on a 120-inch wheelbase, and sold for $850.

LUCK UTILITY — Cleburne, Texas — (1913-1914) — The Cleburne Motor Car Manufacturing Co. built a ½-ton truck. It sold for $750. The four-cylinder engine was under a hood between the individual seats. Other features included a three-speed transmission and shaft drive.

1912 Luck Utility Commercial Roadster (D.J. Kava)

LUVERNE — Luverne, Minnesota — (c. 1912-1925) — This firm began in 1906, evolving out of a carriage-building operation of two brothers, Al and Ed Leicher. The new firm built both autos and trucks. In 1913, they built a motorized fire pumper for the City of Luverne. They stopped building autos in 1917 and trucks in 1923. However, they continued to outfit fire-fighting apparatus, a function the firm still performs.

1917 Luverne One-Ton Farm Truck (DFW)

M

MACCAR — Allentown, Pennsylvania — (1912-1935) — The Maccar Truck Company can be traced to one of the original Mack Brothers. It is best known for its medium and large trucks, although, for a few years, its smallest model was rated at ¾-ton. In 1914, the 1500-pound Model A was $1,650. The same year the Model one-ton, at $1,900 for a chassis, was marketed. Strangely, the "B" designation was also used on 1½- and two-ton models. By 1916, the one-ton was up to $2,100. This configuration remained in the line through the early 1920s, at least.

1914 Maccarr Model A Semi Panel Delivery (OCW)

1914 Maccarr Model A Flare Board Express (OCW)

1914 Maccarr Model A Covered Flare Board (OCW)

1914 Maccarr Model B Chassis (OCW)

MACK — Allentown, Pennsylvania — (1902 to date) — This is one of the best-known of all U.S. trucks, buses, and fire apparatus. Sometimes its smallest chassis would be rated at under one-ton. In the period 1936-1938, Mack Jrs. were marketed in sizes as small as ½-ton; (they were, however, manufactured by Reo, but had minor trim changes). One Mack Jr. was sold as an attractive ½-ton pickup, (and is sought by old truck fans who want to own a Mack, but don't have a large garage).

1936 Mack Junior Milk Delivery Van (DFW/DPL)

1914 Mack Covered Flare Board Express (OCW)

1937 Mack Junior Cab Express (EK)

MAHONING — Youngstown, Ohio — (1904-1905) — Mahoning Motor Car Co. produced a $950 delivery car as part of its four model line. It was powered by a nine horsepower, one-cylinder engine and had an 82 inch wheelbase.

1901 Mahoney Closed Top Delivery Van (JAW)

MAIS — Peru, Indiana/Indianapolis, Indiana — (1911-1917) — Mais Motor Truck Company entered the truck-making business with a lineup of heavy-duty models, but scaled-down to the one-ton class, in 1914 and 1915, when a 1000-pound Flare Board Express was retailed for $825. This truck failed to survive in 1916, when larger models in the 1½- to three-ton range were marketed. The firm lasted until 1917, when the same three "heavies" were offered at identical prices. Mais is best known for being (it is claimed) the first manufacturer to use the principle of internal gear drive. Most of these trucks were powered by four-cylinder power plants mounted under a short hood, behind a rather large radiator. Three-speed transmissions were also employed. The one-ton Flare Board Express was of the eight-post Curtain Top type, which was typical of this era. These posts were attached to a three-panel cargo box at the bottom and supported a long roof, on top, which extended out over the driver's seat, perched atop a platform. Equipment included cowl-mounted headlamps, center controls and artillery spoke wheels.

1914 Mais Covered Flare Board Express (OCW)

MARATHON — Nashville, Tennessee — (1912-1913) — Marathon Motor Works built trucks in a variety of sizes, the smallest of which was rated at ¼-ton. This was listed as the "Runner" model. It was a light delivery with a gasoline fueled engine and an $850 price.

MARMON — Indianapolis, Indiana — (1912-1935) — Nordyke & Marmon, the prestige auto-maker, produced several light-duty trucks. One model was a ¼-ton light delivery van with a T-head four-cylinder engine, three-speed gear box and shaft drive, which had a top speed of 20 m.p.h. The Model 3, of 1913-1914, was a gas-powered ¾-ton selling for $2,500 in chassis-only form. This van had a long 10-foot wheelbase, but a small cargo area.

1914 Marmon Covered Flare Board (OCW)

1914 Marmon Panel Body Delivery (OCW)

MARMON-HERRINGTON — Indianapolis, Indiana/Knoxville, Tennessee — (1931-1963/1973) — Marmon-Herrington Incorporated was formed by auto-maker Walter C. Marmon (see Marmon listing above), when he teamed-up with Colonel Arthur W. Herrington to develop all-wheel-drive trucks, originally for military applications. During the 1930s, the firm — which was based in Indianapolis through 1963 — turned out Reconaissance Cars, Scout Cars and Armoured Vehicles for the United States Army. In 1936, the company started converting "early" Ford V-8 ½-ton trucks into four-wheel-drive vehicles. This phase of the operation prospered throughout World War II and survived long afterwards. The company's rugged, go-anywhere trucks made a major contribution to the Allied war effort and earned an enviable reputation for service and reliability. In the late 1940s, the company was responsible for the "Ranger," a somewhat popular conversion of the 1946-1948 type Ford panel delivery truck into an off-road vehicle. (Ranger, of course, later became the name of a Ford pickup truck line.) Another well-known Marmon-Herrington conversion, which entered production in 1937, was a V-8 Ford-based military ambulance, built off the ½-ton chassis reworked into a semi-forward-control truck with canvas top cab. (The company also carried out a limited number of conversions on Chevrolet, Dodge, IHC and GMC trucks, although it is most commonly associated with Ford.) After World War II, Marmon-Herrington also built a small, multi-stop parcel delivery type truck called the Delivr-All. The first of these was seen about 1945 and the offering lasted until 1952. Later, trolleys and buses were made.

1936 Marmon-Herrington "DeliVr-All" Panel (DFW/BAC)

MARTIN — York, Pennsylvania — (1909-1915) — The Martin Carriage Works built high-wheelers with ½-ton capacity and two-cylinder engines. Models offered in 1910-1912 included the ¾-ton "E" panel ($1,500); the ½-ton "J" panel ($1,400); the ¾-ton "G" full-panel ($1,650); the ¾-ton "F2" shift-top ($1,450); the ¾-ton "G2" full-panel ($1,600); the ¾-ton "G3" full-panel ($1,840); the ¾-ton "G4" full-panel ($1,600) and the "H," a one-ton panel priced at $1,750. However, after 1912, the smallest truck was a one-ton. The Martin name was discontinued in 1915 and replaced by Atlas.

MARYLAND — Luke, Maryland — (1900-1901) — The Maryland Automobile Mfg. Co. sold delivery vans with a 1000-pound payload. They used a two-cylinder, double slide-valve steam engine. The top speed was 30 m.p.h.

MASON — Waterloo, Iowa — (1912-1914) — This company evolved out of Maytag (See separate listing below) and the two are sometimes referred to as Mason-Maytag. The Model 12 was a closed delivery offered at $800 in 1912. It was carried over for 1913-1914 as an open flare board express with similar price.

MAYTAG — Waterloo, Iowa — (1908-1911) — The name survives as a maker of washing machines. The Maytag-Mason Motor Co. built a light auto with a body which could be converted into a light truck.

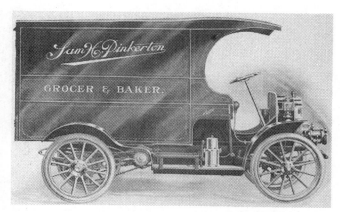

1910 Maytag Model 10 Light Delivery Van (OCW)

1911 Maytag Light Delivery Wagon (DFW/ACTHR)

1910 Maytag Light Express Wagon (DFW/ACTHR)

1911 Maytag Light Delivery Car (DFW/ACTHR)

MAXIM — New York, New York — (1913-1914) — According to *The Complete Encyclopedia of Commercial Vehicles* (Krause Publications), The Maxim Tri-Car Manufacturing Company based the design of its vehicle on the German Phanomobil (a.k.a. "Phanomen"). The Tri-Car was jointly designed by Frenchman Maxim Karminski and German George Peters. This three-wheeler came in several models. For 1913, the Model E was listed as a Delivery having a 500-pound payload rating and carrying a $395 retail price. Listed as a Tri-Car, the Model F, of 1914, was $425. This slightly more substantial vehicle could handle a 750-pound payload. Both versions were powered by an eight-horsepower two-cylinder gasoline engine. The power plant was air-coooled. It drove the front wheel via a single chain. The wheelbase for the original Delivery model was 90 inches. The firm was started, in 1911, at Thompsonville, Connecticut. The original name was Maxim Tri-Car Manufacturing. Sometime in 1913, the company reorganized as Maxim Tri-Car Co., in Port Jefferson (Long Island), New York. The *Manual of Automobile Liability Insurance*, published by the Fidelity and Casualty Company of New York, on January 1, 1916, lists Maxim Tri-Car as a New York City company. This was probably the location of the main sales branch or corporate headquarters. Other features of the Maxim Tri-Car included a massive frame, tiller type steering, "spider" type eight-spoke wheels (two at the rear and one up front), pneumatic tires, and motorcycle type fenders all around.

1911 Maxim Box Body Tricar (OCW/DPL)

1914 Maxim Tricar Delivery Van (OCW)

MAXWELL — Detroit, Michigan — **(1905-1925)** — Starting out as Maxwell-Briscoe and eventually becoming part of Chrysler, the Maxwell Motor Co. produced autos, taxicabs, fire apparatus, delivery vans, and some other light trucks. In terms of total trucks registered in the U.S. in late 1921, Maxwells were tenth from the top.

1909 Maxwell Model A Canopied Express (Wm. Pollock)

1917 Maxwell One-Ton Express (VHTM)

1918 Maxwell One-Ton Covered Express (S. Kellerman)

1922 Maxwell One-Ton Express Wagon (John Lee)

1925 Maxwell Merchant's Car-Panel Body (OCW)

McINTYRE — Auburn, Indiana — **(1909-1915)** — The W. H. McIntyre Co. dated from 1880, building both autos and trucks. Its early trucks were high-wheelers. The company made many, many light-duty commercial styles including an 1800-pound delivery ($800), one-ton delivery ($1,200), 1200-pound delivery ($1,000), 600-pound delivery ($550) and 800-pound chassis ($600).

1912 McIntyre Express (Skip Marketti/ACD Museum)

MEISELBACH — North Milwaukee, Wisconsin — **(1904-1909)** — This company began with a one-tonner powered by a water-cooled, horizontally-opposed two-cylinder engine. It had a friction transmission and chain drive. The price of the one-tonner, in 1908-1909, was $2,000.

MENOMINEE — Menominee, Michigan — **(1913-1918)** — D.F. Poyer & Co., of Menominee, Michigan, built a number of one-ton and under models from its beginning. The Model A, of 1913, was a 1500-pound (¾-ton) that came in chassis ($1,125) or Express ($1,200) forms. Rated for 2000 pounds — or one-ton — was the Model B of the same year. It retailed at $1,400 for the chassis and $1,500 for the Express. Both were carried over, in 1914, as the A-3 and B-3, with similar prices. For 1915, the line was substantially expanded in terms of body styles. For instance, the ¾-ton MA-3 came as a chassis ($1,125), or an Express, Stake or Panel (all ($1,200), while the one-ton Model MB-3 was $1,400 for the chassis and $1,500 for any of the same three other styles. The 1916 line included the ¾-ton Model E and one-ton Model FW, which were $1,125 and $1,575, respectively, for chassis-only editions. In 1917, the firm was reorganized as Menominee Motor Truck Company. The M-EW, a ¾-tonner for $1,425 and the M-FW, a one-tonner for $1,790, were offered as chassis-only that season. In 1918, there were two models, the EW (now uprated to one-ton and priced at $1,650) and a second one-ton ($1,775) called the "Hurry-ton," which was probably a *speedwagon* type of truck.

1914 Menominee Model A-3 Flare Board Express (OCW)

1914 Menominee Model B-3 Flare Board Express (OCW)

MENOMINEE — Clintonville, Wisconsin — (1911-1937) — Named after an Indian tribe, the long-lasting, but relatively obscure truck was built in north-central Wisconsin. It originally offered ¾-ton and one-ton models. By 1923, the range ran from a one-ton up to over-six-tonners. The firm was first known as Menominee Motor Truck Co. In 1928, it became the Utility Supply Co., a subsidiary of Clintonville Four-Wheel-Drive Auto Co.

MERCURY — Chicago, Illinois — (1911-1916) — These were ½-ton high-wheelers, built by the Mercury Manufacturing Company. The first models were a delivery ($750), express ($800) and closed express ($850) powered by a two-cylinder gas engine. In 1912, five 1000-pound models were offered at prices from $750 to $900. In 1914-1915, four versions of the 1000-pound Model P were marketed in the same price range. Strangely, the 1916 line included a small ½-ton Model P delivery ($750), plus a larger electric tractor and a very huge 10-ton chassis.

1914 Mercury Flareboard Express (OCW)

1911 Mercury (Chicago) Flare Board Express (DFW/ATA)

MERCURY — Detroit, Michigan — (1915) — This was a van body on a cyclecar chassis, offered by the Mercury Cyclecar Company. It had a gas-oline engine and a $400 price tag. The engine, which was air-cooled, produced 10 h.p. Drive was taken, from a friction transmission, via long double belts to the rear wheels. It had a 100 inch wheelbase.

MERCURY — Ford of Canada — (1946-1967) -From 1946 to 1957, Canadian Ford dealers sold Ford-type trucks under the Mercury name. They had trim variations from the domestic products, but were basically badge-engineered Fords. The names Monarch and Frontenac were also used, in Canada, for other badge-engineered Ford trucks. For an article on this subject see: *The Best of Old Cars*, Vol. 1,

1949 Mercury (Canadian) M47 Pickup (OCW)

1950 Mercury (Canadian) Stake Bed (OCW)

MERIT — Waterville, Ohio — (1911) — The Waterville Tractor Company built a ½-ton capacity delivery truck. It was designated the Model B and used a two-cylinder, air-cooled gasoline engine. An 84-inch wheelbase was featured, along with friction transmission and double chain drive. The price was $1,000.

MERZ — Indianapolis, Indiana — (1913-1915) — This was a light van body on a cyclecar chassis. It was built by the Merz Cyclecar Company. The vehicle had a seven-foot wheelbase with a 3¼-foot tread. The air-cooled two-cylinder engine generated 10 h.p. Like others of its type, Merz used a friction transmission and belt drive.

MESSERER — Newark, New Jersey — (1898) — This early delivery truck was built by S. Messerer. It had a 1000-pound payload capacity. The 4x6 inch bore and stroke four-cylinder gas engine developed six horsepower at 350 R.P.M. Drive was by six inch pulley

METEOR — Piqua, Ohio — (1913-1932; 1941) — Maurice Wolf's Meteor Co. built phonographs and hearses. In the '20s, its slogan was "Kills 'em with Music and Hauls 'em away." Early models used Continental engines. Later ones were based mostly on Buick or Cadillac running gear. The firm also produced a fine range of ambulances. It later became Miller-Meteor.

1927 Meteor Funeral Car (OCW)

METROPOLITAN — New York, N.Y. — (1917) — Metropolitan Motors produced three ¾-tonners in 1917. The chassis was priced at $895. The Model AA canopy top was $995. Last, but not least, they had the Model AB, a $1,035 full-panel.

METZ — Waltham, Massachusetts — (1916-1917) — Metzer Motor Car Co. had a small 800-pound chassis on the market in 1916. It cost only $535. By 1917, the product line had not grown, but the product had. The sole model, then, was a one-ton priced at $695. This truck was connected to the Hewitt (See separate listing).

MICHAELSON — Minneapolis, Minnesota — (1914) — This cycle car company evolved from a motorcycle firm. The base model, using a 15 h.p. air-cooled engine, sold for $400. A box-bodied Tri-car, tagged at $375, was depicted in the company's catalog, although actual production has not been verified. A pilot model appeared at the Minneapolis Auto Show in Jan. 1914. By the following April, Joseph M. Michaelson left the firm.

1914 Michaelson Box Body Tricar (OCW)

MICHIGAN — Grand Rapids, Michigan — (1915-1921) — The Michigan was a hearse built as an assembled vehicle. It used a six-cylinder Continental power plant and worm drive. "Gothic" style carved sides and stained glass windows were usually featured.

MILBURN — Toledo, Ohio — (1915) — The Milburn Wagon Co. produced a $985 electric-powered 750-pound truck. It had an underslung chassis and 90 inch wheelbase. Solid rubber tires were mounted.

MILLER — Bridgeport, Connecticut — (1907-1908) — This firm produced Model A, B and D sightseeing buses with two-cylinder engines. The smallest sat 12 passengers.

MILLER — Detroit, Michigan — (1913-1914) — This was a ½-ton delivery van made by the Miller Car Co. of Detroit, a branch of the Milwaukee Auto Truck Mfg. Co. This firm also made one of the Champion trucks listed separately in this catalog. A 1914 offering was the Model A, a ½-ton panel with $850 price.

1914 Miller Model A Panel Body (OCW)

MILLER — Bellefontaine, Ohio — (1917-1924) — This coachbuilding firm was founded in 1870 and specialized in funeral vehicles. By 1917, the company was assembling its own distinct "models," which were produced through 1924. Thereafter, conversions were made on numerous different chassis. At the beginning of its motor-hearse experience, Miller bought chassis from Meteor. Fittingly, then, the two firms merged in 1957.

MILWAUKEE — Milwaukee, Wisconsin — (1901-1902) — The Milwaukee Automobile Company built steam passenger cars and two different trucks. Only one fell into the "light-duty" category. It was a light delivery based on the firm's current automobile, which had a two-cylinder, five horse-power engine. It was rated for a payload of 800-pounds.

MINNEAPOLIS — Minneapolis, Minnesota — (1912-1913) — This line of three-wheel delivery vans was built by the Minneapolis Motor Cycle Company. It included a $350 chassis, $395 wood box-body model and $425 metal box-body truck. The designation "14C" was used on all and all shared a payload range rating of 350-400 pounds. Power came from a two-cylinder gas engine.

1914 Minneapolis Box Body Tricar (OCW)

MITCHELL — Racine, Wisconsin — (1903-1923) — This was a passenger car, built by the Mitchell Motor Company. Sometimes, commercial bodies were placed on their chassis. Also, in 1907, the company cataloged a one-ton truck. It sold for $2,000.

1919 Mitchell Panel Delivery (T. Donahue)

MODERN — Bowling Green, Ohio — (1911-1919) — This make was manufactured by the Bowling Green Motor Car Co. Capacities ranged from ½-ton to 3½-ton. In 1913, the 1000-pound BV model sold for $1,325, while the Model AX, a ¾-tonner, was highest at $1,625.

1914 Modern Model F Flare Board (OCW)

1914 Modern Model G Panel Body Delivery (OCW)

MONITOR — Chicago, Illinois — (1910) — The Monitor Automobile Works made a ½-ton wicker delivery van. It was identified as the Model L and sold for $1,050. The engine was a two-cylinder job. Also available was the one-ton Model G Delivery, selling for $1,450.

MONITOR — Janesville, Wisconsin — (1910-1916) — Monitor Automobile Works produced two one-tons in 1911. Both had two-cylinder engines. The B-109 was $1,500 and the D-110 was $1,600. A 1500-pound truck, the A-109 express, was marketed, in 1912, at a price of $1,000. Thereafter, the company produced light-duties in both of these sizes (at around the same prices), plus some heavier models.

1914 Mora Model 24 Standard Open Express Body (OCW)

1914 Monitor Model E Chassis (OCW)

1914 Mora Model 25 Special Body Express

MORELAND — Los Angeles, California — (1912-1941) — This company produced the Model D, a 1500- to 2000-pound chassis in 1914. It was $1,700. In 1915-1916, a one-ton chassis model was also offered. It was priced $1,850 the earlier year, but then dropped to $1,550.

MORT — (see Meteor)

MOTOKART — New York City — (1914) — This box-bodied cyclecar was made by the Tarrytown Motor Car Co. and sold for $400. It was powered by a two-cylinder gas engine and had a load capacity of 500 pounds. Contemporary sources listed it under the Tarrytown Motor Car Co. name.

1914 Monitor Model A Panel Body Delivery (OCW)

MOON — St. Louis, Missouri — (1914-1918) — This was a ½-ton truck, built by the J.W. Moon Buggy Co. It was called the Model A and came as a $1,600 panel for 1914. In 1915, the same model was marketed as a chassis ($1,300), convertible truck ($1,450 and express ($1,550). It was up-rated to 1500-pounds in 1917 and called the "23½ Express," with a price tag of $1,150. In 1918, only two-tonners were made.

1914 Motokart Box Body Delivery (OCW)

MOTORETTE — Hartford, Connecticut — (1913) — These were three-wheeled delivery wagons made by the C.W. Kelsey Manufacturing Co. Both the Model L1 ($450) and Model N1 ($500) were powered by a two-cylinder engine. The first could carry 250-pound loads and the other hauled twice that weight.

1928 Moon Model 672 Chassis-Only (OCW)

MOORE — Philadelphia, Pennsylvania — (1912-1914) — The Moore Motor Truck Co.'s first offering was the Model C, a ¾-tonner. By 1914, the line began at the 1½-ton limit.

MOORE — Syracuse, New York — (1913-1914) — Just to confuse people, this company — with the same trade-name as the previous truck — also built a ¾-ton Model C. But it had an unusual three-cylinder engine, which was air-cooled. Its hood was French styled. Other features included a planetary transmission and double chain drive. It was $1,300. Palmer-Moore was the corporate name. (See separate Palmer-Moore listing)

MORA — Cleveland, Ohio — (1912-1914) — A ¾-ton open express was built by the Mora Power Wagon Company. Called the Model 20, it was a two-cylinder model with a $1,000 price. There was also Models 24 and 25, which were one-tonners in the $1,400-$1,500 price range.

1913 Mottorette Model R-1 Rickshaw (HAC)

MOTOR WAGON — Detroit, Michigan — (1912-1913) — These were light vans, built by the Motor Wagon Co. of Detroit. Both the Express ($610) and Full Panel ($700) were two-cylinder powered and rated for 800-pound loads.

1911 Motor Wagon Light Express Wagon (OCW)

M&P — Detroit, Michigan — (1911-1913) — These were battery-powered trucks which used Westinghouse motors. They were built by the M & P Electric Vehicle Company. Rated at 1500-pounds, the chassis model sold for $1,450.

1914 M & P Flare Board Express (OCW)

1914 M & P Panel Body Delivery (OCW)

MUSKEGON — Muskegon, Michigan — (1917-1920) —The Muskegon Engine Co. is believed to have made one model called the ''20.'' A modern reference says it was a one-tonner, but a contemporary (to the era) insurance guide identifies it as a two-tonner for $2,145. If this is correct, it would not qualify as a ''light-duty.''

MYERS — Pittsburgh, Pennsylvania — (1918-1919) —The E.A. Meyer's Company's smallest model was a one-ton. Not much about this model is known. It is not listed in contemporary insurance guides covering the 1912-1918 period.

742

N

NAPOLEON — Napoleon, Ohio/Traverse City, Michigan — (1917-1922) — This firm offered the Model 1727 in 1917. It was a four-cylinder powered 1,000-pound (½-Ton) truck selling at $735. The gas engine was made by Gray and had overhead valves. Other features included a three-speed gear box and bevel-gear axle.

NASH — Kenosha, Wisconsin — (1927-1954) — Nash produced a one-ton Model 2017 in 1918. It listed for $1,595 in chassis form. The company concentrated on heavier trucks later, but some one-tons were built in the 1920s. After World War II, a ⅔-ton model was built, mainly for export, although it saw limited stateside distribution. It had a six-cylinder OHV engine. The Nash name was also linked to Jeffery, Rambler and AMC/Jeep, which are listed separately in this catalog.

1917 Nash Model 2017 Canopied Express (OCW)

1920 Nash One-Ton Express (John Scott)

1921 Nash One-Ton Express (WOM)

1946 Nash (Customized) Pickup (P.B. Grenier)

NATCO — Bay City, Michigan — (1912-1916) — A one-ton gas engine truck was sold 1913-1916. Known as Model 15, it sold for $1,925 in chassis form.

1914 Natco Type 15 Covered Flare Board Express (OCW)

NELSON & LeMOON CO. — Chicago, Illinois — (1910-1939) — This firm operated under the above name through 1927, and as Nelson & LeMoon Truck Co. thereafter. It claimed to have made a 1906 model, but records start at 1910, in which year a four-cylinder one-ton with double-chain drive was offered. Two trucks of similar capacity, Models D-1 and E-1, were sold at $1,800 in 1914 and 1915, the E-1 continuing, through 1917, at a lower $1,700 price. It used a four-cylinder (3¾x5¼) Continental engine rated for 22.40 h.p. and weighed around 3200 pounds. In 1919-1920, this became the F-1, which was much the same, but about 200 pounds heavier. The G-1, another model with a larger (4⅛x5¼) four — rated at 27.23 h.p. — returned a one-tonner to the line in 1923 and remained through at least 1925. In 1928, six-cylinder Continental engines were adopted for a new, eight-model lineup of smaller trucks. They included a $1,500 one-ton. Later series were made up entirely of larger models.

1914 Nelson & Lemoon Model D-1 Panel (OCW)

NEUSTADT — St. Louis, Missouri — (1911-1914) — This company made motorized fire apparatus as early as 1905. The Model A, a one-tonner, was introduced in 1911. It had a four-cylinder engine and came with either solid or pneumatic tires.

NEWARK — Newark, New Jersey — (1911-1912) — These were small, open vans. They were built by the Newark Automobile Manufacturing Company. Payloads included ½-ton and ¾-ton. They had water-cooled fours, three speed gear boxes and shaft drive. Wheelbases of 96 and 106 inches were available. The 1000-pound Commercial Car had a 1700-pound curb weight and $1,250 price tag.

NEW ERA — Dayton, Ohio — (1911-1912) — This was a three-wheeler, built by the New Era Auto Cycle Company. A one-cylinder, air-cooled engine drove the single rear wheel. The cargo box could handle a 400-pound payload. It had handle-bar steering.

NEW ERA — Joliet, Illinois — (1917) — The New Era Engineering Co. built a gasoline-engine ½-ton Light Delivery that sold for $685. There appears to be no connection between this manufacturer and the earlier company producing tricars under the same name.

NEW YORK — Nutley, New Jersey — (1912) — The New York Motor Works built trucks ranging in size from ¾-ton to five-tons. The smaller models were four-cylinder powered. The company's motto was "Made in the East for the East."

NILES — Niles, Ohio — (1916-1920) — This company built a one-ton through 1918. It was called the Model B and was a four-cylinder truck. The chassis was $1,175 the initial season, $1,500 in 1917 and $1,600 the final year. A 1½-tonner continued to leave the factory thereafter.

NOBLE — Kendallville, Indiana — (1917-1931) — This company produced some one-ton models. Most of its trucks, however, were in the 2½-ton to five-ton range.

NOLAND — Edgewater, Florida — (c. 1985) — Commercial vehicle historian Elliott Kahn says this gas engined utility cart is a three-wheeler which includes four-passenger accomodations (on two bench seats) and a molded cargo bin at the rear of its fiberglass or plastic body. Rack style side-rails appear to be one option intended to increase the cargo capacity.

1985 Noland Covered Utility Cart (EK)

NORTHERN — Detroit, Michigan — (1906-1908) — This was a light delivery van built by the Northern Motor Car Co. Designated the Model C, it used a 20 h.p. two-cylinder engine, planetary transmission and shaft drive. The $1,600 truck rode on a 106 inch wheelbase.

NORWALK — Martinsburg, W. Virgina — 1918-1919 — This company's one-ton truck chassis sold for $1,295 in 1918. It had a four-cylinder Lycoming Model K gasoline engine, three-speed gear box and worm drive. These trucks had a 130 inch wheelbase and did not come with electric lights in a period when most makers offered them.

NYBERG — Chicago, Illinois — (1912-1913) — Nyberg Automobile Works produced a couple of one-ton-or-under commercial vehicles. The 1912 Model 35 was a 1500-pound closed delivery selling for $1,300. Its price rose to $1,500 the next season. In 1912, the Model 38 one-tonner was also marketed. This delivery truck also had a $1,500 price tag.

O

OAKLAND — Pontiac, Michigan -- (1908-1931) — Formed by buggy-maker Edward M. Murphy, Oakland joined General Motors in 1909, shortly before Murphy's passing. Limousine taxicabs were made almost from the beginning. The company became the producer of a medium-priced six in the late teens and was best known for advances in the closed body building field and automotive paint technology. No trucks are known to have been made, but other cabs , with Millsbaugh & Irish bodies, were seen in the 1920s. Also, at least one of the late Oakland V-8s survives today with a combination ambulance/funeral coach body conversion.

1926 Oakland Taxicab (OCW)

OHIO — Cincinnati, Ohio — (1912) — The Ohio Motor Car Company built autos and used the same chassis for a light truck.

O.K. — Detroit, Michigan — (1913-1916) — These were small, open vans built by the O.K. Motor Truck Co.

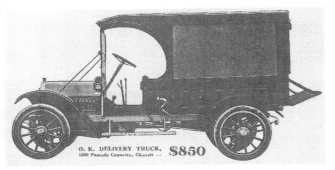

1914 O.K. 1200-Pound Delivery (OCW)

OLD HICKORY — Louisville, Kentucky — (1915-1923) — This was a Southern-built light truck, made by the Kentucky Wagon Manufacturing Company. In 1918, its ¾-ton chassis on a 124-inch wheelbase with a four-cylinder 17 hp. engine, sold for $875.

1918 Old Hickory Covered Flare Board Express (DFW)

OLDSMOBILE — Lansing, Michigan — (1904 - c.1975) — The first of many light-duty commercial vehicles produced by Oldsmobile was a delivery van version of the company's famous Curved Dash model. It appeared as early as 1904. Between 1905 and 1907, the company produced heavier-duty trucks. The firm became a branch of General Motors and, for awhile, stuck chiefly to making passenger cars. However, in 1918, a one-ton truck using an overhead valve four-cylinder Northway engine, came on the market for a short stay. It survived until about 1924, after which time the Oldsmobile truck was seen only in export markets. In the 1930s, Oldsmobile engines were used in some GMC truck models. The company's chassis was also used by some "professional car" builders as a platform for ambulance and hearse conversions. Though never the most popular choice of professional car makers, these conversions were available at least through the mid-1970s from firms like Superior and, especially, Cotner-Bevington. Also of interest, was the development of a prototype Oldsmobile sedan delivery in 1950. Only one of these was ever built. From 1968-1970, the American Quality Coach Co. also produced an airport limousine based on the front-wheel-drive Oldsmobile Toronado. It had twin rear axles, eight doors and seating accomodations for 15 people.

1904 Oldsmobile Box Body Runabout (OCW)

744

1919 Oldsmobile 'Economy' Canopied Express (OCW)

1919 Oldsmobile 1-Ton Rack Body Express (DFW)

1919 Oldsmobile Rack Body Express (C.D. Peck/CPC)

1920 Oldsmobile 1-Ton Canopy Express (J. Vann/CPC)

1920 Oldsmobile 1-Ton Canopied Express (OCW)

1937 Oldsmobile Flat Bed Conversion (B. Maxwell)

1958 Oldsmobile-Comet Funeral Coach (CP)

OLIVER — **Detroit, Michigan** — **(1910-1913)** — The Oliver Motor Car Company built high-wheeled delivery vans.

OLSON — **Garden City, N.Y.** — **(1963-date)** — J.B. Olson was a truck body making concern that produced lightweight aluminum bodies for platforms built by other manufacturers, such as Chevrolet's Step-Van chassis. In 1963, the company was purchased by Grumman Aerospace. A new line of aluminum bodied Grumman Kurbmaster vans was launched. While Olson Kurbmaster trucks used running gear supplied by makers like Ford, Chevrolet and GMC, they were of distinctive design and sold exclusively through Grumman dealers.

1983 Olson Kurbmaster One-Ton Panel Delivery (EK)

OVERLAND — **Toledo, Ohio** — **(1909-1939)** — See the Willys-Overland section in the forward section of the catalog. Trucks bearing only the Overland name were made at various times, but were a Willys-Overland related product.

OWOSSO — **Owosso, Michigan** — **(1910-1914)** — This company's first offering was a one-ton panel delivery. It had a two-cylinder engine that produced 20 h.p. Other features included a planet gear transmission, double chain-drive setup and 106 inch wheelbase. The truck had the engine mounted below its floor. Solid rubber tires were used. Springs were semi-elliptics at all four corners.

1910 Owosso One-Ton Panel Delivery (Steve Schmidt)

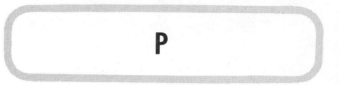

P

PACKARD — **Detroit, Michigan** — **(1905-1923)** — The Packard Motor Car Co. built medium and large trucks in the years indicated; in addition, their large auto chassis were sometimes used for commercial bodies.

1910 Packard Police Patrol Wagon (DFW/MVMA)

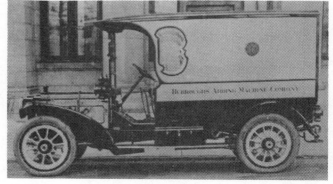

1910 Packard Light Panel Bodied Delivery (DFW/MVMA)

1912 Packard Goodyear Tire Mail Delivery Van (GYTR)

1916 Packard 2000-Pound "ID" Truck Chassis (OCW)

1920 Packard Twin Six Ambulance (DFW/HEPO)

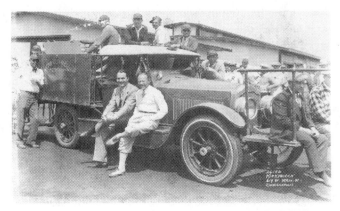

1922 Packard Motion Picture Film Truck (IMSC/DFW)

746

1930 Packard Commercial Chassis (DFW/ASL)

1933 Packard Armored Car (JE/NSPC)

PACO — Chicago, Illinois — (1908) — This was a small delivery van made by the Pietsch Auto & Marine Company.

PAIGE — Detroit, Michigan — (1930-1941) —Graham-Paige Motors Corporation marketed a sedan delivery on their passenger car chassis. Prices in 1930 for the ¾-ton units were: chassis $860; panel delivery, $1,095; and screen delivery, $1,095.

PAK-AGE-CAR — Chicago, Illinois — (1926-1941) — This was a small stand-up van, manufacture of which was associated with a number of prominent names including: Stutz, Auburn and Diamond-T. The vehicles were box-like in appearance and used for home deliveries in cities. Drivers often stood while driving. In the late 1920s, models sold for just under $1,000.

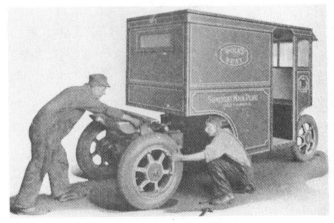

1927 Pak-Age-Car Panel Delivery (DFW/SI)

1927 Pak-Age-Kar Panel Delivery Van (OCW)

1935 Pak-Age-Kar Delivery Van (DFW/MVMA)

1940 Pak-Age-Kar Walk-in Delivery Van (DFW/SI)

PALMER — St. Louis, Missouri — (1912-1918) — This truck, manufactured by the Palmer-Meyer Motor Truck Co., ranged in capacity from ¾-ton to 1½-tons.

PALMER/PALMER-MEYER — St. Louis, Missouri — (1914-1918) — The Palmer-Meyer Motor Truck Company, of St. Louis, Missouri, manufactured both light-duty and heavy-duty commercial vehicles. Some of these are said to have been marketed under the single name Palmer. However, the Fidelity and Casualty Company of New York's January 1, 1916 *Manual of Liability Insurance* listed the brand as Palmer-Meyer and the firm as Palmer-Meyer Motor Car. Early in its history, the company offered a one-ton, gasoline-engined chassis for $1,600. This same type of truck, at the same price, was carried over for 1915. In 1916, the price for a one-ton dropped to $1,350, but a new product was a 1500-pound (¾-ton) chassis-truck for just $950. For 1917 and 1918, the line included a one-ton internal gear chassis-only model with four-cylinder gas engine. Its 1917 price was again $1,350, which climbed to $1,685 in the company's final year. The lightest truck made by the firm (the ¾-ton) was known as the Model B. It had a Platform & Stake body available. A frontal type hood was used. The 1914 one-ton could also be had with a Flare Board Express body. The large cape-type top rested on four sturdy posts at each corner of the express box. At the front, the windshield supported the top above the driver's compartment. Roll-down curtains were provided for weather protection. The engine was a side-valve (L-head) type attached to a three-speed gear box. Double chains carried drive to the rear. Solid tires were mounted on all four wheels. Other features included headlamps and cowl lamps. Shaft drive was adopted in 1915.

1914 Palmer Covered Flare Board Express (OCW)

PALMER-MOORE — Syracuse, New York — (1913-c.-1916) — The Palmer-Moore Company built ¾- and one-ton trucks. In 1916, their ¾-ton Model K sold for $1,150 with a front body. It had a Renault-style hood.

1914 Palmer-Moore Open Flare Board Express (OCW)

1914 Palmer-Moore Model C Platform Stake (OCW)

1914 Palmer-Moore Model C Flare Board Express (OCW)

1914 Palmer-Moore Model C Panel Delivery (OCW)

PATHFINDER — Indianapolis, Indiana — (1912-1914) — The Motor Car Manufacturing Co. built mainly autos, but also sold a light van on their auto chassis.

PATRIOT — Lincoln, Nebraska — (1918-1926) — These were ¾-ton to four-ton trucks built by the Patriot Motors Co. Their models had patriotic names like "Revere," "Lincoln" and "Washington." The Revere was a ¾-ton unit. It had a 129 inch wheelbase, a Continental four-cylinder motor and a dashboard of selected oak, ironbound, with "special provisions for attaching windshield and cab roof irons." The company first operated under the name Hebb Motors Co., introducing its first truck (a 1918 model) on October 1, 1917. In 1920, the name Patriot Motors Co. was adopted and used on trucks produced in Lincoln through 1922. In the latter year, the firm relocated to Havelock, Neb. and took the name Patriot Manufacturing Co. These trucks were marketed with heavy emphasis on agricultural use and were said to be popular with farmers because of the many purpose-built bodies available.

1918 Patriot 1- to 1½-Ton Lincoln Truck (SCC/TL)

PAULDING — St. Louis, Missouri — (1913-1916) — The St. Louis Motor Truck Company built trucks ranging in capacity from less than ½-ton to three-tons.

PENN — Pittsburgh, Pennsylvania — (1911-1913) — This was a light truck version of the auto manufactured by the Penn Motor Car Co.

PERFEX — Los Angeles, California — (1913-1914) — The Perfex Co. built both autos and a ½-ton truck.

1913 Perfex Express Wagon (JDV)

PHILADELPHIA — Philadelphia, Pennsylvania — (1911-1912) — This was a ¾-ton delivery van made by the Philadelphia Truck Company.

PHIPPS-GRINELL — Detroit, Michigan — (1910-1911) — The Phipps-Grinell Auto Co. built a small, battery-powered electric van.

PHOENIX — Phoenixville, Pennsylvania — (1908-1910) — These were high-wheeler delivery trucks produced by the Phoenix Auto Works.

P.H.P. — Westfield, Massachusetts — (1911-1912) — During its short life, the P.H.P. Motor Truck Company built light trucks.

PIERCE-ARROW — Buffalo, New York — (1910-1938) — The Pierce-Arrow Motor Car Co. built a high-quality line of medium and large trucks, and bus chassis, up until the early 1930's. In addition, their passenger car chassis was often used for mounting ambulance, hearse, small bus and fire apparatus bodies. For example, both the Milwaukee and Minneapolis fire departments used substantial numbers of fire apparatus built on Pierce-Arrow chassis.

1933 Pierce-Arrow Hose Truck (DFW/WS)

1935 Pierce-Arrow Sightseeing Tour Bus (DFW/PS)

PITTSBURG — Pittsburgh, Pennsylvania — (1908-1911) — These were light electric trucks built by the Pittsburg Motor Vehicle Co. (the "h" apparently was not used in spelling the city's name at that time).

PLYMOUTH — Toledo, Ohio/Plymouth, Ohio — (1906-1914) — This company built friction-drive trucks. A ½-ton model was sold in 1906-1907. It had a Continental four-cylinder engine and double-chain drive. Most companies did not mate such large engines with friction-drive. By 1908, sightseeing buses with 50 h.p. were available. They held between 12 and 20 passengers. Only two models, including a 26.5 h.p. one-ton with "cyclops" headlight, were 1912 offerings. The one-ton chassis sold for $1,850 in 1914, when two- and three-tonners were also marketed.

1914 Plymouth Model D-3 Covered Flare Board (OCW)

PLYMOUTH — Detroit, Michigan — (1935-1942; 1974 to present) — Chrysler Corporation's economical Plymouth was available in truck models during two separate periods. See the Plymouth section in the forward section of this catalog.

PONTIAC — Pontiac, Michigan — (1927-1928; 1949-1954) — General Motor's Pontiac Division made light-duty trucks, in series production, during two separate periods of time. The company's cars were also the basis for numerous "professional vehicle" conversions. Prototype Pontiac trucks have also been seen. Check the Pontiac section in the forward part of this catalog for more details.

1939 Pontiac Prototype Sedan Delivery (PMD)

POPE-HARTFORD — Hartford, Connecticut — (1906-1914) — The Pope Manufacturing Company built large trucks, and its auto chassis were sometimes fitted with commercial bodies.

1917 Pope-Hartford Motor Ambulance (DFW/HAC)

POWELL — Compton, California — (1954-1956) — The Powell Mfg. Co. built a small pickup based on old Plymouth components. The pickup body's top rail was a long cylinder, rumored to be built for carrying disassembled fly rods.

1955 Powell Sport Wagon (JAG)

1956 Powell Sport Wagon (DFW/HTM)

POWER — Detroit, Michigan — (1917-1923) — Power Truck & Tractor Co. began with a two-ton truck. By 1918, a smaller one-ton was available. It had a four-cylinder engine and lasted until 1921.

PRACTICAL PIGGINS — Racine, Wisconsin — (1913) — The Piggins Motor Truck Co.'s line included a one-ton, gas-engined chassis that sold for $1,750. It used a four-cylinder engine, three-speed gear box and shaft drive system.

PRECEDENT — California — (1984) — The Precedent was a luxury mini-van/limousine unveiled at the National Automobile Dealers Association (NADA) convention in Feb. 1984. It was created by Alain Clenet, who is best known for his Ford-based Neo-Classic car. Artist Mark P. Stehrenberger collaborated with Fred L. Lands, of Lands Design, in Elkhart, Ind., to style the vehicle. Dick Gulstrand, of racing fame, was chassis consultant. The platform of Chevrolet's S-10 pickup was used, in combination with Camaro and Lincoln Continental drivetrain components. The frame and doors were taken from the French-built Citroen, while the chassis and body panels were totally unique.

1984 Precedent Luxury Mini-Van/Limousine (JAG)

PULLMAN — York, Pennsylvania — (1917) — This auto-maker (Pullman Motor Car Corp.) produced the Model 424-32 half-ton truck in 1917. It came in open express ($750) or panel delivery ($775) form.

PURITY — St. Paul, Minnesota — (1914-1915) — The Purity Bread Company apparently built some small electrics for its own use; and then began offering some for sale. These were battery-powered units on a 102 inch wheelbase. Payload capacities were 1200 or 2000 pounds. Pneumatic tires were featured.

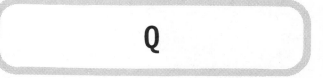

Q

QUAKERTOWN — Quakertown, Pennsylvania — (1916) — Quakertown Auto Manufacturing Co. sold its only commercial vehicle for $500. This was a ½-Ton model with a 35 h.p. four-cylinder engine.

R

RALSTON — Omaha, Nebraska — (1913) — During a short existence, Ralston Motor Company built a ½-ton Open Van. It had a four-cylinder, air-cooled engine, friction transmission, wood frame, 36x2 solid tires and double-chain drive. Price was $750 for the 108 in. wheelbased truck.

RAMBLER — Kenosha, Wisconsin — (1897-1913) — Named for an early bicycle made by Thomas B. Jeffery, the Rambler was Jeffery's first car and became a best-seller. In 1904, a Rambler Delivery Wagon was cataloged. An advertisement said it was fitted with "81 inch wheelbase and four full elliptic springs, insuring safe conveyence for delicate packages." The ad also added that it could "carry one-quarter cubic yards of merchandise, accessible front and rear of wagon." A detachable delivery top was provided with brass sidelamps and a horn. It sold for $850 at the factory. Some Ramblers were also converted into dealer service cars. In 1914, the firm was renamed Jeffery and introduced a ¾-ton express.

1904 Rambler Type 1 Delivery Van (OCW)

1905 Rambler Panel Delivery Van (OCW)

1911 Rambler Model 63 Pickup Conversion (AMC)

RANDOLPH — Flint, Michigan/Chicago, Illinois — (1908-1912/1913) A.K.A. the "Strenuous Randolph," this firm's Model 14 was a one-ton truck with its forward-control driver's bench seat behind a high, flat radiator. A huge headlamp sat, cyclops-style, atop the radiator. Also available were two-cylinder light delivery models. Other features included double chain-drive, solid tires and three-speed gear boxes.

RANIER — Flushing, New York — (1916-1927) — This was a moderately well-known Eastern truck, manufactured by the Ranier Motor Corp. The first model was rated at ½-ton; eventually the firm made trucks up to six-tons in capacity. In 1918, they produced both a ½-ton chassis on a 115-inch wheelbase, selling for $995; and a ¾-ton chassis on a 125-inch wheelbase, selling for $1,150. In 1927, their last year, they produced a ¾-ton chassis, selling for $1,970.

1918 Ranier Screenside Express (DFW/SI)

RAPID — Detroit, Michigan — (1904-1912) — The Rapid Motor Vehicle Co. started out building light vans; and then concentrated on medium-sized trucks. One-tonners were produced as early as 1906. The 1907 line included a one-ton delivery van. By 1909, some 17 different trucks were available, including ambulances and funeral cars. A police patrol wagon was another product that met with some success. By 1909, the line was down to a pair of one-tons and a large 1½-tonner. One-, two- and three-ton trucks were available for 1910. General Motors Truck (GMC) absorbed Rapid in 1912.

1910 Rapid Police Patrol Wagon (DFW/MVMA)

RASSEL — Toledo, Ohio — (1911-1912) — E.C. Rassel Mfg. Co. produced these models. The 1911 Model A truck was a $1,600 one-tonner. It was carried over for 1912 at a $100 higher price. Also available the second year, in chassis form, was the ¾-Ton Model O. It had a $1,500 price tag. Both were gasoline-engined trucks.

READING STEAMER — Reading, Pennsylvania — (1901-1902) — The Steam Vehicle Company of America offered two light enclosed deliveries; the smaller's carrying space was only 48 by 29 by 36 inches, and it sold for $1,200. The larger one's space was 36 by 36 by 51 inches; and it could carry 750 lbs.

REAL — Anderson, Indiana — (1914) — This was a small cyclecar van, built by the H. Paul Prigg Company. It sold for $395. It had a two-cylinder engine, friction transmission and belt drive. The wheelbase was 78 inches. The tread was 36 inches. The frame was made of wood.

RED SHIELD HUSTLER — Detroit, Michigan — (1912) — The Red Shield Hustler Power Company built small high-wheelers, in the 500 to 1200 lb. capacity range. They had two-cylinder engines mounted below the body. A planetary transmission passed drive back to double chains at the rear. Wheelbases of 75 inches and 86 inches were offered in two models.

REGAL — Detroit, Michigan — (1911-1912) Regal Motor Car Co. made some ½-Ton trucks. They were *not* based directly on the Regal automobiles. A wheelbase of 107 inches was used. The power-plant was a 30 horsepower four-cylinder. This model was only built for about one year.

RELAY — Lima, Ohio — (1927-1933) — The Relay Motors Corp. is noted mainly for large trucks. However, in the early 1930s, its smallest model was rated at ¾-ton capacity. This 1931 model used a Continental engine. In earlier years, the firm had offered a six-cylinder engined one-ton truck using a Buda engine and four-speed transmission.

RELIABLE-DAYTON — Chicago, Illinois — (1906-1909) — This firm made a high-wheeler truck. It carried an engine under the seat and featured tiller steering, a transmission with two forward speeds and reverse and a $1,000 list price. The company's main product was passenger cars of similar style.

RENVILLE — Minneapolis, Minnesota — (1912) — These trucks were products of the Renville Buggy Manufacturing Co. A two-cylinder engine was the power plant. The 1500-pound platform model went for $800. The one-ton platform was $1,150.

REO — Lansing, Michigan — (1908-1967) — This firm operated under four names during its long history. It was known as Reo Motor Car Co. from 1908-1939. It then became Reo Motors, Inc., a name that persisted between 1940 and 1957. In the latter year, it became part of White Motor Company known as Reo Division. By 1961, this was modified to Reo Motor Division of White Motor Company. It was a well-known make of truck. In fact, its most reknowned model was the *Reo Speedwagon*, a name which was adopted, later, by a rock musical group that is popular today. (However, the name has been changed in pronunciation to "R-E-O Speedwagon.") In the late 1920s, Reo registrations were fifth highest in the country. The smallest *Reo Speedwagon* was generally rated at one-ton; sometimes ¾-ton. In 1918, Reo's ¾-ton *Speedwagon* chassis on a 128 inch wheelbase sold for $1,100. In the late 1920s, the firm made a "junior" *Speedwagon* rated at ½-ton and up. The Reo Motor Car Co. also produced autos up until the mid-1930s and, in many years, the lightest Reo truck offered was based on the passenger car chassis. For example, in the mid-'30s, the firm built light trucks which were marketed by Mack. The Reo firm built a full range of both truck and bus chassis and is probably better known for its medium-sized units.

1909 Reo Light Flare Board Express (BWA)

1916 Reo Model F ¾-Ton Flare Board Express (OCW)

1918 Reo "Speedwagon" Ambulance (DFW/HCC)

1923 Reo "Speedwagon" Closed Cab Express (F. Morby)

1924 Reo C-Cab Panel Sides Delivery (DFW/HAC)

1925 Reo "Speedwagon" Canopy Top Express (OCW)

1930 Reo Fremont Town Car Delivery (DFW/MVMA)

1931 Reo Cab Express (R. Kingston/DFW)

1932 Reo One-Ton Armored Car (JE/NSPC)

1933 Reo Business Coupe w/Fifth Wheeler (DFW/CSC)

1934 Reo Cab Express (DFW/DPL)

1934 Reo Panel Body Delivery (DJE)

1934 Reo Panel Body Delivery (DFW/DPL)

1940 Reo Model 19AS Express Body (A&A)

752

REPUBLIC — Alma, Michigan — (1913-1929) — These were fairly well-known ''assembled'' trucks, produced by the Republic Motor Truck Co. According to registrations of trucks in use on Dec. 31, 1921, Republics were the second most widely used trucks in the U.S., trailing only Ford. In 1916, their ¾-ton express body truck sold for $995. It was on a 124-inch wheelbase. In 1918, ¾-ton models were offered on both 110-inch and 128-inch wheelbases. Trucks with ¾-ton capacity were offered through 1924, at least. In the mid-1920s the firm moved toward producing larger trucks and, in its last year, was associated with several other well-known makes: Linn (a builder of half-tracks) and American-LaFrance.

1914 Republic Model B Flare Board Express (OCW)

1914 Republic Model B Stake Platform Truck (OCW)

1915 Republic One-Ton Canopy Express (V. Kovlak)

1919 Republic Model 10 One-Ton Platform (Dennis Hurry)

1920 Republic Canopied Express (DFW/WRHS)

1925 Republic Model 10-F ¾-Ton Express (OCW)

REX — Chicago, Illinois — (1921-1923) — One of six trucks made by this firm was a one-tonner. It had a four-cylinder Buda engine. The company was called Royal Rex Motors Co. The firm's logo badge showed a swastika. Many of its worm-drive trucks went into the export market.

REYA — Napolean, Ohio — (1917-1919) — This rarely heard of company produced a one-ton truck.

RIDDLE — Ravenna, Ohio — (1916-1926) — The Riddle Manufacturing Co. was a long-time manufacturer of horse-drawn hearses, which began placing hearse and ambulance bodies on its own motorized chassis. In 1925, their chassis sold for $2,800; their carved hearse, for $4,600; and their limousine hearse, for $5,500.

1921 Riddle Combination Car Ambulance (OCW)

RIKER — Brooklyn, New York — (1898-1903) — These were electric vans built by the Riker Electric Vehicle Company. It was in 1898, that Andrew L. Riker proudly exhibited the first electric truck that he built for B. Altman & Co., of New York City. Much larger trucks were also built, as well as cabs and buses.

1900 Riker Delivery Wagon (HACJ/LIAM)

ROBINSON — Minneapolis, Minnesota — (1909-1920) — Thomas F. Robinson, Robinson-Loomer Truck Co. and Robinson Motor Truck Co. were among names used by this midwestern firm. The "Gopher," an $1,800 one-ton, was the initial product. All of 57 units were made before a switch to larger models only was made.

ROCKNE — South Bend, Indiana - (1932-1933) — This was the name of a Studebaker "companion" model that lasted only two seasons. Trucks were included in the model lineup. See the introduction to the Studebaker section in the forward part of this catalog.

RODEFELD — Richmond, Indiana — (1915-1917) — This firm produced a one-ton, apparently for three years. It was available in "chassis" and "optional" versions. In 1915, the respective prices for the two models were $1,100 and $1,300. In 1916, the chassis dropped $100, the option $150. The line was carried over into 1917 without change.

ROGERS — Omaha, Nebraska — (1912-1914) — The Rogers Motor Car Co. built a ¼-ton truck. This vehicle was actually rated at 600 pounds. A two-cylinder, 18 horsepower gas-engine was used. The light-delivery model sold for $850. It had a 100 inch wheelbase.

ROVAN — Columbus, Ohio — (1911-1914) — This was a light truck with front-wheel-drive produced by the Kinnear Manufacturing Company of Columbus, Ohio and, later, by James Boyd & Brothers, of Philadelphia, Pennsylvania (a firm best known for its fire apparatus). Models with 104 and 124 inch wheelbases were available. They featured a flat, two-cylinder engine, three-speed gear box bolted to the front axle and final worm gear drive. They were rated for ¾-ton and had solid tires. A top speed of 22 miles-per-hour was possible. The standard model sold for $1,600.

1911 Rovan Flare Board Express (JAW)

ROWE — Coatsville, Pennsylvania — (1911-1914) — The Rowe Motor Co. built autos, then introduced trucks. The 1911 line included two 1500-pound deliveries. The first sold for $2,500. A Model A, for $1,800, was the cheaper version. There was also a one-ton Model B delivery for $2,250. Heavier trucks were made in 1912. In 1913, two express trucks fell into our guidelines. One was the new, 1500-pound, $1,800 Model A. Also, the Model B was available at the same price as the 1911 delivery version. In 1914, the name Rowe Motor Manufacturing Co. was adopted and production moved to Downington, Pennsylvania.

1911 Rowe Model A ¾-Ton Covered Express (DJS)

1914 Rowe Flare Board Express (OCW)

1914 Rowe Covered Flare Board Express (OCW)

ROWE — Downington, Pennsylvania — (1914-1925) — Rowe Motor Manufacturing Co. evolved from Rowe Motor Co. (see listing above). For 1914, the Model A (at $1,690) and Model B (at $2,175) were continued as truck chassis. Heavier models were cataloged in 1915 and one of these — the "CW" — was down-rated to one-ton for 1916. In chassis form, it was $2,450. This was carried over for 1917, but the 1918 line started with a two-tonner.

1921 Rowe Vestibule Canopy Delivery (DJS)

R.S. — Reading, Pennsylvania — (1915-1916) — This firm made a three-wheel delivery car in Reading. It used a standard motorcycle engine. The transmission was a three-speed. A chain carried drive power to the single rear wheel.

RUGBY — Detroit, Michigan — (1928-1932) — Trucks of this brand were part of the Durant "family" of cars and commercial vehicles. See Durant in the forward section of this catalog.

RUGGLES — Saginaw, Michigan — (1921-1928) — The Ruggles Motor Truck Co. built trucks in sizes ranging from ¾-ton to three-tons and also built bus chassis. It was used to make models capable of hauling from 16 to 29 people from Point A to Point B. The company made its own engines until 1924.

1922 Ruggles Sightseeing Bus (WJP)

RUSH — Philadelphia, Pennsylvania — (1915-1918) — These were delivery trucks assembled by the Rush Delivery Car Co. The company's 1000-pound chassis sold for $625 in 1916. For 1917, the product line consisted of three versions of the ½-ton Model F. The chassis was $895, the Express $965 and the Panel $985.

$625

1916 Rush Light ½-Ton Delivery Car (WOM)

1917 Rush Light ½-Ton Delivery Car (OCW)

S

SAMPSON — Pittsfield, Massachusetts — (1905-1910) — This company operated in its first location through 1910, then moved west. Most trucks made by Alden Sampson were real "goliaths," but ½-ton and one-ton versions were seen, the smaller truck having an 18 horsepower flat-twin engine and shaft drive.

SAMPSON — Detroit, Michigan — (1910-1913) — The Alden Sampson Mfg. Co. started in Pittsfield, Mass., in 1905. A five-ton truck was the main product. By 1909, models down to one-ton were added. There was also a ½-ton shaft-drive chassis with a two-cylinder, horizontally-opposed power plant developing 18 h.p. Alden Sampson Mfg. Co. relocated to Detroit, Mich. in 1910. There it manufactured and sold a one-ton truck in 1911. This model had a $2,100 price tag. Also available, during the same year, was a ¾-ton delivery model selling for $1,175. This was a rather handsome, open crescent-cab van known as the "Hercules." It used a four-cylinder Continental engine that developed 30 h.p. The ¾-tonner was carried over as a 1913 model, but with a decrease in price to $1,450. By this time, the firm had become part of United Motor Co. and the Sampson nameplate disappeared.

1912 Sampson One-Ton Delivery Van (OCW)

SAMSON — Janesville, Wisconsin — (1920-1923) — The Samson Tractor Co. made a ¾-ton cab-over-engine light-duty truck. It utilized the Chevrolet "490" engine and was intended primarily for farm use. Samson was part of General Motors and, upon its liquidation in 1923, the factory became a Chevrolet assembly plant.

SANBERT — Syracuse, New York — (1911-1912) — The Sanbert-Herbert Company's three-cylinder engined truck was a one-ton available with three body types. The standard delivery was $1,500. The open box model was identically priced. A panel could also be had for $1,625. (Note: Also see Sanford)

SANDOW — Chicago, Illinois — (1914-1928) — This firm sporadically made one-ton trucks, at least through 1921. The Model I, of 1914, sold for $1,800 as a bare chassis. One-tonners returned, in 1917, with the $1,485 Model A. In 1918, the four-cylinder Model G was priced at $2,050. The range continued until 1928 with four-cylinder Buda or Continental engines, apparently including additional one-ton models.

1914 Sandow Model I Panel Delivery (OCW)

SANDUSKY — Sandusky, Ohio — (1911-1914) — For its intial year, the Sandusky Auto Parts & Motor Truck Co. sold only a one-ton closed express which was updated to 1½-tons in 1912. The Model B, of 1914, was another light-duty available as a ¾-ton chassis truck priced at $1 per pound. Common body styles seen on the 1914 chassis included the flare board express and panel delivery van which are both illustrated here. These trucks used the shovel-nose type styling, which was popular in the light-duty truck industry at this time and used by other makers such as IHC. Other features included brass headlights and cowl lamps, wood-spoke wheels and left-hand drive. Double chains were used to carry power to the rear axle. One of the firm's customers was the Catawba Candy Co. of Sandusky.

1914 Sandusky Model B Flare Board (OCW)

1914 Sandusky Model B Panel Delivery (OCW)

SANFORD — Syracuse, New York — (1914-1918) — Sanford Motor Truck Co. offered ¾- and one-ton trucks. In 1914, the one-ton Model K came as a chassis, for $1,660, or as a stake body or flare board, for $1,750. The Model O, of 1915, had a ¾-ton payload rating and a $1,290 chassis price. For $60 extra, an express box could be added. The "O" and "K" were carried over for 1916 at the same prices and the "O" (now considered a ¾- to one-ton) was marketed again, in 1917, with no change in price. Only larger models were included in the 1918 line.

1914 Sanford Model K Flare Board (OCW)

SAUER — New York City — (1911-1918) — This truck was actually a machine imported from Germany, with final assembly taking place here. In its first year of business, a one-ton called the Model A was sold. It was gasoline-engined. The chassis model carried a steep $5,000 price tag. Later models were heavy-duty trucks up to seven-tons.

SAVIANO SCAT — Warren, Michigan — (c. 1955-1960) — Arnold P. Saviano, owner of a tool and die company, created this Jeep-like utility vehicle. It is covered completely in Krause Publication's *Standard Catalog of American Cars 1946-1975*.

SAXON — Detroit, Michigan — (1914-1916) — Automobiles were the Saxon Motor Company's main product, although it also offered light-duty trucks built off the automobile chassis. The company's 400-pound Light Delivery model, of 1915, carried a $395 retail price. It used a gasoline engine. A 500-pound Panel or Curtain Delivery was marketed as the Model 6, in 1917-1918. It sold for $800.

SCHACHT — Cincinnati, Ohio — (1911-1938) — The G.A. Schacht Motor Truck Co. built a moderately well-known truck, although only in their early years were light-duty models offered. In 1911, the firm's first line included the one-ton Model D4 Delivery for $1,385. It had a two-cylinder engine. By 1912, the truck was down-rated to ¾-tons. With a closed delivery body, it cost $1,585. Also available were two ½-tons, the "D" closed delivery (at $975) and the "E" open delivery at $850. For 1913, the D4 was bounced slightly up, to 1800-pounds payload, and cost $1,600 in delivery van form. A chassis model, the "16" was a $2,000 one-tonner. After 1914, only larger trucks were built.

SCHMIDT — Crossing, Illinois — (1911-1913) — Schmidt Brothers Co. made ½-, ¾- and one-ton trucks. The 1911s included the ½-ton Model F Delivery ($975) and a one-ton delivery ($1,325). Both had two-cylinder gas engines. Uprated to ¾-tons, the Model F was priced $1,100 in 1912. Also marketed, in "optional" form, was the 2,000-pound Model C, priced at $1,375. These were carried over, in 1913, at $1,025 for the Model F and $1,375 for the Model C.

SCHNEER — San Francisco, California — (c. 1916) — The J. J. Schneer Company was a short-lived auto manufacturer. Some of their chassis were used for fire apparatus; one restored rig still survives. We don't know whether their light chassis were used for other commercial purposes.

SCHURMEIER — St. Paul, Minnesota — (1911) — The Schurmeier Wagon Company's two-cylinder Model C was a 1500-pound payload truck for $1,800. Contemporary reference sources listed this commercial vehicle for only one year.

SCRIPPS-BOOTH — Detroit, Michigan — (1914-1915) —This auto-maker also produced a Box Body cyclecar having a 750-pound payload rating. It used a 10 horsepower air-cooled twin-cylinder engine that drove through a planetary transmission. The unit had a $395 retail price and featured a 100 inch wheelbase.

SEARS — Chicago, Illinois — (1909-1911) — The Sears was a high-wheeler and was based on the company's similarly configured passenger cars. The commercial model was cataloged as the "Light Farm Wagon." Its features included tiller steering, chain-drive, full-elliptic springs and front and rear fenders. The two-cylinder, horizontally-opposed engine was located under the seat. Like the Sears car, these trucks were marketed through the company's retail merchandise catalogs and were designed to be assembled by the owner. The high-wheel type of vehicle was very popular in rural areas, where roads had not yet been "improved" (paved). The tall, narrow, spoke wheels could wind their way through the deepest mud, muck and mire without getting stuck. In most cases, the wheels were fitted with hard rubber tires, although pneumatic tires were optionally available.

1911 Sear High-Wheeler Farm Wagon (OCW)

SEITZ — Detroit, Michigan — (1911-1913) — Seitz Automobile Transmission Company was another of the lesser known light-duty truck-makers. The 1500-pound Delivery, of 1911, sold for $1,200. Products in 1912 included a 1500-pound Closed Delivery ($1,500) and one-ton truck ($2,000). The latter, coded as the Model C, was carried over in 1913.

SELDEN — Rochester, New York — (1913-1932) — George Selden's claim to fame was his automobile patent which Henry Ford successfully contested. During the controversy, Selden constructed a vehicle from the patent drawings which would have to be considered as a light truck. Interestingly, the truck is now in the Henry Ford Museum at Dearborn, Mich. Later in his life, Selden actively produced larger trucks; his firm's name was the Selden Truck Corporation. In 1918, they produced a ¾-ton chassis, with a 110-inch wheelbase, selling for $1,075.

1877 Selden Motor Wagon Replica (DFW/HFM)

756

1914 Selden Model J Covered Flare Board (OCW)

1914 Selden Model J-L Platform Stake (OCW)

1925 Selden Model 20-6 1-to 1¼-ton Stake Bed (OCW)

SENECA — Fostoria, Ohio — (1917-1918) — A four-post-top commercial vehicle was produced by the Seneca Motor Car Co. in 1917. It had a 1275-pound load capacity and $695 list price. Also available was a vestibuled (closed) version for $725. The firm's 1918 lineup included the $825 Model F ½-ton Open Delivery and $850 Model G ½-ton Panel Delivery, both with a new four-cylinder engine.

SERVICE — Detroit, Michigan/Wabash, Indiana — (1911-1913/1914-1932) — Service Motor Truck Co. started in Detroit. Models for 1911 included the "D" ½-ton delivery ($750); "E" one-ton delivery ($950); "H" nine-passenger bus ($850) and "C" ½-ton Business Car ($850). All used two-cylinder gas engines. In 1912-1913, offerings were the "J" ¾-ton chassis ($1,400) and "K-L" one-ton chassis ($1,550). The firm relocated, to Wabash, Ind., during 1914. That year the "J" (at $1,350) and "K" (at $1,475) were made again. A one-ton Model W chassis with worm drive was $2,000 in 1915. For 1916, two one-ton chassis, the "20" ($1,400) and "W" ($1,300) were available. For 1918, the four-cylinder "220" one-ton chassis (at $1,900) was sold. This truck survived until 1921. Then, only heavier models were made until 1925, when the "25F" and "25H" one-tons bowed.

1914 Service Model J Flare Board Express (OCW)

1915 Service Model J Flare Board Express (DFW)

1914 Service Model K Covered Flare Board (OCW)

1915 Service C-Cab Panel Delivery (JAW)

SHAW — Chicago, Illinois — (1918-1920) — The Walden W. Shaw Livery Co. built taxicabs and automobiles. In 1918, they introduced a line of trucks in both ¾- and two-ton sizes. The light-duty ¾-ton model had a Continental engine, a 116.5 inch wheelbase and $1,650 price tag.

1916 Shaw Model M2 ¾-Ton Stake Body (RAW)

SHELBY — Shelby, Ohio — (1917-1918) — These Shelbys came out a long time before the famous high-performance Mustangs and Dodges. Shelby Tractor and Truck Co. produced them. Both had four-cylinder engines. A ¾-ton chassis was $900. The same price was charged for a nine draw-bar horsepower tractor.

SHERIDAN — Chicago, Illinois — (1916-1917) — The Sheridan Commercial Car Co. made the Model A in 1916. It was a gasoline powered Open Delivery rated for 650-pound payloads and selling for $465. In 1917, the company produced ½-ton stake bed and canopy models for $540 or would sell you a chassis for just $490.

SIEBERT — Toledo, Ohio — (1911-1916) — Two light-duty models, a 1200-pounder and a one-ton, were the first trucks from The Shop of Siebert. A two-cylinder engine powered the smaller model, while the tonner — on a 10-foot wheelbase, used a four-cylinder power plant. The 1914 Model H one-ton flare board truck went for $1,350. In 1915, it was down-rated to a ¾-ton Delivery priced at $1,250. In 1916, the final offering was a $1,350 chassis truck, the Model I. This firm later became a body builder for commercial vehicles, ambulances and funeral cars.

1914 Siebert Model H Covered Flare Board (OCW)

SIGNAL — Detroit, Michigan — (1913-1923) — Starting with a 1½-ton truck, this firm made its ¾-ton light-duty available in 1914 at $1,350 for the chassis. Four one-tons, the D, DL, F and FL were marketed in 1915 at between $1,400 and $1,700. The FS-F, of 1917, was a $1,700 one-ton with a choice of 10- or 12-foot chassis. Also available, concurrently, was the FL one-ton, having a 14-foot chassis and $1,775 price tag. A one-ton "F" returned to the line in 1920. It had a 4⅛x5¼ in. Continental four-cylinder engine that produced 27.23 horsepower and scaled-in at 4,500 pounds. Also available was the lighter (3,575 pound) Model NF, which used the same engine. Both were carried over into 1921. The following season, the NF got a new 22.50 horsepower engine of 3¾x5 inch bore and stroke, which remained available in 1923. By 1924, the company had stopped reporting its models to reference sources like *Branhams*

1914 Signal Screenside Flare Board (OCW)

1914 Signal 1500-Pound Motor Truck Chassis (OCW)

SIMPLO — St. Louis, Missouri — (1908-1909) — The Cook Motor Vehicle Co. built a small delivery van. It had an 86 inch wheelbase and sold for $700. The payload of this vehicle was 1000-lbs. Power came from a 16 h.p. two-cylinder engine. Other features included a friction-drive transmission system and double chains.

SMITH FORM-A-TRUCK — Chicago, Illinois — (1917) — This firm built a unit for attachment to Ford Model Ts. It converted the Model T into a one-ton truck. Ford's entry into the light truck field brought an end to the need for such a unit.

SNYDER — Cleveland, Ohio — (1914) — This was a cyclecar delivery van, produced by the Snyder Motor & Manufacturing Company. It was designed with a 100 inch wheelbase. A water-cooled four-cylinder engine drove through a three-speed transmission, with power carried to the rear via shaft drive. It was priced to sell for $425.

SOULES — Grand Rapids, Michigan — (1905-1915) — Soules Motor Car Co. made a one-ton truck with a horizontally-opposed 22 horsepower two-cylinder engine. It featured shaft drive. After moving to Detroit, the firm apparently continued production, a a line of larger 3-, 4- and 6-tonners was reported for 1915.

1907 Soules Light-Duty Delivery Wagon (JAW)

SOUTH BEND — South Bend, Indiana — (1914-1915) — South Bend Motor Works offfered a ¾-ton Model 28 gas-engined truck in its first season. In chassis form, it sold for $1,375. The following year, a 1½-ton truck was the smallest one from this company.

SOUTHERN — Greensboro, N.C. — (1919-1921) —This company is known to have produced a one-ton truck, but further details about the firm or its product are not known at this time.

SPAULDING — Grinnell, Iowa — (1913) — Grinnell, Iowa's contribution to light-duty trucking was a ¾-ton chassis made by Spaulding Manufacturing Company. It sold for $1,100 and had a gasoline engine.

SPEEDWELL — Dayton, Ohio — (1908-1915) — In its early years, the Speedwell Motor Car Company produced light trucks; later, they switched to building heavier ones.

SPHINX — York, Pennsylvania — (1914-1916) — This short-lived make of light truck was produced by the Sphinx Motor Car Co., of York (a community which contributed more than its share of early auto and truck manufacturers). The three-year-only model was a ½-ton chassis priced at $600. It had a 17 horsepower, four-cylinder Lycoming engine. Other features included a cone type clutch and bevel gear drive.

SPOERER — Baltimore, Maryland — (1914) — This was a light, closed delivery van. It was built by Carl Spoerer's Sons Co. Price for the ¾-ton truck, in its chassis-only form, was $2,250 — not cheap! It had a four-cylinder 8.5-liter engine, 10-foot wheelbase and shaft drive.

1912 Spoerer Model 40C Delivery Wagon (WJP)

SPRINGFIELD — Springfield, Massachusetts — (1901) — This company produced a steam-powered delivery van in ½-ton configuration. For a relatively light-duty machine, it was very complex, having two compound engines, one on each side of the vehicle. A travel range of 50 miles was claimed.

S&S — Cincinnati, Ohio — (1907-1935) — The Sayers and Scoville Co. was probably the best known manufacturer of opulent hearses in the 1920s. Before the turn of the century, the firm was known for its carriages. They came in a wide range of models, some no doubt outfitted on a custom basis. In 1929, for example, they offered six models with six-cylinder engines and seven with eight-cylinder engines. The lowest priced models were $3,300. One reference book added "and up" after prices given for each of the 13 models.

1927 S&S Style 995 DeLuxe Fairview Ambulance (OCW)

ST. LOUIS — St. Louis, Missouri — (1900-1901) — These were light vans made by the St. Louis Motor Carriage Co. They had six horsepower, two-cylinder "pancake" engines, two forward speeds and bevel-gear drive.

STANDARD — Warren, Ohio — (1914) — During its short life, the Standard Motor Truck Co. built trucks between ¾-ton and 3½-ton capacity. Two models called the "A" (2000-pounds) and the "B" (3000-pounds) were marketed. The one-ton Model A, in chassis configuration, carried an $1,800 price tag.

STANLEY — Newton, Massachusetts — (1909-1916) — The Stanley Motor Carriage Co. was well-known for its steamers. They also offered bus and light truck chassis.

1914 Stanley Model 713 Panel Body Delivery (OCW)

1914 Stanley Express Wagon (WOM)

STAR — Elizabeth, New Jersey — (1922-1928) — This nameplate was a part of the "Durant Family" group of automobiles and commercial vehicles. For details, turn to the Durant Family section in the forward part of this catalog.

STAR — Ann Arbor, Michigan — (1914) — No relation to the later Durant products, this firm's Model B could be ordered in two weight classes, both as chassis-only models. The ¾-ton version was $1,500 and the one-ton version was $1,600. Both used gas-fueled power plants.

STAR-TRIBUNE — Detroit, Michigan — (1914) — This company's name sounds like that of a newspaper. Its big news in light-duties was the "O.K." model, a truck chassis with a 1250-lb. payload rating and $850 list price. Also offered was the Model B one-ton chassis. It cost $1,500. Star Tribune Motor Sales Co. was the official corporate title.

STEARNS — Cleveland, Ohio — (1901-1916) — The 1901 Stearns Utility Wagon was advertised as a truck that made "no sound but the slight 'tif-tif' of the engine." Features of the curved-cab delivery featured tiller steering; automatic spark control and an 11 horsepower one-cylinder engine. Its five gallon gas tank was located under the floor. Standard equipment included a top, side curtains, full set of tools, twin oil lamps and a "well-modulated gong." The four-inch diameter pneumatic tires were mounted on 32 inch wheels. A unique idea was that it had no carburetor or mixing chamber. Gas moved directly to the engine through a needle valve with the throttle providing constant fuel mixture. Fuel economy of 20 miles per gallon was claimed. This truck was easy on brake lining wear, too. The engine was used for this function, in addition to the pedal-operated differential brake. The firm also made larger trucks, in later years, under the Stearns name in 1914-1915 and the Stearns-Knight name in 1916.

1901 Stearns Utility Wagon (JAW)

STEEL SWALLOW — **Jackson, Michigan** — **(1908)** — These were small, enclosed vans built by the Steel Swallow Auto Co. They had a seven foot long wheelbase. The engine was a two-cylinder job that generated all of eight horsepower. A friction type transmission was used.

1908 Steel Swallow RFD Postal Delivery Car (WLB)

STEGEMAN — **Milwaukee, Wisconsin** — **(1911-1917)** — This make of truck, produced by the Stegeman Motor Car Co., ranged in size from ¾-ton to five-tons. The firm's first one-ton-and-under model was the $2,250 one-ton chassis sold in 1912. It was carried over, in 1913, being joined by a $1,600 ¾-ton. Both were seen again in 1914. However, the larger truck could, by then, be had in open cab form for a reduced price of $2,100, plus the closed cab chassis at the old price. The ¾-ton lasted until 1915. For 1916, there was a new one-ton at $1,680 for the chassis. Trucks of two-tons and up were available in 1917-1918, but there were no light-duties.

1914 Stegeman Panel Body Delivery (OCW)

1914 Stegeman Covered Flare Board (OCW)

STEINMETZ — **Baltimore, Maryland** — **(1922-1926)** — These were electric trucks, built by the Steinmetz Electric Motor Car Corporation. In the mid-1920s, their ½-ton chassis sold for $1,700; their ¾-ton chassis for $1,850.

1920 Steinmetz Light-Duty Chassis and Cowl (OCW)

1925 Steinmetz Light-Duty Delivery Van (WJP)

STEPHENSON — **Milwaukee, Wisconsin** — **(1912)** — One of three models listed for this Milwaukee, Wis. company was the $2,000 Model B one-ton which came with Express or Stake bodies.

STERLING — **Milwaukee, Wisconsin** — **(1916-1953)** — This make originated as the Germanic-sounding Sternberg truck, which is a rare brand to see today. Due to anti-German sentiment during World War I, the name Sterling Motor Truck Co. was adopted in 1916 (and used in this form through 1933.) During that year, a ¾-ton chassis with a 127 inch wheelbase was available for $895. An electric starter was a $75 option. However, the bulk of the firm's products were larger models. In 1928, Sterling brought out a *speedwagon* type one-tonner. This model made a handsome enclosed panel delivery van. Its styling features included a side hood design with three stacks of short, horizontal louvers, a one-piece windshield, sun visor, drum style headlamps, six-spoke steel ''spider'' wheels and bright metal radiator shell. During 1934, the firm became Sterling Motors Corporation, of Milwaukee. Its later trucks were virtually all larger models, some resembling Brockway and Indiana trucks. In 1951, Sterling was sold to White Motor Co., of Cleveland, Ohio.

759

1916 Sterling 1500-Pound Enclosed Panel (OCW)

1929 Sterling Model DB-7 Panel Delivery (DFW/DPL)

STERNBERG — Milwaukee, Wisconsin — (1908-1915) — This company later became Sterling (See separate listing above). Light-duty models were made some years. One was 1909, when two-cylinder powered ½-ton ($985) and one-ton ($1,650) trucks were offered. Another one-tonner was offered in 1912 at $2,300. Also, in 1915, there was a ½-ton Express or Flare Board model for $875.

STEWART — Cincinnati, Ohio — (1914) — Two one-ton models came from Stewart Iron Works Co., in 1914. Both used two-cylinder gas engines and had $1,150 list prices. The Model C was an Express and the Model D a stake body.

STEWART — Buffalo, New York — (1912-1941) — The Stewart Motor Corp. built a well-known truck, available in a wide range of sizes. A note in one old catalog indicated that Stewart "will have ready for shipment in March 1916, a 1000-lb. truck for $750." In that same year, their ¾-ton chassis on a 118-inch wheelbase sold for $1,290. A 1918 publication indicated they sold a ¾-ton chassis — on a 110-inch wheelbase — for $845. In the early '20s, their lightest models were referred to as "Speed Trucks" and, later in the '20s, as "Buddy Stewarts." From 1926 through 1929, the "Buddy" ¾-ton chassis — powered by a six-cylinder engine — sold for $895. During much of the 1930s, the lightest Stewarts were rated at ½-ton. But by 1936, the Buddy Stewart chassis price had dropped to $495.

1912 Stewart "Chronicle" Panel Delivery (JAW)

760

New Price
$1500
(Chassis)

1914 Stewart 1500-Pound Panel Delivery (OCW)

1914 Stewart Model B Covered Flare Board (OCW)

1914 Stewart Model F Screenside Express (OCW)

1914 Stewart Model A Panel Delivery (OCW)

1926 Stewart Model 16 1-Ton Speed Truck (OCW)

1927 Buddy Stewart Canopy Express (J. Everitt/DFW)

1927 Buddy Stewart 1-Ton Panel Delivery (OCW)

1935 Stewart Light-Duty Panel Delivery (OCW)

1936 Stewart 1-Ton Panel (Sonny Glesbrenner)

1936 Buddy Stewart Panel Delivery (MVMA/DFW)

1936 Buddy Stewart Standard Pickup (MVMA/DFW)

STOUGHTON — Stoughton, Wisconsin — (1920-1928) — The Stoughton Wagon Co. built both conventional trucks (in the one- to two-ton range) and fire apparatus. In 1921, the firm offered its one-ton Model A, with a 3¾x5¼ Midwest four-cylinder engine developing 22.5 horsepower. This rig weighed-in at 3300 pounds. For 1922, the smaller Model C — weighing 2480 pounds — was added. It had a 3½x5 engine, also produced by Midwest Motor Co. and capable of 19.60 horsepower. The "C" actually had a ¾- to 1¼-ton rating, probably based on wheelbase options. It was carried over for 1923 in this manner, but with a smaller 18.23 horsepower engine of 3⅜x4½ inch bore and stroke. For 1924, the truck was available only in its ¾-ton (short wheelbase?) form, in which it scaled-in at 2480 pounds. From this point on, all models seem to be heavy-duty trucks only.

STUDEBAKER — South Bend, Indiana — (1907-1966) — In its early years, Studebaker produced electric Delivery and Truck models of 1½- to 3½-tons. During 1914-1918, a Detroit branch using the name Studebaker Corp. of America produced ¾-ton models. 1915 prices were: (chassis) $1,050; (panel) $1,200 and (express) $1,200. 1916 prices were: (chassis) $985; (panel) $1,085; (express) $1,085 and (baggage) $1,100. 1917 prices were: (combination body) $985 and (panel) $985. 1918 prices were: (chassis) $1,045; (open express) $1,060; (station wagon) $1,085 and (panel delivery) $1,005. The model designation "SF" was used in 1918. There was also a four-cylinder, Model 7 one-tonner in 1917-1918. Additional information about later Studebaker light-duty trucks can be found in the forward section of this catalog.

1914 Sullivan Model 51 Platform Stake (OCW)

SULLIVAN — Rochester, New York — (1910-1923) — This firm was first called Sullivan Motor Car Co. and later Sullivan Motor Truck Co. The name change did not occur until after 1918. An 800-lb. delivery with a 16 horsepower horizontally-opposed twin-cylinder engine was the first Sullivan truck. Its features included a planetary transmission and double chain drive. By 1912, a pair of 1000-1500 pound capacity trucks with different one-cylinder engines was offered. In 1914, the line consisted of four two-cylinder models: the ½-ton Model 20 (chassis $925; panel $1,050); the one-ton Model 51 (chassis $1,050; express $1,100); the one-ton Model 51-D (chassis $1,050; express $1,140) and the one-ton Model 51-J (chassis $1,050; express $1,200). In 1915, the one-ton offering was the Model G, a $1,600 chassis truck. Thereafter, 1½-tonners were the firm's smallest products.

SULTAN — Springfield, Massachusetts — (1911) — Fidelity and Casualty Co. of New York listed this company's taxicab in the truck section of its *Manual of Automobile Liability Insurance* (1916 edition). It was made by Sultan Motor Car Co. The taxi used a gasoline engine and sold for $2,400.

SUPERIOR — Detroit, Michigan — (1911-1913) — In 1911, Superior Motor Car Co. produced a gas engined 1200-pound Delivery which it sold for $1,500. In 1913, the company's product was a one-ton called the Model A. It came with "optional" bodywork for $1,700.

SWEEPLITE — Clearwater, Florida — (c. 1986) — This compact utility vehicle is marketed by American Sweeping Service Co. It uses a John Deere, four-cylinder diesel as its power plant. The circular street sweeping brushes are mounted below the center of the vehicle. On the back is a hydraulically-operated dumpster type box. The cab, which is offset to the left, accomodates only the driver. The engine is mounted directly to the right of the cab. The Coke can on the hood is *not* a factory option.

1986 Sweeplite Utility Dumpster (Elliott Kahn)

T

TARRYTOWN — New York City — (1914) — The Tarrytown Motor Company produced a box-body delivery truck based on its cyclecar. The $400 machine used a two-cylinder gasoline engine. It had a 500-pound load capacity. This model was listed in 1914 only.

TAYLOR — Fremont, Ohio — (1917-1918) — After purchasing the H.G. Burford Co. of Fremont, this firm made trucks up to five-tonners. Its smallest model was a one-ton. Like the rest, it used a four-cylinder Continental engine, Covert gear box and Timken worm-drive rear axle. It had a 130 inch wheelbase.

TERRAPLANE — Detroit, Michigan — (1933-1937) — This nameplate was produced by Hudson Motor Car Co., both as a Hudson model and a separate marque. See the Hudson section in the front of this catalog.

THOMPSON — Providence, Rhode Island — (1905-1906) — Thompson Auto Company's Model A was a steam-powered truck. It used a burner made by Stanley Brothers, the well-known steam car maker. The engine was a 10 horsepower job by Fitzhenry. It had a 96 inch wheelbase, solid tires and an $1,800 price. The only body style was a delivery van.

THORNE — Chicago, Illinois — (1929-c. 1938) — These were stand-up vans, built by the Thorne Motor Corp. They were powered by an 18 horsepower, four-cylinder Continental engine which was front-mounted. It drove via a 90-volt electric motor, just ahead of the rear axle. Lockheed four-wheel brakes were a feature.

1930 Thorne Walk-In Panel Delivery (ATHS/DFW)

762

TIFFIN — Tiffin, Ohio — (1914-1918) — These were light to medium trucks built by the Tiffin Wagon Company. The company's 1914 line included a 1250-pound Model A chassis that sold for $1,600 and another one-ton chassis, the Model G, priced at $2,000. The 1915-1916 pickup sold for $1,600. A one-tonner for $2,000 was continued for these years. The 1916 ¾-ton chassis, with a 110-inch wheelbase, sold for $1,250. The same size truck was also listed in 1918; it rode on 34x4½ pneumatic tires.

1914 Tiffin Model A Platform Stake (OCW)

1914 Tiffin Model G Covered Flare Board (OCW)

TIGER — Detroit, Michigan — (1914-1915) — These were delivery bodies on cyclecar chassis, built by the Automobile Cyclecar Co. They were constructed on an 86 inch wheelbase. The four-cylinder, 12 horsepower engine featured water cooling. Factory list price was $300.

TITAN — Milwaukee, Wisconsin — (1918-1932) — As its name indicates, this firm built huge trucks. A one-ton model was, however, offered in 1925 as the smallest Titan product. It had a four-cylinder, Buda-built engine.

TOLEDO — Toledo, Ohio — (1913) — The Toledo Motor Truck Co. marketed the Model A, a one-ton truck, in 1913. It was gasoline-engine powered. As a chassis-only, it sold for $1,700. Stake or Open Express models were both $1,850. For an extra $100, you could have a full-panel body. A two-tonner was also sold.

TORBENSEN — Bloomfield, New Jersey — (1906-1910) — These were high-wheel ¾-ton vans built by the Torbensen Motor Car Co. The first models used a two-stroke, three-cylinder engine, which was air-cooled. Later, a two-cylinder engine was substituted. Other features were a planetary transmission, double chain drive and a 92 inch wheelbase. By 1907, the firm's two-cylinder Model T was on the market. It was a one-ton having a list price of $1,400. Three years later, another one-tonner — the Torbenson Delivery Truck — became available at no change in price.

1907 Torbenson ¾-Ton Light Delivery Wagon (OCW)

TOURAINE — Philadelphia, Pennsylvania — (1914) — A one-year-only model, Touraine Company's 550-pound Panel Delivery truck carried a $550 price tag.

TOURIST — Los Angeles, California — (1902-1910) — The Auto Vehicle Company produced mainly passenger cars although its chassis were also used for fire apparatus and commercial trucks.

1906 Tourist Light Delivery Car (JDV)

TOWER — Greenville, Michigan — (1917-1923) — In its first year of operations, Tower Motor Truck Company built a four-cylinder light-duty truck. Dubbed the Model A, the gas-engined chassis model had a $1,150 list price. Other trucks made by the firm were heavier-duty models.

TRABOLD — Johnstown, Pennsylvania — (1911-1932) —The first Trabold Truck Manufacturing Co. product was a four-cylinder cab-over-engine truck with chain drive. A Buda-built four-cylinder engine was used in 1913. The company listed several chassis-only models of one-ton and under capacity. They included a $975 three-quarter ton in 1914, a $1,475 tonner the same year, a $1,250 one-ton in 1916 and a ¾- to one-ton priced at $1,150 in 1917. Truck bodies were actually made by the company until 1960.

1914 Trabold Panel Delivery Truck (OCW)

TRACTOR — Atlanta, Georgia — (1912) — Denlock Manufacturing Co. produced the Tractor Truck. But, it was not a "tractor-truck" (as in tractor trailer). It was a one-ton model with a $1,200 price tag. A gas-fired power plant was utilized.

1914 Transit Model E Covered Flare Board (OCW)

TRANSIT — Keene, New Hampshire — (1902) — This truck was built by an auto-maker called Steamobile Co. Chances are good that it was a commercial version of the firm's Steamobile passenger vehicle. The two-cylinder engine cranked out six horsepower, which was transmitted to the rear wheels via a single chain. This was a truck with a rear driving position, the cargo hold being ahead of the operator.

TRANSIT — Louisville, Kentucky — (1912-1916) — Beginnning in the three-ton class, this firm introduced a one-ton in 1913 and the one-ton Model E ($1,200) in 1914 and 1915. This truck had an under-the-floor engine and double chains for drive.

TRANSPORT — Mt. Pleasant, Michigan — (1919-1923) — This firm produced a one-ton called the Model 20 between 1919 and 1921. It had a four-cylinder engine with 22.5 horsepower. The curb weight was 3,070 pounds. The Continental power plant had a 3¾ x 5 inch bore and stroke. This truck was replaced by the Model 15 series, which used the same motor and had a lighter 2775 pound curb weight. A "15A" was added in 1923. The "A" indicated a longer wheelbase. It was about 100 pounds heavier. These two models were built through 1925.

TRAYLOR — Allentown, Pennsylvania — (1920-1928) — Traylor Engineering and Manufacturing Company was primarily in the heavy truck business, but made a one-ton Model A in 1920. It was an assembled unit using a four-cylinder 3¾ x 5⅛ Buda engine that developed 22.5 horsepower. Other components included a Brown-Lipe gear box and Seldon worm-drive rear axle. In 1925, a second one-ton, the Model A, was introduced. It had the same engine and a 300 pound heavier (3800 pounds) curb weight.

TRIANGLE — St. John's, Michigan — (1917-1925) — Triangle Motor Truck Co.'s smallest model, introduced as a ¾-tonner in 1919, was an assembled unit with a Waukesha AC engine. This Model AA was produced as a one-ton from 1920 until 1925, then up-rated to 1½-tons afterwards. The motor had a 3¼ x 5 inch bore and stroke and produced 16.9 horsepower. Shipping weight for the ¾-ton was 2400 pounds and, for the one-ton, 2400-2600 pounds.

TRIUMPH — Chicago, Illinois — (1909-1912) — This was no sports car! Triumph Motor Car Company's first commercial vehicle was a Light-Delivery Van with a two-cylinder, horizontally-opposed Monarch engine below the seat. Other features included a planetary transmission and double chain drive. Air or water cooling systems were optional. They sold for $650 to $850. The company also offered the Model D to one-ton truck buyers. It was also powered by a two-cylinder gas engine and sold for $1,200 in Delivery Van form.

TRIVAN — Frackville, Pennsylvania — (1962-1964) — These were three wheelers (one in the rear), which could carry ½-ton. Built by Roustabout Co., one of their uses was for in-plant hauling of industrial materials. They used a three-speed gear box to transmit power to a single rear wheel. The steel tube frame had an air bag suspension. Production totaled all of 150 units.

1962 Tri-Van ½-Ton 3-Wheel Utility Pickup (JAG)

1963 Tri-Van ½-Ton 3-Wheel Utility Pickup (DJS)

1963 Tri-Van ½-Ton 3-Wheel Utility Pickup (DJS)

TROJAN — Toledo, Ohio — (1914-1920) — Toledo Carriage Woodwork Company made this ¾-tonner. The chassis price was $1,500. A one-ton model was added in 1916, when the firm became Commercial Truck Co. of Cleveland. The larger truck cost $1,600. Both had four-cylinder engines. (Wonder if they developed "Trojan-Horse power?")

TRUMBULL — Bridgeport, Connecticut — (1914-1916) — The Trumball Motor Car Co. also offered a light truck on one of its auto chassis. The ¼-tonner was powered via a 20 horsepower, four-cylinder engine and had a three-speed transmission and shaft drive. The $395 list price was the same one used for Trumbull's Model B and Model 168 roadster passenger cars.

TULSA — Tulsa, Oklahoma — (1913-1916) — The Tulsa Automobile & Manufacturing Co. is believed to have built trucks in the ¾-ton to 1½-ton capacity range. The company's 1913 Model 10 was definitely a ¾-tonner. Its list price was $1,500. The company evolved out of two other firms — Harmon Motor Truck Co. (of Chicago) and Pioneer Automobile Company (of Oklahoma City). A one-ton truck was also produced, according to some sources.

TWIN COACH — Kent, Ohio — (1927-1933) — The Twin Coach Company was formed by William B. Fageol and Frank R. Fageol to produce and market a large, urban transit type bus. Smaller vehicles, which were somewhat a cross between buses and trucks, were produced between 1929 and 1936. Included were a number of one-ton delivery vans that were used by many milk and bakery companies, as well as United Parcel Service. They were walk-in type models with sit-or-stand driving provisions and were available in both electric and gas powered versions. Also optional was the buyer's choice of front or rear wheel drive. Such units were manufactured for about seven years, until this operation was sold to Continental-Divco in 1936. Thereafter, Twin Coach concentrated almost exclusively on the building of larger buses again.

1935 Twin Coach Milk Delivery Van (J. Mattis)

U

UNION — St. Louis, Missouri — (1905) — This was a small, closed van built by the Union Automobile Manufacturing Company. It used a two-cylinder engine that developed 16 horsepower. Other features included a friction type transmission, shaft drive and a 92 inch wheelbase. Solid or pneumatic tires were optional. The list price of the vehicle was $1,275.

1905 Union Light Delivery Car (JAW)

UNITED — Detroit, Michigan — (1914-1915) — This was a delivery van on a cyclecar, built by the National United Service Company. It had a friction type transmission and double chain drive system. The $425 truck rode an eight-foot wheelbase and had a 40 inch tread. The engine was a four-cylinder power plant and used water as its coolant.

UNITED — Grand Rapids, Michigan — (1916-1926) — This firm had four name changes. It began under the name United Motor Truck Co. In 1918, as United Motors Co., it built the four-cylinder Model AX, which was an $1,850-priced one-ton. It became United Motor Products Co. in 1922 and merged with Acme Motor Truck Co. (of Cadillac, Mich.) in 1927. Other one-ton models were built in the 1920s.

URBAN — Louisville, Kentucky — (1911-1918) — These were ½-ton battery electrics, built by the Kentucky Wagon Manufacturing Co., which also built "Old Hickory" trucks. The company's 1913 line was made up of Express ($1,800) and Panel ($1,900) versions of the Model 10 half-ton electric. For 1914, a one-tonner called the Model 20 was retailed at $2,300 for an Express body. A ¾-ton, the Model 15A, came along in 1915. The chassis model was $1,562.50. Express or Panel bodies were $600 more. As its final shot, the company offered three versions of a gas-engined Model M for 1917. The chassis was $825. With a "body-only," this jumped to $865. For $60 more, buyers could get a "body fully-equipped." In 1918, the name Old Hickory (See separate listing) was adopted.

1914 Urban Model 10 Panel Body Delivery (OCW)

1914 Urban Model 20 Covered Flare Board (OCW)

U.S. — Cincinnati, Ohio — (1909-1930) — In its early years, the United States Motor Truck Co. built light models of trucks; then it switched to building heavier ones. One-tons were in the 1911-1912 line. The former was designated the Model A (how original!) and was a $2,000 Delivery. Then along came the Model B (how totally innovative!) for the second year. It was an express model with the same price. Both had two-cylinder gasoline engines. A 20 h.p. two-cylinder "pancake" engine was located under the seat and double chains carried drive to the rear wheels.

UTILITY — Milwaukee, Wisconsin — (1910-1911) — The Stephenson Motor Car Co. built trucks with this brand name. A Model B designation was used for a one-ton Delivery that sold for $1,700 in 1910 and $2,000 in 1911. It featured a four-cylinder gasoline engine, forward-control driving position, friction transmission and double chain drive system.

UTILITY — Gaylord, Michigan — (1912) — Don't confuse this ½-ton chassis model with the Milwaukee-built truck using a similar name one year earlier. This one was produced by Gaylord Motor Car Co. It sold for $1,500.

V

VAN AUKEN — Connersville, Indiana — (1914) — These were small electrics, manufactured by the Van Auken Electric Car Co. Having the oft-used designation "Model A," these were electric-powered chassis-trucks with a 750-pound load capacity and an 80 inch wheelbase. The price was $1,000. General Electric supplied the motor, which provided four forward speeds. A tubular front axle was used. The rear axle was a worm drive unit. The chassis tipped the scales at 1240 pounds.

1914 Van Auken Model A Stake Body (OCW)

VAN DYKE — Detroit, Michigan — (1910-1912) — The Van Dyke Motor Car Co. built delivery vans. All of them had two-cylinder gas-fueled engines. The half-ton was $750 in 1910 and $850 in 1911. Closed delivery models were offered in five configurations during 1912, all with ½-ton payload ratings. They were: Model E-A ($1,000); Model E-C ($975); Model E-D ($1,050); Model E-F ($1,100) and Model E-G ($1,150).

1910 Van Dyke Open Cab Panel Delivery (MVMA/DFW)

VAN-L — Grand Rapids, Michigan — (1911-1912) — This company's name was Van-L Commercial Car Co. As a model name, it sounds like some kind of trim package for a late-model travel van. However, the light-duty product was a rather large one-ton truck with four-cylinder engine, three-speed gear box and double chain drive. In fact, the only thing it had in common with today's vans was a forward-control driving configuration.

VAN WANBEKE — Elgin, Illinois — (1909) — This company produced two Delivery models, of which one — the Model A — had a less-than-one-ton rating. Its load capacity was 1800-pounds; its price a modest $850. H.F. Wambeke & Sons used a two-cylinder gasoline engine in its product.

VEERAC — Minneapolis, Minnesota — (1911-1914) — The Veerac Motor Company built ¾-ton and one-ton trucks, plus an early ½-ton model. The latter, seen only in 1911, was a Delivery for $850. It was called the Model A and, like all of Veerac Motor Company's products, utilized a two-cylinder gasoline engine. For 1912, the 1500-pound truck came in Express ($850); Stake ($875) and Enclosed ($950) models. In 1913, the one-ton Model B was available in Express ($1,125) and Stake ($1,250) styles. The ¾-ton edition of the Model A had a $925 chassis price in 1914, when a platform version of the one-ton Model B sold for $1,125. "Veerac" was an acronym for "valveless explosion every other revolution air-cooled." The company operated in Minneapolis, Minnesota for most of its existence. However, at some point during the 1914 calendar year, the firm transplanted itself to Anoka, Minnesota, where it was to finish out its final year of business. The best known of its commercial vehicle products were the light, open vans, although the Flare Board and Stake Body trucks were popular too. The company's name appeared in large letters prominently on the front of all of the vehicles. They featured a planet gear type of transmission with power carried to the rear of the trucks via a double chain drive system. The twin-cylinder gasoline power plant used in the one-ton model truck was capable of producing 20 horsepower. This vehicle had a wheelbase of 104 inches. A speed governing system, which operated via a cutout in the engine cylinder, limited Veerac trucks to a top speed of 15 miles per hour.

1912 Veerac 1500-Lb. Open Flare Board Express (OCW)

1912 Veerac 1500-Lb. Platform and Stake Body (OCW)

765

1914 Veerac Model B Platform Stake Body (OCW)

VELIE — **Moline, Illinois** — **(1911-1929)** — This well-respected auto-maker produced a one-ton truck in 1914-1915. It was called the Model X and had a chassis price of $2,000. The power plant was a 4⅝ x 5½ bore and stroke four-cylinder producing 34.23 horsepower. Also produced, in 1916-1917, was a ¾-ton Flare Board Express at $890. It had a smaller four-cylinder engine with 3⅛ x 4½ cylinder dimensions and 15.63 horse-power. Shipping weights of the two trucks were far different; 4200 pounds for the larger and 2320 pounds for the smaller. In 1928 and 1929, they offered a ¾-ton chassis, which sold for $1,595. Velie automobile commercial chassis were frequently used to carry ambulance and hearse bodies. In addition, some larger trucks (up to five-tons) were built by the firm.

1914 Velie Model X Open Flare Board Express (OCW)

1914 Velie One-Ton Gravity Dump Truck (OCW)

VIALL — **Chicago, Illinois** — **(1914-1917)** — The lightest truck made by Viall Motor Car Co. fits our criteria for a directory listing. This was a gaso-line-engined one-tonner called the Model B1. As a chassis-model, it sold for $1,400.

VICTOR — **Buffalo, New York** — **(1911-1912)** — It was $1,650 for Victor Motor Truck Company's 1500-pound Model A Delivery in 1911. Buyers who waited until 1912 had to spend $50 (Express or Stake) or $100 (Panel truck) more for carryover versions of the same model. Also seen that sea-son was the one-ton Model B, available in Express or Stake Bed models for $2,100. Bigger — some up to 10 tons — trucks were also Victor-built.

VICTOR — **St. Louis, Missouri** — **(1913-1914)** — These ½-ton capacity electric trucks were made by Victor Automobile Manufacturing Co. They utilized an electric motor manufactured by Westinghouse. Features included a 92 inch wheelbase and $1,500 list price.

VIM — **Philadelphia, Pennsylvania** — **(1914-1923)** — The Touraine Co. made many different light-duty Vims. The sole 1914 product was a $585 Light-Delivery with 14 h.p. Northway four-cylinder gas engine and ½-ton payload. The company listed no 1915 models and built five 1½-ton models in 1916. Then, in 1917, its light-duty activity exploded with a selection of 12 different ½-ton trucks with a full-range of bodies. Vim used the lower letters of the alphabet to code standard type trucks, while the higher ones coded specialty vehicles. In some cases, letters (''U'' for Undertakers' truck) indicated body type. The Model A was a four-door Deluxe with an

$875 price. The Model B was a Deluxe with wire door, tailgate and $855 price tag. There was no Model C, but the Model D, called a ''Standard Deluxe,'' sold for $845. A Salesmans' Express, for $895, was Model E. Model F was an $815 Open Express. There was also a Model G Deluxe Enclosed Cab for $915 and Model H Express with Cab Top for $815. Model J was a Jitney bus for $1,095. Then came the Model M Mail Truck for $905; Model R Fire Truck for $1,505; Model T Taxicab for $1,485 and the aforementioned $995 Model U. In 1918, the ½-ton Vim chassis, on a 108 inch wheelbase, sold for $765, the lowest price for any similar vehi-cle in a trade directory of that era. In the mid-1920s, prices for Vim ¾-ton models were: (chassis) $995; (Open Express) $1,220 and (Closed Panel) $1,260.

1916 Vim Open Can ½-Ton Express (OCW)

1916 Vim Canopy Top Stage Coach (HACJ/LIAM)

VIXEN — **Milwaukee, Wisconsin** — **(1915)** — Davis Manufacturing Com-pany built trucks under this trade-name. The Light Delivery of 1915 held a 400 pound load and cost $395. It used a gas-fueled power plant.

VOLTCAR — **New York, New York** — **(1914-1916)** — Cyclo-Lectric Car Company produced this electric-powered Parcel Delivery Van. Its payload capacity was 800 pounds. The price was $585. Features included a 68 inch wheelbase and worm gear drive.

W

WACHUSETT — **Fitchburg, Massachusetts** — **(1922-1930)** — This com-pany was started by one of the partners that founded New England Truck Co. (NETCO). It was built in a building that Fred Suthergreen built across the street from the NETCO plant. A one-ton model was a conventional type truck manufactured as an ''assembled'' product (one made of parts sourced from other firms). Some features included a Continental power plant, Brown-Lipe transmission and Timken rear axle.

WADE — **Holly, Michigan** — **(1913-1914)** — The Wade Commercial Car Co. made crude-looking high-wheelers with open express bodies. They had an air-cooled, one-cylinder engine mounted under the body. It was linked to a friction drive system and double drive-chains. Perched on a six-foot wheelbase, the $400 model of 1913 carried 800-pound loads. For 1914, the price dropped to $300, the capacity to 500 pounds.

1914 Wade Flare Board Express (OCW)

WAGENHALS — St. Louis, Missouri — (1910-1914) — This firm began as Wagenhals Manufacturing Co. of St. Louis (1910-1911) and, then, moved north to operate as Wagenhals Motor Car Co. in Detroit. The design was a three-wheel delivery with driver *behind* the delivery box. The 1914-1915 Model 20 was available in open- or closed-body form at $690. It had a gas engine and 800-pound payload. Also offered, the second year, was the Model 30. It was an electric priced at $575 and suitable for 800 lb. cargoes. Other features included a planetary transmission and chain-drive to the single rear wheel. The U.S. Post Office used these as mail trucks.

1914 Wagenhals Box Body Tricar (OCW)

WALKER — Chicago, Illinois — (1906-1942) — This was a very well known make of electric truck built by the Walker Vehicle Co. They built trucks in the size range from about ½-ton to seven-tons. In addition to the box-shape one associates with most electrics, Walker also built light delivery trucks with an engine-forward design. They looked like "regular" trucks. In 1916, the ½-ton Model M had an 82 inch wheelbase. It was available with longer wheelbases as well. It had five forward and five reverse speeds and a range of up to 75 miles. In 1918, the ½-ton capacity chassis was on a 93 inch wheelbase. It sold for $1,600 with tires, but without batteries. Beginning in the mid-1920s, the smallest chassis was rated at ¾-ton and sold for about $1,750. There was little change in some Walkers of the 1920s and 1930s, except for updates like pneumatic tires. These were first seen on the light-duties of the 1920s, which had small, dummy hoods. By 1929, the ¾-ton Model 10 Special adopted a full-length hood and more stylish and conventional appearance.

1914 Walker Model G Service Wagon (OCW)

1915 Walker Model G Service Wagon (DPL)

1918 Walker Walk-In Delivery Van (DPL/DFW)

1914 Walker Model F Panel Body (OCW)

1940 Walker UPS Delivery Van (OCW)

WALTHAM — Waltham, Massachusetts — (1906-1908/1922) — Waltham Manufacturing Co. made cyclecars sometimes known as Waltham-Orients. Commercial versions with 600-800 pound payloads were available. They used one- or two-cylinder (6-8 h.p.) engines and friction drive transmission. Eight Light Delivery vans were offered on 98 or 99 inch wheelbases. In 1922, the company — by then reorganized — built a Master Six passenger car. A few of these were converted into *Speedwagons* having commercial type bodies such as the 15-passenger tour bus depicted in the photo below.

1914 Ward Model EO Electric Platform Truck (OCW)

1919 Waltham Speed Wagon Tour Bus (NDC)

WARD — Mt. Vernon, New York — (1910-1934) — Built by the Ward Motor Vehicle Co., this electric was well-known in the East. In 1918, their lightest chassis was rated at ⅜-ton capacity, and was on an 88-inch wheelbase. They also offered a ½-ton model on a 90-inch chassis (as well as other trucks up to five-tons in capacity). During the mid-1920's, they sold a ½-ton chassis for $1,460, and a ¾-ton chassis for $1,770.

1914 Ward Model G2A Covered Flare Board (OCW)

1913 Ward Electric Delivery Van (OHS/DFW)

1914 Ward Model EB Flare Board (OCW)

1914 Ward Model EA Electric Delivery Van (OCW)

1916 Ward Electric Bakery Delivery Van (OCW)

768

1929 Ward Electric Milk Delivery Van (OCW)

WARE — **St. Paul, Minnesota** — **(1912-1915)** — This early type of 4x4 truck was designed by J.J. Ware, founder of Ware Motor Vehicle Company. A prop shaft was used to transmit power from the four-cylinder engine to the rear axle. From there, power dividers on both sides of the differential were connected to long shafts that drove the front axle. The firm — which later became Twin City Four Wheel Drive Co. — made models down to ¾-tons in size.

WARNER — **Beloit, Wisconsin** — **(1917)** — This firm made truck trailers of 1250- to 1500-pound capacity for hauling such things as packages, steers, poles and lumber. Prices ranged from $100 to $325 for these models.

WARREN — **Warren, Ohio** — **(1912-1913)** — The Warren Motor Truck Co. built a ½-ton open express truck. It was called the Model 30. The wheelbase was 110 inches. A 30 h.p. four-cylinder engine supplied the go-power. The firm offered other models through 1916, when a pair of one-tonners were marketed, as well as larger trucks. In chassis form, these 1916 "tonners" were $1,700 and $1,900 respectively.

WARREN — **Detroit, Michigan** — **(1911-1913)** — The Warren light delivery vans were half-tonners and based on the firm's passenger car chassis. They came with open- or closed-body styles. Their "Winged Express" models went for $1,300.

WASHINGTON — **Washington, D.C.** — **(1909-1912)** — These were electrics, ranging from less than ½-ton to two-tons in capacity. They were built by the Washington Motor Vehicle Co. Four models were available, in all. The smallest was rated for 750 pound payloads. They used Edison alkaline batteries that could provide a driving range as high as 50-miles before requiring re-charging.

Washington Open Express (WJP)

WATSON — **Canastota, New York** — **(1916-1925)** — This firm was in business by 1916, making Bottom-Drop and Platform trucks to six-tons. It operated as Watson Wagon Co. until 1919. The name Watson Products Corporation was then used until 1922. In 1923, this was changed to Watson Truck Corporation. For a couple of years, the company's lightest model was rated at ¾-tons. Starting in 1920, Watson Products Co. also built a one-ton Crescent Cab truck. It had a four-cylinder Buda engine, electric lights, left-hand drive and spring-loaded front bumper.

WAVERLY ELECTRIC — **Indianapolis, Indiana** — **(1899-1916)** — Built first by the Indiana Bicycle Company (which eventually became the Waverly Co.) these were moderately well-known electrics. In 1916, their ½-ton chassis on a 90-inch wheelbase sold for $1,800, a price which included: "Top for driver's seat, two head lamps, charging plug, Hubodometer, Sangamo ampere hour meter or regular volt ammeter, bell or horn and regular tool equipment." The price apparently also included a 42-cell, 11-plate battery.

1914 Waverley Panel Body Delivery (OCW)

1914 Waverley Covered Flare Board Express (OCW)

Waverley Electric Screenside Delivery Van (ELC/DFW)

WAYNE — **New York, New York** — **(1914)** — The Wayne Light Commercial Car Company built a truck on a light tricycle chassis. This model had an 800-pound payload rating. An air-cooled two-cylinder engine was the power plant. Belts carried drive to the single rear wheel. Other features included a two-speed gear box and handle-bar steering system. It sold for $495.

WEEKS — Chicago, Illinois — (1907-1908) — These were ½-ton delivery trucks built by the Weeks Commercial Vehicle Co. The body style was that of a closed delivery van. The two-cylinder engine, made by Advance Engine & Manufacturing Co., was positioned below the floorboards. It was vapor-cooled and capable of producing 20 h.p. A friction disc drive system and double-chains completed the powertrain. A curb weight of 1500-pounds was registered.

1907 Weeks Light-Delivery Van (JAW)

WESTCOASTER — Stockton, California — (1927-1975) — Built by the West Coast Machinery Co., these light trucks were mounted on three- and four-wheel chassis. They were used for mail deliveries and by messengers within factories.

WEYHER — Whitewater, Wisconsin — (1910) — This obscure make of small truck was built by Weyher Manufacturing Co. Only a single model, rated for ½-ton, was offered. It had a 16 h.p. twin-cylinder engine, friction transmission and double chain drive. Poised on a 94 inch wheelbase, the water-cooled truck rode on solid rubber tires.

WHIPPET — The Whippet ½-ton chassis with a four-cylinder engine sold for only $380. It was a product of Willys-Overland. See the Willys section in the forward part of this catalog.

WHITE — Cleveland, Ohio — (1900 to date) — Until 1918, White built steam and gas autos, plus trucks. Its first light truck, from 1900, is shown below. It was a Delivery van, probably a half-tonner, with unusual cab. By 1909, the line included ¾-tonners. The gas-engined GBE-GBBE of 1912-1913 was a 1500-pound chassis for $2,100. A ¾-ton on a 133 inch wheelbase still had that price in 1916. In later years, White wasn't viewed as a light-duty producer. However, ¾-tonners were in its line through about 1925 and contributed to the fact that White was America's fifth largest truck-maker (in terms of U.S. registrations) in years such as 1921.

1900 White Steamer Light Delivery Car (JAW)

1909 White ¾-Ton Dealer Service Pickup (DFW/VWC)

1910 White ¾-Ton Domestic Express (DFW/VWC)

1911 White ¾-Ton 9-Passenger Tour Bus (DFW/VWC)

1914 White Model GBBE Covered Flare Board (OCW)

1915 White ¾-Ton Hotel Bus (DFW/VWC)

1915 White Model GBBE ¾-Ton Covered Flare (OCW)

1927 White Model 15A Open Express (J. Markey)

1916 White Panel Delivery (D. Sagvold)

1919 White Deluxe Panel Delivery Van (OCW)

1925 White Model 15 ¾-Ton Covered Flare (OCW)

1920 White Passenger Tour Bus (Strozier Archives)

1926 White Model 15 ¾-Ton Panel Delivery (OCW)

1918 White Passenger Tour Bus (Strozier Arcives)

771

1919 White ¾-Ton Platform Stake Bed (OCW)

WHITE HICKORY — **Atlanta, Georgia** — **(1918)** — A one-ton chassis-truck was produced by White Hickory Wagon Manufacturing Company in 1918. This four-cylinder, called the Model F, sold for $1,800.

WHITESIDES — **Franklin, Indiana** — **(1911-1912)** — This commercial vehicle was a four-cylinder powered one-ton. It used a water-cooled 30 h.p. engine. Body styles available from the Whitesides Commercial Car Company included a flat-bed "dray" model, vestibuled delivery van and stake bed truck. Prices ranged from $1,265 to $1,285.

WHITE STAR — **Brooklyn, New York** — **(1912-1914)** — The White Star Motor & Engineering Company made its one-ton model in 1914. It was gas-engined and weighed-in at 1900-pounds in chassis-only form. Other White Stars were heavier-duty trucks with three- and four-speed gear boxes.

1914 White Star Model 1 Covered Flare Board (OCW)

WICHITA — **Wichita Falls, Texas** — **(1911-1932)** — A one-tonner was about the smallest product of this southwest regional manufacturer. The Model A of 1913-1914 was $1,650, the same price as the chain-drive model of 1915-1916. Also available, in 1915 and 1916, was the wheel-drive Model K. Both had the same prices. In 1917, both models were continued with a higher $1,800 retail price.

1914 Wichita Model A Bottle Body Truck (OCW)

1914 Wichita Model A Platform Stake Truck (OCW)

772

WILCOX — **Minneapolis, Minnesota** — **(1910-1927)** — The H.E. Wilcox Motor Co. built trucks and buses, with the smallest truck rated at ¾-ton capacity. The 1916 Wilcox ¾-ton chassis, on a 120-inch wheelbase, sold for $1,200. In the late 1920s, the firm was reorganized and switched to building buses, mainly for Greyhound.

1914 Wilcox Model L Covered Flare Board (OCW)

1917 Wilcox Petroleum Tank Body Truck (JAW)

WILLYS/WILLYS-OVERLAND — **Terre Haute, Indiana** — **(1903-1963)** — This company, best known for volume production of the Universal Jeeps, built many other types of light-duty commercial vehicles. They are covered in the forward section of this catalog.

WILLET — **Buffalo, New York** — **(1911-1915)** — Prior to 1913, the Willet Engine & Carburetor Co. offered just low-capacity delivery vans with two- or three-cylinder engines. The Model M, a ¾-ton chassis, sold for $1,650 in 1914. For 1915, only the ¾-tonner was made. It featured a 133 inch wheelbase, shaft drive, pneumatic tires and $2,100 price tag.

1914 Willet Model M Screenside Express (OCW)

WILSON — **Detroit, Michigan** — **(1914-1925)** — J.C. Wilson Company made horsedrawn wagons. A Model F one-ton, with four-cylinder power plant, was marketed in 1916 through 1918. It sold for $1,375 the first two years and $1,450 the last year. It came in chassis form and a worm-drive system was used.

1925 Wilson Model C 1-Ton Stake Body (OCW)

WINKLER — **South Bend, Indiana** — **(1911-1912)** — Winkler Brothers Manufacturing Company's truck-line included a one-ton model. It had a 25 h.p. engine, but did not use the three-speed progressive gear box of the firm's larger trucks. Features included a forward-control configuration and open cab styling.

WINTHER — **Kenosha, Wisconsin** — **(1917-1927)** — The Winther Motor Truck Co. built trucks as large as seven tons capacity, as well as automobiles. Most of its smaller trucks were in the range of 1½ to two-tons. However, in 1924, the firm brought a ¾-ton model to market.

WINTON — **Cleveland, Ohio** — **(1896-1924)** — By the end of 1898, Alexander Winton had sold 22 cars. Sales of his product climbed to 850 by 1903. Though passenger cars were the mainstay, Winton at various times built military trucks. The earliest of these was the Wagonette, a 1904 model designed for the U.S. Army Signal Corps. The firm is also said to have moved heavily into military vehicle production during World War I.

1904 Winton Signal Corps Wagonette (SI/OCW)

WISCONSIN — **Loganville, Wisconsin** — **(1912-1926)** — This truck was built by three different firms located in three different Wisconsin communities. In 1916, while being built by the Myers Machine Co., of Sheboygan, a ¾-ton capacity chassis was offered for $1,500.

1918 Wisconsin Petroleum Tank Body Truck (JAW)

WITT-WILL — **Washington, D.C.** — **(1911-1931)** — Most of the Witt-Will Company's products were heavy trucks and beyond the scope of this light-duty truck catalog. However, in 1914 and 1915, there was the Model E-15, a one-ton chassis-truck using a gas-powered engine and priced at $1,850.

1914 Witt-Will Model E-13 Flare Board (OCW)

1914 Witt-Will Model E-13 Panel Body (OCW)

WOLVERINE — **Detroit, Michigan** — **(1918-1922)** — The American Commercial Car Co. built trucks in the ¾-ton to 1½-ton size range. The ¾-tonner was a delivery van with pneumatic tires, offered only until 1918.

WOLVERINE-DETROIT — **Detroit, Michigan** — **(1912-1913)** — The Pratt, Carter, Sigsbee Company produced this brand of truck. The 1912 offering was an open express model with a water-cooled single-cylinder engine, friction transmission and double chain-drive setup. Buyers had the option of ordering solid or pneumatic tires. The express had an 89 inch wheelbase. It sold for $775 in chassis-only configurtaion. For 1913, a ½-ton truck called the Model C was produced. It was a one-cylinder job with a 96 inch wheelbase and worm drive system. It came as a flare board express and had the engine mounted underneath the body.

1914 Wolverine-Detroit Model C Flare Board (OCW)

WONDER — **Chicago, Illinois** — **(c. 1917)** — This company was listed in a 1918 auto insurance manual as maker of two one-ton trucks. The Model 1 Open Truck sold for $800. The Model 2 was a Truck with Top for $850. Both used gas engines.

WOODS — **Havelock and Lincoln, Nebraska** — **(1927-1931)** — Although not thought of, primarily, as a light-duty truck-maker, this firm produced a one-ton truck. The company originally operated as Patriot Manufacturing, in Havelock. It then (1929) became a division of Arrow Aircraft & Motors Corp.

WOOLSTON — **Riverton, New Jersey** — **(1913)** — Another firm whose one-ton and under models was limited to a one-ton truck was C.T. Woolston's company. It came as an express (or pickup) called the Model A. Features included a four-cylinder power plant, three-speed gear box and solid tires. A governor was used to limit the maximum road speed to 15 m.p.h.

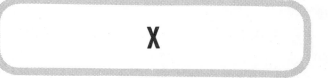

X

XENIA — **Xenia, Ohio** — **(1914)** — This cyclecar came with a delivery box type body. It was powered by a two-cylinder air-cooled engine rated for 10 h.p.. A planet-type transmission passed the motive power to a pair of belts linked to the rearmost wheels. Equipment on the $395 mini-truck included a single headlight.

YELLOW CAB — Chicago, Illinois — (1915-1929) — See Krause Publication's *Standard Catalog of American Cars 1805-1942* for full information on this make of light-duty commercial vehicles.

1923 Yellow Cab Panel Delivery Van (DFW/MCC)

1924 Yellow Cab Panel Delivery Van (Upjohn/DFW)

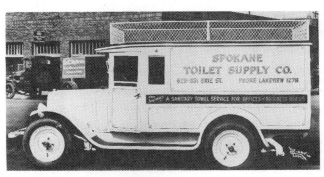

1926 Yellow Cab Panel Delivery Van (OCW)

1926 Yellow-Knight Model T2 One-Ton Chassis (OCW)

Z

ZEITLER & LAMSON — Chicago, Illinois — (1914-1916) — Zeitler & Lamson Motor Truck Company produced a line of five different size and weight class trucks. One of them was a one-ton model priced at $1,550. It used a Continental engine. Production stopped in 1917, but the design was reintroduced under the name King-Zeitler, in 1919.

ZIMMERMAN — Auburn, Indiana — (1912-1916) — This was a ½-ton high-wheeler, built by the Zimmerman Manufacturing Co. It was, of course, based on the firm's passenger car and shared the same two-cylinder engine, planetary transmission and double chain-drive system. Three-quarter elliptic springs were used at the front of the truck, with full-elliptic types at the rear. By 1915, this vehicle was up-rated to 1½-tons, quite a large jump from its introductory form.

(CONTRIBUTORS, from page XIX)

Quill'' award, Fox has contributed articles to a half-dozen national hobby magazines and co-authored Tab Book's *Studebaker—The Complete Story*, in which he wrote the entire truck section. Fred has graduate degrees from the University of California (BS in engineering) and The Pennsylvania State University (MS in engineering). He is a member of Tau Beta Pi, the national engineering honor society. He formerly worked in farming, in chemical sales, as a winery supervisor and as an engineering instructor at Modesto Junior College. Fox belongs to numerous hobby organizations: The Studebaker Drivers Club, Society of Automotive Historians, Horseless Carriage Club of America, Contemporary Historical Vehicle Association, Avanti Owners Association and The Antique Automobile Club of America. Since 1968, he has also held membership in the Studebaker Family National Association. If you haven't guessed, our Studebaker truck section was written (and partly illustrated) by Fred.

JEFF GILLIS did the Durant Family section of this book. After nearly 10 years as a bystander in the old car hobby, Jeff purchased his first true antique car in 1970. It was a 1930 Durant Coach. Over the next six years, he restored the Durant without the aid of a club. This inspired him to form, in 1976, a club called The Durant Family Registry. Its aim was to assist owners of Durant-built cars and trucks. Since that time, the DFR has grown to a sustained membership of 400 hobbyists from all corners of the world. The club magazine, called *Durant's Standard* has received the *Old Cars Weekly* ''Golden Quill'' award several times. In addition to his writing and editing chores for the club, Gillis has contributed articles to *Old Cars Weekly, Car Collector* and other hobby magazines. He participates in hobby events with his Durant and also owns a 1954 Chevrolet two-door sedan.

JOHN A. GUNNELL was born in Staten Island, New York and attended Brooklyn Technical High School to study industrial design. He worked in a variety of fields, spending most years in the grocery industry where he learned about trucks by unloading them. Meanwhile, he studied English, history and fine art, winding up with a Bachelor of Arts degree in art. Writing about antique cars, a favorite subject, as a creative outlet, Gunnell began working as editor of several club publications and *For 'Vettes Only*, the newsletter of the National Corvette Owners Association. In 1978, he was offered a job as technical editor of *Old Cars Weekly* and relocated to Iola, Wisconsin. Since 1975 he has done hundreds of articles, 10 books and edited three *Standard Catalogs*. John owns '36 and '53 Pontiacs, plus a '63 Chrysler 300. He is now looking for just the right '58 Chevy Apache pickup.

BILL SIURU grew up in Detroit during the era when ''Detroit Iron'' was king. Although he was trained as an automotive engineer, Bill was side-tracked into a 24-year career with the U.S. Air Force. There, he was involved in the development of new aircraft as well as missles and spacecraft. However, he never forgot his first love, the automobile. For the past 15 years, he has been both a car collector and restorer. His main interest is the Volvo 1800 model. He is a frequent contributor to numerous car enthusiast publications. Since retiring from the force, Bill has divided his time between writing about cars and aircraft and doing basic research in aerodynamics at the University of Colorado, in Colorado Springs. Bill has written a truck book entitled *Classic Motorbooks Ford Ranchero 1957-1979 Photofacts* and researched the Crosley section of this catalog.

CHARLES WEBB is a freelance writer and member of the Wisconsin Chapter of the Society of Automotive Historians. He is author of *The Investor's Illustrated Guide To American Convertible and Special Interest Automobiles, 1946-1976* and a contributor to *The Standard Catalog of American Cars 1946-1975*. Webb collects vintage truck and car television commercials and sales promotion films. He also writes the ''Cars As The Stars'' video review column for *Old Cars Weekly*. He did the Ford, 1980-1986 Dodge and postwar Plymouth sections of this catalog.

DONALD F. WOOD is a Professor of Transportation in the School of Business at San Francisco State University. He is the co-author of several widely-used college-level textbooks and has served as a consultant to numerous government agencies and private industry. Don writes about old trucks as a hobby. In the past decade, he has written over 50 articles and several books on the development of trucks and trucking. One of his works is *Classic Motorbooks Chevy El Camino 1959-1982 Photofacts*. Professor Wood's important contributions to this catalog included preliminary work on the ''Directory To Additional Light-Duty Truck Manufacturers'' and providing hundreds of photos from his massive collection of commercial vehicle photographs.

R. PERRY ZAVITZ is an acknowledged expert on postwar vehicles and has written numerous specialized articles and book sections covering Canadian models. Perry's special interests include collecting sales literature and factory photos and gathering historical items related to passenger cars, station wagons and crew cab trucks built from 1945 on. He has served as secretary and director of The Society of Automotive Historians and was the first director of the society's Canadian chapter. Perry also writes the long-running and popular column ''Postwar Scripts,'' which appears monthly in *Old Cars Weekly*. He is employed as a television production staff executive. Perry contributed numerous photos of different brands of trucks for this volume. In addition, he rewrote and expanded the Fargo truck section to include data from Canadian sources, such as *Sanford Evans Truck Guides*.

ARTISTS

BOB HOVORKA has done some outstanding automotive artwork that is familiar to car buffs across the country. His ''The Old Filling Station'' feature appears regularly in *Old Cars Weekly*. In addition, he has done several ''Blueprints'' features for *Special Interest Autos* magazine. Hovorka's long list of accomplishments includes other renderings that have appeared in *Car Collector*, as well as on limited-edition posters. Bob's Ford poster, used as a cover on *Old Cars Weekly* during 1984, won an Imperial Palace Moto Award. He is an avowed Jeep enthusiast — as well as Hudson lover — Bob owns a vintage Jeep from the Kaiser-Willys era. The plates covering the 1-5 Vehicle Grading System and the Body I.D. Guides located in front of this catalog are representative of the high-quality artwork that Bob Hovorka has gifted the vintage vehicle hobby with.

BOB LICHTY is in charge of marketing, advertising, public relations and publications for The Flea Marketeers, promoters of the Carlisle (Pennsylvania) collector vehicle shows. These are among the largest such events in the world. Lichty began his career at B.F. Goodrich. He then joined the staffs of several collector publications, did work for Kruse auction company and opened a collector car dealership in California. Later, Bob became advertising manager and art director for *Old Cars Weekly* and *Old Cars Price Guide*. Mr. Lichty has written numerous articles and recently compiled the first-ever directory to hobby events, which was published by Chip and Bill Miller, of Carlisle. For this catalog, we asked Bob to repeat the great ''Body Styles'' drawings he did in a previous *Standard Catalog*, but covering light-duty trucks this time.

SPECIAL THANKS

In addition to the **Marque Researchers** listed above, Krause Publications would like to give special thanks to the following people who went above and beyond the call of duty to help make this catalog possible:

Stan Binnie, Parts of the Past, Waukesha, Wis. (Truck Literature); Terry V. Boyce, Detroit, Mich. (1960-1970s Chevrolet data); George H. Dammann, Crestline Publishing, Sarasota, Fla. (1973-1986 Chevrolet Photos); Bob Hensel, All-Chevy Acres, Brillion, Wis. (Early Chevrolet data and photos); James A. Wren, Automotive Research, Detroit, Mich. (Extensive photos-all marques); Seth Doulton, Golden State Pickup Parts, Santa Barbara, Calif. (proofreading Chevrolet section); LaVon Gray, Bristol, Ind. (IHC ''Red Baby'' sales literature); Jack L. Martin, director, Indy Hall of Fame Museum, Indianapolis, Ind. (photos of Indy 500 Official Trucks); John M. Sawruk, historian, Pontiac Motor Division (photos of prototype Pontiac trucks); Rochelle R. LaDoucher, public relations, GMC Truck & Bus (GMC photos and data); Edward S. Lechtzin, public relations, Chevrolet Motor Division (Chevrolet truck photos); Robert D. Regehr, Route 6 Classics (IHC information); Duane A. Perrin, Manassas, Va., (proof reading Willys-Overland); F. Deney Freeston, Atlanta, Ga. (proof reading Willys-Overland); Jerry Heasley, Pampa, Texas (Ford production data); The Spokesman, Inc., Tulsa, Okla. (general photos); Elliott Kahn, Clearwater Beach, Fla. (directory information).

As with any work of this scope, scores of other researchers, hobbyists, collectors, dealers, historians, writers and experts provided much information without which this catalog would never have become a reality. We'd like to thank everyone who took the time to send letters, notes, memos, clippings and advice. It was impossible to personally answer all of the mail that arrived at the Iola office, but it has all been carefully read and considered in the creation of this book.

REFERENCE SOURCES

GENERAL

A.L.A.M. Handbook to Automobile Specifications. Published by the Association of Licensed Automobile Manufacturers for many years. Originals can be obtained from hobby literature dealers. Some have been reprinted by Classic Motorbooks, Osceola, Wis.

American Funeral Cars and Ambulances Since 1900, by Thomas A. McPherson, Crestline Publishing Co., Sarasota, Fla.

American Truck Spotter's Guide 1966-1980, by Tad Burness, Motorbooks International, Osceola, Wis.

Automobile Trade Journal. These early magazines are great references on trucks. Can be purchased from swap meets or literature dealers.

Best of Old Cars Weekly, Volumes 1-6. Compilations of articles from **Old Cars Weekly**. Includes truck section. Order from Krause Publications, Iola, WI 54990.

Branham Automobile Reference Books. Published annually for many years. A truck section is included. Available from literature dealers.

Complete Encyclopedia of Commercial Vehicles, by G.N. Georgano. By Krause Publications. Out of print. An encyclopedia style reference on trucks, large and small, from around the world. Check used book stores for copies.

The Complete Book of Pickups & Vans, by Petersen Publishing Co., Los Angeles, Calif. A 1972 soft-cover with lots of 1973 model introductory information. Available at swap meets and used book stores.

Edmund's Guides. Published in different editions. Some cover both cars and trucks. Standard and optional equipment and prices. Special editions on trucks, too. From Edmund Publication Corp., West Hempstead, N.Y.

Great American Woodies and Wagons, by Donald J. Narus, Crestline Publishing, Sarasota, Fla.

Lester-Steele Handbook: Automobile Specifications 1915-1942. Many trucks were based on cars. This book reprints the detailed specifications charts from annual "show editions" of trade magazines. By Lester-Steele Publishing, Deerfield Beach, Fla.

Mini-Pickup Trucks, Consumer Guide Publications, Skokie, Ill. Published July 1982. Specifications, prices and option data for new models. Check with Consumer Guides for back issues.

U.S. Military Wheeled Vehicles, by Fred. W. Crismon. From Crestline Publishing Co., Sarasota, Fla.

MOTOR'S Truck Repair Manual. Published annually by MOTOR, The Hearst Corporation, New York, N.Y.

NADA Official Used Car Guides. Published periodically since the 1930s. Include prices, specifications and "used" vehicle values (in year of publication). NADA also published similar "Truck Reference Books." The "Used Car Guides" have a section on trucks. Subscriptions to current editions are available from National Appraisal Guides, Inc., West Covina, Calif.

Official Automobile Guide. These were similar to the NADA Official Used Car Guides described above and particularly well-detailed. A light-duty truck section was included. The publisher was Recording & Statistical Corp.

Pickup and Van Spotter's Guide 1945-1982, by Tad Burness, published by Classic Motorbooks/Motorbooks International, Osceola, Wis.

Production Figure Book For U.S. Cars, by Jerry Heasley. Available from Classic Motorbooks/Motorbooks International, Osceola, Wis.

Red Book Official Used Car Appraisals. These are similar to the NADA used car guides listed above. Published by National Used Car Market Report, Inc., Chicago, Ill.

ONE-MAKE

80 Years of Cadillac-LaSalle, by Walter P. McCall, Crestline Publishing, Co. Sarasota, Fla.

Chevrolet Special Information Catalog. Reprinted by Crank 'En Hope Publications, Blairsville, Pa.

75 Years of Chevrolet, by George H. Dammann, Crestline Publishing Co., Sarasota, Fla.

Chevrolet 1942-1946 Trucks Shop Manual, reprinted by Crank 'En Hope Publications, Blairsville, Pa.

Silver Book: Chevrolet Dealer Guide For Special Bodies & Equipment. These fascinating catalogs have been published annually, for many years, by Verbeist Publishing Co., Grosse Pointe Farms, Mich. Look for them at flea markets.

The History of Hudson, by Donald F. Butler. Crestline Publishing Co., Sarasota, Fla.

The Plymouth-Desoto Story, by Donald F. Butler. Crestline Publishing Co., Sarasota, Fla.

Studebaker: The Complete Story, by Fred K. Fox and William A. Cannon, Tab Books, Blue Ridge Summit, Pa.